D0900029

This Holy Bible belongs to

_____

Presented on

_____

By

_____

_____

THE HOLY BIBLE

BIBLE TEXT

Tyndale House Publishers, Inc.

WHEATON, ILLINOIS

ACKNOWLEDGMENTS

Executive Editors
V. Gilbert Beers
Kenneth N. Taylor

Managing Editor
Ronald A. Beers

Coordinating Editor
Carole Newing Johnson

Features, Notes, and Helps
V. Gilbert Beers

Simplified Living Bible Text
Mark Norton
Kenneth N. Taylor

Design
Timothy R. Botts
Bradford Cathey

Typesetting
Lois Rusch
Dan Beery
Gwen Elliott
Debbie Ingalls

Darcy Kamps
Marlene Muller

Production
Joan Major
James Bolton
Linda Oswald
Marlene S. Muddell
Tan Nguyen
Bill Paetzold
Julee Schwarzburg
Elaine Showers
Stan Michalski

Illustrations
Lee Brubaker
Ron DiCianni
Robert Florczak
Don Gabriel
Blas Gallego
Michael Hackett
Donald Kueker
Al Lorenz
Sergio Martinez
Joseph Miralles

Joan Pelaez
Jeffrey Terreson
Donald Bruckstein

*Special thanks to
the following important
contributors:*
Daniel Partner
Karen Voke
Cynthia Grondahl
Lynn Gabeleck
Philip Comfort
Mark Taylor
Angela Kokes
Susan Krebs
Ginny Olson
Peggy Emigh
Chris Sarros
Kathy Stinnette
Sharon Rasmussen
Vince Morris
Derrick Blanchette
Judith Morse
Sally van der Graaff
Ramona Tucker

WHAT IS THE BIBLE? HOW SHOULD I USE IT?

You are holding the most important book in the world. It will do more for you than any other book.

Why is the Bible so special?
God wrote the Bible. He had helpers. They wrote the words. But God showed them what to write. They wrote what God wanted to say. That's why the Bible is called God's Word.

Who were these people?
God used many kinds of people to help him write the Bible. There were fishermen like Peter and John. Matthew was a tax collector. Luke was a doctor. Paul was a Pharisee, a Jewish religious leader. David was a shepherd boy, then a warrior, then a king. Moses was a slave, then a prince, then a shepherd, then a great leader of God's people. These people did many kinds of work. But they all tried to live the way God wanted. They all wrote what God said.

What does God tell you in the Bible?
God tells you who he is. He tells you how much he loves you. He wants you to see how the world began and how it will end. He tells you how to become his friend. He explains how he will forgive you and how you should forgive others. He also tells you about his Son, Jesus. Jesus came from Heaven to earth. God shows you how to get from earth to Heaven. The Bible also tells you what you should do now, here on earth. God shows you how to please him. He helps you know how to live as you should.

Who is the Bible for?

The Bible is written especially for you. God did not write it for himself. He wrote his Word for his people. When you read the Bible, you learn about God. You'll get to know him. You'll become his friend. You'll learn to do what he wants. You'll learn what it will be like to live with him in Heaven forever. And you'll learn to get ready for Heaven here and now.

What will you find in the Bible?

You'll meet exciting people doing exciting things. You'll meet heroes and villains. You'll watch ordinary people do wonderful things. And you'll watch great people do ordinary things. You'll go with them on great adventures. You'll read about what God did in their lives. You'll listen to what God told them. You'll want to memorize some of the great things God said. These are set apart as key verses. You'll see people make mistakes and sin. You'll learn how they were forgiven. You'll learn how Bible people lived. It was very different from the way you live. You'll fight in battles, ride in chariots, capture walled cities, listen to angels talk, watch dead people come back to life, and walk with Jesus. Walking through the Bible is an adventure you'll never forget.

How should you read your Bible?

Read some each day. Start with the great Bible stories. This Bible shows where they are. As you read, study the pictures. Ask questions. Try to answer the questions with each story. You'll feel like you are there, taking part in each adventure. You'll want to read more than Bible stories. Be sure to read the other parts of the Bible, too, like Psalms and Proverbs.

Memorize a key verse every Monday. Keep saying it every day during the week. Read the special features that show how Bible people lived. These will help you know why people did what they did.

Pray before you read your Bible. Ask God to show you something he wants you to know. When you read, ask what the Bible is saying. Ask what it means. Then ask what you can do about it today.

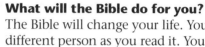

What will the Bible do for you?

The Bible will change your life. You will become a different person as you read it. You will learn that you need Jesus to forgive your sins. You will discover that you need Jesus to be your Savior. You will learn how to please God. You will learn how to live the way God wants. If you live according to what you learn, you will become more honest, more truthful, more faithful, more loving, more kind. You will become a strong Christian. You will build a strong Christian character. This will help you say no to things you should not do. It will help you say yes to things God wants you to do. These are things that are best for you.

The Bible will train you to be God's child. It will prepare you to live in Heaven. It will equip you to live here on earth. It will help you fight temptation and evil. It will help you build a strong family. There are many other wonderful things the Bible will do for you. But it will not do one of these things unless you read it! Start today. Keep it up. You'll soon love the Bible like a best friend.

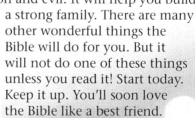

Do you like adventure and excitement? You'll want to read your Bible. It is the greatest adventure book ever written. Here are some of the exciting discoveries you'll find in your Bible. ■ Have you ever seen it rain **fire from the sky**? You will. You'll also see **THE GREATEST FLOOD** ever and the first rainbow when the flood ended. You'll watch a man **wrestle an angel** and win. You'll stand in awe as you watch the world created. And you'll wonder as you see it all come to a dramatic end. You'll watch a million people walk through the sea while God holds the water apart. ■ While walking through the Bible, you'll meet **GIANTS** and **SPIES**, **GENERALS** and **slaves**. You'll watch in amazement as God feeds A MILLION PEOPLE without one grocery store. *A TRUMPET BLAST* helps defeat a city. **A red rope** saves a family during a battle. ■ You'll meet **THE STRONGEST MAN** who ever lived. And you'll wonder how he could be so weak in other ways. You'll see a boy defeat a giant in battle with only a sling. You'll watch him become one of the greatest kings of all time. ■ You'll see *a fiery chariot* pulled by fiery horses going up to Heaven. You'll be amazed to see one man give A HUNDRED MILLION DOLLARS to build God's house. You'll see three young men refuse to bow before a golden statue. Watch when they are thrown into *a blazing furnace*! See them walk out without having their hair or clothes singed. ■ Wise men travel many miles to give precious gifts to a little baby.

But a king hates this baby so much that he kills all the babies in town. When this baby grows up, men give up their jobs to follow him. **THE DEVIL** tries to make a deal with him, but loses. You'll watch him walk on water and feed 5,000 people with a little boy's lunch. You'll watch blind men see, crippled people walk, **dead people** get up and live again . You'll listen to the only person who has ever lived in Heaven. He will tell you how to get there. But you'll feel sad when you see a man sell his best friend for 30 COINS.

■ Have you ever met *an Archangel* ? You'll meet two of them in the Bible. You'll see someone die, with NAILS pounded through his hands. But you'll see him alive again, walking, talking, and eating. You'll watch him rise up through the clouds. You'll see him go back into Heaven. ■ The Bible shows you *shipwrecks* , storms that obey a man's voice, a fish that swallows a man and spits him out again. ■ But most important, when you read your Bible, you'll learn who God is. You'll learn why he loves you and how you can love him, too. You'll learn that he is the same God who made the world and who will end the world. And you'll want very much to go to God's home in H E A V E N where you can live with him forever. ■ This is the greatest adventure book and the greatest lesson book ever written. Be sure to read it. Study the pictures that show what happens. Answer questions about what you have read. You'll never find another book like this. And you'll never be the same again.

1: The Bible translation that is easiest to read and understand. This new Bible text is complete and authoritative. It is written at the third-grade reading level and is verified by the Flesch-Kinkaid readability test. It is based on The Living Bible, the most popular modern translation in the world over the last 20 years. As the text was simplified, it was also updated and revised to be even more accurate to the original languages.

2: Exciting, new, full-color illustrations painted just for this Bible by world-famous artists. Go ahead. Thumb through the pages of this Bible. There has never been such a large, realistic, and archaeologically accurate library of art introduced at one time. There are 180 full-color quality Bible paintings of key Bible events— dramatic, believable, detailed, colorful, with high artistic quality. These take you into the great Bible adventures with key Bible people as if you were there. And these paintings are placed right next to the Bible text they illustrate.

3: Key Bible stories highlighted. Key stories of the Bible are highlighted where they appear in the Bible, making it easy to see them as they fit into the Bible text.

4: Previews. Two types of previews are provided to stir reader interest in the great stories found in the Bible text. First, each Bible story is introduced with a preview. This encourages the reader to read this Bible text. Also, a little feature called "What's next?" wraps up the lesson section for each story. This previews the next Bible story and tells where it can be found.

5: Questions. Stimulating questions appear after the text for each key Bible story, reviewing, discovering values, comparing, contrasting, searching, enriching, building understanding.

6: A timeless Bible truth discovered in each story. A "Discover" feature appears after each Bible story. This helps the reader discover and condense the timeless truth of the Bible story into a phrase or two. This is the essence of what the story teaches and is the foundation for the application feature to follow.

7: Application. Following the Discover feature after each Bible story, there is a feature called "Apply." This helps the reader apply the Bible truth just discovered to everyday living. It has something specific to help change the reader's attitudes or actions, making that Bible truth personal.

JEREMIAH 14

God Loses His Patien

14 This message ca from the Lord. It e was holding back the ra [2]"Judah is full of mo

MARK 1   110

"Someone is coming soon who is far greater than I am. He is so much greater that I am not even worthy to be his slave. [8]I baptize you with water. But he will baptize you with God's Holy Spirit!"

John Baptizes Jesus
[9]Then one day Jesus came from Nazareth in Galilee. He was baptized by John there in the Jordan River. [10]When Jesus came up out of the water, he saw the heavens open. The Holy Spirit in the form of a dove flew down to him. [11]And a voice from Heaven said, "You are my Son, whom I love. I am very pleased with you!"

Satan Tempts Jesus in the Wilderness
[12-13]Right then the Holy Spirit sent Jesus into the desert. There, for 40 days, he was alone except for the desert animals. During that time Satan tried to tempt Jesus to sin. And then the angels came and took care of him.

Jesus Preaches in Galilee
[14]Later on, John was arrested by King Herod. At that time, Jesus went to Galilee to preach God's Good News.
[15]"At last the time has come!" he said. "God's Kingdom is near! Turn from your sins and act on this Good News!"

8: An unbroken chain of the key 300 Bible stories. At the end of each story there is a small feature called "What's next?" This serves two purposes. It offers a preview of what is coming in the next story. But it also connects over 300 stories and their enrichment material in an unbroken chain. This feature also helps the reader, if he wishes, to go straight through the life of Jesus.

---

them or tell them to speak. I didn't give them any messages. They prophesy of visions and revelations they have never seen or heard. They speak lies made up in their own lying hearts. ¹⁵Therefore,

ple. But even then I wouldn't help them. Send the people away from me! Get them out of my sight! ²And they might say to you, 'But where can we go?' If they do, tell them this:

Jesus Calls Four Followers

One day Jesus was walking along the shores of the Sea of Galilee. He saw Simon and his brother Andrew fishing with nets. These men caught ... for a living.

¹⁷Jesus called out to the ... me, follow me! I will make you fishermen for ... souls of men!" ¹⁸At once they left their nets and went along with him.

¹⁹A little farther up the beach, he saw ... bedee's sons, James and John. They ... were in a boat fixing their fishing nets. Jesus called out to them, too. And right ... way, they left their father Zebedee in the boat with the hired men. They went ... with Jesus, too.

Remember: Two men were fishing. Jesus asked them to follow him. Who w... they? What were they doing? (1:...) What did Jesus ask them to do? W... work would they do with him? (1:...) they go with him? (1:18) Jesus asked two other men to follow him. Who were they? (1:19) Did they go with him? (1:20) Why do you think these men gave up their jobs? Why was it more impor... tant to follow Jesus? Would you have done this?

Discover: Following Jesus is more impo... tant than anything else we do.

Apply: Are you trying to follow Jesus ... th? Are you trying to do what he wants? Can you think of anything ... important?

What's next? One minute a woman was in bed with a high fever. The next minute she was well. What ... ed? Read Matthew 8:14-17.

Jesus Teaches with Great Authority

Jesus and his companions went to the ... wn of Capernaum. On Saturday morn... g they went into the Jewish place of

worship, the synagogue. There Jesus preached to the people. ²²They were surprised at his sermon because he spoke as an authority. He didn't try to prove his points by quoting other people. It was quite different from what they were used to hearing!

²³A man with a demon in him was there. He began shouting, ²⁴"Why are you bothering us, Jesus of Nazareth? Have you come to destroy us demons? I know who you are! You are the holy Son of God!"

When we are afraid of something, we should trust Jesus to help us

Don't be afraid. Just trust me.

Mark 5:36

"What sort of new religion is this?" they asked. "Why, even evil spirits obey his orders!"

²⁸The news of what he had done spread quickly through that area of Galilee.

Jesus Heals Simon's Mother-in-Law and Many Others

²⁹⁻³⁰Then they left the synagogue. And Jesus and his disciples went over to Simon and Andrew's home. There they found Simon's mother-in-law sick in bed with a high fever. They told Jesus about her right away. ³¹He went to her bedside. He took her by the hand and helped her to sit up. And the fever suddenly left her! She got up and made dinner for them!

³²⁻³³By sunset the courtyard was filled with the sick and demon-possessed. Their friends had brought them to Jesus for healing. Many people from all over the city of Capernaum gathered outside

---

... ogs
... ild ani-
... "I will
... ate will
... will do
... nasseh,
... n.
... Jerusa-
... ho will
... e? ⁶You
... acks on
... nst you
... always
... will sift
... vill take
... r. And I
... because
... ney will
⁸"There ... ntime I
... nen and
... use pain
... ddenly.
... ck and
... Her sun
... She sits
... r all her

... sadness
... ad died
... ere I go.
... and my
... refusing
... ¹¹Well,
... v how I
... behalf.
... to save

... f north-
... eople's

What Happens When There Is No Water?
JEREMIAH 14:3

Turn on your faucet. Water comes out! There's always more than you need. You never worry about running out of water. It's good water too, good enough to drink. But Bible-time people didn't have all the water they needed. They had no faucets like yours. Bible-time people looked for springs where water flowed from the earth. Brooks and streams of water helped, but they couldn't be counted on. When it rained, or when snow melted, there was often too much water. At other times, brooks or streams dried up.

Some people dug wells. That was hard work. They didn't have good tools. There were no hardware stores where they could buy such things. It took many days to dig a well. Sometimes they had to dig through rock. Cisterns were popular in Bible times. These were big holes, like wells, plastered with lime. People gathered rain water into cisterns. Some cities made aqueducts. These were troughs that carried water a long distance from its source. Without water, people and their animals would die. Aren't you glad you have so much good water? Thank God for it now!

9: Everyday life in Bible times. There are 80 pictorial presentations of everyday life in Bible times. After reading these 80 presentations, a person will know more than most church members about the way Bible-time people lived. In addition, there are large, three-dimensional reconstructions of Bible-time houses, a Bible-time village, and Solomon's Temple.

10: Three-dimensional maps. There are several unusual 3-D maps. You not only see the territory covered by the map, but you see the terrain and buildings as though they were photographed from the air. These 3-D maps help bring important Bible events to life. These are not static two-dimensional maps with dots and masses of color, but living maps that combine events and places.

11: Bible book previews. Each Bible book is introduced with an interesting preview. The preview excites the reader with the adventures to come, highlighting the interest value in that book. But it also helps the reader know more about the setting in which that book was written.

12: Key Bible verses. Dozens of favorite key verses, as found in most good memory programs for children, are highlighted on location, where they appear in the Bible text. A short phrase appears with each verse, summarizing the teaching found in that verse.

GENESIS

Have you ever met a 900-year-old man? You'll meet seven of them in this book. Have you ever seen it rain fire instead of drops of water? You will in Genesis. You'll see the biggest flood that ever was, the first rainbow, and you'll sail on a homemade boat as big as a football field.

You'll meet a slave who became governor in one day. You'll watch a man wrestle an angel. And you'll watch what God did on the very first day.

Genesis tells us how everything began. It starts in the very beginning, before there was a world. No one was there but God. Genesis tells us how God made everything. He made everything you will ever see. And he even made things you will never see.

Genesis is the story of Abraham, his son Isaac, his grandson Jacob and their family. Some day God would make their family into the people of Israel, who would form a great nation. The story of Israel would become the story of the Bible. It would become the story of how Jesus came.

Genesis shows how faithful people trusted God and followed him when their neighbors did not. It will remind you that God does special things through families that follow him.

THROUGH THE BIBLE

///

THE
OLD
TESTAMENT

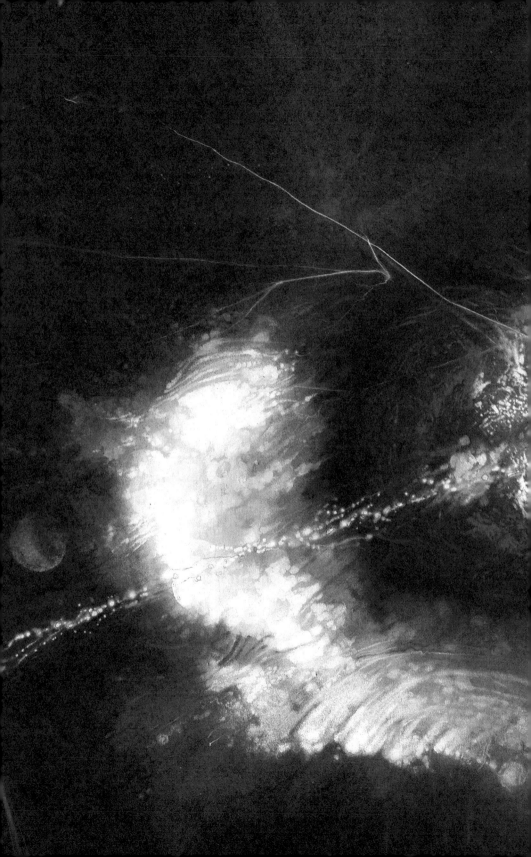

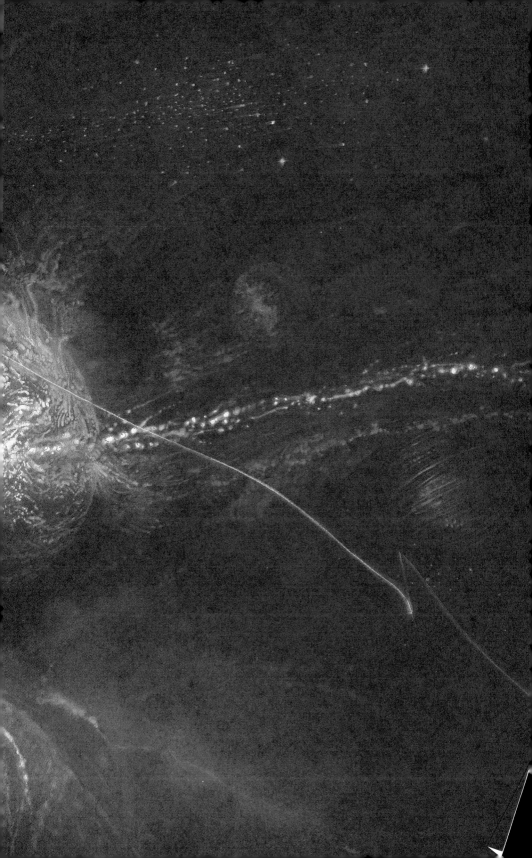

GENESIS

Have you ever met a 900-year-old man? You'll meet seven of them in this book. Have you ever seen it rain fire instead of drops of water? You will in Genesis. You'll see the biggest flood that ever was, the first rainbow, and you'll sail on a homemade boat as big as a football field.

You'll meet a slave who became governor in one day. You'll watch a man wrestle an angel. And you'll watch what God did on the very first day.

Genesis tells us how everything began. It starts in the very beginning, before there was a world. No one was there but God. Genesis tells us how God made everything. He made everything you will ever see. And he even made things you will never see.

Genesis is the story of Abraham, his son Isaac, his grandson Jacob and their family. Some day God would make their family into the people of Israel, who would form a great nation. The story of Israel would become the story of the Bible. It would become the story of how Jesus came.

Genesis shows how faithful people trusted God and followed him when their neighbors did not. It will remind you that God does special things through families that follow him.

God Makes Everything

Would you like to watch God make a world? He takes a little of nothing. Then he says, "Let there be a world!" Suddenly there's a world. Can you do that? Can you make something from nothing?

1 In the beginning God created the heavens and the earth. ²The earth was a shapeless, chaotic mass. The Spirit of God was brooding over the dark vapors.

³Then God said, "Let there be light." And light appeared. ⁴⁵And God was pleased with it and divided the light from the darkness. He called the light "daytime." He called the darkness "nighttime." Together they formed the first day.

[6]And God said, "Let the vapors separate to form the sky above and the oceans below." [7-8]So God made the sky. He divided the vapor above from the water below. This all happened on the second day.

[9-10]Then God said, "Let the water beneath the sky be gathered into oceans. And let the dry land emerge." And so it was. Then God named the dry land "earth." He named the water "seas." And God was pleased. [11-12]And he said, "Let the earth burst forth with every sort of grass and seed-bearing plant. Let it produce fruit trees with seeds inside the fruit. And let these seeds produce the kinds of plants and fruits they came from." And so it was, and God was pleased. [13]This all occurred on the third day.

[14-15]Then God said, "Let bright lights appear in the sky. They will give light to the earth and identify the day and the night. They shall bring about the seasons on the earth, and mark the days and years." And so it was. [16]For God had made two huge lights, the sun and moon, to shine down upon the earth. The larger one, the sun, was to preside over the day. The smaller one, the moon, was to preside through the night. He had also made the stars. [17]God set them in the sky to light the earth. [18]They were to preside over the day and night and to divide the light from the darkness. And God was pleased. [19]This all happened on the fourth day.

[20]Then God said, "Let the waters teem with fish and other life. Let the skies be filled with birds of every kind." [21-22]So God created great sea animals. He made every sort of fish and every kind of bird. And God looked at them with pleasure and blessed them all. "Multiply and stock the oceans," he told them. And to the birds he said, "Let your numbers increase. Fill the earth!" [23]That ended the fifth day.

[24]And God said, "Let the earth bring forth every kind of animal. Let it bring forth cattle and reptiles and wildlife of every kind." And so it was. [25]God made all sorts of wild animals and cattle and reptiles. And God was pleased with what he had done.

[26]Then God said, "Let us make a man—someone like ourselves. He will be the master of all life upon the earth and in the skies and in the seas."

[27]So God made man like his Maker.
Like God did God make man.
Man and maid did he make them.

[28]And God blessed them and told them, "Multiply and fill the earth and subdue it. You are masters of the fish and birds and all the animals.

²⁹And look! I have given you all the plants and all the fruit trees for your food. And I have given all the grass and plants to the animals and birds for their food." ³¹Then God looked over all that he had made. It was excellent in every way. This ended the sixth day.

2 Now at last the heavens and earth were completed, with all that they contained. ²By the seventh day God had finished his task. So he rested from this work he had been doing. ³God blessed the seventh day and declared it holy. For it was the day when he finished this work of creation.

⁴Here is a summary of the events in the creation of the heavens and earth when the Lord God made them.

⁵There were no plants or grain sprouting up across the earth at first. For the Lord God hadn't sent any rain. And there were no people to farm the soil. ⁶(But water welled up from the ground at certain places. Then it flowed across the land.)

- *Remember:* When God was in total darkness, what did he make first? (1:3) What did he make last? (1:27) How many days did it take God to make everything? (1:31) What did God do on the seventh day? (2:3)

- *Discover:* Try to make something from nothing. Can you? Why not?

- *Apply:* Who is the only person who can make something from nothing?

- *What's next?* Two people were never born. How did that happen? Read about it in Genesis 2:7-25. ∎

God Makes Adam and Eve

God made the sun, moon, and stars. He made a beautiful world. He made mountains and seas, plants and animals, birds and fish, and a million other beautiful things. Wasn't this enough? No, he had one more important job to do.

⁷The time came when the Lord God formed a man's body. He made it from the dust of the ground. Then he breathed into it the breath of life. And man became a living person.

⁸Then the Lord God planted a garden in Eden, to the east. And he placed in the garden the man he had formed. ⁹The Lord God planted all sorts of beautiful trees there in the garden. The trees produced the choicest of fruit. At the center of the garden he placed the Tree of Life. He put the Tree of Conscience there also. It gave knowledge of Good and Bad. ¹⁰A river from the land of Eden flowed through the garden to water it. After leaving the garden, the river divided into four branches. ¹¹⁻¹²One of these was named the Pishon. It winds across the entire length of the land of Havilah. In that land nuggets of pure gold are found. Bdellium and lapis lazuli are found there, too. ¹³The second branch is called the Gihon. It crosses the entire length of the land of Cush. ¹⁴The third branch is the Tigris. It flows to the east of the city of Asher. And the fourth is the Euphrates.

[15]The Lord God placed the man in the Garden of Eden as its gardener. He was to tend and care for it. [16-17]But the Lord God warned the man. He said, "You may eat any fruit in the garden except fruit from the Tree of Conscience. You must not eat from that tree. For its fruit will open your eyes. It will make you aware of right and wrong, good and bad. If you eat its fruit, you will be doomed to die."

[18]And the Lord God said, "It isn't good for man to be alone. I will make a companion for him, a helper suited to his needs." [19-20]So the Lord God formed from the soil every kind of animal and bird. He brought them to the man to see what he would call them. Whatever the man called them, that was their name. But still there was no proper helper for the man. [21]Then the Lord God caused the man to fall into a deep sleep. He took one of the man's ribs. Then he closed up the place from which he had taken it. [22]Then he made the rib into a woman, and brought her to the man.

[23]"This is it!" Adam exclaimed. "She is part of my own bone and flesh! Her name is 'woman' because she was taken out of a man." [24]This explains why a man leaves his father and mother. And it tells why he is joined to his wife in such a way that the two become one person. [25]Now the man and his wife were both naked. But neither of them was embarrassed or ashamed.

- *Remember:* Which person was made from dust? (2:7) Which person was made from a rib? (2:21-22) If you had been Adam, what would you have named your three favorite kinds of animals?

- *Discover:* How many different kinds of animals and birds can you name? Make a list so you can count them. God really was creative to make so many kinds of things, wasn't he?

- *Apply:* God made the first people from dust and a rib. He makes the rest of us too. But he does that in a different way. Adam and Eve were not born. We are.

- *What's next?* Have you ever heard of a bad news tree? See Genesis 3. ◼

Adam and Eve Are Tempted

There were two special trees in the Garden of Eden. One was a good news tree. The other was a bad news tree. The good news tree would help Adam and Eve live forever. But what would the bad news tree do?

3 The serpent was the craftiest of all the creatures the Lord God had made. So the serpent came to the woman. "Really?" he asked. "*None* of the fruit in the garden? God says you mustn't eat *any* of it?"

[2-3]"Of course we may eat it," the woman told him. "It's only the fruit from the tree at the *center* of the garden that we must not eat. God says we must not eat it or even touch it. If we do, we will die."

[4]"That's a lie!" the serpent hissed. "You'll not die! [5]God knows very well that as soon as you eat it you will become like him. Your eyes will be opened. You will be able to know good from evil!"

[6]The woman was convinced. How lovely and fresh-looking it was! And it would make her so wise! So she ate some of the fruit and gave some to her husband. He ate it too. [7]And as soon as they ate it, they saw they were naked, and they were embarrassed. So they strung fig leaves together to cover themselves around the hips.

[8]That evening they heard the sound of the Lord God walking in the garden. They hid among the trees. [9]The Lord God called to Adam, "Why are you hiding?"

¹⁰And Adam replied, "I heard you coming. I didn't want you to see me naked. So I hid."

¹¹"Who told you you were naked?" the Lord God asked. "Have you eaten fruit from the tree I warned you about?"

¹²"Yes," Adam said. "But it was the woman you gave me who brought me some. And then I ate it."

¹³Then the Lord God asked the woman, "How could you do such a thing?"

"The serpent tricked me," she replied.

¹⁴So the Lord God said to the serpent, "This is your punishment. You are singled out from among all the tame and wild animals of the whole earth to be cursed. You shall crawl in the dust as long as you live. You will always crawl on your belly. ¹⁵From now on you and the woman will be enemies, as will your offspring and hers. You will strike his heel, but he will crush your head."

¹⁶Then God said to the woman, "You shall bear children in intense pain and suffering. Yet even so, you shall want your husband to love you. And he shall be your master."

¹⁷And God said to Adam, "You listened to your wife. You ate the fruit when I told you not to. Therefore I have placed a curse upon the soil. All your life you will work hard to extract a living from it. ¹⁸It will grow thorns and thistles for you, and you shall eat its grasses. ¹⁹All your life you will sweat to master it, until your dying day. Then you will return to the ground from which you came. For you were made from the ground, and to the ground you will return."

²⁰The man named his wife Eve (meaning "The life-giving one"). For he said, "She shall become the mother of all mankind." ²¹And the Lord God gave clothes to Adam and his wife made from skins of animals.

²²Then the Lord said, "Now the man has become as we are. He knows good from bad. What if he eats the fruit of the Tree of Life and lives forever?" ²³So the Lord God sent him away from the Garden of Eden forever. He sent him out to farm the ground from which he had been taken. ²⁴Thus God expelled him. And God placed mighty angels at the east of the Garden of Eden. They stood with a flaming sword to guard the entrance to the Tree of Life.

- *Remember:* What was the one tree in Eden that was bad for Adam and Eve? Why? (2:17) How was Eve punished for eating the fruit? (3:16) How was Adam punished? (3:17-19)

- *Discover:* What is sin? It's doing what you want when you know that's not what God wants. God must punish us when we sin.

- *Apply:* Is the "fun" of doing something wrong ever worth the hurt of being punished for it?

- *What's next?* So what difference does it make if I get mad at someone? Getting mad changed one man's life. Read about it in Genesis 4:1-16. ■

Cain Kills Abel

Getting mad at his brother got Cain in BIG trouble. This is how it happened.

4 Then Adam lay with Eve his wife. She conceived and gave birth to a son, Cain (meaning "I have created"). For, as she said, "With God's help, I have created a man!" ²Her next child was his brother, Abel.

Abel became a shepherd. Cain was a farmer. ³At harvest time Cain brought the Lord a gift of his farm produce. ⁴Abel brought the fatty cuts of meat from his best lambs, and presented them to the Lord. The Lord accepted Abel's offering, ⁵but not Cain's. This made Cain dejected and very angry. His face grew dark with fury.

⁶"Why are you angry?" the Lord

asked him. "Why is your face so dark with rage? 7It can be bright with joy if you will do what you should! But if you refuse to obey, watch out. Sin is waiting to attack you. It is longing to destroy you. But you can conquer it!"

8One day Cain said to his brother, "Let's go out into the fields." And while they were there, Cain hit his brother and killed him.

9After that the Lord asked Cain, "Where is your brother? Where is Abel?"

"How should I know?" Cain said. "Am I supposed to keep track of him wherever he goes?"

10But the Lord said, "Your brother's blood calls to me from the ground. What have you done? 11You are hereby banished from this ground which you have defiled with your brother's blood. 12No longer will it yield crops for you, even if you toil on it forever! From now on you will be a fugitive and a tramp upon the earth. You will wander from place to place."

13Cain replied to the Lord, "You have punished me more than I can bear. 14For you have sent me away from my farm and from you. You have made me a fugitive. All who see me will try to kill me."

15The Lord replied, "They won't kill you. For I will give seven times your punishment to anyone who does." Then the Lord put a mark on Cain as a warning not to kill him. 16So Cain went out from the presence of the Lord. He settled in the land of Nod, east of Eden.

- *Remember:* Which brother was a farmer? (4:2) Did God refuse Cain's offering because he was a farmer or because he did not obey God? (4:6-7) How did God punish Cain? (4:11-12) Why did this punishment hurt Cain so much? (4:13-14)

- *Discover:* Why did Cain kill Abel? (4:6-8) Are you "mad at" someone? Remember Cain. You could get hurt or hurt someone else.

- *Apply:* Anger is like a mad dog. Unless you tame it, it can hurt you and your friends.

- *What's next?* Why would anyone build a big boat in a desert? Read Genesis 6:5–7:9. ∎

Cain's Family

17Then Cain's wife conceived. She gave him a baby son named Enoch. So when Cain founded a city, he named it Enoch. He named it after his son.

18Enoch was the father of Irad. Irad was the father of Mehujael. Mehujael was the father of Methusael. Methusael was the father of Lamech.

19Lamech married two wives—Adah and Zillah. 20To Adah was born a baby named Jabal. He became the first of the cattlemen and those living in tents. 21His brother's name was Jubal, the first musician. He invented the harp and flute. 22To Lamech's other wife, Zillah, was born Tubal-cain. He opened the first foundry forging tools of bronze and iron.

23One day Lamech said to Adah and Zillah, "Listen to me, my wives. I have killed a youth who attacked and wounded me. 24If anyone kills Cain he will be punished seven times. Anyone taking revenge against me should be punished 77 times!"

Adam's Family

25Later, Eve gave birth to another son and named him Seth (meaning "Granted"). For, as Eve put it, "God has given me another son for the one Cain killed." 26When Seth grew up, he had a son and named him Enosh. It was during his lifetime that men first began to call themselves "the Lord's people."

5 Here is a list of some of the descendants of Adam. When God created man, he made him in God's likeness. 2God created man and woman and blessed them. He called them Man from the start.

3-5*Adam:* Adam was 130 years old when his son Seth was born. Seth was the very image of his father in every way. After Seth was born, Adam lived another 800 years. He produced sons and daughters and died at the age of 930.

6-8*Seth:* Seth was 105 years old when his son Enosh was born. After that he lived another 807 years. He had sons and daughters and died at the age of 912.

9-11*Enosh:* Enosh was 90 years old when his son Kenan was born. After that he lived another 815 years. He had sons and daughters and died at the age of 905.

¹²⁻¹⁴*Kenan:* Kenan was 70 years old when his son Mahalalel was born. After that he lived another 840 years. He had sons and daughters and died at the age of 910.

¹⁵⁻¹⁷*Mahalalel:* Mahalalel was 65 years old when his son Jared was born. After that he lived 830 years. He had sons and daughters and died at the age of 895.

¹⁸⁻²⁰*Jared:* Jared was 162 years old when his son Enoch was born. After that he lived another 800 years. He had sons and daughters and died at the age of 962.

²¹⁻²⁴*Enoch:* Enoch was 65 years old when his son Methuselah was born. After that he lived another 300 years in constant fellowship with God and had sons and daughters. Then, when he was 365, he disappeared. God took him away!

²⁵⁻²⁷*Methuselah:* Methuselah was 187 years old when his son Lamech was born. After that he lived another 782 years.

He had sons and daughters and died at the age of 969.

²⁸⁻³¹*Lamech:* Lamech was 182 years old when his son Noah was born. Lamech named him Noah (meaning "Relief"). For he said, "He will bring us relief from the hard work of farming this ground which God has cursed." After that Lamech lived 595 years. He had sons and daughters and died at the age of 777.

³²*Noah:* Noah was 500 years old and had three sons, Shem, Ham, and Japheth.

The World Becomes Evil

6 Now a population explosion took place upon the earth. It was at this time that beings from the spirit world looked upon the pretty earth women. They took any they desired to be their wives. ³Then the Lord said, "My Spirit must not forever be disgraced in man. He is so evil. I will give him 120 years to mend his ways."

⁴In those days, and even after that, the evil beings from the spirit world were involved with human women. Their children became giants, of whom so many legends are told.

Noah Builds the Ark

Here's a man who built a big boat on dry land. It took him 120 years to build it. Think how many times his friends and neighbors laughed at him. It's no fun to work when your friends and neighbors laugh at you. But Noah did it because he wanted to obey God.

⁵The Lord God saw how wicked people were. He saw that the direction of people's lives was only toward evil. ⁶He was sorry he had made them. It broke his heart.

⁷He said, "I will blot out from the face of the earth all mankind that I created. Yes, and the animals, too, and the reptiles and the birds. I am sorry I made them."

⁸But Noah was a pleasure to the Lord. Here is the story of Noah. ⁹⁻¹⁰He was the only truly righteous man living on the earth at that time. He tried always to live by God's will. He had three sons—Shem, Ham, and Japheth.

¹¹Meanwhile, the crime rate was rising rapidly across the earth. As seen by God, the world was rotten to the core.

12-13God saw how bad it was. He saw that all mankind was vicious and depraved. So he said to Noah, "I have decided to destroy all mankind. For the earth is filled with crime because of man. Yes, I will destroy mankind from the earth. 14Make a boat out of wood. Seal it with tar. And make decks and stalls throughout the ship. 15Make it 450 feet long, 75 feet wide, and 45 feet high. 16Make a skylight all the way around the ship, 18 inches below the roof. Make three decks inside the boat—a bottom, middle, and upper deck. And put a door in the side.

17"Look! I am going to cover the earth with a flood. I am going to destroy every living being. Everything in which there is the breath of life will die. 18But I promise to keep you safe in the ship. You will enter it with your wife and your sons and their wives. 19-20Bring a pair of every animal—a male and a female—into the boat with you. Do this to keep them alive through the flood. Bring in a pair of

each kind of bird and animal and reptile. 21Store away in the boat all the food that they and you will need." 22And Noah did all that God told him.

7 At last the day came when the Lord said to Noah, "Go into the boat. Take all your family. For among all the people of the earth, I consider you alone to be righteous. 2Bring in the animals, too. Bring a pair of each, except those kinds I have chosen for eating and for sacrifice. Take seven pairs of each of them. 3And take seven pairs of every kind of bird. Thus every kind of life will reproduce again after the flood has ended. 4One week from today I will begin 40 days and nights of rain. And all the animals and birds and reptiles I have made will die."

5So Noah did all the Lord commanded him. 6He was 600 years old when the flood came. 7He went on the boat with his wife and sons and their wives, to escape the flood. 8-9With him were all the many kinds of animals. This included those for eating and sacrifice, and those that were not, and the birds and reptiles. They came into the boat in pairs, male and female, just as God told Noah.

- *Remember:* God promised to keep eight people safe in the boat. Who were they? (6:18) How old was Noah when the flood came? (7:6) Why did God protect Noah? (6:8-10) Why did Noah build the big boat? (6:22)

- *Discover:* If your friends were laughing at you, would you keep doing something? Would you keep on doing it if it's something God wants? How long would you keep doing it?

- *Apply:* Which do you want to do more, please your friends or please God? Why?

- *What's next?* Have you ever seen a flood big enough to cover mountains? Read about one in Genesis 7:10–9:17. ∎

God Sends a Great Flood

How would you feel if you and your family were the only people on earth? Here's a family that found themselves alone. There was not one other person on all the earth!

10-12One week later, when Noah was 600 years, two months, and 17 days old, the flood came. The rain came down in mighty torrents from the sky. And the waters under the ground burst forth upon the earth for 40 days and nights. 13But Noah had gone into the boat that very day. He had taken his wife and his sons, Shem, Ham, and Japheth, and their wives. 14-15With them in the boat

were pairs of every kind of animal. There were tame and wild animals. There were reptiles and birds of every sort. 16Two by two they came, male and female, just as God had commanded. Then the Lord God closed the door and shut them in.

17For 40 days the roaring floods prevailed. The water covered the ground and lifted the boat high above the earth. 18As the water rose higher and higher above the ground, the boat floated safely upon it. 19At last the water covered all the high mountains under the whole heaven. 20It stood 22 feet and more above the highest peaks. 21And all living things upon the earth died. The birds, tame and wild animals, the reptiles, and all mankind were killed. 22All that breathed and lived upon dry land died. 23All life on the earth was blotted out—man and animals alike, and reptiles and birds. God destroyed them all, leaving only Noah alive, and those with him in the boat. 24And the water covered the earth 150 days.

8 God didn't forget about Noah and all the animals in the boat! He sent a wind to blow across the waters. Then the floods began to go away. 2The water under the ground stopped gushing. The heavy rains stopped too. 3-4So the flood slowly went away. And 150 days after it began, the boat came to rest upon the mountains of Ararat. 5Three months later, as the waters kept going down, other mountain peaks appeared.

6After another 40 days, Noah opened a window. 7He let a raven go. It flew back and forth until the earth was dry. ⁸Meanwhile he sent out a dove to see if it could find dry ground. ⁹But the dove found no place to land and came back to Noah. The water was still too high. So Noah held out his hand and drew the dove back into the boat.

¹⁰Seven days later Noah let out the dove again. ¹¹This time, toward evening, the bird came back to him with an olive leaf in her beak. So Noah knew that the water was almost gone. ¹²A week later he released the dove again. This time she didn't come back.

¹³Twenty-nine days after that, Noah opened the door to look. The water was gone! ¹⁴Eight more weeks went by. Then at last the earth was dry. ¹⁵⁻¹⁶Then God told Noah, "You may all go out. ¹⁷Release all the animals, birds, and reptiles. That way they will breed and reproduce in great numbers." ¹⁸⁻¹⁹So the boat was soon empty. Noah, his wife, and his sons and their wives all got off. And all the animals, reptiles, and birds followed them. All left the ark in pairs and groups.

²⁰Then Noah built an altar. He sacrificed on it some of the animals and birds God had set apart for that purpose. ²¹And the Lord was pleased with the sacrifice. He said to himself, "I will never again curse the earth. I will never again destroy all living things. I will never do it again, even though man's bent is always toward evil. And even though he does such wicked things from his earliest youth. ²²As long as the earth remains, there will be springtime and harvest. There will be cold and heat, winter and summer, day and night."

9 God blessed Noah and his sons. He told them to have many children and to fill the earth.

²⁻³"All wild animals and birds and fish will be afraid of you," God told him. "For I have placed them in your power. They are yours to use for food. You may also eat grain and vegetables. ⁴But never eat animals unless their lifeblood has been drained off. ⁵⁻⁶And murder is forbidden. Animals who kill people must die. And any man who murders shall be killed. For to kill a man is to kill one made like God. ⁷Yes, have many chil-

dren and fill the earth and subdue it."

⁸Then God told Noah and his sons, ⁹⁻¹¹"I make a solemn promise. This promise is to you and your children and to the animals you brought with you—all these birds and cattle and wild animals. I will never again send another flood to destroy the earth. ¹²And I seal my promise with this sign. ¹³I have placed my rainbow in the clouds. It is a sign of my promise until the end of time, to you and to all the earth. ¹⁴When I send clouds over the earth, the rainbow will be seen in the clouds. ¹⁵I will remember my promise to you and to every being. Never again will the floods come and destroy all life. ¹⁶⁻¹⁷For I will see the rainbow in the cloud. And I will remember my eternal promise to every living being on the earth."

- *Remember:* How long did it rain? (7:17) Rain was not the only water that caused the flood. Where did the other water come from? (7:11) What did Noah build when he left the ark? Why? (8:20-21)

- *Discover:* When we see a rainbow, what promise should we remember?

- *Apply:* A rainbow reminds us that God keeps his promises. Remember to keep your promises too.

- *What's next?* A tower that touches the sky? Who tried to do that? You'll learn about this in Genesis 11:1-9. ■

Noah's Family

¹⁸The names of Noah's three sons were Shem, Ham, and Japheth. (Ham is the ancestor of the Canaanites.) ¹⁹From these three sons of Noah came all the nations of the earth.

²⁰⁻²¹Noah became a farmer. He planted a vineyard, and made wine. One day he became drunk and lay naked in his tent. ²²Ham, the father of Canaan, saw his father naked. He went outside and told his two brothers. ²³Then Shem and Japheth took a robe and held it over their shoulders. Walking backwards into the tent, they let it fall across their father. It covered his nakedness as they looked the other way. ²⁴⁻²⁵Noah awoke from his drunken stupor and learned what Ham, his younger son, had done. Then he cursed Ham's descendants:

"A curse upon the Canaanites,"
   he swore.
"May they be the lowest of slaves
To the descendants of Shem and
   Japheth."

²⁶⁻²⁷Then he said,

"God bless Shem.
May Canaan be his slave.
God bless Japheth.
Let him share the prosperity of Shem,
And let Canaan be his slave."

²⁸Noah lived another 350 years after the flood. ²⁹He was 950 years old at his death.

10 These are the families of Shem, Ham, and Japheth. They were the three sons of Noah. Sons were born to them after the flood.

²The sons of Japheth were: Gomer, Magog, Madai, Javan, Tubal, Meshech, Tiras.

³The sons of Gomer: Ashkenaz, Riphath, Togarmah.

⁴The sons of Javan: Elishah, Tarshish, Kittim, Dodanim.

⁵Their descendants became the maritime nations in various lands, each with a separate language.

⁶The sons of Ham were: Cush, Mizraim, Put, Canaan.

⁷The sons of Cush were: Seba, Havilah, Sabtah, Raamah, Sabteca.

The sons of Raamah were: Sheba, Dedan.

⁸One of the descendants of Cush was Nimrod, who became the first of the kings. ⁹He was a mighty hunter, blessed of God, and his name became famous. People would speak of someone as being "like Nimrod—a mighty hunter, blessed of God." ¹⁰The heart of his empire included Babel, Erech, Accad, and Calneh in the land of Shinar. ¹¹⁻¹²From there he extended his reign to Assyria. He built Nineveh, Rehoboth-Ir, Calah, and Resen (which is located between Nineveh and Calah), the main city of the empire.

¹³⁻¹⁴Mizraim was the ancestor of the people living in these areas: Ludim, Anamim, Lehabim, Naphtuhim, Pathrusim, Casluhim (from whom came the Philistines), and Caphtorim.

¹⁵⁻¹⁹Canaan's oldest son was Sidon, and he was also the father of Heth. These nations came from Canaan: Jebusites, Amorites, Girgashites, Hivites, Arkites, Sinites, Arvadites, Zemarites, Hamathites. Eventually the descendants of Canaan spread from Sidon all the way to Gerar, in the Gaza strip. From there they moved on to Sodom, Gomorrah, Admah, and Zeboiim, near Lasha.

²⁰These, then, were the descendants of Ham, spread abroad in many lands and nations, with many languages.

²¹Eber came from Shem, the oldest brother of Japheth. ²²Here is a list of Shem's other descendants: Elam, Asshur, Arpachshad, Lud, Aram.

²³Aram's sons were: Uz, Hul, Gether, Mash.

²⁴Arpachshad's son was Shelah, and Shelah's son was Eber.

²⁵Two sons were born to Eber: Peleg (meaning "Division," for during his lifetime the people of the world were separated and dispersed), and Joktan (Peleg's brother).

²⁶⁻³⁰Joktan was the father of Almodad, Sheleph, Hazarmaveth, Jerah, Hadoram, Uzal, Diklah, Obal, Abima-el, Sheba, Ophir, Havi-lah, Jobab.

These descendants of Joktan lived all the way from Mesha to the eastern hills of Sephar.

³¹These, then, were the descendants of Shem. They are listed by their political groupings, languages, and locations.

³²All the men listed above came from Noah, through many generations. They lived in the various nations that developed after the flood.

Building a Tower to Touch the Sky

God doesn't usually stop people from making buildings. But here is one building he wouldn't let the builders finish. It was because of the builders, not the building.

11 At that time all mankind spoke one language. ²As the population grew and spread east, a plain was discovered in the land of Babylon. Many people soon lived there. ³⁻⁴The people who lived there began to talk about building a great city. They planned to build a temple tower reaching to the skies. It would be a proud, eternal monument to themselves.

"This will weld us together," they

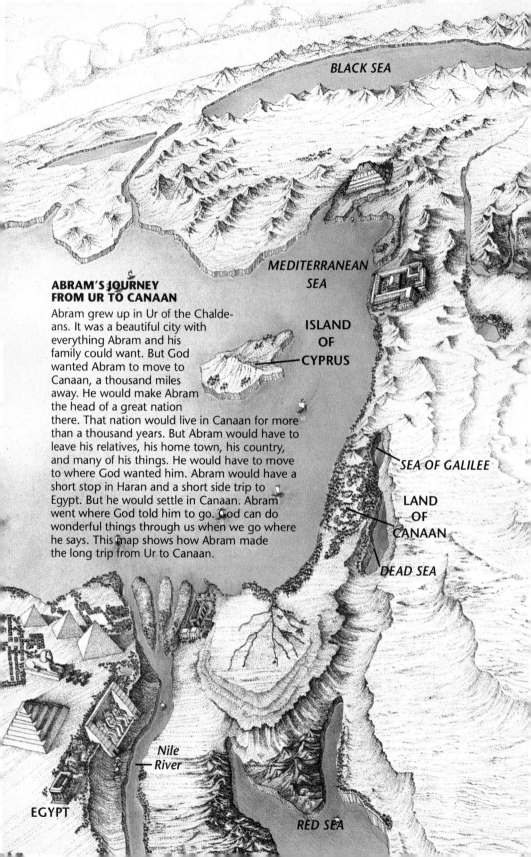

BLACK SEA

MEDITERRANEAN SEA

ABRAM'S JOURNEY FROM UR TO CANAAN

Abram grew up in Ur of the Chaldeans. It was a beautiful city with everything Abram and his family could want. But God wanted Abram to move to Canaan, a thousand miles away. He would make Abram the head of a great nation there. That nation would live in Canaan for more than a thousand years. But Abram would have to leave his relatives, his home town, his country, and many of his things. He would have to move to where God wanted him. Abram would have a short stop in Haran and a short side trip to Egypt. But he would settle in Canaan. Abram went where God told him to go. God can do wonderful things through us when we go where he says. This map shows how Abram made the long trip from Ur to Canaan.

ISLAND OF CYPRUS

SEA OF GALILEE

LAND OF CANAAN

DEAD SEA

Nile River

EGYPT

RED SEA

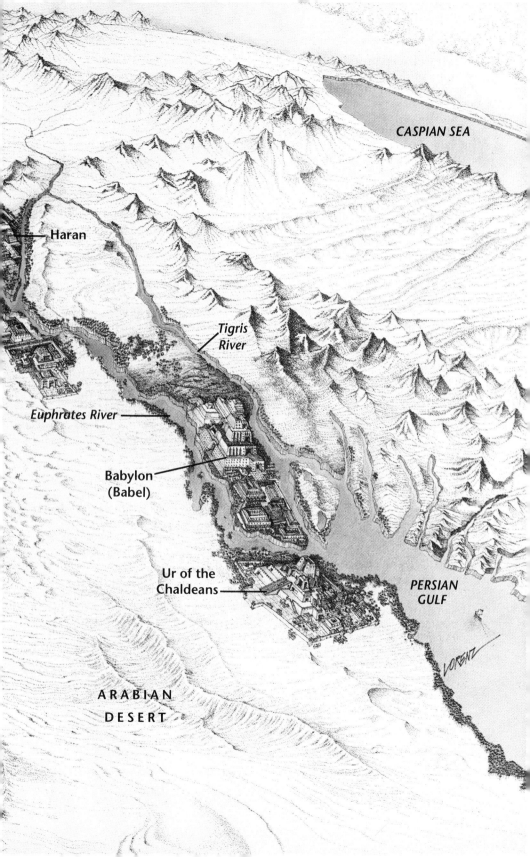

CASPIAN SEA

Haran

Tigris
River

Euphrates River

Babylon
(Babel)

Ur of the
Chaldeans

PERSIAN
GULF

VORENZ

ARABIAN
DESERT

said. "It will keep us from scattering all over the world." So they made great piles of hard brick. And they found tar to use as mortar.

⁵But God came down to see the city and the tower the men were making. ⁶He said, "Look at what they can do because they all speak the same language. Just think of what they will do later! Nothing will be impossible for them! ⁷Come, let us go down and give them different languages. Then they won't understand each other!"

⁸So, that is how God scattered them all over the earth. And that ended the building of the city. ⁹That is why the city was called Babel (meaning "confusion"). It was there that the Lord confused them by giving them many languages. Thus he widely scattered them across the face of the earth.

- *Remember:* How many languages did the people speak when they began their tower? (11:1) Where did these people live? (11:2) Why did they want to build the tower? (11:3-4) Why did God stop the people from building the tower? (11:5-6) How did God stop the people from building the tower? (11:7) What would have happened if they had tried to honor God? Would God have stopped them?

- *Discover:* When we think we're big, we think others are small, even God. Why doesn't God like that?

- *Apply:* God doesn't like pride. When you're proud you're like a balloon with too much air in it. Be careful!

- *What's next?* How would you feel if you had to move all your things to another country? What if you had nothing but carts and wagons? Read about a man who did this in Genesis 11:31–12:9. ■

Shem's Family

¹⁰⁻¹¹Shem's line of descendants included Arpachshad. He was born two years after the flood, when Shem was 100 years old. After that he lived another 500 years and had many sons and daughters.

¹²⁻¹³When Arpachshad was 35 years old, his son Shelah was born. After that he lived another 403 years and had many sons and daughters.

¹⁴⁻¹⁵Shelah was 30 years old when his son Eber was born. He lived 403 years after that, and had many sons and daughters.

¹⁶⁻¹⁷Eber was 34 years old when his son Peleg was born. He lived another 430 years after that. He had many sons and daughters.

¹⁸⁻¹⁹Peleg was 30 years old when his son Reu was born. He lived another 209 years after that and had many sons and daughters.

²⁰⁻²¹Reu was 32 years old when Serug was born. He lived 207 years after that, with many sons and daughters.

²²⁻²³Serug was 30 years old when his son Nahor was born. He lived 200 years after that, with many sons and daughters.

²⁴⁻²⁵Nahor was 29 years old at the birth of his son Terah. He lived 119 years after that and had sons and daughters.

²⁶By the time Terah was 70 years old, he had three sons, Abram, Nahor, and Haran.

²⁷And Haran had a son named Lot. ²⁸But Haran died young. He died in the land where he was born, in Ur of the Chaldeans. His father was still alive.

²⁹Meanwhile, Abram married his half-sister Sarai. His brother Nahor married Milcah. She was the daughter of Haran. She had a sister named Iscah. ³⁰But Sarai was barren. She had no children.

Abram Moves to New Lands

It's moving day without a moving van. You're moving to a new country, but you must walk! And you must not walk faster than your smallest lamb.

³¹Then Terah took his son Abram, his grandson Lot (his son Haran's child), and his daughter-in-law Sarai. He left Ur of the Chaldeans to go to the land of Canaan. But they stopped instead at the city of Haran and settled there. ³²And there Terah died at the age of 205.

12 God had told Abram, "Leave your own country behind you, and your own people. Go to the land I will guide you to. ²If you do, I will cause you to become the father of a great nation. I will bless you and make your name famous. You will be a blessing to many others. ³I will bless those who bless you. I will curse those who curse you. The entire world will be blessed because of you."

⁴So Abram left as the Lord had told him to. And Lot went with him. Abram was 75 years old at that time. ⁵He took his wife Sarai and his nephew Lot. He gathered up all his wealth—the cattle and slaves he had gotten in Haran. And they set out for Canaan and came there at last. ⁶Going through Canaan, they came to a place near Shechem. They set up camp beside the oak at Moreh. The Canaanites lived there at that time.

⁷Then the Lord appeared to Abram and said, "I am going to give this land to your descendants." And Abram built an altar there to the Lord. ⁸After that Abram left that place. He went south to the hilly country between Bethel and Ai. There he made camp. Then he built an altar to the Lord and prayed to him. ⁹Thus he kept going slowly south to the Negeb, pausing frequently.

- *Remember:* Who told Abram to move? (12:1) Who did Abram leave? (12:1) What would God do for Abram if he obeyed? (12:2) Why was it important for Abram to obey God?

- *Discover:* When God says "go," what should we do? When God says "stay," what should we do? God has good things for us when we obey.

- *Apply:* God knows what is best for you. But he can't give you his best unless you obey. Remember this the next time you want to disobey.

- *What's next?* Who do we hurt when we tell a lie? Abram could tell you. Read Genesis 12:10-20. ■

Abram and Sarai Visit Egypt

Abram told a "little" lie to keep out of trouble. But his little lie got him into BIG trouble. Read on to see how many people got hurt with Abram's little lie.

¹⁰There was at that time a bad famine in the land. So Abram went down to Egypt to live. ¹¹⁻¹³But as he came near the border of Egypt, he asked Sarai his wife to tell everyone that she was his sister! "You are very pretty," he told her. "When the Egyptians see you they will say, 'This is his wife. Let's kill him and then we can have her!' But if you say you are my sister, then the Egyptians will treat me

well because of you. They will spare my life!" [14]And sure enough, when they came to Egypt everyone spoke of her beauty. [15]When the palace aides saw her, they praised her to their king, the Pharaoh. She was then taken into his harem. [16]Then Pharaoh gave Abram many gifts because of her. He gave Abram sheep, oxen, donkeys, men and women slaves, and camels.

[17]But the Lord sent a terrible plague on Pharaoh's household on account of her being there. [18]Then Pharaoh called Abram before him and accused him sharply. "What is this you have done to me?" he demanded. "Why didn't you tell me she was your wife? [19]Why were you willing to let me marry her, saying she was your sister? Here, take her and be gone!" [20]And Pharaoh sent them out of the country under armed escort— Abram, his wife, and all his household and the things he owned.

- *Remember:* What was Abram's little lie? (12:11-13) It was half a lie because it was partly true and partly not true. Sarai was his half-sister. But she was still his wife! Is a little lie or a half-lie any better than a big lie? Why not?

- *Discover:* Which of these people were hurt by Abram's little lie—Abram, Sarai, Pharaoh, Pharaoh's people, Abram's servants? How?

- *Apply:* Half a lie is still a lie. Don't think you can get by with a little lie any more than a bigger lie. If Abram couldn't, you can't!

- *What's next?* When a generous uncle and a greedy nephew make a deal, guess what happens? You'll find out in Genesis 13. ■

Lot Leaves Abram

Lot had too many things. Too many things make people feel crowded. That makes people quarrel. Having too many things also makes people want more. Is that why Lot chose the best land for himself?

13 So they left Egypt and went north into the Negeb. Abram went with his wife, and Lot, and all that they owned. He was very rich in livestock, silver, and gold. [3-4]Then they kept going north toward Bethel where he had camped before. They camped between Bethel and Ai. Then they came to the place where he had built the altar. There he again worshiped the Lord.

[5]Lot too was very wealthy. He had sheep and cattle and many servants. [6]But the land could not support both Abram and Lot with all their flocks and herds. There were too many animals and not enough pasture. [7]So fights broke out between the herdsmen of Abram and Lot. This happened despite the danger they all faced from the tribes of Canaanites and Perizzites present in the land. [8]Then Abram talked it over with Lot.

"This fighting between our men has got to stop," he said. "We can't afford to let a rift develop between our clans. Close relatives such as we are must be united! [9]I'll tell you what we'll do. Choose any section of land you want. I will take what's left. If you want that part over there to the east, then I'll stay here in the west. Or, if you want the west, then I'll go over there to the east."

[10]Lot took a long look at the fertile plains of the Jordan River. They were well watered everywhere (this was before the Lord destroyed Sodom and Gomorrah). The whole area was like the Garden of Eden, or like the beautiful land around Zoar in Egypt. [11]So that is what Lot chose—the Jordan valley to the east of them. He went there with his flocks and servants. So he and Abram parted company. [12]Abram stayed in the

land of Canaan. But Lot lived among the cities of the plain. He settled at a place near the city of Sodom. ¹³The men of this area were very wicked. They sinned greatly against the Lord.

¹⁴After Lot was gone, the Lord spoke to Abram. He said, "Look as far as you can see in every way. ¹⁵I am going to give it all to you and your descendants. ¹⁶And I am going to give you so many descendants that, like dust, they can't be counted! ¹⁷Hike in all directions and explore the new land I am giving you." ¹⁸Then Abram moved his tent to the oaks of Mamre, near Hebron. He built an altar to the Lord there.

- *Remember:* What kind of riches did Abram have? (13:2-4) How were his riches different from riches today? What kind of people lived in Sodom? (13:13) Why do you think Lot moved there? (13:10-11)

- *Discover:* Would you rather be like Lot or Abram? Why?

- *Apply:* It's better to be a giver than a taker. What are some ways you can be a giver?

- *What's next?* How would you feel if someone in your family quarreled with you, took the best, and moved away from you? Would you risk your life to help that person? Here's a man who did. Read about him in Genesis 14. ■

Abram Rescues Lot

Lot didn't think he needed his uncle Abram. Sometimes people think that, even about special people. But guess who came to the rescue when Lot needed help?

14 Now war filled the land. Amraphel king of Shinar, Arioch king of Ellasar, Ched-or-laomer king of Elam, and Tidal king of Goiim ²fought against: Bera king of Sodom, Birsha king of Gomorrah, Shinab king of Admah, Shemeber king of Zeboiim, and the king of Bela (later called Zoar).

³These kings (of Sodom, Gomorrah, Admah, Zeboiim, and Bela) mobilized their armies in Siddim Valley (that is, the valley of the Dead Sea). ⁴For 12 years they had all been subject to King Ched-or-laomer. But now, in the 13th year, they rebelled.

⁵⁻⁶One year later, Ched-or-laomer and his allies arrived and the slaughter began. They crushed the following tribes at these places: the Rephaim in Ashteroth-karnaim; the Zuzim in Ham; the Emim in the plain of Kiriathaim; the Horites in Mount Seir, as far as El-paran at the edge of the desert.

⁷Then they swung around to Enmishpat (later called Kadesh). They destroyed the Amalekites, and also the Amorites living in Hazazan-tamar.

⁸⁻⁹But now the other army, that of the kings of Sodom, Gomorrah, Admah, Zeboiim, and Bela (Zoar), unsuccessfully attacked Ched-or-laomer and his allies as they were in the Dead Sea Valley (four kings against five). ¹⁰As it happened, the valley was full of asphalt pits. And as the army of the kings of Sodom and Gomorrah fled, some slipped into the pits. The rest fled to the mountains. ¹¹The victors plundered Sodom and Gomorrah and carried off all their wealth and food. Then they went on their way home. They took Lot with them—Abram's nephew who lived in Sodom—and all he owned. ¹³One of the men who escaped came and told Abram the Hebrew. He was camping among the oaks belonging to Mamre the Amorite (brother of Eshcol and Aner, Abram's allies).

¹⁴When Abram learned that Lot had been captured, he called all the men born into his household. There were 318 of them in all. With them, he chased after the army as far as Dan. ¹⁵He divided his men and attacked during the night from several directions. He then pursued the fleeing army to Hobah, north of Damascus. ¹⁶He got back all the loot that had been taken. He also rescued Lot, and all that Lot owned, including the women and other captives.

¹⁷As Abram came back from his strike against Ched-or-laomer and the other kings at the Valley of Shaveh (later called King's Valley), the king of Sodom came out to meet him. ¹⁸Melchizedek, the king of Salem (Jerusalem), brought Abram bread and wine. He was a priest of the God of Highest Heaven. ¹⁹⁻²⁰Then Melchizedek blessed Abram. He said:

"The blessing of the supreme God, Creator of heaven and earth, be upon you, Abram. And blessed be God, who has given your enemies over to you."

Then Abram gave Melchizedek a tenth of all the loot.

²¹The king of Sodom told him, "Just give me back my people who were captured. Keep for yourself the booty stolen from my city."

²²But Abram replied, "I made a solemn promise to the Lord, the supreme God, Creator of heaven and earth. ²³I will not take so much as a single thread from you. Then you might say, 'Abram is rich because of what I gave him!' ²⁴All I'll accept is what these young men of mine have eaten. But give a share of the loot to Aner, Eshcol, and Mamre, my allies."

• *Remember:* How did Lot get into trouble? (14:11,12) What did Abram do then? (14:14- 16) What do you think of Abram? Would you have done what Abram did?

• *Discover:* Look up Matthew 5:43-44. Who said this? When people turn against us, should we keep on doing good to them?

• *Apply:* We should help others who need us. Sometimes they are our friends. Sometimes they aren't. God helps many people who don't love him.

• *What's next?* How many stars are in the sky? Have you tried to count them? God told a man that his children would be like the stars. Find out why in Genesis 15:1–7. ■

God Makes a Promise to Abram

One night Abram and God had a little talk. Would you like to listen to what they said?

15 After this the Lord spoke to Abram in a vision. He told him, "Don't be fearful, Abram. I will defend you. And I will give you great blessings."

²⁻³But Abram replied, "O Lord God, what good are all your blessings when I have no son? For without a son, some other member of my household will get all my wealth."

⁴Then the Lord told him, "No one else will be your heir. For you will have a son to inherit all you own."

⁵Then God brought Abram outside beneath the night sky. He told him, "Look up into the heavens and count the stars if you can. Your descendants will be like that—too many to count!" ⁶And Abram believed God. Then God considered him righteous on account of his faith.

⁷And he told him, "I am the Lord who brought you out of the city of Ur of the Chaldeans, to give you this land."

• *Remember:* God showed Abram the stars. What did God say? How would Abram's children be like the stars? (15:5) Do you think Abram should believe God? Why?

• *Discover:* Should you ALWAYS believe God's promises? Why?

• *Apply:* God always keeps his promises. So should you!

• *What's next?* Have you ever heard of a woman having a baby for someone else? You'll find out why this happened in Genesis 16. ■

God Shows Abram Strange Things

8But Abram replied, "O Lord God, how can I be sure that you will give it to me?" 9Then the Lord told him to get a three-year-old heifer and a three-year-old female goat. He also told him to get a three-year-old ram, a turtledove, and a young pigeon. 10He told him to slay them. Then he was to cut them apart down the middle and divide the halves. But he was not to divide the birds. 11And when the vultures came down upon the carcasses, Abram shooed them away.

12That evening as the sun was going down, a deep sleep fell upon Abram. He saw a vision of terrible foreboding, darkness, and horror.

13Then the Lord told Abram, "Your descendants will be oppressed as slaves in a foreign land for 400 years. 14But I will punish the nation that makes them slaves. And at the end they will come away with great wealth. 15But you will die in peace, at a ripe old age. 16After four generations they will come back here to this land. For the evil Amorite nations living here now will not be ready to be punished until then."

17As the sun went down and it was dark, Abram saw a smoking firepot and a flaming torch. They passed between the halves of the carcasses. 18So that day the Lord made this covenant with Abram. He said, "I have given this land to your descendants from the Nile River to the Euphrates River. 19-21And I give to them these nations: Kenites, Kenizzites, Kadmonites, Hittites, Perizzites, Rephaim, Amorites, Canaanites, Girgashites, Jebusites."

Sarai Becomes Jealous

Sarai and Abram wanted a baby boy more than anything else in the world. God had said they would have one. But now they were getting too old. Maybe God wouldn't do what he promised. Maybe they should do something to help God. Here's what they did.

16 But Sarai and Abram had no children. So Sarai took her maid, an Egyptian girl named Hagar. 2-3She gave her to Abram to be his second wife.

"The Lord has given me no children," Sarai said to Abram. "So you may sleep with my servant girl, and her children shall be mine."

Abram agreed. (This took place 10 years after Abram had first come to the land of Canaan.) 4So he slept with Hagar, and she conceived. When she learned she was pregnant, she became very proud and arrogant toward her mistress Sarai.

5Then Sarai said to Abram, "It's all your fault. Now this servant girl of mine despises me. And it was I who let her be your wife. May the Lord judge you for doing this to me!"

6"You have my permission to punish the girl as you see fit," Abram replied. So Sarai treated her badly and she ran away.

7The Angel of the Lord found her beside a desert spring along the road to Shur.

8*The Angel:* "Hagar, Sarai's maid, where have you come from? Where are you going?"

Hagar: "I am running away from my mistress."

9-12*The Angel:* "Go back to your mistress and act as you should. For I will make you into a great nation. Yes, you are pregnant and your baby will be a son. You are to name him Ishmael ('God hears'), because God has heard your woes. This son of yours will be a wild one. He will be as free and untamed as a wild donkey! He will be against everyone, and everyone will feel the same toward him. But he will live near the rest of his kin."

13After that Hagar spoke of the Lord

as "the God who looked upon me." For it was he who appeared to her. For she thought, "I saw God and lived to tell it."

¹⁴Later that well was named "The Well of the Living One Who Sees Me." It lies between Kadesh and Bered.

¹⁵So Hagar gave Abram a son. Abram named him Ishmael. ¹⁶Abram was 86 years old at this time.

- *Remember:* Why did Sarai want Hagar to have a baby? (16:1-3) Do you think God wanted this? What kind of trouble did this cause? (16:4-7) Why did Sarai become jealous? (16:4) What do you think Sarai and Abram should have done?

- *Discover:* When we trust God to help us, let's also trust him to do it his way.

- *Apply:* Have you prayed for something? Do you want God to answer his way or your way? Would you like to pray again and ask a different way?

- *What's next?* What would you do if three angels came to your home today? If you want to see what someone else did, read Genesis 18:1-15. ∎

God and Abram Make Promises

17 When Abram was 99 years old, God appeared to him. He told Abram, "I am the Almighty. Obey me and live as you should. ²⁻⁴I will prepare a contract between us. It will promise that I will make you into a mighty nation. In fact you shall be the father of not only one nation, but many nations!" Abram fell face down in the dust as God talked with him.

⁵"What's more," God told him, "I am changing your name. It is no longer 'Abram' ('Exalted Father'), but 'Abraham' ('Father of Nations'), for that is what you will be. I have declared it. ⁶I will give you millions of descendants who will form many nations! Kings shall be among your descendants! ⁷⁻⁸And I will continue this agreement between us generation after generation, forever. It shall be between me and your children as well. It is a contract that I shall be your God and the God of those who come after you. And I will give all this land of Canaan to you and them, forever. I will be your God.

⁹⁻¹⁰"Your part of the contract," God told him, "is to obey. You and your descendants must obey my command that every male among you shall be circumcised. ¹¹This will be the proof that you and they accept this covenant. ¹²Every male shall be circumcised on the eighth day after birth. This applies to every foreign-born slave as well as to those born in your household. This is a permanent part of this contract. It applies to all who come after you. ¹³All must be circumcised. Your bodies will thus show that you are a part of my everlasting covenant. ¹⁴Anyone who refuses these terms shall be cut off from his people. For he has broken my contract."

¹⁵Then God added, "About Sarai your wife. Her name is no longer 'Sarai' but 'Sarah' ('Princess'). ¹⁶I will bless her and give you a son from her! Yes, I will bless her richly. I will make her the mother of nations! Many kings shall come from her."

¹⁷Then Abraham threw himself down in worship before the Lord. But inside he was laughing because he did not believe! "Me, be a father?" he said. "Me at 100 years old? And Sarah, to have a baby at 90?"

¹⁸And Abraham said to God, "Yes, do bless Ishmael!"

¹⁹"No," God replied. "That is not what I said. *Sarah* shall bear you a son, and you are to name him Isaac ('Laughter'). I will sign my covenant with him forever, and with his descendants. ²⁰As for Ishmael, I will bless him also, just as you have asked me to. I will cause him to become a great nation. Twelve princes shall come from him. ²¹But my contract is with Isaac. He will be born to you and Sarah next year at about this time."

²²That ended their talk and God left. ²³Then, that very day, Abraham took Ishmael his son and every other male, either born in his household or bought from outside. He circumcised them just as God had told him to. ²⁴⁻²⁷Abraham was 99 years old at that time. Ishmael was 13. Both were circumcised the same day. So were all the other men and boys of the household, whether born there or bought as slaves.

Angels Visit Abraham

One afternoon three angels came to Abraham's tent. They had good news and bad news. Read on to find the good news. If you want to read about the bad news you will find it in verses 17-23. Did you see that God changed Abram's name to Abraham and Sarai's name to Sarah? You may read about that in Genesis 17:5,15.

18 The Lord came again to Abraham while he was living in the oak grove at Mamre. This is the way it happened. One hot summer day he was sitting at the door of his tent. ²All at once he saw three men coming toward him. He jumped up and ran to meet them and welcomed them.

³⁻⁴"Sirs," he said, "please don't go any farther. Stop awhile and rest here in the shade of this tree. I will get water to refresh your feet, ⁵and a bite to eat to strengthen you. Stay awhile before continuing your journey."

"All right," they said. "Do as you have said."

⁶Then Abraham ran back to the tent and said to Sarah, "Quick! Mix up some pancakes! Use your best flour, and make enough for the three of them!" ⁷Then he ran out to the herd and chose a fat calf. He told a servant to hurry and butcher it. ⁸Soon, he took cheese and milk and the roast veal, and set it before the men. He then stood beneath the trees beside them as they ate.

⁹"Where is Sarah, your wife?" they asked him.

"In the tent," Abraham replied.

¹⁰Then the Lord said, "Next year I will give you and Sarah a son!" Sarah was listening from the tent door behind him. ¹¹Now Abraham and Sarah were both very old. And Sarah was long since past the time when she could have a baby.

¹²So Sarah laughed to herself. "A woman my age have a baby?" she scoffed to herself. "And with a husband as old as mine?"

¹³Then God said to Abraham, "Why did Sarah laugh? Why did she say 'Can an old woman like me have a baby?' ¹⁴Is anything too hard for God? Next year, just as I told you, I will see to it that Sarah has a son."

¹⁵But Sarah denied it. "I didn't laugh," she lied, for she was afraid.

- *Remember:* Where did Abraham live? (18:1) What kind of food did Abraham serve his three visitors? (18:6-8) What good news did they bring? (18:10) Why did Sarah laugh? (18:12) What would you like to tell Sarah about God?

- *Discover:* You must learn to wait for good gifts. Christmas gifts don't come on December 1, do they? God's good gifts don't always come the day you want them either. Are you patient? Will you wait for God?

- *Apply:* Think about something you have prayed for but didn't get. God may not want you to have it. Or he may be saying "wait." Say the word "wait" three times. It's a good word to learn, isn't it?

- *What's next?* Have you ever seen fire come from the sky like rain? Genesis 19:1-29 tells when that happened. ■

Abraham Prays for Sodom

¹⁶Then the men stood up from their meal and started on toward Sodom. Abraham went with them part of the way.

¹⁷"Should I hide my plan from Abraham?" God asked. ¹⁸"For Abraham shall become a mighty nation. And he will be a source of blessing for all the nations of the earth. ¹⁹I have picked him out to have godly descendants. He will have a godly household. They will be men who

are just and good so that I can do for him all I have promised."

²⁰So the Lord told Abraham, "I have heard that the people of Sodom and Gomorrah are very evil. All that they do is wicked. ²¹I am going down to see if these reports are true or not. Then I will know."

²²⁻²³So the other two went on toward Sodom. But the Lord remained with Abraham a while. Then Abraham said to him, "Will you kill good and bad alike? ²⁴Suppose you find 50 godly people there in the city. Will you destroy it, and not spare it for their sakes? ²⁵That wouldn't be right! Surely you wouldn't do such a thing, to kill the godly with the wicked! Why, you would be treating godly and wicked the same! Surely you wouldn't do that! Should not the Judge of all the earth be fair?"

²⁶And God replied, "If I find 50 godly people there, I will spare the entire city for their sake."

²⁷Then Abraham spoke again. "Since I have begun, let me go on and speak further to the Lord, though I am but dust and ashes. ²⁸What if there are only 45? Will you destroy the city for lack of five?"

And God said, "I will not destroy it if I find 45."

God can do anything

Is anything too hard for God?

Genesis 18:14

---

²⁹Then Abraham went further with his request. *"Suppose there are only 40?"*

And God replied, "I won't destroy it if there are 40."

³⁰"Please don't be angry," Abraham pleaded. "Let me speak. *What if only 30 are found there?"*

And God replied, "I won't do it if there are 30 there."

³¹Then Abraham said, "Since I have dared to speak to God, let me continue. *Suppose there are only 20?"*

And God said, "Then I won't destroy it for the sake of the 20."

³²Finally, Abraham said, "Oh, let not the Lord be angry. I will speak but this once more! *What if only 10 are found?"*

And God said, "Then, for the sake of the ten, I won't destroy it."

³³And the Lord went on his way when he had finished his talk with Abraham. And Abraham went back to his tent.

God Destroys Sodom

Suppose some angels came to your house today. What if they said, "Get out of here fast! Something terrible is about to happen!" How fast would you run?

19 That evening the two angels came to the entrance of the city of Sodom. Lot was sitting there as they arrived. When he saw them he stood up to meet them and welcomed them.

²"Sirs," he said, "come to my home. Be my guests for the night. You can get up as early as you like and be on your way again."

"No thanks," they said. "We'll just stretch out here along the street."

³But he was very urgent, until at last they went home with him. He set a great feast before them, complete with freshly baked bread. After the meal, ⁴they prepared to retire for the night. But the men of the city—Sodomites, young and old from all over the city—surrounded the house. ⁵They shouted to Lot, "Bring out those men to us so we can abuse them."

⁶Lot stepped outside to talk to them. He shut the door behind him. ⁷"Please,

men," he begged, "don't do such a wicked thing. ⁸Look, I have two daughters. I'll give them to you to do with as you wish. But leave these men alone. They are under my roof."

⁹"Stand back," they yelled. "Who do you think you are? We let this man settle among us and now he tries to tell us what to do! We'll deal with you far worse than with those other men." And they lunged at Lot and began breaking down the door.

¹⁰But the two men inside reached out and pulled Lot in and bolted the door. ¹¹They blinded the men of Sodom for awhile so that they could not find the door.

¹²"What relatives do you have here in the city?" the men asked. "Get them out of this place—sons, daughters, sons-in-law, or anyone else. ¹³For we will destroy the city. The stench of the place has reached to heaven and God has sent us to destroy it."

¹⁴So Lot rushed out to tell the young men who were to marry his daughters. "Quick, get out of the city! The Lord is going to destroy it." But the young men looked at him as though he were crazy.

¹⁵At dawn the next morning the angels became urgent. "Hurry," they said to Lot. "Take your wife and your two daughters who are here. Get out while you can, or you will be caught when the city is destroyed."

¹⁶When Lot still did not go, the angels seized his hand. They also took the hands of his wife and two daughters. They rushed them to safety outside the city, for the Lord was kind.

¹⁷"Flee for your lives," the angels told him. *"And don't look back.* Escape to the mountains. Don't stay down here on the plain or you will die."

¹⁸⁻²⁰"Oh no, sirs, please," Lot begged. "You've been so kind to me and saved my life. You've granted me such mercy. Let me flee to that little town over there instead of into the mountains. For I fear disaster in the mountains. See, the town is close by and it is just a small one. Please, please, let me go there instead. Don't you see how small it is? And my life will be saved."

²¹"All right," the angel said, "I won't destroy that little town. ²²But hurry! For I can do nothing until you are there." (From that time on that town was named Zoar, meaning "Little City.")

²³The sun was rising as Lot reached the town. ²⁴Then the Lord rained down fire and flaming tar from heaven upon Sodom and Gomorrah. ²⁵He utterly destroyed them, along with the other cities and towns of the plain. All life was wiped out — people, plants, and animals alike.

²⁶Lot's wife looked back as she was following along behind him. And she became a pillar of salt.

²⁷That morning Abraham was up early. He hurried out to the place where he had stood before the Lord. ²⁸He looked out across the plain to Sodom and Gomorrah. In the distance he saw columns of smoke and fumes, as from a furnace, rising from the cities there. ²⁹So God heeded Abraham's plea and kept Lot safe. He removed him from the rainstorm of death that engulfed the cities.

● *Remember:* Who visited Lot at Sodom? (19:1) Why did they tell him to get out of Sodom? (19:13) What did Lot's sons-in-law do about this? (19:14) How fast did Lot leave? (19:16) How did Lot's wife not obey God? (19:26) What kind of people were Lot's family? What do you think about each one?

● *Discover:* God wanted to help Lot and his family. But most of his family wouldn't let him. It's not easy to help people who won't let you help them.

● *Apply:* How can God help us if we don't let him? What does Psalm 119:33-34 tell you about obeying God?

● *What's next?* A new baby for a 100-year-old man? It's true, and it's in Genesis 21:1-21. ■

The Sin of Lot's Daughters

³⁰After that Lot left Zoar, fearful of the people there. He went to live in a cave in the mountains with his two daughters. ³¹One day the older girl said to her sister, "There isn't a man anywhere in this area that our father would let us marry. And our father will soon be too old to have children. ³²Come, let's fill him with wine and then we will sleep with him. That way our clan will not come to an end." ³³So they got him drunk that night. Then the older girl

went in and lay with him. But he did not know she was there.

34The next morning she said to her younger sister, "I slept with my father last night. Let's fill him with wine again tonight. Then you go in and lie with him. That way our family line will not end." 35So they got him drunk again that night. The younger girl went in and lay with him. And, as before, he didn't know that anyone was there. 36And so it was that both girls became pregnant from their father. 37The older girl's baby was named Moab. He became the father of the nation of the Moabites. 38The name of the younger girl's baby was Benammi. He became the father of the nation of the Ammonites.

Abraham Tricks the King

20 Now Abraham moved south to the Negeb. He settled between Kadesh and Shur. One day, when visiting the city of Gerar, 2he said that Sarah was his sister! Then King Abimelech sent for her. He had her brought to him at his palace.

3But that night God came to him in a dream. He told him, "You are a dead man. That woman you took is married."

4But Abimelech had not slept with her yet. So he said, "Lord, will you slay an innocent man? 5He told me, 'She is my sister.' And she herself said, 'Yes, he is my brother.' I was not going to do anything wrong."

6"Yes, I know," the Lord replied. "That is why I held you back from sinning against me. That is why I didn't let you touch her. 7Now restore her to her husband. He will pray for you (for he is a prophet) and you shall live. But if you don't return her to him, you are doomed to death along with all your household."

8The king was up early the next morning. He quickly called a meeting of all the palace staff and told them what had happened. And great fear swept through the crowd.

9-10Then the king called for Abraham. "What is this you've done to us?" he demanded. "What have I done that deserves treatment like this? How could you make me and my kingdom guilty of this great sin? Who would suspect that you would do a thing like this to me? Whatever made you think of this vile deed?"

11-12"Well," Abraham said, "I figured this to be a godless place. 'They will want my wife and will kill me to get her,' I thought. And besides, she *is* my sister. Or at least she is my half-sister (we both have the same father). And I married her. 13And when God sent me far from my childhood home, I told her, 'Have the kindness to mention, wherever we come, that you are my sister.'"

14Then King Abimelech took sheep and oxen and servants—both men and women—and gave them to Abraham. The king also returned Sarah his wife to him.

15"Look my kingdom over, and choose the place where you want to live," the king told him. 16Then he turned to Sarah. "Look," he said. "I am giving your 'brother' 1000 silver pieces as damages for what I did. This will pay for any wrong done. It will settle any claim against me in this matter. Now justice has been done."

17Then Abraham prayed. He asked God to cure the king and queen and the other women of the household, so that they could have children. 18For God had stricken all the women with barrenness to punish Abimelech for taking Abraham's wife.

Isaac Is Born

A baby boy is born. His parents give him a name that means "Laughter." So why aren't they laughing? Why is this boy causing trouble between them?

21 Then God did as he had promised. Sarah became pregnant and gave Abraham a baby son in his old age. And it happened at the time God had said. ³Abraham named him Isaac (meaning "Laughter!"). ⁴⁻⁵Eight days after he was born, Abraham circumcised him, as God required. Abraham was 100 years old at that time.

⁶Sarah said, "God has brought me laughter! All who hear about this shall rejoice with me. ⁷For who would have dreamed that I would ever have a baby? Yet I have given Abraham a child in his old age!"

⁸Time went by and the child grew and was weaned. Abraham gave a party to celebrate the happy occasion. ⁹But Sarah saw Ishmael—the son of Abraham and the Egyptian girl Hagar—teasing Isaac. ¹⁰She turned upon Abraham and demanded, "Get rid of that slave girl and her son. He is not going to share your property with my son. I won't have it."

¹¹This upset Abraham very much. After all, Ishmael was his son too.

¹²But God told Abraham, "Don't be upset over the boy or your slave-girl wife. Do as Sarah says, for Isaac is the son through whom my promise will be fulfilled. ¹³And I will make a nation of the descendants of the slave-girl's son, too. For he also is yours."

¹⁴So Abraham got up early the next morning and prepared food for the trip. He strapped a canteen of water to Hagar's shoulders. Then he sent her away with their son. She walked out into the wilderness of Beersheba, wandering aimlessly.

¹⁵When the water was gone Hagar left the boy in the shade of a bush. ¹⁶She went off and sat down 100 yards or so away. "I don't want to watch him die," she said. Then she burst into tears.

¹⁷God heard the boy crying. And the Angel of God called to Hagar from the sky, "Hagar, what's wrong? Don't be afraid! God has heard the boy's cries as he is lying there. ¹⁸Go and get him and comfort him. I will make a great nation from his descendants."

¹⁹Then God opened her eyes and she saw a well. So she refilled the canteen and gave the boy a drink. ²⁰⁻²¹And God blessed the boy. He grew up in the wilderness of Paran and became an expert archer. And his mother arranged a marriage for him with a girl from Egypt.

- *Remember:* Who named Isaac, and what did his name mean? (21:3) What caused Sarah to be upset with Abraham's other son? (21:9) What did Sarah want Abraham to do? (21:10) Why? What do you think about this? Do you think Sarah was right or wrong? Why?

- *Discover:* Have you ever been jealous and not wanted to share? That's why Sarah wanted to get rid of Hagar and Ishmael. She did not want Ishmael to share Isaac's inheritance. (21:10)

- *Apply:* What if Abraham and Sarah had been poor people? What if they had no money for either son to inherit? How would Sarah have felt different? Refusing to share causes many of our ugly feelings, doesn't it?

- *What's next?* Have you ever said, "I can't do it," but you did it anyway? The next story is about a man who must have said, "I can't do it." ∎

The Agreement at the Well

²²About this time King Abimelech and Phicol, leader of his troops, came to Abraham. They said to him, "It is clear that God helps you in all you do. ²³Swear to me by God's name that you won't

cheat me or my son or my grandson. Promise that you will be on friendly terms with my country, as I have been toward you."

²⁴Abraham replied, "All right, I promise!" ²⁵Then Abraham complained to the king about a well the king's servants had taken away from Abraham's servants.

²⁶"This is the first I've heard of it!" the king exclaimed. "And I have no idea who did it. Why didn't you tell me before?"

²⁷Then Abraham gave sheep and oxen to the king, as sacrifices to seal their pact. ²⁸⁻²⁹He took seven ewe lambs and set them off by themselves. And the king asked, "Why are you doing that?"

³⁰And Abraham said, "They are my gift to you as a public sign that this well is mine."

³¹So from that time on the well was called Beer-sheba ("Well of the Oath"). It marked the place where they made their covenant. ³²Then King Abimelech and Phicol, leader of his army, went home again. ³³Abraham planted a tamarisk tree beside the well. He prayed there to the Lord, calling upon the Eternal God. ³⁴And Abraham lived in the Philistine country for a long time.

Abraham Offers Isaac

Has anyone ever asked you to do something hard? Have you ever said, "I can't do it"? One day God asked Abraham to give up his son. He told Abraham to sacrifice Isaac on an altar. How could he do it? Would Abraham obey? Or would he say, "I can't do it"? This is what Abraham did.

22 Later on, God tested Abraham's faith and obedience.

"Abraham!" God called.

"Yes, Lord?" he replied.

²"Take your only son Isaac whom you love so much. Go to the land of Moriah. Sacrifice him there as a burnt offering upon one of the mountains which I'll point out to you!"

³The next morning Abraham got up early. He chopped wood for a fire upon the altar, and saddled his donkey. He took with him his son Isaac and two young men who were his servants. They started off to the place where God had told Abraham to go. ⁴On the third day of the trip Abraham saw the place in the distance.

⁵"Stay here with the donkey," Abra-ham told the young men. "The boy and I will travel over there and worship. Then we will come right back."

⁶Abraham placed the wood for the burnt offering on Isaac's shoulders. He himself carried the knife and the flint for striking a fire. So the two of them went on together.

⁷"Father," Isaac said, "we have the wood and the flint to make the fire. But where is the lamb for the sacrifice?"

⁸"God will see to it, my son," Abra-ham replied. And they went on.

⁹When they came to the place where God had told Abraham to go, he built an altar. He placed the wood in order, ready for the fire. Then he tied Isaac and laid him on the altar over the wood. ¹⁰Abraham took the knife and

lifted it up to plunge it into his son, to slay him.

¹¹At that moment the Angel of God shouted to him from heaven, "Abraham! Abraham!"

"Yes, Lord!" he answered.

¹²"Lay down the knife. Don't hurt the boy in any way," the Angel said. "For I know that God is first in your life. You have not withheld even your beloved son from me."

¹³Then Abraham saw a ram caught by its horns in a bush. So he took the ram. He sacrificed it instead of his son as a burnt offering on the altar. ¹⁴Abraham named the place "the Lord provides." It still goes by that name to this day.

¹⁵Then the Angel of God called again to Abraham from heaven. ¹⁶"I, the Lord, have sworn by myself that because you have obeyed me and have not withheld even your beloved son from me, ¹⁷I will bless you with great blessings. I will multiply your descendants into countless thousands and millions. They will be like the stars above you in the sky, and like the sands along the seashore. They will conquer their enemies. ¹⁸And your offspring will be a blessing to all the nations of the earth—all because you have obeyed me."

¹⁹So they returned to his young men and traveled home again to Beer-sheba.

- *Remember:* What did God tell Abraham to do to Isaac? (22:2) Did Abraham argue with God? Did he say, "I can't do it"? How did Abraham obey God? (22:3-9) What makes you think Abraham trusted God?

- *Discover:* Would you do ANYTHING God told you to do? Anything?

- *Apply:* God wants you to do three simple things today. They are not hard to do. Will you do them? God wants you to pray. He wants you to read your Bible. He wants you to obey him and your parents. If Abraham could obey God for something tough, can't we obey him for something easy?

- *What's next?* A servant becomes a matchmaker. It's his job to find a wife for another man. You'll read about this in Genesis 24. ■

Nahor's Family

²⁰⁻²³After this, a message arrived that Milcah, the wife of Abraham's brother Nahor, had borne him eight sons. Their names were: Uz, the oldest, Buz, the next oldest, Kemuel (father of Aram), Chesed, Hazo, Pildash, Jidlaph, Bethuel (father of Rebekah).

²⁴He also had four other children from his concubine, Reumah: Tebah, Gaham, Tahash, Maacah.

Sarah Dies

23 When Sarah was 127 years old, she died in Hebron in the land of Canaan. There Abraham mourned and wept for her. ³Then, standing beside her body, he said to the men of Heth:

⁴"Here I am, a visitor in a foreign land. I have no place to bury my wife. Please sell me a piece of ground for this purpose."

⁵⁻⁶"Certainly," the men replied. "You are an honored prince of God among us. It will be an honor to have you choose the finest of our tombs, so that you can bury her there."

⁷Abraham bowed low before them. Then he said, ⁸"Since this is your feeling in the matter, be so kind as to ask Ephron, Zohar's son, ⁹to sell me the cave of Mach-pelah. It is the one down at the end of his field. I will of course pay the full price for it, whatever is publicly agreed upon. It will become a cemetery for my family."

¹⁰Ephron was sitting there among the others. Now he spoke up. He answered Abraham as the others listened, speaking publicly before all the citizens of the town. ¹¹"Sir," he said to Abraham, "please listen to me. I will give you the cave and the field without any charge. Here in the presence of my people, I give it to you free. Go and bury your dead."

¹²Abraham bowed again to the men of Heth. ¹³He said to Ephron, as all listened: "No, let me buy it from you. Let me pay the full price of the field. Then I will bury my dead."

¹⁴⁻¹⁵"Well, the land is worth 400 pieces of silver," Ephron said. "But what is that between friends? Go ahead and bury your dead."

[16]So Abraham paid Ephron the price he had suggested—400 pieces of silver, as publicly agreed. [17-18]This is the land he bought: Ephron's field at Mach-pelah, near Mamre. This included the cave at the end of the field and all the trees in the field. They became his own land as agreed upon in the presence of the men of Heth at the city gate. [19-20]So Abraham buried Sarah there, in the field and cave deeded to him by the men of Heth as a burial plot.

Isaac Gets Married

It was time for Abraham's son Isaac to get married. But there was not one girl in the neighborhood for him to marry. Why? Because the neighbor girls did not believe in God. God had chosen Isaac to be the next leader of his people. So how could Isaac marry a girl who didn't believe in God? Here's what Abraham did about this problem.

24 Abraham was now a very old man. God had blessed him in every way. [2] One day Abraham called his household manager, who was his oldest servant. He said to him,

[3]"Promise by the Lord, the God of heaven and earth, that you will not let my son marry one of these local girls, these Canaanites. [4]Go instead to my homeland. Go to my relatives and find a wife for him there."

[5]"But what if I can't find a girl who will come so far from home?" the servant asked. "Then shall I take Isaac there, to live among your relatives?"

[6]"No!" Abraham warned. "Be careful that you don't do that no matter what. [7]For the Lord God of heaven told me to leave that land and my people. He promised to give me and my children this land. God will send his angel on ahead of you. And he will see to it that you find a girl from there to be my son's wife. [8]If you don't succeed, then you are free from this oath. But you must not take my son there."

[9]So the servant vowed to do what Abraham had told him.

[10]He took with him 10 of Abraham's camels loaded with samples of the best his master owned. He then went to Iraq, to Nahor's village. [11]There he made the camels kneel down outside the town, beside a spring. It was evening, and the women of the village were coming to draw water.

[12]"O Lord, the God of my master," he prayed. "Show kindness to my master Abraham. Help me to fulfill the purpose of my journey. [13]Here I am, standing beside this spring. And the girls of the village are coming out to draw water. [14]This is my request: When I ask one of them for a drink and she says, 'Yes, and I will water your camels too!'—let her be the one you have chosen to be Isaac's wife. That is how I will know."

God sends his angels to help us

God will send his angel on ahead of you.

Genesis 24:7

[15-16]As he was still speaking to the Lord about this, a pretty young girl named Rebekah arrived. She was carrying a water jug on her shoulder. She filled it at the spring. Her father was Bethuel, the son of Nahor and his wife, Milcah. [17]Running over to her, the servant asked her for a drink.

[18]"Of course, sir," she said. Then she quickly lowered the jug for him to drink. [19]Then she said, "I'll draw water for your camels, too, until they have enough!"

[20]So she emptied the jug into the water trough and ran down to the spring

again. She kept carrying water to the camels until they had enough. ²¹The servant said no more. But he watched her closely to see if she would finish the job. In that way, he would know if she was the one. ²²Then at last, when the camels had finished drinking, he gave her a quarter-ounce gold earring and gold bracelets for her wrists.

²³"Whose daughter are you?" he asked. "Would your father have any room to put us up for the night?"

²⁴"My father is Bethuel," she replied. "My grandparents are Milcah and Nahor. ²⁵Yes, we have plenty of straw and food for the camels, and a guest room."

²⁶The man stood there a moment with head bowed. He was worshiping the Lord. ²⁷"Thank you, Lord God of my master Abraham," he prayed. "Thank you for being so kind and true to him. Thank you for leading me straight to the family of my master's relatives."

²⁸The girl ran home to tell her parents. ²⁹⁻³⁰Her brother Laban saw the ring and the bracelets on his sister's wrists. And after hearing her story, he rushed out to the spring where the man was still standing beside his camels. Laban said to him, ³¹"Come and stay with us, friend. Why stand here outside the city? We have a room all ready for you, and a place prepared for the camels!"

³²So the man went home with Laban. Laban gave him straw to bed down the camels. He also gave him feed for them. He supplied water for the camel drivers to wash their feet. ³³Then supper was served. But the old man said, "I don't want to eat until I have told you why I am here."

"All right," Laban said, "tell us your errand."

³⁴"I am Abraham's servant," he said. ³⁵"And the Lord has flooded my master with blessings. He has become a great man among the people of his land. God has given him flocks of sheep and herds of cattle. He has a fortune in silver and gold, and many slaves and camels and donkeys.

³⁶"Now when Sarah, my master's wife, was very old, she gave birth to my master's son. And my master has given him all he owns. ³⁷And my master made me promise not to let Isaac marry one of the local girls. ³⁸He told me to come to his relatives here in this far-off land. I am to bring back a girl from here to marry his son. ³⁹'But what if I can't find a girl who will come?' I asked him. ⁴⁰'She will,' he told me. 'For my Lord, in whose presence I have walked, will send his angel with you. He will make your mission successful. Yes, find a girl from among my relatives. ⁴¹You are under oath to go and ask. If they won't send anyone, then you are freed from your promise.'

⁴²"Well, this evening when I came to the spring I prayed this prayer: 'O Lord, the God of my master Abraham. Please make my mission a success. Please guide me in this way. ⁴³Here I am, standing beside this spring. I will say to some girl who comes out to draw water, "Please give me a drink of water!" ⁴⁴And she will reply, "Yes! And I'll water your camels too!" Let that girl be the one you have selected to be the wife of my master's son.'

⁴⁵"Well, while I was still speaking these words, Rebekah was coming along. She had her water jug on her shoulder. And she went down to the spring and drew water and filled the jug. I said to her, 'Please give me a drink.' ⁴⁶She quickly lifted the jug down from her shoulder so that I could drink. Then she told me, 'Of course, sir, and I will water your camels too!' So she did! ⁴⁷Then I asked her, 'Whose family are you from?' And she told me, 'Nahor's. My father is Bethuel, the son of Nahor and his wife, Milcah.' So I gave her the ring and the bracelets. ⁴⁸Then I bowed my head and worshiped and blessed the Lord, the God of my master Abraham. For he had led me along just the right path to find a girl from the family of my master's brother. ⁴⁹So tell me, yes or no. Will you or won't you be kind to my master and do what is right? When you tell me, then I'll know what my next step should be. I'll know whether to move this way or that."

⁵⁰Then Laban and Bethuel replied,

"The Lord has clearly brought you here, so what can we say? ⁵¹Take her and go! Yes, let her be the wife of your master's son, as the Lord has directed."

⁵²At this reply, Abraham's servant fell to his knees before the Lord. ⁵³Then he brought out jewels set in solid gold and silver for Rebekah, and lovely clothing. And he gave many costly presents to her mother and brother. ⁵⁴Then they had supper, and the servant and the men with him stayed there overnight. But early the next morning he said, "Send me back to my master!"

⁵⁵"But we want Rebekah here at least another 10 days or so!" her mother and brother exclaimed. "Then she can go."

⁵⁶But he pleaded, "Don't hinder my return. The Lord has made my mission a success, and I want to report back to my master."

⁵⁷"Well," they said, "we'll call the girl and ask her what she thinks."

⁵⁸So they called Rebekah. "Are you willing to go with this man?" they asked her.

And she replied, "Yes, I will go."

⁵⁹So they told her good-bye, sending along the woman who had been her childhood nurse. ⁶⁰They blessed her with this blessing as they parted:

"Our sister,
May you become
The mother of many millions!
May your descendants
Overcome all your enemies."

⁶¹So Rebekah and her servant girls mounted the camels and went with him. ⁶²Meanwhile, Isaac, whose home was in the Negeb, had returned to Beer-lahai-roi. ⁶³One evening he was taking a walk out in the fields, thinking about God. As he looked up, he saw the camels coming. ⁶⁴Rebekah saw him and quickly got down from her camel.

⁶⁵"Who is that man walking through the fields to meet us?" she asked the servant.

And he replied, "It is my master's son!" So she covered her face with her veil. ⁶⁶Then the servant told Isaac the whole story.

⁶⁷And Isaac brought Rebekah into his mother's tent, and she became his wife.

He loved her very much. And she was a special comfort to him after the loss of his mother.

- *Remember:* Whom did Abraham send to find Isaac's bride? (24:4) The servant asked God to show him the girl he wanted Isaac to marry. How would God do that? (24:14). Why was the servant wise to ask God's help? Why didn't he do all this himself?

- *Discover:* Which of these words describe Rebekah: serving, kind, helping? (Read 24:18-20) Why was it important for Rebekah to be serving, kind, and helping?

- *Apply:* Think of someone you know who is serving, kind, and helping. Do you like that kind of person? Would you like to be that kind of person? What are some of the things you can do to show that you are serving, kind, and helping?

- *What's next?* Would you trade everything you have for a bowl of stew? Read about a man who did this in Genesis 25:27-34. ▪

Abraham Dies

25 Now Abraham married again. Keturah was his new wife, and she bore him several children: Zimran, Jokshan, Medan, Midian, Ishbak, Shuah. ³Jokshan's two sons were Sheba and Dedan. Dedan's sons were Asshurim, Letushim, and Leummim. ⁴Midian's sons were Ephah, Epher, Hanoch, Abida, and Eldaah.

⁵Abraham deeded all he owned to Isaac. ⁶However, he gave gifts to the sons of his concubines. He then sent them off into the east, away from Isaac.

⁷⁻⁸Then Abraham died, at the ripe old age of 175. ⁹⁻¹⁰And his sons Isaac and Ishmael buried him in the cave of Machpelah near Mamre, in the field Abraham had bought from Ephron the son of Zohar, the Hethite. There Abraham was buried with his wife, Sarah.

¹¹After Abraham's death, God poured out rich blessings upon Isaac. Isaac had now moved south to Beer-lahai-roi in the Negeb.

¹²⁻¹⁵Here is a list, in the order of their births, of the descendants of Ishmael, who was the son of Abraham and Hagar the Egyptian, Sarah's slave girl: Neba-

ioth, Kedar, Abdeel, Mibsam, Mishma, Dumah, Massa, Hadad, Tema, Jetur, Naphish, Kedemah. ¹⁶These 12 sons of his became the founders of 12 tribes that bore their names. ¹⁷Ishmael finally died at the age of 137 and joined his ancestors. ¹⁸These descendants of Ishmael were scattered across the country from Havilah to Shur. This is a little way to the northeast of the Egyptian border in the direction of Assyria. And they were always at war with each other.

Jacob and Esau Are Born

¹⁹This is the story of Isaac's children. ²⁰Isaac was 40 years old when he married Rebekah, the daughter of Bethuel the Aramean from Paddan-aram. Rebekah was the sister of Laban. ²¹Isaac pleaded with the Lord to give Rebekah a child.

For even after many years of marriage she had no children. Then at last she became pregnant. ²²And it seemed as though children were fighting each other inside her!

"I can't endure this!" she exclaimed. So she asked the Lord about it.

²³And he told her, "The sons in your womb shall become two rival nations. One will be stronger than the other. And the older shall be a servant of the younger!"

²⁴And sure enough, she had twins. ²⁵The first was born so covered with reddish hair that one would think he was wearing a fur coat! So they called him "Esau." ²⁶Then the other twin was born with his hand on Esau's heel! So they called him Jacob (meaning "Grabber"). Isaac was 60 years old when the twins were born.

Esau Sells His Birthright

Jacob wanted his brother Esau's birthright. If he had that, he would be head of the family some day. But how could he get it from Esau? Here's how it happened.

²⁷As the boys grew, Esau became a skillful hunter. But Jacob was quiet and liked to stay at home. ²⁸Isaac's favorite was Esau, because of the deer meat he brought home. But Rebekah's favorite was Jacob.

²⁹One day Jacob was cooking stew when Esau came home tired from the hunt.

³⁰*Esau:* "Boy, am I starved! Give me a bite of that red stuff there!" (From this came his nickname "Edom," which means "Red Stuff.")

³¹*Jacob:* "All right, trade me your birthright for it!"

³²*Esau:* "When a man is dying of starvation, what good is his birthright?"

³³*Jacob:* "Well then, vow to God that it is mine!"

And Esau vowed. So he sold all his rights as the oldest son to his younger brother. ³⁴Then Jacob gave Esau bread, peas, and stew. So he ate and drank and went on about his business. He did not seem to care that he had thrown away his birthright.

- *Remember:* Which son was Isaac's favorite? Why? (25:28) What did Easu want from Jacob? (25:30) What did Jacob want from Esau? (25:31) Was Esau sorry that he traded his birthright for Jacob's stew? (25:34)

- *Discover:* Don't pay too much for something just because you want it!

- *Apply:* How much will you pay or give up for something you want? Do you want your friends to like you? Will you give up being God's friend to be their friend?

- *What's next?* Someone is mean to you and tries to hurt you. What would you do? Read what one person did in Genesis 26:12-22. ■

Isaac Tricks the King

26 Now a severe famine was in the land. It was as bad as the one in Abraham's time. So Isaac moved to the city of Gerar where Abimelech, king of the Philistines, lived.

²The Lord appeared to him there and said, "Don't go to Egypt. ³Do as I say and stay here in this land. If you do, I will be with you and bless you. I will give all this land to you and to your descendants, just as I promised Abraham your father. ⁴I will give you as many descendants as there are stars! And I will give them all of these lands. And they shall be a blessing to all the nations of the earth. ⁵I will do this because Abraham obeyed me and my laws."

⁶So Isaac stayed in Gerar. ⁷And when the men there asked him about Rebekah, he said, "She is my sister!" For he feared for his life if he told them she was his wife. He was afraid they would kill him to get her, for she was very pretty. ⁸But sometime later, King Abimelech, king of the Philistines, looked out of a window and saw Isaac and Rebekah loving each other.

⁹Abimelech called for Isaac and exclaimed, "She is your wife! Why did you say she is your sister?"

"Because I was afraid I would be murdered," Isaac replied. "I thought someone would kill me to get her from me."

¹⁰"How could you treat us this way?" Abimelech exclaimed. "Someone might have tried to lie with her, and we would be doomed." ¹¹Then Abimelech made a public statement: "Anyone harming this man or his wife shall die."

Isaac Gives Up His Wells

Isaac had good crops. His flocks and herds did well. He became rich. But his Philistine neighbors became jealous. So they filled his wells with dirt. That was a mean thing to do. What would you like to do to a person who does something mean to you? Read on to find out what Isaac did.

¹²That year Isaac's crops were huge. The yield was 100 times the grain he planted, for the Lord blessed him. ¹³He was soon a man of great wealth and became richer and richer. ¹⁴He had large flocks of sheep and goats, great herds of cattle, and many servants. And the Philistines became jealous of him. ¹⁵So they filled up his wells with earth. They were the wells dug by the servants of his father Abraham.

¹⁶And King Abimelech asked Isaac to leave the country. "Go somewhere else," he said, "for you have become too rich and powerful for us."

¹⁷So Isaac moved to Gerar Valley and lived there instead. ¹⁸And Isaac redug the wells of his father Abraham. They were the ones the Philistines had filled after his father's death. And he gave them the same names they had had before, when his father had named them. ¹⁹His shepherds also dug a new well in Gerar Valley and found a gushing spring.

²⁰Then the local shepherds came and claimed it. "This is our land and our well," they said. They argued over it with Isaac's herdsmen. So he named the well, "The Well of Argument!" ²¹Isaac's men then dug another well, but again there was a fight over it. So he called it, "The Well of Anger." ²²Leaving that one, he dug again, and the local people left him alone at last. So he called it, "The Well of Room Enough for Us at Last!" "For now at last," he said, "the Lord has made room for us and we shall thrive."

- *Remember:* How good were Isaac's crops? (26:12) Isaac's Philistine neighbors were jealous. So what did they do to him? (26:15) Instead of fighting, what did Isaac do? (26:17-22) What would you have done if you were Isaac?

- *Discover:* Sometimes it's better to give up something than to fight for it. Sometimes it's better to be quiet than win an argument.

- *Apply:* The next time you have a fight, stop! Ask: is it worth more to keep a friend or win the fight? The next time someone wants to fight about something, stop! Ask: is this worth the fight?

- *What's next?* Someone hurts you. Then he wants to be a friend. Should you get even? Or should you become friends? Read about what Isaac did in Genesis 26:23-35. ■

Isaac Becomes a Friend

Do you remember the Philistines? They were the nasty neighbors who filled Isaac's wells with dirt. One day the Philistine king came to see Isaac. He brought his army commander with him. Isaac was sure they wanted to cause more trouble. But they didn't. This is what they wanted.

²³When he went to Beer-sheba, ²⁴the Lord appeared to him on the night of his arrival. "I am the God of Abraham your father," he said. "Fear not, for I am with you and will bless you. I will give you so many descendants that they will become a great nation. I will do this because of my promise to Abraham, who obeyed me." ²⁵Then Isaac built an altar and worshiped the Lord. And he settled

there, and his servants dug a well.

²⁶One day Isaac had visitors from Gerar. King Abimelech came with his advisor, Ahuzzath. He also brought Phicol, the leader of his army.

²⁷"Why have you come?" Isaac asked them. "This is clearly no friendly visit, since you kicked me out in a most unkind way."

²⁸"Well," they said, "we can plainly see that the Lord is blessing you. We've decided to ask for a treaty between us. ²⁹Promise that you will not harm us, just as we have not harmed you. In fact, we have done only good to you and have sent you away in peace. We bless you in the name of the Lord."

³⁰So Isaac prepared a great feast for them. And they ate and drank to prepare for the treaty ceremonies. ³¹In the morning, as soon as they were up, they each took solemn oaths to seal a peace treaty. Then Isaac sent them happily home again.

³²That very same day Isaac's servants came to him. They told him they had found water in the well they had been digging. ³³So he named the well, "The Well of the Oath." And the city that grew up there was named "Oath" and is called that to this day.

³⁴Esau, at the age of 40, married a girl named Judith, daughter of Be-eri the Hethite. And he also married Basemath, daughter of Elon the Hethite. ³⁵But Isaac and Rebekah were bitter about his marrying them.

- *Remember:* Which Philistines came to see Isaac? (26:26) Why did Isaac think they wanted more trouble? (26:27) What did these Philistines want? (26:28-29) Isaac could get even. Or he could become a friend. What did he do? (26:30-31) Do you think Isaac did what was best?

- *Discover:* Is it fun to get even with someone who has hurt you? It's more fun to forgive.

- *Apply:* Someone is mean to you and hurts you. Then that person wants to be your friend. What should you do? Read Matthew 6:14,15. What did Jesus say about this?

- *What's next?* A man wears some goat skins to trick his father. Read Genesis 27. ◼

Jacob Deceives Isaac

Isaac is old and almost blind. It is time to give one of his sons his blessing. When Isaac dies, that son will lead the tribe. He will get most of the family money. Isaac plans to give his favorite son Esau the blessing. But Isaac's wife Rebekah comes up with a daring plan. Jacob would get the blessing instead. This is what she does.

27 One day, when Isaac was old and almost blind, he called for Esau his oldest son.

Isaac: "My son?"
Esau: "Yes, father?"
²⁻⁴*Isaac:* "I am an old man now, and expect every day to be my last. Take your bow and arrows out into the fields and get me some deer meat. Prepare it just the way I like it. Then bring it here for me to eat. And I will give you the blessings that belong to you as my first-born son before I die."

⁵Rebekah heard these words. So when Esau left for the field to hunt for the deer, ⁶⁻⁷she called her son Jacob. She told him what his father had said to his brother.

⁸⁻¹⁰*Rebekah:* "Now do exactly as I tell you. Go out to the flocks and bring me two young goats. I will prepare your father's favorite dish from them. Then take it to your father. After he has enjoyed it he will bless *you* before his death, instead of Esau!"

¹¹⁻¹²*Jacob:* "But mother! He won't be fooled that easily. Think how hairy Esau is, and how smooth my skin is! What if my father feels me? He'll

think I'm making a fool of him and curse me instead of blessing me!"

[13]*Rebekah:* "Let his curses be on me, dear son. Just do what I tell you. Go out and get the goats."

[14]So Jacob did as his mother told him. He brought the dressed kids. And she prepared them in his father's favorite way. [15]She took Esau's best clothes, which were there in the house. And she told Jacob to put them on. [16]She made him a pair of gloves from the hairy skin of the young goats. She also fastened a strip of the hide around his neck. [17]Then she gave him the meat, which smelled good, and some fresh-baked bread.

[18]Jacob carried the platter of food into the room where his father was lying.

Jacob: "Father?"

Isaac: "Yes? Who is it, my son—Esau or Jacob?"

[19]*Jacob:* "It's Esau, your oldest son. I've done as you told me to. Here is the tasty meat you wanted. Sit up and eat it, so that you will bless me with all your heart!"

[20]*Isaac:* "How were you able to find it so quickly, my son?"

Jacob: "Because the Lord your God put it in my path!"

[21]*Isaac:* "Come over here. I want to feel you and be sure it really is Esau!"

[22](Jacob goes over to his father. He feels him!)

Isaac: (to himself) "The voice is Jacob's, but the hands are Esau's!"

[23](The ruse convinces Isaac. He gives Jacob his blessings):

[24]*Isaac:* "Are you really Esau?"

Jacob: "Yes, of course."

[25]*Isaac:* "Then bring me the meat, and I will eat it and bless you with all my heart."

(Jacob takes it over to him and Isaac eats. He also drinks the wine Jacob brings him.)

[26]*Isaac:* "Come here and kiss me, my son!"

(Jacob goes over and kisses him on the cheek. Isaac sniffs his clothes, and finally seems convinced.)

[27-29]*Isaac:* "The smell of my son is the good smell of the earth and fields that the Lord has blessed. May God always give you plenty of rain for your crops, and good harvests and grapes. May many nations be your slaves. Be the master of your brothers. May all your relatives bow low before you. Cursed are all who curse you, and blessed are all who bless you."

[30](As soon as Isaac has blessed Jacob, and almost before Jacob leaves the room, Esau arrives, coming in from his hunting. [31]He also has prepared his father's favorite dish and brings it to him.)

Esau: "Here I am, father, with the meat. Sit up and eat it so that you can give me your finest blessings!"

[32]*Isaac:* "Who is it?"

Esau: "Why, it's me, of course! Esau, your oldest son!"

[33](Isaac begins to tremble.)

Isaac: "Then who is it who was just here with meat? For I have already eaten it and blessed him with a blessing I cannot take back."

[34](Esau begins to sob with deep and bitter sobs.)

Esau: "O my father, bless me, bless me too!"

[35]*Isaac:* "Your brother was here and tricked me. He has carried away your blessing."

[36]*Esau:* (bitterly) "No wonder they call him 'The Cheater.' He took my birthright, and now he has stolen my blessing. Oh, haven't you saved even one blessing for me?"

[37]*Isaac:* "I have made him your master. I have given him yourself and all of his relatives as his servants. I have promised him a large amount of grain and wine. What is there left to give?"

[38]*Esau:* "Not one blessing left for me? O my father, bless me too."

(Isaac says nothing as Esau weeps.)

[39-40]*Isaac:* "Yours will be no life of ease and luxury. But you shall hew your way with your sword. For a time you will serve your brother. But you

will at last shake loose from him and be free."

⁴¹So Esau hated Jacob because of what he had done to him. He said to himself, "My father will soon be gone, and then I will kill Jacob." ⁴²But someone got wind of what he was planning and told Rebekah. She sent for Jacob and told him that Esau was planning to kill him.

⁴³"This is what to do," she said. "Flee to your Uncle Laban in Haran. ⁴⁴Stay there with him awhile until your brother's fury is spent. ⁴⁵When he forgets what you have done, then I will send for you. For why should I be bereaved of both of you in one day?"

⁴⁶Then Rebekah said to Isaac, "I'm sick and tired of these local girls. I'd rather die than see Jacob marry one of them."

- *Remember:* What did Isaac tell Esau to do before he gave him the blessing? (27:3-4) What did Rebekah tell Jacob to do to get the blessing? (27:6-10) Why didn't Isaac give Esau a blessing also? (27:33-38) What did Esau want to do to Jacob? (27:41) What did Jacob have to do then? (27:43) How would you have felt if you were Jacob?

- *Discover:* Can family members live together happily when they deceive each other? When Jacob deceived his father, it tore the family apart.

- *Apply:* Are you trying to deceive your parents? Are you trying to trick your brother or sister? Stop! That's what tears a family apart.

- *What's next?* Have you ever seen a stairway that went all the way to heaven? Read in Genesis 28:10-22 about a man who saw one. ▉

Jacob Is Sent Away to Find a Wife

28 So Isaac called for Jacob and blessed him. And he said to him, "Don't marry one of these Canaanite girls. ²Instead, go at once to Paddanaram. Go to the house of your grandfather Bethuel. Marry one of your cousins—your Uncle Laban's daughters. ³God Almighty bless you and give you many children. May you become a great nation of many tribes! ⁴May God pass on to you and to your descendants the mighty blessings promised to Abraham. May you own this land where we now are foreigners, for God has given it to Abraham."

⁵So Isaac sent Jacob away. He went to Paddan-aram to visit his Uncle Laban. Laban was his mother's brother, the son of Bethuel the Aramean.

⁶⁻⁸Esau knew that his father despised the local girls. He saw that his father and mother had sent Jacob to Paddan-aram with his father's blessing, to get a wife from there. And Esau could not help but notice that Jacob had heeded their warning against marrying a Canaanite girl, and had left for Paddan-aram. ⁹So Esau went to his Uncle Ishmael's family. He married another wife from there, besides the wives he already had. Her name was Mahalath, the sister of Nebaioth, and daughter of Ishmael, Abraham's son.

Jacob's Ladder

Jacob had to leave home. He had deceived his father. He had taken the blessing from his brother. The family was divided, so he could not stay. When Jacob stopped for the night, he dreamed of a strange stairway. Sometimes it is called a ladder. It went all the way up to heaven. But look! Someone is on that stairway! And someone at the top is about to speak to Jacob. Listen!

¹⁰So Jacob left Beer-sheba and journeyed toward Haran. ¹¹That night, he stopped to camp at sundown. He found a rock for a headrest and lay down to sleep. ¹²Jacob dreamed that a staircase reached from earth to heaven. He saw the angels of God going up and down upon it.

¹³At the top of the stairs stood the

Lord. "I am the Lord," he said. "I am the God of Abraham, and of your father, Isaac. The ground you are lying on is yours! I will give it to you and to your descendants. ¹⁴For you will have descendants as many as dust! They will cover the land from east to west and from north to south. And all the nations of the earth will be blessed through you and your descendants. ¹⁵Always remember that I am with you. I will protect you wherever you go. And I will bring you back safely to this land. I will be with you always until I have finished giving you all I am promising."

God protects us in strange places

*Always remember that
I am with you. I will protect you
wherever you go.*

Genesis 28:15

---

¹⁶⁻¹⁷Then Jacob woke up. "God lives here!" he exclaimed in terror. "I've stumbled into his home! This is the awesome entrance to heaven!" ¹⁸The next morning he got up very early. He set his stone headrest upright as a memorial pillar, and poured olive oil over it. ¹⁹He named the place Bethel ("House of God"). But the previous name of the nearest town was Luz.

²⁰And Jacob vowed this vow to God: "If God will help and protect me on this journey and give me food and clothes, ²¹and will bring me back safely to my father, then I will choose the Lord as my God! ²²And this pillar shall become a place for worship. And I will give you back a tenth of all you give me!"

- *Remember:* What did Jacob see in his dream? (28:12-13) What did God say? (28:13-15) What did Jacob do the next morning? What did he name this place? Why? (28:18-19) Do you think Jacob chose a good name?

- *Discover:* Bethel means "House of God." Jacob called that place Bethel because God was there. But God is with us everywhere (see verse 15). So wherever you are right now, it is Bethel.

- *Apply:* Read Matthew 28:20. Is Jesus with you right now where you are? Thank him! The next time you think of doing something wrong, stop! Remember that Jesus is there with you.

- *What's next?* What do you say when you meet a cousin for the first time? Read Genesis 29:1-14 to find what Jacob said. ■

Jacob Meets Rachel

Jacob is far from home, alone in a strange land. He must find the woman he should marry. But where will he find her? How should he look for her?

29 Jacob traveled on. At last he came to the land of the East. ²He saw in the distance three flocks of sheep. They were lying beside a well in an open field, waiting to be watered. But a heavy stone covered the mouth of the well. ³The custom was that the stone was not removed until all the flocks were there. After watering them, the stone was rolled back over the mouth of the well again. ⁴Jacob went over to the shepherds and asked them where they lived.

"At Haran," they said.

⁵"Do you know a man there named Laban, the son of Nahor?"

"We sure do."

⁶"How is he?"

"He's well and rich. Look, there comes his daughter Rachel with the sheep."

⁷"Why don't you water the flocks so they can get back to grazing?" Jacob asked. "They'll be hungry if you stop so early in the day!"

8"We don't roll away the stone and begin the watering until all the flocks and shepherds are here," they replied.

9As these words were being spoken, Rachel came with her father's sheep. She was a shepherdess. 10And because she was his cousin—the daughter of his mother's brother—and because the sheep were his uncle's, Jacob went over to the well and rolled away the stone and watered his uncle's flock. 11Then Jacob kissed Rachel and started crying! 12-13He explained about being her cousin on her father's side, and that he was her Aunt Rebekah's son. She quickly ran and told her father, Laban. And as soon as he heard of Jacob's arrival, he rushed out to meet him. He greeted him warmly and brought him home. Then Jacob told him his story.

14"Just think, my very own flesh and blood," Laban said.

● *Remember:* How did Jacob meet Rachel? (29:1-13) What kind of work did Rachel do? (29:9) Why do you think Jacob cried when he talked with Rachel? (29:11) What do you think Rachel thought when Jacob told her who he was? (29:12-13) How do you think God helped Jacob and Rachel meet?

● *Discover:* When God wants us to meet someone, he helps us do it.

● *Apply:* Someday you may get married. Don't worry about who it will be. Start asking God to help you meet the right person. He will.

● *What's next?* It's the morning after the wedding. But a man finds that he did not marry his bride! He married her sister! Read about it in Genesis 29:14b-30. ■

Jacob Marries Rachel

Rachel was a beautiful girl, and Jacob soon fell in love with her. He even promised to work 7 years for his Uncle Laban to marry her. At the end of the 7 years, Jacob and Rachel had a big wedding. But something went wrong. The morning after the wedding, Jacob found that he really did not marry Rachel. He married someone else. Here's what happened.

After Jacob had been there about a month, 15Laban said to him, "Just because we are relatives is no reason for you to work for me without pay. How much do you want?" 16Now Laban had two daughters. Leah was the older and Rachel the younger sister. 17Leah had weak eyes. But Rachel was shapely and in every way a beauty. 18Jacob was in love with Rachel. So he told her father, "I'll work for you seven years if you'll give me Rachel as my wife."

19"Agreed!" Laban replied. "I'd rather give her to you than to someone outside the family."

20So Jacob spent the next seven years working to pay for Rachel. But they seemed to him but a few days, he was so much in love. 21At last the time came for him to marry her.

"I have fulfilled my contract," Jacob said to Laban. "Now give me my wife, so that I can sleep with her."

²²So Laban invited all the men of the settlement to celebrate with Jacob at a big party. ²³But at night, when it was dark, Laban took Leah to Jacob, and he slept with her. ²⁴And Laban gave to Leah a servant girl, Zilpah, to be her maid. ²⁵In the morning Jacob woke up and found Leah next to him!

"What sort of trick is this?" Jacob raged at Laban. "I worked for seven years for Rachel. What do you mean by this trick?"

²⁶"It's not our custom to marry off a younger daughter ahead of her sister," Laban replied smoothly. ²⁷"Wait until the bridal week is over. Then you can have Rachel too. But, you must promise to work for me another seven years!"

²⁸So Jacob agreed to work seven more years. Then Laban gave him Rachel, too. ²⁹And Laban gave to Rachel a servant girl, Bilhah, to be her maid. ³⁰So Jacob slept with Rachel, too. He loved her more than Leah and stayed and worked seven more years.

- *Remember:* Who did Jacob love and want to marry? (29:18) Then why did he marry Leah? (29:22-25) Laban deceived Jacob. What was his reason? (29:26) How long did Jacob have to work for Rachel? (29:30) Why wouldn't you like to have Laban as your uncle?

- *Discover:* When we deceive others, they may deceive us! Jacob had deceived his father. Now his uncle deceived him.

- *Apply:* Jesus said, "Others will treat you as you treat them" (Matthew 7:2). If you deceive, you may be deceived.

- *What's next?* Jacob is going home. But 20 years ago his brother Esau said he would kill Jacob. Will Esau still want to get even? Read what Esau did in Genesis 32–33. ■

Jacob Has Many Children

³¹But because Jacob was slighting Leah, the Lord let her have a child, while Rachel was barren. ³²So Leah became pregnant and had a son, Reuben (mean-ing "God has noticed my trouble"). For she said, "the Lord has noticed my trou-ble. Now my husband will love me." ³³She soon became pregnant again and had another son and named him Simeon (meaning "the Lord heard"). For she said, "the Lord heard that I was unloved, and so he has given me an-other son." ³⁴Again she became preg-nant and had a son, and named him Levi (meaning "Attachment"). For she said, "Surely now my husband will feel affection for me, since I have given him three sons!" ³⁵Once again she was preg-nant and had a son and named him Judah (meaning "Praise"). For she said, "Now I will praise the Lord!" And then she stopped having children.

30 Rachel, realizing she was barren, became jealous of her sister. "Give me children or I'll die," she said to Jacob.

²Jacob flew into a rage. "Am I God?" he flared. "He is the one who has made you barren."

³Then Rachel told him, "Sleep with my servant girl Bilhah. Then her chil-dren will be mine." ⁴So she gave him Bilhah to be his wife, and he slept with her. ⁵And she became pregnant and gave him a son. ⁶Rachel named him Dan (meaning "Justice"). For she said, "God has given me justice, and heard my plea and given me a son." ⁷Then Bilhah, Ra-chel's servant girl, became pregnant again and gave Jacob a second son. ⁸Ra-chel named him Naphtali (meaning "Wrestling"). For she said, "I am in a fierce contest with my sister and I am winning!"

⁹Meanwhile, Leah knew that she wasn't getting pregnant anymore. So she gave her servant girl Zilpah to Jacob, to be his wife. ¹⁰Soon Zilpah had a son. ¹¹Leah named him Gad (meaning "My luck has turned!").

¹²Then Zilpah produced a second son. ¹³Leah named him Asher (meaning "Happy"), for she said, "What joy is mine! The other women will think me blessed indeed!"

¹⁴One day during the wheat harvest, Reuben found some mandrakes grow-ing in a field. He brought them to his mother Leah. Rachel begged Leah to

give some of them to her.

¹⁵But Leah angrily replied, "Wasn't it enough to steal my husband? And now will you steal my son's mandrakes too?"

Rachel said sadly, "He will sleep with you tonight because of the mandrakes."

¹⁶That evening as Jacob was coming home from the fields, Leah went out to meet him. "You must sleep with me tonight!" she said. "For I am hiring you with some mandrakes my son has found!" So he did. ¹⁷And God answered her prayers and she became pregnant again. She gave birth to her fifth son. ¹⁸She named him Issachar (meaning "Wages"). For she said, "God has repaid me for giving my slave girl to my husband." ¹⁹Then once again she became pregnant, with a sixth son. ²⁰She named him Zebulun (meaning "Gifts"). For she said, "God has given me good gifts for my husband. Now he will honor me, for I have given him six sons." ²¹After that she gave birth to a daughter and named her Dinah.

²²Then God remembered about Rachel's plight. He answered her prayers by giving her a child. ²³⁻²⁴So she became pregnant and gave birth to a son. "God has removed the dark slur against my name," she said. And she named him Joseph (meaning "May I also have another!"). For she said, "May the Lord give me another son."

Jacob Becomes Wealthy

²⁵Soon after the birth of Joseph to Rachel, Jacob said to Laban, "I want to go back home. ²⁶Let me take my wives and children and be gone. For I earned them from you. You know how fully I have paid for them with my service to you."

²⁷"Please don't leave me," Laban replied. "A fortune teller that I saw told me that my many blessings are all because of your being here. ²⁸How much of a raise do you need to get you to stay? Whatever it is, I'll pay it."

²⁹Jacob replied, "You know how faithfully I've served you through these many years. And how your flocks and herds have grown! ³⁰For it was little indeed you had before I came. Your wealth has increased greatly. The Lord has

blessed you from all I have done! But now, what about me? When should I provide for my own family?"

³¹⁻³²"What wages do you want?" Laban asked again.

Jacob replied, "If you will do one thing, I'll go back to work for you. Let me go out among your flocks today. Let me remove all the goats that are speckled or spotted, and all the black sheep. Give them to me as my wages. ³³Then if you ever find any white goats or sheep in my flock, you will know that I have stolen them from you!"

³⁴"All right!" Laban replied. "It shall be as you have said!"

³⁵⁻³⁶So that very day Laban went out and formed a flock for Jacob. He took from his herds all the male goats that were ringed and spotted. He also included the females that were speckled and spotted with any white patches, and all of the black sheep. He gave them to his sons to take them three days' distance. But Jacob stayed and cared for Laban's flock. ³⁷Then Jacob took fresh shoots from poplar, almond, and sycamore trees, and peeled white streaks in them. ³⁸He placed these rods beside the watering troughs. That way, Laban's flocks would see them when they came to drink, for that is when they mated. ³⁹⁻⁴⁰So the flocks mated before the white-streaked rods, and their offspring were streaked and spotted. Jacob added these to his flock. Then he divided out the ewes from Laban's flock and took them away from the rams. He let them mate only with Jacob's black rams. Thus he built his flocks from Laban's. ⁴¹Moreover, he watched for the stronger animals to mate. He placed the peeled branches before them, ⁴²but didn't with the feebler ones. So the less healthy lambs were Laban's and the stronger ones were Jacob's! ⁴³As a result, Jacob's flocks increased rapidly. He soon became very wealthy, with many servants, camels, and donkeys.

Jacob Leaves Laban

31 But Jacob learned that Laban's sons were grumbling, "He owes all he has to our father. All his wealth is at our father's expense." ²Soon Jacob noticed a cooling in Laban's attitude toward him.

³The Lord now spoke to Jacob. He told him, "Go back to the land of your fathers, and to your relatives there. I will be with you."

⁴So one day Jacob sent for Rachel and Leah. He asked them to come out to the field where he was with the flocks. ⁵He wanted to talk things over with them.

"Your father has turned against me," he told them. "And now the God of my fathers has come and spoken to me. ⁶You know how hard I've worked for your father. ⁷But he has been unfair. He has broken his wage contract with me again and again and again. But God has not let him do me any harm! ⁸For if he said the speckled animals would be mine, then all the flock produced speckled. And when he changed and said I could have the streaked ones, then all the lambs were streaked! ⁹In this way God has made me wealthy at your father's expense.

¹⁰"And at the mating season, I had a dream. I saw that the he-goats mating with the flock were streaked, speckled, and mottled. ¹¹Then, in my dream, the Angel of God called to me. ¹²He told me that I should mate the white female goats with streaked, speckled, and mottled male goats. 'For I have seen all that Laban has done to you,' the Angel said. ¹³'I am the God you met at Bethel,' he said. 'That is the place where you anointed the pillar and made a vow to serve me. Now leave this country and go back to the land of your birth.'"

¹⁴Rachel and Leah replied, "That's fine with us! There's nothing for us here. None of our father's wealth will come to us anyway! ¹⁵He has reduced our rights to those of foreign women. He sold us, and what he received for us has been spent. ¹⁶The riches God has given you from our father were legally ours and our children's to begin with! So go ahead and do what God has told you to."

Laban Chases Jacob

¹⁷⁻²⁰So one day while Laban was out shearing sheep, Jacob set his wives and sons on camels. He fled without telling Laban. Jacob drove the flocks before him—the flocks he had gotten there at Paddan-aram. He took all he owned and started out to return to his father Isaac in the land of Canaan. ²¹So he fled with all that he owned. And Rachel stole her father's household gods and took them with her. They crossed the Euphrates River and headed for the land of Gilead.

²²Laban didn't learn of their flight for three days. ²³Then, taking several men with him, he set out in hot pursuit. He caught up with them seven days later, at Mount Gilead. ²⁴That night God appeared to Laban in a dream.

"Watch out what you say to Jacob," he was told. "Don't give him your blessing and don't curse him." ²⁵Laban caught up with Jacob as he was camped at the top of a ridge. Laban, meanwhile, camped below him in the mountains.

²⁶"What do you mean by sneaking off like this?" Laban demanded. "Are my daughters prisoners, captured in a battle, that you have rushed them away like this? ²⁷Why didn't you give me a chance to have a farewell party, with singing and harp? ²⁸Why didn't you let me kiss my grandchildren and tell them goodbye? This is a strange way to act. ²⁹I could crush you, but the God of your father appeared to me last night. He told me, 'Be careful not to be too hard on Jacob!' ³⁰But see here—though you feel you must go, and long so intensely for your childhood home—why have you stolen my idols?"

³¹"I sneaked away because I was afraid," Jacob answered. "I said to myself, 'He'll take his daughters from me by force.' ³²But as for your household idols, a curse upon anyone who took them. Let him die! If you find a single thing we've stolen from you, I swear before all these men, I'll give it back without question." For Jacob didn't know that Rachel had taken them.

³³Laban went first into Jacob's tent to search there. Then he went into Leah's, and searched the two tents of the servant girls. But he didn't find them. At last he went into Rachel's tent. ³⁴Rachel was the one who had stolen the idols. She had stuffed them into her camel saddle and

now was sitting on them! So although Laban searched the tents, he didn't find them.

35"Forgive my not getting up, father," Rachel explained. "I'm having my monthly period." So Laban didn't find them.

36-37Now Jacob got mad. "What did you find?" he yelled at Laban. "What is my crime? You have come rushing after me as though you were chasing a criminal. You have searched through everything. Now put what I stole out here in front of us, before your men and mine. Let's look and decide whose it is! 38Twenty years I've been with you. All that time I cared for your ewes and goats so that they produced healthy offspring. And I never touched one ram of yours for food. 39If any were attacked and killed by wild animals, did I show them to you? Did I ask you to reduce the count of your flock? No, I took the loss. You made me pay for every animal stolen from the flocks, whether I could help it or not. 40I worked for you through the scorching heat of the day. I worked through the cold and sleepless nights. 41Yes, 20 years—14 of them earning your two daughters, and six years to get the flock! And you have reduced my wages 10 times! 42In fact, except for the grace of God—the God of my grandfather Abraham, even the glorious God of Isaac, my father—you would have sent me off without a penny to my name. But God has seen your cruelty and my hard work. That is why he appeared to you last night."

43Laban replied, "These women are my daughters, and these children are mine. These flocks and all that you have are mine. So how could I harm my own daughters and grandchildren? 44Come now and we will sign a peace pact, you and I. We will live by its terms."

45So Jacob took a stone and set it up as a monument. 46He told his men to gather stones and make a heap. And Jacob and Laban ate together beside the pile of rocks. 47-48They named it "The Witness Pile"—"Jegar-sahadutha," in Laban's language, and "Galeed" in Jacob's.

"This pile of stones will stand as a witness against us [if either of us crosses this line]," Laban said. 49So it was also called "The Watchtower" (Mizpah). For Laban said, "May the Lord see to it that we keep this bargain when we are out of each other's sight. 50And if you are harsh to my daughters, or take other wives, I won't know, but God will see it. 51-52This heap," Laban went on, "stands between us as a witness of our vows. I will not cross this line to attack you. And you will not cross it to attack me. 53I call upon the God of Abraham and Nahor, and of their father, to destroy either one of us who does."

So Jacob took oath before the mighty God of his father, Isaac, to respect the boundary line. 54Then Jacob made a sacrifice to God there at the top of the mountain. He invited his companions to a feast. After that he spent the night with them on the mountain. 55Laban was up early the next morning. He kissed his daughters and grandchildren. Then he blessed them and went home.

Jacob Meets Esau

Jacob is going home. But he is worried. Twenty years ago his brother Esau swore he would kill Jacob. Would he? Jacob will soon know what Esau will do. So will you as you read this.

32 So Jacob and his household started on again. And the angels of God came to meet him. When he saw them he exclaimed, "God lives here!" So he named the place "God's territory!"

³Jacob now sent messengers to his brother, Esau, in Edom, in the land of Seir. ⁴He sent this message: "Hello from Jacob! I have been living with Uncle Laban until recently. ⁵Now I own oxen, donkeys, sheep, goats, and many servants, both men and women. I have sent these messengers to tell you of my coming. I am hoping that you will be friendly to us."

⁶The messengers came back with news that Esau was on his way to meet Jacob. And he was coming with an army of 400 men! ⁷Jacob was frantic with fear. He divided his household, along with the flocks and herds and camels, into two groups. ⁸For he said, "If Esau attacks one group, perhaps the other can escape."

⁹Then Jacob prayed, "O God of Abraham my grandfather, and of my father Isaac. O Lord who told me to return to the land of my relatives, and said that you would do me good. ¹⁰I am not worthy of the least of all your loving-kindnesses shown me again and again just as you promised me. For when I left home I owned nothing except a walking stick! And now I am two armies! ¹¹O Lord, please deliver me from death at the hand of my brother Esau, for I am afraid. I am afraid that he is coming to kill me and these mothers and my children. ¹²But you promised to do me good. You vowed to multiply my descendants until they become as the sands along the shores—too many to count."

¹³⁻¹⁵Jacob stayed where he was for the night. He prepared a present for his brother Esau: 200 female goats, 20 male goats, 200 ewes, 20 rams, 30 milk camels, with their colts, 40 cows, 10 bulls, 20 female donkeys, 10 male donkeys.

¹⁶He told his servants to drive them on ahead. Each group of animals went by itself, separated by a distance between. ¹⁷He told the men driving the first group that when they met Esau and he asked, "Where are you going? Whose servants are you? Whose animals are these?" ¹⁸they should reply: "These belong to your servant Jacob. They are a present for his master Esau! He is coming right behind us!"

¹⁹Jacob gave the same orders to each driver, with the same message. ²⁰Jacob's plan was to appease Esau with the presents before meeting him face to face! "Perhaps," Jacob hoped, "he will be friendly to us." ²¹So the presents were sent on ahead, and Jacob spent that night in the camp.

²²⁻²⁴But during the night he got up and wakened his two wives and their two servant girls and 11 sons. He sent them across the Jordan River at the Jabbok ford with all that he owned. He then came back again to the camp and was there alone. And a Man wrestled with him until dawn. ²⁵And when the Man saw that he couldn't win the match, he struck Jacob's hip and knocked it out of joint at the socket.

²⁶Then the Man said, "Let me go, for it is dawn."

But Jacob panted, "I will not let you go until you bless me."

²⁷"What is your name?" the Man asked.

"Jacob," was the reply.

²⁸"It isn't anymore!" the Man told him. "It is Israel—one who has power with God. Because you have been strong with God, you shall prevail with men."

²⁹"What is *your* name?" Jacob asked him.

"No, you must not ask," the Man told him. And he blessed him there.

³⁰Jacob named the place "Peniel" ("The Face of God"). For he said, "I have seen God face to face, and yet my life is spared." ³¹The sun rose as he started on, and he was limping because of his hip. ³²That is why even today the people of Israel don't eat meat from near the hip. It is in memory of what happened that night.

33 Then, far in the distance, Jacob saw Esau coming with his 400 men. ²Jacob now put his family into a line. He placed his two servant girls and their children at the head. Leah and her children came next, and Rachel and Joseph were last. ³Then Jacob went on ahead. As he came near his brother he bowed low seven times before him. ⁴And then Esau ran to meet him and hugged him and kissed him. Both of them were in tears!

⁵Then Esau looked at the women and children. He asked, "Who are these people with you?"

"My children," Jacob replied. ⁶Then the servant girls came forward with their children, and bowed low before him. ⁷Next came Leah with her children, and bowed. And finally Rachel and Joseph came and made their bows.

⁸"And what were all the flocks and herds I met as I came?" Esau asked.

And Jacob replied, "They are my gifts, to win your favor!"

⁹"Brother, I have plenty," Esau laughed. "Keep what you have."

¹⁰"No, but please accept them," Jacob said. "What a relief it is to see your friendly smile! I was as frightened of you as though approaching God! ¹¹Please take my gifts. For God has been very good to me and I have enough." So Jacob insisted, and at last Esau took them.

¹²"Well, let's be going," Esau said. "My men and I will stay with you and lead the way."

¹³But Jacob replied, "As you can see, some of the children are small and the flocks and herds have their young. And if they are driven too hard, they will die. ¹⁴So you go on ahead of us. We'll follow at our own pace and meet you at Seir."

¹⁵"Well," Esau said, "at least let me

leave you some of my men to assist you and be your guides."

"No," Jacob urged. "We'll get along just fine. Please do as I suggest."

¹⁶So Esau started back to Seir that same day. ¹⁷Meanwhile Jacob and his household went as far as Succoth. There he built himself a camp, with pens for his flocks and herds. That is why the place is called Succoth, meaning "huts." ¹⁸Then they arrived safely at Shechem, in Canaan, and camped outside the city. ¹⁹He bought the land he camped on from the family of Hamor, Shechem's father, for 100 pieces of silver. ²⁰And there he built an altar and called it "El-Elohe-Israel," "The Altar to the God of Israel."

- *Remember:* Why was Jacob worried? (32:11) What did Jacob do when he met Esau? (33:3) What did Esau do when he met Jacob? (33:4) Did he try to get even? If you were Jacob, what would you say to Esau? If you were Esau, what should you say to Jacob?

- *Discover:* When someone hurts us, we can either get even or forgive. What might have happened if Esau hadn't forgiven Jacob?

- *Apply:* Read Matthew 6:14-15. Why does God tell us to forgive?

- *What's next?* A boy's brothers hate him because of two strange dreams. Read about them in Genesis 37:1-11. ∎

Jacob's Sons Take Revenge

34 One day Dinah, Leah's daughter, went out to visit some of the girls nearby. ²But when Shechem, son of King Hamor the Hivite, saw her, he took her and abused her. ³He fell deeply in love with her, and tried to win her love.

⁴Then he spoke to his father about it. "Get this girl for me," he said. "I want to marry her."

⁵Word soon reached Jacob of what had happened. But his sons were out in the fields herding cattle, so he did nothing until they came back. ⁶⁻⁷Meanwhile King Hamor, Shechem's father, went to talk with Jacob. He arrived just as Jacob's sons came in from the fields. They were too shocked and angry to overlook the insult. It was an outrage against all of them.

⁸Hamor told Jacob, "My son Shechem is truly in love with your daughter. He longs for her to be his wife. Please let him marry her. ⁹⁻¹⁰Moreover, we invite you folks to live here among us and to let your daughters marry our sons. And we will give our daughters as wives for your young men. And you shall live among us wherever you wish and carry on your business among us and become rich!"

¹¹Then Shechem spoke to Dinah's father and brothers. "Please be kind to me and let me have her as my wife," he begged. "I will give whatever you require. ¹²No matter what dowry or gift you demand, I will pay it. Only give me the girl as my wife."

¹³Her brothers then lied to Shechem and Hamor, because of what Shechem had done to their sister. ¹⁴They said, "We couldn't possibly. For you are not circumcised. It would be a disgrace for her to marry such a man. ¹⁵I'll tell you what we'll do. If every man of you will be circumcised, ¹⁶then we will intermarry with you. We will live here and unite with you to become one people. ¹⁷Otherwise we will take her and be on our way."

¹⁸⁻¹⁹Hamor and Shechem gladly agreed. They lost no time in acting upon this request, for Shechem was very much in love with Dinah. He could, he felt sure, sell the idea to the other men of the city. He was highly respected and very popular. ²⁰So Hamor and Shechem appeared before the city council and made their request.

²¹"Those men are our friends," they said. "Let's invite them to live here among us and ply their trade. For the land is large enough to hold them, and we can intermarry with them. ²²But they will only consider staying here on one condition. Every one of us men must be circumcised, the same as they are. ²³But if we do this, then all they have will become ours and the land will be enriched. Come on, let's agree to this so that they will settle here among us."

²⁴So all the men agreed, and all were circumcised. ²⁵But three days later, their wounds were sore and sensitive to every

move they made. Then two of Dinah's brothers, Simeon and Levi, took their swords, and entered the city. No one tried to stop them. They slaughtered every man there, 26including Hamor and Shechem. They rescued Dinah from Shechem's house and returned to their camp again. 27Then all of Jacob's sons went over and plundered the city because their sister had been dishonored there. 28They took all the flocks and herds and donkeys. They took all they could lay their hands on, both inside the city and outside in the fields. 29And they took all the women and children, and wealth of every kind.

30Then Jacob said to Levi and Simeon, "You have made me stink among all the people of this land—all the Canaanites and Perizzites. We are so few that they will come and crush us, and we will all be killed."

31"Should he treat our sister like a prostitute?" they said.

Rachel and Isaac Die

35 "Move on to Bethel now, and settle there," God said to Jacob. "Build an altar to worship me—the God who appeared to you when you fled from your brother Esau."

2So Jacob told all those in his household to destroy the idols they had brought with them. Then he told them to wash themselves and to put on fresh clothing. 3"For we are going to Bethel," he said to them. "And I will build an altar there to the God who answered my prayers in the day of my distress, and was with me on my journey."

4So they gave Jacob all their idols and their earrings. And he buried them beneath the oak tree near Shechem. 5Then they started on again. The terror of God was upon all the cities they journeyed through. And so, they were not attacked. 6At last they came to Luz (also called Bethel), in Canaan. 7And Jacob erected an altar there. He named it "The altar to the God who met me here at Bethel." It was there at Bethel that God appeared to him when he was fleeing from Esau.

8Soon after this Rebekah's old nurse, Deborah, died. She was buried beneath the oak tree in the valley below Bethel. And ever after it was called "The Oak of Weeping."

9Upon Jacob's arrival at Bethel, en route from Paddan-aram, God appeared to him once again and blessed him. 10And God said to him, "You shall no longer be called Jacob ('Grabber'). Your new name is Israel ('One who prevails with God'). 11I am God Almighty," the Lord said to him. "And I will cause you to be fertile and to multiply. You will become a great nation, yes, many nations. Many kings shall be among your descendants. 12And I will pass on to you the land I gave to Abraham and Isaac. Yes, I will give it to you and to your descendants."

13-14After that Jacob built a stone pillar at the place where God had appeared to him. He poured wine over it as an offering to God. He then anointed the pillar with olive oil. 15Jacob named the spot Bethel ("House of God"), because God had spoken to him there.

16Leaving Bethel, he and his household traveled on toward Ephrath (Bethlehem). But Rachel's pains of childbirth began while they were still a long way away. 17After a very hard delivery, the midwife finally exclaimed, "Wonderful—another boy!" 18And with Rachel's last breath (for she died) she named him "Ben-oni" ("Son of my sorrow"). But his father called him "Benjamin" ("Son of my right hand").

19So Rachel died, and was buried near the road to Ephrath (also called Bethlehem). 20And Jacob set up a monument of stones upon her grave. That monument is there to this day.

21Then Israel journeyed on and camped beyond the Tower of Eder. 22It was while he was there that Reuben slept with Bilhah, his father's concubine, and someone told Israel about it.

Here are the names of the 12 sons of Jacob:

23The sons of Leah: Reuben, Jacob's oldest child, Simeon, Levi, Judah, Issachar, Zebulun.

24The sons of Rachel: Joseph, Benjamin.

25The sons of Bilhah, Rachel's servant-girl: Dan, Naphtali.

26The sons of Zilpah, Leah's servant-girl: Gad, Asher.

All these were born to him at Paddan-aram.

27So Jacob came at last to Isaac his father at Mamre in Kiriath-arba (now called Hebron). Abraham also had lived there. 28-29Isaac died soon after that, at the ripe old age of 180. And his sons Esau and Jacob buried him.

Esau's Family

36 Here is a list of the descendants of Esau (also called Edom). 2-3Esau married three local girls from Canaan: Adah (daughter of Elon the Hethite), Oholibamah (daughter of Anah and granddaughter of Zibeon the Hivite), Basemath (his cousin—she was a daughter of Ishmael—the sister of Nebaioth).

4Esau and Adah had a son named Eliphaz. Esau and Basemath had a son named Reuel.

5Esau and Oholibamah had sons named Jeush, Jalam, and Korah. All these sons were born to Esau in the land of Canaan.

6-8Esau gathered together his wives, children, household servants, cattle and flocks. He took all the wealth he had gained in the land of Canaan. He moved away from his brother Jacob to Mount Seir. (There was not land enough to support them both because of all their cattle.)

9Here are the names of Esau's descendants, the Edomites, born to him in Mount Seir:

10-12Descended from his wife Adah, born to her son Eliphaz were: Teman, Omar, Zepho, Gatam, Kenaz, Amalek (born to Timna, Eliphaz's concubine).

13-14Esau also had grandchildren from his wife Basemath. Born to her son Reuel were: Nahath, Zerah, Shammah, Mizzah.

15-16Esau's grandchildren became the heads of clans. They are listed here: the clan of Teman, the clan of Omar, the clan of Zepho, the clan of Kenaz, the clan of Korah, the clan of Gatam, the clan of Amalek.

The above clans were the descendants of Eliphaz, the oldest son of Esau and Adah.

17The following clans were the descendants of Reuel. They were born to Esau and his wife Basemath while they lived in Canaan: the clan of Nahath, the clan of Zerah, the clan of Shammah, the clan of Mizzah.

18-19And these are the clans named after the sons of Esau and his wife Oholibamah (daughter of Anah): the clan of Jeush, the clan of Jalam, the clan of Korah.

20-21These are the names of the tribes that came from Seir, the Horite. This was one of the native families of the land of Seir: the tribe of Lotan, the tribe of Shobal, the tribe of Zibeon, the tribe of Anah, the tribe of Dishon, the tribe of Ezer, the tribe of Dishan.

22The children of Lotan (the son of Seir) were Hori and Heman. (Lotan had a sister, Timna.)

23The children of Shobal: Alvan, Manahath, Ebal, Shepho, Onam.

24The children of Zibeon: Aiah, Anah. (This is the boy who discovered a hot springs in the wasteland while he was grazing his father's donkeys.)

25The children of Anah: Dishon, Oholibamah.

26The children of Dishon: Hemdan, Eshban, Ithran, Cheran.

27The children of Ezer: Bilhan, Zaavan, Akan.

28-30The children of Dishan: Uz, Aran.

31-39These are the names of the kings of Edom (before Israel had her first king):

King Bela (son of Beor), from Dinhabah in Edom.

Succeeded by: King Jobab (son of Zerah), from the city of Bozrah.

Succeeded by: King Husham, from the land of the Temanites.

Succeeded by: King Hadad (son of Bedad), the leader of the forces that defeated the army of Midian when it invaded Moab. His city was Avith.

Succeeded by: King Samlah, from Masrekah.

Succeeded by: King Shaul, from Rehoboth-by-the-River.

Succeeded by: King Baal-hanan (son of Achbor).

Succeeded by: King Hadad, from the city of Pau.

King Hadad's wife was Mehetabel, daughter of Matred and granddaughter of Mezahab.

40-43Here are the names of the sub-tribes of Esau. They lived in the places named after themselves: the clan of Timna, the clan of Alvah, the clan of Jetheth, the clan of Oholibamah, the clan of Elah, the clan of Pinon, the clan of Kenaz, the clan of Teman, the clan of Mibzar, the clan of Magdiel, the clan of Iram.

These, then, are the names of the subtribes of Edom. Each gave its name to the area it occupied. (All were Edomites, descendants of Esau.)

Joseph's Two Strange Dreams

As Jacob's sons grew to be young men, Joseph became his favorite. This made Joseph's older brothers jealous. One day Joseph told the family about two strange dreams. When you read about these dreams, you will see why the dreams divided the family.

37 So Jacob settled again in the land of Canaan, where his father had lived.

2Jacob's son Joseph was now 17 years old. Joseph and his brothers had to shepherd their father's flocks. But Joseph reported to his father some of the bad things his brothers were doing. 3Now as it happened, Israel loved Joseph more than any of his other children. This was because Joseph was born to him in his old age. So one day Jacob gave him a special gift—a brightly colored coat. 4His brothers of course noticed he liked Joseph best. So they hated Joseph. They could not say a kind word to him. 5One night Joseph had a dream and then told it to his brothers. This caused even deeper hatred.

6"Listen to this," he proudly said. 7"We were out in the field binding sheaves. My sheaf stood up, and your sheaves all gathered around it and bowed low before it!"

8"So you want to be our king, do you?" his brothers derided. And they hated him both for the dream and for his cocky attitude. 9Then he had another dream and told it to his brothers. "Listen to my latest dream," he boasted. "The sun, moon, and 11 stars bowed low before me!" 10This time he told his father as well as his brothers. But his father rebuked him. "What is this?" he asked. "Shall I indeed, and your mother and brothers come and bow before you?" 11His brothers were fit to be tied concerning this affair. But his father gave it quite a bit of thought and wondered what it all meant.

- *Remember:* What special gift did Jacob give to Joseph? (37:3) Why do you think he did that? (37:3) What were Joseph's two dreams? (37:7-9). Why did these dreams make his brothers angry? (37:8)

- *Discover:* Playing favorites is like playing with fire. Don't do it! Do you see what happened to Jacob's family? Because Joseph was the favorite, his brothers became jealous, hurt, and angry.

- *Apply:* Do you have a favorite parent? Do you have a favorite brother or sister? Playing favorites can divide a family. Why? Because for every favorite, there is someone in second place. How do you feel when a friend or parent likes someone else better than you? How easy is it to be friends with someone when you are jealous of that person?

- *What's next?* Have you ever heard of anyone who would sell a brother as a slave? You will meet people who did in Genesis 37:12-36. ▨

Joseph's Brothers Sell Him

Joseph was headed for big trouble. He was his father's favorite son. That got him into trouble. His father gave him a special gift. More trouble! Then Joseph dreamed two dreams. He dreamed that his family would bow down to him. That doesn't make angry brothers love you any more, does it? One day Joseph was alone with his brothers. You know something terrible is about to happen, don't you?

¹²One day Joseph's brothers took their father's flocks to Shechem to graze them there. ¹³⁻¹⁴A few days later Israel called for Joseph. He told him, "Your brothers are over in Shechem grazing the flocks. Go and see how they are getting along, and how it is with the flocks. Then bring me word."

"Very good," Joseph replied. So he traveled to Shechem from his home at Hebron Valley. ¹⁵A man noticed him walking in the fields.

"Who are you looking for?" he asked.

¹⁶"For my brothers and their flocks," Joseph replied. "Have you seen them?"

¹⁷"Yes," the man told him, "they are no longer here. I heard your brothers say they were going to Dothan." So Joseph followed them to Dothan and found them there. ¹⁸But when they saw him coming, still far away, they decided to kill him!

¹⁹⁻²⁰"Here comes that master dreamer," they said. "Come on. Let's kill him and toss him into a well. We can tell Father that a wild animal has eaten him. Then we'll see what will become of all his dreams!"

²¹⁻²²But Reuben hoped to spare Joseph's life. "Let's not kill him," he said. "We'll shed no blood. Let's throw him alive into this well here. That way he'll die without our touching him!" (Reuben was planning to get him out later and return him to his father.) ²³So when Joseph got there, they pulled off his brightly colored robe. ²⁴Then they threw him into an empty well. There was no water in it. ²⁵Then they sat down for supper. Suddenly they noticed a string of camels coming toward them in the distance. They were probably Ishmaelite traders who were taking gum, spices, and herbs from Gilead to Egypt.

²⁶⁻²⁷"Look there," Judah said to the others. "Here come some Ishmaelites. Let's sell Joseph to them! Why kill him and have a guilty conscience? Let's not be responsible for his death, for, after all, he is our brother!" And his brothers

agreed. ²⁸So when the traders came by, his brothers pulled Joseph out of the well. They sold him for 20 pieces of silver, and the traders took him along to Egypt. ²⁹Some time later, Reuben (who was away when the traders came by) went back to get Joseph out of the well. When Joseph wasn't there, he ripped at his clothes in pain and frustration.

³⁰"The child is gone. And I, where shall I go now?" he wept to his brothers. ³¹Then the brothers killed a goat and spattered its blood on Joseph's coat. ³²They took the coat to their father and asked him to identify it.

"We found this in the field," they told him. "Is it Joseph's coat or not?" ³³Their father recognized it at once.

"Yes," he sobbed, "it is my son's coat. A wild animal has eaten him. Joseph is without doubt torn in pieces."

³⁴Then Israel tore his clothes and put on sackcloth. He mourned for his son deeply for many weeks. ³⁵His family all tried to comfort him, but it was no use.

"I will die in mourning for my son," he would say. Then he would break down and cry again.

³⁶Meanwhile, in Egypt, the traders sold Joseph to Potiphar. Potiphar was an officer of the Pharaoh—the king of Egypt. Potiphar was captain of the palace guard.

- *Remember:* Why did Joseph's brothers want to kill him? (37:4,8,11) What did they do instead? (37:23-28) Where did the traders take Joseph? (37:28) Did Joseph's brothers think he would die as a slave? How do you know? (37:26-27) How did Joseph's brothers deceive their father, Jacob? (37:31-33)

- *Discover:* It takes a second sin to cover up the first sin. It may take a third to cover up the second. First the brothers sinned by selling their own brother into slavery. Then they had to lie to their father so he wouldn't know what really happened.

- *Apply:* The next time you start to do something wrong, stop! Ask what second sin you may have to do to cover up the first.

- *What's next?* Have you seen someone in double trouble, or even triple trouble? You will in Genesis 39. ◼

Judah and Tamar

38 About this time, Judah left home and moved to Adullam. He lived there with a man named Hirah. ²There he met and married a Canaanite girl— the daughter of Shua. ³⁻⁵They lived at Chezib and had three sons, Er, Onan, and Shelah. These names were given to them by their mother, except for Er, who was named by his father.

⁶When his oldest son, Er, grew up, Judah arranged for him to marry a girl named Tamar. ⁷But Er was a wicked man, and so the Lord killed him.

⁸Then Judah said to Er's brother, Onan, "You must marry Tamar. Our law requires this of a dead man's brother. Her sons from you will be your brother's heirs."

⁹But Onan was not willing to have a child who would not be counted as his own. So, although he married her, whenever he went in to sleep with her, he spilled the sperm on the bed. He did this to prevent her from having a baby which would be his brother's. ¹⁰So far as the Lord was concerned, it was very wrong of him [to deny a child to his deceased brother]. So the Lord killed him, too. ¹¹Then Judah told Tamar, his daughter-in-law, not to marry again at that time. She was to go back to her childhood home and to her parents. She would remain a widow there until his youngest son, Shelah, was old enough to marry her. But he didn't really intend for Shelah to do this. He feared God would kill him, too, just as he had his two brothers. So Tamar went home to her parents.

¹²After some time Judah's wife died. After the time of mourning was over, Judah and his friend Hirah, the Adullamite, went to Timnah to look after the shearing of his sheep. ¹³Someone told Tamar that her father-in-law had left for the sheep-shearing at Timnah. ¹⁴She realized by now that she would not be permitted to marry Shelah, though he was fully grown. She laid aside her widow's clothing and covered herself with a veil to disguise herself. Then she sat beside the road at the entrance to the village of Enaim. This was on the way to Timnah. ¹⁵Judah noticed her as he went

by. He thought she was a prostitute, since her face was veiled. ¹⁶So he stopped and asked her to sleep with him. He did not realize of course that she was his own daughter-in-law.

"How much will you pay me?" she asked.

¹⁷"I'll send you a young goat from my flock," he promised.

"What pledge will you give me, so that I can be sure you will send it?" she asked.

¹⁸"Well, what do you want?" he asked.

"Your seal and your walking stick," she replied. So he gave them to her and she let him come and sleep with her. She became pregnant as a result. ¹⁹After that she went back to wearing her widow's clothing as usual. ²⁰Judah asked his friend Hirah the Adullamite to take the young goat back to her. He was also to pick up the pledges he had given her. But Hirah couldn't find her!

²¹So he asked around of the men of the city, "Where does the prostitute live who is often out beside the road at the entrance of the village?"

"But we've never had a public prostitute here," they said. ²²So he went back to Judah. He told him he couldn't find her. He also told him what the men of the place had said.

²³"Then let her keep them!" Judah exclaimed. "We tried our best. We'll only be laughed at if we go back again."

²⁴About three months later Judah heard news about Tamar, his daughter-in-law. She was pregnant because she had been a prostitute.

"Bring her out and burn her," Judah shouted.

²⁵But as they were taking her out to kill her she sent a message to her father-in-law. She said, "The man who owns this seal and walking stick is the father of my child. Do you recognize them?"

²⁶Judah admitted that they were his. Then he said, "She is more in the right than I am. I refused to keep my promise to give her to my son Shelah." But Judah did not marry her.

²⁷In due season the time of her delivery came. She had twin sons. ²⁸As they were being born, the midwife tied a scarlet thread around the wrist of the child who appeared first. ²⁹But he drew back his hand and the other baby was actually the first to be born. "Where did *you* come from!" she exclaimed. And ever after he was called Perez (meaning "Bursting Out"). ³⁰Then, soon after that, the baby with the scarlet thread on his wrist was born. He was named Zerah.

Potiphar Buys Joseph

Joseph was in trouble. He was a slave in Egypt. Usually slaves in Egypt didn't live long. Then Joseph got into double trouble. His master's wife wanted to pretend that Joseph was her husband. That got Joseph in triple trouble. Here's how it happened.

39 Joseph arrived in Egypt as a captive of the Ishmaelite traders. He was bought as a slave by Potiphar. He was a member of the personal staff of Pharaoh, the king of Egypt. Potiphar was the captain of the king's bodyguard. ²The Lord greatly blessed Joseph there in the home of his master. All he did succeeded. ³Potiphar saw this and knew that the Lord was with Joseph in a very special way.

⁴So Joseph naturally became quite a favorite with him. Soon he was put in charge of Potiphar's household, and all of his business affairs. ⁵At once the Lord began blessing Potiphar for Joseph's sake. All his household affairs began to run smoothly. His crops flourished and his flocks grew. ⁶So Potiphar gave Joseph complete charge over all he owned. He hadn't a worry in the world with Joseph

there, except to decide what he wanted to eat! Joseph, by the way, was a very handsome young man.

7One day at about this time Potiphar's wife began making eyes at Joseph. She asked him to come and sleep with her.

8Joseph refused. "Look," he told her, "my master trusts me with everything in the entire household. 9He himself has no more say here than I have! He has held back nothing from me except you, because you are his wife. How can I do such a wicked thing as this? It would be a great sin against God."

10But she kept on asking day after day. Joseph refused to listen. He kept out of her way as much as possible. 11Then one day he was in the house going about his work. No one else was around at the time. 12She came and grabbed him by the sleeve. "Sleep with me," she demanded. He tore himself away, but as he did, his jacket slipped off. She was left holding it as he fled from the house. 13She saw that she had

his jacket, and that he had fled. 14-15So she began screaming. When the other men around the place came running in to see what had happened, she was crying. "My husband had to bring in this Hebrew slave to insult us!" she sobbed. "He tried to sleep with me. But when I screamed, he ran. And he forgot to take his jacket."

16She kept the jacket. And when her husband came home that night, 17she told him her story.

"That Hebrew slave you've had around here tried to sleep with me. 18I was only saved by my screams. He fled, leaving his jacket behind!"

19Well, when her husband heard his wife's story, he was furious. 20He threw Joseph into prison, where the king's prisoners were kept in chains. 21But the Lord was with Joseph there, too, and was kind to him. He granted him favor with the chief jailer. 22In fact, the jailer soon handed over the entire prison to Joseph's management. All the other

prisoners were under his charge. 23The chief jailer had no more worries after that. Joseph took care of everything. The Lord was with him so that all ran smoothly.

- *Remember:* What kind of work did Potiphar do? (39:1) How did Joseph get into trouble with Potiphar? (39:7-19) Where did Potiphar put Joseph? (39:20) How would you have felt if you were Joseph? How would you have acted? What would you have said to God?

- *Discover:* Things may seem worse before they get better. In prison, Joseph may have wondered how things could get better. But they would. God was there in prison with Joseph!

- *Apply:* If things look bad for you now, remember that God is there with you. Trust him. He may have good surprises for you.

- *What's next?* Have you ever dreamed strange dreams? In Genesis 40 you will read about some really strange ones. ■

Joseph Tells the Meaning of Two Dreams

Joseph was really in trouble! He was a slave. His master's wife lied about him. Now he was in prison. Didn't God love Joseph? Keep asking that as you watch how God made good things come out of bad things in Joseph's life. Here's how these things happened.

40 Some time later the king of Egypt became angry with both his chief baker and his chief butler. He jailed them both in the prison where Joseph was. The prison was in the castle of Potiphar, the captain of the guard. He was also the chief executioner. 4They remained under arrest there for quite some time. Potiphar assigned Joseph to wait on them. 5One night each of them had a dream. 6The next morning Joseph noticed that they looked sad.

7"What in the world is the matter?" he asked.

8And they replied, "We both had dreams last night. But there is no one here to tell us what they mean."

"Interpreting dreams is God's business," Joseph replied. "Tell me what you saw."

9-10The butler told his dream first. "In my dream," he said, "I saw a vine with three branches. They began to bud and blossom. Soon there were clusters of ripe grapes. 11I was holding Pharaoh's wine cup in my hand. So I took the grapes and squeezed the juice into it. I gave it to him to drink."

12"I know what the dream means," Joseph said. "The three branches mean three days! 13Within three days Pharaoh is going to take you out of prison. He will give you back your job again as his chief butler. 14And please have some pity on me when you are back in his favor. Mention me to Pharaoh. Ask him to let me out of here. 15For I was kidnapped from my homeland among the Hebrews. And now this—here I am in jail when I did nothing to deserve it."

16The chief baker saw that the first dream had a good meaning. So he told his dream to Joseph, too.

"In my dream," he said, "there were three baskets of pastries on my head. 17In the top basket were all kinds of bakery goods for Pharaoh. But the birds came and ate them."

18-19"The three baskets mean three days," Joseph told him. "Three days from now Pharaoh will take off your head. He will impale your body on a pole. The birds will come and pick off your flesh!"

²⁰Pharaoh's birthday came three days later. He held a party for all of his officials and household staff. He sent for his chief butler and chief baker. They were brought to him from the prison. ²¹Then he gave the chief butler his former position. ²²But he sentenced the chief baker to be impaled, just as Joseph had predicted. ²³Pharaoh's wine taster, however, forgot all about Joseph. He never gave him another thought.

- *Remember:* Which two men did Joseph meet in prison? (40:1-3) What were their strange dreams? (40:9-11,16-17) What did Joseph say about their dreams? (40:12-13,18-19) Did these things come true? (40:20-22) What did Joseph ask the wine taster to do? (40:14) Did he do it? (40:23) How would you have felt if you were Joseph?

- *Discover:* There may be a good reason for something bad in your life. Don't get angry at every bad thing that happens. Ask God to help something good come from it.

- *Apply:* Has something bad happened to you? Is someone trying to hurt you? Ask God to help something good come from it.

- *What's next?* How could two dreams help a prisoner become governor? They did. Read Genesis 41. ▪

Joseph Becomes Ruler of Egypt

In the morning Joseph was a slave. He woke up in prison. That night he was ruler of Egypt. He went to bed in a palace. It all happened in one day. Here's what happened.

41 One night two years later, Pharaoh dreamed that he was standing on the bank of the Nile River. ²Suddenly, seven sleek, fat cows came up out of the river and began grazing in the grass. ³Then seven other cows came up from the river. But they were very skinny, and all their ribs stood out. They went over and stood beside the fat cows. ⁴Then the skinny cows ate the fat ones! Then Pharaoh woke up!

⁵Soon he fell asleep again and had a second dream. This time he saw seven heads of grain on one stalk. Each kernel was well formed and plump. ⁶Then, suddenly, seven more heads appeared on the stalk. But these were shriveled and withered by the east wind. ⁷And these thin heads swallowed up the seven plump, well-formed heads! Then Pharaoh woke up again and saw it was all a dream. ⁸Next morning, as he thought about it, he became very concerned about what the dreams might mean. He called for all the magicians and sages of Egypt. He told them about it. But not one of them could tell him what his dreams meant. ⁹Then the king's wine taster spoke up. "Today I remember my sin!" he said. ¹⁰"Some time ago you were angry with a couple of us. You put me and the chief baker in jail in the castle of the captain of the guard. ¹¹The chief baker and I each had a dream one night. ¹²We told the dreams to a young Hebrew fellow there. He was a slave of the captain of the guard. And he told us what our dreams meant. ¹³And it happened just as he said. I was given back my position of wine taster. And the chief baker was killed and impaled on a pole."

¹⁴Pharaoh sent at once for Joseph. He was brought hastily from the dungeon. And after a quick shave and change of clothes, he came in before Pharaoh.

¹⁵"I had a dream last night," Pharaoh told him. "And none of these men can tell me what it means. But I have heard that you can interpret dreams. That is why I have called for you."

[16]"I can't do it by myself," Joseph replied. "But God will tell you what it means!"

[17]So Pharaoh told him the dream. "I was standing upon the bank of the Nile River," he said. [18]"Suddenly, seven fat, healthy-looking cows came up out of the river. They began grazing along the river bank. [19]But then seven other cows came up from the river. They were very skinny and bony. In fact, I've never seen such poor-looking cattle in all the land of Egypt. [20]These skinny cattle ate up the seven fat ones that had come out first. [21]And afterwards they were still as skinny as before! Then I woke up.

[22]"A little later I had another dream. This time there were seven heads of grain on one stalk. All seven heads were plump and full. [23]Then, out of the same stalk, came seven withered, thin heads. [24]And the thin heads swallowed up the fat ones! I told all this to my magicians. But not one of them could tell me the meaning."

[25]"Both dreams mean the same thing," Joseph told Pharaoh. "God was telling you what he is going to do here in the land of Egypt. [26]The seven fat cows (and also the seven fat, well-formed heads of grain) mean that there are seven years of prosperity ahead. [27]The seven skinny cows (and also the seven thin and withered heads of grain) show that there will be seven years of famine following the seven years of prosperity.

[28]"So God has showed you what he is about to do. [29]The next seven years will be a period of great prosperity throughout all the land of Egypt. [30]But afterwards there will be seven years of famine so great that all the prosperity will be forgotten and wiped out. Famine will consume the land. [31]The famine will be so terrible that even the memory of the good years will be erased. [32]The double dream gives double impact. It shows that what I have told you is truly going to happen. God has decreed it. And it is going to happen soon. [33]My suggestion is that you find the wisest man in Egypt. Put him in charge of a nationwide farm program. [34-35]Let Pharaoh divide Egypt into five districts. And let the officials of these districts gather into the royal store-houses all the extra crops of the next seven years. [36]That way there will be enough to eat when the seven years of famine come. Otherwise, disaster will surely strike."

[37]Joseph's ideas were well received by Pharaoh and his assistants. [38]They discussed who should be chosen for the job. And Pharaoh said, "Who could do it better than Joseph? For he is a man who is clearly filled with the Spirit of God." [39]Turning to Joseph, Pharaoh said to him, "Since God has revealed the meaning of the dreams to you, you are the wisest man in the country! [40]I hereby appoint you to be in charge of this entire project. What you say goes, throughout all the land of Egypt. I alone will outrank you."

[41-42]Then Pharaoh placed his own signet ring on Joseph's finger as a token of his authority. He dressed him in fine clothing. And he placed the royal gold chain about his neck. He declared, "See, I have placed you in charge of all the land of Egypt."

[43]Pharaoh also gave Joseph the chariot of his second-in-command. Wherever he went the shout arose, "Kneel down!" [44]And Pharaoh said to Joseph, "I, the king of Egypt, swear that you shall have complete charge over all the land of Egypt."

[45]Pharaoh gave him a name meaning "He has the godlike power of life and death!" And he gave him a wife, a girl named Asenath, daughter of Potiphera, priest of Heliopolis. So Joseph became famous throughout the land of Egypt. [46]He was 30 years old as he entered the service of the king. Joseph went out from Pharaoh and began traveling all across the land.

[47]And sure enough, for the next seven years there were bumper crops everywhere. [48]During those years, Joseph collected for the government some of all the crops grown throughout Egypt. He stored them in nearby cities. [49]After seven years of this, the barns were full to overflowing. There was so much that no one kept track of the amount.

[50]During this time before the arrival of the first of the famine years, two sons

were born to Joseph by Asenath, the daughter of Potiphera, priest of the sun god Re of Heliopolis. ⁵¹Joseph named his oldest son Manasseh. (This means "Made to Forget.") Joseph meant that God had made up to him for all the pain of his youth, and for the loss of his father's home. ⁵²The second boy was named Ephraim. (This means "Fruitful.") "For God has made me fruitful in this land of my slavery," he said. ⁵³So at last the seven years of plenty came to an end. ⁵⁴Then the seven years of famine began, just as Joseph had predicted. There were crop failures in all the surrounding countries, too. But in Egypt there was plenty of grain in the storehouses. ⁵⁵The people began to starve. They pleaded with Pharaoh for food, and he sent them to Joseph. "Do whatever he tells you to," he told them.

⁵⁶⁻⁵⁷So now there was famine all over the world. And Joseph opened up the storehouses. He sold grain to the Egyptians. He also sold it to those from other lands who came to Egypt to buy grain from Joseph.

- *Remember:* What did Pharaoh dream? (41:1-7) How did he learn about Joseph? (41:9-13) What did Joseph do that caused Pharaoh to make him ruler of Egypt? (41:39-40). What special job was Joseph to do for Pharaoh? (41:38) If you were Joseph, what would you say in your prayers tonight?

- *Discover:* Joseph told the king, "I can't do this by myself, but God will tell you what it means." (41:16) What did he mean?

- *Apply:* When God does something good for you, don't brag that you did it!

- *What's next?* Have you ever heard of men who didn't know their own brother? You will in Genesis 42. ▪

Joseph's Brothers Buy Grain

Do you remember Joseph's two dreams when he was young? (Genesis 37:6-11) If not, read them again. These dreams made his brothers so angry that they sold him as a slave. They would never bow down before Joseph! That's what they thought. But here they are, bowing before him. Of course they don't know that this Egyptian ruler is Joseph. What do you think will happen now?

42 Jacob heard that there was grain available in Egypt. And he said to his sons, "Why are you standing around looking at one another? ²I have heard that there is grain available in Egypt. Go down and buy some for us before we all starve to death."

³So Joseph's 10 older brothers went down to Egypt to buy grain. ⁴But Jacob wouldn't let Joseph's younger brother Benjamin go with them. He feared some harm might happen to him [as it had to his brother Joseph]. ⁵So it was that Israel's sons arrived in Egypt. They came with many others from many lands to buy food. The famine was as bad in Canaan as it was everywhere else.

⁶Joseph was governor of all Egypt, and in charge of the sale of the grain. So it was to him that his brothers came. They bowed low before him, with their faces to the earth. ⁷Joseph recognized them instantly. But he pretended he didn't.

"Where are you from?" he demanded roughly.

"From the land of Canaan," they replied. "We have come to buy grain."

⁸⁻⁹Then Joseph remembered the dreams of long ago! But he said to them, "You are spies. You have come to see how destitute the famine has made our land."

¹⁰"No, no," they exclaimed. "We have come to buy food. ¹¹We are all brothers and honest men, sir! We are not spies!"

¹²"Yes, you are," he insisted. "You have come to see how weak we are."

¹³"Sir," they said, "there are 12 of us brothers. Our father is in the land of Canaan. Our youngest brother is there with our father. And one of our brothers is dead."

¹⁴"So?" Joseph asked. "What does that prove? You are spies. ¹⁵This is the way I will test your story. I swear by the life of Pharaoh that you are not going to leave Egypt until this youngest brother comes here. ¹⁶One of you go and get your brother! I'll keep the rest of you here, bound in prison. Then we'll find out whether your story is true or not. If you don't have a younger brother, then I'll know you are spies."

¹⁷So he threw them all into jail for three days.

¹⁸The third day Joseph said to them, "I am a God-fearing man. I'm going to give you an opportunity to prove yourselves. ¹⁹I'm going to take a chance that you are honorable. Only one of you shall remain in jail. The rest of you may go on home with grain for your families. ²⁰But bring your youngest brother back to me. In this way I will know whether you are telling me the truth. And if you are, I will spare you." To this they agreed.

²¹Speaking among themselves, they said, "This has all happened because of what we did to Joseph long ago. We saw his terror and anguish and heard his pleadings, but we wouldn't listen."

²²"Didn't I tell you not to do it?" Reuben asked. "But you wouldn't listen. And now we are going to die because we murdered him."

²³Of course they didn't know that Joseph understood them as he was standing there. For he had been speaking to them through an interpreter. ²⁴Now he left the room. He found a place where he could weep. Returning, he selected Simeon from among them. He had him bound before their eyes. ²⁵Joseph then ordered his servants to fill the men's sacks with grain. But he also gave secret orders to put each brother's payment at the top of his sack! He also gave them supplies for their trip. ²⁶So they loaded up their donkeys with the grain and started for home. ²⁷They stopped for the night. And one of them opened his sack to get some grain to feed the donkeys. He found his money in the mouth of the sack!

²⁸"Look," he exclaimed to his brothers, "my money is here in my sack." They were filled with terror. Trembling, they exclaimed to each other. "What is this that God has done to us?" ²⁹So they came to their father, Jacob, in the land of Canaan. They told him all that had happened.

³⁰"The king's chief assistant spoke very roughly to us," they told him. "He took us for spies. ³¹'No, no,' we said, 'we are honest men, not spies. ³²We are 12 brothers, sons of one father. One is dead, and the youngest is with our father in the land of Canaan.' ³³Then the man told us, 'This is the way I will find out if you are what you claim to be. Leave one of your brothers here with me. Take grain for your families and go on home. ³⁴But bring your youngest brother back to me. Then I shall know whether you are spies or honest men. If you prove to be what you say, then I will give you back your brother. And you can come as often as you like to buy grain.'"

³⁵As they emptied out the sacks, there at the top of each was the money paid for the grain! Terror gripped them, as it did their father.

³⁶Then Jacob exclaimed, "You have bereaved me of my children. Joseph didn't come back. Simeon is gone. And now you want to take Benjamin too! Everything has been against me."

³⁷Then Reuben said to his father, "Kill my two sons if I don't bring Benjamin back to you. I'll be responsible for him."

³⁸But Jacob replied, "My son shall not go down with you. His brother Joseph is dead. He alone is left of his mother's children. If anything should happen to him, I would die."

- *Remember:* How many of Joseph's brothers went to Egypt? (42:3) Which brother did not go? Why? (42:4) Which brother did Joseph keep in prison? (42:24) What did the brothers have to do to get Simeon out of prison? (42:19-20) Why do you think Joseph didn't tell his brothers who he was? Why did the brothers think all these things were happening to them? (42:21) Do you think they were starting to feel guilty? (42:21-22)

• *Discover:* Doing wrong makes us feel guilty, doesn't it? Joseph's brothers felt guilty because they sold him. Do you think they should feel guilty? (42:21)

• *Apply:* Do you feel guilty about something you have done wrong? Ask God to forgive you NOW. Then try to correct the wrong you have done.

• *What's next?* Hungry people who are afraid to go to a big banquet? That's true. You'll find out why as you read Genesis 43. ■

Joseph's Brothers Return to Egypt

Here are some men who are really hungry. There's a famine back home. But when they are invited to a big banquet, they are afraid to go. Do you know why?

43 But there was no relief from the terrible famine in the land. ²The grain they had brought from Egypt was almost gone. So their father said to them, "Go again. Buy us a little food."

³⁻⁵But Judah told him, "The man wasn't fooling one bit. And he said, 'Don't ever come back again unless your brother is with you.' We cannot go unless you let Benjamin go with us."

⁶"Why did you ever tell him you had another brother?" Israel moaned. "Why did you have to treat me like that?"

⁷"But the man asked us about our family," they told him. "He wanted to know whether our father was still living. He also asked us if we had another brother. So we told him. How could we know that he was going to say, 'Bring me your brother'?"

⁸Judah said to his father, "Send the boy with me. Then we will be on our way. Otherwise we will all die of starvation—and not only we, but you and all our little ones. ⁹I promise he will be safe. If I don't bring him back to you, then let me bear the blame forever. ¹⁰For we could have gone and come back by this time if you had let him come."

¹¹So their father Israel finally said to them, "If it can't be avoided, then at least do this. Load your donkeys with the best products of the land. Take them to the man as gifts—balm, honey, spices, myrrh, pistachio nuts, and almonds.

¹²Take double money so that you can pay back what was in the mouths of your sacks. It was probably someone's mistake. ¹³And take your brother and go. ¹⁴May God Almighty give you mercy before the man. And may he release Simeon and return Benjamin. And if I must bear the anguish of their deaths, then so be it."

¹⁵So they took the gifts and double money and went to Egypt, and stood before Joseph. ¹⁶Joseph saw that Benjamin was with them. So he said to the manager of his household, "These men will eat with me this noon. Take them home. Prepare a big feast." ¹⁷So the man did as he was told. He took them to Joseph's palace. ¹⁸They were badly frightened when they saw where they were being taken.

"It's because of the money returned to us in our sacks," they said. "He wants to pretend we stole it and seize us as slaves, with our donkeys."

¹⁹As they came to the entrance to the palace, they went over to Joseph's household manager. ²⁰They said to him, "O sir, after our first trip to Egypt to buy food, ²¹as we were going home, we stopped for the night and opened our sacks. The money was there that we had paid for the grain. Here it is. We have brought it back again, ²²along with more money to buy grain. We have no idea how the money got into our sacks."

23"Don't worry about it," the household manager told them. "Your God, even the God of your fathers, must have put it there. We collected your money all right."

Then he released Simeon and brought him out to them. 24They were then conducted into the palace and given water to refresh their feet. And their donkeys were fed. 25Then they got their presents ready for Joseph's arrival at noon, for they were told that they would be eating there. 26When Joseph came home they gave him their presents, bowing low before him.

27He asked how they had been getting along. "And how is your father—the old man you spoke about? Is he still alive?"

28"Yes," they replied. "He is alive and well." Then again they bowed before him.

29Looking at his brother Benjamin, he asked, "Is this your youngest brother, the one you told me about? How are you, my son? God be good to you." 30Then Joseph made a fast exit. He was overcome with love for his brother and had to go out and cry. Going into his bedroom, he wept there. 31Then he washed his face. He came out, keeping himself under control. "Let's eat," he said.

32Joseph ate by himself. His brothers were served at a separate table. And the Egyptians ate at still another. Egyptians despise Hebrews and never eat with them. 33He told each of them where to sit. He seated them in the order of their ages, from the oldest to the youngest. This amazed them all! 34Their food was served to them from Joseph's own table. He gave the largest serving to Benjamin—five times as much as to any of the others! They had a wonderful time talking to each other. And the wine flowed freely!

- *Remember:* What special gifts did the brothers take to Joseph? (43:11-12) Why were the brothers afraid to go to Joseph's banquet? (43:18) How did the brothers sit at the banquet? (43:33) What special kindness did Joseph show to Benjamin? (43:34) What do you think Joseph wanted to say to Benjamin? What do you think he wanted to say to his other brothers?

- *Discover:* Be careful when you get proud. God may humble you or put you down! Do you see Joseph's proud brothers bowing before him? (43:26)

- *Apply:* Have you been put down lately? Maybe you have been proud about something. God may be humbling you.

- *What's next?* Do you like to take tests? Here's one that would really scare you! You wouldn't like it any more than the men who took it in Genesis 44. ▓

Joseph Tests His Brothers

Your teacher may give you a test this week. But not with a silver cup! Joseph had to test his brothers. He had to know if they were sorry for what they had done to him. His silver cup was one way to do it. Find out about the silver cup test as you read on.

44 His brothers were ready to leave. So Joseph ordered his household manager to fill each of their sacks with as much grain as they could carry. He also ordered him to put into the mouth of each man's sack the money he had paid! 2He was also told to put Joseph's own silver cup at the top of Benjamin's sack, along with the grain money. So the household manager did as he was told. 3The brothers were up at dawn and on their way with their loaded donkeys.

4But when they were barely out of the city, Joseph said to his household manager, "Chase after them and stop them. Ask them why they are acting like this when I have been so kind to them. ⁵Ask them, 'What do you mean by stealing my lord's personal silver drinking cup, which he uses for fortune-telling? What a wicked thing you have done!'" ⁶So he caught up with them and spoke to them as Joseph had told him to.

⁷"What in the world are you talking about?" they demanded. "What kind of people do you think we are? How could you accuse us of such a terrible thing as that? ⁸Didn't we bring back the money we found in the mouth of our sacks? Why would we steal silver or gold from your master's house? ⁹If you find his cup with any one of us, let that one die. And all the rest of us will be slaves forever to your master."

¹⁰"Fair enough," the man replied. "But only the one who stole it will be a slave. The rest of you can go free."

¹¹They quickly took down their sacks from the backs of their donkeys. Then they opened them. ¹²He began searching the oldest brother's sack, going on down the line to the youngest. And the cup was found in Benjamin's! ¹³They ripped their clothing in despair. They then loaded the donkeys again, and returned to the city. ¹⁴Joseph was still home when Judah and his brothers arrived. They fell to the ground before him.

¹⁵"What were you trying to do?" Joseph demanded. "Didn't you know such a man as I would know who stole it?"

¹⁶And Judah said, "Oh, what shall we say to my lord? How can we plead? How can we prove our innocence? God is punishing us for our sins. Sir, we have all come back to be your slaves, both we and he in whose sack the cup was found."

¹⁷"No," Joseph said. "Only the man who stole the cup, he shall be my slave. The rest of you can go on home to your father."

¹⁸Then Judah stepped forward and said, "O sir, let me say just this one word to you. Be patient with me for a moment. I know you can doom me in an instant, as though you were Pharaoh himself. ¹⁹"Sir, you asked us if we had a father or a brother. ²⁰We said, 'Yes, we have a father, an old man. And we have a child of his old age, a little one. His brother is dead. He alone is left of his mother's children. And his father loves him very much.' ²¹And you said to us, 'Bring him here so that I can see him.' ²²But we said to you, 'Sir, the boy cannot leave his father, for his father would die.' ²³But you told us, 'Don't come back here unless your youngest brother is with you.' ²⁴So we returned to our father. He told him what you had said. ²⁵And when he said, 'Go back again and buy us a little food.' ²⁶We replied, 'We can't, unless you let our youngest brother go with us. Only then may we come.'

²⁷"Then my father said to us, 'You know that my wife had two sons. ²⁸One of them went away and never came back. He was doubtless torn to pieces by some wild animal. I have never seen him since. ²⁹And if you take away his brother from me also, and any harm befalls him,

I shall die with sorrow.' ³⁰ And now, sir, I cannot go back to my father if the boy is not with us. Our father's life is bound up in the boy's life. ³¹If he sees that the boy is not with us, our father will die. And we will be responsible for bringing down his gray hairs with sorrow to the grave. ³²Sir, I pledged my father that I would take care of the boy. I told him, 'If I don't bring him back to you, I shall bear the blame forever.' ³³Please sir, let me stay here as a slave instead of the boy. Let the boy go back with his brothers. ³⁴For how shall I go back to my father if the boy is not with me? I cannot bear to see what this would do to him."

• *Remember:* What did Joseph put in each grain sack? (44:1) What did he put in Benjamin's sack? (44:2) Which brother wanted to sell Joseph as a slave? (Read Genesis 37:26-27) Which brother begged Joseph for kindness? (44:18) Was this the same brother? Why do you think he has changed so much?

• *Discover:* Be careful what bad things you say about someone. Your words may come back to punish you. Judah once said, "Let's sell Joseph." Now Judah is begging Joseph for their lives.

• *Apply:* Read Psalm 141:3. Ask God to help you be careful about what you say.

• *What's next?* Suppose some people wanted to kill you. So they sold you as a slave. Now you can do anything you want to them. What would you do? Read what Joseph did in Genesis 45. ■

Joseph Forgives His Brothers

The time has come. Joseph's brothers had sold him as a slave. Now he has the power to punish his brothers or forgive them. What do you think he will do?

45 Joseph could stand it no longer. "Out, all of you," he cried out to his attendants. And he was left alone with his brothers. ²Then he wept aloud. His sobs could be heard throughout the palace. And the news was quickly carried to Pharaoh's palace.

³"I am Joseph!" he said to his brothers. "Is my father still alive?" But his brothers couldn't say a word. They were stunned with surprise.

⁴"Come over here," he said. So they came closer. And he said again, "I am Joseph, your brother whom you sold into Egypt! ⁵But don't be angry with yourselves that you did this to me, for God did it! He sent me here ahead of you to preserve your lives. ⁶These two years of famine will grow to seven. During this time there will be neither plowing nor harvest. ⁷God has sent me here to keep you and your families alive, so that you will become a great nation. ⁸Yes, it was God who sent me here, not you! And he has made me a counselor to Pharaoh. I am the manager of this entire nation, ruler of all the land of Egypt.

⁹"Hurry, return to my father and tell him, 'Your son Joseph says, "God has made me chief of all the land of Egypt. Come down to me right away! ¹⁰You shall live in the land of Goshen. That way you can be near me with all your children, your grandchildren, your flocks and herds, and all that you have. ¹¹⁻¹²I will take care of you there."' (You men are witnesses of my promise. And my brother Benjamin has heard me say it.) '"For there are still five years of famine ahead of us. Otherwise you will come to utter poverty along with all your household."' ¹³Tell our father about all my power here in Egypt, and how all obey me. And bring him to me quickly."

¹⁴Then, weeping with joy, he embraced Benjamin, and Benjamin began weeping too. ¹⁵And he did the same with each of his brothers, who found their

tongues at last! ¹⁶The news soon reached Pharaoh—"Joseph's brothers have come." And Pharaoh was very happy to hear it, as were his officials.

¹⁷Then Pharaoh said to Joseph, "Tell your brothers to load their pack animals. They should return quickly to their homes in Canaan. ¹⁸Let them bring your father and all of your families and come here to Egypt to live. Tell them, 'Pharaoh will assign to you the very best land in Egypt. You shall live off the fat of the land!' ¹⁹And tell your brothers to take wagons from Egypt to carry their wives and little ones, and to bring your father here. ²⁰Don't worry about your property, for the best of all the land of Egypt is yours."

²¹So Joseph gave them wagons, as Pharaoh had commanded, and supplies for the trip. ²²He gave each of them new clothes. But to Benjamin he gave five changes of clothes and 300 pieces of silver! ²³He sent his father 10 donkey-loads of the good things of Egypt. He also sent 10 donkeys loaded with grain and all kinds of other food, to eat on his trip. ²⁴So he sent his brothers off.

"Don't quarrel along the way!" was his parting shot! ²⁵They left and went back to the land of Canaan, to Jacob their father.

²⁶"Joseph is alive," they shouted to him. "And he is ruler over all the land of Egypt!" But Jacob's heart was like a stone. He couldn't take it in. ²⁷But when they had given him Joseph's messages, and when he saw the wagons filled with food that Joseph had sent him, his spirit revived.

²⁸And he said, "It must be true! Joseph my son is alive! I will go and see him before I die."

- *Remember:* Did Joseph punish his brothers for selling him? Did he hold a grudge against them? Why didn't he? (45:5-8) Why did Joseph want his father and brothers to move to Egypt? (45:11) What did Joseph send home with the brothers? (45:21-23) What did Jacob think when he heard about Joseph? (45:26-28) What kind of person do you think Joseph was? What do you like best about him?

- *Discover:* Joseph could have held a grudge against his brothers for selling him. He could have punished them. But when you truly forgive, you don't do that. Do you? Did he?

- *Apply:* Are you holding a grudge against someone? Today is a good day to stop.

Take that grudge away. Tell that person you forgive them. Be a Joseph.

- *What's next?* An entire family—children, grandchildren, mothers, fathers, grandfather, uncles, aunts, cousins, nieces, nephews—all move to a foreign country. Read about this in Genesis 46:1–47:12. ∎

Jacob Moves to Egypt

It's moving day. But a moving van doesn't come to Jacob's tent. An entire family is moving. But it's more than one family. Jacob's family is many families with many people. There are almost 80 people who had to move to a new land. Here's how they did it.

46 So Israel set out with all that he owned. He came to Beer-sheba, and offered sacrifices there to the God of his father, Isaac. ²During the night God spoke to him in a vision.

"Jacob! Jacob!" he called.

"Yes?" Jacob answered.

³⁻⁴"I am God," the voice replied, "the God of your father. Don't be afraid to go down to Egypt. I will see to it that you become a great nation there. I will go down with you into Egypt. And I will bring your descendants back again. But you shall die in Egypt with Joseph at your side."

⁵So Jacob left Beer-sheba. And his sons brought him to Egypt. They brought along their little ones and their wives, in the wagons Pharaoh had provided for them. ⁶They brought their livestock, too, and all their belongings accumulated in the land of Canaan. And they came to Egypt. Jacob came with all his children, ⁷sons and daughters, grandsons and granddaughters—all his loved ones.

⁸⁻¹⁴Here are the names of his sons and grandchildren who went with him into Egypt:

Reuben, his oldest son;

Reuben's sons: Hanoch, Pallu, Hezron, and Carmi.

Simeon and his sons: Jemuel, Jamin, Ohad, Jachin, Zohar, and Shaul (Shaul's mother was a girl from Canaan).

Levi and his sons: Gershon, Kohath, Merari.

Judah and his sons: Er, Onan, Shelah, Perez, Zerah (however, Er and Onan died while still in Canaan, before Israel went to Egypt).

The sons of Perez were Hezron and Hamul.

Issachar and his sons: Tola, Puvah, Iob, Shimron.

Zebulun and his sons: Sered, Elon, Jahleel.

¹⁵So these were the descendants of Jacob and Leah, not including their daughter Dinah, born to Jacob in Paddan-aram. They were 33 in all.

¹⁶⁻¹⁷Also with him were:

Gad and his sons: Ziphion, Haggi, Shuni,

Ezbon, Eri, Arodi, and Areli.

Asher and his sons: Imnah, Ishvah, Ishvi,

Beriah, and a sister, Serah.

Beriah's sons were Heber and Malchiel.

¹⁸These 16 persons were the sons of Jacob and Zilpah. Zilpah was the slave-girl given to Leah by her father, Laban:

¹⁹⁻²²Also in the total of Jacob's household were these 14 sons and descendants of Jacob and Rachel:

Joseph and Benjamin;

Joseph's sons, born in the land of Egypt, were Manasseh and Ephraim. (Their mother was Asenath, the daughter of Potiphera, priest of Heliopolis.)

Benjamin's sons: Bela, Becher, Ashbel, Gera, Naaman, Ehi, Rosh, Muppim, Huppim, and Ard.

23-25Also in the group were these seven sons of Jacob and Bilhah. Bilhah was the slave-girl given to Rachel by her father, Laban:

Dan and his son: Hushim.
Naphtali and his sons: Jahzeel, Guni, Jezer, and Shillem.

26So the total number of those going to Egypt, of his own descendants, not counting the wives of Jacob's sons, was 66. 27With Joseph and his two sons included, this total of Jacob's household there in Egypt totaled 70.

28Jacob sent Judah on ahead to tell Joseph that they were on the way, and would soon arrive in Goshen—which they did. 29Joseph jumped into his chariot and went to Goshen to meet his father. They fell into each other's arms and wept a long while.

30Then Israel said to Joseph, "Now let me die, for I have seen you again. Now I know you are alive."

31And Joseph said to his brothers and to all their households, "I'll go and tell Pharaoh that you are here. I will let him know that you have come from the land of Canaan to join me. 32And I will tell him, 'These men are shepherds. They have brought with them their flocks and herds and all they own.' 33When Pharaoh calls for you and asks you about your occupation, 34tell him, 'We have been shepherds from our youth, as our fathers have been for many generations.' When you tell him this, he will let you live here in the land of Goshen." For shepherds were despised and hated in other parts of Egypt.

47 Upon their arrival, Joseph went in to see Pharaoh.

"My father and my brothers are here from Canaan," he reported. "They have come with all their flocks and herds and possessions. They wish to settle in the land of Goshen."

2He took five of his brothers with him, and presented them to Pharaoh.

3Pharaoh asked them, "What is your occupation?"

And they replied, "We are shepherds like our ancestors. 4We have come to live here in Egypt, for there is no pasture for our flocks in Canaan. The famine is very bitter there. We request permission to live in the land of Goshen."

???????????????????????????????????
Someone bought all the land in his country. Then he gave it away. Who was he?

(Read 47:13-31 for the answer.)

???????????????????????????????????

5-6And Pharaoh said to Joseph, "Choose anywhere you like for them to live. Give them the best land of Egypt. The land of Goshen will be fine. And if any of them are capable, put them in charge of my flocks, too."

7Then Joseph brought his father Jacob to Pharaoh. And Jacob blessed Pharaoh.

8"How old are you?" Pharaoh asked him.

9Jacob replied, "I have lived 130 long, hard years. I am not nearly as old as many of my ancestors." 10Then Jacob blessed Pharaoh again before he left.

11So Joseph assigned the best land of Egypt—the land of Rameses—to his father and brothers, just as Pharaoh had commanded. 12And Joseph furnished food to them according to the size of their families.

- *Remember:* What did God say to Jacob on the way to Egypt? (46:2-4) What did Joseph and his father do when they met? (46:29) In what part of Egypt did Joseph want his family to settle? Why? (46:31-34) How was Joseph doing good to those who had done bad to him? Do you think he should have done such good things for his brothers?

- *Discover:* God's way is to do good to others, even those who have hurt us.

- *Apply:* When someone does bad things to you, what should you do? Should you do bad things to them? Or should you do good to them? Read Luke 6:27. Do you do this?

• *What's next?* Before he died, Jacob asked for one promise. Do you know what it is? You will find it in Genesis 49:29–50:14. ◼

The Famine Gets Worse

¹³The famine became worse and worse. All the land of Egypt and Canaan was starving. ¹⁴Joseph collected all the money in Egypt and Canaan in exchange for grain. And he brought the money to Pharaoh's treasure-houses. ¹⁵When the people were out of money, they came to Joseph crying again for food.

"Our money is gone," they said. "But give us bread, for why should we die?"

¹⁶"Well then," Joseph replied, "give me your livestock. I will trade you food in exchange."

¹⁷So they brought their cattle to Joseph in exchange for food. Soon all the horses, flocks, herds, and donkeys of Egypt were in Pharaoh's possession.

¹⁸The next year they came again and said, "Our money is gone, and our cattle are yours. There is nothing left but our bodies and land. ¹⁹Why should we die? Buy us and our land and we will be serfs to Pharaoh. We will trade ourselves for food. Then we will live, and the land won't be abandoned."

²⁰So Joseph bought all the land of Egypt for Pharaoh. All the Egyptians sold him their fields because the famine was so severe. And the land became Pharaoh's. ²¹Thus all the people of Egypt became Pharaoh's serfs. ²²The only land he didn't buy was that belonging to the priests. They were assigned food from Pharaoh and didn't need to sell.

²³Then Joseph said to the people, "See, I have bought you and your land for Pharaoh. Here is grain. Go and sow the land. ²⁴And when you harvest it, a fifth of all you get belongs to Pharaoh. Keep four parts for yourselves to be used for next year's seed. Use it also as food for your households and little ones."

²⁵"You have saved our lives," they said. "We will gladly be the serfs of Pharaoh."

²⁶So Joseph made a law throughout the land of Egypt. It is still the law. It stated that Pharaoh was to receive, as his tax, 20 percent of all the crops except those produced on the land owned by the temples.

Jacob Blesses Joseph's Sons

²⁷So Israel lived in the land of Goshen in Egypt. Soon the people of Israel began to prosper. They multiplied in number very quickly. ²⁸Jacob lived 17 years after his arrival. He was 147 years old at the time of his death. ²⁹As the time drew near for him to die, he called for his son Joseph. He said to him, "Swear to me that you will honor my last request. Do not bury me in Egypt. ³⁰But when I am dead, take me out of Egypt. Bury me beside my ancestors." And Joseph promised. ³¹"Swear that you will do it," Jacob urged. And Joseph did. Soon after that Jacob took to his bed.

48 One day not long after this, word came to Joseph that his father was failing rapidly. So, taking with him his two sons, Manasseh and Ephraim, he went to visit him. ²When Jacob heard that Joseph had come, he gathered his strength. He sat up in the bed to greet him. ³He said to him,

"God Almighty appeared to me at Luz in the land of Canaan and blessed me. ⁴He said to me, 'I will make you a great nation. And I will give this land of Canaan to you and to your children's children. It will be their everlasting possession.' ⁵And now, as to these two sons of yours, Ephraim and Manasseh, born here in the land of Egypt before I arrived, I am adopting them as my own. They will inherit from me just as Reuben and Simeon will. ⁶But any other children born to you shall be your own. They shall inherit Ephraim's and Manasseh's portion from you. ⁷For your mother, Rachel, died after only two children when I came from Paddan-aram. At that time, we were just a short distance from Ephrath. And I buried her beside the road to Bethlehem." ⁸Then Israel looked over at the two boys. "Are these the ones?" he asked.

⁹"Yes," Joseph told him. "These are

my sons whom God has given me here in Egypt."

And Israel said, "Bring them over to me and I will bless them."

¹⁰Israel was half blind with age, so that he could hardly see. So Joseph brought the boys close to him. He kissed and embraced them.

¹¹And Israel said to Joseph, "I never thought that I would see you again. But now God has let me see your children too."

¹²⁻¹³Joseph took the boys by the hand and bowed deeply to him. He led the boys to their grandfather's knees. Ephraim stood at Israel's left hand and Manasseh at his right. ¹⁴But Israel crossed his arms as he stretched them out to lay his hands upon the boys' heads. So his right hand was upon the head of Ephraim, the younger boy. And his left hand was upon the head of Manasseh, the older. He did this purposely.

¹⁵Then he blessed Joseph with this blessing: "May God, the God of my fathers Abraham and Isaac, the God who has shepherded me all my life, wonderfully bless these boys. ¹⁶He is the Angel who has kept me from all harm. May these boys be an honor to my name and to the names of my fathers Abraham and Isaac. And may they become a mighty nation."

¹⁷But Joseph was upset and displeased when he saw that his father had laid his right hand on Ephraim's head. So he lifted it to place it on Manasseh's head instead.

¹⁸"No, Father," he said. "You've got your right hand on the wrong head! This one over here is the older. Put your right hand on him!"

¹⁹But his father refused. "I know what I'm doing, my son," he said. "Manasseh too shall become a great nation. But his younger brother shall become even greater."

²⁰So Jacob blessed the boys that day with this blessing: "May the people of Israel bless each other by saying, 'God make you as prosperous as Ephraim and Manasseh.'" (Note that he put Ephraim before Manasseh.)

²¹Then Israel said to Joseph, "I am about to die. But God will be with you. He will bring you again to Canaan, the land of your fathers. ²²And I have given the choice land of Shekem to you instead of to your brothers. It is your portion of that land which I took from the Amorites with my sword and with my bow."

Jacob Talks about His Sons

49 Then Jacob called together all his sons and said, "Gather around me. I will tell you what is going to happen to you in the days to come. ²Listen to me, O sons of Jacob. Listen to Israel your father.

³"Reuben, you are my oldest son, the child of my vigorous youth. You are the head of the list in rank and in honor. ⁴But you are unruly as the wild waves of the sea. And you shall be first no longer. I am demoting you, for you slept with one of my wives and thus dishonored me.

⁵"Simeon and Levi are two of a kind. They are men of violence and injustice. ⁶O my soul, stay away from them. May I never be a party to their wicked plans. For in their anger they murdered a man and maimed oxen just for fun. ⁷Cursed be their anger, for it is fierce and cruel. Therefore, I will scatter their descendants throughout Israel.

⁸"Judah, your brothers shall praise you. You shall destroy your enemies. Your father's sons shall bow before you. ⁹Judah is a young lion that has finished eating its prey. He has settled down as a lion. Who will dare to rouse him? ¹⁰The scepter shall not depart from Judah until Shiloh comes, whom all people shall obey. ¹¹He has chained his steed to the choicest vine. He has washed his clothes in wine. ¹²His eyes are darker than wine and his teeth are whiter than milk.

¹³"Zebulun shall dwell on the shores of the sea. He shall be a harbor for ships, with his borders extending to Sidon.

¹⁴"Issachar is a strong beast of burden resting among the saddlebags. ¹⁵When he saw how good the countryside was, how pleasant the land, he willingly bent his shoulder to the task. He served his masters with vigor.

¹⁶"Dan shall govern his people like any other tribe in Israel. ¹⁷He shall be a

serpent in the path that bites the horses' heels, so that the rider falls off. ¹⁸I trust in your salvation, Lord.

¹⁹"A marauding band shall stamp upon Gad. But he shall rob and pursue them!

²⁰"Asher shall produce rich foods, fit for kings!

²¹"Naphtali is a deer let loose, producing lovely fawns.

²²"Joseph is a fruitful tree beside a fountain. His branches shade the wall. ²³He has been severely injured by those who shot at him and persecuted him. ²⁴But their weapons were shattered by the Mighty One of Jacob, the Shepherd, the Rock of Israel. ²⁵May the God of your fathers, the Almighty, bless you with blessings of heaven above and of the earth beneath. May he bless you with blessings of the breasts and of the womb. ²⁶May he give you blessings of the grain and flowers, blessings reaching to the utmost bounds of the everlasting hills. These shall be the blessings upon the head of Joseph who was exiled from his brothers.

²⁷"Benjamin is a wolf that prowls. He devours his enemies in the morning. And in the evening he divides the loot."

²⁸So these are the blessings that Israel, their father, blessed his 12 sons with.

Jacob Dies and Is Buried

Jacob will soon die. When he is gone, he wants to be buried back home. If he is, it will mean a lot of time and work for Joseph. But Jacob asks Joseph and his brothers to promise they will do it. Will they?

²⁹⁻³⁰Then he told them, "Soon I will die. You must bury me with my fathers in the land of Canaan. Bury me in the cave in the field of Mach-pelah, facing Mamre. This is the field Abraham bought from Ephron the Hethite for a burial ground. ³¹There they buried Abraham and Sarah, his wife. There they buried Isaac and Rebekah, his wife. And there I buried Leah. ³²It is the cave which my grandfather Abraham bought from the sons of Heth." ³³Then, when Jacob had finished his prophecies to his sons, he lay back in the bed. He breathed his last, and died.

50 Joseph threw himself upon his father's body and wept over him and kissed him. ²Afterwards he told his morticians to embalm the body. ³The embalming process required 40 days, with a period of national mourning of 70 days. ⁴Then, when at last the mourning was over, Joseph approached Pharaoh's staff. He requested them to speak to Pharaoh on his behalf.

⁵"Tell His Majesty," he requested them, "that Joseph's father made Joseph swear to take his body back to the land of Canaan. He must bury him there. Ask His Majesty to permit me to go and bury my father. Assure him that I will come back right away."

⁶Pharaoh agreed. "Go and bury your father as you promised," he said.

⁷So Joseph went, and a great number of Pharaoh's counselors and assistants— all the senior officers of the land. ⁸They went with all of Joseph's relatives—his brothers and their families. But they left their little children and flocks and herds in the land of Goshen. ⁹So a very great number of chariots, cavalry, and people went with Joseph.

¹⁰They arrived at Atad (meaning "Threshing Place of Brambles"), beyond the Jordan River. There they held a very great and solemn funeral service. They observed a seven-day period of lamentation for Joseph's father. ¹¹The local residents, the Canaanites, renamed the place Abel-mizraim (meaning "Egyptian

Mourners"). For they said, "It is a place of very deep mourning by these Egyptians." 12-13So his sons did as Israel told them. They carried his body into the land of Canaan. They buried it there in the cave of Mach-pelah. This was the cave Abraham had bought in the field of Ephron the Hethite, close to Mamre.

14Then Joseph went back to Egypt with his brothers and all who had gone with him to the funeral of his father.

● *Remember:* Only important Egyptians were embalmed when they died. Which Israelite leader was embalmed? (50:2) Who went with Joseph to bury his father? (50:7-9) Did Joseph and his brothers keep their promise to their father? Did they have to do this?

● *Discover:* Joseph's father was dead, so he would not know if Joseph and his brothers kept their promise to him. But they kept it anyway. Promises should be kept, even if the other person isn't there.

● *Apply:* You have promised your parents you will do something (or not do something). But they are not there to watch you. So what difference does it make if you keep that promise?

● *What's next?* A man has every right to punish some people who hurt him. But he doesn't. You'll find out why in Genesis 50:15-26. ■

Joseph Forgives His Brothers

Many years ago Joseph dreamed a dream. His brothers' sheaves of grain bowed down before his sheaf. (Genesis 37:6-7) That meant that some day the brothers would bow down before Joseph, their kid brother. They never wanted to do that. So they sold him as a slave. But Joseph became a powerful ruler in Egypt. He could punish them for what they did. He could kill them or put them in prison for their crime. As long as their father was alive, Joseph would not do that. Now their father was dead. What would Joseph do? Would he get even?

15But now that their father was dead, Joseph's brothers were frightened.

"Now Joseph will pay us back for all the evil we did to him," they said. 16-17So they sent him this message: "Before he died, your father instructed us to tell you to forgive us for the great evil we did to you. We, servants of the God of your father, beg you to forgive us." When Joseph read the message, he broke down and cried.

18Then his brothers came and fell down before him and said, "We are your slaves."

19But Joseph told them, "Don't be afraid of me. Am I God, to judge and punish you? 20God turned into good what you meant for evil. He brought me to this high position I have today so that I could save the lives of many people. 21No, don't be afraid. Indeed, I will take care of you and your families." And he spoke very kindly to them.

22So Joseph and his brothers and their families continued to live in Egypt. Joseph was 110 years old when he died. 23He lived to see the birth of his son Ephraim's children. And the children of Machir, Manasseh's son, played at his feet.

24"Soon I will die," Joseph told his brothers. "But God will surely come and get you and bring you out of this land of Egypt. He will take you back to the land he promised to the descendants of Abraham, Isaac, and Jacob." 25Then Joseph made his brothers promise with an oath that they would take his body back with them when they returned to Canaan. 26So Joseph died at the age of 110. They embalmed him, and his body was placed in a coffin in Egypt.

• *Remember:* Why were Joseph's brothers worried? (50:15) Did he try to punish them or get even with them? What did he say to them? (50:19-21) What would you have done if you were Joseph?

• *Discover:* God is willing to forgive anything we have done if we are sorry and ask him for forgiveness. Should we do less than that for others?

• *Apply:* Does someone want you to forgive them? Will you do it today?

• *What's next?* Four hundred years will go by before our next story, which you will read in Exodus 1. Joseph's family has now grown into a large nation. They have a terrible surprise waiting for them. ■

EXODUS

In Exodus, you'll meet one of the meanest kings on earth. He was so mean that he threw babies into the river to drown. But mean people aren't always smart people. One of the baby boys he tried to kill became his own adopted grandson! That baby boy grew up to be a great man. His name was Moses. He organized the biggest moving day ever.

What would you think if everyone in your town moved on the same day? That would be quite a moving day, wouldn't it? In Exodus, you'll see a million people move at one time. Where are they going? To another country. What are they taking with them? Everything they have. How will they get there? Walk. How long will it take? Forty years.

In Exodus you will see a river turn to blood. You'll see a golden calf, a tent worth millions of dollars, and a pillar of fire that leads people on their trip. In Exodus you'll walk on a dry path through the sea. And you'll see that sea tumble over an army and its chariots. You don't want to miss the excitement of Exodus!

The Hebrews Become Slaves

What kind of work does your father or mother do? How do they dress to go to work? Their work is very different from a Hebrew slave's at this time. These people worked with mud, making bricks. Their bosses beat them with whips. They had to carry heavy loads of brick and mortar. How much money did they make? None! Slaves did not get money for going to work. They did not have nice houses or good food or pretty clothes. Not only that, these people had something much worse happen to them. Let's see what it was.

1 This is the list of the sons of Jacob: Reuben, Simeon, Levi, Judah, Issachar, Zebulun, Benjamin, Dan, Naphtali, Gad, Asher. They went with him to Egypt, with their families.

5So the total number who went with him was 70. (Joseph and his sons were already there.) 6In due season Joseph and each of his brothers died, ending that generation. 7Meanwhile, their

descendants had many children. They increased quickly in number and soon became a large nation. They filled the land of Goshen where they lived.

⁸Then a new king came to the throne of Egypt. He didn't know Joseph. He didn't feel he owed anything to Joseph and his descendants.

⁹He told his people, "The Israelites are becoming too dangerous. There are too many of them. ¹⁰Let's figure out a way to put an end to this. If we don't, and war breaks out, they will join our enemies. They will fight against us and escape out of the country."

¹¹So the Egyptians made slaves of them. They put brutal slave drivers over them. They tried to wear them down under heavy burdens while building the cities of Pithom and Rameses. These cities would be supply centers for the king. ¹²But the worse the Egyptians treated them, the faster the Israelites increased! The Egyptians became alarmed. ¹³⁻¹⁴They made the Hebrew slaves work even harder. They forced them to work long and hard in the fields. They made them carry heavy loads of mortar and brick.

¹⁵⁻¹⁶Then Pharaoh, the king of Egypt, called the Hebrew midwives to him. Their names were Shiphrah and Puah. He told them to kill all Hebrew boys as soon as they were born. They were allowed to let the girls live. ¹⁷But the midwives feared God and didn't obey the king. They let the boys live too.

¹⁸The king called them before him. He asked, "Why have you disobeyed my command? Why have you let the baby boys live?"

¹⁹"Sir," they told him, "the Hebrew women have their babies too fast! We can't get there in time. They are not slow like the Egyptian women!"

²⁰And God blessed the midwives. So the people of Israel kept increasing in number. They became a large nation. ²¹And because the midwives revered God, he gave them children of their own. ²²Then Pharaoh told all of his people to throw newborn Hebrew boys into the Nile River. But the girls, he said, could live.

- *Remember:* The king of Egypt was in charge of armies and chariots. So why was he afraid of the Hebrews? (1:9-10) What did he do to them? (1:11) What happened to the Hebrew boys? (1:22) Do you think your father or mother would like Pharaoh for a boss? Why not?

- *Discover:* When you think something is bad, be thankful it isn't worse!

- *Apply:* Do you grumble about your chores? Do you complain when your mom asks you to clean your room? The next time you feel like complaining, ask yourself, "Would I rather be a Hebrew slave in Egypt?"

- *What's next?* A slave baby becomes a prince. Could that really happen? It did! Read Exodus 2:1-10. ■

Moses Is Born

How could a slave boy become a prince? This is the way it happened.

2 At this time a Hebrew man and woman from the tribe of Levi got married. They had a family, and a baby son was born to them. The baby's mother saw that he was a beautiful baby. So she hid him at home for three months. ³Then it got too hard to hide him. So she made a little boat from papyrus reeds. She covered it with tar so water could not get inside. Then she put the baby in it. And she laid it among the reeds along the river's edge. ⁴The baby's sister watched from a distance to see what would happen to him.

⁵A princess, one of Pharaoh's daughters, came down to bathe in the river. She and her maids were walking along the riverbank. She spied the little boat among the reeds. She quickly sent one of the maids to bring it to her. ⁶When she opened it, there was a baby! And he was crying. This touched her heart. "He must be one of the Hebrew children!" she said.

⁷Then the baby's sister went up to the princess. She asked her, "Shall I go and find one of the Hebrew women to take care of the baby for you?"

⁸"Yes, do!" the princess replied. So the little girl rushed home. She called her mother!

⁹"Take this child home and nurse him for me," the princess told the baby's mother. "I will pay you well!" So she took him home.

¹⁰Later, when he was older, she brought him back to the princess. He became her son. She named him Moses (meaning "to draw out") because she had drawn him out of the water.

- *Remember:* Why did the baby's mother hide him? (1:22) How did she hide him? (2:2-4) Who found the baby boy? How did it happen? (2:5-6) Who took care of the baby until he was older? (2:7-9) Who became the boy's mother then? (2:10) When Moses' mother hid him in the river, what do you think she prayed? Do you think she asked God to keep her boy safe? Do you think she expected him to become a prince of Egypt? God has some good surprises for us, doesn't he?

- *Discover:* God takes care of us. But he doesn't always do it the way we expect. Sometimes he surprises us with something better than we expect.

- *Apply:* Are you praying for God to help you? Are you expecting him to answer your prayer your way? He may surprise you and answer it his way.

- *What's next?* How could a shepherd help an Egyptian prince? You will read about this in Exodus 2:11-22. ■

Moses Runs Away

Moses, the great prince of Egypt, killed a man. He had to run away. Far from home, in the land of Midian, Moses needed someone to help him. He needed someone to give him a home and feed him. But who would do it? You'll learn how a shepherd helps a prince as you read on.

¹¹One day, many years later when Moses had grown up, he went out to visit his fellow Hebrews. He saw the terrible conditions they were under. During his visit he saw an Egyptian knock a Hebrew to the ground. The Egyptian had hit one of Moses' own people! ¹²Moses looked this way and that to be sure no one was watching. Then he killed the Egyptian and hid his body in the sand.

¹³The next day he was out among the Hebrews again. And he saw two of them fighting. "What are you doing? Why are you hitting your own Hebrew brother like that?" he said to the one in the wrong.

¹⁴"Who are you?" the man demanded. "I suppose you think you are *our* prince and judge! Do you plan to kill me as you did that Egyptian yesterday?" When Moses saw that his deed was known, he was afraid. ¹⁵And sure enough, when Pharaoh heard about it he ordered Moses arrested and killed. But Moses ran away into the land of Midian. When he arrived there, he came to a well and sat down beside it. ¹⁶Now a priest of Midian had seven daughters. They came to draw water and fill the water troughs for their father's flocks. ¹⁷But the shepherds chased the girls away. Moses then came to their aid. He rescued them from the shepherds and watered their flocks.

¹⁸They went back to their father, Jethro. He asked, "How did you get the flocks watered so quickly today?"

¹⁹"An Egyptian defended us against the shepherds," they told him. "He drew water for us and watered the flocks."

²⁰"Well, where is he?" their father asked. "Did you just leave him there? Invite him home for supper."

²¹Moses decided to accept Jethro's invitation to live with them. Jethro gave him one of the girls, Zipporah, as his wife. ²²They had a baby named Gershom (meaning "foreigner"). For Moses said, "I am a stranger in a foreign land."

- *Remember:* Why did Moses run away from Egypt? (2:11-15) Who did he meet in Midian? (2:15-18) How did the Midianite shepherd Jethro help Moses? (2:20-22) What if no one in Midian had helped Moses? What would have happened to him? Do you think Moses was thankful for Jethro? Would you be thankful if you were Moses?

- *Discover:* In new places, you may find a friend of God to help you.

- *Apply:* Are you moving to a new town where you will go to a new school? Are you going somewhere you have never been before? You may meet one of God's special friends there. Ask God to help you find that friend.

- *What's next?* A bush that burns and burns, but never burns up? Is that possible? Read Exodus 2:23–4:20. ■

The Burning Bush

Moses saw a burning bush that didn't burn up. He went to see why. This is what he found.

²³Many years later the king of Egypt died. The Israelites were groaning beneath their burdens. They were in deep trouble because of their slavery. They cried bitterly before the Lord. He heard their cries from heaven. ²⁴He remembered his promise to Abraham, Isaac, and Jacob. (He had promised to bring their descendants back into the land of Canaan.) ²⁵Looking down upon them,

he knew that the time had come to rescue them.

3 One day Moses was tending the flock of his father-in-law, Jethro. Jethro was the priest of Midian. Moses was out at the edge of the desert near Horeb, the mountain of God. ²Suddenly the Angel of the Lord appeared to him as a flame of fire in a bush. Moses saw that the bush was on fire. But it didn't burn up. ³⁻⁴So he went over to see why. Then God called out to him,

"Moses! Moses!"

"Who is it?" Moses asked.

⁵"Don't come any closer," God told him. "Take off your shoes, for you are standing on holy ground. ⁶I am the God of your fathers. I am the God of Abraham, Isaac, and Jacob." Moses covered his face with his hands. He was afraid to look at God.

⁷Then God told him, "I have seen the deep sorrows of my people in Egypt. I have heard their pleas for freedom from their harsh slave drivers. ⁸I have come to deliver them from the Egyptians. I will take them out of Egypt into a good land. It is a large land, a land 'flowing with milk and honey.' This is the land where the Canaanites, Hittites, Amorites, Perizzites, Hivites, and Jebusites live. ⁹Yes, the cry of the people of Israel has come to me in heaven. I have seen the heavy work the Egyptians have forced them to do. ¹⁰Now I am going to send you to Pharaoh. You will demand that he let you lead my people out of Egypt."

¹¹"But I'm not the person for a job like that!" Moses exclaimed.

¹²Then God told him, "I really will be with you. I will give you proof that I am the one who is sending you. You shall lead the people out of Egypt. Then you shall worship God here upon this mountain!"

¹³But Moses said, "I could go to the people of Israel. I could tell them that their fathers' God has sent me. But if I do, they will ask, 'Which God are you talking about?' Then what shall I tell them?"

¹⁴"'The one and only God,'" was the reply. "Just say, 'I Am has sent me!' ¹⁵Yes, tell them, 'The Lord, the God of your ancestors Abraham, Isaac, and Jacob, has

sent me to you.' This is my eternal name. It should be used as long as people live on earth.

¹⁶"Now call together all the elders of Israel," God told him. "Tell them about the Lord appearing to you here in this burning bush. Tell them that he said to you, 'I have visited my people. I have seen what is happening to them there in Egypt. ¹⁷I promise to rescue them from the suffering and hurt they are going through. I will take them to the land that now belongs to the Canaanites, Hittites, Amorites, Perizzites, Hivites, and Jebusites. It is a land "flowing with milk and honey."' ¹⁸The elders of the people of Israel will accept your message. They must go with you to the king of Egypt. You will tell him, 'The Lord, the God of the Hebrews, has met with us. He told us to go three days' journey into the desert to sacrifice to him. Tell us we can go.'

God is with us

Then God told him,
"I really will be with you."

Exodus 3:12

---

¹⁹"But I know that the king of Egypt will not let you go except under heavy pressure. ²⁰So I will give him all the pressure he needs! I will destroy Egypt with my miracles. Then at last he will let you go. ²¹And I will see to it that the Egyptians load you down with gifts when you leave. That way you will not go out empty-handed! ²²Every woman will ask for jewels, silver, gold, and the finest of clothes. And her Egyptian master's wife and neighbors will gladly give them. You will clothe your sons and daughters with the best of Egypt!"

4 But Moses said, "They won't believe me! They won't do what *I* tell them to. They'll say, 'The Lord never appeared to you!'"

²"What do you have there in your hand?" the Lord asked him.

And he replied, "A shepherd's rod."

³"Throw it down on the ground," the Lord told him. So he threw it down. It became a serpent, and Moses ran from it!

⁴Then the Lord told him, "Grab it by the tail!" He did, and it became a rod in his hand again!

⁵"Do that, and they will believe you!" the Lord told him. "Then they will know that the Lord, the God of their ancestors Abraham, Isaac, and Jacob, has really appeared to you. ⁶Now reach your hand inside your robe, next to your chest." And when he did, and took it out again, it was white with leprosy! ⁷"Now put it in again," the Lord said. And when he did, and took it out again, it was normal, just as before!

God helps us talk well and do other things well

I will help you speak well.

Exodus 4:12

---

⁸"If they don't believe the first miracle, they will the second," the Lord said. ⁹"And if they don't accept you after these two signs, then take water from the Nile River. Pour it upon the dry land. It will turn to blood."

¹⁰But Moses pleaded, "O Lord, I'm just not a good speaker. I never have been. And I'm not now, even after you have spoken to me. I can't talk very well."

¹¹"Who makes mouths?" the Lord asked him. "Isn't it I, the Lord? Who makes a man so that he can speak or not speak? Who makes him see or not see? Who makes him hear or not hear? ¹²Now go ahead and do as I tell you. I will help you speak well. And I will tell you what to say."

¹³But Moses said, "Lord, please! Send someone else."

¹⁴Then the Lord became angry. "All right," he said, "your brother, Aaron, is a good speaker. He is coming here to look for you. And he will be very happy when he finds you. ¹⁵So I will tell you what to tell him. I will help both of you to speak well. And I will also tell you what to do. ¹⁶He will be your spokesman to the people. And you will be as God to him, telling him what to say. ¹⁷Be sure to take your rod along. For with it you will perform the miracles I have shown you."

¹⁸Moses went home and talked it

over with Jethro, his father-in-law. "If it is alright with you," Moses said, "I will go back to Egypt. I must visit my relatives. I don't even know if they are still alive."

"Go with my blessing," Jethro replied.

¹⁹Before Moses left Midian, the Lord said to him, "Don't be afraid to go back to Egypt. All those who wanted to kill you are dead."

²⁰So Moses took his wife and sons and put them on a donkey. Then he went back to the land of Egypt, holding tightly to the "rod of God"!

- *Remember:* Where was Moses when he saw the burning bush? What was he doing? (3:1) Why did God want Moses to take off his shoes? (3:5) God showed Moses two miracles. What were they?

(4:2-7) Moses carried something special when he went back to Egypt. What was it? (4:20) If God talked to you today, what would you like for him to tell you?

- *Discover:* God doesn't talk to us from burning bushes today. But he does talk to us through the Bible.

- *Apply:* When you read your Bible today, look for one special thing God says.

- *What's next?* Has someone ever yelled at you when you tried to help? This happened to a man in our next story. Read about it in Exodus 5:1–6:1. ■

Moses Arrives in Egypt

²¹The Lord told him, "Go back to Egypt and stand before Pharaoh. Do before

him the miracles I have shown you. But I will make him stubborn so that he will not let the people go. ²²Then you are to tell him, 'The Lord says, "Israel is my oldest son. ²³I have told you to let him go away and worship me, but you have refused. And now see, I will kill your oldest son."'"

²⁴Moses and his family were traveling along. When they stopped for the night, the Lord appeared to Moses. And he threatened to kill him. ²⁵⁻²⁶Then Zipporah his wife took a flint knife. She circumsized her young son and threw the foreskin against Moses' feet. Then she remarked with disgust, "What a bloody husband you've turned out to be!"

Then God let him alone.

²⁷Now the Lord said to Aaron, "Go into the wilderness to meet Moses." So Aaron traveled to Mount Horeb, the mountain of God. He met Moses there, and they greeted each other warmly. ²⁸Moses told Aaron what God had said they must do, and what they were to say. He also told him about the miracles they must do before Pharaoh.

²⁹So Moses and Aaron went back to Egypt. They called the elders of the people of Israel to a council meeting. ³⁰Aaron told them what the Lord had said to Moses. And Moses did the miracles as they watched. ³¹Then the elders believed that God had sent them. The Lord had visited them! He had seen their sorrows! He had decided to save them! Upon hearing this, they all rejoiced. Then they bowed their heads and worshiped.

Making Bricks without Straw

Father wants you to do your chores. That's one job. It's easy. Mother wants you to help with the dishes. That's one job. No problem. God told Moses he had one job for him to do. That doesn't sound like much, does it? But that one job was to take a million slaves from the king of Egypt and lead them to a new country. That's only one job. But it's not easy! Here's how Moses started.

5 After they talked to the elders, Moses and Aaron went to see Pharaoh. They told him, "We bring you a message from the Lord, the God of Israel. He says, 'Let my people go. They must make a holy journey out into the wilderness. They must celebrate a religious feast, and worship me there.'"

²"Is that so?" said Pharaoh. "And who is the Lord, that I should listen to him? Who is he that I should let Israel go? I don't know the Lord. I will not let Israel go."

³But Aaron and Moses persisted. "The God of the Hebrews has met with us," they declared. "We must take a three days' trip into the wilderness. We will sacrifice there to the Lord our God. If we don't obey him, we face death by plague or sword."

⁴⁻⁵"Who do you think you are?" Pharaoh shouted. "Who are you to distract the people from their work? Get back to your jobs!" ⁶That same day Pharaoh sent an order to the officers he had set over the people of Israel. ⁷⁻⁸He said, "Don't give the people any more straw for making bricks! But don't reduce the number of bricks they have to make by a single brick. They must not have enough to do. Otherwise they would not be talking about going out into the wilderness. They would not have time to think about sacrificing to their God.

⁹Load them with work and make them sweat. That will teach them to listen to Moses' and Aaron's lies!"

¹⁰⁻¹¹So the officers told the people: "Pharaoh has given orders. We will give you no more straw. Go and find it wherever you can. But you must make just as many bricks as before!" ¹²So the people scattered everywhere to gather straw.

¹³The slave drivers were very mean. "Make just as many bricks as before," they ordered. ¹⁴Then they whipped the Israelite work crew foremen when they could not keep up. "Why have you made less bricks yesterday and today?" they roared.

¹⁵These foremen went to Pharaoh and pleaded with him. "Don't treat us like this," they begged. ¹⁶"We are given no straw and told to make as many bricks as before. We are beaten for something that isn't our fault. It is the fault of your slave drivers for making such impossible demands."

¹⁷But Pharaoh replied, "You don't have enough work. If you did you would not be saying, 'Let us go and sacrifice to the Lord.' ¹⁸Get back to work. No straw will be given you. And you must deliver the regular number of bricks."

¹⁹Then the foremen saw that they were in big trouble. ²⁰They met Moses and Aaron waiting for them outside the palace. As they came out from their meeting with Pharaoh, ²¹they swore at them. "May God judge you for making us stink before Pharaoh and his people," they said. "You have given them an excuse to kill us!"

²²Then Moses went back to the Lord. "Lord," he protested, "how can you mistreat your own people like this? Why did you ever send me if you were going to do this to them? ²³Ever since I gave Pharaoh your message, he has only been more and more brutal to them. You have not helped them at all!"

6 "Now you will see what I shall do to Pharaoh," the Lord told Moses. "For he must be forced to let my people go. He will not only let them go, but will *drive them out of his land!"*

- *Remember:* Who went with Moses to see Pharaoh? (5:1) Where did Moses get his message for Pharaoh? (5:1) How did Pharaoh make the slaves work harder? (5:7-9) How were these slaves treated? (5:13-14) Moses and Aaron were trying to take these slaves out of Egypt. But what did some of these slaves say to Moses and Aaron? (5:19-21) What would you have thought about these slaves if you were Moses and Aaron?

- *Discover:* Does God want you to help someone? Do it, even if that person doesn't want you to.

- *Apply:* Do you want to help someone know Jesus? That person may yell at you. He may not like you. If you want to please God, don't let that stop you.

- *What's next?* A river turns to blood. Find Exodus 7:8-24 to read about this.

The Hebrews Won't Listen

2-3"I am the Lord, the Almighty God. I appeared to Abraham, Isaac, and Jacob. But I did not reveal my name, the Lord, to them. 4And I entered into a solemn covenant with them. I promised to give them and their descendants the land of Canaan where they were living. 5And now I have heard the groans of the people of Israel, in slavery now to the Egyptians. And I remember my promise.

6"Therefore tell the descendants of Israel that I will use my mighty power. I will perform great miracles to free them from slavery. 7And I will accept them as my people and be their God. And they shall know that I am the Lord their God who has rescued them from the Egyptians. 8-9I will bring them into the land I promised to give to Abraham, Isaac, and Jacob. It shall belong to my people."

So Moses told the people what God had said. But they wouldn't listen anymore. They were too discouraged after what had happened.

10Now the Lord spoke to Moses again. He told him, 11"Go back to Pharaoh. Tell him that he *must* let the people of Israel go."

12"But my own people won't even listen to me anymore," said Moses. "How can I expect Pharaoh to? I'm not a good speaker!"

13Then the Lord ordered Moses and Aaron to go back to the people of Israel and to Pharaoh, king of Egypt. They were to demand that the people be allowed to leave.

Aaron and Moses' Family Record

14These are the names of the heads of the clans of the tribes of Israel.

The sons of Reuben, Israel's oldest son: Hanoch, Pallu, Hezron, Carmi.

15The heads of the clans of the tribe of Simeon: Jemuel, Jamin, Ohad, Jachin, Zohar, Shaul (whose mother was a Canaanite).

16These are the names of the heads of the clans of the tribe of Levi. They are given in the order of their ages: Gershon, Kohath, Merari. (Levi lived 137 years.)

17The sons of Gershon were: Libni, Shime-i (and their clans).

18The sons of Kohath: Amram, Izhar, Hebron, Uzziel. (Kohath lived 133 years.)

19The sons of Merari: Mahli, Mushi.

The above are the families of the Levites, listed according to their ages.

20And Amram married Jochebed, his father's sister. Aaron and Moses were their sons.

Amram lived to the age of 137.

21The sons of Izhar: Korah, Nepheg, Zichri.

22The sons of Uzziel: Misha-el, Elzaphan, Sithri.

23Aaron married Elisheba, the daughter of Amminadab and sister of Nahshon. Their children were: Nadab, Abihu, Eleazar, Ithamar.

24The sons of Korah: Assir, Elkanah, Abiasaph.

These are the families within the clan of Korah.

25Aaron's son Eleazar married one of the daughters of Puti-el, and Phinehas was one of his children. These are all the names of the heads of the clans of the Levites and the families within the clans.

26Aaron and Moses are also in that list. They are the same Aaron and Moses to whom the Lord said, "Lead all the people of Israel out of the land of Egypt." 27They were the ones who went to Pharaoh to ask if they could lead the people from the land. 28-29And to them the Lord said, "I am the Lord. Go in and give Pharaoh the message I have given you."

30This is that Moses who argued with the Lord, "I can't do it. I'm no speaker. Why should Pharaoh listen to *me?*"

Moses' Rod Becomes a Snake

7 Then the Lord said to Moses, "See, I have chosen you to go to Pharaoh. Your brother, Aaron, shall be your spokesman. 2Tell Aaron all that I say to you. He will announce it to Pharaoh. He will demand that the people of Israel be allowed to leave Egypt. 3But I will cause Pharaoh to refuse. He will be stubborn. So I will do many miracles in the land of Egypt. 4Yet even then Pharaoh won't listen to you. So I will crush Egypt with a final blow. Then I will lead my people out. 5The Egyptians will find out that I am indeed God when I show them my power. I will force them to let my people go."

6So Moses and Aaron did as the Lord told them. 7Moses was 80 years old. Aaron was 83 at this time when they went before Pharaoh.

The River That Turned to Blood

What if you saw a man change a stick into a live snake? What if you saw a man touch a river and it suddenly became blood? Would these things scare you? Let's see what the king of Egypt did when he saw these things happen.

8Then the Lord said to Moses and Aaron, 9"Pharaoh will demand that you show him a miracle. He will ask it as proof that God has sent you. When he does, Aaron is to throw down his rod. It will become a snake."

10So Moses and Aaron went in to see Pharaoh. They performed the miracle, as the Lord had told them. Aaron threw down his rod before Pharaoh and his court. And it became a snake. 11Then Pharaoh called in his sorcerers and magicians. They were able to do the same thing with their magic! 12Their rods became snakes, too! But Aaron's snake swallowed theirs! 13Pharaoh's heart was still hard and stubborn. He wouldn't listen, just as the Lord had said. 14The

Lord pointed this out to Moses, that Pharaoh's heart had been unmoved. He knew that Pharaoh would keep on refusing to let the people go.

15"But even so," the Lord said, "go back to Pharaoh in the morning. Be there as he goes down to the river. Stand beside the bank of the river and meet him there. Hold in your hand the rod that turned into a snake. 16Say to him, 'The Lord, the God of the Hebrews, has sent me. I demand that you let his people go to worship him in the wilderness. You would not listen before. 17And now the Lord says this: "You are going to find out that I am God. For I have told Moses to hit the water of the Nile with his rod. The river will turn to blood! 18The fish will die. The river will stink. And the Egyptians won't drink it."'"

¹⁹Then the Lord said to Moses: "Tell Aaron to point his rod toward the waters of Egypt. All its rivers, canals, marshes, and pools will turn to blood. Even the water stored in bowls and pots in the homes will become blood."

²⁰So Moses and Aaron did as the Lord told them. Aaron hit the surface of the Nile with the rod. Pharaoh and all of his officials watched. The river turned to blood. ²¹The fish died and the water smelled so bad that the Egyptians couldn't drink it. And there was blood throughout the land of Egypt. ²²But then the magicians of Egypt used their secret arts. They, too, turned water into blood. So Pharaoh's heart stayed hard and stubborn. He wouldn't listen to Moses and Aaron. This is what the Lord said would happen. ²³So he went back to his palace, unimpressed. ²⁴Then the Egyptians dug wells along the bank of the river to get drinking water. They couldn't drink from the river.

● *Remember:* Whose rod became a snake—Moses' or Aaron's? (7:10) Could anyone else do this miracle? (7:11-12) How did Aaron turn the river into blood? Did he pour something into it? (7:20) What kind of person was Pharaoh? How would you describe him to a friend? (7:13,22)

● *Discover:* Pharaoh saw God's miracles, but he didn't think God was doing them. We are proud and stubborn when we see the things God makes but don't think they are special.

● *Apply:* Which of these is a wonderful work of God: a sunrise, a bird singing, a thunderstorm, a new baby, good food, sleep? Name three more wonderful works of God that you see every day. Thank God each day for these wonderful works, and they will become special to you.

● *What's next?* What would you do with a million frogs? Read Exodus 7:25–8:32. ∎

Pharaoh Learns about God's Power

The king of Egypt was a nasty man. He saw God's miracles. But he didn't think God had done them. So God made life a little harder for this stubborn king. Watch what happened!

²⁵A week went by.

8 Then the Lord said to Moses, "Go in again to Pharaoh. Tell him, 'The Lord says, "Let my people go and worship me. ²If you refuse, I will send millions of frogs. They will invade your land from one end to the other. ³⁻⁴The Nile River will swarm with them. They will come into your houses. They will even come into your bedrooms and right into your beds! Every home in Egypt will be filled with them. They will fill your ovens and your kneading bowls. You and your people will drown in them!"'"

⁵Then the Lord said to Moses, "Tell Aaron to point the rod toward all the rivers, streams, and pools of Egypt. That way there will be frogs in every corner of the land." ⁶Aaron did, and frogs covered the nation. ⁷But the magicians did the same with their secret arts. They, too, caused frogs to come up upon the land.

⁸Then Pharaoh called in Moses and Aaron and begged, "Plead with God to take the frogs away. I will let the people go and sacrifice to him."

⁹"Be so kind as to tell me when you want them to go," Moses said. "Then I will pray that the frogs will die at the time you say. They will die everywhere, except in the river."

¹⁰"Do it tomorrow," Pharaoh said.

"All right," Moses replied, "it shall be as you have said. Then you will know that there is no one like the Lord our God. ¹¹All the frogs will be destroyed, except those in the river."

¹²So Moses and Aaron went out from the presence of Pharaoh. And Moses pleaded with the Lord about the frogs he had sent. ¹³And the Lord did as Moses

promised. Dead frogs covered the land and filled the nation's homes. ¹⁴They were piled into great heaps. And they made a terrible stink all over the land. ¹⁵But when Pharaoh saw that the frogs were gone, he hardened his heart. He refused to let the people go, just as the Lord had predicted.

¹⁶Then the Lord said to Moses, "Tell Aaron to strike the dust with his rod. It will become lice throughout the land of Egypt." ¹⁷So Moses and Aaron did as God ordered. At once lice infested the entire nation. It covered the Egyptians and their animals. ¹⁸Then the magicians tried to do the same thing with their secret arts. But this time they failed.

¹⁹"This is the finger of God," they exclaimed to Pharaoh. But Pharaoh's heart was hard and stubborn. He wouldn't listen to them, just as the Lord had predicted.

²⁰Next the Lord told Moses, "Get up early in the morning. Meet Pharaoh as he comes out to the river to bathe. Say to him, 'The Lord says, "Let my people go and worship me. ²¹If you refuse, I will send swarms of flies throughout Egypt. Your homes will be filled with them. The ground will be covered with them. ²²But it will be very different in the land of Goshen where the Israelites live. No flies will be there. Thus you will know that I am the Lord God of all the earth. ²³For I will make a distinction between your people and my people. All this will happen tomorrow."'"

²⁴And the Lord did as he had said. There were terrible swarms of flies in Pharaoh's palace and in every home in Egypt.

²⁵Pharaoh quickly called Moses and Aaron. He said, "All right, go ahead. Sacrifice to your God. But do it here in the land. Don't go out into the wilderness."

²⁶But Moses replied, "That won't do! Our sacrifices to God are hated by the Egyptians. If we do this right here before their eyes, they will kill us. ²⁷We must

take a three-day trip into the wilderness. We will sacrifice there to the Lord our God, as he commanded us."

²⁸"All right, go ahead," Pharaoh replied. "But don't go too far away. Now, hurry and plead with God for me."

²⁹"Yes," Moses said, "I will ask him to cause the swarms of flies to go away. But I am warning you. You must never again lie to us. You must never promise to let the people go and then change your mind."

³⁰So Moses went out from Pharaoh and asked the Lord to get rid of the flies. ³¹⁻³²And the Lord did as Moses asked. He caused the swarms to go away, so that not one remained. But Pharaoh hardened his heart again. He did not let the people go!

- *Remember:* Name the three terrible plagues mentioned in this story. (8:2, 16, 21) Where did the frogs go when Aaron pointed his rod toward the river? (8:3-4) Did the lice cover just the animals?

Where else did they go? (8:17) The Egyptian magicians did every miracle that Moses and Aaron did, for a while. But suddenly they could not do some miracles. Which was the first one they could not do? (8:17-18). Where was the one place that the plague of flies would not go? (8:22) Why do you think the flies did not go there? What would you like to say to Pharaoh now? What would you like to tell him about God?

- *Discover:* There are some things that only God can do. Can you make a sunset or a cloud? Can you bring a dead person back to life? Even the Egyptian magicians said, "This is the finger of God." (8:19)

- *Apply:* Have you ever looked at something and said, "Only God could have made this"? Name some of these things. How many can you think of?

- *What's next?* Do you think things are getting bad for Pharaoh, king of Egypt? You haven't seen anything yet! Wait until you read Exodus 9–10. ■

The Longest Night

Pharaoh should have had the good sense to stop fighting God and let him do what was best. But he was a stubborn man. He thought he was bigger than God. What do you think? This will help you decide who was bigger.

9 "Go back to Pharaoh," the Lord told Moses. "Tell him, 'The Lord, the God of the Hebrews, demands that you let his people go to sacrifice to him. ²If you refuse, ³the power of God will send a deadly plague. It will destroy your cattle, horses, donkeys, camels, flocks, and herds. ⁴But the plague will affect only the cattle of Egypt. None of the Israelite herds and flocks will even be touched!'"

⁵The Lord announced that the plague would begin the very next day, ⁶and it did. The next morning all the cattle of the Egyptians began dying. But not one of the Israelite herds was even sick. ⁷Pharaoh sent to see whether it was true that none of the Israelite cattle were dead. Yet when he found out that it was so, even

then his mind remained unchanged. He still refused to let the people go.

⁸Then the Lord said to Moses and Aaron, "Take ashes from the kiln. Then have Moses toss them into the sky as Pharaoh watches. ⁹They will spread like fine dust over all the land of Egypt. As a result boils will break out upon people and animals alike, throughout the land."

¹⁰So they took ashes from the kiln and went to Pharaoh. As he watched, Moses tossed them toward the sky. They became boils that broke out on men and animals alike throughout all Egypt. ¹¹The magicians couldn't stand before Moses because of the boils. The boils covered the magicians too. ¹²But the

Lord hardened Pharaoh and made him more stubborn. He refused to listen, just as the Lord had predicted to Moses.

¹³Then the Lord said to Moses, "Get up early in the morning. Go and stand before Pharaoh. Tell him, 'The Lord the God of the Hebrews says, "Let my people go to worship me. ¹⁴This time I am going to send a plague. It will really speak to you and to your servants and to all the Egyptian people. It will prove to you there is no other God in all the earth. ¹⁵I could have killed you all by now. ¹⁶But

I didn't, for I wanted to show my power to you and to all the earth. ¹⁷So you still think you are great, do you? Do you still defy my power? Do you still refuse to let my people go? ¹⁸Well, tomorrow about this time I will send a hailstorm across the nation. It will be such as there has never been since Egypt was founded! ¹⁹Quick! Bring in your cattle from the fields. Every man and animal left out in the fields will die beneath the hail!"'"

²⁰Some of the Egyptians, terrified by this threat, brought their cattle and slaves in from the fields. ²¹But those who had no regard for the word of the Lord left them out in the storm.

²²Then the Lord said to Moses, "Point your hand toward heaven and cause the hail to fall. It will fall over all Egypt. It will fall upon the people, animals, and trees."

²³So Moses held out his hand, and the Lord sent thunder and hail and lightning. ²⁴It was terrible beyond words. Never in all the history of Egypt had there been a storm like that. ²⁵All Egypt lay in ruins. Everything left in the fields, men and animals alike, was killed. The

trees were shattered and the crops were destroyed. ²⁶The only spot in all Egypt without hail that day was the land of Goshen. For that was where the people of Israel lived.

²⁷Then Pharaoh sent for Moses and Aaron. "I see my fault at last," he con-

fessed. "The Lord is right. I and my people have been wrong all along. ²⁸Beg God to end this terrifying thunder and hail. Then I will let you go at once."

²⁹"All right," Moses replied. "As soon as I have left the city I will spread out my hands to the Lord. Then the thunder and hail will stop. This will prove to you that the earth is controlled by the Lord. ³⁰But as for you and your officials, I know that even yet you will not obey him."

³¹All the flax and barley were knocked down and destroyed. The barley was ripe, and the flax was in bloom. ³²But the wheat and the emmer were not destroyed. They were not yet out of the ground.

³³So Moses left Pharaoh and went out of the city. He lifted his hands to heaven to the Lord. The thunder and hail stopped. The rain stopped pouring down. ³⁴But when Pharaoh saw this, he and his officials sinned again. They stubbornly refused to do what they had promised. ³⁵So Pharaoh refused to let the people leave, just as the Lord had predicted to Moses.

10 Then the Lord said to Moses, "Go back again and make your demand upon Pharaoh. But I have hardened him and his officials. I have done this so that I can do more miracles to show my power. ²What stories you can tell your children and grandchildren! You must recount the great things I am doing in Egypt. Tell them what fools I made of the

Egyptians. Remind them of how I proved to you that I am the Lord."

³So Moses and Aaron asked for another meeting with Pharaoh. They told him: "The Lord, the God of the Hebrews, asks, 'How long will you refuse to submit to me? Let my people go so they can worship me. ⁴⁻⁵If you refuse, tomorrow I will cover the entire nation with a thick layer of locusts. You won't even be able to see the ground. And they will destroy all that escaped the hail. ⁶They will fill your palace, and the homes of your officials, and all the houses of Egypt. Never in the history of Egypt has there been a plague like this will be!'" Then Moses stalked out.

⁷The court officials now came to Pharaoh. They asked him, "Are you going to destroy us completely? Don't you know yet that all Egypt lies in ruins? Let the Hebrew *men* go and serve the Lord their God!"

⁸So Moses and Aaron were brought back to Pharaoh. "All right, go and serve the Lord your God!" he said. "But just who is it you want to go?"

⁹"We will go with our sons and daughters, flocks and herds," Moses replied. "We will take everything with us. For we must all join in the holy journey."

¹⁰"In the name of God I will not let you take your little ones!" Pharaoh yelled. "I can see your plot! ¹¹Never! You that are men, go and serve the Lord. For that is what you asked for." Then Pharaoh ordered them to leave.

¹²So the Lord said to Moses, "Hold out your hand over the land of Egypt. This will bring locusts. They will cover the land and eat all that the hail has left."

¹³So Moses lifted his rod. And the Lord caused an east wind to blow all that day and night. When it was morning, the east wind had brought the locusts. ¹⁴And the locusts covered the land of Egypt from border to border. It was the worst locust plague in all Egyptian history. And there will never again be another like it. ¹⁵The locusts covered the face of the earth. They blotted out the sun so that the land was darkened. And they ate every bit of vegetation the hail had left. Not one green thing remained. No trees or plants stood in all the land of Egypt.

¹⁶Then Pharaoh sent an urgent call for Moses and Aaron. He said to them, "I confess my sin against the Lord your God and against you. ¹⁷Forgive my sin only this once. Beg the Lord your God to take away this deadly plague. I promise that I will let you go as soon as the locusts are gone."

¹⁸So Moses went out from Pharaoh and called to the Lord. ¹⁹The Lord sent a very strong west wind. It blew the locusts out into the Red Sea. Not one locust remained in all the land of Egypt! ²⁰But the Lord hardened Pharaoh's heart. He did not let the people go.

²¹Then the Lord said to Moses, "Lift your hands to heaven. Then darkness without a ray of light will descend upon the land of Egypt." ²²So Moses did. And there was thick darkness over all the land for three days. ²³During all that time the people scarcely moved. But all the people of Israel had light as usual.

²⁴Then Pharaoh called for Moses and said, "Go and worship the Lord. But you must let your flocks and herds stay here. You can even take your children with you."

²⁵"No," Moses said. "We must take

our flocks and herds. They will be needed for sacrifices and burnt offerings to the Lord our God. 26Not a hoof shall be left behind. For we must have sacrifices for the Lord our God. And we do not know what he will choose until we get there."

27So the Lord hardened Pharaoh's heart. He would not let them go.

28"Get out of here! Don't let me ever see you again!" Pharaoh shouted at Moses. "The day you do, you shall die."

29"Very well," Moses replied. "I will never see you again."

- *Remember:* Name the terrible plagues mentioned in this story. (9:3,9,18; 10:4,21) What did Moses throw into the sky to cause boils? (9:8-10) What did the hail storm destroy? (9:25-26) What caused Pharaoh to say at last, "I was wrong and God is right?" (9:27-28) Do you think he should have said that before? Why?

- *Discover:* God thought the Hebrew people should be freed from slavery. Pharaoh thought they should stay slaves. Who was right? Who wants what is best for the Hebrews? If you and God don't agree, who is right?

- *Apply:* Do you think God is doing something he shouldn't? If so, don't ask God to change. Ask how you should change. God has a good reason for doing what he does. He wanted what was best for the Hebrews. And he wants what is best for you.

- *What's next?* Why would people paint their doorposts with blood? You'll learn in Exodus 12:1-36. ■

Egypt's Firstborn Will Die

11 Then the Lord said to Moses, "I will send just one more disaster on Pharaoh and his land. After that he will let you go. In fact, he will be anxious to get rid of you. He will almost throw you out of the country! 2Tell all the men and women of Israel to go to their Egyptian neighbors. Tell them to ask for gold and silver jewelry."

3For God caused the Egyptians to have good feelings toward the people of Israel. Moses was a very great man in the land of Egypt. He was respected by Pharaoh's officials and the Egyptian people alike.

4Now Moses said to Pharaoh, "The Lord says, 'About midnight I will pass through Egypt. 5And all the oldest sons shall die in every family in Egypt. This will include everyone. The oldest child of Pharaoh, heir to his throne, will die. So will the oldest child of his lowest slave. Even the firstborn of the animals will die. 6The cry of death will be heard in the whole land of Egypt. Never before has there been such anguish. And it will never be again.

7"'But not a dog shall move his tongue against any of the people of Israel. And none of their animals will die. Then you will know that the Lord makes a distinction between Egyptians and Israelites.' 8All these officials of yours will come running to me. They will bow low and beg, 'Please leave at once. Take all your people with you.' Only then will I go!" Then, red-faced with anger, Moses stomped from the palace.

9The Lord had told Moses, "Pharaoh won't listen. But this will give me the chance to do mighty miracles. Through them I will show my power." 10So Moses and Aaron did these miracles right before Pharaoh's eyes. But the Lord hardened his heart. Pharaoh refused to let the people leave the land.

The First Passover

People over all the land of Goshen are painting their doorposts. But look! They are painting them with blood. And their paintbrushes are plants called hyssop. Why is everyone doing such a strange thing?

12 Then the Lord said to Moses and Aaron, 2"This month will be the first and most important of the whole year. 3-4Announce this to all the people of Israel. Every year, on the 10th day of this month, each family shall get a lamb. If a family is small, let it share the lamb with another small family in the neighborhood. Whether a family should share in this way depends on its size. 5This animal shall be a year-old male. It can be either a sheep or a goat. It cannot have any defects.

6"On the evening of the 14th day of this month, all these lambs shall be killed. 7Their blood will be put on the two side-frames of the door of every home. It will also be put on the panel above the door. Use the blood of the lamb eaten in that home. 8Everyone shall eat roast lamb that night. Unleavened bread and bitter herbs shall be eaten with it. 9The meat must not be eaten raw or boiled. It must be roasted, including the head, legs, heart, and liver. 10Don't eat any of it the next day. If all is not eaten that night, burn what is left.

11"Eat it with your traveling clothes on, prepared for a long trip. Wear your walking shoes and carry your walking sticks in your hands. Eat it quickly. This observance shall be called the Lord's Passover. 12For I will pass through the land of Egypt tonight. I will kill all the oldest sons and firstborn male animals in all the land of Egypt. And I will bring judgment upon all the gods of Egypt. For I am the Lord. 13The blood you have placed on the doorposts will be proof that you obey me. When I see the blood I will pass over you. I will not destroy your firstborn children when I smite the land of Egypt.

14"You shall celebrate this event each year. This is a law that cannot be changed. It will remind you of this fatal night. 15The celebration shall last seven days. For that entire period you are to eat only bread made without yeast. This rule must be obeyed at all times during the seven days of the celebration. Anyone who disobeys shall be expelled from Israel. 16On the first day of the celebration, and again on the seventh day, there will be special religious services for all the people. No work of any kind may be done on those days except the making of food.

17"This yearly 'Feast of Unleavened Bread' will help you always remember today. It will remind you of the day when I brought you out of the land of Egypt. It is a law that you must celebrate this day every year, generation after generation. 18Only bread without yeast may be eaten from the evening of the 14th day of the month until the evening of the 21st day of the month. 19For these seven days there must be no trace of yeast in your homes. During that time anyone who eats anything that has yeast in it shall be expelled from the nation of Israel. These same rules apply to foreigners who are living among you. They apply just as much to foreigners as to those born as Israelites. 20Again I repeat, during those days you must not eat anything made with yeast. Serve only yeastless bread."

21Then Moses called for all the elders of Israel. He said to them, "Go and get lambs from your flocks. Take a lamb for one or more families depending upon the number of persons in the families. Kill the lamb so that God will pass over you and not destroy you. 22Drain the lamb's blood into a basin. Then take a cluster of hyssop branches and dip them into the lamb's blood. Strike the hyssop against the lintel above the door and against the two side panels. That way there will be blood upon them. And none of you shall go outside all night.

23"For the Lord will pass through the land and kill the Egyptians. But he will see the blood on the panel at the top of the door and on the two side pieces. And he will pass over that home. He will not permit the Destroyer to enter and kill your firstborn. 24And remember, this is a changeless law for you and your descendants. 25You shall go into the land that the Lord will give you, just as he promised. And you shall celebrate the Passover there. 26When you do, your children will ask, 'What does all this mean? What is this ceremony about?' 27You will reply, 'It is the celebration of the Lord's passing over us. For he passed over the homes of the people of Israel, though he killed the Egyptians. He passed over our houses and did not come in to destroy us.'" And all the people bowed their heads and worshiped.

28So the people of Israel did as Moses and Aaron had commanded. 29And that night, at midnight, the Lord killed all the firstborn sons in the land of Egypt. All were included, from Pharaoh's oldest son to the oldest son of the captive in the dungeon. All the firstborn of the cattle died too. 30Then Pharaoh and his officials and all the people of Egypt got up in the night. And there was bitter crying all over the land of Egypt. For there was not a house where there was not one dead.

31Pharaoh called for Moses and Aaron during the night. He told them, "Leave us. Please go away, all of you. Go and serve the Lord as you said. 32Take your flocks and herds and be gone. But give me a blessing as you go." 33And the Egyptians were urgent to the people of Israel. They wanted to get them out of the land as fast as possible. For they said, "We are as good as dead."

34The Israelites took with them their bread dough without yeast. They tied their kneading troughs into their spare clothes and carried them on their shoulders. 35And the people of Israel did as Moses said. They asked the Egyptians for silver and gold jewelry and for clothing. 36And the Lord gave the Israelites favor with the Egyptians. They gave them whatever they wanted. The Egyptians were practically stripped of all they owned!

- *Remember:* What makes you think the Passover was important? (12:2) How often were the people to celebrate the Passover? (12:3-4) What kind of animal did these people use for Passover? (12:3-5) What did the people eat at the Passover supper? (12:8) Why do you think they ate this food? How were the people to dress for their Passover supper? (12:11) Why was blood painted on the doorposts? (12:12-13,23) What were the people supposed to remember as they celebrated the Passover? (12:17,25-27) What did the people do when they realized all God had done for them? (12:27)

- *Discover:* God knew how busy his people were each day. But he didn't want them to forget this important day. So he made it a holiday. It was a specific day when the people could rest, worship God, and remember all he had done for them.

- *Apply:* God knows how busy we can get. Are there any holidays or other special days your family has set aside to worship him and remember all he has done for you? Can you name any?

- *What's next?* Watch a million people move at one time. They will do this in the middle of the night. Read Exodus 12:37-51. ∎

The Exodus

A million people are moving. They are taking everything they own. Do they have moving vans? No, they have only carts and wagons. Are they driving to their new home? No, they are walking. What a moving day it is! And it all begins in the middle of the night. Would you like to come along and see what happens? You'll never see a moving day like this again.

[37]That night the people of Israel left Rameses and started for Succoth. There were 600,000 of them, besides all the women and children, going on foot. [38]People of various sorts went with them. And there were flocks and herds—a vast exodus of cattle. [39]When they stopped to eat, they baked bread from the yeastless dough they had brought along. It was yeastless because the people were pushed out of Egypt. They didn't have time to wait for bread to rise to take with them on the trip.

[40-41]The sons of Jacob and their descendants had lived in Egypt 430 years. On the last day of the 430th year, all of the Lord's people left Egypt. [42]This night was selected by the Lord to bring his people out from the land of Egypt. So the

same night was chosen as the date of the yearly celebration of God's deliverance.

[43]Then the Lord said to Moses and Aaron, "These are the rules for observing the Passover. No foreigners shall eat the lamb. [44]But any slave who has been bought may eat it if he has been circumcised. [45]A hired servant or a visiting foreigner may not eat of it. [46]You shall, all of you who eat each lamb, eat it together in one house. You must not carry it outside. And you shall not break any of its bones. [47]All the people of Israel shall observe this memorial at the same time.

[48]"As to foreigners, if they are living with you and want to observe the Passover with you, let all the males be circumcised. Then they may come and celebrate with you. In fact, then they shall be just as though they had been born among you. But no uncircumcised person shall ever eat the lamb. [49]The same law applies to those born in Israel and to foreigners living among you."

[50]So the people of Israel did all that the Lord told Moses and Aaron. [51]That very day the Lord brought out the people of Israel from the land of Egypt. Wave after wave of them crossed the border.

- *Remember:* Where did this great move start and where did the people go first? (12:37) Why were the people moving? Why did they eat bread without yeast? (12:39) Why did God choose this exact night for the people to move? (12:40-42) Moses would lead these people. But who was leading Moses?

- *Discover:* Great leaders like Moses are led by God. To be a great leader, Moses had to be a good follower. He had to follow God's commands.

- *Apply:* Some day you will be a leader. You may be a parent. You may be a teacher. You may run a business. You may be in government. Now is the time to learn to follow God. That's what will help you become a great leader.

- *What's next?* You've seen clouds in the sky, haven't you? But have you ever seen a cloud of fire at night? Have you ever followed a cloud and let it lead you somewhere? You will in Exodus 13:17-22. ∎

Firstborn Dedicated to God

13 The Lord told Moses, "Give to me all of the firstborn sons of Israel. Every firstborn male animal is also mine. They are mine!"

[3]Then Moses said to the people, "This is a day to remember forever. It is the day of leaving Egypt and your slavery. For the Lord has brought you out with mighty miracles. Now remember, during the yearly celebration of this event you are to use no yeast. Don't even have any in your homes. [4-5]Celebrate this day of your exodus at the end of March each year. You will observe this as soon as the Lord brings you into the land of the Canaanites, Hittites, Amorites, Hivites, and Jebusites. This is the land he promised your fathers, a land 'flowing with milk and honey.' [6-7]For seven days you shall eat only bread without yeast. And there must be no yeast in your homes or anywhere within the borders of your land! Then, on the seventh day, a great feast to the Lord shall be held.

[8]"During those celebration days each year you must explain to your children why you are celebrating. It is a celebration of what the Lord did for you when you left Egypt. [9]This yearly memorial week will brand you as his own unique people. It will be as though he had branded his mark of ownership upon your hands or your forehead.

[10]"So celebrate the event each year in late March. [11]And remember, the Lord will bring you into the land he promised to your ancestors long ago. The Canaanites are living there now. [12]When you arrive in that land, all firstborn sons belong to the Lord. So do all the firstborn male animals. And you shall give them to him. [13]A firstborn donkey may be bought back from the Lord. It can be exchanged for a lamb or baby goat. But if you decide not to trade, the donkey shall be killed. However, you *must* buy back your firstborn sons.

[14]"And in the future, when your children ask you, 'What is this all about?' You shall tell them, 'With mighty miracles the Lord brought us out of Egypt from our slavery. [15]Pharaoh wouldn't let us go. So the Lord killed all the firstborn males

throughout the land of Egypt, both of men and of animals. That is why we now give all the firstborn males to the Lord. But all the oldest sons are always bought back.' ¹⁶Again I say, this celebration shall show that you are God's people. It will identify you as if his brand of ownership were placed upon your foreheads. It is a reminder that the Lord brought us out of Egypt with great power."

A Pillar of Cloud and Fire

What would you think if you saw a pillar of cloud on your next trip? It goes before your car. It shows you where to go. You don't need a road map. At night, the cloud becomes a pillar of fire. It keeps on guiding you. Would you think it just happened? Or would you think God was there? This is how God led Moses and his people.

¹⁷⁻¹⁸So at last Pharaoh let the people go.
God did not lead them through the land of the Philistines. That was the most direct route from Egypt to the Prom-ised Land. God felt the people might become discouraged, for they would have to fight their way through. And even though they had left Egypt

armed, he thought they might turn back to Egypt. So instead, God led them along a route through the Red Sea wilderness.

¹⁹Moses took the bones of Joseph with them. Joseph had made the sons of Israel make a vow before God. They promised that they would take his bones with them when God led them out of Egypt. Joseph had been sure that God would someday do this.

²⁰Leaving Succoth, they camped in Etham at the edge of the wilderness. ²¹The Lord guided them by a pillar of cloud during the daytime. He led them by a pillar of fire at night. That way they could travel either by day or by night. ²²The cloud and fire were never out of sight.

● *Remember:* Why didn't God lead his people on the shortest way to the Promised Land? (13:17-18) Moses took some bones with him. Whose bones were they? Why did he take them? (13:19) How did God guide these people? (13:21-22) When it got dark did God take the cloud away? Why not?

● *Discover:* God guides us each day. He guides us in many different ways. What people or things does he use to guide us? We may not have a pillar of cloud or fire. But he is still with us, and he still guides us. He won't leave us.

● *Apply:* Think of every place you have been today. God was already there before you got there. And he was there after you left. Did you talk with him in any of these places?

● *What's next?* You'll want to read about a path that went through the sea. The smallest child could walk on it and not get wet. But the greatest army could not. (Exodus 14) ∎

Crossing the Red Sea

Moses and his people are trapped! God led them to this place. Before them is the sea. There is no way across. Behind them is Pharaoh's army, racing toward them. There is no escape. Why did God get them into this mess? Did he make a mistake? You'll find out as you read on.

14 The Lord now said to Moses, ²"Tell the people to turn toward Pi-hahiroth. It is located between Migdol and the sea. It is opposite Baal-zephon. Tell them to camp there along the shore. ³For Pharaoh will think, 'Those Israelites are trapped now. They are caught between the desert and the sea!' ⁴And once again I will harden Pharaoh's heart and he will chase after you. I have planned this to gain great honor and glory over Pharaoh and all his armies. The Egyptians shall know that I am the Lord."

So they camped where they were told.

⁵Word reached the king of Egypt that the Israelites were not planning to come back to Egypt after three days. They planned to keep on going. When they heard this, Pharaoh and his staff became bold again. "What is this we have done? Why did we let all these slaves get away?" they asked. ⁶So Pharaoh led the chase in his chariot. ⁷He was followed by the pick of Egypt's chariot corps. They drove 600 chariots. Still more chariots were driven by Egyptian officers. ⁸He pursued the people of Israel. They had taken much of the wealth of Egypt with them. ⁹Pharaoh's entire cavalry with horses, chariots, and charioteers joined the chase. The Egyptian army overtook the people of Israel as they were camped beside the shore. The camp was located near Pi-hahiroth. It was across from Baal-zephon.

¹⁰The Egyptian army drew near. The

people of Israel saw them far in the distance, speeding after them. They were filled with fear. They cried out to the Lord to help them.

11Then they turned against Moses. "Have you brought us out here to die in the desert?" they whined. "Did you bring us here because there were not enough graves for us in Egypt? Why did you make us leave Egypt? 12Didn't we tell you, while we were slaves, to leave us alone? We said it would be better to be slaves to the Egyptians than dead in the wilderness."

13But Moses told the people, "Don't be afraid. Just stand where you are and watch. You will see the wonderful way the Lord will rescue you today. The Egyptians you are looking at—you will never see them again. 14The Lord will fight for you. You won't need to lift a finger!"

15Then the Lord said to Moses, "Stop crying out to me! Get the people moving! 16Use your rod. Hold it out over the water, and the sea will open up a path before you. All the people of Israel will walk through on dry ground! 17I will harden the hearts of the Egyptians. Then they will go in after you. But you will see the honor I will get in defeating Pharaoh. I will crush all his armies, chariots, and horsemen. 18And all Egypt shall know that I am the Lord."

19Then the Angel of God, who had been leading the people of Israel, moved the cloud around behind them. 20It stood between the people of Israel and the Egyptians. And that night it changed to a pillar of fire. But it gave darkness to the Egyptians, even as it gave light to the people of Israel! So the Egyptians couldn't find the Israelites!

21Meanwhile, Moses stretched his rod over the sea. The Lord opened up a path through the sea. There were walls of water on each side. And a strong east wind blew all that night. It dried the sea bottom. 22So the people of Israel walked through the sea on dry ground! 23Then the Egyptians followed them. They rode between the walls of water along the bottom of the sea. All of Pharaoh's horses, chariots, and horsemen chased

the people. 24But in the early morning the Lord looked down from the cloud of fire upon the army of Egyptians. Then he began to harass them. 25Their chariot wheels began coming off. And their chariots scraped along the dry ground. "Let's get out of here," the Egyptians yelled. "The Lord is fighting for them and against us."

26All the Israelites came to the other side. Then the Lord said to Moses, "Stretch out your hand again over the sea. The waters will then come back over the Egyptians and their chariots and horsemen." 27Moses did, and the sea went back to normal beneath the morning light. The Egyptians tried to run. But the Lord drowned them in the sea. 28The water covered the path and the chariots and horsemen. All the army of Pharaoh that chased after Israel through the sea drowned. Not one of them survived.

God is on our side, helping us

The Lord will fight for you.

Exodus 14:14

29The people of Israel had walked through on dry land. And the waters had been walled up on either side of them. 30So the Lord saved Israel that day from the Egyptians. And the people of Israel saw the Egyptians dead. They were washed up on the seashore. 31The people of Israel saw the mighty miracle the Lord had done for them against the Egyptians. And they were afraid and revered the Lord. They believed in him and in his servant Moses.

- *Remember:* Who told Moses and his people to camp by the sea? (14:1-2) Why did God do this? Did he make a mistake? (14:3-4) How many chariots did Pharaoh send? (14:7) How did the people of Israel feel when they were trapped? (14:10-12) How did they feel after the Lord saved them? (14:31) What changed their mind? How do you feel when you think God has made a mistake? How do you feel when he makes things turn out right? What changes your mind?

- *Discover:* Do you ever think that no one

can help you? God can! He always knows the way out of your trouble.

- *Apply:* When you're in trouble, what do you do to get out? Start with God. Ask him first to help you. If he can take the people of Israel through the sea, he can take you through your trouble.

- *What's next?* Have you ever been so thirsty you thought you would die? Here are a million thirsty people and not a drop of water! Now what? Read Exodus 15:22-27. ■

Songs to the Lord

15 Then Moses and the people of Israel sang a song to the Lord.

I will sing to the Lord, for he has triumphed gloriously.
He has thrown both horse and rider into the sea.
²The Lord is my strength, my song, and my salvation.
He is my God, and I will praise him.
He is my father's God. I will exalt him.
³The Lord is a warrior.
Yes, the Lord is his name.
⁴He has overthrown Pharaoh's chariots and armies,
He has drowned them in the sea.
The famous Egyptian captains are dead beneath the waves.
⁵The water covers them.
They went down into the depths like a stone.
⁶Your right hand, O Lord, is glorious in power.
It dashes the enemy to pieces.
⁷In the greatness of your majesty
You overthrew all those who rose against you.
You sent forth your anger,
And it burned them up as fire burns up straw.
⁸At the blast of your breath
The waters divided!
They stood as solid walls to hold the seas apart.
⁹The enemy said, "I will chase after them,
Catch up with them, destroy them.
I will cut them apart with my sword
And divide the captured booty."
¹⁰But God blew with his wind,

and the sea covered them.
They sank as lead in the mighty waters.
¹¹Who else is like the Lord among the gods?
Who is glorious in holiness like him?
Who is so awesome in splendor,
A wonder-working God?
¹²You reached out your hand and the earth swallowed them.
¹³You have led the people you bought back.
But in your loving-kindness
You have guided them wonderfully
To your holy land.
¹⁴The nations heard what happened, and they trembled.
Fear has gripped the people of Philistia.
¹⁵The leaders of Edom are appalled.
The mighty men of Moab tremble.
All the people of Canaan melt with fear.
¹⁶Terror and dread have overcome them.
O Lord, because of your great power they won't attack us!
Your people whom you bought
Will pass by them in safety.
¹⁷You will bring them in.
You will plant them on your mountain,
Your own homeland, Lord,
The sanctuary you made for them to live in.
¹⁸The Lord shall reign forever and forever.
¹⁹The horses of Pharaoh, his horsemen, and his chariots
Tried to follow through the sea.
But the Lord let down the walls of water on them.
While the people of Israel walked through on dry land.

²⁰Then Miriam the prophetess, the sister of Aaron, took a tambourine and led the women in dances. ²¹And Miriam sang this song:

Sing to the Lord, for he has won gloriously.
The horse and rider have been drowned in the sea.

Bitter Water at Marah

A million people are walking through the desert. They haven't had a drink of water for three days. How thirsty they must be! They find water at last, but it's bad. They can't drink it. There are no drinking fountains, are there? They're in trouble. They need water. How will they get it?

22Then Moses led the people of Israel on from the Red Sea. They moved out into the wilderness of Shur. They were there three days without water. 23They came to Marah. But they couldn't drink the water because it was bitter. The place was called Marah, because it means "bitter."

24Then the people turned against Moses. "Must we die of thirst?" they demanded.

25Moses pleaded with the Lord to help them. The Lord showed him a tree to throw into the water. As a result, the water became sweet.

It was there at Marah that the Lord gave them the following conditions. They were given to test their commitment to him. 26He said, "You must listen to the voice of the Lord your God, and obey it. You must do what is right. If you do this, I will not make you suffer the diseases I sent on the Egyptians. For I am the Lord who heals you." 27Then they came to Elim where there were 12 springs and 70 palm trees. They camped there beside the springs.

● *Remember:* Why couldn't the people drink the water at Marah? (15:23) Did they pray for God's help? What did they do instead? (15:24) What did Moses do? (15:25) How do you like what the people did? How do you like what Moses did? Which is better? Why?

● *Discover:* God helps us more when we pray than when we complain.

● *Apply:* Do you like to help a friend who complains about the way you help him? Wouldn't you rather help a friend who is glad for your help? Why? When you have a problem do you complain about it or pray about it?

● *What's next?* It's time to get dinner. Does your mother get meat from the sky? Does she gather bread from the ground? You'll read about people who get their food this way in Exodus 16. ■

God Sends Manna and Quail

There wasn't enough food in the desert to feed Moses and all his people. How would you get food if there were no grocery stores and no refrigerators? Where did Moses and his people find food?

16 Now they left Elim and journeyed on into the Sihn Wilderness. It was between Elim and Mt. Sinai. They got there on the 15th day of the second month after leaving Egypt. 2There, too, the people spoke bitterly against Moses and Aaron.

3"Oh, that we were back in Egypt," they moaned. "Oh that the Lord had killed us there! For there we had plenty to eat. But now you have brought us into this wilderness to kill us with starvation."

4Then the Lord said to Moses, "Look, I'm going to rain down food from heaven for them. Everyone can go out each day and gather as much food as he needs. And I will test them in this to see whether they will do what I tell them or not. 5Tell them to gather twice as much as usual on the sixth day of each week."

6Then Moses and Aaron called a

meeting of all the people of Israel. They told them, "This evening you will see that it was the Lord who brought you out of the land of Egypt. 7-9In the morning you will see more of his glory. For he has heard your complaints against him. You aren't really complaining against *us*—who are *we*? The Lord will give you meat to eat in the evening. He will give you bread in the morning. Come now before the Lord. Hear his reply to your complaints."

10So Aaron called them together. And suddenly, out toward the wilderness, there appeared the awesome glory of the Lord. It came from within the guiding cloud.

11-12And the Lord said to Moses, "I have heard their complaints. Tell them, 'In the evening you will have meat. And in the morning you will be stuffed with bread. Then you shall know that I am the Lord your God.'"

13That evening vast numbers of quail came and covered the camp. And in the morning the desert all around the camp was wet with dew. 14When the dew vanished later in the morning it left thin white flakes. They covered the ground like frost. 15When the people of Israel saw it they asked each other, "What is it?"

And Moses told them, "It is the food the Lord has given you. 16The Lord has said for everyone to gather as much as is needed for his household. Take about two quarts for each person."

17So the people of Israel went out and gathered it. Some got more and some less before it melted on the ground. 18And there was just enough for everyone. Those who gathered more had nothing left over and those who gathered little had no lack! Each home had just enough.

19And Moses told them, "Don't leave it overnight."

20But of course some of them wouldn't listen, and left it until morning. When they looked, it was full of maggots and had a terrible odor. And Moses was very angry with them. 21So they gathered the food morning by morning, each home according to its need. And when the sun became hot upon the ground, the food melted and disappeared. 22On the sixth day there was twice as much as usual on the

ground. Four quarts were there for each person instead of two. The leaders of the people came and asked Moses why this had happened.

²³And he told them, "Because the Lord has chosen tomorrow as a day of rest. It is a holy Sabbath to the Lord. On that day we must rest from doing our daily tasks. So cook as much as you want to today. And keep what is left for tomorrow."

²⁴And the next morning the food was wholesome and good. It had no maggots or odor. ²⁵Moses said, "This is your food for today. For today is a Sabbath to the Lord. Thus, there will be no food on the ground today. ²⁶Gather the food for six days. But the seventh is a Sabbath. There will be none there for you on that day."

²⁷But some of the people went out anyway to gather food, even though it was the Sabbath. But there wasn't any.

²⁸⁻²⁹"How long will these people refuse to obey?" the Lord asked Moses. "Don't they know that I am giving them twice as much on the sixth day? That way there will be enough for two days. The Lord has given you the seventh day as a day of Sabbath rest. Stay in your tents. Don't go out to pick up food from the ground that day." ³⁰So the people rested on the seventh day.

³¹And the food became known as "manna" (meaning "What is it?"). It was white, like coriander seed, and flat. It tasted like honey bread.

³²Then Moses gave them this further command from the Lord. They were to collect two quarts of it. It would be kept as a museum specimen forever. That way later generations could see the bread the Lord had fed them with in the wilderness. It would remind them of the time when he brought them from Egypt. ³³Moses told Aaron to get a container and put two quarts of manna in it. He was to keep it in a holy place from generation to generation. ³⁴Aaron did this, just as the Lord had told Moses. And eventually it was kept in the Ark in the Tabernacle.

³⁵So the people of Israel ate the manna for 40 years. They ate it until they came to the land of Canaan. Then, there were crops to eat. ³⁶The container used to measure the manna held about two quarts. It is about a tenth of a bushel.

- *Remember:* When the people had no food, did they pray? What did they do? (16:2-3) What food did God send? How did he send it? (16:13-15,31) Did God give the people just enough food, too much food, or too little food? (16:17-18, 21) Why would you say that all the food we have comes from God?

- *Discover:* God gives us all the food we ever have. God causes all food to grow. We would have no food if he did not help it grow.

- *Apply:* Since everything you eat really comes from God, shouldn't you thank him for your food? Why not do that now? Why not do that before each meal? Don't forget!

- *What's next?* How do you get your drinking water? Do you turn on a faucet? Moses didn't have a faucet. Here's how he did it. (Exodus 17:1-7) ■

Water from a Rock

Do you remember when Moses found water for his million people? (15:25) They are thirsty again. But they have no water. Once more they forget to pray. Once more they complain about God. Would you give people good gifts when they complain about you? Let's see what God does.

17Now, at God's command, the people of Israel left the Sihn desert. They went by easy stages to Rephidim. But upon arrival, there was no water!

²So once more the people growled and complained to Moses. "Give us water!" they wailed.

"Quiet!" Moses said. "Are you trying to test God's patience with you?"

³But they were very thirsty. So they cried out, "Why did you ever take us out of Egypt? Why did you bring us here to die, with our children and cattle too?"

⁴Then Moses pleaded with the Lord. "What shall I do? For they are almost ready to stone me."

⁵⁻⁶Then the Lord said to Moses, "Take the elders of Israel with you. Then lead the people out to Mt. Horeb. I will meet you there at the rock. Strike it with your rod—the same one you struck the Nile with. Water will come pouring out, enough for everyone!" Moses did as he was told, and the water gushed out! ⁷Moses named the place Massah. This means "tempting the Lord to slay us." But sometimes they referred to it as Meribah. This means "argument" or "strife"! It was there that the people of Israel argued against God. They tempted him to slay them by saying, "Is the Lord going to take care of us or not?"

- Remember: Did the people pray to God or complain to Moses? (17:2) Did Moses pray to God or complain to God? (17:4) How did God send water this time? (17:5-6) What two names did people give to this place? What did they mean?

(17:7) What would you like to tell these people about prayer? Is that good advice for you too?

- Discover: God gives us good gifts, even when we don't deserve them.

- Apply: Make a list of the good gifts God has given you this week. Have you thanked him for each?

- What's next? A battle is going to be lost or won. It all depends on the way a man holds up his hands. Read about this in Exodus 17:8-16. ■

Aaron and Hur Help Moses

God asked Moses to do something very strange. But Moses did it!
God asked him to hold his hands up during a battle. Read on to
find out what happened when Moses obeyed.

⁸But now the warriors of Amalek came to fight against the people of Israel at Rephidim. ⁹Moses told Joshua to call the Israelites to arms. They were to fight the army of Amalek.

"Tomorrow," Moses told him, "I will stand at the top of the hill. I will hold the rod of God in my hand!"

¹⁰So Joshua and his men went out to fight the army of Amalek. Meanwhile Moses, Aaron, and Hur went to the top of the hill. ¹¹And as long as Moses held up the rod in his hands, Israel was win-ning. But whenever he rested his arms at his sides, the warriors of Amalek were winning. ¹²Moses' arms became too tired to hold up the rod any longer. So Aaron and Hur rolled a stone for him to sit on. And they stood on each side, holding up his hands until sunset. ¹³As a result, Joshua and his troops crushed the army of Amalek. They put them to the sword.

¹⁴Then the Lord told Moses, "Write this so it cannot be erased. I want you to remember this forever. Tell Joshua that I will blot out every trace of Amalek." ¹⁵⁻¹⁶Moses built an altar there. He called

it "Jehovah-nissi." This means "the Lord is my flag."

"Raise the banner of the Lord!" Moses said. "For the Lord will be at war with Amalek generation after generation."

- *Remember:* Who led the Israelites into battle? (17:9) What helped the Israelites win? What caused them to lose? (17:11) What did Moses hold in his hand? (17:10) How did Joshua help win the battle? (17:10) How did Moses help win the battle? (17:11) How did Aaron and Hur help win the battle? (17:12-13) How did these men need each other? Do you think any of them could have won the battle alone? Why not?

- *Discover:* There are some things we can't do alone. We need others to help us. There are some things we can't do, even with others. We need God to help us.

- *Apply:* Are you trying to do something alone, but you can't do it? Who can help you? Ask him now.

- *What's next?* God offered to make the people of Israel a very special people. All they had to do was one thing. But what was it? Read Exodus 19. ∎

Jethro Visits Moses

18 Word soon reached Jethro, Moses' father-in-law, the priest of Midian. He heard about all the wonderful things God had done for his people and for Moses. He heard how the Lord had brought them out of Egypt.

²Then Jethro took Moses' wife, Zipporah, to him (for he had sent her home). ³He also brought along Moses' two sons. One son was named Gershom. His name means "foreigner." For Moses said when he was born, "I have been wandering in a foreign land." ⁴The other was named Eliezer. His name means "God is my help." For Moses said at his birth, "The God of my fathers was my helper. He delivered me from the sword of Pharaoh." ⁵⁻⁶They came while Moses and the people were camped at Mt. Sinai.

"Jethro, your father-in-law, has come to visit you," Moses was told. "And he has brought your wife and two sons."

⁷Moses went out to meet his father-in-law. He greeted him warmly. They hugged each other and then went into Moses' tent to talk further. ⁸Moses told to his father-in-law all that had happened. He told him what the Lord had done to Pharaoh and the Egyptians in order to deliver Israel. He told about all the problems there had been along the way. He told how the Lord had rescued his people from all of them. ⁹Jethro was very happy about all the Lord had done for Israel. He rejoiced about God's bringing them out of Egypt.

¹⁰"Bless the Lord," Jethro said. "For he has saved you from the Egyptians and from Pharaoh. He has rescued Israel. ¹¹I know now that the Lord is greater than any other god. For he has delivered his people from the proud and cruel Egyptians."

¹²Jethro offered sacrifices to God. After that Aaron and the leaders of Israel came to meet Jethro. They all ate a special meal together before the Lord.

Jethro Gives Moses Good Advice

¹³The next day Moses sat as usual to hear the people's complaints against each other. He listened from morning to evening.

¹⁴Moses' father-in-law saw how much time this was taking. And he said, "Why are you trying to do all this alone? There are people standing here all day long to get your help!"

¹⁵⁻¹⁶"Well, because the people come to me with their disputes. They ask me for God's decisions," Moses told him. "I am their judge. I decide who is right and who is wrong. I also instruct them in God's ways. I apply the laws of God to their particular disputes."

¹⁷"It's not right!" his father-in-law said. ¹⁸"You're going to wear yourself out. And if you do, what will happen to the people? Moses, this job is too heavy a burden for you to handle all by yourself. ¹⁹⁻²⁰Now listen. Let me give you a word of advice, and God will bless you. Be these people's lawyer. Stand as their representative before God. Bring him their questions to decide. You will tell them his decisions. You will teach them God's laws, and show them the principles of godly living.

²¹"But find some capable, godly, honest men who hate bribes to help you. Appoint them as judges, one judge for each 1000 people. Each judge will have 10 judges under him, each in charge of 100. And under each of them will be two judges, each in charge of the affairs of 50 people. Each of these will have five judges beneath him, each helping 10 persons. ²²Let these men do the job of serving the people with justice at all times. Anything that is too important or complicated can be brought to you. But the smaller matters they can take care of themselves. That way it will be easier for you because you will share the burden with them. ²³If you follow this advice, and if the Lord agrees, you will be able to endure the pressures. And there will be peace and harmony in the camp."

²⁴Moses listened to his father-in-law's advice and did what he said. ²⁵He chose able men from all over Israel. He made them judges over the people—thousands, hundreds, fifties, and tens. ²⁶They were always available to bring about justice. They brought the hard cases to Moses but judged the smaller ones themselves.

²⁷Soon after this Moses let his father-in-law go back to his own land.

God Talks to Moses on a Mountain

Would you be willing to do just one thing to be God's special friend? One day God talked to Moses. He said Moses and his people could be his special people. All they had to do was one thing. Do you know what that was? Read on and you will find out.

19The Israelites arrived in the Sinai region three months after the night they left Egypt. ²⁻³After breaking camp at Rephidim, they came to the base of Mt. Sinai. They set up camp there. Moses climbed the rugged mountain to meet with God. From somewhere in the mountain God called to him. He said,

"Give these commands to the people of Israel. Tell them, ⁴'You have seen what I did to the Egyptians. You saw how I brought you to myself as though on eagle's wings. ⁵Now you must obey me and keep your part of my contract with you. If you do, you shall be my own little flock. You will be special among all the nations of the earth, for all the earth is mine. ⁶And you shall be a kingdom of priests to God, a holy nation.'"

⁷Moses came back from the mountain. He called all the leaders of the people to him. He told them what the Lord had said.

⁸They all replied in unison, "We will do all he asks of us." Moses then told the Lord what the people said.

⁹Then God said to Moses, "I am going to come to you in the form of a dark cloud. That way the people themselves can hear me when I talk with you. And then they will always believe you. ¹⁰Go down now and see that the people are ready for my visit. Sanctify them today and tomorrow. Have them wash their clothes. ¹¹Then, the day after tomorrow, I will come down upon Mt. Sinai as all the people watch. ¹²Set boundary lines the people may not pass. Tell them, 'Beware! Do not go up into the mountain or even touch its borders. Whoever does shall die. ¹³No hand shall touch him. If anyone does, he shall be stoned or shot to death with arrows. This will happen whether he is man or animal.' Stay away from the mountain until you hear a ram's horn sounding one long blast. Then gather at the foot of the mountain!"

¹⁴So Moses went down to the people and sanctified them and they washed their clothing.

¹⁵He told them, "Get ready for God's appearance two days from now. Do not sleep with your wives."

¹⁶On the morning of the third day there was a terrific thunder and lightning storm. A huge cloud came down upon the mountain. There was a long, loud blast as from a ram's horn. All the people trembled. ¹⁷Moses led them out from the camp to meet God. They stood at the foot of the mountain. ¹⁸All Mt. Sinai was covered with smoke because the Lord came down upon it in the form of fire. The smoke billowed into the sky as from a furnace. And the whole mountain shook with a violent earthquake. ¹⁹As the trumpet blast grew louder and louder, Moses spoke and God thundered his reply. ²⁰So the Lord came down upon the top of Mt. Sinai. He called Moses up to the top of the mountain, and Moses went up to God.

God does not want us to worship anyone else

Do not worship any other god but me.

Exodus 20:3

---

²¹But the Lord told Moses, "Go back down and warn the people not to cross the borders. They must not come up here to try to see God. For if they do, many of them will die. ²²Even the priests on duty must sanctify themselves, or else I will destroy them."

²³"But the people won't come up into the mountain!" Moses said. "You told them not to! You told me to set borders around the mountain. I declared it off-limits. It is a place for only God."

²⁴But the Lord said, "Go down and bring Aaron back with you. And do not let the priests and the people break across the borders. Do not allow them to try to come up here. If they do, I will punish them."

²⁵So Moses went down to the people and told them what God had said.

● *Remember:* Where was Moses when God talked to him? (19:2-3) What was the one thing God asked the people of Israel to do? (19:5) What would God do for them if they obeyed him? (19:5-6) God told Moses to set a boundary at the bottom of the mountain. The people could not cross it. Why? (19:21) When God asked the people to obey, do you think he was asking them to do too much? What might happen if the people didn't obey? Do you think the "one thing" he asked is too much for us?

● *Discovery:* God wants to help us. But we must do what he says. Our parents want to help us. But we must do what they say.

● *Apply:* Think of three ways God wants to help you. Will you let him do it? How?

● *What's next?* What is the only part of the Bible that God wrote with his own fingers? You'll find out in Exodus 20:1-21. ■

The Ten Commandments

God helped great men write everything in the Bible. But there is one part he wrote with his own finger. Do you know what it is? You will as you read on.

20 Then God gave these laws: ²"I am the Lord your God. I freed you from slavery in Egypt.

³"Do not worship any other god but me.

⁴"You shall not make any idols. Make no images of animals, birds, or fish. ⁵You must never bow or worship an idol in any way. For I, the Lord your God, want you to be mine. I will not share your love with any other god!

"And when I punish people for their sins, the punishment goes on even after they have died. It is suffered by the children, grandchildren, and great-grandchildren of those who hate me.

⁶But I lavish my love upon thousands of those who love me and obey my commands.

⁷"You shall not use the name of the Lord your God irreverently. Nor shall you use it to swear. You will not escape punishment if you do.

⁸"Remember to observe the Sabbath as a holy day. ⁹Six days a week are for your daily duties and your regular work. ¹⁰But the seventh day is a day of Sabbath rest before the Lord your God. On that day you are to do no work of any kind. Nor shall you allow your son, daughter, or slaves to work—whether men or women. Not even your cattle or your houseguests should work. ¹¹For in six days the Lord made the heaven, earth, and sea, and everything in them. But he rested on the seventh day. So he blessed the Sabbath day and set it aside for rest.

¹²"Honor your father and mother. Do this that you may have a long, good life in the land the Lord your God will give you.

¹³"You must not murder.

¹⁴"You must not commit adultery.

¹⁵"You must not steal.

¹⁶"You must not lie.

¹⁷"You must not envy your neighbor's house. You must not want to sleep with his wife. You must not want to own his slaves, oxen, donkeys, or anything else he has."

¹⁸All the people saw the lightning and the smoke rising from the mountain. They heard the thunder and the long trumpet blast. And they stood at a distance, shaking with fear.

¹⁹They said to Moses, "You tell us what God says and we will obey. But don't let God speak directly to us, or it will kill us."

²⁰"Don't be afraid," Moses told them. "For God has come in this way to show you his awesome power. That way, from now on you will be afraid to sin against him!"

²¹As the people stood in the distance, Moses entered into the deep darkness where God was.

● *Remember:* Who gave these 10 special rules? (20:1-2) God pours out his love on certain people. Who are they? (20:6) Would you like to peek ahead a little? Read Exodus 31:18. It will tell you which part of the Bible God wrote with his own finger. Does that make these ten commandments more special to you?

● *Discover:* God gave us his commandments to help us, not hurt us. Why does God want to help us? Because he loves us so much.

● *Apply:* How can we help ourselves most? By doing what God says is best for us. Will you try to do that today?

● *What's next?* Would you talk to a piece of wood or pray to a cow? Who would be dumb enough to do that? in Exodus 32, you'll read about some people who were. ■

Idols and Altars

²²And the Lord told Moses to be his spokesman to the people of Israel. "You are witnesses to the fact that I have made known my will to you from heaven. ²³Remember, you must not make or worship idols made of silver or gold or of anything else!

²⁴"The altars you make for me must be simple altars of earth. Offer upon them your sacrifices to me, your burnt offerings and peace offerings of sheep and oxen. Build altars only where I tell you to, and I will come and bless you there. ²⁵You may also build altars from stone. But if you do, then use only uncut stones and boulders. Do not chip or shape the stones with a tool. That would make them unfit for my altar. ²⁶And do not make steps for the altar. If you do, someone might look up beneath the skirts of your clothing and see your nakedness.

Laws about People

21 "Here are other laws you must obey.

²"If you buy a Hebrew slave, he shall serve only six years. He will be freed in the seventh year. He need pay nothing to regain his freedom.

³"He might have sold himself as a slave and then married after that. If so,

only he shall be freed. But if he was married before he became a slave, then his wife shall be freed with him at the same time. ⁴But perhaps his master gave him a wife while he was a slave. And they might have had sons or daughters. If so, the wife and children shall still belong to the master. And he shall go out by himself free.

⁵"The man might plainly declare, 'I prefer my master, my wife, and my children. I would rather not go free.' ⁶If he does this, then his master shall bring him before the judges. He shall publicly bore his ear with an awl. After that he will be a slave forever.

⁷"If a man sells his daughter as a slave, she shall not be freed at the end of six years as the men are. ⁸If she does not please the man who bought her, then he shall let her be bought back again. But he has no power to sell her to foreigners. For he has wronged her by no longer wanting her after marrying her. ⁹And if he arranges a marriage between a Hebrew slave girl and his son, then he may no longer treat her as a slave girl. He must treat her as a daughter. ¹⁰If he himself marries her and then takes another wife, he may not reduce her food or clothing. He also must not fail to sleep with her as his wife. ¹¹If he fails in any of these three things, then she may leave freely without any payment.

¹²"Anyone who hits a man so hard that he dies shall surely be put to death. ¹³But it might have been accidental—an act of God—and not intentional. If this is true, then I will appoint a place where he can run for safety. ¹⁴However, if a man attacks another on purpose, hoping to kill him, drag him even from my altar, and kill him.

¹⁵"Anyone who hits his father or mother shall surely be put to death.

¹⁶"A kidnapper must be killed, whether he is caught with his victim or has already sold him as a slave.

¹⁷"Anyone who reviles or curses his mother or father shall surely be put to death.

¹⁸"It may happen that two men fight. One might hit the other with a stone or with his fist. He might hurt him so that

he must be confined to bed, but doesn't die. ¹⁹And perhaps later, he might be able to walk again, though with a limp. If all this happens, the man who hit him will be innocent. But he must pay for the loss of the hurt man's time until he is healed. He must also pay any medical expenses.

²⁰"A man might beat his slave to death. This is true whether the slave is male or female. But if he does, he shall surely be punished.

God tells us not to lie

You must not lie.

---

²¹However, if the slave does not die for a couple of days, then the man shall not be punished. This is because the slave is his property.

²²"It may happen that two men will fight. In the process they might hurt a pregnant woman. She might loose her baby, but still live. If this happens, then the man who hurt her shall be fined. He will pay whatever amount the woman's husband shall demand, as long as the judges approve. ²³But if any harm comes to the woman and she dies, he shall be killed.

²⁴"If her eye is injured, injure his. If her tooth is knocked out, knock out his. The payment should be like the harm done. You should take hand for hand, foot for foot. ²⁵Burn should be given for burn, wound for wound, lash for lash.

²⁶"A man might hit his slave in the eye. As a result, the eye might be blinded. If so, then the slave shall go free because of his eye. This is true whether the slave is a man or woman. ²⁷And if a master knocks out his slave's tooth, he shall let him go free to pay for the tooth.

²⁸"If an ox gores a man or woman to death, the ox shall be stoned. Its meat shall not be eaten. But the owner shall not be held. ²⁹This is true except when the owner knows that the ox has gored people in the past and still has not kept it under control. In that case, if it kills someone, the ox shall be stoned. And the owner also shall be killed. ³⁰But the dead man's relatives may accept a fine

instead, if they wish. The judges will determine the amount.

[31]"The same law holds if the ox gores a boy or a girl. [32]But if the ox gores a slave, whether male or female, the slave's master shall be given 30 pieces of silver. Then the ox shall be stoned.

Laws about Property

[33]"A man might dig a well and not cover it. An ox or a donkey might then fall into it. [34]If this happens, the owner of the well shall pay full damages to the owner of the animal. Then the dead animal shall belong to him.

[35]"If a man's ox injures another, and it dies, then the two owners shall sell the live ox. They will divide the price between them. Each shall also own half of the dead ox. [36]But if the ox was known from past experience to gore, and its owner has not kept it under control, then there will not be a division of the income. But the owner of the living ox shall pay in full for the dead ox. Then the dead one shall be his.

22 "A man might steal an ox or sheep and then kill or sell it. If he does, he shall pay a fine of five to one. Five oxen shall be given back for each stolen ox. With sheep, the fine shall be four to one. Four sheep will be given back for each sheep stolen.

[2]"If a thief is caught in the act of breaking into a house and is killed, the one who killed him is not guilty. [3]But if it happens in the daylight, it must be presumed to be murder. The man who kills him is guilty.

"If a thief is captured, he must pay back all that he stole. If he can't, then he must be sold as a slave for his debt.

[4]"If he is caught in the act of stealing a live ox or donkey or sheep or whatever it is, he shall pay double value as his fine.

[5]"Someone might let his animal loose on purpose and it might get into another man's vineyard. Or he might turn it into another man's field to graze. If this happens, then he must pay for all damages. He must give the owner of the field or vineyard an equal amount of the best of his own crop.

[6]"As a field is being burned off, the fire might get out of control. It might go into another field so that the shocks of grain, or the standing grain, are destroyed. If this happens, the one who started the fire will pay back the damages in full.

[7]"Someone might give money or goods to a person to keep for him. That money might be stolen. If the thief is found, he shall pay double. [8]But if no thief is found, then the man to whom the money was given shall be brought before God. There it will be decided whether or not he himself has taken his neighbor's property.

[9]"An ox, donkey, sheep, clothing, or anything else might get lost. The owner might believe he has found it with someone else who denies it. If this happens, both people shall come before God for a decision. The one whom God says is guilty shall pay double to the other.

[10]"A man might ask his neighbor to keep a donkey, ox, sheep, or any other animal for him. It might die, get hurt, or get away. There might be no eyewitness to report just what happened to it. [11]If this is so, then the neighbor must take an oath that he has not stolen it. The owner must accept his word. And he will not have to pay it back. [12]But if the animal or property has been stolen, the neighbor caring for it must repay the owner. [13]If it was attacked by some wild animal, he shall bring the torn carcass to prove it. In such a case he shall not be made to pay it back.

[14]"A man might borrow an animal (or anything else) from a neighbor. It might become injured or killed. And the owner might not be there at the time. If this takes place, then the man who borrowed it must pay for it. [15]But if the owner is there, he need not pay. And if it was rented, then he need not pay. For the animal's possible injury was included in the rental fee.

General Laws

[16]"A man might seduce a girl who is not engaged to anyone. And he might sleep with her. If he does, then he must pay the usual dowry. Then he must accept

her as his wife. ¹⁷But if her father refuses to let her marry him, then he shall pay the money anyway.

¹⁸"A sorceress shall be put to death.

¹⁹"Anyone having sexual relations with an animal shall certainly be killed.

²⁰"Anyone sacrificing to any other god than the Lord shall be killed.

²¹"You must not oppress a stranger in any way. Remember, you yourselves were foreigners in the land of Egypt.

²²"You must not exploit widows or orphans. ²³If you do so in any way, and they cry to me for my help, I will surely give it. ²⁴My anger shall flame out against you. I will kill you with enemy armies. Then your wives will be widows and your children fatherless.

²⁵"If you lend money to a needy fellow-Hebrew, you are not to lend it in the usual way, with interest. ²⁶If you take his clothing as a pledge of his repayment, you must let him have it back at night. ²⁷For it is probably his only warmth. How can he sleep without it? If you don't give it back, and he cries to me for help, I will hear him. And I will be very gracious to him at your expense. For I am very kind.

²⁸"You must not swear using God's name. You must not curse government officials. They are your judges and your rulers.

²⁹"You must be prompt in giving me the tithe of your crops and your wine. You must remember the redemption payment for your oldest son.

³⁰"As to the firstborn of the oxen and the sheep, give it to me on the eighth day. Leave it with its mother for seven days.

³¹"And you are to be holy—my special people. Do not eat any animal that has been attacked and killed by a wild animal. Leave its dead body for the dogs to eat.

23 "Do not pass along untrue reports. Do not cooperate with an evil man by saying on the witness stand what you know is false.

²⁻³"Don't join mobs intent on evil. When on the witness stand, do not be swayed in your testimony by the mood of the majority present. And do not

change what you should say just to help a man because he is poor.

⁴"You might come upon an enemy's ox or donkey that has strayed away. If you do, you must take it back to its owner. ⁵You might see your enemy trying to get his donkey onto its feet beneath a heavy load. If you see him, you must not go on by. You must help him.

⁶"A man's poverty is no excuse for twisting justice against him.

⁷"Keep far away from falsely charging anyone with evil. Never let an innocent person be put to death. I will not stand for this.

⁸"Take no bribes, for a bribe makes you unaware of what you clearly see! A bribe hurts the cause of the person who is right.

⁹"Do not oppress foreigners. You know what it's like to be a foreigner. Remember your own experience in the land of Egypt.

¹⁰"Sow and reap your crops for six years. ¹¹But let the land rest and lie fallow during the seventh year. Let the poor people harvest any volunteer crop that may come up. Leave the rest for the animals to enjoy. The same rule applies to your vineyards and your olive groves.

¹²"Work six days only. Then rest on the seventh day. This is to give your oxen and donkeys a rest. It will be a day of rest for the people in your household. This includes your slaves and visitors.

¹³"Be sure to obey all of these teachings. And remember—never mention the name of any other god.

Three Special Holidays

¹⁴"There are three yearly religious feasts you must celebrate.

¹⁵"The first is the Feast of Unleavened Bread. For seven days you are not to eat bread with yeast, just as I commanded you before. This celebration is to be a yearly event at the regular time in March. This was the month you left Egypt. All must bring me a sacrifice at that time. ¹⁶Then there is the Harvest Feast, when you must bring to me the first of your crops. And, finally, you must celebrate the Feast of Ingathering at the end of the harvest season. ¹⁷At these

three times each year, every man in Israel shall appear before the Lord God.

18"No sacrificial blood shall be offered with leavened bread. No sacrificial fat shall be left unoffered until the next morning.

19"As you reap each of your crops, bring me the best sample of the first day's harvest. It shall be offered to the Lord your God.

"Do not boil a young goat in its mother's milk.

Laws about Enemies

20"See, I am sending an Angel before you. He will lead you safely to the land I have prepared for you. 21Respect him and do all the things he tells you to do. Do not rebel against him, for he will not pardon your sins. I have sent him. He bears my name. 22If you are careful to obey him, doing all I tell you to do, then I will be an enemy to your enemies. 23For my Angel shall go before you. He will bring you into the land of the Amorites, Hittites, Perizzites, Canaanites, Hivites, and Jebusites. You will live there. And I will destroy those people before you.

24"You must not worship the gods of these other nations. You must never sacrifice to them in any way. And you must not follow the evil example of these heathen people. You must fully conquer them and break down their shameful idols.

Serve God Only

25"You shall serve the Lord your God only. Then I will bless you with food and with water. And I will take away sickness from among you. 26Women will not lose their babies. They will have all the children they want. You will live out the full quota of the days of your life.

27"The terror of the Lord shall fall upon all the people whose land you invade. They will flee before you. 28And I will send hornets to drive out the Hivites, Canaanites, and Hittites from before you. 29I will not do it all in one year. For if I did, the land would become a desert. The wild animals would become too many to control. 30But I will drive them out a little at a time. This way

your people will have time to increase enough to fill the land. 31And I will set your borders from the Red Sea to the Philistine coast. Your land will be from the southern deserts as far as the Euphrates River. I will cause you to defeat the people now living in the land. And you will drive them out ahead of you.

32"You must make no promise with them. You must have nothing to do with their gods. 33Don't let them live among you! For I know that they will infect you with their sin of worshiping false gods. That would be an utter disaster to you."

The People Promise to Obey

24 The Lord now told Moses, "Come up here with Aaron, Nadab, Abihu, and 70 of the elders of Israel. All of you except Moses are to worship at a distance. 2Moses alone shall come near to the Lord. And remember, none of the ordinary people are allowed to come up into the mountain at all."

3Then Moses gave the people all the laws and rules God had given him. And the people answered together, "We will obey them all."

4Moses wrote down the laws. And early the next morning he built an altar at the foot of the mountain. He put 12 pillars around the altar because there were 12 tribes of Israel. 5Then he sent some of the young men to sacrifice the burnt offerings and peace offerings to the Lord. 6Moses took half of the blood of these animals. He drew it off into basins. The other half he splashed against the altar.

7And he read to the people the Book he had written. It was called the Book of the Covenant. It contained God's directions and laws. And the people said again, "We promise to obey every one of these rules."

8Then Moses threw the blood from the basins toward the people. Then he said, "This blood confirms the covenant. It seals the covenant the Lord has made with you in giving you these laws."

9Then Moses, Aaron, Nadab, Abihu, and 70 of the elders of Israel went up into the mountain. 10And they saw the God of Israel. Under his feet there seemed to be a pavement of brilliant sapphire stones. They were as clear as the heavens. ¹¹Yet, even though the elders saw God, he did not destroy them. And they had a meal together before the Lord.

Forty Days on the Mountain

¹²And the Lord said to Moses, "Come up to me into the mountain. Remain until I give you the laws and commands I have written on tablets of stone. That way you can teach the people from them." ¹³So Moses and Joshua, his helper, went up into the mountain of God.

¹⁴He told the elders, "Stay here and wait for us until we come back. If there are any problems while I am gone, consult with Aaron and Hur."

¹⁵Then Moses went up the mountain. He vanished into the cloud at the top. ¹⁶The glory of the Lord rested upon Mt. Sinai. And the cloud covered it six days. The seventh day he called to Moses from the cloud. ¹⁷Those at the bottom of the mountain saw the awesome sight. The glory of the Lord on the mountaintop looked like a raging fire. ¹⁸And Moses vanished into the cloud-covered mountaintop. He was there for 40 days and 40 nights.

How to Build the Tabernacle

25 The Lord said to Moses, "Speak to the people of Iśrael. Tell them that all who want to may bring me an offering. They may bring gold, silver, or bronze. They may bring blue cloth, purple cloth, red cloth, fine linen, goats' hair, red-dyed rams' skins, or goatskins. They may also bring acacia wood, olive oil for the lamps, spices for the anointing oil and for the fragrant incense, onyx stones, and stones to be set in the ephod and in the breastplate.

⁸"For I want the people of Israel to make me a holy home. There I will live among them.

⁹"This home of mine shall be called a Tabernacle. I will give you a drawing that shows you how to make it and everything in it.

The Ark

¹⁰"Use acacia wood to make an Ark 3¾ feet long, 2¼ feet wide, and 2¼ feet high. ¹¹Cover it inside and outside with pure gold. Make a molding of gold all around it. ¹²Cast four rings of gold for it. Attach them to the four lower corners. Put two rings on each side. ¹³⁻¹⁴Make poles from acacia wood. Cover them over with gold. Then fit the poles into the rings at the sides of the Ark to carry it. ¹⁵These carrying poles shall never be taken from the rings. They should be left there at all times. ¹⁶When the Ark is finished, place inside it the tablets of stone I will give you. The Ten Commandments will be carved on them.

¹⁷"And make a lid of pure gold. Make it 3¾ feet long and 2¼ feet wide. This is the place of mercy for your sins. ¹⁸Then make two statues of Guardian Angels. Use beaten gold. Place them at the two ends of the lid of the Ark. ¹⁹They shall be one piece with the mercy place. One will be put at each end. ²⁰The Guardian Angels shall be facing each other. They will look down upon the place of mercy. Their wings will spread out above the gold lid. ²¹Install the lid upon the Ark. Place within the Ark the tablets of stone I shall give you. ²²And I will meet with you there. I will talk with you from above the place of mercy between the Guardian Angels. The Ark will contain the laws of my covenant. There I will tell you my commands for the people of Israel.

The Table

²³"Then make a table of acacia wood 3 feet long. Make it 1½ feet wide, and 2¼ feet high. ²⁴Cover it with pure gold. Run a rib of gold around it. ²⁵Put a molding four inches wide around the edge of the top. Run a gold ridge along the molding, all around. ²⁶⁻²⁷Make four gold rings. Put the rings at the outside corner of the four legs, close to the top. These are rings for the poles that will be used to carry the table. ²⁸Make the poles from acacia wood overlaid with gold. ²⁹And make gold dishes, spoons, pitchers, and bowls. ³⁰Always keep the special Bread of the Presence on the table before me.

The Lampstand

[31]"Make a lampstand of pure, beaten gold. The entire lampstand and its decorations shall be one piece—the base, shaft, lamps, and blossoms. [32-33]It will have three branches going out from each side of the center shaft. Each branch must be decorated with three almond flowers. [34-35]The central shaft itself will be decorated with four almond flowers. One must be placed between each set of branches. Also, there will be one flower above the top set of branches. One will also be put below the bottom set. [36]These decorations and branches and the shaft are all to be one piece of pure, beaten gold. [37]Then make seven lamps for the lampstand, and set them so that they reflect their light forward. [38]The snuffers and trays are to be made of pure gold. [39]You will need about 107 pounds of pure gold for the lampstand and its accessories.

[40]"Be sure that everything you make follows the pattern I am showing you here on the mountain.

The Tent

26 "Make the tent for the Tabernacle from 10 colored sheets of fine linen. Make it 42 feet long and 6 feet wide. Dye it blue, purple, and red. Sew figures of Guardian Angels into them. [3]Join five sheets end to end for each side of the tent. This will form two long pieces, one for each side. [4-5]Use loops at the edges to join these two long pieces side by side. There are to be 50 loops on each side, across from each other. [6]Then make 50 gold clasps to fasten the loops. This will make the Tabernacle a single unit.

[7-8]"The roof of the tent is made of goats' hair curtains. There are to be 11 of these curtains. Each one is 45 feet across and 6 feet wide. [9]Connect five of these curtains into one wide section. Use the other six for another wide section. The sixth curtain will hang down across the front of the holy tent. [10-11]Use 50 loops along the edges of each of these two wide pieces. Join the loops together with 50 bronze clasps. Thus the two widths become one. [12]There will be a 1½-foot length of this roof-covering hanging down from the back of the tent. [13]A 1½-foot length will also hang down at the front. [14]On top of these blankets is placed a layer of rams' skins, dyed red. And over them, put a top layer of goatskins. This completes the roof-covering.

[15-16]"The frame of the holy tent shall be made from acacia wood. Each piece of the frame must be 15 feet high and 2¼ feet wide. They should stand upright. [17]Grooves must be put on each side to fit into the next upright piece. [18-19]Twenty of these frames will form the south side of the holy tent. Forty silver bases must be made for the frames to fit into. Two bases will be put under each piece of the frame. [20]On the north side there will also be 20 of these frames. [21]These will have their 40 silver bases. Two bases will support each frame, one under each edge. [22]On the west side there will be six frames. [23]Two frames will stand at each corner. [24]These corner frames will be attached at the bottom and top with clasps. [25]In all, there will be eight frames on that end of the building. Sixteen silver bases will support the frames. There are two bases under each frame.

[26-27]"Make bars of acacia wood to run across the frames. Five bars should be put on each side of the Tabernacle. Also five bars for the rear of the building, facing westward. [28]The middle bar should be put halfway up the frames. It must run all the way from end to end of the Tabernacle. [29]Cover the frames with gold. Make gold rings to hold the bars. Also cover the bars with gold. [30]Set up this tent in the manner I showed you on the mountain.

The Curtains

[31]"Inside the Tabernacle, make a curtain from fine linen. Sew blue, purple, and red Guardian Angels into the cloth. [32]Hang this curtain on gold hooks. The hooks are set into four pillars made from acacia wood overlaid with gold. The pillars are to be set in silver bases. [33]Behind this curtain place the Ark that holds the stone tablets with God's laws. The cur-

tain will divide the Holy Place and the Most Holy Place.

34"Now put the gold lid of the Ark in the Most Holy Place. 35Place the table and lampstand across the room from each other. They must be on the outer side of the veil. The lampstand should stand to the south. The table should stand to the north.

36"Make a screen for the door of the holy tent. Use another curtain of fine linen. Skillfully sew blue, purple, and red thread into it. 37Hang this curtain on gold hooks set into posts made from acacia wood overlaid with gold. The posts are to rest on bronze bases.

The Altar

27 "Using acacia wood, make a square altar. Build it 7½ feet wide and 4½ feet high. 2Make horns for the four corners of the altar. Attach them firmly. And cover everything with bronze. 3The ash buckets, shovels, basins, carcass hooks, and fire pans are all to be made of bronze. 4Make a bronze grating. Put a metal ring at each corner. 5Fit the grating halfway down into the firebox. Rest it upon the ledge built there. 6For moving the altar, make poles from acacia wood overlaid with bronze. 7To carry it, put the poles into the rings at each side of the altar. 8The altar is to be hollow. Make it from planks, just as was shown you on the mountain.

The Courtyard

9-10"Then make a courtyard for the Tabernacle. Enclose it with curtains made from fine-twisted linen. On the south side the curtains will stretch for 150 feet. They will be held up by 20 posts. The posts will fit into 20 bronze post holders. The curtains will be held up with silver hooks. These will be attached to silver rods, attached to the posts. 11It will be the same on the north side of the court. Curtains, 150 feet long, will be held up by 20 posts. The posts will fit into bronze sockets, with silver hooks and rods. 12The west side of the court will be 75 feet wide. It will have 10 posts and 10 sockets. 13The east side will also be 75 feet. 14-15On each side of the entrance

there will be 22½ feet of curtain. It will be held up by three posts. The posts will be fitted into three sockets.

16"The entrance to the court will be a 30-foot-wide curtain. Make it of beautifully embroidered blue, purple, and red fine-twined linen. Attach it to four posts. Support the posts with their four sockets. 17All the posts around the court are to be connected. Connect them with silver rods, using silver hooks. The posts will be supported by solid bronze bases. 18So the entire court will be 150 feet long and 75 feet wide. The curtain walls will be 7½ feet high. Make them from fine-twisted linen.

19"All utensils used in the work of the Tabernacle will be made of bronze. This includes all the pins and pegs for hanging the utensils on the walls.

20"Instruct the people of Israel to bring you pure olive oil. It will be used in the lamps of the Tabernacle. It must burn there all the time. 21Aaron and his sons shall place this eternal flame in the outer holy room. They must tend it day and night before the Lord. It must never go out. This is a lasting rule for the people of Israel.

Clothes for the Priests

28 "Set apart Aaron your brother, and his sons Nadab, Abihu, Eleazar, and Ithamar as holy. They will be priests, to serve me. 2Make special clothes for Aaron. They will show he is set apart to serve God. They must be beautiful clothes that will lend dignity to his work. 3Instruct those to whom I have given special skill as tailors. Tell them to make the clothes that will set him apart from others. That way he may serve me in the priest's office. 4They shall make him a special wardrobe. It will include a chestpiece, an ephod, a robe, an embroidered shirt, a turban, and a sash. They shall also make special clothes for Aaron's sons.

5-6"The ephod shall be made by the most skilled of the workmen. They must use gold, blue, purple, and red threads of fine linen. 7It will consist of two pieces, front and back. These parts will be joined at the shoulders. 8The sash shall be made of the same material. It will be made of threads of gold, blue, purple, and red fine-twisted linen. ⁹Take two onyx stones. Engrave on them the names of the tribes of Israel. ¹⁰Six names shall be on each stone. That way all the tribes are named in the order of their births. ¹¹When engraving these names, do it the same way you would make a seal. Then mount the stones in gold settings. ¹²Fasten the two stones upon the shoulders of the ephod. These will be memorial stones for the people of Israel. Aaron will carry their names before the Lord as a constant reminder. ¹³⁻¹⁴Two chains of pure, twisted gold shall be made. They will be attached to gold clasps on the shoulder of the ephod.

¹⁵"Then, taking great care, make a chestpiece to be used as God's oracle. Use the same gold, blue, purple, and red threads of fine-twisted linen as you did in the ephod. ¹⁶This chestpiece is to be of two folds of cloth. They will form a pouch nine inches square. ¹⁷Attach to it four rows of stones. A ruby, a topaz, and an emerald shall be in the first row. ¹⁸The second row will be carbuncle, a sapphire, and a diamond. ¹⁹The third row will be an amber, an agate, and an amethyst. ²⁰The fourth row will be an onyx, a beryl, and a jasper. All must be set in gold settings. ²¹Each stone will represent one of the tribes of Israel. The name of that tribe will be engraved upon it like a seal.

²²⁻²⁴"Attach the top of the chestpiece to the ephod. Do this with two twisted cords of pure gold. One end of each cord is attached to gold rings. These are placed at the outer top edge of the chest piece. ²⁵The other ends of the two cords are attached to the front edges of the two settings of onyx stones on the shoulder of the ephod. ²⁶Then make two more gold rings. Place them on the two lower, inside edges of the chestpiece. ²⁷Also make two other gold rings. These are for the bottom front edge of the ephod at the sash. ²⁸Now attach the bottom of the chestpiece to the bottom rings of the ephod. Do this by means of blue ribbons. This will prevent the chestpiece from coming loose from the ephod. ²⁹In

this way Aaron shall carry the names of the tribes of Israel on the chestpiece. They will be over his heart (it is God's oracle) when he goes into the Holy Place. Thus the Lord will be reminded of them always. ³⁰⁻³¹Insert into the pocket of the chestpiece the Urim and Thummim. These will be carried over Aaron's heart when he goes in before the Lord. Thus Aaron shall always be carrying the oracle over his heart when he goes in before the Lord.

"The ephod shall be made of blue cloth. ³²It will have an opening for Aaron's head. A woven band will be around this opening, just as around the neck of a coat of mail. That way it will not fray. ³³⁻³⁴The bottom edge of the ephod shall be embroidered. It will have blue, purple, and red pomegranates. These will be alternated with gold bells. ³⁵Aaron shall wear the ephod whenever he goes in to serve the Lord. The bells will tinkle as he goes in and out of the presence of the Lord in the Holy Place. That way he will not die.

³⁶"Next, make a plate of pure gold. Engrave on it, just as you would upon a seal, 'Holy to the Lord.' ³⁷⁻³⁸This plate is to be attached by means of a blue ribbon to the front of Aaron's turban. In this way Aaron will wear it upon his forehead. And thus he will bear the guilt connected with any errors regarding the offerings of the people of Israel. It shall always be worn when he goes into the presence of the Lord. That way the people will be accepted and forgiven.

³⁹"Weave Aaron's embroidered shirt from fine-twisted linen. Use a checkerboard pattern. Make the turban, too, of this linen. And make him an embroidered sash.

⁴⁰"Then, for Aaron's sons, make robes, sashes, and turbans. These will give them honor and respect. ⁴¹Clothe Aaron and his sons with these clothes. Then dedicate these men to their ministry. Anoint their heads with olive oil, thus setting them apart as the priests, my ministers. ⁴²Also make linen undershorts for them. These are to be worn beneath their robes next to their bodies. They will cover between the hips and

knees. [43]These must be worn whenever Aaron and his sons go into the Tabernacle. They also must be worn when they go to the altar in the Holy Place. Otherwise they will be guilty and die. This is a lasting law for Aaron and his sons.

How to Dedicate the Priests

29 "This is the way to dedicate Aaron and his sons as priests. Take a young bull and two rams with no defects. [2]Bake bread made without yeast. Make thin sheets of sweetened bread mingled with oil. And make unleavened wafers with oil poured over them. The various kinds of bread shall be made with finely ground wheat flour. [3-4]Place the bread in a basket. Bring it to the door of the Tabernacle. Also bring the young bull and the two rams.

"Bathe Aaron and his sons there at the door. [5]Then put Aaron's robe on him. Dress him in the embroidered shirt, ephod, chestpiece, and sash. [6]Place on his head the turban with the gold plate. [7]Then take the anointing oil and pour it upon his head. [8]Next, dress his sons in their robes. [9]Put on their woven sashes. Place caps on their heads. They will then be priests forever. Thus you shall set apart Aaron and his sons as holy.

[10]"Then bring the young bull to the Tabernacle. Aaron and his sons shall lay their hands upon its head. [11]And you shall kill it before the Lord, at the door of the Tabernacle. [12]Place its blood upon the horns of the altar. Smear it on with your finger. Pour the rest at the base of the altar. [13]Then take all the fat that covers the inner parts. Also take the gall bladder and two kidneys, and the fat on them. Burn them all upon the altar. [14]Then take the body, including the skin and the dung. Bring it outside the camp. Then burn it as a sin offering.

[15-16]"Next, Aaron and his sons shall lay their hands upon the head of one of the rams as it is killed. Its blood shall also be collected and sprinkled upon the altar. [17]Cut up the ram. Wash off the entrails and the legs. Place them with the head and the other pieces of the body. [18]Then burn it all upon the altar. It is a burnt offering to the Lord, and very pleasant to him.

An Apron for the High Priest

EXODUS 28:5-14

Does your mother wear an apron when she cooks? An apron keeps her clothes from getting dirty. God designed a special apron for the High Priest to wear. It was called an ephod. He did not wear this apron to cook. He wore it because God told him to. It was part of the special clothing God wanted him to wear. This special clothing showed everyone how important the High Priest's work was. It also helped him do God's work. The ephod helped the High Priest know what God wanted. The ephod had 12 precious jewels on it. Each jewel stood for one of Israel's 12 tribes. The ephod also had a pocket. Inside the pocket the High Priest kept the Urim and Thummin. These were probably small stones or precious gems the High Priest used to find out what God wanted. Today we have the Bible to help us know what God wants. We can also pray to God and ask him to help us. We don't need an ephod anymore to know what God wants.

[19-20]"Now take the other ram. Aaron and his sons shall lay their hands upon its head as it is killed. Collect the blood. Place some of it upon the tip of the right ear of Aaron and his sons. Put some of it on their right thumbs and

the big toes of their right feet. Sprinkle the rest of the blood over the altar. [21]Then scrape off some of the blood from the altar. Mix it with some of the anointing oil. And sprinkle it upon Aaron and his sons and upon their clothes. Then they and their clothing shall be made holy to the Lord.

[22]"Then take the fat of the ram. This includes the fat tail and the fat that covers the insides. Take also the gall bladder and the two kidneys and the fat all around them. Also set aside the right thigh. For this is the ram for ordination of Aaron and his sons. [23]Take also one loaf of bread, one cake of shortening bread, and one wafer from the basket of unleavened bread that was placed before the Lord. [24]Place these in the hands of Aaron and his sons. They will wave them in a gesture of offering to the Lord. [25]Afterwards, take them from their hands. Burn them on the altar as a fragrant burnt offering to him. [26]Then take the breast of Aaron's ordination ram. Wave it before the Lord in a gesture of offering. Afterwards, keep it for yourself.

[27]"Give the breast and thigh of the ram for appointing the priests [28]to Aaron and his sons. The people of Israel must always give this portion of their sacrifices—whether peace offerings or thanksgiving offerings. This is their contribution to the Lord.

[29]"These holy clothes of Aaron shall be kept. They will be used for appointing his son who succeeds him. This will be done from generation to generation, for his anointing ceremony. [30]Whoever is the next High Priest after Aaron shall wear these clothes. He will wear them for seven days before beginning service in the Tabernacle and the Holy Place.

[31]"Take the ram used in the ordination ceremony. Boil its meat in a holy area. [32]Aaron and his sons shall eat the meat. They shall also eat the bread in the basket, at the door of the Tabernacle. [33]They alone shall eat those items used in their atonement (that is, in their appointment ceremony). The ordinary people shall not eat them. For these things are set apart and holy. [34]If any of the meat or bread remains until the morning, burn it. It shall not be eaten, for it is holy.

[35]"This, then, is the way you shall ordain Aaron and his sons to their offices. This ordination shall go on for seven days. [36]Every day you shall sacrifice a young bull as a sin offering for atonement. Afterwards, purge the altar by making atonement for it. Pour olive oil upon it to set it apart for my use. [37]Make atonement for the altar and consecrate it to God every day for seven days. After this the altar shall be exceedingly holy. Whatever touches it shall be set apart for God.

The Daily Sacrifices

[38]"Each day offer two yearling lambs upon the altar. [39]One must be offered in the morning and the other in the evening. [40]With one of them offer 3 quarts of finely ground flour. Mix it with 2½ pints of oil, pressed from olives. Also give 2½ pints of wine, as an offering.

[41]Offer the other lamb in the evening for a fragrant offering to the Lord. It will be an offering made to the Lord by fire. Also offer the flour and the wine as in the morning.

[42]"This shall be a daily offering that will be for all time. It must be given at the door of the Tabernacle before the Lord. It is there that I will meet with you and speak with you. [43]I will meet with the people of Israel there. And the Tabernacle shall be made holy by my glory. [44]Yes, I will make the Tabernacle and the altar holy. I will set apart Aaron and his sons. They are my ministers, the priests. [45]And I will live among the people of Israel and be their God. [46]They shall know that I am the Lord their God. I brought them out of Egypt so that I could live among them. I am the Lord their God.

Preparing for Worship

30 "Then make a small altar for burning incense. It shall be made from acacia wood. [2]It is to be 18 inches square and three feet high. Make it with horns

carved from the wood of the altar. They are not to be merely separate parts that are attached. ³Cover the top, sides, and horns of the altar with pure gold. Run a gold molding around the entire altar. ⁴Beneath the molding, on each of two sides, make two gold rings. They will hold the carrying poles. ⁵The poles are to be made of acacia wood overlaid with gold. ⁶Place the altar just outside the veil. It must stand near the place of mercy that is above the Ark that holds the Ten Commandments. I will meet with you there.

⁷"Every morning when Aaron trims the lamps, he shall burn sweet spices on the altar. ⁸Each evening when he lights the lamps, he shall burn the incense before the Lord. This shall go on from generation to generation. ⁹Offer only the incense, burnt offerings, meal offerings, or wine offerings that I tell you.

¹⁰"Once a year Aaron must sanctify the altar. He must place upon its horns the blood of the sin offering for atonement. This shall be a regular, yearly event from generation to generation. For this is the Lord's supremely holy altar."

¹¹⁻¹²And the Lord said to Moses, "Each time you count the people of Israel, tell the men who are counted to give a ransom to the Lord for their souls. This will make sure that there will be no plague among the people when you count them. ¹³His payment shall be half a dollar. ¹⁴All who have reached their twentieth birthday shall give this offering. ¹⁵The rich shall not give more. The poor shall not give less. For it is an offering to the Lord to make atonement for yourselves. ¹⁶Use this money for the care of the Tabernacle. It is to bring you, the people of Israel, to the Lord's attention. It will make atonement for you."

¹⁷⁻¹⁸And the Lord said to Moses, "Make a bronze basin with a bronze pedestal. Put it between the Tabernacle and the altar. Fill it with water. ¹⁹Aaron and his sons shall wash their hands and feet there. ²⁰They must do this when they go into the Tabernacle to appear before the Lord. They must also wash before they go near the altar to burn offerings to the Lord. If they do not, they will die. ²¹These are teachings for Aaron and his sons from generation to generation."

²²⁻²³Then the Lord told Moses to collect the choicest of spices. He needed 18 pounds of pure myrrh, half as much of cinnamon and of sweet cane. ²⁴He also needed the same amount of cassia as of myrrh and 1½ gallons of olive oil. ²⁵The Lord told skilled perfume makers to make all this into a holy anointing oil.

²⁶⁻²⁷"Use this," he said, "to anoint the Tabernacle, the Ark, the table and all its instruments. Put it on the lampstand and all its utensils. Anoint the incense altar, ²⁸the burnt offering altar with all its instruments, and the washbasin and its pedestal. ²⁹Sanctify them, to make them holy. Whatever touches them shall become holy. ³⁰Use it to anoint Aaron and his sons. It will make them holy so that they can serve me as priests. ³¹And say to the people of Israel, 'This shall always be my holy anointing oil. ³²It must never be poured upon an ordinary person. You shall never make any of it yourselves, for it is holy. And it shall be treated by you as holy. ³³Anyone who makes incense like it shall be expelled from Israel. Those who put any of it on someone who is not a priest shall also be expelled.'"

³⁴This is what the Lord told Moses about the incense. He said, "Use sweet spices—stacte, onycha, galbanum, and pure frankincense. Weigh out the same amounts of each. ³⁵Use the usual techniques of the incensemaker. And season it with salt. It shall be a pure and holy incense. ³⁶Beat some of it very fine. Put some of it in front of the Ark where I meet with you in the Tabernacle. This incense is most holy. ³⁷Never make it for yourselves. For it is reserved for the Lord and you must treat it as holy. ³⁸Anyone making it for himself shall be expelled."

Workmen Given Special Skill

31 The Lord also said to Moses, "See, I have chosen Bezalel. (He was the son of Uri, and grandson of Hur, of the tribe of Judah.) ³I have filled him with the Spirit of God. I have given him great wisdom, ability, and skill in building the Tabernacle and all it contains. ⁴He is highly capable as an artistic designer of objects made of gold, silver, and bronze. ⁵He is skilled, too, as a jeweler and in carving wood.

⁶"And I have chosen Oholiab to be his helper. (He is the son of Ahisamach of the tribe of Dan.) Moreover, I have given special skill to all who are known as experts. They will be able to make all the things I have told you to make. ⁷They will build the Tabernacle, the Ark with the place of mercy upon it, and all the furniture of the Tabernacle. ⁸They will make the table and its instruments. They will also make the pure gold lampstand with its instruments. They will make the altar of incense. ⁹They will make the burnt offering altar with its instruments and the laver and its pedestal. ¹⁰They will sew the beautiful, holy clothes for Aaron the priest. They will make the clothes for his sons, so that they can serve as priests. ¹¹They will mix the anointing oil and the sweet-spice incense for the Holy Place. They are to follow exactly the directions I gave you."

Resting on the Sabbath

¹²⁻¹³The Lord then gave these further teachings to Moses. He said, "Tell the people of Israel to rest on my Sabbath day. For the Sabbath is a reminder of the covenant between me and you forever. It helps you to remember that I am the Lord who makes you holy. ¹⁴⁻¹⁵Yes, rest on the Sabbath, for it is holy. Anyone who does not obey this command must die. Anyone who does any work on that day shall be put to death. ¹⁶⁻¹⁷Work six days only. For the seventh day is a special day to remind you of my covenant. It is a weekly reminder forever of my promises to the people of Israel. For in six days the Lord made heaven and earth. And he rested on the seventh day, and was refreshed."

¹⁸Then God finished speaking with Moses on Mount Sinai. And he gave him two tablets of stone. On them, the Ten Commandments were written with the finger of God.

The Golden Calf

Why would someone pretend that a golden calf is God? Who would be that dumb? What about these people?

32 When Moses didn't come back down the mountain right away, the people went to Aaron. "Look," they said, "make us a god to lead us. This man Moses who brought us here from Egypt has disappeared. Something must have happened to him."

²⁻³"Give me your gold earrings," Aaron replied.

So they all did. ⁴Aaron melted the gold. Then he molded and tooled it into the form of a calf. The people exclaimed, "O Israel, this is the god that brought you out of Egypt!"

⁵Aaron saw how happy the people were about it. So he built an altar before the calf. Then he announced, "Tomorrow there will be a feast to the Lord!"

⁶So they were up early the next morning. They started to give burnt offerings and peace offerings to the calf-idol. After

that they sat down to feast and drink at a wild party. This was followed by much immorality.

[7]Then the Lord told Moses, "Quick! Go on down the mountain. The people that you brought from Egypt have defiled themselves. [8]They have quickly abandoned all my laws. They have made themselves a calf. They have worshiped it, and given gifts to it. They are saying, 'This is your god, O Israel! It is he who brought you out of Egypt.'"

[9]Then the Lord said, "I have seen how stubborn and rebellious these people are. [10]Now let me alone. My anger shall blaze out against them and destroy them all. And I will make you, Moses, into a great nation instead of them."

[11]But Moses begged God not to do it. "Lord," he pleaded, "why is your anger so hot? How can you be so angry at your own people? They are the ones whom you brought from the land of Egypt. You saved them with such great power and mighty miracles. [12]Do you want the Egyptians to say, 'God tricked them into coming to the mountains. He did this so that he could slay them. He wanted to destroy them from off the face of the earth'? Turn back from your fierce anger. Don't do this terrible thing against your people! [13]Remember your promise to your servants—to Abraham, Isaac, and Jacob. For you promised, 'I will increase your descendants as the stars of heaven. I will give them all of this land I have promised to your descendants. They shall inherit it forever.'"

[14]So the Lord listened to Moses and spared the people.

[15]Then Moses went down the mountain. He held in his hands the Ten Commandments. These were two stone tablets written on both sides. [16]God himself had written the commands on the tablets.

[17]Joshua heard the noise below them of all the people shouting. He said to Moses, "It sounds as if they are getting ready for war!"

[18]But Moses replied, "No, it's not a cry of victory or defeat. It is the sound of singing."

[19]When they came near the camp, Moses saw the calf and the dancing. In terrible anger he threw the tablets to the ground. And they lay broken at the foot of the mountain. [20]He took the calf and melted it in the fire. When the metal cooled, he ground it into powder. Then he spread it upon the water and made the people drink it.

[21]Then he turned to Aaron. He demanded, "What in the world did the people do to you? Why did you bring such a terrible sin upon them?"

[22]"Don't get so upset," Aaron replied. "You know these people and how wicked they are. [23]They said to me, 'Make us a god to lead us. For something has happened to Moses who led us out of Egypt.' [24]So I told them, 'Bring me your gold earrings' and they brought them to me. I threw them into the fire, and this calf came out!"

[25]Moses saw that the people had sinned greatly, and at Aaron's encouragement. He knew their enemies would laugh at them. [26]He went and stood at the camp entrance. And he shouted, "All of you who are on the Lord's side, come over here and join me." And all the Levites came.

[27]He told them, "The Lord the God of Israel says, 'Get your swords. Go back and forth from one end of the camp to the other. Kill even your brothers, friends, and neighbors.'" [28]So they did. And about 3000 men died that day.

[29]Then Moses told the Levites, "Today you have ordained yourselves for the service of the Lord. For you obeyed him even though it meant killing your own sons and brothers. Now he will give you a great blessing."

[30]The next day Moses said to the people, "You have sinned a great sin. But I will return to the Lord on the mountain. Perhaps I will be able to obtain his forgiveness for you."

[31]So Moses went back to the Lord. He said, "Oh, these people have sinned a great sin. They have made gods of gold. [32]Yet now please forgive their sin. And if not, then blot *me* out of the book you have written."

[33]And the Lord replied to Moses, "Whoever has sinned against me will be blotted out of my book. [34]And now go. Lead the people to the place I told you

about. I assure you that my Angel shall travel on ahead of you. However, when I come to visit these people, I will punish them for their sins."

35And the Lord sent a great plague upon the people because they had worshiped Aaron's calf.

- *Remember:* Who made the golden calf? (32:4) What did he melt to make the calf? (32:2-4) What did these people say this calf had done for them? (32:8) Why do you think God chose Moses instead of Aaron to lead his people? What would you like to say to Aaron about making this golden calf? What would you like to say to the people about worshiping this golden calf?

- *Discover:* Don't let people tempt you to do something God says is wrong. When God punishes you for sinning, don't blame others. Blame yourself.

- *Apply:* "Come on, let's do it," a friend says. "Nobody will know!" What will you say? Who will know? Who will get hurt?

- *What's next?* Have you ever seen a person's face glow? In Exodus 34 you will read of a man who had to put on a veil. His face was so bright no one could look at it. ■

The People Are Sorry

33 The Lord said to Moses, "Lead these people you brought from Egypt. Take them to the land I promised Abraham, Isaac, and Jacob. For I said, 'I will give this land to your descendants.' 2I will send an Angel before you. He will drive out the Canaanites, Amorites, Hittites, Perizzites, Hivites, and Jebusites. 3It is a land 'flowing with milk and honey.' But I will not travel among you. For you are a stubborn, unruly people. And I would be tempted to destroy you along the way."

4When the people heard these stern words, they went into mourning. They

took off all of their jewelry and ornaments.

⁵For the Lord had told Moses to tell them, "You are an unruly, stubborn people. If I were there among you for even a moment, I would destroy you. Remove your jewelry and ornaments until I decide what to do with you." ⁶So, after that, they wore no jewelry.

The Sacred Tent of Meeting

⁷Moses always set up the holy tent (the "Tent for Meeting with God," he called it) far outside the camp. All who wanted to talk with the Lord went out there.

⁸Each time the people saw Moses go into the Tabernacle, they stood. They would rise and stand in their tent doors. ⁹As he entered, the pillar of cloud would come down. It hovered at the door while the Lord spoke with Moses. ¹⁰Then all the people worshiped from their tent doors. They bowed low to the pillar of cloud. ¹¹Inside the tent the Lord spoke to Moses face to face. He spoke with Moses as a man speaks to his friend. Later Moses would go back to the camp. But the young man who helped him, Joshua (son of Nun), stayed behind in the Tabernacle.

Moses Asks to See God

¹²Moses talked there with the Lord. He said to him, "You have been telling me, 'Take these people to the Promised Land.' But you haven't told me whom you will send with me. You say you are my friend, and that I have found favor before you. ¹³Please, if this is really so, guide me clearly along the way you want me to travel. Do this so that I will understand you and do what pleases you. For don't forget that this nation is your people."

¹⁴And the Lord replied, "I myself will go with you and give you success."

¹⁵For Moses had said, "If you aren't going with us, don't let us move a step from this place. ¹⁶If you don't go with us, who will ever know that I and my people have found favor with you? Who will know that we are different from any other people upon the face of the earth?"

¹⁷And the Lord had replied to Moses, "Yes, I will do what you have asked. For you have certainly found favor with me. And you are my friend."

¹⁸Then Moses asked to see God's glory.

¹⁹The Lord replied, "I will make my goodness pass before you. I will announce to you the meaning of my name the Lord. I show kindness and mercy to anyone I want to. ²⁰But you may not see the glory of my face. For man may not see me and live. ²¹However, stand here on this rock beside me. ²²And when my glory goes by, I will put you in the cleft of the rock. I will cover you with my hand until I have passed. ²³Then I will remove my hand. And you shall see my back but not my face."

Moses Talks with God

We can't look at the sun. It shines too brightly. We can't even look at a very bright light. That shines too much also. The leaders of Israel could not look at Moses' face. He had to put on a veil. You'll learn why as you read on.

34 The Lord told Moses, "Prepare two stone tablets like the first ones. I will write upon them the same commands that were on the tablets you broke. ²Be ready in the morning to come up into Mount Sinai. Present yourself to me on the top of the mountain. ³No one shall come with you. No one must be anywhere on the mountain. Do not let the flocks or herds feed close to the mountain."

⁴So Moses took two tablets of stone

like the first ones. He was up early and climbed Mount Sinai, as the Lord had told him to. He carried the two stone tablets in his hands.

5-6Then the Lord came down in the form of a pillar of cloud and stood there with him. He passed in front of him and announced the meaning of his name. "I am the Lord, the merciful and gracious God," he said. "I am slow to anger and rich in steadfast love and truth. 7I, the Lord, show this steadfast love to many thousands by forgiving their sins. Or else I refuse to clear the guilty. I require that a father's sins be punished in the sons and grandsons and even later generations."

8Moses fell down before the Lord and worshiped. 9And he said, "If it is true that I have found favor in your sight, O Lord, then please go with us to the Promised Land. Yes, it is an unruly, stubborn people. But pardon our iniquity and our sins. Accept us as your own."

10The Lord replied, "All right. This is the contract I am going to make with you. I will do miracles such as have never been done before anywhere in all the earth. All the people of Israel shall see the power of the Lord—the terrible power I will display through you. 11Your part of the agreement is to obey all of my commands. Then I will drive out from before you the Amorites, Canaanites, Hittites, Perizzites, Hivites, and Jebusites.

12"Be very, very careful never to compromise with the people there in the land where you are going. If you do, you will soon be following their evil ways. 13Instead, you must break down their heathen altars. Smash the statues they worship. Cut down their shameful idols. 14For you must worship no other gods, but only the Lord. For he is a God who demands total loyalty and devotion.

15"No, do not make a peace treaty of any kind with the people living in the land. They are not faithful to me because they make sacrifices to other gods. If you become friendly with them and one of them invites you to go with him and worship his idol, you are likely to do it. 16And you would accept their daughters, who worship other gods, as wives for your sons. Then your sons would sin against me by worshiping their wives' gods. 17You must have nothing to do with idols.

18"Be sure to celebrate the Feast of Unleavened Bread for seven days, just as I told you. Celebrate it at the dates chosen each year in March. That was the month you left Egypt.

19"Every firstborn male is mine—cattle, sheep, and goats. 20The firstborn colt of a donkey may be bought back by giving a lamb in its place. If you decide not to buy it back, then its neck must be broken. But your sons must all be bought back. And no one shall appear before me without a gift.

21"Even during plowing and harvest times, work only six days. Rest on the seventh.

22"Do not forget to celebrate these three yearly religious festivals: the Festival of Weeks, the Festival of the First Wheat, and the Harvest Festival. 23On each of these three occasions all the men and boys of Israel shall come before the Lord. 24No one will attack and conquer your land when you go up to appear before the Lord your God those three times each year. For I will drive out the nations from before you and enlarge your borders.

25"You must not use leavened bread with your sacrifices to me. None of the meat of the Passover lamb may be kept over until the following morning. 26And you must bring the best of the first of each year's crop to the Tabernacle of the Lord your God. You must not cook a young goat in its mother's milk.

27And the Lord said to Moses, "Write down these laws that I have given you. For they tell the terms of my covenant with you and with Israel."

28Moses was up on the mountain with the Lord for 40 days and 40 nights. And in all that time he neither ate nor drank. At that time God wrote out the Covenant—the Ten Commandments—on the stone tablets.

29Moses didn't know as he came back down the mountain with the tablets that his face glowed from being with

God. ³⁰Because his face was shining, Aaron and the people of Israel were afraid to come near him.

³¹But Moses called them over to him. And Aaron and the leaders of Israel came and talked with him. ³²After that, all the people came to him. He gave them the commands the Lord had given him upon the mountain. ³³When Moses had finished speaking with them, he put a veil over his face. ³⁴But whenever he went into the Tabernacle to speak with the Lord, he removed the veil until he came out again. Then he would pass on to the people whatever God had told him. ³⁵And the people would see his face aglow. After that he would put the veil on again until he went back to speak with God.

● *Remember:* Why did Moses climb back up Mount Sinai? (34:1-2) The Lord came to Moses in a certain form. What was it? (34:5-6) How long was Moses in the mountain? (34:28) What did he not do during those days? (34:28) What caused Moses' face to shine? (34:29) What did Moses wear so people could look at his face? (34:33) When we spend time praying and reading God's Word, do you think that changes us? How?

● *Discover:* Spending time with God makes us more like him.

● *Apply:* Spend more time reading God's Word. Spend more time talking with God. You will become more like God.

● *What's next?* Stop giving! You're giving too much! Nobody ever says that, do they? But a man once had to say it. People gave more than they needed for building God's house. (Exodus 35:1–36:7) ◼

Gifts for the Tabernacle

Moses asked for gifts to build the Tabernacle. That's like someone asking for money to build a new church. People did not have money then. So they brought gold and silver. They brought beautiful cloth and precious stones. They brought many other gifts, too. But before long they brought more than Moses needed. "Stop giving!" Moses said. Here's the way this happened.

35 Now Moses called a meeting of all the people. He told them, "These are the laws of the Lord you must obey.

²"Work six days only. The seventh day is a day of rest, a holy day. It is to be used to worship the Lord. Anyone working on that day must die. ³Don't even light the fires in your homes that day."

⁴Then Moses said to all the people, "This is what the Lord has said. ⁵⁻⁹All of you who wish to, all those with generous hearts, may bring these gifts to the Lord:

Gold, silver, and bronze;
Blue, purple, and red cloth, made of fine-twisted linen or of goats' hair;

Tanned rams' skins and specially treated goatskins;
Acacia wood;
Olive oil for the lamps;
Spices for the anointing oil and for the incense;
Onyx stones and stones to be used for the ephod and chestpiece.

¹⁰⁻¹⁹"Come, all of you who are skilled craftsmen having special talents. Build what God has commanded us:

The Tabernacle tent, and its coverings, clasps, frames, bars, pillars, and bases;
The Ark and its poles;
The place of mercy;

The curtain to enclose the Holy
  Place;
The table, its carrying poles, and all
  of its utensils;
The Bread of the Presence;
Lamp holders, with lamps and oil;
The incense altar and its carrying
  poles;
The anointing oil and sweet incense;
The curtain for the door of the Tab-
  ernacle;
The altar for the burnt offerings;
The bronze grating of the altar, and
  its carrying poles and utensils;
The basin with its pedestal;
The drapes for the walls of the court;
The pillars and their bases;
Drapes for the entrance to the court;
The posts of the Tabernacle court,
  and their cords;
The beautiful clothing for the
  priests, to be used when serving
  in the Holy Place;
The holy clothes for Aaron the
  priest, and for his sons."

20So all the people went to their tents
to prepare their gifts. 21Those whose
hearts were stirred by God's Spirit came
with their offerings. They brought materials for the Tabernacle, its equipment,
and for the holy clothing. 22Both men
and women came, all who had willing
hearts. They brought to the Lord their
offerings of gold jewelry—earrings, rings
from their fingers, necklaces. They
brought gold objects of every kind.
23Others brought blue, purple, and red
cloth made from the fine-twined linen
or goats' hair. Some brought rams' skins
dyed red, and specially treated goatskins. 24Others brought silver and
bronze as their offering to the Lord. And
some brought the acacia wood needed
in the construction.

25The women skilled in sewing and
spinning prepared blue, purple, and red
thread and cloth. They also made fine-
twisted linen. Then they brought them
in. 26Some other women gladly used
their special skill to spin the goats' hair
into cloth. 27The leaders brought onyx
stones to be used for the ephod and the
chestpiece. 28They brought spices, and
oil. These were used for the light, and for

making the anointing oil and the sweet
incense. 29So the people of Israel brought
their freewill offerings to him. Every
man and woman who wanted to help in
the work given to them by the Lord's
command brought their offerings.

30-31And Moses told them, "The Lord
has chosen Bezalel as foreman of the
project. (He was the son of Uri and
grandson of Hur of the tribe of Judah.)
32He will be able to create beautiful
things from gold, silver, and bronze.
33He can cut and set stones like a jeweler
and do beautiful carving. In fact, he has
every needed skill. 34And God has made
him and Oholiab gifted teachers of their
skills to others. (Oholiab is the son of
Ahisamach, of the tribe of Dan.) 35God
has filled them both with special skills.
They are skilled as jewelers and carpenters. They are expert at sewing and
weaving in blue, purple, and red on
linen backgrounds. They excel in all the
crafts we will be needing in the work.

36 "God has given special abilities to
other craftsmen too. They are to
help Bezalel and Oholiab. They will help
build and furnish the Tabernacle." So
Moses told Bezalel and Oholiab and all
others who felt called to the work to
begin. 3Moses gave them the gifts given
by the people. More gifts were collected
each morning.

4-7But at last the workmen all left their
task to meet with Moses. They told him,
"We have more than enough materials
on hand now to complete the job!" So
Moses sent a message around the camp.
He told the people that no more gifts
were needed. Then at last the people
were stopped from bringing more!

• *Remember:* Did Moses tell the people
  they had to give? What did he tell them?
  (35:5) What kind of gifts did Moses
  need? (35:5-9) What were they going to
  make with these gifts? (35:10-19) Some
  people gave themselves and their work
  to the Lord. What would they do?
  (35:30–36:2) Why is it so good to see
  people cheerfully give to the Lord?

• *Discover:* God loves a cheerful giver.
  That's what 2 Corinthians 9:7 tells us.

• *Apply:* Are you a cheerful giver? Do

you like to give to God? Never give with a grumble. Give with a smile. What can you do to be more cheerful about giving?

• *What's next?* Have you ever seen a tent worth a million dollars? You'll see the most beautiful tent ever made as you read Exodus 40. ◼

Preparing to Build the Tabernacle

8-9The skilled weavers first made 10 sheets from fine linen. Then they sewed into them blue, purple, and red Guardian Angels. Each sheet was 42 feet long and 6 feet wide. 10Five of these sheets were attached end to end. Then five others were attached the same way. They formed two long roofsheets. 11-12Fifty blue ribbons were looped along the edges of these two long sheets. Each loop was opposite its mate on the other long sheet. 13Then 50 clasps of gold were made to connect the loops. These tied the two long sheets together. They formed the ceiling of the Tabernacle.

14-15Above the ceiling was a second layer. It was formed by 11 drapes made of goats' hair. They were 45 feet long and 6 feet wide. 16Bezalel joined five of these drapes together to make one long piece. Then he put together six others to make another long piece. 17Then he made 50 loops along the end of each. 18He also made 50 small bronze clasps to join the loops. This attached the drapes firmly to each other.

19The top layer of the roof was made of rams' skins, dyed red, and tanned goatskins.

20For the sides of the Tabernacle he used frames of acacia wood standing on end. 21The height of each frame was 15 feet and the width 2¼ feet. 22Each frame had two clasps joining it to the next. 23There were 20 frames on the south side. 24The bottoms fit into 40 silver bases. Each frame was attached to its base by two clasps. 25-26There were also 20 frames on the north side of the Tabernacle. These also had 40 silver bases. There were two for each frame. 27The west side of the Tabernacle was at its rear. It was made from six frames, 28plus another at each corner. 29These frames, in-

cluding those at the corners, were linked to each other at both top and bottom by rings. 30So, on the west side, there were a total of eight frames. There were 16 silver bases beneath them, two for each frame.

31-32Then he made five sets of bars from acacia wood. He tied the frames together along the sides. There were five for each side of the Tabernacle. 33The middle bar of the five was halfway up the frames, along each side. It ran from one end to the other. 34The frames and bars were all covered with gold. The rings were pure gold.

35The blue, purple, and red inner curtain was made from woven linen. Guardian Angels were skillfully sewed into it. 36The curtain was then attached to four gold hooks. The hooks were then set into four posts of acacia wood. The posts were covered with gold and set into four silver bases.

37Then he made a drapery for the door to the Tabernacle. It was woven from finespun linen. He embroidered it with blue, purple, and red. 38This drapery was connected by five hooks to five posts. The posts and their capitals and rods were overlaid with gold. Their five bases were molded from bronze.

Making the Ark

37Next Bezalel made the Ark. This was made of acacia wood. It was 3¾ feet long, 2¼ feet wide, and 2¼ feet high. 2It was plated with pure gold inside and out. A molding of gold was set all the way around its sides. 3There were four gold rings fastened into its four feet, two rings at each end. 4Then he made poles from acacia wood. He covered them with gold. 5He put the poles into the rings at the sides of the Ark. These were used to carry it.

6Then, from pure gold, he made a lid called "the place of mercy." It was 3¾ feet long and 2¼ feet wide. 7He made two statues of Guardian Angels out of beaten gold. He placed them at the two ends of the gold lid. 8They were molded so that they were actually a part of the gold lid. It was all one piece. 9The Guardian Angels faced each other. Their outstretched wings spread over the place of mercy, looking down upon it.

[10]Then he made a table, using acacia wood. It was 3 feet long, 1½ feet wide, and 2¼ feet high. [11]It was covered with pure gold, with a gold molding all around the edge. [12]A rim 4 inches high was set around the edges of the table. It had a gold molding along the rim. [13]Then he cast four rings of gold. He placed them into the four table legs, [14]close to the molding. They were designed to hold the carrying poles in place. [15]He made the carrying poles of acacia wood covered with gold. [16]Next, using pure gold, he made the bowls, flagons, dishes, and spoons. These were to be placed upon the table.

Making the Lampstand

[17]Then he made the lampstand, again using pure, beaten gold. Its base, shaft, lamp-holders, and decorations of almond flowers were all of one piece. [18]The lampstand had six branches, three from each side. [19]Each of the branches was decorated with identical carvings of blossoms. [20-21]The main stem of the lampstand looked much like the branches. It also had almond blossoms. A flower was on the stem beneath each pair of branches. There was also a flower below the bottom pair and above the top pair. There were four in all. [22]The decorations and branches were all one piece of pure, beaten gold. [23-24]Then he made the seven lamps at the ends of the branches, the snuffers, and the ashtrays. They were all of pure gold. The entire lampstand weighed 107 pounds, all pure gold.

Making the Incense Altar

[25]The incense altar was made of acacia wood. It was 18 inches square and 3 feet high. Its corner-horns were made as part of the altar so that it was all one piece. [26]He covered it all with pure gold. A gold molding ran around the edge. [27]Two gold rings were placed on each side, beneath this molding. These were to hold the carrying poles. [28]The carrying poles were of gold-plated acacia wood.

[29]Then, from sweet spices, he made the holy oil for anointing the priests. He also made the pure incense. He used the techniques of the most skilled perfumers.

Making the Burnt Offering Altar

38 The burnt-offering altar was also made of acacia wood. It was 7½ feet square at the top, and 4½ feet high. [2]There were four horns at the four corners, all of one piece with the rest. This altar was covered with bronze. [3]Then he made bronze utensils: the pots, shovels, basins, meat hooks, and fire pans. They were to be used with the altar. [4]Next he made a bronze grating. It rested on a ledge about halfway up [in the firebox]. [5]Four rings were cast for each side of the grating, to insert the carrying poles. [6]The carrying poles themselves were made of acacia wood, covered with bronze. [7]The carrying poles were inserted into the rings at the side of the altar. The altar was hollow, with plank siding.

[8]The bronze washbasin and its bronze pedestal were cast from solid bronze mirrors. These were donated by the women who assembled at the door to the Tabernacle.

Building the Courtyard

[9]Then he built the courtyard. The south wall was 150 feet long. It was made of drapes woven from fine-twined linen thread. [10]There were 20 posts to hold drapes. The posts had bases of bronze, and silver hooks and rods. [11]The north wall was also 150 feet long. It had 20 bronze posts and bases, and silver hooks and rods. [12]The west side was 75 feet wide. The walls were made from drapes. These were supported by 10 posts and bases, and with silver hooks and rods. [13]The east side was also 75 feet wide.

[14-15]The drapes at either side of the entrance were 22½ feet wide. Each had three posts and three bases. [16]All the drapes making up the walls of the court were woven of fine-twisted linen. [17]Each post had a bronze base. All the hooks and rods were silver. The tops of the posts were overlaid with silver. And the

rods to hold up the drapes were solid silver.

18The drapery covering the entrance to the court was made of fine-twisted linen. It was beautifully embroidered with blue, purple, and red thread. It was 30 feet long and 7½ feet wide. Thus, it was the same as the drapes used on the walls of the court. 19It was supported by four posts. The posts had four bronze bases and silver hooks and rods. The tops of the posts were also silver. 20All the nails used in building the Tabernacle and court were bronze.

21These are the various steps in building the Tabernacle to house the Ark. This was done so the Levites could carry on their ministry. All was done in the order given by Moses. It was supervised by Ithamar, son of Aaron the priest. 22Bezalel was the master craftsman. (He was the son of Uri and grandson of Hur, of the tribe of Judah.) 23He was helped by Oholiab. (Oholiab was the son of Ahisamach of the tribe of Dan.) He too was a skilled craftsman. He was an expert at engraving and weaving. He could sew blue, purple, and red threads into fine linen cloth.

The Materials Used

24The people brought gifts of 3,140 pounds of gold. All of it was used throughout the Tabernacle.

25-26The amount of silver used was 9,575 pounds. This came from the fifty-cent head tax. It was collected from all those who registered in the census who were 20 years old or older. The total came to 603,550 men. 27The bases for the frames of the sanctuary walls and for the posts supporting the veil required 9,500 pounds of silver. Each socket required 95 pounds. 28The silver left over was used for the posts and to overlay their tops. It was also used for the rods and hooks.

29-31The people brought 7,540 pounds of bronze. It was used for casting the bases for the posts at the door to the Tabernacle. It was also used for the bronze altar, the bronze grating, the altar utensils. The bases for the posts supporting the drapes around the court were also bronze. So were all the nails used in the building of the Tabernacle and the court.

Making the Priest's Clothing

39 Then the people made beautiful clothing of blue, purple, and red cloth for the priests. These were to be worn while serving in the Holy Place. This same cloth was used for Aaron's holy clothing. All this was done just the way the Lord told Moses. 2The ephod was made from this cloth too. It was woven from fine-twisted linen thread. 3Bezalel beat gold into thin plates and cut it into wire threads. This he worked into the blue, purple, and red linen. It was a skillful and beautiful piece of workmanship when finished.

4-5The ephod was held together by shoulder straps at the top. It was tied down by an elaborate one-piece woven sash. The sash was made of the same gold, blue, purple, and red cloth cut from fine-twisted linen thread. It was all done just as God had told Moses. 6-7The two onyx stones were attached to the two shoulder straps of the ephod. They were set in gold. The stones were engraved with the names of the tribes of Israel. It was done just as initials are engraved upon a ring. These stones were reminders to the Lord about the people of Israel. All this was done just the way the Lord told Moses.

8The chestpiece was a beautiful piece of work, just like the ephod. It was made from the finest gold, blue, purple, and red linen. 9It was a piece nine inches square, doubled over to form a pouch. 10There were four rows of stones across it. In the first row were a sardius, a topaz, and a carbuncle. 11In the second row were an emerald, a sapphire, and a diamond. 12In the third row were a jacinth, an agate, and an amethyst. 13In the fourth row, a beryl, an onyx, and a jasper. All of them were set in gold filigree. 14The stones were engraved like a seal. They were engraved with the names of the 12 tribes of Israel.

15-18To attach the chestpiece to the ephod, a gold ring was placed at the top of each shoulder strap of the ephod.

From these gold rings two strands of twined gold attached to gold clasps on the top corners of the chestpiece. [19]Two gold rings were also set at the lower edge of the chestpiece. These were on the under side, next to the ephod. [20]Two other gold rings were placed low on the shoulder straps of the ephod. These were close to where the ephod joined its beautifully woven sash. [21]The chestpiece was held securely above the beautifully woven sash of the ephod. This was done by tying the rings of the chestpiece to the rings of the ephod with a blue ribbon.

All this was commanded to Moses by the Lord.

[22]The main part of the ephod was woven, all of blue. [23]There was a hole at the center, just as in a coat of mail, for the head to go through. It was reinforced around the edge so that it would not tear. [24]Pomegranates were attached to the bottom edge of the robe. These were made of linen cloth, embroidered with blue, purple, and red. [25-26]Bells of pure gold were placed between the pomegranates along the bottom edge of the skirt. The bells and pomegranates alternated all around the edge. This robe was worn while Aaron was serving the Lord. It was made just as the Lord had told Moses.

[27]Robes were now made for Aaron and his sons from fine-twined linen thread. [28-29]The chestpiece, the beautiful turbans, the caps, and the underclothes were all made of this linen. The linen belt was beautifully embroidered with blue, purple, and red threads. It was all done just as the Lord had told Moses. [30]Finally, they made the holy plate of pure gold to wear on the front of the turban. It was engraved with the words, "Holy to the Lord." [31]It was tied to the turban with a blue cord, just as the Lord had instructed.

[32]And so at last the Tabernacle was finished. It was done according to all of the Lord's instructions to Moses.

Moses Looks Over the Work

[33-40]Then they brought the entire Tabernacle to Moses:

Furniture; clasps; frames; bars;
Posts; bases; layers of covering for the roof and sides—the rams' skins dyed red, the specially tanned goatskins, and the entrance drape; the Ark with the Ten Commandments in it;
The carrying poles;
The place of mercy;
The table and all its utensils;
The Bread of the Presence;
The pure gold lampstand with its lamps, utensils, and oil;
The gold altar;
The anointing oil;
The sweet incense;
The curtain-door of the Tabernacle;
The bronze altar;
The bronze grating;
The poles and the utensils;
The washbasin and its base;
The drapes for the walls of the court and the posts holding them up;
The bases and the drapes at the gate of the court;
The cords and nails;
All the utensils used there in the work of the Tabernacle.

[41]They also brought for him the beautifully made clothing to be worn while serving in the Holy Place. They brought the holy clothes for Aaron the priest. They also brought the clothes for his sons. They were to be worn when on duty.

[42]So the people of Israel followed all the Lord's instructions to Moses. [43]And Moses inspected all their work. He blessed them because it was all as the Lord had showed him.

The Tabernacle Is Built

You don't use lavers and tables of showbread in your church. You don't use red rams' skins either. But God told his people to use these things in the Tabernacle. He told the people exactly how to build his beautiful tent. Here's what it was like.

40 The Lord now said to Moses, ²"Put together the Tabernacle on the first day of the first month. ³In it, place the Ark that holds the Ten Commandments. And put up the veil to enclose the Ark within the Holy of Holies. ⁴Then bring in the table and place the utensils on it. Bring in the lampstand and light the lamps.

⁵"Place the gold altar for the incense in front of the Ark. Set up the drapes at the door of the Tabernacle. ⁶And place the altar for burnt offerings in front of the entrance. ⁷Set the washbasin between the Tabernacle-tent and the altar. Fill it with water. ⁸Then make the courtyard around the outside of the tent. Hang the curtain-door at the entrance to the courtyard.

⁹"Take the anointing oil. Sprinkle it here and there upon the Tabernacle and everything in it. Sprinkle it on all of the Tabernacle's utensils and parts. Put it on all the furniture. And it shall all become holy. ¹⁰Sprinkle the anointing oil upon the altar of burnt offering and its utensils, making it holy. For the altar shall then become most holy. ¹¹Then anoint the washbasin and its pedestal, making it holy.

¹²"Now bring Aaron and his sons to the door of the Tabernacle. Wash them with water. ¹³Put the holy clothing on Aaron. Anoint him to set him apart to serve me as a priest. ¹⁴Then bring his sons and put their robes upon them. ¹⁵Anoint them as you did their father. Then they may serve me as priests. Their anointing shall be for all time. It will be done from generation to generation. All their children and children's children shall forever be my priests."

¹⁶So Moses did all as the Lord told him to. ¹⁷On the first day of the first month, in the second year, the Tabernacle was put together. ¹⁸Moses set it up by setting its frames into their bases and attaching the bars. ¹⁹Then he spread the coverings over the framework. He put on the top layers, just as the Lord had told him.

²⁰Inside the Ark he placed the stones with the Ten Commandments written on them. He attached the carrying poles to the Ark. And he put the gold lid, the place of mercy, on it. ²¹Then he brought the Ark into the Tabernacle. And he set up the curtain to screen it. He did just what the Lord told him to.

²²Next he placed the table at the north side of the room outside the curtain. ²³He set the Bread of the Presence upon the table before the Lord. He did it all just as the Lord had ordered.

²⁴And he placed the lampstand next to the table, on the south side of the Tabernacle. ²⁵Then he lighted the lamps before the Lord. He followed all the instructions. ²⁶And he placed the gold altar in the Tabernacle next to the curtain. ²⁷He burned upon it the incense made from sweet spices. He did it just as the Lord had ordered.

²⁸He attached the curtain at the door of the Tabernacle. ²⁹He placed the outside altar for the burnt offerings near the entrance. And he offered upon it a burnt offering and a meal offering. He did it just as the Lord had told him.

³⁰Next he placed the washbasin between the tent and the altar. He filled it with water so that the priests could use it for washing. ³¹Moses and Aaron and Aaron's sons washed their hands and feet there. ³²Whenever they walked past the altar to enter the Tabernacle, they stopped and washed. It was done just as the Lord had told Moses.

³³Then he set up the enclosure surrounding the tent and the altar. He also set up the curtain-door at the entrance of the enclosure. So at last Moses finished the work.

³⁴Then the cloud covered the Tabernacle, and the glory of the Lord filled it. ³⁵Moses was not able to enter because the cloud was standing there. The glory of the Lord filled the Tabernacle. ³⁶Whenever the cloud lifted and moved, the people of Israel journeyed onward, following it. ³⁷But if the cloud stayed, they stayed until it moved. ³⁸The cloud rested upon the Tabernacle during the daytime. At night there was fire in the cloud. That way all the people of Israel could see it.

This continued throughout all their journeys.

- *Remember:* Who gave the plans for the Tabernacle? (39:42) Did the workmen follow the plans exactly? (39:43) How did the people know that God was there? (40:34) How did God show the people when they should move? (40:36-38) What would you do if you saw God's special cloud?

- *Discover:* God wants us to make special places where we can worship him.

- *Apply:* The Tabernacle was God's house. Your church is God's house. You go there to talk to God and learn about God. Don't stop going. God's house is a special place.

- *What's next?* How do you move a million-dollar tent? How do you move a tent where God stays? It's not easy. You'll learn how Moses and his people did it in Numbers 10:11-20. ∎

The Tabernacle: God's Tent-House

EXODUS 26–27; 40

Have you ever been to church in a tent? The very first house of God was a very special tent. It was called the Tabernacle. Because it was a tent, the Israelites could carry it with them through the wilderness. They set it up each time they camped. God had told Moses exactly how to make the Tabernacle. It was made of fine cloth, animal skins, silver, gold, and acacia wood. Inside the most holy room of the Tabernacle was the Ark of the Covenant. The Ark held the Ten Commandments that God had given to Moses. God also told Moses exactly how the people were to worship God at his Tabernacle. God wanted a tent-house for himself so that the Israelites would remember that he was always with them. Today we usually go to church in a building. But that doesn't mean that God is not always with us. If you believe in Jesus, God's Son, then he lives inside of you. You are his Tabernacle. You can know that God is with you wherever you go.

LEVITICUS

Moses' people did not learn about God the way you do. Your church building is God's house. God's house was a tent called the Tabernacle.

In Leviticus you will peek into this million-dollar tent. It's God's house for a million people. You don't have that many people in your church, do you? In this million-dollar tent you'll see things you have never seen before. You'll find a golden chest with golden cherubim on it. Their golden wings stretch out to each other. You'll see a golden table with special bread on it. You'll see golden lampstands. But you've never seen lamps like these! Moses' people could not go inside this million-dollar tent. But you can! In Leviticus you can walk into the most beautiful tent ever.

God gave many rules for Moses' people. These rules are in Leviticus. They told Moses' people how to live for God. Some rules seem strange to us today. When Jesus came, he gave us a new and better way to God. So we don't have to follow many of the rules in Leviticus today.

But many things God said in Leviticus will always be important. He said, "Be holy." That means, "Be as much like God as you can." He also said, "Keep away from bad things." That's important to remember.

Leviticus will help you know how Moses' people worshiped God. But it will help you worship God too!

How to Give a Burnt Offering

1 The Lord spoke to Moses from the Tabernacle. 2-3He told him to teach the people of Israel. He said, "When you sacrifice to the Lord, use animals from your herds and flocks.

"If your sacrifice is to be an ox given as a burnt offering, use only a bull. It must have nothing wrong with it. Bring the animal to the door of the Tabernacle. There the priests shall take your gift for the Lord. 4The person bringing it is to lay his hand upon its head. It then becomes his substitute. The death of the animal shall be accepted by God instead of the death of the man who brings it. It shall be the penalty for his sins. ⁵The man shall then kill the animal there before the Lord. Aaron's sons, the priests, shall present the blood before the Lord. They shall sprinkle it upon all sides of the altar at the door of the Tabernacle. ⁶⁻⁷Then the priests shall skin the animal and quarter it. They shall build a wood fire upon the altar. ⁸They shall put the sections of the animal and its head and fat upon the wood. ⁹The internal organs and the legs are to be washed. Then the priests shall burn them upon the altar. They will be a burnt offering with which the Lord is pleased.

¹⁰"If the animal used as a burnt offering is a sheep or a goat, it too must be a male. It must have nothing wrong with it. ¹¹The man who brings it shall kill it before the Lord. He shall do this on the north side of the altar. Aaron's sons, the priests, shall sprinkle its blood back and forth upon the altar. ¹²Then the man shall quarter it. And the priests shall lay the pieces, with the head and the fat, on top of the wood on the altar. ¹³But the internal organs and the legs shall first be washed with water. Then the priests shall burn it all upon the altar as an offering to the Lord. Burnt offerings give much pleasure to the Lord.

¹⁴"If anyone wishes to use a bird as his burnt offering, he may choose either turtledoves or young pigeons. ¹⁵⁻¹⁷A priest shall take the bird to the altar and wring off its head. The blood shall be drained out at the side of the altar. Then the priest shall remove the crop and the feathers. He shall throw them on the east side of the altar with the ashes. Then he shall grasp it by the wings. He shall tear it apart, but not all the way. The priest shall then burn it upon the altar. The Lord will have pleasure in this sacrifice.

How to Give a Grain Offering

2 "A person who wishes to sacrifice a grain offering to the Lord is to bring fine flour. He is to pour olive oil and incense upon it. ²Then he is to take a handful to one of the priests to burn. It will represent the entire amount. And the Lord will be fully pleased. ³The rest of the flour is to be given to Aaron and his sons as their food. But all of it is counted as a holy burnt offering to the Lord.

⁴"If bread baked in the oven is brought as an offering to the Lord, it must be made from finely ground flour. It must be baked with olive oil but without yeast. Wafers made without yeast and spread with olive oil may also be used as an offering. ⁵If the offering is something from the griddle, it shall be made of finely ground flour. It must be without yeast and mingled with olive oil. ⁶Break it into pieces and pour oil upon it. It is a form of grain offering. ⁷If your offering is cooked in a pan, it too shall be made of fine flour. It shall be mixed with olive oil.

⁸"However it is prepared—whether baked, fried, or grilled—you are to bring this grain offering to the priest. He shall take it to the altar to present it to the Lord.

⁹"The priests are to burn only a portion of the offering. But all of it will be fully pleasing to the Lord. ¹⁰The rest belongs to the priests for their own use. But it is all counted as a holy burnt offering to the Lord.

¹¹"Use no yeast with your offerings of flour, for no yeast or honey is allowed in burnt offerings to the Lord. ¹²You may offer yeast bread and honey as thanksgiving offerings at harvesttime, but they must not be given as burnt offerings.

¹³"Every offering must be seasoned with salt. The salt is a reminder of God's covenant.

¹⁴"If you are offering from the first of your harvest, remove the kernels from a fresh ear. Crush and roast them. Then offer them to the Lord. ¹⁵Put olive oil and incense on the offering. For it is a grain offering. ¹⁶Then the priests shall burn part of the bruised grain mixed with oil. With it they must burn all of the incense. It will be a memorial portion before the Lord.

How to Give a Peace Offering

3 "When anyone wants to give an offering of thanksgiving to the Lord, he may use either a bull or a cow. But if the

animal is to be offered to the Lord, it must have nothing wrong with it! ²The man who brings the animal shall lay his hand upon its head. He must then kill it at the door of the Tabernacle. Then Aaron's sons shall throw the blood against the sides of the altar. ³⁻⁵They shall burn before the Lord the fat that covers the inward parts. This includes the two kidneys and the loin-fat on them, and the gallbladder. And it will give the Lord much pleasure.

⁶"If a goat or sheep is used as a thank offering to the Lord, it must have no defect. But it may be either a male or a female. ⁷⁻⁸"If it is a lamb, the man who brings it shall lay his hand upon its head. He must kill it at the door of the Tabernacle. The priests shall throw the blood against the sides of the altar. ⁹⁻¹¹They shall offer all the fat upon the altar. This includes the tail removed close to the backbone and the fat covering the internal organs. The two kidneys with the loin-fat on them and the gallbladder must be burned. These will be given as a burnt offering to the Lord.

¹²"If anyone brings a goat as his offering to the Lord, ¹³he shall lay his hand upon its head. He then must kill it at the door of the Tabernacle. The priest shall throw its blood against the sides of the altar. ¹⁴He shall offer upon the altar the fat that covers the insides. It shall be a burnt offering to the Lord. ¹⁵⁻¹⁶This includes the two kidneys and the loin-fat on them, and the gallbladder. This burnt offering is very pleasing to the Lord. All the fat is the Lord's. ¹⁷This law shall continue from now on throughout your land. You shall eat neither fat nor blood."

How to Give a Sin Offering

4 Then the Lord gave more teachings to Moses.

²"Tell the people of Israel that these are commands for those who sin by accident. ³If a priest sins, even if he does not do it on purpose, he brings guilt upon the people. As a result, he must offer a young bull. It must have nothing wrong with it. It will be a sin offering to

the Lord. ⁴He shall bring it to the door of the Tabernacle. He shall lay his hand upon its head. Then he must kill it there before the Lord. ⁵Then the priest shall take the animal's blood into the Tabernacle. ⁶He shall dip his finger in the blood. And he shall sprinkle it seven times before the Lord. This shall be done in front of the veil that bars the way to the Holy of Holies. ⁷Then the priest shall put some of the blood upon the horns of the incense altar. This stands before the Lord in the Tabernacle. The rest of the blood shall be poured out at the base of the altar for burnt offerings. This stands at the door to the Tabernacle. ⁸Then he shall take all the fat on the entrails. ⁹This includes the two kidneys and the loin-fat on them, and the gallbladder. ¹⁰He shall burn them on the altar of burnt offering. He shall do the same as he would with a bull or cow sacrificed as a thank offering. ¹¹⁻¹²The rest of the young bull shall be carried to a special clean place outside the camp. (This is the place where the ashes from the altar are taken.) The skin, meat, head, legs, internal organs, and intestines are burned there on a wood fire.

¹³"The whole nation of Israel might sin without knowing it. They might do something that the Lord has said not to do. If this happens, then all the people are guilty. ¹⁴When they realize it, they shall offer a young bull for a sin offering. They shall bring it to the Tabernacle. ¹⁵There the leaders of the nation shall lay their hands upon the animal's head. Then they must kill it before the Lord. ¹⁶The priest shall bring its blood into the Tabernacle. ¹⁷He shall dip his finger in the blood. And he shall sprinkle it seven times before the Lord, in front of the veil. ¹⁸Then he shall put blood upon the horns of the altar. This altar stands in the Tabernacle before the Lord. All the rest of the blood shall be poured out at the base of the burnt offering altar. This stands at the door to the Tabernacle. ¹⁹All the fat shall be removed. It must be burned upon the altar. ²⁰He shall follow the same procedure as for a sin offering. In this way the priest shall make atonement for the nation. Then everyone will be forgiven.

21The priest shall then cart the young bull outside the camp. He shall burn it there. He shall treat it just as though it were a sin offering for an individual. But this time it is a sin offering for the whole nation.

22"One of the leaders might sin without knowing it. He might disobey one of God's laws. 23If he does, then as soon as he sees his sin he must bring as his sacrifice a male goat. It must have nothing wrong with it. 24He shall lay his hand upon its head. He shall kill it at the place where the burnt offerings are killed. Then he shall present it to the Lord. This is his sin offering. 25Then the priest shall take some of the blood of this sin offering. He shall place it with his finger upon the horns of the altar of burnt offerings. The rest of the blood shall be poured out at the base of the altar. 26All the fat shall be burned upon the altar. It shall be done just as if it were the fat of the sacrifice of a thank offering. Thus the priest shall make atonement for the leader and his sin. He will then be forgiven.

27"If any one of the common people sins and does not realize it, he is guilty. 28But as soon as he does realize it, he is to bring as his sacrifice a female goat. It must have nothing wrong with it. Its sacrifice shall atone for his sin. 29He shall bring it to the place where the animals for burnt offerings are killed. There he must lay his hand upon the head of the sin offering. Then he must kill it. 30And the priest shall take some of the blood with his finger. He shall smear it upon the horns of the burnt offering altar. Then the priest shall pour out the rest of the blood at the base of the altar. 31All the fat shall be taken off. He shall follow the same procedure as for the thank offering sacrifice. The priest shall burn the fat upon the altar. And the Lord will be pleased by it. Thus the priest shall make atonement for that man, and he will be forgiven.

32"However, if he chooses to bring a lamb as his sin offering, it must be a female. It must have nothing wrong with it. 33He shall bring it to the place where the burnt offerings are killed. He shall lay his hand upon its head. Then he shall kill it there as a sin offering. 34The priest shall take some of the blood with his finger. He shall smear it upon the horns of the burnt offering altar. The rest of the blood shall be poured out at the base of the altar. 35The fat shall be used just as in the case of a thank offering lamb. The priest shall burn the fat on the altar, as in any other sacrifice made to the Lord by fire. Thus the priest shall make atonement for the man. And his sin will be forgiven.

5 "Anyone refusing to give testimony about what he knows about a crime is guilty.

2"Anyone touching anything unclean is guilty. He is guilty even if he was not aware of touching it. The dead body of an animal is unclean and forbidden for food, wild or tame. So is the dead body of a forbidden insect. 3Or if he touches human discharge of any kind, he becomes guilty. He is guilty as soon as he realizes that he has touched it.

4"If anyone makes a rash vow, he is guilty as soon as he realizes what a foolish vow he has taken. This is true whether the vow is good or bad.

5"In any of these cases, he shall confess his sin. 6He shall bring his guilt offering to the Lord. It must be a female lamb or goat. Then the priest shall make atonement for him. And he will be freed from his sin. After that, he need not fulfill the vow.

What to Give If One Is Poor

7"If he is too poor to bring a lamb to the Lord, then he shall bring two turtledoves or two young pigeons. These will serve as his guilt offering. One of the birds shall be his sin offering. The other shall be his burnt offering. 8The priest shall offer as the sin sacrifice whichever bird is handed to him first. He must break its neck. But its head must not be cut from its body. 9Then he shall sprinkle some of the blood at the side of the altar. The rest shall be drained out at the base of the altar. This is the sin offering. 10He shall offer the second bird as a burnt offering. He shall follow the customary rules that have been set forth. So the priest shall make atonement for him and his sin. And he will be forgiven.

¹¹"If he is too poor to bring turtledoves or young pigeons as his sin offering, then he shall bring a tenth of a bushel of fine flour. He must not mix it with olive oil. Neither shall he put any incense on it, for it is a sin offering. ¹²He shall bring it to the priest. The priest shall take out a handful as a memorial portion. He shall burn it on the altar. It shall be done just as any other offering to the Lord made by fire. This will be his sin offering. ¹³In this way the priest shall make atonement for him for any sin of this kind. And he will be forgiven. The rest of the flour shall belong to the priest. It is the same as with the case of the grain offering."

How to Give a Guilt Offering

¹⁴And the Lord said to Moses, ¹⁵"Someone might sin by accident. He might defile what is holy. If he does, then he shall bring a ram without defect. It shall be worth whatever fine you charge against him. It shall serve as his guilt offering to the Lord. ¹⁶And he shall pay for the holy thing he has defiled or the tithe omitted. He must pay for the loss, plus a 20 percent penalty. He shall bring it to the priest. The priest shall make atonement for him with the ram of the guilt offering. And he will be forgiven.

¹⁷⁻¹⁸"Anyone who disobeys some law of God without knowing it is guilty anyway. He must bring his sacrifice of a value determined by Moses. This sacrifice shall be a ram that has nothing wrong with it. It shall be taken to the priest as a guilt offering. With it the priest shall make atonement for him. That way he will be forgiven for whatever it is he has done without knowing it. ¹⁹It must be offered as a guilt offering, for he is guilty before the Lord."

6 And the Lord said to Moses, ²"Someone might sin against me by refusing to bring back a deposit on something borrowed or rented. He might refuse to bring back something entrusted to him. He might rob or oppress his neighbor. ³He might find a lost article and lie about it. He might swear that he doesn't have

it. ⁴⁻⁵If he does these things, then, on the day he is found guilty of any such sin, he shall give back what he took. He shall add a 20 percent fine. And he shall give it to the one he has harmed. On the same day he shall bring his guilt offering to the Tabernacle. ⁶His guilt offering shall be a ram without defect. It must be worth whatever value you demand. He shall bring it to the priest. ⁷And the priest shall make atonement for him before the Lord. Then he will be forgiven."

Rules for Burnt Offerings

⁸Then the Lord said to Moses, ⁹*"Give Aaron and his sons these rules about the burnt offering:*

"The burnt offering shall be left upon the hearth of the altar all night. And the altar fire must be kept burning. ¹⁰The next morning the priest shall put on his linen underclothes. Over them he shall put on his linen outer clothing. He shall clean out the ashes of the burnt offering. And he shall put them beside the altar. ¹¹Then he shall change his clothes and carry the ashes outside the camp. He shall bring them to a special place that is clean. ¹²Meanwhile, the fire on the altar must be kept burning. It must not go out. The priest shall put on fresh wood each morning. He shall lay the daily burnt offering on it. Thus he shall burn the fat of the daily peace offering. ¹³The fire must be kept burning upon the altar at all times. It must never go out.

Rules for Grain Offerings

¹⁴*"These are the rules about the grain offering:*

"Aaron's sons shall stand in front of the altar. There they shall offer it before the Lord. ¹⁵The priest shall then take out a handful of the finely ground flour. He shall mix it with the olive oil and the incense. Then he shall burn it upon the altar as a memorial portion for the Lord. And it will be received with pleasure by the Lord. ¹⁶After taking out this handful, the rest of the flour shall belong to Aaron and his sons for their food. It shall be eaten without yeast in the courtyard of the Tabernacle. ¹⁷(Stress this teaching: if it is baked, it must be without yeast.)

I have given to the priests this part of the burnt offerings made to me. However, all of it is most holy. It is holy, just as is the entire sin offering and the entire guilt offering. [18]It may be eaten by any male descendant of Aaron, any priest, generation after generation. But only the priests may eat these offerings made by fire to the Lord."

[19-20]And the Lord said to Moses, "On the day Aaron and his sons are anointed and inducted into the priesthood, they shall bring to the Lord a regular grain offering. They must bring a tenth of a bushel of fine flour. Half of it is to be offered in the morning. Half is to be offered in the evening. [21]It shall be cooked on a griddle, using olive oil. It shall be well cooked. Then it shall be brought to the Lord. It is an offering that pleases him very much. [22-23]As the sons of the priests replace their fathers, they shall be inducted into office. This shall be done by offering this same sacrifice on the day of their anointing. This is a law that will not change. Each grain offering shall be entirely burned up before the Lord. None of it shall be eaten."

Rules for Sin Offerings

[24]Then the Lord said to Moses, [25]*"Tell Aaron and his sons that these are the teachings about the sin offering:*

"This sacrifice is most holy. It shall be killed before the Lord at the place where the burnt offerings are killed. [26]The priest who performs the ceremony shall eat it in the courtyard of the Tabernacle. [27]Only those who are sanctified—the priests—may touch this meat. If any blood sprinkles onto their clothing, it must be washed in a holy place. [28]Then the clay pot in which the clothing is boiled shall be broken. If a bronze kettle is used, it must be scoured and rinsed out thoroughly. [29]Every male among the priests may eat this offering. But only they, for it is most holy. [30]No sin offering may be eaten by the priests if any of its blood is taken into the Tabernacle to make atonement in the Holy Place. That carcass must be entirely burned with fire before the Lord.

Rules for Guilt Offerings

7 *"Here are the teachings about the most holy offering for guilt:*

[2]"The sacrificial animal shall be killed at the place where the burnt offering sacrifices are slain. Its blood shall be sprinkled back and forth upon the altar. [3]The priest shall offer upon the altar all its fat. This includes the tail, the fat that covers the insides, [4]the two kidneys and the loin-fat, and the gallbladder. All these parts shall be set aside for sacrificing. [5]The priests shall burn them upon the altar as a guilt offering to the Lord. [6]Only males among the priests may then eat the carcass. It must be eaten in a holy place, for this is a most holy sacrifice.

[7]"The same teachings apply to both the sin offering and the guilt offering. The carcass shall be given to the priest who is in charge of the atonement ceremony. It shall be for his food. [8](When the offering is a burnt sacrifice, the priest who is in charge shall also be given the animal's hide.) [9]The priests who present the people's grain offerings to the Lord shall be given whatever remains of the sacrifice after the ceremony is completed. This rule applies whether the sacrifice is baked, fried, or grilled. [10]All other grain offerings are the common property of all sons of Aaron. This is true whether they are mixed with olive oil or dry.

Rules for Peace Offerings

[11]*"Here are the teachings about the sacrifices given to the Lord as special peace offerings:*

[12]"If it is an offering of thanksgiving, unleavened shortbread shall be included with the sacrifice. This shall be given along with unleavened wafers spread with olive oil. Loaves from a batter of flour mixed with olive oil shall also be included. [13]This thanksgiving peace offering shall be given with loaves of leavened bread. [14]Part of this sacrifice shall be given to the Lord. This shall be done by waving it before the altar. Then it shall be given to the assisting priest. He is the one who sprinkles the blood of the animal presented for the sacrifice. [15]The animal shall be sacrificed and presented to the Lord as a peace offering.

This is done to show special thanks to him. Its meat is to be eaten that same day. None is to be eaten the next day.

¹⁶"Someone might bring a sacrifice that is not for thanksgiving, but because of a vow. Or he might simply bring a voluntary offering to the Lord. If he does, then any portion of the sacrifice that is not eaten the first day may be eaten the next day. ¹⁷⁻¹⁸But anything left over until the third day shall be burned. For if any of it is eaten on the third day, the Lord shall not accept it. It shall have no value as a sacrifice. And there shall be no credit to the one who brought it to be offered. The priest who eats it shall be guilty, for it is hated by the Lord. And the person who eats it must answer for his sin.

¹⁹"Any meat that comes into contact with anything that is unclean shall not be eaten. It must be burned. And the meat that may be eaten may only be eaten by a person who is clean. ²⁰Any priest who is unclean but eats the thanksgiving offering anyway shall be cut off from his people. He has defiled what is holy. ²¹Anyone who touches anything that is unclean and then eats the peace offering shall be cut off from his people. This is true whether it is uncleanness from man or beast. He has defiled what is holy."

²²Then the Lord said to Moses, ²³"Tell the people of Israel never to eat fat. This is true whether the fat is from oxen, sheep, or goats. ²⁴The fat of an animal that dies of disease, or is attacked and killed by wild animals, may be used for other purposes. But it must never be eaten. ²⁵Anyone who eats fat from an offering sacrificed by fire to the Lord shall be outlawed from his people.

²⁶⁻²⁷"Never eat blood, whether of birds or of animals. Anyone who does shall be expelled from his people."

²⁸And the Lord said to Moses, ²⁹"Tell the people of Israel that anyone bringing a thanksgiving offering to the Lord must bring it with his own hands. ³⁰He shall bring the offering of the fat and breast. It shall be presented to the Lord by waving it before the altar. ³¹Then the priest shall burn the fat upon the altar.

But the breast shall belong to Aaron and his sons. ³²⁻³³The right thigh shall be given to the officiating priest. ³⁴For I have given the breast and thigh as donations from the people of Israel to the sons of Aaron. Aaron and his sons must always be given this portion of the sacrifice. ³⁵This is their pay! It is to be set apart from the burnt offerings. It must be given to all who have been chosen to serve the Lord as priests. It shall provide for the needs of Aaron and his sons. ³⁶For on the day the Lord anointed them, he commanded that the people of Israel give these portions to them. It is their right forever."

³⁷These were the teachings about the burnt offering, grain offering, sin offering, and guilt offering. These teachings also concern the offering for appointing the priests and the peace offering. ³⁸These teachings were given to Moses by the Lord on Mount Sinai. They were to be passed on to the people of Israel. That way they would know how to offer their sacrifices to God in the Sinai desert.

Aaron and His Sons Become Priests

8 The Lord said to Moses, "Now bring Aaron and his sons to the door of the Tabernacle. They must bring their clothing and the anointing oil. They must also bring the young bull for the sin offering, the two rams, and the basket of bread made without yeast. They must summon all Israel to a meeting there."

⁴So all the people came together. ⁵And Moses said to them, "What I am now going to do has been commanded by the Lord."

⁶Then he took Aaron and his sons. He washed them with water. ⁷And he clothed Aaron with the special clothing. He put on the coat, sash, robe, and the ephod-jacket with its beautifully woven belt. ⁸Then he put on him the chestpiece. He put the Urim and the Thummim inside its pouch. ⁹And he placed on Aaron's head the turban, the holy crown. The sacred gold plate was at its front. Moses did everything as the Lord had told him.

¹⁰Then Moses took the anointing oil.

He sprinkled it upon the Tabernacle itself. Then he put it on each item inside, making them holy. [11]When he came to the altar he sprinkled it seven times. He also sprinkled the utensils of the altar and the washbasin and its pedestal. Thus he sanctified them. [12]Then he poured the anointing oil upon Aaron's head. This set him apart for his work. [13]Next Moses placed the robes on Aaron's sons, with the belts and caps. He did it all as the Lord had told him.

[14]Then he took the young bull for the sin offering. Aaron and his sons laid their hands upon its head [15-16]as Moses killed it. He smeared some of the blood with his finger upon the four horns of the altar. He also put some upon the altar itself. He did this to make it holy. Then he poured out the rest of the blood at the base of the altar. Thus he sanctified the altar, making atonement for it. He took all the fat covering the entrails, the fatty mass above the liver, and the two kidneys and their fat. He burned them all on the altar. [17]The carcass of the young bull, with its hide and dung, was burned outside the camp. It was all done as the Lord had commanded Moses.

[18]Then he presented to the Lord the ram for the burnt offering. Aaron and his sons laid their hands upon its head. [19]And Moses killed it. He then sprinkled the blood back and forth upon the altar. [20]Next he quartered the ram and burned the pieces, the head and the fat. [21]He washed the insides and the legs with water. Then he burned the whole ram on the altar before the Lord. It was a burnt offering that pleased the Lord very much. The Lord's directions to Moses were followed in every detail.

[22]Then Moses presented the other ram, the ram for appointing the priests. Aaron and his sons laid their hands upon its head. [23]Moses killed it and took some of its blood. He smeared it upon the lobe of Aaron's right ear. He put it on the thumb of his right hand. He also put it upon the big toe of his right foot. [24]Next he smeared some of the blood upon Aaron's sons. He put it upon the lobes of their right ears. He also put it upon their right thumbs, and upon the big toes of their right feet. The rest of the blood he sprinkled back and forth upon the altar.

[25]Then he took the fat, the tail and the fat upon the inner organs. He also took the gallbladder, the two kidneys with their fat, and the right shoulder. [26]He placed on top of these one unleavened wafer, one wafer spread with olive oil, and a slice of bread. These were all taken from the basket that had been placed there before the Lord. [27]All this was placed in the hands of Aaron and his sons. They were to present them to the Lord by waving them before the altar. [28]Moses then took it all back from them. He burned it upon the altar, along with the burnt offering to the Lord. And the Lord was pleased by the offering. [29]Now Moses took the breast and presented it to the Lord by waving it before the altar. This was Moses' portion of the ram sacrificed for appointing the priests. He did just as the Lord had told him.

[30]Next he took some of the anointing oil and some of the blood that had been sprinkled upon the altar. He sprinkled it upon Aaron and upon his clothes. He also put it upon his sons and upon their clothes. Thus he made Aaron and his sons and their clothes holy to the Lord's use.

[31]Then Moses said to Aaron and his sons, "Boil the meat at the door of the Tabernacle. Eat it along with the bread that is in the basket for appointing the priests. Do just as I told you to do. [32]Anything left of the meat and bread must be burned."

[33]Next he told them not to leave the Tabernacle door for seven days. After that time their appointment would be completed. It takes seven days. [34]Then Moses stated again that all he had done that day had been commanded by the Lord. It was all done to make atonement for them. [35]And again he warned Aaron and his sons. He told them to stay at the door of the Tabernacle day and night for seven days. "If you leave," he told them, "you shall die. This is what the Lord has said."

[36]So Aaron and his sons did all that the Lord had commanded Moses.

The Priests Begin Their Work

9 On the eighth day of the appointment ceremonies, Moses called Aaron. He also called Aaron's sons and the elders of Israel. ²He told Aaron to take a bull calf from the herd for a sin offering. He also was to take a ram for a burnt offering. Nothing could be wrong with them. He was to offer them before the Lord.

³"And tell the people of Israel," Moses said, "to select a male goat for their sin offering. Choose also a yearling calf and a yearling lamb. They must all be without bodily defect. They shall be for their burnt offering. ⁴In addition, the people are to bring to the Lord a peace offering sacrifice. It must include an ox, and a ram, and a grain offering—flour mingled with olive oil. For today," Moses said, "the Lord will appear to them."

⁵So they brought all these things to the door of the Tabernacle, as Moses had said. And the people came and stood there before the Lord.

⁶Moses told them, "When you have followed the Lord's teachings, his glory will appear to you."

⁷Moses then told Aaron to proceed to the altar. He was to offer the sin offering and the burnt offering. Thus he would make atonement for himself first. Then he would do so for the people. He did just as the Lord had commanded. ⁸So Aaron went up to the altar. He killed the calf as a sacrifice for his own sin. ⁹His sons caught the blood for him. He dipped his finger in it and smeared it upon the horns of the altar. He poured out the rest at the base of the altar. ¹⁰Then he burned upon the altar the fat, kidneys, and gallbladder from this sin offering. He did just as the Lord had told Moses. ¹¹But he burned the meat and hide outside the camp.

¹²Next he killed the burnt offering animal. His sons caught the blood, and he sprinkled it back and forth upon the altar. ¹³They brought the animal to him piece by piece, including the head. He burned each part upon the altar. ¹⁴Then he washed the insides and the legs. He offered these also upon the altar as a burnt offering.

¹⁵Next he sacrificed the people's offering. He killed the goat. Then he offered it in the same way as he had the sin offering for himself. ¹⁶Thus he sacrificed their burnt offering to the Lord. He did it according to the teachings God had given.

¹⁷Then he presented the grain offering. He took a handful and burned it upon the altar. He did this in addition to the regular morning offering.

¹⁸Next he killed the ox and ram. This was the people's peace offering sacrifice. Aaron's sons brought the blood to him. And he sprinkled it back and forth upon the altar. ¹⁹Then he collected the fat of the ox and the ram. This included the fat from their tails and the fat covering the inner organs. He also took the kidneys and gallbladders. ²⁰The fat was placed upon the breasts of these animals. Aaron burned it upon the altar. ²¹But he waved the breasts and right shoulders slowly before the Lord. He did this as a gesture of offering it to him. He did it all just as Moses had commanded.

²²Then, with hands spread out toward the people, Aaron blessed them and came down from the altar. ²³Moses and Aaron went into the Tabernacle. When they came out again, they blessed the people. And the glory of the Lord appeared to the whole assembly. ²⁴Then fire came from the Lord and consumed the burnt offering and fat on the altar. When the people saw it, they all shouted. Then they fell flat upon the ground before the Lord.

Two Priests Are Killed by Fire

10 But Nadab and Abihu, the sons of Aaron, placed unholy fire in their censers. Then they laid incense on the fire and offered the incense before the Lord. This was done contrary to what the Lord had just commanded them! ²So fire blazed forth from the presence of the Lord and destroyed them.

³Then Moses said to Aaron, "This is what the Lord meant when he said, 'I will show myself holy among those who approach me. I will be glorified before all the people.' " And Aaron was speechless.

⁴Then Moses called for Mishael and

Elzaphon, Aaron's cousins, the sons of Uzziel. He told them, "Go and get the charred bodies from before the Tabernacle. Carry them outside the camp."

⁵So they went over and got them. They carried them out in their coats as Moses had told them to.

⁶Then Moses said to Aaron and his sons Eleazar and Ithamar, "Do not mourn. Do not let your hair hang loose as a sign of your mourning. Do not tear your clothes. If you do, God will strike you dead, too. And his wrath will come upon all the people of Israel. But the rest of the people of Israel may lament the death of Nadab and Abihu. They may mourn because of the terrible fire the Lord has sent. ⁷But you are not to leave the Tabernacle under penalty of death. For the anointing oil of the Lord is upon you." And they did as Moses commanded.

⁸⁻⁹Now the Lord told Aaron, "Never drink wine or strong drink when you go into the Tabernacle. If you do, you will die. This rule applies to your sons and to all your descendants to the end of all time. ¹⁰ Your duties shall be to make judgments for the people. You shall teach them the difference between what is holy and what is ordinary. You shall show them the difference between what is pure and what is impure. ¹¹You shall teach them all the laws the Lord has given through Moses."

¹²Then Moses said to Aaron and to his sons who were left, Eleazar and Ithamar, "Offer the grain offering. Take the food that remains after the handful has been offered to the Lord by burning it on the altar. Make sure there is no leaven in it. Then eat it beside the altar. The offering is most holy. ¹³Therefore, you must eat it in the sanctuary, in a holy place. It belongs to you and to your sons, from the offerings to the Lord made by fire. For so I am commanded. ¹⁴The breast and the thigh, which have been offered to the Lord by waving them before him, may be eaten in any holy place. They belong to you and to your sons and daughters for your food. This is your portion of the peace offering sacrifices of the people of Israel. ¹⁵"The people are to bring the thigh

that was set aside. They must also bring the breast that was offered when the fat was burned. These pieces shall be presented before the Lord by waving them. And after that they shall belong to you and your family. For the Lord has commanded this."

¹⁶Then Moses searched everywhere for the goat of the sin offering. He discovered that it had been burned! He was very angry about this with Eleazar and Ithamar, the remaining sons of Aaron.

¹⁷"Why have you not eaten the sin offering in the sanctuary?" he asked. "It is most holy! God has given it to you to take away the sin and guilt of the people. You are to eat it to make atonement for them before the Lord. ¹⁸Its blood was not taken inside the sanctuary. Thus, you should have eaten it there as I ordered you."

¹⁹But Aaron spoke with Moses for his sons. "They offered their sin offering and burnt offering before the Lord," he said. "But if I had eaten the sin offering on such a day as this, would it have pleased the Lord?" ²⁰And when Moses heard that, he was satisfied.

Clean and Unclean Animals

11 Then the Lord said to Moses and Aaron,

²⁻³"Speak to the people of Israel. Tell them which animals may be used for food. They may eat any animal with cloven hooves that chews its cud. ⁴⁻⁷This means that the following may *not* be eaten:

The camel, for it chews the cud but does not have cloven hooves.
The coney, or rock badger, because although it chews the cud, it does not have cloven hooves.
The hare, because although it chews the cud, it does not have cloven hooves.
The swine, because although it has cloven hooves, it does not chew the cud.

⁸"You may not eat their meat or even touch their dead bodies. They are forbidden foods to you.

⁹"As to fish, you may eat whatever has

fins and scales. It does not matter whether it was taken from rivers or from the sea. ¹⁰But all other water creatures are strictly forbidden to you. ¹¹You must not eat their meat or even touch their dead bodies. ¹²I will repeat it again. Any water creature that does not have fins or scales is forbidden to you.

¹³⁻¹⁹"Among the birds, these are the ones you may *not* eat: the eagle, the metire, the osprey, the falcon (all kinds), the kite, the raven (all kinds), the ostrich, the nighthawk, the seagull, the hawk (all kinds), the owl, the cormorant, the ibis, the marsh hen, the pelican, the vulture, the stork, the heron (all kinds), the hoopoe, the bat.

²⁰"No insects may be eaten, ²¹⁻²²with the exception of those that jump. Locusts of all kinds may be eaten. This includes ordinary locusts, bald locusts, crickets, and grasshoppers. ²³All insects that fly and walk or crawl are forbidden to you.

²⁴"Anyone touching their dead bodies shall be defiled until the evening. ²⁵He must wash his clothes right away. He must also isolate himself until nightfall, for he is unclean.

²⁶"You are also defiled by touching any animal with only semiparted hoofs. You are defiled by any animal that does not chew the cud. ²⁷Any animal that walks on paws is forbidden to you as food. Anyone touching the dead body of such an animal will be unclean until evening. ²⁸Anyone carrying away the carcass shall wash his clothes. He will be unclean until evening. For it is forbidden to you.

²⁹⁻³⁰"These are the forbidden small animals that scurry about your feet or crawl upon the ground: the mole, the rat, the great lizard, the gecko, the mouse, the lizard, the snail, the chameleon.

³¹"Anyone touching their dead bodies will be unclean until evening. ³²Anything upon which the carcass falls will be unclean. This includes any article of wood, or of clothing, a rug, or a sack. Anything it touches must be put into water and is unclean until evening. After that it may be used again. ³³If it falls into a pottery bowl, anything in the bowl is unclean. Then you shall smash the bowl. ³⁴If the water used to cleanse the unclean article touches any food, all of it is unclean. Any drink that is in the unclean bowl is also unclean.

³⁵"If the dead body of such an animal touches any clay oven, it is unclean. The oven must be smashed. ³⁶If the body falls into a spring or cistern where there is water, that water is not unclean. Yet anyone who pulls out the carcass is unclean. ³⁷And if the carcass touches grain to be sown in the field, it is not unclean. ³⁸But if the seeds are wet and the carcass falls upon it, the seed is unclean.

³⁹"If an animal that you are allowed to eat dies of disease, anyone touching the carcass will be unclean until evening. ⁴⁰Also, anyone eating its meat or carrying away its carcass shall wash his clothes. He will be unclean until evening.

⁴¹⁻⁴²"Animals that crawl shall not be eaten. This includes all reptiles that slither along upon their bellies as well as those that have legs. No crawling thing with many feet may be eaten, for it is unclean. ⁴³Do not defile yourselves by touching it.

⁴⁴"I am the Lord your God. Keep yourselves pure in these things. Be holy, for I am holy. Therefore do not defile yourselves by touching any of these things that crawl upon the earth. ⁴⁵For I am the Lord who brought you out of the land of Egypt to be your God. You must therefore be holy, for I am holy." ⁴⁶These are the laws about animals, birds, and whatever swims in the water or crawls upon the ground. ⁴⁷These are the distinctions between what is clean and may be eaten, and what is unclean and may not be eaten, among all animal life upon the earth."

Mothers and Childbirth

12 The Lord told Moses to give these teachings to the people of Israel:

²"When a baby boy is born, the mother will be unclean for seven days. She shall be under the same rules as during her monthly period. ³On the eighth day, her son must be circumcised.

[4]Then, for the next 33 days she must not touch anything holy. She must not enter the Tabernacle either.

[5]"When a baby girl is born, the mother's impurity shall last two weeks. During this time she shall be under the same rules as during her period. Then for a further 66 days she shall continue her recovery.

[6]"When these days of cleansing are ended, she must bring a yearling lamb as a burnt offering. She must bring a young pigeon or a turtledove for a sin offering. These teachings are true whether her baby is a boy or a girl.

"She must take them to the door of the Tabernacle to the priest. [7]The priest shall offer them before the Lord and make atonement for her. Then she will be clean again after her bleeding at childbirth.

"These then, are the rules you must follow after childbirth. [8]But if she is too poor to bring a lamb, then she must bring two turtledoves or two young pigeons. One shall be for a burnt offering. The other shall be for a sin offering. The priest shall make atonement for her with these, so that she will be pure again."

Rules about Leprosy

13 The Lord said to Moses and Aaron, "Someone might notice a swelling on his skin. Or he might have a scab or boil or pimple on his skin. If he does, then leprosy is to be suspected. He must be brought to Aaron the priest or to one of his sons. [3]They shall look at the spot. The hair in this spot might turn white. Or the spot might look to be more than skin-deep. If it does, then it is leprosy. And the priest must say he is a leper.

[4]"But the white spot in the skin may not be deeper than the skin. And the hair in the spot may not have turned white. If this is true, then the priest shall isolate him for seven days. [5]At the end of that time, on the seventh day, the priest shall see him again. If the spot has not changed and has not spread in the skin, then the priest must isolate him seven days more. [6]Again on the seventh day the priest shall see him. The marks

of the disease may have become fainter. And the marks may not have spread. If this is true, then the priest shall say he is cured. It was only a scab. The man need only wash his clothes and all shall be normal again. [7] But if the spot spreads in the skin after he has come to the priest to be seen, he must come back to the priest again. [8]The priest shall look again. And if the spot has spread, then the priest must say he is a leper.

[9-10]"When anyone thought to have leprosy is brought to the priest, the priest is to look at him. He will discover if there is a white swelling in the skin. He will see if there are white hairs in the spot and an ulcer developing. [11]If he finds these symptoms, it is a real case of leprosy. And the priest must say he is unclean. The man is not to be set apart to be watched further. He is diseased for sure. [12]But the priest might see that the leprosy has broken out. And he might see it has spread all over his body from head to foot wherever he looks. [13]If this is true, then the priest shall say he is cured of leprosy. For it has all turned white and he is cured. [14-15]But if there is an open sore anywhere, the man shall be declared a leper. It is proved by the open sore. [16-17]But if the raw flesh later changes to white, the leper shall go back to the priest to be seen again. If the spot has indeed turned completely white, then the priest shall say he is cured.

[18]"A man might have a boil on his skin that heals. [19]And it might leave a white swelling or a bright spot, sort of reddish-white. If it does, then the man must go to the priest to be examined. [20]The priest might see that the trouble seems to be down under the skin. And the hair at the spot may have turned white. If this is true, then the priest shall say he is unclean. For leprosy has broken out from the boil. [21]But the priest may also see that there are no white hairs in this spot. And he may see that the spot does not appear to be deeper than the skin. And the color might be gray. If these things are true, then the priest shall isolate him for seven days. [22]If during that time the spot spreads, the priest must say he is a leper. [23]But the bright

spot might not grow any larger. And it might not spread. If this is true, then it is merely the scar from the boil. And the priest shall say that all is well.

²⁴"A man might be burned in some way. And the burned place might become bright reddish-white or white. ²⁵If this happens, then the priest must look at the spot. The hair in the bright spot might turn white. And the problem might seem to be more than skin-deep. If this is true, then it is leprosy that has broken out from the burn. And the priest must say he is a leper. ²⁶But the priest might see that there are no white hairs in the bright spot. And the brightness might appear to be no deeper than the skin. And it might fade. If this is true, then the priest shall isolate him for seven days. ²⁷He shall see him again on the seventh day. If the spot spreads in the skin, the priest must say he is a leper. ²⁸But the bright spot may not move or spread in the skin. And it may be fading. If this is true, then it is simply a scar from the burn. And the priest shall say that he does not have leprosy.

²⁹⁻³⁰"If a man or woman has a sore on the head or chin, the priest must look at him. The infection might seem to be below the skin. And yellow hair might be found in the sore. If this is true, then the priest must say he is a leper. ³¹But the priest's examination might show that the spot is only in the skin. And there might be healthy hair in it. If this is true, then he shall be isolated for seven days. ³²He shall be looked at again on the seventh day. The spot might not have spread. And no yellow hair may have appeared. And the infection might not seem to be deeper than the skin. ³³If this is true, then he shall shave off all the hair around the spot (but not on the spot itself). And the priest shall isolate him for another seven days. ³⁴He shall be looked at again on the seventh day. The spot might not have spread. And it might appear to be no deeper than the skin. If this is true, then the priest shall say he is well. After washing his clothes, he is free. ³⁵But if, later on, this spot begins to spread, ³⁶then the priest must look at him again. And, without waiting

to see if any yellow hair develops, he must say he is a leper. ³⁷But it might appear that the spreading has stopped. And black hairs might be found in the spot. If this is true, then he is healed. He is not a leper. And the priest shall say he is clean.

³⁸"A man or a woman might have white, transparent areas in the skin. ³⁹These spots might grow dimmer with time. If this is true, it is not leprosy. It is an ordinary infection that has broken out in the skin.

⁴⁰"If a man's hair is gone, this does not make him a leper even though he is bald! ⁴¹If the hair is gone from the front part of his head, he simply has a bald forehead. This is not leprosy. ⁴²However, if in the baldness there is a reddish-white spot, it may be leprosy breaking out. ⁴³In that case the priest shall look at him. If there is a reddish-white lump that looks like leprosy, ⁴⁴then he is a leper. The priest must then pronounce him such.

⁴⁵"Anyone who is discovered to have leprosy must tear his clothes. He must let his hair grow in wild disarray. He must cover his upper lip. Then he must call out as he goes, "I am a leper, I am a leper." ⁴⁶As long as the disease lasts, he is unclean. He must live outside the camp.

⁴⁷⁻⁴⁸"A bad disease might be suspected in a woolen or linen garment or fabric, or in a piece of leather or leather-work. ⁴⁹If it has a greenish or a reddish spot in it, then it is probably a bad disease. It must be taken to the priest to be looked at. ⁵⁰The priest shall put it away for seven days. ⁵¹He shall look at it again on the seventh day. If the spot has spread, it is a disease. ⁵²He must burn the clothing, fabric, linen or woolen covering, or leather article. It is contagious and must be destroyed by fire.

⁵³"He might look at it again on the seventh day and see the spot has not spread. ⁵⁴If this is true, then the priest shall order the suspected article to be washed. Then it shall be isolated for seven more days. ⁵⁵After that time the spot still might not have changed its color. It might not even have spread. If this is true, it is a bad disease. It shall be

burned, for the article is infected through and through. ⁵⁶But the priest might see that the spot has faded after the washing. If he does, then he shall cut it out from the garment or leather goods or whatever it is in. ⁵⁷However, if it then reappears, it is a bad disease and he must burn it. ⁵⁸But if after washing it there is no further trouble, it can be put back into service after another washing."

⁵⁹These are the rules for disease in a garment or anything made of skin or leather. They will show whether an object is diseased or not.

When Leprosy Goes Away

14 And the Lord gave Moses these rules for the cleansing of people with leprosy:

³"The priest shall go out of the camp to see him. He will see if the leprosy is gone. ⁴The priest will need two living birds of a kind allowed for food. He will need some cedar wood, a red string, and some hyssop branches. These shall be used for the cleansing ceremony of the one who is healed. ⁵The priest shall then order one of the birds killed. It shall be killed in an earthenware pot held above running water. ⁶The other bird, still living, shall be dipped in the blood. The cedar wood, the red thread, and the hyssop branch shall also be dipped in the blood. ⁷Then the priest shall sprinkle the blood seven times upon the man cured of his leprosy. The priest shall say he is clean. And he shall let the living bird fly into the open field.

⁸"Then the man who is cured shall wash his clothes. He must shave off all his hair. And he must take a bath. Then he may return to live inside the camp. However, he must stay outside his tent for seven days. ⁹The seventh day he shall again shave all the hair from his head, beard, and eyebrows. He must wash his clothes. And he must take a bath. Then he shall be declared fully cured of his leprosy.

¹⁰"The next day, the eighth day, he shall take two male lambs. They must have nothing wrong with them. He shall also take one yearling ewe-lamb without physical defect. And he must take 10 quarts of finely ground flour mixed with olive oil, and a pint of olive oil. ¹¹Then the priest who sees him shall place the man and his offerings before the Lord at the door of the Tabernacle. ¹²The priest shall take one of the lambs and the pint of olive oil. He shall offer them to the Lord as a guilt offering. He shall do this by waving them before the altar. ¹³Then he shall kill the lamb. He shall do this at the place where sin offerings and burnt offerings are killed, there at the Tabernacle. This guilt offering shall then be given to the priest for food. It shall be as in the case of a sin offering. It is a most holy offering. ¹⁴The priest shall take the blood from this guilt offering. He shall smear some of it upon the tip of the right ear of the man being cleansed. He shall put it on the thumb of his right hand. He shall also put it upon the big toe of his right foot.

¹⁵"Then the priest shall take the olive oil. He shall pour it into the palm of his left hand. ¹⁶He shall dip his right finger into it. And he shall sprinkle it with his finger seven times before the Lord. ¹⁷Some of the oil remaining in his left hand shall then be placed by the priest upon the tip of the man's right ear. It shall also be put on the thumb of his right hand and the big toe of his right foot. It shall be done just as he did with the blood of the guilt offering. ¹⁸The rest of the oil in his hand shall be used to anoint the man's head. Thus the priest shall make atonement for him before the Lord.

¹⁹"Then the priest must offer the sin offering. Then again he must perform the rite of atonement for the person being cleansed from his leprosy. After that the priest shall kill the burnt offering. ²⁰He shall offer it along with the grain offering upon the altar. Thus he shall make atonement for the man. And the man shall then be cleansed.

²¹"If he is so poor that he cannot afford two lambs, then he shall bring only one. It must be a male lamb for the guilt offering. It must be presented to the Lord in the rite of atonement by waving it before the altar. Only three quarts of fine white flour will be needed.

It shall be mixed with olive oil, for a grain offering. A pint of olive oil must also be brought.

22"He shall also bring two turtledoves or two young pigeons. He must bring whichever he is able to afford. He must use one of the pair for a sin offering. The other should be used for a burnt offering. 23He shall bring them to the priest at the door of the Tabernacle on the eighth day, for his ceremony of cleansing before the Lord. 24The priest shall take the lamb for the guilt offering and the pint of oil. He shall wave them before the altar as a gesture of offering to the Lord. 25Then he shall kill the lamb for the guilt offering. He shall smear some of its blood upon the tip of the man's right ear. He shall put some upon the thumb of his right hand. He shall also put some upon the big toe of his right foot.

26"The priest shall then pour the olive oil into the palm of his own left hand. 27With his right finger he is to sprinkle some of it seven times before the Lord. 28Then he must put some of the olive oil from his hand upon the tip of the man's right ear. He must put some upon the thumb of his right hand. He must also put some upon the big toe of his right foot. This is to be done just as he did it with the blood of the guilt offering. 29The remaining oil in his hand shall be placed upon the head of the man being cleansed. It shall make atonement for him before the Lord.

30"Then he must offer the two turtledoves or two young pigeons (whichever pair he is able to afford). 31One of the pair is for a sin offering and the other for a burnt offering. They are to be sacrificed along with the grain offering. The priest shall make atonement for the man before the Lord."

32These, then, are the laws for those who are healed of leprosy, but are not able to bring the sacrifices normally needed for the cleansing ceremony.

33-34Then the Lord said to Moses and Aaron, "When you arrive in the land of Canaan which I have given you, I may place a bad disease in some house there. 35Then the owner of the house shall come and report to the priest. He shall say, 'It seems to me that there may be a bad disease in my house!'

36"The priest shall order the house to be emptied before he looks at it. That way everything in the house will not be declared unclean if he decides that there is a bad disease there. 37He might find greenish or reddish streaks in the walls of the house. And the streaks might seem to be beneath the surface. 38If so, he shall close up the house for seven days. 39He shall go back on the seventh day to look at it again. The spots might have spread in the wall. 40If this is true, then the priest shall order the removal of the spotted section of wall. The material must be thrown into an unclean place outside the city. 41Then he shall order the inside walls of the house scraped thoroughly. The scrapings will then be dumped in an unclean place outside the city. 42Other stones shall be brought to replace those that have been removed. New mortar shall be used. The house shall be replastered.

43"But if the spots appear again, 44the priest shall come again and look. If he sees that the spots have spread, it is a bad disease. The house is unclean. 45Then he shall order the house to be destroyed. All of its stones, timbers, and mortar shall be carried out of the city to an unclean place. 46Anyone entering the house while it is closed shall be unclean until evening. 47Anyone who lies down or eats in the house shall wash his clothing.

48"When the priest comes again to look, he may find that the spots have not come back after the fresh plastering. If so, then he shall say the house is cleansed. He shall say the disease is gone. 49He shall also perform the ceremony of cleansing. He shall use two birds, cedar wood, red thread, and hyssop branches. 50He shall kill one of the birds over fresh water in an earthenware bowl. 51-52He shall take the cedar wood, hyssop branch, and red thread, and the living bird. He shall dip them into the blood of the bird that was killed over the fresh water. Then he shall sprinkle the house seven times. In this way the house shall be cleansed. 53Then he shall let the live bird fly away into an open field outside the city. This is the method for making atonement for the house and cleansing it."

⁵⁴These, then, are the laws about the various places where a bad disease may appear. ⁵⁵It might appear in a garment or in a house. ⁵⁶Or it may be in any swelling in one's skin, or a scab from a burn, or a bright spot. ⁵⁷In this way you will know whether something is clean or unclean. That is why these laws are given.

Rules of Health for Men

15 The Lord told Moses and Aaron to give the people of Israel these further teachings:

"Any man who has a genital discharge is unclean. ³This applies not only while the discharge is active. It also applies for a time after it heals. ⁴Any bed he lies on and anything he sits on are unclean. ⁵Thus, anyone touching the man's bed is unclean until evening. He must wash his clothes. And he must take a bath. ⁶Anyone sitting on a seat the man has sat upon while unclean is himself impure until evening. He must wash his clothes. And he must take a bath. ⁷The same teachings apply to anyone touching him. ⁸Anyone he spits on is impure until evening. He must wash his clothes. And he must take a bath. ⁹Any saddle he rides on is unclean. ¹⁰Anyone touching or carrying anything else that was beneath him will be unclean until evening. He must wash his clothes. And he must take a bath. ¹¹If the unclean man touches anyone without first rinsing his hands, that person must wash his clothes. And he must take a bath. He will be unclean until evening. ¹²Any earthen pot touched by the unclean man must be broken. Every wooden utensil must be rinsed in water.

¹³"When the discharge stops, he shall begin a seven-day cleansing ceremony. He shall do this by washing his clothes and bathing in running water. ¹⁴On the eighth day he shall take two turtledoves or two young pigeons. He shall come before the Lord at the door of the Tabernacle. There, he shall give them to the priest. ¹⁵The priest shall sacrifice them there. One shall be sacrificed for a sin

offering. The other shall be given for a burnt offering. Thus the priest shall make atonement before the Lord for the man because of his discharge.

¹⁶"Whenever a man's semen goes out from him, he shall take a complete bath. He will be impure until the evening. ¹⁷Any clothing or bedding the semen spills on must be washed. These objects will remain unclean until evening. ¹⁸After sleeping together, the woman as well as the man must take a bath. They are unclean until the next evening.

Rules of Health for Women

¹⁹"Whenever a woman has her period, she will be in a state of defilement. It will last for seven days afterwards. During that time anyone touching her will be unclean until evening. ²⁰Anything she lies on or sits on during that time will be unclean. ²¹⁻²³Anyone touching her bed or anything she sits upon shall wash his clothes and take a bath. He shall be unclean until evening. ²⁴A man who sleeps with her during this time is unclean for seven days. Every bed he lies upon shall be unclean.

²⁵"Her period might continue after the normal time. Or it might begin at some irregular time during the month. If so, the same rules apply as were given above. ²⁶Anything she lies upon during that time is unclean. It is unclean just as it would be during her normal period. And all she sits on is also unclean. ²⁷Anyone touching her bed or anything she sits on will be unclean. He shall wash his clothes. He shall take a bath. And he shall be unclean until evening. ²⁸Seven days after her period stops, she is no longer unclean.

²⁹"On the eighth day, she shall take two turtledoves or two young pigeons. She shall bring them to the priest at the door of the Tabernacle. ³⁰The priest shall offer one for a sin offering. The other shall be given for a burnt offering. The priest shall make atonement for her before the Lord for her defilement. ³¹In this way you shall cleanse the people of Israel from their defilement. Otherwise they will die because of defiling my Tabernacle that is among them."

³²This, then, is the law for the man who is defiled by a genital disease or by a seminal emission. ³³And this is the law for cleansing from a woman's period. It also provides for anyone who sleeps with her during the period of defilement.

The Day of Atonement

16 After Aaron's two sons died before the Lord, the Lord said to Moses, "Warn your brother Aaron. Tell him not to enter into the Holy Place behind the veil, where the Ark and the place of mercy are, just whenever he chooses. The penalty for entering is death. For I myself am present in the cloud above the place of mercy.

³"Here are the things he must do to enter there. He must bring a young bull for a sin offering. He must bring a ram for a burnt offering. ⁴He must take a bath. Then he must put on the holy linen coat, shorts, belt, and turban. ⁵The people of Israel shall then bring him two male goats for their sin offering. They shall bring a ram for their burnt offering. ⁶First he shall present to the Lord the young bull as a sin offering for himself. With it he shall make atonement for himself and his family. ⁷Then he shall bring the two goats before the Lord at the door of the Tabernacle. ⁸He shall cast lots to determine which is the Lord's and which is to be sent away. ⁹The goat allotted to the Lord shall then be sacrificed by Aaron as a sin offering. ¹⁰The other goat shall be kept alive and placed before the Lord. The rite of atonement shall be performed over it. And it shall then be sent out into the desert as a scapegoat.

¹¹"Aaron shall sacrifice the young bull as a sin offering for himself and his family. ¹²After that, he shall take a censer full of live coals from the altar of the Lord. He shall fill his hands with sweet incense beaten into fine powder. Then he must bring it inside the veil. ¹³There before the Lord he shall put the incense upon the coals. A cloud of incense will cover the mercy place above the Ark. (The Ark contains the stone tablets of the Ten Commandments.) Thus he will not die. ¹⁴And he shall take some of the blood of the young bull. He shall sprinkle it with his finger upon the east side of the mercy place. Then he shall sprinkle the blood seven times in front of it.

¹⁵"Then he must go out and sacrifice the people's sin offering goat. He must bring its blood within the veil. Then he must sprinkle it upon the place of mercy and in front of it. He must do it just as he did with the blood of the young bull. ¹⁶Thus he shall make atonement for the holy place. For it is defiled by the sins of the people of Israel. And thus he shall make atonement for the Tabernacle. For it is located right among them. And it is surrounded by their defilement. ¹⁷Not another soul shall be inside the Tabernacle when Aaron enters to make atonement in the Holy Place. No one shall enter until after he comes out again. He must make atonement for himself and his household and for all the people of Israel. ¹⁸Then he shall go out to the altar before the Lord and make atonement for it. He must smear the blood of the young bull and the goat on the horns of the altar. ¹⁹Then he must sprinkle blood upon the altar seven times with his finger. Thus he shall cleanse it from the sinfulness of Israel. And thus he shall make it holy.

²⁰"He shall complete the rite of atonement for the Holy Place. And the entire Tabernacle and the altar shall be atoned for. Then he shall bring the live goat. ²¹He shall lay both hands upon its head. And he shall confess over it all the sins of the people of Israel. He shall lay all their sins upon the head of the goat. Then he shall send it into the desert. It shall be led by a man chosen for the task. ²²So the goat shall carry all the sins of the people into a land where no one lives. And the man shall let it loose in the wilderness.

²³"Then Aaron shall go into the Tabernacle again. He shall take off the linen clothing he wore when he went behind the veil. And he shall leave them there in the Tabernacle. ²⁴Then he shall bathe in a holy place. He shall put on his clothes again. And he shall go out and sacrifice his own burnt offering for the people. Thus he shall make atonement

for himself and for them. [25]He shall also burn upon the altar the fat for the sin offering.

[26]"(The man who took the goat out into the desert shall wash his clothes. He must also take a bath. Then he may come back into the camp.) [27]And the young bull and the goat used for the sin offering shall be carried outside the camp and burned. This includes the hides and internal organs. Their blood was taken into the Holy Place by Aaron, to make atonement. [28]After that, the person doing the burning shall wash his clothes. He must also take a bath. Then he may go back to camp.

[29-30]"This is a law that will never change: You must do no work on the 25th day of September. You must spend the day in self-examination and humility. This applies whether you are born in the land or are a foreigner living among the people of Israel. This is the day to remember the atonement. It is a day to remember your cleansing in the Lord's eyes from all of your sins. [31]It is a Sabbath of solemn rest for you. You shall spend the day in quiet humility. This is a law that will never change. [32]This ceremony, in later generations, shall be done by the anointed High Priest. He shall be set apart for the Lord's use in place of his ancestor Aaron. He shall be the one to put on the holy linen clothing. [33]He shall make atonement for the holy sanctuary, the Tabernacle, the altar, the priests, and the people. [34]This shall be an everlasting law for you. You shall make atonement for the people of Israel once each year, because of their sins."

And Aaron obeyed all the teachings that the Lord gave to Moses.

Warning against Sacrificing Wrongly

17 The Lord gave to Moses these other teachings for Aaron and the priests and for all the people of Israel:

[3-4]"Any Israelite who sacrifices an ox, lamb, or goat anywhere except at the Tabernacle is guilty of murder. He shall be expelled from his nation. [5] The purpose of this law is to stop the people of Israel from sacrificing in the open fields. It shall cause them to bring their sacrifices to the priest at the door of the Tabernacle. That way they shall burn the fat as a savor the Lord will enjoy. [6]The priest shall be able to sprinkle the blood upon the altar of the Lord at the door of the Tabernacle. He shall burn the fat as a savor the Lord will enjoy. [7]That way the people will not sacrifice to evil spirits out in the fields. This shall be a changeless law for you, from generation to generation. [8-9]I repeat: Anyone who offers a burnt offering or a sacrifice anywhere other than at the door of the Tabernacle, where it will be sacrificed to the Lord, shall be expelled. This is true whether the person is an Israelite or a foreigner living among you.

[10]"And I will turn my face against anyone who eats blood in any form. This is true whether that person is an Israelite or a foreigner living among you. I will expel him from his people. [11]For the life of the flesh is in the blood. And I have given you the blood to sprinkle upon the altar as an atonement for your souls. It is the blood that makes atonement because it is the life. [12]That is the reasoning behind my decree to the people of Israel, that neither they, nor any foreigner living among them, may eat blood. [13]Anyone who goes hunting and kills an animal or bird of a kind allowed for food must pour out the blood and cover it with dust. [14]For the blood is the life. This is true for anyone, whether an Israelite or a foreigner. That is why I told the people of Israel never to eat it. For the life of every bird and animal is its blood. Therefore, anyone who eats blood must be expelled.

[15]"Someone—native born or foreigner—might eat the dead body of an animal that died a natural death. Or he might eat an animal that was killed by wild animals. If he does, then he must wash his clothes. And he must take a bath. He will be unclean until evening. After that he shall be declared cleansed. [16]But if he does not wash his clothes and take a bath, he will suffer the consequences."

Forbidden Sexual Relationships

18 The Lord then told Moses to tell the people of Israel,

"I am the Lord your God. ³Do not act like heathen. Do not act like the people of Egypt, where you lived so long. And do not act like the people of Canaan, where I am going to take you. ⁴⁻⁵You must obey only my laws. You must carry them out in detail. For I am the Lord your God. If you obey them, you will live. I am the Lord.

⁶"None of you shall marry a near relative. For I am the Lord. ⁷Do not disgrace your father by sleeping with your mother. ⁸Do not sleep with any other of your father's wives. ⁹Do not sleep with your sister or half-sister. Do not do it if she is the daughter of your father or your mother. Do not do it if she is brought up in the same household or elsewhere.

¹⁰"You shall not sleep with your granddaughter—the daughter of either your son or your daughter. For she is a close relative. ¹¹You may not sleep with a half-sister—your father's wife's daughter. ¹²You may not sleep with your aunt—your father's sister. For she is so closely related to your father. ¹³You may not sleep with your aunt—your mother's sister. For she is a close relative of your mother. ¹⁴You may not sleep with your aunt—the wife of your father's brother.

¹⁵"You may not marry your daughter-in-law—your son's wife. ¹⁶You may not marry your brother's wife. For she is your brother's. ¹⁷You may not marry both a woman and her daughter or granddaughter. They are near relatives. To do so is horrible sin. ¹⁸You shall not marry two sisters, for they will be rivals. However, if your wife dies, then it is all right to marry her sister.

¹⁹"You must not sleep with a woman who is having her period. ²⁰You must never sleep with anyone else's wife, to defile yourself with her.

²¹"You shall not give any of your children to Molech. You shall not burn them upon his altar. Never profane the name of your God. For I am the Lord.

²²"Homosexuality is completely forbidden. It is a great sin. ²³A man shall not mate with any female animal, thus defiling himself. And a woman must never give herself to a male animal, to mate with it. This is a terrible sin.

²⁴"Do not defile yourselves in any of these ways. These are the things the heathen do. And because they do them, I am going to cast them out from the land into which you are going. ²⁵That entire country is defiled with this kind of activity. That is why I am punishing the people living there. I shall throw them out of the land. ²⁶You must strictly obey all of my laws. You must not do any of these sinful things. These laws apply to you who are born in the nation of Israel. And they also apply to foreigners living among you.

²⁷"Yes, all these sins have been done continually by the people of the land where I am taking you. The land is defiled. ²⁸Do not do these things or I will throw you out of the land. I will throw you out just as I will throw out the nations that live there now. ²⁹⁻³⁰Whoever does any of these terrible deeds shall be expelled from this nation. So be very sure to obey my laws. Do not practice any of these horrible customs. Do not defile yourselves with the evil deeds of those living in the land where you are going. For I am the Lord your God."

Commands for Daily Life

19 The Lord also told Moses to tell the people of Israel, "You must be holy because I, the Lord your God, am holy. You must respect your mothers and fathers. You must obey my Sabbath law. For I am the Lord your God. ³⁻⁴Do not make or worship idols. For I am the Lord your God.

⁵"When you sacrifice a peace offering to the Lord, offer it correctly so that it will be accepted. ⁶Eat it the same day you offer it, or the next day at the latest. Any food remaining until the third day must be burned. ⁷For any of it eaten on the third day is repulsive to me. It will not be accepted. ⁸If you eat it on the third day, you are guilty. For you profane the holiness of the Lord. And you shall be expelled from the Lord's people.

⁹"When you harvest your crops, do

not reap the corners of your fields. Do not pick up stray grains of wheat from the ground. ¹⁰It is the same with your grape crop. Do not strip every last piece of fruit from the vines. And do not pick up the grapes that fall to the ground. Leave them for the poor and for those traveling through. For I am the Lord your God.

¹¹"You must not steal or lie. ¹²You must not swear to a falsehood. This will bring reproach upon the name of your God. For I am the Lord.

¹³"You shall not rob nor oppress anyone. You shall pay your hired workers promptly. If something is due them, do not even keep it overnight.

¹⁴"You must not curse the deaf nor trip up a blind man as he walks. Fear your God. I am the Lord!

¹⁵"Judges must always be just in their sentences. They must not notice whether a person is poor or rich. They must always be perfectly fair.

¹⁶"Do not gossip. Do not falsely accuse your neighbor of some crime. For I am the Lord.

¹⁷"Do not hate your brother. Rebuke anyone who sins. Do not let him get away with it, or you will be equally guilty. ¹⁸Do not seek vengeance. Do not bear a grudge. Love your neighbor as yourself. For I am the Lord.

¹⁹"Obey my laws: Do not mate your cattle with a different kind of animal. Do not sow your field with two kinds of seed. Do not wear clothes made of half wool and half linen.

²⁰"A man might seduce a slave girl. And she might be engaged to be married. If so, then they will be tried in a court. But they will not be put to death, because she is not free. ²¹The man involved shall bring his guilt offering to the Lord at the door of the Tabernacle. The offering shall be a ram. ²²The priest shall make atonement with the ram for the sin the man has committed. Then the sin will be forgiven him.

²³"When you enter the land and have planted all kinds of fruit trees, do not eat the first three crops. They are considered unclean. ²⁴And the fourth year the entire crop shall be devoted to the Lord. It shall

be given to the Lord in praise to him. ²⁵Finally, in the fifth year, the crop is yours.

²⁶"I am the Lord your God! You must not eat meat with undrained blood. And you must not use fortune-telling or witchcraft.

²⁷"You must not trim off your hair on your temples. And you must not clip the edges of your beard, as the heathen do. ²⁸You shall not cut yourselves. And you shall not put tattoo marks upon yourselves in connection with funeral rites. I am the Lord.

²⁹"Do not violate your daughter's holiness by making her a prostitute. Otherwise the land will become full of great wickedness.

³⁰"Keep my Sabbath laws and reverence my Tabernacle. For I am the Lord.

³¹"Do not defile yourselves by asking mediums and wizards for help. For I am the Lord your God.

³²"You shall give due honor and respect to the elderly. You shall do this in the fear of God. I am the Lord.

³³"Do not take advantage of foreigners in your land. Do not wrong them. ³⁴They must be treated like any other citizen. Love them as yourself. Remember that you too were foreigners in the land of Egypt. I am the Lord your God.

³⁵⁻³⁶"You must be fair in judgment. Use accurate measurements—length, weight, and volume. Give full measure. For I am the Lord your God who brought you from the land of Egypt. ³⁷You must heed all of my commands. Carefully obey them. For I am the Lord."

Punishments for Sin

20 The Lord gave Moses these further teachings for the people of Israel:

"Anyone who sacrifices his child as a burnt offering to Molech shall without fail be stoned by his neighbors. This is true whether he is an Israelite or a foreigner living among them. ³And I myself will turn against that man. I will cut him off from all his people. For he has given his child to Molech. Thus he has made my Tabernacle unfit for me to live in. And he has insulted my holy name. ⁴The people of the land might pretend they do not know what the man has done. And they might refuse to put him to death. [5]If so, then I myself will set my face against that man and his family. I will cut him off, along with all others who turn to gods other than me.

[6]"I will set my face against anyone who asks mediums and wizards for help instead of me. I will cut that person off from his people. [7]So sanctify yourselves and be holy. For I am the Lord your God. [8]You must obey all of my commands. For I am the Lord who sanctifies you.

[9]"Anyone who curses his father or mother shall surely be put to death. For he has cursed his own flesh and blood.

[10]"If a man sleeps with another man's wife, both the man and woman shall be put to death. [11]If a man sleeps with his father's wife, he has defiled what is his father's. Both the man and the woman must die, for it is their own fault. [12]And if a man sleeps with his daughter-in-law, both shall be killed. They have brought it upon themselves by defiling each other. [13]The penalty for homosexual acts is death to both parties. They have brought it upon themselves. [14]If a man sleeps with a woman and with her mother, it is a great evil. All three shall be burned alive to wipe out wickedness from among you.

[15]"If a man mates with an animal, he shall be executed and the animal killed. [16]If a woman mates with an animal, kill the woman and the animal. They deserve their punishment.

[17]"If a man sleeps with his sister, whether the daughter of his father or of his mother, it is a shameful thing. They shall publicly be cut off from the people of Israel. He shall bear his guilt. [18]If a man sleeps with a woman during her period, both shall be expelled. For he has uncovered the source of her flow. And she has allowed it.

[19]"A man and his maiden aunt must not sleep together—whether the sister of his mother or of his father. They are near of kin. They shall bear their guilt. [20]If a man sleeps with his uncle's wife, he has taken what belongs to his uncle. Their punishment is that they shall bear their sin and die childless. [21]If a man marries his brother's wife, this is impurity. For he has taken what belongs to his brother. They will be childless.

[22]"You must obey all of my laws. If you do, I will not throw you out of your new land. [23]You must not follow the customs of the nations I will throw out before you. They do all these things I have warned you against. That is the reason I hate them. [24]I have promised you their land. I will give it to you to possess it. It is a land 'flowing with milk and honey.' I am the Lord your God. I have made a distinction between you and the people of other nations.

Keeping close to God will keep you from bad things

Sanctify yourselves and be holy. For I am the Lord your God.

Leviticus 20:7

---

[25]"You shall therefore make a distinction between the birds and animals I have given you permission to eat and those you may not eat. You shall not make yourselves unclean by eating any animal or bird that I have forbidden. You must not eat them, even though the land is full of them. [26]You shall be holy to me, for I the Lord am holy. I have set you apart from all other peoples to be mine.

[27]"A medium or a wizard—whether man or woman—shall surely be stoned to death. They have caused their own doom."

Rules for the Priests

21 The Lord said to Moses: "Tell the priests never to defile themselves by touching a dead person. [2-3]A priest may do this only if the person is a close relative. He may touch his mother, father, son, daughter, or brother. He may also touch an unmarried sister for whom he is responsible. This is because she has no husband. [4]For the priest is a leader among his people. He may not defile himself as an ordinary person can.

[5]"The priests shall not clip bald spots

in their hair or beards. They shall never cut their flesh. ⁶They shall be holy unto their God. They shall not dishonor and profane his name. If they do, they shall be unfit to make food offerings by fire to the Lord their God. ⁷A priest shall not marry a prostitute. He must not marry a woman of another tribe. He also must not marry a divorced woman. For he is a holy man of God. ⁸The priest is set apart to offer the sacrifices of your God. He is holy, for I, the Lord who sanctifies you, am holy. ⁹The daughter of any priest who becomes a prostitute shall be burned alive. She has violated her father's holiness as well as her own.

¹⁰"The High Priest has been anointed with the special anointing oil and wears special clothing. He must not let his hair hang loose in mourning. He must never tear his clothing. ¹¹He must never go into the presence of any dead person— not even his father or mother. ¹²He shall not leave the sanctuary [when on duty]. He must not treat my Tabernacle like an ordinary house. For he is set apart as holy. And the anointing oil of his God is upon him. I am the Lord. ¹³He must marry a virgin. ¹⁴⁻¹⁵He must not marry a widow. He must not marry a woman who is divorced. And he must not marry a prostitute. She must be a virgin from his own tribe. For he must not be the father of children of mixed blood—half priestly and half ordinary."

¹⁶⁻¹⁷And the Lord said to Moses, "Tell Aaron that any of his descendants from generation to generation who have any bodily defect may not offer the sacrifices to God. ¹⁸For instance, a man might be blind or lame. He might have a broken nose or any extra fingers or toes. ¹⁹He might have a broken foot or hand. ²⁰He might have a humped back. He might be a dwarf. He might have a defect in his eye. He might have pimples or scabby skin. Or he might have imperfect testicles. ²¹If any of these are true, then he is not allowed to offer the fire sacrifices to the Lord. This is true even though he is a descendant of Aaron. ²²However, he shall be fed with the food of the priests. He shall eat from the offerings sacrificed to God. He shall eat both from the holy

and most holy offerings. ²³But he shall not go in behind the veil. And he shall not come near the altar. For he has a physical defect. This would defile my sanctuary. For it is the Lord who sanctifies it."

²⁴So Moses gave these teachings to Aaron and his sons and to all the people of Israel.

22 The Lord told Moses, "Tell Aaron and his sons to treat the people's holy gifts with respect. That way they will not to defile my holy name. For I am the Lord. ³A priest who is unclean might sacrifice the animals brought by the people. Or a priest who is unclean might handle the gifts dedicated to the Lord. If he does, then he shall be discharged from the priesthood. For I am the Lord!

⁴"No priest who is a leper or who has a running sore may eat the holy sacrifices until healed. A priest might touch a dead person. He might be defiled by a seminal emission. ⁵He might touch a reptile or other forbidden thing. Or he might touch a person who is unclean for any reason. ⁶If he does any of these things, that priest shall be unclean until evening. He shall not eat of the holy sacrifices until after he has taken a bath that evening. ⁷When the sun is down, he shall be clean again. Then he may eat the holy food, for it is his source of life. ⁸He may not eat any animal that dies of itself or is killed by wild animals. This will defile him. I am the Lord. ⁹Warn the priests to obey these teachings completely. Otherwise they will be declared guilty. And they will die for not obeying these rules. I am the Lord who makes them holy.

¹⁰"No one may eat of the holy sacrifices unless he is a priest. No one visiting the priest, for instance, nor a hired servant, may eat this food. ¹¹However, there is one exception. If the priest buys a slave with his own money, that slave may eat it. And any slave children born in his household may eat it. ¹²If a priest's daughter is married outside the tribe, she may not eat the holy offerings. ¹³But she might be a widow or divorced. And she might have no son to support her. And she may have gone home to her father's

household. If this is true, then she may eat of her father's food again. But otherwise, no one who is not in the priestly families may eat this food.

14"Someone might eat of the holy sacrifices without knowing it. If he does, he shall return to the priest the amount he has used. And he shall add 20 percent. 15The holy sacrifices brought by the people of Israel must not be unclean. They must not be eaten by ordinary persons. For these sacrifices have been offered to the Lord. 16Anyone who does not obey this law is guilty. He is in great danger because he has eaten the holy offerings. For I am the Lord who makes the offerings holy."

Acceptable Animals for Sacrifice

17-18And the Lord said to Moses, "Speak to Aaron and his sons and all the people of Israel. Tell them that an Israelite or other person living among you can offer a burnt offering sacrifice to the Lord. 19But when they do, it must be a male animal without defect. This only will be accepted by the Lord. This is true whether it is to fulfill a promise or is a freewill offering. It must be a young bull or a sheep or a goat. 20Anything that has something wrong with it must not be offered. It will not be accepted.

21"Anyone sacrificing a peace offering to the Lord from the herd or flock must sacrifice an animal that has nothing wrong with it. Otherwise it will not be accepted. This is true whether it is given to fulfill a vow or as a voluntary offering. 22An animal might be blind or disabled or mutilated. It might have sores or the itch or another skin disease. If it has any of these, then it must not be offered to the Lord. It is not a fit burnt offering for the altar of the Lord. 23A young bull or lamb presented to the Lord might have an extra body part. Or it might not have all of its body parts. If either of these is true, then it may be offered as a freewill offering. But it may not be given for a vow. 24An animal that has crushed or castrated genitals shall not be offered to the Lord at any time. 25This applies to the sacrifices made by foreigners among you as well as those made by yourselves.

No defective animal will be accepted for this sacrifice."

26-27And the Lord said to Moses, "When a bullock, sheep, or goat is born, it shall be left with its mother for seven days. From the eighth day onward it is acceptable as a sacrifice by fire to the Lord. 28You shall not kill a mother animal and her offspring the same day. This is true whether the animal is a cow or an ewe. 29-30When you offer the Lord a sacrifice of thanksgiving, you must do it in the right way. You must eat the sacrificial animal the same day it is slain. Leave none of it for the following day. I am the Lord.

31"You must keep all of my commands. For I am the Lord. 32-33You must not treat me as common and ordinary. Revere me and hallow me. For I, the Lord, made you holy to myself. I rescued you from Egypt to be my own people! I am the Lord!"

Special Days

23 The Lord said to Moses, "Announce to the people of Israel that they are to celebrate several yearly feasts of the Lord. These shall be times when all Israel will come together and worship me. 3(These are in addition to your Sabbaths—the seventh day of every week. The Sabbaths are always days of rest in every home. They are days for coming together to worship. They are a time for resting from the normal business of the week.)

4These are the holy feasts that are to be observed each year:

The Passover

5"The Passover of the Lord: This is to be celebrated on the first day of April, beginning at sundown.

The Feast of Unleavened Bread

6"The Feast of Unleavened Bread: This is to be celebrated beginning the day following the Passover. For seven days you must not eat any bread made with yeast. 7On the first day of this feast, you shall gather the people for worship. All ordinary work shall stop. 8You shall do the same on the seventh day of the feast. On each of the days in between you shall make an offering by fire to the Lord.

The Feast of Fruits

9-11*"The Feast of First Fruits:* When you arrive in the land I will give you, you will reap your first harvest. Bring the first sheaf of the harvest to the priest on the day after the Sabbath. He shall wave it before the Lord in a gesture of offering. It will be accepted by the Lord as your gift. 12That same day you shall sacrifice to the Lord a male yearling lamb. It must have nothing wrong with it. It will be a burnt offering. 13A grain offering shall be given with it. It will consist of a fifth of a bushel of finely ground flour mixed with olive oil. It will be offered by fire to the Lord. This will be very pleasant to him. Also offer a drink offering. It shall consist of three pints of wine. 14Until this is done you must not eat any of the harvest for yourselves. You must not eat fresh kernels or bread or parched grain. This is a law that will never change throughout your nation.

The Feast of Pentecost

15-16*"The Harvest Feast (Feast of Pentecost):* Fifty days later you shall bring to the Lord an offering of a sample of the new grain of your later crops. 17This shall consist of two loaves of bread from your homes. It shall be waved before the Lord in a gesture of offering. Bake this bread from a fifth of a bushel of fine flour containing yeast. It is an offering to the Lord of the first sampling of your later crops. 18Along with the bread and the wine, you shall sacrifice as burnt offerings to the Lord seven yearling lambs. These must have nothing wrong with them. You must also give one young bull and two rams. All are fire offerings, very pleasing to the Lord. 19And you shall offer one male goat for a sin offering. Two male yearling lambs shall also be given for a peace offering.

20"The priests shall wave these offerings before the Lord. They shall also wave the loaves that represent the first sampling of your later crops. They are holy to the Lord and shall be given to the priests as food. 21That day shall be a

time of holy assembly of all the people. Do not do any work that day. This is a law to be honored until the end of time. 22When you reap your harvests, you must not reap all the corners of the fields. You must not pick up the fallen grain. Leave it for the poor. And leave it for foreigners living among you who have no land of their own. I am the Lord your God!

The Feast of Trumpets

23-24*"The Feast of Trumpets:* Mid-September is a time for all the people to meet together for worship. It is a time of remembrance. It is to be announced by loud blowing of trumpets. 25Do not do any hard work on that day. But offer a sacrifice by fire to the Lord.

The Day of Atonement

26-27*"The Day of Atonement* follows nine days later. All the people are to come together before the Lord, saddened by their sin. And they shall offer sacrifices by fire to the Lord. 28Do not do any work that day. It is a special day for making atonement before the Lord your God. 29Anyone who does not spend the day in repentance and sorrow for sin shall be expelled from his people. 30-31And I shall put to death anyone who does any kind of work that day. This is a law of Israel to be obeyed until the end of time. 32For this is a Sabbath of rest. In it you shall go without food and be filled with sorrow. This time for atonement begins in the evening. It continues through the next day.

The Feast of Tabernacles

33-34*"The Feast of Shelters:* Five days later, on the last day of September, is the Feast of Shelters. It is to be celebrated before the Lord for seven days. 35On the first day there shall be a holy assembly of all the people. Do not do any hard work that day. 36On each of the seven days of the feast you are to sacrifice an offering by fire to the Lord. The eighth day requires another holy assembly of all the people. At that time there shall again be an offering by fire to the Lord. It is the closing assembly, and no regular work is allowed.

³⁷"These, then, are the regular yearly feasts. They are holy assemblies of all people. In them, offerings to the Lord are to be made by fire. ³⁸These yearly feasts are in addition to your regular Sabbaths—the weekly days of holy rest. The sacrifices made during the feasts are to be in addition to your regular giving and normal fulfillment of your vows.

³⁹"This last day of September is the time to begin to cele-brate this seven-day feast before the Lord. This day comes at the end of your harvesting. Remember that the first and last days of the feast are special days of rest. ⁴⁰On the first day, take branches of fruit trees filled with fruit. Take palm leaves and the branches of leafy trees—such as willows that grow by the brooks. And build shelters with them. Then rejoice before the Lord your God for seven days.⁴¹This seven-day yearly feast is a law from generation to generation. ⁴²During those seven days, all of you who are native Israelites are to live in these shelters. ⁴³The pur-pose of this is to remind the people of Israel, generation after generation, that I rescued you from Egypt. It will remind you of the days when you lived in shel-ters. I am the Lord your God."

⁴⁴So Moses announced these yearly feasts of the Lord to the people of Israel.

The Memorial Offering

24 The Lord said to Moses, "Tell the people of Israel to bring you pure olive oil for an eternal flame. ³⁻⁴It shall be lit in the lampstand of pure gold that stands outside the curtain of the Holy of Holies. Each morning and evening Aaron shall supply it with fresh oil and trim the wicks. It shall be an eternal flame before the Lord from generation to generation.

⁵⁻⁸"Every Sabbath day the High Priest shall take 12 loaves of bread. He shall put them in two rows upon the gold table that stands before the Lord. These loaves shall be baked from finely ground flour. A fifth of a bushel shall be used for each. Pure frankincense shall be sprinkled along each row. This shall be a memorial offering made by fire to the Lord. It is in memory of his everlasting covenant

Seven Golden Lamps

LEVITICUS 24:1-4

What kind of light do you have in your room? When you turn on a switch does the light go on? People of Bible times would be amazed to see a light bulb. They could never believe a house filled with them! In Bible times, people had oil lamps. Most of them were made of clay. They were like a little covered dish. The dish was filled with oil made from olives. An opening at one end had a wick. One end of the wick lay in the olive oil. People lit the other end. That's what gave light. People filled the lamp through an opening in the middle. The Tabernacle had a spe-cial lampstand with seven of these lamps on it. But they were not made of clay. They were made of gold. The stand that held these lamps was also gold. The Lord told Moses exactly how to make this beautiful stand with seven golden lamps. They gave light to the Holy Room inside the Tabernacle so the priests could do their work for God.

with the people of Israel. ⁹The bread shall be eaten by Aaron and his sons, in a place set apart for the purpose. For these are offerings made by fire to the Lord under a permanent law of God. They are most holy."

The Penalty of Cursing God

[10]Out in the camp one day, a young man whose mother was an Israelite and whose father was an Egyptian got into a fight with one of the men of Israel. [11]During the fight the Egyptian man's son cursed God and was brought to Moses for judgment. (His mother's name was Shelomith, daughter of Dibri of the tribe of Dan.) [12]He was put in jail until the Lord would show what to do with him.

[13-14]And the Lord said to Moses, "Take him outside the camp. Tell all who heard him to lay their hands upon his head. Then all the people are to kill him by stoning. [15-16]And tell the people of Israel that anyone who curses his God must pay the penalty. He must die. All the people shall stone him. This law applies to the foreigner as well as to the Israelite who blasphemes the name of the Lord. He must die.

[17]"Also, all murderers must be killed. [18]Anyone who kills an animal [that is not his] shall replace it. [19]The penalty for hurting anyone is to be hurt in exactly the same way. [20]A broken bone must be given for a broken bone. An eye must be given for an eye. A tooth must be given for a tooth. Whatever anyone does to another shall be done to him.

[21]"To repeat, whoever kills an animal must replace it. Whoever kills a man must die. [22]You shall have the same law for the foreigner as for the home-born citizen. For I am the Lord your God."

[23]So they took the youth out of the camp and stoned him until he died. They did just as the Lord had commanded Moses.

Rest for the Land

25 While Moses was on Mount Sinai, the Lord gave him these teachings for the people of Israel:

"When you come into the land I am going to give you, you must let the land rest before the Lord every seventh year. [3]For six years you may sow your field and prune your vineyards and harvest your crops. [4]But during the seventh year the land is to rest before the Lord. You must not cultivate it. Do not sow your crops. Do not prune your vineyards during that entire year. [5]Do not even reap for yourself the volunteer crops that come up. Do not gather the grapes for yourself. For it is a year of rest for the land. [6-7]Any crops that do grow that year shall be free to all. They shall be for you, your servants, your slaves, and any foreigners living among you. Cattle and wild animals alike shall be allowed to graze there.

The Year of Jubilee

[8]"Every fiftieth year, [9]on the Day of Atonement, let the trumpets blow loud and long throughout the land. [10]For the fiftieth year shall be holy. It will be a time to proclaim freedom to all who became slaves because they were in debt. It will be a time for canceling all public and private debts. It will be a year when all the family estates sold to others shall be given back to the original owners or their heirs.

[11]"What a happy year it will be! In it you shall not sow, nor gather crops nor grapes. [12]For it is a holy Year of Jubilee for you. That year your food shall be the volunteer crops that grow wild in the fields. [13]Yes, during the Year of Jubilee everyone shall go home to his original family possession. If he has sold it, it shall be his again! [14-16]In spite of this, the land can be sold or bought during the preceding 49 years. But a fair price shall be decided by counting the number of years until the Jubilee. If the Jubilee is many years away, the price will be high. If it is in a few years, the price will be low. What you are doing is selling the number of crops the land will produce before it is given back.

[17-18]"You must fear your God and not overcharge! For I am the Lord. Obey my laws if you want to live safely in the land. [19]When you obey, the land shall yield bumper crops. You shall eat your fill in safety. [20]But you will ask, 'What will we eat the seventh year? We are not allowed to plant or harvest crops that year.' [21-22]The answer is, 'I will bless you with bumper crops the sixth year. The food will last you until the crops of the eighth year are harvested!' [23]And re-

member, the land is mine, so you may not sell it permanently. You are merely my tenants and sharecroppers!

Rules for Property Owners

24"In every contract of sale there must be a rule that the land can be bought back at any time by the seller. 25If anyone becomes poor and sells some of his land, then his nearest relatives may buy it back. 26But there might not be anyone else to buy it back. And he himself might get together enough money. 27If so, then he must use the number of harvests until the Jubilee to decide its price. He will then buy it back. The owner must take the money and give the land back to him. 28But the original owner might not be able to buy it back. If so, then it shall belong to the new owner until the Year of Jubilee. But at the Jubilee year it must be given back again.

29"If a man sells a house in the city, he has up to one year to buy it back. He has full rights of redemption during that time. 30But if it is not bought back within the year, then it shall belong permanently to the new owner. It does not go back to the original owner in the Year of Jubilee. 31But houses in villages that have no walls are like farmland. They can be bought back at any time. They are always given back to the original owner in the Year of Jubilee.

32"There is one exception: The homes of the Levites, even though in walled cities, may be bought back at any time. 33They must be given back to the original owners in the Year of Jubilee. For the Levites shall not be given farmland like the other tribes. They shall receive only houses in their cities, and the surrounding fields. 34The Levites are not allowed to sell the fields of common land around their cities. These belong to them for all time. They must belong to no one else.

35"If someone close to you becomes poor, you must help him. If he has no home, invite him to yours. 36Fear your God and let your brother live with you. Do not charge him interest on the money you lend him. 37Remember—no

interest! Give him what he needs, at your cost. Do not try to make a profit! 38For I, the Lord your God, brought you out of the land of Egypt to *give* you the land of Canaan and to be your God.

Rules about Slaves

39"If a fellow Israelite becomes poor and sells himself to you, you must not treat him as an ordinary slave. 40Treat him as a hired servant or as a guest. And he shall serve you only until the Year of Jubilee. 41At that time he can leave. He can take his children and go back to his own family and possessions. 42For I brought you from the land of Egypt, and you are my servants. So you may not be sold as ordinary slaves. 43And you may not be treated harshly. Fear your God.

When God lets you have more than someone else, share it

If someone close to you becomes poor, you must help him. If he has no home, invite him to yours.

Leviticus 25:35

44"However, you may buy slaves from the foreign nations living around you. 45And you may buy the children of the foreigners living among you. You may do this even though they have been born in your land. 46They shall be slaves for you to pass on to your children after you. But your brothers, the people of Israel, shall not be treated so.

47"A foreigner living among you might become rich. And an Israelite might become poor. He might sell himself to the foreigner or to the foreigner's family. 48If this happens, then he may be bought back by one of his brothers. 49Or he may be bought back by his uncle, nephew, or anyone else who is a close relative. He may also buy himself back if he can find the money. 50The price of his freedom shall be decided by the number of years left before the Year of Jubilee. It will cost whatever it would cost to hire a servant for that number of years. 51There might still be many years until the Jubilee. If so, he shall pay almost the amount he received when he sold himself. ⁵²But many years might have passed. And perhaps only a few still remain until the Jubilee. If this is true, then he shall repay only a small part of the amount he received when he sold himself. ⁵³He might sell himself to a foreigner. If he does, the foreigner must treat him as a hired servant rather than as a slave or as property. ⁵⁴He might not have been bought back by the Year of Jubilee. If this is true, then he and his children shall be freed at that time. ⁵⁵For the people of Israel are *my* servants. I brought them from the land of Egypt. I am the Lord your God.

Rewards for Obedience

26 "You must have no idols. You must never worship carved images, obelisks, or shaped stones. For I am the Lord your God. ²You must obey my Sabbath laws of rest. You must reverence my Tabernacle. For I am the Lord.

³"If you obey all of my commands, ⁴⁻⁵I shall give you regular rains. All the land will yield bumper crops. The trees will be loaded with fruit long after the normal time! And grapes will still be ripening when sowing time comes again. You shall eat your fill and live safely in the land. ⁶For I will give you peace. And you shall go to sleep without fear. I will chase away the dangerous animals. ⁷You shall chase your enemies. They shall die beneath your swords. ⁸Five of you shall chase a hundred. A hundred of you shall chase ten thousand! You shall defeat all of your enemies. ⁹I will look after you, and multiply you, and fulfill my covenant with you. ¹⁰You shall have such a surplus of crops that you will not know what to do with them when the new harvest is ready! ¹¹And I will live among you and not despise you. ¹²I will walk among you and be your God. And you shall be my people. ¹³For I am the Lord your God who brought you out of the land of Egypt. Now you are slaves no longer. I have broken your chains so that you can walk with dignity.

Results of Disobedience

¹⁴"But you might not listen to me or obey me. ¹⁵And you might reject my laws. ¹⁶If you do, then this is what I will do to you. I will punish you with sudden terrors and panic. You will suffer with tuberculosis and burning fever. You will lose your eyesight. Your life will ebb away. You will sow your crops in vain. Your enemies will eat them. ¹⁷I will set my face against you. And you will flee before your attackers. Those who hate you will rule you. You will even run when no one is chasing you!

¹⁸"And you might still disobey me. If you do, I will punish you seven times more severely for your sins. ¹⁹I will break your proud power. I will make your heavens as iron and your earth as bronze. ²⁰Your strength will be spent in vain. For your land will not yield its crops. And your trees will not bring forth their fruit.

²¹"And even then you might not obey me and listen to me. If this is true, I will send you seven times more plagues because of your sins. ²²I will send wild animals to kill your children and destroy your cattle. They will reduce your numbers so that your roads will be empty.

²³"And even this might not reform you. You might still continue to walk against my wishes. ²⁴If this is true, then I will walk against your wishes. And I, even I, will personally punish you seven times for your sin. ²⁵I will pay you back for breaking my covenant by bringing war against you. You will flee to your cities. And I will send a plague among you there. You will be beaten by your enemies. ²⁶I will destroy your food supply. One oven will be large enough to bake all the bread available for 10 entire families. And you will still be hungry after your food has been given out to you.

²⁷"And if you still will not listen to me or obey me, ²⁸then I will let loose my great anger. I will send you seven times greater punishment for your sins. ²⁹You will eat your own sons and daughters. ³⁰I will destroy the altars on the hills where you worship your idols. I will cut down your incense altars. I will leave your dead bodies to rot among your idols.

And I will hate you. 31I will turn your cities into ruins. I will destroy your places of worship. And I will not respond to your incense offerings. 32Yes, I will destroy your land. Your enemies will live in it. They will be amazed at what I have done to you.

33"I will scatter you out among the nations, destroying you with war as you go. Your land will be desolate and your cities destroyed. 34-35Then at last the land will rest. It will make up for the many years you refused to let it lie idle. For it will lie desolate all the years that you are captives in enemy lands. Yes, then the land will rest and enjoy its Sabbaths! It will make up for the rest you did not give it every seventh year when you lived upon it.

36"And for those who are left alive, I will cause them to be dragged away to distant lands. They will go as prisoners of war and slaves. There they will live in constant fear. The sound of a leaf driven in the wind will send them fleeing as though chased by a man with a sword. They will fall when no one is pursuing them. 37Yes, though none pursue they will stumble over each other in flight, as though fleeing in battle. They will have no power to stand before their enemies. 38You will perish among the nations and be destroyed among your enemies. 39Those left will pine away in enemy lands because of their sins, the same sins as those of their fathers.

Confessed Sin

40-41"But at last they will confess their sins and their fathers' sins of treachery against me. (Because they were against me, I was against them. And I brought them into the land of their enemies.) When at last their evil hearts are humbled, and when they accept the punishment I send them for their sins, 42then I will remember again my promises to Abraham, Isaac, and Jacob. And I will remember the land (and its desolation). 43For the land will enjoy its Sabbaths as it lies desolate. But then at last they will accept their punishment for rejecting my laws and for despising my rule. 44But despite all they have done, I will not

completely destroy them and my covenant with them. For I am the Lord their God. 45For their sakes I will remember my promises to their ancestors to be their God. For I brought their forefathers out of Egypt as all the nations watched in wonder. I am the Lord."

46These were the laws and teachings that the Lord gave to the people of Israel through Moses on Mount Sinai.

Payments to the Lord

27 The Lord said to Moses, "Tell the people of Israel that when a person makes a special vow to give himself to the Lord, he shall give these payments instead. 3A man from the age of 20 to 60 shall pay 25 dollars. 4A woman from the age of 20 to 60 shall pay 15 dollars. 5A boy from five to 20 shall pay 10 dollars. A girl will pay five dollars. 6A boy one month to five years old shall have paid for him 2½ dollars. A girl shall have paid for her 1½ dollars. 7A man over 60 shall pay 7½ dollars. A woman will pay five dollars. 8But if the person is too poor to pay this amount, he shall be brought to the priest. The priest shall talk it over with him. And he shall pay as the priest decides.

9"But if it is an animal that is vowed to be given to the Lord as a sacrifice, it must be given. 10The vow may not be changed. The donor may not change his mind about giving it to the Lord. He may not substitute good for bad or bad for good. If he does, both the first and the second shall belong to the Lord! 11-12But if the animal given to the Lord is not a kind that is allowed as a sacrifice, the owner shall bring it to the priest to value it. And he shall be told how much to pay instead. 13The animal might be a kind that may be offered as a sacrifice. But the man might want to buy it back. If so, then he shall pay 20 percent more than the value set by the priest.

14-15"Someone might donate his home to the Lord. If he does this and then wishes to buy it back, the priest will decide its value. The man shall pay that amount plus 20 percent. Then the house shall be his again.

16"If a man gives any part of his field

to the Lord, its value will be judged by the amount of seed needed to sow it. A section of land that requires 10 bushels of barley seed for sowing is valued at 25 dollars. 17If a man gives his field to God in the Year of Jubilee, then the whole estimate shall stand. 18But if it is after the Year of Jubilee, then the value shall be decided by the number of years until the next Year of Jubilee. 19If the man decides to buy the field back, he shall pay 20 percent, added to what the priest decides. Then the field will be his again. 20But he might decide not to buy the field back. Or he might have sold the field to someone else. If so, then it shall not be given back to him again. 21It shall be freed in the Year of Jubilee. When it is, it shall belong to the Lord as a field devoted to him. And it shall be given to the priests.

22"A man might give to the Lord a field he has bought. And it might not be part of his family possession. 23If this is true, then the priest shall estimate the value until the Year of Jubilee. And he shall give that value to the Lord right away. 24In the Year of Jubilee the field shall be given back to the original owner from whom it was bought. 25All the valuations shall be stated in standard money.

26"You may not give to the Lord the firstborn of any ox or sheep. It is already his. 27But it might be the firstborn of an animal that cannot be sacrificed because it is not on the list of those acceptable to the Lord. If so, then the owner shall pay the priest's estimate of its worth plus 20 percent. Or if the owner does not buy it back, the priest may sell it to someone else. 28However, anything completely devoted to the Lord shall not be sold or bought back. This includes people, animals, or inherited fields. For they are most holy to the Lord. 29No one sentenced by the courts to die may pay a fine instead. He shall surely be put to death.

30"A tenth of the produce of the land, whether grain or fruit, is the Lord's. It is holy. 31If anyone wants to buy back this fruit or grain, he must add a fifth to its value. 32And the Lord owns every tenth animal of your herds and flocks and other tame animals, as they pass by for counting. 33The tenth given to the Lord shall not be chosen on the basis of whether it is good or bad. And there shall be no substitutions. For if there is any change made, then both the original and the substitution shall belong to the Lord. And they may not be bought back!"

34These are the commands the Lord gave to Moses for the people of Israel on Mount Sinai.

NUMBERS

The Book of Numbers is about a long trip. Perhaps you have taken a long trip. Were you gone a week? Perhaps you were gone two weeks!

This is a story about people who took a long trip. They were gone for 40 years! Their trip should have taken two years. But the people did not believe God when he said he would help them. So it took them much longer to get where they were going. Numbers will remind you to believe God when he says, "I will help you."

There were more than a million people on this trip. Moses was the leader. What kinds of things do you see on your trips? Perhaps you see motels and swimming pools. You see cars and gas stations. And you go to interesting places together.

But when you take this trip with Moses and his people, you will meet spies and giants. You will see a bunch of grapes so big that two men must carry it. You will see the ground open up and swallow people. And you will see the strangest medicine of all: a bronze snake. Be sure to travel here with Moses in Numbers.

The People Are Counted

1 The Lord gave these commands to Moses. At the time, Moses was in the Tabernacle in the camp of Israel. They were camped in the wilderness of Sinai. It was the 15th day of April. This was the second year since the Israelites had left Egypt.

2-15The Lord said, "Count all the men 20 years old and older who are able to go to war. Record their tribes and families. You and Aaron are to direct the project. These leaders from each tribe will help you:"

Tribe	Leader
Reuben	Elizur (son of Shedeur)
Simeon	Shelumiel (son of Zurishaddai)
Judah	Nahshon (son of Amminadab)
Issachar	Nethanel (son of Zuar)
Zebulun	Eliab (son of Helon)
Ephraim (son of Joseph)	Elishama (son of Ammihud)
Manasseh (son of Joseph)	Gamaliel (son of Pedahzur)
Benjamin	Abidan (son of Gideoni)
Dan	Ahiezer (son of Ammishaddai)
Asher	Pagiel (son of Ochran)
Gad	Eliasaph (son of Deuel)
Naphtali	Ahira (son of Enan)

¹⁶These were the tribal leaders chosen from among the people.

¹⁷⁻¹⁹ On the same day Moses and Aaron and the leaders called together all the men of Israel. They called all those who were 20 years old or older. They told them to come and register. Each man recorded his tribe and family. They did just as the Lord had told Moses. ²⁰⁻⁴⁶Here is the final count:

Tribe	Total
Reuben (the oldest son of Jacob)	46,500
Simeon	59,300
Gad	45,650
Judah	74,600
Issachar	54,400
Zebulun	57,400
Joseph: Ephraim (son of Joseph)	40,500
Joseph: Manasseh (son of Joseph)	32,200
Benjamin	35,400
Dan	62,700
Asher	41,500
Naphtali	53,400

Grand Total: 603,550

⁴⁷⁻⁴⁹This total does not include the Levites. For the Lord had said to Moses, "Do not include the tribe of Levi in the draft. Do not count them when you take the census. ⁵⁰For the Levites have been given the work connected with the Tabernacle. They shall move it from one place to the next. They are to live near it. ⁵¹Each time the Tabernacle is moved, the Levites are to take it down and set it up again. Anyone else who touches it shall be killed. ⁵²Each tribe of Israel shall have their own camping area with its own flag. ⁵³The Levites' tents shall be pitched around the Tabernacle. They will be like a wall between the people of Israel and God's wrath. They will protect them from his fierce anger against their sins."

⁵⁴All these things that the Lord told Moses were put into effect.

Where the Tribes Camped

2 The Lord gave these other commands to Moses and Aaron. "Each tribe shall have its own tent area. Each shall have its own flagpole and flag. The Tabernacle will be at the center of these tribal areas." ³⁻³¹These are the tribal areas.

Tribe:	Leader:	Location:	Census:
Judah	Nahshon (son of Amminadab)	East side of Tabernacle	74,600
Issachar	Nethanel (son of Zuar)	Next to Judah	54,400

Zebulun	Eliab (son of Helon)	Next to Issachar	57,400

So the total of all those on Judah's side of the camp was 186,400. These three tribes led the way whenever the Israelites traveled to a new campsite.

Reuben	Elizur (son of Shedeur)	South side of Tabernacle	46,500
Simeon	Shelumiel (son of Zurishaddai)	Next to Reuben	59,300
Gad	Eliasaph (son of Reuel)	Next to Simeon	45,650

So the total of the Reuben side of the camp was 151,450. These three tribes were next in line each time the Israelites traveled.

Next in the line of march was the Tabernacle. It was carried by the Levites. When traveling, each tribe stayed under its own flag. They kept apart from other tribes, just as they were in camp.

Ephraim	Elishama (son of Ammihud)	West side of Tabernacle	40,500
Manasseh	Gamaliel (son of Pedahzur)	Next to Ephraim	32,200
Benjamin	Abidan (son of Gideoni)	Next to Manasseh	35,400

So the total on the Ephraim side of the camp was 108,100. They were next in the line of march.

Dan	Ahiezer (son of Ammishaddai)	North side of Tabernacle	62,700
Asher	Pagiel (son of Ochran)	Next to Dan	41,500
Naphtali	Ahira (son of Enan)	Next to Asher	53,400

So the total on Dan's side of the camp was 157,600. They brought up the rear each time Israel traveled. ³²⁻³³So the armies of Israel totaled 603,550. This did not include the Levites. Moses did not count them, for this is what the Lord ordered. ³⁴So the people of Israel set up their camps, each tribe under its own flag. They camped in the places shown by the Lord to Moses.

What the Levites Did

3 When the Lord spoke to Moses on Mount Sinai, ²Aaron's sons were: Nadab (his oldest), Abihu, Eleazar, Ithamar. ³All were anointed as priests. They were set apart to serve at the Tabernacle. ⁴But Nadab and Abihu died before the Lord in the wilderness of Sinai. They were killed when they used unholy fire. They had no children, so this left

only Eleazar and Ithamar to help their father, Aaron.

⁵Then the Lord said to Moses, ⁶"Call the tribe of Levi. Give them to Aaron as his helpers. ⁷⁻⁹They shall do all that he tells them. They shall perform the holy duties at the Tabernacle. This shall be done on behalf of all the people of Israel. For they are given to him to represent all the people of Israel. They are in charge of all the furniture and must maintain the Tabernacle. ¹⁰However, only Aaron and his sons may carry out the duties of the priests. Anyone else who tries to take this office shall be killed."

¹¹⁻¹²And the Lord said to Moses, "I have chosen the Levites. They will take the place of all the oldest sons of the people of Israel. The Levites are mine ¹³in exchange for all the oldest sons. When I killed all the oldest sons of the Egyptians, I took for myself all the firstborn in Israel. The firstborn of both men and animals are mine! I am the Lord."

¹⁴⁻¹⁵The Lord now spoke again to Moses in the Sinai area. He told him, "Count the tribe of Levi. Record each person's clan. Count every male down to one month old." ¹⁶⁻²⁴So Moses did.

Levi's son	Levi's grandsons (clan names)	Census	Leader	Camp Location
Gershon	Libni Shimei	7,500	Elisaph (son of Lael)	West side of Tabernacle

²⁵⁻³⁰These two clans of Levites are to care for the Tabernacle. This includes its coverings, its entry drapes, and the drapes covering the fence around the courtyard. It also includes the screen at the entrance of the courtyard surrounding the Tabernacle, the altar, and all the ropes used to tie the Tabernacle together.

Levi's son	Levi's grandsons (clan names)	Census	Leader	Camp Location
Kohath	Amran Izhar Hebron Uzziel	8,600	Elizaphan (son of Uzziel)	South side of Tabernacle

³¹⁻³⁵These four clans of Levites are to care for the Ark, the table, the lampstand, and the altars. They also are to care for the various items used in the Tabernacle and for the veil. They must do any repairs that are needed on all these items. Eleazar, Aaron's son, shall be the chief manager over the leaders of the Levites. He shall have the special job of overseeing the Tabernacle.

Levi's son	Levi's grandsons (clan names)	Census	Leader	Camp Location
Merari	Mahli Mushi	6,200	Zuriel (son of Abihail)	North side of Tabernacle

³⁶⁻³⁷These two clans are to care for the frames of the Tabernacle building, the posts, and the bases for the posts. They are to maintain all of the equipment needed for their use. They also are in charge of the posts around the courtyard and their bases, pegs, and ropes.

³⁸The area east of the Tabernacle was reserved for the tents of Moses and of Aaron and his sons. They had the final responsibility for the Tabernacle on behalf of the people of Israel. If someone who was not a priest or Levite came into the Tabernacle, he would be killed.

³⁹So all the Levites were 22,000 males one month old and older. They were counted by Moses and Aaron at the command of the Lord.

Levites Take Firstborn Sons Place

⁴⁰Then the Lord said to Moses, "Now count all of the oldest sons in Israel. Include all who are one month old and older. Record them each by name. ⁴¹The Levites shall be mine. I am the Lord! They are to stand for all the oldest sons of Israel. And the Levites' cattle are mine. They are to stand for the firstborn cattle of the whole nation."

⁴²So Moses counted the oldest sons of the people of Israel. He did as the Lord had told him. ⁴³He found the total number of oldest sons one month old and older to be 22,273.

⁴⁴Now the Lord said to Moses, ⁴⁵"Give me the Levites instead of the oldest sons of the people of Israel. Give me the cattle of the Levites instead of the firstborn cattle of the people of Israel. Yes, the Levites shall be mine. I am the Lord. ⁴⁶You must buy back the 273 oldest sons in excess of the number of Levites. ⁴⁷⁻⁴⁸To do this, pay five dollars for each one to Aaron and his sons."

⁴⁹So Moses took redemption money for 273 of the firstborn sons of Israel. This number of sons was in excess of the number of Levites. All the other firstborn sons were already paid for. The Levites had been given to the Lord in their place. ⁵⁰The money collected came to a total of $1,365. ⁵¹And Moses gave it to Aaron and his sons as the Lord had told him.

Jobs for the Kohath Clan

4 Then the Lord said to Moses and Aaron, "Count the Kohath clan of the Levite tribe. ³You shall count all males from ages 30 to 50. Count all those who are able to work in the Tabernacle. ⁴These are their holy duties.

⁵"When the camp moves, Aaron and his sons shall enter the Tabernacle first. They shall take down the veil. They shall cover the Ark with it. ⁶Then they shall cover the veil with goatskin leather. They shall cover the goatskins with a blue cloth. And they shall place the carrying poles of the Ark in their rings.

⁷"Next they must spread a blue cloth over the table. This is the table where the Bread of the Presence is kept. They must place the dishes, spoons, bowls, cups, and the Bread upon the cloth. ⁸They shall spread a red cloth over that. Finally, they shall put a covering of goatskin leather on top of the red cloth. Then they shall insert the carrying poles into the table.

⁹"Next they must cover with a blue cloth the lampstand, the lamps, snuffers, trays, and the container of olive oil. ¹⁰This whole group of objects shall then be covered with goatskin leather. The bundle shall then be placed upon a carrying frame.

¹¹"They must then spread a blue cloth over the gold altar. They must cover it with a covering of goatskin leather. And they must put the carrying poles into the altar. ¹²All of the other utensils of the Tabernacle are to be wrapped in a blue cloth. Then they must be covered with goatskin leather, and placed on the carrying frame.

¹³"The ashes are to be taken from the altar. Then the altar shall be covered with a purple cloth. ¹⁴All of the altar utensils are to be placed upon the cloth. This includes the firepans, hooks, shovels, basins, and other containers. Then a cover of goatskin leather shall be spread over them. Finally, the carrying poles are to be put in place. ¹⁵Aaron and his sons shall finish packing the sanctuary and all the utensils. When they are done, the clan of Kohath shall come. They shall carry the units to wherever the camp is traveling. But they must not touch the holy items. If they do, they will die. This, then, is the holy work of the sons of Kohath.

¹⁶"Aaron's son Eleazar shall be in charge of the oil for the light. He shall also care for the sweet incense, the daily grain offering, and the anointing oil. In fact, his work shall be to manage the whole Tabernacle and all that is in it."

¹⁷⁻¹⁹Then the Lord said to Moses and Aaron, "Don't let the families of Kohath destroy themselves! This is what you must do so that they will not die when they carry the most holy things. Aaron and his sons shall go in with them. They shall point out what each is to carry. ²⁰Otherwise they must never enter the sanctuary for even a moment. If they do, they will look at the holy objects there and die."

Jobs for the Gershon Clan

²¹⁻²³And the Lord said to Moses, "Count the Gershonite clan of the tribe of Levi. Make a record of all the men between the ages of 30 and 50. Count all those who can do the holy work of the Tabernacle. ²⁴These shall be their duties:

²⁵"They shall carry the curtains of the Tabernacle and the Tabernacle itself with its coverings. This includes the goatskin leather roof, and the curtain for the Tabernacle door. ²⁶They are also to carry the drapes covering the courtyard fence, and the curtain across the entrance to the courtyard that surrounds the altar and the Tabernacle. They shall also carry the altar, the ropes, and all the accessories. Their job is to carry these items from one camp to another. ²⁷Aaron or any of his sons may give tasks to the Gershonites. ²⁸But the Gershon-

ites will be directly responsible to Aaron's son Ithamar.

Jobs for the Merari Clan

29"Now take a census of the Merari clan of the Levite tribe. Count all the men from 30 to 50 who are able to do the Tabernacle service. 30-31When the Tabernacle is moved, they are to carry the frames of the Tabernacle, the bars, and the bases. 32They must also carry the frames for the courtyard fence with their bases, pegs, and cords. They must carry all that is connected with their use and repair.

"Assign duties to each man by name. 33The Merari clan will also report to Aaron's son Ithamar."

Counting the Men Who Can Work at the Tabernacle

34So Moses and Aaron and the other leaders counted the Kohath clan. 35They counted all of the men 30 to 50 years of age. But they had to be able to do the work of the Tabernacle. 36The total number was 2,750. 37All this was done to carry out the Lord's commands to Moses. 38-41A similar census of the Gershon clan totaled 2,630. 42-45And the Merari clan numbered 3,200. 46-48Thus Moses and Aaron and the leaders of Israel counted the Levites. They counted all who were 30 to 50 years old. They had to be able to do the work of the Tabernacle. They had to transport it from camp to camp. The total number of Levites was 8,580. 49This census was taken in response to the Lord's command to Moses.

Lepers Must Leave Camp

5 These are more teachings from the Lord to Moses. "Tell the people of Israel that they must send all lepers away from the camp. All who have open sores, or who have been defiled by touching a dead person, must leave. 3This applies to men and women alike. Remove them so that they will not defile the camp. For I live there among you." 4These commands were put into effect.

Consequences of Stealing

5-6Then the Lord said to Moses, "Speak to the people of Israel. Tell them that when anyone sins against another person, he is sinning against the Lord. That person, whether man or woman, is guilty. 7He must confess his sin and make full repayment for what he has stolen. He must add 20 percent. And he must give it back to the person he took it from. 8But the person he wronged might be dead. And there may be no near relative to whom the payment can be made. If this is true, it must be given to the priest. And a lamb must also be given for atonement. 9-10When the people of Israel bring a gift to the Lord, it shall go to the priests."

The Test for an Unfaithful Wife

11-12And the Lord said to Moses, "Speak to the people of Israel. It might happen that a man's wife sleeps with another man. 13But there might be no proof. Maybe there were no witnesses. 14And the husband might be jealous and suspicious. 15If this is true, the man shall bring his wife to the priest. He shall bring an offering for her of a tenth of a bushel of barley meal. It shall be without oil or incense poured on it. This is a suspicion offering. It shall be used to bring out the truth. It will show whether or not she is guilty.

16"The priest shall bring her before the Lord. 17He shall take holy water in a clay jar. He shall mix into it dust from the floor of the Tabernacle. 18He shall untie her hair and put the suspicion offering in her hands. This will show whether or not her husband's suspicions are right. The priest shall stand before her holding the jar of bitter water that brings a curse. 19He shall require her to swear that she is innocent. Then he shall say to her, 'It may be true that no man has slept with you except your husband. If this is so, be free from the effects of this bitter water that causes the curse. 20But it may be that you have slept with another man. 21-22If this is true, then the Lord shall make you a curse among your people. He will make your leg rot away and your body swell.' And the woman shall be made to say, 'Yes, let it be so.' [23]Then the priest shall write these curses in a book. And he shall wash them off into the bitter water. [24]He shall have the woman to drink the water. If she is guilty, it shall become bitter within her.

[25]"Then the priest shall take the suspicion offering from the woman's hand. He shall wave it before the Lord and carry it to the altar. [26]He shall take a handful. It will be a memorial offering. He shall burn the handful upon the altar. Then he shall have the woman drink the water. [27]It might be that she is guilty. She may have been unfaithful to her husband. If this is so, the water will become bitter within her. Her body will swell and her leg will rot. And she shall be a curse among her people. [28]But she might be pure. She may not have slept with another man. If this is so, she shall be unharmed and will soon become pregnant.

[29]"This, then, is the law for dealing with a wayward wife. It is also for a husband who is suspicious of his wife. [30]It shall be used to show whether or not she has been unfaithful to him. The husband shall bring his wife before the Lord. And the priest shall follow these rules. [31]If she is guilty, her husband shall not be brought to trial for causing her disease. For she is the one responsible."

The Nazirite

6 The Lord gave Moses these other teachings for the people of Israel. "Either a man or a woman might take the special vow of a Nazirite. He might set himself apart to the Lord in a special way. [3-4]If he does this, he must not taste strong drink or wine. This is true during the whole time of his special devotion to the Lord. He must not even drink fresh wine, grape juice, grapes, or raisins! He may eat nothing that comes from grape vines. He cannot even eat the seeds or skins!

[5]"Throughout that time he must never cut his hair. For he is holy and set apart for the Lord. That is why he must let his hair grow.

[6-7]"And he may not go near any dead body during the whole time of his vow. He may not even touch the body of his father, mother, brother, or sister. For his promise of special devotion stays in effect. [8]And he is set apart for the Lord throughout that whole time. [9]He might be made unclean by having someone fall dead beside him. If this happens, then seven days later he shall shave his head. He will then be cleansed from his being in the presence of death. [10]The next day, the eighth day, he must take two turtledoves or two young pigeons. He must bring them to the priest at the door of the Tabernacle. [11]The priest shall offer one of the birds for a sin offering. The other shall be given for a burnt offering. This will make atonement for his defilement. He must then renew his vows that day. And he must let his hair begin to grow again. [12]The days of his vow that were fulfilled before his defilement no longer count. He must begin all over again with a new vow. And he must bring a male lamb a year old for a guilt offering.

[13]"When his vow to set himself apart to the Lord is ended, he must go to the door of the Tabernacle. [14]There he must offer a burnt sacrifice to the Lord. It must be a year-old lamb. It must have nothing wrong with it. He must also offer a sin offering, a yearling ewe lamb. It must have nothing wrong with it. He also must offer a peace offering. It shall be a ram without defect. [15]He must give a basket of bread made without yeast. He must offer pancakes made of fine flour mixed with olive oil. He also must bring unleavened wafers spread with oil. With all this, he must bring the usual grain and drink offerings. [16]The priest shall present these offerings before the Lord. First he shall give the sin offering and the burnt offering. [17]Then he shall offer the ram for a peace offering. With that he shall give the basket of bread made without yeast. And finally he shall give the grain offering along with the drink offering.

[18]"Then the Nazirite shall cut his long hair. His hair is the sign of his promise to set himself apart to the Lord. It shall be cut at the door of the Tabernacle. Then the hair shall be put in the fire

under the peace offering sacrifice. [19]After the man's head has been shaved, the priest shall take the roasted shoulder of the lamb. He shall also take one of the pancakes (made without yeast) and one of the wafers (also made without yeast). He shall put them all into the man's hands. [20]Then the priest shall wave it all back and forth before the Lord. This is done as a gesture of offering. All of it is a holy portion for the priest. So are the rib piece and shoulder that were waved before the Lord. After that the Nazirite may again drink wine. For now he is free from his vow.

[21]"These are the rules for a Nazirite. They include his sacrifices at the end of his time of special dedication. With these sacrifices he must bring any further offerings. He may have promised other offerings when he took his vow to become a Nazirite."

How to Bless the People

[22-23]Now the Lord said to Moses, "Speak to Aaron and his sons. Tell them that they are to give this special blessing to the people of Israel. [24-26]'May the Lord bless and protect you. May the Lord's face shine with joy because of you. May he be kind to you. May he show you his favor. May he give you his peace.' [27]This is how Aaron and his sons shall call down my blessings upon the people of Israel. And I myself will bless them."

Gifts for the Tabernacle

7 Moses poured oil on each part of the Tabernacle to make it holy. This included the altar and its utensils. He did this on the day he finished setting it up. [2]Then the leaders of Israel brought their gifts. These men were the chiefs of the tribes. They were the ones who had counted the people. [3]They brought six covered wagons. Each wagon was drawn by two oxen. A wagon came for every two leaders. Thus an ox was brought for each leader. They gave them to the Lord in front of the Tabernacle.

[4-5]"Take their gifts," the Lord told Moses. "And use these wagons for the work of the Tabernacle. Give them to the Levites for whatever needs they may have."

[6]So Moses gave the wagons and the oxen to the Levites. [7]Two wagons and four oxen were given to the Gershon clan for their use. [8]Four wagons and eight oxen were given to the Merari clan. This clan was led by Ithamar, Aaron's son. [9]None of the wagons or teams were given to the Kohath clan. They had to carry their part of the Tabernacle on their shoulders.

[10]The leaders also gave dedication gifts on the day the altar was anointed. They placed them before the altar. [11]The Lord said to Moses, "Let each of them bring his gift on a different day. They shall be for the dedication of the altar."

[12]So Nahshon, the son of Amminadab, brought his gift the first day. He was from the tribe of Judah. [13]He brought a silver platter that weighed three pounds. He also brought a silver bowl of about two pounds. Both were filled with grain offerings of fine flour mixed with oil. [14]He also brought a tiny gold box of incense. It weighed only about four ounces. [15]He brought a young bull, a ram, and a male yearling lamb as burnt offerings. [16]He offered a male goat for a sin offering. [17]For the peace offerings he gave two oxen. He also gave five rams, five male goats, and five male yearling lambs.

[18-23]The next day Nethanel, the son of Zuar, brought his gifts. He was the chief of the tribe of Issachar. His gifts were the same as the ones Nahshon had given the day before.

[24-29]On the third day Eliab, the son of Helon, came with his gifts. He was the chief of the tribe of Zebulun. He brought the same gifts as the others.

[30-35]On the fourth day the gifts were given by Elizur, son of Shedeur. He was the chief of the tribe of Reuben. He brought the same gifts as the others.

[36-41]On the fifth day came Shelumiel, the son of Zurishaddai. He was the chief of the tribe of Simeon. He came with the same gifts.

[42-47]The next day it was Eliasaph's turn, son of Deuel, chief of the tribe of

Gad. He, too, offered the same gifts and sacrifices.

48-53On the seventh day, Elishama, the son of Ammihud, brought his gifts. He was the chief of the tribe of Ephraim. He brought the same gifts as the others.

54-59Gamaliel, son of Pedahzur, came the eighth day with the same gifts. He was a prince of the tribe of Manasseh.

60-65On the ninth day it was Abidan the son of Gideoni, with his gifts. He was the chief of the tribe of Benjamin. He brought the same as those offered by the others.

66-71Ahiezer, the son of Ammishaddai, brought his gifts on the tenth day. He was the chief of the tribe of Dan. His gifts were the same as those given by the others.

72-77Pagiel, son of Ochran, brought his gifts on the eleventh day. He was the chief of the tribe of Asher. He brought the same gifts as the others.

78-83On the twelfth day came Ahira, son of Enan, with his offerings. He was chief of the tribe of Naphtali. His gifts were the same as those brought by the others.

84-86So, at the beginning of the day the altar was anointed. It was dedicated by these gifts from the chiefs of the tribes of Israel. Their combined offerings were as follows:

12 silver platters (each weighing
    about three pounds),
12 silver bowls (each weighing
    about two pounds, so the total
    weight of the silver was about 60
    pounds),
12 gold trays (the trays weighing
    about four ounces apiece, so the
    total weight of gold was about
    three pounds).

87For the burnt offerings they brought:

12 bulls, 12 rams,
12 yearling male goats (with the
    grain offerings that go with them).

For sin offerings they brought:

12 male goats.

88For the peace offerings they brought:

24 young bulls,
60 rams, 60 male goats,
60 male lambs one year old.

89Moses went into the Tabernacle to speak with God. And he heard the Voice speaking to him from above the place of mercy over the Ark. It came from between the statues of the two Guardian Angels.

Setting Up the Lamps

8 The Lord said to Moses, 2"Tell Aaron to light the seven lamps in the lampstand. When he does, he is to set them so that they will throw their light forward."

3So Aaron did this. 4The lampstand, with the flowers on the base and branches, was all made of beaten gold. It was made just as the Lord had shown Moses.

The Levites Are Dedicated

5-6Then the Lord said to Moses, "Now set apart the Levites from the other people of Israel. 7Do this by sprinkling water of cleansing upon them. Then have them shave their whole bodies. Tell them to wash their clothing and themselves. 8Have them bring a young bull and a grain offering of fine flour mingled with oil. They must also bring another young bull for a sin offering. 9Then bring the Levites to the door of the Tabernacle as all the people watch. 10There the leaders of the tribes shall lay their hands upon them. 11And Aaron, with a gesture of offering, shall give them to the Lord. They shall be a gift from the whole nation of Israel. The Levites shall stand in place of all the people in serving the Lord.

12"Next, the Levite leaders shall lay their hands upon the heads of the young bulls. They shall offer them before the Lord. One shall be given for a sin offering. The other shall be offered for a burnt offering. They shall make atonement for the Levites. 13Then the Levites are to be presented to Aaron and his sons. They will be like any other gift to the Lord. They will be given to the priests! 14In this way you shall dedicate the Levites from among the rest of the people of Israel. The Levites shall be mine. 15You shall set them apart as holy. And you shall present them in this way. Then they shall go in and out of the Tabernacle to do their work.

16"They are mine from among all the people of Israel. I have chosen them in place of all the firstborn children of the Israelites. I have taken the Levites to stand in their place. 17For all the firstborn among the people of Israel are mine. This includes both men and animals. I claimed them for myself the night I killed all the firstborn Egyptians. 18Yes, I have chosen the Levites in place of all the oldest sons of Israel. 19And I will give the Levites as a gift to Aaron and his sons. The Levites will carry out the holy duties of the people of Israel in the Tabernacle. They will offer the people's sacrifices. They will make atonement for them. There will be no plagues among the Israelites. But there would be, if the ordinary people went into the Tabernacle."

20So Moses and Aaron and all the people of Israel dedicated the Levites. They carefully followed the Lord's commands to Moses. 21The Levites made themselves pure. And they washed their clothes. Then Aaron gave them to the Lord in a gesture of offering. He then performed the rite of atonement over them to make them pure. 22After that they went into the Tabernacle to help Aaron and his sons. All was done just as the Lord had commanded Moses.

23-24The Lord also told Moses, "The Levites are to begin serving in the Tabernacle at the age of 25. They are to retire at the age of 50. 25-26After they retire they can help with light duties in the Tabernacle. But they will have no regular work."

The Passover Comes Again

9 The Lord gave the following teachings to Moses. He spoke to him while he and the rest of the Israelites were in the Sinai region. It was during the first month of the second year after leaving Egypt.

2-3"The people of Israel must celebrate the Passover every year on April 1. They shall begin their celebration in the evening. Be sure to follow all of my rules for this feast."

4-5So Moses announced that the Passover Feast would begin on the evening of April 1. He announced it there in the Sinai region, just as the Lord had commanded. 6-7But as it happened, some of the men had just attended a funeral. They were unclean because they had touched the dead. So they couldn't eat the Passover lamb that night. They came to Moses and Aaron and explained their problem. They protested because they could not give their sacrifice to the Lord at the proper time.

8Moses said he would ask the Lord about it. 9This was God's reply:

10"Some of the people of Israel might be unclean at Passover time. They might touch a dead body. This might happen now or in the future. Or they might be on a trip and cannot be there. If this happens, they may still celebrate the Passover. But they will do it one month later, 11on May 1. They will begin their celebration in the evening of that day. They are to eat the lamb at that time, with unleavened bread and bitter herbs. 12They must not leave any of it until the next morning. They must not break a bone of it. And they must follow all the regular rules for the Passover.

13"But someone may not be unclean. Or he may not be away on a trip. And he might still refuse to celebrate the Passover at the regular time. If he does this, he shall be expelled from the people of Israel. For he has refused to sacrifice to the Lord at the proper time. Thus he must bear his guilt. 14And a foreigner might live among you. He might want to celebrate the Passover to the Lord. If this is true, he shall follow all these same rules. There is one law for all."

The Pillar of Cloud and Fire

15On the day the Tabernacle was raised the Cloud covered it. That evening the Cloud changed to fire. It stayed that way throughout the night. 16It was always that way. The daytime Cloud changed to fire at night. 17When the Cloud lifted, the people of Israel moved on to wherever it stopped. Then they camped there. 18In this way they traveled at the command of the Lord. They always stopped where he told them to. Then they stayed there as long as the Cloud stayed. ¹⁹If it stayed a long time, then they stayed a long time. But if it stayed only a few days, then they stayed only a few days. For the Lord had told them to do this. ²⁰⁻²¹Sometimes the fire-cloud stayed only during the night and moved on the next morning. But day or night, when it moved, the people broke camp and followed. ²²The Cloud might stay above the Tabernacle two days, a month, or a year. It showed how long the people of Israel would stay. But as soon as it moved, they moved. ²³So it was that they camped or traveled at the command of the Lord. And whatever the Lord told Moses they should do, they did.

The Silver Trumpets

10 Now the Lord said to Moses, "Make two trumpets of beaten silver. They are to be used for calling the people to assemble. They shall also signal the breaking of camp. ³When both trumpets are blown, the people will know that they are to gather at the door of the Tabernacle. ⁴But if only one is blown, then only the chiefs of the tribes of Israel shall come to you.

⁵⁻⁷"One kind of trumpet blast shall be the call to assemble. Another trumpet blast shall be the signal to break camp and move onward. Listen for the travel signal. When it is blown, the tribes camped on the east side of the Tabernacle shall leave first. At the second signal, the tribes on the south shall go. ⁸Only the priests are allowed to blow the trumpets. This is a lasting rule to be followed from now on.

⁹"You will someday arrive in the Promised Land. There you will go to war against your enemies. At that time, God will hear you when you sound the alarm with these trumpets. He will save you from your enemies. ¹⁰Use the trumpets in times of gladness, too. Blow them at your yearly feasts. Blow them at the beginning of each month to rejoice over your burnt offerings and peace offerings. And God will remember his covenant with you. For I am the Lord, your God."

Moving Day for God's House

What would you think if people moved your church to another town? That's what the people of Israel did. But God's house at that time was a big tent. Sometimes it was called the Tabernacle. Here's how they moved it.

¹¹The Pillar of Cloud lifted from the Tabernacle on the 20th day of the second month. This was the second month of the second year since the people of Israel left Egypt. ¹²So the Israelites left the Sinai wilderness. They followed the Cloud until it stopped in the wilderness of Paran. ¹³This was their first trip after hearing the Lord's travel commands.

¹⁴At the head of the march was the tribe of Judah. They were grouped behind its flag. They were led by Nahshon, the son of Amminadab. ¹⁵Next came the tribe of Issachar. It was led by Nethanel, the son of Zuar. ¹⁶And with them came the tribe of Zebulun. They were led by Eliab, the son of Helon.

¹⁷The Tabernacle was taken down. The men of the Gershon and Merari were next in the line of march. These were clans of the tribe of Levi. They carried the Tabernacle upon their shoulders. ¹⁸Then came the flag of the camp of Reuben. Elizur the son of Shedeur was leading his people. ¹⁹Next was the tribe of Simeon. It was headed by Shelumiel,

the son of Zurishaddai. ²⁰They went with the tribe of Gad. Gad was led by Eliasaph, the son of Deuel.

²¹Next came the Kohathites. They carried the items from the inner sanctuary. The Tabernacle would already be put up in its new place by the time they got there. ²²Next in line was the tribe of Ephraim. It was put in groups behind its flag. Ephraim was led by Elishama, the son of Ammihud. ²³They traveled with the tribe of Manasseh. This tribe was led by Gamaliel the son of Pedahzur. ²⁴The tribe of Benjamin also went with them. This tribe was led by Abidan the son of Gideoni. ²⁵Last of all were the tribes headed by the flag of the tribe of Dan. Their leader was Ahiezer, the son of Ammishaddai. ²⁶The tribe of Asher went with them. They were led by Pagiel, the son of Ochran. ²⁷And the tribe of Naphtali went with them. They were led by Ahira, the son of Enan. ²⁸That was the order in which the tribes traveled.

²⁹One day Moses spoke to his brother-in-law, Hobab. He was the son of Jethro, the Midianite. Moses said, "At last we are on our way to the Promised Land. Come with us and we will do you good. For the Lord has given wonderful promises to Israel!"

³⁰But his brother-in-law replied, "No, I must go back to my own land and people."

³¹"Stay with us," Moses pleaded. "For you know the ways of the wilderness. You will be a great help to us. ³²If you come, you will share in all the good things the Lord does for us."

³³They traveled for three days after leaving Mount Sinai. The Ark was at the front of the column. It would show them the place to stop. ³⁴It was daytime when they left. The Cloud moved along ahead of them as they began their march. ³⁵As the Ark was carried forward, Moses cried out, "Arise, O Lord. Scatter your enemies. Let them flee before you." ³⁶And when the Ark was set down he said, "Return, O Lord, to the millions of Israel."

- *Remember:* Where were the Israelites when they moved? Where did they go? (10:12) Was this the first or second time they moved the Tabernacle? (10:13) Who gave the orders? Who told them how to move? (10:14) If you were there, wouldn't you have been afraid of leaving God behind?

- *Discover:* God does not stay in one place only. He goes with us everywhere.

- *Apply:* When you go to a new place, will you pray to God first? How do you know he will be in the new place as much as the old place?

- *What's next?* How does God help us when we have too much work? Read what God did to help Moses. See Numbers 11. ■

Someone to Help Moses

Have you ever had too much work to do? Moses did. This is what God did to help him. Look for that special gift that God gave each of Moses' new helpers.

11 The people were soon complaining about all their troubles. The Lord heard them. His anger flared out against them because of their complaints. And the fire of the Lord began killing those at the far end of the camp. ²They screamed to Moses for help. When he prayed for them the fire stopped. ³After that, the area was known as "The Place of Burning." For there the fire from the Lord burned among them.

⁴⁻⁵Then the Egyptians who had come with them began to long for the good things of Egypt. This added to the discontent of the people of Israel. They wept, "Oh, for a few bites of meat! Oh,

that we had some of the tasty fish we enjoyed so much in Egypt! Remember those cucumbers and melons, leeks, onions, and garlic? 6But now our strength is gone. Day after day we have to eat this manna!"

7The manna was the size of small seeds. It was whitish yellow in color. 8The people gathered it from the ground. They pounded it into flour. Then they boiled it and made cakes from it. The cakes tasted like pancakes fried in oil. 9The manna fell with the dew during the night.

10Moses heard all the families standing around their tent doors weeping. And the anger of the Lord grew hot. Moses also was very angry.

11Moses said to the Lord, "Why pick on me? Why did you give me the burden of a people like this? 12Are they *my* children? Am I their father? Is that why you gave me this job? Am I to nurse them along like babies until we get to the land you promised us? 13Where am I supposed to get meat for all these people? For they whine to me saying, 'Give us meat!' 14I can't carry this nation by myself! The load is far too heavy! 15If you are going to treat me like this, please kill me right now. It will be a kindness! Let me out of this impossible situation!"

16Then the Lord said to Moses, "Call before me 70 of the leaders of Israel. Bring them to the Tabernacle. They are to stand there with you. 17I will come down and talk with you there. And I will take of the Spirit which is on you and put it upon them also. They shall help you lead the people. That way you will not have to do the work alone.

18"Now tell the people to make themselves pure. For tomorrow they shall have meat to eat. Tell them, 'The Lord has heard your complaints. He knows what you left behind in Egypt. He is going to give you meat. You shall eat it, 19-20not for just a day or two. You shall eat it for more than five, 10 or even 20! For one whole month you will have meat. You will eat it until you vomit it from your noses. For you have rejected the Lord who is here among you. And you have wept for Egypt.'"

21But Moses said, "There are 600,000 men alone besides all the women and children. How can you promise them meat for a whole month? 22If we kill all our flocks and herds it won't be enough! We would have to catch every fish in the ocean to fulfill your promise!"

23Then the Lord said to Moses, "When did I become weak? Now you shall see whether my word comes true or not!"

24So Moses left the Tabernacle. He told the people what the Lord had said. Then he called the 70 elders to the Tabernacle. 25And the Lord came down in the Cloud. He talked there with Moses. And the Lord took from the Spirit that was upon Moses. He put it upon the 70 elders. The Spirit rested upon them. And they prophesied for some time.

26But two of the 70 were still in the camp. Their names were Eldad and Medad. When the Spirit rested upon them, they prophesied there. 27Some young men ran and told Moses what was happening. 28Joshua (the son of Nun), one of Moses' special helpers, protested. He said, "Sir, make them stop!"

29But Moses replied, "Are you jealous for my sake? I only wish that all of the Lord's people were prophets. I wish that the Lord would put his Spirit upon them all!" 30Then Moses came back to the camp with the elders of Israel.

31The Lord sent a wind that brought quail from the sea. The wind let the quail fall into the camp and all around it! As far as one could walk in a day in any direction, there were quail flying. They flew three or four feet above the ground. 32So the people caught and killed quail all that day. They kept going through the night and all the next day, too! The least anyone gathered was 100 bushels! Quail were spread out all around the camp. 33But as they began eating the meat, the anger of the Lord rose against the people. He killed large numbers of them with a plague. 34So the name of that place was called, "The Place of the Graves Caused by Lust." This was because they buried people there who had lusted for meat and for Egypt. 35From that place they went to Hazeroth. They stayed there awhile.

- *Remember:* What punishment did God send when the people started complaining? (11:1-3) What did the people want God to do then? (11:4) What kind of food did they eat when they lived in Egypt? (11:5) What kind of food did they eat now? (11:6-9) How did the Lord feel about the complaining? How did Moses feel? (11:10) What kind of helpers did the Lord give Moses? (11:16) What special gift did the Lord give them? (11:17,25) What meat did the Lord send? How did he punish the people with the meat? (11:31-33) What would you like to have told the people when they complained about their food?

- *Discover:* Grumbling and complaining won't solve any of our problems. In fact, it makes things worse. When we need help, we should ask God. This makes things better.

- Apply: What special help do you need today? Could God help you? Will you let him?

- *What's next?* A sister complains about her brother. Then she gets sick. You'll find why when you read Numbers 12. ■

Miriam Gets Leprosy

Have you ever said something mean about your brother or sister? Did anything happen? Perhaps your mother or father punished you. But look what happened to Miriam when she said something mean about her brother Moses! She got a terrible disease. This is the way it happened.

12 One day Miriam and Aaron criticized Moses because his wife was a Cushite woman. ²They said, "Has the Lord spoken only through Moses? Hasn't he spoken through us, too?"

But the Lord heard them. ³⁻⁴He called Moses, Aaron, and Miriam to the Tabernacle. "Come here, you three," he said. So they stood before the Lord. Now Moses was the most humble man on earth.

⁵Then the Lord came down in the Cloud. He stood at the door of the Tabernacle. "Aaron and Miriam, step forward," he commanded. And they did. ⁶And the Lord said to them, "Even with prophets, I usually speak by visions and dreams. ⁷⁻⁸But that is not how I speak with my servant Moses. He is completely at home in my house! With him I speak face to face! And he shall see the very form of God! Why then were you not afraid to criticize him?"

⁹The Lord became very angry with them. Then he went away. ¹⁰As the Cloud moved from above the Tabernacle, Miriam suddenly became white with leprosy. When Aaron saw what had happened, ¹¹he cried out to Moses. "Oh, sir, do not punish us for this sin," he said. "We were fools to do such a thing. ¹²Don't let her be as one dead. Don't let her be like one whose body is half rotted away at birth."

¹³And Moses cried out to the Lord, "Heal her, O God. I beg you!"

¹⁴And the Lord said to Moses, "If her father had but spit in her face she would be unclean seven days. Let her be sent from the camp for seven days. After that she can come back again."

¹⁵So Miriam was sent from the camp for seven days. The people waited until she was brought back in before they traveled again. ¹⁶After that they left Hazeroth. Then they camped in the wilderness of Paran.

- *Remember:* Why did Miriam and Aaron say something bad about Moses? (12:1-2) What happened to Miriam? (12:9) How did Miriam get healed? (12:13) Why do you think Miriam said what she did?

- *Discover:* We should not say mean things about God's helpers. When we do, we may also be saying mean things about God.

• *Apply:* Have you ever said something mean about your minister? Have you ever said something mean about your Sunday school teacher? Have you ever said something mean about your parents? Be careful! God is not pleased when we criticize people who are trying to help him.

• *What's next?* Did you know that God ordered some spies to go into a country? He did! Read about these spies in Numbers 13. ■

The Twelve Spies

Have you ever heard of the Promised Land? That's the place where Moses' people were going. God promised that they could have it. That's why it was called the Promised Land. But there was one problem. People already lived there. What were they like? How many were there? Would they leave? God sent some spies into this land to find out.

13 The Lord now told Moses, ²"Send spies into the land of Canaan. This is the land I am giving to Israel. Send one leader from each tribe."

³⁻¹⁵The Israelites were camped in the wilderness of Paran at the time. Moses did as the Lord had said. He sent these 12 tribal leaders:

Shammua, son of Zaccur, from the tribe of Reuben;

Shaphat, son of Hori, from the tribe of Simeon;

Caleb, son of Jephunneh, from the tribe of Judah;

Igal, son of Joseph, from the tribe of Issachar;

Hoshea, son of Nun, from the half-tribe of Ephraim;

Palti, son of Raphu, from the tribe of Benjamin;

Gaddiel, son of Sodi, from the tribe of Zebulun;

Gaddi, son of Susi, from the tribe of Joseph (actually, the half-tribe of Manasseh);

Ammiel, son of Gemalli, from the tribe of Dan;

Sethur, son of Michael, from the tribe of Asher;

Nahbi, son of Vophsi, from the tribe of Naphtali;

Geuel, son of Machi, from the tribe of Gad.

[16]It was at this time that Moses changed Hoshea's name to Joshua.

[17]Moses sent them out with these commands. "Go north into the hill country of the Negeb," he said. [18]"See what the land is like. See also what the people are like who live there. Notice if they are strong or weak. See if they are many or few. [19]See if the land is fertile or not. Take note of what cities there are. See if they are just villages or if they have walls around them. [20]Take note if the land is rich or poor. See also if there are many trees. Don't be afraid. And bring back some samples of the crops you see." The first of the grapes were being harvested at that time.

[21]So they spied out the land. They went all the way from the wilderness of Zin to Rehob near Hamath. [22]Going north, they passed first through the Negeb and came to Hebron. There they saw the Ahimanites, Sheshites, and Talmites. These are all families descended from Anak. By the way, Hebron was very ancient. It was founded seven years before Tanis in Egypt. [23]Then they came to what is now known as the Valley of Eshcol. There they cut down a cluster of grapes. It was so large that it took two of them to carry it! They carried it on a pole between them. They also took some samples of the pomegranates and figs. [24]The Israelites named the valley "Eshcol" at that time (meaning "Cluster"). They did this because of the cluster of grapes they found!

[25]After 40 days of exploring they came back from their trip. [26]They made their report to Moses, Aaron, and all the people of Israel. The Israelites were waiting in the wilderness of Paran at Kadesh. The spies showed them the fruit they had brought with them.

[27]This was their report: "We came to the land you sent us to see. It is indeed a wonderful country! It is a land 'flowing with milk and honey.' Here [is] some fruit we have brought as proof. [But] the peo-

ple living there are powerful. Their cities have walls around them, and they are very large. What's more, we saw Anakim giants there! [29]The Amalekites live in the south. In the hill country there are the Hittites, Jebusites, and Amorites. Down along the coast of the Mediterranean Sea and in the Jordan River valley live the Canaanites."

[30]But Caleb reassured the people as they stood before Moses. "Let us go up at once and possess it!" he said. "For we are well able to conquer it!"

[31]"Not against people as strong as they are!" the other spies said. "They would crush us!"

[32]So most of the spies were afraid. "The land is full of warriors," they said. "The people are too strong. [33]We saw some of the Anakim there. They came from the ancient race of giants. We felt like grasshoppers beside them. They were so tall!"

- *Remember:* Who gave orders for the spies to go into the land? (13:1) How many spies were there? (13:3) What were the spies to do? (13:17-20) What three kinds of fruit did they bring back? (13:23) Who wanted to go into the land and take it? (13:30) Who did not want to go in? Why? (13:31-33) What would you have wanted to do if you had gone with the spies? Why?

- *Discover:* There are many good things God wants to give us. But sometimes we have to work hard for them. Why? Because we wouldn't appreciate them or take care of them if we didn't work for them.

- *Apply:* God gives us good things to eat. But what do we have to do to get them? He gives us a house to live in. How do we get it? Make a list of some of the good things God gives when we work to get them. Make a list of some of the good things your parents and teachers give when you work to get them.

- *What's next?* Suppose you could not move into a new home for 40 years. How would you feel? That's what you will read about in Numbers 14. ◼

Forty Years in the Wilderness

Back in Egypt the people had houses. They weren't very good, but they were houses. In the wilderness the people lived in tents. But soon they would be moving into new houses in a new land. Then some bad news came. They couldn't move into their new houses for another 40 years. They couldn't move into their new land. They would have to stay in tents in the wilderness. Here's how that happened.

14 Then all the people began weeping aloud. They carried on all night. ²Their voices rose in a great chorus of complaint against Moses and Aaron.

"We wish we had died in Egypt," they wailed. "We even wish we might die here in the wilderness. ³Even that would be better than being taken into this country ahead of us. The Lord will kill us there. Our wives and little ones will become slaves. Let's get out of here. Let's go back to Egypt!" ⁴The idea swept the camp. "Let's elect a leader to take us back to Egypt!" they shouted.

No one is bigger than God

When the Lord is with you, don't be afraid of people who might hurt you.

Numbers 14:9

---

⁵Then Moses and Aaron fell face down on the ground before the people of Israel. ⁶Two of the spies ripped their clothing. Their names were Joshua (the son of Nun) and Caleb (the son of Jephunneh). ⁷They said to all the people, "It is a wonderful country ahead. ⁸And the Lord loves us. He will bring us safely into the land and give it to us. It is *very* fertile, a land 'flowing with milk and honey'! ⁹Oh, do not rebel against the Lord. When the Lord is with you, don't be afraid of people who might hurt you. Don't be afraid of the people of the land. For they are but bread for us to eat!"

¹⁰⁻¹¹But the Israelites only talked of stoning them. Then the glory of the Lord showed itself. The Lord said to Moses, "How long will these people despise me? Will they *never* believe even after all the miracles I have done among them? ¹²I will disown them. I will

destroy them with a plague. I will make your family into a nation far greater than they are!"

¹³"But what will the Egyptians think when they hear about it?" Moses pleaded with the Lord. "They know full well the power you showed in saving your people. ¹⁴They have told this to the people of this land. They are well aware that you are with Israel. They know that you talk with us face to face. They see the pillar of cloud and fire standing above us. And they know that you lead and protect us day and night. ¹⁵Now you might kill all your people. But if you do, the nations that have heard your fame will say, ¹⁶'The Lord had to kill them. He did this because he wasn't able to take care of them in the wilderness. He wasn't strong enough. He wasn't able to bring them into the land he swore he would give them.'

¹⁷⁻¹⁸"Oh, please, show the great power of your patience. Forgive our sins. Show us your steadfast love. Forgive us, even though you have said that you don't let sin go unpunished. Forgive us, even though you punish the father's sin in the children to the third and fourth generation. ¹⁹Oh, I plead with you, pardon the sins of this people. Do it because of your wonderful, steadfast love. Forgive them just as you have forgiven them ever since they left Egypt."

²⁰⁻²¹Then the Lord said, "All right. I will forgive them as you have asked. But I make this promise. It is true that all the earth shall be filled with the glory of the Lord. ²²It is just as true that you will ___ nishment. All these men ___ And all of them saw the ___ both in Egypt and in the ___ n times they refused to ___ bey me. ²³Because of this, ___ n shall even see the land

I promised to their ancestors. ²⁴But my servant Caleb is a different kind of man. He has obeyed me fully. I will bring him into the land he went into as a spy. His descendants shall have their full share in it. ²⁵The Amalekites and the Canaanites live in the valleys. Since you are afraid of them, tomorrow you must turn back into the wilderness. You will travel in the direction of the Red Sea."

²⁶⁻²⁷Then the Lord spoke to Moses and to Aaron. He said, "How long will this wicked nation complain about me? For I have heard all that they have been saying. ²⁸Tell them, 'The Lord promises to do to you what you feared. ²⁹⁻³⁰You will all die here in this wilderness! Not a single one of you 20 years old and older shall enter the Promised Land. This includes all those who have complained against me. Only Caleb (son of Jephunneh) and Joshua (son of Nun) will be allowed to enter it.

³¹"'You said your children would become slaves of the people of the land. Well, instead I will bring *them* safely into the land. They shall inherit what you have rejected. ³²But as for you, your dead bodies shall fall in this wilderness. ³³You must wander in the desert like nomads for 40 years. In this way you will pay for your lack of faith. You will wander until the last of you lies dead in the desert.

³⁴⁻³⁵"'The spies were in the land for 40 days. Thus, you must wander in the wilderness for 40 years. You will wander a year for each day. You will bear the burden of your sins. I will teach you what it means to reject me. I, the Lord, have spoken. Every one of you who has turned against me shall die here in this wilderness.'"

³⁶⁻³⁸Then the 10 faithless spies were struck dead before the Lord. They were punished for causing the people to rebel against the Lord. They had caused the people to be afraid. Of all the spies, only Joshua and Caleb stayed alive. ³⁹What sorrow there was in the camp when Moses told God's words to the people!

⁴⁰They were up early the next morning. They started toward the Promised Land.

"Here we are!" they said. "We know that we have sinned. But now we are ready to go on into the land the Lord has promised us."

⁴¹But Moses said, "It's too late. Now you are disobeying the Lord's orders to go back to the wilderness. ⁴²Don't go ahead with your plan. If you do, you will be crushed by your enemies. For the Lord is not with you. ⁴³Don't you remember? The Amalekites and the Canaanites are there! You have left the Lord. Now he will leave you."

⁴⁴But they went ahead into the hill country. They did this even though neither the Ark nor Moses left the camp. ⁴⁵Then the Amalekites and the Canaanites who lived in the hills came down and attacked them. They chased the Israelites to Hormah.

- *Remember:* What did most of the spies tell the people? (13:32-33) How did the people feel about this? (14:1-3) Where did they want to go? (14:4) How did God punish these people? Who could go into the land? Who could not go into the land? (14:29-30) How long would the people have to stay in the wilderness? (14:34-35) Which spies do you think were right? Why?

- *Discover:* Don't turn against God when he helps you get something special.

- *Apply:* What are some special things God gives you? What other special things do you think he wants to give you? Will you let him do it?

- *What's next?* A big crack opens in the ground. It swallows some people who turn against the Lord. You'll read about this in Numbers 16. ∎

More Rules about Offerings

15 The Lord spoke to Moses. He told him to give these teachings to the people of Israel. "Someday your children will live in the land I am going to give them. ³⁻⁴At this time, they may choose to please the Lord. They might want to offer him a burnt offering or any other offering by fire. When they do this, their sacrifice must be an animal from their flocks of sheep and goats. It may also be from their herds of cattle. Each sacrifice

THE EXODUS AND 40 YEARS IN THE WILDERNESS

The people of Israel were slaves in Egypt. They had been there 400 years. It must have seemed that God had forgotten them. But he hadn't. God had plans for them in Canaan. He would lead them there and would make them a great nation.

Why didn't the people of Israel go straight from Egypt to Canaan? God knew they were not ready to fight the enemies along that route. For 40 years he would lead them through the wilderness where he would help them become an army. At Mount Sinai, God would give them his laws. There he would show them how to make his house, the Tabernacle. The Israelites could not become a great nation without God's laws and God's house.

Sometimes it may seem that the way we are going is the hard way. But if God is leading us, we are going the right way. God's way is always the right way!

EGYPT

GOSHEN

Nile River

MEDITERRANEAN
SEA

LAND OF
CANAAN
(ISRAEL)

KADESH-
BARNEA

WILDERNESS
OF
SIHN

ELIM

MOUNT SINAI

REPHIDIM

RED
SEA

LORENZ

must be given with a grain offering. This is true whether it is an ordinary sacrifice or a sacrifice to fulfill a vow. It is also true of free-will offerings or special sacrifices at the yearly feasts. If a lamb is being sacrificed, use three quarts of fine flour. Mix it with three pints of oil. ⁵Add to this three pints of wine for a drink offering.

⁶"The sacrifice might be a ram. If so, use six quarts of fine flour. Mix it with four pints of oil. ⁷Add to this four pints of wine for a drink offering. This will be a sacrifice that is pleasing to the Lord.

⁸⁻⁹"The sacrifice might be a young bull. If so, then the grain offering with it must be nine quarts of fine flour. This must be mixed with three quarts of oil. ¹⁰Add to this three quarts of wine for the drink offering. This shall be offered by fire as a pleasing fragrance to the Lord.

¹¹⁻¹²"These are the rules for what is to be given with each bull, ram, lamb, or young goat that is sacrificed. ¹³⁻¹⁴These rules apply to native-born Israelites. They also apply to foreigners living among you. These rules are for all who want to please the Lord with sacrifices offered by fire. ¹⁵⁻¹⁶The same law is valid for all, native-born or foreigner. This shall be true for all time. All are the same before the Lord. Yes, one law for all!"

¹⁷⁻¹⁸The Lord also said to Moses at this time, "Speak to the people of Israel. Tell them that they will arrive in the land that I am going to give them. ¹⁹⁻²¹When they do, they must give the Lord a sample of each year's new crops. They must do this by making a loaf. This loaf must be made of coarse flour. The flour must be taken from the first grain that is cut each year. The loaf must be waved back and forth before the altar. This is a way of giving it to the Lord. It is a yearly offering from your threshing floor. This rule must be followed from now on.

²²"By mistake you or those who come after you might fail to carry out all of these rules. You might forget some of these rules the Lord has given over the years through Moses. ²³⁻²⁴If this should happen, and the people know their sin, they must offer one young bull. It must be given for a burnt offering. It will be a pleasant odor before the Lord. It must be

offered along with the usual grain offering and drink offering. One male goat shall also be given for a sin offering. ²⁵And the priest shall make atonement for all of the people of Israel. And they shall be forgiven. For though they sinned, they have atoned for it. They are forgiven through their sacrifice made by fire before the Lord, and by their sin offering. ²⁶All the people shall be forgiven. This includes the foreigners living among them. For all the people are involved in such sin and its forgiveness.

²⁷"The error might be made by just one person. If so, then he shall sacrifice a one-year-old female goat for a sin offering. ²⁸The priest shall make atonement for him before the Lord. Then he shall be forgiven. ²⁹This same law applies to foreigners who are living among you.

³⁰"But someone might sin on purpose. If he does, he is mocking the Lord. He shall be cut off from his people. This is true whether he is a native Israelite or a foreigner. ³¹For he has despised the command of the Lord. He has chosen to disobey his law. Therefore, he must be killed. He must die in his sin."

Punishment for Breaking the Sabbath

³²While the people of Israel were in the wilderness, one of them was caught gathering wood on the Sabbath day. ³³He was taken before Moses and Aaron and the other judges. ³⁴They held him until they could find out the Lord's will for him.

³⁵Then the Lord said to Moses, "The man must die. All the people shall stone him to death outside the camp." ³⁶So they took him outside the camp. There they killed him as the Lord had told them to.

Tassels for Clothes

³⁷⁻³⁸The Lord said to Moses, "Speak to the people of Israel. Tell them to make tassels for the hems of their clothes. This is a lasting rule from now on. Tell them to attach the tassels to their clothes with a blue cord. ³⁹The purpose of this rule is to remind you of the commands of the

Lord. Each time you notice the tassels you will think of God's laws. They will remind you to obey his laws instead of following your own desires. You must not go your own ways, as you used to do in serving other gods. ⁴⁰The tassels will remind you to be holy to your God. ⁴¹For I am the Lord your God who brought you out of the land of Egypt. Yes, I am the Lord, your God."

Korah Rebels

Have you ever heard of a rebel? A rebel doesn't like things the way they are. He wants to change them. Sometimes he wants to change everything now. He can't wait! That's the way it was with Korah, Moses' cousin. Korah teamed up with some rascals named Dathan, Abiram, and On. Then other leaders joined them. Soon 250 leaders rebelled against Moses and Aaron. "We don't want you to lead us anymore," they told Moses. What would you do if you were Moses? This is what Moses did.

16 One day Korah, Dathan, Abiram, and On turned against Moses. Korah was the son of Izhar, grandson of Kohath, a descendant of Levi. Dathan and Abiram were the sons of Eliab. And On was the son of Peleth. All three were from the tribe of Reuben. ²They decided to rebel against Moses. Two hundred and fifty popular leaders joined them. All of them were members of the Council.

³They went to Moses and Aaron. "You have gone too far!" they said. "You are no better than anyone else. Everyone in Israel has been chosen of the Lord. And he is with all of us. What right do you have to be our only leader? What right do you have to claim that we must obey you? What right do you have to act as though you were greater than us? Are we not all people of the Lord?"

⁴When Moses heard what they were saying, he fell face down on the ground. ⁵Then he spoke to Korah and to those who were with him. He said, "In the morning the Lord will show you who are his. He will show you who is holy. He will prove to you whom he has chosen as his priest. ⁶⁻⁷Do this tomorrow. You and all those with you take censers and light them. Put incense in them before the Lord. Then we will find out whom the Lord has chosen. You sons of Levi have gone too far!"

⁸⁻⁹Then Moses spoke again to Korah. "Listen, you Levites," he said. "The God of Israel has chosen you from among all the people of Israel. You have been chosen to be near to the Lord as you work in his Tabernacle. You have been chosen to stand before the people to minister to them. Is that not enough for you? ¹⁰Is it nothing to you that he has given this task to only you Levites? And now are you demanding the priesthood also? ¹¹⁻¹²That is what you are really after! That is why you are revolting against the Lord. And what has Aaron done? Why are you not happy with him?" Then Moses called Dathan and Abiram (the sons of Eliab). But they refused to come.

¹³"Is it a small thing?" they mocked. "Is it a small thing that you brought us out of lovely Egypt? Is it a small thing to kill us here in this wilderness? Is it a small thing that now you want to make yourself our king? ¹⁴What's more, you haven't brought us into the wonderful country you promised. You haven't given us fields and vineyards. Whom are you trying to fool? We refuse to come."

¹⁵Then Moses was very angry and said to the Lord, "Do not accept their

sacrifices! I have never stolen so much as a donkey from them. I have not hurt one of them."

¹⁶And Moses said to Korah, "Come here tomorrow before the Lord. Come with all your friends. Aaron will be here too. ¹⁷Be sure to bring your censers with incense on them. Bring a censer for each man, 250 in all. Aaron will also be here with his."

¹⁸So they did. They came with their censers. They lit them and placed the incense on them. And they stood at the door of the Tabernacle with Moses and Aaron. ¹⁹Meanwhile, Korah had stirred up the whole nation against Moses and Aaron. They all came to watch. Then the glory of the Lord appeared to all the people. ²⁰The Lord said to Moses and Aaron, ²¹"Get away from these people. That way I can destroy them right away."

²²But Moses and Aaron fell face down on the ground before the Lord. "O God, the God of all mankind," they pleaded. "Must you be angry with all the people when one man sins?"

²³⁻²⁴And the Lord said to Moses, "Then tell the people to get away from the tents of Korah, Dathan, and Abiram."

²⁵So Moses rushed over to the tents of Dathan and Abiram. He was followed closely by the 250 Israelite leaders. ²⁶"Quick!" he told the people. "Get away from the tents of these wicked men. Don't touch anything that belongs to them. If you do, you will be included in their sins. And you will be destroyed with them."

²⁷So all the people stood back from the tents of Korah, Dathan, and Abiram. And Dathan and Abiram came out. They stood at the doors of their tents. Their wives and sons and little ones stood with them.

²⁸And Moses said, "By this you shall know that the Lord has sent me. He has told me to do all these things that I have done. I have not done them on my own. ²⁹These men might die a natural death. But if they do, then the Lord has not sent me. ³⁰But the Lord might do a miracle. He might open up the ground and swallow them and all that belongs to them.

And they might go down alive into Sheol. If this happens then you will know that these men have despised the Lord."

³¹He had hardly finished speaking when the ground suddenly split open beneath the rebels. ³²A great crack swallowed them up. It swallowed their tents and families. It swallowed their friends who were standing with them. It swallowed all that they owned. ³³So they went down alive into Sheol. The earth closed upon them, and they died. ³⁴All of the people of Israel fled at their screams. They feared that the earth would swallow them too. ³⁵Then fire came from the Lord. It burned up the 250 men who were offering incense.

³⁶⁻³⁷And the Lord said to Moses, "Speak to Eleazar the son of Aaron the priest. Tell him to pull those censers from the fire. They are holy and set apart for the Lord. He must also scatter the burning incense ³⁸from the censers of these men. They have sinned at the cost of their lives. He shall then beat the metal into a sheet as a covering for the altar. For these censers are holy because they were used before the Lord. And the altar sheet shall be a reminder to the people of Israel."

³⁹So Eleazar the priest took the 250 bronze censers. He beat them out into a sheet of metal to cover the altar. ⁴⁰It was to be a reminder to the people of Israel. It would remind them that no one who was not a descendant of Aaron could come before the Lord to burn incense. If he did, the same thing would happen to him as happened to Korah and his friends. Thus the Lord's directions to Moses were carried out.

⁴¹But the next morning all the people complained again against Moses and Aaron. They said, "You have killed the Lord's people."

⁴²Soon a great, sullen mob formed. Then, as they looked toward the Tabernacle, the Cloud appeared. And the awesome glory of the Lord was seen. ⁴³⁻⁴⁴Moses and Aaron came and stood at the door of the Tabernacle. The Lord said to Moses,

⁴⁵"Get away from these people. Then

I will destroy them." But Moses and Aaron fell face down on the earth before the Lord.

⁴⁶And Moses said to Aaron, "Quick, take a censer. Place fire in it from the altar. Lay incense on it. Then carry it quickly among the people and make atonement for them. For God's anger has gone out among them. The plague has already begun."

⁴⁷Aaron did as Moses told him to. He ran among the people, for the plague had indeed already begun. He put on the incense and made atonement for them. ⁴⁸He stood between the living and the dead. And the plague was stopped. ⁴⁹But not before 14,700 people had died. These dead were in addition to those who had died the day before with Korah. ⁵⁰Then Aaron returned to Moses at the door of the Tabernacle. And so the plague was stopped.

● *Remember:* What did the rebels say to Moses and Aaron? (16:3) What did Moses do first? (16:4) Whose job did Korah want? (16:8-12) How did God show that he had sent Moses? (16:30-33) Who could offer incense to God? (16:40) How would you have felt if you had been Moses? Read some of the things Korah said. How do they show you that he really didn't care about God?

● *Discover:* When we rebel against God and his leaders, we can get into bad trouble.

● *Apply:* Have you ever thought you could do something better than God? Think again! God knows what is best.

● *What's next?* You've seen blossoms and fruit on a fruit tree, haven't you? But have you ever seen these on a wooden stick? You will when you read Numbers 17. ∎

A Rod Like a Fruit Tree

In the spring a tree has blossoms on it. Then later fruit appears. But you never see an old walking stick blooming like a tree, do you? And you never see an old walking stick with fruit on it. This happened one day to Aaron's rod, a walking stick that he carried.

17 Then the Lord said to Moses, "Speak to the people of Israel. Tell them that each of their tribal chiefs is to bring you a wooden rod. It must have his name written upon it. Aaron's name is to be on the rod of the tribe of Levi. ⁴Put these rods in the inner room of the Tabernacle where I meet with you. Put them in front of the Ark. ⁵I will use these rods to show you the man I have chosen. Buds will grow on his rod! Then at last this complaining against you will stop!"

⁶So Moses told the people what to do. Each of the 12 chiefs (including Aaron) brought him a rod. ⁷He put them before the Lord in the inner room of the Tabernacle. ⁸Moses went in the next day. And he found that Aaron's rod, from the tribe of Levi, had budded! It had blossoms on it! And it had ripe almonds hanging from it!

⁹When Moses brought them out to show the others, they stared in disbelief! Then each man except Aaron claimed his rod. ¹⁰The Lord told Moses to place Aaron's rod beside the Ark. It would remind the people of this rebellion. People might still complain about Aaron's authority. But if they did, he was to bring the rod out. He was to show it to the people again to remind them of this event. This would save the people from future disasters. ¹¹So Moses did as the Lord told him.

¹²⁻¹³But the people of Israel only grumbled the more. "We are as good as dead," they whined. "Everyone who even comes close to the Tabernacle dies. Must we all perish?"

- *Remember:* God wanted some men to bring their walking sticks to Moses. Who were they? What were they to write on these rods? (17:1-3) How would God show whom he had chosen to be priest? (17:4-5) What happened to Aaron's rod? (17:7-8) What would you have said if you had been one of these men?

- *Discover:* God can do anything. That's one way we know he is God.

- *Apply:* The next time you pray, remember that God can do anything. That doesn't mean he will do anything. He will do only what he knows is best.

- *What's next?* Moses was a great man, wasn't he? You wouldn't think Moses would disobey God. But he did. You can read about it in Numbers 20:1-13. ■

The Priests' and Levites' Duties

18 The Lord now spoke to Aaron. "You and your sons and your family are responsible for any sins done against the sanctuary," he said. "You will be held responsible for any errors in your priestly work.

2-3"Your kinsmen, the tribe of Levi, are your helpers. But only you and your sons may perform the holy duties in the Tabernacle itself. The Levites must be careful not to touch any of the holy items or the altar. If they do, I will destroy both them and you. 4No one who is not from the tribe of Levi shall help you in any way. 5Don't forget that only the priests are to perform the holy duties. Only they may work within the sanctuary and at the altar. If you follow these rules, the anger of God will never again fall upon any of you. The people of Israel will not be punished for breaking this law. 6I say it again. The Levites are your helpers for the work of the Tabernacle. They are a gift to you from the Lord. 7But you and your sons, the priests, shall handle all the holy service. This includes the altar and all that is within the veil. The priesthood is your special gift of service. Anyone else who tries to perform these duties shall die."

8The Lord gave these further commands to Aaron. "Take all the gifts which are brought to the Lord by the people. I have given them to the priests," he said. "All these gifts given to the Lord belong to you and your sons. They are to be given by waving them before the altar. This is a law for all time. 9The grain offerings, the sin offerings, and the guilt offerings are yours. They are yours, except for the sample given to the Lord by burning upon the altar. All these are most holy offerings. 10They are to be eaten only in a most holy place. They may be eaten only by males. 11All other gifts given to me by waving them before the altar are for you. They may be eaten by your families, sons and daughters alike. All the members of your families may eat these. But those who are unclean may not eat of these.

12"Yours also are the first-of-the-harvest gifts the people bring as offerings to the Lord. These include the best of the olive oil, wine, grain, 13and every other crop. Your families may eat these unless they are unclean at the time. 14-15So all that is dedicated to the Lord shall be yours. This includes the firstborn sons of the people of Israel. It also includes the firstborn of their animals. 16However, you may never take the firstborn sons. Neither may you take the firstborn of any animals that I do not allow for food. Instead, a payment of 2½ dollars must be made for each firstborn child. It is to be brought when he is one month old.

17"However, the firstborn of cows, sheep, or goats may not be bought back. They must be sacrificed to the Lord. Their blood is to be sprinkled upon the altar. Their fat shall be burned as a fire offering. It is very pleasant to the Lord. 18The meat of these animals shall be yours. This includes the breast and right thigh. These are given to the Lord by waving them before the altar. 19Yes, I have given to you all of these 'wave offerings.' They are brought by the people of Israel to the Lord. They are for you and your families as food. This is a lasting contract between the Lord and you. It will also extend to your descendants.

20"You priests may own no property. You may not have any other income. For I am all that you need.

21"As for the tribe of Levi, your relatives, they shall be paid for their service. They shall be paid with the tithes from the whole land of Israel.

22"From now on, Israelites other than the priests and Levites shall not enter the sanctuary. If they do, they shall be judged guilty and die. 23Only the Levites shall do the work there. And they shall be guilty if they fail. This is a lasting law among you. None of the Levites shall own property in Israel. 24For the people's tithes shall belong to the Levites. They shall be offered to the Lord by waving them before the altar. These tithes are their inheritance. Because of this, they have no need for property."

25-26The Lord also said to Moses, "Speak to the Levites. Tell them to give to the Lord a tenth of the tithes they receive. They shall give a tithe of the tithe. It shall be given to the Lord by waving it before the altar. 27The Lord will consider this as your first-of-the-harvest offering to him of grain and wine. It will be as though it were from your own property. 28-29This tithe of the tithe shall be taken from the best part of the tithes you receive as the Lord's portion. Then it shall be given to Aaron the priest. 30It shall be credited to you just as though it were from your own threshing floor and wine press. 31Aaron and his sons and their families may eat it in their homes or anywhere they wish. It is their pay for their service in the Tabernacle. 32You Levites will not be held guilty for taking the Lord's tithes. But you must give the best tenth to the priests. Beware that you do not treat the holy gifts of the people of Israel as if they were common. If you do, you shall die."

What to Do When Defiled

19 The Lord said to Moses and Aaron, "Here are some more of my laws.

"Tell the people of Israel to bring you a red heifer. It must have nothing wrong with it. It must be one that has never been yoked. Give her to Eleazar the priest. He shall take her outside the camp. There someone shall kill her as he watches. 4Eleazar shall take some of her blood upon his finger. He shall sprinkle it seven times toward the front of the Tabernacle. 5Then someone shall burn the heifer as he watches. Her hide, meat, blood, and dung must all be burned. 6Eleazar shall take cedar wood and hyssop branches and red thread. He shall throw them into the burning pile.

7"Then he must wash his clothes. He must take a bath. After that he shall go back to the camp. He will be unclean until the evening. 8The one who burns the animal must also wash his clothes. He must take a bath. He too shall be unclean until evening. 9Then someone who is not unclean shall gather up the ashes of the heifer. He shall place them in some purified place outside the camp. There they shall be kept for the people of Israel. They shall be a source of water for the cleansing ceremonies. This water will be used for taking away sin. 10And

the one who gathers up the ashes of the heifer must wash his clothes. He will be unclean until evening. This is a lasting law for the benefit of the people of Israel. It will also benefit any foreigners living among them.

11"Anyone who touches a dead human body shall be unclean for seven days. 12He shall make himself pure with special water on the third and seventh days. This water has been run through the ashes of the red heifer. After doing this, he will be pure. But it might happen that he does not do this on the third day. If he doesn't, he will be unclean even after the seventh day. 13A person might touch a dead person. If he does not purify himself in the right way, he has defiled the Tabernacle of the Lord. And he shall be expelled from Israel. If the cleansing water was not sprinkled upon him, the defilement continues.

14"A man might die in a tent. If he does, these are the rules you must follow. Everyone who enters the tent shall be unclean for seven days. This includes those who were in the tent at the time of the death. 15Any container in the tent without a lid over it is unclean.

16"Someone out in a field might touch the dead body of a person who has been killed in battle. Or he might touch someone who has died in another way. Or he might even touch a bone or a grave. If any of these things happen, he shall be unclean for seven days. 17To become purified again, take ashes from the red heifer sin offering. Add these to spring water in a kettle. 18Then a person who is not unclean shall take hyssop branches. He shall dip them into the water. Then he shall sprinkle the water upon the tent. He shall sprinkle it upon all the pots and pans in the tent. He shall also sprinkle anyone who has been defiled by being in the tent. This also purifies anyone who has touched a bone. It purifies a person who has touched someone who has been killed or is otherwise dead. It also purifies anyone who has touched a grave. 19This shall take place on the third and seventh days. Then the unclean person must wash his clothes. He must take a bath. And that evening he will be out from under the defilement.

20"But anyone who is unclean and doesn't purify himself shall be expelled. For he has defiled the sanctuary of the Lord. The water to cleanse him has not been sprinkled upon him. Thus he is still unclean. 21This is a law for all time. The man who sprinkles the water must afterwards wash his clothes. Anyone touching the water shall be unclean until evening. 22And anything an unclean person touches shall be unclean until evening."

Moses Disobeys God

Do you always obey? Most of us try. But sometimes we disobey. Even a godly man like Moses disobeyed. When we disobey we may get scolded. But Moses got a much worse punishment when he disobeyed God.

20 The people of Israel came to the wilderness of Zin in April. They camped at Kadesh. It was there that Miriam died and was buried. 2There was not enough water to drink at that place. As a result, the people again rebelled against Moses and Aaron. A great mob formed. 3They held a protest meeting. "We wish that we had died with our dear brothers the Lord killed!" they shouted at Moses. 4"You have brought us into this wilderness on purpose. You brought us here to get rid of us. You even want all our flocks and herds to die. 5Why did you ever make us leave Egypt and bring us here to this evil place? Where is the fertile land of wonderful crops? Where are the figs, vines, and pomegranates you told us about? Why, there isn't even water enough to drink!"

6Moses and Aaron turned away. They went to the door of the Tabernacle. There they fell face down before the Lord. And the glory of the Lord appeared to them.

7And he said to Moses, 8"Get Aaron's rod. Then you and Aaron must call the people. As they watch, speak to that rock over there. Tell it to pour out its water! You will give them water from a rock. There will be enough for all the people and all their cattle!"

9So Moses did as he was told. He took the rod from the place where it was kept before the Lord. 10Then Moses and Aaron called the people to come and gather at the rock. He said to them,

"Listen, you rebels! Must we bring you water from this rock?"

11Then Moses lifted the rod. He struck the rock twice. And water gushed out. The people and their cattle drank.

12But the Lord said to Moses and Aaron, "You did not believe me. And you did not present me as holy in the eyes of the people of Israel. Therefore, you shall not bring them into the land I have promised them!"

13This place was named Meribah. The name means "Rebel Waters." It was named this because the people of Israel fought there against the Lord. And there the Lord showed himself to be holy before them.

- *Remember:* Why did the people rebel against Moses and Aaron? (20:2) Where did Moses and Aaron go for help? (20:6) What did the Lord tell Moses to do to the rock? (20:8) How did Moses disobey? What did he say? What did he do? (20:10-11) How did God punish Moses for disobeying him? (20:12) Why should people get punished for doing wrong things?

- *Discover:* Disobedience brings punishment. We may wish then that we had obeyed.

- *Apply:* Have you been punished lately for disobeying? Was it worth it? Or did you wish you had obeyed? Disobeying hurts you. It hurts your parents. It also hurts God. Remember that the next time you think of disobeying.

• *What's next?* Have you ever asked someone to help you? Did they say no? Here are some people who said no when the Israelites needed help. They even sent an army to say no! Read about this in Numbers 20:14-22. ■

Edom Says No

"Please let us travel through your land," the Israelites said. "No!" the Edomites told them. The Israelites were descendants of Jacob. The Edomites were descendants of Jacob's brother, Esau. You would think the Edomites would be friends. You would think they would say yes. But they didn't. They said no. They even sent an army to say no! Do you think the Israelites will fight? Read on and you will see what happened.

¹⁴While Moses was at Kadesh he sent messengers to the king of Edom. "We are the descendants of your brother, Israel," he said. "You know our sad history. ¹⁵You know how our ancestors went down to visit Egypt. You know how they stayed there a long time. You have heard how they became slaves of the Egyptians. ¹⁶But when we cried to the Lord he heard us. He sent an Angel who brought us out of Egypt. Now we are here at Kadesh. We are camped on the borders of your land. ¹⁷Please let us pass through your country. We will be careful not to go through your planted fields. We will not pass through your vineyards. We won't even drink water from your wells. We will stay on the main road. We will not leave it until we have crossed your border on the other side."

¹⁸But the king of Edom said, "Stay out! You might try to enter my land. But if you do, I will meet you with an army!"

¹⁹"But, sir," protested the Israelite messengers. "We will stay on the main road. We will not even drink your water. If we do, we will pay whatever you ask for it. We only want to pass through. We want nothing else."

²⁰But the king of Edom did not change his mind. "Stay out!" he warned. He got his army ready. He marched to his border with a great force. ²¹⁻²²Edom did not let Israel pass through their country. So Israel turned back. They went from Kadesh to Mount Hor.

• *Remember:* What did Moses ask the king of Edom? (20:17) What did the king tell Moses he would do? (20:18) What did the king do then to keep the Israelites out of his land? (20:20) Did Israel fight? What did they do? (20:21-22) Do you think the king of Edom should have helped the Israelites? Why? Do you think the Israelites should have fought them? Why not?

• *Discover:* There is a time to fight for what is right. And there is a time to walk away without fighting. A wise person knows which is best.

• *Apply:* Pretend that you really need help. You ask a friend and he says no. What would you like to do to that friend? What should you do?

• *What's next?* Do you think a bronze snake could help you get well? Read how a bronze snake helped many Israelites get well. See Numbers 21:4-9. ■

Aaron Dies

²³The Lord spoke to Moses and Aaron at the border of the land of Edom. ²⁴"The time has come for Aaron to die," he said. "Aaron shall not enter the land I have given the people of Israel. The two of you did not fully obey my commands about the water at Meribah. ²⁵Now take Aaron and his son Eleazar. Lead them up onto Mount Hor. ²⁶There you shall take off Aaron's priestly clothing. Put them on Eleazar his son. Aaron shall die there."

²⁷So Moses did as the Lord told him. The three of them went up together into

Mount Hor. All the people watched as they went. 28The three of them reached the top. There Moses took the priestly clothing from Aaron. He put it on his son Eleazar. Aaron died on the top of the mountain. Moses and Eleazar came back. 29The people were told of Aaron's death. They mourned for him for 30 days.

Israelites Defeat King of Arad

21 The king of Arad heard that the Israelites were coming. They were taking the same route as the spies did

before. So he got his army ready. Then he attacked Israel. He took some of the men as prisoners. 2Then the people of Israel made a promise to the Lord. They said, "You are able to help us conquer the king of Arad. If you help us, we will destroy all the cities of this area." 3The Lord listened to them and defeated the Canaanites. The Israelites completely destroyed them and their cities. The name of the region was thereafter called Hormah (meaning "Completely Destroyed").

The Bronze Snake

When you get sick you probably take medicine to get well. Have you ever taken antibiotics? Moses' people did not have medicine like that. So what could they do when snakes bit them? The Lord sent a strange medicine. It was a bronze snake. Here is how it helped the people get well.

4Then the people of Israel went back to Mount Hor. There they turned southward along the road to the Red Sea. They did this to go around the land of Edom. The people were very discouraged. 5They began to complain against God and against Moses. "Why have you brought us out of Egypt to die here in the wilderness?" they asked. "There is nothing to eat here. There is nothing to drink either. We hate this terrible manna."

6So the Lord sent deadly snakes among them to punish them. Many of them were bitten and they died.

7Then the people came to Moses. They cried out, "We have sinned. We have spoken against the Lord and against you. Pray to him to take away the snakes." So Moses prayed for the people.

8Then the Lord told him, "Make a bronze copy of one of these snakes. Put it at the top of a pole. Anyone who is bitten shall live if he simply looks at it!"

9So Moses made the bronze snake. Whenever anyone who had been bitten looked at it, he got better!

• Remember: Why did the people complain again? (21:5) How did God punish them? (21:6) What strong medicine did

God prescribe to help the people get well? (21:8) Did it work? (21:9) If you had been there, would you have looked at the bronze snake?

• Discover: We should listen to God, even when his advice sounds strange.

• Apply: God tells us in the Bible what he wants. Sometimes what he wants seems strange. Jesus said, "Love your enemies." Did he make a mistake when he said that? God never makes a mistake. Listen to him.

• What's next? "Curse these people," a king told a prophet. The prophet didn't want to do it. But the king offered him lots of money. Now would he do it? You'll find out in Numbers 22. ■

On to Moab

10Israel went next to Oboth and camped there. 11Then they went on to Iyeabarim, in the wilderness. This was a short distance east of Moab. 12From there they traveled to the valley of the brook Zared. There they set up camp. 13Then they moved to the far side of the Arnon River, near the borders of the Amorites. The Arnon River is the boundary line between the Moabites and the

Amorites. [14]This fact is mentioned in *The Book of the Wars of the Lord*. There it mentions the valley of the Arnon River and the city of Waheb. [15]It states that they lie between the Amorites and the people of Moab.

[16]Then Israel traveled to Beer. This name means "A Well." This is the place where the Lord told Moses, "Call the people. I will give them water." [17-18]What happened is described in this song the people sang:

> Spring up, O well!
> Sing of the water!
> This is a well
> The leaders dug.
> It was hollowed
> With their staves
> And shovels.

Then they left the desert. They went on through Mattanah, [19]Nahaliel, and Bamoth. [20]Then they came to the valley in the plateau of Moab. This looks over the desert with Mount Pisgah in the distance.

The Israelites Defeat King Sihon

[21]Israel now sent messengers to King Sihon of the Amorites.

[22]"Let us travel through your land," they requested. "We will not leave the road until we have passed beyond your borders. We won't trample your fields. We won't touch your vineyards. We won't drink your water."

[23]But King Sihon refused. Instead he called out his army. He attacked Israel in the wilderness, battling them at Jahaz. [24]But Israel destroyed them. They took their land from the Arnon River to the Jabbok River. They went as far as the borders of the Ammonites. But they were stopped there by the rugged terrain.

[25-26]So Israel captured all the cities of the Amorites and lived in them. This included the city of Heshbon. This had been King Sihon's capital. [27-30]The ancient poets had referred to King Sihon in this poem:

> Come to Heshbon,
> King Sihon's capital,
> For a fire has flamed forth
> And devoured
> The city of Ar in Moab,
> On the heights of the Arnon River.
> Woe to Moab!
> You are finished,
> O people of Chemosh.
> Your sons have fled,
> And your daughters are captured
> By King Sihon of the Amorites.
> He has destroyed
> The little children
> And the men and women
> As far as Dibon, Nophah, and
>   Medeba.

The Israelites Defeat King Og

[31-32]While Israel was there in the Amorite country, Moses sent out spies. They looked over the Jazer area. He then followed up with an armed attack. He captured all of the towns. Thus, he drove out the Amorites. [33]They next turned their attention to the city of Bashan. But King Og of Bashan met them with his army at Edrei. [34]The Lord told Moses not to fear. He told him that the enemy was already conquered! "The same thing will happen to King Og as happened to King Sihon at Heshbon," the Lord assured him. [35]And sure enough, Israel was victorious. They killed King Og, his sons, and his subjects. Not a single survivor was still alive. And Israel took over the land.

King Balak Offers Balaam Money

Will a prophet do something he knows is wrong? Will he do it for lots of money? King Balak thought the prophet Balaam would. So he offered him lots of money to curse Israel. Here's what Balaam did.

22 The people of Israel now traveled to the plains of Moab. They camped east of the Jordan River across from Jericho. ²⁻³King Balak of Moab (the son of Zippor) knew how many Israelites there were. He also learned what they had done to the Amorites. As a result, he and his people were terrified. ⁴They quickly met with the leaders of Midian.

"This mob will eat us like an ox eats grass," they said.

So King Balak ⁵⁻⁶sent messengers to Balaam (son of Beor). He was living in his native land of Pethor. This was near the Euphrates River. He begged Balaam to come and help him.

"A vast number of people has come from Egypt. They cover the face of the earth. And they are headed toward me!" he explained with fear. "Please come.

Curse them for me. That way I will be able to drive them out of my land. For I know what great blessings fall on those whom you bless. I also know that those whom you curse are doomed."

⁷The messengers he sent were some of the top leaders of Moab and Midian. They went to Balaam with money in hand. They urgently explained to him what Balak wanted.

⁸"Stay here tonight," Balaam said. "I'll tell you in the morning what the Lord wants me to say." So they did.

⁹That night God came to Balaam and asked him, "Who are these men?"

¹⁰"They have come from King Balak of Moab," he replied. ¹¹"The king says that a vast number of people from Egypt has come to his border. He wants me to come at once and curse them. He

hopes then that he can defeat them in battle."

¹²"Don't do it!" God told him. "You are not to curse them. For I have blessed them!"

¹³The next morning Balaam told the men, "Go on home! The Lord won't let me do it."

¹⁴So King Balak's messengers went back without him. They told the king what Balaam had said. ¹⁵Balak tried again. This time he sent a larger number of messengers than the former group. ¹⁶⁻¹⁷They came to Balaam with this message:

"King Balak pleads with you to come. He promises you great honors plus any payment you ask. Name your own figure! Only come and curse these people for us."

¹⁸But Balaam replied, "Even if he gave me a palace filled with silver and gold, I could do nothing against the command of the Lord my God. ¹⁹But, stay here tonight. I will find out if the Lord will add any words to what he said before."

²⁰That night God told Balaam, "You may get up and go with these men. But be sure to say only what I tell you to."

²¹So the next morning he saddled his donkey and started off with them. ²²⁻²³But God was angry about Balaam's eager attitude. So he sent an angel to stand in the road to kill him. Balaam and two servants were riding along. Then Balaam's donkey saw the angel of the Lord. He was standing in the road with a drawn sword. The donkey bolted off the road into a field. But Balaam beat her back onto the road. ²⁴Now the angel of the Lord stood at a narrow place. It was a place where the road went between two vineyard walls. ²⁵The donkey saw him standing there. So she squirmed past by pressing against the wall. She crushed Balaam's foot in the process. So he beat her again. ²⁶Then the angel of the Lord moved farther down the road.

He stood in a place so narrow that the donkey couldn't get by at all.

27So she lay down in the road! In a great fit of temper Balaam beat her again with his staff.

28Then the Lord caused the donkey to speak! "What have I done that deserves your beating me these three times?" she asked.

29"Because you have made me look like a fool!" Balaam shouted. "I wish I had a sword with me. If I did, I would kill you."

30"Have I ever done this before?" the donkey asked.

"No," he said.

31Then the Lord opened Balaam's eyes. He saw the angel standing in the roadway with drawn sword. He fell flat on the ground before him.

32"Why did you beat your donkey those three times?" the angel asked. "I have come to stop you because you are headed for doom. 33Three times the donkey saw me. But she shied away from me. If she had not, I would have killed you by now and spared her."

34Then Balaam confessed, "I have sinned. I didn't know you were there. I will go back home if you don't want me to go on."

35But the angel told him, "Go with the men. But say only what I tell you to say." So Balaam went on with them. 36King Balak heard that Balaam was on the way. So he left his city. He went out to meet him at the Arnon River. This was at the border of his land.

37"Why did you delay so long?" he asked Balaam. "Didn't you believe me when I said I would give you great honors?"

38Balaam replied, "I have come. But I can only say what God tells me to say. And that is what I shall speak." 39Balaam went with the king to Kiriathhuzoth. 40There King Balak sacrificed oxen and sheep. He also gave animals to Balaam and the messengers for their sacrifices. 41The next morning Balak took Balaam to the top of Mount Bamoth-baal. From there he could see the people of Israel spread out before him.

• *Remember:* Where was Balak king? (22:2) Why did Balak want Balaam to curse Israel? What did he think it would help him do? (22:5-6) Why was Balaam angry at his donkey? (22:22-27) What did his donkey say to him? (22:28-30) How do you know that Balaam was doing something wrong? (22:34) Balaam would not say anything unless someone special told him what to say. Who was that person? (22:38)

• *Discover:* You should never disobey God, even for the best reward.

• *Apply:* Something looks like fun. But if you do it, you will disobey God. Why should you not do it? What can you do to avoid this temptation?

• *What's next?* A king says, "Do it." God says, "Don't do it." Who is more important? Read in Numbers 23–24 what Balaam did when he had this choice. ■

Who Will Balaam Obey?

"Curse Israel!" King Balak told Balaam. "Don't curse Israel!" God told Balaam. What would you do if you were Balaam? If you obey the king, he can make you rich. If you disobey him, he can cut off your head. This is what Balaam did.

23 Balaam said to the king, "Build seven altars here. Prepare seven young bulls and seven rams for sacrifice."

2Balak did what he told him to do. A young bull and a ram were sacrificed on each altar.

3-4Then Balaam said to the king, "Stand here by your burnt offerings. I will see if the Lord will meet me. Then I will tell you what he says to me." So he went up to a barren height. And God met him there. Balaam told the Lord, "I have prepared seven altars. I have sacri-

ficed a young bull and a ram on each."
⁵Then the Lord gave Balaam a message for King Balak.

⁶When Balaam came back, the king was standing beside the burnt offerings. All the princes of Moab were with him. ⁷⁻¹⁰This was Balaam's message:

"King Balak, king of Moab, has
    brought me
From the land of Aram,
From the eastern mountains.
'Come,' he told me, 'curse Jacob for
    me!
Let your anger rise on Israel.'
But how can I curse
What God has not cursed?
How can I denounce
A people God has not denounced?
I see them from the cliff tops,
I watch them from the hills.
They live alone,
And prefer to stay distinct
From every other nation.
They are as numerous as dust!
They are beyond counting.
If only I could die as happy as an
    Israelite!
Oh, that my end might be like
    theirs!"

¹¹"What have you done to me?" yelled King Balak. "I told you to curse these people. But you have blessed them!"

¹²But Balaam replied, "Can I say anything except what the Lord tells me to?"

¹³Then Balak told him, "Come with me to another place. There you will see only a portion of the nation of Israel. Curse at least that many!"

¹⁴So King Balak took Balaam into the fields of Zophim at the top of Mount Pisgah. He built seven altars there. Then he offered up a young bull and a ram on each altar.

¹⁵Then Balaam said to the king, "Stand here by your burnt offering. I will go to meet the Lord." ¹⁶The Lord met Balaam. And he told him what to say. ¹⁷So he went back to the king and the princes of Moab. They were standing beside their burnt offerings.

"What has the Lord said?" the king asked eagerly.

¹⁸⁻²⁴And he replied,

"Rise up, Balak, and hear:
Listen to me, you son of Zippor.
God is not a man, that he should
    lie.
He doesn't change his mind like
    humans do.
Has he ever promised
Without doing what he said?
Look! I have received a command
    to bless them.
For God has blessed them,
And I cannot reverse it!
He has not seen sin in Jacob.
He will not trouble Israel!
The Lord their God is with them.
He is their king!
God has brought them out of Egypt.
Israel has the strength of a wild ox.
No curse can be placed on Jacob,
And no magic shall be done against
    him.
For now it shall be said of Israel,
'What wonders God has done for
    them!'
These people rise up as a lion.
They shall not lie down
Until they have eaten what they
    capture
And have drunk the blood of the
    slain!"

²⁵"If you aren't going to curse them, at least don't *bless* them!" the king exclaimed to Balaam.

²⁶But Balaam replied, "Didn't I tell you that I must say whatever the Lord tells me to?"

²⁷Then the king said to Balaam, "I will take you to yet another place. Perhaps it will please God to let you curse them from there."

²⁸So King Balak took Balaam to the top of Mount Peor. This mountain overlooked the desert. ²⁹Balaam again told the king to build seven altars. He also told him to prepare seven young bulls and seven rams for the sacrifice. ³⁰The king did as Balaam said. He offered a young bull and ram on every altar.

24 Balaam knew by now that the Lord planned to bless Israel. So he didn't even go to meet the Lord as he had earlier. Instead, he went at once and looked out toward the camp of Israel.

2The camp stretched away across the plains, divided by tribes.

Then the Spirit of God came upon him. 3-9And he spoke this prophecy about them:

"Balaam the son of Beor says,
The man whose eyes are open says,
'I have listened to the word of God,
I have seen what God Almighty
    showed me.
I fell, and my eyes were opened:
Oh, the joys awaiting Israel,
Joys in the homes of Jacob.
I see them spread before me as
    green valleys,
And fruitful gardens by the riverside.
They are as aloes planted by the
    Lord himself.
They are as cedar trees beside the
    waters.
They shall be blessed with an abun-
    dance of water,
And they shall live in many places.
Their king will be greater than Agag.
Their kingdom is exalted.
God has brought them from Egypt.
Israel has the strength of a wild ox,
And shall eat up the nations that
    oppose him.
He shall break their bones in pieces,
And shall shoot them with many ar-
    rows.
Israel sleeps as a lion or a lioness.
Who dares arouse him?
Blessed is everyone who blesses
    you, O Israel,
And curses shall fall upon everyone
    who curses you.'"

10King Balak was filled with rage by now. He struck his hands together in anger and disgust. Then he shouted, "I called you to curse my enemies. Instead you have blessed them three times. 11Get out of here! Go back home! I had planned to promote you to great honor. But the Lord has kept you from it!"

12Balaam replied, "I told your messengers 13that you might give me a palace filled with silver and gold. But even so, I could not go beyond the words of the Lord. I could not say a word of my own. I said that I would say only what the Lord says! 14Yes, now I shall go back to my own people. But first, let me tell you what the Israelites are going to do to your people!"

15-19So he spoke this prophecy to him:

"Balaam the son of Beor is the man
Whose eyes are open!
He hears the words of God
And has knowledge from the Most
    High.
He sees what Almighty God has
    shown him.
He fell, and his eyes were opened:
I see in the future of Israel,
Far down the distant trail,
That there shall come a star from
    Jacob!
This ruler of Israel
Shall smite the people of Moab,
And destroy the sons of Sheth.
Israel shall possess all Edom and
    Seir.
They shall overcome their enemies.
Jacob shall arise in power
And shall destroy many cities."

20Then Balaam looked over at the homes of the people of Amalek. And he prophesied:

"Amalek was the first of the nations,
But its destiny is destruction!"

21-22Then he looked over at the Kenites:

"Yes, you are strongly situated,
Your nest is set in the rocks!
But the Kenites shall be destroyed.
And the mighty army of the king of
    Assyria shall deport you from
    this land!"

23-24He concluded his prophecies by saying:

"Alas, who can live when God does
    this?
Ships shall come from the coasts of
    Cyprus,
And shall oppress both Eber and
    Assyria.
They too must be destroyed."

25So Balaam and Balak went back to their homes.

● *Remember:* Who gave orders to build seven altars, the prophet or the king? (23:1) What did the king tell Balaam to do? What did Balaam do? (23:11) Why do you think Balaam was tempted to do what the king wanted?

- *Discover:* It is better to obey God than to obey a king.

- *Apply:* Why is God even more important than a king? How long will a king help you? How long will God help you?

- *What's next?* The people of Israel get a new leader. Who is he? Read about him in Numbers 27:12-23. ■

The Israelites Worship Baal

25 At this time, Israel was camped at Acacia. Some of the young men began going to wild parties with the local Moabite girls. ²These girls also invited them to attend the sacrifices to their gods. Soon the men were bowing down and worshiping the idols. ³Before long all Israel was joining freely in the worship of Baal. This was a god of Moab. The anger of the Lord became hot against his people.

⁴He gave the following command to Moses:

"Kill all the tribal leaders of Israel. Hang them up before the Lord in broad daylight. That way his fierce anger will turn away from the people."

⁵So Moses ordered the judges to kill all who had worshiped Baal.

⁶But one of the Israelite men insolently brought a Midianite girl into the camp. He did this right before the eyes of Moses and all the people. In fact, he did it just as they were weeping at the door of the Tabernacle. ⁷⁻⁸Phinehas saw this. He was the son of Eleazar and the grandson of Aaron the priest. He jumped up and grabbed a spear. Then he rushed after the man into his tent, where he had taken the girl. He thrust the spear all the way through the man's body. It went through him and into the girl's stomach. So the plague was stopped. ⁹But only after 24,000 people had already died.

¹⁰⁻¹¹Then the Lord said to Moses, "Phinehas has turned away my anger. For he was angry with my anger. He would not tolerate the worship of any God but me. So I have stopped destroying all Israel as I had intended. ¹²⁻¹³Now because of what he has done his descen-

dants shall be priests forever. He has great zeal for his God. And he has made atonement for the people of Israel by what he did."

¹⁴The name of the man who was killed with the Midianite girl was Zimri. He was the son of Salu, a leader of the tribe of Simeon. ¹⁵The girl's name was Cozbi. She was a daughter of Zur, a Midianite prince.

¹⁶⁻¹⁷Then the Lord said to Moses, "Destroy the Midianites. ¹⁸For they are destroying you with their wiles. They are causing you to worship Baal. They are leading you astray. This is true, as you have just seen in the death of Cozbi."

The People Are Counted Again

26 After the plague had ended, The Lord spoke to Moses and to Eleazar (son of Aaron the priest). ²He said, "Count all the men of Israel who are 20 years old or older. Find out how many of each tribe and clan are able to go to war."

³⁻⁴So Moses and Eleazar gave the leaders of Israel instructions for counting the people. The whole nation was camped in the plains of Moab. They were beside the Jordan River, across from Jericho. Here are the results of the census:

⁵⁻¹¹*The tribe of Reuben:* 43,730.

Reuben was Israel's oldest son. In this tribe were the following clans. They were named after Reuben's sons.

The Hanochites were named after their ancestor Hanoch.

The Palluites were named after their ancestor Pallu. In the subclan of Eliab were the families of Nemuel, Abiram, and Dathan. Eliab was one of the sons of Pallu. This Dathan and Abiram went with Korah and turned against Moses and Aaron. They challenged the very authority of God! But the earth opened and swallowed them. And 250 men were destroyed by fire from the Lord that day. This was a warning to the whole nation.

The Hezronites were named after their ancestor Hezron.

The Carmites were named after their ancestor Carmi.

¹²⁻¹⁴*The tribe of Simeon:* 22,200.

In this tribe were the following clans. These were all founded by Simeon's sons.

The Nemuelites were named after their ancestor Nemuel.

The Jaminites were named after their ancestor Jamin.

The Jachinites were named after their ancestor Jachin.

The Zerahites were named after their ancestor Zerah.

The Shaulites were named after their ancestor Shaul.

15-18*The tribe of Gad:* 40,500.

In this tribe were the following clans. They were founded by the sons of Gad.

The Zephonites were named after their ancestor Zephon.

The Haggites were named after their ancestor Haggi.

The Shunites were named after their ancestor Shuni.

The Oznites were named after their ancestor Ozni.

The Erites were named after their ancestor Eri.

The Arodites were named after their ancestor Arod.

The Arelites were named after their ancestor Areli.

19-22*The tribe of Judah:* 76,500.

In this tribe were the following clans. They were named after the sons of Judah. But this did not include Er and Onan. They died in the land of Canaan.

The Shelanites were named after their ancestor Shelah.

The Perezites were named after their ancestor Perez.

The Zerahites were named after their ancestor Zerah.

This census also included the subclans of Perez.

The Hezronites were named after their ancestor Hezron.

The Hamulites were named after their ancestor Hamul.

23-25*The tribe of Issachar:* 64,300.

In this tribe were the following clans. They were named after the sons of Issachar.

The Tolaites were named after their ancestor Tola.

The Punites were named after their ancestor Puvah.

The Jashubites were named after their ancestor Jashub.

The Shimronites were named after their ancestor Shimron.

26-27*The tribe of Zebulun:* 60,500.

In this tribe were the following clans. They were named after the sons of Zebulun.

The Seredites were named after their ancestor Sered.

The Elonites were named after their ancestor Elon.

The Jahleelites were named after their ancestor Jahleel.

28-37*The tribe of Joseph:* 32,500 *in the half-tribe of Ephraim;* 52,700 *in the half-tribe of Manasseh.*

In the half-tribe of Manasseh was the clan of Machirites. They were named after their ancestor Machir.

The subclan of the Machirites was the Gileadites. They were named after their ancestor Gilead.

The following are the tribes of the Gileadites.

The Jezerites were named after their ancestor Jezer.

The Helekites were named after their ancestor Helek.

The Asrielites were named after their ancestor Asriel.

The Shechemites were named after their ancestor Shechem.

The Shemidaites were named after their ancestor Shemida.

The Hepherites were named after their ancestor Hepher. Hepher's son, Zelophehad, had no sons. Here are the names of his daughters: Mahlah, Noah, Hoglah, Milcah, Tirzah.

The 32,500 registered in the half-tribe of Ephraim included the following clans. They were named after the sons of Ephraim.

The Shuthelahites were named after their ancestor Shuthelah. A subclan of the Shuthelahites was the Eranites. They were named after their ancestor Eran. He was a son of Shuthelah.

The Becherites were named after their ancestor Becher.

The Tahanites were named after their ancestor Tahan.

38-41 *The tribe of Benjamin:* 45,600.

In this tribe were the following clans. They were named after the sons of Benjamin.

The Belaites were named after their ancestor Bela.

The following subclans were named after sons of Bela.

The Ardites were named after their ancestor Ard.

The Naamites were named after their ancestor Naaman.

The Ashbelites were named after their ancestor Ashbel.

The Ahiramites were named after their ancestor Ahiram.

The Shuphamites were named after their ancestor Shephupham.

The Huphamites were named after their ancestor Hupham.

42-43 *The tribe of Dan:* 64,400.

In this tribe was the clan of the Shuhamites. They were named after Shuham, the son of Dan.

44-47 *The tribe of Asher:* 53,400.

In this tribe were the following clans. They were named after the sons of Asher.

The Imnites were named after their ancestor Imnah.

The Ishvites were named after their ancestor Ishvi.

The Beriites were named after their ancestor Beriah.

Subclans named after the sons of Beriah were:

The Heberites were named after their ancestor Heber.

The Malchielites were named after their ancestor Malchiel.

Asher also had a daughter named Serah.

48-50 *The tribe of Naphtali:* 45,400.

In this tribe were the following clans. They were named after the sons of Naphtali.

The Jahzeelites were named after their ancestor Jahzeel.

The Gunites were named after their ancestor Guni.

The Jezerites were named after their ancestor Jezer.

The Shillemites were named after their ancestor Shillem.

51 So the total number of the men of draft age throughout Israel was 601,730.

52-53 Then the Lord told Moses to divide the land among the tribes. He was to do this according to their size. This was shown by the census. 54 The larger tribes were to be given more land. The smaller tribes were to receive less land.

55-56 "Let the larger tribes draw lots for the larger sections," the Lord said. "And let the smaller tribes draw for the smaller sections."

57 These are the clans of the Levites counted in the census.

The Gershonites were named after their ancestor Gershon.

The Kohathites were named after their ancestor Kohath.

The Merarites were named after their ancestor Merari.

58-59 These are the families of the tribe of Levi: the Libnites, the Hebronites, the Mahlites, the Mushites, the Korahites.

While Levi was in Egypt, a daughter, Jochebed, was born to him. She became the wife of Amram, son of Kohath. They were the parents of Aaron, Moses, and Miriam. 60 To Aaron were born Nadab, Abihu, Eleazar, and Ithamar. 61 But Nadab and Abihu died. They were killed when they offered incense before the Lord with unholy fire.

62 *The total number of Levites in the census* was 23,000. This included all the males a month old and upward. But the Levites were not included in the total census figure of the people of Israel. For the Levites were given no land when it was divided among the tribes.

63 So these are the census figures as prepared by Moses and Eleazar the priest. They counted the people in the plains of Moab. They were camped beside the Jordan River, just across from Jericho. 64-65 Not one person in this census had been counted in the previous census! The previous census had been taken in the wilderness of Sinai. All who had been counted in that census had died. It was just as the Lord had decreed.

He had said of them, "They shall die in the wilderness." The only exceptions were Caleb (son of Jephunneh) and Joshua (son of Nun).

Zelophehad's Daughters

27 One day the daughters of Zelophehad came to the door of the Tabernacle. They gave a petition to Moses. Eleazar the priest, the tribal leaders, and others were also there. The names of these women were Mahlah, Noah, Hoglah, Milcah, and Tirzah. They were members of the half-tribe of Manasseh (a son of Joseph). Their ancestor was Machir, son of Manasseh. Manasseh's son Gilead was their great-grandfather. His son Hepher was their grandfather. And his son Zelophehad was their father.

3-4"Our father died in the wilderness," they said. "And he was not one of those who died in Korah's revolt against the Lord. He died of a natural death, but he had no sons. Why should the name of our father die out just because he had no son? We feel that we should be given property along with our father's brothers."

5So Moses brought their case before the Lord.

6-7And the Lord replied to Moses, "The daughters of Zelophehad are correct. Give them land along with their uncles. Give them the property that would have been given to their father if he had lived. 8Moreover, this is a general law among you. A man might die and have no sons. If so, then his inheritance shall be passed on to his daughters. 9And if he has no daughter, it shall belong to his brothers. 10And if he has no brother, then it shall go to his uncles. 11But if he has no uncles, then it shall go to the nearest relative."

Joshua Becomes Israel's New Leader

For 40 years Moses had led the people of Israel toward the Promised Land. Now he was almost there. But the Lord would not let him go in because he had disobeyed. What would you say if that happened to you? Would you complain and say it was unfair? What did Moses say?

12One day the Lord said to Moses, "Go up into Mount Abarim. Look across the river. Look out over the land I have given to the people of Israel. 13After you have seen it, you shall die as Aaron your brother did. 14For you did not obey my commands in the wilderness of Zin. When the people of Israel rebelled, you did not glorify me before them. You did not follow my command to order water to come out of the rock." He was speaking of the event at the waters of Meribah ("Place of Strife"). This took place in Kadesh, in the wilderness of Zin.

15Then Moses spoke to the Lord. 16"O Lord, the God of the spirits of all mankind," He said. "Do this before I am taken away. Please choose a new leader for the people. 17He must be a man who will lead them into battle. He must be one who will care for them. That way the people of the Lord will not be as sheep without a shepherd."

18The Lord replied, "Go and get Joshua (son of Nun). He has the Spirit in him. 19Take him to Eleazar the priest. And as all the people watch, charge him with the job of leading the people. 20Publicly give him your authority. That way all the people of Israel will obey him. 21He shall be the one to consult with Eleazar the priest. In this way, he shall get commands from the Lord. The Lord will speak to Eleazar by using the Urim. Eleazar will pass on these commands to Joshua and the people. In this way the Lord will continue to guide them."

²²So Moses did as the Lord told him. He took Joshua to Eleazar the priest. As the people watched, ²³Moses laid his hands upon him. He dedicated him to his position. He did just as the Lord had commanded.

- *Remember:* Why could Moses not go into the Promised Land? (27:14-15) Instead of complaining, what did Moses ask the Lord to do? (27:16-17) What did the Lord say about Joshua? Did he say how brave he was, or how strong he was? (27:18) How would Moses get the people to obey their new leader? (27:20) Who would help Joshua know what the Lord wanted? How? (27:21) Who helps you know what the Lord wants?

- *Discover:* Accept a new leader cheerfully. If you are asked to be the new leader, accept that cheerfully.

- *Apply:* Sometimes your church gets a new pastor. Sometimes your dad's or mom's company gets a new president. This new person needs help. When you become a new leader, you will be glad for others' help.

- *What's next?* Moses was as strong as a young man. So why did he die? Read Deuteronomy 34 for the answer. ■

Daily Offerings

28 The Lord gave Moses these rules to give to the people of Israel. "The offerings which you burn on the altar for me are my food," he said. "They are a pleasure to me. So see to it that they are brought regularly. Make sure they are offered as I have told you.

³"When you make offerings by fire, you shall use yearling male lambs. There must be nothing wrong with them. Two of them shall be offered each day as a regular burnt offering. ⁴One lamb shall be sacrificed in the morning. The other shall be offered in the evening. ⁵With them shall be offered a grain offering. It shall include three quarts of finely ground flour. This shall be mixed with three pints of oil. ⁶This is the burnt offering ordained at Mount Sinai. It is to be offered regularly as a fragrant odor. It is an offering made by fire to the Lord. ⁷Along with it the drink offering shall be given. It shall consist of three pints of strong wine with each lamb. It shall be poured out in the holy place before the Lord. ⁸Offer the second lamb in the evening. It shall be given with the same grain offering and drink offering. It too is a fragrant odor to the Lord. It is an offering made by fire.

Sabbath Offerings

⁹⁻¹⁰"On the Sabbath day, sacrifice two yearling male lambs. They must have nothing wrong with them. These are to be given in addition to the regular offerings. They are to be given with a grain offering. It shall consist of six quarts of fine flour. The flour shall be mixed with oil. The usual drink offering must also be given.

Monthly Offerings

¹¹"Also, on the first day of each month, there shall be an extra burnt offering to the Lord. It shall consist of two young bulls, one ram, and seven male yearling lambs. They must have nothing wrong with them. ¹²Nine quarts of finely ground flour shall be given as a grain offering with each bull. Six quarts of finely ground flour must be given with each ram. ¹³And with each lamb, three quarts of finely ground flour must be given. The flour must be mixed with oil. These will be given for a grain offering. This burnt offering shall be presented by fire. It will please the Lord very much. ¹⁴Along with each sacrifice shall be a drink offering. Six pints of wine shall be offered with each bull. Four pints shall be given for a ram. And three pints shall be offered for a lamb. This, then, will be the burnt offering each month throughout the year.

¹⁵"Also on the first day of each month you shall offer one male goat. It shall be a sin offering to the Lord. This is in addition to the regular daily burnt offering and its drink offering.

Offerings for Passover

¹⁶"On April first you shall celebrate the Passover. This was when the death angel passed over the oldest sons of the Israelites in Egypt. He left them unharmed.

¹⁷On the following day a great, joyous seven-day feast will begin. But no leavened bread shall be served. ¹⁸On the first day of the feast all the people shall be called together before the Lord. No hard work shall be done on that day. ¹⁹You shall offer burnt sacrifices to the Lord. You shall offer two young bulls, one ram, and seven yearling male lambs. All these must have nothing wrong with them. ²⁰⁻²¹With each bull there shall be a grain offering. It must consist of nine quarts of fine flour. It shall be mixed with oil. With the ram, six quarts of flour shall be given. With each of the seven lambs, three quarts of fine flour shall be offered. ²²You must also offer a male goat as a sin offering. This will make atonement for yourselves. ²³These offerings shall be in addition to the usual daily sacrifices. ²⁴This same sacrifice shall be offered on each of the seven days of the feast. They will be very pleasant to the Lord. ²⁵On the seventh day you shall meet together. There shall again be a holy assembly of all the people. During that day you may do no hard work.

Offerings for the Feast of Harvest

²⁶"On the first day of the Harvest Feast all the people must come before the Lord. They must gather for a special assembly. In it they will celebrate the new harvest. On that day you are to present the first of the new crop of grain. It shall be given as a grain offering to the Lord. There is to be no regular work by anyone on that day. ²⁷A special burnt offering shall be offered that day. It will be very pleasant to the Lord. It shall consist of two young bulls, one ram, and seven yearling male lambs. ²⁸⁻²⁹These shall be given with your grain offerings. They shall consist of nine quarts of fine flour mixed with oil with each bull. Six quarts shall be offered with the ram. Three quarts shall be given with each of the seven lambs. ³⁰Also offer one male goat to make atonement for yourselves. ³¹These special offerings are in addition to the regular daily burnt offerings and grain offerings and drink offerings. Make sure that the animals you sacrifice are without defect.

Offerings for the Feast of Trumpets

29 "The Feast of Trumpets shall be celebrated on the 15th day of September each year. There shall be an assembly of all the people on that day. No hard work may be done. ²On that day you shall offer a burnt sacrifice. It shall consist of one young bull, one ram, and seven yearling male lambs. They must have nothing wrong with them. These are sacrifices which the Lord will enjoy. ³⁻⁴A grain offering must also be offered. It shall consist of nine quarts of fine flour with the bull. The flour must be mixed with oil. Six quarts of flour are to be given with the ram. Three quarts of flour are to be given with each of the seven lambs. ⁵In addition, there shall be a male goat sacrificed as a sin offering. It will make atonement for you. ⁶These special sacrifices are in addition to the regular monthly burnt offering for that day. They are also in addition to the regular daily burnt sacrifices. These also are to be offered with their grain offerings and drink offerings. All must be done according to the rules governing them.

Offerings for the Day of Atonement

⁷"Ten days later another meeting of all the people shall be held. This will be a day of humility before the Lord. No work of any kind may be done on this day. ⁸On that day you shall offer a burnt sacrifice to the Lord. It will be very pleasant to him. You must offer one young bull, one ram, and seven yearling male lambs. They must have nothing wrong with them. ⁹⁻¹⁰You must also give the grain offerings that go with them. Nine quarts of fine flour are to be offered with the bull. The flour must be mixed with oil. Six quarts of flour are to be given with the ram. And three quarts are to be offered with each of the seven lambs. ¹¹You are also to sacrifice one male goat for a sin offering. This is in addition to the sin offering of the Day of Atonement. This is offered yearly on that day. The regular daily burnt sacrifices, grain

offerings, and drink offerings must also be given.

Offerings for the Feast of Tabernacles

12"Five days later there shall be yet another assembly of all the people. On that day no hard work shall be done. It is the beginning of a seven-day feast before the Lord. 13You shall give a special burnt sacrifice that day. It will give much pleasure to the Lord. It shall consist of 13 young bulls, two rams, and 14 male yearling lambs. They must have nothing wrong with them. 14These shall be given with the usual grain offerings. Nine quarts of fine flour must be given with each of the 13 young bulls. Six quarts of flour must be given with each of the two rams. 15Three quarts shall be offered with each of the 14 lambs. The flour must be mixed with oil. 16There must also be a male goat sacrificed for a sin offering. This must be offered in addition to the regular daily burnt sacrifice. It shall be given with its grain offerings and drink offerings.

17"On the second day of this seven-day feast you shall sacrifice 12 young bulls, two rams, and 14 male yearling lambs. They must have nothing wrong with them. 18 They shall be given with the usual grain offerings and drink offerings. 19Also, in addition to the regular daily burnt sacrifice, you are to sacrifice a male goat. It shall be given with its grain offering and drink offering. It shall be for a sin offering.

20"On the third day of the feast, offer 11 young bulls, two rams, 14 male yearling lambs. They must each be without defect. 21The usual grain offering and drink offering shall be given with each sacrifice. 22And in addition to the regular daily burnt sacrifices, sacrifice a male goat. It shall be for a sin offering. It shall be given with its usual grain offering and drink offering.

23"On the fourth day of the feast, you are to sacrifice 10 young bulls, two rams, and 14 male yearling lambs. They must each be without defect. 24They shall be offered with their usual grain offerings and drink offerings. 25A male goat shall also be given as a sin offering. The usual grain and drink offerings must be given with it. These must all be offered in addition to the regular daily sacrifices.

26-27"On the fifth day of the feast, sacrifice nine young bulls, two rams, and 14 male yearling lambs. They must have nothing wrong with them. They shall be given with the usual grain offerings and drink offerings. 28Sacrifice a male goat with the usual grain and drink offerings. It shall be a special sin offering. These shall be given in addition to the usual daily sacrifices.

29"On the sixth day of the feast, you must sacrifice eight young bulls, two rams, and 14 male yearling lambs. These must each be without defect. 30These shall be offered along with their usual grain and drink offerings. 31In addition to the usual daily sacrifices, sacrifice a male goat. Offer it with the usual grain and drink offerings. It shall be a sin offering.

32"On the seventh day of the feast, sacrifice seven young bulls, two rams, and 14 male yearling lambs. They must all be without defect. 33Each shall be offered with its usual grain and drink offerings. 34Also sacrifice an extra sin offering of one male goat. Offer it with the usual grain and drink offerings. These shall be given in addition to the regular daily sacrifices.

35"On the eighth day call the people to another assembly. You must do no hard work that day. 36Sacrifice a burnt offering. They are very pleasant to the Lord. Offer one young bull, one ram, and seven male yearling lambs. They must have nothing wrong with them. 37They must be offered with the usual grain and drink offerings. 38Sacrifice also one male goat. Offer it with the usual grain and drink offerings. It shall be for a sin offering. These shall be given in addition to the regular daily sacrifices. 39You must make these sacrifices at your yearly feasts. They must be given in addition to the other sacrifices and offerings. They must not replace other sacrifices given for vows or free-will offerings. You must still offer your other burnt sacrifices, grain offerings, drink offerings, or peace offerings."

⁴⁰So Moses gave all of these commands to the people of Israel.

Rules about Vows

30 Now Moses called the leaders of the tribes. He told them these commands from the Lord. "Someone might make a promise to the Lord. This might be either to do something or to quit doing something. If such a promise is made, it must not be broken. The person making the promise must do exactly as he has said.

³"A woman might promise the Lord to do or not do something. She might still be a girl at home in her father's home. ⁴Her father might hear that she has made a promise with penalties. If he hears this, but says nothing, then her promise shall stand. ⁵But her father might refuse to let her make the promise. Or he might feel that the penalties she has agreed to are too harsh. If this is the case, then her promise shall no longer be valid. Her father must state his disagreement on the first day he hears about it. If he does, then the Lord will forgive her. For her father would not let her do it.

⁶"A girl might take a vow or make a foolish pledge. And later she might marry. ⁷Her husband might learn of her vow. If he says nothing on the day he hears of it, then her vow shall stand. ⁸But her husband might refuse to accept her vow or foolish pledge. If he does, his disagreement makes it void. And the Lord will forgive her.

⁹"But if the woman is a widow or is divorced, she must fulfill her vow.

¹⁰"She might be married and living in her husband's home when she makes the vow. ¹¹And her husband might hear of it. If this happens and he does nothing, the vow shall stand. ¹²But he might refuse to allow it on the first day he hears of it. If he does, then her vow is void. And the Lord will forgive her. ¹³So her husband may either confirm or nullify her vow. ¹⁴But he might say nothing for a day. If this happens, then he has already agreed to it. ¹⁵He might wait more

than a day. Then he might refuse to permit the vow. If he does this, the penalties to which she has agreed shall come upon him. He shall be responsible for the vow."

¹⁶These, then, are the commands the Lord gave Moses. They are for a man and his wife. And they are for a father and his daughter who is living at home.

The War against Midian

31 Then the Lord said to Moses, "Take vengeance on the Midianites. Punish them for leading you into idolatry. Then you must die."

³Moses said to the people, "Some of you must take arms. You must wage the Lord's war against Midian. ⁴⁻⁵Choose 1,000 men from each tribe." So this was done. Out of the many thousands of Israel, 12,000 armed men were sent to battle by Moses. ⁶Phinehas (son of Eleazar the priest) led them into battle. He went with the Ark, and with trumpets blaring. ⁷And every man of Midian was killed. ⁸Among those killed were all five of the Midianite kings. Their names were Evi, Rekem, Zur, Hur, and Reba. Balaam, the son of Beor, was also killed.

⁹⁻¹¹Then the Israelite army took as captives all the women and children. They took the cattle and flocks. They also captured other booty. All of the cities, towns, and villages of Midian were then burned. ¹²The captives and other war loot were gathered. They were brought to Moses and Eleazar the priest. They were brought to the rest of the people of Israel. The people waited on the plains of Moab beside the Jordan River. Their camp was just across from Jericho. ¹³Moses and Eleazar the priest went out to meet the victorious army. All the leaders of the people went with them. ¹⁴But Moses was very angry with the army's leaders.

¹⁵"Why have you let all the women live?" he demanded. ¹⁶"These are the very ones who followed Balaam's advice. They caused the people of Israel to worship idols on Mount Peor. They were the cause of the plague that destroyed us. ¹⁷ Now kill all the boys. Also kill all the women who have slept with a man.

18 Only the little girls may live. You may keep them for yourselves. 19Now you may have killed someone or touched a dead body. If this is true, stay outside of the camp for seven days. Then purify yourselves and your captives on the third and seventh days. 20Remember also to make all your clothing pure. Purify all that is made of leather, goat's hair, or wood."

21Then Eleazar the priest spoke to the men who were in the battle. He said, "This is the command the Lord has given Moses. 22'Anything that will stand heat shall be passed through fire. This includes gold, silver, bronze, iron, tin, or lead. 23This shall be done to make it pure. It must then be further purified with the special water. But anything that won't stand heat shall be purified by the water alone.' 24On the seventh day you must wash your clothes and be purified. Then you may come back into the camp."

Dividing the Loot

25And the Lord spoke to Moses. 26He said, "You and Eleazar the priest are to make a list of all the booty. The leaders of the tribes will help you. This list should include the people and animals. 27Then divide it into two parts. Half of it is for the men who were in the battle. The other half is to be given to the people of Israel. 28But first, the Lord gets a share of it. He shall be given some of the captives, oxen, donkeys, and flocks kept by the army. His share is one out of every 500. 29Give this share to Eleazar the priest. It shall be presented to the Lord by waving it before the altar. 30Also take two percent of all the captives, flocks, and cattle that are given to the people of Israel. Give this to the Levites in charge of the Tabernacle. It is the Lord's portion."

31So Moses and Eleazar the priest did as the Lord told them. 32-35The total booty was 675,000 sheep; 72,000 oxen; 61,000 donkeys; and 32,000 young girls. This was besides the jewelry, clothing, and other booty the soldiers kept for themselves.

36-40So the half given to the army totaled: 337,500 sheep; 36,000 oxen; 30,500 donkeys; 16,000 girls. Of these, 675 sheep, 72 oxen, and 61 donkeys were given to the Lord. And 32 girls were given to the Levites.

41All of the Lord's portion was given to Eleazar the priest. It was done just as the Lord had told Moses.

42-46The half of the booty given to the people of Israel included: 337,500 sheep; 36,000 oxen; 30,500 donkeys; and 16,000 girls. Moses had separated it from the half belonging to the army.

47Following the Lord's directions, Moses gave two percent of these to the Levites.

48-49Then the army leaders came to Moses. They said, "All the men who went out to battle are still alive. Not one of us is missing! 50So we have brought a special thank-offering to the Lord from our loot. The offering included gold jewelry, bracelets, anklets, rings, earrings, and necklaces. This is to make atonement for our souls before the Lord."

51-52Moses and Eleazar the priest received this special offering from the army's leaders. They found its total value to be more than $300,000. 53The soldiers had also kept personal loot for themselves. 54The offering was taken into the Tabernacle. It was kept there before the Lord. It was a memorial for the people of Israel.

Some Tribes Get Their Land

32 The people of Israel came to the land of Jazar and Gilead. The tribes of Reuben and Gad noticed what wonderful sheep country it was. These tribes had very large flocks of sheep. 2So they came before Moses and Eleazar the priest and the other tribal leaders. They said, 3-4"The Lord has used Israel to destroy the people of this whole area. This is the land around Ataroth, Dibon, Jazer, Nimrah, Heshbon, Elealeh, Sebam, Nebo, and Beon. And it is all wonderful sheep country. It is ideal for our large flocks. 5Please let us have this land as our portion. We will take it instead of land on the other side of the Jordan River."

6"Do you plan to sit here while your brothers go across the river? Are you planning to let them do all the fighting?" Moses demanded. 7"Are you trying to discourage the rest of the people? Are you trying to stop them from going across the Jordan? Do you not want them to take the land that the Lord has given them? 8This is the same kind of thing your fathers did! I sent them from Kadesh-barnea to spy out the land. 9They finished their survey. They came back from the valley of Eshcol. But then they discouraged the people from going on into the Promised Land. 10-11 And the Lord's anger was hot against them. He swore that he would punish all those he had rescued from Egypt. Not one of them would see the Promised Land. No one over 20 years of age would see the land he promised Abraham, Isaac, and Jacob. He did this, for they had refused to do what he wanted.

You cannot hide your sins

And you may be sure that your sin will catch up with you.

Numbers 32:23

12"The only exceptions were Caleb (son of Jephunneh the Kenizzite) and Joshua (son of Nun). They had followed the Lord completely. They had urged the people to go on into the Promised Land. 13"The Lord made us wander back and forth in the wilderness for 40 years. We wandered until all that evil generation died. 14But here you are, a brood of sinners doing exactly the same thing! Only there are more of you! So the Lord's anger against Israel will be even worse this time. 15You can turn away from God like this. But if you do, he will make the people stay even longer in the wilderness. You will be responsible for destroying his people! You will bring disaster to this whole nation!"

16"Not at all!" they explained. "We will build sheepfolds for our flocks. We will rebuild cities for our little ones. 17But we ourselves will go over armed. We will go ahead of the rest of the people of Israel. We will fight until we have brought them safely to their inheritance. But first we will need to build walled cities here for our families. This will keep them safe from attack by the local people. 18We will not settle down here until all the people of Israel have received their inheritance. 19We don't want land on the other side of the Jordan. We would rather have it on this side, on the east."

20Then Moses said, "All right. You may do what you have said. Arm yourselves for the Lord's war. 21Keep your troops across the Jordan until the Lord has driven out his enemies. 22Then, when the land is finally conquered, you may come back. Then you will have done what the Lord asks of you. You will have done your duty to the rest of the Israelites. And the land on the eastern side shall be your land. It will be yours from the Lord. 23But you might not do as you have said. If you do not, then you will have sinned against the Lord. And you may be sure that your sin will catch up with you. 24Go ahead and build cities for your families. Build sheepfolds for your sheep. And do all you have said."

25"We will follow your commands exactly," the people of Gad and Reuben replied. 26"Our children, wives, flocks, and cattle shall stay here in the cities of Gilead. 27But all of us who are in the army will go over to battle for the Lord. We will do just as you have said."

28So Moses gave his approval. Then he spoke to Eleazar, Joshua, and the tribal leaders of Israel. 29He said, "All the men of Gad and Reuben shall prepare to fight the Lord's battles. They shall go with you over Jordan. Then, when the land is conquered, you must give them the land of Gilead. 30But if they refuse, then they must take land among the rest of you. They will live in the land of Canaan."

31The tribes of Gad and Reuben said again, "As the Lord has commanded, so we will do. 32We will follow the Lord fully armed into Canaan. But our own land shall be here on this side of the Jordan."

33So Moses gave this land to Gad, Reuben, and the half-tribe of Manasseh. This included the land of King Sihon of the Amorites and of King Og of Bashan. It included all their land and cities.

34-36The people of Gad built these cities: Dibon, Ataroth, Aroer, Atroth-shophan, Jazer, Jogbehah, Beth-nimrah, Beth-haran. They were all fortified cities with sheepfolds.

37-38The children of Reuben built the following cities: Heshbon, Elealeh, Kiriathaim, Nebo, Baal-meon, Sibmah. The Israelites later changed the names of some of these cities they had conquered and rebuilt.

39Then the clan of Machir of the tribe of Manasseh went to Gilead. They conquered it. And they drove out the Amorites who were living there. 40So Moses gave Gilead to the Machirites. And they lived there. 41The men of Jair occupied many of the towns in Gilead. They were another clan of the tribe of Manasseh. They changed the name of their area to Havroth-jair. 42Meanwhile, a man named Nobah led an army to Kenath and the villages around it. He took that land and called the area Nobah. He named it after himself.

How the Israelites Got to the Promised Land

33 This is what happened to the nation of Israel from the time Moses and Aaron led them out of Egypt. 2Moses had written down their movements as the Lord had told him to. 3-4They left the city of Rameses, Egypt, on the first day of April. It was the day after the first Passover. They left proudly, hurried along by the Egyptians. The Egyptians were still burying all their oldest sons. They had been killed by the Lord the night before. The Lord had certainly defeated all the gods of Egypt that night!

5-6After leaving Rameses, they stayed in Succoth. Then they went to Etham, which is at the edge of the wilderness. 7Next, they moved to Pi-hahiroth near Baal-zephon. They camped there at the foot of Mount Migdol. 8From there they went through the middle of the Red Sea. They traveled on for three days into the Etham wilderness. Then they camped at Marah.

9Leaving Marah, they came to Elim. In Elim there are 12 springs of water and 70 palm trees. They stayed there for quite a long time.

10Leaving Elim, they camped beside the Red Sea. 11Then they moved on into the wilderness of Sihn.

12Their next camp was Dophkah. 13Then they stopped at Alush. 14Then they traveled on to Rephidim. There was no water there for the people to drink.

15-37From Rephidim they went to the wilderness of Sinai. From the wilderness of Sinai they went to Kibroth-hattaavah.

From Kibroth-hattaavah they went to Hazeroth.
From Hazeroth they traveled to Rithmah.
From Rithmah they went to Rimmon-parez.
From Rimmon-parez they went to Libnah.
From Libnah they traveled to Rissah.
From Rissah they traveled to Kehelathah.
From Kehelathah they went to Mount Shepher.
From Mount Shepher they went to Haradah.
From Haradah they traveled to Makheloth.
From Makheloth they went to Tahath.
From Tahath they traveled to Terah.
From Terah they went to Mithkah.
From Mithkah they went to Hashmonah.
From Hashmonah they traveled to Moseroth.
From Moseroth they traveled to Bene-jaakan.
From Bene-jaakan they went to Hor-haggidgad.
From Hor-haggidgad they traveled to Jotbathah.
From Jotbathah they went to Abronah.
From Abronah they went to Ezion-geber.
From Ezion-geber they traveled to Kadesh. Kadesh is in the wilderness of Zin.
From Kadesh they went to Mount Hor. This is at the edge of the land of Edom.

38-39They were at the foot of Mount Hor. And Aaron the priest was told by the Lord to go up into the mountain. He went up, and he died there. This happened during the 40th year after the people of Israel had left Egypt. The date of his death was July 15. He was 123 years old.

40It was then that the Canaanite king of Arad heard of the coming Israelites. He lived in the Negeb, in the land of Canaan. 41The Israelites dealt with him. Then they went from Mount Hor. They camped in Zalmonah. 42Then they traveled on to Punon. 43Their next camp was at Oboth. 44Then they stopped at Iye-abarim. This was at the border of Moab. 45From there they went to Dibon-gad. 46Then they went to Almon-diblathaim. 47Next they traveled into the mountains of Abarim, near Mount Nebo. 48And finally they came to the plains of Moab. They camped beside the river Jordan, just across from Jericho. 49While in that area they camped at various places along the Jordan River. They camped from Beth-jeshimoth as far as Abel-shittim, on the plains of Moab.

What to Do in the New Land

50-51While they were camped there, the Lord told Moses to speak to the people of Israel. He said, "You shall pass across the Jordan River. You will enter into the land of Canaan. 52When you do, you must drive out all the people living there. You must destroy all their idols. You must destroy their carved stones and molten images. You must cut down their open-air sanctuaries in the hills. You must destroy all the places where they worship idols. 53I have given the land to you. Take it and live there. 54 You will be given land in proportion to the size of your tribes. The larger sections of land will be divided by lot among the larger tribes. The smaller sections will be divided among the smaller tribes. 55But you might refuse to drive out the people living there. If you refuse, those who are still there will be like hot coals in your eyes. They will be like thorns in your sides. 56And I will destroy you as I had planned for you to destroy them."

The Borders of the New Land

34 The Lord told Moses to speak to the people of Israel: "You shall soon come into the land of Canaan. I am giving you the whole land as your home. These shall be its borders. 3The southern part of the country will be the wilderness of Zin. It runs along the edge of Edom. The southern border will begin at the Dead Sea. 4It will keep going south past Scorpion Pass. It will go in the direction of Zin. Its point farthest south will be Kadesh-barnea. From there it will go to Hazaraddar. Then it will go on to Azmon. 5From Azmon the border will follow the Brook of Egypt down to the Mediterranean Sea.

6"Your western border will be the coastline of the Mediterranean Sea.

7-9"Your northern border will begin at the Mediterranean Sea. It will proceed eastward to Mount Hor. Then it will go to Lebo-Hamath. Then it will proceed on through Zedad and Ziphron to Hazar-enan.

10-11"The eastern border will be from Hazar-enan south to Shepham. Then it will proceed on to Riblah at the east side of Ain. From there it will make a large half-circle. It will first go south. Then it will go west until it touches the southern tip of the Sea of Galilee. 12Then it will follow the Jordan River, ending at the Dead Sea."

13"This is the land you are to divide among yourselves by lot," Moses said. "It is to be divided up among the nine and a half tribes. 14-15The tribes of Reuben, Gad, and the half-tribe of Manasseh have already been given land. It is on the east side of the Jordan, just across from Jericho."

16-28And the Lord said to Moses, "These are the names of the men I have chosen. They will handle the dividing up of the land. Eleazar the priest, Joshua (son of Nun), and one leader from each tribe will do the work. Their names are listed below:

Tribe	Leader
Judah	Caleb (son of Jephunneh)
Simeon	Shemuel (son of Ammihud)
Benjamin	Elidad (son of Chislon)
Dan	Bukki (son of Jogli)
Manasseh	Hanniel (son of Ephod)
Ephraim	Kemuel (son of Shiphtan)

Zebulun	Elizaphan (son of Parnach)
Issachar	Paltiel (son of Azzan)
Asher	Ahihud (son of Shelomi)
Naphtali	Pedahel (son of Ammihud)

²⁹These are the names of the men I have chosen. They will oversee the dividing of the land among the tribes."

Cities for the Levites

35 Israel was camped beside the Jordan on the plains of Moab. They were just across from Jericho. At that time, the Lord said to Moses, ²"Speak to the people of Israel. Tell them to give to the Levites certain cities and pasturelands. It shall be their inheritance. ³These cities are for their homes. The lands around these cities are for their cattle, flocks, and other livestock. ⁴⁻⁵Their gardens and vineyards shall extend 1500 feet out from the city walls in each direction. They will also own another 1500 feet beyond that for pastureland.

⁶"You shall give the Levites the six Cities of Refuge. A person who has killed someone by accident can run there and be safe. The Levites are to be given 42 other cities besides. ⁷In all, there shall be 48 cities with pastureland given to the Levites. ⁸These cities shall be in various parts of the nation. The larger tribes with many cities shall give several to the Levites. The smaller tribes shall give them fewer cities."

Cities of Refuge

⁹⁻¹⁰And the Lord said to Moses, "The people will soon arrive in the land. Tell them that ¹¹Cities of Refuge will be named. Anyone who has killed someone by accident may flee to these cities for safety. ¹²These cities will be places of protection. There the dead man's relatives who want to avenge his death may not touch him. The slayer must not be killed unless a fair trial proves his guilt. ¹³⁻¹⁴Three of these six Cities of Refuge are to be located in the land of Canaan. Three others shall be on the east side of the Jordan River. ¹⁵These are not only for the protection of Israelites. Foreigners and travelers may also find refuge there.

¹⁶"But someone might be struck and killed by a piece of iron. If this happens, it must be presumed to be murder. And the murderer must be killed. ¹⁷Or the slain man might be struck down with a large stone. In such a case, it is murder. And the murderer shall die. ¹⁸The same is true if he is killed with a wooden weapon. ¹⁹The avenger of his death shall kill the murderer when he meets him. ²⁰Someone might kill another out of hatred by throwing something at him. Or someone might ambush another person. ²¹Or he might angrily strike him with his fist so that he dies. If any of these are true, then he is a murderer. The murderer shall be killed by the avenger.

²²⁻²³"But it might be an accident. Perhaps something was thrown without anger. A stone might have been thrown without knowing it would hit anyone. Or a stone might have been thrown without wanting to harm an enemy. Yet still, as a result, a man might have been killed. ²⁴If this happens, then the people shall judge whether or not it was an accident. They shall decide whether he is worthy of death. If he is, they will hand the killer over to the avenger of the dead man. ²⁵It might be decided that it was done by accident. If so, then the people shall save the killer from the avenger. The killer shall be allowed to stay in the City of Refuge. And he must live there until the death of the High Priest.

²⁶"The slayer might leave the city. ²⁷And the avenger might find him outside and kill him. If this happens, it is not murder. ²⁸For the man should have stayed inside the city until the death of the High Priest. But the death of the High Priest might take place. If this happens, the man may go back to his own land and home. ²⁹These are lasting laws for all Israel from generation to generation.

³⁰"All murderers must be killed, but only if there is more than one witness. No man shall die with only one person speaking against him. ³¹Whenever anyone is judged guilty of murder, he must die. No ransom may be taken for him. ³²Nor may a payment be taken from a refugee in a City of Refuge. He cannot pay for his freedom to return to his

home before the death of the High Priest. ³³In this way the land will not be spoiled. For murder spoils the land. No atonement can be made for murder except to kill the murderer. ³⁴You shall not defile the land where you are going to live. For I, the Lord, will be living there too."

Each Tribe's Land to Remain Secure

36 Then the heads of the subclan of Gilead came to Moses. They were from the clan of Machir, of the tribe of Manasseh. Manasseh was one of the sons of Joseph. They brought a petition to Moses and the leaders of Israel. "The Lord told you to divide the land by lot among the people of Israel," they reminded Moses. "And you told us to give the inheritance of our brother Zelophehad to his daughters. ³But they might marry into another tribe. If they do, their land will go with them. Then the land will belong to the tribe into which they marry. In this way the total area of our tribe will be reduced. ⁴It will not even be given back at the Year of Jubilee."

⁵Then Moses replied publicly. He gave them these commands from the Lord. "The men of the tribe of Joseph have a proper complaint," he said. ⁶"This is what the Lord has commanded for the daughters of Zelophehad. 'Let them be married to anyone they like. But they must marry within their own tribe. ⁷In this way none of the land of the tribe will shift to any other tribe. The inheritance of every tribe is to remain forever as it was first given. ⁸This law applies to the girls throughout the tribes of Israel. All girls who are heiresses must marry within their own tribes. That way their land will not leave the tribe. ⁹No inheritance shall move from one tribe to another.'"

¹⁰The daughters of Zelophehad did as the Lord commanded Moses. ¹¹⁻¹² These girls, Mahlah, Tirzah, Hoglah, Milcah, and Noah were married to men in their own tribe of Manasseh. That way their inheritance stayed in their tribe.

¹³These are the commands that the Lord gave to the people of Israel through Moses. He gave them while they were camped on the plains of Moab. They were beside the Jordan River, across from Jericho.

DEUTERONOMY

*For 40 years God had led the Israelites toward
Canaan. He called it the Promised Land. That's
because God promised to give it to them.*

*These people had been slaves in Egypt. God had
helped Moses lead the people out of Egypt. They
took a long trip through the wilderness. It lasted 40
years.*

*On this trip God gave the people some rules. He
told them how they should live. He gave them food
to eat. He helped them build the Tabernacle, God's
tent house.*

*Now the 40-year trip was over. The people were
ready to go into the Promised Land. It wouldn't be
easy. They would have to fight many battles. There
were lots of wicked people in the new land. Do you
suppose some of the Israelite people were afraid?*

*Just before the people went into their new land,
Moses had some important things to tell them. Moses
helped the people know more about themselves. How
had they gotten there? How had God helped them?
Moses also helped the people know more about God.
Who was he? What did he want them to do?*

*In Deuteronomy, you will read about Moses walk-
ing up a mountain to die. He had done a good job
as God's leader. But it was time for a new leader.
You'll meet Joshua, God's new leader. And you'll
learn why God chose him to lead the people into
the Promised Land.*

Moses Talks to the People

1 This book records Moses' address to
the people of Israel. At that time,
they were camped in the valley of the
Arabah. This lay in the wilderness of
Moab, east of the Jordan River. Cities
in the area included Suph, Paran,
Tophel, Laban, Hazeroth, and Dizahab.
The speech was given on February 15.
It was 40 years since the people of Israel
left Mount Sinai. This trip usually
takes only 11 days to travel by foot! The

normal route from Mount Sinai to Kadesh-barnea is by way of Mount Seir. At the time of this address, King Sihon of the Amorites had already been crushed at Heshbon. King Og of Bashan had also been beaten at Ashtaroth, near Edrei. Here is Moses' address to Israel. In it he states all the laws God told him to pass on to them.

Leaders Chosen from Each Tribe

⁶Moses said, "Forty years ago, the Lord our God spoke to us. We were camped at Mount Sinai. He said, 'You have stayed here long enough. ⁷Now go and take the hill country from the Amorites. Take the valley of the Arabah and the Negeb. Conquer all the land of Canaan and Lebanon. Take the whole area from the Mediterranean Sea to the Euphrates River. ⁸I am giving all of it to you! Go in and take it. It is the land the Lord promised to your ancestors. He promised it to Abraham, Isaac, and Jacob, and all of their descendants.'

⁹"At that time I told the people, 'I need help! You are a great burden for me to carry all by myself. ¹⁰The Lord has caused your nation to grow quickly. You have become as many as the stars! ¹¹And may he multiply you a thousand times more! May he bless you as he promised! ¹²But what can one man do to settle all your quarrels and problems? ¹³So choose some men from each tribe who are wise and know a lot about life. I will appoint them as your leaders.'

¹⁴"They agreed to this. ¹⁵So I appointed the men they chose. Some were taken from each tribe. I appointed them to help bring justice. They were in charge of thousands, hundreds, fifties, and tens. Their job was to decide the people's quarrels. They were to help the people in every way. ¹⁶I told them to be perfectly fair at all times, even to foreigners. ¹⁷'When giving your decisions,' I told them, 'never favor a man because he is rich. Be fair to great and small alike. Don't fear their anger. For you are judging in the place of God. Bring me any cases too hard for you. I will handle them.' ¹⁸And I gave them other commands at that time also.

Spies Scout the New Land

¹⁹⁻²¹"Then we left Mount Sinai. We traveled through the great and terrible desert. We came at last to the Amorite hills. This was the place the Lord our God had led us to. We were then at Kadesh-barnea. This is on the border of the Promised Land. I said to the people, 'The Lord God has given us this land. Go and take it as he told us to. Don't be afraid! Don't even doubt!'

²²"But they replied, 'First let's send out spies. They will find the best way to enter the land. They will also help us decide which cities we should capture first.'

²³"This seemed like a good idea. So I chose 12 spies, one from each tribe. ²⁴⁻²⁵They crossed into the hills and came to the Valley of Eshcol. They came back with samples of the local fruit. One look was enough to show us that it was indeed a good land. This was the land the Lord our God had given us.

Israel Refuses to Enter New Land

²⁶But the people refused to go in. They rebelled against the Lord's command. ²⁷"They complained in their tents. They said, 'The Lord must hate us. He brought us here from Egypt to be killed by these Amorites. ²⁸What are we getting into? Our brothers who spied out the land have scared us with their report. They say that the people of the land are tall and strong. They also say that the walls of their cities rise high into the sky! They have even seen giants there. They saw the descendants of the Anakim!'

²⁹"But I said to them, 'Don't be afraid! ³⁰The Lord God is your leader. He will fight for you with his mighty miracles. He will do just as you saw him do in Egypt. ³¹And you know how he has cared for you here in the wilderness. He has cared for you just as a father cares for his child!' ³²But nothing I said did any good.

"They refused to believe the Lord our God. ³³They wouldn't believe even though he had led them all the way. He had chosen the best places for them to camp. He had guided them by a pillar of fire at night. He had led them by a pillar of cloud during the day.

34-35"Well, the Lord heard their complaining and was very angry. He made a promise. No one in that whole generation would live to see the Promised Land. None of them would go into the good land he had promised their fathers. 36Only Caleb (the son of Jephunneh) would enter the land. He had followed the Lord with all his heart. So he would be given some of the land he had walked over. 37"And the Lord was even angry with me because of them. He said to me, 'You shall not enter the Promised Land! 38Instead, your helper, Joshua (the son of Nun), shall lead the people. Encourage him as he gets ready to take over as leader. 39I will give the land to the children they said would die in the wilderness. 40But as for you of the older generation, turn around now. Go on back across the desert toward the Red Sea.

41"Then they confessed, 'We have sinned! We will go into the land. We will fight for it as the Lord our God has told us to.' So they strapped on their weapons. They thought it would be easy to conquer the whole area.

42"But the Lord said to me, 'Tell them not to do it. For I will not go with them. They will be struck down before their enemies.'

43"I told them, but they would not listen. Instead, they rebelled again against the Lord's command. They went on up into the hill country to fight. 44But the Amorites who lived there came out against them. They chased them like bees. They killed them all the way from Seir to Hormah. 45Then they came back and wept before the Lord. But he would not listen. 46So they stayed there at Kadesh for a long time.

Stuck in the Wilderness

2 "Then we turned back across the wilderness toward the Red Sea. We did this because the Lord had told me to. For many years we wandered around in the area of Mount Seir. 2Then at last the Lord said,

3"'You have stayed here long enough. Turn northward. 4Tell the people they will be passing through the country that belongs to the Edomites. The Edomites are their relatives, the descen-

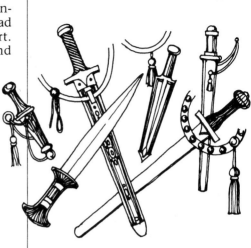

Amorites

DEUTERONOMY 2:24-37

Who were the Amorites? Why were the Israelites to take land from them?

The Amorites were descendants of Noah's grandson, Canaan (Genesis 10:16). They were very evil. Before Moses and his people arrived, the Amorites had captured the land from the Moabites (Numbers 21:26). As the Israelites were traveling to the Promised Land, they asked to go through the Amorites' land safely. They promised they would not eat the Amorites food or drink their water. But Sihon, king of the Amorites, refused. He sent an army to fight Israel (Numbers 21:21-23). The Lord promised to help the Israelites defeat the Amorites. So the Israelites captured their land and some of them then lived there (Numbers 21:24-31).

dants of Esau. They live in Seir. The Edomites will be nervous, so be careful. 5Don't start a fight! For I have given them all the Mount Seir hill country as their homeland. I will not give you even a tiny piece of their land. 6Pay them for any food or water you use. 7The Lord your God has watched over you for all these 40 years. He has blessed you every step of the way as you have wandered in this great wilderness. And you have not needed anything in all that time.'

8"So we passed through Edom where our brothers lived. We crossed the Arabah Road that goes south to Elath and Ezion-geber. Then we traveled northward toward the Moab desert.

9"Then the Lord warned us, 'Don't attack the Moabites either. For I will not give you any of their land. I have given it to the descendants of Lot.'

10"The Emim used to live in that area. They were a very large tribe. They were as tall as the giants of Anakim. 11Both the Emim and the Anakim are often called the Rephaim. But the Moabites call them Emim. 12In earlier days the Horites lived in Seir. But they were driven out by the Edomites, the descendants of Esau. In the same way, Israel would drive out the peoples of Canaan. That land had been given to Israel by the Lord.

13"'Now cross Zered Brook,' the Lord said. And we did.

14-15"So it took us 38 years to get across Zered Brook from Kadesh! For the Lord had promised that this could not happen until all the men had died. This included all the men who 38 years earlier were old enough to fight in battle. Yes, the hand of the Lord was against them until finally all were dead.

16-17"Then at last the Lord spoke to me.

18"'Today Israel shall cross the borders of Moab at Ar. 19They will go into the land of the Ammonites. But do not attack them, for I will not give you any of their land. I have given it to the descendants of Lot.'

20"That area, too, used to be where the Rephaim lived. They are called 'Zamzummim' by the Ammonites. 21They were a large and powerful tribe. They were as tall as the Anakim. But the Lord destroyed them as the Ammonites came in. So the Ammonites lived there in their place. 22The Lord helped the descendants of Esau in a similar way at Mount Seir. They destroyed the Horites who were living there before them. 23A similar thing happened when the people of Caphtor destroyed the tribe of Avvim. They were living in villages scattered across the country as far away as Gaza.

Fighting Battles along the Way

24"Then the Lord said, 'Cross the Arnon River. Go into the land of King Sihon the Amorite. He is the king of Heshbon. Fight against him. Begin to take control of his land. 25Starting today I will make people shake with fear because of you. People throughout the whole earth will dread your coming.'

26"Then from the wilderness of Kedemoth I sent messengers to Sihon. He was the king of Heshbon. They asked for peace. 27"Let us pass through your land,' we said. 'We will stay on the main road. We won't turn off into the fields on either side. 28We will not steal food as we go. We will buy every bite we eat and all we drink. All we want is permission to pass through. 29The Edomites at Seir let us go through their country. So did the Moabites, whose capital is at Ar. We are on our way across the Jordan. We are going to the land the Lord our God has given us.'

30"But King Sihon refused. The Lord your God made him stubborn. The Lord did this so that he could destroy Sihon by the hands of Israel. This has now been done.

31"Then the Lord spoke to me. He said, 'I have begun to give you the land of King Sihon. When you take it, it shall belong to Israel forever.'

32"King Sihon then declared war on us. He got his forces ready at Jahaz. 33-34But the Lord our God crushed him. We conquered all his cities. We destroyed everything and everyone. We left nothing alive 35-36except the cattle. We took them as our reward. We also took booty from the cities we had ransacked. We conquered everything from Aroer to Gilead. This is the area from the edge of the Arnon River valley. It includes all the cities in the valley. Not one city was too strong for us. For the Lord our God gave all of them to us.

37However, we stayed away from the people of Ammon. We stayed away from the Jabbok River and the hill country cities. We avoided all the places the Lord our God had told us not to enter.

3 "Next we turned toward King Og's land of Bashan. He got his army ready right away and attacked us at Edrei. But the Lord told me not to be afraid of him. 'All his people and his land are yours,' the Lord told me. 'You will do to him as you did to King Sihon of the Amorites at Heshbon.' 3So the Lord helped us fight against King Og and his people. We killed them all. 4We conquered all 60 of his cities. This was the whole Argob region of Bashan. 5These were strong cities. They had high walls and barred gates. Of course, we also took all of the towns without walls. 6We destroyed the kingdom of Bashan just as we had destroyed King Sihon's kingdom at Heshbon. We killed all the people. 7But we kept the cattle and loot for ourselves.

8"We now had taken all the land of the two kings of the Amorites east of the Jordan. This included all the land from the valley of the Arnon to Mount Hermon. 9The Sidonians called Mount Hermon 'Sirion.' The Amorites called it 'Senir.' 10We had now conquered all the cities on the plateau. All of Gilead and Bashan as far as the cities of Salecah and Edrei was now ours.

11"By the way, King Og of Bashan was the last of the giant Rephaim. His iron bed is kept in a museum at Rabbah. This is one of the cities of the Ammonites. The bed is 13½ feet long and six feet wide.

Dividing the Land

12"At that time I gave the conquered land to the tribes of Reuben, Gad, and the half-tribe of Manasseh. To the tribes of Reuben and Gad I gave the area beginning at Aroer on the Arnon River. I also gave them half of Mount Gilead, including its cities. 13The half-tribe of Manasseh was given the rest of Gilead. They also received all of the former kingdom of King Og, the Argob region. Bashan is sometimes called 'The Land of the Rephaim.' 14The clan of Jair, of the tribe of Manasseh, took over the whole Argob region (Bashan). This went to the borders of the Geshurites and Maacathites. They renamed their country after themselves. They called it Havvoth-jair (meaning 'Jair's Villages'). It is still known by this name today. 15Then I gave Gilead to the clan of Machir. 16The tribes of Reuben and Gad were given the area that begins at the Jabbok River in Gilead. This was on the Ammonite border. It went from there to the middle of the valley of the Arnon River. 17They were also given the Arabah (or wasteland). This is bordered by the Jordan River on the west. It included the area from Chinnereth to Mount Pisgah and the Dead Sea. The Dead Sea is also called the Sea of the Arabah.

18"At that time I spoke to the tribes of Reuben and Gad and the half-tribe of Manasseh. I reminded them that they could not begin settling down yet. It was true, the Lord had given them the land. But they could not settle there until their armed men led the other tribes across the Jordan. They had to help them conquer the land the Lord was giving them.

19"'But your wives and children,' I told them, 'may live here. They may stay in the cities the Lord has given you. That way they can care for your many cattle. 20After the Lord has given victory to the other tribes, too, then you may come back. You shall help to conquer the land the Lord your God has given them. You must cross the Jordan River to fight. Then you may come back here to your own land.'

Moses Cannot Enter the Land

21Then I said to Joshua, 'You have seen what the Lord your God has done to those two kings. You will do the same to all the kingdoms on the other side of the Jordan. 22Don't be afraid of the nations there, for the Lord your God will fight for you.'

23-25"At that time I made a plea to God. 'O Lord God, please let me cross over into the Promised Land,' I said. 'Let me enter the good land beyond the Jordan River. Let me walk its rolling hills. Please, let me see Lebanon. I want to see the result of all the power you have been showing us. What God in all of heaven or earth can do what you have done for us?'

26"But the Lord was angry with me because of you. So he would not let me cross over. 'Speak of it no more,' he ordered. 27'But go to the top of Mount Pisgah. There you can look out in every direction. From there you will see the land in the distance. But you shall not cross the Jordan River. 28Appoint Joshua to take your place. Then encourage him. For he shall lead the people across to the land. He will conquer the land you will see from the mountaintop.'

29"So we stayed in the valley near Beth-peor.

Obey God

4 "And now, O Israel, listen to these laws I teach you. Obey them if you want to live. Do them if you want to enter the land given you by the Lord God of your fathers. 2Do not add other laws or take away from these. Just obey them, for they are from the Lord your God. 3You have seen what the Lord did to you at Baal-peor. There he destroyed many people for worshiping idols. 4But all of you who were faithful to the Lord your God are still alive today.

5"These are the laws for you to obey. You must begin to follow them when you come to the land where you will live. They are from the Lord our God. He has given them to me to pass on to you. 6If you obey them, you will be known as being wise and smart. The nations nearby will hear these laws. And they will exclaim, 'What other nation is as wise as Israel?' 7What other nation has God among them as the Lord our God is here among us? Who else has a God who is there any time they call upon him? 8And what nation, no matter how great, has laws as fair as these I am giving you today?

9"But watch out! Be very careful never to forget what you have seen God doing for you. May his miracles have a deep effect upon your lives! Tell your

children and your grandchildren about the great miracles he did. 10Tell them about the day you stood before the Lord at Mount Sinai. Tell them about the time he told me, 'Call the people before me. I will teach them. That way they will learn to show respect to me always. That way they will teach my laws to their children.' 11You stood at the foot of the mountain. The mountain burned with fire. Flames shot far into the sky. They were surrounded by black clouds and deep darkness. 12And the Lord spoke to you from the fire. You heard his words but didn't see him. 13He proclaimed the laws you must obey. These are the Ten Commandments. He wrote them on two stone tablets. 14Yes, it was at that time that the Lord spoke to me. He told me to give you these laws. You must obey them when you get to the Promised Land.

Beware of Idols

15"But beware! You didn't see the form of God that day. He spoke to you from the fire at Mount Sinai. 16-17So do not make yourselves unclean by trying to make a statue of God. Do not make an idol in any form. You must not make idols of men, women, animals, or birds. 18Do not make idols of small animals that run along the ground. Do not make idols of fish. 19And do not look up into the sky to worship the sun, moon, or stars. The Lord may allow other nations to get away with this for now, but not you. 20The Lord has rescued you from Egypt. You are to be his special people. You are his very own. 21-22But he was angry with me because of you. He vowed that I could not go over the Jordan River. I cannot go into the good land he has given you. I must die here on this side of the river. 23Beware that you do not break the contract the Lord your God has made with you! You will break it if you make any idols. The Lord your God will not allow this. 24He is like a burning fire! He is a jealous God!

25"In the future, your children and grandchildren will be born. You will have been in the land a long time. And you will defile yourselves by making idols. When this happens, the Lord your God will be very angry because of your sin. ²⁶Heaven and earth will see what you have done. And you shall be quickly destroyed from the land. Soon now you will cross the Jordan River and conquer that land. But your days there will be brief. You will then be completely destroyed. ²⁷For the Lord will scatter you among the nations. And you will be but few in number. ²⁸There, far away, you will worship idols made from wood and stone. You will worship idols that neither see nor hear nor eat nor smell.

²⁹"But you will also begin to search again for the Lord your God. You will find him when you search for him with all your heart and soul. ³⁰And those bitter days will come upon you in the latter times. When they do, you will finally come back to the Lord your God. Then you will listen to what he tells you. ³¹For the Lord your God is merciful. He will not leave you or destroy you. He will not forget the promises he has made to your ancestors.

There Is Only One God

³²"Go back to the time when God created man upon the earth. Search from one end of the heavens to the other. See if you can find anything like this. ³³A whole nation heard the voice of God. You yourselves heard it and lived! ³⁴Where else will you find an example of God's freeing a nation from slavery? Where else can you find a nation saved by God's plagues, mighty miracles, and terror? Yet that is what the Lord your God did for you in Egypt. He did it all right before your very eyes. ³⁵He did these things so you would know that the Lord is God. He did them so you would know that there is no one else like him. ³⁶He let you hear his voice teaching you from heaven. He let you see his great pillar of fire upon the earth. You even heard his words from the center of the fire.

³⁷"He loved your ancestors. So he chose to bless their descendants by bringing you out from Egypt. And he did it with a great display of power. ³⁸He

drove away other nations greater by far than you. And he gave you their land as an inheritance, as it is today. ³⁹This is a wonderful thought! The Lord is God both in heaven and down here upon the earth. There is no God other than he! ⁴⁰You must obey these laws that I will tell you today. That way all will be well with you and your children. And you will live forever in the land the Lord your God is giving you."

Cities of Refuge

⁴¹Then Moses told the people of Israel to set apart three cities east of the Jordan River. ⁴²Anyone who killed someone by accident could run there for safety. ⁴³Bezer was the city chosen for the tribe of Reuben. It was on the plateau in the wilderness. Ramoth was chosen in Gilead. It was for the tribe of Gad. Golan was the city chosen for the tribe of Manasseh. It was in Bashan.

The People Listen to God's Laws

⁴⁴⁻⁴⁶Listed below are the laws Moses gave to the people of Israel. He gave them these laws when they left Egypt. They were now camped east of the Jordan River near the city of Beth-peor. This was the land where the Amorites had once lived under King Sihon. His capital had been Heshbon. He and his people were destroyed by Moses and the Israelites. ⁴⁷Israel conquered his land and that of King Og of Bashan. They were the two Amorite kings east of the Jordan. ⁴⁸Israel also took the area from Aroer at the edge of the Arnon River valley to Mount Sirion. This mountain is also known as Mount Hermon. ⁴⁹They also took the Arabah east of the Jordan River over to the Dead Sea. This is the area below the slopes of Mount Pisgah.

The Ten Commandments

5 Moses kept on speaking to the people of Israel. He said, "Listen carefully now to all these laws God has given you. Learn them, and be sure to obey them!

²⁻³"The Lord our God made a contract with you at Mount Sinai. The contract was *not just with your ancestors. It is with you who are here alive today.* ⁴He spoke

with you face to face from the center of the fire, there at the mountain. ⁵I stood between you and the Lord. For you were afraid of the fire. And you did not go up to him on the mountain. He spoke to me and I passed on his laws to you. This is what he said.

⁶"'I am the Lord your God. I rescued you from slavery in Egypt.

⁷"'Never worship any god but me.

⁸"'Never make idols. Do not worship images, whether of birds, animals, or fish. ⁹⁻¹⁰You shall not bow down to any images. You shall not worship them in any way. For I am the Lord your God. I am a jealous God. I will bring the curse of a father's sins upon his children. It will reach even the third and fourth generations of the children of those who hate me. But I will be kind to a thousand generations of those who love me. I will bless those who keep my commands.

¹¹"'You must never use my name to make a vow you do not intend to keep. I will not overlook that.

¹²"'Keep the Sabbath day holy. This is my command. ¹³Work the other six days. ¹⁴But the seventh day is the Sabbath of the Lord your God. No work shall be done that day by you or by any of your household. Your sons, daughters, servants, oxen, donkeys, and cattle must never work. Even foreigners living among you must obey this law. Everybody must rest as you do. ¹⁵Why should you keep the Sabbath? It is because you were slaves in Egypt. But the Lord your God brought you out with a great display of miracles.

¹⁶"'Honor your father and mother. Remember, this is a command of the Lord your God. If you do so, you shall have a long life. You shall be blessed in the land he is giving you.

¹⁷"'You must not murder.

¹⁸"'You must not sleep with another man's wife.

¹⁹"'You must not steal.

²⁰"'You must not tell lies.

²¹"'You must not want to have another man's wife. You must not envy him for his home, land, servants, oxen, donkeys. You must not want anything else he owns.'

²²"The Lord has given these laws to each one of you. He gave them from the heart of the fire. He gave them from the clouds and thick darkness that were over Mount Sinai. Those were the only commands he gave you at that time. He wrote them out on two stone tablets and gave them to me. ²³But you heard the loud voice from the darkness. And you saw the terrible fire at the top of the mountain. When you did, all your tribal leaders came to me. ²⁴They pleaded, 'Today the Lord our God has shown us his greatness. We have even heard his voice from the heart of the fire. Now we know that a man may speak to God and not die. ²⁵But we will surely die if he speaks to us again. This awesome fire will consume us. ²⁶⁻²⁷What man can hear, as we have, the voice of the living God and live? You go and listen to all that God says. Then come and tell us. We will listen and obey.'

Think often about God's Word

Keep thinking about my commandments.

Deuteronomy 6:6

---

²⁸"And the Lord agreed to your request. He said to me, 'I have heard what the people have said to you. And I agree. ²⁹Oh, that they would always have such a heart for me. Oh, that they would always want to obey my commands. Then all would go well with them in the future. All would go well with their children throughout all generations! ³⁰Go and tell them to go back to their tents. ³¹Then you come back and stand here beside me. I will give you all my commands. Then you shall teach them to the people. And they will obey them in the land I am giving to them.'"

³²So Moses told the people, "You must obey all the commands of the Lord your God. Follow his law in every detail. Do all that he has laid out for you. ³³Only then will you live long and good lives in the land you are to enter and own.

Love God and Obey Him

6 "The Lord your God told me to give you all these commands. You must obey them in the land you will soon be entering. ²The purpose of these laws is to cause you, your children, and your grandchildren to respect the Lord your God. You must do this by obeying all of his laws as long as you live. If you do, you will have long, good years ahead of you. ³Therefore, O Israel, listen closely to each command. Be careful to obey it. Then all will go well with you. And you will have many children. If you obey these commands, you will become a great nation. You will live in a land 'flowing with milk and honey.' It will be just as the God of your fathers promised you.

Teach Your Children to Obey God

⁴"O Israel, listen! The Lord alone is our God. ⁵You must love him with *all* your heart, soul, and might. ⁶Keep thinking about my commandments. ⁷Teach them to your children. Talk about them at home or when you are out walking. Talk about them at bedtime and as soon as you get up in the morning. ⁸Tie them on your finger. Wear them on your forehead. ⁹And write them on the doorposts of your house!

Talk often about God's Word

Teach them to your children. Talk about them at home or when you are out walking. Talk about them at bedtime and as soon as you get up in the morning.

Deuteronomy 6:7

---

¹⁰⁻¹²"The Lord your God will bring you into the land. He will give you the land he promised your ancestors, Abraham, Isaac, and Jacob. He will give you great cities full of good things. These will be cities you did not build. You will also use wells you did not dig. You will enjoy vineyards and olive trees you did not plant. When you have eaten until you can hold no more, then beware. You might forget the Lord. You might forget that he brought you out of the land of Egypt, the land of slavery. ¹³When you are full, do not forget to respect him and serve him. Do not forget to use *his* name alone to endorse your promises.

Good things happen when you please God

When you please God, things will go well for you. Then you will receive the good things God has promised.

Deuteronomy 6:18

---

¹⁴"You must not worship the gods of the nations around you. ¹⁵For the Lord your God who lives among you is a jealous God. His anger may rise quickly against you. And he may wipe you off the face of the earth. ¹⁶You must not provoke him. You must not try his patience as you did when you complained against him at Massah. ¹⁷You must always obey him in all he tells you. ¹⁸When you please God, things will go well for you. Then you will receive the good things God has promised. Only then will you be doing what is right and good in the Lord's eyes. ¹⁹You will also be able to throw out all the enemies living in your land. For the Lord agreed to help you do it.

²⁰"In the years to come your son might ask, 'Why do we have these laws which the Lord our God has given us?' ²¹If he asks this, you must tell him, 'We were Pharaoh's slaves in Egypt. But the Lord brought us out of Egypt. He saved us with great power ²²and mighty miracles. He dealt terrible blows against Egypt and Pharaoh and all his people. We saw it all with our own eyes. ²³He brought us out of Egypt. He saved us so he could give us this land he promised our ancestors. ²⁴And he has told us to obey all of these laws. We are to respect him so that he can keep us alive as he

has until now. 25For it goes well with us when we obey all the laws of the Lord our God.'

Defeat the Enemy Nations

7 "The Lord will soon bring you into the Promised Land. When he does, he will destroy seven nations. They are all greater and stronger than you are. These include the Hittites, the Girgashites, the Amorites, the Canaanites, the Perizzites, the Hivites, the Jebusites.

2"The Lord your God will turn them over to you to be destroyed. When he does, do a complete job of it. Do not make any treaties or show them mercy. Wipe them out completely. 3Do not marry any of them. Do not let your sons and daughters marry their sons and daughters. 4That would surely cause your young people to start worshiping their gods. Then the anger of the Lord would be hot against you. He would surely destroy you.

5"You must break down the heathen altars and shatter the obelisks. You must cut up the shameful images and burn the idols.

6"For you are a holy people. You have been dedicated to the Lord your God. He has chosen you from all the people on the face of the whole earth. You are his own chosen ones. 7He did not choose you because you were a larger nation than any other. You were the smallest of all! 8It was just because he loves you. And he kept his promise to your ancestors. That is why he brought you out of slavery in Egypt. That is why he delivered you with such amazing power and mighty miracles.

9"Know that the Lord your God is the faithful God. He keeps his promises for a thousand generations. He constantly loves those who love him and who obey his commands. 10But those who hate him shall be punished publicly and destroyed. He will deal with them personally. 11So obey all these commands I am giving you today. 12When you obey, the Lord your God will keep his part of the contract. It is a contract which, in his tender love, he made with your fathers. 13And he will love you and

bless you. He will make you into a great nation. He will make you fertile. He will also make your ground and your animals fertile. That way you will have large crops of grain, grapes, and olives. You will have great flocks of cattle, sheep, and goats. You will get all these when you get to the land he promised your fathers. 14You will be blessed above all the nations of the earth. All your men and women will have children. And all of your cattle will have calves. 15 And the Lord will take away all your sickness. He will not let you suffer any of the diseases of Egypt you remember so well. He will give them all to your enemies!

16"You must destroy all the nations the Lord your God delivers into your hands. Have no pity, and do not worship their gods. If you do, it will be a sad day for you. 17Perhaps you will think to yourself, 'How can we ever conquer these nations? They are so much more powerful than we are!' 18But do not be afraid of them! Just remember what the Lord your God did to Pharaoh. Remember what he did to all the land of Egypt. 19 Do you remember the terrors the Lord sent upon them? Your parents saw it with their own eyes. Do you remember the mighty miracles and wonders? Do you remember the power and strength of Almighty God? Do you remember how he used his power to bring you out of Egypt? Well, the Lord your God will use this same might against the people you fear. 20Also, the Lord your God will send hornets to drive out those who hide from you!

21"No, do not be afraid of those nations. For the Lord your God is among you. And he is a great and awesome God. 22He will throw them out a little at a time. He will not do it all at once. For if he did, the number of wild animals would grow too quickly. They would become dangerous to you. 23He will do it slowly. And you will move in against those nations and destroy them. 24He will deliver their kings into your hands. And you will erase their names from the face of the earth. No one will be able to stand against you.

25"Burn their idols. Do not even touch the silver or gold they are made of. Do not take it or it will be a snare to you. It is horrible to the Lord your God. 26Do not bring an idol into your home and worship it. If you do, then your doom is sealed. Hate it completely, for it is a cursed thing.

Do Not Forget God

8 "You must obey all the commands I give you today. If you do, you will not only live, you will multiply. You will go in and take over the land promised to your fathers by the Lord. 2Do you remember how the Lord led you through the wilderness for all those 40 years? Do you remember how he humbled you to find out how you would respond? Do you remember how he tested you to see whether you would obey him? 3Yes, he humbled you by letting you go hungry. Then he fed you with manna. It was a food unknown to both you and your ancestors. He did it to show you that food isn't everything. He wanted you to know that real life comes by obeying every command of God. 4For all these 40 years your clothes haven't grown old. And during this time your feet haven't been blistered or swollen. 5So you should know that the Lord punishes you to help you. He punishes you just as a man punishes his son.

6"Obey the laws of the Lord your God. Walk in his ways and fear him. 7For the Lord your God is bringing you into a good land. It is a land of brooks, pools, gushing springs, valleys, and hills. 8Wheat and barley grow in abundance. It is a land of grape vines, fig trees, pomegranates, olives, and honey. 9It is a land where there is plenty of food. Nothing is lacking. It is a land where iron is as common as stone. The hills are full of copper. 10When you have eaten your fill, praise the Lord your God. For he has given you a good land.

11"But that is the time to be careful! Beware that in your plenty you don't forget the Lord your God. Do not begin to disobey him. 12-13For you might become full and wealthy. And you might

build fine homes to live in. Your flocks and herds may become very large. Perhaps your silver and gold will increase. 14If this happens, watch out that you do not become proud. Do not forget the Lord your God. For he brought you out of your slavery in the land of Egypt. 15Beware that you do not forget the God who led you through the wilderness. It was filled with dangerous snakes and scorpions. And it was very hot and dry. But he gave you water from the rock! 16He fed you with manna in the wilderness! It was a kind of bread unknown before. He gave you this food so that you would become humble. He hoped that your trust in him would grow. He wanted to do you good. 17He wanted you to know that it was not your own power that made you wealthy. 18Always remember that it is the Lord your God who gives you the power to become rich. He does it to fulfill his promise to your ancestors.

19"But you might forget about the Lord your God. You might worship other gods instead, and follow evil ways. If you do, you shall surely die. 20You shall die just as the Lord has caused other nations to die. If you don't obey the Lord your God, death will be your fate, too.

Do Not Forget God's Mercy

9 "O Israel, listen! Today you are to cross the Jordan River. You are to begin to push out the nations on the other side. Those nations are much greater and more powerful than you are! They live in cities with high walls. Among them are the famed Anak giants, against whom none can stand! 3But the Lord your God will go before you. He will be like a raging fire to destroy them. With him, you will quickly conquer them and drive them out.

4"The Lord will do this for you. When he does, do not say to yourselves, 'The Lord has helped us because we are so good!' No, he is doing it because the other nations are so wicked. 5It is not at all because you are such fine, upright people. That is not why the Lord will drive them out from before you! I say it again, it is because the other nations are so wicked. And it is because of his promises to your ancestors, Abraham, Isaac, and Jacob. For these reasons he will do it. [6]I say it yet again. *The Lord your God is not giving you this good land because you are good. For you are not good.* You are a wicked, stubborn people.

[7]"Don't you remember? Oh, never forget it! Don't you remember how angry you made the Lord your God out in the wilderness? Don't you remember how you have rebelled from the day you left Egypt until now? All this time you have turned against him.

[8]"Don't you remember how angry you made him at Mount Sinai? He was ready to destroy you. [9]I was on the mountain at the time. I was getting the contract that the Lord had made with you. It was written on the stone tablets. I was there for 40 days and 40 nights. All that time I ate nothing. I didn't even take a drink of water. [10-11]At the end of those 40 days and nights the Lord gave me the contract. He gave me the tablets on which he had written his commands. These were the commands he had spoken from the mountain while the people watched from below. [12]Then he told me to go down the mountain quickly. The people I had led out of Egypt had sinned greatly. They had quickly turned away from the laws of God. They had made an idol out of metal.

[13-14]"'Let me alone! Then I shall destroy this evil, stubborn people!' the Lord told me. 'I will blot out their name from under heaven. And I will make a mighty nation of you. It will be mightier and greater than they are.'

[15]"I came down from the burning mountain. I held in my hands the two tablets with the laws of God written on them. [16]There below me I could see the calf you had made. You had sinned terribly against the Lord your God. How quickly you turned away from him! [17]I lifted the tablets high above my head. Then I threw them to the ground! I smashed them before your eyes! [18]Then for another 40 days and nights I lay before the Lord. I didn't eat bread or drink water. For you had done what the Lord hated most. Thus you had provoked him to great anger. [19]How I feared for you. For the Lord was ready to destroy you. But that time, too, he listened to me. [20]Aaron was in great danger because the Lord was so angry with him. But I prayed, and the Lord spared him. [21]I took your sin—the calf you had made—and burned it. I ground it into fine dust. Then I threw it into the stream that poured out of the mountain.

[22]"Again at Taberah and once again at Massah you angered the Lord. You did it yet again at Kibroth-hattaavah. [23]At Kadesh-barnea, when the Lord told you to enter the land he had given you, you rebelled. You wouldn't believe that he would help you. You refused to obey him. [24]Yes, you have rebelled against the Lord from the first day I knew you. [25]That is why I fell down before him for 40 days and nights. The Lord was ready to destroy you.

[26]"I prayed to him, 'O Lord God, don't destroy your own people. They are your inheritance. You saved them from Egypt by your mighty power and great strength. [27]Don't notice how rebellious and stubborn these people are. But remember instead your promises to your servants Abraham, Isaac, and Jacob. Oh, please don't notice how wicked and sinful these people are. [28]For if you do, you might destroy them. And the Egyptians will speak among themselves. They will say, "It is because the Lord wasn't able to bring them to the land he promised them." Or they might say, "He destroyed them because he hated them. He brought them into the wilderness to kill them." [29]They are your people. They are your inheritance. You brought them from Egypt by your great power and your mighty arm.'

Ten Commandments Rewritten

10 "At that time the Lord told me to cut two more stone tablets like the first ones. He told me to make a wooden Ark to keep them in. I was then to go back to God on the mountain. [2]He said he would write on the tablets the same commands that were on the tablets I had smashed. He told me to place them in the Ark. [3]So I made an Ark of acacia

wood. I cut out two stone tablets like the first two. Then I took the tablets up on the mountain to God. 4He again wrote the Ten Commandments on them and gave them to me. They were the same commands he had given you from the heart of the fire. They were the laws he gave you from the mountain as you all watched below. 5Then I came down. I put the tablets in the Ark I had made. And they are there to this day. I did just as the Lord told me to do.

6"The people of Israel then went from Be-eroth of Bene-jaakan to Mose-rah. There Aaron died and was buried. His son Eleazar became the next priest.

7"Then they went to Gudgodah. From there they went to Jotbathah, a land of brooks and water. 8It was there that the Lord set apart the tribe of Levi to carry the Ark. It contained the Ten Commandments of the Lord. The Levites were chosen to stand before the Lord. They were to do his work and to bless his name, just as is done today. 9That is why the tribe of Levi does not have a portion of land reserved for it. They will get no property in the Promised Land, as their brother tribes will. For as the Lord told them, he himself is their inheritance.

10"As I said before, I stayed on the mountain before the Lord. I stayed for 40 days and nights the second time, just as I had the first. The Lord again yielded to my pleas and didn't destroy you. 11"But he said to me, 'Get up. Lead the people to the land I promised their fathers. It is time to go in and take it.'

Obey God

12-13"And now, Israel, this is what the Lord your God asks of you. Listen carefully to all he says to you. Obey for your own good the commands I am giving you today. Love the Lord and worship him with all your hearts and souls. 14Earth and highest heaven belong to the Lord your God. 15And yet he rejoiced in your fathers. He loved them so much that he chose you, their children. He chose you to be above every other nation. This fact is clear today. 16So make your sinful hearts clean. Stop being so stubborn.

17"The Lord your God is God of gods and Lord of lords. He is the great and mighty God. He is the God of terror. He plays no favorites. He takes no bribes. 18He gives justice to the fatherless and widows. He loves foreigners and gives them food and clothing. 19You too must love foreigners. You yourselves were foreigners in the land of Egypt. 20You must fear the Lord your God. You must worship him and cling to him. You must take oaths by his name alone. 21He is your praise and he is your God. He is the one who has done mighty miracles you yourselves have seen. 22 When your ancestors went down into Egypt there were only 70 of them. But the Lord your God has made you as many as the stars in the sky!

11 "You must love the Lord your God. Obey every one of his commands. 2Listen! I am not talking now to your children. They have never experienced the Lord's punishments. They have never seen his greatness and his awesome power. 3They weren't there to see the miracles he did in Egypt against Pharaoh and all his land. 4They didn't see what God did to the armies of Egypt. They didn't see how he drowned Egypt's horses and chariots in the Red Sea as they were chasing you. Your children haven't seen how the Lord has kept them powerless against you until this very day! 5They didn't see how the Lord provided through all the years you were in the wilderness. They didn't see how the Lord cared for you until you got here. 6Your children weren't there when Dathan and Abiram (the sons of Eliab, descendants of Reuben) sinned. They didn't see the earth open up and swallow them! They didn't see it swallow their families and tents and all they owned!

Choose a Blessing or a Curse

7"But you have seen these mighty miracles! 8How carefully, then, you should obey these commands I am going to give you today. If you do, you will have the strength to go into the land. You will conquer the land you are about to enter.

⁹If you obey the commands, you will have a long and good life in the land. It is the land the Lord promised to your ancestors and to you, their descendants. It is a wonderful land, 'flowing with milk and honey'! ¹⁰For the land you are about to enter and take is not like the land of Egypt. It is not like the land where you have come from, where irrigation is necessary. ¹¹It is a land of hills and valleys with plenty of rain. ¹²It is a land that the Lord your God personally cares for! His eyes are always upon it, day after day all through the year!

¹³"You must carefully obey all of his commands that I am going to give you today. You must love the Lord your God with all your hearts and souls. You must truly worship him. ¹⁴If you do these things, then he will continue to send both the early and late rains. These will produce rich crops of grain, grapes for your wine, and olive oil. ¹⁵He will give you lush pastures for your cattle to graze in. You will have plenty to eat and be fully content.

¹⁶"But beware that your hearts do not turn from God to worship other gods. ¹⁷For if you do, the anger of the Lord will be hot against you. He will shut the heavens. There will be no rain and no harvest. And you will quickly die from the good land the Lord has given you. ¹⁸So keep these commands in mind. Tie them to your hand to remind you to obey them. Tie them to your forehead between your eyes! ¹⁹Teach them to your children. Talk about them when you are sitting at home. Speak of them when you are out walking, at bedtime, and before breakfast! ²⁰Write them upon the doors of your houses and upon your gates. ²¹If you do this, you and your children will enjoy the good life. This will be true as long as there is sky above the earth. This good life is waiting for you in the land the Lord has promised.

²²"You must carefully obey all the commands I give you. Love the Lord your God. Walk in all his ways. Cling to him. ²³If you do, then the Lord will drive out all the nations in your land. He will do this no matter how much greater and stronger than you they

might be. ²⁴Wherever you go, the land is yours. Your borders will stretch from the southern Negeb to Lebanon. They will stretch from the Euphrates River to the Mediterranean Sea. ²⁵No one will be able to stand against you. For the Lord your God will send fear and dread ahead of you. It will go before you wherever you go. It will happen just as he has promised.

²⁶"I am giving you the choice today between God's blessing or God's curse! ²⁷There will be blessing if you obey the commands of the Lord your God that I am giving you today. ²⁸But there will be a curse if you refuse to do them. You will be cursed if you worship the gods of these other nations. ²⁹The Lord your God shall bring you into the land to take it. When he does, a blessing shall be proclaimed from Mount Gerizim and a curse from Mount Ebal! ³⁰Gerizim and Ebal are mountains west of the Jordan River, where the Canaanites live. They are in the wasteland near Gilgal, where the oaks of Moreh are. ³¹For you are to cross the Jordan. You are to live in the land the Lord is giving you. ³²But you must obey all the laws I am giving you today.

Only One Altar for Sacrifices

12 "These are the laws you must obey when you get to the land. This is the land that the Lord, the God of your fathers, has given you for all time.

²"You must destroy all the heathen altars. Break them down wherever you find them. They might be high in the mountains, up in the hills, or under the trees. ³Break the altars! Smash the obelisks! Burn the shameful images! Cut down the metal idols! Leave nothing even to remind you of them!

⁴⁻⁵"You must not make sacrifices to your God just anywhere. That is how the heathen sacrifice to their gods. Rather, you must build a sanctuary for him. You must put it at the place he himself will choose as his home. ⁶There you shall bring to the Lord your burnt offerings and other sacrifices. There you shall bring your tithes and your offerings. They shall be given by the act of

waving them before the altar. There you shall bring the gifts you promised me and your freewill offerings. There you must bring your offerings of the first-born animals of your flocks and herds. ⁷ There you and your families shall feast before the Lord your God. You shall rejoice in all he has done for you.

⁸"You will no longer go your own way as you do now. Everyone shall not just do whatever he thinks is right. ⁹(For these laws don't go into effect until you get to the land the Lord will give to you.) ¹⁰But you will cross the Jordan River. You will live in the Promised Land. And the Lord will give you rest. He will keep you safe from all your enemies. ¹¹At this time, you must bring all your burnt sacrifices and other offerings to his sanctuary. You shall then go to the place he will choose as his home.

¹²You shall rejoice there before the Lord. You shall do so with your sons and daughters and servants. Remember to invite the Levites to feast with you. For they have no land of their own.

¹³"You are not to sacrifice your burnt offerings just anywhere. ¹⁴You may do so only in the place the Lord will choose. He will pick a place in the land given to one of the tribes. Only there may you offer your sacrifices and bring your offerings. ¹⁵But the meat you eat may be killed anywhere. You will do just as you do now with gazelle and deer. Eat as much of this meat as you wish. Eat it as often as you are able to get it. For the Lord has given it to you. Those who are unclean may eat it too. ¹⁶The only rule is that you are not to eat the blood. Pour it out on the ground like water.

¹⁷"But none of the offerings may be eaten at home. This is true of the tithe of your grain and new wine and olive oil. It includes the firstborn of your flocks and herds. This is true also of anything you have vowed to give the Lord. It includes your freewill offerings. And it includes the gifts to be given to the Lord by waving them before his altar. ¹⁸All these must be brought to the central altar. There you, your children, and the Levites shall eat them before the Lord your God. He will tell you

Burnt Offerings
DEUTERONOMY
12:4-19

When you give offerings to God at church and Sunday school, you usually give money. That helps your church do God's work. If you had lived in Moses' time your offerings would have been burned! That's because people usually brought animals to God's House as an offering instead of money. These animals were killed and their meat was burned on the altar.

The Tabernacle, God's House, had a large altar of wood, covered with bronze or copper. The priest burned offerings on it. Most of the time these offerings were meat. Burning offerings was a way to tell God, "I'm sorry that I have sinned." Since Jesus came, we do not need these altars. We can talk right to Jesus and tell him "I'm sorry." He forgives us.

where this altar must be located. Rejoice before the Lord your God in all you do. ¹⁹By the way, be very careful not to forget about the Levites. Share with them.

20-23"It might happen that the Lord will enlarge your borders. The central altar might then be too far away from you. If this is true, then your flocks and herds may be butchered on your own farms. It may be done, just as you do now with gazelle and deer. And even persons who are unclean may eat them. The only rule is never to eat the blood. The blood is the life. And you shall not eat the life with the meat. 24-25Instead, pour the blood out upon the earth. If you do, all will be well with you and your children. 26-27Only your gifts to the Lord need be taken to the central altar. This includes the offerings you have promised in your vows and your burnt offerings. These may only be sacrificed upon the altar of the Lord your God. The blood will be poured out upon the altar. You will eat the meat.

28"Be careful to obey all of these commands. You must do what is right in the eyes of the Lord your God. If you do, all will go well with you and your children forever. 29He shall destroy the nations in the land where you will live. 30When he does, don't follow their example in worshiping their gods. Do not ask, 'How do these nations worship their gods?' And do not then go and worship as they do! 31You must not insult the Lord your God like that! These nations have done horrible things that he hates. And they do these things in the name of their religion. They have even roasted their sons and daughters in front of their gods. 32Obey all the commands I give you. Do not add to or subtract from them.

Don't Listen to False Prophets

13 "There might be a prophet among you. Or someone might claim to foretell the future by dreams. 2What he predicts might even come true. But he might say, 'Come, let us worship the gods of the other nations.' 3If he does, then don't listen to him. For the Lord is testing you. He wants to find out whether or not you really love him with all your heart and soul. 4You must *never* worship any God but the Lord. Obey only his commands and cling to him.

5"The prophet who tries to lead you astray must be killed. For he has tried to turn you against the Lord your God. This God is the very one who brought you out of slavery in the land of Egypt. By killing him you will clear out the evil from among you.

6-7"Your nearest relative might whisper to you to come and worship these foreign gods. A brother, son, daughter, beloved wife, or closest friend might even do the same. 8If someone does this, then do not say, 'yes.' Don't listen to him. Have no pity. Do not spare that person from the penalty. Don't hide his evil request. 9Put him to death! Your own hand shall be the first upon him to kill him. Then the hands of all the people will follow. 10Stone him to death. For he has tried to draw you away from the Lord your God. This is the very God who brought you from the land of Egypt. He is the one who saved you from the place of slavery. 11Then all Israel will hear about his evil deed. They will fear such wickedness as this among you.

Worship Only God

12-14"You might hear it said about a city in Israel that some people have led others astray. They might be telling the people to worship foreign gods. If you hear this, first check the facts to see if the rumor is true. You might find that such a horrible thing is happening among you. It might be happening in one of the cities the Lord has given you. 15If this is true, you must without fail declare war against that city. You must destroy all the people who live there. You must even kill all of the cattle. 16After that you must pile all the booty into the middle of the street and burn it. Then put the whole city to the torch. Burn it as a burnt offering to the Lord your God. That city shall forever be a lifeless pile. It may never be rebuilt. 17Keep none of the booty! Then the Lord will turn from his fierce anger. He will be merciful to you and have compassion upon you. He will make you a great nation just as he promised your ancestors.

18"The Lord your God will be merciful only if you obey him. You must obey his commands that I am giving you today. You must do that which is right in the eyes of the Lord.

What to Eat and Not Eat

14 "Since you are the people of God, never cut yourselves. The heathen do this when they worship their idols. And never shave the front of your heads for funerals. ²You belong to the Lord your God and him only. He has chosen you to be his own people. You belong to him more than any other nation on the face of the earth does.

³⁻⁵"You are not to eat any animal I have said to be unclean. You may eat the ox, the sheep, and the goat. You may eat the deer, the gazelle, the roebuck, and the wild goat. The ibex, the antelope, and the mountain sheep you may also eat.

⁶"Any animal that has cloven hooves and chews the cud may be eaten. ⁷But if the animal doesn't have both, it may not be eaten. So you may not eat the camel, the hare, or the coney. They chew the cud but do not have cloven hooves. ⁸Pigs may not be eaten. They have cloven hooves, but they do not chew the cud. You may not even touch the dead bodies of such animals.

⁹"Only sea animals with fins and scales may be eaten. ¹⁰All other kinds are unclean.

¹¹⁻¹⁸"You may eat any bird that is clean. But you may not eat the eagle, the vulture, the osprey, the buzzard, or the falcon (any variety). The raven (any variety), the ostrich, the nighthawk, the sea gull, or the hawk (any variety) also must not be eaten. You must not eat the screech owl, the great owl, the horned owl, the pelican, or the vulture. The cormorant, the stork, the heron (any variety), the hoopoe, and the bat are also unclean.

¹⁹⁻²⁰"All insects with wings are unclean for you. They may not be eaten.

²¹"Don't eat anything that has died a natural death. But a foreigner among you may eat it. You may give it or sell it to him. But don't eat it yourself. For you are holy to the Lord your God.

"You must not boil a young goat in its mother's milk.

How to Give to God

²²"You must tithe all of your crops every year. ²³Bring this tithe to eat before the Lord your God. Bring it to the place he shall choose as his sanctuary. This applies to your tithes of grain, new wine, and olive oil. It also applies to the firstborn of your flocks and herds. The purpose of tithing is to teach you always to put God first in your lives. ²⁴The place the Lord chooses for his sanctuary might be far away. It might be too far to carry your tithes to that place. ²⁵If so, then you may sell the tithe of your crops and herds. Take the money to the Lord's sanctuary. ²⁶When you get there, use the money to buy an ox and a sheep. Also buy some wine or beer. Use it to feast there before the Lord your God. Celebrate and rejoice with your family.

²⁷"Don't forget to share your income with the Levites in your area. They have no property or crops as you do.

²⁸"Every third year you are to use your whole tithe for local welfare programs. ²⁹Give it to the Levites who have no inheritance among you. Give it also to foreigners, or to widows and orphans within your city. That way they will eat and be filled. Then the Lord your God will bless you and your work.

Lending Money

15 "At the end of every seventh year you shall cancel all debts! ²Every creditor shall write 'Paid in full' on any bill he holds against a fellow Israelite. For the Lord has released everyone from his debts. ³This release does not apply to foreigners. ⁴⁻⁵No one will become poor because of this law. This is because the Lord will greatly bless you in the land he is giving you. But you must obey this command! You must do just one thing to receive his blessing. You must follow all the commands of the Lord your God that I am giving you today. ⁶If you do, he will bless you as he has promised. You shall lend money to many nations but will never need to borrow! You shall rule many nations, but they shall not rule over you!

7"Soon you will get to the land the Lord will give you. There might be those among you who are poor. If there are, you must not shut your heart or hand against them. 8You must lend them as much as they need. 9Beware! Don't refuse a loan because the year for forgiving debts is close at hand! You might refuse to make the loan. Then the needy man might cry out to the Lord. If he does, it will be counted against you as a sin. 10You must lend him what he needs. And don't moan about it, either! For the Lord will bless you in all you do because of this! 11There will always be some among you who are poor. That is why this command is needed. You must lend to them as they have need.

How to Treat Slaves

12"You might buy a Hebrew slave. The slave might be either a man or a woman. If you do, you must free him after the sixth year you have owned him. 13And don't send him away empty-handed! 14Give him a large farewell present from your flock. Give him gifts from your olive and wine presses. Share with him as the Lord your God has blessed you. 15Remember that you were slaves in the land of Egypt. Remember that the Lord your God rescued you! That is why I am giving you this command.

16"But your Hebrew slave might not want to leave. He might say he loves you. He might enjoy your pleasant home and get along well with you. 17If so, then take an awl and pierce his ear into the door. After that he shall be your slave forever. Do the same with your women slaves. 18But when you free a slave you must not feel bad. Remember that for six years he has cost you less than half the price of a hired hand! And the Lord your God will bless all you do because you have let him go!

Firstborn Animals

19"You shall set aside for God all the firstborn males from your flocks and herds. Do not use the firstborn of your herds to work your fields. Never shear the firstborn of your flocks of sheep and goats. 20Instead, you and your family shall eat these animals. You shall eat them before the Lord your God each year at his sanctuary. 21However, this firstborn animal might have a defect. It might be lame or blind. Or it might have something else wrong with it. If so, you shall not sacrifice it. 22Instead, use it for food for your family at home. Anyone may eat it, just as anyone may eat a gazelle or deer. It may even be eaten by a person who is unclean at the time. 23But do not eat the blood. Pour it out upon the ground like water.

Special Holidays

16 "Never forget to celebrate the Passover during the month of April. That was when the Lord your God brought you out of Egypt by night. 2Your Passover sacrifice shall be either a lamb or an ox. It must be sacrificed to the Lord your God at his sanctuary. 3Eat the sacrifice with unleavened bread. Eat unleavened bread for seven days. It will remind you of the bread you ate as you escaped from Egypt. You will remember that you left Egypt in a great hurry. You went so quickly that there was no time for the bread to rise. Remember that day all the rest of your lives! 4For seven days no trace of yeast shall be in your homes. None of the Passover lamb shall be left until the next morning.

Give generously

Give to God the way God has given to you.

Deuteronomy 16:17

5"The Passover is not to be eaten in your homes. 6It must be eaten at the place the Lord shall choose as his sanctuary. Sacrifice it there on that special evening just as the sun goes down. 7Roast the lamb and eat it, then start back to your homes the next morning. 8For the next six days you shall eat no bread made with yeast. On the seventh day there shall be a quiet gathering of the people. They must gather in each city before the Lord your God. Don't do any work that day.

9"Count seven weeks after the harvest begins. 10At that time, there shall be another feast before the Lord your God. It will be called the Feast of Weeks. At that time, bring to the Lord a freewill offering. Bring an offering that reflects his blessings upon you. Its size shall be judged by the amount of your harvest. 11It is a time to rejoice before the Lord with your family and household. And don't forget to include the local Levites, foreigners, widows, and orphans. Invite them to go with you to the sanctuary. 12Remember! You were a slave in Egypt. Be sure to carry out this command.

13"You must also observe another feast. It will be called the Feast of Shelters. It will run for seven days at the end of the harvest season. This is the time after the grain has been threshed and the grapes pressed. 14It will be a happy time of rejoicing with your family and servants. Don't forget to invite the Levites, foreigners, orphans, and widows of your town.

15"This feast will be held at the Tabernacle. It will be at the place the Lord will show you. This is a time of deep thanks to the Lord for blessing you. Give thanks for the good harvest and his many other blessings. It shall be a time of great joy.

16"Every man in Israel shall appear before the Lord your God three times a year. They must go to the sanctuary for these three feasts:

The Feast of Unleavened Bread
The Feast of Weeks
The Feast of Shelters

"At each of these feasts bring a gift to the Lord. 17Give to God the way God has given to you.

Judges for the People

18"Choose judges and leaders for all the cities the Lord your God is giving you. They will bring justice in every part of the land. 19Never twist justice to help a rich man. Never take bribes. Bribes blind the eyes of the wisest men and corrupt their decisions. 20Justice must prevail.

"That is the only way you will succeed in the land that the Lord your God is giving you.

Feasts
DEUTERONOMY 16:1-17
God commanded the Israelites to have many feasts. These were times for people to get together. People ate, talked, and had fun together. But these were also times to remember God.

There were three important feasts each year. All Israelites had to go to each feast. The Passover was the most important feast. It is still celebrated today. On the Passover, the people of Israel remembered the Exodus, their freedom from slavery in Egypt. Pentecost came at the end of harvest. The first loaves made from the new grain were offered on the altar. On the Day of Atonement, the High Priest went into the Holy of Holies in the Tabernacle or Temple to beg God to forgive the sins of the people.

Do you have special dinners at your church? They are not quite like these feasts. But they are times to get together, eat together, and have fun together. They are also times to think about God together.

21"Never build shameful images beside the altar of the Lord your God. This must never be done, for any reason. 22And never set up stone pillars to worship. For the Lord hates them!

17 "Never sacrifice a sick ox or sheep to the Lord your God. The animals must have nothing wrong with them. For the Lord will not feel honored by such gifts!

2-3"Someone, a man or a woman, might break your covenant with God by worshiping other gods. Or he might worship the sun, moon, or stars. This might happen in any village in your land. I have strictly forbidden these kinds of worship. 4If you hear of this, first check the rumor very carefully. If there is no doubt, 5then those people shall be taken outside the city. There they shall be stoned to death. 6However, never put a man to death on the word of only one witness. There must be at least two or three. 7The witnesses shall throw the first stones. Then all the people shall join in. In this way you will get rid of all the evil among you.

8"A case might come up that is too hard for you to decide. Someone might be accused of murder, but no one can prove it. Or someone's rights might have been violated. In such cases, you shall go to the sanctuary of the Lord your God. 9Bring the case before the priests and Levites. The chief judge on duty at the time will decide. 10His decision cannot be taken back. It must be obeyed to the letter. 11The sentence he gives is to be followed fully. 12The guilty man might refuse to accept what the judge decides. But if he does, the penalty is death. Such sinners must be purged from Israel. 13Everyone will hear about what happened to the man who refused God's verdict. Then they will be afraid to reject a court's judgment.

Choosing a King

14"You shall get to the land the Lord your God will give you. You shall then conquer it. At this time you might begin to think, 'We ought to have a king. All the other nations around us have a king.' 15When this happens, be sure that you choose the king the Lord shall choose. He must be an Israelite, not a foreigner. 16Be sure that he doesn't build up a large stable of horses for himself. He must never send his men to Egypt to raise horses for him there. For the Lord has told you, 'Never go back to Egypt again.' 17He must not have too many wives. If he does, his heart will turn away from the Lord. He must not be too rich, either.

18"Someday a man shall be crowned. He shall sit upon his throne as king. When this happens, he must copy these laws from the book kept by the Levite-priests. 19That copy of the laws shall be his constant companion. He must read from it every day of his life. That way he will learn to respect the Lord his God. And he will obey all of his commands. 20By reading God's laws he will know that he is no better than the rest of his people. It will also keep him from turning away from God's laws, even a little. It will make sure he has a long and good reign. His sons will then follow him upon the throne.

Giving to the Priests and Levites

18 "Remember that the Levite tribe will not be given property like the other tribes. This includes the priests as well. The priests and Levites are to be supported by the sacrifices brought to the altar of the Lord. They will also live on the other gifts the people bring to them. 2They don't need to own property. For the Lord is their property! That is what he promised them! 3The shoulder, the cheeks, and the stomach of every ox or sheep brought for sacrifice must be given to the priests. 4Also, the priests shall receive the harvest samples brought with thanks to the Lord. This includes the first of the grain, the new wine, and the olive oil. It also includes the fleece at shearing time. 5For the Lord your God has appointed the tribe of Levi. He chose them from among all the tribes. They are to serve the Lord for all time.

6-7"Any Levite has the right to come to the sanctuary at any time. He may serve there in the name of the Lord. He has the same rights as his brother Levites who work there regularly. This is true no matter where he lives in the land of Israel. 8He shall be given his share of the sacrifices and offerings. These are his by right, whether he needs them or not.

Don't Do What Bad People Do

9"When you get to the Promised Land you must be very careful. Otherwise you will be corrupted by the horrible customs of the people now living there. 10For example, an Israelite might give his child to be burned to death as a sacrifice to heathen gods. But if anyone should do this, he must be killed. Israelites must never practice black magic. They must never call on evil spirits for aid, or be fortune-tellers. 11They must not be serpent charmers, mediums, or wizards. They must never call forth the spirits of the dead. 12Anyone doing these things is an object of hate to the Lord. The Lord your God will destroy the nations for doing these very things. 13You must walk without sin before the Lord your God. 14The nations you will destroy all do these evil things. But the Lord your God will not allow you to do such things.

A Special Prophet

15"Instead, he will raise up for you a Prophet like me. This prophet will be an Israelite and a man you must listen to and obey. 16For this is what you yourselves begged of God at Mount Sinai. At the foot of the mountain you begged that you might not have to listen to the voice of God again. You did not want to see the awesome fire on the mountain. You were afraid that you might die.

17"'All right,' the Lord said to me. 'I will do as they have requested. 18I will raise up from among them a Prophet. He will be an Israelite like you. I will tell him what to say. He shall be my spokesman to the people. 19I will deal with anyone who will not listen to him and obey his messages from me. 20But any prophet who falsely claims that his message is from me shall die. And any prophet who claims to give a message from other gods must die.' 21You might wonder, 'How shall we know whether the prophecy is from the Lord or not?' 22This is the way to know. The things he prophesies might not happen. If not, it is not the Lord who has given him the message. He has made it up himself. You have nothing to fear from him.

Cities of Refuge

19 "The Lord your God will destroy the nations you will push out. You will soon be living in their cities and homes. 2-3When this happens, you must set apart three Cities of Refuge. That way anyone who kills someone by accident may run to safety. Divide the country into three districts. One of these cities must be in each district. Always keep the roads to these cities in good repair.

4"Here is an example of the purpose of these cities. 5A man might go into the forest with his neighbor to chop wood. The axe head might fly off the handle and kill the man's neighbor. If this happens, he may run to one of those cities and be safe. 6-7Anyone who tries to avenge the death will not be able to. These cities must be scattered around. That way everyone will be close to one of the cities. Otherwise the angry avenger might catch the innocent slayer. He might kill him before he can reach one of the cities. But this man should not die since he has not killed anyone on purpose.

8"The Lord might make your borders bigger as he promised your ancestors. He might give you all the land he promised. 9(Whether he does this depends on your obedience. You must obey all these commands I am giving you today. You must love the Lord your God and walk in his paths.) If your land is made bigger, then you must choose three other Cities of Refuge. 10In this way you will be able to avoid the death of innocent people. And you will not be guilty for allowing innocent people to die.

11"But someone might hate his neighbor. He might spring out of hiding and kill him. Then he might run into one of the Cities of Refuge. 12If this happens, the elders of his hometown ___ ___ for him. They shall bring ___ give him over to the dea___ Then the avenger shall___ pity him! Get rid of a___ Israel! Only then___ you.

14"Y___
Lord y___

do, remember that you must never steal a man's land. You must never move another person's boundary markers.

Rules about Witnesses

¹⁵"Never convict anyone on the word of one witness. There must be at least two, and three is even better. ¹⁶Someone might give false witness. He might claim he has seen someone do wrong when he hasn't. ¹⁷If so, both men shall be brought before the priests and judges on duty at the time. ¹⁸They must be closely questioned. They might discover that the witness was lying. ¹⁹If so, his penalty shall be the punishment he wanted the other man to get. In this way you will get rid of the evil among you. ²⁰Then those who hear about it will be afraid to tell lies on the witness stand. ²¹You shall not show pity to a false witness. Life must be given for life. Eye must be given for eye. Tooth must be given for tooth. Hand must be given for hand. Foot must be given for foot. This is your rule in such cases.

Rules about War

20 "You will soon go to war. You will see before you great numbers of horses and chariots. You will face armies far greater than yours. But when you do, don't be afraid! The Lord your God is with you. He is the same God who brought you safely out of Egypt! ²Before you begin the battle, a priest shall stand before the Israelite army. He shall say,

³"'Listen to me, all you men of Israel! Don't be afraid as you go out to fight today! ⁴For the Lord your God is going with you! He will fight for you against your enemies! And he will give you the victory!'

⁵"Then the officers of the army shall address the men. They will say, 'Has a͟n͟y͟o͟n͟e͟ built a new house but not ？ If so, go home! For you ͟ the battle, and some-dicate it! ⁶Has anyone ͟eyard but not yet ？ If so, go home! ͟d someone ͟ust be-͟d get

married! For you might die in the battle, and someone else would marry your fiancée. ⁸And now, is anyone afraid? If you are, go home before you frighten the rest of us!' ⁹The officers shall finish saying this to their men. Then they will announce the names of the group leaders.

¹⁰"As you come near a city to attack it, first offer it a treaty. ¹¹It might accept the treaty and open its gates to you. If so, then all its people shall become your servants. ¹²But it might refuse and not make peace with you. If so, you must besiege it. ¹³When the Lord your God has given it to you, kill every male in the city. ¹⁴But you may keep for yourselves all the women, children, cattle, and booty. ¹⁵These rules apply only to faraway cities. They do not apply to those in the Promised Land itself.

¹⁶"In the cities within the borders of the Promised Land you are to save no one. Destroy every living thing. ¹⁷Completely destroy the Hittites, the Amorites, the Canaanites, the Perizzites, the Hivites, and the Jebusites. This is the command of the Lord your God. ¹⁸This rule is given to keep you from being tempted into idol worship by the people of the land. They might cause you to take part in their wicked customs. Thus you might sin deeply against the Lord your God.

¹⁹"When you besiege a city, don't destroy the fruit trees. Eat all the fruit you wish. Just don't cut down the trees. They aren't enemies who need to be killed! ²⁰But you may cut down trees that aren't valuable for food. Use them for the siege to make ladders, portable towers, and battering rams.

An Unsolved Murder

21 "You shall soon go into the Promised Land. When you do, a murder victim might be found lying in a field. It might be that no one saw the murder. ²If so, the elders and judges shall measure from the body to the nearest city. ³Then the elders of that city shall take a heifer. It must be one that has never been yoked. ⁴They shall lead it to a valley where there is running water. It must be

a valley that has not been plowed or planted. There they shall break its neck.

5"Then the priests shall come. The Lord your God has chosen them to serve before him. They are to pronounce his blessings and decide lawsuits and punishments. 6The priests shall wash their hands over the heifer. 7They shall say, 'Our hands have not shed this blood. Neither have our eyes seen it. 8O Lord, forgive your people Israel whom you have redeemed. Do not charge them for murdering an innocent man. Forgive us the guilt of this man's blood.' 9In this way you will put away the guilt from among you. You must follow all the Lord's directions.

Marriage and Family

10"You shall soon go to war. And the Lord your God shall deliver your enemies to you. 11When this happens, you might see among the captives a pretty girl. You might want her for your wife. 12If you do, take her home with you. She must shave her head and cut her nails. 13She must change her clothing, laying aside what she was wearing when she was captured. Then she shall stay in your home. She shall be in mourning for her father and mother for a full month. After that you may marry her. 14However, after marrying her you might decide you don't like her. If so, you must let her go free. You may not sell her or treat her as a slave, for you have humiliated her.

15"A man might have two wives. But he might love one and not the other. It may be that both have borne him children. And perhaps the mother of his oldest son is the wife he doesn't love. 16If this is true, he may not give the larger inheritance to his younger son. He may not do this even though this is the son of the wife he loves. 17He must give the normal double portion to his oldest son. He is the beginning of the father's strength. And he owns the rights of a firstborn son. This is true even though he is the son of the wife his father doesn't love.

18"A man might have a stubborn and rebellious son. He might not obey his father or mother, even though they punish him. 19If so, then his father and mother shall take him before the elders of the city. 20Then they must say, 'This son of ours is stubborn and rebellious. He won't obey. He is a worthless drunkard.' 21Then the men of the city shall stone him to death. In this way you shall put away this evil from among you. All the young men of Israel will hear about what happened and will be afraid.

Burying Criminals

22"A man might have done a crime worthy of death. Then he might be killed and hanged on a tree. 23If this happens, his body shall not stay on the tree all night. You must bury him the same day. For anyone hanging on a tree is cursed of God. Don't defile the land the Lord your God has given you.

Helping Neighbors

22 "You might see someone's ox or sheep wandering away. If you do, don't pretend you didn't see it. Take it back to its owner. 2You might not know who the owner is. If so, take it to your farm and keep it there. When the owner comes looking for it, then give it to him. 3The same applies to donkeys, clothing, or anything else you find. Keep it for its owner.

4"You might see someone trying to get an ox or donkey onto its feet. It might have slipped beneath its load. If so, don't look the other way. Go and help!

Other Rules

5"A woman must not wear men's clothing. A man must not wear women's clothing. This is hated by the Lord your God.

6"You might find a bird's nest lying on the ground. Or you might see one in a tree. There might be young ones or eggs in it with the mother sitting in the nest. If so, don't take the mother with the young. 7Let her go, and take only the young. The Lord will bless you for it.

8"Every new house must have a

guardrail around the edge of the flat rooftop. This will stop anyone from falling off. It will keep both the house and its owner free of guilt.

9"Do not plant other crops in the rows of your vineyard. If you do, both the crops and the grapes shall be taken by the priests.

10"Don't plow with an ox and a donkey harnessed together.

11"Don't wear clothing woven from two kinds of thread. Do not weave wool and linen together.

12"You must sew tassels on the four corners of your cloaks.

Breaking Marriage Vows

13-14"A man might marry a girl. Then he might sleep with her. After that he might accuse her of having slept with some other man. He might say, 'She was not a virgin when I married her.' 15If this happens, then the girl's father and mother shall bring proof that she was a virgin. They must bring it to the city judges.

16"Her father shall tell them, 'I gave my daughter to this man to be his wife. Now he hates her. 17-18He accuses her of shameful things. He claims that she was not a virgin when she married him. Yet here is the proof.' And they might then spread before the judges the sheet from her marriage bed with blood on it. If this happens, the judges shall sentence the man to be whipped. 19They will also fine him $100. It shall be given to the girl's father. This man will be punished for falsely accusing a virgin of Israel. She shall remain his wife. He may never divorce her. 20But it may be that what the man says is true. The girl might not have been a virgin. 21If so, the judges shall take the girl to the door of her father's home. There the men of the city shall stone her to death. She has made Israel unclean by her bad crime. She was a prostitute while living at home with her parents. Such evil must be cleansed from among you.

22"A man might be found sleeping with another man's wife. If so, both he and the other man's wife must be killed. In this way evil will be cleansed from Israel. 23-24A girl who is engaged might be seduced within the walls of a city. If so, both she and the man who seduced her shall be taken outside the gates. There they shall be stoned to death. The girl must die because she didn't scream for help. The man must die because he has slept with another man's fiancée. 25-27In this way you will reduce crime among you. But this deed might take place out in the country. If this happens, only the man shall die. The girl is as innocent as a murder victim. For it must be assumed that she screamed, but there was no one to hear her. 28-29A man might sleep with a girl who is not engaged. He might be caught in the act. If so, he must pay a fine to the girl's father and marry her. He may never divorce her. 30A man shall not sleep with his father's widow. For she belonged to his father.

Who Can't Enter the Sanctuary

23 "A man's sex organs might be damaged. If so, he shall not enter the sanctuary. 2A person whose parents were not lawfully married may not enter the sanctuary. His descendants for 10 generations will not be allowed to enter.

3"No Ammonite or Moabite may ever enter the sanctuary, even after the 10th generation. 4There is a reason for this law. These nations did not welcome you with food and water when you came out of Egypt. They even tried to hire Balaam, the son of Beor from Pethor, Mesopotamia. They wanted him to curse you. 5But the Lord would not listen to Balaam. Instead, he turned the intended curse into a blessing for you. This is because the Lord loves you. 6You must never try to help the Ammonites or the Moabites in any way. 7But do not look down on the Edomites and the Egyptians. The Edomites are your brothers, and you lived among the Egyptians. 8The grandchildren of the Egyptians who came with you from Egypt may enter the sanctuary of the Lord.

Keeping the Camp Clean

9-10"When you are at war, the men in the camps must stay away from all evil. A man might become unclean because of a seminal emission during the night. If this happens, he must leave the camp. [11]He must stay outside until the evening. And he must take a bath. Then he may come back at sunset. [12]The toilet area shall be outside the camp. [13]Each man must have a spade as part of his equipment. After relieving himself, he must dig a hole with the spade. In it, he must bury the dung. [14]The camp must be holy, for the Lord walks among you. He is with you to protect you. He is there to cause your enemies to fall before you. But the Lord does not want to see anything indecent. If he does, he will turn away from you.

Other Rules

[15-16]"A slave might escape from his master. If so, you must not force him to go back. Let him live among you in whatever town he chooses. Do not oppress him.

[17-18]"No prostitutes are allowed in Israel. This law applies to both men and women. You must not bring to the Lord any offering from the earnings of a prostitute or a homosexual. For both are hated by the Lord your God.

[19]"Do not demand interest on loans you make to another Israelite. This is true for loans in the form of money, food, or anything else. [20]You may take interest from a foreigner. But you must never take interest from an Israelite. For if you take interest from an Israelite, you will be punished. The Lord your God won't bless you when you get to the Promised Land.

[21]"You might make a vow to the Lord. If you do this, do what you promised him right away. The Lord demands that you fulfill your vows without delay. It is a sin if you don't. [22]But it is not a sin if you never make a vow in the first place! [23] Once you make the vow, you must be careful to do as you have said. For it was your own choice. And you have vowed to the Lord your God.

[24]"You may eat your fill of the grapes from another man's vineyard. But do not take any away in a container. [25]It is the same with someone else's grain. You may eat a few handfuls of it, but don't use a sickle.

24 "A man might not like something about his wife. If so, he may write a letter stating that he has divorced her. He may then give her the letter and send her away. [2]She might then remarry. [3]The second husband might also divorce her, or he might die. [4]If this happens, the former husband may not marry her again. For she has been defiled. This would bring guilt upon the land the Lord your God is giving you.

[5]"A newly married man is not to be drafted into the army. He shall not be given any other special jobs either. He shall be free for a year to be at home, happy with his wife.

[6]"It is illegal to take a millstone as a pledge. For it is a tool by which its owner earns his living. [7]Someone might kidnap a brother Israelite. He might treat him as a slave or sell him. If this happens, the kidnapper must die. You must get rid of this evil among you.

[8]"Be very careful to follow the rules of the priest in cases of leprosy. I have given him guidelines. And you must obey them to the letter. [9]Remember what the Lord your God did to Miriam as you were coming from Egypt.

[10]"If you lend anything to another man, you must not enter his house to get his security. [11]Stand outside! The owner will bring it out to you. [12-13]The man might be poor and give you his cloak as security. If he does, you are not to sleep in it. Take it back to him at sundown. That way he can use it through the night, and he will bless you. And the Lord your God will count it as righteousness for you.

[14-15]"Never oppress a poor hired man. This applies if the man is a fellow Israelite or a foreigner living in your town. Pay him his wage each day before sunset. Since he is poor he will need it right away. If you don't, he may cry out to the Lord. Then it would be counted as a sin against you.

[16]"Fathers shall not be put to death for the sins of their sons. Neither shall sons be killed for the sins of their fathers. Every man worthy of death shall die for his own crime.

[17]"Justice must be given to migrants

and orphans. You must never take a widow's coat in pledge of her debt. ¹⁸Always remember that you were slaves in Egypt. Remember that the Lord your God rescued you. That is why I have given you this command. ¹⁹When taking in your harvest, you might forget to bring in a sheaf from the field. If so, don't go back after it. Leave it for the migrants, orphans, and widows. Then the Lord your God will bless all you do. ²⁰When you beat the olives from your olive trees, don't go over the branches twice. Leave what is left for the migrants, orphans, and widows. ²¹It is the same for the grapes in your vineyard. Do not glean the vines after they are picked. Leave what's left for those in need. ²²Remember that you were slaves in the land of Egypt. That is why I am giving you this command.

25 "A man might be guilty of a crime. The penalty might be a beating. If so, the judge shall command him to lie down. The man shall be beaten in his presence with up to 40 stripes. The number of stripes will be decided by how bad his crime was. But no more than 40 stripes may be given. Otherwise the punishment will seem too severe. And your brother will be degraded in your eyes.

⁴"Don't muzzle an ox as it treads out the grain.

⁵"A man's brother might die without a son. If so, his widow must not marry outside the family. Instead, her husband's brother must marry her and sleep with her. ⁶The first son she bears to him shall be counted as the son of the dead brother. That way his name will not be forgotten. ⁷But the dead man's brother might refuse to do his duty in this matter. He might refuse to marry the widow. If he refuses, then she shall go to the city elders. She shall say to them, 'My husband's brother refuses to let his brother's name continue. He refuses to marry me.' ⁸The elders of the city will then call him. They will talk the matter over with him. He still might refuse. ⁹If so, the widow shall walk over to him in the presence of the elders. She shall pull his sandal from

his foot and spit in his face. She shall then say, 'This is what happens to a man who refuses to build his brother's house.' ¹⁰Ever after this his house shall be called 'the home of the man who had his sandal pulled off!'

¹¹"Two men might have a fight. And the wife of one might help her husband by grabbing the testicles of the other man. ¹²If she does this, her hand shall be cut off without pity.

¹³⁻¹⁵"In all your business deals you must use accurate scales and honest measurements. If you do, you will have a long, good life. You will be blessed in the land the Lord your God is giving you. ¹⁶All who cheat with unjust weights and measurements are hated by the Lord your God.

¹⁷"You must never forget what the people of Amalek did to you as you came from Egypt. ¹⁸Remember that they fought with you. They struck down those who were faint and weary and lagging behind. They showed no respect for God. ¹⁹The Lord your God will soon give you rest from all your enemies in the Promised Land. When he does, you must destroy the name of Amalek from under heaven. Never forget this.

Giving God the First and Best

26 "You shall soon go into the land. You shall conquer it and live there. ²⁻³When this is true, you must give to the Lord the first sample from each yearly harvest. You must present it to him at his sanctuary. Bring it in a basket. Hand it to the priest on duty. Then say to him, 'This gift is an acknowledgement. It shows that the Lord has brought me to the land he promised our ancestors.' ⁴The priest will then take the basket from your hand. He will set it before the altar. ⁵You shall then say before the Lord your God, 'My ancestors were migrant Arameans. They went to Egypt for refuge. They were few in number, but in Egypt they became a mighty nation. ⁶⁻⁷The Egyptians treated us badly and we cried to the Lord God. He heard us and saw our hardship, toil, and oppression. ⁸He brought us out of Egypt

with his powerful hand. He did great and awesome miracles before the Egyptians. ⁹Now he has brought us to this place. He has given us this land "flowing with milk and honey!" ¹⁰And now, O Lord, see! I have brought you a token of the first of the crops. They came from the ground you gave me.' Then place the samples before the Lord your God and worship him. ¹¹After that, go and feast on all the good things he has given you. Celebrate with your family. Also include any Levites or migrants living among you.

¹²"Every third year is a year of special tithing. That year you are to give all your tithes to the Levites, migrants, orphans, and widows. That way they will all be well fed. ¹³Then you shall declare before the Lord your God, 'I have given all of my tithes. They are for the Levites, the migrants, the orphans, and the widows. I have done just as you told me to do. I have not broken or forgotten any of your rules. ¹⁴I have not touched the tithe while I was unclean. I have not touched it while I was in mourning. I have not offered any of it to the dead. I have obeyed the Lord my God and have done all that you commanded me. ¹⁵Look down from your holy home in heaven. Bless your people and the land you have given us. Do just as you promised our ancestors. Make it a land "flowing with milk and honey"!'

Keeping God's Laws

¹⁶"You must obey all of these commands and rules that the Lord your God is giving you today. ¹⁷You have said today that he is your God. You have promised to obey and keep his laws. You have promised to do all he tells you to do. ¹⁸And the Lord has said today that you are his very own people. It is just as he promised. And you must obey all of his laws. ¹⁹If you do, he will make you greater than any other nation. He will let you receive praise, honor, and renown. But to get this honor and renown you must be a holy people to the Lord your God. You must do all that he asks."

The Altar on Mount Ebal

27 Then Moses and the elders of Israel gave the people more laws to obey.

²⁻⁴"You shall soon cross the Jordan River and go into the Promised Land. It is a land 'flowing with milk and honey.' When you cross over, take out boulders from the river bottom. Then pile them into a monument on the other side, at Mount Ebal. Face the stones with a coating of lime. Then write the laws of God in the lime. ⁵⁻⁶And build an altar there to the Lord your God. Use uncut boulders, and on the altar offer burnt offerings to the Lord your God. ⁷Sacrifice peace offerings upon it also. Feast there with great joy before the Lord your God. ⁸Write all of these laws plainly upon the monument."

⁹Then Moses and the Levite-priests spoke to all Israel: "O Israel, listen! Today you have become the people of the Lord your God. ¹⁰So today you must begin to obey all of these commands I have given you."

Staying Away from Sin

¹¹That same day Moses gave this charge to the people.

¹²He said, "You are about to cross into the Promised Land. When you do, the tribes of Simeon, Levi, Judah, Issachar, Joseph, and Benjamin shall stand upon Mount Gerizim. From there they shall proclaim a blessing. ¹³The tribes of Reuben, Gad, Asher, Zebulun, Dan, and Naphtali shall stand upon Mount Ebal. From there they shall proclaim a curse. ¹⁴Then the Levites standing between them shall shout to all Israel,

¹⁵"'The curse of God be upon anyone who makes and worships an idol. This is wrong even if done in secret. It is wrong if the idol is carved of wood or made from metal. For these handmade gods are hated by the Lord.' And all the people shall reply, 'Amen.'

¹⁶"'Cursed is anyone who despises his father or mother.' And all the people shall reply, 'Amen.'

¹⁷"'Cursed is he who moves the boundary marker between his land and his neighbor's.' And all the people shall reply, 'Amen.'

¹⁸"'Cursed is he who takes advantage of a blind man.' And all the people shall reply, 'Amen.'

¹⁹"'Cursed is he who is unjust to the foreigner, the orphan, and the widow.' And all the people shall reply, 'Amen.'

²⁰"'Cursed is he who sleeps with one of his father's wives. For she belongs to his father.' And all the people shall reply, 'Amen.'

²¹"'Cursed is he who mates with an animal.' And all the people shall reply, 'Amen.'

²²"'Cursed is he who sleeps with his sister. This applies if she is a full sister or a half-sister.' And all the people shall reply, 'Amen.'

²³"'Cursed is he who sleeps with his widowed mother-in-law.' And all the people shall reply, 'Amen.'

²⁴"'Cursed is he who secretly kills another.' And all the people shall reply, 'Amen.'

²⁵"'Cursed is he who takes a bribe to kill an innocent person.' And all the people shall reply, 'Amen.'

²⁶"'Cursed is anyone who does not obey these laws.' And all the people shall reply, 'Amen.'

Obedience Brings Blessing

28 "You must fully obey all of these commands of the Lord your God. You must obey the laws I am giving you today. If you do, God will make you into the greatest nation in the world. ²⁻⁶These are the blessings that will come upon you:

Blessings in the city,
Blessings in the field;
Many children,
Ample crops,
Large flocks and herds;
Blessings of fruit and bread;
Blessings when you come in,
Blessings when you go out.

⁷"The Lord will defeat your enemies before you. They will march out together against you but scatter before you in seven directions! ⁸The Lord will bless you with good crops and healthy cattle. He will bless all you do when you get to the land the Lord your God is giving you. ⁹He will change you into a holy people dedicated to himself. This he has promised to do if you will only obey him and walk in his ways. ¹⁰All the nations in the world shall see that you belong to the Lord. And they will stand in awe.

¹¹"The Lord will give you many good things in the land. He will bless you just as he promised. You will have many children, many cattle, and fine crops. ¹²He will let rain fall from the heavens. By it he will give you fine crops every season. He will bless all you do. You shall lend to many nations. But you shall not borrow from them. ¹³You must only listen and obey the commands of the Lord your God. He will make you the head and not the tail. You shall always have the upper hand. ¹⁴But these blessings depend on your not turning aside from the laws I have given you. And you must never worship other gods.

Disobedience Brings Punishment

¹⁵⁻¹⁹"You might not listen to the Lord your God. Perhaps you will not obey these laws I am giving you today. If you do not, then you shall suffer many curses:

Curses in the city,
Curses in the fields,
Curses on your fruit and bread,
The curse of barren wombs,
Curses upon your crops,
Curses upon the fertility of your
    cattle and flocks,
Curses when you come in,
Curses when you go out.

²⁰"For the Lord himself will send his curse upon you. You will be confused. You will fail in all that you do. Then at last you will be destroyed because of the sin of forsaking him. ²¹He will send disease among you. From it you will be destroyed from the face of the land you are about to enter. ²²He will send tuberculosis, fever, infections, plague, and war. He will blight your crops, covering them with mildew. All these bad things will happen until you die.

²³"The heavens above you will be as unyielding as bronze. The earth beneath will be like iron. ²⁴The land will become as dry as dust for lack of rain. Dust storms shall destroy you.

²⁵"The Lord will cause you to be defeated by your enemies. You will march out to battle, but run from your enemies in confusion. You will be tossed to and fro among all the nations of the earth. ²⁶Your dead bodies will be food to the birds and wild animals. And no one will be there to chase them away.

²⁷"He will send upon you Egyptian boils, tumors, scurvy, and itch. There will be no remedies for any of these. ²⁸He will send madness, blindness, fear, and panic upon you. ²⁹You shall grope in the bright sunlight just as the blind man gropes in darkness. You shall not do well in anything you do. You will be taken advantage of and robbed all the time. Nothing will save you.

³⁰"Someone else will marry your fiancée. Someone else will live in the house you build. Someone else will eat the fruit of the vineyard you plant. ³¹Your oxen shall be killed before your eyes. But you won't get a single bite of the meat. Your donkeys will be driven away as you watch. They will never return to you again. Your sheep will be given to your enemies. And there will be no one to protect you. ³²You will watch as your sons and daughters are taken away as slaves. Your heart will break with longing for them. But you will not be able to help them. ³³ A foreign nation you have not even heard of will eat the crops you will have worked so hard to grow. You will always be oppressed and crushed. ³⁴You will go mad because of all the tragedy you see around you. ³⁵The Lord will cover you with boils from head to foot.

³⁶"He will exile you and the king you will choose. You will be taken to a nation of whom neither you nor your ancestors have ever heard. And while in exile you shall worship gods of wood and stone! ³⁷You will become an object of horror. You will be a proverb and a byword among all the nations. You will be known as the nation the Lord thrust away.

³⁸"You will plant much but harvest little. Locusts will eat your crops. ³⁹You will plant vineyards and care for them. But you won't eat the grapes or drink the wine. Worms will destroy the vines. ⁴⁰Olive trees will be growing everywhere, but there won't be enough olive oil to anoint yourselves! For the trees will drop their fruit before it is matured. ⁴¹Your sons and daughters will be snatched away from you as slaves. ⁴²The locusts shall destroy your trees and vines. ⁴³Foreigners living among you shall become richer and richer. You will become poorer and poorer. ⁴⁴They shall lend to you, not you to them! They shall be the head, and you shall be the tail!

⁴⁵"All these curses shall pursue you until you are destroyed. It will all happen because you do not listen to the Lord your God. ⁴⁶These horrors shall come upon you and your descendants as a warning. ⁴⁷⁻⁴⁸You will become slaves to your enemies. This will happen when you fail to praise God for all that he has given you. The Lord will send your enemies against you. You will be hungry, thirsty, naked, and in want of everything. A yoke of iron shall be placed around your neck until you are destroyed!

⁴⁹"The Lord will bring a distant nation against you. It will swoop down upon you like an eagle. It is a nation whose language you don't understand. ⁵⁰It is a nation of fierce and angry men. They will have no mercy upon young or old. ⁵¹They will eat you out of house and home. Your cattle and crops will soon be gone. Your grain, new wine, olive oil, calves, and lambs will all disappear. ⁵²That nation will lay siege to your cities. It will knock down your highest walls. It will break the walls you trust to protect you. ⁵³You will even eat the flesh of your own sons and daughters. This will really happen in the terrible days of siege that lie ahead. ⁵⁴The most gentle man among you will become cruel. He will be cruel to his own brother, his beloved wife, and his children who are still alive. ⁵⁵He will refuse to give them a share of the flesh he is eating. He will eat the flesh of his own children! He will do it because he is starving in the siege of your cities. ⁵⁶⁻⁵⁷The kindest and tenderest woman among you will become cruel. She is so gentle she would

not so much as touch her feet to the ground. But she will refuse to share with her beloved husband, son, and daughter. She will hide from them the afterbirth and the new baby she has borne. She herself will eat them. This will happen because the hunger during the siege will be so horrible. This will be caused by the fear of enemies camped at your gates.

⁵⁸⁻⁵⁹"You might refuse to obey all the laws written in this book. And you might refuse to respect the glorious name of the Lord your God. But if you do, then the Lord will send plagues upon you and your children. ⁶⁰He will bring upon you all the diseases of Egypt. You will suffer from the diseases that you feared so much. They shall plague the land. ⁶¹And that is not all! The Lord will bring upon you every sickness and plague there is. You will suffer diseases not even mentioned in this book. They will destroy you. ⁶²There will be few of you left, though before you were as numerous as stars. All this will happen if you do not listen to the Lord your God.

⁶³"The Lord has rejoiced over you. He has done great things for you. He has multiplied you. But just as he has done these things, so the Lord at that time will rejoice in destroying you. You shall disappear from the land. ⁶⁴For the Lord will scatter you among all the nations. You will be spread from one end of the earth to the other. There you will worship heathen gods. These will be gods that you and your ancestors have not known. They will be gods made of wood and stone! ⁶⁵There among those nations you shall find no rest. But the Lord will give you trembling hearts. You will live in darkness. Your bodies will be wasted from sorrow and fear. ⁶⁶Your lives will hang in doubt. You will live in fear night and day. You will have no reason to believe that you will see the morning light. ⁶⁷In the morning you will say, 'Oh, that night were here!' And in the evening you will say, 'Oh, that morning were here!' You will say this because of the horrors around you. ⁶⁸Then the Lord will send you back to Egypt in ships. You will

make a journey I promised you would never need to make again. There you will try to sell yourselves as slaves. But no one will even want to buy you."

Moses Reviews God's Covenant

29 Moses restated the covenant that the Lord had made with the people of Israel at Mount Sinai. They were in the plains of Moab at the time. ²⁻³He called all Israel before him. Then he told them,

"You have seen the great plagues that the Lord brought upon Pharaoh and his people. You know of the mighty miracles he worked against the land of Egypt. ⁴But even yet the Lord hasn't given you hearts that understand. You still don't have eyes that see or ears that hear! ⁵For 40 years God has led you through the wilderness. During all that time, your clothes haven't become old. Your shoes haven't worn out! ⁶He hasn't let you settle down to grow grain for bread. He hasn't let you grow grapes for wine and strong drink. This is because the Lord your God wants you to know that it is he who takes care of you.

⁷"When we came here, King Sihon of Heshbon and King Og of Bashan came out against us in battle. But we destroyed them! ⁸We took their land. We gave it to the tribes of Reuben, Gad, and the half-tribe of Manasseh. It was given to them as their inheritance. ⁹Therefore, obey the terms of this covenant. If you do, you will succeed in all that you do. ¹⁰All of you are standing today before the Lord your God. Your leaders, the people, your judges, and your officers are all here. ¹¹Your little ones and your wives are present too. Even the foreigners that are among you are here. They chop your wood and carry your water. ¹²You are standing here to enter into a contract with the Lord your God. It is a contract he is making with you today. ¹³He wants to confirm you today as his people. He also wants to confirm that he is your God. It shall be just as he promised your ancestors, Abraham, Isaac, and Jacob. ¹⁴⁻¹⁵This contract is not with you alone as you stand before him

today. It is with all future generations of Israel as well.

16"Surely you remember how we lived in the land of Egypt. You must remember how we left and came safely through the lands of enemy nations. 17You have seen their heathen idols made of wood, stone, silver, and gold. 18Someday some of you might turn away from the Lord our God. You might desire to worship these gods of other nations. It might be a man or woman, family or tribe of Israel. If you do, on that day a root will be planted. It will grow a bitter and deadly fruit.

19"You all hear the warnings of this curse. Let none of you think, 'I shall succeed even though I walk in my own way!' 20For the Lord will not pardon! His anger and jealousy will be hot against that man. And all the curses written in this book shall lie upon him. The Lord will blot out his name from under heaven. 21The Lord will separate that man from all the tribes of Israel. He will pour upon him all the curses that come upon those who break this contract. 22Then your children shall see the devastation of the land. They will see the diseases the Lord will have sent upon it. All your descendants and foreigners who pass by from distant lands shall see its destruction. 23They will see that the whole land is alkali and salt. It will be a burned-over wasteland, unplanted, without crops. It won't have a shred of vegetation. It will be just like Sodom and Gomorrah and Admah and Zeboiim. These cities also were destroyed by the Lord in his anger.

24"'Why has the Lord done this to his land?' the nations will ask. 'Why was he so angry?'

25"And they will be told, 'Because the people of the land broke the contract they made with the Lord. They did not obey the God of their ancestors. They rejected him even after he brought them out of the land of Egypt. 26For they worshiped other gods, breaking his command. 27That is why the anger of the Lord was hot against this land. That is why all his curses broke

forth upon them. 28In great anger the Lord rooted them out of their land. He threw them away into another land. They still live there to this day!'

29"There are secrets the Lord your God has not told us. But these words that he has given are for us and our children to obey forever.

Coming Back to God

30 "When all these things have happened to you, you will meditate upon them. You will remember them as you live among the nations where the Lord your God will send you. 2At that time you might return to the Lord your God. You and your children might then begin to obey all the commands I have given you today. 3If so, then the Lord your God will rescue you from your captivity! He will have mercy upon you. He will come and gather you. He will bring you out of the nations where he will have scattered you. 4Though you are at the ends of the earth, he will go and find you. He will bring you back again 5to the land of your ancestors. You shall own the land again. And he will do you good. He will bless you even more than he did your ancestors! 6He will cleanse your hearts. He will cleanse the hearts of your children and of your children's children. You will love the Lord your God with all your hearts and souls. And Israel shall come alive again!

7-8"You shall return to the Lord. You shall obey all the commands that I gave you today. If you do, the Lord your God will take his curses and turn them against your enemies. Thus he will destroy those who hate and persecute you. 9The Lord your God will bless all that you do. He will give you many children. He will bless you with many cattle and wonderful crops. For the Lord will again rejoice over you as he did over your fathers. 10He will rejoice if you but obey the commands written in this book of the law. He will be glad if you turn to the Lord your God with all your hearts and souls.

Choosing Life or Death

11"Obeying these commands is not something beyond your strength and reach. 12For these laws are not in the far heavens. They are not so distant that you can't hear and obey them. You are not without someone to bring them down to you. 13These laws are not beyond the ocean. They are not so far away that no one can bring you their message. 14They are very close at hand. They are in your hearts and on your lips. So obey them.

Choose to love God and obey him

Choose to love God, to obey him, and to hold on to him.

Deuteronomy 30:20

15"Look, today I have set before you life and death. It all depends on whether you obey or disobey. 16I have commanded you today to love the Lord your God. I have told you to follow his paths and to keep his laws. If you do, you will live and become a great nation. And the Lord your God will bless you and the land you are about to take. 17But your hearts might turn away. And you might not listen. You might be drawn away to worship other gods. 18If this happens, then I declare to you this day that you shall surely die. You will not have a long, good life in the land you are going in to take.

19"I call heaven and earth to witness against you. Today I have set before you life or death. You must choose between a blessing or a curse. Oh, that you would choose life! Oh, that you and your children might live! 20Choose to love God, to obey him, and to hold on to him. For he is your life and the length of your days. You will then be able to live safely in the land the Lord promised your ancestors, Abraham, Isaac, and Jacob."

Joshua Becomes Israel's Leader

31 Moses said all these things to the people of Israel. 2Then he told them, "I am now 120 years old! I am no longer able to lead you. For the Lord has told me that I shall not cross the Jordan River. 3But the Lord himself will lead you. He will destroy the nations living there. And you shall overcome them. Joshua is your new commander, as the Lord has commanded. 4The Lord will destroy the nations living in the land. He will destroy them just as he did Sihon and Og, the Amorite kings. 5The Lord will deliver over to you the people living there. You shall destroy them just as I have told you to do. 6Be strong! Be brave! Do not be afraid of them! For the Lord your God will be with you. He will neither fail you nor forsake you."

7Then Moses called for Joshua. He spoke to him as all Israel watched. He said, "Be strong! Be brave! For you shall lead these people into the land promised by the Lord to their ancestors. See to it that they conquer it. 8Don't be afraid. For the Lord will go before you and will be with you. He will not fail or forsake you."

Moses Writes Down the Laws

9Then Moses wrote out the laws he had already delivered to the people. He gave them to the priests, the sons of Levi. They carried the Ark, which held the Ten Commandments of the Lord. Moses also gave copies of the laws to the elders of Israel. 10-11The Lord commanded that these laws be read to all the people. They were to be read at the end of every seventh year. This was the Year of Release. They were to be read at the Feast of Tabernacles. This is a time when all Israel comes before the Lord at the sanctuary.

12"Call them all together," the Lord said. "Call men, women, children, and foreigners living among you. Call them to hear the laws of God and to learn his will. That way you will respect the Lord your God and obey his laws. 13Do this so that your little children will hear them. They will not have heard these laws. This way they will hear them. And they will learn how to respect the

Lord your God. This must be done as long as you live in the Promised Land."

God Meets with Moses and Joshua

[14]Then the Lord said to Moses, "The time has come when you must die. Call Joshua and come into the Tabernacle. There I will give him his commands." So Moses and Joshua came and stood before the Lord.

[15]He appeared to them in a great cloud at the Tabernacle door. [16]He said to Moses, "You shall die and join your ancestors. After you are gone, these people will begin worshiping foreign gods in the Promised Land. They will forget about me. They will break the contract I have made with them. [17]Then my anger will flame out against them. I will leave them, hiding my face from them. And they shall be destroyed. Trouble will come upon them. They will begin to say, 'God is no longer among us!' [18]I will turn away from them because of their sins in worshiping other gods.

[19]"Now write down the words of this song. Teach it to the people of Israel as my warning to them. [20]I shall bring them into the land I promised their ancestors. It is a land 'flowing with milk and honey.' And they shall become fat and wealthy. But when this happens, they will worship other gods. They will despise me and break my contract. [21]And great disasters will come upon them. At this time, this song will remind them of the reason for their woes. (For this song is a song for all time.) I know now what these people are like. I know this even before they enter the land."

[22]So, on that very day, Moses wrote down the words of the song. Then he taught it to the Israelites. [23]After that he told Joshua (son of Nun) to be strong and brave. He said to him, "You must lead the people of Israel. Bring them into the land the Lord promised them. For the Lord says, 'I will be with you.'"

[24]Moses had finished writing down all the laws that are recorded in this book. [25]Then he spoke to the Levites. They were the ones who carried the Ark containing the Ten Commandments. [26]He told them to put this book of the law beside the Ark. It would be a warning to the people of Israel.

[27]"I know how rebellious and stubborn you are," Moses told them. "Even today you are defiant rebels against the Lord. You are this way while I am still here with you. If you are like this now, how much worse will you be after my death? [28]Now call all the elders and officers of your tribes. I must now speak to them. And call heaven and earth to witness against them. [29]I know that after my death you will defile yourselves. You will turn away from God and his commands. In the days to come evil will crush you. For you will do what the Lord says is evil. Thus you will make him very angry."

Moses' Song

[30]So Moses recited this song to the whole assembly of Israel:

32 "Listen, O heavens and earth!
Listen to what I say!
[2]My words shall fall upon you
Like the gentle rain and dew,
Like rain upon the tender grass,
Like showers on the hillside.
[3]I will proclaim the greatness of the
    Lord.
How glorious he is!
[4]He is the Rock. His work is perfect.
All he does is just and fair.
He is faithful, without sin.
[5]But Israel has become corrupt,
Smeared with sin. They are no
    longer his.
They are a stubborn, twisted genera-
    tion.
[6]Is this the way you treat the Lord?
O foolish people,
Is not God your Father?
Has he not created you?
Has he not established you and
    made you strong?
[7]Remember the days of long ago!
Ask your father and the aged men.
They will tell you all about it.
[8]When God divided up the world
    among the nations,
He gave each of them a supervising
    angel!

⁹But he gave none for Israel,
For Israel was God's own personal
  property!
¹⁰God protected them in the howl-
  ing wilderness
As though they were the apple of
  his eye.
¹¹He spreads his wings over them,
Even as an eagle overspreads her
  young.
She carries them upon her wings,
As does the Lord his people!
¹²When the Lord alone was leading
  them,
And they lived without foreign
  gods,
¹³God gave them fertile hilltops,
Rolling, fertile fields,
Honey from the rock,
And olive oil from stony ground!
¹⁴He gave them milk and meat,
Choice Bashan rams, and goats,
And the finest of the wheat.
They drank the sparkling wine.
¹⁵But Israel was soon overfed.
Yes, they were fat and bloated.
Then, in plenty, they forsook their
  God.
They shrugged away the Rock of
  their salvation.
¹⁶Israel began to follow foreign gods,
And the Lord was very angry.
He was jealous of his people.
¹⁷They sacrificed to heathen gods,
To new gods never before wor-
  shiped.
¹⁸They spurned the Rock who had
  made them.
They forgot it was God who had
  given them birth.
¹⁹God saw what they were doing,
And hated them!
His sons and daughters were mock-
  ing him.
²⁰He said, 'I will leave them.
See what happens to them then!
For they are a stubborn, faithless
  generation.
²¹They have made me very jealous
  of their idols,
Which are not gods at all.
Now I, in turn, will make them
  jealous
By giving my love

To the foolish Gentile nations of
  the world.
²²For my anger has kindled a fire
That burns to the depths of the un-
  derworld,
Consuming the earth and all of its
  crops,
And setting its mountains on fire.
²³I will heap evils upon them
And shoot them down with my ar-
  rows.
²⁴I will waste them with hunger,
Burning fever, and fatal disease.
I will devour them! I will set wild
  beasts upon them,
To rip them apart with their teeth.
And deadly serpents will trouble
  them,
Crawling in the dust.
²⁵Outside, the enemies' sword,
Inside, the plague,
Shall terrorize young men and girls
  alike.
The baby nursing at the breast,
And aged men will suffer.
²⁶I had decided to scatter them to
  distant lands,
So that even the memory of them
Would disappear.
²⁷But then I thought,
"My enemies will boast,
'Israel is destroyed by our own
  might.
It was not the Lord
Who did it!'"'
²⁸Israel is a stupid nation.
They are foolish, without under-
  standing.
²⁹Oh, that they were wise!
Oh, that they could understand!
Oh, that they would know what
  they are getting into!
³⁰How could one single enemy
  chase 1000 of them,
And two put 10,000 to flight,
Unless their Rock had left them,
Unless the Lord had destroyed
  them?
³¹But the rock of other nations
Is not like our Rock.
Prayers to their gods are value-
  less.
³²They act like men of Sodom and
  Gomorrah.

Their deeds are bitter with poison.
³³They drink the wine of serpent
   venom.
³⁴But Israel is my special people,
Sealed as jewels within my treasury.
³⁵Vengeance is mine,
And I decree the punishment of all
   her enemies.
Their doom is sealed.
³⁶The Lord will see his people
   righted,
And will have compassion on them
   when they slip.
He will watch their power ebb away,
Both slave and free.
³⁷Then God will ask,
'Where are their gods,
The rocks they claimed to be their
   refuge?
³⁸Where are these gods now,
To whom they sacrificed their fat
   and wine?
Let those gods arise,
And help them!
³⁹Don't you see that I alone am
   God?
I kill and make live.
I wound and heal.
No one delivers from my power.
⁴⁰⁻⁴¹I raise my hand to heaven
And vow by my existence,
That I will whet the lightning of my
   sword!
And hurl my punishments upon
   my enemies!
⁴²My arrows shall be drunk with
   blood!
My sword devours the flesh and
   blood
Of all the slain and captives.
The heads of the enemy
Are gory with blood.'
⁴³Praise his people,
Gentile nations,
For he will avenge his people,
Taking vengeance on his enemies,
Making his land pure
And his people."

⁴⁴⁻⁴⁵Moses and Joshua had sung all
the words of this song to the people.
⁴⁶Then Moses made these comments:
"Meditate upon all the laws I have
given you today. Pass them on to your
children. ⁴⁷These laws are not mere

words. They are your life! Through
obeying them you will live long, plen-
tiful lives. You will stay in the land you
are going to take across the Jordan
River."

God Tells Moses He Will Soon Die

⁴⁸That same day, the Lord spoke to
Moses. ⁴⁹He said, "Go to Mount Nebo in
the Abarim mountains. It is in the land
of Moab across from Jericho. Climb to
its heights and look out across the
land of Canaan. See the land I am
giving to the people of Israel. ⁵⁰After
you see the land, you must die and
join your ancestors. You must die just
as Aaron, your brother, died in Mount
Hor and joined them. ⁵¹For you dishonored me among the people of Israel at
the springs of Meribah-kadesh. This is
in the wilderness of Zin. ⁵²You will see
spread out before you the land I am
giving the people of Israel. But you will
not enter it."

Moses Blesses All the People

33 This is the blessing Moses, the
man of God, gave to the people of
Israel before his death:

²"The Lord came to us at Mount
   Sinai,
And dawned upon us from Mount
   Seir.
He shone from Mount Paran,
Surrounded by ten thousands of
   holy angels,
And with flaming fire at his right
   hand.
³How he loves his people.
His holy ones are in his hands.
They followed in your steps,
O Lord.
They have received their directions
   from you.
⁴The laws I have given
Are your precious possession.
⁵The Lord became king in Jeru-
   salem,
Elected by a group of the leaders of
   the tribes!
⁶Let Reuben live forever
And may his tribe increase!"

⁷And Moses said of Judah:

"O Lord, hear the cry of Judah
And unite him with Israel.
Fight for him against his enemies."

⁸Then Moses said of the tribe of Levi:

"Give to godly Levi
Your Urim and your Thummim.
You tested Levi at Massah and at
 Meribah.
⁹He obeyed your commands
and destroyed many sinners,
Even his own children, brothers, fa-
 thers, and mothers.
¹⁰The Levites shall teach God's laws
 to Israel.
They shall work before you at the
 incense altar
And the altar of burnt offering.
¹¹O Lord, bless the Levites
And accept the work they do for
 you.
Crush those who are their enemies.
Don't let them rise again."

God will help you at any time

*You can run to God at
any time, and he will put
his arms around you.*

Deuteronomy 33:27

---

¹²Of the tribe of Benjamin, Moses
said:

"He is beloved of God
And lives in safety beside him.
God surrounds him with his loving
 care,
And preserves him from every
 harm."

¹³Of the tribe of Joseph, he said:

"May his land be blessed by God
With the choicest gifts of heaven
And of the earth that lies below.
¹⁴May he be blessed
With the best of what the sun
 makes grow.
May he grow richly month by
 month,
¹⁵With the finest of mountain crops
And of the everlasting hills.
¹⁶May he be blessed with the best
 gifts

Of the earth and its fullness,
And with the favor of God who ap-
 peared
In the burning bush.
Let all these blessings come upon
 Joseph,
The prince among his brothers.
¹⁷He is a young bull in strength and
 splendor,
With the strong horns of a wild ox
To push against the nations every-
 where.
This is my blessing on the multi-
 tudes of Ephraim
And the thousands of Manasseh."

¹⁸Of the tribe of Zebulun, Moses said:

"Rejoice, O Zebulun, you outdoors-
 men,
And Issachar, you lovers of your
 tents.
¹⁹They shall call the people
To celebrate their sacrifices with
 them.
Lo, they taste the riches of the sea
And the treasures of the sand."

²⁰Of the tribe of Gad, Moses said:

"A blessing upon those who help
 Gad.
He crouches like a lion,
With savage arm and face and head.
²¹He chose the best of the land for
 himself
Because it is reserved for a leader.
He led the people
Because he carried out God's penal-
 ties for Israel."

²²Of the tribe of Dan, Moses said:

"Dan is like a lion's cub
Leaping out from Bashan."

²³Of the tribe of Naphtali, Moses said:

"O Naphtali, you are satisfied
With all the blessings of the Lord.
The Mediterranean coast and the
 Negeb
Are your home."

²⁴Of the tribe of Asher:

"Asher is a favorite son,
Esteemed above his brothers.
He bathes his feet in oil.
²⁵May you be protected with strong
 bolts
Of iron and bronze,

And may your strength match the
length of your days!
26There is none like the God of Jerusalem!
He descends from the heavens
In majestic splendor to help you.
27You can run to God at any time,
and he will put his arms around
you.
He thrusts out your enemies before
you.
It is he who cries, 'Destroy them!'
28So Israel dwells safely,

Prospering in a land of corn and
wine,
While the gentle rains descend
from heaven.
29What blessings are yours, O Israel!
Who else has been saved by the
Lord?
He is your shield and your helper!
He is your excellent sword!
Your enemies shall bow low before
you,
And you shall trample on their
backs!"

Moses Dies

You'll learn some amazing things about Moses as you read this
story. There was no one like him. Moses was different in four ways.
Can you find them?

34 Moses climbed from the plains of
Moab. He went to Pisgah Peak in
Mount Nebo, across from Jericho. And
the Lord pointed out to him the Promised Land. They gazed out across Gilead
as far as Dan.

"There is Naphtali. And there is
Ephraim and Manasseh," the Lord told
him. "And across there is Judah, going
all the way to the Mediterranean Sea.
3There is the Negeb and the Jordan Valley. There is Jericho, the city of palm
trees. And there is Zoar."

"That is the Promised Land," the
Lord told Moses. "I promised Abraham,
Isaac, and Jacob that I would give it to
their descendants. Now you have seen
it. But you will not enter it."

Moses, the servant of the Lord, died
in the land of Moab as the Lord had said.
6The Lord buried him in a valley near
Beth-peor in Moab. But no one knows
the exact place.

7Moses was 120 years old when he
died. Yet his eyesight was perfect, and
he was as strong as a young man. 8The
people of Israel mourned for him for 30
days on the plains of Moab.

9Joshua was full of the spirit of wisdom. This was because Moses had laid
his hands upon him. So the people of

Israel obeyed him. They followed the
commands the Lord had given to Moses.

10There has never been another
prophet like Moses. The Lord talked to
him face to face! 11-12And at God's command he did amazing miracles that
have never been equaled.

● *Remember:* Each of these questions will
tell you one way Moses was different
from other people. Who buried Moses?
(34:6) How was Moses like a young
man when he died? (34:7) How was
Moses different from all other prophets?
(34:10) How were Moses' miracles different from all other miracles? (34:11-12)
Would you like to have known Moses?
Why?

● *Discover:* When God is with you, you will
be different from other people. But you
will be different in good ways.

● *Apply:* Do your friends ever tease you because you read the Bible or go to Sunday school? Do they ever tease you
because you're "different"? Let God
make you different. But don't let bad
things make you different.

● *What's next?* Spies go into the Promised
Land. What do you think they will find?
Read Joshua 2 and you will find out. ■

JOSHUA

You'll find adventure in Joshua! A river stops flowing so people can cross. The sun stands still so an army can win a battle. You'll hear a trumpet blast that breaks down a great city wall. And you'll learn how a red rope saved a whole family. Has an angel ever told you to take off your shoes? You'll hear an angel order a great soldier to do that. Do you know why? You will when you read the book of Joshua. This is a true story about brave soldiers and great battles.

The Book of Joshua tells the amazing story of how the Israelites entered the Promised Land and made it their home. The Promised Land was also called the land of Canaan. It was the land God promised to give to the Israelites. Now God was keeping his promise.

The people could have entered the land much sooner. Thirty-nine years before this they were at the same place, ready to go in. But they did not trust God to help them. God punished them by making them wander in the wilderness those 39 years. Now the people were ready to go in again. Would they trust God this time? Read the Book of Joshua to see the great things that happened when the people trusted God.

"Be Brave, Joshua!"

1 So Moses, the Lord's servant, died. After that God spoke to Moses' helper. His name was Joshua. He was the son of Nun. The Lord said to him,

²"Moses my servant is now dead. You are the new leader of Israel. Lead my people across the Jordan River into the Promised Land. ³I say to you what I said to Moses: 'Wherever you go will be part of the land of Israel. ⁴The land all the way from the Negeb desert in the south will be yours. It will be yours from there all the way to the Lebanon mountains in the north. The land from the Mediterranean Sea in the west to the Euphrates River in the east will be yours. This includes all the land of the Hittites.' ⁵No

one will be able to stop you as long as you live. For I will be with you just as I was with Moses. I will never leave you. I will never stop helping you.

God is always with you

I will never leave you. I will never stop helping you.

Joshua 1:5

6"Be strong and brave! You will be a great leader of my people. And they shall conquer all the land I promised to their ancestors. 7You need only be strong and brave. And you must obey to the letter every law Moses gave you. If you are careful to obey every one, you will succeed in all you do. 8Always remind the people about these laws. You yourself must think about them every day and every night. That way you will be sure to obey all of them. For only then will you succeed. 9Be brave! Be strong! Don't ever be afraid or doubt! God is with you wherever you go."

Joshua Gets the People Ready

10-11Then Joshua gave orders to the leaders of Israel. He told them to get the people ready to cross the Jordan River. "In three days we will go across!" he said. "We will conquer and live in the land which God has given us!"

12-13Then he called the leaders of the

tribes of Reuben, Gad, and the half-tribe of Manasseh. He reminded them of their agreement with Moses. "The Lord your God has given you a homeland," Moses had said. "It is here on the east side of the Jordan River. 14Your wives and children and cattle may stay here. But your troops must lead the other tribes across the Jordan River. They must go fully armed. You must help them conquer their land on the other side. 15Stay with them until they finish the conquest. Only then may you settle down here on the east side of the Jordan."

We can be brave and strong because God is with us

Be brave! Be strong! Don't ever be afraid or doubt! God is with you wherever you go.

Joshua 1:9

16To this they fully agreed. They promised to obey their leader Joshua.

17-18"We will obey you just as we obeyed Moses," they said. "And may the Lord your God be with you as he was with Moses. If anyone, no matter who, rebels against your commands, he shall die. So lead on with courage and strength!"

Spies Visit Jericho

Spies sneak into Jericho. But someone sees them. Police come looking for them. Will they get caught? How can they escape?

2 Then Joshua sent two spies from the camp at Acacia to cross the river. They were to check out the land. They were to take a close look at Jericho. They got to an inn owned by a woman named Rahab. She was a prostitute. They were planning to spend the night there. 2But someone ran to the king of Jericho with a report. He told the king that two Isra-

elites had come to the city that evening. He knew that they were probably spies. 3The king sent a group of police to Rahab's home. They demanded that she give them up.

"They are spies," the police said. "They have been sent by the Israelite leaders to find the best way to attack us."

4But she had hidden them. So she

told the officer in charge, "The men were here earlier. But I didn't know they were spies. ⁵They left the city at dusk. The city gates were about to close when they left. I don't know where they went. If you hurry, you can probably catch up with them!"

⁶But actually she had taken them up to the roof. She had hidden them under piles of flax that were drying there. ⁷So the officer and his men went all the way to the Jordan River looking for them. Meanwhile, the city gates were kept shut. ⁸Rahab went up to talk to the men before they went to sleep.

⁹"I know that your God is going to give my country to you," she told them. "We are all afraid of you. We are filled with fear if the word *Israel* is even spoken. ¹⁰For we have heard how the Lord dried up the Red Sea for you when you left Egypt! And we know what you did to Sihon and Og, the two Amorite kings east of the Jordan. We heard how you ruined their land and destroyed their people. ¹¹No wonder we are afraid of you! No one has any fight left after hearing things like that! For your God is the supreme God of heaven. He is not just an ordinary god. ¹²⁻¹³Now I beg for just

one thing. Make a promise to me by the holy name of your God. Tell me that when Jericho is conquered you will let me live. Also let my father and mother, my brothers and sisters, and all their families live. This is only fair after the way I have helped you."

[14]The men agreed. "If you don't give us away, we'll see to it that you are safe. You and your family will not be harmed," they promised. [15]"We'll defend you with our lives." Then she let them down by a rope from a window. Her house was on top of the city wall.

[16]"Run to the mountains," she told them. "Hide there for three days. By then the men who are looking for you will have come back. Then go on your way."

[17-18]But before they left, the men spoke to her. "You must leave this red rope hanging from this window," they said. "And all your relatives must be here inside the house. This includes your fa-

ther, mother, brothers, and anyone else you want to be safe. If not, then we cannot be responsible for you and them. [19]If they go out into the street, we will not be guilty of their blood. But we swear that no one inside this house will be killed or hurt. [20]However, you might betray us. If you do, then we don't have to keep this promise."

[21]"I accept your terms," she replied. And she left the red rope hanging from the window.

[22]The spies went up into the mountains. They stayed there three days, until the search party had gone back to the city. The search party had looked all along the road without success. [23]Then the two spies came down from the mountain and crossed the river. They reported to Joshua all that had happened to them.

[24]"The Lord will give us the whole land for sure," they said. "All the people over there are scared to death of us."

- *Remember:* Why did Joshua send the spies to Jericho? (2:1) How many spies were there? (2:1) Where did Rahab hide the spies? (2:3) Why did Rahab hide the spies? What did she want from them? (2:12-13) Who could be safe when the spies and their army came to Jericho? (2:17-21) How would the spies and their people know who to protect? What should Rahab leave in her window? (2:17-18) Rahab and the spies were enemies. But how did they help each other?

- *Discover:* We can help each other, even though we aren't even friends.

- *Apply:* Suppose you lose your lunch at school. But someone you don't like offers to share lunch with you. Will you do it?

- *What's next?* A river stops flowing to let some people cross. You will read about this in Joshua 3–4. ∎

Crossing the Jordan River

The Israelites must cross the Jordan River to get into their new land. But how will they do it? There are no bridges or boats. The water is too deep and is flowing too fast to swim in. But suddenly the river stops flowing. What is happening?

3 Early the next morning Joshua and all the people of Israel left Acacia. They got to the banks of the Jordan River that evening. They camped there for a few days before crossing. ²⁻⁴On the third day leaders went through the camp. They gave these orders:

"You will see the priests carrying the Ark of God. When you see this, follow them. You have never before been where we are going now. Because of this, they will guide you. However, stay about a half mile behind. Keep a clear space between you and the Ark. Be sure that you don't get any closer."

⁵Then Joshua told the people to make themselves clean. "For tomorrow," he said, "the Lord will do a great miracle."

⁶In the morning Joshua ordered the priests, "Take up the Ark. Then lead us across the river!" And so they started out.

⁷"Today," the Lord told Joshua,

"I will give you great honor. All Israel will know that I am with you just as I was with Moses. ⁸Tell the priests who are carrying the Ark to stop at the edge of the river."

God has something important to tell you

Listen to God!

Joshua 3:9

---

⁹Then Joshua called all the people. He told them, "Listen to God! ¹⁰Today you will know for sure that the living God is among you. You will know that he will, without fail, drive out your enemies. He will drive out the Canaanites, Hittites, Hivites, Perizzites, Girgashites, Amorites, and Jebusites. All the people who now live in your land will be driven out. ¹¹Think of it! The Ark of God will go before you! God himself, who is Lord of the whole earth, will lead you across the river!

¹²"Now choose 12 men for a special task. One must come from each tribe. ¹³⁻¹⁴The priests carrying the Ark will touch the water with their feet. When they do, the river will stop flowing. It will be as though it were held back by a dam. It will pile up as though against an invisible wall!" At that time it was the harvest season. The Jordan River was overflowing all its banks. But the people set out to cross the river. The feet of the priests carrying the Ark touched the water at the river's edge. ¹⁵⁻¹⁶Suddenly, the water began piling up as though against a dam! This happened far up the river at the city of Adam, near Zarethan. And the water below that point flowed on to the Dead Sea. Soon the riverbed was empty. Then the people crossed at a spot where the river was close to Jericho. ¹⁷The priests stood on dry ground in the middle of the Jordan. They were carrying the Ark. They waited as all the people passed by.

4 All the people safely crossed the river. Then the Lord spoke to Joshua. ²⁻³"Speak to the 12 men chosen for a special task," he said. "One must be taken from each tribe. Tell each to take a stone from where the priests are standing in the middle of the Jordan. They

are to carry them out and pile them up. They are to build a monument at the place where you camp tonight."

⁴So Joshua called the 12 men. ⁵He said, "Go out into the middle of the Jordan where the Ark is. Each of you is to carry out a stone on your shoulder. You will get 12 stones in all. One will be taken for each of the 12 tribes. ⁶We will use them to build a monument. In the future your children might ask, 'What is this monument for?' ⁷When they do, you can tell them. You might say, 'It is a reminder for us. It helps us remember that the Jordan River stopped flowing when the Ark of God went across!' The monument will be a lasting reminder to the people of Israel. It will help them remember this great miracle."

⁸So the men did as Joshua told them. They took 12 stones from the middle of the Jordan River. One was taken for each tribe. They did just as the Lord had told Joshua. They carried them to the place where they were camped for the night. There they built a monument. ⁹Joshua also built another monument of 12 stones in the middle of the river. He put it at the place where the priests were standing. It is there to this day. ¹⁰The priests who were carrying the Ark stood in the middle of the river. They stayed there until all the orders of the Lord had been carried out. These orders had been given to Joshua by Moses. Meanwhile, the people had hurried across the riverbed. ¹¹When all were across, the people watched the priests. They carried the Ark up out of the riverbed.

¹²⁻¹³The troops of Reuben, Gad, and the half-tribe of Manasseh led the other tribes. They were fully armed as Moses had ordered. There were 40,000 men in all. They led the Lord's army across to the plains of Jericho.

¹⁴It was a great day for Joshua! The Lord made him great in the eyes of all the people of Israel. They revered him as much as they had Moses. And they respected him deeply all the rest of his life. ¹⁵⁻¹⁶For it was Joshua who issued the orders to the priests carrying the Ark. It was he who gave the Lord's command.

"Come up from the riverbed," the Lord now told him to command them.

[17]So Joshua issued the order. [18]And as soon as the priests came out, the water poured down again as usual. It overflowed the banks of the river as before! [19]This miracle took place on March 25. That day the whole nation crossed the Jordan River. They camped in Gilgal at the eastern edge of the city of Jericho. [20]There the 12 stones from the Jordan were piled up as a monument.

[21]Then Joshua explained again the purpose of the stones. "In the future," he said, "your children might ask you why these stones are here. They might ask you what they mean. [22]When they do, tell them that these stones are to remind you of this miracle. Remember that the nation of Israel crossed the Jordan River on dry ground! [23]Tell them how the Lord our God dried up the river right before our eyes! Tell them how he kept it dry until we were all across! It is the same thing the Lord did 40 years ago at the Red Sea! [24]He did this so all the nations of the earth will know that the Lord is the mighty God. He did it so all of you will worship him forever."

- *Remember:* When did the people learn that God would work a miracle? (3:5) God led the people across the river. But what did he use to lead them? (3:11) How did the river stop? (3:12-17) When did the water flow again? (4:18) Why did Joshua tell some people to bring stones from the river? (4:6-7, 21-24) How many stones were brought from the river? (4:5) Why that number? (4:5) If you had been there, what would you have prayed that night?

- *Discover:* Miracles are special. No human can do a miracle. But they can happen with God's help. Only God can do a miracle.

- *Apply:* Can you do a miracle? Can you command a river to stop? Can you make the sun stand still? Can you make a dead person come back to life? God works miracles.

- *What's next?* What would you do if the commander of God's army stood before you? Read what Joshua did in Joshua 5:13-15. ▪

Joshua Circumcises the Men

5 The nations west of the Jordan River heard that the Lord had dried up the river. They heard that the Israelites had walked across on dry ground. These nations included the Amorites and Canaanites who lived along the Mediterranean coast. When they heard this, their courage melted away. They were frozen with fear!

[2-3]The Lord then told Joshua to set aside a day. On that day all the men and boys of Israel were to be circumcised. It was the second time in Israel's history that this was done. The Lord told them to make flint knives for this purpose. The place where they were circumcised was named "The Hill of the Cut-Off Skin." [4-5]When Israel left Egypt all the men old enough to fight had been circumcised. But that whole generation had died during the years in the wilderness. None of the boys born since that time had been circumcised. That is why they had to do it again at this time. [6]The nation of Israel had gone back and forth across the wilderness for 40 years. They traveled until all the men old enough to fight when they left Egypt were dead. They had not obeyed the Lord. And he vowed that they would not enter the land he had promised to Israel. It was a land that "flowed with milk and honey." [7]So now Joshua circumcised their children. These were the men who had grown up to take their fathers' places.

[8-9]And the Lord said to Joshua, "Today I have ended your shame of not being circumcised." So the place where this was done was called Gilgal. This means "to end." It is still called this today. After the ceremony the whole nation rested in camp. They waited until the raw flesh of their wounds had been healed.

[10]They were camped at Gilgal on the plains of Jericho. While there, they celebrated the Passover during the evening of April 1. [11-12]The next day they began to eat from the gardens and grain fields which they invaded. And they made bread without yeast. The following day no manna fell, and it was never seen again! So from that time on they lived on the crops of Canaan.

Commander-in-Chief of God's Army

The Commander-in-Chief of God's army is standing before Joshua. That's enough to scare the bravest soldier in the world. What should he say? What should he do? What would you do? This is what Joshua said and did.

¹³Joshua was looking out over the city of Jericho. As he stood there, a man appeared nearby with a drawn sword. Joshua went over to him. He asked, "Are you friend or foe?"

¹⁴"I am the Commander of the Lord's army," he replied.

Joshua fell to the ground before him and worshiped him. He said, "Give me your commands."

¹⁵"Take off your shoes," the Commander told him. "For this is holy ground." And Joshua did.

- *Remember:* A man appeared with his sword drawn. What did Joshua ask him? (5:13) What did the man answer? Who was he? (5:14) What did Joshua do then? (5:14) What order did this commander give Joshua? Why was Joshua supposed to take off his shoes? (5:15) What would you say if the commander of God's army told you to do something?

- *Discover:* When God sends someone special, you should listen to that person.

- *Apply:* God sends many special people to help you. Can you make a list of all the people who help you do what God wants? How does each one help you?

- *What's next?* City walls crumbled and fell down. What happened? There was nothing but a trumpet blast and a shout. Read in Joshua 6 how this happened. ■

The Battle for Jericho

This is the strangest battle you will ever see. Soldiers march around and around the city. They don't rush toward the walls. They don't try to climb them. How can they capture a city by doing that?

6 The gates of Jericho were kept tightly shut. The people there were afraid of the Israelites. No one was allowed to go in or out.

²But the Lord said to Joshua, "Jericho and its king are already beaten! So are all its mighty warriors! I have given them to you! ³⁻⁴Your army is to walk around the city once a day for six days. They shall be followed by seven priests walking ahead of the Ark. Each shall carry a trumpet made from a ram's horn. On the seventh day you are to walk around the city seven times. As you walk, the priests shall blow their trumpets. ⁵Then they shall give one long, loud blast. When they do, all the people are to give a mighty shout. And the walls of the city will fall down. Then move in upon the city from every direction."

⁶⁻⁹So Joshua called the priests. He gave them their orders. The armed men would lead the parade. They would be followed by seven priests. The priests would blow on their trumpets as they went. Behind them would come the priests carrying the Ark. They would be followed by a rear guard.

¹⁰"Let there be complete silence except for the trumpets," Joshua told them. "Not a single word from any of you until I tell you to shout. When I do, then *shout!*"

¹¹The Ark was carried around the city once that day. Then everyone went back to the camp again. They spent the night there. ¹²⁻¹⁴At dawn the next morning they went around again. Then they returned again to the camp. They did this for six days.

¹⁵At dawn on the seventh day they started out again. But this time they went around the city not once, but seven times. ¹⁶The seventh time, the priests blew a long, loud trumpet blast. When they did, Joshua yelled to the people, "Shout! The Lord has given us the city!"

¹⁷He had told them before, "Kill everyone except Rahab. And do not kill anyone in her house. For she hid our spies. ¹⁸Don't take any loot. For everything is to be destroyed. If it isn't, disaster will fall upon the whole nation of Israel. ¹⁹But all the silver and gold and bronze and iron will be given to the Lord. These things must be brought into his treasury."

²⁰So, the people heard the trumpet blast. And when they did, they shouted as loud as they could. Suddenly the walls of Jericho crumbled and fell before them. And the people of Israel poured into the city! They attacked from every side and took it! ²¹They killed everyone and destroyed all that was in it.

²²Meanwhile Joshua had said to the two spies, "Keep your promise. Go and rescue Rahab and everyone with her."

²³The young men found her. They saved her and her father, mother, and brothers. They saved all the other relatives who were with her. They were given a place to live outside the camp of Israel. ²⁴Then the Israelites burned the city and all that was in it. They saved only the silver and gold and the bronze and iron utensils. These were kept for the Lord's treasury. ²⁵Thus Joshua saved Rahab. He also saved her relatives who were with her in the house. They still live among the Israelites because she hid the spies sent to Jericho by Joshua.

²⁶Then Joshua declared a terrible curse. It would fall upon anyone who might rebuild Jericho. He warned that when the foundation was laid, the builder's oldest son would die. He also warned that when the gates were set up, his youngest son would die.

²⁷So the Lord was with Joshua. His name became famous everywhere.

- *Remember:* Who planned the battle against Jericho? (6:2) Did Joshua's people do what the Lord said? Did the Lord do what he promised? (6:20) Did Joshua and his people keep their promise to Rahab? (6:22-25) Why do you think keeping promises was important to Joshua and his people?

- *Discover:* Keeping promises is important to us, to others, and to God.

- *Apply:* Have you ever promised something, then broken your promise? The next time you think about breaking a promise, think who you will hurt.

- *What's next?* Nobody likes to be tricked. Do you think an important man like Joshua could be tricked? He was. Read Joshua 9. ∎

Achan Disobeys God

7 But there was sin among the Israelites. God had told them to destroy everything. They were to save only the things reserved for the Lord's treasury. But this order was not obeyed. For Achan took some loot for himself. He was the son of Carmi and the grandson of Zabdi. His great-grandfather was Zerah, of the tribe of Judah. The Lord was very angry with the whole nation of Israel because of this.

²Soon after Jericho's defeat, Joshua called some of his men. He sent them to spy on the city of Ai. This city was located east of Bethel.

³When they got back they spoke to Joshua. "It's a small city," they said. "It won't take more than 2,000 or 3,000 of us to destroy it. There's no point in all of us going there."

⁴So about 3,000 soldiers were sent. But they were soundly defeated. ⁵About 36 of the Israelites were killed during the attack. Many others died while being chased by the men of Ai as far as the quarries. The Israelite army was paralyzed with fear at this turn of events. ⁶Joshua and the elders of Israel tore their clothing. They lay face down before the Ark of the Lord until evening. They threw dust on their heads.

⁷Joshua cried out, "O Lord, why have you brought us over the Jordan River? Have you brought us here to let the

Amorites kill us? Why weren't we content with what we had? Why didn't we stay on the other side? 8O Lord, what am I to do now that Israel has fled from her enemies? 9For the Canaanites and the other nearby nations will hear about it. And when they do, they will surround us. They will attack us and wipe us out. And then what will happen to the honor of your great name?"

10-11But the Lord said to Joshua, "Get up off your face! Israel has sinned and disobeyed my command. Someone has taken loot when I said it was not to be taken. And he has not only taken it, he has also lied about it. He has hidden it among his own things. 12That is why the people of Israel are being defeated. That is why your men are running from their enemies. They are cursed. I will not stay with you any longer unless you get rid of this sin.

13"Get up! Tell the people, 'You must each make yourselves clean. You must do this to get ready for tomorrow. For the Lord your God of Israel says that someone has stolen from him. You cannot defeat your enemies until you deal with this sin. 14In the morning you must come by tribes. The Lord will point out the tribe to which the guilty man belongs. And that tribe must come by its clans. The Lord will point out the guilty clan. And the clan must come by its families. Then each member of the guilty family must come one by one. 15And the one who has stolen that which belongs to the Lord shall be burned with fire. He shall be burned along with all that he has. For he has broken the covenant of the Lord. He has brought trouble upon all of Israel.'"

16So, early the next morning, Joshua brought the tribes of Israel before the Lord. The tribe of Judah was chosen. 17Then he brought the clans of Judah. And the clan of Zerah was singled out. Then the families of that clan were brought before the Lord. And the family of Zabdi was chosen. 18Zabdi's family was brought man by man. His grandson Achan was found to be the guilty one.

Achan's Terrible Punishment

19Joshua said to Achan, "My son, give glory to the God of Israel. Confess your sin. Tell me what you have done."

20Achan replied, "I have sinned against the Lord, the God of Israel. 21For I saw a beautiful robe imported from Babylon. I also saw some silver worth $200, and a bar of gold worth $500. I wanted them so much that I took them. They are hidden in the ground under my tent. The silver is buried deeper than the rest."

22So Joshua sent some men to search for the loot. They ran to the tent. They found the stolen goods hidden there just as Achan had said. The silver was buried under the rest. 23They brought it all to Joshua and laid it on the ground in front of him. 24Then Joshua and all the Israelites took Achan. They took the silver, the robe, and the wedge of gold. They took his sons, his daughters, his oxen, donkeys, sheep, and his tent. They took all that he had! They brought them to the valley of Achor.

25Then Joshua said to Achan, "Why have you brought calamity upon us? The Lord will now bring calamity upon you."

And the men of Israel stoned them to death and burned their bodies. 26Then they piled a great heap of stones upon them. The stones are still there to this day. And even today that place is called "The Valley of Calamity." And so the fierce anger of the Lord was ended.

The Israelites Attack Ai

8 Then the Lord said to Joshua, "Don't be afraid. Don't give up. Take the whole army and go to Ai. It is now yours to conquer. I have given the king of Ai and all of his people to you. 2You shall do to them as you did to Jericho and her king. But this time you may keep the loot and the cattle for yourselves. Set an ambush behind the city."

3-4Joshua sent 30,000 of his bravest troops to hide in ambush close behind the city. They were to be alert for action. He did this before the main army left for Ai.

5"This is the plan," he told them.

"Our main army will attack. When they do, the men of Ai will come out to fight as they did before. And we will run away. 6We will let them chase us until they have all left the city. And they will say, 'The Israelites are running away again! They are afraid just as they were before!' 7Then you will jump up from your ambush and go into the city. For the Lord will give it to you. 8Set the city on fire, as the Lord has commanded. You now have your orders."

9So they left that night. They lay in ambush between Bethel and the west side of Ai. But Joshua and the rest of the army stayed in the camp at Jericho. 10Early the next morning Joshua roused his men and started toward Ai. The elders of Israel went with them. 11-13They all stopped at the edge of a valley north of the city. That night Joshua sent another 5,000 men to join the troops in ambush. They went and joined them on the west side of the city. He himself spent the night in the valley.

14The King of Ai saw the Israelites across the valley. He went out early the next morning. He attacked them at the Plain of Arabah. But of course he didn't know that there was an ambush behind the city. 15Joshua and the Israelite army fled across the desert. They acted like they were badly beaten. 16So all the soldiers in the city were called out to chase after them. The city was left with no one to defend it! 17There was not a soldier left in Ai or Bethel! And the city gates were left wide open!

18Then the Lord said to Joshua, "Point your spear toward Ai. For I will give you the city." Joshua pointed his spear. 19The men in ambush saw his signal. And when they saw it, they jumped up. They poured into the city and set it on fire. 20-21Then the men of Ai looked behind them. They saw smoke from their city filling the sky. And they had nowhere to go. Joshua and the troops who were with him saw the smoke. When they saw it, they knew that their men who had been in ambush were inside the city. So they turned upon the men who were chasing them and began killing them. 22Then the Israelites who were inside the city

came out. They began destroying the enemy from the rear. So the men of Ai were caught in a trap. All of them died! Not one man survived or got away! 23Only the king of Ai lived. But he was captured and brought to Joshua.

24The army of Israel finished killing all the men outside the city. Then they went back and killed all those left inside. 25So all the people of Ai, 12,000 in all, were wiped out that day. 26Joshua kept his spear pointed toward Ai until the last person was dead. 27Only the cattle and the loot were not destroyed. The armies of Israel kept these for themselves. The Lord had told Joshua they could. 28So Ai became a pile of refuse, as it still is today.

29Joshua hanged the king of Ai on a tree until evening. But as the sun was going down, he took down the body. He threw it in front of the city gate. There he piled a great heap of stones over it. The pile can still be seen to this day.

Joshua Reviews God's Laws

30Then Joshua built an altar to the Lord God of Israel at Mount Ebal. 31He did just as Moses had commanded in the book of his laws. "Make me an altar of stones," the Lord had said. "The stones must be neither broken nor carved." Then the priests offered burnt sacrifices and peace offerings to the Lord on the altar. 32And Joshua carved upon the stones of the altar each of the Ten Commandments. He did this as all the people watched.

33Then all the people of Israel divided into two groups. This included the elders, officers, judges, and the foreigners living among them. Half of them stood at the foot of Mount Gerizim. The other half stood at the foot of Mount Ebal. Between them stood the priests with the Ark, ready to give their blessing. This was all done according to the orders given long before by Moses. 34Joshua then read to them all of the blessings and curses of God's covenant. Moses had written these in the book of God's laws. 35Every command Moses had ever given was read before all the people. Everyone was there, even the women and children. The foreigners who lived among the Israelites were also there.

Gibeonites Trick Joshua

Joshua was a brave man and a great soldier. No one should have tricked him. But someone did. Some men lied to Joshua. Because of their lie, Joshua made them a promise he should not have made. Then he learned about their lie. Should Joshua still keep his promise to them? Or could he break his promise because they had lied to him? This is what he did.

9 The kings of that area heard what had happened to Jericho. So they quickly got all their armies together. They got ready to fight for their lives against Joshua and the Israelites. These were the kings of the nations west of the Jordan River. They lived along the shores of the Mediterranean as far north as the Lebanon mountains. These kings ruled the Hittites, Amorites, Canaanites, Perizzites, Hivites, and Jebusites.

3-5The people of Gibeon also heard what had happened to Jericho and Ai. When they heard about it, they resorted to trickery to save themselves. They sent messengers to Joshua. The messengers wore worn-out clothing, as though from a long trip. They wore patched shoes. They had weatherworn saddlebags on their donkeys. They carried old, patched wineskins and dry, moldy bread. 6They went to the camp of Israel at Gilgal. When they got there, they spoke to Joshua and the men of Israel. "We have come from a distant land. We want to make a peace treaty with you," they said.

7The Israelites replied to these Hivites, "How do we know you don't live nearby? For if you do, we cannot make a treaty with you."

8They replied, "We will be your slaves."

"But who are you?" Joshua demanded. "Where do you come from?"

9And they told him, "We are from a very distant country. We have heard of the power of the Lord your God. We heard about all he did in Egypt. 10And we heard about what you did to the two kings of the Amorites. We heard how you defeated Sihon, king of Heshbon, and Og, king of Bashan. 11So our elders and our people told us, 'Prepare for a long trip. Go to the people of Israel. Tell them that our nation will be their servants. And ask for peace.' 12This bread was hot from the ovens when we left. But now, as you see, it is dry and moldy. 13These wineskins were new. But now they are old and cracked. Our clothing and shoes have become worn-out from our long, hard trip."

14-15Joshua and the other leaders believed them in the end. They did not bother to ask the Lord about it. They went ahead and signed a peace treaty. And the leaders of Israel made the agreement with a binding promise.

16Three days later the facts came out. They found out that these men were close neighbors. 17The Israelite army set out at once to check this out. They got to their cities in three days. The names of the cities were Gibeon, Chephirah, Beeroth, and Kiriath-jearim. 18But the cities were not harmed. This was because of the vow which the leaders of Israel had made before the Lord God. The people of Israel were angry with their leaders because of the peace treaty.

19But the leaders replied, "We have made a promise before the Lord God of Israel. We have promised that we will not touch them. So we won't. 20We must let them live. For if we break our promise, the Lord's anger will be upon us."

21So they became servants of the Israelites. They chopped their wood and carried their water.

22Joshua called their leaders. He demanded, "Why have you lied to us? Why did you say that you lived in a distant land? How could you say this when you really live right here among us? 23Now a curse shall be upon you! From this moment you must always furnish us with servants. You must chop wood and carry water for the service of our God."

²⁴They replied, "We did it because we heard that the Lord told Moses to conquer this whole land. We heard you were told to destroy all the people living in it. So we feared for our lives because of you. That is why we have done it. ²⁵But now we are in your hands. You may do with us as you wish."

²⁶So Joshua would not allow the people of Israel to kill them. ²⁷But they chopped wood and carried water for the people of Israel. And they were to be servants at the altar of the Lord. They would work wherever it would be built. (For the Lord hadn't yet told them where to build it.) This arrangement is in force to this very day.

- *Remember:* How did the Gibeonites make Joshua think they came from far away? (9:3-5). What should Joshua and his men have done, but didn't? (9:14-15) What did Joshua and the other leaders say about their promise? Would they keep it? Why? (9:19-20) What did you learn from Joshua about keeping promises?

- *Discover:* Keep your promises, even when you don't want to.

- *Apply:* Yesterday you promised a friend that you would play. Today someone asks you to go to the circus with him or her. What will you do?

- *What's next?* One day the sun and moon stood still. That's because someone prayed that they would. Read about this in Joshua 10. ▪

The Sun and Moon Stand Still

Whoever heard of a time when the sun and moon stood still in the sky? You'll hear about it as you read the following story.

10 Adoni-zedek heard how Joshua had captured and destroyed Ai. He had also heard what he had done at Jericho. Adoni-zedek was the king of Jerusalem. He heard how Joshua had killed Ai's king. He also heard how the people of Gibeon had made peace with Israel and were now their allies. ²After he heard all this, he was very afraid. For Gibeon was a great city. It was as great as the royal cities and much larger than Ai. And its men were known as hard fighters. ³So King Adoni-zedek of Jerusalem sent messengers to several other kings. He sent to King Hoham of Hebron, King Piram of Jarmuth, King Japhia of Lachish, and King Debir of Eglon.

⁴"Come and help me destroy Gibeon," he urged them. "For they have made peace with Joshua and the people of Israel."

⁵So these five Amorite kings combined their armies. They joined to attack Gibeon. ⁶The men of Gibeon quickly sent messengers to Joshua at Gilgal.

"Come and help your servants!" they said. "Come quickly and save us! For all the kings of the Amorites are here with their armies. They live in the hills around us."

⁷So Joshua and the Israelite army left Gilgal. They went to rescue Gibeon.

⁸"Don't be afraid of them," the Lord said to Joshua. "For they are already defeated! I have given them to you to destroy. Not a single one of them will be able to stand up to you."

⁹Joshua traveled all night from Gilgal. He took the enemy armies by surprise. ¹⁰Then the Lord threw them into a panic. And the army of Israel killed great numbers of them at Gibeon. Then they chased the others all the way to Bethhoron and Azekah and Makkedah. They killed them all along the way. ¹¹The enemy raced down the hill toward Bethhoron to get away. But as they ran, the

Lord destroyed them with a great hailstorm. The hail kept falling all the way to Azekah. In fact, more men died from the hail than by the swords of the Israelites.

¹²As the men of Israel were chasing their enemies, Joshua prayed aloud. He said, "Let the sun stand still over Gibeon! Let the moon stand in its place over the valley of Aijalon!"

¹³And the sun and the moon stood still! They didn't move until the Israelite army had finished destroying its enemies! This is told in greater detail in *The Book of Jashar.* So the sun stopped in the heavens. It

stayed there for almost 24 hours! [14]There had never been such a day before. And there has never been such a day since. For on that day, the Lord stopped the sun and moon. And he did it all because of the prayer of one man. But the Lord was fighting for Israel. [15]After that Joshua and his army went back to Gilgal.

- *Remember:* How long did the sun and moon stand still? (10:13) Why did the Lord stop the sun and moon? (10:14) Joshua told his men that they should be strong and courageous. Why? (10:25) What if you had been one of Joshua's soldiers? What would you have said when he prayed for the sun and moon to stand still?

- *Discover:* Nothing is too hard for God to do. He can do anything.

- *Apply:* Have you ever thought nobody could help you? If God can make the sun stand still, he can help you with your problem. Ask him.

- *What's next?* Joshua and his people are winners, aren't they? But these people later became losers. What happened? Read Judges 3:12-31. ■

Five Enemy Kings Are Captured

[16]During the battle the five kings got away. They hid in a cave at Makkedah. [17]The news was brought to Joshua that they had been found. [18]When Joshua heard it, he ordered that a great stone be rolled against the mouth of the cave. Then he set guards there to keep the kings inside.

[19]Then Joshua spoke to the rest of the army. "Go on chasing the enemy," he said. "Cut them down from the rear. Don't let them get back to their cities. The Lord will help you to destroy all of them."

[20]So Joshua and the Israelite army continued the battle. They wiped out the five armies except for a few men. The few left alive managed to reach their walled cities. [21]Then the Israelites went back to their camp at Makkedah. And they hadn't lost a single man! After that no one dared to attack Israel.

[22-23]Joshua now ordered his men to take the stone from the mouth of the

cave. He told them to bring out the five kings. They ruled the cities of Jerusalem, Hebron, Jarmuth, Lachish, and Eglon. [24]Joshua told the captains of his army to put their feet on the kings' necks.

[25]"Don't ever be afraid. Don't ever give up," Joshua said to his men. "Be strong and brave. For the Lord is going to defeat all of your enemies."

[26]With that, Joshua plunged his sword into each of the five kings, killing them. He then hanged them on five trees until evening.

[27]As the sun was going down, Joshua ordered that their bodies be taken down. He ordered them thrown into the cave where they had been hiding. Then a great pile of stones was placed at the mouth of the cave. The pile is still there to this day.

Israel Battles Kings in the South

[28]On that same day Joshua destroyed the city of Makkedah. He killed its king and all who were in it. Not one person in the whole city was left alive. [29]Then the Israelites went to Libnah. [30]There, too, the Lord gave them the city and its king. Every last person was killed. It was just as it had been at Jericho.

[31]From Libnah they went to Lachish and attacked it. [32]And the Lord gave it to them on the second day. Here, too, all the people were killed, just as at Libnah.

[33]During the attack on Lachish, King Horam of Gezer got there with his army. He tried to help defend the city. But Joshua's men killed him and destroyed his whole army.

[34-35]The Israelite army then captured Eglon on the first day. And, as at Lachish, they killed everyone in the city. [36]After leaving Eglon they went to Hebron. [37]They captured it and all of the villages around it. And they killed all the people. Not one person was left alive. [38]Then they turned back to Debir. [39]They quickly captured it with all of its outlying villages. And they killed everyone just as they had at Libnah.

[40]So Joshua and his army conquered the whole country. They took the nations and kings of the hill country. They conquered the Negeb, the lowlands, and

the mountain slopes. They destroyed everyone in the land. They did just as the Lord God of Israel had commanded. [41]They killed their enemies from Kadesh-barnea to Gaza, and from Goshen to Gibeon. [42]This was all done in one campaign. For the Lord God of Israel was fighting for his people. [43]Then Joshua and his army went back to their camp at Gilgal.

The Surprise Attack

11 King Jabin of Hazor soon heard what had happened. When he did, he sent urgent messages to the following kings:

> King Jobab of Madon;
> The king of Shimron;
> The king of Achshaph;
> All the kings of the northern hill country;
> The kings in the Arabah, south of Chinneroth;
> Those in the lowland;
> The kings in the mountain areas of Dor, on the west;
> The kings of Canaan, both east and west;
> The kings of the Amorites;
> The kings of the Hittites;
> The kings of the Perizzites;
> The kings in the Jebusite hill country;
> The Hivite kings in the cities on the slopes of Mount Hermon, in the land of Mizpah.

[4]All these kings called out their armies. They came as one to crush Israel. Their combined troops, and their many horses and chariots, were great in number. They covered the land around the Springs of Merom as far as one could see. [5]For they made their camp at the Springs of Merom.

[6]But the Lord said to Joshua, "Don't be afraid of them. For by this time tomorrow they will all be dead! Hamstring their horses and burn their chariots." [7]Joshua and his troops came to the Springs of Merom suddenly and attacked. [8]And the Lord gave all that great army to the Israelites. They chased them as far as Greater Sidon and a place called

the Salt Pits. They chased them eastward into the valley of Mizpah. Not one enemy troop lived through the battle! [9]Then Joshua and his men did as the Lord had told them. They hamstrung the horses and burned all the chariots.

[10]On the way back, Joshua captured Hazor and killed its king. Hazor had at one time been the capital of all those kingdoms. [11]Every person there was killed and the city was burned.

[12]Then he attacked and destroyed all the other cities of those kings. All the people were killed. It was done just as Moses had commanded long before. [13]However, Joshua did not burn any of the cities built on mounds except for Hazor. [14]All the loot and cattle of the ravaged cities were taken by the Israelites for themselves. But they killed all the people. [15]For so the Lord had commanded his disciple Moses. Moses had passed the command on to Joshua. And Joshua had done as he had been told. He carefully obeyed all of the Lord's commands to Moses.

[16]So Joshua conquered the whole land. He took the hill country, the Negeb, and the land of Goshen. He took the lowlands, the Arabah, and the hills and lowlands of Israel. [17]The Israelites' land now began at Mount Halak, near Seir. It extended from there, to Baal-gad in the valley of Lebanon, at the foot of Mount Hermon. And Joshua killed all the kings of those territories. [18]It took seven years of war to do all of this. [19]None of the cities was given a peace treaty except the Hivites of Gibeon. All of the others were destroyed. [20]For the Lord made the enemy kings want to fight the Israelites instead of asking for peace. So they were killed without mercy, as the Lord had commanded Moses.

[21]During this period Joshua routed all of the giants. These were the descendants of Anak. They lived in the hill country in Hebron, Debir, Anab, Judah, and Israel. He killed them all and destroyed their cities. [22]None was left in all the land of Israel. But some still lived in Gaza, Gath, and Ashdod.

[23]So Joshua took the whole land just

as the Lord had ordered Moses. He gave it to the people of Israel as their inheritance. He divided the land among the tribes. So the land finally rested from its war.

A List of Conquered Kings

12 Here is the list of the kings on the east side of the Jordan River. Their cities were destroyed by the Israelites. The area involved began at the valley of the Arnon River. From there, it stretched all the way to Mount Hermon. It included the cities of the eastern desert.

²The Israelites conquered King Sihon of the Amorites, who lived in Heshbon. His kingdom began at Aroer, on the edge of the Arnon Valley, and at the middle of the valley of the Arnon River. From there, it stretched to the Jabbok River. This river is the border of the Ammonites. This includes half of the present area of Gilead. This land lies north of the Jabbok River. ³Sihon also ruled the Jordan River valley as far north as the western shores of the Lake of Galilee. He also ruled the valley as far south as the Dead Sea and the slopes of Mount Pisgah.

⁴Israel also conquered King Og of Bashan. He was the last of the Rephaim, who lived at Ashtaroth and Edrei. ⁵He ruled a region that began at Mount Hermon in the north. From there, it stretched to Salecah on Mount Bashan in the east. His western border went to the border of the kingdoms of Geshur and Maacah. His kingdom stretched south to include the northern half of Gilead. There his border touched the border of Sihon, king of Heshbon. ⁶Moses and the people of Israel had destroyed these people. And Moses gave the land to the tribes of Reuben and the half-tribe of Manasseh.

⁷Here is another list of the kings destroyed by Joshua and the armies of Israel. These are located on the west side of the Jordan. This land began at Baal-gad in the Valley of Lebanon. From there, it stretched to Mount Halak, west of Mount Seir. This area was given by Joshua to the other tribes of Israel. ⁸⁻²⁴The area included the hill country, the lowlands, and the Arabah. It in-

cluded the mountain slopes, the Judean Desert, and the Negeb.

The people who lived there were the Hittites, the Amorites, the Canaanites, the Perizzites, the Hivites, and the Jebusites. They included the king of Jericho; the king of Ai, near Bethel; the king of Jerusalem; the king of Hebron; the king of Jarmuth; the king of Lachish; the king of Eglon; the king of Gezer; the king of Debir; the king of Geder; the king of Hormah; the king of Arad; the king of Libnah; the king of Adullam; the king of Makkedah; the king of Bethel; the king of Tappuah; the king of Hepher; the king of Aphek; the king of Lasharon; the king of Madon; the king of Hazor; the king of Shimron-meron; the king of Achshaph; the king of Taanach; the king of Megiddo; the king of Kedesh; the king of Jokneam, in Carmel; the king of Dor in the city of Naphathdor; the king of Goiim in Gilgal; and the king of Tirzah. So in all, 31 kings and their cities were destroyed.

Joshua Divides Up the Land

13 Joshua was now an old man. "You are growing old," the Lord said to him. "And there are still many nations to be conquered. ²⁻⁷Here is a list of the areas still to be taken:

Take all the land of the Philistines. Conquer the land of the Geshurites. Take the land now belonging to the Canaanites. It is yours from the brook of Egypt to the southern border of Ekron.
Take the five cities of the Philistines: Gaza, Ashdod, Ashkelon, Gath, Ekron.
Conquer the land of the Avvim in the south.
In the north, take all the land of the Canaanites. This includes Mearah, which belongs to the Sidonians. It stretches north to Aphek at the border of the Amorites.
Conquer the land of the Gebalites on the coast. Take all of the Lebanon mountain area. This includes the land from Baal-gad beneath Mount Hermon in the

south to the entrance of Hamath in the north.

Take all the hill country from Lebanon to Misrephoth-maim. This includes all the land of the Sidonians.

I am ready to drive these people out from before the nation of Israel. So include all this land when you divide it. Divide it among the nine tribes and the half-tribe of Manasseh as I have told you."

The Land East of the Jordan River

[8]The other half of the tribe of Manasseh and the tribes of Reuben and Gad had already received their land. They had received land on the east side of the Jordan. Moses had already given this to them. [9]Their land began at Aroer, on the edge of the valley of the Arnon River. The city in the valley was also theirs. From there, it crossed the tableland of Medeba to Dibon. [10]It also included all the cities of King Sihon of the Amorites. (Sihon had ruled in Heshbon.) The land then stretched as far as the borders of Ammon. [11]It included Gilead and the land of the Geshurites and the Maacathites. All of Mount Hermon and Mount Bashan with its city of Salecah was theirs. [12]All the land of King Og of Bashan was theirs too. Og had ruled in Ashtaroth and Edrei. He was the last of the Rephaim. Moses had attacked them and driven them out. [13]But the people of Israel had not driven out the Geshurites or the Maacathites. They still live there among the Israelites to this day.

Land for Reuben

[14]This is how the land was divided

The Land Given to the Tribe of Levi: Moses hadn't given any land to the tribe of Levi. Instead, they were given the offerings brought to the Lord.

[15]*The Land Given to the Tribe of Reuben:* Moses had given the following area to the tribe of Reuben. The size of its land fit the number of its people. [16]Their land began at Aroer on the edge of the valley of the Arnon River. It stretched past the city of Arnon in the middle of the valley. From there, it extended to beyond the

tableland near Medeba. [17]It included Heshbon and the other cities on the plain. Their names were Dibon, Bamoth-baal, Beth-baal-meon, [18]Jahaz, Kedemoth, Mephaath, [19]Kiriathaim, Sibmah, Zereth-shahar on the mountain above the valley, [20]Beth-peor, Beth-jeshimoth. It also included the slopes of Mount Pisgah.

[21]The land of Reuben also included the cities of the tableland and the kingdom of Sihon. Sihon was the king who had lived in Heshbon. He had been killed by Moses along with the other chiefs of Midian. Their names were Evi, Rekem, Zur, Hur, and Reba. [22]The people of Israel also killed Balaam the magician, the son of Beor. [23]The Jordan River was the western border of the tribe of Reuben.

?????????????????????????????????

When the land was divided, one tribe of Israel was to get meat instead of land. Which tribe was this? What kind of meat did they get?

(Read Joshua 13:8-14 for the answer)

?????????????????????????????????

Land for Gad

[24]*The Land Given to the Tribe of Gad:* Moses also gave land to the tribe of Gad according to the number of its people. [25]This land included Jazer and all the cities of Gilead. It also included half of the land of Ammon as far as Aroer near Rabbah. [26]It extended from Heshbon to Ramath-mizpeh and Betonim. It also stretched from Mahanaim to Lodebar. [27-28]In the valley were Beth-haram, Beth-nimrah, Succoth, and Zaphon. The rest of the kingdom of King Sihon of Heshbon was also there. The Jordan River was the western border. It extended as far as the Lake of Galilee. Then the border turned east from the Jordan River.

Land for the Half-Tribe of Manasseh

[29]*The Land Given to the Half-Tribe of Manasseh:* Moses had given the following land to the half-tribe of Manasseh. He gave it according to their needs. [30]Their

land extended north from Mahanaim. It included all of Bashan, the former kingdom of King Og. It also included the 60 cities of Jair in Bashan. ³¹Half of Gilead and King Og's royal cities of Ashtaroth and Edrei were given to half of the clan of Machir. He was Manasseh's son.

³²That was how Moses divided the land east of the Jordan River. The people were camped there at that time across from Jericho. ³³But Moses had given no land to the tribe of Levi. For, as he had told them, the Lord God was their inheritance. He was all they needed. He would take care of them in other ways.

The Land West of the Jordan River

14 The conquered lands of Canaan were given to the other 9½ tribes of Israel. The land each tribe would get was decided by throwing dice before the Lord. He caused them to turn up in the ways he wanted. Eleazar the priest, Joshua, and the tribal leaders were in charge of all this.

³-⁴Moses had already given land to the 2½ tribes on the east side of the Jordan River. The tribe of Joseph had become two separate tribes, Manasseh and Ephraim. The Levites were given no land at all. They were only given cities in which to live. They were also given the pastures around them for their cattle. ⁵So the land was divided according to the Lord's directions to Moses.

Joshua Blesses Caleb

⁶*The Land Given to Caleb:* A group from the tribe of Judah came to Joshua in Gilgal. They were led by Caleb.

"Do you recall what the Lord said to Moses about you and me?" Caleb asked Joshua. "We were at Kadesh-barnea at the time. ⁷I was 40 years old. Moses had sent us from Kadesh-barnea to spy out the land of Canaan. I reported what I felt was the truth. ⁸But our brothers who went with us scared the people. They made them afraid of going into the Promised Land. But I followed the Lord my God. ⁹So Moses told me, 'The part of Canaan you were just in shall belong to you. It shall belong to your family forever.'

¹⁰"Now, as you see, the Lord has kept me alive from then until now. I have been well for all these 45 years of wandering in the wilderness. And today I am 85 years old. ¹¹I am as strong now as I was when Moses sent us on that journey. And I can still travel and fight as well as I could then! ¹²So I'm asking that you give me the hill country that the Lord promised me. You will remember that as spies we found the Anakim living there. They lived in great, walled cities. But if the Lord is with me, I shall drive them out of the land."

¹³⁻¹⁴So Joshua blessed him and gave him Hebron. It would be his lasting inheritance. For he had followed the Lord God of Israel. ¹⁵Before that time Hebron had been called Kiriath-arba. It was named after a great hero of the Anakim.

And none of the local people tried to stop the Israelites as they settled in the land.

Land for Judah

15 *The Land Given to the Tribe of Judah:* It was chosen by sacred lot. Judah's southern border began at the northern border of Edom. From there, it crossed the Wilderness of Zin. It ended at the northern edge of the Negeb. ²⁻⁴This border began at the south bay of the Dead Sea. It ran along the road going south of Mount Akrabbim. It went on into the Wilderness of Zin to Hezron (south of Kadesh-barnea). It then stretched up through Karka and Azmon. From there, it extended until it reached the Brook of Egypt. It then followed the brook to the Mediterranean Sea.

⁵The eastern border extended along the Dead Sea to the mouth of the Jordan River.

The northern border began at the bay where the Jordan River empties into the Dead Sea. ⁶It crossed to Beth-hoglah. Then it went north of Beth-arabah to the stone of Bohan (son of Reuben). ⁷From that point it went through the Valley of Achor to Debir. There it turned northwest toward Gilgal. It ran across from the slopes of Adummim on the south side of the valley. From there the border extended to the springs at En-shemesh and on to En-rogel. [8]The border then passed through the Valley of Hinnom. It went along the southern shoulder of Jebus. There the city of Jerusalem is located. From there, it stretched west to the top of the mountain above the Valley of Hinnom. Then it went on up to the northern end of the Valley of Rephaim. [9]From there the border extended from the top of the mountain to the spring of Nephtoah. From there, it went to the cities of Mount Ephron before it turned northward. Then it circled around Baalah, which is another name for Kiriath-jearim. [10-11]Then the border circled west of Baalah to Mount Seir. It passed along to the town of Chesalon on the north shoulder of Mount Jearim. Then it went down to Beth-shemesh. Turning northwest again, the borderline proceeded past the south of Timnah. From there, it went to the shoulder of the hill north of Ekron. There it bent to the left, passing south of Shikkeron and Mount Baalah. Turning again to the north, it passed Jabneel. It then ended at the Mediterranean Sea.

[12]The western border was the shoreline of the Mediterranean.

Land for Caleb

[13]*The Land Given to Caleb:* The Lord told Joshua to give some of Judah's land to Caleb (son of Jephunneh). So Caleb was given the city of Arba (also called Hebron). It had been named after Anak's father. [14]Caleb drove out the descendants of the three sons of Anak. Their names were Talmai, Sheshai, and Ahiman. [15]Then he fought against the people living in the city of Debir. Debir was formerly called Kiriath-sepher.

[16]Caleb offered his daughter Achsah to be the wife of anyone who would capture Kiriath-sepher. [17]Othniel (son of Kenaz) was the one who conquered it. He was Caleb's nephew. So Achsah became Othniel's wife. [18-19]She was about to leave home to go with Othniel. At this time, she urged him to ask her father for another field as a wedding present. She got off her donkey to speak to Caleb about this.

"What is it? What can I do for you?" Caleb asked.

And she replied, "Give me another present! For the land you gave me is a desert. Give us some springs too!" Then he gave her the upper and lower springs.

[20]So this was the land given to the tribe of Judah:

[21-32]Many cities of Judah were located along the borders of Edom in the Negeb. Their names were Kabzeel, Eder, Jagur, Kinah, Dimonah, Adadah, Kedesh, Hazor, Ithnan, Ziph, Telem, Bealoth, Hazor-hadattah, Kerioth-hezron (or, Hazor), Amam, Shema, Moladah, Hazar-gaddah, Heshmon, Beth-pelet, Hazar-shual, Beer-sheba, Biziothiah, Baalah, Iim, Ezem, Eltolad, Chesil, Hormah, Ziklag, Madmannah, Sansannah, Lebaoth, Shilhim, Ain, and Rimmon. In all, there were 29 of these cities with villages around them.

[33-36]Some of Judah's cities were located in the lowlands. Their names were Eshtaol, Zorah, Ashnah, Zanoah, En-gannim, Tappuah, Enam, Jarmuth, Adullam, Socoh, Azekah, Shaaraim, Adithaim, Gederah, and Gederothaim. In all, there were 14 of these cities with villages around them.

[37-44]The tribe of Judah also inherited 25 other cities with their villages. Their names were Zenan, Hadashah, Migdal-gad, Dilean, Mizpeh, Joktheel, Lachish, Bozkath, Eglon, Cabbon, Lahmam, Chitlish, Gederoth, Beth-dagon, Naamah, Makkedah, Libnah, Ether, Ashan, Iphtah, Ashnah, Nezib, Keilah, Achzib, and Mareshah.

[45]The land of the tribe of Judah also included all the towns and villages of Ekron. [46]From Ekron the border extended to the Mediterranean. It included the cities along the borders of Ashdod with their nearby villages. [47]It also included the city of Ashdod with its villages. Gaza with its villages as far as the Brook of Egypt were also part of Judah's land. So was the whole Mediterranean coast. It stretched from the mouth of the Brook of Egypt on the south to Tyre on the north.

[48-62]Judah also received 44 cities in the hill country. They were also given

the villages around them. The cities' names were Shamir, Jattir, Socoh, Dannah, Kiriath-sannah (or, Debir), Anab, Eshtemoh, Anim, Goshen, Holon, Giloh, Arab, Dumah, Eshan, Janim, Beth-tappuah, Aphekah, Humtah, Kiriath-arba (or, Hebron), Zior, Maon, Carmel, Ziph, Juttah, Jezreel, Jokdeam, Zanoah, Kain, Gibeah, Timnah, Halhul, Beth-zur, Gedor, Maarath, Beth-anoth, Eltekon, Kiriath-baal (also known as Kiriath-jearim), Rabbah, Beth-arabah, Middin, Secacah, Nibshan, The City of Salt, and En-gedi.

⁶³But the tribe of Judah could not drive out the Jebusites. They lived in the city of Jerusalem. So the Jebusites live there among the people of Judah to this day.

Land for Ephraim

16 *The Southern Border of the Tribes of Joseph:* This includes Ephraim and the half-tribe of Manasseh. This border began at the Jordan River at Jericho. From there, it extended through the wilderness and the hill country to Bethel. It then went from Bethel to Luz. Then it stretched on to Ataroth in the land of the Archites. From there, it turned west to the border of the Japhletites as far as Lower Beth-horon. Then it went to Gezer and on over to the Mediterranean.

⁵⁻⁶*The Land Given to the Tribe of Ephraim:* The eastern border began at Ataroth-addar. From there, it ran to Upper Beth-horon. Then it went on to the Mediterranean Sea. The northern border began at the sea. It ran east past Michmethath. Then it kept going on past Taanath-shiloh and Janoah. ⁷From Janoah it turned south to Ataroth and Naarah. It touched Jericho, and ended at the Jordan River. ⁸The western half of the northern border began at Tappuah. It followed along Kanah Brook to the Mediterranean Sea. ⁹Ephraim was also given some of the cities in the land of the half-tribe of Manasseh. ¹⁰The Canaanites living in Gezer were never driven out. So they still live as slaves among the people of Ephraim.

Land for the Other Half-Tribe of Manasseh

17 *The Land Given to the Half-tribe of Manasseh:* Manasseh was Joseph's oldest son. The clan of Machir had already been given the land of Gilead and Bashan. Machir was Manasseh's oldest son and was the father of Gilead. Gilead and Bashan were on the east side of the Jordan River. They were great warriors. ²So now, land on the west side of the Jordan was given to the other clans of Manasseh. Their names were Abiezer, Helek, Asriel, Shechem, Shemida, and Hepher.

³However, Hepher's son Zelophehad had no sons. He was the grandson of Gilead and the great-grandson of Machir. Thus he was Manasseh's great-great-grandson. Zelophehad had five daughters. Their names were Mahlah, Noah, Hoglah, Milcah, and Tirzah. ⁴These women came to Eleazar the priest and to Joshua and the Israelite leaders. They reminded them,

"The Lord told Moses that we were to receive as much property as the men of our tribe."

⁵⁻⁶The Lord had commanded this through Moses. So these five women were given an inheritance along with their five great-uncles. Manasseh's total inheritance came to 10 sections of land. This was in addition to the land of Gilead and Bashan across the Jordan River. ⁷The northern border of the tribe of Manasseh extended south from the border of Asher. It went to Michmethath, which is east of Shechem. On the south the border went from Michmethath to the Spring of Tappuah. ⁸The land of Tappuah belonged to Manasseh. But the city of Tappuah belonged to the tribe of Ephraim. It was on the border of Manasseh's land. ⁹From the spring of Tappuah the border of Manasseh followed the north bank of the Brook of Kanah. It followed this brook to the Mediterranean Sea. Several cities south of the brook belonged to the tribe of Ephraim. This was true, though they were located in Manasseh's land. ¹⁰The land south of the brook and as far west as the Mediterranean Sea was given to Ephraim. And

the land north of the brook and east of the sea went to Manasseh. Manasseh's northern border was on the border of Asher. Its eastern border was on the border of Issachar.

[11]The half-tribe of Manasseh was also given the following cities. They were situated in the areas given to Issachar and Asher. Their names were Beth-shean, Ibleam, Dor, En-dor, Taanach, and Megiddo. At Megiddo are the three cliffs. These cities came with the villages around them. [12]But the descendants of Manasseh could not drive out the people who lived in those cities. So the Canaanites stayed. [13]Later on, however, the Israelites became stronger. And they forced the Canaanites to work as slaves.

[14]Then the two tribes of Joseph came to Joshua. They asked, "Why have you given us only one portion of land? Do you not see that the Lord has given us a great number of people?"

[15]"The hill country of Ephraim might not be large enough for you," Joshua replied. "But if it isn't, you may clear out the forest land. Clear the land where the Perizzites and Rephaim live."

[16-18]"Fine," said the tribes of Joseph. "For the Canaanites in the lowlands around Beth-shean and the Valley of Jezreel have iron chariots. They are too strong for us."

"Then you shall have the mountain forests," Joshua replied. "And you are a large, strong tribe. So you will surely be able to clear it all and live there. And I'm sure you can drive out the Canaanites from the valleys, too. You can do this even though they are strong and have iron chariots."

Joshua Assigns the Rest of the Land

18 After the conquest all Israel gathered at Shiloh to set up the Tabernacle. They did this even though seven of the tribes of Israel had not yet taken their land. They had not yet conquered the land God had given them.

[3]Then Joshua asked them, "How long are you going to wait? When will you clear out the people living in the land? When will you take the land that the Lord your God has given to you? [4]Choose three men from each tribe. I will send them to scout the untaken areas. They will bring back a report of its size and natural divisions. That way I can divide it for you. [5-6]The scouts will map it into seven sections. Then I will throw the sacred dice to decide which section will be given to each tribe. [7]But remember that the Levites won't receive any land. They are priests of the Lord. That is their great heritage. And of course the tribes of Gad and Reuben and the half-tribe of Manasseh won't get any more land. They already have land on the east side of the Jordan. Moses promised them that they could settle there."

[8]So the scouts went out to map the country. They went out so they could bring back their report to Joshua. Then the Lord could give the sections of land to the tribes. He would do this by the throw of the sacred dice. [9]The men did as they were told. They divided the whole land into seven sections. They listed the cities in each section. Then they went back to Joshua and the camp at Shiloh. [10]There at the Tabernacle at Shiloh the Lord showed Joshua which tribe should have each section. He did this through the sacred lottery.

Land for Benjamin
[11]*The Land Given to the Tribe of Benjamin:*

The section of land given to the families of the tribe of Benjamin lay between the land already given to the tribes of Judah and Joseph.

[12]The northern border began at the Jordan River. From there, it went north of Jericho. Then it went west through the hill country and the Wilderness of Beth-aven. [13]From there, the border went south to Luz (also called Bethel). Then it proceeded down to Ataroth-addar in the hill country south of Lower Beth-horon. [14]There the border turned south. It passed the mountain near Beth-horon. Then it ended at the village of Kiriath-baal (sometimes called Kiriath-jearim). This was one of the cities of the tribe of Judah. This made up the western border.

15The southern border began at the edge of Kiriath-baal. From there, it passed over Mount Ephron to the spring of Naphtoah. 16Then it went down to the base of the mountain beside the valley of Hinnom. This is north of the valley of Rephaim. From there it continued across the valley of Hinnom. It crossed south of the old city of Jerusalem where the Jebusites lived. And it continued down to En-rogel. 17From En-rogel the border proceeded northeast to En-shemesh and on to Geliloth. Geliloth is across from the slope of Adummim. Then it went down to the Stone of Bohan. This stone was named for a son of Reuben. 18There it passed along the north edge of the Arabah. The border then went down into the Arabah. 19It ran south past Beth-hoglah and ended at the north bay of the Dead Sea. This is the southern end of the Jordan River.

20The eastern border was the Jordan River. This was the land given to the tribe of Benjamin. 21-28Twenty-six cities were included in the land given to the tribe of Benjamin. Their names were Jericho, Beth-hoglah, Emek-keziz, Beth-arabah, Zimaraim, Bethel, Avvim, Parah, Ophrah, Chephar-ammoni, Ophni, Geba, Gibeon, Ramah, Beeroth, Mizpeh, Chephirah, Mozah, Rekem, Irpeel, Taralah, Zela, Haeleph, Jebus (or Jerusalem), Gibeah, and Kiriath-jearim. All of these cities were given to the tribe of Benjamin. This also included the villages around them.

Land for Simeon

19 *The Land Given to the Tribe of Simeon:* The tribe of Simeon was given the next parcel of land. It included part of the land already given to Judah. 2-7Their inheritance included 17 cities. It also included the villages around them. The cities' names were Beer-sheba, Sheba, Moladah, Hazar-shual, Balah, Ezem, Eltolad, Bethul, Hormah, Ziklag, Beth-marcaboth, Hazar-susah, Beth-lebaoth, Sharuhen, En-rimmon, Ether, and Ashan. 8The cities as far south as Baalath-beer were also given to the tribe of Simeon. Baalath-beer is also known as Ramah-in-the-Negeb. 9So the Simeon

tribe's inheritance came from what had earlier been given to Judah. For Judah's section had been too large for them.

Land for Zebulun

10*The Land Given to the Tribe of Zebulun:* The third tribe to receive its land was Zebulun. Its border started on the south side of Sarid. 11From there it circled to the west. It went near Mareal and Dabbesheth until it reached the brook east of Jokneam. 12In the other direction, the border line went east to the border of Chisloth-tabor. From there it went to Daberath and Japhia. 13Then it continued east of Gath-hepher, Ethkazin, and Rimmon and turned toward Neah. 14The northern border of Zebulun passed Hannathon and ended at the Valley of Iphtahel. 15-16The cities in these areas, besides those already mentioned, included Kattath, Nahalal, Shimron, Idalah, and Bethlehem. With these cities came the villages around them. In all there were 12 of these cities.

Land for Issachar

17-23*The Land Given to the Tribe of Issachar:* The fourth tribe to be given its land was Issachar. Its borders included 16 cities. Their names were Jezreel, Chesulloth, Shunem, Hapharaim, Shion, Anaharath, Rabbith, Kishion, Ebez, Remeth, En-gannim, En-haddah, Beth-pazzez, Tabor, Shahazumah, and Beth-shemesh. With them came the villages around them. The border of Issachar ended at the Jordan River.

Land for Asher

24-26*The Land Given to the Tribe of Asher:* The fifth tribe to be given its land was Asher. The borders included these cities: Helkath, Hali, Beten, Achshaph, Allammelech, Amad, and Mishal.

The border on the west side went from Carmel to Shihor-libnath. 27Then it turned east toward Beth-dagon. And it went as far as Zebulun in the Valley of Iphtahel. Then it ran north of Beth-emek and Neiel. It then passed to the east of Kabul, 28Ebron, Rehob, Hammon, Kanah, and Greater Sidon. 29Then the border turned toward Ramah and the fortified city of Tyre. It came to the Mediterranean Sea at Hosah. Their land also included Mahalab, Achzib, 30-31Ummah, Aphek, and Rehob. This made an overall total of 22 cities and the villages around them.

Land for Naphtali

32*The Land Given to the Tribe of Naphtali:* The sixth tribe to receive its land was Naphtali. 33Its border began at Judah, at the oak in Zaanannim. It extended across to Adami-nekeb, Jabneel, and Lakkum, ending at the Jordan River. 34The western border began near Heleph. It ran past Aznoth-tabor, then to Hukkok. There it met with the Zebulun border in the south. The border of Asher on the west also came in there. And the Jordan River at the east met them. 35-39There were fortified cities included in this area. They were named Ziddim, Zer, Hammath, Rakkath, Chinnereth, Adamah, Ramah, Hazor, Kedesh, Edrei, Enhazor, Yiron, Migdal-el, Horem, Beth-anath, and Beth-shemesh.

So in all their land included 19 cities with the villages around them.

Land for Dan

40*The Land Given to the Tribe of Dan:* The last tribe to be given its land was Dan. 41-46The cities within its area included Zorah, Eshtaol, Ir-shemesh, Shaalabbin, Aijalon, Ithlah, Elon, Timnah, Ekron, Eltekeh, Gibbethon, Baalath, Jehud, Bene-berak, Gath-rimmon, Me-jarkon, and Rakkon. It also included the area near Joppa. 47-48But some of this land proved hard to conquer. So the tribe of Dan captured the city of Leshem. They killed its people, and lived there. And they called the city "Dan." They named it after their ancestor.

Land for Joshua

49So all the land was divided among the tribes, with the borders given. And the nation of Israel gave a special piece of land to Joshua. 50For the Lord had said that he could have any city he wanted. He chose Timnath-serah in the hill country of Ephraim. He rebuilt it and lived there.

51Eleazar the priest, Joshua, and the leaders of the tribes of Israel supervised the sacred lottery. They divided the land among the tribes. This was done in the Lord's presence. They did it at the door of the Tabernacle at Shiloh.

Cities of Refuge

20 The Lord said to Joshua, 2"Tell the people of Israel to choose now the Cities of Refuge. Do this just as I showed Moses. 3A man might kill someone, but it might be an accident. If so, he can run to one of these cities. There he shall be safe from the relatives of the dead man. They may try to kill him in revenge. 4An innocent killer must go to one of these cities right away. When he gets there, he must meet with the city council. He must explain what happened and they must let him come in. They must give him a place to live among them. 5A relative of the dead man might come to kill him in revenge. If this happens, the innocent killer must not be given to him. This is because the death was by accident. 6The man who killed a person by accident must stay in that city. He must stay until he has been tried by the judges and is found innocent. Then he must live there until the death of the High Priest. This refers to the High Priest who was in office at the time of the accident. But at the priest's death, he is free to go back to his own city and home."

7Three cities were chosen as Cities of Refuge west of the Jordan. Kedesh of Galilee was in the hill country of Naphtali. Shechem was in the hill country of Ephraim. And Kiriath-arba was in the hill country of Judah. This city was also known as Hebron. 8The Lord also told them to choose three more cities for this purpose. They were to be on the east side of the Jordan River, across from Jericho. Bezer was in the wilderness of the land of the tribe of Reuben. Ramoth of Gilead was in the land of the tribe of Gad. And Golan of Bashan was in the land of the tribe of Manasseh. 9These Cities of Refuge were for foreigners living in Israel as well as for the Israelites themselves. Anyone who killed someone by accident could run there for safety. There he would get a fair trial and not be killed in revenge.

Towns for the Levites

21 Then the leaders of the tribe of Levi came to Shiloh. They consulted with Eleazar the priest and with Joshua. The leaders of the various tribes were there also.

2"The Lord told Moses to give cities to us Levites for our homes," they said. "He also told Moses to give us pasture for our cattle."

3So they were given some of the conquered cities with their pastures. 4Thirteen of these cities had been given to the tribes of Judah, Simeon, and Benjamin. These were given to some of the priests of the Kohath clan of the tribe of Levi. They were descendants of Aaron. 5The other families of the Kohath clan were given 10 cities. These cities were from the lands of Ephraim, Dan, and the half-tribe of Manasseh. 6The Gershon clan was given 13 cities. They were chosen by sacred lot in the area of Bashan. These cities were given by the tribes of Issachar, Asher, Naphtali, and the half-tribe of Manasseh. 7The Merari clan received 12 cities. These cities were from the tribes of Reuben, Gad, and Zebulun. 8So the Lord's command to Moses was obeyed. The cities and pastures were chosen by the toss of the sacred dice.

9-16First to receive their cities and pastures were the priests. They were the descendants of Aaron. Aaron was a member of the Kohath clan of the Levites. The tribes of Judah and Simeon gave them the nine cities listed below. The pastures around the cities were included.

Hebron, in the Judean hills, was given as a City of Refuge. It was also called Kiriath-arba. Arba was the father of Anak. But the fields beyond the city and the villages around it were given to Caleb. He was the son of Jephunneh. The other cities were Libnah, Jattir, Eshtemoa, Holon, Debir, Ain, Juttah, and Beth-shemesh.

17-18The tribe of Benjamin gave them four cities. Their pastures were also included. They were called Gibeon, Gaba, Anathoth, and Almon. 19So in all, 13 cities were given to the priests, the descendants of Aaron.

20-22The other families of the Kohath clan were given four cities from the tribe of Ephraim. The pastures around the city were included. The cities were Shechem (a City of Refuge), Gezer, Kibzaim, and Beth-horon.

23-24Four cities and their pastures were given by the tribe of Dan. The cities were Elteke, Gibbethon, Aijalon, and Gath-rimmon.

25The half-tribe of Manasseh gave the cities of Taanach and Gath-rimmon. They gave the pastures around the cities with them. 26These were also given to the rest of the Kohath clan. So the total number of cities with their pastures given to them was 10.

27The descendants of Gershon received two cities from the half-tribe of Manasseh. The pastures of these cities came with them. The Gershonites were another clan of the Levites. They were given Golan, in Bashan (a City of Refuge), and Be-eshterah.

28-29The tribe of Issachar gave four cities: Kishion, Daberath, Jarmuth, and Engannim.

30-31The tribe of Asher gave four cities with their pastures: Mishal, Abdon, Helkath, and Rehob.

32The tribe of Naphtali gave Kedesh, in Galilee (a City of Refuge), Hammoth-dor, and Kartan.

33So 13 cities with their pastures were given to the clan of Gershon.

34-35The rest of the Levites were given four cities by the tribe of Zebulun. These Levites were of the Merari clan. They were given Jokneam, Kartah, Dimnah, and Nahalal.

36-37Reuben gave them Bezer, Jahaz, Kedemoth, and Mephaath. 38-39Gad gave them four cities with their pastures. The cities were Ramoth (a City of Refuge), Mahanaim, Heshbon, and Jazer.

40So the Merari clan of the Levites was given 12 cities in all.

41-42The total number of cities with

their pastures given to the Levites came to 48.

⁴³So in this way the Lord gave the land to Israel. He gave all the land he had promised to their ancestors. They went in and conquered it and lived there. ⁴⁴And the Lord gave them peace, just as he had promised. No one could stand against them. The Lord helped them destroy all their enemies. ⁴⁵Every good thing the Lord had promised them came true.

The Eastern Tribes Settle Down

22 Joshua now called together the troops from the tribes of Reuben, Gad, and the half-tribe of Manasseh. ²⁻³He spoke to them as follows:

"You have done as the Lord's disciple Moses told you. You have obeyed every order I have given you. You have followed every order of the Lord your God. You have not deserted your brother tribes. You did not leave, even though the campaign has lasted for such a long time. ⁴And now the Lord our God has given us success and rest as he promised he would. So go home now to the land given you by the Lord's servant Moses. Go back to the other side of the Jordan River. ⁵Be sure to obey all of the commands Moses gave you. Love the Lord and follow his plan for your lives. Cling to him and serve him with all your heart."

⁶So Joshua blessed them and sent them home. ⁷⁻⁸Moses had given the land of Bashan to the half-tribe of Manasseh. The other half of the tribe was given land on the west side of the Jordan. As Joshua sent away these troops, he blessed them. He told them to share their great wealth with their relatives back home. They were to share their loot of cattle, silver, gold, bronze, iron, and clothing.

⁹So the troops of Reuben, Gad, and the half-tribe of Manasseh left the army of Israel at Shiloh in Canaan. They crossed the Jordan River to their own

homeland of Gilead. ¹⁰Before they went across out of Canaan they built a large monument for all to see. They made it in the shape of an altar.

Cities of Refuge
JOSHUA 20

In Bible times, what happened if you accidentally killed another person? There was a custom that the dead person's closest relative could kill you in revenge. But there was a way of escape.

If you accidentally killed someone, you could run to a city of refuge. There were six of these cities in Israel. You could get a fair trial there. If you really killed the person on purpose, you would be turned over to the one who wanted to kill you. If you were innocent, then you could stay in the city and be safe.

Jesus is like a city of refuge. If you run to him for forgiveness, you will not die because of your sins.

¹¹But the rest of Israel heard about what they had done. ¹²After hearing of it, they gathered an army at Shiloh. They got ready to go to war against their brother tribes. ¹³But they sent a group

led by Phinehas. He was the son of Eleazar the priest. They crossed the river and talked to the tribes of Reuben, Gad, and Manasseh. [14]In this group were 10 leaders of Israel. One was sent from each of the 10 tribes. Each was a clan leader. [15]They got to the land of Gilead. Then they spoke to the tribes of Reuben, Gad, and the half-tribe of Manasseh.

God keeps every promise

You know that all God's promises have come true.

Joshua 23:14

[16]They said, "All the people of the Lord want to know why you are sinning against the God of Israel. They want to know why you are turning away from him. Why have you built an altar to rebel against the Lord? [17-18]Was our guilt at Peor so little that you must rebel again? We still have not yet been cleansed from our sin there. We still bear guilt despite the plague that we suffered. For you know that if you rebel today the Lord will be angry with all of us tomorrow. [19]You might need the altar because your land is unclean. If so, then join us on our side of the river. There the Lord lives among us in his Tabernacle. We will share our land with you. But do not rebel against the Lord by building another altar. There is only one true altar of our God. [20]Don't you remember Achan, the son of Zerah? When he sinned against the Lord, the whole nation was punished! Everyone suffered along with the one man who sinned!"

[21]The people of Reuben, Gad, and the half-tribe of Manasseh answered these leaders. [22-23]They said, "We swear by the Lord, the God of gods. We swear that we have not built the altar to rebel against the Lord. He knows this, and let all Israel know it too! We have not built the altar to sacrifice burnt, grain, or peace offerings. May the curse of God be on us if we did! [24-25]We have done it because we love the Lord. We built it because we fear that in the future your children will forget us. We are afraid they might say

to our children, 'What right do you have to worship the Lord God of Israel? The Lord has put the Jordan River between our people and your people! You have no part in the Lord.' And your children may make our children stop worshiping him. [26-27]So we decided to build the altar. It is a symbol to show our children and your children that we, too, may worship the Lord. We also may bring our burnt offerings and peace offerings. That way your children will not be able to say to ours, 'You have no part in the Lord our God.' [28]They might say this. But if they do, our children can reply, 'Look at the altar of the Lord that our fathers made. It is made like the altar of the Lord. It is not for burnt offerings or sacrifices. It is a symbol of the relationship with God that both of us have.' [29]Far be it from us to turn away from the Lord. We would never rebel against him. We would not build our own altar for burnt or grain offerings, or sacrifices. Only the altar in front of the Tabernacle may be used for that."

[30]Phinehas the priest and the leaders listened to the tribes of Reuben, Gad, and Manasseh. When they had heard them, they were very happy. [31]Phinehas replied to them, "Today we know that the Lord is among us. You have not sinned against the Lord as we thought. Instead, you have saved us from being destroyed!"

[32]Then Phinehas and the 10 leaders went back to the people of Israel. They told them what had happened. [33]And all Israel was glad and praised God. They spoke no more of war against Reuben and Gad. [34]The people of Reuben and Gad named the altar "The Altar of Witness." For they said, "It is a witness between us and them that the Lord is our God too."

Joshua's Final Orders

23 The Lord gave success to the people of Israel against their enemies. Time passed, and Joshua became very old. [2]He called for the leaders of Israel. He called the elders, judges, and officers. He said to them, "I am an old man now. [3]And you have seen all that the Lord your God has done for you during my lifetime. He has fought for you against your enemies. He has given you their land. 4-5And I have divided to you the land of the nations yet untaken. I gave you this land along with the land of those you have already destroyed. All the land from the Jordan River to the Mediterranean Sea shall be yours. For the Lord your God will drive out all the people living there now. You will live there instead. It will all happen just as he has promised you.

6"But be very sure to follow all the laws written in the book of Moses. Do not disobey them the least little bit. 7Be sure that you do not mix with the heathen people still in the land. Do not even mention the names of their gods. Never swear by them or worship them. 8But follow the Lord your God just as you have until now. 9He has driven out great, strong nations from before you. No one has been able to defeat you. 10Each one of you has put to flight a thousand of the enemy. For the Lord your God fights for you. He has done this just as he has promised. 11So be very careful to keep on loving him.

12"You might not keep on obeying him. And you might begin to marry people from the nations around you. 13If this happens, then know for sure that the Lord your God will not be with you. He will no longer chase those nations from your land. Instead, they will be a trap to you. They will be a pain in your side and a thorn in your eyes. And you will disappear from this good land that the Lord your God has given you.

14"Soon I will be going the way of all the earth. I am going to die.

"You know that all God's promises have come true. 15-16The Lord has given you the good things he promised. But just as he gave you good things, he will bring evil upon you if you disobey him. For you might worship other gods. But if you do, he will completely wipe you out. He will push you out of this good land that he has given you. His anger will rise hot against you. And you will quickly die."

Joshua's Good-Bye Speech

24 Then Joshua called all the people of Israel to him at Shechem. He called them along with their leaders. This included the elders, officers, and judges. So they came and presented themselves before God.

2Then Joshua spoke to them. He said, "The Lord God of Israel speaks to you. He says, 'Your ancestors, including Terah the father of Abraham and Nahor, lived east of the Euphrates River. They worshiped other gods. 3But I took your father Abraham from that land across the river. I led him into the land of Canaan. I gave him many descendants through Isaac, his son. 4Isaac's children, whom I gave him, were Jacob and Esau. To Esau I gave the area around Mount Seir. At that time, Jacob and his children went into Egypt.

5"'Then I sent Moses and Aaron to bring terrible plagues upon Egypt. After that I brought my people out as free men. 6But they came to the Red Sea. And the Egyptians chased after them with chariots and cavalry. 7While there, Israel cried out to me. So I put darkness between them and the Egyptians. And I brought the sea crashing in upon the Egyptians, drowning them. You saw what I did! Then Israel lived in the wilderness for many years.

8"'Finally I brought you into the land of the Amorites. This is the land on the other side of the Jordan. They fought against you, but I destroyed them. I gave you their land. 9Then King Balak of Moab started a war against Israel. He asked Balaam, the son of Beor, to curse you. 10But I wouldn't listen to him. Instead I made him bless you. And so I delivered Israel from him.

11"'Then you crossed the Jordan River and came to Jericho. The men of Jericho fought against you. So did many others—the Perizzites, the Canaanites, the Hittites, the Girgashites, the Hivites, and the Jebusites. Each in turn fought against you. But I destroyed them all. 12And I sent hornets ahead of you. They drove out the two kings of the Amorites and their people. It was not your swords or bows that brought you victory!

[13]I gave you land you had not worked for. You took cities you did not build. These are the cities where you are now living. I gave you vineyards and olive groves for food. They are yours, though you did not plant them.'

We should obey God and serve him

As for me and my family, we will serve the Lord.

Joshua 24:15

---

[14]"So respect the Lord. Serve him with all your hearts and minds. Put away forever the idols your ancestors worshiped. Reject the gods they worshiped beyond the Euphrates River and in Egypt. Worship the Lord alone. [15]But you might not want to obey the Lord. If so, then decide today whom you will obey. Will it be the gods of your ancestors beyond the Euphrates? Or will it be the gods of the Amorites here in this land? As for me and my family, we will serve the Lord."

"We Will Obey the Lord!"

[16]And the people said, "We would never forsake the Lord! We would never worship other gods! [17]For the Lord our God is the one who saved our fathers. He brought them from their slavery in the land of Egypt. He is the God who did mighty miracles. He did them before the eyes of Israel, as we traveled through the wilderness. He saved us from our enemies when we passed through their land. [18]It was the Lord who drove out the Amorites. And he drove out the other nations living here in the land. Yes, we choose the Lord! For he alone is our God!"

[19]But Joshua replied to the people, "You are not able to worship the Lord God. For he is holy and jealous. He will not forgive your rebellion and sins. [20]You might forsake him. You might begin to worship other gods. But if you do, he will turn upon you. He will destroy you. He will do this even though he has taken care of you for such a long time."

[21]But the people answered, "We choose the Lord!"

[22]"You have heard yourselves say it," Joshua said. "You have chosen to obey the Lord."

"Yes," they said, "we are witnesses."

[23]"All right," he said, "then you must destroy all the idols you now own. You must obey the Lord God of Israel."

[24]The people replied to Joshua, "Yes, we will worship and obey the Lord alone."

[25]So Joshua made a covenant with them that day at Shechem. He committed them to a lasting contract between themselves and God. [26]Joshua wrote down the people's reply in the book of the laws of God. Then he took a huge stone to remind them. He rolled it under the oak tree that was beside the Tabernacle.

[27]Then Joshua said to all the people, "This stone has heard all the Lord said. It will be a witness against you if you go back on your word."

[28]Then Joshua sent the people away to their own sections of the country.

Joshua Dies at Age 110

[29]Soon after this he died at the age of 110. [30]He was buried on his own land at Timnath-serah. This was in the hill country of Ephraim. His home was on the north side of the mountains of Gaash.

[31]Israel obeyed the Lord while Joshua and the other old men were still living. These men had seen the amazing deeds the Lord had done for Israel.

[32]The bones of Joseph were buried in Shechem. The people of Israel had brought them along when they left Egypt. He was buried in the parcel of ground Jacob had bought from the sons of Hamor. This land was in the area given to the tribes of Joseph.

[33]Eleazar, the son of Aaron, also died. He was buried in the hill country of Ephraim, at Gibeah. This was the city that had been given to his son Phinehas.

JUDGES

Have you ever met a man who could pick up a car and carry it home? Samson could probably have done it. Have you ever seen a little band of 300 men defeat a mighty army of thousands? Gideon's men did it. You'll be surprised at their best weapons, too. They were not swords and spears, but clay pitchers and torches. You'll meet a woman who helped to win a war with a pitcher of milk. You'll see fire come up from a rock while an angel disappears. And you'll learn how a sheepskin sent a soldier into battle.

The Book of Judges is a story about how the Israelites lived once they entered the Promised Land. It tells about heroes. How did some people get to be heroes? They obeyed God. People who obey God have God on their side. If God is on your side, that means he is helping you. If God is helping you, great things can happen in your life.

The Book of Judges also tells about people who tried to be heroes but failed. Why did they fail? They forgot about God and did not obey him. People who disobey God do not have God's help. If God is not helping you, your life is headed for trouble. Samson learned this lesson the hard way.

Brave men and women want to show you how to be a real hero in Judges. Not-so-brave people want to show you what they did wrong so you won't make the same mistakes. Don't keep them waiting.

God Gives Victory

1 After Joshua died, the nation of Israel went to the Lord. They wanted to receive his orders.

"Which of our tribes should be the first to go to war against the Canaanites?" they asked.

²God said, "Judah should go first. And I will give them a great victory."

³But the leaders of the tribe of Judah asked for help. They wanted the tribe of Simeon to go with them. "Join us in clearing out the people living in the land given to us," they said. "Then we will

help you conquer yours." So the army of Simeon went with the army of Judah. 4-6And the Lord helped them defeat the Canaanites and Perizzites. Ten thousand of the enemy were killed at Bezek. King Adoni-bezek got away. But the Israelite army soon caught him. They cut off his thumbs and big toes.

7"I have treated 70 kings in this same way. I have fed them the scraps under my table!" King Adoni-bezek said. "Now God has paid me back." He was taken to Jerusalem, and he died there.

8Judah conquered Jerusalem and killed its people. They set the city on fire. 9After that the army of Judah fought the Canaanites in the hill country. They also fought in the Negeb and on the coastal plains. 10Then Judah marched against the Canaanites in Hebron. This city had once been called Kiriath-arba. They destroyed the cities of Sheshai, Ahiman, and Talmai.

Caleb and His Daughter

11Later they attacked the city of Debir. This city had once been called Kiriath-sepher.

12"Who will lead the attack against Debir?" Caleb challenged them. "Whoever conquers it shall have my daughter Achsah as his wife!"

13Caleb's nephew, Othniel, agreed to lead the attack. He was the son of Caleb's younger brother Kenaz. He conquered the city and won Achsah as his bride. 14They were leaving together for their new home. Just before they went, Achsah urged him to ask her father for another piece of land. She got down from her donkey to speak to Caleb about it.

"What do you wish?" he asked.

15And she replied, "You have been kind enough to give me land in the Negeb. But please give us springs of water too."

So Caleb gave her the upper and lower springs.

Canaanites Left Alive

16The tribe of Judah would soon move into its new land in the Negeb wilderness. This land was south of Arad. When they did, the descendants of Moses' father-in-law went with them. They were members of the Kenite tribe. They left their homes in Jericho, "The City of Palm Trees." And the two tribes lived together. 17After that the army of Judah joined Simeon's. They fought the Canaanites at the city of Zephath. They killed all its people. So now the city is named Hormah. It means "destroyed." 18The army of Judah also conquered the cities of Gaza, Ashkelon, and Ekron. They took all the towns around these cities as well. 19The Lord helped the tribe of Judah destroy the people of the hill country. But they failed to conquer the people of the valley. For the people there had iron chariots.

20The city of Hebron was given to Caleb as the Lord had promised. So Caleb drove out the people of that city. They were descendants of the three sons of Anak.

21The tribe of Benjamin did not push out all the Jebusites living in their part of Jerusalem. They still live there today, mixed with the Israelites.

22-23As for the tribe of Joseph, they attacked the city of Bethel. This city was once known as Luz. And the Lord was with them. First they sent scouts, 24who captured a man coming out of the city. They offered to spare his life and that of his family. But he would have to show them the way through the wall. 25So he showed them how to get in. They killed all the people there except for this man and his family. 26Later the man moved to Syria. He started a city there. He named it Luz, too. That city is called Luz to this day.

27The tribe of Manasseh did not push out the people living in Beth-shean, Taanach, Dor, Ibleam, and Megiddo. And they did not drive them out of the small towns nearby. So the Canaanites stayed there. 28In later years the Israelites became stronger. At that time, they put the Canaanites to work as slaves. But they never did force them to leave the country. 29This was also true of the Canaanites living in Gezer. They still live among the tribe of Ephraim.

30And the tribe of Zebulun did not kill

all the people of Kitron or Nahalol. Instead, they made them their slaves. ³¹⁻³²The tribe of Asher did not drive out the people of Acco, Sidon, Ahlab, Achzib, Helbah, Aphik, or Rehob. So the Israelites still live among the Canaanites. They were the original people of that land. ³³And the tribe of Naphtali did not drive out the people of Bethshemesh or Beth-anath. So these people still live among them as servants.

³⁴As for the tribe of Dan, the Amorites forced them into the hill country. Their enemies wouldn't let them come down into the valley. ³⁵But the Amorites later spread into Mount Heres, Aijalon, and Shaalbim. When they did, the tribe of Joseph conquered them. They made them their slaves. ³⁶The border of the Amorites begins at the ascent of Scorpion Pass. From there it extends to a spot called The Rock. Then it continues upward from there.

Broken Covenant is Announced

2 One day the Angel of the Lord came to Bochim from Gilgal. He spoke to the people of Israel. He said, "I saved you from out of Egypt. I brought you into this land that I promised to your ancestors. I said that I would never break my covenant with you. ²But you were not to make peace treaties with the people living in this land. I told you to destroy their heathen altars. Why have you not obeyed? ³Now you have broken the contract. It is no longer in effect. So I no longer promise to destroy the nations living in your land. Rather, they shall be thorns in your sides. Their gods will be a constant temptation to you."

⁴The people broke into tears as the Angel finished speaking. ⁵So the name of that place was called "Bochim." This name means, "the place where people wept." Then they offered sacrifices to the Lord.

Joshua Dies at Age 110

⁶At the end of the conquest, Joshua sent the armies of Israel home. The tribes moved into their new areas. They took control of the land. ⁷⁻⁹Joshua, the man of God, died at the age of 110. He was buried at the edge of his property in Timnath-heres. This was in the hill country of Ephraim, north of Mount Gaash. The people had stayed true to the Lord while Joshua was alive. They obeyed as long as the old men of his generation were still living. They were the ones who had seen the mighty miracles the Lord had done for Israel.

The People Abandon God

¹⁰But finally all that generation died. And the next generation did not worship the Lord as their God. They did not care about the mighty miracles he had done for Israel. ¹¹They did many things that the Lord had told them not to do. This included worshiping heathen gods. ¹²⁻¹⁴They left the Lord, the God loved and worshiped by their ancestors. They abandoned the God who had brought them out of Egypt. Instead, they were worshiping the idols of the nations around them. So the anger of the Lord burned against all Israel. He left them to the mercy of their enemies. For they had left the Lord. They were worshiping Baal and the Ashtaroth idols.

God Chooses Judges to Rule the People

¹⁵So the nation of Israel went out to battle against its enemies. But when they did, the Lord blocked their path. He had warned them about this. In fact, he had vowed that he would do it. But when the people were in this plight, ¹⁶the Lord raised up judges. They were chosen to save the Israelites from their enemies.

¹⁷Yet even then Israel would not listen to the judges. They broke faith with the Lord by worshiping other gods instead. How quickly they turned away from the true faith of their ancestors! They refused to obey God's commands. ¹⁸ Each judge rescued the people of Israel from their enemies during his lifetime. For the Lord was moved to pity by the groaning of his people under great suffering. So he helped them as long as that judge lived. ¹⁹But when the judge died, the people turned from doing right. And they behaved even worse than their ancestors had. They prayed to heathen gods again.

They threw themselves before them to the ground in humble worship. They stubbornly went back to the evil customs of the nations around them.

20Then the anger of the Lord would flame out against Israel again. He said, "These people have broken the treaty I made with their ancestors. 21Because of this, I will no longer drive out their enemies. I will not drive out the nations left by Joshua when he died. 22Instead, I will use these nations to test my people. I will see if they will obey the Lord as their ancestors did."

23So the Lord left those nations in the land. He did not drive them out. Nor did he let Israel destroy them.

Canaanites Left in the Land

3 Here is a list of the nations the Lord left in the land. He left them to test the new generation of Israel. This new generation had never fought in the wars of Canaan. And God wanted to give the youth of Israel a chance. He wanted them to learn faith and obedience in fighting their enemies. Their enemies were the Philistines (five cities), the Canaanites, and the Sidonians. The Hivites living in Mount Lebanon were also their enemies. They lived from Baal-hermon to the entrance of Hamath. 4These people were a test to the new generation of Israel. They would prove whether or not

the Israelites would obey. The Lord would see if they would follow the commands he had given to them through Moses.

5So Israel lived among the Canaanites, Hittites, Hivites, Perizzites, Amorites, and Jebusites. 6But instead of destroying them, the people of Israel married them. The young men of Israel took their girls as wives. The Israelite girls married their men. And soon Israel was worshiping their gods. 7So the people of Israel were very evil in God's sight. They turned against the Lord their God. They worshiped Baal and the Asheroth idols.

Othniel

8Then the anger of the Lord burned against Israel. And he let King Cushan-rishathaim of eastern Syria conquer them. They were under his rule for eight years. 9But Israel cried out to the Lord. When they did, he gave them Caleb's nephew, Othniel, to save them. He was the son of Kenaz, Caleb's younger brother. 10The Spirit of the Lord took control of him. He reformed and purged Israel. And he led the forces of Israel against the army of King Cushan-rishathaim. When they went out to fight, the Lord helped Israel conquer him.

11Then, for 40 years under Othniel, there was peace in the land. But Othniel died.

Ehud Defeats Moab

Ehud was not a general or a captain. He wasn't even a soldier. But he organized an army and defeated an enemy nation. You'll want to read how he did this.

12And the people of Israel turned once again to their sinful ways. So God helped King Eglon of Moab conquer part of Israel. 13The armies of the Ammonites and the Amalekites helped him. These armies defeated the Israelites. And they took Jericho, often called "The City of Palm Trees." 14For 18 years the people of

Israel had to pay taxes to King Eglon.

15But the people cried to the Lord. And when they did, he sent them a savior. His name was Ehud, and he was left-handed. He was the son of Gera, from the tribe of Benjamin. Ehud was the man chosen to carry Israel's yearly tax money to the capital of Moab. 16Before he went on this trip, he made himself a dagger with two sharp edges. It was 18 inches long. He hid it in his clothing, tied against his right thigh. 17-19After taking the money to King Eglon, he started home again. Eglon, by the way, was very fat! Ehud got outside the city, to the quarries of Gilgal. There, he sent his companions on home. He then went back alone to the king.

"I have a secret message for you," Ehud told him.

The king sent all those who were with him out right away. That way he could talk with Ehud alone. 20Ehud walked over to him as he was sitting in a cool upstairs room. He said to him, "It is a message from God!"

King Eglon stood up at once to receive it. 21Ehud reached under his robe with his strong left hand. He pulled out the dagger with two sharp edges. It was tied against his right thigh. Then he plunged it deep into the king's belly. 22-23The handle of the dagger became hidden beneath the flesh. The fat closed over it as his insides oozed out. Leaving the dagger there, Ehud locked the doors behind him. He then escaped across an upstairs porch.

24The king's servants came back and saw that the doors were locked. So they waited, thinking that perhaps he was using the bathroom. 25But he still didn't come out after a long time. So they became worried and got a key. They opened the door. When they did, they found their king dead on the floor.

26Meanwhile Ehud had escaped past the quarries to Seirah. 27He got to the hill country of Ephraim. Then he blew a trumpet as a call to arms. He quickly gathered an army under his own command.

28"Follow me," he told them. "For the Lord has put your enemies at your mercy!"

The army then went to take the fords of the Jordan River near Moab. They did this to stop anyone from crossing. 29Then they attacked the Moabites. They killed about 10,000 of the strongest of their fighting men. They did not let one escape. 30So Moab was conquered by Israel that day. The land was at peace for the next 80 years.

- *Remember:* God helped Moab conquer Israel. Why? (3:12) How long did the people of Israel have to pay taxes to Moab? (3:14) What was Ehud chosen to do? (3:15) How did Ehud become the leader of Israel in one day? (3:15-27) Was Ehud's victory a big victory or a little victory? How big? How long did it last? (3:28-30)

- *Discover:* God can do big things through unknown people.

- *Apply:* Your friend needs to become God's friend. You could help him or her do it. That's a big job! Do you think God wants to do that big job through you?

- *What's next?* The times of the judges were rough-and-tumble times. They were the "wild west" times of Israel. You wouldn't expect two ladies to lead armies to victory in those times, would you? But they did. Read Judges 4. ■

Shamgar

31The next judge after Ehud was Shamgar. He was the son of Anath. He once killed 600 Philistines with an ox goad. By doing this he saved Israel from disaster.

Deborah and Barak

An army with 900 iron chariots was quite an army in those days. What would it take to kill the general of that army? You wouldn't think a woman with a tent peg could do it, would you?

4 After Ehud's death the people of Israel again sinned against the Lord. ²⁻³So the Lord let them be beaten by King Jabin of Hazor, in Canaan. The commander of his army was Sisera. He lived in Harosheth-hagoiim. He had 900 iron chariots. And he made life very hard for the Israelites for 20 years. But finally they begged the Lord for help.

⁴Israel's leader at that time was Deborah. She was a prophetess. She was the one who brought the people back to God. She was the wife of Lappidoth. ⁵She held court at a place now called "Deborah's Palm Tree." It was between Ramah and Bethel, in the hill country of Ephraim. The Israelites came to her to solve their problems.

⁶One day she called for Barak, the son of Abinoam. He lived in Kedesh, in the land of Naphtali. She said to him, "The Lord God of Israel has ordered you to call out 10,000 men. Call them from the tribes of Naphtali and Zebulun. Lead them to Mount Tabor. ⁷Fight King Jabin's mighty army with all his chariots. They are under General Sisera's command. The Lord says, 'I will draw them to the Kishon River. And you will defeat them there.'"

⁸"I'll go," Barak told her. "But you must go with me!"

⁹"All right," she replied. "I'll go with you. But I'm warning you now. The honor of beating Sisera will go to a woman. It won't go to you!" So she went with him to Kedesh.

¹⁰Barak called the men of Zebulun and Naphtali to meet at Kedesh. Ten thousand men came. And Deborah marched with them. ¹¹Heber, the Kenite, had moved away from the rest of his clan. He had been living in places as far away as the Oak of Zaanannim. This was near Kedesh. The Kenites were the descendants of Moses' brother-in-law Hobab. ¹²General Sisera was told that Barak and his army were camped at Mount Tabor. ¹³When he heard this, he called out his whole army. This included the 900 iron chariots. Then he marched from Harosheth-hagoiim to the Kishon River.

¹⁴Then Deborah said to Barak, "Now is the time for action! The Lord leads on! He has already given Sisera into your hand!"

So Barak led his 10,000 men down the slopes of Mount Tabor into battle.

¹⁵Then the Lord threw the enemy into a panic. Both the soldiers and the chariot drivers were terrified. Sisera leaped from his chariot and got away on foot. ¹⁶Barak and his men chased the enemy and the chariots as far as Harosheth-hagoiim. By this time, Sisera's army was destroyed. Not one man was left alive. ¹⁷Meanwhile, Sisera had escaped to the tent of Jael. She was the wife of Heber the Kenite. There was an agreement between King Jabin of Hazor and the clan of Heber.

¹⁸Jael went out to meet Sisera. She said to him, "Come into my tent, sir. You will be safe here. Don't be afraid." So he went into her tent. And she covered him with a blanket.

¹⁹"Please give me some water," he said. "For I am very thirsty." So she gave him some milk and covered him again.

²⁰"Stand in the door of the tent," he told her. "Someone might come by, looking for me. If they do, tell them that no one is here."

²¹Then Jael took a sharp tent peg and a hammer. She quietly crept up to him as he slept. Then she drove the peg through his temples and into the ground. And so he died, for he was fast asleep.

²²When Barak came by looking for Sisera, Jael went out to meet him. She said, "Come! I will show you the man you are looking for."

So he followed her into the tent. There he found Sisera lying there dead. The tent peg was driven through his temples. ²³So that day the Lord used Israel to subdue King Jabin of Canaan.

²⁴And from that time on Israel became stronger and stronger against King Jabin. In the end, he and all his people were destroyed.

- *Remember:* What caused the people of Israel to be conquered? (4:1) What powerful weapons did Israel's enemies have? (4:2-3) How did Deborah help Israel's army attack? (4:4-9) Who frightened the enemy army? (4:15) How did Jael use a tent peg to kill General Sisera? (4:18-21) What kind of person was Deborah? What kind of person was Jael?

- *Discover:* God can use small things like tent pegs to win big victories.

- *Apply:* You may think God needs dollars to do his work. He does. But pennies, nickels, dimes and quarters make up dollars.

- *What's next?* Would God use wet wool to show someone what he wants? Read about this in Judges 6. ■

The Song of Deborah and Barak

5 Then Deborah and Barak sang this song about the great victory:

²"Praise the Lord!
Israel's leaders bravely led.
The people gladly followed!
Yes, bless the Lord!
³Listen, O you kings and princes,
For I shall sing about the Lord,
The God of Israel.
⁴When you led us out from Seir,
Out across the fields of Edom,
The earth trembled.
And the sky poured down its rain.
⁵Yes, even Mount Sinai quaked
At the presence of the God of Israel!
⁶In the days of Shamgar and of Jael,
The main roads were deserted.
Travelers used the narrow, crooked
side paths.
⁷The number of Israel's people dwindled,
Until Deborah became a mother to
Israel.
⁸When Israel chose new gods,
Everything collapsed.
Our masters would not let us have
A shield or spear.
Among 40,000 men of Israel,
Not a weapon could be found!

⁹How I rejoice
In the leaders of Israel
Who offered themselves so willingly!
Praise the Lord!
¹⁰Let all Israel, rich and poor,
Join in his praises.
This includes those who ride on
white donkeys
And sit on rich carpets.
It even includes those who are poor
and must walk.
¹¹The village musicians
Gather at the village well.
They sing of the triumphs of the
Lord.
Again and again they sing the
ballad
Of how the Lord saved Israel
With an army of peasants!
The people of the Lord
Marched through the gates!
¹²Awake, O Deborah, and sing!
Get up, O Barak!
O son of Abinoam, lead away your
captives!
¹³⁻¹⁴Down from Mount Tabor
marched the noble remnant.
The people of the Lord
Marched down against great odds.
They came from Ephraim and Benjamin,
From Machir and from Zebulun.
¹⁵Down into the valley
Went the princes of Issachar
With Deborah and Barak.
At God's command they rushed
into the valley.
(But the tribe of Reuben didn't go.
¹⁶Why did you sit at home among
the sheepfolds,
Playing your shepherd pipes?
Yes, the tribe of Reuben has an uneasy conscience.
¹⁷Why did Gilead stay across the Jordan,
And why did Dan stay with his
ships?
And why did Asher sit unmoved
Upon the seashore,
At ease beside his harbors?)
¹⁸But the tribes of Zebulun and
Naphtali
Dared to die upon the fields of battle.

¹⁹The kings of Canaan fought in Taa-
nach
By Megiddo's springs,
But did not win the victory.
²⁰The very stars of heaven
Fought Sisera.
²¹The rushing Kishon River
Swept them away.
March on, my soul, with strength!
²²Hear the stamping
Of the horsehoofs of the enemy!
See the prancing of his steeds!
²³But the Angel of the Lord
Put a curse on Meroz.
'Curse them bitterly,' he said,
'Because they did not come to help
the Lord
Against his enemies.'
²⁴Blessed be Jael,
The wife of Heber the Kenite.
Yes, may she be blessed
Above all women who live in tents.
²⁵He asked for water
And she gave him milk in a beauti-
ful cup!
²⁶Then she took a tent pin and a
workman's hammer

And pierced Sisera's temples,
Crushing his head.
She pounded the tent pin through
his head.
²⁷He sank, he fell, he lay dead at her
feet.
²⁸The mother of Sisera watched
through the window
For him to come back.
'Why is his chariot so long in com-
ing?
Why don't we hear the sound of
the wheels?'
²⁹But her maids, and she herself, re-
plied,
³⁰'There is much loot to be divided.
And it takes time.
Each man receives a girl or two.
And Sisera will get beautiful robes.
And he will bring home
Many gifts for me.'
³¹O Lord, may all your enemies
Die as Sisera did.
But may those who love the Lord
Shine as the sun!"

After that there was peace in the land
for 40 years.

God Calls Gideon to Lead Israel

Gideon was a nobody. His family was the poorest in Israel. And his
family thought he was the least important person in the family. So
how does a nobody like Gideon suddenly become a great army
leader?

6 Then the people of Israel began once
again to worship other gods. And
once again the Lord let their enemies
trouble them. This time it was the people
of Midian. They troubled the Israelites
for seven years. ²The Midianites were
very cruel. They were so cruel that the
Israelites fled to the mountains. They
lived in caves and dens. ³⁻⁴Every year, the
Israelites planted their seed. But bands
of thieves from Midian, Amalek, and
other nations came. They destroyed
their crops and plundered their land.
They did this as far away as Gaza. They
left the Israelites nothing to eat. They
even took away all their sheep, oxen,
and donkeys. ⁵These enemy bands came
on camels. The men and their camels
were too many to count! They stayed
until the land was stripped and empty.
⁶⁻⁷So Israel became very poor because of
the Midianites. Then at last the people
of Israel cried out to the Lord for help.

⁸The Lord sent them a prophet. He
said to them, "The Lord God of Israel
brought you out of slavery in Egypt. ⁹He
saved you from the Egyptians. He rescued you from all who were cruel to you.

He drove out your enemies before you. And he gave you their land. 10He told you that he is the Lord your God. He warned you not to worship the gods of the Amorites who live around you on every side. But you have not listened to him."

11But one day the Angel of the Lord came. He sat under the oak tree at Ophrah. This was on the farm of Joash the Abiezrite. Joash's son, Gideon, had been threshing wheat by hand. He was doing it in the bottom of a grape press. This is a pit where grapes were pressed to make wine. He was working there because he was hiding from the Midianites.

12The Angel of the Lord came to him. He said, "Mighty soldier, the Lord is with you!"

13"Stranger," Gideon replied, "you claim that the Lord is with us. But if he is, why has all this happened to us? And where are all the miracles our ancestors have told us about? Why are there no miracles like God did when he brought Israel out of Egypt? Now the Lord has thrown us away. He has let the Midianites ruin us."

14Then the Lord turned to him. He said, "I will make you strong! Go and save Israel from the Midianites! I am sending you!"

15But Gideon replied, "Sir, how can I save Israel? My family is the poorest in the whole tribe of Manasseh. And I am the least thought of in the whole family!"

16Then the Lord said to him, "I will be with you! And you shall quickly destroy the Midianites!"

17Gideon replied, "Is it really true? Are you going to help me like that? If it is true, then do some miracle to prove it! Prove that it is the Lord who is talking to me! 18But stay here until I come back. I will get a present for you."

"All right," the Angel agreed. "I'll stay here until you come back."

19Gideon ran home and roasted a young goat. He also baked some unleavened bread from a bushel of flour. Then he carried the meat in a basket and the broth in a pot. And he took it out to the Angel who was under the oak tree. He gave it to him.

20The Angel said to him, "Put the meat and the bread on that rock over there. Then pour the broth over it."

Gideon did what he was told to do. 21Then the Angel touched the meat and bread with his staff. Fire flamed up from the rock and burned them up! And suddenly the Angel was gone!

God is always with us

I will be with you!

Judges 6:16

22Gideon knew that it had been the Angel of the Lord. So he cried out, "Alas, O Lord God! I have seen the Angel of the Lord face to face!"

23"It's all right," the Lord replied. "Don't be afraid! You shall not die."

24And Gideon built an altar there. He named it "The Altar of Peace with the Lord." The altar is still there in Ophrah in the land of the Abiezrites. 25That night the Lord spoke to Gideon. He told him to hitch his father's best ox to the family altar of Baal. He was to pull it down. He was also to cut down the wooden idol of the goddess Asherah that stood nearby.

26"Replace it with an altar for the Lord your God. Build it here on this hill. Lay the stones with care. Then sacrifice the ox as a burnt offering to the Lord. Use the wooden idol as wood for the fire on the altar."

27So Gideon took 10 of his servants. He did just as the Lord had told him. But he did it at night for fear of the other members of his father's family. He also feared the men of the city. For he knew what would happen if they found out who did it! 28Early the next morning someone found the altar of Baal broken down. And the idol beside it was gone too. A new altar had been built instead. And the remains of a sacrifice were still on it.

29"Who did this?" everyone demanded. Finally they learned that it was Gideon, the son of Joash.

30"Bring out your son!" they shouted to Joash. "He must die for insulting the altar of Baal! He must be punished for cutting down the Asherah idol."

³¹But Joash spoke back to the whole mob, "Does Baal need *your* help? What an insult to a god! You are the ones who should die for insulting Baal! If Baal is really a god, he can take care of himself! He can destroy the one who broke apart his altar!"

³²From then on Gideon was called "Jerubbaal." This was a nickname meaning "Let Baal take care of himself!"

³³Soon after this the armies of Midian, Amalek, and other nations around them met together. They came together in one great army against Israel. They crossed the Jordan and camped in the valley of Jezreel. ³⁴Then the Spirit of the Lord came upon Gideon. He blew a trumpet as a call to arms. And the men of Abiezer came to him. ³⁵ He also sent messengers throughout Manasseh, Asher, Zebulun, and Naphtali. He called out their fighting forces. All of them quickly came.

³⁶Then Gideon said to God, "You seem to be planning to use me to save Israel. You have promised me this! ³⁷But if you are, prove it to me in this way. I'll put some wool on the threshing floor tonight. In the morning I will see if the fleece is wet and the ground is dry. If this happens, I will know you are going to help me!"

³⁸And it happened just that way! He got up the next morning. And he pressed the fleece together. When he did this, he wrung out a whole bowlful of water!

³⁹Then Gideon said to the Lord, "Please don't be angry with me. But let me make one more test. This time let the fleece stay dry while the ground around it is wet!"

⁴⁰So the Lord did as he asked. That night the fleece stayed dry. But the ground was covered with dew!

- *Remember:* How did Israel's enemies hurt them? (6:2-7) The Lord's prophet told the people why they had so much trouble. Why did they? (6:8-10) What did the Lord promise to do for Gideon? (6:14,16) What was the "wet wool" test that Gideon used? What did it show? (6:36-40) How do you think Gideon felt after this test?

- *Discover:* The Lord helps us do things we could never do by ourselves.

- *Apply:* Has your brother or sister ever been sick? You can do many things to help him or her get well, can't you? But don't forget to pray. God does things you can't do.

- *What's next?* An army of only 300 defeats an army of many thousands. How did they do it? Read Judges 7. ■

Gideon's Army of 300

Armies have fought with all kinds of weapons. People who lived a long time ago fought with swords and spears. But here is a battle that Gideon started with trumpets and clay pots. There are thousands of enemy soldiers. Do you think he can win?

7 Gideon and his army got an early start. They went as far as the spring of Harod. The armies of Midian were camped north of them. They were just down in the valley beside the hill of Moreh.

2The Lord then said to Gideon, "There are too many of you! I can't let all of you fight the Midianites. For then the people of Israel will boast to me. They will think that they saved themselves by their own strength! 3Send home any of your men who are afraid."

So 22,000 of them went home. Only 10,000 were left who were willing to fight.

4But the Lord told Gideon, "There are still too many! Bring them down to the spring. I'll show you which ones shall go with you and which ones shall not."

5-6So Gideon assembled them at the water. There the Lord told him, "Divide them into two groups. The group they are in will be decided by the way they drink. In Group 1 will be all the men who cup the water in their hands. They will lift it to their mouths and lap it like dogs. In Group 2 will be those who kneel. They will put their mouths right in the stream."

Only 300 of the men drank from their hands. All the others drank with their mouths right in the stream.

7"I'll conquer the Midianites with these 300 men!" the Lord told Gideon. "Send all the others home!"

8-9So Gideon collected all the clay jars and trumpets they had among them. Then he sent most of the men home. There were only 300 men left with him.

The Midianites were camped in the valley below. And during the night the Lord said to Gideon, "Get up! Take your troops and attack the Midianites. For I will help you defeat them! 10But if you are afraid, first go down to the camp alone. Take along your servant Purah if you like. 11Listen to what they are saying down there! You will be greatly encouraged and be eager to attack!"

So he called Purah. They crept down through the darkness to the outposts of the enemy camp. 12-13The great armies of Midian and Amalek were crowded across the valley like locusts. Other nearby nations had also joined them. Yes, they were like the sand upon the seashore! There were too many camels even to count! Gideon crept up to one of the tents. As he did, a man inside wakened from a bad dream. And he told his friend about it.

"I had this strange dream," he was saying. "There was a huge loaf of barley bread. It came tumbling down into our camp. It hit our tent and knocked it flat!"

14The other soldier replied, "Your dream can mean only one thing! Gideon, the son of Joash, the Israelite, is going to come. He is going to destroy all the armies of Midian!"

15Gideon heard the dream and what it meant. And all he could do was just stand there and worship God! Then he went back to his men. He shouted, "Get up! For the Lord is going to use you to conquer all the armies of Midian!"

16He divided the 300 men into three groups. He gave each man a trumpet and a clay jar with a torch in it. 17Then he told them his plan.

"We will get to the outer posts of the camp," he told them. "When we get there, just do as I do. 18I and the men in my group will blow our trumpets. As soon as we do, blow yours too. Blow them on all sides of the camp. Then shout, 'We fight for God and for Gideon!'"

19-20It was just after midnight and the change of guards. At that time, Gideon crept to the edge of Midian's camp. He took his 100 men with him.

Suddenly they blew their trumpets. They broke their clay jars so that their torches blazed into the night. Then the other 200 of his men did the same. They blew the trumpets in their right hands. And they held the flaming torches in their left hands. They all shouted, "For the Lord and for Gideon!"

21Then they just stood and watched. And the whole enemy army began rushing around in a panic. They were shouting and running away. 22In the confusion the Lord caused the enemy troops to fight and kill each other. This happened from one end of the camp to the other. They ran into the night to places as far as Beth-shittah near Zererah. They went all the way to the border of Abel-meholah near Tabbath.

23Then Gideon sent for the troops of Naphtali, Asher, and Manasseh. He told them

to chase and destroy the fleeing army of Midian. 24Gideon also sent messengers throughout the hill country of Ephraim. There he called troops who took the fords of the Jordan River at Beth-barah. This way he stopped the Midianites from escaping across the river. 25Oreb and Zeeb were caught. They were the two generals of Midian. Oreb was killed at the rock now known by his name. Zeeb was killed at the winepress of Zeeb, as it is now called. And the Israelites took the heads of Oreb and Zeeb across the Jordan to Gideon.

- *Remember:* Why did the Lord want to send some of Gideon's soldiers home? (7:2-3) How did Gideon choose the 300 soldiers who would fight? (7:5-6) What did Gideon's soldiers do to start the battle? (7:19-20) Why did the enemy start fighting each other? (7:21-22) What do you think would have happened here if the Lord had not helped?

- *Discover:* "Can't" becomes "can" when the Lord is helping us.

- *Apply:* "I can't do it!" How many times have you said that? Why not pray and ask God to help you?

- *What's next?* Be careful what you promise! Jephthah made a terrible promise. He had to keep it, too. Read Judges 10:6–11:40. ■

Gideon's Wise Answer

8 But the tribal leaders of Ephraim were very angry with Gideon.

"Why didn't you send for us?" they demanded. "You should have told us when you first went to fight the Midianites!"

2-3But Gideon said, "God let you catch Oreb and Zeeb! They are the generals of the army of Midian! What have I done to compare with that? Your actions at the end of the battle were very important. Your work was even more important than ours at the beginning!" So they calmed down.

Chasing Zebah and Zalmunna

4Gideon now crossed the Jordan River with his 300 men. They were very tired. But they were still chasing the enemy. 5He asked the men of Succoth for food. "We are tired from chasing after Zebah and Zalmunna, the kings of Midian," he said.

6But the leaders of Succoth replied, "You haven't caught them yet! We could feed you, but you might fail. If this happens, they'll come back and destroy us."

7Then Gideon warned them, "The Lord will deliver them to us. And when he does, I will come back. I will tear your flesh with the thorns and briars of the wilderness."

8Then he went up to Penuel. He asked for food there, too. But he got the same answer. 9And he said to them also, "This will be all over soon. And when it is, I will come back. I will break down this tower."

10By this time King Zebah and King Zalmunna with 15,000 troops were in Karkor. That was all that was left of the allied armies of the east. For 120,000 had already been killed. 11Then Gideon circled around by the caravan route east of Nobah and Jogbehah. He struck at the Midianite army in surprise raids. 12The two kings fled, but Gideon chased and caught them. He routed their whole force. 13Later, Gideon went back by way of Heres Pass. 14There he caught a young man from Succoth. He made him write down the names of the 77 leaders of the city.

15He then went back to Succoth. "You mocked me," he said. "And you said that I would never catch King Zebah and King Zalmunna. You did not give us food when we were tired and hungry. Well, here they are!"

16Then he took the leaders of the city. He scraped them to death with wild thorns and briars. 17He also went to Penuel. He knocked down the city tower. And he killed all the men of the city.

18Then Gideon spoke to King Zebah and King Zalmunna. He said, "What were the men like that you killed at Tabor?"

They replied, "They were dressed just like you. They looked like sons of kings!"

19"They must have been my brothers!" Gideon exclaimed. "I swear that if you hadn't killed them I wouldn't kill you."

20Then he turned to Jether, his oldest son. He told him to kill them. But the boy was young and was afraid to.

21Then Zebah and Zalmunna said to Gideon, "You do it! We would rather be killed by a man!" So Gideon killed them. And he took the ornaments from their camels' necks.

"Gideon, Be Our King!"

22Now the men of Israel said to Gideon, "Be our king! You and your sons and all your descendants shall be our rulers. For you have saved us from Midian."

23-24But Gideon replied, "I will not be your king, nor shall my son. The Lord is your King! But I have one request. Give me all the earrings collected from your fallen foes." The troops of Midian all wore gold earrings. For they were Ishmaelites.

25"Gladly!" they replied. Then they

spread out a sheet. Everyone was to throw into it the gold earrings he had gathered. 26In all they were worth about $25,000. This did not even include the crescents and pendants. Neither did it include the royal clothing of the kings or the chains around the camels' necks. 27Gideon made an ephod from the gold. He put it in Ophrah, his hometown. But all Israel soon began worshiping it. So it became an evil deed that Gideon and his family did.

Gideon Dies

28That is the true story of how Midian was subdued by Israel. Midian never recovered. And the land was at peace for 40 years. It was peaceful for the rest of Gideon's life. 29He went home 30and had 70 sons. For he married many wives. 31He also had a concubine in Shechem. She bore him a son named Abimelech. 32Gideon finally died, an old, old man. He was buried in the tomb of his father, Joash. The tomb was in Ophrah, in the land of the Abiezrites.

33But as soon as Gideon was dead, the Israelites began to worship idols. They set up Baal-berith as their god. 34And they no longer thought of the Lord as their God. They forgot him even though he had rescued them from enemies on every side. 35And they did not show any kindness to the family of Gideon. They forgot him, even though he had done so much for them.

Abimelech Tries to Become King

9 One day Gideon's son Abimelech visited his uncles in Shechem. These were his mother's brothers.

2"Go talk to the leaders of Shechem," he said. "Ask them if they want to be ruled by 70 kings or by one man. See if they want to be ruled by Gideon's 70 sons or by me! I am your own flesh and blood!"

3So his uncles went to the leaders of the city. They told them of Abimelech's plans. They saw that his mother was a native of their town. So they went along with it. 4They gave him money from the temple offerings of the idol Baal-berith. He used it to hire some reckless men.

They agreed to do whatever Abimelech told them to. 5He took them to his father's home at Ophrah. There they killed all 70 of his half brothers. Only the youngest escaped and hid. His name was Jotham. 6Then the people of Shechem and Beth-millo called a meeting. They gathered under the oak beside the fort at Shechem. There they chose Abimelech to be their king.

????????????????????????????????

Who killed 70 of his brothers?
(Read Judges 9:1-6 for the answer)

????????????????????????????????

7Jotham heard about this. So he went to the top of Mount Gerizim. From there, he shouted to the men of Shechem. He said, "If you want God's blessing, listen to me! 8Once upon a time the trees decided to elect a king. First they asked the olive tree, 9but it refused.

"'Both God and man are blessed by the oil I make. Should I quit making it just to wave back and forth over the other trees?' it asked.

10"Then they said to the fig tree, 'You be our king!'

11"But the fig tree also refused. 'Should I quit making fruit just to lift my head above all the other trees?' it asked.

12"Then they said to the grapevine, 'You reign over us!'

13"But the grapevine replied, 'I make the wine that cheers both God and man. Shall I stop making it just to be greater than all the other trees?'

14"Then all the trees finally turned to the thorn bush. 'You be our king!' they said.

15"And the thorn bush replied, 'If you really want me, come and humble yourselves in my shade! If you refuse, let fire flame forth from me. It will burn down the great cedars of Lebanon!'

16"Now make sure you are doing the right thing. Have you done right in making Abimelech your king? Have you been fair to Gideon and all of his family? 17My father fought for you. He risked his life and saved you from the Midianites. 18Yet you have rebelled against him. And you have killed his 70 sons upon a single stone. Now you have chosen Abimelech to be your king. He was only the son of Gideon's slave girl. And you chose him just because he is your relative. ¹⁹Are you sure you have done right by Gideon and his family? If so, then may you and Abimelech have a long and happy life together. ²⁰But it may be that you have not been fair to Gideon. If this is true, then may Abimelech destroy the people of Shechem and Beth-millo! And may they destroy Abimelech!"

²¹Then Jotham ran away. He went to live in Beer, for he was afraid of his brother, Abimelech. ²²⁻²³Three years passed. And God stirred up trouble between King Abimelech and the people of Shechem. So the people rebelled. ²⁴In the events that followed, Abimelech and the people of Shechem were punished. For Abimelech had killed Gideon's 70 sons. And the people of Shechem had helped him. ²⁵The men of Shechem set an ambush for Abimelech. They set it along the trail at the top of the mountain. They waited there for him to come along. As they waited, they robbed everyone else who passed that way. But someone warned Abimelech about their plot.

²⁶At that time Gaal moved to Shechem with his brothers. He was the son of Ebed. He soon became one of the leading people there. ²⁷During the harvest feast at Shechem that year the wine flowed freely. The feast was held in the temple of the local god. During the feast everyone began cursing Abimelech. ²⁸"Who is Abimelech?" Gaal shouted. "And why should he be our king? Why should we be his servants? He and his friend Zebul should be *our* servants. Down with Abimelech! ²⁹Make me your king. If you do, you'll soon see what happens to Abimelech! I'll tell Abimelech, 'Get up an army! Come on out and fight!'"

³⁰But Zebul heard what Gaal was saying. He was the mayor of the city. And he was very angry. ³¹He sent messengers to Abimelech in Arumah. He told him, "Gaal, son of Ebed, has come to live in Shechem. He moved here with his relatives. They are getting the city to rebel against you. ³²Come by night with an army. Hide out in the fields. ³³In the morning, as soon as it is light, storm the city. He and those who are with him will come out against you. When they do, you can do with them as you wish!"

³⁴So Abimelech and his men marched through the night. They split into four groups and surrounded the city. ³⁵The next morning Gaal sat at the city gates. He was talking about various things with the local leaders. At this time, Abimelech and his men began their march upon the city.

³⁶When Gaal saw them, he exclaimed to Zebul, "Look over at that mountain! Doesn't it look like people coming down?"

"No!" Zebul said. "You're just seeing shadows that look like men!"

³⁷"No, look over there," Gaal said. "I'm sure I see people coming toward us. And look! There are others coming along the road past the oak of Meonenim!"

³⁸Then Zebul turned on him in triumph. "Now where is that big mouth of yours?" he demanded. "Who was it who said, 'Who is Abimelech? Why should he be our king?' The men you taunted are right outside the city! Go on out and fight!"

³⁹So Gaal led the men of Shechem into the battle. They fought with Abimelech, ⁴⁰but were beaten. Many of the men of Shechem were left wounded all the way to the city gate. ⁴¹Abimelech was living at Arumah at this time. And Zebul drove Gaal and his relatives out of Shechem. He wouldn't let them live there any more.

⁴²The next day the men of Shechem went out to battle again. But someone had told Abimelech about their plans. ⁴³So he divided his men into three groups. And they hid in the fields. The men of the city went out to attack. But Abimelech and his men jumped up from their hiding places. Then they began killing the people of Shechem. ⁴⁴Abimelech stormed the city gate. He did this to keep the men of Shechem from getting back in. His other two groups cut the people down in the fields. ⁴⁵The battle went on all day before Abimelech finally took the city. He killed all its people and

leveled it to the ground. ⁴⁶The people at the nearby town of Migdal saw what was happening. So they took refuge in the fort next to the temple of Baal-berith.

⁴⁷⁻⁴⁸Abimelech learned of this. And he led his forces to Mount Zalmon. There he began chopping a bundle of firewood. He put it upon his shoulder. "Do as I have done," he told his men. ⁴⁹So each of them quickly cut a bundle of wood. Then they carried it back to the town. They followed Abimelech's example. The bundles were piled against the walls of the fort. Then they were set on fire. So all the people inside died. There were about 1,000 men and women.

⁵⁰Abimelech next attacked the city of Thebez, and took it. ⁵¹But there was a fort inside the city. All the people ran into it. They blocked the gates and climbed to the rooftop to watch. ⁵²Abimelech was getting ready to burn it down. ⁵³But a woman on the roof threw down a millstone. It landed on Abimelech's head and crushed his skull.

⁵⁴"Kill me!" he groaned to his armor-bearer. "Never let it be said that a woman killed Abimelech!"

So the young man stabbed him with his sword, and he died. ⁵⁵His men saw that he was dead. So they broke up and went back to their homes. ⁵⁶⁻⁵⁷Thus God punished both Abimelech and the men of Shechem. For they had sinned by murdering Gideon's 70 sons. So the curse of Jotham, Gideon's son, came true.

Tola and Jair

10 After Abimelech's death, the next judge of Israel was Tola. He was the son of Puah and the grandson of Dodo. He was from the tribe of Issachar. But he lived in the city of Shamir in the hill country of Ephraim. ²He was Israel's judge for 23 years. When he died, he was buried in Shamir. ³He was succeeded by Jair, a man from Gilead. Jair judged Israel for 22 years. ⁴His 30 sons rode around together on 30 donkeys. And they owned 30 cities in the land of Gilead. These cities are still called "The Cities of Jair." ⁵When Jair died he was buried in Kamon.

Jephthah's Foolish Vow

Jephthah asked the Lord to help him win a big battle. If he did, Jephthath would do something special for the Lord. So Jephthah made a promise. It was a foolish promise. That promise made him hurt his only daughter.

⁶Then the people of Israel turned away from the Lord again. They worshiped the heathen gods Baal and Ashtaroth. They also bowed to the gods of Syria, Sidon, Moab, Ammon, and Philistia. But not only this; they no longer worshiped the Lord at all. ⁷⁻⁸This made the Lord very angry with his people. So he let the Philistines and the Ammonites torment them. These attacks took place east of the Jordan River. This was the land of the Amorites. It was also known as Gilead. ⁹Attacks also took place in Judah, Benjamin, and Ephraim. For the Ammonites crossed the Jordan to attack the Israelites. This went on for 18 years. ¹⁰Finally the Israelites turned to the Lord again. They begged him to save them.

"We have sinned against you. We have forsaken you as our God. And we have worshiped idols," they confessed.

¹¹But the Lord replied, "Didn't I save you from the Egyptians? Didn't I deliver you from the Amorites, the Ammonites, and the Philistines? ¹²Didn't I save you from the Sidonians, the Amalekites, and the Maonites? Has there ever been a time when you cried out to me that I haven't

rescued you? 13Yet you continue to leave me. You go and worship other gods. So go away! I won't save you anymore! 14Go and cry to the new gods you have chosen! Let them save you in your hour of distress!"

15But they pleaded with him again. They said, "We have sinned. Punish us in any way you think best. Only save us once more from our enemies."

16Then they destroyed their foreign gods. And they worshiped only the Lord. And he felt sorry for them when he saw their suffering. 17The armies of Ammon were called out in Gilead at that time. They got ready to fight Israel's army at Mizpah.

18"Who will lead our forces against the Ammonites?" the leaders of Gilead asked each other. "Whoever will lead us shall be our king!"

11 Now Jephthah was a great warrior. He was from the land of Gilead. But his mother was a prostitute. His father's name was Gilead. He had many other sons by his wife. When these half brothers grew up, they chased Jephthah out of the country.

"You'll not get any of our father's property," they said. "You're the son of another woman." 3So Jephthah ran from his father's home. He lived in the land of Tob. Soon he had quite a band of reckless men as his followers. They lived off the land as bandits. 4It was about this time that the Ammonites began their war against Israel. 5The leaders of Gilead sent for Jephthah. 6They begged him to come and lead their army against the Ammonites.

7But Jephthah said to them, "Why do you come to me when you hate me? You have driven me out of my father's house! Why come now when you're in trouble?"

8"Because we need you," they replied. "Come and be our leader against the Ammonites. If you do, we will make you the king of Gilead."

9"Sure!" Jephthah said. "Do you expect me to believe that?"

10"We swear it," they replied. "We promise with a solemn oath."

11So Jephthah agreed to help them.

He was made their leader and king. The contract was made before the Lord in Mizpah. All the people were there to see it. 12Then Jephthah sent messengers to the king of Ammon. He asked why Israel was being attacked. 13The king of Ammon claimed that the land belonged to the people of Ammon. He said it had been stolen from them. The Israelites took it when they came from Egypt. He claimed the whole area from the Arnon River to the Jabbok and the Jordan.

"Give us back our land in peace," he demanded.

14-15Jephthah replied, "Israel did not steal the land. 16This is what happened. The people of Israel traveled from Egypt after crossing the Red Sea. They got to Kadesh. 17From there, they sent a message to the king of Edom. They asked him if they could pass through his land. But the king would not let them pass through. Then they asked the king of Moab if they could pass through his land. His answer was the same. So the people of Israel stayed in Kadesh.

18"Finally they went around Edom and Moab. They traveled through the wilderness. They followed the eastern border. Then at last they got beyond the border of Moab at the Arnon River. But they never once crossed into Moab. 19Then Israel sent messengers to King Sihon of the Amorites. He lived in Heshbon. They asked if they could cross through his land to get to their land.

20"But King Sihon didn't trust Israel. So he called out an army at Jahaz and attacked them. 21-22But the Lord our God helped Israel defeat King Sihon and all your people. So Israel took over all of your land from the Arnon River to the Jabbok. They took it all from the wilderness to the Jordan River.

23"So you see, it was the Lord God of Israel who took away the land from the Amorites. And it was he who gave it to Israel. Why, then, should we give it back to you? 24You keep whatever your god Chemosh gives you. We will keep whatever the Lord our God gives us! 25And besides, just who do you think you are? Are you better than King Balak, the king of Moab? Did he try to recover his land after Israel defeated him? No, of course not. ²⁶But now after 300 years you make an issue of this! Israel has been living here for all that time. They have spread across the land from Heshbon to Aroer. And they live all along the Arnon River. Why have you made no effort to recover it before now? ²⁷No, I have not sinned against you. Rather, you have wronged me by coming to war against me. But the Lord will soon show whether Israel or Ammon is right."

²⁸But the king of Ammon did not listen to Jephthah's message.

²⁹At that time the Spirit of the Lord came upon Jephthah. He led his army across the land of Gilead and Manasseh. They marched past Mizpah in Gilead and attacked the army of Ammon. ³⁰⁻³¹During this time Jephthah made a vow to the Lord. He knew that God would help Israel conquer the Ammonites. And he expected to return home in peace. But when this took place, he promised he would make a burnt offering to the Lord. And he would take the first person coming out of his house to meet him as that sacrifice!

³²So Jephthah led his army against the Ammonites. And the Lord gave him the victory. ³³He destroyed the Ammonites with a terrible slaughter. He destroyed them all the way from Aroer to Minnith. This included 20 cities. He attacked them as far away as Vineyard Meadow. Thus the Ammonites were subdued by the people of Israel.

³⁴Then Jephthah went home to his daughter. She was his only child. She ran out to meet him. She was playing on a tambourine and dancing for joy. ³⁵When he saw her, he tore his clothes in pain.

"Alas, my daughter!" he cried out. "You have brought me to the dust. For I have made a vow to the Lord, and I cannot take it back."

³⁶And she said, "Father, you must do whatever you promised the Lord. For he has given you a great victory over the Ammonites. ³⁷But first let me go up into the hills. I will roam with my girlfriends for two months. I will weep because I'll never marry."

38"Yes," he said. "Go."

And so she did. She cried in sorrow for two months with her friends. 39Then she went back to her father. And he did as he had promised. So she was never married. After that this became a custom in Israel. 40All the young girls went away for four days each year. And there they mourned the fate of Jephthah's daughter.

- *Remember:* What vow or promise did Jephthah make to the Lord? (11:30-31) Who came from his house first? (11:34) How did Jephthah feel about keeping his promise? (11:35) How did his daughter feel about him keeping it? (11:36-37) How would you have felt if you had been Jephthah? How would you have felt if you had been his daughter?

- *Discover:* Don't make foolish promises.

- *Apply:* "Do you promise?" a friend asks. Before you say yes, remember Jephthah and his daughter. Then pray!

- *What's next?* God said one boy should never get a haircut. Why would God say that? Read Judges 13. ∎

Jephthah Attacks Ephraim

12 Then the tribe of Ephraim called out its army at Zaphon. And they sent a message to Jephthah. "Why didn't you call for us to help you fight against Ammon?" they asked. "We are going to burn down your house, with you in it!"

2"I called you, but you refused to come!" Jephthah said. "You failed to help us in our time of need. 3So I risked my life and went to battle without you. And the Lord helped me to conquer the enemy. Is that anything for you to fight us about?"

4Then Jephthah became angry at the taunt of Ephraim. They had said that the men of Gilead were outcasts and the scum of the earth. So he called out his army and attacked the army of Ephraim. 5He captured the fords of the Jordan behind the army of Ephraim. Those who escaped from Ephraim tried to cross the river to their land. But when they did, the Gilead guards stopped them.

"Are you a member of the tribe of Ephraim?" they asked. If they said no, 6then the guards demanded, "Say 'Shibboleth.'" But if they were from Ephraim they could not say the *SH*. They would say, "Sibboleth" instead of "Shibboleth." If this happened, they were dragged away and killed. So 42,000 people of Ephraim died there at that time.

7Jephthah was Israel's judge for six years. At his death he was buried in one of the cities of Gilead.

Ibzan, Elon, and Abdon

8The next judge was Ibzan. He lived in Bethlehem. 9-10He had 30 sons and 30 daughters. He married his daughters to men outside his clan. And he brought in 30 girls to marry his sons. He judged Israel for seven years before he died. He was buried at Bethlehem.

11-12The next judge was Elon from Zebulun. He judged Israel for 10 years. He was buried at Aijalon in Zebulun.

13Next was Abdon from Pirathon. He was the son of Hillel. 14He had 40 sons and 30 grandsons. They rode on 70 donkeys. He was Israel's judge for eight years. 15Then he died and was buried in Pirathon, in Ephraim. This was the hill country of the Amalekites.

Samson Is Born

A fire is burning. An angel rises out of the fire. He goes up into heaven. What would you think? What would you say?

13 Once again Israel sinned by worshiping other gods. So the Lord let them be conquered by the Philistines. They ruled Israel for 40 years.

2-3Then one day the Angel of the Lord came to the wife of Manoah. Manoah was from the tribe of Dan. He and his wife lived in the city of Zorah. She had no children. But the Angel said to her, "You have not been able to have any children. But you will soon have a son! 4Don't drink any wine or beer. And don't eat any food that you're not supposed to. 5Your son's hair must never be cut. For he shall be a Nazirite. He shall be a special servant of God from the day he is born. And he will begin to rescue Israel from the Philistines."

6The woman ran and told her husband. "A man from God came to me," she said. "And I think he must be the Angel of the Lord. For he was almost too bright to look at. I didn't ask where he was from. And he didn't tell me his name. 7But he told me, 'You are going to have a baby boy!' And he told me not to drink any wine or beer. And I am not to eat food that isn't kosher. For the baby is going to be a Nazirite. He will be set apart to God. He will be set apart from the day of his birth until his death!"

8Then Manoah prayed, "O Lord, please! Let the man from God come back to us again. Give us more orders about the child you are going to give us." 9The Lord answered his prayer. And the Angel of God came once again to his wife. At the time, she was out sitting in the field. But again she was alone. Manoah was not with her. 10So she quickly ran and found her husband. She told him, "The same man is here again!"

11Manoah ran back with his wife. He asked, "Are you the man who talked to my wife the other day?"

"Yes," he replied, "I am."

12So Manoah asked him, "Can you give us any special orders? Can you tell us how we should raise the baby after he is born?"

13-14And the Angel replied, "Be sure that your wife follows the orders I gave her. She must not eat grapes or raisins. She must not drink any wine or beer. And she must not eat anything she isn't supposed to."

15Then Manoah said to the Angel, "Please stay here! We will get you something to eat."

16"I'll stay," the Angel said. "But I won't eat anything. However, you might wish to bring something. If so, bring an offering to sacrifice to the Lord." Manoah didn't yet know that he was the Angel of the Lord.

17Then Manoah asked him for his name. "All this shall come true and the baby will be born," he said to the Angel. "But when it happens, we will want to tell people who told us about it!"

18"Don't even ask my name," the Angel replied. "For it is a secret."

19Then Manoah took a young goat and a grain offering. He offered it as a sacrifice to the Lord. And the Angel did a strange and wonderful thing! 20The flames from the altar lept up toward the sky. And as Manoah and his wife watched, the Angel went up in the fire! Manoah and his wife fell face down on the ground. 21And that was the last they ever saw of him. It was then that Manoah knew that it had been the Angel of the Lord.

22"We will die," Manoah cried out to his wife. "For we have seen God!"

23But his wife said, "The Lord might decide to kill us. But if he wanted to, he wouldn't have taken our burnt offerings. He wouldn't have come to us and told us this wonderful thing. And he wouldn't have done these miracles."

24When her son was born they named him Samson. And the Lord blessed him as he grew up. 25And the Spirit of the Lord began to excite him. This happened while he was at the parade grounds of the army of the tribe of Dan. This was between the cities of Zorah and Eshtaol.

- *Remember:* Why did Israel need a strong leader? (13:1) The Angel of the Lord appeared one day. He told a woman her son would rescue Israel. But why should this son never get a haircut? (13:5) How did this Angel go back into heaven? (13:20-21) The Angel of the Lord is really God. Who said this? (13:22) Would you listen if God was there talking with you? What do you think he would say?

- *Discover:* Manoah needed a special visit from God to talk to him. But we can listen to God and talk with him today.

- *Apply:* Do you have a Bible? When you read it, you can listen to what God says. Do you pray? You can talk with God.

- *What's next?* Would you like to meet a man who killed a lion with his bare hands? You will in Judges 14. ■

Samson Gets Married

Do you have a big brother? What would you think of him if he killed a lion with his bare hands? Samson did this. Keep reading, and you will learn how strong Samson really was.

14 One day Samson was in Timnah. And he noticed a certain Philistine girl. ²When he got home he spoke to his father and mother. He told them that he wanted to marry her. ³They did not want him to do this at all.

"Why don't you marry an Israelite girl?" they asked. "Why must you go and get a wife from these heathen Philistines? Isn't there one girl among all the people of Israel you could marry?"

But Samson told his father, "She is the one I want. Get her for me."

⁴His father and mother didn't know that the Lord was behind the request. For God was setting a trap for the Philistines. At that time, they were the rulers of Israel.

⁵Samson and his parents were on their way to Timnah. As they went, a young lion attacked Samson. This happened in the vineyards just outside the town. ⁶At that moment the Spirit of the Lord came strongly upon him. He had no weapon. So he ripped the lion's jaws apart! And he did it as easily as though it were a young goat! But he didn't tell his father or mother about it. ⁷When they got to Timnah, he talked with the girl. He found her to be just what he wanted. So wedding plans were made.

⁸He went back to Timnah for the wedding. On his way, he turned off the path. He went to look at the dead body of the lion he had killed. He found a swarm of bees in it. And there was some honey in it, too! ⁹He took some of the honey with him. He ate it as he went. And he gave some of it to his father and mother. But he didn't tell them where he had gotten it.

¹⁰⁻¹¹His father went to make final plans for the marriage. At this time, Samson threw a party for 30 young men of the village. This was the custom of the day. ¹²Samson asked if they would like to hear a riddle. They all said that they would.

"You might solve my riddle during these seven days of the feasting," he said. "And if you do, I'll give you 30 plain robes. I'll give you 30 fancy robes as well. ¹³But you might not be able to solve it. If not, then you must give robes to me!"

"All right," they agreed. "Let's hear it."

¹⁴This was his riddle: "Food came out of the eater, and sweetness from the strong!" Three days later they were still trying to figure it out.

¹⁵On the fourth day they spoke to his new wife. They said, "Get the answer from your husband. If you don't, we'll

burn down your father's house with you in it. Were we invited to this party just to make us poor?"

¹⁶So Samson's wife broke down in tears before him. She said, "You don't love me at all! You hate me! For you have told a riddle to my people. But you haven't even told me the answer."

"I haven't told it to my father or mother. Why should I tell you?" he replied.

¹⁷So she cried whenever she was with him. She kept it up for the rest of the feast. At last, on the seventh day, he told her the answer. She, of course, then gave the answer to the young men. ¹⁸So before sunset of the seventh day they gave him their reply.

"What is sweeter than honey?" they asked. "And what is stronger than a lion?"

"You made my wife tell you. That is the only way you could have found the answer to my riddle!" he fumed.

¹⁹Then the Spirit of the Lord came upon him. He went to the city of Ashkelon. While there, he killed 30 men. He took their clothing. Then he gave it to the young men who had told

B. Gallego

him the answer to his riddle. But he was angry about it. So he left his wife. And he went back home to live with his father and mother. ²⁰So his wife was married instead to another young man. She was married to the one who had been best man at Samson's wedding.

- *Remember:* What did Samson's parents tell him that he should not do? (14:1-3) What weapon did Samson use to kill the lion? (14:5-6) What was Samson's riddle? (14:12-14,16) How would you like Samson to be your minister? What would you want him to do differently?

- *Discover:* God gives us good gifts, but we don't always use them well.

- *Apply:* God may allow some of your neighbors to make lots of money. Can you think of some ways they use money that do not make God happy? Do you ever use your money unwisely?

- *What's next?* Today you will make many choices. Tomorrow you will make many other choices. In Judges 16:1-21 you will learn about a man who made some very bad choices. You'll see how those choices hurt him. ■

Samson Kills Many Enemies

15 Later on Samson took a young goat as a present to his wife. He went during the wheat harvest. He wanted to sleep with her. But her father would not let him in.

²"I really thought you hated her," he said. "So I let her marry your best man. But look, her sister is prettier than she is. Marry her instead."

³Samson was very angry. "You can't blame me for what happens now," he shouted.

⁴So he went out and caught 300 foxes. He tied their tails together in pairs. And he tied a torch between each pair. ⁵Then he lit the torches. He let the foxes run through the fields of the Philistines. This burned their grain to the ground. All the sheaves and shocks of grain were burned up. It also destroyed their olive trees.

⁶"Who did this?" the Philistines demanded.

"Samson!" was the reply. "He did it because his wife's father gave her to an-

other man." So the Philistines came and got the girl and her father. They burned them alive.

⁷"Now my anger will strike again!" Samson vowed. ⁸So he attacked the Philistines with great fury. He killed many of them. Then he went to live in a cave in the rock of Etam. ⁹The Philistines in turn sent a huge posse into Judah and raided Lehi.

¹⁰"Why have you come here?" the men of Judah asked.

And the Philistines replied, "We came to capture Samson. We want to do to him as he has done to us."

¹¹So 3,000 men of Judah went down to get Samson. They found him at the cave in the rock of Etam.

"What are you doing to us?" they demanded of him. "Don't you know that the Philistines are our rulers?"

But Samson replied, "I only paid them back for what they did to me."

¹²⁻¹³"We have come to capture you," the men of Judah told him. "We must take you to the Philistines."

"All right," Samson said. "But promise me that you won't kill me yourselves."

"No," they replied, "we won't do that."

So they tied him with two new ropes and led him away. ¹⁴Samson and his captors went to Lehi. As they got there, the Philistines shouted with glee. But then the strength of the Lord came upon Samson. The ropes with which he was tied snapped like thread! They fell from his wrists! ¹⁵Then he picked up a donkey's jawbone that was lying on the ground. And he killed 1,000 Philistines with it. ¹⁶⁻¹⁷Tossing away the jawbone, he remarked,

"Heaps upon heaps,
All with a donkey's jaw!
I've killed 1,000 men,
All with a donkey's jaw!"

The place has been called "Jawbone Hill" ever since.

¹⁸But now Samson was very thirsty. So he prayed to the Lord. He said, "You have given me a great victory today! Through me you have delivered Israel! After all this, must I die of thirst? Must I

now fall to the mercy of these heathen?" ¹⁹So the Lord caused water to gush out from a hollow in the ground. And Samson's spirit was revived as he drank. Then he named the place "The Spring of the Man Who Prayed." That spring is still there to this day.

²⁰Samson was Israel's leader for the next 20 years. But the Philistines still ruled the land.

Samson's Foolish Choices

Pretend that you are at an intersection in the road. One way says "bad choice—you'll get hurt." The other way says "good choice—you'll be helped." Which way should you go? Watch to see which way Samson went.

16 One day Samson went to the Philistine city of Gaza. He spent the night there with a prostitute. ²Word soon spread that he had been seen in the city. So the police were alerted. And many men of the city lay in wait all night at the city gate. They planned to capture him if he tried to leave.

B. Gallego

"In the morning," they thought, "there will be more light. Then we'll find him and kill him."

³Samson stayed in bed with the girl until midnight. Then he went out to the city gates. He lifted them, with the two gateposts, right out of the ground. He put them on his shoulders. And he carried them to the top of the mountain across from Hebron!

⁴Later on he fell in love with a girl named Delilah. She lived over in the valley of Sorek. ⁵The five leaders of the Philistine nation went to see her. They told her to find out from Samson what made him so strong. That way they would know how to capture him and keep him tied up.

"Each of us will give you $1,000 for this job," they promised.

⁶So Delilah begged Samson to tell her his secret. *"Please* tell me, Samson," she pleaded. "Tell me why you are so strong. I don't think anyone could ever capture you!"

⁷"Well," Samson replied, "someone might tie me with seven raw-leather bowstrings. If they did, I would become as weak as anyone else."

⁸So they brought her the seven bowstrings. While he slept she tied him with them. ⁹Some men were hiding in the next room. As soon as she had tied him up she exclaimed,

"Samson! The Philistines are here!"

Then he snapped the bowstrings like cotton thread. And so his secret was not found out.

¹⁰After that Delilah said to him, "You are making fun of me! You told me a lie! *Please* tell me how you can be captured!"

¹¹"Well," he said, "someone might tie me with brand new ropes. The ropes must never have been used. If this is done, I will be as weak as other men."

¹²So that time, as he slept, Delilah took new ropes. She tied him with them. The men were hiding in the next room, as before. Again Delilah shouted,

"Samson! The Philistines have come to capture you!"

But he broke the ropes from his arms like spiderwebs!

¹³"You have mocked me again! You have told me more lies!" Delilah complained. "Now tell me how you can *really* be captured."

"Well," he said, "someone might weave my hair into your loom! If this is done, I will be as weak as other men."

¹⁴So while he slept, she did just that. Then she screamed, "The Philistines have come, Samson!" He woke up and yanked his hair away, breaking the loom.

¹⁵"How can you say you love me?" she whined. "You don't even confide in me! You've made fun of me three times

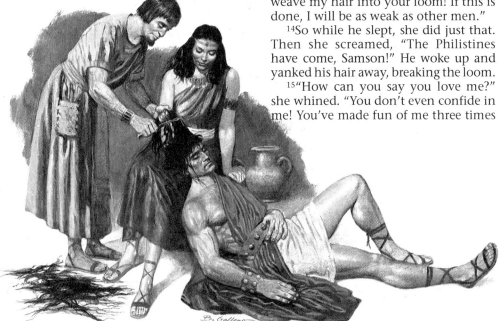

B. Gallego

now! And you still haven't told me what makes you so strong!"

16-17She nagged at him every day until he couldn't stand it any longer. In the end, he told her his secret.

"My hair has never been cut," he confessed. "For I've been a Nazirite to God since before my birth. If my hair were cut, my strength would leave me. I would become as weak as anyone else."

18Delilah saw that he had told her the truth at last. So she sent for the five Philistine leaders.

"Come just this once more," she said. "For this time he has told me his secret."

So they brought the money with them. 19She lulled him to sleep with his head in her lap. And they brought in a barber who cut off his hair. Delilah could see that his strength was leaving him.

20Then she screamed, "The Philistines are here! They have come to capture you, Samson!" He woke up and thought, "I will do as before. I'll just shake myself free." But he didn't know that the Lord had left him. 21So the Philistines captured him. They gouged out his eyes and took him to Gaza. There he was tied with bronze chains. They made him grind grain in the prison. 22But before long his hair began to grow again.

- *Remember:* What did the Philistine leaders want Delilah to do for them? (16:5) How did she try to learn Samson's secrets? (16:6-15) What did Samson choose to tell Delilah? (16:16-17) Why was that foolish? How did this choice hurt him? (16:21) What would you have liked to say to Samson about his choices?

- *Discover:* Good choices will bring good things. Bad choices will bring bad things.

- *Apply:* Someone will say, "Come on, let's do it!" Ask, "Is this a good choice or a bad one? Is this a choice God wants me to make?"

- *What's next?* Samson pushes an entire building down. Read Judges 16:22-31. ■

Samson Pulls Down a Temple

The strongest man in the world needed a little boy to lead him. That's because Samson was blind. The Philistines cut out his eyes. Now they were making fun of him. This strongest man looked very weak now. But what could Samson do?

23-24The Philistine leaders had a great feast to enjoy the capture of Samson. The people made sacrifices to their god Dagon. And they praised him.

"Our god has given our enemy Samson to us!" they said. For he was now in chains. "He killed many of us! He was the scourge of our nation! But now he is in our power!" 25-26The people were half-drunk by now. They demanded, "Bring out Samson. We want to have some fun with him!"

So he was brought from the prison. They made him stand at the center of the temple. He stood between the two pillars that held up the roof. Samson spoke to the boy who was leading him by the hand. He said, "Put my hands against the two pillars. I want to rest against them."

27By then the temple was filled with people. The five Philistine leaders were there. And there were 3,000 people in the balconies. They were watching Samson and making fun of him.

28Then Samson prayed to the Lord. He said, "O Lord, remember me! Please give back my strength one more time. Do this so that I may pay back the Philistines. Let me be avenged for the loss of at least one of my eyes."

29Then Samson pushed against the

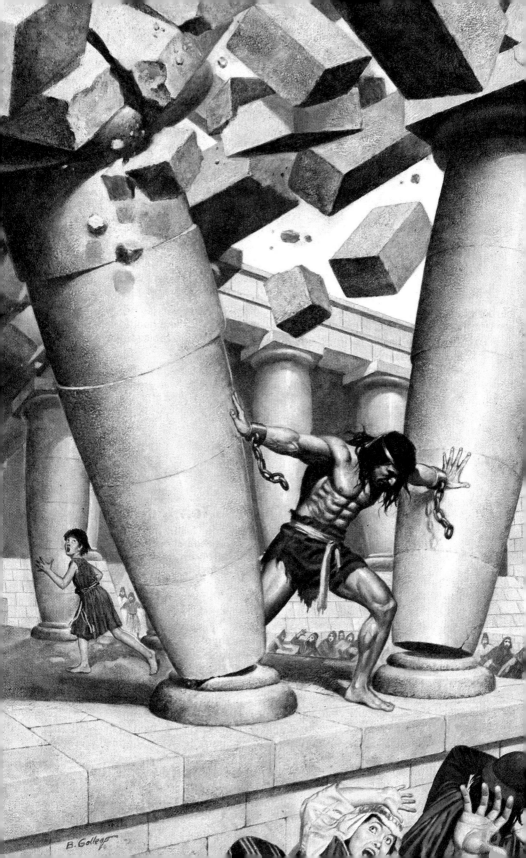

B. Gallego

pillars with all his might.

³⁰"Let me die with the Philistines," he prayed.

And the temple crashed down upon the Philistine leaders and all the people. He killed more at his death than those he had killed during his whole lifetime. ³¹Later, his brothers and other relatives came down to get his body. They brought him back home. They buried him between Zorah and Eshtaol. They put him where his father, Manoah, was buried. He had led Israel for 20 years.

- *Remember:* Samson made some bad choices. Do you remember some of them? (16:16-17) Staying with Delilah was a bad choice. How did she hurt him? (16:18-21) Why did the Philistines have a big party? (16:23-25) How did Samson get even with the Philistines? (16:27-30) Why was getting even not so good for Samson?

- *Discover:* Getting even can hurt us as much as the other person.

- *Apply:* Have you thought of getting even with someone? How would you do it? Ask first how you could get hurt, too. Then don't do it.

- *What's next?* It isn't easy to leave your home, is it? It isn't easy to go to live in another country. Read Ruth 1. It's about a young lady who left her home and country to live with a special person. ■

Micah's Idol Collection

17 In the hill country of Ephraim lived a man named Micah.

²One day he spoke to his mother. He said, "Remember that money you thought was stolen from you? You were cursing about it. Well, I stole it!"

"God bless you for telling me," his mother said. ³So he gave her back the money.

"I am going to give it to the Lord. It will be a credit for your account," she said. "I'll have an idol carved for you.

And I will cover it with the silver."

4-5So his mother took a fifth of it to a silversmith. The idol he made from it was put in Micah's shrine. Micah had many idols. He also had an ephod and some teraphim. He appointed one of his sons as the priest. 6For in those days Israel had no king. Everyone did what they wanted to. They did what seemed right in their own eyes.

7-8One day a young priest came from the town of Bethlehem, in Judah. He came to that area of Ephraim. And he was looking for a good place to live. He happened to stop at Micah's house as he was traveling through.

9"Where are you from?" Micah asked him.

And he replied, "I am a priest from Bethlehem, in Judah. I am looking for a place to live."

10-11"Well, stay here with me," Micah said. "You can be my priest. I will give you $100 a year. I will also give you a new suit and your board and room." The young man agreed to this. And he became like one of Micah's sons. 12So Micah made him his personal priest.

13"I know the Lord will really bless me now!" Micah exclaimed. "Now I have a real priest working for me!"

The Danites Steal Micah's Idols

18 As has already been stated, there was no king in Israel at that time. The tribe of Dan was trying to find a place to settle. They had not yet driven out the people living in the land given to them. 2So the men of Dan chose five army heroes. They came from the cities of Zorah and Eshtaol. They went as scouts to spy out the land they would settle in. They traveled through the hill country of Ephraim. When they got there, they stayed at Micah's home. 3They noticed the young Levite's accent. So they took him aside. They asked him, "What are you doing here? Why did you come?" 4He told them about his contract with Micah. He told them that he was his personal priest.

5"Well, then," they said, "ask God whether or not our trip will be successful."

6"Yes," the priest replied, "all is well. The Lord is taking care of you."

7So the five men went on to the town of Laish. They saw how safe everyone felt. And they were very rich. They lived quietly and were not ready for an attack. There were no tribes in the area strong enough to try it. They lived a long way from their relatives in Sidon. And they had little or no contact with the nearby villages. 8So the spies went back to their people in Zorah and Eshtaol.

"What about it?" they were asked. "What did you find?"

9-10And the men replied, "Let's attack! We have seen the land and it is ours for the taking. It is a broad, fertile, and wonderful place. It's a real paradise! The people aren't even ready to defend themselves! Come on, let's go! For God has given it to us!"

11So 600 armed troops of the tribe of Dan set out from Zorah and Eshtaol. 12They camped first at a place west of Kiriath-jearim in Judah. This place is still called "The Camp of Dan." 13Then they went on up into the hill country of Ephraim.

As they passed the home of Micah, 14the five spies spoke to the others. "There is a shrine in there," they said. "It has an ephod and some teraphim. It also has many plated idols. It's obvious what we ought to do!"

15-16So the five men went over to the house. All the armed men stood just outside the gate. They talked to the young priest. And they asked him how he was getting along. 17Then the five spies went into the shrine. They took the idols, the ephod, and the teraphim.

18"What are you doing?" the young priest demanded. For he saw them carrying them out.

19"Be quiet and come with us," they said. "Be a priest to all of us. Wouldn't it be better for you to be a priest to a whole tribe in Israel? Don't settle for serving just one man in his private home!"

20The young priest was then quite happy to go with them. And he took along the ephod, the teraphim, and the idols. 21They started on their way again. But they put their children, cattle, and household goods at the front of the column. ²²They went quite a distance from Micah's home. But then Micah and some of his friends came after them. ²³They called out to them, telling them to stop.

"What do you want? Why are you chasing after us like this?" the men of Dan demanded.

²⁴"What do you mean, 'What do I want'!" Micah shouted. "You've taken away all my gods and my priest! I have nothing left!"

²⁵"Be careful how you talk," the men of Dan replied. "We might get angry and kill every one of you."

²⁶So the men of Dan kept going. Micah saw that there were too many of them for him to handle. So he turned and went back home.

²⁷Then the men of Dan went on to the city of Laish. They brought with them Micah's idols and the priest. When they got there, there weren't even any guards. They went in and killed all the people. Then they burned the city to the ground. ²⁸There was no one to help the people there. They were too far away from Sidon, and they had no local friends. They did not have any dealings with anyone. This happened in the valley next to Beth-rehob. Then the people of the tribe of Dan rebuilt the city and lived there. ²⁹The city was named "Dan" after their ancestor, Israel's son. But it had originally been called Laish.

³⁰Then they set up the idols. They chose a man named Jonathan. He was a son of Gershom and grandson of Moses! They made him and his sons their priests. Members of this family were priests until the city was conquered by its enemies. ³¹So the tribe of Dan worshiped Micah's idols. They did this as long as the Tabernacle was at Shiloh.

A Horrible Crime

19 At this time Israel did not have a king. There was a man from the tribe of Levi. He lived on the far side of the hill country of Ephraim. He brought home a girl from Bethlehem in Judah to be his concubine. ²But she became angry with him and ran away. She went back to her father's home in Bethlehem. And she was there about four months. ³Then her husband went to see her. He took along a servant and an extra donkey. He wanted to try to win her back again. When he got to her home, she let him in. And when her father saw him, he welcomed him. ⁴Her father urged him to stay awhile. So he stayed three days. And they all had a very pleasant time.

⁵On the fourth day they were up early, ready to leave. But the girl's father wanted them to have breakfast first. ⁶Then he pleaded with him to stay one more day. This was because they were having such a good time. ⁷At first the man refused. But his father-in-law kept urging him. And in the end, he gave in. ⁸The next morning they were up early again. But again the girl's father pleaded, "Stay just today. You can leave sometime this evening." So they had another day of feasting.

⁹Later, the man, his wife, and his servant were getting ready to go. But his father-in-law said, "Look, it's getting late. Stay just tonight. We will have a pleasant evening together. Then tomorrow you can get up early and be on your way."

¹⁰But this time the man would not stay. So they left. They got as far as Jerusalem before dark. Jerusalem was called Jebus at that time. ¹¹His servant said to him, "It's getting too late to travel. Let's stay here tonight."

¹²⁻¹³"No," his master said. "We can't stay in this heathen city where there are no Israelites. We will go on to Gibeah, or possibly Ramah."

¹⁴So they went on. The sun was setting just as they came to Gibeah. This was a village of the tribe of Benjamin. ¹⁵So they went there for the night. But no one invited them in. So they camped in the village square. ¹⁶Just then an old man came by. He was on his way home from his work in the fields. He was originally from the hill country of Ephraim. But he was living now in Gibeah. He lived there even though it was in the land of Benjamin. ¹⁷He saw the travelers camped in the square. And he asked

them where they were from and where they were going.

¹⁸"We're on the way home from Bethlehem, in Judah," the man replied. "I live on the far edge of the Ephraim hill country, near Shiloh. But no one has taken us in for the night. ¹⁹We even have food for our donkeys. And we have plenty of food and wine for ourselves."

²⁰"Don't worry," the old man said. "Be my guests. For you must not stay here in the square. It's too dangerous."

²¹So he took them home with him. He fed their donkeys while they rested. After that they had supper together. ²²They were starting to relax and enjoy themselves. But a gang of wicked men gathered around the house. They started beating at the door. They yelled at the old man. They told him to bring out the man who was staying with him. They wanted to rape him. ²³The old man stepped outside to talk to them.

"No, my brothers, don't do such a terrible thing!" he begged. "For he is my guest. ²⁴Here, take my virgin daughter and this man's concubine. I'll bring them out. You can do whatever you like to them. But don't do such a thing to this man."

²⁵But they wouldn't listen to him. Then the girl's husband pushed her out to them. And they abused her all night. They took turns raping her until morning. Finally, just at dawn, they let her go. ²⁶She fell down at the door of the house and lay there until it was light. ²⁷Her husband opened the door to be on his way. He found her there. She had fallen down in front of the door. Her hands were digging into the threshold.

²⁸"Well, come on," he said. "Let's get going."

But there was no answer, for she was dead. So he threw her across the donkey's back and took her home. ²⁹When he got there he took a knife. He cut her body into 12 parts. Then he sent one piece to each tribe of Israel. ³⁰The whole nation was called to action against the men of Benjamin because of this awful deed.

"There hasn't been such a horrible crime since Israel left Egypt," every-one said. "We've got to do something about it!"

Israel Attacks the Tribe of Benjamin

20 The whole nation of Israel gathered before the Lord at Mizpah. They sent their leaders and 450,000 troops to gather there. They came from as far away as Dan and Beersheba, and everywhere in between. They even came from across the Jordan in the land of Gilead. ³Word of this meeting of Israelites at Mizpah soon got to the land of Benjamin. The chiefs of Israel now called for the murdered woman's husband. They asked him just what had happened.

⁴"One evening we came to Gibeah, a village in Benjamin," he began. ⁵"That night the men of Gibeah came to the house. They planned to kill me. And they raped my wife until she was dead. ⁶So I cut her body into 12 pieces. Then I sent the pieces throughout the land of Israel. I did this because these men have done a terrible thing. ⁷Now then, people of Israel, tell me what you think! Give me your advice!"

⁸⁻¹⁰They answered as one person. They said, "We must punish the village of Gibeah. Not one of us will go home until we have done this. A 10th of the army will be chosen by lot. They will be a supply line to bring us food. The rest of us will destroy Gibeah for this terrible deed."

¹¹So the whole nation united in this task.

¹²Then messengers were sent to the tribe of Benjamin. They asked, "Did you know about the terrible thing that was done among you? ¹³Give up these evil men from the city of Gibeah. Then we will be able to execute them. That way we will purge Israel of her evil." But the people of Benjamin wouldn't listen. ¹⁴⁻¹⁵Instead, 26,000 of them went to Gibeah. They went there to join the 700 local fighting men. Together they planned to defend the city against the rest of Israel. ¹⁶Among all these there were 700 left-handed soldiers. They could sling stones at a target and hit

within a hair's breadth. They never missed! ¹⁷The army of Israel numbered 400,000 men. This did not include the men of Benjamin.

¹⁸Before the battle the Israelite army went to Bethel. They went there to ask counsel from God. "Which tribe shall lead us against the people of Benjamin?" they asked.

And the Lord replied, "Judah shall go first."

¹⁹⁻²⁰So the whole army left early the next morning. They went to Gibeah to attack the men of Benjamin. ²¹But the men defending the village stormed out. They killed 22,000 Israelites that day. ²²⁻²⁴Then the Israelite army wept before the Lord until evening. They asked him, "Shall we fight further against our brother Benjamin?"

And the Lord said, "Yes." So the men of Israel took courage. They went out again the next day to fight at the same place. ²⁵And that day they lost another 18,000 men. And they were all skilled swordsmen.

²⁶Then the whole army went up to Bethel. They wept there before the Lord and fasted until evening. They gave burnt sacrifices and peace offerings. ²⁷⁻²⁸The Ark of God was in Bethel in those days. Phinehas, the son of Eleazar and grandson of Aaron, was the priest.

The men of Israel asked the Lord, "Shall we go out again? Shall we fight against our brother Benjamin, or shall we stop?"

And the Lord said, "Go! Tomorrow I will see to it that you defeat the men of Benjamin."

²⁹So the Israelite army set an ambush all around the village. ³⁰Then they went out again on the third day. And they set themselves in their usual battle formation. ³¹The army of Benjamin came out of the town to attack. When they did, the Israelite forces ran away. In this way, Benjamin was drawn away from the town as they chased after Israel. And as before, Benjamin began to kill the men of Israel. They did this along the roadway running between Bethel and Gibeah. About 30 of the men of Israel died.

³²Then the army of Benjamin shouted, "We're beating them again!" But the armies of Israel had planned to run away. They wanted the army of Benjamin to chase them. That way they would be drawn away from the town. ³³So the main army of Israel reached Baal-tamar. At that point it turned and attacked. And the 10,000 men in ambush west of Geba jumped up from where they were. ³⁴They advanced against the rear of the army of Benjamin. The Benjaminites still didn't know that they were about to be destroyed. ³⁵⁻³⁹So the Lord helped Israel defeat Benjamin. And the Israelite army killed 25,100 men of Benjamin that day. They left only a small group of them alive.

Summary of the Battle: The army of Israel ran from the men of Benjamin. They did this to give the ambush more room to work. The men of Benjamin killed about 30 of the Israelites. They were sure that they would kill many Israelites just as they had before. But then the men in ambush rushed into the village. They killed everyone in it. Then they set it on fire. A great cloud of smoke poured into the sky. It signalled the Israelite army to turn around and attack the army of Benjamin. ⁴⁰⁻⁴¹They looked behind them and they were terrified. They saw that their city was on fire. And they knew they were in serious trouble. ⁴²So they ran toward the wilderness. But the Israelites chased after them. And the men who had set the ambush came out. They joined the attack from behind. ⁴³They made a circle around the army of Benjamin east of Gibeah. They then killed most of them there. ⁴⁴Eighteen thousand of the Benjamin troops died in that day's battle. ⁴⁵The rest of the army ran into the wilderness. They went toward the rock of Rimmon. But 5,000 were killed along the way, and 2,000 more near Gidom.

⁴⁶⁻⁴⁷So the tribe of Benjamin lost 25,000 brave warriors that day. That left only 600 men who got to the rock of Rimmon. They lived there for four months. ⁴⁸Then the Israelite army went back. They killed all the people of the tribe of Benjamin. This included men,

women, children, and cattle. And they burned down every city and village in the whole land.

Wives for the Men of Benjamin

21 The leaders of Israel had made a vow at Mizpah. They promised never to let their daughters marry a man from the tribe of Benjamin. ²And now the Israelite leaders met at Bethel. They sat before God until evening. They cried bitterly.

³"O Lord God of Israel," they cried out. "Why has this happened? How is it that now one of our tribes is missing?"

⁴The next morning they were up early. They built an altar. And on it, they offered sacrifices and peace offerings. ⁵They said among themselves, "We held our council before the Lord at Mizpah. When we met, was any tribe of Israel not there?" At that time it was agreed that anyone who refused to come must die. They agreed this by solemn oath. ⁶There was deep sadness throughout all Israel. This was because they had lost their brother tribe, Benjamin.

"Gone," they kept saying to themselves. "A whole tribe of Israel has been cut off and is gone. ⁷And how shall we get wives for the few who are still alive? We promised by the Lord that we would not give them our daughters."

⁸⁻⁹Then they thought again of their oath to kill anyone who did not come to Mizpah. And they found that no one had come from Jabesh-gilead. ¹⁰⁻¹²So they sent 12,000 of their best soldiers to destroy the people of Jabesh-gilead. All the men, married women, and children were killed. But the young virgins that could be married were saved. There were 400 of these. And they were brought to the camp at Shiloh.

¹³Then Israel chose a group to carry a message of peace. They went to the small group of the men of Benjamin at Rimmon Rock. ¹⁴The 400 girls were given to them as wives. And they went back to their homes. But there were not enough of these girls for all of them. ¹⁵What a sad time it was in Israel in those days! For the Lord had separated the tribes of Israel.

¹⁶"What shall we do for wives for the others?" the leaders asked. "All the women of the tribe of Benjamin are dead. ¹⁷There must be some way to get wives for them. That way the whole tribe of Israel will not be lost for all time. ¹⁸But we can't give them our own daughters. We have made a solemn oath. We have promised that anyone who does this shall be cursed of God."

¹⁹Suddenly someone thought of a yearly religious feast. It was observed in the fields of Shiloh, between Lebonah and Bethel. They held the feast along the east side of the road that goes from Bethel to Shechem.

²⁰They spoke to the men of Benjamin who still needed wives. "Go and hide in the vineyards," they told them. ²¹"And the girls of Shiloh will come out for their dances. When they do, rush out and catch them. Take them home with you to be your wives! ²²Their fathers and brothers will come to us in protest. When they do, we will speak to them. We will tell them, 'Please let them have your daughters. For we didn't find enough wives for them when we destroyed Jabesh-gilead. And you couldn't have given your daughters to them without being guilty.'"

²³So the men of Benjamin did as they were told. They took the girls who took part in the dance. They carried them off to their own land. Then they rebuilt their cities and lived in them. ²⁴So the people of Israel went back to their homes.

²⁵There was no king in Israel in those days. And every man did whatever he thought was right.

RUTH

Ruth lived during the time of the Judges. It was a bad time to live. People lived a rough-and-tumble life. This was the "Wild West" days of the Bible, when people often took the law into their own hands. But the story of Ruth is a sweet story about a loving, unselfish young lady. Ruth was like a star shining in a dark sky. Ruth was like a beautiful flower blooming in a mud puddle. There is only one other book in the Bible about a woman. Her name was Esther. She was an Israelite in a foreign land. Ruth was a foreigner in Israel.

Ruth was such a wonderful person that thousands of parents have named their daughters after her. Do you know someone named Ruth? Ruth's story is about faithfulness and loyalty. It is about an unselfish young lady who became the great-grandmother of King David. Hundreds of years later a baby named Jesus would be born in Bethlehem. Ruth was his great-great-great grandmother with a dozen or more greats added. You'll want to read about Ruth. Who knows? Someday you may name your daughter after her!

Ruth Goes Home with Naomi

Naomi and her husband lived in Moab. That was a foreign country. People there did not believe in God. While they were there, Naomi's husband died. Then her two married sons died. You can imagine how sad she felt about that. Naomi was alone in Moab with her two Moabite daughters-in-law. Naomi needed a loyal friend. Were these Moabite girls her friends?

1 This happened long ago when the judges ruled in Israel. A man named Elimelech, from Bethlehem, left the country of Israel. He did this because there was a famine there. He moved to the land of Moab. His wife, Naomi, went with him. And they brought their two sons, Mahlon and Chilion. ³While they lived there, Elimelech died. So Naomi was left with her two sons.

4-5These young men, Mahlon and Chilion, married girls from Moab. Their names were Orpah and Ruth. But later, both men died. So Naomi was left alone, without her husband or sons. 6-7She decided to go back to Israel with her daughters-in-law. She had heard that the Lord had blessed his people. She was told that the Lord had once again given them good crops.

When we love someone we want to be with them

I want to go wherever you go.
I want to live wherever you live.
Your people shall be my people.
And your God shall be my God.

Ruth 1:16

8But after they had begun their homeward journey, she changed her mind. She spoke to her two daughters-in-law. She said, "Why don't you go back to your parents' homes instead of coming with me? And may the Lord reward you. You have been faithful to your husbands and to me. 9And may he bless you with another happy marriage." Then she kissed them. And they all broke down and cried.

10"No," they said. "We want to go with you to your people."

11But Naomi replied, "It is better for you to go back to your own people. Do I have younger sons who could grow up to be your husbands? 12No, my daughters, go back to your parents' homes. I am too old to have a husband. And what if that were possible? What if I did become pregnant tonight and sons were born? 13Even if this happened, would you wait for them to grow up? No, of course not, my daughters. Oh, how I grieve for you! I am sad that the Lord has punished me in a way that hurts you too."

14And again they cried together. So Orpah kissed her mother-in-law goodbye. She went back to her childhood home. But Ruth held on to Naomi. She would not leave her.

15"See," Naomi said to her. "Your sister-in-law has gone back to her people and to her gods. You should do the same."

16But Ruth replied, "Don't make me leave you. I want to go wherever you go. I want to live wherever you live. Your people shall be my people. And your God shall be my God. 17I want to die where you die and be buried there. May the Lord do terrible things to me if I let anything but death come between us!"

18Naomi saw that Ruth had made up her mind. She saw that nothing could make her leave. So she stopped urging her to go. 19And they both came to Bethlehem. When they got there, the whole village was stirred by their coming.

"Is it really Naomi?" the women asked.

20But she told them, "Don't call me Naomi. Call me Mara." Naomi means "pleasant." But Mara means "bitter." "Almighty God has dealt me bitter blows," she said. 21"I went out full and the Lord has brought me home empty. Why should you call me Naomi? For the Lord has turned his back on me! He has sent great calamity my way!"

22They came from Moab and got to Bethlehem at the beginning of the barley harvest.

- *Remember:* Why did Naomi ask her daughters-in-law to go home to Moab? (1:8-13) Which one went home? Which one stayed with Naomi? (2:14) Why did Ruth go with Naomi? (1:16-17) Which of these words tells about Ruth—angry, loyal, or dishonest? Why?

- *Discover:* A true friend is a loyal friend. A true family member is a loyal family member.

- *Apply:* Someone at school makes fun of your brother or sister. Are you loyal to your family? What should you do?

- *What's next?* Have you ever needed a friend? Ruth did. This friend helped her when she really needed help. Read Ruth 2. ■

Ruth Gleans in the Fields

Gleaning was no fun. Poor people walked behind reapers in grain fields. They picked up wheat or barley grains the reapers missed. That's how gleaners got their food. This was what Ruth had to do. There were no grocery stores in her day.

2 Now Naomi had a relative there in Bethlehem. He was a very rich man. His name was Boaz.

²One day Ruth spoke to Naomi. She said, "Let me go out into the fields. Perhaps someone will be kind to me. Maybe he will let me glean the grain dropped by the reapers."

Naomi said, "All right, dear daughter. Go ahead."

³So she did. And as it happened, the field where she found herself belonged to Boaz. He was a close relative of Naomi's husband.

⁴⁻⁵Boaz came out from the city while she was there. After greeting his reapers he spoke to his foreman. "Hey, who's that girl over there?" he asked.

⁶And the foreman replied, "It's that girl from the land of Moab. She came back with Naomi. ⁷She asked me this morning if she could pick up the grain dropped by the reapers. She has been at it ever since. She has only taken a few minutes' rest over there in the shade."

⁸⁻⁹Boaz went over and talked to her. "Listen, my child," he said to her. "Stay right here with us to glean. Don't think of going to any other fields. Stay right behind my women workers. I have warned the young men not to bother you. When you are thirsty, go and help yourself to the water."

¹⁰⁻¹¹She thanked him warmly. "How can you be so kind to me?" she asked. "You must know I am only a foreigner."

"Yes, I know," Boaz replied. "I also know about the love and kindness you have shown your mother-in-law. You helped her even after the death of your husband. And I heard how you left your father and mother in your own land. You did this to come here to live among strangers. ¹²May the Lord God of Israel bless you for it. May you find shelter in the Lord. For you have come under his wings to take refuge."

¹³"Oh, thank you, sir," she replied. "You are so good to me! And I'm not even one of your workers!"

¹⁴At lunch time Boaz called to her, "Come and eat with us."

So she sat with his reapers. And he gave her more food than she could eat. ¹⁵She went back to work again. And when she did, Boaz told his young men to let her glean right among the sheaves. They were not to stop her. ¹⁶He even told them to snap off some heads of barley. They were to drop them on purpose for her to glean. And they were not to say anything about it. ¹⁷So she worked there all day. And in the evening she beat out the barley she had gleaned. It came to a whole bushel! ¹⁸She carried it back into the city and gave it to her mother-in-law. She also brought home what was left of her lunch.

¹⁹"So much!" Naomi exclaimed. "Where in the world did you glean today? Praise the Lord for whoever was so kind to you." So Ruth told her mother-in-law all about it. And she mentioned that the owner of the field was Boaz.

²⁰"Praise the Lord for a man like that! God has been kind to us and to your dead husband!" Naomi cried excitedly. "Why, that man is one of our closest relatives!"

²¹"Well," Ruth said, "he told me to

come back. He said to stay close behind his reapers until the whole field is harvested!"

²²"This is wonderful!" Naomi exclaimed. "Do as he has said. Stay with his girls right through the whole harvest. You will be safer there than in any other field!"

²³So Ruth did. She gleaned with them until the end of the barley harvest. Then she gleaned with them during the wheat harvest too.

● *Remember:* Did Naomi tell Ruth to gather grain? Or did Ruth want to do it? (2:2) How was Boaz kind to Ruth? (2:8-9, 14-16) How do you know that Ruth was thankful? (2:10-11) How was Ruth kind to Naomi? (2:10-12) How do you think Boaz would have treated Ruth if she had been mean to Naomi? What did you learn about kindness from Ruth and Boaz?

● *Discover:* Kind people are often rewarded with kindness.

● *Apply:* Do you want others to be kind to you? Be kind to others first. Then others will want to be kind to you. Think of someone who has been kind to you this week. Will you do something kind to that person today?

● *What's next?* There are many ways to say, "Let's get married." You will read about a very different way in Ruth 3–4. ▪

Ruth Marries Boaz

Here is a young woman who asks an older man to marry her. But she asks him because her mother-in-law tells her to do it. Will the man say yes?

3 One day Naomi spoke to Ruth. "My dear, it is time that I found a husband for you," she said. "It is time you were happily married. ²The man I'm thinking of is Boaz! He has been so kind to us and is a close relative. I happen to know that he will be winnowing barley tonight out on the threshing-floor. ³Now do what I tell you. Take a bath and put on some perfume. Dress up in some nice clothes. Then go on down to the threshing-floor. But don't let him see you until he has finished his supper. ⁴Notice where he lies down to sleep. Then go and lift the cover off his feet and lie down there. He will tell you what to do about getting married."

⁵And Ruth replied, "All right. I'll do whatever you say."

⁶⁻⁷So she went down to the threshing-floor that night. She did all that her mother-in-law had told her. Boaz ate a good meal. After he was finished he lay down beside a heap of grain. And there he went to sleep. Then Ruth came quietly. She lifted the covering off his feet and lay there. ⁸Suddenly, around midnight, he woke up. He sat up, startled. There was a woman lying at his feet!

⁹"Who are you?" he demanded.

"It's I, sir, Ruth," she replied. "Make me your wife according to God's law. For you are my close relative."

¹⁰"Thank God for a girl like you!" he exclaimed. "For you are being even kinder to Naomi now than before. Surely you would rather marry a younger man, even though poor. But you have put aside your personal desires. ¹¹Now don't worry about a thing, my child. I'll handle all the details. Everyone knows what a wonderful person you are. ¹²But there is one problem. It's true that I am a close relative. But there is someone else who is closer to you than I am. ¹³Stay here tonight. In the morning I'll talk to him. If he will marry you, fine. Let him do his duty. But if he won't, then I will. I swear this by the

name of the Lord. Now lie down until the morning."

¹⁴So she lay at his feet until the morning. But she was up early, before daybreak. He had said to her, "Don't let it be known that a woman was here at the threshing-floor."

¹⁵⁻¹⁸"Bring your shawl," he told her. Then he tied up a bushel and a half of barley in it. It was a present for her mother-in-law. He laid it on her back. Then she went back to the city.

"Well, what happened, dear?" Naomi asked her when she got home. Ruth told Naomi everything. She gave her the barley

from Boaz. She also mentioned his remark that she mustn't go home without a gift.

Then Naomi said to her, "Just be patient until we hear what happens. Boaz won't rest until he has followed through on this. He'll settle it today."

4 So Boaz went down to the market. There he found the relative he had spoken of.

"Say, come over here," he called to him. "I want to talk to you a minute."

So they sat down together. ²Then Boaz called for 10 of the chief men of the village. He asked them to sit as witnesses.

³Boaz said to his relative, "You know Naomi. She is the one who came back to us from Moab. She is selling our brother Elimelech's property. ⁴I felt that I should speak to you about it. That way you can buy it if you wish. And these chief men will stand as witnesses. If you want it, let me know right away. For if you don't take it, I will. You have the first right to buy it and I'm next."

The man replied, "All right, I'll buy it."

⁵Then Boaz told him, "If you buy the land from Naomi, you must also marry Ruth. That way she can have children. They will then carry on her husband's name and inherit the land."

⁶"Then I can't do it," the man replied. "For her son would become an heir to my property too. You buy it."

⁷In those days there was the custom in Israel that a man who gave up a right to buy something was to pull off his sandal. Then he was to hand it to the person he was giving his right to. This made the transfer of his right public and legal. ⁸So, as the man said to Boaz, "You buy it," he drew off his sandal.

⁹Then Boaz spoke to the witnesses and to the crowd standing there. "You have seen that today I have bought all the property of Elimelech, Chilion, and Mahlon, from Naomi," he said. ¹⁰"And with it, I have bought Ruth the Moabitess. She is the widow of Mahlon. And she will be my wife. That way she can have a son. And he will carry on the family

name for her dead husband."

¹¹And all the people standing there and the witnesses replied, "We are witnesses. This woman will now come into your home. May the Lord give her as many children as Rachel and Leah! For the whole nation of Israel came from them! May you be a great man in Bethlehem. ¹²Perez, the son of Tamar and Judah, had many honored descendants. May the Lord give you as many from this young woman! And may they be just as honored!"

¹³So Boaz married Ruth. And when he slept with her, the Lord gave her a son.

¹⁴And the women of the city said to Naomi, "Bless the Lord! For he has given you this little grandson. May he be famous in Israel. ¹⁵May he restore your youth. And may he take care of you in your old age. For he is the son of your daughter-in-law who loves you so much. And she has been kinder to you than seven sons!"

¹⁶⁻¹⁷Naomi took care of the baby. And the other women said, "Now at last Naomi has a son again!"

And they named him Obed. He was the father of Jesse and grandfather of King David.

¹⁸⁻²²This is the family tree of Boaz. It begins with his ancestor Perez: Perez, Hezron, Ram, Amminadab, Nashon, Salmon, Boaz, Obed, Jesse, David.

- *Remember:* Who told Ruth to get married? What did she say? (3:1-4) Did Ruth argue with Naomi? What did she say to her? (3:5) How did Ruth ask Boaz to marry her? What did she do? (3:6-9) What did Boaz say about this? (3:10-12) How did Boaz publicly arrange to marry Ruth? (4:1-12) A famous king became the grandson of Ruth's and Boaz's son. Who was he? (4:17) Do you think King David liked the story of his great-grandparents' marriage? Do you think he told it to his children?

- *Discover:* Ruth and Boaz were very unselfish people. God blessed them. Their son became the grandfather of the most famous king in the Bible. God does special things for unselfish people.

- *Apply:* Do something unselfish today that will please your mother or father. Do this even though you may not want to.

- *What's next?* A woman gives her son to someone else. You'll learn why in 1 Samuel 1. ▪

FIRST SAMUEL

This is a book of high adventure. Get ready to see a young boy challenge a nine-foot-high giant to a fight. You'll also see a young man and his armor bearer fight a whole army. You'll listen quietly as God talks with a boy one night. You'll read about two of the best friends who ever lived. You'll see a king who begs a witch to help him, and a beautiful young lady who stops a big fight. In 1 Samuel you'll meet warriors called Philistines. You'll see them capture God's golden chest, but then try desperately to give it back. First Samuel is a book about brave heroes and cowardly villains. It is a book about a shepherd boy who becomes king.

First Samuel is about a change of leaders. Israel had been ruled by judges. But the people wanted a king, so God let them have a king. First Samuel tells about the failures of the first king, Saul. He failed because he did not obey and trust God. God wanted a king who would obey him and trust him. That's why he chose David to be the next king. He wants us to obey him and trust him, too. The adventures of Saul and David are exciting! But they also help you know what you should do for God.

Samuel Is Born

How much would you give to God? Would you give all your money? Would you give your best toys? Here is a story about a woman who gave her little boy to God. She gave God what she loved most.

1 This is the story of Elkanah. He was a man of the tribe of Ephraim. He lived in Ramathaim-zophim. This was in the hills of Ephraim.

His father's name was Jeroham.

His grandfather was Elihu.
His great-grandfather was Tohu.
His great-great-grandfather was Zuph.

²He had two wives, Hannah and

Peninnah. Peninnah had some children, but Hannah had none.

³Each year Elkanah and his families went to the Tabernacle at Shiloh. There they worshiped the Lord of the heavens. They sacrificed to him. The priests on duty then were the two sons of Eli. Their names were Hophni and Phinehas. ⁴The day came when Elkanah gave his sacrifice. When he did this, he always gave a share of meat to Peninnah and her children. ⁵But he always gave a special share of the meat to Hannah. He did this because he loved her and because the Lord had kept her from having children. ⁶But Peninnah made matters worse by making fun of Hannah. She did this because Hannah had no children. ⁷Every year it was the same. Peninnah laughed at her as they went to Shiloh. She made Hannah cry so much she could not eat.

⁸"What's the matter, Hannah?" Elkanah would ask. "Why aren't you eating? Why make such a fuss over having no children? Isn't having me better than having 10 sons?"

⁹One evening after supper Hannah went over to the Tabernacle. Eli the priest was sitting at his normal place beside the door. ¹⁰She was in deep sorrow. She was crying as she prayed to the Lord.

¹¹And she made a promise to the Lord. "O Lord of heaven," she said. "Please, look down upon my sorrow. Please, answer my prayer and give me a son. If you do, then I will give him back to you. He'll be yours for his whole lifetime. And his hair shall never be cut."

¹²⁻¹³Eli saw her mouth moving as she prayed to herself. Since he heard no sound, he thought she had been drinking.

¹⁴"Must you come here drunk?" he shouted. "Throw away your wine!"

¹⁵⁻¹⁶"Oh no, sir!" she replied. "I'm not drunk! But I am very sad. I was pouring out my heart to the Lord. Please don't think that I am drunk!"

¹⁷"In that case," Eli said, "cheer up! May the Lord give you what you asked for, whatever it is!"

¹⁸"Oh, thank you, sir!" she said. So she went back happy, and began to eat her meals again.

¹⁹⁻²⁰The whole family was up early the next morning. They went to the Tabernacle to worship the Lord once more. Then they went back home to Ramah. And when Elkanah slept with Hannah, the Lord did not forget what she had asked for. In due time, a baby boy was born to her. She named him Samuel. His name means "asked of God." For she said, "I asked the Lord for him."

²¹⁻²²The next year Elkanah and Peninnah and her children went on the yearly trip to the Tabernacle. But they went without Hannah. She told her husband, "Wait until the baby is ready to eat food. Then I will take him to the Tabernacle and leave him there."

²³"Well, do what you think is best," Elkanah agreed. "May the Lord's will be done."

So she stayed home until the baby was able to eat solid food. ²⁴Then they took him to the Tabernacle in Shiloh. He was still a very small boy at the time. They also brought along a three-year-old bull for the sacrifice. A bushel of flour and some wine were brought for other offerings. ²⁵After the sacrifice they took the child to Eli.

²⁶"Sir, do you remember me?" Hannah asked him. "I am the woman who stood here that time praying to the Lord! ²⁷I asked him to give me this child. And he has given me what I asked for! ²⁸Now I am giving him to the Lord for as long as he lives." So she left him there at the Tabernacle for the Lord to use.

• *Remember:* Why was Hannah so sad? (1:1-7) What did Hannah want? (1:11) What did Hannah promise to do if God gave her a son? (1:11) What did Hannah name her baby? Why? (1:19-20) Hannah gave Samuel to someone. Who? Why did she do this? (1:27) How important was God to Hannah? How do you know that?

• *Discover:* God gives us his best. Shouldn't we want to give God our best?

• *Apply:* When you read your Bible or pray, do you give your best time of the day to God? Or do you do these things when you have nothing else to do? How can you do better? Do you do your best work for God or for yourself? How can you do better?

- *What's next?* God talks to a young boy instead of an important man. Why? You'll find out in 1 Samuel 3. ◾

Hannah's Prayer of Thanks

2 This was Hannah's prayer:
"How I rejoice in the Lord!
How he has blessed me!
Now I have an answer for my
    enemies,
For the Lord has solved my problem.
How I rejoice!
²No one is as holy as the Lord!
There is no other God,
Nor any Rock like our God.
³Quit acting so proud!
The Lord knows what you have
    done,
And he will judge your deeds.
⁴Those who were mighty are
    mighty no more!
Those who were weak are now
    strong.
⁵Those who were well are now
    starving.
Those who were starving are fed.
The barren woman now has seven
    children.
She with many children has no
    more!
⁶The Lord kills,
The Lord gives life.
⁷Some he causes to be poor
And others to be rich.
He cuts one down
And lifts another up.
⁸He lifts the poor from the dust.
Yes, he lifts them from a pile of
    ashes.
And treats them as princes
Sitting in the seats of honor.
For all the earth is the Lord's
And he has set the world in order.
⁹He will protect his godly ones,
But the wicked shall be silenced in
    darkness.
No one shall succeed by strength
    alone.
¹⁰Those who fight against the Lord
    shall be broken.

He thunders against them from
    heaven.
He judges throughout the earth.
He gives mighty strength to his
    King,
And gives great glory to his
    anointed one."

¹¹So they went home to Ramah without Samuel. And the child became the Lord's helper. He helped Eli the priest in the Tabernacle.

Samuel Serves the Lord

¹²Now the sons of Eli were evil men. They didn't love the Lord. ¹³⁻¹⁴They often sent their servants to the people who were offering sacrifices. The meat of the sacrificed animal would be boiling in a pot. The servants would put a three-pronged hook into the pot. Then they would demand that the meat it brought up be given to Eli's sons. They treated all the Israelites this way when they came to Shiloh to worship. ¹⁵Sometimes the servants would come even before the fat had been burned on the altar. They would demand raw meat before it was boiled. They did this so they could roast it.

**Be glad when God does
good things for you**

How I rejoice in the Lord!

1 Samuel 2:1

---

¹⁶The man offering the sacrifice might say, "Take as much as you want. But the fat must first be burned as the law says it should." But though the offerer might say this, the servants would not agree. They would say,

"No! Give it to us now! If you don't, we'll take it by force."

¹⁷So the sin of these young men was very great in the eyes of the Lord. They did not show respect for the people's offerings to the Lord.

¹⁸Samuel, though only a child, was the Lord's helper. He wore a little linen robe just like the priest's. ¹⁹Each year his mother made a little coat for him. She brought it to him when she came with her husband for the sacrifice. ²⁰Before

they went back home, Eli would bless Elkanah and Hannah. He asked God to give them other children. They would take the place of this one they had given to the Lord. 21And the Lord gave Hannah three sons and two daughters. Meanwhile, Samuel grew up in the service of the Lord.

22Eli was now very old. But he knew what was going on around him. He knew that his sons were doing things that were wrong. They were even sleeping with the young women who helped at the door of the Tabernacle!

23-25"I have been hearing bad reports from the Lord's people," Eli told his sons. "Why are you doing all these bad things? It is a bad thing to make the Lord's people sin. Ordinary sin will be punished greatly. But you will be punished even more! This sin of yours has been done against the Lord!" But they wouldn't listen to their father. For the Lord was already planning to kill them.

26Little Samuel was growing in two ways. He was getting taller. And he was becoming the peoples' favorite. He was favored by the Lord!

A Prophet Speaks to Eli

27One day a prophet came to Eli. He gave him this message from the Lord. "Did I not show my power when the people of Israel were slaves in Egypt?" he asked. 28"Did I not choose your ancestor Levi from among all his brothers to be my priest? Was he not chosen to give sacrifices on my altar and to burn incense?

Did I not choose him to wear a priestly robe as he served me? And did I not give the sacrifices to you priests? 29Then why are you so greedy for all the other offerings which are brought to me? Why have you honored your sons more than me? You and they have become fat! You have eaten from the best of the offerings of my people!

30"Therefore, I, the Lord God of Israel, make a promise. I once said that your branch of the tribe of Levi could always be my priests. But, even so, what you are doing cannot go on. I will honor only those who honor me. I will hate those who hate me. 31I will put an end to your family. They will no longer serve as priests. Every member will die before his time. None shall live to be old. 32You will want all the riches I will give my people. But you and your family will be in distress and need. Not one of them will live out his days. 33Those who are left alive will live in sadness and grief. And their children shall die by the sword. 34I will prove that what I have said will come true! I will cause your two sons, Hophni and Phinehas, to die on the same day!

35"Then I will choose a faithful priest. He will serve me and do whatever I tell him to do. I will bless his descendants. And his family shall be priests to my kings forever. 36Then your descendants shall bow before him. They will beg him for money and food. 'Please!' they will say. 'Give me a job among the priests. That way I will have enough to eat.'"

God Speaks to Samuel

Eli was the most important priest in all Israel. Samuel was only a little boy who helped Eli. One night God gave an important message. He didn't speak to Eli. He spoke to Samuel. You'll find out why as you read on.

3 Meanwhile, little Samuel was helping the Lord by serving Eli. Messages from the Lord were very rare in those days. 2-3One night, Eli went to bed and Samuel was sleeping in the Temple near

the Ark. Eli was very old and almost blind by now. 4-5That night, the Lord called out, "Samuel! Samuel!"

"Yes?" Samuel replied. "What is it?" He jumped up and ran to Eli. "Here I am.

What do you want?" he asked.

"I didn't call you," Eli said. "Go on back to bed." So he did. 6Then the Lord called again, "Samuel!" And again Samuel jumped up and ran to Eli.

"Yes?" he asked. "What do you need?"

"No, I didn't call you, my son," Eli said. "Go back to bed."

7Samuel had never had a message from the Lord before. 8So now the Lord called the third time. Once more Samuel jumped up and ran to Eli.

"Yes?" he asked. "What do you need?"

Then Eli knew it was the Lord who had spoken to the child. 9So he said to Samuel, "Go and lie down again. If he calls you again, say, 'Yes, Lord, I'm listening.'" So Samuel went back to bed.

10And the Lord came and called as before, "Samuel! Samuel!"

And Samuel replied, "Yes, Lord, I'm listening."

11Then the Lord said to Samuel, "I am going to do a shocking thing in Israel.

12I am going to do all the things I warned Eli about. 13I have warned him and his whole family. I have told him I will punish them because his sons do not respect God. But still Eli does not stop them. 14So I have made a promise. The sins of Eli and his sons shall never be forgiven by sacrifices and offerings."

15Samuel stayed in bed until morning. Then he opened the doors of the Temple as usual. He was afraid to tell Eli what the Lord had said to him. 16-17But Eli called him.

We should listen to God

If he calls you again, say,
"Yes, Lord, I'm listening."

1 Samuel 3:9

"My son," he said, "what did the Lord say to you? Tell me everything. And may God punish you if you hide anything from me!"

18So Samuel told him what the Lord had said.

"It is the Lord's will," Eli replied. "Let him do what he thinks best."

¹⁹As Samuel grew, the Lord was with him. And the people listened to what he said. ²⁰All the people of Israel knew that Samuel was going to be a prophet of the Lord. ²¹⁻⁴:¹Then the Lord began to give messages to him there at the Tabernacle in Shiloh. And he passed them on to the people of Israel.

- *Remember:* How was Samuel helping the Lord at the Tabernacle? (3:1) How many times did the Lord call to Samuel? Who did Samuel think was calling each time? (3:4-10) What did the Lord say to Samuel? (3:11-14) Why did people listen to Samuel as he grew older? (3:19) God

had something important to say. But he said it to a young boy. Why? Because God knew the young boy would listen. Do you spend time each day listening for God?

- *Discover:* God doesn't speak to us with a human voice today. He speaks to us from the pages of the Bible. That is his Word to us.

- *Apply:* How can you listen to God today? Read your Bible. God will tell you something important as you read it. It doesn't matter if you are old or young. What matters is that you are ready for God to talk to you.

- *What's next?* The Ark of the Covenant is stolen from Israel. Read about this in 1 Samuel 4. ■

The Ark Is Stolen

The Ark was the most important object in Israel. It was a golden chest that held the Ten Commandments. God wrote these commandments with his own finger. Israel could not lose something this important. If they did, it would seem that God had left them. But they did lose it. This is how it happened.

4 At that time Israel was at war with the Philistines. The Israelite army was camped near Ebenezer. The Philistines were camped at Aphek. ²And the Philistines defeated Israel. They killed 4,000 of them. ³After the battle was over, the army of Israel went back to their camp. There the leaders talked about why the Lord had let them be beaten. "Let's bring the Ark here from Shiloh," they said. "We will carry it into battle with us. If we do, the Lord will be with us. He will surely save us from our enemies."

⁴So they sent for the Ark of the Lord of heaven who sits above the angels. Hophni and Phinehas, the sons of Eli, came with it into the battle. ⁵The Israelites saw the Ark coming. And their shout of joy was very loud. It was so loud that

it almost made the ground shake!

⁶"What's going on?" the Philistines asked. "What's all the shouting about over in the camp of the Hebrews?"

They were told it was because the Ark of the Lord had come. ⁷So they became afraid.

"God has come into their camp!" they cried out. "We're in trouble! We have never had to face anything like this before! ⁸Who can save us from these mighty gods of Israel? They are the same gods who destroyed the Egyptians. They destroyed them with plagues when Israel was in the wilderness. ⁹Fight as you never have before, O Philistines. For if we don't, we will become their slaves just as they have been ours."

¹⁰So the Philistines fought hard and Israel was beaten again. In fact, 30,000

men of Israel died that day. The rest of them ran to their tents. ¹¹The Ark of God was taken captive. And Hophni and Phinehas were killed in the battle.

¹²A man from the tribe of Benjamin ran from the battle. He got to Shiloh that same day. He had torn his clothes and put dirt on his head. ¹³Eli was waiting beside the road to hear the news of the battle. He was afraid for the safety of the Ark of God. The messenger came from the battle. He told the people what had happened. Then a great cry arose throughout the city.

¹⁴"What is all the noise about?" Eli asked. And the messenger rushed over to Eli. He told him what had happened. ¹⁵Eli was 98 years old and was blind.

¹⁶"I have just come from the battle. I was there today," he told Eli. ¹⁷"Israel has been beaten. Thousands of the Israelite troops died in the battle. Hophni and Phinehas were killed too. And the Ark has been taken."

¹⁸When the messenger told him what had happened to the Ark, Eli fell backward. He fell from his seat beside the gate. And his neck was broken by the fall. So he died, for he was old and fat. He had judged Israel for 40 years.

Ichabod Is Born

¹⁹Eli's daughter-in-law, Phinehas's wife, was going to have a baby soon. She heard that the Ark had been taken. She also heard that her husband and father-in-law were dead. With this news, her labor pains suddenly began. ²⁰Just before she died, a baby boy was born. The women who were helping her told her it was a boy. They told her everything was all right. But she did not reply or respond in any way. ²¹⁻²²Then she said, "Name the child 'Ichabod.' For Israel's glory is gone." Ichabod means "there is no glory." She named him this because the Ark of God had been taken. She also said it because her husband and father-in-law were dead.

- *Remember:* Who were the armies of Israel fighting? (4:1) Why did the Israelites take the Ark into battle? (4:3) Who won that battle? How was the Ark captured? (4:10-11) Four people in Eli's family died that day. Who were they? (4:11,18-20) Why did Phinehas's wife name her baby Ichabod? (4:21-22) It seemed to these people that God had left them. That would make anyone sad, wouldn't it?

- *Discover:* Things seem dark when we think God is not with us. Things seemed dark to Eli's family when they thought God was not with them. God is not with us when we refuse to invite him to be with us. The Israelites brought the Ark with them into battle, but they forgot to ask God to come along. They thought the Ark was all they needed.

- *Apply:* We are like the Israelites when we carry our Bibles somewhere but forget to ask God to come also. Do you feel like God is with you today? If you think he isn't, things may seem dark or sad. Did you ask him to be with you this morning? If you didn't, stop right now. Ask him!

- *What's next?* Everywhere the stolen Ark goes, people get sick and die. What's happening? Read 1 Samuel 5. ■

Philistines Are Punished

If you do something wrong, how are you punished? The Philistines captured the Ark—the golden chest with the Ten Commandments inside. But God did not want them to have it. This is the way God punished them.

5 The Philistines took the Ark of God from the battle at Ebenezer. They brought it to the temple of their idol Dagon. This temple was in the city of Ashdod. ³The people in the city went to see the Ark the next morning. But they saw that Dagon had fallen with his face to the ground! The idol was bowing before the Ark of the Lord! So they set him up again. ⁴But the next morning the people found the same thing. The idol had fallen facedown before the Ark of the Lord again! This time the idol's head and hands were broken off. They were lying in the doorway. Only the trunk of his body had not been broken. ⁵To this day, Dagon's worshipers will not step on the doorway of his temple in Ashdod.

⁶Then the Lord began to kill the people of Ashdod with a plague. The people of nearby towns were also dying. ⁷The people soon saw what was happening. So they said, "We can't keep the Ark of the God of Israel here any longer. If we do, we will all die along with our god Dagon."

⁸So they called a meeting of the leaders from the five Philistine cities. They came together to decide what to do with the Ark. They decided to take it to Gath. ⁹But when the Ark got to Gath, the Lord began killing its people. Both young and old people died of the plague. And there was great panic. ¹⁰So they sent the Ark to Ekron. But when the people of Ekron saw it coming they were afraid. They cried out, "They are bringing the Ark of the God of Israel here to kill us, too!"

¹¹So they called all the leaders again. They begged them to send the Ark back to its own country. They were afraid that the whole city would die. For the plague had already begun. And great fear was sweeping across the city. ¹²Those who didn't die were deathly sick. There was crying all around the city.

- *Remember:* Where did the Philistines take the Ark first? (5:1-2) What happened to the statue of Dagon then? (5:3-4) What happened to the people then? (5:6) How did the people try to get the Ark away from them? (5:8-12) Why do you think the Philistines were so afraid of the Ark now? (5:11-12) What advice would you have given to them? Why?

- *Discover:* The Philistines thought they had beaten God because they had taken the Ark. They were making fun of God by making fun of the Ark. But no one can defeat God.

- *Apply:* Do you know someone who makes fun of God or the Bible? From where you are, it may seem that God isn't doing anything about it. But he is! The person who thinks he is stronger than God will one day discover how strong God really is.

- *What's next?* The Philistines give some special gifts. Golden rats and golden tumors! Read 1 Samuel 6:1–7:4. ■

The Ark Comes Back

God punished the Philistines as long as they kept the Ark. Before long they couldn't wait to send it home to Israel. "What gift should we send along with it?" they asked. They wanted to send a gift that said, "We were wrong. We're sorry." This is what they sent.

6 The Ark stayed in the Philistine country for seven months. ²Then the Philistines called for their priests and diviners. They asked them, "What shall we do about the Ark of God? How shall we send it back to its own land? And when we do, what sort of gift shall we send with it?"

³"Yes, it should be sent back with a gift," they were told. "Send a guilt offering so that the plague will stop. Then, if it doesn't, you will know God didn't send the plague upon you after all."

⁴⁻⁵"What guilt offering shall we send?" they asked.

And they were told, "Send five gold models of the tumor caused by the plague. And send five gold models of rats. This is because rats have ravaged the whole land. They have overrun the capital cities and villages alike. Send these gifts and then praise the God of Israel. If you do, then maybe he will stop punishing you and your god. ⁶Don't be stubborn and rebel as Pharaoh and the Egyptians did. They wouldn't let Israel go. So God destroyed them with dreadful plagues. ⁷Now build a new cart. Hitch two cows to it that have just had calves. Choose cows that have never been yoked before. Then shut their calves away from them in the barn. ⁸Put the Ark of God on the cart. Put it beside a chest with the gold models of the rats and tumors in it. Then let the cows go wherever they want to. ⁹They might cross the border of our land and go into Beth-shemesh. If they do, then you will know that it was God who brought this plague upon us. But they might not. The cows might go back to their calves. If this happens, then we will know that the plague was not sent by God at all. We will know that the plague just happened by chance."

¹⁰So these orders were carried out. Two cows with newborn calves were hitched to the cart. Then their calves were shut up in the barn. ¹¹Then the Ark of the Lord and the chest with the gold

rats and tumors were put on the cart. ¹²And sure enough, the cows went straight along the road toward Beth-shemesh. They did not turn right or left. And they mooed all the way there. The Philistine leaders followed them as far as the border of Beth-shemesh. ¹³At the time, the people of Beth-shemesh were harvesting wheat in the valley. When they saw the Ark, they went wild with joy!

¹⁴The cart came into the field of a man named Joshua. It stopped there beside a large rock. So the people broke up the wood of the cart for a fire. They killed the cows. Then they sacrificed them to the Lord as a burnt offering. ¹⁵Several men of the tribe of Levi came. They lifted the Ark and the chest with the gold rats and tumors from the cart. They then laid them on the rock. And many burnt sacrifices were given to the Lord that day by the men of Beth-shemesh.

¹⁶The five Philistine leaders watched for awhile. Then they went back to Ekron that same day. ¹⁷The five gold models of tumors were a guilt offering to the Lord. They were sent by the Philistine leaders from the five capital cities. These five cities were Ashdod, Gaza, Ashkelon, Gath, and Ekron. ¹⁸The gold rats were a guilt offering to God for the other Philistine cities. These included the walled cities and the country towns near the five capitals. By the way, the large rock at Beth-shemesh can still be seen in the field of Joshua. ¹⁹But the Lord killed 70 of the men of Beth-shemesh because they looked into the Ark. And the people mourned because the Lord had killed so many people.

²⁰"Who is able to stand before the Lord, this holy God?" they cried out. "Where can we send the Ark from here?"

²¹So they sent messengers to the people at Kiriath-jearim. They told them that the Philistines had brought back the Ark of the Lord.

"Come and get it!" they begged.

7 So the men of Kiriath-jearim came. They took the Ark to the hillside home of Abinadab. They chose his son Eleazar to be in charge of it. ²The Ark stayed there for 20 years. During that time all Israel was sad. It seemed to the people that the Lord had left them.

● *Remember:* The Philistine priests told their leaders how to return the Ark. What gifts did they describe? (6:4-5) What were they to do with cows and a cart? (6:7-9) What did the Israelites do when the Ark came back? (6:14-15)

Why did 70 Israelites die that day? (6:19) What did the others say? (6:20) What would you have thought of the Ark after these things happened?

- *Discover:* God punishes people when they do wrong. He punished the Philistines, the enemy. But he also punished his own people when they did wrong and looked inside the Ark.

- *Apply:* Are you doing something that God does not like? Are you about to do something you know is wrong? Stop! Tell God you're sorry. Ask him to forgive you. Do it now.

- *What's next?* If you want to learn how prayer and thunder helped win a battle, read 1 Samuel 7:3-14. ■

God Sends Thunder

"God will save you from the Philistines," Samuel told his people. How? The Philistines had better weapons. They had a better army. But Samuel and his people had something the Philistines did not have. Read on to learn what that was.

³At that time Samuel spoke to them. "Are you serious about wanting to return to the Lord?" he asked. "If you are, get rid of your idols and choose to obey only the Lord. Then he will save you from the Philistines."

⁴So they destroyed their idols of Baal and Ashtaroth. And they worshiped only the Lord.

⁵Then Samuel told them, "Come to Mizpah. There I will pray to the Lord for you."

⁶So they went there and had a great ceremony. They drew water from the well and poured it out before the Lord. They also went without food all day. This was done to show they were sorry for their sins. It was at Mizpah that Samuel became Israel's judge.

⁷The Philistine leaders heard about

the great crowds at Mizpah. So they called out their army and advanced. The Israelites were afraid when they heard the Philistines were coming.

⁸"Plead with God to save us!" they begged Samuel.

⁹So Samuel took a baby lamb. He offered it to the Lord as a whole burnt offering. Samuel begged him to help Israel and the Lord answered him. ¹⁰Samuel was sacrificing the burnt offering before the Lord. At that time, the Philistines arrived for battle. Then the Lord spoke with a mighty voice of thunder from heaven. This threw the enemy into confusion. As a result, the Israelites defeated them. ¹¹They chased them from Mizpah to Beth-car. And they killed them all along the way. ¹²Samuel then took a stone. He put it between Mizpah and Jeshanah. He named it Ebenezer. This name means, "the Stone of Help." For he said, "The Lord has helped us!" ¹³So the Philistines were beaten. And they didn't invade Israel again at that time. The Lord was against them through the rest of Samuel's lifetime. ¹⁴The Israelite cities between Ekron and Gath were now taken back for Israel. These cities had been taken by the Philistines. The Israelite army rescued them from their Philistine captors. And there was peace between Israel and the Amorites in those days.

- *Remember:* Samuel told his people that God would rescue them. But they had to do two things. What? (7:3) What did the people do then? (7:4) Samuel said he would do something for the people at Mizpah. What? (7:5) Samuel asked God to save his people from the Philistines. What did God send? (7:10) How long did Samuel serve God as judge? (7:15) Would you rather have a big army and the best weapons, or have God helping you? Why?

- *Discover:* God is more powerful than big armies or fearsome weapons. He is more powerful than anything people have. And he wants to use this power to help those who obey him.

- *Apply:* Do you need help? Ask God! Do it now! He can help you in wonderful

ways. He is more powerful than anything else in the world.

- *What's next?* Where is the man who is to become king? He's hiding! Read 1 Samuel 9–10. ■

Samuel the Circuit Rider

¹⁵Samuel was Israel's judge for the rest of his life. ¹⁶He went on a circuit every year. He set up his court first at Bethel, then Gilgal, and then Mizpah. Cases of dispute were brought to him in each of those cities. People also came from all the area around them. ¹⁷Then he would go back to Ramah. This was his home. He would hear cases there too. And he built an altar to the Lord at Ramah.

Israel Demands a King

8 In his old age, Samuel retired. Then he set up his sons as judges in his place. ²Joel and Abijah, his oldest sons, held court in Beersheba. ³But they were not like their father. They were greedy for money. They took bribes and were not fair when they judged people. ⁴Finally the leaders of Israel met in Ramah to talk about this problem with Samuel. ⁵They told him that things were not the same since he retired. They told him that his sons were not good men.

"Give us a king like all the other nations have," they pleaded. ⁶Samuel was very upset. So he went to the Lord for advice.

⁷"Do as they say," the Lord replied. "For I am the one they are rejecting, not you. They do not want me to be their king any longer. ⁸Ever since I brought them from Egypt they have forsaken me. They have followed other gods time after time. Now they are doing the same thing to you. ⁹Do as they ask you to. But warn them about what it will be like to have a king!"

¹⁰So Samuel told the people what the Lord had said.

¹¹"You might insist on having a king," Samuel said. "But if you do, he will take your sons. And he will make them run in front of his chariots. ¹²Some of them will be made to lead his troops into battle. Others will work as slaves.

They will be forced to plow in the royal fields. Then they will harvest his crops without pay. They will also be forced to make his weapons and chariot equipment. ¹³He will take your daughters from you. He will force them to cook and bake for him. They will be forced to make perfumes for him. ¹⁴He will take away the best of your fields, vineyards, and olive groves. And he will give them to his friends. ¹⁵He will take a tenth of your harvest. And he will give it to his favorites. ¹⁶He will demand your slaves and the finest of your children. He will use your animals for his personal gain. ¹⁷He will demand a tenth of your flocks, and you shall be his slaves. ¹⁸You will shed tears because of this king you are asking for. But when you do, the Lord will not help you."

¹⁹But the people did not listen to Samuel's warning.

"Even so, we still want a king," they said. ²⁰"For we want to be like the nations around us. He will rule us and lead us into battle."

²¹So Samuel told the Lord what the people had said. ²²And the Lord replied again, "Then do as they say. Give them a king."

So Samuel agreed and sent the men home again.

Saul Becomes King

Saul didn't really want to be king. So he hid! But someone found him. Did Samuel still let the people make him king?

9 Kish was a rich man from the tribe of Benjamin. He was the son of Abiel and grandson of Zeror. He was the great-grandson of Becorath, and great-great-grandson of Aphiah. ²His son Saul was the most handsome man in Israel. He was head and shoulders taller than anyone else in the land!

³One day Kish's donkeys ran away. So he sent Saul and a servant to look for them. ⁴They traveled all through the hill country of Ephraim. They went to the land of Shalisha and to the Shaalim area. They also walked the whole land of Benjamin. But they couldn't find the donkeys anywhere. ⁵Finally, they came to the land of Zuph. There Saul spoke to the servant. "Let's go home," he said. "By now my father will be more worried about us than about the donkeys!"

⁶But the servant said, "I've just thought of something! There is a prophet who lives here in this city. He is held in high honor by all the people. All that he says comes true! Let's go and find him. Maybe he can tell us where the donkeys are."

⁷"But we don't have anything to pay him with," Saul replied. "Even our food is gone. We don't have a thing to give him."

⁸"Well," the servant said, "I have a dollar! We can at least offer it to him and see what happens!"

⁹⁻¹¹"All right," Saul agreed. "Let's try it!"

So they started toward the city where the prophet lived. They climbed a hill on their way there. As they went, they saw some young girls going out to draw water. Saul asked them if they knew if the seer was in town. (In those days prophets were called seers. "Let's go and ask the seer," people would say. We call this kind of person a prophet now.)

¹²⁻¹³"Yes," they replied, "stay right on this road. He lives just inside the city gates. He has just come back from a trip. He came back to take part in a sacrifice up on the hill. So hurry! He'll probably be leaving about the time you get there. And the guests can't eat until he comes and blesses the food."

¹⁴So they went into the city. Just as they entered the gates, they saw Samuel. He was coming toward them, about to

go up the hill. 15The Lord had spoken to Samuel just the day before.

16"Be ready about this time tomorrow," the Lord had said. "I will send you a man from the land of Benjamin. You are to anoint him as the leader of my people. He will save them from the Philistines. For I have looked down on them in mercy. I have heard their cry."

17When Samuel saw Saul the Lord said, "That's the man I told you about! He will rule my people."

18Just then Saul walked up to Samuel. He asked, "Can you please tell me where the prophet's house is?"

19"I am the prophet!" Samuel replied. "Go on up the hill ahead of me. We'll eat there together. In the morning I will tell you what you want to know. Then I will send you on your way. 20And don't worry about those donkeys that were lost three days ago. They have been found. And anyway, you own all the wealth of Israel now!"

21"Pardon me, sir," Saul replied. "I'm from the tribe of Benjamin. It's the smallest tribe in Israel. And my family is the smallest in the whole tribe! You must have the wrong man!"

22Then Samuel took Saul and his servant into the great hall. He put them at the head of the table. He honored them above the 30 special guests that were there. 23Samuel then ordered the chef to bring Saul the best piece of meat. He was to give him the piece set aside for the guest of honor. 24So the chef brought it in and placed it before Saul.

"Go ahead and eat it," Samuel said. "I was saving it for you before I invited these others!"

So Saul ate with Samuel. 25After the feast, they went back to the city. Samuel took Saul up to the porch on the roof. He talked with him there. 26-27The next morning at daybreak, Samuel called up to him. "Get up," he said. "It's time you were on your way!"

So Saul got up and walked with Samuel to the edge of the city. They got to the city walls. Then Samuel told Saul to send his servant on ahead. Samuel said, "I have a special message for you from the Lord."

10 Then Samuel took a bottle of olive oil. He poured it over Saul's head. Then he kissed him on the cheek. Samuel said,

"I am doing this because the Lord has chosen you! You are to be the king of his people, Israel! 2After you leave me, you will see two men beside Rachel's tomb at Zelzah. This is in the land of Benjamin. They will tell you that your father's donkeys have been found. They will also say your father is worried about you. He is asking, 'How am I to find my son?' 3You will then go on to the oak of Tabor. There you will see three men coming toward you. They will be on their way to worship God at the altar at Bethel. One will be bringing three young goats. Another will have three loaves of bread. And the third will have a bottle of wine. 4They will greet you and offer you two of the loaves. You are to take them. 5After that you will come to Gibeath-elohim. It is also known as "God's Hill." There is a Philistine outpost there. As you get there you will meet a band of prophets. They will be coming down the hill playing a psaltery, a timbrel, a flute, and a harp. They will be prophesying as they come.

6"At that time the Spirit of the Lord will come upon you. You will prophesy with them. And you will feel and act like a new person. 7From that time on you should do what seems best to you. The Lord will be with you and he will guide you. 8Then go to Gilgal. Wait there seven days for me. For I will be coming to sacrifice burnt offerings and peace offerings. I will give you further orders when I get there."

9Saul said good-bye and started his journey. At that time, God gave Saul a new heart. And all of Samuel's prophecies came true that day. 10Saul and his servant came to the Hill of God. There they saw the prophets coming toward them. The Spirit of God came upon Saul. And he too began to prophesy.

11His friends heard about it. And they exclaimed, "What? Saul a prophet?" 12And one of the neighbors added, "With a father like his?" That is the origin of the proverb, "Is Saul a prophet too?"

[13]When Saul had finished prophesying he climbed the hill to the altar.

[14]"Where in the world did you go?" Saul's uncle asked him.

And Saul replied, "We went to look for the donkeys. But we couldn't find them. So we went to the prophet Samuel to ask him where they were."

[15]"Oh? And what did he say?" his uncle asked.

[16]"He said the donkeys had been found!" Saul replied. But Saul didn't tell him that he had been chosen as king!

[17]Samuel now called a meeting of all Israel at Mizpah. [18-19]He gave them this message from the Lord God: "I brought you from Egypt. I rescued you from the Egyptians. I saved you from all of the nations that were bothering you. But though I have done so much for you, you have rejected me. You have said, 'We want a king instead!' All right, then, present yourselves before the Lord. Come by tribes and clans."

[20]So Samuel called the tribal leaders together before the Lord. The tribe of Benjamin was chosen by sacred lot. [21]Then he brought each family of the tribe of Benjamin before the Lord. The family of the Matrites was chosen. And finally the sacred lot chose Saul, the son of Kish. But when they looked for him, he was not there!

[22]So they asked the Lord, "Where is he? Is he here among us?"

And the Lord replied, "He is hiding in the baggage."

[23]So they found him and brought him out. He stood head and shoulders above anyone else.

[24]Then Samuel spoke to all the people. "This is the man the Lord has chosen as your king," he said. "There isn't his equal in all of Israel!"

And all the people shouted, "Long live the king!"

[25]Samuel told the people what the rights and duties of a king were. He wrote them down in a book. He put it in a special place before the Lord. Then Samuel sent the people home again.

[26]Saul went back home to Gibeah. And a band of men went with him. They were brave men whose hearts the Lord had touched. [27]There were, however, some troublemakers. They said, "How can this man save us?" They hated him and refused to bring him gifts. But Saul took no notice.

- *Remember:* Was Saul ugly or handsome? Tall or short? (9:2) Why did Saul and his servant visit Samuel? (9:6) How did Samuel make Saul the honored guest at the banquet? (9:22-24) How did Samuel tell Saul that he would be king? (10:1) How would Saul know that this was true? (10:2-8) How do you know that Saul did not want to be king? (10:22) But did he become king?

- *Discover:* Sometimes God has a special job for you. Will you take it? Will you do it?

- *Apply:* If God asked you to do a special job, would you be ready? Here are some things you can do to prepare for the work he has for you: (1) be sure you know God by believing in his Son Jesus Christ; (2) be sure you know what God wants by reading your Bible each day; (3) be sure to talk with God each day; and (4) be sure you obey God each day, even in the little things.

- *What's next?* A king does not obey. Why not? Read 1 Samuel 13:1-15. ■

Saul Launches a Surprise Attack

11 At this time Nahash led the Ammonites against the Israelite city of Jabesh-gilead. But the people of Jabesh asked for peace. "Leave us alone and we will be your servants," they said.

[2]"All right," Nahash said. "But only on one condition. I will gouge out the right eye of every one of you! This will bring disgrace upon all Israel!"

[3]"Give us seven days! We will see if we can get some help!" replied the elders of Jabesh. "Perhaps none of our brothers will come and save us. If they won't, we will agree to your terms."

[4]A messenger ran to Gibeah, Saul's hometown. He told the people about their trouble. Everyone there broke into tears.

[5]Saul was out plowing in the field. When he got back to town he asked,

"What's the matter? Why is everyone crying?"

So they told him about the message from Jabesh. 6Then the Spirit of God came strongly upon Saul. He became very angry. 7He took two oxen and cut them into pieces. Then he sent messengers to carry them through all Israel.

"Someone might refuse to follow Saul and Samuel to battle. But if he does, this is what will happen to his oxen!" he said. God caused the people to be afraid of Saul's anger. So they came to him as one man. 8He counted them in Bezek. He found that there were 300,000 of them. And this was in addition to 30,000 from Judah.

9So he sent the messengers back to Jabesh-gilead. They said, "We will rescue you before tomorrow noon!" What joy there was in that city when that message got there!

10The men of Jabesh then told their enemies, "We give up. Tomorrow we will come out to you. You can do to us as you wish."

11But early the next morning Saul got there. He had divided his army into three groups. He made a surprise attack against the Ammonites. And he slaughtered them all morning. The Ammonite army was badly scattered. In fact, no two of them were left together!

12Then the people spoke to Samuel. They asked, "Where are the men who said that Saul shouldn't be our king? Bring them here and we will kill them!"

13But Saul replied, "No one will be put to death today. For today the Lord has rescued Israel!"

14Then Samuel said to the people, "Come! Let us all go to Gilgal. There we will agree to obey Saul as our king."

15So they went to Gilgal. And in a solemn ceremony before the Lord they crowned him king. Then they offered peace offerings to the Lord. And Saul and all Israel were very happy.

Samuel Reminds the People to Obey God

12 Then Samuel spoke to the people again.

"Look," he said, "I have done as you asked. I have given you a king. 2I have chosen him ahead of my own sons. Now I stand here, an old, gray-haired man. I have been in public service from the time I was a boy. 3Now speak to me as I stand before the Lord and before his chosen king. Whose ox or donkey have I stolen? Have I ever lied to you? Have I ever been unfair to you? Have I ever taken a bribe? Tell me and I will make right whatever I have done wrong."

4"No," they replied. "You have never lied to us. You have never been unfair to us in any way. You have never taken even a single bribe."

5"The Lord and his chosen king are my witnesses," Samuel said. "You can never accuse me of robbing you."

"Yes, it is true," they replied.

6"It was the Lord who chose Moses and Aaron," Samuel said. "He brought your ancestors out of the land of Egypt.

7"Now stand here before the Lord. I will remind you of all the good things he has done. This includes what he has done for you and for your ancestors.

8"Long ago, the Israelites were in Egypt. They cried out to the Lord. So he sent Moses and Aaron to bring them into this land. 9But the people soon forgot about the Lord their God. So he let them be conquered by Sisera, the general of King Hazor's army. The Philistines and the king of Moab also came and conquered them.

10"Then they cried to the Lord again. They confessed their sins, for they had turned away from him. They had even worshiped the Baal and Ashtaroth idols. And they pleaded, 'We will worship you and you alone! Please rescue us from our enemies!' 11Then the Lord sent Gideon, Barak, Jephthah, and Samuel to save you. And then you lived in safety.

12"But then you were afraid of Nahash, the king of Ammon. So you came to me. You said you wanted a king to reign over you. But the Lord your God was already your King. In fact, he has always been your King. 13All right, here is the king you have chosen. Look him over. You have asked for him. Now the Lord has given you what you asked for.

14"Now maybe you will fear and worship the Lord. Perhaps you will listen to his commands and not rebel against him. And perhaps both you and your king will follow the Lord your God. If this happens, then all will be well. [15]But you might rebel against the Lord's commands. Perhaps you will refuse to listen to him. If so, then his hand will be heavy upon you. It will be as it was upon your ancestors.

[16]"Now watch as the Lord does great miracles. [17]You know that it does not rain at this time of the year. It is now the time of the wheat harvest. But I will pray for the Lord to send thunder and rain today. When he does, you will know how bad it was for you to ask for a king!"

[18]So Samuel called to the Lord. And the Lord sent thunder and rain. All the people were very much afraid of the Lord and of Samuel.

[19]"Pray for us so we won't die!" they cried out to Samuel. "For now we have added to all our other sins by asking for a king."

[20]"Don't be afraid," Samuel told them. "You have done wrong. But make sure now that you worship the Lord with all your hearts. Don't turn your back on him in any way. [21]Other gods can't help you. [22]The Lord will not leave his chosen people. If he did, he would dishonor his great name. He made you a special nation for himself. And he did it just because he wanted to!

Keep on praying for each other

I will not sin by forgetting to pray for you.

1 Samuel 12:23

---

[23]"As for me, I will not sin by forgetting to pray for you. I will keep on teaching you those things which are good and right.

[24]"Trust in the Lord. Worship him with all your hearts. Think of all the great things he has done for you. [25]But if you keep on sinning, you and your king will be destroyed."

Saul's Foolish Mistake

A king is the most powerful person in the land. So why does he need to obey? Who does he need to obey? King Saul could answer both questions. He refused to obey and something terrible happened.

13 By this time Saul had been king for one year. At this time, [2]he chose 3,000 special troops. He took 2,000 of them with him to Michmash and Mount Bethel. The other 1,000 stayed with Jonathan, Saul's son. They stayed in Gibeah in the land of Benjamin. The rest of the army was sent home. [3-4]Then Jonathan attacked and destroyed the Philistines at Geba. The news spread quickly through the land of the Philistines. So Saul sounded the call to arms throughout Israel. He told the people that he had destroyed the Philistines at Geba. He also warned his men that the Philistines really hated them now! So the whole Israelite army was called out again. They came together at Gilgal. [5]The Philistines called out a mighty army. It had 3,000 chariots, 6,000 horsemen, and as many soldiers as sand along the seashore. They made their camp at Michmash east of Beth-aven.

[6]The men of Israel saw the huge enemy army. And they knew they were in trouble. So they tried to hide in caves, thickets, and among the rocks. They even hid in tombs and wells. [7]Some of them crossed the Jordan River. They ran to the land of Gad and Gilead. Meanwhile, Saul stayed at Gilgal. All those who were with him were shaking with

fear. [8]Samuel had told Saul to wait seven days for him to come. But seven days had passed and Samuel still hadn't come. Saul's troops were quickly slipping away. [9]So Saul decided to sacrifice the burnt offering and the peace offerings himself. [10]But just as he was finishing, Samuel got there. Saul went out to meet him and to get a blessing from him. [11]But Samuel said, "What is this you have done?"

"Well," Saul replied, "I saw that my men were leaving me. You didn't come at the time you said you would. And the Philistines are at Michmash. They are ready for battle. [12]So I said, 'The Philistines are ready to march against us! And I haven't even asked for the Lord's help!' So I offered the burnt offering without waiting for you to come."

[13]"You fool!" Samuel exclaimed. "You have disobeyed the command of the Lord your God. He was planning to make you and your descendants kings of Israel for all time. [14]But now your kingly line must end. For the Lord wants a man who will obey him. And he has found the man he wants. He has already chosen him as king over his people. For you have not obeyed the Lord's command."

[15]Samuel then left Gilgal. From there he went to Gibeah in the land of Benjamin.

Saul counted the soldiers who were still with him. He found only 600 left!

- *Remember:* Why were the Israelites so afraid of the Philistine army? (13:5-6) What did the Israelite soldiers do then? (13:6,7) What had Samuel told Saul to do? (13:8) How did Saul disobey God's commands that Samuel gave? (13:8-9) How would God punish Saul for disobeying? (13:14) Why do you think it was so important for King Saul to obey God?

- *Discover:* Saul had a big problem. An enemy army was ready to attack and his

friends were deserting him. But Saul decided to solve the problem his way. God had told him what to do, but God's way didn't seem right. Doing things God's way may not always seem the best way at first, but it is.

- *Apply:* Obey God at all times, and especially when things get tough. Disobeying God only makes things worse.

- *What's next?* Two young men fight an entire army. Read 1 Samuel 14:1-23. ■

An Army without Weapons

[16]Saul and Jonathan and these 600 men set up their camp in Geba. This town was in the land of Benjamin. But the Philistines stayed at Michmash. [17]Three groups of raiders soon left the camp of the Philistines. One went toward Ophrah in the land of Shual. [18]Another went to Beth-horon. The third moved toward the border above the valley of Zeboim. This was near the desert.

[19]There were no blacksmiths at all in the land of Israel in those days. The Philistines wouldn't let them live or work there. They were afraid they would make swords and spears for the Israelites. [20]The Israelites might need to sharpen their plowshares, discs, axes, or sickles. If they did, they had to take them to a Philistine blacksmith. [21]The blacksmiths' charges were as follows:

For sharpening a plow point, 60¢
For sharpening a disc, 60¢
For sharpening an axe, 30¢
For sharpening a sickle, 30¢
For sharpening an ox goad, 30¢

[22]So there was not a single sword or spear in the whole army of Israel that day. Saul and Jonathan were the only ones who had real weapons. [23]The mountain pass at Michmash had meanwhile been taken by a group from the Philistine army.

Jonathan's Brave Fight

Who could be braver than an entire army? Jonathan was. Who would dare fight an entire army? Jonathan did. Who could cause an entire army to run away? Jonathan did.

14 A day or so later, Prince Jonathan spoke to his bodyguard. "Come on," he said. "Let's cross the valley to the camp of the Philistines." But he didn't tell his father that he was leaving.

²Saul and his 600 men were camped at the edge of Gibeah. They were set up around the pomegranate tree at Migron. ³Among his men was Ahijah the priest. He was the son of Ahitub, Ichabod's brother. Ahitub was the son of Phinehas and the grandson of Eli. Eli had been the priest of the Lord in Shiloh.

No one knew that Jonathan had gone. ⁴To reach the Philistine camp, Jonathan had to go over a narrow pass. It ran between two rocky peaks. These peaks were named Bozez and Seneh. ⁵The peak on the north was in front of Michmash. The southern peak was in front of Geba.

⁶"Yes," Jonathan had said to his bodyguard. "Let's go across to those heathen. Perhaps the Lord will do a miracle for us. It doesn't matter to him how many enemy troops there are!"

⁷"Fine!" the bodyguard replied. "Do as you think best. I'm with you heart and soul, whatever you decide."

⁸"All right, then this is what we'll do," Jonathan told him. ⁹"When they see us, they might say, 'Stay where you are or we'll kill you!' If they do, then we will stop and wait for them. ¹⁰But they might say, 'Come on up and fight!' If so, then we will do just that. For it will be God's signal that he will help us beat them!"

¹¹When the Philistines saw them coming they shouted, "Look!" The Israelites are coming out of their holes!" ¹²Then they shouted to Jonathan, "Come on up here. We'll show you how to fight!"

"Come on, climb right behind me," Jonathan said to his bodyguard. "The Lord will help us beat them!"

¹³So they climbed up on their hands and knees. And the Philistines fell back as Jonathan and his bodyguard killed them right and left. ¹⁴They killed about 20 men in all. Their bodies were scattered over about half an acre of land. ¹⁵Suddenly panic broke out in the Philistine army. Even the raiding parties panicked. And just then there was a great earthquake. This made their terror even worse.

¹⁶Saul's lookouts in Gibeah saw a strange sight. The great army of the Philistines began to melt away in all directions.

¹⁷"Find out who isn't here," Saul ordered. They checked, and found that Jonathan and his bodyguard were gone. ¹⁸"Bring the Ark of God," Saul shouted to Ahijah. For the Ark was among the people of Israel at that time. ¹⁹But while Saul was talking to the priest, the shouting in the Philistine camp grew louder and louder. "Quick! What does God say?" Saul demanded.

²⁰Then Saul and his 600 men rushed out to the battle. They found the Philistines killing each other! There was great confusion all around them. ²¹ And the Hebrews who had been forced to join the Philistine army revolted. They joined up with the Israelite army. ²²Finally even the men hiding in the hills joined the battle. For they saw that the Philistines were running away. ²³So the Lord saved Israel that day. And the battle kept going out beyond Beth-aven.

● *Remember:* Why did Jonathan leave Saul's camp? (14:1) Who went with him? (14:1) Jonathan expected someone to help them. Who? What might he do? (14:6) How would Jonathan and his bodyguard know if God would help them? What test did they have? (14:8-10) What did God do to cause the Philistines to panic? (14:15) How did this help Saul and his men defeat the Philistines? (14:20-23) Do you think Jonathan would have been this brave if he had not trusted God to help him?

- *Discover:* We are braver when we know that God is with us. If we are doing what is right, we know he will help us do more than we can do by ourselves.

- *Apply:* Are you ever afraid of something? Are you afraid of someone? Are you afraid when it is dark? Are you afraid in a strange place? Ask God to help you.

Then trust him to help you. You will be much braver when you do.

- *What's next?* Have you ever made a foolish promise, then wished you had not made it? Perhaps you saw that this foolish promise would hurt you. King Saul made a foolish vow or promise. Read about it in 1 Samuel 14:24-46. ■

Saul's Foolish Promise

Saul made a foolish promise. Sometimes it is called a vow. "Why did I make such a foolish vow?" Saul must have wondered later. Everyone else could see how foolish it was. His vow didn't help anyone. But it hurt lots of people. It almost killed his brave son. This is what happened.

24-25Saul had declared, "A curse upon anyone who eats before evening. No one may eat before I have full revenge on my enemies." So no one ate all day. They did not even eat the honeycomb they found in the forest. 26They all were afraid of Saul's curse. 27But Jonathan had not heard his father's command. So he dipped a stick into a honeycomb. And when he had eaten the honey he felt much better. 28Then someone told him that his father had made a curse. It would fall on anyone who ate food that day. As a result, all the men were tired and weak.

29"That's foolish!" Jonathan said. "A command like that only hurts us. See how much better I feel now that I have eaten this little bit of honey. 30The people should have been allowed to eat freely. They could have eaten the food they found among our enemies. If they had, think how many more we could have killed!"

31But hungry as they were, they killed the Philistines all day. They chased them from Michmash to Aijalon. As the day wore on, they grew more and more faint. 32That evening they were starving. So they flew upon the battle loot. They butchered the sheep, oxen, and calves. Then they ate the raw, bloody meat. 33Someone told Saul what was happening. He told Saul the people were sin-

ning against the Lord by eating blood.

"That is very wrong," Saul said. "Roll a great stone over here. 34Go out among the troops. Tell them to bring the oxen and sheep here to kill and drain them. Tell them not to sin against the Lord by eating the blood." So that is what they did.

35And Saul built an altar to the Lord. This was his first.

36After that Saul said, "Let's chase the Philistines all night. We shall destroy every last one of them."

"Fine!" his men replied. "Do as you think best."

But the priest said, "Let's ask God first."

37So Saul asked God, "Shall we go after the Philistines? Will you help us defeat them?" But the Lord made no reply all night.

38Then Saul said to the leaders, "Something's wrong! We must find out what sin was done today. 39I will make a promise by the name of the God who saved Israel. Even if the sinner is my own son Jonathan, he shall surely die!" But no one would tell him what the trouble was.

40Then Saul said, "Jonathan and I will stand over here. All of you stand over there." And the people agreed.

41Then Saul said, "O Lord God of Israel, why haven't you answered my question? What is wrong? Are Jonathan and I guilty? Or is the sin among the others? O Lord God, show us who is guilty." And Jonathan and Saul were chosen by sacred lot as the guilty ones. The people were shown to be innocent.

42Then Saul said, "Now draw lots between me and Jonathan." And Jonathan was chosen as the guilty one.

43"Tell me what you've done," Saul demanded of Jonathan.

"I tasted a little honey," Jonathan said. "It was only a little bit on the end of a stick. But now I must die."

44"Yes, Jonathan," Saul said, "you must die. May God strike me dead if you are not killed for this."

45But the troops said, "Jonathan saved Israel today! Shall he die? Far from it! We promise by the life of God that not one hair on his head will be touched. For he has been used by God to do a great miracle today." So the people rescued Jonathan.

46Then Saul called back the army. And the Philistines went back home.

- *Remember:* What was Saul's foolish vow? (14:24-25) How did Jonathan feel about Saul's vow? (14:29-30) How did the foolish vow hurt the army? (14:31-33) How did it almost kill Jonathan? (14:34-44) Who rescued Jonathan? Why? (14:45) Was it really necessary for Saul to make a vow? Why or why not?

- *Discover:* Vows should not be broken, so be careful what vows or promises you make!

- *Apply:* The next time you're about to say, "I promise," stop! Ask yourself, "Is this a good promise or a foolish promise? Do I really need to say this? Who will it hurt? Who will it help? If it's a promise, God expects me to keep it."

- *What's next?* Biggest isn't always best. But would you choose a shepherd boy to be your next king? God did. Read 1 Samuel 16:1-13. ∎

Saul's Army Is Successful

47And now Saul was secure as the king of Israel. So he sent the Israelite army out in every direction. He sent them out to

fight Moab, Ammon, Edom, the kings of Zobah, and the Philistines. And wherever he turned, he succeeded. 48He did great deeds. He conquered the Amalekites. And he saved Israel from all those who had ruled over them.

49Saul had three sons, Jonathan, Ishvi, and Malchishua. He also had two daughters, Merab and Michal. 50-51Saul's wife was Ahinoam, the daughter of Ahimaaz. And the general of his army was his cousin Abner, his uncle Ner's son. Abner's father, Ner, and Saul's father, Kish, were brothers. Both were the sons of Abiel.

52The Israelites fought with the Philistines throughout Saul's lifetime. And Saul took all the brave, strong young men into his army.

Saul Fails to Obey

15One day Samuel said to Saul, "I crowned you king of Israel because God told me to. Now be sure that you obey him. 2This is his command to you: 'I have decided to punish the nation of Amalek. They would not let my people cross their land when Israel came from Egypt. 3Now go and destroy the whole Amalek nation. Destroy their men, women, babies, and little children. Kill all their oxen, sheep, camels, and donkeys.'"

4So Saul called out his army at Telaim. There were 200,000 troops. And these were in addition to 10,000 men from Judah. 5The Amalekites were camped in the valley below them. 6Saul sent a message to the Kenites. He told them to get out from among the Amalekites. If they didn't come out, they would die with them. "For you were kind to the people of Israel when they came out of the land of Egypt," he explained. So the Kenites packed up and left.

7Then Saul defeated the Amalekites. He chased and killed them all the way from Havilah to Shur, east of Egypt. 8He captured Agag, the king of the Amalekites. But he killed everyone else. 9But Saul and his men kept the best of the sheep and oxen. They also kept the fattest of the lambs. In fact, they took all that they wanted. They destroyed only what was worthless or of poor quality.

¹⁰Then the Lord said to Samuel, ¹¹"I am sorry that I ever made Saul king. For again he has refused to obey me."

Samuel was deeply moved when he heard what God was saying. He was so upset that he cried to the Lord all night. ¹²Early the next morning he went out to find Saul. Someone said that he had gone to Mount Carmel. He had gone there to build a monument to himself. And from there he had gone on to Gilgal. ¹³When Samuel found him, Saul greeted him happily.

"The Lord bless you!" he said. "I have carried out all the Lord's commands!"

¹⁴"Then what is all that bleating of sheep I hear?" Samuel demanded. "What about all the oxen I hear mooing?"

¹⁵"The army took them. They kept the best of the sheep and oxen," Saul admitted. "But they are going to sacrifice them to the Lord your God. We have destroyed everything else."

¹⁶Then Samuel said to Saul, "Stop! Listen to what the Lord told me last night!"

"What was it?" Saul asked.

¹⁷Samuel said, "When you were humble, God made you king of Israel. ¹⁸Then he gave you a job to do. He told you, 'Go and completely destroy the Amalekites. Do not let any person or animal among them live.' ¹⁹Why didn't you obey the Lord? Why did you take this loot? Why did you do just what God said not to?"

²⁰"But I *have* obeyed the Lord," Saul insisted. "I did what he told me to. I brought King Agag alive, but I killed everyone else. ²¹I let my troops keep the best of the sheep and oxen. But they demanded it. And they took them to sacrifice to the Lord."

²²Samuel replied, "What pleases the Lord the most? Does he want your burnt offerings and sacrifices? Or does he want your obedience? It is much better to obey the Lord than to give him an offering. It is much better to listen to him than to offer him something. ²³Refusing to obey is as bad as the sin of witchcraft. Being stubborn is as bad as worshiping idols. You have not obeyed the word of the Lord. Because of this, he has rejected you from being king."

Saul Pleads for Forgiveness

²⁴"I have sinned," Saul finally said. "Yes, I have disobeyed your orders. I have failed to obey the command of the Lord. I was afraid of the people and did what they demanded. ²⁵Oh, please forgive my sin. Go with me now to worship the Lord."

²⁶But Samuel replied, "It's no use! You have not obeyed the command of the Lord. Because of this, he has rejected you from being the king of Israel."

²⁷Samuel turned to go. As he did, Saul grabbed at him and tried to hold him back. In doing this, he tore Samuel's robe.

God is more pleased by what we do for him than what we give to him

It is much better to obey the Lord than to give him an offering.

1 Samuel 15:22

---

²⁸And Samuel said to him, "See? The Lord has torn the kingdom of Israel from you today. He has given it to a man who is better than you are. ²⁹And he who is the glory of Israel is not lying! And he will not change his mind, for he is not a man!"

³⁰Then Saul begged again, "I have sinned! But at least honor me before the leaders! Honor me before my people by going with me to worship the Lord your God."

³¹So Samuel finally agreed and went with him.

³²Then Samuel said, "Bring King Agag to me." Agag came all full of smiles. He thought, "Surely the worst is over! They will soon let me go!" ³³But Samuel said, "Your sword has killed the sons of many mothers. Now your mother shall be childless." And Samuel chopped him in pieces before the Lord at Gilgal. ³⁴Then Samuel went home to Ramah. And Saul went back to Gibeah. ³⁵Samuel never saw Saul again, but he mourned for him all the time. And the Lord was sorry that he had ever made Saul king of Israel.

Samuel Anoints David

God told Samuel to anoint one of Jesse's sons to be the next king. But which one? God didn't tell him that. And Jesse had seven sons! Which one did God want?

16 Finally the Lord said to Samuel, "You have mourned long enough for Saul. I have rejected him as king of Israel. Now take a bottle of olive oil. Go to Bethlehem and find a man named Jesse. I have chosen one of his sons to be the new king."

²But Samuel asked, "How can I do that? If Saul hears about it, he will kill me."

"Take a young cow with you," the Lord replied. "Say that you have come to make a sacrifice to the Lord. ³Then call Jesse to the sacrifice. I will show you which of his sons to anoint."

⁴So Samuel did as the Lord had told him to. When he got to Bethlehem, the elders of the city came to meet him. They were afraid.

"What is wrong?" they asked. "Why have you come?"

⁵But he replied, "All is well. I have come to sacrifice to the Lord. Make yourselves clean. Then come with me to the sacrifice."

Samuel purified Jesse and his sons, and he invited them, too. ⁶When they got there, Samuel saw Eliab. He thought, "Surely this is the man the Lord has chosen!"

⁷But the Lord said to Samuel, "Don't judge by a man's face or height. This is not the man I have chosen. I don't make decisions the way you do! People accept

others by the way they look on the outside. But I look inside a person. I look at a person's heart and thoughts."

⁸Then Jesse called his son Abinadab to step forward. He told him to walk in front of Samuel. But the Lord said, "This is not the right man either."

**God looks at our hearts
rather than our looks**

People accept others by the way they look on the outside. But I look inside a person. I look at a person's heart and thoughts.

1 Samuel 16:7

---

⁹Next Jesse called Shammah. But the Lord said, "No, this is not the one." In the same way all seven of his sons showed themselves to Samuel. And each one was rejected.

¹⁰⁻¹¹"The Lord has not chosen any of them," Samuel told Jesse. "Are these all there are?"

"Well, there is the youngest," Jesse replied. "But he's out in the fields watching the sheep."

"Send for him at once," Samuel said. "For we will not sit down to eat until he gets here."

¹²So Jesse sent for him. He was a fine-looking boy. He had a ruddy face and pleasant eyes. And the Lord said, "This is the one. Anoint him."

¹³So David stood there among his brothers. And Samuel took the olive oil he had brought. He poured it on David's head. And the Spirit of the Lord came upon him. And the Lord gave him great power from that day onward. Then Samuel went back to Ramah.

- *Remember:* To what city did God tell Samuel to go? Why? (16:1) Why did Samuel think God might choose Eliab to be king? What did God say about that? (16:6-7) Which brother was anointed to be the next king? (16:13) What did you learn here about David? (16:10-13) What happened to David after he was anointed? (16:13) If you were a king, would you want God's power more than your own power? Why?

- *Discover:* When God gives you a job, he will also give you the power to do it. It doesn't matter how young or old you are. When God chose David to be king, he gave David power to do the job.

- *Apply:* Think of two things God wants you to do. Does he want you to play an instrument for him? Does he want you to be kind to an unkind boy or girl? Does he want you to tell other people about Jesus? If that's what he wants you to do, he will give you the power to do it. Ask him.

- *What's next?* When you are sick you usually take medicine. When King Saul got sick, he ordered harp music. Read 1 Samuel 16:14-23. ▪

David Plays Music for Saul

King Saul had a bad spirit bothering him. He was often depressed and afraid. What would help him? Harp music. Who would play for him? The next king!

¹⁴But the Spirit of the Lord had left Saul. And instead, the Lord sent a tormenting spirit. It filled Saul with sadness and fear. ¹⁵⁻¹⁶Some of Saul's helpers thought of a cure.

"We'll find a good harpist," they said.

"He will play for you when the tormenting spirit is bothering you. The harp music will quiet you. You'll soon be well again."

¹⁷"All right," Saul said. "Find me a harpist."

¹⁸One of them said he knew a young fellow in Bethlehem. He was the son of a man named Jesse. He was a good harp player. Besides that he was handsome, brave, and strong. And he had good, solid judgment. "What's more," he added, "the Lord is with him."

¹⁹So Saul sent messengers to Jesse. He asked that he send his son David, the shepherd. ²⁰Jesse responded by sending David. He also sent a young goat and a donkey carrying a load of food and wine. ²¹From the instant he saw David, Saul admired and loved him. And David became his bodyguard.

²²Then Saul wrote to Jesse, "Please let David join my staff. I am very fond of him."

²³David would play his harp when the tormenting spirit from God bothered Saul. Then Saul would feel better and the spirit would go away.

- *Remember:* What cure did the king's helpers suggest for Saul's troubles? (16:16)

Who became Saul's harpist? (16:18-19) How did Saul feel about David? What other work did David do for Saul? (16:21-22) Did David's music help the king? (16:23) What would Saul have thought had he known David would take his place as king? What do you think he would have done?

- *Discover:* Some day David would be king instead of Saul. Now he was content to serve the king. Now he would learn to follow and serve. Before we can be a leader we must learn to follow and serve. We must be willing to help those who are our leaders now.

- *Apply:* Right now, today, you may be serving and following. You're going to school. You're helping others. Don't be sorry. You may be learning to be a leader. Do your best at what you're doing now. Some day you'll be glad you did.

- *What's next?* A young boy and a giant man fight. Who do you think will win? Read 1 Samuel 17. ■

David Fights Goliath

A young man goes out to fight a giant. If he loses, his entire army loses. How would you like to be David? You're fighting to save your own life. But you're also fighting to save hundreds of others, too. What would you do? This is what David did.

17 The Philistines now called their army for battle. They camped between Socoh and Azekah. ²Saul then called his army to meet at the Valley of Elah. ³So the Philistines and Israelites faced each other on opposite hills. A valley lay between the two armies.

⁴⁻⁷Then Goliath came out of the Philistine ranks to face Israel's army. He was a Philistine champion from Gath. Goliath was a giant of a man! He was over nine feet tall! He wore a bronze helmet, a 200-pound coat of mail, and bronze leggings. He carried a bronze spear several inches thick. It was tipped with a 25-pound iron spearhead. His bodyguard walked ahead of him with a huge shield.

⁸He stood and shouted across to the Israelites. "Do you need a whole army to settle this?" he yelled. "I will fight for the Philistines. You choose someone to fight for you. Then we will settle this in single combat! ⁹If your man kills me, then we will be your slaves. But if I kill him, then you must be our slaves! ¹⁰I defy the armies of Israel! Send me a man who will fight with me!"

¹¹Saul and the Israelite army heard this. They were very worried and afraid. ¹²David had seven older brothers. Their father, Jesse, was quite old by now. He was a member of the tribe of Judah. He and his family lived in Bethlehem. ¹³Jesse's three oldest sons were Eliab,

Abinadab, and Shammah. They had already joined Saul's army and were there to fight the Philistines. 14-15David was the youngest son and was on Saul's staff on a part-time basis. He went back and forth to Bethlehem to help his father with the sheep. 16For 40 days, twice a day, morning and evening, the Philistine giant strutted before the armies of Israel.

17One day Jesse spoke to David. "Take this bushel of roasted grain and these 10 loaves of bread," he said. "Bring them to your brothers. 18Give this cheese to their captain. See how your brothers are getting along. Then bring us back a letter from them!"

19Saul and the Israelite army were camped at the Valley of Elah.

20So David left the sheep with another shepherd. And he left early the next morning with the gifts. He came to the edge of the camp. Just then, the Israelite army was leaving for the battlefield. The soldiers were shouting their battle cries. 21Soon the Israelite and Philistine forces stood facing each other. 22David left his things with the man in charge of supplies. Then he hurried out to the ranks to find his brothers. 23As he was talking with them, he saw Goliath the giant step out from the Philistine troops. Goliath shouted his challenge to the army of Israel. 24As soon as they saw him, the Israelite army began to run away in fear.

25"Have you seen the giant?" the soldiers asked. "He has made fun of the whole army of Israel. And have you heard about the reward the king will give the man who kills him? The king will give him one of his daughters for a wife! And his whole family will be free from paying taxes!"

26David talked to some others standing there. He wanted to see if this was true. "What will a man get for killing this Philistine? What is the reward for ending his insults to Israel?" he asked them. "Who is this heathen Philistine, anyway? Who is he to defy the armies of the living God?" 27And he got the same reply as before.

28But David's oldest brother, Eliab, heard David talking like that. And he was very angry. "What are you doing around here, anyway?" he demanded. "What about the sheep you're supposed to be taking care of? I know what a cocky boy you are! You just want to see the battle!"

29"What have I done now?" David replied. "I was only asking a question!"

30So he walked over to some others nearby. He asked them the same thing. They gave him the same answer. 31They finally saw what David meant and someone told King Saul. Then the king sent for him.

32"Don't worry about a thing," David told him. "I'll take care of this Philistine!"

33"Don't be foolish!" Saul replied. "How can you fight with a man like him? You are only a boy. He has been in the army *since* he was a boy!"

34But David would not give up. "I am the shepherd of my father's sheep," he said. "Lions and bears come and take lambs from the flock. 35But when they do, I go after them with a club. I take the lambs right from their mouths! If they turn on me, I catch them by the jaw and club them to death. 36I have done this to both lions and bears. And I'll do it to this heathen Philistine too. For he has insulted the armies of the living God! 37The Lord has saved me from the claws and teeth of the lion and the bear. And he also will save me from this Philistine!"

Saul finally agreed. "All right, go ahead," he said. "May the Lord be with you!"

38-39Then Saul gave David his own armor. He gave him a bronze helmet and a coat of mail. David put it on and strapped the sword over it. He took a step or two to see what it was like. He had never worn such things before. "I can hardly move!" he said. So he took them off again. 40Then he picked up five smooth stones from a stream. He put them in his shepherd's bag. And armed only with his staff and sling, he went out to meet Goliath. 41-42Goliath walked out toward David with his shieldbearer ahead of him. He laughed at the little red-cheeked boy that had come out to meet him!

43"Am I a dog?" he roared at David. "Is that why you come at me with a stick?" And he cursed David by the names of his gods. 44"Come over here," Goliath yelled. "I'll give your flesh to the birds and wild animals."

45David shouted in reply, "You come to me with a sword and spear. But I come to you in the name of the Lord of the armies of heaven and of Israel. I come in the name of the God whom you have defied. 46Today the Lord will conquer you. I will kill you and cut off your head. I will give the dead bodies of *your* men to the birds and wild animals. Then the whole world will know that there is a God in Israel! 47And Israel will learn a great lesson. The Lord doesn't need weapons to do what he wants. He can work without the help of human strength! He will give you to us!"

48-49As Goliath came near, David ran out to meet him. He reached into his shepherd's bag and took out a stone. He hurled it from his sling. It hit the Philistine in the forehead. The stone sank in, and the giant fell on his face to the ground. 50-51So David killed the Philistine giant with a sling and a stone. Since he had no sword, he ran over and pulled

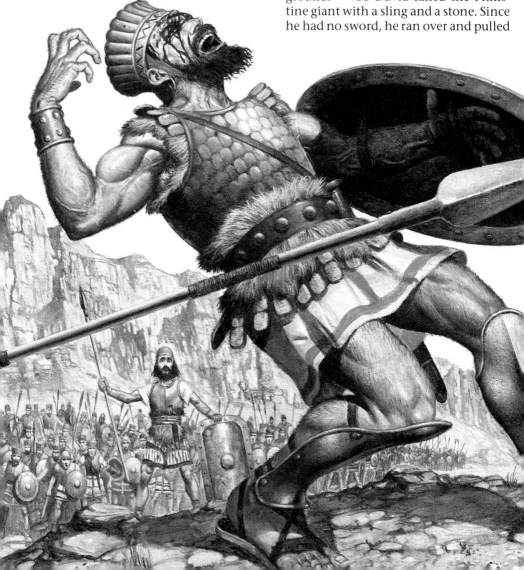

Goliath's from its sheath. He then killed him with it and cut off his head. The Philistines saw that their champion was dead. So they turned and ran.

God does not need our things to make him strong

The Lord doesn't need weapons
to do what he wants.
He can work without the help
of human strength!

1 Samuel 17:47

Saul Is Impressed by David

⁵²Then the Israelites gave a great shout of triumph. They rushed after the Philistines. They chased them as far as Gath and the gates of Ekron. The bodies of the dead and wounded Philistines were all along the road to Shaaraim. ⁵³Then the Israelite army went back. And they plundered the deserted Philistine camp.

⁵⁴Later David took Goliath's head to Jerusalem. But he stored Goliath's armor in his tent.

⁵⁵As Saul was watching David go out to fight Goliath, he spoke to Abner. Abner was the general of his army. "Abner, what sort of family does this young boy come from?" he asked.

"I really don't know," Abner said.

⁵⁶"Well, find out!" the king told him.

⁵⁷After David had killed Goliath, Abner brought him to Saul. He was carrying the Philistine's head in his hand.

⁵⁸"Tell me about your father, my boy," Saul said.

And David replied, "His name is Jesse. We live in Bethlehem."

● *Remember:* What kind of man was Goliath? How would you describe him to your friends? (17:4-7) What did Goliath say to the Israelite army? (17:8-10) Why didn't someone fight him? (17:11) Why was David visiting the army camp? (17:12-18) Why wasn't David afraid of Goliath? (17:34-37) What weapons did David use to fight Goliath? (17:40) What special help did David have that Goliath did not have? (17:45-47) What do you like about David? What do you not like about Goliath?

● *Discover:* It is better to have less with God than to have more without God. Goliath had the finest weapons, but he didn't have God. David had only a sling

and five stones, but he had God on his side. And you know who won!

- *Apply:* Goliath was a champion warrior. No one thought David could beat him. No one except God. Do you have to do something this week that seems impossible? Have you asked God to help you? With God on your side you can do it!

- *What's next?* What does it really mean to be best friends? Jonathan and David could tell you. Read 1 Samuel 18:1. ■

David and Jonathan Become Friends

David was a brave young man. He fought a giant with a sling and stones. King Saul's son Jonathan was also a brave young man. He fought an army with only his bodyguard. Soon these two became best friends.

18 King Saul finished talking with David. Then David met Jonathan, the king's son. Right away there was a bond of love between them. Jonathan promised to be his blood brother. ⁴He sealed his promise by giving him his robe, sword, bow, and belt.

- *Remember:* How long did it take David and Jonathan to become friends? (18:1-3) What tells you they were such good friends? (18:1-3) What did Jonathan give David to show his friendship? (18:4) Why

B. Gallego

do you think David and Jonathan liked each other so much?

- *Discover:* How do you become a best friend? By showing love to someone else. Best friends do the best things for you. Jonathan showed he was a best friend by giving his best gifts to David.

- *Apply:* What three things do you like best about your best friends? Do you think they like the same three things about you? Do for your best friends what you would like your best friends to do for you.

- *What's next?* A king becomes jealous of a young soldier. What will happen to the soldier? Read 1 Samuel 18:4-16. ■

Saul Becomes Jealous of David

King Saul ruled over all Israel. He had everything he wanted. David worked for Saul. He was one of Saul's army officers. But Saul was jealous of David. He wanted something David had. What could that be?

King Saul now kept David with him. He wouldn't let him go back home any more. ⁵He was Saul's special helper. David always succeeded in doing all that he was told to do. So Saul made him a commander of his troops. This pleased the army and general public alike. ⁶After David had killed Goliath, the army went home. Women came out from all the towns along the way. They came out to cheer for King Saul. They were singing and dancing for joy. They were playing tambourines and cymbals.

⁷But this was their song: "Saul has killed his thousands, and David his ten thousands!"

⁸Of course, Saul was very angry. "What's this?" he said to himself. "They credit David with ten thousands and me with only thousands. Next they'll be making him their king!"

⁹So from that time on King Saul was jealous of David. ¹⁰The very next day the tormenting spirit from God came upon Saul. And he began to rave like a madman. David began to soothe him by playing the harp. David played his harp whenever this happened. Saul had a spear in his hand at the time. ¹¹⁻¹²Suddenly he threw it at David. He tried to pin him to the wall. But David jumped aside and got away. This happened another time, too, for Saul was afraid of David. He was jealous because the Lord

had left him and was now with David. ¹³Finally Saul banned him from his presence. He also demoted him to the rank of captain. But this put David more than ever in the public eye.

¹⁴David continued to succeed in all that he did. For the Lord was with him. ¹⁵⁻¹⁶When King Saul saw this, he became even more afraid of him. But all Israel and Judah loved him, for he was as one of them.

- *Remember:* Who was glad when David was promoted to commander? (18:5) What made Saul jealous of David? (18:6-8) What did Saul try to do to David? Why? (18:9-13) Why did David succeed? Who was with him? (18:14) How did Saul let his jealousy hurt himself? What would you say to him about his jealousy? Who did he hurt more, David or himself?

- *Discover:* Jealousy always hurts you more than the person you are jealous of.

- *Apply:* Are you jealous of someone? Why? If you are jealous, you probably want something that person has. What is it? Is it something to play with? Is it money? Or is it something like popularity? Whatever it is, try praising God that this person has what you don't. Then be thankful for all you do have. Then you may stop being jealous.

- *What's next?* A brave soldier escapes somewhere into the night. Read 1 Samuel 19. ■

David Marries
Saul's Daughter, Michal

¹⁷One day Saul spoke to David. "I am ready to give you my oldest daughter Merab as your wife," he said. "But first you must prove yourself to be a real soldier. You must fight the Lord's battles." For Saul thought to himself, "I'll send him out against the Philistines. They will kill him for me. Then I won't have to do it myself."

¹⁸"Who am I that I should be the king's son-in-law?" David said. "My father's family is nothing!"

¹⁹The time came for the wedding. But Saul married her to Adriel instead of David. He was a man from Meholath. ²⁰In the meantime Saul's daughter Michal had fallen in love with David. And Saul was happy when he heard about it.

²¹"Here's another chance to see him killed by the Philistines!" Saul said to himself. But to David he said, "You can be my son-in-law after all! I will give you my youngest daughter."

²²Then Saul spoke to his men. He told them to speak to David in private. They were to tell David that Saul and his men really liked him. They were to encourage David to try and become Saul's son-in-law.

²³But David replied, "I am a poor man from an unknown family. How could I find enough dowry to marry the daughter of a king?"

²⁴Saul's men reported this back to him. ²⁵So Saul told them, "Tell David that the only dowry I need is 100 dead Philistines! I just want to get back at my enemies." But Saul hoped that David would be killed in the fight.

²⁶David was happy to take up the offer. So, before the time was up, ²⁷he

and his men went out. They killed 200 Philistines. Then they gave the foreskins to King Saul for proof. So Saul gave Michal to him.

²⁸The king saw how much the Lord was with David. He also saw how all the people loved him. ²⁹Because of this, Saul became even more afraid of him. And he grew to hate him more with each passing day. ³⁰Whenever the Philistine army attacked, David succeeded against them. In fact, he was the best of all Saul's officers. So David's name became very famous throughout the land.

Saul Tries to Kill David

At last his jealousy made him try to kill David. Saul wanted to murder the man who helped him the most. David was not Saul's enemy. He was Saul's best helper. Why would a man want to kill his best helper?

19 Saul now urged his aides and his son Jonathan to kill David. But Jonathan was a close friend of David's. ²So he told David what his father was planning. "Tomorrow morning," he warned him, "you must find a hiding place out in the fields. ³I'll ask my father to go out there with me. I'll talk to him about you. Then I'll tell you everything I can find out."

⁴The next morning Jonathan and his

father talked together. Jonathan spoke well of David. And he begged Saul not to be against David.

"He's never done anything to harm you," Jonathan pleaded. "He has always helped you in any way he could. 5Have you forgotten about the time he risked his life to kill Goliath? Don't you remember how the Lord brought a great victory to Israel as a result? You were very happy about it then. Why should you now murder an innocent man? There is no reason for it at all!"

6Finally Saul agreed. He promised, "As the Lord lives, he shall not be killed."

7After that, Jonathan called David. He told him what had happened. Then he took David to Saul and everything was fine between them. 8War broke out shortly after that. David led his troops against the Philistines. He killed many of them and chased their whole army away.

9-10But one day Saul was sitting at home, listening to David playing the harp. Suddenly the tormenting spirit from the Lord came upon him. Saul had his spear in his hand. He threw it at David, trying to kill him. But David got out of the way and ran into the night. He left the spear stuck in the wooden timbers of the wall. 11Saul sent troops to watch David's house. They were to kill him when he came out in the morning.

"You must leave tonight!" Michal warned him. "If you don't, you'll be dead by morning."

12So she helped him get down to the ground through a window. 13Then she took an idol and put it in his bed. She covered it with blankets. And she put its head on a pillow of goat's hair. 14The soldiers came to catch David and take him to Saul. But when they got there, Michal told them he was sick. She told them he couldn't get out of bed. 15Saul told them to bring him in his bed. Then he would kill him. 16So they came to carry him out. But they found that it was only an idol!

17"Why have you lied to me?" Saul shouted at Michal. "How could you let my enemy escape?"

"I had to," Michal replied. "He said he would kill me if I didn't help him."

18In that way David got away. He went to Ramah to see Samuel. He told him all that Saul had done to him. So Samuel took David with him to live at Naioth.

Saul Begins to Prophesy

19The report reached Saul that David was at Naioth in Ramah. 20So Saul sent soldiers to capture him. But when they got there, they saw Samuel and the other prophets prophesying. Then the Spirit of God came upon them. And they began to prophesy too. 21Saul heard what had happened. So he sent other soldiers. But they, too, prophesied! The same thing happened a third time! 22Then Saul himself went to Ramah. He came to the great well in Secu.

"Where are Samuel and David?" he demanded.

Someone told him they were at Naioth. 23But on the way to Naioth the Spirit of God came upon Saul. He too began to prophesy! 24He tore off his clothes. And he lay naked all day and all night. He prophesied with Samuel's prophets, and his men were amazed!

"What!" they exclaimed. "Is Saul a prophet too?"

- *Remember:* Who tried to stop Saul from killing David? (19:1-5) What did Saul promise? (19:6) Did Saul keep his promise? (19:9-10) What do you think kept Saul from keeping his promise? What did Saul do that almost killed David? (19:9-10) How did David's wife help him escape? (19:11-17) Where did David go when he escaped? (19:18) How would this story change if Saul had kept his promise to Jonathan? (19:6)

- *Discover:* Saul's jealousy became so bad it made him want to kill someone. Jealousy eats away at us until we do foolish and terrible things.

- *Apply:* Are you jealous of someone? Stop! Start doing something nice for that person right away. If you don't ask God to help you take your jealousy away, you may do something foolish. Remember Saul.

- *What's next?* Would you betray your best friend to become king? That's what Jonathan had to decide. Read 1 Samuel 20. ■

Jonathan Warns David

King Saul hated David and wanted to kill him. If he did, his son Jonathan would be the next king. If Saul didn't kill him, David would be the next king. Jonathan knew that. Would Jonathan betray his best friend so he could become king?

20 David now fled from Naioth in Ramah and found Jonathan.

"What have I done?" he exclaimed. "Why does your father want to kill me so badly?"

²"That's not true!" Jonathan protested. "I'm sure he's not planning any such thing. He always tells me everything he's going to do. He even tells me the little things. I know he wouldn't hide something like this from me. It just isn't so."

³"Of course you don't know about it!" David fumed. "Your father knows about our friendship. So he has said to himself, 'I'll not tell Jonathan. Why should I hurt him?' But the truth is, I am only a step away from death! I swear it by the Lord and by your own soul!"

⁴"Tell me what I can do," Jonathan begged.

⁵And David replied, "Tomorrow the feast of the new moon begins. Always before, I've been with your father at this feast. But tomorrow I'll hide in the field. I'll stay there until the evening of the third day. ⁶Your father might ask where I am. If he does, tell him that I asked to go home to Bethlehem. Tell him I had to go there for a yearly family reunion. ⁷He might say, 'Fine!' If he does, then I'll know that all is well. But if he is angry, then I'll know that he is planning to kill me. ⁸Do this for me as my sworn brother. Or else kill me yourself if I have sinned against your father. But don't betray me to him!"

⁹"Of course not!" Jonathan exclaimed. "Look, wouldn't I say so if I knew that my father was planning to kill you?"

¹⁰Then David asked, "How will I know whether or not your father is angry?"

¹¹"Come out to the field with me," Jonathan replied. And they went out there together.

¹²Then Jonathan told David, "I will make a promise by the Lord God of Israel. About this time tomorrow I will talk to my father about you. I will do this by the next day at the latest. Then I will let you know right away how he feels about you. ¹³He might be angry and want you killed. If so, then may the Lord kill me if I don't tell you. That way you can escape and live. May the Lord be with you as he used to be with my father. ¹⁴And remember, you must always show the love and kindness of the Lord to me. ¹⁵And you must also show it to my children. Remember this after the Lord has destroyed all of your enemies."

¹⁶So Jonathan made a covenant with the family of David. And David promised he would fulfill it. He swore a terrible curse against himself if he didn't do what he promised. That curse would also go against his descendants. ¹⁷But Jonathan made David swear to it again. This time he swore by his love for him. For he loved him as much as he loved himself.

¹⁸Then Jonathan said, "Yes. They will miss you tomorrow when your place at the table is empty. ¹⁹By the day after tomorrow, everyone will be asking about you. So be at the hideout where you were before, over by the stone pile. ²⁰I will come out and shoot three arrows in front of the pile. I will pretend that I am shooting at a target. ²¹Then I'll send a boy to bring the arrows back. You might hear me tell him, 'They're on this side.' If so, then you will know that all is well. It will be a sign that there is no trouble. ²²But I might tell him, 'Go farther. The arrows are still ahead of you.' If you hear this, it will mean that you must leave right away. ²³And may the Lord make us keep our promises to each other. For he has heard us make them."

²⁴⁻²⁵So David hid himself in the field. The new moon feast began and the king sat down to eat. He took his usual place against the wall. Jonathan sat

across from him. Abner was sitting beside Saul. But David's place was empty. ²⁶Saul didn't say anything about it that day. He thought that something had happened so that David was unclean. Yes, surely that must be it! ²⁷But his place was still empty the next day. So Saul asked Jonathan, "Why hasn't David been here for dinner? He hasn't been here either yesterday or today."

²⁸⁻²⁹"He asked me if he could go to Bethlehem," Jonathan replied. "He wanted to take part in a family feast. His brother asked that he be there, so I told him to go ahead."

³⁰Saul boiled with rage. "You son of a disobedient woman!" he yelled at him. "I know you're on David's side. You want him to be king in your place! You bring shame on yourself and your mother! ³¹As long as David is alive, you'll never be king. Now go! Get him so I can kill him!"

³²"But what has he done?" Jonathan demanded. "Why should he be put to death?"

³³Then Saul threw his spear at Jonathan, trying to kill him. At last Jonathan knew that his father really wanted to kill David. ³⁴Jonathan left the table in fierce anger. He would not eat all that day. He was ashamed of what his father wanted to do to David.

³⁵The next morning, as agreed, Jonathan went out into the field. He took a young boy with him to gather his arrows.

³⁶"Start running," he told the boy. "That way you will be able to find the arrows as I shoot them." So the boy ran and Jonathan shot an arrow beyond him. ³⁷The boy had almost reached the arrow. Jonathan shouted, "The arrow is still ahead of you. ³⁸Hurry, hurry, don't wait." So the boy quickly picked up the arrow. Then he ran back to his master. ³⁹He, of course, didn't know what Jonathan meant. Only Jonathan and David knew. ⁴⁰Then Jonathan gave his bow and arrows to the boy. He told him to take them back to the city.

⁴¹As soon as the boy was gone, David came out. He had been hiding near the south edge of the field. Both of them were crying as they said goodbye. David cried the most. ⁴²At last Jonathan said to David, "Cheer up! We have given each other into God's hands for all time. And we have done the same with our children." So they left each other. David went away and Jonathan went back to the city.

- *Remember:* What tests did Jonathan and David plan to see if Saul wanted to kill David? (20:5-13, 18-23) Jonathan knew that David would be the next king. How do you know that? (20:14-15) How did Saul show that he wanted to kill David? (20:24-33) Did Jonathan betray David? (20:35-41) Would you say that Jonathan was selfish or unselfish? Would you say he was a good friend or a bad friend? What is one of the things you can do to be a good friend?

- *Discover:* A good friend is always a good friend, even when it hurts him. Jonathan remained David's good friend, even though David would become king instead of him.

- *Apply:* Do you have a good friend? How much of a good friend are you? Would you remain a good friend even if it hurts you?

- *What's next?* A man murders 85 priests for doing something good. Read 1 Samuel 22. ■

David Eats the Holy Bread

21 David went to the city of Nob to see Ahimelech, the priest. Ahimelech was afraid when he saw him.

"Why are you alone?" he asked. "Why is no one with you?"

²"The king has sent me on a private matter," David said. "He told me not to tell anybody why I am here. I have told my men where to meet me later. ³Now, what is there to eat? Give me five loaves of bread or anything else you can."

⁴"We don't have any regular bread," the priest replied. "But there is the holy bread. I guess you can have it. But your young men cannot have slept with any women for awhile."

⁵"Don't worry," David replied. "I never let my men run wild when they

have work to do. They stay clean even on normal trips. On this trip, it is even more important!"

⁶There was no other food around. So the priest gave him the holy bread. This was the Bread of the Presence. It was put before the Lord in the Tabernacle. It had just been replaced that day with fresh bread.

⁷It happened that Doeg the Edomite was there at the time. He had come to purify himself. He was Saul's chief herdsman.

⁸David asked Ahimelech if he had a spear or sword he could use. "The king's orders are very important," David told him. "I left in such a hurry that I came away without a weapon!"

⁹"Well," the priest said, "I have the sword of Goliath, the Philistine. He was the man you killed in the Valley of Elah. It is wrapped in a cloth in the clothes closet. Take that if you want it. There is nothing else here."

"Just the thing!" David replied. "Give it to me!"

¹⁰Then David hurried on. He was afraid of Saul. From there, he went to King Achish of Gath. ¹¹But Achish's officers weren't happy about his being there. "Isn't he the top leader of Israel?" they asked. "Isn't he the one the people honor at their dances? Don't they sing about him? 'Saul has slain his thousands and David his ten thousands!'"

¹²David heard these comments. And he was afraid of what King Achish might do to him. ¹³So he pretended to be crazy! He scratched on doors and let his spit flow down his beard. ¹⁴⁻¹⁵Finally King Achish said to his men, "Must you bring me a madman? We already have enough of them around here! Should such a fellow as this be my guest?"

The Murder of the Priests

Saul was jealous of David. He wanted people to say good things about him instead of David. Saul was so jealous he wanted to kill David. He even wanted to kill people who helped David. Look what happens here.

David Hides in a Cave

22 So David left Gath and escaped to the cave of Adullam. His brothers and other relatives soon joined him there. ²Then others began coming until David was the leader of about 400 men. The men who came were often in some kind of trouble. Perhaps they were in debt. Or maybe they weren't happy with Saul's leadership. ³Later David went to Mizpeh in Moab. He asked if his father and mother could live there under royal protection. David wanted them to be safe until he knew what God was going to do. ⁴They stayed in Moab during the period that David was living in the cave.

⁵One day the prophet Gad told David to leave the cave. He told him to go back to the land of Judah. So David went to the forest of Hereth. ⁶The news that David had come back to Judah soon got to Saul. He was in Gibeah at the time. He was sitting under an oak tree playing with his spear. His officers were standing around him.

⁷"Listen here, you men of Benjamin!" Saul exclaimed when he heard the news. "Has David promised you fields and vineyards? Has he given you a command in his army? ⁸Why are you against me? Not one of you has ever told me that my own son is on David's side. You're not even sorry for me. Think of it! My own son is helping David to come and kill me!"

⁹⁻¹⁰Then Doeg the Edomite spoke up. He was standing there with Saul's men. "I was at Nob," he said. "While I was there, I saw David talking to Ahimelech the priest. Ahimelech spoke with the Lord to find out what David should do.

Then he gave him food and the sword of Goliath the Philistine."

11-12King Saul called Ahimelech and his family right away. He also called all the other priests at Nob. When they got there, Saul shouted at him. "Listen to me, you son of Ahitub!" he said.

"What is it?" said Ahimelech.

13"Why have you and David turned against me?" Saul demanded. "Why did you give him food and a sword? Why did you talk to God for him? Why did you help him to revolt against me? Now he is about to come here and attack me!"

14"But sir," Ahimelech replied, "isn't David your most faithful servant? Why, he is your own son-in-law! He is the captain of your bodyguard! He is an honored member of your own family! 15This was not the first time I had spoken to God for him. It is unfair of you to accuse me and my family in this matter. We knew nothing of any plot against you."

16"You shall die, Ahimelech!" the king shouted. "And your whole family will die with you!" 17He ordered his bodyguards, "Kill these priests! They have taken David's side. They knew he was running away from me, but they didn't tell me!"

But the soldiers would not kill the priests.

18Then the king said to Doeg, "You do it."

So Doeg turned on them and killed them. He killed 85 priests in all. And they were all wearing their priestly robes. 19Then he went to Nob, the city of the priests. There he killed the priests' families. He killed men, women, children, and babies. He also killed all the oxen, donkeys, and sheep. 20Only Abiathar got away and ran to David. He was one of the sons of Ahimelech.

21Abiathar told David what Saul had done. 22And David exclaimed, "I knew it! When I saw Doeg there, I knew he would tell Saul! Now I have caused the death of all of your father's family. 23Stay here with me. I'll protect you with my own life. Any harm to you will be over my dead body."

● *Remember:* Saul complained to his soldiers. What about? (22:7-8) Doeg told Saul a secret. What was it? (22:9-10) Why did Saul order the 85 priests killed? (22:11-18) Who wouldn't kill them? (22:17) Who did kill them? (22:18) Who else does Doeg kill? (22:19) Who escaped? Where did he go? (22:20-23) Would Doeg have killed these people if Saul had not been jealous?

● *Discover:* Saul's jealousy allowed Doeg to murder 85 priests and their families. Jealousy may seem harmless at first, but when it grows it causes all kinds of evil. Saul didn't murder these people himself, but he allowed a wicked man to do it. That's just as bad as doing it himself.

● *Apply:* Are you jealous of someone? You wouldn't hurt that person, would you? But would you be glad if that person was hurt? That's just as bad as hurting that person. Are you jealous because someone has something you don't have? You wouldn't take it, would you? But would you be glad if someone else took it or the person lost it? That's just as bad as taking it yourself.

● *What's next?* What do you think of a traitor? You'll see two cities filled with traitors in 1 Samuel 23. ■

Traitors Turn against David

Nobody likes a traitor. A traitor only pretends to be a friend. But he will help enemies hurt you. David and his men rescued some people when the Philistines were robbing them. Would they ever betray David? Would they tell King Saul where David was hiding? Let's see what these people did.

David Protects the Town of Keilah

23 One day news came to David that the Philistines were at Keilah. They were robbing the threshing floors there.

2David asked the Lord, "Shall I go and attack them?"

"Yes, go and save Keilah," the Lord told him.

3But David's men said, "We're afraid even here in Judah. We don't want to go to Keilah to fight the whole Philistine army!"

4David asked the Lord again. The Lord again replied, "Go down to Keilah. I will help you conquer the Philistines."

5They went to Keilah and defeated the Philistines. They also took their cattle. And so the people of Keilah were saved. 6Abiathar the priest went to Keilah with David. He took his ephod with him to get answers for David from the Lord. 7Saul soon learned that David was at Keilah.

"Good!" he said. "We've got him now! God has given him to me. He has trapped himself in a walled city."

8So Saul called out his whole army. He planned to march to Keilah and attack David and his men. 9But David learned of Saul's plan. So he told Abiathar the priest to bring the ephod. He told him to ask the Lord what he should do.

10"O Lord God of Israel," David said. "I have heard that Saul is planning to come. He plans to destroy Keilah because I am here. 11Will the men of Keilah give me up to him? And will Saul actually come, as I have heard? O Lord God of Israel, please tell me."

And the Lord said, "He will come."

12"And will these men of Keilah give me up to Saul?" David asked.

And the Lord replied, "Yes, they will give you up."

13So David and his men left Keilah. They began roaming the countryside. By then there were about 600 of them.

Word soon reached Saul that David had escaped. So he didn't go there after all. 14-15David now lived in the wilderness caves in the hill country of Ziph. One day near Horesh he got the news that Saul was on the way to Ziph. Saul was looking for him and wanted to kill him. Saul hunted him day after day. But the Lord didn't let him find him.

16Prince Jonathan now went to find David. He met him at Horesh and encouraged him in his faith in God.

17"Don't be afraid," Jonathan told him. "My father will never find you! You are going to be the next king of Israel! I will be second to you. My father is well aware of this." 18So the two of them renewed their pact of friendship. And David stayed at Horesh while Jonathan went home.

19But now the men of Ziph went to Saul in Gibeah. They told him where David was.

"We know where he is hiding," they said. "He is in the caves of Horesh on Hachilah Hill. This is down in the southern part of the desert. 20Come on down, sir. We will catch him for you. Then your fondest wish will be fulfilled!"

21"Well, praise the Lord!" Saul said. "At last someone has had pity on me! 22Go and check again to be sure of where he is staying. And check with the one who has seen him there. For I know that he is very crafty. 23Find his hiding places. Then come back and give me a more definite report. If you do this, I'll go with you. And if he is in the area at all, I'll find him! I'll get him if I have to search every inch of the whole land!"

24-25So the men of Ziph went back home. But David heard that Saul was on his way to Ziph. So he and his men went even farther into the wilderness of Maon. This was in the southern part of the desert. But Saul followed them there. 26He and David were now on opposite sides of a mountain. Saul and his men began to close in. David tried his best to escape, but it was no use. ²⁷But just then a message reached Saul that the Philistines were raiding Israel again. ²⁸So Saul quit the chase and went back to fight the Philistines. Ever since that time the place where David was camped has been called, "The Rock of Escape!" ²⁹David then went to live in the caves of Engedi.

- *Remember:* What did David do to help the people of Keilah? (23:1-6) Who told David to do this? (23:2) Would these people betray David after David had helped them? Would they tell King Saul that he was there? (23:10-11) How did Saul's son Jonathan show that he was David's friend? (23:16-18) Were the people of Ziph David's friends or were they traitors? What did they do? (23:19-20) What saved David? (23:26-28) What must you do to keep others from calling you a traitor?

- *Discover:* A traitor pretends to be a friend but will hurt you to help himself. Nobody trusts a traitor.

- *Apply:* Do you ever try to hurt a friend? Does a friend ever try to hurt you? Do you ever try to hurt someone in your family? That's being a traitor, isn't it?

- *What's next?* David could get even with Saul. But he doesn't. Why not? Read 1 Samuel 24. ◼

David Refuses to Get Even

Saul hunted David like a wild animal. He wanted to kill him. While Saul was looking for David he went into a cave. He was alone. The soldiers were outside. He didn't know David was hiding there. David could kill Saul easily. This was the time to get even. Did David do it?

24 Saul came back from his battle with the Philistines. And he was told that David had gone into the wilderness of Engedi. ²So he took 3,000 special troops. He went to search for David among the rocks and wild goats of the desert. ³There is a place where the road passes some sheepfolds. At that place, Saul went into a cave to go to the bathroom. But as it happened, David and his men were hiding in the cave!

⁴"Now's your time!" David's men whispered to him. "Today is the day the Lord was talking about. He said, 'I will put Saul into your power, to do with as you wish'!" Then David crept forward. He quietly cut off the bottom of Saul's robe! ⁵But then his conscience began bothering him.

⁶"I shouldn't have done it," he said to his men. "It is a serious sin to attack God's chosen king in any way."

⁷⁻⁸These words of David persuaded his men not to kill Saul.

Saul left the cave and went on his way. Then David came out and shouted after him, "My lord the king!" And when Saul looked around, David bowed low before him.

⁹⁻¹⁰Then he shouted to Saul, "Some people say I am trying to hurt you. Why do you listen to them? This very day you have seen it isn't true. For the Lord placed you at my mercy back there in the cave. Some of my men told me to kill you. But I let you live! For I said, 'I will never harm him. He is the Lord's chosen king.' ¹¹See what I have in my hand? It is the hem of your robe! I cut it off, but I didn't kill you! Doesn't this prove to you that I am not trying to hurt you? Can't you see that I have not sinned against you? I am innocent, even though you have been trying to kill me!

¹²"The Lord will decide between us. Perhaps he will kill you for what you are trying to do to me. But I will never hurt you. ¹³As that old proverb says, 'From wicked people come wicked deeds.' But even though you have been wicked, I'll not touch you. ¹⁴And who is the king of Israel trying to catch, anyway? Should he spend his time chasing me? I am as worthless as a dead dog or a flea! ¹⁵May

B. Gallego

the Lord judge as to which of us is right. And may he punish the one who is guilty. He is my lawyer and defender. He will rescue me from your power!"

¹⁶Saul called back, "Is it really you, my son David?" Then he began to cry. ¹⁷ And he said to David, "You are a better man than I am. You have repaid me good for evil. ¹⁸Yes, you have been very kind to me today. For the Lord gave me into your hand. But you didn't kill me. ¹⁹Who else in all the world would let his enemy get away when he had him in his power? May the Lord reward you well for the kindness you have shown me today. ²⁰And now I know that you are surely going to be king. Israel shall be yours to rule. ²¹Please, make a promise to me by the Lord! Promise that when you become king you will not kill my family. Please, do not destroy my line of descendants!"

²²So David promised, and Saul went home. But David and his men went back to their cave.

- *Remember:* How many soldiers did Saul take with him? (24:2) How could David get even with Saul? What did his men want him to do? (24:3-4) How did David show that he would not get even with him? (24:4-15) What did Saul do then? (24:16-19) What did Saul ask David to promise? (24:20-21) Did David promise? (24:22) Why didn't David ask Saul to promise not to hurt him? Did Saul keep his other vows and promises? Because David did not get even, Saul said David would be king. (24:20) Why do you think he said that?

- *Discover:* Anyone can get even. Only a special person will refuse to get even. David was a special person. God had chosen him to be the next king.

- *Apply:* Has someone hurt you or said something bad about you? Would you like to get even? Don't! Be a special person like David.

- *What's next?* Who could stop a mighty warrior who was very angry from fighting? Read 1 Samuel 25. ∎

Abigail Stops a Fight

It's easy to get into a fight. It's harder to stop one. Here's how a beautiful lady stopped a fight that was about to happen and was about to hurt a lot of people.

25 Shortly after that Samuel died. And all Israel gathered for his funeral. They buried him in his family plot at Ramah.

Meanwhile David went down to the wilderness of Paran. ²A wealthy man from Maon owned a sheep ranch there, near the village of Carmel. He had 3,000 sheep and 1,000 goats. He was at his ranch at this time for the sheep shearing. ³His name was Nabal. His wife was a beautiful and very smart woman. Her name was Abigail. The man was a descendant of Caleb. But he was stubborn and bad-mannered.

⁴David heard that Nabal was shearing his sheep. ⁵So he sent 10 of his young men to Carmel to give him a message. ⁶"May God prosper you and your family and multiply all you own," they said. ⁷"We are told that you are shearing your sheep and goats. While your shepherds have lived among us, we have never harmed them. We have not stolen anything from them the whole time they have been in Carmel. ⁸Ask your young men. They will tell you if this is true or not. We have come at a time of feasting. For this reason, be kind to us and to your son David. Please give us a present of whatever is at hand."

⁹The young men gave David's message to Nabal. They waited for his reply.

¹⁰"Who is this fellow David?" he sneered. "Who does this son of Jesse think he is? There are lots of servants these days who run away from their masters. ¹¹Should I take my bread and my water? Should I take the meat that I've killed for my shearers? Should I give it to a gang which comes from who knows where?"

¹²So David's messengers went back. They told him what Nabal had said.

¹³"Get your swords!" was David's reply as he strapped on his own. Four hundred of them started off with David. Two hundred stayed behind to guard their gear.

¹⁴Meanwhile, one of Nabal's men went and spoke to Abigail. "David sent men from the wilderness to talk to our master," he told her. "But Nabal insulted them and taunted them. ¹⁵⁻¹⁶But David's men were very good to us. We never suffered any harm from them. In fact, day and night they protected us and the sheep. Nothing was stolen from us the whole time they were with us. ¹⁷You'd better think fast. For there is going to be trouble for our master and his whole family. He's such a stubborn man! No one can even talk to him!"

¹⁸Then Abigail quickly took 200 loaves of bread and two barrels of wine. She killed and dressed five sheep. She also took two bushels of roasted grain, 100 raisin cakes, and 200 fig cakes. Then she packed it all onto donkeys.

¹⁹"Go on ahead," she said to her young men. "I will follow." But she didn't tell her husband what she was doing. ²⁰Then she rode down the trail on her donkey. As she was riding, she met David coming toward her.

²¹David had been saying to himself, "A lot of good it did us to help Nabal! We protected his flocks in the wilderness. Not one thing was lost or stolen! But he has given me bad for good. All that I get for my trouble is insults. ²²May God curse me if even one of his men is alive by tomorrow morning!"

²³When Abigail saw David, she quickly got down. She bowed low before him.

²⁴"I accept all blame in this matter, my lord," she said. "Please listen to what I have to say. ²⁵Nabal is a bad-tempered fool. Please don't listen to what he said. He is a fool, just like his name means. But I didn't see the messengers you sent. ²⁶Sir, the Lord has kept you from taking revenge with your own hands. I pray by the life of God, and your life too, that all your enemies shall be as cursed as Nabal is. ²⁷And now, here is a gift I have brought to you and your young men. ²⁸Forgive me for my boldness in coming out here. The Lord will surely reward you and your descendants with a kingship for all time. For you are fighting his battles. As long as you live, people will never find any wrong in you. ²⁹You might even be chased by those who seek your life. But even so, you are safe in the care of the Lord your God. It is just as though you were safe inside his purse! But the lives of your enemies shall disappear like stones from a sling! ³⁰⁻³¹The Lord shall do all the good things he promised you. And he shall make you king of Israel. When this happens, you won't want to carry the guilt of a murderer! You won't want to be known as one who took the law into his own hands! And when the Lord has done these great things for you, please remember me!"

³²David replied to Abigail, "Bless the Lord God of Israel! He has sent you to meet me today! ³³Thank God for your good sense! Bless you for keeping me from murdering the man! I have been saved from taking revenge with my own hands. ³⁴I swear by the Lord, the God of Israel! He has kept me from hurting you. You might not have come out to meet me. But if you hadn't, not one of Nabal's men would be alive tomorrow morning."

³⁵Then David took her gifts. He told her to go back home without fear. For he would not kill her husband. ³⁶When she got home she found that Nabal had thrown a big party. He was very drunk. So she didn't tell him about her meeting with David until the next morning. ³⁷⁻³⁸By that time he was sober. When his wife told him what had happened, he had a stroke. And he lay there unable to move for about 10 days. Then he died, for the Lord killed him.

³⁹When David heard that Nabal was dead, he said, "Praise the Lord! God has paid back Nabal and kept me from doing it myself. He has been punished for his sin."

Then David wasted no time in sending messengers to Abigail. He sent them to ask her to marry him. ⁴⁰The messengers went to Carmel and told her why they had come. ⁴¹She quickly agreed to David's request. ⁴²She got ready without delay. And she took along five of her serving girls as helpers. She got on her donkey and followed the men back to David. So she became his wife.

David Also Marries Ahinoam

⁴³David also married Ahinoam from Jezreel. ⁴⁴King Saul, meanwhile, had forced David's wife Michal to marry a man from Gallim. His name was Palti. He was the son of Laish.

- *Remember:* What kind of person was Nabal? (25:3,14-17,25) What kind of person was Abigail? (25:3,34) Why did David want to fight Nabal? (25:9-13) What did Abigail do to stop David? (25:18-31) What gifts did Abigail take to David? Why? (25:18) Would you call Nabal a troublemaker or a peacemaker? Would you call Abigail a troublemaker or a peacemaker? Why?

- *Discover:* Read Matthew 5:9. What did Jesus say about peacemakers—people who strive for peace? Peacemaking brings happiness. If you want to be happy, don't be a troublemaker. Be a peacemaker. Be like Abigail.

● *Apply:* The next time you do something that would start trouble, stop! Don't do it. Be a peacemaker, not a troublemaker.

● *What's next?* "I won't try to hurt you anymore," Saul says to David. Why can't David believe him? Read 1 Samuel 26. ■

David Sneaks into Saul's Camp at Night

Some people can be trusted with anything. Other people can't be trusted with anything. But how do you know? This is a story about David and King Saul. One man could be trusted with anything. One could not. This story will tell you which man could be trusted and which could not.

26 Now the men from Ziph came back to Saul at Gibeah. They told him that David had gone back to the wilderness. They said he was hiding on Hachilah Hill. ²So Saul took his elite group of 3,000 troops. And he went to hunt him down. ³⁻⁴Saul camped along the road at the edge of the wilderness where David was hiding. But David knew of Saul's coming. So he sent out spies to watch his movements.

⁵⁻⁷David slipped over to Saul's camp one night to look around. King Saul and General Abner were sleeping. They were inside a ring formed by the sleeping soldiers.

"Any volunteers to go down there with me?" David asked Ahimelech and Abishai. Ahimelech was a Hittite and Abishai was Joab's brother and the son of Zeruiah.

"I'll go with you," Abishai replied. So David and Abishai went to Saul's camp and found him asleep. His spear was in the ground beside his head.

⁸"God has put your enemy within your power this time for sure," Abishai whispered to David. "Let me go and put that spear through him. I'll pin him to the earth with it. I'll not need to strike a second time!"

⁹"No," David said. "Don't kill him. For who can be innocent after attacking the Lord's chosen king? ¹⁰Surely God will strike him down someday. Or he will die in battle or of old age. ¹¹But God forbid that I should kill the man he has chosen to be king! But we will take his spear and his jug of water and then get out of here!"

¹²So David took the spear and jug of water. They got away without anyone seeing them or even waking up. For the Lord had put them in a sound sleep. ¹³They climbed the mountain slope across from the camp. They walked until they were at a safe distance.

¹⁴Then David shouted down to Abner and Saul, "Wake up, Abner!"

"Who is it?" Abner demanded.

¹⁵"Well, Abner, you're a great soldier, aren't you?" David said. "Where in all Israel is there anyone as great? So why haven't you guarded your master the king? Last night someone came to kill him! ¹⁶This isn't good at all! I swear by the Lord that you ought to die for being so careless. Where is the king's spear? Where is the jug of water that was beside his head? Look and see!"

¹⁷⁻¹⁸Saul knew David's voice. He said, "Is that you, my son David?"

And David replied, "Yes, sir, it is. Why are you chasing me? What have I done? What is my crime? ¹⁹Perhaps the Lord has stirred you up against me. If so, then let him take my peace offering. But perhaps this is just the plan of a man. If so, then may he be cursed by God. For you have driven me out of my home. I can no longer be with the Lord's people. And you have sent me away to worship heathen gods. ²⁰Must I die on foreign soil, far from the presence of the Lord? Why should the king of Israel come out to hunt my life like a partridge on the mountains?"

²¹Then Saul confessed, "I have done wrong. Come back home, my son. I'll no longer try to harm you. For you saved my life today. I have been a fool, and very, very wrong."

²²"Here is your spear, sir," David replied. "Let one of your young men come over and get it. ²³The Lord gives his own reward for doing good and for being loyal. I did not kill you even when the Lord placed you in my power. ²⁴Now may the Lord save my life, even as I have saved yours today. May he rescue me from all my troubles."

²⁵And Saul said to David, "Blessings on you, my son David. You shall do great deeds. You shall be a great conqueror."

Then David went away and Saul went back home.

- *Remember:* When David and Abishai went into Saul's camp, what were Saul's soldiers doing? (26:5-7) Why didn't David kill Saul? Saul was there to kill him. This was a good time to get even. (26:8-11) What did David do instead? (26:12-20) Saul confessed that he had been wrong. He asked David to come home. (26:21-25) Why didn't David go home with him? Could he trust Saul to keep his promise? Why not? Could Saul trust David? How do you know?

- *Discover:* We trust people who show they can be trusted. We stop trusting people who show they can't be trusted. David showed he could be trusted. Saul showed he could not be trusted.

- *Apply:* Do your parents trust you? Do your friends trust you? Each time they do, do you show them you can be trusted? The next time they trust you, remember David and Saul. Show them they can trust you.

- *What's next?* Saul visits a witch one night. Why would the king do that? Read 1 Samuel 28. ■

David Lives among the Philistines

27 But David thought to himself, "Someday Saul is going to get me. I'll try my luck among the Philistines. Saul will give up someday and quit hunting for me. Then I will finally be safe again."

2-3 So David took his 600 men and their families. They all went to live at Gath under the protection of King Achish. He had his two wives with him. They were Ahinoam of Jezreel and Abigail of Carmel, Nabal's widow. 4 Word soon reached Saul that David had fled to Gath. So he quit hunting for him.

5 One day David spoke to Achish. "My lord, we would rather live in one of the country towns," he said. "If you think well of me, please let us move. Why should we live here in the royal city with you?"

6 So Achish gave him Ziklag. This town still belongs to the kings of Judah to this day. 7 They lived there among the Philistines for a year and four months. 8 He and his men went to raid the Geshurites, the Girzites, and the Amalekites. These were people who had lived near Shur. This was along the road to Egypt. They had lived there ever since ancient times. 9 They didn't leave one person alive in the villages they hit. They took for themselves their sheep, oxen, donkeys, camels, and clothing. Then they would go back to see Achish.

10 "Where did you make your raid today?" Achish would ask.

David would reply, "We went against the south of Judah. We also raided the people of Jerahmeel and the Kenites."

11 No one was left alive to come to Gath and tell where he had really been. This happened again and again while he was living among the Philistines. 12 Achish believed David. He thought that the Israelites must hate him by now. "Now he will have to stay here!" the king thought. "He will serve me forever!"

Saul Visits a Witch

Saul was terrified. The Philistine army was ready to fight. Saul was not ready. What should he do? Saul had not pleased the Lord, so the Lord did not help him. Who could tell him what to do next? Saul could have gone to many good people for advice. Instead, he went to see a witch.

28 About that time the Philistines called out their armies. They were planning for another war with Israel.

"Come and help us fight," King Achish said to David and his men.

2 "Good," David agreed. "You will soon see what a help we can be to you."

"If you are, you shall be my bodyguard for life," Achish told him.

3 Meanwhile, Samuel had died. And all Israel had mourned for him. He was buried in Ramah, his hometown. King Saul had banned all mediums and wizards from the land of Israel.

4 The Philistines set up their camp at Shunem. Saul and the armies of Israel were at Gilboa. 5-6 Saul saw the great army of the Philistines. And he was very afraid. He asked the Lord what he should do. But the Lord would not answer him. He gave him no answer by dreams, or by Urim, or by the prophets. 7-8 Saul then ordered his aides to try to find a medium. He wanted to ask her what to do. They found one at Endor. Saul disguised himself by wearing normal clothing instead of his royal robes. He went to the woman's home at night. He took two of his men with him.

"I've got to talk to a dead man," he pleaded. "Will you call his ghost up?"

9 "Are you trying to get me killed?" the woman demanded. "You know that Saul has had all of the witches killed.

You are spying on me."

[10]But Saul promised that he wouldn't tell on her.

[11]Finally the woman said, "Whom do you want me to bring up?"

"Bring me Samuel," Saul replied.

[12]When the woman saw Samuel, she screamed. "You've lied to me!" she cried. "You are Saul!"

[13]"Don't be afraid!" the king told her. "What do you see?"

"I see a ghost coming up out of the earth," she said.

[14]"What does he look like?"

"He is an old man wrapped in a robe."

Saul knew that it was Samuel. So he bowed low before him.

[15]"Why have you troubled me by bringing me back?" Samuel asked Saul.

"Because I am in deep trouble," he replied. "The Philistines are at war with us. God has left me and won't speak to me by prophets or dreams. So I have called for you to ask you what to do."

[16]But Samuel replied, "Why ask me if the Lord has left you? Why bother me if he has become your enemy? [17]He has done just as he said he would. He has taken the kingdom from you. And he has given it to your rival, David. [18]All this has come upon you because you did not obey the Lord's orders. You did not do what he told you when he was so angry with Amalek. [19]What's more, the whole Israelite army will be destroyed by the Philistines tomorrow. And you and your sons will be here with me."

[20]Saul now fell full length upon the ground. He could not move because he was afraid of Samuel's words. He was also faint with hunger. He had eaten nothing all day. [21]The woman saw how afraid Saul was. So she said, "Sir, I obeyed your command at the risk of my life.

22Now do what I say. Let me give you some food to eat. It will give you back your strength for the trip to camp."

23But he refused. His servants joined the woman in asking him to eat. So he finally gave in. He got up and sat on the bed. 24The woman had been fattening a calf. So she hurried out and killed it. She kneaded dough and baked unleavened bread. 25She brought the meal to the king and his men, and they ate it. Then they went out into the night.

- *Remember:* Why was Saul so afraid? (28:4-6) The Lord didn't answer Saul when he asked for help. Why not? (28:18) Where did Saul go for advice then? (28:7-8) Saul could have gone to wise people for advice. He could have gone to godly men. Instead, he went to a witch, or medium. What does this tell you about Saul? What kind of man was he?

- *Discover:* We show our character by the people we trust for advice. Saul trusted a witch for advice.

- *Apply:* When you're in trouble, whose advice do you want? You will show what kind of person you are by the kind of person you ask for advice. Ask God for wisdom. And ask people who know God for advice.

- *What's next?* An army does not want help from strong soldiers. Why not? Read 1 Samuel 29–30. ∎

David Leaves the Philistines

David had a problem. He had been hiding from King Saul, who wanted to kill him. At last he hid with the Philistines, Israel's enemies. One day the Philistines went to fight the Israelites. How could David go with them and fight his own people? But how could he refuse? The Philistines would think he was a traitor. What should he do?

29 The Philistine army now gathered at Aphek. The Israelites camped at the springs in Jezreel. 2The Philistine captains led their troops by hundreds and thousands. David and his men marched at the back with King Achish.

3But the Philistine commanders spoke to Achish. "What are these Israelites doing here?" they demanded.

King Achish told them, "This is David. He is the runaway servant of King Saul of Israel. He's been with me for years. I've never found one fault in him since he came."

4But the Philistine leaders were angry. "Send them back!" they demanded. "They aren't going into the battle with us. They'll turn against us! What better way is there for him to make up with King Saul than by turning against us in the battle? 5This is the same man the women of Israel sang about in their dances. 'Saul has slain his thousands and David his ten thousands!' they used to sing."

6So Achish called David and his men. "I swear by the Lord," he told them. "You are some of the finest men I've ever met. I think you should go with us. But my commanders do not agree. 7Please don't upset them, but go back quietly."

8"What have I done to deserve this treatment?" David demanded. "Why can't I fight your enemies?"

9But Achish said, "You are as pleasing to me as an angel of God. But my commanders are afraid to have you with them in the battle. 10Now get up early in the morning. Leave as soon as it is light."

11So David headed back into the land of the Philistines. And the Philistine army went on to Jezreel.

30 Three days later David and his men got back to their city of Ziklag. They found that the Amalekites had raided the city. They had burned it to the ground! 2And they had taken all the women and children! 3David and his men looked at the ruins. They saw what had happened to their families. 4Then they cried until they could cry no more. 5David's two wives, Ahinoam and Abigail, were among those who had been taken. 6David was very worried. His own men began talking about killing him. They were very angry and sad because of what had happened to their children. But David took strength from the Lord.

7Then he said to Abiathar the priest, "Bring me the oracle!" So Abiathar brought it.

8David asked the Lord, "Shall I chase them? Will I catch them?"

And the Lord told him, "Yes, go after them! You will get everything back that was taken from you!"

9-10So David and his 600 men set out after the Amalekites. They got to Besor Brook. At the brook, 200 of the men were too tired to go across. But the other 400 kept going. 11-12Along the way they found an Egyptian boy in a field. They brought him to David. He had not had any food or drink for three days and nights. So they gave him part of a fig cake, two cakes of raisins, and some water. His strength soon came back.

13"Who are you? Where did you come from?" David asked him.

"I am an Egyptian. I was the servant of an Amalekite," he replied. "My master left me behind three days ago because I was sick. 14We were on our way back from raiding the Cherethites in the Negeb. We had raided the south of Judah and the land of Caleb. And we had just burned Ziklag."

15"Can you tell me where they went?" David asked.

The young man replied, "Swear by God's name that you will not kill me. And promise you will not give me back to my master. If you promise this, then I will guide you to them."

16So he led them to the Amalekite camp. They were spread out across the fields. They were eating and drinking and dancing with joy. They had a huge amount of loot! They had taken it from the Philistines and from the men of Ju-

dah. 17David and his men rushed in among them. They fought with them all that night and the whole next day until evening. No one got away except 400 young men who fled on camels. 18-19David got back all they had taken. The men found their families and all they owned. And David rescued his two wives. 20His troops rounded up all the flocks and herds. They drove them on ahead of them. "These are all yours personally, as your reward!" they told David.

21They came to Besor Brook. There they met the 200 men who had been too tired to go on. David greeted them joyfully. 22But some of the other men with David spoke up. "They didn't go with us," they said. "So they can't have any of the loot. Give them their wives and their children and tell them to be gone."

23But David said, "No, my brothers! The Lord has kept us safe and helped us defeat the enemy. 24Do you think that anyone will listen to you when you talk like this? We share and share alike. Those who go to battle must share with those who guard the equipment."

25From then on David made this a law for all of Israel. It is still followed to this day.

David Sends a Present to Judah

26When he got back to Ziklag, he sent part of the loot to the elders of Judah. "Here is a present for you. It was taken from the Lord's enemies," he wrote them. 27-31 The gifts were sent to the elders in the following cities: Bethel, South Ramoth, Jattir, Aroer, Siphmoth, Eshtemoa, Racal, the cities of the Jerahmeelites, the cities of the Kenites, Hormah, Borashan, Athach, and Hebron.

• Remember: Did David and his men start out to battle with the Philistines? (29:1-2) Who stopped them? Who sent them back? Why? (29:3-11) What terrible thing happened while David was away? (30:1-6) Who did David ask for advice? (30:7-8) How did David and his men find the Amalekites? (30:9-19) What new rule did David make about sharing with others? (30:21-25) Do you like this rule? Why?

- *Discover:* When Saul needed advice he asked a witch (1 Samuel 28:3-25). When David needed advice, he asked the Lord. Saul was defeated. David was victorious. The Lord has the best answers.

- *Apply:* When you have a problem, whose advice do you seek? Bad people give bad advice. Godly people give good advice. Ask God and godly persons.

- *What's next?* King Saul kills himself. Why? Read 1 Samuel 31. ■

Saul Dies in Battle

King Saul was fighting the Philistines, his enemies. Suddenly he killed himself with his own sword. Why would a king do that?

31 Meanwhile the Philistines had begun to fight against Israel. And the Israelites ran from them. Many of them were killed on Mount Gilboa. ²The Philistines closed in on Saul. They killed his sons Jonathan, Abinidab, and Malchishua.

³⁻⁴Then the archers overtook Saul and wounded him badly. He groaned to his bodyguard, "Kill me with your sword. Don't let these heathen Philistines capture me and torture me." But his bodyguard was afraid to do it. So Saul took his own sword. He fell on the point of the blade, and it pierced him through. ⁵His bodyguard saw that he was dead. So he also fell upon his sword and died with him. ⁶So Saul, his bodyguard, his three sons, and his troops died together that same day.

⁷There were Israelites on the other side of the valley. There were others that lived beyond the Jordan. They heard that their comrades had been beaten. They heard that Saul and his sons were dead. So they ran from their cities. And the Philistines took them and lived in them.

⁸The next day the Philistines went out to strip the dead. They found the bodies of Saul and his three sons on Mount Gilboa. ⁹They cut off Saul's head and stripped off his armor. Then they spread the news of Saul's death in the temples of their idols. They spread the news to the people throughout their land.

¹⁰His armor was placed in the temple of Ashtaroth. His

body was hung on the wall of Beth-shan.
¹¹But the people of Jabesh-gilead heard what the Philistines had done. ¹²So warriors from that town traveled all night to Beth-shan. They took down the bodies of Saul and his sons from the wall. Then they brought them back to Jabesh. There they burned them. ¹³Then they buried their remains under the oak tree at Jabesh and fasted for seven days.

- *Remember:* The Philistines killed three of Saul's sons. Who were they? (31:2) Why did Saul ask his armor bearer to kill him? (31:3-4) Who killed Saul? (31:4) What did the Philistines do with Saul's body? (31:8-10) What did the people of Jabesh-gilead do? (31:11- 13) Read 1 Samuel 11 to see why they liked Saul so much.

- *Discover:* Saul commanded his armor bearer to kill him (31:3-4). If he did, he would be murdering his king. If he didn't, he would be disobeying his king. The armor bearer refused to kill his king because murder is sin. We should never sin, no matter who tells us to do it. We must never sin, even if a very important person orders us to do it.

- *Apply:* Your best friend says, "Let's do it!" But doing that is a sin. Don't do it! A movie star or star athlete does something that looks exciting. But it is sin. Don't do it, just because that person does it!

- *What's next?* For seven years a king is a king, but not completely a king. Read 2 Samuel 5:1-12. ▨

SECOND
SAMUEL

King David was the most powerful king Israel ever had. People call David's reign the Golden Age of Israel because he helped Israel become a great nation. But it wasn't easy. The Book of 2 Samuel tells the adventures of how David became king. You'll read about many of the brave things he did. You'll also read about some foolish things he did. This will help you understand the way God wants you to live.

In this book you'll see him running for his life from his own son. You'll see him scolded by a prophet for sinning. You'll see his men slinking home half-naked with beards half shaved off. And you'll see David pleading with God for the lives of his people. But you'll also see King David at his best. You'll watch as David is crowned king of all the land. You'll wonder why he was kind to a crippled grandson of the man who tried to kill him. You'll be amazed to see him forgive a man who cursed him. And you'll watch David cry when Absalom dies, even though Absalom had tried to kill him. This is mostly a book about David and his people. You'll want to get to know David. When you do, you'll know why the Lord loved him so much.

1 At this time, Saul was dead. David had just come back to Ziklag after destroying the Amalekites. Three days later, a man came from the Israelite army. His clothes were torn and dirt was on his head as a sign of mourning. He fell to the ground before David in deep respect.

³"Where do you come from?" David asked.

"From the Israelite army," he replied.
⁴"What happened?" David de-

manded. "Tell me how the battle went."

And the man replied, "Our whole army fled. Thousands of men are dead and wounded on the field. And Saul and his son Jonathan have been killed."

⁵"How do you know they are dead?"
⁶"I was on Mount Gilboa and saw Saul there leaning against his spear. The enemy chariots were closing in on him. ⁷When he saw me he told me to come to him.

⁸"'Who are you?' he asked.

"'An Amalekite,' I replied.

9"'Come and put me out of my pain,' he begged. 'I am badly hurt and am almost dead already.'

10"So I killed him, for I knew he couldn't live. Then I took his crown and one of his bracelets to bring to you, my lord."

11David and his men tore their clothes in sorrow when they heard the news. 12They mourned and cried and fasted all day for Saul and his son Jonathan. They also cried for the nation of Israel, the Lord's people. They cried for all the men of Israel who had died that day.

13Then David turned to the young man who had brought the news. "Where are you from?" he asked.

And he replied, "I am an Amalekite."

14"Why did you kill God's chosen king?" David demanded.

15Then he said to one of his young men, "Kill him!" So he ran him through with his sword, and he died.

16"You have spoken against yourself," David said. "You are guilty of your own death. You said yourself that you killed God's chosen king."

David's Song for Saul and Jonathan

17-18Then David wrote a funeral song for Saul and Jonathan. He ordered that it be sung throughout Israel. It is quoted here from the book *Heroic Ballads*.

19O Israel, your pride and joy lies
  dead upon the hills.
Mighty heroes have fallen.
20Don't tell the Philistines, or they
  will rejoice.
Hide it from the cities of Gath and
  Ashkelon,
Or the heathen nations will laugh
  in triumph.
21O Mount Gilboa,
Let there be no dew nor rain upon
  you.
Let no crops of grain grow on your
  slopes.
For there the mighty Saul has died.
He is God's chosen king no more.
22Both Saul and Jonathan killed
  their strongest foes.

They did not come back from battle
  empty-handed.
23How much they were loved! How
  great they were,
Both Saul and Jonathan!
They were together in life and in
  death.
They were faster than eagles,
  stronger than lions.
24But now, O women of Israel, weep
  for Saul.
He made you rich
With fine clothing and gold ornaments.
25These mighty heroes have fallen
  in the middle of the battle.
Jonathan is slain upon the hills.
26How I cry for you, my brother
  Jonathan.
How much I loved you!
And your love for me was deeper
Than the love of women!
27The mighty ones have fallen!
They are stripped of their weapons,
  and dead.

Judah Crowns David King

2David then asked the Lord, "Shall I move back to Judah?"

And the Lord replied, "Yes."

"Which city shall I go to?"

And the Lord replied, "Hebron."

2So David went up to Hebron with his two wives. One was Ahinoam from Jezreel. The other was Abigail, the widow of Nabal from Carmel. 3David also brought his men and their families with him to Hebron. 4Then the leaders of Judah came to David. They crowned him king of Judah.

David heard that the men of Jabeshgilead had buried Saul. 5So he sent them this message. "May the Lord bless you for being so loyal to your king," he said. "You have been kind to him by giving him a good burial. 6May the Lord be loyal to you in return! May he reward you with his love! And I too will be kind to you because of what you have done. 7Now be strong and brave, for Saul is dead. Be like the tribe of Judah, who have chosen me as their new king."

Abner Crowns Ish-bosheth King

[8]But Abner, Saul's commander, had gone to Mahanaim. There they had crowned Saul's son Ish-bosheth as king. [9]His land included Gilead, Ashuri, and Jezreel. It also included Ephraim, the tribe of Benjamin, and the rest of Israel. [10-11]Ish-bosheth was 40 years old at the time. He ruled in Mahanaim for two years. At that time, David was ruling in Hebron. He was the king of Judah for 7½ years.

Civil War Begins

[12]One day General Abner led some of Ish-bosheth's troops from Mahanaim. They went up to Gibeon. [13]General Joab led David's troops out to meet them. Joab was the son of Zeruiah. They met at the pool of Gibeon. There they sat facing each other from across the pool. [14]Then Abner said to Joab, "Let's watch some swordplay between our young men!"

Joab agreed. [15]So twelve men were chosen from each side to fight each other. [16]Each one grabbed his enemy by the hair. Each then thrust his sword into the other's side. In the end, all of them died. The place has been known ever since as "Field of Swords."

[17]The two armies began to fight each other that day. In the end, David's men defeated Abner and the men of Israel. [18]Joab's brothers, Abishai and Asahel, were also in the battle. Asahel could run like a deer, [19]and he began chasing Abner. He wouldn't stop for anything. He kept on chasing after Abner alone.

[20]Abner looked behind and saw him coming. So he called out to him, "Is that you, Asahel?"

"Yes," he called back, "it is."

[21]"Go after someone else!" Abner warned. But Asahel did not listen and kept on coming.

[22]Again Abner shouted to him, "Get away from here. If you don't, I will have to kill you! Then I won't ever be able to face your brother Joab again."

[23]But he would not turn away. So Abner stabbed him through the belly with the butt end of his spear. It went right through his body and came out his back. He stumbled to the ground and died there. Everyone stopped when they came to the place where he lay.

[24]Now Joab and Abishai set out after Abner. The sun was just going down as they got to Ammah Hill near Giah. This lay along the road into the Gibeon desert. [25]Abner's troops from the tribe of Benjamin met there at the top of the hill. [26]Abner shouted down to Joab, "Must our swords keep on killing each other? How long will it be before you tell your men to stop? Tell them to stop chasing their brothers."

[27]Joab shouted back, "I swear this by the name of God. Even if you hadn't spoken, we all would have gone home tomorrow morning." [28]Then he blew his trumpet. And his men stopped chasing the troops of Israel.

[29]That night Abner and his men went back across the Jordan Valley. They crossed the river. Then they traveled all the next morning until they got to Mahanaim. [30]Joab and his men went back home, too. There Joab made a count of his men. He found that only 19 were missing, in addition to Asahel. [31]But 360 of Abner's men were dead. All of them were from the tribe of Benjamin. [32]Joab and his men took Asahel's body to Bethlehem. They buried him there beside his father. Then they traveled all night and got to Hebron at daybreak.

David Becomes Stronger

3 That was the beginning of a long war between the families of Saul and David. David's position now became stronger and stronger. But Saul's family became weaker and weaker.

[2]Several sons were born to David while he was at Hebron. The oldest was Amnon, born to his wife Ahinoam. [3]His second son, Chileab, was born to Abigail. She was the widow of Nabal of Carmel. The third was Absalom, born to Maacah. She was the daughter of King Talmai of Geshur. [4]The fourth was Adonijah. He was born to Haggith. Then Shephatiah was born to Abital. [5]And Ithream was born to Eglah.

[6]As the war went on, Abner became a powerful leader among Saul's followers. [7]Now Saul had once had a concubine whose name was Rizpah. She was the

daughter of Aiah. Ish-bosheth accused Abner of sleeping with her. He asked, "Why did you sleep with my father's concubine?" 8Abner was very angry.

"Am I a dog from Judah to be kicked around like this?" he shouted. "I have done a great deal for you and your father! I have not betrayed you into David's hands! Is this my reward? How could you now find fault with me about some woman? 9-10May God curse me if I don't help David now! I will do all I can to take the kingdom away from you. David will rule all the way from Dan to Beersheba. It will be just as the Lord said."

11Ish-bosheth made no reply, for he was afraid of Abner.

12Then Abner sent messengers to David to discuss a deal. He would give the kingdom of Israel over to David. But David had to make him the commander of the armies of Israel and Judah.

13"All right," David replied. "But I will not talk unless you bring my wife Michal, Saul's daughter." 14David then sent this message to Ish-bosheth. "Give me back my wife Michal," he said. "I bought her with the lives of 100 Philistines."

15So Ish-bosheth took her away from her husband. His name was Paltiel, son of Laish. 16He went along behind her as far as Behurim, crying as he went. Then Abner told him, "Go on home now." So he went back home.

17At that time, Abner spoke with the leaders of Israel. He reminded them that for a long time they had wanted David as their king.

18"Now is the time!" he told them. "For the Lord has said, 'David is the one I have chosen. He will save my people from the Philistines. He will rescue them from all their enemies.'"

19Abner also talked to the leaders of the tribe of Benjamin. Then he went to Hebron. He told David of his progress with the people of Israel and Benjamin. 20There were 20 men with him. And David prepared a feast for them.

21As Abner left, he made a promise to David. "I will call a meeting of all the people of Israel," he said. "Then they will choose you as their king, as you've wanted for so long." So David let Abner go home in safety.

Joab Kills Abner in Revenge

22But just after Abner left, Joab and some of David's troops came home from a raid. They brought a great deal of loot with them. 23Joab was told that Abner had just been there. He heard that Abner had visited the king and been sent away in peace. 24-25So Joab rushed to the king. "What have you done?" he demanded. "Why did you let him get away? You know that he came to spy on us! You must know that he plans to come back and attack us!"

26Then Joab sent messengers to catch up with Abner. They were to tell him to come back. They found him at the well of Sirah. And he came back with them. But David knew nothing about it. 27When Abner got to Hebron, Joab took him aside at the city gate. He acted as if he wanted to speak with him alone. But then he pulled out a dagger. He killed him in revenge for the death of his brother Asahel.

28David heard about this. And he declared, "I make this promise by the name of the Lord. I and my people are innocent of this crime against Abner. 29Joab and his family are the guilty ones. May each of his children be victims of cancer! May they be lepers! May they be sterile! May they die of hunger! Or may they be killed by the sword!"

30So Joab and his brother, Abishai, killed Abner. They did it because Abner had killed their brother, Asahel, at the battle of Gibeon.

31Then David spoke to Joab and to those who were with him. "Go into deep mourning for Abner," he said. And King David himself walked behind the body to the burial site. 32They buried Abner in Hebron. And the king and all the people cried beside the grave.

33-34"Should Abner have died like a fool?" the king mourned.

"Your hands were not bound.
Your feet were not tied.
You were murdered.
You were the victim of a wicked
    plot."

And all the people cried again for him. 35-36David had refused to eat anything the day of the funeral. And now everyone begged him to take a bite of supper. But David promised that he would eat nothing until sundown. This pleased his people! And everything else he did pleased them too! 37So the whole nation, both Judah and Israel, understood. They knew by David's actions that he was not guilty of Abner's death.

38And David spoke to his people. "A great leader and a great man has fallen today in Israel," he said. 39"And even though I am God's chosen king, I am weak! I can do nothing with these two sons of Zeruiah. May the Lord repay bad men for their bad deeds."

King Ish-bosheth Is Murdered

4 King Ish-bosheth heard about Abner's death at Hebron. And he was frozen with fear. His people were also very afraid. 2-3The command of the Israelite troops then fell to two brothers. Their names were Baanah and Rechab. They were captains of King Ish-bosheth's raiding groups. They were the sons of Rimmon, who was from Beeroth in Benjamin. People from Beeroth are counted as Benjaminites. This is true even though they fled to Gittaim and live there now.

4There was a little lame grandson of King Saul's. His name was Mephibosheth. He was the son of Prince Jonathan. He was five years old when news came that Saul and Jonathan were dead. The news of Israel's defeat at the battle of Jezreel had reached the capital. So the child's nurse grabbed him and ran. But she fell and dropped him as she was running. Because of this, he became lame.

5Rechab and Baanah came to King Ish-bosheth's home. They got there at noon as he was taking a nap. 6-7They walked into the kitchen as though to get a sack of wheat. But then they went into his bedroom. They murdered him and cut off his head. They took his head and ran across the desert that night and escaped. 8They brought the head to David at Hebron.

"Look!" they exclaimed. "Here is the head of Ish-bosheth. He was the son of your enemy Saul who tried to kill you. Today the Lord has given you revenge upon Saul and his family!"

9But David replied, "I swear this by the Lord who saved me from my enemies! 10At another time, someone told me, 'Saul is dead!' He thought he was bringing me good news. But I killed him. That is how I paid him for his 'glad tidings.' 11And I shall do much more to you! This is because bad men have killed a good man! They have killed him in his own house and on his bed! Shall I not demand your lives?"

12So David ordered his young men to kill them. And they did. They cut off their hands and feet. Then they hanged their bodies beside the pool in Hebron. They took Ish-bosheth's head. They buried it in Abner's tomb in Hebron.

David Becomes King of All Israel

For seven years David had been king. But he was king of only part of Israel, not all of it. There was another king, named Ish-bosheth. When he died, David could at last become king of all Israel. Would he? Or would something stop him?

5 Leaders of all the tribes of Israel now came to David at Hebron. There they promised him that they would be loyal.

"We are your blood brothers," they said. 2"Even when Saul was our king you were our real leader. The Lord has said that you should be the shepherd and leader of his people."

3So David made a contract with the leaders of Israel before the Lord. And they crowned him king of Israel there at Hebron. [4-5]He had already been the king of Judah for seven years. He began his rule there at the age of 30. He then ruled 33 years in Jerusalem as king of both Israel and Judah. So he ruled for 40 years in all.

[6]David now led his troops to Jerusalem. They went to fight against the Jebusites who lived there.

"You'll never come in here," they told him. "Even the blind and lame could keep you out!" For they thought they were safe. [7]But David and his troops captured the city of Zion with its great walls. Now it is called the City of David.

[8]The insults from the defenders of the city came to David. And he told his troops, "Go up through the water tunnel into the city. Destroy those 'lame' and 'blind' Jebusites. How I hate them." That is the origin of the saying, "Even the blind and the lame could conquer you!"

[9]So David moved into Zion with its strong walls. He called it the City of David. He built up the area around it. He began at the old Millo section of the city. Then he built northward toward the present city center. [10]So David became greater and greater, for the Lord God of heaven was with him.

[11]Then King Hiram of Tyre sent cedar lumber, carpenters, and masons. They were sent to build a palace for David. [12]David now knew why the Lord had made him the king. It was clear why the Lord had blessed his kingdom so much. It was because God wanted to be kind to Israel. He wanted to show love to his chosen people.

- *Remember:* Who pledged their loyalty to David at Hebron? (5:1) How long had David been king of Judah? (5:4-5) How much longer was he king of all Israel? (5:5) How did David capture Jerusalem? (5:6-9) Why did the Lord make David king? Why did he bless David's kingdom so much? (5:12) Did David know this?

- *Discover:* Sometimes God gives us important work to do. But he is not trying to make us important. He wants to help his people. God made David king. But he was not trying to make David important. He was trying to help his people. David

was the best person to help his people (read 5:12 again).

- *Apply:* When God gives you an important job to do, don't think he is making you important. He wants you to help others.

- *What's next?* King David wants to take God's Ark of the Covenant to a better place. But God says no. Why? Read 2 Samuel 6. ▨

God Instructs David in Battle

[13]After moving from Hebron to Jerusalem, David married more wives. And he had many sons and daughters. [14-16]These are his children who were born at Jerusalem. Their names are Shammua, Shobab, Nathan, Solomon, Ibhar, Elishua, Nepheg, Japhia, Elishama, Eliada, Eliphelet.

[17]The Philistines heard that David had been crowned king of Israel. So they tried to capture him. But David was told that they were coming. And he went down into the stronghold. [18]The Philistines came and spread out across the valley of Rephaim.

[19]Then David asked the Lord, "Shall I go out and fight against them? Will you defeat them for me?"

And the Lord replied, "Yes, go ahead. For I will give them to you."

[20]So David went out. He fought with them at Baal-perazim and defeated them. "The Lord did it!" he exclaimed. "He burst through my enemies like a raging flood." So he named the place "Bursting." [21]At that time David and his men took away many idols that the Philistines had left. [22]But the Philistines came back. Again they spread out across the valley of Rephaim.

[23]David asked the Lord what to do. And the Lord replied, "Don't attack them from the front. Go behind them and come out by the balsam trees. [24]You will hear a sound like marching feet in the tops of the balsam trees. When you hear the sound, attack! For it will show that the Lord has made the way for you. And he will destroy them."

[25]So David did as the Lord had ordered him. And he destroyed the Philistines all the way from Geba to Gezer.

David Brings the Ark to Jerusalem

The Ark was holy. It was God's special golden chest. There was a right way to handle it and a wrong way to handle it. God had told his people the right way. When King David tried to handle it the wrong way, something terrible happened.

6 Then David called out 30,000 special troops. He led them to Baal-judah to bring home the Ark of the Lord. The Lord's seat is above the Guardian Angels on the Ark. ³The Ark was put on a new cart. It was taken from the hillside home of Abinadab. It was driven by Abinadab's sons, Uzzah and Ahio. ⁴Ahio was walking in front. ⁵He was followed by David and the other leaders of Israel. They were happily waving branches of juniper trees. And they were playing every kind of musical instrument before the Lord. They played on lyres, harps, tambourines, castanets, and cymbals.

⁶But when they got to the threshing floor of Nacon, the oxen stumbled. So Uzzah put out his hand to steady the Ark. ⁷Then the anger of the Lord flared out against Uzzah. The Lord killed him for doing this. So he died there beside the Ark. ⁸David was angry at what the Lord had done. He named the spot "The Place of Wrath upon Uzzah." It is still called this to this day.

⁹David was now afraid of the Lord. He asked, "How can I ever bring the Ark home?" ¹⁰So he decided against taking it to the City of David. He took it instead to the home of Obed-edom, who had come from Gath. ¹¹It stayed there for three months. And the Lord blessed Obed-edom and all his family.

¹²David heard this. So he brought the Ark to the City of David with great joy. ¹³When the men carrying the Ark had gone six steps, they stopped and waited. Then David sacrificed an ox and a fat lamb. ¹⁴And David danced before the Lord with all his might. He was wearing priests' clothing. ¹⁵So Israel brought home the Ark of the Lord. They did it with much shouting and blowing of trumpets.

¹⁶But as the Ark came into the city, Michal, Saul's daughter, watched from a window. She saw King David leaping and dancing before the Lord. And she was filled with hate for him.

¹⁷The Ark was put inside the tent that David had made for it. And he sacrificed burnt offerings and peace offerings to the Lord. ¹⁸Then he blessed the people in the name of the Lord of heaven. ¹⁹He gave gifts to everyone, men and women alike. He gave each a loaf of bread, some wine, and a cake of raisins. When it was all over, everyone went home. ²⁰And David went home to bless his family.

But Michal came out to meet him. She said in disgust, "How great the king of Israel looked today! He took off his clothes in front of the girls along the street! He acted like a common fool!"

²¹David said, "I was dancing before the Lord. He chose me above your father and his family! He chose me as the leader of Israel, the people of the Lord! So I am happy to act like a fool. For I have done it to show my joy in the Lord. ²²Yes, and I am happy to look even more foolish than this! But the girls of whom you spoke will still respect me!"

²³And Michal never had any children to the day she died.

- *Remember:* How was the Ark carried from Abinadab's home? (6:3) How were David and the other leaders praising God? (6:5) But what terrible thing happened? What stopped David from bringing the Ark to the City of David? (6:6-9) Read 1 Chronicles 15:13-15. David learned the right way to carry the Ark, the way God commanded. This time he would bring the Ark to the City of David. No one was hurt. What did you learn about doing things God's way?

• *Discover:* There is a right way to do God's work—the way he tells us. Doing God's work our way gets us into trouble.

• *Apply:* Does God want you to do something for him? Does he want you to tell others about Jesus? Does he want you to help at Sunday school or church? Does he want you to sing or play your instrument? Remember to do God's work God's way, not your way. Ask him to help you.

• *What's next?* Why is a king so kind to a crippled boy? Read 2 Samuel 9. ■

7 So the Lord finally sent peace upon the land. And Israel was no longer at war with the nations nearby. ²So David said to Nathan the prophet, "Look! Here I am living in this great cedar palace! But the Ark of God is out in a tent!"

³"Go ahead with what you

have in mind," Nathan replied. "For the Lord is with you."

⁴But that night the Lord said to Nathan, ⁵"Tell my servant David not to do it! ⁶For I have never lived in a temple. My home has always been a tent. It has been so ever since I brought Israel out of Egypt. ⁷And I have never once complained to Israel's leaders, the shepherds of my people. I have never asked them, 'Why haven't you built me a great cedar temple?'

⁸"Now go. Give this message to David from the Lord of heaven. 'I chose you to be the leader of my people Israel,' he said. 'And at that time, you were just a shepherd. You were watching your sheep in the pasture. ⁹I have been with you wherever you have gone. I have destroyed your enemies. And I will make your name greater yet! You will be one of the most famous men in the world!

¹⁰⁻¹¹I have chosen a homeland for my people. And they will never have to move! It will be their own land, where the heathen nations won't bother them. The nations won't trouble them as they did when the judges ruled my people. There will be no more wars against you. Your descendants shall rule this land for many years to come! ¹²For when you die, I will put one of your sons upon your throne. And I will make his kingdom strong. ¹³He is the one who shall build me a temple. And I will keep his kingdom for all time. ¹⁴I will be his father and he shall be my son. If he sins, I will use other nations to punish him. ¹⁵But my love and kindness shall not leave

him. I will not take it as I took it from Saul, the king who came before you. [16]Your family shall rule my kingdom for all time.'"

[17]So Nathan went back to David. He told him all the Lord had said.

God is great

You are so great, Lord!

2 Samuel 7:22

---

[18]Then David went into the Tabernacle. He sat there before the Lord. He prayed, "O Lord God, why have you given your blessings to me? I am such a small person! [19]And now you promise to give me even more! You speak of giving me a kingdom that will be for all time! Such kindness is far beyond what any man could give! O Lord God! [20]What can I say? For you know what I am like! [21]You are doing all these things just because you promised to. You do them just because you want to! [22]You are so great, Lord! We have never heard of a god like you. Really, there is no other god.

David Claims God's Promise

[23]What other nation in all the earth has been given such blessings as Israel, your people? For you have saved your chosen nation in order to bring glory to your name. You have done great miracles to destroy Egypt and its gods. [24]You chose Israel to be your people forever. And you became our God.

[25]"And now, Lord God, do for me and my family as you have promised. [26]Then you will be honored for all time. For you have made Israel your people. And you have built my kingdom and they will rule before you. [27]O Lord of heaven, God of Israel! You have shown me that I am the first of a family of rulers. And they will rule your people for all time. That is why I have been brave enough to pray this prayer to you. [28]For you are indeed God. And your words are truth. You have promised me these good things. [29]So do as you have promised! Bless me and my family forever! May they rule on and on before you! For you, Lord God, have promised it."

David Strengthens His Kingdom

8 After this David humbled the Philistines. He did this by taking Gath, their largest city. [2]He also conquered the land of Moab. He divided his enemies by making them lie down side by side in rows. Two-thirds of each row, as measured with a tape, were killed. One-third were allowed to live. They became David's servants and paid him taxes each year.

[3]He also destroyed the forces of King Hadadezer. He was the son of Rehob and the king of Zobah. David fought him in a battle at the Euphrates River. [4]David killed 1,700 horsemen and 20,000 foot soldiers. Then he made all of the chariot horses lame except for 100 teams. [5]He also killed 22,000 Syrians from Damascus. They had come to help Hadadezer. [6]David placed several army groups in Damascus. And the Syrians became David's subjects. They brought him yearly tribute money. So the Lord gave him victory wherever he turned. [7]David brought the gold shields to Jerusalem. They had been used by King Hadadezer's officers. [8]He also carried back to Jerusalem a very large amount of bronze. This came from Hadadezer's cities of Betah and Berothai.

[9]King Toi of Hamath heard about David's victory over the army of Hadadezer. [10]So he sent his son Joram to praise him. This was because Hadadezer and Toi were enemies. He gave David gifts made from silver, gold, and bronze. [11-12]David gave all of these to the Lord. He also gave him all the other silver and gold he had taken. It had come from Syria, Moab, Ammon, the Philistines, Amalek, and King Hadadezer.

[13]So David became very famous. After this, he destroyed 18,000 Edomites at the Valley of Salt. [14]Then he placed army groups in Edom. That way the whole nation was forced to pay tribute money to Israel. This was another example of how the Lord gave him victory wherever he went.

[15]David ruled with justice over Israel. He was fair to everyone. [16]The general of his army was Joab. He was the son of Zeruiah. And his recorder was Jehosha-

phat. He was the son of Ahilud. [17]Zadok and Ahimelech were the High Priests. Zadok was the son of Ahitub. Ahimelech was the son of Abiathar. And Seraiah was the king's private secretary. [18]Benaiah was captain of his bodyguard. He was the son of Jehoiada. And David's sons were his helpers.

David Is Kind to Mephibosheth

Mephibosheth was King Saul's grandson. All of Saul's sons were dead. His other grandsons were dead. Mephibosheth was the only one from Saul's family who could still become king. When Mephibosheth was called for by King David, he was afraid. Would David kill him? Most kings would do that.

9 One day David began wondering if any of Saul's family was still alive. He wanted to be kind to them as he had promised Prince Jonathan. [2]He heard about a man named Ziba. He had been one of Saul's servants. So David called him.

"Are you Ziba?" the king asked.

"Yes, sir, I am," he replied.

[3]The king then asked him, "Is anyone left from Saul's family? If so, I want to fulfill a sacred promise by being kind to him."

"Yes," Ziba replied. "Jonathan's lame son is still alive."

[4]"Where is he?" the king asked.

"In Lo-debar," Ziba told him. "At the home of Machir."

[5-6]So King David sent for Mephibosheth. He was Jonathan's son and Saul's grandson. Mephibosheth came in great fear. He greeted the king and was very humble. He bowed low before him.

[7]But David said, "Don't be afraid! I've asked you to come so that I can be kind to you. This is because of my promise to your father Jonathan. I will give you all the land of your grandfather Saul. And you shall live with me here at the palace!"

[8]Mephibosheth fell to the ground before the king. "Should the king show kindness to a dead dog like me?" he said.

[9]Then the king called Saul's servant Ziba. "I have taken all that belonged to Saul and his family," he said. "I have given it your master's grandson. [10-11]You and your sons and servants are to farm the land for him. You will grow food for his family. But he will live here with me."

Ziba had 15 sons and 20 servants. He replied, "Sir, I will do all you have said."

And from that time on, Mephibosheth ate with King David. It was as though he were one of his own sons. [12]Mephibosheth had a young son, Mica. All the family of Ziba became Mephibosheth's servants. [13]But Mephibosheth moved to Jerusalem to live at the palace. He was lame in both feet.

- *Remember:* King Saul had tried many times to kill David. Why did David want to be kind to Saul's family? Why not get even? (9:1) How did David find Mephibosheth? (9:2-4) How did David show kindness to Mephibosheth? (9:5-11) What do you think of David for doing this? What do other people think of you when you are kind?

- *Discover:* David was kind to Mephibosheth because he had promised Jonathan that he would be kind to all his relatives. (Read 1 Samuel 20:14-17.) We should be kind to others, even our enemies.

- *Apply:* David promised his best friend that he would be kind to his family. Think of some other good reasons to be kind to others. What are they? Remember these reasons the next time you are tempted to be unkind.

- *What's next?* Some men visit a king. But he shaves half of each man's beard to insult them. Read 2 Samuel 10. ◼

A King Makes Fun of David's Men

All the men of Israel wore beards. No man would think of shaving his beard. But the Syrian king wanted to make fun of David's men. So he shaved half of each man's beard and cut their robes off at the waist. This made David very angry. What do you think he did?

10 Some time after this the Ammonite king died. His son Hanun took his place.

²"I am going to show special respect for him," David said. "His father Nahash was always very loyal and kind to me." So David sent messengers to speak to Hanun. They told him how sorry David was about his father's death.

³But Hanun's officers didn't trust them. "These men aren't here to honor your father!" they said. "David has sent them to spy out the city! He wants to come and take it!"

⁴So Hanun took David's men. He shaved off half their beards. He cut their robes off at the hips. Then he sent them home half naked. ⁵David heard what had happened. So he told them to stay at Jericho until their beards grew out. This was because the men were ashamed of the way they looked.

⁶Now the people of Ammon saw how angry they had made David. So they hired 20,000 Syrian soldiers. They came from the lands of Rehob and Zobah. The king of Maacah sent 1,000. And 10,000 came from the land of Tob. ⁷⁻⁸David heard about this. So he sent Joab and the whole Israelite army to attack them. The Ammonites defended the gates of their city. The Syrians from Zobah, Rehob, Tob, and Maacah fought in the fields. ⁹Joab soon saw that he would have to fight on two fronts. So he chose the best fighters in his army. He put them under his personal command. Then he took them out to fight the Syrians in the fields. ¹⁰He left the rest of the army to his brother Abishai. They were to attack the city.

¹¹"I might need help against the Syrians. If I do, come out and help me," Joab told him. "And the Ammonites might be too strong for you. If so, I will come and help you. ¹²Courage! We must really act like men today! We must be strong if we are going to save our people and the cities of our God. May the Lord's will be done."

¹³Then Joab and his troops attacked. And the Syrians began to run away. ¹⁴When the Ammonites saw the Syrians running, they ran too. They went into their city. After that Joab went back to Jerusalem. ¹⁵⁻¹⁶The Syrians now knew that they were no match for Israel. So they came together again and were joined by more Syrian troops. These were called by Hadadezer from the other side of the Euphrates River. These troops came to Helam under the command of Shobach. He was the commander of all Hadadezer's armies.

¹⁷David heard what was happening. So he personally led the Israelite army to Helam. There the Syrians attacked him. ¹⁸But again the Syrians ran from the Israelites. This time they left 700 chariot drivers dead on the field. Also, 40,000 horsemen died that day. And General Shobach was among them. ¹⁹Hadadezer's allies saw that the Syrians had been beaten. So they made peace with David and became his servants. And the Syrians were afraid to help the Ammonites anymore after that.

- *Remember:* Why did David send men to see Hanun? (10:1-2) Why did Hanun make fun of David's men? (10:3) What did he do to them? (10:4) What else did the Ammonites do to David? (10:6) What did David do then? (10:7-19) Do you think Hanun wished then he had not made fun of David's men?

- *Discover:* Before you do something wrong, think what could happen. Do you really want to do this? Would the punishment be worth the risk? If you think first about the punishment, you won't be as eager to do wrong things.

- *Apply:* The next time you are tempted to do wrong, stop! Think about the way you could be punished. Is it worth it?

- *What's next?* A kind man murders a loyal soldier. Why would he do that? Read 2 Samuel 11. ∎

David and Bathsheba

King David had everything he could want. He was the most powerful king in that part of the world. He had a beautiful palace and lots of money. He loved God and tried to please him. What more could he want? But David wanted one more thing. That got him into deep trouble.

11 Spring was the normal time for kings to go to war. So at that time, David sent Joab and the Israelite army to destroy the Ammonites. They began by laying siege to the city of Rabbah. But David stayed in Jerusalem.

²One night he couldn't get to sleep. So he went for a walk on the roof of the palace. As he looked out over the city, he noticed a very pretty woman. She was taking her evening bath. ³He sent to find out who she was. He was told that she was Bathsheba, the daughter of Eliam. She was the wife of Uriah. ⁴Then David sent messengers to bring her to him. When she came, he slept with her. (She had just purified herself from her monthly period.) Then she went back home.

5She soon found out that she was pregnant. So she sent a message to David to tell him.

6So David wrote a letter to Joab. He said, "Send me Uriah the Hittite." 7When Uriah got there, David asked him how Joab and the army were doing. He also asked how the war was going. 8Then he told him to go home and relax. And he sent a present to him at his home. 9But Uriah didn't go there. He stayed that night at the gateway of the palace. He slept there with the other servants of the king.

10David heard what Uriah had done. So he called him and asked, "What's the matter with you? Why didn't you go home to your wife last night? You have been away for a long time!"

11Uriah replied, "The Ark and the army are far from home. The general and his officers are camping out in open fields. How could I go home to enjoy a good meal? How could I go and sleep with my wife? I swear that I will never be guilty of acting like that."

12"Well, stay here tonight," David told him. "Tomorrow you may go back to the army."

So Uriah stayed around the palace. 13David invited him to dinner and got him drunk. But even then he didn't go home that night. Again he slept at the door to the palace.

14Finally the next morning David wrote a letter to Joab. He gave it to Uriah to deliver. 15The letter told Joab to put Uriah at the front of the battle. He was to send him where the fighting was hottest. Then he was to pull back and leave him there to die! 16So Joab sent Uriah to a spot close to the city. He knew that the enemies' best men were fighting there. 17And Uriah was killed along with several other Israelite soldiers.

18Joab sent a report to David of how the battle was going. 19-21And he told his messenger, "The king might be angry. He might ask, 'Why did the troops go so close to the city? Didn't they know there would be shooting from the walls?

Wasn't Abimelech killed at Thebez by a woman who threw down a millstone on him?' If the king speaks like this, tell him, 'Uriah was killed too.'"

22So the messenger went to Jerusalem. He gave the report to David.

23"The enemy came out against us," he said. "We chased them back to the city gates. 24Then the men on the wall attacked us. And some of our men were killed. Uriah the Hittite is dead too."

25"Well, tell Joab not to be upset," David said. "The sword kills one as well as another! Fight harder next time, and conquer the city. Tell him he is doing well."

26Bathsheba heard that her husband was dead. So she mourned for him. 27Then, when the time of mourning was over, David sent for her. He brought her to the palace and she became one of his wives. And she gave birth to his son. But the Lord was very angry with what David had done.

- *Remember:* David took another man's wife. What was her name? (11:3) Why was this wrong? (11:2-4) How did David arrange for Uriah to be killed? (11:14-21) What did the Lord think of David's sins? (11:27) What do you think of David's sins?

- *Discover:* One sin is bad enough. But sometimes we try to cover up one sin with another one. Before long, we are in deep trouble. That's what happened to David.

- *Apply:* It's easy to do something wrong. It's also easy to tell "a little lie" to try to cover it up. The second sin tries to cover the first sin. But what covers the second sin? Another sin. Before long, you're really in trouble. The next time you are tempted to do wrong, think of what you may have to do to keep others from knowing about it. Also think of the trouble this could lead you into. Then don't do it!

- *What's next?* A man dared to tell a king, "You are wrong! You have sinned!" He could be killed for that. Read 2 Samuel 12:1-25. ∎

Nathan Scolds David

No one dared to scold a king. No one dared to tell a king that he had done something wrong. No one dared to tell a king that he would be punished. But Nathan dared to do all these things. David could kill him for doing this. But what did he do?

12 So the Lord sent the prophet Nathan. He told David this story. "There were two men in a certain city. One was very rich. He owned many flocks of sheep and herds of goats. ³The other was very poor. He owned nothing but a little lamb. It was his children's pet. He fed it from his own plate and let it drink from his own cup. He cuddled it in his arms like a baby daughter. ⁴Then a guest came to the home of the rich man. But he did not take a lamb from his own flocks to feed the traveler. Instead, he took the poor man's lamb. He roasted it and served it."

⁵After hearing this story, David was very angry. "I promise this by the living God!" he said. "The man who did that should be put to death! ⁶He should pay four lambs to the poor man. They will pay for the lamb he stole and for his lack of pity."

⁷Then Nathan said to David, "*You* are that rich man! The Lord God of Israel says, 'I made you king of Israel. I saved you from the power of Saul. ⁸I gave you this palace and many wives. I gave you the kingdoms of Israel and Judah. And I would have given you much, much more! ⁹Why, then, have you hated the laws of God? Why have you done this evil deed? You have murdered Uriah and stolen his wife! ¹⁰Therefore murder shall be a threat in your family from this day on. You have shown that you don't respect me! You have stolen Uriah's wife! ¹¹I promise that because of this, your own family will rebel against you. I will give your wives to another man. And he will go to bed with them in public view. ¹²You did it in secret. But I will do this to you openly. It will be done in the sight of all Israel.'"

¹³"I have sinned against the Lord," David said to Nathan.

Then Nathan replied, "Yes, but the Lord has forgiven you. You won't die for this sin. ¹⁴But you have given the Lord's enemies a chance to hate and curse him. Because of this, your child shall die."

¹⁵Then Nathan went to his home. And the Lord made Bathsheba's baby very sick. ¹⁶David begged the Lord to let the child live. He lay all night before the Lord on the bare earth. And he would not eat. ¹⁷The leaders of the nation pleaded with him to get up. They begged him to eat with them. But he would not. ¹⁸Then, on the seventh day, the baby died. David's men were afraid to tell him.

"He was so broken up about the baby being sick," they said. "What will he do to himself when we tell him the child is dead?"

¹⁹David saw them whispering. So he knew what had happened.

"Is the baby dead?" he asked.

"Yes," they replied, "he is." ²⁰Then David got up off the ground. He washed himself, brushed his hair, and changed his clothes. Then he went into the Tabernacle to worship the Lord. After that he went back to the palace and ate. ²¹His men were amazed.

"We don't understand you," they told him. "While the baby was still living, you wept and would not eat. Now the baby is dead. But you have stopped mourning and you are eating again."

²²David replied, "I fasted and cried while the child was alive. For I said, 'Maybe the Lord will be kind to me. Maybe he will let the child live.' ²³But why should I fast when he is dead? Can I bring him back again? I shall someday die and go to him, but he shall not come back to me."

²⁴Then David comforted Bathsheba. And when he slept with her, she got pregnant. She had a baby boy and named him Solomon. And the Lord loved the baby. ²⁵So the Lord sent blessings through Nathan the prophet. David called the baby Jedidiah. This means "Beloved of the Lord." This was because of the Lord's interest in the child.

- *Remember:* What story did Nathan tell David?(12:1-2) Who sent him to tell this story? (12:1-4) What did David say about the rich man in that story? (12:5-6) What did David do wrong? How would God punish him?
(12:7-14) Do you think David should have been punished? Why?

- *Discover:* Sin brings punishment.

- *Apply:* Should bad people be punished for doing bad things? Should good people be punished for doing bad things? Should you be punished for doing bad things? Next time you think about doing something bad, ask if you should be punished for doing it. Then don't do it!

- *What's next?* A son turns against his own father. He even wants to kill his father. Read 2 Samuel 15. ■

David Conquers the Ammonites

26-27At this time, Joab and the Israelite army were ending their siege of Rabbah. This was the capital of Ammon. Joab sent messengers to David. "Rabbah and its water supply are ours!" he said. 28"Now bring the rest of the army and finish the job. That way you will get the credit for the victory instead of me."

29-30So David led his army to Rabbah and took it. Huge amounts of loot were carried back to Jerusalem. David took the king of Rabbah's crown. It was made from solid gold and was set with gems. He put it on his own head. 31He made slaves of the people of the city. He made them work with saws, picks, and axes. He made them work in the brick kilns. That is the way he treated all of the cities of the Ammonites. Then David and the army went back to Jerusalem.

Amnon Rapes Tamar

13 Prince Absalom, David's son, had a beautiful sister named Tamar. And Prince Amnon fell in love with her. Amnon was Tamar's half brother. 2He wanted her so badly that he became sick. But he had no way of talking to her. This was because the girls and young men were kept apart. 3But Amnon had a very clever friend. His friend's name was Jonadab. He was Amnon's cousin, the son of David's brother Shimeah.

4One day Jonadab said to Amnon, "What's the trouble? Why should the son of a king look so sad morning after morning?"

So Amnon told him, "I am in love with Tamar, my half sister."

5"Well," Jonadab said, "I'll tell you what to do. Go back to bed and pretend you are sick. Your father will come to see you. When he does, ask him to let Tamar come. Tell him you want her to make some food for you. Tell him you'll feel better if she feeds you."

6So Amnon did as he said. When the king came to see him, Amnon asked him for this favor. He asked that his sister Tamar be allowed to come. He wanted her to cook some good food for him to eat. 7David agreed and sent word to Tamar. He told her to go to Amnon's room. She was to make some food for him. 8So she did as she was told and went into his bedroom. That way he could watch her mix some dough. Then she baked some special bread for him. 9But when she set the serving tray before him, he refused to eat!

"Everyone get out of here," he told his servants. So they all left the room.

10Then he said to Tamar, "Now bring me the food here in my bedroom. Feed it to me." So Tamar took it to him. 11But as she stood there in front of him, he grabbed her. He demanded, "Come to bed with me, my darling."

12"Oh, Amnon," she cried. "Don't be foolish! Don't do this to me! You know what a crime it is in Israel. 13Where could I go in my shame? And you would be called a fool in Israel. Please, just speak to the king about it. He will let you marry me."

14But he wouldn't listen to her. And since he was stronger than she, he forced her. 15Then suddenly his love turned to hate. Now he hated her more than he had loved her.

"Get out of here!" he snarled at her.

16"No, no!" she cried. "To reject me now is a worse crime than the other you did to me."

But he wouldn't listen to her. [17-18]He shouted for his valet. He demanded, "Throw this woman out! Then lock the door behind her!"

So he put her out. She was wearing a long robe with sleeves. This was the custom for daughters of the king who had not slept with a man. [19]Now she tore the robe and put ashes on her head. And with her head in her hands, she went away crying.

Absalom Murders Amnon

[20]Her brother Absalom asked her, "Is it true that Amnon slept with you? Don't be so upset. It's all in the family anyway. It's not anything to worry about!"

So Tamar lived in her brother Absalom's rooms. She was a sad and lonely woman.

[21-24]When King David heard what had happened, he was very angry. But Absalom said nothing about it to Amnon. However, he hated him with a deep hatred. This was because of what he had done to his sister. Two years passed. It was time for Absalom's sheep to be sheared at Baal-hazor in Ephraim. At that time, Absalom invited his father and all his brothers to come. They would have a feast at that happy time. [25]The king replied, "No, my son. We might all come. But if we did, we would be too much of a burden on you."

Absalom pressed him, but he wouldn't come. But he sent his thanks. [26]"Well, then," Absalom said. "You might not be able to come. But how about sending my brother Amnon instead?"

"Why Amnon?" the king asked.

[27]Absalom kept asking his father and finally the king agreed. He let all of his sons go, including Amnon.

[28]Absalom told his men, "Wait until Amnon gets drunk. Then, at my signal, kill him! Don't be afraid. I'm the one who gives the orders around here. This is a command! Take courage and do it!"

[29-30]So they murdered Amnon. Then the other sons of the king jumped on their mules and ran. As they were on the way back to Jerusalem, a report reached David. "Absalom has killed all of your sons," the report said. "Not one is left alive!"

[31]The king jumped up and ripped off his robe. Then he fell to the ground. His men also tore their clothes in horror and sorrow.

[32-33]But just then Jonadab got there. He was the son of David's brother Shimeah. He said, "No, not all have been killed! It was only Amnon! Absalom has been plotting this ever since Amnon slept with Tamar. No, no! Your sons aren't all dead! It was only Amnon."

[34]Meanwhile Absalom escaped. Now the watchman on the Jerusalem wall saw a great crowd coming toward the city. They were traveling along the road at the side of the hill.

[35]"See!" Jonadab told the king. "There they are now! Your sons are coming, just as I said."

[36]When they got there, they were crying loudly. The king and his officials cried with them. [37-39]Absalom ran to King Talmai of Geshur, the son of Ammihud. Absalom stayed there for three years. After a time, David became used to Amnon's death. Then he wished, day after day, that his son Absalom would come home.

A Widow Asks the King for Help

14 General Joab saw how much the king wanted to see Absalom. [2-3]So he sent for a woman of Tekoa. She was known for having great wisdom. He told her to ask to speak with the king. He told her what to say to him.

"Pretend you are in mourning," Joab told her. "Wear mourning clothes and mess up your hair. Act as if you have been very sad for a long time."

[4]The woman went to see the king. When she got there, she fell face down on the floor in front of him. She cried out, "O king! Help me!"

[5-6]"What's the trouble?" he asked.

"I am a widow," she replied. "My two sons had a fight out in the field. Since no one was there to stop them, one of them was killed. [7]Now the rest of the family says I must give up my other son. They want to kill him for murdering his brother. But if I do that, I will have no one left. And my husband's name will be lost from the face of the earth."

8"Leave it with me," the king told her. "I'll see to it that no one touches him."

9"Oh, thank you, my lord," she replied. "I'll take the blame if you are accused for helping me like this."

10"Don't worry about that!" the king replied. "If anyone doesn't like it, bring him to me. I promise you he will not complain again!"

11Then she said, "Please make a promise to me by God's name. Promise that you won't let anyone hurt my son. I don't want anyone else to die."

"I promise by God's name," he replied. "Not a hair of your son's head shall be hurt!"

12"Please let me ask one more thing of you!" she said.

"Go ahead," he replied. "Speak!"

13"You have promised to do a great deal for me. Why don't you do as much for all the people of God?" she asked. "You have shown yourself to be wrong by making this decision. Have you not refused to bring home your own son? 14All of us must die some day. Our lives are like water that is poured out on the ground. It cannot be gathered up again. You should find a way to bring your son back from his exile. If you do, God will bless you with a longer life. 15-16I have come to plead with you for my son. I did this because my life and my son's life have been threatened. And I said to myself, 'Perhaps the king will listen to me. Maybe he will rescue us from those who would end our life in Israel. 17Yes, the king will give us peace again.' I know that you are like the angel of God. I know that you can tell good from evil. May God be with you."

18"I want to know one thing," the king replied.

"Yes, my lord?" she asked.

19"Did Joab send you here?"

And the woman replied, "How can I deny it? Yes, Joab sent me and told me what to say. 20He did it in order to place the matter before you in a new light. But you are as wise as an angel of God! You know about all that happens!"

21So the king sent for Joab. He told him, "All right, go and bring back Absalom."

22Joab fell to the ground before the king. He blessed him and said, "At last I know that you like me! For you have given me what I asked!"

23Then Joab went to Geshur. And he brought Absalom back to Jerusalem.

Absalom and David Meet Again

24"He may go to his own rooms," the king ordered. "But he must never come here. I refuse to see him."

25Now no one in Israel was as handsome as Absalom. And no one else was given as much praise. 26He cut his hair only once a year. And he cut it then only because it weighed three pounds. It was too much of a load to carry around! 27He had three sons and one daughter, Tamar. She was a very pretty girl.

28Absalom was in Jerusalem for two years and still hadn't seen the king. 29So he sent for Joab. He asked him to go to the king for him. But Joab wouldn't come. Absalom sent for him again. But again he refused to come.

30So Absalom spoke to his servants. "Go and set fire to that barley field of Joab's next to mine," they said. So they did this.

31Then Joab went to Absalom. He demanded, "Why did your servants set my field on fire?"

32And Absalom replied, "Because I wanted you to go to the king for me. I wanted to ask him why he brought me back from Geshur. Why did he send for me if he didn't want to see me? I might as well have stayed there. Let me speak with the king. He might find that I am guilty of murder. If he does, then let him kill me."

33So Joab told the king what Absalom had said. Then at last David called Absalom. He came and bowed low before the king, and David kissed him.

Absalom Rebels

For four years, Absalom planned to rebel against his father David. Slowly he began to convince people he would make a better king than David. After a while, many were on his side. They wanted him to be king. But Absalom would have to kill his father to be king. Would anyone be that bad?

15 Absalom then bought a great chariot and chariot horses. He hired 50 footmen to run ahead of him. ²He got up early every morning and went out to the gate of the city. Often people would come to bring cases to the king for trial. Absalom called them over and showed an interest in their problems.

³He would say, "I can see that you are right in this matter. It's too bad the king has no one to help with these cases. ⁴I surely wish I were the judge. Then anyone with a problem could come to me. I would give him justice!"

⁵And when anyone came to bow to him, Absalom wouldn't let him. He shook his hand instead! ⁶So in this way Absalom stole the hearts of all the people of Israel.

⁷⁻⁸After four years, Absalom spoke to the king. "Let me go to Hebron," he said. "I must sacrifice to the Lord to fulfill a promise. I made the promise while I was at Geshur. I said that if he brought me back to Jerusalem, I would sacrifice to him."

⁹"All right," the king told him. "Go and fulfill your promise."

So Absalom went to Hebron. ¹⁰But while he was there, he sent spies to every part of Israel. He did this to turn them against the king. "You will soon hear trumpets," his message read. "When you do, you will know that Absalom has been crowned in Hebron." ¹¹He took 200 men from Jerusalem with him as guests. But they did not know what he was planning to do. ¹²While he was offering the sacrifice, he sent for Ahithophel. He was one of David's counselors who lived in Giloh. Ahithophel agreed to support Absalom. So did more and more others. So the rebel group became very strong.

¹³A messenger soon came to Jerusalem to tell King David. "All Israel has joined Absalom," he said. "They have rebelled against you!"

¹⁴"Then we must run at once!" David said right away. "If we don't, it will be too late! We must get out of the city before he gets here. If we do, both we and the city of Jerusalem will be saved."

¹⁵"We are with you," his men replied. "Do as you think best."

¹⁶So the king and his family left at once. He left no one behind except 10 of his young wives. He left them there to keep the palace in order. ¹⁷⁻¹⁸As they left, David stopped at the edge of the city. He let his troops move past him to lead the way. There were 600 Gittites with him from Gath. And the Cherethites and Pelethites were also with him.

¹⁹⁻²⁰But suddenly the king turned to Ittai. He was the captain of the 600 Gittites. David said to him, "What are you doing here? Go on back with your men to Jerusalem, to your king. For you are a guest in Israel, a foreigner in exile. It seems but yesterday that you came. Now today should I force you to wander with us? We don't even know where we are going! Go on back and take your troops with you. May the Lord be merciful to you."

²¹But Ittai replied, "I make this promise by the name of God and by your own life! Wherever you go, I will go. I will stay with you no matter what happens. I will stay with you if it means life or death."

²²So David replied, "All right, come with us." Then Ittai and his 600 men and their families went along.

²³There was deep sadness in the city as the king passed by. He and his men crossed Kidron Brook and went out into the country. ²⁴Abiathar and Zadok and the Levites took the Ark of God. They set it down beside the road until all had passed. ²⁵⁻²⁶Then, following David's orders, Zadok took the Ark back into the

city. "If the Lord is pleased with me," David said, "he will bring me back. He will let me see the Ark and the Tabernacle once again. But maybe he is finished with me. If so, let him do what seems best to him."

27Then the king told Zadok, "Look, here is my plan. Go back to the city with your son Ahimaaz. Take Abiathar's son Jonathan along with you. 28I will stop at the ford of the Jordan River. I will wait there for a message from you. Tell me what has happened in Jerusalem before I go into the wilderness."

29So Zadok and Abiathar carried the Ark of God back into the city and stayed there.

30David walked up the road that led to the Mount of Olives. He cried as he went. His head was covered and his feet were bare. These were signs of his mourning. The people who were with him covered their heads. And they also cried as they climbed the mountain. 31Someone told David that Ahithophel, his advisor, was helping Absalom. When David heard this, he prayed to the Lord. He said, "O Lord, please make Ahithophel give Absalom bad advice!" 32They got to the spot on the Mount of Olives where people worshiped God. David found Hushai the Archite waiting for him there. He had torn his clothing and dirt was on his head.

33-34But David told him, "If you go with me, you will only be a burden. Go back to Jerusalem. Tell Absalom, 'I will counsel you as I did your father.' Then you can make Ahithophel's advice seem useless. 35-36Zadok and Abiathar, the priests, are there. Tell them the plans that are being made to capture me. They will send their sons Ahimaaz and Jonathan to find me. They will tell me what is going on."

37So David's friend Hushai went back to the city. He got there the same time Absalom did.

- *Remember:* How did Absalom win the people over to him? (15:1-6) How did Absalom make himself king? (15:7-12) Did David fight Absalom? What did he do? (15:13-14) How did Hushai help David? (15:32-37) What kind of person

was Absalom? Why isn't he the kind of friend you would like to have?

- *Discover:* Absalom was the most handsome man in Israel. (14:25) But he murdered his half brother. He set fire to a friend's field. He rebelled against his father. He even wanted to kill his own father. Good looks don't make good people. Good-looking people may do good things or bad things. People who are not so good-looking may do good things or bad things. We can do good no matter how we look.

- *Apply:* Do you ever wish you were more beautiful or handsome? Do you ever wish you were bigger or smaller? Do you ever wish you looked different? You can do good things no matter how you look. Doing good is more important than looking good. Try to do one more good thing today.

- *What's next?* A man curses his king and throws stones at him. What will happen to him? Read 2 Samuel 16:5-14. ■

Ziba Joins David

16 David went past the top of the Mount of Olives. Just then, Ziba caught up with him. Ziba was the manager of Mephibosheth's land. He was leading two donkeys. They were loaded with 200 loaves of bread and 100 cakes of raisins. They also carried 100 bunches of grapes and a small barrel of wine.

2"What are these for?" the king asked Ziba.

And Ziba replied, "The donkeys are for your people to ride on. The bread and summer fruit are for the young men to eat. The wine is to be taken with you into the wilderness. It will help any who become weak."

3"And where is Mephibosheth?" the king asked him.

"He stayed at Jerusalem," Ziba replied. "He said, 'Now I'll get to be king! Today I will get back the kingdom of my father, Saul.'"

4"In that case," the king told Ziba, "I give you all he owns."

"Thank you, thank you, sir," Ziba replied.

Shimei Insults David

Who would dare curse his king and throw stones at him? Shimei did. He even called King David a murderer. Surely King David or his men would kill Shimei for doing this. But they didn't. Why?

⁵David and his party came to Bahurim. As they drew near, a man came out of the village cursing them. His name was Shimei, the son of Gera. He was a member of Saul's family. ⁶He threw stones at the king and his officers. But all the mighty warriors gathered around David.

⁷⁻⁸"Get out of here, you murderer, you scoundrel!" he shouted at David. "The Lord is paying you back for murdering King Saul and his family. You stole his throne! Now the Lord has given it to your son Absalom! At last you will taste some of your own medicine, you murderer!"

⁹"Why should this dead dog curse my lord the king?" Abishai demanded. "Let me go over and cut off his head!"

¹⁰"No!" the king said. "Maybe the Lord has told him to curse me. If so, who am I to say no? ¹¹My own son is trying to kill me. This Benjaminite is only cursing me. Let him alone, for no doubt the Lord has told him to do it. ¹²And perhaps the Lord will see that I am being wronged. In the end, he may bless me because of these curses."

¹³So David and his men went on. Shimei kept pace with them on a nearby hillside. And he cursed them as he went. He threw stones at David and tossed dust into the air. ¹⁴The king and those with him were tired when they got to Bahurim. So they stayed there awhile and rested.

- *Remember:* How did Shimei insult David? What did he do and say? (16:5-8,13) Who wanted to kill him? (16:9) Why didn't David let him do it? (16:10-12) Was David right or wrong? Should he have punished Shimei? What would you have advised David to do?

- *Discover:* Read Matthew 5:39. Jesus said we should not fight evil with evil. We should not do bad things to stop bad things. David refused to murder Shimei.

We should not fight one sin by doing another sin.

- *Apply:* Has someone hurt you or made fun of you? Don't try to hurt or make fun of that person. Has someone said something bad about you? Don't say something bad about that person. Instead, pray for him.

- *What's next?* A prince's long hair gets him into trouble. Read 2 Samuel 17:24–19:8. ∎

Absalom Seizes the Throne

¹⁵At that time, Absalom and his men got to Jerusalem. Ahithophel was with them. ¹⁶When David's friend, Hushai the Archite, got there, he went to see Absalom right away.

"Long live the king!" he exclaimed. "Long live the king!"

¹⁷"Is this the way to treat your friend David?" Absalom asked him. "Why aren't you with him?"

¹⁸"Because I work for the man who is chosen by the Lord and by Israel," Hushai replied. ¹⁹"And anyway, why shouldn't I? I helped your father and now I will help you!"

²⁰Then Absalom turned to Ahithophel. He asked him, "What shall I do next?"

²¹Ahithophel told him, "Go and sleep with your father's wives. For he has left them here to keep the house. All Israel will then know that you have offended him beyond being forgiven. Then they will all come and follow you."

²²So a tent was set up on the roof of the palace. There everyone could see it. And Absalom went into the tent to sleep with his father's wives. ²³Absalom did whatever Ahithophel told him to, just as David had. For every word Ahithophel spoke seemed wise. His advice seemed as though it had come right from the mouth of God.

Absalom Follows Bad Advice

17 "Now," Ahithophel said, "give me 12,000 men. We will start out after David tonight. 2-3I will come upon him while he is tired and weak. He and his men will be thrown into a panic and everyone will run away. I will kill only the king. Then I will let all those who are with him live and bring them to you."

4Absalom and all the elders of Israel approved of the plan. 5But Absalom said, "Ask Hushai the Archite what he thinks about this."

6When Hushai got there, Absalom told him what Ahithophel had said.

"What is your opinion?" Absalom asked him. "Should we follow Ahithophel's advice? If not, speak up."

7"Well," Hushai replied, "this time I think Ahithophel has made a mistake. 8 You know your father and his men. They are mighty warriors and are upset. They are probably like a mother bear who has been robbed of her cubs. And your father is an old soldier. He probably won't be spending the night among the troops. 9He has probably already hidden in some pit or cave. If you chase him, he might come out and attack. And some of your men might fall. If this happens, there will be panic among your men. Everyone will start shouting that your men are being killed. 10Then even the bravest of them will be frozen with fear. This will happen even though they have hearts of lions. For all Israel knows what a mighty man your father is. And they all know how brave his soldiers are.

11"I think you should call out the whole army of Israel. Bring them from as far away as Dan and Beersheba. That way you will have a huge army. And you should personally lead the troops. 12Then when we find him we can destroy his whole army. Not one of them will be left alive. 13And maybe David will have escaped into some city. If so, you will have the whole army of Israel there at your command. Then we can take ropes and drag the walls of the city into the nearest valley. We'll be able to work until every stone is torn down."

14Then Absalom and all the men of Israel agreed. "Hushai's advice is better than Ahithophel's," they said. The Lord had arranged to defeat the plan of Ahithophel. This was because Ahithophel had really given the better plan. The Lord did this to bring disaster on Absalom! 15Then Hushai reported to Zadok and Abiathar, the priests. He told them what Ahithophel had said. And he also told them the plan that he himself had given.

16"Quick!" he told them. "Find David. Tell him not to stay at the ford of the Jordan River tonight. He must go across into the wilderness beyond right away. If he doesn't, he will die, and his whole army with him."

17Jonathan and Ahimaaz had been staying at En-rogel. That way they would not be seen coming to and from the city. A servant girl carried the messages to them. And they then took the messages to King David. 18But a boy saw them leaving En-rogel to go to David. And he told Absalom about it. They escaped to Bahurim where a man hid them inside a well in his back yard. 19The man's wife put a cloth over the top of the well. She put grain on it to dry in the sun. That way no one thought they were there.

20Absalom's men came. They asked her if she had seen Ahimaaz and Jonathan. She told them they had crossed the brook and were gone. They looked for them but they couldn't find them. So they went back to Jerusalem. 21Then the two men crawled out of the well and hurried on to King David. "Quick!" they told him. "Cross the Jordan tonight!" And they told him how Ahithophel had advised that he be captured and killed. 22So David and all the people with him went across during the night. They were all on the other side before dawn.

23At that time, Ahithophel saddled his donkey and went to his hometown. He set all his affairs in order. Then he hanged himself. So he died and was buried beside his father. He did this because Absalom and the men of Israel did not listen to him.

Absalom Is Defeated

A great battle is fought. But everyone loses. Absalom loses the battle and his life. Joab wins the battle but loses his job. David wins the battle but loses his son Absalom. Israel loses 20,000 strong young men. Did anyone win anything?

²⁴David soon got to Mahanaim. Meanwhile, Absalom had called out the whole army of Israel. And he was leading the men across the Jordan River. ²⁵Absalom had chosen Amasa as general of the army. He was to take Joab's place. Amasa was Joab's second cousin. His father was Ithra, an Ishmaelite. His mother was Abigail, the daughter of Nahash. She was the sister of Joab's mother, Zeruiah. ²⁶Absalom and the Israelite army now camped in the land of Gilead.

²⁷When David got to Mahanaim, he was warmly greeted by Shobi, Machir, and Barzillai. Shobi was the son of Nahash of Rabbah, an Ammonite. Machir was the son of Ammiel of Lodebar. Barzillai was a Gileadite of Rogelim. ²⁸⁻²⁹They brought David and those with him mats to sleep on. They brought cooking pots and serving bowls. And they gave them wheat and barley flour, roasted grain, beans, lentils, honey, butter, and cheese. They said, "You must be very tired, hungry, and thirsty. You have made a long march through the wilderness."

18 David now chose leaders over groups of 1,000 and over groups of 100. ²Joab led one-third of the men. Another third of them were put under Joab's brother, Abishai. He was the son of Zeruiah. And a third were put under Ittai, the Gittite. The king planned to lead the army himself. But his men would not let him.

³"You must not do it!" they said. "We might have to turn and run. Half of us might even die! But that will mean little to them. They will be looking only for you. You are worth 10,000 of us! It is better that you stay here in the city. From here, you can send us help if we need it."

⁴"Well, whatever you think best," the king replied. So he stood at the gate of the city as all the troops passed by.

⁵And the king spoke to Joab, Abishai, and Ittai. "For my sake, deal gently with young Absalom," he commanded. And all the troops heard the king give them this charge.

⁶So the battle began in the forest of Ephraim. ⁷And the Israelite troops were beaten back by David's men. Many men were killed. In fact, 20,000 men laid down their lives that day. ⁸The battle raged all across the land. And more men died in the forest than were killed in battle. ⁹During the battle Absalom came upon some of David's men. So he ran away on his mule. The mule went under the thick branches of a great oak tree. There Absalom's hair got caught in the branches. His mule went on, leaving him hanging in the air. ¹⁰One of David's men saw him and told Joab.

¹¹"What? You saw him there and didn't kill him?" Joab demanded. "I would have given you a reward! I would have made you an officer!"

¹²"I wouldn't do it for any reward," the man replied. "We all heard the king speak to you and Abishai and Ittai. He said, 'For my sake, please don't hurt young Absalom.' ¹³And I might have betrayed the king by killing his son. But

the king would find out who did it. And if this happened, you yourself would be the first to accuse me."

¹⁴"Enough of this nonsense!" Joab said. And he took three daggers. He plunged them into the heart of Absalom. For Absalom was still alive as he hung from the oak. ¹⁵Ten young men who carried Joab's armor then gathered around Absalom. They hit him and killed him. ¹⁶Then Joab blew the trumpet. So his men stopped chasing the army of Israel. ¹⁷They threw Absalom's body into a deep pit in the forest. Then they put a great pile of stones over it. And the army of Israel ran to their homes.

¹⁸Absalom had built a monument to himself in the King's Valley. He had said, "I have no sons to carry on my name." He called it "Absalom's Monument," as it is still known today.

¹⁹Then Zadok's son Ahimaaz said, "Let me run to King David. I will bring him the good news. I will tell him that the Lord has saved him from his enemy Absalom."

²⁰"No," Joab told him. "It wouldn't be good news to the king that his son is dead. You can be my messenger some other time."

²¹Then Joab called a man from Cush. "Go tell the king what you have seen," he said. The man bowed and ran off.

²²But Ahimaaz pleaded with Joab, "Please let me go too."

"No, we don't need you now, my boy," Joab replied. "There is no further news to send."

²³"Yes, but let me go anyway," he begged.

And Joab finally said, "All right, go ahead." Then Ahimaaz took a shortcut across the plain. So he got there ahead of the man from Cush. ²⁴David was sitting at the gate of the city. The watchman climbed the stairs to his post at the top of the wall. From there he could see a man running toward them.

²⁵He shouted the news down to David. The king replied, "If he is alone, he has news."

As the messenger came closer, ²⁶the watchman saw another man running toward them. He shouted down, "Here comes another one."

And the king replied, "He will have more news."

²⁷"The first man looks like Ahimaaz, the son of Zadok," the watchman said.

"He is a good man. He must be coming with good news," the king replied.

²⁸Then Ahimaaz cried out to the king, "All is well!" He bowed low with his face to the ground. Then he said, "Blessed be the Lord your God! He has destroyed the rebels who dared to stand against you."

²⁹"What of young Absalom?" the king demanded. "Is he all right?"

"When Joab told me to come, there was a lot of shouting. I didn't know what was happening," Ahimaaz answered.

³⁰"Wait here," the king told him. So Ahimaaz stepped aside.

³¹Then the man from Cush got there. He said, "I have good news for my lord the king. Today the Lord has saved you from all those who turned against you."

³²"What about young Absalom? Is he all right?" the king demanded.

And the man replied, "May all of your enemies be as that young man is!"

B. Gallego

³³Then the king broke into tears. He went up to his room over the gate. He cried as he went, "O my son Absalom, my son, my son Absalom. If only I could have died for you! O Absalom, my son, my son."

19 Word soon reached Joab that the king was mourning for Absalom. ²The people heard of the king's deep grief for his son. And the joy of that day's victory turned into deep sadness. ³The whole army crept back into the city. They walked as though they were ashamed. They acted like they had been beaten in battle.

⁴The king covered his face with his hands. He kept on weeping, "O my son Absalom! O Absalom my son, my son!"

⁵Then Joab went to the king's room. He said to him, "We saved your life today! We saved the lives of your sons,

your daughters, your wives, and concubines! And yet you act like this! You have made us feel ashamed. You act like we have done something wrong. ⁶You seem to love those who hate you, and hate those who love you. It seems like we don't mean anything to you. If Absalom had lived and all of us had died, you would be happy. ⁷Now go out there and praise the troops. For I make this promise by the name of the Lord. If you don't, not one of them will stay for the night! Then you will be worse off than you have ever been in your whole life."

David Returns to Jerusalem

⁸⁻¹⁰So the king went out and sat at the city gates. The news spread in the city that he was there. Soon everyone went to him.

- *Remember:* David told Joab, Abishai, and Ittai how to deal with Absalom. What did he say? (18:5) What did Joab do when he caught Absalom? (18:14-17) Was David happy that his troops won the battle? (18:32-33) What advice did Joab give to David? (19:1-7) What did David do then? (19:8)

- *Discover:* Absalom's rebellion hurt himself, his father, the army, and the nation. Rebellion hurts everyone. Nobody wins!

- *Apply:* The next time you feel rebellious against your parents, remember Absalom.

- *What's next?* Brave men risk their lives for a drink of water. But no one drinks it. Read 2 Samuel 23:8-23. ■

At that time, the people were arguing all across the nation. "Why don't we bring David back to be our king?" was the question everywhere. "He saved us from our enemies, the Philistines. We made Absalom our king instead and chased David out of the country. But now Absalom is dead. Let's ask David to come and be our king again."

¹¹⁻¹²Then David sent Zadok and Abiathar the priests to speak to the elders of Judah. "Why are you the last ones to call back your king?" he asked. "For all Israel is ready, and only you are holding out. Yet you are my own brothers! You are my own tribe, my own flesh and blood!"

¹³And he told them to tell Amasa, "You are my nephew. And may God strike me dead if I do not appoint you. You will be the commander of my army in place of Joab." ¹⁴Then Amasa spoke to all the leaders of Judah. And they all agreed that David should be king. They sent word to the king, "Come back to us. Bring back all those who are with you."

¹⁵So the king started back to Jerusalem. On his way, he came to the Jordan River. The men of Judah had come to Gilgal to meet him. They came to bring him across the river. ¹⁶Then Shimei came across with the men of Judah to welcome King David. He was the son of Gera the Benjaminite. He was the man from Bahurim. ¹⁷A thousand men from the tribe of Benjamin were with him. This included Ziba, the servant of Saul. And Ziba's 15 sons and 20 servants were there too. They rushed down to the Jordan to get there ahead of the king. ¹⁸They all worked hard carrying the king's family and troops across. They helped them in every way they could.

As the king was crossing, Shimei fell down before him. ¹⁹He pleaded, "My lord the king, please forgive me. Forget what I did when you left Jerusalem. ²⁰For I know very well how much I sinned. That is why I have come here today. I am the very first person in all the tribe of Joseph to greet you."

²¹Abishai asked, "Shall not Shimei die? He cursed the Lord's chosen king!"

²²"Don't talk to me like that!" David exclaimed. "This is not a day for killing but for joy! I am once more king of Israel!"

²³Then, turning to Shimei, he vowed, "You will not be killed."

²⁴⁻²⁵Now Mephibosheth came from Jerusalem to meet the king. He was Saul's grandson. He had not washed his feet or clothes for a long time. And he had not trimmed his beard since the day the king left Jerusalem.

"Why didn't you come with me, Mephibosheth?" the king asked him.

²⁶And he replied, "My lord, O king, my servant Ziba lied to me. I told him, 'Saddle my donkey so that I can go with the king.' For as you know I am lame. ²⁷But Ziba has told lies about me. He told you that I refused to come. But I know that you are as an angel of God, so do what you think best. ²⁸I and all my relatives could expect only death from you. But instead you have honored me! You have let me eat at your own table! So how can I complain?"

²⁹"All right," David replied. "You and Ziba will divide the land between you."

³⁰"Give him all of it," Mephibosheth said. "I am content just to have you back again!"

³¹⁻³²Barzillai came from Rogelim to bring the king across the river. He had fed the king and his army during their exile in Mahanaim. He was very old now, about 80, and very rich.

³³"Come across with me and live in Jerusalem," the king said to Barzillai. "I will take care of you there."

³⁴"No," he replied. "I am far too old for that. ³⁵I am 80 years old today. Food and wine are no longer tasty. I am too old to hear the voices of men and women singers. I would only be a burden to my lord the king. ³⁶Just to go across the river with you is all the honor I need! ³⁷Let me return again to die in my own city. For there my father and mother are buried. But here is Chimham. Let him go with you. Give him all the good things you want to give him."

³⁸"Good," the king agreed. "Chimham shall go with me. I will do for him what I would have done for you."

³⁹So all the people crossed the Jordan with the king. And after David had kissed and blessed Barzillai, he went home. ⁴⁰The king then went on to Gilgal, taking Chimham with him. And most of Judah and half of Israel were there to greet him. ⁴¹But the men of Israel complained to the king. This was because only men from Judah had brought him and his family across the Jordan.

⁴²"Why not?" the men of Judah replied. "The king is one of our own tribe. Why should this make you angry? We have charged him nothing. He hasn't fed us or given us gifts!"

⁴³"But there are 10 tribes in Israel," the others replied. "So we have 10 times as much right in the king as you do. Why didn't you invite the rest of us? And, remember, we were the first to speak of bringing him back to be our king again."

The argument kept going back and forth. And the men of Judah were very rough in their replies.

Sheba Rebels against David

20 Then a hothead whose name was Sheba blew a trumpet. Sheba was the son of Bichri, a Benjaminite. He yelled, "We want nothing to do with David! Come on, you men of Israel. Let's get out of here. He's not our king."

²So all except Judah and Benjamin turned around. They turned from David and followed Sheba! But the men of Judah stayed with their king. They went with him from the Jordan to Jerusalem. ³David went home to his palace in Jerusalem. He had left 10 wives to keep the palace in order. He ordered that they be put in a house under guard. Their needs were to be cared for. But David would no longer sleep with them as his wives. So they lived as widows until they died.

⁴Then the king ordered Amasa to call out the army of Judah. He was to do this within three days and then report back at that time. ⁵So Amasa went out to call the troops. But it took him longer than the three days he had been given.

⁶Then David said to Abishai, "Sheba is going to hurt us more than Absalom did. Quick, take my bodyguard and chase after him. Catch him before he gets into a walled city where we can't get him."

⁷So Abishai and Joab set out after Sheba. They went with men from Joab's army and the king's own bodyguard. ⁸⁻¹⁰As they got to the great stone in Gibeon, they came face to face with Amasa. Joab was wearing his uniform with a dagger tied to his side. He stepped forward to greet Amasa. As he did this, he took the dagger from its sheath. "I'm glad to see you, my brother," Joab said. He took him by the beard with his right hand. He did this as though he was going to kiss him. Amasa didn't see the dagger in Joab's left hand. Then Joab stabbed him in the stomach with it. And his insides gushed out onto the ground. He did not need to stab him again, and Amasa died there. Joab and his brother, Abishai, left him lying there. Then they went after Sheba.

¹¹One of Joab's young officers shouted to Amasa's troops. He said, "If you are for David, come and follow Joab."

¹²But Amasa lay in his blood in the middle of the road. Joab's young officers saw that a crowd was coming to stare at him. So they dragged him off the road into a field. Then they threw a coat over him. ¹³With the body out of the way, everyone went on with Joab to capture Sheba.

¹⁴Meanwhile Sheba had traveled

across Israel. He planned to call his own clan of Bichri to fight. They lived at the city of Abel in Beth-maacah. ¹⁵When Joab's army got there, they set up camp around Abel. They built a mound against the city wall and began battering it down.

¹⁶But a wise woman in the city called out to Joab. "Listen to me, Joab," she said. "Come over here so I can talk to you."

¹⁷As he came near, the woman asked, "Are you Joab?"

And he replied, "I am."

¹⁸So she told him, "There used to be a saying. It said, 'If you want to settle an argument, ask advice at Abel.' For we always give wise counsel. ¹⁹You are destroying an old and peaceful city. It is a city that has been loyal to Israel. Should you destroy what is the Lord's?"

²⁰And Joab replied, "That isn't it at all. ²¹All I want is a man named Sheba. He is from the hill country of Ephraim. He has started a revolt against King David. If you will give him up to me, we will leave the city in peace."

"All right," the woman replied. "We will throw his head over the wall to you."

²²Then the woman went to the people with her wise advice. They cut off Sheba's head and threw it out to Joab. And he blew the trumpet and called his troops back from the attack. Then they went back to the king at Jerusalem.

²³Joab was commander of the army, and Benaiah was in charge of the king's bodyguard. ²⁴Adoram was in charge of the forced labor groups. Jehoshaphat was the historian who kept the records. ²⁵Sheva was the secretary, and Zadok and Abiathar were the chief priests. ²⁶Ira the Jairite was David's personal chaplain.

Saul's Sons Are Executed

21 There was a famine during David's reign. It lasted year after year for three years. And David spent much time in prayer about it. Then the Lord said, "The famine is because of the guilt of Saul and his family. It is because they killed the Gibeonites."

²So King David called the Gibeonites. They were not part of Israel. They were what was left of the nation of the Amorites. Israel had sworn not to kill them. But Saul had tried to wipe them out.

³David asked them, "What can I do for you to free ourselves of this guilt? What can I do to make you ask God to bless us?"

⁴"Well, money won't do it," the Gibeonites replied. "And we don't want to see Israelites killed in revenge."

"What can I do, then?" David asked. "Just tell me and I will do it for you."

⁵⁻⁶"Well, then," they replied, "give us seven of Saul's sons. Give us the sons of the man who did his best to destroy us. We will hang them before the Lord in Gibeon, the city of King Saul."

"All right," the king said. "I will do it."

⁷He saved Jonathan's son Mephibosheth, who was Saul's grandson. He did this because of the oath between himself and Jonathan. ⁸But he gave them Saul's two sons Armoni and Mephibosheth. Their mother was Rizpah, the daughter of Aiah. He also gave them the five adopted sons of Michal. She had raised them for Saul's daughter Merab. Merab was the wife of Adriel. ⁹Then the men of Gibeon killed them on the mountain before the Lord. So all seven of them died together. This happened at the beginning of the barley harvest.

¹⁰Then Rizpah spread sackcloth upon a rock. She stayed there through the whole harvest season. Rizpah was the mother of two of the men. She stayed there to stop the vultures from eating their bodies during the day. She also stopped the wild animals from eating them at night. ¹¹David learned about what she had done. ¹²⁻¹⁴So he had the men's bones buried in the grave of Saul's father, Kish. At the same time he sent a request to the men of Jabesh-gilead. He asked them to bring him the bones of Saul and Jonathan. They had stolen their bodies from the public square at Beth-shan. There the Philistines had hung them up after they had died in battle on Mount Gilboa. So their bones were brought to him. Then at last God answered prayer and ended the famine.

The Battle of the Giants

¹⁵Once again the Philistines were at war with Israel. One day, David and his men were in the thick of the battle. During the fight, David became tired and weak. ¹⁶Ishbi-benob closed in on David and was about to kill him. He was a giant whose speartip weighed more than 12 pounds. He also was wearing a new suit of armor. ¹⁷But Abishai, the son of Zeruiah, came to his rescue. He killed the Philistine. After that David's men said, "You are not going out to battle again! Why should we risk snuffing out the light of Israel?"

¹⁸Later, Sibbecai the Hushathite killed Saph, another giant. This happened during a war with the Philistines at Gob. ¹⁹Elhanan killed the brother of Goliath the Gittite. This happened at yet another time, but at the same place. This giant's spearhandle was as huge as a weaver's beam! ²⁰⁻²¹One time the Philistines and the Israelites were fighting at Gath. There was a giant with six fingers on each hand and six toes on each foot. He stood out and made fun of Israel. But David's nephew Jonathan killed him. He was the son of David's brother Shimei. ²²These four were from the tribe of giants in Gath. They were killed by David's troops.

David's Song of Praise

22 David sang this song to the Lord. He sang it after the Lord had rescued him from Saul. He also sang it after being saved from all his other enemies.

²"The Lord is my rock,
My fortress and my Savior.
³I will hide in God,
Who is my rock and my refuge.
He is my shield
And my salvation,
My refuge and high tower.
Thank you, O my Savior,
For saving me from all my enemies.
⁴I will call upon the Lord,
Who is worthy to be praised.
He will save me from all my enemies.
⁵The waves of death were all around me.
Floods of evil burst upon me.

⁶I was trapped and bound
By hell and death.
⁷But I called upon the Lord in my distress,
And he heard me from his Temple.
My cry reached his ears.
⁸Then the earth shook and trembled.
The foundations of the heavens quaked
Because of his wrath.
⁹Smoke poured from his nostrils.
Fire leaped from his mouth.
It burned up all before him,
Setting fire to the world.
¹⁰He bent the heavens down and came to earth.
He walked upon dark clouds.
¹¹He rode upon the glorious—
On the wings of the wind.
¹²Darkness surrounded him,
And clouds were thick around him.
¹³The earth was radiant with his brightness.
¹⁴The Lord thundered from heaven.
The God above all gods gave out a mighty shout.
¹⁵He shot forth his arrows of lightning
And routed his enemies.
¹⁶By the blast of his breath
Was the sea split in two.
The bottom of the sea appeared.
¹⁷From above, he rescued me.
He drew me out from the waters.
¹⁸He saved me from powerful enemies,
From those who hated me
And from those who were too strong for me.
¹⁹They came upon me
In the day of my calamity,
But the Lord was my salvation.
²⁰He set me free and rescued me,
For I was his delight.
²¹The Lord rewarded me for my goodness,
For my hands were clean.
²²And I have not departed from my God.
²³I knew his laws,
And I obeyed them.
²⁴I was perfect in obedience
And kept myself from sin.

25That is why the Lord has done so much for me,
For he sees that I am clean.
26You are merciful to the merciful.
You show your perfections
To the blameless.
27To those who are pure,
You show yourself pure.
But you destroy those who are evil.
28You will save those in trouble,
But you bring down the haughty.
For you watch their every move.
29O Lord, you are my light!
You make my darkness bright.
30By your power I can crush an army.
By your strength I leap over a wall.
31God's way is perfect.
His word is true.
He puts a shield in front of all who hide behind him.

God protects us

He puts a shield in front of all who hide behind him.

2 Samuel 22:31

32Our Lord alone is God.
We have no other Savior.
33God is my strong fortress.
He has made me safe.
34He causes the good to walk a steady tread
Like mountain goats upon the rocks.
35He gives me skill in war
And strength to bend a bow of bronze.
36You have given me the shield of your salvation.
Your gentleness has made me great.
37You have made wide steps for my feet,
To keep them from slipping.
38I have chased my enemies
And destroyed them.
I did not stop till all were gone.
39I have destroyed them
So that none can rise again.
They have fallen beneath my feet.
40For you have given me strength for the battle.
You have caused me to subdue

All those who rose against me.
41You have made my enemies
Turn and run away.
I have destroyed them all.
42They looked in vain for help.
They cried to God,
But he refused to answer.
43I beat them into dust.
I crushed and scattered them
Like dust along the streets.
44You have preserved me
From the rebels of my people.
You have preserved me
As the head of the nations.
Foreigners shall serve me
45And shall quickly submit to me
When they hear of my power.
46They shall lose heart
And come, trembling,
From their hiding places.
47The Lord lives.
Blessed be my Rock.
Praise to him,
The Rock of my salvation.
48Blessed be God
Who destroys those who oppose me
49And rescues me from my enemies.
Yes, you hold me safe above their heads.
You deliver me from violence.
50No wonder I give thanks to you, O Lord, among the nations.
No wonder I sing praises to your name.
51He gives great deliverance to his king.
And he shows mercy to his anointed,
To David and his family,
Forever."

David's Last Words

23 These are the last words of David:
"David, the son of Jesse, speaks.
David, the man to whom God gave such great success;
David, the anointed of the God of Jacob;
David, sweet psalmist of Israel:
2The Spirit of the Lord spoke by me,
And his word was on my tongue.
3The Rock of Israel said to me:
'One shall come who rules righteously,

Who rules in the fear of God.
⁴He shall be as the light of the
    morning.
He shall be like a cloudless sunrise
When the tender grass
Springs forth upon the earth.
He shall be as sunshine after rain.'
⁵And it is my family
He has chosen!
Yes, God has made
An everlasting covenant with me.

His agreement is eternal, final,
    sealed.
He will constantly look after
My safety and success.
⁶But the godless are as thorns to be
    thrown away.
For they tear the hand that touches
    them.
⁷One must be armed to chop them
    down.
They shall be burned."

David's Men Bring Water from Bethlehem

Bethlehem, David's childhood home, had been captured by the
Philistines. One day David longed for a drink of water from Bethlehem. Three of his bravest men fought their way to the well and
brought water to David. But David would not drink it. Why?

⁸These are the names of the Top Three.
They were the most heroic men in
David's army. The first was Josheb-
basshebeth from Tahchemon. He was
also known as Adino the Eznite. He
once killed 800 men in one battle.

⁹Next in rank was Eleazar. He was the
son of Dodo and grandson of Ahohi. He
was one of the three men who stood
with David. They held back the Philistines when the rest of the Israelite army
ran. ¹⁰He killed the Philistines until his
hand was too tired to hold his sword.
And the Lord gave him a great victory.
The rest of the army did not come back
until it was time to collect the loot!

¹¹⁻¹²After him was Shammah. He was
the son of Agee from Harar. Once during
a Philistine attack all his men ran away
and left him. He stood alone at the center of a field of lentils. He beat back the
Philistines alone! And God gave him a
great victory.

¹³Once, three of The Thirty went
down at harvest time to visit David. The
Thirty were the top officers of the Israelite army. The Philistines were then
camped in the valley of Rephaim. And
at that time, David was living in the cave
of Adullam. ¹⁴David was in a safe place,

for Philistine soldiers had taken the
nearby city of Bethlehem.

¹⁵David said, "How thirsty I am! I
would love some good water from the
city well!" The well was near the city
gate.

¹⁶So the three men broke through the
Philistine ranks. They drew water from
the well and brought it to David. But he
refused to drink it! Instead, he poured it
out before the Lord.

¹⁷"No, my God," he exclaimed, "I
cannot do it! This is the blood of these
men who have risked their lives."

¹⁸⁻¹⁹One of those three men was
Abishai. He was the brother of Joab, the
son of Zeruiah. Of the three that went
for the water, he was the greatest. Once
he took on 300 of the enemy by himself
and killed them all! He became as famous as The Three. But he was not actually one of them. He was the greatest of
The Thirty and he was their leader. The
Thirty were the top officers of the army.

²⁰There was also Benaiah, the son of
Jehoiada. He was a heroic soldier from
Kabzeel. Benaiah killed two giants, the
sons of Ariel of Moab. Another time he
went down into a pit. There was slippery
snow on the ground. He took on a lion

that was caught there and killed it. 21Another time he killed an Egyptian warrior who was armed with a spear. But he was armed only with a staff. He grabbed the spear from the Egyptian's hand and killed him with it. 22These were some of the deeds that gave Benaiah almost as much fame as the Top Three. 23He was one of the greatest of The Thirty. But he was not actually one of the Top Three. And David made him chief of his bodyguard.

• *Remember:* Who were the three bravest men in David's army? (23:8-12) Where and when did these three visit David? (23:13) David was hiding from Saul at this time. Why didn't David just go to Bethlehem for a drink? (23:13-14) Who went to Bethlehem? What did they do there? (23:16) Did David drink the water? Why not? What did he do with it? (23:16-17) Would you have done what David did? Or would you drink the water?

• *Discover:* Some gifts are special. David wanted to honor the Lord with his special gift. We should honor God with all our gifts, but especially with our special gifts.

• *Apply:* Do you have a special gift? Can you sing better, play better, or do something better than others? Let God use your special gift. Honor him with it.

• *What's next?* Why did a king buy a threshing floor when he didn't want to thresh there? Read 2 Samuel 24. ■

David's Thirty Mighty Men

24-39Asahel, the brother of Joab, was also one of The Thirty. Others were:

Elhanan (son of Dodo) from Bethlehem;
Shammah from Harod;
Elika from Harod;
Helez from Palti;
Ira (son of Ikkesh) from Tekoa;
Abiezer from Anathoth;
Mebunnai from Hushath;
Zalmon from Ahoh;
Maharai from Netophah;
Heleb (son of Baanah) from Netophah;
Ittai (son of Ribai) from Gibeah, of the tribe of Benjamin;
Benaiah of Pirathon;
Hiddai from the brooks of Gaash;
Abi-albon from Arbath;
Azmaveth from Bahurim;
Eliahba from Shaalbon;
The sons of Jashen;
Jonathan;
Shammah from Harar;
Ahiam (the son of Sharar) from Harar;
Eliphelet (son of Ahasbai) from Maacah;
Eliam (the son of Ahithophel) from Gilo;
Hezro from Carmel;
Paarai from Arba;
Igal (son of Nathan) from Zobah;
Bani from Gad;
Zelek from Ammon;
Naharai from Beeroth, the armor-bearer of Joab (son of Zeruiah);
Ira from Ithra;
Gareb from Ithra; and
Uriah the Hittite. There were 37 in all.

David Buys a Threshing Floor

Counting people is usually not wrong. But counting people for the wrong reason is. David counted people for the wrong reason. What was it?

24 Once again the Lord became angry with the nation of Israel. So he caused David to harm them by counting all the people. "Go and count the people of Israel and Judah," the Lord told him.

2So the king spoke to Joab, commander of his army. He said, "Count all the people. Count them from one end of the nation to the other. That way I will know how many of them there are."

3But Joab replied, "May God give you 100 times more people! And may you live to see the day when this happens! But why do you want to do such a thing? You have no right to rejoice in their strength."

4But the king's command overruled Joab's words. So Joab and the other army officers went out to count the people of Israel. 5First they crossed the Jordan and camped at Aroer. This is south of the city that lies in the middle of the valley of Gad, near Jazer. 6Then they went to Gilead in the land of Tahtim-hodshi. From there they went to Dan-jaan and around to Sidon. 7Then they went to the great city of Tyre. They visited all the cities of the Hivites and Canaanites. Then they went south to Judah as far as Beersheba. 8They went through the whole land. They finished counting the people in nine months and twenty days. 9And Joab told the king the number of the people. There were 800,000 men of fighting age in Israel. There were 500,000 of that age in Judah.

10But after he had counted the people, David became worried. He said to the Lord, "What I did was very wrong. Please forgive this foolish sin of mine."

11The next morning the word of the Lord came to the prophet Gad. He was David's contact with God.

The Lord said to Gad, 12"Tell David that I will give him three choices."

13So Gad came to David. He said to him, "You have three choices. You may choose seven years of famine across the land. You may choose to run from your enemies for three months. Or you may choose to suffer three days from a plague. Which will it be? Think this over. Let me know what answer to give to God."

14"This is a hard decision," David replied. "But it is best that we be punished by the Lord. His mercy is great. This is better than being punished by other people."

15So the Lord sent the plague upon Israel that morning. It lasted for three days. And 70,000 men died throughout the nation. 16The death angel was about to destroy Jerusalem. But the Lord was sorry for what was happening. So he told the angel to stop. The angel was by the threshing floor of Araunah the Jebusite at the time.

17When David saw the angel, he spoke to the Lord. "Look," he said, "I am the one who has sinned! What have these people done? Let your anger be only against me and my family."

18That day Gad came to David. He said to him, "Go and build an altar to the Lord. Build it on the threshing floor of Araunah the Jebusite." 19So David went to do what the Lord had told him. 20Araunah saw the king and his men coming toward him. So he came forward and fell flat on the ground. He put his face in the dust.

21"Why have you come?" Araunah asked.

And David replied, "To buy your threshing floor. I must build an altar to the Lord. Then he will stop the plague."

22"Use anything you like," Araunah told the king. "Here are oxen for the burnt offering. You can use the threshing tools and ox yokes for wood. Build a fire on the altar with them. 23I will give it all to you! And may the Lord God accept your sacrifice."

24But the king said to Araunah, "No, I will not have it as a gift. I must buy it. I don't want to give the Lord burnt offerings that have cost me nothing."

So David paid him for the threshing floor and the oxen. 25And David built an altar there to the Lord. He offered burnt offerings and peace offerings. And the Lord answered his prayer, and the plague was stopped.

● *Remember:* Who warned David not to count the people? (24:3) Why did he say it was wrong? (24:3) How many men of military age were there? (24:9) Why did David feel sorry for what he had done? (24:10) What three punishments did the Lord offer? (24:12-13) Which one did David choose? (24:14-15) Why did David want to build an altar at Araunah's threshing floor? (24:16-21) David's pride got him into deep trouble. He was proud of the size of his army. He depended on that. He forgot to depend on God more than numbers.

- *Discover:* We must never be proud of our own strength, or money, or abilities. God wants us to depend on him.

- *Apply:* The next time you are proud of what you are or what you have, stop! Have you forgotten to depend on God? Have you forgotten that all you have comes from him? Thank God instead of forgetting about him.

- *What's next?* Two sons claim to be king. But both can't reign. Which one will be king? Read 1 Kings 1. ■

FIRST KINGS

Have you ever fed some birds? In 1 Kings some birds feed a man. You'll meet the wisest man of all, who did some of the dumbest things of all. You'll see fire come down from the sky and burn stones and water. You'll see a barrel of flour and a jar of oil that never get empty.

In 1 Kings, Solomon becomes king when his father David dies. He becomes a rich and powerful king with a kingdom much bigger than David's. And he builds the most beautiful building in the world, the Temple.

Solomon was a man who had everything. He started well, but he became too rich. Before long, this wise king was doing foolish things. He forgot to live for God. So did his son Rehoboam. When Solomon died, his kingdom died too. You'll learn from Solomon that it's not smart to live without God. God is more important than all the money and things in the world.

Solomon Becomes King

King David was now very old. His son Adonijah wanted to be the next king. But David didn't know it. David didn't want Adonijah to be king. He had promised that someone else would be king. What happened when David found out?

1 In his old age King David had to stay in his bed. They piled up many blankets on him. But still he was always cold.

²"There is a cure for this," his servants told him. "You must find a young virgin to be your concubine and nurse. She will lie in your arms and keep you warm."

³⁻⁴So they searched the country from one end to the other. They wanted to find the most beautiful girl in all the land. Abishag, from Shunam, was chosen. They brought her to the king. She took care of the king and waited on him. And she lay in his arms to warm him. But she had no intimate relations with the king.

⁵David and his wife Haggith had a son named Adonijah. He decided to crown himself king in place of his aged father. So he hired chariots and drivers. And he got 50 men to run down the streets in front of him. ⁶Now his father,

King David, had never tried to stop him. He never asked him, "Why are you doing these things?" Adonijah was a very handsome man. And he was born next after Absalom. ⁷He talked to General Joab, son of Zeruiah, and Abiathar the priest. And they agreed to help him become king. ⁸But many leaders stayed loyal to King David. These included the priests Zadok and Benaiah and the prophet Nathan. Shimei, Rei, and David's army chiefs also stayed loyal. They would not support Adonijah.

⁹Adonijah went to En-rogel. There he sacrificed sheep, oxen, and fat young goats at the Serpent's Stone. Then he called all his brothers, the other sons of King David. He also called the rulers and leaders of Judah. He asked them all to come to watch him become king. ¹⁰But he did not ask Nathan the prophet, Benaiah, or the loyal army officers. He didn't ask his brother Solomon either.

¹¹Then Nathan the prophet went to Bathsheba. She was the mother of Solomon. He asked her, "Did you know what Haggith's son, Adonijah, is doing? He has made himself king! And our lord David doesn't even know about it! ¹²You must save your own life and the life of your son Solomon. To do this, do just as I say! ¹³Go at once to King David. Ask him, 'My lord, didn't you make a promise to me? Didn't you say that my son Solomon would be the next king? Didn't you tell me he would sit on your throne? If you promised this, then why is Adonijah now ruling?' ¹⁴And while you are still talking, I'll come. I'll tell him that all you've said is true."

¹⁵So Bathsheba went into the king's bedroom. He was an old, old man now. And Abishag was caring for him. ¹⁶Bathsheba bowed low before him.

"What do you want?" he asked her.

¹⁷She replied, "My lord, you made a promise to me by the Lord your God. You promised that my son Solomon would be the next king. You told me he would sit on your throne. ¹⁸But instead, Adonijah is the new king! And you don't even know about it! ¹⁹He is celebrating his kingship by sacrificing oxen, fat goats, and many sheep. He has asked all your sons to come. He has also asked Abiathar the priest and General Joab. But he didn't ask Solomon. ²⁰And now, my lord the king, all Israel is waiting for you to decide. You must say if Adonijah is the one you have chosen to be king. ²¹If you don't act, my son Solomon and I will be arrested. Then we will be killed as criminals as soon as you die."

²²⁻²³While she was speaking, the king's servants spoke to him. "Nathan the prophet is here to see you," they said.

Nathan came in and bowed low before the king. ²⁴He asked, "My lord, have you chosen Adonijah to be the next king? Is he the one you have chosen to sit upon your throne? ²⁵Today he was crowned as king. He did this by sacrificing oxen, fat goats, and many sheep. And he has invited your sons to come to the feast. He also invited General Joab and Abiathar the priest. They are feasting and drinking with him. And they are shouting, 'Long live King Adonijah!' ²⁶But Zadok the priest and Benaiah and Solomon and I weren't invited. ²⁷Did you know about all this? For you haven't told anyone what you've decided. You haven't said which of your sons will be the next king."

²⁸"Call Bathsheba," David said. So she came back in and stood before the king.

²⁹And the king promised, "The Lord has saved me from every danger. As he lives, I make this promise to you. ³⁰I promise that your son Solomon shall be the next king. He shall sit on my throne. This shall happen just as I promised you before by the Lord God of Israel."

³¹Then Bathsheba bowed low before him again. "Oh, thank you, sir," she said. "May my lord the king live forever!"

³²"Call Zadok the priest," the king ordered. "Also call Nathan the prophet, and Benaiah."

When they got there, ³³he spoke to them. "Take Solomon and my officers to Gihon," he ordered. "Solomon is to ride on my personal mule. ³⁴Zadok the priest and Nathan the prophet are to anoint him there as king of Israel. Then blow the trumpets and shout, 'Long live King Solomon!' ³⁵When you bring him back here, put him upon my throne. He will be the new king. For I have chosen him as king of Israel and Judah."

³⁶"Amen! Praise God!" replied Benaiah. Then he added, ³⁷"May the Lord be with Solomon as he has been with you. And may God make Solomon's reign even greater than yours!"

³⁸So Zadok the priest, Nathan the prophet, Benaiah, and David's bodyguard took Solomon to Gihon. And Solomon rode on King David's own mule. ³⁹At Gihon, Zadok took a bottle of sacred oil from the Tabernacle. He poured it over Solomon. Then the trumpets were blown. And all the people shouted, "Long live King Solomon!"

⁴⁰Then they all went back with him to Jerusalem. And they made a joyful noise all along the way.

⁴¹Now Adonijah and his guests were just finishing their feast. They heard the trumpets and shouting in the distance.

"What's going on?" Joab demanded. "Why is there so much noise in the city?"

⁴²While he was still speaking, Jonathan rushed in. Jonathan was the son of Abiathar the priest.

"Come in," Adonijah said to him. "For you are a good man. You must have good news."

⁴³"Our lord King David has made Solomon king!" Jonathan shouted. ⁴⁴⁻⁴⁵"The king sent him to Gihon. And he sent Zadok the priest and Nathan the prophet with him. He was guarded by Benaiah and the king's own bodyguard. And he rode on the king's own mule. Zadok and Nathan have anointed him as the new king! They have just gone back to Jerusalem. The whole city is full of joy. That's what all the noise is. ⁴⁶⁻⁴⁷Solomon is sitting on the throne. And all the people are telling King David what a good thing he's done. They are saying, 'May God bless Solomon even more than he has blessed you! May God make Solomon's reign

even greater than yours!' And the king is lying in bed worshiping God. ⁴⁸He is saying, 'Blessed be the Lord God of Israel! He has chosen one of my sons to sit upon my throne! And I am still alive to see it!'"

⁴⁹⁻⁵⁰Then Adonijah and his guests jumped up from the feast. They ran away in panic. They were afraid they would be killed! Adonijah ran into the Tabernacle. There he caught hold of the horns of the holy altar. ⁵¹Word reached Solomon that Adonijah was in the Tabernacle. And Adonijah sent a message asking Solomon not to kill him. ⁵²Solomon said, "If he behaves himself, he will not be hurt. But if he does not, he shall die." ⁵³So King Solomon called him. And they brought him down from the altar. He came to bow low before the king. Then Solomon sent him away.

"Go on home," he said.

- *Remember:* Who tried to make himself king? (1:5) How had his father David disciplined him when he grew up? (1:6) Who told David what Adonijah was doing? (1:11-27) Who became Israel's new king instead of Adonijah? (1:34,39) Why did Adonijah run to the Tabernacle? What did he do there? (1:49-51) What did Solomon say to Adonijah? (1:53)

- *Discover:* Sometimes we can't have what we want simply because of the way we act. Adonijah wanted to be king. As David's oldest living son, he probably would have become the next king if he had been less greedy and more obedient. The way he acted, he didn't deserve to be king.

- *Apply:* Is there something you'd like to be? Is there something you'd like your parents to do for you? Have you first treated your parents the way you should? Have you acted in a way that would make your parents want to do this for you?

- *What's next:* If God said you could have anything you want, what would you choose? Read 1 Kings 3:3-15 to see what Solomon wanted. ▪

David's Instructions for Solomon

2 The time for King David's death was near. So he gave his son Solomon his last commands.

2"I am going where every man on earth must some day go. I am counting on you to be a strong and worthy leader. 3Obey the laws of God and follow all his ways. Keep each of his commands written in the law of Moses. That way you will prosper in all you do. You will succeed wherever you turn. 4If you do this, then the Lord will fulfill the promise he gave me. He promised that one of my descendants would always be the king of Israel. But this will only happen if my descendants watch their step. They must all be faithful to God. If they are, my family will always rule in Israel.

5"Now listen to my orders. You know that Joab murdered my two generals, Abner and Amasa. He acted as if it was an act of war. But he did it in a time of peace. 6You are a wise man and will know what to do. Don't let him die in peace. 7But be kind to the sons of Barzillai the Gileadite. Make them permanent guests of the king. They took care of me when I ran from your brother Absalom. 8And do you remember Shimei, the son of Gera? He is the Benjaminite from Bahurim. He cursed me as I was going to Mahanaim. But he came down to meet me at the Jordan River. And I promised I wouldn't kill him. 9But that promise doesn't bind you! You are a wise man. You will know how to arrange a bloody death for him."

10Then David died and was buried in Jerusalem. 11He had ruled over Israel for 40 years. Seven of them were spent in Hebron and 33 in Jerusalem. 12And Solomon became the new king. He took his father David's place. And he had strong control of his kingdom.

Solomon's Enemies Are Killed

13One day Adonijah came to see Solomon's mother, Bathsheba. Adonijah was the son of Haggith.

"Have you come to make trouble?" she asked him.

"No," he replied. "I come in peace.

14As a matter of fact, I have a favor to ask of you."

"What is it?" she asked.

15"All was going well for me," he said. "The kingdom was mine. Everyone expected me to be the next king. But the tables are turned. Everything went to my brother instead. For that is the way the Lord wanted it. 16But now I have just a small favor to ask of you. Please don't turn me down."

"What is it?" she asked.

17"Speak to King Solomon on my behalf," he said. "I know he will do anything you ask. Ask him to give me Abishag, the Shunammite, as my wife."

18"All right," Bathsheba replied, "I'll ask him."

19So she went to ask the favor of King Solomon. The king stood up from his throne as she came in. Then he bowed low to her. He ordered that a throne for his mother be put beside his. So she sat at his right hand.

20"I have one small request to make of you," she said. "I hope you won't turn me down."

"What is it, my mother?" he asked. "You know I won't refuse you."

21"Then let your brother Adonijah marry Abishag," she replied.

22"Are you crazy?" he demanded. "If I were to give him Abishag, I would be giving him the kingdom too! For he is my older brother! He and Abiathar the priest and General Joab would take over!" 23-24Then King Solomon swore with a great oath. "May God strike me dead if Adonijah does not die this very day!" he said. "For he has made a plot against me! I promise this by the living God. For the Lord has given me the throne of my father David. He has given me this kingdom he promised me."

25So King Solomon sent Benaiah to kill him. And he killed Adonijah with a sword.

26Then the king said to Abiathar the priest, "Go back to your home in Anathoth. You should be killed, too. But I won't do it now. For you carried the Ark of the Lord during my father's reign. And you suffered right along with him in all his troubles."

²⁷Solomon made Abiathar give up his place as priest of the Lord. So he fulfilled the promise of the Lord at Shiloh about the family of Eli.

²⁸When Joab heard about Adonijah's death he ran to the Tabernacle for safety. Joab had joined Adonijah's revolt, though not Absalom's. In the Tabernacle, he caught hold of the horns of the altar. ²⁹When news of this got to King Solomon, he sent Benaiah to kill him.

³⁰Benaiah went into the Tabernacle. He said to Joab, "The king says to come out!"

"No," he said, "I'll die here."

So Benaiah went back to the king for new orders.

³¹"Do as he says," the king replied. "Kill him there beside the altar and bury him. Then I and my father's family will not be guilty of his murders. ³²He killed two men who were better than he was. One was Abner, commander of the army of Israel. The other was Amasa, commander of the army of Judah. The Lord will hold Joab guilty for the murders of both of them. For my father David did not know he had killed them. ³³May Joab and his family be guilty of these murders for all time! May the Lord declare David and his family free of guilt! May they rule in peace for all time!"

³⁴So Benaiah went back to the Tabernacle and killed Joab. He was buried beside his house in the desert.

³⁵Then the king chose Benaiah as commander of the army. And he chose Zadok as priest in place of Abiathar.

³⁶⁻³⁷The king now sent for Shimei. He told him, "Build a house here in Jerusalem. Do not step outside the city. If you do, you will die. The moment you go beyond Kidron Brook, you will die. And it will be your own fault."

³⁸"All right," Shimei replied. "I'll do what you say." So he lived in Jerusalem for a long time.

³⁹But three years later two of Shimei's slaves ran away. They went to King Achish of Gath. Shimei learned where they were. ⁴⁰So he saddled a donkey and went to Gath to visit the king. And when he found his slaves, he took them back to Jerusalem.

⁴¹Solomon heard that Shimei had left Jerusalem. He knew he had gone to Gath and come back. ⁴²So the king sent for Shimei. He said, "I made you promise in the name of God to stay in Jerusalem. I warned that if you didn't, you would die. You said, 'Very well, I will do as you say.' ⁴³Then why did you not do what you said you would? Why did you not obey my command? ⁴⁴And what about all the bad things you did to my father, King David? May the Lord take revenge on you! ⁴⁵But may I be given God's rich blessings! And may one of David's family always sit on this throne!"

⁴⁶Then, at the king's command, Benaiah took Shimei outside. There he killed him.

So Solomon's grip upon the kingdom became strong.

3 Solomon made a treaty with Pharaoh, the king of Egypt. To do this he married one of his daughters. He brought her to Jerusalem to live in the City of David. At this time Solomon was building his palace and the Temple. He was also finishing the wall around the city.

²At that time the people sacrificed their offerings on altars in the hills. This was because the Temple of the Lord hadn't yet been built.

Solomon Asks for Wisdom

Have you ever read a story about a person who was granted one wish? God told Solomon he could have anything he wanted. What would you say if God offered you anything you wanted? What would you choose? What did Solomon choose?

³Solomon loved the Lord and followed all of his father David's orders. But he still gave sacrifices and burned incense in the hills. ⁴The most famous of the hilltop altars was at Gibeon. The king went there and sacrificed 1,000 burnt offerings! ⁵The Lord spoke to him in a dream that night. He told him to ask for anything he wanted. And he promised it would be given to him!

⁶Solomon replied, "You were very kind to my father David. He was honest and true and faithful to you. He obeyed all your commands. And you are still being kind to him. For you have given him a son to be king after him. ⁷O Lord my God, you have made me king in place of my father David. But I am like a little child who doesn't know his way around. ⁸And here I am among your own chosen people. It is a great nation! There are too many people to count! ⁹Please give me wisdom. Help me understand how to rule your people well. Help me know what is right and what is wrong. How can I do these things by myself?"

God helps us understand what we should do and should not do

Help me know what is right and what is wrong.

1 Kings 3:9

---

¹⁰The Lord was happy with his reply. He was glad that Solomon had asked for wisdom. ¹¹So he replied, "You did not ask for a long life. You did not ask for riches for yourself. You did not ask me to defeat your enemies. Instead, you asked for wisdom in ruling my people. ¹²Yes, I'll give you what you asked for! I will make you wiser than anyone else ever has been or will be! ¹³And I will also give you what you didn't ask for. I will give you riches and honor! And not a king in all the world will be as famous as you! ¹⁴I ask that you follow me and obey my laws. You must do just as your father David did. And if you do, I will give you a long life."

¹⁵Then Solomon woke up and saw it had been a dream. He went back to Jerusalem and went into the Tabernacle. He stood there before the Ark of the Covenant of the Lord. And there he sacrificed burnt offerings and peace offerings. Then he invited all his officials to a great banquet.

- *Remember:* What did the Lord offer Solomon? (3:5) What did Solomon ask the Lord to give him? (3:9) Was the Lord pleased with this? Because he was pleased with Solomon's answer, what else did the Lord say he would give Solomon? (3:10-14) Do you think Solomon asked for the right thing? Why?

- *Discover:* When you pray, ask God to give you what will please him most, not what will please you most. He may even give you more than you ask, but don't expect it.

- *Apply:* The next time you pray, ask, "Am I asking God for something he wants me to have?" Be sure you do.

- *What's next?* Two women both say they are a baby's mother. How could anyone decide which one was right? Solomon will show you how he decided. Read 1 Kings 3:16-28. ■

Solomon Shows How Wise He Is

Two women came to King Solomon one day. Each said she was the mother of the same baby. Which one was right? How could anyone decide who was telling the truth? How could Solomon know for sure? Read about what he did.

¹⁶Soon after that two young prostitutes came to the king. They had a problem that needed to be solved. ¹⁷⁻¹⁸"Sir," one of them began, "we live in the same house. I had a baby while this woman was there with me. When it was three days old, this woman's baby was born too. ¹⁹But her baby died during the night. She rolled over on it in her sleep and killed it. ²⁰Then she got up during the night. She took my son from beside me while I was asleep. She laid her

dead child in my arms. Then she took my baby to sleep beside her. ²¹And in the morning when I tried to feed my baby it was dead! But when it became light, I saw that it wasn't my son at all."

²²Then the other woman said, "No! The living baby is mine! The dead baby is yours!"

"No!" the first woman said. "The dead one is yours! The living one is mine!" And so they argued back and forth before the king.

²³Then the king said, "Let's get the facts straight. Both of you claim the living child. Each of you says the dead child belongs to the other. ²⁴All right, bring me a sword." So a sword was brought to the king. ²⁵Then he said, "Divide the living child in two! Give half to each of these women!"

²⁶The woman who was the mother of the child loved him very much. So she cried out, "Oh no, sir! Give her the child. Don't kill him!"

But the other woman said, "All right. It won't be yours or mine. Divide it between us!"

²⁷Then the king said, "Give the baby to the woman who wants him to live. She is the mother!"

²⁸Word of the king's decision spread quickly through the nation. All the people were amazed. They saw the great wisdom God had given him.

- *Remember:* Why were the two women quarreling? (3:17-21) What did Solomon do next? (3:23-25) How did Solomon learn who was the real mother? (3:26-27) What did people around the country think about this? (3:28) Do you think Solomon made the right decision? Do you think he was truly wise?

- *Discover:* Being smart doesn't make you wise. A wise person knows how to make choices that will (1) uncover the truth,

(2) show what is fair and right, or
(3) help others.

- *Apply:* You may be the smartest person in school. But you show you are wise when you make wise choices. If you choose to do foolish things, you are not being wise. Choose what will please God most.

- *What's next?* A king builds the most beautiful building in the world. Read how he did it in 1 Kings 5:1–6:7.■

Solomon's Cabinet Members

4 King Solomon ruled over all Israel. Here is a list of his leading officers.

Azariah (son of Zadok) was the High Priest.

Elihoreph and Ahijah (sons of Shisha) were secretaries.

Jehoshaphat (son of Ahilud) was the court historian. He was in charge of the court records.

Benaiah (son of Jehoiada) was commander of the army.

Zadok and Abiathar were priests.

Azariah (son of Nathan) was secretary of state.

Zabud (son of Nathan) was the king's personal priest. He was also Solomon's special friend.

Ahishar was the manager of palace affairs.

Adoniram (son of Abda) was manager of public works.

????????????????????????????????????

Who cooked 30 cows and 100 sheep each day to feed his household?

(Read 4:20-23 for the answer.)

????????????????????????????????????

7There were also 12 officers of Solomon's court. One man was chosen from each tribe. Their job was to collect food from the people for the king and his family. Each of them collected food for one month of the year.

8-19These are the names of the 12 officers.

Ben-hur was governor of the hill country of Ephraim.

Ben-deker was in charge of Makaz, Shaalbim, Beth-shemesh, and Elon-beth-hanan.

Ben-hesed was governor over Arubboth. This included Socoh and all the land of Hepher.

Ben-abinadab was over the highlands of Dor. He married Solomon's daughter, the princess Taphath.

Baana (son of Ahilud) was in charge of Taanach and Megiddo. He was also over all of Beth-shean near Zarethan below Jezreel. And he governed the land from Beth-shean to Abel-meholah and over to Jokmeam.

Ben-geber was the governor of Ramoth-gilead. This included the villages of Jair (the son of Manasseh) in Gilead. He was also in charge of the land of Argob in Bashan. This included 60 walled cities with bronze gates.

Ahinadab (the son of Iddo) was governor of Mahanaim.

Ahimaaz was in charge of the area of Naphtali. He married Princess Basemath, another of Solomon's daughters.

Baana (son of Hushai) was over the areas of Asher and Bealoth.

Jehoshaphat (son of Paruah) governed the area of Issachar.

Shimei (son of Ela) was in charge of the area of Benjamin.

Geber (son of Uri) was the governor of Gilead. This included the land of King Sihon of the Amorites and King Og of Bashan.

A general manager was put over these officials and their work.

Solomon's Kingdom

20There were many people in the land of Israel and Judah at this time. They were a rich and happy nation. 21King Solomon ruled a great region. It began at the Euphrates River. From there it went to the land of the Philistines. Its southern border stretched as far as the borders of Egypt. The people of the lands around sent taxes to Solomon. And they served him through his whole lifetime.

²²Much food was needed every day to feed Solomon and all those who ate at his table. Each day they used 195 bushels of fine flour and 390 bushels of meal. ²³They ate 10 grain-fed oxen, 20 pasture-fed cattle, and 100 sheep. And at times they also ate deer, gazelles, roebucks, and fat birds.

²⁴Solomon ruled over all the kingdoms west of the Euphrates River. He ruled from Tiphsah to Gaza. And there was peace in the whole land.

²⁵During Solomon's life, all of Judah and Israel lived in peace and safety. Each family had its own home and garden.

²⁶Solomon owned 40,000 chariot horses. And he hired 12,000 chariot drivers. ²⁷Each month the tax officials brought food for King Solomon and his court. ²⁸They also brought the barley and straw for the royal horses in the stables.

Solomon Is Famous for His Wisdom

²⁹God gave Solomon great wisdom. He was able to understand many things. He had a mind with broad interests. ³⁰In fact, his wisdom was greater than that of any of the wise men of the East. It was also greater than the wisdom of the wise men of Egypt. ³¹He was wiser than Ethan the Ezrahite. He was wiser than Heman, Calcol, and Darda, the sons of Mahol. And he was famous among all the nations around Israel. ³²He was the author of 3,000 proverbs and wrote 1,005 songs. ³³He was a great naturalist. He taught about the many kinds of plants. He taught about the great cedars of Lebanon and the tiny hyssop that grows in the wall. He taught about all the other plants as well. He also knew about animals, birds, snakes, and fish. ³⁴And kings from many lands sent their people to him for his advice.

Solomon Builds the Temple

What is the most beautiful building you have ever seen? You have probably never seen a building as beautiful as Solomon's Temple. This is what it was like.

5 King Hiram of Tyre had always been a friend of David's. And Hiram heard that David's son Solomon was the new king of Israel. So he sent messengers to bring his good wishes to Solomon. ²⁻³Solomon replied by telling Hiram about the Temple of the Lord he wanted to build. His father, David, had not been able to build it. This was because of the many wars going on. He had been waiting for the Lord to give him peace.

⁴"But now," Solomon said to Hiram, "the Lord my God has given Israel peace on every side. I have no foreign enemies or rebels among my people. ⁵So I am planning to build a Temple for the Lord my God. I will build it just as he told my father I should. For the Lord told him, 'I will put your son on your throne. And he shall build me a Temple.' ⁶Now please help me with this project. Send your woodsmen to the mountains of Lebanon. Tell them to cut cedar timber for me. I will send my men to work beside them. I will pay your men whatever wages you ask. For no one in Israel can cut timber like the people of Sidon!"

⁷Hiram was very happy with the message from Solomon. "Praise the Lord!" he said. "He has given David a wise son to be king of the great nation of Israel." ⁸Then he sent his reply to Solomon. "I have received your message," he said. "I will do as you have asked about the timber. I can supply both cedar and cypress. ⁹My men will bring the logs from the Lebanon mountains to the Mediterranean Sea. There they will build them into rafts. We will float them along the coast to the place you need them. Then we will break the rafts apart and deliver

the timber to you. You can pay me with food for my family."

¹⁰So Hiram cut for Solomon as much cedar and cypress timber as he wanted. ¹¹To pay him back, Solomon sent him food for his family. Each year he sent 125,000 bushels of wheat and 96 gallons of pure olive oil. ¹²So the Lord gave great wisdom to Solomon just as he had promised. And Hiram and Solomon made a treaty of peace.

¹³Then Solomon called up 30,000 workers from all over Israel. ¹⁴He sent 10,000 of them to Lebanon each month. That way each man was a month in Lebanon and two months at home. Adoniram was the general manager of this labor camp. ¹⁵Solomon also had 80,000 stonecutters. They cut the stone in the hill country. And he had 70,000 other workers to carry the stones. ¹⁶He put 3,300 foremen over the workers. ¹⁷The king told them to cut and shape huge blocks of fine stone. These stones were for the foundation of the Temple. ¹⁸Men from Gebal helped Solomon's and Hiram's builders. They helped them to cut the timber and make the boards. They also helped them make the stones for the Temple.

6 So Solomon began to build the Temple. He began the work in the spring of the fourth year of his reign. This was 480 years after the people of Israel left their slavery in Egypt. ²The Temple was 90 feet long, 30 feet wide, and 45 feet high. ³All along the front of the Temple was a porch. It was 30 feet long and 15 feet deep. ⁴Narrow windows were put in the Temple.

⁵Side rooms were built along the full length of the Temple. They were put on both sides against the outer walls. ⁶These rooms were three stories high. The lower floor was 7½ feet wide. The second floor was 9 feet wide. And the upper floor was 10½ feet wide. The rooms were tied to the walls of the Temple. This was done resting beams on blocks built out from the wall. That way the beams were not put into the walls themselves.

⁷The stones used in building the Temple were already finished at the quarry. So the whole building was built without the sound of hammer or axe. No such sounds were heard at the building site.

- *Remember:* Which king helped Solomon build the Temple? What did he give Solomon? (5:1-9) How did Solomon pay for this material? (5:11) Name one or two of the jobs men did to build the Temple. (5:15-18) What did they do about the noise when they built the Temple? Why do you think they did that? (6:7) Why do you think Solomon made God's house a special place?

- *Discover:* God's house should be a special place. You can help to make it a special place.

- *Apply:* The next time you go to church, ask, "Am I quiet in God's house when I should be? Do I help to keep it clean? Do I want to make God's house special?" Then do it!

- *What's next?* A queen gives someone lots of money. Why does she do that? Read 1 Kings 10:1-13. ■

The Temple Is Finished

⁸There was a door to the bottom floor of the side rooms. It was on the right side of the Temple. There were winding stairs going up to the second floor. Then another flight of stairs led from the second to the third. ⁹After building the Temple, Solomon paneled it all with cedar. This included the beams and pillars. ¹⁰As was said before, there were side rooms on each side of the building. They were tied to the Temple walls by cedar timbers. Each story of the annex was 7½ feet high.

¹¹⁻¹²Then the Lord sent this message to Solomon. It was about the Temple he was building. "You must do as I tell you," he said. "You must follow all my commands and orders. If you do, I will do what I told your father David I would do. ¹³I will live with the people of Israel and never leave them."

¹⁴At last the Temple was finished. ¹⁵The inside was paneled with cedar. It was cedar from floor to ceiling! And the floors were made of cypress boards. ¹⁶The Most Holy Place was also paneled from floor to ceiling with cedar boards. This room was 30 feet square. It was at the far end of the Temple. ¹⁷The rest of the Temple, other than the Most Holy Place, was 60 feet long. ¹⁸The cedar paneling was laid over the stone walls everywhere. It was carved with rosebuds and open flowers.

¹⁹The inner room was where the Ark of the Covenant of the Lord was placed. ²⁰It was 30 feet long, 30 feet wide, and 30 feet high. Its walls and ceiling were covered with pure gold. And Solomon made a cedarwood altar for this room. ²¹⁻²²Then he covered the inside of the rest of the Temple with pure gold. This included the cedar altar. And he made gold chains. These would guard the door to the Most Holy Place.

²³⁻²⁸Solomon put two statues of Guardian Angels in the inner room. They were made from olive wood. They were each 15 feet high. They were put so that their outer wings reached from wall to wall. Their inner wings touched each other at the center of the room. Each wing was 7½ feet long. So each angel measured 15 feet from wing tip to wing tip. The two angels were the same size in every way. Each of them was covered with gold.

²⁹Figures of angels, palm trees, and open flowers were carved on all the walls of both rooms of the Temple. ³⁰And the floor of both rooms was covered with gold.

³¹The doorway to the inner room was a five-sided opening. ³²Its two olivewood doors were carved with figures. The figures were of Guardian Angels, palm trees, and open flowers. They also were covered with gold.

³³Then he made square doorposts of olive wood. They were for the doorway to the Temple. ³⁴There were two folding doors of cypress wood. Each door was hinged to fold back upon itself. ³⁵Angels, palm trees, and open flowers were carved on these doors. Then they were covered with gold.

³⁶The wall of the inner court had three layers of cut stone. Over that was put one layer of cedar beams.

³⁷The foundation of the Temple was laid in the fourth year of Solomon's reign. It was in the month of May. ³⁸And the building was finished in the 11th year of his reign. It was in the month of November. So it took seven years to build the Temple.

Solomon Builds His Palace

7 Then Solomon built his own palace. It took 13 years to build.

²One of the rooms in the palace was called the Hall of the Forest of Lebanon. It was huge! It was 150 feet long, 75 feet wide, and 45 feet high. The great cedar ceiling beams rested upon four rows of cedar pillars. ³⁻⁴There were 45 windows in the hall. They were set in three rows. One row was above the other, five to a row. They faced each other from three walls. ⁵Each of the doorways and windows had a square frame.

⁶Another room was called the Hall of Pillars. It was 75 feet long and 45 feet wide. It had a porch in front. It was covered by a canopy that was held up by pillars.

⁷There was also the Throne Room or

Judgment Hall. That was where Solomon sat to hear legal matters. It was paneled with cedar from floor to ceiling.

⁸His living quarters were built around a courtyard behind this hall. They were all paneled in cedar. He made rooms of the same size in the palace he built for Pharaoh's daughter. She was one of his wives. ⁹These buildings were built from huge, fine stones. They were cut to measure. ¹⁰The foundation stones were 12 to 15 feet across. ¹¹The huge stones in the walls were also cut to measure. They were topped with cedar beams. ¹²The Great Court had three courses of cut stone in its walls. These were topped with cedar beams. It was built just like the inner court of the Temple and the porch of the palace.

Equipment for the Temple

¹³King Solomon then asked for a man named Hiram to come from Tyre. He was a skilled craftsman in bronze work. ¹⁴He was half Jewish. His mother was a widow of the tribe of Naphtali. His father had been a craftsman in bronze work from Tyre. So he came to work for King Solomon.

¹⁵He cast two hollow bronze pillars. Each was 27 feet high and 18 feet around. The walls were three inches thick. ¹⁶⁻²²He made two capitals from melted bronze to put at the top of the pillars. Each was 7½ feet high. The upper part of each capital was shaped like a lily. This part was six feet high. Each capital was covered with a net made out of seven bronze chains. They also had 400 pomegranates on them. These were set in two rows. Hiram set these pillars at the door of the Temple. The one on the south was called the Jachin Pillar. The one on the north was called the Boaz Pillar.

²³Then Hiram cast a round bronze tank. It was 7½ feet high and 15 feet from brim to brim. It was 45 feet all the way around it. ²⁴Just below the rim were two rows of ornaments. They were set an inch or two apart. They were cast from bronze along with the tank. ²⁵It rested on 12 bronze oxen. They stood tail to tail. Three faced to the north and three to the south. Three faced to the west and

three to the east. ²⁶The sides of the tank were four inches thick. Its brim was shaped like a goblet. It could hold up to 12,000 gallons.

The Biggest Washbowl in the World
1 KINGS 7:23-26

When your great-grandfather was a boy, many people washed their hands in a washbowl. They did not have nice bathrooms like yours. King Solomon made the biggest washbowl in the world. Sometimes it is called the Laver or the Molten Sea. It stood in the courtyard of the Temple, south of the altar. This big bowl was made of bronze and rested on the backs of 12 giant oxen, also made of bronze. The bowl held 12,000 gallons of water. That's as big as some swimming pools! Priests who worked in the Temple washed their hands and feet in this bowl. We're not exactly sure why. But when priests washed their hands here it was not just to get their hands clean. It was also a way of saying that they wanted their hearts and minds to be clean to do God's work. We don't need to wash in a bowl to say that. But we may want to ask God to make us clean inside so we can do his work. That's good to do each day, isn't it?

²⁷⁻³⁰Then he made 10 four-wheeled movable stands. Each was six feet square and 4 ½ feet high. They were made by putting square side panels on a frame. These side panels had carved lions, oxen, and angels on them. Above and below the lions and oxen were wreath designs. Each of these movable stands had four bronze wheels and bronze axles. At each corner of the stands were supporting posts. These posts were made of bronze. They also had wreath designs on each side. ³¹On top of each stand was a bowl 1½ feet high. The bowl was 2¼ feet deep. It had wreath designs carved on the frame. The panels of the frame were square, not round.

³²The stands rode on four wheels. They were tied to axles that had been cast as part of the stands. The wheels were 27 inches high. ³³They were similar to chariot wheels. All the parts of the stands were cast from melted bronze. This included the axles, spokes, rims, and hubs. ³⁴There were supports at each of the four corners of the stands. These, too, were cast with the stands. ³⁵A nine-inch rim was put around the top of each stand. It was all cast as one piece with the stand. ³⁶Figures of Guardian Angels, lions, and palm trees were made. Wreath designs were put around them. These were put on the borders of the band where there was room. ³⁷All 10 stands were the same size. They were made just the same, for each was cast from the same mold.

³⁸Then he made 10 brass bowls and put them on the stands. Each bowl was six feet square. Each held 240 gallons of water. ³⁹Five of these bowls were put on the left side of the Temple. The other five were put on the right side of the Temple. The tank was in the southeast corner, on the right-hand side of the room. ⁴⁰Hiram also made the pots, shovels, and basins that were needed. He at last finished the work in the Temple of the Lord. This work had been given to him by King Solomon.

⁴¹⁻⁴⁶Here is a list of the items he made.

He made two pillars,
A capital at the top of each pillar,
And chain nets covering the bases
   of the capitals.

He made 400 pomegranates in two
   rows around the chain nets.
They covered the bases of the
   two capitals.
He made 10 movable stands hold-
   ing 10 vats,
One large tank and 12 oxen under
   it,
Pots,
Shovels,
Basins.

All these things were made of polished bronze. They were cast on the plains of the Jordan River between Succoth and Zarethan. ⁴⁷The total weight of these pieces was not known. This was because they were too heavy to weigh!

⁴⁸All the tools and furniture used in the Temple were made of solid gold. This included the altar and the table where the Bread of the Presence was put. ⁴⁹The lampstands were also made of gold. Five were put on the right side and five on the left. These stood in front of the Most Holy Place. The flowers, lamps, tongs, ⁵⁰cups, snuffers, basins, spoons, firepans were also gold. So were the hinges of the doors to the Most Holy Place. The main entrance doors of the Temple also had golden hinges. Each of these was made of solid gold.

⁵¹The Temple of the Lord was finished at last! David, Solomon's father, had set aside some silver, gold, and special dishes for the Temple. So Solomon brought these into the treasury of the Temple.

The Ark Is Brought to the Temple

8 Then Solomon called a meeting at Jerusalem. All the leaders of Israel were to come. This included the heads of all the tribes and clans. They came to watch him move Ark of the Covenant of the Lord. They were moving it from the tent in the City of David to the Temple. ²This event took place at the time of the Tabernacle Feast. It was during the month of October. ³⁻⁴At this time, the priests carried the Ark to the Temple. They also brought all the holy furniture that had been in the Tabernacle. ⁵King Solomon and all the people gathered before the Ark. They sacrificed so many sheep and oxen that they couldn't count them.

⁶Then the priests took the Ark into the Most Holy Place. They put it there under the wings of the mighty angels. ⁷The angels had been made so their wings spread out. They hung over the spot where the Ark would be placed. So now their wings hung over the Ark and its carrying poles. ⁸The poles were so long that they stuck out past the angels. They could be seen from the next room, but not from the outer court. They are still there to this day. ⁹There was nothing in the Ark at that time except the two stone tablets. Moses had put them there at Mount Sinai after the Israelites left Egypt. This was the time when the Lord made his covenant with the people of Israel.

¹⁰*Look! The priests are coming from the Most Holy Place! And a bright cloud fills the Temple!* ¹¹*The priests have to go outside because the glory of the Lord fills the whole building!*

¹²⁻¹³Now King Solomon prayed this prayer.

"The Lord has said that he would
  live in the thick darkness.
But, O Lord, I have built you a
  lovely home on earth. It is a
  place for you to live for all time."

¹⁴Then the king turned around. He faced the people as they stood before him. He blessed them.

¹⁵"Blessed be the Lord God of Israel," he said. "He has done today what he promised my father, David. ¹⁶For he said to him, 'I brought my people from Egypt. But I didn't choose a place for my Temple. Instead, I chose a man to be the leader of my people.' ¹⁷This man was my father, David. He wanted to build a Temple for the Lord God of Israel. ¹⁸But the Lord told him not to. 'I am glad you want to do it,' he said. ¹⁹'But your son is the one who shall build my Temple.' ²⁰And now the Lord has done what he promised. I have followed my father as king of Israel. And now this Temple has been built for the Lord God of Israel. ²¹And I have made a place in the Temple for the Ark. In it is the covenant made by the Lord with our fathers. He made this covenant with them when he brought them out of Egypt."

Solomon Dedicates the Temple

²²⁻²³As all the people watched, Solomon stood before the altar of the Lord. His hands were spread out toward heaven. And he said, "O Lord God of Israel! There is no god like you in heaven or earth! You are loving and kind. You keep your promises to your people if they do their best to do your will. ²⁴Today you have made your promise come true. This was the promise made to my father, David, who was your servant. ²⁵And now, O Lord God of Israel, fulfill your other promise to him. You said, 'Your descendants must obey me as you have obeyed me. If they do, then one of them shall always sit upon the throne of Israel.' ²⁶Yes, O God of Israel, fulfill this promise too.

²⁷"But is it possible that God would live on earth? Why, even the skies and the highest heavens cannot hold you! This Temple I have built will not be able to hold you either! ²⁸And yet, O Lord my God, you have heard and answered what I asked. ²⁹Please watch over this Temple night and day. For this is the place you have promised to live. Please listen to my prayers here, whether by night or by day. ³⁰Listen to every prayer of the people of Israel. Listen to them when they face this place to pray. Yes, hear in heaven where you live. And when you hear, forgive.

³¹"A man might be accused of doing something wrong. Then he might come and stand here before your altar. He might promise that he didn't do it. ³²If this happens, hear him in heaven and do what is right. Judge whether he did it or not.

³³⁻³⁴"And your people might sin and their enemies defeat them. If so, hear them from heaven. Forgive them if they turn to you again. Listen to them if they say you are their God. Bring them back again to this land which you have given to their fathers.

³⁵⁻³⁶"And there might be no rain because of their sin. If so, hear them from heaven. Forgive them when they pray toward this place and praise your name. And after you have punished them, help them to do what is right. Send rain upon

the land that you have given your people.

37"There might be a famine in the land. It might be caused by plant disease or locusts or caterpillars. Or maybe Israel's enemies will besiege one of her cities. Or the people might be struck by a plague. Any of these things might happen. 38Then maybe the people will see their sin. They might pray toward this Temple. 39If they do, hear them from heaven. Forgive and answer all who confess their sin. For you know each heart. 40In this way they will always learn to respect you. They will respect you as they live in this land that you have given their fathers.

**God keeps his promises,
so we should praise him**

*I will praise the Lord because
he has kept his promises.*

1 Kings 8:56

41-42"And foreigners might hear of your great name. Perhaps they will come from faraway lands to worship you. For they shall hear of your great name and mighty miracles. They might come and pray toward this Temple. 43If they do, listen to them from heaven. Answer their prayers. All the nations of the earth will know your name. All will fear your name just as your own people Israel do. And all the earth will know that this is your Temple.

44"You might send your people out to battle against their enemies. At that time, they might pray to you. Maybe they will look toward your chosen city of Jerusalem. They might pray toward this Temple that I have built in your name. 45If they do, hear their prayer and help them.

46"They might sin against you (and who doesn't?). Maybe you will become angry with them. You might let their enemies lead them away as captives to some foreign land. That place might be far or near. 47At that time, they might come to their senses. Maybe they will turn to you. They might cry to you, saying, 'We have sinned. We have done wrong.' 48Perhaps they will honestly come back to you. They might pray toward this

land that you have given their fathers. They might turn toward this city of Jerusalem that you have chosen. They might bow toward this Temple that I have built for your name. 49If they do this, hear their prayers from heaven where you live. And help them.

50"Forgive your people for all of their evil deeds. Make their captors merciful to them. 51For they are your people. You brought them out from the Egyptian furnace. 52May your eyes be open and your ears listening to their pleas. O Lord, hear and answer them whenever they cry out to you. 53For you brought our fathers out of the land of Egypt. And then you told your servant Moses that you had chosen Israel. You chose them from among all the nations of the earth. You picked them to be your own special people."

54-55Solomon had been kneeling. His hands were stretched toward heaven. As he finished this prayer, he stood before the altar of the Lord. He cried out this blessing upon all the people of Israel.

56"I will praise the Lord because he has kept his promises. He has given rest to his people Israel. Not one promise has failed of all those given by his servant Moses. 57May the Lord our God be with us as he was with our fathers. May he never leave us. 58May he make us want to do his will in everything. May he help us to obey all the commands he gave our ancestors. 59And may my prayer be always before him day and night. That way he will help me and all of Israel with our daily needs. 60May people all over the earth know that the Lord is God! May they know that there is no other god at all! 61O my people, may you live good lives before the Lord our God. May you always obey his laws and commands. May you always do just as you are doing today."

62-63Then the king and all the people dedicated the Temple. They sacrificed peace offerings to the Lord. They offered a total of 22,000 oxen! And they gave 120,000 sheep and goats! 64The king set aside the court in front of the Temple. It would be used for the burnt offerings, grain offerings, and the fat of the peace offerings. This was because the bronze altar was too small to handle so many animals. [65]The feast lasted for 14 days. And a great crowd came from one end of the land to the other. [66]After this Solomon sent the people home. They were happy for all the goodness that the Lord had shown to his servant David. They praised him for what he had done for his people Israel. And they blessed the king.

God's Warning to Solomon

9 So Solomon had finished building the Temple. He also had finished the palace and all the other buildings he had planned. [2-3]At that time, the Lord came to him the second time. The first time had been at Gibeon. He said to him,

"I have heard your prayer. I have made this Temple holy that you have built. And I have put my name here forever. I will always watch over it and have joy in it. [4]And you must live in honesty and truth as your father, David, did. You must always obey me. [5]If you do, then your descendants will be the kings of Israel for all time. I will do just as I promised your father, David. I told him, 'One of your sons shall always be upon the throne of Israel.'

[6]"But maybe you or your children will turn away from me. You might worship other gods. You might not obey my laws. [7]If this happens, then I will take the people of Israel away from this land. I will take them from this Temple which I have made holy for my name. I will throw them out of my sight! Israel will become a joke to the nations. They will become an example and proverb of sudden disaster. [8]This Temple will become a heap of ruins. Everyone passing by will be amazed. They will whistle with amazement! They will ask, 'Why has the Lord done such things to this land and this Temple?' [9]And the answer will be, 'The people of Israel left the Lord their God. They did this even though he brought them out of the land of Egypt. They worshiped other gods instead. That is why the Lord has brought this evil upon them.'"

Solomon's Other Projects

[10]By the end of 20 years, Solomon had built the Temple and the palace. [11-12]At that time, he gave 20 cities to King Hiram of Tyre. These cities were in the land of Galilee. Solomon gave them as payment for the cedar and cypress lumber and the gold Hiram had sent him. He had given it for the building of the palace and Temple. Hiram came from Tyre to see the cities. But he wasn't at all pleased with them.

[13]"What sort of deal is this, my brother?" he asked. "These cities are a wasteland!" And they are still known as "The Wasteland" today. [14]For Hiram had sent gold to Solomon valued at $3,500,000!

[15]Solomon had called up forced labor to build the Temple and his palace. This labor was also used to build Fort Millo and the wall of Jerusalem. They built the cities of Hazor, Megiddo, and Gezer as well. [16]Gezer was the city the king of Egypt conquered and burned. He had killed all the Israelite people there. Later he gave the city to his daughter as a dowry. She was one of Solomon's wives. [17-18]So now Solomon rebuilt Gezer. He also rebuilt Lower Beth-horon, Baalath, and Tamar, a desert city. [19]He built cities for grain storage. He built cities in which to keep his chariots. He built cities for homes for his cavalry and chariot drivers. And he built resort cities near Jerusalem and in the Lebanon mountains. He put others elsewhere throughout the land.

[20-21]Solomon called up his labor forces from the nations he conquered. These included the Amorites, Hittites, Perizzites, Hivites, and Jebusites. The people of Israel had not been able to wipe them all out in Joshua's day. These people are still used as slaves even today. [22]Solomon didn't take any Israelites for this work. But they became soldiers, officials, army officers, chariot commanders, and horsemen. [23]And there were 550 men of Israel who oversaw the labor forces.

[24]King Solomon moved Pharaoh's daughter from the City of David. This was the old section of Jerusalem. He moved

her to the new rooms he had built for her in the palace. Then he built Fort Millo.

²⁵After the Temple was finished, Solomon offered burnt offerings and peace offerings. He did this three times a year on the altar he had built. And he also burned incense upon it.

²⁶King Solomon had a shipyard in Ezion-geber near Eloth. This was on the Red Sea in the land of Edom. There he built a fleet of ships.

²⁷⁻²⁸King Hiram had sailors who knew much about the sea. He sent them to sail with Solomon's men. They used to sail back and forth from Ophir. They brought gold to King Solomon. They brought back several million dollars of gold each trip.

The Queen of Sheba Visits Solomon

When a queen visits the wisest, richest, most powerful king, what gift does she bring?

10 The queen of Sheba heard how the Lord had blessed Solomon with wisdom. So she decided to test him with some hard questions. ²She came to Jerusalem with a long train of camels. They carried spices, gold, and jewels. She told him all her problems. ³Solomon answered all her questions. Nothing was too hard for him. For the Lord gave him the right answers every time. ⁴She soon saw that all she had ever heard about his great wisdom was true. She also saw the great palace he had built. ⁵She saw the foods on his table. She saw his many servants who stood around in beautiful clothes and his cupbearers. She saw the many offerings he sacrificed by fire to the Lord. After seeing all this, there was no more spirit in her!

⁶She exclaimed to him, "All I heard in my own country about your wisdom is true! ⁷I didn't believe it until I came. But now I have seen it for myself! And really! I had not heard about half of it! Your wisdom and riches are greater than anything I've ever heard of! ⁸Your people are happy. Your palace servants are content. But how could it be otherwise? For they stand here day after day listening to your wisdom! ⁹Blessed be the Lord your God who chose you. Praise be to him who set you on the throne of Israel. How the Lord must love Israel! For he gave you to them as their king! And you give your people a just, good government!"

¹⁰Then she gave the king a gift of $3,500,000 in gold. She also gave him many spices and precious jewels. In fact, it was the largest single gift of spices King Solomon had ever been given.

¹¹And King Hiram's ships brought gold to Solomon from Ophir. When they came, they also brought along a great supply of algum trees and jewels. ¹²Solomon used the algum wood to make pillars for the Temple and the palace. He also used it to make harps and harpsichords for his choirs. Never before or since has there been such a supply of beautiful wood.

¹³Solomon gave gifts for the gifts from the queen of Sheba. He gave her all she asked him for. This was besides the presents he had already planned to give her. Then she and her servants went back to their own land.

- *Remember:* Why did the queen of Sheba visit Solomon? (10:1) Where did Solomon get the right answers to her questions? Who told him? (10:3) Did the queen think Solomon's people were happy? What did she say? (10:8-9) What did the queen give Solomon? (10:10) What did Solomon give the queen? (10:13) The people who lived there with Solomon seemed to be happy. Why? Was it his money? Or was it something else? What?

- *Discover:* People like to be with a truly wise person.

- *Apply:* You can be a wise person if you know what God says and what God wants. Solomon was wise because God

helped him. Read your Bible often. That's where you will learn what God says and wants.

- *What's next:* The man who has everything forgets who gave it to him. Terrible things will happen. Read 1 Kings 11:1-13. ▪

Solomon's Great Riches

¹⁴Each year Solomon was brought gold worth $250,000,000. ¹⁵This was besides sales taxes and profits he made from trade. He traded with the kings of Arabia and the leaders of other lands nearby. ¹⁶⁻¹⁷Solomon had some of the gold beaten into 200 large shields. Gold worth $6,000 went into each large shield. He also made 300 small gold shields. Gold worth $1,800 was used in each one. And he kept them in his palace in the Hall of the Forest of Lebanon.

¹⁸He also made a huge ivory throne. He covered it with pure gold. ¹⁹It had six steps and a rounded back. On each side was an armrest, and a lion was standing on each side. ²⁰And there were two lions on each step. There were 12 in all. There was no other throne in all the world so great as that one.

²¹All of King Solomon's cups were of solid gold. All the dishes in the Hall of the Forest of Lebanon were made of solid gold. Silver wasn't used because it wasn't thought to be of much value!

²²King Solomon had a fleet of trading ships. They went with King Hiram's ships. Every three years a great load of gold, silver, ivory, apes, and peacocks came to Israel's ports.

²³So King Solomon was richer and wiser than all the kings of the earth. ²⁴Great men from many lands came to speak to him. They came to listen to his God-given wisdom. ²⁵They brought him yearly tribute. They brought it in silver and gold dishes, beautiful cloth, myrrh, spices, horses, and mules.

²⁶Solomon built up a great stable of horses. He also had many chariots and horsemen. He had 1,400 chariots in all. And he had 12,000 horsemen. They lived

in the chariot cities and with the king at Jerusalem. [27]Silver was as common as stones in Jerusalem in those days. And cedar was of no greater value than the common sycamore! [28]Solomon's horses were brought to him from Egypt and southern Turkey. There his servants bought them at good prices. [29]An Egyptian chariot delivered to Jerusalem cost $400. The horses were valued at $150 each. Many of these were then resold to the Hittite and Syrian kings.

Solomon Turns from God

A man who has everything should not want more, should he? King Solomon had everything a king could want. Did he want more? Was he grateful for what he had?

11 King Solomon married many other girls besides the Egyptian princess. Many of them came from nations where idols were worshiped. These nations were Moab, Ammon, Edom, and Sidon. They also came from the Hittites. [2]Now the Lord had told his people not to marry into those nations. This was because the women they married would get them to worship their gods. But Solomon did it anyway. [3]He had 700 wives and 300 concubines. And sure enough, they turned his heart away from the Lord. [4]As Solomon grew old, his wives caused him to worship other gods. So he didn't trust only in the Lord as his father, David, had done. [5]Solomon worshiped Ashtoreth, the goddess of the Sidonians. And he worshiped Milcom, the god of the Ammonites. [6]Solomon did what was wrong. He did not follow the Lord as his father, David, did. [7]He even built a temple for Chemosh on the Mount of Olives. This was across the valley from Jerusalem. Chemosh was the god of Moab. He built another for Molech, the god of the Ammonites. [8]Solomon built these temples for his foreign wives. They wanted to use them for burning incense and sacrificing to their gods.

[9-10]The Lord was very angry with Solomon about this. For now Solomon had turned from obeying the Lord God of Israel. He did this even though the Lord had come to him twice. The Lord had warned Solomon not to worship other gods. But he hadn't listened. [11]So now the Lord said to him, "You have not kept our agreement. You have not obeyed my laws. So I will take the kingdom away from you. I will take it from your family and give it to someone else. [12-13]But I won't do this while you are still alive. I will wait for the sake of your father, David. But I will take the kingdom away from your son. And even so I will let him be king of one tribe. I do this for David's sake. And I do it for the sake of Jerusalem, my chosen city."

- *Remember:* Where did Solomon get many of his wives? Why was this wrong? (11:1-2) What terrible thing did these women do to Solomon? (11:3-8) What did God think about this? How did God punish Solomon? (11:9-11) What advice would you have given Solomon? What did he do wrong? What should he have done? Solomon started out as a wise king. But he stopped being wise when he stopped putting God first. He was not wise to always want more.

- *Discover:* We should be happy and content with the wonderful things God gives us. We should not always want more.

- *Apply:* Do you want something more right now? Do you want it so much that you are not happy with what you already have? Thank God right now for what he has given you.

- *What's next?* For 80 years Israel had been one of the finest kingdoms. But trouble was coming. Something terrible was about to happen. Read 1 Kings 12:1-24. ▉

Solomon's Enemies

[14]So the Lord caused Hadad the Edomite to grow in power. And Solomon became afraid. For Hadad was a member of the

royal family of Edom. [15]Years before, David had been in Edom with Joab. They were there to arrange for the burial of some Israelite soldiers. The soldiers had died there in battle. At that time, the Israelite army had killed nearly every male in the country. [16-18]It took six months to do this. But they finally killed all the males except Hadad. A few royal servants got away. They then took Hadad to Egypt. He was a very small child at the time. They slipped out of Midian and went to Paran. There others joined them and went with them to Egypt. While in Egypt, Pharaoh gave them homes and food.

[19]Hadad became one of Pharaoh's closest friends. And he gave him a wife. She was the sister of Queen Tahpenes. [20]She gave him a son, Genubath. He was raised in Pharaoh's palace among Pharaoh's own sons. [21]Hadad, there in Egypt, heard that David and Joab were both dead. So he asked Pharaoh if he could go back to Edom.

[22]"Why?" Pharaoh asked him. "What don't you have here? What haven't I given you?"

"Everything is great," he replied. "But even so, I'd like to go back home."

[23]Another of Solomon's enemies whom God raised to power was Rezon. He was one of the officials of King Hadadezer of Zobah. He had left his post and run from the country. [24]He then became the leader of a gang of bandits. They ran with him to Damascus, where he later became king. They had all escaped from Zobah when David destroyed it. [25]During Solomon's lifetime, Rezon and Hadad were his enemies. They hated Israel a great deal.

[26]Another rebel leader was Jeroboam. He was the son of Nebat. He came from the city of Zeredah in Ephraim. His mother was Zeruah, a widow. [27-28]This is the story of how he turned against the king. Solomon was building Fort Millo. And he was fixing the walls of the city his father had built. Jeroboam was a very capable man. Solomon saw that he was a good worker. So he put him in charge of his labor groups from the tribe of Joseph.

[29]One day Jeroboam was leaving Jerusalem. The prophet Ahijah from Shiloh met him. He had put on a new robe for the occasion. He called Jeroboam aside to talk to him. The two of them were alone in the field. [30]And Ahijah tore his new robe into 12 parts. [31]Then he said to Jeroboam, "Take 10 of these pieces. For the Lord God of Israel has spoken. He says, 'I will take the kingdom from Solomon. And I will give 10 of the tribes to you! [32]But I will leave him one tribe. I do this for the sake of my servant David. I also do it for the sake of Jerusalem. I have chosen Jerusalem above all the other cities of Israel. [33]For Solomon has turned away from me. He worships Ashtoreth, the goddess of the Sidonians. He worships Chemosh, the god of Moab. He also worships Milcom, the god of the Ammonites. He has not followed my paths. He has not done what I consider right. He has not kept my laws and commands as his father, David, did. [34]But I will not take the kingdom from him now. I will wait, for the sake of my servant David. He was my chosen one. He obeyed my commands. For his sake, I will let Solomon rule for the rest of his life.

[35]"'But I will take away the kingdom from his son. I will give 10 of the tribes to you. [36]His son shall have the other tribe. That way the descendants of David will still rule in Jerusalem. For this is the city where I have chosen to put my name. [37]And I will put you on the throne of Israel. I will give you power over them. [38]You must listen to what I tell you. You must walk in my path and do what is right. You must obey my commands as my servant David did. If you do, then I will bless you. And your descendants shall rule Israel for all time. I once made this same promise to David. [39]But because of Solomon's sin, I will punish the descendants of David. But I will not punish them for all time.'"

[40]Solomon tried to kill Jeroboam. But Jeroboam ran to King Shishak of Egypt. He stayed there until the death of Solomon.

Solomon's Death

[41]The rest of what Solomon did and said is written in the book *The Acts of Solomon.* [42]He ruled in Jerusalem for 40 years. [43]Then he died and was buried in the city of his father, David. And his son Rehoboam ruled in his place.

The Kingdom Splits in Two

King Solomon was dead. He had ruled 40 years. Now his son Rehoboam was king. But his people were not happy. Solomon had made life hard for them. They begged Rehoboam not to be as harsh as Solomon. Read what happened when he wouldn't listen to them.

12 Rehoboam was made king at Shechem. And all Israel came for the ceremony. 2-4Jeroboam heard about the plans from his friends. He was still in Egypt where he had run from King Solomon. They told him to go, so he joined the rest of Israel at Shechem. While there, he got the people to make demands of Rehoboam.

"Your father was a hard master," they told Rehoboam. "You might not treat us any better than he did. And if you don't, we don't want you as our king."

5"Give me three days to think this over," Rehoboam replied. "Come back then for my answer." So the people left.

6Rehoboam talked it over with the old men. They had counseled his father Solomon.

"What do you think I should do?" he asked them.

7And they replied, "You should give them a nice answer. Agree to be kind to them and serve them well. If you do, you can be their king for all time."

8But Rehoboam did not listen to the old men. He called in the young men with whom he had grown up.

9"What do you think I should do?" he asked them.

10And the young men replied, "Tell them, 'You might think my father was hard on you! But I'll be even harder! 11Yes, my father was harsh. But I'll be even harsher! My father used whips on you. But I'll use scorpions!'"

12Jeroboam and the people came back three days later. 13-14When they did, the new king answered them roughly. He did not listen to the old men's advice. He followed the advice of the young men. 15So the king did not listen to the people's demands. But the Lord's hand was in it. He caused the new king to do this. He did it to make his promise to Jeroboam come true. This was the promise he made through Ahijah, the prophet from Shiloh.

16-17The people saw that the king meant what he said. It was clear that he would not listen to them. So they began shouting, "Down with David and all his family! Let's go home! Let Rehoboam be king of his own family!"

And they all left him except for the tribe of Judah. Judah stayed loyal and made Rehoboam their king. 18King Rehoboam sent Adoram to call up men from the other tribes. Adoram was in charge of the draft. When Adoram went, a great mob stoned him to death. King Rehoboam got away by chariot and ran to Jerusalem. 19Since then, Israel has been against the family of David.

20The people of Israel heard that Jeroboam had come back from Egypt. So he was asked to come before an open meeting of all the people. And there he was made king of Israel. Only the tribe of Judah stayed under the kingship of David's family.

21When King Rehoboam got to Jerusalem, he called his army. This included all the men of Judah and Benjamin. There were 180,000 special troops. He wanted to force the rest of Israel to make him their king. 22But God sent this message to Shemaiah, the prophet.

23-24"Speak to Rehoboam the son of Solomon, king of Judah," he said. "And speak to all the people of Judah and Benjamin too. Tell them that they must not fight against their brothers, the people of Israel. Tell them all to go home. I wanted all this to happen to Rehoboam." So the army went home as the Lord had commanded.

- *Remember:* What did Jeroboam and his friends want King Rehoboam to change? (12:2-4) What did Rehoboam's older advisers tell him? Did he listen to them? (12:6-8) What did his younger advisers tell him? Did he listen to them? (12:9-15) Ten tribes refused to serve Rehoboam. What did they do about a king? (12:16-20) Rehoboam was ready to go to war against the 10 tribes. Why didn't he? (12:21-24) Do you think Rehoboam should have listened to the young advisers or the older advisers? Why?

- *Discover:* Listen to good advice. It will keep you out of a lot of trouble. How do you know good advice when you hear it? Good advice seeks to help people, not hurt them. It seeks peace, not conflict. Which of Rehoboam's advisers was trying to do this, the older ones or the younger ones?

- *Apply:* Older people have been around longer than you have. They don't always have the best advice, but they have seen more things happen. Listen carefully when your parents, pastor, or teachers give you advice. Then ask, "How will this help others? Will it bring peace or more fighting?"

- *What's next?* Why would any king say that a golden calf is God? Read 1 Kings 12:25–13:7. ▨

Jeroboam Makes Two Golden Calves

The kingdom of Israel had divided. Jeroboam was king of the northern part. He wanted his people to stay away from Jerusalem, the capital of the southern part. Two golden calves helped them stay away. How did they do that?

²⁵Jeroboam now built the city of Shechem. It was in the hill country of Ephraim. It became his capital. Later he built Penuel. ²⁶Jeroboam thought, "I must be very careful. If I'm not, the people will want one of David's family as their king. ²⁷Jerusalem is where the Temple is. My people are still going to Jerusalem to offer sacrifices and worship at the Temple. When they do, they will become friends with King Rehoboam. Then they will kill me and ask him to be their king instead."

²⁸Jeroboam went to his men for advice. And the king had two gold calf-idols made. He told the people, "It's too much trouble to go to Jerusalem to worship. From now on these will be your gods. They were the ones who saved you from slavery in Egypt!"

²⁹One of these calf-idols was put in Bethel. The other was placed in Dan. ³⁰This was of course a great sin. For the people worshiped them. ³¹Jeroboam made shrines on the hills. He also chose priests from among all the people. He even chose those who were not from the priestly tribe of Levi. ³²⁻³³Jeroboam also said that the yearly Tabernacle Feast would be held at Bethel. It would be held on November 1. This was a date he decided on himself. It would be similar to the yearly feast at Jerusalem. He himself offered sacrifices upon the altar to the calves at Bethel. And he also burned incense to them. And it was there at Bethel that he chose priests. They would serve in the shrines on the hills.

13 At the feast, Jeroboam went up to the altar. He was going to burn incense to the gold calf-idol. Just then, a prophet of the Lord walked up to him. The prophet was from Judah. ²Then, at the Lord's command, the prophet shouted, "O altar, the Lord says this! A child named Josiah shall be born into the family line of David. He shall sacrifice the priests upon you. These are the priests from the shrines on the hills who come here to burn incense. And men's bones shall be burned upon you."

³Then he gave proof that his message was from the Lord. "This altar will split apart!" he said. "The ashes on it will spill to the ground!"

⁴The king was very angry with the prophet for saying this. He shouted to his guards, "Arrest that man!" He shook his fist at him. But the king's arm became frozen that way! He couldn't pull it back again! ⁵At the same time, the altar cracked wide open! And the ashes poured out! It all happened just as the prophet said it would. This was the prophet's proof that God had been speaking through him.

6"Oh, please, please!" the king cried out to the prophet. "Beg the Lord your God to heal my arm."

The prophet prayed to the Lord. And the king's arm became normal again.

7Then the king spoke with the prophet. "Come to the palace with me," he said. "Rest awhile and have some food. I'll give you a reward because you healed my arm."

- *Remember:* Why didn't Jeroboam want his people to go to Jerusalem? (12:26-27) What did he make to keep them away? How would these idols keep them away? (12:28-29) What other things did Jeroboam do to turn people from God? (12:30-31) How did God show Jeroboam that he was unhappy with these things? (13:1-5) What advice would you have given Jeroboam?

- *Discover:* God made Jeroboam king, but Jeroboam turned his people against God. We should never try to hurt God, especially with the gift he gives us.

- *Apply:* What has God given you or your family? It may be a nice car, a nice home, or anything else that you enjoy. Do you use that to help God or hurt God? Do you remember God when you are using that, or do you forget God? Thank God for the things he has given you. Decide now, today, that you will help him with these things and not hurt him.

- *What's next?* You have fed birds, haven't you? But have birds ever fed you? You'll read about some birds that feed a man. Read 1 Kings 17:1-6. ■

A Prophet Dies for Disobeying

8But the prophet said to the king, "I would never go into your palace! I wouldn't go even if you gave me half of it! I wouldn't eat or even drink water in this place! 9For the Lord has given me strict orders. I am not to eat anything or drink any water while I'm here. And I am not to go back to Judah by the road I came on."

10So he went back another way.

11As it happened, there was an old prophet living in Bethel. His sons went home and told him what the prophet from Judah had done. They also told him what he had said to the king.

12"Which way did he go?" the old prophet asked. So they told him.

13"Quick, saddle the donkey," the old man said. And when they had saddled the donkey for him, 14he rode after the prophet. He found him sitting under an oak tree.

"Are you the prophet who came from Judah?" he asked him.

"Yes," he replied, "I am."

15Then the old man said to the prophet, "Come home with me and eat."

16-17"No," he replied, "I can't. For I cannot eat anything or drink any water at Bethel. The Lord strictly warned me against it. He also told me not to go home by the same road I came on."

18But the old man said, "I am a prophet too, just as you are. And an angel gave me a message from the Lord. I am to take you home with me and give you food and water."

But the old man was lying to him. 19So they went back together. And the prophet ate some food and drank some water at the old man's home.

20While they were sitting at the table, a message from the Lord came to the old man. 21-22The old prophet shouted at the prophet from Judah. He said, "The Lord says that you have not obeyed his clear command. For you have come here. You have eaten and drunk water in the place he told you not to. So your body shall not be buried in the grave of your fathers."

23After finishing the meal, the old man saddled the prophet's donkey. 24-25Then the prophet started off again. But as he was traveling, a lion came out and killed him. His body lay there on the road. And the donkey and the lion stood beside it. Those who came by saw the body lying in the road. And they saw the lion standing there beside it. So they told the people in Bethel what they had seen. And that was where the old prophet lived.

26The old prophet heard what had happened. So he exclaimed, "It is the prophet who disobeyed the Lord's command! The Lord fulfilled his warning by causing the lion to kill him."

27Then he said to his sons, "Saddle my donkey!" And they did.

28He found the prophet's body lying in the road. The donkey and lion were still standing there beside it. For the lion had not eaten the body nor attacked the donkey. 29So the prophet laid the body upon the donkey. He took it back to the city to cry over it and bury it.

30He laid the body in his own grave. Then he said, "Alas, my brother!"

31After that he spoke to his sons. "When I die," he said, "bury me in the grave where the prophet is buried. Lay my bones beside his bones. 32For the Lord told him to shout against the altar in Bethel. And his curse against the shrines in Samaria shall surely come about."

33But Jeroboam did not turn from his evil ways. He did not change even after the prophet's warning. Instead, he made more priests than ever from the common people. And he chose them to offer sacrifices to idols in the shrines on the hills. Anyone who wanted to could be a priest. 34This was a great sin. And because of it, Jeroboam's kingdom was destroyed. And all of his family died.

Jeroboam's Son Dies

14 Jeroboam's son Abijah now became very sick. 2So Jeroboam spoke to his wife. "Put on a disguise," he said. "That way no one will know you are the queen. Go to Ahijah the prophet at Shiloh. He is the man who told me that I would become king. 3Take him a gift of 10 loaves of bread, some fig bars, and a jar of honey. Then ask him whether the boy will get better."

4So his wife went to Ahijah's home at Shiloh. He was an old man now and could no longer see. 5But the Lord told him that the queen would come. He said she would pretend to be someone else. He told Ahijah that her son was very sick. So Ahijah knew she would ask about her son. And the Lord told him what to tell her.

6Ahijah heard her at the door. So he called out, "Come in, wife of Jeroboam!

Why are you pretending to be someone else?" Then he told her, "I have sad news for you. 7Give your husband this message from the Lord God of Israel. The Lord said, 'I chose you from the ranks of the common people. I made you king of Israel. 8I took the kingdom away from the family of David and gave it to you. But you have not obeyed my commands as my servant David did. His heart's desire was always to obey me. He wanted to do whatever I wanted him to. 9But you have done more evil than all the other kings before you. You have made other gods! You have made me very angry with your gold calves! And you have refused to respect me. 10So I will bring disaster upon your home. I will destroy all of your sons. I will kill this boy who is sick and all those who are well. I will sweep away your family as a stable hand shovels out dung. 11I make this promise! Those of your family who die in the city shall be eaten by dogs. And those who die in the field shall be eaten by birds.'"

12Then Ahijah said to Jeroboam's wife, "Go on home. When you step into the city, the child will die. 13All of Israel will mourn for him and bury him. But he is the only member of your family who will come to a quiet end. For this child is the only good thing that the Lord God of Israel sees in the whole family of Jeroboam. 14And the Lord will raise a king over Israel. And he will destroy the family of Jeroboam. 15Then the Lord will shake Israel like a reed whipped about in a stream. He will uproot the people of Israel from this good land of their fathers. He will scatter them beyond the Euphrates River. For they have made the Lord angry by worshiping idols. 16He will leave Israel because Jeroboam sinned. And he made all of Israel sin along with him."

17So Jeroboam's wife went back to Tirzah. And the child died just as she walked through the door of her home. 18And there was mourning for him throughout the land. It all happened just as the Lord had said through Ahijah.

19Everything else that Jeroboam did was written down. This includes the wars he fought and the other events of his reign. It is all written in *The Annals of the Kings of Israel.* 20Jeroboam ruled 22 years. When he died, his son Nadab took the throne.

Rehoboam Rules Judah

21Meanwhile, Rehoboam the son of Solomon was king in Judah. He was 41 years old when he began to reign. He was on the throne 17 years in Jerusalem. This was the city where the Lord had chosen to live. He chose it out of all the cities in Israel. Rehoboam's mother was Naamah, an Ammonite woman. 22During his reign the people of Judah did what was wrong. They acted like the people of Israel. They made the Lord angry with their sin. For it was even worse than that of their ancestors. 23They built shrines and obelisks and idols. They put them on every high hill and under every green tree. 24There were even male prostitutes throughout the land. And the people of Judah became as bad as the heathen nations. They were as bad as the nations the Lord drove out to make room for his people.

?????????????????????????????????
Someone forced his grandmother to stop being queen. Why did he do that?
(Read 15:9-15 for the answer.)
?????????????????????????????????

25Then King Shishak of Egypt attacked and conquered Jerusalem. This happened in the fifth year of Rehoboam's reign. 26He took the treasures from the Temple and the palace. He stole everything! This included all the gold shields Solomon had made. 27After that Rehoboam made bronze shields to replace the gold ones. The palace guards used those instead. 28When the king went to the Temple, the guards marched before him. Then they took the shields back to the guard chamber.

29The other events in Rehoboam's reign are written in *The Annals of the Kings of Judah.* 30There was constant war between Rehoboam and Jeroboam. 31When Rehoboam died he was buried among his ancestors in Jerusalem. His mother was Naamah the Ammonitess. And his son Abijam took the throne.

Abijam Rules Judah

15 Abijam became the king of Judah. He began his reign during the 18th year of Jeroboam's reign in Israel. Abijam ruled in Jerusalem for three years. Abijam's mother was Maacah, the daughter of Abishalom. 3He was as great a sinner as his father was. And his heart was not right with God, as King David's had been. 4But despite Abijam's sin, the Lord did not end the royal line of David. The Lord did not destroy Abijam because of his love for David. 5For David had obeyed God during his whole lifetime. There was only one time that David did not obey the Lord. That was when he sinned against Uriah the Hittite. 6During Abijam's reign there was constant war between Israel and Judah. 7The rest of Abijam's history is recorded in *The Annals of the Kings of Judah.* 8When he died he was buried in Jerusalem. Then his son Asa ruled in his place.

Asa Rules Judah

9Asa became king of Judah in the 20th year of Jeroboam's reign over Israel. 10He reigned 41 years in Jerusalem. His grandmother was Maacah, the daughter of Abishalom. 11He pleased the Lord like his ancestor King David. 12He killed all the male prostitutes. And he got rid of all the idols his father had made. 13He deposed his grandmother Maacah as queen-mother. This was because she had made an idol. Asa cut it down and burned it at Kidron Brook. 14But the shrines on the hills were not all taken down. For Asa did not know that these were wrong. 15Asa and his father had given some silver and gold articles to the Lord. So Asa put all these special things into the Temple.

16There was war between King Asa of Judah and King Baasha of Israel. 17King Baasha built the walled city of Ramah. He wanted to try and cut off all trade with Jerusalem. 18Then Asa took all the silver and gold left in the Temple treasury. He also took all the treasures of the palace. He gave them to his servants to take to Damascus. He sent them to King Ben-hadad of Syria. He sent this message:

19"Let us be friends just as our fathers were. I am sending you a present of gold and silver. Now break your treaty with King Baasha of Israel. That will force him to leave me alone."

20Ben-hadad agreed. He sent his armies against some of the cities of Israel. He destroyed Ijon, Dan, Abel-beth-maacah, and all of Chinneroth. He also conquered all the cities in the land of Naphtali. 21Baasha was sent word of the attack. So he stopped building the city of Ramah and went back to Tirzah. 22Then King Asa gave an order to all the people of Judah. He asked every able-bodied man to help destroy Ramah. He wanted to haul away its stones and timbers. Then King Asa used these materials to build the city of Geba in Benjamin. He also used them in the city of Mizpah.

23The rest of Asa's biography is found in *The Annals of the Kings of Judah.* This includes his victories and the names of the cities he built. In his old age he caught a disease in his feet. 24And when he died, he was buried in the royal cemetery in Jerusalem. Then his son Jehoshaphat became the new king of Judah.

Nadab Rules Israel

25Meanwhile over in Israel, Nadab had become king. He was the son of Jeroboam. He ruled for two years. His rule began in the second year of King Asa's reign. 26But Nadab was not a good king. Like his father he worshiped many idols. And he led all of Israel into sin.

27Then Baasha made a plot against him. Baasha was the son of Ahijah, from the tribe of Issachar. He killed Nadab while he was with the Israelite army. They were attacking the Philistine city of Gibbethon at the time. 28So Baasha took Nadab's place as the king of Israel in Tirzah. This happened during the third year of the reign of King Asa of Judah. 29He killed all of the descendants of King Jeroboam right away. That way not one of the royal family was left. It happened just as the Lord said it would.

The Lord had predicted this through Ahijah the prophet from Shiloh. 30Jeroboam had made the Lord God of Israel angry. He had sinned and led the rest of Israel into sin. That is why his family was killed.

Baasha Rules Israel

31More details of Baasha's reign are written in *The Annals of the Kings of Israel.*

32-33There was war between King Asa of Judah and King Baasha of Israel. Baasha reigned for 24 years. 34But he disobeyed the Lord all that time. He followed the evil paths of Jeroboam. For he led the people of Israel into the sin of worshiping idols.

16 The Lord sent a message of judgment to King Baasha at this time. It was spoken by the prophet Jehu.

2"I lifted you out of the dust," the message said. "I made you king of my people Israel. But you have walked in the evil paths of Jeroboam. You have made my people sin, and I am angry! 3So now I will destroy you and your family. I will do just as I did with the family of Jeroboam. 4-7Those of your family who die in the city will be eaten by dogs. Those who die in the fields will be eaten by the birds."

The message was sent to Baasha and his family. This was because he had made the Lord angry by all his evil deeds. He was just as bad as Jeroboam. He didn't learn from seeing the Lord kill Jeroboam's family for their sins.

The rest of Baasha's biography are written in *The Annals of the Kings of Israel.* This includes all his deeds and victories.

Elah Rules Israel

8Elah, Baasha's son, became the king of Israel. He began his rule during the 26th year of the reign of King Asa of Judah. But he reigned only two years. 9Then General Zimri turned against him. He was in charge of half the royal chariot troops. One day King Elah was half-drunk. He was at the home of Arza, who was the manager of the palace. This took place in the capital city of Tirzah. 10Zimri simply walked in and struck him down and killed him. This happened during the 27th year of the reign of King Asa of Judah. Then Zimri declared himself to be the new king of Israel.

[11]He killed the whole royal family right away. He did not leave a single male child. He even killed distant family and friends. [12]So Zimri destroyed all of Baasha's family. It happened just as the Lord said it would through the prophet Jehu. [13]It happened because of the sins of Baasha and his son Elah. For they had led Israel into worshiping idols. And the Lord was very angry about it. [14]The rest of the history of Elah's reign is written in *The Annals of the Kings of Israel.*

Zimri Rules Israel

[15-16]But Zimri lasted only seven days. For the army of Israel heard that Zimri had killed the king. They were attacking the Philistine city of Gibbethon at the time. They decided on General Omri as their new ruler. He was the commander of the army. [17]So Omri led the army of Gibbethon to besiege Tirzah, Israel's capital. [18]Zimri saw that the city had been taken. So he went into the palace and burned it over him. He died there in the flames. [19]For he, too, had sinned like Jeroboam. He had worshiped idols and had led the people of Israel to sin with him. [20]The rest of the story of Zimri and his treason are written in *The Annals of the Kings of Israel.*

Omri Rules Israel

[21]But now the kingdom of Israel was split in two. Half the people were loyal to General Omri. The other half followed Tibni, the son of Ginath. [22]But General Omri won and Tibni was killed. So Omri ruled by himself.

[23]Omri became king of Israel. At that time, King Asa of Judah had been king for 31 years. Omri ruled for 12 years, six of them in Tirzah. [24]Then Omri bought the hill now known as Samaria. He bought it from its owner, Shemer. He paid him $4,000 for it and built a city on it. He called it Samaria in honor of Shemer. [25]But Omri was worse than any of the kings before him. [26]He worshiped idols as Jeroboam had. And he led Israel into this same sin. So God was very angry. [27]The rest of Omri's history is recorded in *The Annals of the Kings of Israel.* [28]When Omri died he was buried in Samaria. His son Ahab became king in his place.

Ahab Rules Israel

[29]So Ahab became the king of Israel. At that time, King Asa of Judah had been on the throne 38 years. Ahab reigned for 22 years in Samaria. [30]But he was even more wicked than his father Omri. He was worse than any other king of Israel! [31]And as though that were not enough, he married Jezebel. She was the daughter of King Ethbaal of the Sidonians. Then he began to worship Baal. [32]First he built a temple and an altar for Baal in Samaria. [33]Then he made other idols. He did more to anger the Lord God of Israel than any of the other kings of Israel before him.

[34]It was during his reign that Hiel, a man from Bethel, rebuilt Jericho. When he laid the foundations, his oldest son, Abiram, died. When he finally set up its gates, his youngest son, Segub, died. For this was the Lord's curse upon Jericho. It had been spoken by Joshua, the son of Nun.

Ravens Feed Elijah

There was a terrible famine in the land. It seemed that no one had food. Where did Elijah get something to eat? Who gave it to him? How did God take care of his prophet?

17 Elijah was a prophet from Tishbe in Gilead. He spoke to King Ahab. "This will happen as surely as the Lord God of Israel lives," he said. "There won't be any dew or rain for several years! The land will be dry until I say the word!"

[2]Then the Lord said to Elijah, [3]"Go to the east. Hide by Cherith Brook. Stay at a place east of where it enters the Jordan River. [4]Drink from the brook and eat what the ravens bring you. I have commanded them to feed you."

⁵So he did as the Lord had told him to and camped beside the brook. ⁶The ravens brought him bread and meat each morning and evening. And he drank from the brook.

- *Remember:* Elijah told King Ahab about God's punishment for him and his people. What was it? (17:1) Without rain or dew, there would be no crops. Without crops, there would be no food. How did God feed Elijah? (17:2-6) What do you think Elijah would say to you about God's care?

- *Discover:* God takes care of his people. Sometimes he has unusual ways to do it.

- *Apply:* Do you ever worry that you won't have enough to eat? Do you ever worry that you won't have clothes or a place to live? Remember Elijah! God may not feed you or clothe you the way you expect. But he will give you what you need. Trust him.

- *What's next?* A woman has almost nothing to eat. But she never is hungry. What happens? Read 1 Kings 17:7-24. ■

Elijah Helps a Poor Widow

A widow had only enough flour and oil to make one last piece of bread. Then she had nothing more. She could have starved to death. "Make that piece of bread for me," Elijah told her. "Then you will have plenty to eat." How could that have happened? Did she believe him? Did she do it?

⁷But after awhile the brook dried up. For there was no rain anywhere in the land.

⁸⁻⁹Then the Lord said to him, "Go and live in the village of Zarephath. It is near the city of Sidon. There is a widow there who will feed you. I have given her my orders."

¹⁰So he went to Zarephath. As he got to the gates of the city he saw a widow gathering sticks. He asked her for a cup of water.

¹¹She went to get it. And he called to her, "Bring me a bite of bread too."

¹²But she said, "I promise this by the Lord your God. I don't have a single piece of bread in the house. And I have only a handful of flour left. And I have just a little cooking oil in the bottom of the jar. I was just getting a few sticks to cook this last meal. Then my son and I must die of hunger."

¹³But Elijah said to her, "Don't be afraid! Go ahead and cook that 'last meal.' But bake me a little loaf of bread first. After that there will still be enough food for you and your son. ¹⁴For this is what the Lord God of Israel says: 'That jar will always have plenty of flour in it! That bottle will never be empty of oil! This will be true until the Lord sends rain and the crops grow again!'"

¹⁵So she did as Elijah said. And she and Elijah and her son ate from her supply of flour and oil as long as it was needed. ¹⁶No matter how much they used, there was always plenty left! It was just as the Lord had promised through Elijah!

¹⁷But one day the woman's son became sick and died.

¹⁸"O man of God," she cried. "What have you done to me? Have you come here to punish my sins by killing my son?"

¹⁹"Give him to me," Elijah replied. And he took the boy's body from her. He carried it upstairs to the guest room where he lived. He laid the body on his bed. ²⁰Then he cried out to the Lord, "O Lord my God! Why have you killed the son of this widow with whom I am staying?"

²¹He stretched himself upon the child three times. And he cried out to the Lord, "O Lord my God! Please let this child's spirit come back to him."

²²The Lord heard Elijah's prayer! The spirit of the child came back! And he became alive again! ²³Then Elijah took him downstairs and gave him to his mother.

"See! He's alive!" he said.

²⁴"Now I know for sure that you are a prophet," she told him. "I now know that what you say is from the Lord!"

- *Remember:* Where did Elijah find the widow? What was she doing? (17:10) What did he ask her to do? (17:10-11) What was the widow's problem? (17:12) Elijah told the woman to bake some bread with the flour and oil she had left. But who must eat first? Why do you think he did it that way? (17:13) How long did the woman have plenty to eat? (17:16) How else did Elijah help the woman and her son? (17:17-24) Do you think the woman trusted God from that time on? Why?

- *Discover:* God gives us food and clothing and a place to live. You may not have as much as you want, but have you ever had less than you need to live? Trust God to give you what you need, not what you want.

- *Apply:* Make a list of things you want. Next to it make a list of things you really need. How is the list different? Thank God for giving you what you really need.

- *What's next?* Fire comes down from heaven and burns up rocks and water. What's happening? Read 1 Kings 18. ■

Elijah Defeats the Prophets of Baal

The Israelites were trying to worship God and Baal. But God said they must choose. They could not worship both. One day Elijah had a test. The true God would send fire from heaven. The prophets of Baal prayed to their god. Nothing happened. Then Elijah prayed to his God. Did he answer? What happened?

18 Three years later the Lord spoke to Elijah. He said, "Go and tell King Ahab that I will soon send rain again!"

²So Elijah went to tell him. Meanwhile the famine had become very bad in Samaria.

³⁻⁴The man in charge of Ahab's palace was Obadiah. He was a true follower of the Lord. Queen Jezebel had once tried to kill all of the Lord's prophets. At that time, Obadiah had hidden 100 of them in two caves. He put 50 prophets in each cave. Then he fed them with bread and water.

⁵So Elijah went to see King Ahab. At the same time, Ahab spoke to Obadiah. "We must check every stream and brook," he said. "We must try to find grass to save at least some of my horses and mules. You go one way. I'll go the other. That way we'll search the whole land."

⁶So they did, each going alone. ⁷Suddenly Obadiah saw Elijah coming toward him! Obadiah knew him at once and fell to the ground before him.

"Is it really you, my lord Elijah?" he asked.

⁸"Yes, it is," Elijah replied. "Now go and tell the king I am here."

⁹"Oh, sir," Obadiah said. "If I tell Ahab that, he will have me killed! What have I done that you should send me to my death? ¹⁰The king has looked in every nation and kingdom on earth to find you. And each time he was told 'Elijah isn't here.' And King Ahab made the kings of those nations promise they were telling the truth. ¹¹And now you say, 'Go and tell him Elijah is here'! ¹² But as soon as I leave you, the Spirit of the Lord might carry you away. And when Ahab comes and can't find you, he will kill me. Yet I have been a true servant of the Lord all my life. ¹³Has no one told you about the time when Queen Jezebel was trying to kill the Lord's prophets? I hid 100 of them in two caves. And I fed them with bread and water. ¹⁴And now you say, 'Go tell the king that Elijah is here'! Sir, if I do that, I'm dead!"

¹⁵But Elijah said, "I promise that I will show myself to Ahab today. I promise this by the Lord God of the armies of heaven. For I stand in his presence."

¹⁶So Obadiah went to tell Ahab that Elijah had come. And Ahab went out to meet him.

¹⁷"So it's you, is it? It's the man who

brought this famine on Israel!" Ahab said when he saw him.

18"You're talking about yourself," Elijah said. "For you and your family have not obeyed the Lord. You have worshiped Baal instead. 19Now bring all the people of Israel to Mount Carmel. Bring along all 450 prophets of Baal who are supported by Jezebel. And bring the 400 prophets of Asherah too."

20So Ahab called all the people and the prophets to Mount Carmel.

21Then Elijah talked to them. "How long will you try to serve both Baal and the Lord?" he asked the people. "If the Lord is God, *follow* him! But if Baal is God, then follow *him!*"

22Then Elijah spoke again. "I am the only prophet of the Lord who is left," he told them. "But Baal has 450 prophets. 23Now bring two young bulls. The prophets of Baal may choose the one they wish. They shall cut it into pieces and lay it on the wood of their altar. But they shall not put any fire under the wood. I will prepare the other young bull. I will lay it on the wood on the Lord's altar. And I will put no fire under it. 24Then pray to your god, and I will pray to the Lord. The god who answers by sending fire to light the wood is the true God!" And all the people agreed to this test.

25Then Elijah turned to the prophets of Baal. "You first," he said. "For there are many of you. Choose one of the bulls and prepare it. Then call to your god. But don't put any fire under the wood."

26So they prepared one of the young bulls and put it on the altar. They called to Baal all morning, shouting, "O Baal, hear us!" But there was no reply of any kind. Then they began to dance around the altar. 27About noon, Elijah began mocking them.

"You'll have to shout louder than that to make your god hear you!" he said. "Maybe he is talking to someone! Or perhaps he is out sitting on the toilet! Or maybe he is away on a trip! Or perhaps he is asleep and needs to be wakened!"

28So they shouted louder. They cut themselves with knives and swords. And their blood gushed out. This was one of

their customs. 29They raved all afternoon until the time of the evening sacrifice. But there was no reply, no voice, no answer.

30Then Elijah called to the people, "Come over here."

And they all crowded around him. He fixed the altar of the Lord that had been torn down. 31He took 12 stones. There was one stone for each of the tribes of Israel. 32He used the stones to rebuild the Lord's altar. Then he dug a trench about three feet wide around the altar. 33He piled wood upon the altar. He cut the young bull into pieces and laid them on the wood.

"Fill four barrels with water," he said. "Then pour the water over the meat and the wood."

After they had done this he said, 34"Do it again." And they did.

"Now, do it once more!" And they did. 35And the water ran off the altar and filled the trench.

36It was the normal time for offering the evening sacrifice. So Elijah walked up to the altar. He prayed, "O Lord God of Abraham, Isaac, and Israel! Prove today that you are the God of Israel. Show these people that I am your servant. Prove that I have done all this at your command. 37O Lord, answer me! Answer me so these people will know that you are God. Let them know that you have brought them back to yourself."

38Then, suddenly, fire flashed down from heaven! It burned up the young bull, the wood, the stones, and the dust! It even burned all the water in the ditch!

39When the people saw it, they fell on their faces to the ground. They shouted, "The Lord is God! The Lord is God!"

40Then Elijah told them to grab the prophets of Baal. "Don't let a single one get away," he commanded.

So they caught them all. Elijah took them to Kishon Brook and killed them there.

41Then Elijah said to Ahab, "Go and enjoy a good meal! For I hear a mighty rainstorm coming!"

42So Ahab made a feast. But Elijah climbed to the top of Mount Carmel. He

got down on his knees, with his face between his knees. ⁴³Then he said to his servant, "Go and look out toward the sea."

He did and came back to Elijah. He told him, "I didn't see anything."

Then Elijah told him, "Go again, and again, and again. Go seven times!"

⁴⁴On the seventh time, his servant told him, "I saw a little cloud. It was about the size of a man's hand. It was coming up from the sea."

Then Elijah shouted, "Hurry to Ahab. Tell him to get into his chariot and get down the mountain. If he doesn't, he'll be stopped by the rain!"

⁴⁵And sure enough, the sky was soon black with clouds. And a heavy wind brought a great rainstorm. Ahab left in a hurry for Jezreel. ⁴⁶And the Lord gave special strength to Elijah. He was able to run ahead of Ahab's chariot to the gates of the city!

● *Remember:* How long had the land been without rain? (18:1) Who was Obadiah? How had he helped God's prophets? (18:3-4) Elijah told Obadiah to get King Ahab. Why was Obadiah afraid? (18:9-12) What was the test to decide who was the true God? (18:21-24) What happened when the prophets of Baal prayed to their god? (18:25-29) What happened when Elijah prayed? (18:30-38) Which do you think was real, God or Baal? Why?

● *Discover:* God is the true God and the only real God. We must worship him. Don't worship anyone or anything else.

● *Apply:* Which do you love more, God or things? Which do you love more, God or TV? How will you show God today that you love him more? How much time will you spend with him?

● *What's next?* When does a whisper speak louder than a violent wind or raging fire? Read 1 Kings 19:1-18 to find out. ■

God Whispers to Elijah

Elijah felt sorry for himself. He thought he was the only one who loved God. He even thought that God would not take care of him. Then God spoke to Elijah. What do you think he said?

19 Ahab told Queen Jezebel what Elijah had done. He told her that Elijah had killed the prophets of Baal. ²When she heard this, she sent a message to Elijah. "You killed my prophets," she said. "Now I make this promise, by the gods. I am going to kill you by this time tomorrow night."

³So Elijah ran for his life. He went to Beersheba, a city of Judah, and left his servant there. ⁴Then he went on alone into the wilderness. He traveled all day. Then he sat down under a broom bush and prayed that he might die.

"I've had enough," he told the Lord. "Take away my life. I've got to die sometime, and it might as well be now."

⁵Then he lay down and slept under the broom bush. But as he was sleeping, an angel touched him. The angel told him to get up and eat! ⁶He looked around. He saw some bread baking on hot stones and a jar of water! So he ate and drank and lay down again.

⁷Then the angel of the Lord came again. He touched him and said, "Get up and eat some more. For there is a long journey ahead of you."

⁸So he got up and ate and drank. The food gave him strength to travel 40 days and 40 nights to Mount Sinai. This was the mountain of God. ⁹And he lived there in a cave.

But the Lord said to him, "What are you doing here, Elijah?"

¹⁰He replied, "I have worked very hard for the Lord God of the heavens. But the people of Israel have broken their covenant with you. They have torn down your altars. They have

killed your prophets. Only I am left! And now they are trying to kill me too!"

¹¹"Go out and stand before me on the mountain," the Lord told him. And as Elijah stood there the Lord passed by. A mighty wind hit the mountain. It was such a blast that the rocks were torn loose! But the Lord was not in the wind. After the wind, there was an earthquake. But the Lord was not in the earthquake. ¹²And after the earthquake, there was a fire. But the Lord was not in the fire. And after the fire, there was the sound of a gentle whisper. ¹³When Elijah heard it, he wrapped his face in his scarf. He went out and stood at the entrance of the cave.

And a voice said, "Why are you here, Elijah?"

¹⁴He replied again, "I have worked hard for the Lord God of heaven's armies. But the people have broken their covenant with you. They have torn down your altars. They have killed every one of your prophets but me. And now they are trying to kill me too."

¹⁵Then the Lord told him, "Go back by the desert road to Damascus. When you get there, anoint Hazael to be king of Syria. ¹⁶Then anoint Jehu to be king of Israel. He is the son of Nimshi. And anoint Elisha to replace you as my prophet. He is the son of Shaphat of Abel-meholah. ¹⁷Anyone who gets away from Hazael shall be killed by Jehu. And those who get away from Jehu shall be killed by Elisha! ¹⁸And by the way, there are 7,000 men in Israel who have never bowed to Baal!"

● *Remember:* What did Queen Jezebel say she would do to Elijah? Why? (19:1-2) What did Elijah do? (19:3-4) Do you think Elijah felt sorry for himself? Why do you think this? (19:3-4) Where did God send Elijah? (19:5-8) What three violent things did God send? Was God in any of them? (19:11-12) What came next? Was God in the whisper? (19:12-13) What important work did God give to Elijah? (19:15-18) Do you think Elijah should have felt sorry for himself? Would God take care of him? Did God still have important work for him to do?

● *Discover:* Do you ever feel sorry for yourself? Do you ever think that God is not helping you? Remember Elijah! God is always there, taking care of you. He never leaves you alone.

● *Apply:* The next time you feel sorry for yourself, stop! Praise God that he is there. Thank God that he is helping you. You won't feel sorry for yourself then.

● *What's next?* It's time for someone to take Elijah's place. Who will he pick? Read 1 Kings 19:19-21. ■

Elijah Gives His Coat to Elisha

Elijah was one of the greatest prophets who ever lived. But he was getting old. Who would do his work when he was gone? One day Elijah threw his coat on a younger man named Elisha. That was a way to say, "You will do my work when I'm gone. Come with me now and learn how." What do you think Elisha did?

¹⁹So Elijah went and found Elisha. He was plowing a field with 11 other teams of oxen ahead of him. He was at the end of the line with the last team. Elijah went over to him. He threw his coat across his shoulders and walked away again.

²⁰Elisha left the oxen standing there and ran after Elijah. He said to him, "First let me go and say good-bye to my father and mother. Then I'll go with you!"

Elijah replied, "Go on back! I won't get in your way."

²¹Elisha then went back to his oxen. He killed them. And he used wood from the plow to build a fire to roast their meat. He passed around the meat to the other plowmen. They all had a great feast. Then he went with Elijah, as his helper.

● *Remember:* What was Elisha doing when Elijah found him? (19:19) How many teams were plowing? Where was Elisha in the line? (19:19) What did Elijah do? (19:19) What did Elisha do then? (19:20-21) What do you think Elisha will learn from Elijah? Do you think that will help him do God's work better?

● *Discover:* You can do God's work better if you let others help you.

● *Apply:* Do you want to please God? Do you want to help God do his work? Ask your parents or Sunday school teacher or pastor to show you how.

● *What's next?* A wicked king wants to buy a neighbor's vineyard. But the neighbor says no, he won't sell. What do you think the king will do next? Read 1 Kings 21. ■

God Gives Israel Victory over Syria

20 King Ben-hadad of Syria now called out his army. He had 32 kings and their armies under him. They had many chariots and horses. And they attacked Samaria, the Israelite capital. ²⁻³He sent this message into the city to King Ahab of Israel. "Your silver and gold are mine," he said. "I will also take the best of your wives and children!"

⁴"All right, my lord," Ahab replied. "All that I have is yours!"

⁵⁻⁶Soon Ben-hadad's messengers came back again with another message. "You must not only give me your silver, gold, wives, and children," he said. "But about this time tomorrow I will send my men to search your palace. They will also search the homes of your people. They will take away whatever they like!"

⁷Then Ahab called his advisors. "Look what this man is doing," he said to them. "He is looking for trouble. I have already said he could have my wives and children and silver and gold. I have given these to him just as he demanded."

⁸"Don't give him anything more," the elders advised.

⁹So he spoke to the messengers from Ben-hadad. "Bring my lord the king this message," he said. "Tell him I will give him all he asked for the first time. But his men may not search the palace. And they may not search the homes of the people." So the messengers went back to Ben-hadad.

¹⁰Then the Syrian king sent this message to Ahab. "I am going to destroy Samaria," he

said. "I am going to turn it into handfuls of dust! If I don't do this, may the gods destroy me!"

11The king of Israel said, "Don't count your chickens before they hatch!"

12This reply of Ahab's was sent to Ben-hadad and the other kings. It got there as they were drinking in their tents.

"Prepare to attack!" Ben-hadad told his officers.

13Then a prophet came to see King Ahab. He gave him this message from the Lord. "Do you see all these enemy armies?" he said. "I will give them all to you today. Then at last you will know that I am the Lord."

14Ahab asked, "How will he do it?"

And the prophet replied, "The Lord says, 'By the officers from the provinces.'"

"Shall we attack first?" Ahab asked.

"Yes," the prophet said.

15So he called out the officers from the provinces. There were 232 of them. Then he called out the rest of his army of 7,000 men. 16About noon the first of Ahab's troops marched out of the city. At the time, Ben-hadad and his 32 kings were still drinking themselves drunk.

17As they came near, Ben-hadad's scouts reported to him. "Some troops are coming!" they said.

18"Take them alive," Ben-hadad commanded. "Take them if they have come for truce or for war."

19By now Ahab's whole army had joined the attack. 20Each one killed a Syrian soldier. Suddenly the whole Syrian army panicked and ran. The Israelites chased them. But King Ben-hadad and a few others got away on horses.

21 Most of the horses and chariots were captured. And most of the Syrian army was killed.

22Then the prophet spoke to King Ahab. He said, "Get ready for another attack by the king of Syria."

23For after their defeat, Ben-hadad's officers spoke to the king. "The Israelite God is a god of the hills," they said. "That is why they won. But we can beat them easily on the plains. 24Only this time replace the kings with generals!

25Call out another army like the one you lost. Give us the same number of horses, chariots, and men. Then we will fight against them in the plains. There's not a shadow of a doubt that we will beat them." So King Ben-hadad did as they said. 26The next year he called up the Syrian army again. And he marched out against Israel. This time the attack was at Aphek. 27Israel then called out its army. They set up supply lines and moved into the battle. But the Israelite army looked like two little flocks of baby goats. And the great Syrian army filled the countryside!

28Then a prophet went to the king of Israel. He brought this message from the Lord: "The Syrians have said, 'The Lord is a God of the hills. He is not a God of the plains.' So I will help you beat this great army. And you shall know that I am the Lord."

29The two armies camped across from each other for seven days. On the seventh day the battle began. And the Israelites killed 100,000 Syrian soldiers that first day. 30The rest ran behind the walls of Aphek. But the wall fell on them and killed another 27,000. Ben-hadad ran into the city. He hid there in the inner room of one of the houses.

31"Sir," his officers said to him. "We have heard that the kings of Israel are very merciful. Let us wear sackcloth and put ropes on our heads. Then let us go out to King Ahab. Let us see if he will let you live."

32So they went to the king of Israel. They begged, "Your servant Ben-hadad pleads, 'Let me live!'"

"Oh, is he still alive?" the king of Israel asked. "He is my brother!"

33The men were quick to grab this straw of hope. So they hurried to clinch the matter. They said, "Yes, your brother Ben-hadad!"

"Go and get him," the king of Israel told them. And when Ben-hadad got there, he asked him up into his chariot!

34Ben-hadad told him, "I will give back the cities my father took from your father. And you may set up trading posts in Damascus, as my father did in Samaria."

35Then the Lord spoke to one of the prophets. He told him to say to another man, "Strike me with your sword!" But the man would not do it.

36Then the prophet told him, "You have not obeyed the voice of the Lord. Because of this, a lion shall kill you as soon as you leave me." And sure enough, as he turned to go a lion attacked and killed him.

37Then the prophet turned to another man. He said, "Strike me with your sword." And he did, wounding him.

38The prophet waited for the king beside the road. He put a bandage over his eyes so the king wouldn't know him.

39As the king passed by, the prophet called out to him. "Sir," he said. "I was in the battle. And a man brought me a prisoner. He said, 'Keep this man. If he gets away, you must die, or else pay me $2,000!' 40But while I was busy, the prisoner got away!"

"Well, it's your own fault," the king replied. "You'll have to pay."

41Then the prophet took the bandage from his eyes. And the king knew him as one of the prophets. 42Then the prophet said, "The Lord says this: 'You have saved the man I said must die. So now you must die in his place. And your people shall die instead of his.'"

43So the king of Israel went home to Samaria. He was angry and sullen.

Ahab Steals Naboth's Vineyard

King Ahab wanted Naboth's vineyard. But Naboth did not want to sell. The story should have ended there. But Ahab wanted the vineyard so much he became angry and upset. He would have done anything to get it. But what did he do?

21 Naboth, a man from Jezreel, had a vineyard. It was at the edge of the city near King Ahab's palace. 2One day the king talked to him about selling him this land.

"I want it for a garden," the king explained. "It is so near to the palace." So he offered to pay him money for it. Or, if Naboth wanted, he would give him a better piece of land in trade.

3But Naboth replied, "Not on your life! That land has been in my family for years!"

4So Ahab went back to the palace angry and sullen. He would not eat. And he went to bed with his face to the wall.

5"What in the world is the matter?" his wife, Jezebel, asked him. "Why aren't you eating? What has made you so upset and angry?"

6"I asked Naboth to sell me his vineyard. I also offered to trade for it. But he wouldn't do it!" Ahab told her.

7"Are you the king of Israel or not?" Jezebel demanded. "Get up and eat. Don't worry about it. I'll get you Naboth's vineyard!"

8So she wrote letters in Ahab's name. She sealed them with his seal. Then she sent them to the leaders of Jezreel. This was the city where Naboth lived. 9In her letter she commanded: "Call the citizens together for fasting and prayer. Then call Naboth. 10And find two scoundrels who will accuse him of cursing God and the king. Then take him out and kill him."

11The city fathers did what the queen told them to. 12They called the meeting and put Naboth on trial. 13Two scoundrels accused him of cursing God and the king. Then he was dragged outside the city and stoned to death. 14The city officials then sent word to Jezebel that Naboth was dead.

15When Jezebel heard the news, she spoke to Ahab. "You know the vineyard Naboth wouldn't sell you?" she asked. "Well, you can have it now! He's dead!"

16So Ahab went down to the vineyard to claim it.

¹⁷But the Lord said to Elijah, ¹⁸"Go to Samaria to meet King Ahab. He will be at Naboth's vineyard. He will be about to claim it as his own. ¹⁹Give him this message from me: 'Isn't killing Naboth bad enough? Must you rob him too? Because you have done this, dogs shall lick your blood outside the city! They shall lick your blood just as they licked the blood of Naboth!'"

²⁰"So my enemy has found me!" Ahab said to Elijah.

"Yes," Elijah answered. "I have come to place God's curse upon you. For you have done what is wrong. ²¹The Lord is going to bring great harm to you. He will sweep you away! He will not let a single male in your family live! ²²He is going to destroy your family. He will do just as he did with the families of King Jeroboam and King Baasha. For you have made him very angry. And you have led all of Israel into sin. ²³The Lord has also told me that the dogs of Jezreel shall tear apart the body of your wife, Jezebel. ²⁴The members of your family who die in the city shall be eaten by dogs. And those who die in the country shall be eaten by vultures."

²⁵No king had ever been as bad as Ahab. For his wife, Jezebel, encouraged him to do every sort of evil. ²⁶He was guilty because he worshiped idols. This was the same thing Amorites did. And for that reason, the Lord had chased the Amorites out of the land. The Lord had done this to make room for the people of Israel. ²⁷When Ahab heard these prophecies, he tore his clothing. He put on rags, fasted, and slept in sackcloth. And he was very humble.

²⁸Then another message came to Elijah. ²⁹"Do you see how Ahab has humbled himself before me?" the Lord said. "Because he has done this, I will not do what I promised during his lifetime. It will happen to his sons. I will destroy his descendants."

- *Remember:* Why did King Ahab want Naboth's vineyard? (21:1-2) Why didn't Naboth want to sell it? (21:3) How did Ahab feel about that? What did he do? (21:4) What did Queen Jezebel do to help Ahab get the vineyard? (21:7-15) Was Ahab happy with this? Did he scold her for murdering Naboth? (21:16) How would Ahab be punished for doing this? (21:17-24) What kind of person was Ahab? (21:25-26) Why wouldn't Ahab be a good friend?

- *Discover:* When we want something too much, we may try to get it the wrong way. Ahab and Jezebel used lies, stealing, and even murder to get the vineyard.

- *Apply:* Do you want something? How much do you want it? What would you do to get it? If you're ever tempted to lie or steal or cheat or hurt someone to get something, stop! Don't do those things. God will punish you if you do.

- *What's next?* God's prophet warns the king not to do something. Will the king listen? Read 1 Kings 22:1-40. ■

Ahab Dies in Battle

If God told you, "Don't do this. If you do, it will kill you," would you still do it? God sent a prophet to King Ahab to tell him, "Don't do this. If you do, you will get killed." Do you think Ahab still did it?

22 For three years there was no war between Syria and Israel. ²During the third year, King Jehoshaphat of Judah visited King Ahab of Israel. ³At this time, Ahab spoke to his advisors. He said, "Did you know that the Syrians still control our city of Ramoth-gilead? And we're sitting here doing nothing about it!"

⁴Then he turned to Jehoshaphat. He asked him, "Will you send your army with mine? Will you help me to get Ramoth-gilead back?"

And King Jehoshaphat of Judah

Ships
1 KINGS
22:48

In a world where there were no planes, trains, or automobiles, a ship was really the only way to travel to faraway lands. It was sure a lot faster than walking, and you could carry more home with you! Ships are not mentioned much in the Bible. Paul sailed on a Roman ship that was wrecked in a storm. Jonah tried to run away from God on a ship. He also got into a storm. Solomon had a fleet of ships.

King Jehoshaphat built a fleet of ships, too. He wanted to send his ships off to find the beautiful things that the men on Solomon's ships found. But his ships were destroyed before they could sail, probably from a great storm or battle.

Ships at this time were sailing ships made of wood. Some ships had long oars so that slaves could row in calm water. Fleets of ships helped a country be rich. They could sail to faraway lands and find beautiful treasures. But life was not easy on these ships. There was not a lot of food, and the sailors were often on the water for months at a time without ever seeing land. Sailing was also dangerous. Many Bible-time ships were lost in storms.

replied, "Of course! You and I are brothers. My people are yours to command. And my horses are at your service. 5But we should ask the Lord first," he added. "We should do this to be sure of what he wants."

6So King Ahab called his 400 heathen prophets. He asked them, "Shall I attack Ramoth-gilead, or not?" And they all said, "Yes, go ahead. For God will help you conquer it." 7But Jehoshaphat asked, "Isn't there a prophet of the Lord here? I'd like to ask him too."

8"Well, there is one," King Ahab replied. "But I hate him. He never predicts anything good. He always has something gloomy to say. His name is Micaiah, the son of Imlah."

"Oh, come now!" Jehoshaphat replied. "Don't talk like that!"

9So King Ahab called to one of his servants, "Go get Micaiah. Hurry!"

10The two kings were dressed in their royal robes. They were sitting on thrones on the threshing floor. This was near the city gate. All the prophets were standing in front of the kings speaking messages from God. 11One of the prophets, Zedekiah, made some iron horns. He was the son of Chenaanah. He said, "You will use these horns to push the Syrians around. And the Lord promises that you will destroy them."

12And all the others agreed. "Go ahead and attack Ramoth-gilead," they said. "For the Lord will cause you to triumph!"

13A messenger went to get Micaiah. He told him what the other prophets were saying. And he urged Micaiah to say the same thing.

14But Micaiah told him, "I make this promise. I will say only what the Lord tells me to!"

15When he arrived, the king asked him, "Micaiah, shall we attack Ramoth-gilead, or not?"

"Why, of course! Go right ahead!" Micaiah told him. "You will have a great victory, for the Lord will cause you to conquer!"

¹⁶"How many times must I tell you to speak only what the Lord tells you to?" the king demanded.

¹⁷Then Micaiah told him, "I saw all Israel scattered upon the mountains. They were like sheep without a shepherd. And the Lord said, 'Their king is dead. Send them to their homes.'"

¹⁸Ahab turned to Jehoshaphat and complained. "Didn't I tell you this would happen?" he said. "He *never* tells me anything good. It's *always* bad."

¹⁹Then Micaiah said, "Listen to this word from the Lord. I saw the Lord sitting on his throne. The armies of heaven stood around him.

²⁰"Then the Lord said, 'Who will trick Ahab into going to die at Ramoth-gilead?'

"They talked about it, but couldn't decide. ²¹Then one angel said to the Lord, 'I'll do it!'

²²"'How?' the Lord asked.

"And he replied, 'I will go as a lying spirit. I will speak in the mouths of all his prophets.'

"And the Lord said, 'That will do it. You will succeed. Go ahead.'

²³"Don't you see? The Lord has put a lying spirit in the mouths of all these prophets. But the fact is that the Lord has planned trouble for you."

²⁴Then Zedekiah walked over. He was the son of Chenaanah. He slapped Micaiah on the face.

"When did the Spirit of the Lord leave me?" he demanded. "And when did he start speaking only to you?"

²⁵And Micaiah replied, "You will have the answer to your question. It will be clear when you find yourself hiding in an inner room."

²⁶Then King Ahab ordered Micaiah's arrest.

"Take him to Amon, the mayor of the city, and to my son Joash. ²⁷Tell them, 'The king says to put this fellow in jail. Feed him with bread and water until I come home in peace. Give him just enough to keep him alive.'"

²⁸"Perhaps you will come back in peace," Micaiah replied. "If you do, it will prove that the Lord has not spoken through me." Then he turned to the people standing nearby. He said, "Take note of what I've said."

²⁹So King Ahab of Israel and King Jehoshaphat of Judah led their armies to Ramoth-gilead.

³⁰Ahab said to Jehoshaphat, "You wear your royal robes. But I'll not wear mine!"

So Ahab went into the battle dressed like any soldier. ³¹For the king of Syria had given his 32 chariot captains special orders. They were to fight no one except King Ahab himself. ³²⁻³³They saw King Jehoshaphat in his royal robes. So they thought, "That's the man we're after." Then they turned around to chase him. But when Jehoshaphat shouted who he was, they turned back! ³⁴But someone shot an arrow at random. And it hit King Ahab between the joints of his armor.

"Take me out of the battle," he groaned to his chariot driver. "For I am badly wounded."

³⁵The battle became more and more intense as the day wore on. And King Ahab went back in. He was propped up in his chariot. And the blood from his wound ran down onto the floorboards. Finally, toward evening, he died. ³⁶⁻³⁷Just as the sun was going down the cry ran through his troops. "It's all over! Go back home! The king is dead!"

And his body was taken to Samaria and buried there. ³⁸His chariot and armor were washed beside the pool of Samaria. This was where the prostitutes bathed. While there, dogs came and licked the king's blood. It happened just as the Lord said it would.

³⁹The rest of Ahab's history is written in *The Annals of the Kings of Israel*. This includes the story of his ivory palace and the cities he built. ⁴⁰So Ahab was buried among his ancestors. And Ahaziah, his son, became the new king of Israel.

• *Remember:* What did King Ahab ask King Jehoshaphat to do? (22:3-4) What did Jehoshaphat say he would do? (22:4) But what did he want to do first? (22:5) Who advised Ahab at first? What do you think of these prophets? (22:6,10-12) What advice did Micaiah give? What did Ahab think of it? (22:17-26) What did Ahab and Jehoshaphat do? Did they accept God's advice? (22:29-31) What happened to Ahab? Was Micaiah right? (22:32-38) What do you think Ahab should have done? Why?

- *Discover:* Listen to God's advice. He knows exactly what you should and shouldn't do.

- *Apply:* God has lots of good advice for us in the Bible. Read the Bible each day. When you do, ask, "What should I do about this?"

- *What's next?* Horses appear from the sky pulling a chariot. And they are blazing with fire. What's happening? Read 2 Kings 2:1-14. ■

Jehoshaphat Rules Judah

[41]Meanwhile Jehoshaphat had become king of Judah. He was the son of Asa. He became king during the fourth year of King Ahab's reign in Israel. [42]Jehoshaphat was 35 years old when he became king. He reigned in Jerusalem for 25 years. His mother was Azubah, the daughter of Shilhi. [43]He did as his father Asa had done. He obeyed the Lord in all but one thing. He did not destroy the shrines on the hills. So the people sacrificed and burned incense there. [44]He also made peace with Ahab, the king of Israel. [45]The rest of the wars and deeds of Jehoshaphat are written in *The Annals of the Kings of Judah.*

[46]He also got rid of all the male prostitutes. For some still lived there from the days of his father Asa. [47]There was no king in Edom at that time, only a deputy. [48]King Jehoshaphat built great ships to sail to Ophir for gold. But they never got there. They were wrecked at Ezion-geber. [49]Ahaziah, King Ahab's son, wanted to help Jehoshaphat. He wanted to send some of his men along on the ships. But Jehoshaphat had refused his offer.

[50]King Jehoshaphat died and was buried with his ancestors in Jerusalem. This was the city of his forefather, David. Then his son Jehoram became king of Judah.

Ahaziah Rules Israel

[51]Ahaziah, Ahab's son, became king over Israel. He became king during the 17th year of the reign of King Jehoshaphat of Judah. He reigned in Samaria for two years. [52-53]But he was not a good king. He followed in the steps of his father and mother. And he did the same things as King Jeroboam. He led Israel into the sin of worshiping idols. So Ahaziah made the Lord God of Israel very angry.

SECOND KINGS

Have you ever seen a chariot and horses of fire? You will in this book. You'll not only see one, you'll even see a whole army of them! You'll watch a man go to heaven in a whirlwind. Second Kings is filled with adventure and excitement. There are armies and battles, dramatic miracles and interesting people.

This book continues the story of 1 Kings. It is a story that lasted 200 years. But it is a sad story. The beautiful kingdom of Israel that once put God first is now breaking apart. Why? You've guessed the reason already. The people had forgotten about God. In fact, many were even disobeying God on purpose. Two great prophets, Elijah and Elisha, were two lights in this dark time. These men, who had nothing, showed how great God is. Evil kings and queens, who seemed to have everything, showed how weak and helpless they really were. When you read 2 Kings, you'll want to shout, "God is great. I need him!"

King Ahaziah Dies for His Sin

1 After King Ahab died, the nation of Moab broke away from Israel's rule. They would not pay tribute to Israel any longer.

²Ahaziah was Israel's new king. He fell off the upstairs porch of his palace at Samaria. And he was badly hurt. So he sent messengers to the temple of the god Baal-zebub at Ekron. He sent them to ask if he would get better.

³But an angel of the Lord came to Elijah the prophet. "Go and meet the messengers," the angel said. "Ask them, 'Is it true that there is no God in Israel? Is that why you are going to Baal-zebub, the god of Ekron? Is that why you are going to him to ask if the king will get better? 4-5Because King Ahaziah has done this, he will surely die. The Lord says that he will never leave the bed he is lying on.'"

When Elijah told the messengers this, they went back to the king right away.

"Why have you come back so soon?" he asked them.

⁶"A man came up to us," they said. "He told us to go back to the king. He said to give you this message from the Lord: 'Why are you asking questions of Baal-zebub, the god of Ekron? Is it because there is no God in Israel? Now, since you have done this, you will surely die. You will not leave the bed you are lying on.'"

⁷"Who was this man?" the king demanded. "What did he look like?"

⁸"He was a hairy man," they replied. "He wore a wide leather belt."

"It was Elijah the prophet!" the king exclaimed. ⁹Then he sent an army captain with 50 soldiers to arrest him. They found him sitting on top of a hill. The captain said to him, "O man of God! The king has commanded you to come along with us."

¹⁰But Elijah replied, "Perhaps I am a man of God. If so, let fire come down from heaven. Let it destroy you and your 50 men!" Then lightning struck them and killed them all!

¹¹So the king sent another captain with 50 men. The captain said, "O man of God! The king says that you must come down right away."

¹²Elijah replied, "Perhaps I am a man of God. If so, let fire come down from heaven. Let it destroy you and your 50 men!" And again the fire from God burned them up.

¹³Once more the king sent 50 men. But this time the captain fell to his knees before Elijah. He pleaded with him, "O man of God! Please save my life. And please, save the lives of these, your 50 servants. ¹⁴Have mercy on us! Don't destroy us as you did the others."

¹⁵Then the angel of the Lord spoke to Elijah. "Don't be afraid," the angel said. "Go with him." So Elijah went to the king.

¹⁶"Why did you send messengers to Baal-zebub, the god of Ekron? Why did you try to ask Baal-zebub about your sickness?" Elijah demanded. "Is it because there is no God in Israel to ask? Because you have done this, you will surely die! You shall not leave this bed."

¹⁷So Ahaziah died as the Lord had promised through Elijah. Then his brother Joram became the new king. This was because Ahaziah did not have a son to be king after him. This happened in the second year of the reign of King Jehoram of Judah. Jehoram was the son of Jehoshaphat. ¹⁸The rest of the history of Ahaziah's reign is written in *The Annals of the Kings of Israel.*

A Whirlwind Takes Elijah Away

There was a man who never died. His name was Elijah. This is the way God took him to heaven. You'll find it a very exciting way to go!

2 Now the time came for the Lord to take Elijah to heaven. The Lord was going to take him to heaven by means of a whirlwind! Elijah spoke to Elisha as they left Gilgal. "Stay here," he said. "For the Lord has told me to go to Bethel."

But Elisha replied, "I promise this before God. I won't leave you!"

So they went on together to Bethel. ³The school of young prophets at Bethel came out to meet them. They asked Elisha, "Did you know that the Lord is going to take Elijah away from you today?"

"Yes, I know," Elisha said. "But don't talk about it."

⁴Then Elijah said to Elisha, "Please stay here in Bethel. For the Lord has sent me to Jericho."

But Elisha replied again, "I promise this before God. I won't leave you!" So they went on together to Jericho.

⁵Then the school of young prophets at Jericho came to Elisha. They asked him, "Do you know that the Lord is going to take away your master today?"

"Will you please be quiet?" he commanded. "Of course I know it!"

⁶⁻⁷Then Elijah said to Elisha, "Please stay here. For the Lord has sent me to the Jordan River."

But Elisha replied as before, "I make this promise before God. I won't leave you!"

So they went on together and stood beside the Jordan River. Fifty of the young prophets watched from a distance. ⁸Then Elijah folded his cloak together. Then he

hit the water with it. The river divided and they went across on dry ground!

⁹When they got to the other side Elijah turned to Elisha. "What wish shall I give you before I am taken away?" he asked.

Elisha said, "Please give me double the prophetic power you have had."

¹⁰"You have asked a hard thing," Elijah replied. "If you see me when I am taken from you, then you will get what you asked. But if not, you won't."

¹¹They were walking along, talking. Then suddenly a chariot of fire came. It was pulled by horses of fire. It drove between them and separated them. Then Elijah was carried by a whirlwind into heaven.

¹²Elisha saw it and cried out, "My father! My father! The chariots of Israel and their horsemen!"

As they went out of sight he tore his robe. ¹³⁻¹⁴Then he picked up Elijah's cloak. He went back to the bank of the Jordan River. And he hit the water with it.

"Where is the Lord God of Elijah?" he cried out. The water divided and Elisha went across on dry ground!

- *Remember:* Three times Elijah told Elisha to stay behind while he went on. What did Elisha answer each time? Why did he answer that way? (2:1-7) Two groups of young prophets told Elisha that Elijah would be taken away. Who were they? (2:1-7) What special gift did Elisha ask of Elijah? (2:9) Did he get it? How do you know? (2:10-12)

- *Discover:* 50 young prophets saw a special miracle when Elijah was taken to heaven. God shows us special miracles each day when we look at his creation.

- *Apply:* Have you seen a sunrise? That's a miracle of creation. Have you seen a baby? That's another miracle of creation. Can you name three other special miracles that God lets you see each day?

- *What's next?* A woman gets into big trouble. She can't pay her bills. So a man is ready to sell her sons as slaves. What can she do? Read 2 Kings 4:1-7. ■

The Young Prophets Insist on Looking for Elijah

¹⁵The young prophets of Jericho saw what had happened. So they exclaimed, "The spirit of Elijah rests upon Elisha!"

They went to meet him and greeted him with respect.

¹⁶"Sir," they said, "just say the word. If you do, 50 of our best athletes will search the wilderness for your master. Perhaps the Spirit of the Lord has left him on some mountain. Or maybe he put him in some ravine."

"No," Elisha said, "don't bother."

¹⁷But they kept asking until he could not refuse. So he said, "All right, go ahead." Then 50 men looked for Elijah for three days. But they didn't find him.

¹⁸Elisha was still at Jericho when they got back. "Didn't I tell you not to go?" he said.

Elisha Brings God's Healing to the Water

¹⁹Now a group of the city leaders from Jericho came to see Elisha. "We have a problem," they told him. "This city is in a nice place, as you can see. But the water is bad. It causes our land to grow very poor crops."

²⁰"Well," he said, "bring me a new bowl filled with salt." So they brought it to him.

²¹Then he went out to the city well and threw the salt in. He said, "The Lord has healed these waters. They shall no longer cause death or keep the land from growing crops."

²²And sure enough! The water was made pure, just as Elisha had said.

Elisha Is Laughed At

²³From Jericho he went to Bethel. As he was walking along the road, a gang of young men began making fun of him. They had come from the city. They made fun of him because his head was bald. ²⁴He turned around and cursed them in the name of the Lord. Suddenly two female bears came out of the woods. The bears tore up 42 of them. ²⁵Then he went to Mount Carmel and finally went back to Samaria.

Elisha Helps King Jehoshaphat

3 Ahab's son Joram became king over Israel. He began his reign during the 18th year of King Jehoshaphat's reign in Judah. He ruled for 12 years. His

capital was Samaria. ²He was a very bad man. But he was not as bad as his father and mother had been. At least he tore down the pillar to Baal that his father had made. ³But he still held on to the great sin of Jeroboam, the son of Nebat. He had led the people of Israel into the worship of idols.

⁴King Mesha of Moab and his people were sheep ranchers. They paid Israel a yearly tribute of 100,000 lambs. They also paid the wool of 100,000 rams. ⁵But after Ahab's death, the king of Moab broke from Israel's rule. ⁶⁻⁸So King Joram called the Israelite army. And he sent this message to King Jehoshaphat of Judah.

"The king of Moab has turned against me," he said. "Will you help me fight him?"

"Of course I will," Jehoshaphat replied. "My people and horses are yours to command. What are your battle plans?"

"We'll attack from the wilderness of Edom," Joram replied.

⁹Their two armies were also joined by troops from Edom. They went on a route through the wilderness for seven days. But there was no water for the men or their pack animals.

¹⁰"Oh, what shall we do?" the king of Israel cried out. "The Lord has brought us here to let the king of Moab defeat us."

¹¹But Jehoshaphat, the king of Judah, spoke up. "Isn't there a prophet of the Lord with us?" he asked. "If so, we can find out what to do!"

"Elisha is here," said one of Israel's officers. Then he added, "He was Elijah's helper."

¹²"Fine," Jehoshaphat said. "He's just the man we want." So the kings of Israel, Judah, and Edom went to talk with Elisha.

¹³"I want no part of you," Elisha said to King Joram of Israel. "Go to the false prophets of your father and mother!"

But King Joram replied, "No! For it is the Lord who has called us here to be destroyed by the king of Moab!"

¹⁴"I make this promise before the Lord God. I wouldn't even talk to you if King Jehoshaphat of Judah wasn't here," Elisha replied. ¹⁵"Now bring me someone to play the lute." As the lute was played, the message of the Lord came to Elisha.

The Lord Sends Water

¹⁶"The Lord says to dig holes in this dry valley. The holes will hold the water he will send. ¹⁷You won't see wind or rain. But this valley will be filled with water! You will have plenty for yourselves and for your animals! ¹⁸But this is only the beginning. For the Lord will help you beat the army of Moab! ¹⁹You will conquer the best of their cities. You will even capture the cities with walls around them. And you will ruin all their good land with stones."

²⁰And sure enough, the next day water came! It came when the morning sacrifice was given. It was flowing from the direction of Edom. Soon there was water everywhere.

²¹The people of Moab heard about the three armies marching against them. So they called out every man who could fight, old and young. And they set up along their borders. ²²But early the next morning the sun looked red as it shone across the water!

The Moabites See Blood

²³"Blood!" they exclaimed. "The three armies have attacked and killed each other! Let's go and collect the loot!"

²⁴When they got to the Israelite camp, the army of Israel rushed out. They began killing the Moabites. So the army of Moab ran away. Then the men of Israel moved forward into the land of Moab. They destroyed everything as they went. ²⁵They destroyed the cities and threw stones on every good piece of land. They filled up the wells and cut down the fruit trees. In the end, only Fort Kir-hareseth was left. But even that finally fell to them.

²⁶The king of Moab saw that the battle had been lost. So he led 700 of his swordsmen in a last rush. He tried to break through to the king of Edom. But he failed. ²⁷Then he took his oldest son. This son would have been the next king. And he killed him and sacrificed him as a burnt offering upon the wall. As a result, there was great anger against Israel. So the army of Israel turned back and went to their own land.

Elisha Helps a Poor Widow

A poor woman got into trouble when her husband died. He owed some money. But she didn't have any. So the man who lent it said he would sell her sons as slaves. The woman begged Elisha for help. But what could he do? Watch and see!

4 One day the wife of one of the prophets came to Elisha. She came to tell him that her husband had died. He was a man who had loved God, she said. But he had owed some money when he died. Now the man he owed it to was demanding it back. If she didn't pay, he said he would take her two sons as his slaves.

²"What shall I do?" Elisha asked. "How much food do you have in the house?"

"Nothing at all! All I have is a jar of olive oil," she replied.

³"Then find as many pots and pans as you can. Borrow them from your friends and neighbors," he said. ⁴"Go into your house with your sons. Shut the door behind you. Then pour olive oil from your jar into the pots and pans. Set them aside as they are filled!"

⁵So she did. Her sons brought the pots and pans to her. And she filled one after another! ⁶Soon every container was full to the brim!

"Bring me another jar," she said to her sons.

"There aren't any more!" they told her. And then the oil stopped flowing!

⁷She told the prophet what had happened. And he said to her, "Go and sell the oil. Pay your debt. And you will still have money left for you and your sons to live on!"

- *Remember:* How did this poor woman get into debt? (4:1) What would happen if she could not pay the money back? (4:1) What one thing did the woman own? (4:2) What did Elisha tell her to do with it? (4:3-4) How did this help her get out of debt? (4:5-7) Do you think this woman was thankful? Do you think she thanked God for helping her?

- *Discover:* God can do wonderful things for us if we follow his commands.

- *Apply:* God gave us many commands in the Bible. Read two of them in Mark 12:30-31. Will you do that?

- *What's next?* Someone gives a special room to a man who doesn't have one. Read 2 Kings 4:8-17.

A Room for Elisha

Elisha was a prophet who traveled from place to place. A woman and her husband wanted to help him. So they fixed a special room for him. He could stay there whenever he came to this area. Did he do that?

⁸One day Elisha went to Shunem. An important woman of the city asked him in to eat. After that he stopped there for dinner whenever he passed that way.

⁹She said to her husband, "I'm sure this man who stops in from time to time is a holy prophet. ¹⁰Let's make a little room for him on the roof. We can put a bed, a table, a chair, and a lamp in the room. Then he will have a place to stay when he comes by."

¹¹⁻¹²Once Elisha was resting in the room. He called his servant Gehazi. "Tell the woman I want to speak to her," he said.

So he called her and she came. [13]Then Elisha said to Gehazi, "Tell her we are thankful. For she has been very kind to us. Ask her what we can do for her. Does she want me to put in a good word for her to the king? Does she want a favor from the general of the army?"

"No," she replied, "I am happy with things as they are."

[14]"What can we do for her?" he asked Gehazi after she left.

He said, "She doesn't have a son. And her husband is an old man."

[15-16]"Call her back again," Elisha told him.

When she came back, he talked to her as she stood in the door. "Next year at about this time you shall have a son!"

"O man of God!" she exclaimed. "Don't lie to me like that!"

[17]But it was true. The woman had a baby boy the next year. It all happened just as Elisha had promised it would.

- *Remember:* What did the woman and her husband do for Elisha? (4:8-9) What did God do for this woman and her husband? (4:10-17) Why do you think God did this? God gave the couple much money. They gave something good to God's helper. Then God gave them a son.

- *Discover:* God loves to give good gifts to us. We should love to give good gifts to him and his helpers.

- *Apply:* Do you love to give to God? You should, because God has given much to you. Sometimes he will give even more when you give to him. But don't give to God just to get him to give more. Give because he has already given you much.

- *What's next?* A boy dies. Can Elisha do anything about that? Read 2 Kings 4:18-37. ■

Elisha Raises a Boy from the Dead

The woman and man who built a special room for Elisha had a son. But when the child was older he suddenly died. What happened then? What did Elisha do when the boy died? How did he help then?

¹⁸One day when her child was older, he went out to see his father. His father was out working with the harvesters. ¹⁹There in the field, the boy got a bad headache. "My head! My head!" he moaned. His father told one of the servants to carry him home to his mother.

²⁰So he took him home, and his mother held him on her lap. But around noon he died. ²¹She carried him up to the bed of the prophet and shut the door. ²²Then she sent a message to her husband. "Send one of the servants and a donkey," she said. "I will hurry to the prophet and come right back."

²³"Why today?" he asked. "This isn't a feast day."

But she said, "It's important. I must go."

²⁴So she saddled the donkey and said to the servant, "Hurry! Don't slow down for my comfort unless I tell you to."

²⁵As she came near Mount Carmel, Elisha saw her in the distance. He said to Gehazi, "Look, that woman from Shunem is coming. ²⁶Run and meet her. Ask her what the trouble is. See if her husband is all right and if the child is well."

"Yes," she told Gehazi, "all is well."

²⁷But then she came to Elisha at the mountain. She fell to the ground before him and caught hold of his feet. Gehazi began to push her away. But the prophet said, "Let her alone. Something is both-

ering her deeply. And the Lord hasn't told me what it is."

²⁸Then she said, "It was you who said I would have a son. And I begged you not to lie to me!"

²⁹Then he said to Gehazi, "Quick, take my staff! Don't talk to anyone along the way. Hurry! Lay the staff upon the child's face."

³⁰But the boy's mother said, "I make this promise before God. I won't go home without you." So Elisha went with her.

³¹Gehazi went on ahead. He laid the staff upon the child's face. But nothing happened. There was no sign of life. He went back to meet Elisha. "The child is still dead," he told him.

³²When Elisha got there, the child was dead. He was still lying there on the prophet's bed. ³³He went in and shut the door behind him. He prayed to the Lord. ³⁴Then he lay upon the child's body. He put his mouth upon the child's mouth. He put his eyes upon the child's eyes. And he put his hands upon the child's hands. And the child's body began to grow warm again! ³⁵Then the prophet went down and walked back and forth in the house a few times. He went back upstairs and stretched himself again upon the child. This time the little boy sneezed seven times! And he opened his eyes!

³⁶Then the prophet called Gehazi. "Call

her!" he said. Gehazi called her and she came in. "Here's your son!" Elisha said.

37She fell to the floor at his feet. Then she picked up her son and went out.

- *Remember:* How did the boy get sick? (4:18-21) What did the boy's mother do about this? (4:22-28) How did Elisha help God bring the boy back to life? (4:29-35) Could you bring a dead person back to life? Elisha couldn't do it himself either. Who really brought the boy back to life?
- *Discover:* God can do anything, even bring a dead person back to life.
- *Apply:* Do you ever think your problem is too big for God? Nothing is too big or too hard for God!
- *What's next?* How can a little slave girl help an army general get well? Read 2 Kings 5:1-14. ■

The Poisonous Stew

38Elisha now went back to Gilgal. But there was a famine in the land. One day he was teaching the young prophets. He said to Gehazi, "Make some stew for supper for these men."

39One of the young men went out into the field to find vegetables. He came back with some wild gourds. He cut them up and put them into a kettle. But he didn't know that they had poison in them. 40After the men had eaten a bite or two they cried out, "Oh, sir! There's poison in this stew!"

41"Bring me some meal," Elisha said. He threw it into the kettle. And he said, "Now it's all right! Go ahead and eat!" And then it didn't hurt them.

Miracle Food for 100 Prophets

42One day a man from Baal-shalishah brought Elisha a sack of fresh corn. He also brought 20 loaves of barley bread. They were made from the first grain of his harvest. Elisha told Gehazi to use it to feed the young prophets.

43"What?" Gehazi exclaimed. "Feed 100 men with only this?"

But Elisha said, "Go ahead. For the Lord says there will be plenty for all. There will even be some left over!"

44And sure enough, there was. It happened just as the Lord had promised!

Naaman Is Healed

In Bible times, leprosy was a terrible disease. People had no way to get well because there was no cure. Sometimes they had to leave home and family and live alone. Naaman was general of Syria's army, but he had leprosy. One day his little slave girl told about a man who could heal him. Did he listen to her? Did he go to see the man?

5 The king of Syria had great respect for Naaman. He was the commander of the king's army. He had led the king's troops to many great victories. So he was a great hero, but he was a leper. 2Bands of Syrians had invaded the land of Israel. And among their captives was a little girl. She had been given to Naaman's wife as a maid.

3One day the little girl spoke to her mistress. "I wish my master would go to see the prophet in Samaria," she said. "He would heal him of his leprosy!"

4Naaman told the king what the little girl had said.

5"Go and visit the prophet," the king told him. "I will send a letter for you to carry to the king of Israel."

So Naaman started out. He took gifts of $20,000 in silver and $60,000 in gold. He also brought 10 suits of clothing. 6The letter to the king of Israel said: "The man bringing this letter is my servant Naaman. I want you to heal him of his leprosy."

7The king of Israel read it and tore his

clothes. He said, "This man sends me a leper to heal! Am I God, that I can kill and give life? He is only trying to get an excuse to invade us again."

8But Elisha the prophet heard about the king of Israel's plight. So he sent this message to him: "Why are you so upset? Send Naaman to me. He will learn that there is a true prophet of God here in Israel."

9So Naaman came with his horses and chariots. He stood at the door of Elisha's home. 10Elisha sent a messenger out to speak with him. The messenger told him to go and wash in the Jordan River seven times. He promised that if he did this, he would be healed of his leprosy! 11But Naaman was angry and went away.

"Look," he said, "I thought at least he would come out and talk to me! I thought he would wave his hand over the leprosy. I thought he would call upon the name of the Lord his God and heal me! 12The Abana River and Pharpar River of Damascus are clean. They're better than all the rivers of Israel put together! If it's rivers I need, I'll wash at home. I'll get rid of my leprosy there." So he went away very angry.

13But his officers tried to reason with him. They said, "The prophet might have told you to do some great thing. If he had, wouldn't you have done it? So why don't you do what he says? He simply says to go and wash and be cured!"

14So Naaman went down to the Jordan River. He dipped himself seven times as the prophet had told him to. And his skin became as healthy as a little child's! He was healed!

- *Remember:* The little slave girl said a man could heal Naaman. Who was he? (5:3) How did Naaman arrange a visit to Israel? (5:4-7) What did Elisha say that Naaman must do to get well? (5:10) What did Naaman think about that? (5:11-13) How was Naaman healed? (5:14) What did you learn here about obeying God?

- *Discover:* If we want God to help us we must obey him, no matter what he says. Naaman did not want to obey. What God wanted seemed foolish to him. But when he obeyed, he was healed.

- *Apply:* When you read your Bible today, write down one thing you find in it that God wants you to do. Do you want to do it? If you don't, do it anyway!

- *What's next?* Something terrible happens to a greedy man. Read 2 Kings 5:15-27.

Elisha's Greedy Servant

Naaman had leprosy, a terrible disease. He would have given anything to be healed. But no man could heal him. Only God could do that. When Elisha told Naaman what to do, God healed him. Naaman was so grateful that he wanted to give Elisha lots of money. Did he take it?

15Then he and his whole party went back to find the prophet. They stood humbly before him. And Naaman said, "Now I know that there is no God in all the world except in Israel! Now please take my gifts."

16Elisha replied to Naaman, "I make this promise before the Lord my God. I will not take your gifts."

Naaman tried to make him take the gifts. But he wouldn't do it. 17"Well," Naaman said, "all right. But please give me two mule loads of dirt. I will take it back to Syria with me. From now on I'll never offer burnt offerings or sacrifices to other gods. I'll only offer them to the Lord. 18However, may the Lord pardon me this one thing. My master the king

goes into the temple of the god Rimmon. As he worships there, he leans on my arm. May the Lord pardon me when I bow too!"

¹⁹"All right," Elisha said. So Naaman started home again.

²⁰Gehazi was Elisha's servant. And he said to himself, "My master should have taken this man's gifts. He shouldn't have sent him away without taking them. I will chase after him and get something from him."

²¹Gehazi soon caught up with him. Naaman saw him coming. So he jumped down from his chariot and ran to meet him.

"Is everything all right?" he asked.

²²"Yes," he said, "but my master has sent me with a message. Two young prophets from the hills of Ephraim just came. He would like $2,000 in silver and two suits to give them."

²³"Take $4,000," Naaman said. He gave him two fine robes and tied up the money in two bags. He gave them to two of his servants to carry back with Gehazi. ²⁴They got to the hill where Elisha lived. There Gehazi took the bags from the servants. Then he sent the men back. And he hid the money in his house.

²⁵He soon went in to see his master. Elisha asked, "Where have you been, Gehazi?"

"I haven't been anywhere," he replied.

²⁶But Elisha asked him, "Don't you know that I know what you did? I was with you in spirit when you went to meet Naaman. I saw him as he stepped down from his chariot to meet you! This isn't the time to get money, clothing, olive farms, and vineyards. It isn't the time to get sheep, oxen, and servants. ²⁷Because you have done this, Naaman's leprosy shall be upon you! It will also be upon your children and your children's children for all time!"

And Gehazi walked from the room a leper. His skin was as white as snow.

- *Remember:* What did Naaman say to Elisha when he was healed? (5:15) What did Naaman want to do for Elisha? (5:15) Did Elisha accept Naaman's gifts? (5:16) (5:8) Why did Gehazi chase after Naaman? (5:20) What two lies did Gehazi tell? (5:22,25) How was Gehazi punished? (5:27)

- *Discover:* Gehazi lied to Naaman to get the money, then lied to Elisha to cover up his first lie. When you tell one lie, you may have to tell another lie to cover it.

- *Apply:* The next time you are tempted to lie, stop! You may have to tell a bigger lie. And you may be punished.

- *What's next?* A young man sees an army with fiery chariots and horses. Read 2 Kings 6:1-17. ■

A Servant Sees a Fiery Army

The king of Syria was angry at Elisha. He wanted to kill him. So he sent an army. Elisha's servant was afraid. What could two men do against a whole army? Then Elisha prayed and the servant saw an army with fiery horses and chariots.

6 One day the young prophets came to Elisha. They told him, "As you can see, the place we live in is too small. Tell us if we should build a new one down beside the Jordan River. There are plenty of logs to build with down there."

"All right," he told them, "go ahead." ³"Please, sir, come with us," someone said. "I will," he said.

⁴When they got to the Jordan, they began cutting down trees. ⁵But as one of them was chopping, his axhead fell into the river.

"Oh, sir!" he cried, "I borrowed that ax!"

⁶"Where did it fall?" the prophet asked. The youth showed him the place. So Elisha cut a stick and threw it into the water. The axhead rose to the surface and floated! ⁷"Grab it," Elisha said to him. And he did.

⁸Once the king of Syria was at war with Israel. And he said to his officers, "We will set up our camp at this place."

⁹Elisha warned the king of Israel right away. "Don't go near that place!" he said. "The Syrian army is planning to set up camp there!"

¹⁰The king sent a scout to see if Elisha was right. Sure enough, he had saved him from trouble. This happened several times.

¹¹The king of Syria was angry about this. He called together his officers. And he demanded, "Which of you is the traitor? Who has been telling the king of Israel about my plans?"

¹²"It's not us, sir," one of the officers replied. "Elisha, the prophet, tells the king of Israel everything. He even knows the words you speak in your own bedroom!"

¹³"Go and find out where he is. We'll send troops to catch him!" the king exclaimed.

The report soon came back, "Elisha is at Dothan."

¹⁴So one night the king of Syria sent a great army to surround the city. They went with many chariots and horses. ¹⁵The prophet's servant got up early the next morning and went outside. He saw troops, horses, and chariots everywhere.

"My master!" he cried out to Elisha. "What shall we do now?"

¹⁶"Don't be afraid!" Elisha told him. "For our army is bigger than theirs!"

¹⁷Then Elisha prayed, "Lord, open his eyes. Let him see!" And the Lord opened the young man's eyes. He saw that the mountain was covered with horses and chariots of fire!

- *Remember:* Which countries were at war? (6:8) Which king did Elisha help? How? (6:9-10) How did the king of Syria try to stop Elisha? (6:13-14) What did Elisha pray? (6:17) What did Elisha's servant see? (6:17) Do you think God can protect his people? How do you know?

- *Discover:* God is more powerful than the most powerful army. He will protect us when he knows that is best.

- *Apply:* When was the last time you were afraid of something? Did you think no one could help you? God can! Remember that the next time you are afraid.

- *What's next?* An entire army suddenly becomes blind. Read 2 Kings 6:18-23. ■

The Blind Army

An army came to kill Elisha. Elisha prayed to God for help. Read on to see what God did.

¹⁸The Syrian army advanced upon them. But Elisha prayed, "Lord, please make them blind." And he did.

¹⁹Then Elisha went out to them. He told them, "You've come the wrong way! This isn't the right city! Follow me and I will take you to the man you're looking for." And he led them to Samaria!

²⁰As soon as they got there Elisha prayed. He said, "Lord, now open their eyes. Let them see." And the Lord did. They saw that they were in Samaria, the capital city of Israel!

²¹The king of Israel saw them there. So he shouted to Elisha, "Oh, sir! Shall I kill them? Shall I kill them?"

²²"Of course not!" Elisha told him. "Do we kill prisoners of war? Give them food and drink and send them home again."

²³So the king made a great feast for them. Then he sent them home to their king. After that the Syrian raiders stayed away from the land of Israel for a while.

- *Remember:* What did Elisha ask God to do? Did he? (6:18) How did Elisha capture the whole army? (6:19-20) How was Elisha kind to these soldiers? (6:21-23) How did this bring peace for a while?

(6:23) Which helped bring peace more, fighting or showing kindness?

• *Discover:* You won't always win by fighting. Sometimes you win by being kind to your enemies.

• *Apply:* Read Matthew 5:43-48. What did Jesus say about being kind to enemies? The next time you want to get even with someone, don't do it. Be kind instead. See what happens.

• *What's next?* Four sick people keep a whole city from starving. Read 2 Kings 6:24–7:20. ■

Four Lepers Visit an Enemy Camp

The Syrian army was camped around Israel's capital city, Samaria. The people of Samaria could not get out to find food. They were starving. Suddenly one day four lepers helped the whole city have plenty of food. Here's how they did it.

²⁴Later, however, King Ben-hadad of Syria called out his whole army. Then he went and besieged Samaria. ²⁵As a result there was a great famine in the city. After a while even a donkey's head sold for $50! And a pint of dove's dung brought three dollars!

²⁶⁻³⁰One day the king of Israel was walking along the wall of the city. And a woman called to him, "My lord the king! Help me!"

"If the Lord doesn't help you, what can I do?" he said. "I have neither food nor wine to give you. However, what's the problem?"

She replied, "This woman said we should eat my son one day and her son the next. So we boiled my son and ate him. The next day I said, 'Kill your son. That way we can eat him.' But she hid him."

When the king heard this he tore his clothes. The people saw through the rip he had torn. And he was wearing a robe made of sackcloth next to his skin.

³¹"May God kill me if I don't kill Elisha this very day," the king said.

³²Elisha was sitting in his house. He was meeting with the elders of Israel. At that time, the king sent a messenger to call him. But before the messenger got there Elisha spoke to the elders. He said, "This murderer has sent a man to kill me. When he gets here, shut the door.

Keep him out. For his master will soon follow him."

³³While Elisha was still saying this, the messenger got there. And the king came right after him.

"The Lord has caused this mess," the king stormed. "Why should I expect any help from him?"

7 Elisha replied, "This is what the Lord says! By this time tomorrow two gallons of flour will be sold for a dollar! Four gallons of barley grain will be sold for the same!"

²The officer helping the king said, "That could never happen! It couldn't happen if the Lord made windows in the sky!"

But Elisha replied, "You will see it happen. But you won't be able to buy any of it!"

³Now there were four lepers sitting outside the city gates.

"Why sit here until we die?" they asked each other. ⁴"We'll starve if we stay here. And we'll starve if we go back into the city. So we might as well go out to the Syrian camp. If they let us live, so much the better. But if they kill us, we would have died anyway."

⁵So that evening they went out to the camp of the Syrians. But there was no one there! ⁶The Lord had made the whole Syrian army hear the noises of a great army. They had heard the clatter of speeding chariots. They had also

heard a loud galloping of horses. "The king of Israel has hired the Hittites and Egyptians to attack us," they cried out. ⁷So they panicked and ran into the night. They left their tents, horses, donkeys, and everything else.

⁸So the lepers got to the empty camp. And they went into one tent after another. They ate food and drank wine. They took silver, gold, and clothes and hid them. ⁹Finally they said to each other, "This isn't right. This is great news, and we aren't sharing it with anyone! Even if we wait until morning, some bad thing will happen to us. Come on! Let's go back and tell the people at the palace!"

¹⁰So they went back to the city. They told the watchmen they had gone out to the Syrian camp. And they told them that no one was there! The horses and donkeys were tied. The tents were all in order. But there was not a soul around. ¹¹Then the watchmen shouted the news to those in the palace.

¹²The king got out of bed and spoke to his officers. "I know what has happened," he said. "The Syrians know we are starving. So they have left their camp and have hidden in the fields. They think we will be tricked into leaving the city. Then they will attack us and get in. And they will make us their slaves."

¹³One of his officers replied, "We'd better send out scouts to see. Let them take five of the horses. Something might happen to the animals. But it won't be a great loss. If they stay here, they will die with the rest of us anyway!"

¹⁴Four chariot-horses were found. And the king sent out two chariot drivers. They went to see where the Syrians had gone. ¹⁵They followed the Syrian army all the way to the Jordan River. They found a trail of clothing and equipment all the way there. It was thrown away by the Syrians in their hurry to get away. The scouts went back and told the king. ¹⁶And the people of Samaria rushed out. They plundered the camp of the Syrians. So it was true that two gallons of flour sold that day for one dollar! And four gallons of barley sold for the

same! It happened just as the Lord said it would!

¹⁷The king chose his special helper to control the traffic at the gate. But he was knocked down and trampled. He was killed as the people rushed out. The day before, Elisha had said this would happen. He had said it when the king came to arrest him. ¹⁸And the prophet had told the king that flour and barley would be cheap the next day.

¹⁹The king's officer had replied, "That could never happen! It couldn't happen even if the Lord opened the windows of heaven!"

And the prophet had said, "You will see it happen. But you won't be able to buy any of it!"

²⁰And he couldn't. For the people trampled him to death at the gate!

- *Remember:* How did the Syrian king bring a famine to Samaria? (6:24-25) What kind of food were people eating? (6:25-30) The king was angry at God. How did he want to hurt God? (6:31-33) Who trusted God for help? (7:1-12) Who didn't? (6:33; 7:1-2) Who was right? How did four lepers help the whole city get that food? (7:3-10) How did God chase the Syrian army away? (7:6) Elisha said the city would have plenty of food. Could anyone think that God would give them food this way?

- *Discover:* God takes care of us in unusual ways.

- *Apply:* Do you ever worry about something? Do you ever wonder how God could possibly help you get what you need? He can! But he will do it his way.

- *What's next?* A little boy becomes king. How could that happen? Read 2 Kings 11. ■

A Woman Gets Her Land Back

8 Elisha had warned the woman whose son he had brought back to life. "Take your family and move to some other country," he had said. "For the Lord has called down a famine on Israel. And it will last for seven years."

²So the woman took her family. She went to live in the land of the Philistines for seven years. ³After the famine ended,

she went back to the land of Israel. And she went to see the king about getting back her house and land. ⁴Just as she came in, the king was talking with Gehazi, Elisha's servant. He was saying, "Tell me some stories of the great things Elisha has done." ⁵And Gehazi was telling the king about the time when Elisha brought a little boy back to life. At that very moment, the mother of the boy walked in!

"Oh, sir!" Gehazi exclaimed. "Here is the woman now! And this is her son! He is the very one Elisha brought back to life!"

⁶"Is this true?" the king asked her. And she told him that it was. So he sent one of his officials with her. He was to see that she was given all she had owned. He also saw that she got the value of the crops harvested while she was gone.

Hazael Commits Murder

⁷After that Elisha went to Damascus, the capital of Syria. King Ben-hadad was there and he was sick. Someone told the king that the prophet had come.

8-9The king heard the news. So he said to Hazael, "Take a gift to the man of God. Tell him to ask the Lord whether I will get well again."

So Hazael took 40 camel-loads of the best produce of the land. He brought them as gifts for Elisha. He said to him, "I have come for your son Ben-hadad, the king of Syria. He wants to know if he will get better."

10And Elisha replied, "Tell him, 'Yes.' But the Lord has shown me that he will surely die!"

11Elisha stared at Hazael until he became ashamed. Then Elisha started crying.

12"What's the matter, sir?" Hazael asked him.

Elisha replied, "I know the bad things you will do to the people of Israel. You will burn their forts! You will kill the young men! You will throw their babies against the rocks! And you will rip open the bellies of pregnant women!"

13"Am I a dog?" Hazael asked him. "I would *never* do that sort of thing!"

But Elisha replied, "The Lord has shown me that you will be king of Syria."

14Then Hazael went back to the king. The king asked him, "What did he tell you?"

And Hazael replied, "He told me that you would get better."

15But the next day Hazael took a blanket. He dipped it in water. And he held it over the king's face until he died. And Hazael became king instead.

Two Evil Kings for Judah

16King Jehoram became the king of Judah. He was the son of King Jehoshaphat. He began his reign during the fifth year of King Joram's reign in Israel. Joram was the son of Ahab. 17Jehoram was 32 years old when he became king of Judah. And he ruled in Jerusalem for eight years. 18But he was as wicked as Ahab and the other kings of Israel. He even married one of Ahab's daughters. 19But even then God did not destroy Judah. This was because God had made a promise to his servant David. He promised that he would watch over and guide David's family. He promised he would not destroy Judah.

20During Jehoram's reign, the people in Edom broke from Judah's rule. They chose their own king. 21King Jehoram tried to stop them, but he failed. He crossed the Jordan River and attacked the city of Zair. But he was quickly surrounded by the army of Edom. Under cover of night he broke through their ranks. But his army left him and ran. 22So Edom has been free from Judah's rule to this day. Libnah also broke from Israel's rule at that time.

23The rest of the history of King Jehoram is written in *The Annals of the Kings of Judah.* 24-25He died and was buried in the royal cemetery. This is in the City of David, the old section of Jerusalem.

Then his son Ahaziah became the new king of Judah. He became king in the 12th year of King Joram's reign in Israel. Joram of Israel was the son of Ahab. 26Ahaziah was 22 years old when he began to rule. But he reigned only one year in Jerusalem. His mother was Athaliah. She was the granddaughter of King Omri of Israel. 27He was a bad king, just as all of King Ahab's family was. For he was related to Ahab by marriage.

28Ahaziah joined King Joram of Israel, the son of Ahab, at Ramoth-gilead. They made war there against Hazael, the king of Syria. King Joram was wounded in the battle. 29So he went to Jezreel to rest and get better from his wounds. While he was there, King Ahaziah of Judah came to visit him. Ahaziah was the son of Jehoram of Judah.

Jehu Will Be King

9Meanwhile Elisha had called one of the young prophets.

"Get ready to go to Ramoth-gilead," he told him. "Take this bottle of oil with you. 2Find Jehu. He is the son of Jehoshaphat, the son of Nimshi. Call him into a private room away from his friends. 3Pour the oil over his head. Tell him that the Lord has chosen him to be the king of Israel. Then run for your life!"

4So the young prophet did as he was told. He went to Ramoth-gilead. 5And he found Jehu sitting with the other army officers.

"I have a message for you, sir," he said.

"For which one of us?" Jehu asked.

"For you," he replied.

⁶So Jehu left the others and went into the house. The young man poured the oil over his head. And he said, "The Lord God of Israel says, 'I anoint you king of the Lord's people, Israel. ⁷You are to destroy the family of Ahab. You will avenge the murder of my prophets. You will avenge all my other people who were killed by Jezebel. ⁸The whole family of Ahab must be wiped out. Every male must die, no matter who. ⁹I will destroy the family of Ahab. They will be destroyed like the family of Jeroboam, the son of Nebat. I will destroy them as I destroyed the family of Baasha, the son of Ahijah. ¹⁰Dogs shall eat Ahab's wife Jezebel at Jezreel. And no one will bury her.'"

Then he opened the door and ran.

¹¹Jehu went back to his friends. And one of them asked him, "What did that crazy man want? Is everything all right?"

"You know very well who he was and what he wanted," Jehu replied.

¹²"No, we don't," they said. "Tell us."

So he told them what the man had said. He told them that he had been anointed king of Israel!

¹³They quickly carpeted the bare steps with their coats. And they blew a trumpet, shouting, "Jehu is king!"

Jehu Kills Joram and Ahaziah

¹⁴That is how Jehu turned against King Joram. Jehu was the son of Jehoshaphat, the son of Nimshi. King Joram had been with the army at Ramoth-gilead. He was defending Israel against the forces of King Hazael of Syria. ¹⁵But he had gone to Jezreel to let his wounds heal.

"You want me to be king," Jehu said to the men who were with him. "So don't let anyone go to Jezreel. Don't let anyone tell the king what we have done."

¹⁶Then Jehu jumped into a chariot. He rode to Jezreel himself to find King Joram. He was lying there wounded. King Ahaziah of Judah was there too. For he had gone to visit him. ¹⁷The watchman on the Tower of Jezreel saw Jehu and his company coming. He shouted, "Someone is coming."

"Send out a rider. Find out if he is friend or foe," King Joram shouted back. ¹⁸So a soldier rode out to meet Jehu.

Messengers

2 KINGS 9:17-19

Today the phone may ring. A friend has some news for you. She is a messenger. She can give you her message without leaving her room. We send messages today by computer, fax machine, telephone, television, radio, and many other ways. People in Bible times had none of these. They had nothing but people to take a message. So a messenger ran, or rode a camel or donkey, with the message. Ordinary people could not afford a messenger. Only kings or other rich people could afford to send someone. The next time you make a phone call or send a letter, remember Bible-time messengers. How would you like to run to another state with your message? God has called us to be his messengers. We have good news about Jesus. When we tell someone what Jesus can do for him, we take God's message to that person. You can be God's messenger! You can take the best news in the world to someone else.

"The king wants to know if you are friend or foe," he demanded. "Do you come in peace?"

Jehu replied, "What do you know about peace? Get behind me!"

The watchman called out to the king. He told him that the messenger had met them but was not coming back. ¹⁹So the king sent out a second rider. He rode up to them. He demanded in the name of the king to know if they were friends or not.

Jehu answered, "What do you know about friends? Get behind me!"

²⁰"He isn't coming back either!" the watchman exclaimed. "It must be Jehu, for he is driving so fast."

²¹"Quick! Get my chariot ready!" King Joram commanded.

Then he and King Ahaziah of Judah rode out to meet Jehu. They met him at the field of Naboth. ²²There King Joram demanded, "Do you come as a friend, Jehu?"

Jehu replied, "How can there be friendship? For the bad things your mother Jezebel did are all around us!"

²³Then King Joram pulled the chariot-horses around and fled. He shouted to King Ahaziah, "There is treachery, Ahaziah! Treason!"

²⁴Then Jehu drew his bow with his full strength. And he shot Joram between the shoulders. The arrow hit his heart and he sank down dead in his chariot.

²⁵Jehu said to Bidkar, his helper, "Throw him into the field of Naboth. Long ago you and I were riding along behind his father Ahab. And the Lord told me that this would happen. ²⁶The Lord said, 'I will repay him here on Naboth's land. I will pay him back for the murder of Naboth and his sons.' So throw him out on Naboth's field, just as the Lord said."

²⁷Meanwhile, King Ahaziah of Judah had fled along the road to Beth-haggan. Jehu rode after him, shouting, "Shoot him too."

So they shot him in his chariot. He was hit at the place where the road climbs to Gur, near Ibleam. He was able to go on as far as Megiddo, but died there. ²⁸His men took him by chariot to Jerusalem. There they buried him in the royal cemetery. ²⁹Ahaziah's reign over Judah had begun in the 12th year of the reign of King Joram of Israel.

Wicked Queen Jezebel's Terrible Death

³⁰Jezebel heard that Jehu had come to Jezreel. So she painted her eyelids and fixed her hair and sat at a window. ³¹Jehu entered the gate of the palace. And she shouted at him, "How are you today, you murderer! You son of a Zimri who murdered his master!"

³²He looked up and saw her at the window. He shouted, "Who is on my side?" And two or three servants looked out at him.

³³"Throw her down!" he yelled.

So they threw her out the window. Her blood spattered against the wall and on the horses. And she was trampled by the horses' hoofs.

³⁴Then Jehu went into the palace for lunch. After he ate, he said, "Someone go and bury this cursed woman. For she is the daughter of a king."

³⁵So they went out to bury her. But they found only her skull, her feet, and her hands.

³⁶They went back and told him. He said, "That is just what the Lord said would happen. He told Elijah the prophet that dogs would eat her flesh. ³⁷He said that her body would be scattered like dung upon the field. And he said no one would be able to tell whose body it was."

Jehu Kills Ahab's Family

10 Then Jehu wrote a letter to the city council of Samaria. He also wrote to those who guarded Ahab's 70 sons. All of them were living in Samaria.

²⁻³"When you get this letter, choose the best of Ahab's sons. Make him your king. Then get ready to fight for his throne. For you have chariots and horses. And you have a walled city and an armory."

⁴But they were too afraid to do it. "Two kings couldn't stand against this man! What can we do?" they said.

5So the manager of the palace and the city manager met with the city council. They also met with the men who guarded Ahab's sons. They sent him this message:

"Jehu, we are your servants. We will do anything you tell us to. We have decided that you should be our king. You will be king instead of one of Ahab's sons."

6Jehu sent them this message: "Maybe you are on my side. Perhaps you plan to obey me. If so, bring the heads of your master's sons to me at Jezreel. Come at about this time tomorrow."

These 70 sons of King Ahab had been living with the chief men of the city. They had been raised in their homes since childhood. 7After getting the letter, all 70 of Ahab's sons were killed. Their heads were packed into baskets and sent to Jehu at Jezreel. 8A messenger told Jehu that the heads of the king's sons had come. So Jehu told them to put them in two piles at the city gate. They were to be left there until the next morning.

9-10In the morning he went out. And he spoke to the crowd that had gathered around them. "You aren't to blame," he told them. "I turned against my master and killed him. But I didn't kill his sons! The Lord has done that. For everything he says comes true. He spoke through his servant Elijah. He said this would happen to Ahab's family."

11Jehu then killed all the rest of Ahab's family in Jezreel. He also killed all his officials, friends, and chaplains. Finally, no one was left who had been close to him in any way. 12Then he set out for Samaria. He stayed that night at a shepherd's inn along the way. 13While he was there he met the brothers of King Ahaziah of Judah.

"Who are you?" he asked them.

And they replied, "We are brothers of King Ahaziah. We are going to Samaria. We want to see the sons of King Ahab and the Queen Mother, Jezebel."

14"Grab them!" Jehu shouted to his men. And he took them out to the well. There he killed all 42 of them.

15As he left the inn, he met Jehonadab, the son of Rechab. He was coming to meet him. After they had greeted each other, Jehu spoke to him. "Are you as loyal to me as I am to you?" he asked.

"Yes," Jehonadab replied.

"Then give me your hand," Jehu said. And he helped him into the royal chariot.

16"Now come along with me," Jehu said. "See how much I have done for the Lord." So Jehonadab rode along with him. 17When he got to Samaria he killed all Ahab's friends and relatives. He did just as Elijah, speaking for the Lord, had promised.

Jehu Kills the Priests of Baal

Then Jehu called a meeting of all the people of the city. He said to them, "Ahab hardly worshiped Baal at all. I am going to worship him much more! 18-19Call all the prophets and priests of Baal. Call together all his worshipers. See to it that every one of them comes. For we worshipers of Baal are going to have a great feast. Then we will celebrate and praise him. Any of Baal's worshipers who don't come will be killed."

But Jehu's plan was to kill them. 20-21He sent messengers throughout all Israel calling those who worshiped Baal. They all came and filled the temple of Baal from one end to the other. 22He spoke to the man in charge of the robes. "Be sure that every worshiper wears one of the special robes," he said.

23Then Jehu and Jehonadab, son of Rechab, went into the temple. They went there to speak to the people. "Check to be sure that only those who worship Baal are here," they said. "Don't let anyone in who worships the Lord!"

24The priests of Baal began offering sacrifices and burnt offerings. At this time, Jehu surrounded the building with 80 of his men. He told them, "Don't let anyone get away! If you do, you'll pay with your own life!"

25When he had finished sacrificing the burnt offering, Jehu went out. He said to his men, "Go in and kill all of them. Don't let a single one get away."

So they killed them all and dragged

their bodies outside. Then Jehu's men went into the inner temple. ²⁶They pulled out the pillar used for the worship of Baal. Then they burned it. ²⁷They wrecked the temple and made it into a public toilet. It is still used for this today. ²⁸Thus Jehu destroyed every trace of Baal from Israel. ²⁹But he didn't destroy the gold calves at Bethel and Dan. This was the great sin of Jeroboam, the son of Nebat. For it caused all the people of Israel to sin.

³⁰After this the Lord said to Jehu, "You have done well. You have followed my orders to destroy the family of Ahab. Because of this I will reward you. I will make your son, your grandson, and your great-grandson kings of Israel."

³¹But Jehu didn't follow the Lord God of Israel with all his heart. He still worshiped Jeroboam's gold calves. They had been the cause of great sin in Israel.

³²⁻³³At about that time the Lord began to cut down the size of Israel. King Hazael took some of the country east of the Jordan River. He took all of Gilead, Gad, and Reuben. He took parts of Manasseh. This land started at the Aroer River in the valley of the Arnon. It went from there to Gilead and Bashan.

³⁴The rest of Jehu's deeds are written in *The Annals of the Kings of Israel.* ³⁵When Jehu died, he was buried in Samaria. His son Jehoahaz became the new king. ³⁶Jehu ruled as king of Israel for 28 years. His capital was Samaria.

Joash Becomes King

Who would want a little boy to be king? Many of the people did. That's why he became king. It all happened in one day. This is how it happened.

11 Now Athaliah, the mother of King Ahaziah of Judah, heard that her son was dead. So she killed all his children. ²⁻³His year-old son Joash was the only one who got away. Joash was saved by his Aunt Jehosheba. She was King Ahaziah's sister and a daughter of King Jehoram. She stole him away from among the rest of the king's children. They were all about to be killed. She hid him and his nurse in a storeroom of the Temple. They lived there for six years while Athaliah ruled as queen.

⁴In the seventh year, Jehoiada the priest called the officers of the palace guard. He also called the queen's bodyguard. He met them in the Temple. He made them promise to keep a secret. And he showed them the king's son.

⁵Then he gave them their orders. "A third of those on duty on the Sabbath are to guard the palace," he said. ⁶⁻⁸"The other two-thirds shall stand guard at the Temple. Surround the king, weapons in hand. Kill anyone who tries to break through. Stay with the king at all times."

⁹So the officers did what Jehoiada told them to do. They brought to Jehoiada the men who were going off duty on the Sabbath. And those who were coming on duty then came too. ¹⁰He gave them spears and shields from the Temple's supply. These weapons had belonged to King David. ¹¹The guards stood across the front of the sanctuary. They stood with their weapons ready. They surrounded the altar, which was near Joash's hiding place.

¹²Then Jehoiada brought out the young prince. He put the crown on his head. He gave him a copy of the Ten Commandments. And he anointed him as king. Then everyone clapped and shouted, "Long live the king!"

¹³⁻¹⁴Athaliah heard the noise and she ran into the Temple. She saw the new king standing beside the pillar. It was the custom to stand there when being crowned king. He was surrounded by

her bodyguard and many trumpeters. Everyone was full of joy and they were blowing trumpets.

"Treason! Treason!" she screamed. And she began to tear her clothes.

¹⁵"Get her out of here," shouted Jehoiada to the officers of the guard. "Don't kill her here in the Temple. But kill anyone who tries to save her."

¹⁶So they took her to the palace stables and killed her there.

¹⁷Jehoiada made a treaty between the Lord, the king, and the people. They agreed that they would be the Lord's people. He also made a contract between the king and the people. ¹⁸Everyone went over to the temple of Baal and tore it down. They broke down the altars and images. And they killed Mattan, the priest of Baal, in front of the altar. And Jehoiada set guards at the Temple of the Lord. ¹⁹Then he led the king from the Temple. They went past the guardhouse and into the palace. The officers and the guards and all the people went with the new king. And he sat upon the king's throne.

²⁰So everyone was happy. And the city became peaceful after Athaliah's death.

²¹Joash was seven years old when he became king.

- *Remember:* Who did Athaliah murder? (11:1) But which grandson was not murdered? Why not? (11:2-3) How did the priest help to make little Joash the king? (11:4-12) How did Jehoiada the priest help the people turn to God? (11:17) How old was Joash when he became king? (11:21) What kind of person was Athaliah? What kind of person was Jehoiada?

- *Discover:* Wicked people will be punished. Athaliah was punished for being so wicked.

- *Apply:* Every day the newspapers tell about wicked people who do wicked things. They will be punished. Be sure you don't do something that God must punish you for.

- *What's next?* A king is punished. Who would dare do that? Read 2 Chronicles 26. ■

Joash Rules Judah

12 Joash became king of Judah seven years after Jehu became king of Israel. He ruled in Jerusalem for 40 years. His mother was Zibiah, from Beersheba. ²As long as the High Priest Jehoiada taught him, Joash did what was right. ³Yet even so he didn't destroy the shrines on the hills. And the people still sacrificed and burned incense there.

4-5One day King Joash said to Jehoiada, "The Temple building needs to be fixed. If anyone brings a gift to the Lord, use it to fix the Temple. This includes what is brought for regular taxes. It also includes what is brought for special gifts."

Godly teachers help us please God

As long as the High Priest Jehoiada taught him, Joash did what was right.

2 Kings 12:2

6But in the 23rd year of his reign the Temple was still not fixed. 7So Joash called Jehoiada and the other priests. He asked them, "Why haven't you done anything about the Temple? Now don't use any more money for your own needs. From now on it must all be spent on fixing the Temple."

8So the priests agreed to set up a special fund to fix the Temple. The money in it would not go through their hands. That way, it couldn't be used to care for their personal needs. 9Jehoiada the priest made a hole in the lid of a large chest. He put the chest to the right of the altar at the Temple door. The doorkeepers put all the people's gifts into it. 10When the chest became full, the king's secretary and the High Priest counted it. They put it into bags. 11-12Then they gave it to the building managers. They used it to pay the carpenters, masons, and quarrymen. They paid timber dealers and stone traders with it. They also used it to buy the other things needed to fix the Lord's Temple. 13-14It was not used to buy silver cups, gold snuffers, bowls, or trumpets. It was only used to fix the building. 15They did not make the building managers tell how the money was spent. This was because they were honest and faithful men. 16Some of the money was given for guilt and sin offerings. This was given to the priests for their own use. It was not put into the chest.

17About this time, King Hazael of Syria went to war against Gath and took it. Then he moved on toward Jerusalem to attack it. 18King Joash took all the holy objects that his ancestors had put in the Temple. This included all the things given by Jehoshaphat, Jehoram, and Ahaziah, the kings of Judah. It also included the things he himself had given. He took all the gold in the Temple and the palace. And he sent it to Hazael. So Hazael called off the attack.

19The rest of the history of Joash is recorded in *The Annals of the Kings of Judah.* 20But his officers turned against him. They killed him in his royal house at Millo on the road to Silla. 21The killers were Jozachar and Jehozabad. Jozachar was the son of Shimeath. Jehozabad was the son of Shomer. Both of them were Joash's trusted servants. He was buried in the royal cemetery in Jerusalem. And his son Amaziah became the new king.

Jehoahaz Rules Israel

13Jehoahaz became the king of Israel. He was the son of Jehu. He began his reign during the 23rd year of King Joash's reign in Judah. He reigned over Israel for 17 years. 2But he was a bad king. He followed the wicked paths of Jeroboam, who had caused Israel to sin. 3So the Lord was very angry with Israel. He let King Hazael of Syria and his son Ben-hadad conquer them again and again.

4But Jehoahaz prayed for the Lord's help. And the Lord listened to him. For the Lord saw how badly the king of Syria was treating Israel. 5So the Lord chose leaders among the Israelites. They saved them from the rule of the Syrians. Then Israel lived in peace again as they had in former days. 6But they kept sinning. They kept following the evil ways of Jeroboam. And they kept worshiping the goddess Asherah at Samaria. 7All that was left of Jehoahaz's army were 50 horsemen, 10 chariots, and 10,000 soldiers. This was because the king of Syria had killed the others. He had stepped on them like dust under his feet.

8The rest of the history of Jehoahaz is recorded in *The Annals of the Kings of Israel.*

Jehoash Rules Israel

9-10Jehoahaz died and was buried in Samaria. Then his son Jehoash ruled in Samaria in his place. He was king for 16 years. He came to the throne in the 37th year of King Joash of Judah. 11But he was a bad man. Like Jeroboam, he tempted the people to worship idols. And he led them into sin. 12The rest of the history of Jehoash is written in *The Annals of the Kings of Israel.* This includes his wars against King Amaziah of Judah. 13Jehoash died and was buried in Samaria with the other kings of Israel. Jeroboam II became the new king.

The Death of a Powerful Prophet

14When Elisha was in his last illness, King Jehoash came to him. He was sad and cried over him.

"My father! My father! You are the strength of Israel!" he cried.

15Elisha told him, "Get a bow and some arrows." So Jehoash got them.

16-17"Open that eastern window," he ordered.

Then he told the king to put his hand upon the bow. And Elisha laid his own hands upon the king's hands.

"Shoot!" Elisha commanded. So he did.

Then Elisha said, "This is the Lord's arrow! It is full of victory over Syria! For you will conquer the Syrians at Aphek. 18Now pick up the other arrows. Then hit them against the floor."

So the king picked them up and hit the floor three times. 19But the prophet was angry with him. "You should have hit the floor five or six times!" he said. "If you had, you would have completely destroyed Syria. But now you will beat them only three times."

20-21So Elisha died and was buried.

In those days, groups of Moabite bandits invaded the land each spring. One day, some men were burying a friend. But they saw a group of these bandits. So they quickly threw his body into the tomb of Elisha. The body touched Elisha's bones. And suddenly the dead man came alive! He jumped to his feet!

22King Hazael of Syria had troubled Israel during the whole reign of King Jehoahaz. 23But the Lord was kind to the people of Israel. They were not totally wiped out. For God had pity on them. He helped them because of his contract with Abraham, Isaac, and Jacob. 24Then King Hazael of Syria died. And his son Ben-hadad became king in his place.

25King Jehoash of Israel had three major victories against the Syrians. In those battles he took back cities that his father had lost to Ben-hadad.

Amaziah Rules Judah

14 Amaziah, the son of Joash, became king of Judah. He became king during the second year of the reign of King Joash of Israel. 2Amaziah was 25 years old at the time. And he ruled in Jerusalem for 29 years. His mother was Jehoaddin, a native of Jerusalem. 3He was a good king in the Lord's sight. But he was not quite like his ancestor David. But he was as good a king as his father Joash. 4However, he didn't destroy the shrines on the hills. So the people still sacrificed and burned incense there.

???????????????????????????????
Which dead man brought another dead man back to life?
(Read 13:14-21 for the answer.)
???????????????????????????????

5Amaziah gained firm control of the kingdom of Judah. Then he killed the men who had murdered his father. 6But he didn't kill their children. For the Lord had made a command in the law of Moses. He had said that fathers shall not be killed for their children. And children shall not be killed for the sins of their fathers. Everyone must pay for his own sins. 7Once Amaziah killed 10,000 Edomites in Salt Valley. He also conquered Sela and changed its name to Joktheel. It is still called this to this day.

8One day he sent a message to King Joash of Israel. Joash of Israel was the son of Jehoahaz and the grandson of Jehu. He told him to call out his army. Then he dared him to come and fight.

9But King Joash replied with a story. He said, "The thistle of Lebanon made a demand of the mighty cedar tree.

'Give your daughter to be a wife for my son,' the thistle said. But just then a wild animal passed by. He stepped on the thistle and crushed it into the ground! ¹⁰You have destroyed Edom and are very proud about it. But I advise you to be content with your glory and stay home! Why bring trouble for both yourself and Judah?"

¹¹But Amaziah would not listen. So King Joash of Israel called out his army. The battle began at Beth-shemesh. This was one of the cities of Judah. ¹²Judah was beaten and the army ran for home. ¹³King Amaziah was captured. Then the army of Israel marched on Jerusalem. They broke down its wall from the Gate of Ephraim to the Corner Gate. This was about 600 feet in length. ¹⁴King Joash took many hostages. He took all the gold and silver from the Temple and palace treasuries. He also took the gold cups. Then he went back to Samaria.

¹⁵The rest of the history of Joash is recorded in *The Annals of the Kings of Israel.* This includes his war with King Amaziah of Judah. ¹⁶When Joash died, he was buried in Samaria with the other kings of Israel. And his son Jeroboam became the new king.

¹⁷Amaziah lived 15 years longer than Joash of Israel. ¹⁸The rest of his deeds are recorded in *The Annals of the Kings of Judah.* ¹⁹There was a plot against his life in Jerusalem. So he ran to Lachish. But his enemies sent men to kill him there. ²⁰His body was brought back to Jerusalem on horses. And he was buried in the royal cemetery. This was in the City of David section of Jerusalem.

²¹Then his son Uzziah became the new king at the age of 16. ²²After his father's death, he built Elath. And he brought it back under Judah's rule.

Jeroboam II Rules Israel

²³Meanwhile, over in Israel, Jeroboam II had become king. He began his reign during the 15th year of King Amaziah's reign in Judah. Jeroboam's reign lasted 41 years. ²⁴But he was as evil as Jeroboam I, the son of Nebat. For he led Israel into the sin of worshiping idols. ²⁵Jeroboam II took back the lost land of Israel between Hamath and the Dead Sea. He did just as the Lord God of Israel had promised. The Lord had spoken through Jonah, the son of Amittai. He was the prophet from Gathhepher. ²⁶The Lord had seen the suffering of Israel. She had no one to help her. ²⁷And he had not yet promised he would blot out the name of Israel. So he used King Jeroboam II to save her.

²⁸The rest of Jeroboam's biography is recorded in *The Annals of the Kings of Israel.* This includes his deeds, his great power, and his wars. It recounts how he won back Damascus and Hamath. These cities had been taken by Judah. ²⁹When Jeroboam II died, he was buried with the other kings of Israel. And his son Zechariah became the new king of Israel.

Uzziah Rules Judah

15Uzziah, the son of Amaziah, became king of Judah. This was during King Jeroboam's 27th year. Uzziah was 16 years old at the beginning of his reign. He ruled for 52 years in Jerusalem. His mother's name was Jecoliah. She was from Jerusalem. ³Uzziah was a good king. He pleased the Lord just as his father Amaziah had. ⁴But like the kings before him, he didn't destroy the shrines on the hills. So the people kept sacrificing and burning incense there. ⁵The Lord struck Uzziah with leprosy. It lasted until the day he died. So he lived in a house by himself. During this time, his son Jotham was the acting king. ⁶The rest of the history of Uzziah is recorded in *The Annals of the Kings of Judah.* ⁷When Uzziah died, he was buried in the City of David. And his son Jotham became king after him.

Zechariah Rules Israel

⁸Zechariah, the son of Jeroboam, became king of Israel. He ruled for six months in Samaria. He began his reign in the 38th year of King Uzziah of Judah. ⁹But Zechariah was a bad king in the Lord's sight, just like his ancestors. Like Jeroboam I, the son of Nebat, he tempted Israel to worship idols. ¹⁰Then Shallum, the son of Jabesh, turned against him. He killed him at Ibleam and took the crown himself. ¹¹The rest of the

history of Zechariah's reign is found in *The Annals of the Kings of Israel.* [12]So the Lord's word to Jehu came true. He had promised that Jehu's son, grandson, and great-grandson would be kings of Israel.

Shallum Rules Israel

[13]So Shallum, the son of Jabesh, became king of Israel. He ruled for one month in Samaria. He became king in the 39th year of King Uzziah of Judah. [14]A month after Shallum became king, Menahem came to Samaria from Tirzah. Menahem was the son of Gadi. He killed Shallum and took the throne. [15]More about King Shallum and his reign are written in *The Annals of the Kings of Israel.*

[16]Menahem destroyed the city of Tappuah and all the land around it. This was because its people did not accept him as their king. He killed all the people. He even ripped open the women who were going to have babies.

Menahem Rules Israel

[17]So Menahem became the king of Israel. He reigned for 10 years in Samaria. He began his reign during King Uzziah's 39th year as king of Judah. [18]But Menahem was a bad king. He worshiped idols, as King Jeroboam I had done so long before. And he led the people of Israel into great sin. [19-20]Then King Pul of Assyria invaded the land. But King Menahem gave him a gift of $2,000,000. So Pul turned around and went back home. Menahem got this money by taxing the rich people in Israel. He demanded that they each give $2,000 for a special tax. [21]The rest of the history of King Menahem is written in *The Annals of the Kings of Israel.* [22]When he died, his son Pekahiah became the new king.

Pekahiah Rules Israel

[23]So Pekahiah, the son of Menahem, became the king of Israel. He reigned for two years in Samaria. At that time, King Uzziah had been the king of Judah for 50 years. [24]But Pekahiah was a bad king. He supported the idol-worship begun by Jeroboam I, the son of Nebat. Jeroboam had led Israel down that evil trail long before.

[25]Then Pekah, the son of Remaliah, turned against him. Pekah was the general of his army. He took 50 men from Gilead and killed him in the palace at Samaria. Argob and Arieh were also killed in the revolt. So Pekah became the new king. [26]The rest of the history of King Pekahiah is written in *The Annals of the Kings of Israel.*

Pekah Rules Israel

[27]So Pekah, the son of Remaliah, became the king of Israel. He reigned for 20 years in Samaria. At that time, King Uzziah had been the king of Judah for 52 years. [28]Pekah, too, was a bad king. He followed the example of Jeroboam I, the son of Nebat. And he led all of Israel into the sin of worshiping idols. [29]During Pekah's reign, King Tiglath-pileser led an attack against Israel. He took the cities of Ijon, Abel-beth-maacah, Janoah, Kedesh, Hazor, Gilead, Galilee. He took all the land of Naphtali. And he brought the people with him to Assyria as captives. [30]Then Hoshea, the son of Elah, turned against Pekah. He killed him and became king in his place. So Hoshea became the king of Israel. At that time, King Jotham, the son of Uzziah, was the king in Judah. He had been king there for 20 years.

[31]The rest of the history of Pekah's reign is written in *The Annals of the Kings of Israel.*

Jotham Rules Judah

[32-33]Now Jotham, the son of King Uzziah, became the king in Judah. He was 25 years old when he became king. He reigned for 16 years in Jerusalem. His mother's name was Jerusha. She was a daughter of Zadok. When he became king, King Pekah, the son of Remaliah, was the king of Israel. He had been king there for two years. [34-35]Jotham was a good king. Like his father Uzziah, he followed the Lord. But he didn't destroy the shrines on the hills. So the people kept sacrificing and burning incense there. During King Jotham's reign the upper gate of the Temple was built. [36]The rest of Jotham's history is written in *The Annals of the Kings of Judah.* [37]In those

days the Lord caused King Rezin of Syria and King Pekah of Israel to attack Judah. ³⁸When Jotham died he was buried with the other kings of Judah in the royal cemetery. This was in the City of David section of Jerusalem. Then his son Ahaz became the new king.

Ahaz Rules Judah

16 So Ahaz, the son of Jotham, became the King of Judah. He was 20 years old when he began his reign. At that time, King Pekah, son of Remaliah, had been king in Israel for 17 years. Ahaz ruled for 16 years in Jerusalem. ²But he did not follow the Lord as his ancestor David had. ³He was as wicked as the kings of Israel. He even killed his own son! He gave him as a burnt sacrifice to the gods! This was a heathen custom of the nations around Judah. And the Lord destroyed those nations when the people of Israel entered the land. ⁴He also sacrificed and burned incense at the shrines on the hills. And he gave sacrifices at the many altars in the groves of trees.

???????????????????????????????????

Who burned his own son in a fire?

(Read 16:1-4 for the answer.)

???????????????????????????????????

⁵Then the kings of Syria and Israel made war against Ahaz. King Rezin was the king of Syria. King Pekah, the son of Remaliah, was the king of Israel. They besieged Jerusalem, but they did not take it. ⁶But at that time, King Rezin took back the city of Elath for Syria. He drove out the people of Judah and sent Syrians to live there. And they live there to this day. ⁷King Ahaz sent a messenger to King Tiglath-pileser of Assyria. He begged him to help him fight the armies of Syria and Israel. ⁸Ahaz took the silver and gold from the Temple and palace. Then he sent it as a payment to the Assyrian king. ⁹So the Assyrians attacked Damascus, the capital of Syria. They took away the people of the city as captives. And they sent

people from Kir to live there. At that time, King Rezin of Syria was killed.

¹⁰Now King Ahaz went to Damascus to meet with King Tiglath-pileser. While he was there, he saw an altar in a heathen temple. He drew up a plan and made a sketch of this altar. And he sent it back to Uriah the priest. ¹¹⁻¹²Uriah built one just like it by following this plan. It was ready for the king when he got back from Damascus. So Ahaz dedicated it with sacrifices. ¹³The king gave a burnt offering and a grain offering. Then he poured out a drink offering over it. And he sprinkled the blood of peace offerings on it. ¹⁴Then he took the old bronze altar from the front of the Temple. It had stood between the Temple door and the new altar. He put it on the north side of the new altar. ¹⁵He told Uriah the priest to use the new altar. He was to use it for burnt offerings and the evening grain offerings. He was to use it for the king's burnt offerings and grain offerings. And he was to use it for the offerings of the people. This included their drink offerings. The blood from the sacrifices was to be sprinkled over the new altar. So the old altar was used only for asking questions of God.

"The old bronze altar," he said, "will be only for my use."

¹⁶Uriah the priest did as King Ahaz told him. ¹⁷Then the king took the wheeled stands in the Temple apart. He took off their side panels. He took off the bowls they held up. He also took the great tank from the backs of the bronze oxen. He put it on the stone pavement. ¹⁸He also took away the passage he had made between the palace and the Temple. He did this out of respect for the king of Assyria.

¹⁹The rest of the history of the reign of King Ahaz is written in *The Annals of the Kings of Judah.* ²⁰When Ahaz died he was buried in the royal cemetery. It was in the City of David sector of Jerusalem. And his son Hezekiah became the new king.

Israel Is Taken into Captivity

If God said, "Do this," would you do it? If God said, "Don't do that," would you listen and obey? God told Israel, "Obey me" and "Don't worship other gods." That wasn't asking too much, was it? So what did Israel do? They disobeyed God and worshiped other gods. Now what do you think God did?

17 Hoshea, the son of Elah, became the king of Israel. He reigned nine years in Samaria. He became king during the 12th year of King Ahaz of Judah. Hoshea did what the Lord said was wrong. But he was not as bad as some of the other kings of Israel.

³King Shalmaneser of Assyria attacked and defeated King Hoshea. So Israel had to pay heavy yearly taxes to Assyria. ⁴Then Hoshea turned against the king of Assyria. He asked King So of Egypt to help him break free of Assyria's power. But the king of Assyria found out about his plans. Hoshea also did not pay his yearly tribute to Assyria. So the king of Assyria put him in prison for not obeying.

⁵Now the land of Israel was filled with Assyrian troops for three years. They were there to attack Samaria, the capital city of Israel. ⁶Samaria was finally taken in the ninth year of King Hoshea's reign. And the people of Israel were sent off to Assyria. Some were put in colonies in the city of Halah. Others were sent to the banks of the Habor River in Gozan. And others were settled among the cities of the Medes.

⁷This trouble came upon Israel because the people worshiped other gods. They had sinned against the Lord their God. He was the God who had brought them out of their slavery in Egypt. ⁸They had followed the evil customs of the nations around them. They acted just like the people the Lord had thrown out before them. ⁹The people of Israel had also done many wrong things in secret. They had built altars to other gods throughout the land. ¹⁰They had put obelisks and idols on every hill and under every green tree. ¹¹They had burned incense to the gods of the nations around them. They were acting like the people the Lord had pushed out when the Israelites came. So the people of Israel had done many bad things. And the Lord was very angry. ¹²Yes, they worshiped idols. And they did this even when the Lord warned them not to.

¹³Again and again the Lord had sent prophets to warn both Israel and Judah. They had told them to turn from their sinful ways. They had warned them to obey the commands he had given to their ancestors. ¹⁴But Israel wouldn't listen. The people were as stubborn as their ancestors. They refused to believe in the Lord their God. ¹⁵They rejected his laws and the covenant he had made with their ancestors. They refused to listen to all his warnings. In their foolishness they worshiped heathen idols. And they did this even though the Lord had warned them not to. ¹⁶They did not obey the commands of the Lord their God. And they made two calves from melted gold. They made shameful idols. They worshiped Baal and the sun, moon, and stars. ¹⁷They even burned their own sons and daughters to death on the altars of Molech! They spoke with fortune tellers and used magic. They sold themselves to evil. So the Lord was very angry. ¹⁸He swept them from his sight. In the end, only the tribe of Judah was left in the land.

¹⁹But even Judah did not obey the commands of the Lord their God. They walked in the same evil paths as Israel. ²⁰So the Lord rejected all the descendants of Jacob. He punished them by giving them to their enemies to be destroyed. ²¹For Israel split off from the kingdom of David. And they chose Jeroboam I, the son of Nebat, as their king. Then Jeroboam drew Israel away from following the Lord. He made them sin a great sin. ²²The people of Israel never quit doing the bad things that Jeroboam led them into. ²³So the Lord finally swept them away. He did just as all his prophets had warned. Israel was carried

off to the land of Assyria. And they are still there to this day.

Israel Resettled by Foreigners

24And the king of Assyria took groups of people from Babylon, Cuthah, Avva, Hamath, and Sepharvaim. He sent them to the cities of Samaria. They were sent to take the place of the people of Israel.

So the Assyrians took over Samaria and the other cities of Israel. 25But these Assyrian people did not worship the Lord when they first came. So the Lord sent lions among them to kill some of them.

26Then they sent a message to the king of Assyria. "We people in Israel don't know the laws of the god of the land," they said. "He has sent lions among us to destroy us. This is because we have not worshiped him."

27-28So the king of Assyria sent one of the priests from Samaria back to Israel. He sent him to teach the new people there the laws of the god of the land. So one of them went back to Bethel. He taught the people from Babylon how to worship the Lord.

29But these foreigners also worshiped their own gods. They put them in the shrines on the hills near their cities.

30Those from Babylon worshiped idols of their god Succoth-benoth. Those from Cuth worshiped their god Nergal. And the men of Hamath worshiped Ashima. 31The gods Nibhaz and Tartak were worshiped by the Avvites. And the people from Sephar even burned their own children. They burned them on the altars of their gods Adrammelech and Anammelech. 32They also worshiped the Lord. And they chose priests from among themselves. These priests gave sacrifices to the Lord on the hill-

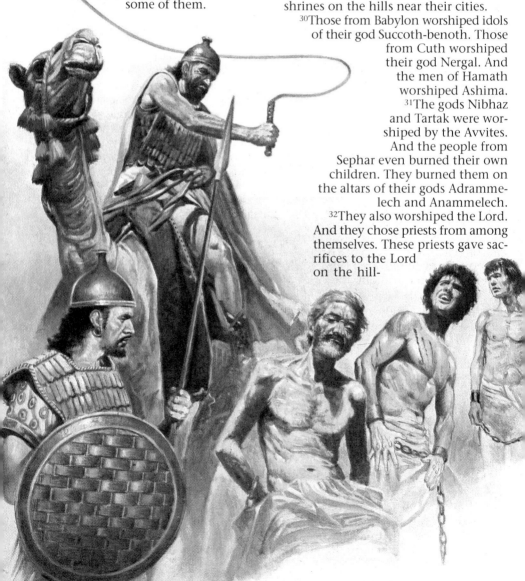

top altars. ³³But they kept following the religious customs of the nations they came from. ³⁴And this is still going on among them today. They follow their old customs. They don't really worship the Lord. And they do not obey the laws he gave to the descendants of Jacob. Jacob's name was later changed to Israel. ³⁵⁻³⁶For the Lord had made a contract with them. They were never to worship or make sacrifices to any heathen gods. They were to worship only the Lord. For he had brought them out of the land of Egypt. And he had saved them with great miracles and power. ³⁷The descendants of Jacob were to obey all of God's laws. And they were *never* to worship other gods.

³⁸For God had said, "You must never forget the covenant I made with you. Never worship other gods. ³⁹You must worship only the Lord. He will save you from all your enemies."

⁴⁰But Israel didn't listen. And the people kept worshiping other gods. ⁴¹So these people from Babylon worshiped the

Lord. But they also worshiped their idols. And to this day their descendants do the same thing.

- *Remember:* Which enemy attacked Israel? (17:3) When Israel rebelled, what did Assyria do? (17:4-6) Why did God punish Israel this way? (17:7-18) Read 17:38, then read Exodus 20:3-6. What did God tell his people to do? What did he warn his people not to do? Do you think they were foolish to disobey God and worship other gods? What would you like to say to these people?

- *Discover:* Don't make anything else more important than God.

- *Apply:* Is God really first in your life? Are you putting anything else ahead of him? Is this really more important than God?

- *What's next?* One angel defeats an entire army. Read Isaiah 36–37. ■

Hezekiah Rules Judah

18 Hezekiah, the son of Ahaz, became the king of Judah. This happened in the third year of Hoshea, the son of Elah, king of Israel. Hezekiah was 25 years old when he became king. He reigned for 29 years in Jerusalem. His mother's name was Abijah. She was the daughter of Zechariah. Hezekiah did what the Lord said was right. He did just as his ancestor David had done. ⁴He got rid of the shrines on the hills. He broke down the obelisks. He knocked down the shameful idols of Asherah. And he broke up the bronze serpent that Moses had made. He did this because the people of Israel had begun to worship it. They were burning incense to it. They did this even though it was just a piece of bronze. ⁵Hezekiah trusted very strongly in the Lord God of Israel. In fact, none of the kings before or after him were as close to God as he was. ⁶For he followed the Lord in everything. He obeyed all of God's commands to Moses. ⁷So the Lord was with him and blessed all he did. Then he turned against the king of Assyria.

And he did not pay tribute any longer. [8]He also conquered the Philistines as far distant as Gaza and its suburbs. He destroyed cities both large and small.

[9]During the fourth year of Hezekiah's reign, king Shalmaneser of Assyria attacked Israel. And he began a siege on the city of Samaria. At this time, King Hoshea of Israel had reigned there for seven years. [10]Three years later Samaria fell. This was during the sixth year of King Hezekiah's reign. It was also the ninth year of the reign of King Hoshea of Israel. [11]At that time, the king of Assyria sent the Israelites to Assyria. He put some of them in the city of Halath. He sent others to places along the Habor River in Gozan. And others he put in the cities of the Medes. [12]This was because they had refused to listen to the Lord their God. They had not done what he had told them to do. Instead, they had forgotten his covenant. They had disobeyed all the laws given to them by Moses the servant of the Lord.

[13]Later, Sennacherib of Assyria captured all the walled cities of Judah. This happened during the 14th year of King Hezekiah's reign. [14]So King Hezekiah sent a message to the king of Assyria at Lachish. "I have done wrong," he said. "I will pay whatever tribute you demand if you will only go away." The king of Assyria then asked for $1,500,000. [15]Hezekiah gave him all the silver stored in the Temple. He also emptied the palace treasury. [16]He even took the gold from the Temple doors. He also took the gold from the doorposts he had covered with gold. He gave it all to the Assyrian king.

The Assyrians Threaten to Conquer Judah

[17]But even then, the king of Assyria sent his field marshal. He also sent his chief treasurer and his chief of staff from Lachish. And these men came with a great army. They camped along the highway beside the field where cloth was bleached. They were near the conduit of the upper pool. [18]They demanded that King Hezekiah come out to speak to them. But instead he sent Eliakim, who was his business manager. He also sent Shebnah, his secretary, and Joah, his royal historian.

[19]Then the Assyrian general sent this message to King Hezekiah. He said, "The great king of Assyria says: 'No one can save you from my power! [20-21]You need more than just promises of help before turning against me. Which of your friends will give you more than words? Egypt? Perhaps you should lean on Egypt. But if you do, she will be like a stick that breaks under your weight! And after breaking, it will pierce your hand! The Egyptian Pharaoh will never help you! [22]And you might say, "We're trusting the Lord to rescue us." But if you do, just remember that he is the one whose hilltop altars you've destroyed. For you make everyone worship at the altar in Jerusalem!' [23]I'll tell you what. Make a bet with my master, the king of Assyria! If you have 2,000 men left who can ride horses, we'll give you the horses! [24]Your army is so small that you are no threat at all. You can't even defeat one of Assyria's least important officers. Even if Egypt gives you horses and chariots, it will do no good. [25]And do you think we have come here on our own? No! The Lord sent us and told us, 'Go and destroy this nation!'"

[26]Then Eliakim, Shebnah, and Joah spoke to them. "Please speak in Aramaic, for we understand it," they said. "Don't use Hebrew, for the people standing on the walls will hear you."

[27]But the Assyrian general replied, "Has my master sent me to speak only to you and to your master? Hasn't he sent me to the people on the walls too? For they are doomed with you to eat their own dung and drink their own urine!"

[28]Then the Assyrian messenger shouted in Hebrew to the people on the wall. "Listen to the great king of Assyria!" he said. [29]"Don't let King Hezekiah fool you. He will never be able to save you from my power. [30]Don't let him fool you into trusting in the Lord to save you. [31-32]Don't listen to King Hezekiah. Surrender! You can live in peace here in your own land. And soon I will take you

to another land just like this one. It will be a land with rich crops, grain, grapes, olive trees, and honey. All of this instead of death! Don't listen to King Hezekiah when he tries to tell you that the Lord will save you. ³³Have the gods of other nations ever saved their people from Assyria? ³⁴What happened to the gods of Hamath, Arpad, Sepharvaim, Hena, and Ivvah? Did they save Samaria? ³⁵What god has ever been able to save any nation from my power? So what makes you think the Lord can save Jerusalem?'"

³⁶But the people on the wall stayed silent. For the king had told them to say nothing. ³⁷Then Hezekiah's messengers went to him with their clothes torn. The first was Eliakim, the son of Hilkiah, who was the business manager. With him were Shebnah, the king's secretary, and Joah, the son of Asaph, the historian. They told him what the Assyrian general had said.

Isaiah Tells of God's Plan to Save Judah

19 King Hezekiah heard their report. Then he tore his clothes and put on sackcloth. And he went into the Temple to pray. ²Then he told Eliakim and Shebnah to dress themselves in sackcloth. He told some of the older priests to do the same. And he sent them to Isaiah the prophet. He was the son of Amoz. So they took him this message:

³"King Hezekiah says, 'This is a day of trouble, insult, and dishonor. It is sad, like when a child is ready to be born, but the mother is too weak to deliver it. ⁴ Yet perhaps the Lord your God has heard the Assyrian general. Maybe he has heard him making fun of the living God. Maybe he will punish him. Oh, pray for the few of us who are left.'"

⁵⁻⁶Isaiah replied, "The Lord says, 'Don't be afraid of the words these Assyrians have spoken against me.' ⁷For the king of Assyria will get bad news from home. And he will decide to go back there. Then the Lord will make sure that he is killed when he gets there."

⁸Then the Assyrian general went back to his king at Libnah. For he had heard that the king had left Lachish. ⁹Soon after this, news reached the king. King Tirhakah of Ethiopia was coming to attack him. He was about to leave to meet the attack. But he sent back this message to King Hezekiah:

¹⁰"Don't be fooled by that god you trust in. Don't believe it when he says that I won't conquer Jerusalem. ¹¹You know what the kings of Assyria have done wherever they have gone. They have completely destroyed everything. Why would you be any different? ¹²Have the gods of the other nations saved them? Where were the gods of Gozan, Haran, Rezeph, and Eden in the land of Telassar? The former kings of Assyria destroyed them all! ¹³What happened to the king of Hamoth and the king of Arpad? What happened to the kings of Sepharvaim, Hena, and Ivvah?"

Hezekiah Asks God for Help

¹⁴Hezekiah took the letter from the messengers. He read it. Then he went over to the Temple and spread it out before the Lord. ¹⁵Then he prayed this prayer:

"O Lord God of Israel! You sit on your throne high above the angels. You alone are the God of all the kingdoms of the earth. You created the heavens and the earth. ¹⁶Bend low, O Lord, and listen. Open your eyes, O Lord, and see. Listen to the insults this man has made to the living God. ¹⁷Lord, it is true that the kings of Assyria have destroyed all those nations. ¹⁸And they have burned their idol-gods. But they weren't gods at all. They were just things made of wood and stone. And they were made by the hands of mere men. ¹⁹O Lord our God, please save us from his power! Then all the kingdoms of the earth will know that you alone are God."

God Promises Safety for Jerusalem

²⁰Then Isaiah sent this message to Hezekiah: "The Lord God of Israel says, 'I have heard you! ²¹And this is my reply to King Sennacherib. The virgin daughter of Zion isn't afraid of you! The daughter of Jerusalem laughs and makes fun of you. ²²Whom have you insulted and raised your voice against? And toward

whom have you felt so proud? It is the Holy One of Israel!

23"'You have boasted, "My chariots have conquered the highest mountains. Yes, they have taken the peaks of Lebanon. I have cut down the tallest cedars and choicest cypress trees. I have conquered the farthest borders. 24I have drunk from the wells I have conquered. I have destroyed the strength of Egypt just by walking by!"

25"'Don't you know that it is I, the Lord, who lets you do these things? I allowed you to conquer all those walled cities! 26So of course the nations you conquered had no power against you! They were like grass under the hot sun. They were like grain rotting before it is half-grown. 27I know everything about you. I know all your plans and where you are going next. I also know the bad things you have said about me. 28And I know of your pride against me. So I am going to put a hook in your nose. I'll put a bridle in your mouth. And I'll turn you back on the road by which you came. 29And this is the proof that I will do as I have promised. This year my people will eat the volunteer wheat. And they will use it as seed for next year's crop. And in the third year they will have a rich harvest.

30"'O my people Judah! Those of you who have escaped the siege shall become a great nation again. You shall be rooted deeply in the soil. And you shall bear fruit for God. 31A few of my people shall become strong in Jerusalem. The Lord wants very much to make this happen.

32"'And I command the king of Assyria not to enter this city. He shall not stand before it with a shield. He shall not build a ramp against its wall. He won't even shoot an arrow into it. 33He shall go back by the road he came. 34For I will defend and save this city. I will do it for the sake of my own name. And I will do it for the sake of my servant David.'"

35That very night the angel of the Lord killed 185,000 Assyrian troops. Their dead bodies were seen all across the land the next morning.

36Then King Sennacherib went back to Nineveh. 37He went to worship in the temple of his god Nisroch. As he was worshiping, his sons Adrammelech and Sharezer killed him. They escaped into eastern Turkey, the land of Ararat. And his son Esarhaddon became the new king.

Hezekiah Gets Sick

King Hezekiah got very sick. He was going to die. Then Hezekiah prayed. He begged the Lord to help him get well. Read on to see what happened.

20 Hezekiah now became deathly sick. And Isaiah the prophet went to visit him.

"Set your affairs in order. Get ready to die," Isaiah told him. "The Lord says you won't get better."

2Hezekiah turned his face to the wall.

3"O Lord!" he pleaded. "Remember how I've always tried to obey you? Remember how I've tried to please you in everything I do?" Then he broke down and cried.

4So before Isaiah had left the courtyard, the Lord spoke to him again.

5"Go back to Hezekiah, the leader of my people. Tell him that the Lord God of his ancestor David has heard his prayer. Tell him the Lord has seen his tears. I will heal him! Three days from now he will be out of bed and at the Temple! 6I will add 15 years to his life. And I will save him and this city from the king of Assyria. I will do this for the glory of my own name. And I will do it for the sake of my servant David."

7Isaiah then told Hezekiah to boil some dried figs. He told him to make a paste of them and spread it on the boil. And he got better!

8Meanwhile, King Hezekiah had said to Isaiah, "Do a miracle! Prove to me that the Lord will heal me. Prove that I will be able to go to the Temple again three days from now."

9"All right, the Lord will give you a proof," Isaiah told him. "Do you want the shadow on the sundial to go forward 10 points? Or do you want it to go backward 10 points?"

10"The shadow always moves forward," Hezekiah replied. "Make it go backward."

11So Isaiah asked the Lord to do this. And he caused the shadow to move 10 points backward on the sundial of Ahaz!

- *Remember:* Who told Hezekiah that he would die? (20:1) What did Hezekiah do when he heard this? (20:2-3) How did God answer Hezekiah's prayer? (20:4-5) Why did God do this? (20:6) What miracle did Isaiah do to prove that God would make him well? (20:8-11) Do you think it pays to pray? Do you think God really answers prayer? Why do you think this?
- *Discover:* God hears our prayers and answers them. But he answers the way he thinks is best for us.
- *Apply:* Are you praying for something? Ask yourself what God thinks is best for you. That may tell you how God will answer.
- *What's next?* Workmen are repairing a building. They find an old scroll. But it suddenly becomes the most important thing in the land. Read 2 Chronicles 34. ◼

Babylonians Visit Hezekiah

12At that time Merodach-baladan sent messengers with greetings and a gift to Hezekiah. He was the son of King Baladan of Babylon. He did this because he had learned of Hezekiah's sickness. 13Hezekiah welcomed them and showed them all his treasures. He showed them the silver, gold, spices, aromatic oils, and the armory. He showed them everything.

14Then Isaiah went to King Hezekiah. He asked him, "What did these men want? Where are they from?"

"From far away in Babylon," Hezekiah replied.

15"What have they seen in your palace?" Isaiah asked.

And Hezekiah replied, "Everything. I showed them all my treasures."

????????????????????????????????????
Which boy became king when he was only 12?
(Read 21:1-6 for the answer.)
????????????????????????????????????

16Then Isaiah said to Hezekiah, "Listen to the word of the Lord. 17The time will come when everything in this palace shall be taken to Babylon. All the treasures of your ancestors will be taken. Nothing shall be left behind. 18Some of your own sons will be taken away and made into eunuchs. They will serve in the palace of the king of Babylon."

19"All right," Hezekiah replied. "If this is what the Lord wants, it is good." But he was really thinking, "At least there will be peace for the rest of my own life!"

20The rest of the history of Hezekiah is recorded in *The Annals of the Kings of Judah.* This includes his great deeds and the pool and the conduit he made. And it tells about how he brought water into the city. 21When he died, his son Manasseh became the new king.

Manasseh Rules Judah

21 Manasseh was 12 years old when he became king of Judah. He ruled for 55 years in Jerusalem. His mother's name was Hephzibah. He did things that the Lord had said were wrong. He did the same things the other nations had done. And those nations were thrown out of the land before the Israelites. 3-5He rebuilt the hilltop shrines that his father Hezekiah had destroyed. He built altars for Baal. And he made a shameful Asherah idol. He did just as Ahab the king of Israel had done. Heathen altars were even put in the Temple of the Lord! These altars were built for the sun god, moon god, and the gods of the stars. They were in the very city and building that the Lord had chosen to

honor his own name. ⁶And Manasseh sacrificed one of his own sons. He gave him as a burnt offering on a heathen altar. He did black magic and used fortune telling. He also used mediums and wizards. So the Lord was very angry. For Manasseh was a bad man in God's sight. ⁷He even set up a shameful Asherah idol in the Temple. He put it in the very place the Lord had spoken to David and Solomon about. He had said, "I will put my name for all time in this Temple. I will put my name in Jerusalem. This is the city I have chosen. I have chosen it from all the cities of Israel. ⁸But the people of Israel must follow the commands I gave them through Moses. If they do, I will never again make them leave the land of Israel."

⁹But the people did not listen to the Lord. And Manasseh tempted them to do evil. They did even more evil than the nations around them had done. And they did this even though the Lord had destroyed those nations. He had destroyed them for their evil ways. And he had pushed them out before the people of Israel.

¹⁰Then the Lord gave this message through the prophets.

¹¹"King Manasseh has done bad things," they said. "He is even more wicked than the Amorites who were in this land long ago. He has led the people of Judah to worship idols. ¹²Because of this, I will bring trouble upon Jerusalem and Judah. It will be very bad. In fact, the ears of those who hear about it will tingle. ¹³I will punish Jerusalem as I did Samaria. I will punish her as I did King Ahab of Israel and his family. I will wipe away the people of Jerusalem. I will do it as a man wipes a dish and turns it upside down to dry. ¹⁴Then I will leave even those few of my people who are left. And I will hand them over to their enemies. ¹⁵For they have done great evil. They have made me angry ever since I brought their ancestors from Egypt."

¹⁶But Manasseh didn't just worship idols. And he didn't just lead the people to worship them. He also murdered many people who hadn't done anything

wrong. And Jerusalem was filled with the bodies of the people he killed.

¹⁷The rest of the history of Manasseh's sinful reign is written in *The Annals of the Kings of Judah.* ¹⁸When he died he was buried in the garden of his palace at Uzza. And his son Amon became the new king.

Amon Rules Judah

¹⁹⁻²⁰Amon was 22 years old when he became king of Judah. He ruled as king for two years in Jerusalem. His mother's name was Meshullemeth. She was the daughter of Haruz. She was from Jotbah. ²¹He did all the bad things his father had done. He worshiped the same idols. ²²And he turned his back on the Lord God of his ancestors. He refused to listen to God's commands. ²³But his servants turned against him. They killed him in the palace. ²⁴Then a group of the people killed the men who had killed the king. Then they put Amon's son Josiah upon the throne. ²⁵The rest of Amon's deeds are written in *The Annals of the Kings of Judah.* ²⁶He was buried in a tomb in the garden of Uzza. And his son Josiah became the new king.

Josiah Becomes King When He Is Eight

22 Josiah was eight years old when he became king of Judah. He ruled for 31 years in Jerusalem. His mother's name was Jedidah. She was the daughter of Adaiah of Bozkath. ²Josiah did what the Lord said was right. He followed in the steps of his ancestor, King David. He obeyed the Lord in all that he did.

³⁻⁴In the 18th year of his reign, King Josiah sent Shaphan to the Temple. Shaphan was the son of Azaliah, the son of Meshullam. He was Josiah's secretary. Josiah sent him with orders for Hilkiah, the High Priest.

"Take the money given to the priests at the door of the Temple. It is given to them when the people come to worship. ⁵⁻⁶Give this money to the building manager. That way he will be able to hire carpenters and masons. They will fix the Temple. They will also use the money to buy lumber and stone."

[7]The building managers didn't have to tell how they spent the money. This was because they were honest men.

Josiah Discovers a Book of the Law

[8]One day Hilkiah the High Priest went to Shaphan the secretary. "I have found a scroll in the Temple!" he said. "It has God's laws written on it!"

He gave the scroll to Shaphan to read. [9-10]So Shaphan told the king about the repairs at the Temple. And he also told him about the scroll found by Hilkiah. Then Shaphan read it to the king. [11]When the king heard what was written in it, he tore his clothes in fear. [12-13]He commanded his men to ask the Lord, "What shall we do?" These men were Hilkiah the priest, and Shaphan, and Asaiah, the king's helper. Ahikam (Shaphan's son) and Achbor (Michaiah's son) were also with them. Josiah continued, "We have not been following the commands of this book. The Lord must be very angry with us! Neither we nor our ancestors have followed his commands!"

[14]So these men went to the Mishneh section of Jerusalem. They were Hilkiah the priest, Ahikam, Achbor, Shaphan, and Asaiah. They went there to find Huldah the prophetess. She was the wife of Shallum. Shallum was the son of Tikvah, the son of Harhas. He was in charge of the palace tailor shop. [15-16]She gave them this message from the Lord God of Israel.

"Tell the king that I am going to destroy this city and its people," the Lord said. "I will do it just as I said in that book you read. [17]For the people of Judah have thrown me aside. They have worshiped other gods. They have made me very angry. And my anger can't be stopped! [18-19]But you were sorry. You humbled yourself before the Lord. You listened when you read the book and its warnings. For you knew that this land would be cursed and become empty. And you have torn your clothing and cried before me. You showed how sorry you were for your sin. Because of this, I will listen to you. [20]The death of this nation will not happen until after you die. You will not see the trouble that I will bring on this place."

So they took the message to the king.

Josiah Obeys God's Law and Destroys Idol Worship

23 Then the king sent for the elders. And he sent for the other leaders of Judah and Jerusalem. He told them all to go to the Temple with him. So all the priests and prophets came. All the people, small and great, of Jerusalem and Judah came too. They all met there at the Temple. They came to hear the king read the whole book of God's laws. This was the scroll that had been found in the Temple. [3]Josiah stood beside a pillar in front of the people. There he and his people promised to obey the Lord at all times. And they promised to do all that the book commanded.

Together let's promise God that we will obey him

There he and his people promised to obey the Lord at all times.

2 Kings 23:3

---

[4]Then the king gave orders to Hilkiah the High Priest. He also gave orders to the rest of the priests and the guards of the Temple. He told them to destroy all the things used to worship Baal and Asherah. He told them to get rid of things used to worship the sun, moon, and stars. The king had all these things burned. The fire was set in the fields of the Kidron Valley outside Jerusalem. Then he carried the ashes to Bethel. [5]He killed the heathen priests. These priests had been chosen by the kings of Judah before Josiah. They were killed because they had burned incense to false gods. They had done this in the shrines on the hills of Judah and Jerusalem. They had also offered incense to Baal. They had burned it to the sun, moon, stars, and planets. [6]He took away the shameful idol of Asherah from the Temple. He took it outside Jerusalem to Kidron Brook. There he burned it and beat it to dust. Then he

threw the dust on the graves of the common people. [7]He also tore down the houses of male prostitutes around the Temple. This was where the women wove robes for the Asherah idol.

[8]He brought back to Jerusalem the priests of the Lord. They were living in other cities of Judah. He tore down all the shrines on the hills where they had burned incense. He tore them down as far away as Geba and Beersheba. He also destroyed the shrines at the door of the palace of Joshua. He was the former mayor of Jerusalem. This home was on the left side as one enters the city gate. [9]These priests did not serve at the altar of the Lord in Jerusalem. But they did eat with the other priests.

????????????????????????????????
Which king was king only three months?
(Read 23:31-33 for the answer.)
????????????????????????????????

[10]Then the king destroyed the altar of Topheth. This was in the Valley of the Sons of Hinnom. That way no one could ever use it again. No one could burn his son or daughter to death on it as a sacrifice to Molech. [11]He tore down the statues of horses and chariots. These were near the door of the Temple. They were next to the rooms of Nathan-melech the eunuch. These had been given by former kings of Judah to the sun god. [12]Then he tore down the altars on the palace roof. They were above the Ahaz Room. They had been built by the kings of Judah. Josiah also destroyed the altars that Manasseh had built. These were in the two courts of the Temple. Josiah smashed them to bits and threw the pieces into Kidron Valley.

[13]Next he took away the shrines on the hills east of Jerusalem. These were the ones south of Destruction Mountain. Solomon had built these shrines. One of them was for Ashtoreth, the goddess of Sidon. He had built another for Chemosh, the god of Moab. He had built yet another for Milcom, the god of the Ammonites. [14]He smashed the obelisks and cut down the shameful idols of Asherah.

Then he made these places unclean by scattering human bones over them. [15]He also tore down the altar and shrine at Bethel. This was the one that Jeroboam I had made when he led Israel into sin. He crushed the stones to dust. And he burned the shameful idol of Asherah.

[16]As Josiah was looking around, he saw some graves in the side of the mountain. He ordered his men to bring out the bones in them. They burned them there on the altar at Bethel. They did this to make it unclean. It happened to Jeroboam's altar just as the Lord's prophet had said it would.

[17]"What is that monument over there?" Josiah asked.

And the men of the city told him. "It is the grave of the prophet who came from Judah," they said. "He promised that what you have just done would happen here at the altar at Bethel!"

[18]So King Josiah replied, "Leave it alone. Don't disturb his bones."

So they didn't burn his bones or those of the prophet from Samaria.

[19]Josiah broke down the shrines on the hills in all of Samaria. They had been built by the kings of Israel. And they had made the Lord very angry. But now Josiah crushed them into dust. He did everywhere just as he had done at Bethel. [20]He killed the priests of the heathen shrines on their own altars. And he burned human bones on the altars to make them unclean. Finally he went back to Jerusalem.

[21]The king then gave orders for his people to observe the Passover feast. They were to do as the Lord their God told them in *The Book of the Covenant.* [22]There had not been a Passover feast like that since the days of the judges of Israel. And there was never another like it in all the years of the kings of Israel and Judah. [23]This Passover was in the 18th year of the reign of King Josiah. The feast took place in Jerusalem.

[24]Josiah also killed the mediums and wizards. He got rid of every kind of idol worship. He did this both in Jerusalem and throughout the land. For Josiah wanted to follow all the laws written in the book. This was the scroll that Hilkiah

the priest had found in the Temple. ²⁵There was no other king who so completely turned to the Lord. He followed all the laws of Moses. And no king since Josiah has obeyed the Lord as completely.

²⁶But the Lord still did not hold back his great anger against Judah. The Lord's anger was caused by the bad things King Manasseh had done. ²⁷For the Lord had said, "I will destroy Judah! I will destroy her just as I have destroyed Israel. I will throw away my chosen city of Jerusalem. I will get rid of the Temple that I said was mine."

²⁸The rest of the deeds of Josiah were written in *The Annals of the Kings of Judah.* ²⁹In those days King Neco of Egypt went out to help the king of Assyria. He set out to meet him at the Euphrates River. Then King Josiah went out with his troops to fight King Neco. But King Neco defeated him at Megiddo and killed him. ³⁰His officers took his body back in a chariot from Megiddo to Jerusalem. There they buried him in the grave he had chosen. His son Jehoahaz was chosen by the nation as its new king.

Jehoahaz Rules Judah

³¹⁻³²Jehoahaz was 23 years old when he became king of Judah. He ruled in Jerusalem for three months. His mother's name was Hamutal. She was the daughter of Jeremiah of Libnah. Jehoahaz did what was wrong in the sight of the Lord. He did just like most of the other kings before him. ³³Pharaoh-Neco put him in jail at Riblah in Hamath. He did this to stop him from ruling in Jerusalem. And he made the people of Judah pay him a total of $230,000. ³⁴The Egyptian king then chose Eliakim to rule in Jerusalem. He was another of Josiah's sons. Then he changed Eliakim's name to Jehoiakim. Then he took King Jehoahaz to Egypt, where he died. ³⁵Jehoiakim taxed the people to get the money that the Pharaoh had asked for.

Jehoiakim Rules Judah;
Babylon Invades Judah

³⁶⁻³⁷Jehoiakim became king of Judah when he was 25 years old. He ruled for 11 years in Jerusalem. His mother's name was Zebidah. She was the daughter of Pedaiah of Rumah. Jehoiakim did what was wrong in the sight of the Lord. He was just like most of the other kings of Judah before him.

24 During the reign of King Jehoiakim, King Nebuchadnezzar of Babylon attacked Jerusalem. Jehoiakim gave up and paid him tribute for three years. But then he broke away from Babylon's rule. ²And the Lord sent bands of Chaldeans, Syrians, Moabites, and Ammonites against Judah. He did this to destroy the nation. It happened just as the Lord had warned through his prophets. ³⁻⁴It is clear that these troubles came on Judah at the Lord's command. He had decided to wipe Judah out of his sight. He did this because of the many sins of Manasseh. For Manasseh had filled Jerusalem with blood. And the Lord would not forgive it.

⁵The rest of the history of Jehoiakim is written in *The Annals of the Kings of Judah.* ⁶When he died, his son Jehoiachin became the new king. ⁷The Egyptian Pharaoh never came back after that. This was because the king of Babylon took the whole land of Egypt. This included all the land from the Brook of Egypt to the Euphrates River.

Jehoiachin Rules Judah;
Babylon Invades Judah Again

⁸⁻⁹So Jehoiachin became the next king of Judah. He became king when he was 18 years old. He ruled for three months in Jerusalem. His mother's name was Nehushta. She was the daughter of Elnathan, a man from Jerusalem.

¹⁰During his reign the armies of King Nebuchadnezzar of Babylon attacked the city of Jerusalem. ¹¹Nebuchadnezzar himself came during the siege. ¹²And King Jehoiachin, all of his officials, and the queen mother gave in to him. The surrender was accepted by the Babylonians. Then Jehoiachin was put in prison in Babylon. This happened during the eighth year of Nebuchadnezzar's reign.

¹³The Babylonians took home all the treasures from the Temple. They also took everything from the royal palace. And they cut apart all the gold bowls in

the Temple. King Solomon of Israel had put these in the Temple. He did this because the Lord told him to. [14]King Nebuchadnezzar took 10,000 captives from Jerusalem. This included all the princes. It also included the best of the soldiers, craftsmen, and smiths. So only the poorest and least skilled people were left in the land. [15]Nebuchadnezzar took King Jehoiachin to Babylon. He also took his wives and officials, and the queen mother. [16]He took 7,000 of the best troops. And he brought along 1,000 craftsmen and smiths. All of these were strong and fit for war. [17]Then the king of Babylon chose King Jehoiachin's great-uncle, Mattaniah, to be the next king. He changed his name to Zedekiah.

Zedekiah Rules Judah; Babylon Conquers Judah

[18-19]So Zedekiah became the new king of Judah. He was 21 years old when he became king. He ruled for 11 years in Jerusalem. His mother's name was Hamutal. She was the daughter of Jeremiah of Libnah. Zedekiah did what was wrong in the sight of the Lord. He ruled just like Jehoiakim before him. [20]So the Lord was very angry. And he destroyed the people of Jerusalem and Judah. But now King Zedekiah turned against the king of Babylon.

25 Then King Nebuchadnezzar of Babylon called out his whole army. He laid siege to Jerusalem. He came on March 25 of the ninth year of Zedekiah's reign in Judah. [2]The siege went on into the 11th year of his reign.

????????????????????????????????????
Which king watched while his sons were executed, then had his eyes put out?
(Read 25:1-7 for the answer.)
????????????????????????????????????

[3]The last food in the city was eaten on July 24. [4-5]And that night the king and his troops made a hole in the inner wall. They ran out through it toward the Arabah. They went through a gate that was between the double walls near the

king's garden. The Babylonian troops camped around the city went after him. They caught him in the plains of Jericho. And all his men ran away.

The Babylonians Demolish Jerusalem

[6]He was taken to Riblah. There he was tried and sentenced before the king of Babylon. [7]He was forced to watch as his sons were killed before his eyes. Then his eyes were put out. And he was tied with chains and taken away to Babylon.

[8]General Nebuzaradan was the captain of the royal bodyguard. He came to Jerusalem from Babylon on July 22. This was during the 19th year of King Nebuchadnezzar's reign. [9]He burned down the Temple and the palace. He also burned down all the other houses of any worth. [10]He then had the Babylonian army tear down the walls of Jerusalem. [11]The rest of the people in the city were all taken away into Babylon. This included the Jewish traitors who supported the king of Babylon. [12]But the poorest of the people were left to farm the land.

[13]The Babylonians broke up the bronze pillars of the Temple. They cut up the bronze tank and its bases. And they carried all the bronze to Babylon. [14-15]They took all the pots, shovels, firepans, snuffers, and spoons with them. They also took other bronze items used for the sacrifices. The gold and silver bowls, and all that was gold and silver, were also taken. [16]The bronze they found was too heavy to weigh. There were the two pillars and the great tank and its bases. All of these were made for the Temple by King Solomon. [17]Each pillar was 27 feet high. There were 4½-foot capitals at the top of each one. There was a net design on each capital. And all around each capital were figures of pomegranates.

[18]The general took Seraiah, the chief priest, to Babylon as a captive. He also took his helper Zephaniah and the three Temple guards. [19]The general also took other people from Jerusalem. He took a commander of the army of Judah. He took the man who chose people for the

army. He took five of the king's counselors. And he took 60 other men in the city. He found all of these hiding in the city. ²⁰They were taken by General Nebuzaradan to the king of Babylon at Riblah. ²¹There they were put to death by the sword.

So Judah was sent away from its land.

Judah's Last Hope

²²Then King Nebuchadnezzar chose Gedaliah as governor over the people left in Judah. He was the son of Ahikam and the grandson of Shaphan. ²³There were still some army leaders left in Judah. They learned that the king of Babylon had chosen Gedaliah as governor. So some of these leaders and their men joined him at Mizpah. These leaders included Ishmael, Johanan, Seraiah, Jaazaniah, and their men. Ishmael was the son of Nethaniah. Johanan was the son of Kareah. Seraiah was the son of Tanhumeth the Netophathite. And Jaazaniah was the son of Maachathite. ²⁴Gedaliah told them to give themselves up. He told them to do what the Babylonians said. If they did this, he would let them live in the land. He promised they would not be kicked out. ²⁵But seven months later, Ishmael went to Mizpah with 10 men. Ishmael was a member of the royal line. He killed Gedaliah and his court. This included both the Jews and the Babylonians.

²⁶Then all the men of Judah and the army leaders ran in panic to Egypt. They were afraid of what the Babylonians would do to them.

²⁷King Jehoiachin was set free from prison on the 27th day of the last month. This was during his 37th year in Babylon as a captive.

This happened during the first year of King Evil-merodach's reign in Babylon. ²⁸He treated Jehoiachin kindly. He treated him better than all the other kings who were prisoners in Babylon. ²⁹Jehoiachin was given nice clothes to put on. He put away his prison clothes for good. And for as long as he lived, he ate at the king's table. ³⁰The king also gave him a cash allowance for the rest of his life.

FIRST CHRONICLES

In 1 Chronicles you will meet mighty warriors such as Benaiah the giant killer. You'll see an angel standing between heaven and earth with his sword drawn. You'll watch a king put a 75-pound crown of gold and jewels on his head. And you'll wonder as you see a man give $100,000,000 of his own money to build a house for God that he will never see.

First Chronicles tells the story of King David and his family. It is the same story told in 1 and 2 Samuel, but seen through different eyes. This book tells much about the Temple and how people worshiped there. It tells the good things about David, but almost never tells the bad things about him. Those were told in 1 and 2 Samuel. It is the story of how David was made king, how he ruled, and how his kingdom went to his son Solomon. If David is one of your heroes, you will want to read 1 Chronicles.

Adam's Descendants

1 Adam was the father of Seth. Seth was the father of Enosh. Enosh was the father of Kenan. Kenan was the father of Mahalalel. Mahalalel was the father of Jared. Jared was the father of Enoch. Enoch was the father of Methuselah. Methuselah was the father of Lamech. Lamech was the father of Noah. Noah was the father of Shem, Ham, and Japheth.

5-9The sons of Japheth were Gomer, Magog, Madai, Javan, Tubal, Meshech, and Tiras.

The sons of Gomer were Ashkenaz, Diphath, and Togarmah.

The sons of Javan were Elishah, Tarshish, Kittim, and Rodanim.

The sons of Ham were Cush, Mizraim, Canaan, and Put.

The sons of Cush were Seba, Havilah, Sabta, Raama, and Sabteca.

The sons of Raama were Sheba and Dedan.

10Another of the sons of Cush was Nimrod. He became a great hero.

11-12The clans named after the sons of Mizraim were the Ludites, the Anamites, the Lehabites, the Naphtuhites, the Pathrusites, the Caphtorites, and the Casluhites. The Casluhites were the ancestors of the Philistines.

13-16Among Canaan's sons were Sidon and Heth. Sidon was his firstborn.

Canaan was also the ancestor of the Jebusites, Amorites, Girgashites, Hivites, Arkites, Sinites, Arvadites, Zemarites, and Hamathites.

17The sons of Shem were Elam,

Asshur, Arpachshad, Lud, Aram, Uz, Hul, Gether, and Meshech.

¹⁸Arpachshad's son was Shelah. Shelah's son was Eber.

¹⁹Eber had two sons. One was named Peleg. His name means "Divided." He was called this because people started speaking different languages during his lifetime. Peleg's brother was named Joktan.

²⁰⁻²³The sons of Joktan were Almodad, Sheleph, Hazarmaveth, Jerah, Hadoram, Uzal, Diklah, Ebal, Abimael, Sheba, Ophir, Havilah, and Jobab.

²⁴⁻²⁷So the son of Shem was Arpachshad. The son of Arpachshad was Shelah. The son of Shelah was Eber. The son of Eber was Peleg. The son of Peleg was Reu. The son of Reu was Serug. The son of Serug was Nahor. The son of Nahor was Terah. The son of Terah was Abram. Abram was later known as Abraham.

²⁸⁻³¹Abraham's sons were Isaac and Ishmael.

Ishmael's oldest son was Nebaioth. His other sons were Kedar, Adbeel, Mibsam, Mishma, Dumah, Massa, Hadad, Tema, Jetur, Naphish, and Kedemah.

³²Abraham also had sons by his wife Keturah. Their names were Zimram, Jokshan, Medan, Midian, Ishbak, and Shuah.

Jokshan's sons were Sheba and Dedan.

³³The sons of Midian were Ephah, Epher, Hanoch, Abida, and Eldaah. These were Abraham's children by his wife Keturah.

³⁴Abraham's son Isaac had two sons, Esau and Israel.

³⁵The sons of Esau were Eliphaz, Reuel, Jeush, Jalam, and Korah.

³⁶The sons of Eliphaz were Teman, Omar, Zephi, Gatam, Kenaz, Timna, and Amalek.

³⁷The sons of Reuel were Nahath, Zerah, Shammah, and Mizzah.

³⁸⁻³⁹The sons of Esau also included Lotan, Shobal, Zibeon, Anah, Dishon, Ezer, and Dishan. Esau's daughter was named Timna. Lotan's sons were named Hori and Homam.

⁴⁰The sons of Shobal were Alian, Manahath, Ebal, Shephi, and Onam. Zibeon's sons were Aiah and Anah.

⁴¹Anah's son was Dishon. The sons of Dishon were Hamran, Eshban, Ithran, and Cheran.

⁴²The sons of Ezer were Bilhan, Zaavan, and Jaakan. Dishan's sons were Uz and Aran.

⁴³Here is a list of the names of the kings of Edom. These kings reigned before the kingdom of Israel began.

Bela, the son of Beor, was the king of Edom. He lived in the city of Dinhabah.

⁴⁴When Bela died, Jobab became the new king. He was the son of Zerah from Bozrah.

⁴⁵When Jobab died, Husham became the king. He was from the country of the Temanites.

⁴⁶When Husham died, Hadad became king. He was the son of Bedad. Bedad was the one who destroyed the army of Midian. The battle took place in the fields of Moab. Hadad ruled from the city of Avith.

⁴⁷When Hadad died, Samlah came to the throne. He was from the city of Masrekah.

⁴⁸When Samlah died, Shaul became the new king. He was from the river town of Rehoboth.

⁴⁹When Shaul died, Baal-hanan became king. He was the son of Achbor.

⁵⁰When Baal-hanan died, Hadad became king. He ruled from the city of Pai. His wife was Mehetabel. She was the daughter of Matred. Matred was the daughter of Mezahab.

⁵¹⁻⁵⁴At the time of Hadad's death, the chiefs of Edom were Timna, Aliah, Jetheth, Oholibamah, Elah, Pinon, Kenaz, Teman, Mibzar, Magdiel, and Iram.

Jacob's Descendants

2 The sons of Israel were Reuben, Simeon, Levi, Judah, Issachar, Zebulun, Dan, Joseph, Benjamin, Naphtali, Gad, and Asher.

³Judah had three sons by Bathshua. She was a girl from Canaan. His sons' names were Er, Onan, and Shelah. But the oldest son, Er, was very wicked. So the Lord killed him.

⁴Then Er's widow, Tamar, had twin

sons. Their names were Perez and Zerah. Judah was their father. So Judah had five sons.

⁵The sons of Perez were Hezron and Hamul.

⁶The sons of Zerah were Zimri, Ethan, Heman, Calcol, and Dara.

⁷Achan was the son of Carmi. He was the man who robbed God. He made great trouble for his nation.

⁸Ethan's son was Azariah.

⁹The sons of Hezron were Jerahmeel, Ram, and Chelubai.

¹⁰Ram was the father of Amminadab. Amminadab was the father of Nahshon, a leader of Israel.

¹¹Nahshon was the father of Salma. Salma was the father of Boaz.

¹²Boaz was the father of Obed. Obed was the father of Jesse.

¹³Jesse's first son was Eliab. His second son was Abinadab. His third son was Shimea. ¹⁴His fourth son was Nethanel. His fifth son was Raddai. ¹⁵His sixth son was Ozem. And his seventh son was David. ¹⁶He also had two girls by the same wife. They were named Zeruiah and Abigail.

Zeruiah's sons were Abishai, Joab, and Asahel.

¹⁷Abigail had a son named Amasa. Her husband was Jether from the land of Ishmael.

¹⁸Caleb was the son of Hezron. He had two wives, Azubah and Jerioth. Azubah's children were Jesher, Shobab, and Ardon.

¹⁹After Azubah's death, Caleb married Ephrath. She gave him a son named Hur.

²⁰Hur's son was Uri. Uri's son was Bezalel.

²¹Hezron married Machir's daughter at the age of 60. She gave him a son called Segub. Machir was also the father of Gilead.

²²Segub was the father of Jair. Jair ruled 23 cities in the land of Gilead. ²³But Geshur and Aram took these cities from him. They also took Kenath and the 60 villages around it.

²⁴Soon after his father Hezron's death, Caleb married Ephrathah. She was his father's widow. She gave birth to Ashhur, the father of Tekoa.

²⁵These are the sons of Jerahmeel. He was the oldest son of Hezron. Jerahmeel's oldest son was Ram. His other sons were Bunah, Oren, Ozem, and Ahijah.

²⁶Jerahmeel's second wife Atarah was the mother of Onam.

²⁷The sons of Ram were Maaz, Jamin, and Eker.

²⁸Onam's sons were Shammai and Jada. Shammai's sons were Nadab and Abishur.

²⁹The sons of Abishur and his wife Abihail were Ahban and Molid.

³⁰Nadab's sons were Seled and Appaim. Seled died without children. ³¹But Appaim had a son named Ishi. Ishi's son was Sheshan. Sheshan's son was Ahlai.

³²Shammai's brother Jada had two sons, Jether and Jonathan. Jether died without children. ³³But Jonathan had two sons named Peleth and Zaza.

³⁴⁻³⁵Sheshan had no sons. But he had several daughters. He gave one of his daughters to be the wife of Jarha. Jarha was his Egyptian servant. And they had a son named Attai.

³⁶Attai's son was Nathan. Nathan's son was Zabad. ³⁷Zabad's son was Ephlal. Ephlal's son was Obed. ³⁸Obed's son was Jehu. Jehu's son was Azariah. ³⁹Azariah's son was Helez. Helez's son was Eleasah. ⁴⁰Eleasah's son was Sismai. Sismai's son was Shallum. ⁴¹Shallum's son was Jekamiah. Jekamiah's son was Elishama.

⁴²The oldest son of Caleb was Mesha. Caleb was Jerahmeel's brother. Mesha was the father of Ziph. Ziph was the father of Mareshah. And Mareshah was the father of Hebron.

⁴³The sons of Hebron were Korah, Tappuah, Rekem, and Shema.

⁴⁴Shema was the father of Raham. Raham was the father of Jorkeam. Rekem was the father of Shammai.

⁴⁵Shammai's son was Maon. Maon was the father of Bethzur.

⁴⁶Caleb's concubine Ephah bore him Haran, Moza, and Gazez. Haran also had a son named Gazez.

⁴⁷The sons of Jahdai were Regem, Jotham, Geshan, Pelet, Ephah, and Shaaph.

⁴⁸⁻⁴⁹Caleb had another concubine named Maacah. She gave him sons named Sheber, Tirhanah, Shaaph, and Sheva. Shaaph was the father of Madmannah. Sheva was the father of Machbenah and of Gibea. Caleb also had a daughter, whose name was Achsah.

⁵⁰⁻⁵¹The sons of Hur were Shobal, Salma, and Hareph. (Hur was the oldest son of Caleb and Ephrathah.) Shobal was the father of Kiriath-jearim. Salma was the father of Bethlehem. And Hareph was the father of Beth-gader.

⁵²Shobal's sons included Kiriath-jearim and Haroeh. Horoeh was the ancestor of half of the Menuhoth tribe.

⁵³The families of Kiriath-jearim were the Ithrites, the Puthites, the Shumathites, and the Mishraites. From the Mishraites came the Zorathites and Eshtaolites.

⁵⁴The descendants of Salma were his son Bethlehem, the Netophathites, Atrothbeth-joab, half the Manahathites, and the Zorites. ⁵⁵They also included the families of the writers living at Jabez. These were the Tirathites, Shimeathites, and Sucathites. All these are Kenites who descended from Hammath. Hammath was the founder of the family of Rechab.

David's Descendants

3 King David's oldest son was Amnon. He was born to his wife, Ahinoam of Jezreel.

The second son was Daniel. His mother was Abigail from Carmel.

²The third son was Absalom. He was the son of his wife Maacah. Maacah was the daughter of King Talmai of Geshur.

The fourth son was Adonijah, the son of Haggith.

³The fifth son was Shephatiah, the son of Abital.

The sixth son was Ithream, the son of his wife Eglah.

⁴These six were born to him in Hebron. David reigned there 7½ years. Then he moved the capital to Jerusalem. There he reigned another 33 years.

⁵These are the children born to David while he was in Jerusalem. His wife Bathsheba became the mother of his sons Shimea, Shobab, Nathan, and Solomon. Bathsheba was the daughter of Ammiel.

⁶⁻⁸David also had nine other sons. They were named Ibhar, Elishama, Eliphelet, Nogah, Nepheg, Japhia, Elishama, Eliada, and Eliphelet.

⁹This list does not include the sons of his concubines. David also had a daughter, Tamar.

¹⁰⁻¹⁴These are the descendants of King Solomon. Rehoboam was the father of Abijah. Abijah's son was Asa. Asa's son was Jehoshaphat. Jehoshaphat's son was Joram. Joram's son was Ahaziah. Ahaziah's son was Joash. Joash's son was Amaziah. Amaziah's son was Uzziah. Uzziah's son was Jotham. Jotham's son was Ahaz. The son of Ahaz was Hezekiah. Hezekiah's son was Manasseh. Manasseh's son was Amon. And Amon's son was Josiah.

¹⁵The sons of Josiah were Johanan, Jehoiakim, Zedekiah, and Shallum.

¹⁶The sons of Jehoiakim were Jehoiachin and Zedekiah.

¹⁷⁻¹⁸These are the sons who were born to King Jehoiachin. They were born during the years that he was in Babylon. Their names were Shealtiel, Malchiram, Pedaiah, Shenazzar, Jekamiah, Hoshama, and Nedabiah.

¹⁹⁻²⁰Pedaiah was the father of Zerubbabel and Shimei.

Zerubbabel's children were Meshullam, Hananiah, Hashubah, Ohel, Berechiah, Hasadiah, and Jushab-hesed. He also had a daughter named Shelomith.

²¹⁻²²Hananiah's sons were Pelatiah and Jeshaiah. Jeshaiah's son was Rephaiah. Rephaiah's son was Arnan. Arnan's son was Obadiah. Obadiah's son was Shecaniah. Shecaniah's son was Shemaiah. Shemaiah had six sons. Their names were Hattush, Igal, Bariah, Neariah, and Shaphat.

²³Neariah had three sons. Their names were Elioenai, Hizkiah, and Azrikam.

²⁴Elioenai had seven sons. Their names were Hodaviah, Eliashib, Pelaiah, Akkub, Johanan, Delaiah, and Anani.

Judah's Descendants

4 Judah's descendants were Perez, Hezron, Carmi, Hur, and Shobal.

²Shobal's son Reaiah was the father of Jahath. Jahath was the ancestor of Ahumai and Lahad. These were known as the Zorathite clans.

³⁻⁴Hur was the firstborn of Ephrathah. And he was the father of Bethlehem. Hur's three sons were Etam, Penuel, and Ezer. The sons of Etam were Jezreel, Ishma, and Idbash. Hazzelelponi was Etam's daughter. Penuel was the father of Gedor. Ezer was the father of Hushah.

⁵Ashhur was the father of Tekoa. He had two wives named Helah and Naarah.

⁶Naarah gave him Ahuzzam, Hepher, Temeni, and Haahashtari. ⁷Helah gave him Zereth, Izhar, and Ethnan.

⁸Koz was the father of Anub and Zobebah. He was also the ancestor of the clan named after Aharhel. Aharhel was the son of Harum.

⁹Jabez was better known than any of his brothers. His mother named him Jabez because she had such a hard time at his birth. Jabez means "Distress."

¹⁰He was the one who prayed to the God of Israel. "Oh, that you would bless me and help me in my work!" he said. "Please be with me in all that I do! Keep me from all evil and trouble!" And God did for him what he asked.

¹¹⁻¹²The descendants of Recah were Chelub, Eshton, and Tehinnah. Chelub was the brother of Shuhah. And Chelub had a son named Mehir. Mehir was the father of Eshton. Eshton was the father of Bethrapha, Paseah, and Tehinnah. Tehinnah was the father of Irnahash.

¹³The sons of Kenaz were Othniel and Seraiah.

Othniel's sons were Hathath and Meonothai.

¹⁴Meonothai was the father of Ophrah.

Seraiah was the father of Joab. Joab was the ancestor of the people of Craftsman Valley. It was called that because many craftsmen lived there.

¹⁵Caleb was the son of Jephunneh. The sons of Caleb were Iru, Elah, and Naam.

The sons of Elah included Kenaz.

¹⁶Jehallel's sons were Ziph, Ziphah, Tiria, and Asarel.

¹⁷Ezrah's sons were Jether, Mered, Epher, and Jalon.

Mered married Bithiah, an Egyptian princess. She was the mother of Miriam, Shammai, and Ishbah. Ishbah was an ancestor of Eshtemoa.

¹⁸Eshtemoa's wife was a Jewess. She was the mother of Jered, Heber, and Jekuthiel. Jered was the ancestor of the Gedorites. Heber was the ancestor of the Socoites. Jekuthiel was the ancestor of the Zanoahites.

¹⁹Hodiah's wife was the sister of Naham. One of her sons was the father of Keilah the Garmite. Another of her sons was the father of Eshtemoa the Maacathite.

²⁰The sons of Shimon were Amnon, Rinnah, Ben-hanan, and Tilon.

The sons of Ishi were Zoheth and Ben-zoheth.

²¹⁻²²Shelah was the son of Judah. Shelah's sons were Er, Laadah, Jokim, the men from Cozeba, Joash, and Saraph. Er was the father of Lecah. Laadah was the father of Mareshah. Saraph was a ruler in Moab before he went back to Lehem. These names all come from very old records. ²³These clans were known for their pottery, gardening, and planting. They all worked for the king.

Simeon's Descendants

²⁴The sons of Simeon were Nemuel, Jamin, Jarib, Zerah, and Shaul.

²⁵Shaul's son was Shallum. Shallum's son was Mibsam. And Mibsam's son was Mishma.

²⁶Mishma's son was Hammuel. Hammuel was the father of Zaccur. Zaccur was the father of Shimei.

²⁷Shimei had 16 sons and six daughters. But none of his brothers had large families. They all had fewer children than was normal in Judah.

²⁸Shimei's children lived at Beersheba, Moladah, and Hazar-shual. ²⁹They also lived at Bilhah, Ezem, Tolad, ³⁰Bethuel, Hormah, and Ziklag. ³¹Others of them settled at Beth-marcaboth,

Hazar-susim, Beth-biri, and Shaaraim. These cities were under their control until the time of David.

32-33Their descendants also lived in or near Etam, Ain, Rimmon, Tochen, and Ashan. Some were as far away as Baalath. These facts are recorded in their family history.

34-39These are the names of some of the clan chiefs. Their families became very large. So they went to the east side of Gedor Valley. They went there in search of pasture for their flocks. Their names were Meshobab, Jamlech, Joshah, Joel, Jehu, Elioenai, Jaakobah, Jeshohaiah, Asaiah, Adiel, Jesimiel, Benaiah, and Ziza. Ziza was the son of Shiphi. Shiphi was the son of Allon. Allon was the son of Jedaiah. Jedaiah was the son of Shimri. Shimri was the son of Shemaiah.

40-41They found good pastures, and everything was quiet and peaceful. But the land belonged to the descendants of Ham.

So during the reign of King Hezekiah of Judah these princes invaded the land. The broke down the tents and houses of the descendants of Ham. They killed the people of the land and took the land for themselves.

42Later, 500 of these people from the tribe of Simeon went to Mount Seir. Their leaders were Pelatiah, Neariah, Rephaiah, and Uzziel. They were all sons of Ishi.

43There they killed the few living members of the tribe of Amalek. And they have lived there ever since.

Reuben's Descendants

5 The oldest son of Israel was Reuben. But he dishonored his father by sleeping with one of his father's wives. Because of this, his birthright was given to his brother, Joseph. So the family record doesn't name Reuben as the oldest son.

2Joseph was given the birthright. But Judah was a powerful tribe in Israel. And from the tribe of Judah came a prince.

3Reuben was the firstborn of Israel's sons. The sons of Reuben were Hanoch, Pallu, Hezron, and Carmi.

4These are Joel's descendants. Joel's son was Shemaiah. Shemaiah's son was Gog. Gog's son was Shimei.

5Shimei's son was Micah. Micah's son was Reaiah. Reaiah's son was Baal.

6Baal's son was Beerah. He was a prince of the tribe of Reuben. He was taken captive by King Tilgath-pilneser of Assyria.

7-8His relatives became heads of clans. They were included in the family record. Their names were Jeiel, Zechariah, and Bela. Bela was the son of Azaz. Azaz was the son of Shema. Shema was the son of Joel.

These Reubenites lived in Aroer. They settled as far away as Mount Nebo and Baal-meon.

9Joel had great herds of animals. He pastured them eastward to the edge of the desert. He went as far as the Euphrates River. They went there because there were too many animals in the land of Gilead.

10During the reign of King Saul, the men of Reuben defeated the Hagrites in war. They moved into their tents and houses on the eastern edge of Gilead.

Gad's Descendants

11Across from them lived the people of Gad. They lived in the land of Bashan. The people of Gad were spread as far as Salecah.

12Joel was the greatest. He was followed by Shapham, also Janai and Shaphat. 13Their relatives were Michael, Meshullam, Sheba, Jorai, Jacan, Zia, and Eber. These men were the heads of the seven clans.

14The descendants of Buz were Jahdo, Jeshishai, Michael, Gilead, Jaroah, Huri, Abihail. These are listed in order of their generations.

15Ahi was the son of Abdiel and grandson of Guni. He was the leader of the clan. 16The clan lived in and around Gilead. They also lived in the land of Bashan. And they lived throughout the whole pasture country of Sharon. 17All were included in the family history of Gad. This was made while King Jotham ruled in Judah. This was also the time King Jeroboam ruled in Israel.

[18]There were 44,760 armed and trained men in the army of Reuben, Gad, and the half-tribe of Manasseh. [19]They declared war on the Hagrites, the Jeturites, the Naphishites, and the Nodabites. [20]They cried out to God to help them. And he did, for they trusted in him. So the Hagrites and all their allies were beaten. [21]The booty included 50,000 camels, 250,000 sheep, 2,000 donkeys, and 100,000 captives. [22]A great number of the enemy also died in the battle. This was because God was fighting against them. So the Reubenites lived in the land of the Hagrites. It was their land until the time of the exile.

Manasseh's Descendants

[23]The half-tribe of Manasseh spread through the land from Bashan. They went as far as Baal-hermon, Senir, and Mount Hermon. They also had very many people.

[24]The chiefs of their clans were Epher, Ishi, Eliel, Azriel, Jeremiah, Hodaviah, Jahdiel.

Each of these men was well known as a warrior and leader. [25]But they were not true to the God of their fathers. Instead they worshiped the idols of the people whom God had destroyed. [26]So God caused King Pul of Assyria to invade the land. (King Pul was also known as Tilgath-pilneser III.) He sent the men of Reuben, Gad, and the half-tribe of Manasseh from their land. They took them to Halah, Habor, Hara, and the Gozan River. They still live there to this day.

Levi's Descendants

6 The names of the sons of Levi were Gershon, Kohath, and Merari.

[2]Kohath's sons were Amram, Izhar, Hebron, and Uzziel.

[3]Amram's children were Aaron, Moses, and Miriam.

Aaron's sons were Nadab, Abihu, Eleazar, and Ithamar.

[4-15]Eleazar was the father of Phinehas. Phinehas was the father of Abishua. Abishua was the father of Bukki. Bukki was the father of Uzzi.

Uzzi was the father of Zerahiah. Zerahiah was the father of Meraioth. Meraioth was the father of Amariah. Amariah was the father of Ahitub. Ahitub was the father of Zadok. Zadok was the father of Ahimaaz. Ahimaaz was the father of Azariah. Azariah was the father of Johanan. Johanan was the father of Azariah. Azariah was the High Priest in Solomon's Temple at Jerusalem. He was the father of Amariah. Amariah was the father of Ahitub. Ahitub was the father of Zadok. Zadok was the father of Shallum. Shallum was the father of Hilkiah. Hilkiah was the father of Azariah. Azariah was the father of Seraiah. Seraiah was the father of Jehozadak. Jehozadak went into exile with the people of Judah and Jerusalem. The Lord sent them into captivity under Nebuchadnezzar.

[16]The sons of Levi were Gershon, Kohath, and Merari.

[17]The sons of Gershon were Libni and Shimei.

[18]The sons of Kohath were Amram, Izhar, Hebron, and Uzziel.

[19-21]The sons of Merari were Mahli and Mushi.

This is a list of the clans of the Levites. They are listed by the father of each clan.

Gershon was the father of Libni. Libni was the father of Jahath. Jahath was the father of Zimmah. Zimmah was the father of Joah. Joah was the father of Iddo. Iddo was the father of Zerah. Zerah was the father of Jeatherai.

[22-24]Kohath's son was Amminadab. Amminadab's son was Korah. Korah's son was Assir. Assir's son was Elkanah. Elkanah's son was Ebiasaph. Ebiasaph's son was Assir. Assir's son was Tahath. Tahath's son was Uriel. Uriel's son was Uzziah. Uzziah's son was Shaul.

[25-27]Elkanah's sons were Amasai and Ahimoth. Ahimoth's son was Elkanah. The son of Elkanah was Zophai. The son of Zophai was Nahath. Nahath's son was Eliab. The son of Eliab was Jeroham. Jeroham's son was Elkanah. And Elkanah's son was Samuel.

²⁸The sons of Samuel were Joel and Abijah. Joel was the oldest. Abijah was the second.

²⁹⁻³⁰These are the descendants of Merari. Merari's son was Mahli. Mahli's son was Libni. Libni's son was Shimei. Shimei's son was Uzzah. Uzzah's son was Shimea. Shimea's son was Haggiah. Haggiah's son was Asaiah.

³¹King David chose songleaders and choirs. Their job was to praise God in the Tabernacle. They began their ministry after David had put the Ark there. ³²Later, Solomon built the Temple at Jerusalem. At that time, the choirs carried on their work there.

³³⁻³⁸These are the names of the choir leaders and their ancestors. Heman the singer was from the clan of Kohath. Heman was the son of Joel. Joel was the son of Samuel. Samuel was the son of Elkanah III. Elkanah III was the son of Jeroham. Jeroham was the son of Eliel. Eliel was the son of Toah. Toah was the son of Zuph. Zuph was the son of Elkanah II. Elkanah II was the son of Mahath. Mahath was the son of Amasai. Amasai was the son of Elkanah I. Elkanah I was the son of Joel. Joel was the son of Azariah. Azariah was the son of Zephaniah. Zephaniah was the son of Tahath. Tahath was the son of Assir. Assir was the son of Ebiasaph. Ebiasaph was the son of Korah. Korah was the son of Izhar. Izhar was the son of Kohath. Kohath was the son of Levi. Levi was the son of Israel.

³⁹⁻⁴³Heman's helper was Asaph. Asaph's group served at the right hand of Heman's. Asaph was the son of Berechiah. Berechiah was the son of Shimea. Shimea was the son of Michael. Michael was the son of Baaseiah. Baaseiah was the son of Malchijah. Malchijah was the son of Ethni. Ethni was the son of Zerah. Zerah was the son of Adaiah. Adaiah was the son of Ethan. Ethan was the son of Zimmah. Zimmah was the son of Shimei. Shimei was the son of Jahath. Jahath was the son of Gershon. Gershon was the son of Levi.

⁴⁴⁻⁴⁷Heman's second helper was Ethan. He was from the clan of Merari. He and his group stood on Heman's left.

Ethan was the son of Kishi. Kishi was the son of Abdi. Abdi was the son of Malluch. Malluch was the son of Hashabiah. Hashabiah was the son of Amaziah. Amaziah was the son of Hilkiah. Hilkiah was the son of Amzi. Amzi was the son of Bani. Bani was the son of Shemer. Shemer was the son of Mahli. Mahli was the son of Mushi. Mushi was the son of Merari. Merari was the son of Levi.

⁴⁸The other Levites were given the other jobs in the Tabernacle. ⁴⁹But only Aaron and his descendants were the priests. Their work included sacrificing burnt offerings and incense. They did all the work of the inner sanctuary, the Holy of Holies. They also did all the work of the yearly Day of Atonement for Israel. They made sure all the things commanded by Moses, God's servant, were done.

⁵⁰⁻⁵³These are the descendants of Aaron. Aaron's son was Eleazar. Eleazar's son was Phinehas. Phinehas's son was Abishua. Abishua's son was Bukki. Bukki's son was Uzzi. Uzzi's son was Zerahiah. Zerahiah's son was Meraioth. Meraioth's son was Amariah. Amariah's son was Ahitub. Ahitub's son was Zadok. Zadok's son was Ahimaaz.

⁵⁴This is a record of the cities and land given to the descendants of Aaron. They were members of the Kohath clan. Their land was chosen first among the Levites.

⁵⁵⁻⁵⁷In Judah, the priests were given Hebron and the pastures around it. It was one of the Cities of Refuge. But the fields and suburbs near Hebron were given to Caleb. He was the son of Jephunneh. ⁵⁸⁻⁵⁹Aaron's descendants were also given Libnah, Jattir, Eshtemoa, Hilen, Debir, Ashan, Beth-shemesh. These cities were given with the pastures around them. ⁶⁰The tribe of Benjamin gave them the cities of Geba, Alemeth, and Anathoth. These were given with the pastures around them.

These Kohath clans were given a total of 13 cities.

⁶¹Lots were then drawn to choose land for the rest of Kohath's descendants. They were given 10 cities in the land of the half-tribe of Manasseh.

⁶²The clans of Gershon were given 13

cities. They were in the Bashan area. These cities were given by the tribes of Issachar, Asher, Naphtali, and Manasseh.

⁶³The subclans of Merari were given 12 cities. They were given by the tribes of Reuben, Gad, and Zebulun.

⁶⁴⁻⁶⁵Cities and pastures were given to the Levites from the tribes of Judah, Simeon, and Benjamin. These cities have already been mentioned.

⁶⁶⁻⁶⁹The tribe of Ephraim gave cities and pastures to the clans of Kohath. They gave them Shechem in the hill country of Ephraim. This was a City of Refuge. They also gave them Gezer, Jokmeam, Beth-horon, Aijalon, and Gath-rimmon.

⁷⁰The rest of the Kohath clans were given cities from the western half-tribe of Manasseh. They gave them the cities of Aner and Bileam. These cities were given with the pastures around them.

⁷¹The clan of Gershon was given cities by the eastern half-tribe of Manasseh. They were given Golan, in Bashan, and Ashtaroth. These cities were given with their pastures.

⁷²The tribe of Issachar gave them Kedesh, Daberath, ⁷³Ramoth, and Anem. The pastures of each city were also given.

⁷⁴The tribe of Asher gave them Abdon, Mashal, ⁷⁵Hukok, and Rehob. The pastures came with the cities.

⁷⁶The tribe of Naphtali gave them Kedesh in Galilee. They also gave Hammon and Kiriathaim. The pastures came with the cities.

⁷⁷The Merari clan was also given cities and pastures. The tribe of Zebulun gave them Jokneam, Kartah, Rimmono, and Tabor with their pastures.

⁷⁸⁻⁷⁹The tribe of Reuben also gave cities to the clan of Merari. They gave them Bezer, which was a desert town. They also gave them Jahzah, Kedemoth, and Mephaath. These cities were given along with their pastures. They were located across the Jordan from Jericho.

⁸⁰The tribe of Gad gave them Ramoth in Gilead and Mahanaim. ⁸¹They also gave them Heshbon and Jazer. Each city was given with the pastures around it.

Issachar's Descendants

7 The sons of Issachar were Tola, Puah, Jashub, Shimron.

²Each of the sons of Tola was the head of a subclan. They were Uzzi, Rephaiah, Jeriel, Jahmai, Ibsam, and Shemuel.

At the time of King David, 22,600 soldiers came from these families.

³Uzzi's son was Izrahiah. Israhiah's sons were Michael, Obadiah, Joel, and Isshiah. All five of his sons were clan chiefs. ⁴At the time of King David, there were 36,000 soldiers among their descendants. This was because all five of them had several wives and many sons. ⁵The total number of soldiers from all the clans of Issachar was 87,000. They were all brave fighters. All of them are included in the family record.

Benjamin's Descendants

⁶The sons of Benjamin were Bela, Becher, and Jediael.

⁷The sons of Bela were Ezbon, Uzzi, Uzziel, Jerimoth, and Iri.

These five mighty soldiers were chiefs of clans. They had 22,034 soldiers as their descendants. All of them were recorded in the family history.

⁸The sons of Becher were Zemirah, Joash, Eliezer, Elioenai, Omri, Jeremoth, Abijah, Anathoth, Alemeth.

⁹At the time of David there were 20,200 soldiers among their descendants. They were led by their clan chiefs.

¹⁰The son of Jediael was Bilhan.

The sons of Bilhan were Jeush, Benjamin, Ehud, Chenaanah, Zethan, Tarshish, Ahishahar.

¹¹They were the chiefs of the clans of Jediael. Their descendants included 17,200 soldiers at the time of King David.

¹²The sons of Ir were Shuppim and Huppim. Hushim was one of the sons of Aher.

Naphtali's Descendants

¹³The sons of Naphtali were Jahziel, Guni, Jezer, and Shallum. They were descendants of Jacob's wife Bilhah.

Manasseh's Descendants

¹⁴Two of Manasseh's sons were Asriel and Machir. They were born of his

concubine from Aram. Machir became the father of Gilead.

¹⁵It was Machir who found wives for Huppim and Shuppim. Machir's sister was Maacah. Another descendant was Zelophehad. He had only daughters and no sons.

¹⁶Machir's wife, also named Maacah, bore him a son. She named him Peresh. His brother's name was Sheresh. Sheresh had sons named Ulam and Rakem. ¹⁷Ulam's son was Bedan.

These were the sons of Gilead. Gilead was the son of Machir. Machir was the son of Manasseh. ¹⁸Hammolecheth, Machir's sister, bore Ishhod, Abiezer, and Mahlah.

¹⁹The sons of Shemida were Ahian, Shechem, Likhi, and Aniam.

Ephraim's Descendants

²⁰⁻²¹The sons of Ephraim were Shuthelah, Bered, Tahath, Eleadah, Tahath, Zabad, Shuthelah, Ezer, and Elead.

Elead and Ezer tried to steal cattle at Gath. But they were killed by the local farmers. ²²Their father Ephraim mourned for them a long time. And his brothers tried to comfort him. ²³After that his wife had a son. Ephraim called him Beriah. This name means "a tragedy." He named him this because of what had happened.

²⁴Ephraim's daughter's name was Sheerah. She built Lower and Upper Beth-horon and Uzzen-sheerah.

²⁵⁻²⁷This is Ephraim's line of descent.

Ephraim was the father of Rephah.
Rephah was the father of Resheph.
Resheph was the father of Telah.
Telah was the father of Tahan.
Tahan was the father of Ladan.
Ladan was the father of Ammihud.
Ammihud was the father of Elishama.
Elishama was the father of Nun.
Nun was the father of Joshua.

²⁸One border of Ephraim's land was made by Bethel and the towns around it. The eastern border was made by Naaran. The western border was Gezer and its villages. The last border was at

Shechem and the villages nearby. It went as far as Ayyah and its towns.

²⁹The tribe of Manasseh were descendants of Joseph the son of Israel. They had the cities of Beth-shean, Taanach, Megiddo, and Dor. This also included the areas around them.

Asher's Descendants

³⁰The sons of Asher were Imnah, Ishvah, Ishvi, and Beriah. Their sister was Serah.

³¹The sons of Beriah were Heber and Malchiel. Malchiel was the father of Birzaith.

³²Heber's sons were Japhlet, Shomer, and Hotham. Shua was their sister.

³³Japhlet's sons were Pasach, Bimhal, and Ashvath.

³⁴His brother Shomer's sons were Rohgah, Jehubbah, and Aram.

³⁵The sons of his brother Hotham were Zophah, Imna, Shelesh, and Amal.

³⁶⁻³⁷The sons of Zophah were Suah, Harnepher, Shual, Beri, Imrah, Bezer, Hod, Shamma, Shilshah, Ithran, and Beera.

³⁸The sons of Ithran were Jephunneh, Pispa, and Ara.

³⁹The sons of Ulla were Arah, Hanniel, and Rizia.

⁴⁰These descendants of Asher were heads of clans. They were all skilled soldiers and chiefs. They had 26,000 soldiers among their descendants. These were recorded in the family history.

Benjamin's Descendants

8 Benjamin was the father of Bela. Bela was Benjamin's first son. Ashbel was his second son. Aharah was his third son. Nohah was Benjamin's fourth son. Rapha was his fifth son.

³⁻⁵The sons of Bela were Addar, Gera, Abihud, Abishua, Naaman, Ahoah, Gera, Shephuphan, Huram.

⁶⁻⁷These were the sons of Ehud. They were chiefs of the clans living at Geba. They were captured in war and sent away to Manahath. They were Naaman, Ahijah, and Gera. Gera was also called Heglam. He was the father of Uzza and Ahihud.

⁸⁻¹⁰Shaharaim divorced his wives Hushim and Baara. But he had children

in the land of Moab by Hodesh, his new wife. His sons were Jobab, Zibia, Mesha, Malcam, Jeuz, Sachia, Mirmah.

These sons all became chiefs of subclans.

[11]His wife Hushim had borne him Abitub and Elpaal.

[12]The sons of Elpaal were Eber, Misham, Shemed. Shemed built Ono and Lod and the villages nearby.

[13]His other sons were Beriah and Shema. They were chiefs of clans living in Aijalon. They chased out the people of Gath.

[14]Elpaal's sons also included Ahio, Shashak, and Jeremoth.

[15-16]The sons of Beriah were Zebadiah, Arad, Eder, Michael, Ishpah, and Joha.

[17-18]The sons of Elpaal also included Zebadiah, Meshullam, Hizki, Heber, Ishmerai, Izliah, and Jobab.

[19-21]The sons of Shimei were Jakim, Zichri, Zabdi, Elienai, Zillethai, Eliel, Adaiah, Beraiah, and Shimrath.

[22-25]The sons of Shashak were Ishpan, Eber, Eliel, Abdon, Zichri, Hanan, Hananiah, Elam, Anthothijah, Iphdeiah, and Penuel.

[26-27]The sons of Jeroham were Shamsherai, Shehariah, Athaliah, Jaareshiah, Elijah, and Zichri.

[28]These were the chiefs of the subclans living at Jerusalem.

[29]Jeiel lived at Gibeon where he was the leader. His wife's name was Maacah.

[30-32]Jeiel's oldest son was named Abdon. His other sons were Zur, Kish, Baal, Nadab, Gedor, Ahio, Zecher, and Mikloth. Mikloth was the father of Shimeah.

All of these families lived together near Jerusalem.

[33]Ner was the father of Kish. Kish was the father of Saul.

Saul's sons were Jonathan, Malchishua, Abinadab, and Eshbaal.

[34]The son of Jonathan was Mephibosheth.

The son of Mephibosheth was Micah.

[35]The sons of Micah were Pithon, Melech, Tarea, and Ahaz.

[36]Ahaz was the father of Jehoaddah. Jehoaddah was the father of Alemeth, Azmaveth, and Zimri. Zimri's son was Moza.

[37]Moza was the father of Binea. Binea's sons were Raphah, Eleasah, and Azel.

[38]Azel had six sons. Their names were Azrikam, Bocheru, Ishmael, Sheariah, Obadiah, and Hanan.

[39]Azel's brother Eshek had three sons. Ulam was his first son. Jeush came second. Eliphelet was his third son.

[40]Ulam's sons were great soldiers. They were expert marksmen with their bows. These men had 150 sons and grandsons. They were all from the tribe of Benjamin.

The Exiled People Return Home

9 The family tree of every person in Israel was recorded in *The Annals of the Kings of Israel.*

Judah was exiled to Babylon because the people worshiped idols.

[2]The first to come back and live again in their cities were families from the tribes of Israel. With them came some priests, Levites, and Temple servants.

[3]Then some families from the tribes of Judah, Benjamin, Ephraim, and Manasseh came to Jerusalem.

[4]One family was that of Uthai. He was the son of Ammihud, son of Omri, son of Imri, son of Bani. He was of the clan of Perez. Perez was a son of Judah.

[5]The Shilonites were another family to come back. They included Asaiah and his sons. Asaiah was Shilon's oldest son.

[6]There were also the sons of Zerah. These included Jeuel and his relatives. There were 690 of them in all.

[7-8]From the tribe of Benjamin came Sallu. He was the son of Meshullam. Meshullam was the son of Hodaviah. Hodaviah was the son of Hassenuah. With him came Ibneiah and Elah. Ibneiah was the son of Jeroham. And Elah was the son of Uzzi. Uzzi was the son of Michri. Meshullam also came back. He was the son of Shephatiah. Shephatiah was the son of Reuel. And Reuel was the son of Ibnijah.

[9]These men were all chiefs of clans. A total of 956 Benjaminites came back.

[10-11]The priests who came back were

Jedaiah, Jehoiarib, and Jachin. Azariah also came back. He was the son of Hilkiah. Hilkiah was the son of Meshullam. Meshullam was the son of Zadok. Zadok was the son of Meraioth. Meraioth was the son of Ahitub. He was the chief custodian of the Temple.

¹²Another of the priests who came back was Adaiah, the son of Jeroham. Jeroham was the son of Pashhur. Pashhur was the son of Malchijah.

Another priest was Maasai, the son of Adiel. Adiel was the son of Jahzerah. Jahzerah was the son of Meshullam. Meshullam was the son of Meshillemith. Meshillemith was the son of Immer.

¹³In all, 1,760 priests came back to Jerusalem.

¹⁴Among the Levites who came back was Shemaiah, the son of Hasshub. Hasshub was the son of Azrikam. Azrikam was the son of Hashabiah. Hashabiah was a descendant of Merari.

¹⁵⁻¹⁶With him, came Bakbakkar, Heresh, Galal, and Mattaniah. Mattaniah was the son of Mica. Mica was the son of Zichri. Zichri was the son of Asaph. Obadiah, the son of Shemaiah, also came back. Shemaiah was son of Galal. Galal was the son of Jeduthun. Berechiah, the son of Asa, also came. Asa was the son of Elkanah. Elkanah lived in the area of the Netophathites.

¹⁷⁻¹⁸The gatekeepers were Shallum, Akkub, Talmon, and Ahiman. Shallum was the chief gatekeeper. All of these men were Levites. They are still in charge of the eastern royal gate. ¹⁹Shallum's ancestry went back through Kore and Ebiasaph to Korah. He and his close relatives the Korahites were in charge of the sacrifices. They also protected the sanctuary. Their ancestors had once managed and guarded the Tabernacle. ²⁰Phinehas was the first director of this group in ancient times. He was the son of Eleazar the priest. And the Lord was with him.

²¹At that time Zechariah had the job of guarding the door to the Tabernacle. Zechariah was the son of Meshelemiah. ²²There were 212 doorkeepers in those days. They were chosen from their villages on the basis of their family history. And they were chosen by David and Samuel because they were faithful. ²³They and their descendants were in charge of the Lord's Tabernacle. ²⁴They were assigned to each of the four sides: east, west, north, and south. ²⁵And their relatives in the villages were told to help them from time to time. They served for seven days at a time.

²⁶The four head gatekeepers, all Levites, were in an office of great trust. They were in charge of the rooms and treasuries in the Tabernacle of God. ²⁷ Because of their important positions, they lived near the Tabernacle. They opened the gates each morning. ²⁸Some of them were told to care for the vessels used in the sacrifices and worship. They checked them in and out so they wouldn't lose them. ²⁹Some were in charge of the furniture and the items in the sanctuary. Others took care of the supplies, such as fine flour, wine, incense, and spices.

³⁰Other priests prepared the spices and incense.

³¹And Mattithiah had the job of making the flat cakes for grain offerings. He was a Levite and the oldest son of Shallum the Korahite.

³²Some members of the Kohath clan were in charge of making the special bread each Sabbath.

³³⁻³⁴The singers were all Levites. They lived in Jerusalem at the Temple. They were on duty at all hours. They were free from other jobs and were chosen by their family history.

Saul's Family Tree

³⁵⁻³⁷Jeiel lived in Gibeon. His wife was Maacah. He had many sons. Their names were Gibeon, Abdon, Zur, Kish, Baal, Ner, Nadab, Gedor, Ahio, Zechariah, and Mikloth. Abdon was the oldest.

³⁸Mikloth lived with his son Shimeam in Jerusalem near his relatives.

³⁹Ner was the father of Kish. Kish was the father of Saul. Saul was the father of Jonathan, Malchi-shua, Abinadab, and Eshbaal.

⁴⁰Jonathan was the father of Mephibosheth.

Mephibosheth was the father of Micah.

⁴¹Micah was the father of Pithon, Melech, Tahrea, and Ahaz.

⁴²Ahaz was the father of Jarah.

Jarah was the father of Alemeth, Azmaveth, and Zimri.

Zimri was the father of Moza.

⁴³Moza was the father of Binea, Rephaiah, Eleasah, and Azel.

⁴⁴Azel had six sons. Their names were Azrikam, Bocheru, Ishmael, Sheariah, Obadiah, and Hanan.

Saul Dies and David Becomes King

10 The Philistines attacked and beat the Israelite troops. They turned and ran. They were killed on the slopes of Mount Gilboa. ²They caught up with Saul and his three sons, Jonathan, Abinadab, and Malchi-shua. They killed them all. ³Saul had been hard-pressed with heavy fighting all around him. Then the Philistine archers shot and wounded him.

⁴He cried out to his bodyguard, "Quick! Kill me with your sword! Do it before these heathen catch and torture me."

But the man was afraid to do it. So Saul took his own sword. He fell against its point and it pierced his body. ⁵His bodyguard saw that Saul was dead. So he killed himself in the same way. ⁶So Saul and his three sons died together. The whole family was wiped out in one day.

⁷The Israelites in the valley below the mountain heard that their troops had been beaten. And they heard that Saul and his sons were dead. So they left their cities and ran. And the Philistines came and lived in them. ⁸The Philistines went back the next day. They planned to strip the bodies of the men killed in action. They wanted to gather the booty from the battlefield. At this time, they found the bodies of Saul and his sons. ⁹So they took off Saul's armor and cut off his head. Then they showed them all through the nation. And they celebrated the news before their idols. ¹⁰The Philistines put his armor in the temple of their gods. And they nailed his head to the wall of Dagon's temple.

¹¹But the people of Jabesh-gilead heard what the Philistines had done to Saul. ¹²So their heroic soldiers went out to the battlefield. They brought back Saul's body and the bodies of his three sons. Then they buried them under the oak tree at Jabesh. And there they mourned and fasted for seven days.

¹³Saul died because he didn't obey the Lord. And he had asked advice of a medium. ¹⁴He did not ask the Lord to guide him. So the Lord killed him. And he gave the kingdom to David, the son of Jesse.

David Conquers Jerusalem

11 Then the leaders of Israel went to David at Hebron. They told him, "We are your relatives. ²Even when Saul was king, you led our armies to battle. And it was you who brought them safely back again. The Lord your God has told you, 'You shall be the shepherd of my people Israel. You shall be their king.'"

³So David made a contract with them before the Lord. And they made him king of Israel, just as the Lord had told Samuel. ⁴Then David and the leaders went to Jerusalem. This city used to be called Jebus. The Jebusites lived there. They were the original people of the land. ⁵⁻⁶But the people of Jebus did not let them enter the city. So David took the walled city of Zion. It was later called the City of David. And he said to his men, "The first man to kill a Jebusite shall be made commander!" Joab, the son of Zeruiah, was the first. So he became the general of David's army. ⁷David lived in the walled city. That is why that area of Jerusalem is called the City of David. ⁸He extended the city out around the walled area. And Joab rebuilt the rest of Jerusalem. ⁹David became more and more famous and powerful. For the Lord of the heavens was with him.

David's Bravest Warriors

¹⁰These are the names of some of the bravest of David's soldiers. They had told the leaders of Israel to make David

their king. It happened just as the Lord had said it would.

¹¹Jashobeam, from Hachmon, was the leader of The Top Three. These were the greatest heroes among David's men. He once killed 300 men with his spear.

¹²The second of The Top Three was Eleazar. He was the son of Dodo. Dodo was a member of the clan of Ahoh. ¹³He was with David in the battle against the Philistines at Pasdammim. The Israelite army was in a barley field and had begun to run away. ¹⁴But he held his ground in the middle of the field. He took it back and killed the Philistines. And the Lord saved them with a great victory.

????????????????????????????????????
Two men each fought 300 men at one time. Who were they?

(Read 11:10-20 for the answer.)

????????????????????????????????????

¹⁵Another time, three of The Thirty went to David while he was hiding in the cave of Adullam. The Philistines were camped in the Valley of Rephaim. ¹⁶David was in the stronghold at the time. An outpost of the Philistines had been set up at Bethlehem. ¹⁷David wanted a drink from the Bethlehem well beside the gate. He mentioned this to his men. ¹⁸⁻¹⁹So these three broke through to the Philistine camp. They drew some water from the well. Then they brought it back to David. But he would not drink it! Instead he poured it out as an offering to the Lord. He said, "God forbid that I should drink it! It is the very blood of these men who risked their lives to get it."

²⁰Abishai, Joab's brother, was commander of The Thirty. He had gained his place among The Thirty by killing 300 men at one time with his spear. ²¹He was the chief and the most famous of The Thirty. But he was not as great as The Top Three.

²²Benaiah killed the two famous giants from Moab. Benaiah's father was a mighty soldier from Kabzeel. He also killed a lion in a slippery pit when there

was snow on the ground. ²³Once he killed an Egyptian who was 7½ feet tall. And his spear was as thick as a weaver's beam. But Benaiah went up to him with only a club in his hand. He pulled the spear away from him and used it to kill him. ²⁴⁻²⁵He was nearly as great as The Three. And he was very famous among The Thirty. David made him captain of his bodyguard.

²⁶⁻⁴⁷This is a list of other famous soldiers among David's men.

Asahel was Joab's brother.
Elhanan was the son of Dodo from Bethlehem.
Shammoth was from Harod.
Helez was from Pelon.
Ira was the son of Ikkesh. He was from Tekoa.
Abiezer was from Anathoth.
Sibbecai was from Hushath.
Ilai was from Ahoh.
Maharai was from Netophah.
Heled was the son of Baanah. He was from Netophah.
Ithai was the son of Ribai. He was a Benjaminite from Gibeah.
Benaiah was from Pirathon.
Hurai was from near the brooks of Gaash.
Abiel was from Arbath.
Azmaveth was from Baharum.
Eliahba was from Shaalbon
The sons of Hashem were from Gizon.
Jonathan was the son of Shagee. He was from Harar.
Ahiam was the son of Sacher. He was from Harar.
Eliphal was the son of Ur.
Hepher was from Mecherath.
Ahijah was from Pelon.
Hezro was from Carmel.
Naarai was the son of Ezbai.
Joel was the brother of Nathan.
Mibhar was the son of Hagri.
Zelek was from Ammon.
Naharai was from Beeroth. He was General Joab's bodyguard.
Ira was from Ithra.
Gareb was from Ithra.
Uriah was a Hittite.
Zabad was the son of Ahlai.
Adina was the son of Shiza. He was

from the tribe of Reuben. He was among the 31 leaders of Reuben.
Hanan was the son of Maacah.
Joshaphat was from Mithna.
Uzzia was from Ashterath.
Shama and Jeiel were the sons of Hotham. They were from Aroer.
Jediael was the son of Shimri.
Joha was Jediael's brother. He was from Tiza.
Eliel was from Mahavi.
Jeribai and Joshaviah were the sons of Elnaam.
Ithmah was from Moab.
Eliel, Obed, and Jaasiel were from Mezoba.

More Warriors Join David

12 These are the names of the famous soldiers who joined David at Ziklag. This was while he was hiding from King Saul. ²All of them were expert archers and slingers. They could use their left hands as well as their right! Like King Saul, they were all of the tribe of Benjamin.

³⁻⁷Their chief was Ahiezer, the son of Shemaah. He was from Gibeah. His brother Joash also came. There were also Jeziel and Pelet. They were the sons of Azmaveth. And Beracah came too, along with Jehu from Anathoth, and Ishmaiah from Gibeon. Ishmaiah was a brave soldier rated as high or higher than The Thirty. Jeremiah, Jahaziel, Johanan, and Jozabad also came. Jozabad was from Gederah. With them came Eluzai, Jerimoth, Bealiah, Shemariah, and Shephatiah. Shephatiah came from Haruph. Elkanah, Isshiah, Azarel, Joezer, Jashobeam came too. They were all Korahites. Joelah and Zebadiah, the sons of Jeroham, came from Gedor.

⁸⁻¹³Great and brave soldiers from the tribe of Gad also went to David in the wilderness. They were experts with both shield and spear. They were as fierce as lions. And they could run as swiftly as deer upon the mountains.

Ezer was their chief.
Obadiah was second in command.
Eliab was third in command.
Mishmannah was fourth in command.

Jeremiah was fifth in command.
Attai was sixth in command.
Eliel was seventh in command.
Johanan was eighth in command.
Elzabad was ninth in command.
Jeremiah was 10th in command.
Machbannai was 11th in command.

¹⁴These men were army officers. The weakest was worth 100 normal men! The strongest was worth 1,000! ¹⁵They crossed the Jordan River during a time of flooding. They took the lowlands on both the east and west banks.

¹⁶Others came to David from Benjamin and Judah. ¹⁷David went out to meet them. He said, "You might have come to help me. If so, we are friends. But you may have come to betray me to my enemies when I am innocent. If so, then may the God of our fathers see and judge you!"

¹⁸Then the Holy Spirit came upon them. And Amasai, a leader of The Thirty, replied,

"We are yours, David.
We are on your side, son of Jesse.
Peace, peace be unto you.
And peace be to all who help you.
For your God is with you."

So David let them join him. And he made them captains of his army.

¹⁹Some men from Manasseh left the Israelite army and joined David. This happened when he was going into battle with the Philistines against King Saul. But the Philistine generals would not let David and his men go with them. After much talking they sent them back. They were afraid that David and his men would fight for King Saul.

²⁰Here is a list of the men from Manasseh. They went with David as he was on his way to Ziklag. Their names were Adnah, Jozabad, Jediael, Michael, Jozabad, Elihu, and Zillethai. Each was a high-ranking officer of Manasseh's troops. ²¹They were brave and able soldiers. They helped David when he fought against the Amalekite raiders at Ziklag.

²²More men joined David almost every day. Soon he had a great army. They were the army of God. ²³Here is the

record of men who joined David at Hebron. They all wanted to see David become king instead of Saul. This was just as the Lord had said it would happen.

24-37From Judah, 6,800 troops came. They were armed with shields and spears.

From the tribe of Simeon came 7,100 good soldiers.

From the Levites came 4,600.

From the priests there were 3,700 troops. These men were descendants of Aaron. They were under the command of Zadok and Jehoiada. Zadok was a very brave young man. He and 22 members of his family were officers of the fighting priests.

From the tribe of Benjamin there were 3,000. This was the same tribe Saul was from. Most of that tribe stayed with Saul.

From the tribe of Ephraim came 20,800 mighty soldiers. Each was famous in the clan he came from.

From the half-tribe of Manasseh, 18,000 were sent. They went just to help David become king.

From the tribe of Issachar, there were 200 leaders of the tribe. Their relatives came with them. All of them were men who understood what Israel needed to do.

From the tribe of Zebulun came 50,000 trained soldiers. They were fully armed and loyal to David.

From Naphtali there were 1,000 officers and 37,000 troops. They brought shields and spears with them.

From the tribe of Dan there were 28,600 troops. All of them were ready for war.

From the tribe of Asher, there were 40,000 trained and ready troops.

From the other side of the Jordan River there came 120,000 troops. They brought every kind of weapon with them. These men came from the tribes of Reuben and Gad and the half-tribe of Manasseh.

38All of these men came to Hebron ready for battle. They came there just to make David the king of Israel. In fact, all of Israel was ready for this change. 39They feasted and drank with David for three days. For a feast had been made for their coming. 40People brought food on donkeys, camels, mules, and oxen. They brought it from nearby and from as far as Issachar, Zebulun, and Naphtali. Great supplies of flour, fig cakes, raisins, wine, oil, cattle, and sheep were brought. They were to be used in a great feast. This was because joy had spread throughout the land.

David Celebrates But Uzza Dies

13 First David spoke with all of his army officers. 2Then he spoke to all the men of Israel who were there.

"You think that I should be your king," he said. "And the Lord our God agrees with you. So let us send messages to our brothers throughout the land of Israel. This should include the priests and Levites. Invite them to come and join us. 3And let us bring back the Ark of our God. For we have forgotten it ever since Saul became king."

4Everyone agreed with him. They all believed it was the right thing to do. 5So David called the people of Israel from all across the nation. That way they could be there when the Ark of God was brought from Kiriath-jearim.

6Then David and all Israel went to Kiriath-jearim in Judah. They went there to bring back the Ark of the Lord. The Lord sits on it between the angels. 7It was taken from the house of Abinadab on a new cart. Uzza and Ahio drove the oxen. 8Then David and all the people danced before the Lord with great joy. They danced to singing and music by zithers, harps, tambourines, cymbals, and trumpets. 9When they came to the threshing-floor of Chidon, the oxen stumbled. Uzza reached out his hand to steady the Ark. 10Then the anger of the Lord blazed out against Uzza. And he killed him because he had touched the Ark. And so he died there before God. 11David was angry at the Lord for what he had done to Uzza. So he named the place "The Outbreak Against Uzza." And it is still called that to this day.

¹²Now David was afraid of God. And he asked, "How shall I ever get the Ark of God home?"

¹³Finally he decided to take it to the home of Obed-edom the Gittite. He did this instead of bringing it to the City of David. ¹⁴The Ark stayed there with the family of Obed-edom for three months. And the Lord blessed him and his family.

God Blesses David

14 King Hiram of Tyre sent masons and carpenters. They were to help build David's palace. He also supplied David with much cedar lumber. ²David now knew why the Lord had made him king. He now knew why the Lord had made his kingdom so great. It was for a special reason. It was to give joy to God's people!

³After David moved to Jerusalem, he married more wives. He became the father of many sons and daughters.

⁴⁻⁷These are the names of the sons born to him in Jerusalem: Shammua, Shobab, Nathan, Solomon, Ibhar, Elishua, Elpelet, Nogah, Nepheg, Japhia, Elishama, Beeliada, and Eliphelet.

David Conquers the Philistines

⁸The Philistines heard that David was Israel's new king. So they called out their army to capture him. But David learned that they were on the way. So he called together his own army. ⁹The Philistines were raiding the Valley of Rephaim. ¹⁰ David said to the Lord, "I might go out and fight them. But if I do, will you give me the victory?"

And the Lord replied, "Yes, I will."

¹¹So he attacked them at Baal-perazim and wiped them out. He said, "God has used me to sweep away my enemies like water bursting through a dam!" That is why the place has been known as Baal-perazim ever since. That name means "The Place of Breaking Through."

¹²After the battle the Israelites picked up many idols left by the Philistines. But David ordered them burned.

¹³Later the Philistines raided the valley again. ¹⁴Again David asked God what to do.

The Lord replied, "Go around by the mulberry trees. Attack from there. ¹⁵You will hear a sound like marching in the tops of the mulberry trees. That is your signal to attack. For God will go before you and destroy the enemy."

???????????????????????????????????

Which man died because he touched a golden chest?

(Read 13:6-11 for the answer.)

???????????????????????????????????

¹⁶So David did as the Lord commanded him. And he cut down the army of the Philistines. He chased them all the way from Gibeon to Gezer. ¹⁷David's fame spread everywhere. And the Lord caused all the nations to fear him.

The People Celebrate When the Ark Comes Back

15 David now built several palaces for himself in Jerusalem. And he also built a new Tabernacle to house the Ark of God. ²He gave these orders: "We will soon move the Ark to its new home. When we do, no one but the Levites may carry it. For God has chosen them for this work. They are to serve him for all time."

³Then David called all Israel to Jerusalem. They were to celebrate the bringing of the Ark into the new Tabernacle. ⁴⁻¹⁰This is a list of the priests and Levites that were there.

There were 120 from the clan of Kohath. Uriel was their leader.
There were 220 from the clan of Merari. Asaiah was their leader.
There were 130 from the clan of Gershon. Joel was their leader.
There were 200 from the subclan of Elizaphan. Shemaiah was their leader.
There were 80 from the subclan of Hebron. Eliel was their leader.
There were 112 from the subclan of Uzziel. Amminadab was their leader.

¹¹Then David called for Zadok and Abiathar, the High Priests. He also called for the Levite leaders. Their names were Uriel, Asaiah, Joel, Shemaiah, Eliel, and Amminadab.

¹²"You are the leaders of the clans of the Levites," he told them. "Now make yourselves pure with all your brothers. That way you may go with the Ark of the Lord, the God of Israel. That way you may bring it to the place I have made for it. ¹³The Lord destroyed us before because you, the Levites, did not carry it. We did not ask the Lord how we should carry the Ark."

????????????????????????????????????

Which woman hated her husband because she saw him dancing?

(Read 15:25-29 for the answer.)

????????????????????????????????????

¹⁴So the priests and the Levites made themselves pure by doing the proper things. They had to be pure to bring home the Ark of the Lord God of Israel. ¹⁵Then the Levites carried the Ark on their shoulders with its carrying poles. They did just as the Lord had ordered Moses.

¹⁶King David also ordered the Levite leaders to organize an orchestra. They played loudly on psaltries, harps, and cymbals. They also sang joyful songs. ¹⁷Heman, Asaph, and Ethan were the heads of the musicians. Heman was the son of Joel. Asaph was the son of Berechiah. Ethan was the son of Kushaiah, from the clan of Merari.

¹⁸Men were chosen as their helpers. Their names were Zechariah, Jaaziel, Shemiramoth, Jehiel, Unni, Eliab, Benaiah, Maaseiah, Mattithiah, Eliphelehu, Mikneiah, Obed-edom and Jeiel. They served as the doorkeepers.

¹⁹Heman, Asaph, and Ethan were chosen to sound the bronze cymbals. ²⁰Zechariah, Aziel, Shemiramoth, Jehiel, Unni, Eliab, Maaseiah, and Benaiah played lyres. ²¹Mattithiah, Eliphelehu, Mikneiah, Obed-edom, Jeiel, and Azaziah were the harpists. ²²The song leader was Chenaniah, the chief of the Levites. He was chosen for his skill. ²³Berechiah and Elkanah were guards for the Ark. ²⁴Shebaniah, Joshaphat, Nethanel, Amasai, Zechariah, Benaiah, and Eliezer blew the trumpets. They were all priests. They were to march at the front of the procession. And Obed-edom and Jehiah guarded the Ark.

²⁵Then David went with great joy to the home of Obed-edom. The elders of Israel and the high officers of the army went with him. They all went to bring the Ark to Jerusalem. ²⁶And God didn't destroy the Levites who were carrying the Ark. So they sacrificed seven bulls and seven lambs. ²⁷Now David was dressed in a fine linen robe. So were the Levites carrying the Ark, the singers, and Chenaniah the song leader. David also wore a linen ephod. ²⁸So the leaders of Israel took the Ark to Jerusalem with shouts of joy. They blew the horns and trumpets. They clashed the cymbals. And they played loudly on the harps and zithers.

²⁹The Ark finally came to Jerusalem. And David's wife Michal watched from a window. She was the daughter of King Saul. As she watched David dancing like a madman, she felt hate for him.

David Praises God with a Song

16 So they brought the Ark of God into a special tent. David had made this tent just for the Ark. And the leaders of Israel gave burnt offerings and peace offerings to God. ²At the end of these offerings David spoke to the people. He blessed them in the name of the Lord. ³Then he gave gifts to every person there, men and women alike. He gave them each a loaf of bread, some wine, and a cake of raisins.

⁴He chose certain of the Levites to serve before the Ark. They were to give praise and thanks to the Lord God of Israel. And they were to ask for his blessings on his people. ⁵Asaph was the leader of this group. His job was to sound the cymbals. His helpers were Zechariah, Jehiel, Shemiramoth, Jehiel, Mattithiah, Eliab, Benaiah, Obed-edom, and Jeiel. They played the harps and zithers. ⁶The

priests Benaiah and Jahaziel played their trumpets regularly before the Ark.

[7]At that time David began the custom of using choirs in the Tabernacle. They were used to sing thanks to the Lord. Asaph was the leader of this choir of priests.

[8]"Oh, give thanks to the Lord and
    pray to him," they sang.
"Tell the peoples of the world
About his mighty doings.
[9]Sing to him! Yes, sing his praises!
And tell of his great works.
[10]Glory in his holy name.
Let all rejoice who seek the Lord.
[11]Seek the Lord! Yes, seek his
    strength!
And seek his face without tiring.
[12-13]O descendants of his servant
    Abraham,
O chosen sons of Jacob,
Remember his mighty miracles!
Never forget his great miracles!
And remember his power.
[14]He is the Lord our God!
His power is seen throughout the
    earth.
[15]Remember his covenant forever.
Do not forget the words he com-
    manded
To a thousand generations.
[16]Remember his agreement with
    Abraham,
And his oath to Isaac.
[17]Do not forget his promise to Jacob.
He promised Israel
With an everlasting promise.
[18]'I will give you the land of Ca-
    naan,' he said.
'It will be your inheritance.'
[19]Israel was once few in number.
    Oh, so few!
They were just strangers in the
    Promised Land.
[20]They wandered from country to
    country,
From one kingdom to another.
[21]But God didn't let anyone harm
    them.
Even kings were killed who sought
    to hurt them.
[22]'Don't harm my chosen people,'
    he declared.

'These are my prophets. Do not
    touch them.'
[23]Sing to the Lord, O earth!
Declare each day that he is the one
    who saves!
[24]Show his glory to the nations!
Tell everyone about his miracles.
[25]For the Lord is great and should
    be highly praised.
He is to be held in awe above all
    gods.
[26]The other so-called gods are demons.
But the Lord made the heavens.
[27]Majesty and honor march before
    him.
Strength and gladness walk beside
    him.
[28]O people of all nations of the
    earth,
Ascribe great strength and glory to
    his name!

God deserves our praise

*Yes, the Lord deserves your
praise. So praise him!*

1 Chronicles 16:29

---

[29]Yes, the Lord deserves your praise.
So praise him!
Bring an offering and come before him.
Worship the Lord when clothed
    with holiness!
[30]Tremble before him, all the earth!
The world stands unmoved.
[31]Let the heavens be glad, the earth
    rejoice.
Let all the nations say, 'It is the
    Lord who reigns.'
[32]Let the great seas roar!
Let the countryside and everything
    in it rejoice!
[33]Let the trees in the woods sing for
    joy before the Lord!
For he comes to judge the earth.
[34]Oh, give thanks to the Lord, for
    he is good.
His love and his kindness go on for-
    ever.
[35]Cry out to him, 'Oh, save us, God
    of our salvation.
Bring us safely back from among
    the nations.
Then we will thank your holy name.

We will triumph in your praise.'
36Blessed be the Lord God of Israel,
Forever and ever."

And all the people shouted "Amen!"
and praised the Lord.

37David had Asaph and his fellow
Levites serve at the Tabernacle. They did
whatever needed to be done each day.
38This group included Obed-edom and
Hosah. Obed-edom was the son of Jeduthun. And 68 others helped them as
guards.

39Meanwhile the old Tabernacle of
the Lord was still used. It was on the
hill of Gibeon. David left Zadok the
priest to serve the Lord there. The
priests who worked under Zadok served
there too. 40They sacrificed burnt offerings to the Lord each morning. They
also gave them each evening. They
made the sacrifices on the altar set
aside for that purpose. They did just
as the Lord had commanded Israel.
41David also chose Heman and Jeduthun to give thanks to the Lord. He also
chose several others by name to help
them. They were to praise the Lord for
his constant love and mercy. 42They
used their trumpets and cymbals. They
played as the singers sang loud praises
to God. And Jeduthun's sons were chosen as guards.

43At last the celebration ended and
the people went back to their homes.
And David went to bless his own family.

God Makes a Promise to David

17 David had been living in his new
palace for some time. And he said
to Nathan the prophet, "Look! I'm living
here in a cedar-paneled home. But the
Ark of the Covenant of God is out there
in a tent!"

2And Nathan replied, "Carry out your
plan in every detail. For it is the will of
the Lord."

3But that same night God spoke to
Nathan. 4"Go!" the Lord said. "Give my
servant David this message: 'You are not
to build my temple! 5I've lived in a tent
ever since Israel left Egypt. I've gone
from one tent to another all this time.
6In all that time I never told any of the

leaders of Israel to build me a cedar-lined
temple.'

7"Tell my servant David, 'The Lord of
heaven says this to you. I took you from
being a shepherd. I made you the king
of my people. 8And I have been with you
everywhere you've gone. I have destroyed your enemies. And I will make
your name as great as the greatest of the
earth. 9And I will give a lasting home to
my people Israel. I will plant them in
their land. They will not be troubled any
more. The wicked nations won't conquer them as they did before. They
won't trouble them as they did 10when
the judges ruled them. I will conquer all
of your enemies. And I now make a
special promise. I will cause your descendants to be kings of Israel just as you are.

11"'Someday your time here on earth
will be over and you will die. At that
time, I will put one of your sons on your
throne. And I will make his kingdom
strong. 12He is the one who shall build
me a temple. And I will make his royal
line last for all time. 13I will be his father.
And he shall be my son. I will never take
away my mercy and love from him. I will
never treat him as I treated Saul. 14I will
put him over my people. He will rule
over the kingdom of Israel for all time.
And his descendants will always be
kings.'"

15So Nathan told King David all that
the Lord had said.

David Accepts God's Promise

16Then King David went in and sat before
the Lord. He said, "Who am I, O Lord
God? What is my family that you have
given me all this? 17For you have already
done great things for me. But they are
nothing compared to what you have
promised in the future! O Lord God, you
have promised that future generations
of my children will be kings too! You
speak as though I were someone very
great. 18What else can I say? You know
that I am but a dog. But you have chosen
to honor me! 19O Lord, you have given
me many great promises. And you have
given them just because you want to be
kind to me. You have given them because
of your own great heart. 20O Lord, there

is no one like you. There is no other God. In fact, we have never even heard of another god like you!

21"And what other nation in all the earth is like Israel? You have made a special nation. And you have saved it from Egypt. And you did it so that the people could be your people. And you made a great name for yourself. You did great miracles in driving out the nations from before your people. 22You have said that your people Israel belong to you for all time. And you have become their God.

23"You promised that I and my children will always rule this nation. And now, do as you have promised, Lord. 24And may this bring eternal honor to your name. Prove to everyone that you always do what you say. They will exclaim, 'The Lord of heaven is indeed the God of Israel!' And Israel shall always be ruled by my children and their descendants! 25Now I have the courage to pray to you. For you have told me this. 26God himself has promised this good thing to me! 27May this blessing rest upon my children for all time. For when you give a blessing, Lord, it is an eternal blessing!"

David Conquers Many Enemies

18 David finally conquered the Philistines. He took control of Gath and all the towns around it. 2He also conquered Moab. And he made its people send him money every year. 3David fought against King Hadadezer of Zobah. He fought against him as far as Hamath. At that time Hadadezer was trying to spread his kingdom to the Euphrates River. 4David captured 1,000 of his chariots, 7,000 cavalry, and 20,000 troops. He crippled most of the chariot teams. But he kept 100 chariot teams for his own use.

5The Syrians came from Damascus to help King Hadadezer. But David killed 22,000 of them. 6Then he put a group of his troops in Damascus, the Syrian capital. So the Syrians, too, had to send David large amounts of money every year. And the Lord gave David victory everywhere he went. 7He brought the gold shields of King Hadadezer's officers

to Jerusalem. 8He also brought a great amount of bronze from Hadadezer's cities of Tibhath and Cun. King Solomon later melted the bronze and used it for the Temple. He molded it into the bronze tank and the pillars. He also used it for the items used in offering sacrifices on the altar.

9King Tou of Hamath learned that King David had destroyed Hadadezer's army. 10So he sent his son Hadoram to greet King David. He praised him for his success. And he gave him many gifts of gold, silver, and bronze. He wanted to make a treaty with David. For Hadadezer and Tou had been enemies. There had been many wars between them. 11King David dedicated these gifts to the Lord. He did the same with the silver and gold he took from other nations. Those nations were Edom, Moab, Ammon, Amalek, and the Philistines.

12Abishai then destroyed 18,000 Edomites in the Valley of Salt. Abishai was the son of Zeruiah. 13He put army groups in Edom. And they forced the Edomites to pay large amounts of money to David every year. This is just another example of how the Lord gave David victory after victory. 14David reigned over all of Israel and was a just ruler.

15Joab was commander of the army. He was the son of Zeruiah. Jehoshaphat was the historian. He was the son of Ahilud. 16Zadok and Ahimelech were the head priests. Zadok was the son of Ahitub. Ahimelech was the son of Abiathar. Shavsha was the king's special helper. 17 Benaiah was in charge of the king's bodyguard. He was the son of Jehoiada. The bodyguard was made up of the Cherethites and Pelethites. David's sons were his chief helpers.

David Defends the Honor of His People

19 King Nahash of Ammon died. So his son Hanun became the new king.

2-3Then David said, "I am going to show friendship to Hanun. This is because of all the kind things his father did for me."

So David sent a kind message to

Hanun at the death of his father. David's messengers went to King Hanun. But Hanun's counselors warned him.

Spies

1 CHRONICLES 19:1-5

Bible-time battles were not fought with swords and spears only. Spies were important. Men were sent ahead of the warriors to see what they could learn about the enemy. Spies had two jobs to do. The first was to look for strengths and weaknesses in enemy defenses. Joseph accused his brothers of being spies, looking for Egypt's weaknesses (Genesis 42:8-9). Joshua sent two spies into Jericho to see where it was weak (Joshua 2:1). Spies sometimes had a second job. When Absalom rebelled against his father, King David, he sent spies throughout the land. Their job was to spread lies about David. They turned people against the king. Satan can use these same two tactics to defeat Christians. Our only defense is to ask God for his help.

"Don't fool yourself!" they said. "Don't believe that David has sent these men to honor your father! They are here to spy out the land! That way they will be able to come in and conquer it!"

⁴So King Hanun made fun of King David's messengers. He shaved their beards and cut their robes off at the hips. Then he sent them back to David in shame. ⁵David heard what had happened. So he sent a message to his messengers. They were very ashamed of how they looked. He told them to stay at Jericho until their beards could grow out again. ⁶King Hanun soon saw his mistake. And he sent $2,000,000 to buy the help of troops, chariots, and cavalry. They came from Mesopotamia, Aram-maacah, and Zobah. ⁷He hired 32,000 chariots. He also hired the support of the king of Maacah and his whole army. These forces camped at Medeba. And there the troops King Hanun had called out from his cities joined them.

⁸David soon learned about this. So he sent Joab and the best soldiers of Israel. ⁹The army of Ammon went out to meet them. And they began the battle at the gates of the city of Medeba. Meanwhile, the forces hired by Hanun from Syria were out in the field. ¹⁰Joab saw that the enemy forces were both in front of and behind him. So he divided his army. And he sent one group to fight the Syrians. ¹¹The other group moved against the Ammonites. The second group was under the command of Joab's brother Abishai.

¹²"The Syrians might be too strong for me. If so, come and help me," Joab told his brother. "But the Ammonites might be too strong for you. If so, I'll come and help you. ¹³ Be brave! Let us act like men! Let us save our people and the cities of our God! And may the Lord do what is best."

¹⁴So Joab and his troops attacked the Syrians. And the Syrians turned and ran. ¹⁵The Ammonites were under attack by Abishai's troops. They saw that the Syrians were running. So they ran into the city. Then Joab went back to Jerusalem.

¹⁶After their defeat, the Syrians called for more troops. They came from east of the Euphrates River. These were led by Shophach, King Hadadezer's army commander. ¹⁷⁻¹⁸This news soon got to David. So he called out all Israel to fight.

He crossed the Jordan River and fought the enemy troops. But the Syrians again ran from David. And he killed 7,000 chariot drivers and 40,000 of their troops. He also killed Shophach, the commander of the Syrian army. ¹⁹Then King Hadadezer's troops gave in to King David. And they became his subjects. Never again did the Syrians help the Ammonites in their battles.

David Defeats the Ammonites

20 Spring was the season when wars usually began. So the next spring Joab led the Israelite army against Ammon. He had many successful attacks against the cities and villages there. After destroying them, he surrounded Rabbah and took it. Meanwhile, David had stayed in Jerusalem. ²Later David came to the battle. He took the crown from the head of the king of Rabbah. And he put it on his own head. It was made of gold inlaid with gems. And it weighed 75 pounds! David also took many valuable things from the city. ³He drove the people from the city. And he set them to work with saws, iron picks, and axes. This was his custom with all the conquered Ammonite peoples. Then David and all his army went back to Jerusalem.

David Fights the Philistines

⁴The next war was against the Philistines at Gezer. But Sibbecai killed one of the sons of the giant, Sippai. Sibbecai was from Hushath. So the Philistines gave up. ⁵During another war with the Philistines, Elhanan killed Lahmi. Elhanan was the son of Jair. Lahmi was the brother of Goliath the giant. The handle of his spear was like a weaver's beam! ⁶⁻⁷Later, Israel fought another battle at Gath. There was a giant there whose father was also a giant. He had six fingers on each hand and six toes on each foot. And he made fun of Israel. But he was killed by David's nephew Jonathan. He was the son of David's brother Shimea. ⁸These giants were descendants of the giants of Gath. And they were killed by David and his soldiers.

David Counts the People and God Sends a Plague

21 Then Satan brought trouble on Israel. For he made David decide to count all the people.

²"Count all the people in the land. Then bring me the totals," he told Joab and the other leaders.

³But Joab did not think this was a good idea. "The Lord might make his people grow 100 times. And if he did, would they not all be yours? So why are you asking us to do this? Why must you cause Israel to sin?"

⁴But the king won the argument. So Joab did as he was told. He traveled all through Israel and came back to Jerusalem. ⁵Joab counted 1,100,000 men of fighting age in Israel and 470,000 in Judah. ⁶But he didn't count the tribes of Levi and Benjamin. This was because he was so upset at what the king had made him do.

⁷And God was not happy because David had counted the people. So he punished Israel for it.

⁸But David said to God, "I am the one who has sinned. Please forgive me. For I know now how wrong I was to do this."

⁹Then the Lord spoke to Gad, David's personal prophet. ¹⁰⁻¹¹He said, "Go and tell David, 'The Lord has given you three choices. Which will you choose? ¹²You may have three years of famine. You may have three months of attack by the enemies of Israel. Or you may have three days of deadly plague. In the plague, the Lord's angel will bring death to the land. Think it over. Let me know what answer to give the one who sent me.'"

¹³"This is a hard thing to decide," David replied. "But let me fall into the hands of the Lord. This is better than falling into the power of men. For God's mercies are very great."

¹⁴So the Lord sent a plague upon Israel. As a result, 70,000 men died. ¹⁵During the plague God sent an angel to destroy Jerusalem. But then he felt such pity that he changed his mind. He commanded the destroying angel, "Stop! It is enough!" The angel of the Lord was standing near Jerusalem at the time. He was by the threshing-floor of Araunah the Jebusite. ¹⁶David saw the angel of the

Lord standing between heaven and earth. The angel's sword was drawn. And he was pointing it toward Jerusalem. So David and the elders of Israel clothed themselves in sackcloth. And they fell to the ground before the Lord.

¹⁷And David said to God, "I am the one who sinned. I am the one who ordered the people to be counted. But what have these sheep done? O Lord my God, destroy me and my family. But do not destroy your people."

¹⁸Then the angel of the Lord spoke to Gad. He told him to order David to build an altar to the Lord. He was to build it at the threshing-floor of Araunah the Jebusite. ¹⁹⁻²⁰So David went to see Araunah. He was threshing wheat at the time. Araunah saw the angel as he turned. And his four sons ran and hid. ²¹Then Araunah saw the king coming. So he left the threshing-floor and bowed to the ground before King David.

²²David said to Ornan, "Let me buy this threshing-floor from you at its full price. Then I will build an altar to the Lord. And the plague will stop."

²³"Take it, my lord. Use it as you wish," Ornan said to David. "Take the oxen, too. Use them for burnt offerings. Use the threshing tools for wood for the fire. And use the wheat for the grain offering. I give it all to you."

²⁴"No," the king replied, "I will buy it for the full price. I cannot take what is yours and give it to the Lord. I will not offer a burnt offering that has cost me nothing!"

²⁵So David paid Ornan $4,300 in gold. ²⁶And he built an altar to the Lord there. He sacrificed burnt offerings and peace offerings upon it. And he called out to the Lord. And the Lord answered by sending down fire from heaven. He burned up the offering on the altar. ²⁷Then the Lord commanded the angel to put back his sword into its sheath. ²⁸David saw that the Lord had answered his prayer. So he sacrificed to him again. ²⁹The Tabernacle and altar made by Moses in the wilderness were on the hill of Gibeon. ³⁰But David didn't have time to go there to plead before the Lord. For he was afraid of the drawn sword of the angel of the Lord.

David Gets the Materials Ready for the Temple

22 Then David said, "This is the place where the Temple of the Lord will be built! It will be built at Araunah's threshing-floor. And the altar for Israel's burnt offerings will be put here!"

²David now called all the foreigners who lived in Israel. He had them make blocks of squared stone for the Temple. ³They also made iron into the many nails that would be needed. They would be used in the doors, the gates and for the clamps. And they melted so much bronze that it was too much to weigh. ⁴The men of Tyre and Sidon brought great rafts of cedar logs to David.

⁵"Solomon my son is young and tender," David said. "The Temple of the Lord must be a great building. It must be famous throughout the world! So I will start to get ready for it now."

So David gathered the building materials before his death. ⁶Then he told his son Solomon to build a temple for the Lord God of Israel.

⁷"I wanted to build it myself," David told him. ⁸"But the Lord said not to do it. 'You have killed too many men in great wars,' he told me. 'You have made the ground red with blood. So you are not to build my Temple. ⁹But I will give you a son,' he told me. 'He will be a man of peace. For I will give him peace with his enemies in the lands nearby. His name shall be Solomon. This name means "Peaceful." And I will give peace to Israel during his reign. ¹⁰He shall build my Temple. He shall be as my own son. And I will be his father. I will cause his sons and his descendants to reign. They will be kings over every generation of Israel.'

¹¹"So now, my son, may the Lord be with you. May he prosper you as you do what he told you to do. May you build the Temple of the Lord. ¹²And may the Lord give you good judgment. May you follow all his laws when he makes you king of Israel. ¹³For you must obey the laws and commands that he gave to Israel through Moses. And if you do, you will succeed in all you do.

Be strong and brave! Don't ever be afraid and discouraged!

14"By hard work I have collected many building materials. I have several billion dollars worth of gold. I've collected millions in silver. And there is so much iron and bronze that I haven't even weighed it. I have also gathered timber and stone for the walls. This is at least a beginning. It is something with which to start. 15And you have many skilled stonemasons and carpenters. You have craftsmen of every kind! 16They are expert gold and silver smiths. And they know how to work bronze and iron. So get to work! And may the Lord be with you!"

17Then David ordered all the leaders of Israel to help his son in this project. 18"The Lord your God is with you," he said. "He has given you peace with the nations around us. For I have conquered them in the name of the Lord and for his people. 19Now try with every fiber of your being to obey the Lord your God. If you do, you will soon bring the Ark into the Temple of the Lord! And you will bring all the other holy articles with it!"

David Gives the Levites Their Jobs

23 By this time David was an old man. So he stepped down from the throne. And he chose his son Solomon as the new king of Israel. 2He called all the leaders of Israel. He also called all the priests and Levites. They came for the ceremony to crown Solomon king. 3At this time, the men of the tribe of Levi who were 30 years or older were counted. The total came to 38,000.

4-5David said, "From the Levites, take 24,000 of them to oversee the work at the Temple. And 6,000 will be bailiffs and judges. And 4,000 will be temple guards. And 4,000 will praise the Lord with musical instruments. They will play the instruments I have made."

6Then David divided them into three main groups. The groups were named after the sons of Levi. There was the Gershon clan, the Kohath clan, and the Merari clan.

7Subgroups were made of the Gershon clan. They were named after his sons Ladan and Shimei. 8-9These subgroups were further divided into six groups. These were named after the sons of Ladan and Shimei. Ladan's sons were Jehiel the leader, Zetham, and Joel. Shimei's sons were Shelomoth, Haziel, and Haran.

10-11The subclans of Shimei were named after his four sons. They were Jahath, Zizah, Jeush, and Beriah. Jahath was the first son. Zizah was the next son. And Jeush and Beriah made up just one subclan. This was because neither had many sons.

????????????????????????????????
Who gathered billions of dollars in gold to build the Temple, but said it was only a start?

(Read 22:11-16 for the answer.)

????????????????????????????????

12The clan of Kohath was divided into four groups. They were named after his sons Amram, Izhar, Hebron, and Uzziel. 13Amram was the ancestor of Aaron and Moses. Aaron and his sons were set apart as priests. They served in the holy work of sacrificing the people's offerings to the Lord. They served the Lord at all times. And they made blessings in the Lord's name.

14-15Moses was the special man of God. He and his sons were included with the tribe of Levi. His sons were named Gershom and Eliezer. 16Gershom's sons were led by Shebuel. 17Eliezer's only son was Rehabiah. He was the leader of his clan, for he had many children.

18The sons of Izhar were led by Shelomith.

19The sons of Hebron were led by Jeriah. Amariah was second in command. Jahaziel was third in command. And Jekameam was fourth in command.

20The sons of Uzziel were led by Micah. Isshiah was the second in command.

21The sons of Merari were Mahli and Mushi. The sons of Mahli were Eleazar and Kish. 22Eleazar died without any sons. And his daughters were married to their cousins, the sons of Kish. 23Mushi's sons were Mahli, Eder, and Jeremoth.

²⁴So the Levites were counted and listed. They counted all the men of Levi, 20 years old or older. They were listed under the names of these clans and subclans. And they were all given work at the Temple. ²⁵For David said, "The Lord God of Israel has given us peace. And he will always live in Jerusalem. ²⁶Now the Levites will no longer need to carry the Tabernacle from place to place. And they won't need to carry its tools either."

²⁷David was the one who ordered the tribe of Levi to be counted. It was one of the last things he did before his death. ²⁸The work of the Levites was to help the priests. The priests were the descendants of Aaron. The Levites helped them make the sacrifices at the Temple. They also did the custodial work. And they helped perform the rituals for making people pure. ²⁹They made the Bread of the Presence. They provided the flour for the grain offerings. And they baked the wafers made without yeast. These were either fried or mixed with olive oil. They also checked all the weights and measures. ³⁰Each morning and evening they stood before the Lord. They sang thanks and praise to him. ³¹They helped in the special sacrifices of burnt offerings and the Sabbath sacrifices. They helped at the new moon feasts and at all the other feasts too. There were always as many Levites there as were needed for the event. ³²They took care of the Tabernacle and the Temple. And they helped the priests in whatever way they could.

David Divides the Priests into Groups and Gives Them Jobs

24 The priests were the descendants of Aaron. They were divided into two clans. The clans were named after Aaron's sons, Eleazar and Ithamar.

Nadab and Abihu were also sons of Aaron. But they died before their father did. And they had no children. So only Eleazar and Ithamar were left to carry on. ³Zadok and Ahimelech helped David. Zadok was the leader of the Eleazar clan. Ahimelech was the leader of the Ithamar clan. David divided Aaron's descendants into many groups. Each group was given certain duties. And they each served at certain times. ⁴Eleazar's descendants were divided into 16 groups. Ithamar's descendants were divided into eight groups. There were more leaders among the clan of Eleazar.

⁵All jobs were given to the groups by coin-toss. That way no one could complain about their work. Many famous men and high officials of the Temple were chosen from each clan. ⁶Shemaiah was a Levite and the son of Nethanel. He acted as recording secretary. He wrote down the names of the priests and their jobs. He did this in front of the king and a group of leaders. The leaders were Zadok the priest and Ahimelech. Ahimelech was the son of Abiathar. The other heads of the priests and Levites were also there. Two groups from the clan of Eleazar and one from the clan of Ithamar were chosen for each job.

⁷⁻¹⁸The work was given in this order. It was decided by coin-toss.

The first group chosen was led by Jehoiarib.
The second group was led by Jedaiah.
The third group was led by Harim.
The fourth group was led by Seorim.
The fifth group was led by Malchijah.
The sixth group was led by Mijamin.
The seventh group was led by Hakkoz.
The eighth group was led by Ahijah.
The ninth group was led by Jeshua.
The 10th group was led by Shecaniah.
The 11th group was led by Eliashib.
The 12th group was led by Jakim.
The 13th group was led by Huppah.
The 14th group was led by Jeshebeab.
The 15th group was led by Bilgah.
The 16th group was led by Immer.
The 17th group was led by Hezir.
The 18th group was led by Happizzez.
The 19th group was led by Pethahiah.
The 20th group was led by Jehezkel.
The 21st group was led by Jachin.
The 22nd group was led by Gamul.
The 23rd group was led by Delaiah.
The 24th group was led by Maaziah.

¹⁹Each group carried out the Temple duties it was given. This work had been given by God to their ancestor Aaron long before.

²⁰These were the other descendants of Levi. Amram's descendant was Shubael. Shubael's descendant was Jehdeiah. ²¹The Rehabiah group was led by his oldest son Isshiah. ²²The Izhar group was led by Shelamoth. And his descendant was Jahath. ²³The sons of Hebron were Jeriah, Amariah, Jahaziel, and Jekameam. Jeriah was Hebron's oldest son. Amariah was his second son. Jahaziel was his third son. Jekameam was his fourth son.

²⁴⁻²⁵The Uzziel group was led by his son Micah. Micah's son was Shamir. Micah's brother was Isshiah. Isshiah's son was Zechariah.

²⁶⁻²⁷The Merari group was led by his sons Mahli and Mushi. Jaaziah's group was led by his son Beno. It included his brothers Shoham, Zaccur, and Ibri. ²⁸⁻²⁹Mahli's descendants were Eleazar and Kish. Eleazar had no sons. Kish had sons and Jerahmeel was one of them. ³⁰The sons of Mushi were Mahli, Eder, and Jerimoth.

These were the descendants of Levi in their various clans. ³¹Like the descendants of Aaron, they were given their duties by coin-toss. No privileges were given to those with age or rank. It was done in front of King David, Zadok, and Ahimelech. The leaders of the priests and the Levites were also there.

The Musicians' Duties

25 David and the army commanders then chose men to prophesy. They were to prophesy to the music of zithers, harps, and cymbals. These men were from the groups of Asaph, Heman, and Jeduthun. Here is a list of their names and their work.

²Under Asaph were his sons Zaccur, Joseph, Nethaniah, and Asharelah. Asaph prophesied for David and directed his sons.

³Under Jeduthun were his six sons. They led in giving thanks and praising the Lord. They did this to the music of the zither. Their names were Gedaliah,

Zeri, Jeshaiah, Shimei, Hashabiah, and Mattithiah.

⁴⁻⁵Under the direction of Heman were his sons. Heman was the king's private chaplain. His sons were Bukkiah, Mattaniah, Uzziel, Shebuel, Jerimoth, Hananiah, Hanani, Eliathah, Geddalti, Romamti-ezer, Joshbekashah, Mallothi, Hothir, and Mahazioth. God had honored Heman with 14 sons and three daughters. ⁶⁻⁷Their music ministry included the playing of cymbals, harps, and zithers. All were under their father as they did this work in the Tabernacle.

Asaph, Jeduthun, and Heman reported directly to the king. They and their families were all trained in singing praises to the Lord. Each one of them was a master musician. There were 288 in all. ⁸The singers were given their term of service by coin-toss. It didn't matter how old or great they were.

⁹⁻³¹The first toss fell to Joseph of the Asaph clan. It included 12 of his relatives.
The second fell to Gedaliah. From his group 12 were chosen.
The third fell to Zaccur. From his group 12 were chosen.
The fourth fell to Izri. From his group 12 were chosen.
The fifth fell to Nethaniah. From his group 12 were chosen.
The sixth fell to Bukkiah. From his group 12 were chosen.
The seventh fell to Jesharelah. From his group 12 were chosen.
The eighth fell to Jeshaiah. From his group 12 were chosen.
The ninth fell to Mattaniah. From his group 12 were chosen.
The 10th fell to Shimei. From his group 12 were chosen.
The 11th fell to Azarel. From his group 12 were chosen.
The 12th fell to Hashabiah. From his group 12 were chosen.
The 13th fell to Shubael. From his group 12 were chosen.
The 14th fell to Mattithiah. From his group 12 were chosen.

The 15th fell to Jeremoth. From his group 12 were chosen.

The 16th fell to Hananiah. From his group 12 were chosen.

The 17th fell to Joshbekasha. From his group 12 were chosen.

The 18th fell to Hanani. From his group 12 were chosen.

The 19th fell to Mallothi. From his group 12 were chosen.

The 20th fell to Eliathah. From his group 12 were chosen.

The 21st fell to Hothir. From his group 12 were chosen.

The 22nd fell to Giddalti. From his group 12 were chosen.

The 23rd fell to Mahazioth. From his group 12 were chosen.

The 24th fell to Romamti-ezer. From his group 12 were chosen.

The Duties of the Temple Guard

26 The temple guards were from the Asaph division of the Korah clan. The captain of the guard was Meshelemiah. He was the son of Kore.

2-3The men under him were his sons. The oldest was Zechariah. Jediael was the second. Zebadiah was the third. Jathniel was the fourth. Elam was the fifth. Jehohanan was the sixth. Eliehoenai was the seventh.

4-5The sons of Obed-edom were also chosen as Temple guards. Shemaiah was the oldest. Jehozabad was the second. Joah was the third. Sacar was the fourth. Nethanel was the fifth. Ammiel was the sixth. Issachar was the seventh. Peullethai was the eighth.

What a blessing God gave him with all those sons!

6-7Shemaiah's sons were all able men. For this reason, they were all leaders in their clan. Their names were Othni, Rephael, Obed, and Elzabad.

Their brave brothers were Elihu and Semachiah. They were also very able men.

8All of these sons and grandsons of Obed-edom were capable men. They were all very good at their work. There were 62 of them in all. 9Meshelemiah's 18 sons and brothers, too, were real leaders. 10Hosah chose Shimri as the leader

among his sons. He chose him even though he was not the oldest. Hosah was from the Merari clan. 11The names of some of his other sons were Hilkiah, Tebaliah, and Zechariah. Hilkiah was the second. Tebaliah was the third. Zechariah was the fourth. Hosah's sons and brothers numbered 13 in all.

12The groups of Temple guards were named after the leaders. Like the other Levites, they were chosen to work at the Temple. 13They were given guard duty at the various gates by coin toss. It didn't matter how great or famous their family was. 14-15Shelemiah and his group were chosen to watch the east gate. Zechariah was Shelemiah's son. He was chosen to watch the north gate. He was a man of great wisdom. Obed-edom and his group were chosen to guard the south gate. His sons were given charge of the storehouses. 16Shuppim and Hosah were chosen to watch the west gate. They also were to guard the Shallecheth Gate on the upper road. 17Six guards were sent daily to the east gate. Four were sent to the north gate. Four were sent to the south gate. And two were sent to each of the storehouses. 18Six guards were sent each day to the west gate. Four were sent to the upper road. And two were sent to the nearby areas. 19The Temple guards were chosen from the clans of Korah and Merari.

The Duties of the Other Officials

20-22Another group of Levites were led by Ahijah. They were given the care of the Temple treasury. They took care of the gifts brought to the Lord. These men were from the clan of Gershon. They were from the subclan of Ladan. Their names were Zetham and Joel, the sons of Jehieli. 23-24Shebuel was the chief officer of the treasury. He was a descendant of Gershom. Gershom was the son of Moses. Shebuel was in charge of the subclans named after Amram, Izhar, Hebron, and Uzziel.

25Shebuel's relatives descended from Eliezer. Eliezer's son was Rehabiah. Rehabiah's son was Jeshaiah. Jeshaiah's son was Joram. Joram's son was Zichri. Zichri's son was Shelomoth. 26Shelomoth and his brothers were chosen to care for the gifts given to the Lord by King David. They cared for the gifts from the other leaders of the nation too. These leaders were officers and generals of the army. 27For these men gave their war loot to help support the Temple. 28Shelomoth and his brothers also cared for the items given to the Lord by Samuel the prophet. They cared for the gifts given by Saul the son of Kish. They cared for the gifts given by Abner the son of Ner. And they cared for the gifts given by Joab the son of Zeruiah. They cared for gifts from anyone who was important in Israel.

29Chenaniah and his sons were chosen as judges. They were from the subclan of Izhar. 30Hashabiah and 1,700 of his clansmen were from the family of Hebron. They were all able men. They were put in charge of the land of Israel west of the Jordan River. They oversaw the Lord's work there. And they made sure the laws of God and the king were followed. 31-32According to the records, Jerijah was the leader of the clan of Hebronites. In the 40th year of King David's reign, a search was made of the records. Able men of the clan of the Hebronites were found at Jazer in Gilead. Jerijah had 2,700 relatives who were all very capable men. Under Jerijah's leadership, they were put in charge of Reuben, Gad, and the half-tribe of Manasseh. They oversaw the Lord's work there. And they also took care of the king's business east of the Jordan.

The Commanders of the Army

27 The Israelite army was divided into 12 groups. Each group had 24,000 troops. This included officers and other leaders. Each group was called up for active duty one month each year. Here is the list of the units and their group commanders.

2-3The commander of the first group was Jashobeam. He had charge of 24,000 troops. They were on duty the first month of each year.

4The commander of the second group was Dodai. He was a descendant of Ahohi. He had charge of 24,000 troops. They were on duty the second month of each year. Mikloth was the first officer in his group.

5-6The commander of the third group was Benaiah. His 24,000 men were on duty the third month of each year. He was the son of Jehoiada the High Priest. He was also the chief of The Thirty. These were the greatest soldiers in David's army. His son Ammizabad later took his place as group commander.

7The commander of the fourth group was Asahel. He was the brother of Joab. He was later replaced by his son Zebadiah. He had 24,000 men under him. They were on duty the fourth month of each year.

8The commander of the fifth group was Shamuth from Izrah. He had 24,000 men under him. They were on duty the fifth month of each year.

9The commander of the sixth group was Ira. He was the son of Ikkesh from Tekoa. He had 24,000 men under him. They were on duty the sixth month of each year.

10The commander of the seventh group was Helez from Pelona in Ephraim. He had 24,000 men under him. They were on duty the seventh month of each year.

11The commander of the eighth group was Sibbecai. He was of the Hushite subclan from Zerah. He had 24,000 men under him. They were on duty the eighth month of each year.

12The commander of the ninth group was Abiezer. He was from Anathoth in the tribe of Benjamin. He commanded 24,000 troops. They were on duty during the ninth month of each year.

13The commander of the 10th group was Maharai. He was from Netophah in Zerah. He had 24,000 men under him. They were on duty the 10th month of each year.

14The commander of the 11th group was Benaiah. He was from Pirathon in Ephraim. He had 24,000 men under him. They were on duty during the 11th month of each year.

15The commander of the 12th group was Heldai. He was from Netophah in the area of Othniel. He commanded 24,000 men. They were on duty during the 12th month of each year.

Officers of the Tribes

16-22The top officers of the tribes of Israel were as follows.

Over Reuben was Eliezer. He was the son of Zichri.

Over Simeon was Shephatiah. He was the son of Maacah.

Over Levi was Hashabiah. He was the son of Kemuel.

Over the descendants of Aaron was Zadok.

Over Judah was Elihu. He was a brother of King David.

Over Issachar was Omri. He was the son of Michael.

Over Zebulun was Ishmaiah. He was the son of Obadiah.

Over Naphtali was Jeremoth. He was the son of Azriel.

Over Ephraim was Hoshea. He was the son of Azaziah.

Over the half-tribe of Manasseh was Joel. He was the son of Pedaiah.

Over the other half of Manasseh, in Gilead, was Iddo. He was the son of Zechariah.

Over Benjamin was Jaasiel. He was the son of Abner.

Over Dan was Azarel. He was the son of Jeroham.

23David only counted those who were 20 years old or older. This was because the Lord had promised there would be as many people as the stars. 24Joab began to count the people. But he never finished it. For the anger of God broke out upon Israel. The final total was never put into the records of King David.

Administrators of the Kingdom

25Azmaveth was the chief in charge of the palace treasuries. He was the son of Adiel. Jonathan (son of Uzziah) was chief of the regional treasuries. These were in the cities, villages, and forts of Israel. 26Ezri was manager of the laborers on the king's estates. He was the son of Chelub. 27Shimei from Ramath oversaw the king's vineyards. And Zabdi from Shiphma was in charge of making and storing wine. 28Baal-hanan from Gedera was in charge of the king's olive yards. He was also in charge of his sycamore trees. These were in the lowlands bordering Philistine lands. Joash had charge of the supplies of olive oil.

29Shitrai was in charge of the cattle on the Plains of Sharon. Shitrai was from the Plains of Sharon. Shaphat had charge of those in the valleys. He was the son of Adlai. 30Obil had charge of the camels. He was from the land of Ishmael. Jehdeiah from Meronoth had charge of the donkeys. 31The sheep were under the care of Jaziz the Hagrite. These men were King David's overseers.

32The attendant to the king's sons was Jonathan, David's uncle. He was a wise counselor and an educated man. Jehiel was their tutor. He was the son of Hachmoni.

33Ahithophel advised the king. Hushai the Archite was the king's friend. 34Ahithophel was helped by Jehoiada and by Abiathar. Jehoiada was the son of Benaiah. Joab was commander of the Israelite army.

David and Solomon Discuss Plans for the Temple

28 David now called all of his officials to Jerusalem. He called the political leaders. He called the commanders of the 12 army groups and the other army officers. He called those in charge of his property and livestock. And he called all the other leaders in his kingdom. 2He rose and stood before them. And he spoke to them as follows:

"My brothers and my people! It was my desire to build a temple. It was to be a place for the Ark of the Covenant of the Lord to rest. It was to be a place for our God to live in. I have now collected all that is needed for the building. 3But God has told me, 'You are not to build my temple. For you are a soldier and have shed much blood.'

4"But the Lord God of Israel has chosen me. He chose me from among all my father's family. He chose me to begin a line that will rule Israel for all time. He

If you look for him,
you will find him.

1 Chronicles 28:9

has chosen the tribe of Judah. And from the families of Judah, he chose my father's family. And from among his sons, the Lord chose me. And he has made me king over all Israel. 5The Lord has given me many children. But from among my sons he has chosen Solomon. He will succeed me on the throne of his Kingdom of Israel. 6He has told me, 'Your son Solomon shall build my Temple. For I have chosen him as my son. And I will be his father. 7He must keep on obeying my commands and laws as he has until now. If he does, I will make his kingdom last for all time.'"

8Then David turned to Solomon. He said, "I speak to you here before the leaders of Israel. We stand before the people of God, and in the sight of our God. Here I am telling you to search out every command of the Lord. That way you may keep ruling this good land. That way you may leave it to your children to rule for all time. 9Solomon, my son, get to know the God of your fathers. Worship and serve him with a clean heart and a willing mind. For the Lord sees every heart. He knows every thought. If you look for him, you will find him. But if you forget him, he will throw you aside. 10So be very careful. For the Lord has chosen you to build his holy Temple. Be strong and do as he commands."

11Then David gave Solomon the plans for the Temple and the area around it. There were plans for the treasuries. There were plans for the upstairs rooms and the inside rooms. There were plans for the sanctuary and the place of mercy. 12He also gave Solomon his plans for the outer court and the outside rooms. There were plans for the Temple storage areas. There were plans for the treasuries to store gifts given by famous people. For the Holy Spirit had given David all these plans. 13The king

also passed on to Solomon directions about the work of the groups of priests and Levites. And he gave directions about each item in the Temple. These were the items to be used for worship and sacrifice.

14David weighed out enough gold and silver to make these items. 15He also weighed out the gold needed for the lampstands and lamps. He also weighed

Golden Meat Hooks
1 CHRONICLES 28:17

Have you ever seen a solid gold meat hook? You would if you could visit the Temple. Priests handled meat for burnt offerings in the Temple with these hooks.

Before meat was offered on the altar, it was boiled in a pot. While it was boiling, the priests sent a servant with a hook. The servant dug the hook into the meat and pulled. The meat that came off with the hook was given to the priests to eat. The priests did not get paid money for working at the Temple. So this was how the priests got some of their food.

The meat hooks were an important part of the sacrifices. The meat hooks were also an important part of helping the priests get enough food to eat. Some ordinary things have an extraordinary purpose in serving God, don't they?

out the silver for the silver lampstands and lamps. Each was made according to how it would be used. 16He weighed out the gold for the table. This was the table for the Bread of the Presence. He also weighed out the gold for the other gold tables. And he weighed the silver for the silver tables. ¹⁷Then he weighed out the gold for the solid gold hooks. These were used in handling the meat from sacrifices. He also weighed the metal for the basins, cups, and bowls of gold and silver. ¹⁸Finally, he weighed out the gold for the altar of incense and for the gold angels. These were the angels whose wings were stretched over the Ark of the Covenant of the Lord.

Others may want to serve God because of the way we serve him

Who will do what I have done? Who will give himself and all that he has to the Lord?

1 Chronicles 29:5

---

¹⁹"Every part of this plan is in writing," David told Solomon. "For the hand of the Lord was upon me. He gave me knowledge about everything in the plan." ²⁰Then he continued, "Be strong and brave! And get to work! Don't be scared by the size of the task. For the Lord my God is with you. He will not leave you. He will see to it that all is finished in the right way. ²¹And these groups of priests and Levites will serve in the Temple. Others with skills of every kind will help. The army and the whole nation are at your command."

The People Bring Gifts for the Temple

29 Then King David turned to the whole assembly. He said, "God has chosen my son Solomon to be the next king of Israel. He is still young and has a lot to learn. The work ahead of him is huge. For the temple he will build is not just another building. It is for the Lord God himself! ²I have worked hard to gather the materials for building it. I have gathered enough gold, silver, bronze, and iron. There is also enough wood. There is enough onyx, other precious stones, costly jewels, and marble. ³And now I am giving all my own treasures to help in the building. This is

---

We should give because we want to give

Everyone was happy for this chance to give.

1 Chronicles 29:9

---

because of my devotion to the Temple of God. I give this over and above the materials I have already gathered. ⁴⁻⁵These personal gifts consist of millions of dollars of gold from Ophir. There are huge amounts of silver. This metal is to be used to cover the walls of the buildings. It will also be used for the gold and silver designs. Now then, who will do what I have done? Who will give himself and all that he has to the Lord?"

⁶⁻⁷Then the clan leaders, the heads of the tribes, the army officers, and the officers of the king got together. They promised huge sums of gold and silver. They also promised 675 tons of bronze and 3,750 tons of iron. ⁸They also gave great amounts of jewelry. These were put in the Temple treasury with Jehiel. Jehiel was a descendant of Gershon. ⁹Everyone was happy for this chance to give. And King David was moved with deep joy.

David Praises God

¹⁰David was still in front of the whole assembly. And he spoke his praises to the Lord. "O Lord God of our father Israel," he prayed. "Praise your name for ever and ever! ¹¹Yours is the mighty power and glory and victory and majesty. Everything in the heavens and earth is yours, O Lord. And this is your kingdom. We adore you as being in control of everything. ¹²Riches and honor come from you alone. And you are the Ruler of all mankind. Your hand controls power and might. And you are the one who makes men great and gives strength. ¹³O our God, we thank you and praise your great name. ¹⁴But who am I? And who are my people? Who are we to be allowed to give anything to you? Everything we have has come from you! We only give you what is yours already! ¹⁵For we are here for but a moment. We are strangers in the land as our fathers were before us. Our days

on earth are like a shadow. They are gone so soon without a trace. [16]O Lord our God! All this material gathered to build a temple for your holy name comes from you! It all belongs to you! [17]I know, my God, that you test men to see if they are good. For you enjoy good men. I have done all this with good motives. I have watched your people give their gifts with joy.

**God owns everything
in the heavens and earth**

*Everything in the heavens and
earth is yours, O Lord.*

1 Chronicles 29:11

---

[18]"O Lord, God of our fathers Abraham, Isaac, and Israel! Make your people always want to obey you. And see to it that their love for you never changes. [19]Give my son Solomon a good heart toward God. That way he will want to obey you in the smallest detail. And he will look forward to building your Temple. He will finish the Temple for which I have prepared."

[20]Then David said to all the people, "Give praise to the Lord your God!" And they did. They bowed low before the Lord and the king.

[21]The next day they brought 1,000 young bulls, 1,000 rams, and 1,000 lambs. They gave them as burnt offerings to the Lord. They also gave drink offerings. And they gave many other sacrifices on behalf of all Israel. [22]Then they feasted and drank before the Lord with great joy.

And again they crowned King David's son Solomon as their king. They anointed him before the Lord as their leader. And they anointed Zadok as their priest. [23]So God chose Solomon to take the throne of his father David. He succeeded in all he did. And all the people of Israel obeyed him. [24]The national leaders, the army officers, and his brothers all were loyal to King Solomon. [25]The Lord made him popular with all the people of Israel. And he gained even more wealth and honor than his father.

David Dies at an Old Age

[26-27]David was king of the land of Israel for 40 years. He ruled in Hebron for seven of those years. Then he reigned in Jerusalem for 33 years. [28]He died at an old age. He was rich and honored. And his son Solomon ruled in his place. [29]The deeds of King David have been written in the history of Samuel the prophet. David's deeds have been recorded in the history written by Nathan the prophet. They have also been written in the history written by the prophet Gad. [30]These records tell of his reign and of his power. They tell all that happened to him and to Israel. They also record what happened to the kings of the nearby nations.

SECOND
CHRONICLES

Have you ever seen fire come down from Heaven? You will in 2 Chronicles. You'll also see a horse barn with 4,000 stalls. And you'll be amazed at the beautiful Temple of God, with its walls and ceiling made of pure gold. It cost billions of dollars and took 150,000 people to make it. In this book, you'll meet the richest and wisest king in the world.

Second Chronicles is the story of the glory of Solomon. He became the king who had everything. But when Solomon became too rich, he turned away from God. His great nation divided and became weak. You'll cry a little when you see Jerusalem captured and the beautiful Temple destroyed. But at the end of this book you will see that God is still with his people, even though they turned against him. You'll be glad to learn that God is still with us, too.

Solomon Asks God for Wisdom

1 King David's son Solomon was now the only ruler of Israel. For the Lord his God had made him a great king. 2-3He called all the army officers and judges to Gibeon. He also called all the other leaders of Israel. He led them up to the hill to the old Tabernacle. It had been built by Moses, the Lord's servant. He had made it while he and the Israelites were in the desert. 4There was another Tabernacle in Jerusalem. It was built by King David for the Ark of God. He put the Ark there when he moved it from Kiriath-jearim. 5-6The bronze altar made by Bezalel still stood in front of the old Tabernacle. (Bezalel was the son of Uri. And Uri was the son of Hur.) Now Solomon and the people he had asked to come stood before it. And he sacrificed on it 1,000 burnt offerings to the Lord.

7That night God spoke to Solomon. He told him, "Ask me for anything. I will give it to you!"

8Solomon replied, "O God! You have been so kind and good to my father David. And now you have given me the kingdom. 9This is all I want! For you have fulfilled your promise to David my father. You have made me king over a nation full of people. Israel has as many people as the earth has dust! 10Now give me wisdom and knowledge to rule them properly. For who can rule such a great nation by himself?"

11God replied, "You want to help your people more than anything else. You didn't ask for riches and honor for yourself. And you didn't ask me to curse your enemies. You didn't even ask for a long life. But you asked for wisdom and knowledge to lead my people. 12Yes, I will give you the wisdom and knowledge you asked for! And I will also give you riches and honor! You will have more of these than any other king before you! There will never again be such a great king in all the world!"

??????????????????????????????????
Which man owned 12,000 horses?

(Read 1:14-17 for the answer.)

??????????????????????????????????

¹³Solomon then left the Tabernacle. He went down the hill and went back to Jerusalem to rule Israel. ¹⁴He built up a huge force of 1,400 chariots. And he called up 12,000 cavalry to guard the cities where the chariots were kept. Some of them, of course, were stationed at Jerusalem near the king. ¹⁵During Solomon's reign, silver and gold were common. They were as common in Jerusalem as rocks on the road! And cedar lumber was used like common sycamore! ¹⁶Solomon sent horse traders to Egypt. There they bought whole herds at cheap prices. ¹⁷At that time Egyptian chariots sold for $400 each and horses for $100. This was the price when they were brought to Jerusalem. Many of these were then resold to the kings of the Hittites and Syria.

Solomon Makes Plans for Building the Temple

2 Solomon now decided to build a temple for the Lord. He decided to build a palace for himself too. ²To do this they would need a force of 70,000 laborers and 80,000 stonecutters in the hills. They would also need 3,600 foremen to manage the others. ³Solomon sent a messenger to King Hiram at Tyre. He asked for shipments of cedar lumber. Hiram had once given such lumber to David when he was building his palace.

⁴"I am about to build a temple for the Lord my God," Solomon told Hiram. "It will be a place where I can burn incense and sweet spices before God. At this temple, we will show the special bread. We will give burnt offerings each morning and evening. We will give them on the Sabbaths. We will give offerings at the new moon feasts. And we will give them at other regular feasts of the Lord our God as well. For God wants Israel to always celebrate these special times. ⁵It is going to be a great temple. This is because he is a great God. He is greater than any other. ⁶But who can ever build him a worthy home? Not even the highest heaven would be great enough! And who am I to be allowed to build a temple for God? But it will be a place to worship him.

⁷"So send me skilled craftsmen. Send me workers in gold and silver. Send brass and iron workers, too. Send me weavers to make purple, red, and blue cloth. Send skilled carvers. They will work beside the craftsmen of Judah and Jerusalem. These have been chosen by my father David. ⁸Also send me cedar trees and fir trees. And send algum trees from the Forests of Lebanon. For your men are the best lumbermen in the world! I will send my men to help them. ⁹A huge amount of lumber will be needed. For the temple I am going to build will be large. It will also be very beautiful. ¹⁰I will pay your men 20,000 sacks of crushed wheat. I will give them 20,000 barrels of barley. I will also give them 20,000 barrels of wine and 20,000 barrels of olive oil."

¹¹King Hiram sent a message to King Solomon. "The Lord must love his people!" he said. "That is why he has made you their king! ¹²Praise to the Lord God of Israel! He is the one who made the heavens and the earth! He has given to David a wise and understanding son. You will build God's Temple and a royal palace for yourself.

God Sends a Master Craftsman

¹³"I am sending you a master craftsman. His name is Huramabi. He is a wise man, ¹⁴the son of a Jewish woman from Dan in Israel. His father is from here in Tyre. He is skillful at working with gold and silver. He also does fine work with brass and iron. He knows all about stonework, carpentry, and weaving. And he is an expert in the dyeing of purple, blue, and red cloth. He is a carver besides, and an inventor! He will work

with your craftsmen. He will teach those chosen by my lord David, your father. [15]So send along the wheat, barley, olive oil, and wine you promised. [16]We will begin cutting wood from the Lebanon mountains. We will cut as much as you need. We will bring it to you in log rafts across the sea to Joppa. From there you can take the logs inland to Jerusalem."

[17]Solomon now counted all the foreigners in the country. He did just as his father David had done. He found that there were 153,600 of them. [18]He chose 70,000 as laborers and 80,000 as loggers. He also chose 3,600 as foremen.

The Construction Begins

3 Finally the building of the Temple began. It was in Jerusalem at the top of Mount Moriah. There the Lord had spoken to Solomon's father, King David. This was where the threshing-floor of Araunah the Jebusite had been. David had chosen it as the site for the Temple. [2]The actual building began on the 17th day of April. This was in the fourth year of King Solomon's reign.

[3]The base was 90 feet long and 30 feet wide. [4]A covered porch ran along the whole 30-foot width of the Temple. The inner walls and ceiling were covered with pure gold! The roof was 180 feet high.

[5]The main part of the Temple was paneled with cypress wood. This wood was covered with pure gold. And it had palm trees and chains carved on it. [6]Pretty jewels were put into the walls to add to the beauty. The gold, by the way, was of the best. It came from Parvaim. [7]All the walls, beams, doors, and thresholds in the Temple were plated with gold. And angels were carved on the walls.

[8]Inside the Temple, at one end, was the most sacred room. This was the Holy of Holies. It was 30 feet square. This too was covered with the finest gold. It was valued at millions of dollars. [9]Gold nails were used. They each weighed 26 ounces. The upper rooms were also covered with pure gold.

[10]Inside the Holy of Holies, Solomon put two statues of angels. Huramabi covered them with gold. [11-13]They stood on the floor facing the outer room. Their wings stretched wingtip to wingtip across the room. They reached from wall to wall. [14]Across the entrance to this room he put a curtain of blue and red linen. It had angels sewn into it.

[15]At the front of the Temple were two pillars. They were 52½ feet high. At the top of each was a 7½-foot capital. The capitals flared out to the roof. [16]Huramabi made chains and put them on top of the pillars. There were 100 gold pomegranates tied to the chains. [17]Then he set up the pillars at the front of the Temple. One was on the right. The other was on the left. And he gave them names. Jachin was the one on the right. And Boaz was the one on the left.

Huramabi's Skillful Work

4 He also made a bronze altar. It was 30 feet long, 30 feet wide, and 15 feet high. [2]Then he made a huge round tank. It was 15 feet across from rim to rim. The rim stood 7½ feet above the floor. And the tank was 45 feet around. [3]The tank had two rows of gourd designs around its base. These were cast as part of the tank. [4]The tank stood on 12 metal oxen facing outward. Three faced to the north. Three faced to the west. Three faced to the south. And three faced to the east. [5]The walls of the tank were five inches thick. They flared out like the cup of a lily. It held 3,000 barrels of water.

[6]He also made 10 bowls for water to wash the offerings. Five were put to the right of the huge tank. Five were put to the left of it. The priests used the tank for their own washing. They did not use the bowls.

[7]Carefully doing what God had ordered, he then made 10 gold lampstands. He put them in the Temple. Five were set against each wall. [8]He also built 10 tables. He put five against each wall on the right and left. And he molded 100 solid gold bowls. [9]Then he built a court for the priests. He also made the public court. He covered the doors of these courts with bronze. [10]The huge tank was in the southeast corner of the outer room

of the Temple. [11]Huramabi also made the needed pots, shovels, and basins. These would be used in making the sacrifices.

So at last he finished the work given to him by King Solomon.

[12-16]He built the two pillars.

He made the two flared capitals on the tops of the pillars.

He made the two sets of chains on the capitals.

He made the 400 pomegranates. They hung from the two sets of chains on the capitals.

He made the bases for the bowls and the bowls themselves.

He made the huge tank and the 12 oxen under it.

He made the pots, shovels, and meat hooks.

Huramabi made all these items for King Solomon. And he used polished bronze. [17-18]The king did the casting at the claybanks of the Jordan valley. This was between Succoth and Zeredah. They used so much bronze that it was too heavy to weigh. [19]Solomon commanded that all the furniture of the Temple be made of gold. This included the utensils and the altar. It also included the table for the Bread of the Presence. [20]The lamps and lampstands were to be made of gold. [21]The flower designs and tongs were to be gold. [22]The lamp snuffers, basins, spoons, and firepans all were to be made of solid gold. Even the doorway of the Temple was covered with gold. So were the main door and the inner doors to the Holy of Holies.

5 So the Temple was finally finished. Then Solomon brought in the gifts given to the Lord by his father, King David. They were stored in the Temple treasury.

The Ark Is Brought to the Temple

[2]Solomon now called all the leaders of Israel to Jerusalem. He called all the heads of the tribes and clans. They came to move the Ark. It would be taken from the Tabernacle in the City of David. And it would be moved to its new home in the Temple. [3]This feast took place in October. It was the time of the yearly Feast of Tabernacles. [4-5]As the leaders of Israel watched, the Levites lifted the Ark. They carried it out of the Tabernacle. And they brought all the other holy vessels with it. [6]King Solomon sacrificed sheep and oxen before the Ark. The other leaders made the offerings with him. They offered so many animals that no one tried to keep count!

[7-8]Then the priests carried the Ark into the inner room of the Temple. This was the Holy of Holies. And they put it under the angels' wings. Their wings spread over the Ark and its carrying poles. [9]The poles were so long that their ends could be seen from the outer room. But they could not be seen from the outside doorway.

The Ark is still there at the time of this writing. [10]Nothing was in the Ark but the two stone tablets. Moses had put them there at Mount Sinai. That was when the Lord made a covenant with the people of Israel. At that time, they were just leaving Egypt.

[11-12]Then the priests went out from the Holy of Holies. They all had made themselves pure no matter what clan they were from. And the Levites praised the Lord as the priests came out! The singers were Asaph, Heman, and Jeduthun. And all their sons and brothers were with them. They were dressed in fine linen robes. And they stood at the east side of the altar. Along with the choir, 120 priests blew their trumpets. Others were playing cymbals, lyres, and harps. [13-14]The band and chorus sang and played as one. Together they praised and thanked the Lord. They sang songs with the sound of trumpets and the clashing of cymbals. And they played other musical instruments loudly. All were praising and thanking the Lord. The theme was "The Lord is so good! His loving-kindness lasts for all time!"

And at that moment the glory of the Lord filled the Temple. It came as a bright cloud. It filled the Temple so that the priests could not do their work.

Solomon Blesses the People

6 This is the prayer prayed by Solomon at that time.

"The Lord has said that he would
   live in the thick darkness.
But I have made a Temple for you,
   O Lord! It is a place for you to
   live in for all time!"

[3]Then the king turned around to the people. They stood to be blessed by him. [4]"Blessed be the Lord God of Israel," he said to them. "He is the God who talked to my father David. And now he has fulfilled the promise he made to him. For the Lord told him, [5-6]'I have never before chosen a special city. I have never chosen a place where my name will be honored. I have not done this since bringing my people from the land of Egypt. And never before have I chosen a king for my people Israel. But now I have chosen Jerusalem as that city. And I have chosen David as that king.'

[7]"My father David wanted to build this Temple. [8]But the Lord said not to. The Lord told him that it was good to want to build it. [9]But he was not the one chosen to do it. His son was chosen for that task. [10]And now the Lord has done what he promised. For I have become king in my father's place. I have built the Temple for the Name of the Lord God of Israel. [11]And I have put the Ark there. And in the Ark is the Covenant between the Lord and his people Israel."

Solomon Dedicates the Temple to the Lord

[12-13]As he spoke, Solomon was standing in front of the people. He stood on a platform in the center of the outer court. It was in front of the altar of the Lord. The platform was made of bronze. It was 7½ feet square and 4½ feet high. Now, as all the people watched, he knelt down. He reached out his arms toward heaven and prayed this prayer.

[14]"O Lord God of Israel," he prayed. "There is no God like you in heaven and earth. You are the God who keeps his kind promises. You keep your promises to all who obey you and try to do your will. [15]And you have kept your promise to my father David. It is clear by what you have done today. [16]And now, O God of Israel, carry out your other promise to him. Fulfill your promise that David's family shall always rule over Israel. Help them always to rule if they obey your laws as David did. [17]Yes, Lord God of Israel! Please fulfill this promise too. [18]But will God really live upon the earth with men? Why, even the heavens cannot hold you! How much less this Temple I have built!

[19]"How I pray that you will hear my prayers, O Lord my God! Listen to my prayer that I am praying to you now! [20-21]Look down and bless this Temple day and night. Bless this place where you have promised to put your name. Always hear the prayers I will pray to you as I face toward this place. Yes, hear and answer them! Listen to my prayers. Listen to the prayers of your people Israel. Listen when they pray toward this Temple. Yes, hear us from heaven. And when you hear, forgive.

[22]"A person might do something wrong to another person. As a result he must go before the altar. There he might swear he didn't do it. [23]If this happens, hear from heaven. Punish him if he is lying. Or show him innocent if he didn't do it.

[24]"Your people Israel might be beaten by their enemies. This might happen because they have sinned against you. But they might turn to you and call themselves your people. Perhaps they will pray to you here in this Temple. [25]If they do, then listen to them from heaven. Forgive their sins. And give them back this land you gave to their fathers.

[26]"Maybe the skies will be shut. Perhaps there will be no rain because of our sins. But then we might pray toward this Temple. Maybe we will claim you as our God. Perhaps we will turn from our sins because you have punished us. [27]If this happens, then listen from heaven. Forgive the sins of your people. And teach them what is right. Send rain upon this land that you have given to your people.

[28]"There might be a famine in the land. There might be plagues or crop disease. There might be attacks of locusts

or caterpillars. Or there might be enemies in the land attacking our cities. ²⁹If this happens, listen to every person's prayer. Hear the people's private sorrows. Listen also to all the public prayers. ³⁰Hear from heaven where you live and forgive. Give each person what he deserves. For you know the hearts of all people. ³¹Then they will respect you for all time. They will always walk where you tell them to go.

God will forgive our sins when we are sorry and ask him to forgive

If my people are sorry for their sins, they must pray. They must turn from their sin. They must search for me. Then I will forgive them.

2 Chronicles 7:14

---

³²"And foreigners might hear of your power. Perhaps they will come from far-away lands. Maybe they will come to worship your great name. They might turn and pray toward this Temple. ³³If they do, hear them from heaven where you live. Do what they ask of you. Then all the people of the earth will hear of your fame. They will all respect you just as your people Israel do. And they too will know that this Temple I have built is truly yours.

³⁴"Your people might go out at your command to fight their enemies. And they might pray toward this city of Jerusalem that you have chosen. They might turn to this Temple that I have built for your name. ³⁵If they do, then hear their prayers from heaven. Give them success in battle.

³⁶"Perhaps your people will sin against you. (And who has never sinned?) And you might become angry with them. Maybe you will let their enemies defeat them. Perhaps you will let them take your people away as captives. Your people might be brought to some other nation near or far. ³⁷⁻³⁸But when they get to that land of exile, they might turn to you again. Maybe they will face toward this land you gave their fathers. Perhaps they will turn toward this city and your Temple I have built. They might plead with you with all their hearts to forgive them. ³⁹If this happens, then hear from heaven where you live. Help them. Forgive your people who have sinned against you.

⁴⁰"Yes, O my God, be wide awake! Listen to all the prayers made to you in this place. ⁴¹And now, O Lord God, arise! Enter this resting place of yours. This is where the Ark of your strength has been put. Let your priests, O Lord God, be clothed with salvation. Let your people have joy in the kind deeds you do. ⁴²O Lord God, do not ignore me. Do not turn your face away from me, your chosen king. Oh, remember your love for David and your kindness to him."

God's Glory Fills the Temple

7 As Solomon finished praying, fire flashed down from heaven! It burned up all the sacrifices! And the glory of the Lord filled the Temple. The priests couldn't even go in! ³All the people had been watching. And now they fell flat on the ground. They worshiped and thanked the Lord.

"How good he is!" they said. "He is always so loving and kind."

⁴⁻⁵Then the king and all the people dedicated the Temple. They did this by sacrificing burnt offerings to the Lord. King Solomon's gift for this purpose was 22,000 oxen and 120,000 sheep. ⁶The priests were standing at their posts of duty. And the Levites were playing their song of thanks. This song was called "His Loving-kindness Is Forever." They used the musical instruments King David himself had made. David had once used them to praise the Lord. Then the priests blew the trumpets. And all the people stood again. ⁷Solomon made the inner court of the Temple holy. They used it that day as a place of sacrifice. This was because there were too many sacrifices for the bronze altar.

⁸For the next seven days they celebrated the Tabernacle Feast. Large crowds came in from all over Israel. They came from as far away as Hamath

in the north. And they came from the brook of Egypt in the south. ⁹A final service was held on the eighth day. ¹⁰Then on October 7, Solomon sent the people home. They were happy because the Lord had been so good to David and Solomon. And the Lord had been good to his people Israel.

God Speaks to Solomon

¹¹So Solomon finished building the Temple and his own palace. He did all that he had planned to do.

¹²One night the Lord came to Solomon. He told him, "I have heard your prayer. And I have chosen this Temple. It is the place where I want you to sacrifice to me. ¹³I might shut up the heavens so that there is no rain. I might command the locust swarms to eat up all your crops. Or I might send a plague among you. ¹⁴But if my people are sorry for their sins, they must pray. They must turn from their sin. They must search for me. If they do, I will hear them from heaven. Then I will forgive them. And I will heal their land. ¹⁵I will listen, wide awake, to every prayer made in this place. ¹⁶For I have chosen this Temple. I have made it holy to be my home for all time. My eyes and my heart shall always be here.

¹⁷"As for yourself, you must follow me as your father David did. ¹⁸If you do, then you and your descendants will always be the kings of Israel. ¹⁹But you might not follow me. You might not follow the laws I have given you. Perhaps you will even worship idols. ²⁰If this happens, then I will send my people from this land. It is the land that I have given them. And this Temple shall be broken down. This will happen even though I have made it holy for myself. And I will make it a public horror and a place of shame. ²¹It will not be famous. Instead, all who pass by will be amazed.

"'Why has the Lord done such a terrible thing? Why has he destroyed this land and this Temple?' they will ask.

²²"And the answer will be, 'Because his people left the Lord God of their fathers. They left the God who brought them out of the land of Egypt. And they worshiped other gods instead. That is why he has done all this to them.'"

Solomon's Building Activities

8 It was now 20 years since Solomon had become king. The Lord's Temple and Solomon's royal palace were finished. ²So Solomon rebuilt the cities that King Hiram of Tyre had given to him. And he sent some of the people of Israel to live in them. ³At this time, Solomon also fought against the city of Hamath-zobah. He took that city. ⁴He built Tadmor in the desert. And he built cities in Hamath as supply centers. ⁵He built walls around the cities of upper Beth-horon and lower Beth-horon. He also put barred gates on them. This was because both cities were supply centers. ⁶He also built Baalath and other supply centers. And he built cities where his chariots and horses were kept. He built to his heart's desire. He built in Jerusalem and Lebanon. He built throughout his whole kingdom!

⁷⁻⁸He began to call out people as slave workers. These people were from the Hittites, Amorites, Perizzites, Hivites, and Jebusites. They were from the nations that the Israelites had not wiped out. This practice still is done to this day. ⁹But he didn't make slaves of any of the Israelite people. He used Israelites as soldiers, officers, charioteers, and horsemen. ¹⁰Also, 250 of them were officials. They were in charge of all public affairs.

¹¹Solomon moved his wife from the City of David section of Jerusalem. She was Pharaoh's daughter. He moved her to the new palace he had built for her. For he said, "She must not live in King David's palace. For the Ark of the Lord was there. And it is holy ground."

¹²Then Solomon sacrificed burnt offerings to the Lord. He gave them on the altar he had built in front of the Temple. ¹³The number of sacrifices was not the same from day to day. He followed the laws Moses had given. There were more sacrifices on the Sabbaths. There were special sacrifices on new moon feasts. There were also special

sacrifices at the three yearly feasts. These were the Passover Feast, the Feast of Weeks, and the Feast of Tabernacles. ¹⁴He gave the priests their jobs with the chart made by his father David. He also gave the Levites their work of praise and of helping the priests. And he told the gatekeepers which gates they were to guard. ¹⁵Solomon followed all David's orders about these things. He also gave the people in charge of the treasury their jobs. ¹⁶Thus Solomon finished building the Temple.

¹⁷⁻¹⁸Then he went to the seaport towns of Ezion-geber and Eloth. These towns were in Edom. He went there to send off a fleet of ships given to him by King Hiram. King Hiram's crews knew a lot about sailing. So they went along with King Solomon's men. These ships went to Ophir. And they brought back several million dollars of gold on each trip!

The Queen of Sheba Visits King Solomon

9 The queen of Sheba heard of Solomon's great wisdom. So she came to Jerusalem. She wanted to test him with hard questions. A large group of servants went with her. They brought camel-loads of spices, gold, and jewels. ²And Solomon answered all her problems. Nothing was hidden from him. He could explain everything to her. ³Soon she saw how wise he really was. She saw the beauty of his palace. ⁴She saw how good the food was at his tables. She saw how many servants and advisors he had. She saw their uniforms and his stewards in full dress. And she saw the size of the men in his bodyguard. When she saw all this, she could hardly believe it!

⁵Finally she turned to the king. "Everything I heard about you in my own country is true!" she said. ⁶"I didn't believe it until I got here and saw it with my own eyes. Your wisdom is far greater than I could ever have thought. ⁷These men of yours are very blessed! For they can stand here and listen to you talk! ⁸Blessed be the Lord your God! How he must love Israel to give them a king like you! He wants them to be a great, strong nation for all time."

⁹She gave the king a gift of over $1,000,000 in gold. She gave him great amounts of spices. They were of very high quality. She also gave him many, many jewels.

¹⁰King Hiram's and King Solomon's crews brought gold from Ophir. They also brought sandalwood and jewels. ¹¹The king used the sandalwood to

Tribute
2 CHRONICLES
9:13-14

When a neighboring king became too strong, he might demand a tribute from the nations around him. That was payment to keep peace with him. Solomon ruled over a large kingdom. He was not a warrior like his father David. But he was a powerful king. Neighboring kings did not want to fight him. So Solomon promised not to go to battle against them if they paid him a tribute. Each year these kings paid Solomon millions of dollars worth of gold (9:13). They also gave him many other gifts as tribute—gifts like precious jewels and spices, beautiful wood, and even rare animals (9:21). Many kings brought these gifts themselves. They wanted to see Solomon and learn what made him so wise and powerful. It is easy to see why King Solomon became even richer and stronger.

make steps for the Temple and the palace. And he used it to make harps and lyres for the choir. Never had there been such nice instruments in all the land of Judah!

¹²King Solomon gave the queen of Sheba gifts. They were of the same value as the gifts she had brought to him. He also gave her everything else she asked for! Then she and her people went back to their own land.

Solomon's Riches

¹³⁻¹⁴Solomon was sent $250,000,000 worth of gold each year. It came from the kings of Arabia. It also came from many other lands that paid yearly tribute to him. Besides this, his merchants and traders also sent him gold. ¹⁵He used some of the gold to make 200 large shields. Each was worth $100,000. ¹⁶And he also made 300 smaller shields. Each was worth $50,000. The king placed these in the Forest of Lebanon Room in his palace. ¹⁷He also made a huge ivory throne covered with pure gold. ¹⁸It had gold armrests. Each was flanked by a gold lion. It had a footstool of gold. And six gold steps led up to it. ¹⁹Gold lions also stood at each side of each step. No other throne in all the world could be compared with it! ²⁰King Solomon's cups were all solid gold. So was all the furniture in the Forest of Lebanon Room. Silver was too cheap to count for much in those days!

²¹Every three years the king sent his ships to Tarshish. He used sailors given by King Hiram. From there he brought back gold, silver, ivory, apes, and peacocks.

²²So King Solomon was richer and wiser than any other king in all the earth. ²³Kings from every nation came to visit him. They came to hear the wisdom God had put into his heart. ²⁴Each brought him yearly tribute of silver and gold bowls. They also brought clothing, armor, spices, horses, and mules.

²⁵In addition, Solomon had 4,000 stalls of horses and chariots. And he also had 12,000 horsemen. These were in the chariot cities and Jerusalem. Their job was to protect the king. ²⁶He ruled over all kings and kingdoms beginning at the Euphrates River. His rule stretched to the land of the Philistines. It went as far away as the border of Egypt. ²⁷Silver became as common in Jerusalem as stones in the road! And cedar was used as though it were common sycamore.

Solomon's Death

²⁸Horses were brought to him from Egypt and other lands.

²⁹The rest of Solomon's deeds are written in the history of Nathan the prophet. They can also be found in the prophecy of Ahijah the Shilonite. And his deeds relating to Jeroboam are recorded in the visions of Iddo. Jeroboam was the son of Nebat.

³⁰So Solomon ruled over all Israel for 40 years. He reigned from Jerusalem. ³¹Then he died and was buried in Jerusalem. And his son Rehoboam became the new king.

Rehoboam Becomes King but Follows Bad Advice

10 All the leaders of Israel came to Shechem. They came to see Rehoboam become king. ²⁻³Meanwhile, friends of Jeroboam sent word to him of Solomon's death. Jeroboam was the son of Nebat. He was in Egypt at the time. He had gone there to get away from King Solomon. He now went quickly back to Israel. He was there at the crowning of Rehoboam. He led the people's demands on Rehoboam.

⁴"Your father was a hard master," they said. "Be easier on us than he was. If you do, we will let you be our king!"

⁵Rehoboam told them to come back in three days. Then he would tell them what he had decided. ⁶He talked about their demands with the old men. These were the men who had advised his father Solomon.

"What shall I tell them?" he asked.

⁷"You want to be their king," they replied. "So you will have to give them a good reply. Treat them kindly."

⁸⁻⁹But he did not listen to their advice. He asked the young men what they thought. These were the young men

who had grown up with Rehoboam. "What do you think I should do?" he asked. "Shall I be easier on them than my father was?"

¹⁰"No!" they replied. "Tell them, 'You might think my father was hard on you. But just wait and see what I'll be like!' Tell them, 'My little finger is thicker than my father's loins! ¹¹I am going to be tougher on you, not easier! My father used whips on you. But I'll use scorpions!'"

¹²So Jeroboam and the people came back in three days. They came to hear what King Rehoboam had decided. ¹³He spoke roughly to them. For he did not listen to the advice of the old men. ¹⁴And he followed the advice of the younger ones.

"My father gave you heavy burdens. But I will give you heavier ones!" he told them. "My father punished you with whips. But I will punish you with scorpions!"

A Revolt in the Kingdom

¹⁵So the king turned down the people's demands. God caused him to do this. He did this to fulfill his promise to Jeroboam. This promise was given by Ahijah the Shilonite. ¹⁶The people saw what the king was saying. So they turned their backs and left him.

"Forget David and his family!" they shouted angrily. "We'll get someone else to be our king. Let Rehoboam rule his own tribe of Judah! Let's go home!" So they did.

¹⁷The people of the tribe of Judah stayed loyal to Rehoboam. ¹⁸After that, King Rehoboam sent out Hadoram. He went to call out forced labor groups from the other tribes of Israel. But the people stoned him to death. When this news reached King Rehoboam, he jumped into his chariot. And he fled to Jerusalem. ¹⁹Israel has not been ruled by a descendant of David to this day.

The Lord Tells Rehoboam
Not to Fight

11 Rehoboam got back to Jerusalem. He called out the armies of Judah and Benjamin. There were 180,000 men.

And he declared war against the rest of Israel. He wanted to try to keep the kingdom from splitting into two.

²But the Lord spoke to Shemaiah the prophet.

³"Go and speak to King Rehoboam of Judah," he said. "Talk to Solomon's son, and to the people of Judah and of Benjamin."

⁴"Tell them, 'The Lord says not to fight against your brothers. Go home. For I wanted this to happen.'" So they obeyed the Lord. And they did not fight against Jeroboam.

⁵⁻¹⁰Rehoboam stayed in Jerusalem. He built walls and gates around many cities of Judah to protect himself. These cities were Bethlehem, Etam, Tekoa, Beth-zur, Soco, Adullam, Gath, Mareshah, Ziph, Adoraim, Lachish, Azekah, Zorah, Aijalon, and Hebron.

¹¹He also made the forts stronger. And he sent groups of soldiers under their officers to man them. He supplied them with food, olive oil, and wine. ¹²Shields and spears were put in armories in every city. This was done to make the cities safer. For only Judah and Benjamin stayed loyal to him.

The Priests and Levites
Move to Judah

¹³⁻¹⁴The priests and Levites from the other tribes now left their homes. They moved to Judah and Jerusalem. This was because King Jeroboam had sent them away. He told them to stop being priests of the Lord. ¹⁵He chose other priests. They told the people to worship idols instead of God. They told them to sacrifice to idols of goats and calves. Jeroboam put these idols on the tops of hills. ¹⁶Laymen, too, from all over Israel began moving to Jerusalem. There they could worship the Lord God of their fathers. And there they could make sacrifices to him. ¹⁷This made the kingdom of Judah stronger. So King Rehoboam was king for three years with few problems. During those years he tried to obey the Lord. He tried to do as King David and King Solomon had done.

Rehoboam's Wives and Children

18Rehoboam married his cousin Mahalath. She was the daughter of David's son Jerimoth and of Abihail. Abihail was the daughter of David's brother Eliab. 19Three sons were born from this marriage. Their names were Jeush, Shemariah, and Zaham.

20Later he married Maacah. She was the daughter of Absalom. The children she bore him were Abijah, Attai, Ziza, and Shelomith. 21He loved Maacah more than any of his other wives and concubines. He had 18 wives and 60 concubines. They bore him 28 sons and 60 daughters. 22Maacah's son Abijah was his favorite. So he planned to make him the next king. 23He very wisely scattered his other sons throughout the land. He put them in charge of the walled cities in Judah and Benjamin. He gave them large salaries. And he gave them each several wives.

Egypt Conquers Jerusalem

12 But when Rehoboam was still popular and powerful, he left the Lord. And the people followed him in this sin. 2As a result, King Shishak of Egypt attacked Jerusalem. This happened in the fifth year of King Rehoboam's reign. 3He attacked with 1,200 chariots and 60,000 horsemen. There were so many soldiers they couldn't be counted! Among them were Egyptians, Libyans, Sukkiim, and Ethiopians. 4He quickly took Judah's walled cities and soon came to Jerusalem.

5The prophet Shemaiah now met with Rehoboam. The leaders from every part of Judah were also there. They had fled to Jerusalem for safety. Shemaiah told them, "The Lord says, 'You have left me. So I have left you! I have given you to Shishak!'"

6Then the king and the leaders of Israel confessed their sins. They said, "The Lord is right in doing this to us!"

7And the Lord saw them humble themselves. So he sent Shemaiah to them. He said, "You have humbled yourselves. So I will not completely destroy you. Some of you will get away. I will not use Shishak to pour out my anger on Jerusalem. 8But you must pay yearly tribute to him. Then you will see how much better it is to serve me than to serve him!"

9So King Shishak of Egypt conquered Jerusalem. He took away all the treasures of the Temple and of the palace. He also took all Solomon's gold shields. 10King Rehoboam made bronze shields to use in their place. He gave them to the care of the captain of his bodyguard. 11When the king went to the Temple, the guards would carry them. Then they would bring them back to the armory. 12When the king humbled himself, the Lord's anger was turned aside. He didn't totally destroy Judah. In fact, the economy of Judah stayed strong. This was true even after Shishak invaded Judah.

Rehoboam's Reign

13King Rehoboam reigned 17 years in Jerusalem. This was the city God had chosen to live in. He chose it out of all the other cities of Israel. Rehoboam had become king at the age of 41. His mother's name was Naamah the Ammonitess. 14But he was a bad king. For he never did really decide to please the Lord. 15The deeds of Rehoboam are recorded in the history written by Shemaiah the prophet. His deeds were also recorded by Iddo the seer. And they appear in *The Family Register.*

There were continual wars between Rehoboam and Jeroboam. 16When Rehoboam died he was buried in Jerusalem. And his son Abijah became the new king.

Abijah Defeats Jeroboam

13 Abijah became the new king of Judah in Jerusalem. He became king in the 18th year of King Jeroboam's reign in Israel. He lasted three years. His mother's name was Micaiah. She was the daughter of Uriel of Gibeah.

Early in his reign war broke out between Judah and Israel. 3Judah was led by King Abijah. He had an army of 400,000 able soldiers. He went out to fight twice as many Israelite troops. The Israelite army was made up of strong, brave men. They were led by

King Jeroboam. [4]The army of Judah came to Mount Zemaraim. This was in the hill country of Ephraim. There King Abijah shouted to King Jeroboam and the Israelite army.

[5]"Listen!" he said. "Don't you know that the Lord God of Israel made a promise to David's family? He promised they would always be the kings of Israel. [6]Your King Jeroboam is a mere servant of David's son. And he was a traitor to his master. [7]Then a whole gang of worthless rebels joined him. They rejected Solomon's son Rehoboam. For he was young and afraid. And he couldn't stand up to them. [8]Do you really think you can defeat the kingdom of the Lord? It is led by a descendant of David! Your army is twice as large as mine. But you are cursed with those gold calves you have with you. They are the ones that Jeroboam made for you. And he calls them your gods! [9]And you have sent away the priests of the Lord and the Levites. You have chosen heathen priests instead. You act just like the people of other nations. You make into a priest anybody who comes with a young bull and seven rams to sacrifice. Anyone at all can be a priest of these false gods of yours!

[10]"But as for us, the Lord is our God. And we have not left him. Only the descendants of Aaron are our priests. And the Levites alone may help them in their work. [11]They burn sacrifices to the Lord every morning and evening. These are burnt offerings and offerings of sweet incense. And they put the Bread of the Presence on the holy table. The gold lampstand is lighted every night. For we are careful to follow the orders of the Lord our God. But you have forgotten him. [12]So you see, God is with us. He is our Leader. His priests will lead us into battle against you. They will blow trumpets as they go. O people of Israel, do not fight against the Lord God of your fathers! For you will not win!"

[13-14]Meanwhile, Jeroboam had sent out part of his army. They went around behind the men of Judah to ambush them. So Judah was surrounded. The enemy was all around them. Then they cried out to the Lord for mercy. And the priests blew the trumpets. [15-16]The men of Judah began to shout. And as they shouted, God turned the tide of the battle. He used King Abijah and Judah's army to defeat King Jeroboam and Israel's army. [17]And the army of Judah killed 500,000 troops of Israel that day.

[18-19]So Judah defeated Israel. They did it by depending upon the Lord God of their fathers. They chased King Jeroboam's troops. And they took some of his cities. These cities were Bethel, Jeshanah, Ephron, and their suburbs. [20]King Jeroboam of Israel never regained his power during Abijah's lifetime. And in time, the Lord struck him and he died.

[21]Meanwhile, King Abijah of Judah became very strong. He married 14 wives. And he had 22 sons and 16 daughters. [22]His deeds and speeches are recorded in the prophet Iddo's *History of Judah.*

Asa Rules Judah

14 King Abijah was buried in Jerusalem. Then his son Asa became the new king of Judah. There was peace in the land for the first 10 years of his reign. [2]This was because Asa was careful to obey the Lord his God. [3]He broke down the heathen altars on the hills. And he broke down the pillars. He chopped down the shameful Asherim idols. [4]He demanded that the whole nation obey the commands of the Lord God of their ancestors. [5]Also, he took away the sun-images from the hills. And he took down the incense altars from all of Judah's cities. That is why God gave his kingdom peace. [6]This made it possible for him to build walled cities throughout Judah.

[7]"Now is the time to build. For the Lord is blessing us with peace. This is because we have obeyed him," he told his people. "Let us build cities. And let us build walls, towers, gates, and bars to protect them." So they went ahead with this building with great success.

[8]King Asa's army was 300,000 strong. They were armed with light shields and spears. His army of Benjaminites numbered 280,000. They were armed with

large shields and bows. Both armies were made up of well-trained, brave men.

9-10But now he was attacked by an army of 1,000,000 troops. They came from Ethiopia with 300 chariots. They were under the leadership of General Zerah. They came toward the city of Mareshah, in the valley of Zephathah. King Asa sent his troops to fight with them there.

11"O Lord!" he cried out to God. "No one else can help us! Here we are, powerless against this mighty army. Oh, help us, Lord our God! For we trust in you alone to save us. And in your name we attack this great army. Don't let mere men defeat you!"

12Then the Lord defeated the Ethiopians. Asa and the army of Judah won. And the Ethiopians ran for their lives. 13The army of Judah chased them as far as Gerar. And the whole Ethiopian army was wiped out. Not one man was left! For the Lord and his army killed them all. Then the army of Judah carried off many things. 14While they were at Gerar they attacked all the cities in that area. And fear from the Lord came upon the people there. As a result, great amounts of plunder were taken from these cities too. 15They not only plundered the cities. They also destroyed the camps where the shepherds lived. And they took great herds of sheep and camels. After this, they went back to Jerusalem.

Asa Destroys the Idols and Rebuilds the Altar

15 Then the Spirit of God came upon Azariah. He was the son of Oded. 2He went out to meet King Asa as he came back from the battle.

"Listen to me, Asa! Listen, armies of Judah and Benjamin!" he shouted. "The Lord will stay with you as long as you stay with him! When you look for him, you will find him. But if you leave him, he will leave you. 3For some time, the people in Israel haven't worshiped the true God. And they have not had a true priest to teach them. They have lived without God's laws. 4But at times they have turned again to the Lord God of Israel. In their trouble, they have looked

for him. And in such times, he has helped them. 5But when they rebelled against God there was no peace. Problems troubled the nation on every hand. Crime was seen everywhere. 6There were wars with other nations. There were battles between Israelite cities. For God was giving them all sorts of trouble. 7But you men of Judah, keep up the good work. Don't get discouraged. For you will be given a reward."

8When King Asa heard this message from God, he took courage. He broke down all the idols in the land of Judah and Benjamin. He destroyed the idols in the cities he had taken in Ephraim. And he rebuilt the altar of the Lord in front of the Temple.

9Then he called all the people of Judah and Benjamin. He also called all the people who had come from Israel. Many had come from the lands of Ephraim, Manasseh, and Simeon in Israel. They came when they saw that the Lord God was with King Asa. 10They all came to Jerusalem in June of the 15th year of King Asa's reign. 11There they sacrificed 700 oxen and 7,000 sheep to the Lord. It was part of the plunder they had taken in the battle. 12Then they made a contract to worship only the Lord God of their fathers. 13They agreed that anyone who did not do this must die. This was true whether they were old or young, man or woman. 14They shouted out their oath of loyalty to God. They did this with trumpets blaring and horns sounding. 15All were happy for this covenant with God. For they had entered into it with all their hearts and wills. They wanted him above all else, and they found him! And he gave them peace throughout the nation.

16King Asa even took his mother Maacah from her place as queen mother. This was because she made an Asherah idol. He cut down the idol. And he crushed and burned it at Kidron Brook. 17Over in Israel the idol temples were not taken down. But in Judah and Benjamin the heart of King Asa was perfect before God. He followed God through his lifetime. 18He found the silver and gold bowls his father had given to the Lord.

And he brought them back to the Temple. ¹⁹So there was no more war until the 35th year of King Asa's reign.

Asa Forgets God

16 In the 36th year of King Asa's reign, King Baasha of Israel declared war on him. He built the walled city of Ramah to control the road to Judah. ²Then Asa took the silver and gold from the Temple and the palace. He sent it to King Ben-hadad of Syria at Damascus. He also sent a message.

³"Your father and my father once had a treaty. Let us renew this treaty," he said. "See, here is silver and gold. It is to encourage you to break your treaty with King Baasha of Israel. That way he will have to leave me alone."

⁴Ben-hadad agreed to King Asa's treaty. He called out his armies to attack Israel. They destroyed the cities of Ijon, Dan, and Abel-maim. He also destroyed all of the supply centers in Naphtali. ⁵King Baasha of Israel heard what was happening. So he stopped building Ramah. And he gave up his plan to attack Judah. ⁶Then King Asa and the people of Judah went out to Ramah. They carried away the building stones and timbers. And they used them to build Geba and Mizpah instead.

The Lord helps those who trust him

He tries to find people who have given their hearts to him. He wants to show his great power in helping them.

2 Chronicles 16:9

---

⁷About that time the prophet Hanani came to King Asa. He said, "You have put your trust in the king of Syria. You did not trust in the Lord your God. Because of this, the army of the king of Syria has escaped from you. ⁸Don't you remember what happened to the Ethiopians and Libyans? Don't you remember what I did to their great army? Don't you remember what I did with all their chariots and horsemen? But you depended on the Lord then. And he

gave them all into your hand. ⁹For the eyes of the Lord search back and forth across the whole earth. He tries to find people who have given their hearts to him. He wants to show his great power in helping them. What a fool you have been! From now on you shall have wars."

¹⁰Asa was very angry with the prophet for saying this. So he threw him into jail. And Asa was cruel to all the people at that time.

¹¹The rest of the deeds of Asa are written in *The Annals of the Kings of Israel and Judah.* ¹²In the 39th year of his reign, Asa got a bad disease in his feet. But he didn't go to the Lord with the problem. He went to the doctors instead. ¹³⁻¹⁴So he died in the 41st year of his reign. He was buried in his own tomb. He had cut it out for himself in Jerusalem. He was laid on a bed perfumed with sweet spices and ointments. And his people burned much incense for him at his funeral.

Jehoshaphat Rules Judah

17 Then his son Jehoshaphat became the king. He called out Judah's army for war against Israel. ²He put army groups in all of the walled cities of Judah. And he put them in various other places across the country. He also sent army groups to the cities of Ephraim his father had taken.

³The Lord was with Jehoshaphat. This was because he followed in the good footsteps of his father's early years. And he did not worship idols. ⁴He obeyed the commands of his father's God. He was not like the people across the border in the land of Israel. ⁵So the Lord made his kingship in Judah strong and secure. All the people of Judah paid their taxes. So he became very rich as well as being very popular. ⁶He boldly followed the paths of God. He even knocked down the heathen altars on the hills. And he destroyed the Asherim idols.

⁷⁻⁹In the third year of his reign he began to teach the people about God. He sent out top officials as teachers in all the cities of Judah. These men included

Ben-hail, Obadiah, Zechariah, Nethanel, and Micaiah. He also used the Levites for this purpose. These included Shemaiah, Nethaniah, Zebadiah, Asahel, Shemiramoth, Jehonathan, Adonijah, Tobijah, and Tobadonijah. The priests, Elishama and Jehoram, also taught the people. They carried copies of *The Book of the Law of the Lord*. They took them to all the cities of Judah. And they taught the Scriptures to the people.

¹⁰Then the fear of the Lord fell upon all the kingdoms around them. None of them dared to fight against King Jehoshaphat.

¹¹Even some of the Philistines brought him gifts and yearly tribute. And the Arabs gave him 7,700 rams and 7,700 male goats. ¹²So Jehoshaphat became very strong. And he built walled cities and supply cities throughout Judah.

¹³His public works program was also large. And he had a huge army stationed at Jerusalem, his capital. ¹⁴⁻¹⁵There were 300,000 troops from Judah there under General Adnah. Next in command was Jehohanan. He had an army of 280,000 men. ¹⁶Next was Amasiah, the son of Zichri, with 200,000 troops. He was a man of unusual piety. ¹⁷Benjamin supplied 200,000 men armed with bows and shields. They were under the command of Eliada, a great general. ¹⁸His second in command was Jehozabad. He led 180,000 trained men. ¹⁹These were the troops in Jerusalem. Others were sent by the king to man the walled cities throughout the nation.

Jehoshaphat and Ahab Join Forces

18 King Jehoshaphat of Judah was a very rich and popular king. He made a treaty by marriage with King Ahab of Israel. He arranged for his son to marry King Ahab's daughter. ²A few years later he went down to Samaria to visit King Ahab. King Ahab gave a great party for him and his servants. He killed many sheep and oxen for the feast. Then he asked King Jehoshaphat to fight with him against Ramoth-gilead.

³⁻⁵"Why, of course!" King Jehosha-

phat replied. "I'm with you all the way. My troops are at your command! But let's check with the Lord first."

So King Ahab called 400 of his heathen prophets. He asked them, "Shall we go to war with Ramoth-gilead or not?"

And they replied, "Go ahead! God will give you a great victory!"

⁶⁻⁷But Jehoshaphat wasn't sure. "Isn't there some prophet of the Lord around here too?" he asked. "I'd like to ask him the same question."

"Well," Ahab told him, "there is one. But I hate him. He never prophesies anything good! His name is Micaiah, the son of Imlah."

"Oh, come now, don't talk like that!" Jehoshaphat said. "Let's hear what he has to say."

⁸So the king of Israel called one of his servants. "Quick! Go and get Micaiah, the son of Imlah," he ordered.

⁹The two kings were sitting on thrones in their royal robes. They were at an open place near the Samaria gate. And all the "prophets" were prophesying before them. ¹⁰One of them was Zedekiah, the son of Chenaanah. He made some iron horns for the occasion. And he said, "The Lord says you will gore the Syrians to death with these!"

¹¹And all the others agreed. "Yes!" they said. "Go up to Ramoth-gilead and take it. For the Lord will help you to win the battle."

¹²The man who went to get Micaiah told him what was happening. He filled him in on what the prophets were saying. They were saying that the war would end in triumph for the king.

"I hope you will agree with them," the man said. "I hope you predict that the king will win."

¹³But Micaiah replied, "I make this promise before God. Whatever God says is what I will say."

¹⁴So Micaiah came before the king. And the king spoke to him. "Micaiah," he said, "shall we go to war against Ramoth-gilead or not?"

And Micaiah replied, "Sure, go ahead! It will be a great victory!"

¹⁵"Look here!" the king said sharply.

"I have told you to speak nothing but what the Lord tells you. How many times must I say this?"

¹⁶Then Micaiah told him, "In my vision I saw all of Israel. They were scattered on the mountain. They were like sheep without a shepherd. And the Lord said, 'Their master has been killed. Send them home.'"

¹⁷"Didn't I tell you?" the king of Israel said to Jehoshaphat. "He does it every time. He *never* prophesies *anything* but trouble against me."

¹⁸"Listen to what else the Lord has told me," Micaiah said. "I saw the Lord upon his throne. He had a great army of angels all around him.

¹⁹⁻²⁰"And the Lord said, 'Who can get King Ahab to fight against Ramoth-gilead? Do this so he will go and be killed there.'

"The angels didn't agree about who should go. But finally an angel stepped forward before the Lord. He said, 'I can do it!'

"'How?' the Lord asked him.

²¹"He replied, 'I will be a lying spirit. I will speak in the mouths of the king's prophets!'

"'It will work,' the Lord said. 'Go and do it.'

²²"The Lord has put a lying spirit in the mouths of these prophets of yours. And he will do just the opposite of what they are telling you!"

²³Then Zedekiah, the son of Chenaanah, walked up to Micaiah. He slapped him across the face. "You liar!" he yelled. "When did the Spirit of the Lord leave me and enter you?"

²⁴"You'll find out soon enough," Micaiah replied. "You will know when you are hiding in an inner room!"

²⁵"Arrest this man!" the king of Israel ordered. "Take him back to Governor Amon and to my son Joash. ²⁶Tell them, 'The king says to put this man in prison. Feed him with bread and water until I come back from the battle!'"

²⁷Micaiah replied, "You might come back safely. But if you do, the Lord has not spoken through me." Then he turned to those around them. He said, "Take note of what I have said."

Ahab Dies in Battle

²⁸So the king of Israel and the king of Judah led their armies to Ramoth-gilead. ²⁹The king of Israel spoke to Jehoshaphat. "I'll dress so that no one will know me," he said. "But you put on your royal robes." So that is what they did.

³⁰Now the king of Syria had given orders to his chariot drivers. He told them, "Only try to kill the king of Israel!"

³¹The Syrian chariot drivers saw King Jehoshaphat of Judah in his royal robes. So they chased after him. They thought he was the man they were after. But Jehoshaphat cried out to the Lord to save him. And the Lord made the chariot drivers see their mistake. ³²They saw that he was not the king of Israel. So they stopped chasing him. ³³But one of the Syrian soldiers shot an arrow at the Israelite troops. And it hit the king of Israel. It hit him between the lower armor and the breastplate. "Get me out of here," he groaned to the driver of his chariot. "I am badly wounded." ³⁴The battle grew hotter and hotter all that day. King Ahab went back in to fight the Syrians. He was propped up in his chariot. But just as the sun sank into the western skies, he died.

The Prophet Jehu Has a Message for Jehoshaphat

19 King Jehoshaphat of Judah went back home, unhurt. ²The prophet Jehu, the son of Hanani, went out to meet him.

"Should you be helping the wicked? Should you love those who hate the Lord?" he asked him. "Because of what you have done, God's anger is upon you. ³But there are some good things about you. You have rid the land of the shame idols. And you have tried to be faithful to God."

Jehoshaphat Appoints Judges

⁴So Jehoshaphat made no more trips to Israel after that. He stayed quietly at Jerusalem. Later he went out again among the people. He traveled from Beersheba to the hill country of Ephraim. He encouraged his people to worship the God of their ancestors. ⁵He

chose judges throughout the nation in all the larger cities. ⁶He said to them:

"Watch your step! I have not chosen you. God is the one who chose you. And he will stand beside you. He will help you give justice in each case that comes before you. ⁷Be very much afraid to decide against what God tells you. For God's judges must always judge fairly. They must not play favorites. And they must never take bribes."

⁸Jehoshaphat set up courts in Jerusalem, too. He chose the judges from among the Levites, priests and clan leaders. ⁹He gave them these orders. "You are to act always in the fear of God, with honest hearts," he said. ¹⁰"A case might be sent to you by the judges out in the country. They might send you a murder case. Or maybe some of God's laws have been disobeyed. You are to help them to decide justly. You must do this so the wrath of God doesn't come down upon you and them. If you do this, you will have done the job God gave you."

¹¹Then he chose Amariah the High Priest. He was to judge in the court of final appeal in religious cases. And Jehoshaphat chose Zebadiah, the son of Ishmael. He was a ruler in Judah. He was to judge in the court of final appeal in all civil cases. The Levites were to work as their helpers. "Don't be afraid in your stand for truth and honesty! And may God use you to defend the innocent!" was his final word to them.

God Gives Jehoshaphat a Victory

20 Later some other nations came to fight against Jehoshaphat and Judah. They were the Moabites, Ammonites, and the Meunites. ²Word came to Jehoshaphat that a great army was coming. It was coming from beyond the Dead Sea from Edom. It was already at Hazazon-tamar. This place was also called Engedi. ³Jehoshaphat was badly shaken by this news. So he turned to beg for help from the Lord. He told all the people of Judah to go without food for a time. They did this to show they were sorry for their sins. And they wanted God to know they wanted his help. ⁴People from all across the nation came to

Jerusalem to pray together. ⁵Jehoshaphat stood before the people. They gathered at the new court of the Temple. And he prayed this prayer:

⁶"O Lord God of our fathers! You are the only God in all the heavens! You are the Ruler of all the kingdoms of the earth! You are so powerful, so mighty! Who can stand against you? ⁷O our God! Didn't you drive out the heathen who lived in this land when your people came? And didn't you give this land to the descendants of your friend Abraham for all time? ⁸Your people settled here and built this Temple for you. ⁹We truly believe that in a time like this we can call on you for help. When we are faced with any problem such as war we can call on you. When we suffer from disease or famine we can call on you. We can stand here before this Temple and before you. For you are here in this Temple. And we can cry out to you to save us. And you promised that you would hear us and save us.

¹⁰"And now see what the armies of Ammon, Moab, and Mount Seir are doing. You wouldn't let our ancestors attack those nations when Israel left Egypt. So we went around them and didn't destroy them. ¹¹Now see how they reward us! For they have come to throw us out of the land you have given us. ¹²O our God, won't you stop them? We have no way to protect ourselves against this mighty army. We don't know what to do. But we are looking to you."

¹³People from all over Judah stood before the Lord. They stood with their little ones, wives, and children. ¹⁴And the Spirit of the Lord came upon one of the men standing there. His name was Jahaziel. He was the son of Zechariah. Zechariah was the son of Benaiah. Benaiah was the son of Jeiel. Jeiel was the son of Mattaniah the Levite. And Mattaniah was one of the sons of Asaph.

¹⁵"Listen to me!" he said. "Listen, all you people of Judah and Jerusalem. And listen, O king Jehoshaphat. The Lord says, 'Don't be afraid! Don't be frozen by this mighty army! For the battle is not yours, but God's! ¹⁶Tomorrow, go down

and fight them! You will find them coming up the slopes of Ziz. This is at the end of the valley that opens into the wilderness of Jeruel. ¹⁷But you will not need to fight!

Booty
2 CHRONICLES 20:25
Why were warriors in Bible times so willing to fight in a bloody war? Some liked the adventure of fighting. Others wanted to protect their honor. But everyone wanted to protect homes, families, and possessions. If men didn't fight, enemies would probably kill them, make their wives and children slaves, and take everything else that they had. The loser lost cattle and grain and anything else that the winner could carry away. Since there were no banks, soldiers often carried their gold or silver into battle. Stripping dead soldiers gave the winning warriors food, swords, spears, clothing, gold and silver, jewels, and armor. Jehoshaphat and his soldiers won so many valuable things that it took three days to carry it all away (20:25).

Take your places. Stand quietly. And see the great things God will do for you! O people of Judah and Jerusalem, don't be afraid! And don't be discouraged! Go out there tomorrow, for the Lord is with you!'"

¹⁸Then King Jehoshaphat fell to the ground with his face to the earth. And all the people of Judah and Jerusalem did the same. And they worshiped the Lord. ¹⁹Then the Levites of the Kohath clan and the Korah clan stood. They began to praise the Lord God of Israel with songs of praise. Their songs rang out strong and clear.

²⁰Early the next morning the army of Judah went out into the wilderness of Tekoa. On the way Jehoshaphat stopped and spoke to them. "Listen to me, O people of Judah and Jerusalem," he said. "Believe in the Lord your God and you shall have success! Believe his prophets and everything will be all right!"

²¹He talked with the leaders of the people. And they decided that there should be a choir leading the march. They were to be clothed in holy clothing. And they were to sing the song "His Loving-kindness Is Forever" as they walked. They were to praise and thank the Lord! ²²And so they began to sing and to praise the Lord. At that moment, the Lord caused the enemy armies to begin fighting each other. And the armies of Ammon, Moab, and Mount Seir destroyed each other! ²³For the Ammonites and Moabites turned against the army from Mount Seir. And they killed every one of them. And when they had finished that job, they turned against each other! ²⁴The army of Judah came to the tower that looks out over the wilderness. And as far as they could look there were dead bodies lying on the ground. Not a single one of the enemy was left alive! ²⁵King Jehoshaphat and his people went out to plunder the bodies. They came away loaded with money, clothing, and jewels. These were taken from the dead men. They found so much that it took them three days to take it all away! ²⁶On the fourth day they gathered in the Valley of Blessing. This valley is called this to this day. And how they praised the Lord!

27Then they went back to Jerusalem with Jehoshaphat leading them. They were full of joy. For the Lord had saved them from their enemies. 28They marched into Jerusalem and went to the Temple. A band of harps, lyres, and trumpets played as they went. 29And as had happened before, the fear of God fell upon the kingdoms around them. For they heard that the Lord himself had fought against Israel's enemies. 30So Jehoshaphat's kingdom was quiet. For his God had given him rest.

Jehoshaphat's Reign

31King Jehoshaphat became king of Judah when he was 35 years old. He reigned 25 years in Jerusalem. His mother's name was Azubah. She was the daughter of Shilhi. 32He was a good king, just as his father Asa was. He tried hard to follow the Lord. 33But he did not destroy the idol shrines on the hills. And the people never really decided to follow the God of their ancestors.

34All the events of Jehoshaphat's reign are written in the history of Jehu the son of Hanani. This is included in *The Annals of the Kings of Israel.*

35But at the end of his life, Jehoshaphat made a treaty with Ahaziah. Ahaziah was the king of Israel. He was a very wicked man. 36They made ships in Ezion-geber to sail to Tarshish. 37Then Eliezer prophesied against Jehoshaphat. Eliezer was the son of Dodavahu from Mareshah. Eliezer told him, "You have made an agreement with King Ahaziah. Because of this, the Lord has destroyed your work." So the ships met disaster and never got to Tarshish.

Jehoram Rules Judah and Displeases God

21 Jehoshaphat died and was buried in the cemetery of the kings in Jerusalem. His son Jehoram became the new ruler of Judah. 2Jehoram's brothers were Azariah, Jehiel, Zechariah, Azariah, Michael, and Shephatiah. These were all sons of Jehoshaphat. 3-4Their father had given each of them gifts of money and jewels. They were also put in charge of some of Judah's walled cities. But Je-

hoshaphat gave the kingship to Jehoram because he was the oldest. But when Jehoram became king, he killed all of his brothers. He also killed many other leaders of Israel. 5He was 32 years old when he began to reign. And he ruled eight years in Jerusalem. 6But he was as wicked as the kings who were over in Israel. Yes, he was as wicked as Ahab! For Jehoram had married one of the daughters of Ahab. And his whole life was full of doing bad things. 7But the Lord still did not end the line of David. For he had made a covenant with David. He had promised always to have one of his descendants on the throne.

8At that time the king of Edom broke from Judah's rule. He claimed he was free of Judah. 9Jehoram attacked him with his full army. He brought all of his chariots, marching by night. And he almost beat him. 10But to this day Edom has been free of Judah's rule. Libnah also broke from Judah's rule. This was because Jehoram had turned away from the Lord God of his fathers. 11What's more, Jehoram made idol shrines in the mountains of Judah. And he led the people of Jerusalem in worshiping idols. In fact, he forced his people to worship them.

12Then Elijah the prophet wrote him a letter. "The Lord God of your ancestor David sends you this message," he wrote. "You have not followed in the good ways of your father Jehoshaphat. And you have not followed the good ways of King Asa. 13But you have been as bad as the kings in Israel. You have made the people of Jerusalem and Judah worship idols. This is just as it was in the times of King Ahab. And you have killed your brothers, who were better than you. 14Because of this, now the Lord will destroy your nation with a great plague. You, your children, your wives, and all that you have will get sick. 15You will be sick with a stomach disease and your bowels will rot away."

16Then the Lord made the Philistines and the Arabs angry with Jehoram. These nations lived near the Ethiopians. 17They marched against Judah and broke across the border. They took all that was of value in the king's palace. This included his sons and wives. Only his youngest son, Ahaziah, got away.

?????????????????????????????????
Which grandmother tried to kill all of her grandsons?
(Read 22:10-12 for the answer.)
?????????????????????????????????

[18]It was after this that the Lord made Jehoram sick. The Lord gave him a stomach disease that could not be cured. [19]At the end of two years, his intestines came out. And he died with great suffering. They didn't even have the normal ceremony at his funeral. [20]He was 32 years old when he began to reign. He reigned in Jerusalem eight years. And when he died, no one cried for him. He was buried in Jerusalem. But he was not put in the royal cemetery.

Ahaziah Rules Judah and Follows Evil Advice

22 Then the people of Jerusalem chose Ahaziah as their new king. Ahaziah was Jehoram's youngest son. The attacking bands of Arabs had killed all his older sons. [2]Ahaziah was 22 years old when he began to reign. He ruled for one year in Jerusalem. His mother's name was Athaliah. She was the granddaughter of Omri. [3]Ahaziah also walked in the evil ways of Ahab. For his mother encouraged him in doing wrong. [4]Yes, he was as bad as Ahab. For Ahab's family became his advisors after his father's death. And they led him on to ruin.

[5-6]Following their evil advice, Ahaziah made a treaty with King Joram of Israel. Joram was the son of Ahab. He was at war with King Hazael of Syria at Ramoth-gilead at the time. Ahaziah led his army there to join the battle. King Joram of Israel was wounded and went to Jezreel to get better. Ahaziah went to visit him. [7]But this turned out to be a deadly mistake. For God had decided to punish Ahaziah for his treaty with Joram. It was during this visit that Ahaziah went out with Joram to challenge Jehu. Jehu was the son of Nimshi. The Lord had chosen Jehu to end the family line of Ahab.

[8]Jehu was hunting down and killing the family and friends of Ahab. As he did this, he met King Ahaziah's nephews. These were princes of Judah. And he killed them.

A Baby Prince Is Rescued

[9]Then Jehu and his men went to look for Ahaziah. They found him hiding in the city of Samaria. So they brought him to Jehu, who killed him. Even so, Ahaziah was given a royal burial. This was because he was the grandson of King Jehoshaphat. And Jehoshaphat had been a man who served the Lord. But none of Ahaziah's sons lived to succeed him as king. Only Joash got away and lived. [10]This was because their grandmother Athaliah killed them. She did this when she heard the news of her son Ahaziah's death.

[11]Joash was saved by his Aunt Jehoshabeath. She was King Ahaziah's sister. She was a daughter of King Jehoram and the wife of Jehoiada the priest. Joash was hidden away in a storage room in the Temple. [12]Joash stayed hidden in the Temple for six years. During that time, Athaliah ruled as queen. He was cared for by his nurse, and by his aunt and uncle.

Young Joash Becomes King

23 In the seventh year of Queen Athaliah's reign, Jehoiada the priest got up his courage. And he spoke to some of the army officers. They were Azariah, Ishmael, Azariah, Maaseiah, and Elishaphat. Azariah was the son of Jeroham. Ishmael was the son of Jehohanan. Azariah was the son of Obed. Maaseiah was the son of Adaiah. Elishaphat was the son of Zichri. [2-3]These men went across the nation in secret. They told the Levites and clan leaders about Jehoiada's plans. And they called them to come to Jerusalem. The leaders came and promised to support the young king. He was still in hiding at the Temple.

"At last the time has come for the king's son to reign!" Jehoiada said. "The Lord has made a promise. He promised that a descendant of King David shall be our king. And this will be true again. ⁴This is what we'll do. A third of you priests and Levites come off duty on the Sabbath. But this time you will stay at the entrance as guards. ⁵⁻⁶Another third will go over to the palace. And the other third will be at the Lower Gate. Everyone else must stay in the outer courts of the Temple. This is what God's laws demand. For only the priests and Levites on duty may go into the Temple itself. For they are holy. ⁷You Levites, form a bodyguard for the king. Use your weapons and kill any person that shouldn't enter the Temple. Stay right beside the king."

⁸So the plans were made. The Levites and the leaders of Judah did just as Jehoiada had ordered. The three leaders led the priests coming for duty that Sabbath. And they led those whose week's work was done. These were the priests going off duty. For Jehoiada the chief priest didn't let them go home. ⁹Then Jehoiada gave spears and shields to all the army officers. These had once belonged to King David. They were stored in the Temple. ¹⁰These officers were fully armed. They formed a line from one side to the other in front of the Temple. That line then stretched around the altar in the outer court. ¹¹Then they brought out the little prince. They put the crown on his head. They handed him a copy of God's law. And they made him their king.

Jehoiada and his sons anointed him. As they did, a great shout went up. "Long live the king!" they said.

Queen Athaliah Is Killed

¹²Queen Athaliah heard all the noise. She also heard the shouts of praise to the king. So she ran over to the Temple to see what was going on. And there stood the king by his pillar at the entrance. And there were army officers and trumpeters all around him. People from all over the land were happy. They were blowing trumpets and singers were singing. And an orchestra was leading the people in a great psalm of praise.

Athaliah ripped her clothes. And she screamed, "Treason! Treason!"

¹³⁻¹⁴"Take her out and kill her," Jehoiada the priest shouted to the army officers. "Don't do it here at the Temple. And kill anyone who tries to help her."

¹⁵⁻¹⁷So the crowd opened up for them to take her out. And they killed her at the palace stables.

The People Turn to God

Then Jehoiada made a solemn promise to the Lord. He, the king, and the people all agreed to be the Lord's. And all the people rushed over to the temple of Baal. They knocked it down and broke up the altars. They knocked down the idols. And they killed Mattan the priest of Baal before his altar. ¹⁸Jehoiada now chose the Levite priests as guards. He also chose them to give the burnt offering to the Lord. For this is what the law of Moses said to do. He gave the same jobs to the Levite clans that King David had. They sang with joy as they worked in God's house. ¹⁹The guards at the Temple gates kept out all that was not holy. They kept out everyone who didn't belong there.

When we work in God's house, we should be happy

They sang with joy as they worked in God's house.

2 Chronicles 23:18

---

²⁰Then they took the king from the Temple. All the army officers, nobles, governors, and all the people went along. They made their way from the Upper Gate to the palace. There they seated the king upon his throne. ²¹So all the people of the land were full of joy. And the city was quiet and peaceful because Queen Athaliah was dead.

Joash Repairs the Temple

24 Joash was seven years old when he became king. He reigned 40 years in Jerusalem. His mother's name was Zibiah. She was from Beersheba. ²Joash tried hard to please the Lord as long as Jehoiada the priest was alive. ³Jehoiada

chose two wives for Joash. And Joash had sons and daughters.

⁴Later on Joash decided to repair the Temple. ⁵He called the priests and Levites. And he gave them orders.

"Go to all the cities of Judah," he said. "Collect offerings for the building fund. Then we will be able to keep the Temple in good repair. Get at it right away. Don't delay." But the Levites took their time.

⁶So the king called for Jehoiada the High Priest. He asked him, "Why haven't you sent the Levites out? Why haven't they gone to collect the Temple taxes? They must get them from the cities of Judah and from Jerusalem. The tax law given by Moses the servant of the Lord must be enforced. That way the Temple can be fixed up."

⁷⁻⁸The followers of wicked Athaliah had ruined the Temple. The things that were used to worship God had been taken out. They had been taken to the temple of Baal. So now the king ordered that a chest be made. It was to be set outside the Temple gate. ⁹Then an order was sent to all the cities of Judah. It was sent throughout Jerusalem. It told the people to bring a tax to the Lord. This was the tax that Moses the servant of God had demanded of Israel. ¹⁰And all the leaders and the people were glad. They brought the money and put it in the chest until it was full.

¹¹Then the Levites carried the chest to the king's officers. There the secretary and the High Priest's helper counted the money. Then they took the chest back to the Temple again. This went on day after day. And money kept on pouring in. ¹²The king and Jehoiada gave the money to the building managers. They hired masons and carpenters to fix the Temple. They also hired metal workers. They made items of iron and brass. ¹³So the work went forward. And the Temple was soon in much better shape than before. ¹⁴They finished the work. And the rest of the money was brought to the king and Jehoiada. They used it for making the gold and silver spoons and bowls used for incense. They also made the tools used in the sacrifices.

Burnt offerings were given at the proper times during the life of Jehoiada the priest. ¹⁵He lived to a very old age. But he finally died at 130 years of age. ¹⁶He was buried in the City of David among the kings. This was because he had done so much good for Israel, God, and the Temple.

Jehoiada Dies and Joash Sins

¹⁷⁻¹⁸But after his death, the leaders of Judah came to King Joash. They tempted him to forget the Temple of the God of their ancestors. And they led him to worship shame idols instead! So the anger of God came down upon Judah and Jerusalem again. ¹⁹God sent prophets to bring them back to the Lord. But the people wouldn't listen.

²⁰Then the Spirit of God came upon Zechariah, Jehoiada's son. He called a meeting of all the people. He stood before them upon a platform. And he said to them, "God wants to know why you are disobeying his commands. For when you do, everything you try fails. You have left the Lord, and now he has left you."

²¹Then the leaders plotted to kill Zechariah. Finally King Joash himself ordered him to be killed in the Temple court. ²²That was how King Joash paid Jehoiada back for his love and loyalty— He killed his son! Zechariah's last words were, "O Lord! See what they are doing and pay them back."

²³A few months later the Syrian army came. They conquered Judah and Jerusalem. They killed all the leaders of the nation. And they sent back great amounts of booty to the king of Damascus. ²⁴It was a great triumph for the tiny Syrian army. But the Lord let the great army of Judah be beaten by them. This was because they had forsaken the Lord God of their ancestors. In that way God judged Joash. ²⁵When the Syrians left, they left Joash badly wounded. His own officials decided to kill him. This was because he had murdered the son of Jehoiada the priest. They killed him as he lay in bed. They buried him in the City of David. But they did not put him in the cemetery of the kings. ²⁶The men

who killed him were Zabad and Jehozabad. Zabad's mother was Shimeath, a woman from Ammon. Jehozabad's mother was Shimrith, a woman from Moab.

27If you want to read about the sons of Joash, see *The Annals of the Kings*. This also records the curses put on Joash and the fixing of the Temple.

When Joash died, his son Amaziah became the new king.

Amaziah Rules Judah, Doing Both Good and Evil

25 Amaziah was 25 years old when he became king. He reigned 29 years in Jerusalem. His mother's name was Jehoaddan. She was a native of Jerusalem. 2Amaziah did what was right. But he did not always want to! 3After he became king, he killed the men who had killed his father. 4But he didn't kill their children. For he followed the command of the Lord written in the law of Moses. It says that the fathers shall not die for the children's sins. And the children shall not die for the father's sins. No, everyone must pay for his own sins.

5-6Another thing Amaziah did was to organize the army. He chose leaders of each clan from Judah and Benjamin. Then he counted the people. He found that he had an army of 300,000 men 20 years old and older. All were trained and skilled in the use of spear and sword. He also paid $200,000 to hire 100,000 strong soldiers from Israel.

7But a prophet came with a message from the Lord. "Sir, do not hire troops from Israel," he said. "For the Lord is not with them. 8You might let them go with your troops to battle. But if you do, you will be beaten no matter how well you fight. For God has the power to help you or defeat you."

9"But the money!" Amaziah said. "What shall I do about that?"

And the prophet replied, "The Lord is able to give you much more than this!"

10So Amaziah sent them home again to Ephraim. This made them very angry. They took it as an insult. 11Then Amaziah took courage and led his army

to the Valley of Salt. There he killed 10,000 men from Seir. 12Another 10,000 were taken alive to the top of a cliff. They were thrown down so they were crushed on the rocks below.

13Meanwhile, the army of Israel that had been sent home raided some of Judah's cities. These cities were near Beth-horon toward Samaria. They killed 3,000 people and carried off much booty.

14King Amaziah came back from beating the Edomites. He brought with him idols taken from the people of Seir. He set them up as gods and bowed before them. And he burned incense to them! 15This made the Lord very angry. So he sent a prophet to Amaziah. "Why have you worshiped these gods?" he asked. "They couldn't even save their own people from you."

16"Since when have I asked your advice?" the king said. "Be quiet now before I have you killed."

The prophet left with a warning. "I know that God will destroy you," he said. "For you have worshiped these idols. And you have not listened to my advice."

17King Amaziah of Judah now took the advice of his counselors. He declared war on King Joash of Israel. Joash was the son of Jehoahaz and the grandson of Jehu.

God can help us win or lose

For God has the power to help you or defeat you.

2 Chronicles 25:8

18King Joash replied with this parable. "Out in the Lebanon mountains a thistle made a demand of a cedar tree. He said, 'Give your daughter in marriage to my son.' Just then a wild animal came by and stepped on the thistle, crushing it! 19You are very proud about your defeat of Edom. But my advice is to stay home. Don't bother me. If you do, you and all Judah will get badly hurt."

20But Amaziah didn't listen. And God was planning to destroy him. This was because he had worshiped the gods of Edom. ²¹The armies met at Beth-shemesh in Judah. ²²Judah was beaten and its army fled home. ²³King Joash of Israel captured King Amaziah of Judah. He took him as a prisoner to Jerusalem. Then King Joash ordered 200 yards of Jerusalem's walls to be broken down. They broke it down from the gate of Ephraim to the Corner Gate. ²⁴He carried off all the treasures and gold bowls from the Temple. He also took the treasures from the palace. And he took hostages, including Obed-edom, and went back to Samaria.

²⁵But King Amaziah of Judah lived 15 years longer than King Joash of Israel. ²⁶The complete life of King Amaziah is written in *The Annals of the Kings of Judah and Israel.* ²⁷This includes a report of how Amaziah turned away from God. It tells how his people turned against him in Jerusalem. And it tells how he ran to Lachish. But they went after him and killed him there. ²⁸They brought him back on horses to Jerusalem. And they buried him in the royal cemetery.

A King Turns into a Leper

God gave King Uzziah everything a king could want. But that wasn't enough for Uzziah. He wasn't satisfied just to be king. He also wanted to do what the priests did. He wanted to burn incense in the Temple. "Get out! Get out!" the priests begged. "God does not want you here." But the king stubbornly refused. Suddenly something happened to the king. At once he knew he had made a terrible mistake. But it was too late.

26 The people of Judah now crowned Uzziah as their new king. He was only 16 years old at the time. ²After his father's death, he rebuilt the city of Eloth. He brought it back under Judah's rule. ³In all, he reigned 52 years in Jerusalem. His mother's name was Jecoliah. She was from Jerusalem. ⁴He followed in the footsteps of his father, Amaziah. He was, in general, a good king in the Lord's sight.

⁵While Zechariah was alive Uzziah was always eager to please God. Zechariah was a man who had special words from God. When the king followed the paths of God, he succeeded. For God blessed him.

⁶He declared war on the Philistines. He took the city of Gath and broke down its walls. He did the same to Jabneh and Ashdod. Then he built new cities in the Ashdod area. He also built in other parts of the Philistine country. ⁷God helped him with his wars against the Philistines. He helped him in his battles with the Arabs of Gur-baal. And he helped him in his wars with the Meunites. ⁸The Ammonites paid yearly tribute to him. And his fame spread even to Egypt. For he was very powerful.

⁹He built towers in Jerusalem at the Corner Gate and the Valley Gate. He built another at the turning of the wall. ¹⁰He also built forts in the Negeb. And he dug many wells. For he had great herds of cattle. These were out in the valleys and on the plains. He was a man who loved the soil. So he had many farms and vineyards. These were both on the hillsides and in the rich valleys.

¹¹He organized his army into groups. Men were drafted under quotas set by Jeiel. He was the secretary of the army. Maaseiah, his helper, worked with him. The commander was General Hananiah. ¹²There were 2,600 brave clan leaders to lead these groups. ¹³The army was made up of 307,500 men. They were all strong soldiers. ¹⁴Uzziah gave them

shields, spears, helmets, coats of mail, bows, and slingstones. ¹⁵And he built clever devices to fight with. They were designed by clever men and made in Jerusalem. These devices shot arrows and huge stones from the towers and walls. So he became very famous. For the Lord helped him until he became very powerful.

¹⁶But when he became powerful, he became proud. He sinned against the Lord his God. He did this by going into the holy sanctuary of the Temple. And there he burned incense on the altar. ¹⁷⁻¹⁸Azariah the High Priest went in after him. He took 80 other priests with him, all brave men. They told him to get out.

"It is not for you, Uzziah, to burn incense," they said. "That is the work of the priests alone. Only the sons of Aaron are set apart for this work. Get out! For you don't belong here. The Lord will not honor you for this!"

¹⁹Uzziah was angry. He would not set down the incense burner he was holding. But look! Suddenly leprosy was on his forehead! ²⁰When Azariah and the others saw it, they rushed him out. In fact, he himself wanted to get out too! This was because the Lord had struck him.

²¹So King Uzziah was a leper until the day he died. He had to live alone. He was cut off from his people and from the Temple. His son Jotham became vice-regent. He was in charge of the king's affairs. And he oversaw the judging of the people of the land.

²²Other details of Uzziah's reign are recorded by the prophet Isaiah, the son of Amoz. ²³When Uzziah died, he was buried in the royal cemetery. They put him there even though he was a leper. And his son Jotham became the new king.

- *Remember:* How long was Uzziah king? (26:3) Was he mostly a good king or a bad king? (26:4-5) What good things did God help Uzziah do? (26:6-15) How did Uzziah change? (26:16) How did Uzziah sin against God? (26:16-19) How did God punish Uzziah for his sin? (26:19-21) Do you think Uzziah should have been satisfied with all he had? Why was it wrong for him to want what he should not have?

- *Discover:* Be satisfied with what God has given you. If you want more, be sure it's something God wants you to have.

- *Apply:* Make a list of special things God has given you. Don't forget parents, home, good food, and clothing. What else do you want? Ask, "Is this something God wants me to have?"

- *What's next?* The people of Israel are captured and taken to a strange land. Read 2 Kings 17. ■

King Jotham Follows God

27 Jotham was 25 years old when he became king. He ruled for 16 years in Jerusalem. His mother was Jerushah. She was the daughter of Zadok. ²He followed the good example of his father Uzziah. Uzziah had been a good king, though he had sinned by burning incense in the Temple. But even though Jotham was a good king, his people became very sinful.

³He built the Upper Gate of the Temple. He also rebuilt the walls on the hill where the Temple was. ⁴And he built cities in the hill country of Judah. He built forts and towers on the wooded hills.

⁵His war against the Ammonites was successful. In fact, for the next three years he was sent a yearly tribute from them. It included $200,000 in silver, 10,000 sacks of wheat, and 10,000 sacks of barley. ⁶King Jotham became powerful. This was because he followed the path of the Lord his God.

⁷The rest of his history is written in *The Annals of the Kings of Israel and Judah.* This includes his wars and other deeds. ⁸He was 25 years old when he began to reign. And he reigned 16 years in Jerusalem. ⁹When he died, he was buried in Jerusalem. And his son Ahaz became the new king.

Ahaz Angers God

28 Ahaz was 20 years old when he became king. He ruled 16 years in Jerusalem. But he was a bad king. He was not like his ancestor King David. ²For he followed the example of the kings in Israel. And he worshiped the idols of Baal. ³He even went out to the Valley of Hinnom. And he did not just burn incense to the idols. He even sacrificed his own children in the fire! He did just like the heathen nations that were thrown out of the land. The Lord had thrown them out to make room for Israel. ⁴He sacrificed and burned incense at the idol shrines. These were on the hills and under every green tree.

⁵That is why the Lord God let the king of Syria defeat him. And he sent many of his people away to Damascus. The armies from Israel also killed many of his troops. ⁶On a single day, Pekah, the son of Remaliah, killed 120,000 of his bravest soldiers. This was because they had turned away from the Lord God of their fathers. ⁷Then Zichri killed the king's son Maaseiah. Zichri was a great soldier from Ephraim. Zichri also killed the palace manager Azrikam and the king's second-in-command Elkanah. ⁸The armies from Israel captured 200,000 Judean women and children. They also took great amounts of booty. They took it all back to Samaria.

⁹But Oded, a prophet of the Lord, was there in Samaria. He went out to meet the army as it came home.

"Look!" he said. "The Lord God of your fathers was angry with Judah. So he let you capture them. But you have killed them with no mercy. And all heaven is troubled. ¹⁰Now are you going to make slaves of these people from Judah and Jerusalem? What about your own sins against the Lord your God? ¹¹Listen to me and send these relatives of yours home. For now the fierce anger of the Lord is upon *you.*"

¹²Some of the top leaders of Ephraim agreed with the prophet. These men were Azariah, Berechiah, Jehizkiah, and Amasa. Azariah was the son of Johanan. Berechiah was the son of Meshillemoth. Jehizkiah was the son of Shallum. And Amasa was the son of Hadlai.

¹³"You must not bring the captives here!" they said. "If you do, the Lord will be angry. And this sin will be added to our many others. We are in enough trouble with God as it is."

¹⁴So the army officers gave the captives and booty to the leaders. They were to decide what to do. ¹⁵Then the four men who were named gave the clothing to the women and children who needed it. They gave them shoes, food, and wine. They put those who were sick and old on donkeys. And they took them back to their families in Jericho. Jericho was also known as the City of Palm Trees. Then they went back to Samaria.

Ahaz Nails the Temple Shut

¹⁶About that time King Ahaz of Judah asked the king of Assyria to help him. He wanted help fighting against the armies of Edom. For Edom was attacking Judah and taking many people as slaves. ¹⁷⁻¹⁸Meanwhile, the Philistines had invaded the lowland cities and the Negeb. They had already taken Beth-shemesh, Aijalon, Gederoth, Soco, Timnah, and Gimzo. They took these cities with the villages around them. And the Philistines were living there. ¹⁹For the Lord brought Judah very low. This was because of the bad deeds of King Ahaz of Israel. For he had caused the people of Judah to sin. And he had not been faithful to the Lord. ²⁰Tilgath-pilneser, the king of Assyria, came. But he caused trouble for King Ahaz instead of helping him. ²¹Ahaz had given him the Temple gold and the palace treasures. But even that did no good.

²²In this time of trouble, King Ahaz was even more unfaithful to the Lord. ²³He gave sacrifices to the gods of Damascus who had beaten him. He felt that these gods had helped the kings of Syria. And he believed they would help him too if he sacrificed to them. But instead, they were the ruin of Ahaz and all his people. ²⁴The king took the gold bowls from the Temple. He slashed them to pieces. And he nailed the door of the Temple shut. That way no one could worship there. And he made altars to the heathen gods in every corner of Jerusalem. ²⁵And he did the same in every city of Judah. And he made the Lord God of his fathers very angry.

²⁶The other details of his life are recorded in *The Annals of the Kings of Judah and Israel.* ²⁷When King Ahaz died, he

was buried in Jerusalem. But he was not put in the royal tombs. His son Hezekiah became the new king.

Hezekiah Opens God's House

29 Hezekiah was 25 years old when he became the king of Judah. He reigned 29 years in Jerusalem. His mother's name was Abijah. She was the daughter of Zechariah. ²His reign was good in the Lord's sight. It was just as his ancestor David's had been.

³Hezekiah opened the doors of the Temple and fixed them. He did this in the very first month of his first year as king. ⁴⁻⁵He called the priests and Levites to meet him. They came to the open space east of the Temple. And there Hezekiah spoke to them.

"Listen to me, you Levites," he said. "Make yourselves pure and make the Temple of the Lord God of your ancestors holy. Clean all the trash from the holy place. ⁶For our fathers have done a deep sin before the Lord our God. They left the Lord and his Temple. They turned their backs on it. ⁷The doors have been shut tight. The flame that was always supposed to burn has been put out. And the incense and burnt offerings have not been given. ⁸Therefore, the anger of the Lord has been upon Judah and Jerusalem. He has caused us to be objects of horror and shame as you see us today. ⁹Our fathers have been killed in war. Our sons, daughters, and wives have been taken captive because of this.

¹⁰"But now I want to make a covenant with the Lord God of Israel. That way his fierce anger will turn away from us. ¹¹My children, don't forget your duties any longer. For the Lord has chosen you to serve him and to burn incense."

¹²⁻¹⁴Then the Levites went into action.

From the Kohath clan came Mahath and Joel. Mahath was the son of Amasai. Joel was the son of Azariah.

From the Merari clan came Kish and Azariah. Kish was the son of Abdi. Azariah was the son of Jehallelel.

From the Gershon clan came Joah and Eden. Joah was the son of Zimmah. Eden was the son of Joah.

From the Elizaphan clan came Shimri and Jeuel.

From the Asaph clan came Zechariah and Mattaniah.

From the Hemanite clan came Jehuel and Shimei.

From the Jeduthun clan came Shemaiah and Uzziel.

¹⁵They in turn called their fellow Levites. They made themselves pure. And they began to clean up and make the Temple pure and holy. They did just as the king had commanded them. For he was speaking for the Lord. ¹⁶The priests cleaned up the inner room of the Temple. They brought out into the court all the dirt and decay they found there. The Levites then took it out to the brook Kidron. ¹⁷This all began on the first day of April. And by the eighth day they had reached the outer court. And the outer court took eight days to clean up. So the whole job was finished in 16 days.

¹⁸Then they went back to the palace. There they gave King Hezekiah a full report. "We have finished cleaning the Temple," they said. "We have cleaned the altar of burnt offerings and its tools. We have also cleaned the table of the Bread of the Presence and its tools. ¹⁹What's more, we have found and made holy all the things thrown away by King Ahaz when he closed the Temple. They are beside the altar of the Lord."

The Temple Is Consecrated

²⁰Early the next morning King Hezekiah went to the Temple. He went with the city officials. ²¹They took seven young bulls, seven rams, seven lambs, and seven male goats. They were for a sin offering for the nation and for the Temple.

He told the priests to sacrifice them on the altar of the Lord. The priests were descendants of Aaron. ²²So they killed the young bulls. And the priests took the blood and sprinkled it on the altar. They killed the rams and sprinkled their blood on the altar. And they did the same with the lambs. ²³The male goats were for the sin offering. They were brought before the king and his officials. They laid their hands on them. 24Then the priests killed the animals. They made a sin offering with their blood upon the altar. They did this to bring forgiveness for all Israel. They did just as the king had commanded. For the king had said that the burnt and sin offerings must be given for the whole nation.

25-26He told Levites at the Temple to form an orchestra. They were to use cymbals, psalteries, and harps. This was

???????????????????????????????????
Which king gave a present of 1,000 bulls and 7,000 sheep to his people?

(Read 30:23-27 for the answer.)

???????????????????????????????????

to follow the orders of David and the prophets Gad and Nathan. They had been given their orders from the Lord. The priests formed a trumpet group. 27Then Hezekiah ordered the burnt offering to be put on the altar. So the sacrifice began. The instruments began to play songs of the Lord. And the trumpets began to blow. 28Through the ceremony everyone worshiped the Lord. The singers sang. And the trumpets blew. 29After that the king and his servants bowed low before the Lord in worship. 30Then King Hezekiah ordered the Levites to sing before the Lord. They sang some of the psalms of David and of the prophet Asaph. The Levites sang gladly! And they bowed their heads and worshiped.

31"The Temple has now been made holy to the Lord," Hezekiah said. "Now bring your sacrifices and thank offerings." So the people brought their sacrifices and thank offerings. They brought them from every part of the nation. And those who wanted to brought burnt offerings too. 32-33In all, there were 70 young bulls for burnt offerings, 100 rams, and 200 lambs. In addition, 600 oxen and 3,000 sheep were brought as holy gifts. 34But there

were too few priests to prepare the burnt offerings. So their brothers the Levites helped them until the work was finished. Later more priests came to work. The Levites were more ready to cleanse themselves than the priests were. 35There were many burnt offerings. And the usual drink offering was given with each. Many peace offerings were given too. In this way, the Temple was opened up for use. And the sacrifices were given once again. 36Hezekiah and all the people were very happy. For God had done this very quickly.

Passover—A Happy Time Again

30 King Hezekiah now sent letters to all the people of Israel and Judah. He also sent them to Ephraim and Ma-nasseh. He called everyone to come to the Temple at Jerusalem. There they would celebrate the yearly Passover Feast. 2-3The king, his officers, and the people of Jerusalem had agreed to celebrate the Passover in May. The normal time for this feast was April. But they chose May because not enough priests were ready at the earlier time. And there wasn't enough time to call the people to Jerusalem. 4The king and his advisors agreed in this matter. 5So they sent a message about the Passover Feast throughout Israel. It was sent from Dan to Beersheba. Everyone was invited to come. They had not kept this feast in great numbers as the law commanded.

6"Come back to the Lord God of Abraham, Isaac, and Israel," the king's letter said. "Do this so that he will come back to us. For we have escaped from the power of the kings of Assyria. 7Do not be like your fathers and brothers. For they sinned against the Lord God of their fathers. And as a result, they were destroyed. 8Do not be stubborn, as they were. But give yourselves to the Lord. Come to his Temple which he has made holy for all time. Worship the Lord your God. Do this so that his fierce anger will turn away from you. 9Turn to the Lord again. If you do, your brothers and children will be treated with mercy by their captors.

And they will be able to come back to this land. For the Lord your God is full of kindness and mercy. He will not keep on turning his face from you. He won't do this if you come back to him."

[10]So the messengers went from city to city. They went to Ephraim and Manasseh and as far as Zebulun. But for the most part people only laughed at them! [11]But some from the tribes of Asher, Manasseh, and Zebulun turned to God. And they came to Jerusalem. [12]But in Judah the whole nation felt a strong desire to obey the Lord's orders. These were the orders given by the king and his officers. [13]And so it was that a very large crowd came to Jerusalem. They came in the month of May for the Passover Feast. [14]They set to work and broke down the heathen altars in Jerusalem. They knocked down all the incense altars. And they threw them into Kidron Brook.

[15]On the first day of May the people killed their Passover lambs. Then the priests and Levites became ashamed of themselves. For they had not taken an active part in the feast. So they made themselves holy. And they brought burnt offerings into the Temple. [16]They stood at their posts as commanded by the law of Moses the man of God. And the priests sprinkled the blood given to them by the Levites.

[17-19]People came from Ephraim, Manasseh, Issachar, and Zebulun. And many of them were unclean. This was because they had not done the special things to become pure. So the Levites killed their Passover lambs for them. They did this to make them pure. Then King Hezekiah prayed for them. And they were allowed to eat the Passover anyway. They did this even though it was against God's rules. But Hezekiah said, "May the good Lord forgive everyone who decides to follow the Lord God of his fathers. May the Lord forgive him, even though he is not properly cleansed for the feast." [20]And the Lord listened to Hezekiah's prayer. And he did not destroy them.

[21]So the people of Israel observed the Passover at Jerusalem. The feast went on for seven days with great joy.

Meanwhile the Levites and priests praised the Lord. They did this with music and cymbals day after day. [22]King Hezekiah praised the Levites for their good work.

So for seven days the feast kept going. Peace offerings were given. And the people confessed their sins to the Lord God of their fathers. [23]The people kept on celebrating with great joy. So they decided to continue the feast for another seven days. [24]King Hezekiah gave the people 1,000 young bulls for offerings. He also gave 7,000 sheep. The princes gave 1,000 young bulls and 10,000 sheep. At this time another large group of priests stepped forward. They came and made themselves holy before the Lord.

[25]Then the people of Judah were filled with deep joy. So were the priests, the Levites, the foreign residents, and the visitors from Israel. [26]Jerusalem hadn't seen a feast like this since the days of King David's son Solomon! [27]Then the priests and Levites stood and blessed the people. And the Lord heard their prayers from his holy temple in heaven.

Hezekiah and the People Worship Again

31 After the Passover a great campaign against idol worship was begun. The people went out to the cities of Judah, Benjamin, Ephraim, and Manasseh. They tore down the idol altars, the pillars, and the shame images. They destroyed all the other heathen centers of worship. Then the people from the northern tribes went back to their own homes.

[2]Hezekiah now put the priests and Levites into service groups. Some were to offer the burnt offerings and peace offerings. Some were to worship and give thanks and praise to the Lord. [3]Hezekiah gave animals for the daily morning and evening burnt offerings. He gave animals for the weekly Sabbath offerings and the monthly new moon festivals. He also gave animals for the

other yearly feasts. He gave what was commanded by the law of God.

⁴Hezekiah gave an order to the people in Jerusalem. He told them to bring a tenth of what they had. They were to give it to the priests and Levites. That way they wouldn't need other work outside the Temple. But they could give themselves fully to their work as commanded in the law of God. ⁵⁻⁶The people gave right away and freely. They gave of the first of their crops and grain, new wine, and olive oil. They gave of their money and everything else. They gave a tenth of all they owned. The law said this much was to be given to the Lord their God. Everything was laid out in great piles. Some people had moved to Judah from Israel. And some of the people of Judah lived in the country. But they also brought in a tenth of their cattle and sheep. A tenth of the things given to the Lord were also brought. These things were piled in great heaps. ⁷⁻⁸The first of these offerings was brought in June. And the piles kept on growing until October. Hezekiah and his officials came and saw these huge piles. And how they blessed the Lord and praised his people!

⁹"Where did all this come from?" Hezekiah asked the priests and Levites.

¹⁰Azariah the High Priest from the clan of Zadok spoke. "The people have brought their offerings," he said. "We have been eating from these stores of food for many weeks. But all this is left over! For the Lord has blessed his people."

¹¹Hezekiah decided to make storerooms in the Temple. ¹²⁻¹³All the supplies given to the Lord were brought into the Lord's house. Conaniah the Levite was put in charge. He was helped by his brother Shimei. They were both helped by Jehiel, Azaziah, Nahath, Asahel, Jerimoth, Jozabad, Eliel, Ismachiah, Mahath, and Benaiah.

These jobs were given by King Hezekiah and Azariah the High Priest.

¹⁴⁻¹⁵Kore, the son of Imnah was a Levite. He was the gatekeeper at the East Gate. He was put in charge of giving the offerings to the priests. His faithful helpers were Eden, Miniamin, Jeshua, Shemaiah, Amariah, and Shecaniah. They brought the gifts to the clans of priests in their cities. They gave them to young and old alike. ¹⁶But the priests on duty at the Temple were supplied from there. They and their families were given what they needed. So they were not included in the plan to deliver supplies. ¹⁷⁻¹⁸The priests were listed in the records by clans. The Levites 20 years old and older were listed under the names of their work groups. A regular supply of food was given to the families of priests. They had no other way to get food. For their time was given to the service of the Temple. ¹⁹One of the priests was chosen in each of the cities of the priests. He was to give food and other supplies to all priests in the area. He was also to give supplies to all the Levites.

²⁰In this way King Hezekiah sent supplies throughout all Judah. He did what was just and fair in the sight of the Lord his God. ²¹He worked very hard to bring respect to the Temple, the law, and godly living. And he was very successful.

An Angel Fights for Judah

32 Some time later after this good work of King Hezekiah, King Sennacherib of Assyria invaded Judah. He surrounded the walled cities. And he planned to place them under tribute. ²It soon became clear that Sennacherib wanted to attack Jerusalem. ³So Hezekiah called his princes and officers for a council of war. It was decided to plug the springs outside the city. ⁴They put a huge crew of men to work. They blocked the springs off. And they cut off the brook that ran through the fields.

"Why should the king of Assyria come and find water?" they asked.

⁵Then Hezekiah made his defenses stronger. He fixed the wall where it was broken down. And he added towers to the wall. He made a second wall outside the first one. He also made Fort Millo in the City of David stronger. And he made many weapons and shields. ⁶He called out an army and chose officers. He

called them to the plains outside the city. And he gave them this speech.

7"Be strong. Be brave," he said. "Do not be afraid of the king of Assyria or his mighty army. For there is someone with us who is far greater than he is! 8He has a great army. But they are all just men. But we have the Lord our God to fight our battles for us!" This made the army feel better.

9King Sennacherib of Assyria was camped around the city of Lachish. He sent messengers with this message. They brought it to King Hezekiah and the people of Jerusalem.

10"King Sennacherib of Assyria asks, 'Do you think you can live through my attack of Jerusalem? 11King Hezekiah is trying to tell you to commit suicide by staying there. You will die of hunger and thirst! And he promises that "the Lord our God will deliver us from the king of Assyria"! 12Don't you know that Hezekiah is the person who destroyed all the idols? He commanded Judah and Jerusalem to use only the one altar at the Temple! And he told you to burn incense on it alone! 13Don't you know about the record that I and the other kings of Assyria have? We have never yet failed to conquer a nation we attacked! The gods of those nations weren't able to save their lands! 14Name just one time when anyone was able to stop us! What makes you think your God can do any better? 15Don't let Hezekiah fool you! Don't believe him. I say it again! No god of any nation has ever yet been able to save his people from me or my ancestors. How much less your God?'" 16So the messenger laughed at the Lord God and God's servant Hezekiah.

17King Sennacherib also sent letters laughing at the Lord God of Israel.

"The gods of all other nations failed to save their people from me," he wrote. "The God of Hezekiah will fail too!"

18The messengers who brought the letters shouted out in Hebrew. They shouted threats to the people on the walls of the city. They tried to scare them. 19These messengers talked about the God of Jerusalem. They acted just as

though he were one of the heathen gods. They laughed at him like he was a handmade idol!

20Then King Hezekiah and Isaiah the prophet, the son of Amoz, prayed to God in heaven. 21And the Lord sent an angel. He destroyed the Assyrian army with all its officers and generals! So Sennacherib went back home in deep shame to his own land. And when he got home he went to the temple of his god. And some of his own sons killed him there. 22That is how the Lord saved Hezekiah and the people of Jerusalem. And now there was peace at last in Judah.

23From then on King Hezekiah was given respect by the nations around them. And many gifts for the Lord were sent to Jerusalem. Many rich gifts were sent to King Hezekiah, too.

Hezekiah Gets a Second Chance

24But about that time Hezekiah became very sick. He prayed to the Lord. And the Lord healed him with a miracle. 25But Hezekiah wasn't really thankful. He didn't give God the praise he deserved. For he had become proud. So the anger of God was on him and on Judah and Jerusalem. 26But finally Hezekiah and the people of Jerusalem became humble. So the anger of the Lord did not fall on them while Hezekiah was alive.

27So Hezekiah became very rich and was highly honored. He had to build special treasury buildings. These were for his silver, gold, precious stones, and spices. They also stored his shields and gold bowls. 28-29He also built many storehouses for his grain, new wine, and olive oil. And he had many stalls for his animals. And he made pens for the great flocks of sheep and goats he bought. And he took control of many towns. For God had given him great riches. 30He dammed up the Upper Spring of Gihon. And he brought the water down to the west side of Jerusalem. This was the City of David section of the city. He succeeded in all that he did.

31But messengers came from Babylon to find out about his being healed. And

God left him to himself. He wanted to test him to see what he was really like.

³²The rest of the story of Hezekiah is written in *The Book of Isaiah*. This was written by Isaiah the prophet, the son of Amoz. Hezekiah's story is also found in *The Annals of the Kings of Judah and Israel*. ³³So Hezekiah died. He was buried in the royal cemetery among the other kings. And all Judah and Jerusalem honored him at his death. Then his son Manasseh became the new king.

King Manasseh's Heart Is Changed

33 Manasseh was only 12 years old when he became king. And he reigned for 55 years in Jerusalem. ²But it was an evil reign. For he tempted his people to worship the idols of the heathen nations. These nations were destroyed by the Lord when the people of Israel entered the land. ³He rebuilt the heathen altars his father Hezekiah had destroyed. These were the altars of Baal and the shame images. He also worshiped the sun, moon, and stars. ⁴⁻⁵He even built heathen altars in both courts of the Temple of the Lord. These were used to worship the sun, moon, and stars. He did this in the very place where the Lord had said he would be honored for all time. ⁶And Manasseh sacrificed his own children as burnt offerings. This was done in the Valley of Hinnom. He spoke with spirit-mediums, too. And he hired fortune tellers and sorcerers. He encouraged every sort of evil. And this made the Lord very angry.

⁷Think of it! He put an idol in the very Temple of God! He put it where God had told David and his son Solomon he would be. He had said, "I will be honored here in this Temple and in Jerusalem for all time. This is the city I have chosen to be honored. It will be honored above all the other cities of Israel. ⁸And you must only obey my commands. You must follow all the laws and commands given to you by Moses. If you do, I won't ever again send Israel from this land. For this is the land I gave your ancestors."

⁹But Manasseh encouraged the people of Judah and Jerusalem to do bad things. And they did even more evil than the other nations. These other nations were the ones the Lord destroyed when Israel entered the land. ¹⁰Both Manasseh and his people did not listen to the warnings the Lord sent them. ¹¹So God sent the Assyrian armies. They caught him with hooks. They tied him with bronze chains. And they took him away to Babylon. ¹²Then at last he came to his senses. He cried out humbly to God for help. ¹³And the Lord listened and answered his prayer. He let him go back to Jerusalem and to his kingdom! Finally Manasseh knew that the Lord was really God!

¹⁴After this he rebuilt the outer wall of the City of David. And he fixed the wall, starting west of the Spring of Gihon in the Kidron Valley. He worked from there to the Fish Gate. Then he worked around Citadel Hill. At that point the wall was built very high. And he sent his army generals to live in all of the walled cities of Judah. ¹⁵He also took the foreign gods from the hills. And he took his idol from the Temple. He tore down the altars he had built on the mountain where the Temple stood. He got rid of the altars that were in Jerusalem. He dumped them outside the city. ¹⁶Then he fixed the altar of the Lord. And he gave sacrifices on it. He gave peace offerings and thanksgiving offerings. And he demanded that the people of Judah worship the Lord God of Israel. ¹⁷But the people still gave offerings on the altars in the hills. But these were only made to the Lord their God.

¹⁸The rest of Manasseh's deeds are all written in *The Annals of the Kings of Israel*. This record includes his prayer to God. And it records God's reply through the prophets. ¹⁹His prayer and the way God answered it are recorded in *The Annals of the Prophets*. This includes an account of his sins and errors. There is a list of the hills where he built idols. It also tells where he set up shame idols and graven images. This of course was before he had the great change in his heart.

Evil Amon Rules Judah

20-21When Manasseh died, he was buried under his own palace. His son Amon became the new king. Amon was 22 years old when he began to reign in Jerusalem. But he lasted for only two years. 22It was an evil reign. It was like the early years of his father Manasseh.

For Amon sacrificed to all the idols just as his father had. 23But he didn't change as his father did. Instead, he sinned more and more. 24At last his own officers killed him in his palace. 25But some of the people killed the men who had killed King Amon. And they made his son Josiah the new king.

The Book of the Law Is Found

Pretend that there is only one Bible in the world. It has been lost for many years. Then one day some people find it! That's what happened in this story. The Book of the Law was the only part of the Bible Josiah's people had. But they didn't even know they had it. People had not been reading it. They had lost the only copy that they had. But one day some people found it. What would they do with it?

34 Josiah was only eight years old when he became king. He reigned for 31 years in Jerusalem. 2His was a good reign. He followed the good example of his ancestor King David. 3When he was 16 years old he began to search for the God of his ancestor David. This was in the eighth year of his reign. And four years later he began to clean up Judah and Jerusalem. He broke down the heathen altars and the shame idols on the hills. 4He went out to watch as the altars of Baal were knocked apart. He made sure the pillars above the altars were chopped down. And he ground the shame idols into dust. Then he scattered that dust over the graves of those who had sacrificed to them. 5Then he burned the bones of the heathen priests on their own altars. He did this to clear the people of Judah and Jerusalem from their guilt. This was the guilt from their sin of idol worship.

6Then he went to the cities of Manasseh, Ephraim, and Simeon. He even went to faraway Naphtali. And he did the same thing there. 7He broke down the heathen altars. He ground the shame idols to powder. And he chopped down the pillars. He did this everywhere in the whole land of Israel. Then he went back to Jerusalem.

8So he finished cleaning the idols from the land. And he made the Temple pure again. Then during the 18th year of his reign he chose three men to fix the Temple. The first was Shaphan the son of Azaliah. The second was Maaseiah, the governor of Jerusalem. And the third was Joah, the son of Joahaz. He was the city treasurer. 9They set up a plan to collect gifts for the Temple. The money was collected at the Temple gates. The Levites on guard duty there took them. Gifts were brought by all the people who came. They brought gifts from Manasseh and Ephraim. They brought them from other parts of Israel, too. And gifts were brought by the people of Jerusalem. The money was taken to Hilkiah the High Priest to be counted. 10-11Then it was used by the Levites. They paid carpenters and stonemasons. And they bought building materials. This included stone building blocks, timber, lumber, and beams. He now rebuilt

what earlier kings of Judah had torn down.

¹²The men worked very hard under their leaders, Jahath and Obadiah. These men were Levites of the clan of Merari. Zechariah and Meshullam, of the clan of Kohath, were the building managers. The Levites who were skilled musicians played music while the work went on. ¹³Other Levites told the unskilled laborers what to do. They carried in the materials to the workmen. Still others helped as accountants, managers, and carriers.

¹⁴One day Hilkiah the High Priest was at the Temple. He was counting the money collected at the gates. And he found an old scroll. It was a copy of the laws of God as given to Moses!

15-16"Look!" Hilkiah said to Shaphan, the king's secretary. "See what I have found in the Temple! These are the laws of God!" Hilkiah gave the scroll to Shaphan. And Shaphan took it to the king. He also brought his report that the work was going well. This was the work of rebuilding the Temple.

17"The money chests have been opened and counted," he said to the king. "And the money has been put into the hands of the overseers and workmen."

18Then he told the king about the scroll. And he told how Hilkiah had found it. So he read it to the king. 19The king heard God's laws. And he saw what they asked God's people to do. So he ripped his clothing in despair. 20And he called Hilkiah and Ahikam. Ahikam was the son of Shaphan. He called Abdon, the son of Micah. He called Shaphan the treasurer. And he called Asaiah, the king's personal advisor.

21"Go to the Temple and pray to the Lord for me!" the king told them. "Pray for all those left in Israel and Judah! For this scroll tells us why the Lord is angry. It tells us why his great anger has been poured out on us. It is because our ancestors have not obeyed the laws that are written here."

22So the men went to Huldah the prophetess. She was the wife of Shallum. Shallum was the son of Tokhath. And Tokhath was the son of Hasrah. Shallum was the king's tailor. He lived in the second ward. They told her of the king's trouble. 23And she replied, "The Lord God of Israel says, 24'Yes, I will destroy this city and its people. All the curses written in the scroll will come true. 25For my people have left me. They have worshiped heathen gods. And I am very angry with them for their deeds. Therefore, my anger is poured out on this place.'

26"But the Lord also says this to the king of Judah. He is the one who sent you to ask me about this. Tell him the Lord God of Israel says, 27'You are sorry. And you have humbled yourself before God. You listened when you heard my words against this city and its people.

You have torn your clothing in despair. And you have cried before me. I have heard you, says the Lord. 28So I will wait to send the promised trouble upon this city and its people. I will not send it until after you die.'" So they brought back to the king this word from the Lord. 29Then the king called all the elders of Judah and Jerusalem. 30He called the priests and Levites. He called all the people great and small. He wanted them to go with him to the Temple. There the king read the scroll to them. This was the covenant of God that was found in the Temple. 31As the king stood before them, he made a promise to the Lord. He promised to follow his commands with all his heart and soul. And he promised to do what was written in the scroll. 32He told everyone in Jerusalem and Benjamin to make this promise to God. And all of them did.

33So Josiah got rid of all the idols from the land of Israel. And he made all of the people worship the Lord their God. And during the rest of his life they served the Lord. They served the God of their ancestors.

- *Remember:* What did King Josiah do to stop idol worship? (34:1-7) What did he do to help the Temple, God's house? (34:8-13) What did Hilkiah, the High Priest, find? (34:14) Where did he send the scroll? (34:15-16) What did the king do when he heard God's laws? (34:19-21) How would God punish the people for disobeying him? (34:22-25) Why would this not happen while Josiah was alive? (34:26-28) How did Josiah help others know what God said? (34:29-32) Why do you think Josiah pleased God?

- *Discover:* We please God when we obey his Word. We will be punished when we disobey his Word.

- *Apply:* Think of two things the Bible tells you to do. Will you obey them? If you can't think of two things, read Ephesians 6:1-2. Or read the Ten Commandments in Exodus 20.

- *What's next?* The great city of Jerusalem is destroyed. Read 2 Chronicles 36. ■

Josiah Celebrates Passover

35 Then Josiah observed the Passover feast in Jerusalem. This took place on the first day of April. The Passover lambs were killed that evening. ²He also gave the priests their duties. He encouraged them to begin their work at the Temple again. ³The Levites were set apart for the Lord's work. They were the religious teachers in Israel. Josiah said to them:

"The Ark is now in Solomon's Temple. You don't need to carry it back and forth on your shoulders. So spend your time serving the Lord and his people. ⁴⁻⁵Form the service groups of your ancestors. Do the jobs that were given to you by King David and his son Solomon. Help the people in their family groups. Help them as they bring their offerings to the Temple. ⁶Kill the Passover lambs and make yourselves pure. Get ready to help the people who come. Follow all of the orders of the Lord through Moses."

⁷Then the king gave 30,000 lambs and young goats. These were for the people's Passover offerings. He also gave 3,000 young bulls. ⁸The king's officials gave gifts to the priests and Levites freely. Hilkiah, Zechariah, and Jehiel were the overseers of the Temple. They gave the priests 2,600 sheep and goats. And they gave 300 oxen as Passover offerings. ⁹The Levite leaders gave 5,000 sheep and goats, and 500 oxen. These Levite leaders were Conaniah, Shemaiah, and Nethanel. Hashabiah, Jeiel, and Jozabad also gave. They gave these animals to the Levites for their Passover offerings.

¹⁰When everything was ready, the priests stood in their places. The Levites were in service groups as the king had ordered. ¹¹The Levites killed the Passover lambs and brought the blood to the priests. They sprinkled it on the altar as the Levites took off the animal skins. ¹²They piled up the dead animals for each tribe to give its burnt sacrifices to the Lord. They did just as it is written in the law of Moses. They did the same with the oxen. ¹³Then they roasted the Passover lambs. They boiled the holy offerings in pots, kettles, and pans. And they hurried them out to the people to eat. They did it all as directed by the laws of Moses. ¹⁴After that the Levites made a meal for themselves and for the priests. For they had been busy from morning till night. They had worked all day offering the fat of the burnt offerings.

¹⁵The singers, the sons of Asaph, were in their places. They followed the rules made by King David, Asaph, Heman, and Jeduthun the king's prophet. The gatekeepers guarded the gates. They didn't need to leave their posts of duty. For their meals were brought to them by their Levite brothers. ¹⁶The whole Passover Feast was finished in that one day. All the burnt offerings were sacrificed upon the altar of the Lord. They had done it just as Josiah had ordered.

¹⁷Everyone in Jerusalem took part in the Passover Feast. This was followed by the Feast of Unleavened Bread for the next seven days. ¹⁸Never, since the time of Samuel the prophet, had there been such a Passover. None of the kings of Israel had ever had a Passover Feast like this one. So many of the priests and Levites were there. And people came from Jerusalem and from all parts of Judah. They even came from over in Israel. ¹⁹This all happened in the 18th year of the reign of Josiah.

Josiah Dies in Battle

²⁰After this, King Neco of Egypt led his army to Carchemish. This was on the Euphrates River. And Josiah declared war on him.

²¹But King Neco sent messengers to Josiah with a message. "I don't want a fight with you, O king of Judah!" he said. "I have come only to fight the power with which I am at war. Leave me alone! God has told me to hurry! Don't meddle with God. If you do, he will destroy you. For he is with me."

²²But Josiah would not turn back. Instead he led his army into the battle at the Valley of Megiddo. He laid aside his royal robes so that the enemy wouldn't know him. Josiah did not believe that Neco's message was from

God. ²³The enemy archers hit King Josiah with their arrows. And they wounded him badly.

"Take me out of the battle," he said to his men.

²⁴⁻²⁵So they lifted him out of his chariot. The put him in his second chariot. And they brought him back to Jerusalem where he died. He was buried there in the royal cemetery. And all Judah and Jerusalem mourned for him. This even included Jeremiah the prophet. And the Temple choirs sang for him. To this day they still sing sad songs about his death. For these songs of sorrow were among the official songs of lament.

²⁶⁻²⁷The other deeds of Josiah all are written in *The Annals of the Kings of Israel and Judah*. This record includes his good deeds. And it tells how he followed the laws of the Lord.

Jerusalem Is Destroyed

Jerusalem had been the capital of Israel and then Judah for almost 500 years. Then enemies destroyed it, broke down its walls, and burned the Temple. This is the way it happened.

36 Josiah's son Jehoahaz was chosen as the new king. ²He was 23 years old when he began to rule. But his reign lasted only three months. ³Then he was deposed by the king of Egypt. He demanded a yearly tribute of $230,000 from Judah.

⁴The king of Egypt now chose Eliakim as the new King of Judah. Eliakim was the brother of Jehoahaz. Eliakim's name was changed to Jehoiakim. Jehoahaz was taken to Egypt as a prisoner. ⁵Jehoiakim was 25 years old when he became king. He ruled for 11 years in Jerusalem. But his reign was an evil one. ⁶Finally, Nebuchadnezzar king of Babylon conquered Jerusalem. He took away the king in chains to Babylon. ⁷Nebuchadnezzar also took some of the gold bowls and other items from the Temple. He put them in his own temple in Babylon. ⁸The rest of the deeds of Jehoiakim are written in *The Annals of the Kings of Judah*. This record includes all the bad things he did. His son Jehoiachin became the new king.

⁹Jehoiachin was 18 years old when he became king. But he lasted only three months and 10 days. It was an evil reign in the Lord's sight. ¹⁰The following spring he was called to Babylon by King Nebuchadnezzar. Many treasures from the Temple were taken away to Babylon at that time. King Nebuchadnezzar chose Jehoiachin's brother Zedekiah as the new king of Judah and Jerusalem.

¹¹Zedekiah was 21 years old when he became king. He ruled 11 years in Jerusalem. ¹²His reign, too, was evil in the Lord's sight. For he did not listen to Jeremiah the prophet. He gave Zedekiah messages from the Lord. ¹³Zedekiah broke from King Nebuchadnezzar's rule. He did this even though he had made a promise to be loyal. Zedekiah was a hard and stubborn man. For he would not obey the Lord God of Israel.

¹⁴All the leaders of Judah worshiped the idols of the nations around them. Even the High Priests did this! In this way they made the Temple of the Lord in Jerusalem unclean. ¹⁵The Lord God of their fathers sent his prophets to warn them. For he loved his people and his Temple. ¹⁶But the people laughed at the messengers of God. They would not listen to their words. They mocked the prophets until the Lord's anger could not be held back. There was no longer any hope for them.

¹⁷Then the Lord brought the king of Babylon against them. He killed their young men. He even went after them into the Temple. He had no pity on them. He killed even young girls and old men. The Lord used the king of Babylon to punish them. ¹⁸He took home with him all the items used in the Temple. He took the treasures from both the Temple and the palace. And he took with him all the royal princes. ¹⁹Then his army burned the Temple. And they broke down the walls of Jerusalem. They burned all the palaces. And they destroyed all the Temple furniture and tools. ²⁰Those who were not killed were taken away to Babylon. They were slaves to the king and his sons. They served there until the kingdom of Persia conquered Babylon.

God Fulfills His Promises

²¹Thus the word of the Lord spoken through Jeremiah came true. He had said that the land must rest for 70 years. This would make up for the years the people did not observe the Sabbath.

²²⁻²³But the Lord stirred the spirit of King Cyrus of Persia. This happened in Cyrus's first year as king. He sent this message throughout his kingdom. And he put it into writing. He said:

"The Lord God of heaven has made me great. All the kingdoms of the earth have been given to me. He has ordered me to build him a Temple in Jerusalem, in the land of Judah. All among you who are the Lord's people go back to Israel. Build this temple. And may the Lord be with you."

This made the words of Jeremiah the prophet come true.

Remember: Two of Josiah's sons became kings. Who were they? Which was made king by the king of Egypt? (36:1-4) Two of Jehoiachin's sons became kings. Who were they? Which was made king by the king of Babylon? (36:9-10) What were Zedekiah's people doing wrong? (36:14-16) How did God punish these people? How would this story have been different if God's people had obeyed him?

- *Discover:* Obeying God brings happiness. Disobeying him brings punishment and sadness.

- *Apply:* Are you really happy? Ask, "Am I obeying God or disobeying him?" If you're not happy, perhaps you are not doing what he wants.

- *What's next?* The people of Israel were captives in Babylon for 70 years. Now they can go home. Read Ezra 1–2. ■

EZRA

If you want to read about dangerous trips to far-away places, read Ezra. If you like to read about treasure, read Ezra. You'll see thousands of gold and silver things, captured many years before in battle. You'll see people carry these things hundreds of miles through strange country. You'll see a caravan of 42,360 people and thousands of horses, camels, and donkeys.

The people of Israel had been captured years before and taken to Babylon. But then a new king became ruler over Babylon. He let the Israelites go home. The Book of Ezra tells about the plans for this long trip. It gives us lists of the treasures that had been captured. It tells us who went on this adventure back to Jerusalem and what happened when they got there.

The Israelites Return Home

Suppose someone captures you and takes you far away to a strange land. The people there rule over you. They tell you what to do. But suppose the ruler of that land says you can go home. How would you feel? Now you know how the Israelites felt when King Cyrus said they could go home.

1 It was the first year of the reign of King Cyrus of Persia. At that time the Lord fulfilled Jeremiah's prophecy. He did this by giving King Cyrus the desire to send this message throughout his empire. This message was also put in the royal records.

²"Cyrus, king of Persia, hereby says this: The Lord, the God of heaven, gave me my great empire. He has now told me to build him a Temple in Jerusalem. This city is in the land of Judah. ³All Jews in my kingdom may now go back to Jerusalem. They may rebuild the Temple of the Lord. For he is the God of Israel and of Jerusalem. May his blessings rest upon you. ⁴Those Jews who do not go should give to pay for the needs of those who do. They should supply them with silver and gold. They should give them clothing and supplies for the trip. And they should give special gifts for the Temple."

⁵Then the leaders of the tribes of Judah and Benjamin got ready to go. So did the priests, Levites, and whoever else

God gave the desire to go. They got ready to go back to Jerusalem at once to rebuild the Temple. ⁶All the Jews who chose to stay in Persia gave them whatever help they could. They sent them with gifts for the Temple.

⁷King Cyrus himself gave them gold bowls and other valuable items. King Nebuchadnezzar had taken these items from the Temple at Jerusalem. And he had put them in the temple of his own gods. ⁸He told Mithredath, the treasurer of Persia, to give these gifts to Sheshbazzar. Sheshbazzar was the leader of the Jews who were going back to Judah.

⁹⁻¹⁰Cyrus gave many valuable items. He gave 1,000 gold trays and 1,000 silver trays. He gave 29 censers, 30 bowls of solid gold, and 2,410 silver bowls. These bowls were of various designs. He also gave 1,000 other items. ¹¹In all there were 5,469 gold and silver items. These were given to Sheshbazzar to take back to Jerusalem.

2 Here is the list of the Jews who went back to Jerusalem. Some of them also went to the other cities of Judah. They went back to the cities from which their parents had been taken. They had been taken away to Babylon by King Nebuchadnezzar.

²The leaders were Zerubbabel, Jeshua, Nehemiah, Seraiah, Reelaiah, Mordecai, Bilshan, Mispar, Bigvai, Rehum, and Baanah.

Here is a list of those who went back. They are listed by their subclans.

³⁻³⁵From the subclan of Parosh came 2,172.

From the subclan of Shephatiah came 372.

From the subclan of Arah came 775.

From the subclan of Pahath-moab came 2,812. These were the descendants of Jeshua and Joab.

From the subclan of Elam came 1,254.

From the subclan of Zattu came 945.

From the subclan of Zaccai came 760.

From the subclan of Bani came 642.

From the subclan of Bebai came 623.

From the subclan of Azgad came 1,222.

From the subclan of Adonikam came 666.

From the subclan of Bigvai came 2,056.

From the subclan of Adin came 454.

From the subclan of Ater came 98. These were the descendants of Hezekiah.

From the subclan of Bezai came 323.

From the subclan of Jorah came 112.

From the subclan of Hashum came 223.

From the subclan of Gibbar came 95.

From the subclan of Bethlehem came 123.

From the subclan of Netophah came 56.

From the subclan of Anathoth came 128.

From the subclan of Azmaveth came 42.

From the subclans of Kiriath-arim, Chephirah, and Beeroth came 743.

From the subclans of Ramah and Geba came 621.

From the subclan of Michmas came 122.

From the subclans of Bethel and Ai came 223.

From the subclan of Nebo came 52.

From the subclan of Magbish came 156.

From the subclan of Elam came 1,254.

From the subclan of Harim came 320.

From the subclans of Lod, Hadid, and Ono came 725.

From the subclan of Jericho came 345.

From the subclan of Senaah came 3,630.

³⁶⁻³⁹Here is a record of the priests who came back.

From the families of Jedaiah of the subclan of Jeshua came 973.

From the subclan of Immer came 1,052.

From the subclan of Pashhur came 1,247.

From the subclan of Harim came 1,017.

40-42Here is a record of the Levites who came back.

From the families of Jeshua and Kadmiel of the subclan of Hodaviah came 74.
From the choir members from the clan of Asaph came 128.
From the descendants of the gatekeepers came 139. These were the families of Shallum, Ater, Talmon, Akkub, Hatita, and Shobai.

43-54These families of the Temple workers came back: Ziha, Hasupha, Tabbaoth, Keros, Siaha, Padon, Lebanah, Hagabah, Akkub, Hagab, Shamlai, Hanan, Giddel, Gahar, Reaiah, Rezin, Nekoda, Gazzam, Uzza, Paseah, Besai, Asnah, Meunim, Nephisim, Bakbuk, Hakupha, Harhur, Bazluth, Mehida, Harsha, Barkos, Sisera, Temah, Neziah, and Hatipha.

55-57Descendants of King Solomon's officials also made the trip. They were Sotai, Hassophereth, Peruda, Jaalah, Darkon, Giddel, Shephatiah, Hattil, Pochereth-hazzebaim, and Ami.

58The Temple workers and the descendants of Solomon's officers numbered 392.

59Another group came back to Jerusalem at this time from the Persian cities. They came from Tel-melah, Tel-harsha, Cherub, Addan, and Immer. But they had lost their family records. So they could not prove that they were really Israelites. 60This group included the subclans of Delaiah, Tobiah, and Nekoda. In all there were a total of 652.

61Three subclans of priests also went back to Jerusalem. These subclans were Habaiah, Hakkoz, and Barzillai. Barzillai married one of the daughters of Barzillai the Gileadite. Then he took her family name. 62-63But they too had lost their family records. So the leaders did not let them serve as priests. They would not even let them eat the priests' share of food. This food came from the sacrifices. They had to wait for the matter to be settled with the Urim and Thummim. This way they would find out from God if they were priests or not.

64-65So a total of 42,360 people went back to Judah. Besides these, 7,337 slaves and 200 choir members also went. Among these, there were both men and women. 66-67They took with them 736 horses and 245 mules. They also took 435 camels and 6,720 donkeys.

68Some of the leaders gave gifts to rebuild the Temple. 69Each one gave as much as he could. The total worth of their gifts came to $300,000 of gold and $170,000 of silver. They also gave 100 robes for the priests.

70So the priests and Levites went to live in the cities of Judah where they came from. The singers, the gatekeepers, and the Temple workers also went to the cities of Judah from which they had come. And the rest of the people did the same.

- *Remember:* Who was king of Persia at this time? (1:1) Which prophet had said that Cyrus would send the Israelites home? (1:1) According to Cyrus, who gave him his empire? (1:2) Who gave money and gifts to the Jews who returned? (1:6-7) What did Cyrus give? (1:7-11) How many people returned to Jerusalem? (2:64-65) How do you think these people felt when they got home to Jerusalem? What is the first thing you would have done when you got there?

- *Discover:* Many years before God said the Israelites would come home. He said he would not forget them. God always keeps his promises. But he keeps them when he thinks the time is best.

- *Apply:* Did you pray for something yesterday? Do you think you should have it today? Wait for God.

- *What's next?* Some people cried when they saw the new Temple. Why would they do that? Read Ezra 3. ■

The New Temple

The foundation of the new Temple was laid. Some people shouted for joy. Other people cried. Why were some very happy and some very sad?

3 By the month of September, the people were living in their hometowns. At that time, they all went to Jerusalem. Jeshua with his fellow priests and Zerubbabel with his clan called the people together. Jeshua the priest was the son of Jozadak. Zerubbabel was the son of Shealtiel. They rebuilt the altar of the God of Israel. And they sacrificed burnt offerings on it. They followed the laws of Moses, the man of God. ³The altar was rebuilt on its old site. And it was used right away. They used it for the morning and evening burnt offerings to the Lord. For the people were afraid of attack from their enemies.

⁴And they observed the Feast of Tabernacles. They did this by the laws of Moses. And they gave the burnt offerings needed for each day of the feast. ⁵They also gave the special sacrifices needed for the Sabbaths. They followed all the laws for the new moon feasts. And they did the same for the other yearly feasts of the Lord. Freewill offerings of the people were also given. ⁶So the priests began sacrificing the burnt offerings to the Lord. This began on the 15th day of September. This happened before they began building the base of the Temple.

⁷Then they hired masons and carpenters. They bought cedar logs from the people of Tyre and Sidon. They paid them with food, wine, and olive oil. The logs were brought down from the Lebanon mountains. They were floated along the coast of the Mediterranean Sea to Joppa. King Cyrus had included this supply of lumber in his grant.

⁸The actual building of the Temple began in June. This was during the second year of their coming to Jerusalem. The workers were all those who had come back from Babylon. And they were under the direction of Zerubbabel and Jeshua. Zerubbabel was the son of Shealtiel. Jeshua was the son of Jozadak. Jeshua's fellow priests and the Levites also helped to direct the work. The Levites who were 20 years old or older were chosen to manage the workers. ⁹The work of managing the project was given to Jeshua, Kadmiel, and Henadad. Their sons and relatives helped them. All of these men were Levites.

¹⁰The builders finished the base of the Temple. When they did, the priests put on their official robes. And they blew their trumpets. The descendants of Asaph crashed their cymbals to praise the Lord. This was the way ordained by King David. ¹¹They sang songs of praise and thanks to God. They sang this song: "He is good! His love and mercy toward Israel will last for all time." Then all the people gave a great shout. They praised God because the base of the Temple had been laid.

¹²But many of the priests and Levites and other leaders cried out loud. These were the old men who remembered Solomon's great Temple. But the others were shouting for joy! ¹³So the shouting and the crying mixed together in a loud noise. It could be heard far away!

- *Remember:* Where did the people get the logs to build the Temple? How did they pay for them? (3:7) What did the priests do when the foundation was finished? (3:10-11) Who shouted for joy when they saw the foundation? (3:11) Who cried when they saw the foundation? Why? (3:12) The young people were thankful to have any Temple. They had never had one. The older people had long ago had a much nicer Temple. So they cried when they saw this. Don't you think everyone should have been thankful?

- *Discover:* Be thankful for God's gifts, no matter how small or great.

- *Apply:* Do you have less than some friends? Thank God for what you have. Don't cry for what you don't have.

- *What's next?* A man begs to go home. Read Nehemiah 1:1–2:8. ■

Enemies Try to Stop the Rebuilding

4 The enemies of Judah and Benjamin heard that the exiles had come back, and they heard they were rebuilding the Temple. ²So they came to Zerubbabel and the other leaders. And they said, "Let us work with you. For we are just like you. We want to worship your God with you. We have sacrificed to him ever since King Esar-haddon of Assyria brought us here."

³But Zerubbabel and Jeshua and the other Jewish leaders spoke to them. "No," they replied. "You may have no part in this work. The Temple of the God of Israel must be built by the Israelites. It must be done just as King Cyrus has commanded."

⁴·⁵Then the local people tried to discourage the people of Israel. They tried to make them afraid by telling lies about them to King Cyrus. This went on during his whole reign. And it lasted until King Darius took the throne.

King Artaxerxes Stops the Work

⁶And after that, King Ahasuerus began to reign. And they wrote him a letter against the people of Judah and Jerusalem. ⁷They did the same thing during the reign of Artaxerxes. Bishlam, Mithredath, and Tabeel and their men wrote a letter in the Aramaic language. They sent it to the king. And it was translated for him. ⁸·⁹Governor Rehum and Shimshai, who was a scribe, also took part in the plot. So did several judges and other local leaders. The Persians, the Babylonians, and the men of Erech and Susa also took part. ¹⁰So did men from several other nations. These men had been taken from their own lands by the great and noble Osnappar. They had been sent to live in Jerusalem and Samaria. Others were living in nearby lands west of the Euphrates River.

¹¹Here is the letter they sent to King Artaxerxes:

"Dear sir. Greetings from your loyal people west of the Euphrates River. ¹²Some time ago, Jews were sent to Jerusalem from Babylon. They are now rebuilding this evil city. Throughout history they have been known to disobey! They have already built the city's walls. And they have rebuilt the base of the Temple. ¹³But we want to give you this warning. This city might soon be rebuilt. But if it is, it will cause you much trouble. For the Jews will then break away from your rule. And they will refuse to pay their taxes to you.

¹⁴"We are grateful to you as our king. And we do not want to see the Jews dishonor you. So we have decided to send you this message. ¹⁵We think that you should look into the ancient records. You will find there that Jerusalem is a city that does not obey. In fact, it was destroyed because of this. It has always disobeyed the kings and countries that were over it. ¹⁶We want to give you this warning. This city might be rebuilt. And its walls might soon be finished. But if this happens, you will lose all of your empire beyond the Euphrates River."

¹⁷Then the king sent this reply to Governor Rehum and Shimshai the scribe. It was also sent to their friends in Samaria. It was for all those in the area west of the Euphrates River.

¹⁸"Gentlemen: Greetings! The letter you sent has been translated and read to me. ¹⁹I have ordered a search made of the records. And I have found that Jerusalem has at times not obeyed the kings over it. In fact, refusing to obey is normal there! ²⁰I find that there have been some very great kings in Jerusalem. They have ruled the whole land beyond the Euphrates River. They have been paid great amounts in tribute, custom, and toll. ²¹Therefore, I command these men to stop their work. And I will look into the matter some more. ²²Do not delay! For we must not let this problem get out of control!"

²³This letter from King Artaxerxes was read to Rehum and Shimshai. And they hurried to Jerusalem. They made the Jews stop building. ²⁴So the work ended until the second year of the reign of King Darius of Persia.

The Rebuilding Continues

5 But there were prophets in Jerusalem and Judah at that time. They were Haggai and Zechariah. Zechariah was

the son of Iddo. They brought messages from the God of Israel to Zerubbabel and Jeshua. Zerubbabel was the son of Shealtiel. And Jeshua was the son of Jozadak. They encouraged them to begin building again! So they did. And the prophets helped them.

3But Tattenai, Shethar-bozenai, and their friends heard about this. Tattenai was the governor of the lands west of the Euphrates. They soon went to Jerusalem. They asked, "Who said you could rebuild this Temple? Who said you could finish these walls?"

4They also asked for a list of names. They wanted a list of all the men who were working on the Temple. 5But the Lord was taking care of this problem. So our enemies did not make us stop building. They let us keep on while King Darius looked into the matter.

Enemies Report to King Darius

6The Governors Tattenai and Shethar-bozenai sent King Darius a letter. They did this with the support of other officials as well.

7"To King Darius:

"Greetings!

8"We want to tell you what is happening in Jerusalem. We went to the building site of the Temple of the God of Judah. It is being built with huge stones. And timber is being laid in the city walls. The work is going forward with great energy and success. 9We asked the leaders, 'Who said you could do this?' 10And we demanded their names so that we could tell you. 11Their answer was, 'We are the servants of the God of heaven and earth. We are rebuilding the Temple that was here many years ago. It was built by a great king of Israel. 12But our ancestors made the God of heaven angry. So he left them and let King Nebuchadnezzar destroy this Temple. He allowed his people to be sent away into Babylonia.'

13"But they say that King Cyrus of Babylon made a law. They claim this law states that the Temple should be rebuilt. The law was made during the first year of Cyrus's reign. 14They say King Cyrus sent back gold and silver bowls. These were the ones Nebuchadnezzar took

from the Temple in Jerusalem. He took them and put them in the temple of Babylon. They say these items were given into the charge of a man named Sheshbazzar. King Cyrus chose this man as the governor of Judah. 15The king told him to bring the bowls back to Jerusalem. He told him to rebuild the Temple of God there. 16So Sheshbazzar came and laid the base of the Temple at Jerusalem. And the people have been working on it ever since. But it is not yet finished. 17We ask that you look in the royal library of Babylon. Find out if King Cyrus ever made such a law. Then let us know what you want us to do."

King Darius Approves the Rebuilding

6 So King Darius gave orders to look through the library of Babylon. This was where the records were kept.

2The record was found in the palace at Ecbatana. This was in the province of Media. This is what it said:

3"This is the first year of the reign of King Cyrus. A law has been made about the Temple of God at Jerusalem. This is where the Jews give their sacrifices. This Temple is to be rebuilt. Its base is to be strongly laid. The height will be 90 feet and the width will be 90 feet. 4There will be three layers of huge stones in the base. This will be topped with a layer of new timber. All costs will be paid by the king. 5And the gold and silver bowls shall be taken back to Jerusalem. They shall be put into the Temple as they were before. These were the bowls that Nebuchadnezzar took from the Temple of God."

6So King Darius II sent this message to Governor Shethar-bozenai. It also went to the other officials west of the Euphrates.

"Do not stop the building of the Temple. Build it where it was before. 7Don't stop the governor of Judah and the other leaders in their work. 8You are to pay the building costs right away. Pay them from my taxes taken in the lands you control. 9Give the priests in Jerusalem young bulls, rams, and lambs. These will be for burnt offerings to the God of heaven. Give them wheat, wine, salt, and olive oil each day without fail. ¹⁰Then they will be able to offer good sacrifices to the God of heaven. And they will pray for me and my sons. ¹¹Anyone who tries to change this message shall be punished. He shall have the beams pulled from his house. Those beams shall be used to build a gallows. And the offender will be hanged on it. His house shall be made into a pile of rubble. ¹²The Lord God has chosen the city of Jerusalem. He will destroy any king and any nation that changes this command. He will punish anyone who destroys this Temple. I, Darius, have made this law. Let it be obeyed without fail!"

The Temple Is Completed and Dedicated

¹³Governors Tattenai and Shethar-bozenai obeyed the command of King Darius. Their friends did the same.

¹⁴So the Jewish leaders kept on with their work. They were greatly helped by the preaching of the prophets Haggai and Zechariah. Zechariah was the son of Iddo.

The Temple was finally finished. It was built as it had been commanded by God. It was also done to obey the laws made by Cyrus, Darius, and Artaxerxes. These were kings of Persia. ¹⁵The Temple was finished on February 18. This was in the sixth year of the reign of King Darius II.

¹⁶The Temple was then given to God with great joy. It was dedicated by the priests, the Levites, and all the people. ¹⁷During the dedication feast 100 young bulls, 200 rams, and 400 lambs were offered. And 12 male goats were given as a sin offering. One was given for each of the 12 tribes of Israel. ¹⁸Then the priests and Levites were divided into their service groups. They did the work of God as it was given in the laws of Moses.

The People Celebrate Passover

¹⁹The Passover was observed on the first day of April. ²⁰For by that time many priests and Levites had made themselves pure. ²¹⁻²²So the whole nation of Israel worshiped the Lord God with joy. And some of the heathen people who now lived in Judah joined them. They turned from their sinful ways. They all ate the Passover feast together. Then they observed the Feast of Unleavened Bread for seven days. There was great joy in the land. For the Lord had caused the king of Assyria to be kind to Israel. He had helped them to rebuild the Temple.

Ezra Comes to Teach

7 Here is the genealogy of Ezra. He traveled from Babylon to Jerusalem. He did this during the reign of King Artaxerxes of Persia.

Ezra was the son of Seriah.
Seriah was the son of Azariah.
Azariah was the son of Hilkiah.
Hilkiah was the son of Shallum.
Shallum was the son of Zadok.
Zadok was the son of Ahitub.
Ahitub was the son of Amariah.
Amariah was the son of Meraioth.
Meraioth was the son of Zerahiah.
Zerahiah was the son of Uzzi.
Uzzi was the son of Bukki.
Bukki was the son of Abishua.
Abishua was the son of Phinehas.
Phinehas was the son of Eleazar.
Eleazar was the son of Aaron, the chief priest.

⁶Ezra was a teacher of Jewish law. He knew the laws of the Lord very well. These were the laws that Moses had given to the people of Israel. He asked to be allowed to go back to Jerusalem. And the king let him do this. For the Lord his God was blessing him. ⁷⁻⁹Many people went along with him. Priests, Levites, singers, gatekeepers, and Temple workers went too. They left Babylon in the month of March. This was in the seventh year of the reign of Artaxerxes. They got to Jerusalem in the month of August. For the Lord gave them a good trip. ¹⁰Ezra had chosen to study and obey the laws of the Lord. He planned to become a teacher of Scripture. He wanted to teach God's laws to the people.

King Artaxerxes Writes to Ezra

¹¹King Artaxerxes gave this letter to Ezra the priest. He was a student of God's laws.

12"From: Artaxerxes, the king of kings.

"To: Ezra the priest, the teacher of the laws of the God of heaven.

13"I make this law for any Jew in my kingdom. This includes the priests and Levites. Any of them may go back to Jerusalem with you. 14I and my Council of Seven instruct you to take a copy of God's laws to Judah and Jerusalem. And you must send back a report of the progress being made there. 15We will also send silver and gold with you. You shall take it to Jerusalem. We are giving it as an offering to the God of Israel.

To be a good Bible teacher, you must study the Bible and obey it

Ezra had chosen to study and obey the laws of the Lord. He wanted to teach God's laws to the people.

Ezra 7:10

16"You are to collect Temple offerings of silver and gold. Collect them from the Jews and their priests. Do this in all of the provinces of Babylon. 17These funds are to be used to buy oxen, rams, and lambs. Also buy grain offerings and drink offerings. These shall be given upon the altar of your Temple. Do this when you get to Jerusalem. 18The money that is left over may also be used. Use it in a way you and your brothers feel is the will of your God. 19And take the gold bowls with you. Take the other items we are giving you as well. They are for the Temple of your God at Jerusalem. 20You might run short of money for building the Temple. Or you might have other needs. If you do, take funds from the royal treasury.

21"I, Artaxerxes the king, make this law. I am sending it to all the treasurers in the lands west of the Euphrates River. 'You are to give Ezra what he asks of you. For he is a priest and teacher of the laws of the God of heaven. 22Give him up to $200,000 in silver. Give him 1,225 bushels of wheat. Supply him with 990 gallons of wine. Give him any amount

of salt. 23And give him whatever else the God of heaven needs for his Temple. For why should we take a chance? If we don't help them, God might get angry at the king and his sons. 24I also make this law. It applies to priests, Levites, and choir members. It also applies to gatekeepers, Temple attendants, or other workers in the Temple. They shall not pay taxes of any kind.'

25"And you, Ezra, are to use the wisdom God has given you. Use it to choose judges and other leaders. They will govern all the people west of the Euphrates River. They might not know the laws of your God. If they don't, you are to teach them. 26Someone might not obey the laws of your God. Or he might not obey the laws of the king. If this happens, he shall be punished. He might be put to death right away. Or perhaps he shall be sent from the land. Or maybe all that he owns shall be taken from him. Or he might be put in prison."

Ezra Praises God

27Well, praise the Lord God of our ancestors! He made the king want to rebuild the Temple of the Lord in Jerusalem! 28And praise God for showing such kindness to me! He honored me before the king and his Council of Seven! He honored me before all of his mighty princes! I was given great honor because the Lord my God was with me. And I called some of the leaders of Israel to go with me to Jerusalem.

The Exiles Who Returned with Ezra

8 These are the names and records of the leaders who went with me. They came from Babylon during the reign of King Artaxerxes.

2-14From the clan of Phinehas came Gershom.
From the clan of Ithamar came Daniel.
From the subclan of David of the clan of Shecaniah came Hattush.
From the clan of Parosh came Zechariah and 150 other men.
From the clan of Pahath-moab came Eliehoenai and 200 other

men. Eliehoenai was the son of
Zerahiah.
From the clan of Shecaniah came
the son of Jahaziel and 300 other
men.
From the clan of Adin came Ebed
and 50 other men. Ebed was the
son of Jonathan.
From the clan of Elam came Jeshaiah and 70 other men. Jeshaiah
was the son of Athaliah.
From the clan of Shephatiah came
Zebadiah and 80 other men. Zeb-
adiah was the son of Michael.
From the clan of Joab came
Obadiah and 218 other men.
Obadiah was the son of Jehiel.
From the clan of Bani came She-
lomith and 160 other men.
Shelomith was the son of Josi-
phiah.
From the clan of Bebai came Zecha-
riah and 28 other men. Zecha-
riah was the son of Bebai.
From the clan of Azgad came Joha-
nan and 110 other men. Johanan
was the son of Hakkatan.
From the clan of Adonikam came
Eliphelet, Jeuel, Shemaiah, and
60 other men. They came at a
later time.
From the clan of Bigvai came Uthai,
Zaccur, and 70 other men.

Ezra Goes to Jerusalem

15We gathered at the Ahava River. We
camped there for three days. I went over
the lists of the people and the priests
who had come. And I found that not
one Levite had come along! 16So I sent
for Eliezer, Ariel, Shemaiah, Elnathan,
Jarib, Elnathan, Nathan, Zechariah, and
Meshullam. These were the Levite leaders. I also sent for Joiarib and Elnathan.
These were very wise men. 17I sent them
to Iddo. This was the leader of the Jews
at Casiphia. So they all went to see Iddo
and his brothers and the Temple workers. They asked them to send us priests
for the Temple of God at Jerusalem.
18And God was good! He sent us an able
man named Sherebiah. And 18 of his
sons and brothers came along. He was a
very wise man. And he was a descen-

dant of Mahli. Mahli was the son of
Levi. And Levi was the son of Israel.
19God also sent Hashabiah. And he sent
Jeshaiah with 20 of his sons and brothers. Jeshaiah was a descendant of Merari.
20And 220 Temple workers came too.
The Temple workers were helpers to the
Levites. This job in the Temple was first
given by King David. These 220 men
were all listed by name.

????????????????????????????????

In Ezra's time, which were the six kinds of people who never had to pay taxes?

(Read 7:21-24 for the answer.)

????????????????????????????????

21Then I declared a fast while we were
at the Ahava River. This would help us
to humble ourselves before our God. We
prayed that he would give us a good trip.
We prayed that our children and our
goods would be safe as we went. 22For I
was ashamed to ask the king for soldiers
and cavalry. They might have gone with
us to keep us safe from the enemies
along the way. But we had told the king
that our God would keep us safe. This
was because we all worshiped him. We
told him that trouble could come only
to those who had left him! 23So we fasted
and begged God to take care of us. And
he did.
24I chose 12 leaders of the priests.
They were Sherebiah, Hashabiah, and
10 other priests. 25They were in charge
of moving the silver and gold. This
included the gold bowls and other
items. These had been given by the king
and his council. Some of them had also
been given by the leaders and people
of Israel. They were to be given to the
Temple of God. 26-27I weighed the money
as I gave it to them. I found it to total
$1,300,000 in silver and $200,000 in
silver utensils. And there were many
millions in gold. There were also 20 gold
bowls. They were worth a total of
$100,000. There were also two pretty
pieces of brass. These were worth as
much as gold. 28I made these men holy
to the Lord. Then I made the treasures
holy to the Lord. This included the

equipment and money and bowls. These had been given as freewill offerings to the Lord God of our fathers.

29"Guard these treasures well!" I told them. "Give them without a penny lost to the leaders at Jerusalem. This includes the priests, the Levite leaders, and the elders of Israel. There they will be put in the treasury of the Temple."

?????????????????????????????????

Which man pulled hair from his own beard and head? Why did he do that?

(Read 9:1-3 for the answer.)

?????????????????????????????????

30So the priests and the Levites took this job. They were in charge of taking these things to God's Temple in Jerusalem. 31We broke camp at the Ahava River at the end of March. Then we started off to Jerusalem. And God kept us safe. He saved us from enemies and bandits along the way. 32So at last we came safely to Jerusalem.

33The silver, gold, and other items were weighed in the Temple. This work was done by Meremoth, Eleazar, Jozabad, and Noadiah. Meremoth was the son of Uriah the priest. Eleazar was the son of Phinehas. Jozabad was the son of Jeshua. And Noadiah was the son of Binnui. All of these men were Levites. We weighed the silver and gold on the fourth day after we got there. 34A record was made for each item. And the weight of the gold and silver was noted.

35Then everyone in our party gave burnt offerings to the God of Israel. We gave 12 oxen for the nation of Israel. We also gave 96 rams and 77 lambs. And we gave 12 goats as a sin offering. 36The king's laws were given to the governors of the lands west of the Euphrates River. And then they helped to rebuild the Temple of God.

Ezra Confesses His People's Sin

9 But then the Jewish leaders came to speak to me. They said that many of the Jewish people were doing bad things. They had taken up the bad customs of the people in the land. Even some of the priests and Levites were doing this! They were all acting like the Canaanites, Hittites, Perizzites, Jebusites, Ammonites, Moabites, Egyptians, and Amorites. 2The men of Israel had married girls from these nations. They had taken them as wives for their sons. So the holy people of God were made unclean by these mixed marriages. And the leaders were worse than anyone else!

3When I heard this, I tore my clothing. I pulled hair from my head and beard. And I sat down very confused. 4There were many who feared the God of Israel because of this sin. They came and sat with me until the time of the evening burnt offering.

5Finally I stood before the Lord in great shame. Then I fell to my knees and lifted my hands to the Lord. 6I cried out, "O my God, I am ashamed! I blush to lift up my face to you. For our sins are piled higher than our heads. And our guilt is as big as the heavens. 7Our whole history has been one of sin. That is why we, our kings, and our priests were killed by heathen kings. That is why we were captured, robbed, and shamed, just as we are today. 8But now we have been given a moment of peace. For you have let a few of us come back to Jerusalem from our exile. You have given us a moment of joy and new life in our slavery. 9For we were slaves. But you have shown us love and mercy. You did not keep us slaves for all time. Instead, you caused the kings of Persia to be kind to us. They have even helped us in rebuilding the Temple of our God. And they have helped by giving us Jerusalem as a walled city in Judah.

10"And now, O God, what can we say after all of this? For once again we have left you! Once again we have broken your laws! 11The prophets warned us that the land of promise was unclean. It was made unclean by the evil deeds of the people living there. From one end to the other it is filled with evil. 12You told us not to let our daughters marry their sons. You warned us not to let our sons marry their daughters. We were not to help those nations in any way. You told us to follow this rule. And if we did, you said we would become a rich nation. And you said we would leave our riches to our children for all time. ¹³But we were punished in exile because we were wicked. And we have been punished far less than we should have been. Yet now you have let some of us come back to our land. ¹⁴But we have broken your commands again. We have married people who do these bad things. Surely your anger will destroy us now! Not even the few of your people left will get away! ¹⁵O Lord God of Israel, you are a just God. What hope can we have if you give us justice? For we stand here before you in our sin."

The People Confess Their Sin

10 I lay on the ground in front of the Temple. I was crying and praying. And I was making this confession. Soon a large crowd of men, women, and children gathered around me. And they cried with me.

²Then Shecaniah spoke to me. He was the son of Jehiel of the clan of Elam. He said, "We admit our sin against God. For we have married these heathen women. But there is hope for Israel in spite of this. ³For we agree before our God to divorce our heathen wives. We will send them away with our children. We will follow your commands. And we will follow the commands of the others who fear our God. We will obey the laws of God. ⁴Be brave and tell us how to make things right. We will do all that you say."

⁵So I stood up. And I made all the people of Israel promise to do as Shecaniah had said. I made the leaders of the priests and Levites swear that they would do this. And they all agreed. ⁶Then I went into the room of Jehohanan in the Temple. I would not eat any food and drink. For I was mourning because of the sin of the people.

⁷⁻⁸Then an order was sent throughout Judah and Jerusalem. It called everyone to come to Jerusalem within three days. It said that the leaders and elders had made a rule. Anyone who did not come would be expelled from Israel. ⁹So within three days all the men of Judah and Benjamin had come. This was on the fifth day of December. They sat in the open space before the Temple. They were shaking because it was a serious matter. They were upset because the rain was falling hard. ¹⁰Then I, Ezra the priest, stood and said to them:

"You have sinned! For you have married heathen women. Now we are even more guilty before God than we were before. ¹¹Confess your sin to the Lord God of your fathers. Do what he asks! Set yourselves apart from the heathen people around you. Set yourselves apart from these women."

¹²Then all the men spoke up. They said, "We will do what you have said. ¹³But this can't be done in a day or two. For there are many of us who have sinned this way. And it is raining very hard. So we can't stay out here much longer. ¹⁴Let our leaders set up trials for us. Everyone who has a heathen wife will come at the right time. He will come with the elders and judges of his city. Then each case will be decided. And the problem will be cleared up. That way the fierce anger of God will be turned away from us."

¹⁵Only Jonathan, Jahzeiah, Meshullam, and Shabbethai were against this course of action. Jonathan was the son of Asahel. Jahzeiah was the son of Tikvah. And Shabbethai was a Levite.

God Forgives the People

¹⁶⁻¹⁹So this was the plan that was followed. Some of the clan leaders and I were chosen as judges. We began our work on December 15. We finished by March 15.

This is the list of priests who had married heathen wives. They promised to divorce their wives, and they admitted their guilt. They did this by offering rams as sacrifices. These priests were Maaseiah, Eliezer, Jarib, and Gedaliah.

²⁰From the sons of Immer were Hanani and Zebadiah.

²¹From the sons of Harim were Maaseiah, Elijah, Shemaiah, Jehiel, and Uzziah.

²²From the sons of Pashhur were Elioenai, Maaseiah, Ishmael, Nethanel, Jozabad, and Elasah.

²³The Levites who were guilty were

Jozabad, Shimei, Kelaiah, Pethahaiah, Judah, and Eliezer. Kelaiah was also called Kelita.

²⁴Of the singers, there was Eliashib.
Of the gatekeepers, there were Shallum, Telem, and Uri.

²⁵Here is the list of people who were found guilty.

From the clan of Parosh were Ramiah, Izziah, Malchijah, Mijamin, Eleazar, Hashabiah, and Benaiah.

²⁶From the clan of Elam were Mattaniah, Zechariah, Jehiel, Abdi, Jeremoth, and Elijah.

²⁷From the clan of Zattu were Elioenai, Eliashib, Mattaniah, Jeremoth, Zabad, and Aziza.

²⁸From the clan of Bebai were Jehohanan, Hananiah, Zabbai, and Athlai.

²⁹From the clan of Bani were Meshullam, Malluch, Adaiah, Jashub, Sheal, and Jeremoth.

³⁰From the clan of Pahath-moab were Adna, Chelal, Benaiah, Maaseiah, Mattaniah, Bezalel, Binnui, and Manasseh.

³¹⁻³²From the clan of Harim were Eliezer, Isshijah, Malchijah, Shemaiah, Shimeon, Benjamin, Malluch, and Shemariah.

³³From the clan of Hashum were Mattenai, Mattattah, Zabad, Eliphelet, Jeremai, Manasseh, and Shimei.

³⁴⁻⁴²From the clan of Bani were Maadai, Amram, Uel, Banaiah, Bedeiah, Cheluhi, Vaniah, Meremoth, Eliashib, Mattaniah, Mattenai, Jaasu, Bani, Binnui, Shimei, Shelemiah, Nathan, Adaiah, Machnadebai, Shashai, Sharai, Azarel, Shelemiah, Shemariah, Shallum, Amariah, and Joseph.

⁴³From the clan of Nebo were Jeiel, Mattithiah, Zabad, Zebina, Jaddai, Joel, and Benaiah.

⁴⁴Each of these men had heathen wives. And many of them had children by these wives.

NEHEMIAH

Nehemiah was an Israelite. He was the cupbearer to King Artaxerxes, the king of Persia. The cupbearer tasted the king's food and drink to make sure it wasn't poisoned.

Nehemiah liked the king, but he really wanted to go back home to Israel. His family was part of the group of captives that decided to stay in Persia and not return to Israel with Ezra. But Nehemiah wanted to go. And God helped him go home. He helped him return to the city of Jerusalem. He helped him rebuild the walls that had been torn down by enemy armies. This is a book about a great building project. But it is also a book about enemies who tried to stop Nehemiah from rebuilding the walls of Jerusalem. They tried everything. But God wanted the walls built. So they were built. When the work was done, Nehemiah and his friends dedicated the walls to God.

Nehemiah Begs to Go Home

Nehemiah begged God to help him talk with the king. Then he begged the king to send him home to Jerusalem. He wanted to rebuild the walls. Nehemiah was only a servant. Did the king let him do this?

1 These are the words of Nehemiah, the son of Hecaliah.

I, Nehemiah, was in the palace at Shushan. It was in December of the 20th year of King Artaxerxes' reign in Persia. ²One of my fellow Jews was named Hanani. He came to visit me with some men who had come from Judah. I asked them about how things were going in Jerusalem.

"How are they getting along?" I asked. "How are the Jews who went back to Jerusalem?"

³"Well," they said, "things are not good. The wall of Jerusalem is still torn down. And the gates are burned down."

⁴When I heard this, I sat down and cried. In fact, I would not eat for several days. I spent the time in prayer to the God of heaven.

⁵"O Lord God!" I cried out. "O great and awesome God! You keep your

promises! And you are so loving and kind to those who love and obey you! Hear my prayer! 6-7Listen carefully to what I say! Look down and see me praying night and day for your people Israel. I know that we have sinned against you. Yes, I and my people have not obeyed the commands you gave us. These are the commands you gave through your servant Moses. 8But, please remember what you told Moses! You said,

"'If you sin, I will scatter you among the nations. 9But you might still come back to me and obey my laws. You might do this even though you are sent away to the corners of the earth. And if you come back to me, I will bring you back to Jerusalem. For Jerusalem is the place in which I have chosen to live.'

10"We are your servants. We are the people you saved by your great power. 11O Lord, please hear my prayer! Listen to the prayers of those of us who love to honor you. Please help me now as I go to ask the king for a great favor. Put it into his heart to be kind to me."

At that time, I was working as the king's cupbearer.

2 One day I was serving the king his wine. It was in April, four months later. He asked me, "Why are you so sad? You aren't sick, are you? You look like a man with deep troubles." For until then I had always been happy when I was with him. I was very afraid. 3But I said, "Sir, why shouldn't I be sad? For the city of my ancestors is in ruins. And the gates have been burned down."

4"Well, what should be done?" the king asked.

I made a quick prayer to the God of heaven. Then I said, "Perhaps you will look upon me with your royal favor. If you do, please send me to Judah. I want to rebuild the city of my fathers!"

5-6The queen was sitting beside the king at the time. And the king replied, "How long will you be gone? When will you come back?"

So it was agreed! And I set a time when I would leave!

7Then I asked the king one more thing. "If it please the king," I said, "give me letters to the governors west of the Euphrates River. Tell them to let me go through their lands on my way to Judah. 8Also send a letter to Asaph. He is the manager of the king's forests. Tell him to give me wood for beams. I will need the wood for gates in the fort near the Temple. I will also need it for the city walls and for a house for myself."

And the king gave me what I asked. For God was being kind to me.

• *Remember:* Who was the king of Persia? (1:1) What caused Nehemiah to cry and pray? (1:2-4) What kind of work did Nehemiah do for the king? (1:11–2:1) What did Nehemiah ask the king to do? (2:4) Did the king do it? (2:8) Was Nehemiah willing to do something to help God answer his prayers? What did he want to do?

• *Discover:* When you pray for God to do something, be willing to help him do it.

• *Apply:* Have you ever asked God to help a friend know Jesus? Are you ready to tell your friend about Jesus? Get ready to help God when you pray. Get ready to be a part of God's answer to prayer through you.

• *What's next?* One dark night some men slipped out of the city quietly. They walked along its broken walls. What were they doing? Read Nehemiah 2:9-20. ■

A Night Visit at the Walls

One night Nehemiah and some friends slipped out of Jerusalem. Quietly they went along the broken walls of the city. They wanted to see just how bad the walls were. But they didn't want their enemies to know what they were doing. What a terrible mess they saw. It looked impossible. Did Nehemiah still want to rebuild the walls when he saw this mess?

⁹I got to the land west of the Euphrates River. And I gave the king's letters to the governors there. The king, I should add, had sent along army officers and troops! They came along to keep me safe. ¹⁰But Sanballat and Tobiah heard that I had come. Sanballat was a Horonite. Tobiah was an Ammonite who was a government official. They were very angry that anyone wanted to help Israel.

¹¹⁻¹²So I came to Jerusalem. Three days after I got there, I went out during the night. I took only a few men with me. I hadn't yet told anyone why I had come. I hadn't told anyone about the plans for Jerusalem that God had put into my heart. I was riding on my donkey and the others were on foot. ¹³We went out through the Valley Gate toward the Jackal's Well. From there we went over to the Dung Gate. There we saw the broken walls and burned gates. ¹⁴⁻¹⁵Then we went to the Fountain Gate and to the King's Pool. But my donkey couldn't get through the rubble. So we went around the city. I followed the brook, checking the wall. Then we came back in again at the Valley Gate.

¹⁶The city leaders did not know I had been out there or why. For I had not told anyone about my plans. I had not told the leaders. And I had not spoken to the people who would be doing the work.

¹⁷But now I went and spoke to them. "You know full well the sad story of our city," I said. "It is in ruins and its gates are burned down. Let us rebuild the wall of Jerusalem! Let us get rid of this shame!"

¹⁸Then I told them about the desire God had put into my heart. I told them of my words with the king. And I told them the plan to which he had agreed.

They replied at once, "Good! Let's rebuild the wall!" And so the work began.

¹⁹But Sanballat, Tobiah, and Geshem the Arab heard of our plan. They laughed at us and said, "What are you doing? Why are you rebelling against the king like this?"

²⁰But I replied, "The God of heaven will help us. We, his servants, will rebuild this wall. But you may have no part in this work."

- *Remember:* Who was angry at Nehemiah? Why? (2:10) What did Nehemiah do one night? (2:11-15) What did he tell the officials that they must do? (2:17) Did they want to rebuild the walls? (2:18) Who would help Nehemiah and his friends with the walls? (2:20) Do you think Nehemiah would build the walls if he knew God wasn't helping? Why not?

- *Discover:* Before you start anything for God, make sure God will help you. He will if it pleases him.

- *Apply:* Is there something you want to do for God? What is it? Does God want you to do it? If you don't think he does, don't start. If you think he does, get going!

- *What's next?* Strong men made fun of Nehemiah. What would he do? Read Nehemiah 4. ∎

The Builders of the City Wall

3 Eliashib the High Priest and the other priests worked together. They rebuilt the wall as far as the Tower of the Hundred and the Tower of Hananel. Then they rebuilt the Sheep Gate. They hung its doors. And they dedicated it to the Lord. ²Men from the city of Jericho worked next to them. Beyond them was the work crew led by Zaccur. Zaccur was the son of Imri.

³The Fish Gate was built by the sons of Hassenaah. They did the whole thing. They cut the beams, hung the doors, and made the bolts and bars. ⁴Meremoth

fixed the next section of wall. He was the son of Uriah. Uriah was the son of Hakkoz. Beyond Meremoth were Meshullam and Zadok. Meshullam was the son of Berechiah. And Berechiah was the son of Meshezabel. Zadok was the son of Baana. ⁵Next were the men from Tekoa. But their leaders were lazy and didn't help.

⁶The Old Gate was fixed by Joiada and Meshullam. Joiada was the son of Paseah. Meshullam was the son of Besodeiah. They laid the beams and set up the doors. They also put in the bolts and bars. ⁷Next to them were Melatiah and Jadon. Melatiah was from Gibeon. Jadon was from Meronoth. And men from Gibeon and Mizpah worked with them. They lived in that area. ⁸Uzziel was a goldsmith by trade. He was the son of Harhaiah. But he too worked on the wall. Beyond him was Hananiah. He was a maker of perfumes. Repairs were not needed from there to the Broad Wall.

⁹Rephaiah was the son of Hur. He was the ruler of half of Jerusalem. He was next down the wall from them. ¹⁰Jedaiah was the son of Harumaph. He fixed the wall beside his own house. Next to him was Hattush. Hattush was the son of Hashabneiah. ¹¹Then came Malchijah and Hasshub. Malchijah was the son of Harim. Hasshub was the son of Pahathmoab. They fixed the Furnace Tower and a part of the wall. ¹²Shallum and his daughters fixed the next section. Shallum was the son of Hallohesh. He was the ruler of the other half of Jerusalem.

¹³The people from Zanoah were led by Hanun. They built the Valley Gate and hung the doors. They also put in the bolts and bars. Then they fixed the 1,500 feet of wall to the Dung Gate.

¹⁴The Dung Gate was fixed by Malchijah. Malchijah was the son of Rechab. He was the ruler of the Bethhaccherem area. After building the gate, he hung the doors. And he put in the bolts and bars.

¹⁵Shallum was the son of Col-hozeh. He was the ruler of the Mizpah area. He fixed the Fountain Gate. He rebuilt it, roofed it, and hung its doors. He also put in its locks and bars. Then he began to fix the wall at the Pool of Siloam. He worked from there to the king's garden. And he fixed the stairs that go down from the City of David section of Jerusalem. ¹⁶Next to him was Nehemiah. Nehemiah was the son of Azbuk. He was the ruler of half the Beth-zur area. He built the wall across from the royal cemetery. He went as far as the man-made pool and the House of Heroes. ¹⁷Next was a group of Levites. They worked under Rehum. Rehum was the son of Bani. Then came Hashabiah. He was the ruler of half the Keilah area. He oversaw the building of the wall in his own area. ¹⁸Next down the line were his clan brothers. They were led by Bavvai. Bavvai was the son of Henadad. He was the ruler of the other half of the Keilah area.

¹⁹Next to them the workers were led by Ezer. Ezer was the son of Jeshua. He was the ruler of another part of Mizpah. They also worked on the wall across from the Armory. This is where the wall turns. ²⁰Next to him was Baruch. Baruch was the son of Zabbai. He built from the turn in the wall to the home of Eliashib the High Priest. ²¹Meremoth was the son of Uriah. Uriah was the son of Hakkoz. He built the wall across from the door of Eliashib's house. From there he built to the side of the house.

²²Then came the priests from the plains outside the city. ²³Their names were Benjamin, Hasshub, and Azariah. Azariah was the son of Maaseiah. Maaseiah was the son of Ananiah. They fixed the wall next to their own houses. ²⁴Next was Binnui. He was the son of Henadad. He built the wall from Azariah's house to the corner. ²⁵Palal was the son of Uzai. He carried on the work from the corner. He built from there to the base of the upper tower. This tower was on the king's castle beside the prison yard. Next was Pedaiah. He was the son of Parosh.

²⁶The Temple workers living in Ophel also fixed the wall. They built as far as the East Water Gate and the Projecting Tower. ²⁷Then came the Tekoites. They fixed the wall across from the Castle Tower. From there they went over to the wall of Ophel. ²⁸The priests fixed the wall beyond the Horse Gate. Each one

did the part just across from his own house.

²⁹Zadok also rebuilt the wall next to his own house. Zadok was the son of Immer. Beyond him was Shemaiah. Shemaiah was the son of Shecaniah. He was the gatekeeper of the East Gate. ³⁰Next were Hananiah, Hanun, and Meshullam. Hananiah was the son of Shelemiah. Hanun was the sixth son of Zalaph. Meshullam was the son of Berechiah. They built next to their own houses. ³¹Malchijah was one of the goldsmiths. He fixed the wall as far as the house of the Temple workers and traders. This was across from the Muster Gate. Then he built to the upper room at the corner. ³²The other goldsmiths and traders finished the wall from that corner to the Sheep Gate.

Nehemiah Builds the Walls

Has someone ever made fun of you or bullied you? Did you want to quit doing something for God because they did this? Sanballat and Tobiah made fun of Nehemiah for rebuilding the walls. Then they tried to scare Nehemiah by getting ready to fight. They thought they could make him quit. Did it work?

4 Sanballat was very angry when he learned that we were fixing the wall. He flew into a rage. He made fun of us and laughed at us. And so did his friends and the Samaritan army officers. "What do these poor, weak Jews think they are doing?" he laughed. "Do they think they can build this wall? Do they think they will soon offer sacrifices? And look at those burned stones they are using! They are pulling them out of the broken walls. And they're using them again!"

³Tobiah was standing beside Sanballat. He said, "A fox might walk along the top of their wall. But if it did, the wall would fall down!"

⁴Then I prayed, "Hear us, O Lord God! For we are being laughed at. May their laughing fall back upon their own heads! May they become captives in a foreign land! ⁵Do not forget their sin. Do not blot it out. For they have mocked you in mocking us. For we are building your wall."

⁶At last the wall was built to half its old height. It was around the whole city! For the workers had worked hard.

⁷But Sanballat and Tobiah heard that the work was going ahead. The Arabians, Ammonites, and Ashdodites also heard this. They heard that the breaks in the wall were being fixed. And they became very angry. ⁸They planned to lead an army against Jerusalem. They wanted to cause trouble there. ⁹But we prayed to our God. And we guarded the city day and night. We did this to keep the city safe.

¹⁰Then some of the leaders said, "The people are getting tired. There is too much trash to be taken away. We can never get it done by ourselves." ¹¹Meanwhile, our enemies were planning to swoop down upon us and kill us. They wanted to end our work. ¹²The people who lived in the nearby cities went home for visits. And our enemies tried to talk them out of going back to Jerusalem. ¹³So I chose armed guards from each family. I put them in the cleared spaces behind the walls.

¹⁴Then I looked over the problem. I called the leaders and the people. And I spoke to them. "Don't be afraid!" I said. "Remember the Lord. He is great and strong! Fight for your friends, your families, and your homes!"

¹⁵Our enemies learned that we knew of their plot. They found that God had ruined their plan. Now we all went back

to our work on the wall. ¹⁶But from then on, only half worked. The other half stood guard behind them. ¹⁷The masons and laborers worked with weapons near them. ¹⁸Or they worked with swords tied to their sides. The trumpeter stayed with me to sound the alarm.

¹⁹"The work is so spread out," I told them. "We are spread out far from each other. So listen for the sound of the trumpet. If you hear it, rush to where I am. And God will fight for us."

²⁰⁻²¹We worked early and late. We worked from sunrise to sunset. Half the men were always on guard. ²²I told those living outside the walls to move into Jerusalem. That way their servants could go on guard duty. And they could also work during the day. ²³During this time we never took off our clothes except for washing. This included me, my brothers, the servants, and the guards who were with me. And we carried our weapons with us at all times.

- *Remember:* Who made fun of Nehemiah? Why do you think they did this? (4:1-3) What did Nehemiah do first? (4:4-5) Who plotted to lead an army against Jerusalem? (4:7-8) What did Nehemiah do? (4:9) How did Nehemiah and his people guard themselves at work? (4:15-23) Nehemiah did

not depend on weapons only. He always prayed first. Why do you think this was a good idea?

- *Discover:* You must never stop helping God because someone makes fun of you.

- *Apply:* Has anyone made fun of you because you are a Christian? Or because you read your Bible or pray? Or because you don't do the bad things some of your friends do? Pray first, and ask God to help you be strong enough to keep doing what you know is right.

- *What's next?* Some men plan to kill Nehemiah. What should he do? Read Nehemiah 6:1–7:4. ■

Nehemiah Defends the Poor

5 About this time there was a great protest from the people. They were angry with some of the rich Jews. These Jews were taking advantage of them. ²⁻⁴Families were running out of money for food. The parents sometimes had to sell their children as slaves in order to eat. They had to borrow money from rich people. But they might not be able to pay it back. So the rich people would take their fields, vineyards, and homes. Some couldn't even borrow. For they had already borrowed to the limit to pay their taxes.

⁵"We are their brothers! Our children are just like theirs," the people said. "But we must sell our children as

slaves to get enough money to live. We have already sold some of our daughters. And we don't have the money to buy them back. This is because these men have taken our fields too."

⁶I was very angry when I heard this. ⁷So I thought about the problem. Then I spoke out against these rich leaders.

"What is this you are doing?" I demanded. "You are charging your fellow Israelites too much interest for your loans!"

Then I called a public trial to deal with them.

⁸At the trial I shouted at them. "The rest of us are doing all we can to help our Jewish brothers!" I said. "They have come back from exile. They were slaves in faraway lands. But you are making them slaves again. How often must we buy them back?"

They didn't say anything to defend themselves.

⁹Then I spoke some more. "What you are doing is very evil!" I said. "Should you not fear our God? Don't we have enough enemies around us who are trying to destroy us? ¹⁰The rest of us are lending money and grain to our fellow Jews. But we are not charging any interest. I beg you, gentlemen, stop this business of charging interest. ¹¹Give back their fields, vineyards, olive groves, and homes to them. Do it this very day. Drop your claims against them."

¹²So they agreed to do it. They said they would help their brothers. And they stopped making them give their lands and their children as security for their loans. Then I called the priests. I made these men promise to do what they said. ¹³And I put a curse of God on those who did not do it.

"You might fail to keep this promise," I declared. "But if you do, may God destroy your homes! And may he destroy all you own!"

All the people shouted, "Amen." And they praised the Lord. And the rich men did as they had promised.

¹⁴I was governor of Judah for 12 years. This was from the 20th to the 32nd year of King Artaxerxes' reign. During that time, my helpers and I were not paid for our work. We took no help from the people of Israel. ¹⁵This was not like the governors before us. They had demanded food and wine and $100 a day in cash. These leaders had put the people at the mercy of those who helped them. And these helpers had taken advantage of them. But I obeyed God and did not act that way. ¹⁶I stayed at work on the wall. And I did not buy any land. I also made my helpers spend time on the wall. ¹⁷And even so, I often fed 150 Jewish leaders at my table. And I also fed leaders from other lands! ¹⁸The food needed for each day was one ox and six fat sheep. We also ate many tame birds. And we needed a huge supply of all kinds of wines every 10 days. But I did not make a special tax against the people. For they were already having a hard time. ¹⁹O my God, please do not forget all that I've done for these people. Bless me for it!

Nehemiah Finishes the Walls

Nehemiah's enemies tried everything to stop him. They did not want him to rebuild the walls. First, they made fun of him. That didn't work. Then they tried to kill him. They lied about him. They tried to get him to do something wrong. Did any of these work?

6 Sanballat, Tobiah, and Geshem the Arab found out that we had almost finished the wall. The rest of our enemies also heard this. But we had not yet hung all the doors of the gates. ²They sent me a message. They asked me to meet them in one of the towns on the Plain of Ono. But I knew they were trying to kill me. ³So I sent them back a message.

"I am doing a great work!" I said. "Why should I stop to come and visit with you?"

⁴Four times they sent the same message. Each time I gave the same answer. ⁵⁻⁶The fifth time, Sanballat's servant came. He had an open letter in his hand. This is what it said:

"There is a report that says the Jews are going to break from Persia's rule. It says that is why you are building the wall. Geshem says this report is true. He claims you plan to be their king. ⁷He also reports that you have chosen prophets. He says they are speaking for you in Jerusalem. They are saying, 'Look! Nehemiah is just the man we need!'

"I am going to pass along this report to King Artaxerxes! Maybe you should come and talk it over with me. That is the only way you can save yourself!"

⁸My reply was, "I know you are lying. There isn't one bit of truth to the whole story. ⁹You're just trying to scare us into stopping our work." O Lord God, please give me strength!

¹⁰A few days later I went to visit Shemaiah. He was the son of Delaiah. And Delaiah was the son of Mehetabel. He said he was getting a message from God.

"Let us hide in the Temple and bolt the door," he said. "For they are coming tonight to kill you."

¹¹But I said, "Should I run away from danger? I am the governor! And I could go into the Temple. But I am not a priest. So if I went there, I would give up my life. No, I won't do it!"

¹²⁻¹³Then I knew that God had not spoken to him. I knew that Tobiah and Sanballat had hired him to scare me. They wanted to make me sin by running to the Temple. Then they would be able to accuse me.

¹⁴"O my God!" I prayed. "Don't forget all the evil of Tobiah and Sanballat. Don't forget the evil of Noadiah the prophetess. Don't forget the evil of all the other prophets who have tried to stop me."

¹⁵The wall was finally finished in early September. This was just 52 days after we had begun!

¹⁶Our enemies and the nations around us heard about it. They were afraid and ashamed. For they knew that the work had been done with our God's help. ¹⁷During those 52 days many letters were sent to Tobiah. These letters were sent by the rich leaders of Judah. ¹⁸For many in Judah were loyal to Tobiah. This was because his father-in-law was Shecaniah the son of Arah. And Tobiah's son Jehohanan was married to the daughter of Meshullam. Meshullam was the son of Berechiah. ¹⁹They all told me what a good man Tobiah was. Then they told him all that I had said. And Tobiah sent many letters to scare me.

7 So the wall was finished. And we had hung the doors in the gates. Then we chose the gatekeepers, singers, and Levites. ²I put my brother Hanani and Hananiah in charge of Jerusalem. Hananiah was the commander of the fortress. He was a very faithful man. He respected God more than most people do. ³I told them not to open the Jerusalem gates until well after sunrise. And I told them to close and lock them while the guards were still on duty. I also ordered that the guards live in Jerusalem. And I told them that they must be on duty at regular times. Each person who lived near the wall was to guard the wall near his own

home. ⁴For the city was large. But there were few people living there. There were only a few houses in the city.

● *Remember:* Who were three of Nehemiah's worst enemies? (6:1) How did they try to kill him? (6:2-4) What lie did these people tell against Nehemiah? (6:6-7) Why? (6:9) How did they try to trick Nehemiah into doing something wrong? (6:10-13) What did Nehemiah say to them? What do you think would have happened if Nehemiah had listened to their lies and threats? Would he have finished the wall? Why not?

● *Discover:* Bad people want to stop God's work. They will do bad things to stop it.

● *Apply:* Some people will do anything to keep you from helping God. Don't listen to them! Don't do what they say!

● *What's next?* A queen gets into big trouble! Read Esther 1. ■

Nehemiah Registers the People

⁵Then the Lord spoke to me. He told me to call all the leaders of the city. I was also to call all the other people too. They were to come to register. For I had found the family records of those who had come back to Judah before. This is what was written there:

⁶"This is a list of the names of the Jews who came back to Judah. They came back after being exiled by King Nebuchadnezzar of Babylon.

⁷"Their leaders were Zerubbabel, Jeshua, Nehemiah, Azariah, Raamiah, Nahamani, Mordecai, Bilshan, Mispereth, Bigvai, Nehum, and Baanah.

"These are the others who came back at that time.

⁸⁻³⁸From the subclan of Parosh came 2,172.

From the subclan of Shephatiah came 372.

From the subclan of Arah came 652.

From the families of Jeshua and Joab came 2,818. They were of the subclan of Pahath-moab.

From the subclan of Elam came 1,254.

From the subclan of Zattu came 845.

From the subclan of Zaccai came 760.

From the subclan of Binnui came 648.
From the subclan of Bebai came 628.
From the subclan of Azgad came 2,322.
From the subclan of Adonikam came 667.
From the subclan of Bigvai came 2,067.
From the subclan of Adin came 655.
From the family of Hezekiah of the subclan of Ater came 98.
From the subclan of Hashum came 328.
From the subclan of Bezai came 324.
From the subclan of Hariph came 112.
From the subclan of Gibeon came 95.
From the subclans of Bethlehem and Netophah came 188.
From the subclan of Anathoth came 128.
From the subclan of Beth-azmaveth came 42.
From the subclans of Kiriath-jearim, Chephirah, and Beeroth came 743.
From the subclans of Ramah and Geba came 621.
From the subclan of Michmas came 122.
From the subclans of Bethel and Ai came 123.
From the subclan of Nebo came 52.
From the subclan of Elam came 1,254.
From the subclan of Harim came 320.
From the subclan of Jericho came 345.
From the subclans of Lod, Hadid, and Ono came 721.
From the subclan of Senaah came 3,930.

39-42"Here is a list of the priests who came back.

From the family of Jeshua of the subclan of Jedaiah came 973.
From the subclan of Immer came 1,052.
From the subclan of Pashhur came 1,247.
From the subclan of Harim came 1,017.

43-45"Here is a list of the Levites.

From the family of Kadmiel came 74. These were of the subclan of Hodevah and the clan of Jeshua.
From the choir members of the clan of Asaph came 148.
From the clans of Shallum came 138. These were all gatekeepers.

46-56"This is a list of the subclans of Temple helpers. There were descendants of Ziha, Hasupha, Tabbaoth, Keros, Sia, Padon, Lebana, Hagaba, Shalmai, Hanan, Giddel, Gahar, Reaiah, Rezin, Nekoda, Gazzam, Uzza, Paseah, Besai, Asnah, Meunim, Nephushesim, Bakbuk, Hakupha, Harhur, Bazlith, Mehida, Harsha, Barkos, Sisera, Temah, Neziah, and Hatipha.

57-59"This is a list of the descendants of Solomon's officials. They all came back to Judah. They were Sotai, Sophereth, Perida, Jaala, Darkon, Giddel, Shephatiah, Hattil, Pochereth-hazzebaim, and Amon.

60"In all, the Temple helpers and the descendants of Solomon's servants numbered 392."

61Another group came back to Jerusalem at that time. They came from the Persian cities of Tel-melah, Tel-harsha, Cherub, Addon, and Immer. But they had lost their family records. They could not prove that they were Jews. 62These were the subclans of Delaiah, Tobiah, and Nekoda. From these subclans came a total of 642 people.

63There were also the subclans from Hobaiah, Hakkoz, and Barzillai. These subclans of priests could not find their family records. Barzillai married one of the daughters of Barzillai the Gileadite. Then he took her family name. 64-65So these subclans could not serve as priests. They could not even eat the priests' share of food from the sacrifices. They had to consult the Urim and Thummim to hear from God. They were to find out that way if they really were priests.

66There was a total of 42,360 people who came back to Judah at that time. 67There were also 7,337 slaves and 245 choir members. This included both men and women. 68-69They took with them 736 horses and 245 mules. They also brought 435 camels and 6,720 donkeys.

[70]Some of their leaders gave gifts for the work. The governor gave $5,000 in gold and 50 gold bowls. He also gave 530 sets of clothing for the priests. [71]The other leaders gave a total of $100,000 in gold and $77,000 in silver. [72]The common people gave $100,000 in gold and $70,000 in silver. They also gave 67 sets of clothing for the priests.

[73]The priests and the Levites now went back to their hometowns throughout Judah. The gatekeepers, the choir members, the Temple attendants, and the rest of the people did the same. But during the month of September they came back to Jerusalem.

Ezra Reads the Law

8 Now in mid-September all the people gathered at the plaza. This was in front of the Water Gate. They asked Ezra to read them the law of God. Ezra was their religious leader. These laws were the ones God had given to Moses.

So Ezra the priest brought out the scroll of Moses' laws. He stood on a wooden stand made just for this reading. That way everyone could see him as he read. He faced the square in front of the Water Gate. He read from early morning until noon. Everyone stood up as he opened the scroll. And all who were old enough to understand listened closely. To his right stood Mattithiah, Shema, Anaiah, Uriah, Hilkiah, and Maaseiah. To his left were Pedaiah, Mishael, Malchijah, Hashum, Hash-baddenah, Zechariah, and Meshullam.

[6]Then Ezra praised the Lord, the great God. And all the people said, "Amen." And they lifted their hands toward heaven. Then they bowed and worshiped the Lord with their faces toward the ground.

[7-8]As Ezra read from the scroll, the Levites went among the people. They told the people what the words of the law meant. The Levites who did this were Jeshua, Bani, Sherebiah, Jamin, Akkub, Shabbethai, Hodiah, Maaseiah, Kelita, Azariah, Jozabad, Hanan, and Pelaiah. [9]All the people began crying when they heard the commands of the law.

Then Ezra the priest and I as governor spoke to the people. So did the Levites who were helping me. We said, "Don't cry on such a day as this! For today is a holy day before the Lord your God. [10]It is a time to feast with a good meal. It is a time to send gifts to those in need. You must not be sad! The joy of the Lord is your strength!"

**Do you want to grow stronger?
Be happy doing what God wants**

The joy of the Lord is your strength!

Nehemiah 8:10

---

[11]And the Levites spoke to the people, too. They told them, "That's right! Don't cry! For this is a day of holy joy. It is not a day of sadness."

[12]So the people went away to feast and to send gifts to the needy. It was a time of great joy. This was because they had heard and understood God's words.

[13]The next day the clan leaders, the priests, and the Levites met with Ezra. They went over the law in greater detail. [14]As they studied it, they saw what the Lord had told Moses. They saw that the people of Israel were to live in tents. They were to do this during the Feast of Tabernacles. This feast was to be held that month. [15]He had said that a message should be sent to the cities of the land. This message was to be sent to Jerusalem first. The people were told to go to the hills. They were to get branches from olive, myrtle, palm, and fig trees. They were to use these branches to make huts. And they were to live in them during the feast.

[16]So the people went out and cut branches. Some used them to build huts on the roofs of their houses. Others built them in their courtyards. Some put them in the court of the Temple. Others made them on the plaza beside the Water Gate. Still others put them in the Ephraim Gate Plaza. [17]They lived in these huts for the seven days of the feast. And everyone was filled with joy! This had not been done since the days of Joshua. [18]Ezra read from the scroll on each of the seven days of the feast. On

the eighth day there was a solemn closing service. The laws of Moses said to do this.

Ezra Leads the People in Confession

9 On October 10 the people gathered together again. This time they fasted. They dressed in sackcloth. And they put dirt in their hair. They did this to show that they were sad. And the Israelites set themselves apart from all foreigners. ³The laws of God were read out loud to them for two or three hours. Then they took turns confessing their own sins. They also confessed the sins of their ancestors. And everyone worshiped the Lord their God. ⁴Some of the Levites were on the platform. They praised the Lord God with songs of joy. These men were Jeshua, Kadmiel, Bani, Shebaniah, Bunni, Sherebiah, Bani, and Chenani.

God made everything, and he takes care of it

You are the only God.
You made the skies and heavens.
You made the earth and seas
and all that is in them.
You take care of it all.

Nehemiah 9:6

---

⁵Then the Levite leaders called out to the people. They said, "Stand up! Praise the Lord your God! For he lives for all time. Praise his great name! It is far greater than we can think or say."

The leaders in this part of the service were Jeshua, Kadmiel, Bani, Hashabneiah, Sherebiah, Hodiah, Shebaniah, and Pethahiah.

⁶Then Ezra prayed, "You are the only God. You made the skies and heavens. You made the earth and seas and all that is in them. You take care of it all. And all the angels of heaven worship you.

⁷"You are the Lord God who chose Abram. You brought him from Ur of the Chaldeans. And you gave him his new name, Abraham. ⁸He was faithful to you. So you made a contract with him. You promised to give him and his descendants a homeland for all time. This was the land of the Canaanites, Hittites, Amorites, Perizzites, Jebusites, and Girgashites. And now you have done what you promised. For you are always true to your word.

⁹"You saw the troubles and sorrows of our ancestors in Egypt. You heard their cries from beside the Red Sea. ¹⁰You did great miracles against Pharaoh and his people. For you knew how badly the Egyptians were treating them. You made it so everyone knew your name. You did this by doing those great deeds. ¹¹You divided the sea for your people. And they went across it on dry land! And then you destroyed their enemies in the depths of the sea. They sank like stones under the mighty waters. ¹²You led our ancestors by a pillar of cloud during the day. You led them by a pillar of fire at night. That way they could find their way.

¹³"You came down on Mount Sinai. You spoke to them from heaven. And you gave them good laws and true commands. ¹⁴These included the laws about the holy Sabbath. You commanded them to obey them all. You did this through Moses your servant.

¹⁵"You gave them bread from heaven when they were hungry. And you gave them water from the rock when they were thirsty. You commanded them to go in and conquer the land you had promised to give them. ¹⁶But our ancestors were proud and stubborn people. They would not listen to your commands.

¹⁷"They would not obey. They forgot the miracles you did for them. Instead, they broke away from you. They chose a leader to take them back as slaves to Egypt! But you are a God of forgiveness. You are always ready to forgive. You are kind and full of mercy. You are slow to become angry. You are full of love and mercy. You didn't leave them, ¹⁸even though they made a calf-idol. They said, 'This is our God! He brought us out of Egypt!' They sinned in so many ways. ¹⁹But in your great mercy you didn't leave them to die in the wilderness! The

pillar of cloud led them forward day by day. And the pillar of fire showed them the way through the night. 20You sent your good Spirit to teach them. You did not stop giving them bread from heaven. And he always gave you water for their thirst. 21For 40 years you fed them in the desert. They needed nothing in all that time. Their clothes didn't wear out. And their feet didn't swell!

22"Then you helped them conquer great kingdoms and many nations. You put your people in every corner of the land. They took over the whole land of King Sihon of Heshbon and King Og of Bashan. 23You caused the Israelites to have many children. You brought them into the land you had promised to their ancestors. 24You conquered whole nations before them. Even the kings and the people of the Canaanites could not stop you! 25Your people took walled cities and rich land. They took over houses full of good things. They had wells and vineyards and olive groves. And they had many, many fruit trees. So they ate and were full. And they enjoyed all your blessings.

26"But despite all this, they did not obey. They broke away from you. They threw away your law. They killed the prophets who told them to come back to you. And they did many other bad things. 27So you gave them to their enemies. But in their time of trouble they cried to you. You heard them from heaven. In great mercy you sent them saviors. These people saved them from their enemies. 28But when all was going well, your people turned to sin again. And once more you let their enemies conquer them. Yet at times your people came back to you. They cried to you for help. Then once more you listened from heaven. And in your great mercy you saved them! 29You punished them so they would obey your laws. They should have obeyed them. But they were proud and wouldn't listen. They kept on in their sin. 30You were patient with them for many years. You sent your prophets to warn them about their sins. But still they wouldn't listen. So once again you let the heathen nations conquer them.

31But in your great mercy you did not destroy them. You never gave up on them for all time. What a kind God you are! How full of mercy you are!

32"And now, O great and awesome God! You always keep your promises of love and kindness. Please do not let all the hardships we have gone through become as nothing to you. Great trouble has come upon us. It has come upon our kings and princes. It has come upon our priests and prophets. Our ancestors suffered too. We have had troubles from the days when the kings of Assyria first triumphed over us until now. 33Every time you punished us you were being fair. We have sinned so badly that you gave us only what we deserved. 34Our kings, princes, priests, and ancestors didn't obey your laws. They didn't listen to your warnings. 35They did not worship you despite the great things you did for them. They forgot the great goodness you showed them. You gave them a large, fat land. But they would not turn from their sin.

36"So now we are slaves here in this land of plenty! This is the very land that you gave to our ancestors! We are slaves with plenty all around us! 37The rich crops of this land go into the hands of other kings. They are the kings whom you have let conquer us because of our sins. They have power over our bodies and our cattle. We do what they ask us to. And we are very sad. 38Because of all this, we again promise to serve the Lord! We and our princes and Levites and priests put our names to this covenant."

The People Agree to Obey

10 I, Nehemiah the governor, signed the covenant. The others who signed it were Zedekiah, Seraiah, Azariah, Jeremiah, Pashhur, Amariah, Malchijah, Hattush, Shebaniah, Malluch, Harim, Meremoth, Obadiah, Daniel, Ginnethon, Baruch, Meshullam, Abijah, Mijamin, Maaziah, Bilgai, and Shemaiah. All of these men were priests.

9-13These were the Levites who signed. They were Jeshua, Binnui, Kadmiel, Shebaniah, Hodiah, Kelita, Pelaiah, Hanan, Mica, Rehob, Hashabiah,

Zaccur, Sherebiah, Shebaniah, Hodiah, Bani, and Beninu. Jeshua was the son of Azaniah. Binnui was the son of Henadad.

14-27The political leaders who signed were Parosh, Pahath-moab, Elam, Zattu, Bani, Bunni, Azgad, Bebai, Adonijah, Bigvai, Adin, Ater, Hezekiah, Azzur, Hodiah, Hashum, Bezai, Hariph, Anathoth, Nebai, Magpiash, Meshullam, Hezir, Meshezabel, Zadok, Jaddua, Pelatiah, Hanan, Anaiah, Hoshea, Hananiah, Hasshub, Hallohesh, Pilha, Shobek, Rehum, Hashabnah, Maaseiah, Ahiah, Hanan, Anan, Malluch, Harim, and Baanah.

28These men signed the covenant for all the rest of the people. They signed it for the common people and the priests. They signed it for the Levites and the gatekeepers. They signed it for the choir members and the Temple servants. They signed it for all the rest of the people with their wives, sons, and daughters. These people were old enough to understand. And they had set themselves apart from the heathen people of the land. They had done this so they could serve God. 29For we all agreed to obey this covenant. And we promised to accept the curse of God if we did not obey God's laws. These were the laws given by his servant Moses.

30We also agreed not to let our daughters marry non-Jewish men. And we would not let our sons marry non-Jewish girls.

31We knew that the heathen people in the land might bring some grain. Or they might bring some other produce. They might want to sell it on the Sabbath or on any other holy day. But if they did this, we agreed not to buy it. And we agreed not to do any work every seventh year. And we promised to forgive and cancel the debts of our brother Jews on that year.

32We also agreed to charge ourselves yearly with a Temple tax. This was so there would be money to take care of the Temple of our God. 33For we needed supplies of the special Bread of the Presence. And we needed grain offerings and burnt offerings. These were for the Sabbaths, the new moon feasts, and the yearly feasts. We needed to buy the other things needed for the work of the Temple. And we also needed items for making Israel clean before God.

34Then we tossed a coin. This was to decide who would bring the wood for the burnt offerings. It was to be brought by the families of priests, Levites, and leaders. Each family was to bring it at the same time each year. This wood was for the burnt offerings at the Temple. This was part of the law.

35We also agreed always to bring the first part of every crop to the Temple. This included ground crops and the produce from fruit and olive trees.

36We agreed to give to God our oldest sons. We agreed to give the firstborn of all our cattle, herds, and flocks. We did just as the law says. We gave them to the priests who serve in the Temple of our God. 37They stored the produce in the Temple of our God. They stored the best of our grain crops. They took the first of our fruit. And they stored the first of the new wine and olive oil. And we promised to bring to the Levites a tenth of what grew on our land. The Levites took in these tithes in the small towns. 38A priest would be with the Levites as they took these tithes. The priest was a descendant of Aaron. A tenth of all that was taken as tithes was brought to the Temple. It was then put in the storage rooms. 39The people and the Levites were to bring these offerings to the Temple. The law told them to do this. They were to bring offerings of grain, new wine, and olive oil. They were to put them in the holy storage rooms. These supplies were used by the priests, the gatekeepers, and the choir singers.

So we agreed not to forget the Temple of our God.

The People Move into the New City

11 The Israelite leaders were living in Jerusalem at this time. But now the people cast lots. They chose a tenth of the people from the other cities and towns of Judah and Benjamin. These were sent to live in Jerusalem, the Holy

City, too. ²Some who moved to Jerusalem at this time were volunteers. They were honored by the people.

³These are the names of the area leaders who came to Jerusalem. But most of the leaders still lived in their own homes in the cities of Judah. These leaders included priests, Levites, and Temple workers. There were also descendants of Solomon's servants.

⁴⁻⁶These are the leaders from the tribe of Judah who came to Jerusalem. There was Athaiah, the son of Uzziah. Uzziah was the son of Zechariah. Zechariah was the son of Amariah. Amariah was the son of Shephatiah. Shephatiah was the son of Mahalalel. Mahalalel was a descendant of Perez. There was also Maaseiah, the son of Baruch. Baruch was the son of Col-hozeh. Col-hozeh was the son of Hazaiah. Hazaiah was the son of Adaiah. Adaiah was the son of Joiarib. Joiarib was the son of Zechariah. Zechariah was the son of the Shilonite. There were 468 descendants of Perez who lived in Jerusalem.

⁷⁻⁹These are the leaders from the tribe of Benjamin who came to Jerusalem. There was Sallu, the son of Meshullam. Meshullam was the son of Joed. Joed was the son of Pedaiah. Pedaiah was the son of Kolaiah. Kolaiah was the son of Maaseiah. Maaseiah was the son of Ithiel. Ithiel was the son of Jeshaiah. There were also 968 descendants of Gabbai and Sallai. Their chief was Joel. Joel was the son of Zichri. Joel's helper was Judah, the son of Hassenuah.

¹⁰⁻¹⁴These are the leaders from among the priests. There was Jedaiah, the son of Joiarib. There was Jachin. And there was Seraiah, the son of Hilkiah. Hilkiah was the son of Meshullam. Meshullam was the son of Zadok. Zadok was the son of Meraioth. Meraioth was the son of Ahitub the chief priest. In all, there were 822 priests working at the Temple under these men. And there were 242 priests under Adaiah, the son of Jeroham. Jeroham was the son of Pelaliah. Pelaliah was the son of Amzi. Amzi was the son of Zechariah. Zechariah was the son of Pashhur. Pashhur was the son of Malchijah. There were also 128 men un-

der Amashsai, the son of Azarel. Azarel was the son of Ahzai. Ahzai was the son of Meshillemoth. Meshillemoth was the son of Immer. Amashsai's helper was Zabdiel, the son of Haggedolim.

¹⁵⁻¹⁷These are the Levite leaders. There was Shemaiah, the son of Hasshub. Hasshub was the son of Azrikam. Azrikam was the son of Hashabiah. Hashabiah was the son of Bunni. There were also Shabbethai and Jozabad. They were in charge of the work outside the Temple. And there was Mattaniah, the son of Mica. Mica was the son of Zabdi. Zabdi was the son of Asaph. Mattaniah was the one who began the services of thanks with prayer. Bakbukiah and Abda were Mattaniah's helpers. Abda was the son of Shammua. Shammua was the son of Galal. Galal was the son of Jeduthun. ¹⁸In all, there were 284 Levites in Jerusalem.

¹⁹There were also 172 gatekeepers. These were led by Akkub, Talmon, and others of their clan. ²⁰The other priests, Levites, and people lived at the places where their family land was. ²¹But the Temple workers all lived in Ophel. Their leaders were Ziha and Gishpa.

²²⁻²³The manager of the Levites in Jerusalem was Uzzi. He was also manager of those serving at the Temple. Uzzi was the son of Bani. Bani was son of Hashabiah. Hashabiah was the son of Mattaniah. Mattaniah was the son of Mica. They were all descendants of Asaph. His clan became the singers in the Tabernacle. Asaph was chosen by King David. David also set the pay scale of the singers.

²⁴Pethahiah helped in all the king's work. He was the son of Meshezabel. Meshezabel was a descendant of Zerah. Zerah was a son of Judah.

²⁵⁻³⁰Some of the people of Judah lived in small cities and the towns around them. Some lived in Kiriatharba, Dibon, Jekabzeel, and the towns nearby. Some lived in Jeshua, Moladah, Beth-pelet, Hazar-shual, Beersheba, and the towns around them. Some lived in Ziklag, Meconah, En-rimmon, Zorah, Jarmuth, Zanoah, Adullam, and the towns around them. Some live in

Lachish and its nearby fields. Others lived in Azekah and its towns.

So the people spread from Beersheba to the valley of Hinnom.

31-35The people of the tribe of Benjamin lived at Geba, Michmash, Aija, Bethel, and the towns around them. Some lived in Anathoth, Nob, Ananiah, Hazor, and Ramah. Others lived in Gittaim, Hadid, Zeboim, Neballat, Lod, and Ono. Ono was the Valley of the Craftsmen.

36Some of the Levites who lived in Judah were sent to live with the tribe of Benjamin.

The Priests and Levites

12 These are the priests who went with Zerubbabel and Jeshua. Zerubbabel was the son of Shealtiel. These priests were Seraiah, Jeremiah, Ezra, Amariah, Malluch, Hattush, Shecaniah, Rehum, Meremoth, Iddo, Ginnethoi, Abijah, Mijamin, Maadiah, Bilgah, Shemaiah, Joiarib, Jedaiah, Sallu, Amok, Hilkiah, and Jedaiah.

8The Levites who went with them were Jeshua, Binnui, Kadmiel, Sherebiah, Judah, and Mattaniah. Mattaniah was the one in charge of the service of thanks.

9Bakbukiah and Unni, their relatives, helped Mattaniah during the service.

10-11Jeshua was the father of Joiakim. Joiakim was the father of Eliashib. Eliashib was the father of Joiada. Joiada was the father of Jonathan. Jonathan was the father of Jaddua.

12-21The following were the clan leaders of the priests. They served under the High Priest Joiakim.

Meraiah was leader of the Seraiah clan.
Hananiah was leader of the Jeremiah clan.
Meshullam was leader of the Ezra clan.
Jehohanan was leader of the Amariah clan.
Jonathan was leader of the Malluchi clan.
Joseph was leader of the Shebaniah clan.
Adna was leader of the Harim clan.

Helkai was leader of the Meraioth clan.
Zechariah was leader of the Iddo clan.
Meshullam was leader of the Ginnethon clan.
Zichri was leader of the Abijah clan.
Piltai was leader of the Moadiah and Miniamin clans.
Shammua was leader of the Bilgah clan.
Jehonathan was leader of the Shemaiah clan.
Mattenai was leader of the Joiarib clan.
Uzzi was leader of the Jedaiah clan.
Kallai was leader of the Sallai clan.
Eber was leader of the Amok clan.
Hashabiah was leader of the Hilkiah clan.
Nethanel was leader of the Jedaiah clan.

22A record of the heads of the clans of the priests and Levites was made. This was done during the reign of King Darius of Persia. This was in the days of Eliashib, Joiada, Johanan, and Jaddua. These were all Levites. 23In *The Book of the Chronicles* the Levite names were recorded. They were recorded down to the days of Johanan, the son of Eliashib.

24The chiefs of the Levites at that time were Hashabiah, Sherebiah, and Jeshua. Jeshua was the son of Kadmiel.

Their relatives helped them during the services of praise and thanks. They did just as they were told by David, the man of God.

25The gatekeepers were in charge of the storerooms at the gates. They were Mattaniah, Bakbukiah, Obadiah, Meshullam, Talmon, and Akkub.

26These were the men who were active in the time of Joiakim. Joiakim was the son of Jeshua. Jeshua was the son of Jozadak. They were active when I was the governor. And at that time, Ezra was the priest and teacher of religion.

The Dedication of the City Wall

27During the dedication of the new Jerusalem wall, all the Levites came to Jerusalem. They came to help in the services. They took part in the joy with their songs of thanks. And they played cymbals, psaltries, and harps. ²⁸The choir members also came to Jerusalem from the towns nearby. And they came from the towns of the Netophathites. ²⁹They also came from Beth-gilgal and the area of Geba and Azmaveth. For the singers had built their own towns as suburbs of Jerusalem. ³⁰The priests and Levites first gave themselves to the Lord. Then they did the same with the people, the gates, and the wall.

³¹⁻³²I led the leaders of Judah to the top of the wall. I divided them into two choirs. They stood in long lines. They were to walk opposite ways along the top of the wall. They were to sing songs of thanks as they went. One group went to the right toward the Dung Gate. It was made up of half of the leaders of Judah. ³³These included Hoshaiah, Azariah, Ezra, and Meshullam. ³⁴Also among them were Judah, Benjamin, Shemaiah, and Jeremiah.

³⁵⁻³⁶The priests who played the trumpets were Zechariah, Shemaiah, Azarel, Milalai, Gilalai, Maai, Nethanel, Judah, and Hanani. Zechariah was the son of Jonathan. Jonathan was the son of Shemaiah. Shemaiah was the son of Mattaniah. Mattaniah was the son of Micaiah. Micaiah was the son of Zaccur. Zaccur was the son of Asaph. They used the musical instruments made by King David. Ezra the priest led this group. ³⁷They went to the Fountain Gate. Then they went straight ahead and climbed the stairs. These are the ones that go up beside the castle to the old City of David. Then they went to the Water Gate on the east.

³⁸The other group went around the other way to meet them. I was a member of this group. We walked from the Tower of Furnaces to the Broad Wall. ³⁹Then we went from the Ephraim Gate to the Old Gate. We passed the Fish Gate and the Tower of Hananel. And we went on to the gate of the Tower of the Hundred. Then we went on to the Sheep Gate. And we stopped at the Prison Gate.

⁴⁰⁻⁴¹Both choirs then went to the

Squeezing Grape Juice
NEHEMIAH 13:15

Your mother probably doesn't squeeze juice from oranges or other fruit the way they did it in Bible times. People then squeezed grapes by stamping on them with their bare feet. Lots of juice squished up between their toes! People in Israel had many vineyards. These are the fields where grapes grow. Grapes were an important crop. The juice was often made into wine. When grapes were brought from the vineyard, they were dumped into a large stone tank. There was a large wooden pole over it. Ropes hung from the pole. Men held onto the ropes while they stamped their feet on the grapes. The juice ran from a hole in the bottom of the tank into a smaller stone tank. People dipped up the juice and put it in pots or bottles made from animal skins. Would you like to squish grapes this way? Would you like a glass of fresh grape juice from this Bible-time juicer?

Temple. Those with me were joined by the priests who played the trumpets. These were Eliakim, Maaseiah, Miniamin, Micaiah, Elioenai, Zechariah, and Hananiah. ⁴²We were also joined by the singers. These were Maaseiah, Shemaiah, Eleazar, Uzzi, Jehohanan, Malchijah, Elam, and Ezer.

They sang loudly and clearly. Jezrahiah was their leader.

⁴³Many sacrifices were offered on that joyful day. For God had given us cause for great joy. The women and children were happy too. The joy of the people of Jerusalem was heard far away!

The People Show Appreciation

⁴⁴On that day men were chosen to be in charge of the treasuries. They also took care of the wave offerings and the tithes. They took in the offerings of firstfruits. They collected these from the farms as the laws of Moses told them to. These offerings were given to the priests and Levites. The people of Judah were happy to give these things. For the priests and Levites served at the Temple. ⁴⁵The singers and gatekeepers also helped them to worship God. They helped in the rites for becoming pure. This was done by the laws of David and his son Solomon. ⁴⁶In the days of David and Asaph the custom began of having choir directors. They led the choirs in hymns of praise and thanks to God. ⁴⁷So now the people brought a daily supply of food for the members of the choir. They also brought food to the gatekeepers and the Levites. The Levites, in turn, gave to the priests part of what they had been given.

Foreigners Are Sent Away

13 On that same day the laws of Moses were read to the people. They found that the Ammonites and Moabites should not be allowed to worship at the Temple. ²For they had not been friendly to the people of Israel. Instead, they had hired Balaam to curse them. But God had turned the curse into a blessing. ³When this rule was read, the foreigners were sent away from the group right away.

⁴Before this happened, Eliashib was the priest in charge of the Temple. He was also a good friend of Tobiah's. ⁵He had made a storage room into a guest room for Tobiah. The room had once been used for storing grain offerings and incense. It had been used to store bowls and tithes of grain. They had stored new wine and olive oil in it. Moses had said that these offerings belonged to the priests and Levites. They were also for the members of the choir and the gatekeepers.

⁶I was not in Jerusalem at the time. For I had gone back to Babylon. I went there in the 32nd year of the reign of King Artaxerxes. But later he allowed me to go back again to Jerusalem. ⁷When I came back to Jerusalem, I learned of this evil deed of Eliashib. I heard that he had made a guest room in the Temple for Tobiah. ⁸I was very angry! I threw out all of Tobiah's things from the room. ⁹Then I had the room cleaned. And I brought back the Temple bowls, the grain offerings, and the incense.

The People Take Care of the Levites

¹⁰I also learned that the Levites had not been given what was due them. Because of this they had gone home to their farms. The choir singers who led the worship services had also gone home. ¹¹I spoke to the leaders right away. I asked them, "Why haven't you taken care of the Temple?" Then I called all the Levites back again. I gave them to their proper work. ¹²And once more all the people of Judah began bringing their tithes. These were offerings of grain, new wine, and olive oil. They brought them to the Temple treasury.

¹³I put Shelemiah the priest in charge of the storage rooms. Zadok the scribe and Pedaiah the Levite worked with him. I chose Hanan as their helper. Hanan was the son of Zaccur. Zaccur was the son of Mattaniah. These men were known to be fair. Their job was to give out the food to the Levites. They had to do this fairly.

¹⁴O my God, remember this good deed! Do not forget all that I have done for the Temple!

Nehemiah Stops Work on the Sabbath

¹⁵One day I was on a farm. I saw some men treading winepresses on the Sabbath. They were also bringing in sheaves of grain. They were loading their donkeys with wine, grapes, and figs. And they took these things into Jerusalem that day. So I warned them in public about doing this. ¹⁶There were also some men from Tyre. They brought in fish and all sorts of wares. They sold them on the Sabbath to the people of Jerusalem.

¹⁷Then I spoke to the leaders of Judah. I asked, "Why are you working on the Sabbath? ¹⁸Wasn't it enough that your fathers did this sort of thing? They brought these bad days upon us and upon our city! And now you are bringing more anger on the people of Israel. You do this by allowing people to buy and sell on the Sabbath."

¹⁹So I commanded that the gates of the city be shut on Friday evenings. They were not to be opened until the Sabbath had ended. And I sent some of my servants to guard the gates. That way no goods could be brought in on the Sabbath day. ²⁰The traders camped outside Jerusalem once or twice. ²¹But I spoke sharply to them. I said, "What are you doing out here? Why are you camping around the wall? If you do this again, I will arrest you!" And that was the last time they came on the Sabbath.

²²Then I commanded the Levites to make themselves pure. I told them to guard the gates. They were to make sure that the Sabbath day was kept holy. Remember this good deed, O my God!

Have mercy on me! Do this according to your great goodness.

Nehemiah Gets Tough

²³Then I saw that some of the Jews had married women from Ashdod, Ammon, and Moab. ²⁴Many of their children spoke in the language of Ashdod. They couldn't even speak the language of Judah! ²⁵So I spoke to these parents. I cursed them and even punched a few of them! I knocked them around and pulled out their hair! And they made a promise before God. They said that they would not let their children marry non-Jews.

²⁶"Wasn't this King Solomon's problem?" I demanded. "There was no king who was as great as he was. God loved him and made him the king over all Israel. But even so he was led to worship idols by foreign women. ²⁷Do you think that we will let you do this sinful thing?"

²⁸One of the sons of Jehoiada had married a daughter of Sanballat the Horonite. Jehoiada was the son of Eliashib the High Priest. So I chased him out of the Temple. ²⁹Remember them, O my God! For they have made the priesthood unclean. They have made the promises of the priests and Levites into lies. ³⁰So I sent away all the foreigners. And I gave jobs to the priests and Levites. I made sure that each knew his work. ³¹They supplied wood for the altar at the proper times. They took care of the sacrifices and the first offerings of every harvest. Remember me, my God, with your kindness!

ESTHER

Would you like to read a story like this? A poor orphan girl is chosen to be queen of a great empire. But an evil man plots to kill all the queen's people. The queen has a party and at just the right time tells the king about the evil plot. The evil man is hanged. Swords are given to the queen's people. They fight and win. The beautiful queen is a heroine. This is the story of the Book of Esther.

This book is about an Israelite girl whose family had been captured and brought to Babylon. Now her parents are dead, and she lives with her Uncle Mordecai. One day Esther is chosen to become queen. Because she is queen, she is able to save the Jewish people from an evil plot.

There are two books in the Bible named for women. The Book of Ruth is about a foreign girl from Moab. Because she took care of her Israelite mother-in-law, a man fell in love with her. The Book of Esther is about an Israelite girl who was a captive in Persia, a foreign land. Because the king fell in love with her, she saved her people.

Trouble in the Palace

Bible-time kings could do almost anything they wanted. They could decide if a person would live or die. Everyone was expected to obey a king. But one day Queen Vashti refused to obey the king. What did he do?

1 It was the third year of the reign of King Ahasuerus. He was king of the great empire of Media-Persia. His empire had 127 provinces, and it stretched from India to Ethiopia. This was the year of the great feast at Shushan Palace. The king asked all his governors, advisors, and army officers to come. They came from every part of Media-Persia. ⁴The feast lasted for six months! During that time, King Ahasuerus showed his great riches. And he proved to everyone how great his empire was.

⁵When it was all over, the king gave a special party. This was for the palace servants and officials. Everyone came,

janitors and cabinet officials alike. They came for seven days of feasting. This feast was held in the courtyard of the palace garden. 6The garden was hung with white and blue curtains. The curtains were tied to silver rings with ribbons of white and purple. The silver rings were set into marble pillars. There were gold and silver benches. These stood on floors of black, red, white, and yellow marble. 7Drinks were served in gold goblets of many designs. And there was plenty of royal wine to drink. The king was feeling very generous. 8The king commanded the servants to serve each person as much wine as he wanted. But they were not to force anyone to take more than he pleased. The king had told his servants to let everyone decide this for himself.

9Queen Vashti gave a party for the women of the palace at the same time.

10On the final day the king was feeling high. He was half-drunk from wine. He spoke to the seven eunuchs who were his personal servants. Their names were Mehuman, Biztha, Harbona, Bigtha, Abagtha, Zethar, and Carkas. 11He told them to bring Queen Vashti to him. She was to wear the royal crown on her head. He wanted all the men to see how pretty she was. For she was a very pretty woman. 12So they went and gave the king's order to Queen Vashti. But she would not come. The king was very angry. 13-15He spoke to his lawyers, for he did nothing without their advice. They were men of wisdom. They also knew about Persian law and justice. And the king trusted what they had to say. These men were Carshena, Shethar, Admatha, Tarshish, Meres, Marsena, and Memucan. They were seven of the greatest men in Media-Persia. They were the king's personal friends and the chief officers of the empire.

"What shall we do about this?" he asked them. "What does the law say must be done to Queen Vashti? She did not obey the king's orders. And those orders were properly sent through his servants."

16Memucan answered for the others, "Queen Vashti has done wrong to the king. But she also has done wrong to every person of your empire! 17For women all around will begin to disobey their husbands. They will do this when they learn what Queen Vashti has done to you. 18This very day, all our wives will hear what the queen did. And they will start talking to us husbands the same way. There will be trouble and anger throughout your empire. 19We suggest that you make a royal law. It should be a law of the Medes and Persians that can never be changed. It should state that Queen Vashti be sent away from you for all time. And you shall choose another queen who is better than she. 20This law should be sent throughout your great kingdom. If you do this, wives everywhere will show respect for their husbands!"

21The king and all his advisors thought this made good sense. So he did what Memucan told him to do. 22He sent letters to all the provinces. These were sent out in all the local languages. The letters said that men should rule and take charge of their homes.

- *Remember:* What kind of party did the king give? (1:1-8) What did the king ask Queen Vashti to do? (1:11) What did the queen do about that? (1:12) What did the king do to Queen Vashti then? (1:12-21) Who do you think was wrong, the king or queen? Why do you think so?

- *Discover:* God can help good things to come from bad. The king's bad choices and Vashti's refusal to obey a king paved the way for Esther to become queen. That made it possible for her to save the Jewish people.

- *Apply:* Is something bad happening to you today? Ask God what good may come from it. Then depend on him to work it out.

- *What's next?* An orphan girl becomes queen. Read Esther 2. ∎

Esther Becomes Queen

Esther was an orphan girl. Her cousin Mordecai took care of her. She was also a captive in a foreign land. What hope did she have? But one day she became queen. How did that happen?

2 But King Ahasuerus's anger cooled off before long. And he became sad over the loss of Vashti. He knew that he would never see her again.

²So his advisors said, "Let us go and find all the pretty girls in the empire. Let us bring them to the king for his pleasure. ³We will appoint men in each province. They will choose pretty young girls for the royal harem. They will be brought to Hegai, the eunuch in charge. He will see that they are given beauty treatments. ⁴After that, you will choose the girl you like the most. Then she will be queen instead of Vashti."

This idea made the king very happy. So he did what they said right away.

⁵Now there was a certain Jew at the palace named Mordecai. He was the son of Jair. Jair was the son of Shimei. Shimei was the son of Kish. He was a Benjaminite. ⁶He had been captured when Jerusalem was destroyed by King Nebuchadnezzar. He was taken to Babylon along with King Jehoiachin of Judah and many others. ⁷This man had a pretty young cousin named Hadassah. She was also called Esther. Her father and mother were dead. So Mordecai had adopted her into his family and raised her as his own daughter. ⁸Now Esther was brought to the king's harem at Shushan Palace. Many other young girls were brought there with her. This was because of the king's law. ⁹Hegai was in charge of the harem. He liked Esther very much and did his best to make her happy. He ordered special food for her. And he gave her special beauty treatments. He also gave her seven girls from the palace as her maids. And he gave her the best room in the harem. ¹⁰Esther hadn't told anyone that she was a Jewess. This was because Mordecai had said not to. ¹¹He came every day to the court of the harem to ask about Esther. He wanted to find out what was happening to her.

¹²⁻¹⁴Before being taken to the king's bed, the girls were given beauty treatments for one year. For the first six months they were treated with oil of myrrh. For the last six months they were treated with special perfumes and ointments. Then each girl's turn came for spending the night with King Ahasuerus. She could choose any clothing and jewelry that she thought would make her more beautiful. She was taken to the king's room in the evening. The next morning she was sent to the second harem. This was where the king's wives lived. There she was under the care of Shaashgaz. He was another of the king's eunuchs. There she would live for the rest of her life. She would probably never see the king again. She would only see him if he liked her a lot. Then he might send for her by name.

¹⁵Esther's turn came to go to the king. She took the advice of Hegai, the eunuch in charge of the harem. She dressed as he told her to. And all the other girls exclaimed with delight when they saw her. ¹⁶So Esther was taken to the palace of the king. This was in January of the seventh year of his reign. ¹⁷Well, the king loved Esther more than any of the other girls. He liked her so much that he set the royal crown on her head. He made her queen instead of Vashti. ¹⁸To celebrate this, he threw another big party. He asked all his officials and servants to come. And he gave rich gifts to everyone.

¹⁹Later the king asked for a second group of pretty girls. By that time Mordecai had become a government official. ²⁰Esther still hadn't told anyone she was a Jewess. For she was still doing what Mordecai told her. She still obeyed him just as she had in his home.

● *Remember:* What was Esther's other name? (2:7) Who helped Esther? (2:9)

Why did the king make Esther queen? (2:17)

- *Discover:* One day Esther was an ordinary person. The next day she was queen of the empire. Sometimes God helps ordinary people become very important people. But when he does, he has a good reason.

- *Apply:* If God gives you something important to do, it may not be because you are better than someone else. It may be that he has an important job for you. Accept it. Thank him for it. Do it well.

- *What's next?* Queen Esther risks her life for her people. Read Esther 3–4. ■

Mordecai Saves the King's Life

[21]One day Mordecai was on duty at the palace. At that time, two of the king's eunuchs were angry at the king. So they made a plan to kill him. Their names were Bigthan and Teresh. They were guards at the palace gate. [22]Mordecai heard about the plan and told Queen Esther. Esther told the king about it. She also told the king that Mordecai had reported it. [23]The king checked to see if the story was true. The two men were found guilty and were hung on a gallows. This was all recorded in the book of the history of King Ahasuerus's reign.

Haman Tricks the King

The king loved his beautiful Queen Esther. Nobody would dare hurt her. But the wicked prime minister, Haman, tricked the king. He got the king to sign a death order against all Jews. He didn't know that Queen Esther was a Jew. What happened when the king found out he had ordered the queen's death?

3 Soon after this King Ahasuerus chose Haman as Prime Minister. Haman was the son of Hammedatha the Agagite. He was the most powerful official in the empire next to the king himself. [2]Now all the king's officers bowed before him with deep respect. They did this whenever he passed by. This was what the king had commanded them to do. But Mordecai would not bow down to him.

[3-4]"Why are you not obeying the king's command?" the others asked day after day. But still he would not do it. Finally they spoke to Haman about it. They wanted to see if Mordecai could get away with it because he was a Jew. This was the reason Mordecai had given for not bowing down. [5-6]Haman was very angry but decided not to punish just Mordecai. He made a plan to destroy all of Mordecai's people, the Jews. He wanted to destroy all the Jews in the whole kingdom of Ahasuerus.

[7]The best time for destroying the Jews was found by throwing dice. This was done in April of the 12th year of the reign of Ahasuerus. February of the next year was the date chosen for this action.

[8]Haman now went to the king about the matter. "There is a certain race of people in your kingdom," he said. "Their laws are not like those of any other nation. And they refuse to obey the king's laws. Therefore, it is not in the king's interest to let them live. [9]If it please the king, make a law that they be destroyed. I will pay $20 million into the royal treasury. It will pay for the expense of destroying these people."

[10]The king agreed to Haman's plan. And he took his ring from his finger and gave it to Haman. [11]"Keep the money," he said. "But go ahead and do as you like with these people. Do what you think is best."

[12]Two or three weeks later, Haman called in the king's secretaries. He had them write letters to the officials throughout the empire. He sent letters to each province in its own language. These letters were signed in the name of

King Ahasuerus. And they were sealed with his ring.

[13]They were then sent by messengers to all the provinces of the empire. They said the Jews must all be killed. This included young and old, women and children. This was to happen on the 28th day of February of the following year. And the property of the Jews was to be given to those who killed them. [14]"A copy of this law," the letter stated, "must be read in every province. It must be made known to all the people. That way they will be ready to kill the Jews when the day comes." [15]The law went out by the king's fastest messengers. But it was made known in the city of Shushan first. Then the king and Haman sat down to drink. But the city fell into confusion and panic.

4 Mordecai soon learned what had been done. So he tore his clothes and put on sackcloth and ashes. He went out into the city, crying with a loud and bitter wail. [2]Then he stood outside the gate of the palace. For no one was allowed to go in while wearing mourning clothes. [3]And throughout all the provinces there was great mourning among the Jews. There was much fasting, crying, and despair at the king's law. Many wore sackcloth and put ashes on their heads.

[4]Esther's maids and eunuchs came and told her about Mordecai. She was deeply troubled and sent clothing to him. She wanted him to wear it instead of the sackcloth. But he would not put it on. [5]Then Esther sent for Hathach. He was one of the king's eunuchs. He had been chosen as her special servant. She told him to go out to Mordecai. He was to find out what the trouble was and why he was acting like that. [6]So Hathach went out to the city square. He found Mordecai just outside the palace gates. [7]He heard the whole story from him. He also heard about the $20 million Haman had promised the king to destroy the Jews. [8]Mordecai also gave Hathach a copy of the king's law. It was the law that said all the Jews must die. Mordecai told him to show it to Esther and to tell her what was happening. He told him to tell Esther that she should go to the king to plead for her people. [9]So Hathach went to Esther with Mordecai's message. [10]Esther told Hathach to go back to speak with Mordecai.

[11]"All the world knows the law of this land," she said. "Anyone who goes into the king's inner court without being called must die. That person shall live only if the king holds out his golden scepter. This is true with man or woman. And the king has not called for me to come to him in more than a month."

[12]So Hathach gave Esther's message to Mordecai.

[13]Mordecai then sent a reply to Esther. "Do you think you will be free from this law there in the palace?" he asked. "Do you think you will get away when all other Jews are killed? [14]You might keep quiet at a time like this. If you do, God will save the Jews some other way. But you and your family will die. And who knows? God may have made you queen so you could help at this time!"

God may help you get a job so you can help him

God may have made you queen so you could help at this time!

Esther 4:14

[15]Then Esther sent a message back to Mordecai.

[16]"Go and bring together all the Jews of Shushan," she said. "Fast for me. Do not eat or drink for three days, night or day. I and my maids will do the same. Then I will go in to see the king. I will do this even though it is not allowed. And if I die, I die."

[17]So Mordecai did just what Esther told him to.

● *Remember:* Why didn't Mordecai bow before Haman? (3:4) What lie did Haman tell the king about the Jews? (3:8-9) What did the king tell him to do to the Jews? (3:11) How did Esther learn about the king's order? (4:1-9) Why could Esther be killed if she went to the king? (4:11) What did Mordecai say that helped her decide to go? (4:13) What kind of person was Esther? What makes you think so?

- *Discover:* Sometimes there is a special reason why you are at a certain place at a certain time.

- *Apply:* Do you have a special friend? Perhaps God has made you friends so you can tell this person about Jesus. Have you

just moved? Perhaps God has something special he wants you to do in this new place. Look for it!

- *What's next?* Throughout the empire, Esther's people will soon be murdered. How can she stop it? Read Esther 5–7. ■

Queen Esther Defeats Haman

The king has given a law. The Jews will all be murdered on a certain day. No one can change the king's law. So what can Esther do? How can she stop this?

5 Three days later Esther put on her royal robes. She went into the inner court. This was just beyond the royal hall of the palace. There the king was sitting on his royal throne. ²And when he saw Queen Esther standing there in the inner court, he called to her. He held out the golden scepter to her. So Esther went near and touched its tip.

³Then the king asked her, "What do you wish, Queen Esther? What have you come to ask me? I will give it to you, even if it is half the kingdom!"

⁴And Esther replied, "My king, if it pleases you, I want you and Haman to come to a banquet. I have made it ready for you today."

⁵The king turned to his servants. "Tell Haman to hurry!" he said. So the king and Haman came to Esther's banquet.

⁶During the wine course the king spoke to Esther. "Now tell me what you really want," he said. "I will give it to you, even if it is half of the kingdom!"

⁷⁻⁸Esther replied, "I hope Your Majesty loves me and wants to give what I ask. I want you to come again with Haman tomorrow. I shall make another banquet ready for you. And tomorrow I will explain what this is all about."

⁹What a happy man Haman was as he left the banquet! He saw Mordecai there at the gate. He was not standing up or bowing before him. And this made Haman very angry. ¹⁰But he did not do anything. He went on home and called all his friends and Zeresh, his wife. ¹¹He

bragged to them about his riches and his many children. He boasted of the jobs the king had given him. He was proud that he had become the greatest man in the kingdom next to the king himself.

¹²Then he said, "Yes, and Esther the queen asked only me and the king to a banquet! And she asked us to come again tomorrow! ¹³But yet," he added, "all this is nothing. For I see Mordecai the Jew just sitting there in front of the king's gate. And still he will not bow down to me!"

¹⁴Then Zeresh, his wife, and all his friends spoke up. "Get a 75-foot-high gallows ready," they said. "In the morning ask the king to let you hang Mordecai on it. When this is done, you can go on your merry way with the king to the banquet." This made Haman very happy. So he ordered the gallows built.

6 That night the king had trouble sleeping. So he decided to read for awhile. He ordered the records of his kingdom from the library. In them he came across the story about Mordecai. It told of how Mordecai had reported the plot of Bigthana and Teresh. These men were two of the king's eunuchs, watchmen at the palace gates. They had made a plan to kill the king.

³"What reward did we ever give Mordecai for this?" the king asked.

His servants said, "Nothing!"

⁴"Who is on duty in the outer court?" the king asked. Now, as it happened, Haman had just come into the outer

court of the palace. He was there to ask the king to hang Mordecai from the gallows he was building.

⁵So the servants said to the king, "Haman is out there."

"Bring him in," the king ordered. ⁶So Haman came in. The king asked him, "What should I do to honor a man who truly pleases me?"

Haman thought to himself, "Whom would he want to honor more than me?" ⁷⁻⁸So he replied, "Bring out some of the royal robes the king himself has worn. Bring out the king's own horse and the royal crown. ⁹Tell one of the king's most noble princes to put the royal robes on the man. Have this prince lead him through the streets on the king's own horse. Have him shout, 'This is the way the king honors those who truly please him!'"

¹⁰"Very good!" the king said to Haman. "Hurry and take these robes and my horse. Do just as you have said. Do this for Mordecai, the Jew who sits at the king's gate. Do it all just as you have said."

¹¹So Haman took the robes and put them on Mordecai. He put him on the king's own horse. And he led him through the streets of the city. He shouted, "This is the way the king honors those who truly please him."

¹²After this Mordecai went back to his job. But Haman went home in great shame. ¹³Haman told Zeresh his wife and all his friends what had happened. They said, "Mordecai is a Jew. If this is so, you will never succeed in your plans against him. To keep on going against him might end in your death."

¹⁴They were still talking about this when the king's messengers came. They brought Haman quickly to the banquet Esther had made.

7 So the king and Haman came to Esther's banquet. ²Again, during the wine course, the king spoke to her. "What is it that you wanted, Queen Esther?" he asked. "What do you wish?

5"What are you talking about?" King Ahasuerus asked. "Who would dare touch you?" 6Esther replied, "This wicked Haman is our enemy." Then Haman grew pale with fear before the king and queen. 7The king jumped to his feet and went out into the palace garden. Haman stood up to cry for his life to Queen Esther. For he knew that he was doomed to die. 8In despair he fell upon the couch where Queen Esther was resting. Just then, the king came back from the palace garden. "Will he even sleep with the queen?" the king roared. "Will he do it right here in the palace? Will he do it before my very eyes?" Right then the death veil was put over Haman's face. 9Then Harbona, one of the king's servants, spoke up. "Sir, Haman has just had a 75-foot gallows made," he said. "He made it to hang Mordecai, the man who saved the king from being killed! It stands in Haman's courtyard."

"Hang Haman on it," the king ordered.

10So they did, and the king's anger was put at rest.

I will give it to you, even if it is half of my kingdom!"

3At last Queen Esther said, "Perhaps I have won your favor, O king. And perhaps this will make Your Majesty happy. Please, save my life and the lives of my people. 4For I and my people have been sold to those who will destroy us. We are doomed to be destroyed and killed! If we were only to be sold as slaves, maybe I could stay quiet. But even then there would be great damage to the king. The damage would be so great that no amount of money could begin to cover it."

- *Remember:* When Esther went to see the king, how did he welcome her? (5:1-2) How do you know that the king loved Esther? (5:3-6) What did Haman plan to do to Mordecai? (5:14) But what stopped Haman from killing Mordecai? Why did the king honor Mordecai? (6:1-12) How was Haman punished? (7:9-10) Do you think Haman deserved it? Why?

- *Discover:* The bad things we plan for others may come back to hurt us.

- *Apply:* Do you wish something bad would happen to someone? Be careful! It could happen to you! Pray for that person instead.

- *What's next?* A rich man loses everything he has. What will he do? What will he say to God? Read Job 1:1–2:10. ∎

A New Law to Protect the Jews

8 That same day King Ahasuerus gave all that Haman owned to Queen Esther. Then Mordecai was brought before the king. For Esther had told the king that he was her cousin and foster father. ²The king took off his ring, which he had taken back from Haman. He gave it to Mordecai and chose him as Prime Minister. And Esther told Mordecai to manage all of Haman's property for her.

³Now once more Esther came before the king. She fell down at his feet. She begged him with tears to stop Haman's plot against the Jews. ⁴And again the king held out the golden scepter to Esther. So she rose and stood before him. ⁵Esther said, "If it pleases Your Majesty, and if you love me, please send out a new law. Do this to stop Haman's law to destroy the Jews throughout your kingdom. ⁶For how can I stand seeing my people killed?"

⁷Then King Ahasuerus spoke to Queen Esther and Mordecai the Jew. "I have given Esther the palace of Haman," he said. "And he has been hanged on the gallows because he tried to destroy you. ⁸Now go ahead. Send a message to the Jews. Tell them whatever you want to in the king's name. And seal it with the king's ring so that it cannot be stopped."

⁹⁻¹⁰The king's secretaries were called right away. It was now the 23rd day of the month of July. They wrote as Mordecai spoke. They sent this law to the Jews. And they sent it to the princes of all the provinces from India to Ethiopia. There were 127 provinces in all. The law was written in the languages of all the people of the kingdom. Mordecai wrote in the name of King Ahasuerus. And he sealed the message with the king's ring.

He sent the letters by fast messengers. They rode on camels and mules used in the king's service. ¹¹This law allowed the Jews to defend their lives and their families. It allowed them to destroy all the forces against them. And they were allowed to take the property of their enemies. ¹²The day set for this was the 28th day of February! This law was to be in effect throughout all the provinces of King Ahasuerus. ¹³These letters also said that a copy of this law had to be read to all the people. That way the Jews would be ready to stand against their enemies. ¹⁴So the mail went out quickly. It was carried by the king's messengers and speeded by the king's command. The same law was also given at Shushan Palace.

¹⁵Then Mordecai put on the royal robes of blue and white. He wore a great crown of gold. And he wore an outer cloak of fine linen and purple. He went out from the king. And he went through the city streets filled with shouting people. ¹⁶And the Jews had joy and gladness. And they were honored everywhere. ¹⁷And to every city and province the king's law was brought. And the Jews were filled with joy and declared a feast. Many people of the land acted like they were Jews. This was because they were afraid of what the Jews might do to them.

The Jews Defeat Their Enemies

9 So the 28th day of February came. This was the day the two laws of the king were to be put into effect. This was the day the Jews' enemies had hoped to destroy the Jews. But it did not turn out that way. The Jews gathered in their cities throughout all the king's provinces. They came together to defend themselves against any who might try to hurt them. But no one tried. For they were very afraid of the Jews. ³And all the rulers of the provinces helped the Jews. They did this because they were afraid of Mordecai. ⁴Mordecai was a mighty name in the king's palace. And his fame was known throughout all the provinces. For he had become

more and more powerful.

⁵But the Jews went ahead on that day and killed their enemies. ⁶They even killed 500 men in Shushan. ⁷⁻¹⁰They also killed the 10 sons of Haman, the Jews' enemy. Haman was the son of Hammedatha. His sons were named Parshandatha, Dalphon, Aspatha, Poratha, Adalia, Aridatha, Parmashta, Arisai, Aridai, and Vaizatha.

But they did not try to take all that Haman owned.

¹¹Late that evening the king was told how many were killed in Shushan. ¹²He called for Queen Esther. "The Jews have killed 500 men in Shushan alone," he said. "They have also killed Haman's 10 sons. If they have done that here, I wonder what has happened in the rest of the provinces! But now, what more do you want? It will be given to you. Tell me and I will do it."

¹³And Esther said, "If it pleases Your Majesty, let the Jews here in Shushan do tomorrow as they have done today. And let Haman's 10 sons be hanged on the gallows."

¹⁴So the king agreed and the law was read in Shushan. And they hung up the bodies of Haman's 10 sons. ¹⁵Then the Jews at Shushan came together the next day also. And they killed 300 more men. But again they took no property.

A New Celebration Feast

¹⁶The other Jews in the king's provinces also had come together. They had fought for their lives and killed their enemies. They had killed 75,000 of those who hated them. But they did not take their goods. ¹⁷Out in the provinces this was done on the 28th day of February. The next day they rested. And they celebrated their victory with feasting and gladness. ¹⁸But the Jews at Shushan went on killing their enemies the second day also. But they rested the next day. They feasted and were glad. ¹⁹Now the Jews in the towns throughout Israel have a yearly feast. And on the second day they rejoice and send gifts to each other. They still do this today.

²⁰Mordecai wrote a history of all these events. And he sent letters to the Jews near and far. They were sent throughout all the king's provinces. ²¹He told them to make a yearly feast on the last two days of the month. ²²He told them to celebrate with feasting and gladness. And they were to give gifts to each other. For in these days, the Jews were saved from their enemies. Their sorrow was turned to gladness. And their mourning was turned to happiness.

²³So the Jews did what Mordecai said. They made this a yearly custom. ²⁴⁻²⁵It would remind them of Haman, the son of Hammedatha the Agagite. He was a great enemy of all the Jews. It would remind them that he had tried to destroy them. It would remind them that the matter came before the king. And they would remember the new law that was made. This law caused Haman and his sons to be hanged on the gallows. They would remember that these days were chosen by the throw of the dice. ²⁶That is why this feast is called "Purim." The word for "throwing dice" in Persian is *pur*. ²⁷All the Jews in the empire agreed to start this feast. And they promised to pass it on to their descendants and to all who became Jews. They said they would never fail to celebrate these two days each year. ²⁸It would be a yearly event from generation to generation. It would be observed by every family throughout the empire. That way the Jews would never forget what had happened.

²⁹⁻³¹Queen Esther also wrote a letter supporting Mordecai's letter about the Feast of Purim. Esther was the daughter of Abihail. But she was later adopted by Mordecai the Jew. Letters were also sent to all the Jews throughout the kingdom of Ahasuerus. They brought messages of goodwill. They made sure everyone knew about the yearly Feast of Purim. This feast was called for by both Mordecai the Jew and Queen Esther. The Jews themselves had also decided on this feast. It would help them remember the time of their fasting and prayer. ³²So the command of Esther showed that these dates were right. All this was written down in the records.

God Rewards Mordecai

10 King Ahasuerus collected tribute from everywhere in the empire. Even lands far away on the seacoast had to pay him tribute. ²His great deeds are written in *The Book of the Chronicles of the Kings of Media and Persia*. The full account of Mordecai's honors given him by the king were also written there. ³Mordecai the Jew was the Prime Minister. He had power next to that of King Ahasuerus himself. He was, of course, very great among the Jews. He was loved by all his countrymen. This was because he did his best for his people. And he was a friend at court for all of them.

JOB

Have you ever seen 11,000 camels, donkeys, sheep, and oxen? You would have if you had visited Job. These animals, head to tail, would form a line 20 miles long! It would take almost all day to walk from one end of the line to the other. Animals in Job's time were like what money in the bank is today. People then didn't have money like ours. There were no coins, paper money, checks, or banks. There were no stocks or bonds or savings accounts. Rich people then had lots of animals, servants and slaves, and gold and silver. Job had 11,000 animals, a beautiful home, and a lovely family. He probably had lots of gold and silver, too. Job had everything a person could want. But he lost it all in one day. Would he curse God or praise God? The Book of Job shows what Job did when he lost everything he owned. Someday you may lose something very important to you. If you do, you'll want to remember what you read in the Book of Job.

Job Loses Everything

What would you say if you lost everything you own? Would you be angry at God? The story of Job is a story of a rich man who had everything. But one day he lost it all. Then he became very sick. Would he get angry at God? Would you?

1 A man named Job lived in the land of Uz. He was a good man who respected God. And he stayed away from doing wrong. 2-3He had a large family of seven sons and three daughters. He was very rich. He owned 7,000 sheep, 3,000 camels, 500 teams of oxen, and 500 female donkeys. He also had many servants. He was, in fact, the greatest man in that whole area.

4Job's sons used to take turns having feasts at their homes. They asked all their brothers and sisters to come. At these feasts they would eat and drink with great joy. ⁵These feasts sometimes lasted several days. But when the feasts ended, Job would call all his children and make them pure. He got up early in the morning and offered a burnt offering for each of them. For Job said, "Perhaps my sons have sinned. Maybe they have turned from God in their hearts." Job did this at every feast.

God gives us everything we have

I was born naked. I will die naked. The Lord gave me everything I have.

Job 1:21

---

⁶One day the angels came before the Lord. And Satan, the Accuser, came with them.

⁷"Where have you come from?" the Lord asked Satan.

"I've come from the earth," Satan said. "I've been watching everything that's going on."

⁸Then the Lord asked Satan, "Have you seen my servant Job? He is the finest man in all the earth. He is a good man who respects God. And he has nothing to do with evil."

⁹"Why shouldn't he obey you when you pay him so well?" Satan said. ¹⁰"You have always kept him safe. And you have kept his home and property from harm. You have helped him succeed in all that he does. Look how rich he is! No wonder he worships you! ¹¹But just take away his wealth. If you do, you'll see him curse you to your face!"

¹²⁻¹³So the Lord said to Satan, "All right. You can do anything you want to with all he owns. But you must not hurt him."

So Satan went away. And sure enough, soon after this, trouble came to Job. Job's sons and daughters were feasting at the oldest brother's house. ¹⁴⁻¹⁵A messenger rushed to Job's home with the news. "Your oxen were plowing," he said. "And the donkeys were feeding beside them. But the Sabeans raided us!

They drove away all the animals. And they killed all your servants except me. I am the only one left."

¹⁶This messenger was still speaking when another one came with more bad news. "The fire of God has fallen from heaven!" he said. "It burned up your sheep and all the herdsmen. I am the only one who escaped to tell you."

¹⁷This man was still talking when yet another messenger ran in. "Three bands of Chaldeans have driven off your camels," he said. "They have killed your servants. I am the only one who escaped to tell you."

¹⁸As he was still speaking, another came up. "Your sons and daughters were feasting in their oldest brother's home," he said. ¹⁹"A mighty wind blew in from the desert. It hit the house and the roof fell in on them. They are all dead! I am the only one who escaped to tell you."

²⁰Then Job stood up and tore his robe in grief. He fell down upon the ground before God. ²¹Job said, "I was born naked. I will die naked. The Lord gave me everything I have. It was his to take away. Blessed be the name of the Lord!"

²²Although Job lost everything, he did not blame God. That would have been a sin.

2 Now the angels came again to stand before the Lord. And Satan came with them.

²"Where have you come from?" the Lord asked Satan.

"I've come from the earth," Satan replied. "I've been watching all that's going on there."

³"Have you seen my servant Job?" the Lord asked. "He is the finest man in all the earth. He is a good man who respects God. And he turns away from all evil, even though I let you bring trouble upon him. And you did this when he didn't deserve it. But still he has kept his faith in me."

⁴⁻⁵"Skin for skin," Satan replied. "A man will give anything to save his life. But if you make his body sick, he will curse you to your face!"

⁶"Do with him as you please," the Lord said. "But do not kill him."

⁷So Satan went out from the Lord.

And he gave Job a bad case of boils. He had boils from head to foot! [8]Then Job took a broken piece of pottery. He used it to scrape himself. And he sat among the ashes.

[9]His wife said to him, "Are you still trying to be godly? God has done all this to you! Curse him and die!"

[10]But Job said, "You talk like some heathen woman. Shall we take only good things from the hand of God? Shall we never take any bad things?" So in all this Job did nothing wrong.

- *Remember:* What kind of person was Job? (1:1) What kind of riches did Job own? How were his things different from your family's things? (1:2-3) Why do you think Job was a godly man? (1:1,5) What did God let Satan do to Job the first time? (1:6-19) Did Job get angry at God? (1:20-22) What else did God let Satan do to Job? (2:1-8) Did Job get angry at God? (2:9-10) What do you think of Job now? Why?

- *Discover:* God gave you everything you have (1:21). You would have nothing without him.

- *Apply:* Have you or your family lost something? Don't get angry at God. He is the one who gave it to you. He can help you the most. Ask him.

- *What's next?* God gives Job twice as much as he had. Why? Read Job 42. ■

Job's Friends Come to Comfort Him

[11]Three of Job's friends heard of all the trouble Job was having. They agreed to go from their homes to see Job. They wanted to comfort him. Their names were Eliphaz the Temanite, Bildad the Shuhite, and Zophar the Naamathite. [12]Job was so changed that they hardly knew him. They cried loudly because they were sad. They tore their clothes and threw dust into the air. And they put dirt on their heads to show how sorry they were. [13]Then they sat on the ground with him for seven days and nights. No one spoke a word! They saw that his suffering was too great for words.

Job Wishes He Had Died at Birth

3 At last Job spoke, and he cursed the day he was born.

[2-3]"Let the day I was born be cursed," he said. "And curse the night when people said, 'It's a boy!' [4]Let that day be forgotten for all time. Let it be lost even to God. Let it be lost in eternal darkness. [5]Yes, let the darkness take it for its own. And may a black cloud put it in shadow. [6]May that day be taken off the calendar. May it never again be counted among the days of that year. [7]Let that night be sad and without joy. [8]Let those who are good at cursing curse it. [9]Let the stars of the night fall from the sky. Let it want to see light but never see it. Let it never see the morning light. [10]Curse it for not closing my mother's womb. Curse it for letting me be born to come to all this trouble.

It is wrong for us to blame God for our trouble

Although Job lost everything,
he did not blame God.
That would have been a sin.

Job 1:22

---

[11]"Why didn't I die when I was born? [12]Why did the midwife let me live? Why did my mother nurse me at her breasts? [13]If only I had died at birth! Then I would be quiet now, asleep and at rest. [14-15]I would be asleep with princes and kings with all their greatness. I would be at rest with rich princes whose castles are full of riches. [16]Oh, to have died when I was born! I wish I had never breathed or seen the light. [17]For when you die the wicked stop bothering you. And in death, tired people can rest. [18]Even prisoners are at rest there. There is no cruel jailer to curse them. [19]Both rich and poor alike are there. And the slave is free at last from his master.

[20-21]"Oh, why should light and life be given to those who suffer? Why should life be given to those who want to die? Why should life be given to those who look for death as others look for food or money? [22]What a relief when at last they die! [23]God might give a man a sad life.

Why is such a man allowed to be born? ²⁴I cannot eat because I am crying. My groans pour out like water. ²⁵What I always feared has happened to me. ²⁶I was not fat and lazy, yet trouble has come to me."

Eliphaz Gives Advice

4 Then Eliphaz spoke to Job:
²"Will you let me say a word? For who could keep from speaking out? ³⁻⁴In the past, you have told many hurting people to trust in God. You have helped those who are weak or falling. You have encouraged those who lie crushed on the ground. You have helped those who are tempted to give up. ⁵But now when

---

God sends rain so plants can grow

God sends the rain upon the earth to water the fields.

Job 5:10

---

you have trouble, you faint and break.

⁶"Shouldn't you still trust in God? Shouldn't you believe that God will take care of those who are good? ⁷⁻⁸Stop and think! Have you ever known a truly good person who was punished? Experience teaches that it is those who sin that are punished. ⁹They die under the hand of God. ¹⁰Though they are as strong as young lions, they shall all be broken and killed. ¹¹Like old, weak lions they shall starve. And all their children shall be scattered.

¹²"This truth was given me in secret. It was whispered in my ear. ¹³It came in a nighttime vision as others slept. ¹⁴Suddenly, fear took hold of me. I shook with terror. ¹⁵As a spirit passed before my face my hair stood up on end. ¹⁶I felt that the spirit was there. But I couldn't see it standing there. Then out of the silence came this voice:

¹⁷"'Is mere man more fair than God? Is he more pure than his Creator?'

¹⁸⁻¹⁹"God cannot even trust his own messengers. Even angels make mistakes! And men are made of dust! They are even less worthy of trust. They are crushed to death as easily as moths! ²⁰They are alive in the morning but by

evening they are dead. They are gone forever with hardly a thought from anyone. ²¹Their candle of life is snuffed out. They die and no one cares.

5 "They cry for help but no one listens. They turn to their gods, but none gives them help. ²They die frustrated. They are overcome by their own anger. ³Those who turn from God may be blessed for awhile. But then sudden disaster comes. ⁴Their children are cheated, with no one to defend them. ⁵Their harvests are stolen. Their riches satisfy the thirst of many others, not themselves! ⁶Sadness comes upon them to punish them for sowing seeds of sin. ⁷Mankind heads for sin and sadness just as flames shoot up from a fire.

⁸"My advice to you is this: Go to God and confess your sins to him. ⁹For he does great miracles. He does so many marvels they cannot be counted. ¹⁰God sends the rain upon the earth to water the fields. ¹¹He blesses the poor and humble. And he takes those who suffer to a safe place.

¹²"He stops the plans of crafty men. ¹³They are caught in their own traps. He gets in the way of their plans. ¹⁴They walk around like blind men in the daylight. They see no better in the daytime than at night.

¹⁵"God saves the fatherless and the poor from these cruel men. ¹⁶And so at last the poor have hope. And the teeth of the wicked are broken.

¹⁷"How blessed is the man whom God corrects! Oh, do not run from the discipline of the Lord when you sin. ¹⁸For though he wounds, he binds and heals again. ¹⁹He will save you again and again so that no evil can touch you.

²⁰"He will keep you from death when there is no food. He will save you from the power of the sword in time of war. ²¹You will be safe from the lies of others. There is no need to fear the future.

²²"You shall laugh at war and hunger. Wild animals will leave you alone. ²³Dangerous animals will be at peace with you.

²⁴"You need not worry about your

home while you are gone. Nothing shall be stolen from your barns.

25"Your sons shall become important men. You shall have as many descendants as there is grass! 26You shall live a long, good life. It shall be like standing grain. You will not be harvested until it is time! 27I have found from experience that all of this is true. For your own good, listen to what I have said."

Job Wonders Why He Is Suffering

6 Then Job answered him:

2"Oh, if only my sadness and troubles could be weighed. 3For they are heavier than the sand of 1,000 seashores. That is why I spoke so rashly. 4For the Lord has struck me down with his arrows. He has sent his poisoned arrows deep within my heart. All God's terrors are set against me. 5-7When wild donkeys bray, it is because their grass is gone. Oxen do not low when they have food. A man complains when there is no salt in his food. And how tasteless is the uncooked white of an egg! I am never hungry when I look at it. I gag at the thought of eating it!

8-9"Oh, that God would give the thing I want the most. I want to die under his hand. That way I will be free from his painful grip. 10This, at least, gives me comfort despite all the pain. I know that I have not denied the words of the holy God. 11Oh, why does my strength keep me alive? How can I be patient until I die? 12Am I unfeeling, like stone? Is my body made of brass? 13For I am helpless. I have no hope.

14"One should be kind to a fainting friend. But you have accused me without the slightest fear of God. 15-18My brother, you are like a brook. It floods when there is ice and snow. But in hot weather, it is no longer there. The caravans turn aside to find water. But there is nothing there to drink, and so they die. 19-21Caravans from Tema and from Sheba stop for water there. But their hopes are dashed. And so my hopes in you are dashed. For you turn away from me in terror and you do not help. 22But why? Have I ever asked you for even a small thing? Have I begged you for a

present? 23Have I ever asked for your help? 24All I want is a clear answer. Then I will keep quiet. Tell me, what have I done wrong?

25-26"It is wonderful to speak the truth. But your words against me are not based on fact. Are you going to condemn me just because I cried out in pain? 27That would be like hurting a helpless orphan or selling a friend. 28Look at me! Would I lie to your face? 29Stop thinking I am guilty, for I am righteous. Don't be so unfair! 30Don't I know what is right and what is wrong? Would I not tell you if I had sinned?

7 "How mankind must struggle. A man's life is long and hard. It is like that of a slave. 2How he longs for the day to end. How he grinds on to the end of the week and his pay. 3And so I also have been given months of trouble. I have been given these long and weary nights. 4When I go to bed I think, 'Oh, that it were morning!' And then I toss till dawn.

???????????????????????????????

Whose hair stood on end when he dreamed about a ghost?

(Read Job 4:12-21 for the answer.)

???????????????????????????????

5"My skin is filled with worms and blackness. My flesh breaks open, full of pus. 6My life drags by, day after hopeless day. 7My life is but a breath, and nothing good is left. 8You see me now, but not for long. Soon you'll look upon me dead. 9I shall be like a cloud that vanishes. Those who die go away forever—just like that. 10They are gone from their family and their home for all time. They shall never be seen again. 11Ah, let me tell you about my pain. Let me be free to speak out of the trouble of my soul.

12"O God, am I some monster that you never let me alone? 13-14Even when I try to forget my pain in sleep, you give me nightmares. 15I would rather be choked to death than go on and on like this. 16I hate my life. Oh, let me alone for these few last days. 17What is mere man that you should spend your time hurting him? 18Must you be his judge every morning? Must you test him every moment of the day? ¹⁹Why won't you let me alone, even long enough to spit?

²⁰"Has my sin hurt you, O God, Watcher of mankind? Why have you made me your target? Why have you made my life so heavy a burden to me? ²¹Why not just forgive my sin and take it all away? For all too soon I'll lie down in the dust and die. When you look for me, I shall be gone."

Bildad Gives Advice

8 Then Bildad spoke to Job:
²"How long will you go on like this, Job? How long will you blow words around like wind? ³Is God unfair? ⁴Your children might sin against him. If they did, he would punish them. ⁵But you might beg Almighty God for them. ⁶And if you were pure and good, he would hear your prayer. He would answer you and bless you with a happy home. ⁷And though you started with little, you

---

God does many wonderful miracles

God does great miracles,
too many to count.

Job 9:10

---

would end with much.

⁸"Read the history books and see. ⁹For we were born but yesterday and know so little. Our days here on earth pass as quickly as shadows. ¹⁰But the wisdom of the past will teach you. The knowledge of others will speak to you. It will remind you that ¹¹⁻¹³those who forget God have no hope. They are like rushes without any mud to grow in. They are like grass without water to keep it alive. It begins to wither even before it is cut. ¹⁴A man without God is trusting in a spider's web. Everything he counts on will fall apart. ¹⁵If he counts on his home, it won't last. ¹⁶At dawn he seems so strong, like a green plant. His branches spread across the garden. ¹⁷His roots are in the stream, down among the stones. ¹⁸But when he dies, he isn't even missed! ¹⁹That is all he can look forward to! And others

spring up from the earth to take his place!

²⁰"But look! God will not throw away a good man. And he will not bless people who do wrong. ²¹He will yet fill your mouth with laughter and your lips with shouts of joy. ²²Those who hate you shall be full of shame. And the wicked will be destroyed."

Job Has More Questions

9 Then Job answered:
²"Yes, I know all that. You're not telling me anything new. But how can a man be truly good in the eyes of God? ³God might choose to argue with him. And if he does, can a man answer even one of 1,000 questions he asks? ⁴For God is so wise and so mighty. Who has ever fought against him with success?

⁵"Suddenly he moves the mountains. He turns them over in his anger. ⁶He shakes the earth to its base. ⁷The sun won't rise, the stars won't shine, if he commands it so! ⁸Only he has stretched the heavens out and walked along the seas. ⁹He made the Bear, Orion, and the Pleiades. He made the constellations in the skies.

¹⁰"God does great miracles, too many to count. ¹¹He moves along, but I don't see him go. ¹²When he sends death to snatch a man away, who can stop him? Who dares to ask him, 'What are you doing?'

¹³"And God does not keep back his anger. The pride of man breaks before him. ¹⁴And who am I that I should try to argue with Almighty God? Who am I to even reason with him? ¹⁵Even if I were without sin, I wouldn't say a word. I would only cry for mercy. ¹⁶And even if my prayers were answered, I could hardly believe that he had heard my cry. ¹⁷For he is the one who destroys. He gives me wounds without a cause. ¹⁸He will not let me breathe, but fills me with bitter sorrows. ¹⁹He alone is strong and fair.

²⁰"But I? Am I righteous? My own mouth says no. Even if I were perfect, God would prove me wicked. ²¹And even if I am innocent, I dare not think of it. I despise what I am. ²²Good or evil,

it is all the same to him. For he destroys both the good and the evil man. ²³He will laugh when trouble crushes the good man. ²⁴The whole earth is in the hands of the wicked. God blinds the eyes of the judges and lets them be unfair. If not he, then who?

²⁵"My life passes swiftly away. It is filled with pain. ²⁶My years disappear like swift ships, like the eagle that swoops upon its prey.

²⁷"I might choose to forget my complaints against God. I might do this to end my sadness and be cheerful. ²⁸But then he would pour even greater sorrows upon me. For I know that you will not consider me to be good, O God. ²⁹But you will judge me. So what's the use of trying? ³⁰I might even wash myself with purest water. I might cleanse my hands with lye to make them clean. ³¹But even so, you would throw me into the ditch and mud. And even my clothing would be less dirty than you think me to be!

³²⁻³³"And I cannot defend myself. For you are no mere man as I am. If you were, then we could talk about it fairly. But there is no umpire between us. There is no middleman, no mediator to bring us together. ³⁴Oh, let him stop beating me. Then I would not need to live in fear of his punishment. ³⁵Then I could speak to him without fear. I could tell him boldly that I am not guilty.

10 "I am tired of living. Let me complain freely. I will speak in my sorrow and pain. ²I will say to God, 'Don't just condemn me! Tell me *why* you are doing it! ³Is it really right to punish me, a man you have made? Is it right to send joy and riches to the wicked? ⁴⁻⁷Are you unfair like men? Must you punish me for sins you know I've not done? Is it because you know no one can save me from your hand?

⁸"You have made me. Yet you destroy me. ⁹Oh, please remember that I'm made of dust. Will you change me back again to dust so soon? ¹⁰You have already poured me from bottle to bottle like milk. You have curdled me like cheese. ¹¹You gave me skin and flesh and knit together bones and sinews.

¹²You gave me life and were so kind and loving to me. I was safe in your care.

¹³⁻¹⁴"Your real reason for making me was to destroy me if I sinned. You made me so you could refuse to forgive my sin. ¹⁵Just the smallest sin and I am done for. And if I'm good, that doesn't count. I am frustrated. ¹⁶I start to get up off the ground. But you jump on me like a lion and quickly finish me off. ¹⁷Again and again you witness against me. You pour

????????????????????????????????
Which Bible-time man said that he wished he had never been born?
(Read Job 10:13-22 for the answer.)
????????????????????????????????

out more and more anger upon me. You bring fresh armies against me.

¹⁸"Why then did you even let me be born? Why didn't you let me die at birth? ¹⁹Then I would not have suffered like this. I would have gone right from the womb to the grave. ²⁰⁻²¹Can't you see how little time I have left? Oh, let me alone that I may have a little moment of comfort. Let me rest before I leave for the land of darkness and the shadow of death, never to come back. ²²It is a land as dark as midnight. It is a land of the shadow of death. Confusion rules there and the brightest light is dark as midnight."

Zophar Gives Advice

11 Then Zophar spoke to Job:
²"Shouldn't someone stop you from saying all these words? Is a man proved right by all this talk? ³Should I stay quiet while you brag? When you mock God, shouldn't someone make you ashamed? ⁴You claim you are pure in the eyes of God! ⁵Oh, that God would speak and tell you what he thinks! ⁶Oh, that he would make you truly see yourself. For he knows all that you've done. Listen! God is doubtless punishing you far less than you deserve!

⁷"Do you know the mind and purposes of God? Will long searching make them known to you? Do you know

enough to judge the Almighty? 8He is as pure as heaven is high. But who are you? His mind is deeper than deep. What can you know in comparison to him? 9His Spirit is wider than the earth and the sea. 10He rushes in and makes an arrest and calls the court to order. Who is going to stop him? 11For he knows all the sins of mankind. He sees all sin without even looking.

12"Mere man is as likely to be wise as a wild donkey's colt is likely to be born a man!

13-14"You might turn to God and stretch out your hands to him. But before you do, get rid of your sins. Leave all wrong deeds behind you. 15Only then can you walk forward to God without fear. For you will be without the sin that makes you unclean. 16Only then can you forget your misery. It will all be in the past. 17And your life will be without any clouds. The darkness will be as bright as morning!

18"You will be brave because you will have hope. You will take your time and rest in safety. 19You will lie down without fear. And many will look to you for help. 20But the wicked shall find no way to escape. Their only hope is death."

Job Wants to Hear from God

12 Then Job answered him: 2"Yes, I know that you know everything! All wisdom will die with you! 3Well, I know a few things myself. You are no better than I am. And who doesn't know these things you've been saying? 4I was the man who begged God for help, and God answered me. But my neighbors just laugh at me. Yes, I am a righteous man. But now they just laugh at me. 5The rich laugh at those in trouble. They are quick to look down on all those in need. 6Robbers become rich. Go ahead and make God angry! It makes no difference! He will supply your every need anyway!

7-9"Who doesn't know that the Lord does things like that? Ask the dumbest beast. He knows that it is so. Ask the birds—they will tell you. Or let the earth teach you, or the fish of the sea. 10For the soul of every living thing is in the hand of God. So is the breath of all mankind. 11Just as my mouth can taste good food, so my mind tastes truth when I hear it. 12And as you say, older men like me are wise. They understand. 13But true wisdom and power are God's. He alone knows what we should do. He alone understands.

14"And how great is his strength! What he destroys can't be rebuilt. When he closes in on a man, there is no escape. 15He holds back the rain, and the earth becomes a desert. He sends the storms and floods the ground. 16Yes, with him is strength and wisdom. Those who tell lies and those who are lied to are both his slaves.

17"He makes fools of counselors and judges. 18He makes kings into slaves and frees their servants. 19Priests are led away as slaves. He overthrows the strong. 20He takes away the voice of preachers. He takes away the wisdom of the elders. 21He looks down on princes and makes the strong weak. 22He floods the darkness with light, even the dark shadow of death. 23He raises up a nation and then destroys it. He makes it great, and then makes it into nothing. 24-25He takes away the understanding of princes and kings. He leaves them wandering, lost and groping, without a guiding light.

13 "Look, I have seen many things such as you describe. I understand what you are saying. 2I know as much as you do. I'm not stupid. 3Oh, how I wish I could speak to the Almighty. I want to talk this over with God himself. 4For you do not understand the whole thing. You are doctors who don't know what they are doing. 5Oh, please be quiet! That would be your highest wisdom.

6"Listen to me now. Listen to the reasons for what I think. Listen to my cries.

7"Must you go on 'speaking for God'? He never once has said the things that you are putting in his mouth. 8Does God want your help if you are going to twist the truth for him? 9Be careful that he doesn't find out what you are doing! Or do you think you can fool God as well as men? 10No, you will be in trouble with him if you use lies to try to help him out. 11Doesn't his majesty strike fear into your heart? How can you do this thing? 12These great words you have spoken are worth about as much as ashes. Your defense of God is as weak as a clay vase!

13"Be silent now and let me alone, that I may speak. And I am willing to face what God might do to me. 14Yes, I will take my life in my hands and say what I really think. 15God may kill me for saying this. In fact, I expect him to. But even so, I am going to argue my case with him. 16This at least will be in my favor, that I am not godless. For I won't be sent from him right away. 17Listen closely to what I am about to say. Hear me out.

18"This is my case: I know that I am righteous! 19Who can argue with me over this? If you could prove me wrong, I would stop defending myself and die.

20"O God, there are two things I beg you to do to me. Only then will I be able to face you. 21Please stop doing these terrible things to me. Stop making me afraid with your awesome presence. 22Then call to me to come. How quickly I will answer! Or let me speak to you, and you give me an answer. 23Tell me, what have I done wrong? Help me! Point out my sin to me. 24Why do you turn away from me? Why hand me over to my enemy? 25Would you blame a leaf that is blown about by the wind? Will you chase dry, useless straws?

26"You write down bitter things against me. You bring up all the sins of my youth. 27-28You send me to prison and shut me in on every side. I am like a fallen, rotten tree. I am like a coat that has been eaten by moths.

14 "How weak man is! How few days he has to live! And how full of trouble those days are! 2He blossoms for a moment, like a flower, and then withers. Like the shadow of a passing cloud, he is quickly gone. 3Must you be so harsh with weak men and demand an accounting from them? 4How can you demand purity in one born impure? 5You have given mankind such a short life. Months are all you give him! Not one bit longer may he live. 6So give him a little rest, won't you? Turn away your

angry look. Let him have a few moments of relief before he dies.

7"For there is hope for a tree if it's cut down. It sprouts again and grows tender, new branches. 8-9Its roots may have grown old in the earth. And its stump may have decayed. But still it may sprout and bud again at the touch of water, like a new seedling. 10But when a man dies and is buried, where does his spirit go? 11-12Water disappears from a lake. And rivers disappear in the dry season. So a man lies down for the last time. He does not get up again until the heavens are no more. He shall not wake up, or be roused from his sleep. 13Oh, that you would hide me with the dead. Forget me there until your anger ends. But mark your calendar to think of me again!

14"If a man dies, shall he live again? This thought gives me hope. So that in all my pain I wait for sweet death to come! 15You would call and I would come. You would reward all I do. 16But now, instead, you give me only a few steps upon the stage of life. And you see every sin I do. 17You bundle them all together against me.

18-19"Mountains wear away and disappear. Water grinds the stones to sand. Rivers tear away the soil. So every hope of man is worn away. 20-21Always you are against him, and then he passes off the scene. You make him old and wrinkled, then send him away. He never knows if his sons are honored. He never knows if they fail and face trouble. 22For him there is only sorrow and pain."

Eliphaz Speaks Again but Says Nothing New

15 Then Eliphaz answered him: 2"You are supposed to be a wise man. Yet you give us all this foolish talk. You are nothing but a windbag. 3It isn't right to speak so foolishly. What good do such words do? 4-5Have you no fear of God? Do you have no respect for him? Your sins are telling your mouth what to say! Your words are based on clever lies. 6But why should I condemn you? Your own mouth does!

7-8"Are you the wisest man alive? Were

you born before the hills were made? Have you heard the secret counsel of God? Are you called into his counsel room? Do you know all wisdom? ⁹What do you know more than we do? What do you understand that we don't? ¹⁰On our side are aged men much older than your father! ¹¹Is God's comfort too little for you? Is his gentleness too rough?

¹²"What is this you are doing? Why do you get carried away by your anger, with flashing eyes? ¹³And you turn against God and say all these evil things against him. ¹⁴What man in all the earth can be as pure and righteous as you claim to be? ¹⁵Why, God doesn't even trust the angels! Even the heavens can't be pure compared with him! ¹⁶How much less someone like you, who is corrupt and sinful. You drink in sin as a sponge soaks up water!

¹⁷⁻¹⁹"Listen, and I will answer you from my own experience. It is supported by the wise men who have been told this same thing from their fathers. Our ancestors to whom alone the land was given have passed this wisdom to us.

²⁰"A wicked man is always in trouble in his life. ²¹He is surrounded by terrors. If there are good days, they will soon be gone. ²²He dares not go out into the darkness. If he does, he might be murdered. ²³⁻²⁴He wanders around begging for food. He lives in fear, distress, and pain. His enemies conquer him as a king defeats his foes. ²⁵⁻²⁶Armed with his tin shield, he clenches his fist against God. He shouts at the Almighty, stubbornly fighting him.

²⁷⁻²⁸"This wicked man is fat and rich. He has lived in cities after killing off their people. ²⁹But he will not keep on being rich. And he won't get more things. ³⁰No, darkness shall overtake him forever. The breath of God shall destroy him. The flames shall burn up all he has.

³¹"Let him no longer trust in foolish riches. Let him no longer lie to himself. For the money he trusts in will be his only reward. ³²Before he dies, all this will become clear to him. For all he counted on will be gone. ³³It will fall to the ground like a dried grape. How little will

come of his hopes! ³⁴For the godless are barren. They can produce nothing truly good. God's fire burns them with all they own. ³⁵The only thing they can make is sin. Their hearts give birth only to wickedness."

Job Tells His Friends That They Are No Help

16 Then Job answered:

²"I have heard all this before. What poor comforters all of you are. ³Won't you ever stop your flow of foolish words? What have I said that makes you speak so much? ⁴But perhaps I'd speak the same as you, if you were I and I were you. I would speak my judgments against you and shake my head at you. ⁵But no! I would speak in such a way that it would help you. I would try to take away your sadness.

⁶"But now my sadness stays no matter how I defend myself. And it doesn't help if I refuse to speak. ⁷For God has ground me down and taken away my family. ⁸O God, you have turned me to skin and bones. They say this is proof of my sins. ⁹God hates me and tears at my skin in anger. He has bitten me with his teeth. And he watches to kill any sign of life. ¹⁰These 'comforters' have great jaws to swallow me. They slap my cheek. My enemies gather themselves against me. ¹¹And God has given me over to sinners. He has put me into the hands of the wicked.

¹²"I was living quietly until he broke me apart. He has taken me by the neck and dashed me to pieces. Then he hung me up as his target. ¹³His archers stand all around me. They shoot me with their arrows. The ground is wet from my blood. ¹⁴Again and again he attacks me, running upon me like a giant. ¹⁵Here I sit in sackcloth. I have laid all hope in the dust. ¹⁶My eyes are red with crying. On my eyelids is the shadow of death.

¹⁷"Yet I am innocent, and my prayer is pure. ¹⁸O earth, do not hide my blood. Let it protest for me.

¹⁹"Yet even now the Witness to my innocence is there in heaven. My Advocate is there on high. ²⁰My friends laugh at me. But I pour out my tears to God.

21I plead that he will listen as a man would listen to his neighbor. 22For all too soon I must go down that road from which I shall never come back.

17"I am sick and near death. The grave is ready to take me in. 2There are mockers all around me. I see them everywhere. 3-4Will no one prove my innocence? But you, O God, have kept them from knowing this. Oh, do not let them win. 5If they take bribes to lie about their friends, their children shall go blind.

6"He has made the people laugh at me. They spit in my face. 7My eyes are dim with crying and I am but a shadow of my former self. 8Fair-minded men are amazed when they see me.

"Yet, the innocent shall come out on top, above the godless. 9The righteous shall move onward and forward. Those with pure hearts shall become stronger and stronger.

10"As for you, all of you, please go away. For I do not find a wise man among you. 11My good days are in the past. My hopes have left me. My heart's desires are broken. 12They say that night is day and day is night. How they turn the truth around!

13-14"If I die, I go out into darkness. I call the grave my father. And I call the worm my mother and my sister. 15Where then is my hope? Can anyone find any? 16No, my hope will go down with me to the grave. We shall rest together in the dust!"

Bildad Says Job Must Deserve This Punishment

18 Then Bildad spoke again:
2"Who are you trying to fool? Speak some sense if you want us to answer! 3Have we become like animals to you, stupid and dumb? 4Just because you tear your clothes in anger, is this going to start an earthquake? Shall we all go and hide?

5"The truth remains that if you do not prosper, it is because you are wicked. And your bright flame shall be put out. 6There will be darkness in every home where there is wickedness.

7"The long steps of the wicked man will be made short. He will know his failing strength. 8-9He walks into traps, and robbers will attack him. 10There is a booby trap in every path he takes. 11He has good cause for fear. His enemy is close behind him!

12"His strength is lost because of hunger. Trouble stands ready to jump on him. 13His skin is eaten by disease. Death shall eat him. 14The wealth he trusted in shall reject him. And he shall be brought down to the King of Fears. 15His home shall burn under a fiery rain of brimstone. 16He shall die from the roots up. All his branches will be cut off.

17"All memory of his life will die from the earth. No one will remember him. 18He will be driven out from the kingdom of light into darkness. He will be chased out of the world. 19He will have neither son nor grandson left, nor any other relatives. 20Old and young alike will be amazed at what happens to him. 21Yes, that is what happens to sinners, to those who reject God."

Job Is Impatient but Believes in God

19 Then Job answered him:
2"How long are you going to trouble me? How long will you try to break me with your words? 3Ten times now you have said I am a sinner. Why aren't you ashamed to deal with me so harshly? 4And if indeed I was wrong, you have yet to prove it. 5You think yourselves so great? Then prove my guilt!

6"The fact of the matter is that God has overthrown me. He has caught me in his net. 7I scream for help and no one hears me. I cry, but get no justice. 8God has blocked my path and turned my light to darkness. 9He has taken away my glory. He has taken the crown from my head. 10He has broken me down on every side, and I am done for. He has destroyed all hope. 11His anger burns against me. He counts me as an enemy. 12He sends his troops to surround my tent.

13"He has sent away my brothers and my friends. 14My relatives have not helped me. My friends have all left me. 15Those living in my home, even my servants, think of me as a stranger. I am like a foreigner to them. ¹⁶I call my servant, but he doesn't come. I even beg him! ¹⁷My own wife and brothers refuse to see me. ¹⁸Even young children look down on me. When I stand to speak, they laugh.

¹⁹"My best friends hate me. Those I loved have turned against me. ²⁰I am skin and bones. I have escaped death by the skin of my teeth.

²¹"Oh, my friends, pity me. For the angry hand of God has touched me. ²²Why must you hurt me as God does? Why aren't you satisfied with my pain? ²³⁻²⁴Oh, that I could write my words with

---

**Although our bodies die,
God will raise them up again**

*And I know that after this body
has died, I shall see God!*

Job 19:26

---

an iron pen in the rock forever.

²⁵"But as for me, I know that my Redeemer lives. I know that he will stand upon the earth at last. ²⁶And I know that after this body has died, I shall see God! ²⁷Then he will be on *my* side! Yes, I shall see him. He will not be a stranger! He will be my friend! What a great hope!

²⁸"How dare you go on hurting me as though I were proven guilty? ²⁹I warn you, you are in danger of being punished!"

Zophar Gives Job a Hard Time

20 Then Zophar spoke to Job:
²"I hurry to make this answer. I have the answer for you. ³You have tried to make me feel ashamed of myself for calling you a sinner. But my spirit won't let me stop.

⁴"You know that man has been on the earth for a long time. ⁵And all this time, the triumph of the wicked has been short-lived. And the joy of the godless has lasted only for a moment. ⁶The godless might be as proud as the heavens. And he might walk with his nose in the air. ⁷But he shall die, cast away like his own dung. Those who knew him will wonder where he has gone. ⁸He will fade

like a dream. ⁹Neither his friends nor his family will ever see him again.

¹⁰"His children shall beg from the poor. Their hard work shall pay for his sins. ¹¹Though still a young man, his bones shall lie in the dust.

¹²"He enjoyed the taste of his wickedness. He let it melt in his mouth. ¹³He sipped it slowly, so it would not be gone. ¹⁴But the food he has eaten turns sour within him. ¹⁵He will vomit all that he ate. God won't let him keep it down. ¹⁶It is like poison and death to him. ¹⁷He shall not enjoy the goods he stole. They will not be butter and honey to him after all. ¹⁸His work shall not be rewarded. Riches will give him no joy. ¹⁹For he has been cruel to the poor. He has taken their homes. He will never get better. ²⁰Though he was always greedy, now he has nothing. Nothing is left of all the things he dreamed of. ²¹His riches will stop because he stole whenever he could.

²²"He shall run into trouble at the peak of his powers. All the wicked shall destroy him. ²³Just as he is about to fill his belly, God will rain down anger upon him. ²⁴He will be chased and knocked down. ²⁵The arrow is pulled from his body. And the shining point comes out from his gall. The fears of death are upon him.

²⁶"His treasures will be lost in deepest darkness. A raging fire will burn his goods. It will burn all that he has left. ²⁷The heavens will show his sins. And the earth will speak against him. ²⁸His riches will disappear under the anger of God. ²⁹This is what waits for the wicked man. For God makes it ready for him."

Job Tells His Friends That They Don't Understand God

21 Then Job answered:
²⁻³"Listen to me. Let me speak, and after that, you can laugh some more.

⁴"My complaint is against God, not man. No wonder my spirit is so troubled. ⁵Look at me in horror, and lay your hand upon your mouth. ⁶Even I am afraid when I see myself. Fear takes hold of me and I shake.

⁷"The truth is that the wicked live on

to a good old age. They become great and powerful. [8]They live to see their children grow old around them. They see their grandchildren, too. [9]Their homes are safe from every fear. And God does not punish them. [10]Their cattle produce many calves. [11]They have many happy children. [12-13]They spend their time singing and dancing. They are rich and can have anything they want. They succeed to the end. [14]All this despite the fact that they ordered God away. This happens even though they wanted no part of him and his ways.

[15]"'Who is Almighty God?' they laugh. 'Why should we obey him? What good will it do us?'

[16]"Look, everything the wicked touch has turned to gold! But I refuse even to deal with people like that. [17]Yet the wicked get away with it every time. They never have trouble. God skips them when he gives out his sorrows and anger. [18]Are they driven before the wind like straw? Are they carried away by the storm? Not at all!

[19]"'Well,' you say, 'at least God will punish their children!' But I say that God should punish the man who sins, not his children! Let him feel the punishment himself. [20]Yes, let him be destroyed for his sin. Let him drink deeply of the anger of the Almighty. [21]For when he is dead, then he will never again be able to enjoy his family.

[22]"But who can talk back to God, the supreme Judge? [23-24]He destroys those who are healthy, rich, and fat. [25]God also destroys those who are very poor. He destroys those who have never known anything good. [26]Both alike are buried in the same dust. Both are eaten by the same worms.

[27]"I know what you are going to say. [28]You will tell me of rich and wicked men who came to trouble because of their sins. [29]But I tell you to ask anyone who has been around. He can tell you the truth. [30-32]He can tell you that the evil man is often allowed to get away in the day of trouble. No one speaks against him openly. No one pays him back for what he has done. And an honor guard keeps watch at his grave. [33]A great funeral parade walks in front and behind him as the soft earth covers him. [34]How can you comfort me when what you say is so wrong?"

Eliphaz Wants Job to Give In

22 Then Eliphaz spoke again:
[2]"Is mere man of any worth to God? Even the wisest is of value only to himself! [3]Is it any pleasure to the Almighty if you are righteous? Would it be any gain to him if you were perfect? [4]Is it because you are good that he is hurting you? [5]Not at all! It is because of your sin! Your sins are endless!

[6]"For instance, you might have refused to loan money to needy friends. You might have demanded that they give you all their clothing as a pledge. Yes, you must have stripped them to the bone. [7]You must not have given water to the thirsty and bread to the hungry. [8]But no doubt you gave important men anything they wanted. And you let the rich live wherever they chose. [9]You sent widows away without helping them. And you broke the arms of orphans. [10-11]That is why there are now traps and sudden fears all around you. That is why you see only darkness and waves of trouble.

[12]"God is so great! He is higher than the heavens. He is higher than the stars. [13]But you reply, 'That is why he can't see what I am doing! How can he judge through the thick darkness? [14]For thick clouds swirl about him so that he cannot see us. He is way up there, walking in the heavens.'

[15-16]"Don't you know that those walking the old ways of sin are taken away in youth? Don't you know that the base of their lives is washed out for all time? [17]For they said to God, 'Go away, God! What can you do for us?' [18]God forbid that I should say a thing like that. Yet they forgot that he had filled their homes with good things. [19]And now the righteous shall see them destroyed. The innocent shall laugh at the wicked. [20]'See,' they will say, 'the last of our enemies have been burned in the fire.'

[21]"Quit arguing with God! Agree with him and you will have peace at last! His favor will surround you. All you have to

do is admit that you were wrong. 22Listen to his teachings and store them in your heart. 23You go back to God and put right all the wrong in your home. If you do, then you will be forgiven. 24You might give up your lust for money and throw your gold away. 25If you do, then the Almighty himself shall be your treasure. He will be your fine silver!

26"Then you will find joy in the Lord and look up to God. 27You will pray to him, and he will hear you. And you will fulfill all your promises to him. 28Whatever you wish will happen! And the light of heaven will shine upon the road ahead of you. 29You might be attacked and knocked down. But you will know that there is someone who will lift you up again. Yes, he will save the humble 30and help even sinners by your pure hands."

Job Wants to Talk to God

23 Then Job answered:
2"My complaint today is still a bitter one. And my punishment is far worse than my sin deserves. 3Oh, if only I knew where to find God. I wish I could go to his throne and talk with him there. 4-5I would tell him all about my side of the story. I would listen to his answer and know what he wants. 6Would he just overpower me with his greatness? No, he would listen kindly. 7Fair and honest men could reason with him and be forgiven by my Judge.

8"I look but I do not find him. I look for him here and there. But he is not to be seen. 9I look for him in his workshop in the North. But I cannot find him there. Nor can I find him in the South. There, too, he hides himself. 10But he knows everything that is happening to me. And when he has tested me, he will say I am innocent. He will say I am as pure as solid gold!

11"I have stayed in God's paths, following his steps. I have not turned aside. 12I have not refused his commands. I have enjoyed them more than my daily food. 13But even so, his thoughts about me stay the same. And who can turn him from his plans? What he wants to do, he does. 14So he will do to me all he has planned, and there is more ahead. 15"No wonder I am so afraid when I

stand before him. When I think of it, fear takes hold of me. 16-17God has given me a weak heart. He, the Almighty, has made me afraid. He has put darkness all around me. There is thick darkness everywhere.

24 "Why doesn't God open the court and listen to my case? Why must the godly wait for him in vain? 2For a crime wave has come upon us. Landmarks have been moved. Flocks of sheep are stolen. 3Even the donkeys of the poor and fatherless are taken. Poor widows must given the little they have as a pledge to get a loan. 4The needy are kicked aside. They must get out of the way. 5The poor must spend all their time just keeping soul and body together. They are like the wild donkeys in the desert. They are sent into the desert to search for food for their children. 6They eat what they find that grows wild. They must even glean the vineyards of the wicked. 7All night they lie naked in the cold. They sleep without clothing or blankets. 8They are wet with the showers of the mountains. And they live in caves because they don't have a home.

9"The wicked take fatherless children from their mother's breasts. They take a poor man's baby as a pledge for a loan of money or grain. 10That is why they must go about naked and without clothing. They are forced to carry food while they are starving. 11They are forced to press out the olive oil without tasting it. They have to tread out the grape juice as they suffer from thirst. 12The bones of the dying cry from the city. The wounded cry for help. Yet God does not hear their moaning.

13"The wicked rebel against the light. They do not know what is right and good. 14-15They are murderers who rise in the early dawn to kill the poor and needy. At night they steal and sleep with other mens' wives. They wait for the dark of evening. They say, 'This is when no one will see me.' They put masks on their faces so no one will know them. 16They break into houses at night. They sleep in the daytime. They do not know the light. 17The black night is like morning to them. They make friends with the terrors of the darkness.

¹⁸"But how quickly they disappear from the face of the earth. Everything they own is cursed. They leave nothing for their children. ¹⁹Death consumes sinners as drought and heat consume snow. ²⁰Even the sinner's own mother shall forget him. Worms shall feed sweetly on him. No one will remember him any more. For wicked men are broken like a tree in the storm. ²¹For they are unfair toward the childless who have no sons to protect them. They will not help the needy widows.

²²⁻²³"Yet sometimes it seems as though God helps the rich by his power. It seems like he gives them life when anyone else would die. God gives them strength and helps them in many ways. ²⁴But though they are great now, they shall be gone like all others. In a moment they will be cut off like heads of grain. ²⁵Can anyone claim that it happens any other way? Who can prove me a liar and claim that I am wrong?"

Bildad Says
No One Can Stand Before God

25 Then Bildad answered: ²"God is powerful and dreadful. He keeps the peace in heaven. ³Who is able to count his many angels? And his light shines down on all the earth. ⁴How can mere man stand before God and claim to be righteous? Who in all the earth can brag that he is clean? ⁵God is so great that even the moon and stars are less than nothing compared to him. ⁶How much less is man, who is but a worm in his sight?"

Job Does Not Agree
with His Friends

26 Then Job answered: ²"What wonderful helpers you all are! And how you have helped me in my great need! ³How you have helped me see the light! What wise things you have said! ⁴How did you ever think of all these wise words?

⁵⁻⁶"The dead stand naked. They shake before God in the place where they go. ⁷God stretches out heaven over empty space. He hangs the earth upon nothing.

Olive Oil
JOB 24:11

If someone said "oil" you would probably think first of the motor oil Dad or Mom puts into the car. Oil in Bible times was not that kind of oil at all. The oil we use in a car is pumped up from the ground. Sometimes gasoline is made from it. But most Bible-time oil was made from olives. People picked the olives just before they were ripe and squeezed the olive oil from them. Sometimes they did this by stamping on the olives with their feet. Sometimes they put the olives into a stone press like the one in the picture and squeezed the oil out. Each year a good olive tree would grow enough olives to make 10-15 gallons of olive oil. This oil was often as important in Bible times as gold and silver. Olive oil was burned in lamps. It was also used in cooking and making bread. When a king was anointed, a high priest poured olive oil on his head. It was used in medicines. And it was important in some offerings in the Tabernacle and Temple. Having no oil was almost as bad as having no water.

8He wraps the rain in his thick clouds. And the clouds are not split by the weight. 9He blankets his throne with his clouds. 10He sets a border for the ocean. Yes, he even sets a border for the day and the night. 11The pillars of heaven shake before him. 12And by his power the sea grows calm. He is skilled at crushing its pride! 13The heavens are made beautiful by his Spirit. He stabs the swiftly gliding snake.

14"These are some of the small things he does. These are just a whisper of his power. Who then can stand against his thunder?"

Job Defends Himself

27 Then Job gave a final defense:

2"I promise this before the living God. He is the one who has taken away my rights. He is the Almighty God who has made my soul bitter. 3I make this promise for as long as I live. I promise this as long as I have breath from God. 4My lips shall speak no evil. My tongue shall speak no lies. 5I will never, never agree that you are right. Until I die I will defend my innocence. 6I am *not* a sinner. I repeat it again and again. My heart is clean and does not trouble me. 7Those who say otherwise are my enemies. They are bad men.

8"But what hope has the godless when God cuts him off and takes away his life? 9Will God listen to his cry when trouble comes upon him? 10For he does not delight himself in the Almighty. He does not listen to God except in times of trouble.

11"I will teach you about God. 12But really, I don't need to. For you yourselves know as much about him as I do. Yet you are saying all these useless things to me.

13"This is what is waiting for the wicked from the hand of God. 14If he has many children, they will die in war or starve to death. 15Those who live shall be brought down to the grave by disease. And there will be no one to cry for them. They will not even have their wives.

16"The evil man may collect money like dust. He may have closets full of clothing. 17Yes, he may order them from his own tailor. But the innocent shall wear that clothing. And the righteous shall divide his silver among them. 18Every house built by the wicked is as weak as a spider web. They are as full of cracks as a leafy shelter!

19"He goes to bed rich but wakes up to find all his riches gone. 20Terror comes after him. He is blown away in the storms of the night. 21The east wind carries him away and he is gone. It sweeps him out of his place. 22For God shall hurl the wind at him with no mercy. He longs to run from its power. 23It claps its hands to make fun of him. It whistles at him as he runs from his place.

28 "Men know how to mine silver and make gold pure. 2They know how to dig iron from the earth. They know how to melt copper from stone. 3-4Men know how to put light into darkness. They know how to sink a mine shaft into the earth. They know how to search the earth and explore its deep secrets. Into the black rock, men go down on ropes. They are shadowed by death. And they swing back and forth.

5"Men know how to grow food on the surface of the earth. But underneath the earth is fire.

6"They know how to find sapphires and gold dust. 7They find treasures that no bird of prey can see, no eagle's eye observe. 8For they are deep within the mines. No wild animal has ever walked upon those treasures. No lion has set his paw there. 9Men know how to tear apart flinty rocks. They know how to turn the roots of mountains. 10They drill tunnels in the rocks and lay bare precious stones. 11They dam up streams of water and pan the gold.

12"Men can do all these things. But they don't know where to find wisdom and understanding. 13They don't know how to get it. In fact, it is not to be found among the living.

14"'It's not here,' the oceans say. The seas reply, 'Nor is it here.'

15"It cannot be bought for gold or silver. 16It cannot be bought for all the gold of Ophir. It cannot be bought for precious onyx stones or sapphires. 17Wisdom is far better than gold and glass. It cannot be bought for jewels mounted in fine gold. ¹⁸Coral or crystal is worthless in trying to get it. Its price is far above rubies. ¹⁹Topaz from Ethiopia cannot buy it, nor even the purest gold.

²⁰"Then where can we get it? Where can it be found? ²¹For it is hid from the eyes of all mankind. Even the sharp-eyed birds in the sky cannot see it.

²²"But Death speaks of knowing something about it! ²³⁻²⁴And God surely knows where it is to be found. For he looks throughout the whole earth, under all the heavens. ²⁵He makes the winds blow and sets the borders of the oceans. ²⁶He makes the laws of the rain and a path for the lightning. ²⁷He knows where wisdom is and tells all who will listen. He made it and tested it over and over. ²⁸And this is what he says to all mankind: 'Look, to fear the Lord is true wisdom. To stop doing evil is real understanding.'"

Job Continues to Talk

29 Job continued to speak: ²"Oh, for the years gone by when God took care of me. ³Oh, for the times when he lighted the way before me. Then I walked safely through the darkness. ⁴Yes, I wish for my early years. Then the friendship of God was felt in my home. ⁵The Almighty was still with me and my children were around me. ⁶Then all my work succeeded. Even the rock poured out streams of olive oil to me!

⁷"Those were the days when I went out to the city gate. I took my place among the honored elders. ⁸The young saw me and stepped aside. Even the old stood up in respect at my coming. ⁹The princes stood in silence and laid their hands on their mouths. ¹⁰The highest officials of the city stood and were quiet. ¹¹All took joy in what I said. All who saw me spoke well of me.

¹²"For I, as an honest judge, helped the poor in their need. I helped the children who had no fathers to help them. ¹³I helped those who were ready to die, and they blessed me. And I caused the widows' hearts to sing for joy. ¹⁴All I did was fair and honest, for righteousness was my clothing! ¹⁵I served as eyes

for the blind and feet for the lame. ¹⁶I was as a father to the poor. I saw to it that even strangers were given a fair trial. ¹⁷I knocked out the fangs of men who were godless and cruel. I made them drop their victims.

¹⁸"I thought, 'Surely I shall die quietly in my nest after a long, good life.' ¹⁹For everything I did prospered. The dew lay all night on my fields and watered them. ²⁰Fresh honors were given me all the time. And my skills were always kept fresh and new. ²¹Everyone listened to me and valued my advice. They were silent until I spoke. ²²And after I spoke, they spoke no more. For my counsel gave them what they needed. ²³They wished for me to speak as those in drought-time wish for rain. They waited with open mouths. ²⁴When they were down-hearted, I smiled. That made them feel better and lightened their spirits. ²⁵I told them what they should do. I corrected them as their chief, or as a king teaches his army. And I comforted those who mourned.

30 "But now those younger than I laugh at me. These are young men whose fathers are less than my dogs. ²Their backs are no longer strong. So their strength is useless to me. ³They are thin with the lack of good food. They have been thrown out into deserts and the wastelands. ⁴They eat roots and leaves. ⁵They have been sent to live far from other people. Men shouted after them as after thieves. ⁶So now they live in deep and dry riverbeds. They live in caves and among the rocks. ⁷They sound like animals among the bushes. They huddle together for shelter under the nettles. ⁸These sons of theirs have also turned out to be fools. Yes, they are children of no name. They are thrown out from where most people live.

⁹"Now they make fun of me with songs! I am a joke among them! ¹⁰They look down on me and won't come near me. They don't even mind spitting in my face. ¹¹For God has put my life in trouble. These young men have humbled me. And now they do and say what they want in front of me. ¹²They trip me and lay traps in my path. ¹³They block

my road and do everything they can to make my trouble worse. They know very well that I have no one to help me. ¹⁴They come at me from all directions. They rush upon me when I am down.

¹⁵"I live in terror now. They show me no respect. My success is gone like a cloud before a strong wind. ¹⁶My heart is broken. Sadness takes up my days. ¹⁷My weary nights are filled with pain. It is as though something were chewing at my bones. ¹⁸All night long I toss and turn. My clothing binds around me. ¹⁹God has thrown me into the mud. I have become as dust and ashes.

²⁰"I cry to you, O God. But you don't answer me. I stand before you and you don't bother to look. ²¹You have become cruel toward me. You torture me with great power and effect. ²²You throw me into the whirlwind. You dissolve me in the storm. ²³And I know that your purpose for me is death. ²⁴Surely no one hurts a broken man. He cries for help in his deep trouble.

²⁵"And did I not weep for those in trouble? Wasn't I deeply sorry for the needy? ²⁶I therefore looked for good to come. But evil came instead. I waited for the light. But darkness came. ²⁷My heart is troubled and restless. Waves of pain have come upon me. ²⁸⁻²⁹I am black, but not from sunburn. I stand up and cry to the assembly for help. But I might as well save my breath. For I am thought to be a brother to jackals and a friend to ostriches. ³⁰My skin is black and peeling. My bones burn with fever. ³¹The voice of joy and gladness has turned to crying.

31 "I made a covenant with my eyes not to look with lust upon a girl. ²⁻³I know full well that Almighty God above sends trouble on those who do. ⁴He sees everything I do and every step I take.

⁵"Perhaps I have lied and deceived others. ⁶But God knows that I am innocent. ⁷⁻⁸Or maybe I have stepped off God's pathway. Perhaps my heart has lusted for what my eyes have seen. Or maybe I am guilty of some other sin. If this is so, then let someone else harvest the crops I have planted. Let all that I have planted be dug up.

⁹"Or perhaps I have wanted another man's wife. ¹⁰If so, then may I die. And may my wife be in another man's home. May someone else become her husband. ¹¹For lust is a shameful sin. It is a crime that should be punished. ¹²It is a great fire that destroys to hell. It would dig up all I have planted.

¹³"I might have been unfair to my servants. ¹⁴But if so, how could I face God? What could I say when he asked me about it? ¹⁵For God made me and made my servant too. He created us both.

¹⁶"I might have hurt the poor, or caused widows to cry. ¹⁷Or perhaps I did not give food to hungry orphans. ¹⁸But we have always cared for orphans in our home. We treated them as our own children. ¹⁹⁻²⁰Or I might have seen someone freezing. Perhaps I did not give him clothing or fleece from my sheep to keep him warm. ²¹Or maybe I was unfair to an orphan because I thought I could get away with it. ²²If I have done any of these things, then let my arm be torn from its socket! Let my shoulder be pulled out of place! ²³Rather that than face the judgment sent by God. I dread that more than anything else. For if the power of God is against me, what hope is there?

²⁴"I might have put my trust in money. ²⁵Perhaps my being happy depends on being rich. ²⁶Or I might have looked at the sun shining in the skies. I might have looked at the moon walking down her silver pathway. ²⁷And maybe my heart has been secretly tempted. Maybe I have worshiped them by kissing my hand to them. ²⁸This, too, must be punished by the judges. For if I had done such things, I would have been unfaithful to the God of heaven.

²⁹"Perhaps I have felt joy when an enemy was hurt. ³⁰But really, I have never cursed anyone or asked for revenge. ³¹Maybe one of my servants has gone hungry. ³²But I have never turned away even a stranger! I have opened my doors to all. ³³Or perhaps, like Adam, I have tried to hide my sins. ³⁴Maybe I was afraid of the crowd and its hate. So perhaps I did not admit my sin and did not

go outside. ³⁵Oh, that there were someone who would listen to me. I wish someone would try to see my side of this argument. Look, I will sign my name to defend myself. Now let the Almighty show me that I am wrong. Let *him* agree to the judgments made against me by my enemies. ³⁶I would treasure it like a crown.

³⁷Then I would tell him just what I have done and why. I would give my case as a man he listens to.

³⁸⁻³⁹"My land might accuse me because I stole the fruit it grows. Or perhaps I have murdered its owners to get their land for myself. ⁴⁰If so, then let thistles grow on that land instead of wheat. Let weeds grow instead of barley."

Job's words are ended.

Elihu Becomes Angry

32 The three men would not speak to Job any more. This was because he kept saying he had done nothing wrong.

²Then Elihu became angry because Job would not admit he had sinned. Job would not admit that God had a good reason for punishing him. Elihu was the son of Barachel, the Buzite. He was of the Clan of Ram. ³But he was also angry with Job's three friends. They had not been able to answer what Job had said. But they still judged him. ⁴Elihu had waited until now to speak because the others were older than he.

⁵But when he saw that they had no further reply, he spoke out in anger. ⁶He said, "I am young and you are old. So I held back and did not dare to tell you what I think. ⁷For those who are older are said to be wiser. ⁸⁻⁹But it is not mere age that makes men wise. Rather, it is the spirit in a man. It is the breath of the Almighty that makes him wise. ¹⁰So listen to me awhile and let me tell you what I think.

¹¹⁻¹²"I have waited a long time. I have listened to what all of you had to say. But not one of you has made Job admit that he is a sinner. And none of you have proved that he is. ¹³And don't tell me, 'Only God can make the sinner admit his sin.' ¹⁴If Job had been talking to me,

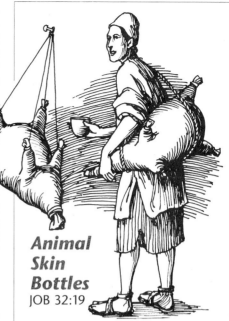

Animal Skin Bottles
JOB 32:19

How many bottles do you think you have in your house? Try counting them. What is in each of them? Most Bible-time bottles were not like the ones you just counted. Your bottles are made of glass or plastic. They hold many different kinds of things. Most Bible-time bottles were animal skins, sewed around the edges to leave one opening. The animal skin is called leather. Most of these leather bottles came from goats. People filled them with water, milk, or wine. Sometimes the leather bottle was even used as a butter churn. The cream was shaken in it until it became butter. As these leather bottles were used, they stretched. When they stretched too much, they broke. Leather bottles were often carried on a person's back. They did not break as easily as a clay pot or jar. Glass was made in Bible times, but it cost too much for the average person. Tiny glass flasks were used only for expensive perfume. How would you like to drink a whole "bottle" of milk? You'd be quite full, wouldn't you?

I would not answer with that kind of logic!

¹⁵"You sit there confused. You have nothing more to say. ¹⁶Shall I then still wait when you are silent? ¹⁷No, I will give my answer too. ¹⁸For I am full of words. And the spirit inside me pushes me to speak. ¹⁹I am like a wine bottle without a hole! My words are ready to burst out! ²⁰I must speak to find relief. So let me give my answers. ²¹⁻²²Don't ask that I be careful for fear I will put someone down. Don't make me flatter anyone. Let me be honest or God might strike me dead.

33 "Please listen, Job, to what I have to say. ²I have begun to speak. Now let me keep on. ³I will speak the truth with an honest heart. ⁴For the Spirit of God has made me. And the breath of the Almighty gives me life. ⁵Don't wait to answer me if you can.

⁶"Look, I am the one you were wishing for. I am someone to stand between you and God. I will be both his lawyer and yours. ⁷You need not be afraid of me. I am not some famous person to make you afraid. I, too, am made of common clay.

⁸"You have said it in my hearing. Yes, you've said it again and again. ⁹'I am pure. I am innocent. I have not sinned.' ¹⁰You say God is looking very closely to find a single sin. You say he wants to count you as his enemy. ¹¹'He puts my feet in chains,' you say. 'And he watches every move I make.'

¹²"All right, here is my reply. In this very thing, you have sinned by speaking of God that way. For God is greater than man. ¹³Why should you fight against him just because he does not explain what he does?

¹⁴"For God speaks again and again. ¹⁵He speaks in dreams and in visions of the night. He speaks when deep sleep falls on men as they lie on their beds. ¹⁶He opens their ears in times like that. And he gives them wisdom and teaching. ¹⁷⁻¹⁸He helps them to change their minds. He keeps them from pride. He warns them of judgment of sin. And he keeps them from falling into some trap. ¹⁹Or God might send sickness and pain. He might do this even though no bone is broken. ²⁰He might do this so that a man loses all taste for food. He might make a man not want the sweetest dessert. ²¹He becomes thin, mere skin and bones. ²²And he comes near to death.

²³⁻²⁴"But a messenger from heaven might come to speak to him as a friend. He might come to show him what is right. And then God might pity him. And he might say, 'Set him free. Do not make him die. For I have found a way to pay for his life.' ²⁵Then his body will become as healthy as a child's. It will become firm and strong again. ²⁶And when he prays to God, God will hear and answer. He will take him in with joy. And he will send him back to his work. ²⁷And he will declare to his friends, 'I sinned. But God let me go. ²⁸He did not let me die. I will go on living in the realm of light.'

²⁹"Yes, God often does these things for man. ³⁰He brings back his soul from the pit. He does this so that he may live. ³¹Mark this well, O Job. Listen to me, and let me say more. ³²But if you have anything to say at this point, go ahead. I want to hear it. For I want to prove you are innocent. ³³But if not, then listen to me. Keep silence and I will teach you wisdom!"

Elihu Has Part of the Answer

34 Then Elihu said:

²"Listen to me, you wise men. ³We can choose the sounds we want to listen to. We can choose the taste we want in food. ⁴And we should choose to follow what is right. But first of all we must decide what is good. ⁵For Job has said, 'I am innocent. But God says I'm not. ⁶I am called a liar, even though I am innocent. I am punished, even though I have not sinned.'

⁷⁻⁸"Who else is as proud as Job? He must have spent much time with evil men. ⁹For he said, 'Why waste time trying to please God?'

¹⁰"Listen to me, you with wisdom. Surely everyone knows that *God doesn't sin!* ¹¹Rather, he punishes the sinners. ¹²There is no truer statement than this:

God is never wicked or unfair. [13]He alone has power over the earth. He gives justice to the world. [14]God might choose to take away his Spirit. [15]But if he did, all life would die. And mankind would turn again to dust.

[16]"Listen now and try to understand. [17]Could God rule if he hated justice? Are you going to condemn the Almighty Judge? [18]Are you going to condemn this God? He is the one who says to kings and nobles, 'You are wicked and unfair!' [19]For he doesn't care how great a man may be. He doesn't listen any more to the rich than to the poor. He made them all. [20]In a moment they die. At midnight great and small shall suddenly pass away. They might be taken by no human hand.

[21]"For God watches the deeds of all mankind. He sees them all. [22]No darkness is thick enough to hide evil men from his eyes. [23]So there is no need to wait for some great crime before a man is called before God in judgment. [24]Without making a big deal over it, God breaks the greatest of men. And he puts others in their places. [25]He watches what they do. And in a single night he overturns them and destroys them. [26]Or he openly strikes them down as wicked men. [27]For they turned aside from following him. [28]They caused the cry of the poor to come to the ears of God. Yes, he hears the cries of those being hurt. [29-30]Yet when he chooses not to speak, who can speak against him? Again, he may stop a bad man from ruling. And thus he might save a nation from ruin. But he can destroy a whole nation just as easily.

[31]"Why don't people say to their God, 'We have sinned. But now we will stop'? [32]Or, 'We know not what evil we have done. Only tell us, and we will stop at once'?

[33]"Must God fit his justice to your demands? Must he change the order of the world to make you happy? The answer must be clear even to you! [34-35]Anyone even half-bright will agree with me. They will see that you, Job, are speaking like a fool. [36]You should be punished greatly for the wicked way you have talked about God. [37]For now you have added rebellion and pride to your other sins."

35 Then Elihu said:
[2-3]"Do you think it is right for you to claim, 'I haven't sinned. But I'm no better off before God than if I had'?

[4]"I will answer you and all your friends, too. [5]Look up there into the sky, high above you. [6]If you sin, does that shake the heavens? Does it knock God from his throne? You might even sin again and again. But what effect will it have upon him? [7]Or if you are good, is this some great gift to him? [8]Your sins may hurt another man. Or perhaps your good deeds may help him. [9-10]The oppressed may cry under their wrongs. They might groan under the power of the rich. But none of them cry to God. None ask, 'Where is God my Maker who gives songs in the night? [11]Where is God who makes us a little wiser than the animals and birds?'

[12]"But someone might cry out this question to him. And if he does, God never answers by instant punishment of the tyrants. [13]But it is false to say he doesn't hear those cries. [14-15]And it is even more false to say that he doesn't see what is going on. He *does* bring about justice at last if you will only wait. But do you cry out against him because he does not answer right away? [16]Job, you have spoken like a fool."

Elihu Continues to Defend God

36 Then Elihu said:
[2]"Let me go on. I will show you the truth of what I am saying. For I have not finished defending God! [3]I get my knowledge from far away. I will defend the goodness of my Maker. [4]I am telling you the honest truth. For I am a man of well-rounded knowledge.

[5]"God is almighty and yet does not hate anyone! And he is perfect in his understanding. [6]He does not reward the wicked with his blessings. But he gives them their full share of punishment. [7]He does not forget the good men. But he honors them by putting them upon kingly thrones. [8]Troubles might come upon them. They might become slaves or they might suffer. [9]But then he takes

the trouble to tell them the reason. He tells them what they have done wrong. Or he shows them how they have acted proudly. ¹⁰He helps them hear his teachings to turn away from their sin.

¹¹"Then they might listen and obey him. And if they do, they will be given success throughout their lives. ¹²But if they won't listen to him, they shall die in battle. Or they shall die because they have no good sense. ¹³But the godless harvest his anger. They do not even go back to him when he punishes them. ¹⁴They die young after lives of sin with prostitutes in the idol shrines. ¹⁵God saves people by giving them trouble! This makes them listen to him!

We can never know all about God

God is so great that we cannot begin to know all about him.

Job 36:26

---

¹⁶"How he wanted to pull you away from danger into a wide and pleasant valley! How he wanted to give you success there! ¹⁷But now you are given the punishment evil people should have. ¹⁸Watch out! Don't let your anger at others lead you into laughing at God! Don't let your suffering make you bitter toward the only one who can save you. ¹⁹Do you think that if you shout loudly at God, he will be ashamed and repent? Will this put an end to your troubles?

?????????????????????????????????
Who fills his hands with lightning bolts?

(Read Job 36:30-33 for the answer.)

?????????????????????????????????

²⁰"Do not wish for the dark of night. Do not wish for a chance to sin. ²¹Turn back from evil. For God sent this suffering to stop you from getting into a life of evil.

²²"Look, God is all-powerful. Who is a teacher like him? ²³Who can say that what he does is bad or wrong? ²⁴Instead, praise him for the mighty works he is known for. ²⁵Everyone has seen these things from a distance.

²⁶"God is so great that we cannot begin to know all about him. The number of his years cannot be found out. ²⁷He draws up the water vapor and then makes it into rain. ²⁸And the skies pour it down as rain. ²⁹Can anyone really understand the spreading of the clouds? Can anyone understand the thunders within? ³⁰See how he spreads the lightning around him. See how he blankets the tops of the mountains. ³¹By his great powers in nature he punishes or blesses the people. He can give them more food than they need. ³²He fills his hands with lightning bolts. He throws each at its target. ³³We feel his presence in the thunder. Even the cattle know when a storm is coming.

37 "My heart shakes at this. ²Listen, listen to the thunder of his voice. ³It rolls across the heavens, and his lightning flashes out in every direction. ⁴After that comes the roaring of the thunder. This is the great voice of his majesty. ⁵His voice is great in the thunder. We cannot know the greatness of his power. ⁶For he makes snow, showers, and storms to fall upon the earth. ⁷Man's work stops at such times so that all men may see his power. ⁸The wild animals hide in the rocks or in their dens.

⁹"From the south comes the rain. From the north comes the cold. ¹⁰God blows upon the rivers, and even the widest rapids freeze. ¹¹He loads the clouds with water. And they send forth his lightning. ¹²The lightning bolts are sent by his hand. They do what he commands throughout the earth. ¹³He sends the storms as punishment. Or he sends his kindness to give comfort.

¹⁴"Listen, O Job! Stop and think about the great works of God. ¹⁵Do you know how God controls all nature? Do you know how he causes the lightning to flash out of the clouds? ¹⁶⁻¹⁷Do you understand how he hangs the clouds with such skill? Do you know why you become hot when the south wind blows? And do you know why everything becomes still? ¹⁸Can you spread out the great skies as he does?

19-20"You who think you know so much! Teach the rest of us how we should go before God. For we are too stupid to know! With your wisdom, would we then dare to go before him? Well, does a man wish to be eaten alive? 21For we cannot look at the sun. It is too bright when the winds have cleared away the clouds. 22And neither can we gaze at the terrible brightness of God breaking forth from heaven. He is clothed in the brightest of light. 23We cannot even think of the power of the Almighty. Yet he is so fair and merciful that he does not destroy us. 24No wonder men everywhere fear him! For he does not respect the world's wisest men!"

The Lord Speaks to Job

38 Then the Lord answered Job from the whirlwind:

2"Why are you making my purpose unclear by saying things that are not true? 3Now get ready to fight. For I am going to demand some answers from you. And you must reply.

4"Where were you when I laid the foundation for the earth? Tell me, if you know so much! 5Do you know who marked off its size? Do you know who surveyed it? 6-7What supports its foundations? Who laid its cornerstone as the morning stars sang together? Who did this as all the angels shouted for joy?

8-9"Who made the borders of the seas when they gushed from the depths? Who clothed them with clouds and thick darkness? 10Who stopped them by giving them shores? 11Who said, 'You may come here, but no farther! This is where your proud waves shall stop!'?

12"Have you ever once commanded the morning to come? Have you caused the dawn to rise in the east? 13Have you ever told the daylight to spread to the ends of the earth? Have you ever told it to end the wickedness of night? 14Have you ever dressed the dawn in red? 15Have you troubled the hideouts of wicked men? Have you stopped the arm raised to strike?

16"Have you found the springs from which the seas come? Have you walked in the sources of their depths? 17-18Do you know where the gates of Death are? Do you know the ends of the earth? Tell me about it if you know! 19Where does the light come from? And how do you get there? Or tell me about the darkness. Where does it come from? 20Can you find its borders, or go to its source? 21But of course you know all this! For you were born before it was all created! And you know so very much!

22-23"Have you seen the treasuries of the snow? Or have you seen where hail is made and stored? I have stored it for the time when I will need it in war. 24How do you get to the place where light comes from? Where is the home of the east wind? 25-27Who dug the valleys for the torrents of rain? Who laid out the path for the lightning? Who caused the rain to fall upon the dry deserts? Who gives the dry ground water so that tender grass springs up?

28"Has the rain a father? Where does dew come from? 29Who is the mother of the ice and frost? 30For the water changes and turns to ice as hard as rock.

31"Can you hold back the stars? Can you stop Orion or Pleiades? 32Can you make the seasons come at the right time? Can you guide the constellation of the Bear with her stars across the heavens? 33Do you know the laws of the universe? Do you know how the heavens affect the earth? 34Can you shout to the clouds and make it rain? 35Can you make lightning strike? Can you cause it to strike where you want it to?

36"Who gave the heart wisdom? Who gave knowledge to the mind? 37-38Who is wise enough to count all the clouds? Who can let the rain fall when everything is dusty and dry? 39-40Can you stalk prey like a lioness? Can you feed the young lions as they lie in their dens? Can you feed them as they lie in wait in the jungle? 41Who provides for the ravens when their young cry out to God? Who gives them food as they struggle up from their nest in hunger?

39 "Do you know how mountain goats give birth? Have you ever seen the deer give birth to her fawn? 2-3Do you count the months until they give birth? Do you tell them when to stop carrying their burden? ⁴Their young grow up in the open field. Then they leave their parents and come back to them no more.

⁵"Who makes the wild donkeys wild? ⁶I have put them in the wilderness. I have given them salt plains to live in. ⁷For they hate the noise of the city. They want no drivers shouting at them! ⁸The mountain ranges are their pasture. There they look for every blade of grass.

⁹"Will the wild ox be your happy servant? Will he stay beside your feeding crib? ¹⁰Can you use a wild ox to plow with? Will he pull the harrow for you? ¹¹Because he is so strong, will you trust him? Will you let him decide where to work? ¹²Can you send him out to bring in the grain?

¹³"The ostrich flaps her wings but has no true motherly love. ¹⁴She lays her eggs on top of the earth, to warm them in the dust. ¹⁵She forgets that someone may step on them and crush them. She forgets that the wild animals might destroy them. ¹⁶She forgets her young as though they weren't her own. She is not sad when they die. ¹⁷For God has not given her wisdom. ¹⁸But when she jumps up to run, she passes the fastest horse with its rider.

¹⁹"Have you given the horse strength? Have you clothed his neck with a flying mane? ²⁰Have you made him able to jump forward like a locust? His majestic snorting is something to hear! ²¹⁻²³He paws the earth and rejoices in his strength. When he goes to war, he is not afraid. He does not run away, though the arrows rattle against him. He does not flee, though the flashing spear and javelin fly toward him. ²⁴Fiercely he paws the ground. And he rushes forward into battle when the trumpet blows. ²⁵At the sound of the horn he shouts, 'Aha!' He smells the battle when far away. He has joy in the shouts of battle and the roar of the captain's commands.

²⁶"Do you know how a hawk flies? Do you know how she spreads her wings to the south? ²⁷Is it at your command that the eagle rises high upon the cliffs to make her nest? ²⁸She lives upon the cliffs, making her home in her mountain fortress. ²⁹From there she sees her prey while it is far away. ³⁰Her young gulp down blood. For she goes where the dead are."

40 The Lord went on: ²"Do you still want to argue with the Almighty? Or will you give in? Do you have the answers to all these questions?"

Job Replies to God

³Then Job replied to God:

⁴"I am nothing. How could I ever find the answers? I lay my hand upon my mouth in silence. ⁵I have said too much already."

The Lord Speaks from the Whirlwind

⁶Then the Lord spoke to Job again from the whirlwind:

⁷"Stand up like a man and brace yourself for battle. Let me ask you a question, and give me the answer. ⁸Are you going to reject my justice and judge me? Then do you want me to say you are right? ⁹Are you as strong as God? Can you shout as loudly as he? ¹⁰All right then, put on your robes of state. Put on your honor and greatness. ¹¹Let your anger out. Let it overflow against the proud. ¹²Make the proud humble by just looking at them. Walk over the wicked where they stand. ¹³Knock them into the dust, stone-faced in death. ¹⁴If you can do that, then I will agree with you. I will agree that your own strength can save you.

¹⁵"Take a look at the hippopotamus! I made him, too, just as I made you! He eats grass like an ox. ¹⁶See his powerful body and the muscles of his belly. ¹⁷His tail is as straight as a cedar. The muscles of his thighs are tightly knit together. ¹⁸His back is as straight as a tube of brass. His ribs are like iron bars. ¹⁹How fierce he is among all of God's creation. So let whoever hopes to master him bring a sharp sword! ²⁰The mountains offer their best food to him. These are the hills where the wild animals play. ²¹He lies down under the lotus plants. He is hidden by the reeds. ²²He is covered by their

shade among the willows there beside the stream. ²³He is not troubled by raging rivers. He is not afraid when the swelling Jordan rushes down on him. ²⁴No one can catch him off guard. No one can put a ring in his nose and lead him away.

41 "Can you catch a crocodile with a hook and line? Can you put a rope around his tongue? ²Can you tie him with a rope through the nose? Can you stab his jaw with a spike? ³Will he beg you to stop? Will he try to trick you into letting him go? ⁴Will he agree to let you make him your slave for life? ⁵Can you make a pet of him like a bird? Can you give him to your little girls to play with? ⁶Do fishermen sell him at the market? ⁷Will his hide be hurt by darts, or his head with a spear?

⁸"You might lay your hands upon him. But you will long remember the battle that follows! And you will never try it again! ⁹No, it's useless to try to catch him. It is scary even to think about it! ¹⁰No one dares to stir *him* up, let alone try to catch him. And if no one can stand before *him,* who can stand before *me?* ¹¹I owe no one anything. Everything under the heavens is mine.

¹²"I should also tell you about the great strength in his legs and body. ¹³Who can cut his hide? Who dares come within reach of his jaws? ¹⁴For his teeth are terrible. ¹⁵⁻¹⁷His scales are his pride. They make a tight seal so no air can get between them. And nothing can cut through them.

¹⁸"When he sneezes, the sunlight sparkles. It is like lightning across the spray. His eyes glow like sparks. ¹⁹Fire leaps from his mouth. ²⁰Smoke flows from his nostrils. It is like steam from a boiling pot that is fired by dry rushes. ²¹Yes, his breath would set coals on fire. Flames leap from his mouth.

²²"The great strength in his neck brings terror wherever he goes. ²³His flesh is hard and firm, not soft and fat. ²⁴His heart is hard as rock, just like a millstone. ²⁵When he stands up, the strongest are afraid. Terror grips them. ²⁶No sword can stop him. No spear or dart or pointed shaft can hurt him. ²⁷⁻²⁸Iron is nothing but straw to him. And brass is like rotten wood. Arrows cannot make him run. Slingstones are as useless as straw. ²⁹Clubs do no good. And he laughs at the javelins thrown at him. ³⁰His belly is covered with scales as sharp as pottery shards. They tear up the ground as he drags through the mud.

³¹⁻³²"He makes the water boil when he moves. He stirs up the depths. He leaves shining waves of foam behind him. One would think the sea was made of frost! ³³There is nothing else so fearless anywhere on earth. ³⁴Of all the beasts, he is the proudest. He is the king of all that he sees."

God Gives Job Good Gifts

Job was a rich man. God gave him all that he owned. But then he lost everything. He could praise God for giving him things or curse God for taking things away. Job praised God. What would God do then?

42 Then Job replied to God:
²"I know that you can do anything. No one can stop any of your plans. ³You asked who it was who questioned your plans so foolishly. It is I. I was talking about things I knew nothing about. I really did not understand. These are things far too great for me to know.

⁴"You said, 'Listen and I will speak! Let me put the questions to you! See if you can answer them!'

⁵"But now I say, 'I had heard about

you before. But now I have seen you. 6And I detest myself and repent in dust and ashes.'"

7The Lord had finished speaking with Job. So he said to Eliphaz:

"I am angry with you and with your two friends. For you have not been right in what you have said about me, as my servant Job was. 8Now take seven young bulls and seven rams. Go to my servant Job and offer a burnt offering for yourselves. My servant Job will pray for you. And I will hear his prayer for you. I won't destroy you as I should because of your sin. For you failed to speak truly about my servant Job."

9So Eliphaz, Bildad, and Zophar did as the Lord told them. And the Lord heard Job's prayer for them. 10When Job had prayed for his friends, the Lord gave him back his riches and joy! In fact, the Lord gave him twice as much as before! 11Then all of his brothers, sisters, and friends came. They feasted with him in his home. They comforted him for all his sorrow. They comforted him because of all the trials the Lord had given him. And each of them brought him a gift of money and a gold ring.

12So the Lord blessed Job at the end of his life more than at the beginning. For now he had 14,000 sheep, 6,000 camels, 1,000 teams of oxen, and 1,000 female donkeys.

13-14God also gave him seven more sons and three more daughters.

The names of his daughters were Jemima, Kezia, and Keren.

15And in all the land there were no other girls as pretty as Job's daughters. And their father put them into his will along with their brothers.

16Job lived 140 years after that. He lived to see his grandchildren and great-grandchildren too. 17Then at last he died, an old, old man. He had lived a long, good life.

- *Remember:* Who said he was sorry because he talked about things he didn't understand? (42:1-6) God was angry at three men. Who were they? Why was he angry at them? (42:9) What did they do so that God would forgive them? (42:8-10) What good things happened to Job after that? (42:11-17) When Job lost everything was it better to praise God or curse God? Why? Would you have done this?

- *Discover:* Don't get angry at God for what you don't have. Praise God for what you do have.

- *Apply:* Do you see others who have more than you? Do you ever complain to God about this? Don't! Thank God for what you have. Will he give you more? Maybe. Maybe not. But you should still be grateful for what you have, so thank him.

- *What's next?* A man is forgiven when a burning coal touches his lips. Read Isaiah 6. ■

PSALMS

Do you have hymnals in your church? These are books with songs of praises to God. Do you have chorus books in your Sunday school room? These are also books with songs of praises to God. The Book of Psalms is another book of songs that praise God. King David and his friends wrote these songs. They were sung in the Temple in Jerusalem. They were sung in the synagogues throughout the ancient world. They were sung for many years after King David's time. You probably have memorized some favorite psalms, such as Psalm 23. You'll want to memorize other favorite verses marked in this Bible. Some psalms tell about a Savior who will come. They were written about a thousand years before Jesus. How did David and his friends know about Jesus? God told them. As you read the Book of Psalms, imagine young David playing his harp. Imagine him singing psalms to his sheep. Imagine also God's people singing these psalms at the great Temple in Jerusalem. You may want to make up your own songs with some psalms. Try it!

Pleasing God

1 Oh, the joys of those who do not listen to the advice of evil people!
They do not hang around with sinners.
They do not laugh at the things of God.
²But they take joy in doing all God wants them to.
They think about God's laws day and night.
They think about ways to follow him more closely.
³They are like trees along a river.
They have sweet fruit each season without fail.
Their leaves never get dry and fall off.
All that they do succeeds.
⁴But for sinners, what a different story! They blow away like chaff before the wind.
⁵They are not safe on Judgment Day.
They shall not stand among the godly.
⁶For the Lord watches over godly men.
But godless people will be destroyed.

Greater than Kings

2 The nations are foolish to be angry
at the Lord!
How strange that men should try to
trick God with their plans!
²For the kings of the earth get ready to
fight.
The leaders make plans against the
Lord and his King.
³"Come, let us break his chains!" they
say.
"Let us free ourselves from being
God's slaves!"
⁴But God in heaven just laughs!
He laughs at all their weak plans.
⁵And then in fierce anger he warns
them.
He fills them with fear.

Listen to God, not evil people

*Oh, the joys of those who
do not listen to the advice of
evil people.They think about
God's laws day and night.*

Psalm 1:1-2

---

⁶For the Lord says, "This is the King of
my choice.
I have put him on the throne in
Jerusalem, my holy city."
⁷His chosen one says, "I will tell you
the plans of God.
For the Lord has said to me, 'You
are my Son.
This is the day you will be crowned
king.
Today I am giving you your glory.
⁸Only ask and I will give you all the
nations of the world.
⁹Rule them with an iron rod.
Smash them like clay pots!'"
¹⁰O kings and rulers of the earth!
Listen while there is time.
¹¹Serve the Lord with great respect.
Be happy, but shake before him.
¹²Fall down before his Son.
Show him respect before you die.
He can quickly become angry.
I am warning you! His anger will
soon begin!
But oh, the joys of those who trust in
him!

The Only Winner

3 O Lord, so many are against me.
So many are trying to hurt me.
I have so many enemies.
²So many say that God will never help
me.

God protects us

Lord, you protect me like a shield.

Psalm 3:3

---

³But Lord, you protect me like a shield.
You are my glory and my only hope.
You alone can lift my head, now
bowed in shame.
⁴I cried out to the Lord.
He heard me from his Temple in
Jerusalem.
⁵Then I lay down and slept in peace
and woke up safely.
For the Lord was watching over me.
⁶And now 10,000 enemies are all
around me.
But still I am not afraid.
⁷I will cry to him, "Arise, O Lord!
Save me, O my God!"
And he will slap them in the face.
He will laugh at them.
He will break off their teeth.
⁸For salvation comes from God.
What joy he gives to all his people!

Who Can Keep Us Safe?

4 O God, answer me when I call to
you. Help me in my trouble and
pain.
Have mercy on me and hear my
prayer.
²The Lord God asks, "People, how
long will you make my glory
into shame?
How long will you worship these
silly idols?
How long will you believe what is
not true?"
³The Lord has chosen for himself
those who are loyal to him.
Therefore he will listen to me.
He will answer when I call to him.
⁴Stand before the Lord in awe.
Do not sin against him.
Lie quietly on your bed thinking
about him.
⁵Put your trust in the Lord.

Give him pleasing sacrifices.
⁶Many say that God will never help us.
  Prove them wrong, O Lord!
  Let the light of your face shine
    down on us.
⁷Yes, you have given me great gladness.
  It is far greater than their joys at
    harvest time.
  I have more joy than they do as
    they look at their rich crops.
⁸I will lie down in peace and sleep.
  For though I am alone, O Lord, you
    will keep me safe.

God Hates Lies

5 O Lord, hear me praying.
  Listen to my cry, O God my King.
For I will never pray to anyone but
    you.
³Each morning I will look to you in
    heaven.
  I will tell you what I need.
  I will pray with all my heart.
⁴You are never happy with what is
    wicked.
  You cannot stand even the smallest
    sin.
⁵Proud sinners will not live when you
    look at them.
  For how you hate their evil deeds!
⁶You will destroy them for their lies.
How you hate all murder and
    deception!
⁷But as for me, I will come into your
    Temple.
  You will protect me by your mercy
    and love.
I will worship you with deep respect.
⁸Lord, lead me as you promised me
    you would.
  Otherwise my enemies will conquer
    me.
Tell me clearly what to do.
  Show me which way to turn.
⁹For they cannot speak one truthful
    word.
  Their hearts are filled to the brim
    with wickedness.
  Their plans stink of sin and death.
  Their tongues are filled with lies.
¹⁰O God, declare them guilty!
  Catch them in their own traps.
Let them fall under the weight of their
    own sins.

For they rebel against you.
¹¹But make everyone rejoice who puts
    his trust in you.
  Keep them shouting for joy because
    you defend them.
Fill all who love you with your
    happiness.
¹²For you bless the godly man, O Lord.
  You protect him with your shield of
    love.

God Hears My Prayers

6 Lord, don't punish me in the heat
  of your anger.
²Pity me, O Lord, for I am weak.
  Heal me, for my body is sick.
³I am upset and troubled.
  My mind is filled with fear and
    gloom.
Oh, help me soon!
⁴Come, O Lord, and make me well.
  In your kindness save me.
⁵For if I die, I cannot give you glory.
  I cannot praise you in front of my
    friends.
⁶I am worn out with pain.
  Every night my pillow is wet with
    tears.
⁷My eyes are growing old and dim
    with sadness.
  For my enemies trouble me.
⁸Go, leave me now, you men of evil
    deeds.
  For the Lord has heard my crying.
⁹He has heard my calls for help.
  He will answer all my prayers.
¹⁰All my enemies shall be suddenly
    without honor.
  They will be full of fear and shame.
  God will turn them back in shame.

The Perfect Judge

7 I am depending on you, O Lord my
  God.
  I look to you to save me from my
    enemies.
²Don't let them jump on me as a lion
    would.
  Don't let them drag me away with
    no one to save me.
³It would be different, Lord, if I were
    doing bad things.
⁴I may have paid back evil for good.

Or maybe I have hurt someone I
    didn't like.
5If so, it would be right for you to let
    my enemies destroy me.
    It would be right for them to crush
      me to the ground.
    It would be good for them to
      trample my life in the dust.

We should tell others about him

*O Lord, I will praise you with all
my heart! I will tell everyone
about the great things you do.*

Psalm 9:1

6But Lord!
    Rise up in anger against my
      enemies!
Wake up!
    Demand justice for me, Lord!
7-8Gather all peoples before you.
    Sit high above them and judge their
      sins.
But show everyone I am not guilty.
    Prove my honor and truth before
      them all.
9End all wickedness, O Lord.
Bless all who truly worship God.
    For you are the righteous God.
You look deep within the hearts of
    men.
    You see all their plans and thoughts.
10God is my shield.
    He will defend me.
He saves those whose hearts and lives
    are true and right.
11God is a judge who is always fair.
    He is angry with the wicked every
      day.
12If they are not sorry, he will sharpen
    his sword and kill them.
    He has bent and strung his bow.
13He has fitted it with deadly arrows.
    They are made from shafts of fire.
14The wicked man makes an evil plan.
    He works out its dark details.
    He brings about his tricks and lies.
15Let him fall into his own trap.
16May the bad things he plans for
    others come upon himself.
    Let him die.
17Oh, how thankful I am to the Lord
    because he is so good.

I will sing praise to the name of the
    Lord who is above all lords.

Why God Made Us

8 O Lord our God, the glory of your
name fills all the earth.
    Your greatness overflows the
      heavens.
2You have taught little children to
    praise you.
    May their example shame and
      silence your enemies!
3I look up into the night skies.
    I see the work of your fingers.
    I see the moon and the stars you
      have made.
4And I cannot understand how you
    can bother with mere man.
    I don't know why you pay any
      attention to him!
5Yet you have made him only a little
    lower than the angels.
    You have put a crown of glory and
      honor on his head.
6You have put him in charge of all you
    have made.
    Everything is put under his control.
7He is in charge of all the sheep and
    oxen.
    He has power over wild animals,
      too.
8He rules the birds and fish.
    You have put him over the life in
      the sea.
9O Lord, our Lord, the glory of your
    name fills the earth.

God Does Not Ignore Us—
He Hears Us

9 O Lord, I will praise you with all
my heart!
    I will tell everyone about the great
      things you do.
2I will be filled with joy because of you.
    I will sing your praises, O Lord God
      above all gods.
3My enemies will fall back and die in
    your presence.
4You have listened to my troubles.
    You have helped me with my work.
You have said from your throne that it
    is good.
5You have judged the nations and
    destroyed the wicked.

You have blotted out their names
  for all time.
⁶O enemies of mine, you are doomed
  forever.
  The Lord will destroy your cities.
  Even the memory of them will
  disappear.
⁷⁻⁸But the Lord lives on forever.
  He sits upon his throne.
  He judges the nations of the world
  fairly.
⁹All who are hurt and troubled may
  come to him.
  He is their place of rest in times of
  trouble.
¹⁰All those who know your mercy,
  Lord, will look to you for help.
  For you have never yet forsaken
  those who trust in you.
¹¹Oh, sing out your praises to the God
  who lives in Jerusalem.
  Tell the world about his great deeds.
¹²He brings revenge against the
  murderer.
  He has an open ear to those who
  cry to him for justice.
He does not ignore the prayers of men
  in trouble.
  He does not close his ear when they
  call to him for help.
¹³And now, O Lord, have mercy on me.
See how I suffer at the hands of those
  who hate me!
  Lord, save me from the jaws of
  death.
¹⁴Help me, so that I can praise you.
  I will praise you in front of all the
  people at Jerusalem's gates.
I will rejoice that you have rescued me.
¹⁵The nations fall into the pits they
  have dug for others.
  The trap they set has snapped on
  them.
¹⁶The Lord is famous for the way he
  punishes the wicked.
  He catches them in their own traps!
¹⁷The wicked shall be sent away to hell.
  This is the fate of all the nations
  who forget the Lord.
¹⁸For the needs of the needy shall not
  be ignored forever.
  The hopes of the poor shall not
  always be crushed.

¹⁹O Lord, rise up and punish the
  nations.
  Don't let them laugh at you!
²⁰Make them shake in fear.
  Put the nations in their place.
Then at last they will know they are
  only weak men.

Will the Wicked Succeed?

10Lord, why are you standing so far
  away?
  Why do you hide when I need you
  the most?
²Come and deal with all these proud
  and wicked men.
  They take advantage of the poor
  without mercy.
Pour on these men the bad things
  they planned for others!
³For these men brag about all the bad
  things they do.
  They hate God and bless those who
  are greedy.
  Their only goal in life is money.
⁴These wicked men are very proud.
  They seem to think that God is
  dead.
  They wouldn't think of looking for
  him!
⁵Yet there is success in all they do.
  Their enemies fall before them.
They do not see your punishment
  waiting for them.
⁶They brag that neither God nor man
  can ever keep them down.
  They think that no matter what,
  somehow they'll find a way!
⁷Their mouths are full of lies.
  They are always bragging of their
  evil plans.
⁸They hide in dark alleys of the city.
And there they murder those who pass
  by.
⁹Like lions they crouch silently.
  They wait to jump upon the poor.
Like hunters they catch their victims
  in their traps.
¹⁰The poor are crushed by their great
  strength.
  They fall under their blows.
¹¹"God isn't watching," they say to
  themselves.
  "He'll never know!"
¹²O Lord, rise up!

O God, crush them!
Don't forget the poor or anyone else
  in need.
[13]Don't let the wicked get away with
  this!
  For they think that God will never
  stop them.
[14]Lord, you see what they are doing.
  You have noted each evil act.
  You know what trouble and grief
  they have caused.
  Now punish them.
O Lord, the poor man trusts himself to
  you.
  You are known as the helper of the
  helpless.

We should sing praises to God

I will sing to the Lord. For he
has blessed me so much.

Psalm 13:6

---

[15]Break the arms of these wicked men.
  Go after them until the last of them
  is destroyed.
[16]The Lord is King forever and ever.
  Those who follow other gods shall
  be swept from his land.
[17]Lord, you know the hopes of humble
  people.
  Surely you will hear their cries.
  Surely you will comfort their hearts
  by helping them.
[18]You will be with the orphans and all
  who are oppressed.
  That way evil men will no longer
  make them afraid.

God Sees It All

11 How dare you tell me, "Run to
   the mountains for safety"?
For I am trusting in the Lord!
[2]The wicked have strung their bows.
  They have drawn their arrows tight
  against the bowstrings.
  They have aimed at the people of
  God from their hiding places.
[3]"Law and order no longer stand," we
  are told.
  "What can the righteous do but run
  away?"
[4]But the Lord is still in his holy temple.
  He still rules from heaven.

He closely watches everything that
  happens here on earth.
[5]He puts the righteous and the wicked
  to the test.
  He hates those loving violence.
[6]He will rain down fire and brimstone
  on the wicked.
  He will burn them with his burning
  wind.
[7]For God is good, and he loves
  goodness.
  The godly shall see his face.

Can I Trust God?

12 Lord! Help!
   Godly men are very hard to find.
Where in all the world can they be
  found?
[2]Everyone lies to his neighbor.
  There are no honest people left.
[3-4]But the Lord will cut off all lying lips.
  He will destroy those who say, "We
  will lie all we want.
  Our lips are our own. Who can stop
  us?"
[5]The Lord says, "I will rise up!
  I will help the poor and needy.
  I will save them as they have
  wanted me to."
[6]The Lord's promise is sure.
  He speaks no word without
  thinking about it.
  All he says is purest truth.
  His word is like silver refined seven
  times.
[7]O Lord, you will keep your people
  away from bad men.
[8]They prowl around on every side.
  And sin is praised throughout the
  land.

I Need Help

13 How long will you forget me,
   Lord?
Will you forget me forever?
How long will you look the other way
  when I am in need?
[2]How long must I hide pain in my
  heart?
How long shall my enemy have the
  upper hand?
[3]Answer me, O Lord my God!
  Give me light in my darkness.
If you don't, I will die.

⁴Don't let my enemies say, "We have
      beaten him!"
   Don't let them be glad that I am
      down.
⁵But I will trust in you forever.
   I will always trust in your mercy.
   I will have joy in your salvation.
⁶I will sing to the Lord.
   For he has blessed me so much.

Foolish or Wise?

14 That man is a fool who says,
      "There is no God!"
   Anyone who talks like that is evil.
   He cannot really be a good person
      at all.
²The Lord looks down from heaven on
      all mankind.
   He looks to see if there are any who
      are wise.
   He looks for all who want to please
      God.
³But no, all have strayed away.
   All are rotten with sin.
   Not one is good, not one!
⁴They eat my people like bread.
   They don't even think of praying!
Don't they really know any better?

The Lord is always near us

*I am always thinking of the
Lord. And because he is so near,
I never need to stumble or fall.*

Psalm 16:8

---

⁵Terror shall grip them.
   For God is with those who love him.
⁶He is the place of safety for the poor
      and humble.
   He saves them when evil men
      oppress them.
⁷Oh, that the time of their rescue were
      already here!
   Oh, that God would come from
      Zion to save his people!
What gladness there will be when the
      Lord saves Israel!

What Makes Someone Good?

15 O Lord, who may find shelter in
      your Tabernacle?
   Who may live on your holy hill?

²Only a person who does what is right.
   Only a person with a pure heart.
³He doesn't lie about others.
   He never listens to gossip.
   He doesn't harm his neighbor.
⁴He always speaks out against sin.
   And he confronts those who are
      doing it.
He commends the faithful followers of
      the Lord.
   And he keeps a promise even if it
      ruins him.
⁵He does not crush those who owe
      him money.
   He never lies about the innocent,
      even when bribes are offered.
Such a man shall stand firm forever.

Being God's Friend

16 Save me, O God, because I have
      come to you for refuge.
²I said to him, "You are my Lord.
   I have no other help but yours."
³I want the company of the godly
      people in the land.
   They are the true nobles.
⁴Those choosing other gods shall all be
      filled with sorrow.
   I will not offer the sacrifices they do.
   I will never even speak the names
      of their gods.
⁵The Lord himself is all I need.
   He is my food and drink, my
      highest joy!
   He guards all that is mine.
⁶He sees that I am given pleasant
      brooks and meadows!
   He has given me a beautiful portion!
⁷I will bless the Lord who counsels me.
   He gives me wisdom in the night.
   He tells me what to do.
⁸I am always thinking of the Lord.
   And because he is so near, I never
      need to stumble or fall.
⁹Heart, body, and soul are filled with
      joy.
   ¹⁰For you will not leave me among
      the dead.
   You will not let your loved one rot
      in the grave.
¹¹You have let me know the joys of life.
   You have given me the joy of being
      close to you.

Seeing God Face to Face

17 I am begging for your help,
O Lord. For I have been honest
and have done what is right.
You must listen to the cry of my heart!
²Declare me not guilty, Lord.
For you are always fair.
³You have tested me and seen that I
am good.
You have come even in the night.
And you have found nothing
wrong.
You know that I have told the truth.
⁴I have followed your commands.
I have not gone along with cruel
and evil men.
⁵My feet have not slipped from your
paths.
⁶Why am I praying like this?
Because I know you will answer me,
O God!
Yes, listen as I pray.
⁷Show me your strong love in great
ways.
You save all those who ask for your
help against their enemies.
⁸Protect me as you would the pupil of
your eye.
Hide me in the shadow of your wings
as you fly over me.
⁹My enemies are all around me.
They have murder in their eyes.
¹⁰They have no pity and they are
proud.
Listen to their bragging.
¹¹They close in on me.
They are ready to throw me to the
ground.
¹²They are like lions that want to tear
me apart.
They are like young lions hiding
and waiting their chance.
¹³⁻¹⁴Lord, rise up and stand against
them.
Push them back!
Come and save me from these men of
the world.
Their only desire is earthly gain.
You have filled these men with your
treasures.
Even their children and
grandchildren are rich.
¹⁵But as for me, my joy is not in riches.
I have joy in seeing you.

I am happy knowing all is well
between us.
And when I awake in heaven, I will be
happy.
For I will see you face to face.

God Cares for Us

18 Lord, how I love you!
For you have done such great
things for me.
²The Lord is my fort where I can enter
and be safe.
No one can follow me in and kill
me.
He is a rugged mountain where I hide.
He is my Savior, a rock where none
can reach me.
He is a tower of safety.
He is my shield.
He is like the strong horn of a fighting
bull.
³All I need to do is cry to him.
Oh, praise the Lord!
I am saved from all my enemies!
⁴Death tied me with chains.
Floods of the ungodly sent a great
attack against me.
⁵I was trapped and helpless.
I fought against the ropes that drew
me on to death.

God Hears Us

⁶In my pain I begged the Lord for help.
And he heard me from heaven.
My cry reached his ears.
⁷Then the earth rocked and reeled.
The mountains shook and trembled.
How they shook, for he was angry!
⁸Flames leaped from his mouth.
They set the earth on fire.
Smoke blew from his nose.
⁹He bent the heavens down and came
to help me.
Thick darkness was under his feet.
¹⁰He rode on a mighty angel.
He sped swiftly to help me with
wings of wind.
¹¹He covered himself with darkness.
He hid his coming with dense
clouds.
They were as dark as dirty waters.
¹²Suddenly the brightness of the Lord
broke through the clouds.

It came with lightning and a
　　mighty storm of hail.
13The Lord thundered in the heavens.
　　The God above all gods has spoken.
Oh, the hailstones! Oh, the fire!
14He flashed his fearful arrows of
　　lightning.
　　He chased away all my enemies.
　　See how they run!
15Then you gave your command, O
　　Lord.
　　And the sea went back from the
　　shore.
At the blast of your breath the deep
　　sea was opened.
16He reached down from heaven.
　　He took me and pulled me out of
　　my great trials.
　　He rescued me from deep waters.
17He saved me from my strong enemy.
　　He delivered me from those who
　　hated me.
I was helpless in their hands.
18On the day when I was weakest, they
　　attacked.
　　But the Lord held me steady.
19He led me to a safe place.
　　He did this because he loves me.
20The Lord rewarded me for doing
　　right.
　　He blessed me for being pure.
21For I have followed his commands.
　　I have not sinned by turning away
　　from him.
22I kept close watch on all his laws.
　　I did not refuse a single one.
23I did my best to keep them all.
　　I held myself back from doing
　　wrong.
24And so the Lord has paid me with
　　his blessings.
　　For I have done what is right.
　　And I am pure of heart.
This he knows, for he watches my
　　every step.
25Lord, how merciful you are to those
　　who show mercy.
　　And you do not punish those who
　　run from evil.
26You give blessings to the pure.
　　But you give pain to those who
　　leave your paths.
27You help the humble.

But you judge the proud and
　　haughty.
28You have turned on my light!
　　The Lord my God has made my
　　darkness turn to light.
29Now in your strength I can climb
　　any wall.
　　I can attack any soldier.
30What a God he is!
　　How perfect he is in every way!
　　All his promises prove true.
He is a shield for all who hide behind
　　him.
31For who is God except our Lord?
　　Who but he is as a rock?
32He fills me with strength.

Our prayers go all the way to heaven

*In my pain I begged the Lord for
help. And he heard me from
heaven. My cry reached his ears.*

Psalm 18:6

He keeps me safe wherever I go.
33He gives me the sure feet of a
　　mountain goat.
　　He leads me safely along the top of
　　the cliffs.
34He gets me ready for battle.
　　He gives me the strength to draw
　　an iron bow!

God Supports Us

35You have given me your salvation as
　　my shield.
　　Your right hand, O Lord, holds me
　　up.
　　Your gentleness has made me great.
36You have made wide steps under my
　　feet.
　　That way I need never slip.
37I chased my enemies and caught up
　　with them.
　　I did not turn back until all were
　　conquered.
38I pinned them to the ground.
　　All were helpless before me.
　　I put my feet upon their necks.
39For you have armed me with strong
　　armor for the battle.
My enemies shake before me and fall
　　beaten at my feet.
40You made them turn and run.

I destroyed all who hated me.
⁴¹They shouted for help.
But no one dared to save them.
They cried to the Lord.
But he refused to answer them.
⁴²So I crushed them fine as dust.
And I threw them to the wind.
I threw them away like dirt from the
floor.

**The world around us shows
that God created it**

*The heavens are telling the glory
of God. They are a great display
of what God can do.*

Psalm 19:1

---

⁴³⁻⁴⁵You gave me victory in every battle.
The nations came and served me.
Even those I didn't know before
come now and bow before me.
Foreigners who have never seen me
give in without a fight.
They come shaking from their walled
cities.
⁴⁶God is alive!
Praise him who is the great rock of
safety.
⁴⁷He is the God who pays back those
who harm me.
He defeats the nations before me.
⁴⁸He saves me from my enemies.
He holds me safely out of their
reach.
He saves me from these powerful
enemies.
⁴⁹For this, O Lord, I will praise you
among the nations.
⁵⁰Many times you have saved me, the
king you chose.
You have been loving and kind to
me.
And you will do the same to my
descendants.

More Valuable Than Gold

19The heavens are telling the glory
of God.
They are a great display of what
God can do.
²Day and night they keep on telling
about God.
³⁻⁴They don't make a sound or speak a
word.

They are silent in the skies.
But their message reaches out to all
the world.
The sun lives in the heavens where
God put it.
⁵It moves out across the skies.
It shines like a bridegroom going to
his wedding.
It is like a joyous runner looking
forward to a race!
⁶The sun crosses the heavens from end
to end.
Nothing can hide from its heat!
⁷⁻⁸God's laws are perfect.
They protect us and make us wise.
They give us joy and light.
⁹God's laws are pure, eternal, and just.
¹⁰God's laws are more desirable than
gold.
They are sweeter than honey in a
honeycomb.
¹¹For they warn us away from harm.
And they give success to those who
obey them.
¹²But how can I ever know what sins
are hiding in my heart?
Set me free from these hidden sins.
¹³And keep me from doing wrong
things on purpose.

**The Bible is worth more than gold
and is sweeter than honey**

*God's laws are more desirable
than gold. They are sweeter than
honey in a honeycomb.*

Psalm 19:10

Help me to stop doing them.
Only then can I be free of guilt.
And then I will be innocent of great
crimes.
¹⁴I want my words and thoughts to
please you.
O Lord, you are my Rock and my
Redeemer.

When We Are in Trouble,
God Is There

20In your day of trouble, may the
Lord be with you!
May the God of Jacob keep you
from all harm.
²May he send you help from his
sanctuary in Zion.

³May he remember with joy the
gifts you have given him.
May he never forget your sacrifices
and burnt offerings.
⁴May he give you your heart's desire.
May he fulfill all your plans.

We should want to please God

*I want my words and thoughts
to please you.*

Psalm 19:14

---

⁵May there be shouts of joy when we
hear the news of your victory.
May there be flags flying with
praise to God for all he has done.
May he answer all your prayers!
⁶"God save the king!" I know he does!
He hears me from highest heaven.
And he sends great victories.
⁷Some nations brag of armies and
weapons.
But our boast is in the Lord our God.
⁸Those nations will collapse and die.
But we will rise to stand firm and
sure!
⁹Give victory to our king, O Lord.
Oh, hear our prayer.

Thanking God for His Answers

21 The king rejoices in your
strength, O Lord!
He bursts with gladness every time
you save him!
²You have given him his heart's desire.
You have not held back what he
asked for.
³You welcomed him to the throne
with many blessings.
You set a crown of solid gold on his
head.
⁴He asked for a long, good life.
And you have given him what he
asked for.
The days of his life stretch on forever.
⁵You have given him fame and honor.
You have clothed him with honor
and praise.
⁶You have filled him with happiness
that will never end.
You have made him glad because
you were with him.
⁷And the king trusts in the Lord.
So he will never stumble or fall.

He stands on the love of the God who
is above all gods.
⁸Your hand, O Lord, will find your
enemies.
It will catch all who hate you.
⁹⁻¹⁰When you come, they will be
destroyed.
They will be burned in the hot fire
of your presence.
The Lord will destroy them and their
children.
¹¹For these men plot against you,
Lord.
But they cannot succeed.
¹²They will turn and run when they
see your arrows aimed at them.
¹³Accept our praise, O Lord, for all
your great power.
We will write songs to sing of your
mighty acts!

Everyone Hates Me—Does God?

22 My God, my God, why have you
left me?
Why do you refuse to help me?
Why don't you even listen to my
groans?
²Day and night I keep on crying for
your help.
But there is no answer.
³⁻⁴For you are holy.
The praises of our fathers
surrounded your throne.
They trusted you and you helped
them.
⁵You heard their cries for help and
saved them.
They were never let down when
they asked for your help.
⁶But I am a worm, not a man.
I am hated by my own people and
by all mankind.
⁷Everyone who sees me laughs and
sneers.
⁸"Is this the one who gave his burden
to the Lord?" they laugh.
"Is this the one who says the Lord
loves him?
We'll believe it when we see God
save him!"
⁹⁻¹¹Lord, how you have helped me
before!
You took me safely from my
mother's womb.

And you brought me through the
years of childhood.
I have depended upon you since birth.
You have always been my God.
Don't leave me now, for trouble is near.
No one else can possibly help.
¹²I am surrounded by fearsome
enemies.

The Lord is ruler over everything

The Lord is King and
rules the nations.

Psalm 22:28

They are as strong as the giant bulls
from Bashan.
¹³They come at me with open jaws.
They are like roaring lions attacking
their prey.
¹⁴My strength has drained away like
water.
And all my bones are out of joint.
My heart melts like wax.
¹⁵My strength has dried up like
sun-baked clay.
My tongue sticks to my mouth.
For you have laid me in the dust of
death.
¹⁶The enemy circles me like a pack of
dogs.
They have pierced my hands and
feet.
¹⁷I can count every bone in my body.
See these men of evil gloat and
stare.
¹⁸They divide my clothes among them
by a toss of the dice.
¹⁹O Lord, don't stay away.
O God my Strength, hurry to help
me.
²⁰Rescue me from death.
Spare my life from all these evil
men.
²¹Save me from these lions' jaws.
Deliver me from the horns of these
wild oxen.
Yes, God will answer me and rescue
me.
²²I will praise you to all my brothers.
I will stand up before the people.
And I will tell them of the great
things you have done.
²³"Praise the Lord, each one of you
who fears him," I will say.

"Each of you must fear and respect
his name.
Let all Israel sing his praises.
²⁴For he has not ignored my cries of
deep despair.
He has not turned and walked away.
When I cried to him, he heard and
came."
²⁵Yes, I will stand and praise you
before all the people.
I will fulfill my promises in front of
those who respect your name.
²⁶The poor shall eat and have enough.
All who look for the Lord shall find
him.
And they shall praise his name.
Their hearts shall rejoice with
everlasting joy.
²⁷The whole earth shall see it and go
back to the Lord.
The people of every nation shall
worship him.

The Lord takes good care of us

The Lord is my Shepherd.
So I have everything I need.

Psalm 23:1

---

²⁸The Lord is King and rules the
nations.
²⁹Both proud and humble together
shall worship him.
All who are human shall bow
before him.
³⁰Our children too shall serve him.
For they shall hear from us about
the wonders of the Lord.
³¹People yet unborn shall hear of the
miracles he did for us.

The Good Shepherd

23 The Lord is my Shepherd.
So I have everything I need!
²He lets me rest in the meadow grass.
He leads me beside the quiet
streams.
³He gives me new strength.
He helps me do what honors him
the most.
⁴I may walk through the dark valley of
death.
But even then I will not be afraid.
For you are close beside me.

And you are guarding and guiding
all the way.
[5]You give me good food in the house
of my enemies.
You have welcomed me as your
guest.
Blessings overflow all around me!
[6]Your goodness and kindness shall be
with me all of my life.
And then I will live with you
forever in your home.

Who Owns the World?

24 The earth belongs to the Lord!
Everything in all the world is
his!
[2]He is the one who pushed the oceans
back.
It was he who made the dry land
appear.
[3]Who may climb the mountain of
God?
Who may go to the place where he
lives?
Who may stand before the Lord?
[4]Only those with pure hands and
hearts.
They must not lie or be dishonest.
[5]God will give his own goodness to
them as his blessing.
It will be planted in their lives by
God himself!
[6]These are the ones who are allowed to
stand before the Lord.
And they will worship the God of
Jacob.
[7]Open up, O ancient gates!
Let the King of Glory in.
[8]Who is this King of Glory?
He is the Lord, strong and mighty.
He cannot be beaten in battle.
[9]Yes, open wide the gates!
Let the King of Glory in.
[10]Who is this King of Glory?
The Commander of all of heaven's
armies!
He is the King of Glory!

God Will Be My Guide

25 To you, O Lord, I pray.
[2]Don't fail me, Lord, for I am
trusting you.
Don't let my enemies succeed.
Don't give them victory over me.

[3]No one who trusts you will ever be
ashamed.
But all who harm the innocent
shall be defeated.
[4]Show me the path where I should go,
O Lord.
Point out the right road for me to
walk.
[5]Lead me. Teach me.
For you are the God who saves me.
I have no hope except in you.
[6-7]Overlook my youthful sins, O Lord!
Look at me instead through eyes of
mercy and forgiveness.
Look through eyes of love and
kindness.

The Lord owns everything

The earth belongs to the Lord!
Everything in all the world is his!

Psalm 24:1

---

[8]The Lord is good.
He is glad to teach the proper path
to all who go astray.
[9]He will teach the ways that are right
and best.
He will lead all those who humbly
turn to him.
[10]The paths of the Lord are full of his
kindness and truth.
This is given to all who obey his
commands.
[11]But Lord, my sins!
How many they are!
Oh, forgive them for the honor of
your name.
[12]Where is the man who fears the
Lord?
God will teach him how to choose
the best.
[13]He shall live within God's circle of
blessing.
And his children shall inherit the
earth.
[14]Friendship with God is given to
those who respect him.
With them alone he shares the
secrets of his promises.
[15]My eyes are ever looking to the Lord
for help.
For he alone can save me.
[16]Come, Lord, and show me your
mercy.

For I am helpless and in deep pain.
¹⁷My problems go from bad to worse.
Oh, save me from them all!
¹⁸See my sorrows.
Feel my pain.
Forgive my sins.
¹⁹See how many enemies I have!
Take note of how much they hate me!
²⁰Save me from them!
Deliver my life from their power!
Oh, let it never be said that I trusted you for no reason!
²¹Give me Goodness and Honesty as my bodyguards.
For I trust that you will take care of me.
²²I look for you to save Israel from all her troubles.

On God's Side

26 Do not listen to the charges against me, Lord.
For I have tried to keep your laws.
And I have trusted you without turning back.
²Question me, O Lord, and see that this is so.
Test my motives and desires, too.
³For I have taken your kindness and truth as my ideals.
⁴I do not have fellowship with tricky, two-faced men.
They are false and pretend they are good.

We should love to go to church

Lord, I love your home.

Psalm 26:8

---

⁵I hate the places where sinners meet.
I refuse to enter them.
⁶I wash my hands to prove my innocence.
I come before your altar.
⁷I am singing a song of thanks.
I am telling about your miracles.
⁸Lord, I love your home.
I love this place where the brightness of your presence lives.
⁹⁻¹⁰Don't treat me as a common sinner or murderer.
Don't treat me like one who plots against the innocent.

Don't treat me like one who asks for bribes.
¹¹No, I am not like that, O Lord.
I try to walk a straight and narrow path.
I try to do what is right.
Therefore in mercy save me.
¹²I praise the Lord before all the people.
I praise him for keeping me from slipping and falling.

Why Should I Be Afraid?

27 The Lord is my light and my salvation.
He protects me from danger.
So whom shall I fear?
²Evil men come to destroy me.
But they stumble and fall!
³Yes, a mighty army might march against me.
But my heart shall know no fear!
I know that God will save me.
⁴I want this one thing from God.
This is the thing I seek most of all.
I want to live in the Lord's house all my life.
I want to live near him every day.
I want to delight in his glory.
⁵There I'll be when troubles come.
And there he will hide me.
He will set me on a high rock.
⁶I'll be out of reach of all my enemies.
Then I will bring him sacrifices.
I will sing his praises with much joy.
⁷Listen to my begging, Lord!
Be merciful and send the help I need.
⁸My heart hears you speak.
You say, "Come and talk with me, O my people."
And my heart responds, "Lord, I am coming."
⁹Oh, do not hide yourself.
For I am trying to find you.
Do not reject your servant in anger.
You have been my help in all my trials before.
Don't leave me now.
Don't forsake me, O God of my salvation.
¹⁰For my father and mother might leave me.
But you would welcome and comfort me.
¹¹Tell me what to do, O Lord.

Make it plain because enemies are
all around me.
¹²Don't let them get me, Lord!
Don't let me fall into their hands!
For they accuse me of things I never did.
And all the while they are planning
cruel deeds.
¹³I am hoping the Lord will save me
again.
I expect to live to see his goodness
to me once more.
¹⁴Don't be impatient.
Wait for the Lord.
He will come and save you!
Be brave and take courage!
Yes, wait and he will help you.

Prayer Is Powerful

28 I beg you to help me, Lord. For
you are my Rock of safety.
If you do not answer me
I might as well give up and die.
²Lord, I lift my hands to heaven!
I cry out for your help.
Oh, listen to my cry.
³Don't punish me with all the wicked
ones.
They speak so sweetly to their
neighbors.
But at the same time they plan to
murder them.

The Lord doesn't stay angry very long

His anger lasts a moment.
His favor lasts for a lifetime!

Psalm 30:5

---

⁴Give them the punishment they so
richly deserve!
Measure it out to them according to
what they do.
Pay them back for all their evil
deeds.
⁵They care nothing for God.
They do not care what he has done
or what he has made.
Therefore God will break them down
like old buildings.
And they will never be rebuilt again.
⁶Oh, praise the Lord!
For he has listened to my cries!
⁷He is my strength and my shield from
every danger.
I trusted in him and he helped me.

Joy rises in my heart!
I burst out in songs of praise to him.
⁸The Lord protects his people.
He gives victory to his chosen king.
⁹Defend your people, Lord.
Defend and bless your chosen ones.
Lead them like a shepherd.
Carry them forever in your arms.

Nature Speaks of God

29 Praise the Lord, you angels of his.
Praise his glory and his strength.
²Praise him for his great glory, the
glory of his name.
Come before him clothed in holy
clothing.
³The voice of the Lord echoes from the
clouds.
The God of glory thunders through
the skies.
⁴His voice is so powerful!
It is full of majesty.
⁵⁻⁶It breaks down the cedars.
It splits the giant trees of Lebanon.
It shakes Mount Lebanon and Mount
Sirion.
They leap and skip before him like
young calves!
⁷The voice of the Lord thunders
through the lightning.
⁸It resounds through the deserts.
It shakes the wilderness of Kadesh.
⁹The voice of the Lord spins and
topples the mighty oaks.
It strips the forests bare.
They whirl and sway beneath the blast.
But in his temple all are praising,
"Glory, glory to the Lord."
¹⁰At the Flood the Lord showed his
control of all creation.
Now he still proves his power.
¹¹He will give his people strength.
He will bless them with peace.

Saved from the Grave

30 I will praise you, Lord!
For you have saved me from my
enemies.
You refuse to let them triumph over
me.
²O Lord my God, I begged you.
And you gave me my health again.
³You brought me back from the brink
of the grave.

You delivered me from death itself.
And here I am alive!
⁴Oh, sing to him, you saints of his.
Give thanks to his holy name.

The Lord will help us be brave

*Cheer up! Be brave! Take courage
if you are trusting in the Lord.*

Psalm 31:24

---

⁵His anger lasts a moment.
His favor lasts for a lifetime!
Crying may go on all night.
But in the morning there is joy.
⁶⁻⁷In my prosperity I said, "This is
forever.
Nothing can stop me now!
The Lord has shown me his favor.
He has made me steady as a
mountain."
Then, Lord, you turned your face away
from me.
You cut off your river of blessings.
Suddenly my courage was gone.
I was afraid and full of panic.
⁸I cried to you, O Lord. I cried:
⁹"What will you gain, O Lord, from
killing me?
How can I praise you then to all my
friends?
How can my dust in the grave
speak out?
How can it tell the world about
how faithful you are?
¹⁰Hear me, Lord!
Oh, have pity and help me."
¹¹Then he turned my sorrow into joy!
He took away my clothes of
mourning.
And he dressed me with joy!
¹²Now I can sing glad praises to the
Lord.
I can sing instead of lying in silence
in the grave.
O Lord my God, I will keep on
thanking you forever!

Believe, No Matter What

31 Lord, I trust in you alone.
Don't let my enemies defeat me.
Rescue me because you are the God
who always does what is right.
²Answer quickly when I cry to you.
Bend low and hear my whispered cry.

Be for me a great Rock of safety from
my enemies.
³Yes, you are my Rock and my fortress.
Honor your name by leading me
out of this danger.
⁴Pull me from the trap my enemies
have set for me.
For you alone are strong enough.
⁵⁻⁶Into your hand I commit my spirit.
You have saved me, O God who
keeps his promises.
I worship only you.
How you hate all those who
worship idols.
For those are not true gods.
⁷I am full of joy because of your mercy.
For you have listened to my
troubles.
And you have seen the crisis in my
soul.
⁸You have not handed me over to my
enemy.
But you have given me open
ground in which to move.
⁹⁻¹⁰O Lord, have mercy on me in my
pain.
My eyes are red from crying.
My health is broken from sorrow.
I am becoming weak with grief.
My years are made short.
They are drained away because of
sadness.
My sins have taken away my strength.
I stoop with sorrow and with shame.
¹¹All my enemies think badly of me.
And so do my neighbors and
friends.
They hate it when they meet me.
And they look the other way when
I go by.
¹²I am forgotten like a dead man.
I am like a broken pot that is
thrown away.
¹³I heard the lies about me.
I heard the slanders of my enemies.
Everywhere I looked I was afraid.
For they were plotting against my life.
¹⁴⁻¹⁵But I am trusting you, O Lord.
I said, "You alone are my God.
My times are in your hands.
Rescue me from those who hunt me
down.
¹⁶Let your favor shine again on your
servant.

Save me just because you are so kind!
[17]Don't shame me, O Lord!
  Please answer when I call to you for
    help.
But let the wicked be shamed by what
    they trust in.
  Let them lie silently in their graves.
[18]Let their lying lips be made quiet at
    last.
  These are the lips of proud men.
  They accuse honest men of evil
    deeds."
[19]Oh, how great is your goodness!
  You have stored up great blessings
    for those who trust you.
  You give these blessings in the sight
    of all people.
[20]Hide your loved ones in the shelter
    of your presence.
  Hide them safe beneath your hand.
  Keep them safe from all evil men.
[21]Blessed is the Lord!
  For he has shown me his never-
    failing love.
It protects me like the walls of a fort!
[22]I spoke too quickly when I said, "The
    Lord has left me."
  For you heard my cry and answered
    me.
[23]Oh, love the Lord, all of you who are
    his people.
  For the Lord protects those who are
    loyal to him.
  But he punishes all who proudly
    reject him.
[24]Cheer up! Be brave!
  Take courage if you are trusting in
    the Lord.

God Forgives

32 What happiness for those whose
  guilt has been forgiven!
  What joy when sins are covered over!
What relief for those who have
    confessed their sins!
  What peace when God has cleared
    their record!
[3]There was a time when I wouldn't
    admit what a sinner I was.
  But not telling the truth made me
    sad.
  It filled my days with trouble.
[4]All day and all night your hand was
    heavy on me.

My strength left me like water on a
    sunny day.
[5]But I finally confessed all my sins to
    you.
  I stopped trying to hide them.
I said to myself, "I will confess them
    to the Lord."
  And you forgave me!
All my guilt is gone.

**The Lord teaches good things
and gives good advice**

*"I will teach you," says the Lord.
"I will guide you along the best
path for your life. I will advise
you and watch your progress."*

Psalm 32:8

---

[6]Each believer should confess his sins
    to God.
  He should do this when he is aware
    of them.
  He should do this while there is
    time to be forgiven.
Judgment will not touch him if he
    does.
[7]You are my hiding place from every
    storm of life.
  You even keep me from getting into
    trouble!
You surround me with songs of victory.
[8]"I will teach you," says the Lord.
  "I will guide you along the best
    path for your life.
  I will advise you and watch your
    progress."
[9]Don't be like a senseless horse or
    mule.
  It needs a bit in its mouth to keep it
    in line!
[10]Many sorrows come to the wicked.
  But love follows those who trust in
    the Lord.
[11]So rejoice in him, all those who are
    his!
  Shout for joy, all those who try to
    obey him!

Who Is in Charge?

33 Let all the joys of the godly well
  up in praise to the Lord!
  It is right to praise him.

[2]Play joyful songs of praise on the lyre and harp.
[3]Write new songs of praise to him.
Play them with skill on the harp.
Sing them with joy.
[4]For all God's words are right.
And all he does is worthy of our trust.
[5]He loves whatever is just and good.
And the earth is filled with his tender love.
[6]He merely spoke, and the heavens were formed.
All the stars appeared at his command.
[7]He made the oceans and set their borders.
[8]Let everyone in all the world fear the Lord.
Let men, women, and children stand in awe of him.
[9]For when he spoke, the world began!
It appeared at his command!
[10]And with a breath he can scatter the nations who hate him.
[11]But his own plan stands forever.
His purposes are the same for every generation.

We should watch what we say

Don't let your tongue say anything evil. Don't let your lips tell a lie.

Psalm 34:13

---

[12]Blessed is the nation whose God is the Lord.
Blessed are the people he has chosen as his own.
[13-15]The Lord looks down on mankind from heaven where he lives.
He has made their hearts.
And he closely watches all that they do.
[16-17]The best-equipped army cannot save a king.
For great strength is not enough to save anyone.
A war horse is a poor risk for winning victories.
It is strong, but it cannot save.
[18-19]But the eyes of the Lord are watching over those who respect him.

He looks for those who trust in his steady love.
He will keep them from death even in times of hunger!
[20]We depend upon the Lord alone to save us.
Only he can help us.
He protects us like a shield.
[21]No wonder we are happy in the Lord!
For we are trusting him.
We trust his holy name.
[22]Yes, Lord, let your constant love surround us.
For our hope is in you alone.

How to Trust God

34 I will praise the Lord no matter what happens.
I will always speak of his glories and grace.
[2]I will brag of all his kindness to me.
Let all who are discouraged take heart.
[3]Let us praise the Lord together and exalt his name.
[4]For I cried to him and he answered me!
He freed me from all my fears.
[5]Others were happy because of what he did for them.
Their faces were not sad and downcast!
[6]This poor man cried to the Lord.
And the Lord heard him and saved him from his troubles.
[7]For the Lord saves those who respect him.
The Angel of the Lord guards them.
[8]Oh, put God to the test and see how kind he is!
Happy are those who trust in him.
[9]If you belong to the Lord, respect him.
For everyone who does this has all he needs.
[10]Even strong young lions sometimes go hungry.
But those who respect the Lord will never lack any good thing.
[11]Sons and daughters, come and listen.
Let me teach you the importance of fearing the Lord.
[12]Do you want a long, good life?
[13]Then don't let your tongue say anything evil.

Don't let your lips tell a lie.
¹⁴Turn from all known sin.
And spend your time in doing good.
Try to live in peace with everyone.
Work hard at it!
¹⁵For the Lord sees those who live
good lives.
And he listens when they cry to
him.
¹⁶But the Lord is against those who do
evil.
He will make sure they are
forgotten forever.
¹⁷Yes, the Lord hears the good man
when he calls for help.
He saves him out of all his troubles.
¹⁸The Lord is close to those whose
hearts are breaking.
He saves those who are sorry for
their sins.
¹⁹The good man does not escape all
troubles.
But the Lord helps him in each and
every one.
²⁰Not one of his bones is broken.
²¹Trouble will surely overtake the
wicked.
Those who hate the good suffer great
punishment.
²²But as for those who serve the
Lord, he will redeem them.
Everyone who takes refuge in him will
be freely forgiven.

When People Aren't Fair

35 O Lord, fight those fighting
against me.
Declare war on them for their
attacks on me.
²Put on your armor and take your
shield.
Protect me by standing in front.
³Lift your spear in my defense.
For those who chase me are getting
very close.
Let me hear you say that you will save
me from them.
⁴Dishonor those who are trying to
kill me.
Turn them back and confuse them.
⁵Blow them away like chaff in the
wind.
Blow them on wind sent by the
Angel of the Lord.

⁶Make their path dark and slippery
before them.
Send the Angel of the Lord after
them.
⁷For I did them no wrong.
But they laid a trap for me.
They dug a pitfall in my path.
⁸Let them be overtaken by sudden
ruin.
Let them be caught in their own
net and destroyed.
⁹But I will rejoice in the Lord.
He shall save me!
¹⁰From the bottom of my heart praise
rises to him.
Where is his equal in all of heaven
and earth?
Who else protects the weak and
helpless from the strong?
Who saves the poor and needy
from those who would rob them?
¹¹These evil men promise that lies are
true.
They accuse me of things I have
never even heard about.
¹²I do them good, but they return me
harm.
I am sinking down to death.
¹³When they were ill, I mourned
before the Lord in sackcloth.
I asked him to make them well and I
would not eat.
I prayed for them with all my heart.
But God did not listen.
¹⁴I went about sadly as though it were
my friend or brother.
I cried as though it were my mother
who was near to death.
¹⁵But now that I am in trouble they
are glad.
They come together in meetings.
They speak with lies against me.
I didn't even know some of those who
were there.
¹⁶For they gather with the worthless
fellows of the town.
They spend their time cursing me.
¹⁷Lord, how long will you stand there,
doing nothing?
Act now and save me.
For I have but one life.
And these young lions are out to get it.
¹⁸Save me, and I will thank you before
all the people.

I will speak before the largest crowd
I can find.
¹⁹Don't give victory to those who fight
me without any reason!
Don't let them rejoice at my fall.
Instead, let them die.
²⁰They don't talk of peace and doing
good.
They talk of plots against innocent
men.
They plan to hurt those who are
minding their own business.
²¹They shout that they have seen me
doing wrong!
"Aha!" they say. "With our own eyes
we saw him do it."
²²Lord, you know all about it.
Don't stay silent!
Don't leave me now!
²³Rise up, O Lord my God, and avenge
me.
²⁴Declare me "not guilty," for you
are just.
Don't let my enemies rejoice over me
in my troubles.
²⁵Don't let them say, "Aha!
Our wish against him will soon
come about!"
Don't let them say, "At last we have
him!"
²⁶Let those who boast against me be
ashamed.
They were happy when I suffered
my troubles.
May they be stripped bare of all they
own.
²⁷But give great joy to all who wish me
well.
Let them shout, "Great is the Lord
who enjoys helping his child!"
²⁸And I will tell everyone how great
and good you are.
I will praise you all day long.

God's Goodness Is Great

36 Sin hides deep in the hearts of
the wicked.
It urges them on to do evil all day
long.
They have no fear of God to hold
them back.
²Instead they think they can hide their
evil deeds.

They think they can sin and not get
caught.
³Everything they say is crooked and
false.
They are no longer wise and good.
⁴They lie awake at night to hatch their
evil plans.
They do not plan how to keep away
from wrong.
⁵Your steadfast love, O Lord, is as great
as all the heavens.
Your faithfulness reaches beyond
the clouds.
⁶Your justice is as solid as God's
mountains.
Your purposes are full of wisdom.
They are as full of wisdom as the
oceans are with water.
You are concerned for men and
animals alike.
⁷How precious is your constant love, O
God!
All people take refuge in the
shadow of your wings.
⁸You feed them with blessings from
your own table.
You let them drink from your rivers
of delight.
⁹For you are the Fountain of life.
Our light is from your light.
¹⁰Pour out your unfailing love on
those who know you!
Never stop giving your blessings to
those who want to do your will.
¹¹Don't let these proud men trample
me.
Don't let their wicked hands push
me around.
¹²Look! They have fallen.
They are thrown down and will not
rise again.

Keep Doing Good

37 Never envy the wicked!
²Soon they fade away like grass
and disappear.
³Trust in the Lord instead.
Be kind and good to others.
Then you will live safely here in the
land.
You will succeed in all you do,
feeding in safety.
⁴Be delighted with the Lord.

Then he will give you all your
heart's desires.
⁵Give all you do to the Lord.
Trust him to help you do it, and he
will.
⁶Your innocence will be clear to
everyone.
He will deliver you with the blazing
light of justice.
It will shine down as from the
noonday sun.
⁷Rest in the Lord.
Wait patiently for him to act.
Don't be envious of evil men who
prosper.
⁸Stop your anger! Turn off your wrath.
Don't fret and worry. It only leads
to harm.
⁹For the wicked shall be destroyed.
But those who trust the Lord shall
be given every blessing.
¹⁰Only a little while and the wicked
shall disappear.
You will look for them and not find
them.
¹¹The Lord shall bless those who are
humble before him.
He shall give them wonderful peace.
¹²⁻¹³The Lord is laughing at those who
plot against the godly.
For he knows their judgment day is
coming.
¹⁴Evil men take aim to kill the poor.
They are ready to kill all those who
do right.
¹⁵But their swords will be plunged into
their own hearts.
And all their weapons will be
broken.
¹⁶It is better to have little and be godly
than to own an evil man's riches.
¹⁷For the strength of evil men shall be
broken.
But the Lord takes care of those he
has forgiven.
¹⁸Day by day the Lord sees the good
deeds of godly men.
And he gives them eternal rewards.
¹⁹He cares for them when times are
hard.
Even in famine, they will have
enough.
²⁰But evil men shall die.

These enemies of God will dry up
like grass.
They will float away like smoke.
²¹Evil men borrow and "cannot pay it
back"!
But the good man gives back what
he owes with extra besides.
²²Those blessed by the Lord shall
inherit the earth.
But those cursed by him shall die.

If you let the Lord help you, he will

Give all you do to the Lord.
Trust him to help you do it,
and he will.

Psalm 37:5

---

²³The steps of good men are directed
by the Lord.
He takes joy in each step they take.
²⁴If they fall it isn't deadly.
For the Lord holds them with his
hand.
²⁵I have been young and now I am old.
And I have never seen the Lord
leave a man who loves him.
I have not seen the children of the
godly go hungry.
²⁶Instead, the godly are able to be
generous.
They are free with their gifts and
loans to others.
And their children are a blessing.
²⁷So if you want an eternal home,
leave your evil.
Give up your sinful ways and live
good lives.
²⁸For the Lord loves justice and
fairness.
He will never leave his people.
They will be kept safe forever.
But all who love wickedness shall
die.
²⁹The godly shall be firmly planted in
the land.
And they will live there forever.
³⁰⁻³¹The godly man is a good counselor.
For he is just and fair and knows
right from wrong.
³²Evil men spy on the godly.
They wait for an excuse to accuse
them.
And then they demand their death.

33But the Lord will not let these evil men succeed.

He will not let the godly be condemned when they are brought to trial.

34Don't be impatient for the Lord to act!

Keep traveling steadily along his pathway.

In the end he will honor you with every blessing.

And you will see the wicked destroyed.

35-36I myself have seen it happen.

A proud and evil man towered like a cedar of Lebanon.

But when I looked again, he was gone!

I searched but could not find him!

37But the good man—what a different story!

The good man has a wonderful future ahead of him.

For him, there is a happy ending.

38But evil men shall be destroyed.

And their descendants shall be cut off.

39The Lord saves the godly!

He is their salvation and their refuge when trouble comes.

40Because they trust in him, he helps them.

He delivers them from the plots of evil men.

Confessing Our Sin

38 O Lord, don't punish me while you are angry!

2Your arrows have struck deep.

Your blows are crushing me.

3-4Because of your anger, my body is sick.

My health is broken beneath my sins.

They are like a flood, higher than my head.

They are a burden too heavy to bear.

5-6My wounds are infected and full of pus.

Because of my sins, I am bent and racked with pain.

My days are filled with trouble.

7My loins burn with fever.

My whole body is sick.

8I am tired and crushed.

I groan in despair.

9Lord, you know how I wish for my health once more.

You hear my every sigh.

10My heart beats wildly and my strength fails.

I am going blind.

11My loved ones and friends stay away.

They are afraid of the sickness I have.

Even my own family stands at a distance.

12Meanwhile my enemies are trying to kill me.

They plan to ruin me.

They spend all their waking hours planning evil deeds.

13-14But I am deaf to all their threats.

I am silent before them as a man who cannot speak.

I have nothing to say.

15For I am waiting for you, O Lord my God.

Come and protect me.

16Put an end to their pride.

Do not let them gloat when I am cast down!

17How often I find myself about to sin.

This source of sorrow always stares me in the face.

18I confess my sins.

I am sorry for what I have done.

19But many enemies hate me with energy.

They hate me though I have done nothing to deserve it.

20They repay me evil for good.

They hate me for standing for the right.

21Don't leave me, Lord.

Don't go away!

22Come quickly!

Help me, O my Savior.

Life Is Short—
So What's Important?

39 I said to myself, "I'm going to stop sinning by what I say!

I'll keep quiet, especially when the ungodly are around me."

2-3So I stood there silently.

I did not even say anything good.

And the turmoil within me grew to
the bursting point.
The more I thought, the hotter the
fires grew inside.
Then at last I spoke with God.
⁴Lord, help me to know how short my
time on earth will be.
Help me to know that I am here for
but a moment.
⁵⁻⁶My life is no longer than my hand!
My whole lifetime is but a moment
to you.
Proud man! Frail as breath! A shadow!
And all his busy rushing ends in
nothing.
He heaps up riches for someone else to
spend.
⁷And so, Lord, my only hope is in you.
⁸Save me from being overpowered by
my sins.
For even fools will mock me then.
⁹Lord, I am speechless before you.
I will not open my mouth to speak
one word.
For my punishment is from you.
¹⁰Lord, don't hit me anymore.
I am tired beneath your hand.
¹¹You punish a man for his sins and he
is destroyed.
For he is as weak as a moth-eaten
cloth.
Yes, man is weak as breath.
¹²Hear my prayer, O Lord.
Listen to my cry!
Don't sit back, not seeing my tears.
For I am your guest.
I am a traveler passing through the
earth.
I am just as all my fathers were.
¹³Spare me, Lord! Let me get better!
Let me be happy again before my
death.

Obeying by Waiting

40 I waited patiently for God to
help me.
Then he listened and heard my cry.
²He lifted me out of the pit of despair.
He pulled me from the bog and the
mud.
He set my feet on a hard, firm path.
He steadied me as I walked along.
³He has given me a new song to sing.
It is a song of praises to our God.

Now many will hear of the great
things he did for me.
They will stand in awe before the
Lord.
They will put their trust in him.
⁴Many blessings are given to those
who trust the Lord.
Happy are those who put no confidence in those who are proud.
Many blessings are given to those
who don't trust in idols.

**Doing what God wants
should make us happy**

*I am so happy to do what you
want, my God. For your law is
written on my heart!*

Psalm 40:8

---

⁵O Lord my God, you have done great
things for us.
And you are always thinking about
us.
Who else can do such great things?
No one else can be compared with
you.
There isn't time to tell of all your
wonderful deeds.
⁶It isn't sacrifices and offerings that
you really want from your
people.
Burnt animals bring no special joy to
your heart.
But you have accepted the offer of
my lifelong service.
⁷Then I said, "See, I have come.
I am here just as all the prophets
foretold.
⁸I am so happy to do what you want,
my God.
For your law is written on my
heart!"
⁹I have told everyone the good news
that you forgive people's sins.
I have not been afraid to do this.
You know this well, O Lord.
¹⁰I have not kept this good news
hidden in my heart.
But I have proclaimed your love
and truth to all the people.
¹¹O Lord, don't hold back your tender
mercies from me!
My only hope is in your love and
faithfulness.

¹²Without your mercy, I die.
　For great problems are piled higher
　　than my head.
Meanwhile my sins have all caught up
　　with me.
　There are too many to count.
　And I am ashamed to look up.
My heart is weak within me.
¹³Please, Lord, rescue me!
　Quick! Come and help me!
¹⁴⁻¹⁵Confuse them! Turn them around!
　Knock down all those who are
　　trying to destroy me.
　Disgrace these scoffers and shame
　　them!
¹⁶But may the joy of the Lord be given
　to all who love him.
　They will always love you for
　　saving them.
　May they constantly say, "How
　　great God is!"
¹⁷I am poor and weak.
　But the Lord is thinking about me
　　right now!
O my God, you are my helper.
　You are my Savior.
Come quickly and save me.
　Please don't wait!

God: The Only True Friend

41 God blesses those who are kind
　to the poor.
　He helps them out of their troubles.
²He protects them and keeps them
　　alive.
　He honors them in front of the
　　people.
　He destroys the power of their
　　enemies.
³He nurses them when they are sick.
　He soothes their pains and worries.
⁴"O Lord," I prayed, "be kind and
　　heal me.
　For I have confessed my sins."
⁵But my enemies say, "May he soon
　　die and be forgotten!"
⁶They act friendly when they come to
　　visit me while I am sick.
　But all the time they hate me.
They are glad that I am lying there on
　　my bed of pain.
　And when they leave, they laugh
　　and mock.

⁷They whisper together about what
　　they will do when I am dead.
⁸"He is going to die," they say.
　"He'll never get out of that bed!"
⁹Even my best friend has turned
　　against me.
　He was a man I completely trusted.
How often we ate together.
¹⁰Lord, don't you desert me!
　Be kind, Lord, and make me well
　　again.
That way I can pay them back!
¹¹I know you are pleased with me.
　For you haven't let my enemies
　　triumph over me.
¹²You have kept me alive because I was
　　honest.
　You have let me come near you.
¹³Bless the Lord, the God of Israel!
　He lives from everlasting ages past.
　And he will live on into everlasting
　　ages ahead.
Amen and amen!

Why Am I So Sad?

42 As the deer pants for water, so I
　wish for you, O God.
²I thirst for God, the living God.
Where can I find him to come and
　　stand before him?
³Day and night I cry for his help.
　And all the while my enemies make
　　fun of me.
"Where is this God of yours?" they
　　laugh.
⁴⁻⁵Take courage, my soul!
　Do you remember those great times
　　of worship?
　But how could you ever forget them!
You led a great procession to the
　　Temple on feast days.
You sang with joy, praising the Lord.
Why then be downcast?
　Why be discouraged and sad?
Hope in God!
　I shall yet praise him again.
　Yes, I shall again praise him for his
　　help.
⁶Yet I am standing here sad and
　　gloomy.
　But I will think about your kindness.
You have been good to this lovely
　　land.
　Here the Jordan River flows.

And here Mount Hermon and
    Mount Mizar stand.
⁷All your waves and billows have gone
    over me.
    Floods of sadness pour on me like a
    great waterfall.
⁸Yet day by day the Lord also pours
    out his love on me.
    And through the night I sing his
    songs.
I pray to God who gives me life.
⁹"O God my Rock," I cry.
    "Why have you left me?
Why must I suffer these attacks from
    my enemies?"
¹⁰Their taunts cut me like a deadly
    wound.
    Again and again they ask, "Where
    is that God of yours?"
¹¹But, O my soul, don't be discouraged.
Don't be upset. Expect God to act!
He is my help!
He is my God!

God Makes Me Smile Again

43 O God, defend me from the
charges of merciless liars.
    ²For you are God, my only place of
    safety.
Why have you tossed me aside?
    Why must I cry because my
    enemies hate me?
³Oh, send out your light and your
    truth.
    Let them lead me.
    Let them lead me to your Temple.
It is on your holy mountain, Zion.
⁴There I will go to the altar of God.
    I will go with great joy.
I will praise him with my harp.
    O God, my God!
⁵O my soul, why be so gloomy and
    sad?
    Trust in God!
I shall again praise him for his help.
    He will make me smile again.
    For he is my God!

God Alone Can Save Us

44 O God, we have heard of the
miracles you did long ago.
Our fathers have told us how you
    drove the heathen nations from
    this land.

You gave it all to us!
The people of Israel spread from one
    end of the country to the other.
³They did not conquer by their own
    strength and skill.
    But they won it by your mighty
    power.
    They conquered because you smiled
    on them and loved them.
⁴You are my King and my God.
    Promise victories for your people.
⁵For it is only by your power that we
    conquer.
    It is through your name that we
    tread down our enemies.
⁶I do not trust my weapons.
    They could never save me.
⁷Only you can give us the victory over
    those who hate us.
⁸My constant boast is in God.
    I can never thank you enough!
⁹And yet for a time, O Lord, you have
    tossed us aside.
    You have not honored us.
    You have not helped us in our
    battles.
¹⁰You have actually fought against us.
    You have defeated us before our
    enemies.
Our enemies have invaded our land.
    They have looted our villages.
¹¹You have treated us like sheep about
    to be killed.
    You have scattered us among the
    nations.
¹²You sold us for a small amount of
    money.
    You valued us at nothing at all.
¹³The neighboring nations laugh and
    mock us.
    This is because of all the evil you
    have sent.
¹⁴You have made the name *Israel* a
    word of shame.
    It is known among all the nations
    and hated by all.
¹⁵⁻¹⁶I am always mocked and cursed by
    my enemies.
    ¹⁷And all this has happened, Lord,
    despite our loyalty to you.
We have not sinned against your
    covenant.
    ¹⁸Our hearts have not left you!

We have not left your path by a
single step.
¹⁹If we had, we would understand why
you have punished us.
We would understand your sending
us into darkness and death.
²⁰We might have turned away from
worshiping our God.
Or perhaps we were worshiping
idols.

God will protect me and keep me safe

*God is our refuge and strength.
He is a tested help in times of
trouble.*

Psalm 46:1

---

²¹But if so, would God not know it?
Yes, he knows the secrets of every
heart.
²²But that is not our case.
For we are facing death threats
because of serving you!
We are like sheep waiting to be
killed.
²³Wake up! Rouse yourself!
Don't sleep, O Lord!
Have you thrown us out forever?
²⁴Why do you look the other way?
Why don't you see our sorrows and
trouble?
²⁵We lie face down in the dust.
²⁶Rise up, O Lord, and come and
help us.
Save us by your constant love.

The King's Wedding

45 My heart is overflowing with
beautiful thoughts!
I will write a lovely poem to the King.
For I am full of words.
I am like the fastest writer pouring
out his story.
²You are the fairest of all!
Your words are filled with grace.
God himself is blessing you forever.
³Arm yourself, O Mighty One.
You are so great, so powerful!
⁴And in your majesty go on to victory.
Defend truth, humility, and justice.
Go forth to do great deeds!
⁵Your arrows are sharp in your
enemies' hearts.

They fall before you.
⁶Your throne, O God, goes on forever.
Justice is your royal scepter.
⁷You love what is good and hate what
is wrong.
Therefore God has given you great
gladness.
He has given you more than
anyone else.
⁸Your clothes are perfumed with
myrrh, aloes, and cassia.
You live in palaces of inlaid ivory.
And lovely music is being played
for your enjoyment.
⁹Kings' daughters are among your
concubines.
Standing beside you is the queen.
She wears jewelry of fine gold from
Ophir.
¹⁰⁻¹¹"I advise you, O daughter.
Do not worry about your parents far
away.
Your royal husband delights in your
beauty.
Respect him, for he is your master.
¹²The people of Tyre will give you
many gifts.
The richest people of our day will
ask for your favors."
¹³The bride, a princess, waits within
her chamber.
She is robed in beautiful clothing
woven with gold.
¹⁴Lovely she is, led beside her maids of
honor to the king!
¹⁵What a joyful, glad procession as
they enter in the palace gates!
¹⁶"Your sons will someday be kings
like their father.
They shall sit on thrones around
the world!
¹⁷"I will cause your name to be
honored in all generations.
The nations of the earth will praise
you forever."

God Is on Our Side

46 God is our refuge and strength.
He is a tested help in times of
trouble.
²And so we need not be afraid.
Not even if the world blows up.
Not even if the mountains crumble
into the sea.

³Let the oceans roar and foam.
  Let the mountains tremble!
⁴There is a river of joy flowing through
    the city of our God.
  It is the holy home of the God
    above all gods.
⁵God himself is living in that city.
  Therefore it stands unmoved
    despite the trouble everywhere.
He will not wait to give his help.
⁶The nations rant and rave in anger.
  But when God speaks, the earth
    melts.
  And kingdoms fall into ruin.
⁷The Commander of the armies of
    heaven is here among us.
  He, the God of Jacob, has come to
    save us.
⁸Come, see the great things that our
    God does.
  See how he brings ruin upon the
    world.
⁹See how he causes wars to end
    throughout the earth.
  See how he breaks and burns every
    weapon.
¹⁰"Stand silent! Know that I am God!
  I will be honored by every nation in
    the world!"
¹¹The Commander of the heavenly
    armies is here among us!
  He, the God of Jacob, has come to
    rescue us!

God Is the Great King

47 Come, everyone, and clap for joy!
    Shout triumphant praises to the
      Lord!
²For the Lord is great beyond words.
  He is the God above all gods.
  He is the great King of all the earth.
³He subdues the nations before us.
⁴He will choose his best blessings for
    his people.
  He will give the very best to those
    he loves.
⁵God has gone up with a mighty shout.
  He has ascended with trumpets
    blaring.
⁶⁻⁷Sing out your praises to our God,
    our King.
  Yes, sing your highest praises to our
    King.
He is the King of all the earth!

Sing thoughtful praises!
⁸He rules all the nations.
  He sits on his holy throne.
⁹The Gentile rulers of the world have
    joined with us.
  They too are praising him, the God
    of Abraham.
For the battle shields of all the armies
    of the world are his trophies.
  He is highly honored everywhere.

God Protects Jerusalem

48 How great is the Lord!
    How much we should praise him.
He lives upon Mount Zion in
    Jerusalem.
  ²What a glorious sight!
See Mount Zion rising north of the
    city.
  It is high above the plains for all to
    see.
Mount Zion is the joy of all the earth.
  It is the home of the great King.
³God himself is the defender of
    Jerusalem.

**Being quiet helps us learn
more about God**

*Stand silent!
Know that I am God!*

Psalm 46:10

---

⁴The kings of the earth have come
    together to see the city.
⁵They are amazed at the sight.
  And they hurry home again.
⁶They are afraid of what they have
    seen.
  They are filled with panic like a
    woman giving birth!
⁷For God destroys the biggest warships
    with a breath of wind.
⁸We have heard of the city's glory.
  It is the city of our God.
He is the Commander of the armies of
    heaven.
  And now we see it for ourselves!
God has set up Jerusalem forever.
⁹Lord, we are here in your Temple.
  We think about your kindness and
    your love.
¹⁰Your name is known throughout the
    earth, O God.
  You are praised everywhere.

For you have given salvation to the
  world.
¹¹O Jerusalem, rejoice!
  O people of Judah, rejoice!
For God will see to it that you are
  finally treated fairly.
¹²Go, look the city over!
  Walk around and count her many
    towers!
¹³Note her walls and tour her palaces.
  That way you can tell your children.
¹⁴For this great God is our God forever
  and ever.
  He will be our guide until we die.

Money Can't Save You

49 Listen, everyone!
  High and low, rich and poor,
    listen to my words.
³For they are wise and filled with
  insight.
⁴I will tell the answer to one of life's
  great problems.
  I will give this answer in song and
    with harps.
⁵There is no need to fear when times
  of trouble come.
  Do not fear even though enemies
    are all around!
⁶They trust in their riches.
  They brag about how rich they are.
⁷But not one of them can save his
  brother from sin.
  He cannot do this though he is as
    rich as a king!
  For God's forgiveness does not
    come that way.
⁸⁻⁹For a soul is too precious to be
  bought by earthly riches.
  No amount of money can keep a
    soul out of hell.

Even the Rich and Wise Die

¹⁰Rich man! Proud man! Wise man!
  You must die like all the rest!
You have no greater lease on life than
  foolish, stupid men.
  You must leave your riches to
    others.
¹¹You name your estates after
  yourselves.
  You do this as though your lands
    could be forever yours.

You live like you could live on them
  for all time.
¹²But man with all his pride must die
  like any animal.
¹³This is how foolish these men are.
  But after they die they will be
    known for their wisdom.

We have always been sinners

*I was born a sinner. Yes, I sinned
from the moment I was born!*

Psalm 51:5

---

¹⁴Death is the shepherd of all
  mankind.
  And those who are evil will be the
    slaves of those who are good.
For the power of their riches is gone
  when they die.
  They cannot take it with them.
¹⁵But as for me, God will save my soul
  from the power of death.
  For he will take me in.
¹⁶So do not be sad when evil men
  grow rich.
  Do not be dismayed when they
    build their lovely homes.
¹⁷For when they die, they carry
  nothing with them!
  Their honors will not follow them.
¹⁸A man might call himself happy all
  through his life.
  And the world might loudly clap at
    his success.
¹⁹Yet in the end he dies like everyone
  else.
  He also must enter eternal darkness.
²⁰For man with all his pride must die
  like any animal.

God Wants Our True Thanks

50 The mighty God, the Lord, has
  called all mankind from east to
    west!
²God's light shines from the Temple
  on Mount Zion.
³He comes with the noise of thunder.
  There is a burning fire all around
    him.
  A great storm blows round about
    him.
⁴He has come to judge his people.
  To heaven and earth he shouts out.

⁵He says, "Gather together my own
  people.
  Call those who have promised to
    obey me."
⁶God will judge them with complete
  fairness.
  For all heaven declares that he is
    just.
⁷O my people, listen!
  For I am your God.
O Israel, listen!
  Here are my charges against you.
⁸I have no problem with the sacrifices
  you bring to my altar.
  For you bring them as you should.
⁹But it isn't bulls and goats that I
  really want from you.
¹⁰⁻¹¹For all the animals of field and
  forest are mine!
  The cattle on 1,000 hills are mine!
  And all the birds upon the
    mountains belong to me!
¹²If I were hungry, I would not
  mention it to you.
  For all the world is mine and all
    that is in it.
¹³No, I don't need your sacrifices of
  flesh and blood.
¹⁴⁻¹⁵What I want from you is your true
  thanks.
  I want you to do all the things you
    promised.
  I want you to trust me in your
    times of trouble.
  I want to save you, and you can
    give me glory.
¹⁶But God speaks to evil men.
  He tells them to stop reading his
    laws.
  He tells them to stop asking for his
    promises.
¹⁷For you have refused my discipline.
  You have not obeyed my laws.
¹⁸You see a thief and help him.
  And you spend your time with evil
    men.
¹⁹You curse and lie.
  Bad words stream from your
    mouths.
²⁰You tell lies about your own brother.
²¹I stayed silent. You thought I didn't
  care.
  But now your time of punishment
    has come.

And I list all the above charges
  against you.
²²This is the last chance for all of you
  who have forgotten God.
  For I will tear you apart.
No one will be able to help you then.
²³But true praise is a worthy sacrifice.
  This really honors me.
Those who walk my paths will be
  saved by the Lord.

A Prayer of Forgiveness

51 O loving and kind God, have
  mercy.
  Have pity upon me.
Take away the awful stain of my sin.
²Oh, wash me, clean me from this
  guilt.
  Let me be pure again.
³For I admit my shameful deed.
  It troubles me day and night.
⁴It is against you and you alone that I
  sinned.
  You saw it all, and your sentence

The Lord can make a clean heart in us

*Create in me a new, clean heart,
O God. Fill it with clean
thoughts and right desires.*

Psalm 51:10

---

against me is just.
⁵I was born a sinner.
  Yes, I sinned from the moment I
    was born!
⁶You deserve honesty from the heart.
  Yes, you deserve complete
    truthfulness.
Oh, give me this wisdom.
⁷Sprinkle me with the cleansing blood.
  Then I shall be clean again.
Wash me and I shall be whiter than
  snow.
⁸And after you have punished me, give
  me back my joy again.
⁹Don't keep looking at my sins.
  Take them away from your sight.
¹⁰Create in me a new, clean heart,
  O God.
  Fill it with clean thoughts and right
    desires.
¹¹Don't send me away from you
  forever.

Don't take your Holy Spirit from
me.
12Give me back again the joy of your
salvation.
And make me want to obey you.
13Then I will teach your ways to other
sinners.
They, guilty like me, will come back
to you.
14-15Don't sentence me to death.
O my God, you alone can save me.
Then I will sing of your forgiveness.
For my lips will be opened.
Oh, how I will praise you!
16You don't want me to pay for my sin.
If you did, how gladly would I pay
for it!
You don't want offerings burned
before you on the altar.
17It is a broken spirit you want.
You want me to be sorry for my sin.
A broken heart, O God, you will not
ignore.
18And Lord, don't punish Israel for my
sins.
Help your people and protect
Jerusalem.
19And when my heart is right,
Then you will rejoice in the good
that I do.
Then you will be happy with the bulls
I bring to sacrifice upon your altar.

God Punishes the Wicked

52 You call yourself a *hero*, do you?
You *brag* about this evil deed of
yours against God's people.
2You are sharp as a tack in planning
your evil tricks.
3How you love wickedness, far more
than good!
And you love lying more than truth!
4You love to tell lies about people.
You love to say anything that will
do harm.
You are a man with a lying tongue.
5But God will strike you down.
He will pull you from your home.
He will drag you away from the
land of the living.
6The followers of God will see it
happen.
They will watch in awe.
Then they will laugh.

7They will say, "See what happens to
those who despise God.
See the punishment for those that
trust in their riches.
They become ever more bold in their
wickedness."
8But I am like a sheltered olive tree.
I am protected by the Lord himself.
I trust in the mercy of God forever
and ever.
9O Lord, I will praise you forever and
ever.
I will praise you for your
punishment.
And I will wait for your mercies.
For everyone knows what a merciful
God you are.

Sin Keeps Us from God

53 Only a fool would say to himself,
"There is no God."
And why does he say it?
It is because he has a wicked heart.
And he does dark and evil deeds.
His life is full of sin.
2God looks down from heaven.
He looks among all mankind.
He tries to find a single one who does
right.
He looks for one who really seeks
for God.
3But all have turned their backs on
him.
They are dirty with sin.
They are rotten through and
through.
Not one is good, not one!
4How can this be?
Can't they understand anything?
For they eat my people like bread.
And they refuse to come to God.
5But soon great terror will fall on them.
God will scatter the bones of these,
your enemies.
They are doomed, for God has
rejected them.
6Oh, that God would come from Zion
now and save Israel!
For the Lord himself must restore
them.
Only then can they ever be really
happy again.

God Is My Keeper

54 Come with great power, O God, and save me!
Defend me with your might!
²Oh, listen to my prayer.
    ³For violent men have risen against me.
    Ruthless men are seeking my life.
    They care nothing for God.
⁴But God is my helper.
    He is a friend of mine!
⁵He will cause the evil deeds of my enemies to fall back upon them.
Do as you promised.
    Put an end to these wicked men, O God.
⁶Gladly I bring my sacrifices to you.
    I will praise your name, O Lord, for it is good.
⁷God has saved me from all my trouble.
    He has triumphed over my enemies.

When Friends Hurt Us

55 Listen to my prayer, O God.
Don't hide yourself when I cry to you.
²Hear me, Lord! Listen to me!
    For I groan and cry in my sadness.
³My enemies shout against me.
    They threaten me with death.
They surround me with terror and plot to kill me.
    Their anger and hatred rise up to grab me.
⁴My heart is in pain within me.
    Great fear has power over me.
⁵Shaking and terror overwhelm me.
⁶Oh, for wings like a dove.
    Oh, to fly away and rest!
⁷I would fly to the far-off deserts and stay there.
⁸I would flee to some refuge from all this storm.
⁹O Lord, make these enemies start to fight each other.
    Destroy them with their own violence.
¹⁰They guard their walls night and day against invaders.
    But their real problem is inside.
    Wickedness is in the heart of the city.
¹¹There is murder and robbery there.

There is cheating in the markets
    and wherever you look.
¹²It was not an enemy who made fun of me.
    If it had been, I could have taken it.
    I could have hidden and escaped.
¹³But it was you, a man like myself.
    It was my companion and my friend.

God will always listen to our prayers

But I will call upon the Lord to save me. And he will do it. I will pray morning, noon, and night. And he will hear and answer.

Psalm 55:16-17

---

¹⁴What fellowship we once had!
    What wonderful talks we had!
We walked together to the Temple of the Lord on holy days.
¹⁵Let death take them and cut them down while they are strong.
    For there is sin in their homes.
    They are dirty to the depths of their souls.
¹⁶But I will call upon the Lord to save me.
    And he will do it.
¹⁷I will pray morning, noon, and night.
I will beg aloud with God.
    And he will hear and answer.
¹⁸The tide of battle runs strongly against me.
    For so many are fighting against me.
    But he will still save me.
¹⁹God himself will answer them!
    This is God from everlasting ages past!
For they refuse to fear him or even honor his commands.
²⁰This friend of mine betrayed me.
    And I was at peace with him at the time.
    He broke his promises.
²¹His words were oily smooth.
    But in his heart was war.
His words were sweet.
    But underneath were knives.
²²Give your burdens to the Lord.
    He will carry them.
He will not let the godly slip or fall.

²³He will send my enemies to the pit
of destruction.
Murderers and liars will not live out
half their days.
But I am trusting you to save me.

God Is on My Side

56 Lord, have mercy on me.
All day long the enemy troops
press in.
So many are proud to fight against
me.
How they want to conquer me!
³⁻⁴But when I am afraid, I will trust in
you.
Yes, I will trust the promises of God.
And since I am trusting him, what can
mere man do to me?
⁵They are always twisting what I say.
All their thoughts look for ways to
harm me.
⁶They meet together to perfect their
plans.
They hide beside the trail.
They listen for my steps.
They wait there to kill me.
⁷They expect to get away with it.
Don't let them, Lord.
In anger, throw them to the ground.
⁸You have seen me tossing and
turning through the night.
You have collected all my tears.
You have kept them in your bottle!
You have recorded every one in
your book.
⁹The very day I call for help, the tide
of battle turns.
My enemies turn and run!
This one thing I know: God is for me!
¹⁰⁻¹¹I am trusting God.
Oh, praise his promises!
I am not afraid of anything mere man
can do to me!
Yes, praise his promises.
¹²I will surely do what I have
promised, Lord.
And I will thank you for your help.
¹³For you have saved me from death.
You have kept my feet from
slipping.
Now I can walk before the Lord in the
land of the living.

Greater than Heaven—
Higher than the Skies

57 O God, have pity, for I am
trusting you!
I will hide under the shadow of your
wings until this storm is past.
²I will cry to the God of heaven.
He does such wonders for me.
³He will send down help from heaven.
He will save me because of his love
and faithfulness.
He will rescue me from these liars.
They want so badly to destroy me.
⁴Enemies are all around me like fierce
lions.
Their teeth are as sharp as spears
and arrows.
Their tongues are like swords.
⁵Lord, be praised above the highest
heavens!
Show your glory high above the
earth.
⁶My enemies have set a trap for me.
Great fear takes hold of me.
They have dug a pit in my path.
But look! They themselves have
fallen into it!
⁷O God, my heart is quiet and
confident.
No wonder I can sing your praises!
⁸Wake up, my soul!
Rise up, O harp and lyre!
Let us greet the morning with song!
⁹I will thank you throughout the land.
I will sing your praises among the
nations.
¹⁰Your kindness and love are as big as
the heavens.
Your faithfulness is higher than the
skies.
¹¹Yes, be exalted, O God, above the
heavens.
May your glory shine throughout
the earth.

God Cares about
Right and Wrong

58 Justice?
You leaders don't even know the
meaning of the word!
Fairness?
Which of you has any left?
Not one!
All your dealings are crooked.

You give "justice" in exchange for
  bribes.
³These men are born sinners.
  They lie from their earliest words!
⁴⁻⁵They are poisonous as deadly snakes.
  They are cobras that close their ears
    to the most expert of charmers.
⁶O God, break off their fangs.
  Tear out the teeth of these young
    lions, Lord.
⁷Let them disappear like water into
    thirsty ground.
  Make their weapons useless in their
    hands.
⁸Let them be like snails.
  They turn into slime.
Let them be like those who die at birth.
  They never see the sun.
⁹God will sweep away both old and
    young.
He will destroy them quickly,
  faster than a cooking pot feels the
    fire under it.
¹⁰The godly shall rejoice when the
    right wins.
  They shall walk in fields of dead,
    wicked men.
¹¹Then at last everyone will know that
    good is rewarded.
  They will know that there is a God
    who judges justly here on earth.

God Is Safety in a Wicked World

59 O my God, save me from my
    enemies.
  Protect me from these who have
    come to destroy me.
²Keep me safe me from these
    murderers.
³They hide, trying to take my life.
  Strong men are out there waiting.
  And not, O Lord, because I've done
    them wrong.
⁴Yet they get ready to kill me.
  Lord, wake up!
  See what is happening!
  Help me!
⁵And O Lord, God of heaven's armies!
  O God of Israel!
Rise up and punish the heathen
    nations around us.
  Do not let these evil men live!
⁶At evening they come to spy.

They sneak around like dogs that
    prowl the city.
⁷I hear them shouting insults and
    cursing God.
  "No one will hear us," they think.
⁸Lord, laugh at them!
  And scoff at the nations around us,
    too.
⁹O God my Strength!
  I will sing your praises.
  For you are my place of safety.
¹⁰My God is changeless in his love for
    me.
  He will come and help me.
  He will let me see my wish come
    true upon my enemies.
¹¹Don't kill them, but stagger them
    with your power.
Bring them to their knees.
  For my people soon forget such
    lessons.
Bring them to the dust, O Lord our
    shield.
¹²⁻¹³They are proud, cursing liars.
  Angrily destroy them. Wipe them
    out.
  And let the nations find out, too.
Let them know that God rules in Israel.
  Tell them he will rule throughout
    the world.
¹⁴⁻¹⁵Let these evil men sneak back at
    evening.
  Let them prowl the city all night
    before they are happy.
  Let them howl like dogs looking for
    food.
¹⁶But as for me, I will sing each
    morning.
  I will sing about your power and
    mercy.
For you have been my high tower of
    refuge.
  You have been a place of safety in
    the day of my trouble.
¹⁷O my Strength, to you I sing my
    praises.
  For you are my high tower of safety.
  You are my God of mercy.

Real Help Comes from God

60 O God, you have rejected us
    and broken our defenses.
  You have become angry and left us.
Lord, restore us again to your love.

²You have caused this nation to shake
with fear.
You have torn it apart.
Lord, heal it now.
For it is shaken to its depths.
³You have been very hard on us.
You have made us stumble beneath
your blows.
⁴⁻⁵But you have given us a flag to
follow.
All who love truth will run to it.
Then you can save your dear people.
Use your strong right arm to save us.
⁶⁻⁷God has promised to help us.
He has vowed it by his holiness!
No wonder I praise him!
"Shechem, Succoth, Gilead,
Manasseh—still are mine!" he
says.
"Judah shall keep on producing
kings.
And Ephraim will produce great
soldiers.
⁸Moab shall become my lowly servant,
and Edom my slave.
And I will shout in triumph over
the Philistines."
⁹⁻¹⁰Who will bring me in triumph into
Edom's strong cities?
God will!
He who threw us off!
He who left us to our foes!
¹¹Yes, Lord, help us against our
enemies.
For man's help is useless.
¹²With God's help we shall do mighty
things.
For he will trample down our
enemies.

God Hears Us Wherever We Are

61 O God, listen to me!
Hear my prayer!
²For wherever I am, I will cry to you
for help.
I will do this though far away at the
ends of the earth.
I will call on you when my heart is
weak and afraid.
Lead me to the mighty, towering Rock
of safety.
³For you are my place of safety and
rest.

You are a high tower where my
enemies can never reach me.
⁴I shall live forever in your tabernacle.
Oh, to be safe under the shelter of
your wings!
⁵For you have heard my promises,
O God.
I have promised to praise you every
day.
And you have given me great
blessings.
You save these blessings for those who
respect your name.
⁶You will give me added years of life.
You will live for many generations.
⁷And I shall live before the Lord
forever.
Oh, send your love and truth to
guard and watch over me.
⁸I will praise your name always.
I will do as I promised, praising you
each day.

God Is in Control

62 I stand silently before the Lord.
I wait for him to save me.
For salvation comes from him alone.
²Yes, he alone is my Rock.
He is my rescuer, defense, and
fortress.
Why then should I be tense with fear
when troubles come?
³⁻⁴But what is this?
They pick on me at a time when my
rule is weak.
They plan my death and speak lies.
They try to force me from the
throne.
They are so friendly to my face.
But they curse me in their hearts!
⁵I stand silently before the Lord.
I wait for him to rescue me.
For salvation comes from him alone.
⁶Yes, he alone is my Rock.
He is my rescuer, defense, and
fortress.
Why then should I be tense with fear
when troubles come?
⁷My protection and success come from
God alone.
He is my place of safety.
He is a Rock where no enemy can
reach me.

⁸O my people, trust him all the time.
  Tell him what you need, for he can
    help!
⁹The greatest of men or the lowest are
    nothing in his sight.
  They weigh less than air on scales.
¹⁰Don't become rich by cheating and
    stealing.
  If you become rich, don't be proud.
¹¹⁻¹²God has said it many times.
  Power belongs to him alone.
Also, O Lord, steadfast love belongs to
    you.
  He rewards each one of us
    according to what we deserve.

I Want to Be Near God

63 O God, my God!
   How I look for you!
  How I thirst for you in this dry and
    weary land.
It is a land where there is no water.
  How I want to find you!
²How I wish I could go into your
    sanctuary.
  How I want to see your strength
    and glory.
³Your love and kindness are better to
    me than life itself.
  How I praise you!
⁴I will bless you as long as I live.
  I will lift up my hands to you in
    prayer.
⁵At last I shall be really happy.
  I will praise you with great joy.
⁶I lie awake at night thinking of you.
⁷I think of how much you have
    helped me.
  How I rejoice through the night!
I rest under the shadow of your wings.
⁸I follow close behind you.
  I am safe beside your strong right
    arm.
⁹But there are those who plan to
    destroy me.
  They shall go down to the depths of
    hell.
¹⁰They are doomed to die by the sword.
  They will become the food of
    jackals.
¹¹But I will rejoice in God.
  All who trust in him are happy.
  But liars shall be made silent.

When People Make Traps

64 Lord, listen to my troubles.
   Oh, save my life from the plans
    of these wicked men.
³They cut me down with sharp
    tongues.
  They aim their bitter words like
    arrows straight at my heart.
⁴They hide and shoot at the innocent.
  Suddenly the deed is done.
  But they are not afraid.
⁵They encourage each other to do evil.
  They meet in secret to set their
    traps.
"He will never notice them here," they
    say.
⁶They keep a sharp lookout for
    chances to do wrong.
  They spend long hours making evil
    plans.
⁷But God himself will shoot them
    down.
  Suddenly his arrow will wound
    them.
⁸They will stagger backward.
  They will be destroyed by those
    they spoke against.
All who see it happening will laugh at
    them.
⁹Then everyone shall stand in awe.
  They will admit the greatness of
    God's deeds.
At last they will know what great
    things he does.
¹⁰And the godly shall have joy in the
    Lord.
  They will trust and praise him.

Giving Thanks to God

65 O God in Zion, we wait before
   you in silent praise.
  In this way, we fulfill our promise.
  And you answer prayer.
So all mankind will come to you with
    their requests.
³Though sins fill our hearts, you
    forgive them all.
⁴How happy are those who live with
    you!
  How happy are those who live in
    the holy tabernacle courts!
  What joys wait for us among all the
    good things there!

⁵With great power you will save us
from our enemies.
You are the God who saves us!
You are the only hope of all mankind
in the world and far away upon the
sea.
⁶He formed the mountains by his
mighty strength.
⁷He quiets the raging oceans and all
the world's trouble.

**When we keep sins,
they hurt our prayers**

*He would not have listened if
I had not confessed my sins.*

Psalm 66:18

---

⁸At the corners of the earth the acts of
God shall amaze everyone.
The dawn and sunset shout for joy!
⁹He waters the earth to make it grow
trees and grass.
The rivers of God will not run dry!
He gets the earth ready for his people.
He sends them rich harvests of
grain.
¹⁰He waters the ground with plenty of
rain.
Showers soften the earth.
They melt the clods of dirt.
And they cause seeds to grow across
the land.
¹¹⁻¹²Then he crowns it all with green.
He makes rich pastures in the
wilderness.
Hillsides blossom with joy.
¹³The pastures are filled with flocks of
sheep.
And the valleys are filled with grain.
All the world shouts with joy and
sings.

We Are in God's Hand

66 Sing to the Lord, all the earth!
²Sing of his great name!
Tell the world how wonderful he is.
³How great are your deeds, O God!
How great is your power!
No wonder your enemies give in!
⁴All the earth shall worship you and
sing of your glories.
⁵Come, see the things God has done.
See the great miracles that happen
to his people!

⁶He made a dry road through the sea
for them.
They went across on foot.
What joy there was that day!
⁷Because of his great power he rules
forever.
He watches every movement of the
nations.
O rebel lands, he will break your pride.
⁸Let everyone bless God and sing his
praises.
⁹For he holds our lives in his hands.
And he holds our feet to the path.
¹⁰You have made us pure with fire,
O Lord.
You have burned us like silver in a
furnace.
¹¹You captured us in your net.
And you put great loads on our
backs.
¹²You sent troops to ride across our
broken bodies.
We went through fire and flood.
But in the end, you brought us into
riches.
¹³Now I have come to your Temple.
I bring burnt offerings to fulfill my
promises.
¹⁴For I was once in trouble.
And I promised you many offerings.
¹⁵That is why I am bringing you these
animals.
I bring fat male goats, rams, and
calves.
The smoke of their sacrifice shall rise
before you.
¹⁶Come and hear, all of you who
respect the Lord.
I will tell you what he did for me.
¹⁷For I cried to him for help with
praises on my tongue.
¹⁸He would not have listened if I
had not confessed my sins.
¹⁹But he listened to me!
He heard my prayer!
²⁰Blessed be God, who didn't turn
away when I was praying.
I praise him, for he didn't refuse me
his kindness and love.

A Missionary Psalm

67 O God, in mercy bless us.
Let your face beam with joy as
you look down at us.

2Send us around the world with the news of your power.

Send us to tell everyone about your good plan for all mankind.

3How everyone throughout the earth will praise the Lord!

4How glad the nations will be! They will sing for joy!

This is because you are their King. And you will give true justice to your people.

5Praise God, O world!

May all the peoples of the earth give thanks to you.

6-7For the earth has given rich harvests.

God, even our own God, will bless us. And people from faraway lands will worship him.

God: The Great Provider

68 Rise up, O God! Scatter all your enemies! Chase them all away!

2Drive them off like smoke before a wind.

Melt them like wax in a fire!

Let the wicked die in the presence of God.

3But may the godly man have joy! May he rejoice and be merry!

4Sing praises to the Lord!

Raise your voice to him who rides the clouds!

Your name is the Lord.

Oh, have joy because he is here.

5He is a father to the fatherless.

He gives justice to the widows, For he is holy.

6He gives families to the lonely.

He sets prisoners free from jail.

And they go, singing with joy!

But for rebels there is hunger and trouble.

7O God, you led your people through the wilderness.

8And the earth and the heavens shook.

Mount Sinai trembled before you, the God of Israel.

9-10You sent plenty of rain upon your land, O God.

You sent it to refresh it in its weariness!

There your people lived.

For you gave them this home when they had nothing.

11-13The Lord speaks. The enemy flees.

The women at home cry out the happy news:

"The armies that came to destroy us have fled!"

Now all the women of Israel are dividing the booty.

See them sparkle with jewels of silver and gold.

They are covered all over as wings cover doves!

14God scattered their enemies.

They were like snowflakes melting in the forests of Zalmon.

15-16O mighty mountains in Bashan!

O great and many-peaked ranges!

You should be jealous of Mount Zion.

For this is the mount where God has chosen to live forever.

17The Lord has too many chariots to count around him.

He moves on from Mount Sinai.

And he comes to his holy temple high upon Mount Zion.

18He climbs the heights, leading many captives in his train.

He takes gifts for men, even those who once were rebels.

God will live among us here.

19What a great Lord!

He carries our troubles each day.

And he gives us our salvation.

20He frees us!

He saves us from death.

21But he will crush his enemies.

For they will not leave their guilty, stubborn ways.

22The Lord says, "Come," to all his people's enemies.

They are hiding on Mount Hermon's highest slopes.

They hide deep within the sea!

23His people must destroy them.

They must cover your feet with their blood.

Dogs will eat them.

24The procession of God my King moves onward to the sanctuary.

25Singers lead the way.

Musicians take up the rear.

Girls playing the timbrels walk in
between.
26Let all the people of Israel praise the
Lord.
For he is Israel's fountain.
27The little tribe of Benjamin leads the
way.
The princes and elders of Judah are
right behind.
The princes of Zebulun and
Naphtali are with them.
28Call up all your power.
Show your strength, O God.
For you have done such great
things for us.
29The kings of the earth are bringing
their gifts.
They are carrying them to your
Temple in Jerusalem.
30Rebuke our enemies, O Lord.
Bring them under your power.
Scatter all who like to fight in war.
31Egypt will send gifts of rich metals.
Ethiopia will stretch out her hands
to God in praise.
32Sing to the Lord, O kingdoms of the
earth.
Sing praises to the Lord!
33Praise him who rides upon the
ancient heavens.
Praise the Lord whose mighty voice
thunders from the sky.
34Power belongs to God!
His greatness shines down on Israel.
His strength is mighty in the
heavens.
35What respect we feel!
We kneel here before him in the
sanctuary.
The God of Israel gives strength to his
people.
Praise be to God!

A Sea of Trouble

69 Save me, O my God.
The floods have risen around me.
Deeper and deeper I sink in the mud.
The waters rise all around me.
3I have cried until I am very tired.
My throat is dry and hoarse.
My eyes are swollen with crying.
I am waiting for my God to act.
4I cannot even count all those who
hate me.

And they hate me without any
reason.
They are men who have power.
They plan to kill me though I am
innocent.
They demand that I be punished for
what I didn't do.
5O God, you know so well how stupid
I am.
And you know all my sins.
6O Lord God of the armies of heaven!
Don't let me be a stumbling block
to those who trust in you.
O God of Israel!
Don't let me cause them to be
confused.
7I am cursed and shamed for your sake.
8Even my own brothers pretend they
don't know me!
9My love for God and his work burns
hot within me.
And I support your cause.
So your enemies make fun of me.
And in doing this, they make fun of
you.
10How they mock me when I mourn!
How they laugh as I fast before the
Lord!
11How they talk about me when I wear
sackcloth!
I wear it to show that I am humble.
I want to show that I am sorry for
my sins.
12I am the talk of the town.
I am in the songs of the drunks.
13But I keep right on praying to you,
Lord.
For now is the time!
You are bending down to hear!
You are ready with a supply of love
and kindness.
Now answer my prayer and save me as
you promised.
14Pull me out of this mud.
Don't let me sink in.
Rescue me from those who hate me.
Save me from the deep waters I
am in.
15Don't let the floods drown me.
Don't let the ocean swallow me.
Save me from the pit that threatens
me.
16O Lord, answer my prayers.
For your love is wonderful.

And there is always more than enough
of your mercy!
It is so tender and so kind.
¹⁷Don't hide from me.
For I am in deep trouble.
Quick! Come and save me.
¹⁸Come, Lord, and rescue me.
Buy me back from all my enemies.
¹⁹You know how they talk about me.
You know how they dishonor me.
You see them all and know what
each has said.
²⁰Their lack of respect has broken my
heart.
My spirit is heavy within me.
If even one would show some pity!
If even one would comfort me!
²¹For food they give me bitter gall.
For my awful thirst they give me
vinegar.
²²Let their joys turn to ashes.
Let their peace be lost.
²³Let darkness, blindness, and great
weakness be theirs.
²⁴Pour out your anger on them.
Burn them with the fierceness of
your anger.
²⁵Let their homes be broken down and
empty.
²⁶For they attack the one you have
beaten.
They laugh at the pain of the one
you have cut.
²⁷Pile their sins high and do not
overlook them.
²⁸Let these men be taken from the list
of the living.
Do not give them the joys of life
with the righteous.
²⁹But rescue me, O God, from my
poverty and pain.
³⁰Then I will praise God with my
singing!
My thanks will be his praise.
³¹That will please him more than
sacrificing a bull or an ox.
³²The humble shall see their God at
work for them.
No wonder they will be so glad!
All who look for God shall live in joy.
³³For the Lord hears the cries of his
needy ones.
He does not look the other way.
³⁴Praise him, all heaven and earth!

Praise him, all the seas and all that
is in them!
³⁵For God will save Jerusalem.
He rebuilds the cities of Judah.
His people shall live in them.
³⁶Their children shall inherit the land.
All who love his name shall live
there safely.

A Short Prayer for Help

70 Rescue me, O God!
Lord, hurry to help me!
²⁻³They are after my life.
They take joy in hurting me.
Confuse them! Shame them! Stop
them!
Don't let them keep on making fun
of me!
⁴But fill the followers of God with joy.
Let those who love your salvation
speak up.
Let them say, "What a wonderful
God he is!"
⁵But I am in deep trouble.
Rush to help me.
For only you can help and save me.
O Lord, don't wait!

Young or Old—God Helps

71 Lord, you are my place of safety!
Don't let me down!
²Save me from my enemies.
For you are just!
Rescue me! Bend down your ear.
Listen to me and save me.
³Be to me a great protecting Rock.
Be a place where I am always
welcome.
Keep me safe from all attacks.
For you have given the order to
save me.
⁴Save me, O God, from these unjust
and cruel men.
⁵O Lord, you alone are my hope.
I've trusted you from childhood.
⁶Yes, you have been with me from
birth.
You have helped me constantly.
No wonder I am always praising you!
⁷Many stand amazed at my success.
But I succeed because you are my
mighty helper.
⁸All day long I'll praise and honor you,
O God.

For you have done great things for
me.

⁹And now, in my old age, don't set me
aside.

Don't leave me now when my
strength is failing.

¹⁰My enemies are whispering, ¹¹"God
has left him!

Now we can get him.

There is no one to help him now!"

¹²O God, don't stay away!

Come quickly! Help!

¹³Cover them with failure and shame.

Destroy these enemies of mine!

¹⁴I will keep on looking for you to
help me.

I praise you more and more.

¹⁵I cannot count the times when you
have saved me from danger.

I tell everyone about how good you
are.

I tell them of your constant, daily
care.

¹⁶I walk in the strength of the Lord
God.

I tell everyone that you alone are
just and good.

¹⁷O God, you have helped me since I
was a child.

I have always told others of the
great things you do.

¹⁸And now that I am old and gray,
don't leave me.

Give me time to talk to this new
generation.

Let me talk to their children too!

Let me tell them about all your
mighty miracles.

¹⁹Your power and goodness, Lord,
reach to the highest heavens.

You have done such great things.

Where is there another God like you?

²⁰You have let me sink down deep in
big problems.

But you will bring me back to life
again.

You will bring me up from deep in
the earth.

²¹You will give me greater honor than
before.

You will turn again and comfort me.

²²I will praise you with music.

I will tell how you are faithful to all
your promises.

For you are the Holy One of Israel.

²³I will shout and sing your praises for
saving me.

²⁴I will talk to others all day long
about your fairness.

I will tell them of your goodness.

For all who tried to hurt me have been
made ashamed.

The Perfect King

72 O God, help the king to judge as
you would.

And help his son to walk in
godliness.

²Help him to give justice to your
people.

Help him to be fair even to the poor.

³May the mountains and hills bring
forth riches.

May they flourish because of his
good reign.

⁴Help him to defend the poor and
needy.

And help him to crush their
enemies.

⁵May the poor and needy respect you
always.

May they look to you as long as sun
and moon are in the skies!

Yes, for all time!

⁶May the reign of this son of mine be
gentle and fruitful.

May it be like the rains of spring
upon the grass!

May it be like showers that water
the earth!

⁷May all good men grow rich in his
reign.

May there be peace to the end of
time.

⁸Let him reign from sea to sea.

Let him rule from the Euphrates
River to the ends of the earth.

⁹The desert nomads shall bow before
him.

His enemies shall fall face down in
the dust.

¹⁰Kings along the Mediterranean coast
will bring their gifts.

So will the kings of Tarshish and
the islands.

And even those from Sheba and
from Seba.

¹¹Yes, kings from everywhere!

All will bow before him!
All will serve him!
¹²He will take care of the helpless.
He will help the poor when they
    cry to him.
For they have no one else to defend
    them.
¹³He feels pity for the weak and needy.
And he will rescue them.
¹⁴He will save them from violence.
For their lives are precious to him.
¹⁵And he shall live.
And to him will be given the gold
    of Sheba.
And there will always be praise for
    him.
His people will bless him all day long.
¹⁶Bless us with rich crops throughout
    the land.
May they even grow on the
    highland plains.
May there be fruit like that of
    Lebanon.
May the cities be as full of people as
    the fields are of grass.
¹⁷His name will be honored for all
    time.
It will keep on going like the sun.
And all will be blessed in him.
All nations will praise him.
¹⁸Blessed be the Lord God, the God of
    Israel.
Only he does such great things!
¹⁹Blessed be his great name forever!
Let the whole earth be filled with
    his glory.
Amen and amen!
²⁰This ends the psalms of David, the
    son of Jesse.

Why Are Wicked People Rich?

73 How good God is to Israel!
How kind he is to those who
    have pure hearts.
²But as for me, I came so close to the
    edge of the cliff!
My feet were slipping and I was
    almost gone.
³For I was jealous of those who were
    rich.
I wanted to be like the proud and
    wicked.
⁴Yes, all through life their road is
    smooth!

They grow sleek and fat.
⁵They aren't always in trouble.
They don't have problems like
    everyone else.
⁶So their pride sparkles like a jeweled
    necklace.
And their clothing is woven of
    cruelty!
⁷These people have all their hearts
    could ever wish for!
⁸They laugh at God and make threats
    against his people.
How proudly they speak!
⁹They brag against the very heavens.
And their words march through the
    earth.
¹⁰And so God's people are sad and
    confused.
They drink it all in.
¹¹"Does God know what is going on?"
    they ask.
¹²"Look at these men of pride.
They never have to work hard.
They live lives of ease.
And all the time they get richer."
¹³Have I been wasting my time?
Why take the trouble to be pure?
¹⁴All I get out of it is trouble.
I have problems every day and all
    day long!
¹⁵I might have really said that.
But then I would have been a
    traitor to your people.
¹⁶Yet it is so hard to explain!
Why do those who hate the Lord
    prosper?
¹⁷Then one day I went into God's
    sanctuary to think.
I thought about the future of these
    evil men.
¹⁸What a slippery path they are on!
Suddenly God will send them sliding
    over the edge of a cliff.
They will fall down to their
    destruction.
¹⁹All their happiness will end in an
    instant.
And then they must face an
    eternity of terror.
²⁰Their present life is only a dream!
They will wake up to the truth!
They will wake up from a dream of
    things that never really were!

²¹When I saw this, what sadness filled
my heart!
²²I saw myself so stupid and with no
wisdom.
I must seem like an animal to you,
O God.
²³But even so, you love me!
You are holding my right hand!
²⁴You will keep on guiding me all my
life.
You will guide me with your wisdom and counsel.
And then you will welcome me into
the glories of heaven!
²⁵Whom have I in heaven but you?
And I desire no one on earth as
much as you!
²⁶My health fails and my spirits droop.
But God still remains!
He is the strength of my heart.
He is mine forever!
²⁷But those who do not worship God
will die.
For he destroys those serving other
gods.
²⁸But as for me, I get as close to him as
I can!
I have chosen him.
And I will tell everyone about the
ways he saves me.

Remember Your Promises, O Lord

74 O God, why have you thrown us
away forever?
Why is your anger hot against us?
We are the sheep of your own pasture.
²Remember that we are your people.
We are the ones you chose in times
of old.
You took us from slavery.
And you made us the best of your
possessions.
You chose Jerusalem as your home on
earth!
³Walk through the awful ruins of the
city.
See what the enemy has done to
your sanctuary.
⁴There they shouted their battle cry.
And they made idols to show their
victory.
⁵⁻⁶Everything lies in shambles.

It is like a forest chopped to the
ground.
They came with their axes and
hammers.
They smashed and chopped the
carved paneling.
⁷They set the sanctuary on fire.

**The Lord controls everything because
he made everything**

*You control both day and night.
That's because you made
the sun and stars.*

Psalm 74:16

They broke it to the ground.
This was your sanctuary, Lord!
⁸"Let's wipe out every trace of God,"
they said.
They went through the whole
country.
They burned down the meeting places
where we worshiped you.
⁹⁻¹⁰There is nothing left to show that
we are your people.
The prophets are gone.
And who can say when it all will
end?
How long, O God?
How long will you let our enemies
dishonor your name?
Will you let them get away with
this forever?
¹¹Why do you wait?
Why hold back your power?
Throw your fist and give them a final
blow.
¹²God is my King from ages past.
You have helped me everywhere in
the land.
¹³⁻¹⁴You divided the Red Sea with your
strength.
You crushed the sea-god's heads!
You gave him to the desert tribes to
eat!
¹⁵At your command the springs burst
forth.
And they gave your people water.
Then you dried a path for them.
And they walked across the ever-
flowing Jordan.
¹⁶You control both day and night.

That's because you made the sun
and stars.
17All nature is within your hands.
You make the summer and the
winter too.
18Lord, see how these enemies laugh at
you.
O Lord, a proud nation has misused
your name.
19O Lord, save me!
Protect your turtledove from the
hawks.
Save your beloved people from
these beasts.
20Remember your promise!
For the land is full of darkness and
cruel men.
21O Lord, don't let your people be
insulted forever.
Give these poor and needy ones a
reason to praise your name!
22Rise up, O God!
State your case against our enemies.
Remember the insults they have
made against you.
23Don't overlook the cursing of these
enemies of yours.
It grows louder and louder.

Wicked People Will Be Judged

75 How we thank you, Lord!
Your mighty miracles give proof
that you care.
2"Yes," the Lord replies.
"And when I am ready, I will
punish the wicked!
3The earth shakes and all its people
live in turmoil.
But still its pillars are firm.
For I have set them in place."
4I warned the proud people to stop
being so proud!
I told the wicked to stop looking
around with no respect.
5I warned them to stop being stubborn
and proud.
6-7For power does not come from
the earth.
Power comes only from God.
He lifts one up and puts down
another.
8In the Lord's hand there is a cup.
It is full of pale and sparkling wine.

It is his judgment.
It will be poured out on the wicked
of the earth.
They must drink that cup until it's
empty.
9But as for me, I shall always praise the
God of Jacob.
10"I will cut off the strength of evil
men," says the Lord.
"I will increase the power of good
men in their place."

God Is Great

76 God is well known in Judah and
in Israel.
2His home is in Jerusalem.
He lives upon Mount Zion.
3There he breaks the weapons of our
enemies.
4The everlasting mountains cannot
compare with you in glory!
5The mightiest of our enemies are
conquered.
They lie before us in the sleep of
death.
Not one can lift a hand against us.
6When you spoke, God of Jacob,
horses and riders fell.
7No wonder you are feared so much!
Who can stand before an angry God?
8You pronounce sentence on them
from heaven.
The earth shakes and stands silently
before you.
9You stand up to punish the evildoers.
And you defend the humble people
on the earth.
10Man's weak anger will bring you
glory.
You will use it as an ornament!
11Fulfill all the promises you have
made to the Lord your God.
Let everyone bring him gifts.
He should be respected and feared.
12For he cuts down princes.
And he does great things to the
kings of the earth.

God Helps in Hard Times

77 I cried to the Lord.
I call and call to him.
Oh, that he would listen!
2I am in deep trouble.

I need his help so much.
All night long I pray.
I lift my hands to heaven, begging.
There can be no joy for me until he
acts.
³I think of God and groan.
I need his help so badly.
⁴I cannot sleep until you act.
I am too troubled even to pray!
⁵I keep thinking of the good old days
of the past.
⁶Then my nights were filled with
joyous songs.
I search my soul and think about
the difference now.
⁷Has the Lord sent me away forever?
Will he never again help me?
⁸Is his love and kindness gone forever?
Has his promise failed?
⁹Has he forgotten to be kind to one so
undeserving?
Has he slammed the door in anger
on his love?
¹⁰And I said, "This is my fate!
The love of God has changed to
hate."
¹¹I remember the miracles he did for
me so long ago.
¹²Those great deeds are always in my
thoughts.
I cannot stop thinking about them.
¹³O God, your ways are holy.
Where is there any other as great as
you?
¹⁴You are the God of miracles and
wonders!
You still show your awesome power.
¹⁵You have saved us by your strength.
You have bought us, the sons of
Jacob and Joseph.
¹⁶When the Red Sea saw you, how it
was afraid!
It shook to its very bottom!
¹⁷The clouds poured down their rain.
The thunder rolled and crackled in
the sky.
Your lightning flashed.
¹⁸There was thunder in the whirlwind.
The lightning lighted up the world!
The earth trembled and shook.
¹⁹Your road led by a pathway through
the sea.
It was a pathway no one knew was
there!

²⁰You led your people along that road
like a flock of sheep.
Moses and Aaron were their
shepherds.

A History Lesson Teaches Us What to Do

78 O my people, listen to my
teaching.
Open your ears to what I am saying.
²⁻³For I will show you lessons from our
history.
I will tell stories handed down to us
from our parents.
⁴I will teach these truths to you.
That way you will be able to tell
your children.
You will describe the great deeds of the
Lord.
You will tell them about the mighty
miracles he did.
⁵For he gave his laws to Israel.
He commanded our fathers to teach
them to their children.
⁶This was so they could teach their
children too.
Thus his laws pass down from
generation to generation.
⁷In this way each generation has been
able to obey his laws.
And they have set their hope anew
on God.
They have not forgotten his great
miracles.
⁸Thus they did not need to be as their
fathers were.
They did not need to be stubborn,
rebellious, and unfaithful.
They did not refuse to give their
hearts to God.
⁹The people of Ephraim were fully
armed.
But they turned their backs and ran
from battle.
¹⁰They did this because they didn't
obey his laws.
They refused to follow his ways.
¹¹⁻¹²And they forgot about God's great
miracles.
They could not remember what
God had done for their fathers in
Egypt.
¹³For he divided the sea before them
and led them through!

The water stood banked up along both sides of them!

¹⁴In the daytime he led them by a cloud.

At night he led them by a pillar of fire.

¹⁵He split open the rocks in the wilderness.

And he gave them plenty of water. It came as though rushing from a spring.

¹⁶Streams poured from the rock! They flowed out like a river!

¹⁷Yet the people kept on rejecting God. They sinned against the God who is above all gods.

¹⁸They murmured and complained. They asked for other food than God was giving them.

¹⁹⁻²⁰They even spoke against God himself.

"Why can't he give us good food as well as water?" they said.

²¹The Lord heard them and was angry. The fire of his anger burned against Israel.

²²This was because they didn't believe in God.

And they didn't trust in him to care for them.

²³He even commanded the skies to open.

He opened the windows of heaven.

²⁴And he sent down manna for their food.

He gave them bread from heaven!

²⁵They ate angels' food! He gave them all they could hold.

²⁶He sent the mighty east wind. And he guided the south wind by his mighty power.

²⁷He rained down birds as thick as dust. He sent clouds of them like sands along the shore!

²⁸He caused the birds to fall to the ground among the tents.

²⁹The people ate their fill. He gave them what they asked for.

³⁰They ate, and the meat was still in their mouths.

³¹But the anger of the Lord rose against them.

And he killed the finest of Israel's young men.

³²Yet even so the people kept on sinning.

They would not believe in God's miracles.

³³So he cut their lives short. He gave them years of fear and trouble.

³⁴Then at last he had broken them. And they walked awhile behind him.

How earnestly they turned around and followed him!

³⁵Then they remembered that God was their Rock.

They knew that their Savior was the God above all gods.

³⁶But it was only with their words that they followed him.

They still did not follow him with their hearts.

³⁷Their hearts were far away. They did not keep their promises.

³⁸Yet he was merciful to them. He forgave their sins and didn't destroy them all.

Many and many a time he held back his anger.

³⁹For he remembered that they were merely men.

He knew they were gone in a moment like a breath of wind.

⁴⁰Oh, how often they rebelled against him in those desert years!

And how this made his heart sad!

⁴¹Again and again they turned away. They tempted God to kill them.

It was hard for God to give them his blessings.

⁴²They forgot his power and love. They forgot how he had saved them from their enemies.

⁴³They forgot the plagues he sent upon the Egyptians in Tanis.

⁴⁴They did not remember how he turned their rivers into blood.

No one in all Egypt could drink the water!

⁴⁵They forgot how he sent big swarms of flies to fill the land.

They forgot how the frogs had covered all of Egypt!

⁴⁶He gave their crops to caterpillars. Their harvest was eaten by locusts.

47He destroyed their grapevines with
  hail.
  He broke down their sycamores
  with sleet.
48Their cattle died in the fields.
  They were killed by huge hailstones
  from heaven.
Their sheep were killed by lightning.
49He loosed on them his fierce anger.
  He sent them sorrow and trouble.
He sent against them a band of
  destroying angels.
  50He let his anger run free.
And he did not spare the Egyptians'
  lives.
  He let them die of plagues and
  sickness.
51Then he killed the oldest son in each
  Egyptian family.
  He killed the beginning of their
  strength and joy.
52But he led forth his own people like
  a flock.
  He guided them safely through the
  wilderness.
53He kept them safe, so they were not
  afraid.
  But the sea closed in on their
  enemies and overcame them.
54He brought them to the border of his
  land of blessing.
  He led them to this land of hills he
  made for them.
55He drove out the nations in the land.
  He gave each tribe of Israel a place
  as its home.
56He did all this for them.
  But still they rebelled against the
  God above all gods.
  And they would not to follow his
  commands.
57They turned back from entering the
  Promised Land.
  They disobeyed as their fathers had.
  Like a crooked arrow, they missed
  the target of God's will.
58They made him angry by making
  idols.
  And they made altars to other gods.
59When God saw their deeds, his anger
  was strong.
  And he hated his people.
60Then he left his Tabernacle at Shiloh.
  He had lived there among mankind.

61And he let his Ark be captured.
  He gave up his glory into enemy
  hands.
62He caused his people to be killed
  because his anger was strong.
63Their young men were killed by fire.
  Their girls died before they were old
  enough to marry.
64The priests were killed.
  And their widows died before they
  could even cry.
65Then the Lord rose up as though
  waking from sleep.
  He was like a mighty man aroused
  by wine.
66He stood and routed his enemies.
  He drove them back and sent them
  to eternal shame.
67But he rejected Joseph's family, the
  tribe of Ephraim.
  68He chose the tribe of Judah
  instead.
  And he chose Mount Zion, which
  he loved.
69There he built his towering temple.
  It was solid and as strong as the
  heavens and the earth.
70He chose his servant David.
  He took him from feeding sheep.
71-72He called him from following the
  ewes with lambs.
  God gave David to his people as
  their shepherd.
  He took care of them with a true
  heart and skillful hands.

Life Is Not Fair, but God Is

79 O God, your land has been
  conquered by the heathen
  nations.
  Your Temple is defiled.
  And Jerusalem is a heap of ruins.
2The bodies of your people are not
  buried.
  They are food for birds and animals.
3The enemy has killed all the people
  of Jerusalem.
  Blood has flowed like water.
  No one is left even to bury them.
4The nations all around us laugh.
  They pile up contempt on us.
5O Lord, how long will you be angry
  with us?
  Will you be angry forever?

Will your jealousy burn till every
hope is gone?
⁶Pour out your anger on the godless
nations.
These kingdoms refuse to pray.
They will not call on your name.
Do not destroy us!
⁷They have destroyed your people
Israel.
They have gone into every home.
⁸Oh, do not hold us guilty for our
former sins!
Let your mercies meet our needs.
For we are brought low to the dust.
⁹Help us, God of our salvation!
Help us for the honor of your name.
Oh, save us and forgive our sins.
¹⁰Why should the heathen nations be
allowed to laugh?
Why should they be allowed to say,
"Where is their God?"
Avenge this killing of your people!
¹¹Listen to the sighing of the prisoners.
Listen to those condemned to die.
Show the greatness of your power
by saving them.
¹²O Lord, repay these nations seven
times over.
Punish them for scorning you.
¹³We your people are the sheep of your
pasture.
We will thank you forever and ever.
We will praise your greatness from
generation to generation.

God Will Help Us Trust Him

80 O Shepherd of Israel!
You lead Israel like a flock.
O God enthroned above the Guardian
Angels!
Bend down your ear and listen as I
beg.
Show your power and bright glory.
²Let Ephraim, Benjamin, and
Manasseh see you rouse yourself.
Let them see you use your mighty
power to save us.
³Turn us again to yourself, O God.
Look down on us in joy and love.
Only then shall we be saved.
⁴O Lord, God of heaven's armies!
How long will you be angry and
reject our prayers?
⁵You have fed us with sorrow and tears!

⁶You have made us the scorn of the
neighboring nations.
They laugh among themselves.
⁷Turn us again to yourself, O God of
Hosts.
Look down on us in joy and love.
Only then shall we be saved.
⁸You brought us from Egypt.
You treated us like we were a tender
vine.
You drove away the heathen from
your land and planted us.
⁹You cleared the ground and tilled the
soil.
And we took root and filled the
land.
¹⁰The mountains were covered with
our shadow.
We were like the mighty cedar trees.
¹¹We covered the whole land.
We lived from the Mediterranean
Sea to the Euphrates River.
¹²But now you have broken down our
walls.
You have left us without protection.
¹³The boar from the forest roots
around us.
And the wild animals feed on us.
¹⁴Come back, O God of the armies of
heaven.
We beg you to bless us.
Look down from heaven and see our
plight.
Come and take care of this your
vine!
¹⁵Protect what you yourself have
planted.
Save this son you have raised for
yourself.
¹⁶For we are chopped and burned by
our enemies.
May they die at your frown.
¹⁷Strengthen the man you love.
Lift up the son of your choice.
¹⁸And we will never leave you again.
Call us to life again and we will
trust in you.
¹⁹Turn us again to yourself, O God of
heaven's armies.
Look down on us, your face aglow
with joy and love.
Only then shall we be saved.

A Psalm for Special Times

81 The Lord makes us strong!
Sing praises! Sing to Israel's God!
²Sing along with the drums.
Pluck the sweet lyre and harp.
³Sound the trumpet!
Come to the joyous feasts.
Come at full moon, new moon, and
the other holidays.
⁴For God has given us these times of
joy.
They are part of the law of Israel.
⁵He gave them to remind us of his war
against Egypt.
There we were slaves on foreign
soil.
I heard a voice in an unknown
language.
It said,

Listen to the Lord

⁶"Now I will lift this load from your
shoulder.
I will free your hands from their
heavy tasks."
⁷He said, "You cried to me in trouble,
and I saved you.
I answered from Mount Sinai where
the thunder hides.
I tested your faith at Meribah.
This was when you complained there
was no water.
⁸Listen to me, O my people!
Listen while I give you stern
warnings.
O Israel, if you will only listen!
⁹You must never worship any other
gods.
You must not ever have an idol in
your home.
¹⁰For it was I who brought you out of
the land of Egypt.
I am the Lord your God.
Only test me!
Open your mouth wide.
See if I won't fill it.
You will get every blessing you can use!
¹¹"But no, my people won't listen.
Israel doesn't want me around.
¹²So I am letting them go their blind
and stubborn way.
I am letting them live as they want
to.

¹³"But oh, that my people would listen
to me!
Oh, that Israel would follow me,
walking in my paths!
¹⁴How quickly then I would conquer
her enemies!
How soon my hands would be
upon her foes!
¹⁵Those who hate the Lord would bow
before him.
Their destruction would last for all
time.
¹⁶But he would feed you with the best
of foods.
He would satisfy you with honey
for the taking."

God Will Judge

82 God stands up to open heaven's
court.
He pronounces judgment on the
judges.
²How long will you judges refuse to
listen to truth?
How long will you do favors for the
wicked?
³Give fair judgment to the poor man.
Help the fatherless and the abused.
⁴Rescue the poor and helpless from
the hands of evil men.
⁵But you are so foolish and ignorant!
You are in complete darkness!
And so, the foundations of society are
shaken to the core.
⁶I have called you all "gods."
I have called you "sons of the Most
High."
⁷But in death you are mere men.
You will fall as any prince, for all
must die.
⁸Stand up, O God, and judge the earth.
For all of it belongs to you.
All nations are in your hands.

Tell the World God Is Good

83 O God, don't sit by and do
nothing.
Do not stay silent when we pray.
Answer us! Deliver us!
²Don't you hear the noise of your
enemies?
Don't you see what they are doing?

These are proud men who hate the
    Lord.
    3They are full of craftiness.
They make evil plans against your
    people.
    They plot to slay your precious ones.
4"Come," they say.
    "Let us wipe out Israel as a nation.
    We will destroy her very memory."
5This was their decision at their
    meeting.
    They signed a treaty to fight against
    Almighty God.
6These were Ishmaelites, Edomites,
    Moabites, and Hagrites.
    7These were people from the lands
    of Gebal, Ammon, Amalek,
    Philistia and Tyre.
8Assyria has joined them, too.
And they have joined with the
    descendants of Lot.
9Do to them as once you did to
    Midian.
    Defeat them as you did Sisera and
    Jabin at the river Kishon.
10Do to them as you did to your
    enemies at Endor.
    Their dead bodies still make the soil
    rich.
11Make their mighty nobles die as
    Oreb did, and Zeeb.
    Let all their princes die like Zebah
    and Zalmunna.
12They once said, "Let us take these
    pastures of God!"
13O my God, blow them away like dust.
    Blow them like chaff before the
    wind.
14Destroy them as a forest fire that
    roars across a mountain.
    15Chase them with your fiery
    storms and tornados.
16Make them a disgrace, O Lord.
    Destroy them until they know your
    power and name.
17Make them fail in all that they do.
    Let them be ashamed and afraid.
18Teach them you alone, the Lord, are
    God.
    Teach them that you are above all
    gods.
    Show that you are in charge of all
    the earth.

God Delights in Us When
We Trust in Him

84 How lovely is your Temple,
O Lord of the armies of heaven.
2I wish I could enter your courtyard.
    Yes, I faint with wishing!
I want so much to come near to the
    Living God.
3Even the sparrows and swallows are
    welcome there.
    They come and nest among your
    altars.
    And there they have their young.
O Lord of heaven's armies, my King
    and my God!
    4How happy are those who can live
    in your Temple.
    What joy for those who sing your
    praises.
5Happy are those who are strong in
    the Lord.
    What joy for those who want to
    follow your steps.
6They walk through the Valley of
    Crying.
    And it will become a place of
    springs.
    There, pools of blessing collect after
    rains!
7They will grow constantly in strength.
    And each of them is asked to meet
    with the Lord in Zion.
8O Lord, God of the heavenly armies,
    hear my prayer!
    Listen, God of Israel.
9O God, our Defender and our Shield!
    Have mercy on the one you have
    chosen as your king.
10A single day spent in your Temple is
    sweet.
    It is better than a thousand
    anywhere else!
I want to be a doorman in the Temple
    of my God.
    I would rather this, than live in
    palaces of the wicked.
11For the Lord God is our Light and
    Shield.
    He gives us grace and glory.
No good thing will he withhold.
    He will give to those who walk
    along his paths.
12O Lord of the armies of heaven!
    Blessed are those who trust in you.

Peace Comes When
We Follow God

85 Lord, you have poured out great blessings on this land!
You have brought back the wealth of Israel.
[2]You have forgiven the sins of your people.
Yes, you have covered over each one.
[3]So all your blazing anger is now ended.
[4]Now bring us back to loving you, O Lord.
That way you will never need to be angry with us again.
[5]Will you be always angry?
Will you be angry to distant generations?
[6]Oh, call us back to where we were!
Then your people will rejoice in you again.
[7]Pour out your love and kindness on us, Lord.
And give us your salvation.
[8]I am listening carefully to all the Lord is saying.
For he speaks peace to his people, his saints.
All they need to do is stop their sinning.
[9]Surely his salvation is near to those who respect him.
Our land will be filled with his glory.
[10]Mercy and truth have met together.
Grim justice and peace have kissed!
[11]Truth rises from the earth.
Righteousness smiles down from heaven.
[12]Yes, the Lord pours down his blessings on the land.
And it gives forth its rich crops.
[13]Justice goes before him.
It makes a pathway for his steps.

There Is Only One True God

86 Bend down and hear my prayer, O Lord.
Answer me, for I am deep in trouble.
[2]Protect me from death.
For I try to follow all your laws.

Save me, for I am serving you and trusting you.
[3]Be merciful, O Lord!
For I am looking up to you with hope.
[4]Give me happiness, O Lord!
For I worship only you.
[5]O Lord, you are so good and kind.
You are so ready to forgive.
You are so full of mercy for all who ask for help.
[6]Listen closely to my prayer, O God.
Hear my urgent cry.
[7]I will call to you whenever trouble strikes.
And you will help me.
[8]Where among the heathen gods is there a god like you?
Where are their miracles like yours?

We should obey God

Tell me where you want me to go. And I will go there.

Psalm 86:11

---

[9]All the nations were made by you.
They will come and bow before you, Lord.
They will praise your great and holy name.
[10]For you are great and do great miracles.
You alone are God.
[11]Tell me where you want me to go.
And I will go there.
May I always show respect for your name.
[12]With all my heart I will praise you.
I will give glory to your name forever.
[13]For you love me so much!
You are always so kind!
You have saved me from deepest hell.
[14]O God, proud men hate me.
Violent, godless men are trying to kill me.
[15]But you are merciful and gentle, Lord.
You are slow in getting angry.
You are full of constant love and truth.
[16]So look down in pity.
Give strength to your servant and save me.

¹⁷Send me a sign of your favor.
   Those who hate me will see it.
   And they will lose face when you
      help and comfort me.

Jerusalem: A City Loved by God

87 High on his holy mountain
      stands Jerusalem.
   It is the city of God.
   It is the city he loves more than any
      other!
³O city of God, what stories are told of
      you!
⁴Now I might mention the names of
      Egypt and Babylonia.
   I might speak of Philistia and Tyre.
   I might even talk about faraway
      Ethiopia.
When I do, someone brags about the
      land of his birth.
⁵But someday the highest honor will
      be to be a native of Jerusalem!
   For the God above all gods will
      bless this city.
⁶He will register her people.
   He will put a mark beside the
      names of those who were born
      here.
⁷And at the feasts they will sing.
   They will say, "All my heart is in
      Jerusalem."

God Understands When You are Hurting

88 O Lord, God of my salvation!
      I have cried before you day and
      night.
²Now hear my prayers.
   Oh, listen to my cry.
³For my life is full of troubles.
   And death draws near.
⁴They say my life is leaving me.
   They say I am a hopeless case.
⁵They have left me here to die.
   They have left me like those killed
      in battle.
I am like those from whom your
      mercies are removed.
⁶You have thrown me down to the
      darkest depths.
   ⁷Your anger lies very heavy on me.
Wave after wave comes over me.
⁸You have made my friends to hate me.
   They have all gone away.

I am in a trap with no way out.
⁹My eyes grow dim with crying.
   Each day I beg your help.
O Lord, I lift my hands to you for
      mercy.
¹⁰Soon it will be too late!
   Of what use are your miracles when
      I am in the grave?
How can I praise you then?
¹¹Can those in the grave declare your
      love and kindness?
   Can they tell people about how
      faithful you are?
¹²Can the darkness speak of your
      miracles?
   Can anyone in the Land of Death
      talk about your help?
¹³O Lord, I ask for my life.
   I will keep on asking day by day.
¹⁴O Lord, why have you thrown my
      life away?
   Why are you turning your face
      from me?
   Why do you look the other way?
¹⁵From my youth I have been sickly
      and ready to die.
   I stand helpless before your terrors.
¹⁶Your fierce anger has come over me.
   Your terrors have cut me off.
¹⁷They flow around me all day long.
   ¹⁸Lovers and friends are all gone.
   There is only darkness all around.

God Keeps Promises Forever

89 Forever I will sing about the
      tender kindness of the Lord!
   Young and old shall hear about
      your blessings.
²Your love and kindness are forever.
   Your truth lasts as long as the
      heavens.
³⁻⁴The Lord God says, "I have made an
      agreement.
   I have spoken with my chosen
      servant David.
   I have promised to make his
      descendants kings forever.
   They will rule on his throne, from
      now until eternity!"
⁵All heaven shall praise your miracles,
      O Lord.
   Armies of angels will praise you for
      being so faithful.

⁶For who in all of heaven can be
    compared with God?
  What great angel is at all like him?
⁷The most powerful angels are afraid
    of him.
  Who is so respected by his servants
    as he is?
⁸O Lord, Commander of the heavenly
    armies!
  Where is there any other Mighty
    One like you?
  Faithfulness is your very character.
⁹You rule the oceans when their waves
    rise in storms.
  You speak, and they lie still.
¹⁰You have cut proud Egypt to pieces.
  Your enemies are scattered by your
    awesome power.
¹¹The heavens are yours, the world,
    everything.
  For you created them all.
¹²You created north and south!
  Mount Tabor and Mount Hermon
    are full of joy.
  They are glad you are their maker!
¹³Your arm is so strong!
  And so is your hand!
  Your right hand is lifted high in
    great strength.
¹⁴⁻¹⁵Your throne is made on two strong
    pillars.
  The one is Justice and the other
    Righteousness.
  Mercy and Truth walk before you as
    your helpers.
  Happy are those who hear the joyful
    blast of the trumpet.
  For they shall walk in the light of
    your presence.
¹⁶They praise your perfect name.
  They rejoice in your goodness.
¹⁷You are their strength. What glory!
  Our power is based on your favor!
¹⁸Yes, our protection is from the Lord
    himself.
  He, the Holy One of Israel, has
    given us our king.
¹⁹In a vision you spoke to your
    prophet.
  You said, "I have chosen a fine
    young man to be king.
  I chose him from the common
    people.
²⁰He is my servant David!

I have anointed him with my holy
    oil.
²¹I will steady him and make him
    strong.
  ²²His enemies shall not outwit him.
  And the wicked shall not overpower
    him.
²³I will beat down his enemies before
    him.
  I will destroy those who hate him.
²⁴I will protect and bless him always.
  I will surround him with my love.
  He will be great because of me.
²⁵He will rule from the Euphrates River.
  He will reign to the Mediterranean
    Sea.
²⁶And he will cry to me, 'You are my
    Father.
  You are my God and my Rock of
    Salvation.'
²⁷"I will treat him as my firstborn son.
  I will make him the greatest king in
    all the earth.
²⁸I will love him forever and be kind
    to him always.
  My covenant with him will never
    end.
²⁹He will always have a descendant
    who is king.
  His throne will be as endless as the
    days of heaven.
³⁰⁻³²His children might forget my laws.
  They might not obey them.
  And if so, then I will punish them.
³³But I will never take away all my
    love from them.
  I will not let my promise fail.
³⁴No, I will not break my covenant.
  I will not take back one word of
    what I said.
³⁵⁻³⁶For I have made a promise to
    David.
  And a holy God can never lie!
  I said his family would rule forever.
  I promised his throne would
    continue to the end of time.
³⁷His rule shall last as long as the
    moon!
  The moon is my faithful witness in
    the sky."
³⁸Then why throw me off, rejected?
  Why be so angry with the one you
    chose as king?

39Have you taken back your promise to
David?
For you have thrown his crown in
the dust.
40You have broken down the walls
keeping him safe.
You have ruined every fort
defending him.
41Everyone who comes along has
robbed him.
And his neighbors stand by and
make fun.
42You have made his enemies strong
against him.
You have made them happy.
43You have knocked down his sword.
You have refused to help him in
battle.
44You have ended his greatness.
You have thrown down his throne.
45You have made him old before his
time.
You have made him a public shame.
46O Lord, how long will this go on?
Will you hide yourself from me
forever?
How long will your anger burn like
fire?
47Oh, remember how short you have
made man's life.
Is it an empty, futile life you give
the sons of men?
48No man can live forever. All will die.
Who can save his life from the
power of death?
49Lord, where is the love you used to
have for me?
Where is your kindness that you
promised to David?
You promised it to him!
50Lord, see how all the people are
looking down on me.
51Your enemies joke about me.
I am the one you chose as their king.
52And yet, blessed be the Lord forever!
Amen and amen!

Life Is Short,
but God's Kingdom Is Eternal

90 Lord, through all the
generations you have been our
home!
2You were there before the mountains
were made.

Anointing
PSALM 89:20

What would you think if someone
poured a cup of oil on your head?
If you lived in Bible times, this could
be a sign of great honor. It was
called *anointing*. A prophet or priest
poured olive oil from an animal
horn. He poured it on the anointed
person's head. Sometimes the oil
had spices mixed with it. From that
time on, the anointed person had a
special job to do for God. He could
be a king, a priest, or a prophet. But
he belonged to God. Many of the
kings of Israel were anointed. God
commanded Samuel to anoint
David as the next king (1 Samuel
16:13). Sometimes objects were
anointed. That showed they were
to be used only for God's work. The
Tabernacle and its furniture were
anointed (Exodus 30:26-28). We no
longer need to be anointed with olive oil today. Instead, God pours his
Spirit on us so we may do special
jobs for him. If you want to do a
special job for God, ask him to
anoint you with his Holy Spirit.

You were there before the earth was
formed.
You are God without beginning or
end.
³You speak, and man turns back to
dust.
⁴A thousand years are like yesterday to
you!
They are like a single hour!
⁵⁻⁶We glide along through time as
quickly as a racing river.
And we disappear as fast as a dream.
We are like grass that is green in the
morning.
But it is cut down before the
evening shadows fall.
⁷We die beneath your anger.
We are overwhelmed by your wrath.
⁸You spread out our sins before you.
You see all our secret sins.
⁹No wonder the years are hard here
under your anger.
All our days are filled with crying.

**When the Lord is with us
we should not be afraid**

*Now you don't need to be afraid
of the dark. You don't need to
fear the dangers of the day, either.*

Psalm 91:5

---

¹⁰Seventy years are given us!
And some may even live to eighty.
But even the best of these years are
often empty.
They are years full of pain.
Soon they disappear, and we are
gone.
¹¹Who can know the terrors of your
anger?
Which of us can fear you as he
should?
¹²Teach us to count our days.
Help us to know how few they are.
Show us how to spend them as we
should.
¹³O Lord, come and bless us!
How long will you wait?
Turn away your anger from us.
¹⁴Show love to us when we are very
young.
Give us constant joy to the end of
our lives.

¹⁵Give us as much gladness as we had
sadness before!
Take the bad years and give us good
ones.
¹⁶Let us see your miracles again.
Let our children see great things.
Let them see the miracles you used
to do.
¹⁷Let the Lord our God help us.
Let him give us success.
May he make all we do last forever.

Safe from Danger

91 We live under the shadow of the
Almighty.
We are sheltered by the God who is
above all gods.
²This I say, that he alone is my safe
place.
He is my God, and I am trusting
him.
³For he saves you from every trap.
He rescues you from the deadly
plague.
⁴He will shield you with his wings!
They will shelter you.
His faithful promises are your armor.
⁵Now you don't need to be afraid of
the dark.
You don't need to fear the dangers
of the day, either.
⁶You need not fear the plagues of
darkness.
And don't be afraid of troubles in
the morning.
⁷One thousand might fall at my side.
Ten thousand might be dying
around me.
But even so, the evil will not touch me.

**The Lord sends his angels
to watch over us**

*For he orders his angels to
protect you.*

Psalm 91:11

---

⁸I will see how the wicked are
punished.
But I will not share it.
⁹For the Lord is my place of safety!
I choose the God above all gods to
shelter me.
¹⁰How then can evil overtake me?
How can any plague come near?

¹¹For he orders his angels to protect
you.
¹²They will steady you with their
hands.
They will keep you from falling on
rocks on the trail.
¹³You can safely meet a lion.
You can even step on poisonous
snakes.
Yes, you can even trample them
under your feet!
¹⁴For the Lord says, "Because he loves
me, I will rescue him.
I will make him great because he
trusts in my name.
¹⁵When he calls on me, I will answer.
I will be with him in trouble.
I will save him and honor him.
¹⁶I will satisfy him with a full life.
I will give him my salvation."

A Song for the Lord's Day

92 It is good to say thank you to the
Lord.
It is great to sing praises to him.
²Every morning tell him, "Thank you
for your kindness."
Every evening be happy because he
is so faithful.
³Sing his praises.
Play music from the harp and lute
and lyre.
⁴You have done so much for me,
O Lord.
No wonder I am glad!
No wonder I sing for joy.
⁵O Lord, what miracles you do!
And how deep are your thoughts!
⁶Unthinking people do not
understand them!
No fool can understand this:
⁷The wicked seem to grow like
weeds.
But still, there is only eternal death
ahead of them.
⁸But the Lord is praised in the heavens
forever.
⁹His enemies and sinners shall be
scattered.
¹⁰But you have made me as strong as a
wild bull.
How fresh I am because of your
blessings!

¹¹I have heard the doom of my
enemies spoken.
And I have seen them destroyed.
¹²But the godly shall grow like palm
trees.
They shall grow as tall as the cedars
of Lebanon.

We should thank and praise the Lord

It is good to say thank you
to the Lord. It is great to sing
praises to him.

Psalm 92:1

---

¹³For they are planted into the Lord's
own garden.
They are under his personal care.
¹⁴Even in old age they will still bear
fruit.
Even then they will be growing and
green.
¹⁵This honors the Lord.
It proves his faithful care.
He is my shelter.
There is nothing but goodness in
him!

Our Almighty God

93 The Lord is King!
He is clothed in greatness and
strength.
The world is his throne.
²O Lord, you have ruled from the
everlasting past.
³The mighty oceans thunder to
praise you.
⁴You are greater than all the waves
pounding the seashores!
⁵Your royal laws cannot be changed.
Holiness is forever the keynote of
your reign.

God Will Deal with the Wicked

94 Lord God, you are the one who
punishes evil!
Let your glory shine out.
Rise up and judge the earth.
Give the proud the punishment they
should get.
³Lord, how long will you let the
wicked win?
⁴Hear their proud words!
See how proud they act!

How these men of evil brag!
5See them hurting your people, O Lord.
They are taking advantage of those
you love.
6-7They murder widows, foreigners,
and orphans.
They say, "The Lord isn't looking."
They think, "Besides, he doesn't
care."
8These people are fools!
9Is God deaf and blind?
Didn't he make ears and eyes?
10He punishes the nations!
Won't he also punish you?
He knows everything!
Doesn't he also know what you are
doing?
11The Lord knows how weak the
thoughts of people are.
12-13So he helps us by punishing us.
This makes us follow his paths.
It gives us rest from our enemies.
For God traps them and destroys
them.

We should sing to the Lord

Oh, come, let us sing to the Lord!
Psalm 95:1

14The Lord will not leave his people.
For they are his prize.
15Judgment will again be fair.
And all those who obey will be glad.
16Who will keep me safe from the
wicked?
Who will be my shield?
17I would have died unless the Lord
had helped me.
18I screamed, "I'm slipping, Lord!"
And he was kind and saved me.
19Lord, when doubts fill my mind,
quiet me.
When my heart is troubled, give me
hope and cheer.
20Will you let evil leaders rule?
Will you protect them?
Will you let wrong overcome the
right?
21-22Do you like it when the innocent
are sent to die?
No, of course not!
The Lord my God is my fortress.
He is the mighty Rock where I can
hide.

23God has made the sins of evil men to
come back upon them!
He will destroy them by their own
plans.
The Lord our God will cut them off.

Let's Worship God

95 Oh, come, let us sing to the Lord!
Give a happy shout in honor of
the Rock of our salvation!
2Come before him with thankful
hearts.
Let us sing him psalms of praise.
3For the Lord is a great God.
He is the great King of all gods.
4He controls the depths of the earth.
He holds up the highest mountains.
All of these are his.
5He made the sea and formed the land.
They too are his.
6Come, kneel before the Lord our
Maker.
7For he is our God.
We are his sheep.
And he is our Shepherd.
Oh, that you would hear him calling
you.
Oh, that you would come to him!
8Don't harden your hearts.
Don't do as Israel did at Meribah
and Massah.
9For there your fathers doubted me.
And they had seen so many of my
miracles before.
My patience was tried by their
complaints.
10The Lord God says, "For 40 years I
watched them in disgust.
Their thoughts and hearts were far
away from me.
They would not obey my laws.
11Therefore, I rose in mighty anger.
I swore that they would never enter
the Promised Land.
I promised they would not come to
the place of rest I planned for
them."

How Can I Praise God?

96 Sing a new song to the Lord!
Sing it all around the world!
2Sing out his praises! Bless his name.
Each day tell someone that he saves.

3Speak of his great acts throughout the
    earth.
    Tell everyone about the great things
        he does.
4For the Lord is great beyond saying it.
    He is greatly to be praised.
Worship only him among the gods!
    5For the gods of other nations are
        merely idols.
    But our God made the heavens!
6Honor and majesty surround him.
    Strength and beauty are in his
        Temple.

Tell others how wonderful the Lord is

*Tell everyone about the great
things he does.*

Psalm 96:3

7O nations of the world!
    Confess that God alone is great and
        strong.
8Give him the glory he deserves!
    Bring your offering and come to
        worship him.
9Worship the Lord in the beauty of
        holiness.
    Let the earth shake before him.
10Tell the nations that the Lord reigns!
    He rules the world.
His power can never be overthrown.
    He will judge all nations fairly.
11Let the heavens be glad, the earth
        rejoice.
    Let the roaring seas show his glory.
12Praise him for the growing fields.
    For they prove his greatness.
Let the trees of the forest rustle with
        praise.
        13For the Lord is coming to judge
            the earth.
        He will judge the nations fairly and
            with truth!

God Is Awesome and Just

97 The Lord is King!
    Let all the earth rejoice!
    Tell the farthest islands to be glad.
2Clouds and darkness are all around
        him.
    Goodness and justice are the
        foundation of his throne.
3Fire goes forth before him.
    It burns up all his enemies.

4His lightning flashes out across the
        world.
    The earth sees it and shakes.
5The mountains melt like wax before
        the Lord.
    He is Lord of all the earth.
6The heavens declare his perfect
        goodness.
    Every nation sees his glory.
7Let those who worship idols be
        disgraced.
    Put down all who brag about their
        worthless gods.
    For every god must bow to him!
8-9Jerusalem has heard of your justice,
        Lord.
    So have all the other cities of Judah.
They are glad that you rule over the
        whole earth.
    They are happy that you are far
        greater than these other gods.
10The Lord loves those who hate evil.
    He protects the lives of his people.
    He saves them from the wicked.
11Light is planted for the godly.
    Joy is given to the good.
12May all who are godly be happy in
        the Lord.
    May they crown him, our holy God.

A Song of Joy and Victory

98 Sing a new song to the Lord.
    Tell about his mighty deeds!
For he has won a great victory.
    He won it by his power and
        holiness.
2-3He has announced this victory.
    He has shown it to every nation.
He has fulfilled his promise to be kind
        to Israel.
    The whole earth has seen God's
        salvation of his people.
4That is why the earth breaks out in
        praise to God!
    That is why it sings for joy!
5Sing your praises to him!
    Sing with music from the harp.
6Let the cornets and trumpets shout!
    Make a joyful noise before the Lord,
        the King!
7Let the sea in all its greatness roar
        with praise!
    Let the earth and all those living on
        it shout.

Let them say, "Glory to the Lord."
8-9Let the waves clap their hands in
glee.
Let the hills sing out their songs of
joy before the Lord.
For he is coming to judge the world
with perfect justice.

God Is Fair and Holy

99 The Lord is King!
Let the nations shake before
him!
He sits between the Guardian Angels.
Let the whole earth tremble.
2The Lord sits in majesty in Zion.
He is above all rulers of the earth.
3Let them respect your great and holy
name.
4This mighty King always gives justice.
Fairness is found in all that he does.
He judges fairly throughout Israel.
5Praise the Lord our holy God!
Bow low before his feet.
6Moses and Aaron cried to him for
help.

We belong to the Lord

*The Lord is God! He made us
and we are his.*

Psalm 100:3

So did Samuel, his prophet.
And the Lord answered them.
7He spoke to them from the pillar of
cloud.
And they did what he told them to.
8O Lord our God!
You answered them and forgave
their sins.
But you punished them when they
went wrong.
9Praise the Lord our God!
Worship at his holy mountain in
Jerusalem.
For he is holy.

Come Before God and Praise Him

100 Shout with joy before the
Lord, O earth!
2Obey him gladly.
Come before him, singing with joy.
3Try to know what this means: the
Lord is God!
He made us and we are his.

We are his people, the sheep of his
pasture.
4Go through his open gates with great
thanks.
Go into his courts with praise.
Give thanks to him and bless his
name.
5For the Lord is always good.
He is always loving and kind.
And his faithfulness goes on and on.
It reaches to all generations.

Living a Clean Life for God

101 I will sing about your love and
kindness, Lord.
I will praise you for your justice.
I will sing your praises!
2I will try to walk a blameless path.
But how I need your help!
I need it most in my own home.
For there I wish to act as I should.
3Help me to refuse the low and bad
things.
Help me to hate all crooked deals of
every kind.
Help me to have no part in them.
4I will reject all selfishness.
I will stay away from every evil.
5I will not let anyone secretly put
down his neighbor.
I will not allow pride.
6I will make the godly of the land my
heroes.
I will invite them to my home.
Only those who are truly good shall be
my servants.
7But I will not let liars stay in my
house.
8My daily task will be to catch evil
people.
I will free the city of God from their
power.

When We Need Help

102 Lord, hear my prayer!
Listen to my cry!
2Don't turn away from me in this time
of trouble.
Bend down your ear and give me
speedy answers.
3-4For my days float away like smoke.
My health is broken, and my heart
is sick.

It is trampled like grass and is dried
   up.
My food is without taste.
   I have lost my desire to eat.
⁵I am reduced to skin and bones.
   This is because of all my groaning
   and sadness.
⁶I am like a vulture in a far-off
   wilderness.
   I am like an owl alone in the desert.
⁷I lie awake, lonely as a single sparrow
   on the roof.
⁸My enemies laugh at me day after day.
   They curse at me.
⁹⁻¹⁰I eat ashes instead of bread.
   My tears run down into my drink.
Your anger is against me.
   For you have rejected me and
   thrown me out.
¹¹My life is passing as fast as the
   evening shadows.
   I am drying up like grass.
¹²But you, Lord, are a famous King
   forever.
   Your fame will be known to every
   generation.
¹³I know that you will come and have
   mercy on Jerusalem.
   And now is the time to pity her.
   Now is the time you promised help.
¹⁴For your people love every stone in
   her walls.
   They love every grain of dust in her
   streets.
¹⁵Now let the rulers of the nations
   shake before the Lord.
   Let them tremble before his glory.
¹⁶For the Lord will rebuild Jerusalem!
   He will come in his glory!
¹⁷He will listen to the prayers of the
   poor.
   For he is never too busy to hear
   what they say.
¹⁸I am writing this down.
   I want future generations to praise
   the Lord.
   I want them to remember all that
   he has done.
And a people that shall be created
   shall praise the Lord.
¹⁹Tell them that God looked down
   from his temple in heaven.
²⁰He heard the cries of his people in
   slavery.

They were children of death, and
   he let them go.
²¹⁻²²So many went to the Temple in
   Jerusalem.
They went there to praise him.
And his praises were sung throughout
   the city.
   And many rulers throughout the
   earth came to worship him.
²³He has cut me down in middle life.
   He has made my days short.
²⁴But I cried to him, "O God!
   You live forever and ever!

God never grows old or dies

But you never grow old. You are
forever, and your years never end.

Psalm 102:27

Don't let me die half through my
   years!
²⁵In ages past you laid the foundations
   of the earth!
   You made the heavens with your
   hands!
²⁶They shall die, but you go on forever.
   They will grow old like worn-out
   clothing.
You will change them like a man
   putting on a new shirt.
   You will throw away the old one.
²⁷But you never grow old.
   You are forever, and your years
   never end.
²⁸But our families will keep living.
   Generation after generation will
   live by your hand."

God's Great Love for Us

103 I bless the holy name of God
   with all my heart.
²Yes, I will bless the Lord.
   I will not forget the great things he
   does for me.
³He forgives all my sins.
   He heals me.
⁴He brings me out from hell.
   He surrounds me with love and
   tender mercies.
⁵He fills my life with good things!
   My youth is made new like the
   eagle's!
⁶He gives justice to all who are treated
   unfairly.

7He showed his will and nature to
  Moses and the people of Israel.
8He is merciful and tender toward
  those who don't deserve it.
  He is slow to get angry and full of
  kindness and love.
9He never holds a grudge.
  He does not stay angry forever.
10He has not punished us as we
  deserve for all our sins.
  11For he has mercy toward those
  who fear and honor him.
His mercy is as great as the height of
  the heavens above the earth.
12He has taken our sins far away
  from us.
  He has taken them as far as the east
  is from the west.

God is like a kind father

He is like a father to us.
He is tender and kind
to those who honor him.

Psalm 103:13

13He is like a father to us.
  He is tender and kind to those who
  honor him.
14For he knows we are but dust.
  15He knows that our days are few
  and short.
  They are like grass and flowers.
16They are blown by the wind and
  gone forever.
17-18But the love of the Lord lasts
  forever.
  He will always love those who
  honor him.
  He will save the grandchildren of
  those who obey him!
19The Lord has made the heavens his
  throne.
  From there he rules over all there
  is.
20Bless the Lord, you mighty angels.
  Bless him, you who carry out his
  orders.
  Praise him as you listen for each of
  his commands.
21Yes, bless the Lord, you armies of
  angels.
  Praise him, you who serve him all
  the time.

22Let everything everywhere bless the
  Lord.
  And how I bless him too!

God Takes Care of His World

104 I bless the Lord!
     O Lord my God, how great
       you are!
You are clothed with honor, greatness,
  and light!
  You stretched out the starry curtain
  of the heavens.
3You cut out the surface of the earth to
  make the seas.
  The clouds are your chariots!
  You ride upon the wings of the
  wind!
4The angels are your messengers.
  They are your servants of fire!
5You put the world together so that it
  would never fall apart.
6You clothed the earth with floods of
  waters.
  You even covered up the mountains!
7-8You spoke, and the water went into
  the ocean beds.
  Mountains rose and valleys sank to
  the levels you commanded.
9And then you set a border for the seas.
  You did this so they would never
  again cover the earth.
10He put springs in the valleys.
  And he made the streams that pour
  from the mountains.
11They give water for all the animals to
  drink.
  There the wild donkeys quench
  their thirst.
12The birds build nests beside the
  streams.
  And they sing among the branches
  of the trees.
13He sends rain upon the mountains.
  He fills the earth with fruit.
14The tender grass grows up at his
  command to feed the cattle.
  There are fruit trees, vegetables, and
  grain for man to grow.
15There is wine to make him glad.
  There is olive oil as lotion for his
  skin.
  There is bread to give him strength.
16The Lord planted the cedars of
  Lebanon.

They are tall and growing.
¹⁷There the birds make their nests.
The storks nest in the firs.
¹⁸High in the mountains are pastures
for the wild goats.
Rock-badgers burrow in among the
rocks.
They find a safe place there.
¹⁹He told the moon to mark the
months.
And he told the sun to mark the
days.
²⁰He sends the night and darkness.
This is when all the forest folk
come out.
²¹Then the young lions roar for their
food.
But they still need the Lord's help.
²²At dawn they sneak back into their
dens to rest.
²³And men go off to work until the
evening shadows fall again.
²⁴O Lord, what different kinds of
things you have made!
And in wisdom you have made
them all!
The earth is full of your riches.
²⁵There before me lies the mighty
ocean.
It is full of life of every kind.
There is life, both great and small.
²⁶And look! See the ships!
And over there, the whale you
made to play in the sea.
²⁷Every one of these depends on you
to give them daily food.
²⁸You supply it, and they gather it.
You open wide your hand to feed
them.
And they have enough from what
you give.
²⁹But if you turn away from them,
then all is lost.
You might gather up their breath.
But then they die and turn again to
dust.
³⁰Then you send your Spirit.
And new life is born.
It builds up all the living of the
earth.
³¹Praise God forever!
How he must rejoice in all his work!
³²The earth shakes when he looks at it.

The mountains burst into flame at
his touch.
³³I will sing to the Lord as long as I
live.
I will praise God to my last breath!
³⁴May he be pleased by all these
thoughts about him.
For he is the source of all my joy.
³⁵Let all die who will not praise him.
But I will praise him.
Praise the Lord!

Remember God's Miracles

105 Thank the Lord for all the great
things he does.
Tell them to all the nations.
²Sing his praises!
Tell everyone about his miracles.
³Glory in the Lord.
O worshipers of God, be full of joy.
⁴Search for him and for his strength.
And keep on searching!
⁵⁻⁶Think of the mighty deeds he did
for us.
We are his chosen ones.
We are the children of God's servant
Abraham, and of Jacob.
Remember how he destroyed our
enemies.
⁷He is the Lord our God.
His goodness is seen throughout
the land.
⁸⁻⁹One thousand generations might
pass.
But he will never forget his promise.
He will not forget his covenant
with Abraham and Isaac.
¹⁰⁻¹¹He will not forget his promises
to Jacob.
This is his treaty with the people of
Israel:
"I will give you the land of Canaan.
It will be yours for all time."
¹²He said this when there were only a
few of them.
At that time, they were only visitors
in Canaan.
¹³Later they were sent out among the
nations.
They were driven from one
kingdom to another.
¹⁴But the Lord did not let anyone hurt
them.
He warned kings not to touch them.

And he destroyed many a king who tried!

15"Do not touch my chosen people," he warned.

"And do not hurt my prophets."

16He called for a famine on the land of Canaan.

He cut off its food supply.

17Then he sent Joseph as a slave to Egypt.

He went there to save his people from hunger.

18There in prison they hurt his feet with chains.

They put his neck in an iron collar.

19But then God's time finally came.

Oh, how God tested his patience!

20Then the king sent for him and set him free.

21He was put in charge of all that the king owned.

22He had power to put the king's servants in prison.

He was a teacher for the king's advisors.

23Then Jacob (Israel) came to Egypt.

And he lived there with his sons.

24Soon the people of Israel had many children.

They became a greater nation than their rulers.

25At that point God turned the Egyptians against them.

They hated them and made them slaves.

26But God sent Moses as his servant.

And he sent Aaron with him.

27They called down plagues on the land of Egypt.

28They did all that the Lord told them.

He sent thick darkness through the land.

29He turned the nation's water into blood.

He poisoned the fish.

30Then frogs invaded the land in great numbers.

They were found even in the king's private rooms.

31When Moses spoke, the flies and other insects swarmed.

They came in great clouds from one end of Egypt to the other.

32Instead of rain he sent down a killing hail.

Lightning flashes held the nation in terror.

33Their grape vines and fig trees were ruined.

All the trees lay broken on the ground.

34He spoke, and many locusts came.

35They ate up everything green.

They destroyed all the crops.

36Then he killed the oldest child in each Egyptian home.

He destroyed their pride and joy!

37He brought his people safely out from Egypt.

They left, loaded with silver and gold.

There were no sick and feeble folk among them then.

38Egypt was glad when they were gone.

For they were very afraid of them.

39He spread out a cloud above them.

It was to shield them from the burning sun.

He gave them a pillar of flame at night.

It lit the way before them.

40They asked for meat.

So he sent them quail.

He gave them manna, bread from heaven.

41He opened up a rock.

And water rushed out to form a river.

It flowed through the dry and empty land.

42For the Lord remembered his holy promises.

These were the ones he made to Abraham his servant.

43So he brought his chosen ones singing into the Promised Land.

44He gave them the lands of the Gentiles.

And their growing crops came with it.

They ate what others planted.

45This was done to make them faithful.

It was to help them obey his laws.

Praise the Lord!

God Always Forgives

106 Praise the Lord!
Thank you, Lord!
How good you are!

Your love for us goes on forever.
²Who can ever list the great miracles
of God?
  Who can ever praise him even half
  enough?
³Happiness comes to those who are
fair to others.
  Joy is given to those who are always
  kind and good.
⁴Remember me, too, O Lord!
  Remember me as you bless and save
  your people.
⁵Let me share in your chosen ones'
riches.
  Let me share in all their joys.
  Let me have some of the glory you
  give to them.
⁶Both we and our fathers have sinned
so much.
⁷They weren't impressed by the
wonder of your miracles in Egypt.
  They soon forgot your many acts of
  kindness to them.
Instead they broke away from you at
the Red Sea.
⁸But even so you saved them.
  You saved them to defend the
  honor of your name.
  You rescued them to show your
  power to all the world.
⁹You commanded the Red Sea to
divide.
  You made a dry road across its
  bottom.
  Yes, it was as dry as any desert!
¹⁰Thus you saved them from their
enemies.
¹¹Then the water fell back.
  It covered the road and drowned
  their enemies.
  Not one lived to tell of it!
¹²Then at last his people believed him.
  Then they finally sang his praise.
¹³Yet how quickly they forgot again!
  They wouldn't wait for him to act.
¹⁴They demanded better food.
  They tested God's patience to the
  breaking point.
¹⁵So he gave them what they wanted.
  But he sent them leanness in their
  souls.
¹⁶They were jealous of Moses.
  Yes, they were jealous of Aaron, too.

Aaron was the man chosen by God as
his priest.
¹⁷Because of this, the earth opened up.
  It swallowed Dathan, Abiram, and
  his friends.
¹⁸And fire fell from heaven to burn
  these wicked men.
    ¹⁹⁻²⁰For they wanted a statue of an
    ox that eats grass.
  They wanted that instead of God
  himself.
²¹⁻²²Thus they broke away from their
  Savior, even though he had done
  such great miracles in Egypt and
  at the Sea.
²³So the Lord was going to kill them
all!
  But Moses, his chosen one, stepped
  into the gap.
He stood between the people and their
God.
  He begged the Lord to turn from his
  anger.
  He asked him not to destroy them.
²⁴They would not go into the
Promised Land.
  For they wouldn't believe his
  promise to care for them.
²⁵Instead, they pouted in their tents.
  They cried and did not follow his
  command.
²⁶Then he promised that they would
  die in the wilderness.
    ²⁷He swore to send their children
    away.
  They would be sent to faraway
  lands as prisoners.
²⁸Then our fathers joined the
  worshipers of Baal at Peor.
  They even gave sacrifices to the
  dead!
²⁹With all these things they made God
  angry.
  And so a plague broke out upon
  them.
³⁰The plague grew worse until Phineas
  stood up.
  He killed the ones whose sin had
  made the plague start.
³¹For this good deed Phineas will be
  remembered forever.
³²At Meribah, too, Israel made God
  angry.

And they got Moses into bad trouble.

³³For he got angry and spoke foolishly.

³⁴And Israel did not destroy the nations in the land.

They did not do as God had told them to.

³⁵But they lived with the heathen.

And they learned their evil ways.

³⁶They made sacrifices to their idols.

And they were led away from God.

³⁷⁻³⁸They even sacrificed their little children to demons.

They sacrificed them to the idols of Canaan.

They killed little babies who had done nothing wrong.

And with this murder, they made the land unclean.

³⁹Their evil deeds made them dirty.

For their love of idols was evil in God's sight.

⁴⁰That is why the Lord's anger burned against his people.

That is why he hated them.

⁴¹⁻⁴²That is why he let the heathen nations crush them.

They were ruled by those who hated them.

They were pushed around by their enemies.

⁴³Again and again he saved them from slavery.

But they just kept on rebelling against him.

They were finally destroyed by their sin.

We must be sure to thank the Lord

*Say thank you to the Lord
for being so good!
Thank him for always being
so loving and kind.*

Psalm 107:1

---

⁴⁴Yet, even so, he listened to their cries.

He heard them in their trouble and sadness.

⁴⁵He remembered his promises to them.

And he let up because of his great love.

⁴⁶He made even their enemies who captured them to pity them.

⁴⁷O Lord God, save us!

Bring us from the nations!

That way we will be able to thank your holy name.

Then we will be able to rejoice and praise you.

⁴⁸Blessed be the Lord, the God of Israel!

Praise be to him forever and ever.

Let all the people say, "Amen!"

Praise the Lord!

Give Thanks Always

107 Say thank you to the Lord for being so good!

Thank him for always being so loving and kind!

²Has the Lord saved you? Then speak out!

Tell others he has saved you from your enemies.

³He brought the exiles back to Israel.

He brought them from the corners of the earth.

⁴They were wandering without a home in the desert.

⁵They were hungry and thirsty and faint.

⁶"Lord, help!" they cried, and he did!

⁷He led them straight to safety.

He gave them a good place to live.

⁸Oh, that these men would praise the Lord for his love!

Oh, that they would bless him for his great deeds!

⁹For he gives drink to the thirsty soul.

He fills the hungry soul with goodness.

¹⁰Who are these who sit in darkness?

Who sits in the shadow of death?

Who is crushed by sadness and slavery?

¹¹They rebelled against the Lord.

They made fun of the God above all gods.

¹²That is why he broke them with hard work.

They fell and none could help them stand again.

¹³Then they cried to the Lord in their troubles.

And he turned and saved them!

¹⁴He led them from the darkness.

He broke their chains and set them
   free!
15Oh, that these men would praise the
   Lord for his love!
   Oh, that they would bless him for
   his great deeds!
16For he broke down their prison gates
   of brass.
   He cut apart their iron bars.
17Others, the fools, were sick because
   of their sinful ways.
18They didn't even want to eat
   anymore.
   And they were about to die.
19Then they cried to the Lord in their
   troubles.
   He helped them and saved them.
20He spoke, and they were healed.
   He pulled them from the door of
   death.
21Oh, that these men would praise the
   Lord for his love!
   Oh, that they would bless him for
   his great deeds!
22Let them tell him thank you as their
   sacrifice.
   Let them sing about his great deeds.
23And then there are the sailors sailing
   the seven seas.
   They sailed the trade routes of the
   world.
24They, too, see the power of God in
   action.
25He calls to the storm winds.
   The waves rise high.
26Their ships are tossed to the heavens.
   Then they sink again to the depths.
   The sailors shake in fear.
27They reel and stagger like drunks.
   They are about to go crazy.
28Then they cry to the Lord in their
   trouble.
   And the Lord turns and saves them.
29He calms the storm and stills the
   waves.
30What a blessing is that still sea!
   It is quiet as he brings them safely
   into harbor!
31Oh, that these men would praise the
   Lord for his love!
   Oh, that they would bless him for
   his great deeds!
32Let them praise him before all the
   people.

Let them praise him before the
   leaders of the nation.
33He dries up rivers.
34He turns the good land of the wicked
   into deserts of salt.
35Again, he turns deserts into rich,
   watered valleys.
36He brings the hungry to settle there
   and build their cities.
37He brings them to plant their fields
   and vineyards.
   He helps them harvest rich crops!
38How he blesses them!
   They raise big families there, and
   many cattle.
39But others become poor through
   trouble and sorrow.
   40For God pours contempt upon the
   proud.
   He makes princes to wander among
   ruins.
41But he saves the poor who are godly.
   He gives them many children and
   riches.
42Good men everywhere will see it and
   be glad.
   But evil men are made silent.
43Listen, if you are wise.
   Hear what I have to say.
   Think about the love of the Lord!

With God, We Can

108 O God, my heart is ready to
   praise you!
   I will sing and rejoice before you.
2Wake up, O harp and lyre!
   We will meet the morning with
   song.
3I will praise you everywhere around
   the world.
   I will praise you in every nation.
4For your love is great beyond measure.
   It is as high as the heavens.
Your faithfulness reaches the skies.
5His glory is far bigger than the
   heavens.
   It towers above the earth.
6Hear the cry of your beloved child.
   Come with mighty power and
   save me.
7God has given holy promises.
   No wonder I am so full of praise!
He has promised to give us the land of
   Shechem.

He also has promised us Succoth
Valley.
8"Gilead is mine to give to you," he
says.
"I give you Manasseh as well.
The land of Ephraim is my helmet.
Judah is my scepter.
9But Moab and Edom are hated.
And I will shout in triumph over
the Philistines."
10Who but God can give me strength?
Who but he can help me take these
walled cities?
Who else can lead me into Edom?
11Lord, have you thrown us away?
Have you left our army?
12Oh, help us fight against our
enemies.
For men are useless helpers in a
fight.
13But with the help of God we shall do
mighty acts.
For he walks over our enemies.

Help Me, O Lord!

109 O God of my praise!
Don't stand silent and far away.
2The wicked are telling lies about me.
3They have no reason to hate and
fight me.
But still, they do!
4I love them and pray for them.
But even then, they are trying to
destroy me.
5They give me bad when I give them
good.
They hate me when I love them.
6Show them how it feels!
Let lies be told about them.
Bring them to court before an
unfair judge.
7And let him be declared guilty in
court.
Count his prayers as sins.
8Let his years be few and short.
Let others step forward to take his
place.
9-10May his children become fatherless.
May his wife become a widow.
May they be sent out from the ruins
of their home.
11May people take all that he owns.
May strangers spend all he has
earned.

12-13Let no one be kind to him.
Let no one pity his fatherless
children.
May they die!
May his family name be forgotten
in one generation.
14Punish the sins of his father and
mother.
Don't overlook them.
15Think always about the bad things
he has done.
Make his name be forgotten by
everyone.
16For he did not give kindness to
others.
He took advantage of those in need.
He pushed those with broken hearts
to death.
17He loved to curse others.
Now you curse him.
He never blessed others.
Now don't you bless him.
18Cursing is as much a part of him as
his clothing.
He drank it like he drinks water.
He ate it like rich food.
19Now may those curses come back on
him.
May they stick to him like his
clothing or his belt.
20This is the Lord's punishment on my
enemies.
They tell lies about me and want to
kill me.
21But as for me, O Lord, treat me as
your child.
Deal with me as one who bears
your name!
Because you are so kind, O Lord, save
me.
22-23I am slipping down the hill to
death.
My life is like a grasshopper
brushed from a man's arm.
24My knees are weak from fasting.
I am skin and bones.
25I am a symbol of failure to all
mankind.
When they see me they shake their
heads.
26Help me, O Lord my God!
Save me because you are loving and
kind.
27Do it in front of the people.

That way all will see that you have
    done it.
28Then let them curse me if they like.
    I won't mind that if you are
    blessing me!
For then all their work to destroy me
    will fail.
    And I shall go right on with joy!
29Make them fail in all they do.
    Dress them with shame.
30But I will give thanks to the Lord.
    I will praise him before everyone.
31For he stands beside the poor and
    hungry.
    He saves them from their enemies.

Jesus Christ, The Messiah

110 The Lord God said to my Lord,
    "Sit at my right hand.
    I will defeat your enemies.
    I will make them bow low before
    you."
2The Lord has put your throne in
    Jerusalem.
    From there you are to rule over
    your enemies.
3Your people shall come to you on the
    day you come to power.
    They shall come dressed in holy
    altar robes.
And your strength shall be new each
    day.
    It will come like the morning dew.
4The Lord has made a promise.
    And he will not take it back now.
You will be a priest forever like
    Melchizedek.
5God stands beside you to keep you
    safe.
    He will strike down many kings in
    the day of his anger.
6He will punish the nations.
    He will fill them with their dead.
    He will crush many heads.
7But he himself shall be fresh.
    He will drink from springs along
    the way.

All God Does Is Good

111 Praise the Lord!
    I want to thank God before his
    people.
    I want to praise him for his mighty
    miracles.

All who are thankful should think on
    them with me.
3For his miracles show his honor.
    They prove his majesty and eternal
    goodness.
4Who can forget the wonders he does?
    Who can forget his deeds of mercy
    and grace?
5He gives food to those who trust him.
    He never forgets his promises.
6He has shown his great power to his
    people.
    He did this by giving them the land
    of Israel.
    He did this even though it was the
    home of many nations.
7All he does is just and good.
    And all his laws are right.
8For they are formed from truth and
    goodness.
    And they will stand firm forever.
9He has paid a full ransom for his
    people.
    Now they are always free to come
    to the Lord.
What a holy and great name he has!
10How can men be wise?
    The only way to begin is by
    respecting God.
For growth in wisdom comes from
    obeying his laws.
    Praise his name forever.

God Takes Care of
Those Who Obey

112 Praise the Lord!
    For all who fear God will be
    happy.
Those who trust in him will be blessed.
    Yes, happy is the man who loves to
    obey his commands.
2His children shall be honored
    everywhere.
    Good men's sons will be blessed.
3He himself shall be rich.
    His good deeds will never be
    forgotten.
4Darkness might overtake him.
    But then light will come bursting in.
The Lord is kind and full of mercy.
5And all goes well for the good man.
    He does his business with fairness.
6Such a man will not be destroyed by
    trouble.

He will be remembered forever.
⁷He is not afraid of bad news.
He does not live in fear of what
may happen.
For he is settled in his mind.
He knows that the Lord will take
care of him.

We should praise God at all times

*Praise the Lord from
sunrise to sunset!*

Psalm 113:3

---

⁸That is why he is not afraid.
But he can calmly face his enemies.
⁹He gives freely to those in need.
His deeds will never be forgotten.
He shall have power and honor.
¹⁰Evil men will be angry when they
see this.
They will grind their teeth in anger.
They will sneak away, their hopes
destroyed.

God Cares about Everyone

113 Praise the Lord!
O servants of the Lord, praise
his name.
²Blessed is his name forever and ever.
³Praise the Lord from sunrise to
sunset!
⁴For he is high above the nations.
His glory is far greater than the
heavens.
⁵Who can be compared with God
enthroned on high?
⁶Far below him are the heavens and
the earth.
He stoops down to look.
⁷He lifts the poor from the dirt.
He takes the hungry from the
garbage dump.
⁸He sets them among princes!
⁹He gives children to the childless wife.
And now she is a happy mother.
Praise the Lord!

Celebrate God's Great Work

114 Long ago the Israelites escaped
from Egypt.
They came from that land of a
foreign language.

²And the land of Israel became God's
new home and kingdom.
³The Red Sea saw them coming.
And it quickly broke apart in front
of them.
The Jordan River opened up a path
for them to cross.
⁴The mountains skipped like rams!
The little hills jumped like lambs!
⁵What's wrong, Red Sea, that made
you cut yourself in two?
What happened, Jordan River, to
your waters?
Why were they held back?
⁶Why, mountains, did you skip like
rams?
Why, little hills, did you jump like
lambs?
⁷Shake, O earth, for the Lord is here!
Tremble before the God of Jacob.
⁸For he brought rushing streams from
dry rock!

God Lives

115 Make your name great, not
ours, O Lord!
Make everyone praise your love and
truth.
²Why let the nations say, "Their God
is dead!"
³For he is in the heavens and does
as he wishes.
⁴Their gods are just manmade things.
They are made of silver and of gold.
⁵They can't talk with their mouths!
They can't see with their eyes!
⁶And they can't hear or smell.
⁷They can't use their hands or feet.
They can't even speak!
⁸There are those who make and
worship the idols.
But they are just as foolish as their
idols!
⁹O Israel, trust in the Lord!
He is your helper.
He is your shield.
¹⁰O priests of Aaron, trust in the Lord!
He is your helper.
He is your shield.
¹¹All of you, his people, trust in him.
He is your helper.
He is your shield.
¹²The Lord is always thinking about us.
He will surely bless us.

He will bless the people of Israel.
He will bless the priests of Aaron.
¹³He will bless all who respect him.
¹⁴May the Lord richly bless both you
and your children.
¹⁵Yes, the Lord made heaven and earth.
And he will personally bless you,
too!
¹⁶The heavens belong to the Lord.
But he has given the earth to all
mankind.
¹⁷The dead cannot sing praises to the
Lord on earth.
¹⁸But we can! We praise him forever!
Praise the Lord!

God Saves Us; Let's Worship Him

116 I love the Lord because he
hears my prayers.
²He bends down and listens.
So I will pray as long as I breathe!
³Death stared me in the face.
I was afraid and sad.
⁴Then I cried, "Lord, save me!"
⁵How kind he is!
How good he is!
This God of ours is so merciful!
⁶The Lord protects the simple and the
childlike.
I was facing death and then he
saved me.
⁷Now I can rest.
For the Lord has done this miracle
for me.
⁸He has saved me from death.
He has dried my eyes from tears.
He has kept my feet from stumbling.
⁹I shall live close to the Lord!
I shall live with him here on earth!

God hears our prayers

I love the Lord because he hears

my prayers.

Psalm 116:1

---

¹⁰⁻¹¹I was sad and discouraged.
I thought, "They are lying when
they say I will get better."
¹²But now what can I give the Lord?
He has done so much for me!
¹³I will bring him an offering of wine.
I will praise his name for saving me.
¹⁴I will bring him the sacrifice I
promised.

I will do this in front of all the
people.
¹⁵His loved ones are very special to
him.
He does not lightly let them die.
¹⁶O Lord, you have freed me from my
chains.
I will serve you forever.
¹⁷I will worship you always.
I will give you a sacrifice of thanks.
¹⁸⁻¹⁹Here I am in the courts of the
Temple in Jerusalem.
Here, before all the people, I will
fulfill my promise.
I will pay everything I promised to the
Lord.
Praise the Lord!

Praise God for His Love

117 Praise the Lord, all nations
everywhere!
Praise him, all the peoples of the
earth!
²For he loves us very dearly.
And his truth goes on forever.
Praise the Lord!

God's Love Never Fails

118 Oh, thank the Lord, for he's so
good!
His love and kindness last forever.
²Let all the people of Israel praise him.
Let them say, "His love and
kindness last forever."
³And let the priests of Aaron join them.
Let them say, "His love and
kindness last forever."
⁴Then let the Gentile believers speak
up.
Let them say, "His love and
kindness last forever."
⁵In my trouble I prayed to the Lord.
He answered me and saved me.
⁶He is for me!
How can I be afraid?
What can mere man do to me?
⁷The Lord is on my side.
He will help me.
Let those who hate me be careful.
⁸It is better to trust in the Lord than in
men.
⁹It is best to look to the Lord for
safety.

This is better than looking to the greatest king!

[10]All the powerful nations attack me.
But I will march out behind his flag and destroy them.

God's Word will help us live a clean life

How can a young person stay pure? By reading your Word and doing what it says.

Psalm 119:9

---

[11]Yes, they surround and attack me.
But with his flag flying above me I will cut them off.
[12]They swarm around me like bees.
They burn against me like a roaring flame.
But under his flag I shall destroy them.
[13]You did your best to kill me, O my enemy.
But the Lord helped me.
[14]He is my strength and song in the heat of battle.
And now he has given me the victory.
[15-16]Songs of joy are sung.
They are sung at the news of our rescue.
They are sung in the homes of the godly.
The strong arm of the Lord has done great things!
[17]I shall not die but live to tell of all his deeds.
[18]The Lord has punished me.
But he has not handed me over to death.
[19]Open the gates of the Temple.
I will go in and give him my thanks.
[20]Those gates are the way into the Lord's presence.
Only the godly go in there.
[21]O Lord, thank you for answering my prayer.
Thank you so much for saving me.
[22]The builders threw away a stone.
But that stone has become the capstone of the arch!
[23]This is the Lord's doing.
And it is wonderful to see!

[24]This is the day the Lord has made.
We will rejoice and be glad in it.
[25]O Lord, please help us.
Save us! Give us success!
[26]Blessed is the one who is coming.
He is the one sent by the Lord.
We bless you from the Temple.
[27-28]The Lord God is our light.
I present to him my sacrifice on the altar.
For you are my God.
And I shall give you this thanks and praise.
[29]Oh, give thanks to the Lord, for he is so good!
For his love and kindness last forever.

Happiness Is Obeying God

119 Happy are all who follow the laws of God.
[2]Happy are all who search for God.
They always choose to do his will.
[3]They do not do evil.
And they walk only in his paths.
[4]You have given us your laws to obey.
[5]Oh, how I want to follow them!
[6]Then I will not be ashamed.
For I will have a clean record.
[7]I will thank you with an honest heart.
For now I know that your laws are fair.
[8]I will obey you!
Oh, don't leave me.
Don't let me slip back into sin again.

How Can I Be Pure?

[9]How can a young person stay pure?
By reading your Word and doing what it says.
[10]I have tried my best to find you.
Don't let me wander from your truths.
[11]I have thought much about your words.
I have stored them in my heart.
That way they will hold me back from sin.
[12]Blessed Lord, teach me your rules.
[13]I have said your laws over and over.
[14]I am more happy with them than with riches.

¹⁵I will think about them.
　I will give them my full respect.
¹⁶I will delight in them and not forget
　them.

God Provides a Plan for Our Lives

¹⁷Bless me with life.
　Do this so I can keep on obeying
　you.
¹⁸Open my eyes to see wonderful
　things in your Word.
¹⁹I am just a traveler here on earth.
　I need a map to show me the way.
　And your commands are my chart
　and guide.
²⁰I wish for your laws more than I can
　tell.
²¹You put down the proud who don't
　obey your commands.
²²Don't let them hate me for
　obeying you.
²³For even princes sit and talk against
　me.
　But I will still follow your plans.
²⁴Your law is my light and my
　counselor.

God Helps Us Follow Him

²⁵I am completely discouraged.
　I lie down in the dust.
　Pick me up with your Word.
²⁶I told you my plans and you
　answered me.
　Now tell me what you want me to
　do.
²⁷Make me understand what you want.
　For then I shall see your miracles.
²⁸I cry because I am sad.
　My heart is heavy with sorrow.
　Encourage and cheer me with your
　words.
²⁹⁻³⁰Keep me far from every wrong.
　Help me to obey your laws.
　Do this even though I don't deserve it.
　For I have chosen to do right.
³¹I cling to your commands.
　I follow them as closely as I can.
　Lord, don't let me make a mess of
　things.
³²Help me to want your will!
　If you do, I will follow your laws
　even more closely.

How Can I Please God?

³³⁻³⁴Just tell me what to do and I will
　do it, Lord.
　As long as I live I'll obey with all
　my heart.
³⁵Make me walk along the right paths.
　For I know how delightful they
　really are.
³⁶Help me to want to obey more than
　making money!
³⁷Turn me away from wanting any
　other plan than yours.
　Bring my heart back toward you.
³⁸Tell me that your promises are for
　me.
　For I trust and respect you.
³⁹How I hate being laughed at for
　obeying.
　For your laws are right and good.

God Helps Us Obey Him

⁴⁰⁻⁴²I want so much to obey them!
　Therefore in fairness make my life
　new.
For this was your promise.
　Yes, Lord, you promised to save me!
Now spare me by your kindness and
　your love.
　Then I will have an answer for
　those who make fun of me.
　For I trust your promises.
⁴³May I never forget your words.
　For they are my only hope.
⁴⁴⁻⁴⁶Therefore I will keep on obeying
　you forever.
　I am free within the limits of your
　laws.
I will speak to kings about their value.
　And they will listen with interest
　and respect.
⁴⁷How I love your laws!
　How I enjoy your commands!
⁴⁸"Come, come to me," I call to them.
　For I love them and will let them
　fill my life.

God Comforts Us

⁴⁹⁻⁵⁰Never forget your promises to me
　your servant.
　For they are my only hope.
They give me strength in all my
　troubles.
　How they refresh me and give me
　strength!

⁵¹Proud men think badly of me for
   obeying God.
 But I will not change my mind.
⁵²From when I was a child I have tried
   to obey you.
 Your Word has been my comfort.
⁵³I am very angry with those who
   don't obey your commands.
  ⁵⁴For these laws have been my
   source of joy.
 They have given me a reason to
   sing in this life.
⁵⁵I obey them even at night.
 I keep my thoughts, O Lord, on you.
⁵⁶What a blessing this has been to me.
 I seek always to obey.

God, I Want to Follow You

⁵⁷The Lord is mine!
 And I promise to obey!
⁵⁸With all my heart I want your
   blessings.
 Be merciful just as you promised.
⁵⁹⁻⁶⁰I thought about the wrong way I
   was headed.
 I turned around and came running
   back to you.
⁶¹Evil men have tried to drag me into
   sin.
 But I am firmly tied to your laws.
⁶²At midnight I will rise up.
 I will give thanks to you for your
   good laws.
⁶³Anyone is my brother who respects
   the Lord.
 I am a friend to all who trust the
   Lord and obey him.
⁶⁴O Lord, the earth is full of your love
   and kindness!
 Teach me your good paths.

Punishment Teaches Us
to Follow God

⁶⁵Lord, I am overflowing with your
   blessings.
 You have given me all you
   promised.
⁶⁶Now teach me good judgment as
   well as knowledge.
 For your laws are my guide.
⁶⁷I used to wander off until you
   punished me.
 Now I closely follow all you say.
⁶⁸You are good and do only good.

 Make me follow your lead.
⁶⁹Proud men have made up lies about
   me.
 But the truth is that I obey your
   laws with all my heart.
⁷⁰Their minds are dull and stupid.
 But I have sense enough to follow
   you.
⁷¹⁻⁷²The punishment you gave me was
   good.
 It was the best thing that could
   have happened to me.
 For it taught me to obey your laws.
They are more precious than millions
   in silver and gold!

Delight in God's Law

⁷³You made my body, Lord.
 Now give me sense to obey your
   laws.
⁷⁴There are those who fear and trust in
   you.
 They will welcome me, for I too
   trust in your Word.
⁷⁵⁻⁷⁷I know, O Lord, that your laws are
   right.
 Your punishment was right and did
   me good.
Now let your love and kindness
   comfort me.
 Do just as you promised.
Surround me with your tender mercies
   that I may live.
 For your law is my joy.
⁷⁸Let the proud be disgraced.
 For they have cut me down with all
   their lies.
 But I will think always upon your
   laws.
⁷⁹Let all others join me who trust and
   respect you.
 We will talk together about your
   laws.
⁸⁰Help me to love your every wish.
 Then I will never have to be
   ashamed of myself.

Be Patient, God Will Hear You

⁸¹I faint for your salvation.
 But I expect your help, for you have
   promised it.
⁸²My eyes are straining to see your
   promises come true.

When will you comfort me with
your help?
83I am like a wineskin, shriveled in the
smoke.
I am tired of waiting.
But still I cling to your laws and
obey them.
84How long must I wait?
When will you punish those who
persecute me?
85-86These proud men hate your truth
and laws.
They have dug deep pits for me to
fall into.
Their lies have brought me into deep
trouble.
Help me, for you love only truth.
87They have almost finished me off.
But I refuse to give in and disobey
your laws.
88In your kindness, save my life.
Then I can keep on obeying you.

Remember God's Promises

89Forever, O Lord, your Word stands
firm in heaven.
90-91Your faithfulness is true for every
generation.
It is like the earth you make.
It is held up by your command.
For everything serves your plans.
92I would have despaired and died.
But your laws were my deepest joy.
93I will never lay aside your laws.
For you have used them to give me
joy and health.
94I am yours! Save me!
For I have tried to do what you
wanted.
95The wicked hide along the way to
kill me.
But I will quietly keep my mind
upon your promises.

God Gives Us Wisdom

96Nothing is perfect except your words.
97Oh, how I love them!
I think about them all day long.
98They make me wiser than my
enemies.
For they are my guide at all times.
99Yes, I am wiser than my teachers.
For I am ever thinking of your rules.

100They make me even wiser than old
men.
101I have refused to walk the paths of
evil.
For I will stay obedient to your
Word.
102-103No, I haven't turned away from
what you taught me.
Your words are sweeter than honey.
104Only your rules can give me
wisdom and understanding.
So no wonder I hate every false
teaching.

God's Word Lights Our Way

105Your words are a lamp to light the
path ahead of me.
They keep me from stumbling and
falling.
106I've said it once, and I'll say it again
and again.
I will obey these wonderful laws of
yours.
107I am close to death at the hands of
my enemies.
Oh, give me back my life again.
Do for me just as you promised.

**God's Word shows us the
right things to do**

*Your words are a lamp to light
the path ahead of me.*

Psalm 119:105

108Take my grateful thanks.
Please, tell me what you want of me.
109My life hangs in the balance.
But I will not stop obeying your
laws.
110The wicked have set traps for me
along your path.
But I will not turn aside.
111Your laws are my joyous treasure
forever.
112I will obey you until I die.

Why Should I Obey God?

113I hate those who have not decided
whether or not to obey you.
But my choice is clear!
I love your law!
114You are my place of safety and my
shield.

Your promises are my only source
of hope.
[115]Be gone, you evil-minded men!
Don't try to stop me from obeying
God's commands.
[116]Lord, you promised to let me live!
Never let it be said that God failed
me.
[117]Hold me safe above the heads of all
my enemies.
Then I can keep on obeying your
laws.
[118]But you have rejected all who reject
your laws.
They are only fooling themselves.
[119]The wicked are the scum you skim
off and throw away.
No wonder I love to obey your laws!
[120]I shake in fear of you.
I fear your punishments.

Lord, Give Me Common Sense
[121]Don't leave me to the mercy of my
enemies.
For I have done what is right.
I have been perfectly fair.
[122]Promise you will bless me!
Don't let the proud oppress me!
[123]My eyes grow dim because I want
you so much.
I want you to fulfill your promise to
save me.
[124]Lord, deal with me in love and
kindness.
Teach me, your servant, to obey.
[125]For I am your servant.
Therefore give me common sense.
Help me apply your rules to all I do.
[126]Lord, it is time for you to act.
For these evil men have broken
your laws.
[127]I love your commands more than
the finest gold.
[128]Every law of God is right, whatever
it concerns.
I hate every other way.

God's Laws Are Perfect
[129]Your laws are wonderful!
No wonder I obey them.
[130]As your plan unfolds, even the
simple can understand it.
[131]No wonder I wait for each of your
commands.

[132]Come and have mercy on me.
For this is your way with those who
love you.
[133]Guide me with your laws.
That way I will not be overcome by
evil.
[134]Save me from the oppression of evil
men.
Then I can obey you.
[135]Look down in love upon me.
Teach me all your laws.
[136]I cry because your laws are
disobeyed.
[137]O Lord, you are just and your
punishments are fair.
[138]Your demands are just and right.
[139]I am angry because my enemies
have not obeyed your laws.
[140]I have tested your promises.
That is why I love them so much.
[141]I am worthless and hated.
But I don't hate your laws.
[142]Your justice is forever.
For your laws are always fair.
[143]In my distress and pain your
commands comfort me.
[144]Your laws are always fair.
Help me to understand them, and I
shall live.

God's Laws Never Change
[145]I am praying with all my heart.
Answer me, O Lord, and I will obey
your laws.
[146]"Save me!" I cry,
"for I am obeying your laws."
[147]It is early in the morning before the
sun is up.
And I am praying and showing you
how much I trust in you.
[148]I stay awake through the night.
I think about your promises.
[149]You are so loving and kind.
So listen to me and make me well
again.
[150]Here come these lawless men to
attack me.
[151]But you are near, O Lord.
All your commands are based on
truth.
[152]I have known from childhood that
your will never changes.

God Gives Us Strength When We Are Tempted

¹⁵³Look down upon my sadness and save me.
For I am obeying your commands.
¹⁵⁴Yes, save me and give me back my life.
Do just as you have promised.
¹⁵⁵The wicked are far from being saved.
For they do not care for your laws.
¹⁵⁶Lord, how great is your mercy.
Oh, give me back my life again.
¹⁵⁷My enemies are so many.
They try to make me disobey.
But I have not walked away from what you want.
¹⁵⁸I hate these traitors.
For they don't care about your laws.
¹⁵⁹Lord, see how much I really love your demands.
Now give me back my life and health.
Do this because you are so kind.
¹⁶⁰There is truth in all your laws.
Your decrees are eternal.

God Gives Us Peace

¹⁶¹Great men have persecuted me.
They have not had good reasons to do it.
But I stand in awe of only your words.
¹⁶²I rejoice in your laws.
To me they are like a great treasure.
¹⁶³How I hate all lies and falsehoods.
But how I love your laws.
¹⁶⁴I will praise you seven times a day.
I do this because of your wonderful laws.
¹⁶⁵Those who love your laws have great peace.
They do not stumble and fall.
¹⁶⁶I wish for your salvation, Lord.
And so I have obeyed your laws.
¹⁶⁷I have looked for your commands.
And I love them very much.
¹⁶⁸Yes, I have looked hard for them.
You know this because you know all that I do.

God Stands Ready to Help You

¹⁶⁹O Lord, listen to my prayers.
Give me the common sense you promised.
¹⁷⁰Hear my prayers.
Save me as you said you would.
¹⁷¹I praise you for letting me learn your laws.
¹⁷²I will sing about their wonder.
For each of them is just.
¹⁷³Stand ready to help me.
For I have chosen to follow your will.
¹⁷⁴O Lord, I have wished for your salvation.
And your law is my delight.
¹⁷⁵If you will let me live, I will praise you.
Let your laws always help me.
¹⁷⁶I have wandered away like a lost sheep.
Please, come and find me.
For I have not turned away from your commands.

God Will Help

120 In my troubles I begged God to help me, and he did!
²Deliver me, O Lord, from liars.
³O lying tongue, what shall be your fate?
⁴You shall be pierced with sharp arrows.
You shall be burned with glowing coals.
⁵⁻⁶I live here among these haters of the Lord.
They are men of Meshech and Kedar.
I am tired of being here among these men who hate peace.
⁷I am for peace, but they are for war.
My voice goes unheard in their meetings.

God Guards Us

121 Shall I look to the mountains for help?
²No! My help comes from the Lord.
He is the one who made the mountains!
And he made the heavens too!
³⁻⁴He will never let me stumble, slip, or fall.
For he is always watching, never sleeping.
⁵The Lord himself is caring for you!
He is your helper and defender.

⁶He protects you day and night.
⁷He keeps you from all evil.
He preserves you from death.
⁸He always keeps his eye upon you.
As you come and go, he always
guards you.

Worshiping with God's People

122 I was glad when they said to
me,
"Let's go to the Temple of the Lord."
²⁻³Now we are standing here inside the
crowded city.
⁴All Israel, the Lord's people, have
come to worship.
They come as the law tells them to.
They come to thank and praise the
Lord.
⁵Look! There are the judges holding
court.
They stand beside the city gates.
They decide all the people's
arguments.
⁶Pray for the peace of Jerusalem.
May all who love this city prosper.
⁷O Jerusalem, may there be peace
within your walls.
May there be wealth in your palaces.
⁸This I ask for the sake of all my
brothers.
I ask it also for my friends who live
here.
⁹And may there be peace in Jerusalem.
That way the Temple of the Lord
will be safe.

God Is Merciful

123 O God on the throne in
heaven!
I lift my eyes to you.
²We look to the Lord our God for his
mercy and kindness.
We look just as a servant keeps his
eyes upon his master.
We wait like a slave girl who waits
for a command from her mistress.
³⁻⁴Have mercy on us, Lord, have mercy.
For we are tired of being made
fun of.
We are tired of the laughs of the
rich and proud.

God Is on Our Side

124 What if the Lord had not been
on our side?
Let all Israel say this!
What if the Lord had not been on our
side?
²⁻³We would have been swallowed
alive by our enemies.
We would have been destroyed by
their anger.
⁴⁻⁵We would have drowned under their
rage.
We would have been buried under
their pride.
⁶Blessed be the Lord who has not let
them devour us.
⁷We have escaped with our lives.
We are like a bird that escapes from a
hunter's trap.
The trap is broken and we are free!
⁸Our help is from the Lord who made
heaven and earth.

God Is Our Protector

125 Those who trust in the Lord
are as steady as Mount Zion.
They are not moved when troubles
come.
²The mountains surround and protect
Jerusalem.
And so the Lord surrounds and
protects his people.
³For the wicked shall not rule the
godly.
For then the godly would be forced
to do wrong.
⁴O Lord, do good to those who are
good.
Bless those whose hearts are right
with the Lord.
⁵But lead evil men to death.
And let Israel have quietness and
peace.

Tears Turn to Joy

126 The Lord brought back his
exiles to Jerusalem.
And it was like a dream!
²How we laughed and sang for joy!
And the other nations spoke among
themselves.
They said, "What great things the
Lord has done for them!"
³Yes, what great things!

What wonder! What joy!
⁴May we be made fresh as by streams
in the desert.
⁵Those who plant tears shall harvest
joy.
⁶Yes, they go out crying.
They carry seed for planting.
But they come back singing.
And they are carrying their harvest!

God Makes Life Worthwhile

127 The Lord must build a house.
If he doesn't, the builders'
work is useless.
The Lord must protect a city.
If he doesn't, guards will do it no
good.
²You might live in fear of starving to
death.
But if so, it is stupid to work hard
from morning until night.
For God wants his loved ones to get
their proper rest.
³Children are a gift from God.
They are his reward.
⁴Children born to a young man are
like sharp arrows to defend him.
⁵Happy is the man who has his
quiver full of them.
That man shall have the help he needs.
His sons will stand with him as he
talks to his enemies.

A Family Blessing

128 Happy are those who respect
and trust the Lord!
May all who obey him be blessed!
²Their reward shall be riches and
happiness.
³Your wife shall be happy in your
home.
And look at all those children!
There they sit around the dinner table.
They are as strong and healthy as
young olive trees.
⁴That is God's reward to those who
respect and trust him.
⁵May the Lord bless you with heaven's
blessings.
And may he give you human joys
as well.
⁶May you live to enjoy your
grandchildren!
And may God bless Israel!

God Will Deal with Your Enemies

129 I have been treated badly for
my whole life.
Let Israel say this again!
²I have been treated badly for my
whole life.
But still I have not been destroyed!
My enemies have never been able to
finish me off!
³⁻⁴My back is cut to ribbons with their
whips.
But still, the Lord is good.
For he has snapped the chains around
me.
Evil men had bound me with them.
⁵May all who hate Jerusalem be
brought defeat and shame.
⁶⁻⁷May they be like grass in shallow
soil.
It turns yellow when half-grown.
It goes unseen by the harvester.
It is looked down upon by the
binder.
⁸And may those passing by not bless
them.
May they never say, "The Lord's
blessings be upon you.
We bless you in the name of the
Lord."

God Forgives

130 O Lord, I cry for your help!
I cry out from the depths of
despair.
²I say, "Hear me! Answer! Help me!"
³⁻⁴Lord, do you keep in mind all our
sins?
If you do, who can ever get an
answer to his prayers?
But you forgive! What a great thing
this is!
⁵That is why I wait for you.
I trust God to help.
For he has promised to help me.
⁶I want him more than guards want
dawn to come.
⁷O Israel, hope in the Lord!
For he is loving and kind.
And he comes to us with loads of
salvation.
⁸He himself shall buy Israel from her
slavery to sin.

A Psalm of Contentment

131 Lord, I am not proud.
I don't think myself better than
others.
I don't pretend to "know it all."
²I am quiet now before the Lord.
I am just as a child who is weaned
from the breast.
Yes, my begging has been stilled.
³O Israel, you too should quietly trust
in the Lord.
You should trust him now and
always.

Honor God and He Will Honor You

132 Oh Lord, do you remember
David?
Do you remember all the troubles
he suffered?
²⁻⁵He couldn't sleep as he thought
about his promise to the Lord.
He promised to build a home for
the Ark of the Lord.
He promised to make a Temple for
the Mighty One of Israel.
⁶First the Ark was in Ephrathah.
Then it was moved to the
countryside of Jaar.
⁷But now it will be settled in the
Temple.
It will be in God's home here on
earth.
That is where we will go to worship
him.
⁸Rise up, O Lord!
Enter your Temple with the Ark.
It is the symbol of your power.
⁹We will clothe the priests in white.
This is the symbol of all purity.
May our nation shout for joy.
¹⁰Do not reject your servant David.
He is the king you chose for your
people.
¹¹You promised him that his son
would sit on his throne.
And surely you will never go back
on a promise!
¹²You also promised that David's
family would always rule in
Jerusalem.
But his descendants must obey your
covenant.
¹³O Lord, you have chosen Jerusalem
as your home.

¹⁴"This is my home where I shall live,"
you said.
"For I have always wanted it this
way.
¹⁵I will make this city rich.
I will give plenty of food to her
poor.
¹⁶I will dress her priests with salvation.
Her saints shall shout for joy.
¹⁷David's power shall grow.
For I have promised for him a
mighty Son.
¹⁸I'll clothe his enemies with shame.
But he shall be a great King."

Living Together in Peace

133 How pleasant it is when
brothers live in harmony!
²For harmony and peace are precious.
They are as precious as fragrant
anointing oil.
This oil was poured over Aaron's head.
It ran down onto his beard.
Then it flowed onto the border of
his robe.
³Harmony is as refreshing as the dew
on Mount Hermon.
And God has given this blessing to
Jerusalem.
It is the blessing of life forever.

Worship the Lord

134 Oh, bless the Lord!
You who serve him as
watchmen in the Temple,
praise him!
²Lift your hands in holiness and bless
the Lord.
³The Lord bless you from Zion.
For the Lord made heaven and
earth.

Our God Is Real

135 Praise the Lord!
²Yes, let his people praise him.
Let them sing praises as they stand
in his Temple courts.
³Praise the Lord because he is so good.
Sing to his wonderful name.
⁴For the Lord has chosen Israel as his
people.
⁵I know the greatness of the Lord.

I know he is far greater than any
    other god.
⁶He does whatever pleases him!
    He controls all of heaven and earth.
    He controls the deepest seas.
⁷He makes mists rise throughout the
    earth.
    He sends the lightning to bring
    down the rain.
    He sends the winds from his
    treasuries.
⁸He destroyed the oldest child in each
    Egyptian home.
    And he killed the firstborn of their
    flocks.
⁹He did great miracles in Egypt.
    He did them before Pharaoh and all
    his people.
¹⁰He destroyed great nations.
    He killed mighty kings.
¹¹He killed Sihon, king of the Amorites.
    And he killed Og, the king of
    Bashan.
    And he destroyed the kings of
    Canaan.
¹²He gave their land as an eternal gift
    to his people Israel.
¹³O Lord, your name will go on forever.
    Your fame is known to every
    generation.
¹⁴For the Lord will defend his people.
    He will show love to his servants.
¹⁵The heathen worship idols made by
    men.
    They are made of gold and silver.
¹⁶These idols have mouths that don't
    talk.
    They have eyes that don't see.
¹⁷They have ears that cannot hear.
    They cannot even breathe.
¹⁸Those who make them become like
    them!
    And so do all who trust in them!
¹⁹O Israel, bless the Lord!
    High priests of Aaron, bless his
    name.
²⁰O Levite priests, bless the Lord!
    Oh, bless his name!
    Praise him, all who trust and
    respect him.
²¹All people of Jerusalem, praise the
    Lord!
    For he lives here in Jerusalem.
    Praise the Lord!

Never-Ending Love

136 Oh, give thanks to the Lord,
    for he is good.
    His love continues forever.
²Give thanks to the God of gods.
    For his love continues forever.
³Give thanks to the Lord of lords.
    For his love continues forever.
⁴Praise him who alone does mighty
    miracles.
    For his love continues forever.
⁵Praise him who made the heavens.
    For his love continues forever.
⁶Praise him who planted the water
    within the earth.
    For his love continues forever.
⁷Praise him who made the heavenly
    lights.
    For his love continues forever.
⁸He made the sun to rule the day.
    For his love continues forever.
⁹He made the moon and stars to rule
    at night.
    For his love continues forever.
¹⁰Praise the God who killed the
    firstborn of Egypt.
    For his love to Israel continues
    forever.
¹¹⁻¹²He brought them out with mighty
    power.
    They came out with upraised fist to
    strike their enemies.
    For his love to Israel continues
    forever.
¹³Praise the Lord who opened the Red
    Sea.
    He made a dry path before them.
    For his love continues forever.
¹⁴He led them safely through.
    For his love continues forever.
¹⁵But he drowned Pharaoh's army in
    the sea.
    For his love to Israel continues
    forever.
¹⁶Praise him who led his people
    through the wilderness.
    For his love continues forever.
¹⁷Praise him who saved his people.
    He delivered them from the power
    of mighty kings.
    For his love continues forever.
¹⁸He killed famous kings who were
    their enemies.

For his love to Israel continues forever.
[19]He killed Sihon, king of Amorites.
For God's love to Israel continues forever.

We can't hide from God

I can never be lost to your Spirit!
I can never get away
from my God!

Psalm 139:7

---

[20]He killed Og, king of Bashan.
For his love to Israel continues forever.
[21]God gave the land of these kings to Israel.
He gave it as a gift for all time.
For his love to Israel continues forever.
[22]Yes, he gave a lasting gift to his servant Israel.
For his love continues forever.
[23]He remembered our utter weakness.
For his love continues forever.
[24]He saved us from our enemies.
For his love continues forever.
[25]He gives food to every living thing.
For his love continues forever.
[26]Oh, give thanks to the God of heaven.
For his love continues forever.

Song of the Captives

137 Crying, we sat beside the rivers of Babylon.
We were there, thinking of Jerusalem.
[2]We have put away our lyres.
We have hung them on the branches of the willow trees.
[3-4]For how can we sing?
Yet our captors demand that we sing for them.
They want to hear the happy songs of Zion!
[5-6]Could I ever forget you, O Jerusalem?
If I do, let my hand forget its skill upon the harp.
Could I forget to love her more than my highest joy?
If I do, let me never sing again.

[7]O Lord, do not forget what these Edomites did.
They were happy on that day when Babylon took Jerusalem.
"Break her to the ground!" they yelled.
[8]O Babylon, evil beast, you shall be destroyed.
Blessed is the man who destroys you as you have destroyed us.
[9]Blessed is the man who takes your babies.
Blessed is he who smashes them against the rocks!

God Hears and Answers Us

138 Lord, with all my heart I thank you.
I will sing your praises.
I will sing them before armies of angels.
[2]I face your Temple as I worship.
I give thanks to you for all your love.
I praise you for being so faithful.
For your promises are backed by the honor of your name.
[3]When I pray, you answer me.
You help me by giving me the strength I need.
[4]Every king in all the earth shall give you thanks, O Lord.
For all of them shall hear your voice.
[5]Yes, they shall sing about the Lord's glorious ways.
For his glory is very great.
[6]Yet though he is so great, he respects the humble.
But proud men must keep their distance.
[7]I have troubles all around me.
But you will bring me safely through them.
You will clench your fist against my angry enemies!
Your power will save me.
[8]The Lord will work out his plans for my life.
For your love, Lord, continues forever.
Don't leave me, for you made me.

God Knows All about You

139 O Lord, you have tested my heart.
You know everything about me.
²You know when I sit or stand.
When far away, you know my every thought.
³You clear the path ahead of me.
You tell me where to stop and rest.
Every moment you know where I am.
⁴You know what I am going to say.
You know this even before I say it!
⁵You go in front of me.
And you also follow me.
You put your hand of blessing on my head.
⁶This is too wonderful to believe!

God Goes with You

⁷I can *never* be lost to your Spirit!
I can *never* get away from my God!
⁸If I go up to heaven, you are there.
If I go down to the place of the dead, you are there.
⁹I might ride the morning winds.
I might sail to the farthest oceans.
¹⁰But even there, your hand will guide me.
Even there, your strength will support me.
¹¹I might try to hide in the darkness.
But the night becomes light around me.
¹²For even darkness cannot hide from God.
To you the night shines as bright as day.
Darkness and light are both the same to you.

God Made You Just Right

¹³You made all the parts of my body.
You put them together in my mother's womb.
¹⁴Thank you for making me so wonderfully!
It is amazing to think about!
Your workmanship is wonderful!
How well I know it!
¹⁵You were there while I was being made!
¹⁶You saw me before I was born.
You planned each day of my life before I began to breathe.

Every day was recorded in your book!
¹⁷⁻¹⁸How precious this is, Lord!
How great to know you think about me all the time!

God created us

You made all the parts of my body. You put them together in my mother's womb.

Psalm 139:13

I can't even count how many times your thoughts turn toward me.
And when I wake in the morning, you are still thinking of me!

God, Please Correct Me When I'm Wrong

¹⁹Surely you will kill the wicked, Lord!
Away with men who kill others!
²⁰They make fun of your name.
They stand in pride against you.
How silly can they be?
²¹O Lord, shouldn't I hate those who hate you?
Shouldn't I be upset about them?
²²Yes, I hate them!
For your enemies are my enemies too.
²³Search me, O God, and know my heart.
Test my thoughts.
²⁴Point out anything you find in me that makes you sad.
Lead me along the path of everlasting life.

A Prayer for Protection from Our Enemies

140 O Lord, save me from evil men.
Preserve me from the violent.
²They plot and stir up trouble all day long.
³Their words sting like deadly snakes.
⁴Keep me out of their power.
Save me from their violence.
For they are making evil plans against me.
⁵These proud men have set a trap to catch me.
They hang a noose to yank me up.

They want to leave me hanging in
the air.
They hide with a net to throw over me.
They want to hold me helpless in
its meshes.
6-8O Lord and Savior, my God and my
shield!
Hear me as I pray!
Don't let these wicked men succeed.
Don't let them be happy and proud.
9Let their plots fall back on them!
Let them be destroyed by the evil
they have planned for me.
10Let burning coals fall down on their
heads.
Throw them into the fire.
Put them into deep pits they can't
get out of.
11Don't let liars prosper here in our
land.
Quickly punish them.
12But the Lord will surely help those
they hurt.
He will protect the rights of the
poor.
13Surely the godly are thanking you.
For they shall live close to you.

When You're Facing
Temptation and Criticism

141 Quick, Lord, answer me—for I
have prayed.
Listen when I cry to you for help!
2Think of my prayer as my evening
sacrifice.
View it as incense blowing up to
you.
3Help me, Lord, to keep my mouth
shut.
Help me to keep my lips sealed.
4Take away my lust for evil things.
Don't let me want to be with
sinners.
Don't let me do what they do.
5Let the godly beat me!
It will be a kindness!
If they punish me, it is like medicine!
Don't let me refuse it.
But I am in constant prayer against
the wicked and their deeds.
6-7Their leaders someday will be
condemned.
Their bones will be spread across
the ground.

Then these men will finally listen to
me.
They will know that I am trying to
help them.
8I look to you for help, O Lord God.
You are my safe place.
Don't let them kill me.
9Keep me out of their traps.
10Let them fall into their own snares.
Please, help me to get away.

When You Feel Trapped

142 How I pray to God.
How I ask for his mercy.
I pour out my troubles before him.
3For I am overcome and in deep
trouble.
You alone know which way I should
turn.
You know how to miss the traps my
enemies have set for me.
4There's one just over there to the
right!
No one gives me a passing thought.
No one will help me.
No one cares a bit what happens to
me.
5Then I prayed to the Lord.
"Lord," I said, "you alone can keep
me safe.
6Hear my cry, for I am very low.
Save me from those who try to hurt
me.
For they are too strong for me.
7Bring me out of prison so that I
can thank you.
The godly will rejoice with me for
all your help."

When You're Weak and Scared

143 Hear my prayer, O Lord.
Answer my cry.
For you are faithful to your
promises.
2Don't bring me to trial!
For as compared with you, no one
is perfect.
3My enemies chased and caught me.
They have knocked me to the
ground.
They force me to live in the darkness.
They want to put me in the grave.
4I am losing all hope.

I am frozen with fear.
⁵I remember the great miracles you did.
    You did them in days of long ago.
⁶I reach out for you.
    I thirst for you as dry land thirsts
        for rain.
⁷Come quickly, Lord!
    Answer me, for I am getting sadder
        each day.
    Don't turn away from me or I shall
        die.
⁸Let me see your kindness to me in the
        morning.
    For I am trusting you.
Show me where to walk.
    For my prayer is sincere.
⁹Save me from my enemies.
    O Lord, I run to you to hide me.
¹⁰Help me to do your will.
    For you are my God.
Lead me in good paths.
    For your Spirit is good.
¹¹Lord, saving me will bring glory to
        your name.
    Bring me out of all this trouble.
    For you always keep your promises.
¹²And you show love and kindness to
        me.
    So cut off all my enemies.
    Destroy those who are trying to
        hurt me.
    For I am your servant.

Rejoice in God's Care

144 Bless the Lord who is my Rock.
        He gives me strength and skill
            in battle.
²He is always kind and loving to me.
    He is my fortress.
    He is my tower of strength and
        safety.
He is the one who saves me.
    He stands before me as a shield.
    He puts my people under me.
³O Lord, what is man that you even
        notice him?
    Why bother at all with the human
        race?
⁴For man lives little longer than a
        breath.
    His days pass by like a shadow.
⁵Bend down from the heavens, Lord,
    and come.

The mountains smoke at your
        touch.
⁶Shoot your lightning, your arrows,
        Lord.
    Shoot them upon your enemies and
        scatter them.
⁷Reach down from heaven and save
        me.
    Deliver me from deep waters.
    Save me from the power of my
        enemies.
⁸Their mouths are filled with lies.
    They promise that lies are true.
⁹I will sing you a new song, O God.
    I will sing with a ten-stringed harp.
¹⁰For you give victory to kings!
    You are the one who will save your
        servant David.
    You will save him from the deadly
        sword.
¹¹Save me from these enemies!
    Deliver me from these liars.
    Free me from these cheating men.
¹²The land where the Lord is God will
        be full of joy!
Sons will be strong and tall.
    They will be like growing plants.
Daughters will be pretty.
    They will be like the pillars of a
        palace wall.
¹³Barns will be full to the brim.
    There will be crops of every kind.
    There will be sheep by the
        thousands out in our fields.
¹⁴There will be oxen loaded down with
        produce.
No enemy will attack the walls.
    There will be peace everywhere.
    No crimes will be found in our
        streets.
¹⁵Yes, happy are those whose God is
        the Lord.

A Magnificent God

145 I will praise you, my God and
        King.
    I will bless your name each day and
        forever.
³Great is the Lord!
    So greatly praise him!
    His greatness is beyond even
        knowing it!
⁴Let each generation teach its children.

Let them tell of the great things he does.
[5]I will think about your glory and power.
I will remember your greatness and miracles.
[6]People will talk about your great deeds everywhere.
I will tell everyone of your greatness.
[7]Everyone will tell about how good you are.
They will sing about your fairness.
[8]The Lord is kind and full of mercy.
He is slow to get angry, full of love.
[9]He is good to everyone.
His love is found in all he does.
[10]All living things shall thank you, Lord.
And your people will bless you.
[11]They will talk about the greatness of your kingdom.
They will talk about how you've shown your power.
[12]They will tell about your miracles.
They will remember the power and glory of your reign.
[13]For your kingdom never ends.
You rule over every generation.
[14]The Lord lifts the fallen.
He helps those bent under their loads.
[15]The eyes of all mankind look up to you for help.
You give them their food as they need it.
[16]You always feed the hungry.
And you give water to every living thing.
[17]The Lord is fair in all he does.
He is always full of kindness.
[18]He is close to all who call on him sincerely.
[19]He gives those who respect him what they want.
He always helps those who trust him.
He hears their cries for help and saves them.
[20]He keeps safe all those who love him.
But he destroys the wicked.
[21]I will praise the Lord.
I will call on all men everywhere.
I will tell them to praise his holy name forever.

God's Help Is All You Need

146 Praise the Lord!
Yes, really praise him!
[2]I will praise him as long as I live.
Yes, I'll even praise him with my dying breath.
[3]Don't look to men for help.
Their greatest leaders fail.
[4]For every man must die.
His breathing stops and life ends.
In a moment all he planned for himself is over.
[5]But happy is the man who has the God of Jacob as his helper.
What joy for those who hope in the Lord.
[6]He is the God who made both earth and heaven.
He made the seas and all that is in them.
He is the God who keeps every promise.
[7]He gives justice to the poor.
He gives food to the hungry.
He sets the prisoners free.
[8]And he opens the eyes of the blind.
He lifts burdens from those bent down under their loads.
For the Lord loves good men.
[9]He protects the people visiting our land.
He takes care of the orphans and widows.
But he turns the plans of the wicked upside down.
[10]The Lord will rule for all time.
O Jerusalem, your God is King in every generation!
Praise the Lord!

Yes, Praise the Lord!

147 Praise the Lord!
Yes, praise the Lord!
How good it is to sing his praises!
How delightful, and how right!
[2]He is rebuilding Jerusalem.
He is bringing the exiles back home.
[3]He heals those with broken hearts.
He ties up their hurts and wounds.
[4]He counts the stars and calls them all by name.
[5]How great he is!
His power cannot be stopped!
His understanding has no limits.

⁶The Lord helps the humble.
  But he brings the wicked down into
    the dust.
⁷Sing out your thanks to him.
  Sing praises to our God.
  Sing praises with the harp.
⁸He covers the heavens with clouds.
  He sends down the showers.
  He makes the green grass grow in
    mountain pastures.
⁹He feeds the wild animals.
  The young ravens cry to him for
    food.
¹⁰The speed of a horse is nothing to
    him.
  How small to him is man's strength!
¹¹But his joy is in those who respect
    him.
  He helps those who trust in his love.
¹²Praise him, O Jerusalem!
  Praise your God, O Zion!
¹³For he has built your gates against all
    enemies.
  And he has blessed your children.
¹⁴He sends peace across your nation.
  He fills your barns with the finest
    wheat.
¹⁵He sends his orders to the world.
  How fast his word flies!
¹⁶He sends the snow in all its lovely
    whiteness.
  He scatters the frost upon the
    ground.
¹⁷He throws the hail to the earth.
  Who can stand before his freezing
    cold?
¹⁸But then he calls for warmer weather.
  The spring winds blow.
  And all the river ice is broken.
¹⁹He has made known his laws and
    feasts to Israel.
  ²⁰He has not done this with any
    other nation.
  They have not known his
    commands.
Praise the Lord!
  Yes, praise the Lord!

Let All Creation Give Praise

148 Praise the Lord, O heavens!
Praise him from the skies!
²Praise him, all his angels, all the
  armies of heaven.

³Praise him, sun and moon and all
  you twinkling stars.
⁴Praise him, skies above.
  Praise him, vapors high above the
    clouds.
⁵Let everything he has made give
    praise to him.
  For he gave the command, and
    they came into being.
⁶He made them stay for all time.
  His orders will never be taken back.
⁷And praise him down here on earth.
  Praise him, you creatures of the
    ocean.
⁸Let fire and hail obey him.
  Let snow, rain, wind, and weather
    all obey.
⁹Let the mountains and hills praise
    him!
  Praise him, fruit trees and cedars!
¹⁰Let the wild animals and cattle, the
    snakes and birds praise him.
¹¹Let kings and all the people give him
    praise.
  Praise him, rulers and judges!
¹²Young men and maidens, old men
    and children, all praise him.
¹³All praise the Lord together.
  For he alone is worthy.
His glory is far greater than all of earth
    and heaven.
¹⁴He has made his people strong.
  He has honored his godly ones.
  They are the people of Israel.
  They are the people closest to him.
Praise the Lord!
  Yes, praise the Lord!

God Enjoys Us

149 Praise the Lord!
Yes, praise the Lord!
Sing him a new song.
  Sing his praises, all his people.
²O Israel, have joy in your Maker.
  O people of Jerusalem, be happy in
    your King.
³Praise his name with dancing.
  Play songs on the drums and lyre.
⁴⁻⁵For the Lord enjoys his people.
  He will save the humble.
Let his people rejoice in this honor.
  Let them sing for joy as they lie on
    their beds.
⁶⁻⁷Adore him, O his people!

And take a double-edged sword.
Use it to bring his punishment on
the nations.
⁸Tie up their kings and leaders with
iron chains.
⁹And bring about their punishments.
He is the glory of his people.
Praise the Lord!
Yes, praise him!

Praise the Lord, One and All

150 Praise the Lord!
Yes, praise the Lord!
Praise him in his Temple.
Praise him in the heavens he made
with mighty power.
²Praise him for his mighty works.
Praise his greatness, which is
beyond compare.

³Praise him with the trumpet and with
lute and harp.

**We should join all God's
creation in praising him**

*Let everything alive give praises
to the Lord! You, too, praise him!*

Psalm 150:6

⁴Praise him with the drums and
dancing.
Praise him with stringed instruments and horns.
⁵Praise him with the cymbals.
Yes, play loud clanging cymbals.
⁶Let everything alive give praises to
the Lord!
You, too, praise him!
Praise the Lord!

PROVERBS

Who is the wisest person you know? Is it your pastor, or a neighbor, or a teacher? Is it one of your parents? It's fun to listen to wise people say wise things. It's even more fun when you know these wise sayings will help you. One time, thousands of years ago, a queen traveled many miles to listen to the wisest man in the world. This wise man was Solomon. The queen stayed with Solomon for quite some time. And she brought him millions of dollars in gold and other special gifts. She just wanted to listen to all his wise sayings. She knew this would help make her wise. Then, when she had a problem, she would have a better chance at solving it. You can sit and listen to this wise man Solomon. You, too, can work at becoming wise. And you don't have to pay millions of dollars, either. All you need to do is read the Book of Proverbs. Solomon wrote most of the wise sayings in this book. So spend a few minutes with Solomon each day. As you do, you'll be surprised that these proverbs are written for people just like you!

The Reason for Proverbs

1 These are the proverbs of King Solomon of Israel, David's son.

2He wrote them to teach his people how to live. He wanted them to have self-control and wisdom. 3He wanted them to have understanding. He desired them to be just and fair in all they did. 4"I want to make the simpleminded wise!" he said. "I want to warn young people about some problems they will face. 5-6I want those already wise to become even wiser. I want them to become leaders by seeing the truth in these wise words."

Wisdom Keeps You Out of Trouble

7-9How does a person become wise? The first step is to trust and respect the Lord!

Only fools won't let anyone teach them. Listen to your father and mother. What you learn from them will help you greatly. It will gain you many honors.

10Sinners might say to you, "Come and join us." But if they do, turn your back on them! 11"We'll hide and rob and kill," they say. 12"Good or bad, we'll treat them all alike. 13And the loot we'll get! All kinds of stuff! 14Come on, join us. We'll split with you in equal shares."

How does a person become wise? The first step is to trust and respect the Lord!

Proverbs 1:7

¹⁵Don't do it, son! Stay far from people like that! ¹⁶For crime is their way of life. Murder is what they do best. ¹⁷When a bird sees a trap being set, it stays away. ¹⁸But not these people—they trap themselves! They lay a booby trap for their own lives. ¹⁹This is what happens to all who live by violence and murder. They will die a violent death.

Wisdom Demands Your Attention

²⁰Wisdom shouts in the streets wanting to be heard. ²¹She calls out to the crowds along Main Street. She calls to the judges in their courts. She calls out to everyone in all the land! ²²"You foolish people!" she cries. "How long will you go on being fools? How long will you laugh at wisdom and fight the facts? ²³Come here and listen to me! I'll pour out the spirit of wisdom upon you. I will make you truly wise. ²⁴I have called you so often, but still you won't come. I have begged, but it hasn't done any good. ²⁵For you have not listened to my coun-

Listen to your father and mother. What you learn from them will help you greatly.

Proverbs 1:8-9

sel and advice. ²⁶Someday you'll be in trouble, and I'll laugh! Do you laugh at me now? Later, I'll laugh at you! ²⁷A storm of terror will be all around you. Pain and trouble will engulf you. ²⁸And then I will not answer your cry for help. It will be too late, even though you look for me with all your heart.

²⁹"For you closed your eyes to the facts. You did not choose to respect and trust the Lord. ³⁰You turned your back on me, laughing at my advice. ³¹So you

must eat the bitter fruit of having your own way. You will find all the terrors of the pathway you have chosen. ³²For you turned away from me, to death. Your own laziness will kill you. Fools! ³³But all who listen to me shall live in peace and safety. They shall live their lives, unafraid."

Wisdom Comes from God

2 Every young person should listen to me and obey my orders. If he does, he will be given wisdom and good sense. ³⁻⁵Yes, you might want to be wiser, with deeper understanding. If you do, look for wisdom as you would for lost money or hidden treasure. Then wisdom will be given you and knowledge of God himself. You will soon learn how important it is to respect the Lord and trust in him.

⁶For the Lord gives wisdom! His every word is a treasure of knowledge. ⁷⁻⁸He gives good sense to the godly, his saints. He is their shield, guarding their pathway. ⁹He shows how to know right from wrong. He teaches how to find the right decision every time. ¹⁰For wisdom and truth will enter the very center of your being. They will fill your life with joy. ¹¹⁻¹³You will be given the sense to stay away from evil people. They want you to join them in doing bad things. They turn from God's ways to walk down dark and evil paths. ¹⁴They take joy in doing wrong. For they really enjoy their sins. ¹⁵All that they do is crooked and wrong.

¹⁶⁻¹⁷Only wisdom from the Lord can save a man from tempting words of prostitutes. These girls have left their husbands. They have ignored the laws of God. ¹⁸Their houses lie along the road to death and hell. ¹⁹The men who enter them are doomed. None of these men will ever be the same again.

²⁰Follow the steps of the godly instead. Stay on the right path! ²¹For only good people enjoy life to the full. ²²Evil people lose the good things they might have had. And they themselves shall be destroyed.

Wisdom Is Worth More than Precious Jewels

3 My son, never forget the things I've taught you. If you want a long and good life, closely follow my teachings. [3]Never get tired of being loyal and kind. Hold on to these things with all your strength. Write them deep within your heart. [4-5]Perhaps you want favor with both God and people. You might want to be known for good judgment and common sense. If so, then trust the Lord with all your heart. Don't ever trust yourself. [6]In all you do, put God first. He will direct you and crown your efforts with success.

[7-8]Don't be proud and sure of your own wisdom. Instead, trust and respect the Lord. Always turn your back on evil. When you do, you will find new health and strength.

[9-10]Honor the Lord by giving him the first part of all your income. Then he will fill your barns with wheat and barley. Your wine vats will overflow with the finest wines.

Put God first

In all you do, put God first. He will direct you and crown your efforts with success.

Proverbs 3:6

[11-12]Young person, do not hate it when God punishes and corrects you. For his punishment is proof of his love. A father punishes a child he loves to make him better. And the Lord corrects you for the same reason.

[13-15]The person who knows right from wrong and has good judgment is happy. In fact, he is happier than the person who is very rich! For such wisdom is far more valuable than precious jewels. Nothing else compares with it. [16-17]Wisdom gives a long, good life, riches, honor, pleasure, and peace. [18]Wisdom is a tree of life to those who eat her fruit. Happy is the person who keeps on eating it.

[19]The Lord's wisdom made the earth. His knowledge made all the universe and space. [20]The deep fountains of the earth were broken open by his knowledge. And the skies poured down rain by his understanding.

Accept God's punishment and learn from it

Do not hate it when God punishes and corrects you. For his punishment is proof of his love.

Proverbs 3:11-12

---

[21]Have two goals: wisdom and common sense. Don't let them slip away! [22]For they fill you with living energy. And they bring you honor and respect. [23]They keep you safe from defeat and disaster. And they guard you from stumbling off the trail. [24-26]With them on guard you can sleep without fear. You don't need to be afraid of trouble or the plans of wicked people. For the Lord is with you. He will always protect you.

[27-28]Don't hold back from paying back the money you owe. Don't say, "Some other time" if you can pay now. [29]Don't make evil plans against your neighbor. He is trusting you. [30]Don't get into needless fights. [31]Don't be jealous of violent people. Don't copy their ways. [32]For such people are hated by the Lord. But he gives his friendship to the godly.

[33]The curse of God is on the wicked. But his blessing is on the upright. [34]The Lord mocks at mockers. But he always helps the humble. [35]The wise are given honor. But fools are given shame!

You Can Learn Wisdom

4 Young men, listen to me as you would to your father. Listen, and grow wise, for I speak the truth. Don't turn away. [3]For I, too, was once a son and the companion of my father. I also was tenderly loved by my mother as an only child. [4]He told me never to forget his words. "If you follow them," he said, "you will have a long and happy life. [5]Learn to be wise," he said. "And gain good judgment and common sense! I cannot say this enough times!"

6Hang on to wisdom; she will protect you. Love her; she will guard you.

7Getting wisdom is the most important thing you can do! And with your wisdom, develop common sense and good judgment. 8-9If you love wisdom, she will love you. Hold her fast, and she will lead you to great honor. She will put a beautiful crown on your head. 10My son, listen to me and do as I say. If you do, you will have a long, good life.

God sees everything you do

God is closely watching you. He weighs carefully all that you do.

Proverbs 5:21

11I want you to learn this fact: a life of doing right is the wisest life there is. 12If you live that kind of life, you'll not limp or stumble as you run. 13Carry out my orders. Don't forget them. For they will lead you to real living.

14Don't do as the wicked do. 15Stay away from their meeting places. Turn away and go somewhere else. 16For evil people can't sleep until they've done their evil deed for the day. They can't rest unless they cause someone to stumble and fall. 17They eat and drink wickedness and violence!

18But the good person walks along in the light of God's favor. The dawn gives way to morning splendor. 19But the evil person stumbles in the dark.

20Listen, son of mine, to what I say. Listen carefully. 21Keep these thoughts ever in mind. Let them go deep within your heart. 22For they will mean real life and radiant health for you.

23Above all else, guard your heart. For your heart runs everything else in your life. 24Run from the careless kiss of a prostitute. Stay far from her. 25Look straight ahead. Don't even turn your head to look. 26Watch your step. Stick to the path and be safe. 27Don't sidetrack. Pull back your foot from danger.

Run from Sin; Keep Yourself Clean

5Listen to me, my son! I know what I am saying. Listen! 2Watch yourself, or you might say something you shouldn't. You might tell some important information to the wrong person. 3For the lips of a prostitute are as sweet as honey. Smooth flattery is how she makes her money. 4But afterwards only a bitter conscience is left to you. It is as sharp as a double-edged sword. 5She leads you down to death and hell. 6For she does not know the path to life. She staggers down a crooked trail. She doesn't even know where it goes.

7Young men, listen to me. Never forget what I'm about to say. 8Run from her! Don't go near her house. 9If you do, you might fall to her temptation and lose your honor. Then you will give the rest of your life to the cruel and merciless. 10If you fall, strangers will get your riches. And you will become a slave of foreigners. 11Afterwards you will groan in pain. You will live in shame, for disease will consume your body. 12You will say, "Oh, if only I had listened! If only I had not gone my own way! 13Oh, why wouldn't I take advice? Why was I so stupid? 14For now I must face public shame."

15Drink from your own well, my son. Be faithful and true to your wife. 16Why should you give children to women of the street? 17Why share your children with those outside your home? 18Be happy, yes, rejoice in the wife of your youth. 19Let her breasts and tender embrace make you happy. Let her love alone fill you with joy. 20Why delight yourself with prostitutes, holding what isn't yours? 21For God is closely watching you. He weighs carefully all that you do.

22The wicked person is doomed by his own sins. They are ropes that catch and hold him. 23He shall die because he will not listen to the truth. He has let himself be led away into great foolishness.

Run from Foolishness

6Son, do not sign a loan for someone you hardly know. Don't promise to pay his debt. If you do, you will be in big trouble. 2You may have trapped yourself by your agreement. 3Quick! Get out of it if you possibly can! Swallow your pride. Don't let shame stand in the way. Go and beg to have your name taken off the loan. ⁴Don't put it off. Do it now! Don't rest until you do. ⁵Get out of this trap now! Save yourself like a deer that escapes from a hunter or a bird from the net.

⁶Take a lesson from the ants, you lazy fellow. Learn from their ways and be wise! ⁷They have no king to make them work. ⁸But they work hard all summer. They gather food for the winter. ⁹But you, all you do is sleep. When will you wake up? ¹⁰"Let me sleep a little longer!" you say. Sure, just a little more! ¹¹And as you sleep, poverty sneaks up on you like a robber. Hunger attacks you in its full armor.

¹²⁻¹³Let me describe for you a worthless and wicked person. First, he is a constant liar. He tells the truth to his friends only with eyes and feet and fingers. ¹⁴He is always thinking up new ways to cheat people. He stirs up trouble everywhere. ¹⁵But he will be destroyed suddenly. He will be broken beyond any hope of healing.

¹⁶⁻¹⁹For there are six things the Lord hates—no, seven. He hates pride, lying, murdering, evil plans, eagerness to do wrong, a false witness, and planting trouble among brothers.

Your Parents' Advice Is a Beam of Light

²⁰Young person, obey your father and your mother. ²¹Take to heart all of their advice. Keep in mind all that they tell you. ²²Every day and all night long their counsel will lead you and save you from harm. When you wake up in the morning, let their teachings guide you into the new day. ²³For their advice is a beam of light. It shines into the dark corners of your mind. It will warn you of danger and give you a good life. ²⁴Their counsel will keep you far away from prostitutes, with all their lies. It will keep you from the unfaithful wives of other men.

²⁵Don't lust for their beauty. Don't let their coyness tempt you. ²⁶For a prostitute will make a man poor. And a married woman who sleeps with another man may cost him his very life.

²⁷Can a person hold fire against his chest and not be burned? ²⁸Can he walk on hot coals and not blister his feet? ²⁹So it is with the man who sleeps with another man's wife. He shall not go unpunished for this sin. ³⁰A thief might be excused if he steals when he is starving! ³¹But even so, he is fined seven times as much as he stole. It may mean selling all he has in his house to pay it back.

³²But the man is a fool who sleeps with a woman who is not his wife. For he destroys his own soul. ³³He will suffer wounds and constant shame. ³⁴For the woman's husband will be jealous and very angry. And he will have no mercy on you when he comes looking for you. ³⁵You won't be able to buy him off no matter what you offer.

Keep Yourself Pure

7 Follow my advice, my son. Always keep it in mind and stick to it. ²Obey me and live! Guard my words as the most valuable thing you own. ³Write them down. Keep them deep in your heart. ⁴Love wisdom like a sweetheart. Make her a beloved member of your family. ⁵Let her hold you back from affairs with other women. Let her keep you from listening to their false words.

⁶I was looking out the window of my house one day. ⁷I saw a simple man. He was a young man who had no common sense. ⁸⁻⁹He was walking down the street at dusk. He was going to the house of a wayward girl, a prostitute. ¹⁰She came up to him, saucy and pert. She was dressed to excite him. ¹¹⁻¹²She was the forward, coarse type. She is often seen in the streets and markets. She stands at every corner asking men to be her lovers.

¹³She put her arms around him and kissed him. And she said, "I was just coming to look for you. And here you are! ¹⁴⁻¹⁷Come home with me. I'll fix you a nice dinner. My bed is spread with lovely, colored sheets of finest linen imported from Egypt. It is perfumed with myrrh, aloes, and cinnamon. ¹⁸Come on, let's take our fill of

love until morning. ¹⁹My husband is away on a long trip. ²⁰He has taken a wallet full of money with him. He won't come back for several days."

²¹So she coaxed him with her pretty speech. And in the end, he gave in to her. He couldn't resist her flattery. ²²He followed her as an ox going to the butcher. He went like a deer walking into a trap. ²³He was like a deer waiting to be killed with an arrow through its heart. He was as a bird flying into a snare. He did not know what would happen to him there.

²⁴Listen to me, young men! Not only listen, but obey! ²⁵Don't let your desires get out of hand. Don't let yourself think about her. Don't go near her. Stay away from where she walks. If you don't, she will tempt you. ²⁶For she has been the ruin of many men. A great many men have been her victims. ²⁷If you want to find the road to hell, look for her house.

Wisdom Gives Good Advice

8 Can't you hear the voice of wisdom? She is standing at the city gates. She is calling at every fork in the road. She is waiting at the door of every house. Listen to what she says: ⁴⁻⁵"Listen, men!" she calls. "How foolish you are! Let me give you understanding. O foolish ones, let me show you common sense! ⁶⁻⁷Listen to me! For I have important truth for you. All that I say is right and true. For I hate lies and every kind of cheating. ⁸My advice is pure and good. There is nothing of evil in it. ⁹My words are plain and clear to anyone whose mind is open! ¹⁰My teaching is far more valuable than silver or gold."

¹¹For the value of wisdom is far above rubies. Nothing can be compared with it! ¹²Wisdom and good judgment live together. For wisdom knows where to find knowledge. ¹³If anyone respects and fears God, he will hate evil. For wisdom hates pride, cheating, and lying of every kind.

¹⁴⁻¹⁶"I, Wisdom, give good advice and common sense. Because of my strength, kings reign in power, and rulers make fair laws. ¹⁷I love all who love

me. Those who look for me shall surely find me. ¹⁸Riches, honor, justice, and goodness are mine to give away. ¹⁹My gifts are better than the purest gold or silver! ²⁰My paths are those of justice and right. ²¹Those who love and follow me are indeed rich. I fill their banks and storehouses. ²²The Lord made me in the beginning. I was there before he made anything else. ²³From ages past, I am. I was there before the earth began. ²⁴I lived before the oceans were made. I was there before the springs bubbled forth their waters onto the earth. ²⁵Before the mountains and the hills were made, I was there. ²⁶Yes, I was born before God made the earth and fields. I was there before he made the first handfuls of soil.

²⁷⁻²⁹"I was there when he made the heavens. I was born before he formed the great springs at the bottom of the oceans. I was there when he set the limits of the seas. I gave them his orders not to spread beyond their borders. I was there when he made the blueprint for the earth and oceans. ³⁰I was the craftsman at his side. I was his constant joy. I loved always being in his presence. ³¹And how happy I was with what he created. I loved his wide world and all his family of mankind! ³²And so, young people, listen to me. For how happy are all who follow my teachings.

³³"Listen to my counsel and be wise. Oh, don't refuse it! ³⁴Happy is the person who wants to be with me so much that he watches for me at my gates! Blessed is he who waits for me outside my home! ³⁵For whoever finds me finds life. He wins approval from the Lord. ³⁶But the one who misses me has hurt himself beyond repair. Those who don't listen to me show that they love death."

Knowing God Results in Wisdom

9 Wisdom has built a palace supported on seven pillars. ²She has made a great banquet and mixed the wines. ³She has sent out her maidens inviting all to come. She calls out from the busiest places in the city. ⁴"Come, you simple ones without good judgment," she

says. ⁵"Come to wisdom's banquet and drink the wines that I have mixed. ⁶Leave behind your foolishness and begin to live. Learn how to be wise."

⁷⁻⁸If you put down a fool, you will only get a rude answer. Yes, he will snarl at you. So don't bother with him. He will only hate you for trying to help him. But a wise person, when rebuked, will love you all the more. ⁹Teach a wise person, and he will be even wiser. Teach a good person, and he will learn more. ¹⁰For the respect and fear of God are basic to all wisdom. Knowing God results in every other kind of understanding. ¹¹"I, Wisdom, will make the hours of your day more useful. I will make the years of your life more fruitful." ¹²Wisdom is its own reward. If you laugh at her, you hurt only yourself.

¹³A prostitute is loud and brash. She never has enough of lust and shame. ¹⁴She sits at the door of her house. Or she stands at the street corners of the city. ¹⁵She whispers to men going by. She talks to those minding their own business. ¹⁶"Come home with me," she says to simple men. ¹⁷"Stolen melons are the sweetest. Stolen apples taste the best!" ¹⁸But they don't know that her former guests are now in hell.

God's Wisdom Is for Everyone

10 Happy is the man with a level-headed child. But the mother of a rebel is sad.

²Riches gained by cheating don't bring happiness that lasts. But right living does.

³The Lord will not let a good person starve to death. And he won't let the wicked person's riches continue forever.

⁴Lazy people are soon poor. Hard workers get rich.

⁵A wise youth makes hay while the sun shines. But what a shame to see a lad who sleeps away his chances for success.

⁶The good person is covered with blessings from head to foot. But an evil person is always cursing his luck.

⁷We all have happy memories of good people gone to their reward. But the names of wicked people stink after they are gone.

⁸The wise person is glad to be taught. But a fool who tries to stand alone falls flat on his face.

⁹A good person has firm footing. But a thief will slip and fall.

¹⁰Winking at sin leads to sorrow. But bold reproof leads to peace.

¹¹There is living truth in what a good person says. But the mouth of the evil person is filled with curses.

¹²Hatred stirs old quarrels. But love overlooks insults.

¹³People with common sense are looked up to as counselors. But those without it are beaten as servants.

¹⁴A wise person holds his tongue. Only a fool blurts out all that he knows. That only leads to sorrow and trouble.

¹⁵The rich person's wealth is his only strength. The poor person's poverty is his only curse.

¹⁶The good person's earnings help the cause of good. The evil person wastes his money on sin.

¹⁷Anyone who wants to be corrected is on the path to life. Anyone who refuses correction has lost his chance.

¹⁸To hide hatred is to be a liar. To tell lies about another person is to be a fool.

¹⁹Don't talk too much. If you do, you will put your foot in your mouth. Be wise and turn off the flow!

²⁰When a good person speaks, he is worth listening to. But the words of fools are a dime a dozen.

²¹A godly person gives good advice. But a rebel is destroyed by lack of common sense.

²²The Lord's blessing is our greatest wealth. All our work adds nothing to it!

²³A fool has fun by being bad. A wise person has fun by being wise!

²⁴The wicked person's fears will all come true. So will the good person's hopes.

²⁵Disaster strikes like a cyclone, and the wicked are whirled away. But the good person has a strong anchor.

²⁶A lazy fellow is a pain to his employers. He is like smoke in their eyes or vinegar that sets the teeth on edge.

²⁷Respect for God adds hours to each day. So how can the wicked expect a long, good life?

²⁸The hope of good people is eternal happiness. The hopes of evil people are all worthless.

²⁹God protects the good. But he destroys the wicked.

³⁰The good shall never lose God's blessings. But the wicked shall lose everything.

³¹The good person gives wise advice. But the liar's counsel is not heard.

³²The upright say words that are helpful. But the wicked speak words of rebellion.

God Hates Cheating

11 The Lord hates cheating and loves honesty.

²Proud people end in shame. But the humble become wise.

³A good person is led by his honesty. But the evil person is destroyed by his dishonesty.

⁴Your riches won't help you on Judgment Day. Only righteousness counts then.

⁵Good people are directed by their honesty. But the wicked shall fall under their load of sins.

God wants us to be honest

The Lord hates cheating and loves honesty.

Proverbs 11:1

---

⁶The good person's goodness saves him. The evil person's cheating is his undoing.

⁷When an evil person dies, his hopes all die too. For they are based on this earthly life.

⁸God saves good people from danger. But he lets the wicked fall into it.

⁹The evil person destroys his neighbor with evil words. But through knowledge, the good person gets away.

¹⁰The whole city celebrates a good person's success. They are also happy at the godless person's death.

¹¹The good influence of godly people helps a city to prosper. But the moral decay of the wicked drives it downhill.

¹²To argue with a neighbor is foolish. A person with good sense holds his tongue.

¹³A gossip goes around spreading lies. But a person who is worthy of trust tries to quiet them.

¹⁴Without wise leadership, a nation is in trouble. But with good counselors there is safety.

¹⁵Be sure you know a person well before you vouch for his credit! It is better to refuse than to suffer later.

¹⁶Honor goes to kind and good women. But only money goes to cruel people.

¹⁷Your own soul is fed when you are kind. It is destroyed when you are cruel.

¹⁸The evil person gets rich for the moment. But the good person's reward lasts forever.

¹⁹The good person finds life. But the evil person finds only death.

²⁰The Lord hates the stubborn. But he takes joy in those who are good.

²¹You can be very sure the evil person will not go unpunished forever. And you can also be very sure God will save the children of the godly.

²²A beautiful woman with no modesty is like a fine gold ring in a pig's nose.

²³The good person can look forward to happiness. But the wicked can expect only anger and trouble.

²⁴⁻²⁵It is possible to give away and become richer! It is also possible to hold on too tightly and lose everything. Yes, the generous person shall be rich! By watering others, he waters himself.

God helps us do good things

A godly person is like a tree that bears life-giving fruit.

Proverbs 11:30

---

²⁶People curse the person who holds his grain for higher prices. But they bless the person who sells it to them in their time of need.

²⁷If you search for good, you will find God's favor. If you search for evil, you will find his curse.

²⁸Trust in your money and down you go! Trust in God and grow like a tree!

²⁹The fool who makes his family angry will have nothing good left in the end. He shall be the servant of a wiser person.

³⁰A godly person is like a tree that bears life-giving fruit. And all who teach wisdom are wise.

³¹The godly shall be rewarded here on earth. But how much more the wicked will be punished!

Avoid Mistakes by Gaining Wisdom

12 To learn you must want to be taught. To refuse teaching is stupid.

²The Lord blesses good people and condemns the wicked.

³Wickedness never brings real success. Only the godly will truly succeed.

⁴A worthy wife is her husband's joy and crown. The other kind destroys his strength. She tears down everything he does.

⁵A good person's mind is filled with honest thoughts. An evil person's mind is full of lies.

⁶The wicked accuse. The godly defend.

⁷The wicked shall die. The godly shall stand.

We should listen to good advice

A wise person listens to others.

Proverbs 12:15

---

⁸Everyone loves someone with good sense. But a person with an evil mind is hated.

⁹A person might have to get his hands dirty to eat. But he is better off than the one who is too proud to work and goes hungry.

¹⁰A good person is concerned for the welfare of his animals. But even the kindness of godless people is cruel.

¹¹Hard work means success. Only a fool wastes his time.

¹²Thieves are jealous of each other's loot. But good people long to help each other.

¹³Lies will get anyone into trouble. But honesty is its own defense.

¹⁴Telling the truth gives great joy to a person. Hard work gives back many blessings to him.

¹⁵A fool thinks he needs no advice. But a wise person listens to others.

¹⁶A fool is quick-tempered. A wise person stays cool when he is insulted.

¹⁷A good person is known by his truthfulness. A false person is known by his cheating and lies.

¹⁸Some people like to make cutting remarks. But the words of the wise soothe and heal.

¹⁹Truth stands the test of time. But lies are soon brought into the open.

²⁰Deceit fills hearts that are planning evil. Joy fills hearts that are planning for good!

God wants us to keep our promises

God delights in those who keep their promises.

Proverbs 12:22

---

²¹No real harm befalls the good. But there is constant trouble for the wicked.

²²God delights in those who keep their promises. He hates those who don't.

²³A wise person doesn't show his knowledge. But a fool shows everyone his foolishness.

²⁴Work hard and become a leader. Be lazy and never succeed.

²⁵Fearful hearts are very heavy. But a word of help does wonders!

²⁶The good person asks advice from friends. The wicked plunge ahead and fall.

²⁷A lazy person won't even dress the game he gets while hunting. But the diligent person makes good use of all he finds.

²⁸The path of the godly leads to life. So why fear death?

Following God's Word Leads to Success

13 A wise youth accepts his father's rebuke. A young mocker doesn't listen.

²The good person wins his case by

careful argument. The evil-minded person only wants to fight.

³Self-control means controlling the tongue! A quick answer can ruin everything.

⁴Lazy people want much but get little. But diligent people succeed in all they do.

Control your anger

A wise person controls his temper. He knows that anger causes mistakes.

Proverbs 14:29

---

⁵A good person hates lies. Wicked people lie all the time and soon come to shame.

⁶A person's goodness helps him all through life. But evil people are destroyed by their wickedness.

⁷Some rich people are poor and some poor people have great riches!

⁸Being kidnapped and held for ransom never worries the poor person!

⁹The good person's life is full of light. The sinner's road is dark and gloomy.

¹⁰Pride leads to arguments. Be humble, take advice, and become wise.

¹¹Riches from gambling quickly disappear. Riches from hard work grow every day.

¹²When hope seems far off the heart becomes sick. But when dreams come true at last, there is life and joy.

¹³Despise God's Word and find yourself in trouble. Obey it and succeed.

¹⁴The advice of a wise person refreshes like water from a mountain spring. Those who hear it find out about the pitfalls ahead.

¹⁵A person with good sense is loved. A cheating person must walk a rocky road.

¹⁶A wise person thinks ahead. A fool doesn't, and even brags about it!

¹⁷A messenger that cannot be trusted can cause a lot of trouble. Good communication makes progress happen.

¹⁸If you refuse teaching, you will end up in poverty and shame. If you accept it, you are on the road to fame.

¹⁹It is pleasant to see plans develop. That is why fools refuse to give them up even when they are wrong.

²⁰Be with wise people and become wise. Be with evil people and become evil.

²¹Curses chase sinners, while blessings chase the righteous!

²²When a good person dies, he leaves an inheritance to his grandchildren. But when a sinner dies, his riches are stored up for the godly.

²³A poor person's farm may have good soil. But injustice robs him of its riches.

²⁴If you refuse to discipline your son, it proves you don't love him. For if you love him, you will be prompt to punish him.

²⁵The good person eats to live, while the evil person lives to eat.

Anger Causes Mistakes

14 A wise woman builds her house. But a foolish woman tears hers down by her own efforts.

²To do right honors God. To sin is to hate him.

³A rebel's foolish talk should prick his own pride! But the wise person's speech is respected.

⁴An empty stable stays clean. But there is no income from an empty stable.

⁵A truthful witness never lies. A false witness always lies.

⁶A mocker never finds the wisdom he claims he is looking for. But it comes easily to the people with common sense.

⁷If you are looking for advice, stay away from fools.

⁸The wise person looks ahead. The fool attempts to fool himself and won't face facts.

⁹The common bond of rebels is their guilt. The common bond of godly people is good will.

¹⁰Only the person involved can know his own bitterness or joy. No one else can really share it.

¹¹The work of the wicked will pass away. The work of the godly will grow.

¹²Before every person there lies a wide and pleasant road. It seems right but ends in death.

¹³Laughter cannot hide a heavy heart.

When the laughter ends, the grief stays behind.

¹⁴The backslider gets bored with himself. The godly person's life is exciting.

¹⁵Only a simple person believes all he's told! A wise person understands the need for proof.

¹⁶A wise person is cautious and avoids danger. A fool plunges ahead with great confidence.

¹⁷A short-tempered person is a fool. He hates the person who is patient.

¹⁸The simple person is crowned with folly. The wise person is crowned with knowledge.

¹⁹Evil people shall bow before the godly.

²⁰⁻²¹Even his own neighbors hate the poor person. And the rich have many "friends." But to hate the poor is to sin. Blessed are those who help them.

²²Those who plan evil shall wander away and be lost. But those who plan good shall be given mercy and quietness.

²³Work brings profit. Talk brings poverty!

²⁴Wise people are praised for their wisdom. Fools are hated for their folly.

²⁵A witness who tells the truth saves good people from being sentenced to death. But a false witness is a traitor.

²⁶Respect for God gives people deep strength. His children have a place of safety and security.

Godliness helps us be great

Godliness makes a nation great. But sin will bring any people down.

Proverbs 14:34

²⁷Respect for the Lord is a fountain of life. Its waters keep people from death.

²⁸A nation with many children is a king's glory. A nation that is shrinking is his doom.

²⁹A wise person controls his temper. He knows that anger causes mistakes.

³⁰A relaxed attitude lengthens a person's life. Jealousy rots it away.

³¹Anyone who oppresses the poor is insulting God who made them. To help the poor is to honor God.

³²The godly have a place of safety when they die. But the wicked are crushed by their sins.

³³Wisdom lives in the hearts of people with common sense. But it must shout loudly before fools will hear it.

³⁴Godliness makes a nation great. But sin will bring any people down.

³⁵A king rejoices in servants who know what they are doing. He is angry with those who cause trouble.

God Delights in Our Prayers

15 A gentle answer turns away anger. But harsh words cause fights.

²A wise teacher makes learning a joy. A bad teacher speaks foolish things.

³The Lord is watching everywhere. He keeps his eye on both the evil and the good.

Answer angry words with kind ones

A gentle answer turns away anger. But harsh words cause fights.

Proverbs 15:1

⁴Gentle words cause life and health. Complaining brings sadness and trouble.

⁵Only a fool despises his father's advice. A wise son considers each word he hears.

⁶There is treasure in being good. But trouble follows the wicked everywhere.

⁷Only the good can give good advice. Rebels just can't do it.

⁸The Lord hates the gifts of the wicked. But he takes joy in the prayers of his people.

⁹⁻¹⁰The Lord hates the deeds of the wicked. But he loves those who try to be good. If they stop trying, the Lord will punish them. If they rebel against that punishment, they will die.

¹¹The depths of hell are open to God's knowledge. How much more the hearts of all mankind!

¹²A mocker stays away from wise people because he hates to be scolded.

¹³A happy face means a glad heart. A sad face means a breaking heart.

[14] A wise person is hungry for truth. But the mocker feeds on trash.

[15] When people are gloomy, everything seems to go wrong. When they are cheerful, everything seems right!

[16] It is better to have only a little with respect for God than to have great treasure and trouble with it.

[17] It is better to eat soup with someone you love than steak with someone you hate.

[18] A quick-tempered person starts fights. A cool-tempered person tries to stop them.

[19] A lazy fellow has trouble all through life. The good person's path is easy!

[20] A good son makes his father glad. A wicked son makes his mother sad.

If you're proud, you'll get hurt

Pride will destroy you.
It will make you fall.

Proverbs 16:18

---

[21] If someone enjoys folly, something is wrong! The sensible stay on the pathways of right.

[22] Plans go wrong with too few counselors. Many counselors bring success.

[23] Everyone enjoys giving good advice. How wonderful it is to be able to say the right thing at the right time!

[24] The road of the godly leads upward, leaving hell behind.

[25] The Lord destroys the possessions of the proud, but cares for widows.

[26] The Lord hates the thoughts of the wicked. But he takes joy in kind words.

[27] Dishonest money brings grief to all the family. But hating bribes brings happiness.

[28] A good person thinks before he speaks. Evil people pour out their evil words without a thought.

[29] The Lord is far from the wicked. But he hears the prayers of the righteous.

[30] Pleasant sights and good reports give happiness and health.

[31-32] If you learn from good criticism, you will become wise. But to reject good criticism is to hurt yourself and your own best interests.

[33] Humility and respect for the Lord will make you both wise and honored.

The Proud Man Runs into Trouble

16 We can make our plans, but the final outcome is in God's hands.

[2] We can always "prove" that we are right. But is the Lord convinced of this?

[3] Give your work to the Lord, then it will succeed.

[4] The Lord has made everything for his own purposes. And he has made the wicked for punishment.

[5] The Lord hates pride. Take my word for it: proud people shall be punished.

[6] Sin is made right by mercy and truth. Evil is avoided by respect for God.

[7] When a person is trying to please God, God makes even his worst enemies to be at peace with him.

[8] A little gained honestly is better than great riches gotten by dishonest means.

[9] We should make plans, but count on God to lead us.

[10] God will help the king to judge the people fairly. There need be no mistakes.

[11] The Lord demands fairness in every business deal. He made this rule.

[12] It is a bad thing for a king to do evil. His right to rule depends upon his fairness.

[13] The king rejoices when his people are truthful and fair.

[14] The anger of the king is a messenger of death. And a wise person will appease it.

[15] Many favors are showered on those who please the king.

[16] How much better is wisdom than gold! How much better is understanding than silver!

[17] The path of the godly leads away from evil. He who follows that path is safe.

[18] Pride will destroy you. It will make you fall.

[19] Better poor and humble than proud and rich.

[20] God blesses those who obey him.

Happy is the person who puts his trust in the Lord.

²¹The wise person is known by his common sense. And a pleasant teacher is the best.

²²Wisdom is a fountain of life to those who have it. But a fool's burden is his folly.

You will be happy when you obey God and trust him

God blesses those who obey him. Happy is the person who puts his trust in the Lord.

Proverbs 16:20

---

²³From a wise mind comes careful and persuasive speech.

²⁴Kind words are like honey. They are nice to hear and they bring health.

²⁵Before every person there lies a wide and pleasant road he thinks is right. But this road ends in death.

²⁶Hunger is good if it makes you work to satisfy it!

²⁷Hands without any work to do are used by the devil. Lips with nothing good to say are the devil's mouthpiece.

²⁸An evil person plants trouble. Gossip pulls the best of friends apart.

²⁹Wickedness loves company and leads others into sin.

³⁰The wicked person stares into space with pursed lips. He is deep in thought, planning his evil deeds.

³¹White hair is a crown of glory and is seen most among the godly.

³²It is better to be slow-tempered than famous. It is better to have self-control than to control an army.

³³We toss the coin, but it is the Lord who controls its decision.

True Friends Are Loyal

17 A dry crust eaten in peace is better than steak every day along with argument and strife.

²A wise slave will rule his master's wicked sons and share their estate.

³Silver and gold are made pure by fire. But it is God who makes hearts pure.

⁴The wicked enjoy fellowship with others who are wicked. Liars enjoy liars.

⁵Laughing at the poor is like laughing at the God who made them. He will punish those who rejoice at others' troubles.

⁶An old man's grandchildren are his crowning glory. A child's glory is his father.

⁷Truth from a rebel or lies from a king are both unexpected.

⁸A bribe works like magic. Whoever uses it will prosper!

⁹Love forgets mistakes. Nagging about them parts the best of friends.

¹⁰A few words of rebuke to a person of common sense is very helpful. It is more effective than a hundred lashes on the back of a rebel.

¹¹The wicked live to rebel. They shall be punished greatly.

¹²It is safer to meet a bear robbed of her cubs than a fool caught in his folly.

¹³If you repay evil for good, a curse is upon your home.

¹⁴It is hard to stop a quarrel once it starts, so don't let it begin.

A friend keeps on being a friend at all times

A true friend is always loyal.

Proverbs 17:17

---

¹⁵The Lord despises those who say that bad is good and good is bad.

¹⁶It is senseless to pay tuition to educate a rebel who has no heart for truth.

¹⁷A true friend is always loyal. And a brother is born to help in time of need.

¹⁸It is poor judgment to sign another's loan. It is dangerous to become responsible for his debts.

¹⁹Sinners love to fight. The person who brags is looking for trouble.

²⁰An evil person is afraid of everyone. He runs into constant trouble.

²¹It's no fun to be a rebel's father.

²²A cheerful heart does good like medicine. But a broken spirit makes one sick.

²³It is wrong to accept a bribe to twist justice.

²⁴Wisdom is the main goal of sensible

people. But a fool's goals are at the ends of the earth!

²⁵A bad son is a grief to his father. He is a bitter blow to his mother.

²⁶How shortsighted to fine the godly for being good! How foolish it is to punish nobles for being honest!

²⁷⁻²⁸The person of few words and a settled mind is wise. Therefore, even a fool is thought to be wise when he is silent. It pays him to keep his mouth shut.

Get the Facts before Deciding

18 The selfish person argues against every sound principle of conduct. He is always demanding his own way.

²A rebel doesn't care about the facts. All he wants to do is yell.

³Sin brings shame.

⁴A wise person's words express deep streams of thought.

⁵It is wrong for a judge to help the wicked and condemn the innocent.

⁶⁻⁷A fool gets into fights all the time. His mouth is his undoing! His words bring danger to him.

⁸What tasty morsels rumors are. They are eaten with great joy!

⁹A lazy person is brother to the person who destroys things.

¹⁰The Lord is a strong fortress. The godly run to him and are safe.

¹¹The rich person thinks of his riches as a strong defense. He thinks they are a high wall of safety. What a dreamer!

¹²Pride ends in destruction. Humility ends in honor.

¹³What a shame to decide before knowing the facts! Yes, how stupid!

¹⁴A person's courage can sustain his broken body. But when courage dies, what hope is left?

¹⁵The smart person is always open to new ideas. In fact, he looks for them.

¹⁶A gift does wonders. It will bring you before important people!

¹⁷Any story sounds true until someone tells the other side and sets the record straight.

¹⁸A coin toss ends arguments. It settles disputes between powerful opponents.

¹⁹It is hard to win back the friendship of an offended brother. It is harder than capturing a city with great walls around it. His anger shuts you out like iron bars.

²⁰The ability to give wise advice gives joy like a good meal!

²¹Those who love to talk will suffer

"Pretend" friends are not good friends

Some people only pretend to be friends. But a true friend sticks closer than a brother.

Proverbs 18:24

---

the consequences. People have died for saying the wrong thing!

²²The man who finds a wife finds a good thing. She is a blessing to him from the Lord.

²³The poor person begs, and the rich person answers with insults.

²⁴Some people only pretend to be friends. But a true friend sticks closer than a brother.

A Lazy Man Goes Hungry

19 It is better to be poor and honest than to be rich and dishonest.

²It is dangerous and sinful to rush into the unknown.

³A person may ruin his chances by his own foolishness. Then he might blame it on the Lord!

⁴A rich person has many "friends." The poor person has none left.

⁵Punish false witnesses. Track down liars.

⁶Many beg favors from a person who is generous. Everyone is his friend!

⁷A poor person's own brothers turn away from him in shame. How much more his friends! He calls after them, but they are gone.

⁸He who loves wisdom loves his own best interest and will be a success.

⁹A false witness shall be punished. A liar shall be caught.

¹⁰It doesn't seem right for a fool to succeed! It is wrong for a slave to rule over princes!

¹¹A wise person holds back his anger and overlooks insults. This is to his credit.

¹²The king's anger is as dangerous as a lion's. But his approval is as refreshing as the dew on grass.

¹³A rebellious son is a trouble to his father. A nagging wife annoys like constant dripping.

¹⁴A father can give his sons homes and riches. But only the Lord can give them good wives.

¹⁵A lazy person sleeps soundly, and he goes hungry!

¹⁶Keep the commandments and keep your life. Hating them means death.

¹⁷When you help the poor you are lending to the Lord. He pays wonderful interest on your loan!

¹⁸Discipline your son in his early years while there is hope. If you don't, you will ruin his life.

¹⁹A person with a hot temper must suffer his own penalty. You can't do much to help him. If you try once, you must try a dozen times!

²⁰Get all the advice you can and be wise the rest of your life.

²¹People can make many plans. But only the Lord's plans will always happen.

²²Kindness makes people attractive. And it is better to be poor than dishonest.

²³Respect for God gives life, happiness, and safety from harm.

²⁴Some people are so lazy they won't even feed themselves!

²⁵Punish a mocker, and others will learn from his example. Reprove a wise person, and he will be the wiser.

²⁶A son who hurts his father or mother is a public shame.

²⁷Stop listening to teaching that doesn't agree with what you know is right.

²⁸A worthless witness cares nothing for truth. He enjoys his sinning too much.

²⁹Mockers and rebels shall be severely punished.

Your Actions Tell a Lot about You

20 Wine gives false courage. Hard liquor leads to fights. What fools people are to let it master them! It makes them stagger drunkenly down the street!

²The king's anger is like that of a roaring lion. To make him angry is to risk your life.

³It is an honor for someone to stay out of a fight. Only fools insist on arguing.

⁴If you won't plow in the cold, you won't eat at the harvest.

⁵Good advice lies deep within a counselor's heart. But the wise person will draw it out.

⁶Most people will tell you what loyal friends they are. But are they telling the truth?

⁷It is a wonderful thing to have an honest father.

⁸A king sitting as judge weighs all the evidence carefully. He decides what is

---

What you do shows what kind of a person you are

The way someone behaves shows what kind of person he is.

Proverbs 20:11

---

true and what is false.

⁹Who can ever say, "I have made my heart clean. I am without sin"?

¹⁰The Lord despises every kind of cheating.

¹¹The way someone behaves shows what kind of person he is. He is known by whether he does what is pure and right.

¹²You might have good eyesight and good hearing. If so, thank God who gave them to you.

¹³If you love sleep, you will end in poverty. Stay awake, work hard, and there will be plenty to eat!

¹⁴"Totally worthless!" says the buyer as he haggles over the price. But afterwards he brags about his bargain!

¹⁵Good sense is far better than gold or precious jewels.

¹⁶It is risky to make loans to strangers!

¹⁷Some people enjoy cheating. But the cake they buy with "dirty money" will turn to gravel in their mouths.

¹⁸Don't go ahead with your plans without the advice of others. Don't go to war until they agree.

¹⁹Don't tell your secrets to a gossip unless you want them broadcast to the world.

²⁰God puts out the light of the person who curses his father or mother.

²¹Quick riches are not a blessing in the end.

²²Don't repay evil for evil. Wait for the Lord to handle the matter.

²³The Lord hates all cheating and dishonesty.

²⁴The Lord is directing our steps. So why try to understand all that happens along the way?

²⁵It is foolish to make a promise to the Lord before counting the cost.

²⁶A wise king stamps out crime by severe punishment.

²⁷A person's conscience is the Lord's lamp. It brings his hidden motives to the light.

²⁸If a king is kind, honest, and fair, his kingdom stands safely.

²⁹The glory of young men is their strength. The glory of old men is their experience.

³⁰Punishment that hurts chases evil from the heart.

Learn by Listening

21 Just as water is turned into ditches, so the Lord directs the king's thoughts. He turns them wherever he wants to.

²We can justify our every deed. But God looks at our motives.

³God is more pleased when we are just and fair than when we give him gifts.

⁴Pride, lust, and evil actions are all sin.

⁵Steady plodding brings wealth and success. Looking for fast money makes people poor.

⁶Dishonest gain will never last, so why take the risk?

⁷The wicked are unfair. So their violence comes back and destroys them.

⁸A person is known by his actions. An evil person lives an evil life. A good person lives a godly life.

⁹It is better to live in an attic than with a crabby woman in a lovely home.

¹⁰An evil person loves to hurt others. Being a good neighbor is out of his line.

¹¹The wise person learns by listening. The simple person can learn only by seeing mockers punished.

¹²God, the Righteous One, knows what is going on in the homes of the wicked. He will bring the wicked to judgment.

¹³He who shuts his ears to the cries of the poor will be ignored in his own time of need.

¹⁴An angry person is made silent by giving him a gift!

¹⁵A good person loves justice. But it is a calamity to those who do evil.

Don't say things that will get you into trouble

Be careful what you say. That will keep you out of trouble.

Proverbs 21:23

---

¹⁶The person who strays away from common sense will end up dead!

¹⁷A person who loves pleasure becomes poor. Wine and luxury are not the way to riches!

¹⁸The wicked will finally lose. The righteous will finally win.

¹⁹Better to live in the desert than with a complaining woman.

²⁰The wise person saves for the future. But the foolish person spends whatever he gets.

²¹The person who tries to be good and kind finds life, goodness, and honor.

²²The wise person conquers the strong person and levels his defenses.

²³Be careful what you say. That will keep you out of trouble.

²⁴Mockers are proud and haughty.

²⁵⁻²⁶The lazy person wishes for many things. But his hands refuse to work. He is greedy to get. But the godly love to give!

²⁷God hates the gifts of evil people. He especially hates it if they are trying to bribe him!

²⁸No one believes a liar, but everyone respects the words of an honest person.

²⁹An evil person is stubborn. But a

godly person will think about his decision.

³⁰No one, no matter how clever, can stand against the Lord.

³¹Go ahead and get ready for the conflict. But victory comes from God.

Giving to the Poor Can Make You Happy

22 If you must choose, take a good name rather than great riches. For to be held in loving respect is better than silver and gold.

²The rich and the poor are alike before the Lord who made them all.

³A wise person sees the problems ahead and gets ready for them. The simple person goes blindly on and suffers as a result.

⁴True humility and respect for the Lord lead a person to riches, honor, and long life.

⁵The rebel walks a thorny, hard road. The person who values his soul will stay away.

⁶Teach a child how to choose the right path. When he is older, he will still be on it.

⁷Just as the rich rule the poor, so the borrower is servant to the lender.

⁸The unjust tyrant will harvest disaster. His reign of terror shall end.

⁹Happy is the generous person, the one who feeds the poor.

¹⁰Throw out the mocker, and you will be rid of tension and fighting.

¹¹He who values grace and truth is the king's friend.

¹²The Lord preserves the upright. But he ruins the plans of the wicked.

¹³The lazy person is full of excuses. "I can't go to work!" he says. "If I go outside, I might meet a lion in the street and be killed!"

¹⁴A prostitute is a dangerous trap. Those cursed of God are caught in it.

¹⁵A youngster's heart is filled with rebellion. But punishment will drive it out of him.

¹⁶He who gains by hurting the poor or bribing the rich shall end in poverty.

¹⁷⁻¹⁹Listen to this wise advice: Trust in the Lord. Follow it closely, for it will do you good. Then you can pass it on to others.

²⁰⁻²¹In the past, haven't I been right? Then believe what I am telling you now. Share it with others.

Choose the right path as a child, and it will shape your whole life

Teach a child how to choose the right path. When he is older, he will still be on it.

Proverbs 22:6

---

²²⁻²³Don't rob the poor and sick! For the Lord is their defender. If you hurt them, he will punish you.

²⁴⁻²⁵Keep away from angry, short-tempered people. If you don't, you will learn to be like them. And thus, you will put your soul in danger.

²⁶⁻²⁷Unless you have the extra cash on hand, don't sign a loan. Why risk all you own? They'll even take your bed!

²⁸Do not move the ancient boundary marks. That is stealing.

²⁹Do you know a hard-working person? He shall be successful and stand before kings!

Criticism Can Help You

23 When eating with a rich person, be on your guard. Don't stuff yourself, even though it all tastes so good. For he is trying to bribe you. No good is going to come of his invitation.

⁴⁻⁵Don't weary yourself trying to get rich. Why waste your time? For riches can disappear as though they had the wings of a bird!

⁶⁻⁸Don't spend time with evil people. Don't wish for their favors and gifts. Their kindness is a trick. They want to use you as their pawn. The good food they serve will turn sour in your stomach. You will vomit it and have to take back your words of thanks for their "kindness."

⁹Don't waste your breath on a rebel. He will despise the wisest advice.

¹⁰⁻¹¹Don't steal the land of orphans by moving their boundary marks. For their Redeemer is strong. He himself will accuse you.

¹²Don't refuse to accept correction. Get all the help you can.

¹³⁻¹⁴Don't fail to correct your children. Good discipline won't hurt them. They won't die if you use a stick on them! But it may help to keep them out of hell.

¹⁵⁻¹⁶My son, how I will rejoice if you become a man of common sense. Yes, my heart will thrill to your thoughtful, wise words.

¹⁷⁻¹⁸Don't envy evil people, but keep on respecting the Lord all the time. For surely you have a wonderful future ahead of you. There is hope for you yet!

¹⁹⁻²¹O my son, be wise and stay in God's paths. Don't spend time with drunks and gluttons. For they are on their way to becoming poor. And remember that too much sleep clothes a person with rags. ²²Listen to your father's advice. Don't hate your old mother's experience. ²³Get the facts at any price. Hold on tightly to all the good sense you can get. ²⁴⁻²⁵The father of a godly man has cause for joy. What pleasure a wise son is! So give your parents joy!

²⁶⁻²⁸O my son, trust my advice. Stay away from prostitutes. For a prostitute is a deep and narrow grave. Like a robber, she waits for her victims as one after another become unfaithful to their wives.

Discipline helps us much more than it hurts us

Don't fail to correct your children. Good discipline won't hurt them. But it may help to keep them out of hell.

Proverbs 23:13-14

---

²⁹⁻³⁰Whose heart is filled with pain and sorrow? Who is always fighting? Who is the person with bloodshot eyes and many wounds? It is the one who spends long hours in the taverns. He tries out all the new mixtures. ³¹Don't let the sparkle and the smooth taste of strong wine trick you. ³²For in the end it bites like a poisonous snake. It stings like an adder. ³³Your eyes will see strange things. And your mind will be confused. You will say foolish, silly things that would shame you to no end when sober. ³⁴You will stagger like a sailor tossed at sea, clinging to a swaying mast. ³⁵And after that you will say, "I didn't even know it when they beat me up! Let's go and have another drink!"

Evil Plans Are As Bad As Evil Actions

24 Don't be jealous of godless people. Don't even enjoy their company. ²For they spend their days planning violence and cheating.

³⁻⁴Any good project is built by wise planning. It becomes strong through common sense. It really helps to know all the facts.

⁵A wise person is mightier than a strong person. Wisdom is mightier than strength.

⁶Don't go to war without wise guidance. There is safety in many counselors.

⁷Wisdom is too much for a rebel. He'll not be chosen as a counselor!

⁸To plan evil is as wrong as doing it.

⁹The rebel's schemes are sinful. And the mocker brings trouble on all mankind.

¹⁰You are a poor person if you can't stand the pressure of trouble.

¹¹⁻¹²Rescue those who are unjustly sent to their death. Don't stand back and let them die. Don't try to say you didn't know about it. For God, who knows all hearts, knows yours. He knows that you knew! And he will reward everyone according to his deeds.

¹³⁻¹⁴My son, honey whets the appetite and so does wisdom! When you enjoy becoming wise, there is hope for you! A bright future lies ahead!

¹⁵⁻¹⁶O evil person, leave the good person alone. Stop trying to cheat him out of his rights. Even though you trip him up seven times, this good person will rise up each time! But one problem is enough to knock you down.

¹⁷Do not be happy when your enemy meets trouble. Let there be no gladness when he falls. ¹⁸For the Lord may be

unhappy with you. And he may stop punishing him!

19-20Don't be jealous of the wicked. Don't wish you had his riches. For the evil person has no future. His candle will be blown out.

21-22My son, watch your step before the Lord and the king. And don't spend time with troublemakers. For you will go down with them to sudden disaster. And who knows where it all will end?

23It is wrong to punish the poor and let the rich go free. 24Someone might say to the wicked, "You are innocent." But if he does, he shall be cursed by the people of many nations. 25Blessings shall be given to those who rebuke sin with no fear.

26It is an honor to be given an honest and frank answer.

27Build your business first, before building your house.

28-29Don't testify spitefully against an innocent neighbor. Why lie about him? Don't say, "Now I can pay him back for all his meanness to me!"

30-31I walked by the field of a lazy person. I saw that it was overgrown with thorns. It was covered with weeds. And its walls were all broken down. 32-34Then, as I looked, I learned this lesson. Too much sleep means that poverty will break in upon you. It will come suddenly like a robber, and violently like a bandit.

Keep Your Promises

25 These proverbs of Solomon were found and copied by the servants of King Hezekiah of Judah.

2-3It is God's privilege to hide things. It is the king's privilege to find and invent. You cannot know the height of heaven! You cannot measure the size of the earth! You can never know all that goes on in the king's mind!

4-5When you take away dross from silver, you have pure silver ready for the silversmith. When you take away corrupt people from the king's court, his reign will be just and fair.

6-7Don't ask the king to see you as though you were some powerful prince. It is best to wait to be invited. Don't push

forward, or you may be sent back to the end of the line! Then you will be shamed in public.

8-10Don't be hotheaded and rush to court! You may start something you can't finish. You may go down before your neighbor in shameful defeat. So talk about the matter with him privately. Don't tell anyone else, or he might accuse you of slander. Then you won't be able to take back what you said.

11Timely advice is as lovely as gold apples in a silver basket.

12It is a badge of honor to accept valid criticism.

13A faithful worker is as refreshing as a cool day in hot summer.

Choose the right words to say

Timely advice is as lovely as gold apples in a silver basket.

Proverbs 25:11

14Don't promise a gift and then not give it. That is like a cloud blowing over a desert without dropping any rain.

15Be patient and you will finally win. For a soft tongue can break hard bones.

16Do you like honey? Don't eat too much of it. If you do, it will make you sick!

17Don't visit your neighbor too often. If you do, you will wear out your welcome!

18Telling lies about someone is as harmful as hitting him with an axe. It is like wounding him with a sword. It is like shooting him with a sharp arrow.

19Putting confidence in an unworthy person is like chewing with a sore tooth. It is like trying to run on a broken foot.

20Don't be happy and sing songs to someone who is sad. It is as bad as stealing his jacket in cold weather. It is like rubbing salt in his wounds.

21-22If your enemy is hungry, give him food! If he is thirsty, give him something to drink! This will make him feel ashamed of himself. And God will reward you.

23As a wind from the north brings cold, so a harsh answer causes anger!

²⁴It is better to live in an attic than in a beautiful home with a cranky woman.

²⁵Good news from far away is like cold water to the thirsty.

²⁶A godly person might compromise with the wicked. But if he does, it is like making a fountain dirty or putting mud in a spring.

²⁷It is harmful to eat too much honey. It is also bad for people to think about all the honors they deserve!

²⁸A person without self-control is without defense. He is like a city with its walls broken down.

Rebels Are Impossible

26 Honor doesn't go with fools any more than snow with summer or rain with harvest!

²An undeserved curse has no effect. Its intended victim will be no more hurt by it than by a sparrow. It will not hurt him any more than a swallow flying through the sky.

³Guide a horse with a whip and a donkey with a bridle! And lead a rebel with a rod to his back!

⁴⁻⁵When arguing with a rebel, don't use foolish arguments as he does. If you do, you will become as foolish as he is! Prick his pride with silly replies!

⁶It is foolish to trust a rebel to take a message. It is as foolish as cutting off your feet and drinking poison!

⁷In the mouth of a fool a proverb becomes as useless as a frozen leg.

⁸Honoring a rebel will backfire like a stone tied to a slingshot!

⁹A rebel will misapply an illustration. Its point will no more be felt than a thorn in the hand of a drunk.

¹⁰The master may get better work from an untrained apprentice than from a skilled rebel!

¹¹As a dog goes back to his vomit, so a fool repeats his folly.

¹²There is one thing worse than a fool. That is a person who is proud.

¹³The lazy person won't go out and work. "There might be a lion outside!" he says. ¹⁴He sticks to his bed like a door to its hinges! ¹⁵He is too tired even to lift his food from his dish to his mouth!

¹⁶Yet in his own opinion he is smarter than seven wise men.

¹⁷Entering an argument that isn't any of your business is as foolish as yanking a dog's ears.

¹⁸⁻¹⁹A person might be caught lying to his neighbor. And he might say, "I was just fooling." But if he does this, he is like a madman throwing around firebrands, arrows, and death!

²⁰Fire goes out for lack of fuel. And tensions go away when gossip stops.

²¹A quarrelsome person starts fights as easily as a match sets fire to paper.

²²Gossip is a tasty morsel eaten with great joy.

²³Pretty words may hide a wicked heart. They are like the pretty glaze that covers a common clay pot.

²⁴⁻²⁶A person with hate in his heart may sound pleasant enough. But don't believe him. For he is cursing you in his heart. He might pretend to be kind. But his hatred will finally come to light for all to see.

²⁷The person who sets a trap for others will get caught in it himself. Roll a boulder down on someone, and it will roll back and crush you.

²⁸Flattery is a form of hatred and wounds cruelly.

Jealousy Is Dangerous

27 Don't brag about what you will do tomorrow. Wait and see what happens.

²Don't praise yourself. Let others do it.

³A rebel's frustrations are heavier than sand and rocks.

⁴Jealousy is more dangerous and cruel than anger.

⁵Open rebuke is better than hidden love!

⁶Wounds from a friend are better than kisses from an enemy!

⁷Even honey seems tasteless to a person who is full. But if he is hungry, he'll eat anything!

⁸A person who strays from home is like a bird that wanders from its nest.

⁹Friendly suggestions are as pleasant as perfume.

¹⁰Never leave a friend, either yours or your father's. Then you won't need to go

Don't praise yourself

> *Don't praise yourself.*
> *Let others do it.*
>
> Proverbs 27:2

to a distant relative for help in your time of need.

11My son, how happy I will be if you turn out to be sensible! It will be a public honor to me.

12A sensible person watches for problems ahead and gets ready to meet them. The simple person never looks and suffers for it.

13The world's poorest credit risk is the person who agrees to pay a stranger's debts.

14You might shout a pleasant greeting to a friend too early in the morning. And if you do, he will count it as a curse!

15A constant dripping on a rainy day and a cranky woman are much alike! 16You can no more stop her complaints than you can stop the wind.

17People can help each other, just as iron sharpens iron.

18A workman may eat from the orchard he tends. Anyone who protects another's interests should be rewarded.

19A mirror reflects a person's face. But what he is really like is shown by the kind of friends he chooses.

20Ambition and death are alike in this way: neither is ever happy.

Your friends reflect what you are

> *A mirror reflects a person's face.*
> *But what he is really like is*
> *shown by the kind of friends*
> *he chooses.*
>
> Proverbs 27:19

21The purity of silver and gold can be tested over a fire. But a person is tested by his reaction to people's praise.

22You can't separate a rebel from his foolishness though you crush him to powder.

23-24Riches can disappear fast. And the king's crown doesn't stay in his family forever. So watch your business interests closely. Know the state of your flocks and your herds. 25-27Then there will be enough lambs' wool for clothing. There will be enough goats' milk for food for all your family after the hay is harvested. This is when the new crop appears, and the mountain grasses are gathered in.

Admit Your Mistakes

28 The wicked run when no one is chasing them! But the godly are as bold as lions!

2When there is moral rot within a nation, its government falls easily. But with honest, sensible leaders there is strength.

3A poor person might take advantage of those even poorer. If he does, he is like a flood sweeping away their last hope.

4To complain about the law is to praise wickedness. To obey the law is to fight evil.

5Evil people don't understand the importance of justice. But those who follow the Lord are very concerned about it.

6It is better to be poor and honest than to be rich and a cheater.

7Young people who are wise obey the law. A son who is a member of a lawless gang is a shame to his father.

8Income from hurting the poor will end up in the hands of someone who pities them.

9God doesn't listen to the prayers of those who disobey the law.

10A curse on those who lead the godly astray. But people who help the upright to do good shall be given a good reward.

11Rich people are proud. But their real poverty is clear to the poor.

12When the godly are successful, everyone is glad. When the wicked succeed, everyone is sad.

13A person who refuses to admit his mistakes can never be successful. But if he admits and leaves them, he gets another chance.

14Blessed is the person who respects God. But the person who doesn't care is headed for trouble.

¹⁵A wicked ruler is as dangerous to the poor as a lion or bear attacking them.

¹⁶Only a stupid prince will oppress his people. But a king will have a long reign if he hates dishonesty and bribes.

¹⁷A murderer's conscience will drive him into hell. Don't stop him!

¹⁸Good people will be saved from harm. But cheaters will be destroyed.

¹⁹Hard work brings prosperity. Playing around brings poverty.

You are wise when you control your anger

A person who can't control his anger is foolish. A person who controls his anger is wise.

Proverbs 29:11

---

²⁰The person who wants to do right will get a rich reward. But the person who wants to get rich quick will quickly fail.

²¹Giving special treatment to rich people is a clear case of selling one's soul for a piece of bread.

²²Trying to get rich quick is evil and leads to poverty.

²³In the end, people like frankness more than flattery.

²⁴A person might rob his parents and say, "What's wrong with that?" If he does, he is no better than a murderer.

²⁵Greed causes fighting. Trusting God leads to success.

²⁶A person is a fool to trust himself! But those who use God's wisdom are safe.

²⁷If you give to the poor, your needs will be supplied! But a curse upon those who close their eyes to poverty.

²⁸When the wicked prosper, good people go away. When the wicked meet disaster, good people come back.

God Rewards Fairness

29 A person might be corrected often, but he might not listen to criticism. This person will suddenly be broken. He will never have another chance.

²With good people in power, everyone is happy. But with the wicked in power, everyone groans.

³A wise son makes his father happy. But a boy who hangs around with prostitutes shames him.

⁴A just king gives strength to his nation. But one who demands bribes destroys it.

⁵⁻⁶Flattery is a trap. Evil people are caught in it. But good people stay away and sing for joy.

⁷The good person knows the poor person's rights. The godless don't care.

⁸Fools start fights everywhere. But wise people try to keep peace.

⁹There's no use arguing with a fool. He only rages and laughs. Then tempers begin to burn.

¹⁰The godly pray for those who long to kill them.

¹¹A person who can't control his anger is foolish. A person who controls his anger is wise.

¹²A wicked ruler will have wicked servants on his staff.

¹³Rich and poor are alike in this way: each depends on God for light.

¹⁴A king who is fair to the poor shall have a long reign.

¹⁵Scolding and spanking a child helps him to learn. Left to himself, he brings shame to his mother.

¹⁶When rulers are wicked, their people are too. But good people will live to see the tyrant's downfall.

¹⁷Discipline your son, and he will give you happiness and peace of mind.

¹⁸Where there is ignorance of God, crime runs wild. But what a wonderful thing it is for a nation to know and keep his laws.

¹⁹Sometimes mere words are not enough. Discipline is needed. For the words may not be listened to.

²⁰There is more hope for a fool than for a person of quick temper.

²¹Pamper a servant from childhood, and he will expect you to treat him as a son!

²²A hot-tempered person starts fights. He gets into all kinds of trouble.

²³Pride ends in a fall, but humility brings honor.

²⁴A person who helps a thief must really hate himself! For he knows it might bring trouble, but does it anyway.

²⁵Fear of people is a dangerous trap. But to trust in God means safety.

²⁶Do you want justice? Don't beg for it from the judge. Ask the Lord for it!

²⁷The good hate the badness of the wicked. The wicked hate the goodness of the good.

Baffling and Wonderful Things

30 These are the words of Agur, the son of Jakeh. They were spoken to Ithiel and Ucal.

²I am tired out, O God, and ready to die. I am too stupid even to call myself a human being! ³I cannot understand people, let alone God. ⁴Who else but God goes back and forth to heaven? Who else holds the wind in his fists? Who wraps up the oceans in his coat? Who but God has created the world? If there is any other, what is his name? What is his Son's name, if you know it?

⁵Every word of God proves true. He defends all who come to him for protection. ⁶Do not add to his words, or he might rebuke you. And you might be found a liar.

⁷O God, I beg two favors from you before I die. ⁸First, help me never to tell a lie. Second, give me neither poverty nor riches! Give me just enough to satisfy my needs! ⁹For if I grow rich, I may become content without God. And if I am too poor, I may steal. That way I might insult God's holy name.

Amazing Things

¹⁰Never falsely accuse a person to his employer. If you do, he might curse you for your sin.

¹¹⁻¹²There are those who curse their father and mother. They think they are innocent even though they have done many sins. ¹³⁻¹⁴They are proud beyond saying it! They have no respect for anyone! They devour the poor with teeth as sharp as knives!

¹⁵⁻¹⁶There are two things that are never satisfied. They are like a leech, forever wanting more. No, there are three things! No, four! Hell, the barren womb, a barren desert, and fire.

¹⁷A person who laughs at his father and hates his mother shall have his eye plucked out by ravens and eaten by vultures.

¹⁸⁻¹⁹There are three things too great for me to understand. No, there are four!

How an eagle glides through the sky;
How a serpent crawls upon a rock;
How a ship finds its way across the heaving ocean;
The growth of love between a man and a girl.

²⁰A prostitute sins and then says, "What's wrong with that?"

²¹⁻²³There are three things that make the earth shake. No, there are four it cannot stand!

A slave who becomes a king;
A rebel who prospers;
A bitter woman when she finally marries;
A servant girl who marries the husband of her mistress.

²⁴⁻²⁸There are four things that are small but very wise!

Ants: they aren't strong, but they store up food for the winter.
Cliff badgers: they are delicate little animals. They stay safe by living among the rocks.
The locusts: though they have no leader, they stay together in swarms.
The lizards: they are easy to catch and kill. But they are found even in kings' palaces!

²⁹⁻³¹There are three stately monarchs in the earth. No, there are four!

The lion, king of the animals—he won't turn aside for anyone;
The peacock;
The male goat;
A king as he leads his army.

³²You might have been a fool by being proud or planning evil. Don't brag about it! Cover your mouth with your hand in shame.

³³The churning of cream yields butter. And a blow to the nose causes bleeding. In the same way, anger causes fights.

31 These are the wise sayings of King Lemuel of Massa. They were taught to him at his mother's knee.

²O my son, whom I have given to the Lord! ³Do not spend your time with women. This is the royal pathway to destruction.

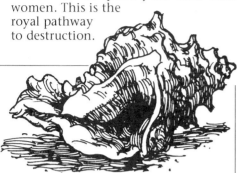

Purple
PROVERBS 31:22

What is your favorite color? Why? Purple was special in Bible times. This purple was a bright red-purple, not a soft violet. Kings often wore purple robes. Only the very rich could afford to buy purple. The dye for purple came from the murex shellfish in the sea. To get the dye, the murex shell had to be broken. A tiny amount of the valuable dye was taken from a gland in the neck of the shellfish. Thousands of murex shellfish were needed for a tiny amount of dye. An entire robe dyed purple was very expensive. That's why only kings or very wealthy people could afford purple. Purple was used in the Tabernacle furnishings and the High Priest's clothes. It was used also for the veil of the Temple. Lydia, Paul's friend, sold purple dye (Acts 16:14). Today a purple shirt or dress wouldn't cost any more than a green one. We don't use murex shellfish for our purple colors now. But whenever you read about someone with purple in Bible times, you know that person had lots of money or a very special gift.

⁴And it is not for kings, O Lemuel, to drink wine and whiskey. ⁵For if they drink they may forget their duties. They may not be able to give justice to those who are oppressed. ⁶⁻⁷Hard liquor is for sick people at the brink of death. Wine is for those in deep depression. Let them drink to forget their poverty and misery.

⁸You should defend those who cannot help themselves. ⁹Yes, speak up for the poor and helpless. See to it that they get justice.

¹⁰If you can find a truly good wife, she is worth more than precious gems! ¹¹Her husband can trust her. And she will richly satisfy his needs. ¹²She will not hinder him but help him all her life. ¹³She finds wool and flax and busily spins it. ¹⁴She buys imported foods brought by ship from distant ports. ¹⁵She gets up before dawn to make breakfast for her household. She plans the day's work for her servant girls. ¹⁶She goes out to inspect a field and buys it. With her own hands she plants a vineyard. ¹⁷She is a hard worker. ¹⁸And she watches for bargains. She works far into the night!

¹⁹⁻²⁰She sews for the poor and helps those in need. ²¹She has no fear of winter for her household. For she has made warm clothes for all of them. ²²She also makes beautiful covers for her bed. Her own clothing is nicely made, a purple gown of pure linen. ²³Her husband is well known. He sits in the council chamber with the other civic leaders. ²⁴She makes belted linen robes to sell to the traders.

²⁵She is a woman of strength and dignity. And she has no fear of old age. ²⁶When she speaks, her words are wise. Kindness is the rule for all she says. ²⁷She watches carefully all that goes on throughout her household. She is never lazy. ²⁸Her children stand and praise her. So does her husband. He praises her with these words: ²⁹"There are many fine women in the world. But you are the best of them all!"

³⁰Charm can deceive, and beauty doesn't last. But a woman who fears and respects God shall be greatly praised. ³¹Praise her for the many fine things she does. These good deeds of hers shall bring her honor from great people.

ECCLESIASTES

Why do we make so many mistakes? Why do we do so many foolish things? Have you ever said, "I wish I had not done that"? Or, "Why did I do that? I should have known better." You won't touch a hot stove if you listen to someone who has already been burned. Ecclesiastes is a book that will keep you from getting burned. It will help you choose what is best for you. The wisest man who ever lived wrote it. He wrote it when he was old. He had everything. He had done everything. Now he's telling us what works and what doesn't work. He's telling us what looked good but really wasn't. He's telling us what didn't look like much but was really wonderful. Solomon wants to have a little talk with you. He wants to keep you from doing many of the foolish things he did. He wants the very best for you. Listen to Solomon! You'll be glad you did.

Is Life Worth Living?

1 These are the words of the Preacher. He is the son of David, king in Jerusalem.

²In my opinion, nothing is worthwhile. Everything is useless. ³⁻⁷For what does a person get for all his hard work?

Fathers, sons, and then grandsons come and go. But nothing ever changes. The sun rises and sets. Then it hurries around to rise again. The wind blows south and north, here and there. It twists back and forth and gets nowhere. The rivers run into the sea. But the sea is never full. And the water goes back again to the rivers. Then it flows again to the sea. ⁸⁻¹¹Everything is weary beyond saying it. Everything is tiresome. No matter how much we see, we are never happy. No matter how much we hear, we are not content.

History just repeats itself. Nothing is really new. It has all been done or said before. What can you point to that is new? How do you know it wasn't around long ages ago? We don't remember what happened in those early times. And in the future no one will remember what we have done back here.

Being Smart Isn't Everything

¹²⁻¹⁵I, the Preacher, was king of Israel. I was living in Jerusalem. And I set out to understand everything in the world. I found that man's life, which God has given to him, is not a happy one. It is all useless, chasing the wind. What is wrong cannot be righted. It is water over the dam. And there is no use thinking of what might have been.

¹⁶⁻¹⁸I said to myself, "Look, I know more than any of the kings before me in

Jerusalem. I have greater wisdom and knowledge." So I worked hard to be wise instead of foolish. But now I know that even this was like chasing the wind. For the more my wisdom, the more my grief. To increase knowledge only increases suffering.

Having a Good Time Isn't Everything

2 I said to myself, "Come now, enjoy life! Enjoy yourself to the full." But I found that this, too, was useless. For it is silly to be laughing all the time. What good does it do?

³So after a lot of thinking, I decided to try the road of drink. But I still held tight to my course of seeking wisdom.

Next I changed my course again. I followed the path of folly. I wanted to see how happy I could be.

⁴⁻⁶So I tried to find joy in building many things. I built homes, vineyards, gardens, parks, and orchards for myself. I made big pools to hold water for my gardens.

⁷⁻⁸Next I bought slaves, both men and women. Other slaves were born within my household. I also bred great herds and flocks. I had more than any of the kings before me. I collected silver and gold as taxes from many kings and countries.

In the cultural arts, I started men's and women's choirs and orchestras.

And then there were my many beautiful concubines.

⁹So I became greater than any of the kings in Jerusalem before me. And with it all I stayed clear-eyed. That way I could evaluate all these things. ¹⁰Anything I wanted I took. I did not stop myself from any joy. I even found great pleasure in hard work. This pleasure was, indeed, my only reward for all my labors.

Hard Work Isn't Everything

¹¹But as I looked at all I had tried, it was all so useless! It was like chasing the wind. There was nothing really worthwhile anywhere.

¹²Now I began to compare the virtues of wisdom and folly. And anyone else would come to the same conclusion I did. ¹³⁻¹⁴They would see that wisdom is of more value than foolishness. Wisdom is better just as light is better than darkness. For the wise man sees, while the fool is blind. And yet I saw that there was one thing that happened to wise and foolish alike. ¹⁵Just as the fool will die, so will I. So of what value is all my wisdom? Then I saw that even wisdom is useless. ¹⁶For the wise and the fool both die. And in the days to come both will be forgotten. ¹⁷So now I hate life because it is all so useless! All is foolishness, chasing the wind.

¹⁸And I am disgusted about this. For I must leave the fruits of all my hard work to others. ¹⁹And who can tell whether my son will be a wise man or a fool? And yet all I have will be given to him. How discouraging!

²⁰⁻²³So I turned in sadness from hard work. I saw that it wasn't the answer to my search for happiness. For I might spend my life searching for wisdom, knowledge, and skill. But then I must leave all of it to someone who hasn't done a day's work in his life. He inherits all my efforts, free of charge. This is not only foolish but also unfair. So what does a man get for all his hard work? He lives through days full of sorrow and grief. And he suffers through restless, bitter nights. It is all completely useless!

Pleasure Comes from God

²⁴⁻²⁶So I decided there was nothing for a man to do but enjoy his food and drink and his job. Then I saw that even this pleasure is from the hand of God. For who can eat or enjoy apart from him? For God gives those who please him wisdom, knowledge, and joy. But if a sinner becomes rich, God takes the riches away from him. And he gives it to those who please him. So here, too, we see an example of foolishly chasing the wind.

There's a Right Time for Everything

3 There is a right time for everything:
²There is a time to be born.
There is a time to die.

There is a time to plant.
There is a time to harvest.
[3]There is a time to kill.
There is a time to heal.
There is a time to destroy.
There is a time to rebuild.
[4]There is a time to cry.
There is a time to laugh.
There is a time to grieve.
There is a time to dance.
[5]There is a time for scattering stones.
There is a time for gathering stones.
There is a time to hug.
There is a time not to hug.
[6]There is a time to find.
There is a time to lose.
There is a time for keeping.
There is a time for throwing away.
[7]There is a time to tear.
There is a time to repair.
There is a time to be quiet.
There is a time to speak up.
[8]There is a time for loving.
There is a time for hating.
There is a time for war.
There is a time for peace.

God Is in Control

[9]What does one really get from hard work?

[10]I have thought about all the various kinds of work God has given to mankind. [11]He has made all things good in their own time. God has put eternity in the hearts of men. But, even so, many cannot see the whole scope of God's work from beginning to end. [12]So I conclude that, first, there is nothing better for a man than to be happy. He should enjoy himself as long as he can. [13]Second, he should eat and drink and enjoy the fruits of his work. For these are gifts from God.

[14]And I know that whatever God does is final. Nothing can be added or taken from it. God does all this so that man will respect him.

[15]Whatever is has been long ago. And whatever is going to be has been before. God will make happen again what already happened in the faraway past.

[16]Moreover, I notice that all over the earth justice is giving way to crime. Even the courts of law are corrupt. [17]I said to myself, "In due season God will judge all that man does. He will judge both good and bad."

[18]And then I saw that God was letting the world go on its sinful way. He was doing that to test mankind. He wanted men themselves to see that they were no better than animals. [19]For men and animals both breathe the same air. And both of them die. So mankind has no real advantage over the beasts. What a strange thing! [20]All go to one place. They all come from dust, and they will all go back to dust when they die. [21]For who can prove that the spirit of man goes upward? And who can prove that the spirit of an animal goes downward into dust? [22]So I saw that there is nothing better for men than that they should be happy in their work. For that is what they are here for. And no one can bring them back to life to enjoy what will be in the future. So let them enjoy it now.

I Would Rather Be Dead

4 Next I saw all the oppression and sadness throughout the earth. The oppressed shed tears and no one was helping them. Their oppressors had powerful friends on their side. [2]So I felt that the dead were better off than the living. [3]And most lucky of all are those who have never been born. For they have never seen all the evil throughout the earth.

[4]Then I saw that the basic reason for success is the driving force of jealousy! But this, too, is useless, chasing the wind! [5-6]The fool won't work and almost starves. But he feels that it is best to be lazy and barely get by. He thinks this is better than to work hard. This is because in the long run it is all so useless.

[7]I also saw another piece of foolishness on the earth. [8]This is the case of a man who is quite alone. He has no sons or brothers. But he works hard to keep getting more riches. And to whom will he leave it all? And why is he giving up so much now? It is all so useless and sad!

Going It Alone Isn't the Answer

⁹Two can do more than twice as much as one. And the results can be much better. ¹⁰If one falls, the other pulls him up. But if a man falls when he is alone, he's in trouble.

**Team up with someone
and you'll get more done**

Two can do more than twice as much as one. And the results can be much better.

Ecclesiastes 4:9

---

¹¹Also, on a cold night, two under the same blanket get warmth from each other. But how can one be warm alone? ¹²And one standing alone can be attacked and beaten. But two can stand back-to-back and win! Having three is even better. For a cord with three strands is not easy to break.

Success Doesn't Last

¹³A young man might be poor but wise. He is better off than an old and foolish king who won't listen to advice. ¹⁴Such a boy could come from prison and succeed. He might even become king, though born with nothing in his pockets. ¹⁵Everyone is eager to help a youth like that. They might even help him to take the throne. ¹⁶He might become the leader of millions of people and be loved by all. But, then, younger people might grow up around him and reject him! So again, it is all foolishness, chasing the wind.

Have Respect for God

5 As you go into the Temple, keep your ears open and your mouth shut! Don't be a fool who doesn't even know it is sinful to make rash promises to God. For he is in heaven and you are only here on earth. So let your words be few. Being too busy gives you bad dreams. In the same way, being a fool makes you talk far too much! ⁴You might talk to God and make a promise to him. If you do this, don't wait to do it. For God has no pleasure in fools. Keep your promise to him. ⁵You might not promise to do anything. This is better than saying you will and then not doing it. ⁶⁻⁷If you make a promise and don't fulfill it, your mouth is making you sin. Don't try to defend yourself to God's messenger. Don't try to tell him that the promise you made was all a mistake. That would make God very angry. And he might destroy your success. Dreaming instead of doing is foolish. And there is ruin in a flood of empty words. Respect God, instead.

⁸You might see some poor man being oppressed by the rich. Or you might see justice fail somewhere in the land. If you see this, don't be surprised! For every official is under orders from higher up. And the higher officials look up to their leaders. And so the matter of injustice is lost in red tape and excuses. ⁹And over them all is the king. Oh, for a king who is devoted to his country! Only he can bring order from this chaos.

¹⁰He who loves money shall never have enough. How foolish it is to think that riches can make you happy! ¹¹The more you have, the more you spend. You will spend right up to the limits of your income. So what is the advantage of riches? It just gives you the chance to watch it run through your fingers! ¹²The man who works hard sleeps well whether he eats little or much. But the rich must worry and have a hard time sleeping.

¹³⁻¹⁴There is another great problem I have seen everywhere. Savings are often put into deals that turn sour. Soon there is nothing left to leave to one's son. ¹⁵The man who speculates is soon back to where he began, with nothing. Even though he has worked hard, he leaves just as he came. ¹⁶This, as I said, is a very great problem. For all his hard work has been for nothing. He has been working for the wind. It is all blown away. ¹⁷All the rest of his life he is under a cloud. He is gloomy, sad, and angry.

Enjoying Life Is a Gift from God

¹⁸Well at least one thing is good. It is good for a man to eat well and drink a good glass of wine. It is good for him to accept what life has given him. It is good

for him to enjoy his work, whatever his job may be. And may he enjoy these things for however long the Lord lets him live. 19-20And, of course, it is very good if a man has riches from the Lord. And it is good if he has good health to enjoy them. To enjoy your work and to accept what you have in life is a gift from God. The person who does that will not need to look sadly on his past. For God gives him reasons for joy.

Is Life Really Worth Living?

6 Yes, but there is a very great evil that I have seen everywhere. 2God has given to some men very great riches and honor. They can have anything they want! But God doesn't give them the health to enjoy it. They die and others get it all! This is unfair! It just doesn't make sense!

3A man might have 100 sons and as many daughters. And he might live to be very old. But he leaves so little money at his death that his children can't even bury him. I say that he would be better off born dead. 4His birth would then be useless and end in darkness. He would die without even a name. 5He would have never seen the sun or even known it was there. But that is better than to be an old, unhappy man. 6A man might live for 1,000 years twice over. But if he is never happy, well, what's the use?

7-8Wise men and fools alike spend their lives looking for food. Both never seem to get enough. Both have the same problem. But the poor man who is wise lives a far better life. 9A bird in the hand is worth two in the bush. Mere dreaming of nice things is foolish. It's chasing the wind.

10All things that happen were planned long ago. Each man is what he was created to be. So there's no use arguing with God about it.

11The more words you speak, the less they mean. So why bother to speak at all?

12We have only a few days of our empty lifetimes. So who can say how one's days can best be spent? Who can know what will be best for the future

after he is gone? For who knows the future?

Some Tips for a Meaningful Life

7 A good name is better than the best perfume.

The day one dies is better than the day he is born! 2It is better to spend your time at funerals than at feasts. For you are going to die. And it is a good thing to think about it while there is still time. 3Sorrow is better than laughter. For sadness has a good influence on us. 4Yes, a wise man thinks much of death. But the fool thinks only of having a good time now.

5It is good to be criticized by a wise man. This is better than being praised by a fool! 6For a fool's praise goes as quickly as paper in fire. It is silly to listen to it.

7The wise man is turned into a fool by a bribe. It destroys his understanding.

8Finishing is better than starting! Patience is better than pride! 9Don't let your temper flare quickly. That is being a fool.

10Don't wish for "the good old days." For you don't know whether they were any better than these!

11To be wise is as good as being rich. In fact, it is better. 12You can get anything by either wisdom or money. But being wise has many advantages.

13See the way God does things, and do what he does. Don't fight the facts of nature. Who can make straight what he has made crooked? 14Enjoy success whenever you can. When hard times come, know that God gives hard times as well as good times. Everyone should know that nothing is sure in this life.

15-17In this silly life I have seen everything. I have seen that some of the good die young. I have seen that some of the wicked live on and on. So don't be too good or too wise! Why destroy yourself? On the other hand, don't be too wicked either. Don't be a fool! Why should you die before your time?

18Take care of every task that comes along. And if you respect God, you can expect his blessing.

19A wise man is stronger than the mayors of 10 big cities! 20There is not a single man in all the earth who is always good and never sins.

²¹⁻²²Don't listen in when you aren't supposed to! You may hear your servant cursing you! For you know how often you yourself curse others!

²³I have tried my best to be wise. I said, "I will be wise." But it didn't work. ²⁴Wisdom is far away and very hard to find. ²⁵I looked everywhere. I wanted to find wisdom and the reason for things. I wanted to prove to myself that foolishness is wicked and crazy.

²⁶A prostitute is more bitter than death. May it please God that you escape from her. But sinners don't get away from her traps.

²⁷⁻²⁸"This is one thing I have learned," says the Preacher. "I found this out step by step. I came to this after studying hard. I found that truly good men are very hard to find. Such people are just one in 1,000!

²⁹"And I found that God made men to be good. But each has turned away to follow his own downward road."

Obey the Law

8 How wonderful to be wise and understand things. How good it is to be able to look at them and find out what they mean. Wisdom lights up a man's face. Wisdom softens its hardness.

²⁻³Obey the king as you have promised to do. Don't always try to get out of doing your duty, even when it's not fun. For the king punishes those who disobey. ⁴The king's command is backed by great power. No one can stand against it or question it. ⁵Those who obey him will not be punished. The wise man will find a time and a way to do what he says. ⁶⁻⁷Yes, there is a time and a way for all things. This is true even though man's trouble lies heavy on him. For how can he keep away from what he doesn't know will happen?

⁸No one can hold back his spirit from leaving. No one has the power to stop his day of death. For you cannot get out of dying. A man's wickedness is not going to help him then.

Obey God

⁹⁻¹⁰I have thought deeply about all that goes on here in the world. I have thought about how some have the power to hurt each other. I have seen wicked men buried. Their friends leave the graveyard after the burial. And they have already forgotten all the dead man's evil deeds! This evil man is praised in the very city where he did so many bad things! How strange! ¹¹God does not always punish sinners right away. So people feel it is safe to do wrong. ¹²A man might sin 100 times and still live. But I know very well that those who respect God will be better off. ¹³Those who respect God are not like the wicked. The wicked will not live long, good lives. Their days shall pass away quickly. Their lives will pass as shadows because they don't respect God.

¹⁴But there is a strange thing happening here on the earth. God seems to treat some good men as though they are wicked. And at times it seems that some wicked men are treated like they are good. This is all very confusing!

God Sees Everything

¹⁵Then I decided to spend my time having fun. I felt that there was nothing better to do than eat, drink, and enjoy life. Then joy will help mankind do all the hard work that God gives them.

¹⁶⁻¹⁷In my search for wisdom I saw all that was going on across the earth. Things were happening without stopping, day and night. Of course, only God can see everything. Even the wisest man who says he knows everything doesn't!

Life Is Worth Living; Do It Well

9 This, too, I carefully studied. I found that godly and wise men are in God's will. But still, no one knows if he will help him or not. All is chance! ²⁻³The same God confronts everyone, whether good or bad. It seems so unfair that one end comes to all. That is why men are not more careful to be good. But instead they choose their own crazy paths. For they have no hope. There is nothing but death ahead anyway.

⁴There is hope only for the living. It

is better to be a live dog than a dead lion! ⁵For the living at least know that they will die! But the dead know nothing. They don't even have their memories. ⁶Whatever they did in their lifetime is long gone. They can no longer love, hate, or envy. They have no part in anything here on earth anymore. ⁷So go ahead—eat, drink, and enjoy life. For it seems to make no difference to God! ⁸Wear fine clothes, with a dash of cologne! ⁹Live happily with the woman you love through the few days of life. For the wife God gives you is your best reward down here for all your earthly work. ¹⁰Whatever you do, do well. For in death, where you are going, there is no working or planning. There is no knowing or understanding.

¹¹Again I looked around the earth. And I saw that the fastest person does not always win the race. I saw that the strongest man doesn't always win the battle. I saw that wise men are often poor. And I found that men with great skill are not always famous. But it is all by chance. You succeed by being at the right place at the right time. ¹²A man never knows when he is going to run into bad luck. He is like a fish caught in a net. He is like a bird caught in a trap.

¹³Here is another thing that I have seen as I have watched human actions. ¹⁴There was a small city with only a few people living in it. A great king came with his army and attacked it. ¹⁵There was in the city a wise man, very poor. He knew what to do to save the city. And so it was saved. But after that no one thought any more about him. ¹⁶I saw that wisdom is better than strength. But even so, if the wise man is poor, he will be hated. And all the wise things he says will not be heard. ¹⁷But even so, the quiet words of a wise man are better than the shout of a king of fools. ¹⁸Wisdom is better than weapons of war. But one sinner can spoil much good.

Behave Wisely

10 Dead flies will cause even a bottle of perfume to stink! Yes, a small mistake can destroy much wisdom and honor. ²A wise man's heart leads him to do right. A fool's heart leads him to do evil. ³You can spot a fool just by the way he walks down the street!

⁴If the boss is angry with you, don't quit! A quiet spirit will quiet his bad temper.

⁵There is another unfair thing I have seen in the world. It has to do with kings and rulers. ⁶I have seen foolish men given great power. And I have seen rich men not given the respect they deserve! ⁷I have even seen servants riding! And I have seen princes walk like servants!

Do your best!

Whatever you do, do well.

Ecclesiastes 9:10

---

⁸⁻⁹Dig a well and fall into it! Break down an old wall and be bitten by a snake! When working in a quarry, stones will fall and crush you! There is danger in each stroke of your axe!

¹⁰A dull axe needs great strength. Be wise and sharpen the blade.

¹¹When the horse is stolen, it is too late to lock the barn.

¹²⁻¹³It is pleasant to listen to wise words. But a fool's speech brings him to ruin. He begins with a foolish idea. So his conclusion is sheer madness. ¹⁴A fool knows all about the future. And he tells everyone in detail! But who can really know what is going to happen? ¹⁵A fool gets upset by a little work. So then he has no strength for the smallest thing.

¹⁶⁻¹⁷How terrible it is for the land whose king is a child. How bad it is for the land whose leaders are drunk in the morning. Happy is the land whose king is a nobleman. Happy is the land whose leaders work hard before they feast and drink. And then they only eat to gain strength for the work ahead! ¹⁸Laziness lets the roof leak. And soon the rafters begin to rot. ¹⁹A party gives laughter, and wine gives happiness. And money gives all these things! ²⁰Never curse the king, not even in your thoughts. Never curse a rich man, either. For a little bird will tell them what you've said.

Keep It Up; God Will Honor You

11 Give freely, for your gifts will come back to you later. [2]Divide your gifts among many. For in the days ahead you yourself may need help.

[3]When the clouds are heavy, the rains come down. When a tree falls, whether south or north, it will lie where it falls. [4]If you wait for things to be perfect, you will never get anything done. [5]God's ways are hard to understand. They are as hard to find as the pathway of the wind. And they are as hard to understand as how a human spirit is put into a baby. [6]Keep on planting your seed. For you never know which will grow. Perhaps all of it will.

Enjoy Life Fully

[7]It is a great thing to be alive! [8]If a person lives to be very old, let him rejoice in every day of life. But let him also remember that eternity is far longer. Remind him that everything down here is useless in comparison.

[9]Young man, it's good to be young! Enjoy every minute of it! Do all you want to. Take in all you can. But know that you must account to God for all you do. [10]So put away grief and pain. But remember that bad mistakes can be made while you are young. And those mistakes might affect your whole life ahead.

Honor God Whether You Are Young or Old

12 Don't let the joy of being young make you forget about your Creator. Honor him in your youth before the hard years come. Then you won't enjoy living any more. [2]It will be too late then to try to remember him. The sun and light and moon and stars will be dim to your old eyes. And there will be no silver lining left among your clouds. [3]For there will come a time when your limbs will shake with age. Your strong legs will become weak. And your teeth will be too

---

Don't forget about God!

Don't let the joy of being young make you forget about your Creator.

Ecclesiastes 12:1

---

few to do their work. And you will be blind too. [4]Then let your lips be tightly closed while eating. For your teeth will be gone! And you will wake up at dawn with the first note of the birds. But you will be deaf and tuneless, with weak voice. [5]You will be afraid of heights and of falling. You will be a withered old man with white hair. You will limp along as you walk. Your desire will be gone. You will be standing at death's door. Then you will go to your everlasting home. And the mourners will walk along the streets.

We are on earth to honor and obey God

Honor God and obey his commands. This is really the reason you are here.

Ecclesiastes 12:13

---

[6]Yes, remember your Creator now while you are young. Remember him before the silver cord of life snaps. Look to him before the gold bowl is broken. Remember him before the pitcher is broken at the fountain. Look to him before the wheel is broken at the well. [7]Then the dust goes back to the earth as it was. And the spirit goes back to God who gave it. [8]All is useless, says the Preacher. It is all useless!

Fear God and Obey Him

[9]But the Preacher was wise. So he went on teaching the people all he knew. And he collected proverbs and put them in order. [10]For the Preacher was not just a wise man. He was also a good teacher. He didn't just teach what he knew to the people. He taught them in an interesting way. [11]The wise man's words are like spurs that push a horse to act. They nail down important truths. Students are wise who learn what their teachers tell them.

[12]But, my son, be warned. There is no end to the writing of books. Studying them can go on forever and become very tiring!

[13]Here is my final advice: honor God and obey his commands. This is really the reason you are here. [14]For God will judge us for all the things we do. He will judge us for every hidden thing, good or bad.

SONG OF
SOLOMON

Some day you may fall in love and get married. Many people do. This is a book about love. A husband and his bride tell about their exciting, wonderful romance. They tell what love really is. It's much different from what TV says about love. Solomon called this book Song of Songs. You may not find this book as exciting as books with adventure stories. But it is an important book for people who are ready to fall in love. It is also important for better understanding God's great love for his people.

The Wedding Day

1 This is King Solomon's greatest song. *The Girl:* 2"Kiss me again and again. For your love is sweeter than wine. 3How good your cologne smells! How great is your name! No wonder all the young girls love you! 4Take me with you. Come, let's run! The king has brought me into his palace. How happy we will be! Your love is better than wine. No wonder all the young girls love you! 5I am dark but lovely, O girls of Jerusalem! I am as tanned as the dark tents of Kedar. But I am as lovely as the silken tents of Solomon!

6"Don't look down on me, you city girls. Don't hate me just because my skin is so dark and tanned. My brothers were angry with me. They sent me out into the sun to tend the vineyards. But see what it has done to me!

7"Tell me, O one I love! Where are you leading your flock today? Where will you be at noon? For I will come and join you there. Then I won't have to wander among the flocks of your friends."

King Solomon: 8"You are the most beautiful woman in all the world! And to find me, just follow the trail of my flock to the shepherds' tents. There you may feed your sheep and their lambs. 9What a lovely mare you are, my love! 10How lovely your cheeks are, with your hair falling down upon them! How shapely is your neck with that long string of jewels. 11We shall make you gold earrings and silver beads."

The Girl: 12"The king lies on his bed. He is thrilled by the scent of my perfume. 13My loved one is like a sack of myrrh lying between my breasts. 14He is like a bouquet of flowers in the gardens of Engedi."

King Solomon: 15"How pretty you are, my love! Oh, how pretty! Your eyes are soft like doves."

The Girl: 16"How handsome you are, my lover! And you are so pleasant! Our bed is made in the soft grass. 17We are shaded by cedar trees and firs."

2 *The Girl:* "I am the rose of Sharon, the lily of the valley."

King Solomon: 2"Yes, you are a lily among thorns. So you are, compared with any other girls!"

The Girl: 3"My lover is an apple tree. He is the finest in the orchard. He is finer than any of the other young men. I am sitting in his much-loved shade. His fruit is sweet to eat. ⁴He brings me to the banquet hall. Everyone can see how much he loves me. ⁵Oh, feed me with your love. Feed me with your 'raisins' and your 'apples.' For I am sick with love. ⁶His left hand is under my head. And with his right hand he holds me.

Don't be ashamed to let others know that you love someone

Everyone can see how much he loves me.

Song of Solomon 2:4

The Girl Speaks to Her Friends: ⁷"O girls of Jerusalem, I charge you! Promise this by the gazelles and deer in the park. Do not wake my feelings of love until I am ready!"

Memories of Courtship

The Girl: ⁸"Ah, I hear my lover! Here he comes, jumping upon the mountains. He is leaping over the hills. ⁹My lover is like a gazelle or young deer. Look, there he is behind the wall! Now he is looking in at the windows!

¹⁰"My lover said to me, 'Rise up, my love! Come away with me, my fair one! ¹¹For the winter is past. And the rain is over and gone. ¹²The flowers are springing up. And the time of the singing of birds has come. Yes, spring is here. ¹³The leaves are coming out. And the grapevines are in blossom. How sweet they smell! Rise up, my love! Come away with me, my fair one!'"

King Solomon: ¹⁴"My dove is hiding behind some rocks. She is just behind an outcrop of the cliff. Call to me, and let me hear your lovely voice. Let me see your pretty face. ¹⁵The little foxes are ruining the vineyards. Catch them, for the grapes are all in blossom."

The Girl: ¹⁶"My lover is mine and I am his. He is feeding among the lilies! ¹⁷He is there until dawn comes. Then the shadows will flee away. Come to me, my lover! Be like a gazelle or a young stag on the rough mountains."

3 *The Girl:* "One night my lover was missing from my bed. I got up to look for him but couldn't find him. ²I went

out into the streets of the city. I walked the roads to look for him. But I could not find him. ³The police stopped me. I said to them, 'Have you seen him anywhere? Have you seen this one I love so much?' ⁴Soon after this I found him. And I held him tight. I would not let him go until I had brought him into my childhood home. I brought him into my mother's old bedroom. ⁵I charge you, O women of Jerusalem! Promise this by the gazelles and deer of the park. Do not wake my feelings of love before I am ready!"

Memories of Engagement

The Young Women of Jerusalem: ⁶"Who is this sweeping in from the deserts? He is like a cloud of smoke along the ground! He smells of myrrh and incense. He smells of every other spice that can be bought! ⁷Look, it is the chariot of Solomon! Sixty of his strongest men are around it. ⁸They are all skilled swordsmen and good bodyguards. Each one has his sword upon his thigh. They are ready to defend their king against any attack in the night. ⁹King Solomon made himself a chariot from the wood of Lebanon. ¹⁰Its posts are silver. Its canopy is made of gold. The seat on it is purple. And the back is inlaid with these words: 'With love from the girls of Jerusalem!'"

The Girl: ¹¹"Go out and see King Solomon, O young women of Zion! See the crown his mother gave him on his wedding day. This was his day of joy and gladness."

4 *King Solomon:* "How pretty you are, my love! Oh, how pretty! Your eyes are soft like doves. Your hair falls across your face like flocks of goats. They are like goats that dance across the hills of Gilead. ²Your teeth are white like sheep's wool, newly shaved and washed. They are perfectly matched. Not a single one is missing. ³Your lips are like a thread of red. How beautiful your mouth is. Your pretty cheeks are a matched pair behind your hair. ⁴Your neck is shapely like the tower of David. It is jeweled with a thousand heroes' shields. ⁵Your breasts are like twin fawns of a gazelle, feeding among the lilies. ⁶I will go to the mountain of myrrh and to the hill of incense. I will lie there until the morning dawns and the shadows flee away. ⁷You are so pretty, my love. Every part of you is beautiful.

⁸"Come with me from Lebanon, my bride. We will look down from the top of the mountain. We will look from the top of Mount Hermon. There the lions have their dens and panthers prowl. ⁹You have stolen my heart, my lovely one, my bride. I am overcome by one glance of your eyes. I am taken by a single bead of your necklace. ¹⁰How sweet is your love, my darling, my bride. How much better it is than mere wine. The perfume of your love is sweeter than all the richest spices. ¹¹Your lips, my dear, are made of honey. Yes, honey and cream are under your tongue. And the smell of your clothes is like the scent of the mountains and cedars of Lebanon.

¹²"My darling bride is like a private garden. She is like a spring that no one else can have. She is a fountain of my own. ¹³⁻¹⁴You are like a lovely orchard growing sweet fruit. And the rarest of perfumes grow there. Nard and saffron, calamus and cinnamon all grow there. And there is perfume from every other incense tree. There is also myrrh and aloes. And every other lovely spice grows there too. ¹⁵You are a garden fountain! You are a well of living water! You are as fresh as the streams from the Lebanon mountains."

The Girl: ¹⁶"Come, north wind, wake up! Come, south wind, blow on my garden. Blow its lovely perfume to my lover. Let him come into his garden and eat its sweetest fruits."

5 *King Solomon:* "I am here in my garden, my darling, my bride! I gather my myrrh with my spices. I eat my honeycomb with my honey. I drink my wine with my milk."

The Young Women of Jerusalem: "Oh, lover and beloved! Eat and drink! Yes, drink deeply!"

A Disturbing Dream

The Girl: ²"One night as I was sleeping, my heart woke up in a dream. I heard the voice of my lover. He was knocking at my bedroom door. 'Open to me, my darling, my lover, my lovely dove,' he said. 'For I have been out in the night. And I am covered with dew.'

³"But I said, 'I have undressed. Shall I get dressed again? I have washed my feet. Should I get them dirty again?'

⁴"My lover tried to unlock the door. And my heart was thrilled within me. ⁵I jumped up to open it. My hands dripped with perfume as I pulled back the bolt. ⁶I opened to my lover, but he was gone. My heart stopped. I looked for him but couldn't find him anywhere. I called to him, but there was no answer. ⁷The guards found me. They hit and hurt me. The watchman on the wall tore off my veil. ⁸Make this promise to me, O women of Jerusalem! If you find my lover, tell him that I am sick with love."

The Young Women of Jerusalem: ⁹"O woman of rare beauty! What is it about your loved one that is better than any other? What about him makes you command us in this way?"

The Girl: ¹⁰"My lover is tanned and handsome. He is better than 10,000 others! ¹¹His head is purest gold. And he has wavy hair, as black as a raven. ¹²His eyes are like doves beside the water brooks. They are deep and quiet. ¹³His cheeks are like sweetly scented beds of spices. His lips are like perfumed lilies. His breath is like myrrh. ¹⁴His arms are round bars of gold set with topaz. His body is bright ivory covered with jewels. ¹⁵His legs are like pillars of marble set in sockets of finest gold. They are like the cedars of Lebanon! None can compare with him. ¹⁶His mouth is sweet and lovable in every way. Such, O women of Jerusalem, is my lover and my friend."

6 *The Young Women of Jerusalem:* "O rarest of beautiful women! Where has your loved one gone? We will help you find him."

The Girl: ²"He has gone down to his garden, to his spice beds. He has gone to pasture his flock and to gather the lilies. ³I am my lover's and he is mine. He pastures his flock among the lilies!"

A Bowl of Bible Fruit
SONG OF SOLOMON 7:12

Do you ever have a bowl of fruit in your house? If you do, what's in it? You probably have an apple, a banana, a pear or peach, some grapes, and an orange. You might also have plums, tangerines, or cherries. But if you lived in Israel in Bible times, you would not have so many kinds of fruit. Grapes, figs, and olives were the most common fruit then. Because there wasn't always lots of water, grape juice became an important drink.

Fresh fruit spoiled quickly, so dried fruit was popular. Figs, dates, and raisins are mentioned often in the Bible. When dried, they could be carried on long trips or kept through the winter. Pomegranates were a favorite fresh fruit. They are about the size of an apple. Inside are many little pockets of sweet juice. They were so popular then that little pomegranate decorations hung on the high priest's robe (Exodus 28:33-34).

Fruit wasn't just used for eating. Oil from olives was used in lamps for light. Olive oil was also used as hand lotion.

Wow! What a Beautiful Bride

King Solomon: 4"O my darling, you are as pretty as the lovely land of Tirzah. Yes, you are as beautiful as Jerusalem. Oh, how you capture my heart! 5Look the other way, for your eyes have overcome me! Your hair falls across your face. It is like a flock of goats dancing down the slopes of Gilead. 6Your teeth are white as freshly washed lambs. They are perfectly matched, and not one is missing. 7Your cheeks are matched loveliness behind your hair. 8I have 60 other wives, all queens. I have 80 concubines. And there are virgins available to me beyond counting them. 9But you, my dove, my perfect one, are the only one among them all. You have no equal! The women of Jerusalem were full of joy when they saw you. Even the queens and concubines praise you. 10'Who is this?' they ask. 'She rises like the dawn. She is as fair as the moon. She is as pure as the sun. She is so wonderfully pretty!'"

The Girl: 11"I went down into the orchard of nut trees. I went out to the valley to see the springtime there. I wanted to see if the grapevines were budding yet. I wanted to see if the pomegranates had blossoms. 12Before I knew it, I was very homesick. I wanted to be back among my own people."

The Young Women of Jerusalem: 13"Come back to us, O girl of Shulam. Come back so we can see you once again."

The Girl: "Why should you look for a girl from Shulam? Why should you want to look at her?"

7 *King Solomon:* "How pretty are your dancing feet, O queenly maiden! Your rounded thighs are like jewels. They are the work of the most skilled of craftsmen. 2Your navel is lovely, like a goblet filled with wine. Your waist is like a heap of wheat set about with lilies. 3Your two breasts are like two fawns, yes, lovely twins. 4Your neck is shapely like an ivory tower. Your eyes are like the pools in Heshbon by the gate of Bath-rabbim. Your nose is shapely like the tower of Lebanon looking over Damascus.

5"As Mount Carmel crowns the mountains, so your hair is your crown.

The king is held captive in your queenly tresses.

⁶"Oh, how delightful you are. How pleasant, O love, for utter delight! ⁷You are tall and slim like a palm tree. Your breasts are like its clusters of dates. ⁸I said, I will climb up into the palm tree. I will take hold of its branches. Now may your breasts be like grape clusters. May the scent of your breath be like apples. ⁹And may your kisses be as exciting as the best of wine, smooth and sweet. They cause the lips of those who are asleep to speak."

The Bride Tells of Her Love

The Girl: ¹⁰"I belong to my lover, and I am the one he desires. ¹¹Come, my lover, let us go out into the fields. Let us stay in the villages. ¹²Let us get up early and go out to the vineyards. Let us see if the vines have budded. Let us see if the blossoms have opened. Let us see if the pomegranates are in flower. And there I will give you my love. ¹³There the mandrakes give forth their scent. The rarest fruits are at our doors, the new as well as the old. For I have stored them up for my lover."

8 *The Girl:* "Oh, if only you were my brother. Then I could kiss you no matter who was watching. And no one would laugh at me. ²I would bring you to my childhood home. And there you would teach me. I would give you spiced wine to drink, sweet pomegranate wine. ³His left hand would be under my head. And his right hand would hold me tight. ⁴Promise me this, O women of Jerusalem! Do not to wake up my feelings of love until I am ready."

The Power of Love

The Young Women of Jerusalem: ⁵"Who is this coming up from the desert? Who is that leaning on her lover?"

King Solomon: "I woke up your love under the apple tree. It was there that your mother gave birth to you. ⁶Put me like a seal over your heart. Place me like a seal over your arm. For love is strong as death. And jealousy is as cruel as the grave. It flashes fire, the very flame of the Lord. ⁷Many waters cannot quench the flame of love. Neither can the floods drown it. If a man tried to buy it with all he owned, he couldn't do it."

The Girl's Brothers: ⁸"We have a little sister too young for breasts. What shall we do if someone asks to marry her? ⁹If she is a virgin, we will put silver towers on her. If she is not, we will enclose her with cedar boards."

The Girl: ¹⁰"I am a virgin. And my breasts are like towers. And I have found favor in my lover's eyes. ¹¹Solomon had a vineyard at Baal-hamon. He rented it out to some farmers there. The rent was 1,000 pieces of silver from each. ¹²But as for my own vineyard, you, O Solomon, shall have my 1,000 pieces of silver. And I will give 200 pieces to those who care for it. ¹³O my lover, how good that your friends listen to your voice. Let me hear it too! ¹⁴Come quickly, my lover. Be like a gazelle or young deer on the mountains of spices."

ISAIAH

Hundreds of years before Jesus came, Isaiah talked about him. He told how Jesus would be crucified. How could Isaiah do this? God knew all of these things, and he told Isaiah. In Isaiah's book you'll see other wonderful things. You'll watch angel-like creatures called seraphs. You'll see them use their six wings. You'll see the Temple shake when they sing. You'll be amazed to see a mighty army defeated. But not one weapon is used against them.

Isaiah lived in Judah, the southern kingdom of the Israelites. At that time, people did what they wanted, not what God wanted. They sinned against God. They did many wicked things. Isaiah said God would punish them. He said that one day the Babylonians would capture them. Then the Israelites would wish they had obeyed God. Isaiah also said that many years later a Savior would come. He would die to save his people from their sins. You'll be amazed to read what Isaiah said about this Savior.

God's Message to His People

1 These are the messages that came to Isaiah, the son of Amoz. They told what was going to happen to Judah and Jerusalem. They came in visions he saw during the reigns of King Uzziah, King Jotham, King Ahaz, and King Hezekiah. These kings all ruled over Judah. God showed Isaiah what was going to happen in the days ahead.

²Listen, O Heaven and earth! Listen to what the Lord is saying:

"I raised and cared for my children. I tenderly watched them grow. But they have turned against me. ³Even the donkey and the ox know their owner. They are happy with his care for them. But my people Israel don't know me! No matter what I do for them, they still don't care."

⁴Oh, what a sinful nation they are! They walk bent-backed under their load of guilt. Their fathers before them were evil too. Born to be bad, they have turned their backs upon the Lord. They have hated the Holy One of Israel. They have cut themselves off from his help.

⁵⁻⁶Oh, my people, haven't you had enough of punishment? Why will you force me to whip you again and again? Must you forever turn against me? From head to foot you are sick and weak and faint. You are covered with bruises and

welts and infected wounds. They are not cleaned and tied up in bandages. ⁷Your country lies in ruins. Your cities are burned. While you watch, strangers from other lands are coming here. They are destroying all they see. ⁸You stand there helpless and alone. You look like a watchman's shack that stands alone in the field when the harvest is over.

⁹The Lord Almighty might not have saved the few of us who are left. If he hadn't, we would have all been wiped out. We would have been like Sodom and Gomorrah. ¹⁰That is a good comparison! Listen, you leaders of Israel! Listen, you men of Sodom and Gomorrah. Hear me, as I call you now! Listen to the Lord. Hear what he is telling you! ¹¹"I am sick of your sacrifices. Don't bring me any more of them. I don't want your fat rams. I don't want to see the blood from your offerings. ¹²⁻¹³Who wants your sacrifices when you aren't sorry for your sins? The incense you bring me stinks in my nose. Your holy feasts of the new moon and the Sabbath are all false! All your special days for fasting, even your most holy meetings, are lies! I want nothing more to do with them. ¹⁴I hate them all. I can't stand the sight of them. ¹⁵From now on, when you pray with your hands stretched out to Heaven, I won't look or listen. Even though you make many prayers, I will not hear. For your hands are the hands of murderers. They are covered with the blood of your victims.

¹⁶"Oh, wash yourselves! Be clean! Let me no longer see you doing all these wicked things. Quit your evil ways. ¹⁷Learn to do good and be fair. Learn to help the poor, the fatherless, and widows.

¹⁸"Come, let's talk this over!" says the Lord. "No matter how deep the stain of your sins, I can take it out. I can make you as clean as freshly fallen snow. Even if you are stained as red as crimson, I can make you white as wool! ¹⁹All you have to do is let me help you! All you have to do is obey! If you do, then I will make you rich! ²⁰But you might choose to keep on turning your backs on me. You might not listen to me at all. If you do this, you

will be killed by your enemies! I, the Lord, have spoken."

²¹Jerusalem was once a faithful wife! But now she is a prostitute! She runs after other gods! Once she was "The City of Fair Play." But now she is a gang of murderers. ²²Once she was like pure silver. Now she is mixed with other worthless metals! Once she was so pure. But now she is like wine with water in it! ²³Your leaders are wicked. They spend much of their time with thieves. All of them take bribes and won't help the widows and orphans. ²⁴Because of this, the Lord, the Mighty One of Israel, speaks up! He says: "I will pour out my anger on you. You are now my enemies! ²⁵I myself will melt you in a pot. I will then skim off the dirt and sludge that floats to the top.

²⁶"And after that I will give you good judges. I will give you wise counselors like those you used to have. Then your city shall again be called 'The City of Justice.' Again it will be known as 'The Faithful Town.'"

²⁷Those who come back to the Lord he will buy back. Those who are fair and good shall be saved. ²⁸But all sinners shall die, for they will not come to me. ²⁹Shame will cover all of you. You will blush to think of all those times you bowed to idols. ³⁰You will die like a withered tree or a garden without water. ³¹The strongest among you will disappear like burning straw. Your evil deeds are the spark that sets the straw on fire. And no one will be able to put the fire out.

Walk in God's Light

2 This is another message to Isaiah from the Lord. It is a message about Judah and Jerusalem.

²In the last days Jerusalem and the Temple will be the most important place in the world. People from many lands will go there to worship the Lord.

³"Come!" all the people will say. "Let us go up the mountain of the Lord. Let us go to the Temple of the God of Israel. There he will teach us his laws, and we will obey them." For in those days the world will be ruled from Jerusalem. ⁴The

Lord will settle all fights between nations. All the nations will make their weapons of war into tools to be used for peace. Then at last all wars will stop. And all training for war will end. ⁵O Israel, come. Let us walk in the light of the Lord! Let us obey all his laws!

⁶The Lord has turned away from you because you welcome foreigners from the East. They practice magic and talk with evil spirits. They do just as the Philistines do.

⁷Israel has great treasures of silver and gold. They have many horses and chariots. ⁸But they also have many idols! The land is full of them! They are made by people, but you bow down to them! ⁹Small and great, all bow before them. God will not forgive you for this sin.

¹⁰Crawl into the caves in the rocks. Hide there in terror from his great power. ¹¹For the day is coming when your proud looks will be brought low. The Lord alone will be praised and lifted up. ¹²On that day the Lord Almighty will move against the proud. He will bring them down to the dust. ¹³All the tall cedars of Lebanon and all the mighty oaks of Bashan shall bend low. ¹⁴All the high mountains and hills will be destroyed. ¹⁵And he will knock down every high tower and wall. ¹⁶All the proud ocean ships and small harbor boats shall be crushed before the Lord that day. ¹⁷All the glory of mankind will bow low. The pride of men will lie in the dust. And the Lord alone will be praised and lifted up. ¹⁸And all idols will be sent away and totally destroyed.

¹⁹The Lord will stand up from his throne to shake up the earth. His enemies will crawl with fear into the holes in the rocks. They will hide in the caves because of the glory of his power and greatness. ²⁰Then at last they will leave their gold and silver idols to the moles and bats. ²¹They will crawl into the caverns. They will hide among the jagged rocks at the tops of the cliffs. They will try to get away from the terror of the Lord. They will try to hide from his glory when he rises to terrify the earth. ²²Oh, how small man is! He is as weak as his breath! Don't ever put your trust in him!

A Well-Earned Punishment

3 The Lord will cut off the food and water supplies from Jerusalem and Judah. ²And he will kill her leaders. He will destroy her armies, judges, prophets, and elders. ³He will kill the leaders of her army. He will also kill her businessmen, lawyers, magicians, and politicians. ⁴Israel's kings will be like babies. They will rule like children. ⁵Everyone will be against someone else. Neighbors will fight against neighbors. Young people will not obey those who are over them. Criminals will laugh at good men.

⁶In those days a man will turn to his brother. He might say, "You have some extra clothing. You be our king and take care of this mess!"

⁷"No!" he will reply. "I cannot be of any help! I have no extra food or clothes. Don't ask me to try and help!"

⁸Israel's government will be in total ruin. This is because the Jews have spoken out against their Lord. They will not turn and worship him. They offend his glory. ⁹The very look on their faces gives them away. It shows that they are guilty. And they are just like the people of Sodom. They are proud of their great sin! They aren't even ashamed of it. What a terrible thing! They have brought great trouble on themselves.

¹⁰But all is well for the godly man. Tell him, "What a reward you are going to get!" ¹¹But say to the wicked, "Your death is sure. You too shall get what you deserve. You have earned your punishment, and it is on the way."

¹²O my people! Can't you see what fools your rulers are? They are so weak! They are so foolish! Are they true leaders? No, they are just misleading you! They are leading you down the path to certain doom.

¹³The Lord stands up to judge the people! He takes his place in court. He is proving his case against his people! ¹⁴The elders and the princes will be first to feel his anger. This is because they have taken advantage of the poor. They have filled their barns with stolen grain. And they have taken it from helpless poor people!

¹⁵"How dare you grind my people in

the dust like that?" the Lord Almighty will ask.

[16]Next he will judge the proud women of Jerusalem. They walk around with their proud noses in the air. They wear bracelets on their ankles that tinkle as they walk. They look around and flirt with their eyes. They try to catch the glances of men. [17]The Lord will send a plague of scabs to cover their heads! He will make all their hair fall out. [18]They won't walk around proudly any more. For the Lord will strip away their beauty and their jewelry. [19]He will take away their necklaces and bracelets. He will take off their shiny veils. [20]Gone shall be their scarves and ankle chains. They will have no headbands, earrings, and perfumes. [21]Their rings, jewels, [22]party clothes, nightgowns, capes, fancy combs, and purses will all be gone. [23]Their mirrors, pretty dresses, and veils will all be taken away. [24]Instead of smelling of sweet perfume, they'll stink. For belts they'll wear ropes. Their well-set hair will all fall out. They'll wear sacks instead of robes.

All their beauty will be gone. All that will be left to them is shame. [25-26]Their husbands will die in battle. The women will sit on the ground crying.

God's Holy People

4 At that time there will be very few men left alive. Seven women will fight over each man! They will say, "Let us all marry you! We will buy our own food and clothing. Just let us be called by your name. That way we won't be laughed at for not getting married."

[2]At that time the Lord's Branch will be beautiful and great. And the land will produce for them its richest crops and sweetest fruit. [3]Those who are left in Jerusalem will be God's holy people. They will be those recorded as being still alive in Jerusalem. [4]The sin of the women of Jerusalem will be washed away. Jerusalem will be made clean by judgment and fire. [5]Then the Lord will provide shade for all Jerusalem. He will shade every home and all its public grounds. He will provide a canopy of smoke and cloud throughout the day.

He will give clouds of fire at night. They will cover the Glorious Land. [6]They will protect it from daytime heat. They will shelter it from rains and storms.

Sour Grapes in God's Garden

5 Now I will sing a song about his vineyard to the one I love. My loved one has a vineyard on a very rich hill. [2]He plowed it and took out all the rocks. And he planted his vineyard with the best vines. He built a watchtower and cut a winepress in the rocks. Then he waited for the harvest. But the grapes that grew were wild and sour. They were not at all the sweet ones he had expected.

[3]Now, men of Jerusalem and Judah, you have heard the case! You be the judges! [4]What more could I have done? Why did my vineyard give me wild grapes instead of sweet? [5]I will tear down the fences. I will let my vineyard go to pasture. I will let it be trampled by cattle and sheep. [6]I won't prune it or hoe it. I'll let it be overgrown with weeds and thorns. I will command the clouds not to rain on it any more.

[7]I have given you the story of God's people. They are the vineyard that I spoke about. Israel and Judah are his pleasant and rich hill! He expected them to give a crop of justice. But he found bloodshed instead. He expected goodness. But instead, the cries of deep oppression met his ears. [8]You buy up land so others have no place to live. Your homes are built on great estates so you can be alone in the midst of the earth! [9]But the Lord Almighty has promised your awful fate. I heard him say this with my own ears! "Many a beautiful home will lie empty," he said. "Their owners will either be killed or gone. [10]An acre of vineyard will not produce a gallon of juice! Ten bushels of seed will yield a one-bushel crop!"

[11]It is a bad thing that you get up early in the morning to look for strong drink. And then you drink late into the night! I am warning you men who get drunk all the time! [12]You play lovely music at your grand parties. The orchestras are superb! But for the Lord you have no thought or care. [13]Therefore I will send

you into exile far away. This is because you neither know nor care that I have done so much for you. Your great and honored men will starve. And the common people will die of thirst.

¹⁴Hell is licking its chops waiting for Jerusalem. Her great and small shall be swallowed up. ¹⁵At that time the proud shall be brought down to the dust. And they shall be made humble. ¹⁶But the Lord Almighty is lifted up above all. For he alone is holy, just, and good. ¹⁷In those days flocks will feed among the ruins. Lambs and calves and baby goats will pasture there!

¹⁸Woe to those who drag their sins behind them like a bull on a rope. ¹⁹They even laugh at the Holy One of Israel. They even dare the Lord to punish them! "Hurry up and punish us, O Lord," they say. "We want to see what you can do!" ²⁰They say that what is right is wrong. And they claim that what is wrong is right. They say that black is white and white is black. They claim that bitter is sweet and sweet is bitter.

²¹I am warning those who think they are so wise and clever! ²²I am warning those who are "heroes" when it comes to drinking. They brag about the liquor they can hold! ²³They take bribes to turn justice upside down. They let the wicked go free and put innocent men in jail. ²⁴Therefore God will deal with them and burn them. They will disappear like straw set on fire. Their roots will rot and their flowers wither. For they have thrown away the laws of God! They have hated the Word of the Holy One of Israel! ²⁵That is why the anger of the Lord is hot against his people. That is why he has reached out his hand to smash them. The hills will shake. And the rotting bodies of his people will be thrown as garbage in the streets. But even so, his anger is not ended. His hand is heavy on them still.

²⁶He will send a signal to the nations far away. He will call to those at the ends of the earth. And they will come racing toward Jerusalem. ²⁷They will never get tired or stumble. They will never stop!

Their belts are tight, their bootstraps strong. They run without stopping for rest or for sleep. ²⁸Their arrows are sharp. Their bows are bent. Sparks fly from their horses' hooves. And the wheels of their chariots spin like the wind. ²⁹They roar like lions and pounce on their prey.

Jewelry
ISAIAH 3:16-24
What jewelry have you seen in the store? Most stores have rings, bracelets, necklaces, and pins. Some are made of gold, silver, or other metals. Many pieces of jewelry are set with precious stones. Perhaps your mother has a diamond ring. She may even have a ruby or emerald one. In Bible times people wore jewelry, too. They had rings, bracelets, necklaces, and pins, just as we do. Many women wore ankle bracelets. But some even wore nose rings! They were very much in style. Some people used jewelry to show off. They wanted to say, "Look at me! I'm rich!" God didn't like that. Read Isaiah 3:16-24 and you'll see how much God hated the people who showed off with their jewelry and fine clothes. When the jewelry and fine things were gone, these people wouldn't look so good! God doesn't want us to use the pretty things he has given us to show off. When we try to look nice to help others see God in us, God is pleased. Try to spend as much time making your heart and thoughts attractive as you spend making your body attractive.

They take hold of my people and carry them off as captives. There is no one to save them. ³⁰They growl over their victims like the roaring of the sea. Over all Israel lies a cloud of darkness and sadness. And the heavens are black.

God Calls Isaiah

Pretend that one morning, as you get to church, you suddenly see God sitting on a beautiful throne. Where the choir usually sits, there are six big creatures instead. They look like angels. Then they cover their faces with their wings and begin to sing a very beautiful song that shakes your church. Then your whole church is filled with smoke. That's what Isaiah saw when he went to the Temple one day. What do you think he did then?

6 The year King Uzziah died I saw the Lord! He was sitting on a lofty throne. And the Temple was filled with his glory. ²Flying about him were mighty, six-winged angels of fire. Two of their wings covered their faces. With two others, they covered their feet. And with the other two they flew. ³In a great chorus they sang, "Holy, holy, holy is the Lord of Heaven's armies. The whole earth is filled with his glory." ⁴Such singing it was! It shook the Temple to the ground! And suddenly the whole sanctuary was filled with smoke.

God is greater than anyone or anything

Holy, holy, holy is the Lord of Heaven's armies. The whole earth is filled with his glory.

Isaiah 6:3

⁵Then I said, "I will surely die! For I am a sinner, and my mouth isn't pure. And I live among a people who are also sinful. But I have looked upon the King, the Lord of Heaven's armies!"

⁶Then one of the mighty angels flew over to the altar. And with a pair of tongs, he picked out a burning coal. ⁷He touched my lips with it. Then he said, "Now you are not guilty. Your mouth is pure because this coal has touched your lips. Your sins are all forgiven."

⁸Then I heard the Lord speaking. "Whom shall I send as a messenger to my people?" he asked. "Who will go and speak for me?"

And I said, "Lord, I'll go! Send me."

⁹And he said, "Yes, go. But tell my people this: 'You have heard my words many times. But still you don't understand them! You have watched me do my miracles. But still you don't know what they mean!' ¹⁰Make their minds dull! Close their ears! Shut their eyes! I don't want them to see or to hear or to understand. I don't want them to turn to me for healing."

¹¹Then I said, "Lord, how long will it be before they are ready to listen?"

And he replied, "Not until their cities are destroyed! There won't be a person left. The whole country will be a wasteland. ¹²And they will all be taken away as slaves to other countries far away. All the land of Israel will be empty! ¹³Yet a tenth of them, just a few, will survive. Israel will be attacked again and again and destroyed. But Israel will be like a tree cut down, whose stump still lives to grow again."

● *Remember:* What happened to Isaiah when King Uzziah died? What did he see? (6:1-4) Why was Isaiah afraid?

(6:5) How were Isaiah's sins forgiven? What happened? (6:6-7) How did the Lord call Isaiah? What did the Lord want him to do? (6:8-13) Do you think Isaiah was glad to do special work for God? Why?

- *Discover:* God has special work for us to do. But first he wants to forgive our sins.

- *Apply:* Would you like to do something special for God? First, ask him to forgive you for bad things you have done. Then you will be clean inside and ready to respond if God chooses you.

- *What's next?* Before a man was born, God chose him for very special work. What was that work? Read Jeremiah 1 ▣

Immanuel—God Is with Us

7 Now Ahaz was the son of Jotham. And Jotham was the son of Uzziah. During the reign of Ahaz, Jerusalem was attacked by King Rezin of Syria and King Pekah of Israel. King Pekah was the son of Remaliah. But Jerusalem was not taken. The city stood up to the attack. ²The news had come to the royal court, "Syria has joined with Israel to fight against us!" When they heard this, the hearts of the king and his people shook with fear. They shook like the trees of a forest shake in a storm.

³Then the Lord said to Isaiah, "Go out and talk with King Ahaz. Take Shear-jashub, your son, with you. You will find Ahaz at the end of the aqueduct that leads to the upper pool. He will be near the road that leads down to the bleaching field. ⁴Tell him to stop worrying. Tell him he doesn't need to be afraid. The anger of kings Rezin and Pekah is no reason to fear. ⁵Yes, the kings of Syria and Israel are coming against you.

⁶"They say, 'We will attack Judah. We will throw her people into panic. Then we'll fight our way into Jerusalem. We will choose the son of Tabeel as their king.'

⁷"But the Lord God says, 'This plan will not succeed. ⁸For Damascus will be the capital of Syria alone. King Rezin's kingdom will not get any bigger. And within 65 years Ephraim, too, will be crushed and broken. ⁹Samaria is the cap-

ital of Ephraim alone. And King Pekah's power will not increase. You don't believe me? If you want me to keep you safe, you must believe what I say.'"

¹⁰Not long after this, the Lord sent another message to King Ahaz.

¹¹"Ask me for a sign, Ahaz," he said. "I will prove that I will crush your enemies as I have said. Ask anything you like, in Heaven or on earth."

¹²But the king would not do it. "No," he said. "I'll not bother the Lord with anything like that."

¹³Then Isaiah said, "Ahaz, son of David, aren't you content to try my patience? You are trying the Lord's patience as well! ¹⁴All right then, the Lord himself will choose the sign. A child shall be born to a virgin! And she shall call him Immanuel. This name means, 'God is with us.' ¹⁵⁻¹⁶This son will soon be eating curds. And by the time he knows right from wrong, the two kings you fear so much will both be dead. And the lands of Israel and Syria will both be empty.

¹⁷"But later on, the Lord will bring a terrible curse on you. And that curse will also fall on your nation and your family. There will be a great terror in the land! Such terror has not been known since Solomon's kingdom was divided into Israel and Judah. At that time, the mighty king of Assyria will come with his great army!"

¹⁸At that time the Lord will whistle for the army of Upper Egypt. He will call Assyria too. They will swarm down upon you like flies and destroy you. They will act like bees, stinging to kill. ¹⁹They will come in great numbers. They will spread across the whole land. Even the desolate valleys, caves, and thorny parts will be filled with them! They will spread out across your rich farm land. ²⁰In that day the Lord will take this "razor." He will use these Assyrians to shave off all you have. You will lose your land, your crops, and your people.

²¹⁻²²When they finally stop, the whole nation will be a pasture. Whole flocks and herds will be destroyed. And a farmer will be lucky to have a cow and two sheep left. But his animals will yield plenty of milk. And everyone left in the

LIVING IN A BIBLE-TIME HOUSE

If you lived in a Bible-time house, your life would be much different from what it is today. Most houses had only two or three rooms. The walls were made of rocks. Even the floor was dirt or rocks. Rooftops were used like a deck or patio today. On a hot evening, people sat on the flat roof to do their chores. Windows were just holes in the walls with wooden poles across them to keep people and animals out. There was very little furniture and no carpeting. A mat or two might be on the floor. People had no electricity in those days. Think of all the things you have that use electricity. There was no running water. So there were no tubs or showers and no toilets. Women carried water into the house in clay jars. Do you see the woman grinding flour? She will bake bread in the oven near her. She will use sticks to heat the oven. Think about all the ways your day would be different in a Bible-time house.

land will live on milk and wild honey. ²³At that time the vineyards will become full of thorns. ²⁴All the land will be one great briar patch. It will be a hunting ground overrun by wildlife. ²⁵No one will go to the rich hillsides where the gardens once grew. For thorns will cover them. Cattle, sheep, and goats will graze there.

Isaiah Predicts Assyria Will Invade

8 Again the Lord sent me a message: "Take a large scroll and make a sign with it. Write on it the name of the son I am going to give you. Use capital letters! His name will be Maher-shalal-hash-baz. This name means 'Your enemies will soon be destroyed.'" ²I asked Uriah the priest and Zechariah the son of Jeberechiah to watch me write it. Both were known as honest men. They could tell everyone that I had written it before the child was even on the way. ³Then I slept with my wife, and she gave me a son. And the Lord said, "Call him Maher-shalal-hash-baz. ⁴His name carries a prophetic message. Soon, the king of Assyria will attack Damascus and Samaria. He will take these cities and carry away their riches. This will happen before this child is even old enough to say 'Daddy' or 'Mommy.'"

⁵Then the Lord spoke to me again. He said:

⁶"The people of Jerusalem are planning to refuse my gentle care. They are afraid of King Rezin and King Pekah. ⁷⁻⁸Therefore I will overwhelm my people with Euphrates' mighty flood. The king of Assyria and all his mighty armies will attack them. The river will overflow all its channels. It will sweep into your land of Judah flooding it from end to end. O Immanuel!"

⁹⁻¹⁰Do your worst, O Syria and Israel, our enemies. But you will not succeed. You will be crushed! Listen to me, all you enemies of ours. Get ready for war against us and die! Yes! Die! Call your councils of war, and die! Make your plans of attack, and die! For God is with us.

¹¹The Lord has said in strongest terms: "Don't go along with the plans of Judah.

Don't look to Assyria for help. ¹²Don't let people call you a traitor for staying true to God. Don't you panic as so many of your neighbors are doing. Don't worry about Syria and Israel attacking you. ¹³Don't fear anything except the Lord of the armies of Heaven! If you fear him, you need fear nothing else. ¹⁴⁻¹⁵He will be your safety. But Israel and Judah have refused his care. They have fallen against the Rock of their salvation. They lie crushed under it. God's presence among them has been a danger to them! ¹⁶Write down all these things I am going to do," says the Lord. "Seal them up for the future. Give them to some godly man to pass on to godly men in the future."

¹⁷I will wait for the Lord to help us, though he is hiding now. My only hope is in him. ¹⁸I and the children God has given me have special names. They tell the Lord's plans for his people. Isaiah means "The Lord will save his people." Shear-jashub means "A remnant shall return." And Maher-shalal-hash-baz means "Your enemies will soon be destroyed." ¹⁹So why are you trying to find out the future by talking to witches and mediums? Don't listen to their whisperings. Can the living find out the future from the dead? Why not ask your God?

²⁰"Check these witches' words against the Word of God!" he says. "Their messages may well be different than mine. If so, it is because I have not sent them. For they have no light or truth in them. ²¹My people will be led away captive. They will stumble along, tired and hungry. They will shake their fists at Heaven. They will curse their King and their God. ²²Wherever they look there will be trouble, pain, and dark despair. And they will be thrust out into the darkness."

The Coming Messiah

9 But, that time of trouble and despair shall not go on forever. Soon the land of Zebulun and Naphtali will be under God's judgment. But in the future these very lands will be filled with glory. This is Galilee of the Gentiles, where the road to the sea runs. ²The people who walk in

darkness shall see a great Light. This Light will shine on all those who live in the land of the shadow of death. ³For Israel will be great once again, filled with joy. They will be happy like harvesters when the harvesttime has come. They will be like men dividing up the plunder they have won. ⁴For God will break the chains that tie up his people. He will throw away the whip that beats them. It will happen as it did when he destroyed the Midianites with Gideon's little band. ⁵In that day of peace there won't be any need for armor or weapons. There won't be any uniforms of war stained with blood. All such things will be burned.

⁶For unto us a child is born. Unto us a son is given. And the government shall be upon his shoulders. He will be called "Wonderful Counselor," "The Mighty God," "The Everlasting Father," "The Prince of Peace." ⁷His peaceful government will never end. He will rule with perfect fairness from the throne of his father David. He will bring true justice and peace to all the nations of the world. This will happen because the Lord has decided to do it!

⁸⁻¹⁰The Lord has spoken out against proud Israel. For they claim that they will rebuild their land better than before. They say this even though their land lies in ruins now! They see that their sycamore trees are cut down. But they plan to plant cedars in their place! ¹¹⁻¹²The Lord gives this answer to Israel's bragging: He will bring their enemies against them. The Syrians will attack from the east. And the Philistines will come from the west. With sharp teeth they will devour Israel. And even then the Lord's anger against you will not be satisfied. His fist will still be lifted to smash you. ¹³For after all this punishment you will not repent and turn to the Lord. ¹⁴⁻¹⁵Therefore the Lord will destroy the leaders of Israel. He will get rid of Israel's lying prophets. And he will do this in one day! ¹⁶For the leaders of his people have led them down the paths of ruin.

¹⁷That is why the Lord has no joy in their young men. He will show no mercy to even the widows and orphans. For they are all wicked liars with dirty mouths. That is why his anger is not yet satisfied. And that is why his fist is still lifted to smash them all. ¹⁸He will burn up all this wickedness, these thorns and briars. And the flames will burn the forests too. The fire will send a great cloud of smoke up from their burning. ¹⁹⁻²⁰The land is blackened by that fire. It is destroyed by the anger of the Lord of Heaven's armies. The people are fuel for the fire. Each fights against his brother to steal his food. But none of them will ever have enough. Finally they will even eat their own children! ²¹Manasseh against Ephraim and Ephraim against Manasseh. And both of them will fight against Judah. Yet even after all of this, God's anger is not yet satisfied. His hand is still lifted to crush them.

God Will Protect His People

10 "I give this warning to you unjust judges," says the Lord. "I am warning those who make unfair laws. ²There is no justice for the poor, the widows, and orphans. Yes, it is true! They even rob the widows and fatherless children.

³"Oh, what will you do when I visit you? What will you do when I send destruction on you from a far-off land? To whom will you turn then for your help? Where will your treasures be safe? ⁴I will not help you. You will stumble along as prisoners. Or you will lie among those who are dead. And even then my anger will not be satisfied. My fist will still be lifted to hit you. ⁵⁻⁶Assyria is the whip of my anger. Her strength is my weapon against this godless nation. She will make them her slaves. She will plunder them and trample them like dirt under her feet. ⁷But the king of Assyria will not know that it is I who sent him. He will think he is attacking my people as part of his plan to conquer the world. ⁸He will declare that every one of his princes will soon be a king, ruling a conquered land.

⁹"'We will destroy Calno just as we did Carchemish,' he will say. 'Hamath will go down before us as Arpad did. And we will destroy Samaria just as we did Damascus. ¹⁰Yes, we have finished off

many a kingdom. And their idols were far greater than those in Jerusalem and Samaria. [11]After we have defeated Samaria and her idols, we will destroy Jerusalem with hers.'"

[12]The Lord will use the king of Assyria to do what he wants. But then he will turn on the Assyrians and punish them too. For they are very proud.

[13]They boast, "We have won these wars by our own power and wisdom. We are great and wise. By our own strength we broke down the walls. We destroyed the people and carried off their treasures because we are strong. [14]In our greatness we have robbed their nests of riches. We have taken up kingdoms as a farmer gathers eggs. No one can move a finger or open his mouth to stop us!"

[15]But the Lord says, "Shall the axe brag of more power than the man who uses it? Is the saw greater than the man who saws? Can a rod strike unless a hand is moving it? Can a cane walk by itself?"

[16]You have done a great deal of evil bragging, O king of Assyria! So the Lord of Hosts will send a plague among your proud troops. He will strike them down! [17]God is the Light and Holy One of Israel. He will be the fire and flame that will destroy them. In a single night he will burn those thorns and briars. He will destroy the Assyrians who destroyed the land of Israel. [18]Assyria's great army is like a glorious forest. But it will all be destroyed. The Lord will destroy them, soul and body. They will be like a sick man who wastes away. [19]Only a few from all that mighty army will be left. There will be so few that a child could count them!

[20]Then at last those left in Israel and in Judah will trust the Lord. They will look to the Holy One of Israel. They won't be afraid of the Assyrians. [21]A few of them will come back to the mighty God. [22]Israel is now as many as the sands along the shore. But only a few of them will be left to return at that time. God has rightly decided to destroy his people. [23]Yes, the Lord God has already decided to destroy them.

[24]Therefore the Lord God says, "O my people in Jerusalem! Don't be afraid of the Assyrians when they oppress you. For they will do just as the Egyptians did long ago. [25]It will not last very long. In a little while my anger against you will end. And then it will rise against them to destroy them."

[26]The Lord Almighty will send his angel. He will kill them in a mighty slaughter. It will be like the time when Gideon triumphed over Midian at the rock of Oreb. Or it will be like the time God drowned the Egyptian armies in the sea. [27]On that day God will end the slavery of his people. He will break the chains off their necks. He will free them as he promised.

[28-29]Look, the mighty armies of Assyria are coming! Now they are at Aiath, now at Migron. They are storing some of their weapons at Michmash. And they are crossing over the pass. They are staying overnight at Geba. Fear strikes the city of Ramah. All the people of Gibeah are running for their lives. Gibeah is the city of Saul. [30]Well may you scream in terror, O people of Gallim. Shout out a warning to Laish. For the mighty army comes. O poor Anathoth, what a fate is yours! [31]There go the people of Madmenah, all running. And the people of Gebim are getting ready to run. [32]But the enemy stops at Nob for the rest of that day. He shakes his fist at Jerusalem on Mount Zion.

[33]Then, look, look! The Lord is chopping down the mighty tree! He is destroying all of that great army. Great and small alike, both officers and men are falling! [34]He, the Mighty One, will cut down the enemy. He will do it like a woodsman cuts down the forest trees in Lebanon.

God Promises a Perfect Leader

11 The royal line of David will be cut off, chopped down like a tree. But from the stump will grow a Shoot. Yes, a new Branch will grow from the old root. [2]And the Spirit of the Lord shall rest upon him. This is the Spirit of wisdom, insight, counsel, and might. It is the Spirit of knowledge and of the fear of the Lord. [3]His joy will be in obeying the Lord. He will not judge by the way

things look. He won't make judgments just by what people say. ⁴But he will defend the poor. He will rule against the wicked who oppress them. ⁵For he will be clothed with fairness and with truth.

⁶In that day the wolf and the lamb will lie down together. And the leopard and goats will be at peace. Calves and fat cattle will be safe among lions. And a little child shall lead them all. ⁷The cows will graze among bears. Cubs and calves will lie down side by side. And lions will eat grass like the cows. ⁸Babies will crawl safely among deadly snakes. And a little child who puts his hand into a nest of adders will not be hurt. ⁹Nothing will hurt or destroy in all my holy mountain. And as the waters fill the sea, the earth will be full of the knowledge of the Lord.

¹⁰It was the Lord who created the royal line of David. And in that day, he will be a flag of salvation to all the world. The nations will run to him. For the land where he lives will be a wonderful place. ¹¹At that time the Lord will bring back a few of his people. This will be the second time he has done this. He will bring them back to the land of Israel. They will come from Assyria, Upper and Lower Egypt, Ethiopia, Elam, Babylonia, and Hamath. And they will come from all the coastal lands far away. ¹²He will raise a flag among the nations for them to run to. He will gather the scattered Israelites from the ends of the earth. ¹³Then at last Israel and Judah will stop being jealous of each other. They will not fight each other any more. ¹⁴Together they will fight against the nations living in their land. They will join hands to destroy those on the east and on the west. And they will control the nations of Edom and Moab and Ammon.

¹⁵The Lord will dry a path through the Red Sea. And he will wave his hand over the Euphrates. He will send a mighty wind to divide it into seven streams. He will do this so it can be easily crossed. ¹⁶He will make a highway from Assyria

Banners
ISAIAH 11:10-12

Have you seen pictures on football helmets or basketball uniforms? Teams like to use pictures of lions, bears, tigers, and other fierce things. These pictures tell people which team the players are on. They also say to the team and fans, "We're tough!" or "Let's get excited about our team!" Bible-time tribes and armies put pictures on flags attached to poles. These were called banners or standards. People who belonged to an army, a tribe, or clan within a tribe would gather around their banner. They would also carry their banner at the head of the group to get their people excited about their group or to keep them together. When Moses led the Israelites across the wilderness, each tribe had a banner.

Isaiah said that someday Jesus would be a banner of salvation. Someday people from all nations will rally around him. Let's get excited about living on Jesus' team!

for the remnant there. He will do just as he did long ago when Israel came back from Egypt.

Singing God's Praise

12 On that day you will say, "Praise the Lord! He was angry with me. But now he comforts me. ²See, God has come to save me! I will trust and not be afraid. For the Lord is my strength and song. He is my salvation. ³Oh, the joy of drinking deeply from the Fountain of Salvation!"

⁴In that wonderful day you will say, "Thank the Lord! Praise his name! Tell the world about his great love. How great he is!" ⁵Sing to the Lord, for he has done great things. Make his praise be known around the world. ⁶Let all the people of Jerusalem shout his praise with joy. For great and mighty is the Holy One of Israel, who lives among you.

Babylon Will Be Destroyed

13 This is the vision God showed Isaiah, the son of Amoz. This vision was all about Babylon's doom.

²See the flags waving as their enemy attacks. Shout to them, O Israel! Wave them on as they march against Babylon. Cheer for them as they go to destroy the palaces of the rich and strong. ³I, the Lord, have set apart these armies to do this. I have called those who take joy in their strength to do this work. I do this to satisfy my anger. ⁴Hear the loud noise on the mountains! Listen as the armies march! It is the tumult and the shout of many nations. The Lord Almighty has brought them here. ⁵He has brought them from countries far away. They are his weapons against you, O Babylon. They carry his anger with them. And they will destroy your whole land.

⁶Scream in terror, for the Lord's time has come. This is the time for the Almighty to crush you. ⁷Your arms lie frozen with fear. The strongest hearts melt ⁸and are afraid. Fear grips you with terrible pangs, like those of a woman in labor. You look at each other, helpless. The flames of the burning city reflect off your pale faces. ⁹For see, the day of the Lord is coming. This is the terrible day

of his fierce anger. The land shall be destroyed and all the sinners with it. ¹⁰The heavens will be black above them. No light will shine from stars or sun or moon.

¹¹And I will punish the world for its evil. I will judge the wicked for their sin. I will crush the pride of the proud man. I will put down the selfishness of the rich. ¹²Few will live when I have finished up my work.

Men will be as rare as gold. They will be of greater value than the gold of Ophir. ¹³For I will shake the heavens in my fierce anger. And the earth will move from its place in the skies.

¹⁴The armies of Babylon will run until tired. They will run back to their own land like deer chased by dogs. They will wander like sheep without their shepherd. ¹⁵Those who don't run will be killed. ¹⁶Their little children will be dashed to death against the stones. This will happen right in front of their eyes! Their homes will be sacked. And their wives will be raped by the attacking armies. ¹⁷For I will stir up the Medes against Babylon. No amount of silver or gold will buy them off. ¹⁸The attacking armies will have no mercy on the young people of Babylon. They will kill all the babies and children.

¹⁹And so Babylon, the greatest of kingdoms, will be totally destroyed. It will be like Sodom and Gomorrah were when God sent fire from Heaven. ²⁰Babylon will never rise again. Generation after generation will come and go. But the land will never again be lived in. The nomads will not even camp there. The shepherds won't let their sheep stay overnight. ²¹The wild animals of the desert will make it their home. The houses will be haunted by howling creatures. Ostriches will live there, and demons will come there to dance. ²²Hyenas and jackals will live in the palaces. Babylon's days are few in number. Her time of doom will soon be here.

God Promises to Love His People

14 But the Lord will have mercy on the people of Israel. They are still his special ones. He will bring them back to

settle once again in the land of Israel. And many nations will come and join them there. And they will be their loyal friends. 2The nations of the world will help them to come back. And those coming to live in their land will serve them. Those who made Israel their slaves will be the slaves of Israel. Israel shall rule over all her enemies!

3In that wonderful day the Lord will give his people rest from sorrow and fear. They will be free from slavery and chains. 4And you will laugh at the king of Babylon and say, "You bully, you! At last you have what was coming to you! 5For the Lord has crushed your wicked power. He has broken your evil rule." 6You hit my people with blows that never stopped. You held many nations in your angry grip. You didn't show mercy to those under your rule. 7But at last the whole earth is at rest and quiet! All the world begins to sing! 8Even the trees of the woods sing out in joyous song. Even the fir trees and cedars of Lebanon sing out: "Your power is broken. No one will bother us now. At last we have peace!"

9Dead people crowd to meet you as you enter their world. World leaders and earth's greatest kings, long dead, are there to see you. 10With one voice they all cry out, "Now you are as weak as we are!" 11Your strength and power are gone. They are buried with you. All the pleasant music in your palace has stopped playing. Now maggots are your sheet! Worms are your blanket!

12How you are fallen from Heaven, O star of the morning, son of dawn! How you are cut down to the ground. This happened even though you were great against the nations of the world. 13For you said to yourself, "I will go up to Heaven and rule the angels. I will take the highest throne. I will rule on the Mount of Assembly far away in the north. 14I will climb to the highest heavens and be like the Most High." 15But instead, you will be brought down to the pit of hell. You will go down to its lowest depths. 16Everyone there will stare at you. They will ask, "Can this be the one who shook the earth? Can this

be the one who ruled the kingdoms of the world? 17Can this be the one who destroyed the world? Is this the one who broke down its greatest cities? Is this the one who had no mercy on his prisoners?"

18The kings of the nations lie in stately glory in their graves. 19But your body is thrown out like a broken branch. It lies in an open grave. It is covered with the dead bodies of those killed in battle. It lies as a carcass in the road. It is trampled and torn up by horses' hoofs. 20No grave stone will be made for you. For you have destroyed your nation and killed your people. Your son will not follow you as the king. 21Kill the children of this sinner. Do not let them rise and conquer the land. Do not let them rebuild the cities of the world.

22"I, myself, have risen against him," says the Lord. "I will cut off his children and grandchildren from ever sitting on his throne. 23I will make Babylon into an empty land fit only for owls. It will be full of swamps and marshes. I will sweep the land with the broom of destruction," says the Lord. 24He has taken an oath to do it! For this is his purpose and plan. 25"I have decided to break the Assyrian army when they are in Israel. I will crush them on my mountains. My people shall no longer be their slaves. 26This is my plan for the whole earth. I will do it by my mighty power that reaches all around the world. 27The Lord, the God of battle, has spoken! Who can change his plans? When his hand moves, who can stop him?"

What God Will Do to the Philistines

28This is the message that came to me the year King Ahaz died:

29Don't be too happy, Philistines! Don't rejoice that the king who struck you is dead. That rod is broken, yes. But his son will be a greater enemy to you than his father ever was! From the snake will be born an adder. He will be a fiery serpent to destroy you! 30I will shepherd the poor of my people. They shall graze in my pasture! The needy shall lie down in peace. But as for you, I will wipe you out with famine and the sword. ³¹Cry out loud, Philistine cities, for you are doomed. All your nation is doomed. For a great army is coming down from the north against you. ³²What then shall we tell the reporters? Tell them that the Lord has built Jerusalem. Tell them that the poor of his people will find a safe place inside her walls.

What God Will Do to the Moabites

15 Here is God's message to Moab: In one night your cities of Ar and Kir will be destroyed. ²Your people in Dibon will go mourning to their temples. They will cry for what happened to Nebo and Medeba. They shave their heads in sadness and cut off their beards. ³They wear sackcloth through the streets. And from every home comes the sound of crying. ⁴The cries from the cities of Heshbon and Elealeh are heard far away. Those cries are heard even in Jahaz. The bravest soldiers of Moab cry out in great fear.

⁵My heart cries for Moab! His people run to Zoar and Eglath. Crying, they climb the upward road to Luhith. And their crying will be heard all along the road to Horonaim. ⁶Even the Nimrim River is empty! The grassy banks are dried up. And the tender plants are gone. ⁷The desperate refugees take only the things they can carry. And they run across the Brook of Willows. ⁸The whole land of Moab is a land of crying from one end to the other. ⁹The stream near Dibon will run red with blood. But I am not through with Dibon yet! Lions will hunt down the ones still living. They will kill both those who escape and those who stay in the city.

16 Moab's refugees at Sela send lambs as tribute to the king of Judah. ²The women of Moab are left at the fords of the Arnon River. They are like birds without a home. ³Messengers from Moab bring the gift to Jerusalem. And they beg for advice and help. "Give us sanctuary. Protect us. Do not turn us over to our enemies. ⁴⁻⁵Let our outcasts stay among you. Hide them from our enemies! God will reward you

for your kindness to us. You should let Moab's exiles settle among you. Then when the terror is past, God will set up David's throne forever. And on that throne he will place a just and righteous King."

⁶Is this proud Moab, about which we heard so much? His pride is all gone now! ⁷So all of Moab cries out loud. Yes, Moab, you will cry for destroyed Kir-hareseth. ⁸You will weep for the empty farms of Heshbon. You will cry for the vineyards at Sibmah. The enemy warlords have cut down the best of the grapevines. Their armies spread out as far as Jazer in the deserts. They are camped even down to the sea. ⁹So I cry for Jazer and the vineyards of Sibmah. My tears shall flow for Heshbon and Elealeh. For their summer fruits and harvests have been destroyed. ¹⁰Gone now is the gladness. Gone is the joy of harvest. The happy singing in the vineyards will be heard no more. The treading out of the grapes in the wine presses has stopped forever. I have ended all their harvest joys.

¹¹I will cry, and cry some more, for Moab. And my sadness for Kir-hareseth will be very great. ¹²The people of Moab will desperately pray to their idols at the tops of the hills. But it will do no good. They will cry to their gods in their idol temples. But none will come to save them. ¹³⁻¹⁴All this concerning Moab has been said before. But now the Lord says that within three years, the glory of Moab shall be ended. This will happen without fail! Few of all its people will be left alive.

What God Will Do to the Syrians

17 This is God's message to Damascus, the capital of Syria:

"Look, Damascus is gone! It is no longer a city. It has become a heap of ruins! ²The cities of Aroer are empty. Sheep pasture there, lying quiet and unafraid. There is no one to chase them away. ³The strength of Israel and the power of Damascus will end. And the remnant of Syria shall be destroyed. For as Israel's glory left, so will theirs," says the Lord Almighty. ⁴"Yes, the glory of

Israel will be very dim when poverty stalks the land. [5]Israel will be as empty as the harvested grain fields in the Valley of Rephaim. [6]Oh, a very few of her people will be left. They will be like a few stray olives left on the trees after the harvest. There will be just two or three on the highest branches and four or five out on the tips of the limbs. That is how it will be in Damascus and Israel. They will be stripped bare of people. Only a few of the poor will still be there."

[7]Then at last they will think of God their Creator. They will have respect for the Holy One of Israel. [8]They will no longer ask their idols for help in that day. They will not bow down to what their hands have made! They will no longer have respect for the images of Ashtaroth and the sun-idols.

[9]Their largest cities will be as empty as the distant wooded hills. They will become like the empty cities of the Amorites. They were deserted when the Israelites came so long ago. [10]Why? Because you have turned from the God who can save you. He is the Rock who can hide you. So, you might plant a wonderful, rare crop of great value. [11]And it might grow so well that it blossoms on the very morning that you plant it. But you will never harvest it. Your only harvest will be grief and pain.

[12]Look, see the armies coming toward God's land. [13]They roar like breakers rolling up on a beach. But God will silence them. They will run, scattered like chaff by the wind. They will whirl like dust before a storm. [14]In the evening Israel waits in terror. But by dawn her enemies are dead. This is the just reward of those who plunder and destroy the people of God.

What God Will Do to the Ethiopians

18 Ah, land beyond the upper reaches of the Nile! There winged sailboats glide along the river! [2]Land that sends messengers in fast boats down the Nile! Let fast messengers go back to you. You are a strong and powerful nation feared far and wide. You are a conquering nation whose land the upper Nile divides. And this is the message sent to you:

[3]I will raise my battle flag upon the mountain. When I do, let all the world take notice! When I blow the trumpet, listen! [4]For the Lord has told me this: "Let your mighty army now go against the land of Israel. God will watch quietly from his Temple in Jerusalem. He will be at peace as on a pleasant summer day. He will be at rest as on a lovely autumn morning during harvest." [5]But before you have begun the attack, he will cut you off. While your plans are ripening like grapes, he will cut you off like he might prune a tree. He will snip off the shoots. [6]Your mighty army will be left dead on the field. They will be eaten by the mountain birds and wild animals. The vultures will tear bodies all summer. And the wild animals will chew on bones all winter. [7]But the time will come when gifts will be brought to the Lord of Heaven's armies. They will come from people that are tall and smooth skinned. They are a strong and mighty nation. Their people speak a foreign language. They are a terror to all both far and near. And their land is divided by the rivers. They will bring gifts to the Lord Almighty in Jerusalem. For this is the place of his name.

What God Will Do to the Egyptians

19 This is God's message for Egypt:
Look, the Lord is coming against Egypt. He is riding on a swift cloud. The idols of Egypt shake. The hearts of the Egyptians melt with fear. [2]"I will set them to fighting against each other," says the Lord Almighty. "Brother will fight against brother. Neighbor will fight against neighbor. City will fight against city. Province will fight against province. [3]Her wise counselors are all at a loss of what to do. They beg with their idols for wisdom. They call on mediums, wizards, and witches to show them what to do. [4]I will hand Egypt over to a hard master. I will put them under a cruel king."

[5]And the waters of the Nile will fail to rise and flood the fields. The ditches

will be parched and dry. 6Their channels will be fouled with rotting reeds. 7All green things along the riverbank will wither and blow away. All crops will die. Everything will die. 8The fishermen will cry, for they won't have any work. Those who fish with hooks and those who use the nets will all be unemployed. 9The weavers will have no flax or cotton, for the crops will fail. 10Great men and small, all will be crushed and broken.

11What fools the counselors of Zoan are! Their best counsel to the king of Egypt is stupid and wrong. Will they still brag of their wisdom? Will they dare tell Pharaoh about the long line of wise men they have come from? 12What has happened to your "wise counselors," O Pharaoh? Where has their wisdom gone? If they are wise, let them tell you what the Lord is going to do to Egypt. 13The "wise men" from Zoan are also fools. And those from Memphis are totally misled. They are the best you can find. But they have ruined Egypt with their foolish counsel. 14The Lord has sent a spirit of foolishness on them. He has made all their advice to be wrong. They make Egypt stagger like a sick drunkard. 15Egypt cannot be saved by anything or anybody. No one can show her the way.

16In that day the Egyptians will be as weak as women. They will huddle in fear under the uplifted fist of God. 17Just to speak the name of Israel will strike deep fear in their hearts. For the Lord Almighty has laid his plans against them.

18At that time five of the cities of Egypt will follow the Lord Almighty. And they will begin to speak the Hebrew language. One of these will be Heliopolis, "The City of the Sun." 19There will be an altar to the Lord in the heart of Egypt in those days. And a monument will be built to the Lord at its border. 20This will be for a sign of loyalty to the Lord Almighty. And they will cry to the Lord for help against those who oppress them. When they do, the Lord will send them a Savior, and he will save them. 21In that day the Lord will make himself known to the Egyptians. Yes, they will know the Lord. They will give their sacrifices and offerings to him. They will make promises to God and keep them. 22The Lord will knock Egypt down. But then he will lift her up again! For the Egyptians will turn to the Lord. And he will listen to their cries and heal them.

23In that day Egypt and Assyria will be connected by a highway. And the Egyptians and the Assyrians will move freely between their lands. And they shall worship the same God. 24And Israel will be their friend. The three will be together, and Israel will be a blessing to them. 25For the Lord will bless Egypt and Assyria because of their friendship with Israel. He will say, "Blessed be Egypt, my people. Blessed be Assyria, the land I have made. Blessed be Israel, for you are my own!"

Isaiah Goes Barefoot

20 Sargon was the king of Assyria. He sent the commander of his army against the Philistine city of Ashdod. He went there and captured it. 2The Lord told Isaiah, the son of Amoz, to take off his clothing. He was even to take off his shoes. Then he was to walk around naked and barefoot. And Isaiah did as he was told.

3Then the Lord said, "My servant Isaiah is a symbol. He has been walking naked and barefoot for the last three years. He is a symbol of the troubles I will bring upon Egypt and Ethiopia. 4For the king of Assyria will take them away as prisoners. He will make them walk naked and barefoot to the shame of Egypt. Both young and old will walk around, naked below the waist. 5-6Then how upset the Philistines will be! For they counted on 'Ethiopia's power.' And they looked to their 'powerful friend,' Egypt! They will say, 'If this can happen to Egypt, what chance do we have?'"

God Tells Isaiah His Plans for Babylon, Edom, and Arabia

21 This is God's message about Babylon:

Disaster is roaring down upon you from the desert. It is like a whirlwind sweeping from the Negeb. 2I see an awesome vision! Oh, the horror of it all!

God is telling me what he is going to do. I see you plundered and destroyed. Elamites and Medes will take part in the siege. Babylon will fall! Then the groaning of all the nations she enslaved will end. ³My stomach cramps and burns with pain. Sharp pangs of fear are on me. They are like the pains of a woman giving birth to a child. I faint when I hear what God is planning. I am afraid. I am blinded with dismay. ⁴My mind reels. My heart races. I am gripped by awful fear. Sleep at night was once so pleasant. But now that is gone. I lie awake, shaking.

⁵Look! They are getting a great banquet ready! They load the tables with food. They pull up their chairs to eat. But then, quick, quick, grab your shields! Get ready for the battle! You are being attacked!

⁶⁻⁷Meanwhile in my vision the Lord had told me, "Put a watchman on the city wall. He should shout out what he sees. When he sees riders in pairs on donkeys and camels, tell him, 'This is it!'"

⁸⁻⁹So I put the watchman on the wall. And at last he shouted, "Sir, day after day and night after night I have been here at my post. Now at last, look! Here come riders in pairs!"

Then I heard a Voice shout out, "Babylon is fallen! And all the idols of Babylon lie broken on the ground."

¹⁰O my people, you are threshed and winnowed. I have told you all that the Lord Almighty, the God of Israel, has said.

¹¹This is God's message to Edom:

Someone from among you keeps calling to me. "Watchman, what of the night? Watchman, what of the night? How much time is left?" ¹²The watchman replies, "Your judgment day is dawning now. Turn again to God, so that I can give you better news. Seek for him, then come and ask again!"

¹³This is God's message about Arabia:

O caravans from Dedan, you will hide in the deserts of Arabia. ¹⁴O people of Tema, bring food and water to these tired wanderers! ¹⁵They have run

Weaving Cloth
ISAIAH 19:9

When you need new clothes, Mom or Dad goes to the store with you and buys them. Today we have hundreds of kinds and colors of cloth. But if you had lived in Bible times, getting clothes was not this easy. First you would need to make your own thread! This was done by spinning together sheeps' wool, goats' hair, flax, or cotton. Then you would have to weave these threads together to make a piece of cloth.

This weaving was done on a loom. Weaving cloth could take many, many days of hard work. So people did not have many clothes. A person who wanted clothes with colors would need to find dye and dye each bunch of thread. Some dyes, like purple, were hard to find. They cost so much that only kings and very wealthy people could afford them. The next time you look in your closet, thank God for your beautiful clothes! Even a Bible-time prince or princess would like to have what you have!

from drawn swords and sharp arrows. They have escaped the terrors of war! [16]"But in a long year the power of the enemy will end," says the Lord. "The mighty tribe of Kedar will be destroyed. [17]Only a few of its strong archers will live through it." The Lord, the God of Israel, has spoken.

What God Will Do to Jerusalem

22 This is God's message about Jerusalem:

What is happening? Where is everyone going? Why are they running to the rooftops? What are they looking at? [2]The whole city is in terrible uproar. What's the trouble in this busy, happy city? Bodies are lying everywhere! They were killed by plague and not by sword. [3]All your leaders run. They give up without a fight. The people slip away, but they are captured too. [4]Let me alone to cry. Don't try to comfort me. Let me cry for my people as I watch them being destroyed. [5]Oh, what a day of crushing trouble! What a day of confusion and terror from the Lord God of Heaven's armies! The walls of Jerusalem are broken. And the cry of death echoes from the mountains. [6-7]Elamites are the archers. Syrians drive the chariots. The men of Kir hold up the shields. They fill your choicest valleys and crowd against your gates.

[8]God has taken away his protecting care. You run to the armory for your weapons! [9-11]You inspect the walls of Jerusalem to see what needs fixing! You check over the houses and tear some down for stone. You need it for fixing the walls. Between the city walls, you build a pool to store water from the lower pool! But all your great plans will not succeed. For you never ask for help from God. And it is he who has let this happen to you. He is the one who planned it long ago. [12]The Lord God called you to repent, to cry and mourn. He wanted you to shave your heads in sorrow for your sins. He told you to wear clothes made of sackcloth to show how sorry you were. [13]But instead, you sing and dance and play, and feast and drink. "Let us eat, drink, and enjoy life," you say. "What's the difference! For tomorrow we die." [14]The Lord Almighty has shown me that this sin will not be forgiven until the day you die.

[15-16]The same Lord God of the armies of Heaven has told me to go and say to Shebna, the palace manager: "And who do you think you are? Why are you building this beautiful tomb in the rock for yourself? [17]For the Lord who allowed you to be rich will throw you away. He will send you into captivity, O strong man! [18]He will pick you up in his hands like a ball. Then he'll toss you away into a far-off land. There you will die, O great one! You bring shame on your nation!

[19]"Yes, I will drive you out of office," says the Lord. "I will pull you down from your high position. [20]And then I will call my servant Eliakim, the son of Hilkiah. He will take your place. [21]He shall have your uniform and title and authority. And he will be a father to the people of Jerusalem and all Judah. [22]I will give him charge over all my people. Whatever he says will be done. None will be able to stop him. [23-24]I will make of him a strong and steady peg to support my people. They will load him with work to do. And he will be an honor to his family name." [25]But the Lord will pull out that other peg! It seems to be so firmly fastened to the wall! But it will come out and fall to the ground. And all it supports will fall with it. This will happen, for the Lord has spoken.

What God Will Do to the Evil City Tyre

23 This is God's message to Tyre: Cry out, O ships of Tyre, as you come home from distant lands! Cry for your harbor, for it is gone! The rumors that you heard in Cyprus are all true. [2-3]Deathly silence is all around. Stillness reigns where once your hustling port was full of ships from Sidon. They brought goods from far across the ocean. They brought them all the way from Egypt and along the Nile. You were the trading center of the world! [4]Be full of shame, O Sidon, stronghold of the sea. For you are childless now! [5]When Egypt hears the news, there will be great sor-

row. [6]Flee to Tarshish, men of Tyre, crying as you go. [7]This silent ruin is all that's left of your once joyous land. What a history was yours! Think of all the colonists you sent to distant lands!

[8]Who has brought this trouble on Tyre? She was the empire builder and top trader of the world! [9]The Commander of the armies of Heaven has done it to destroy your pride! He has done it to show his contempt for all the greatness of mankind. [10]Sail on, O ships of Tarshish, for your harbor is gone. [11]The Lord holds out his hand over the seas. He shakes the kingdoms of the earth. He has spoken out against this great trading city. He has destroyed its strength.

[12]He says, "Never again, daughter of Sidon, will you rejoice. Never again will you be strong. Even if you flee to Cyprus, you will find no rest."

[13]The Assyrians will not destroy Tyre. It will be the Babylonians who give Tyre to the wild beasts. They will lay siege to it and destroy its palaces. They will make it a heap of ruins. [14]Wail, you ships that ply the oceans. For your home port is destroyed!

[15-16]For 70 years Tyre will be forgotten. Then, in the days of another king, the city will come back to life again. She will sing sweet songs as a prostitute does as she walks the streets looking for her long lost lovers. [17]Yes, after 70 years, the Lord will revive Tyre. But she will be no different than she was before. She will go back again to all her evil ways around the world. [18]Yet her businesses will someday bring their profits to the Lord! Their riches will not be stored up. They will be used for good food and fine clothes for the priests of the Lord!

Trouble Is Coming!

24 Look! The Lord is turning the land of Judah upside down. He is making it a great and empty wasteland. See how he is emptying out all its people. He is scattering them over the face of the earth. [2]Priests and people, servants and masters, slave girls and mistresses—none will be left. Buyers and sellers, lenders and borrowers, bankers and debtors—he will send them all away. [3]The land will be emptied and looted. The Lord has spoken! [4-5]The land suffers for the sins of its people. The earth dries up, the crops die, the skies refuse to rain. The land is made unclean by crime. The people have twisted the laws of God. They have broken his everlasting commands. [6]Therefore, the curse of God is upon them. They are left empty, destroyed by the drought. Few will be left alive.

[7]All the joys of life will go. The grape harvest will fail. The wine will be gone. The merrymakers will sigh and mourn. [8]The chords of the harp and timbrel are heard no more. The happy days are ended. [9]No more are the joys of wine and song. Strong drink turns bitter in the mouth.

???????????????????????????????????
How will the earth be like a drunk man or a tent in a storm?

(Read 24:17-20 for the answer.)

???????????????????????????????????

[10]The city lies in chaos. Every home and shop is locked up tight to keep out robbers. [11]Mobs form in the streets, crying for wine. Joy has left the land. Gladness has been sent away. [12]The city is left in ruins. Its gates are beaten down. [13]Throughout the land the story is the same. Only a few people are left.

[14]But all who are left will shout and sing for joy. Those in the west will praise the majesty of God. [15-16]And those in the east will respond with praise. Hear them singing to the Lord from the ends of the earth. They are singing praises to the Righteous One!

But my heart is heavy with grief. For evil still rules, and cheating is all around. [17]Terror and pits and traps still wait for you, O people of the earth. [18]When you run in terror, you will fall into a pit. If you get away from the pit, you will step into a trap. For destruction falls from the heavens upon you. The world is shaken under you. [19]The earth has broken up. The earth is terribly shaken. Everything is lost, abandoned, and confused. [20]The world staggers like a drunkard. It shakes like a tent in a storm. It falls and will not rise again. For the sins of the earth are very great.

²¹On that day the Lord will punish the fallen angels in the heavens. He will judge the proud rulers of the nations on earth. ²²They will be rounded up like prisoners. They will be put in a dungeon until they are tried and condemned. ²³Then the Lord of Heaven's armies will sit on his throne in Zion. And he will rule with power in Jerusalem. He will rule in the sight of all the elders of his people. There will be such glory that the sun and moon will seem to fade away.

A Day of Rejoicing

25 O Lord, I will honor and praise your name, for you are my God. You do such wonderful things! You planned them long ago. And now you have made them happen, just as you said! ²You turn mighty cities into heaps of ruins. The strongest forts are turned to rubble. Beautiful palaces in distant lands disappear. They will never be rebuilt. ³Therefore strong nations will shake with fear before you. Ruthless nations will obey and glorify your name.

If we want peace, we must trust God

He will keep in perfect peace all those who trust in him.

Isaiah 26:3

---

⁴But to the poor, O Lord, you are a refuge from the storm. You are a shadow from the heat. You are a shelter from cruel men. They are like a driving rain that melts down an earthen wall. ⁵As a hot, dry land is cooled by clouds, you will cool the pride of cruel nations. ⁶Here in Jerusalem the Lord Almighty will spread a great feast. It will be for everyone around the world. It will be a tasty feast of good food. There will be clear, well-aged wine and choice beef. ⁷At that time he will remove the cloud of gloom. The canopy of death that hangs over the earth will be lifted. ⁸He will swallow up death forever. The Lord God will wipe away all tears. He will take away all insults and mockery against his land

and people forever. The Lord has spoken! He will surely do it!

⁹In that day the people will proclaim, "This is our God in whom we trust. He is the one for whom we waited. Now at last he is here." What a day of joy that will be! ¹⁰For the Lord's good hand will rest upon Jerusalem. And Moab will be crushed like straw under his feet. It will be left there to rot. ¹¹God will push them down just as a swimmer pushes down the water with his hands. He will end their pride and all their evil works. ¹²The high walls of Moab will be broken into dust.

The People Sing

26 Listen to them singing! At that time, the whole land of Judah will sing this song:

"Our city is strong! We are surrounded by the walls of his salvation!" ²Open the gates to everyone. For all may enter in who love the Lord. ³He will keep in perfect peace all those who trust in him. He will bless those whose thoughts turn often to him. ⁴Trust in the Lord God always. For in the Lord is your strength. ⁵He humbles the proud and brings the proud city to the dust. Its walls come crashing down. ⁶He gives it to the poor and needy for their use.

⁷But for good men the path is not uphill and rough! The Lord makes the road smooth before them. ⁸O Lord, we love to do your will! Our heart's desire is to bring glory to your name. ⁹All night long I look for you. Earnestly I search for God. For you will come to punish the earth! Only then will people turn away from wickedness and do what is right.

¹⁰Your kindness to the wicked doesn't make them good. They keep on doing wrong and take no notice of your majesty. ¹¹They do not listen when you threaten. They will not look to see your upraised fist. Show them how much you love your people. Perhaps then they will be ashamed! Yes, let them be burned up by the fire saved for your enemies.

¹²Lord, give us peace. For all we have and are has come from you. ¹³O Lord our God, once we worshiped other gods. But

now we worship you alone. [14]Those we served before are dead and gone. Never again will they come back. You came against them and destroyed them. And now they are long forgotten. [15]O praise the Lord! He has made our nation very great. He has widened the borders of our land!

[16]Lord, in their trouble they looked for you. When you punished them, they whispered a desperate prayer. [17]How we missed your presence, Lord! We suffered as a woman giving birth who cries and rolls around in pain. [18]We too have rolled around in pain. But it did not help at all. No salvation has come from all our efforts. [19]But we have this to live by: We know that those who belong to God shall live again. Their bodies shall rise again! Those who dwell in the dust shall awake and sing for joy! For God's light of life will fall like dew upon them!

[20]Go home, my people, and lock the doors! Hide for a little while until the Lord's anger has passed. [21]Look! The Lord is coming from the heavens. He is coming to punish the people of the earth for their sins. The earth will no longer hide the murderers. The guilty will be found!

God Stops Feeling Angry

27 In that day the Lord will take his terrible, swift sword. And he will judge leviathan, the swiftly moving serpent. He will punish leviathan, the coiling, writhing serpent, the dragon of the sea.

[2]In that day of Israel's freedom let this be their song:

[3]"Israel is my vineyard. I, the Lord, will tend the fruitful vines. Every day I'll water them. Day and night I'll watch to keep all enemies away. [4-5]My anger against Israel is gone. If I find thorns and briars bothering her, I will burn them up. I will spare only those enemies who give in and beg for peace. I will save only those who ask for my protection." [6]The time will come when Israel will take root. She will bud and blossom and fill the whole earth with her fruit!

[7-8]Has God punished Israel as much as he has punished her enemies? No, for he has destroyed her enemies. But he has punished Israel just a little. He sent her far from her own land as though blown away in a storm from the east. [9]And why did God do it? It was to wash away her sins. It was to get rid of all her idol altars and idols. They will never be worshiped again. [10]Her walled cities will be silent and empty, and her houses will be silent. The streets will be overgrown with grass. Cows will graze through the city. They will munch on twigs and branches.

[11]My people are like the dead branches of a tree. They have been broken off and used to burn under the pots. They are a foolish nation, a witless, stupid people. For they turn away from God. Therefore, he who made them will not have pity on them. He will not show them his mercy. [12]Yet the time will come when the Lord will gather them together. He will call them one by one like handpicked grain. He will choose them from here and there. He will pick them from his great threshing floor. It reaches all the way from the Euphrates River to the Egyptian border. [13]In that day the great trumpet will be blown. And many who are dying among their enemies, Assyria and Egypt, will be saved. They will be brought back to Jerusalem to worship the Lord in his holy mountain.

A Wonderful Teacher

28 I am warning the city of Samaria, surrounded by her rich valley. Samaria is the pride and joy of the drunks of Israel! Her beauty is fading away fast. She is the pride of a nation of men lying drunk in the streets! [2]For the Lord will send the mighty army of Assyria against you. Like a mighty hailstorm he will burst upon you. He will dash you to the ground. [3]The proud city of Samaria will be thrown to the ground. She will be trampled under the enemies' feet. Yes, she is the joy of the drunks of Israel! [4]She was once a great city. She was surrounded by a rich valley. But her fading beauty will suddenly be gone! It will be snatched away like an early fig that is picked and gobbled up!

[5]Then at last the Lord Almighty himself will be their crowning glory. He will

be the shining diadem to his people who are left. ⁶He will make your judges want to bring justice. He will give great courage to your soldiers who are fighting before your gates. ⁷But Jerusalem is now led by drunks! Her priests and prophets reel and stagger. They make stupid errors and mistakes. ⁸Their tables are covered with vomit. Dirt and filth are all around.

⁹"Who does Isaiah think he is!" the people say. "Who is he to speak to us like this! Are we little children? Are we just barely old enough to talk? ¹⁰He tells us everything over and over again! He tells us a line at a time and in such simple words!"

¹¹But they won't listen. The only language they can understand is punishment! So God will punish them by sending foreigners against them. They are people who speak strange languages! Only then will they listen to him! ¹²They could have rest in their own land if they would obey him. They could have peace if they were kind and good. He told them that, but they wouldn't listen to him. ¹³So the Lord will spell it out for them again. He will say it over and over in simple words whenever he can. Yet over this simple message they will stumble and fall. They will be broken, trapped, and captured.

¹⁴Therefore hear the word of the Lord, you mocking rulers in Jerusalem.

¹⁵You have made a deal with Death, you say. You sold yourselves to the devil for his help against the Assyrians. "They can never touch us!" you say. "For we are under the care of one who will trick and fool them."

¹⁶But the Lord God says, "See, I am placing a Foundation Stone in Jerusalem. It is a firm, tested, precious Cornerstone that is safe to build on. He who believes need never run away again. ¹⁷I will take the measuring line of justice. I will use it to check the foundation wall you built. It looks so fine, but it is so weak a storm of hail will knock it down! The enemy will come like a flood and sweep it away. And you will be drowned. ¹⁸I will take away your deal with Death and the devil. And when the enemy floods in, you will be trampled into the

ground. ¹⁹Again and again that flood will come and carry you off. Then at last you will know that my terrible warnings were all true!"

²⁰The bed you have made is far too short to lie on. The blankets are too narrow to cover you. ²¹The Lord will come suddenly and in anger. He will come like he did at Mount Perazim and Gibeon. He will do a strange thing. He will destroy his own people! ²²So stop laughing. If you don't, your punishment may be made even greater. For the Lord God has clearly told me that he will crush you.

²³⁻²⁴Listen to me! Listen as I beg before you. Does a farmer always plow and never plant? Is he forever digging the soil and never planting it? ²⁵Does he not finally plant his many kinds of grain? Does he not plant each in its own section of his land? ²⁶He knows just what to do, for God has made him see and understand. ²⁷He doesn't thresh all grains the same. A sledge is never used on dill. It is beaten out with a stick. A threshing wheel is never rolled on cummin. It is beaten softly with a flail. ²⁸Bread grain is easily crushed. So he doesn't keep on pounding it. ²⁹The Lord Almighty is a good teacher. He gives the farmer the wisdom he needs.

No One Can Hide from God

29 How terrible it will be for Jerusalem, the city of David. Year after year you make your many offerings. ²But I will send heavy judgment on you. And there will be great crying and sadness. You shall become like an altar covered with blood. ³I will be your enemy. I will surround Jerusalem and lay siege against it. I will build forts around it to destroy it. ⁴Your voice will whisper like a ghost from the earth where you lie buried.

⁵But suddenly your cruel enemies will be driven away. They will be like chaff before the wind. ⁶In an instant, I, the Lord of Heaven's armies, will come upon them. I will come with thunder, earthquake, whirlwind, and fire. ⁷And all the nations fighting Jerusalem will vanish like a dream! ⁸A hungry man dreams of eating but is still hungry. A thirsty man

dreams of drinking but is still faint from thirst when he wakes up. And so your enemies will dream of great victory, but it will never happen.

⁹Are you amazed? Don't you believe it? Then go ahead and be blind if you must! You are stupid, and not from drinking, either! Stagger, and not from wine! ¹⁰For the Lord has poured out upon you a spirit of deep sleep. He has closed the eyes of your prophets. ¹¹All of these future events are a sealed book to them. You might try and give it to someone who can read. But he will say, "I can't read it. It's sealed up." ¹²You might then give it to another. But he will say, "Sorry, I can't read."

¹³And so the Lord says, "These people say they are mine. But they do not obey me. Their worship is just words they have learned by rote. ¹⁴Because of this, I will take terrible vengeance on these hypocrites. Their wisest men will be shown to be fools."

¹⁵How terrible it will be for those who try to hide their plans from God. They try to keep him from knowing what they are doing! "God can't see us," they say to themselves. "He doesn't know what is going on!" ¹⁶How stupid can they be! Isn't he greater than you? He is the Potter. You are just the jars of clay he makes! Will you say to him, "He didn't make us"? Does a machine call its inventor dumb?

¹⁷Soon the wilderness of Lebanon will be a fruitful field again. It will be a rich and beautiful forest. ¹⁸In that day the deaf will hear the words of a book. And out of their gloom and darkness the blind will see my plans. ¹⁹The humble will be filled with fresh joy from the Lord. And the poor shall praise the Holy One of Israel. ²⁰Bullies and mockers will be gone away. And all those who make evil plans will be killed. ²¹The violent man who fights at the drop of a hat will be gone. The man who waits to beat up the judge who sentenced him will be gone. And the men who make excuses to be unfair will be here no more.

²²So the Lord who saved Abraham says: "My people will no longer be afraid or ashamed. ²³For they will see the grow-ing birth rate. They will see that the economy is strong and growing. And then they will respect my name and rejoice in it. They will praise the Holy One of Israel and stand in awe of him. ²⁴Those in error will believe the truth. And those who complain will want to learn!

God Is Waiting

30 "How terrible it will be for my children who rebel," says the Lord. "You ask advice from everyone but me. Then you decide to do what I don't want you to do. You join yourselves with people who don't believe. In this way, you pile up your sins. ²For without asking me you have gone down to Egypt to find help. You have put your trust in Pharaoh for his protection. ³But in trusting Pharaoh, you will be let down. You will be put to shame. For he can't do what he promises to do. ⁴For his power just reaches to Zoan and Hanes. ⁵And this treaty will all turn out to your shame. He won't help one little bit!"

⁶See them moving slowly across the terrible desert to Egypt. Donkeys and camels are loaded down with treasure to pay for Egypt's help. On through the badlands they go. Lions and swift, deadly snakes live there. And Egypt will give you nothing for all this! ⁷For Egypt's promises are useless! I call her "The Reluctant Dragon"!

⁸Now go and write down this word of mine about Egypt. That way people will be able to read it until the end of time. It will be a sign to prove Israel's unbelief. ⁹For if you don't write it, they will say I never warned them. "Oh no!" they'll say. "You never told us that!"

For they are stubborn rebels. ¹⁰⁻¹¹They tell my prophets, "Shut up! We don't want any more of your reports!" Or they say, "Don't tell us the truth. Tell us nice things. Tell us lies. Forget all this gloom. We've heard more than enough about your 'Holy One of Israel.' We're tired of what he has to say."

¹²This is the reply of the Holy One of Israel:

"You hate what I tell you. You trust in false prophets and their lies. And you won't turn away from your sin. [13]Because of this, trouble will come upon you suddenly. It will come upon you like a bulging wall that cracks and falls. In one moment it comes crashing down. [14]God will smash you like a broken dish. He will not act with mercy. There will be no large pieces left. There won't be one big enough to carry coals from the fire. There won't be one large enough to carry a little water from the well." [15]For the Lord God, the Holy One of Israel, says: "Only by coming back to me will you be saved. Only by waiting for me will you be rescued. In quietness and confidence is your strength." But you'll have none of this.

[16]"No," you say. "We will get our help from Egypt. They will give us swift horses for riding to battle." Yes, you will see swiftness all right! But it will be the swiftness of your enemies chasing you! [17]One of them will chase a thousand of you! Five of them will scatter you until not two of you are left together. You will be like lonely trees on the distant mountains. [18]Yet the Lord still waits for you to come to him. He wants so much to show you his love. He will conquer you to bless you, just as he said. For the Lord is faithful to his promises. Blessed are all those who wait for him to help them.

[19]O my people in Jerusalem, you shall cry no more. For he will surely be kind to you at the sound of your cry. He will answer you. [20]He feeds you with the bread of trouble and water of pain. But he will be with you to teach you. With your own eyes you will see your Teacher. [21]And perhaps you will leave God's paths and go astray. If you do, you will hear a Voice behind you. It will say, "No, this is the way. Walk here." [22]And you will destroy all your silver idols and gold images. You will throw them out like dirty things you hate to touch. "Ugh!" you'll say to them. "Be gone!"

[23]Then God will bless you with rain at planting time. He will give you rich harvests. And there will be plenty of pasture for your cows. [24]The oxen and young donkeys that plow the ground will eat grain. And the grain's chaff will blow away in the wind. [25]At that time, God will step in to destroy your enemies. He will give you streams of water. They will flow down each mountain and every hill. [26]The moon will be as bright as the sun. And the sun's light in one day will be brighter than it is in seven days now! It will be like this when the Lord begins to heal his people. He will cure the wounds he gave them.

[27]See, the Lord comes from far off. He is burning with anger, and thick smoke is all around him. His lips are filled with anger. His words burn like fire. [28]His anger pours out like floods upon them all, to sweep them all away. He will divide out the proud nations. He will put bridles on them and lead them off to their doom.

[29]But the people of God will sing a song of solemn joy. They will sing songs like those sung on the nights of holy feasts. His people will have gladness of heart. They will have joy like when a flutist leads a pilgrim band to Jerusalem. He leads them to the Mountain of the Lord, the Rock of Israel. [30]And the Lord shall cause his great voice to be heard. He shall crush down his mighty arm on his enemies. He will do it with angry flames and tornados. He will do it with terrible storms and huge hailstones. [31]The voice of the Lord shall punish the Assyrians, who had been his rod of punishment. [32]And when the Lord beats them, his people will rejoice with music and song. [33]The funeral fire has long been ready for Molech, the Assyrian god. It is piled high with wood. The breath of the Lord will set it all on fire. It will be like fire from a volcano.

The Sword of God

31 How terrible it will be for those who run to Egypt for help! How terrible for those who trust Egypt's mighty cavalry and chariots! Instead they should look to the Holy One of Israel and ask him for help. [2]In his wisdom, he will send great evil on his people. He will not change his mind. He will rise against them for the evil they have done. And he will crush their friends too. [3]For these Egyptians are mere men, not God! Their horses are weak flesh, not mighty spirits! The Lord will clench his fist against them. And when he does, they will stumble. They will fall among those they are trying to help. Everything will fail together.

4-5But the Lord has told me this: "A lion, even a young one, might kill a sheep. And when he does, he does not listen to the shepherd's shouts and noise. He goes right on and eats. In the same way, the Lord will come and fight at Jerusalem. He will not be frightened away! He, the Lord Almighty, will hover over Jerusalem as birds hover round their nests. And he will defend the city and save it."

6O my people, though you are such wicked rebels, come! Return to God. 7I know a great day will soon come. On that day you will throw away your gold idols and silver images. These you have made in your sinfulness.

8"The Assyrians will be destroyed, but not by swords of men. The 'sword of God' will hit them. They will panic and run. And the strong young Assyrians will be taken away as slaves. 9Even their generals will shake with terror. They will run when they see the battle flags of Israel," says the Lord. For the flame of God burns brightly in Jerusalem.

A Promise of Peace

32 Look, a righteous King is coming, with honest princes! 2He will shelter Israel from the storm and wind. He will refresh her as a river in the desert. He will be like the cooling shadow of a mighty rock in a hot, dry land. 3Then at last the eyes of Israel will open wide to God. His people will listen to his voice. 4Even the hotheads among them will be full of understanding. And those who cannot speak clearly will speak out plainly.

5In those days the ungodly will not be heroes! Rich cheaters will not be spoken of as good men! 6Everyone will know an evil man when he sees him. Hypocrites will fool no one at all. Their lies about God and their cheating of the hungry will be plain for all to see. 7The

smooth tricks of evil men will be shown to all. So will all the lies they use to oppress the poor in the courts. 8But good men will be kind to others. They will be blessed of God for all they do.

9Listen, you women who sit around in lazy ease. Listen to me and I will tell you your reward. 10In a short time, suddenly you'll care, O careless ones. This will happen in just a little more than a year! For the crops of fruit will fail. The harvest will not take place. 11Shake, O women of lazy ease. Throw off your careless unconcern. Strip off your pretty clothes. Wear sackcloth for your grief. 12Beat your breasts in sadness for those rich farms of yours. For they will soon be gone. Mourn for those fruitful vines of other years. 13For your lands will be full of thorns and briars. Your joyous homes and happy cities will be gone. 14Palaces and mansions will all be made empty. Even the crowded cities will have no one in them. Wild herds of donkeys and goats will graze upon the mountains by the watchtowers. 15It will be like this until at last the Spirit is poured down on us from Heaven. Then once again rich crops will grow. 16Then justice will rule through all the land. 17And out of justice will come peace. Quietness and peace will reign forever.

18My people will live in safety, quietly at home. 19But the Assyrians will be destroyed and their cities laid low. 20And God will greatly bless his people. Wherever they plant, rich crops will spring up. And their flocks and herds will graze in green pastures.

God's Great Forgiveness

33 How terrible it will be for you, Assyrians! For you have destroyed everything around you. But you have never suffered the pain yourselves. You expect others to keep their promises to you. But you don't keep your own promises! Now you, too, will be attacked and destroyed.

2But to us, O Lord, be merciful! For we have waited for you. Be our strength each day. Be our salvation in the time of trouble. 3The enemy runs at the sound of your voice. When you stand up, the nations flee. ⁴Swarms of locusts can quickly strip the fields and vines. In the same way, Jerusalem will strip the fallen army of Assyria!

⁵The Lord is very great and lives in Heaven. He will make Jerusalem the home of fairness and goodness. ⁶A great store of salvation is saved up for Judah in a safe place. There is also plenty of wisdom and knowledge and respect for God.

⁷But now your messengers cry in bitter sadness. For Assyria has refused their cry for peace. ⁸Your roads lie in ruins. Travelers go by way of back roads. The Assyrians have broken their peace pact. They care nothing for the promises they made in the presence of witnesses. They have no respect for anyone. ⁹All the land of Israel is in trouble. Lebanon has been destroyed. Sharon has become a wilderness. Bashan and Carmel are plundered.

¹⁰But the Lord says, "I will stand up and show my power and might. ¹¹You Assyrians will gain nothing by all your efforts. Your own breath will turn to fire and kill you. ¹²Your armies will be burned to lime. They will be like thorns cut down and tossed into the fire. ¹³Listen to what I have done, O nations far away! And you that are near, admit that I am strong!"

¹⁴The sinners among my people shake with fear. "Which one of us can live here?" they cry. "Who can live here with this Fire that burns on and on?" ¹⁵I will tell you who can live here. Those who are honest and fair can live here. I accept those who don't make money by cheating. I accept those who hold back from taking bribes. I accept those who will not listen to people who plan murder. I accept those who shut their eyes to all sin. ¹⁶People like these shall live on high. The rocks of the mountains will be their place of safety. Food will be given to them. And they will have all the water they need.

¹⁷Your eyes will see the King in his beauty. You will see the highlands of Heaven far away. ¹⁸Your mind will think back to this time of terror. It is a time when Assyrian officers wait outside your walls. They are counting your towers and seeing how much they will get from your fallen city. ¹⁹But soon they will all be gone. These people speak a strange language you can't understand. But they will soon be gone.

²⁰Instead you will see Jerusalem at peace. It will be a place where God is worshiped. It will be a city quiet and unmoved. ²¹The glorious Lord will be to us as a wide river of protection. He will be a river no enemy can cross. ²²For the Lord is our Judge. He is our Lawgiver and our King. He will care for us and save us. ²³The enemies' sails hang loose on broken masts with useless tackle. Their treasure will be divided by the people of God. Even the lame will win their share. ²⁴The people of Israel will no longer say, "We are sick and helpless." For the Lord will forgive them their sins and bless them.

Come and Listen!

34 Come and listen, O nations of the earth. Let the world and everything in it hear my words. ²For the Lord is angry at the nations. His anger is against their armies. He will totally destroy them and kill them all. ³Their dead will be not be buried. And the stink of rotting bodies will fill the land. The mountains will flow with their blood. ⁴At that time the heavens above will melt away. They will disappear just like a rolled-up scroll. And the stars will fall like leaves. They will fall like ripe fruit from the trees.

⁵And when my sword has finished its work in the heavens, then watch. For it will fall upon Edom, the people I have doomed. ⁶The sword of the Lord is full of blood. It is covered with flesh. It is as though it was used for killing lambs and goats for sacrifice. For the Lord will kill a great sacrifice in Edom. He will kill many people there. ⁷The strongest will die, young boys and soldiers, too. The land will be soaked with blood. And the soil will be made rich with fat. ⁸For it is the time of vengeance. It is the time when Edom will be paid back for what she did to Israel. ⁹The streams of Edom will be filled with burning pitch. The

ground will be covered with fire.

¹⁰This judgment on Edom will never end. Its smoke will rise up forever. The land will lie empty for many generations. No one will live there anymore. ¹¹There the hawks and porcupines will live. And the owls and ravens will build their nests there. For God will look at that land. And he will find that it deserves to be destroyed. He will test its rulers and find them worthy of death. ¹²It will be called "The Land of Nothing." And its princes soon will all be gone. ¹³Thorns will overrun the palaces. Nettles will grow in its forts. It will become a house for jackals and a home for ostriches. ¹⁴The wild animals of the desert will live there with wolves and hyenas. Their howls will fill the night. There the night-monsters will scream at each other. And the demons will come there to rest. ¹⁵There the owl will make her nest and lay her eggs. She will hatch her young and nestle them under her wings. And the hawks will come there, each one with its mate. ¹⁶Look in the Book of the Lord and see all that he will do. He will not miss one detail! Not one hawk will be there without a mate. For the Lord has said it. And his Spirit will make it all come true. ¹⁷He has measured and divided the land. He has given it to all those wild animals. They shall own it for all time.

Streams in the Desert

35 Even the wilderness and desert will rejoice in those days. The desert will blossom with flowers. ²Yes, there will be many flowers and much singing and joy! The deserts will become as green as the Lebanon mountains. They will be as lovely as Mount Carmel's pastures and Sharon's meadows. For the Lord will show his glory there. Everyone will see the greatness of our God.

³With this news bring cheer to all discouraged ones. ⁴Encourage those who are afraid. Tell them, "Be strong! Don't be afraid! For your God is coming to destroy your enemies. He is coming to save you." ⁵And when he comes, he will open the eyes of the blind. He will

unstop the ears of the deaf. ⁶The lame man will leap up like a deer. And those who could not speak will shout and sing! Springs will burst forth in the wilderness, and streams in the desert. ⁷The dry ground will become a pool. There will be springs of water in the thirsty land. Where desert jackals lived, there will be reeds and rushes!

⁸And a main road will go through that

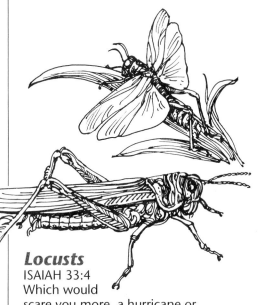

Locusts

ISAIAH 33:4

Which would scare you more, a hurricane or some locusts? Hurricanes, tornadoes, and earthquakes scare us today. But if you lived in Bible times, locusts would scare you just as much. Perhaps more! A locust looks something like a grasshopper. Sometimes locusts multiplied until they became huge swarms of thousands. These swarms swept across the countryside in dark clouds, eating every plant. There were no crops left. Without food, the people often starved. A swarm of locusts was as bad as an invading army. Nothing was scarier than seeing a dark cloud of locusts coming your way. A swarm of locusts was one of the worst plagues in the world at that time.

once-empty land. It will be named "The Holy Highway." No evil-hearted men may walk upon it. God will walk there with you. Even the most stupid cannot miss the way. ⁹No lion will hide along its course. And there won't be any other dangers. Only the people God has bought from slavery will travel there. ¹⁰Those who are set free by the Lord will go home along that road to Jerusalem. They will sing songs of endless joy as they go. For them all sadness and crying will be gone forever. Only joy and gladness will be there.

An Angel Destroys an Army

The Assyrian army was one of the most powerful armies in the world. Judah's army was small and weak. How could little Judah fight big Assyria? It seemed hopeless. But God promised that Assyria would not conquer Judah. How would that happen?

36 Sennacherib, the king of Assyria, came to fight against the walled cities of Judah. He attacked and conquered them. He did this in the 14th year of King Hezekiah's reign. ²Then he sent his personal messenger with a great army from Lachish. He sent them to talk with King Hezekiah in Jerusalem. He camped near the outlet of the upper pool. This was along the road going past the field where cloth is bleached.

³Eliakim, Hilkiah's son, was the prime minister of Israel at that time. Shebna was the king's scribe. Joah, Asaph's son, was the royal secretary. They got together and went out of the city to meet with him. ⁴The Assyrian messenger told them to bring a message to Hezekiah. He said, "The mighty king of Assyria says you are a fool. The king of Egypt will never help you. ⁵What are the Pharaoh's promises worth? Mere words won't make up for his lack of strength. But you look to him for help. And you have broken from my rule! ⁶Egypt is a dangerous friend. She is like a sharp stick. It will pierce your hand if you lean on it. That has happened to all who have ever asked her for help. ⁷But perhaps you say, 'We are trusting in the Lord our God!' Oh? Isn't he the one your king insulted? Didn't he tear down his temples and altars in the hills? Didn't he make everyone in Judah worship only at the altars here in Jerusalem? ⁸⁻⁹My master, the king of Assyria, wants to make a little bet with you! He thinks you don't have 2,000 men left in your whole army! If you do, he will give you 2,000 horses for them to ride on! With that tiny army, how can you think of fighting the army of Assyria? You wouldn't have a chance against the smallest and weakest group of my master's troops! For you'll get no help from Egypt. ¹⁰What's more, do you think I have come here without the Lord's telling me to take this land? The Lord said to me, 'Go and destroy it!'"

¹¹Then Eliakim, Shebna, and Joah said to him, "Please talk to us in Aramaic. For we understand it quite well. Don't speak in Hebrew, for the people on the wall will hear."

¹²But he replied, "My master wants everyone in Jerusalem to hear this. This message isn't just for you. He wants them to know that you need to give up. If you don't, this city will be put under siege. Everyone will soon be so hungry that they will eat their own dung. They will be so thirsty that they will drink their own urine."

¹³Then he shouted in Hebrew to the Jews listening on the wall. He said, "Hear the words of the great king, the king of Assyria:

¹⁴"Don't let Hezekiah fool you. Nothing he can do will save you. ¹⁵Don't let

him talk you into trusting in the Lord. Don't let him tell you that the Lord won't let you be defeated by Assyria. 16Don't listen to Hezekiah. This is what the king of Assyria is offering you: You must give me a present as a sign that you have given up. You must open Jerusalem's gates and come out. Then I will let you each have your own farm and garden and water. 17But I will arrange to take you away to a country very similar to this one. It is a land where there are rich crops of grain and grapes. It will be a land of plenty. 18Don't let Hezekiah take all this away from you! Don't let him tell you the Lord will save you from our armies. Have any other nation's gods ever stopped the armies of Assyria? 19Don't you remember what I did to Hamath and Arpad? Did their gods save them? And what about Sepharvaim and Samaria? Where are their gods now? 20Of all the gods of these lands, which one has ever saved their people from my power? Name just one! And do you think this God of yours can save Jerusalem from me? Don't be foolish!"

21But the people were silent and didn't answer. For Hezekiah had told them to say nothing. 22Then Eliakim, Shebna, and Joah went back to Hezekiah. They had ripped their clothes to show how upset they were. And they told King Hezekiah all that had happened.

37 King Hezekiah was told what happened at the meeting. He tore his robes and dressed in coarse cloth used for making sacks. This was a sign that he was humble and sad. Then he went over to the Temple to pray. 2Meanwhile he sent Eliakim, Shebna, and the older priests to Isaiah the prophet, son of Amoz. They all wore sackcloth. 3They brought him this message from Hezekiah:

"This is a day of trouble and great insults to God. It is a very serious time. It is like when a woman is in heavy labor, but the child does not come. 4But maybe the Lord heard the insults the king of Assyria's messenger gave. He laughed out loud at the living God! Surely God won't let him get away with this. Surely God will punish him for those words.

Oh, Isaiah, pray for those of us who are left!"

5So they took the king's message to Isaiah.

6Then Isaiah sent King Hezekiah this message: "Don't be upset by this speech from the servant of the king of Assyria. Don't worry about his insults to God. 7For a report from Assyria will soon reach the king. It will say that he is needed at home right away. So he will go back to his own land. And when he gets there, I will have him killed."

8-9Now the Assyrian messenger left Jerusalem. He went to talk with his king. The king had left Lachish and was attacking Libnah. But then the Assyrian king heard that Tirhakah was attacking him. Tirhakah was the crown prince of Ethiopia. He was leading an army against the Assyrians from the south. When the king heard this, he sent messengers back to Jerusalem. They brought Hezekiah this message:

10"Don't let this God you trust in fool you. Don't promise your people that Jerusalem will not be captured by the king of Assyria! 11Just remember what has happened wherever the kings of Assyria have gone. They have crushed everyone who has stood against them. Do you think you will be any different? 12Did their gods save the cities of Gozan, Haran, or Rezeph? Were the people of Eden in Telassar saved by their gods? No, the Assyrian kings completely destroyed them! 13Don't forget what happened to the kings of Hamath and Arpad. And remember what happened to the kings of the cities of Sepharvaim, Hena, and Ivvah."

14King Hezekiah read this letter. And right away he went over to the Temple. He spread the letter out before the Lord. 15Then he prayed, saying, 16-17"O Lord, Almighty God of Israel! You are the one who sits between the Guardian Angels! You alone are God of all the kingdoms of the earth. You alone made Heaven and earth. Listen as I beg. See me as I pray. Look at this letter from King Sennacherib. For he has laughed at the living God. 18It is true, O Lord, that the kings of Assyria have destroyed all those nations. It happened just as the letter says it did. ¹⁹They destroyed those nations and threw their gods into the fire. For they weren't gods at all but merely idols. They were carved by men from wood and stone. So of course the Assyrians could destroy them! ²⁰O Lord our God! Save us so that all the kingdoms of the earth will know that you are God. Show them that you are the only God!"

²¹Then Isaiah, the son of Amoz, sent a message to King Hezekiah. He said: "The Lord God of Israel has spoken. He says, 'This is my answer to your prayer against Sennacherib, Assyria's king.

²²"'The Lord says: My people laugh at you. They mock and shake their heads at you in scorn. ²³Who is it you laughed at? Whom did you make fun of? At whom did you direct your violence and pride? It was against the Holy One of Israel! ²⁴You have sent your messengers to laugh at the Lord. You brag, "I came with my mighty army against the nations of the west. I cut down the tallest cedars and cypress trees. I conquered their highest mountains and destroyed their thickest forests."

²⁵"'You boast of wells you've dug in many a conquered land. You brag that Egypt with all its armies is no problem for you! ²⁶But do you not yet know that it was I who decided all this long ago? You don't know that it was I who gave you all this power from ancient times? I have caused all this to happen as I planned. I let you crush walled cities into ruined heaps. ²⁷That's why their people had so little power! That's why they were so easy for you to conquer! They were as helpless as the grass. They were like the tender plants you trample down under your feet. They were like grass on the housetops, burnt yellow by the sun. ²⁸But I know you well. I know about your comings and goings and all you do. I know the way you have raged against me. ²⁹I know about your anger against the Lord. I heard it all! And because of it, I have put a hook in your nose. I have put a bit in your mouth. I have led you back to your own land by the same road you came.'"

³⁰Then God said to Hezekiah: "Here is proof that I am the one who has saved this city from Assyria. This year he will stop his attack. It is now too late to plant your crops. But you will have volunteer grain this fall. It will give you enough seed for a small harvest next year. And two years from now you will be living in luxury again. ³¹And you who are left in Judah will take root again in your own soil. You will grow and multiply. ³²For a remnant shall go out from Jerusalem to fill the land. The power of the Lord Almighty will cause all this to happen.

³³"As for the king of Assyria, his armies shall not enter Jerusalem. They shall never shoot their arrows there. They shall not march outside its gates. And they shall never build up an earthen ramp against its walls. ³⁴He will go back to his own country by the road he came on. He will not enter this city, says the Lord. ³⁵For my own honor I will defend it. And I will rescue it in memory of my servant David."

³⁶That night the Angel of the Lord went out to the camp of the Assyrians. He killed 185,000 soldiers. When the living wakened the next morning, all these lay dead before them. ³⁷Then Sennacherib, king of Assyria, went back to his own country. He went back to his capital city of Nineveh. ³⁸And one day he went to worship in the temple of Nisroch his god. While he was there, his sons Adrammelech and Sharezer killed him with their swords. Then they escaped into the land of Ararat. And Esarhaddon, his son, became king.

- *Remember:* Who was the king of Judah at this time? (36:1) Which country invaded Judah? (36:1) How did the Assyrians make fun of God? (36:20) When King Hezekiah came to God, was he proud or humble? How do you know? (37:1) How did one angel defeat the entire Assyrian army? (37:36) If you had to choose, would you rather have God on your side or a big army? Why?

- *Discover:* No one is more powerful than God, not even the biggest army on earth.

- *Apply:* Are you worried about something? Ask God to help you first. Do you need something? Ask God to help you.

Are you afraid of something? Ask God to help you.

• *What's next?* A man is about to die, but then God lets him live 15 more years. Why? Read 2 Kings 20:1-11. ■

A King Asks for a Miracle

38 It was just before all this that Hezekiah became deathly sick. And Isaiah the prophet, the son of Amoz, went to visit him. He gave him this message from the Lord:

"Set your affairs in order, for you are going to die. You will not get better from this sickness."

²When Hezekiah heard this, he turned his face to the wall. Then he prayed:

³"O Lord, don't you remember how true I've been to you? Have you forgotten how I've always tried to obey you?" Then he broke down with great sobs.

⁴So the Lord sent another message to Isaiah:

⁵"Go and speak to Hezekiah. Tell him that the Lord God of his forefather David hears him praying. Tell him that I see his tears and will let him live 15 more years. ⁶I will save him and this city from the king of Assyria. I will defend and help him. ⁷And here is proof of what I say: ⁸I will send the sun backwards 10 degrees as measured on Ahaz's sundial!"

So the sun went backwards 10 degrees just as the Lord said!

⁹When King Hezekiah was well again, he wrote this poem. It told about his experience.

¹⁰"My life is but half done, and I must leave it all. I am robbed of my normal years. Now I must enter the gates of the grave. ¹¹Never again will I see the Lord in the land of the living. Never again will I see my friends in this world. ¹²My life is blown away like a shepherd's tent. It is cut short like when a weaver stops his work at the loom. In one short day my life hangs by a thread.

¹³"All night I cried. It was like being torn apart by lions. ¹⁴I chattered like a swallow and mourned like a dove. My eyes grew tired of looking up for help. 'O God!' I cried. 'I am in trouble! Help

me!' ¹⁵But what can I say? For he himself has sent this sickness. All my sleep has fled because of my soul's sadness. ¹⁶O Lord, your discipline is good. It leads to life and health. Oh, heal me and make me live!

¹⁷"Yes, now I see it all. It was good for me to suffer like this. For you have lovingly saved me from death. You have forgiven all my sins. ¹⁸For dead men cannot praise you. They cannot be filled with hope and joy. ¹⁹The living, only the living, can praise you as I do today. One generation makes known your faithfulness to the next. ²⁰Think of it! The Lord healed me! Every day of my life I will sing my songs of praise in the Temple. I will sing along with the orchestra."

²¹(Isaiah had also spoken to Hezekiah's servants. He said, "Make an ointment of figs and spread it over the boil. Then he will get well again."

²²And then Hezekiah had asked, "What sign will the Lord give me? How will he prove that he will heal me?")

Messengers from Babylon

39 Soon after this, the king of Babylon sent Hezekiah a present. This king was named Merodach-baladan. He was the son of Baladan. With the present, he also sent his best wishes. For he had heard that Hezekiah had been very sick and now was well again. ²This made Hezekiah very happy. So he took the messengers from Babylon on a tour of the palace. He showed them his treasure house full of silver, gold, spices, and perfumes. He took them into his jewel rooms too. He opened to them all his treasures. He showed them everything.

³Then Isaiah the prophet came to the king. He said, "What did they say? Where are they from?"

"From far away in Babylon," Hezekiah replied.

⁴"How much have they seen?" asked Isaiah.

And Hezekiah replied, "I showed them all I own. I showed them all my priceless treasures."

⁵Then Isaiah gave him this message from the Lord:

⁶"The time is coming when all you

have will be carried off to Babylon. This includes all the treasures stored up by your fathers. Nothing will be left. [7]And some of your own sons will become slaves. Yes, they will be eunuchs in the palace of the king of Babylon."

[8]"All right," Hezekiah replied. "Whatever the Lord says is good. At least there will be peace during my lifetime!"

God Will Feed His Flock

40 "Comfort, yes, comfort my people," says your God. [2]"Speak tenderly to Jerusalem. Tell her that her sad days are gone. Tell her that her sins are forgiven. Let her know that I have punished her in full for all her sins."

[3]Listen! I hear the voice of someone shouting. It says, "Make a road for the Lord through the wilderness. Make him a straight, smooth road through the desert. [4]Fill the valleys. Level the hills. Straighten out the crooked paths. And smooth off the rough spots in the road. [5]The glory of the Lord will be seen by all mankind together." The Lord has spoken, and so it shall be.

[6]The voice says, "Shout!"

God's Word will never be destroyed

The grass dries up and the flowers fade. But the Word of our God shall stand forever.

Isaiah 40:8

"What shall I shout?" I asked.

"Shout that man is like the grass that dies away. All his beauty fades like dying flowers. [7]The grass dries up, the flower fades under the breath of God. And so it is with weak man. [8]The grass dries up and the flowers fade. But the Word of our God shall stand forever."

[9]O Crier of good news, shout to Jerusalem from the mountains! Shout louder, don't be afraid! Tell the cities of Judah, "Your God is coming!" [10]Yes, the Lord God is coming with mighty power. He will rule with awesome strength. See, his reward is with him. He will give to each just as he has done. [11]He will feed his flock like a shepherd. He will carry the lambs in his arms. And he will gently lead the mothers with their young.

[12]Who else has held the oceans in his hands? Who else has measured off the heavens with his ruler? Who knows the weight of all the earth? Who weighs the mountains and the hills? [13]Who can advise the Spirit of the Lord? Or who can be his teacher or give him counsel? [14]Has he ever needed anyone's advice? Did he need instruction as to what is right and best? [15]No, for all the peoples of the world are nothing compared with him. They are but a drop in the bucket. They are just specks of dust on the scales. He picks up the islands as though they had no weight at all. [16]Lebanon's forests don't have enough wood to burn a sacrifice big enough to honor him. All of Lebanon's animals aren't enough to offer to our God. [17]All the nations are like nothing to him. In his eyes they are less than nothing. They are just emptiness and foam.

[18]How can we describe God? With what can we compare him? [19]Can we compare him to an idol? Is he like an idol made from a mold, overlaid with gold? Is he like an idol with silver chains around its neck? [20]The poor may not be able to buy expensive gods like that. But they find a tree free from rot. Then they pay someone to carve a face on it. And that's their god. It is a god that cannot even move!

[21]Are you so ignorant? Are you so deaf to the words of God—the words he gave before the world began? Have you never heard nor understood? [22]It is God who sits above the circle of the earth. (The people below must seem to him like grasshoppers!) He is the one who stretches out the heavens like a curtain and makes his tent from them. [23]He dooms the great men of the world and brings them all to naught. [24]They hardly get started, barely take root, when he blows on them and their work withers, and the wind carries them off like straw.

[25]"With whom will you compare me? Who is my equal?" asks the Holy One. [26]Look up into the heavens! Who created all these stars? As a shepherd leads his sheep, calling each by its pet name, and counts them to see that none are

lost or strayed, so God does with stars and planets!

²⁷O Jacob, O Israel, how can you say that the Lord doesn't see your troubles and isn't being fair? ²⁸Don't you yet understand? Don't you know by now that the everlasting God, the Creator of the farthest parts of the earth, never grows faint or weary? No one can fathom the depths of his understanding. ²⁹He gives power to the tired and worn out. He gives strength to the weak. ³⁰Even the youths shall be exhausted, and the young men will all give up. ³¹But they that wait upon the Lord shall renew their strength. They shall mount up with wings like eagles. They shall run and not be weary. They shall walk and not faint.

Don't Be Afraid, Israel!

41 "Listen in silence before me, O lands beyond the sea. Bring your strongest arguments. Come now and speak. The court is ready for your case.

²"Who has stirred up this one from the east? Victory meets him at every step! Who, indeed, but the Lord? God has given him victory over many nations. He has let him trample kings underfoot. He has allowed him to put whole armies to the sword. ³He chases them away and goes on safely, though the paths he treads are new. ⁴Who has done such mighty deeds? Who directs the affairs of mankind as they march by? It is I, the Lord. I am the First and Last. I alone am he."

⁵The lands beyond the sea watch in fear. They wait for word of Cyrus's new campaigns. Remote lands shake and get ready for war. ⁶⁻⁷The craftsmen rush to make new idols to protect them. The carver hurries the goldsmith. And the molder helps at the anvil. "Good," they say. "It's coming along fine. Now we can solder on the arms." Carefully they join the parts together. Then they tie the thing in place so it won't fall over!

⁸"But as for you, O Israel, you are mine. You are my chosen ones. For you are Abraham's family, and he was my friend. ⁹I have called you back from the ends of the earth. I told you that you had

to serve me alone. For I have chosen you and will not throw you away. ¹⁰Don't be afraid, for I am with you. Do not be dismayed, for I am your God. I will strengthen you. I will help you. I will uphold you with my strong right hand.

¹¹"See, all your angry enemies lie confused and broken. Anyone who stands against you will die. ¹²You will look for your enemies, but you won't find them. ¹³I am holding you by your right hand. It is I, the Lord your God. And I tell you not to be afraid. I am here to help you. ¹⁴Even though you are hated, don't be afraid, O Israel. For I will help you. I am the Lord, your Redeemer. I am the Holy One of Israel. ¹⁵You shall be a new and sharp threshing tool. You will tear all your enemies apart. You will make chaff out of mountains. ¹⁶You shall throw them into the air. And the wind shall blow them all away. Whirlwinds shall scatter them. And the joy of the Lord shall fill you. You shall glory in the God of Israel.

God helps tired and weak people

He gives power to the tired and worn out. He gives strength to the weak.

Isaiah 40:29

---

¹⁷"The poor and needy look for water and find none. Their tongues are dry from thirst. But I will answer when they cry to me. I, Israel's God, will not ever leave them. ¹⁸I will open up rivers for them on high plateaus! I will give them fountains of water in the valleys! In the deserts will be pools of water. Rivers fed by springs shall flow across the dry ground. ¹⁹I will plant trees on dry, empty land. There will be cedars, myrtle, olive trees, the cypress, fir, and pine. ²⁰Everyone will see this miracle. And they will know that it is God who did it, Israel's Holy One.

²¹"Can your idols make such claims as these? Let them come and show what they can do! God, the King of Israel, says all this. ²²Let them try to tell us what happened in years gone by. Let them tell us what will happen in the future. ²³Yes,

that's it! If you are gods, tell what will happen in the days ahead! Or do some mighty miracle that will amaze us. 24But no! You are less than nothing. You can do nothing at all. Anyone who chooses you needs to have his head examined!

25"But I have stirred up Cyrus from the north and east. He will come against the nations and call on my name. And I will give him victory over kings and princes. He will walk on them as a potter tramples clay.

26"Who but I have told you this would happen? Who else predicted this, making you admit that he was right? No one else! None other said one word! 27I was the first to tell Jerusalem, 'Look! Look! Help is on the way!' 28Not one of your idols told you this. Not one gave any answer when I asked. 29See, they are all foolish, worthless things. Your idols are all as empty as the wind.

God's Chosen One

42 "See my servant, whom I uphold. He is my Chosen One, and I delight in him. I have put my Spirit upon him. And he will show justice to the nations of the world. 2He will be gentle. He will not shout or argue in the streets. 3He will not break the bruised reed. He will not put out the dimly burning flame. He will help the faint of heart. He will strengthen those tempted to despair. He will see full justice given to all who have been wronged. 4He won't be content until truth and goodness rule the earth. He won't rest until even distant lands have put their trust in him."

5The Lord God made the heavens and stretched them out. He made the earth and everything in it. He gives life and breath and spirit to everyone in all the world. He is the one who says to his Servant,

6"I the Lord have called you to show what it means to be righteous. I will guard and support you. For I have given you to my people. You are the personal proof of my agreement with them. You shall also be a light to guide the nations to me. 7You will open the eyes of the blind. You will set free those who sit in prison darkness. 8I am the Lord! That is my name. And I will not give my glory to anyone else. I will not share my praise with carved idols. 9Everything I have said has come true. And now I will speak again. I will tell you the future before it happens."

10Sing a new song to the Lord. Sing his praises, all you who live on the earth! Sing, O sea! Sing, all you who live in distant lands beyond the sea! 11Join in the chorus, you desert cities of Kedar and Sela! And you, too, dwellers in the mountains. 12Let the western coastlands glorify the Lord. Let them sing of his mighty power.

13The Lord will be a mighty warrior, full of anger toward his enemies. He will give a great shout and will surely win. 14He has been silent for a long time. He has held himself back. But now he will let his anger go. He will groan and cry like a woman delivering her child. 15He will level the mountains and hills and destroy their greenery. He will dry up the rivers and pools. 16He will bring blind Israel along a path they have not seen before. He will make the darkness bright before them. He will smooth and straighten out the road ahead. He will not leave them. 17But those who trust in idols and call them gods will be greatly disappointed. They will be turned away.

People Who Can't See God

18Oh, how blind and deaf you are toward God! Why won't you listen? Why won't you see? 19Who in all the world is as blind as my own people? And they are supposed to be my messengers of truth! Who is so blind as my "dedicated one," the "servant of the Lord"? 20You see and understand what is right. But you won't listen to it or do it. You hear, but you won't obey.

21The Lord has magnified his law and made it truly great. Through it he had planned to show the world that he is righteous. 22But what a sight his people are! And they were supposed to show the world the glory of his law. They are robbed, enslaved, imprisoned, and trapped. They are fair game for all, with no one to help them. ²³Won't even one of you learn these lessons from the past? Won't any of you see the ruin that waits for you up ahead? ²⁴Who let Israel be robbed and hurt? Did not the Lord? It is the Lord they sinned against. For they would not go where he sent them. They would not listen to his laws. ²⁵That is why God poured out such anger on his people. That is why he destroyed them in battle. They have been set on fire and burned. But still they don't see the reason why. They don't see that it is God who does this. They don't understand that he wants them to repent.

No Other Savior

43 But now the Lord who made you, O Israel, is speaking up. He says, "Don't be afraid, for I have bought you from sin and slavery. I have called you by name. You are mine. ²You might go through deep waters and great trouble. But I will be with you. You might go through rivers of hardship. But I won't let you drown! You might walk through the fire of oppression. But you will not be burned up. The flames will not consume you. ³For I am the Lord your God, your Savior. I am the Holy One of Israel. I gave Egypt and Ethiopia and Seba to Cyrus in exchange for your freedom. I gave them to buy you back. ⁴Others died that you might live. I traded their lives for yours. This is because you are precious to me. You are honored, and I love you.

⁵"Don't be afraid, for I am with you. I will gather you from east and west. ⁶I will bring you from north and south. I will bring my sons and daughters back to Israel from the farthest corners of the earth. ⁷All who claim me as their God will come. For I have made them for my glory. I created them! ⁸Bring them back to me. Bring those who have eyes but are blind and those who have ears but are deaf."

⁹Gather the nations together! Which of all their idols ever has foretold such things? Which can predict a single day ahead? Where are the witnesses of anything they said? They might have no witnesses. But if so, they must confess that only God can prophesy.

¹⁰"But I have witnesses, O Israel!" says the Lord. "You are my witnesses and my servants. I chose you to know and to believe me. I chose you to understand that I alone am God. There is no other God. There never was and never will be. ¹¹I am the Lord, and there is no other Savior. ¹²Whenever you have thrown away your idols, I have shown you my power. With one word I have saved you. You have seen me do it. You are my witnesses that it is true. ¹³From eternity to eternity I am God. No one can stand in the way of what I do."

God Forgets the Sins of His People

¹⁴The Lord, your Redeemer, the Holy One of Israel, says:

"For your sakes I will send an army against Babylon. It will walk in, almost untouched. The boasts of the Babylonians will turn to cries of fear. ¹⁵I am the Lord, your Holy One. I am Israel's Creator and King. ¹⁶I am the Lord, who opened a way through the waters. I made a path right through the sea. ¹⁷I called forth the mighty army of Egypt with all its chariots and horses. And now they lie under the waves, dead. Their lives are snuffed out like candlewicks.

God is with us

Don't be afraid,
for I am with you.

Isaiah 43:5

---

¹⁸"But forget all that. It is nothing compared to what I'm going to do! ¹⁹For I'm going to do a brand new thing. See, I have already begun! Don't you see it? I will make a road through the wilderness of the world. On it, my people will travel home. And I will create rivers for them in the desert! ²⁰The wild animals in the fields will thank me, the jackals and ostriches too. They will thank me for giving them water in the wilderness. Yes, there will be springs in the desert. That way my people, my chosen ones, can be

refreshed. ²¹I have made Israel for myself. And these my people will someday honor me before the world.

²²"But O my people, you won't ask for my help. You have grown tired of me! ²³You have not brought me the lambs for burnt offerings. You have not honored me with sacrifices. Yet my requests for offerings and incense have been very few! I have not treated you as slaves. ²⁴You have brought me no sweet-smelling incense. And you have not pleased me with the sacrificial fat. No, you have only given me your sins. You have made me tired with all your faults.

²⁵"I, yes, I alone am the one who cleans away your sins. I do it for my own sake. And I will never think of them again once I've done it. ²⁶Oh, remind me of this promise of forgiveness. For we must talk about your sins. Plead your case before me. Ask me to forgive you. ²⁷From the very first your ancestors sinned against me. All your forebears sinned against my law. ²⁸That is why I have put down your priests and destroyed Israel. That is why I have left her to shame.

Idols Are False Gods

44 Listen to me, O my servant Israel. Listen, O my chosen ones.

²The Lord made you and will help you. He says, "O servant of mine, don't be afraid. O Jerusalem, my chosen ones, don't be afraid. ³For I will give you plenty of water for your thirst. I will water your dry fields. And I will pour out my Spirit and my blessings on your children. ⁴They shall thrive like watered grass. They will be like willows on a riverbank. ⁵'I am the Lord's,' they'll proudly say. 'I am from Israel,' they will brag. Then they'll write the name of God on their hands."

⁶The Lord says, "I am Israel's Redeemer, the Lord Almighty. I am the First and the Last. There is no other God. ⁷Who else can tell you what is going to happen in the days ahead? Let them tell you if they can and prove their power. Let them do as I have done since ancient times. ⁸Don't be afraid. Haven't I said from ages past that I would save you?

You are my witnesses. Is there any other God? No! None that I know about! There is no other Rock!"

⁹What fools they are who manufacture idols for their gods. Their hopes will never be answered. They themselves are witnesses that this is so. For their idols neither see nor know. No wonder those who worship them are so ashamed. ¹⁰Who but a fool would make his own god? Who would make an idol that can't help him a bit? ¹¹All who worship these will stand before the Lord in shame. They will stand there along with all these carpenters. They are just men, but they claim to have made a god. Together they will stand in terror. ¹²The metal-smith stands at his forge to make an axe. He pounds on it with all his might. He grows hungry and thirsty, weak and faint. ¹³Then the woodcarver takes the axe and uses it to make an idol. He measures and marks out a block of wood. And he carves the figure of a man. Now he has a wonderful idol that can't so much as move from where it is placed. ¹⁴He cuts down cedars. He chooses the cypress and the oak. He plants the ash in the forest to be nourished by the rain. ¹⁵And after his care, he uses part of the wood to make a fire. He uses it to warm himself and to bake his bread. And then he takes the rest of it and makes himself a god. He actually makes a god for men to worship! An idol to fall down before and praise! ¹⁶Part of the tree he burns to roast his meat. He uses it to keep him warm and fed and well content. ¹⁷And with what's left he makes his god, a carved idol! He falls down before it and worships it and prays to it. "Deliver me," he says. "You are my god!"

¹⁸How stupid and foolish! God has shut their eyes so that they cannot see. He has closed their minds from understanding. ¹⁹The man never stops to think. He never says, "Why, it's just a block of wood! I've burned it for heat. I've used it to bake my bread and roast my meat. How can the rest of it be a god? Should I fall down before a chunk of wood?" ²⁰The poor fool feeds on ashes. He is trusting what can never give him any help at all. Yet he cannot bring

himself to ask, "Is this thing a lie? Is this idol that I'm holding in my hand not a real god?"

21"Listen, Israel, for you are my servant. I made you, and I will not forget to help you. 22I've cleaned away your sins. They are gone like morning mist at noon! Oh, come back to me, for I have paid the price to set you free."

23Sing, O heavens, for the Lord has done this great thing. Shout, O earth! Break forth into song, O mountains and forests. Sing out, yes, every tree! For the Lord has rescued Jacob. And he is glorified in Israel. 24The Lord, your Redeemer made you. And he says, "All things were made by me. I alone stretched out the heavens. By myself I made the earth and everything in it.

25"I am the one who shows what liars all false prophets are. I cause something else to happen than the things they say. I make wise men give opposite advice to what they should. I do this to show they are fools. 26But what my prophets say will happen, I cause to happen. When they say Jerusalem will be saved, it shall be done. When they say the cities of Judah will be full once again, it will happen! 27When I speak to the rivers and say, 'Be dry!' they shall be dry. 28When I say of Cyrus, 'He is my shepherd,' he will certainly do as I say. And Jerusalem will be rebuilt and the Temple restored, for I have spoken it."

The One, True God

45 This is the Lord's message to Cyrus, God's anointed. I have chosen him to conquer many lands. God shall give his right hand great power. And he shall crush the strength of mighty kings. God shall open the gates of Babylon to him. The gates shall not be shut against him any more. 2"I shall go before you, Cyrus. I shall level the mountains. I shall smash down the city gates of brass and iron bars. 3And I shall give you treasures hidden in the darkness, secret riches. And you will know that I am doing this. I am the Lord, the God of Israel. I am the one who calls you by your name.

4"And why have I chosen you for this work? I have done it for the sake of Jacob. He is my servant, Israel, my chosen one. I called you by name when you didn't know me. 5I am the Lord. There is no other God. I will make you strong and send you out to victory. I will do this even though you don't know me. 6All the world from east to west will know there is no other God. I am the Lord and there is no one else. I alone am God. 7I form the light and make the dark. I send good times and bad. I, the Lord, am the one who does these things. 8Open up, O heavens. Let the skies pour out their goodness. Let salvation and goodness sprout up together from the earth. I, the Lord, created them.

Making Idols

ISAIAH 44:9-20

God made the world. He made the sun, moon, and stars. The Bible tells us so. But did you make God? Of course not! Some Bible-time people tried to make their own gods. Isaiah tells how they did it. They made their own axe. Then they cut down a tree with this axe. They carved a figure from a block of wood from this tree. They burned the scraps of wood. They prayed to this block of wood. Why did they pray to this part of the wood? Why didn't they pray to the scraps they burned? Would you want to pray to something you made? Or would you rather pray to the God who made you? Which do you think could help you more?

9"How terrible it will be for the man who fights with his Creator. Does the pot argue with its maker? Does the clay argue with the one who shapes it? Does it say, 'Stop, you're doing it wrong!' Or does the pot say, 'How clumsy can you be!'? 10Does the baby just being born turn to his father and mother and say, 'Why have you produced me? Can't you do anything right at all?'"

11The Lord, the Holy One of Israel, says: "What right have you to question what I do? Who are you to command me concerning the work of my hands? 12I have made the earth and created man upon it. With my hands I have stretched out the heavens. And I made all the millions of stars. 13I have raised up Cyrus to fulfill my righteous purpose. And I will direct all his paths. He shall restore my city and free my captive people. And he won't even do it for a reward!"

14The Lord says: "The Egyptians, Ethiopians, and Sabeans shall be subject to you. They shall come to you with all their products. And all of them shall be yours. They shall follow you as prisoners in chains. They shall fall down on their knees before you. And they shall say, 'The only God there is, is your God!'"

15Truly, O God of Israel, Savior, you work in strange, mysterious ways. 16All who worship idols shall be ashamed. 17But Israel shall be saved by the Lord with eternal salvation. They shall never be let down by their God through all eternity. 18For the Lord made the heavens and earth. And he put everything in place. He made the world to be lived in, not to be an empty chaos. "I am the Lord," he says. "And there is no other! 19I make big promises in public. I do not whisper them in some dark corner so no one can know what I mean. And I didn't tell Israel to ask me for what I didn't plan to give! No, for I, the Lord, speak only the truth.

20"Gather together and come, you nations that escape from Cyrus's hand. What fools they are who carry around the wooden idols. How foolish to pray to gods that cannot save! 21Talk together and argue your case. Prove to me that worshiping idols pays! Who but God has

said that these things about Cyrus would come true? What idol ever told you these things would happen? For there is no other God but me, no, not one! I am a just God and a Savior. 22Let all the world look to me for salvation! For I am God. There is no other. 23I have sworn that every knee in the world shall bow to me. And every tongue will swear to obey me. And I will not go back on my word, for it is true.

24"In the Lord is all my righteousness and strength," the people shall say. And all who were angry with him shall come to him and be ashamed. 25But with the Lord's help, all the people of Israel shall be made good. And they will praise his name.

Who Can Compare to God?

46 The idols of Babylon, Bel and Nebo, are being hauled away on ox carts! But look! The beasts are stumbling! The cart is turning over! The gods are falling out onto the ground! Is that the best that they can do? They cannot even save themselves from such a fall! How can they save their worshipers from Cyrus?

3"Listen to me, all Israel who are left. I have created you and cared for you since you were born. 4I will be your God through all your lifetime. Yes, I will be with you even when your hair is white with age. I made you and I will care for you. I will carry you along and will be your Savior.

5"With what in all of Heaven and earth do I compare? Whom can you find who is as great as I am? 6Will you compare me with an idol made with silver and gold? They hire a goldsmith to take your riches and make a god from it! Then they fall down and worship it! 7They carry it around on their shoulders. And when they set it down, it stays there. It can't even move! And when someone prays to it, there is no answer. For it cannot get him out of his trouble.

8"Don't forget this, O guilty ones. 9And don't forget the many times I clearly told you what was going to happen in the future. For I am God, I only. And there is no other like me. 10For I can tell you what is going to happen. All I say will come to pass, for I do whatever I wish. ¹¹I will call that swift bird of prey from the east. I will call that man Cyrus from far away. And he will come and do my bidding. I have said I would do it, and I will. ¹²Listen to me, you stubborn, evil men! ¹³For I am offering to save you. This is not in the distant future, but right now! I am ready to save you, and I will restore Jerusalem and Israel, who is my glory.

God's Revenge

47 "O Babylon, the unconquered, come sit in the dust. For your days of glory, pride, and honor are ended. O Babylon, never again will you be the lovely princess, tender and pretty. ²Take heavy millstones and grind the corn. Take off your veil. Strip off your robe. Show yourself to the public. ³You shall be naked and full of shame. I will take vengeance upon you and will not let up."

⁴So speaks our Redeemer, who will save Israel from Babylon's mighty power. The Lord Almighty is his name. He is the Holy One of Israel.

⁵"Sit in darkness and silence, O Babylon. Never again will you be called 'The Queen of Kingdoms.' ⁶For I was angry with my people Israel. So I punished them a little by letting them fall into your hands, O Babylon. But you showed them no mercy. You have made even the old folks carry heavy burdens. ⁷You thought your reign would never end, Queen Kingdom of the world. You didn't care a bit about my people. And you didn't think about what might happen to those who do them harm.

⁸"You are a kingdom mad with pleasure, living at ease. You brag that you are the greatest in the world. Listen to the sentence of my court upon your sins. You say, 'I alone am God! I'll never be a widow. I'll never lose my children.' ⁹Well, those things shall come upon you in one moment. You shall become a widow in one day. And you shall lose your children despite all your magic.

¹⁰"You felt safe in all your wickedness. 'No one sees me,' you said. Your 'wisdom' and 'knowledge' have caused you to turn away from me. And now you claim that you yourself are the Lord! ¹¹That is why trouble shall overtake you suddenly. It will come so fast that you won't know where it comes from. And there will be no way then to clean away your sins.

??????????????????????????????????
Which great world power will never again be called "The Queen of Kingdoms"?
(Read 47:5 for the answer.)
??????????????????????????????????

¹²"Call out the demons you've worshiped all these years. Call on them to help you strike deep terror into many hearts again. ¹³You have advisors by the ton. They try to tell you what the future holds. ¹⁴But they are as useless as dried grass burning in the fire. They cannot even save themselves! You'll get no help from them at all. Theirs is no fire to sit beside to make you warm! ¹⁵And all your friends of childhood days shall slip away and disappear. They won't be able to help you either.

No Peace for the Wicked

48 "Hear me, my people! You promise to follow the Lord without meaning a word of it. Then you boast of living in the Holy City. And you brag about depending on the God of Israel. ³Time and again I told you what was going to happen in the future. My words were scarcely spoken when I did just what I said. ⁴I knew how hard and stubborn you are. Your necks are as unbending as iron. Your heads are as hard as brass. ⁵That is why I told you ahead of time what I was going to do. That way you could never say, 'My idol did it. My carved image commanded it to happen!' ⁶You have heard what I said would happen and you have seen it fulfilled. But you refuse to agree it is so. Now I will tell you new things I haven't said before. I will tell you secrets you haven't heard.

⁷"Then you can't say, 'We knew that all the time!'

⁸"Yes, I'll tell you new things. For I know so well what traitors you are. You have been rebels from early childhood. You are rotten through and through. ⁹But for my own sake, I will hold back my anger. For the honor of my name, I will not wipe you out. ¹⁰I refined you in the furnace of suffering. But I found no silver there. You are worthless, with nothing good in you at all. ¹¹Yet for my own sake I will save you from my anger. I will not destroy you. For if I did, the heathen would claim their gods had conquered me. I will not let them have my glory.

¹²"Listen to me, my people, my chosen ones! I alone am God. I am the First. I am the Last. ¹³It was my hand that laid the foundations of the earth. The palm of my right hand spread out the heavens above. I spoke and they came into being.

¹⁴"Come, all of you, and listen. Among all your idols, which one has ever told you this: 'The Lord loves Cyrus. He will use him to put an end to the empire of Babylonia. He will conquer the armies of the Chaldeans'? ¹⁵But I am saying it. I have called Cyrus. I have sent him on this errand. And I will make him succeed.

¹⁶"Come closer and listen. I have always told you plainly what would happen. I have told you clearly so that you could understand." And now the Lord God and his Spirit have sent me with this message:

¹⁷"I am the Lord, your Redeemer. I am the Holy One of Israel. I am the one who punishes you for your own good. I lead you along the paths that you should follow.

¹⁸"Oh, that you had listened to my laws! Then you would have had peace flowing like a gentle river. And great waves of righteousness would have poured from you. ¹⁹Then you would have become as numerous as the sands along the seashores of the world. There would have been too many to count. And there would have been no need for your destruction."

²⁰Yet even now, be free from your captivity! Leave Babylon, singing as you go. Shout to the ends of the earth! Tell everyone that the Lord has bought back his servants. ²¹They were not thirsty when he led them through the deserts. He divided the rock, and water gushed out for them to drink.

²²"But there is no peace for the wicked," says the Lord.

A Light for the World

49 Listen to me, all of you in far-off lands. The Lord called me before my birth. From within the womb he called me by my name. ²God will make my words of judgment sharp as swords. He has hidden me in the shadow of his hand. I am like a sharp arrow in his quiver.

³He said to me: "You are my servant. You are Israel, and you shall bring me glory."

⁴I replied, "But my work for them seems useless. I have spent my strength for them, but they have not listened. Yet I leave it all with God for my reward."

⁵The Lord formed me from my mother's womb to serve him. He called me to restore to him his people Israel. He has given me the strength to perform this work. And he has honored me for doing it! ⁶He says, "You shall do more than restore Israel to me. I will make you a Light to the nations of the world. You will bring my salvation to them too."

⁷The Lord is the one who saves you. He is the Holy One of Israel. He speaks to the one who is hated and rejected by mankind. He speaks to the one who is held under the heel of the world's rulers. He says, "Kings shall stand up when you pass by. Princes shall bow low because the Lord has chosen you. He is the faithful Lord. He is the Holy One of Israel. And it is he who chooses you."

Comfort for God's People

⁸⁻⁹The Lord says, "Your prayer has come at a good time. I will keep you from harm. I will give you as a token and pledge to Israel. You are proof that I will reestablish the land of Israel. You are proof that I will give it to its own people again. Through you I am saying to the prisoners of darkness, 'Come out! I am giving you your freedom!' They will be

my sheep, grazing in green pastures and on the grassy hills. ¹⁰They shall neither hunger nor thirst. The hot sun and dry desert winds will not reach them any more. For the Lord in his mercy will lead them beside the cool waters. ¹¹And I will make my mountains into level paths for them. The highways shall be raised above the valleys. ¹²See, my people shall come back from far away. They shall come from north and west and south."

¹³Sing for joy, O heavens! Shout, O earth! Break forth with song, O mountains! For the Lord has comforted his people. And he will have mercy on them in their sadness.

¹⁴Yet they say, "The Lord left us. He has forgotten us."

¹⁵"Never! Can a mother forget her little child? Can she forget her love for her own son? Yet even if that should be, I will not forget you. ¹⁶See, I have written your name upon my palm. And here in front of me is a picture of Jerusalem's walls in ruins. ¹⁷Soon your rebuilders shall come and chase away those destroying you. ¹⁸Look and see, for the Lord has promised that all your enemies shall come and be your slaves. They will be like jewels to display. They will be like bridal ornaments.

¹⁹"Even the most desolate parts of your empty land shall soon be crowded with your people. And the enemies who made you their slaves shall be far away. ²⁰The generations born in exile shall come back. They shall say, 'We need more room! It's crowded here!' ²¹Then you will think to yourself, 'Who has given me all these? For most of my children were killed. And the rest were carried away into exile, leaving me here alone. Who bore these? Who raised them for me?'"

²²The Lord God says, "See, I will give a signal to the Gentiles. And they shall carry your little sons back to you in their arms. They shall carry your daughters on their shoulders. ²³Kings and queens shall serve you. They shall care for all your needs. They shall bow to the earth before you. They shall lick the dust from off your feet. Then you shall know I am

Don't Borrow Here!
ISAIAH 50:1

Have you ever borrowed something? What was it? You returned it when you promised, didn't you? Sometimes moms and dads borrow money. They need extra money to buy a house or a car. Many people have always had debts, even in Bible times. Some rates of interest then were very high, from 20 percent to 50 percent. The prophets said it was wrong to charge high rates of interest. Israelites were told not to charge fellow Israelites any interest. But many people did not listen. They charged high interest anyway. People who could not pay their debts were in big trouble. Sometimes they were thrown into prison until they could pay. And prisoners were often bound in stocks, like in the picture. But since they could not earn money in prison to pay their debt, they often stayed there. Sometimes a son, daughter, or slave had to work off the debt. That usually meant they became slaves, since it took so long to pay off the debt. If you lived in Bible times, it was a good idea not to borrow money. It's a good idea to be careful what you borrow even today!

the Lord. Those who wait for me shall never be ashamed."

24Who can steal the prey from the hands of a mighty man? Who can demand that a tyrant let his captives go? 25But the Lord says, "Even the captives of the most mighty shall all be freed. For I will fight those who fight you. And I will save your children. 26I will feed your enemies with their own flesh. And they shall be drunk with rivers of their own blood. All the world shall know that I, the Lord, am your Savior and Redeemer. I am the Mighty One of Israel."

God's Servant Obeys

50 The Lord asks, "Did I sell you to my creditors? Is that why you aren't here? Or is your mother gone because I divorced her and sent her away? No, you went away as captives because of your sins. And your mother, too, was taken in payment for your sins. 2Was I too weak to save you? Is that why the house is silent and empty when I come home? Do I no longer have the power to save? No, that is not the reason! For I can rebuke the sea and make it dry! I can turn the rivers into deserts, covered with dying fish. 3I am the one who sends the darkness out across the skies."

4The Lord God has given me his words of wisdom. He does this so I will know what I should say to all these tired ones. Morning by morning he wakens me. He opens my understanding to his will. 5The Lord God has spoken to me. And I have listened. I do not rebel or turn away. 6I give my back to the whip. I turn my cheeks to those who pull out the beard. I do not hide from shame. They spit in my face.

7Because the Lord God helps me, I will not be sad. Therefore, I have set my face like flint to do his will. And I know that I will triumph. 8He who gives me justice is near. Who will dare to fight against me now? Where are my enemies? Let them appear! 9See, the Lord God is for me! Who shall declare me guilty? All my enemies shall be destroyed. They will be like old clothes eaten up by moths!

10Who among you fears the Lord and obeys his Servant? If such men walk in darkness, let them trust in the Lord. If they live without one ray of light, let them rest in their God. 11But see here, you who live in your own light. You warm yourselves by your own fires and not by God's. You will live among many sorrows.

The People Must Fear God

51 "Listen to me, all who hope to be saved! Listen, all of you who seek the Lord! Consider the quarry from which you were mined. Think about the rock from which you were cut! Yes, think about your ancestors Abraham and Sarah, from whom you came. You worry about being so small and few. But Abraham was only *one* when I called him. But when I blessed him, he became a great nation." 3And the Lord will bless Israel again. He will make her deserts blossom. Her dry desert will become as beautiful as the Garden of Eden. Joy and gladness will be found there. There will be many thanks and lovely songs.

4Listen to me, my people! Listen, O Israel! For I will see that right wins in the end. 5My mercy and justice are coming soon. Your salvation is on the way. I will rule the nations. They shall wait for me and wish for me to come. 6Look high in the skies and watch the earth under them. For the skies shall disappear like smoke. The earth shall wear out like a piece of clothing. And the people of the earth shall die like flies. But my salvation lasts forever. My righteous rule will never die. It will never end.

7"Listen to me, you who know right from wrong. Listen, all who love my laws in your hearts. Don't be afraid of people's scorn or their lies about you. 8For the moth shall destroy them like clothing. The worm shall eat them like wool. But my justice and mercy shall last forever. And my salvation shall reach to every generation."

9Wake up, O Lord! Rise up and robe yourself with strength. Rouse yourself as in the days of old when you judged Egypt, the dragon of the Nile. 10Are you not the same today? Are you not the mighty God who dried up the sea? Are you not the one who made a path right through it for your people? ¹¹The time will come when God's people will all come home again. They shall come with singing to Jerusalem. They shall come, filled with joy and gladness. Sadness and crying will all disappear.

¹²"I, even I, am he who comforts you. I am the one who gives you all this joy. So what right have you to be afraid of mortal men? They dry up like the grass and disappear! ¹³And yet you have no fear of God, your Maker. You have forgotten him! He is the one who spread the stars in the skies and made the earth. Will you be in constant fear of men's oppression? Will you fear their anger all day long? ¹⁴Soon, soon all you slaves shall be let go. Prisons, hunger, and death are not in your future. ¹⁵For I am the Lord your God. I am the Lord Almighty. I dried a path for you right through the sea, between the roaring waves. ¹⁶And I have put my words in your mouth and hidden you safe within my hand. I planted the stars in place and molded the earth. I am the one who says to Israel, 'You are mine.'"

¹⁷Wake up, wake up, Jerusalem! You have drunk enough from the cup of God's anger. You have drunk to the dregs the cup of terror. You have squeezed out the last drops. ¹⁸Not one of her sons is left alive to help or tell her what to do. ¹⁹These two things have been your lot: ruin and destruction. Yes, famine and the sword. And who is left to feel sorry for you? Who is left to comfort you? ²⁰For your sons have fainted and lie in the streets. They are helpless like wild goats caught in a net. The Lord has poured out his anger and rebuke upon them. ²¹But listen now to this, suffering ones. Listen, you who are full of troubles. ²²The Lord speaks to you. He is the Lord your God who cares for his people. "See, I take from your hands the terrible cup," he says. "You shall drink no more of my anger. It is gone at last. ²³But I will put that terrible cup into the hands of those who hurt you. I will punish those who trampled your souls in the dust. I will hurt those who walked on your backs."

God Will Bring His People Home

52 Wake up, wake up, Jerusalem! Dress yourselves with strength from God. Put on your beautiful clothes, O Jerusalem, Holy City. For those who turn from God will no longer enter your gates. ²Rise from the dust, Jerusalem. Take off the slave bands from your neck, O captive daughter. ³For the Lord says, "I sold you into exile. But I asked no fee from your oppressors. Now I can take you back again and owe them not a cent! ⁴My people were abused without cause by Egypt and Assyria. And I have saved them.

⁵"And now, what is this?" asks the Lord. "Why are my people slaves again? Why are they oppressed without excuse? Those who rule them shout in joy. And my name is laughed at every day. ⁶Therefore I will show my name to my people. And they shall know the power in that name. Then at last they will know that it is I who speak to them."

⁷How beautiful upon the mountains are the feet of those who bring good news. They carry the happy news of peace and salvation. This is the news that the God of Israel reigns. ⁸The watchmen shout and sing with joy. For they see the Lord God bringing his people home again. ⁹Let the ruins of Jerusalem break into joyous song. For the Lord has comforted his people. He has bought back Jerusalem. ¹⁰The Lord has bared his holy arm before the eyes of all the nations. The ends of the earth shall see the salvation of our God.

¹¹Go now, leave your bonds and slavery. Put Babylon and all it stands for far behind you. It is unclean to you. You are the holy people of the Lord. Make yourselves pure, all you who carry home the vessels of the Lord. ¹²You shall not leave in haste, running for your lives. For the Lord will go ahead of you. And he, the God of Israel, will protect you from behind.

Someone to Pay for Our Sins

¹³See, my Servant shall prosper. He shall be highly praised. ¹⁴⁻¹⁵Yet many shall be amazed when they see him. Yes, even far-off nations and their kings will see

him. They shall stand speechless in front of him. For they shall see and understand what they had not been told before. They shall see my Servant beaten and bloody. He will be so beaten up that one would hardly know it was a person. And so shall he make many nations clean.

53 But, oh, how few believe it! Who will listen? To whom will God reveal his saving power? ²In God's eyes he was like a tender green shoot. He was a sprout from a root in dry ground. But in our eyes there was no beauty at all. There was nothing to make us want him. ³We hated him and rejected him. He was a man of great sadness. And he knew the bitterest of grief. We turned our backs on him. We looked the other way when he went by. He was hated, and we didn't care.

⁴Yet it was *our* grief he carried. It was *our* sorrows that weighed him down. And we thought his troubles were a punishment from God for his *own* sins! ⁵But he was wounded and bruised for *our* sins. He was beaten that we might have peace. He was lashed, and we were healed! ⁶*We* have all strayed away like sheep! *We* left God's paths to follow our own. Yet God laid on *him* the guilt and sins of every one of us!

Look for God now!

Look for the Lord while you can find him. Call for him now while he is near.

Isaiah 55:6

---

⁷He was oppressed and he was abused, yet he never said a word. He was brought as a lamb to be killed. And he was quiet like a sheep before her shearers. He stood silent before the ones judging him. ⁸From prison and trial they led him away to his death. But who among the people of that day knew it was their sins that he was dying for? Who knew that he was suffering their punishment? ⁹He was buried like a criminal, but in a rich man's grave. But he had done no wrong and had never spoken an evil word.

¹⁰Yet it was the Lord's good plan to bruise him and fill him with grief. But his soul shall be made an offering for sin. And then he shall have many children and heirs. He shall live again. And God's plans shall succeed through him. ¹¹And he shall see all that has been done by the pain of his soul. Then he shall be happy. And by his experience, my righteous Servant shall make many clean before God. For he shall carry all their sins. ¹²Therefore, I will give him the honors of one who is great. This is because he has poured out his soul unto death. He was counted as a sinner. He carried the sins of many. And he prayed to God for sinners.

Everlasting Love

54 Sing, O childless woman! Break out into loud and joyful song, Jerusalem! For she was once left alone. But now she has more blessings than she whose husband stayed! ²Make your house bigger. Build on more rooms. Spread out your home! ³For you will soon be bursting at the seams! And your descendants will possess the cities left behind during the exile. They will rule the nations that took their lands.

⁴Don't be afraid! You won't live in shame any more. The shame of your youth and the sorrows of widowhood will be forgotten. ⁵For your Creator will be your "husband." The Lord Almighty is his name. He is your Redeemer, the Holy One of Israel. He is the God of all the earth. ⁶For the Lord has called you back from your sadness. He has come back to you, a young wife left by her husband. ⁷He says, "For a short time I left you. But with great love I will take you back. ⁸In a moment of anger I turned my face a little while. But with everlasting love I will have pity on you."

⁹"In the time of Noah I promised I would never again let a flood cover the earth. I promised I would never destroy all its life. So now I promise that I will never again pour out my anger on you. ¹⁰For the mountains may depart and the hills disappear. But my kindness shall not leave you. My promise of peace for you will never be broken," says the Lord who has mercy upon you.

¹¹"O my troubled people, I will rebuild you on a foundation of sapphires. I will make the walls of your houses from precious jewels. ¹²I will make your towers of sparkling agate. I will build your gates and walls of shining gems. ¹³And all your people shall be taught by me. And they shall prosper in all they do. ¹⁴You will live under a government that is just and fair. Your enemies will stay far away. You will live in peace. Terror shall not come near. ¹⁵If any nation comes to fight you, it will not be sent by me to punish you. Therefore, it will be chased away, for I am on your side. ¹⁶I have created the smith who blows the coals under the forge. He is the one who makes the weapons of war. And I have created the armies that destroy. ¹⁷But in that coming day, no weapon turned against you shall succeed. And you will have justice against every courtroom lie. This is the heritage of the servants of the Lord. This is the blessing I have given you," says the Lord.

A Promise of Joy and Peace

55 "Say there! Is anyone thirsty? Come and drink! Come even if you have no money! Come, take your choice of wine and milk. It's all free! ²Why spend your money on food that doesn't give you strength? Why pay for groceries that do you no good? Listen, and I'll tell you where to get good food that fills the soul!

³"Come to me with your ears wide open. Listen, for the life of your soul is at stake. I am ready to make an everlasting covenant with you. I want to give you all the unfailing love that I had for King David. ⁴He proved my power by conquering foreign nations. ⁵You also will command the nations. And they will come running to obey. They will not obey because of your own power or goodness. They will obey because I, the Lord your God, have given you glory."

⁶Look for the Lord while you can find him. Call for him now while he is near. ⁷Let men throw off their wicked deeds. Let them put out of their minds the very thought of doing wrong! Let them turn to the Lord that he may have mercy upon them. Let them turn to our God, for he will forgive! ⁸This plan of mine is not a plan you might work out. My thoughts are not the same as yours! ⁹For just as the heavens are higher than the earth, my ways are higher than yours. And my thoughts are higher than yours.

God's ways are higher than ours

For just as the heavens are higher than the earth, my ways are higher than yours. And my thoughts are higher than yours.

Isaiah 55:9

---

¹⁰"The rain and snow come down from Heaven. They stay on the ground to water the earth. They cause the grain to grow. And they make seed for the farmer and bread for the hungry. ¹¹It is the same with my Word. I send it out, and it always produces fruit. It shall do all I want it to. It will grow everywhere I plant it. ¹²You will live in joy and peace. The mountains and hills and the trees of the field will rejoice. All the world around you will be full of joy. ¹³Where once were thorns, fir trees will grow. Where briars grew, the myrtle trees will sprout up. This miracle will make the Lord's name very great. It will be an everlasting sign of God's power and love.

God Will Come to the Rescue

56 "Be just and fair to all," the Lord God says. "Do what's right and good, for I am coming soon to save you. ²Blessed is the man who does not work on my Sabbath days of rest. Happy is the man that honors those days. And blessed is the man who stops himself from doing wrong.

³"And my blessings are for Gentiles, too, when they accept the Lord. Don't let them think that they are just second-class. And this promise is for the eunuchs too. They can be as much mine as anyone. ⁴For I say this to the eunuchs who keep my Sabbaths holy. I say this

for those who do things that please me and obey my laws. ⁵I will give them a place in my house, within my walls. I will give them more honor than the honor of having sons and daughters. For the name that I will give them is an everlasting one. It will never disappear.

⁶"The Gentiles too will join the people of the Lord. They will serve him and love his name. The Lord will bless those who are his servants. He will include those who observe the Sabbath. And those who have accepted his covenant and promises will belong to him. ⁷I will also bring them to my holy mountain of Jerusalem. I will make them full of joy within my House of Prayer.

"I will accept their sacrifices and offerings. For my Temple shall be called 'A House of Prayer for All People'!" ⁸The Lord God brings back the outcasts of Israel. And he says, "I will bring others, too, besides my people Israel."

⁹Come, wild animals of the field. Come, tear apart the sheep. Come, wild animals of the forest, eat my people. ¹⁰For the leaders of my people are blind to every danger. And these are the Lord's watchmen, his shepherds! They are foolish and give no warning when danger comes. They love to lie there. They love to sleep, to dream. ¹¹And they are as greedy as dogs, never content. They are stupid shepherds who only look after their own interests. Each tries to get as much as he can for himself from every possible source.

¹²"Come," they say. "We'll get some wine and have a party. Let's all get drunk. This is really living. Let it go on and on, and tomorrow will be even better!"

A Reward for Those Who Love God

57 Many good men die. The godly often die before their time. And no one seems to care or wonder why. No one seems to know that God is taking them away from evil days ahead. ²For the godly who die shall rest in peace.

³"But you, come here, you witches' sons! Come, you children of prostitutes! ⁴Who do you laugh at? Who do you make faces at, sticking out your tongues? You children of sinners and liars! ⁵You worship your idols with great zeal. You bow to them under the shade of every tree. And you kill your children as human sacrifices down in the valleys. You do this under overhanging rocks. ⁶Your gods are the smooth stones in the valleys. You worship them, and they, not I, are your reward. Does all this make me happy? ⁷⁻⁸You have been unfaithful to me on the tops of the mountains. For you worship idols there. Behind closed doors you set your idols up. You worship these gods instead of me. This is like sleeping with someone you aren't married to! For you are giving these idols your love instead of loving me. ⁹You have taken incense and perfume to Molech as your gift. You have traveled far to find new gods to love. ¹⁰You grew tired in your search, but you never gave up. You made yourselves strong and went on. ¹¹Why were you more afraid of them than of me? How is it that you didn't give me a second thought? Is it because I've been too gentle that you have no fear of me?

¹²"Your 'righteousness' and your 'good works' will not save you. ¹³Let's see if all your idols can help you when you cry to them to save you! They are so weak that the wind can carry them off! A breath can puff them away. But he who trusts in me shall own the land and inherit my Holy Mountain. ¹⁴I will say, 'Rebuild the road! Clear away the rocks and stones. Build a highway for my people to come home from captivity.'"

¹⁵The Lord is great and lives forever. He is the Holy One. He says, "I live in a high and holy place. And there those with sad and humble spirits live with me. I give the humble new strength. And I give new courage to those with hearts that are sorry for their sins. ¹⁶For I will not fight against you forever. I won't always show my anger. If I did, all mankind would die. All of the same souls that I have made would soon be gone. ¹⁷I was angry and punished these greedy men. But they went right on sinning. They did whatever their evil heart wanted. ¹⁸I have seen what they do. But

I will heal them anyway! I will lead them and comfort them. I will help them to mourn and to confess their sins. ¹⁹Peace, peace to them, both near and far. For I will heal them all. ²⁰But those who still reject me are like the restless sea. It is never still but always churns up sludge and dirt. ²¹There is no peace for them!"

God Tells the People to Share

58 "Shout with the voice of a trumpet blast. Tell my people of their sins! ²Yet they act so holy and religious! They come to the Temple every day. They are so happy to hear the reading of my laws. They act just like they want to obey them! They act like they don't hate the commands of their God! How worried they are about doing their worship just right. Oh, how they love the Temple services!

³"'We have fasted before you,' they say. 'Why aren't you impressed? Why don't you see our sacrifices? Why don't you hear our prayers? We have given up so much for you, and you don't even notice it!' I'll tell you why! Because you are living in evil pleasure even while you are fasting. And you keep right on taking advantage of your workers. ⁴Look, what good is fasting when you keep on fighting and arguing? This kind of fasting will never get you anywhere with me. ⁵Is this what I want? Do I want you to do penance, bowing like reeds in the wind? Do I want you to put on sackcloth and cover yourselves with ashes? Is this what you call fasting?

⁶"No, the kind of fast I want is that you stop hurting those who work for you. I want you to treat them fairly and give them what they earn. ⁷I want you to share your food with the hungry. I want you to bring them right into your own homes! I want you to help those who are helpless, poor, and needy. Put clothes on those who are cold. And don't hide from relatives who need your help.

⁸"If you do these things, God will shed his light upon you. He will heal you. Your godliness will lead you forward. Goodness will be a shield before you. And the glory of the Lord will pro-

tect you from behind. ⁹Then, when you call, the Lord will answer you. 'Yes, I am here,' he will quickly reply. All you need to do is to stop taking advantage of the weak. And you must stop telling lies about people to get them in trouble!

¹⁰"Feed the hungry! Help those in trouble! Then your light will shine out from the darkness. And the darkness around you shall be as bright as day. ¹¹And the Lord will guide you and satisfy you with all good things. He will keep you healthy too. And you will be like a well-watered garden. You will be like a spring that never runs dry. ¹²Your sons will rebuild the empty ruins of your cities. And you will be known as 'The People Who Rebuild Their Walls and Cities.'

God gives us all we need

And the Lord will guide you and satisfy you with all good things.
Isaiah 58:11

---

¹³"You must keep the Sabbath holy. You must not just have your own fun. Don't just do your business on that day. But enjoy the Sabbath. Speak of it with joy as the Lord's holy day. Honor the Lord in what you do. Do not follow your own desires, and don't talk about foolish things. ¹⁴Then the Lord will be your joy. And I will make sure you get your full share of the blessings I promised to Jacob, your father." The Lord has spoken.

The Lord Tells His People to Obey

59 Listen now! The Lord isn't too weak to save you. And he isn't getting deaf! He can hear you when you call! ²But the trouble is that your sins have cut you off from God. Because of sin, he has turned his face away from you. And now he won't listen anymore. ³For your hands are those of murderers. And your fingers are dirty with sin. You lie and grumble and try to stop the good. ⁴No one cares about being fair and true. Your lawsuits are based on lies. You spend your time planning evil deeds and doing them. ⁵You spend your time and energy making evil plans that end up in deadly actions. ⁶You cheat and shortchange everyone. Everything you do is filled with sin. You are well known for your violence. ⁷Your feet run to do evil and rush to murder. Your thoughts are only of sinning. And wherever you go you leave behind a trail of sadness and death. ⁸You don't know what true peace is. And you don't know what it means to be just and good. You always do wrong, and those who follow you won't have any peace either.

⁹It is because of all this evil that you aren't finding God's blessings. That's why he doesn't punish those who hurt you. No wonder you are in darkness when you expected light. No wonder you are walking in the gloom. ¹⁰No wonder you grope like blind men and stumble along in broad daylight. Yes, you can't even see at brightest noontime. It seems to you like it is the darkest night! No wonder you are like dead bodies when compared with strong young men! ¹¹You roar like hungry bears. You moan with mournful cries like doves. You look for God to save you, but he doesn't. He has turned away. ¹²For your sins keep piling up before the righteous God. They stand and testify against you.

Yes, we know what sinners we are. ¹³We know that we always disobey. We have denied the Lord our God. We know what rebels we are and how unfair we are. For we carefully plan our lies. ¹⁴Our courts stand against the good man. We don't even know what fairness is! Truth falls dead in the streets, and justice is outlawed.

¹⁵Yes, truth is gone, and anyone who tries a better life is soon attacked. The Lord saw all the evil. And he was upset to find no steps taken against sin. ¹⁶He saw no one was helping you. And he was amazed that no one came to help. Therefore, he himself stepped in to save you. He did this through his mighty power and justice. ¹⁷He put on righteousness as a coat of armor and the helmet of salvation on his head. He dressed himself with robes of vengeance and godly anger. ¹⁸He will pay back his enemies for their evil deeds. He will turn his anger against enemies in distant lands. ¹⁹Then at last they will respect and glorify the name of God from west to east. For he will come like a flood tide driven by the Lord's breath. ²⁰He will come as a Redeemer to those in Zion who have turned away from sin.

²¹"As for me, this is my promise to them," says the Lord. "My Holy Spirit shall not leave them. And they shall want the good and hate the wrong. This will also be true for their children and grandchildren forever.

The Glory of the Lord

60 "Rise up, my people! Let your light shine for all the nations to see! For the glory of the Lord is streaming from you. ²Darkness as black as night shall cover all the peoples of the earth. But the glory of the Lord will shine from you. ³All nations will come to your light. Mighty kings will come to see the glory of the Lord upon you.

⁴"Lift up your eyes and see! For your sons and daughters are coming home to you from distant lands. ⁵Your eyes will shine with joy. Your hearts will be excited. For traders from around the world will come to you. They will bring you riches from many lands. ⁶Great herds of camels will travel to you. They will come from Midian and Sheba, and Ephah too. They will bring gold and incense to add to the praise of God. ⁷The flocks of Kedar shall be given to you. The rams of Nabaioth will be used on my altars. And I will glorify my Temple in that day.

⁸"And who are these who fly like a cloud to Israel? Who are those who are like doves going to their nests? ⁹I have set aside the ships of many lands, the very best. I will use them to bring the sons of Israel home again from far away. And they will bring their riches with them. For the Holy One of Israel is known around the world. And he has honored you in the eyes of all.

¹⁰"Foreigners will come and build your cities. Presidents and kings will send you help. For I once destroyed you in my anger. But then I will have mercy on you through my grace. ¹¹Your gates will stay wide open around the clock. They will take in the wealth of many

lands. The kings of the world will do what you ask of them. ¹²For the nations who aren't your friends shall die. They shall be destroyed. ¹³The glory of Lebanon will be yours to make my sanctuary beautiful. You will use the forests of firs, pines, and box trees. My Temple will be great and glorious.

¹⁴"The sons of Gentiles will come and bow before you! They will kiss your feet! They will call Jerusalem 'The City of the Lord.' They will call it 'The Glorious Mountain of the Holy One of Israel.'

¹⁵"Though once hated by all, you will be beautiful forever. You will be a joy for all the peoples of the world. For I will make you so. ¹⁶Powerful kings and mighty nations shall give you their best goods. They will satisfy your every need. And you will know at last that I, the Lord, am your Savior and Redeemer. You will finally know that I am the Mighty One of Israel. ¹⁷I will take your brass and give you gold instead. I will trade your iron for silver. I will take your wood and give you brass. I will replace your stones with iron. Peace and goodness shall rule over you! ¹⁸Violence will disappear out of your land. All wars will end! Your walls will be 'Salvation' and your gates 'Praise.'

¹⁹"No longer will you need the sun or moon to give you light. For the Lord your God will be your everlasting light. And he will be your glory. ²⁰Your sun shall never set. The moon shall not go down. For the Lord will be your everlasting light. Your days of mourning all will end. ²¹All your people will be good. They will finally own their land forever. For I will plant them there with my own hands. This will bring me glory and honor. ²²The smallest family shall grow into a clan. The tiniest group shall be a mighty nation. I, the Lord, shall make it happen when it is time."

Caravans
ISAIAH 60:6

When you go on a trip, you get into the family car and drive on an expressway. Your car has a heater to keep you warm and possibly an air conditioner for summer. You may have a radio or tape deck in your car for music when you drive. The seats in your car are soft, like the sofa in your living room. But travel in Bible times was not that easy. If you wanted to travel far away, you would probably join a caravan. It wasn't safe to travel alone, so people often traveled together in large groups called caravans. Robbers hid along the road. They often hurt or killed a lone traveler. Then they stole the person's money or things. Caravans that went far away often used camels. Caravans that went nearby used donkeys. Sometimes people walked. Camels were the semi-trucks of Bible times. They carried spices, gold, nuts and other goods from one place to another. Donkeys were the pickup trucks of Bible times. Next time you go on a long trip, ask Mom or Dad to take a camel or donkey. Do you think they will? If you do, you'll be glad for your family car!

Good News

61 The Spirit of the Lord God is upon me. For the Lord has chosen me to bring good news to the suffering and poor. He has sent me to comfort those with broken hearts. He has told me to tell the captives that they are free. He has sent me to open the eyes of the blind. ²I am to tell those who mourn that the time of God's favor to them has come. And the day of his anger to their enemies has arrived. ³To all who mourn in Israel he will give beauty for ashes. He will give them joy instead of mourning. He will give them praise instead of sadness.

For God has planted them like strong and graceful oaks for his own glory.

⁴And they shall rebuild the ancient ruins. They will repair the cities that were destroyed long ago. They will fix them, though they have lain broken for so long. ⁵Foreigners shall be your servants. They shall feed your flocks and plow your fields. They will also take care of your vineyards. ⁶You shall be called priests of the Lord, the helpers of God. You shall be fed with the treasures of the nations. And you shall have glory in their riches. ⁷You shall not have shame and dishonor anymore. Instead, you shall have a double portion of prosperity and joy.

⁸"For I, the Lord, love justice. I hate robbery and wrong. I will faithfully reward my people for their suffering. And I will make an everlasting covenant with them. ⁹Their descendants shall be known and honored among the nations. All shall know that they are a people God has blessed."

¹⁰Let me tell you how happy God has made me! For he has dressed me with clothes of salvation. He has put around me the robe of righteousness. I am like a bridegroom in his wedding suit. Or I am like a bride with her jewels. ¹¹The Lord will show the nations of the world his justice. All will praise him. His righteousness shall be like a budding tree. It will be like a garden in early spring, full of young plants springing up everywhere.

Isaiah's Prayer

62 My heart longs for Jerusalem. So I will not stop praying for her. I will not stop crying out to God on her behalf. I won't stop until she shines forth in his righteousness. I won't stop until she is glorious in his salvation. ²The nations shall see your goodness. Kings shall be blinded by your glory. And God will give you a new name. ³He will hold you up in his hands for all to see. You will be like a beautiful crown for the King of kings. ⁴Never again shall you be called the "Land That God Forgot." Your new name will be "The Land of God's Delight" and "The Bride." This is because the Lord delights in you. And he will claim you as his own. ⁵Your children will take care of you, O Jerusalem. They will do it with joy like that of a young man who marries a virgin. And God will rejoice over you as a bridegroom with his bride.

⁶⁻⁷O Jerusalem, I have set people on your walls. They shall cry to God all day and all night. They will pray that his promises will be fulfilled. Take no rest, all you who pray. And give God no rest until he saves Jerusalem. Do not stop until he makes her respected throughout the earth. ⁸The Lord made a promise to Jerusalem with all his honesty. He said, "I will never again give you to your enemies. Never again shall foreign soldiers come and take away your grain and wine. ⁹You planted and grew it. So you shall keep it, praising God. Within the Temple courts you yourselves shall drink the wine you pressed."

¹⁰Go out! Go out! Prepare the roadway for my people to come home! Build the roads! Pull out the boulders! Raise the flag of Israel!

¹¹See, the Lord has sent his messengers to every land. They say, "The Lord your God is coming to save you. And he will bring you many gifts." ¹²And they shall be called "The Holy People" and "The Lord's Redeemed." Jerusalem shall be called "The Land of Desire" and "The City God Has Blessed."

The Lord Is Loving and Kind

63 Who is this who comes from Edom, from the city of Bozrah? Who is coming with his beautiful clothes of deep red? Who is this in royal robes, marching in the greatness of his strength?

"It is I, the Lord, promising you salvation. I, the Lord, am the one who is mighty to save!"

2"Why are your clothes so red? They look like you have come from treading out the grapes."

3"I have trodden the winepress alone. No one was there to help me. In my anger I have trodden my enemies like grapes. In my anger I trampled my foes. It is their blood you see upon my clothes. 4For the time has come for me to avenge my people. It is time to save them from the hands of their oppressors. 5I looked but no one came to help them. I was amazed and surprised. So I took vengeance on them alone. Without help, I gave them their judgment. 6I crushed the heathen nations in my anger. And I made them stagger and fall to the ground."

7I will tell of the love of God. I will praise him for all he has done. I will rejoice in his great goodness to Israel. He has been kind because of his mercy and love. 8He said, "They are my very own. Surely they will not be false again." And he became their Savior. 9In all their pain he was put through pain. And he personally saved them. In his love and pity he rescued them. He lifted them up and carried them through all the years.

10But they rebelled against him and grieved his Holy Spirit. That is why he became their enemy and fought against them. 11Then they remembered those days of old. They remembered when Moses, God's servant, led his people out of Egypt. And they cried out, "Where is the one who brought Israel through the sea, with Moses as their shepherd? Where is the God who sent his Holy Spirit to be among his people? 12Where is he whose mighty power divided the sea before them? Where is the one who acted when Moses lifted up his hand? Where is the one who made his name great forever? 13Who led them through the bottom of the sea? Like fine horses racing through the desert, they never stumbled. 14They were like cattle grazing in the valleys. The Spirit of the Lord gave them rest. Thus he gave himself a great name."

15O Lord, look down from Heaven. See us from your holy, glorious home. Where is the love that you used to show us? Where is your power, your mercy, and your compassion? Where are they now? 16Surely you are still our Father! Abraham and Jacob might even disown us. But still you would be our Father, our Redeemer from ages past. 17O Lord, why have you made our hearts hard? Why have you made us sin and turn against you? Come back and help us. For we who belong to you need you so. 18We controlled Jerusalem for such a short time! And now our enemies have destroyed her. 19O God, why do you treat us as though we weren't your people? Why do you treat us like a heathen nation that never called you "Lord"?

God Is Like a Potter

64 Oh, that you would burst forth from the skies and come down! How the mountains would shake in your presence! 2The burning fire of your glory would burn down the forests. It would boil the oceans dry! The nations would shake before you. Then your enemies would learn the reason for your fame! 3It was like that before when you came down. For you did great things beyond our highest thoughts. And how the mountains shook! 4For since the world began no one has seen or heard of such a God as ours. He helps and works for those who wait for him! 5You welcome those who do good with joy. You bless those who follow godly ways.

But we are not godly. We are constant sinners and have been all our lives. Therefore your anger is heavy on us. How can people like us be saved? 6We are all infected and impure with sin. We put on our robes of righteousness, but we find they are dirty rags. Like the leaves in fall, we fade, dry up, and fall down. And our sins, like the wind, blow us away. 7Yet no one calls on your name. No one begs you for mercy. Therefore, you have turned away from us. And you have turned us over to our sins.

8And yet, O Lord, you are our Father. We are the clay and you are the Potter. We are all made by your hand. 9Oh, don't be so angry with us, Lord. Don't remember our sins forever. Oh, look and see that we are all your people.

10Your holy cities are destroyed. Jerusalem is an empty wilderness. 11Our holy, beautiful Temple where our fathers praised you is burned down. And all the things of beauty are destroyed. 12After all of this, must you still refuse to help us, Lord? Will you stand silent and still punish us?

The New Heavens and the New Earth

65 The Lord says, "People who never before asked about me are now looking for me. Nations that never looked for me before are now finding me.

2"But my own people have turned away from me. They have done this even though I have spread out my arms to welcome them. They follow their own evil paths and thoughts. 3All day long they insult me to my face. They do this by worshiping idols in many gardens. And they burn incense on the rooftops of their homes. 4At night they go out among the graves and caves to worship evil spirits. And they eat pork and other forbidden foods. 5Yet they say to one another, 'Don't come too close! If you do, you'll make me unclean! For I am holier than you!' Day in and day out they make me angry.

6"See, this is what I have to say. It is all written out before me. 'I will not stand silent. I will pay them back. Yes, I will pay them back! 7I won't just pay them back for their own sins. I will charge them with the sins of their fathers too,' says the Lord. 'For they also burned incense on the mountains. And they insulted me upon the hills. I will pay them back in full.'

8"But I will not destroy them all," says the Lord. "For good grapes are found among a cluster of bad ones. Someone will say, 'Don't throw them all away. There are some good grapes there!' So I will not destroy all Israel. For I still have some true servants there. 9I will save a remnant of my people to own the land of Israel. Those I choose will inherit it and serve me there. 10And I will bless my people who have looked for me. The plains of Sharon shall again be filled with flocks. And the valley of Achor shall be a place to pasture herds.

11"But most of you have forsaken the Lord and his Temple. And you worship the gods of 'Fate' and 'Destiny.' 12I will give you to the sword. And you shall suffer a dark end. For when I called, you didn't answer. When I spoke, you wouldn't listen. You sinned before my very eyes, choosing to do what you know I hate."

13The Lord God says, "You shall starve. But my servants shall eat. You shall be thirsty while they drink. You shall be sad and ashamed. But they shall be full of joy. 14You shall cry in sorrow and despair, while they sing for joy. 15Your name shall be a curse word among my people. For the Lord God will kill you. And he will call his true servants by another name.

16"The time will come when those who make a promise shall swear by the God of Truth. For I will put aside my anger and forget the evil that you did. 17For see, I am creating new heavens and a new earth! They will be so wonderful that no one will even think about the old ones anymore. 18Be glad! Rejoice forever in my creation. Look! I will recreate Jerusalem as a place of happiness. And her people shall be a joy! 19And I will rejoice in Jerusalem and in my people. And the voice of crying shall not be heard there any more.

20"No longer will babies die when only a few days old. No longer will men be thought to be old at 100! Only sinners will die that young! 21-22In those days, when a man builds a house, he will keep on living in it. It will not be destroyed by enemy armies as in the past. My people will plant vineyards and eat the fruit themselves. Their enemies will not steal it. For my people will live as long as trees. And they will long enjoy their hard-won gains. 23Their harvests will not be eaten by their enemies. Their children will not be born to die young. For they are the children of those the Lord has blessed. And their children, too, shall be blessed. 24I will answer them before they even call to me. While they are still talking to me about their needs, I will go ahead and answer their prayers! 25The wolf and lamb shall feed together. The lion shall eat straw as the ox does. Deadly snakes shall never bite again! In those days nothing shall be hurt or destroyed in all my holy mountain," says the Lord.

The World Will
See God's Goodness

66 "Heaven is my throne and the earth is my footstool. What Temple can you build for me as good as that? 2My hand has made both earth and skies, and they are mine. Yet I will look with pity on the man who has a humble and a contrite heart. I will be kind to the one who respects my word.

3"But those who choose their own ways are cursed. Those who take joy in their sins will be punished. God will not accept their offerings. Such men might sacrifice an ox on the altar of God. But it would be no better to the Lord than a human sacrifice! They might sacrifice a lamb or bring an offering of grain. But it is as hated by God as putting the blood of a pig on his altar! They might come and burn incense to him. But he counts it the same as though they blessed an idol. 4I will send great troubles upon them. I will send them all the things they are afraid of. For when I called them, they would not answer. And when I spoke to them, they would not hear. Instead, they did wrong before my eyes. They chose to do what they knew I hated."

5Hear the words of God, all you who fear him. Shake as you hear his words: "Your brothers hate you. They throw you out for being loyal to my name. 'Glory to God,' they laugh. 'Be happy in

the Lord!' But they shall be put to shame.

6"What is all the trouble in the city? What is that terrible noise from the Temple? It is the voice of the Lord taking vengeance on his enemies.

7-8"Who has heard or seen anything as strange as this? For in one day, suddenly, a nation, Israel, shall be born. It will happen even before the birth pains come. In a moment, just as Israel's pain starts, the baby is born. The nation begins. 9Shall I bring her to the point of birth and then not deliver?" asks the Lord your God. "No! Never!

10"Rejoice with Jerusalem, all you who love her. Be glad with her, all you who cried for her. 11Take great joy in Jerusalem. Drink deeply of her glory. Drink like a baby at a mother's breasts. 12Success shall overflow Jerusalem like a river," says the Lord. "For I will send it. The riches of the Gentiles will flow to her. Her children shall be nursed at her breasts. They will be carried on her hips and bounced on her knees. 13I will comfort you there as a little one is comforted by its mother."

God answers prayer while we pray or even before we pray

I will answer them before they even call to me. They will just be talking to me about their needs. And I will go ahead and answer their prayers!

Isaiah 65:24

14When you see Jerusalem, your heart will be full of joy. Health will be yours. All the world will see the good hand of God upon his people. And they will see his anger against his enemies. 15For see, the Lord will come with fire. He will come with swift chariots of doom. And he will pour out the fury of his anger. He will shout his hot rebuke with flames of fire. 16For the Lord will punish the world by fire and by his sword. And those killed by the Lord shall be many!

17"Some worship idols hidden behind a tree in the garden. They feast there on pork and mouse and all forbidden meat. But they will come to an evil end," says the Lord. [18]"I see what they are doing. I know what they are thinking. So I will call all nations and people against Jerusalem. And there they shall see my glory. [19]I will perform a mighty miracle against them. And I will send those who escape as missionaries to the nations. They will go to Tarshish, Put, Lud, Meshech, Rosh, Tubal, and Javan. They will go to the lands beyond the sea. They will tell those who have not heard of my fame or seen my glory. There they shall declare my glory to the Gentiles. [20]And they shall bring back all your brothers from every nation. They will be a gift to the Lord. They will send them gently on horses and in chariots. They will come in litters and on mules and camels. They will come to my holy mountain, to Jerusalem," says the Lord. "It will be like the offerings flowing into the Temple of the Lord at harvest. They are carried in vessels made holy to the Lord. [21]And I will set aside some of those coming back. They will be my priests and Levites," says the Lord.

[22]"My new heavens and earth shall always be. And in the same way, you shall surely always be my people. You shall have a name that shall never disappear. [23]All mankind shall come to worship me. They will come every Sabbath and every new moon. [24]They shall go out and look at the dead bodies of those who have sinned against me. The worms that eat their bodies shall never die. Their fire shall not be put out. And they shall be a hated sight to everyone."

JEREMIAH

When you first read Jeremiah, you may think it's a sad book. The prophet tells his people many unhappy things that may happen. Those sad things won't happen if they stop worshiping idols and turn to God. That's simple, isn't it? But they didn't do it. So these sad things did happen to them. You'll find exciting times of adventure in Jeremiah, too. You'll listen to God command a young man to do some special work. You'll watch brave people rescue the prophet from a deep and muddy well. You'll see an evil king burn a scroll that had the words of God written on it. You'll watch a man wear a heavy ox yoke to teach his people a lesson. Jeremiah may not make you happy when you read it. But in it you'll find some very important lessons.

God Calls Jeremiah

"Do my work!" God told Jeremiah. "I'm too young," Jeremiah answered. What do you think God said to that?

1 These are God's messages to Jeremiah, the son of Hilkiah. He belonged to the family of priests from Anathoth in the land of Benjamin. The first of these messages came to him in the 13th year of Josiah, king of Judah. ³Others came during the reign of Josiah's son Jehoiakim. Messages also came at other times up until the 11th year of Zedekiah, the son of Josiah. That year was the year that Jerusalem fell to Babylon. And at that time the people were taken away as slaves.

⁴The Lord said to me, ⁵"I knew you before you were shaped in your mother's womb. Before you were born I set you apart. I chose you as my spokesman to the world."

⁶"O Lord God!" I said. "I can't do that! I'm far too young! I'm only a youth!"

⁷"Don't say that," he replied. "For you will go where I send you. And you will say what I tell you to. ⁸And don't be afraid of the people. For I, the Lord, will be with you and see you through."

⁹Then the Lord reached out and touched my mouth. He said, "See, I have put my words in your mouth! ¹⁰Today your work begins. You shall warn the nations and the kingdoms of the world.

I will do everything according to the words I speak through your mouth. I will tear down some nations and destroy them. But I will plant others and take care of them. I will make them strong and great."

¹¹Then the Lord said to me, "Look, Jeremiah! What do you see?"

And I said, "I see a whip made from the branch of an almond tree."

¹²And the Lord replied, "That's right. And it means that I will surely carry out my threats."

¹³Then the Lord asked me, "What do you see now?"

And I said, "I see a pot of boiling water. It is tipping toward the south. It is spilling over Judah."

¹⁴"Yes," he said. "Terror from the north will boil out on all the people of this land. ¹⁵I am calling the armies of the kingdoms of the north. They will come to Jerusalem. They will set their thrones at the gates of the city and all along its walls. And they will rule all the other cities of Judah, too. ¹⁶This is the way I will punish my people for turning from me. They turned and worshiped other gods. Yes, they bowed to idols they made with their own hands! ¹⁷Get up and get dressed. Go out and tell them whatever I tell you to say. Don't be afraid of them or I will make a fool of you in front of them. ¹⁸For see, today I have made you safe from their attacks. They cannot hurt you. You are strong like a walled city that cannot be taken. You are like an iron pillar and heavy gates of brass. All the kings of Judah won't be able to stand against you. Its officers, priests, and people will not be able to touch you. ¹⁹They will try, but they will fail. For I am with you," says the Lord. "I will rescue you."

- *Remember:* How long had God known Jeremiah? (1:4-5) What kind of work did God tell Jeremiah to do? (1:5) What excuse did Jeremiah give? (1:6) Why should Jeremiah not be afraid? (1:7-10, 17-19) When God is with you, why should you not be afraid to do his work?

- *Discover:* When you work for God, he will take care of you. Don't be afraid.

- *Apply:* Are you ever afraid to tell others that Jesus loves them? Are you ever afraid to pray at church? Are you ever afraid to invite someone to Sunday school? Don't be afraid. This is God's work. He will take care of you.

- *What's next?* A king burns an important book. Read Jeremiah 36. ■

God's Rebellious People

2 Again the Lord spoke to me. ²He said, "Go and shout this in Jerusalem's streets. The Lord says, 'I remember how much you wanted to please me as a young bride long ago. I remember how you loved me and followed me even through dry deserts. ³In those days Israel was a holy people. They were the first of my children. All who harmed them were counted deeply guilty. And great trouble came on anyone who touched them.'"

⁴⁻⁵"O Israel," says the Lord, "why did your fathers leave me? What sin did they find in me that turned them away? What changed them into fools who worship idols? ⁶They forgot that it was I, the Lord, who brought them safely out of Egypt. They forgot that I led them through the wilderness. It was a land of deserts and rocks. It was a place of thirst and death. And no one lives there or even travels through. ⁷And I brought them into a fruitful land. I brought them there to eat of its bounty and goodness. But they made it into a land of sin and corruption. And they turned my land into an evil thing. ⁸Even their priests cared nothing for the Lord. And their judges didn't listen to me. Their rulers turned against me. And their prophets worshiped Baal and wasted their time on nonsense.

⁹"But I will not give you up. I will beg you to come back to me. And I will keep on begging! Yes, even with your children's children in the years to come!

¹⁰⁻¹¹"Look closely all around you. See if you can find another nation that has traded in its old gods for new ones. They are loyal even though their gods are nothing. Send to the west to the island of Cyprus. Send to the east to the deserts of Kedar. See if anyone there has ever

heard so strange a thing as this. And yet my people have given up their great God for silly idols! ¹²The heavens are shocked at such a thing. They fall back in horror and dismay. ¹³For my people have done two evil things. They have turned away from me, the Fountain of Life-giving Water. And they have made for themselves cracked tanks that can't hold water!

¹⁴"Why has Israel become a nation of slaves? Why is she captured and led far away?

¹⁵"I see great armies marching on Jerusalem. They come with mighty shouts to destroy her. They plan to leave her cities in ruins, burned and empty. ¹⁶I see the armies of Egypt rising against her. They are marching from their cities of Memphis and Tahpanhes. They plan to destroy Israel's glory and power. ¹⁷And you have brought this on yourselves. You have done this by sinning against the Lord your God. You turned from him when he wanted to lead you and show you the way!

¹⁸"What have you gained by your treaties with Egypt and Assyria? ¹⁹Your own wickedness will punish you. You will see what a bad thing it is to turn against the Lord your God. You will see how bad it is to leave him without fear," says the Lord of Heaven's armies. ²⁰"Long ago you shook off my yoke and broke away from my ties. You would not obey me. On every hill and under every tree you've bowed low before idols.

²¹"How could this happen? How could this be? For when I planted you, I chose my seed so carefully. I planted only the very best! Why have you become this race of sinful men? ²²No amount of soap or lye can make you clean. You are stained with guilt that cannot ever be washed away. I see it always before me," the Lord God says. ²³"You say it isn't so? Do you claim you haven't worshiped idols? How can you say a thing like that? Go and look in any valley in the land! Face the awful sins that you have done. You are like a restless female camel, looking for a male! ²⁴You are a wild donkey, sniffing the wind at mating time. Who can hold back your lust? Any male that wants you need not look. For you just come running to him! ²⁵Why don't you turn from all this running after other gods? But you say, 'Don't waste your breath. I've fallen in love with these strangers. I can't stop loving them now!'

²⁶⁻²⁷"Like a thief, the only shame that Israel knows is getting caught. Your kings, princes, priests, and prophets are all alike in this. They call a carved wooden post their father. And for their mother they have an idol made from stone. Yet in times of trouble they cry to me to save them! ²⁸Why don't you call on these gods you have made? When danger comes, let them save you if they can! For you have as many gods as there are cities in Judah. ²⁹Don't come to me. You are all rebels," says the Lord. ³⁰"I have punished your children, but it did them no good. They still will not obey. And you have killed my prophets as a lion kills its prey.

³¹"O my people, listen to the words of God. Have I been unjust to Israel? Have I been like a desert to them? Have I been like a land of darkness and evil? Why then do my people say, 'At last we are free from God! We won't have anything to do with him again!'? ³²How can you disown your God like that? Can a girl forget her jewels? What bride will seek to hide her wedding dress? Yet for years on end my people have forgotten me. And I am the most precious of their treasures.

³³"How you plot and plan to tempt your lovers! The best of prostitutes could learn a lot from you! ³⁴Your clothing is stained with the blood of the innocent and the poor. Proudly you murder without any reasons. ³⁵And yet you say, 'I haven't done anything to make God angry. I'm sure he isn't upset!' I will punish you even more because you say, 'I haven't sinned!'

³⁶"First here, then there, you jump around. You go from one nation to another for help. But it's all no good. Your new friends in Egypt will fail you just as Assyria did before. ³⁷You will be left in despair and cover your face with your hands. For the Lord has rejected the ones

that you trust. You will not succeed even with their help.

3 "Now a man might divorce a woman. And that woman might then get married again. But the man is never to take her back again. This is because she has been corrupted. But you have left me and married many lovers. Yet still I have asked you to come to me again," the Lord says. 2"Is there a single clean spot in all the land? Is there any place you haven't made dirty by worshiping these other gods? You sit like a prostitute beside the road waiting for a man! You sit alone like a Bedouin in the desert. You have made the land dirty by playing the prostitute. 3That is why even the spring rains have failed. For you are a prostitute and you aren't even ashamed. 4-5And yet you say to me, 'O Father, you have always been my Friend. Surely you won't be angry about such a little thing! Surely you will just forget it!' So you talk and keep right on doing all the evil that you can."

The People Give Up God for Idols

6This message came to me during the reign of King Josiah.

The Lord said, "Have you seen what Israel does? She is like an unfaithful wife. She gives herself to other men at every chance. Israel has worshiped other gods on every hill and under every shady tree. 7I thought that someday she would come back to me. I hoped that once again she would be mine. But she didn't come back. And her faithless sister Judah saw the sin of Israel. 8But she didn't even notice. And she even saw that I divorced faithless Israel. But now Judah has left me too. She has made herself a prostitute. For she also has gone to other gods to worship them. 9She treated it all so lightly. To her it was nothing at all that she should worship idols made of wood and stone. And so the land was made dirty and unclean. 10Then this faithless one came back to me. But she only pretended to be sorry," says the Lord God. 11"In fact, faithless Israel is less guilty than Judah!

12"So, go and speak to Israel. Say to them, 'O Israel, my sinful people, come home to me again. For I am full of mercy. I will not be angry with you forever. 13Only admit that you are guilty. Admit that you turned against the Lord your God. Admit that you were unfaithful and worshiped idols under every tree. Confess that you refused to follow me.' 14O sinful children, come home, for I am your Master. And I will bring you again to the land of Israel. I will bring one from here and two from there. I will bring you from wherever you are scattered. 15And I will give you leaders after my own heart. They will guide you with wisdom and understanding.

16"Someday your land will once more be filled with people," says the Lord. "Then you will no longer wish for 'the good old days of long ago.' You will no longer wish for the times when you had the Ark of God's covenant. Those days will not be missed or even thought about. And the Ark will not be rebuilt. For the Lord himself will be among you. 17The whole city of Jerusalem will be known as the throne of the Lord. All nations will come to him there. And they will no longer follow their evil desires. 18At that time the people of Judah and of Israel will come. They will return together from their exile in the north. And they will come to the land I gave their fathers forever. 19And I thought how good it would be for you to be here among my children. I planned to give you part of this good land. It is the finest in the world. I looked forward to your calling me 'Father.' And I thought that you would never turn away from me again. 20But you have betrayed me. You have gone off and given yourself to many foreign gods. You have been like a faithless wife who leaves her husband."

21I hear a voice high upon the windswept mountains. It is crying and crying. It is the sons of Israel who have turned their backs on God. They have wandered far away. 22"O my sinful children, come back to me again. And I will heal you from your sins."

And they reply, "Yes, we will come. For you are the Lord our God. 23We are tired of worshiping idols on the hills. We are tired of bowing to idols on the mountains. It is all a lie. Only the Lord our God can ever give Israel help and salvation. 24Since childhood we have seen our fathers waste all they had on priests and idols. They threw away their flocks and herds and sons and daughters. 25We lie in shame and in dishonor. For we and our fathers have sinned from childhood against the Lord our God. We have not obeyed him."

God Asks His People to Obey

4 "O Israel, you must truly come back to me. You must throw away all your idols. 2You must swear by me alone, the living God. And you must begin to live good, honest, clean lives. If you do these things, then you will be a testimony to the nations of the world. And they will come to me and glorify my name."

3The Lord speaks to the men of Judah and Jerusalem. He says, "Plow up the hardness of your hearts. Otherwise the good seed will be wasted among the thorns. 4Make your minds and hearts clean, not just your bodies. If you don't, my anger will burn you to a crisp for all your sins. And no one will be able to put the fire out.

5"Shout to Jerusalem and to all Judea! Tell them to sound the alarm throughout the land. 'Run for your lives! Run to the walled cities!' 6Send a signal from Jerusalem: 'Flee now, don't delay!' For I the Lord am bringing terrible destruction on you from the north." 7A lion, a destroyer of nations, stalks from his den. And he is headed for your land. Your cities will lie in ruins, and they will be empty. 8Put on clothes of mourning and cry out with broken hearts. For the fierce anger of the Lord has not stopped yet. 9"In that day," says the Lord, "the king and the princes will shake in fear. And the priests and the prophets will be frozen in terror."

10Then I said, "But Lord, the people have been confused by what you said. For you promised great blessings on Jerusalem. Yet the sword is even now lifted to strike them dead!"

11-12At that time he will send a burning wind. It will blow from the desert upon them. And he will announce their judgment. This wind won't come in little gusts. It will come in a roaring blast! 13The enemy shall roll down upon us like a storm wind. His chariots are like a whirlwind. His steeds are faster than eagles. How terrible it will be for us, for we are ruined!

14"O Jerusalem, make your hearts clean while there is still time. You can still be saved by throwing out your evil thoughts. 15From Dan and from Mount Ephraim your judgment has been announced. 16Warn the other nations that the enemy is coming from a distant land. And they will shout against Jerusalem and the cities of Judah. 17They surround Jerusalem like shepherds moving in on some wild animal! For my people have sinned against me," says the Lord. 18"Your ways have brought this down upon you. It is a bitter dose of your own medicine. And it will strike deep within your hearts."

19My heart, my heart, I roll around in pain. My heart pounds within me. I cannot be still because I have heard the enemies' battle cries. O my soul, I have heard the blast of the enemies' trumpets. 20Wave upon wave of destruction rolls over the land. It keeps coming until the land lies in complete ruin. Suddenly, in a moment, every house is crushed. 21How long must this go on? How long must I see war and death all around me?

22"You will see it until my people leave their foolish ways," says the Lord. "For they will not listen to me. They are dull, foolish children who have no understanding. They are smart enough at doing wrong. But for doing right they have no talent at all."

23I looked down on their land. Everything was in ruins as far as I could see. And all the heavens were dark. 24I looked at the mountains and saw that they shook. 25I looked, and all the people were gone. And the birds of the heavens had flown away.

26The rich valleys had become a wilderness. And all the cities were broken down before the Lord. They had been crushed by his fierce anger. 27The Lord's promise of destruction covers the whole land.

"Yet," he says, "there will be a few of my people left. 28The earth shall mourn. The heavens shall be draped with black. This will happen because of my decree against my people. I have made up my mind and will not change it."

29All the people run in terror from the cities. They hear the noise of marching armies coming near. The people hide in the bushes and run to the mountains. All the cities are empty. All the people have fled in terror. 30Why do you put on your most beautiful clothing? Why do you put on your jewelry and brighten your eyes with mascara? It will do you no good! Your enemies hate you and will kill you.

31I have heard great crying. It sounded like that of a woman giving birth to her first child. It is the cry of my people gasping for breath. They are begging for help. They lie on the ground before their murderers.

No Respect for God

5 The Lord says, "Run up and down through every street in all Jerusalem. Look high and low and try to find even one person who is fair and honest! Search every square! And if you find just one, I'll not destroy the city! 2Even when they make promises, they all tell lies."

3O Lord, you are looking for faithful people. You have tried to get your people to be honest, for you have punished them! But still they won't change! You have destroyed them, but they will not turn from their sins. They are determined not to repent. Their faces are set as hard as rock.

4Then I said, "But what can we expect from the poor and ignorant? They don't know the ways of God. How can they obey him?

5"So I will go now to their leaders, the men who are leaders. I will speak to them, for they know the ways of the Lord. They all know about the judgment that follows sin." But they too had totally turned away from their God.

6So I will send upon them the wild fury of the "lion from the forest." The "desert wolves" shall jump on them. And a "leopard" shall hide around their cities. And all who go out shall be torn apart. For their sins are very many and great.

7"How can I forgive you? For even your children have turned away from me. Even they worship gods that are not gods at all. I fed my people until they were full. And they thanked me by worshiping other gods! 8They are well-fed, lusty horses, each calling for his neighbor's wife. 9Shall I not punish them for this? Shall I not send my vengeance on such a nation as this? 10Go down the rows of the vineyards and destroy them! But leave a scattered few to live. Strip the branches from each vine, for they are not the Lord's.

11"For the people of Israel and Judah are full of sin against me," says the Lord. 12They have lied and said, "He won't bother us! No evil will come upon us! There will be neither hunger nor war! 13God's prophets," they say, "are windbags full of words. They have no divine power or authority. Their claims of judgment will fall on themselves, not us!"

14So this is what the Lord of Heaven's armies says to his prophets: "Because of talk like this, I shall take your words and turn them into raging fire. I shall burn up these people like kindling wood. 15See, I will bring a distant nation against you, O Israel," says the Lord. "It is a mighty nation. It is an ancient nation whose language you don't know. 16Their weapons are deadly. Their men are all mighty. 17And they shall eat your harvest and your children's bread. They will take your flocks of sheep and herds of cattle. Yes, they will harvest all your grapes and figs. And they shall sack your walled cities that you think are safe. 18But I will not completely blot you out." So says the Lord.

19"And your people will ask, 'Why is the Lord doing this to us?' And you shall say, 'You turned away from him. And you gave yourselves to other gods while in your land. Now you must be slaves to foreigners in their lands.'

20"Make this announcement to Judah and to Israel:

²¹"'Listen, O foolish people. Listen, all of you who have no sense. You have eyes, but you do not see. You have ears, but you do not listen. ²²Don't you have any respect at all for me?' the Lord God asks. 'How can it be that you don't even shake in my presence? I set the shorelines of the world by my commands. The oceans, though they toss and roar, can never pass those bounds. Isn't such a God to be feared and worshiped?'

²³⁻²⁴"But my people have sinful hearts. They have turned against me and gone off to worship idols. I am the one who gives them rain each year in spring and fall. And I am the one who sends the harvest. But still they have no respect for me. ²⁵And so I have taken away these great blessings from them. This sin has robbed them of all of these good things.

²⁶"Among my people are wicked men. They hide and wait for victims like a hunter in a hideout. They set their traps for men. ²⁷Like a coop full of chickens their homes are full of evil plans. And the result? Now they are great and rich. ²⁸They are well fed and well dressed. And there is no limit to their wicked deeds. They refuse to be fair to orphans. And they never defend the rights of the poor. ²⁹Should I sit back and act as though nothing is going on?" the Lord God asks. "Shouldn't I punish a nation such as this?

³⁰"A horrible thing has happened in this land! ³¹The priests are ruled by false prophets. And my people like it that way! But your judgment is sure.

One Last Warning

6 "Run, people of Benjamin! Run for your lives! Flee from Jerusalem! Sound the alarm in Tekoa. Send up a smoke signal at Beth-haccherem. Warn everyone that a powerful army is on the way from the north. And it's coming to destroy this nation! ²We are helpless like a girl, pretty and gentle. But we are sure to be destroyed! ³Evil shepherds shall surround you. They shall set up camp around the city. And they will divide your pastures for their flocks. ⁴Watch them get ready for battle. At noon it

Makeup
JEREMIAH 4:30

Makeup in Bible times looked quite different from today. Bible-time women did not buy makeup in stores. It did not come in fancy packages with fancy names. Most came from minerals. A woman who used makeup often had a palette with the different colors on it. Or she might keep them in little jars. She mixed the paints and put them on with spoons, spatulas, and sticks. Her mirror was made of brass or bronze, polished so much that she could see her face in it.

There are at least 18 kinds of perfume mentioned in the Bible. Perfume was very popular. It came from spices and was usually mixed with olive oil or animal fat. Since it was hard to take a bath, people often used perfume to hide body odor. Egyptian women used lots of cosmetics. But Israelite women who used too much color on their faces were thought to be worldly. Wouldn't these people be surprised to see all the makeup at stores today? Jeremiah told the women of Jerusalem that no makeup can change the way you are on the inside. Only God can do that. To be beautiful on the inside means to be good, honest, kind, and loving. Those are the kind of good looks that impress God.

begins. It goes on all afternoon until the evening shadows fall. [5]'Come!' they say. 'Let us attack by night and destroy her palaces!'"

[6]For the Lord of Heaven's armies has spoken to them. He says, "Cut down her trees for battering rams. Smash down the walls of Jerusalem. This is the city to be punished. For she is wicked through and through. [7]She spouts evil like a fountain! Her streets echo with the sounds of violence. Her sickness and wounds are always in front of me.

[8]"This is your last warning, O Jerusalem. If you don't listen, I will empty the land. [9]Disaster on disaster shall happen to you. Even the few who stay in Israel shall be attacked again," the Lord Almighty has said. "For the men who pick grapes check each vine to pick what they have missed. In the same way, the few of my people that are left shall be destroyed again."

[10]But who will listen when I warn them? Their ears are closed and they will not listen. The word of God has made them angry. They don't want to hear it at all.

[11]For all this I am full of the anger of God against them. I am tired of holding it in. "I will pour my anger out over Jerusalem, even on the children playing in the streets. I will pour it out on the meetings of young men. I will pour it out against husbands and wives and grandparents. [12]Their enemies shall live in their homes. They shall take their fields and wives. For I will punish the people of this land," the Lord has said. [13]"They are all cheaters and liars. They are that way, from the smallest of them right to the top! Yes, even my prophets and priests! [14]You can't heal a wound by saying it's not there! Yet the priests and prophets promise peace when war is everywhere. [15]Were my people ashamed when they worshiped idols? No, not at all! They didn't even blush. Therefore they shall lie among the dead. They shall die beneath my anger."

[16]Yet the Lord begs you still: "Ask where the good road is. Look for the godly paths you used to walk in. Yes, follow the paths you walked in days of long ago. Travel there, and you will find rest for your souls. But you say, 'No, that is not the road we want!' [17]I set watchmen over you. They warned you, 'Listen for the sound of the trumpet! It will let you know when trouble comes.' But you said, 'No! We won't listen!'

[18-19]"This, then, is my law against my people. Listen to it, faraway lands. Listen to it, O my people in Jerusalem. Listen to it, all the earth! I will bring evil against this people. It will be the fruit of their own sin because they will not listen to me. They reject my law. [20]There is no use now in burning sweet incense from Sheba before me! Keep your rich perfumes! I cannot accept your offerings. They have no sweet smell for me. [21]I will make the pathway of my people like an obstacle course. Fathers and sons shall stumble. Neighbors and friends shall fall down together." [22]The Lord God says, "See the armies marching from the north. A great nation is rising up against you. [23]They are a cruel nation. And they are fully armed and ready to fight! The noise of their army is like a roaring sea!"

[24]We have heard how strong their armies are. And we are weak with fear. Fear and pain have gripped us like a woman having a baby. [25]Don't go out to the fields! Don't walk the roads! For the enemy is everywhere, ready to kill. We are afraid at every turn.

[26]O Jerusalem, you are the pride of my people. Put on mourning clothes and sit in ashes. Cry bitterly like you would for an only son. For suddenly the destroying armies will be upon you.

[27]"Jeremiah, I have made you a judge of the value of metals. Now you may test my people and see what they are worth. Listen to what they are saying. Watch what they are doing. [28]Are they not the worst of rebels? Are they not full of evil talk against the Lord? They are as stubborn and proud as brass. They are as hard and cruel as iron. [29]The bellows are blowing hard. The refining fire is getting hotter. But it can never make them clean. For there is no pureness in them to bring out. Why keep on trying to

clean them any more? All is dirt and trash. No matter how hot the fire, they keep doing wicked things. [30]I must label them 'Rejected Silver.' And I have thrown them away."

False Worship

7 Then the Lord said to Jeremiah, [2]"Go over to the door of the Temple of the Lord. Give this message to the people: 'O Judah, listen to this message from God. Listen to it, all of you who worship here.'" [3]The Lord, the God of Israel says: "Even now, you might stop doing evil things. If you do, I will let you stay in your own land. [4]But don't be fooled by those who lie to you. Don't listen to those who say, 'The Temple of the Lord is here! God will never let Jerusalem be destroyed.' [5]You may stay only if you stop your wicked thoughts and deeds. And you must be fair to others. [6]You must stop taking advantage of orphans, widows, and foreigners. And you must stop your murdering. You must stop bowing to idols as you do now to your own harm. [7]If you do all these things, then I will let you stay in this land. This is the land that I gave to your fathers to keep forever.

[8]"You think that because the Temple is here, you will never suffer? Don't fool yourselves! [9]Do you really think that you can steal, murder, sleep around, and lie? Do you think you can worship Baal and all of those new gods of yours? [10]How can you do that and then come to stand before me in my Temple? How can you even think of saying, 'We are saved'? And then you go right back to all these evil things again! [11]Is my Temple just a hideout for robbers, in your eyes? For I see all the evil going on in there.

[12]"Go to Shiloh, the city I first honored with my name. See what I did to her because of the sin of my people Israel. [13-14]And now," says the Lord, "I will do the same thing here. I will destroy her because of all this evil you have done. Again and again I spoke to you about it. I got up early and called out. But you would not hear or answer. Yes, I will destroy this Temple, as I did in Shiloh. This Temple is called by my name, which you trust for help. And I gave this place to you and your fathers. [15]I will soon send you into exile. I will do it just as I did to your brothers, the people of Israel.

[16]"Pray no more for these people, Jeremiah. Don't cry for them or beg me to help them. For I will not listen. [17]Don't you see what they are doing in the cities of Judah? Can't you see what is going on in the streets of Jerusalem? [18]No wonder my anger is so great! Watch how the children gather wood and the fathers build fires. Look, the women are making cakes to give to the Queen of Heaven and their other idols. [19]Am I the one that they are hurting?" asks the Lord. "Most of all they hurt themselves. And they do this to their own shame." [20]So the Lord God says, "I will pour out my anger. Yes, I will send my fury on this place. I will strike down people, animals, trees, and plants. They will all be burned by the hot fire of my anger."

[21]The Lord, the God of Israel says, "Take away your offerings and sacrifices! [22]I never really wanted sacrifices from your fathers. When I led them out of Egypt, I didn't really want their offerings. That was not the point of my command. [23]I wanted them to *obey* me! And I promised to be their God if they would obey my commands. I asked them to be my people. I told them that if they did as I said, all would be well!

[24]"But they wouldn't listen. They kept on doing whatever they wanted to. They kept on following their own evil thoughts. They went backward instead of forward. [25]Ever since your fathers left Egypt, I have kept sending them my prophets. I have done this again and again. [26]But they wouldn't listen or even try to hear. They are hard and stubborn. They are even worse than their fathers were.

[27]"Tell them all that I will do to them. But don't expect them to listen. Cry out your warnings. But don't expect them to listen and obey. [28]Say to them, 'This is the nation that will not obey the Lord its God. These are the people who refuse to be taught. She is a nation that is living a lie.

²⁹"'O Jerusalem, shave your head in shame. Cry alone upon the mountains. For the Lord has rejected this people who make him so angry.' ³⁰For the people of Judah have sinned before my very eyes," says the Lord. "They have set up their idols right in my own Temple, making it unclean. ³¹They have built the altar called Topheth in the Valley of Ben-hinnom. And there they burn their little children as sacrifices to their gods. This is a deed so horrible I've never even thought of it! ³²The time is coming," says the Lord, "when that valley's name will be changed. It will no longer be called Topheth or the Valley of Ben-hinnom. Its name will be changed to the Valley of Killing. For there will be many dead people in Jerusalem. There will be so many that there won't be room enough for all the graves. And they will dump the bodies in that valley.

³³"The bodies of my people shall be food for the birds and animals. And no one shall be left to scare them away. ³⁴I will end the happy singing and laughter in Jerusalem. I will stop the happy voices of brides and grooms in the streets of Judah's cities. For all the land shall lie empty and silent.

8 "Then," says the Lord, "the enemy shall break open the graves. They shall dig up the bones of the kings and princes of Judah. They shall dig up the bones of the priests, prophets, and people. ²They shall spread the bones out on the ground before the sun and moon and stars. These are the gods of my people! These are the gods whom they have loved and worshiped. Their bones shall not be gathered up again or buried. They shall be scattered like dung upon the ground. ³And the people of Judah who are still alive shall wish they were dead. They would rather die than to live where I will send them," says the Lord.

The People Believe Lies

⁴⁻⁵"Once again give them this message from the Lord: 'When a person falls, he jumps up again. A person might be walking on the wrong road and find his mistake. And then he goes back to the fork where he made the wrong turn. But these people keep on going along their evil path. They do this even though I warn them. ⁶I listen to their words, and what do I hear? Is anyone sorry for sin? Does anyone say, "What a terrible thing I have done"? No, all are running down the path of sin as fast as a horse to the battle! ⁷The stork knows the time to fly south for the winter. So does the turtledove, the crane, and the swallow. They all go at God's chosen time each year. But not my people! They don't listen to the laws of God.

⁸"'How can you say, "We understand his laws"? Your teachers have twisted them up to mean what I never said! ⁹These wise teachers of yours will be shamed for this sin by being forced to leave their homeland. For they have rejected the word of the Lord. Are they then so wise? ¹⁰I will give their wives and their farms to others. For all of them have one purpose in mind. They want to get what isn't theirs. This includes the great and the small, prophets and priests. ¹¹They give useless medicine for my people's terrible wounds. For they tell them all is well when that isn't so at all! ¹²Are they ashamed because they worship idols? No, not in the least. They don't even know how to blush! That is why I will see to it that they lie among the fallen. I will visit them with death. ¹³Their figs and grapes will disappear. All their fruit trees will die. And all the good things I made for them will soon be gone.'"

¹⁴Then the people will say, "Why should we wait here to die? Come, let us go to the walled cities and die there. For the Lord our God has promised our judgment. He has given us a cup of poison to drink for all our sins. ¹⁵We expected peace, but no peace came. We looked for health, but there was only terror."

¹⁶The noise of war comes from the northern border. The whole land shakes at the coming of the terrible army. For the enemy is coming! It is destroying the land and everything in it. It is devouring the cities and people alike.

¹⁷"For I will send these enemy troops among you. And they will be like deadly snakes that you cannot charm. No mat-

ter what you do, they will bite you. And then you shall die."

¹⁸My pain is beyond healing. My heart is broken. ¹⁹Listen to the crying of my people all across the land.

"Where is the Lord?" they ask. "Has God left us?"

"Oh, why have they made me angry? Why do they bow before their carved idols? Why do they do their strange, evil rites?" the Lord replies.

²⁰"The harvest is finished. The summer is over, and we are not saved."

²¹I cry for the hurt of my people. I stand amazed and silent with sadness. ²²Is there no medicine in Gilead? Is there no doctor there? Why doesn't God do something? Why doesn't he help?

Jeremiah Cries

9 Oh, I wish my eyes were a fountain of tears. If they were, I would cry forever! I would cry day and night for my people who have died! ²Oh, that I could go away and forget them. Oh, that I could live in some wayside shack in the desert. For my people are all cheating liars.

³"They bend their tongues like bows to shoot their arrows of untruth. They care nothing for right and go from bad to worse. They care nothing for me," says the Lord.

⁴"Watch out for your neighbor! Watch out for your brother! All of them take advantage of one another. And they tell their lies about each other. ⁵With skillful tongues they fool and cheat each other. They wear themselves out with all their sinning.

⁶"They pile evil upon evil, lie upon lie. And they totally refuse to come to me," says the Lord.

⁷Therefore, the Lord says, "See, I will melt them in a cooking pot of pain. I will refine them and test them like metal. What else can I do with them? ⁸For their tongues aim lies like poisoned spears. They speak cleverly to their neighbors while planning to kill them. ⁹Should I not punish them for such things as this?" asks the Lord. "Shall I not make them pay for their deeds?"

¹⁰Sobbing and crying, I point to their mountains and pastures. For now they are empty, without a living soul. Gone is the lowing of cattle. Gone are the birds and wild animals. All have gone away.

¹¹"And I will turn Jerusalem into piles of broken-down houses. It will be a place where only jackals have their dens. The cities of Judah shall be ghost towns, with no one living in them."

¹²Who is wise enough to understand all this? Where is the Lord's messenger to explain it? Why is the land a desert so that no one dares even to travel through?

¹³"Because," the Lord replies, "my people have not obeyed my laws. ¹⁴Instead, they have done whatever they wanted. They have worshiped the idols of Baal, as their fathers told them to." ¹⁵So now, this is what the Lord, the God of Israel, says: "Look! I will feed them with bitterness. And I will give them poison to drink. ¹⁶I will scatter them around the world. And they will be strangers in distant lands. Even there the sword of destruction shall chase them. They will have no rest until I have totally destroyed them."

¹⁷⁻¹⁸The Lord says, "Send for the mourners! Quick! Begin your crying! Let the tears flow from your eyes. ¹⁹Hear Jerusalem crying in despair. 'We are ruined! Disaster has befallen us! We must leave our land and homes!'" ²⁰Listen to the words of God, O women who cry. Teach your daughters to cry, and your neighbors too. ²¹For death has crept in through your windows into your homes. He has killed off the flower of your youth. Children no longer play in the streets. The young men don't meet anymore in the markets.

²²"Tell them this," says the Lord. "Bodies shall be scattered across the fields like dung. They shall be spread out like sheaves after the mower. And no one will bury them."

²³The Lord says, "Don't let the wise man rest in his wisdom. Don't let the strong man rest in his strength. And don't let the rich man rest in his riches. ²⁴Let them boast only that they truly know me. Let them brag that they know that I am the Lord of justice and

goodness. Let them boast about my love, which stands firm. And let them brag that I love to be this way.

25-26"A time is soon to come," says the Lord. "And I will punish all those who are circumcised in body but not in spirit. This includes Egyptians, Edomites, Ammonites, Moabites, and Arabs. And yes, it includes even you people of Judah. For all these pagan nations also circumcise themselves. But you must circumcise your hearts by loving me. If you don't, your circumcision is only a heathen rite like theirs."

The God of Creation

10 Hear the word of the Lord, O Israel: 2-3"Don't act like the people who make horoscopes. Don't try to read your future in the stars! Don't be afraid of the things they predict. For it is all a pack of lies. Their ways are foolish. They cut down a tree and use it to carve an idol. 4They cover it with gold and silver. And they fasten it in place with hammer and nails. They do this so it won't fall over! 5And there stands their god like a helpless scarecrow in a garden! It cannot speak. And it must be carried, for it cannot walk. Don't be afraid of such a god. It can't harm you or help you."

6O Lord, there is no other god like you. For you are great, and your name is full of power. 7Who would not fear you, O King of nations? And that title belongs to you alone! Among all the wise men of the earth there is no one like you.

8The wisest of men who worship idols are stupid and foolish. 9They bring beaten sheets of silver from Tarshish. They bring gold from Uphaz. And they give them to skillful goldsmiths to make their idols. Then they dress these gods in royal purple robes that expert tailors make.

10But the Lord is the only true God. He is the living God, the everlasting King. The whole earth shall shake at his anger. The world shall hide before his fury.

11Say this to those who worship other gods: "Your so-called gods shall vanish from the earth. For they have not made the heavens and earth." 12But our God made the earth by his power and wisdom. By his knowledge he hung the stars in space. And he stretched out the heavens. 13It is his voice that echoes in the thunder of the storm clouds. He causes mist to rise upon the earth. He sends the lightning and brings the rain. And from his treasuries he brings the wind.

14But foolish men without knowledge of God bow before their idols. It is a shameful business that these men are in. For what they make are lies. They are gods without life or power in them. 15All are worthless and silly. They will be crushed when their makers die. 16But the God of Jacob is not like these foolish idols. He is the Creator of all, and Israel is his chosen nation. He is known as the Lord of Heaven's armies.

17"Pack your bags," he says. "Get ready now to leave. The siege will soon begin. 18For suddenly I'll fling you from this land. And I'll pour great troubles down upon you. At last you shall feel my anger!"

19Deep is my wound. My sadness is great. My sickness cannot be cured. But I must bear it. 20My home is gone. My children have been taken away. And I will never see them again. There is no one left to help me rebuild my home. 21The shepherds of my people have lost their senses. They no longer follow God or ask his will. Therefore they die, and their flocks are scattered. 22Listen! Hear the terrible sound of great armies coming from the north. The cities of Judah shall become dens of jackals.

23O Lord, I know it is not in the power of man to plan his life. 24So you correct me, Lord. But please be gentle. Don't do it in your anger, for I would die. 25Pour out your anger on the nations who don't obey the Lord. For they have destroyed Israel. And they have made a wasteland of this whole land.

Remember God's Promise

11 Then the Lord spoke to Jeremiah once again. He said, "Speak to the men of Judah and all the people of Jerusalem. Remind them that I made a contract with their fathers. And the man who does not obey it is cursed! ⁴For I spoke to them at the time I brought them out of slavery in Egypt. I told them to obey me and do whatever I commanded them. If they obeyed, I promised that they and all their children would be mine. And I promised that I would be their God. ⁵And now, Israel, obey me," says the Lord. "Obey me, so that I can do for you the great things I promised I would. I want to give you a land that 'flows with milk and honey,' as it is today."

Then I replied, "So be it, Lord!"

⁶Then the Lord said, "Speak this message in Jerusalem's streets. Go from city to city throughout the land and speak to the people. Tell them to remember the covenant that their fathers made with God. And to do all the things they promised him they would. ⁷For I made promises to your fathers when I brought them out of Egypt. And I have kept on telling them over and over again until this day. I said, 'Obey my every command!' ⁸But your fathers didn't do it. They wouldn't even listen. Each followed his own stubborn will and proud heart. Because they would not obey, I did to them all the evils stated in the contract."

⁹Again the Lord spoke to me. He said, "I have found a plot against me among the men of Judah and Jerusalem. ¹⁰They have gone back to the sins of their fathers. They will not listen to me, and they are worshiping idols. The agreement I made with their fathers is broken and canceled." ¹¹So the Lord says, "I am going to bring trouble upon them. And they shall not get away. They might cry for mercy. But I will not listen to their cries. ¹²Then they will pray to their idols and burn incense before them. But that cannot save them from their time of pain and despair. ¹³O my people, you have as many gods as there are cities. And your altars to Baal are along every street in Jerusalem.

¹⁴"So Jeremiah, don't pray any more for these people. And don't cry or beg for them. For I will not listen to them. I won't even listen when they are in bad

Is That Piece of Wood God?
JEREMIAH 10:3-5

What would you think if someone said your chair was God? Or what if she said your bike was God? What about your table? Is it God? Of course not! If you pretended that your bike was God, your bike would be called an idol. In Bible times many people made statues from wood, stone, or gold. Then they would bow down to the statue and pretend that it was God. The statue might look like a person or an animal. Sometimes they tried to worship both the real God and the idol at the same time.

God won't accept that kind of worship. The idol came from a piece of wood. The wood came from a tree. God made the tree. So how can the wood be God? It can't. Don't worship things God made. Worship the God who made the things! Some people today treat money as if it was God. Money seems more important to them than God. To other people, TV seems more important than God. Be sure that God is first in your life. Don't let money or TV or anything else become more important to you than God. If that happens, you will be an idol worshiper just like the people in Jeremiah's day.

enough trouble to beg me for help. [15]What right do my beloved people have now to come to my Temple? For they have been unfaithful and worshiped other gods. Can promises and sacrifices now stop your death? Can they give you life and joy again?"

[16]The Lord used to call you his green olive tree. You were beautiful to see and full of good fruit. But now he has sent the anger of your enemies to burn you up. He has sent them to leave you broken and burned. [17]Israel and Judah have been wicked. They have offered incense to Baal. And now the Lord who planted the tree has ordered it cut down.

[18]Then the Lord told me all about their plans. He showed me all their evil plots. [19]I had been as trusting as a lamb or ox on the way to be killed. I didn't know that they were planning to kill me! "Let's destroy this man and all his messages," they said. "Let's kill him so that his name will be forever lost."

[20]O Lord of Heaven's armies, you are fair and just. See the hearts and motives of these men. Pay them back for all that they have planned! I look to you for justice.

[21-22]And the Lord replied, "The men of the city of Anathoth shall be punished. For they have made plans to kill you. They will tell you not to prophesy in God's name on pain of death. And so their young men shall die in battle. Their boys and girls shall starve. [23]Not one of these plotters of Anathoth shall live. For I will bring a great disaster upon them. Their time has come."

Jeremiah Complains to God

12 O Lord, you always give me justice when I bring a case before you to decide. Now let me bring you this complaint. Why are the wicked so rich? Why are evil men so happy? [2]You plant them. They take root and their business grows. Their profits get bigger, and they are rich. They say, "Thank God!" But in their hearts they give no credit to you. [3]But as for me, you know my heart. Lord, you know how much it longs for you. But I am poor, O Lord! Drag them off like helpless sheep to be killed. Judge them, O God!

[4]How long must this land of yours put up with all their sins? Even the grass of the field groans and cries over their wicked deeds! The wild animals and birds have moved away. They have left the land empty. Yet the people say, "God won't bring judgment on us. We're very safe!"

[5]The Lord said to me, "You have become tired after racing with these weak men of Anathoth. So how will you race against horses? How will you run against the king? How about his court and all his evil priests? If you stumble and fall on open ground, what will you do in Jordan's jungles? [6]Even your own family has turned against you. They have planned to call for a mob to kill you. Don't trust them, no matter how nicely they speak. Don't believe them."

God Gets Angry at His People

[7]Then the Lord said, "I have left my people. I have given my dearest ones to their enemies. [8]My people have roared at me like a lion of the forest. So I have treated them as though I hated them. [9]My people have fallen. I will bring upon them swarms of vultures and wild animals. These will pick the flesh from their bodies.

[10]"Many foreign rulers have come into my vineyard. They have trampled down the vines. They have turned all its beauty into dry desert. [11]They have made it empty and dead. I hear its mournful cry. The whole land is empty and no one cares. [12]Destroying armies plunder the land. The sword of the Lord kills from one end of the nation to the other. Nothing shall get away. [13]My people have planted wheat but harvested thorns. They have worked hard, but it does them no good. They shall harvest a crop of shame. For the fierce anger of the Lord is upon them."

[14]And now the Lord says this to the evil nations. He speaks to the nations all around the land he gave his people Israel. He says, "See, I will force you from your land. And I will force Judah from hers, too. [15]But after that I will come

back. I will show love to all of you. And I will bring you home to your own land again. ¹⁶And these heathen nations might quickly learn my people's ways. They might turn and claim me as their God instead of Baal. Baal is the god they taught my people to worship. If they do this, then they shall be strong among my people. ¹⁷But any nation that does not obey me will be thrown out again and destroyed," says the Lord.

Good for Nothing

13 The Lord said to me, "Go and buy a linen belt and wear it. But don't wash it. Don't put it in water at all." ²So I bought the belt and put it on. ³Then the Lord's message came to me again. This time he said, ⁴"Take the belt out to the Euphrates River. Hide it in a hole in the rocks."

⁵So I did. I hid it as the Lord had told me to. ⁶Then, a long time after this, the Lord spoke to me again. He said, "Go out to the river again and get the belt." ⁷And I did. I dug it out of the hole where I had hidden it. But now it was rotten and falling apart. It was totally useless!

⁸⁻⁹Then the Lord said, "This shows how I will rot the pride of Judah and Jerusalem. ¹⁰This evil nation will not listen to me. It follows its own evil desires and worships idols. Therefore, it shall become like this belt. It will be rotten and good for nothing. ¹¹A belt is made to cling to a man's waist. This is how I made Judah and Israel cling to me," says the Lord. "They were my people, an honor to my name. But then they turned away.

¹²"Tell them this. 'The Lord God of Israel says, "All your wine jugs will be full of wine."' And they will reply, 'Of course, you don't need to tell us how rich we will be!' ¹³Then tell them, '"That's not what I mean. I mean that I will fill everyone living in this land with drunkenness. The king sitting on David's throne will be confused. So will the priests and prophets, and all the people. ¹⁴And I will smash fathers and sons against each other," says the Lord. "I will not let pity or mercy save them from total destruction."'"

¹⁵Oh, that you were not so proud and stubborn! Then you would listen to the Lord, for he has spoken. ¹⁶Give glory to the Lord your God before it is too late. Praise him before he causes deep darkness to fall upon you. It will be so dark that you will stumble and fall upon the dark mountains. When you look for light, you will find only darkness. ¹⁷Do you still refuse to listen? Then my lonely, sad heart shall mourn because of your pride. My eyes will overflow with tears. This is because the Lord's flock shall be carried away as slaves.

¹⁸Say to the king and the queen mother, "Come down from your thrones. Sit in the dust! For your crowns are taken off your heads. They are no longer yours." ¹⁹The cities of the Negeb have closed their gates against the enemy. These cities lie well to the south of Jerusalem. They must defend themselves, for Jerusalem cannot help. And all Judah shall be taken away as slaves.

²⁰See the armies marching from the north! Where is your flock, Jerusalem? Where is the beautiful flock he gave you to take care of? ²¹How will you feel when he lets nations you thought were your friends rule over you? You will roll around in pain like a woman having a child. ²²And you might ask yourself, "Why is all this happening to me?" It is because of the greatness of your sins. That is why you have been raped and destroyed by the invading army. ²³Can the Ethiopian change the color of his skin? Can a leopard take away his spots? No, of course not! Well then, can you, who are so used to doing evil, now start being good?

²⁴⁻²⁵"You have put me out of your mind. You have put your trust in false gods. So I will scatter you like chaff blown by strong winds off the desert. Then this is what you will get. I have measured it out especially for you. ²⁶I myself will bring you to total shame. ²⁷I am very much aware of your sins. I know about how you have been unfaithful to me. I know about your idol worship in the fields and on the hills. How terrible it will be for you, O Jerusalem! How long will it be before you are pure?"

God Loses His Patience

14 This message came to Jeremiah from the Lord. It explained why he was holding back the rain.

2"Judah is full of mourning," says the Lord. "Business in the land has come to a stop. All the people lie down on the ground. And a great cry rises from Jerusalem. 3The nobles send servants for water from the wells. But all the wells are dry. The servants come back, troubled and desperate. They cover their heads in sadness. 4The ground is dry and cracked because there is no rain. The farmers are afraid. 5The deer leaves her fawn because there is no grass. 6The wild donkeys stand on the bare hills panting like thirsty jackals. They strain their eyes looking for grass to eat. But there is none to be found."

7O Lord, we have sinned greatly against you! But please help us for the sake of your own name! 8O Hope of Israel, why are you a stranger to us? Our Helper in times of trouble, why are you like one who just passes through the land? Why are you just stopping for the night? 9Are you also confused? Are you helpless to save us? O Lord, you are right here among us, and we carry your name. We are known as your people. O Lord, don't leave us now!

10But the Lord replies, "You have loved to wander far from me. You have not tried to follow in my paths. Now I will no longer accept you as my people. Now I will remember all the evil you have done. And I will punish your sins."

11The Lord told me again, "Don't ask me anymore to bless this people. Don't pray for them anymore. 12When they stop eating, I will not even look their way. When they give their sacrifices to me, I will not accept them. I will give them war, hunger, and disease for their trouble!"

13Then I said, "O Lord God, their prophets are telling them that all is well. They tell the people that no war or hunger will come. They tell the people you will surely send them peace, that you will bless them."

14Then the Lord said, "The prophets are telling lies in my name. I didn't send them or tell them to speak. I didn't give them any messages. They prophesy of visions and revelations they have never seen or heard. They speak lies made up in their own lying hearts. 15Therefore, the Lord says, I will punish these lying prophets. For they have spoken in my name, though I did not send them. They say no war or hunger shall come. But by war and hunger they themselves shall die! 16And the people who listen to them will die of hunger and war. Their bodies shall be thrown out into the streets of Jerusalem. There shall be no one to bury them. Husbands, wives, sons, and daughters will all be gone. For I will pour out great punishment upon them for their sins.

17"So now tell them this: 'Night and day my eyes shall overflow with tears. I cannot stop my crying. For my people have been run through with a sword. And they lie deeply wounded on the ground. 18If I go out in the fields, there lie the bodies of those the sword has killed. And if I walk in the streets, there lie those dead from hunger and disease. And yet the prophets and priests alike travel through the whole country. They tell everyone that everything is all right. But they are speaking of things they know nothing about.'"

19"O Lord," the people will cry, "have you completely rejected Judah? Do you hate Jerusalem? Even after punishment, will there be no peace? We thought, 'Now at last he will heal us. At last he will tie up our wounds.' But no peace has come. And there is only trouble and fear all around. 20O Lord, we admit that we are wicked. And we know that our fathers were wicked, too. 21Do not hate us, Lord. Forgive us for the sake of your own name. Don't shame yourself and the throne of your glory! Don't forget your promise to bless us! 22What heathen god can give us rain? Who but you alone, O Lord our God, can do such things as this? Therefore we will wait for you to help us."

Jerusalem, A City in Trouble

15 Then the Lord said to me, "Moses and Samuel might even stand before me begging me to help these people. But even then I wouldn't help them. Send the people away from me! Get them out of my sight! ²And they might say to you, 'But where can we go?' If they do, tell them this: 'Those who are supposed to die will die. Those who must die by the sword will die by the sword. Those who must starve will die with hunger. And those who will go as captives will be sent to a distant land.' ³I will choose over them four kinds of destroyers," says the Lord. "The sword will kill. The dogs will tear. And the vultures and wild animals will finish up what's left. ⁴I will punish you so badly that your fate will terrify the nations of the world. I will do this because of the bad things Manasseh, son of Hezekiah, did in Jerusalem.

⁵"Who will feel sorry for you, Jerusalem? Who will cry for you? Who will even bother to ask how you are? ⁶You have left me and turned your backs on me. So I will clench my fists against you to destroy you. I am tired of always giving you another chance. ⁷I will sift you at the gates of your cities. I will take from you all that you hold dear. And I will destroy my own people because they will not turn back to me. They will not turn from all their evil ways. ⁸There shall be many widows. At noontime I will bring death to the young men and sorrow to their mothers. I will cause pain and fear to fall upon them suddenly. ⁹The mother of seven gets sick and faints, for all her sons are dead. Her sun is gone down while it is yet day. She sits childless and ashamed now. For all her children have been killed."

¹⁰Then Jeremiah said, "What sadness is mine, my mother. Oh, that I had died at birth. For I am hated everywhere I go. I am not a creditor soon to demand my money. And I am not a debtor refusing to pay. But still, they all curse me. ¹¹Well, let them curse! Lord, you know how I have begged with you on their behalf. You know how I have begged you to save these enemies of mine."

¹²⁻¹³"Can a man break bars of northern iron or bronze? This people's

What Happens When There Is No Water?
JEREMIAH 14:3

Turn on your faucet. Water comes out! There's always more than you need. You never worry about running out of water. It's good water too, good enough to drink. But Bible-time people didn't have all the water they needed. They had no faucets like yours. Bible-time people looked for springs where water flowed from the earth. Brooks and streams of water helped, but they couldn't be counted on. When it rained, or when snow melted, there was often too much water. At other times, brooks or streams dried up.

Some people dug wells. That was hard work. They didn't have good tools. There were no hardware stores where they could buy such things. It took many days to dig a well. Sometimes they had to dig through rock. Cisterns were popular in Bible times. These were big holes, like wells, plastered with lime. People gathered rain water into cisterns. Some cities made aqueducts. These were troughs that carried water a long distance from its source. Without water, people and their animals would die. Aren't you glad you have so much good water? Thank God for it now!

stubborn will can't be broken either. So, because you have sinned against me, I will give your treasures to the enemy. [14]I will have your enemies take you as slaves. They will take you to a land where you have never been before. For my anger burns like fire, and it shall consume you."

God's Word feeds our souls like good food

Your words are what keep me going. They are food to my hungry soul.

Jeremiah 15:16

---

[15]Then Jeremiah replied, "Lord, you know it is for you that I am suffering. They are hurting me because I have spoken your word to them. Don't let them kill me! Save me from their hands. Give them what they deserve! [16]Your words are what keep me going. They are food to my hungry soul. They bring joy to my sad heart and delight me. How proud I am to bear your name, O Lord. [17-18]I have not joined the people in their glad feasts. I sit alone beneath the hand of God. I burst with anger at their sins. Yet you have failed me in my time of need! You have let them keep right on with all their sins. Will they never stop hurting me? Your help is as uncertain as a seasonal mountain stream. It is sometimes a flood, sometimes as dry as a bone."

[19]The Lord replied, "Stop this foolishness and talk some sense! Only if you come back and trust me will I let you be my spokesman. You are to change *them,* not let them change *you!* [20]They will fight against you like an army against a high city wall. But they will not conquer you. For I am with you to protect and save you," says the Lord. [21]"Yes, I will surely save you from these wicked men. I will rescue you from their cruel hands."

People Try to Run Away from God

16 At another time God spoke to me. He said, [2]"You must not marry and have children here. [3]For children will be born in this city. And their mothers and fathers shall live here. [4]But they shall die

from terrible diseases. No one shall cry for them or bury them. But their bodies shall lie on the ground to rot and make the soil rich. They shall die from war and hunger. And their bodies shall be picked apart by vultures and wild animals. [5]Do not mourn or cry for them. For I have taken away my help and my peace from them. I have taken away my love and my mercy. [6]Both great and small shall die in this land. They will not be buried, and no one will mourn for them. Their friends shall not cut themselves or shave their heads as signs of sorrow. (This is their heathen custom.) [7]No one shall comfort the mourners with a meal. No one shall send them a cup of wine showing sadness for their parents' death.

[8]"Don't join them any more in their feasts and parties. Don't even eat a meal with them. Do this as a sign to them of these sad days ahead." [9]For the Lord, the God of Israel, says: "In your own lifetime, I will end all joy in this land. I will do this before your very eyes. There will be no happy songs or marriage feasts. There will be no songs of brides and grooms.

[10]"And you shall tell the people all these things. And they will ask, 'Why has the Lord said such bad things against us? What have we done to deserve such punishment? What is our sin against the Lord our God?' [11]Then tell them that the Lord's reply is this: 'Because your fathers forgot me. They worshiped other gods and served them. They did not keep my laws. [12]And you have been worse than your fathers were! You follow evil to your heart's content. And you will not listen to me. [13]Therefore, I will throw you out of this land. I will chase you into a foreign land. It will be a land where neither you nor your fathers have been before. There you can go ahead and worship your idols all you like. And I will give you no favors!'

[14-15]"But there will come a great day," says the Lord. "At that time, everyone will be talking about the great things God will do. He will bring his people home from a nation in the north. He will bring them back from many other lands where he scattered them. You won't look

back anymore to the time when I saved you from your slavery in Egypt. That mighty miracle will hardly be spoken of any more. Yes, I will bring you back again," says the Lord. "I will bring you to this same land I gave your fathers.

[16]"Now I am sending for many fishermen. They will fish you from the deeps where you are hiding from my anger. I am sending for hunters to chase you down like deer in the forests. They will chase you like mountain goats on the high peaks. You might run to get away from my judgment. But I will find you and punish you. [17]For I am closely watching you, and I see every sin. You cannot hope to hide from me.

[18]"And I will punish you twice for each of your sins. For you have made my land unclean with your idols. And you have filled it up with all your evil deeds."

[19]O Lord, you are my Strength and Fortress. You are my Refuge in the day of trouble. Nations from around the world will come to you. They will say, "Our fathers have been foolish. For they have worshiped useless idols! [20]Can men make God? The gods they made are not real gods at all."

[21]"And when they come in that spirit, I will show them my power and might. I will help them understand at last that I alone am God.

A Green and Growing Tree

17 "My people sin just like they were commanded to. They act like their evil deeds were laws cut with an iron pen on their stony hearts. They act like their sins are cut with a diamond point on the corners of their altars. [2-3]Their youths do not forget to sin. They worship idols under each tree. They do it high in the mountains or in the open country down below. And so I will give all your treasures to your enemies. That shall be the price you pay for all your sins. [4]And the rich promises I made to you will slip out of your hand. And I will send you away as slaves to your enemies in distant lands. For you have built the fire of my anger that shall burn forever."

The Sabbath
JEREMIAH 17:21-27
How would you feel if you had to work all day and all night? How long could you do this without falling asleep? God made us so we could work. But he also made us so we must rest. That's why you have recess and lunchtime at school. That's why you sleep at night.

God rested on the seventh day of the creation week. He called that day the Sabbath. God told us to rest on the seventh day of the week too. That shows us how important the Sabbath is to God. The Sabbath became a special day to worship God. The Israelites worshiped in the Temple in Jerusalem. But when it was destroyed, they worshiped in synagogues like the one in the picture.

In Old Testament times, the Sabbath was always on Saturday. Most Christians today choose Sunday to worship the Lord. That's because Christ rose from the dead on Sunday. God still wants you to have a day to rest. And he wants you to worship him on his day. Will you?

[5] The Lord says, "Cursed are those who put their trust in people. Cursed are those who turn their hearts away from God. [6] He is like a stunted shrub in the desert. He has no hope for the future. He lives on salty plains in the dry wilderness. Good times pass him by forever.

[7] "But happy is the man who trusts in the Lord. Happy is he who has made the Lord his hope and strength. [8] He is like a tree planted by a river. The roots of such a tree reach deep into the water. So it will not be bothered by the heat. It won't be worried by long months without rain. Its leaves stay green. And it goes right on growing its sweet fruit.

[9] "The heart, more than anything else, is very wicked. No one can really know how bad it is! [10] Only the Lord knows! He searches all hearts and looks into the deepest motives. That way he can give to each person his right reward. He can give to him according to how he has lived.

[11] "A mother bird might hatch an egg she never laid. But that young bird will soon leave her and fly away. A man who gets his riches by cheating is like that. Sooner or later he will lose all his riches. And at the end of his life he will be a poor old fool."

[12] But our place of safety is your throne—eternal, high and great. [13] O Lord, the Hope of Israel, all who turn away from you shall be shamed. They are made for earth and not for glory. For they have turned from the Lord, the Fountain of living waters. [14] Lord, you alone can heal me. You alone can save. And my praises are for you alone.

[15] Men laugh at me. And they say, "What is this word of the Lord you keep talking about? You say these threats are really from God. But if they are, why don't they come true?"

[16] Lord, I don't want the people crushed by trouble. The plan is yours, not mine. It is your message I've given them, not my own. I don't want them to die! [17] Lord, don't leave me now! You alone are my hope. [18] Bring confusion and trouble on all who try to hurt me. But please give me peace. Yes, bring double punishment upon them!

The Lord's Warning

[19] Then the Lord said to me, "Go and stand in the gates of Jerusalem. Go first to the gate where the king goes out. Then stand at each of the other gates, too. [20] Say to all the people, 'Hear the word of the Lord. Listen, all you kings of Judah. Listen, all the people of this nation and Jerusalem. [21-22] The Lord is warning you to listen and live. Don't do work on the Sabbath day, but make it a holy day. I gave this command to your fathers. [23] But they didn't listen or obey. They would not listen and learn.

[24] "'You must turn and obey me,' says the Lord. 'And do not work on the Sabbath day. Make it a special day, set apart and holy. [25] If you do this, then this nation shall be here for all time. There shall always be sons of David sitting on the throne here in Jerusalem. There shall always be kings and princes riding among the people. And this city of Jerusalem shall stand forever. [26] People shall come from all around Jerusalem. They shall come from the cities of Judah and Benjamin. They shall come from the Negeb and from the lowlands west of Judah. And they will bring their burnt offerings and grain offerings and incense. They will bring their sacrifices to praise the Lord in his Temple.

[27] "'But you might choose not to listen to me. You might decide not to keep the Sabbath holy. You might keep on trading goods through the gates of Jerusalem on the Sabbath. You might just treat it like any other day. But if you do this, then I will set fire to these gates. The fire shall spread to the palaces and burn them down. No one shall be able to put out the raging flames.'"

No One Listens to Jeremiah

18 Here is another message to Jeremiah from the Lord. The Lord says, [2] "Go down to the shop where clay pots and jars are made. I will talk to you there." [3] I did as the Lord told me. And I found the potter working at his wheel. [4] But the jar that he was making didn't turn out as he wanted. So he pressed it into a lump and started again.

[5] Then the Lord said, [6] "O Israel, can't

I do to you as this potter has done to his clay? The clay is in the power of the potter's hand. In the same way, you are under the power of my hand. [7]I am the one who says that a nation or kingdom is to be taken up and destroyed. [8]But that nation might turn from its evil ways. If it does, then I will not destroy it as I had planned. [9]I am the one who says that a nation will become strong and great. [10]But that nation might change its mind and turn to evil. It might stop obeying me. If it does, then I will change my mind too. I will not bless that nation as I had said I would.

[11]"Therefore, go and warn all Judah and Jerusalem. Say to them, 'Hear the word of the Lord. I am planning evil against you now instead of good. Turn back from your evil paths and do what is right.'"

[12]But they replied, "Don't waste your breath. We don't plan to do what God says. We will keep on living as we want to. We will live free from any rules and laws. We will do whatever we want, no matter how wicked!"

[13]Then the Lord said, "Even among the heathen, no one has ever heard of such a thing! My people have done something too bad to understand. [14]The snow never melts high up in the Lebanon mountains. The cold, flowing streams from the crags of Mount Hermon never run dry. [15]These can be counted on. But not my people! For they have left me and turned to foolish idols. They have turned away from the ancient highways of good. And they walk the muddy paths of sin. [16]Therefore, their land shall become empty. And all who pass by will gasp and shudder. They will shake their heads in amazement at its total desolation. [17]I will scatter my people before their enemies. I will scatter them like the east wind scatters dust. And in all their trouble I will turn my back on them. I will refuse to notice their trouble."

[18]Then the people said, "Come, let's get rid of Jeremiah. We have our own priests and wise men and prophets. We don't need his advice. Let's silence him so he won't speak against us anymore.

Clay Pots and Potter's Wheels
JEREMIAH 18:1-10

Find all the different kinds of pots, pans, vases, and china in your house. You have many beautiful things, don't you? Today you have kettles made of copper or stainless steel. You have china and vases with bright colors. You have many kinds of glass. Bible-time people did not have all these beautiful things. Glass was hard to make, so they did not have much of it. Most pottery was made of clay. A person who made it was called a potter. He used a potter's wheel to turn the clay. Then he shaped it with his hands. Sometimes he did not like what he had made. So he squished the clay together and started over. When he finished, he baked the pot in a kiln. That was an oven heated by a fire. That made the clay hard. God said he is like a potter. He made his people. So he can do with them what he thinks is best.

Let's get rid of him so he won't bother us again."

¹⁹O Lord, help me! See what they are planning to do to me! ²⁰Should they give me evil for good? They have set a trap to kill me. But I spoke well of them to you. I tried to defend them from your anger. ²¹Now, Lord, let their children starve to death! And let the sword pour out their blood! Let their wives be widows! And let them lose all their children! Let their men die in plagues. Let their young men die in battle! ²²Let screaming be heard from their homes as troops of soldiers come suddenly upon them. For they have dug a pit for me to fall in. They have hidden traps along my path. ²³Lord, you know all their murderous plans against me. Don't forgive them. Don't wash away their sin. But let them die before you. Deal with them in your anger.

Jerusalem Will Be Destroyed

19 The Lord said, "Buy a clay jar. Take it out into the valley of Ben-hinnom by the east gate of the city. Take some of the elders of the people and some of the older priests with you. Speak to them whatever words I give you."

³Then the Lord spoke to them. He said, "Listen to the word of the Lord! Listen, kings of Judah and people of Jerusalem! The Lord, the God of Israel, says, 'I will bring terrible evil upon this place. It will be so terrible that the ears of those who hear it will prickle. ⁴For Israel has turned from me. They have turned this valley into a place of shame and sin. The people burn incense to idols. These are idols that none of their fathers ever worshiped before. And they have filled this place with the blood of children. ⁵They have built high altars to Baal. And there they burn their sons in sacrifice. This is something I never told them to do. I never even thought of it! ⁶"'A day is soon coming,' says the Lord. 'On that day, this valley shall no longer be called Topheth or Ben-hinnom Valley. It will be known as the Valley of Killing. ⁷For I will upset the battle plans of Judah and Jerusalem. I will let enemy armies kill you here. I will

leave your dead bodies for vultures and wild animals to feed upon. ⁸And I will wipe Jerusalem off the earth. Everyone will gasp with amazement at all that I have done to her. ⁹I will see to it that your enemies surround the city. They will stay until all the food in the city is gone. And those inside will begin to eat their own children and friends.'

¹⁰"And now, Jeremiah, as these men watch, smash the jar you brought with you. ¹¹Say to them, 'This is the message to you from the Lord of Heaven's armies. He says, "You can see this jar broken on the ground. In the same way, I will break the people of Jerusalem. And as this jar cannot be fixed, neither will they. The killing will be terrible! There won't even be room enough to bury all the people. So their bodies will be piled in this valley. ¹²And as it will be in this valley, so it will be in Jerusalem. For I will fill Jerusalem with dead bodies too. ¹³And I will make all the homes in Jerusalem unclean. I will do the same with the palace of the kings of Judah. I will reject the places where incense was burned to your star gods. I will declare unclean the places you poured out drink offerings to them."'"

¹⁴Jeremiah came back from Topheth where he had given this message. Then he stopped in front of the Temple of the Lord. There he spoke to all the people. ¹⁵He said, "The Lord, the God of Israel, says: 'I will bring upon this city all the evil I promised. It will be the same in all the towns around her as well. This is because you have not listened to the Lord.'"

Jeremiah Is Arrested

20 Now Pashhur, the son of Immer, heard what Jeremiah was saying. Pashhur was the priest in charge of the Temple of the Lord. ²So he arrested Jeremiah and had him whipped and put in the stocks. The stocks stood at the Benjamin Gate near the Temple. ³He left him there all night.

The next day Pashhur finally let him go. When he did, Jeremiah said, "Pashhur, the Lord has changed your name. He says from now on to call you 'The

Man Who Lives in Fear.' 4For the Lord will send terror on you and all your friends. And you will see them die by the swords of their enemies. 'I will hand over Judah to the king of Babylon,' says the Lord. 'And he shall take away these people as slaves to Babylon and kill them. 5And I will let your enemies loot Jerusalem. All the famous treasures of the city shall be carried off to Babylon. This includes the jewels and gold and silver of your kings. 6And Pashhur, you and all your family shall become slaves in Babylon. And you will die there in that land. And those to whom you lied will suffer with you. You told them that everything would be all right.'"

7O Lord, you tricked me when you promised me your help. I have to give them your messages because you are stronger than I am. But now everyone in the city is laughing at me. I am mocked by all. 8You have never once let me speak a word of kindness to them. Always it is disaster and horror. No wonder they laugh and mock and make my name a household joke. 9And I can't quit! I might say I'll never again mention the Lord. I might try to never again speak in his name. But then his word in my heart is like fire that burns in my bones. And I can't hold it in any longer. 10Yet on every side I hear their threats, and I am afraid. "We will report him to the rulers," they say. Even those who were my friends are watching me. They are waiting for me to make a mistake. "He will trap himself," they say. "Then we will get our revenge on him."

11But the Lord stands beside me like a great warrior. Before him, the Mighty, Terrible One, they shall fall down. They cannot defeat me. They shall be shamed and made humble. Their shame shall never be forgotten. 12O Lord of Heaven's armies! You know those who are good. You study the deepest thoughts of our hearts and minds. Let me see your revenge on them. For I have given my cause to you. 13Therefore, I will sing out in thanks to the Lord! Praise him! For he has saved me, poor and needy, from my enemies.

14Yet, cursed be the day that I was born! 15Cursed be the man who brought my father the news that a son was born. 16Let that messenger be destroyed like the cities of old that God overthrew without mercy. Terrify him all day long with battle shouts. 17For he did not kill me at my birth! Oh, that I had died within my mother's womb. Oh, how I wish that it had been my grave! 18Why was I ever born? For my life has been but trouble and sorrow and shame.

God's Answer to the King Is No

21 Then King Zedekiah sent Pashhur and Zephaniah the priest to Jeremiah. Pashhur was the son of Malchiah. Zephaniah was the son of Maaseiah. They begged, "Ask the Lord to help us. For Nebuchadnezzar, king of Babylon, has declared war on us! 2Perhaps the Lord will be kind to us. Maybe he will do a mighty miracle as he did in olden times. Perhaps he will force Nebuchadnezzar to withdraw his army."

3-4Jeremiah replied, "Go back to King Zedekiah. Tell him the Lord God of Israel says, 'I will make all your weapons useless against the king of Babylon. You won't be able to stand against the Chaldeans attacking you. In fact, I will bring your enemies right into the heart of this city. 5And I myself will fight against you. For I am very angry with my people. 6And I will send a terrible plague on this city. Both men and animals shall die. 7And finally I will give King Zedekiah himself into the hands of King Nebuchadnezzar of Babylon. I will give all those left alive in the city into his hands. And he will kill them without pity or mercy.'

8"Tell these people, 'The Lord says: "Take your choice of life or death! 9Stay here in Jerusalem and die. You will be killed by your enemies. You will be killed by hunger and disease. Or you can go out and give in to the Babylonian army and live. 10For I have set my face against this city. I will be its enemy and not its friend," says the Lord. It shall be captured by the king of Babylon. And he shall burn it down to ashes.'

11"And to the king of Judah, the Lord says: 12'I am ready to judge you because of all the evil you are doing. Quick! Give justice to these you judge! Begin doing what is right. If you don't, my burning anger will flash out upon you. It will be like a fire no man can put out. ¹³I will fight against this city of Jerusalem. It brags, "We are safe. No one can touch us here!" ¹⁴And I myself will destroy you for your sinfulness,' says the Lord. 'I will light a fire in the forests that will burn up everything in its path.'"

Evil Kings Will Be Judged

22 Then the Lord said to me, "Go over and speak to the king of Judah. Say to him, ²'Listen to this message from God, O king of Judah. Listen as you sit on David's throne. And let your servants and your people listen too.

³"'The Lord says, "Be fair-minded. Do what is right! Help those in need of justice! Quit your evil deeds! Protect the rights of immigrants, orphans, and widows. Stop murdering the innocent! ⁴You must put an end to all these terrible things you are doing. If you do, then I will save this nation. And once more kings will sit on David's throne. And there shall be riches for all. ⁵You might choose not to act on this warning. But if you do, then I make this promise by my own name," says the Lord. "I promise that this palace shall be destroyed."'"

⁶For this is the Lord's message about the palace. He says, "I love you as much as fruitful Gilead and the green forests of Lebanon. But I will destroy you and leave you empty. No people will live in your land. ⁷I will call for a group of men. They will bring their tools and tear you down. They will tear out all of your fine cedar beams and throw them on the fire. ⁸People from many nations will pass by the ruins of this city. They will say to one another, 'Why did the Lord do it? Why did he destroy such a great city?' ⁹And the answer will be, 'Because the people living here forgot the Lord their God. They did not keep their agreement with him. They turned from him and worshiped idols.'"

¹⁰Don't cry for the dead! Instead cry for the captives led away! For they will never come back to see their land again.

¹¹For the Lord speaks about Jehoahaz. He became king after his father, King Josiah. And he was taken away as a captive. ¹²The Lord says, "He shall die in a distant land. And he shall never again see his own country.

¹³"And how terrible it will be for you, King Jehoiakim! For you are building your great palace with forced labor. By not paying wages you are building injustice into its walls. You are putting oppression into its doors and ceilings. ¹⁴You say, 'I will build a great palace with huge rooms. It will also have many windows. I will panel it with sweet-smelling cedar. And I will paint it a lovely red.' ¹⁵But a beautiful palace does not make a great king! Why did your father, Josiah, reign so long? Because he was just and fair in all he did. That is why God blessed him. ¹⁶He saw to it that justice and help were given to the poor and needy. So all went well for him. This is how a man lives close to God. ¹⁷But you! You are full of selfish greed and are not honest! You murder the innocent and oppress the poor. And your rule is cruel and ruthless."

¹⁸This is God's punishment against King Jehoiakim. He followed his father, Josiah, on the throne. The Lord says, "His family will not cry for him when he dies. His people will not even care that he is dead. ¹⁹He shall be buried like a dead donkey. He shall be dragged out of Jerusalem. And he shall be thrown on the garbage dump beyond the gate! ²⁰Cry, for your friends and allies are gone. Look for them in Lebanon. Shout for them at Bashan. Seek them at the fording points of Jordan. See, they are all destroyed. Not one is left to help you! ²¹When you were rich I warned you. But you replied, 'Don't bother me.' Since childhood you have been that way. You just won't listen! ²²And now all your friends have disappeared with a puff of wind. All your friends are taken off as slaves. Surely at last you will see your wickedness and be ashamed. ²³It's very nice to live in a beautiful palace among the cedars of Lebanon. But soon you will cry and groan in pain. You will suffer like a woman who is having a baby.

24-25"And I have a word for you, Jehoiachin, son of Jehoiakim, king of Judah. Even if you were the signet ring on my right hand, I would pull you off. I would give you to those who want to kill you. I would give you over to Nebuchadnezzar, king of Babylon, and his mighty army. 26I will throw you and your mother out of this country. And you will die in a foreign land. 27You will never again come back to the land you love. 28Jehoiachin is like a broken dish that is thrown away. He and his children will be taken away to distant lands.

29"O earth, earth, earth! Hear the word of the Lord! 30The Lord says, 'Record this man Jehoiachin as having no children. For none of his children shall ever sit upon the throne of David. None of them shall ever rule in Judah. His life will amount to nothing.'"

A Perfect King Will Come

23 The Lord says, "I will send disaster upon the leaders of my people. I will destroy the shepherds of my sheep. For they have hurt and scattered the very ones they were to care for. 2You did not lead my flock to safety. Instead, you have left them and driven them to destruction. And now I will pour out judgment upon you for the evil you have done to them. 3And I will gather together the few that are left of my flock. I will bring them from wherever I have sent them. I will lead them back into their own fold. And they shall have many children and increase. 4And I will choose good shepherds to care for them. And they shall not need to be afraid again. All of them shall be watched over at all times.

5-6"For a great day is coming," says the Lord. "At that time, I will place a righteous Branch upon King David's throne. He shall be a King who shall rule with wisdom and justice. He will make goodness rule everywhere on the earth. And this is his name: The Lord Our Righteousness. At that time Judah will be saved and Israel will live in peace.

7"A day is soon coming," says the Lord. "At that time, people will no longer make promises by 'the Lord who saved Israel from the land of Egypt.' 8Instead, they will make promises by 'the Lord who brought Israel back from exile in Babylon.'"

Signing Your Name

JEREMIAH 22:24

Each time your mother writes a letter, she signs her name. Each time your father writes a check, he signs his name. Perhaps you sign your name on school papers or a birthday card. In Bible times, most people could not write. Many kings and officials could not write. They could not sign their own names. So they had people carve little pictures on a ring. Some called this a signet ring. The king or official stamped his signet ring in soft clay. The clay hardened with the little pictures in it. No one else could have the same pictures. That was the person's signature, the way he signed his name. The signet ring was one of the most important things a person owned. It showed others who he was. King Jehoiachin was a wicked person. What if he were God's own signet ring? God said he would be ashamed of him. He would take him off and throw him away.

A Warning about False Prophets

9My heart is broken for the false prophets. They are full of lies. I wake up afraid and stagger like a drunk does from wine. This is because I know of the terrible judgment waiting for them. For God has spoken holy words of judgment against them. ¹⁰The land is full of unfaithful people! And the curse of God is on it. The land itself is mourning. The pastures are dried up. For the prophets do evil and their power is used wrongly.

¹¹"The priests are like the prophets. They are all ungodly, wicked men. I have seen their evil deeds right here in my own Temple," says the Lord. ¹²"Therefore, their paths will be dark and slippery. They will be chased down dark trails, and they will fall. For I will bring evil upon them. And I will make sure they pay in full for all their sins.

You cannot hide from God

Can anyone hide from me? Am I not everywhere in Heaven and earth at the same time?

Jeremiah 23:24

---

¹³"I knew the prophets of Samaria were very evil. I saw them prophesy by Baal. And they led my people Israel into sin. ¹⁴But the prophets of Jerusalem are even worse! The things they do are horrible. They sleep with women who aren't their wives. And they love to be dishonest. They help those who are doing evil instead of stopping them. These prophets are as bad as the men of Sodom and Gomorrah were."

¹⁵Therefore the Lord says, "I will feed them with bitter food. I will give them poison to drink. For it is because of them that wickedness fills this land. ¹⁶This is my warning to my people," says the Lord of Heaven's armies. "Don't listen to these false prophets when they speak to you. Do not let them fill you with useless hopes. They are making up all that they say. They do not speak for me! ¹⁷They keep saying to these rebels who hate me, 'Don't worry! All is well!' And they say, 'The Lord has said you shall have peace!'

¹⁸"But do any of these prophets live close to God? Are they close enough to God to hear what he is saying? Has even one of them cared enough to listen? ¹⁹See, the Lord is sending a great whirlwind to sweep away these wicked men. ²⁰The full punishment for their sins will be carried out. For the terrible anger of

the Lord will not stop until then. Later, when Jerusalem has fallen, you will see what I mean.

²¹"I have not sent these prophets, yet they claim to speak for me. I gave them no message, yet they say their words are mine. ²²If they were mine, they would try to turn my people from their evil ways. ²³Am I a God who is only in one place? Do they think I cannot see what they are doing? ²⁴Can anyone hide from me? Am I not everywhere in Heaven and earth at the same time?

²⁵"'Listen to the dream I had from God last night,' they say. And then they go on to lie in my name. ²⁶How long will this go on? If they are 'prophets,' they are prophets of lies. They make up everything they say. ²⁷They tell these false dreams to try to get my people to forget me. They do this in the same way as their fathers did. For they turned away to the idols of Baal. ²⁸Let these false prophets tell their dreams. And let my true prophets faithfully speak my every word. There is a difference between chaff and wheat! ²⁹Does not my word burn like fire?" asks the Lord. "Is it not like a mighty hammer that smashes the rock to pieces? ³⁰⁻³¹So I stand against these 'prophets' who get their messages from each other. These smooth-tongued 'prophets' say, 'This message is from God!' ³²Their made-up dreams are lies that lead my people into sin. I did not send them. And they have no message at all for my people," says the Lord.

³³"One of the people might come to question you. Or one of their 'prophets' or priests might speak to you. They might ask, 'Well, Jeremiah, what is the sad news from the Lord today?' If they do this, you shall say, 'What sad news? You are the sad news! For the Lord has thrown you away!' ³⁴There are those who joke about 'today's sad news from God.' These people include false prophets and priests and the people, too. But I will punish them and their families for this. ³⁵You may ask each other, 'What is God's message? What is he saying?' ³⁶But stop using this term, 'God's sad news.' For what is sad is you and your lying. You twist my words. And you

make up 'messages from God' that I didn't even speak. [37]You may ask Jeremiah with respect, 'What is the Lord's message? What has he said to you?' [38-39]But I have warned you not to make fun of him. I have warned you not to ask him about 'today's sad news from God.' And if you don't listen, then I, the Lord God, will get rid of you. I will throw you out of my presence. I will also throw out this city I gave to you and your fathers. [40]And I will bring disgrace upon you forever. You shall never forget your shame."

Good Figs, Bad Figs

24 Nebuchadnezzar, king of Babylon, captured Jehoiachin. Jehoiachin was the son of Jehoiakim, king of Judah. Nebuchadnezzar sent him to Babylon along with the princes of Judah. He took the skilled carpenters and blacksmiths along too. At that time, the Lord gave me this vision. [2]I saw two baskets of figs. They were in front of the Temple in Jerusalem. In one basket there were fresh figs. But in the other the figs were spoiled and moldy. They were too rotten to eat. [3]Then the Lord said to me, "What do you see, Jeremiah?"

I replied, "I see figs. Some of them are very good and some are very bad."

[4-5]Then the Lord said, "The good figs stand for those taken away to Babylon. I have done it for their good. [6]I will see that they are well treated. And I will bring them back here again. I will help them and not hurt them. I will plant them and not pull them up. [7]I will give them hearts that listen to me. They shall be my people and I will be their God. For they shall come back to me with great joy.

[8]"But the rotten figs stand for Zedekiah, king of Judah. They stand for his officials and all the people of Jerusalem left here in this land. And they also stand for those who live in Egypt. I will treat them like spoiled figs, too bad to use. [9]I will make them hated by every nation of the earth. They shall be laughed at and cursed wherever I send them. [10]And I will send war, hunger, and disease among them. It will keep coming until

they are destroyed from the land of Israel. They will no longer live in this land which I gave to them and to their fathers."

Disaster Ahead!

25 This message came from the Lord to Jeremiah. It was for all the people of Judah. It came during the fourth year of the reign of King Jehoiakim. He was the king of Judah and the son of Josiah. This was the year Nebuchadnezzar, king of Babylon, began his reign.

[2-3]"For the past 23 years God has been sending me his messages," Jeremiah said. "They began in the 13th year of the reign of Josiah, king of Judah. I have faithfully passed them on to you. But you haven't listened. [4]Again and again down through the years, God has sent you his prophets. But you have not listened to them. [5]Each time the message was this: 'Turn from the evil road you are traveling. Stop the evil things you are doing. Only then can you keep on living here in this land. Only then will you keep the land the Lord gave to you and your ancestors forever. [6]Don't make me angry by worshiping idols. But if you are true to me, then I'll not hurt you. [7]But you won't listen. You have gone ahead and made me angry by worshiping idols. So you have caused all the evil that has come your way.'"

[8-9]And now the Lord God says, "You have not listened to me. So I will gather together all the armies of the north. They will fight under the command of Nebuchadnezzar, king of Babylon. I have chosen him as my helper. I will bring them all against this land and its people. He also will fight against the other nations near you. And I will destroy you. Your name will be laughed at forever. [10]I will take away your joy and gladness. I will take away your wedding feasts. Your businesses shall fail. And all your homes shall lie in silent darkness. [11]This whole land shall become an empty wasteland. All the world will be shocked at the disaster that happens to you. Israel and her neighbors shall serve the king of Babylon for 70 years.

[12]"Then, these years of slavery will

end. And I will punish the king of Babylon and his people for their sins. I will make the land of Babylon an empty waste forever. ¹³I will bring upon them all the terrors I have promised in this book. I will punish them with all the penalties spoken by Jeremiah against the nations. ¹⁴For many nations and great kings shall make the Babylonians their slaves. They will be slaves, just as they made my people their slaves. I will punish them according to how they treated my people."

A Whirlwind of Anger

¹⁵For the Lord God said to me, "Take from my hand this wine cup. It is filled to the brim with my anger. Make all the nations to whom I send you drink from it. ¹⁶They shall drink from it and stagger. They will be made crazy by the death blows I send down upon them."

¹⁷So I took the cup of anger from the Lord. And I made all the nations drink from it. This included every nation God sent me to. ¹⁸I went to Jerusalem and to the cities of Judah. Their kings and princes drank of the cup. So from that day until this they have been ruined, hated, and cursed. ¹⁹⁻²⁰I went to Egypt, and Pharaoh, his servants, the princes, and the people also drank from that terrible cup. They did this along with all the foreign people living in the land. So did all the kings of the land of Uz. The kings of the Philistine cities also drank from it. These were the cities of Ashkelon, Gaza, Ekron, and what is left of Ashdod. ²¹I went to the nations of Edom, Moab, and Ammon. ²²I visited all the kings of Tyre and Sidon. I also went to the kings of the lands across the sea. ²³I went to Dedan, Tema, and Buz, and the other heathen there. ²⁴I went to all the kings of Arabia and the nomadic tribes of the desert. ²⁵I visited all the kings of Zimri, Elam, and Media. ²⁶I went to all the kings of the northern countries. I went to lands far and near, one after the other. I went to all the kingdoms of the world. And finally, the king of Babylon drank from this cup of God's anger.

²⁷"Tell them, 'The Lord of Heaven's armies has spoken. He says, "Drink from this cup of my anger. Drink from it until you are drunk and vomit. Drink until you fall down and can't get up. For I am sending terrible wars upon you."'
²⁸Maybe they will refuse to drink from the cup. If they do, tell them, 'The Lord of Heaven's armies says you must drink it! You cannot escape! ²⁹I have begun to punish my own people. So why should I let you go free? No, you shall not escape my punishment. I will call for war against all the peoples of the earth.'

³⁰"So speak against them. Tell them the Lord shouts against his own land. He shouts from his holy temple in Heaven. He shouts against all those living on the earth. He shouts like the harvesters who tread the juice from the grapes. ³¹That cry of judgment will reach the farthest ends of the earth. For the Lord has a strong case against all the nations. He will kill all the wicked. ³²'See,' says the Lord, 'the punishment shall go from nation to nation. A great whirlwind of anger shall rise against the farthest corners of the earth.' ³³On that day those the Lord has killed shall fill the earth from one end to the other. No one shall mourn for them. No one shall gather up the bodies to bury them. They shall make the earth rich."

³⁴Cry and moan, O evil shepherds. Let the leaders of mankind beat their heads upon the stones. For their time has come to be killed and scattered. They shall fall and break like fine pottery. ³⁵And you will find no place to hide. There will be no way to escape.

³⁶Listen to the fearful cries of the shepherds. Listen to the leaders shouting in despair. For the Lord has spoiled their pastures. ³⁷People now living in peace will be cut down by the anger of the Lord. ³⁸He has left his den like a lion seeking to kill. Their land has been made into an empty wasteland by fighting armies. This is because of the fierce anger of the Lord.

Jeremiah Almost Dies!

26 This message came to Jeremiah from the Lord. It came during the first year of the reign of Jehoiakim. Jehoiakim was the son of Josiah, the king of Judah.

2The Lord says, "Stand out in front of the Temple of the Lord. Speak to all the people who have come there to worship. They have come from many parts of Judah. Give them the whole message. Don't leave out one word of all I have for them to hear. 3For perhaps they will listen. Maybe they will turn from their evil ways. If they do, then I can stop the punishment I have planned for them. I am ready to pour it out on them because of their evil deeds. 4Tell them the Lord says, 'You must listen to me and obey the laws I have given you. 5You must listen to my servants, the prophets. For I sent them again and again to warn you. But you would not listen to them. 6If you don't do this, then I will destroy this Temple. I will destroy it as I destroyed the Tabernacle at Shiloh. I will make Jerusalem a curse word in every nation of the earth.'"

7-8Jeremiah finished his message. He said everything the Lord had told him to. But the priests and false prophets were very angry. And all the people in the Temple mobbed him. They shouted, "Kill him! Kill him! 9What right do you have to say this? How can you say the Lord will destroy this Temple like the one at Shiloh?" they yelled. "What do you mean by saying Jerusalem will be destroyed? How can you say there will be no one left here?"

10The high officials of Judah heard what was going on. They rushed over from the palace. They sat down at the door of the Temple to hold court. 11Then the priests and the false prophets accused Jeremiah to the officials and people. "This man should die!" they said. "You have heard with your own ears what a traitor he is. For he has spoken against this city."

12Then Jeremiah spoke in his defense. "The Lord sent me," he said, "to prophesy against this Temple and this city. He gave me every word that I have spoken. 13But you must stop your sinning. You must begin to obey the Lord your God. If you do, he will stop all the punishment he has predicted. 14As for me, I am helpless and in your power. Do with me as you think best. 15But there is one thing sure. If you kill me, you will be killing an innocent man. The guilt will lie upon you and this city. It will lie upon every person living in it. For the Lord sent me to speak every word that you have heard."

16Then the officials and people spoke to the priests and false prophets. They said, "This man does not deserve to die. For he has spoken to us in the name of the Lord our God."

17Then some of the wise old men stood. They spoke to all the people standing around.

18They said, "The decision is right. For back in the days of King Hezekiah of Judah, Micah prophesied to us. He told the people what God said. He said, 'This hill shall be plowed like an open field. This city of Jerusalem shall be broken into piles of stone. And a forest shall grow at the top where the great Temple now stands!' 19But did King Hezekiah and the people kill him for saying this? No, they turned from their sin and worshiped the Lord. They begged the Lord to have mercy on them. And the Lord held back the terrible punishment he had planned for them. We could kill Jeremiah for giving us the messages of God. But then, who knows what God will do to us!"

20Another prophet of the Lord spoke against Jerusalem at the same time. His name was Uriah, the son of Shemaiah. He was from Kiriath-jearim. 21King Jehoiakim, his army officers, and the officials heard what he was saying. So the king sent to have him killed. Uriah heard about it and ran away to Egypt. 22Then King Jehoiakim sent Elnathan, the son of Achbor, to Egypt. He went with several other men to capture Uriah. 23They took him prisoner and brought him back to King Jehoiakim. The king killed him with a sword. And he buried him in an unmarked grave.

24But Ahikam, the son of Shaphan, stood with Jeremiah. He was the royal secretary. He made sure the court did not turn him over to the mob to kill him.

The People Will Be Slaves

27 This message came to Jeremiah from the Lord. It came at the beginning of the reign of Jehoiakim. Jehoiakim was the son of Josiah, king of Judah.

²The Lord says, "Make a yoke and tie it on your neck with leather thongs. Tie it there as you would strap a yoke on an ox. ³Then send messages to the kings of Edom, Moab, Ammon, Tyre, and Sidon. Send the messages through their servants in Jerusalem. ⁴Say to them, 'Tell your masters that the Lord, the God of Israel, sends you this message:

⁵"'By my great power I have made the earth. I have made all mankind and every animal. And I give these things of mine to anyone I want to. ⁶So now I have given all your countries to King Nebuchadnezzar of Babylon. He is my helper. And I have handed over to him all your cattle for his use. ⁷All the nations shall serve him and his son and his grandson. They will serve Babylon until his time is up. Then many nations and great kings shall conquer Babylon. And they shall make him their slave. ⁸Give in to him and serve him. Put your neck under Babylon's yoke! I will punish any nation refusing to be his slave. I will send war, hunger, and disease upon that nation. I will do this until he has conquered it.

⁹"'Do not listen to your false prophets. Don't listen to fortune-tellers, dreamers, mediums, and magicians. Don't listen to those who say the king of Babylon won't make you his slaves. ¹⁰For they are all liars. You might follow their advice. You might refuse to give in to the king of Babylon. But if you do, I will drive you out of your land. And I will send you far away to die. ¹¹But the people of any nation might give in to the king of Babylon. If they do, they will be allowed to stay in their own country. He will let them farm the land as usual.'"

¹²Jeremiah spoke all these words to Zedekiah, king of Judah. "If you want to live, give in to the king of Babylon," he said. ¹³"Why do you and your people want to die? Why should you choose war and hunger and disease? For the Lord has promised these to every nation that will not give in to Babylon. ¹⁴Don't listen to the false prophets, for they are liars. They keep telling you that the king of Babylon will not conquer you. ¹⁵'I have not sent them,' says the Lord. 'They are telling you lies in my name. If you keep listening to them, I must drive you from this land to die. I will send you away, and all these "prophets" too.'"

¹⁶I spoke again and again to the priests and all the people. I told them, "The Lord says, 'Don't listen to your prophets. They are telling you that soon the gold dishes from the Temple will be brought back from Babylon. It is all a lie. ¹⁷Don't listen to them. Give in to the king of Babylon and live. For if you don't, this whole city will be destroyed. ¹⁸If they are really God's prophets, let them pray to the Lord of Heaven's armies. Let them pray for the gold dishes still here in the Temple. Let them pray for the dishes in the palace of the king of Judah and in the palaces in Jerusalem. 'Let them pray that these will not be carried away with you to Babylon!'

¹⁹⁻²¹"The Lord of Heaven's armies says this about the things left in Jerusalem. 'There are pillars of bronze standing before the Temple. There is the great bronze basin in the Temple court with the metal stands. There are many other worship objects left here. They were left by Nebuchadnezzar when he took away all the important people of Judah and Jerusalem. He took them all to Babylon, along with Jehoiachin, the son of Jehoiakim, king of Judah. ²²But these things will still be carried away to Babylon. And they will stay there until I send for them. Then I will bring them all back to Jerusalem again.'"

A False Prophet

28 It was the fourth year of the reign of Zedekiah, king of Judah. On a December day that same year Hananiah, the son of Azzur, spoke to me in the Temple. He spoke to me while all the priests and people listened. Hananiah was a false prophet from Gibeon.

²He said, "The Lord of Heaven's armies, the God of Israel, says this: 'I have

lifted the yoke of the king of Babylon from your necks. ³Within two years I will bring back all the Temple treasures. These are the things that Nebuchadnezzar carried off to Babylon. ⁴I will bring back King Jehoiachin, the son of Jehoiakim, king of Judah. And I will bring back all the other captives sent away to Babylon,' says the Lord. 'I will surely lift the yoke put on your necks by the king of Babylon.'"

⁵Then Jeremiah spoke to Hananiah. He did this in front of all the priests and people. ⁶He said, "Amen! May your prophecies come true! I hope the Lord will do all you say. I hope he will bring back from Babylon the treasures of this Temple. And I hope he will bring all our loved ones, too. ⁷But listen now to the words I speak to you. I am speaking in front of all these people. ⁸The ancient prophets before us spoke against many nations. They always warned of war, hunger, and plague. ⁹So a prophet who foretells peace has to prove that God has really sent him. Only when his message comes true can it be known that he really is from God."

¹⁰Then Hananiah, the false prophet, took the yoke off Jeremiah's neck and broke it. ¹¹And Hananiah spoke again to the crowd that had gathered. He said, "The Lord has promised that in two years he will free the nations now under King Nebuchadnezzar of Babylon." At that point Jeremiah walked out.

¹²Soon after this the Lord gave this message to Jeremiah. ¹³"Go and tell Hananiah that the Lord says, 'You have broken a wooden yoke. But these people have yokes of iron on their necks.' ¹⁴The Lord, the God of Israel, says: 'I have put a yoke of iron on the necks of all these nations. I have forced them into slavery to Nebuchadnezzar, king of Babylon. And nothing will change this prophecy. For I have even given him all your flocks and herds.'"

¹⁵Then Jeremiah spoke again to Hananiah, the false prophet. He said, "Listen, Hananiah, the Lord has not sent you. And the people are believing your lies. ¹⁶Therefore the Lord says you must

die. This very year your life will end. This is because you have turned against the Lord."

¹⁷And sure enough, two months later Hananiah died.

Yokes
JEREMIAH 27:1-8
Oxen and cattle were used in Bible times to pull plows. When two oxen were hitched to one plow, they were held together by a yoke. This was a large piece of wood. It reached across the necks of both animals. A loop of rope, leather, or wood was fastened around each neck. The plow was hitched to the middle of the yoke. It was usually made of wood. Jesus and Joseph were carpenters, so they probably made many yokes. Sometimes yokes were put on people captured in battle. God told Jeremiah to put on a yoke to show that Judah should let Babylon capture them. If they tried to fight Babylon, they would get into big trouble.

More Warnings about False Prophets

29 Jehoiachin the king, the queen mother, and their court officials had been sent to Babylon by Nebuchadnezzar. The tribal officers and craftsmen had been taken with them. Jeremiah wrote them a letter from Jerusalem. He addressed it to the elders, priests, and prophets of Israel. It was written to the common people, too. ³He sent the letter with Elasah and Gemariah. Elasah was the son of Shaphan. Gemariah was the son of Hilkiah. They went to Babylon as King Zedekiah's messengers to Nebuchadnezzar. And this is what the letter said:

**When we really look for God
we will find him**

*You will find me when
you look for me.*

Jeremiah 29:13

---

⁴"The Lord, the God of Israel, sends this message. It is for all the captives he has sent to Babylon from Jerusalem.

⁵The Lord says, "Build homes and plan to stay. Plant vineyards, for you will be there many years. ⁶Marry and have children. Then find mates for them and have many grandchildren. Multiply! Don't dwindle away! ⁷Work for the peace and strength of Babylon. Pray for her, for if Babylon has peace, so will you."

⁸The Lord, the God of Israel, says: "Don't let the false prophets and mediums who are there among you fool you. Don't listen to the dreams that they make up. ⁹For they tell lies in my name. I have not sent them," says the Lord. ¹⁰"The truth is this. You will be in Babylon for 70 years. But then I will come to you. I will do for you all the good things I have promised. And I will bring you home again. ¹¹For I know the plans I have for you," says the Lord. "They are plans for good and not for evil. I want to give you a future and a hope. ¹²In those days when you pray, I will listen. ¹³You will find me when you look for me. I will be there, if you look for me with all your heart.

¹⁴"Yes," says the Lord, "I will be found by you. I will end your slavery and give back your riches. I will gather you out of the nations where I sent you. I will bring you back home again to your own land.

¹⁵"But now, you listen to the false prophets among you. And you claim the Lord has sent them. ¹⁶⁻¹⁷So I will send war, hunger, and disease upon the people left here in Jerusalem. Your relatives who were not sent to Babylon will suffer.

So will the king who sits on David's throne. I will make them like rotting figs, too bad to eat. ¹⁸And I will scatter them around the world. And every nation they are put in will curse them and laugh at them. ¹⁹For they will not listen to me. They won't listen, even though I spoke to them again and again through my prophets."

²⁰Therefore listen to the word of God. Listen, all you Hebrew captives over there in Babylon. ²¹The Lord, the God of Israel, says this about your false prophets. Their names are Ahab, the son of Kolaiah, and Zedekiah, the son of Maaseiah. They are speaking lies to you in my name. The Lord says, "Look, I am turning them over to Nebuchadnezzar. He will kill them in front of all the people. ²²These prophets shall become a symbol of all evil. When anyone wants to curse someone he will say, 'The Lord make you like Zedekiah and Ahab. The king of Babylon burned them alive!' ²³For these men have done a terrible thing among my people. They have slept with their neighbors' wives and have lied in my name. I know, for I have seen all they do," says the Lord.

²⁴And say this to Shemaiah the dreamer. ²⁵"The Lord, the God of Israel, says: 'You have written a letter to Zephaniah the priest. He is the son of Maaseiah. And you sent copies to all the other priests. You also had copies sent to everyone in Jerusalem. ²⁶In this letter you said to Zephaniah, "The Lord has chosen you to replace Jehoiada as priest in Jerusalem. And it is your job to stop any madman who claims to be a prophet. You are to put him in the stocks and collar. ²⁷Why haven't you done something about this false prophet Jeremiah of Anathoth? ²⁸For he has written to us here in Babylon saying that our captivity will be long. He says we should build permanent homes and plan to stay many years. He says we should plant fruit trees. For we will be here to eat the fruit from them for a long time to come."'"

²⁹Zephaniah took the letter over to Jeremiah and read it to him. ³⁰Then the Lord gave this message to Jeremiah. ³¹"Send an open letter to all the exiles

in Babylon. Tell them this: 'The Lord says that Shemaiah has spoken to you when he didn't send him. He has fooled you into believing his lies. ³²So I will punish him and his family. None of his children shall see the good I have waiting for my people. For he has taught you to turn against the Lord.'"

Bringing Back the People

30 This is another of the Lord's messages to Jeremiah.

²"The Lord God of Israel says, 'Make a record of all I have said to you. ³For the time is coming when I will make everything good. It will be as it was before for Israel and Judah. I will bring them home to this land that I gave to their fathers. They shall own it and live here again.'

⁴"And write this also about Israel and Judah:

⁵"'Where shall we find peace?' they cry. There is only fear and shaking. ⁶Do men give birth? Then why do they stand there like women in labor? Their faces are pale, and their hands are pressed against their sides.

⁷"In all history, has there ever been a time of such terror? It is a time of trouble for my people Israel. It is a time like they have never known before. Yet God will save them! ⁸For on that day I will break the yoke from their necks," says the Lord of Heaven's armies. "I will snap their chains. And foreigners shall no longer be their masters! ⁹For they shall serve the Lord their God. And they shall serve David their king. I will raise him up for them," says the Lord.

¹⁰"So don't be afraid, my servant. Don't be sad, O Israel. For I will bring you home again from distant lands. I will bring your children from their exile. They shall have rest and quiet in their own land. And no one will make them afraid. ¹¹For I am with you and I will save you," says the Lord. "I might destroy the nations where I scatter you. But I will not destroy you. I will punish you. Yes, you will not go unpunished.

¹²"For your sin is a bruise that will not heal. It is a terrible wound. ¹³There is no one to help you or to bind up your wound. And no medicine does any

good. ¹⁴All your lovers have left you. They don't care anything about you anymore. For I have wounded you cruelly. I have hurt you as though I were your enemy. I have wounded you without mercy. I acted as though I were your worst enemy. For your sins are so many and your guilt so great.

¹⁵"Why do you protest your punishment? Your sin is so bad that your sorrow should never end! It is because your guilt is great that I have had to punish you so much.

¹⁶"But in that coming day, all who are hurting you shall be destroyed. And all your enemies shall be slaves. Those who rob you shall be robbed. And those attacking you shall be attacked. ¹⁷I will give you back your health again and heal your wounds. Now you are called 'The Outcast' and 'Jerusalem, the Place Nobody Wants.'

¹⁸"But," says the Lord, "I will bring you home again from your captivity. I will give you back your fortunes. And Jerusalem will be rebuilt upon her ruins. The palace will be rebuilt as it was before. ¹⁹The cities will be filled with joy and great thanks. And I will make the number of my people grow. I will make them a great and honored nation. ²⁰Their children shall prosper as in David's reign. Their nations shall be made strong before me. And I will punish anyone who hurts them. ²¹They will have their own ruler again. He will not be a foreigner. And I will invite him to be a priest at my altar. He shall come close to me. For who would dare to come unless asked? ²²And you shall be my people, and I will be your God."

²³Suddenly the terrible whirlwind of the Lord roars with fury. It shall burst upon the heads of the wicked. ²⁴The Lord will not call off the fierceness of his anger. It will keep on until it has finished all the terrible punishment he has planned. Later on you will understand what I am telling you.

God Still Loves the People

31 "At that time," says the Lord, "all Israel shall know me as the Lord. They shall act like my people. ²I will care

for them as I did those who escaped from Egypt. I showed them my mercies in the wilderness, when Israel looked for rest." ³For long ago the Lord said to Israel: "I have always loved you and will always love you. With love I have drawn you to me. ⁴I will rebuild your nation, O virgin of Israel. You will again be happy and dance with the timbrels. ⁵Again you will plant your vineyards upon the mountains of Samaria. And you will eat from your own gardens there.

God keeps on loving us. He always has and always will

I have always loved you and will always love you. With love I have drawn you to me.

Jeremiah 31:3

---

⁶"The day shall come when watchmen on the hills of Ephraim will call out. They will say, 'Arise! Let us go up to Zion to the Lord our God.'"

⁷For the Lord says, "Sing with joy for all that I will do for Israel. She is the greatest of the nations! Shout out with praise and joy, 'The Lord has saved his people, Israel!' ⁸For I will bring them from the north and from earth's farthest ends. I will not forget their blind and lame. I will bring their young mothers with their little ones. And I won't forget those about to give birth. It will be a great company who comes. ⁹Tears of joy shall stream down their faces. And I will lead them home with great care. They shall walk beside the quiet streams and not stumble. For I am a Father to Israel, and Ephraim is my oldest child."

¹⁰Listen to this message from the Lord, you nations of the world. Tell it to everyone everywhere. "The Lord who scattered his people will gather them back together again. He will watch over them like a shepherd does his flock. ¹¹He will save Israel from those who are too strong for them! ¹²They shall come home and sing songs of joy upon the hills of Zion. They shall rejoice over the goodness of the Lord. He will give them good crops of wheat, wine, and oil. And he will give them healthy flocks and herds. Their life shall be like a watered garden. And all their sadness shall be gone. ¹³The young girls will dance for joy. And the men, old and young, will take their part in all the fun. For I will turn their mourning into joy. I will comfort them and make them rejoice. For their captivity with all its sadness will be behind them. ¹⁴The priests will feast with the many offerings brought to them at the Temple. I will satisfy my people with my bounty," says the Lord.

¹⁵The Lord spoke to me again. "In Ramah there is bitter crying. Rachel is crying for her children. She cannot be comforted, for they are gone." ¹⁶But the Lord says, "Don't cry anymore, for I have heard your prayers. You will see your children again. They will come back to you from the distant land of the enemy. ¹⁷There is hope for your future," says the Lord. "And your children will come again to their own land.

¹⁸"I have heard Israel groaning, 'You have punished me greatly. But I needed it all. I needed it like a calf needs to be trained for the yoke. Turn me again to you and restore me. For you alone are the Lord, my God. ¹⁹I turned away from God, but I was sorry later. I kicked myself for being so stupid. I was very ashamed of all I did in younger days.'"

²⁰And the Lord says, "Israel is still my son, my darling child. I had to punish him, but I still love him. I long for him and will surely have mercy on him.

²¹"As you travel into exile, set up road signs pointing back to Israel. Mark your pathway well. For you shall come back again, O virgin Israel. You will return to your cities here. ²²How long will you wander back and forth, O wayward daughter? For the Lord will cause something new and different to happen. Israel will turn and look for God."

²³The Lord, the God of Israel, says, "I will bring them back again. And they shall speak out in Judah and her cities. They shall say, 'The Lord bless you, O righteous city, O holy hill!' ²⁴And city dwellers, farmers, and shepherds alike shall live together in peace. ²⁵For I have given rest to the tired and joy to all who are sad."

26Then Jeremiah woke up. "Such sleep is very sweet!" he said.

27The Lord says, "The time will come when I will make the number of people here grow quickly. And I will cause the number of cattle here in Israel to increase. 28In the past I destroyed the nation, but now I will carefully build it up. 29The people shall no longer say, 'Children pay for their fathers' sins.' 30For everyone shall die for his own sins. The person eating sour grapes is the one whose teeth are set on edge."

31The Lord says, "Someday I will make a new contract. I will make this contract with the people of Israel and Judah. 32It won't be like the one I made with their fathers when I brought them out of Egypt. This was a contract they broke. And so they forced me to reject them," says the Lord. 33"But this is the new contract I will make with them. I will write my laws on their hearts. I will do this so they shall want to honor me. Then they shall truly be my people and I will be their God. 34At that time I will no longer have to warn my people to seek the Lord. Everyone, both great and small, shall really know me," says the Lord. "And I will forgive and forget their sins."

35The Lord gives us sunlight in the daytime. And he gives us the moon and stars to light the night. It is he who stirs the sea to make the roaring waves. He is called the Lord of Heaven's armies.

36He says, "I am not likely to do away with these laws of nature. And I am less likely to forget my people Israel! 37I will never throw them away forever for their sins! Not until the heavens are measured would I even think of it! Not until the base of the earth is explored would I consider it!

38-39"For the time is soon coming," says the Lord. "All Jerusalem shall be rebuilt for the Lord. The building will start from the Tower of Hananel at the northeast corner. And it will go to the Corner Gate at the northwest. And from the Hill of Gareb at the southwest, the building will go across to Goah on the southeast. 40And the whole city shall be holy to the Lord. This includes the graveyard and ash dump in the valley. It includes all the fields out to the brook of Kidron. It includes the area from the Kidron to the Horse Gate on the east side of the city. It shall never again be captured or destroyed."

Jeremiah Buys a Field

32 The following message came to Jeremiah from the Lord. It came in the 10th year of the reign of Zedekiah, king of Judah. This was also the 18th year of Nebuchadnezzar's reign. 2At this time Jeremiah was in the prison under the palace. And the Babylonian army was attacking Jerusalem. 3King Zedekiah had put Jeremiah in prison. He did this because Jeremiah said the city would be conquered by the king of Babylon. 4Jeremiah also said that King Zedekiah would be taken prisoner. He said Zedekiah would be taken before the king of Babylon to be tried and sentenced.

5"He will take you to Babylon. He will put you in prison there for many years. And you will stay there until you die. Why fight the facts? You can't win! Give up now!" Jeremiah had told him again and again.

6-7Then this message from the Lord came to Jeremiah. The Lord said, "Your cousin Hanamel, the son of Shallum, will soon come. He will ask you to buy the farm he owns in Anathoth. According to the law you have the first chance to buy it. And you must refuse it before it is offered to anyone else."

8So Hanamel came, as the Lord had said he would. He came and visited me in the prison. "Buy my field in Anathoth, in the land of Benjamin," he said. "For the law gives you the first right to buy it." Then I knew that the message I had heard was really from the Lord.

9So I bought the field, paying Hanamel 17 pieces of silver. 10I signed and sealed the deed of purchase before witnesses. I weighed out the silver and paid him. 11Then I took the sealed deed with the terms and conditions. I also took the unsealed copy. 12And in front of my cousin Hanamel, I handed the papers to Baruch. The witnesses who had signed the deed were also there.

And so were the prison guards. Baruch was the son of Neriah. Neriah was the son of Mahseiah. ¹³And I spoke to him as they all listened.

¹⁴I said, "The Lord, God of Israel, says: 'Take this sealed deed. And take the copy, too. Put them into a pottery jar to keep them for a long time.' ¹⁵For the Lord, God of Israel, says, 'In the future these papers will be valuable. Someday people will again own property here in this country. They will again buy and sell houses and vineyards and fields.'"

¹⁶Then after I had given the papers to Baruch I prayed.

God can do anything

Is there anything too hard for me? No!

Jeremiah 32:27

¹⁷I said, "O Lord God! You have made the heavens and earth by your great power. Nothing is too hard for you! ¹⁸You are loving and kind to thousands. But children suffer for their fathers' sins. You are the great and mighty God, the Lord of Heaven's armies. ¹⁹You have all wisdom and do great and mighty miracles. For your eyes are open to all the ways of men. And you reward everyone according to his life and deeds. ²⁰You have done great things in the land of Egypt. They are things still remembered to this day. And you have continued to do great miracles in Israel and all around the world. You have made your name very great, as it is today.

²¹"You brought Israel out of Egypt with mighty miracles. You saved them with great power and terror. ²²You gave Israel this land that you promised their fathers long ago. It is a wonderful land that 'flows with milk and honey.' ²³Our fathers came and conquered it and lived in it. But they would not obey you or follow your laws. They have hardly done one thing you told them to. That is why you have sent all this terrible evil upon them. ²⁴See how the ramps have been built against the city walls. The Babylonians shall conquer the city by sword, hunger, and disease. Everything has

happened just as you said it would. It has happened as you decided it should! ²⁵But still you tell me to buy the field. You tell me to pay good money for it in front of these people. You do this even though the city will belong to our enemies."

²⁶Then this message came to Jeremiah: ²⁷"I am the Lord, the God of all mankind. Is there anything too hard for me? No! ²⁸I will give this city to the Babylonians. I will give it to Nebuchadnezzar, king of Babylon. He shall conquer it. ²⁹And the Babylonians outside the walls shall come in and set fire to the city. They shall burn down all these houses where the roofs have been used for evil. They were used to offer incense to Baal. They were used to pour out drink offerings to other gods. These things made my anger grow! ³⁰For Israel and Judah have done nothing but wrong since their earliest days. They have made me angry with all their evil deeds. ³¹From the time this city was built until now it has done nothing but make me angry. So I am determined to get rid of it.

³²"The sins of Israel and Judah stir me up. The sins of the people, of their kings, officers, priests, and prophets make me angry. ³³They have turned their backs on me and will not turn back. Day after day, year after year, I taught them right from wrong. But they would not listen or obey. ³⁴They have even made my own Temple unclean. They have worshiped their evil idols there. ³⁵And they have built high altars to Baal in the Valley of Hinnom. There they have burnt their children as sacrifices to Molech. This is something I never commanded. I could not even think of asking it! What a terrible evil to cause Judah to sin so greatly!

³⁶"Now therefore the Lord God of Israel says this about this city. It will fall to the king of Babylon through warfare, hunger, and disease. ³⁷But I will bring my people back again. I bring them back from all the lands where in my anger I will send them. I will bring them back to this very city. And I will make them live in peace and safety. ³⁸They shall be my people and I will be their God. ³⁹And I will give them one heart and mind to

worship me forever. It will be for their own good and for the good of all their descendants.

⁴⁰"And I will make an everlasting covenant with them. I will promise never again to leave them. I will only do good to them. I will put a desire into their hearts to worship me. And they shall never leave me. ⁴¹I will be happy to do them good. And I will bring them back to this land with great joy. ⁴²I have sent all these terrors and evils upon them. But then I will do all the good I have promised them.

⁴³"This land is now destroyed and owned by the Babylonians. Men and animals alike are all gone. But then, fields will again be bought and sold in this land. ⁴⁴Yes, fields shall once again be bought and sold! Deeds shall be signed and sealed and witnessed. This shall happen in the country of Benjamin and here in Jerusalem. It shall happen in the cities of Judah and in the hill country. It shall happen in the Philistine plain and the Negeb too. For someday I will bring wealth and success back to them."

A Wonderful Promise

33 While Jeremiah was still in jail, the Lord sent him this second message.

²The Lord says, "The Lord is the Maker of Heaven and earth. The Lord is his name. He says, ³'Ask me, and I will tell you some great secrets. They are about what is going to happen here. ⁴You have torn down the houses of this city, and the king's palace too. You have done this for materials to make the walls stronger. For the weapons of the enemy are pounding against them. ⁵But still the Babylonians will get in. And the men of this city are already as good as dead. For I have decided to destroy them in my great anger. I have left them because they are so wicked. And I will not pity them when they cry for help.'

⁶"Even so, the time will come when I will heal Jerusalem. And I will give her prosperity and peace. ⁷I will rebuild the cities of both Judah and Israel. And I will give them back their riches. ⁸I will wash away all their sins against me. And I will

forgive them. ⁹Then this city will be an honor to me. It will give me joy. It will give me glory before all the nations of the earth! The people of the world will see the good I do for my people. And they will shake with awe and respect!

¹⁰⁻¹¹"The happy voices of brides and grooms will sing again in this empty land. The happy songs of those bringing offerings of thanks to the Lord will be heard again. The people will sing, 'Praise the Lord! For he is good, and his mercy lasts forever!' For I will make this land happier and richer than it has ever been before. ¹²This land is now as good as empty. Every man and animal and city will soon be gone. But this land will once more see shepherds leading sheep and lambs. ¹³Once again their flocks will prosper in the mountain villages. Once more they will graze near the cities east of the Philistine plain. They will prosper in all the cities of the Negeb and in the land of Benjamin. They will graze near Jerusalem and in all the cities of Judah. ¹⁴Yes, the day is coming soon," says the Lord. "At that time I will give Israel and Judah all the good I promised them.

¹⁵"At that time I will bring to the throne the true Son of David. And he shall rule fairly. ¹⁶In that day the people of Judah and Jerusalem shall live in safety. Their motto will be, 'The Lord is our righteousness!' ¹⁷For from then on, David shall forever have a son sitting on Israel's throne. ¹⁸And there shall always be Levites to offer burnt offerings and meal offerings. They shall give the sacrifices to the Lord."

¹⁹Then this message came to Jeremiah from the Lord. ²⁰⁻²¹The Lord says, "You know I have made a covenant with the day and the night. According to the agreement, day and night always come at the right time. This covenant can never be broken! In the same way, my covenant with David, my servant, can never be broken. David shall always have a son to reign upon his throne. And my covenant with the Levite priests, my helpers, cannot be broken either. ²²The stars cannot be counted. And the sand on the seashores cannot be measured. In

the same way, the line of David my servant will grow and grow. And the line of the Levites who serve me will be made great."

²³The Lord spoke to Jeremiah again. He said, ²⁴"Have you heard what people are saying? They say that the Lord chose Judah and Israel and then left them! They are laughing at Israel. They say that she isn't worthy to be counted as a nation. ²⁵⁻²⁶But this is the Lord's reply: 'I could never totally reject my people! I would change my laws of night and day before I did that! I will never leave the people of Israel or David, my servant. I will never change the plan that his child will rule the descendants of Israel. Instead I will cause them to prosper once again. And I will have mercy on them.'"

King Zedekiah Will Be Captured

34 This is the message that came to Jeremiah from the Lord. It came when Nebuchadnezzar, king of Babylon, came and fought against Jerusalem. All the armies from the kingdoms he ruled came with him. They also attacked the other cities of Judah.

²The Lord says, "Go speak to Zedekiah, king of Judah. Tell him that the Lord says this: 'I will give this city to the king of Babylon. And he shall burn it down. ³You shall not get away. You shall be captured and taken before the king of Babylon. He shall pronounce sentence against you. And you shall be sent as a prisoner to Babylon. ⁴But listen to this, O Zedekiah, king of Judah. God says you won't be killed in war. ⁵But you will die quietly among your people. And they will burn incense in your memory. They will treat you just as they did your fathers. They will cry for you and say, "Alas, our king is dead!" This I have promised, says the Lord.'"

⁶So Jeremiah gave the message to King Zedekiah. ⁷At this time the Babylonian army was attacking Jerusalem, Lachish, and Azekah. These were the only walled cities of Judah still standing.

Slaves Will Be Free

⁸This is the message that came to Jeremiah from the Lord. It came after King Zedekiah of Judah had freed all the slaves in Jerusalem. ⁹For King Zedekiah had told everyone to free his Hebrew slaves, both men and women. He had said that no Hebrew should be the master of another Hebrew. This was because all of them were brothers. ¹⁰The princes and all the people had obeyed the king's command. They had freed all their slaves. But this action did not last very long. ¹¹They changed their minds and made their servants slaves again. ¹²That is why the Lord gave this message to Jerusalem.

¹³The Lord, the God of Israel, says: "I made a covenant with your fathers long ago. I did this when I brought them from their slavery in Egypt. ¹⁴I told them that every Hebrew slave must be freed after serving six years. But this was not done. ¹⁵A short time ago you began doing what was right. You did as I commanded you and freed your slaves. You had promised me in my Temple that you would do it. ¹⁶But now you have taken back your promise. You have made my name unclean by not keeping your promise. You have made the slaves you set free into slaves again."

¹⁷So the Lord says, "You have not listened to me. You have not let your Hebrew slaves go free. So I will give you over to the power of death by war and hunger and disease. And I will scatter you over all the world as exiles. ¹⁸⁻¹⁹You have not kept the terms of our contract. So I will cut you apart just as you cut apart the calf you killed to make your promise to me. You walked between its halves to say you would keep your promise. Yes, I will butcher you, for you have broken your promise. I will do this whether you are princes, court officials, priests, or people. ²⁰I will give you to your enemies, and they shall kill you. I will feed your dead bodies to the vultures and wild animals. ²¹And I will give Zedekiah, king of Judah, to the army of Babylon. And all your leaders will be taken with the king. I will do this even though the armies of Babylon have left the city for a little while. ²²I will call the Babylonian armies back again. And they will fight against it. They will capture

this city and burn it. And I will see to it that the cities of Judah are totally destroyed. I will make sure they are left empty without a living soul in them."

Some Obey, Some Disobey

35 This is the message the Lord gave Jeremiah. He gave it when Jehoiakim, the son of Josiah, was the king of Judah.

²The Lord says, "Go to the town where the families of the Rechabites live. Invite them to come to the Temple. Take them into one of the inner rooms and offer them a drink of wine."

³So I went over to see Jaazaniah, the son of Jeremiah. This Jeremiah was the son of Habazziniah. I brought him and all his brothers and sons to the Temple. Members of all the Rechabite families were there. ⁴I brought them to the room used by the sons of Hanan the prophet. Hanan was the son of Igdaliah. This room was next to the one used by the palace official. It was right above the room of Maaseiah, the son of Shallum. Maaseiah was the temple doorman. ⁵I set cups and jugs of wine before them. And I asked them to have a drink. ⁶But they would not do it.

"No," they said. "We don't drink. This is because Jonadab our father, the son of Rechab, commanded us not to drink. This includes all of our descendants forever. ⁷He also told us not to build houses, but to always live in tents. And he told us not to plant crops or vineyards and not to own farms. He said that if we obeyed, we would live long, good lives in our own land. ⁸And we have obeyed him in all these things. We

have never had a drink of wine since then. And our wives, our sons, and our daughters haven't either. ⁹We haven't built houses or owned farms or planted crops. ¹⁰We have lived in tents and have obeyed all the commands of Jonadab our father. ¹¹But Nebuchadnezzar, king of Babylon, came to this land and we were afraid. So we decided to move to Jerusalem. That's why we are here."

¹²Then the Lord gave this message to Jeremiah:

¹³"The Lord, the God of Israel, says: 'Go and speak to Judah and Jerusalem. Ask them to learn a lesson from the families of Rechab. ¹⁴They don't drink because their father told them not to. But I have spoken to you again and again. But still you won't listen or obey. ¹⁵I have sent you prophet after prophet to tell you to turn back from your wicked ways. I have told you again and again to stop worshiping other gods. I told you that if you obeyed, I would let you live in this land. I promised you peace here in the land I gave to you and your fathers. But you wouldn't listen or obey. ¹⁶The families of Rechab have obeyed their father completely. But you have refused to listen to me.' ¹⁷So the Lord of Heaven's armies, the God of Israel, says: 'You have not listened or answered when I have called. So I will send upon Judah and Jerusalem all the evil I have ever threatened.'"

¹⁸⁻¹⁹Then Jeremiah turned to the Rechabites. He said, "The Lord, the God of Israel, has a word for you. You have obeyed your father in every way. Because of this, he shall always have descendants who will worship me."

The King Burns Jeremiah's Scroll

God gave some messages to Jeremiah. Jeremiah told Baruch what these messages were. Baruch was a scribe. He wrote God's messages on a scroll. Books at that time were written by hand. They were written on scrolls made of long pieces of animal skin or papyrus. But after the king listened to these messages, he cut up the scroll. He burned the pieces in a fire. Then he tried to arrest Jeremiah and Baruch. He wanted to destroy God's Word. Could he? Did he?

36 This message came to Jeremiah from the Lord. It came in the fourth year of King Jehoiakim's reign. He was the king of Judah and the son of Josiah.

²The Lord says, "Get a scroll. Write down all my messages against Israel, Judah, and the other nations. Begin with the first message back in the days of Josiah. Then write down every one of them. ³Show the people of Judah on paper all the bad things I will do to them. Then they will turn from their sins. And then I will be able to forgive them."

⁴So Jeremiah sent for Baruch, the son of Neriah. And Baruch wrote down all the words as Jeremiah spoke them.

⁵When they had finished, Jeremiah spoke to Baruch. He said, "I am a prisoner here. ⁶So you read the scroll in the Temple. Read it on the next day of fasting. For on that day people will be there from all over Judah. ⁷Perhaps even yet they will turn from their evil ways. Maybe they will ask the Lord to forgive them before it is too late. Perhaps they will be saved, even though God's curses have been spoken against them."

⁸Baruch did as Jeremiah told him to. He read all these messages to the people at the Temple. ⁹This happened on the day of fasting held in December. This was in the fifth year of the reign of King Jehoiakim, the son of Josiah. People came from all over Judah to attend the services at the Temple that day. ¹⁰Baruch went to the office of Gemariah the scribe. Gemariah was the son of Shaphan. Baruch went there to read the scroll. This room was just off the upper assembly hall of the Temple. It was near the door of the New Gate.

¹¹Micaiah, the son of Gemariah, was there and he heard the messages from God. ¹²After that, Micaiah went down to the palace. And once there, he went to the room where the leaders were meeting. Elishama the scribe was there. Delaiah, Elnathan, Gemariah, and Zedekiah were also there. Delaiah was the son of Shamaiah. Elnathan was the son of Achbor. Gemariah was the son of Shaphan. Zedekiah was the son of Hananiah. There were also others there who held similar positions. ¹³Micaiah told them about the messages Baruch was reading to the people. ¹⁴⁻¹⁵So the officials sent a man named Jehudi to ask Baruch to come. They wanted Baruch to read the messages to them, too. So Baruch read Jeremiah's words to them.

¹⁶By the time he finished they were very afraid. "We must tell the king," they said. ¹⁷"But first, tell us how you got these messages. Did Jeremiah himself tell them to you?" ¹⁸So Baruch told them that Jeremiah had dictated them to him word by word. Then he had written them down in ink on the scroll. ¹⁹"You and Jeremiah both hide," the leaders said to Baruch. "Don't tell a soul where you are!" ²⁰Then the officials hid the scroll in the room of Elishama the scribe. And they went to tell the king.

²¹The king sent Jehudi to get the scroll. Jehudi brought it from Elishama the scribe. He read it to the king as all his officials stood by. ²²The king was in a winter room in the palace. He was sitting in front of a fireplace. This was because it was December and cold. ²³After Jehudi finished reading three or four columns, the king would take out his knife. He would cut off the section that had just been read and throw it into the fire. He did this until the whole scroll was burned up. ²⁴⁻²⁵And no one said anything except Elnathan, Delaiah, and Gemariah. They begged the king not to

burn the scroll. But he wouldn't listen to them. The rest of the king's officials were not afraid or angry at what he had done.

²⁶Then the king told Jerahmeel, Seraiah, and Shelemiah to arrest Baruch and Jeremiah. Jerahmeel was a member of the royal family. Seraiah was the son of Azriel. And Shelemiah was the son of Abdeel. But the Lord hid Jeremiah and Baruch!

²⁷After the king burned the scroll, the Lord spoke to Jeremiah. ²⁸He said, "Get another scroll. Write everything again just as you did before. ²⁹And send this message to the king. The Lord says, 'You burned the scroll because it said the king of Babylon would destroy this land. ³⁰And now the Lord adds this word about you, Jehoiakim, king of Judah. None of your sons shall sit on David's throne. Your dead body shall lie out in the hot sun and frosty nights. ³¹I will punish you and your family because of their sins. All of your officials will be punished, too. I will pour out upon them all the evil I promised. And this evil will also fall upon all the people of Judah and Jerusalem. For none of you would listen to my warnings.'"

³²Then Jeremiah took another scroll. He dictated again to Baruch all that he had written before. But this time the Lord added a lot more!

- Remember: Whose messages were written on the scroll? (36:1) Who spoke the messages and who wrote them down? (36:4) Where did Baruch read these messages? (36:5-6,8) What did the king do when he heard these messages? (36:21-23) What did Jeremiah do about this? (36:32) What would you like to tell the king? Can he destroy God's Word?

- Discover: No one can destroy God's Word. Someone can burn a Bible, but they can't burn every Bible in the world.

- Apply: Thank God now for his Word, the Bible. He has given it to you. He has given it to the world. The world will always have the Bible.

- What's next? A man is put into a deep and dirty well. How can he ever get out? He does! Read Jeremiah 37:1–38:13. ∎

Ebed-Melech Rescues Jeremiah

This is a story about a brave man named Ebed-melech. He stayed friends with Jeremiah, even though Jeremiah was the most unpopular man in Jerusalem. He even told the king that he was doing wrong to Jeremiah. That takes courage, doesn't it? Did the king listen to him?

37 Nebuchadnezzar chose Zedekiah, the son of Josiah, to rule over Judah. He did not make Jehoiachin, Jehoiakim's son, the new king. ²But King Zedekiah did not listen to what the Lord said through Jeremiah. And the people still left in the land didn't listen either. ³But even so, King Zedekiah sent Jehucal and Zephaniah the priest to ask Jeremiah to pray for them. Jehucal was the son of Shelemiah. Zephaniah was the son of Maaseiah. ⁴Jeremiah had not been put in prison yet. So he could come and go as he wanted to.

⁵The army of Pharaoh Hophra of Egypt came to the southern border of Judah. They were there to help Jerusalem, which was under attack by Babylon. The Babylonian army soon heard that the Egyptians were there. So they left Jerusalem to fight the Egyptians.

⁶Then the Lord sent this message to Jeremiah. ⁷"The Lord, the God of Israel, says: 'Speak to the king of Judah. He wants you to ask me what is about to happen. Tell him that Pharaoh's army is about to run back to Egypt! They did come up here to help you, but they won't succeed. The Babylonians shall beat them and send them running home. ⁸These Babylonians shall capture this city and burn it to the ground. ⁹Don't fool yourselves that the Babylonians are gone for good. They aren't! ¹⁰You might even destroy the whole Babylonian army! There might just be a handful of soldiers left lying wounded in their tents. But still, they would stagger out and defeat you! Still, they would put this city to the torch!'"

¹¹The Babylonian army had left Jerusalem to fight Pharaoh's army. ¹²At that time, Jeremiah left the city too. He planned to visit the land of Benjamin. He wanted to see the land he had bought. ¹³But as he was walking through the Benjamin Gate, a guard grabbed him. He claimed that Jeremiah was a traitor. He thought Jeremiah was going to join the Babylonians. The guard making the arrest was Irijah, the son of Shelemiah. Shelemiah was the son of Hananiah.

¹⁴"That's not true!" Jeremiah said. "I'm not planning to do any such thing!"

But Irijah wouldn't listen. He took Jeremiah before the city officials. ¹⁵-¹⁶They were angry with Jeremiah. So they had him beaten and put into the prison. This was under the house of Jonathan the scribe. Jeremiah was kept there for several days. ¹⁷But after a while King Zedekiah sent for him to come to the palace secretly. The king asked him if there was any recent message from the Lord. "Yes," said Jeremiah, "there is! You shall be defeated by the king of Babylon!"

¹⁸Then Jeremiah asked the king why he had been put in prison. "What have I ever done to deserve this?" he asked the king. "What crime did I do? Have I done anything against you? Have I done anything against your officials or the people? ¹⁹Where are those prophets now who told you that the king of Babylon would not come? ²⁰Listen, O my lord the king! I beg you, don't send me back to that prison. If you do, I'll die there."

²¹Then King Zedekiah ordered that Jeremiah not be put back in prison. He put him in the palace prison instead. He ordered that Jeremiah be given a small loaf of fresh bread every day. They were to do this as long as there was any left in the city. So Jeremiah was kept in the palace prison.

38 But Shephatiah, Gedaliah, Jucal, and Pashhur heard what Jeremiah was telling the people. Shephatiah was the son of Mattan. Gedaliah was the son of Pashhur. Jucal was the son of Shele-miah. And Pashhur was the son of Malchiah. ²Jeremiah was saying that everyone in Jerusalem would die by sword, hunger, or disease. But he said that those who gave in to the Babylonians would live. ³He also claimed that the city of Jerusalem would surely be captured by the king of Babylon. ⁴So these four men went to see the king. They said, "Sir, this man must die! His words will make the few soldiers we have left afraid. He will make all the people afraid too. Soon they will all want to give up! This man is a traitor."

⁵So King Zedekiah agreed. "All right," he said. "Do as you like. I can't stop you."

⁶They took Jeremiah from his prison room. They lowered him by ropes into an empty well in the prison yard. The well belonged to Malchiah. He was a member of the royal family. There was no water in it. But there was a thick layer of mud at the bottom. And Jeremiah sank down into it.

⁷Ebed-melech the Ethiopian heard that Jeremiah was in the well. Ebed-melech was an important palace official. ⁸When he heard this, he ran out to the Gate of Benjamin. The king was holding court there that day.

⁹"My lord the king!" he said. "These men have done a very evil thing! It was very bad for them to put Jeremiah into the well. He will die there of hunger. For almost all the bread in the city is gone."

¹⁰Then the king told Ebed-melech to call 30 men. He was to take them with him and pull Jeremiah out before he died. ¹¹So Ebed-melech took his 30 men. He went to a room used for storing used clothing. There he found some old rags and clothes. He took them to the well and lowered them to Jeremiah on a rope. ¹²Ebed-melech called down to Jeremiah. He said, "Put these rags under your armpits. They will protect you from the ropes." Then Jeremiah got ready to be pulled out. ¹³They pulled him out and brought him back to the palace prison. And it was there that he stayed.

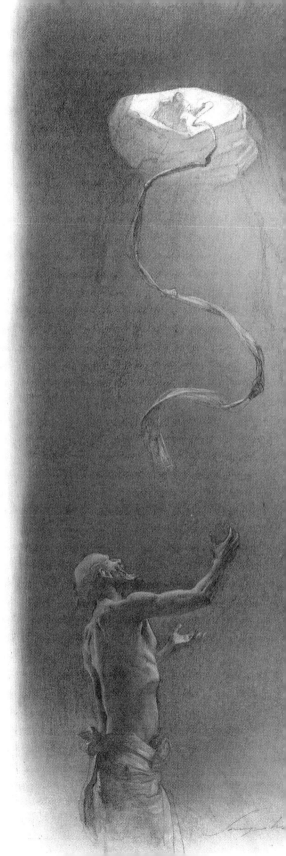

- *Remember:* What message did the Lord give to Jeremiah? (37:7-10) Why did the people of Jerusalem not want to hear this? How was Jeremiah punished? (37:15-17; 38:6) How did Ebed-melech show that he was brave? (38:7-13) Ebed-melech took sides with Jeremiah when others hated him. He could have been hurt. Do you think your friends would do that if you got into big trouble?

- *Discover:* Always take the right side, even if you could get hurt.

- *Apply:* Is someone at school unpopular? Why? Do people make fun of this person? Why? If you think this person is right, should you be on his side? Should you be his friend? Why?

- *What's next?* A man has the best food in the country. But he won't eat it. Read Daniel 1. ◼

Zedekiah Questions Jeremiah

¹⁴One day King Zedekiah sent for Jeremiah. He wanted to meet him at the side door of the Temple.

"I want to ask you something," the king said. "And don't you try to hide the truth!"

¹⁵Jeremiah said, "If I tell you the truth, you will kill me. And you won't listen to me anyway."

¹⁶So King Zedekiah made a promise before God his Creator. He promised that he would not kill Jeremiah. And he promised that he wouldn't give him to the men who wanted him dead.

¹⁷Then Jeremiah said to Zedekiah, "The Lord, the God of Israel, says: 'You might choose to surrender to Babylon. If you do, you and your family shall live. And the city will not be burned. ¹⁸But you might refuse to surrender. If you do, this city shall be set on fire by the Babylonian army. And you will not be able to get away.'"

¹⁹"But I am afraid to surrender," the king said. "For the Babylonians will hand me over to the people of Israel who are on their side. And who knows what they will do to me?"

²⁰Jeremiah replied, "You won't be given into their hands if you obey the Lord. Your life will be saved, and all will go well for you. ²¹⁻²²But if you don't

surrender, all the women left in your palace will be brought out. They will be given to the officers of the Babylonian army. And these women will laugh at you bitterly. 'Fine friends the Egyptians turned out to be,' they'll say. 'They have failed you and left you to your fate!' ²³All your wives and children will be led out to the Babylonians. And you will not get away. You will be caught by the king of Babylon. And this city will be burned to the ground."

²⁴Then Zedekiah said to Jeremiah, "Don't tell anyone you told me this! ²⁵My officials might hear that I talked with you. And they might threaten you with death unless you tell them what we talked about. ²⁶If this happens, just say that you begged me for help. Tell them you were afraid you would be put back in the prison in Jonathan's house. Tell them you were afraid you would die there."

²⁷And sure enough, soon the city officials came to Jeremiah. They asked him why the king had called for him. So he said what the king had told him to. And they left without finding out the truth. The words between Jeremiah and the king had not been heard by anyone. ²⁸And Jeremiah stayed in the prison yard until the day Jerusalem was captured.

Jerusalem Is Captured

39 King Nebuchadnezzar and all his army came back to Jerusalem again. They camped around the city and kept supplies from getting in. This happened in January of King Zedekiah's ninth year as king of Judah. ²Two years later, in the month of July, they broke down the wall. Soon after that, the city fell. ³All the officers of the Babylonian army went into the city. They sat in triumph at the middle gate. Nergal-sharezer of Samgar was there. And so was Nebo-sarsechim, who was a chief officer. Nergal-sharezer, the king's chief officer, was also there, along with many others.

⁴King Zedekiah and his soldiers found out that the city was lost. So they fled during the night. They went out through the gate between the two walls

behind the palace garden. Then they went across the fields toward the Jordan valley. 5But the Babylonians saw the king and chased after him. They caught him on the plains of Jericho. They brought him to Nebuchadnezzar, the king of Babylon. At that time he was at Riblah, in the land of Hamath. There at Riblah, Nebuchadnezzar judged Zedekiah. 6The king of Babylon killed all of Zedekiah's children. He also killed all the nobles of Judah. And he made Zedekiah watch the whole thing. 7Then he cut out Zedekiah's eyes and bound him in chains. He sent him away to Babylon as a slave.

8Meanwhile the army burned Jerusalem, including the palace. And they tore down the walls of the city. 9Then Nebuzaradan and his men sent the people left in Jerusalem to Babylon. This included the people of Judah who had joined the side of Babylon. Nebuzaradan was the captain of the guard. 10He left only a few people in the land of Judah. And they were of the poorest people in the land. He gave these poor people fields and vineyards.

11-12Meanwhile King Nebuchadnezzar had told Nebuzaradan to find Jeremiah. "See that he isn't hurt," he said. "Look after him well and give him all he wants." 13So Nebuzaradan, Nebushazban, Nergal-sharezer, and the other officials did as the king had commanded. Nebuzaradan was the captain of the guard. Nebushazban was the chief of the eunuchs. Nergal-sharezer was the king's advisor. 14They sent soldiers to bring Jeremiah out of the prison. And they put him in the care of Gedaliah, the son of Ahikam. Ahikam was the son of Shaphan. They told Gedaliah to take him back to his home. And Jeremiah lived there among the people left in the land.

15The Lord gave this message to Jeremiah before the Babylonians got there. It came while he was still in prison. 16The Lord says, "Send this word to Ebed-melech the Ethiopian: 'The Lord, the God of Israel, says: "I will do to this city all that I said I would. I will destroy it before your eyes. 17But I will save you. You shall not be killed by those you fear so much. 18You have trusted in me. So I will save your life and keep you safe."'"

Jeremiah Is Set Free

40 Nebuzaradan, captain of the guard, took Jeremiah to Ramah. He brought him along with all the people of Judah who were being sent to Babylon. But then at Ramah he set him free.

2-3The captain called for Jeremiah. He said, "The Lord your God has brought this disaster on this land. He has done just as he said he would. For these people have sinned against the Lord. That is why it happened. 4Now I am going to take off your chains and let you go. If you want to come with me to Babylon, fine. I will see that you are well cared for. But if you don't want to come, don't. The world is before you. Go where you want to. 5If you decide to stay, then go back to Gedaliah. He has been chosen as governor of Judah by the king of Babylon. Stay there with the few people he rules. But it's up to you. Go where you like."

Then Nebuzaradan gave Jeremiah some food and money and let him go. 6So Jeremiah went back to Gedaliah. He lived in Judah with the people who were left in the land.

7Now there were some leaders of the army of Judah still there in the land. They heard that King Nebuchadnezzar had chosen Gedaliah as governor. He was to rule over the poor of the land who were left behind. Nebuchadnezzar had not sent everyone to Babylon. 8These leaders from Judah's army came to see Gedaliah at Mizpah. This was the town he used as his capital. These are the names of the leaders who came: Ishmael, Johanan and Jonathan, Seraiah, the sons of Ephai, and Jezaniah. Ishmael was the son of Nethaniah. Johanan and Jonathan were the sons of Kareah. Seraiah was the son of Tanhumeth. Ephai was a Netophathite. Jezaniah was the son of a Maacathite. With these leaders came all their men. 9And

Gedaliah told them it would be safe to surrender to the Babylonians.

"Stay here and serve the king of Babylon," he said. "If you do, all will go well for you. [10]As for me, I will stay at Mizpah. I will speak to the Babylonians for you when they come to see how I am doing. Settle in any city you wish and live off the land. Harvest the grapes and summer fruits and olives and store them away."

[11]Many people from Judah had run to Moab, Ammon, and Edom. But they heard that some people were still left in Judah. They found out that the king of Babylon had not taken them all away. And they heard that Gedaliah was the governor. [12]They all began to come back to Judah from their hiding places. They stopped at Mizpah to talk about their plans with Gedaliah. Then they went out to the empty farms. They gathered a great harvest of wine grapes and other crops.

[13-14]But soon after this Johanan, the son of Kareah, came to Mizpah. He brought along some of the other leaders from Judah's army. They warned Gedaliah that Baalis, king of the Ammonites, wanted to kill him. They said Baalis had sent Ishmael, the son of Nethaniah, to do it. But Gedaliah didn't believe them. [15]So Johanan asked to speak with Gedaliah alone. And Johanan said he would kill Ishmael secretly.

"Why should we let him come and murder you?" Johanan asked. "What will happen then to the people of Judah who have come back? Why should the few that are left be scattered and lost?"

[16]But Gedaliah said, "I will not let you do any such thing. For I am sure you are lying about Ishmael."

The Governor Dies

41 But in October, Ishmael came to Mizpah and brought 10 men with him. Ishmael was the son of Nethaniah. And Nethaniah was the son of Elishama. Ishmael was a member of the royal family and one of the king's top officials. Gedaliah asked Ishmael and his men to come to dinner. [2]So they all came and sat down to eat. But Ishmael and his men suddenly jumped up. They pulled out their swords and killed Gedaliah. [3]Then they killed all the leaders of Judah who were in Mizpah with Gedaliah. And they killed the Babylonian soldiers who were there, too.

[4-5]The next day, 80 men came to Mizpah from Shechem, Shiloh, and Samaria. At this time, the outside world still didn't know what had happened. These 80 men wanted to worship at the Temple of the Lord. They had shaved off their beards. They had torn their clothes and cut themselves. And they were bringing offerings and incense. [6]Ishmael went out from the city to meet them. He was crying as he went. When he came to them he said, "Oh, come and see what has happened to Gedaliah!"

[7]So they all went quickly into the city. Then Ishmael and his men killed all but 10 of them. And they threw their bodies into a well. [8]The 10 men who were not killed had spoken to Ishmael. They had promised to bring him their stores of wheat, barley, oil, and honey. [9]The well where the bodies were dumped had been made by King Asa. He made it when he built up Mizpah to protect himself against Baasha, king of Israel.

[10]Ishmael made captives of all the people in Mizpah. He captured the king's daughters and all the people under Gedaliah's care. These people had been put under Gedaliah by Nebuzaradan, captain of the guard. Soon after this, Ishmael took his captives with him toward the land of the Ammonites.

[11]But Johanan, the son of Kareah, heard what Ishmael had done. So he called the rest of the leaders of Judah's army. [12]They took all their men and set out to stop him. They caught up with him at the pool near Gibeon. [13-14]The people with Ishmael shouted for joy when they saw Johanan and his men. They left Ishmael and ran to meet Johanan.

[15]Meanwhile Ishmael got away with eight of his men. They went into the land of the Ammonites.

[16-17]Then Johanan and his men went to the village of Geruth Chimham. This village was near Bethlehem. They took

with them all those they had saved. There were soldiers, women, children, and eunuchs among them. And they got ready to leave for Egypt. [18]This was because they were afraid of what the Babylonians would do. They would soon find out that Ishmael had killed Gedaliah, the governor. And Gedaliah had been chosen by the Babylonian king.

Don't Go to Egypt!

42 Then Johanan and the army captains came to Jeremiah. All the people, great and small, were there with them. [2]They said, "Please pray for us to the Lord your God. For we are only a tiny number compared to what we were before. You know this as well as we do. [3]Beg the Lord your God to show us what to do. Ask him to tell us where to go."

[4]"All right," Jeremiah said. "I will ask him. Then I will tell you what he says. I will hide nothing from you."

[5]Then they said to Jeremiah, "We might not obey what the Lord says we should do. But if we don't obey him, may the curse of God be on us! [6]If we like it or not, we will obey the Lord our God. He is the one to whom we send you with our request. For if we obey him, everything will turn out well for us."

[7]Ten days later the Lord gave his answer to Jeremiah. [8]So he called for Johanan and the captains of his forces. He called for all the people, great and small. [9]And he said, "You sent me to the Lord, the God of Israel, with your request. And this is his answer:

[10]"The Lord says, 'Stay here in this land. If you do, I will bless you. And no one will hurt you. For I am sorry for all the trouble I have had to give to you. [11]Don't be afraid of the king of Babylon anymore. For I am with you to rescue you. I will keep you safe from his hand. [12]And I will show mercy to you by making him kind. He will not kill you or make slaves of you. But he will let you stay here in your land.'

[13-14]"But you might not obey the Lord. You might say, 'We will not stay here.' You might decide to go down to Egypt. For it is a place you think is safe from war and hunger. [15]But if you do

this, then this is what the Lord says to you. Listen, O people of Judah! The Lord, the God of Israel, says: 'You might choose to go down to Egypt. [16]But if you do, the war and hunger you fear will follow close behind you. And you will die there. [17]That is what will happen to all who go to live in Egypt. Yes, you will die from sword, hunger, and disease. None of you will get away from the evil I will bring upon you there.'

[18]"For the Lord, the God of Israel, says: 'My anger was once poured out on the people of Jerusalem. In the same way, it will be poured out on you when you get to Egypt. You will be welcomed with hatred. You will be cursed and looked down upon. And you will never again see your own land.' [19]For the Lord has said: 'O people of Judah, do not go to Egypt!'"

Jeremiah said, "Never forget the warning I have given you today. [20]If you go, it will be at the cost of your lives. For you lied when you sent me to pray for you. You said, 'Just tell us what God says, and we will do it!' [21]And today I have told you what he said. But you will not obey any more now than you did the other times. [22]So know for sure that you will die by sword, hunger, and disease in Egypt. For you have decided to go there."

The People Won't Believe

43 Jeremiah finished giving this message from God to all the people. [2-3]Then Azariah, Johanan, and the other proud men spoke up. Azariah was the son of Hoshaiah. Johanan was the son of Kareah. These men said to Jeremiah, "You lie! The Lord our God didn't tell us not to go to Egypt! Baruch, the son of Neriah, has plotted against us. He told you to say this so that we would stay here. Then we would be killed or carried off to Babylon as slaves."

[4]So Johanan and the leaders of Judah's army and all the people did not obey. They did not listen to the Lord and stay in Judah. [5]All of them now started off for Egypt. All those who had come back from hiding in nearby lands went too. Johanan and the other captains

were in command. 6In the crowd were men, women, and children. The king's daughters were there. And so were all those whom Nebuzaradan had left with Gedaliah. They even forced Jeremiah and Baruch to go with them. 7And so they came to Egypt at the city of Tahpanhes. For they would not obey the Lord.

8Then at Tahpanhes, the Lord spoke to Jeremiah again. 9The Lord said, "Call together the men of Judah. Then take some large rocks. Bury them in the clay of the brick pavement. Do this at the door of Pharaoh's palace here in Tahpanhes. And do it all as the people watch you. 10Then tell the men of Judah this: 'The Lord, the God of Israel, says: "I will surely bring Nebuchadnezzar, king of Babylon, here to Egypt. For he is my servant. I will set his throne upon these stones that I have hidden. He shall spread his royal tent over them. 11And when he comes, he shall destroy the land of Egypt. He shall kill all those I want killed. He shall capture all those I want captured. And many shall die of plague. 12He will set fire to the temples of the gods of Egypt. And he will burn their idols. He will carry off the people as his captives. And he shall plunder the land of Egypt as a shepherd picks fleas from his cloak! And he himself shall leave unhurt. 13He shall break down the stone pillars standing in the city of Heliopolis. And he shall burn down the temples of the gods of Egypt."'"

God Gets Angry

44 This is a message that God gave to Jeremiah. It was for all the people of Judah living in Egypt. It was for the people of Judah in Migdol, Tahpanhes, and Memphis.

2-3"The Lord, the God of Israel, says: 'You saw what I did to Jerusalem. You saw what I did to all the cities of Judah. Because of all their wickedness they lie in heaps and ashes. They are empty, without a living soul. For my anger rose high against them for bowing to other gods. They worshiped "gods" that neither you nor any of your fathers ever knew.

4"'I sent my servants, the prophets, to protest over and over again. I sent my servants to beg them not to do this thing I hate. 5But they wouldn't listen. They wouldn't turn back from their wicked ways. They have kept on giving sacrifices to these "gods." 6And so my anger boiled over. It fell like fire on the cities of Judah. It poured into the streets of Jerusalem. And these cities are empty and ruined to this day.'

?????????????????????????????????

Why did God get so angry at his people that he burned their cities into heaps of ashes?

(Read 44:2-6 for the answer.)

?????????????????????????????????

7"And now the Lord, the God of Israel, asks you: 'Why are you destroying yourselves? For not one of you who has come here from Judah shall live. Not a man, woman, or child among you will survive. Even the babies will all die. 8For you are making me angry with your idols. First you made them, and now you worship them here in Egypt. You burn incense to them, too! You are causing me to destroy you. I will make you a curse. I will make you a stench in the noses of all the nations of the earth. 9Have you forgotten the sins of your fathers? Don't you remember the sins of the kings and queens of Judah? Have you forgotten your own sins? Don't you remember the sins of your wives in Judah and Jerusalem? 10And until this very hour, no one has even said he was sorry! No one has wanted to come back to me. No one wants to follow the laws I gave you and your fathers before you.'

11"Therefore the Lord, the God of Israel, says: 'My face is full of anger. And I will destroy every one of you! 12I will take these people of Judah who came here to Egypt and burn them up. They shall fall here in Egypt, killed by hunger and the sword. All shall die, from the least important to the greatest. They shall be hated and cursed by the people around them. 13I will punish them in Egypt just as I punished them in Jerusalem. I will do it by the sword, hunger, and disease. [14]Not one of them shall escape from my anger except those who are sorry they came. And those who are sorry must go back again to their own land.'"

[15]There were men there who knew that their wives had burned incense to idols. And there were also many of the women present. It was a great crowd of people from Judah who were in Egypt. They said to Jeremiah:

[16]"We will not listen to your false 'Messages from God'! [17]We will do whatever we want to. We will burn incense to the Queen of Heaven. We will sacrifice to her just as much as we like. We will do just as we and our fathers before us have done. Our kings and princes have always done it in the cities of Judah. They even did it in the streets of Jerusalem. For in those days we had plenty to eat. And we were well off and happy! [18]But we stopped burning incense to the Queen of Heaven. And we stopped worshiping her. Ever since then, we have been in great trouble. And we have been destroyed by the sword and hunger."

[19]"And," the women said, "our husbands knew what we were doing all along. They knew we were worshiping the Queen of Heaven. They knew we were pouring out our drink offerings to her. They saw us making cakes for her with her image on them. Would we do this without our husbands knowing it and helping us? Of course not!"

[20]Then Jeremiah spoke to all of them, men and women alike. He spoke to all who had answered him.

[21]Jeremiah said, "Do you think the Lord didn't know what you were doing? Do you think he was blind to the deeds of your fathers? Do you think he couldn't see what your kings and princes were doing? Do you think he didn't know the people were burning incense to idols? Do you think he didn't see this in the cities of Judah and Jerusalem? [22]He could no longer stand all the bad things you were doing. That is why he made your land a great and empty ruin. That is why it is cursed and empty, as it is today. [23]These terrible things have happened to you because you have burned incense to idols. You have sinned against the Lord and would not obey him."

[24]Then Jeremiah spoke to them all. The women were there along with the men. Jeremiah said, "Listen to the word of the Lord! Listen, all you people of Judah who are here in Egypt! [25]The Lord, the God of Israel, says: 'Both you and your wives have said that you will not stop doing evil. You will not stop worshiping and giving sacrifices to the Queen of Heaven. And you have proved this by your actions. So go ahead! Keep all your promises to her!' [26]But listen to the word of the Lord! These words are for all you people of Judah living in Egypt: 'I make this promise by my great name,' says the Lord. 'It will do you no good to look for help and blessing from me any more. Never come to me saying, "O Lord our God, help us!" [27]For I will watch over you, but *not* for good! I will see to it that bad things happen to you. You shall be destroyed by war and hunger until all of you are dead.

[28]"'Only those who go back to Judah shall escape my anger. And there will only be a few of you who go back! But all who do not go back shall find out if I tell the truth! [29]And I give you this proof that all I have said will happen to you. [30]I will turn Pharaoh Hophra, king of Egypt, over to those who want to kill him. It will be just as it was when I turned Zedekiah, king of Judah, over to Nebuchadnezzar, king of Babylon.'"

45 This is the message Jeremiah gave to Baruch. He gave it in the fourth year of the reign of King Jehoiakim, the son of Josiah. This was after Baruch had written down all God's messages as Jeremiah dictated them to him.

[2]"O Baruch, the Lord God of Israel says this to you: [3]'You have said, "How terrible it is for me! Don't I have troubles enough already? And now the Lord has added more! I am tired of my own crying. I find no rest."' [4]But tell Baruch this. 'The Lord says: "I will destroy this nation that I built. I will wipe out what I made. [5]Are you looking for great things for yourself? Don't do it! For I will bring great evil upon all these people. But I

will keep you safe wherever you go. This will be your reward.""'"

A Message to the Egyptians

46 Here are the messages given to Jeremiah concerning foreign nations:

²This message was given against Egypt. It came at the time of the battle of Carchemish. This happened near the Euphrates River. There Pharaoh Necho, king of Egypt, and his army were beaten by Nebuchadnezzar, king of Babylon. This was in the fourth year of Jehoiakim's reign. Jehoiakim was the son of Josiah, king of Judah.

³"Buckle on your armor, you Egyptians. And go into battle! ⁴Harness the horses and get ready to climb on them. Put on your helmets and sharpen your spears. Put on your armor. ⁵But look! The Egyptian army runs in terror. The strongest of its soldiers run without looking back. Yes, terror shall surround them on every side," says the Lord. ⁶"The swift will not get away. Neither shall the strongest soldiers. In the north, by the river Euphrates, they have stumbled and fallen.

⁷"What is this mighty army? It is rising like the Nile at flood time. It is flooding all the land. ⁸It is the Egyptian army. It brags that it will cover the earth like a flood, beating down every enemy. ⁹Then come, O horses and chariots and mighty soldiers of Egypt! Come, all of you from Cush and Put and Lud! Come, all you who handle the shield and bend the bow! ¹⁰For this is the day of the Lord, the Lord of Heaven's armies. It is a day of revenge upon his enemies. The sword shall kill until it is satisfied. Yes, it will kill until it is drunk with your blood. For the Lord will be given a sacrifice today. It will be given in the north country beside the river Euphrates! ¹¹Go up to Gilead for medicine, O daughter of Egypt! Yet there is no cure for your wounds. You might use many medicines, but there is no healing for you. ¹²The nations have heard of your shame. The earth is filled with your cry of despair and defeat. Your strongest soldiers will stumble across each other and fall together."

¹³Then God gave Jeremiah this message. It is about the coming of Nebuchadnezzar, king of Babylon, to attack Egypt.

¹⁴"Shout it out in Egypt. Tell it in the cities of Migdol, Memphis, and Tahpanhes! Call out your army for battle. For the sword of death shall kill all around you. ¹⁵Why has Apis, your bull god, run away in terror? Because the Lord knocked him down before your enemies. ¹⁶Many people shall fall down in great piles. Then there will be only a few people of Judah left. They will say, 'Come, let us go back again to Judah where we were born. Let's get away from all this killing here!'

¹⁷"Give Pharaoh Hophra a new name. Call him 'The Man with No Power But with Plenty of Noise!'"

¹⁸The King's name is the Lord of Heaven's armies. He says, "One is coming against Egypt who is as tall as Mount Tabor. He is as big as Mount Carmel by the sea! ¹⁹Pack up your things! Get ready to leave for exile, you people of Egypt. For the city of Memphis shall be destroyed. Not a person will be left alive. ²⁰⁻²¹Egypt is as sleek as a heifer. But a gadfly sends her running. And it is a gadfly from the north! Even her famous soldiers have become like scared calves. They turn and run, for it is the day of great trouble for Egypt. It is a time of great punishment. ²²⁻²³Silent as a snake gliding away, Egypt runs. The attacking army marches in. The soldiers cut down your people like woodsmen who clear a forest of its trees. ²⁴Egypt is as weak as a girl before these men from the north."

²⁵The Lord, the God of Israel, says: "I will punish Amon, the god of Thebes. I will punish all the gods of Egypt. I will punish Pharaoh too, and all who trust in him. ²⁶I will give them into the hands of those who want them killed. I will give them to Nebuchadnezzar, king of Babylon, and his army. But after that the land shall be healed from the pain of war.

²⁷"But don't you be afraid, O my people who go back to your own land. Don't

be upset and sad. For I will save you from far away. And I will bring your children from a distant land. Yes, Israel shall come back and be at rest. And nothing shall make her afraid. 28Don't be afraid, O Jacob, my servant," says the Lord. "For I am with you. I will destroy all the nations to which I have sent you. But I will not destroy you. I will punish you, but only enough to correct you."

A Message to the Philistines

47 This is God's message to Jeremiah about the Philistines of Gaza. It was given before the city was captured by the Egyptian army.

2"The Lord says: 'A flood is coming from the north. It will overflow the land of the Philistines. It will destroy their cities and everything in them. Strong men will scream in terror. And everyone in the land will cry. 3Hear the galloping hoofs and rumbling wheels as the chariots go rushing by. Fathers run without looking back at their helpless children. 4For the time has come when all the Philistines will be destroyed. And their friends from Tyre and Sidon will fall with them. For the Lord is destroying the Philistines, those people from Caphtor. 5The cities of Gaza and Ashkelon will be cut to the ground. They will lie broken and in ruins. O descendants of the Anakim, how you will cry and mourn!

6"'O sword of the Lord, when will you be at rest again? Go back into your sheath. Rest and be still! 7But how can it be still when the Lord has sent it on a mission? For the city of Ashkelon and those living along the sea must be destroyed.'"

The Proud Moabites Are Doomed

48 This is the message of the Lord of Heaven's armies, the God of Israel. It is given against the land of Moab.

"How terrible it will be for the city of Nebo. For it shall lie in ruins. The city of Kiriathaim and its forts are captured. 2-4No one will ever brag about Moab any more. For there is a plot against her life. In Heshbon plans have been made to destroy her. 'Come,' they say, 'we will cut her off from being a nation.' In the town of Madmen all is quiet. And then the roar of battle will go against Horonaim. For all Moab is being destroyed. Her crying will be heard as far away as Zoar. 5Her people will climb the hills of Luhith, crying bitterly. And cries of terror will rise to them from the city below. 6Run for your lives! Hide in the wilderness! 7For you trusted in your riches and skill. Therefore, you shall die. Your god Chemosh shall be taken away to distant lands! And his priests and princes shall be taken with him.

8"All the villages and cities shall be destroyed. For the Lord has said it. 9Oh, that Moab had wings! Then she could fly away. For her cities shall be left without anyone living. 10Those who don't attack you with their swords shall be cursed. For that would be refusing to do the work God has given them!

11"From her earliest history Moab has lived there. It has not been troubled by any invasions. She is like wine that has not been poured from jar to jar. She is smooth and smells sweet. But now she shall be poured out into exile! 12There is a time coming soon," the Lord has said. "At that time, I will send enemies. They will spill her out from jar to jar. And then they will break all the jars! 13Then at last Moab will be ashamed of her idol Chemosh. They will be ashamed like Israel was of her calf-idol at Bethel.

14"Do you remember that boast of yours? You said, 'We are heroes, mighty men of war!' 15But now Moab is to be destroyed. Her destroyer is on the way. Her best children will soon die," says the King, the Lord of Heaven's armies. 16"Disaster is coming fast to Moab. 17"O friends of Moab, cry for her! See how the strong, the beautiful is broken! 18Come down from your glory and sit in the dust, O people of Dibon. For those destroying Moab shall destroy Dibon too. And they shall tear down all her towers. 19Those in Aroer are afraid and stand beside the road to watch. They shout to those who are running from Moab, 'What has happened there?'

20"And they reply, 'Moab lies in ruins. Cry out loud and wail. Tell it by the banks of the Arnon River. Tell everyone that Moab is destroyed.'

²¹"All the cities of the plains lie in ruins too. For God's judgment has been poured out on them all. Holon and Jahzah and Mephaath have been judged. ²²So have Dibon and Nebo and Beth-diblathaim. ²³Kiriathaim and Beth-gamul and Beth-meon are destroyed. ²⁴And Kerioth and Bozrah have fallen. All the cities of the land of Moab, far and near, lie in ruins.

²⁵"The strength of Moab is ended. Her horns are cut off. Her arms are broken. ²⁶Let her stagger and fall like a drunk. For she has sinned against the Lord. Moab shall sit in her own vomit. She shall be looked upon with scorn by all. ²⁷For you laughed at Israel and robbed her. And you were happy at her fall.

²⁸"O people of Moab, run from your cities. Go and live in the caves like doves. For they nest in the clefts of the rocks. ²⁹We have all heard of the pride of Moab, for it is very great. We know her pride and her arrogant heart. ³⁰I know her pride," the Lord has said. "But her bragging is false, and now she is helpless. ³¹Yes, I cry for Moab. My heart is broken for the men of Kir-heres.

³²"O men of Sibmah, you were rich in vineyards. I cry for you even more than for Jazer. For the destroyer has cut off your spreading vines. He has taken your grapes and summer fruits. He has picked you bare! ³³Joy and gladness are gone from fruitful Moab. The presses yield no wine. No one treads the grapes with shouts of joy. There is shouting, yes, but not the shouting of joy. ³⁴Instead the awful cries of terror and pain rise from all over the land. You can hear the cries from Heshbon to Elealeh and Jahaz. You can hear them from Zoar to Horonaim and Eglath-shelishiyah. The pastures of Nimrim are empty now."

³⁵For the Lord says, "I have put a stop to Moab's worshiping false gods. I have stopped them from burning incense to idols. ³⁶My heart is sad for Moab and Kir-heres. For now all their riches are gone. ³⁷They shave their heads and beards in sadness. They slash their hands and put on clothes of sackcloth.

³⁸Crying and sadness will be in every Moabite home and on the streets. For I have crushed Moab like an old, thrown away bottle. ³⁹How it is broken! Hear the cries! See the shame of Moab! For she is a sign of horror. And her neighbors laugh at her now.

⁴⁰"A vulture circles above the land of Moab," says the Lord. ⁴¹"Her cities are fallen. Her walled cities are taken. The hearts of her strongest soldiers fail with fear. They are like women in the pains of giving birth. ⁴²Moab shall no longer be a nation. For she has boasted against the Lord. ⁴³Fear and traps shall be your lot, O Moab," says the Lord. ⁴⁴"He who runs shall fall in a trap. He who gets away from the trap shall run into a snare. I will see to it that you do not get away. For the time of your judgment has come. ⁴⁵They run to Heshbon, not able to go farther. But a fire comes from Heshbon, the home of Sihon. Fire burns the land from end to end with all its sinful people.

⁴⁶"How terrible it will be for you, O Moab. The people of the god Chemosh are destroyed. And your sons and daughters are taken away as slaves. ⁴⁷But in the last days," says the Lord, "I will bring Moab back."

Here the prophecy about Moab ends.

A Message to the Ammonites

49 "What is this you are doing? Why are you living in the cities of Judah? Aren't there enough people from Judah to fill them up? Didn't they get these cities from me? You are the people who worship Milcom. Why then have you taken over Gad and all its cities? ²I will punish you for this," the Lord says. "I will soon destroy your city of Rabbah. It shall become an empty pile of rubble. And all the towns nearby shall be burned. Then Israel shall come and take back her land from you again. You pushed her out of her land. And now she shall push you out," says the Lord.

³"Cry out, O Heshbon, for Ai is destroyed! Weep, daughter of Rabbah! Put on clothes for crying. Cry and wail, hiding in the hedges. For your god Milcom shall be sent away along with his princes

and priests. ⁴You are proud of your rich valleys, but they will soon be ruined. O wicked daughter, you trusted in your riches. You thought no one could ever hurt you. ⁵But see, I will bring terror upon you," says the Lord of Heaven's armies. "For all your neighbors shall drive you from your land. And no one shall help your people as they run. ⁶But later I will give back the riches of the Ammonites," says the Lord.

A Message to the Edomites

⁷The Lord says, "Where are all your wise men of days gone by? Is there not one left in all of Teman? ⁸Run away to the farthest parts of the desert, O people of Dedan. For when I punish Edom, I will punish you! ⁹⁻¹⁰Those who gather grapes leave hardly any for the poor. Even thieves don't take everything! But I will strip bare the land of Esau. And there will be no place to hide. Her children, her brothers, and her neighbors will all be destroyed. And she herself will die too. ¹¹But I will take care of the children who are left without fathers. And let your widows depend upon me."

¹²The Lord says to Edom: "If the innocent must suffer, how much more must you! You shall not go without being punished! You must drink this cup of judgment! ¹³For I promise this by my own name," says the Lord. "I promise that Bozrah shall become a pile of ruins. She will be cursed and laughed at. And the cities around her shall be empty wastelands forever."

¹⁴I have heard this message from the Lord. He said, "I have sent a messenger to call the nations together against Edom. They will gather together and destroy her. ¹⁵I will make her weak among the nations and hated by all," says the Lord. ¹⁶"You have been fooled by your pride. You live there in the mountains of Petra. You hide in the clefts of the rocks. You live among the peaks with the eagles. But even so, I will bring you down," says the Lord.

¹⁷"It will be terrible for Edom. All who go by will be amazed. They will gasp when they see it. ¹⁸Your cities will become silent. They will be like Sodom and Gomorrah and the towns nearby," says the Lord. "No one will live there anymore. ¹⁹I will send against them one who will come like a lion. He will come from the wilds of Jordan stalking the

Sackcloth
JEREMIAH 49:3
When Bible-time people mourned, they put on sackcloth. They mourned when someone died. They also mourned when something sad happened to the city or country. Sometimes a person wore sackcloth to show God he was sorry. Sackcloth was made of goat hair or camel hair. It was rougher than sheep's wool. It did not feel as good as wool or cotton. Sackcloth was probably black. Sometimes people today wear black clothing to mourn. Why was it called sackcloth? Some grain sacks were made from the same material. How would you like to wear sackcloth to school today? Jeans look and feel much better, don't they? Aren't you glad you have clothing that looks and feels good? Thank God for it!

sheep in the fold. Suddenly Edom shall be destroyed. I will send the person of my choice to destroy the Edomites. For who is like me, and who can call me to account? What shepherd can stand against me?"

²⁰Listen well, for the Lord will surely

do this to Edom. He will also do this to the people of Teman. Even little children will be taken away as slaves! It will be a sad thing to see. ²¹The earth shakes with the noise of Edom's fall. The cry of the people is heard as far away as the Red Sea. ²²The one who will come will fly as fast as a vulture. He will spread his wings against Bozrah. Then the courage of the strongest soldiers will melt away. They will be afraid like a woman in labor.

A Message to Damascus

²³"The cities of Hamath and Arpad are full of fear. For they have heard the news of their judgment. Their hearts are troubled like a wild sea in a great storm. ²⁴Damascus has become weak. All of her people turn to run. Fear, pain, and sadness have a hold on her like a woman in labor. ²⁵O famous city, city of joy, you are all alone now! ²⁶Your young men lie dead in the streets. Your whole army shall be destroyed in one day," says the Lord of Heaven's armies. ²⁷"And I will start a fire at the edge of Damascus. And it shall burn up the palaces of Benhadad."

A Message to Kedar and Hazor

²⁸This prophecy is about Kedar and the kingdoms of Hazor. They will be destroyed by Nebuchadnezzar, king of Babylon. For the Lord will send him to destroy them.

²⁹"Their flocks and their tents will be captured," says the Lord. "And so will all their household goods. Their camels will be taken away. And all around will be the shouts of panic. 'We are surrounded and can't get away!' they will cry. ³⁰Run for your lives," says the Lord. "Go deep into the deserts, O people of Hazor. For Nebuchadnezzar, king of Babylon, has made plans against you. And he is getting ready to destroy you.

³¹"Go!" said the Lord to King Nebuchadnezzar. "Attack those rich Bedouin tribes living alone in the desert. They don't have a care in the world. They brag that they can stand all by themselves. They claim that they need neither walls nor gates. ³²Their camels and cattle shall all be yours. And I will scatter these

heathen to the winds. From all directions I will bring trouble upon them.

³³"Hazor shall be a home for wild animals of the desert. No one shall ever live there again. It shall be empty and ruined forever."

A Message to Elam

³⁴God's message against Elam came to Jeremiah. It came in the beginning of the reign of Zedekiah, king of Judah.

³⁵"The Lord says, 'I will destroy the army of Elam. ³⁶And I will scatter the people of Elam to the four winds. They shall be sent to countries all around the world. ³⁷My anger will bring great evil upon Elam,' says the Lord. 'I will cause her enemies to wipe her out. ³⁸And I will set my throne in Elam,' says the Lord. 'I will destroy her king and princes. ³⁹But in the latter days I will bring the people back,' says the Lord."

A Message to Babylon

50 This is the message from the Lord against Babylon. It was spoken by Jeremiah the prophet.

²"Tell all the world that Babylon will be destroyed. Her god Marduk will be put to shame! ³For a nation shall come down upon her from the north. It will come with such power that no one shall live in her again. All shall be gone. Both men and animals shall run away.

⁴"Then the people of Israel and Judah shall join together. They shall cry and seek the Lord their God. ⁵They shall ask the way to Jerusalem and start back home again. 'Come,' they will say, 'let us join ourselves to the Lord. Let us make a promise to him that will never be broken again.'

⁶"My people have been lost sheep. Their shepherds led them the wrong way. Then they turned them loose in the mountains. My people lost their way and didn't remember how to get back home. ⁷Everyone who found them destroyed them. And those who destroyed them said, 'We are allowed to attack them freely. For they have sinned against the Lord, the God of justice.'

⁸"But now, run from Babylon, the land of the Chaldeans. Lead my people

home again. ⁹For see, I am calling up an army of great nations from the north. I will bring them against Babylon to attack her. And she shall be destroyed. The enemies' arrows go straight to the mark. They do not miss! ¹⁰And Babylon shall be sacked until everyone has more than enough loot," says the Lord.

¹¹"You were once glad, O Babylonians. You plundered my people and are fat like cows fed in rich pastures. And you neigh like strong horses. ¹²But your mother shall be full of shame. For you shall become the weakest of the nations. You shall become a wilderness, a dry and desert land. ¹³Because of the anger of the Lord, Babylon shall become empty wasteland. All who pass by shall be amazed. And they shall laugh at her for all her wounds.

¹⁴"Yes, get ready to fight with Babylon, all you nations round about. Let the archers shoot at her. Don't hold back any of your arrows. For she has sinned against the Lord. ¹⁵Shout against her from every side. Look! She surrenders! Her walls have fallen down. The Lord has taken revenge. Do to her as she has done! ¹⁶Let the farmhands all leave the land. Let them run back to their own lands as the enemies come.

¹⁷"The Israelites are like the sheep that lions chase. First the king of Assyria ate them up. Then Nebuchadnezzar, the king of Babylon, crunched their bones." ¹⁸Therefore the Lord, the God of Israel, says: "Now I will punish the king of Babylon and his land. I will punish him just as I punished the king of Assyria. ¹⁹And I will bring Israel home again to her own land. They will feed in the fields of Carmel and Bashan. They will be happy once more on Mount Ephraim and Mount Gilead. ²⁰In those days," says the Lord, "no sin shall be found in Israel or in Judah. For I will forgive the few Israelites I keep alive.

²¹"Go up, O my soldiers, against the land of Merathaim. Go and fight against the people of Pekod. Yes, march against Babylon, the land of rebels. It is a land that I will judge! Kill them off as I have ordered you. ²²Let there be the shout of battle in the land. And let it be a shout

of great destruction. ²³Babylon, the strongest hammer in all the earth, lies broken. Babylon is a ruin among the nations! ²⁴O Babylon, I have set a trap for you and you are caught. For you have fought against the Lord.

?????????????????????????????????
Which kingdom was like the biggest hammer on earth?
(Read 50:22-25 for the answer.)
?????????????????????????????????

²⁵"The Lord has opened his weapon rooms. He has brought out weapons to send his anger upon his enemies. The terrible things that happen to Babylon will be the work of the Lord God. ²⁶Yes, come against her from distant lands. Break open her storerooms of grain. Knock down her walls and houses. Smash them into heaps of ruins. Totally destroy her! Let nothing be left. ²⁷Don't even let her cattle stay alive! Kill them all! For the time has come for Babylon to be destroyed.

²⁸"But my people will run away. They will escape back to their own country. They will tell how the Lord their God has showed his anger. He has turned against those who destroyed his Temple.

²⁹"Send out a call for archers to come to Babylon. Surround the city so that none can get away. Do to her as she has done to others. For she has proudly stood against the Lord, the Holy One of Israel. ³⁰Her young men will fall in the streets and die. Her soldiers will all be killed. ³¹For see, I am against you, O people so proud. And now your day of judgment has come. ³²Land of pride, you will stumble and fall. And no one will lift you up again. For the Lord will light a fire in the cities of Babylon. And those fires will burn everything around them."

³³"The Lord says, 'Wrong has been done to the people of Israel and Judah. Their enemies hold them and will not let them go.' ³⁴But their Redeemer is strong. His name is the Lord of Heaven's armies. He will speak for them and see that they are set free. He will send them to live again in quietness in Israel.

"As for the people of Babylon, there

is no rest for them! [35]The sword of death shall cut at the people of Babylon," says the Lord. "It shall kill the people of Babylon. It shall destroy her princes and wise men too. [36]All her wise counselors shall become fools! Terror shall take hold of her strongest soldiers! [37]War shall destroy her horses and chariots. And her friends from other lands shall become as weak as women. Her treasures shall all be robbed. [38]Even her water supply will fail. And why? Because the whole land is full of idols. The people are madly in love with them.

[39]"So the city of Babylon shall become the home of ostriches and jackals. It shall be a home for the wild animals of the desert. Never again shall it be lived in by human beings. It shall lie empty forever. [40]The Lord says that he will destroy Babylon. He will destroy it just like he destroyed Sodom and Gomorrah. No one has lived in those cities since. And no one will live again in Babylon.

[41]"See them coming! It is a great army from the north! And there are many kings among them. They were called by God from many lands. [42]They are fully armed for killing. They are cruel and show no mercy. Their battle cry roars like the surf against the shoreline. O Babylon, they ride against you fully ready for the battle."

[43]The king of Babylon heard the message. And his hands fell helpless at his sides. Feelings of terror grabbed him like the fear of a woman in labor.

[44]"I will send enemies against Babylon. They will come suddenly, like a lion from the jungles of Jordan. I will chase her from her land. And I will choose leaders to rule over them. For who is like me? What ruler can stand against my will? Who can question what I choose to do?"

[45]Listen to the plan of the Lord against Babylon. For even little children shall be taken away as slaves. Oh, the horror! Oh, the terror!   [46]The whole earth shall shake at Babylon's fall. And her cry of pain shall be heard around the world.

Our Great and Mighty God

51 The Lord says, "I will stir up an enemy against Babylon. And they shall destroy her. [2]Foreigners shall come and sift her out. Then the wind shall blow her away. They shall come from every side. They shall rise against her in her day of trouble. [3]The arrows of the enemy shall strike down the bowmen of Babylon. They shall pierce her soldiers through their coats of mail. No one shall be saved. Both young and old alike shall be killed. [4]They shall fall down dead in the land of Babylonia. They will be slashed to death in her streets. [5]For the Lord of Heaven's armies has not left Israel and Judah. He is still their God. But the land of Babylonia is filled with sin against the Holy One of Israel."

[6]Run away from Babylon! Save yourselves! Don't get trapped! If you stay, you will be destroyed. For soon God will take revenge on all of Babylon's sins. [7]Babylon has been like a gold cup in the Lord's hands. She was a cup from which he made the whole earth drink and go mad. [8]But now, suddenly Babylon too has fallen. Cry for her. Give her medicine. Perhaps she can yet be healed. [9]We would help her if we could. But nothing can save her now. Let her go. Leave her and go back to your own land. For God is judging her from Heaven. [10]The Lord has taken revenge for us. Come, let us tell those in Jerusalem about all that the Lord has done.

[11]Sharpen the arrows! Lift up the shields! For the Lord has stirred up the spirit of the kings of the Medes. They will march on Babylon and destroy her. This is his revenge on those who did bad things to his people. This is his punishment on those that made his Temple unclean. [12]Get your defenses ready, Babylon! Set many watchmen on your walls. Send out a trap, for the Lord will do what he has said about Babylon. [13]O rich center of trade, your end has come. The thread of your life is cut. [14]The Lord of Heaven's armies has made this promise by his own name. He says, "Your cities shall be filled with enemies. They will be like fields filled with locusts in a plague.

They shall lift to the skies their mighty shouts of victory."

¹⁵God made the earth by his power and wisdom. He stretched out the heavens by his knowledge. ¹⁶When he speaks, there is thunder in the heavens. He causes the vapors to rise around the world. He brings the lightning with the rain. He sends the winds from his storerooms. ¹⁷Compared to him, all men are stupid beasts. They have no wisdom at all! The silversmith is made dull by the images he makes. For in making them he lies. He calls them gods when there is not a breath of life in them at all! ¹⁸Idols are nothing! They are lies! And the time is coming when God will come and destroy them all. ¹⁹But the God of Israel is no idol! For he made everything there is. And Israel is his nation. He is known as the Lord of Heaven's armies.

²⁰"Cyrus is God's ax and sword. I will use you," says the Lord. "You shall break nations in pieces. You shall destroy many kingdoms. ²¹With you I will crush armies. I will destroy the horse and his rider. I will destroy the chariot and the chariot driver. ²²Yes, and the common people will die too—old and young, boys and girls. ²³Shepherds and their flocks will be destroyed. So will farmers and their oxen. Captains and rulers will also fall. ²⁴I will pay back Babylon for all the evil they have done to my people. And I will do it before your very eyes," says the Lord.

²⁵"For see, I am against you, O mighty mountain, Babylon! You are the destroyer of the earth! I will lift my hand against you. I will roll you down from your heights. Then I will leave you, a burnt-out mountain. ²⁶You shall be empty forever. Even your stones shall never be used for building again. You shall be totally wiped out."

²⁷Tell many nations to get ready for war on Babylon. Sound the battle cry. Bring out the armies of Ararat, Minni, and Ashkenaz. Choose a leader and bring many horses! ²⁸Bring against her the armies of the kings of the Medes and their generals. And bring along all the armies of the lands they rule.

²⁹Babylon shakes and rolls around in pain. For all that the Lord has planned against her will happen. Babylon will be left empty without a living person. ³⁰Her strongest soldiers no longer fight. They stay in their houses. Their courage is gone. They have become weak like women. The invaders have burned the houses and broken down the city gates. ³¹Messengers from every side come running to the king. They tell him all is lost! ³²All the escape routes are blocked. There is no way out! The walls and towers are burning. And the army is in panic.

³³For the Lord, the God of Israel, says: "Babylon is like the wheat on a threshing floor. In just a little while the harvest will begin."

³⁴⁻³⁵The people of Judah in Babylon say, "Nebuchadnezzar has eaten and crushed us. He has emptied out our strength. He has eaten us like a great monster. He has filled his belly with our riches. He has cast us out of our own country. May Babylon be paid back for all she did to us! May she be paid back for all the blood she spilled!"

³⁶And the Lord replies, "I will be your lawyer. I will plead your case. I will give your enemies what they deserve. I will dry up her river and her water supply. ³⁷And Babylon shall become a heap of ruins, haunted by jackals. It shall be a land terrible to look at. It shall be empty, without a living person. ³⁸In their drunken feasts, the men of Babylon roar like lions. ³⁹And they lie down drunk with all their wine. As they sleep, I will make another kind of feast for them. I will make them drink until they faint on the floor. There they will sleep forever. They will never wake up again," says the Lord. ⁴⁰"I will bring them like lambs to be killed. They will be like rams and goats.

⁴¹"How Babylon is fallen! Great Babylon, you were praised by all the earth! Now the world can hardly believe its eyes at Babylon's fall! ⁴²The sea has risen upon Babylon. She is covered by its waves. ⁴³Her cities lie in ruins. She is a dry wilderness where no one lives. Travelers don't even pass by there. ⁴⁴And I will punish Bel, the god of Babylon. I will make him give up what he has

taken. The nations shall no longer come and worship him. The wall of Babylon has fallen.

⁴⁵"O my people, run away from Babylon. Save yourselves from the anger of the Lord. ⁴⁶But don't panic when you hear the first story of enemy armies. For stories will keep coming year after year. Then there will be a time of civil war. The governors of Babylon fight against each other. ⁴⁷For the time is surely coming when I will punish this great city and all her idols. Her dead shall lie in the streets. ⁴⁸Heaven and earth shall be happy. For out of the north shall come armies against Babylon," says the Lord. ⁴⁹"Just as Babylon killed the people of Israel, so must she be killed. ⁵⁰Go, you who escaped the sword! Don't stand and watch. Run while you can! Remember the Lord, and go home to Jerusalem far away!"

⁵¹"We are very ashamed. The Temple of the Lord has been made unclean by people from Babylon."

⁵²"Yes," says the Lord. "But the time is coming when the idols of Babylon will be destroyed. All through the land will be heard the groans of the wounded. ⁵³Babylon might be as powerful as Heaven. She might even make herself much stronger! But even so, she shall die," says the Lord.

⁵⁴"Listen! Hear the cry of great destruction out of Babylon! ⁵⁵For the Lord is destroying Babylon. Her mighty voice is quiet as the waves roar in upon her. ⁵⁶Enemy armies come and kill her strong men. All her weapons break in her hands. For the Lord God gives just punishment. And he is giving Babylon all that she deserves. ⁵⁷I will make drunk her princes, wise men, rulers, captains, and soldiers. They shall sleep and not wake up again!" says the King, the Lord of Heaven's armies. ⁵⁸"For the wide walls of Babylon shall be broken to the ground. And her high gates shall be burned down. The builders from many lands have worked for nothing. For all their work shall be destroyed by fire!"

⁵⁹This message came during the fourth year of Zedekiah's reign. It came to Jeremiah to give to Seraiah, the son of Neriah. Neriah was the son of Mahseiah.

The message was about Seraiah's capture and exile to Babylon. He was taken along with Zedekiah, king of Judah. Seraiah was a leader of Zedekiah's army. ⁶⁰Jeremiah wrote on a scroll all the terrible things God had planned for Babylon. ⁶¹⁻⁶²He gave the scroll to Seraiah. And Jeremiah said to him, "When you come to Babylon, read what I have written. Then say to the Lord, 'You have said that you will destroy Babylon. And you will do it so that no living creature will be left. You have said it will be left empty forever.' ⁶³Then, when you have finished reading the scroll, tie a rock to it. Throw it into the Euphrates River. ⁶⁴And say, 'So shall Babylon sink, never to float again. For I am bringing great evil upon her.'"

This ends Jeremiah's messages.

52 Zedekiah was 21 years old when he became king. He ruled 11 years in Jerusalem. His mother's name was Hamutal. She was the daughter of Jeremiah of Libnah. ²But he was a wicked king, just as Jehoiakim had been. ³Things became very bad at the end of his reign. Then the Lord, in his anger, caused Zedekiah to rebel against the king of Babylon. In the end, he and the people of Israel were sent from Jerusalem and Judah. They were taken away as captives to Babylon.

⁴Nebuchadnezzar, king of Babylon, came with all his army against Jerusalem. He built forts and ramps around it. This happened in the ninth year of Zedekiah's reign. It was the 10th day of the 10th month of that year. ⁵Nebuchadnezzar camped around the city for two years. ⁶Then finally, the hunger in the city was very great. All of the food was gone. This happened in the ninth day of the fourth month. ⁷Then the people in the city tore a hole in the city wall. And all the soldiers ran away during the night. They went out by the gate between the two walls near the king's gardens. They made a dash for it across the fields, toward Arabah.

⁸But the Babylonian soldiers chased them. They caught King Zedekiah in the fields near Jericho. For all his army had run away from him. ⁹They brought

Zedekiah to the king of Babylon. He was staying in the city of Riblah in the kingdom of Hamath. And there judgment was passed upon Zedekiah. ¹⁰Nebuchadnezzar had Zedekiah's sons and all the princes of Judah killed. This was done right in front of Zedekiah. ¹¹Then his eyes were cut out. And he was taken in chains to Babylon. There they put him in prison for the rest of his life.

¹²Nebuzaradan was the captain of the guard in Babylon's army. He was sent to Jerusalem. He went there on the 10th day of the fifth month. This was during the 19th year of Nebuchadnezzar's reign in Babylon. ¹³He burned the Temple and the palace and all the larger homes. ¹⁴And he set the army to work tearing down the walls of the city. ¹⁵Then he took many people to Babylon as captives. He took along some of the poorest of the people. He also brought those who lived through the fall of Jerusalem. He brought those who had left Zedekiah to help the Babylonian army. And he brought the tradesmen who were left. ¹⁶But he left some of the poorest people there. They were given charge over the farms and vineyards.

¹⁷The Babylonians took apart the two large bronze pillars. These stood at the door of the Temple. They took apart the bronze basin and bronze bulls on which it stood. They took these and carted them off to Babylon. ¹⁸They also took all the bronze pots and kettles. They took the ash shovels used at the altar. They took the snuffers, spoons, and bowls. And they took all the other items used in the Temple. ¹⁹They also took the firepans. And they took the solid gold and silver candlesticks, and the cups and bowls.

²⁰The two great pillars, the basin, and the 12 bulls were very heavy. They were so heavy they could not weigh them. These had been made in the days of King Solomon. ²¹The pillars were each 27 feet high and 18 feet around. They were hollow, with 3-inch walls. ²²The top 7½ feet of each column had bronze carvings. And there was a network of bronze pomegranates. ²³There were 96 pome-

Cutting Out Eyes
JEREMIAH 52:8-11

Jeremiah had warned King Zedekiah to surrender to the king of Babylon. If he didn't, he would have big trouble. But Zedekiah would not listen. Then one day Nebuchadnezzar, king of Babylon, caught him. Nebuchadnezzar killed Zedekiah's sons. He made Zedekiah watch. Then he cut out Zedekiah's eyes. He could never see again. As long as he lived he would always remember his sons being killed. Blinding prisoners was a common punishment in Bible times. When the Philistines captured Samson, they gouged out his eyes (Judges 16:21). There was an Ammonite king named Nahash. He said he would gouge out the right eye of every person in Jabesh-gilead (1 Samuel 11:2). King Saul rescued this city, so the people were not blinded. Blinding was only one way prisoners were tortured. If you were a soldier, would you fight hard so you would not be captured?

granates on the sides. On the network round about there were 100 more.

²⁴⁻²⁵The captain of the guard took many prisoners. He took Seraiah the chief priest and Zephaniah his helper. He took the three chief temple guards

and one of the leaders of the army. He took seven of the king's special advisors found in the city. He took the secretary of the general of Israel's army, who recruited the soldiers. He also brought 60 other important men that he found hiding. 26He took them to the king of Babylon at Riblah. 27There the king killed them all.

This is how the nation of Judah came to an end.

28The first captives were taken to Babylon in the seventh year of Nebuchadnezzar's reign. The number taken at this time was 3,023. 29Then 11 years later 832 more were taken. 30Five years after that Nebuchadnezzar sent Nebuzaradan to Jerusalem. And Nebuzaradan took 745 prisoners. There were 4,600 captives in all.

31In Babylon, Jehoiachin, king of Judah, was in prison for 37 years. Evil-merodach became king of Babylon in that year. On February 25, after 37 years in prison, Evil-merodach was kind to Jehoiachin. He decided to bring him out of prison. 32He spoke kindly to him. He was kinder to him than any of the other kings in Babylon. 33He gave him new clothes. And he fed him from the king's kitchen as long as he lived. 34And he was given a regular allowance to pay for his daily needs until he died.

LAMENTATIONS

Have you ever cried because you were sad? What happened? Did your pet die? Did someone in your family get hurt or die? We cry when we lose someone we love. We cry when we lose something special. In this book Jeremiah cries. He cries because his beautiful city of Jerusalem has been destroyed. He had been told for years that this would happen. That's because the people kept turning away from God. They kept sinning. If they had stopped, God wouldn't have destroyed the city. But they didn't. Sin makes people or nations weak. The Kingdom of Judah, where Jeremiah lived, was weak. So the Babylonians came in. They conquered Judah. They destroyed Jerusalem. They blinded King Zedekiah. Now Jeremiah is crying. These things did not need to happen. If only the people had stopped sinning! Are you doing things God doesn't like? Stop! You may cry when someone gets hurt. And that someone could be you!

Jeremiah's Great Sadness

1 Jerusalem's streets were once full of people, but they are silent now. She is like a widow broken with sadness. She sits alone in her mourning. She was once the queen of nations, but now she is a slave.

²She cries through the night. Tears run down her cheeks. Among all her lovers there is no one to help her. All her friends are now her enemies.

³Why is Judah led away as a slave? Because of all the wrong she did to others. She made others her slaves. Now she sits far away from home, and there is no rest for her. Those who chased her have now caught her.

⁴The roads to Jerusalem are sad. They are no longer filled with happy people. No one walks on them on their way to the Temple feasts. The city gates are silent, and no one passes through them. Jerusalem's priests groan, and her young girls have been dragged away. Jerusalem cries in grief and sadness.

⁵Her enemies now rule over her. For the Lord has punished Jerusalem for all her sins. Her young children are taken far away as slaves.

⁶All her beauty and her greatness are gone. Her princes are like starving deer that look for food. They are like helpless game too weak to keep on running from their enemies.

7And in all Jerusalem's sadness she remembers happy days of long ago. She thinks of all the joys she had before her enemy struck her down. And now there is no one to help her.

8For the sins of Jerusalem were very great. So now she is thrown away like dirty rags. All who honored her hate her now. For they have seen her naked and ashamed. She groans and hides her face.

9Jerusalem made herself dirty by all her sins. She would not face the fact that punishment was sure to come. Now she lies in the gutter. And there is no one left to lift her out. "O Lord," she cries, "see how much I am suffering. The enemy has won."

10Her enemies have plundered her completely. They have taken all the valuable things she had. She has seen foreign nations make her holy Temple unclean. They were foreigners who should never have gone into your Temple.

11Jerusalem's people groan and cry for bread. They have sold all they have for food to gain a little strength. "Look, O Lord," she prays, "and see how I'm hated."

12"Is it nothing to you, all you who pass by? Look and see if there is any sadness as great as mine. For the Lord has done terrible things to me in the day of his anger.

???????????????????????????????????

To which city did God send fire that burned within its bones?

(Read 1:12-14 for the answer.)

???????????????????????????????????

13"He has sent fire from heaven that burns within my bones. He has put a pitfall in my path and turned me back. He has left me sick and sad, all day, every day.

14"He wove my sins into ropes to tie me to a yoke of slavery. He took away my strength and gave me to my enemies. I am helpless in their hands.

15"The Lord has trampled all my strong men. A great army has come at his command to crush the noblest youth. The Lord has trampled his beloved city as grapes in a winepress.

16"For all these things I cry. Tears flow down my cheeks. My Comforter is far away. And he alone is the one who could help me. My children have no future. We are a conquered land.

17"Jerusalem begs for help, but no one comforts her. For the Lord has spoken. He has said, 'Let her neighbors be her enemies! Let her be thrown out like dirty rags!'

18"And the Lord is right, for we have sinned. And yet, O people everywhere, see my pain and sadness. For my children are taken far away as slaves to distant lands.

19"I begged my friends for their help. But my hope in them was useless. They could not help at all. And my priests and elders couldn't help either. They were starving in the streets. They were looking through the garbage dumps for bread.

20"See my pain, O Lord! My heart is broken. And my soul has given up hope. For I have sinned terribly against you. In the streets the sword waits for me. At home, disease and death are there.

21"Hear my groans! And there is no one to help. All my enemies have heard my troubles. And they are glad to see what you have done. And yet, O Lord, a new time will surely come, for you have promised it. At that time you will do to them as you have done to me.

22"Look also on their sins, O Lord. Punish them as you have punished me. For my tears are many, and my heart is weak."

God Hates Sin

2 A cloud of anger from the Lord hangs over Jerusalem. The fairest city of Israel lies in the dust of the earth. It has been thrown from the heights of heaven at his command. In his day of great anger he has shown no mercy even to his Temple.

2The Lord without mercy has destroyed every home in Israel. In his anger he has broken every tower and wall. He has brought the kingdom to dust. He has brought all its rulers low.

3All the strength of Israel is gone under his anger. He has taken away his protection as the enemy attacks. God burns across the land of Israel like a raging fire.

⁴He bends his bow against his people as though he were an enemy. His strength is used against them to kill their finest youth. His anger is poured out like fire upon them.

⁵Yes, the Lord has conquered Israel like an enemy. He has destroyed her forts and palaces. Sadness and tears are his gift for Jerusalem.

⁶He has broken down his Temple. He did it as though it were a shelter of leaves and sticks in a garden! No longer can the people keep their holy feasts and Sabbaths. Kings and priests together fall before his anger.

⁷The Lord has rejected his own altar. This is because he hates the false "worship" of his people. He has given their palaces to their enemies. And they have parties in the Temple as Israel used to do on days of holy feasts!

⁸The Lord decided to destroy Jerusalem. He laid out a plan that could not be changed. And the towers and walls fell down before him.

⁹Jerusalem's gates are useless. All their locks and bars are broken. For he has crushed them. Her kings and princes are now slaves in far-off lands. They have no temple for worship. They don't have a divine law to govern them. And there is no prophetic vision to guide them.

¹⁰The elders of Jerusalem sit upon the ground in silence. They are dressed in sackcloth. They throw dust on their heads in sadness and despair. The young girls of Jerusalem hang their heads in shame.

¹¹I have cried until the tears no longer come. My heart is broken and my spirit poured out. For I see what has happened to my people. Little children and tiny babies are dying in the streets.

¹²"Mama, Mama, we want food," they cry. Then they die in their mothers' arms. Their lives leave them like those wounded in battle.

¹³In all the world has there ever been such sadness? O Jerusalem, what can I compare your pain to? How can I comfort you? For your wound is as deep as the sea. Who can heal you?

¹⁴Your "prophets" have said so many foolish things. They have told you many lies. They have not tried to hold you back from slavery. They never pointed out your sins. They lied and said that everything was fine.

¹⁵All who pass by laugh at Jerusalem. They shake their heads and say, "Is this the city called 'Most Beautiful in All the World'? Is this the city known as the 'Joy of All the Earth'?"

¹⁶All your enemies make fun of you. They hiss and grind their teeth at you. They say, "We have destroyed her at last! We have waited a long time for this! Now it is finally here! With our own eyes we've seen her fall."

¹⁷But it is the Lord who did it, just as he had warned. He has fulfilled the promises of judgment he made so long ago. He has destroyed Jerusalem without mercy. He has caused her enemies to be happy and brag of their power.

¹⁸Then the people cried before the Lord. O walls of Jerusalem, let tears fall down upon you like a river. Give yourselves no rest from crying day or night.

¹⁹Get up in the night and cry to your God. Pour out your hearts like water to the Lord. Lift up your hands to him. Beg for your children as they faint with hunger in the streets.

²⁰O Lord, think! These are your own people to whom you are doing this. Shall mothers eat their little children? Shall they eat those they bounced on their knees? Shall priests and prophets die within the Temple of the Lord?

²¹See them lying in the streets, old and young, boys and girls. They have been killed by the enemies' swords. You have killed them, Lord, in your anger. You have killed them without mercy.

²²You have called for this trouble on purpose. When you were angry none got away or stayed. All my little children lie dead upon the streets before the enemy.

One Ray of Hope

3 I am the man who has seen the judgment from the rod of God's anger. ²He has brought me into deep darkness. He has shut out all light. ³He has turned against me. Day and night his hand is heavy on me. ⁴He has made me old and has broken my bones.

⁵He has built forts against me. He has put pain and trouble all around me. ⁶He buried me in dark places, like those long dead. ⁷He has walled me in. I cannot get away. He has tied me with heavy chains. ⁸And though I cry and shout, he will not hear my prayers! ⁹He has shut me into a place of high, smooth walls. He has filled my path with traps.

¹⁰He hides like a bear, like a lion, waiting to attack me. ¹¹He has dragged me into the brush and torn me with his claws. He has left me bleeding and helpless.

Every day God has a wonderful new way to say "I love you"

The Lord never stops loving us. He keeps on showing us mercy. His love and kindness begin fresh each day.

Lamentations 3:22-23

---

¹²He has bent his bow and aimed it right at me. ¹³He has sent his arrows deep into my heart.

¹⁴My own people laugh at me. All day long they sing their songs to make fun of me.

¹⁵He has filled me with bitter food. He has given me a cup of deep sadness to drink. ¹⁶He has made me eat gravel and broken my teeth. He has rolled me in ashes and dirt. ¹⁷O Lord, all peace and all riches have long since gone. For you have taken them away. I have forgotten what it means to be happy. ¹⁸All hope is gone. My strength has turned to water, for the Lord has left me. ¹⁹Oh, remember the suffering you have given to me! ²⁰For I can never forget these awful years. Always my soul will live in total shame.

²¹Yet there is one ray of hope! ²²The Lord never stops loving us. He keeps on showing us mercy. That alone has kept us from total destruction. ²³Great is his faithfulness. His love and kindness begin fresh each day. ²⁴My soul claims the Lord as my part. Therefore I will hope in him. ²⁵The Lord is good to those who wait for him. He is kind to those who look for him. ²⁶It is good to hope and wait quietly for the Lord to save you.

²⁷It is good for a young man to be corrected. ²⁸For it causes him to sit apart in silence under the Lord's demands. ²⁹It causes him to lie facedown in the dust. Then at last there is hope for him. ³⁰Let him turn the other cheek to those who strike him. Let him take their awful insults. ³¹For the Lord will not leave him forever. ³²God gives him grief and sadness. But he will show love too. He will do this by the greatness of his love and kindness. ³³For he does not enjoy hurting men and causing sadness.

³⁴⁻³⁶But you have crushed the poor of the world under your feet. You have taken from the poor their God-given rights. You have failed to be just and fair. No wonder the Lord has had to punish you! ³⁷For who can act against you unless the Lord lets them do it? ³⁸It is the Lord who helps one and harms another.

³⁹Why then should we complain when we are punished for our sins? ⁴⁰Let us look closely at ourselves instead. Let us be sorry for our sins and turn back to the Lord. ⁴¹Let us lift our hearts and hands to him in heaven. ⁴²For we have sinned. We have turned against the Lord, and he has not forgiven it.

⁴³You have drowned us by your anger, Lord. You have killed us without mercy. ⁴⁴You have hidden yourself as with a cloud. And now our prayers do not reach through to you. ⁴⁵You have made us like garbage among the nations. ⁴⁶All our enemies have spoken out against us. ⁴⁷We are filled with fear, for we are trapped and destroyed.

⁴⁸⁻⁴⁹My eyes flow day and night with streams of tears. I cry this way for my broken people. ⁵⁰Oh, that the Lord might look down from heaven. Oh, I wish he would listen to my cry! ⁵¹My heart is breaking over what is happening to the young girls of Jerusalem.

⁵²My enemies chased me as though I were a bird. And I had never harmed them. ⁵³They threw me in a well and put a rock over the opening. ⁵⁴The water

flowed above my head. I thought, "This is the end!" 55But I called on your name, O Lord. I cried out from deep within the well. 56And you heard me! You listened to my begging. You heard my crying! 57Yes, you came at my cry and told me not to be afraid.

58O Lord, you are my lawyer! Speak for me in court! For you have bought back my life. 59You have seen the wrong they did to me. Be my Judge, to prove me right. 60You have seen the evil plans my enemies have made against me. 61You have heard the bad names they have called me. 62You know all that they say about me. You have heard all their secret plans. 63See how they laugh and sing with joy as they plan my death.

64O Lord, pay them back well for all the evil they have done. 65Harden their hearts and curse them, Lord. 66Chase after them hotly and wipe them off the earth. Let them never again be seen under the heavens of the Lord.

God Is No Longer Angry

4 The finest gold has lost its shine! For the golden Temple walls are broken in the streets! 2The finest of our youth were once precious as gold. But now they are treated as if they were clay pots. 3-4Even the jackals feed their young. But my people, Israel, don't feed theirs. They are like cruel desert ostriches. They don't hear their babies' cries for food. The children's tongues stick in their mouths because they are thirsty. There is not a drop of water left. Babies cry for bread, but no one can give them any. 5Those who used to eat all they wanted are begging for any food they can find. Those brought up in palaces now dig in garbage pits for food. 6For the sin of my people is greater than that of Sodom. And there disaster struck in a moment without the hand of man.

7Our princes were lean and tanned, the finest of men. 8But now their faces are as black as charcoal. No one can even tell who they are. Their skin has become wrinkled and dry as wood. 9Those killed by the sword are lucky! That is much better than dying of hunger. 10Good women have cooked and eaten their own children. That is how they lived through the siege.

11But now at last the anger of the Lord is satisfied. His anger has been poured out. He started a fire in Jerusalem that burned it down to the ground. 12Not a king in all the earth would have thought an enemy could break down Jerusalem's gates! 13But God let it happen because of the sins of her prophets and priests. They had made the city unclean by shedding innocent blood. 14Now these same men are staggering through the streets. They are covered with blood, making all they touch unclean.

**Discipline helps us grow
the right way**

*It is good for a young man to be
corrected.*

Lamentations 3:27

15"Get away!" the people shout at them. "You are unclean!" They run away to distant lands. And they wander there among the foreigners. But none will let them stay. 16The Lord himself has punished them. He no longer helps them. The priests and elders are no longer honored.

17We look for our friends to come and save us. But all that looking will do no good. The nation we had hoped would help us makes no move at all.

18We can't go into the streets without danger to our lives. Our end is near! We have only a few days left. 19Our enemies are faster than the eagles. If we run to the mountains, they will find us. If we hide in the wilderness, they are waiting for us there. 20Our king, the Lord's chosen, was caught in their traps. Yes, even our king has been taken! We once bragged that with him we could stand against any nation on earth!

21Are you happy, O people of Edom? Are you full of joy in the land of Uz? But you, too, will feel the terrible anger of the Lord. 22The judgment for Israel's sins will end. But Edom's judgment will never end.

Jeremiah Prays

5 O Lord, remember all that has happened to us. See what sadness we must feel! ²Our homes and our nation are filled with foreigners. ³We are all orphans. Our fathers are dead and our mothers are widowed. ⁴We must even pay for water to drink. Our fuel is sold to us at the highest of prices. ⁵We bow our necks under the victors' feet. All we have to look forward to is work without end. ⁶We beg for bread from Egypt, and from Assyria too.

⁷Our fathers sinned but died before the hand of judgment fell. We have suffered the judgment that they deserved!

⁸Our former servants have become our masters. There is no one left to save us. ⁹We went into the wilderness to hunt for food, risking death from enemies. ¹⁰Our skin was black from hunger. ¹¹They rape the women of Jerusalem and the girls in Judah's cities.¹²Our princes are hanged by their thumbs. Even old men are treated with hate. ¹³They take away the young men to grind their grain. Even the little children stagger under heavy loads.

¹⁴The old men don't sit in the city gates any more. The young no longer dance and sing. ¹⁵The joy of our hearts has ended. Our dance has turned to death. ¹⁶Our glory is gone. The crown is fallen from our head. We are suffering like this for our sins. ¹⁷Our hearts are faint and tired. Our eyes can hardly see. ¹⁸Jerusalem and the Temple of the Lord are empty. Only wild animals are there, hiding in the ruins.

¹⁹O Lord, you always stay the same! Your throne will stand from generation to generation. ²⁰Why do you forget us forever? Why do you leave us alone for so long? ²¹Turn us around and bring us back to you again! That is our only hope! Give us back the joys we used to have! ²²Or have you totally left us? Are you angry with us still?

Stepping on Your Neck

LAMENTATIONS 5:5

Do you have a favorite basketball or football team? Suppose this team plays a game. But they lose. Suddenly the captain gets down on his knees. He puts his head on the ground. The captain of the other team puts his foot on the losing captain's neck. This was often done in Bible times when someone won a battle. The winning king put his foot on the losing king's neck. That was his way of showing people that he had won. Sometimes he did much worse things. He might have cut out the loser's eyes or torn off his skin. These kings played rougher than our pro teams, didn't they?

EZEKIEL

One day the king of Babylon sent soldiers to Jerusalem. They captured the city. They took many Jewish people back to Babylon. Daniel and his three friends were among those captives. Eight years later, the king of Babylon sent his army again. They took more Jewish people to Babylon. This time, Ezekiel was among them. Ezekiel had been a priest in the Temple in Jerusalem. Now he became a prophet in Babylon. Ezekiel told his people that they had sinned. That was why they were captured. If they wanted to go home, they had to turn to the Lord.

Ezekiel used many strange word pictures when he talked to his people. He told them about a great storm with fire flashing in a cloud. He talked about angelic beings with four faces and two pairs of wings. He told about a man who ate a scroll that tasted like honey. He also talked about a valley of bones. These bones came together to make skeletons. Then the skeletons became live people.

As a prophet, Ezekiel was not always popular. He had to tell his people about their sins. And no one likes to hear about the wrong things they do. Ezekiel had to show his people that forgetting about God leads to trouble. As you read the Book of Ezekiel, pretend that this wise prophet is talking to you. Are you remembering God each day? Are you living in a way that pleases him? Remember what happened to Ezekiel's people when they didn't.

A Fiery Cloud

1 I am Ezekiel, the son of Buzi the priest. I was living with the Jewish exiles beside the Chebar Canal in Babylon. One day, the heavens suddenly opened up and I saw visions from God.

This happened late in June, when I was 30 years old. ⁴I saw, in this vision, a great storm coming toward me from the north. The storm was pushing a huge cloud of fire in front of it. The fire inside the cloud flashed the whole time. And in the fire there was something that shone like polished brass.

5Then four strange shapes came from the center of the cloud. They looked like men. 6But each had four faces and two pairs of wings! 7Their legs were like those of men. But their feet were like calves' feet. And they shone like polished brass. 8And under each of their wings I could see human hands.

9The four living beings were joined wing to wing. And they flew straight forward without turning. 10Each had the face of a man in front. The face of a lion was on the right side of his head. The face of an ox was on the left side. And the face of an eagle was at the back. 11Each had two pairs of wings spreading from the middle of his back. One pair stretched out to touch the wings of living beings on each side. The other pair covered his body. 12Wherever the spirit went, they went. They always went straight forward without turning.

13Going up and down among them were other creatures. They glowed like bright coals of fire or torches in the night. And it was from these that the lightning flashed. 14The living beings darted to and fro, as fast as lightning.

15As I looked at all of this, I saw four wheels on the ground under them. There was one wheel belonging to each. 16The wheels looked as if they were made of polished amber. And each wheel was made with a second wheel crosswise inside. 17They could go in any of the four directions without having to face around. 18The four wheels had rims and spokes. And the rims were filled with eyes around their edges.

19-21When the four living beings flew forward, the wheels moved forward with them. When they flew upward, the wheels went up too. When the living beings stopped, the wheels stopped. The spirit of the four living beings was in the wheels. So wherever the spirit went, the wheels and the living beings went too.

22The sky above them looked like it was made of crystal. It was so beautiful, I can't even talk about it.

23Under the sky I could see the two living beings. Each of their wings stretched out to touch the wings of the other. And each had two wings covering his body. 24And as they flew, their wings roared like waves against the shore. They sounded like the voice of God. Or perhaps it sounded like the shouting of a great army. When they stopped, they let down their wings. 25And every time they stopped, there came a voice from the crystal sky above them.

26Now high in the sky was what looked like a throne. It was made of beautiful blue sapphire stones. And someone who looked like a Man sat on it.

27-28From his waist up, he seemed to be all glowing bronze. He was shining like fire. And from his waist down he seemed to be burning. And there was glowing light like a rainbow all around him. That was the way the glory of the Lord looked to me. And when I saw it, I fell facedown on the ground. And I heard the voice of someone talking to me.

God Calls Ezekiel

2 And he said, "Stand up, son of dust. I want to speak with you."

2And the Spirit came into me as he spoke. And he put me on my feet.

3"Son of dust," he said, "I am sending you to the nation of Israel. They are a nation that sins against me. They and their fathers have sinned against me until this very hour. 4For they are a stubborn people with stiff necks. But I am sending you to give them my messages. They are the messages of the Lord God. 5They might listen, or they might not. For remember, they are rebels. But at least they will know they have had a prophet among them.

6"Son of dust, don't be afraid of them. Don't be afraid even though their threats are sharp. Don't run even if they sting like scorpions. Don't be upset by their dark looks. For remember, they are rebels! 7You must give them my messages whether they listen or not. But they won't, for they are total rebels. 8Listen, son of dust, to what I say to you. Don't you be a rebel too! Open your mouth and eat what I give you."

9-10Then I looked and saw a hand holding a scroll out to me. It had writing on both sides. Then he opened up the scroll. And I saw that it was full of warnings and judgments.

God Makes Ezekiel His Watchman

3 And he said to me, "Son of dust, eat what I am giving you. Eat this scroll! Then go and give its message to the people of Israel."

²So I took the scroll.

³"Eat it all," he said. And when I ate it, it tasted sweet like honey.

⁴Then he said, "Son of dust, I am sending you to the people of Israel. You will bring them my messages. ⁵I am not sending you to some distant land where you don't know the language. ⁶I am not sending you to tribes with strange and hard words. If I did, they would listen! ⁷I am sending you to the people of Israel. And they won't listen to you! For they have never listened to me! The whole lot of them are hard and stubborn. ⁸But see, I have made you hard and stubborn too. You are as tough as they are. ⁹I have made your forehead as hard as rock. So don't be afraid of them. Don't fear their angry looks. Don't run from them even though they are such rebels."

¹⁰Then he added, "Son of dust, let all my words sink into your heart first. Listen to them carefully for yourself. ¹¹Then, go to your people in Babylon. They might listen, or they might not. But tell them: 'This is what the Lord God says!'"

¹²Then the Spirit lifted me up and the glory of the Lord began to move away. At the same time, I heard the sound of a great earthquake. ¹³It was the noise of the wings of the living beings and the wheels under them.

¹⁴⁻¹⁵The Spirit lifted me up and took me away to Tel Abib. This was another colony of Jewish exiles beside the Chebar River. I was very unhappy and angry. But the hand of the Lord was strong upon me. And I sat there in shock for seven days.

¹⁶At the end of the seven days, the Lord spoke to me. ¹⁷He said, "Son of dust, I have chosen you as a watchman for Israel. I will send warnings to you for my people. When you get a warning,

pass it on to them right away. ¹⁸You might refuse to warn the wicked when I want you to. You might refuse to say, 'You will soon be punished by death. So turn from your sins and save your life.' And they might die in their sins because you didn't speak up. But if this happens, I will punish you. I will demand your blood for theirs. ¹⁹But you might speak up and warn them. And they might keep on sinning and not turn from their sins. If they do this, they will die in their sins. But you will be free of guilt. For you have done all you could. ²⁰A good man might begin to sin. And you might not warn him of what will happen if he keeps on sinning. Then the Lord might destroy him. The good deeds he did before won't help him. And he shall die in his sin. But you will be guilty of his death because you didn't speak up. And I will punish you for it. ²¹But you might warn him and he might turn from his sins. If this happens, he shall live. And you will have saved your own life too."

²²I felt the Lord's hand was upon me there. And he said to me, "Go out into the valley. I will talk to you there." ²³So I got up and went. And oh, I saw the glory of the Lord there! It was just like my first vision! And I fell with my face on the ground.

²⁴Then the Spirit came into me and set me on my feet. He talked to me and said, "Go, shut yourself up in your house. ²⁵I will make it so you can't move at all. That way you won't be able to leave. ²⁶I will make your tongue stick to the roof of your mouth. That way you won't be able to speak. You won't be able to tell the people to repent, for they are rebels. ²⁷But every time I give you a message, then I will set your tongue free. Then I will let you speak, and you shall say, 'The Lord God says this!' Let anyone listen who wants to, but don't make them listen. For they are rebels.

Ezekiel Draws a Picture

4 "And now, son of dust, take a large brick. Lay it in front of you and draw a map of the city of Jerusalem on it. Draw a picture of a ramp being built up against the city. Put enemy camps

around it and battering rams against the walls. ³And put an iron plate between you and the city, like a wall of iron. Show how an enemy army will capture Jerusalem!

"There is special meaning in each detail of what I have told you to do. For it is a warning to the people of Israel.

⁴⁻⁵"Now lie on your left side for 390 days. Do this to show that Israel will be punished for 390 years by exile. Each day you lie there stands for a year of punishment ahead for Israel. ⁶After that, turn over and lie on your right side for 40 days. This will stand for the years of Judah's punishment. Each day will stand for one year.

⁷"Then you will show what it will be like in Jerusalem during the siege. Lie there with your arm uncovered. This will stand for great strength and power in the attack against her. This will show that she will be destroyed. ⁸And I will make it so you can't move at all. You won't be able to turn over from one side to the other. You will be this way until you have finished all the days of the siege.

⁹"During the first 390 days, eat bread made of flour. Mix the flour from wheat, barley, beans, lentils, and spelt. Mix the various kinds of flour together in a barrel. ¹⁰You are to eat eight ounces of this flour each time. And you are to eat one meal each day. ¹¹And use one quart of water a day. Don't use more than that. ¹²Each day take flour from the barrel. Cook it as you would cook barley cakes. While all the people are watching, bake it over a fire. Use dried human dung to burn in your fire instead of wood. ¹³For the Lord says, 'Israel shall eat unclean bread in the Gentile lands to which I send them!'"

¹⁴Then I said, "O Lord God, must I be made unclean by cooking with dung? For I have never been unclean before in all my life. I have never eaten any animal that died of sickness. I haven't eaten any animal that I found hurt or dead. I haven't eaten any of the animals our law says not to eat."

¹⁵Then the Lord said, "All right. You may use cow dung instead of human dung."

¹⁶Then he told me, "Son of dust, bread will be hard to find in Jerusalem. It will be weighed out with great care and eaten with fear. The water will be given out by the drop. And the people will drink it with care. ¹⁷I will make sure the people won't have enough bread and water. They will look at one another in terror. They will waste away because of their sins.

A Crazy Haircut

5 "Son of dust, take a sharp sword. Use it as a barber's razor to shave your head and beard. Use scales to weigh the hair into three equal parts. ²Put a third of it at the center of your map of Jerusalem. After your siege, burn it there. Scatter another third across your map. Then slash at it with a knife. Scatter the last third to the wind. For I will chase my people with the sword. ³Keep just a bit of the hair and tie it up in your robe. ⁴Then take a few hairs out and throw them into the fire. For a fire shall come from the few left and destroy all Israel."

⁵⁻⁷The Lord God says, "This shows what will happen to Jerusalem. For she has turned away from my laws. She has been even more wicked than the nations around her." ⁸So the Lord God says, "I, even I, am against you. And I will punish you while all the nations watch. ⁹I will do this because of the terrible sins you have done. I will punish you more terribly than I have ever done before or ever will again. ¹⁰Fathers will eat their own sons. And sons will eat their fathers. And those who live through it will be scattered all over the world.

¹¹"For I promise you this. You have made my Temple unclean with idols and evil sacrifices. Therefore I will not spare you or pity you at all. ¹²One-third of you will die from hunger and disease. One-third will be killed by the enemy. And one-third I will scatter to the winds. I will send the sword of the enemy chasing after you. ¹³Then at last my anger will be used up. And all Israel will know that when I say something will happen, it will happen.

¹⁴"So I will make an example of you in front of all the nations. I will show this to everyone who goes past the ruins of your land. ¹⁵Everyone in the whole world will laugh at you. You will become an example to everyone. They will see what happens when the Lord punishes a nation. I, the Lord, have spoken it!

¹⁶"I will shoot deadly arrows of hunger at you. And I will shoot to kill! The hunger will get worse and worse. In the end, every bit of bread will be gone. ¹⁷And not just hunger will come. Wild animals will also attack and kill you. Disease and war will walk around your land. And the sword of the enemy will kill you. I, the Lord, have spoken it!"

Ezekiel Talks to the Mountains

6 Again a message came from the Lord. ²"Son of dust," the Lord said, "look over toward the mountains of Israel. Then speak out against them. ³Say to them, 'O mountains of Israel! Hear the message of the Lord God against you. And hear this word against the rivers and valleys. I, even I the Lord, will bring war upon you to destroy your idols. ⁴⁻⁷All your cities will be smashed and burned. And the idol altars will be left empty. Your gods will be broken apart. The bones of their worshipers will lie scattered among the altars. Then at last you will know I am the Lord.

⁸"'But I will let a few of my people get away. They will be scattered among the nations of the world. ⁹Then when they are exiled among the nations, they will remember me. For I will take away their unfaithful hearts. I will take away their love of idols. And I will blind their lustful eyes that look after other gods. Then at last they will hate themselves for all this sin. ¹⁰They will know that I alone am God. And they will know that I wasn't lying when I told them all this would happen to them.'"

¹¹The Lord God says, "Raise your hands in horror. Shake your head with deep sadness. Then say, 'We are sorry for all the evil we have done!' For you are going to die from war and hunger and disease. ¹²Disease will strike down those in exile. War will destroy those in the

land of Israel. And any who stay will die by hunger and war. So at last I will satisfy my anger on you. ¹³Your dead will lie among your idols and altars on every hill

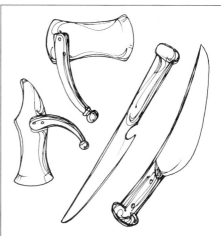

Shave and Haircut
EZEKIEL 5:1

Did your father shave this morning? If he did, he probably used an electric razor or a safety razor. Did he get a haircut this week? If so, the barber probably used electric clippers and scissors. But in Bible times, there were no scissors, safety razors, or electric shavers. There was no electricity! Men who shaved their faces used large knives made of bronze. And they looked into mirrors of polished bronze. These mirrors were about as clear as mirrors today that have been covered by mist from the shower.

Egyptian men shaved their beards and often their heads. Joseph had to shave before he went to see Pharaoh (Genesis 41:14). But most Israelite men had beards. That was the custom. Maybe it was because they didn't like shaving their face with those large bronze knives!

and mountain. They will lie under every green tree where they burned incense to their gods. And you will know that I alone am God. ¹⁴I will crush you and make your cities empty. I will do this from the wilderness in the south to Riblah in the north. Then you will know I am the Lord."

Jerusalem Will Be Punished

7 This further message came to me from God: ²"Say to Israel, 'Wherever you look, your land is finished. Look east, west, north, or south. ³No hope is left. For I will pour out my anger on you for bowing to idols. ⁴I will turn my eyes away and show no pity. I will pay you back in full. And you shall know I am the Lord.'"

⁵⁻⁶The Lord God says, "With one blow after another I will finish you. The end has come. Your final doom is waiting. ⁷O Israel, the day of your destruction is here. The time has come. The day of trouble nears. It is a day of shouts of pain, not shouts of joy! ⁸⁻⁹Soon I will pour out my anger. I will let it finish punishing you for all your evil deeds. I will not spare or pity you. And you will know that I, the Lord, am doing it. ¹⁰⁻¹¹The day of judgment has come. The morning is here! For your wickedness and pride have run their course and reached their climax. None of these rich and wicked men of pride shall live. All your bragging will die away. And no one will be left to cry for you.

¹²"Yes, the time has come. The day draws near. There will be nothing to buy or sell. For the anger of God is on the land. ¹³And even if a trader lives, his business will be gone. For God has spoken against all the people of Israel. All will be destroyed. Not one of those whose lives are filled with sin will live through it.

¹⁴"The trumpets shout to Israel's army, 'Call out your armies!' But no one listens, for my anger is against them all. ¹⁵If you go outside the walls, there stands the enemy to kill you. If you stay inside, hunger and disease will kill you. ¹⁶Any who get away will be lonely as mourning doves hiding on the mountains. Each will hide there, crying for his sins. ¹⁷All hands and knees shall be as weak as water. ¹⁸You shall dress yourselves with sackcloth. Horror and shame shall cover you. You shall shave your heads in sad-

ness and because you are sorry for your sins.

¹⁹"Throw away your money! Throw it out like useless garbage. For it will have no value in that day of anger. It will neither satisfy nor feed you. For your love of money is the reason for your sin. ²⁰I gave you gold to use to make the Temple beautiful. But you used it instead to make idols! Therefore, I will take it all away from you. ²¹I will give it to foreigners and to wicked men as booty. They shall make my Temple unclean. ²²I will not look when they dirty it, and I will not stop them. Like robbers, they will take the treasures and leave the Temple in ruins.

²³"Bring out chains for my people, for the land is full of bloody crimes. Jerusalem is filled with violence, so I will make her people slaves. ²⁴I will crush your pride. I will do it by bringing to Jerusalem the worst of the nations. They will live in your homes. They will break down the towers and walls you are so proud of. And they will make your Temple an unclean place. ²⁵For the time has come for Israel to be cut off. You will ask for peace, but you won't get it. ²⁶⁻²⁷Trouble upon trouble will come upon you. Disaster upon disaster will follow you! You will wish you had a prophet to guide you. But the priests and elders and the kings and princes will be helpless. They will stand there crying in despair. The people will shake with fear. For I will do to them the evil they have done. I will give them just what they deserve. And they shall know that I am the Lord."

The Sins of the People

8 It was late in August of the sixth year of King Jehoiachin's captivity. I was talking with the elders of Judah in my home. And the power of the Lord God fell upon me. ²I saw what appeared to be a Man. From his waist down, he was made of fire. From his waist up, he was all amber-colored brightness. ³He put out what seemed to be a hand and took me by the hair. And the Spirit lifted me up into the sky. It seemed to transport me to Jerusalem, to the entrance of the north gate. And there I saw the large idol

that had made the Lord so angry. ⁴Suddenly the glory of the God of Israel was there. It was just as I had seen it before in the valley.

⁵He said to me, "Son of dust, look toward the north." So I looked just to the north of the altar gate. And in the entrance stood the idol.

⁶And he said, "Son of dust, do you see what they are doing? Do you see what great sins the people of Israel are doing? They are pushing me right out of my Temple! But come, and I will show you greater sins than these!"

⁷Then he brought me to the door of the Temple court. And from there, I could see an opening in the wall.

⁸"Now dig into the wall," he said. I did, and found a door to a hidden room.

⁹"Go in," he said. "See the wickedness going on in there!"

¹⁰So I went in. The walls were covered with pictures of all kinds of snakes and lizards. And all the idols worshiped by the people of Israel were carved there too. ¹¹Seventy elders of Israel were standing there. Jaazaniah, the son of Shaphan, was with them. And they were worshiping the pictures! Each of them held a censer of burning incense. So there was a thick cloud of smoke above their heads.

¹²Then the Lord said to me, "Son of dust, have you seen what the elders of Israel are doing in their minds? For they say, 'The Lord doesn't see us. He has gone away!'" ¹³Then he added, "Come! I will show you greater sins than these!"

¹⁴He brought me to the north gate of the Temple. There sat women crying for Tammuz, their god.

¹⁵"Have you seen this?" he asked. "But I will show you greater evils than these!"

¹⁶Then he brought me into the inner court of the Temple. There at the door, between the porch and bronze altar, were about 25 men. They were standing with their backs to the Temple of the Lord. They were facing to the east, worshiping the sun!

¹⁷"Have you seen this?" he asked. "Is it nothing to the people of Judah that they do these terrible sins? They lead the whole nation into idol worship. They lift up their noses at me and wake up my anger against them. ¹⁸So, I will deal with them in anger. I will neither pity nor spare them. And even if they shout out for mercy, I will not hear them."

Some Wicked People Die

9 Then he thundered, "Call those to whom I have given the city! Tell them to bring their weapons with them!"

²Six men came when he called. They came from the upper north gate, each one with his sword. One of them wore linen clothing. And he carried a writer's case strapped to his side. They all went into the Temple and stood beside the bronze altar. ³And the glory of the God of Israel rose from between the Guardian Angels where it had rested. And it stood above the door to the Temple.

And the Lord called to the man with the writer's case. ⁴He said to him, "Walk through the streets of Jerusalem. Put a mark on the foreheads of the men who are sad because of all the sins they see around them."

⁵Then I heard the Lord speak to the other men. He said, "Follow him through the city. Kill everyone whose forehead isn't marked. Do not spare or pity them. ⁶Kill them all, old and young, girls, women and little children. But don't touch anyone with the mark. And begin right here at the Temple." And so they began by killing the 70 elders.

⁷And he said, "Make the Temple dirty and unclean! Fill its courts with the bodies of those you kill! Go!" And they went throughout the city and did as they were told.

⁸While they were obeying their orders, I was alone. I fell to the ground on my face and cried out. I said, "O Lord God! Will your anger against Jerusalem wipe out everyone left in Israel?"

⁹But he said to me, "The sins of the people of Israel and Judah are very great. All the land is full of murder and unfairness. For they say, 'The Lord doesn't see it! He has gone away!' ¹⁰And so I will not spare them or have any pity on them.

And I will pay them back for all they have done."

[11]Just then the man carrying the writer's case came back. And he said, "I have finished the work you gave me to do."

Burning Coals
Thrown over the City

10 Suddenly I saw a throne of beautiful blue sapphire in the sky. It was above the heads of the Guardian Angels.

[2]Then the Lord spoke to the man in linen clothing. He said, "Go in between the whirling wheels under the Guardian Angels. Take a handful of glowing coals and scatter them over the city."

So he did this as I watched. [3]The Guardian Angels were standing at the south end of the Temple when the man went in. And the cloud of glory filled the inner court. [4]Then the glory of the Lord rose from above the Guardian Angels. It went over to the door of the Temple. The Temple was filled with the cloud of glory. And the court of the Temple was filled with the brightness of the Lord. [5]And the sound of the wings of the Guardian Angels was loud. It was like the voice of Almighty God when he speaks. It could be heard clear out in the outer court.

[6]The Lord had told the man in linen clothing to go between the Guardian Angels. He had told him to take some burning coals from between the wheels. So the man went in and stood beside one of the wheels. [7-8]And one of the Guardian Angels reached out his hand. Each of the mighty Angels had, under his wings, what looked like human hands. The Angel took some live coals from the flames between the Angels. And the Angel put them into the hands of the man in linen clothes. The man then took them and went out.

[9-13]Each of the four Guardian Angels had a wheel beside him. And each wheel had a second wheel spinning crosswise within. They sparkled like chrysolite, giving off a greenish-yellow glow. Because of the way these wheels were made, the Angels could go straight forward in each of four directions. They did not turn when they changed direction. But they could go in any of the four ways their faces looked. Each of the four wheels was covered with eyes. This included the rims and the spokes. [14]Each of the four Guardian Angels had four faces. The first was that of an ox. The second was a man's face. The third was a lion's face. And the fourth was an eagle's face.

[15-16]These were the same beings I had seen beside the Chebar Canal. And when they rose into the air, the wheels went with them. The wheels stayed beside them as they flew. [17]When the Guardian Angels stood still, so did the wheels. For the spirit of the Guardian Angels was in the wheels.

[18]Then the glory of the Lord moved from the door of the Temple. It went and stood above the Guardian Angels. [19]And as I watched, the Guardian Angels flew to the east gate of the Temple. Their wheels flew beside them. And the glory of the God of Israel was above them.

[20]I had seen these same living beings under the God of Israel beside the Chebar Canal. I knew they were the same. [21]For each had four faces and four wings. And they had what looked like human hands under their wings. [22]Their faces too were the same as the faces of those I had seen at the Canal. And they traveled straight ahead, just as the others did.

God Will Bring His People Back

11 Then the Spirit lifted me and brought me over to the east gate of the Temple. There I saw 25 of the city's leaders. This included two officers, Jaazaniah and Pelatiah. Jaazaniah was the son of Azzur. Pelatiah was the son of Benaiah. Then the Spirit said to me, "Son of dust, these are the men who are doing so much evil. They give wicked advice to the people in this city. [3]For they say to the people, 'It is time to rebuild Jerusalem. For our city is an iron shield. It will protect us from all harm.' [4]Therefore, son of dust, speak against them loudly and clearly."

[5]Then the Spirit of the Lord came upon me. He told me to say, "The Lord

says to the people of Israel: 'Is that what you are saying? Yes, I know it is, for I know every thought that comes into your minds. 6You have murdered many and filled your streets with the dead.'

7"Therefore the Lord God says, 'You think this city is an iron shield? No, it isn't! It will not keep you safe. Your dead will lie inside the city's walls. But you will be dragged out and killed. 8The war you have been so afraid of will get you,' says the Lord God. 9"I will take you from Jerusalem and hand you over to foreigners. And they will carry out my judgments against you. 10You will be killed all the way to the borders of Israel. And you will know I am the Lord. 11No, this city will not be an iron shield for you. You will never be safe inside her walls. I will chase you even to the borders of Israel. 12And you will know I am the Lord. You have not obeyed me. But instead, you have copied the nations all around you.'"

13While I was still telling them this, Pelatiah suddenly died. Then I fell to the ground on my face. I cried out, "O Lord God! Are you going to kill everyone in all Israel?"

14Again a message came from the Lord. 15He said, "Son of dust, the people left in Jerusalem are talking about the Jews in Babylon. They are saying, 'The Lord has sent them to Babylon because they were so wicked. Now the Lord has given us their land!'

16"But tell the exiles that the Lord God says, 'I have scattered you in the countries of the world. But I will keep you safe while you are there. 17I will bring you back from the nations where you are scattered. And I will give you the land of Israel once again. 18And when you come back, you will get rid of all this idol worship. 19I will give you one heart and a new spirit. I will take from you your hearts of stone. And I will give you tender hearts of love for God. 20So you will obey my laws and be my people. And I will be your God. 21But there are those now in Jerusalem who love their idols. I will pay them back fully for their sins," the Lord God says.

22Then the Guardian Angels lifted their wings. They rose into the air with their wheels beside them. And the glory of the God of Israel stood above them. 23Then the glory of the Lord rose from over the city. And it stood above the mountain on the east side.

24After that the Spirit of God carried me back again to Babylon. He brought me to the Jews in exile there. That is how the vision of my visit to Jerusalem ended. 25And I told the Jews in Babylon all that the Lord had shown me.

Ezekiel Digs a Tunnel

12 Again a message came to me from the Lord. 2"Son of dust," he said. "You live with people who could know the truth if they wanted to. But they just don't want to! They could hear me if they would listen. But they just won't do it. 3This is because they are rebels. So now show them what it will be like to be exiled. Pack whatever you can carry on your back and leave your home. Go somewhere else. Go in the daylight so they can see. For perhaps even yet they will think about what this means. They might still listen, even though they are such rebels. 4Bring your baggage outside your house during the daylight so they can watch. Then leave the house at night. Do just as captives do when they march to distant lands. 5Dig a tunnel through the city wall while they are watching. Carry your baggage out through the hole. 6As they watch, lift your pack to your shoulders. Then walk away into the night. Cover your face so you can't see the ground. All this is a sign to the people of Israel. It will show them that evil will come upon Jerusalem."

7So I did as I was told. I brought my pack outside in the daylight. I packed all I could take into exile. In the evening I dug through the wall with my hands. I went out into the darkness with my pack on my shoulder. And the people watched the whole thing. 8The next morning this message came to me from the Lord:

9"Son of dust, the people of Israel have asked what all this means. 10Tell them the Lord God says it is a message to King Zedekiah in Jerusalem. Tell them it is a message to all the people of Israel. [11]Tell them you did this to show them what is going to happen. For they shall be driven out of their homes and sent away into exile.

[12]"Even King Zedekiah shall go out at night through a hole in the wall. He shall take only what he can carry with him. He will cover his face so he won't be able to see. [13]I will capture him in my net. And I will bring him to Babylon, the land of the Chaldeans. But he shall not see that land, though he shall die there. [14]I will scatter his servants and guards to the four winds. And I shall send the sword after them. [15]I will scatter them among the nations. Then they shall know I am the Lord. [16]But I will spare a few of them from death by war and hunger and disease. I will save them to tell the nations how wicked they have been. And they shall know I am the Lord."

[17]Then this message came to me from the Lord.

[18]"Son of dust," he said, "shake as you eat your meals. Drink your water with care as though it were your last. [19]And tell the people what the Lord God says. They shall save their food and eat it with great care. They will sip their tiny rations of water in great despair. They will suffer this way because of all their sins. [20]Your cities shall be destroyed and your farms empty. And you shall know I am the Lord."

[21]Again a message came to me from the Lord. [22]"Son of dust," he said. "What is that proverb they quote in Israel? 'As the days pass, they make liars out of every prophet.'" [23]The Lord God says, "I will put an end to this proverb. And they will soon stop saying it. Give them this one instead: 'The time has come for all these prophecies to be fulfilled.'

[24]"There will no more lies that claim you will be safe in Jerusalem. [25]For I am the Lord! What I say will happen. There will be no more delays, O rebels of Israel! I will do it in your own lifetime!" says the Lord God.

[26]Then this message came: [27]"Son of dust, the people of Israel say, 'His visions won't come true for a long, long time.'

[28]Therefore say to them, 'The Lord God says, "All delay has ended! I will do it now!"'"

False Teachers Get in Trouble

13 Then this message came to me: [2-3]"Son of dust, speak against the false prophets of Israel. They are making up their own visions. They say they have messages from me, but I never told them anything at all. Oh, it will be terrible for them!

[4]"O Israel, these 'prophets' of yours are useless. They are as useless as foxes for fixing your walls! [5]O evil prophets, what have you ever done to build up the walls of Israel against her enemies? What have you done to build up Israel in the Lord? [6]Instead you have lied. You said, 'My message is from God!' But God did not speak to you. And yet you expect him to do what you say will happen. [7]You claimed to see 'visions' from the Lord! You said you heard messages from God. But I never spoke to you at all!"

[8]So the Lord God says, "I will destroy you for these 'visions' and lies. [9]My hand shall be against you. And you shall be cut off from among the leaders of Israel. I will blot out your names. And you will never see your own country again. You shall know I am the Lord. [10]For these evil men lie to my people. They say, 'God will send peace.' But this is not my plan at all! My people build a thin and weak wall. And these prophets praise them for it! They cover it with whitewash!

[11]"Tell these evil builders that their wall will fall. A heavy rainstorm will wash it away. Great hailstones and mighty winds will knock it down. [12]And when the wall falls, the people will cry out. They will say, 'Why didn't you tell us that it wasn't good enough? Why did you whitewash it and cover up its weak spots?' [13]Yes, it will surely fall!" The Lord God says, "I will sweep it away with a great flood of anger. I will break it down with hailstones of wrath. [14]I will break down your whitewashed wall. It will fall on you and crush you. And you shall know I am the Lord. [15]Then at last my anger against the wall will be completed. And I will say, 'The wall and its builders

both are gone. ¹⁶For they were lying prophets.' They claimed Jerusalem would have peace when there is no peace," says the Lord God.

¹⁷"Son of dust, speak out against the women prophets too. For they act like the Lord has given them his messages, too. ¹⁸Tell them, 'The Lord God says: "How terrible it will be for you women! You are leading my people into great sin. You are lying to both young and old alike. You tell them to tie magic charms on their wrists. You give them magic veils in order to trap them. You destroy the lives of my people but then try to save your own! ¹⁹You turn my people away from me. And you get paid a few handfuls of barley for it! You have led those to death who should not die! And you have promised life to those who should not live. You have lied to my people. And how they love it!"'"

²⁰And so the Lord says, "I will crush you! For you hunt my people's souls with all your magic charms. I will tear off the charms. I will set my people free like birds from cages. ²¹I will tear off the magic veils and save my people from you. They will no longer be hurt by you. And you shall know I am the Lord. ²²Your lies have made the righteous give up when I didn't want them to. And you have helped the wicked by promising life even though they keep on sinning. ²³But you won't lie any more. No longer will you talk of seeing 'visions' that you never saw. And you won't practice your magic. For I will save my people from your hands by destroying you. And you shall know I am the Lord."

God Hates Idols

14 Then some of the elders of Israel came to me. They asked me for a message from the Lord. ²This is the message that came to me to give to them.

³"Son of dust, these men worship idols in their hearts. So should I let them ask me anything? ⁴Tell them, 'The Lord God says: "I the Lord will punish anyone in Israel who worships idols and then comes to ask my help. ⁵For I hope to win back the hearts of those who have turned from me to idols."'

⁶⁻⁷"So warn them that the Lord God says: 'Repent and destroy your idols. Stop worshiping them in your hearts. I the Lord will punish everyone who turns away from me for idols. This is true for the people of Israel or the foreigners living among you. Those who reject me for idols and then come to a prophet for my help shall be punished. ⁸I will turn upon him and destroy him. I will make a bad example of him. And you shall know I am the Lord. ⁹And if one of the false prophets gives him a message, it is a lie. His prophecy will not come true. And I will stand against that "prophet." I will destroy him from among my people Israel. ¹⁰False prophets and liars will all be punished for their sins. These are just evil people who say they want to hear my words. ¹¹I will punish them so the people of Israel will learn not to leave me. That way they will not be made dirty with sin any longer. They will be my people and I their God.' This is what the Lord says."

¹²Then this message of the Lord came to me: ¹³"Son of dust, the people of a land might sin against me. If they do, then I will crush them with my fist. I will break off their food supply. And I will send hunger to destroy both man and animal. ¹⁴Noah, Daniel, and Job might be there during this time of punishment. But if they were, only they would be saved by their goodness. And I would destroy the rest of Israel," says the Lord God.

¹⁵"I might send dangerous wild animals into the land. They might come to devour the land. ¹⁶And these three good men might be there. But even then, the Lord God swears that it would do no good. Their presence would not save the people from their death. Those three only would be saved. But the land would be destroyed.

¹⁷"Or I might bring war against that land. I might tell the enemy armies to come and destroy everything. ¹⁸And these three men might be there in the land. But the Lord God says that they alone would be saved.

¹⁹"And I might pour out my anger by sending a plague into the land. And the

plague might kill man and animal alike. 20And Noah, Daniel, and Job might be living there. But the Lord God says that only they would be saved because of their goodness."

21And the Lord says, "Four great punishments are coming to Jerusalem. They will come and destroy all life. These punishments are war, hunger, wild beasts, and plague. 22Some people might live through them. They might then come here to join you in Babylon. If they do, you will see with your own eyes how wicked they are. Then you will know it was right for me to destroy Jerusalem. 23You will agree with my judgment, when you meet them. You will agree that all these things are being done to Israel for a good reason."

A Useless Vine

15 Then this message came to me from the Lord: 2"Son of dust, what good are vines from the forest? Are they as useful as trees? Are they even as useful as a single branch? 3No, for vines can't be used even for making pegs to hang up pots and pans! 4All they are good for is firewood. And even so, they burn quite badly! 5-6So they are useless both before and after being put in the fire!

"This is what I mean," the Lord God says. "The people of Jerusalem are like the vines of the forest. They are useless before being burned. And they are not even useful as firewood! 7And I will set myself against them. I will make sure that if they get away from one fire, they will fall into another. And then you shall know I am the Lord. 8And I will make the land empty because they worship idols," says the Lord God.

Terrible Sins

16 Then again a message came to me from the Lord: 2"Son of dust," he said. "Speak to Jerusalem about her sins. 3Tell her that the Lord God says: 'You are no better than the people of Canaan. Your father must have been an Amorite! And your mother must have been a Hittite! 4When you were born, no one took care of you. When I first saw you, your cord was not cut. You had not been washed or rubbed with salt. No one had put any clothes on you. 5No one even wanted to help you. No one pitied you or cared for you. On that day when you were born, you were dumped out in a field. You were left there to die.

6-7"But I came by and saw you there. You were covered with your own blood. And I said, "Live! Grow like a plant in the field!" And you did! You grew up and became tall, slender and supple. You were a jewel among jewels. Then you reached the age of womanhood. Your breasts were full and your hair had grown. Yet you were naked.

8"'Later, I passed by and saw you again. And you were old enough to be married. So I wrapped my cloak around you. And I legally promised to marry you. I signed a covenant with you, and you became mine. 9-10Then, after the marriage, I gave you pretty clothes of linen and silk. Your clothes had designs sewn into them. And I gave you sandals made of dolphin hide. 11I gave you lovely bracelets and pretty necklaces. 12I gave you a ring for your nose and two more for your ears. I gave you a lovely tiara for your head. 13And so you were made pretty with gold and silver. And your clothes were silk and linen with pretty designs sewn in them. You ate the best foods and became prettier than ever. You looked like a queen, and so you were! 14You were well known among the nations for your beauty. It was perfect because of all the gifts I gave you,' says the Lord God.

15"'But you thought you could get along without me. You trusted in your beauty instead. And you gave yourself as a prostitute to every man who came along. Your beauty was his for the asking. 16You used the lovely things I gave you for making idol shrines. You used them to make your bed tempting to other men. Who could ever think of doing such a thing? There has never been anything like it before! 17You took the very jewels and gold and silver I gave to you. And you made statues of men and worshiped them. This is as bad as sleeping with a man who is not your husband! 18You used the pretty clothes I gave you with designs sewn on them. And you covered your idols with them! You used my oil and incense to worship them! [19]You gave them the fine flour and oil and honey I gave you! Have you ever heard of such a thing? [20]You took the sons and daughters I had given you. And you sacrificed them to your gods. So now they are gone. Wasn't it enough that you should be a prostitute? [21]Must you also kill my children by giving them to idols?

[22]"'You have been unfaithful to me for all these years. But you never think of those days long ago. You can't remember when you were naked and covered with blood.

[23-24]"'Oh, how terrible it will be for you! For you did many other evil things against me. You built a large place to worship false gods. You have built idol altars on every street! [25]And there you gave your beauty to every man who came by. You have been unfaithful to me time after time. [26]And you gave yourself to lustful Egypt. You made a treaty with her. And this has made me very angry.

[27]"'So now I have crushed you with my fist. I have made your country small. I have given you into the hands of the Philistines, who hate you. And even they are ashamed of you.

[28]"'You have been a prostitute with the Assyrians too. You did this by making a treaty with them. And you worshiped their gods, too. It seems that you can never find enough new gods. After being unfaithful with them, you still weren't happy. [29]So you worshiped the gods of that great land of Babylon. And you still weren't happy. [30]What a dirty heart you have!' says the Lord God. 'For you have done so many terrible things. You are like a prostitute that has no shame. [31]You build your idol altars on every street. You have been worse than a prostitute. You want to sin so badly that you have not even charged for your love! [32]Yes, you are like an unfaithful wife. You are like a woman who lives with other men instead of her own husband. [33-34]Prostitutes charge men for what they give. Men pay them with many gifts. But not you! You give them

gifts! You pay them to come to you! So you are different from other prostitutes. But you had to pay them, for no one wanted you.

[35]"'O prostitute, hear the word of the Lord!' [36]The Lord God says, 'I see your dirty sins. I see how you worship your idols. You even kill your own children as sacrifices to your gods. [37]So this is what I am going to do. I will call all your friends and lovers together. These are the lovers you have sinned with. They include those you loved and those you hated. And I will make you naked before them, that they may see you. [38]I will punish you like a woman who has murdered someone. I will treat you like a woman who has been unfaithful to her husband and is living with other men. [39]I will give you to your lovers, these many nations, to be destroyed. And they will knock down your temples and idol altars. They will strip you and leave you naked. They will take your pretty jewels and leave you ashamed. [40-41]They will burn your homes, punishing you before the eyes of many women. Yes, I will make sure you stop worshiping other gods. I will stop you from paying your friends for their love.

[42]"'Then at last my anger against you will die away. My jealousy against you will end. Then I will be quiet and not be angry with you anymore. [43]But you don't remember how helpless you were as a child. And you have made me angry by all the evil things you do. So I will pay you back for all of your sins,' says the Lord. 'For you have done many evil things. But beyond that, you aren't even thankful for all I have done for you.

[44]"'"Like mother, like daughter!" That is what everyone will say of you. [45]For your mother hated her husband and her children. And now, you do too. And you are just like your sisters. For they hated their husbands and their children. Truly, your mother must have been a Hittite! And your father must have been an Amorite!

[46]"'Your older sister is Samaria. She is living with her daughters north of you. Your younger sister is Sodom and her daughters, in the south. [47]You have not

just sinned like they did. No, that was nothing to you! In a very short time you sinned far more than they did!

48"'I tell you the truth!' the Lord God says. 'Sodom and her daughters have never been as bad as you and your daughters. 49Your sister Sodom's sins were pride, laziness, and too much food. And the poor and needy suffered outside her door. 50She worshiped many idols as I watched. So then I crushed her.

51"'Even Samaria has not done half the sins you have! You have worshiped idols far more than your sisters have. They seem almost good compared to you! 52Don't be surprised when their punishment is less than yours. For your sins are so bad that compared to you, your sisters seem innocent! 53But someday I will give back the fortunes of Sodom and Samaria. And I will do the same for Judah too. 54Your punishment will help to comfort them. This is because yours will be much worse than theirs.

55"'Yes, your sisters, Sodom and Samaria, will be brought back. All their people will be restored. And Judah, too, will prosper in that day. 56In your proud days, you hated and looked down upon wicked Sodom. 57But now your wickedness is even worse! And it has been shown to the whole world! Now you are the one who is hated and looked down upon. You are looked down upon by Edom and all her neighbors. You are even looked down upon by the Philistines! 58This is part of your punishment for all your sins,' says the Lord.

59-60"For the Lord God says, 'I will pay you back for your broken promises. You lightly broke your promises to me. But I will keep the promise I made to you when you were young. I will make a covenant with you that will last forever. 61You will remember with shame all the evil you have done. And you will be overcome by my favor. For I will take your sisters, Samaria and Sodom. And I will make them your daughters. I will give them to you to rule over. You will know you don't deserve this kind act. For you did not keep my covenant. 62I will make my covenant again with you.

And you will know I am the Lord. 63You have done many terrible things. But even so, I will be kind to you again. You will remember your sins and cover your mouth in silence. You will be full of shame when I forgive you for all that you have done,' says the Lord God."

The Great Eagle

17 Then this message came to me from the Lord: 2"Son of dust, give this riddle to the people of Israel. 3-4There was a great eagle, with broad wings. It was full of many-colored feathers. This eagle came to Lebanon. He picked off the shoot at the top of the tallest cedar tree. Then he carried it into a city filled with traders. 5There he planted it in rich ground beside a wide river. There it would grow as fast as a willow tree. 6It took root and grew. It became a low but spreading tree that turned toward the eagle. It grew strong branches and lush leaves. 7But then another great eagle came along. And the tree sent its roots and branches out toward him instead. 8It turned to the other eagle even though it was already in good soil. It did this even though it already had plenty of water to make lush leaves and fruit."

9The Lord God asks, "Shall I let this tree grow? No! I will pull it out, roots and all! I will cut off its branches and let its leaves wither and die. It will pull out easily enough. It won't take a big crew or big machines to do that. 10Though the tree began so well, will it keep on growing? No, it will dry up completely when the east wind touches it. It will die in the same rich soil where it had grown so well."

11Then this message came to me from the Lord: 12-13"Ask these rebels of Israel: 'Don't you know what this riddle of the eagles means? I will tell you. Nebuchadnezzar, king of Babylon, came to Jerusalem. He was the first of the two eagles. He took away Judah's king and princes. These were her topmost buds and shoots. Then he brought them to Babylon. Nebuchadnezzar made a covenant with a member of the royal family. This was King Zedekiah. He had promised to stay loyal to Babylon. He took a small tree and planted it in rich ground beside a broad river. He also took away the top men of Judah's government. ¹⁴That way Judah would not be strong again and try to break away from Babylon. But by keeping her promises, Judah could be respected and keep her name.

¹⁵"'But even so, Zedekiah broke from Babylon's rule. He sent messengers to Egypt to ask for a great army. He asked for many horses to fight against Nebuchadnezzar. But will Judah prosper after breaking all her promises like that? Will she succeed? ¹⁶No! For as I live,' says the Lord, 'the king of Israel shall die. Nebuchadnezzar will pull out the tree, roots and all! Zedekiah shall die in Babylon. He will die in the land of the king who gave him his power. He will die in the land of the one whose covenant he broke. ¹⁷Pharaoh and all his mighty army won't be able to help Judah. The king of Babylon will attack Jerusalem again. And he will take many lives. ¹⁸For the king of Judah broke his promise after saying he would obey. Therefore he shall not get away.'"

¹⁹The Lord God says, "As I live, surely I will punish him. For he broke the promise he made in my name. ²⁰I will throw my net over him. And he shall be caught in my trap. I will bring him to Babylon. I will punish him there for betraying me. ²¹And all the best soldiers of Israel will be killed by the sword. And those still in the city will be scattered to the four winds. Then you will know that I, the Lord, have spoken these words."

²²⁻²³The Lord God says, "I will take a tender sprout from the top of a tall cedar. I will plant it on the top of Israel's highest mountain. It shall become a tall cedar. It shall grow great branches and bring forth seed. Animals of every sort will gather under it. Its branches will shelter every kind of bird. ²⁴And everyone shall know that it is I, the Lord, who cuts down the high trees. Everyone shall know that I lift up the low. They shall know that I make the green tree dry up and the dead tree grow. I, the Lord, have said that I would do it, and I will."

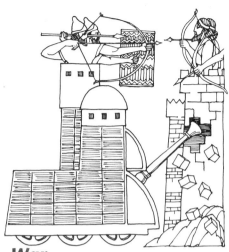

War

EZEKIEL 17:15-18

Bible-time soldiers and warriors would be amazed to see tanks, airplanes, radar, bombs, and guns! Wars were fought then with swords, spears, bows, and arrows. Assyrians and Babylonians built some machines for war. There were no engines in them, though. So men pushed these machines. Some of them had a big beam of wood called a battering ram. Men pushed the battering ram against the gate of the city to break it down. Some machines were like crude little tanks. These protected soldiers from enemy arrows.

A king did not usually say to another king, "We're going to war against you." He led his soldiers to a city. Then he surrounded the city and demanded that it surrender. If it did not, the soldiers tried to break down the gate. Sometimes they would camp around the city for months. The people in the city could not get out to get food. If they did not surrender, they starved. The enemy army would attack the city when the people inside were very hungry and weak. This is what happened to Jerusalem when the Babylonians attacked it.

Turn and Live!

18 Then the Lord's message came to me again. [2]"Son of dust," he said. "What is that proverb they quote in Israel? 'The children are punished for their fathers' sins.' [3]I tell you the truth," says the Lord God. "You will not use this proverb anymore in Israel. [4]For all souls are mine to judge, fathers and sons alike. And my rule is this: It is for a man's own sins that he will die.

[5]"But a man might be just. And he might do what is lawful and right. [6]Perhaps he never went out to the mountains to feast before idols and worship them. Maybe he has never slept with a woman who was not his wife. Or he might not have sinned against any of God's laws. [7]He might be kind to the people he lends money to. He might refuse to hold on to the things given to him in pledge by poor people. Perhaps he gives food to the hungry and gives clothes to those in need. [8]He might give loans without interest. He might stay away from all sin. Perhaps he is honest and fair when judging others. [9]Perhaps he obeys all my laws. If anyone does these things, then he is just. And he shall surely live," says the Lord.

[10]"But that man might have a son who is a robber or murderer. And he might not do anything he is supposed to. [11]He might not obey the laws of God. And he might even worship idols on the mountains. Perhaps he sleeps with women other than his wife. [12]He might take advantage of the poor and helpless. He might rob those who owe him money. He might not let them buy back what they have given him in pledge. Perhaps he is a man who loves idols and worships them. [13]He might loan out his money at interest. But if he does all these things, shall that man live? No! He shall surely die. And it is his own fault.

[14]"But, in turn, this sinful man might have a son. And this son might see all his father's wickedness. And he might fear God and decide against that kind of life. [15]He might not go up on the mountains to feast before the idols and worship them. And he might refuse to sleep with women other than his wife. [16]Per-

haps he is fair to those who borrow from him, and doesn't rob them. And maybe he feeds the hungry and clothes the needy. [17]He might help the poor and refuse to loan money at interest. And he might choose to obey all my laws. If this happens, then he shall not die because of his father's sins. He shall surely live. [18]But his father shall die for his own sins. This is because he is cruel and robs and does wrong.

[19]"'What?' you ask. 'Doesn't the son pay for his father's sins?' No! For if the son does what is right, he shall surely live. [20]The one who sins is the one who dies. The son shall not be punished for his father's sins. And the father won't be punished for his son's. The good person will be rewarded for his own goodness. And the wicked person will be punished for his wickedness. [21]But a wicked person might turn away from all his sins. And he might begin to obey my laws and do what is just and right. If he does this, he shall surely live and not die. [22]All his past sins will be forgiven. And he shall live because of his goodness.

[23]"Do you think I like to see the wicked person die?" asks the Lord. "Of course not! I only want him to turn from his wicked ways and live. [24]But, if a good person turns to sinning, should he be allowed to live? No, of course not. All the good things he did before will be forgotten. And he shall die for his sins.

[25]"Yet you say, 'The Lord isn't being fair!' Listen to me, O people of Israel. Am I the one who is unfair, or is it you? [26]A good man might turn away from being good, begin to sin, and die in his sins. If this happens, then he shall die for the evil he has done. [27]And a wicked person might turn away from his sin and obey the law and do right. If he does this, then he shall save his soul. [28]For he has thought it over. He has decided to turn from his sins and live a good life. So he shall surely live. He shall not die.

[29]"And yet the people of Israel keep saying, 'The Lord is not fair!' O people of Israel, it is you who are not fair, not I. [30]I will judge each of you, O Israel. I will punish or reward each according to his own actions. Oh, turn from your sins

while there is yet time. 31Put them behind you and receive a new heart and a new spirit. For why will you die, O Israel? 32I do not enjoy seeing you die," the Lord God says. "Turn, turn and live!

A Death Song

19 "Sing this death song for the leaders of Israel: 2What a woman your mother was! She was like a mother lion! Her children were like lion's cubs! 3One of her cubs, King Jehoahaz, grew into a strong young lion. He learned to catch prey and became a man-eater. 4Then the nations called out their hunters. They trapped him in a pit and brought him in chains to Egypt.

5"Israel, the mother lion, saw that all her hopes for him were gone. So she took another of her cubs, King Jehoiachin. She taught him to be 'king of the beasts.' 6He became a leader among the lions and learned to catch prey. And he too became a man-eater. 7He destroyed the palaces of the nations around him. And he ruined their cities. Their farms and crops were destroyed. Everyone in the land shook with terror when they heard him roar. 8Then the armies of the nations surrounded him. They came at him from every side. They trapped him in a pit and caught him. 9They pushed him into a cage and brought him before the king of Babylon. He was held captive so that his voice could never again be heard on the mountains of Israel.

10"Your mother was like a vine beside a river. It had lush, green leaves because of all the water. 11Its strongest branch became a ruler's scepter. And it was very great. It towered above the others and could see things from far away. 12But the vine was pulled up in anger and thrown down to the ground. Its branches were broken and dried up by a strong wind from the east. The fruit was destroyed by fire. 13Now the vine is planted in the wilderness. And there the ground is hard and dry. 14It is dying from within. No strong branch is left. The fulfillment of this sad prophecy has already begun. Yet there is still more ahead."

God Says, "Remember!"

20 Late in July, some of the elders of Israel came to ask for orders from the Lord. They came to me six years after King Jehoiachin was captured. They stood in front of me waiting for the Lord's reply.

2Then the Lord gave me this message: 3"Son of dust, speak to the elders of Israel. Tell them, 'The Lord God says: "How dare you come to ask my help? I promise that I will tell you nothing."' 4Judge them, son of dust. Condemn them. Tell them about all the sins of this nation. Remind them of the times of their fathers until now. 5-6Tell them, 'The Lord God says: "I chose Israel and showed myself to her in Egypt. And I made a promise to her and her descendants. I told them that I would bring them out of Egypt to a land I had found for them. It was a good land, flowing with milk and honey. It was the best of all lands anywhere."'

7"Then I said to them, 'Get rid of every idol. Do not make yourselves dirty by worshiping the Egyptian gods. For I am the Lord your God.' 8But they turned against me and would not listen. They didn't get rid of their idols or give up the gods of Egypt. Then I thought, I will pour out my anger on them. I will fulfill my anger against them while they are still in Egypt.

9-10"But I didn't do it, for I acted to protect the honor of my name. If I had destroyed them, the Egyptians would have laughed at Israel's God. For it would have looked like I couldn't keep them from being hurt. So I brought my people out of Egypt right in front of the Egyptians' eyes. From there, I led them into the wilderness. 11There I gave them my laws which bring life to those who obey them. 12And I gave them the Sabbath, a day of rest. This day came every seventh day. It was a symbol between them and me. It was to remind them that it was I, the Lord, who saved them. It would help them remember that they were truly my people.

13"But Israel sinned against me. There in the wilderness they would not obey my laws. They would not obey my rules, even though obeying them meant life. And they misused my Sabbaths. Then I thought, I will pour out my anger upon them. I wanted to destroy them completely in the desert.

¹⁴"But again I did not do it. This was to protect the honor of my name. For if I had destroyed them, the nations who saw me bring them out of Egypt would not have understood. They would have said that I was too weak to take care of them. They would think that was the reason I destroyed them. ¹⁵But I made a promise to them in the wilderness. I told them I would not bring them into the land I had given them. It was a land full of milk and honey. It was the best land on earth. ¹⁶I made this promise because they laughed at my laws. They would not do what I asked them to. And they did not keep my Sabbaths. Their hearts were with their idols! ¹⁷But even so, I did not kill them. I didn't finish them off in the wilderness.

¹⁸"Then I spoke to their children. I said: 'Don't follow your fathers' footsteps. Don't sin with their idols. ¹⁹For I am the Lord your God. Follow my laws. Keep my rules. ²⁰Keep my Sabbaths holy. For they are a symbol of the contract between us. They are to help you remember that I am the Lord your God.'

²¹"But their children, too, turned against me. They would not keep my laws. And these were the laws designed to bring life. And they did not keep my Sabbaths holy. So then I said, 'Now at last I will pour out my anger upon you in the wilderness.'

²²"But even so, again I did not judge them. I did this to protect my name among the nations. For they had seen my power in bringing them out of Egypt. ²³⁻²⁴But I made a promise against them while they were in the wilderness. I promised that I would scatter them, sending them to the ends of the earth. I did this because they did not obey my laws. But they laughed at them instead. And they did not keep my Sabbaths holy. Instead they wished for their fathers' idols. ²⁵I let them start customs and laws that were worthless. By keeping such laws they could never gain life.

²⁶I let them dirty themselves with the very gifts I gave them. They burnt their firstborn children as offerings to their gods! I let them do this hoping they would draw back in horror. I hoped that they would come to know that I alone am God.

²⁷⁻²⁸"Son of dust, speak to my people, Israel. Tell them that the Lord God says: 'Your fathers were always unfaithful to me. They were this way even after I brought them into the land I promised them. For they gave sacrifices and incense on every high hill and under every tree! They made me angry as they gave their sacrifices to those "gods." They brought their perfumes and incense. And they poured out their drink offerings to them! ²⁹I said to them, "What is this place of sacrifice where you go?" And so it is still called "The Place of Sacrifice." That is how it got its name.

³⁰"'The Lord God wants to know something. He wants to know if you are going to dirty yourselves like your fathers did. He wonders if you plan to keep on worshiping idols. ³¹For you might offer gifts to them. And you might give your little sons to be burned to ashes as you do even today. But if you do, shall I listen to you? Should I come and help you, Israel? As I live,' the Lord God says, 'I will not give you any message. I won't speak, even though you have come to me to ask.

³²"'What you have in mind will not be done. You want to be like the nations all around you. You want to serve gods of wood and stone. ³³I will rule you with an iron fist. I will govern you with great anger and with power. ³⁴With strength and anger I will bring you out from the lands where you are scattered. ³⁵⁻³⁶And I will bring you into my desert judgment hall. I will judge you there and get rid of the rebels. I will do just as I did in the wilderness after I brought you out of Egypt. ³⁷I will count you carefully and let only a few come back. ³⁸And the others I will get rid of. These are the rebels and all those who sin against me. They shall not enter Israel. But I will bring them out of the countries where

they have been taken. And when that happens, you will know I am the Lord.

³⁹"'Listen, O Israel,' says the Lord God. 'If you insist on worshiping your idols, go right ahead. But then don't bring your gifts to me as well! Such disrespect of my holy name must stop!

⁴⁰"'For at Jerusalem in my holy mountain,' says the Lord, 'all Israel shall worship me. There I will accept you. I will demand that you bring me your offerings and the finest of your gifts. ⁴¹I will bring you back from exile. And then you will be like an offering of incense to me. And the nations will see the great change in your hearts. ⁴²I will bring you home to the land I promised your fathers. And then you will know I am the Lord. ⁴³Then you will look back at all your sins. You will hate yourselves because of the evil you have done. ⁴⁴I will honor my name by blessing you. And I will do this even though you are so wicked. Then, O Israel, you will know I am the Lord.'"

⁴⁵Then this message came to me from the Lord: ⁴⁶"Son of dust, look toward Jerusalem. Speak out against it and the forest lands of the Negeb. ⁴⁷Prophesy to it, 'Hear the word of the Lord! I will set you on fire, O forest. And every tree will die, green and dry alike. The terrible flames will not be put out. And they will burn the world. ⁴⁸And all the world will see that I, the Lord, have set the fire. It shall not be put out.'"

⁴⁹I then said, "O Lord God. They say of me, 'He only talks in riddles!'"

Ezekiel's Glittering Sword

21 Then this message came to me from the Lord: ²"Son of dust, look toward Jerusalem. Speak against Judah and against my Temple! ³For the Lord says, 'I am against you, Israel. I will take out my sword and destroy your people. I will kill good and bad alike. ⁴I will not save even the righteous. I will make a clean sweep throughout the land. I will go from the Negeb to your northern borders. ⁵All the world shall know that it is I, the Lord. My sword is in my hand. I will not put it away again until its work is done.'

⁶"Cry out before the people, son of dust. Groan in your bitter pain. Sigh with grief and a broken heart. ⁷They might ask you why. If they do, tell them, 'Because of the bad news that God has given me. When it comes true, the bravest heart will melt with fear. All strength will disappear. Every spirit will faint. Strong knees will shake and become as weak as water.' And the Lord God says, 'Your doom is on the way. My judgments will soon be fulfilled!'"

⁸Then again this message came to me from God: ⁹⁻¹¹"Son of dust, tell them this, 'A sword is being sharpened. It is being polished for terrible killing. Now will you laugh? For those far stronger than you have died under its power. It is ready now to hand to the killer.' ¹²Son of dust, with crying, beat on your thigh. For that sword shall kill my people and all their leaders. All alike shall die. ¹³It will put them all to the test. And what chance do they have?" the Lord God asks.

¹⁴"Speak to them in this way: Clap your hands loudly. Then take a sword and hold it up two times, then three times. This will stand for the terrible killing they will soon see! ¹⁵Let their hearts melt with fear. For a sword shines at every gate. It flashes like lightning. It is as sharp as a razor for killing. ¹⁶O sword, cut to the right. Then cut to the left. Cut wherever you will, wherever you want. ¹⁷And as you speak, keep on clapping your hands. You have told the people that I, the Lord, will punish Jerusalem. And by doing this I will satisfy my anger."

¹⁸Then this message came to me. The Lord said: ¹⁹⁻²⁰"Son of dust, make a map. Trace two routes on it for the king of Babylon to follow. One should go to Jerusalem and the other to Rabbah in Transjordan. And put a signpost at the fork in the road from Babylon. ²¹For the king of Babylon stands at a fork. He doesn't know whether to attack Jerusalem or Rabbah. He will call his magicians to try to decide. They will cast lots by shaking arrows from the quiver. They will sacrifice to idols and look at the liver of their sacrifice. ²²And they will decide

to turn toward Jerusalem! With battering rams they will go against the gates, shouting for the kill. They will build towers and build a ramp against the walls to reach the top. ²³Jerusalem won't understand how this could happen. How could the magicians make this terrible mistake? For Babylon is Judah's friend. She has promised to help and defend Jerusalem! But the king of Babylon will think only of the times the people turned against him. He will attack and defeat them."

²⁴The Lord God says, "Again and again your guilt cries out against you. You sins are done out in the open without shame. Wherever you go, you sin. Whatever you do, all is filled with sin. And now the time of your punishment has come.

²⁵"O King Zedekiah, evil prince of Israel, your day of judgment is here. ²⁶Take off your jeweled crown," the Lord God says. "The old order changes. Now the poor are lifted up. And the rich are brought very low. ²⁷I will overturn the kingdom again and again. Even the new order that comes will not succeed. It will only succeed when the Man who has a right to it comes. And I will give it all to him.

²⁸"Son of dust, speak to the Ammonites too. For they laughed at my people in their time of trouble. Tell them this: 'My shining sword is out of its sheath. It is sharp and polished. And it flashes like lightning. ²⁹Your magicians and false prophets have told you lies of safety and success. They say that your gods will save you from the king of Babylon. In this way, they have caused your death along with all the other wicked. For when the day of final judgment has come, you will be wounded unto death. ³⁰Shall I put my sword away before I deal with you? No, I will destroy you in your own country where you were born. ³¹I will pour out my anger on you. I will blow upon the fire of my anger until it burns out of control. I will put you into the hands of cruel men skilled in destruction. ³²You are the fuel for the fire. Your blood will be spilled in your own country. And

you will be wiped out. Your memory will be lost from history. For I, the Lord, have spoken it.'"

God Lists the People's Sins

22 Now another message came from the Lord. He said: ²"Son of dust, declare that Jerusalem is the City of Murder. Tell everyone about her terrible deeds. ³She is the City of Murder, judged guilty. She is the City of Idols, dirty and foul. ⁴You, Jerusalem, are guilty of both murder and idolatry. Now comes your day of judgment. You have reached the limit of your years. I will make all the nations laugh at you. You will be looked down upon by all the nations of the world. ⁵Near and far they will mock you. You will be known as a city of trouble.

⁶"Every leader in Israel who lives within your walls is bent on murder. ⁷Fathers and mothers are ignored by their children. Visitors are forced to pay you for their 'protection.' Orphans and widows are wronged and oppressed. ⁸The things of God are all hated. No one keeps my Sabbaths. ⁹Prisoners are falsely accused and sent to their death. Every mountaintop is filled with idols. Loose and sinful acts are done everywhere. ¹⁰There are men who sleep with their fathers' wives. Others sleep with women during their periods. ¹¹It is common to sleep with a neighbor's wife or a daughter-in-law. Some even sleep with their half sisters. ¹²Hired murderers are everywhere. People make money by charging unfair interest. And they get rich by taking advantage of their neighbors. They never even think of me and my commands," the Lord God says.

¹³"But now I snap my fingers. I call a stop to your cheating and killing. ¹⁴How strong and brave will you be then, in my day of judgment? For I, the Lord, have spoken. And I will do all that I have said. ¹⁵I will scatter you throughout the world. I will burn out the wickedness within you. ¹⁶You will be put to shame among the nations. And you shall know I am the Lord."

¹⁷Then the Lord said this, ¹⁸⁻²⁰"Son of dust, the people of Israel are worthless. They are like the waste metal that is left

when silver is melted. They are the dross, mixed from the brass, tin, iron, and lead. So now the Lord God says, 'You are worthless dross. So I will bring you to my furnace in Jerusalem. I will melt you there with the heat of my anger. 21I will blow the fire of my wrath upon you. 22And you will melt like silver in fierce heat. Then you will know that I, the Lord, have poured my anger upon you.'"

23Again the message of the Lord came to me. The Lord said, 24"Son of dust, speak to the people of Israel. Say to them, 'In the day of my anger you shall be like a desert without rain. 25Your "prophets" have worked against you like lions looking for food. They devour many lives. They take treasures and steal riches. They cause many widows to be here in the land. 26Your priests have not obeyed my laws. They have made my Temple and my holiness unclean. To them the things of God are no more important than any daily task. They have not taught my people what is right and what is wrong. And they have not kept my Sabbath days holy. So my holy name has been made unclean among them. 27Your leaders are like wolves. They tear apart their victims. And they destroy lives to get rich. 28Your "prophets" tell about false visions. They speak false messages they claim are from God. But the Lord hasn't spoken one word to them. Thus they fix the walls with whitewash! 29Even the common people rob the poor and needy. And they force visitors in the land to pay them money.

30"'I looked everywhere to find a good person. I needed someone who could build the wall of goodness that guards the land. I looked for someone to stand in the gap and defend you from my just attacks. But I couldn't find anyone.' 31And so the Lord God says, 'I will pour out my anger upon you. I will burn you with the fire of my anger. I will give you the full penalty for all your sins.'"

Two Sisters

23 The Lord's message came to me again. He said, 2-3"Son of dust, there were two sisters. As young girls, they became prostitutes in Egypt.

4-5"The older girl was named Oholah. Her sister was Oholibah. (I am really speaking of Samaria and Jerusalem!) I married them. And they gave me sons and daughters. But then Oholah turned to other gods instead of me. She gave her love to the Assyrians, her neighbors. 6For they were all good-looking young men, captains and commanders. They wore handsome blue uniforms. And they dashed around on their horses. 7And so she sinned with them, the best men of Assyria. She worshiped their idols, making herself unclean. 8For when she left Egypt, she did not stop being a prostitute. She was still as loose as she was in her youth. At that time, the Egyptians had poured out their lusts upon her. They had touched her and slept with her.

9"And so I gave her into the evil hands of the Assyrians. For she loved their gods so much. 10They stripped her and killed her. And they took away her children as their slaves. Her name was known to every woman in the land as a sinner. Everyone knew that she had gotten what she deserved.

11"Oholibah (Jerusalem) saw what had happened to her sister. But she went right ahead in the same way. And she sinned even more than her sister! 12She gave herself to her Assyrian neighbors. She gave herself to those handsome young men on fine horses. They were army officers in handsome uniforms. 13I saw the way she was going. She was following right along behind her older sister.

14-15"She was in fact more sinful than Samaria. For she fell in love with pictures she saw painted on a wall! They were pictures of Babylonian soldiers. They wore striking red uniforms, with handsome belts. And they had flowing turbans on their heads. 16When she saw these paintings, she wished to give herself to the men in the pictures. So she sent messengers to Babylon to ask them to come to her. 17And they came and slept with her. They made her unclean in their bed of love. But after that she hated them and broke off all relations with them.

¹⁸"And I hated her, just as I hated her sister. This was because she flaunted herself before them. And she gave herself to their lusts. ¹⁹⁻²⁰But that didn't bother her. She turned to even greater sins. She slept with the lustful men she remembered from her youth in Egypt. ²¹In that way she celebrated those former days. For then as a young girl you gave yourself to Egypt.

²²"And now, O Oholibah (Jerusalem), you once turned away from your lovers. But the Lord God says that he will raise them against you. ²³For the Babylonians will come from Pekod and Shoa and Koa. And all the Assyrians will come with them. They are handsome young men of high rank, riding their horses. ²⁴They will come against you from the north. They will bring chariots, wagons, and a great army. They will be ready for attack. They will surround you on every side with armored men. And I will let them do with you as they wish. ²⁵And I will send my jealousy and my anger against you. They will cut off your nose and ears. Those who live through the first attack will be killed. Your children will be taken away as slaves. And everything left will be burned. ²⁶They will strip you of your clothes and jewels.

²⁷"This is how I will stop the sins you brought from the land of Egypt. You won't want Egypt and her gods anymore." ²⁸For the Lord God says, "I will surely give you over to your enemies. I will give you to those you hate. ²⁹They will be cruel to you and rob you of all you own. They will leave you naked and bare. And the shame of your sin shall be shown to all the world.

³⁰"You brought all this upon yourself! You did it by worshiping the gods of other nations. You made yourself unclean by worshiping all their idols. ³¹You have followed in your sister's footsteps. So I will punish you with the same terrors that destroyed her. ³²Yes, the terrors that fell upon her will fall upon you. And the cup from which she drank was full and large. All the world will laugh at you for your trouble. ³³You will stagger like a drunk under the blows of sadness and pain. You will fall just as your sister Samaria did. ³⁴In deep pain you will drink that cup of terror to the very bottom. You will lick the inside to get every drop. For I have spoken," says the Lord. ³⁵"You have forgotten me and turned your backs on me. So now you must bear the fruit of all your sin.

³⁶"Son of dust, you must judge Jerusalem and Samaria. You must show them all the bad things they have done. ³⁷For they have been unfaithful to me by worshiping idols. And they have killed their own children. They have burned them as sacrifices on their altars. And I was the one who gave them these children! ³⁸On the same day they made my Temple unclean. And they did not keep my Sabbaths holy. ³⁹For they killed their children in front of their idols. Then, on the same day, they came into my Temple to worship! That is how much respect they have for me!

⁴⁰"You even sent for priests from distant lands. You asked them to come with other gods for you to serve. So they came, and you welcomed them! You took a bath and painted your eyelids. Then you put on your finest jewels for them. ⁴¹You sat together on a bed with pretty designs sewn on it. And you put my incense and my oil on a table spread before you. ⁴²From your room came the sound of many men in a wild party. They were loose men and drunks from the wilderness. They put bracelets on your wrists and pretty crowns upon your head. ⁴³Will they sleep with these old washed-up prostitutes? ⁴⁴Yet that is what they did. They went in to them, to Samaria and Jerusalem, these shameless prostitutes. They went to them with all the energy of lustful men who visit prostitutes. ⁴⁵But good people everywhere will judge them for what they really are. They are unfaithful wives and murderers. They will punish them with the judgments the law demands."

⁴⁶The Lord God says, "Bring an army against them! Hand them out to be crushed and hated! ⁴⁷For their enemies will stone them and kill them with swords. They will kill their children and burn their homes. ⁴⁸In this way I will make sin and idol worship stop in the

land. My judgment will be a lesson against idolatry for all to see. ⁴⁹For you will be paid back for being unfaithful and worshiping idols. You will suffer the full judgment. And you will know that I alone am God."

A Cooking Pot

24 One day late in December another message came to me from the Lord. It came during the ninth year of King Jehoiachin's exile in Babylon.

²"Son of dust," he said. "Write down this date. For on this day, the king of Babylon has attacked Jerusalem. ³And now give this story to these sinners, Israel. Tell them, 'The Lord God says: Put a pot of water on the fire to boil. ⁴Fill it with the best sheep meat. Take the rump and shoulder and all the most tender cuts. ⁵Use only the best sheep from the flock. Then pile up fuel on the fire under the pot. Boil the meat well, until the flesh falls off the bones.'

⁶"For the Lord God says, 'How terrible it will be for Jerusalem, City of Murderers! You are a pot that is full of rust and wickedness. So take out the meat chunk by chunk in the order it comes. None of it is better than any other. ⁷For her wickedness is found in all of it. She murders without any shame. She leaves blood on the rocks in open view for all to see. She does not even try to cover it. ⁸And I have left it there, uncovered. It shouts to me against her. It wakes up my anger and my desire for revenge.

⁹"'How terrible it will be for Jerusalem, City of Murderers. I will pile on the wood under her. ¹⁰Let the fire roar and the pot boil. Cook the meat well. Then empty the pot and burn the bones. ¹¹Now set it empty on the coals to burn away the rust and dirt. ¹²But all this doesn't help at all. All the rust and dirt are still there even after burning in the hottest fire. ¹³It is the rust and dirt of worshiping your idols. I wanted to clean you and you did not let me. So now stay dirty until my anger has brought all its terrors upon you! ¹⁴I, the Lord, have spoken it. It shall come to pass and I will do it.'"

¹⁵Again a message came to me from the Lord. He said, ¹⁶"Son of dust, I am going to take away your lovely wife. Suddenly, she will die. Yet you must show no sadness. Do not cry at all. Let there be no tears. ¹⁷You may sigh, but only quietly. Let there be no crying at her grave. Don't bare your head or feet. And don't take the food brought to you by friends."

???????????????????????????????????

Why could Ezekiel not show any sorrow when his wife died?

(Read 24:16-24 for the answer.)

???????????????????????????????????

¹⁸I said this to the people in the morning. And in the evening my wife died. The next morning I did all the Lord had told me to.

¹⁹Then the people said, "What does all this mean? What are you trying to tell us?"

²⁰⁻²¹And I answered, "The Lord told me to speak to the people of Israel. He says, 'I will destroy my lovely Temple, the strength of your nation. And your sons and daughters in Judea will be killed by the sword. ²²And you will do as I have done. You may not cry in public. You may not comfort yourself by eating the food brought to you by friends. ²³Your head and feet shall not be bared. You shall not mourn or cry. But you will be sorry for your sins. And you will cry alone for all the evil you have done. ²⁴Ezekiel is an example to you,' the Lord God says. 'You will do as he has done. And when that time comes, then you will know I am the Lord.'"

²⁵"Son of dust, I will take the Temple from Jerusalem. It is the joy of their hearts and their glory. It is the joy of their wives, their sons, and their daughters. ²⁶On that day, a man will escape from Jerusalem. He will start on a journey to come to you in Babylon. He will tell you what has happened there. ²⁷And on the day he gets here, your voice will come back. That way you will be able to talk with him. And you will be a symbol for these people. And they shall know I am the Lord."

Thieves in the Desert

25 Then the Lord's message came to me again. He said, [2]"Son of dust, look toward the land of Ammon. Speak against its people. [3]Tell them, 'Listen to what the Lord God says. You laughed when my Temple was broken down. You mocked Israel in her pain. You laughed at Judah when she was marched away captive. [4]So now I will call Bedouins from the desert to the east. They will come and overrun your land. They will set up their camps among you. They will harvest all your fruit and steal your dairy cattle. [5]I will turn the city of Rabbah into a pasture for camels. All the country of the Ammonites will become a wasteland. And there, flocks of sheep will graze. Then you will know I am the Lord.'

[6]"For the Lord God says, 'You clapped and cheered with joy when my people were destroyed. [7]So now I will lay my hand heavily upon you. I will give you to many nations to be destroyed. I will cut you off from being a nation. I will destroy you. Then you shall know I am the Lord.'

[8]"And the Lord God says, 'The Moabites have spoken badly of Judah. They have said Judah is no better off than any other nation. [9-10]So now I will open up the eastern flank of Moab. I will wipe out her frontier cities, the glory of the nation. These cities are Beth-jeshimoth, Baal-meon, and Kiriathaim. And Bedouin tribes from the desert to the east will pour in upon her. It will happen to Moab, just as it will to Ammon. And Moab will no longer be counted among the nations. [11]Thus I will bring down my judgment on Moab. And they shall know I am the Lord.'

[12]"And the Lord God says, 'The people of Edom have sinned greatly. They have taken revenge on the people of Judah. [13]So now I will smash Edom with my fist! I will wipe out her people, her cattle, and her flocks. The sword will destroy everything from Teman to Dedan. [14]By the hand of my people, Israel, this shall be done. They will carry out my revenge.'

[15]"And the Lord God says, 'The Philistines have acted against Judah out of revenge. They have hated Judah for many years. [16]So now I will shake my fist over the land of the Philistines. I will wipe out the Cherithites. And I will totally destroy the people along the seacoast. [17]I will bring terrible revenge on them. I will do this to punish them for what they have done. And when all this happens, then they shall know I am the Lord.'"

A City Will Be Ruined

26 Another message came to me from the Lord. It came on the first day of the month. It was during the 11th year of King Jehoiachin's time in Babylon.

[2]"Son of dust," he said. "Tyre was happy about the fall of Jerusalem. They said, 'Ha! She had control over the rich north-south trade routes. These routes ran along the coast and along the Jordan River. But now her control has been broken. And now I am in control! Because Jerusalem is destroyed, I shall become rich!'

[3]"So now the Lord God says, 'I stand against you, Tyre. I will bring nations against you like ocean waves. [4]They will destroy the walls of Tyre and tear down her towers. I will scrape away her soil and make her a bare rock! [5]Her island shall become empty. It will be a place for fishermen to spread their nets. For I have spoken it,' says the Lord God. 'Tyre shall become the prey of many nations. [6]Her mainland city shall die by the sword. Then they shall know I am the Lord.'

[7]"For the Lord God says, 'I will bring Nebuchadnezzar, king of Babylon. He is the king of kings from the north. He will come against Tyre with a great army. He will bring horses and chariots. [8]First he will destroy your suburbs. Then he will attack your mainland city. He will build a ramp up to your walls. He will raise a roof of shields against it. [9]He will set up battering rams against your walls. He will break down your forts with hammers. [10]The hoofs of his horses will choke the city with dust. And your walls will shake as the horses gallop through

your broken gates. And they will pull chariots behind them. [11]Horsemen will take every street in the city. They will kill your people. And your famous, huge pillars will fall down.

[12]"They will take all your riches and objects of trade. They will break down your walls. They will destroy your lovely homes. They will throw your stones and timber and even your dust into the sea. [13]I will stop the music of your songs. No more will there be the sound of harps among you. [14]I will make your island a bare rock. It will be a place for fishermen to spread their nets. You will never be built again. For I, the Lord, have spoken it.' So says the Lord. [15]The whole country will shake with your fall. The wounded will scream as the killing goes on.

[16]"Then all the seaport rulers shall come down from their thrones. They will lay aside their robes and rich clothing. They will sit on the ground shaking with fear at what they have seen. [17]And they shall cry for you. And they will sing this song: "O mighty island city! Your power at sea once brought fear to those on the mainland. O how you have disappeared from the seas! [18]How the islands shake at your fall! They watch full of sadness and fear."'

[19]"For the Lord God says, 'I will destroy Tyre to the ground. You will sink under the terrible waves of enemy attack. Great seas shall swallow you. [20]I will send you to the pit of hell. You will lie there with those of long ago. Your city will lie in ruins, dead. You will be like those who entered the world of the dead long ago. No one will ever live in you again. And there will be no beauty here in the land of those who live. [21]I will bring you to a terrible end. No matter how hard they look, no one will be able to find you,' says the Lord."

A Great Seaport City

27 Then this message came to me from the Lord. [2]"Son of dust," he said. "Sing this sad song for Tyre:

[3]"O mighty seaport city, trading center of the world, the Lord God speaks. You say, "I am the most beautiful city in all the world." [4]You have marked your borders out in the sea. Your builders have made you great. [5]You are like a ship built of finest fir from Senir. They took a cedar from Lebanon to make a mast for you. [6]They made your oars from oaks of Bashan. The walls of your cabin are of cypress from the southern coast of Cyprus. [7]Your sails are made of Egypt's finest linens. You stand under tents bright with purple and red dyes from eastern Cyprus.

[8]"Your sailors come from Sidon and Arvad. Your helmsmen are skilled men from Zemer. [9]Wise old craftsmen from Gebal do the caulking. Ships come from every land with all their goods to trade.

[10]"Your army includes men from distant Paras, Lud, and Put. They serve you well. It is a feather in your cap to have their shields hang upon your walls. It is the greatest of honors. [11]Men from Arvad and from Helech are the guards on your walls. Your towers are manned by men from Gamad. Their shields hang row on row upon the walls. They make your glory perfect.

[12]"From Tarshish come all kinds of riches to your markets. They bring silver, iron, tin, and lead. [13]Traders from Javan, Tubal, and Meshech bring slaves and bronze dishes. [14]From Togarmah, come chariot horses and mules.

[15]"Traders come to you from Rhodes. And many coastlands are at your service. They pay you in ebony and ivory. [16]Edom sends her traders to buy your many wares. They bring emeralds, purple dyes, and fine linen. They bring jewelry of coral and agate. [17]Judah and the cities in Israel once sent traders with wheat from Minnith and Pannag. And they also brought honey, oil, and balm. [18]Damascus also comes. She brings wines from Helbon. And she brings white Syrian wool to trade for all the rich goods you make. [19]Vedan and Javan bring Arabian yarn, wrought iron, cassia, and calamus. [20]Dedan brings rich cloths used for riding.

[21]"The Arabians and Kedar's rich princes bring you lambs, rams, and goats. [22]The traders of Sheba and Raamah come with all kinds of spices. They also bring jewels and gold. [23]Haran,

Canneh, Eden, Asshur, and Chilmad all send their wares. ²⁴They bring fine fabrics to trade. They bring blue cloth and many-colored carpets. They are tied with cords and made secure. ²⁵The ships of Tarshish are your ocean caravans. Your island warehouse is filled to the brim!

²⁶"'But now your statesmen bring your ship of state into a great storm! Your mighty ship flounders in the heavy eastern wind. And you break apart in the middle of the seas! ²⁷Everything is lost. Your riches and wares, your sailors and pilots are gone. So are your ship builders, traders, and soldiers. And all the people sink into the sea on the day of your ruin.

²⁸"'The cities nearby shake at the sound as your pilots shout with fear. ²⁹All your sailors out at sea come to land. They look at the mainland shore. ³⁰They cry bitterly and throw dust on their heads. They sit in the ash heaps. ³¹They shave their heads in sadness. They put on sackcloth. They cry for you with bitter hearts and deep sadness.

³²"'And they sing this song in their sadness: "Where in all the world was there such a great city as Tyre? And how fast she was destroyed in the sea! ³³Your trade satisfied the hunger of many nations. Kings at the ends of the earth were happy with the riches you sent them. ³⁴Now you lie broken under the sea. All your riches and your trade have died with you. ³⁵All who live along the coast watch, amazed. Their kings are afraid and watch with twisted faces. ³⁶The traders of the nations shake their heads. For your downfall was terrible. You have forever died away.""'

A Proud King Will Fall

28 Here is another message given to me from the Lord. ²⁻³"Son of dust," he said. "Say to the prince of Tyre, 'The Lord God says: You are so proud you think you are God! You sit on the throne of a god. You live on your island home in the middle of the seas. You are only a man and not a god. But you brag that you are like God. You are wiser than Daniel. For no secret is hidden from you. ⁴You have used your wisdom and

knowlege to become very rich. You have gold, silver, and many treasures. ⁵Yes, your wisdom has made you very rich and very proud.'

⁶"So now the Lord God says, 'You claim that you are as wise as God. ⁷So now an enemy army shall suddenly draw their swords against your wisdom. They shall come and destroy your greatness! ⁸They will bring you to the pit of hell. And you shall die like those cut with many wounds. You will die there on your island in the middle of the seas. ⁹Then will you brag like a god? No! For these enemies won't think you are a god. They will see you as a mere man! ¹⁰You will die like an outcast at the hands of enemies. For I have spoken it,' the Lord God says."

¹¹Then this further message came to me from the Lord. ¹²"Son of dust," he said. "Cry for the king of Tyre. Tell him, 'The Lord God says: You were the perfection of wisdom and beauty. ¹³You were in Eden, the garden of God. Your clothing was sewn with every precious stone. Your clothes were full of rubies, topaz, diamonds, chrysolite, onyx, jasper, sapphires, carbuncles, and emeralds. They were all put in pretty settings of fine gold. They were given to you on the day you were created. ¹⁴I chose you to be the Guardian Angel. You were allowed into the holy mountain of God. You walked among the stones of fire.

¹⁵"'You were perfect in all you did from the day you were created. But then a time came when wrong was found in you. ¹⁶Your great riches filled you with pride and you sinned. So now, I throw you out of the mountain of God like a common sinner. I destroyed you, O Guardian Angel. I sent you from the middle of the stones of fire. ¹⁷Your heart was filled with pride because of all your beauty. You made your wisdom evil for the sake of your glory. So now I have thrown you to the ground. I have made you helpless before the curious gaze of kings. ¹⁸You made your holiness dirty with lust for gain. So I brought fire from your own actions. And I let it burn you to ashes on the earth. I did this in the sight of all those watching. ¹⁹All who

know you are amazed at your fall. You are an example of horror. You are destroyed forever.'"

20Then another message came to me from the Lord: 21"Son of dust, look toward the city of Sidon. Speak against it. Say to it, 22'The Lord God says: I am your enemy, O Sidon. I will prove my power over you. I will destroy you and show my holiness to you. Then all who see shall know I am the Lord. 23I will send disease and an army to destroy. The wounded shall be killed in your streets by troops on every side. Then you shall know I am the Lord. 24No longer will Israel's neighbors prick and tear at Israel like thorns and briars. Then they shall know I am the Lord.

25"'The people of Israel will once more live in their own land. This is the land I gave their father Jacob. For I will gather them back again from distant lands where I have scattered them. And I will show the nations of the world my holiness among my people. 26They will live safely in Israel. They will build their homes and plant their vineyards. I will punish all the nations around them that treated them with such hate. Then they shall know I am the Lord their God.'"

A King Like a Dragon

29 This message came to me from the Lord. These words came late in December during the 10th year of King Jehoiachin's exile.

2"Son of dust," the Lord said. "Look toward Egypt and speak against Pharaoh her king. Speak against all her people. 3Tell them that the Lord God says: 'I am your enemy, Pharaoh, king of Egypt. You are a great dragon lying between your rivers. For you have said, "The Nile is mine. I have made it for myself!" 4I will put hooks into your jaws. I will pull you onto the land with fish sticking to your sides. 5And I will leave you and all the fish in the desert to die. And you won't be buried. For I have given you as food to the wild animals and birds.

6"'Your strength failed when Israel called on you for help. Because of this, all of you shall know I am the Lord. 7Israel leaned on you, but you broke

under her hand. You were like a cracked walking stick. You pulled her shoulder out of joint. You made her stagger with the pain. 8So now the Lord God says: I will bring an army against you, O Egypt. They will destroy both your men and herds. 9The land of Egypt shall become an empty land. And the Egyptians will know that I, the Lord, have done it.

??????????????????????????????????

Which king did God say was like a mighty dragon lying in the middle of the river?

(Read 29:2-5 for the answer.)

??????????????????????????????????

10"'You once said, "The Nile is mine! I made it!" So now I am against you and your river. I will destroy the land of Egypt, from Migdol to Syene. You will be destroyed as far south as the border of Ethiopia. 11For 40 years not a soul will pass that way. There will be no men or animals. It will be completely empty. 12I will make Egypt empty. And she will have empty nations all around her. Her cities will be like a wasteland for 40 years. I will send the people of Egypt to other lands.

13"'But the Lord God makes this promise. At the end of 40 years he will bring the Egyptians home again. They will come from the nations to which they will be sent. 14And I will give back the wealth of Egypt. I will bring her people back to the land of Pathros in southern Egypt where they were born. But she will be a weak and small kingdom. 15She will be the lowest of all the nations. Never again will she raise herself above the other nations. Never again will Egypt be great enough for that.

16"'Israel will no longer look for any help from Egypt. She might think of asking for it. But she will remember her sin of asking for it before. Then Israel will know that I alone am God.'"

17This message came to me from the Lord. It came in the 27th year of King Jehoiachin's exile. It was around the middle of March.

18"Son of dust," he said. "The army of King Nebuchadnezzar of Babylon fought hard against Tyre. The soldiers' heads were bald from carrying heavy baskets of dirt. Their shoulders were raw and sore from carrying stones for attacking the city. And Nebuchadnezzar got no pay for his work. So he could not pay the army for all their work." 19So the Lord God says, "I will give the land of Egypt to Nebuchadnezzar, king of Babylon. He will carry off her riches, taking all she has. He will use it to pay his army. 20Yes, I have given him the land of Egypt for his salary. He was working for me during those 13 years at Tyre," says the Lord. 21"And the day will come when I will bring back the old glory of Israel. Then at last her words will be respected. And Egypt shall know I am the Lord."

A Day of Clouds and Gloom

30 This is another message from the Lord! 2-3"Son of dust, speak out!" he said. "Tell them that the Lord God says, 'Cry out loud! For the terrible day is almost here. This is the day of the Lord. It is a day of clouds and gloom. It is a day of despair for the nations! 4A sword shall fall on Egypt. The dead shall cover the ground. Her riches have been taken away. Her foundations have been broken up. The land of Cush has been plundered. 5For all the nations who are their friends shall die in that war. This includes Cush, Put, Lud, Arabia, and Libya.'"

6For the Lord says, "All Egypt's friends shall fall. And the pride of Egypt's power shall come to an end. From Migdol to Syene they shall die by the sword. 7She will be empty. And all the nations around her will be empty too. Her cities will be in ruins. And they will have other ruined cities all around them. 8I will set Egypt on fire and destroy her friends. Then they will know I am the Lord. 9At that time I will send fast messengers. They will bring a message of panic to the Ethiopians. Great fear shall come to them at that time of Egypt's judgment. This will all come true."

10For the Lord God says, "Nebuchadnezzar, king of Babylon, will destroy the people of Egypt. 11He and his armies are sent to destroy the land. They are the terror of the nations! They shall fight against Egypt and cover the ground with the dead. 12I will dry up the Nile. I will sell the whole land to wicked men. I will destroy Egypt and everything in it. And I will use foreign enemies to do it. I, the Lord, have spoken it.

13"And I will smash the idols of Egypt and the images at Memphis. And there will be no king in Egypt. The people will do whatever they like!

14"The cities of Pathros, Zoan, and Thebes shall lie in ruins by my hand. 15And I will pour out my anger on Pelusium. This is the strongest fort in Egypt. And I will stamp out the people of Thebes. 16Yes, I will set fire to Egypt. Pelusium will be racked with pain. Thebes will be torn apart. Memphis will be in terror every day. 17The young men of Heliopolis and Bubastis shall die by the sword. And the women will be taken away as slaves. 18When I come to break the power of Egypt, it will be a dark day for Tahpanhes too. A dark cloud will cover her. And her daughters will be taken away as captives. 19So I will punish Egypt greatly. And they shall know I am the Lord."

20This message came to me about a year later. It was around the middle of March of the 11th year of King Jehoiachin's exile.

21"Son of dust," the Lord said. "I have broken the arm of Pharaoh, king of Egypt. It has not been set or put into a cast. So it is not strong enough to hold a sword." 22For the Lord God says, "I am against Pharaoh, king of Egypt. And I will break both his arms. I will break the strong one and the one that was broken before. And I will make his sword fall to the ground. 23I will send the Egyptians away to many lands. 24And I will make the arms of the king of Babylon strong. I will put my sword in his hand. But I will break the arms of Pharaoh, king of Egypt. And he shall groan before the king of Babylon. He will be like one who has been wounded unto death. 25I will make the hands of the king of Babylon strong. But the arms of Pharaoh fall useless to his sides. Yes, I will put my sword into the hand of the king of Babylon.

And he will swing it over the land of Egypt. Then Egypt shall know I am the Lord. 26I will send the Egyptians among the nations. Then they shall know I am the Lord."

A Magnificent Tree Cut Down

31 This message came to me from the Lord. It came in the middle of May. It was the 11th year of King Jehoiachin's exile.

2-3"Son of dust," he said. "Speak to Pharaoh, king of Egypt, and all his people. Say to them, 'You are like Assyria once was. You are a great and strong nation. You are like a cedar of Lebanon. It is full of thick branches and casts deep forest shade. Its top is high up among the clouds. 4Its roots dig deep into the rich earth. It gives streams of water to all the trees around it. 5It grows far above all the other trees. It grows long thick branches because of all the water at its roots. 6The birds nest in its branches. And in its shade the flocks and herds give birth to young. All the great nations of the world live in its shadow. 7It is strong and beautiful, for its roots go deep to water. 8This tree is taller than any other in the garden of God. No cypress tree has branches as big as it does. No tree can compare with its beauty. 9All the other trees of Eden were jealous of it. This is because of the greatness I gave it.

10"'But Egypt has become proud,' the Lord God says. 'She has set herself high above the others, reaching to the clouds. 11So now I will give her into the hands of a mighty nation. This nation will punish her to the amount her sin deserves. I, myself, will cut her down. 12A foreign army from Babylon will attack her land. This nation is known as the terror of the nations. Babylon will cut her down and leave her fallen on the ground. Her branches will be spread out everywhere. They will be across the mountains and valleys and rivers of the land. All those who live in her shade will go away. They will leave her lying there, fallen. 13The birds will pull off her twigs. The wild animals will lie among her branches. 14Let no other nation be proud for its own success. Such a nation might be higher than the clouds, but it will be judged. Such a nation will go to the grave along with all the proud men of the world.'

15"The Lord God says, 'When she fell, I made the oceans mourn for her. I held back their tides. I dressed Lebanon in black and caused the trees of Lebanon to cry. 16I made the nations shake with fear at the sound of her fall. For I threw her down to the grave with all the others like her. And all the other proud trees of Eden are comforted to find her there with them. 17Her friends, too, are all destroyed. They die with her. They are going down with her to the grave.

18"'O Egypt, you are great among the trees of Eden, the nations of the world. And you will be brought down to death with all these other nations. You will be among the nations you hate, killed by the sword. This is what will happen to Pharaoh and all his people,' says the Lord."

Lion or Crocodile?

32 This message came to me from the Lord. It came in the middle of February during the 12th year of King Jehoiachin's exile.

2"Son of dust," the Lord said. "Mourn for Pharaoh, king of Egypt. Say to him, 'You think of yourself as a strong young lion among the nations. But you are just a crocodile along the banks of the Nile. You just make bubbles and make the stream muddy.'

3"The Lord God says, 'I will send a great army to catch you with my net. I will pull you out. 4I will leave you stranded on the land to die. And all the birds of the heavens will land on you. The wild animals of the whole earth will eat you until they are full. 5And I will cover the hills with your flesh. I will fill the valleys with your bones. 6And I will make the earth wet with your gushing blood. It will fill valleys to the tops of the mountains. 7I will blot you out. I will hide the heavens and darken the stars. I will cover the sun with a cloud. The moon shall not give you her light. 8Yes, darkness will be all across your land. Even the bright stars will be dark above you.

9"'When I destroy you, sadness will be in many hearts. Distant nations you have never seen will cry for you. 10Yes, fear shall strike in many lands. Their kings shall be afraid because of all I do to you. They shall shake with fear when I lift my sword before them. They shall fear for their lives on the day of your fall.'

God wants bad people to come to him before they die

I am not happy when the wicked die. I want the wicked to turn from their evil ways and live.

Ezekiel 33:11

11"For the Lord God says, 'The sword of the king of Babylon shall come upon you. 12I will destroy you with Babylon's mighty army. It will smash the pride of Egypt and all her people. All will die. 13I will destroy all your flocks and herds that graze beside the streams. Neither man nor animal will stir up those waters anymore. 14So the waters of Egypt will be clear. They will flow as smoothly as olive oil,' the Lord God says. 15'I will destroy Egypt and wipe out everything she has. Then she shall know that I, the Lord, have done it. 16Yes, cry for the sadness of Egypt. Let all the nations cry for her and for her people,' says the Lord."

17Two weeks later, another message came to me from the Lord. He said, 18"Son of dust, cry for the people of Egypt. Cry also for the other strong nations. Send them down to the grave among the dead. 19Cry out to them, 'What nation is as beautiful as you, O Egypt? But your judgment is the grave. You will be laid beside the people you hate.' 20The Egyptians will die with the people killed by the sword. For the sword is drawn against the land of Egypt. She will be drawn down to judgment. 21The strong soldiers in the grave will welcome her as she goes there with all her friends. She will lie there beside the nations she once hated. She will lie down with others who died by the sword.

22"The princes of Assyria lie dead there. The graves of her people are all around them. They were killed by the sword. 23Their graves are in the depths of the pit. Their friends lie all around the grave. All these strong men once struck fear into the hearts of everyone. But now they are dead at the hands of their enemies.

24"Great kings of Elam lie there with their people. They once made the nations afraid while they were alive. But now they lie undone in the place of the dead. Their fate is the same as that of other men. 25They have a resting place among the dead. And the graves of their people are around them. Yes, they made the nations afraid while they lived. But now they lie in shame in the pit. They have been killed by the sword.

26"The princes of Meshech and Tubal are there. And the graves of their armies are all around them. All of them worshiped idols. They once struck fear into the hearts of all. Now they lie dead. 27They are buried in a common grave. They are not buried like heroes who are buried in great honor. They don't have their weapons beside them. Their shields do not cover them. And they don't have their swords under their heads. While they lived, they made everyone afraid. 28'Now you will lie crushed and broken among idol worshipers. You will lie among those who are killed by the sword.'

29"Edom is there with her kings and her princes. They were strong, but they too lie among the others whom the sword has killed. They lie with the idol worshipers who have gone down to the pit. 30All the princes of the north are there. So are the people from Sidon. All of them are dead. Once a terror, now they lie in shame. They bring their shame with them down to the pit. They go there with all the others who are dead.

31"When Pharaoh gets there, he will be comforted to find that he is not alone. He will find others there who had their armies destroyed," says the Lord God.

³²"For I have caused my terror to fall upon all the living. And Pharaoh and his army shall lie among the idol worshipers who are killed by the sword."

God Will Be the Judge

33 Once again a message came to me from the Lord. He said, ²"Son of dust, speak to your people. Say to them, 'I will bring an army against a country. So the people of that land should choose a watchman. ³He will look for the army that is coming. When he sees the enemy, he should blow the alarm to warn his people. ⁴Some might hear the alarm but do nothing about it. Well, if they die, it is their own fault. ⁵For they heard the warning but wouldn't listen. If they had listened to the warning, they would have saved their lives. ⁶But the watchman might see the enemy coming. And he might not sound the alarm and warn the people. If this happens, the watchman is guilty for their deaths. They will die in their sins. But I will charge the watchman with their deaths.'

⁷"So it is with you, son of dust. I have chosen you as the watchman for the people of Israel. So listen to what I say and warn them for me. ⁸I might say to the wicked, 'O wicked man, you will die!' But you might not tell him what I say. And as a result, he does not repent. If this happens, that wicked person will die in his sins. But I will hold you guilty for his death. ⁹But you might warn him to turn from his sins, and he might refuse. If this happens, he will die in his sin. And you will not be guilty.

¹⁰"The Lord God says, 'O people of Israel, I hear you saying, "Our sins are heavy upon us. We are dying of our guilt. How can we live?"' ¹¹Tell them, 'I make this promise to you. I am not happy when the wicked die. I want the wicked to turn from their evil ways and live. Turn, turn from your wickedness. For why do you want to die, O Israel? ¹²For the good works of a righteous man will not save him if he turns to sin. And the sins of an evil man will not destroy him if he turns from his sins.'

¹³"I have said the good man will live. But he might sin, thinking his past

Watchmen and Watchtowers
EZEKIEL 33:1-6

An enemy army could not fly over a Bible-time city. There were no airplanes. Armies could not drive up fast. There were no tanks or cars. Armies had to march toward a city on foot or horseback. It was important for the city to know that an army was coming. It took time for their army to get ready. So cities often had watchtowers. Usually these watchtowers were built on the city wall. A watchman stayed in the tower. He watched for armies. When he saw one coming, he blew his trumpet. Soldiers ran home. They got their swords and spears, bows and arrows. If the watchman didn't warn his people, many would die. If the people didn't listen to his warning, they would be in trouble.

God told Ezekiel to be a watchman for the Israelite people. But Ezekiel wasn't supposed to watch for enemy armies. He was to watch out for another kind of enemy even more dangerous than an army. That enemy was sin. When Ezekiel saw the people sinning, he knew they would get hurt. Ezekiel had to warn them about this. God was the only weapon to help them fight this kind of enemy.

goodness will save him. But if he does this, then none of his good deeds will be remembered. I will destroy him for his sins. ¹⁴And I might tell the wicked man he will die. But then he might turn from his sins. He might do what is fair and right. ¹⁵He might give back a pledge given to him by a borrower. Or he might give back what he has stolen. Perhaps he will walk along the paths of right, not doing evil. If this happens, he shall surely live. He shall not die. ¹⁶None of his past sins shall be brought up against him. For he has turned to the good and shall surely live.

¹⁷"And yet your people are saying the Lord isn't fair. The real trouble is that they aren't fair. ¹⁸For I say again, the good man might turn to evil. If this happens, he shall die. ¹⁹But the wicked man might turn from his sins. He might choose to do what is fair and just. If this happens, then he shall live. ²⁰Yet you are saying the Lord isn't fair. But I will judge each of you according to your deeds."

The People Don't Listen to Ezekiel

²¹It was the 11th year of our exile, late in December. At that time, a man escaped from Jerusalem and came to speak to me. He said, "The city has fallen!" ²²Now the hand of the Lord was upon me the evening before. He had made it so I could speak again by the time the man got there.

²³Then this message came to me: ²⁴"Son of dust, there are just a few people of Judah living among the ruined cities. They keep saying, 'Abraham was only one man. But he was given the whole land! We are many, so we should be able to get it back!' ²⁵But the Lord God says, 'You have no power, for you do evil! You eat meat with the blood still in it. You worship idols and murder people. Do you think I'll let you have the land? ²⁶You are murderers! You are idol worshipers! You sleep with people you aren't married to! Should you own this land?'

²⁷"Tell them, 'The Lord God says, "I make this promise. Surely those living in the ruins shall die by the sword. Those living in the open fields shall be eaten by wild animals. And those in the forts and caves shall die of disease. ²⁸I will destroy the land and her pride. And her power shall come to an end. The mountain villages of Israel shall be ruined. No one will even travel through them! ²⁹I shall ruin the land because of their sins. Then they shall know I am the Lord."'

³⁰"Son of dust, your people are talking behind your back. They talk about you in their houses. They whisper about you at the doors. They say, 'Come on, let's have some fun! Let's go hear him tell us what the Lord is saying!' ³¹So they come as though they want to hear. They sit in front of you like they are listening. But they don't plan to do what I tell them to. They talk very sweetly about loving the Lord. But with their hearts they love their money. ³²To the people, you are like someone who sings lovely songs. You are like someone with a beautiful voice. They think of you like they would a person who plays an instrument well. They hear what you say. But they don't do anything about it! ³³But all these terrible things will happen to them. They surely will happen! Then they will know a prophet has been among them."

God's Flock

34 Then this message came to me from the Lord. He said, ²"Son of dust, speak against the leaders of Israel. They are the shepherds of my people. Say to them, 'The Lord God says to you: How terrible it will be for you shepherds! For you feed yourselves instead of your flocks. Shouldn't shepherds feed the sheep? ³You eat the best food. You wear the finest clothes. But you let your flocks starve! ⁴You haven't taken care of the weak. You haven't tended the sick. You haven't bound up the broken bones. You never go looking for those who have wandered away and are lost. Instead, you have ruled them with force and cruelty. ⁵So they were scattered, without a shepherd. They have become a prey to every animal that comes along. ⁶My sheep wandered through the mountains and hills. They walked over the face of the earth. But there was no one to look for them or care about them.

⁷"So now, O shepherds, hear the

word of the Lord! [8]I make this promise,' says the Lord God. 'You left my flock. You left them to be attacked and destroyed. You were no real shepherds at all. For you didn't even look for them. You fed yourselves and let them starve. [9-10]Because of this, I am against the shepherds. They will be guilty for what has happened to my flock. I will take away their right to feed the flock. I will take away their right to eat. I will save my flock from being taken for their food.'

[11]"For the Lord God says, 'I will look for and find my sheep. [12]I will be like a shepherd looking for his flock. I will find my sheep and save them. I will save them from the places where they are scattered. [13]And I will bring them back from among the people and nations where they were. I will bring them back home to their own land of Israel. I will feed them on the mountains of Israel. I will lead them by the rivers where the land is rich and good. [14]Yes, I will give them good pasture on the high hills of Israel. There they will lie down in peace and feed in rich mountain pastures. [15-16]I myself will be the Shepherd of my sheep. I will let them lie down in peace,' the Lord God says. 'I will look for my lost ones, those who ran away. And I will bring them safely home again. I will put splints and bandages on their broken legs. And I will heal the sick among them. I will destroy the powerful, fat shepherds. I will feed them, yes! But I will feed them only punishment!

[17]"'And as for you, my flock, I will judge you,' the Lord God says. 'I will separate good from bad, sheep from goats.

[18]"'O evil shepherds! Is it not enough for you to keep the best of the pastures for yourselves? Must you then trample down what you can't use? Is is not enough that you take the best water for yourselves? Must you then muddy the rest with your feet? [19]All that's left for my flock is what you've trampled down. All they have to drink is water that you've made dirty.'

[20]"So now the Lord God says, 'I will judge between these fat shepherds and their thin sheep. [21]For these shepherds push and crowd my sick and hungry flock. And now they're scattered far away. [22]So I myself will save my flock. They won't be picked on and destroyed anymore. And I will notice which is fat and which is thin. And I know why they are that way!

[23]"'And I will set one Shepherd over all my people, even my Servant David. He shall feed them and be a Shepherd to them.

[24]"'And I, the Lord, will be their God. And my Servant David shall be a Prince among my people. I, the Lord, have spoken it.

[25]"'I will make a peace treaty with them. I will send away the dangerous animals from the land. That way my people will be able to camp safely in the wildest places. And they will sleep safely in the woods. [26]I will make my people and their homes around my hill a blessing. And there shall be showers of blessing. For I will not shut off the rains but send them in their seasons. [27]Their fruit trees and fields will yield rich crops. And everyone will live in safety. I will break off their chains of slavery. I will save them from those who took advantage of them. And they shall know I am the Lord. [28]Other nations will no longer conquer them. And wild animals will never again attack. The people shall live in safety. No one shall make them afraid.

[29]"'And I will raise up a Vine in Israel. I will do this so my people will never again go hungry. And they will never again be shamed by heathen conquest. [30]In this way they will know that I, the Lord their God, am with them. They will know that they, the people of Israel, are my people,' says the Lord God. [31]'You are my flock, the sheep of my pasture. You are my people, and I am your God.' This is what the Lord says."

Edom Will Be Ruined

35 Again a message came from the Lord. He said, [2]"Son of dust, look toward Mount Seir. Speak against the people saying, [3]'The Lord God says: I am against you! I will smash you with my fist and destroy you. [4-5]You hate my people Israel. So I will destroy your cities and make you desolate. Then you shall know I am the Lord. You killed my people when they were helpless. You turned on them when I had punished them for all their sins. 6So I make this promise now. Since you enjoy blood so much, I will give you a bloodbath. Your turn has come! 7I will wipe out the people of Mount Seir. I will kill off all those who try to get away. And I will catch all those who come back. 8I will fill your mountains with the dead. Your hills, your valleys, and your rivers will be filled with those the sword has killed. 9Never again will you revive. You will be silent and empty forever. Your cities will never be rebuilt. Then you shall know I am the Lord.

10"For you said, "Both Israel and Judah shall be mine. We will take control of them. What do we care that God is there?" 11So now I, the Lord, make this promise. I will pay back your angry deeds with mine. I will punish you for all your acts of envy and of hate. And I will honor my name in Israel by what I do to you. 12And you shall know that I have heard each evil word you spoke against the Lord. You said, "His people are helpless. They are food for us to eat!" 13Saying that, you spoke against the Lord. And I have heard it all!

14"The whole world will rejoice when I destroy you. 15You were happy when Israel was destroyed. Now I will be happy when the same thing happens to you! You will be wiped out, O people of Mount Seir. This includes all of you who live in Edom! And then you will know I am the Lord!'

A Promise of Good Times

36 "Son of dust, speak to Israel's mountains. Tell them, 'Listen to this message from the Lord.

2"'Your enemies have laughed at you. They took your ancient land as their own. 3They have destroyed you on every side. They sent you away as slaves to many lands. You are laughed at and slandered. 4So now, O mountains of Israel, hear the word of the Lord God. He is speaking to the hills and mountains, dales and valleys. He is speaking to the

ruined farms and the empty cities. They were destroyed and mocked by heathen nations all around. 5My anger is on fire against these nations, especially Edom. They took my land for themselves with great joy. They did not show any respect for me.'

6"So now speak to the hills and mountains, dales and valleys of Israel. Say to them, 'I, the Lord, am full of anger. For you suffered shame before the nations around you. 7So I make this promise with hand held high. Those nations are going to have their turn of being covered with shame. 8But for Israel good times will soon come back. There will be heavy crops of fruit to get ready for my people. And they will be coming home again soon! 9See, I am for you! I will come and help you as you get the ground ready and plant your crops. 10I will make the number of people grow in all Israel. The ruined cities will be rebuilt and filled with people. 11Not only the people, but your flocks and herds will also grow fast. O mountains of Israel, again you will be filled with homes. I will do even more for you than I did before. Then you shall know I am the Lord. 12My people will walk upon you once again. And you will belong to them again. You will no longer be a place for burning their children on idol altars.'

13"The Lord God says, 'Now the other nations make fun of you. They are saying, "Israel is a land that kills her own people!" 14But they will not say this anymore. More and more children will be born. And your babies will not die when they are small,' says the Lord. 15"Those heathen nations won't laugh anymore. For you will no longer be a nation of sinners,' the Lord God says."

16Then this further word came to me from the Lord. He said, 17"Son of dust, this happened a long time ago. The people of Israel once lived in their own country. But they made it unclean by doing evil things. To me their worship was as bad as dirty rags. 18They made the land unclean with murder and idol worship. So I poured out my anger on them. 19And I sent them away to many lands. That is how I punished them for the evil way they lived. [20]My people were scattered out among the nations. But then they gave me a bad name. This is because the nations said, 'These are the people of the Lord. But the Lord couldn't keep them from getting hurt!' [21]I am troubled that the nations speak about me this way. My people have given me a bad name throughout the world.

[22]"Now say to the people of Israel, 'The Lord God says: I am bringing you back again. But I am not doing it because you deserve it. I am doing it to protect my holy name. For you have given me a bad name among the nations. [23]I will honor my great name, that you defiled. And the people of the world shall know I am the Lord. I will be honored before their eyes by saving you from exile among them. [24]For I will bring you back home again to the land of Israel.

[25]"'Then it will be as though I poured clean water on you. For you will be clean. Your dirtiness will be washed away. Your idol worship will be gone. [26]And I will give you a new heart with new and right desires. I will put a new spirit inside of you. I will take out your stony heart of sin. In its place, I'll give you a new heart of love. [27]And I will put my Spirit within you. Then you will obey my laws and do whatever I command.

[28]"'And you shall live in Israel. This is the land that I gave your fathers long ago. I will be your God. And you shall be my people. [29]I will wash away your sins. I will make sure there are no droughts or famines. [30]I will give you huge harvests from your fruit trees and fields. And never again will the other nations laugh at your land for its famines. [31]Then you will remember your past sins. You will hate yourselves for all the evils you did. [32]But always remember this! It is not for your own sakes that I will do this, but for mine. O my people Israel, be ashamed of all that you have done!

[33]"'The Lord God says: I will make you clean from all your sins. I will bring you home again to Israel and rebuild the ruins. [34]Land will be planted again that during the exile lay empty. It was an empty wilderness. All who passed by were shocked to see how your land was ruined. [35]But when I bring you back, they will say, "This empty land has become like Eden's garden! The ruined cities are rebuilt with walls around them. And they are filled with people!" [36]Then the nations all around will know about me. They will know that I, the Lord, rebuilt the ruins. They will know that I planted rich crops in the wilderness. For I, the Lord, have promised it. And I will do it.'

[37-38]"The Lord God says, 'I am ready to hear Israel's prayers for these blessings. I am ready to give them what they ask for. Just let them ask, and I will give them many children. The nation will be full, like Jerusalem's streets are full of sheep at sacrifice time. The ruined cities will be crowded once more. Then everyone will know I am the Lord.'"

Dried Bones

37 The power of the Lord came upon me. And I was carried away by the Spirit of the Lord. He took me to a valley full of old, dry bones. The bones were scattered everywhere across the ground. He led me around among them. [3]Then he said:

"Son of dust, can these bones become people again?"

I replied, "Lord, you alone know the answer to that."

[4]Then he told me to speak to the bones. He told me to say, "O dry bones! Listen to the words of God. [5]For the Lord God says, 'See! I am going to make you live and breathe again! [6]I will put new flesh and muscles on you. I will cover you with skin. I will put breath into you and you shall live. Then you shall know I am the Lord.'"

[7]So I spoke these words from God, just as he told me to. And suddenly there was a rattling noise from all across the valley. And the bones of each body came together. They attached to each other as they used to be. [8]As I watched, the muscles and flesh formed over the bones. Then skin covered them. But the bodies still had no breath. [9]Then he told me to call to the wind. He told me to say, "Come from the four winds, O Spirit.

Breathe on these dead bodies. Make it so they are alive again." [10]So I spoke to the winds as he told me to. Then the bodies began to breathe. They became alive and stood up. They made up a very great army.

[11]Then he told me what the vision meant. "These bones," he said, "stand for all the people of Israel. They say, 'We have become a heap of dried-out bones. All hope is gone.' [12]But tell them, 'I, the Lord, will open your graves of exile. I will cause you to rise again. I will help you come back to the land of Israel.' [13]And, then at last, O my people, you will know I am the Lord. [14]I will put my Spirit into you. You shall live and come home again to your own land. Then you will know that I, the Lord, have done just what I promised you.'"

Ezekiel's Carved Stick

[15]Again a message from the Lord came to me. He said, [16]"Take a stick and carve some words on it. Write, 'This stick stands for Judah and her tribes.' Then take another stick and carve these words on it: 'This stick stands for all the other tribes of Israel.' [17]Now hold them together in your hand as one stick. [18-20]Hold the sticks so the people can see what you are doing. Then tell them, "The Lord God says: 'I will take the tribes of Israel. I will join them to Judah. I will make them one stick in my hand.'"

[21]For the Lord God says, "I am calling the people of Israel from the nations. I am bringing them home from around the world to their own land. [22]I will make them into one nation. One king shall be king of them all. They won't be divided into two nations any longer. [23]They shall stop worshiping idols. And they won't do their other sins. For I will save them from all this. Then they shall truly be my people and I their God.

[24]"And David, my Servant, shall be their King, their only Shepherd. And they shall obey my laws and all my wishes. [25]They shall live in the land of Israel where their fathers lived. This is the land I gave my servant Jacob. They and their children after them shall live there. And their grandchildren will live there after them. This will go on forever. And my Servant David shall be their Prince forever. [26]And I will make a covenant of peace with them. It will be a treaty that will never end. I will bless them and make them grow in numbers. I will put my Temple among them forever. [27]And I will make my home among them. Yes, I will be their God. And they shall be my people. [28]And my Temple will stay among them forever. Then the nations will know that I, the Lord, have chosen Israel as my very own."

Ezekiel's Message to Gog

38 Here is another message to me from the Lord. [2-3]"Son of dust," he said. "Look to the north toward the land of Magog. Speak against Gog king of Meshech and Tubal. Tell him that the Lord God says, 'I am against you, Gog. [4]I will put hooks into your jaws and pull you to your judgment. I will call out your troops and horsemen. I will make you a mighty army, all fully armed. [5]Peras, Cush, and Put shall join you too. And they will bring all their weapons with them. [6]Gomer and all his armies will also come. So will the armies of Togarmah, from the distant north. There will also be many others. [7]Get ready! Keep your army ready. You are their leader, Gog!

[8]"'A long time from now you will be called to action. In distant years you will swoop down onto the land of Israel. At that time, it will be lying in peace. Its people will have come back from many lands. [9]You and all your friends, a great army, will roll down upon them. You will come like a storm and cover the land like a cloud. [10]For at that time an evil thought will have come to your mind. [11]You will have said, "Israel is a land with no defenses! None of its villages have walls around them. I will march against her and destroy these people living in peace! [12]I will go to those once-empty cities that are now filled with people again. For the people of Israel have come back from all the nations. I will take great amounts of loot and many slaves. For the people are rich with cattle now. And the whole earth looks to them!"

13"'But Sheba and Dedan will ask, "Who are you to rob them of silver and gold? Who are you to drive away their cattle? Who are you to take their goods and make them poor?" The trading princes of Tarshish will also ask this. These are nations who trade with Israel.'

14"The Lord God says to Gog, 'My people will be living in peace in their land. At that time, you will get yourself ready. 15-16You will come from all over the north. You will bring your great army of horses. You will cover the land like a cloud. This will happen in the distant future. It will take place in the last years of history. I will bring you against my land. And my holiness will be proved in your destruction before their eyes. Then all the nations will know that I am God.'

17"The Lord God says, 'I spoke of you long ago through the prophets of Israel. I said that after many years had passed, I would bring you against my people. 18But when you come to destroy the land of Israel, my anger will rise! 19For I am a jealous God with blazing anger. And I promise a mighty shaking in the land of Israel on that day. 20All living things shall shake in fear at my presence. Mountains shall be thrown down. Cliffs shall tumble. Walls shall crumble to the earth. 21I will call every kind of terror against you,' says the Lord God. 'You will fight against yourselves in deadly combat! 22I will fight you with sword, disease, floods, hailstones, fire, and brimstone! 23In this way I will show how great I am. I will bring honor to my name. All the nations of the world will hear what I have done. And they shall know that I am God!'

God's Holiness

39 "Son of dust, speak this also against Gog. Tell him, 'I stand against you, Gog. You are the leader of Meshech and Tubal. 2I will turn you and drive you toward the mountains of Israel. I will bring you from the distant north. And I will destroy 85 percent of your army in the mountains. 3I will knock your weapons from your hands and leave you helpless. 4You and all your

armies will die upon the mountains. I will give you to the vultures and wild animals to eat. 5You will never reach the cities. You will fall in the open fields. For I have spoken,' the Lord God says. 6'And I will rain down fire on Magog. I will rain it down on all your friends who live safely on the coasts. And they shall know I am the Lord.

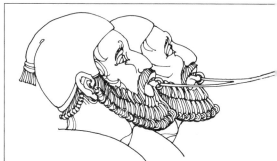

Hooks in Their Faces
EZEKIEL 38:4
Have you ever caught a fishhook in your finger? If you have, you know how much it hurts. People in Bible times put hooks through the nose or jaw of a bull. This helped them lead the bull. Assyrian kings often pushed hooks through the lips of a prisoner. Then they fastened a rope to the hook and pulled the prisoner. The prisoner was often the king they had defeated. An Assyrian king did this to King Manasseh of Judah (2 Chronicles 33:11). It hurt a king badly to lose a battle. But think how much more this hurt!

7"'In this way I will make my holy name known among my people Israel. I will not let it be laughed at anymore. And the nations, too, shall know I am the Lord, the Holy One of Israel. 8That day of judgment will come. Everything will happen just as I have said it would.

9"'The people of the cities of Israel will go out. They will pick up your shields and bucklers, bows and arrows, javelins and spears. They will use them to burn for fuel. There will be enough to last them seven years. 10For seven years they will need nothing else for their fires. They won't cut wood from the fields or forests. For these weapons will give them all they need. They will use the tools of war belonging to those who attacked them.

11"'And I will make a great graveyard for Gog and his armies. I will put it in the Valley of the Travelers, east of the Dead Sea. It will block the path of the travelers. There Gog and all his armies will be buried. And they will change the name of the place to 'The Valley of Gog's Army.' 12It will take seven months for the people of Israel to bury the bodies. 13Everyone in Israel will help. It will be a great victory for Israel on that day. On that day, I shall prove my glory,' says the Lord. 14'At the end of the seven months, they will choose a group of men. These men will look for any dead bodies left and will bury them. That way the land will be made clean. 15-16If anyone sees some bones, he will put up a marker beside them. That way the buriers will see them. Then they will take them to the Valley of Gog's Army to bury them. A city named Hamonah will be there! And so the land will finally be made clean.'

17"And now, son of dust, call all the birds and animals. Say to them, 'Gather together for a great feast. Come from far and near to the mountains of Israel. Come, eat the flesh and drink the blood! 18Eat the flesh of mighty men! Drink the blood of princes! They are the rams, the lambs, the goats, and the fat young bulls of Bashan for my feast! 19Fill yourselves with flesh until you are too full. Drink blood until you are drunk. This is the sacrifice I have made ready for you. 20Feast at my banquet table. Feast on horses, riders, and brave soldiers,' says the Lord God.

21"In this way I will show my glory among the nations. All shall see the punishment of Gog. And they will know that I have done it. 22And from then on, the people of Israel will know I am the Lord their God. 23And the nations will know why Israel was sent away to exile. It was punishment for sin, for they were unfaithful to their God. So I turned my face away from them and let their ene-mies destroy them. 24I turned my face away. I punished them according to how bad their sins were.

25"But now," the Lord God says, "I will end the captivity of my people. I will have mercy on them and give them back their wealth. For I am concerned about what people think of my name! 26Their time of shame will all be in the past. They will be home again, in peace and safety in their own land. No one will bother them or make them afraid. 27I will bring them home from the lands of their enemies. And my glory shall be clear to all the nations when I do it. Through them I will prove my holiness before the nations. 28Then my people will know I am the Lord their God. They will know that I sent them away to exile. And they will know that it was I who brought them home again. I will leave none of them exiled among the nations. 29And I will never hide my face from them again. For I will pour out my Spirit upon them," says the Lord God.

The New Temple

40 It was early in April during the 25th year of our exile. This was the 14th year after Jerusalem was captured. At that time, the hand of the Lord came upon me. 2In a vision he took me to the land of Israel. He set me down on a high mountain. There I saw what looked like a city across from me. 3Going nearer, I saw a man whose face shone like bronze. He was standing beside the Temple gate. He held a measuring tape and a measuring stick in his hand.

4He said to me, "Son of dust, watch and listen. Take to heart everything I show you. For you have been brought here so I can show you many things. And then you are to go back to the people of Israel. You will tell them all you have seen." 5The man began to measure the wall around the outside of the Temple area. He used his measuring stick, which was 10½ feet long. He told me, "This wall is 10½ feet high and 10½ feet wide." 6Then he took me over to the passage that goes through the eastern wall. We climbed the seven steps into the entrance. Then he measured the entry hall of the passage. It was 10½ feet wide.

7-12I walked on through the passage. And I saw that there were three guardrooms on each side. Each of these rooms was 10½ feet square. There was a distance of 8¾ feet along the wall between them. In front of these rooms was a low wall 18 inches high and 18 inches wide. Beyond the guardrooms was a 10½-foot doorway. It opened into a 14-foot hall with 3½-foot columns. Beyond this hall, at the inner end of the passage, was the entrance to the gate. This was 22¾ feet wide and 17½ feet long.

13Then he measured the outside width of the passage. He measured across the roof from the outside doors of the guardrooms. This distance was 43¾ feet. 14Then he measured the pillars on each side of the porch to be about 100 feet high. 15The full length of the entrance passage was 87½ feet from one end to the other. 16There were windows that narrowed inward through the walls. They were along both sides of the passage and along the guardroom walls. The windows were also in the exit and in the entrance halls. The pillars were decorated with palm tree carvings.

17And so we passed through the passage to the court inside. A stone pavement ran around the inside of the walls. And 30 rooms were built against the walls. They opened onto this pavement. 18This was called "the lower pavement." It went out from the walls into the court just as far as the passage did.

19Then he measured across to the wall on the other side of this court. This was called "the outer court" of the Temple. He found that the distance was 175 feet. 20As I followed, he left the eastern passage. He went over to the passage through the northern wall. Then he measured it. 21Here, too, there were three guardrooms on each side. All the measurements were the same as for the east passage. It was 87½ feet long and 43¾ feet from side to side across the top of the guardrooms. 22There were windows, an entry hall, and the palm tree decorations. It was just the same as on the east side. There were seven steps

leading up to the doorway to the entry hall inside.

23At the north entry, there was an inner wall straight across from the gate. There was also a passage through this wall to an inner court. It was just as it was on the east side. The distance between the two passages was 175 feet. 24Then he took me around to the south gate. He measured the various parts of its passage. He found they were just the same as in the others. 25It had windows along the walls as the others did. And it had an entry hall. And like the others, it was 87½ feet long and 43¾ feet wide. 26It, too, had a stairway of seven steps leading up to it. And there were palm tree carvings along the walls. 27And again, one might walk through the passage into the court. After crossing the court, he would come to the inner wall. Again, there was a passage through it to the inner court. And the distance between the passages was 175 feet.

28Then he took me over to the inner wall and its south passage. He measured this passage. He found it was the same as the passages of the outer wall. 29-30Its guardrooms, pillars, and entrance and exit hall were the same as the others. So were the windows along its walls and entry. And, like the others, it was 87½ feet long by 43¾ feet wide. 31The only difference was that it had eight steps leading up to it instead of seven. It had palm tree carvings on the pillars, just like the others.

32Then he took me along the court to the eastern entrance of the inner wall. He measured it too. It was the same size as the others. 33Its guardrooms, pillars, and entrance hall were just like those of the other passages. And there were windows along the walls and in the entry hall. And it was 87½ feet long by 43¾ feet wide. 34Its entry hall faced the outer court. And there were palm tree carvings on its columns. But there were eight steps instead of seven going up to the entrance.

35Then he took me around to the north gate of the inner wall. And it was the same size as all the others. 36The guardrooms, pillars, and entry hall of this passage were the same as the others. It was 87½ feet long and 43¾ feet wide. ³⁷Its entry hall faced toward the outer court. It had palm tree carvings on the walls of each side of the passage. There were eight steps leading up to the entrance.

³⁸But a door led from its entry hall into a side room. There the sacrifices were washed before being taken to the altar. ³⁹On each side of the entry hall of the passage there were two tables. There the animals for sacrifice were killed. They were for the burnt offerings, sin offerings, and guilt offerings to be given in the Temple. ⁴⁰Outside the entry hall there were two more tables. They were set on each side of the stairs going up to the north entrance. ⁴¹So, in all there were eight tables. Four were inside and four were outside. These were where the sacrifices were cut up and made ready. ⁴²There were also four stone tables. The butchering knives and other tools were laid on them. These tables were about 2⅝ feet square and 1¾ feet high. ⁴³There were hooks, 3 or 4 inches long. These were fastened along the walls of the entry hall. And on the tables the flesh of the offering was to be laid.

⁴⁴In the inner court there were two one-room buildings. One was beside the northern entrance, facing south. The other was beside the southern entrance, facing north.

⁴⁵And he said to me, "The building beside the inner northern gate is for the priests who take care of the building. ⁴⁶The building beside the inner southern entrance is for the priests in charge of the altar. These are the descendants of Zadok. For they alone may come near to the Lord to serve to him."

⁴⁷Then he measured the inner court in front of the Temple. He found it to be 175 feet square. There was an altar in the court, standing in front of the Temple. ⁴⁸⁻⁴⁹Then he brought me to the entrance hall of the Temple. Ten steps led up to it from the inner court. Its walls went up on either side to form two pillars. Each of them was 8¾ feet thick. The entrance was 24½ feet wide

with 5¼-foot walls. Thus the entry hall was 35 feet wide and 19¼ feet long.

The Holy of Holies

41 After that he brought me into the Holy Place. This is the large main room of the Temple. He measured the pillars that formed its doorway. They were 10½ feet square. ²The entrance hall was 17½ feet wide and 8¾ feet deep. The holy place itself was 70 feet long by 35 feet.

³Then he went into the inner room at the end of the Holy Place. He measured the columns at the entrance. He found them to be 3½ feet thick. Its doorway was 10½ feet wide. There was a hallway 12¼ feet deep behind it. ⁴The inner room was 35 feet square. "This," he told me, "is the Most Holy Place."

⁵Then he measured the wall of the Temple. He found that it was 10½ feet thick. It had a row of rooms along the outside. Each room was 7 feet wide. ⁶These rooms were in three stories, one above the other. There were 30 rooms in each story. The whole building was supported by beams. It was not attached to the Temple wall for support. ⁷Each floor was wider than the one below it. This was because the Temple wall got narrower as it rose higher. A stairway at the side of the Temple led up from floor to floor.

⁸I saw that the Temple was built on a terrace. The bottom row of rooms went out 10½ feet onto the terrace. ⁹The outer wall of these rooms was 8¾ feet thick. This left a free space of 8¾ feet out to the edge of the terrace. It was the same on both sides.

¹⁰There was another row of rooms down in the inner court. They were 35 feet away from the terrace, on both sides of the Temple. ¹¹Two doors opened from the tiers of rooms to the terrace yard. This yard was 8¾ feet wide. One door faced north and the other south.

¹²A large building stood on the west. It faced the Temple courtyard. It was 122½ feet wide by 157½ feet long. Its walls were 8¾ feet thick. ¹³Then he measured the Temple and the courtyards right around it. The area was 175 feet

square. ¹⁴The inner court at the east of the Temple was also 175 feet wide. ¹⁵⁻¹⁶The building west of the Temple, including its two walls, was the same.

The Holy Place and the Holy of Holies and the entry hall were paneled. And all three had recessed windows. The inner walls of the Temple were paneled with wood above and below the windows. ¹⁷⁻¹⁸The space above the door leading into the Holy of Holies was also paneled. The walls were decorated with carvings of Guardian Angels, each with two faces. There were also palm trees set between the Guardian Angels. ¹⁹⁻²⁰One face, that of a man, looked toward the palm tree on one side. The other face, that of a young lion, looked toward the palm tree on the other side. And so it was, all around the inner wall of the Temple.

²¹There were square doorposts at the doors of the Holy Place. In front of the Holy of Holies was what looked like an altar. But it was made of wood. ²²This altar was 3½ feet square and 5¼ feet high. Its corners, base, and sides were all of wood. "This," he told me, "is the Table of the Lord."

²³Both the Holy Place and the Holy of Holies had double doors. ²⁴Each door had two swinging sections. ²⁵The doors of the Holy Place were decorated with Guardian Angels and palm trees. These were just like those on the walls. And there was a wooden canopy over the entry hall. ²⁶There were recessed windows and carved palm trees on both sides of the entry hall. The carved palm trees were in the hallways beside the Temple. And they were on the canopy over the entrance.

The Priests' Rooms

42 Then he led me out of the Temple. He took me back to the inner court. We went to the rooms north of the Temple yard, and to another building. ²This group of structures was 175 feet long by 87½ feet wide. ³The rows of rooms behind this building were on the inner wall of the court. The rooms were in three stories. They looked out over the outer court on one side. There was a 35-foot strip of inner court on the other

side. ⁴A 17½-foot walk ran between the building and the stories of rooms. This went the whole length, with the doors of the building facing north. ⁵The upper two stories of rooms were not as wide as the lower ones. This was because the upper stories had wider walkways beside them. ⁶And the building was not built with beams like those in the outer court. So the upper stories were set back from the ground floor.

⁷⁻⁸The north stories of rooms, next to the outer court, were 87½ feet long. They were only half as long as the inner wing that faced the Temple court. This was 175 feet long. But a wall extended from the end of the shorter wing, parallel to the longer wing. ⁹⁻¹⁰There was an entrance from the outer court to these rooms from the east. Across from the Temple there was a similar building made of two units of rooms. This was on the south side of the inner court. It was between the Temple and the outer court. And it was designed the same as the other. ¹¹There was a walk between the two wings of the building. It was the same as in the other building across the court. It was the same length and width. And it had the same exits and doors. These units were exactly the same. ¹²And there was a door from the outer court at the east.

¹³Then he said, "These north and south stories of rooms facing the Temple yard are holy. The priests shall offer up the sacrifices to the Lord. Then they shall eat of the most holy offerings in these rooms. They shall also store the cereal offerings, sin offerings, and guilt offerings there. For these rooms are holy. ¹⁴When the priests leave the Holy Place they must change their clothes. They must do this before going out to the outer court. They must take off the special robes they wear while giving sacrifices. This is because these robes are holy. They must put on other clothes before going into the parts of the building open to the people."

¹⁵He finished measuring these places. Then he led me out through the east passage to measure the whole Temple area. ¹⁶⁻²⁰He found that it was in the form

of a square. It was 875 feet long on each side. There was a wall all around it. It kept it apart from the places ordinary people could go.

Ezekiel Writes Down Some Rules

43 After that he brought me out again to the passage through the outer wall. This was the one leading to the east. ²And I saw the glory of the God of Israel coming from the east. The sound of his coming was like the roar of rushing waters. And the whole landscape lighted up with his glory. ³It was just as I had seen it in the other visions. The first time I was by the Chebar Canal in Babylon. Then I saw it later at Jerusalem when he came to destroy the city. And I fell down before him with my face in the dust. ⁴And the glory of the Lord came into the Temple through the eastern passage.

⁵Then the Spirit took me up. And he brought me into the inner court. The glory of the Lord filled the Temple. ⁶And I heard the Lord speaking to me from within the Temple. The man who had been measuring was still standing beside me.

⁷And the Lord spoke to me. "Son of dust," he said. "This is the place of my throne and my footstool. And here I shall stay. I will live among the people of Israel forever. They and their kings will not defile my holy name any more. They won't worship other gods or the pillars made by their kings. ⁸They once built their idol temples beside mine. They put only a wall between them! And there, they worshiped their idols. They defiled my holy name by such wickedness. So I destroyed them in my anger. ⁹Now let them put away their idols and the pillars built by their kings. And I will live among them forever.

¹⁰"Son of dust, tell the people of Israel about the Temple I have shown you. Tell them what it looks like. Tell them the way it is made. Then they will be ashamed of all their sins. ¹¹And if they are truly ashamed, then tell them how it was made. Tell them about its doors and entrances. Tell them everything about it. Write out all the directions and the rules

for them to keep. ¹²And this is the basic law of the Temple: Holiness! The whole top of the hill where the Temple is built is holy. Yes, this is the first law of my Temple.

¹³"And this is the size of the altar. The base is 21 inches high, with a 9-inch rim around its edge. The rim extends 21 inches beyond the altar on all sides. ¹⁴The first stage of the altar is a stone platform 3½ feet high. This platform is 21 inches narrower than the base block on all sides. Rising from this is a narrower platform. This is 21 inches narrower on all sides, and 7 feet high. ¹⁵From it a still narrower platform rises 7 feet. This is the top of the altar. It has four horns that stand 21 inches above the corners. ¹⁶This top platform of the altar is 21 feet square. ¹⁷The platform under it is 24½ feet square. It has a 10½-inch curb around the edges. The whole platform extends out from the top 21 inches on all sides. On the east side are steps to climb the altar."

¹⁸"Son of dust," he said to me. "The Lord God says: This is the size of the altar to be made in the future. It will be built for the burning of offerings. And blood will be sprinkled on it. ¹⁹At that time the Zadok family is to be given a bull for a sin offering. The members of the Zadok family of the Levite tribe are my special priests. ²⁰You shall take some of its blood and smear it on the four horns of the altar. Smear it on the four corners of the top platform. Then smear some in the curb around it. This will make the altar clean and holy. ²¹Then take the bull for the sin offering. Burn it at the chosen place outside the Temple area.

²²"The second day, sacrifice a young male goat for a sin offering. It must have nothing wrong with it. It cannot be sick or deformed. It cannot have any cuts or scars. In this way the altar shall be made clean, as it was by the bull. ²³Finish this ceremony to make the altar clean. Then offer another perfect bull and a perfect ram from the flock. ²⁴Present them before the Lord. The priests shall sprinkle salt upon them as a burnt offering.

²⁵"Every day for seven days sacrifices

must be made. You must give a male goat, a bull, and a ram from the flock. These shall be given as a sin offering. These animals must not have anything wrong with them. ²⁶Do this each day for seven days to make the altar pure and clean. It this way, you will make it holy to the Lord. ²⁷On the eighth day, and on each day after that, the priests will sacrifice offerings on the altar. They shall give burnt offerings and thank offerings from the people. Then I will accept you," says the Lord God.

What the Priests Should Do

44 Then the Lord brought me back to the eastern passage in the outer wall. But it was closed. ²And he said to me, "This gate shall stay closed. It shall never be opened. No man shall pass through it. For the Lord, the God of Israel, entered here. And so it shall stay shut. ³Only the prince may sit inside the passage to feast there before the Lord. But he shall come and go only through the entry hall of the passage."

⁴Then he brought me through the north passage to the front of the Temple. I looked and saw that the glory of the Lord filled the Temple. And I fell to the ground with my face in the dust.

⁵And the Lord said to me, "Son of dust, look around carefully. Use your eyes and ears. Listen to all I tell you about the laws and rules of the Temple of the Lord. Note carefully who may come to the Temple. Remember who is not allowed to come into it. ⁶And say to the people of Israel, 'The Lord God says: O Israel, you have sinned greatly. ⁷For you have let foreigners come into my Temple. These are people who have no heart for God! You do this, as you offer me my food, the fat and the blood. Thus you have broken my covenant in addition to all your other sins. ⁸You have not kept the laws I gave you concerning these holy things. For you have hired foreigners to take charge of my Temple.'"

⁹The Lord God says, "Foreigners must never go into my Temple. Keep them out if they have not been circumcised and do not love the Lord. ¹⁰And there were men of the tribe of Levi who turned

against me. They did this when Israel strayed away from God to idols. These people must be punished for being unfaithful. ¹¹They may be Temple guards and gatemen. They may kill the animals brought for burnt offerings. They may come there to help the people. ¹²But they once encouraged the people to worship other gods. Long ago they caused Israel to fall into deep sin. So now I have lifted my hand and made a promise," says the Lord God. "I have promised that they must be punished. ¹³They shall not come near me to serve as priests. They may not touch any of my holy things. For they must bear their shame for all their sins. ¹⁴They are the Temple caretakers. They must keep the buildings clean and in good shape. And they are to help the people in a general way.

¹⁵"But the sons of Zadok, of the tribe of Levi, are my priests. They kept serving in the Temple even when Israel left me for idols. These men shall be my special priests. They shall stand before me to offer the fat and blood of the sacrifices," says the Lord God. ¹⁶"They shall enter my Temple. They shall come to my Table to serve me. They shall do all that I want them to do.

¹⁷"They must wear only linen clothing when they go into the inner court. They must wear no wool while on duty in the inner court or in the Temple. ¹⁸They must wear linen turbans and linen trousers. They must not wear anything that would cause them to sweat. ¹⁹When they go back to the outer court, they must take off the clothes they wear while serving me. They must leave them in the holy rooms. There they must put on other clothes. If they don't, they could hurt the people by touching them with this clothing.

²⁰"They must not let their hair grow too long. But they are not to shave it all off either. They are allowed haircuts that are not too short. ²¹No priest may drink wine before coming to the inner court. ²²He may marry only a Jewish girl, or the widow of a priest. He may not marry a woman who is divorced.

²³"He shall teach my people what is

holy and what is not holy. He shall teach them what is right and what is wrong.

24"They will serve as judges. They will solve the problems among my people. What they decide must be based on my laws. The priests themselves shall obey my rules at all the holy feasts. They shall make sure that the Sabbath is kept as a holy day.

25"A priest must not make himself unclean by going near a dead person. He may only do this if it is his father, mother, child, brother, or unmarried sister. In such cases it is all right. 26But after that he must wait seven days before he is clean. Then he will be able to do his Temple duties again. 27The first day he comes back he must offer a sin offering for himself. He must do this before he goes into the inner court and the sanctuary." the Lord God says.

28"As to property, they shall not own any. For I am their heritage! That is enough!

29"Their food shall be the sacrifices brought to the Temple by the people. They shall eat of the cereal offerings, the sin offerings, and the guilt offerings. Whatever anyone gives to the Lord shall belong to the priests. 30The first of the fruits harvested each season shall go to the priests. All the gifts for the Lord shall go to them too. The first samples of each harvest of grain shall be given to the priests. That way the Lord will bless your homes. 31Priests may never eat meat from any bird or animal that dies a natural death. They must not eat animals that die after being attacked by other animals.

Some Land for the Lord

45 "You shall divide the land among the tribes of Israel. But first you must give a section of it to the Lord as his holy part. This piece shall be 8⅓ miles long and 6⅔ miles wide. It shall all be holy ground.

2"A section of this land, 875 feet square, shall be set aside for the Temple. Another 87½-foot strip all around is to be left empty. 3The Temple shall be built within the area which is 8⅓ miles long and 3⅓ miles wide. 4All this section shall be holy land. It will be used by the priests, who serve in the Temple. It will be used for their homes and for my Temple.

5"The strip next to it is 8⅓ miles long and 3⅓ miles wide. This land shall be where the Levites live. These are the Levites who work at the Temple. 6Next to the holy lands will be an area 8⅓ miles by 1⅔ miles. This for a city open to everyone in Israel.

7"Two special sections of land shall be set apart for the prince. They will be on each side of the holy lands and city. It will be the same length as the holy lands. Its eastern and western borders will be the same as those of the tribal sections. 8This shall be the prince's land. My princes shall no longer oppress and rob my people. They shall give the rest of the land to the people. They shall give a part of it to each tribe."

9For the Lord says to the rulers, "Stop robbing and cheating my people out of their land. Stop sending them from their homes. Always be fair and honest. 10You must use honest scales, honest bushels, honest gallons. 11A homer, about five bushels, shall be your standard unit of measure. You shall use this for both liquid and dry measures. Another unit of measure shall be the ephah, about one half bushel, for dry measure. And the bath, about 17 quarts, shall be used for liquid. 12The unit of weight shall be the silver shekel, about half an ounce. It must always be changed for 20 gerahs, no less. Five shekels shall be valued at five shekels, no less. And 10 shekels at 10 shekels! Fifty shekels shall always equal one mina.

13"This is the tax you must give to the prince. You must give a bushel of wheat or barley for every 60 you harvest. 14You must give him one percent of your olive oil. 15From each 200 sheep in all your flocks, give him one sheep. These are the meal offerings, burnt offerings, and thank offerings. They will bring forgiveness to those who bring them," says the Lord God. 16"All the people of Israel shall bring their offerings to the prince.

17"The prince shall give the people sacrifices for public worship. He shall supply sin offerings, burnt offerings, meal offerings, drink offerings, and thank offerings. These will be used to bring the people of Israel close to God. This shall be done at the time of the religious feasts. It shall be done at the new moons, Sabbaths, and all other feasts.

[18]The Lord God says, "Give a young bull on each New Year's Day. It must have nothing wrong with it. Sacrifice it to make the Temple pure. [19]The priest shall take some of the blood of this sin offering. He shall put it on the doorposts of the Temple. He shall put it on the four corners of the base of the altar. And he shall put it on the walls at the entry of the inner court. [20]Do this also on the seventh day of that month. This is for anyone who has sinned by accident. That way the Temple will be kept holy.

[21]"On the 14th day of the same month, you shall celebrate the Passover. It will be a seven-day feast. Only bread without yeast shall be eaten during those days. [22]On the day of Passover the prince shall give a young bull. It will be a sin offering for himself and all the people of Israel. [23]On each of the seven days of the feast he shall prepare a burnt offering to the Lord. This daily offering will be seven young bulls and seven rams. These animals must have nothing wrong with them. A male goat shall also be given each day for a sin offering. [24]And the prince shall give one half bushel of grain with each bull and ram. This will be for a meal offering. He shall also give three quarts of olive oil for each half bushel of flour.

[25]"Early in October celebrate the yearly feast of shelters. This feast lasts for seven days. At this time, the prince shall give these same sacrifices. They are for the sin offering, burnt offering, meal offering, and oil offering.

Special Offerings

46 The Lord God says, "Do this at the eastern entrance of the inner wall. It shall be closed during the six work days. But open it on the Sabbath. Also open it on the days of the new moon

How Far, How Much?

EZEKIEL 45:10-12

Does your Mother make cakes or pies or pancakes? If she does, she uses a measuring cup and some measuring spoons. She may measure flour with the measuring cup. She measures other things with special teaspoons or tablespoons. Have you measured something with a tape measure or ruler? If so, you look for the number of inches, feet, centimeters, or meters. Bible-time people had different measures. A homer was about 6 1/2 bushels of liquid or dry things. A bath was a tenth of a homer of liquid. An ephah was a tenth of a homer of dry things. Things were weighed by shekels, not pounds or ounces. A shekel was about a half ounce. Fifty shekels were a maneh. You may find many other Bible words such as cubit, furlong, talent, and omer. Each one tells how far, how long, or how much. Instead of using a yardstick, how would you like to measure something with a cubit stick? Would you like to see how much candy you could buy at the store with a talent? What would Dad say if you asked how many furlongs per hour he was driving? Or what would the clerk at the store say if you asked for a bath of milk?

feasts. ²The prince shall enter the outside entry hall of the passage. Then he shall go to the inner wall at the other end. At this time, the priest offers his burnt offering and peace offering. He shall worship inside the passage and then go back to the entrance. This shall not be closed until evening. ³The people shall worship the Lord in front of this passage on the Sabbaths. They shall also do this on the days of the new moon feasts.

⁴"The prince shall give a burnt offering to the Lord on the Sabbath days. It shall be six lambs and a ram. These animals must have nothing wrong with them. ⁵He shall give a meal offering of one half bushel of flour. This will go with the ram. He can give any amount of flour he wants to for each lamb. And he shall bring three quarts of olive oil for each half bushel of flour. ⁶At the new moon feast, he shall bring one young bull. It must be perfect in every way. He must also bring six lambs and one ram. These must have nothing wrong with them. ⁷With the young bull, he must bring one half bushel of flour. This will be for a meal offering. With the ram must bring one half bushel of flour. With the lamb he is to bring whatever he is willing to give. With each half bushel of grain he is to bring three quarts of olive oil.

⁸"The prince shall go in at the entry hall of the passageway. And he shall go out the same way. ⁹The people shall come in through the north passage to sacrifice during the feasts. But they must go out through the south passage. Those coming in from the south must go out by the north. They must never go out the same way they came in. They must always use the opposite passage to leave. ¹⁰The prince shall enter and leave with the common people at these times.

¹¹"At the special feasts the meal offering shall be one half bushel with the young bull. It shall be one half bushel with the ram. It shall be as much as the prince is willing to give with each lamb. And three quarts of oil must be given with each half bushel of grain. ¹²The prince might offer an extra burnt offering or peace offering to the Lord. If so, the inner eastern gate shall be opened up for him to come in. And he shall offer his sacrifices just as on the Sabbaths. Then he shall turn around and go out. Then the passage shall be shut behind him.

¹³"Each morning a lamb must be sacrificed. This lamb must be one year old. It is a burnt offering to the Lord. ¹⁴⁻¹⁵And there must be a meal offering each morning. It shall be made of five pounds of flour. One quart of oil is to be mixed with it. This is a lasting law. The lamb, the grain offering, and the olive oil shall be given every morning. This sacrifice is to be given every day.

¹⁶The Lord says, "The prince might give a gift of land to one of his sons. If so, it will belong to his son forever. ¹⁷But he might give a gift of land to one of his servants. If so, the servant may keep it only until the Year of Release. This is every seventh year. At that time the servant is set free. Then the land goes back to the prince. Only gifts to his sons are lasting. ¹⁸And the prince may never take anyone's land by force. If he gives land to his sons, it must be from his own land. For I don't want my people losing their land and having to move away."

¹⁹⁻²⁰After that, we went through the door in the wall. It was at the side of the main passage. He led me through the entrance to the block of holy rooms that faced north. There, at the far west end of these rooms, I saw a special place. My guide told me that this is where the priests boil meat. This is the meat of the trespass and sin offerings. And it is here that they bake the flour of the flour offerings into bread. They do it here so they won't have to carry the sacrifices through the outer court. This is done to keep from hurting the people.

²¹⁻²²Then he brought me to the outer court again. He led me to each of the four corners of the court. I saw a small court in each corner. They were 70 feet long by 52½ feet wide. These courts were enclosed by walls. ²³Around the inside of these walls there was a row of brick boiling pans. And under the pans, there were ovens. ²⁴These courts were

for the Temple helpers, the Levites. They were to use them to boil people's sacrifices.

The River of Healing

47 Then he brought me back to the door of the Temple. I saw a stream flowing eastward from under the Temple. It passed to the right of the altar. That is, it flowed on the altar's south side. ²Then he brought me outside the wall through the north passage. We went around to the eastern entrance. And there I saw the stream. It was flowing along on the south side of the eastern passage. ³He took me 1,500 feet east along the stream and told me to go across. He measured it as we went. At that point the water was up to my ankles. ⁴He measured off another 1,500 feet and told me to cross again. This time the water was up to my knees. ⁵After another 1,500 feet it was up to my waist. Another 1,500 feet and it had become a deep river. It was so deep I would have had to swim to get across. It was too deep to cross on foot.

⁶He told me to keep in mind what I had seen. Then he led me back along the bank. ⁷And now, to my surprise, many trees were growing on both sides of the river!

⁸He told me, "This river flows east through the desert. It flows through the Jordan Valley to the Dead Sea. There it will heal the salty waters and make them fresh and pure. ⁹Everything touching the water of this river shall live. There will be many fish in the Dead Sea. For its waters will be healed. Wherever this water flows, everything will live. ¹⁰Fishermen will stand along the shores of the Dead Sea. They will fish all the way from Engedi to Eneglaim. The shores will be filled with nets drying in the sun. Fish of every kind will fill the Dead Sea. It will be just like the Mediterranean! ¹¹But the marshes and swamps will not be healed. They will still be salty. ¹²All kinds of fruit trees will grow along the riverbanks. The leaves will never turn brown and fall. And there will always be fruit. There will be a new crop every month without fail! For they are watered by the river flowing

Making Bread
EZEKIEL 46:19-20

Does your mother ever make bread? Most of the time she probably buys bread at the store. It comes in a package. Usually the company that makes it puts its name on the package. If your mother lived in Bible times, she would bake bread almost every day. There were a few bakers, but they usually made bread only for kings or rich people. The mother, or a daughter, ground barley or wheat grains between two round stones called millstones. Then she mixed water and some olive oil with it and kneaded it with her hands. Sometimes a piece of yesterday's dough was put into the mixture. This helped the dough to rise. It made the bread more fluffy. Bread was shaped like a dinner plate. But it was only as thick as your finger. Bread was baked in a clay oven or over a fire. Making bread was hard work. It took a long time to make enough to feed a big family.

from the Temple. The fruit will be for food and the leaves for medicine."

¹³The Lord God says, "Here are orders for dividing the land among the 12 tribes of Israel. The tribe of Joseph shall

be given two sections. This includes both Ephraim and Manasseh. [14]The rest of the tribes will be given an equal share. I made a promise to your fathers with my hand raised high. I promised to give the land to your fathers. And now, you shall inherit it.

[15]"The northern border will run from the Mediterranean toward Hethlon. Then it will go on through Labweh to Zedad. [16]It will stretch from there to Berothah and Sibraim. These are on the border between Damascus and Hamath. Then finally the border will go to Hazer-hatticon. This is on the border of Hauran. [17]So the northern border will begin at the Mediterranean Sea. It will run to Hazar-enan. It will follow the border with Damascus. The border with Hamath will be to the north.

[18]"The eastern border will run south from Hazar-enan to Mount Hauran. There it will bend to the west toward the Jordan. It will reach the Jordan at the southern tip of the Sea of Galilee. It will follow down along the Jordan River separating Israel from Gilead. Then it will go past the Dead Sea to Tamar.

[19]"The southern border will go west from Tamar to the springs at Meribath-kadesh. Then it will follow the course of the Brook of Egypt to the Mediterranean.

[20]"On the west side, the Mediterranean itself will be your border. From the southern border to the the northern border, the sea will mark your western border.

[21]"Divide the land within these borders among the tribes of Israel. [22]Take the land as an inheritance for yourselves. Take it for the foreigners who live among you with their families. All children born in the land have a right to the land. This is true even if their parents are foreigners. They should have the same rights your own children have. [23]All these foreigners are to be given land with the tribes they now live among.

The Land Is Divided

48 "Here is the list of the tribes and the land each is to get. Give Dan the land beginning at the northwest bor-

der. This is on the Mediterranean Sea. From there, the border shall go across to Hethlon and then to Lebo-hamath. Then it shall go to Hazar-enan on the border with Damascus. Then it shall stretch toward the north, near Hamath. These are Dan's borders from the east side to the west side. [2]Asher's land lies south of Dan's. It will share a border with Dan from east to west. [3]Naphtali's land lies south of Asher's. It will border with Asher from east to west. [4]Then comes Manasseh, south of Naphtali. It will border with Manasseh from east to west. [5-7]Next, to the south, is Ephraim. And Reuben and Judah are south of Ephraim. All have the same borders on the east and the west.

[8]"South of Judah is the land set aside for the Temple. It has the same eastern and western borders as the tribal areas. The Temple is at the center between the borders. [9]This Temple area will be 8⅓ miles long and 6⅔ miles wide.

[10]"There is another strip of land 8⅓ miles long by 3⅓ miles wide. It runs north to south. This land surrounds the Temple. [11]It is for the sons of Zadok who obeyed me. They didn't sin when the people of Israel and the rest of their tribe of Levi did. [12]This is their special part of the land when the land is divided. It is the most holy land of all. Next to it lies the area where the other Levites will live. [13]It will be of the same size and shape as the first. Together they measure 8⅓ miles by 6⅔ miles. [14]None of this special land shall ever be sold or traded. None of it shall be used by others. For it belongs to the Lord, and it is holy.

[15]"There is a strip of land 8⅓ miles long by 1⅔ miles wide. This lies to the south of the Temple section. It is for the people to use. They shall use it for homes, pastures, and parks, with a city in the center. [16]The city itself is to be 1½ miles square. [17]Open land for pastures shall surround the city for about a 10th of a mile. [18]Outside the city is a garden area belonging to the city. It is for use by all the people. This land stretches east and west for three miles beside the holy grounds. [19]It is open to anyone working in the city. It doesn't

matter what part of Israel he comes from.

²⁰"The whole area, including holy lands and city lands, is 8⅓ miles square.

²¹⁻²²"The land on both sides of this area shall belong to the prince. This land goes clear out to the eastern and western borders of Israel. This land lies between the sections given to Judah and Benjamin. It is 8⅓ miles square on each side of the holy and city lands.

²³"The land given to the rest of the tribes is as follows. Benjamin's land stretches across the whole country of Israel. It goes from its eastern border clear across to the western border. ²⁴South of Benjamin's area lies that of Simeon. It has the same eastern and western borders as the other areas. ²⁵Next is Issachar's land. It has the same eastern and western borders as the others. ²⁶Then comes Zebulun's land. It also extends all the way across. ²⁷⁻²⁸Then comes Gad's land. It has the same eastern and western borders as the others. But its southern border runs from Tamar

to the Spring at Meribath-kadesh. Then it follows the Brook of Egypt to the Mediterranean. ²⁹This is the land to be given to each tribe," says the Lord God.

The City Gates

³⁰⁻³¹"Each city gate will be named in honor of one of the tribes of Israel. On the north side, with its 1½-mile wall, there will be three gates. One will be named for Reuben, one for Judah, and one for Levi. ³²On the east side, with its 1½-mile wall, there will be three more. The gates will be named for Joseph, Benjamin, and Dan. ³³The south wall, also the same length, will have three gates. They will be named for Simeon, Issachar, and Zebulun. ³⁴On the 1½ miles of the west side, there will be three more gates. They will be named for Gad, Asher, and Naphtali.

³⁵"The distance around the city is six miles. And the name of the city will be 'The City of God.'"

DANIEL

Daniel was a teenager when King Nebuchadnezzar and his armies attacked the city of Jerusalem. Daniel and thousands of others were captured and taken to Babylon. His mother and father probably weren't there to tell him what he should do in this strange land. But Daniel decided to do what God wanted. The king soon noticed that Daniel was a good man. He saw that God was with him. Daniel became an important man in Babylon. One day the king put him over all the other officials.

You'll see many wonderful things happen in this book. You'll see a man sleep with hungry lions and not get hurt. You'll watch men walk in a blazing furnace and not get burned. You'll see a king eat grass. And you'll watch a great hand write on a wall. The Book of Daniel tells about many exciting things that happened in Daniel's day. But Daniel also tells about exciting things that haven't happened yet but will someday. How did Daniel know what would happen in the future? God told him. Daniel helps us know that no matter how bad things look, behind it all God is in control of all history.

Daniel Refuses to Eat the King's Food

Daniel was a captive in a strange land. He could have been fed bread and water. Or he could have starved. Instead, he was given the best food and wine in the country. But Daniel didn't want to eat it. He thought God did not want him to have it. Now what would happen?

1 Babylon's King Nebuchadnezzar attacked Jerusalem with his armies. This happened three years after King Jehoiakim began to rule in Judah. And the Lord gave Nebuchadnezzar victory over Jehoiakim. After conquering Jerusalem, he went home to Babylon. He took along some of the holy cups from the Temple of God. He put them in the temple of his god in the land of Shinar.

3-4Ashpenaz was in charge of the people who worked at Nebuchadnezzar's palace. Nebuchadnezzar ordered him to choose some of the boys he had brought back from Judah. These were young men of Judah's royal family. Ashpenaz was ordered to teach them the Chaldean language and literature. "Pick strong, healthy, good-looking boys," he said. "They should read books about many things. They must be smart, alert, and have common sense. And they should have good manners so they will look good around the palace."

5The king put them in a three-year training program. During that time, he gave them the best food and wine from his own kitchen. He wanted to make them his counselors when they graduated.

6Daniel, Hananiah, Mishael, and Azariah were four of the young men chosen. They were all from the tribe of Judah. 7But their teacher gave them Babylonian names. Their names were as follows:

Daniel was called Belteshazzar.
Hananiah was called Shadrach.
Mishael was called Meshach.
Azariah was called Abednego.

8But Daniel decided not to eat the king's food and wine. He asked his teacher if he could eat other things instead. 9God had helped his teacher understand Daniel and what he believed. 10But he was afraid to do what Daniel had asked him to do.

"I'm afraid you will become pale and thin," he said. "You will look weak compared with the other youths your age. Then the king will cut my head off for not doing my work."

11Daniel talked it over with the steward. He was chosen by their teacher to look after Daniel, Hananiah, Mishael, and Azariah. 12Daniel asked if they could eat special food for 10 days as a test. During that time they would eat only vegetables and water. 13Then, at the end of this time, the steward could see how they looked. He could compare them with the other young men who ate the king's rich food. After this, he could decide whether or not to let them continue their diet.

14The steward finally agreed to the test. 15Well, at the end of the 10 days, Daniel and his three friends looked very healthy. They looked better than the young men who had been eating the king's food! 16So after that the steward fed them only vegetables and water!

17God gave these four young men the ability to learn very fast. They soon learned all the literature and science of the time. And God gave Daniel a special ability to understand the meanings of dreams and visions.

18-19Then the three-year training period was finished. And their teacher brought all the young men to the king for exams. King Nebuchadnezzar had long talks with each of them. But none of them impressed him as much as Daniel, Hananiah, Mishael, and Azariah. So they were put on his regular staff of advisers. 20In all things that needed knowledge and common sense, the king found the advice of these young men to be excellent. Their advice was 10 times better than that of all the magicians and fortune tellers in his kingdom.

21Daniel was the king's counselor until the first year of the reign of King Cyrus.

• *Remember:* Which king attacked the city of Jerusalem? (1:1-2) Where did he take his captives? (1:1-2) What was Daniel chosen to do? (1:3-4) What special food was given to Daniel? (1:5) What did Daniel decide to do about this food and wine? (1:8) What test did he suggest? How did it work? (1:11-16) What did the king think about Daniel? What work did he give him? (1:17-21) How did Daniel honor God? How did God honor Daniel?

• *Discover:* God rewards and honors those who honor him.

• *Apply:* Do your friends want you to do things God doesn't want you to do? Who do you want to please more, your friends or God? God will honor you if you please him and honor him.

• *What's next?* A king dreams a strange dream but can't remember it. Can anyone tell him what he dreamed? One man can. Read Daniel 2. ■

Daniel Tells the King What He Dreamed

Could you tell your mother or father what they dreamed last night? No one could do that, right? One night Daniel's king had a strange dream. But he couldn't remember it. Could anyone tell him what he dreamed? Daniel did!

2 One night Nebuchadnezzar had a terrible dream. When he woke up, he was shaking with fear. And to make matters worse, he couldn't remember his dream! This happened in the second year of his reign. So Nebuchadnezzar called in all his magicians and astrologers. He demanded that they tell him what his dream had been.

"I've had a terrible dream," he said as they stood before him. "And I can't remember what it was. Tell me, for I fear some trouble is coming soon. I need to know what it means right away."

4Then the magicians spoke to the king in Aramaic. They said, "Sir, tell us the dream. Then we can tell you what it means."

5But the king replied, "I tell you, I can't remember it! You had better tell me what it was and what it means. If you don't, I'll have you torn limb from limb! And I'll destroy all your houses, too! 6But if you tell me what the dream was, I will give you many gifts. And if you tell me the meaning of the dream, I will give you great honor. So, begin!"

7They said again, "We don't even know what the dream was! How can we tell you what it means?"

8-9The king replied, "I can see your trick! You're trying to stall for time. You're planning to make up some story to make me happy. You hope that things will change soon. But my mind is made up! You must tell me what the dream is before you tell me what it means. If you don't, I won't be able to believe you when you tell me what it means."

10The magicians said to the king, "No one can tell others what they have dreamed! And there isn't a king in all the world who would ask such a thing! 11This thing that the king wants cannot be done! No one except the gods can tell you your dream. And they are not here to help."

12When he heard this, the king became very angry. He sent out orders to kill all the wise men of Babylon. 13And Daniel and his friends were rounded up with the others to be killed.

14Arioch, the commander of the king's guard, came to kill them. But Daniel spoke to him with great wisdom. He asked, 15"Why is the king so angry? What is the matter?"

Then Arioch told him all that had happened.

16So Daniel went in to see the king. "Give me a little time," he said. "Then I will tell you the dream and what it means."

17Then he went home and told his friends, Hananiah, Mishael, and Azariah. 18They asked the God of heaven to show them his mercy. They asked him to tell them the secret. Then they would not have to die with the others. 19That night in a vision God told Daniel what the king had dreamed.

Then Daniel praised the God of heaven. 20He said, "Praise to the name of God forever! He alone has all wisdom and all power. 21World events are under his control. He gets rid of kings and puts others on their thrones. He gives wise men their wisdom and gives scholars their knowledge. 22He reveals secrets beyond the understanding of any man. He knows all hidden things, for he is light. He conquers darkness. 23I thank and praise you, O God of my fathers. You have given me wisdom and good health. And now I understand the king's dream and what it means."

24Then Daniel went in to see Arioch. He was the one who had been ordered to kill the wise men of Babylon. Daniel said, "Don't kill them. Take me to the king. I will tell him what he wants to know."

25Then Arioch brought Daniel in to the king. Arioch said, "Here is one of the Jewish captives. He will tell you your dream!"

26The king said to Daniel, "Is this true? Can you tell me what my dream was and what it means?"

27Daniel replied, "No wise man, astrologer, or magician can tell the king such things. 28But there is a God in heaven who reveals secrets. He has told you in your dream what will happen in the future. This was your dream:

29"You dreamed of things that are going to happen. He who reveals secrets was speaking to you. 30But remember, I'm not wiser than anyone else because I know about your dream. God showed it to me so I could help you.

31"O king, you saw a huge and powerful statue of a man. It was shining brightly in the sun. It was awesome and terrible. 32The head of the statue was made of pure gold. Its chest and arms were made of silver. Its belly and thighs were made of brass. 33Its legs were made of iron. And its feet were made partly of iron and partly of clay. 34But as you watched, a Rock was cut from the mountain. But it was not done by human hands. It came flying toward the statue. It crushed the feet of iron and clay. 35Then the whole statue fell into a pile of iron, clay, brass, silver, and gold. Its pieces were crushed as small as dust. And the wind blew them all away. But the Rock that knocked the statue down became a great mountain. It was so great that it covered the whole earth.

36"That was the dream. Now this is what it means.

37"Your Majesty, you are a king over many kings. The God of heaven has given you your kingdom, power, strength, and glory. 38You rule lands and peoples that are far away. Even animals and birds are under your control. You are the head of gold on the statue.

39"But your kingdom will come to an end. Then another world power will rise up to take your place. This kingdom will not be as great as yours. Then that king-dom will also fall. And a third great power will rise to rule the world. This power is represented by the bronze belly of the statue. 40After it falls, the fourth kingdom will rise and be as strong as iron. It will smash, bruise, and conquer. 41-42The feet and toes you saw stand for a fifth kingdom. This kingdom will be divided, just as the feet were part iron and part clay. Some parts of it will be as strong as iron. But other parts of it will be as weak as clay. 43The feet of iron and clay also show that these kingdoms will try to make themselves strong. They will do this by making treaties with each other. They will plan marriages between their rulers. But this will not succeed, for iron and clay don't mix.

44"In the time of those kings, the God of heaven will set up a new kingdom. It will be a kingdom that can't be de-stroyed. No one will ever conquer it. It will crush all these kingdoms into noth-ingness. But it shall stand forever! It shall never be destroyed! 45That is the meaning of the Rock cut from the mountain without human hands doing it. This Rock will crush the iron and brass, the clay, the silver, and the gold.

"Thus the great God has shown what will happen in the future. You know I have described your dream as you saw it. So now you can also believe the expla-nation I have given."

46Then Nebuchadnezzar fell to the ground in front of Daniel and worshiped him. He commanded his people to offer sacrifices. He told them to burn sweet incense before him.

47"Truly, O Daniel," the king said, "your God is the God of gods! He is the Ruler of kings! He is the Revealer of secrets! For he has told you this secret."

48Then the king made Daniel very great. He gave him many valuable gifts. He chose him to be ruler over the whole province of Babylon. Daniel became the chief over all his wise men.

49Then Daniel asked the king to choose Shadrach, Meshach, and Abed-nego as his helpers. They were in charge of all the affairs of the province of Bab-ylon. Daniel served as chief adviser in the king's court.

- *Remember:* Why was the king afraid? (2:1) Why did he plan to kill his advisers? What could they not do? (2:1-12) Who did Daniel ask for help? (2:18) Daniel told the king what he dreamed and what it meant. How did he honor God by doing this? (2:27- 28) How did the king honor God because Daniel honored God? (2:47) How would this story be different if Daniel had not asked God for help? How would it be different if he had not honored God?

- *Discover:* God helps us when we ask him. But we must tell others that he did it, not that we did it. Then they will honor God, too.

- *Apply:* Has God done something special for you? Did you tell your friends that you did it? Or did you tell them that God did it?

- *What's next?* Three men are thrown into a fiery furnace. But they are not burned. Read Daniel 3. ▓

The Fiery Furnace

Have you ever touched a lighted match or a hot stove? What happened? Were you burned? What do you think would happen if you were thrown into a raging fire? That happened to Daniel's three friends. But they were not burned. Why not?

3 King Nebuchadnezzar made a gold statue 90 feet high and 9 feet wide. He set it up on the Plain of Dura, in the province of Babylon. ²Then he sent messages to all the princes, governors, captains, judges, treasurers, counselors, sheriffs, and rulers. He sent these messages to all the provinces of his kingdom. He asked them all to come to the dedication of his statue. ³Then they all came and stood in front of it. ⁴A herald shouted out, "O people of all nations! Here is the king's command.

⁵"When the band strikes up, you are to fall flat on the ground. You are to worship King Nebuchadnezzar's gold statue. ⁶Anyone who does not obey will be thrown into a flaming furnace."

⁷Then the band began to play. And everyone fell down and worshiped the statue.

⁸Some officials went to the king. They told him that some of the Jews were not bowing down to worship!

⁹They said to him, ¹⁰"O king, you made a law for everyone to obey. You said that everyone would hear the band play. And then everyone was supposed to fall down and worship the gold statue. ¹¹You said that anyone who did not do this would be thrown into a flaming furnace. ¹²But there are some Jews out there who have not obeyed you. Their names are Shadrach, Meshach, and Abednego. They are important officers here in Babylon. They refuse to serve your gods or to worship the gold statue."

¹³Then Nebuchadnezzar became very angry. He ordered Shadrach, Meshach, and Abednego to be brought in before him.

¹⁴He spoke to Shadrach, Meshach, and Abednego. "Is this true?" he asked. "Is it true that you won't serve my gods or worship the statue? ¹⁵I'll give you one more chance. When the music plays, if you worship the statue, all will be well. But if you don't bow down, you will be thrown into a flaming furnace. And what god can save you out of my hands then?"

¹⁶Shadrach, Meshach, and Abednego gave him this answer. "O Nebuchadnezzar," they said. "We are not afraid of what will happen to us. ¹⁷If we are thrown into the flaming furnace, our God can save us. And he will save us out of your hand, O king. ¹⁸But if he doesn't, even then we will never serve your gods.

And we will never worship the gold statue you have made."

¹⁹Then Nebuchadnezzar became very angry at Shadrach, Meshach, and Abednego. He commanded that the furnace be heated up seven times hotter than usual. ²⁰He called for some of the strongest men of his army. He told them to tie up Shadrach, Meshach, and Abednego. Then he commanded that they be thrown into the fire. ²¹So they tied them tightly with ropes. Then they threw them into the furnace with their clothes on. ²²The king, in his anger, had told his men to make the furnace extra hot. So flames leaped out and killed the soldiers as they threw them in! ²³Shadrach, Meshach, and Abednego fell down into the roaring flames.

²⁴But suddenly, as he was watching, Nebuchadnezzar jumped up! He was amazed! He shouted to his advisers, "Didn't we throw three men into the furnace?"

"Yes," they said, "we did indeed, Your Majesty."

²⁵"Well, look!" Nebuchadnezzar shouted. "I see four men, untied, walking around in the fire. They aren't even hurt by the flames! And the fourth looks like a god!"

²⁶Then Nebuchadnezzar came as close as he could to the open door of the flaming furnace. He yelled, "Shadrach, Meshach, and Abednego, servants of the Most High God! Come out! Come here!" So they stepped out of the fire.

²⁷Then the princes, governors, captains, and counselors crowded around them. They saw that the fire hadn't touched them. Not a hair of their heads was burned. Their clothes weren't burned either. And they didn't even smell like smoke!

²⁸Then Nebuchadnezzar said, "Praise to the God of Shadrach, Meshach, and Abednego. He sent his angel to save his servants when they did not obey the king's command. They were willing to die rather than serve or worship any god except their own. ²⁹So now, I will make a new law. It will go against any person who speaks a word against the God of Shadrach, Meshach, and Abednego.

Such a person will be torn limb from limb. And his house will be broken into a pile of rubble. For no other God can do what this one does."

³⁰Then the king promoted Shadrach, Meshach, and Abednego in the province of Babylon.

- *Remember:* Why did the king throw Daniel's three friends into a fiery furnace? What did they do? (3:8-12) How do you know that God was helping them? (3:21-26) How did the king praise God for what he had done? (3:28-30) What difference did it make for the three men to worship God only? What do you think would have happened if they had worshiped the statue instead?

- *Discover:* Worship God only. Don't think about what you may get. Think about pleasing him, no matter what happens.

- *Apply:* Will you please God today, even if you think you could get hurt? Please him! Sometimes you may get hurt. Sometimes you may get wonderful gifts. Please him no matter what happens.

- *What's next?* A giant hand writes on a wall. Read Daniel 5. ■

The King Dreams about a Tree

4 Nebuchadnezzar the king wrote a letter. He sent it to people of every language in every nation of the world. The letter said:

Greetings!

²All of you should know the strange thing the Most High God did to me. ³It was a great and mighty miracle! And now I know for sure that his kingdom will last for all time. He rules forever and ever.

⁴I, Nebuchadnezzar, was living in peace and strength. ⁵Then one night I had a dream that made me very afraid. ⁶I called in all the wise men of Babylon to tell me the meaning of my dream. ⁷The magicians, astrologers, and fortune tellers came to hear about my dream. But they didn't know what it meant. ⁸At last Daniel came in. I named Daniel "Belteshazzar" after my god. The spirit of the holy gods lives in him. So I told him my dream.

⁹"O Belteshazzar, you are a master

magician. I know that the spirit of the holy gods is in you. No secret is too great for you to find out. Tell me what my dream means.

10-11"I saw a very tall tree out in a field. It grew higher and higher into the sky. At last it could be seen by everyone. 12Its leaves were fresh and green. And its branches were heavy with fruit. It had enough fruit for everyone to eat. Wild animals rested in its shade. And the birds lived in its branches. All the world was fed from it. 13Then as I lay there dreaming, I saw one of God's angels coming down from heaven.

14"He shouted, 'Cut down the tree! Chop off its branches! Shake off its leaves! Scatter its fruit! Get the animals out from under it. Send the birds from its branches. 15But leave its stump and roots in the ground. Put a band of iron and brass around the stump. Let it stay in the ground with tender grass all around it.

???????????????????????????????????
What king lived with wild animals and ate grass?
(Read 4:31-33 for the answer.)
???????????????????????????????????

"'Let the dew of heaven water the man. Let him eat grass with the wild animals! 16For seven years let him have the mind of an animal instead of a man.

17"'For this has been declared by messengers. It has been demanded by the Holy Ones. This order is given so all the world will know that the Most High rules the kingdoms of the world. He gives kingdoms to anyone he wants to. He can even give power to the weakest of men!'

18"O Belteshazzar, that was my dream. Now tell me what it means. For no one else can help me. All the wisest men of my kingdom have failed me. But you can tell me, for the spirit of the holy gods is in you."

Daniel Explains the Dream
19Then Daniel sat there stunned and silent for an hour. He was greatly troubled about the meaning of the dream. Finally

the king asked him to speak. The king said, "Belteshazzar, don't be afraid to tell me what it means."

Daniel replied, "Oh, I wish the things foretold in this dream would not happen to you! I wish they would happen to your enemies instead. 20For the tree you saw growing so tall is a picture of you, Your Majesty. The tree reached high into the heavens for all the world to see. 21It had fresh green leaves, loaded with fruit for all to eat. The wild animals lived in its shade. Its branches were full of birds. 22That tree is you! For you have grown strong and great. Your greatness reaches up to the heavens. Your rule stretches to the ends of the earth.

23"Then you saw God's angel coming down from heaven. The angel said, 'Cut down the tree and destroy it. But leave the stump and the roots in the earth with tender grass around it. Put a band of iron and brass around it. Let him be wet with the dew of heaven. For seven years let him eat grass with the animals of the field.'

24"Your Majesty, the Most High God has ordered this. So it will surely happen. 25Your people will throw you out of your palace. You will live in the fields like an animal. You will eat grass like a cow. Your back will be wet with dew from heaven. For seven years this will be your life. Then you will learn that the Most High God rules the kingdoms of men. He gives power to anyone he chooses. 26But the stump and the roots were left in the ground! This means that you will get your kingdom back again. But this will happen only when you have learned that God rules.

27"O King Nebuchadnezzar, listen to me. Stop sinning. Do what you know is right. Be merciful to the poor. Perhaps even yet God will save you."

The Dream Comes True
28But all this happened to Nebuchadnezzar. 29It happened 12 months after he had this dream. One day he was walking on the roof of the royal palace in Babylon. 30He said to himself, "I, by my own power, have built this great city. I have built it to be my home and the capital of my kingdom."

³¹As he was still speaking these words, a voice called down to him from heaven. "O King Nebuchadnezzar," it said, "listen to this message! You are no longer the ruler of this kingdom. ³²You will be forced out of the palace to live with the animals in the fields. You will eat grass like the cows for seven years. Then you will know that God gives kingdoms to anyone he chooses."

³³That very same hour this prophecy was fulfilled. Nebuchadnezzar was chased from his palace and ate grass like the cows. His body was wet with dew. His hair grew as long as eagles' feathers. His nails were like birds' claws.

³⁴At the end of seven years I, Nebuchadnezzar, looked up to heaven. And then my sanity came back. I praised and worshiped the Most High God. I honored him who lives forever. His rule is everlasting, and his kingdom eternal. ³⁵All the people of the earth are nothing compared to him. He can do whatever he thinks is best. This is true among the angels of heaven, as well as here on earth. No one can stop him or challenge him. No one can say to him, 'What do you mean by doing these things?' ³⁶When my mind came back to me, so did my honor and glory and kingdom. My counselors and officers came back to me. I was made the head of my kingdom again. I was given even greater honor than before.

³⁷Now, I, Nebuchadnezzar, praise and honor the King of Heaven. He is the Judge of all. His every act is right and good. For he is able to take those who walk proudly and push them into the dust!

Strange Writing on the Wall

One night the king and a thousand officers were eating dinner. The king wanted to do something exciting, so he and his officers drank from the golden Temple cups. While they drank, they praised idols instead of God. Suddenly a giant hand began to write on the wall. But no one could read the writing. The king offered great power and riches to anyone who could read the writing. Do you think anyone could do it?

5 Belshazzar the king asked 1,000 of his officers to come to a great feast. They all drank a lot of wine. ²⁻⁴While Belshazzar was drinking, he remembered some special gold and silver cups. These cups had been taken from the Temple in Jerusalem by Nebuchadnezzar. He had brought them to Babylon many years before this. Belshazzar ordered that these holy cups be brought in to the feast. When they came, he and his princes, wives, and concubines drank from them. And they made toasts to their idols of gold and silver, brass and iron, wood and stone.

⁵They were drinking from these cups when suddenly they saw the fingers of a man's hand. The hand was writing on the plaster of the wall across from the lampstand. The king himself saw the fingers as they wrote. ⁶He was so afraid that his knees knocked together. His legs began to give way under him.

⁷"Bring the magicians and astrologers!" he screamed. "Bring the Chaldeans! Whoever reads that writing on the wall will be honored. I will reward anyone who can tell me what it means. He will be dressed in purple robes of royal honor. A gold chain will be put around his neck. He will become the third ruler in the kingdom!"

⁸But when they came, none of them could understand the writing. None of them could tell him what it meant.

⁹The king grew more and more afraid, and his face showed his fear. His officers were also very shaken. ¹⁰But then the

queen mother heard what was happening. She rushed to the banquet hall. She said to Belshazzar, "Calm yourself, Your Majesty. Don't be so pale and scared about this. ¹¹There is a man in your kingdom who has in him the spirit of the holy gods. In the days of your father this man was found to be full of wisdom. It is as though he were himself a god. He was the chief of all the magicians and astrologers of Babylon. ¹²Call for this man, Daniel. He was called Belteshazzar by the king. His mind is filled with divine knowledge and understanding. He can interpret dreams, explain riddles, and solve hard problems. He will tell you what the writing means."

¹³So Daniel was rushed in to see the king. The king asked him, "Are you Daniel? Are you the one brought from Israel by King Nebuchadnezzar? ¹⁴I have heard that you have the spirit of the gods within you. And I have heard that you are filled with wisdom. ¹⁵My wise men and astrologers have tried to read that writing on the wall. They have tried to tell me what it means. But they can't do it. ¹⁶I am told you can solve all kinds of problems. Please tell me the meaning of those words. If you do, I will dress you in purple robes. I will put a gold chain around your neck. And I will make you the third ruler in the kingdom."

¹⁷Daniel answered, "Keep your gifts or give them to someone else. But I will tell you what the writing means. ¹⁸Nebuchadnezzar was the king before you. The Most High God gave him a great kingdom with much glory and honor. ¹⁹He gave him such power that all the nations of the world shook before him. The king killed anyone he didn't like. And he honored anyone he happened to like. At his whim rulers rose or fell. ²⁰His heart and mind were hardened in pride. So God took him from his royal throne and took away his glory. ²¹He was chased out of his palace into the fields. His thoughts and feelings became those of an animal. He lived among the wild donkeys. He ate grass like the cows. And his body was wet with the dew of heaven. Then at last he knew that the Most High rules over the kingdoms of men. He chooses anyone he wants to reign over them.

²²"And you, O Belshazzar, have become king after him. You knew all this, but you have not been humble. ²³For you have defied the Lord of Heaven. You have taken these special cups from his Temple. You and your officers and wives and concubines have been drinking wine from them. And as you drank, you praised gods of silver, gold, brass, iron, wood, and stone. These gods neither see nor hear nor know anything at all. But you have not praised God who gives you the breath of life! You have not praised the One who controls your destiny! ²⁴⁻²⁵And so God sent those fingers to write this message: 'Mene, Mene, Tekel, Parsin.'

²⁶"This is what these words mean: Mene means 'numbered.' God has numbered the days of your reign, and they are ended. ²⁷Tekel means 'weighed.' You have been weighed in God's balances and have failed the test. ²⁸Parsin means 'divided.' Your kingdom will be divided and given to the Medes and Persians."

²⁹Then at Belshazzar's command, Daniel was dressed in purple. A gold chain was hung around his neck. And he was made the third ruler in the kingdom.

³⁰That very night Belshazzar, the king of Babylon, was killed. ³¹And Darius the Mede took the city and became king. He began reigning at the age of 62.

- *Remember:* Who was king at this time? (5:1) What kind of party did he have? What did he do to make the party more exciting? (5:2-4) Why was the king suddenly afraid? (5:5-6) What did he promise to anyone who could tell what the writing meant? (5:7) Who told him? What did the writing mean? (5:17-28) What happened later that night? (5:30-31) What kind of person was Daniel? What kind of person was King Belshazzar? Which would you rather be like? Why?

- *Discover:* Don't want to be like bad people. Want to be like godly people.

- *Apply:* Who are your heroes? What kind of people are they like? Are they godly? If not, you'd better get some new heroes!

- *What's next?* Hungry lions won't eat a man. Why? Read Daniel 6. ∎

Daniel in the Lions' Den

Some men were jealous. They thought Daniel would get more power than they would get. So they planned a trap. Daniel was thrown into a den of hungry lions. Would God protect him?

6Darius divided the kingdom into 120 provinces, each under a governor. 2The 120 governors were put under three great rulers. Daniel was chosen as one of the three great rulers. This helped the king rule the kingdom more wisely. And it kept him from being cheated by his governors.

3Daniel soon proved he was more capable than all the other rulers and governors. The king began to think of putting Daniel in charge of the whole empire.

4This made the other rulers and governors very jealous. They began looking for something that Daniel was doing wrong. Then they planned to complain to the king about him. But they couldn't find anything to criticize! He was faithful and honest and made no mistakes. 5So they said, "We will never find a way to accuse Daniel! But we must find something. Our only chance to get him is through his religion!"

We should pray each day, as Daniel did

He prayed there three times a day, just as he always had.

Daniel 6:10

6They decided to go to the king and say, "King Darius, live forever! 7We rulers, governors, and counselors have decided that you should make a new law. This law will go into effect for the next 30 days. During this time no one may ask a favor of God or man except from you. If they do, they will be thrown to the lions. 8Your Majesty, we ask that you might sign this law. Sign it so that it cannot be canceled or changed. It will be a 'law of the Medes and Persians' that cannot be canceled."

9So King Darius signed the law.

10But even though Daniel knew about the new law, he went home and prayed. He bowed down as usual in his upstairs bedroom. He opened its windows toward Jerusalem. He prayed there three times a day, just as he always had.

11Then the men went to Daniel's house. They found him praying there, asking favors of his God. 12They rushed back to the king and reminded him about his law. "Haven't you signed a new law?" they asked. "This law does not allow people to pray to any god or man except you. And this law lasts for 30 days. Anyone who does not obey it will be thrown to the lions!"

"Yes," the king replied, "it is 'a law of the Medes and Persians.' It cannot be changed or canceled."

13Then they told the king, "Daniel is not obeying your law. He is asking favors of his God three times a day."

14When he heard this, the king was very mad at himself for signing the law. He wanted to save Daniel with all his heart. He spent the rest of the day trying to get Daniel out of trouble.

15In the evening the men came again to the king. They said, "Your Majesty, there is nothing you can do. You signed the law, and it cannot be changed."

16So at last the king gave the order for Daniel's arrest. Then he was taken to the den of lions. The king said to him, "May your God, whom you worship, save you." And then they threw him in. 17A stone was brought and put over the mouth of the den. The king sealed it with his own signet ring and with that of his government. So no one could save Daniel from the lions.

18Then the king went back to his palace. He did not eat dinner that night. He refused his usual entertainment. And he didn't sleep all night. 19Very early the next morning he hurried out to the lions' den. 20He called out in sorrow, "O Daniel, you are a servant of the living God! Was your God, whom you worship, able to save you from the lions?"

21Then he heard a voice! "Your Majesty, live forever!" It was Daniel! 22"My

God has sent his angel. He shut the lions' mouths so that they can't touch me. I am innocent before God. And I have not done anything wrong to you."

23The king was beside himself with joy. He ordered Daniel lifted from the den. And not a scratch was found on him because he believed in his God.

24Then the king gave a command to bring the men who had accused Daniel. They were throw into the den along with their children and wives. And the lions jumped on them and tore them apart!

25-26After that King Darius wrote this message. He sent it to everyone in his empire.

"Greetings! I command that everyone in my kingdom shall shake with fear before the God of Daniel. For his God is the living, unchanging God. His kingdom shall never be destroyed. And his power shall never end. 27He saves his people and keeps them from harm. He does great miracles in heaven and earth. It is he who saved Daniel from the power of the lions."

28So Daniel was honored during the reign of Darius. He was also honored in the reign of Cyrus the Persian.

- *Remember:* Why were some men jealous of Daniel? (6:3-4) How did they try to hurt Daniel? (6:4-8) Daniel could be killed if he prayed. Did he? (6:10) How did the king feel about throwing Daniel into the lions' den? (6:14,18-20) Who shut the lions' mouths? (6:22) How was God praised because of Daniel? Why do you think Daniel kept on praying? Why didn't he stop when he knew he could be killed?

- *Discover:* Don't stop praying for anyone or anything. Daniel didn't.

- *Apply:* Are you too tired to pray? Are you ashamed to pray when a friend is near? Are you too busy to pray? Remember Daniel! Pray anyway!

- *What's next?* A man is swallowed by a great fish. Read Jonah 1–2. ■

Daniel Dreams about Four Beasts

7One night Daniel had a dream, and he wrote it down. It came during the first year of Belshazzar's reign over the Babylonian Empire. This is what he saw:

2In my dream I saw a great storm on a mighty ocean. Strong winds were blowing from every direction. 3Then four huge animals came up out of the water. Each was different from the other. 4The first was like a lion, but it had eagle's wings! And as I watched, its wings were pulled off so that it could no longer fly. It was left standing on the ground, on two feet, like a man. And a man's mind was given to it. 5The second animal looked like a bear with its paw raised, ready to strike. It held three ribs between its teeth. And I heard a voice saying to it, "Get up! Devour many people!" 6The third of these strange animals looked like a leopard. But on its back it had wings like those of birds. It had four heads! And great power over all mankind was given to it.

7Then, as I watched in my dream, a fourth animal rose up out of the ocean. It was too terrible to describe and it was very strong. It devoured some of its victims by tearing them apart with its huge iron teeth. It crushed others under its feet. It was far more brutal and vicious than any of the other animals. And it had 10 horns.

8I was looking at the horns. Then suddenly another small horn appeared among them. Three of the first ones were yanked out, roots and all, to give it room. This little horn had a man's eyes and a bragging mouth.

9I watched as thrones were put in place. And the Ancient of Days sat down to judge. His clothing was as white as snow. His hair was like the whitest wool. He sat on a fiery throne brought in on flaming wheels. 10And a river of fire flowed from before him. Millions of angels served him. Hundreds of millions of people stood before him. They were waiting to be judged. Then the court began its session, and the books were opened.

11As I watched, the brutal fourth animal was killed. Its body was burned because of its pride against God. It was also punished for the bragging of its little horn. 12As for the other three animals, their kingdoms were taken from them.

But they were allowed to live a short time longer.

¹³Next I saw the coming of a Man, or so he seemed to be. He was brought there on clouds from heaven. He came to the Ancient of Days and was presented to him. ¹⁴He was given the ruling power and glory over all the nations of the world. All people of every language had to obey him. His power is eternal. And his government shall never fall.

The Dream Is Explained

¹⁵I was confused and disturbed by all I had seen. ¹⁶So I went to one of those standing beside the throne. I asked him the meaning of all these things. And he explained them to me:

¹⁷"These four huge animals stand for four kings. They will someday rule the earth. ¹⁸But in the end the people of the Most High God shall rule the world forever."

¹⁹Then I asked about the fourth animal, the one so brutal and shocking. It had great iron teeth. And its brass claws tore men apart and killed them. ²⁰I asked, too, about the 10 horns. I asked about the little horn that came up and destroyed three others. This little horn had eyes and a loud, bragging mouth. It was stronger than the others. ²¹For I had seen this horn fighting against God's people and winning. ²²But then the Ancient of Days came to help his people. He gave them worldwide power.

²³"This fourth animal," he told me, "is the fourth world power that will rule the earth. It will be more brutal than any of the others. It will devour the whole world. It will destroy everything that stands in its way. ²⁴His 10 horns are 10 kings that will rise out of his empire. Then another king will arise. He will be more brutal than the other 10. He will destroy three of them. ²⁵He will defy the Most High God. He will persecute God's people and wear them down. And he will try to change all laws, morals, and customs. God's people will be helpless in his hands for 3½ years.

²⁶"But then the Ancient of Days will come and open his court of justice. He will take all power from this terrible king

and shall destroy him. ²⁷Then all nations under heaven shall be given to the people of God. They shall rule all things forever. And all rulers shall serve and obey them."

²⁸That was the end of the dream. When I woke up, I was greatly troubled. My face was pale with fear. But I told no one what I had seen.

Daniel Dreams about a Ram and a Goat

8 In the third year of the reign of King Belshazzar, I had another dream. It was similar to the first.

²This time I was at Susa, the capital in the province of Elam. I was standing beside the Ulai River. ³As I was looking around, I saw a ram with two long horns. It was standing on the riverbank. As I watched, one of these horns began to grow. It soon became longer than the other. ⁴The ram butted everything out of its way. No one could stand against it or help its victims. It did whatever it wanted to and became very great.

⁵I was wondering what this could mean. Then, suddenly a buck goat came from the west. It ran so fast that it didn't even touch the ground. This goat had one very large horn between its eyes. ⁶It rushed at the two-horned ram. ⁷And the closer he came, the angrier he was. He charged into the ram and broke off both his horns. Now the ram was helpless. The buck goat knocked him down and trampled him. No one rescued him.

⁸The winner became both proud and powerful. But suddenly, at the height of his power, his horn was broken. And in its place grew four good-sized horns pointing in four directions. ⁹One of these, growing slowly at first, soon became very strong. It attacked the south and east, and fought against the land of Israel. ¹⁰It fought against the people of God and defeated some of their leaders. ¹¹It even challenged the Commander of the army of heaven. It did so by canceling the daily sacrifices offered to him. And it also defiled his Temple. ¹²But the army of heaven was kept from destroying him for this sin. As a result, truth and

goodness became weak, and evil triumphed and prospered.

¹³Then I heard two of the holy angels talking to each other. One of them said, "How long will it be until the daily sacrifice is restored again? How long until the destruction of the Temple is avenged? How long until God's people triumph?"

¹⁴The other replied, "Twenty-three hundred days must first go by."

Gabriel Explains the Dream

¹⁵I was trying to understand the meaning of this vision. Suddenly a man stood in front of me. Or at least he looked like a man. ¹⁶And I heard a man's voice calling from across the river. He said, "Gabriel, tell Daniel the meaning of his dream."

???????????????????????????????????
Which two archangels spoke to Daniel?

(Read 8:15-18 and 10:13 for the answer.)
???????????????????????????????????

¹⁷So Gabriel started toward me. But as he came, I was too afraid to stand. I fell down with my face to the ground. "Son of man," he said. "Let me help you understand your vision. The events you have seen will not take place until the end times come."

¹⁸Then I fainted, lying face downward on the ground. But he woke me up with a touch and helped me to my feet. ¹⁹"I am here," he said, "to tell you what is going to happen in the last days. It will be a time of terror.

²⁰"The two horns of the ram you saw are the kings of Media and Persia. ²¹The shaggy-haired goat is the nation of Greece. Its long horn stands for the first great king of that country. ²²You saw the horn break off and four smaller horns take its place. This means that the Grecian Empire will break into four parts with four kings. None of them will be as great as the first.

²³"Toward the end of their kingdoms, an angry king shall rise to power. He will have great knowledge. ²⁴His power will

be great. But it will be satanic strength and not his own. He will prosper wherever he turns. He will destroy all those who stand against him. Even if their armies are strong, he will conquer God's people.

²⁵"He will be a master of deception. He will defeat many by catching them off guard. Without warning he will destroy them. He will think he is so great that he will even take on the Prince of Princes in battle. But in so doing he will seal his own doom. For he shall be destroyed by God.

²⁶"And then in your vision you heard about the 2,300 days. These days must pass before the rights of worship are restored. This number is literal, and means just that. But none of these things will happen for a long time. So don't tell anyone about them yet."

²⁷Then I grew faint and was sick for several days. After that I was up and around again. And I did my duties for the king. But I was greatly troubled by the dream and did not understand it.

Daniel Prays for His People

9 It was now the first year of the reign of King Darius. He was the son of Ahasuerus. Darius was a Mede but became king in Babylon. ²In that first year of his reign, I, Daniel, was reading the Book of Jeremiah the prophet. As I read, I learned that Jerusalem must lie empty for 70 years. ³So I prayed to the Lord God. I asked him to end our captivity and send us back to our own land.

As I prayed, I fasted and wore rough sackcloth. And I sat in ashes. ⁴I confessed my sins and those of my people.

"O Lord," I prayed, "you are a great and awesome God. You always fulfill your promises of mercy to those who love you and keep your laws. ⁵But we have sinned so much. We have sinned against you and scorned your commands. ⁶We have refused to listen to your servants the prophets. You sent them to us again and again down through the years. They brought our messages to our kings and princes and to all the people. But we didn't listen to them.

⁷"O Lord, you are righteous. But as for

us, we are ashamed of our sin. Yes, all of us, the men of Judah, the people of Jerusalem, and all Israel. We have been scattered everywhere because of our sin against you. 8O Lord, we and our kings and princes and fathers are ashamed because of our sins.

9"But the Lord our God is merciful. He forgives even those who have sinned against him.

10"O Lord our God, we have disobeyed you. We have not obeyed all the laws you gave us through your servants, the prophets. 11All Israel has disobeyed. We have turned away from you. We haven't listened to your voice. And so the awesome curse of God has crushed us. This is the curse written in the laws of Moses your servant. 12And you have done just as you warned us you would do. For never in history has there been a disaster like what happened at Jerusalem to us and our rulers. 13Every curse against us written in the laws of Moses has come true. All the evils he promised have come. But even so we still refuse to turn from our sins. We still don't satisfy the Lord our God and do what is right.

14"And so the Lord crushed us. He is fair in all he does. But still we would not obey. 15O Lord our God, you brought lasting honor to your name when you brought your people from Egypt. What a great display of power! Lord, do it again! We have sinned so much and are full of wickedness. 16Yet because of all your faithful mercies, Lord, please turn away your anger from Jerusalem. For the heathen mock at you because your city lies in ruins for our sins.

17"O our God, hear your servant's prayer! Listen as I beg! Let your face shine again with peace and joy upon your empty sanctuary. Do this for your own glory, Lord.

18"O my God, bend down your ear and listen to my cry. Open your eyes and see our sadness. See how your city lies in ruins. For everyone knows that it is yours! We don't ask because we deserve help. We ask only because you are so full of mercy.

19"O Lord, hear! O Lord, forgive! O Lord, listen to me and act! Don't wait.

Michael and Gabriel
DANIEL 8:16–11:1

Do you have a friend named Michael? Perhaps that is your name. Do you have a friend named Gabriel? Michael and Gabriel were angels. But they were more important than most angels. Sometimes Michael is called an archangel. That meant he was one of the greatest angels. He may even be the greatest angel. Someday he will lead an angel army against Satan. Michael's army will defeat Satan and his army (Revelation 12:7-9). Gabriel was one of the greatest angels, too. Some think he was also an archangel. God sent Gabriel to Mary (Luke 1:26-28). He told Mary that she would be Jesus' mother. God also sent Gabriel to Zacharias (Luke 1:19). He told Zacharias that he would have a son. His son would be John the Baptist. Gabriel said that he lives with God (Luke 1:19). He said that God had sent him. He certainly is very important, isn't he? Michael and Gabriel both talked with Daniel (8:16-18; 9:21; 10:13,21; 11:1). What they said must be very important! Don't you think Daniel listened carefully?

Do this for your own sake, O my God. Do it because your people and your city bear your name."

Gabriel Tells Daniel the Plan

[20]I kept praying and confessing my sin and the sins of my people. I asked the Lord my God to look to Jerusalem, his holy mountain. [21]As I prayed, Gabriel flew swiftly to me. He is the angel I had seen in the earlier vision. This happened at the time of the evening sacrifice. [22]He said to me, "Daniel, I am here to help you understand God's plans. [23]The moment you began praying a command was given. I am here to tell you what it was. For God loves you dearly. Listen, and try to understand the meaning of the vision that you saw!

[24]"The Lord has commanded 490 years of further punishment upon Jerusalem and your people. Then at last they will learn to stay away from sin. And their guilt will be cleansed. Then the kingdom of everlasting righteousness will begin. And the Most Holy Place will be rebuilt, as the prophets have said. [25]Now listen! A command will be given to rebuild Jerusalem. Then from that time until the Anointed One comes, 49 years plus 434 years will pass. Jerusalem's streets and walls will be rebuilt despite the terrible times.

[26]"After the time of 434 years, the Anointed One will be killed. He will not get his kingdom. And a king will arise whose armies will destroy the city and the Temple. They will be destroyed as with a flood. War and its miseries are decreed from that time to the very end. [27]This king will make a seven-year treaty with the people. But after half that time, he will break his promise. Then he will stop the Jews from all their sacrifices and their offerings. Finally, to end all his terrible deeds, the Enemy shall defile the Temple of God. But in God's time and plan, his judgment will be poured out upon this evil one."

Daniel Sees a Heavenly Messenger

10 Daniel, also called Belteshazzar, had another vision. This one came in the third year of the reign of Cyrus, king of Persia. It was about things that would happen in the future. There would be times of great trouble, with wars and sadness. This time, Daniel understood what the vision meant.

[2]I, Daniel, saw this vision. At the time, I had been in mourning for three full weeks. [3]All that time I ate neither wine nor meat. I neither washed nor shaved nor combed my hair.

[4]Then one day early in April, I had this vision. I was standing beside the great Tigris River. [5-6]As I stood there, I looked up. And suddenly there stood before me a person dressed in linen clothes. He had a belt of purest gold around his waist. And his skin was glowing and lustrous! From his face came blinding flashes like lightning. And his eyes were pools of fire. His arms and feet shone like polished brass. His voice was like the roaring of a great crowd of people.

[7]I, Daniel, alone saw this great vision. The men with me saw nothing. But they were suddenly filled with terror and ran to hide. [8]So I was left alone. When I saw this vision, my strength left me. I grew pale and weak with fear.

[9]Then he spoke to me. And I fell to the ground, facedown in a deep faint. [10]But a hand touched me and lifted me to my hands and knees. [11]And I heard his voice. "O Daniel, you are greatly loved by God," he said. "Stand up and listen carefully, for God has sent me to you." So I stood up, still shaking with fear.

[12]Then he said, "Don't be afraid, Daniel. For your request has been heard in heaven. It was answered the very first day you began to fast before the Lord and pray for understanding. That very day I was sent here to meet you. [13]But for 21 days the Evil Spirit who rules the kingdom of Persia blocked my way. Then Michael, one of the top officers of the heavenly army, came to help me. So I was able to get past these spirit rulers of Persia. [14]Now I am here to tell you what will happen to your people, the Jews. This will happen in the end times. For the fulfillment of this prophecy is many years away."

¹⁵All this time I was looking down, unable to speak a word. ¹⁶Then someone who looked like a man touched my lips. And I could talk again. Then I said to the messenger from heaven, "Sir, I am terrified by the way you look. I have no strength. ¹⁷How can such a person as I even talk to you? For my strength is gone, and I can hardly breathe."

¹⁸Then the one who seemed to be a man touched me again. I felt my strength come back. ¹⁹"God loves you very much," he said. "Don't be afraid! Calm yourself. Be strong!"

Suddenly, as he spoke these words, I felt stronger. So I said to him, "Now you may speak, sir. For you have given me strength."

²⁰⁻²¹He replied, "Do you know why I have come? I am here to tell you what is written in the 'Book of the Future.' Then, when I leave, I will go again to fight my way back. I will have to get past the prince of Persia and then the prince of Greece. Only Michael will be there to help me. Michael is the angel who guards your people, Israel.

The Messenger Predicts the Future

11 "I was the one sent to help Darius the Mede in the first year of his reign. ²But now I will show you what the future brings. Three more Persian kings will reign. Then a fourth will come, far richer than the others. He will use his riches to gain power. And he will plan a war against Greece.

³"Then a mighty king will rise in Greece. This king will rule a great kingdom and do all that he sets out to do. ⁴But at the height of his power, his kingdom will break apart. It will be divided into four weaker nations, not even ruled by his sons. For his empire will be torn apart and given to others. ⁵One of them, the king of Egypt, will increase in power. But this king's own officials will turn against him. They will take away his kingdom and make it still more powerful.

⁶"Several years later a treaty will be made between the king of Syria and the king of Egypt. The daughter of the king of Egypt will be married to the king of Syria. This will be done to bring peace. But she will lose her power, and so will he and their child. As a result, her hopes will be ruined. And so will those of her father, the king of Egypt. ⁷But then her brother will take over as king of Egypt. He will raise an army against the king of Syria. He will march against him and defeat him. ⁸When he comes back again to Egypt, he will carry back their idols with him. He will also bring priceless gold and silver dishes. For many years afterward he will leave the Syrian king alone.

⁹"Meanwhile, the king of Syria will invade Egypt briefly. Then he will soon go back again to his own land. ¹⁰⁻¹¹But the sons of this Syrian king will build a great army. This army will swarm across Israel into Egypt, to a fortress there. Then the king of Egypt will rally against the great forces of Syria and defeat them. ¹²Filled with pride after this great victory, he will kill many thousands of his enemies. But his success will be short-lived.

¹³"A few years later the Syrian king will come back with a strong army. It will be far greater than the one he lost. ¹⁴And other nations will join him in a crusade against Egypt. People among your own people, the Jews, will join them, fulfilling prophecy. But they will not succeed. ¹⁵Then the Syrian king and his friends will come. They will lay siege to a walled city in Egypt and capture it. The proud armies of Egypt will go down to defeat.

¹⁶"The Syrian king will march onward. None will be able to stop him. And he will also enter 'The Glorious Land' of Israel and wreck it. ¹⁷This will be his plot for conquering all Egypt. He, too, will make a treaty with the Egyptian king by giving him a daughter in marriage. She will work for him from within. But the plan will fail.

¹⁸"After this he will turn to the coastal cities and conquer many. But a general will stop him and cause him to retreat in shame. ¹⁹He will turn homeward again but will have trouble on the way and disappear.

²⁰"His successor will be remembered

as the king who sent a tax collector into Israel. But after a very brief reign, he will die in a secret way. He won't die either in a battle or in a riot.

21"Next to come to power will be an evil man. He will not come from the royal line. But during a crisis he will take over the kingdom by flattery and intrigue. 22Then all his enemies will be swept away before him. This will include a leader of the priests. 23His promises will be worthless. From the first his method will be lies and deceit. With just a handful of followers, he will become strong. 24He will enter the richest areas of the land without warning. He will do something never done before. He will take the property of the rich and scatter it out among the people. With great success he will besiege and capture powerful cities. But this will last for only a short while. 25Then he will stir up his courage. He will raise a great army against Egypt. And Egypt, too, will raise a mighty army. But it won't be effective, for plots against him will succeed.

26"Those of his own household will bring his downfall. His army will leave him, and many will be killed.

27"Both these kings will be making evil plans against each other when they meet. They will try to cheat each other. But it will make no difference. Neither can succeed until God's chosen time has come.

28"The Syrian king will then go home with great riches. He will first march through Israel and destroy it. 29Then at the chosen time he will again turn his armies to the south. He will do just as he had threatened. But now it will be a very different story from those first two times. 30-31For Roman warships will scare him off. And he will withdraw and go back home. The Syrian king will be angry because he had to retreat. So he will again wreck Jerusalem and pollute the sanctuary. He will put a stop to the daily sacrifices. And he will worship idols inside the Temple. He will leave godless Jews in power when he leaves. These men have turned against their fathers' faith. 32He will flatter those who hate the things of God. He will win them over to his side. But the people who know their God shall be strong and do great things.

33"Those with spiritual understanding will teach many people in those days. But they will be in constant danger. Many of them will die by fire and sword, or be jailed and robbed. 34When they fall, they will get a little help. Some ungodly men will join them. They will pretend to offer a helping hand, only to take advantage of them.

35"And some who are most gifted in the things of God will stumble and fall. But this will only refine them and make them pure. Then their trials will be over at God's chosen time.

36"The king will do whatever he wants. He will claim to be greater than every god there is. He will laugh at the God of gods. And he will prosper until his time is up. For God's plans cannot be shaken. 37He will have no regard for any god. This includes the gods of his fathers and the god loved by women. For he will brag that he is greater than them all. 38Instead of these, he will worship the Fortress god. This is a god his fathers never knew. He will give this god costly gifts! 39Claiming this god's help, he will have great success against the strongest forts. He will honor those who submit to him. He will give them positions of power. He will divide the land to them as their reward.

40"Then at the time of the end, the king of Egypt will attack him again. But the king of Syria will react with the strength of a whirlwind. His great army and navy will crush him with their might. 41He will invade various lands on the way, including Israel, the Pleasant Land. He will overthrow the governments of many nations. Moab, Edom, and most of Ammon will escape. 42But Egypt and many other lands will be taken. 43He will capture all the treasures of Egypt. And the Libyans and Ethiopians shall be his servants.

44"But then news from the east and north will alarm him. He will go back in great anger to destroy as he goes. 45He will stop between Jerusalem and the sea and there pitch his royal tents. But while he is there his time will suddenly run out. There will be no one to help him.

A Message about the End of Time

12 "At that time Michael will come. He is the mighty angel who stands guard over your nation. He will fight for you in heaven against satanic forces. And there will be a time of trouble for the Jews. It will be greater than any previous suffering in Jewish history. But all of your people whose names are written in the Book will be saved.

²"And many of those whose bodies lie dead and buried will rise up. Some will rise to everlasting life and some to shame and everlasting contempt.

³"And those who are wise, the people of God, shall shine as brightly as the sun. And those who turn many to righteousness will glitter like stars forever.

⁴"But Daniel, keep this prophecy a secret. Seal it up so that it will not be understood until the end times. Then travel and education shall be greatly increased!"

⁵Then I, Daniel, looked and saw two men on each bank of a river. ⁶And one of them spoke to the man in linen clothes. He was standing now above the river. He asked him, "How long will it be until all these terrors end?"

⁷When he replied, he lifted both hands to heaven. And he made a prom-ise by him who lives forever and ever. He said that they would not end until 3½ years have passed. By then, the power of God's people would have been crushed.

⁸I heard what he said, but I didn't understand what he meant. So I said, "Sir, how will all this finally end?"

⁹But he said, "Go now, Daniel. What I have said is not to be understood until the time of the end. ¹⁰Many shall be made pure by great trials and troubles. But the wicked shall continue in their wickedness. And none of them will understand. Only those who are willing to learn will know what it means.

When we win people to God, we shine like stars

And those who turn many to righteousness will glitter like stars forever.

Daniel 12:3

---

¹¹"The daily sacrifices will be stopped. Then 1,290 days will pass. And the Horrible Thing will be set up to be worshiped. ¹²Those who wait and stay until 1,335 days have passed will be happy!

¹³"But go on now to the end of your life and your rest. For you will rise again and have your full share of those last days."

HOSEA

Does God love you? Of course he does! Does he still love you when you sin? Yes! Does he still love you when you turn away from him? Yes! Hosea is a book that tells how much God loves his people. He loves them even when they turn away from him. Hosea's marriage is an object lesson. His wife ran away to love other men. She got into trouble. She was sold as a slave. But Hosea bought her back. That showed how much he loved her. God did that, too. His people sinned. They turned away from him. But Jesus died for them and for us. That shows how much God loves us. Hosea lived in the Northern Kingdom, called Israel. This was almost 200 years after the whole nation of Israel divided into two parts: a Northern Kingdom, which was still called Israel, and a Southern Kingdom, called Judah. People in Hosea's land were very wicked. But God loved them. He kept on loving them, even when they kept on running away from him. That tells you how much God loved Israel. It also tells you how much God loves us.

Hosea's Wife and Children

1 These are the messages from the Lord to Hosea, the son of Beeri. They came during the reigns of these four kings of Judah: Uzziah, Jotham, Ahaz, and Hezekiah. During that time, Jeroboam, the son of Joash, was the king in Israel.

²Here is the first message.

The Lord said to Hosea, "Go and marry a girl who is a prostitute. Some of her children will be born to you from other men. This will show how my people have been untrue to me. They have been unfaithful to me by worshiping other gods."

³So Hosea married Gomer, daughter of Diblaim. She gave birth to a son.

⁴⁻⁵And the Lord said, "Name the child Jezreel. For in the Valley of Jezreel I am about to punish King Jehu's kingdom. I will do this to avenge the murders he committed. In fact, I will put an end to Israel as a kingdom. I will break the power of the nation in the Valley of Jezreel."

⁶Soon Gomer had another child. This

one was a daughter. And God said to Hosea, "Name her Lo-ruhamah. This means 'No more mercy.' For I will have no more mercy upon Israel. I will not forgive her again. 7But I *will* have mercy on the tribe of Judah. I will free her from her enemies. I will do so without any help from her armies or weapons."

8Once Lo-ruhamah was no longer a baby, Gomer gave birth to a son. 9And God said, "Call him Lo-ammi. This means 'Not my people.' For Israel is not mine, and I am not her God.

10"Yet the time will come when Israel shall prosper and become a great nation. In that day her people will be too many to count. They will be as many as the grains of sand along a seashore! Then I will not say to them, 'You are not my people.' I will tell them, 'You are my sons, children of the Living God.' 11Then the people of Judah and Israel will unite and have one leader. They will come back from exile together. What a day that will be! God will plant his people in the rich soil of their own land again.

Punishment and Forgiveness

2 "O Jezreel, give your brother and sister new names. Call your brother Ammi. This means 'You are my people.' Name your sister Ruhamah. This means 'The one I love.' For now God will have mercy upon her!

2"Beg with your mother, for she has become another man's wife. I am no longer her husband. Beg her to stop being a prostitute. Beg her to quit giving herself to others. 3If she doesn't, I will strip her as naked as she was on the day she was born. I will cause her to waste away and die of thirst. She will be like a land full of hunger and drought. 4And I will not give special favors to her children as I would to my own. For they are not my children. They belong to other men.

5"For their mother has slept with other men. She did a very shameful thing. She said, 'I'll run after other men. I'll sell myself to them for food and drinks and clothes.'

6"But I will fence her in with briars and thornbushes. I'll block the road before her to make her lose her way. 7When she runs after her lovers she will not catch up with them. She will look for them but not find them. Then she will think, 'I might as well go back to my husband. I was better off with him than I am now.'

8"She doesn't know that all she has, has come from me. It was I who gave her all the gold and silver she used in worshiping her god!

9"But now I will take back the wine and ripened corn I gave her. I will take the clothes I gave her to cover her nakedness. I will no longer give her rich harvests of grain and grapes. 10Now I will show her naked in public for all her lovers to see. And no one will be able to save her from my hand.

11"I will put an end to all her parties, holidays, and feasts. 12I will destroy her vineyards and her orchards. She claims these are gifts her lovers gave her. I will let them grow into a jungle. Wild animals will eat their fruit.

13"I will punish her for all the incense she burned to Baal, her idol. I will punish her for the times she put on earrings and jewels and went out looking for her lovers. I will punish her because she left me.

14"But I will court her again and bring her into the wilderness. And I will speak to her tenderly there. 15There I will give back her vineyards to her. I will transform her Valley of Troubles into a Door of Hope. She will respond to me there. She will sing with joy as in days long ago in her youth. She will sing as in the days after I had freed her from captivity in Egypt.

16"In that day," says the Lord, "she will call me 'My Husband' instead of 'My Master.' 17O Israel, I will cause you to forget your idols. Their names will not be spoken anymore.

18"At that time I will make peace between you and the wild animals, birds, and snakes. None will ever fear any of the others again. And I will destroy all weapons. All wars will end.

"Then you will lie down in peace and safety, unafraid. 19And I will tie you to me forever. You will be bound with chains of goodness and justice and love and mercy. 20I will marry you in faithfulness and love. And you will really know me then as you never have before.

21-22"In that day," says the Lord, "I will answer the begging of the sky for clouds. It will pour down water on earth in answer to its cry for rain. Then the earth can answer the cry of the grain, grapes, and olive trees for water and dew. And the whole chorus will sing together that 'God plants!' He has given all!

23"At that time I will plant a crop of Israelites. I will raise them for myself! I will pity those who are 'not pitied.' I will say to those who are 'not my people,' 'Now you are my people.' And they will reply, 'You are our God!'"

Hosea Brings Gomer Back Home

3 Then the Lord said to me, "Go, and get your wife again. Bring her back to you and love her. Do this even though she loves to sleep with other men. For the Lord still loves Israel. Even though she has turned to other gods and offered them gifts, he still loves her."

2So I bought her back from her slavery. She was worth just a few dollars and eight bushels of barley. 3And I said to her, "You must live alone for many days. Do not go out with other men or be a prostitute. I will wait for you."

4This shows that Israel will be a long time without a king or prince. And they will also be without an altar, temple, priests, or even idols!

5Afterward they will come back to the Lord their God. They will come back to the Messiah, their King. And they will come humbly, bowing to the Lord. And they will get his blessings in the end times.

God's Case against Israel's Sins

4 Hear the word of the Lord, O people of Israel! The Lord has filed a lawsuit against you. Here are the charges: "There is no faithfulness. There is no kindness. There is no knowledge of God in your land. 2You swear and lie and kill. You steal and sleep around. There is violence everywhere, with one murder after another.

3"That is why your land is not rich. It is filled with sadness. All living things

grow sick and die. The animals, the birds, and even the fish begin to disappear.

4"Don't point your finger at someone else! Don't try to pass the blame to him! Look, priest, I am pointing my finger at *you*. 5As a sentence for your crimes, you

????????????????????????????????

How much did Hosea pay for his wife?

(Read 3:1-2 for the answer.)

????????????????????????????????

priests will stumble in broad daylight. You will stumble then like you do at night. And so will your false 'prophets.' And I will destroy your mother, Israel. 6My people are destroyed because they don't know me. And it is all your fault, you priests. For you yourselves don't even know me. So now, I will not recognize you as my priests. Since you have forgotten my laws, I will 'forget' to bless your children. 7The more my people multiplied, the more they sinned against me. I will make them ashamed of themselves.

8"The priests rejoice in the sins of the people. They lap them up and lick their lips for more! 9And so is the saying, 'Like priests, like people.' Because the priests are wicked, the people are wicked. So now, I will punish both priests and people for all their wicked deeds. 10They will eat and still be hungry. Though they do a big business as prostitutes, they will have no children. For they have left me and turned to other gods.

11"Wine, women, and song have robbed my people of their understanding. 12For they are asking a piece of wood to tell them what to do. 'Divine Truth' comes to them through tea leaves! Longing after idols has made them foolish. For they have been like prostitutes. They serve other gods, turning from me. 13They sacrifice to idols on the tops of mountains. They go up into the hills to burn incense in the pleasant shade of trees.

"There your daughters turn to prostitution. And your brides sleep with other men. 14But why should I punish them?

For you men are doing the same thing. You commit sin with prostitutes and temple prostitutes. Fools! Your doom is sealed! For you refuse to understand.

We should try to get to know the Lord

Oh, that we might know the Lord! Let us try our best to know him. And he will come to us as surely as the coming of dawn.

Hosea 6:3

---

¹⁵"Israel acts like a prostitute, but may Judah stay far from such a life! O Judah, don't go up to worship at Gilgal and Bethel. Don't go there and just pretend to worship me! Their worship is mere pretense. ¹⁶Don't be like Israel, stubborn as a heifer. They resist the Lord's attempts to lead them into green pastures. ¹⁷Stay away from her, for she is married to idols.

¹⁸"The men of Israel get drunk and go out looking for prostitutes. Their love for shame is greater than their love for honor.

¹⁹"So a mighty wind will sweep them away. They will die in shame because they sacrifice to idols.

The Verdict Is In: Guilty

5 "Listen to this, you priests and all of Israel's leaders. Listen, all you men of the royal family. You are doomed! For you have led the people astray with idols at Mizpah and Tabor. ²And you have dug a deep pit to trap them at Acacia. But never forget! I will settle with all of you for what you've done.

³"I have seen your evil deeds, Israel. You have left me as a prostitute leaves her husband. You are full of sin and dirt. ⁴Your deeds won't let you come to God again. For the spirit of unfaithfulness is deep within you. And you cannot know the Lord.

⁵"The very pride of Israel speaks against her in my court. She will stumble under her load of guilt. And Judah, too, shall fall. ⁶Then at last they will come with their flocks and herds to sacrifice to God. But it will be too late. They will not

find him. He has left them, and they are left alone.

⁷"For they have been unfaithful to the Lord. You have borne children that aren't his. Suddenly they and all their riches will disappear. ⁸Sound the alarm! Warn with trumpet blasts in Gibeah and Ramah, and on over to Beth-aven. Shake, land of Benjamin! ⁹Hear these words, Israel. When your day of punishment comes, you will become a pile of rubble.

¹⁰"The leaders of Judah have become thieves. So I will pour my anger down upon them like a waterfall. ¹¹And Ephraim will be crushed and broken by my sentence. I will do this because she is determined to follow idols. ¹²I will destroy her as a moth does wool. I will take away Judah's strength.

¹³"Ephraim and Judah will see how sick they are. And Ephraim will turn to Assyria, to the great king there. But he won't be able to help or cure.

¹⁴"I will tear Ephraim and Judah as a lion rips apart its prey. I will carry them off and chase all rescuers away.

¹⁵"I will leave them until they admit their guilt. I will go back to my home until they ask me for help. For as soon as trouble comes, they will look for me and speak to me.

6 "They will say, 'Come, let us go to the Lord. It is he who has torn us. So now he will heal us. He has wounded us. So now he will bind us up. ²In just a couple of days, he will set us on our feet again to live in his kindness! ³Oh, that we might know the Lord! Let us try our best to know him. And he will come to us as surely as the coming of dawn. He will come as surely as the rain of early spring.'

God Wants Israel's Love

⁴"O Ephraim and Judah, what shall I do with you? For your love vanishes like morning clouds. It passes away like dew. ⁵I sent my prophets to warn you of your judgment. I have warned you with the words of my mouth. I have threatened you with death. Suddenly, without warning, my judgment will strike you. It

will come just as surely as day follows night.

6"I don't want your sacrifices. I want your love. I don't want your offerings. I want you to know me.

7"But like Adam, you broke my covenant. You refused my love. 8Gilead is a city of sinners, tracked with footprints of blood. 9Her people are gangs of robbers. They attack their victims. Packs of priests murder along the road to Shechem. They practice every kind of sin. 10Yes, I have seen a horrible thing in Israel. I have seen Ephraim chasing other gods and Israel full of sin.

11"O Judah, there is a rich harvest of punishment waiting for you. And I wanted so much to bless you!

Israel: Always Missing the Target

7 "I wanted to forgive Israel, but her sins were far too great. No one can even live in Samaria without being a liar, a thief, and a bandit!

2"Her people never seem to know that I am watching them. Their sinful deeds give them away on every side. I see them all. 3The king is glad about their wickedness. The princes laugh about their lies. 4They are all unfaithful to their wives. As a baker's oven is always burning, so are these people always burning with lust.

5"On the king's birthday, the princes get him drunk. He makes a fool of himself. And he drinks with those who laugh at him. 6Their hearts blaze like a furnace with a plot of murder. Their plot burns through the night. And in the morning it flames forth like raging fire.

7"They kill their kings one after another. And none cries out to me for help.

8"My people mix with the heathen. They pick up their evil ways. Thus they have become as useless as a half-baked cake!

9"Worshiping foreign gods has stolen their strength. But they don't know it. Ephraim's hair is turning gray. And he doesn't even know how weak and old he is. 10His pride in other gods has openly judged him. Yet he doesn't go back to his God. He doesn't even try to find him!

11"Ephraim is a silly, senseless dove. She calls to Egypt and flies to Assyria.

12But as she flies, I throw my net over her. I bring her down like a bird from the sky. I will punish her for all her evil ways.

13"How terrible it will be for my people who have left me. Let them die, for they have sinned against me. I wanted to save them, but their hard hearts would not accept the truth. 14They lie there sleepless with fear. But they won't ask for my help. Instead, they worship heathen gods. They ask them for crops and for riches.

15"I have helped them and made them strong. But now they turn against me.

16"They look everywhere except to the Most High God. They are like a crooked bow that always misses its target. Their leaders will die by the sword of the enemy because they don't respect me. And all Egypt will laugh at them.

A Prediction of Captivity

8 "Sound the alarm! They are coming! Like a vulture, the enemy comes down upon the people of God. For they have broken my treaty and turned against my laws.

2"Now Israel begs with me. She says, 'Help us, for you are our God!' 3But it is too late! Israel has thrown away her chance. And now her enemies will chase her. 4She has chosen kings and princes, but not with my consent. She has cut herself off from my help. Her people have worshiped the idols they made from their silver and gold.

5"O Samaria, I reject this calf-idol you have made. My anger burns against you. How long will it be before one honest man is found among you? 6When will you admit that this calf was made by human hands? It is not God! Therefore, it must be smashed to pieces.

7"They have planted the wind. And they will harvest the whirlwind. Their cornstalks stand there dry and sickly, with no grain. If there is any, foreigners will eat it.

8"Israel is destroyed. She lies among the nations as a broken pot. 9She is a lonely, wandering wild donkey. The only friends she has are those she hires. Assyria is one of them.

¹⁰"She hires 'friends' from many lands to help her. But I will send her off to exile. Then she will be free of the burden of her king! ¹¹Ephraim has built many altars. But they don't use them to worship me! They are altars of sin! ¹²Even if I gave her 10,000 laws, she'd say they weren't for her. She'd say they were for someone far away. ¹³Her people love to make sacrifices and eat the meat. But to me their sacrifices are worthless! For I am not happy with their sins and will punish them. They will go back as slaves to Egypt.

¹⁴"Israel has built great palaces. Judah has made great defenses for her cities. But they have forgotten their Maker. So now I will send down fire on those palaces. And I will burn those walls and forts."

Wandering without God

9 O Israel, rejoice no more as others do. For you have left your God. And you have sacrificed to other gods on every threshing floor.

²So now your harvests will be small. Your grapes will die on the vine.

³You may no longer stay here in this land of God. You will be carried off to Egypt and Assyria. There you will live on scraps of food. ⁴There you will not be allowed to pour out wine for sacrifice to God. For no sacrifice that is offered there will please him. It will be dirty, just as the food of mourners is. All who eat such sacrifices are unclean. They may eat this food to feed themselves. But they must not offer it to God. ⁵What then will you do on holy days? What will you do on days of feasting to the Lord? ⁶For you will be slaves in Assyria. Who will get all the things you left behind? Egypt will! She will gather your dead. Memphis will bury them. And thorns and thistles will grow up among the ruins.

⁷The time of Israel's punishment has come. The day of judgment is almost here. Soon Israel will know it all too well. "The prophets are crazy." "The inspired men are mad." Yes, so they laugh. For the nation is weighed down with sin. It shows only hatred for those who love God.

⁸I chose the prophets to guard my people. But the people have blocked them at every turn. They have shown their hatred in front of everyone, even in the Temple of the Lord. ⁹The things my people do are as sinful as what they did in Gibeah long ago. The Lord does not forget. He will surely punish them.

¹⁰"O Israel, how well I remember those first sweet days! In those days I led you through the wilderness. Your love was so fresh! It was so satisfying! It was like the early figs of summer in their first season! But then you left me for Baal-peor. You gave yourselves to other gods. And soon you were as bad as they were. ¹¹The glory of Israel flies away like a bird. Your children will die at birth or even die in the womb. ¹²And if your children grow, I will take them from you. All are doomed. Yes, it will be a sad day when I turn away and leave you alone."

¹³In my vision I have seen the sons of Israel doomed. The fathers are forced to lead their sons to die. ¹⁴O Lord, what shall I ask for your people? I will ask for women that don't give birth. I will ask for mothers that cannot give milk.

¹⁵"All their wickedness began at Gilgal. There I began to hate them. I will drive them from my land because they worship idols. I won't love them any more. For all their leaders are rebels. ¹⁶Ephraim is doomed. The roots of Israel are dried up. She shall bear no more fruit. And if she gives birth, I will kill even her beloved child."

¹⁷My God will destroy the people of Israel. For they will not listen or obey. They will be wandering Jews, homeless among the nations.

A Vine Full of Sin

10 How rich Israel is! She is like a vine filled with fruit! But the more riches I give her, the more she pours on the altars of her heathen gods. The richer the harvests I give her, the more beautiful the idols she makes. ²The hearts of her people are false toward God. They are guilty and must be punished. God will break down their heathen altars and smash their idols.

³Then they will say, "We turned from

the Lord. So he took away our king. But what's the difference? We don't need one anyway!"

⁴They make promises they don't intend to keep. So now judgment will spring up among them like deadly weeds in the field. ⁵The people of Samaria are afraid that their calf-god idols at Beth-aven could be hurt. The priests and people, too, cry over the loss of their gods. ⁶Their idol will be taken with them when they go as slaves to Assyria. It will be a present to the great king there. Ephraim will be laughed at for trusting in this idol. Israel will be put to shame. ⁷As for Samaria, her king will disappear. He will be like a chip of wood on an ocean wave. ⁸And the idol altars of Aven at Bethel where Israel sinned will crumble. Thorns and thistles will grow up around them. And the people will cry to the mountains and hills. They will ask them to fall on them and crush them.

⁹"O Israel, ever since that awful night in Gibeah, there has been only sin, sin, sin! You have made no progress whatever. Was it not right that the men of Gibeah were wiped out? ¹⁰I will come against you for your sin. I will make the nations' armies punish you.

¹¹"Ephraim is used to treading out the grain. It's an easy job that she loves. I have never put her under a heavy yoke before. I have spared her tender neck. But now I will harness her to the plow and harrow. Her days of ease are gone.

¹²"Plant the good seeds of righteousness. And you will harvest a crop of my love. Plow the hard ground of your hearts. For now is the time to seek the Lord. Seek until he comes and showers salvation upon you.

¹³"But you have planted wickedness and raised a crop of sins. You have earned the full reward of trusting in a lie. You believed that military strength could make a nation safe!

¹⁴"So now the terrors of war shall come upon your people. All your forts will fall. It will happen as it did at Beth-arbel, which Shalman destroyed. Even mothers and children were dashed to death there. ¹⁵That will be your fate, too, you people of Israel. This all will happen

because of your great wickedness. In one morning the king of Israel shall be destroyed.

God Still Loves Israel

11 "When Israel was a child I loved him as a son. And I brought him out of Egypt. ²But the more I called to him, the more he turned away. He sacrificed to Baal and burnt incense to idols. ³I trained him from the time he was a baby. I taught him to walk. I held him in my arms. But he doesn't know or even care that it was I who raised him.

⁴"As a man leads his favorite ox, I led Israel with my ropes of love. I loosened his muzzle so he could eat. I myself have stooped and fed him. ⁵But my people shall go back as slaves to Egypt. For they won't come back to me.

⁶"War will swirl through their cities. Their enemies will crash through their gates. They will trap them in their own forts. ⁷For my people are determined to turn against me. And so I have sent them to be slaves. And no one shall set them free.

⁸"Oh, how can I give you up, my Ephraim? How can I let you go? How can I forsake you like Admah and Zeboiim? My heart cries out within me. How I want to help you! ⁹No, I will not punish you as much as I really should. This is the last time I will destroy Ephraim. For I am God and not man. I am the Holy One living among you. I did not come to destroy you.

¹⁰"For the people shall walk after the Lord. I shall roar like a lion at their enemies. And my people shall come home, shaking from the west. ¹¹Like a flock of birds, they will come from Egypt. They will come like doves flying from Assyria. I will bring them home again. It is a promise from the Lord."

¹²Israel surrounds me with lies and deceit. But Judah still trusts in God and is faithful to the Holy One.

God Wants the People to Come Back to Him

12 Israel feeds on the wind. She even chases the wind! For she has given gifts to Egypt and Assyria to get their help. But in return she gets their worthless promises.

²But the Lord is bringing a lawsuit against Judah. Jacob will be justly punished for his ways. ³When he was born, he struggled with his brother. When he became a man, he even fought with God. ⁴Yes, he wrestled with the Angel and won. He cried and begged for a blessing from him. He met God there at Bethel, face to face. God spoke to him there. ⁵This God is the Lord of Heaven's armies. The Lord is his name.

⁶Oh, come back to God. Live by the rule of love and justice. Always expect much from him, your God.

⁷But no, my people are like traders selling from dishonest scales. They love to cheat. ⁸Ephraim brags, "I am so rich! I have gotten it all by myself!" But riches can't make up for sin.

⁹"I am the same Lord who saved you from slavery in Egypt. I am the one who will make you live in tents again. You will live in tents, just as you do each year at the Tabernacle Feast. ¹⁰I sent my prophets to warn you with many visions, parables, and dreams."

¹¹But the sins of Gilgal get worse just the same. Row upon row of altars are used for sacrifices to your idols. They stand there like furrows in a field. And Gilead, too, has many fools who worship idols. ¹²Jacob fled to Syria and earned a wife by tending sheep. ¹³Then the Lord led his people out of Egypt by a prophet. He guided and kept them safe. ¹⁴But Ephraim has made the Lord angry. The Lord will sentence him to death as payment for his sins.

How Much Does It Weigh?

HOSEA 12:7

Do you have a bathroom scale that you step on? If you do, it tells you how much you weigh. Mother or father may have other scales in the house. Father may have some that weigh fish when he goes fishing. Mother may have some that weigh letters. They tell how much postage to put on the letter. In Bible times there were no scales like these. People used balances, like the one in the picture. On one side they put weights. Each was exactly a certain amount. On the other side they put the object to be weighed. When both sides weighed the same, the two sides were even. They were "balanced." But some people cheated. Their weights were smaller than they should have been. So whatever was weighed was less, too! People got less than they should have. God did not like that. God tells us to be fair. He tells us not to cheat.

God Is Angry

13 Long ago when Israel spoke, the nations shook with fear. For he was a mighty prince. But he worshiped Baal and brought about his own doom.

²And now the people disobey more and more. They melt their silver to mold into idols. They use their skillful hands to make these idols. "Sacrifice to these!" they say. And the men kiss idols shaped like calves! ³They shall disappear like morning mist. They shall be like dew that quickly dries away. They shall blow away like chaff taken by the wind. They shall disappear like smoke from a chimney.

⁴"I alone am God, your Lord. I have been your God ever since I brought you out from Egypt. You have no God but me, for there is no other Savior. ⁵I took care of you in the wilderness, that dry

and thirsty land. 6But when you had eaten and were satisfied, you became proud and forgot me. 7So I will come upon you like a lion or leopard looking for food. 8I will claw you like a bear whose cubs have been taken away. I will devour you like a lion.

9"O Israel, if I destroy you, who can save you? 10Where is your king? Why don't you call on him for help? Where are all the leaders of the land? You asked for them. Now let them save you! 11I gave you kings in my anger. Now in my anger I have taken them away. 12Israel's sins are harvested and stored away for punishment.

13"New birth is offered to him. But he is like a child refusing to be born. How stubborn! How foolish! 14Shall I buy him back from hell? Shall I ransom him from Death? O Death, bring forth your terrors so he can taste them! O Grave, show him your plagues! For I will not show mercy!

15"He was called the most fruitful of all his brothers. But the east wind from the desert will blow hard upon him. It will dry up his land. All his flowing springs and green oases will dry away. He will die of thirst. 16Samaria must bear her guilt. For she turned against her God. Her people will be killed by the enemy army. Her babies will be dashed to death against the ground. Her pregnant women will be ripped open with a sword."

God Offers Forgiveness

14 O Israel, come back to the Lord, your God. For you have been crushed by your sins. 2Bring your requests to the Lord. Come to him and say, "O Lord, take away our sins. Have mercy on us and accept us. And we will offer you the sacrifice of praise. 3Assyria cannot save us in battle. Our own strength can't save us either. Never again will we call the idols we have made 'our gods.' For in you alone, O Lord, the helpless find mercy."

4"Then I will cure you from worshiping idols. I will make you a faithful people. And my love will know no bounds, for my anger will be gone forever! 5I will

---

**If we want to be good,
we will follow the Lord**

*For the paths of the Lord
are true and right. Good people
walk along them.*

Hosea 14:9

---

refresh Israel like the dew from heaven. She will blossom like the lily. She will root deeply in the soil like cedars in Lebanon. 6Her branches will spread out as beautiful as olive trees. She will be as fragrant as the forests of Lebanon. 7Her people will come home from exile far away. They will rest under my shadow. They will be a watered garden and blossom like grapes. They will be as fragrant as the wines of Lebanon.

8"O Israel! Stay away from idols! I am alive and strong! I look after you and care for you. I am like an evergreen tree. I will give fruit to you throughout the year. My mercies never fail."

9Whoever is wise, let him understand these things. Whoever is smart, let him listen. For the paths of the Lord are true and right. Good people walk along them. But those who turn against God will fall down in them.

JOEL

Joel was a prophet. He lived about 800 years before Jesus came, and preached to the people of the Southern Kingdom, called Judah. A great swarm of locusts came upon the land. They ate all the crops. People would not have enough food. Joel said God was punishing his people. They had turned away from God. The people must obey God. If they kept on disobeying him, he would send an army of soldiers. They would hurt the people much worse than the locusts had. Joel also told the people that the Holy Spirit would come someday. How did he know this 800 years before it happened? God told him. Joel also talks about a time when God will judge all people. At that time God will punish those who have turned away from him. He will reward those who have obeyed him. Don't you think we should listen to Joel's warnings?

A Plague of Locusts

1 This message came from the Lord to Joel, son of Pethuel.

²Listen, you aged men of Israel! Everyone, listen! In all your lifetime, have you ever heard of such a thing? ³In years to come, tell your children about it. Pass the awful story down from father to son. ⁴After the cutter-locusts finish eating your crops, the swarmer-locusts will take what's left! After them will come the hopper-locusts! And then the stripper-locusts too!

⁵Wake up and cry, you drunks! For all the grapes are ruined. And all your wine is gone! ⁶A great army of locusts covers the land. It is a terrible army, too large to count. They have teeth as sharp as those of lions! ⁷They have ruined my vines. They have stripped the bark from the fig trees.

⁸Cry out with sadness. Cry like a virgin whose fiancé is dead. ⁹The offerings of grain and wine are gone. The priests are starving. Hear the crying of these servants of God. ¹⁰The fields are bare of crops. Sorrow and sadness are everywhere. The grain, the grapes, the olive oil are gone.

¹¹You farmers should stand shocked and stricken. You vinedressers should be crying. Cry for the wheat and the barley, too. For they are gone. ¹²The grapevines are dead. The fig trees are dying. The

pomegranates wither. The apples shrivel on the trees. All joy has withered with them.

Joel Tells the People to Repent

13O priests, dress yourselves in sackcloth. O servants of my God, lie all night before the altar, crying. For there are no more offerings of grain and wine for you. 14Call everyone to stop eating. Call a serious meeting. Gather the elders and all the people into the Lord's Temple. And cry before him there.

God promised that the Holy Spirit would come

I will pour out my Spirit on all of you!

Joel 2:28

15Alas, this terrible day of punishment is on the way. Destruction from the Almighty is almost here! 16Our food will disappear before our eyes. All joy and gladness will be ended in the Temple of our God. 17The seed rots in the ground. The barns and granaries are empty. The grain has dried up in the fields. 18The cattle groan with hunger. The herds stand perplexed, for there is no pasture for them. The sheep are in misery.

19Lord, help us! For the heat has dried up the pastures. The heat has burned up all the trees. 20Even the wild animals cry to you for help. For there is no water for them. The creeks are dry, and the pastures are scorched.

Judgment Will Come

2 Sound the alarm in Jerusalem! Let the trumpet blast be heard upon my holy mountain! Let everyone shake in fear. For the day of the Lord's judgment is coming.

2It is a day of darkness and gloom. It is a day of black clouds and thick darkness. What a mighty army! It covers the mountains like night! How great, how powerful these "people" are! No one like them has ever been seen before. No one like them will ever be seen again! 3Fire goes before them and follows them on every side! Ahead of them the land lies fair as Eden's Garden in all its beauty. But they destroy it to the ground. Not one thing escapes. 4They look like tiny horses, and they run as fast. 5Look at them leaping along the tops of the mountain! Listen to the noise they make. It's like the rumbling of chariots or the roar of a crackling fire. It's like a mighty army moving into battle.

6Fear grips the waiting people. Their faces grow pale with fright. 7These "soldiers" charge like infantry. They scale the walls like trained commandos. Straight forward they march, never breaking ranks. 8They never crowd each other. Each is right in place. No weapon can stop them. 9They swarm upon the city. They run upon the walls. They climb up into the houses, coming like thieves through the windows. 10The earth shakes before them. The heavens tremble. The sun and moon cannot be seen. The stars are hidden.

11The Lord leads them with a shout. This is his mighty army, and they follow his orders. The day of the judgment of the Lord is an awesome, terrible thing. Who can endure it?

Return to the Lord

12That is why the Lord says, "Turn to me now. Turn while there is still time. Give me all your hearts. Come with fasting, crying, and mourning. 13Let your guilt tear at your hearts and not at your clothes." Go back to the Lord your God, for he is kind and full of mercy. He is not easily angered. He is full of kindness. He does not want to punish you.

14Who knows? Perhaps even yet he will decide to leave you alone. Perhaps he will give you a blessing instead of his terrible curse. Perhaps he will give you a great blessing. Then you can offer your grain and wine to the Lord as before!

15Sound the trumpet in Zion! Call everyone to stop eating. Gather all the people together for a serious meeting. 16Bring everyone. Bring the elders, the children, and even the babies. Call the groom from his quarters. Call the bride from her rooms.

17The priests will stand between the people and the altar, crying. And they will pray, "Save your people, O our God. Don't let the heathen rule them, for they belong to you. Don't let them be disgraced by the heathen. For they say, 'Where is this God of theirs? How weak and helpless he must be!'"

The Fields Turn Green Again

18Then the Lord will pity his people. He will want to honor the people of his land! 19He will reply, "See, I am sending you much corn and wine and oil. It will fully satisfy your need. No longer will the nations laugh at you. 20I will remove these armies from the north. I will send them far away. I will turn them back into the deserts where they will die. Half shall be driven into the Dead Sea, and the rest into the Mediterranean. Then their rotting stink will rise upon the land. The Lord has done a mighty miracle for you."

21Fear not, my people. Be glad now and rejoice. For he has done amazing things for you. 22Let the flocks and herds forget their hunger. The pastures will turn green again. The trees will bear their fruit. The fig trees and grapevines will give fruit again. 23Rejoice, O people of Jerusalem! Rejoice in the Lord your God! For the rains he sends are signs of his forgiveness. Once more the autumn rains will come, as well as those of spring. 24The threshing floors will pile high again with wheat. The presses will overflow with olive oil and wine.

25"And I will give you back the crops the locusts ate! 26Once again you will have all the food you want.

"Praise the Lord, who does these miracles for you. Never again will my people know disaster like this! 27And you will know that I am here among my people Israel. You will know that I alone am the Lord your God. And my people shall never again be dealt a blow like this.

God Will Pour Out His Spirit

28"I will pour out my rains again. Then I will pour out my Spirit on all of you! Your sons and daughters will prophesy. Your old men will dream dreams. Your

A Threshing Floor

JOEL 2:23-26

Where do you get your bread? Probably Mother buys a loaf at the store. The store gets it from a bakery. The bakery makes it from flour that came from a miller. He has ground the wheat into flour. But the miller must get the wheat from farmers. If you could visit the farm where this wheat is grown, you would see huge combines. A farmer drives a combine through the wheat field. It cuts the stalks, and beats the heads of grain from them. It blows the chaff away and puts the grains of wheat into a truck. All the farmer does is drive the combine.

But you would not have seen any of this in Bible times. Farmers then cut the stalks of grain with sickles. They held the sickles in their hands. They carried bundles of stalks to a threshing floor. This was a large, flat dirt area bigger than your house. Animals pulled a heavy threshing sledge over the stalks. The sledge was like a wagon without wheels. This beat the grains of wheat from the stalks. The stalks were broken into small pieces. This was called chaff. The farmer waited until the wind blew. Then he picked up the chaff and grain with a large wooden fork. He threw it up into the air. The wind blew the chaff away. The grain fell back to the ground. The farmer did this many times. He wanted all the chaff to blow away. Throwing the grain up like this was called winnowing. A Bible-time farmer would be amazed to see a combine.

young men will see visions. ²⁹And I will pour out my Spirit on your slaves, both men and women. ³⁰And I will put strange symbols in the earth and sky. There will be blood and fire and pillars of smoke.

³¹"The sun will be turned into darkness. And the moon will be turned to blood. This will happen before the great and terrible Day of the Lord comes.

³²"Everyone who calls on the name of the Lord will be saved. Even in Jerusalem some will escape, just as the Lord has promised. For he has chosen some to survive.

Bad News for Israel's Enemies

3 "At that time, I will restore Judah and Jerusalem," says the Lord. ²"I will gather the armies of the world into the 'Valley Where the Lord Judges.' I will punish them there for harming my people and dividing up my land.

³"They divided up my people as their slaves. They traded a young lad for a prostitute. They sold a little girl for wine enough to get drunk. ⁴Tyre and Sidon, don't you try to interfere! Are you trying to take revenge on me, you cities of Philistia? Beware! I will strike back swiftly.

⁵"You have taken my silver and gold and all my precious treasures. You have carried them off to your heathen temples. ⁶You have sold the people of Judah and Jerusalem to the Greeks. They took them far from their own land. ⁷But I will bring them back again from all these places. And I will pay you back for all that you have done. ⁸I will sell your sons and daughters to the people of Judah. And they will sell them to the Sabeans far away. This is a promise from the Lord."

⁹Announce this far and wide. Get ready for war! Get your best soldiers. Collect all your armies. ¹⁰Melt your plowshares into swords. Beat your pruning hooks into spears. Let the weak be strong. ¹¹Gather together and come, all nations everywhere. And now, O Lord, bring down your soldiers!

¹²"Collect the nations. Bring them to the Valley of Jehoshaphat. For there I will judge them all. ¹³Now let the sickle do its work. The harvest is ripe and waiting. Tread the winepress. For it is full to overflowing with the wickedness of these men."

¹⁴Many, many are waiting in the valley for their destruction! For the Day of the Lord is near, in the Valley of Judgment.

Israel, God Is Your Refuge and Strength

¹⁵The sun and moon will be darkened. The stars will hold back their light. ¹⁶The Lord shouts from his Temple in Jerusalem. And the earth and sky begin to shake. But to his people Israel, the Lord will be very gentle. He is their Refuge and Strength.

¹⁷"Then you will know that I am the Lord your God. I am the God of Zion, my holy mountain. Jerusalem will be mine forever. The time will come when no foreign armies will pass through her any more.

¹⁸"Sweet wine will drip from the mountains. The hills will flow with milk. Water will fill the dry streambeds of Judah. A fountain will flow from the Lord's Temple to water Acacia Valley. ¹⁹Egypt will be destroyed, and Edom, too. I will destroy them because they were cruel to the people of Judah.

²⁰"But Israel and Jerusalem will prosper forever. ²¹For I will avenge the blood of my people. I will not forgive their enemies of their guilt. For my home is in Jerusalem with my people."

AMOS

Amos was a poor shepherd. He also had a part-time job punching holes in sycamore fruit. This fruit was punched when it was green. It would not get ripe without a hole in it. Sycamore fruit looked like figs. Poor people ate it. Perhaps no one else wanted it. God gave Amos a new job. He called Amos to be a prophet. He told Amos what to say. Amos left his home south of Jerusalem. He went to the Northern Kingdom to preach. Rich people there were stealing from poor people. They cheated the poor people. Amos warned these rich people that God would punish them for not helping those who needed help. He told them to turn to God. That's good advice for us, too!

God Punishes Israel's Neighbors

1 Amos was a herdsman living in the village of Tekoa. All day long he sat on the hillsides watching the sheep. He kept them from straying.

²One day, in a vision, God spoke to him. He told him what was going to happen to his nation, Israel. This vision came to him at the time Uzziah was king of Judah. At the same time, Jeroboam the son of Joash was king of Israel. This was two years before the earthquake.

This is his report of what he saw and heard. The Lord roared like a lion from his Temple on Mount Zion. And suddenly the rich pastures of Mount Carmel withered and dried. And all the shepherds mourned.

³The Lord says, "The people of Damascus have sinned again and again. I will not forget it. I will not let her go unpunished any more. For they have beaten my people in Gilead as grain is beaten with a threshing sledge. ⁴So I will set fire to King Hazael's palace. I will destroy the strong fort of Ben-hadad. ⁵I will snap the bars that locked the gates of Damascus. I will kill her people as far away as the plain of Aven. And the people of Syria shall come back to Kir as slaves." The Lord has spoken.

⁶The Lord says, "Gaza has sinned again and again. I will not forget it. I will not let her go unpunished any more. For she sent my people into exile. She sold them as slaves in Edom. ⁷So I will set fire to the walls of Gaza. All her forts shall be destroyed. ⁸I will kill the people of Ashdod and destroy Ekron. I will destroy the king of Ashkelon. All Philistines left will die." The Lord has spoken.

⁹The Lord says, "The people of Tyre have sinned again and again. I will not forget it. I will not let them go unpunished any more. For they broke their treaty with their brother, Israel. They

attacked and conquered him. They led him into slavery in Edom. ¹⁰So I will set fire to the walls of Tyre. All its forts and palaces will burn down."

¹¹The Lord says, "Edom has sinned again and again. I will not forget it. I will not let him go unpunished any more. For he chased his brother, Israel, with the sword. He showed him no mercy. ¹²So I will set fire to Teman. All the forts of Bozrah will burn down."

Sin keeps good people apart

For how can we walk together with your sins between us?

Amos 3:3

---

¹³The Lord says, "The people of Ammon have sinned again and again. I will not forget it. I will not let them go unpunished any more. For in their wars in Gilead to enlarge their borders they committed cruel crimes. They ripped open pregnant women with their swords.

¹⁴"So I will set fire to the walls of Rabbah. All the forts and palaces will burn down. There will be wild shouts of battle like a whirlwind in a mighty storm. ¹⁵And their king and his princes will go into exile together." The Lord has spoken.

2 The Lord says, "The people of Moab have sinned again and again. I will not forget it. I will not let them go unpunished any more. For they ruined the tombs of the kings of Edom. They have no respect for the dead. ²Now in return I will send fire upon Moab. It will destroy all the palaces in Kerioth. Moab will fall as the soldiers shout and trumpets blare. ³And I will destroy their king. I will kill all his leaders." The Lord has spoken.

⁴The Lord says, "The people of Judah have sinned again and again. I will not forget it. I will not let them go unpunished any more. For they have rejected the laws of God, refusing to obey him. They have hardened their hearts and sinned as their fathers did. ⁵So I will destroy Judah with fire. I will burn down all Jerusalem's palaces."

God Punishes Israel, Too

⁶The Lord says, "The people of Israel have sinned again and again. I will not forget it. I will not let them go unpunished any more. For money they are unfair to the poor. They have sold into slavery the poor who can't pay back the money they owe. They trade them for a pair of shoes. ⁷They trample the poor into the dust. They kick aside the humble.

"And a man and his father sleep with the same temple-girl. When they do so, they make my holy name dirty. ⁸At their religious feasts they dress in clothing stolen from people who owed them money. In my own Temple they offer sacrifices of wine they bought with stolen money.

⁹"Yet think of all I did for them! I cleared the land of the Amorites before them! The Amorites were as tall as cedar trees and strong as oaks! But I lopped off their fruit and cut their roots. ¹⁰I brought you out from Egypt. I led you through the desert for 40 years. Then you took the land of the Amorites. ¹¹And I chose your sons to be Nazirites and prophets. Can you deny this, Israel?" asks the Lord. ¹²"But you caused the Nazirites to sin by urging them to drink your wine. And you silenced my prophets, telling them, 'Shut up!'

¹³"So now I will make you groan as a wagon groans, loaded with sheaves. ¹⁴Your fastest soldiers will stumble as they run away. The strong will all be weak. And the great ones can no longer save themselves. ¹⁵The archer's aim will fail. The fastest runners won't be fast enough to get away. And even the best of horsemen won't be able to outrun the danger then. ¹⁶The bravest of your mighty men will drop their weapons. They will run for their lives that day." The Lord God has spoken.

Sinful People Cannot Walk with God

3 Listen! This is your doom! It is spoken by the Lord against both Israel and Judah. It is spoken against the whole family I brought from Egypt.

²"Of all the peoples of the earth, I have chosen you alone. That is why I

must punish you even more for all your sins. ³For how can we walk together with your sins between us?

⁴"Would I be roaring like a lion unless I had a reason? The fact is, I am getting ready to punish you. Even a young lion, when it growls, shows it is ready for its food. ⁵A trap doesn't snap shut unless it is stepped on. Your punishment is well deserved. ⁶The alarm has sounded. Listen and fear! For I, the Lord, am sending disaster into your land.

⁷"But always, first of all, I warn you through my prophets. This I now have done."

⁸The Lion has roared. Shake in fear. The Lord God has sounded your doom. I dare not refuse to tell about it.

⁹"Call together the Assyrian and Egyptian leaders. Tell them, 'Take your seats now on the mountains of Samaria. Look at the scandalous sight of all Israel's crimes.' ¹⁰My people have forgotten what it means to do right," says the Lord. "Their beautiful homes are full of the loot from their thefts. ¹¹So now," the Lord God says, "an enemy is coming! He is surrounding them. He will shatter their forts and plunder those beautiful homes."

¹²The Lord says, "A shepherd tried to save his sheep from a lion. But it was too late. He snatched from the lion's mouth two legs and a piece of ear. So it will be when the Israelites in Samaria are finally saved. All they will have left is half a chair and a tattered pillow.

¹³"Listen to this! Speak it throughout Israel!" says the Lord of Heaven's armies. ¹⁴"I will punish Israel for her sins. And on that same day I will also destroy the idol altars at Bethel. The horns of the altar will be cut off and fall to the ground.

¹⁵"And I will destroy the beautiful homes of the rich. I will destroy their winter mansions and their summer houses. And I will crush their ivory palaces."

God Punishes the People; They Still Sin

4 Listen to me, you "fat cows" of Bashan living in Samaria. Some of you women encourage your husbands to rob the poor and crush the needy. Yet you never have enough to drink! ²The Lord God has sworn by his holiness that someday you will be taken away. He will put hooks in your noses and lead you away like cattle. They will drag the last of you away with fishhooks! ³You will be hauled from your beautiful homes. You will be tossed out through the nearest hole in the wall. The Lord has said it.

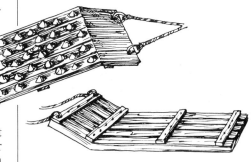

Threshing Sledge
AMOS 1:3
Farmers in Bible times had no combines, as farmers today do. They brought their sheaves of grain to a threshing floor. This was a flat area of hard dirt, bigger than your house. Animals pulled a wooden sledge over the sheaves. This sledge was made of wood planks. It had rocks or pieces of iron under it. The rocks or iron tore up the sheaves. It beat the grain from the sheaves. Nobody would like to be a sheaf of grain under a threshing sledge. The people of Damascus had hurt God's people like a threshing sledge would tear the sheaves. God said he would punish them for doing that.

⁴Go ahead and sacrifice to idols at Bethel and Gilgal. Keep on doing wrong things. Your sins are getting worse and worse. Give sacrifices each morning.

Bring your tithes twice a week! ⁵Give all the proper sacrifices and give extra offerings. How you pride yourselves and brag about it everywhere!

⁶"I sent you hunger," says the Lord. "But it did no good. You still would not come back to me. ⁷I ruined your crops by holding back the rain three months before the harvest. I sent rain on one city but not another. While rain fell on one field, another was dry and withered. ⁸People from two or three cities would make a long journey. They would look for a drink of water in a city that had rain. But there wasn't ever enough. Even then you wouldn't come back to me," says the Lord.

⁹"I sent blight on your farms and your vineyards. The locusts ate your figs and olive trees. And still you wouldn't come back to me," says the Lord. ¹⁰"I sent you plagues like those of Egypt long ago. I killed your young men in war and drove away your horses. The stink of death was terrible to smell. And yet you refused to come. ¹¹I destroyed some of your cities, as I did Sodom and Gomorrah. And those still left are half burned. And still you won't come back to me," says the Lord.

God knows everything that we think

He knows your every thought.
Amos 4:13

---

¹²"So now I will bring upon you all the evils I have spoken of. Get ready to meet your God in judgment, Israel. ¹³For you are dealing with the One who formed mountains and made the winds. He knows your every thought. He turns the morning to darkness. He crushes down the mountains under his feet. He is the Lord of Heaven's armies."

A Sad Song of Grief

5 Sadly I sing this song of grief for you, O Israel.

²"Beautiful Israel lies broken and crushed on the ground and cannot rise. No one will help her. She is left alone to die." ³This is what the Lord God says. "From the city that sends 1,000 men to battle, only 100 will come back. From the city that sends 100, only 10 will come back alive."

⁴The Lord says to the people of Israel, "Seek me and live. ⁵Don't seek the idols of Bethel, Gilgal, or Beersheba. For the people of Gilgal will be carried off to exile. And those of Bethel will surely be sad."

⁶Seek the Lord and live. If not, he will sweep like fire through Israel and burn her up. None of the idols in Bethel can put it out.

⁷O evil men, you make "justice" a bitter pill for the poor. You don't even know what "righteousness" and "fair play" mean!

⁸Seek him who created the Seven Stars and the constellation Orion. Seek him who turns darkness into morning and day into night. Seek him who calls forth water from the ocean and pours it out as rain upon the land. The Lord is his name. ⁹With blinding speed he brings destruction on the strong.

¹⁰How you hate honest judges! How you hate people who tell the truth! ¹¹You trample on the poor. You steal their smallest crumb by all your taxes. So you will never live in the beautiful stone houses you are building. You will never drink the wine from the vineyards you are planting.

¹²For many and great are your sins. I know them all so well. You are the enemies of all that is good. You take bribes. You refuse to give justice to the poor. ¹³The wise will not try to stop the Lord when he punishes you.

¹⁴Be good, run from evil, and live! Then the Lord of Heaven's armies will truly be your Helper. ¹⁵Hate evil and love what is good. Judge others fairly. Then maybe the Lord God might yet have mercy on his people who stay.

¹⁶So the Lord God says this: "There will be crying in all the streets. Call for the farmers to cry with you too. Call for professional mourners to wail and lament. ¹⁷There will be sadness and crying in every vineyard. For I will pass through and destroy. ¹⁸You say, 'If only the Day of the Lord were here. Then God would save us from all our enemies.' But you

have no idea what you ask. For that day will *not* bring light and wealth. It will only bring darkness and doom! How terrible the darkness will be for you. Not a ray of joy or hope will shine. ¹⁹In that day you will be like a man who is chased by a lion and is met by a bear. You will be like a man in a dark room who leans against a wall and puts his hand on a snake. ²⁰Yes, that will be a dark and hopeless day for you.

²¹"I hate it when you pretend to 'honor' me. I hate your 'religious' feasts and serious meetings. ²²I will not accept your burnt offerings and thank offerings. I will not look at your offerings of peace. ²³Away with your hymns of praise. They are just noise to my ears. I will not listen to your music, no matter how lovely it is.

²⁴"I want to see a mighty flood of justice. I want to see a waterfall of doing good.

²⁵⁻²⁷"You sacrificed to me for 40 years while you were in the desert, Israel. But always your real interest has been in your heathen gods. You carried along images of Sakkuth your king and Kaiwan, your god of the stars. So I will send them into captivity with you. You will take them far to the east of Damascus," says the Lord of Heaven's armies.

God Hates Israel's Pride

6 Woe to those living richly in Jerusalem and Samaria. They have become so famous and popular among the people of Israel. ²Go over to Calneh and see what happened there. Then go to great Hamath and down to Gath in the Philistines' land. Once they were better and greater than you. But look at them now. ³You push away all thought of punishment awaiting you. But by your deeds you bring the Day of Judgment near.

⁴You lie on ivory beds with wealth all around you. You eat the meat of the tenderest lambs and the choicest calves. ⁵You sing idle songs to the sound of the harp. You think yourselves to be great musicians, as great as King David was. ⁶You drink wine by the bucketful and perfume yourselves with sweet perfumes. You do not care that your broth-

ers need your help. ⁷So you will be the first to be taken as slaves. Suddenly your parties will end.

⁸The Lord has promised this by his own name. He says, "I hate the pride and false glory of Israel. I hate their beautiful homes. I will give this city to her enemies."

⁹If there are only 10 people left and one house, they too will die. ¹⁰A man's uncle will be the only one left to bury him. He will go in to carry his body from the house. And he will ask the only one still alive inside, "Are any others left?" And the answer will be, "No." And he will add, "Shhh . . . don't say the name of the Lord. He might hear you."

We should hate bad, love good, and treat others fairly

Hate evil and love what is good. Judge others fairly.

Amos 5:15

---

¹¹The Lord commanded that homes both great and small should be smashed to pieces. ¹²Can horses run on rocks? Can oxen plow the sea? It is stupid even to ask. But it is no more stupid than what you do to make a mockery of justice. ¹³And it is just as stupid as your rejoicing in how great you are. In fact, you are less than nothing. How stupid to pride yourselves in your own feeble power!

¹⁴"O Israel, I will bring against you a nation that will bitterly oppress you. You will be oppressed from the north and south. You will suffer from Hamath to the brook of Arabah." The Lord of Heaven's armies says this.

Amos Sees Locusts, Fire, and a Plumbline

7 This is what the Lord God showed me in a vision. He was building a great swarm of locusts to destroy all the main crop. This crop was supposed to go to the king. ²The locusts ate everything in sight. Then I said, "O Lord God, please forgive your people! Don't send them this plague! If you turn against Israel, what hope is there? For Israel is so small!"

³So the Lord gave in and did not fulfill the vision. "I won't do it," he told me.

⁴Then the Lord God showed me a fire he had made to punish them. It had burned up the waters and was devouring the whole land.

⁵Then I said, "O Lord God, please don't do it. If you turn against them, what hope is there? For Israel is so small!"

⁶Then the Lord turned from this plan too. He said, "I won't do that either."

⁷Then he showed me another vision. The Lord was standing beside a wall built with a plumbline. He was checking it with a plumbline to see if it was straight. ⁸And the Lord said to me, "Amos, what do you see?"

I answered, "A plumbline."

And he replied, "I will test my people with a plumbline. I will no longer turn away from punishing them. ⁹The idol altars and temples of Israel will be destroyed. And I will destroy the family of King Jeroboam by the sword."

¹⁰Then Amaziah, the priest of Bethel, heard what Amos was saying. He rushed a message to Jeroboam, the king. "Amos is a traitor to our nation," he said. "He is planning your death. This cannot happen. It will lead to rebellion all across the land. ¹¹He says you will be killed. And he says Israel will be sent far away into slavery."

¹²Then Amaziah sent orders to Amos, "Get out of here, you prophet, you! Run to the land of Judah and prophesy there! ¹³Don't bother us here with your visions. Do not speak here in the capital where the king lives!"

¹⁴But Amos replied, "I am not really one of the prophets. I do not come from a family of prophets. I am just a herdsman and fruit-picker. ¹⁵But the Lord took me from caring for the flocks. He told me, 'Go and speak to my people Israel.'

¹⁶"Now, therefore, listen to this message to you from the Lord. You say, 'Don't prophesy against Israel.' ¹⁷The Lord has a reply. 'Because you won't listen, your wife will become a prostitute in this city. Your sons and daughters will be killed. And your land will be divided up. You yourself will die in a heathen land. And the people of Israel will become slaves in another land.'"

Amos Sees a Basket of Fruit

8 Then the Lord God showed me another a vision. I saw a basket full of ripe fruit.

²"What do you see, Amos?" he asked.

I replied, "A basket full of ripe fruit."

Then the Lord said, "This fruit stands for my people Israel. They are ripe for punishment. I will not put off their punishment again. ³The riotous sound of singing in the Temple will turn to crying then. Dead bodies will be scattered all around. They will be carried out of the city in silence." The Lord has spoken.

⁴Listen, you traders who rob the poor. Listen, you who trample on the needy. ⁵You're the ones who want the Sabbath and the religious holidays to end. Then you can get out and start cheating again, using your dishonest scales. ⁶You are those who make slaves of the poor. You buy them for a piece of silver or a pair of shoes. Then you turn and sell them your moldy wheat.

⁷The Lord, the Pride of Israel, has made a promise. He says, "I won't forget your deeds! ⁸The land will shake as it waits for judgment. Everyone will mourn. It will rise like the river Nile at floodtime. It will toss about and sink again. ⁹At that time I will make the sun go down at noon. I will darken the earth in the daytime. ¹⁰And I will turn your parties into times of mourning. Your songs of joy will be turned to cries of fear. You will wear funeral clothes and shave your heads as signs of sadness. It will be as if your only son had died. Bitter, bitter will be that day.

¹¹"Soon," says the Lord God, "I will send a famine on the land. This will not be a famine of bread or water. It will be a famine of hearing the Lord's messages. ¹²Men will wander everywhere from sea to sea, seeking the Word of the Lord. They will look, running here and going there, but will not find it. ¹³Pretty girls and fine young men alike will thirst for the Word of God. But they will not find

it. They will become tired and weary. ¹⁴And those who worship the idols of Samaria, Dan, and Beersheba will fall. They will never rise again."

Israel Will Be Destroyed

9 I saw the Lord standing beside the altar. He said, "Smash the tops of the pillars. Shake the Temple until the pillars crumble. Shake it until the roof crashes down upon the people below. Though they run, they will not get away. They all will be killed.

²"Though they dig down to hell, I will reach down and pull them up. Though they climb into the heavens, I will bring them down. ³Though they hide among the rocks at Carmel, I will find them. Though they hide at the ocean's bottom, I will send the sea-serpent after them. It will bite and destroy them. ⁴Though they want to go into exile, they will be killed there. I will see to it that they are given evil and not good."

⁵The Lord of Heaven's armies touches the land, and it melts. All its people mourn. It rises like the river Nile in Egypt and then sinks again. ⁶The upper stories of his home are in the heavens. The first floor is on earth. He calls for the vapor to rise from the ocean. He pours it down like rain upon the ground. The Lord is his name.

⁷"O people of Israel, are you any more to me than the Ethiopians are? Have not I, who brought you out of Egypt, done as much for other people too? I brought the Philistines from Caphtor and the Syrians out of Kir.

⁸"The eyes of the Lord God are watching Israel, that sinful nation. I will root her up and scatter her across the world. Yet I have promised that this rooting out will not last forever. ⁹For I have commanded that Israel be sifted by the other nations. She will be sifted as grain is sifted in a sieve. Yet not one true kernel will be lost. ¹⁰All the sinners who think they are safe will die by the sword.

God Will Rebuild Israel

¹¹"At that time I will rebuild David's City, which is now lying in ruins. It will

Funerals
AMOS 8:9-10

Have you ever seen a funeral? Most funerals today are held at a church or a funeral home. The body is dressed well and put into an expensive box called a casket. The funeral may be held several days after the person dies. At the funeral people sing hymns, pray, and preach. Sometimes the body is cremated. That means it is burned and the ashes are kept or scattered in a certain place.

In Bible-time Israel, people who died were buried within a few hours. Often they wrapped the body in strips of cloth. But they did not use a casket. Sometimes friends and neighbors went with a person to bury the dead. Friends and neighbors were with the widow at Nain (Luke 7:12). Sometimes professional mourners would come to the home. They would cry and moan for the dead. Sometimes people showed they were sad by wearing sackcloth. Or they put ashes on their heads and stopped eating for a while. Let's be glad we can sing about Jesus at funerals. Christians live with Jesus when they die. That's something to sing about, isn't it?

return to its former glory. ¹²Israel will take what is left of Edom. Israel will also get all the nations that belong to me." For so the Lord, who plans it all, has said.

¹³"The time will come when there will be plenty of crops. Then, the time of harvest will end just before the farmer starts to plant another crop. And the grapes on the hills of Israel will drip sweet wine! ¹⁴I will give back the fortunes of my people Israel. They will rebuild their ruined cities and live in them again. They will plant vineyards and gardens. They will eat their crops and drink their wine. ¹⁵I will firmly plant them there in the land that I have given them. They will not be uprooted again," says the Lord your God.

OBADIAH

Do you know anyone who is proud? Are you ever proud? Proud people think they are bigger or better than others. God does not like us to be proud. He does not like nations to be proud. Obadiah's short book is about a proud nation called Edom. The man who started the nation of Edom was Esau. Esau lived over 1000 years before Obadiah. Esau's brother was Jacob. Jacob started the nation of Israel. So you would think these nations would be friends. But the Edomites did not like the Israelites. They would not be friends. They were too proud. Do you remember when Moses led the Israelites from Egypt? They wanted to go through Edom to the Promised Land. But the Edomites would not let them. Now, many years later, Obadiah wrote his short book about these people. He told them they were too proud. He told them God would punish them. Let's remember Obadiah's book when we think we're bigger or better than someone else.

Edom Will Be Destroyed

1 In a vision the Lord God showed Obadiah the future of Edom.

A report has come from the Lord. God has sent a messenger to the nations with a message. He says to them, "Listen! You are to send your armies against Edom and destroy her!

²"I will cut you down to size among the nations, Edom. I will make you small and hated by all.

³"You are proud because you live in those high cliffs. 'Who can ever reach us way up here!' you brag. Don't fool yourselves! ⁴You might fly as high as eagles. You might build your nest among the stars. Still, I will bring you down," says the Lord.

⁵"It would be far better for you if thieves had come to rob you. For they would not take everything! It would be better for you if your vineyards were robbed of all their fruit. For at least the gleanings would be left! ⁶Every nook and cranny will be searched and robbed. Every treasure will be found and taken.

⁷"All your friends will turn against you. They will push you out of your land. They will promise peace while planning to destroy you. Your trusted friends will set traps for you. All you do to stop them will fail. ⁸In that day not

one wise man will be left in all of Edom!" The Lord has said it. "For I will make the wise men of Edom stupid. ⁹The strongest soldiers of Teman will be confused. They won't be able to stop the slaughter.

¹⁰"And why? Because of what you did to your brother Israel. Now your sins will be hung out for all to see. Ashamed and defenseless, you will be cut off forever.

The People of Israel Move Home

¹¹"For you turned from Israel in his time of need. You refused to lift a finger to help him. His enemies carried off his wealth and divided Jerusalem among them. But you did not try to stop them. In fact, you were one of his enemies.

We should not be glad when someone is in trouble

You should not have been happy when he was in trouble. You should not have laughed at him in his time of need.

Obadiah 1:12

---

¹²"You should not have done it. You should not have rejoiced when they took him off to foreign lands. You should not have been happy when he was in trouble. You should not have laughed at him in his time of need. ¹³You yourselves went into the land of Israel and robbed him. You made yourselves rich at his expense. ¹⁴You stood at the crossroads and killed those trying to get away. You caught those who got away and gave them to their enemies.

¹⁵"The Lord's punishment will soon come to all Gentile nations. As you have done to Israel, so will it be done to you. Your acts will come back upon your own heads. ¹⁶You drank my cup of punishment on my holy mountain. The nations around you will drink it too. Yes, they will drink and stagger back. They will disappear from history and no longer be nations.

¹⁷"But Jerusalem will become a place of safety, a way of escape. Israel will take the land once again. ¹⁸Israel will be a fire that sets the dry fields of Edom aflame. And no one will survive," for the Lord has spoken.

¹⁹"Then my people who live in the Negeb shall occupy Edom's hill country. Those living in Judean lowlands shall own the Philistine plains. They shall retake the fields of Ephraim and Samaria. And the people of Benjamin shall own Gilead.

²⁰"The Israelite exiles shall come back. They will take the Phoenician coastal strip. Their land shall stretch as far north as Zarephath. Those exiled in Asia Minor shall come back to their homeland. They shall conquer the Negeb's outlying villages. ²¹For deliverers will come to Jerusalem and rule all Edom. And the Lord shall be King!"

JONAH

Did any of your friends ever run away from home? You would never do that, would you? Jonah writes about the time he tried to run away from God. He didn't want to do some chores God gave him. So he ran away. But Jonah forgot something. You can't run away from God! God is everywhere. Wherever you go, God is already there. You'll want to read about the great storm God sent. You'll want to see the big fish God sent that swallowed Jonah. But God is also there with the fish. You'll see how God rescues Jonah from the fish. And you'll watch Jonah hurry to do God's chores! Jonah learned two important words while he was in the fish. Listen! Obey! It's important for us to listen to God. It's also important to obey him.

A Big Fish Swallows Jonah

Jonah tried to run away from God. He couldn't do that, of course. God can see us wherever we are. Jonah tried to hide inside a ship. But God sent a big storm. It looked as if the ship would sink. Jonah knew that God had found him. When the sailors threw Jonah overboard, God sent a big fish. It swallowed Jonah. What would happen now?

1 The Lord sent this message to Jonah, the son of Amittai.

2 "Go to the great city of Nineveh. Give them this message from the Lord: 'I am going to destroy you. For your wickedness rises up before me. It smells to highest Heaven.'"

3 But Jonah was afraid to go. So he ran away from the Lord. He went down to the seacoast, to the port of Joppa. He found a ship that was leaving for Tarshish. He bought a ticket and went on board. He went into the lower part of the ship to hide from the Lord.

4 The ship set sail for Tarshish. But suddenly the Lord created a great wind over the sea. It caused a huge storm that was about to send them to the bottom. 5 The sailors were afraid for their lives. So they shouted to their gods for help. And they threw the cargo overboard to lighten the ship. And all this time Jonah was sound asleep down in the hold.

6 So the captain went down after him. "What do you mean by this?" he roared. "How can you sleep at a time like this?

Get up and pray to your god! See if he will have mercy on us and save us!"

7Then the crew decided to draw straws. They wanted to see who had offended the gods and caused this terrible storm. And Jonah drew the short one.

8"What have you done," they asked, "to bring this awful storm upon us? Who are you? What is your work? What country are you from?"

9-10And he said, "I am a Hebrew. I worship the Lord, the God of Heaven. He is the one who made the earth and sea." Then he told them he was running away from the Lord.

Worship and praise God

I will never worship anyone but you! For how can I thank you enough for all you have done? I will surely keep my promises.

Jonah 2:9

The men were very afraid when they heard this. "Oh, why did you do it?" they shouted. 11"What should we do to you to stop the storm?" For it was getting worse and worse.

12"Throw me out into the sea," he said. "Then it will become calm again. For I know this terrible storm has come because of me."

13They tried harder to row the boat ashore, but they couldn't make it. The storm was too fierce to fight against. 14Then they shouted out a prayer to the Lord, Jonah's God. "O Lord," they begged, "don't make us die for this man's sin. Don't hold us guilty for his death, for it is not our fault. You have sent this storm upon him for your own good reasons."

15Then they picked up Jonah and threw him overboard into the raging sea. And suddenly, the storm stopped!

16The men stood there in awe before the Lord. And they made sacrifices to him and promised to serve him.

17Now the Lord had arranged for a great fish to swallow Jonah. And Jonah was inside the fish three days and three nights.

2Then Jonah prayed to the Lord his God from inside the fish.

2He said, "In my great trouble I cried to the Lord, and he answered me. From the depths of death I called out to you. And Lord, you heard me! 3You threw me into the ocean depths. I sank down into the floods of waters and was covered by wild waves. 4Then I said, 'O Lord, you have rejected me and thrown me away. How shall I ever again see your holy Temple?'

5"I sank under the waves. Death was very near. The waters closed above me. The seaweed wrapped itself around my head. 6I went down to the bottom of the ocean floor. I was locked out of life. I was imprisoned in the land of death. But, O Lord my God, you have snatched me from the pit of death!

7"When I had lost all hope, I turned my thoughts once more to the Lord. And my earnest prayer went to you in your holy Temple. 8Those who worship false gods have turned their backs on the Lord!

9"But I will never worship anyone but you! For how can I thank you enough for all you have done? I will surely keep my promises. For my deliverance comes from the Lord alone."

10Then the Lord ordered the fish to spit up Jonah on the beach. And it did.

- *Remember:* Where did God tell Jonah to go? (1:1-2) What did God want Jonah to do there? (1:1-2) So why didn't Jonah do it? (1:3) What happened to the ship? (1:4-5) Why did the sailors throw Jonah overboard? (1:7-15) How long was Jonah in the big fish? (1:17) What did he do there? (2:1-9) How did he get out of the fish? (2:10) Do you think Jonah will do what God wants now? Why?

- *Discover:* Don't try to run away from God. You can't because God is everywhere.

- *Apply:* Do you ever try to hide from your parents when you do something wrong? Don't try to hide from God.

It's much better to do what God wants. Then you don't need to hide from him. And if God wants you to do something, he will help you do it. Why would he ask you to do something and then not help you? The next time you think you can hide from God, remember Jonah.

● *What's next?* A man gets angry when God is kind to some people. Read Jonah 3–4. ■

Jonah Preaches at Nineveh

Jonah didn't want to obey God. He didn't want to go to Nineveh to preach. But a big storm and three days in a fish's belly changed Jonah's mind. Now he wanted to obey God. He went to Nineveh. He preached. He told the people they were bad and that God was going to destroy their city. Imagine Jonah's surprise when the people begged God to forgive them! Most preachers would have been happy about that. But Jonah wasn't. He was angry at God. Now God would not destroy Nineveh. What would people think of Jonah then? Jonah had a problem, didn't he? Let's see how God dealt with his problem.

3 Then the Lord spoke to Jonah again. "Go to that great city, Nineveh," he said. "Warn them of their judgment, as I told you to before!"

³So Jonah obeyed and went to Nineveh. Now Nineveh was a very large city with many towns around it. It was so large that it would take three days to walk through it.

⁴⁻⁵Jonah went into the city and began to preach. And on the very first day the people turned from their sins. Jonah shouted to the crowds that gathered around him. He said, "Forty days from now Nineveh will be destroyed!" They believed him and called everyone to stop eating. From the king on down, everyone put on sackcloth.

⁶Nineveh's king heard what Jonah was saying. So he stepped down from his throne right away. He laid aside his royal robes and put on sackcloth. Then he went and sat in ashes. ⁷The king and his nobles sent a message throughout the city. "Let no one, not even the animals, eat or drink anything. ⁸Everyone must wear sackcloth and cry out to God. And let everyone turn from his evil ways, his violence, and robbing. ⁹Who can tell? Perhaps even yet God will decide to let us live. Maybe he will hold back his fierce anger from destroying us."

¹⁰And God saw that they had put a stop to their evil ways. So he decided not to destroy them.

4 This change of plans made Jonah very angry. ²He complained to the Lord about it. He said, "This is exactly what I thought you'd do, Lord. I told you this when I was there in my own country. That's why I ran away to Tarshish. For I knew you were a kind God. I knew you were merciful and slow to get angry. I knew how easily you could cancel your plans for destroying these people.

³"Please kill me, Lord. I'd rather be dead than alive."

⁴Then the Lord said, "Is it right to be angry about this?"

⁵So Jonah went out and sat sulking on the east side of the city. He made a leafy shelter to shade him from the sun. He sat there and waited to see if anything would happen to the city. ⁶Then the leaves of the shelter withered in the heat. So the Lord made a vine to grow up quickly. It spread its broad leaves over Jonah's head to shade him. This made a cool place for him to sit in. And Jonah was very pleased to have such a shelter.

⁷But God also prepared a worm! The next morning the worm ate through the

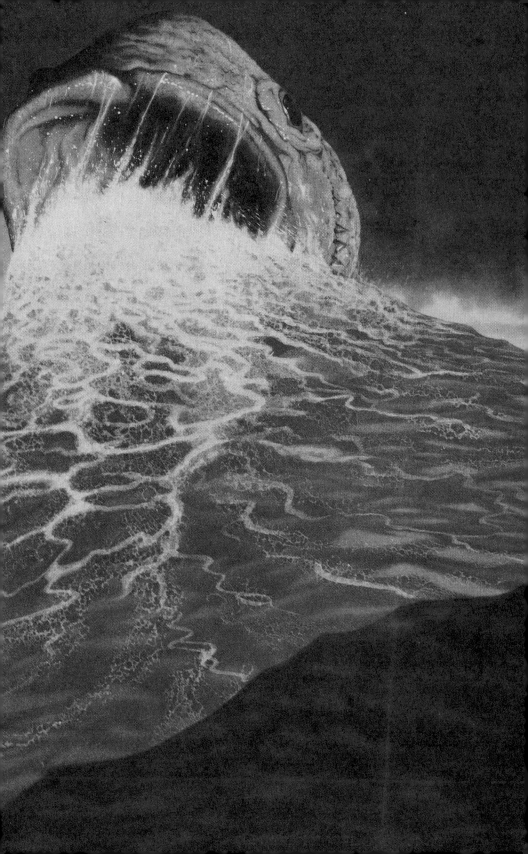

stem of the plant. As a result, it withered away and died.

⁸The sun rose higher and got hotter. And God ordered a scorching east wind to blow on Jonah. The sun beat down upon his head until he grew faint. So he wanted to die. He said, "Death is better than this!"

⁹And God spoke to Jonah. He said, "Is it right for you to be angry because the plant died?"

"Yes," Jonah said, "it is. It is right for me to be angry enough to die!"

¹⁰Then the Lord said, "You felt sorry for the plant when it was destroyed. Yet you didn't even do any work to put it there. And the plant is, at best, short-lived. ¹¹So why shouldn't I feel sorry for a great city like Nineveh? For there are many animals living there. And it has 120,000 people who don't know right from wrong."

● *Remember:* What did God tell Jonah to do at Nineveh? (3:1-2) Did he do it? (3:3) What did the people do when they heard Jonah? (3:4-9) When the people repented, what did God decide to do? (3:10) How did Jonah feel about God's kindness? (4:1-3) How did God show Jonah that he was wrong? (4:4-10) What would you like to say to Jonah about this?

● *Discover:* Don't ask God to hurt someone, even your enemy. Ask God to help that person instead.

● *Apply:* Think of someone who has tried to hurt you. Honestly, would you like to see God hurt that person? Stop! Pray for that person right now. Ask God to help that person.

● *What's next:* An angel tells someone about a special baby. Read Luke 1:1-25. ■

MICAH

Micah's country had many rich people who lived in beautiful homes. There were many poor people, too. But the rich people wanted to be richer. So they stole from the poor people. And the poor became even poorer. That made God angry. So Micah warned the rich people who were doing wrong. He told them they were not pleasing God. He told them God would punish them.

But Micah also told them about God's love. He told the people who were doing wrong that God loved them. He just didn't love their sins. And if they stopped doing wrong and started loving God again, he would save them from the terrible things that were about to happen to them because of their sins. Micah lived about 700 years before Jesus came. But he told about a time when Jesus would be born. He would be born in the town of Bethlehem. He would come to save his people from their sins. How did Micah know this? God told him. Why did God tell Micah this? So that all who read the Book of Micah can see how much God loves us, how much he hates sin, and how much he wants us to live in a way that pleases him.

Dark Days Ahead for Israel and Judah

1 These are messages that the Lord gave to Micah. Micah lived in the town of Moresheth during the reigns of Jotham, Ahaz, and Hezekiah. They were all kings of Judah. The messages came to Micah in the form of visions. They were given for both Samaria and Judah.

²Listen! Let all the people of the world listen! For the Lord in his holy Temple makes judgment against you!

³Look! He is coming! He leaves his throne in Heaven and comes to earth. He walks on the mountaintops. ⁴They melt under his feet. They flow into the valleys like melting wax. They look like water pouring down a hill.

⁵And why is this happening? It is because of the sins of Israel and Judah. It is because of the sins being done in the capital cities, Samaria and Jerusalem.

⁶So now the whole city of Samaria will crumble into a pile of rubble. It will

become an open field. And her streets will be plowed up for planting grapes! The Lord will tear down her wall and her forts. He will dig up their foundations. The stones will fall into the valleys below. 7All her carved images will be smashed to pieces. Her idol temples, built with the gifts of worshipers, will all be burned.

8I will cry and lament, howling like a jackal. I will be as sad as an ostrich crying in the desert at night. I will walk naked and barefoot in sadness and shame. 9For my people's wound is far too deep to heal. The Lord stands ready at Jerusalem's gates to punish her. 10How terrible it will be for the city of Gath! Cry out, men of Bakah! In Beth-le-aphrah, roll in the dust in your suffering and shame. 11There go the people of Shaphir. They are taken away as slaves. They are stripped, naked, and ashamed. The people of Zaanan don't dare to go outside their walls. The foundations of Beth-ezel are swept away. 12The people of Maroth vainly hope for better days. But only destruction awaits them in Jerusalem.

13Quick! Use your fastest chariots and run, O people of Lachish. For you were the first city of Judah to follow Israel in her sin. Then all the cities of the south began to follow your example. 14Write off Moresheth of Gath. There is no hope of saving her. The town of Achzib has lied to the kings of Israel. For she promised help she cannot give. 15You people of Mareshah will be a prize to your enemies. He who is the pride of Israel will hide at Adullam.

16Cry, cry for your little ones. For they are taken away. You will never see them again. They have gone as slaves to distant lands. Shave your heads in sadness.

God Punishes Injustice

2 How terrible it will be for you who lie awake at night, planning evil! You rise at dawn to carry out your plans. You do whatever you can get away with. 2You want a certain piece of land or someone else's house. So you take it by cheating, threats, and violence.

3But the Lord God says, "I will reward your evil with evil. Nothing can stop me.

Never again will you be proud after I am through with you. 4Then your enemies will laugh at you and mock you. They will say what you are thinking, 'We are finished, ruined. God has taken our land and sent us far away. He has given what is ours to others.'" 5Others will set your boundaries then. The People of the Lord will live where they are sent.

6"Don't say such things," the people say. "That sort of talk is shameful. Such troubles surely will not come our way."

7Is that the right reply for you to make, O House of Jacob? Do you think the Spirit of the Lord likes to talk so roughly? No! His threats are for your own good. They are made to get you on the right path again.

8Yet to this very hour my people rise against me. For you steal the shirts right off the backs of those who trusted you.

9You have driven the widows out of their homes. You have stripped their children of every God-given right. 10Up! Begone! This is no more your land and home. For you have filled it with sin, and it will vomit you out.

11"I'll preach to you the joys of wine and drink," you say. Yes, these are words you like to hear. But they are the words of a drunken, lying prophet!

A Hopeful Promise about the Messiah

12The Lord God says, "The time will come, O Israel, when I will gather those who remain. I will bring them together again like sheep in a fold. 13The Messiah will lead you out of exile. He will bring you through the gates of the cities in which you were slaves. He will bring you back to your own land. Your King will go before you. The Lord will lead on!"

God Punishes the Leaders

3 Listen, you leaders of Israel. You are supposed to know right from wrong. 2Yet you are the very ones who hate good and love evil. You skin my people and strip them to the bone.

3You devour them, beat them, break their bones. You chop them up like meat for the cooking pot. 4And then you beg the Lord for his help in times of trouble!

Do you really expect him to listen? He will look the other way! ⁵You false prophets! You lead his people astray! You cry "Peace" to those who give you food! You threaten those who will not pay!

This is God's message to you: ⁶"The night will close about you and cut off all your visions. Darkness will cover you. You will not hear a word from God. The sun will go down upon you and your day will end. ⁷Then at last you will cover your faces in shame. And you will admit that your messages were not from God."

⁸But as for me, I am filled with power. The Spirit of the Lord is upon me. I will announce God's punishment on Israel for her sins.

⁹Listen to me, you leaders of Israel. Listen, all who hate justice and love unfairness. ¹⁰You fill Jerusalem with murder and sin of every kind. ¹¹You take bribes. You priests and prophets won't preach and prophesy until you're paid. And yet you pretend to depend upon the Lord. You say, "All is well. The Lord is here among us. No harm can come to us." ¹²It is because of you that Jerusalem will be plowed like a field. It will become a pile of rubble. The mountaintop where the Temple stands will be overgrown with brush.

Someday the Lord Will Be King

4 But in the last days Mount Zion will be the best-known mountain in the world. It will be praised by all nations. People from all over the world will make journeys there.

²"Come," they will say to one another. "Let us visit the mountain of the Lord. Let us see the Temple of the God of Israel. He will tell us what to do, and we will do it." In those days the whole world will be ruled by the Lord from Jerusalem! He will announce his laws from there.

³He will make peace among all the nations. They will beat their swords into plowshares. They will make their spears into pruning hooks. Nations will no longer fight one another. For all war will end. There will be worldwide peace. All

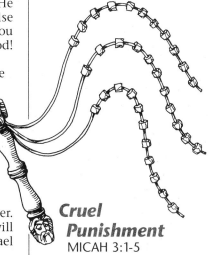

Cruel Punishment
MICAH 3:1-5

Some kinds of punishments in Bible times were very cruel. Stephen was stoned (Acts 7:57-60). People threw big rocks at him until he died. And when King Adoni-bezek was captured by the Israelites, his thumbs and big toes were cut off. He had done this to seventy kings (Judges 1:3-7). Jesus was flogged—beaten by a whip with sharp metal at the ends. He had a crown of thorns jammed over his head. And his hands and feet were nailed to the cross. Some had their heads cut off with a sword or an ax. Samson's eyes were gouged out (Judges 16:21). Ish-bosheth's murderers had their hands cut off (2 Samuel 4:12). Nebuchadnezzar said he would tear some people apart (Daniel 2:5).

Micah was telling the leaders of Israel that they were doing these terrible things to innocent people! The leaders of Israel had become evil, and they would punish good people who didn't help them do evil. Today there are still bad people who try to get good people to do bad. But God tells us always to be good, even if it hurts. One day he will punish all bad and evil people in a way that is even worse than what you just read about. God won't let evil go on forever.

the military schools and training camps will be closed down.

⁴Everyone will live quietly in his own home in peace. For there will be nothing to fear. The Lord himself has promised this. ⁵So we will follow the Lord our God forever. And we will do this even though all the nations around us worship idols!

⁶In that coming day, the Lord says he will bring back his people. Oh, his people will become sick and lame and without a home. ⁷But he will make them strong again when he brings them home. They will be a mighty nation. And the Lord himself will be their King. He will rule from Mount Zion forever. ⁸O Jerusalem, you are the tower over God's people. Your power will come back to you again.

But for Now . . . Suffering

⁹But for now, you cry out in fear. Where is your king to lead you? He is dead! Where are your wise men? All are gone! Pain has taken you over like a woman in labor. ¹⁰Groan in your terrible pain, O people of Zion. For you must leave this city and live in the fields. You will be sent far away to Babylon. But there the Lord will save you. He will free you from your enemies.

¹¹True, many nations have gathered together against you. They are eager to destroy you. ¹²But they do not know the thoughts of the Lord or understand his plan. For the time will come when the Lord will gather together the enemies of his people. They will be gathered like sheaves upon the threshing floor. They will be helpless before Israel.

¹³Rise, thresh, O daughter of Zion. I will give you horns of iron and hooves of brass. You will trample to pieces many people. You will give their riches as offerings to the Lord of all the earth.

A Ruler Will Come
from Bethlehem

5 Call out your armies! The enemy comes against Jerusalem! With a rod they shall strike the Judge of Israel on the face.

²"O Bethlehem Ephrathah, you are but a small Judean village. Yet you will be the birthplace of my King who lives from everlasting ages!" ³God will give up his people to their enemies for awhile. Then she who is to give birth will have her son. And at last his people who were in exile will come home. They will rejoin their brothers in their own land.

⁴And he will stand and feed his flock. He will do it with the Lord's strength. And he will bring glory to the name of the Lord his God. His people will stay there in peace. For he will be greatly honored all around the world. ⁵He will be our Peace. The Assyrians will invade our land and march across our hills. Then he will choose seven shepherds to watch over us. And he will choose eight princes to lead us. ⁶They will rule Assyria with drawn swords. They will enter the gates of the land of Nimrod. He will save us from the Assyrians when they attack our land.

⁷Then Israel will refresh the world like gentle dew or rain showers. ⁸And Israel will be as strong as a lion. The nations will be like helpless sheep before her! ⁹She will stand up to her enemies. All of them will be wiped out.

¹⁰"At that same time," says the Lord, "I will destroy all your weapons. ¹¹I will tear down your walls. I will break down the defenses of your cities. ¹²I will put an end to all witchcraft. There will be no more fortune tellers to talk to. ¹³And I will destroy all your idols. Never again will you worship what you have made. ¹⁴For I will get rid of the heathen shrines from among you. And I will destroy the cities where your idol temples stand.

¹⁵"I will pour out my anger on the nations who will not obey me."

God Has a Case
against His People

6 Listen to what the Lord is saying to his people.

The Lord says, "Stand up and state your case against me. Let the mountains and hills listen to what you have to say."

²And now, O mountains, listen to the Lord's complaint! For he has a case against his people Israel! He will judge them to the full. ³He says, "O my people, what have I done that makes you turn

away from me? Tell me why your patience is all gone! Answer me! ⁴For I brought you out of Egypt and cut your chains of slavery. I gave you Moses, Aaron, and Miriam to help you.

⁵"Don't you remember, O my people? Don't you remember how Balak, king of Moab, tried to destroy you? He tried to get Balaam, son of Beor, to curse you. But I made him bless you instead. That is the kindness I showed you again and again. Have you no memory at all of what happened at Acacia and Gilgal? Don't you remember how I blessed you there?"

⁶"How can we make up to you for what we've done?" you ask. "Shall we bow before the Lord with offerings of young calves?"

Oh no! ⁷For if you offered him thousands of rams, would that please him? Would he be happy with thousands of rivers of olive oil? If you sacrificed your oldest child, would that make him glad? Then would he forgive your sins? Of course not!

⁸No, he has told you what he wants. Be fair. Do what is right. Be kind, even to people who don't deserve it. Then walk humbly with your God.

⁹The Lord's voice calls out to all Jerusalem. Listen to the Lord if you are wise! The armies of destruction are coming. The Lord is sending them. ¹⁰For your sins are very great. Will those who get rich by cheating never be stopped? The homes of the wicked are full of ungodly treasures and false scales. ¹¹Shall I say "Good!" to all your traders who cheat their customers? How could God be just while saying that? ¹²Your rich men are wealthy through force and violence. Your people are so used to lying that their tongues can't tell the truth!

¹³"So now I will wound you!" says the Lord. "I will make your hearts suffer for all your sins. ¹⁴You will eat but never have enough. Hunger pangs and emptiness will still be there. And though you try to save your money, it will come to nothing. And what little you succeed in saving I'll give to those who conquer you! ¹⁵You will plant crops but not harvest them. You will press out the oil from the olives. But you will not get enough to anoint your-

self! You will trample the grapes but get no juice to make your wine.

¹⁶"The only commands you keep are those of Omri. The only example you follow is that of Ahab! So I will make an awesome example of you. I will destroy you. All the world will laugh at you. All who see you will snicker and sneer!"

Hard Times for Everyone

7 How terrible it is for me! It is hard to find an honest man. It's as hard as finding grapes and figs when harvest days are over. There is not a cluster of grapes to eat! There is not a single fig, no matter how much I want them! The good men have gone from the earth. Not one fair and just man is left. They are all murderers. They even turn against their own brothers.

The Lord wants us to be good to all

Be fair. Do what is right. Be kind, even to people who don't deserve it.

Micah 6:8

---

³They go at their evil deeds with both hands. How skilled they are in using them! The governor and judge alike demand bribes. The rich man pays them off and tells them whom to ruin. Justice is twisted between them. ⁴Even the best of them are as prickly as briars. The straightest is more crooked than a hedge of thorns. But your judgment day is coming soon. Your time of punishment is almost here. Confusion, destruction, and terror will be yours.

⁵Don't trust anyone. Don't trust your best friend. Don't trust even your wife! ⁶For the son hates his father. The daughter won't listen to her mother. The bride curses her mother-in-law. Yes, a man's enemies will be found in his own home.

God Will Forgive
and Show His Goodness

⁷As for me, I look to the Lord for his help. I wait for God to save me. He will hear me. ⁸Do not rejoice against me, O my enemy. For though I fall, I will rise again!

When I sit in darkness, the Lord himself will be my light. [9]I will be patient while the Lord punishes me. For I have sinned against him. Then he will defend me from my enemies. He will punish them for all the evil they have done to me. God will bring me out of my darkness into the light. And I will see his goodness. [10]Then my enemy will see that God is for me. He will be ashamed for having said, "Where is that God of yours?" With my own eyes I see them trampled down like mud in the street.

[11]Your cities, people of God, will be rebuilt. They will be much larger and stronger than before. [12]People of many lands will come and honor you. They will come from Assyria to Egypt, and from Egypt to the Euphrates. They will come from sea to sea and from distant hills and mountains.

[13]But before these blessings come, Israel will be destroyed. This will happen because her people were so wicked. [14]O Lord, come and rule your people. Lead your flock. Make them live in peace and success. Let them enjoy the pastures of Bashan and Gilead as they did long ago.

[15]"Yes," replies the Lord, "I will do mighty miracles for you. They will be like those when I brought you out of slavery in Egypt. [16]All the world will stand amazed at what I will do for you. They will be ashamed for thinking they were so strong. They will stand in silent awe, deaf to all around them." [17]They will see what snakes they are. They are like worms crawling from their holes. They will come shaking from their forts to meet the Lord our God. They will fear him. They will stand in awe.

[18]Where is another God like you? You are a God who forgives the sins of his people. You cannot stay angry with your people. For you love to be kind. [19]Once again you will have mercy on us. You will tread our sins under your feet. You will throw them deep into the ocean! [20]You will bless us as you promised Jacob long ago. You will set your love upon us, as you promised our father Abraham!

NAHUM

God is good. But God can get angry. Sin and wickedness make him angry. The Israelites had sinned. They had turned against God. So he let Assyria conquer them. But Assyria was wicked. The people were cruel. Now God was angry at Assyria's wickedness. He would punish them, too. Through Nahum, God told Assyria how it would happen. He would destroy their city, Nineveh. This happened in 612 B.C., just the way God said it would. God knows exactly what will happen in the future. That's because he is God!

God Is Patient and Powerful

1 This is the vision God gave to Nahum, who lived in Elkosh. In this vision he saw that Nineveh would be destroyed.

²God is jealous over those he loves. That is why he judges those who hurt them. He furiously destroys their enemies. ³He is slow in getting angry. But when he does get angry, his power is terrible. He will punish those who are guilty. He shows his power in the cyclone and the raging storms. Clouds are just the dust under his feet! ⁴At his command the oceans and rivers become dry sand. The lush pastures of Bashan and Carmel fade away. The green forests of Lebanon dry up. ⁵In his presence mountains shake and hills melt. The earth crumbles, and its people are destroyed.

⁶Who can stand before an angry God? His anger is like fire. The mountains tumble down before it.

⁷The Lord is good. When trouble comes, he is the place to go! And he knows everyone who trusts in him! ⁸But he sweeps away his enemies with a terrible flood. He chases after them all night long.

Happy Times Are Ahead for Judah

⁹What are you thinking of, Nineveh, to stand against the Lord? He will stop you with one blow. He won't need to strike again. ¹⁰He tosses his enemies into the fire like a bunch of thorns. They burst into flames and burn like straw. ¹¹Who is this king of yours who dares to make plans against the Lord? ¹²But the Lord is not afraid of him! "Let him try to build a great army," the Lord says. "It will be cut off and it will vanish.

"O my people, I have punished you enough! ¹³Now I will break your chains. I will set you free from slavery to this Assyrian king." ¹⁴And to the king he says, "Your kingdom will end. Your sons will never sit upon your throne. And I will destroy your gods and temples. And I will bury you! For how you stink with sin!"

15See, the messengers come running down the mountains with glad news. "No more will the enemy bother you. They have been wiped out. You are safe!" O Judah, set aside a day of special thanks. Worship only the Lord, as you have promised. For this enemy from Nineveh will never come again. He is cut off forever. He will never be seen again.

We should thank God for protecting us

No more will the enemy bother you. You are safe! Set aside a day of special thanks. Worship only the Lord, as you have promised.

Nahum 1:15

Nineveh Will Fall

2 Nineveh, you are finished! You are already surrounded by enemy armies! Sound the alarm! Man the fortress! Gather your defenses, full force. Keep a sharp watch for the enemy attack to begin! 2For the land of God's people lies empty and broken after your attacks. But the Lord will bring their honor and power back again!

3Shields flash red in the sunlight! The attack begins! See their bright red uniforms! See their shining chariots moving forward side by side! 4Your own chariots race along the streets and through the squares. They dart like lightning and look like torches. 5The king shouts for his officers. They stumble in their hurry. They rush to the walls to set up their defenses. 6But it is too late! The river gates are open! The enemy has come in! The palace is in panic!

7The queen of Nineveh is brought out naked to the streets. She is led away like a slave. All her maidens follow behind, crying. Listen to them mourn like doves and beat their breasts! 8Nineveh is like a leaking water tank! Her soldiers slip away, leaving her. She cannot hold them back. "Stop, stop," she shouts. But they keep on running.

9Take the silver! Take the gold! There seems to be no end of treasures. Her great, uncounted riches are taken away. 10Soon the city is an empty shambles. Hearts melt in horror. Knees shake. Her people stand pale-faced and trembling.

11Where now is that great Nineveh? It used to be the lion of the nations, full of fight and pride. It was a place where the old and feeble were safe. It was a place where the young and tender could live unafraid.

12O Nineveh, once-mighty lion! You crushed your enemies to feed your children and your wives. You filled your city and your homes with captured goods and slaves.

13But now the Lord of Heaven's armies have turned against you. He destroys your weapons. Your chariots stand there, silent and unused. Your finest young men lie dead. Never again will you bring back slaves from conquered nations. Never again will you rule the earth.

Total Destruction

3 How terrible it will be for you, Nineveh, City of Blood! You are full of lies and treasures taken in war. 2Listen! Hear the crack of the whips as the chariots rush forward against her. Hear the wheels rumbling and horses' hooves pounding. Hear the chariots clattering as they bump wildly through the streets! 3See the flashing swords and shining spears in the arms of the horsemen! The dead are lying in the streets. There are piles of bodies everywhere. Men stumble over them, jump to their feet, and fall again.

4All this because Nineveh sold herself to the enemies of God. O beautiful and faithless city! She was a mistress of deadly charms. She tempted the nations with her beauty. Then she taught them all to worship her false gods. She seduced people everywhere.

5"No wonder I stand against you," says the Lord of Heaven's armies. "And now all the earth will see you naked and ashamed. 6I will cover you with filth. I will show the world how really evil you are." 7All who see you will shrink back in horror. They will say, "Nineveh lies in ruin." Yet no one anywhere is sad about it!

⁸Are you any better than Thebes? She was protected by the Nile and the sea. ⁹Ethiopia and the whole land of Egypt were her friends. She could call on them for help. And she could call on Put and Libya, too. ¹⁰But still Thebes fell and her people were led off as slaves. Her babies were dashed to death against the stones of the streets. Soldiers drew straws to see who would get her officers as servants. All her leaders were bound in chains.

¹¹Nineveh, too, will stagger like a drunk. She will hide herself in fear. ¹²All your forts will fall. They will be devoured like first-ripe figs. For these figs fall into the mouths of those who shake the trees. ¹³Your troops will be as weak and helpless as women. The gates of your land will be opened wide to the enemy. They will be set on fire and burned. ¹⁴Get ready for the siege! Store up water! Strengthen the forts! Make many bricks for fixing your walls! Go into the pits to trample the clay. And then make molds for the bricks.

¹⁵But in the middle of your work, the fire will burn you. The sword will cut you down. The enemy will devour you like young locusts that eat up everything. There is no getting away, though you multiply like grasshoppers. ¹⁶Traders, as many as stars, filled your city with great riches. But your enemies will swarm like locusts and carry it away. ¹⁷Your officials are like grasshoppers sitting on stone walls on a cold day. When the sun comes up and warms the earth, they will leave.

¹⁸O Assyrian king, your princes lie dead in the dust. Your people are scattered across the mountains. There is no shepherd now to gather them. ¹⁹There is no healing for your wound. It is far too deep to cure. All who hear about your destruction will clap their hands for joy. For who has not suffered from your cruelty?

HABAKKUK

Do you ever ask why some things happen? Why did someone lose his job? Why did someone get hurt? Why did someone die? Why? Why? Why? Habakkuk asks God why. Why doesn't God answer me when I pray? Why doesn't God punish wicked people for their sin? Why does God let wicked people hurt good people? God answers Habakkuk. Sinners will be punished. Wicked people who hurt others will also be punished. Habakkuk learns that God is in control of everything. He doesn't always do things the way we think they should be done. But he is always right and fair. He always does what is best at the best time.

Habakkuk Has Questions for God

1 This is the message that came to the prophet Habakkuk. He was given this message in a vision from God.

²O Lord, how long must I call for help before you will listen? I shout to you, but it does no good. There is no answer. "Help! Murder!" I cry. But no one comes to save me. ³Must I forever see this sin and sadness all around me?

Wherever I look I see oppression and cheating. I see men who love to argue and to fight. ⁴The law is not kept. There is no justice given in the courts. For there are far more wicked people than righteous.

God Answers

⁵The Lord replied, "Look! You will be amazed at what I am about to do! And I am going to do it in your own lifetime. You will have to see it to believe it. ⁶I am raising a new force on the world scene, the Babylonians. They are a cruel and violent nation. They will march across the world and conquer it. ⁷They are known for being cruel. They will do as they like. No one will be able to stop them. ⁸Their horses are faster than leopards. They are a fierce people, fiercer than wolves at dusk. Their horsemen will come from a distant land. Like eagles they will come swooping down on their prey. ⁹All their enemies will melt away in terror when they come. They will collect captives like sand.

¹⁰"They will laugh at kings and princes. They will laugh at their forts and defenses. They will simply pile up dirt against their walls and capture them! ¹¹They will sweep past like the wind and be gone. But they are guilty, for power is their god."

More Questions

¹²O Lord my God, my Holy One, are you not eternal? Is your plan in all of this to wipe us out? Surely not! O God our Rock, you have raised up these Babylonians to correct us. They will punish us for our

awful sins. ¹³We are wicked, but they far more! Will you stand by while they swallow us up? Should you be silent while the wicked destroy those who are better than they?

¹⁴Are we but fish, to be caught and killed? Are we but creeping things that have no leader to defend us? ¹⁵Must we be strung up on their hooks? Must we be caught in their nets, while they rejoice? ¹⁶Then they will worship their nets and burn incense before them! "These are the gods who make us rich," they'll say.

¹⁷Will you let them get away with this forever? Will they succeed forever in their wars?

God Explains His Ways to Habakkuk

2 I will climb my watchtower now. I will wait to see what answer God will give to my complaint.

²The Lord said to me, "Write my answer on a billboard. Make it large and clear. Then anyone can read it at a glance and rush to tell the others. ³These things I plan won't happen right away. Slowly, steadily, surely, the time is coming when the vision will be fulfilled. If it seems slow, do not despair. For these things will surely come to pass. Just be patient! They will not be overdue a single day!

If we live rightly and trust God, we will live forever

The righteous person trusts in me and lives!

Habakkuk 2:4

---

⁴"Take note of this! Wicked people trust in themselves and fail. They do like these Babylonians do. But the righteous person trusts in me and lives! ⁵What's more, these proud Babylonians are made weak by all their wine. In their greed they have collected many nations. But like death and hell, they are never content. ⁶The time is coming when all their captives will laugh at them. They will say, 'You robbers! At last justice has caught up with you! Now you will get what's coming to you!'

⁷"Suddenly those you have stolen money from will rise up in anger. They will turn on you and take all you have, while you stand there helpless. ⁸You have ruined many nations. Now they will ruin you. You murderers! You have filled the countryside and cities with trouble.

⁹"How terrible it will be for you! For you have gotten rich by doing evil. You tried to live beyond the reach of danger. ¹⁰By the murders you commit you have shamed your name. And you have sinned against your own selves. ¹¹The very stones in the walls of your homes cry out against you. The beams in the ceilings echo what they say.

¹²"How terrible it will be for you! For you build cities with money gained from murder and robbery! ¹³Has not the Lord said that godless nations' gains will turn to ashes? They work so hard, but all of it will soon be gone!

¹⁴"The earth will be filled with a knowledge of the Lord's glory. The earth will be filled as the waters fill the sea.

¹⁵"How terrible it will be for you! For you have made your neighboring lands stagger like a drunk. You make them drunk and then take joy in their nakedness and shame. ¹⁶Soon your own glory will become shame. Drink down God's judgment on yourselves. Stagger and fall! ¹⁷You cut down the forests of Lebanon. Now you will be cut down! You terrified the wild animals you caught in your traps. Now terror will strike you because of all the murdering you did.

¹⁸"What help can be found in worshiping all your man-made idols? How stupid it is to think that they could help! What fools you were to trust what you yourselves had made. ¹⁹How terrible it will be for you! For you command your wooden idols to rise up and save you. How terrible it will be for those who call out to stone idols for answers. Can images speak for God? They are covered with gold and silver. But there is no life at all inside!

²⁰"But the Lord is in his holy Temple. Let all the earth be silent before him."

Habakkuk's Prayer

3 This is the prayer of triumph that Habakkuk sang before the Lord.

2O Lord, now I have heard your report. I worship you in awe for the fearful things you are going to do. In this time of our deep need, begin again to help us. Help us as you did in years gone by. Show us your power to save us. In your anger, remember mercy.

3I see God moving across the deserts from Mount Sinai. His brightness fills the earth and sky. His glory fills the heavens. The earth is full of his praise! What a great God he is! 4From his hands flash rays of light. He rejoices in his awesome power. 5Plagues march before him. Diseases follow close behind. 6He stops. He stands still for a moment, gazing at the earth. Then he shakes the nations. He scatters the everlasting mountains and flattens the hills. His power is just the same as always! 7I see the people of Cushan and of Midian in mortal fear.

8-9Was it in anger, Lord, that you struck the rivers and parted the sea? Were you angry with them? No, you were sending your chariots of salvation! Everyone saw your power! Then springs burst forth on the earth at your command! 10The mountains watched and shook. Onward swept the raging water. The mighty deep cried out. 11The lofty sun and moon began to fade. They were hidden by your bright arrows and flashing spear.

12You marched across the land in awesome anger. You trampled down the nations in your wrath. 13You went out to save your chosen people. You crushed the head of the wicked. You destroyed him from head to toe. 14They came out like a whirlwind. They thought Israel would be easy to destroy. But you destroyed them with their own weapons.

15Your horsemen marched across the sea. The mighty waters piled high. 16I shake when I hear all this. My lips quiver with fear. My legs give way under me. I shake in terror. I will quietly wait for the day of trouble to come upon our enemies.

17When it happens, the fig trees will be destroyed. No blossoms or fruit will be left. The olive crops will all fail, and the fields will lie empty. The flocks will die in the fields, and the cattle barns will be empty. 18Even when all this happens, I will rejoice in the Lord. I will be happy in the God of my salvation. 19The Lord God is my strength. He will give me the speed of a deer. He will bring me safely over the mountains.

(*A note to the choir director:* This song is to be sung with stringed instruments.)

ZEPHANIAH

Josiah was only eight years old when he became king of Judah. But there was much sin in Judah then. Rich people stole from poor people. Many turned away from God. When Josiah was 16, he tried to help his people come back to God. He tore down idols. He fixed God's house, the Temple. God's Word was found and read. During this time, Zephaniah was a prophet in Judah. He helped Josiah turn people toward God. He warned that God would judge Judah's sin. Someday God would judge all people.

Someday the Day of the Lord will come. It will be a time when God does something special. Zephaniah brings some wonderful promises from God. A special king will come. Jesus would be this special king. That was good news for people who had not had many good kings. It's good news for us, too!

A Grim Prediction for Judah

1 Zephaniah was given a message from the Lord.

Zephaniah was Cushi's son. Cushi was Gedaliah's son. Gedaliah was Amariah's son. Amariah was Hezekiah's son. Zephaniah lived during the reign of Josiah, the king of Judah. Josiah was the son of Amon.

²"I will sweep away everything in all your land," says the Lord. "I will destroy it to the ground. ³I will sweep away both men and animals alike. Mankind and all the idols he worships will be gone. Even the birds of the air and the fish in the sea will die. ⁴I will crush Judah and Jerusalem and everyone who worships Baal. I will put an end to the priests who worship idols. Even the memory of them will be gone. ⁵They go up on their roofs and bow to the sun, moon, and stars. They 'follow the Lord,' but worship Molech too! I will destroy them. ⁶I will destroy those who once worshiped the Lord, but now have turned away. I will destroy those who never loved him and never wanted to love him."

⁷Stand silent in the presence of the Lord. For the awesome day of his judgment is coming. The Lord is ready to sacrifice his people, Judah. And he has chosen the ones who will kill them. ⁸"On that Day of Judgment I will punish the leaders of Judah. And I will punish all others wearing heathen clothing. ⁹Yes, I will punish those who follow heathen customs. I will punish those who worship idols in their temples. They fill the temples of their gods with violence and lies. ¹⁰A cry of alarm will begin at the

farthest gate of Jerusalem. The noise will get closer as the enemy army gets closer.

¹¹"Cry in sorrow, you people of Jerusalem. All you greedy merchants and traders will die. So will the bankers who charge high interest.

¹²"I will search Jerusalem with lanterns. I will find and punish those who keep on in their sins. They don't think about God. And they think he will leave them alone. ¹³Their property will be taken over by the enemy. They won't be able to live in the new homes they have built. They will never drink wine from the vineyards they have planted.

The Lord will help us when we are humble and not proud

Beg him to save you, all who are humble and want to obey.

Zephaniah 2:3

---

¹⁴"That terrible day is near. It is coming very quickly. It is a day when strong men will cry bitterly. ¹⁵It is a day when God's anger will be poured out. It is a day of terrible trouble and suffering. It is a day of ruin, destruction, and darkness. It is a day of clouds, blackness, ¹⁶trumpet calls, and battle cries. Down go the walled cities and strongest forts!

¹⁷"I will make you as helpless as a blind man looking for a path. For you have sinned against the Lord. Your blood will be poured out on the dust. Your bodies will lie there rotting on the ground."

¹⁸Your silver and gold will not help you on that terrible day. You cannot buy your way out of it. For the whole land will be burned by his fire. He will make a complete end of all the earth.

Change Your Ways; God May Save You

2 Come together and pray, you shameless nation. ²Pray while there still is time left. Pray before judgment begins and your chance is blown away like chaff in the wind. Look to the Lord before the terrible day of God's anger begins. ³Beg him to save you, all who are humble and want to obey.

Walk humbly and do what is right. Perhaps even yet the Lord will save you from his anger.

Punishment for Judah's Neighbors

⁴Gaza, Ashkelon, Ashdod, Ekron, and cities in Philistia will be destroyed. ⁵How terrible it will be for you Philistines living on the coast and in Canaan. For the judgment is against you too. The Lord will destroy you until not one of you is left. ⁶The coastland will become a pasture for shepherds and sheep.

⁷There those left of the tribe of Judah will find pasture. They will lie down to rest in the empty houses in Ashkelon. For the Lord God will visit his people in kindness. He will bring their wealth and success back again.

⁸"I have heard the people of Moab laughing at my people. I know that Ammon planned to take their land. ⁹So now," says the Lord, the God of Israel, "Moab and Ammon will be destroyed. They will become like Sodom and Gomorrah. They will become a place of thorns, salt pits, and desolation. Those of my people who are left will rule over them."

¹⁰They will be paid back for all their pride. For they have laughed at the people who belong to the Lord of Heaven's armies. ¹¹The Lord will do terrible things to them. He will wipe out all the gods of foreign powers. And everyone will worship him, each in his own land throughout the world.

¹²You Ethiopians, too, will be killed by his sword. ¹³And so will the lands of the north. He will destroy Assyria and make its great capital, Nineveh, a wilderness. ¹⁴That once proud city will become a pasture for sheep. All sorts of wild animals will have their homes in her. Hedgehogs will burrow there. The vultures and owls will live among the ruins of her palaces. All her cedar paneling will lie open to the wind.

¹⁵This is the fate of that great city. She said, "In all the world there is no city as great as I." But now, see how she has become a place of ruins. She has become a place where wild animals

live! Everyone passing that way will shake his head in disbelief.

Judgment for Jerusalem

3 How terrible it will be for sinful Jerusalem! For she is a city of violence and crime. ²In her pride she won't even listen to God's voice. No one can tell her anything. She refuses to listen and be corrected. She does not trust the Lord or seek for God.

³Her leaders are like roaring lions hunting for their victims. They try to get everything they can. Her judges are like hungry wolves at evening time. By sunrise there is no trace left of their prey.

⁴Her "prophets" are liars seeking their own gain. Her priests make the Temple unholy by disobeying God's laws.

⁵But the Lord is there within the city. And he does no wrong. Day by day his justice is more clear. But no one listens to him. And the wicked know no shame.

⁶"I have destroyed many nations. I have left their streets in silent ruin. Their cities are empty. There is no one left to remember what happened. ⁷I thought, 'Surely they will listen to me now. Surely they will listen to my warnings. I won't need to strike again.' But no! They keep on with their evil ways from morning to night." ⁸But the Lord says, "Be patient. The time is coming soon when I will judge these evil nations. For I have decided to gather together the kingdoms of the earth. Then I will pour out my anger upon them. All the earth will be burned by my raging fire.

A Promise of Hope

⁹"At that time I will purify all the people. Then they all will worship the Lord together. ¹⁰My scattered people who live beyond the rivers of Ethiopia will come to me. They will bring their offerings. They will ask me to be their God again. ¹¹And then you will no longer need to be ashamed of yourselves. For you will no longer be rebels against me. I will get rid of all the proud people from among

you. There will be no pride on my holy mountain. ¹²Those who are left will be the poor and the humble. They will trust in the name of the Lord. ¹³They will not be sinners, full of lies and cheating. They will live quietly, in peace and in safety. And no one will make them afraid."

¹⁴Sing, O daughter of Zion! Shout, O Israel! Be glad and rejoice with all your heart, O daughter of Jerusalem. ¹⁵For the Lord will take away his hand of judgment. He will scatter the armies of your enemy. And the Lord himself, the King of Israel, will live among you! At last your troubles will be over. You do not need to be afraid anymore.

We may please God enough to cause him to sing

He will rejoice over you with great gladness. Is that a happy choir I hear? No, it is the Lord himself singing a happy song!

Zephaniah 3:17-18

---

¹⁶On that day Jerusalem will be told, "Cheer up! Don't be afraid! ¹⁷⁻¹⁸For the Lord your God has come to live among you. He is a mighty Savior. He will give you victory. He will rejoice over you with great gladness. He will love you and not judge you." Is that a happy choir I hear? No, it is the Lord himself singing a happy song!

"I have helped those who were sad and wounded. ¹⁹And I will punish all who have hurt you. I will save the weak and helpless ones. I will bring together those who were chased away. I will give honor to my former exiles.

²⁰"At that time, I will gather you together and bring you home again. I will give you a good name. Your name will be known among all the peoples of the earth. And they will praise you. For I will restore your fortunes before your very eyes," says the Lord.

HAGGAI

Where do you go to church and Sunday school? What kind of building do you have? Your church building is God's house. King Solomon built a beautiful Temple for God. But the Babylonians destroyed it when they captured Judah. Now, 70 years later, a king lets some Jews come home. He lets them rebuild the Temple. They start. But then they stop. They have many excuses for not building God's house. Haggai tells them that they must build God's house. God will not bless them until they do. As you read Haggai, ask how you treat God's house. Do you take good care of it? Will you?

Let's Rebuild the Temple

1 Haggai was given a message from the Lord.

Haggai the prophet gave this message to Zerubbabel. Zerubbabel was the son of Shealtiel, and was the governor of Judah. And Haggai gave this message to Joshua. Joshua was the son of Josedech and was the High Priest.

He gave this message in the month of August. This was during the second year of the reign of King Darius I.

²The Lord has a question. He asks, "Why is everyone saying it's not the right time to rebuild my Temple?

³⁻⁴"Is it then the right time for you to live in fine homes? You have fine homes, while the Temple lies in ruins. ⁵Look what's happening! ⁶You plant much but harvest little. You have hardly enough to eat or drink. You don't have enough clothes to keep you warm. Your money is gone as quickly as it comes. It is as though you were putting it into pockets filled with holes!

⁷"Think it over," says the Lord of Heaven's armies. "Think about how you have acted. Then think about what has happened as a result! ⁸Then go up into the mountains. Bring down timber and rebuild my Temple. I will be happy with it. I will appear there in my glory," says the Lord.

⁹"You hope for much but get so little. And when you bring it home, I blow it away. It doesn't last at all. Why? Because my Temple lies in ruins, and you don't care. Your only concern is with your own fine homes. ¹⁰That is why I am holding back the rains from heaven. That is why I am giving you so few crops. ¹¹Your land won't be given rain. Your grain, grapes, olives, and all your other crops will dry up. You and all your cattle will starve. Everything you have worked so hard to get will be ruined."

¹²Then the few people there in the land obeyed Haggai's message from the Lord. Among them were Zerubbabel and Joshua. Zerubbabel, the son of Shealtiel, was the governor of Judah. And Joshua, the son of Josedech, was the High Priest. They all began to worship the Lord their God.

¹³Then the Lord spoke to them. He again sent the message through Haggai, his messenger. The Lord said, "I am with you. I will bless you." ¹⁴⁻¹⁵And the Lord gave them a desire to rebuild his Temple. So they all gathered in September of the second year of King Darius's reign. And they offered their help.

God Promises to Bless His People

2 The Lord also sent them this message through Haggai. It came in October of the same year.

²The Lord said, "Ask this question of the governor and the High Priest. Ask it of everyone left in the land.

³"'Who among you can remember the Temple as it was before?' How great it was! Compared to the old Temple, the new one is nothing, is it? ⁴But take courage, O Zerubbabel and Joshua. O people, be brave. Take courage and work, for I am with you," says the Lord of Heaven's armies. ⁵"For I promised when you left Egypt that my Spirit would stay with you. So don't be afraid.

God is with us, so we should be brave and do our work

Be brave. Take courage and work, for I am with you.

Haggai 2:4

---

⁶"For the Lord of Heaven's armies makes this promise: 'In just a little while I will begin to shake the heavens and the earth. I will shake the oceans and the dry land, too. ⁷I will shake all nations. And the Desire of All Nations will come to this Temple. And I will fill this place with my glory,' says the Lord. ⁸⁻⁹'The glory of this Temple in the future will be great. It will have greater glory than the first one! For I have plenty of silver and gold to do it! And here I will give peace,'" says the Lord.

¹⁰The Lord gave another message to Haggai the prophet. It came in December, during the second year of King Darius's reign.

¹¹"Ask the priests this question about the law. ¹²'Suppose one of you is carrying a holy sacrifice in his robe. Suppose his robe happens to touch some bread or wine or meat. Will these also become holy?'"

"No," the priests replied. "Holiness does not pass to other things that way."

¹³Then Haggai asked, "Suppose someone touches a dead person. And by doing that he becomes unholy. Then suppose he touches something else. Does the thing he touches become unholy?"

And the priests answered, "Yes."

¹⁴Haggai then made his meaning clear. He spoke for the Lord. "You people," he said, "were living unholy lives. These lives made your sacrifices unholy. And not only them, but everything else you did as a 'service' to me. ¹⁵And so everything you did went wrong. But all is different now because you have begun to build the Temple. ¹⁶⁻¹⁷Before, when you hoped for a crop of 20 bushels, there were only 10. When you hoped for 50 gallons from the olive press, there were only 20. I rewarded all your labor with rust, mildew, and hail. Yet, even so, you would not come back to me," says the Lord.

¹⁸⁻¹⁹"But now note this. From today, this 24th day of the month, I will bless you. I will do this because the base of the Lord's Temple is finished. So from this day onward I will bless you. I am giving you this promise now! It is yours, even before you have begun to rebuild the Temple structure! It is yours, even before you have harvested all your crops. This includes your grapes, figs, pomegranates, and olives. From this day I will bless you."

²⁰Another message came to Haggai from the Lord that same day.

²¹"Give Zerubbabel, the governor of Judah, a message. Say to him, 'I am about to shake the heavens and the earth. ²²I am going to overthrow thrones. I will destroy the strength of the kingdoms of the nations. I will overthrow their armies. And everyone will kill one another. ²³When that happens, I will honor you, O Zerubbabel my servant. You will be like a signet ring upon my finger. For I have specially chosen you,'" says the Lord of Heaven's armies.

ZECHARIAH

*Zechariah lived about the same time as Haggai.
Both men told their people to rebuild God's house,
the Temple. It had been destroyed many years before
by the Babylonians. But now they could rebuild it.
So why didn't they do it? There were many excuses.
Zechariah and Haggai did not think any of them
were good excuses. God would bless his people when
they built his house. Zechariah also tells about the
time when Jesus will come. He tells how Jesus will
ride into Jerusalem on a donkey. He tells how Jesus
will be betrayed for 30 pieces of silver. He tells how
the 30 pieces will be used to buy a potter's field. But
Zechariah lived 500 years before Jesus came. Only
God could have told him these things.*

Return to the Lord

1 Zechariah was given messages from the Lord. He was the son of Berechiah. Berechiah was the son of Iddo. These messages came in November, during the second year of King Darius's reign.

²The Lord was very angry with your fathers. ³But he will turn to you again. And he will favor you if only you come back to him. ⁴Don't be like your fathers were! The earlier prophets asked them to turn from all their evil ways.

"Come back to me," the Lord God said. But they wouldn't listen. They paid no attention at all.

⁵⁻⁶Your fathers and their prophets are now long dead. But remember the lesson they learned: *God's Word stands forever!* It caught up with them and punished them. Then at last they turned from their sins.

"We have gotten what we deserved from God," they said. "He has done just as he warned us he would."

Zechariah Sees a Man among the Trees

⁷Another message from the Lord came to Zechariah. He was the son of Berechiah. Berechiah was the son of Iddo. The message came the next February, still in the second year of King Darius's reign.

⁸During the night I had a vision from God. I saw a man sitting on a red horse. They were standing among the myrtle trees beside a river. Behind him were other horses, red and bay and white. Each horse had a rider.

⁹An angel stood beside me. I asked him, "Sir, what are all those horses for?"

"I'll tell you," he replied.

¹⁰Then the rider on the red horse gave

me an answer. He said, "The Lord has sent them to patrol the earth for him."

¹¹Then the other riders gave a report to the Angel of the Lord. "We have patrolled the whole earth. Everywhere there is prosperity and peace."

¹²When he heard this, the Angel of the Lord prayed. He said, "O Lord of Heaven's armies! You have been angry with Jerusalem and Judah's cities for 70 years. How long will it be until you again show mercy to them?"

¹³The Lord answered the angel who stood beside me. He spoke words of comfort.

¹⁴Then the angel said, "Shout out this message from the Lord! He says, 'Don't you think I care about what has happened to Judah and Jerusalem? I am as jealous as a husband for his captive wife. ¹⁵I am very angry with the heathen nations sitting around at ease. But I was only a little angry with my people. For the nations hurt them far too much.' ¹⁶So the Lord makes says this, 'I have come to Jerusalem with mercy. My Temple will be rebuilt,' says the Lord of Heaven's armies. 'So will the whole city of Jerusalem.' ¹⁷Say it again! 'The Lord of Heaven's armies says that the cities of Israel will be rebuilt. The Lord will again comfort Jerusalem. He will bless her and live in her.'"

Zechariah Sees Four Horns and Four Blacksmiths

¹⁸Then I looked and saw four animal horns!

¹⁹"What are these?" I asked the angel. He replied, "They stand for four world powers. They are the nations that have scattered Judah, Israel, and Jerusalem."

²⁰Then the Lord showed me four blacksmiths.

²¹"What have these men come to do?" I asked.

The angel replied, "They have come to take hold of the four horns that scattered Judah. They will hammer them on the anvil and throw them away."

Zechariah Sees a Man with a Yardstick

2 Then I looked around me again. I saw a man carrying a yardstick in his hand.

²"Where are you going?" I asked.

"I'm going to measure Jerusalem," he said. "I want to see whether it is big enough for all the people!"

³Then the angel who was talking to me went away. As he left, he met another angel coming toward him.

⁴"Give a message to this young man," said the other angel. "Jerusalem will be full of people! She will not have any walls. Yet all the people and all their many cattle will be safe. ⁵For the Lord himself will be a wall of fire around Jerusalem. He will be the glory of the city."

⁶⁻⁷The Lord has a message to the exiles in Babylon. "Come, flee from the land of the north," says the Lord. "I scattered you to the winds. But I will bring you back again. Come away, come to Jerusalem now!"

⁸"The Lord of Glory has sent me against the nations that hurt you. For he who hurts you, hurts what is most precious to the Lord!

⁹"I will smash them with my fist! Their slaves will be their rulers! *Then you will know it was the Lord who sent me.* ¹⁰Sing, Jerusalem, and rejoice! For I have come to live among you," says the Lord. ¹¹⁻¹²"At that time many nations will follow the Lord. And they too will be my people. I will live among them all. *Then you will know it was the Lord who sent me to you.* And Judah will be the Lord's special place in the Holy Land. For God will once more choose to bless Jerusalem.

¹³"Be silent, all mankind, before the Lord. For he has been called from his holy dwelling."

Zechariah Sees the High Priest

3 Then the Angel showed me another vision. I saw Joshua the High Priest standing before the Angel of the Lord. And Satan was there too. He was at the Angel's right hand. He was accusing Joshua of many things.

²And the Lord said to Satan, "I rebuke you, Satan. For I have decided to be merciful to Jerusalem and Joshua. They are like a burning stick pulled out of the fire."

³Joshua's clothing was dirty as he stood before the Angel of the Lord. ⁴Then the Angel said to the others standing there, "Take off his dirty clothing." And turning to Joshua he said, "See, I have taken away your sins. And now I am giving you these fine new clothes."

⁵⁻⁶Then I said, "Could he also have a clean turban on his head?" So they gave him one.

Then the Angel of the Lord spoke very seriously to Joshua. He said, ⁷"The Lord of Heaven's armies is making a declaration. He says, 'Follow the paths I set for you. Do all I tell you to do. Then I will put you in charge of my Temple, to keep it holy. And I will let you come into my presence with these angels. ⁸Listen to me, O Joshua the High Priest. Listen, all you other priests. You are signs of the good things to come. Don't you see? Joshua stands for my servant the Branch, whom I will send. ⁹He will be the Foundation Stone of the Temple that Joshua is standing beside. I will write a message on it seven times. It will say, *I will take away the sins of this land in a single day.* ¹⁰After that,' the Lord says, 'you will all live in peace. Each of you will have your own home. And you will be able to ask your neighbors to enjoy it with you.'"

Zechariah Sees the Golden Lampstand

4 Then the angel who had been talking with me came back. He woke me up like a man is awakened from sleep.

²"What do you see now?" he asked.

I answered, "I see a gold lampstand holding seven lamps. At the top there is a bowl for the olive oil. This oil feeds the lamps. It flows into them through seven tubes. ³And I see two olive trees carved upon the lampstand. There is one on each side of the bowl. ⁴What is it, sir?" I asked. "What does this mean?"

⁵"Don't you know?" the angel asked.

"No, sir," I said, "I don't."

⁶Then he said, "This is God's message to Zerubbabel: 'You will not succeed by your own strength and power. You will succeed because of my Spirit, even though you are few and weak.' This is what the Lord of Heaven's armies says. ⁷So no mountain, however high, can stand before Zerubbabel! For it will flatten out before him! And Zerubbabel will finish building this Temple. When this happens, there will be shouts of thanks for God's mercy and grace."

**Don't try to succeed
unless God is helping you**

*You will not succeed by your
own strength and power.
You will succeed because of
my Spirit, even though you are
few and weak.*

Zechariah 4:6

---

⁸I was given another message from the Lord.

⁹It said, "Zerubbabel laid the foundation of this Temple. And he will finish it. Then you will know these messages are from the Lord of Heaven's armies. ¹⁰Do not look down on this small beginning. For the eyes of the Lord rejoice to see the work begin. They see the plumbline in the hand of Zerubbabel. For these seven lamps stand for the eyes of the Lord. These eyes see all around the world."

¹¹Then I asked about the two olive trees on each side of the lampstand. ¹²And I asked about the two olive branches. These branches emptied oil into gold bowls through two gold tubes.

¹³"Don't you know?" he asked.

"No, sir," I said.

¹⁴Then he told me, "They stand for two special men. They have been chosen to serve the Lord of all the earth."

Zechariah Sees a Flying Scroll

5 I looked up again and saw a scroll flying through the air.

²"What do you see?" he asked.

"A flying scroll!" I replied. "It seems to be about 30 feet long and 15 feet wide!"

3"This scroll," he said, "stands for God's curse. This curse is going out over the whole land. It says that all who

Chariots
ZECHARIAH 6:1-8

Important people like presidents usually ride in big, long cars. They are called limousines. In Bible times there were no limousines. Some kings had only a horse or a donkey. But most kings had a chariot. Sometimes other important people had chariots, too. When people saw a chariot, they knew the man in it was important. Chariots helped people go places fast. Chariots were also used in battles. They were pulled by one or two horses. Chariots were used like tanks are used today. It was hard to fight a man in a fast-moving chariot. You wouldn't want a soldier in a chariot to chase you, would you? But it might be fun to ride in a chariot.

steal and lie have been sentenced to death.

4"I am sending this curse into the home of every thief. And it will go to everyone who swears falsely by my name. And my curse will stay upon his

home and destroy it." The Lord of Heaven's armies has spoken.

Zechariah Sees a Flying Basket
5Then the angel left me for awhile. But he came back and said, "Look up! Something is flying through the sky!"

6"What is it?" I asked.

He replied, "It is a bushel basket filled with sin. It's the sin that everyone throughout the land is doing."

7Suddenly the heavy lead cover on the basket was lifted off. I could see a woman sitting inside the basket!

8He said, "The woman stands for wickedness." Then he pushed her back into the basket. And he clamped down the heavy lid again.

9Then I saw two women flying toward us. They had wings like those of a stork. They took the bushel basket and flew off with it, high in the sky.

10"Where are they taking her?" I asked the angel.

11He replied, "To Babylon, where they will build a temple for the basket. People will worship it there!"

Zechariah Sees Four Chariots
6Then I looked up again and saw four chariots. They were coming from between what looked like two mountains made of brass. 2The first chariot was pulled by red horses. The second one was pulled by black ones. 3The third was pulled by white horses. And the fourth was pulled by dappled-gray horses.

4"And what are these, sir?" I asked the angel.

5He replied, "These are the four heavenly spirits. They stand before the Lord of all the earth. They are going out to do his work. 6The chariot pulled by the black horses will go north. And the one pulled by white horses will follow it there. The dappled-gray horses will go south."

7The red horses were impatient to get going. They were eager to patrol back and forth across the earth. So the Lord said, "Go! Begin your patrol." So they left at once.

⁸Then the Lord called to me. He said, "Those who went north have carried out my judgment. My anger is now satisfied."

The Symbolic Crowning of Joshua

⁹The Lord gave me another message.

¹⁰⁻¹¹He said, "Heldai, Tobijah, and Jedaiah is coming from Babylon. They will bring gifts of silver and gold from the Jews exiled there. The same day they come, meet them at the home of Josiah. Josiah is Zephaniah's son. They will stay there. Take their gifts. Use them to make a crown from the silver and gold. Then put the crown on the head of Joshua the High Priest. Joshua is Josedech's son. ¹²Tell him what the Lord says: 'You stand for the Man who will come. His name is "The Branch." He will grow up from himself. And he will build the Temple of the Lord. ¹³To him belongs the royal title. He will rule both as King and as Priest. And there will be perfect harmony between his two roles!'

¹⁴"Then put the crown in the Temple of the Lord. May it honor those who gave it: Heldai, Tobijah, Jedaiah, and also Josiah. ¹⁵Those who have come from so far away stand for many others. For one day they will come from distant lands to rebuild the Lord's Temple. And when this happens, you will know that the Lord has sent me. All this will happen if you obey the commands of the Lord your God."

Be Just and Kind

7 Another message came to me from the Lord. It came in November, during the fourth year of King Darius's reign.

²The Jews at Bethel had sent a group of men to Jerusalem. This group was headed by Sharezer and Regem-melech. They came to the Temple to seek the Lord's blessing. ³And they had a question for the priests and prophets. They wanted to know if they should keep up an old custom. It was the custom of fasting and mourning during the month of August.

⁴The Lord gave them an answer.

⁵He said, "When you go back to Bethel, you must speak to all your people and priests. Say to them, 'Think back to those 70 years of exile. During that time, you fasted and mourned in August and October. But did you do it for me? No, not at all! ⁶And even now in your holy feasts to God, you don't think of me. ⁷Many years ago the prophets warned you about this. At that time Jerusalem and her suburbs were wealthy and filled with people. Back then, the prophets warned them that this would lead to their ruin.'"

⁸⁻⁹Then this message from the Lord came to Zechariah. "Tell them to be honest and fair," the Lord said. "Tell them not to take bribes. They must be merciful and kind to everyone. ¹⁰Tell them to stop taking advantage of widows and orphans. Tell them to be fair to foreigners and poor people. They must stop making evil plans against each other. ¹¹Your fathers would not listen to this message. They turned away. They put their fingers in their ears to keep from hearing me. ¹²They hardened their hearts like stone. They refused to hear the law and the words the Lord had given them. And these were sent to them by his Spirit through the prophets! That is why such great anger came down on them from God. ¹³I called, but they would not listen. So when they cried to me, I turned away. ¹⁴I scattered them as with a whirlwind among the distant nations. Their land became empty. No one even traveled through it. The Pleasant Land became barren."

Judah Will Be Blessed

8 Again the Lord's message came to me. ²The Lord of Heaven's armies says, "I have a burning love for Jerusalem. And I am very angry. Jerusalem's enemies have done too much to her. ³Now I am going to come back to my land. And I myself will live in Jerusalem. Then Jerusalem will be called 'The Faithful City.' And she will be called 'The Holy Mountain'

and 'The Mountain of the Lord of Heaven's Armies.'"

⁴The Lord says that Jerusalem will have peace. Once again old men and women will hobble through her streets on canes. ⁵And the streets will be filled with boys and girls at play.

⁶The Lord says, "This probably seems unbelievable to you. This is because you are not great. But it is no great thing for me. ⁷You can be sure that I will save my people from east and west. ⁸I will bring them home again to live safely in Jerusalem. They will be my people. And I will be their God in truth and justice!"

⁹The Lord says, "Get on with the job and finish it! You have been listening long enough! You have not done anything since you laid the Temple's foundation. The prophets have told you about the blessings that await you when it's finished. ¹⁰Before the work began there were no jobs and poor wages. There was no safety at all. If you left the city, you could not be sure you would ever come back. This was because there was so much crime.

¹¹"But it is all so different now!" says the Lord of Heaven's armies. ¹²"For I am planting peace and success among you. Your crops will prosper. The grapevines will be weighted down with fruit. The ground will be rich, with plenty of rain. All these blessings will be given to the people left in the land. ¹³'May you be as poor as Judah,' the heathen used to say! But no longer! For now Judah is a word of blessing, not a curse. 'May you be as rich and happy as Judah is,' they'll say. So don't be afraid or sad! Get on with building the Temple! ¹⁴⁻¹⁵If you do, I will surely bless you. And don't think that I might change my mind. I did what I said I would when your fathers made me angry. I promised to punish them! And I won't change this decision of mine to bless you. ¹⁶But you must do your part. Tell the truth! Be fair! Live at peace with everyone! ¹⁷Don't harm others! Don't swear that something is true when it isn't! How I hate all these things!" says the Lord.

¹⁸Another message came to me from the Lord of Heaven's armies.

¹⁹The Lord said, "The fasts you kept in July, August, October, and January are now ended. They will be changed to happy feasts if you love truth and peace! ²⁰⁻²¹People from around the world will come to Jerusalem. They will come from many cities to attend these feasts. People will write their friends in other cities. They will say, 'Let's go to Jerusalem. Let's ask the Lord to bless us and be merciful to us. I'm going! Please come with me. Let's go now!' ²²Yes, many people, even strong nations, will come to the Lord in Jerusalem. They will ask for his blessing and help. ²³In those days 10 men from different nations will clutch the robe of one Jew. And they will say, 'Let us be with you. For we know that God is with you.'"

Israel's Enemies Will Be Punished

9 This is the message about God's curse on the lands of Hadrach and Damascus. For the Lord is closely watching all mankind, as well as Israel.

²"How terrible it will be for Hamath, near Damascus. And Tyre and Zidon are doomed, even though they are very wise. ³Tyre has made herself ready to fight. She has become so rich that silver is like dirt to her. And fine gold is like dust in the streets. ⁴Yet the Lord will give her up. And he will throw her walls and forts into the sea. And she will be set on fire and burned to the ground.

⁵"Ashkelon will see it happen and be filled with fear. Gaza will huddle in fear. Ekron will shake with terror. Their hopes that Tyre might stop the enemy will all be destroyed. Gaza will be conquered, and her king will be killed. Ashkelon will be totally destroyed.

⁶"Foreigners will take over the city of Ashdod. She is the richest city of the Philistines. ⁷I will take her idol worship out of her mouth. I will pull from her teeth the sacrifices she eats with blood. Everyone left will worship God. They will be taken into Israel as a new family. The Philistines of Ekron will marry the Jews. This will be just as the Jebusites did so long ago. ⁸And I will surround my Temple like a guard. I will keep armies from coming into Israel. I am closely

watching their movements. And I will keep them away. No foreign armies will again overrun my people's land.

The King Is Coming

⁹"Rejoice greatly, O my people! Shout with joy! For look, your King is coming! He is the Righteous One, the Victor! Yet he is lowly, riding on a donkey's colt! ¹⁰I will disarm all peoples of the earth, including my people in Israel. And the King will bring peace among the nations. His realm will stretch from sea to sea. It will reach from the river to the ends of the earth.

¹¹"I have saved you from death in a waterless pit. I did this because of the covenant I made with you. And this covenant was sealed with blood. ¹²Come to the place of safety, all you prisoners. For there is yet hope! I am making you a promise right now. I will give you two mercies for each one of your troubles! ¹³Judah, you are my bow! Israel, you are my arrow! Both of you will be my sword. You'll be like the sword of a mighty soldier fighting the sons of Greece."

¹⁴The Lord will lead his people as they fight! His arrows will fly like lightning. The Lord God will sound the trumpet call. He will go out against his enemies like a whirlwind from the desert. ¹⁵He will defend his people, and they will overcome their enemies. They will tread them under their feet. They will taste victory and shout with triumph. They will kill all their enemies. ¹⁶⁻¹⁷The Lord their God will save his people in that day. He will be like a Shepherd caring for his sheep. They will shine in his land as jewels in a crown. How great it all will be! There will be plenty of grain and grapes. It will make the young men and girls happy.

God's Promises for Israel and Judah

10 Ask the Lord for rain in the springtime. And he will answer with lightning and showers. Every field will become a rich pasture. ²How foolish to ask the idols for anything like that! The words of fortune tellers are all lies. What comfort is there in promises that don't

come true? Judah and Israel have been led astray. They wander like lost sheep. Everyone attacks them, for they have no shepherd to protect them.

³"My anger burns against your 'shepherds' who are your leaders. I will punish them. For the Lord of Heaven's armies has come to help his flock of Judah. I will make them strong like a proud horse in battle. ⁴From them will come the Cornerstone. He will be the Peg on which all hope hangs. He will be the Bow that wins the battle. He will be the Ruler over all the earth. ⁵They will be mighty soldiers for God. They will grind their enemies' faces into the dust. The Lord is with them as they fight. Their enemy is doomed.

⁶"I will make Judah strong. Yes, and I will do the same for Israel. I will restore them because I love them. It will be as though I had never given them up. For I, the Lord their God, will hear their cries. ⁷They will be like mighty soldiers. They will be happy, like people with wine. Their children, too, will see the mercies of the Lord and be glad. Their hearts will rejoice in the Lord. ⁸When I whistle to them, they'll come running. For I have bought them back again. Only a few still remain. But their nation will grow again to the size it once was. ⁹In the past I scattered them like seeds among the nations. But they will remember me and come back again to God. With all their children, they will come home again to Israel. ¹⁰I will bring them back from Egypt and Assyria. I will make a home for them in Gilead and Lebanon. There will hardly be room for all of them! ¹¹They will pass safely through the sea of trouble. For the waves will be held back. And the Nile River will become dry. The rule of Assyria and Egypt over my people will end."

¹²The Lord says, "I will make my people strong with power from me! They will go wherever they wish. And wherever they go they will be under my personal care."

11 Open your doors to judgment, O Lebanon. You will be destroyed as though by fire raging through your forests. ²Cry, O cypress trees, for all the

ruined cedars. The tallest and most beautiful of them are fallen. Cry in fear, you oaks of Bashan, as you watch the forests cut down. ³Listen to the cries of Israel's leaders, those evil shepherds. For their riches are gone. Hear the young lions roaring. They are crying princes. For their great Jordan Valley lies in ruins.

The Two Shepherds

⁴The Lord my God said to me, "Go and take a job as a shepherd. Your flock should be made fat to be killed. ⁵This will show how my people have been bought and killed by evil leaders. And these leaders go unpunished! They sell their people and say, 'Thank God, now I am rich!' ⁶I won't spare them either," says the Lord. "I will let them fall into the hands of their own wicked leaders. And their leaders will kill them. They will turn the land into a wilderness. I will not protect it from them."

⁷So I took two shepherd's staffs. I named one Grace and the other Union. And I fed the flock as I had been told to do. ⁸And I got rid of their three evil shepherds in one month. But I became impatient with these sheep. And they were tired of me.

⁹So I told them, "I won't be your shepherd any more. If you die, you die. If you are killed, I don't care. Go ahead and destroy yourselves!"

¹⁰And I took my staff called Grace and snapped it in two. This showed that I had broken my agreement to lead and protect them. ¹¹That was the end of the agreement. Those who bought and sold sheep saw what I did. They knew that God was telling them something through this.

¹²Then I spoke to their leaders. I said, "If you like, give me my pay. Give me whatever I am worth. But only if you want to."

So they counted out 30 little silver coins as my wages.

¹³And the Lord told me, "Use it to buy a field from the pottery makers. This is the great price at which they valued me!"

I took the 30 coins. And I threw them into the Temple for the pottery makers.

¹⁴Then I broke my other staff, Union. I did this to show that the brotherhood between Judah and Israel was broken.

¹⁵Then the Lord told me to go again and get a shepherd's job. This time I was to act the part of a worthless, wicked shepherd.

¹⁶And he said, "This is also supposed to show something. It will show how I will give this nation a worthless shepherd. He will not care for the dying ones. He won't look after the young. He will not heal the broken bones or feed the healthy ones. He will not carry the lame that cannot walk. Instead, he will eat the fat ones. He will even tear off their feet. ¹⁷How terrible it will be for this worthless shepherd! For he doesn't care for the flock. God's sword will cut his arm and pierce through his right eye. His arm will become useless and his right eye blinded."

God Defends His People

12 The Lord says that this is what will happen to Israel. This is the Lord who stretched out the heavens. It was he who laid the earth's foundation. This is the Lord who made the spirit of man within him.

²"Jerusalem will be a cup of poison to the nations that come against her. And when armies come against Jerusalem, they will come against Judah. ³Jerusalem will be a heavy stone. She will be a burden to the world. The nations of the earth will come together to try to move her. But they will all be crushed.

⁴"In that day," says the Lord, "I will make fools of the armies coming against her. I will watch over the people of Judah. But I will make all her enemies blind.

⁵"Those in Judah will say, 'The people of Jerusalem are strong. For their strength is in the Lord their God.'

⁶"In that day I will make those in Judah like a little fire. But that little fire will set the forest aflame. They will burn up all the nations around them. But Jerusalem will stand unmoved. ⁷The Lord will give victory to the rest of Judah first. Then Jerusalem will be victorious.

And the people of Jerusalem and the royal line of David won't be proud.

8"The Lord will defend the people of Jerusalem. The weakest among them will be as strong as King David! And the royal line will be great like God. They will be like the Angel of the Lord who goes before them! 9For my plan is to destroy all the nations that come against Jerusalem.

10"Then I will pour out the spirit of grace and prayer. It will come upon all the people of Israel and Jerusalem. They will look on the one they have pierced. They will mourn for him as for an only son. They will grieve for him as for an oldest child who died. 11There will be great sadness and mourning in Jerusalem at that time. It will be even greater than the mourning for the godly King Josiah. Josiah was killed in the valley of Megiddo.

12-14"All of Israel will cry in deep sadness. The whole nation will be bowed down with grief. The king, prophets, priests, and people will be sad. Each family will go into mourning. Everyone will face their sadness alone.

God's Fountain of Forgiveness

13 "At that time a Fountain will be opened to those in Israel and Jerusalem. This Fountain will make them clean from all their sins."

2The Lord of Heaven's armies says, "In that day I will destroy every form of idol worship in the land. Even the names of the idols will be forgotten. All false prophets and fortune tellers will be wiped out. 3And if anyone begins false prophecy again, his own parents will kill him! 'You must die,' they will tell him. 'For you are speaking lies in the name of the Lord.'

4"No one will brag then about being a prophet! No one will wear prophet's clothes to try to fool the people any more.

5"'No,' he will say, 'I am not a prophet. I am a farmer. Farming has been my work from my earliest youth.'

6"If someone asks, 'Then what are these scars on your chest and your back?'

He will say, 'I got into a fight at the home of a friend!'

7"Awake, O sword, against my Shepherd. This man is my friend," says the Lord of Heaven's armies. "Strike down the Shepherd and the sheep will scatter. But I will come back and comfort and care for the lambs. 8Two-thirds of all the nation of Israel will be cut off and die. But a third will be left in the land. 9I will bring the third that stay through the fire. In this way I will make them pure. They will be refined and made pure by fire. They will be made pure just as gold and silver are. They will call on my name, and I will hear them. I will say, 'These are my people.' And they will say, 'The Lord is our God.'"

The Lord Will Rule over All the Earth

14 Watch, for the day of the Lord is coming soon! On that day the Lord will gather together the nations to fight Jerusalem. The city will be taken, the houses looted, the loot divided, and the women raped. Half the people will be taken away as slaves. Half will remain in what is left of the city.

3Then the Lord will go out ready for war. He will fight against those nations. 4That day his feet will stand upon the Mount of Olives, east of Jerusalem. And the Mount of Olives will split apart. The split will make a very wide valley running from east to west. For half the mountain will move toward the north. The other half will move toward the south. 5You will escape through that valley. For it will reach across to the city gate. Yes, you will get away just as your people did long ago. They ran from the earthquake in the days of Uzziah, king of Judah. Then the Lord my God will come. And all his saints and angels will come with him.

6The sun and moon and stars will no longer shine. 7Yet there will be daylight all the time! Only the Lord knows how! There will be no normal day and night. At evening time it will still be light. 8Life-giving waters will flow out from Jerusalem. Half of the waters will flow toward the Dead Sea. And half will flow toward the Mediterranean. They will flow at all times, both in winter and in summer.

⁹And the Lord will be King over all the earth. In that day there will be one Lord. His name alone will be worshiped. ¹⁰All the land from Geba (Judah's northern border) will be one great plain. That plain will stretch all the way to Rimmon (Judah's southern border). But Jerusalem will be on an elevated site. It will cover a great area. It will be all the way from Benjamin's Gate to the site of the old gate. And it will extend to the Corner Gate. Then it will be from the Tower of Hananel to the king's winepresses. ¹¹And Jerusalem will be full of people and safe at last. It will never again be cursed or destroyed.

¹²And the Lord will send a plague on all the people who fought Jerusalem. They will become like walking dead men. Their eyes will shrivel in their sockets. Their tongues will decay in their mouths.

¹³They will be driven by fear and terror. The Lord will cause them to panic. They will fight against each other in hand-to-hand combat. ¹⁴The people of Judah will fight at Jerusalem. The riches of all the nearby nations will be gathered. They will get great amounts of gold and silver and fine clothing. ¹⁵This same plague will strike all the animals in the enemy camp. This includes horses, mules, camels, and donkeys.

¹⁶In the end, there will be some nations left. They will go up to Jerusalem each year to worship the King, the Lord of Heaven's armies. They will celebrate a time of thanks. ¹⁷No nation in all the world will refuse to come to Jerusalem. For if they don't worship the King, the Lord, they will have no rain. ¹⁸But if Egypt does not come, God will punish her with some other plague. ¹⁹Egypt and the other nations will all be punished if they refuse to come.

²⁰In that day the horses' bells will have written on them, "Holy to the Lord." And the cooking pots in the Lord's Temple will be as holy as the bowls beside the altar. ²¹Every container in Jerusalem and Judah will be holy to the Lord. All who come to worship may use any of them free of charge. They may boil their sacrifices in them. No more unholy people will go into the Temple of the Lord of Heaven's armies!

MALACHI

There are two ways for God's people to live. They can obey God and do what pleases him. Or they can live like they don't care about God. Malachi's people were living like they didn't care about God. Many years before, they had been captured. They were taken to Babylon. There they lived and worked, far from home. But God let them come home again. They rebuilt the Temple. They worshiped God there. But they became bored. They lost their excitement to live for God. Malachi told them to get back to God. He told about a Savior who was coming. He would bring hope for the future. We know that this Savior is Jesus. Jesus wants us to obey God and please him. He wants to help us live with God forever. He does not want us to live like we have forgotten about him or don't care about him.

God Loves His People

1 Here is the Lord's message to Israel. It was sent through the prophet Malachi.

²⁻³"I have loved you very deeply," says the Lord.

But you say, "Really? When was this?"

This is the Lord's reply: "I showed my love for you by loving your father, Jacob. But I didn't have to. I even rejected his brother, Esau. I have destroyed Esau's mountain country. I have given his land to the jackals of the desert. ⁴And suppose his children should say, 'We will rebuild the ruins.' Then the Lord would say, 'You can try to if you like. But I will destroy it again.' For their country is named 'The Land of Wickedness.' And their people are called 'Those Whom God Does Not Forgive.'"

⁵O Israel, lift your eyes to see what God is doing around the world. Then you will say, "Truly, the Lord's great power goes far beyond our borders!"

The Priests Don't Measure Up to God's Standards

⁶"A son honors his father, and a servant honors his master. I am your Father and Master. Yet, O priests, you don't honor me! You look down on my name."

"Who? Us?" you say. "When do we ever look down on your name?"

⁷"When you offer unclean sacrifices on my altar."

Then you say, "Unclean sacrifices? When have we ever done a thing like that?"

"You do it every time you say, 'Don't bother bringing anything very good to offer to God!' ⁸You lead the people astray. You say, 'Lame animals are all right to give on the Lord's altar. Even the sick and the blind ones are all right.' And you claim this isn't evil? Try it on your governor sometime. Give him gifts like that. Then see how happy he is!

⁹"'God have mercy on us,' you say. 'God be kind to us!' But then you bring a gift that he would not accept. Why should he show you any favor at all?

¹⁰"Oh, to find one priest among you who would refuse this kind of sacrifice! I have no pleasure in you," says the Lord of Heaven's armies. "I will not accept your offerings.

¹¹"But my name will be honored by the Gentiles from morning till night. They will offer sweet incense and pure offerings in honor of my name. For my name will be great among the nations," says the Lord. ¹²"But you dishonor my name. You say that my altar is not important. You tell people to bring cheap, sick animals to offer on it.

¹³"You say, 'Oh, it's hard to serve the Lord and do what he asks.' And you don't follow the rules he has given you to obey. Think of it! Stolen animals, lame and sick, given as offerings to God! Should I accept such offerings as these?" asks the Lord. ¹⁴"Cursed is that man who promises a fine ram and gives a sick one instead. Should the Lord accept such a sacrifice? For I am a Great King," says the Lord of Heaven's armies. "My name will be greatly honored among the Gentiles."

God Warns His Priests

2 Listen, you priests, to this warning from the Lord. He says, "You must change your ways and give glory to my name. If not, I will send terrible punishment upon you. Instead of giving you blessings, I will give you curses. Indeed, I have cursed you already. For you haven't shown respect for the things that are most important to me.

³"Take note that I will punish your children after you are gone. I will spread on your faces the dung of these animals you offer me. And I will throw you out like dung. ⁴Then at last you will know it was I who sent you this warning. I am warning you to follow the covenant I made with your father Levi," says the Lord. ⁵"The purpose of this covenant was to give you life and peace. You were to follow it and show respect for me. ⁶The priests passed on to the people all the truth they got from me. They did not lie or cheat. They walked with me, living good and righteous lives. They turned many from their lives of sin.

⁷"The lips of priests should flow with the knowledge of God. Then people should come to them to learn God's laws. The priests are the messengers of the Lord. People should come to them for guidance. ⁸But they shouldn't come to you! For you have left God's paths. Your 'guidance' has caused many to stumble in sin. You have damaged the covenant of Levi," says the Lord. ⁹"So now I have made you hated by all the people. For you have not obeyed me. You let your friends break the law without correcting them."

Be Faithful to Your Wives

¹⁰We are children of the same father, Abraham. We are all created by the same God. And yet we are faithless to each other. We have broken the covenant of our fathers! ¹¹In Judah, in Israel, and in Jerusalem, there is evil. The men of Judah have defiled God's holy and beloved Temple. They did this by marrying heathen women who worship idols. ¹²May the Lord cut off from his covenant everyone who has done this!

¹³Yet you cover the altar with your tears. You are upset that the Lord doesn't notice your offerings anymore. You are bothered that you are not getting blessings from him. ¹⁴"Why has God left us?" you ask. I'll tell you why. It is because the Lord has seen your evil in divorcing your wives. They had been faithful to you through the years. They were your companions that you promised to care for and keep. ¹⁵You were united to your wife by the Lord. When you married, the two of you became one person in God's sight. And what does he want? Godly children from your union. So guard your passions! Keep faith with the wife of your youth.

[16]For the Lord, the God of Israel, hates divorce. And he hates people who are cruel. So control your passions. Let no one divorce his wife.

[17]You have made the Lord tired with your words.

"Made him tired?" you ask. "How have we made him tired?"

You have done this by saying that evil is good. You have claimed that evil pleases the Lord! You have said that God won't punish us because he doesn't care.

The Coming of the Messiah

3 "Listen! I will send my messenger before me to prepare the way. And then the One you are looking for will come suddenly to his Temple. He is the Messenger of God's covenant. He will bring you great joy. Yes, he is surely coming," says the Lord. [2]"But who can live when he appears? Who can endure his coming? For he is like a hot fire used to purify precious metal. And he can make the dirtiest clothes white again! [3]Like a refiner of silver, he will make the dross burn away. He will purify the Levites, the servants of God. He will refine them like gold or silver. Then, they will do their work for God with pure hearts. [4]Then the Lord will enjoy the offerings from the people of Judah and Jerusalem. The offerings brought to him will be accepted, as they once were long ago. [5]At that time my judgments will be quick and sure. I will quickly judge wicked men who trick the innocent. I will judge people who are unfaithful to their wives. I will punish liars. I will judge all those who cheat their hired hands. I will judge those who hurt widows and orphans. I will punish those who cheat strangers. And I will judge those who do not fear me," says the Lord.

[6]"For I am the Lord. I never change. That is why you are not already destroyed. For my mercy lasts forever.

The People Rob God

[7]"You have not followed my laws from earliest time. Yet you may still come back to me," says the Lord. "Come and I will forgive you.

"But you say, 'We have never even gone away!'

[8]"Will a person rob God? Of course not! But yet you have robbed me!

"But you ask, 'What do you mean? When did we ever rob you, Lord?'

God never changes

For I am the Lord. I never change.

Malachi 3:6

"You robbed me by not giving the tithes and offerings due to me. [9]And so the awesome curse of God is upon you. For your whole nation has been robbing me. [10]Bring all of your tithes into the storehouse for me. Then there will be enough food in my Temple. If you do, I will open up the windows of Heaven for you. I will pour out great blessings. You won't have enough room to take it all in!

"Try it! Let me prove it to you! [11]Your crops will be large. I will guard them from insects and disease. Your grapes won't dry up before they get ripe," says the Lord. [12]"And all nations will call you blessed. You will be a land that is full of happiness. These are the promises of the Lord of Heaven's armies.

[13]"You have said bad things against me," says the Lord.

"But you say, 'What do you mean? What have we said that was bad?'

When we give our offerings to God, he will bless us

Bring all of your tithes into the storehouse for me. If you do, I will open up the windows of Heaven for you. I will pour out great blessings. You won't have enough room to take it all in!

Malachi 3:10

[14-15]"Listen! You have said, 'It is foolish to worship God and obey him. What good does it do to obey his laws? What good does it do to mourn for our sins? As far as we can see, it is the proud who are blessed. For those who do evil prosper. And those who laugh at God are never punished.'"

The Faithful Few

[16]Then those who feared and loved the Lord spoke of him to one another. And the Lord had a Book of Remembrance drawn up. In this book he wrote the names of those who respected and loved him.

[17]"They will be mine," says the Lord. "In that day they will be my very own. I will show mercy to them, just as a man shows mercy to a son who obeys him. [18]Then you will see how God treats good and bad people. You will see how God treats those who serve him and those who don't.

The Great Judgment Day of the Lord

4 "Watch now!" the Lord says. "The day of judgment is coming, burning like a furnace. Proud and evil people will be burned up like straw. They will be burned like a tree, roots and all.

[2]"But for you who fear my name, the Sun of Righteousness will rise. He will come with healing in his wings. And you will go free, jumping with joy like calves let out to pasture. [3]Then you will walk on the wicked as if they were ashes under your feet," says the Lord. [4]"Remember to obey my laws. I gave them to all Israel through my servant Moses on Mount Sinai.

[5]"See, I will send you another prophet like Elijah. He will come before the great and terrible judgment day of God. [6]His preaching will bring fathers and children together again. They will be of one mind and heart. For they will know that they must turn from their sins. If they don't, I will come and bring a curse to their land."

THE
NEW
TESTAMENT

MATTHEW

Suppose you wanted someone to write a book about your life. What kind of person would you choose? Would you choose a person everyone hated? Would you choose a person who cheated others? Would you choose a person who worked for your enemies? That's what Jesus did. He chose Matthew to follow him. Later Matthew wrote a book about the life of Jesus. This was Matthew's most important work for Jesus.

When Jesus first met Matthew, he was a tax collector. His name then was Levi. He was an Israelite. But he made his own people pay taxes to the Romans. The Romans were enemies. They had captured Matthew's people. They ruled over them. The Israelites hated anyone who helped the Romans. So they hated Matthew.

When Matthew met Jesus, he changed. He became a disciple. He stopped cheating people and started doing good. He worked with Jesus and followed him for three years, until Jesus went back to Heaven. That's why he could write a book about Jesus.

This is the book Matthew wrote. He wrote it to help the Jews in Israel know Jesus better. Do you think Matthew's book about Jesus will help you know Jesus better, too?

Jesus' Family Tree

1 These are the ancestors of Jesus Christ. He was a descendant of King David and of Abraham.

2Abraham was the father of Isaac. Isaac was the father of Jacob. Jacob was the father of Judah and his brothers.

3Judah was the father of Perez and Zerah. Tamar was their mother. Perez was the father of Hezron. Hezron was the father of Aram.

4Aram was the father of Amminadab. Amminadab was the father of Nahshon. Nahshon was the father of Salmon.

⁵Salmon was the father of Boaz. Rahab was his mother. Boaz was the father of Obed. Ruth was his mother. Obed was the father of Jesse.

⁶Jesse was the father of King David. David was the father of Solomon. His mother was the widow of Uriah.

⁷Solomon was the father of Rehoboam. Rehoboam was the father of Abijah. Abijah was the father of Asa.

⁸Asa was the father of Jehoshaphat. Jehoshaphat was the father of Joram. Joram was the father of Uzziah.

⁹Uzziah was the father of Jotham. Jotham was the father of Ahaz. Ahaz was the father of Hezekiah.

¹⁰Hezekiah was the father of Manasseh. Manasseh was the father of Amon. Amon was the father of Josiah.

¹¹Josiah was the father of Jehoiachin and his brothers. They were born at the time of the exile to Babylon.

¹²Jehoiachin was the father of Shealtiel. Shealtiel was the father of Zerubbabel.

¹³Zerubbabel was the father of Abiud. Abiud was the father of Eliakim. Eliakim was the father of Azor.

¹⁴Azor was the father of Zadok. Zadok was the father of Achim. Achim was the father of Eliud.

¹⁵Eliud was the father of Eleazar. Eleazar was the father of Matthan. Matthan was the father of Jacob.

¹⁶Jacob was the father of Joseph. Joseph was the husband of Mary, the mother of Jesus the Messiah.

¹⁷So there were 14 generations from Abraham to King David. There were 14 from King David's time to the exile. And there were 14 from the exile in Babylon to the time of Christ.

An Angel Visits Joseph

Joseph was worried. He was engaged to Mary. But he learned that she was going to have a baby. He knew he was not the father. Mary said that God was the baby's father. But who would believe that? Mary could be punished for this. But Joseph loved Mary. He did not want her hurt. He would quietly break their engagement. Then something happened. An angel came to Joseph. This is what the angel said.

¹⁸These are the facts about the birth of Jesus Christ. His mother, Mary, was engaged to be married to Joseph. She was still a virgin, but she found out she was going to have a baby. She became pregnant by the Holy Spirit. ¹⁹Joseph, her fiancé, was a good and kind man. He decided to break the engagement, but to do it quietly. He didn't want to shame her in public.

²⁰He lay awake thinking about this. Then he fell into a dream, and saw an angel standing beside him. "Joseph, son of David," the angel said. "Don't be afraid to take Mary as your wife! For the child within her is from the Holy Spirit. ²¹She will have a Son, and you shall name him Jesus. This means 'Savior,' for he will save his people from their sins. ²²This will fulfill God's message through his prophet. He said, ³'Listen! The virgin shall have a child! She shall give birth to a Son. And he shall be called "Emmanuel." This means, "God is with us."'"

²⁴Then Joseph woke up. And he did just as the angel commanded him. He brought Mary home to be his wife. ²⁵But he did not sleep with her until her Son was born. And Joseph named the baby "Jesus."

Escape to Egypt

What would you think of someone who killed lots of babies? A king wanted to kill only one baby. But he didn't know which one. So he killed all the babies in town. Here's how it happened.

¹³After they were gone, an Angel of the Lord spoke to Joseph in a dream. "Get up and go to Egypt with the baby and his mother," the angel said. "Stay there until I tell you to come back. For King Herod will try to kill the child." ¹⁴That same night he left for Egypt with Mary and the baby. ¹⁵They stayed there until King Herod's death. This fulfilled the prophet's words: "I have called my Son from Egypt."

¹⁶Herod was very angry when he learned that the wise men had disobeyed him. So he sent soldiers to Bethlehem. He ordered them to kill every baby boy two years old and under. He told them to check in the town and on the nearby farms. For the wise men had told him the star first appeared to them two years before. ¹⁷This brutal action of Herod's fulfilled the words of Jeremiah. He said, ¹⁸"Screams of pain come from Ramah. There is much crying and sadness. Rachel is crying for her children. She cannot be comforted, for they are dead."

¹⁹When Herod died, an Angel of the Lord spoke to Joseph in a dream. He was still in Egypt at the time. The angel said, ²⁰"Get up and take the baby and his mother back to Israel. Those who were trying to kill the child are dead."

²¹So he went back to Israel right away with Jesus and his mother. ²²But on the way he became afraid. This was because he heard that the new king was Herod's son, Archelaus. Then, in another dream, he was warned not to go to Judea. So they went on to Galilee instead. ²³They went to the town of Nazareth and settled there. This fulfilled the words of the prophets about the Messiah. They had said, "He shall be called a Nazarene."

- *Remember:* Who talked to Joseph in a dream? (2:13) What did he tell Joseph to do? Why? (2:13) Did Joseph do it? (2:14) Who killed all the babies of Bethlehem? (2:16) Whom do you think he really wanted to kill? (2:13) Why would Jesus be called a Nazarene? (2:23)

- *Discover:* Look up Jeremiah 31:15 in your Bible. Jeremiah said this 600 years before this story happened. How do you think he knew what to say?

- *Apply:* God knows what will happen 600 years from now. He also knows what will happen next week. He knows what will happen next year. He knows what will happen when you grow up. Why is that a good reason to trust in God and pray to him?

- *What's next?* Where did Jesus grow up? What kind of boy was he? Do you think you would have liked him? Would you like to know? You'll find out in Luke 2:39-40. ■

John the Baptist Preaches about Jesus

3 While they were living in Nazareth, John the Baptist began preaching in the Judean desert. He said, ²"Turn from your sins! Turn to God! For the Kingdom of Heaven is coming soon." ³Isaiah the prophet had told about John's preaching long before! He had written, "I hear a shout from the wilderness. It says, 'Make a road ready for the Lord. Smooth out the path where he will walk.'"

⁴John's clothing was made out of camel's hair. He wore a leather belt around his waist. His food was locusts and wild honey. ⁵People from Jerusalem and from all over the Jordan Valley came to hear him preach. In fact, people came from every part of Judea! ⁶When they confessed their sins, he baptized them in the Jordan River.

⁷Many of the Pharisees and Sadducees came to the place John was preaching. John said to them, "You sons of snakes! Who said that you could escape the coming anger of God? ⁸Prove that you have turned from sin by doing good deeds. ⁹Don't think you can get by as

you are! Don't think, 'We are safe because we are Jews, descendants of Abraham.' That proves nothing. God can change these rocks here into Jews!

10"And even now the axe of God's judgment is lifted to chop down trees. Every tree that doesn't bear fruit will be chopped and burned in the fire.

11"With water I baptize those who turn away from their sins. But someone else is coming who is far greater than I am. He is so great that I am not worthy to carry his shoes! He shall baptize you with the Holy Spirit and with fire. 12He will separate the chaff from the grain. He will burn the chaff with never-ending fire. And he will store away all the grain."

John Baptizes Jesus

Have you ever seen someone baptized? After Jesus was baptized, something wonderful happened. What was it?

13Then Jesus went from Galilee to the Jordan River. He went there to be baptized by John. 14John didn't want to do it.

"This isn't proper," he said. "I am the one who needs to be baptized by you."

15But Jesus said, "Please do it. For I must do all that is right." So then John baptized him.

16After his baptism, Jesus came up out of the water. Just then, the heavens were opened to him! And he saw the Spirit of God coming down in the form of a dove. 17And a voice from Heaven said, "This is my Son whom I love. I am very pleased with him."

- *Remember:* Who baptized Jesus? (3:13) Where? (3:13) Why do you think John

didn't want to baptize Jesus? (3:14) Someone looked like a dove. Who was this? (3:16) What did God say about Jesus? (3:17) How do you think Jesus pleased God?

- *Discover:* Would you like for God to say that you please him? He has three special gifts for you if you please him. Read about them in Ecclesiastes 2:26.

- *Apply:* Think of three things you can do to please God. Will you do one today, one tomorrow, and one the next day?

- *What's next?* Are you ever tempted to do something wrong? Jesus was tempted, too. But did he do something wrong? Read Matthew 4:1-11. ■

Jesus Is Tempted

Could anyone get Jesus to do something wrong? Satan tried. Did his plan work?

4 Then Jesus was led out into the desert by the Holy Spirit. He went there to be tempted by Satan. 2For 40 days and 40 nights he ate nothing. And he became very hungry. 3Then Satan tempted him to get food. He told Jesus to change stones into loaves of bread.

"It will prove you are the Son of God," he said.

4But Jesus told him, "No! For the Scriptures tell us that bread won't feed men's souls. Obedience to every word of God is what we need."

5Then Satan took him to

Jerusalem. He led Jesus to the roof of the Temple. [6]"Jump off," he said. "Prove you are the Son of God. For the Scriptures say, 'God will send his angels. They will lift you up in their hands. And you will not strike your foot on a rock.' The angels will keep you from being smashed on the rocks below."

[7]Jesus said, "The Scriptures also say not to test the Lord your God!"

[8]Next Satan took him to the top of a very high mountain. He showed him the nations of the world and all their glory. [9]"I'll give it all to you!" he said. "All you have to do is bow down and worship me."

[10]"Get out of here, Satan!" Jesus told him. "The Scriptures say, 'Worship only the Lord God. Obey only him.'"

[11]Then Satan went away. And angels came and took care of Jesus.

- *Remember:* Where was Jesus when Satan tempted him? (4:1) Jesus didn't eat for a long time. How long? (4:2) Satan tempted Jesus to get food. How? (4:3) How did Jesus say no to Satan? (4:4) Satan tempted Jesus another way. How? (4:5-6) How did Jesus say no to Satan? (4:7) Satan tempted Jesus to worship him. How? (4:8-9) How did Jesus say no to Satan? (4:10) Were you cheering for Jesus or Satan? Why?

- *Discover:* Jesus said no to Satan's temptations three times. Each time he gave an answer from the Bible. Is that a good way for you to say no to temptation too?

- *Apply:* Memorize a good Bible verse today. Have you memorized John 3:16? If not, memorize it first. Then memorize John 14:15. The next time you are tempted to do wrong, repeat some of the Bible verses you have learned. This will help you.

- *What's next?* Who followed Jesus first? You'll find out in John 1:35-51. ∎

Jesus Tells People to Turn to God

12-13When Jesus heard that John had been arrested, he left Judea. He went back home to Nazareth in Galilee. But soon he moved to Capernaum, beside the Lake of Galilee. This was close to Zebulun and Naphtali. 14This fulfilled Isaiah's words:

15-16"The land of Zebulun and land of Naphtali are beside the Lake. They lie along the Jordan River. This is Galilee, where so many foreigners live. There the people who sat in darkness have seen a great Light. They sat in the land of death. But the Light broke through upon them."

17From then on, Jesus began to preach. He said, "Turn from sin! Turn back to God! For the Kingdom of Heaven is near."

Four Fishermen Follow Jesus

18One day he was walking along the beach beside the Lake of Galilee. He saw two brothers out in a boat fishing with a net. Their names were Simon, also called Peter, and Andrew. These men caught fish for a living.

We should be kind to others

Happy are the kind and merciful. For they shall be shown mercy.

Matthew 5:7

19Jesus called out, "Come along with me! I will show you how to fish for the souls of men!" 20They left their nets at once and went with him.

21A little farther up the beach he saw two other brothers. Their names were James and John. They were sitting in a boat with their father, Zebedee. They were fixing their fishing nets. He called out to them and asked them to come too. 22At once they stopped their work. And, leaving their father behind, they went with him.

Jesus Preaches and Heals the Sick

23Jesus traveled all through Galilee teaching in the Jewish synagogues. He went everywhere, preaching the Good News about the Kingdom of Heaven.

And he healed every kind of sickness and disease. 24The report of his miracles spread far beyond the borders of Galilee. Sick people were soon coming to be healed from as far away as Syria. And whatever their sickness or pain, he healed them all. He even healed people who had demons in them. And He healed people who were crazy or para-lyzed. 25Great crowds followed him wherever he went. People came from Galilee, the Ten Cities, and Jerusalem. They came from all over Judea. They even came from across the Jordan River.

The Sermon on the Mount

5 One day, Jesus looked out and saw the crowds around him. So he went up the hillside with his disciples. He sat down and taught them there.

3"Happy are those who know how sinful they are!" he told them. "For the Kingdom of Heaven belongs to them. 4Happy are those who mourn and are sad! For they shall be comforted. 5Happy are the humble and lowly! For the whole world belongs to them.

6"Happy are those who want to be fair and good. For they shall be satisfied. 7Happy are the kind and merciful. For they shall be shown mercy. 8Happy are those whose hearts are pure. For they shall see God. 9Happy are those who work hard to bring peace. For they shall be called the sons of God. 10Happy are those who are treated badly because they are good. For the Kingdom of Heaven is theirs.

11"You might be laughed at and treated badly because you follow me. Others might even lie about you. But if this happens, great! 12Be happy about it! Be very glad! For a great reward is waiting for you up in Heaven. And remember, the ancient prophets were treated badly, too.

Be Like Salt and Light

13"You are the salt of the world, to make it a good place. If you lose your flavor, what will happen to the world? And you yourselves will be thrown away! You will be trampled underfoot as useless. 14You are the world's light. You are a city on a hill. You glow in the night for all to see. ¹⁵⁻¹⁶Don't hide your light! Let it shine for all. Let your good deeds glow for all to see. That way they will praise your heavenly Father.

God's Laws Are Important

¹⁷"Don't think I've come to cancel the laws of Moses and the words of the prophets. No, I came to fulfill them. I came to make them all come true. ¹⁸I tell you the truth! Every law in the Book will continue until its purpose is achieved. ¹⁹Someone might break the smallest command. Or he might teach others to do this. But if he does, he shall be the least in the Kingdom of Heaven. But someone might teach God's laws and obey them. If he does, he shall be great in the Kingdom of Heaven.

We do good things so that people will praise God

Don't hide your light! Let it shine for all. Let your good deeds glow for all to see. That way they will praise your heavenly Father.

Matthew 5:15-16

---

²⁰"But I warn you, your goodness must be greater than that of the Pharisees. If it isn't, you won't be able to get into the Kingdom of Heaven at all!

Don't Let Anger Get the Best of You

²¹"Under the laws of Moses the rule was, 'If you murder, you must die.' ²²But I have added to that rule. I say that if you are only *angry,* you are in danger of judgment! You might call your friend a fool. If you do, you are in danger of being brought before the court. And if you curse him, you are in danger of the fires of hell.

²³"Suppose you are standing before the altar in the Temple. You are offering a sacrifice to God. And suddenly you remember that a friend has something against you. ²⁴If this happens, leave your sacrifice there beside the altar. Go and say you are sorry and make up to him. Then come and give your sacrifice to God. ²⁵Come to terms quickly with your enemy before it is too late. If you don't, he might drag you into court. You might be thrown into a prison for owing him money. ²⁶And you will stay there until you have paid the last penny!

Jesus Teaches about Adultery

²⁷"The laws of Moses said, 'You must not commit adultery.' ²⁸But I say that a man might just look at a woman with lust in his eye. If he does, he has already committed adultery with her in his heart. ²⁹So if your eye causes you to sin, cut it out and throw it away. Better for part of you to be destroyed than for all of you to be thrown into hell. ³⁰And if your hand causes you to sin, cut it off and throw it away. Better that than find yourself in hell.

³¹"The law of Moses says, 'Someone might want to get rid of his wife. If he does, he can do this by giving her a divorce letter.' ³²But I say that a man who divorces his wife causes her to commit adultery if she remarries. And the man who marries her commits adultery, too. There is only one good reason for a man to divorce his wife. That is if she sleeps with another man.

A Promise Is Enough

³³"Again, the law of Moses says, 'You shall not break your promises to God. You must fulfill them all.' ³⁴But I say, Don't make any promises! And even to say 'By heavens!' is a holy promise to God. For the heavens are God's throne. ³⁵And if you say 'By the earth!' it is a holy promise. For the earth is his footstool. And don't swear 'By Jerusalem!' For Jerusalem is the capital of the great King. ³⁶Don't even swear 'By my head!' For you can't turn one hair white or black. ³⁷Say just a simple 'Yes, I will' or 'No, I won't.' Your word is enough. To strengthen your promise with a promise shows that something is wrong.

Do Good to Those Who Wrong You

38"The law of Moses says, 'A man might gouge out another man's eye. If this happens, he must pay with his own eye. If a tooth gets knocked out, knock out the tooth of the one who did it.'39But I say don't stand against violence! If you are slapped on one cheek, turn the other one, too. 40Someone might order you to come to court. And your shirt might be taken from you. If this happens, give your coat, too. 41A soldier might demand that you carry his gear for a mile. If this happens, carry it for two. 42Give to those who ask. Don't turn away from those who want to borrow.

Don't stop loving someone who hurts you

Love your enemies, too! Pray for those who treat you badly!

Matthew 5:44

43"There is a saying, 'Love your friends and hate your enemies.' 44But I say love your enemies, too! Pray for those who treat you badly! 45In that way you will be acting as true sons of your Father in Heaven. For he gives his sunlight to both the evil and the good. He sends rain on the just and on the unjust, too. 46If you love only those who love you, what good is that? Even bad people do that much. 47If you are friendly only to your friends, how are you different from anyone else? Even the heathen do that. 48But you are to be perfect, even as your Father in Heaven is perfect.

Help Others without Bragging

6 "Take care! Don't do your good deeds in front of people so they will admire you. If you do, you will lose the reward from your Father in Heaven. 2You might decide to give a gift to a beggar. If you do, don't shout about it like the hypocrites do. They blow trumpets in the synagogues and streets! They want everyone to see the good things they do! I tell you the truth! They have been given all the reward they will ever get. 3But when you do a kind thing for someone,

keep it a secret. Don't tell your left hand what your right hand is doing. 4And your Father, who knows all secrets, will reward you.

Jesus Teaches about Prayer

5"Let me teach you about prayer. When you pray, don't be like the hypocrites. They pretend to be godly by praying in front of everyone. They pray on street corners and in the synagogues. That way everyone can see them. Truly, that is all the reward they will ever get. 6But when you pray, go away by yourself, all alone. Shut the door behind you. Pray to your Father in secret. And your Father, who knows your secrets, will reward you.

7-8"Don't say the same prayer over and over as the heathen do. They think prayers are answered only by saying them again and again. Remember, your Father knows just what you need. He knows it even before you ask him!

9"Pray like this: 'Our Father in Heaven, we honor your holy name. 10We ask that your kingdom will come now. May your will be done here on earth, just as it is in Heaven. 11Give us our food again today, as usual. 12And forgive us our sins, just as we have forgiven those who have sinned against us. 13Don't bring us into temptation. But keep us safe from the Evil One. Amen.' 14-15Your heavenly Father will forgive you if you forgive those who sin against you. But if you won't forgive them, he won't forgive you.

If You Fast, Do It in Secret

16"Now, let me teach you about fasting. You might decide to take a fast, not eating food for a spiritual reason. If you do, don't do it in front of people. This is what the hypocrites do. They try to look weak and messy so people will feel sorry for them. Truly, that is the only reward they will ever get. 17But when you fast, put on festive clothing. 18That way no one will know you are hungry. Only your Father will know, for he knows every secret. And he will reward you.

19"Don't store up treasures here on earth. For they can rust away or they might be stolen. 20Store them in Heaven where they will never lose their value. And there, they are safe from robbers. ²¹If your treasures are in Heaven, your heart will be there, too.

²²"If your eye is pure, there will be sunshine in your soul. ²³But your eye might be clouded with evil thoughts and desires. If so, you are in deep spiritual darkness. And oh, how deep that darkness can be!

²⁴"You cannot serve two masters: God and money. For you will hate one and love the other.

Serve God, Not Money

²⁵"So my advice is: Don't worry about things. Don't worry about food, drink, and clothes. For you already have life and a body. They are much more important than what to eat and wear. ²⁶Look at the birds! They don't worry about what to eat. They don't need to plant or harvest food. For your heavenly Father feeds them. And you are much more important to him than they are. ²⁷Will all your worries add a single moment to your life?

²⁸"And why worry about your clothes? Look at the field lilies! They don't worry about theirs. ²⁹Yet King Solomon in all his glory was not dressed as nicely as they. ³⁰God cares for the flowers that are here today and gone tomorrow. Won't he more surely care for you, O men of little faith?

³¹⁻³²"So don't worry at all about having enough food and clothing. Why be like the heathen? For they take pride in all these things. And they are very worried about them, too. But your heavenly Father already knows that you need them. ³³Give him first place in your life. Live as he wants you to. Then he will give all these things to you as well.

³⁴"So don't be worried about tomorrow. God will take care of your tomorrow, too. Live one day at a time.

Don't Criticize Others

7 "Don't judge others. Then you won't be judged. ²For others will treat you the way you treat them. ³And why worry about a speck of dust in the eye of a brother? First check to see the big stick

Fasting
MATTHEW 6:17

Do you like to eat? How many meals do you eat each day? How would you like to stop eating all day? How would you like to stop eating for many days? Bible-time people sometimes did this. Some people do this today. It is called fasting. Moses, Elijah, and Jesus fasted for 40 days. How would you like to stop eating for 40 days? Some Bible-time people fasted because there was not enough food. Others fasted because they were upset about something. Hannah fasted because she did not have children (1 Samuel 1:8). King David fasted when his baby boy was sick. He prayed that God would make him well again (2 Samuel 12:16). Some fasted to show their love to God. Others fasted when they prayed for something special.

Many people fast today in order to spend more time with God. Instead of eating, they can spend that time praying and reading the Bible. Jesus said that if you fast, don't be a show-off. If you fast to impress others, then you are showing off. If you fast to spend more time with God, then you are doing it for the right reason.

Leprosy
MATTHEW 8:1-4

What is the worst disease today? Is it AIDS? Is it cancer? Many people die each year from these diseases. In Bible times people did not know about AIDS. Cancer was not common. The worst disease then was called leprosy. Some leprosy was probably just a bad skin infection. Other leprosy was so bad that a person's skin rotted. People were terrified that they would catch leprosy from a leper. So lepers usually had to live by themselves. What a lonely life to be sick and have to stay away from your mother, father, and other loved ones. When lepers met people, they had to shout, "Unclean!" It was hard for lepers to earn money to buy food. Who would have wanted to hire them? So most had to beg. If lepers got well, they had to show themselves to a priest. If the priest said the leper was well, he could live with others again. Leviticus 14:1-32 tells what the leper had to do to prove he was completely well. Be glad you're not a Bible-time leper! It was a very sad way to live.

of wood in your own. ⁴Don't say, 'Friend, let me help you get that speck out of your eye.' You can't even see because of the piece of wood in your own! ⁵Hypocrite! First get rid of the stick of wood in your eye. Then you can see to help your brother.

⁶"Don't give holy things to sinful men. Don't give pearls to pigs! They will trample on the pearls. Then they will turn and attack you.

God Gives Good Gifts
⁷"Ask, and you will be given what you ask for. Look hard, and you will find. Knock, and the door will be opened. ⁸For everyone who asks, receives. Anyone who looks, finds. If only you will knock, the door will open up. ⁹Suppose a child asks his father for a loaf of bread. Will he be given a stone instead? ¹⁰Suppose he asks for fish. Will he be given a deadly snake? Of course not! ¹¹You sinful men even know how to give good gifts to your children. So won't your Father in Heaven be sure to give good gifts to those who ask him for them?

¹²"Do for others what you want them to do for you. This is the meaning of the laws of Moses and the words of the prophets.

Jesus Talks about the Way to Heaven
¹³"Heaven can be entered only through the narrow gate! The highway to hell is wide. Its gate is big enough for the many who choose its easy way. ¹⁴But the Gateway to Life is small. That road is narrow. And only a few ever find it.

Actions Speak Louder than Words
¹⁵"Be careful of false teachers. They come dressed up like harmless sheep. But they are wolves who will tear you apart. ¹⁶You can identify a tree by its fruit. In the same way, you can know false teachers by the way they act. Do people pick grapes from thorn bushes? Can figs be picked from thistles? ¹⁷Good fruit trees grow good fruit. But bad trees grow bad fruit. ¹⁸A good tree will always produce good fruit. And a bad tree will

always produce bad fruit. [19]So the trees having the bad fruit are chopped down and thrown on the fire. [20]Yes, the way to know a tree or a person is by the kind of fruit produced.

[21]"Not all who sound religious are really godly people. They might call me 'Lord, Lord.' But still they won't enter the Kingdom of Heaven. For the important thing is that they obey my Father in Heaven. [22]At the Judgment many will tell me, 'Lord, Lord, we told others about you. We used your name to cast out demons. We also did many other great miracles.' [23]But I will say, 'You have never been mine. Go away, for your deeds are evil.'

Listen to Jesus and Obey Him

[24]"All who listen to my teachings and follow them are wise. They are like a man who builds his house on solid rock. [25]The rain might fall down like a waterfall. The floods might rise. The storm winds might beat against his house. But it won't fall down, for it is built on rock.

[26]"Some others might hear my teachings, but not do them. They are foolish, like a man who builds his house on sand. [27]For the rains and floods will come. And storm winds will beat against his house. And it will fall with a great crash." [28]The crowds were amazed at Jesus' sermons. [29]For he taught as one who had great authority. He did not teach like the other Jewish leaders.

Two Men Believe and Are Healed

8 Large crowds followed Jesus as he came down the hillside.

[2]Then a man with leprosy came up to him. He knelt in front of Jesus, worshiping. "Sir," the leper said, "if you want to, you can heal me."

[3]Jesus touched the man. "I want to," he said. "Be healed!" And right away the leprosy was gone!

[4]Then Jesus said to him, "Don't stop to talk to anyone. Go right over to the priest. He will check to see if you are healed. And take with you the special offering. It is required by Moses' law for lepers who are healed. Give it to show everyone that you are healed."

Treat others nicely

Others will treat you the way
you treat them.

Matthew 7:2

[5-6]When Jesus came to Capernaum, a Roman army captain came to him. He begged him to come to his home and heal his servant boy. The boy was in bed paralyzed and in great pain.

[7]"Yes," Jesus said, "I will come and heal him."

[8-9]Then the officer said, "Sir, I am not worthy to have you in my home. And you don't really need to come. You can just stand here and say, 'Be healed.' If you do, my servant will get better! I know, because I am under the power of the officers over me. And I have power over my soldiers. I might say to one, 'Go.' And he will go. I might say to another, 'Come.' And he will come. And I might say to my slave boy, 'Do this or that.' And he does it. And I know you have power to tell his sickness to go. And it will go!"

[10]Jesus stood there amazed! He turned to the crowd. Then he said, "I haven't seen faith like this in all the land of Israel! [11]And I tell you the truth! Many Gentiles like this Roman officer shall come from all over the world. They will sit down in the Kingdom of Heaven with Abraham, Isaac, and Jacob. [12]And many an Israelite shall be thrown into outer darkness. They will be put in the place of crying and pain. Yes, this will happen to those for whom the Kingdom was made!"

[13]Then Jesus said to the Roman officer, "Go on home. What you have believed has happened!" And the boy was healed that same hour!

Jesus Heals a Sick Woman

Have you ever been sick? It's no fun, is it? Jesus came to Peter's house one day. But Peter's mother-in-law was sick. She was in bed with a high fever. She wanted to get dinner for Jesus. But she was too sick. So Jesus did something special for her.

[14]Then Jesus came to Peter's house. And Peter's mother-in-law was in bed with a high fever. [15]But when Jesus touched her hand, the fever left her. And she got up and made a meal for them!

[16]That evening several people with demons in them were brought to Jesus. And when he spoke a single word, all the demons left. And all the sick were healed. [17]This fulfilled the words of Isaiah, "He took our sicknesses. He bore our diseases."

- *Remember:* Whose house did Jesus visit? (8:14) Who was sick? (8:14) What was wrong? (8:14) What did Jesus touch? (8:15) What happened to the woman when Jesus touched her? (8:15) What did the woman do for Jesus then? (8:15) Why was this a special thing to do for him?

- *Discover:* When Jesus healed this woman she said thank you. She said it by getting dinner for Jesus. That's one good way to say thank you, isn't it?

- *Apply:* Do your parents do special things for you? Say thank you by doing something special for them. Can you think of something good to do today?

- *What's next?* The worst disease in the world in Jesus' time was leprosy. There was no cure. A man with leprosy finds Jesus and begs to be healed. Can Jesus heal him? Will he? Read Mark 1:40-45. ■

The Cost of Following Jesus

[18]Jesus saw how large the crowd was getting. So he told his disciples to get ready to go to the other side of the lake.

[19]Just then one of the Jewish religious teachers came up. He said to Jesus, "Teacher, I will follow you no matter where you go!"

[20]But Jesus said, "Foxes have dens to live in. And birds have nests to live in. But I have no home of my own. I have no place to lay my head."

[21]Another of his disciples came up. He said, "Sir, when my father is dead, then I will follow you."

[22]But Jesus told him, "Follow me now! Let those who are spiritually dead bury their own dead."

The Disciples Are Amazed by Jesus' Power

[23]Then he got into a boat. He started across the lake with his disciples. [24]Suddenly a terrible storm came up. Its waves were higher than the boat. But Jesus was asleep.

[25]The disciples went to him and woke him up. "Lord, save us!" they shouted. "We're sinking!"

[26]But Jesus answered, "O you men of little faith! Why are you so afraid?" Then he stood up and spoke to the wind and waves. The storm stopped! The sea was calm! [27]The disciples just sat there, in awe! "Who is this?" they asked themselves. "Even the winds and the sea obey him!"

Jesus Heals a Man with Demons

[28]They came to the other side of the lake, in the country of the Gadarenes. There, two men with demons in them met him. They lived in a graveyard. They were so dangerous that no one could go through that area.

[29]They began shouting at him, "What do you want with us, O Son of God? You have no right to trouble us yet."

[30]A herd of pigs was feeding in the distance. [31]So the demons begged, "If you send us out, send us into that herd of pigs."

[32]"All right," Jesus told them. "Come out."

So they came out of the men and went into the pigs. The whole herd rushed over a cliff and drowned in the water below. [33]The herdsmen ran to the nearest city with the story of what had happened. [34]All the people came rushing out to see Jesus. They begged him to go away and leave them alone.

Jesus Heals a Paralyzed Man

9 So Jesus climbed back into a boat. He went across the lake to Capernaum, where he was living at the time.

²Soon some men brought him a paralyzed boy on a mat. Jesus saw their faith. So he said to the sick boy, "Cheer up, son! For I have forgiven your sins!"

³Some of the religious leaders heard this. "Blasphemy!" they said among themselves. "This man is saying he is God!"

⁴Jesus knew what they were thinking. So he asked them, "Why are you thinking such evil thoughts? ⁵⁻⁶I, the Messiah, have the power on earth to forgive sins. But talk is cheap. Anybody could say that. So I'll prove it to you by healing this man." Then he turned to the paralyzed man. He said, "Pick up your sleeping mat and go on home. For you are healed."

⁷And the boy jumped up and left!

⁸A chill of fear swept through the crowd. They saw this happen right before their eyes! How they praised God for giving such power to a man!

Jesus Asks Matthew to Follow Him

Most of the Jews hated tax collectors. One day Jesus met a tax collector. What did Jesus say? What did he do?

⁹As Jesus was going on down the road, he saw a tax collector. His name was Matthew. He was sitting at a tax collection booth. "Come and be my disciple," Jesus said to him. And Matthew jumped up and went along with him.

¹⁰Later, Jesus and his disciples ate dinner at Matthew's house. Many tax collectors and "sinners" were there as guests!

¹¹The Pharisees were angry. "Why does your teacher eat with men like that?" they asked.

¹²Jesus heard them ask this. "People who are well don't need a doctor!" he replied. "It's the sick people who do!" ¹³Then he added, "Go and learn the meaning of this verse of Scripture: 'It isn't your sacrifices and your gifts I want. I want you to show mercy.' For I have not come to call those who think they are righteous. I have come to call back to God those who know they are sinners."

- *Remember:* What kind of work did Matthew do? (9:9) Where did he work? (9:9) What did Jesus ask Matthew to do? (9:9) Where did Jesus have dinner that night? (9:10) Who else was at that dinner? (9:10) Did Jesus hate this tax collector? Why not? Should we hate people Jesus loves?

- *Discover:* If Jesus loves someone, we should not hate that person. We should love that person the way Jesus does.

- *Apply:* Do you hate someone? Is there someone you really don't like? Do you think Jesus loves that person? What would Jesus want you to do?

- *What's next?* "I can't do anything." Have you ever said something like that? What do you think Jesus would say about those words? Read about a man who said "I can't" in John 5:1-9. ■

Jesus Answers Questions about Fasting

¹⁴One day the disciples of John the Baptist came to Jesus. They asked him, "Why don't your disciples fast? We do, and so do the Pharisees."

¹⁵"Should the bridegroom's friends mourn while he is with them? Should they go without food at wedding time?" Jesus asked. "But the time is coming when I will be taken from them. Then there will be time for them to go without food.

¹⁶"Who would patch an old piece of clothing with unshrunk cloth? For the patch would tear away and make the hole worse. ¹⁷And who would use old

wineskins to store new wine? For the old skins would burst with the pressure. The wine would be spilled and the skins ruined. Only new wineskins are used to store new wine. That way both will continue to be good."

Two Wonderful Miracles

[18]As he was saying this, the rabbi of the local synaogue came. He bowed down to Jesus and said, "My little daughter has just died. But you can bring her back to life again. All you have to do is come and touch her."

[19]So Jesus and the disciples went to the rabbi's home. [20]As they went, a woman came up behind Jesus. This woman had been sick for 12 years with internal bleeding. In the crowd, she quietly touched a tassel of his robe. [21]She thought, "If I only touch him, I will be healed."

[22]Jesus turned around and spoke to her. "Daughter," he said, "all is well! Your faith has healed you." And the woman was well from that moment.

[23]Jesus came to the rabbi's home. And he saw the noisy crowds and heard the funeral music. [24]He said, "Get them out. For the little girl isn't dead. She is only sleeping!" The people there all laughed and sneered at him!

[25]The crowd was finally outside. And Jesus went in to where the little girl was lying. He took her by the hand, and she jumped up! She was all right again! [26]The news of this great miracle spread all around the land.

Blind Men See and a Speechless Man Talks

[27]As Jesus was leaving her home, two blind men followed along behind. They shouted, "O Son of King David, have mercy on us."

[28]They went right into the house where he was staying. And Jesus asked them, "Do you believe I can make you see?"

"Yes, Lord," they told him, "we do."

[29]Then he touched their eyes. And he said, "Because of your faith it will happen."

[30]And suddenly they could see! Jesus warned them not to tell anyone about it. [31]But instead they spread his fame all over the town.

[32]Leaving that place, Jesus met a man who couldn't speak. He couldn't speak because a demon was inside him. [33]So Jesus cast out the demon, and right away the man could talk. How the crowds were amazed! "Never in all our lives have we seen anything like this," they said.

[34]But the Pharisees said, "He can cast out demons because he has a demon himself. He has Satan, the demon king, in him!"

Jesus Needs More Workers

[35]Jesus went to all the cities and villages of that area. He taught in all the Jewish synagogues. He told the people the Good News about the Kingdom. And wherever he went he healed people of every sort of sickness. [36]And what pity he felt for the crowds that came! This was because their problems were so great. And they didn't know what to do or where to go for help. They were like sheep without a shepherd.

[37]"The harvest is so great. But the workers are so few," he told his disciples. [38]"So pray to the one in charge of the harvesting. Ask him to find more workers for his harvest fields."

Jesus Sends Out the Disciples

10 Jesus called his 12 disciples to him. He gave them the authority to cast out evil spirits. He gave them the power to heal every kind of sickness and disease.

[2-4]Here are the names of his 12 disciples. There were Simon, also called Peter, and his brother Andrew. There were James and John, the sons of Zebedee. There were Philip, Bartholomew, and Thomas. There was Matthew, the tax collector. There was James, Alphaeus' son. There were Thaddaeus and Simon. Simon was a member of "The Zealots." And there was Judas Iscariot, the one who betrayed Jesus.

⁵Jesus sent them out with these orders: "Don't go to the Gentiles or the Samaritans. ⁶Only go to the people of Israel. They are God's lost sheep. ⁷Go and tell them that the Kingdom of Heaven is near. ⁸Heal the sick, raise the dead, cure the lepers, and cast out demons. Give as freely as you have received!

Tell others you are Jesus' friend

Someone might say he is my friend in front of many people. If so, I will say he is my friend before my Father in Heaven.

Matthew 10:32

⁹"Don't take any money with you. ¹⁰Don't carry a duffle bag with extra clothes and shoes. Don't even bring a walking stick. For those you help should feed and care for you. ¹¹When you enter a city or village, look for a godly man. Stay in his home until you leave for the next town. ¹²When you ask to stay at someone's home, be friendly. ¹³If it turns out to be a godly home, give it your blessing. If not, keep the blessing. ¹⁴A city or home might not welcome you. If this happens, shake off the dust of that place from your feet as you go. ¹⁵Truly, the wicked cities of Sodom and Gomorrah will be better off at Judgment Day than they.

Not Everyone Will Like You

¹⁶"I am sending you out as sheep among wolves. Be as wise as snakes and harmless as doves. ¹⁷But be careful! For you will be arrested and tried in court. You will be beaten in the synagogues. ¹⁸Yes, and you must stand trial before governors and kings for my sake. This will give you the chance to tell them about me. Yes, in this way you will witness to the world.

¹⁹"When they arrest you, don't worry about what to say at your trial. For you will be given the right words at the right time. ²⁰And it won't be you doing the talking. It will be the Spirit of your heavenly Father speaking through you!

²¹"Men will turn against their own brothers and send them to be killed. Fathers will turn against their own children. Children will turn against their parents and send them to die. ²²Everyone shall hate you because you belong to me. But all of you who are faithful to the end shall be saved.

²³"When you are treated badly in one city, go to the next! I will come back before you have gone to them all!

²⁴"A student is not greater than his teacher. A servant is not above his master. ²⁵The student shares his teacher's fate. The servant shares his master's! I, the master of the household, have been called 'Satan.' How much more will they say the same of you! ²⁶But don't be afraid of those who try to scare you. For the time is coming when the truth will be shown. Their secret plans will be known to everyone.

²⁷"What I tell you now in the darkness, shout out loud when morning comes! What I whisper in your ears, shout from the housetops!

Don't Be Afraid of the People Who Don't Like You

²⁸"Don't be afraid of those who can kill only your bodies. They can't touch your souls! Fear only God, who can destroy both soul and body in hell. ²⁹Not one sparrow can fall to the ground without your Father knowing it. And what do they cost? You can buy two for a penny! ³⁰And the very hairs of your head are all counted. ³¹So don't worry! You are worth more to him than many sparrows.

³²"Someone might say he is my friend in front of many people. If so, I will say he is my friend before my Father in Heaven. ³³But someone might say he doesn't know me. If so, I will say I don't know him before my Father in Heaven.

³⁴"Don't think that I came to bring peace to the earth! No, I have brought a sword instead. ³⁵I have come to set a man against his father. I will set a daughter against her mother. I will set a daughter-in-law against her mother-in-law. ³⁶A man's worst enemies will be right in his own home! ³⁷You might love your father and mother more than you love me. But

if so, you are not worthy of being mine. You might love your son or daughter more than me. But if so, you are not worthy of being mine. [38]You might not take up your cross and follow me. But if so, you are not worthy of being mine.

God Has a Reward for Us

[39]"If you hold on to your life, you will lose it. But if you give it up for me, you will save it.

[40]"Those who welcome you are welcoming me. And when they welcome me they are welcoming God who sent me. [41]You might welcome a prophet because he is a man of God. If so, you will be given the same reward a prophet gets. And you might welcome good and godly men because they are good. If so, you will be given a reward like theirs.

[42]"And you might give a cup of cold water to a little child because you are my disciples. If so, you will surely be rewarded."

John the Baptist Has Questions about Jesus

11 Jesus finished giving these orders to his 12 disciples. Then he went to preach and teach in the towns of Galilee.

[2]John the Baptist was now in prison. He had heard about all the miracles Jesus was doing. So he sent his disciples to speak to Jesus. [3]They asked, "Are you the one we are waiting for? Or shall we keep on looking?"

[4]Jesus told them, "Go back to John. Tell him about the miracles you've seen me do. [5]Tell him that blind people can now see! Tell him that lame people are now walking without help! Tell him about the cured lepers! Tell him about those once deaf who can hear! Tell him about those once dead who are living! And tell him about my preaching the Good News to the poor. [6]Then give him this message, 'Blessed are those who don't doubt me.'"

Is John the Baptist Crazy? Is Jesus a Glutton?

[7]When John's disciples had gone, Jesus began talking about him to the crowds. "You went out into the barren desert to see John. When you went there, what did you expect him to be like? Did you expect him to be like grass blowing in the wind? [8]Or did you expect to see a man dressed like a prince in a palace? [9]Or did you expect a prophet of God? Yes, and he is more than just a prophet! [10]For John is the man spoken of in the Scriptures. He is a messenger to come before me. He was to tell about my coming. He was to get people ready to receive me.

[11]"I tell you the truth. Of all men ever born, none has been greater than John the Baptist. And yet, he who is least in the Kingdom of Heaven will be greater than he is! [12]From the time John the Baptist began his work until now, many have been crowding toward the Kingdom of Heaven. And people using force have been trying to take the Kingdom. [13]For all the laws and prophets looked forward to the Messiah until John came. [14]And if you are willing to hear what I say, he is Elijah. He is the one the prophets said would come at the time the Kingdom begins. [15]If ever you were willing to listen, listen now!

[16]"What shall I say about this nation? These people are like children playing. They say to their friends, [17]'We played wedding and you weren't happy. So we played funeral but you weren't sad.' [18]For John the Baptist doesn't even drink wine. Also, he often goes without food. And you say, 'He's crazy.' [19]I, the Messiah, feast and drink. And you complain that I am 'a glutton and a drinking man'! You say I like to 'hang around with the worst sort of sinners.' But wisdom is proved by the things it does."

A Warning for Those Who Do Not Believe

[20]Then Jesus spoke against the cities where he had done most of his miracles. He did this because they hadn't turned to God.

[21]"How terrible it will be for you, Chorazin! How terrible it will be for you, Bethsaida! I did many miracles in your streets. I might have done the same in wicked Tyre and Sidon. If I had, their people would have turned from their sins long ago. They would have been

ashamed and humble. ²²Truly, Tyre and Sidon will be better off on the Judgment Day than you! ²³And Capernaum, though highly honored, shall go down to hell! For I did many miracles in you. If I had done the same in Sodom, they would have turned from their sins. And Sodom would still be here today! ²⁴Truly, Sodom will be better off at the Judgment Day than you."

If you love Jesus you'll help him

Anyone who isn't helping me is against me.

Matthew 12:30

---

²⁵And Jesus prayed this prayer: "O Father, Lord of Heaven and earth! Thank you for hiding the truth from those who think themselves so wise. And thank you for showing the truth to little children. ²⁶Yes, Father, for it pleased you to do it this way!

²⁷"Everything has been given to me by my Father. Only the Father knows the Son. And the Son knows the Father. The Son also shows the Father to some people. And through the Son they also know the Father. ²⁸Come, all who work so hard under heavy burdens. Come to me and I will give you rest. ²⁹Do the work I have for you and let me teach you. For I am gentle and humble in spirit. And you will find rest for your souls. ³⁰For the work I ask you to do is easy. And the burdens I give you are light."

Jesus Talks about the Sabbath

12 One day, Jesus was walking through some fields of grain. His disciples were with him at the time. It was on the Sabbath, the Jewish day of worship. And his disciples were hungry. So they began breaking off heads of wheat and eating the grain.

²But some Pharisees saw them do it. "Your disciples are breaking the law," they said. "They are harvesting grain on the Sabbath."

³But Jesus said to them, "What did King David do when he and his friends were hungry? Haven't you ever read about it? ⁴David went into the Temple. He took the holy bread that only the

priests were allowed to eat. Then he and his friends ate it. That was breaking the law, too. ⁵And haven't you ever read the law of Moses? The priests on duty in the Temple are to work on the Sabbath. But the priests don't sin by doing that. ⁶And truly, one is here who is greater than the Temple! ⁷The Scriptures say, 'I want you to be merciful more than I want your offerings.' You should learn what this means! If you knew, you would not have judged those who were not guilty! ⁸For I, the Messiah, am master even of the Sabbath."

Jesus Heals a Man's Hand on the Sabbath

⁹Then he went over to the synagogue. ¹⁰He saw a man there with a crippled hand. The Pharisees asked Jesus, "Is it right to heal on the Sabbath day?" They were, of course, hoping he would say yes. That way they could arrest him! ¹¹This was his answer: "Suppose you had just one sheep. And suppose it fell into a well on the Sabbath. Would you work to save it on that day? Of course you would! ¹²And a person is more important than a sheep! Yes, it is right to do good on the Sabbath." ¹³Then he said to the man, "Hold out your arm." And as he did, his hand became normal. It was just like the other one!

¹⁴Then the Pharisees called a meeting. They wanted to plan Jesus' arrest and death.

Jesus Is the Chosen, Beloved One

¹⁵But he knew what they were planning. So he left the synagogue, and many followed him. He healed all the sick among them. ¹⁶But he told them not to spread the news about his miracles. ¹⁷This fulfilled the prophecy of Isaiah about him:

¹⁸"Look at my Servant.
See my Chosen One.
He is my Beloved, in whom my soul delights.
I will put my Spirit upon him.
And he will judge the nations.
¹⁹He does not fight or shout.
He does not raise his voice!
²⁰He does not crush the weak,
Or quench the smallest hope.

He will end all war with his final
victory.
²¹And his name shall be the hope
Of all the world."

Where Does Jesus Get His Power?

²²Then a man with a demon was brought to Jesus. He was both blind and unable to talk. And Jesus healed him so that he could both talk and see. ²³The crowd was amazed. "Maybe Jesus is the Messiah!" they said.

²⁴But the Pharisees heard about the miracle. And they said, "He can cast out demons because he is Satan, king of devils."

²⁵Jesus knew their thoughts. So he said, "A divided kingdom ends in ruin. A city or home divided against itself cannot stand. ²⁶And if Satan is casting out Satan, he is fighting himself. He is destroying his own kingdom. ²⁷You claim I am casting out demons by the powers of Satan. But if I am, what power do your own people use when they cast them out? Let them answer to what you are saying! ²⁸But suppose I am casting out demons by the Spirit of God. If that is true, then the Kingdom of God has come among you. ²⁹One cannot rob Satan's kingdom without first tying Satan up. Only then can his demons be thrown out! ³⁰Anyone who isn't helping me is against me.

³¹⁻³²"Even blasphemy against me or any other sin can be forgiven. Only speaking against the Holy Spirit shall never be forgiven. It won't be forgiven either in this world or in the world to come.

³³"A tree is known by its fruit. A tree that is good produces good fruit. Poor trees don't produce good fruit. ³⁴You snakes! You are evil men! How can men like you say what is good and right? For a man's speech begins in his heart. ³⁵A good man's speech shows the rich treasures within him. An evil-hearted man is filled with poison, and his speech proves it. ³⁶And I tell you the truth! You must give account on Judgment Day for every careless word you speak. ³⁷The words you say now will decide how you will be judged later. You might be proved

innocent by them. Or you might be proved guilty."

Religious Leaders Ask Jesus for a Miracle

³⁸One day some of the Jewish leaders came to Jesus. There were some Pharisees among them. They asked him to show them a miracle.

³⁹⁻⁴⁰But Jesus said, "Only an evil, faithless nation would ask for more proof. And none will be given except what happened to Jonah the prophet! Jonah was in the great fish for three days and three nights. In the same way, I shall be in the grave three days and three nights. ⁴¹The men of Nineveh shall rise against this nation at the Judgment. They will be the ones to judge you. For when Jonah preached to them, they repented. They turned to God from all their evil ways. And now someone greater than Jonah is here. But you will not believe him. ⁴²The Queen of Sheba shall rise against this nation in the Judgment. She will be the one to judge you. For she came from a distant land to hear the wisdom of Solomon. And now someone greater than Solomon is here. But you will not believe him.

⁴³⁻⁴⁵"This evil nation is like a man with a demon in him. For if the demon leaves, it goes into the deserts for a while. It looks for rest but it finds none. Then it says, 'I will go back to the man I came from.' So it goes back and finds the man's heart clean but empty! Then the demon finds seven other spirits more evil than itself. All of them enter the man and live in him. And so he is worse off than before."

Jesus Talks about His Real Family

⁴⁶⁻⁴⁷Jesus was speaking in a crowded house. At the time, his mother and brothers were outside. They wanted to talk with him. Someone told him they were there. ⁴⁸So he said, "Who is my mother? Who are my brothers?" ⁴⁹He pointed to his disciples. "Look!" he said. "These are my mother and brothers." ⁵⁰Then he added, "Anyone who obeys my Father in Heaven is my brother, sister, and mother!"

A Story about a Farmer

Do you like to listen to stories? Jesus told many stories. They are called parables. Jesus used these stories to teach important lessons to those who listened to them. These stories can teach us, too. This story is about soil, or dirt. It's also about seeds and the farmer who plants them. Can you figure out what Jesus is trying to teach in this story?

13 Later that same day, Jesus left the house and went down to the shore. ²There, a great crowd soon gathered. So Jesus got into a boat and taught from it. The people listened from the beach. ³He used many stories to teach the people.

"A farmer was planting grain in his fields," he said. ⁴"He was throwing the seed across the ground. Some of it fell beside a path. And the birds came and ate it. ⁵Some fell on rocky ground where the soil was very shallow. The plants grew up quickly in the shallow soil. ⁶But the hot sun soon burned them and they died. This was because they had such small roots. ⁷Other seeds fell among thorns. And the thorns soon grew up and choked out the tender grain. ⁸But some seeds fell on good soil. These grew a crop that was 30, 60, or even 100 times what he had planted. ⁹If you have ears, listen!"

¹⁰Later his disciples came to him. "Why do you always teach with these stories?" they asked. "They are hard to understand."

¹¹Then he said, "Only you are allowed to know about the Kingdom of Heaven. Others cannot know about these secret things. ¹²For the person who has something will be given more. He will have more than he needs. But some people don't have much. And even the little they have will be taken away. ¹³That is why I use these stories. It is so people will hear and see but not really understand.

¹⁴"This fulfills the words of Isaiah: 'They hear, but don't understand. They look, but don't see! ¹⁵For their hearts are fat and heavy. Their ears are dull. And they have closed their eyes in sleep. ¹⁶So they won't see and hear and understand. They won't turn to God again and let me heal them.'

But blessed are your eyes, for they see. And blessed are your ears, for they hear. ¹⁷Many a prophet and godly man has wished to see what you have seen. Many have wanted to hear what you have heard.

¹⁸"This is what the story about the farmer means. ¹⁹What does the soil by the hard path stand for? It stands for the person who hears the Good News about the Kingdom and doesn't understand it. Then Satan comes and takes the seeds from his heart before they can grow. ²⁰What does the shallow, rocky soil stand for? It stands for the person who hears the message and receives it with joy. ²¹But he doesn't have much depth in his life. So the seeds don't root very deeply. And when trouble comes his joy soon fades away. When he is treated badly because of his beliefs, he drops out. ²²What does the ground covered with thistles stand for? It stands for a man who hears the message. But the cares of this life and his love for money choke out God's Word. As a result, he does less and less for God. ²³What does the good soil stand for? It stands for the heart of a man who listens to the message and understands it. He goes out and brings 30, 60, or even 100 others into the Kingdom."

- *Remember:* What kinds of soil are mentioned? (13:4-7) What happened to the seeds in each kind of soil? (13:4-7) Which kind of soil had a good crop? (13:8) God's Word, the Bible, is like seed. Your heart is like the soil. When will God's Word grow in your heart? (13:23) Which of these four kinds of hearts would please God most? Why?

- *Discover:* God's Word grows in our hearts when we accept it. It will not grow when we reject it.

- *Apply:* What do you think when you read your Bible? Are you glad to read it? Or do you read it just to please someone? Ask God to show you something special. He will.

- *What's next?* Someone lights a lamp. Then he puts a box over it. Would you do that? Read Mark 4:21-25. ■

A Story about Weeds

²⁴Here is another story Jesus told. "The Kingdom of Heaven is like a farmer," Jesus said. "He was planting good seed in his field. ²⁵But one night while he slept, his enemy came to his field. He planted thistles in the field of wheat. ²⁶When the crop began to grow, the thistles grew, too.

²⁷"The farmer's men came to him. 'Sir,' they said. 'The field you planted with choice seed is full of thistles!'

²⁸"'An enemy has done it!' he exclaimed.

"'Shall we pull out the thistles?' they asked.

²⁹"'No,' he replied. 'You'll hurt the wheat if you do. ³⁰Let both grow together until the harvest. I will tell the harvesters to sort out the thistles and burn them. Then they will put the wheat in the barn.'"

A Story about a Tiny Seed

³¹⁻³²Here is another of his stories. "The Kingdom of Heaven is like a tiny mustard seed planted in a field," he said. "It is the smallest of all seeds. But it grows to be a large plant. It becomes a tree where birds can build their nests."

A Story about Baking Bread

³³He also used this story. "The Kingdom of Heaven is like a woman making bread," he said. "She takes a measure of flour and mixes in the yeast. Soon the yeast spreads to every part of the dough."

³⁴Jesus always used such stories when teaching the people. In fact, he never spoke to them without using at least one story. ³⁵The prophet had said that Jesus would use such stories. For this was said through the prophet: "I will speak by using stories. I will tell about things hidden since the beginning of time."

Jesus Explains His Stories

³⁶Then, leaving the crowds outside, Jesus went into the house. His disciples went with him. They asked him what the story of the thistles and the wheat meant.

³⁷"All right," he said, "I am the farmer who plants the choice seed. ³⁸The field is the world. And the seed stands for the people of the Kingdom. The thistles are the people who belong to Satan. ³⁹The enemy who planted the thistles among the wheat is the devil. The harvest is the end of the world. And the harvesters are the angels.

⁴⁰"In this story the thistles are sorted out and burned. The same thing will happen at the end of the world. ⁴¹I will send my angels at that time. They will sort out everything that causes sin. And they will sort out all who are evil. ⁴²They will throw them into the fire and burn them. At that time, there will be crying and grinding of teeth. ⁴³Then the godly shall shine as the sun in their Father's Kingdom. Let those with ears, listen!

A Story about Hidden Treasure

⁴⁴"The Kingdom of Heaven is like a treasure a man found in a field. In his joy, he sold all he had to get the money to buy the field. And with the field, he got the treasure, too!

A Story about a Pearl

Pretend that everything you own is in one big pile. Pretend that you sell it all. You have nothing left but the money. What would you buy with that money? This tells what one man bought.

45"Again, the Kingdom of Heaven is like a pearl trader looking for choice pearls. 46He found a pearl of great value. So he sold all he owned to buy it!

- *Remember:* What did the man do for a living? (13:45) What did he want to find? (13:45) What did he find? (13:46) How much did he sell? (13:46) What did he buy with the money? (13:46) Why do you think he did this? What did Jesus compare this to? (13:45)

- *Discover:* Jesus is worth more than everything in this world. We should be willing to give up anything for him.

- *Apply:* Is Jesus worth more than TV? Is he worth more than your toys? How much time do you spend with your TV? How much time do you spend with your toys? How much time do you spend with Jesus?

- *What's next?* How are we like a net full of fish? Jesus tells us. Read Matthew 13:47-52. ■

A Story about Some Fish

We don't look like fish, do we? We don't smell like fish either! So how are we like fish? Jesus tells us.

47-48"Again, the Kingdom of Heaven is like a fisherman. He throws a net into the water and catches fish of every kind. Some are good, but some are useless. When the net is full, he drags it up onto the beach. He sits down and sorts out the good fish into crates. Then he throws the others away. 49That is the way it will be at the end of the world. The angels will come and sort out the godly people. 50Then they will take the wicked and throw them into the fire. At that time, there shall be crying and grinding of teeth. 51Do you understand?"

"Yes," they said, "we do."

52Then he added, "Those who teach the Jewish law and learn about the kingdom have double treasure. They have the treasure of the Old Covenant and the treasure of the New!"

- *Remember:* What does this fisherman catch? What kinds of fish are in his net? (13:47-48) How are angels like this fisherman? What will they do? (13:49) What will they do with wicked people? (13:50) Jesus will not take wicked people into his kingdom. He will take only those people who have accepted him as Savior.

- *Discover:* Wicked people will not live with God in Heaven. Only people who love God and try to please him will live in Heaven.

- *Apply:* Do you love God? Have you accepted Jesus as Savior? If you have, he has taken your sins away. Are you living for Jesus? If you are, then you will be trying your best to make him happy and obey his Word, the Bible.

- *What's next:* A big storm comes while Jesus and his disciples are out on the lake. The boat starts to sink. Read Mark 4:35-41 to find out what happens. ■

The People of Jesus' Hometown Doubt Him

53-54Jesus finished saying these things. Then he went back to his hometown, Nazareth in Galilee. He taught there in the synagogue. And he amazed everyone with his wisdom and his miracles.

55"How is this possible?" the people asked. "He's just a carpenter's son. We know Mary his mother. We know his brothers, James, Joseph, Simon, and Judas. 56And his sisters, they all live here.

How can he be so great?" 57And they became angry with him!

Then Jesus told them, "A prophet is honored everywhere except in his own town! He is never honored by his own people!" 58And so he did only a few great miracles there. This was because they didn't believe in him.

Herod Kills John the Baptist

14 At that time, King Herod heard about Jesus. 2He said to his men, "This must be John the Baptist, come back to life again. That is why he can do these miracles." 3For Herod had arrested John and put him in prison. Herod had done this because of his wife Herodias. Herodias was his brother Philip's ex-wife. 4And John had told him it was wrong for him to marry her. 5He would have killed John but was afraid of a riot. For all the people believed John was a prophet.

6But at a birthday party for Herod, Herodias' daughter danced for him. And he was very pleased by her dancing. 7So he promised to give her anything she wanted. 8Urged by her mother, the girl asked for John the Baptist's head on a tray.

9The king was upset by what she asked. But he had made a promise. And he didn't want to back down in front of his guests. So he gave the order for John to be killed.

10So John was beheaded in the prison. 11His head was brought on a tray and given to the girl. She then took it to her mother.

12John's disciples came for his body and buried it. Then they came to tell Jesus what had happened.

Jesus Feeds 5,000 People

13When Jesus heard the news, he went off by himself. He took a boat to a remote area to be alone. But the crowds saw where he was going. So they followed him by land from many villages.

14So when Jesus came out of the wilderness, a great crowd was waiting for him. He took pity on them and healed their sick.

15That evening the disciples came to him. They said, "It is already past time for supper. But there is nothing to eat here in the desert. Send the crowds away so they can go to the villages and buy some food."

16But Jesus said, "There is no need for that. You feed them!"

17"What!" they exclaimed. "We have just five small loaves of bread and two fish!"

18"Bring them here," he said.

19Then he told the people to sit down on the grass. He took the five loaves and two fish. He looked up into the sky and asked God's blessing on the meal. Then he broke the loaves apart. He gave them to the disciples to give to the people. 20And they all ate until they were full! And when the scraps were picked up, there were 12 basketfuls left over! 21About 5,000 men were in the crowd that day! And there were many women and children, too.

Jesus Walks on Water

Have you ever seen anyone walk across a lake? Have you ever tried to do this? Don't! But you'll read here about someone who did!

22Right after this, Jesus told his disciples to get into their boat. They were to cross over to the other side of the lake. Jesus stayed for awhile to get the people started home.

23-24Then Jesus went up into the hills to pray. Night came, and out on the lake the disciples were in trouble. For the wind had risen and they were in a heavy storm.

25About four o'clock in the morning Jesus came to them. And he was walking on the water! 26They screamed in fear, for they thought he was a ghost.

27But Jesus spoke to them to comfort them. "Don't be afraid!" he said.

28Then Peter called to him, "Sir, is it really you? If it is, tell me to come over to you. Let me walk on the water."

29"All right," the Lord said, "come along!"

So Peter went over the side of the boat. And he walked on the water toward Jesus. 30But then he looked around at the high waves. He was very afraid and began to sink. "Save me, Lord!" he shouted.

31So Jesus reached out his hand and saved him. "O man of little faith," Jesus said. "Why did you doubt me?" 32And when they had climbed back into the boat, the wind stopped.

33The others sat there, full of awe. "You really are the Son of God!" they exclaimed.

- *Remember:* What time of the day or night did this story happen? (14:23,25) Why were the disciples having trouble with their boat? (14:24) What did the disciples do when they saw Jesus walking on the water? (14:26) Who else tried to walk on the water? (14:28) Why couldn't he keep doing it? (14:30-31) Pretend you are Peter. How would you feel walking on the stormy lake? Why would you want Jesus out there with you?

- *Discover:* The disciples said that Jesus was God's Son. Why do you think they said that?

- *Apply:* Jesus is God's Son. He knows God better than anyone else. Wouldn't you like to read what he says about God? It's in your Bible.

- *What's next?* What if a person told everyone in the hospital to get well at once? What do you think would happen? Read Mark 6:53-56. ∎

Jesus Heals Everyone Who Touches Him

34They landed at Gennesaret. 35The news of their coming spread quickly throughout the city. Soon people were telling everyone to bring in their sick to be healed. 36The sick begged him to let them touch even the tassel of his robe. And all who did were healed.

God's Rules Are the Ones That Count

15 Some Pharisees and other Jewish leaders came from Jerusalem to speak to Jesus.

2"Why don't your disciples obey the old Jewish laws?" they demanded. "For they don't wash their hands before they eat." 3Jesus replied, "And why do your traditions break the commands of God? 4God's law says, 'Honor your father and mother. Anyone who curses his parents must die.' 5-6But you say, 'Your parents might be in need. But you may give their support money to God instead.' By your man-made rule, you nullify the direct command of God. For he says you should honor and care for your parents. 7You hypocrites! Isaiah was right when he spoke about you. 8He said, 'These people say they honor me. But their hearts are far away. 9Their worship is worthless. For they teach their man-made laws instead of those from God.'"

What You Say and Think Matter to God

10Then Jesus called to the crowds. "Listen to what I say," he said. "Try to understand me. 11You aren't made unholy by eating without washing your hands! It is what you say and think that makes you unclean."

12Then the disciples came to him. They said, "You made the Pharisees angry by saying that."

13-14Jesus replied, "Every plant not planted by my Father shall be rooted up. So don't listen to them. They are blind guides leading the blind. And both will fall into a ditch."

15Then Peter said, "You said we don't need to wash our hands before we eat. But the tradition says we are supposed to. Tell us what you mean."

16"Don't you understand?" Jesus asked him. 17"Anything you eat passes through your stomach and out again. 18But evil words come from an evil heart. This makes the man who says them unholy. 19For from the heart come evil thoughts, murder, adultery, theft, lying, and slander. 20These are what make a man unholy. But there is nothing unholy about eating without washing your hands first!"

A Woman's Faith Pleases Jesus; He Heals Her Daughter

[21]Jesus then left that part of the country. He walked to the area around Tyre and Sidon.

[22]A woman from Canaan was living there. She came to him, begging, "Have mercy on me, O Lord, King David's Son! For my daughter has a demon in her. And it torments her all the time."

[23]But Jesus gave her no answer. He did not even speak a word. Then his disciples urged him to send her away. "Tell her to get going," they said. "She is bothering us with all her begging."

[24]Then he said to the woman, "I was sent to help the Jews. They are the lost sheep of Israel. I was not sent to the Gentiles."

[25]But she came and bowed down in front of him. She begged again, "Sir, help me!"

[26]"It isn't right to take bread from children and throw it to the dogs," he said.

[27]"Yes, it is!" she said. "Even puppies under the table eat the crumbs that fall."

[28]"Woman," Jesus told her, "you have great faith. So I will do what you ask." And her daughter was healed right then.

Jesus' Miracles Amaze the Crowds

[29]Jesus now went back to the Sea of Galilee. He climbed a hill and sat there. [30]And a great crowd brought him their lame, blind, and crippled. They brought him those who couldn't speak, and many others. They laid them before Jesus, and he healed them all. [31]What a sight it was! People who hadn't ever said a word were talking loudly! The crippled were walking and jumping around! Those who had been blind were looking all around! The crowds were amazed, and they praised the God of Israel.

Bread and Fish for 4,000 People

[32]Then Jesus called his disciples to him. "I'm sorry for these people," he said. "They've been here with me for three days now. And they have nothing left to eat. I don't want to send them away hungry. For if I do, they'll faint on the way home."

[33]The disciples replied, "There are so many people here! Where could we get enough food here in the desert for all of them?"

[34]Jesus asked them, "How much food do you have?"

They replied, "We have seven loaves of bread and a few small fish!"

Evil words show a person's evil heart

But evil words come from an evil heart. This makes the man who says them unholy.

Matthew 15:18

---

[35]Then Jesus told all of the people to sit down on the ground. [36]He took the seven loaves and the fish. He gave thanks to God for them and broke them into pieces. Then he gave them to the disciples who gave them to the crowd. [37-38]And everyone ate until full. There were 4,000 men besides all the women and children! When they were finished, the scraps were picked up. There were seven basketfuls left over!

[39]Then Jesus sent the people home. He got into the boat and crossed to Magadan.

The Jewish Leaders Ask Again for a Miracle

16 One day the Pharisees and Sadducees came to see Jesus. They wanted to test him to see if he really was the Messiah. So they asked him to do some great wonder in the skies as a sign.

[2-3]He replied, "You are good at reading the weather signs of the skies. A red sky tonight means fair weather tomorrow. A red sky in the morning means bad weather all day. But you can't read the clear signs of the times! [4]This evil, unfaithful nation is asking for a strange sign in the heavens. But no more proof will be given except the miracle that happened to Jonah." Then Jesus walked out on them and went away.

Beware of Wrong Teaching

5They all went across the lake. When they got there, the disciples found they had forgotten to bring food.

6"Watch out!" Jesus warned them. "Be careful of the yeast of the Pharisees and Sadducees."

7They thought he was saying this because they had forgotten to bring bread.

8Jesus knew what they were thinking. So he said, "O men of little faith! Why are you so worried about having no food? 9Won't you ever understand? Don't you remember the 5,000 I fed with five loaves? Don't you remember all the food that was left over? 10Don't you remember the 4,000 I fed, and all that was left? 11How could you even think I was talking about food? But again I say, 'Be careful of the yeast of the Pharisees and Sadducees.'"

12Then at last they understood what he meant. The *yeast* stood for the *wrong teachings* of the Pharisees and Sadducees.

Peter Says Jesus Is the Messiah

13Then Jesus went to the area of Caesarea Philippi. He asked his disciples, "Who do the people say that I am?"

14"Well," they replied, "some say you are John the Baptist. Some say you are Elijah. Others say you are Jeremiah or one of the other prophets."

15Then he asked them, "Who do *you* think I am?"

16Simon Peter answered, "You are the Messiah, the Son of the living God."

17"God has blessed you, Simon, son of Jonah," Jesus said. "For my Father in Heaven has told you this. This truth has not come from any human source. 18You are Peter, a rock. And upon this rock I will build my church. And all the powers of hell shall not stand against it. 19And I will give you the keys of the Kingdom of Heaven. All the doors you lock on earth shall be locked in Heaven. And all the doors you open on earth shall be open in Heaven!"

20Then he warned the disciples not to tell others that he was the Messiah.

Jesus Begins to Talk about His Death

21From then on Jesus began to speak clearly to his disciples. He told them he would go to Jerusalem. And he told them what would happen to him there. He told them that he would suffer at the hands of the Jewish leaders. He told them he would be killed. And he told them he would be raised to life again three days later.

22But Peter took him aside to speak with him. "Heaven forbid, sir," he said. "This is not going to happen to you!"

23Then Jesus turned on Peter. "Get away from me, you Satan!" he said. "You are a dangerous trap for me. You are thinking from a human point of view, and not from God's."

24Then Jesus said to the disciples, "Do you want to be my followers? If you do, you must deny yourselves. You must take up your cross and follow me. 25For anyone who keeps his life for himself shall lose it. And anyone who loses his life for me shall find it again. 26What good is it if you gain the whole world and lose eternal life? What could ever be as good as eternal life? 27For I, the Messiah, shall come with my angels in my Father's glory. I will judge each person according to his deeds. 28And some of you standing here now will live to see me coming in my Kingdom."

Jesus Is Made Glorious

17Six days later Jesus took Peter, James, and his brother John. He brought them to the top of a high and lonely hill. 2As they watched, he changed so that his face shone like the sun. And his clothing became shining white.

3Suddenly Moses and Elijah came. And they were talking with him. 4Peter blurted out, "Sir, it's wonderful that we can be here! If you want me to, I'll build three shelters. I'll make one for you, one for Moses, and one for Elijah."

5But even as he said it, a bright cloud came over them. A voice from the cloud said, "This is my Son whom I love. I am very pleased with him. Obey him."

6At this the disciples fell face down on the ground. They were very afraid. 7Then Jesus came over and touched them. "Get up," he said. "Don't be afraid."

8And when they looked, only Jesus was with them.

9So they went back down the mountain. As they went, Jesus told them not to tell anyone what they had seen. They were to keep it a secret until after he had risen from the dead.

10His disciples asked, "Why do the Jewish leaders say Elijah must come back before the Messiah comes?"

11Jesus replied, "They are right. Elijah must come and set everything in order. 12In fact, he has already come, but no one knew him. He was treated badly by many. And I, the Messiah, shall also suffer at their hands."

13Then the disciples knew he was speaking of John the Baptist.

Jesus Heals a Boy with a Demon

14When they got to the bottom of the hill, a huge crowd was waiting for them. A man came and knelt before Jesus. He said, 15"Sir, have mercy on my son. For he has seizures and he suffers a great deal. He often falls into the fire or into the water. 16So I brought him to your disciples, but they couldn't help him."

17Jesus replied, "Oh, you stubborn, faithless people! How long shall I bear with you? Bring him here to me." 18Then Jesus spoke to the demon in the boy and it left him. From that moment the boy was well.

19After that the disciples asked Jesus, "Why couldn't we cast that demon out?"

20"Because of your little faith," Jesus told them. "Suppose you had faith even as small as a tiny mustard seed. If you did, you could say to this mountain, 'Move!' And it would move far away. Nothing would be too hard to do. 21But this kind of demon won't leave unless you have prayed and gone without food."

Jesus Reminds the Disciples of His Death

22-23One day they came together in Galilee. And Jesus said to them, "I am going to be given to those who will kill me. On the third day after I am killed I will be brought back to life again." And the disciples' hearts were filled with sadness and fear.

Peter Finds Tax Money Inside a Fish

24When they got to Capernaum, the Temple tax collectors came to Peter. They asked him, "Doesn't your master pay taxes?"

25"Of course he does," Peter replied.

Then he went into the house to talk to Jesus about it. But before he had a chance to speak, Jesus asked him, "What do you think, Peter? Do kings demand taxes from their own people or from conquered foreigners?"

26-27"They demand taxes from foreigners," Peter replied.

"Well, then," Jesus said, "the people are free! But we don't want to offend them. So go down to the shore and throw in a line. Open the mouth of the first fish you catch. You will find a coin to cover the taxes for both of us. Take it and pay them."

Who Is the Greatest?

Do you ever think you are better than someone else? If so, why? Do you have more money? Do you live in a better house? Do you have better clothes? Do you think you are smarter? This is what Jesus wants to tell you.

18 About that time the disciples went to Jesus. They wanted to know which of them would be greatest in the Kingdom of Heaven.

²Jesus called a small child over to him. He set the child down among them. ³Then he said, "You must turn to God from your sins. And you must become like little children. If you don't, you will never get into the Kingdom of Heaven. ⁴The one who humbles himself like this little child is the greatest in the Kingdom of Heaven. ⁵And anyone who welcomes a little child in my name is welcoming me and caring for me. ⁶But suppose one of you caused one of these little ones to lose his faith in me. If you did, it would be better for you to have a rock tied to your neck and be thrown into the sea.

⁷"How terrible it will be for the world because of all its evils. People will always be tempted to do wrong. But how terrible it will be for the person who does the tempting. ⁸So if your hand or foot causes you to sin, cut it off and throw it away. It is better to enter Heaven crippled than to be in hell with both of your hands and feet. ⁹And if your eye causes you to sin, gouge it out and throw it away. It is better to enter Heaven with one eye than to be in hell with two.

- *Remember:* What did the disciples ask Jesus? (18:1) Who did Jesus say is greatest? (18:4) Do you know someone who is humble? What is that person like?

- *Discover:* The greatest people in the world are those who please Jesus.

- *Apply:* Whenever you begin to do something, do you ask if it would please Jesus? Are there some things Jesus wants you to do better? Start doing them today.

- *What's next?* How many times should you forgive a person? Read Matthew 18:21-35. ■

A Story about a Lamb

There are 99 sheep safe inside. There is one little lamb lost outside. Will the shepherd stay with the 99? Or will he go to look for the one?

¹⁰"Be careful that you don't look down upon a single one of these children. For I tell you that in Heaven their angels can speak directly to my Father. ¹¹And I, the Messiah, came to save the lost.

¹²"Suppose a man has 100 sheep. And suppose one wanders away and is lost. What will he do? Won't he leave the 99 others? Won't he go out into the hills to look for the lost one? ¹³And if he finds it, he will rejoice over it. He will be happier over the one than over the 99 others safe at home! ¹⁴Just so, it is not my Father's will that even one of these little ones should die.

- *Remember:* When the man watching his sheep learned that one of his sheep was lost, what did he do? (18:12) What did the man do when he found it? (18:13) Does God want even one little child to be lost from him? (18:14) Why not? What does this tell you about God?

- *Discover:* God loves children and all people. He does not want one child or one person to be lost from knowing him as Savior.

- *Apply:* God wants you to live with him one day in Heaven. He sent Jesus to help you get there. If you say yes to Jesus you will. If you say no to Jesus you won't.

● *What's next?* Jesus heals a blind man. Why should that cause trouble? Read John 9. ▉

What Do You Do If Someone's Sin Hurts You?

¹⁵"If a brother sins against you, go to him in private. Speak with him about the wrong thing he has done. If he listens and confesses it, you have won back a brother. ¹⁶But if not, then take one or two others with you. Go back to him again, proving everything you say by these witnesses. ¹⁷If he still won't listen, then take your case to the church. If he won't listen to the church's decision, then the church should expell him. ¹⁸And I tell you the truth! Whatever you bind on earth is bound in Heaven. Whatever you free on earth will be freed in Heaven.

¹⁹"I also tell you this. Suppose two of you agree down here on earth about something you ask for. If this is so, my Father in Heaven will do it for you. ²⁰For where two or three gather together because they are mine, I will be right there among them."

A Story about Forgiving

If someone did something bad to you, would you forgive him? Would you forgive him a hundred times? How much should we forgive? This is what Jesus said.

²¹Then Peter came to Jesus. "Sir, how often should I forgive a brother who sins against me?" he asked. "Should I forgive him seven times?"

²²"No!" Jesus replied, "seventy times seven!

²³"The Kingdom of Heaven is like a king. This king decided to bring his accounts up to date. ²⁴One of his servants was brought in who owed him $10 million! ²⁵He couldn't pay. So the king ordered him to be sold to pay back what he owed. He also ordered the man's wife and children and all he owned to be sold.

²⁶"But the servant fell down before the king. His face was in the dust. He said, 'Oh, sir, be patient with me. I will find a way to pay it all.'

²⁷"Then the king was filled with pity for him. So he let his servant go and said he didn't have to pay back his debt.

²⁸"But when the servant left the king, he went to a man who owed him $2,000. He grabbed the man by the throat. And he demanded he pay his debt right away.

²⁹"The man fell down before him. He begged him for a little time. 'Be patient and I will pay it,' he begged.

³⁰"But the servant wouldn't wait for his money. He had the man arrested. And he put him jail until the debt would be paid in full.

³¹"Then the man's friends went to the king. They told him what had happened. ³²And the king called before him the servant he had forgiven. He said, 'You evil-hearted servant! I forgave you a huge debt, just because you asked me to. ³³Shouldn't you have had mercy on others, just as I had mercy on you?'

Only Jesus can save people from sin

And I, the Messiah, came to save the lost.

Matthew 18:11

³⁴"Then the angry king sent the man to prison. And he would stay there until he had paid every last penny. ³⁵This is what my heavenly Father will do to you if you don't forgive your brothers."

● *Remember:* Who asked Jesus about forgiving? (18:21) How many times should we forgive? What did Jesus say? What do you think he meant by that? (18:22) In the story Jesus told, how much did the man owe the king? (18:24) What did the king say he would do to the man and his family? (18:25) Why didn't he? What did the king do to the man instead? (18:26-27) When this man was forgiven, what did he do to another man who owed him money? (18:28-30) What did the king do when he heard about this? What will God do if we don't forgive others? (18:35) Do you think the king did the right thing? Why? Would you have done this if you were the king?

- *Discover:* We must forgive others when they ask for forgiveness.

- *Apply:* Do you hate someone? Is there someone you won't forgive? Read this story again. What does God want you to do?

- *What's next?* What is the difference between a friend and a good friend? Jesus tells you in Luke 10:25-37. ■

Jesus Talks about Marriage and Divorce

19 After Jesus had finished this address, he left Galilee. He circled back to Judea from across the Jordan River. ²Great crowds followed him, and he healed their sick. ³Some Pharisees came to speak to him. They tried to trap him into saying something that would ruin him.

"Do you allow divorce?" they asked.

⁴"Don't you read the Scriptures?" he replied. "In them it is written that in the beginning God created man and woman. ⁵⁻⁶It says that a man should leave his father and mother. And he should be forever united to his wife. The two shall become one. No longer two, but one! And no man may tear apart what God has joined together."

⁷"Then, why," they asked, "did Moses say that a man may divorce his wife? He said a man could do this by writing his wife a divorce letter."

⁸Jesus replied, "Moses did that because of your hard and evil hearts. But it was not what God had planned in the beginning. ⁹And I tell you the truth! Anyone who divorces his wife and marries another commits adultery. The only exception is when his wife has been unfaithful to him."

¹⁰Jesus' disciples then said to him, "If that is how it is, it is better not to marry!"

¹¹"Not everyone can accept these words," Jesus said. "Only those whom God helps will receive them. ¹²Some are born without the ability to marry. Some are made that way by men. Some don't marry for the sake of the Kingdom of Heaven. Let anyone who can, accept this statement."

Jesus Loves the Children

¹³Little children were brought for Jesus to lay his hands on them and pray. But the disciples scolded those who brought them. "Don't bother him," they said.

¹⁴But Jesus said, "Let the little children come to me. Don't stop them. For the Kingdom of Heaven belongs to such as these." ¹⁵And he put his hands on their heads and blessed them before he left.

Jesus Speaks to the Rich Young Man

¹⁶Someone came to Jesus with this question. He said, "Good master, what must I do to have eternal life?"

¹⁷"When you call me good you are calling me God," Jesus replied. "For God alone is truly good. But you can get to Heaven if you keep God's commands."

¹⁸"Which ones?" the man asked.

And Jesus replied, "Don't murder. Don't commit adultery. Don't steal. Don't lie. ¹⁹Honor your father and mother. And love your neighbor as yourself!"

Anyone who wants to be in Heaven must come to Jesus like a little child

Jesus said, "Let the little children come to me. Don't stop them. For the Kingdom of Heaven belongs to such as these."

Matthew 19:14

---

²⁰"I've always obeyed every one of them," the youth replied. "What else must I do?"

²¹Jesus told him, "If you want to be perfect, sell everything you have. Give the money to the poor. And you will have treasure in Heaven. Then come and follow me." ²²But when the young

man heard this, he went away sadly. This was because he was very rich.

²³Then Jesus said to his disciples, "I tell you the truth! It is hard for a rich man to get into the Kingdom of Heaven. ²⁴I say it again! It is very hard for a camel to go through the eye of a needle. But it is even harder for a rich man to enter the Kingdom of God!"

²⁵These words were hard for the disciples to understand. "Then who in the world can be saved?" they asked.

²⁶Jesus looked at them intently. Then he said, "Humanly speaking, no one. But with God, everything is possible."

²⁷Then Peter said to him, "We left everything to follow you. What will we get out of it?"

²⁸And Jesus replied, "I, the Messiah, shall sit on my throne in the Kingdom. And you my disciples shall sit on 12 thrones judging the 12 tribes of Israel. ²⁹And some might give up their homes, brothers, sisters, fathers, mothers, wives, children, or property, to follow me. They shall be given 100 times as much in return. And they shall have eternal life. ³⁰But many who are first now will be last then. And some who are last now will be first then."

A Story about a Vineyard

Two people do the same work. One gets more money than the other. "That's not fair!" someone says. "Yes it is," Jesus said. How can he say that? How could it be fair? Here's the answer.

20 Here is another story about the Kingdom of Heaven. "The owner of an estate went out early one morning. He needed to hire workers to harvest his field. ²He agreed to pay them $20 a day and sent them out to work.

³"A couple of hours later he saw some men standing around in the marketplace. They had nothing to do. ⁴So he sent them also into his fields. He told them he would pay them whatever was right at the end of the day. ⁵At noon he did the same thing. And he did it again around three o'clock in the afternoon.

⁶"At five o'clock that evening he was in town again. He saw some more men standing around. He asked them, 'Why haven't you been working today?'

⁷"'Because no one hired us,' they replied.

"'Then go on out and join the others in my fields,' he told them.

⁸"That evening he told the paymaster to call the men in and pay them. He was to begin by paying the last men first. ⁹When the men hired at five o'clock were paid, each was given $20. ¹⁰Then the men hired earlier came to get their pay. They thought that they would get much more. But they, also, were paid $20.

¹¹⁻¹²"They were upset! They said, 'Those men worked only one hour. But you've paid them just as much as us. And we worked all day in the scorching heat.'

¹³"'Friend,' he answered one of them, 'I did you no wrong! Didn't you agree to work all day for $20? ¹⁴Take it and go. It is my desire to pay all the same. ¹⁵Is it against the law to give away my money if I want to? Should you be angry because I am kind?' ¹⁶And so it is that the last shall be first, and the first, last."

● *Remember:* How much did the first workers get? How long did they work for it? (20:1-2) When did the other workers start? (20:3-7) When did the owner pay everyone? What did he pay everyone? (20:8-10) Did he pay anyone less than they agreed? Did he pay anyone more than they deserved? Who? The man paid everyone as much as they agreed to work for. He was fair to them. But he gave some people extra. He was generous with them.

- *Discover:* We must always pay as much, or do as much, as we agree. That's fair. But sometimes we like to pay more, or do more, than we agree. That's generous. God is fair. He is also generous!

- *Apply:* The next time you say, "It's not fair," stop and think. Did someone do less than you agreed? Did they do exactly what you agreed? Or did they do even more than you agreed? It's not fair if it's less. It is fair if it's the same. It's generous if it's more.

- *What's next?* A blind man calls for help. He wants Jesus. Will Jesus hear? Read Mark 10:46-52. ◼

Jesus Talks about His Death

17Now Jesus was on his way to Jerusalem. He took the 12 disciples aside. 18He told them about what would happen to him when they got there.

"I will be turned in to the chief priests and other Jewish leaders. They will condemn me to die. 19And they will hand me over to the Romans. I will be laughed at and killed on a cross. Then on the third day I will rise to life again."

James and John's Mother Asks for a Favor

20Then the mother of James and John, the sons of Zebedee, came to Jesus. She brought her sons with her to ask Jesus a favor.

21"What is it that you want?" he asked.

She replied, "In your Kingdom, please let one of my sons sit at your right. And please let the other sit at your left."

22But Jesus told her, "You don't know what you are asking!" Then he turned to James and John. He asked them, "Can you drink the terrible cup I am going to drink?"

"Yes," they replied, "we are able!"

23"You shall indeed drink from it," he told them. "But I have no right to say who will sit on the thrones next to mine. Those places are given by my Father."

If You Want to Be Great, Learn to Serve

24The other 10 disciples were angry. For they heard what James and John had asked for.

25But Jesus called them together. He said, "Among the heathen, kings are tyrants. And each minor ruler lords it over those under him. 26But among you it is quite different. Anyone wanting to be a leader among you must be your servant. 27And if you want to be right at the top, you must serve like a slave. 28You must do just as I do. For I, the Messiah, did not come to be served. Instead, I came to serve. And I came to give my life as a ransom for many."

Jesus Heals Two Blind Men

29Jesus and the disciples were leaving the city of Jericho. And a great crowd followed along behind them.

30Two blind men were sitting beside the road. When they heard that Jesus was coming that way, they began shouting. "Sir, King David's Son!" they cried. "Have mercy on us!"

31The crowd told them to be quiet. But they only yelled louder.

32-33Then Jesus came to the place where they were. He stopped in the road and called, "What do you want me to do for you?"

"Sir," they said, "we want to see!"

34Jesus was moved with pity for them, so he touched their eyes. And right away they could see, and they followed him.

Jesus Rides into Jerusalem

Why did people throw their coats on the ground? Why did they throw them in front of a donkey?

21 Jesus and his disciples drew near to Jerusalem. They were near the town of Bethphage on the Mount of Olives. And Jesus sent two of them into the village ahead.

2"Just as you arrive," he said, "you will see a donkey tied there. It will have its colt standing beside it. Untie them and bring them here. 3Someone might ask you what you are doing. If they do, just say, 'The Master needs them.' Then there will be no trouble."

4This was done to fulfill the words of the prophet. He said, 5"Tell Jerusalem her King is coming to her! He is riding humbly on a donkey's colt!"

6The two disciples did as Jesus said. 7They brought the animals to him. And they threw their coats over the colt for him to ride on. 8And some in the crowd threw down their coats along the road ahead of him. Others cut branches from the trees and spread them out before him.

9Then the crowds pushed on ahead and pressed along behind. They shouted, "God bless King David's Son! God's Man is here! Bless him, Lord! Praise God in highest Heaven!"

10The whole city of Jerusalem was stirred as he entered. "Who is this?" they asked.

11And the crowds replied, "It's Jesus! He is the prophet from Nazareth up in Galilee."

- *Remember:* Why did Jesus ride a donkey into Jerusalem? (21:4-5) What did people throw in front of Jesus' donkey? (21:8) What did the people say about Jesus? (21:9) The people were excited. They thought Jesus would become King of Israel. But Jesus is God's Son. He is not just a king. He is King over all the earth.

- *Discover:* Jesus rules over everything! He is King over all kings. See Revelation 19:16.

- *Apply:* Before you go to sleep tonight, spend some time praising God. Why? Because he made you! Because he made

Heaven! Because one day he will rule over all Heaven and earth!

- *What's next?* Would you steal something from God? Read about some people who tried in Mark 12:1-12. ∎

Jesus Cleans Out the Temple

12Jesus went into the Temple area. He drove out all who were buying and selling there. He knocked over the tables of the money changers. He pushed over the benches of those who were selling doves.

13"The Scriptures say my Temple is to be a place of prayer," he said. "But you have turned it into a den of robbers."

14And now the blind and crippled came to him. He healed them there in the Temple. 15The chief priests and other Jewish leaders saw these miracles. They heard even the children in the Temple shouting, "God bless the Son of David." So these leaders were upset and angry. They asked him, "Do you hear what these children are saying?" 16"Yes," Jesus replied. "Didn't you ever read the Scriptures? For they say, 'Even little babies shall praise him!'"

17Then he went back to Bethany, where he stayed overnight.

If They Really Believe, the Disciples Can Do Miracles Too

18In the morning he was going back to Jerusalem, and he was hungry. 19On the way, he saw a fig tree beside the road. He went over to see if there were any figs on it. But there were only leaves. Then he said to it, "Never bear fruit again!" And soon the fig tree withered up.

20The disciples were amazed. "How did the fig tree wither so quickly?" they asked.

21Then Jesus told them, "I tell you the truth! You must have faith and you must not doubt. Then you will do things like this and much more. You might even say to this Mount of Olives, 'Move over into the ocean.' And it will go there. 22You

will be given anything you ask for in prayer, if you believe."

Who Gives Jesus His Authority?

[23]So Jesus went back to the Temple and began teaching. And the chief priests and other Jewish leaders came up to him. They wanted to know who gave him the authority to throw out the merchants the day before.

[24]"I'll tell you if you answer one question first," Jesus replied. [25]"Was John the Baptist sent from God or not?"

They talked it over among themselves. "We might say he came from God," they said. "But then he will ask why we didn't believe what John said. [26]And if we deny that God sent him, we'll be mobbed. For all the people believe John was a prophet." [27]So they finally said, "We don't know!"

And Jesus said, "Then I won't answer your question either."

A Story about Two Sons

[28]"But what do you think about this?" Jesus asked. "A man with two sons told the older boy, 'Son, go out and work on the farm today.' [29]'I won't,' he answered. But later he changed his mind and went. [30]Then the father told the youngest, 'You go!' And he said, 'Yes, sir, I will.' But then he didn't go. [31]Which of the two obeyed his father?"

They replied, "The first, of course."

Then Jesus explained his meaning: "Surely evil men and prostitutes will get into the Kingdom before you do. [32]For John the Baptist told you to repent and turn to God, but you wouldn't. But the tax collectors and prostitutes did repent. And even after you saw this, you still would not repent and believe him.

A Story about Wicked Farmers

[33]"Now listen to this story. A certain landowner planted a vineyard with a hedge around it. He built a platform for the watchman. He leased the vineyard to some farmers on a sharecrop basis. Then he went away to live in another country.

[34]"The time of the grape harvest came. So he sent his agents to the farmers to collect his share. [35]But the farmers attacked his men. They beat one, killed one, and stoned another.

[36]"Then he sent a larger group of his men to collect for him. But the results were the same. [37]Finally the owner sent his son, thinking they would surely respect him.

[38]"But these farmers saw the son coming. And they said among themselves, 'Here comes the heir to this vineyard. Come on, let's kill him and get it for ourselves!' [39]So they dragged him out of the vineyard and killed him.

[40]"When the owner comes back, what do you think he will do to those farmers?"

[41]The Jewish leaders replied, "He will put the wicked men to a horrible death. Then he will lease the vineyard to others who will pay him right away."

[42]Then Jesus asked them, "Haven't you ever read in the Scriptures? It says, 'The stone rejected by the builders has been made the cornerstone. What an amazing thing the Lord has done!'

[43]"I am telling you about the Kingdom of God. It shall be taken away from you. But it will be given to a nation that will give God his share of the crop. [44]All who stumble on this rock of truth shall be broken. But those it falls on will be scattered like dust."

[45]The chief priests and other Jewish leaders understood that Jesus was talking about them. They saw that they were the farmers in his story. [46]They wanted to get rid of him. But they were afraid to try because of the crowds. For all the people believed Jesus was a prophet.

A Story about a Wedding

Suppose the president or prime minister invited you to dinner. Would you go? Or would you laugh? This is a story about a king who invited some people to dinner. But they laughed at him. What would he do?

22 Jesus told several other stories to show what the Kingdom of Heaven is like.

"For instance," he said, "the Kingdom is like the story of a king. This king made a great wedding dinner for his son. ³Many guests were asked to come. The banquet was made ready. Then the king sent messengers to tell everyone it was time to come. But all of them refused! ⁴So he sent other servants to tell them, 'Everything is ready! The roast is in the oven. Hurry!'

⁵"But the guests he had asked to come just laughed. They went on about their business. One went to his farm, another went to his store. ⁶Others beat up his messengers and treated them badly. They even killed some of them.

⁷"Then the angry king sent out his army. He destroyed the murderers and burned their city. ⁸And he said to his servants, 'The wedding feast is ready. The guests I have asked to come aren't worthy of the honor. ⁹Now go out to the street corners and invite everyone you see.'

¹⁰"So the servants did, and brought in all they could find. They brought good and bad alike. And the banquet hall was filled with guests. ¹¹So the king came in to meet the guests. But he saw a man who wasn't wearing the wedding robe provided for him.

¹²"'Friend,' he asked, 'why are you here without a wedding robe?' And the man had no answer.

¹³"Then the king said to his servants, 'Tie him up, hand and foot. Then throw him out into the outer darkness. In that place, there is much crying and grinding of teeth.' ¹⁴For many are called, but few are chosen."

- *Remember:* A king invited people to dinner. What did they do? (22:1-6) Who did he invite next? (22:8-10) This is a story about Heaven. God has invited many people to come and live with him. But most of them laugh at him. They want to go to Heaven their own way, not God's way. So God invites others who will come his way.

- *Discover:* We must go to Heaven God's way. He invites us to come. We must accept. We cannot get into God's home our own way.

- *Apply:* The Bible tells us God's way to Heaven. We go there by accepting Jesus as Savior. Are you trying to get to Heaven by just being good? Are you trying to get there another way? It won't work.

- *What's next?* When is a penny worth more than a bag of money? Jesus will tell you in Luke 21:1-4. ∎

Pharisees Try to Trap Jesus with Questions about Taxes

¹⁵Then the Pharisees met together. They wanted to find some way to trap Jesus into saying something wrong. They wanted some excuse to arrest him. ¹⁶So they sent some of their men along with the Herodians. And they said to him, "Sir, we know you are very honest. We know that you teach the truth no matter what the cost. You have no fear and you aren't looking for favor. ¹⁷Now tell us, is it right to pay taxes to Rome or not?"

¹⁸But Jesus saw what they were after. "You hypocrites!" he exclaimed. "Who are you trying to fool with your trick questions? ¹⁹Here, show me a coin." And they handed him a penny.

²⁰"Whose picture is stamped on it?" he asked them. "And whose name is this under the picture?"

²¹"Caesar's," they replied.

"Well, then," he said, "give it to Caesar if it is his. And give to God everything that belongs to God."

²²His reply surprised and amazed them. So they went away.

Sadducees Try to Trick Jesus with Questions about the Resurrection

23But that same day some of the Sadducees came to Jesus. The Sadducees claim there is no resurrection after death. They said, 24"Sir, Moses told us what to do if a man died without children. Moses said that his brother should marry the widow. And their children would get all the dead man's property. 25Well, we had among us a family of seven brothers. The first of these men married and then died, without children. So his widow became the second brother's wife. 26This brother also died without children. So the wife was passed to the next brother. This happened again and again until she had been the wife of each of them. 27And then she also died. 28So whose wife will she be after the resurrection? For she was the wife of all seven of them!"

29But Jesus said, "Your thinking is full of errors. This is because you don't know the Scriptures. And you don't believe in God's power! 30For in the resurrection there is no marriage. Everyone is like the angels in Heaven. 31But now let us look at your doubt about the resurrection of the dead. Don't you ever read the Scriptures? Have you not read, 32'I am the God of Abraham, Isaac, and Jacob'? So God is not the God of the dead, but of the living."

What Is the Most Important Commandment?

33The crowds were amazed by his answers. 34-35But the Pharisees weren't! They saw that he had confused the Sadducees with his answer. So they thought up a question of their own to ask him. One of them, a lawyer, spoke up. He said, 36"Sir, which is the most important command in the laws of Moses?"

37Jesus said, "'Love the Lord your God with all your heart, soul, and mind.' 38-39This is the first and greatest command. The second most important is similar: 'Love your neighbor as much as you love yourself.' 40All the other commands come from these two laws. And all the demands of the prophets come from them, too. Keep only these two and you will find that you are obeying all the others."

The Religious Leaders Can't Answer Jesus' Question

41The Pharisees were all around him. So Jesus asked them a question: 42"What about the Messiah? Whose son is he?"

"The son of David," they replied.

43"Then why does David call him 'Lord'?" Jesus asked. "And David was speaking under the power of the Holy Spirit. For David said, 44'God said to my Lord, "Sit at my right hand until I put your enemies under your feet."'

45"Since David called him 'Lord,' how can he be just his son?"

46They had no answer. And after that no one dared ask him any more questions.

Jesus Warns the People about the Religious Leaders

23 Then Jesus spoke to the crowds, and to his disciples. He said, 2"You would think these Jewish leaders and these Pharisees were Moses! For they keep making up so many laws. 3And of course you should obey their every desire! It may be all right to do what they say. But above anything else, don't follow their example. For they don't do what they tell you to do. 4They load you down with demands that cannot be kept. They themselves don't even try to keep them.

5"Everything they do is done for show. They act holy by wearing little prayer boxes on their arms. And they make the tassels on their robes longer. 6And how they love to sit at the head table at banquets! They love to sit in the reserved seats in the synagogue! 7How they enjoy the respect given to them on the streets! They love to be called 'Rabbi' and 'Master'! 8Don't ever let anyone call you that. For only God is your Rabbi. All of you are on the same level, as brothers. 9And don't speak to anyone here on earth as 'Father.' For only God in Heaven should be spoken to like that. 10And don't be called 'Master.' For only one is your master, the Messiah.

11"The more humble your service to others, the greater you are. To be the greatest is to be a servant. 12But those who think themselves great shall be made humble. And those who humble themselves shall be honored.

Seven Woes Against the Religious Leaders

13-14"How terrible it will be for you, Pharisees! How terrible it will be for all you other religious leaders! You are hypocrites! You won't let others enter the Kingdom of Heaven. And you won't go in yourselves. And you pretend to be holy! You make long, public prayers in the streets. But at the same time, you are kicking widows out of their homes. Hypocrites! 15Yes, it will be terrible for you hypocrites. For you go to great lengths to make one believer. But then you turn him into twice the son of hell you are yourselves. 16Blind guides! It will be terrible for you! For you make rules so that you can get away with lying. You say a promise made 'By God's Temple' means nothing. You claim you can break such a promise. But you say a promise made 'By the gold in the Temple' cannot be broken! 17Blind fools! Which is greater, the gold, or the Temple that makes the gold holy? 18And you say a promise 'By the altar' can be broken. But you say a promise 'By the gifts on the altar' cannot be broken! 19Blind guides! For which is greater, the gift on the altar, or the altar itself that makes the gift holy? 20Suppose you make a promise 'By the altar.' If so, you are promising by the altar and everything on it. 21And suppose you make a promise 'By the Temple.' If so, you are promising by the Temple and by God who lives in it. 22And suppose you make a promise 'By heavens.' If so, you are promising by the Throne of God and by God himself.

23"Yes, it will be terrible for you, Pharisees! It will be terrible for all you religious leaders! You are all hypocrites! For you tithe down to the last mint leaf in your garden. But you don't do the important things. You don't uphold justice. You don't do acts of mercy. And you have no faith. Yes, you should tithe. But you shouldn't leave out the more important things. 24Blind guides! You strain out a gnat and swallow a camel.

25"It will be terrible for you, Pharisees! It will be terrible for all you other religious leaders! You are hypocrites! You are so careful to polish the outside of the cup. But the inside is dirty with cheating and greed. 26Blind Pharisees! First clean out the inside of the cup. Then the whole cup will be clean.

27"How terrible it will be for you Pharisees and religious leaders! You are like whitewashed tombs. You are bright and clean on the outside. But you are full of dead men's bones. All kinds of unclean things are on the inside! 28You try to look like holy men. But under your white robes are hearts dirty with every kind of sin.

We must love God with all we are

Jesus said, "Love the Lord your God with all your heart, soul, and mind."

Matthew 22:37

29-30"Yes, how terrible it will be for you, Pharisees! How terrible it will be for all you religious leaders! You are hypocrites! For you build monuments to the prophets killed by your fathers. You lay flowers on the graves of the godly men they destroyed. You say, 'We surely would never have acted like our fathers did.'

31"In saying that, you accuse yourselves of being the sons of wicked men. 32And you are following in their steps. You are doing just the things they once did. 33You snakes! You children of vipers! How shall you escape the judgment of hell?

34"I will send you prophets, wise men, and inspired writers. But you will kill some on a cross. You will rip open the backs of others with whips in your synagogues. You will chase them from city to city. 35You will become guilty of all the blood of godly men who have been murdered. The list begins with righteous Abel. And it goes to Zechariah, the son of Barachiah. He was killed by you between the Temple and the altar. 36Yes, all the judgment of the centuries shall break upon your heads!

37"O Jerusalem, Jerusalem! She is the

city that kills the prophets God sends to her! How often I have wanted to gather your children together. I wanted to do this like a hen gathers her chicks under her wings. But you wouldn't let me. ³⁸And now your house is left to you, empty and destroyed. ³⁹For I tell you the truth! You will not see me again until you can say, 'Blessed is he who comes in the name of the Lord.'"

Jesus Tells about the Future

24 Jesus began to leave the Temple grounds and his disciples came along. They wanted to take him on a tour of the Temple buildings.

²But he told them, "All these buildings will be knocked down. Not one stone will be left on top of another!"

³"When will this happen?" the disciples asked him later. They were sitting on the slopes of the Mount of Olives. "What events will show that you are coming back? How will we know the end of the world is near?"

⁴Jesus told them, "Don't let anyone fool you. ⁵For many will come claiming to be the Messiah. And they will lead many astray. ⁶You will hear about wars beginning. But this alone does not mean I am coming. These must come, but the end is not yet. ⁷The nations and kingdoms of the earth will rise against each other. There will be famines and earthquakes in many places. ⁸But all this will be only the beginning of the horrors to come.

⁹"Then all over the world you will be hated because you are mine. You will be treated badly and even killed. ¹⁰Many of you will fall back into sin. Some of you will even betray and hate each other. ¹¹And many false prophets will come. They will lead many astray. ¹²Sin will be everywhere. It will cool the love of many. ¹³But those who stand to the end shall be saved.

¹⁴"And the Good News about the Kingdom will be preached throughout the whole world. All nations will hear it. Then, finally, the end will come.

¹⁵"You will see the horrible thing told about by Daniel the prophet. It will be standing in a holy place. Let the reader understand this! ¹⁶Then those in Judea must run to the Judean hills. ¹⁷Those on their porches must not even go inside to pack before they go. ¹⁸Those working in the fields should not go home for their clothes.

¹⁹"And how terrible it will be for pregnant women! How terrible it will be for those with babies! ²⁰And pray that you won't have to run during the winter. Just hope you won't have to flee on the Sabbath. ²¹For there will be trouble like the world has never before seen. And the world will never see such trouble again.

²²"In fact, unless those days are shortened, all mankind will die. But they will be shortened for the sake of God's chosen people.

Jesus Tells about His Return

²³"At that time, someone might say, 'The Messiah has come to such and such a place.' If someone says this, don't believe it. ²⁴For false Christs shall come. And there will be many false prophets. They will do great miracles. Even God's chosen ones might even be tricked. ²⁵See, I have warned you!

²⁶"Suppose someone tells you the Messiah has come back. Suppose you are told he is out in the desert. If this happens, don't even bother to go and look. And suppose someone says the Messiah is hiding at a certain place. If you hear this, don't believe it! ²⁷For lightning flashes across the sky from east to west. And in the same way, I will come back. ²⁸And wherever the dead animal is, there the vultures will gather.

²⁹"Right after the trouble of those days the sun will be made dark. The moon will not give light. The stars will seem to fall from the heavens. And all the heavenly bodies will be shaken.

³⁰"And then at last the signal of my coming will appear in the heavens. There will be deep sadness all around the earth. And the nations of the world will see me come in the clouds of Heaven. I will come with power and great glory. ³¹And I shall send forth my angels with the sound of a mighty trumpet blast. And they shall gather my chosen ones. They shall bring them from the farthest

ends of the earth and Heaven.

³²"Now learn a lesson from the fig tree. There is a time when her branch is tender and the leaves begin to sprout. You know that this happens when summer is almost here. ³³In the same way, you will see all these things beginning to happen. And you will know that my coming is near. At that time, I will be right at the door! ³⁴Then at last this age will come to its end.

³⁵"Heaven and earth will disappear, but my words stand forever.

Jesus Says to Always Be Watching for His Return

³⁶"But no one knows the date and hour when the end will be. Not even the angels know this. No, not even God's Son knows this. Only the Father knows.

³⁷"At the time the Messiah returns people will be at ease. It will be like it was in the days of Noah. ³⁸In the days before the flood, the world was at ease. People ate, drank, and had weddings right up to the flood. But then the flood came upon them suddenly! ³⁹People refused to believe the flood was coming until it came. And then it was too late! It washed them all away. The same thing will happen when I come back.

⁴⁰"Two men will be working together in the fields. One will be taken. The other will be left behind. ⁴¹Two women will be going about their household work. One will be taken. The other will be left behind.

⁴²"So be ready at all times. For you don't know what day your Lord is coming.

⁴³"A person can avoid trouble from robbers by keeping watch for them. ⁴⁴In the same way, you can avoid trouble by always being ready for my coming.

⁴⁵"Are you a wise and faithful servant of the Lord? Have I given you the task of taking care of my household? Have I asked you to feed my children day by

day? ⁴⁶Blessings on you if I come and find you doing your work. ⁴⁷I will put such faithful ones in charge of all that I own!

⁴⁸"But suppose you say to yourself, 'My Lord won't be coming for a while.' ⁴⁹Suppose you begin treating your fellow servants badly. And what if you start getting drunk all the time? ⁵⁰Your Lord will come when you aren't ready. ⁵¹He will whip you badly. And he will send you off to the Judgment of the hypocrites. In that day, there will be much crying and grinding of teeth.

A Story about Ten Bridesmaids

25 "The Kingdom of Heaven is like the story of 10 bridesmaids. They took their lamps and went to meet the bridegroom. ²⁻⁴But only five of them were wise. They filled their lamps with oil. But the other five were foolish and forgot.

⁵⁻⁶"The bridegroom was late in coming. So they lay down to rest until midnight. Then they were woken by a shout, 'The bridegroom is coming! Come out and welcome him!'

⁷⁻⁸"All the girls jumped up and trimmed their lamps. Then the five who didn't have any oil begged the others to share with them. This was because their lamps were going out.

⁹"But the others said, 'We don't have enough. Go instead to the shops and buy some.'

¹⁰"But while they were gone, the bridegroom came. Those who were ready went in with him to the marriage feast. And the door was locked after them.

¹¹"Later, the other five came back. They stood outside, calling, 'Sir, open the door for us!'

¹²"But he called back, 'Go away! It is too late!'

¹³"So stay awake and be ready. For you do not know the date or moment of my coming.

A Story about Talents

God gives each of us certain talents, or abilities. We can do some things well. What do you do well? He also gives us special gifts. What do you do with them? Do you use them in a way that makes God happy? Here is a story about using talents.

¹⁴"The Kingdom of Heaven is like the story of a man going into another country. He called together his servants. And he loaned them money to invest for him while he was gone.

¹⁵"He gave $5,000 to one, $2,000 to another, and $1,000 to the last. He gave them money according to their skills. Then he left on his trip. ¹⁶The man who was given $5,000 went right to work. He went into business and soon earned another $5,000. ¹⁷The man with $2,000 went right to work, too. And soon he earned another $2,000.

¹⁸"But the man who was given $1,000 dug a hole in the ground. Then he hid the money there to keep it safe.

¹⁹"After a long time their master came back from his trip. He called them in to report on the money he had given them to use. ²⁰The man to whom he had given $5,000 brought him $10,000.

²¹"His master praised him for good work. 'You have been faithful in handling this small amount,' he told him. 'So now I will give you much more to work with. Begin the jobs I have given to you.'

²²"Next came the man who had been given $2,000. He said, 'Sir, you gave me $2,000 to use. And now I have doubled it.'

²³"'Good work,' his master said. 'You are a good and faithful servant. You have been faithful over this small amount. So now I will give you much more.'

²⁴⁻²⁵"Then the man with the $1,000 came. He said, 'Sir, I knew you were a hard man. And I was afraid you would rob me of what I earned. So I hid your money in the earth and here it is!'

²⁶"But his master replied, 'Wicked man! Lazy slave! You knew I would ask for your profit. ²⁷But you should at least have put my money into the bank. That way I could have made some money as interest. ²⁸Take the money from this man and give it to the man with the $10,000. ²⁹For the man who uses well what he is given shall be given more. He shall have all that he needs. But for the unfaithful man, even the little he has shall be taken from him. ³⁰And throw the useless servant out into outer darkness. In that place, there shall be much crying and grinding of teeth.'

- *Remember:* How much money did the man give each servant? (25:15) How did each man use the money? (25:16-18) How did the man reward the first two servants? Why? (25:19-23) How did he punish the third servant? Why? (25:24-28) What did the man say about a person who uses his talents well? What about a person who does not use his talents well? (25:29) Do you think this is true? Why?

- *Discover:* God gives each person special talents. Use them well or you will lose them.

- *Apply:* Make a list of your best talents. What do you think you do well? Write down what others say you do well. Beside each one write how you are using it. Now write how you should use it. Will you?

- *What's next?* A man agrees to "sell" his best friend. What happens? Read Luke 22:1-6. ■

The Sheep and the Goats: The Final Judgment

³¹"But I, the Messiah, shall come in my glory. And all the angels shall come with me. Then I shall sit upon my throne of glory. ³²And all the nations shall be brought together before me. And I will

sort out the people as a shepherd sorts the sheep from the goats. ³³I will put the sheep at my right hand. And I will put the goats at my left.

³⁴"Then I, the King, shall speak to those at my right. I will say, 'Come, blessed of my Father. Come into the Kingdom prepared for you from the beginning of the world. ³⁵For I was hungry and you fed me. I was thirsty and you gave me water. I was a stranger and you asked me to come to your homes. ³⁶I was naked and you put clothes on me. I was sick and in prison, and you came to visit me.'

³⁷"Then these righteous ones will reply, 'Sir, when did we ever see you hungry and feed you? When did we see you thirsty and give you anything to drink? ³⁸When did we find you as a stranger, and help you? When did we find you naked, and put clothes on you? ³⁹When did we ever see you sick or in prison, and visit you?'

⁴⁰"And I, the King, will tell them, 'You did these things for these my brothers. And in helping them, you were serving me!' ⁴¹Then I will turn to those on my left. I will say, 'Away with you, you cursed ones. Go into the fire prepared for the devil and his demons. ⁴²For I was hungry and you wouldn't feed me. I was thirsty, and you wouldn't give me a drink. ⁴³I was a stranger, and you would not take me in. I was naked, and you wouldn't give me clothes. I was sick, and in prison, but you didn't visit me.'

⁴⁴"Then they will reply, 'Lord, when did we ever see you hungry and not feed you? When did we see you thirsty and not give you a drink? When did we see you as a stranger and not take you in? When did we see you naked and not give you clothes? When did we see you sick or in prison and not visit you?'

⁴⁵"And I will answer, 'You would not help the least of these my brothers. When you didn't help them, you were refusing to help me.'

⁴⁶"And they shall go away into punishment forever. But the righteous will go into everlasting life."

Weddings
MATTHEW 25:1-13

Have you ever been to a wedding? How was the bride dressed? Was there a party or reception after the wedding? Things were different in Bible times. Girls and boys did not go on dates. Parents, especially fathers, usually decided whom their children would marry. After a bride was chosen, the couple was "betrothed." It was something like being engaged today. There was no wedding ceremony like we have today. No minister married them. There was no church. On the wedding day, the bride and bridegroom dressed in fine clothes. Some friends took the bridegroom to the bride's home. This often took place at night, so they carried lamps or torches. Friends played musical instruments as they went. It was a very happy time. The bridegroom then took the bride and their friends to his home or to his father's home. There they had a great wedding feast. Sometimes this lasted for a week. A wedding was a wonderful occasion for friends and family to get together.

A Plot to Kill Jesus

26 Jesus finished this talk with his disciples. Then he told them, 2"As you know, the Passover Feast begins in two days. At that time, I shall be turned in and put to death on a cross."

3At that very moment the chief priests and other Jewish leaders were meeting. They were at the home of Caiaphas the High Priest. 4They wanted to find ways of catching Jesus quietly and killing him. 5"But not during the Passover Feast," they agreed. "For if we did it then, there would be a riot."

A Woman Pours Expensive Perfume on Jesus

6Jesus now went to Bethany, to the home of Simon the leper. 7While he was eating, a woman came in. She had a bottle of very expensive perfume. And she poured it over his head.

8-9The disciples were upset. "What a waste of good money," they said. "Why, she could have sold it for a fortune. And she could have given the money to the poor."

10Jesus knew what they were thinking. He said, "Why are you saying these things? For she has done a good thing for me. 11You will always have the poor among you. But you won't always have me. 12She has poured this perfume on me to get my body ready to be buried. 13And she will always be remembered for this deed. The story of what she has done will be told throughout the whole world. She will be known wherever the Good News is preached."

Judas Agrees to Betray Judas

14Then Judas Iscariot went to the chief priests. Judas was one of the 12 apostles. 15He asked, "How much will you pay me to get Jesus into your hands?" They gave him 30 silver coins to do the job. 16From that time on, Judas watched for a chance to turn Jesus over to them.

The Disciples Get Ready for Passover

17It was the first day of the Passover Feast. That day bread made with yeast was taken from every Jewish home. At this time, the disciples came to Jesus. They asked, "Where shall we plan to eat the Passover?"

18He replied, "Go into the city and see a certain man. Tell him, 'Our Master says that his time has come. He wants to eat the Passover meal with his disciples at your house.'" 19So the disciples did as he told them. And they made the supper there.

Jesus and the Disciples Eat the Last Supper

20-21That evening he sat eating with the 12 disciples. He said, "One of you will betray me."

22Sadness filled their hearts. And each one asked, "Am I the one?"

23He replied, "It is the one I served first. 24For I must die just as the prophets said I would. But it will be terrible for the man who betrays me. It would be better for that man if he had never been born."

25Judas, also, asked him, "Rabbi, am I the one?" And Jesus had told him, "Yes, you are the one."

26As they were eating, Jesus took a small loaf of bread. He blessed it and broke it apart. Then he gave it to the disciples. He said, "Take it and eat it, for this is my body."

27And he took a cup of wine. He gave thanks for it. Then he gave it to them to drink. He said, "Each one of you drink from it. 28For this is my blood which will seal the New Covenant. It is poured out to forgive the sins of many. 29Mark my words. I will not drink wine again until I drink it with you in my Father's Kingdom."

30Then they sang a hymn and went out to the Mount of Olives.

Jesus Tells His Disciples They Will Desert Him

31Jesus said to them, "Tonight you will all leave me. For it is written in the Scriptures that God will strike the Shepherd. And the sheep of the flock will be scattered. 32But then I will be brought back to life again. And I will go to Galilee and meet you there."

33Peter said, "I will never leave you! I won't, even if everyone else does!"

³⁴"I tell you the truth," Jesus said. "This very night you will pretend you don't know me. And you will do it three times before the cock crows at dawn!"

³⁵"I would die first!" Peter said. And all the other disciples said the same thing.

Jesus Prays in the Garden

³⁶Then Jesus brought them to a garden grove called Gethsemane. He told them to sit down and wait while he went to pray. ³⁷He took with him Peter and Zebedee's two sons, James and John. He began to be filled with sadness and despair.

³⁸Then he told them, "My soul is crushed with sadness. I am at the point of death. Please stay here. Stay awake with me."

³⁹He went forward a little. There, he fell face down on the ground. And he prayed, "My Father! If it can be done, let this cup be taken away from me. But I want what you want. I will do your will, not mine."

⁴⁰Then he went back to the three disciples. And he found them asleep. "Peter," he called, "couldn't you stay awake with me for one hour? ⁴¹Stay awake and pray. If you don't, you won't be able to stand when you are tempted. For your spirit wants to do what is right. But your body is very weak!"

⁴²Again he left them and prayed, "My Father! If this cup cannot be taken until I drink it all, your will be done."

⁴³He went back to them again. But again, he found them sleeping. Their eyes were very heavy. ⁴⁴So he went back to pray a third time. And he said the same things again.

⁴⁵Then he came back to the disciples. "Sleep on now, and take your rest," he said. "But no! The time has come! I am given into the hands of evil men! ⁴⁶Wake up! Let's be going! Look! Here comes the man who is betraying me!"

Judas Betrays Jesus

Some leaders wanted to kill Jesus. They were afraid that if people followed Jesus, they would stop following them. They were jealous. They didn't care if he was God's Son. They would kill him anyway. You would not think that a friend of Jesus would help these wicked leaders. But he did.

⁴⁷While he was still saying this, Judas came to the garden. And he brought with him a great crowd armed with swords and clubs. They had been sent by the Jewish leaders. ⁴⁸Judas had told them to arrest the man he greeted. He would greet Jesus to show he was the one they wanted. ⁴⁹So Judas went straight over to Jesus. He said, "Hello, Master!" And he hugged him in a friendly way.

⁵⁰Jesus said, "My friend, go ahead. Do what you have come for." Then the others grabbed him.

⁵¹One of the men with Jesus pulled out a sword. And he cut off the ear of the High Priest's servant.

⁵²"Put away your sword," Jesus told him. "Those using swords will get killed. ⁵³Don't you know that I could call on my Father? He could send thousands of angels to keep us safe! And he could send them right away! ⁵⁴But if I did this, how would the Scriptures be fulfilled? For they foretold what is happening now."

⁵⁵Then Jesus spoke to the crowd. "Am I some dangerous criminal?" he asked. "Is that why you armed yourselves with swords and clubs to arrest me? I was with you, teaching in the Temple. But you didn't stop me then. ⁵⁶But this is all happening to fulfill the words of the prophets."

At that point, all the disciples left him and ran away.

- *Remember:* Who was the man who betrayed Jesus? (26:47) Who came with Judas? (26:47) What did one man do to try to help Jesus? (26:51) That man was Peter. Who did he hurt? (26:51) What did Jesus tell Peter? (26:52) Would you want to be a Judas to your friends? Why not?

- *Discover:* When you love someone, don't hurt that person.

- *Apply:* Do you love your parents? Don't hurt them. Do you love Jesus? Don't hurt him. Do you love your brothers or sisters? Don't hurt them. Who else do you love? Don't hurt them.

- *What's next?* Religious leaders beat Jesus with their fists. Why? Read Mark 14:53-65. ■

The High Priest Questions Jesus

⁵⁷Then the mob took him to the home of Caiaphas, the High Priest. All the Jewish leaders were meeting there. ⁵⁸Meanwhile, Peter was following behind the crowd. He came to the courtyard of the High Priest's house and went in. He sat there with the soldiers. He wanted to know what was going to happen to Jesus.

⁵⁹The chief priests were all there. In fact, the whole Jewish Supreme Court was there! They were looking for witnesses who would lie about Jesus.

They wanted to make a case against him that would result in his death. ⁶⁰⁻⁶¹They did find many who agreed to tell lies about Jesus. But their stories didn't agree.

Finally two men were found. They said, "This man said, 'I am able to destroy the Temple of God. Then I will build it again in three days.'"

⁶²Then the High Priest stood up. He said to Jesus, "Well, what about it? Did you say that, or didn't you?" ⁶³But Jesus didn't say a word.

Then the High Priest said to him, "I make this demand in the name of the living God. Tell us if you are the Messiah, the Son of God!"

⁶⁴"Yes," Jesus said, "I am. And in the future you will see me, the Messiah. I will be sitting at the right hand of God. I will come back on the clouds of Heaven."

⁶⁵⁻⁶⁶Then the High Priest tore at his own clothing. He shouted, "Blasphemy! We don't even need any other witnesses. You have heard him say it! What do you think?"

They shouted, "He is guilty! He should be put to death!"

⁶⁷Then they spat in his face. They hit him and slapped him. ⁶⁸They said, "Prophesy to us, you Messiah! Who hit you that time?"

Peter Denies that He Knows Jesus

What if a friend said he did not know you? What would you think of him? Peter was Jesus' friend. But that's what he did. He said he didn't even know Jesus. He even cursed and swore about it.

⁶⁹Meanwhile, Peter was sitting in the courtyard. And a girl came over to him. She said, "You were with Jesus. For both of you are from Galilee."

⁷⁰But Peter denied it loudly. "I don't know what you are talking about!" he said.

⁷¹Later, out by the gate, another girl saw him. She spoke to those standing around. "This man was with Jesus of Nazareth," she said.

⁷²Again Peter denied it. "I don't know the man," he said. And this time he swore to it!

⁷³After a while others standing there came over to Peter. They said, "We know you are one of his disciples. We can tell by your Galilean accent."

⁷⁴Peter began to curse and swear. "I don't know the man," he said.

And just then the cock crowed. ⁷⁵Then Peter remembered Jesus' words. He had said, "Before the cock crows, you will deny me three times." So Peter went away, crying bitterly.

- *Remember:* How many times did people ask if Peter had been with Jesus? (26:69, 71,73) What did Peter say each time? (26:70,72,74) What happened when the rooster crowed? (26:75) Why do you think Peter cried? How do you think he felt?

- *Discover:* Are you ever ashamed of Jesus? You will feel sad if you are.

- *Apply:* Are you ever ashamed to say you read your Bible? Are you ever ashamed to say that you pray? Are you ever ashamed to tell friends you love Jesus? If you are, you should cry about it. How do you think this makes Jesus feel?

- *What's next?* A man hangs himself on a tree. Why? Read Matthew 27:1-10. ■

Judas Hangs Himself

Judas was Jesus' friend. But he betrayed Jesus. Now Jesus would die. What did Judas say about that?

27 When it was morning, the chief priests and Jewish leaders met again. They wanted to find a way to make the Romans sentence Jesus to die. ²So they sent him in chains to Pilate, the Roman governor.

³About that time, Judas saw that Jesus had been sentenced to die. Judas was the disciple who had betrayed him. He changed his mind and was very sad about what he had done. So he brought the money back to the chief priests.

⁴"I have sinned," he said. "For I have betrayed an innocent man."

"That's your problem," they replied.

⁵So Judas threw the money onto the floor of the Temple. Then he went out and hanged himself. ⁶The chief priests picked the money up. "We can't keep the money for the Temple," they said. "It's against our laws to take money paid for murder."

⁷They talked it over. In the end, they decided to buy a field with it. They bought a field where potters found their clay. They made it into a graveyard for burying foreigners who died in Jerusalem. ⁸That is why the graveyard is still called "The Field of Blood."

⁹This fulfilled the prophecy of Jeremiah. He said, "They took the 30 pieces of silver. This was what the people of Israel thought he was worth. ¹⁰They bought a field from the potters, as the Lord commanded me."

- *Remember:* How did Judas show that he was sorry? Find four ways. (27:3-5) What did the priests do with Judas's money? (27:7) Judas was very sorry for hurting Jesus. Were the priests sorry too?

- *Discover:* When we have done something wrong, we should be sorry.

- *Apply:* What did you do this week that did not please God? Have you told him you are sorry? Why not do that now?

- *What's next?* Jesus' own people wanted to kill him. But the Roman governor did not. Read what happened in John 18:28-40. ■

Pilate Wants to Free Jesus but Doesn't

¹¹Now Jesus was standing before Pilate, the Roman governor. "Are you the Jews' Messiah?" the governor asked him.

"Yes," Jesus replied.

¹²Then the chief priests and other Jewish leaders accused him. But Jesus didn't say a word.

¹³"Don't you hear what they are saying?" Pilate demanded.

¹⁴But much to the governor's surprise, Jesus said nothing.

15Now the governor had a yearly custom. Each year during the Passover Feast, he let one Jewish prisoner go free. And the people chose which prisoner it would be. 16That year there was a notorious prisoner named Barabbas. 17The crowds had gathered in front of Pilate's house that morning. So he asked them, "Which prisoner shall I set free? Should I give you Barabbas? Or should I give you Jesus, your Messiah?" 18Pilate knew very well that the Jewish leaders were jealous of Jesus. He knew they had arrested Jesus because he was so popular with the people.

19Just then, Pilate's wife sent him a message. The message read: "Leave that good man alone. For I had a terrible dream about him last night."

20But the Jewish leaders spoke to the crowd. They persuaded them to ask for Barabbas's release and for Jesus' death. 21Then the governor asked, "Which of these two shall I set free?" And the crowd shouted back their answer: "Barabbas!"

22"Then what shall I do with Jesus, your Messiah?" Pilate asked.

And they shouted, "Crucify him!"

23"Why?" Pilate demanded. "What has he done wrong?" But they kept shouting, "Crucify him! Crucify him!"

24When Pilate saw that he wasn't getting anywhere. And a riot was starting to develop. So he sent for a bowl of water. Then he washed his hands before the crowd. He said, "I am innocent of this good man's blood. You are all guilty of his blood!"

25And the mob yelled back, "His blood be on us and on our children!"

26So Pilate set Barabbas free. But he had Jesus whipped and sent him away to be crucified.

The Soldiers Make Fun of Jesus

27But first they took him into the armory. There, they called out the whole company of soldiers. 28They stripped him and put a red robe on him. 29They made a crown from long thorns and put it on his head. They put a stick in his right hand for a scepter. And they bowed before him to make fun of him. "Hail, King of the Jews," they yelled. 30They spat on him and grabbed the stick from his hands. They beat him on the head with it.

31After the mockery, they took off the robe. They put his own garment on him again. And they took him out to crucify him.

They Take Jesus Away to Crucify Him

32They made their way to the place where Jesus would be killed. On the way, they came across a man from Cyrene, in Africa. His name was Simon. They forced him to carry Jesus' cross. 33Then they went out to an area known as Golgotha. The name means "Skull Hill." 34And there, the soldiers gave him drugged wine to drink. But when he had tasted it, he would not drink it.

Jesus Is Crucified

God had a plan. He would send his Son to earth. His Son would die for us. People who accept his Son would go to Heaven. It's hard to understand. But that was God's plan. That's why Jesus died on the cross. No one should have made fun of him!

35After they crucified him, the soldiers threw dice. In this way, they divided his clothes among themselves. 36Then they sat around and watched him as he hung there. 37And they put a sign above his head. It read: "This is Jesus, the King of the Jews."

38Two robbers were also crucified that morning. One was on either side of him. 39And the people who passed by made fun of him. They said, [40]"So! You can destroy the Temple and build it again in three days, can you? Well, then, come on down from the cross if you are the Son of God!"

[41-43]And the chief priests and Jewish leaders also mocked him. "He saved others," they laughed. "But he can't save himself! So you are the King of Israel, are you? Come down from the cross and we'll believe you! He trusted God. Let God show he is king by saving him! Didn't he say, 'I am God's Son'?"

[44]And the robbers beside him also made fun of him.

[45]That afternoon, the whole earth was covered with darkness. It was dark for three hours, from noon until three o'clock.

[46]About three o'clock, Jesus shouted, "Eli, Eli, lama sabachthani?" This means, "My God, my God, why have you forsaken me?"

[47]Some of the people there didn't understand. They thought he was calling for Elijah. [48]One of them ran and filled a sponge with sour wine. He put it on a stick and held it up to him to drink. [49]But the rest said, "Leave him alone. Let's see whether Elijah will come and save him."

[50]Then Jesus shouted out again, gave up his spirit, and died.

[51]Right then, the curtain in the Temple was torn apart from top to bottom. The earth shook, and rocks broke apart. [52]Tombs opened, and many godly men and women who had died came back to life again. [53]After Jesus' resurrection, they left the graveyard and went into Jerusalem. They showed themselves to many people there.

[54]The soldiers were terrified by the earthquake and all that had happened. They exclaimed, "Surely this was God's Son."

[55]Many women were there, watching from a distance. They had come down from Galilee with Jesus to care for him. [56]Among them were Mary Magdalene and Mary the mother of James and Joseph. The mother of James and John, the sons of Zebedee, was there, too.

- *Remember:* Three kinds of people made fun of Jesus as he died. Who were they? (27:39,41-44) What time of day did Jesus die? (27:46) Four great things happened when Jesus died. What were they? (27:51-53) What did the soldiers say about Jesus then? (27:54) They probably wished they could change some things. They wished they had not beat Jesus. They wished they had not spit on him. They wished they had not made fun of him.

- *Discover:* God sent Jesus because he loved us. Jesus died on the cross because he loved us. We should accept him as our Savior because we love him and he loves us. See John 3:16.

- *Apply:* Do you love your mom or dad when they do something special for you? Do you thank them? Thank God for sending Jesus. Thank Jesus for dying for you. Ask Jesus to be your Savior.

- *What's next?* When Jesus died, a man asked if he could bury him. Who was he? Read Luke 23:50-56. ■

Joseph Places Jesus' Body in a Tomb

[57]In the evening, a rich man from Arimathea came to the cross. His name was Joseph. He was one of Jesus' followers. [58]He went to Pilate and asked for Jesus' body. So Pilate gave an order to release the body to him. [59]Joseph took the body and wrapped it in a clean linen cloth. [60]He put it in his own new tomb. And he rolled a great stone across the door as he left. [61]Both Mary Magdalene and the other Mary were sitting nearby, watching.

The Religious Leaders Seal and Guard the Tomb

[62]On the next day, the chief priests and Pharisees went to Pilate. [63]They said, "Sir, that liar once said, 'After three days I will come back to life again.' [64]So we ask that you seal the tomb until the third day. That will keep his disciples from coming and stealing his body. And they won't be able to tell everyone he came back to life! If that happens, we'll

be worse off than we were in the beginning."

65"Use your own Temple police," Pilate told them. "They can guard it safely enough."

66So they sealed the stone in front of the tomb's door. And they posted guards to keep anyone from getting in.

Jesus Comes Back to Life!

28 It was early on Sunday morning. The new day was just dawning. And Mary Magdalene and the other Mary went out to the tomb.

2Suddenly there was a great earthquake. For an Angel of the Lord came down from Heaven. He rolled aside the stone and sat on it. 3His face shone like lightning. And his clothes were a shining white. 4The guards shook with fear when they saw him. They fell into a dead faint.

When we obey and follow Jesus, he will always stay with us

Then teach these new disciples to obey all the commands I have given you. And be sure of this thing! I am with you always, even to the end of the world.

Matthew 28:20

5Then the angel spoke to the women. "Don't be afraid!" he said. "I know you are looking for Jesus, who was crucified. 6But he isn't here! For he has come back to life again. It has happened, just as he said it would. Come in and see where his body was lying. 7And now, go quickly and tell his disciples that he has risen from the dead. Tell them he is going to Galilee to meet them there. That is my message to them."

8The women ran from the tomb. They were afraid, but also filled with joy. They rushed to find the disciples to give them the angel's message. 9And as they were running, suddenly Jesus was there in front of them!

"Good morning!" he said. And they fell to the ground before him. They held his feet and worshiped him.

10Then Jesus said to them, "Don't be afraid! Go tell my brothers to leave at once for Galilee. I will meet them there."

The Guards Lie about What Happened

11So the women went back into the city. Meanwhile, some of the Temple police who were guarding the tomb had gone back, too. They went to the chief priests and told them what had happened. 12-13A meeting of all the Jewish leaders was called. They decided to bribe the police to say they had all fallen asleep. They were to say that Jesus' disciples came during the night and stole his body.

14"The governor might hear about it," the Council said. "But if he does, we'll stand up for you. That way everything will be all right."

15So the police took the bribe. And they did what they were told to do. Their story spread widely among the Jews. It is still believed by them to this very day.

The Disciples Are Commanded to Tell Others about Jesus

16Then the 11 disciples left for Galilee. They went to the mountain where Jesus had said they would find him. 17There they met him and worshiped him. But some of them weren't sure it really was Jesus!

18He told his disciples, "I have been given all power in Heaven and earth. 19So now go and make disciples in all the nations. Baptize them into the name of the Father, the Son, and the Holy Spirit. 20Then teach these new disciples to obey all the commands I have given you. And be sure of this thing! I am with you always, even to the end of the world."

MARK

When Mark was a boy he lived in a big house. He lived with his mother, Mary. People went there to talk and pray. They told many stories about Jesus. Mark knew these people. He heard their stories. He learned much about Jesus. Jesus may have gone there too. If he did, Mark listened to him. He talked with him. He learned many things from Jesus.

When Mark was old enough, he went on a missionary trip. He went with Paul and his cousin Barnabas. They went to tell people about Jesus. But Mark got homesick, or scared, or tired. He wanted to go home. Paul didn't like that. He did not want Mark on his next trip. So Mark went next time with his cousin. This time he was a good helper.

Mark wrote this book about Jesus. In this book you'll see a storm obey Jesus. You'll hear him order demons out of a man. And you'll see them obey. In Mark you'll watch Jesus make a blind man see. You'll even see a dead man come back to life. You must not miss Mark! It's exciting.

John the Baptist
Prepares the Way for Jesus

1 This is the wonderful story of Jesus the Messiah, the Son of God.

²In the Book of Isaiah, God said that he would send his Son to earth. He also promised that a special messenger would come before him. This messenger would get the world ready for his Son's coming.

³"This messenger will live out in the desert," Isaiah said. "He will tell people to turn from their sins. That way they will be ready for the Lord's coming."

⁴This messenger was John the Baptist. He lived out in the desert. And he taught that all people should be baptized. They were to do this to show everyone that they had turned their backs on sin. And that way, God would forgive them of their sins. ⁵People came all the way from Jerusalem into the Judean desert to hear John. In fact, they came from all over Judea! When they confessed their sins he baptized them in the Jordan River. ⁶His clothes were woven from camel's hair. And he wore a belt made out of leather. He ate locusts and wild honey for his food. ⁷This is what he said:

"Someone is coming soon who is far greater than I am. He is so much greater that I am not even worthy to be his slave. ⁸I baptize you with water. But he will baptize you with God's Holy Spirit!"

John Baptizes Jesus

⁹Then one day Jesus came from Nazareth in Galilee. He was baptized by John there in the Jordan River. ¹⁰When Jesus came up out of the water, he saw the heavens open. The Holy Spirit in the form of a dove flew down to him. ¹¹And a voice from Heaven said, "You are my Son, whom I love. I am very pleased with you!"

Satan Tempts Jesus in the Wilderness

¹²⁻¹³Right then the Holy Spirit sent Jesus into the desert. There, for 40 days, he was alone except for the desert animals. During that time Satan tried to tempt Jesus to sin. And then the angels came and took care of him.

Jesus Preaches in Galilee

¹⁴Later on, John was arrested by King Herod. At that time, Jesus went to Galilee to preach God's Good News.

¹⁵"At last the time has come!" he said. "God's Kingdom is near! Turn from your sins and act on this Good News!"

Jesus Calls Four Followers

Four men are working hard. They have jobs to do. Then Jesus comes. "Give up your jobs," Jesus tells them. "Follow me." Will they do it?

¹⁶One day Jesus was walking along the shores of the Sea of Galilee. He saw Simon and his brother Andrew fishing with nets. These men caught fish for a living.

¹⁷Jesus called out to them, "Come, follow me! I will make you fishermen for the souls of men!" ¹⁸At once they left their nets and went along with him.

¹⁹A little farther up the beach, he saw Zebedee's sons, James and John. They were in a boat fixing their fishing nets. ²⁰Jesus called out to them, too. And right away, they left their father Zebedee in the boat with the hired men. They went with Jesus, too.

- *Remember:* Two men were fishing. Jesus asked them to follow him. Who were they? What were they doing? (1:16-17) What did Jesus ask them to do? What work would they do with him? (1:17) Did they go with him? (1:18) Jesus asked two other men to follow him. Who were they? (1:19) Did they go with him? (1:20) Why do you think these men gave up their jobs? Why was it more important to follow Jesus? Would you have done this?

- *Discover:* Following Jesus is more important than anything else we do.

- *Apply:* Are you trying to follow Jesus each day? Are you trying to do what he wants? Can you think of anything more important?

- *What's next?* One minute a woman was in bed with a high fever. The next minute she was well. What happened? Read Matthew 8:14-17. ■

Jesus Teaches with Great Authority

²¹Jesus and his companions went to the town of Capernaum. On Saturday morning they went into the Jewish place of worship, the synagogue. There Jesus preached to the people. ²²They were surprised at his sermon because he spoke as an authority. He didn't try to prove his points by quoting other people. It was quite different from what they were used to hearing!

²³A man with a demon in him was there. He began shouting, ²⁴"Why are you bothering us, Jesus of Nazareth? Have you come to destroy us demons? I know who you are! You are the holy Son of God!"

²⁵Jesus commanded the demon to be quiet and to come out of the man. ²⁶At that moment the evil spirit screamed and shook the man violently. But then the demon left him. ²⁷The people there were amazed. They began to talk about what had happened.

"What sort of new religion is this?" they asked. "Why, even evil spirits obey his orders!"

²⁸The news of what he had done spread quickly through that area of Galilee.

Jesus Heals Simon's Mother-in-Law and Many Others

²⁹⁻³⁰Then they left the synagogue. And Jesus and his disciples went over to Simon and Andrew's home. There they found Simon's mother-in-law sick in bed with a high fever. They told Jesus about her right away. ³¹He went to her bedside. He took her by the hand and helped her to sit up. And the fever suddenly left her! She got up and made dinner for them!

³²⁻³³By sunset the courtyard was filled with the sick and demon-possessed. Their friends had brought them to Jesus for healing. Many people from all over the city of Capernaum gathered outside

the door to watch. ³⁴So Jesus healed great numbers of sick people that evening. And he ordered many demons to come out of their victims. But he did not let the demons speak. This was because they knew who he was.

Jesus Travels and Preaches

³⁵The next morning he was up long before daybreak. He went out alone into the wilderness to pray.

³⁶⁻³⁷Later, Simon and the others went out to find him. They said to him, "Everyone is asking for you."

³⁸But he replied, "We must go on to other towns as well. We must give my message to them too, for that is why I came."

³⁹So he traveled throughout the area of Galilee. He preached in the synagogues. And he set many free from the power of demons.

Jesus Heals a Leper

How would you feel if you had the worst disease in the world? How much would you give to be healed? A man with leprosy came to Jesus one day. He had the worst disease in the world. He begged Jesus to heal him. Could Jesus do it? Did he do it?

⁴⁰Once a leper came and knelt in front of him. He begged Jesus to heal him. "If you want to, you can make me well again," he said.

⁴¹Jesus was moved with pity. So he touched him and said, "I want to! Be healed!" ⁴²Right away the leprosy was gone! The man was healed!

⁴³⁻⁴⁴Jesus then told him sternly, "Go and let the priest examine you right away. Don't stop to speak to anyone along the way. Take along the offering Moses ordered for lepers who have been healed. That way everyone will have proof that you are well again."

⁴⁵But as the man went on his way he began to shout the good news. He told everyone that he had been healed. As a result, great crowds soon surrounded Jesus. And he couldn't openly go to any of the cities. He had to stay out in the barren wastelands. And people from everywhere came to him there.

- *Remember:* Did the leper want to be healed? How do you know? (1:40) Did he really believe Jesus could heal him? How do you know? (1:40) Did Jesus want to heal him? How do you know? (1:41) How should the man thank God? (1:44) Why didn't Jesus want him to tell others? What happened to Jesus? (1:45) Suppose you had the worst disease in the world. Suppose Jesus healed you. Would you want to offer a gift to God? What would you want to give him?

- *Discover:* When Jesus does something special, we should give God our thanks. We may also give him other special gifts.

- *Apply:* Has Jesus forgiven your sins? Has he become your Savior? Think of special ways you can thank God. Think of special gifts you can give God.

- *What's next?* Some men can't get near Jesus. So they tear a hole in a roof. What happens then? Read Mark 2:1-12. ∎

A Hole in the Roof

Some men carried a friend. They wanted Jesus to heal him. But there were too many people in the house where Jesus was speaking. They had to see Jesus. What did they do?

2 Several days later he went back to Capernaum. The news of his coming spread quickly through the city. ²Soon the house where he was staying was packed with visitors. There were so many that there wasn't room for a single person more. There wasn't room even outside the door. And he preached the Word to them. ³Four men came carrying a paralyzed man on a stretcher. ⁴They couldn't get to Jesus through the crowd. So they dug through the clay roof above his head. Then they let the sick man down on his stretcher. That way they set him down right in front of Jesus.

⁵Jesus saw how much they believed that he would help. So he said to the sick man, "Son, your sins are forgiven!"

⁶But some of the Jewish religious leaders sitting there heard what he said. They said among themselves, ⁷"What? This is blasphemy! Does he think he is God? For only God can forgive sins."

⁸Jesus could read their minds. So he said to them at once, "Why does this bother you? ⁹⁻¹¹I, the Messiah, have the power on earth to forgive sins. But talk is cheap. Anybody could say that. So I'll prove it to you by healing this man." Then, he turned to the paralyzed man. He said, "Pick up your stretcher and go on home. For you are healed!"

¹²The man jumped up and took his stretcher with him. And he pushed his way through the amazed onlookers. Then how they praised God! "We've never seen anything like this before!" they all shouted.

- *Remember:* How many men carried their sick friend? (2:3) Why couldn't the men get to Jesus? (2:4) What did they do then? (2:4) Was everyone happy when the man was healed? Who wasn't happy? Why? (2:6-7) Why could Jesus heal a person? Why could he forgive sins? (2:8-11) Could you do that? Why not?

- *Discover:* These four men cared a lot about their sick friend. So they helped him. They took him to Jesus.

- *Apply:* Do you have a friend who is sick or hurt or needs some help? What can you do for your friend? Be like the four men in this story. Do something to show you care. You might even have a chance to bring them to Jesus.

- *What's next?* People hated tax collectors. Did Jesus hate them too? Read Matthew 9:9-13. ■

Jesus Eats Supper at Matthew's House

¹³Then Jesus went out to the seashore again. And he preached to the crowds that gathered around him. ¹⁴As he was walking up the beach he saw Levi, the son of Alphaeus. He was sitting at his tax collection booth. "Come with me," Jesus told him. "Come be my disciple."

And Levi jumped to his feet and went along.

¹⁵That night Levi asked his fellow tax collectors and other known sinners to be his dinner guests. He wanted them to meet Jesus and his disciples. There were many men of this type among the crowds that followed him. ¹⁶Some of the Jewish religious leaders saw him eating with these sinful men. So they said to his disciples, "How can he stand it? How can he eat with such sinful people?"

¹⁷Jesus heard what they were saying. And he told them, "Sick people need the doctor, not healthy ones! I haven't come to tell good people to repent. I have come to save the bad ones."

Why Don't the Disciples Fast?

¹⁸John's disciples and the Jewish leaders sometimes fasted. That is, they went without food as part of their religion. One day some people came to Jesus. They asked why his disciples didn't do this too.

¹⁹Jesus replied, "Do friends of the bridegroom refuse to eat at the wedding

feast? Should they be sad while he is with them? [20]But someday he will be taken away from them. Then it will be time for them to mourn. [21]Besides, going without food is part of the old way of doing things. It is like patching an old garment with unshrunk cloth! What happens? The patch pulls away and leaves the hole worse than before. [22]You know better than to put new wine into old wineskins. They would burst. The wine would be spilled out and the wineskins ruined. New wine needs fresh wineskins."

Jesus Answers Questions about the Sabbath

[23]One Sabbath day Jesus and his disciples were walking through some fields. The disciples were hungry. So they broke off heads of wheat and ate the grain.

[24]Some of the Jewish religious leaders saw this. They said to Jesus, "They shouldn't be doing that! It's against our laws to work by harvesting grain on the Sabbath."

[25-26]But Jesus replied, "Didn't you ever hear about the time King David and his men were hungry? Abiathar was the High Priest then. David went into the house of God. And he ate the special bread only priests were allowed to eat. He also gave some to his friends. That was against the law, too. [27]But the Sabbath was made to serve man. Man was not made to serve the Sabbath. [28]And I, the Messiah, have power to decide what men can do on Sabbath days!"

Jesus Heals a Crippled Hand

You would be happy if a sick person was healed, wouldn't you? Why would anyone be angry about that? But some men got angry at Jesus for doing just this. They even wanted to kill him. Why?

3 While in Capernaum Jesus went to the synagogue again. He saw a man there with a crippled hand.

[2]Since it was the Sabbath, Jesus' enemies watched him closely. Would he heal the man's hand? If he did, they planned to arrest him!

[3]Jesus asked the man to come and stand in front of the people. [4]Then he turned to his enemies. He asked them, "Is it all right to do kind deeds on Sabbath days? Or is this a day for doing harm? Is it a day to save lives? Or is it a day to destroy them?" But they wouldn't answer him. [5]He looked around at them angrily. He was very upset that they didn't care about people's needs. Then Jesus said to the man, "Reach out your hand." The man did, and right away his hand was healed!

[6]At once the Pharisees went away. They met with the Herodians to make plans for killing Jesus.

- *Remember:* Why do you think Jesus' enemies wanted to arrest him? What were they waiting for him to do? These people thought you should not do any work on the Sabbath. They thought healing was work. So they thought Jesus should not heal on the Sabbath. They would rather see the sick man stay sick. (3:2) What did Jesus ask his enemies? (3:4) How do you know these people were hard-hearted? (3:5) Why do you think Jesus was angry at these men? (3:5) Would you be angry at them? Why?

- *Discover:* Any time is the right time to help someone.

- *Apply:* We must have rules. They show us what is usually best. Talk with your parents about this story. Are there times when we must break a rule to help someone?

- *What's next?* A man is healed. Jesus never touched him. He never even saw him. How did it happen? Read Luke 7:1-10. ■

Large Crowds Follow Jesus

7-8Meanwhile, Jesus and his disciples went to the shore of the lake. But a huge crowd followed them there. The people came from all over Galilee, Judea, Jerusalem, and Idumea. They also came from beyond the Jordan River. Some even came from as far away as Tyre and Sidon. The news about his miracles had spread far and wide. As a result, many people came to see him for themselves.

9He told his disciples to bring a boat around. He wanted it standing ready to rescue him in case he was crowded off the beach. 10For there had been many healings that day. As a result, many sick people were crowding around him. They were all trying to touch him.

11When people with demons in them saw Jesus, they fell down before him. They cried out, "You are the Son of God!" 12But he warned them not to make him known.

Jesus Chooses the Twelve Disciples

13After that he went up into the hills. He called certain people he had specially chosen. He asked them to come and join him there. So they followed him there. 14-15Then he chose 12 of them to be his disciples. These would go out to preach and to cast out demons. 16-19These are the names of the 12 he chose. There was Simon, whom he renamed "Peter." There were James and John, the sons of Zebedee. Jesus called them the "Sons of Thunder." There were Andrew, Philip, and Bartholomew. There were Matthew and Thomas. There was James, the son of Alphaeus. There were Thaddaeus and Simon. This Simon was a member of a political party that wanted to overthrow the Romans. And there was Judas Iscariot, who later betrayed him.

Religious Leaders Say Jesus Is Possessed by Satan

20Then Jesus went back to the house where he was staying. And the crowds began to gather again. Soon the house was full of visitors. He couldn't even find time to eat. 21His friends heard what was happening. So they came to try to take him home with them.

"He's out of his mind," they said.

22But some Jewish teachers of religion came from Jerusalem. They said, "His trouble is that he's possessed by Satan, king of demons. That's why demons obey him."

23Jesus called these men over. He spoke to them using proverbs they all understood. He asked, "How can Satan cast out Satan? 24A kingdom divided against itself will fall. 25A home filled with strife and division destroys itself. 26And if Satan is fighting against himself, how could he get anything done? He would never survive. 27A strong man must be tied up before his house can be robbed. In the same way, Satan must be tied up before his demons can be cast out.

28"I tell you the truth! Any sin of man can be forgiven, even blasphemy against me. 29But blasphemy against the Holy Spirit can never be forgiven. It is an eternal sin."

[30]He told them this because they were saying he did his miracles by Satan's power. In doing this, they denied that Jesus acted by the Holy Spirit's power.

Jesus Talks about His True Family

[31-32]Now Jesus' mother and brothers came to see him. He was in a crowded house where he was teaching. They sent word for him to come out and talk with them. "Your mother and brothers are outside," he was told. "They want to see you."

[33]He replied, "Who is my mother? Who are my brothers?" [34]He looked at the people around him. And he said, "These are my mother and brothers! [35]Anyone who does God's will is my brother, and my sister, and my mother."

A Story about Four Kinds of Soil

4 Once again Jesus was teaching on the shores of the lake. And a great crowd had gathered around him. So he got into a boat and sat down and talked from there. [2]His usual method of teaching was to tell the people stories. One of them went like this:

[3]"Listen! A farmer decided to plant some grain. So he went out to scatter it across his field. [4]Some of it fell on a path. And the birds came and ate it off the hard ground. [5-6]Some of it fell on thin soil with rock under it. It grew up quickly enough. But soon it dried up under the hot sun and died. This was because the roots were too shallow. [7]Other seeds fell among the thorns. The thorns shot up and crowded out the young plants. So in the end, they produced no grain. [8]But some of the seeds fell into good soil. They produced 30 times as much as he had planted. Some of it produced even 60 or 100 times as much! [9]If you have ears, listen!"

Jesus Explains the Story about the Soil

[10]Later, Jesus was alone with the 12 disciples and some others. They asked him, "What does your story mean?"

[11-12]He replied, "You are allowed to know some truths about the Kingdom of God. But these truths are hidden to those outside the Kingdom. I do this so that: 'They might see and hear. But they won't understand or turn to God. Otherwise they might turn, and be forgiven for their sins.'"

[13]Then Jesus said, "Can't you understand this simple story? How then will you understand all the others I am going to tell?

[14]"The farmer I talked about is anyone who brings God's message to others. He is trying to plant good seed within their lives. [15]What does the hard pathway stand for? It stands for the hard hearts of some of those who hear God's message. Satan comes right away to make them forget it. [16]What does the rocky soil stand for? It stands for the hearts of those who hear the message with joy. [17]But, like young plants in such soil, their roots don't go very deep. At first they get along fine. But when hard times come, they give up.

[18]"What does the thorny ground stand for? It stands for the hearts of people who listen to the Good News and receive it. [19]But soon other things get in the way. They begin to wish for the joys of being rich and successful. They begin to want nice things. These things crowd out God's message from their hearts. And in the end, no crop is produced.

[20]"What does the good soil stand for? It stands for the hearts of those who truly accept God's message. They produce a rich harvest for God. They produce 30, 60, or even 100 times as much as was planted in their hearts."

A Story about a Lamp

Why do you turn on a light? You want to see, don't you? Would you put a box over your light? It would light the inside of the box. But the room would still be dark. So why turn on the light?

²¹Then Jesus said, "Suppose someone lights a lamp. Does he put a box over it to shut out the light? Of course not! The light couldn't be seen or used. A lamp is placed on a stand to shine and be useful.

²²"All that is now hidden will someday come to light. ²³If you have ears, listen! ²⁴And be sure to put into practice what you hear. The more you do this, the more you will understand what I tell you. ²⁵To him who has something, more shall be given. But from he who has little, even more shall be taken away.

- *Remember:* Why wouldn't you put a box over a light? (4:21) Why do you use a light? (4:21) What should you do with your ears? (4:23) God's Word is a light. See Psalm 119:105. Don't do anything that keeps you from seeing God's truth. Don't do anything that keeps you from listening to God's truth.

- *Discover:* God's Word is a light. Look for it. Then look at it. Read it. Listen to it. Try

to understand it. Then it will show you how to live.

- *Apply:* Do you read your Bible each day? That's the only way God can show you how to live. Do you ask him to help you understand it? Ask: what is it saying to me? What does this mean to me? What should I do about it?

- *What's next?* If it's not big, it's not important! Is that true? Read what Jesus said in Mark 4:30-34. ■

A Story about Planting Seeds

²⁶"Here is another story that shows what the Kingdom of God is like.

"A farmer planted his field ²⁷and went away. As time passed, the seeds grew and grew without his help. ²⁸For the soil made the seeds grow. First a leaf-blade pushed through. Later the wheat-heads formed, and finally the grain became ripe. ²⁹Then the farmer came with his sickle and harvested it."

A Story about a Tiny Seed

A mustard seed is so tiny you can hardly see it. So it can't do much, can it? So why would Jesus tell a story about this tiny seed?

³⁰Jesus asked, "How can I describe the Kingdom of God? What story shall I use to tell you about it? ³¹⁻³²It is like a tiny mustard seed! This is one of the smallest of seeds. But it grows to become one of the largest of plants. It has long branches where birds can build their nests."

³³He used many such stories to teach the people. He taught them as much as they were ready to understand. ³⁴In fact,

he taught in public only by using stories. But when he was alone with his disciples, he explained his meaning to them.

- *Remember:* How big is a mustard seed? (4:31-32) How big is a mustard plant? What can it hold in its branches? (4:31-32) Why did Jesus tell these stories? (4:33-34) What do you think he is saying in this story?

- *Discover:* God can make big things come from tiny things.

- *Apply:* Your smallest prayer can have big answers. Your smallest work for God can have big things come from it. You may be young, but God can do great things through you.

- *What's next?* Would you sell everything you have to buy one thing? Read Matthew 13:45-46. ■

Jesus Stops a Storm

Think of the worst storm you have seen. What happened? What if you had said "stop" to the storm? Would it have stopped? Jesus said "stop" to a storm one day. Let's see what happened.

³⁵Evening was coming on. And Jesus said to his disciples, "Let's cross to the other side of the lake." ³⁶So they took him just as he was and started out. They left the crowds behind, though other boats followed. ³⁷But soon a terrible storm came up. High waves began to break into the boat. Soon, it was almost full of water and about to sink. ³⁸Jesus was asleep at the back of the boat with his head on a cushion. They woke him up, shouting, "Teacher! Don't you even care that we are all about to drown?"

³⁹Then he spoke to the wind and the sea. He said, "Quiet down!" Suddenly, the wind fell! And there was a great calm!

⁴⁰And he asked them, "Why were you so afraid? Don't you have confidence in me yet?"

⁴¹The disciples were filled with awe. They said among themselves, "Who is this man? Even the winds and seas obey him!"

- *Remember:* How do you know this was a bad storm? (4:37) Why did the disciples ask Jesus if he cared about them? (4:38) What did Jesus say to the storm? (4:39) What did the

storm do? (4:39) How did the disciples feel when they saw this? (4:41) What did they say? What would you have said?

- *Discover:* The winds and seas obey Jesus. So does the rest of nature. What does that tell you about who Jesus is?

- *Apply:* If the wind and seas and the rest of nature obey Jesus, why don't we obey him? Think of one thing Jesus would like for you to do most. Why don't you do it?

- *What's next?* Have you ever seen a demon? One day Jesus met a man. He had a demon in him. What would you do if you met a man like this? Read Mark 5:1-20. ■

Jesus Heals a Man with Demons

It would not be fun to meet a demon, would it? It would not be fun to meet a man with a demon in him. Would you be afraid? What would you say? This is what Jesus said.

5 They came to the other side of the lake. Just then, a man with a demon in him ran out from a graveyard. This happened just as Jesus was climbing from the boat.

³⁻⁴This man lived among the gravestones. He was so strong that no one could tie him up. He could break out of anything, even chains! No one was strong enough to control him. ⁵All day

long and through the night he would wander among the tombs. Or he would run around in the wild hills. He would scream and cut himself with sharp pieces of stone.

⁶The man saw Jesus when he was still far out on the water. He had run to meet him, and fell down before him.

⁷⁻⁸Then Jesus spoke to the demon within the man. "Come out, you evil spirit!" he commanded.

It gave a terrible scream. It cried, "What are you going to do to me, Jesus, Son of the Most High God? For God's sake, don't torture me!"

⁹"What is your name?" Jesus asked.

"My name is Legion," the demon replied. "For there are many of us here in this man." ¹⁰Then the demons begged him not to send them to some faraway place.

¹¹Now there was a huge herd of hogs feeding on the hill above the lake. ¹²"Send us into those hogs," the demons begged.

¹³And Jesus gave them permission. Then the evil spirits came out of the man and went into the hogs. The whole herd ran down the steep hillside into the lake. And they all drowned.

¹⁴The herdsmen ran to the nearby towns and countryside. They spread the news as they ran. Everyone rushed out to see for themselves. ¹⁵And a large crowd soon gathered where Jesus was. They saw the man sitting there, fully clothed and perfectly sane. But they were very afraid. ¹⁶Those who saw what happened told everyone about it. ¹⁷And the crowd began begging Jesus to go away and leave them alone! ¹⁸So

he got back into the boat. The man who had been freed from the demons begged Jesus to let him go along. ¹⁹But Jesus said no.

"Go home to your friends," he told him. "Tell them what great things God has done for you. Tell them how merciful he has been."

²⁰So the man started off to visit the Ten Towns of that region. And he told everyone about the great things Jesus had done for him. All the people there were amazed by his story.

- *Remember:* Where was the man with the demons living? (5:1-3) Would you have been afraid of this man? Why? Why do you think others were afraid of him? (5:3-5) What did Jesus tell the demon to do? (5:7-8) Why do you think the demon was afraid of Jesus? (5:7-8) Was there more than one demon in the man? (5:9) Where did Jesus send the demons? What happened to them? (5:13) What happened to the man then? (5:15) Where did Jesus tell the man to go? What did he tell him to do? (5:19-20)

- *Discover:* All Jesus had to do was speak and the demons ran away. He didn't even have to fight. Demons are afraid of Jesus. They know Jesus is God and more powerful than they are. They know Jesus is more powerful than Satan, who rules the demons.

- *Apply:* When you become scared thinking about Satan or demons, pray to Jesus right away. Say his name. This will help you remember that Satan and his demons run when Jesus is near.

- *What's next?* A woman touches Jesus' clothes. Something special happens. What? Read Mark 5:21-34. ■

A Woman Touches Jesus' Clothes

A sick woman reached out to touch Jesus. Look what happened!

²¹Now Jesus went back across to the other side of the lake by boat. And a great crowd gathered around him on the shore.

²²The leader of the local synagogue came and fell down before him. The man's name was Jairus. ²³He begged

Jesus to heal his little daughter.

"She is at the point of death," he said. "Come and put your hands on her. Please, make her live."

²⁴Jesus went with him, and the crowd followed behind. ²⁵In the crowd was a woman who had been sick for 12 years. She was bleeding inside her body. ²⁶She had suffered much from many doctors through the years. She had become poor by paying them and she was still no better. In fact, she was worse. ²⁷She had heard all about the great miracles Jesus did. That is why she came up behind him through the crowd and touched his clothes.

²⁸For she thought to herself, "I must just touch his clothes. If I do, I will be healed." ²⁹And as soon as she touched him, the bleeding stopped. Right away, she knew she was well!

³⁰Jesus knew at once that healing power had gone out from him. So he turned around in the crowd. Then he asked, "Who touched my clothes?"

³¹His disciples said to him, "All this crowd is pressing around you. How can you ask who touched you?"

³²But he kept on looking around to see who had done it. ³³Then the frightened woman came and fell at his feet. She was shaking because she knew she was healed. She told him what she had done. ³⁴And Jesus said to her,

"Daughter, your faith has made you well. Go in peace, and be free of your disease."

- *Remember:* How long had this woman been bleeding? (5:25) Why didn't she go to a doctor? (5:26) Why did she touch Jesus' clothes? (5:27-28) What happened when she did that? (5:29) What did Jesus say to the woman? (5:34) What do you think the woman told Jesus then?

- *Discover:* Jesus has special power. He can do many things that we can't do. He will do special things for us. But we must believe that he will (5:34).

- *Apply:* Turn on a light switch. What happens? The switch lets power into the light bulb. Pray. What happens? Prayer lets Jesus' power into your life.

- *What's next?* A dead girl comes back to life. No one thought it could happen. But it did. Read Luke 8:40-56. ■

Jairus's Daughter Dies and Lives Again

³⁵He was still talking to her when messengers came from Jairus's home. "It is too late," they said. "Your daughter is already dead. There is no point in Jesus' coming now."

³⁶But Jesus did not listen to them. He said to Jairus, "Don't be afraid. Just trust me."

³⁷Then Jesus stopped the crowd. He

only let Peter, James, and John go on with him to Jairus's home. ³⁸When they got there, Jesus saw that all was in great confusion. People were crying out loud and wailing. ³⁹So he went inside and spoke to the people.

When we are afraid of something, we should trust Jesus to help us

Don't be afraid. Just trust me.

Mark 5:36

"Why all this crying and noise?" he asked. "The child isn't dead. She is only asleep!"

⁴⁰They laughed at him, but he told them all to leave. Then he took the little girl's father and mother and his three disciples. And he went into the room where she was lying.

⁴¹⁻⁴²Taking her by the hand he said to her, "Get up, little girl!" She was 12 years old. And she jumped up and walked around! Her parents just couldn't get over it. ⁴³Jesus told them not to tell anyone about what had happened. Then he told them to give the girl something to eat.

The People of Nazareth Will Not Believe

6Soon after this Jesus left that part of the country. He went back to Nazareth with his disciples. This was his hometown. ²⁻³The next Sabbath he went to the synagogue to teach. The people were amazed at his wisdom and his miracles. For he was just a local man like themselves.

"He's no better than we are," they said. "He's just a carpenter, Mary's boy. He's the brother of James and Joseph, Judas and Simon. And his sisters live right here among us." And they became angry with him!

⁴Then Jesus told them, "A prophet is honored everywhere except in his hometown. He is never respected among his relatives and by his own family." ⁵And because of their unbelief he didn't do any great miracles among them. He only put his hands on a few sick people and healed them. ⁶And he could hardly accept the fact that they wouldn't believe in him.

Then he went out among the villages, teaching.

The Disciples Get an Assignment from Jesus

⁷He called his 12 disciples together and sent them out two by two. He gave them the power to cast out demons. ⁸⁻⁹He said to them, "Take nothing with you except a walking stick. Don't take any food or a knapsack. Don't take any money. Don't even take an extra pair of shoes or a change of clothes.

¹⁰"Stay at one home in each village," he said. "Don't move around from house to house while you are there. ¹¹You might come to a village that won't accept you or listen to you. If so, shake off the dust from your feet as you leave. It is a sign that you have left it to its fate."

¹²So the disciples went out. They told everyone they met to turn from sin. ¹³And they cast out many demons and healed many sick people. They poured olive oil over them.

Herod Kills John the Baptist

If you visited a king and he offered to give you anything in his kingdom, what would you choose? Here is a story about someone who had that choice, but made a terrible decision.

¹⁴King Herod soon heard about Jesus. For his miracles were talked about everywhere. The king thought Jesus was John the Baptist come back to life again. So the people were saying, "No wonder he can do such miracles." ¹⁵Others thought

Jesus was Elijah the ancient prophet, now come to life again. Still others claimed he was a new prophet like the great ones of the past.

¹⁶"No," Herod said, "it is John, the man I beheaded. He has come back from the dead."

¹⁷⁻¹⁸For Herod had sent soldiers to arrest John and put him in prison. He did this because John kept saying it was wrong for him to marry Herodias. She had once been his brother Philip's wife. ¹⁹Herodias wanted John killed in revenge. But unless Herod gave the order, she could not have him killed. ²⁰And Herod respected John. He knew John was a good and holy man. So he kept him under his protection. Herod always got a little upset when he talked with John. But even so, Herod liked to listen to him.

²¹But Herodias's chance finally came. It was Herod's birthday. So he threw a party for his officials and army officers. He also invited the leaders of Galilee. ²²⁻²³Herodias' daughter came in and danced before them. And she greatly pleased them all.

"Ask me for anything you like," the king promised. "I'll give you anything, even up to half of my kingdom!"

²⁴She went out and spoke to her mother. She told her, "Ask for John the Baptist's head!"

²⁵So she hurried back to the king. "I want the head of John the Baptist," she said. "I want it right now, on a tray!"

²⁶The king was very upset because she asked for John's death. But he didn't want to break his promise in front of his guests. ²⁷So he sent one of his bodyguards to the prison. He told him to cut off John's head and bring it to him. The soldier killed John in the prison. ²⁸They brought back his head on a tray and gave it to the girl. Then she took it to her mother.

²⁹John's disciples heard what had happened. So they came for his body and buried it in a tomb.

- *Remember:* Why did Herod put John in prison? (6:17-18) Why did Herod's wife want to kill John? (6:19) So why didn't Herod kill John at first? (6:20) What fool-ish promise did Herod make? (6:21-23) What strange gift did Herod give on his birthday? (6:25-28) Why do you think Herod was sorry? How could he have kept out of this trouble?

- *Discover:* Don't make foolish promises. You will be sorry when you have to keep them.

- *Apply:* Did you ever wish you had not promised something? The next time you start to make a promise, stop! Don't make it unless you want to keep it.

- *What's next?* How many hungry people could you feed with your lunch at school? Two? 10? 100? Could you feed 5,000? Jesus fed 5,000 people with one boy's lunch. Read John 6:1-15. ■

A Miracle Picnic for 5,000 People

³⁰Now the apostles came back to Jesus from their tour. They told him all they had done. They told him what they had said to the people they visited.

³¹Then Jesus suggested, "Let's get away from the crowds for a while and rest." For so many people were coming and going that they hardly had time to eat. ³²So they left by boat for a quieter spot. ³³But many people saw them leaving. So they ran on ahead along the shore. And they met them as soon as they landed. ³⁴So the usual crowd was there as he stepped from the boat. And Jesus had pity on them because they were like sheep without a shepherd. He taught them many things they needed to know.

³⁵⁻³⁶Late in the afternoon his disciples came to him. They said, "Tell the people to go away to the nearby villages and farms. Tell them to buy themselves some food. For there is nothing to eat here in this place. And it is getting late."

³⁷But Jesus said, "You feed them."

"With what?" they asked. "It would take a fortune to buy food for all this crowd!"

³⁸"How much food do we have?" he asked. "Go and find out."

They came back with the report. There were five loaves of bread and two fish. ³⁹⁻⁴⁰Then Jesus told the crowd to sit down. Soon colorful groups of 50 or 100 were sitting on the green grass.

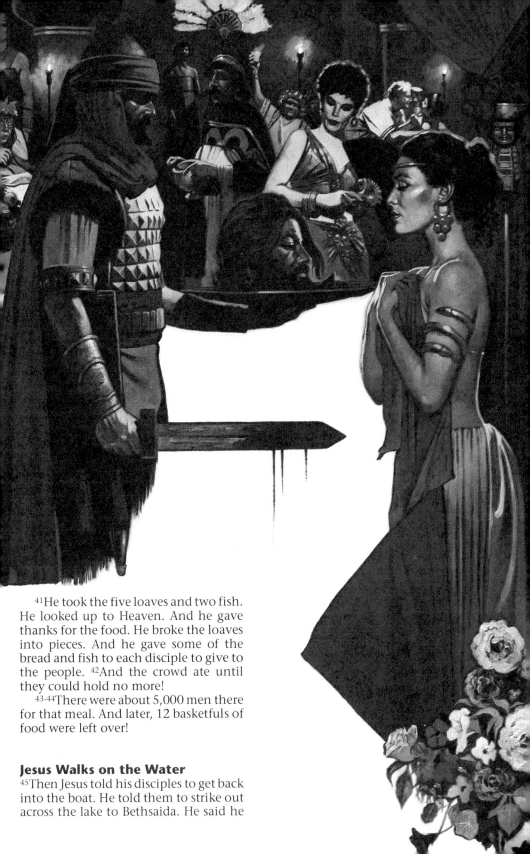

⁴¹He took the five loaves and two fish.
He looked up to Heaven. And he gave
thanks for the food. He broke the loaves
into pieces. And he gave some of the
bread and fish to each disciple to give to
the people. ⁴²And the crowd ate until
they could hold no more!

⁴³⁻⁴⁴There were about 5,000 men there
for that meal. And later, 12 basketfuls of
food were left over!

Jesus Walks on the Water

⁴⁵Then Jesus told his disciples to get back
into the boat. He told them to strike out
across the lake to Bethsaida. He said he

would join them later. He himself stayed to get the people started on their way home.

⁴⁶After that he went up into the hills to pray. ⁴⁷During the night, he was still alone on the land. The disciples were in their boat out in the middle of the lake. ⁴⁸But Jesus saw that they were having trouble. They were rowing hard and struggling against the wind and waves.

About three o'clock in the morning he walked out to them on the water. He started to go past them. ⁴⁹But they saw something walking beside them on the water. They were very afraid, thinking it was a ghost. ⁵⁰For they all saw him.

But he spoke to them at once. "It's all right," he said. "It is I! Don't be afraid." ⁵¹Then he climbed into the boat and the wind stopped!

They just sat there, unable to take it in! ⁵²For they still didn't know who he was, even after the miracle the evening before! For they didn't want to believe!

Jesus Heals Many Sick People

There were no hospitals in Bible times. There were no drugstores. There were very few doctors. There were no good medicines. So how did people get well? Most of them didn't. Many people died when they were young. That's why people begged Jesus to heal them!

⁵³They came to Gennesaret on the other side of the lake. They tied up the boat ⁵⁴and climbed out.

The people standing around there knew who he was right away. ⁵⁵They ran through the whole area to spread the news that he had come. And they began to bring sick people to him on mats and stretchers. ⁵⁶They went to villages and cities and out on the farms. And wherever he went they laid the sick in the marketplaces and streets. They begged him to let them at least touch the fringes of his clothes. And as many as touched him were healed.

- *Remember:* Where were Jesus and his friends? (6:53) How did they get there? (6:53) What happened when he got there? (6:54-56) How were the people healed? What did Jesus do? (6:56) What if you had been sick? What would you have asked Jesus to do?

- *Discover:* Who *really* heals us when we're sick? Doctors help. Hospitals help. Nurses help. Mom and Dad help. Medicines help. But God heals us.

- *Apply:* The next time you're sick, think about this. Let the doctor help you all he can. Let your parents help you all they can. Take your medicine. But ask God to heal you. Then don't forget to thank him.

- *What's next?* How would you feel if you could not hear anything? What if you could not talk either? Would you want someone to heal you? Read Mark 7:31-37. ■

Looking Holy Doesn't Matter; Honor God with Your Actions

7 One day some Jewish religious leaders came from Jerusalem. They wanted to find out more about Jesus. ²They saw that some of his disciples didn't follow all the usual rituals before eating. ³For the Jews will never eat until they have washed their arms to the elbows. This is what their ancient traditions say they must do. This is true especially of the Pharisees who are very strict. ⁴When they come home from the market they must always wash before eating any food. This is an example of the many rules they have followed for centuries. And they still follow them. They also have a ritual for cleansing pots, pans, and dishes.

⁵So the religious leaders asked, "Why don't your disciples follow our customs? For they eat without first washing their hands."

⁶⁻⁷Jesus replied, "You hypocrites!

Isaiah the prophet described you very well. He said, 'These people speak nicely about the Lord. But they don't love him at all. Their worship is a lie. For they claim that God commands the people to obey their petty rules.' How right Isaiah was! 8For you don't obey God's specific orders. But you follow your own traditions instead. 9You reject God's laws for the sake of following your man-made traditions.

10"For instance, Moses gave you this law from God: 'Honor your father and mother.' He said that anyone who speaks against his father or mother must die. 11But you say it is all right for a man to ignore his needy parents. You claim it is fine for him to say, 'Sorry, I can't help you! For I have given to God what I could have given to you.' 12-13And so you break the law of God in order to protect your man-made tradition. And this is only one example. There are many, many others."

14Then Jesus called to the crowd to come and hear. "All of you listen," he said. "Try to understand. 15-16Your souls aren't hurt by what you eat. They are hurt by what you think and say!"

17Then he went into a house to get away from the crowds. His disciples asked him what he meant by what he had just said.

18"Don't you understand either?" he asked. "Can't you see that what you eat won't harm your soul? 19For food doesn't come in contact with your heart. It only passes through the stomach and out again." By saying this he showed that every kind of food is kosher.

20And then he added, "It is the thoughtlife that makes a person unclean. 21For out of men's hearts come evil thoughts of lust, theft, murder, and adultery. 22The heart is the source of greed, wickedness, lying, lewdness, envy, slander, pride, and all other evil. 23All these bad things come from within. They are what pollute you and make you unfit for God."

Jesus Sends a Demon Out of a Girl

24Then he left Galilee and went to the region of Tyre and Sidon. He tried to keep it a secret that he was there, but couldn't. For as usual the news of his coming spread fast.

25Right away a woman came to him whose little girl had a demon in her. The woman had heard about Jesus. So she came and fell at his feet. 26She begged him to set her child free from the demon. But she was a Gentile from Syrian Phoenicia.

27Jesus told her, "First I should help my own family, the Jews. It isn't right to take the children's food and throw it to the dogs."

28She replied, "That's true, sir. But even the puppies are given some scraps from the children's plates."

29"Good!" he said. "You have answered well. So I will heal your little girl. Go on home, for the demon has left her!"

30When she got home, her little girl was lying quietly in bed. And the demon was gone.

Jesus Helps a Man Hear

Listen! Do you hear the birds sing? Do you hear Mother talk to you? Do you hear music playing? What other things do you like to hear? What if you couldn't hear any of these? What if you couldn't hear anything? What if you couldn't talk well either? Would you want someone to help you?

31From Tyre he went to Sidon. Then he went back to the Sea of Galilee by way of the Ten Towns. 32A deaf man with a speech problem was brought to him. Everyone begged Jesus to lay his hands on the man and heal him.

[33]Jesus led him away from the crowd. He put his fingers into the man's ears. Then he spat and touched the man's tongue with the spittle. [34]Then, looking up to Heaven, he sighed. And he commanded, "Open!" [35]Right away the man could hear perfectly and speak plainly!

[36]Jesus told the crowd not to spread the news. But the more he told them this, the more they talked about it. [37]For they were overcome with utter amazement. Again and again they said, "Everything he does is wonderful. He even heals those who are deaf and can't talk!"

- *Remember:* What was wrong with the sick man? (7:32) Did he ask Jesus to help him? Why didn't he? Who did? (7:32) How did Jesus heal him? (7:33-34) Why do you think he did that? Why do you think the people told others? Why didn't they keep this a secret? (7:36-37) If you had seen this, would you have told others about Jesus? Why?

- *Discover:* Some news is too good to keep, especially news about Jesus. We must share it with others.

- *Apply:* Do you think Jesus is special? Do you think he loves you? Has he done something special for you and me? Can you really keep this a secret? What can you do to tell others?

- *What's next?* One minute a man is blind. The next minute he can see. What happened? Read Mark 8:22-26. ■

Another Mealtime Miracle

8One day about this time another great crowd gathered. But the people ran out of food again. So Jesus called his disciples to talk about it.

"I pity these people," he said. "They have been here three days and have nothing left to eat. [3]If I send them home without feeding them, they will faint along the road! For some of them have come a long way."

[4]"Are we supposed to find food for them here in the desert?" his disciples asked.

[5]"How many loaves of bread do you have?" he asked.

"Seven," they replied. [6]So he told the crowd to sit down on the ground. Then he took the seven loaves. He thanked God for them. Then he broke them into pieces and passed them to his disciples. And the disciples gave them to the people. [7]A few small fish were found, too. So Jesus also blessed these and told the disciples to serve them.

[8-9]And the whole crowd ate until they were full. After that he sent the people home. There were about 4,000 people in the crowd that day. They picked up the scraps after the meal. And there were seven very large basketfuls left over!

The Religious Leaders Want Another Miracle

[10]Right after this he got into a boat with his disciples. They set sail for the area of Dalmanutha.

[11]The local Jewish leaders soon learned that Jesus had come. So they came to argue with him.

"Do a miracle for us," they said. "Make something happen in the sky. Then we will believe in you."

[12]He sighed deeply when he heard this. Then he said, "I will not do this. How many more miracles do you people need?"

Watch Out for Wrong Teaching

[13]So he and his disciples got back into the boat and left them. Then he crossed to the other side of the lake. [14]But the disciples had forgotten to stock up on food before they left. So they only had one loaf of bread in the boat.

[15]As they were crossing, Jesus spoke to them very seriously. He said, "Be careful about the yeast of King Herod and of the Pharisees."

[16]"What does he mean?" the disciples asked each other. They thought he must be talking about their forgetting to bring bread.

[17]Jesus knew what they were saying. So he said to them, "No, that isn't it at all! Can't you understand? Are your hearts too hard to take it in? [18]'Your eyes are to see with. Why don't you look? Why don't you open your ears and listen?' Don't you remember anything at all?

[19]"What about the 5,000 men I fed with five loaves of bread? How many basketfuls of scraps did you pick up after that?"

"Twelve," they said.

[20]"And when I fed the 4,000 with seven loaves, how much was left?"

"Seven basketfuls," they said.

[21]"And yet you think I'm worried that we have no bread?"

Jesus Heals a Blind Man

Close your eyes. Or put on a blindfold. How would you feel if you could not see anything—no colors, none of your favorite people, no favorite things? If you are blind you already know how it feels! This is a story about a man who was blind. But some friends begged Jesus to heal him. Did he?

[22]Then they came to Bethsaida. While there, some people brought a blind man to Jesus. They begged him to touch and heal him. [23]Jesus took the blind man by the hand and led him out of the village. He spat on his eyes and laid his hands over them.

"Can you see anything now?" Jesus asked him.

[24]The man looked around. "Yes!" he said. "I see men! But I can't see them very clearly. They look like trees walking around!"

[25]Then Jesus put his hands over the man's eyes again. The man looked around intently, and soon was completely healed. He saw everything clearly, drinking in the sights around him.

[26]Jesus sent him home to his family. "Don't even go back to the village first," he said.

- *Remember:* Where did Jesus meet the blind man? (8:22) How did he find his way to Jesus? (8:22) What did Jesus do? (8:23) Why do you think Jesus did it this way? Why didn't he just heal the man? What do you think the man said when he got home? What would you have said?

- *Discover:* One minute makes a big difference when Jesus is with you!

- *Apply:* Is something bothering you? Is something wrong? Ask Jesus to help you. If he can heal a blind man, he can help you with your problem, too. Nothing is too little or too big for him to do.

- *What's next?* Suddenly a man begins to shine like the sun. His face and clothes shine like a bright light. What is happening? Read Luke 9:28-36. ■

Peter Says Jesus Is the Messiah

[27]Jesus and his disciples now left Galilee. They went from there to the villages of Caesarea Philippi. As they were walking along he asked them, "Who do the people think I am? What are they saying about me?"

[28]"Some of them think you are John the Baptist," the disciples replied. "Others say you are Elijah. And some think you are another ancient prophet come back to life again."

[29]Then he asked, "Who do you think I am?" Peter replied, "You are the Messiah." [30]But Jesus warned them not to tell anyone!

Jesus Begins to Talk about His Death

[31]Then he began to tell them about the terrible things he would suffer. He told them that he would be rejected by the Jewish leaders. He told them that he would be killed. Then he said he would rise again three days later. [32]He talked about it quite clearly with them. So Peter took him aside and scolded him. "You shouldn't say things like that," he told Jesus.

[33]Jesus turned and looked at his disciples. Then he said to Peter very sternly,

"Satan, get behind me! You are looking at this only from a human point of view. You must look at it from God's."

What It Really Means to Follow Jesus

³⁴Then he called his disciples and the crowds. He told them to come over and listen. "One of you might want to be my follower," he told them. "If so, you must put aside your own desires. You must pick up your cross and follow me closely. ³⁵If you want to save your life, you will lose it. Only by giving up your life for my sake and the sake of the Good News can you save it.

³⁶"What good is it if a man gains the whole world and loses his soul? ³⁷For is anything worth more than his soul? ³⁸You might be ashamed of me and my message in these days of unbelief and sin. But if you are, I will be ashamed of you when I come back. And I will come in the glory of my Father, with the holy angels."

9 Jesus went on to say, "I tell you the truth. Some of you standing here will live to see the Kingdom of God come in great power!"

The Transfiguration

²Six days later Jesus took Peter, James, and John to the top of a mountain. No one else went with them.

Suddenly his face began to shine with glory. ³His clothes became a bright and shining white. They were far brighter than anyone on earth could ever make them! ⁴Then Elijah and Moses appeared and began talking with Jesus!

⁵"Teacher, this is wonderful!" Peter exclaimed. "We will make three booths here. We will build one for each of you!"

⁶He said this just to be talking, for he didn't know what else to say. And they were all very afraid.

⁷But while he was still speaking these words, a cloud covered them. The cloud blotted out the sun. A voice from the cloud said, "This is my Son whom I love. Listen to him."

⁸Then the three disciples looked around them. Moses and Elijah were

suddenly gone. Only Jesus was still there with them.

⁹So they began their journey down the mountain. As they walked, Jesus told them to keep what they had seen a secret. He told them not to tell anyone about it until he had risen from the dead. ¹⁰So they kept it to themselves, but they often talked about it. They wondered what he meant by "rising from the dead."

¹¹So they said to Jesus, "The Jewish teachers say that Elijah must come before the Messiah. Why do they say this?" ¹²⁻¹³Jesus replied, "Yes, Elijah must come first. He must make the way ready for the Messiah. He has, in fact, already come! He was treated very badly, just as the prophets said he would be." Then Jesus asked them, "Why did the prophets say that the Messiah would suffer? Why did they say he would be treated with hate?"

Jesus Can Heal a Boy; Why Can't the Disciples?

¹⁴At the bottom of the mountain they found a great crowd. They were standing all around the other nine disciples. Some of the Jewish leaders were arguing with them. ¹⁵The crowd watched Jesus in awe as he came toward them. Then they ran to meet him. ¹⁶"What's all the arguing about?" he asked.

¹⁷One of the men in the crowd spoke up. "Teacher," he said, "I brought my son for you to heal. He can't talk because he has a demon in him. ¹⁸When the demon takes control of him it throws him to the ground. It makes him foam at the mouth. It makes him grind his teeth and become stiff. So I begged your disciples to cast out the demon. But they couldn't do it."

¹⁹Jesus said to his disciples, "Oh, what tiny faith you have! How much longer must I be with you until you believe? How much longer must I be patient with you? Bring the boy to me."

²⁰So they brought the boy to Jesus. But when he saw Jesus, the demon took control of the boy. The boy was thrown to the ground and was rolling around. And he was foaming at the mouth.

²¹"How long has he been this way?" Jesus asked the father.

And he replied, "Since he was very small. ²²The demon often makes him fall into the fire or into water to kill him. Oh, have mercy on us and do something if you can."

²³"If I can?" Jesus asked. "Anything is possible if you have faith."

²⁴The father replied, "I do have faith! Oh, help me to have more!"

²⁵Jesus saw that the crowd was growing. So he spoke to the demon.

"O demon, you make this boy deaf and dumb!" he said. "I command you to come out of this child and stay out!"

²⁶Then the demon screamed loudly. He again made the boy roll around wildly. But then the demon left him. The boy lay there quietly. He didn't make a move. It looked as if he was dead. A murmur ran through the crowd, "He is dead." ²⁷But Jesus took him by the hand and helped him to his feet. The boy stood up and was all right! ²⁸After that, Jesus was alone in the house with his disciples. They asked him, "Why couldn't we cast that demon out?"

²⁹Jesus replied, "This kind of demon can come out only with much prayer."

Jesus Predicts His Death a Second Time

³⁰⁻³¹Leaving that region, they went through Galilee. There, Jesus tried to stay away from the crowds of people. This was because he wanted to spend more time with his disciples, teaching them. He would say to them, "I, the Messiah, will be betrayed and killed. Then three days later I will come back to life again."

The Disciples Argue about Being the Greatest

³²But they didn't understand what he was saying. And they were afraid to ask him what he meant.

³³And so they came to Capernaum. They soon settled into the house where they were to stay. Then Jesus asked them, "What were you talking about out on the road?"

Booths Made of Branches
MARK 9:5

Do you like parties? Have you ever been at a party that went on for a week? The Israelites had three big feasts each year. Sometimes they were called festivals. They were something like parties, but not exactly. People stopped work. They went to Jerusalem. They talked and ate together for a week. They had lots of fun. But they also did many things to worship God.

One of these feasts was called the Feast of Tabernacles. It was a time to thank God for all good things. When the harvest was done, people came together to thank God. They ate and talked together. They sang and danced folk dances. They read the Bible. They visited the Temple. During the week, people lived in little booths they had made. These were made of tree branches. These booths reminded them of the time long before when the Israelite slaves escaped from Egypt. They did not have homes then. They lived in tents in the wilderness. Israelites wanted to remember this each year. This reminded them to be thankful for their homes. Are you thankful for your house? This might be a good time to thank God for it.

³⁴But they were ashamed to answer. For they had been arguing about which of them was the greatest!

Jesus Teaches His Disciples about Humility

³⁵He sat down and called them around him. "Anyone wanting to be the greatest must be the least," he said. "The greatest must be the servant of all!"

³⁶Then he brought a little child and took the child into his arms. He said to them, ³⁷"Welcome the little children like this in my name. For in doing this, you will be welcoming me. And anyone who welcomes me is welcoming my Father who sent me!"

Jesus Says to Accept Others Who Do Miracles in His Name

³⁸One of his disciples, John, came to Jesus one day. He said, "Teacher, we saw a man using your name to cast out demons. But we told him not to, for he isn't one of our group." ³⁹"Don't tell him not to!" Jesus said. "For no one doing miracles in my name will quickly turn against me. ⁴⁰Anyone who isn't against us is for us. ⁴¹I tell you the truth! Someone might give you a cup of water because you belong to me. And if he does, he won't lose his reward. ⁴²But someone might cause someone who believes in me to lose faith. If he does this, it would be better for that man if he was thrown into the sea. Yes, thrown into the sea with a huge stone tied around his neck!

Stand Strong against Temptation

⁴³⁻⁴⁴"If your hand does wrong, cut it off. Better live forever with one hand than be thrown into the fires of hell with two! ⁴⁵⁻⁴⁶If your foot carries you toward evil, cut it off! Better be lame and live forever than have two feet that carry you to hell.

⁴⁷"And if your eye is sinful, gouge it out. Better enter the Kingdom of God half-blind than have two eyes and see the fires of hell. ⁴⁸For in hell, the worm never dies and the fire never goes out. ⁴⁹There, all will be burned with fire.

⁵⁰"Good salt is worthless if it loses its saltiness. It can't season anything. So don't lose your flavor! Live in peace with each other."

Jesus Teaches about Marriage and Divorce

10 Then Jesus left Capernaum and went southward to the Judean borders. He went from there into the area east of the Jordan River. As always, great crowds were following him. And as usual, he taught them.

²Some Pharisees came to see Jesus. They asked him, "Do you allow divorce?" Of course they were trying to trap him.

³"What did Moses say about divorce?" Jesus asked them.

⁴"He said it was all right," they replied. "He said that all a man has to do is write his wife a letter of dismissal."

⁵"And why did he say that?" Jesus asked. "I'll tell you why! It was because the people's hearts were so hard! ⁶⁻⁷But it certainly isn't God's way. From the very first God made man and woman. And he made them to be joined together permanently in marriage. So a man is to leave his father and mother. ⁸And he and his wife are married so that they are no longer two, but one. ⁹And no man may break apart what God has joined together."

¹⁰Later, Jesus was alone with his disciples in the house. And they brought up the subject again.

The way to be great is to serve others

*The greatest must be
the servant of all!*

Mark 9:35

---

¹¹He told them, "Suppose a man divorces his wife to marry someone else. If he does this, he commits adultery against her. ¹²And suppose a wife divorces her husband and gets married again. If she does this, she, too, commits adultery."

Jesus and the Children

Does God have time for children? Or is he too busy? Would he tell you, "Don't bother me"? The disciples thought Jesus was too busy for children. They said, "Don't bother him." But this is what Jesus did.

¹³One day, some mothers brought their children to Jesus to bless them. But the disciples sent them away. They told the mothers not to bother Jesus.

¹⁴But Jesus saw what was happening. And he was very much upset with his disciples. He said to them, "Let the children come to me. For the Kingdom of God belongs to such as they. Don't send them away! ¹⁵I tell you the truth. All people must come to God as little children. If they don't, they will never be allowed into his Kingdom."

¹⁶Then he took the children into his arms. He put his hands on their heads and he blessed them.

● *Remember:* Who told the children to go away? Why? (10:13) How did Jesus feel about this? (10:14) How do you know that Jesus wants children to come to him? (10:14) What did Jesus do to show that he loves children? (10:16) How do you think these children felt about Jesus after this? How would you have felt?

● *Discover:* Jesus loves children. He loves you!

● *Apply:* Jesus loves you very much. He wants you to love him too.

● *What's next?* A man asks, "What shall I do to get to Heaven?" How would you answer? Read Luke 18:18-30 to see what Jesus said. ■

A Lesson about Money and Following Jesus

¹⁷As he was starting out on a trip, a man came running to him. This man knelt

down and asked, "Good Teacher, what must I do to get to Heaven?"

¹⁸"Why do you call me good?" Jesus asked. "Only God is truly good! ¹⁹But as for your question, you know the commandments. You shall not murder. You shall not commit adultery. You shall not steal, lie, or cheat. You shall respect your father and mother."

²⁰"Teacher," the man replied, "I've never broken any of those laws."

²¹Jesus felt love for this man as he looked at him. "You lack only one thing," he told him. "Go and sell all you have. Give the money to the poor. And you shall have treasure in Heaven. Then come and follow me."

²²Then the man's face fell and he went sadly away. This was because he was very rich.

²³Jesus watched him go, and then he turned around. He said to his disciples, "It's very hard for the rich to get into the Kingdom of God!"

²⁴The disciples were very amazed by these words. So Jesus said, "Dear children, it is hard for rich people to enter the Kingdom of God. ²⁵It is very hard for a camel to go through the eye of a needle. But it is even harder for a rich man to enter the Kingdom of God."

²⁶The disciples were even more amazed! "Then who in the world can be saved, if not a rich man?" they asked.

²⁷Jesus looked at them intently. Then he said, "Without God, it is impossible. But with God all things are possible."

²⁸Then Peter said, "We've given up everything to follow you!"

²⁹And Jesus replied, "Let me tell you this!

You may have given up many things. You may have given up home, brothers, sisters, mother, father, children, or land. And you may have done this because you love me. You may have wanted to tell others the Good News. [30]But those who have done this will get back 100 times what they gave. They will be given back homes, brothers, sisters, mothers, children, and land. But they will also be given persecution!

"All these people will be his here on earth. And in the world to come they shall have eternal life. [31]But many people who seem to be important now will be the least important then. Many who are thought to be least here shall be the greatest there."

Jesus Talks about His Death for the Third Time

[32]Now Jesus and his disciples were on the way to Jerusalem. And Jesus was walking along ahead. As the disciples followed, they became afraid and full of dread.

Then Jesus took them aside. He told all that was going to happen to him when they got to Jerusalem.

[33]"When we get there," he told them, "I, the Messiah, will be arrested. I will be taken before the chief priests and the Jewish leaders. They will sentence me to die and hand me over to the Romans to be killed. [34]They will laugh at me and spit on me. They will beat me with their whips and kill me. But after three days I will come back to life again."

True Greatness Comes from Serving Others

[35]Then James and John, the sons of Zebedee, came over to Jesus. They spoke to him in a low voice. "Master," they said, "we want you to do us a favor."

[36]"What is it?" he asked.

[37]"We want to sit on the thrones next to yours in your Kingdom," they said. "One of us wants to sit at your right and the other at your left!"

[38]But Jesus answered, "You don't know what you are asking! Are you able to drink from the bitter cup of sorrow I must drink from? Are you able to be baptized with the baptism of suffering I must be baptized with?"

[39]"Oh, yes," they said, "we are!"

And Jesus said, "You shall indeed drink from my cup. And you shall be baptized with my baptism. [40]But I do not have the right to put you on thrones next to mine. Those choices have already been made."

[41]The other disciples found out what James and John had asked. And they were very upset with them. [42]So Jesus called them together around him. He said, "As you know, great kings of the earth lord it over the people. [43]But among you it is different. Whoever wants to be great among you must be your servant. [44]And whoever wants to be greatest of all must be the slave of all. [45]For even I, the Messiah, am not here to be served. I have come to help others, and to give my life as a ransom for many."

Jesus Heals Blind Bartimaeus

"Help me!" a blind man cries to Jesus. "Shut up!" some people tell him. Will Jesus listen to him? Or will he also tell the man to be quiet?

[46]And so they came to Jericho. Later, as they left town, a great crowd was following them. Now as it happened, there was a blind beggar there named Bartimaeus. He was the son of Timaeus. He was sitting beside the road as Jesus went by.

[47]Bartimaeus heard that Jesus from Nazareth was near. So he began to shout

out, "Jesus, Son of David! Have mercy on me!"

⁴⁸"Shut up!" some of the people yelled at him.

But he only shouted the louder, again and again. "O Son of David!" he cried. "Have mercy on me!"

⁴⁹When Jesus heard him, he stopped there in the road. He said, "Tell him to come here."

So they called the blind man. "You lucky fellow," they said. "Come on, he's calling you!" ⁵⁰Bartimaeus yanked off his old coat and threw it aside. He jumped up and came to Jesus.

⁵¹"What do you want me to do for you?" Jesus asked.

"O Teacher," the blind man said, "I want to see!"

⁵²And Jesus said to him, "All right, it's done. Your faith has healed you."

And right away the blind man could see. And he followed Jesus down the road!

- *Remember:* What was the blind man's name? (10:46) What did he ask Jesus to do? (10:47) What did some people say to the blind man? (10:48) Did Jesus listen to the man? Did he help him? (10:49) Jesus said that something healed the man. What was it? (10:52) Why do you think the man followed Jesus after he was healed? Why didn't he just go home?

- *Discover:* Jesus can do great things for us. But we must believe that he will.

- *Apply:* Would you like Jesus to do something special for you? Be sure it's something God wants. Then ask Jesus to help you. And believe that he will.

- *What's next?* Why would a rich little man climb up into a big tree? Read Luke 19:1-10. ∎

Crowds Welcome Jesus to Jerusalem

11 They came to Bethphage and Bethany on the outskirts of Jerusalem. These towns were at the Mount of Olives. From there, Jesus sent two of his disciples on ahead.

²"Go into that village over there," he told them. "Just as you enter you will see a colt tied up that has never been ridden. Untie him and bring him here. ³Someone might ask you what you are doing. If so, just say, 'Our Master needs him and will bring him back soon.'"

We must first forgive others, then God will forgive us

But when you pray, first forgive anyone you are holding a grudge against. That way your Father in Heaven will forgive your sins too.

Mark 11:25

---

⁴⁻⁵So the two men went and found the colt standing in the street. It was tied up outside a house. So they went and began untying it. Some men who were standing there asked, "What are you doing? Why are you untying that colt?"

⁶So they said what Jesus had told them to, and then the men agreed.

⁷So the colt was brought to Jesus. And the disciples threw their coats across its back for him to ride on. ⁸Then many in the crowd spread out their coats along the road before him. Others threw down leafy branches from the fields.

⁹He was in the center of the parade. There were crowds ahead of him and behind him. All of them shouted, "Hail to the King! Praise God for him who comes in the name of the Lord! ¹⁰Praise God for the return of our father David's kingdom. Hail to the King of the universe!"

¹¹And so Jesus entered Jerusalem and went into the Temple. He looked around carefully at everything and then left. For now it was late in the afternoon. Jesus then went out to Bethany with his 12 disciples.

Jesus Clears the Temple

¹²The next morning as they left Bethany, Jesus felt hungry. ¹³A little way off he saw a fig tree in full leaf. So he went over to see if he could find any figs on it. But no, there were only leaves. This was because it was too early in the season for fruit.

¹⁴Then Jesus said to the tree, "You shall never bear fruit again!" And the disciples heard him say it.

15When they got back to Jerusalem, Jesus went to the Temple. He drove out the people who were buying and selling there. He knocked over the tables of the money changers. And he pushed over the stalls of those selling doves. 16He stopped everyone from bringing in things to sell there.

17He told them, "It is written in the Scriptures: 'My Temple is to be a place of prayer for all nations.' But you have turned it into a den of robbers."

18Soon the chief priests and other Jewish leaders heard what he had done. So they began to plan how best to get rid of him. They had to figure out a secret plan that wouldn't make the people angry. This was because the people were so amazed by Jesus' teaching.

19That evening as usual they left the city.

How Should You Pray?

20On the next morning, the disciples passed the fig tree Jesus had cursed. They saw that it was withered from the roots! 21Then Peter remembered what Jesus had said to the tree the day before. He said, "Look, Teacher! The fig tree you cursed has died!"

22-23In reply Jesus said, "All you need is a little faith in God. This is the truth! If you have faith, you can even give commands to this Mount of Olives. You might say, 'Rise up and fall into the Mediterranean.' And if you do, your command will be obeyed. You just need to really believe and have no doubt! 24Listen to me! You might pray for anything. And if you believe, you will have it. It's yours! 25But when you pray, first forgive anyone you are holding a grudge against. That way your Father in Heaven will forgive your sins too."

The Religious Leaders Question Jesus' Authority

26-28By this time they had come to Jerusalem again. And as he was walking through the Temple area, the Jewish leaders came up to him. They demanded, "What's going on here? Who

Money Changers
MARK 11:15

In Jesus' time Israelites did not have paper money, like dollar bills. They used coins. At the Temple they needed coins to pay taxes and to buy animals. They paid a tax each year to the Temple. It was like a church offering, except they *had* to pay it. It helped take care of the building and the priests. People paid this tax with coins. They also sacrificed animals at the Temple. They used coins to buy the animals from merchants. But there was a problem. They could not use certain coins to pay the tax and buy animals. Coins with the Roman emperor's picture could not be used. The emperor pretended he was a god. The Israelites thought his picture was an idol. They would not accept coins like this in the Temple. So money changers set up booths. They exchanged the right kind of coins for the ones that could not be used. But they cheated the people when they did this. Jesus did not want the money changers in the Temple. One time he chased them out. He said God's house is a place to worship God. It should not be a big shopping mall. It should never be a place to cheat people.

gave you the authority to drive out the merchants?"

²⁹Jesus replied, "I'll tell you if you answer one question! ³⁰What about John the Baptist? Was he sent by God, or not? Answer me!"

³¹They talked it over among themselves. "We might say that God sent him. But then he will say, 'All right, why didn't you accept him?' ³²On the other hand, we might say God didn't send him. But then the people will start a riot." This was because the people all believed that John was a prophet.

³³So they said, "We can't answer. We don't know."

To which Jesus replied, "Then I won't answer your question either!"

A Story about a Farm

Who would try to steal something from God? Who would try to kill his son? Some people did. Jesus told a story about them.

12 Here are some of the stories Jesus gave to the people at that time.

"A man planted a vineyard," Jesus said. "He built a wall around it. Then he dug a pit for pressing out the grape juice. He also built a watchman's tower. Then he leased the farm to tenant farmers and moved to another country. ²At harvest time he sent one of his men to collect his share of the crop. ³But the farmers beat up the man and sent him back empty-handed.

⁴"The owner then sent another of his men. He was treated even worse than the first one. He came back with a serious head injury. ⁵The next man he sent was killed. Then later, others were either beaten or killed. ⁶In the end there was only one left. It was his only son. So the man finally sent his son. He thought they would surely respect him.

⁷"But the farmers saw him coming. They said, 'He will own the farm when his father dies. Come on, let's kill him! Then the farm will be ours!' ⁸So they caught him and murdered him. Then they threw his body out of the vineyard.

⁹"What do you suppose the owner will do when he hears what happened? He will come and kill them all. Then he will lease the vineyard to others. ¹⁰Don't you remember reading this verse in the Scriptures? 'The Rock the builders threw away became the cornerstone. It became the most honored stone in the building!

¹¹This is what the Lord is doing. And it is an amazing thing to see.'"

¹²The Jewish leaders wanted to arrest him then and there. They knew that he was pointing at them. They were the wicked farmers in his story. But they were afraid to touch him for fear of the people. So they left him and went away.

- *Remember:* Who owned this farm? Who did the farming? (12:1-2) How did the owner try to get his share of the crops? What did the wicked farmers do each time? (12:3-6) How would the owner punish the wicked farmers? (12:9) Who were the wicked farmers? Why did they hate Jesus? (12:12) The religious leaders, like the wicked farmers, had killed many prophets. They did not like to hear God's truth. They would kill Jesus. They did not like to hear Jesus tell how wrong they were.

- *Discover:* God expects us to use his earth wisely. He expects us to use his Word wisely. He expects us to treat his Son well.

- *Apply:* God gave us a beautiful world. We should not abuse it. God gave us his Word, the Bible. We should share it. God gave us his Son. We should follow him and obey him.

- *What's next?* Some men try to trick Jesus. But Jesus stops their trick with one small coin. How do you think he does this? Read Mark 12:13-17. ■

Jesus Talks about Caesar and God

Some men came to Jesus. They asked him a question. It was a trick! If he said yes, people would get mad at him. If he said no, people would get mad at him. What did he do?

13But they sent other religious and political leaders to talk with him. They tried to trap him into saying something that would get him in trouble.

14"Teacher," these spies said, "we know you tell the truth no matter what! You aren't swayed by the opinions and desires of men. You always teach the ways of God. Now tell us, is it right to pay taxes to Rome, or not?"

15Jesus saw their plan to trick him. So he said, "Show me a coin and I'll tell you."

16So they handed a coin to him. Then he asked, "Whose picture and title is on this coin?" They answered, "Caesar's."

17"All right," he said. "If it is his, give it to him. But everything that belongs to God must be given to God!" And they were amazed at his answer.

- *Remember:* Some men tried to trick Jesus. What did they ask him? (12:14) Whose picture was on the coin? (12:16) What should people give to the emperor, or government? (12:17) What should people give to God? (12:17) Should we pay tax money to our government? Should we pay money to help God's work?

- *Discover:* We should help our government and God. Each is important.

- *Apply:* Do you give part of your money to God? You should! When you earn money, you must give part of it to your government. You can't just say, "I won't do it." Neither should you say, "I won't give part of my money to God."

- *What's next?* A king invites some people to eat with him. But these people laugh at him! What will he do? Read Matthew 22:1-14. ■

The Sadducees Ask Tricky Questions about the Resurrection

18Then the Sadducees stepped forward. They believed that no person will rise from the dead. This is what they asked:

19"Teacher, Moses gave us a law for men who die without children. He said that the dead man's brother should marry his widow. Then she will have children in his brother's name. 20-22Now suppose there were seven brothers. The oldest brother married a woman. But then he died and left no children. So the second brother married the widow. But soon he died too and left no children. Then the next brother married her and died without children. This happened again and again, until all of them were dead. But still there were no children. Then, last of all, the woman died too.

23"We want to know whose wife she will be when they rise from the dead. For she was the wife of all of them."

24Jesus replied, "Your trouble is that you don't know the Scriptures. And you don't know the power of God either. 25For when these seven brothers and the woman rise from the dead, they won't be married. They will be like the angels.

26"But you don't believe people will rise from the dead anyway! Have you never read in the Book of Exodus about Moses and the burning bush? God said to Moses, 'I *am* the God of Abraham. I *am* the God of Isaac. I *am* the God of Jacob.'

27"God was telling Moses that these men were still very much alive. For he would not have said, 'I *am* the God' of those who don't exist! God is the God of the living, not of the dead. You Sadducees don't have the truth!"

What Is the Most Important Commandment?

28One of the teachers of religion came to Jesus. He had been standing there while Jesus argued with the Pharisees and Sadducees. He saw that Jesus had answered wisely. So he asked, "Of all the commands, which is the most important?"

29Jesus replied, "The one that says, 'Hear, O Israel! The Lord our God is the one and only God. 30And you must love him with all your heart and soul and mind and strength.'

³¹"The second is, 'You must love others as much as yourself.' No other commands are greater than these."

³²The teacher of religion replied, "Sir, you have spoken a true word. For you have said that there is only one God and no other. ³³And I know it is important to love him with all my heart, mind, and strength. And I know I should love others as myself. I also know that these things are more important than giving sacrifices on the altar of the Temple."

³⁴Jesus saw that the man had given him a wise answer. So he said to him, "You are not far from the Kingdom of God." And after that, no one dared ask him any more questions.

Jesus Has a Question for the Religious Leaders

³⁵Later, Jesus was again teaching the people in the Temple area. He asked them, "Your teachers say the Messiah must be a descendant of King David. Why do they say this? ³⁶For David himself said, 'God said to my Lord, "Sit at my right hand. Stay there until I put your enemies under your feet."' And the Holy Spirit was speaking through him when he said it. ³⁷David called the Messiah his Lord. So how can the Messiah be his *son?*"

This sort of thinking delighted the crowd. So they listened to him with great interest.

Jesus Warns the People against the Religious Leaders

³⁸Jesus taught them many other things at this time.

"Beware of the teachers of religion!" he warned. "For they love to wear the robes of the rich and scholarly. They love it when everyone bows to them as they walk through the markets. ³⁹They love to sit in the best seats in the synagogues. They like to sit at the places of honor at banquets. ⁴⁰But they also cheat widows out of their homes. And they have no shame about it! Then they cover up how sinful they really are. They do this by pretending to be pious

by praying long prayers in public. Because of this, their punishment will be the greater."

A Poor Widow Gives More than the Rich Do

⁴¹Then Jesus went over to the collection boxes in the Temple. He sat and watched as the crowds dropped in their money. Some who were rich put in large amounts. ⁴²Then a poor widow came and dropped in two pennies.

⁴³⁻⁴⁴Jesus called his disciples over to him. "That poor widow has given more than all those rich men put together!" he said. "They gave just a little of their extra fat. But she gave up her last penny."

Jesus Tells about the Future

13 Jesus was leaving the Temple that day. One of his disciples said, "Teacher, what beautiful buildings these are! Look at the decorated stonework on the walls."

²Jesus replied, "Yes, look! For not one stone will be left upon another, except as ruins."

³⁻⁴Later on, Jesus was sitting alone on the slopes of the Mount of Olives. He was across the valley from Jerusalem. At that time, Peter, James, John, and Andrew went to him. They asked him, "Just when is all this going to happen to the Temple? Will there be some warning ahead of time?"

⁵So Jesus said to them, "Don't let anyone trick you. ⁶For many will come claiming they are your Messiah. And they will lead many astray. ⁷Wars will break out near and far. But this is not the signal of the end-time.

⁸"For nations and kingdoms will proclaim war against each other. And there will be earthquakes in many lands, and famines. These are just signs of the early stages of the trouble ahead. ⁹But when these things begin to happen, watch out! For you will be in great danger. You will be dragged before the courts. You will be beaten in the synagogues. You will be accused before governors and kings of being my followers. This is your chance to tell them

the Good News. ¹⁰And the Good News must first be made known in every nation before the end comes. ¹¹But when you are arrested and stand trial, don't worry about what to say. Just say what God tells you to. Then you will not be speaking, but the Holy Spirit will.

¹²"Brothers will turn each other in to be killed. Fathers will turn against their own children. And children will turn their parents in to be killed. ¹³Everyone will hate you because you are mine. But all who stand to the end and do not turn against me shall be saved.

¹⁴"You will see the horrible thing standing in the Temple. You who read this should pay attention! At that time, run to the Judean hills if you can. ¹⁵⁻¹⁶Hurry! You might be on your rooftop porch. If so, don't even go back into the house. You might be out in the fields. If so, don't even go back for your money or clothes.

¹⁷"It will be terrible for pregnant women in those days. It will be terrible for mothers nursing their children. ¹⁸And pray that you will not have to run away during the winter. ¹⁹For those days will be terrible. No such days have ever been since the beginning of God's creation. And such days will never be again. ²⁰But the Lord will shorten that time of trouble. If he didn't, not a soul in all the earth would live. For the sake of his chosen ones he will limit those days.

Jesus Tells about His Return

²¹"At that time someone might say, 'This is the Messiah.' Or another might say, 'That person is the Messiah.' If you hear this, don't listen at all. ²²For there will be many false Messiahs and false prophets. They will do great miracles that might even trick God's own children. ²³Take care! I have warned you!

²⁴"After this trouble comes, then the sun will grow dim. The moon will not shine. ²⁵The stars will fall from the sky. And the heavens will shake.

²⁶"Then all mankind will see me, the Messiah. I will come in the clouds with great power and glory. ²⁷I will send out the angels to gather my chosen ones

from all over the world. They will bring them from the farthest ends of earth and Heaven.

²⁸"Now, here is a lesson from a fig tree. There is a time when its buds become tender and its leaves begin to sprout. When this happens, you know that spring has come. ²⁹In the same way, there will be a time when you see these things happening. When this happens, you can be sure that my coming is very near. You will know that I am right at the door!

³⁰"Yes, these are the events that will signal the end of the age. ³¹Heaven and earth shall disappear. But my words stand sure forever.

Jesus Says to Be Ready for His Return

³²"However, no one knows the day or hour when these things will happen. The angels in Heaven don't even know. I myself don't know. Only the Father knows. ³³And since you don't know when it will happen, stay ready. Be on the watch for my coming.

³⁴"My coming is like a man who went on a trip to another country. He laid out his employees' work for them to do while he was gone. And he told the gatekeeper to watch for his return.

³⁵⁻³⁷"Keep a sharp lookout! For you do not know when I will come. I might come at evening, at midnight, early dawn, or late daybreak. Don't let me find you sleeping. Watch for my return! This is my message to you and to everyone else."

A Plot to Kill Jesus

14 The Passover Feast began two days later. This was a yearly Jewish holiday. During the celebration no bread made with yeast was eaten. The chief priests and other Jewish leaders were still making plans. They were looking for a chance to arrest Jesus in secret. Then they hoped to put him to death.

²"But we can't do it during the Passover," they said. "If we do, there will be a riot."

A Gift of Love for Jesus

[3]Meanwhile Jesus was in Bethany, at the home of Simon the leper. During supper a woman came in with a flask of expensive perfume. Then, breaking the seal, she poured it over his head.

[4-5]Some of those at the table were upset about this. They thought it was a great "waste."

"Why, she could have sold that perfume for a fortune!" they snarled. "Then she could have given the money to the poor!"

[6]But Jesus said, "Let her alone. Why speak against her for doing a good thing? [7]You always have the poor among you. You can help them whenever you want to. But I won't be here much longer.

[8]"She has done what she could. She has anointed my body ahead of time for being buried. [9]I tell you this in solemn truth. The Good News will be preached throughout the world. And this woman's deed will be remembered and praised by all those who hear it."

Judas Agrees to Betray Jesus

[10]Then Judas Iscariot, one of his disciples, went to the chief priests. He went there to plan how to turn Jesus over to them.

[11]He told the chief priests why he had come. They were excited and happy and promised him a reward. So he began looking for the right time and place to betray Jesus.

The Last Supper

"One of you will betray me," Jesus said. His friends were sad. "Am I the one?" each asked. "All of you will leave me," Jesus said later. Good friends don't run away, do they? They don't betray their friend. Would Jesus' friends really do this?

[12]It was the first day of the Passover. This was the day the lambs were sacrificed. The disciples asked Jesus where he wanted to eat the Passover supper. [13]He sent two of them into Jerusalem to get ready.

"As you go," he told them, "you will see a man coming toward you. This man will be carrying a pot of water. Follow him. [14]At the house he enters, speak to the man in charge. Tell him, 'Our Master sent us to see the room you have ready for us. We will eat the Passover supper there this evening!' [15]He will take you upstairs to a large room all set up. Make our supper there."

[16]So the two disciples went on ahead into the city. They found everything as Jesus had said. And they made the Passover supper.

[17]In the evening Jesus came with the other disciples. [18]They sat down around the table to eat. And Jesus said, "I tell you the truth. One of you will betray me. And it is one of you who is here eating with me."

[19]A great sadness came over them. One by one they asked him, "Am I the one?"

[20]He replied, "It is one of you 12 eating with me now. [21]I must die, as the prophets promised long ago. But, oh, how sad it will be for the man who betrays me! It would have been better if he had never been born!"

[22]As they were eating, Jesus took bread. He asked God's blessing on it. Then he broke it in pieces and gave it to them. He said, "Eat it. This is my body."

[23]Then he took a cup of wine. He gave thanks to God for it and gave it to them. And they all drank from it. [24]Then he said to them, "This is my blood, poured out for many. It seals the new agreement between God and man. [25]I tell you the truth. I shall never again taste wine until the day I drink it in the Kingdom of God."

²⁶Then they sang a hymn and went out to the Mount of Olives.

²⁷"All of you will leave me," Jesus told them. "For God has said through the prophets, 'I will kill the Shepherd. And the sheep will scatter.' ²⁸After I am raised to life again, I will go to Galilee and meet you there."

²⁹Peter said to him, "I will never leave you no matter what the others do!"

³⁰"Peter," Jesus said, "tonight you will say you don't know me. You will do this three times before the rooster crows twice."

³¹"No!" Peter exploded. "Not even if I have to die with you! I'll *never* deny you!" And all the others promised the same.

- *Remember:* What was this supper called? (14:12) What did Jesus say one of his friends would do? (14:18) When Jesus broke the bread, what did he say? When he gave the disciples the cup, what did he say? (14:22-24) How does this remind you of communion in your church? Jesus told one disciple that he would deny him three times. Who was he? (14:30) Peter thought he would never deny Jesus. He would never pretend that he did not know Jesus. But he did!

- *Discover:* Sometimes Jesus' friends pretend they don't even know him.

- *Apply:* Your friends at school make fun of church and Sunday school. Or they make fun of Jesus. Would you say, "I'm Jesus' friend"? Would you say, "I go to Sunday school every Sunday"? Or would you be quiet?

- *What's next?* Do you ever fall asleep when you should be praying? Read about some of Jesus' friends who did this in Luke 22:39-46. ∎

Jesus Prays in the Garden of Gethsemane

³²And now they came to an olive grove called the Garden of Gethsemane. He said to his disciples, "Sit here while I go and pray."

³³He took Peter, James, and John with him. Jesus then began to be filled with horror and deepest sadness. ³⁴And he said to them, "My soul is crushed by sadness. I am at the point of death. Stay here and watch with me."

³⁵He went on a little further and fell to the ground. He prayed that if it were possible the hour awaiting him might never come.

³⁶"Father, Father," he said, "everything is possible for you. Take away this cup from me. Yet I want your will, not mine."

³⁷Then he went back to the three disciples and found them asleep.

"Simon!" he said. "Asleep? Couldn't you watch with me even one hour? ³⁸Watch with me and pray. If you don't, the Tempter will overpower you. For though the spirit is willing enough, the body is weak."

³⁹And he went away again and prayed the same thing as before. ⁴⁰Again he went back to them and found them sleeping. For they were very tired. And they didn't know what to say.

⁴¹Then he came back to them a third time. "Sleep on," he said. "Get your rest! But no! The time for sleep has ended! Look! I am betrayed into the hands of wicked men. ⁴²Come! Get up! We must go! Look! My betrayer is here!"

The Mob Arrests Jesus

⁴³And then, while he was still speaking, Judas came with a crowd of men. They were armed with swords and clubs. They were sent by the chief priests and other Jewish leaders.

⁴⁴Judas had told them, "You will know which one to arrest. For I will go over and greet him. Then you can take him easily." ⁴⁵So as soon as they got there he walked up to Jesus. "Master!" he said. Then he hugged him as though he were a good friend. ⁴⁶Then the mob arrested Jesus and held him fast. ⁴⁷But one of the disciples pulled out a sword. He slashed at the High Priest's servant, cutting off his ear.

⁴⁸Jesus asked them, "Am I some dangerous robber, that you come like this? Why do you carry swords and clubs to capture me? ⁴⁹Why didn't you arrest me in the Temple? I was there teaching every day. But these things are happening to fulfill the prophecies about me."

⁵⁰Meanwhile, all his disciples had run away. ⁵¹⁻⁵²There was, however, a young man following along behind. He was dressed only in a linen nightshirt. When the mob tried to grab him, he got away. But his clothes were torn off in the process. So he ran away completely naked.

Jesus Is Taken before the Rulers

Religious leaders should love God's Son. They shouldn't beat God's Son with their fists. But these religious leaders did. They hated Jesus. Do you know why?

⁵³Jesus was taken to the High Priest's home. And all the chief priests and other Jewish leaders soon gathered there. ⁵⁴Peter followed far behind. Then he slipped inside the gates of the High Priest's home. He sat there beside a fire among the servants.

⁵⁵Inside, the chief priests and the whole Jewish Supreme Court were trying to find something against Jesus. They wanted to find something that would be bad enough to put him to death. But they couldn't find anything wrong with him. ⁵⁶Many people told lies about Jesus to get him into trouble. But none of their stories agreed.

⁵⁷Finally some men stood up to lie about him. They said, ⁵⁸"We heard him say, 'I will destroy this Temple made with human hands. And in three days I will build another, made without human hands!'" ⁵⁹But even then they didn't get their stories straight!

⁶⁰Then the High Priest stood up before the Court. He asked Jesus, "Do you refuse to answer this charge? What do you have to say for yourself?"

⁶¹To this Jesus said nothing.

Then the High Priest asked him. "Are you the Messiah, the Son of God?"

⁶²Jesus said, "I am. You will someday see me sitting at the right hand of God. And I will come back to earth in the clouds of Heaven."

⁶³⁻⁶⁴Then the High Priest tore at his clothes. "What more do we need?" he cried. "Why wait for witnesses? You have heard his blasphemy. What is your verdict?" Everyone said that Jesus was guilty and that he should die.

⁶⁵Then some of them began to spit at him. They covered his eyes and began to hit his face with their fists.

"Who hit you that time, you prophet?" they laughed. The guards then led him away and beat him.

- *Remember:* What were the religious leaders trying to do to Jesus? (14:55) Why were they not getting what they wanted at first? (14:56, 59) What did the High Priest ask Jesus? (14:61) What did Jesus say? (14:62) Who voted to kill Jesus? Why? (14:63-64) Only God's Son could bring dead people back to life. He did many other miracles. But these people did not believe what they saw. Do you?

- *Discover:* Jesus is God's Son. Only God's Son could do the things that he did.

- *Apply:* Can you make a blind person see? Can you make a storm stop? Can you bring a dead person back to life? Can you drive demons from a man? Jesus did all these things. They show that he is God's Son. Believe him when he says he is.

- *What's next?* Are you ever ashamed to say you're Jesus' friend? Peter was. Read about Peter's bad morning in Matthew 26:69-75. ■

Peter Says He Doesn't Know Jesus

⁶⁶⁻⁶⁷Meanwhile Peter was below in the courtyard. One of the maids who worked for the High Priest saw Peter. He was warming himself at the fire.

She looked at him closely. Then she said, "You were with Jesus, the Nazarene."

⁶⁸Peter said it wasn't true. "I don't know what you're talking about!" he said. Then he walked over to the edge of the courtyard.

Just then, a rooster crowed.

⁶⁹The maid saw him standing there and began telling the others. "There he is!" she said. "There's that disciple of Jesus!"

⁷⁰Again Peter said it wasn't true.

A little later others standing around the fire turned to Peter. "You are one of them!" the said. "For you are from Galilee!"

⁷¹He began to curse and swear. "I don't even know this fellow you are talking about," he said.

⁷²And then the rooster crowed the second time. Suddenly Jesus' words flashed through Peter's mind. He had said, "Before the cock crows twice, you will deny me three times." And he began to cry.

Pilate Questions Jesus about the Charges against Him

15 Early in the morning the Supreme Court met to talk about what they should do. This included the chief priests, elders, and teachers of religion. They decided to send Jesus under armed guard to Pilate, the Roman governor.

²Pilate asked him, "Are you the King of the Jews?"

"Yes," Jesus replied, "it is as you say."

³⁻⁴Then the chief priests claimed that Jesus had done many crimes. So Pilate asked him, "Why don't you say something? What about all these charges against you?"

⁵But Jesus said no more, much to Pilate's amazement.

Pilate Wants to Free Jesus but Is Afraid of the Mob

⁶Now, Pilate had a custom at Passover time. Each year he set one Jewish prisoner free. He would set free any prisoner the people asked for. ⁷One of the prisoners at that time was Barabbas. He was charged along with others for murder during a rebellion.

⁸Now a mob began to crowd in toward Pilate. They asked him to set a prisoner free as usual.

⁹"How about giving you the 'King of Jews'?" Pilate asked. "Is he the one you want set free?" ¹⁰For he knew by now that Jesus had been framed by the chief priests. He saw that they were doing this because they were jealous of him.

¹¹But at this point the chief priests stirred up the crowd. They got the crowd to demand that Pilate set Barabbas free instead of Jesus.

¹²"I might set Barabbas free," Pilate said to them. "But if so, what shall I do with this man you call your king?"

¹³They shouted back, "Crucify him!"

¹⁴"But why?" Pilate demanded. "What has he done wrong?" They roared even louder, "Crucify him!"

¹⁵Now Pilate was afraid of a riot. So to make the people happy, he set Barabbas free. Then he ordered that Jesus be beaten with a leaded whip. And he handed Jesus over to be crucified.

Roman Soldiers Beat Jesus

Jesus was the most important person in the world. He was God's Son. He came from Heaven. He wanted to help people get to Heaven. So everyone should love him. Everyone should be happy to listen to him. But look what some people did!

¹⁶⁻¹⁷Then the Roman soldiers took him into the barracks of the palace. They called out the whole palace guard. They dressed him in a purple robe. And they made a crown of sharp thorns and put it on his head. ¹⁸Then they cheered, yelling, "Yea! King of the Jews!" ¹⁹They beat him on the head with a cane and

spat on him. They made fun of him by bowing down to "worship" him.

²⁰They finally got tired of their sport. So they took off the purple robe and put his own clothes on him again. Then they led him away to be crucified.

²¹A man named Simon of Cyrene was coming in from the country just then. He was forced to carry Jesus' cross. Simon is the father of Alexander and Rufus.

²²And they brought Jesus to a place called Golgotha. The name Golgotha means "skull." ²³They offered him wine drugged with bitter herbs. But he would not drink it. ²⁴Then they crucified him and threw dice for his clothes.

- *Remember:* The Roman soldiers made fun of Jesus. Can you find six ways? (15:16-19) Who helped carry Jesus' cross? (15:21) Where was Jesus crucified? (15:22,24) What happened to Jesus' clothes? (15:24) What do you think of the Roman soldiers there? What would you like to say to them?

- *Discover:* Jesus came from Heaven. He wants to help you get to Heaven. Don't turn against him. Listen to him. Only he can show you the way.

- *Apply:* Pretend that a king walks into your house. "Come to my palace," he says. "Eat with me and stay with me." Would you make fun of him? Would you spit at him? Would you beat him? Or would you listen to him?

- *What's next?* A person dies. When he does, there is an earthquake. Dead people get up and walk. Read Matthew 27:35-56. ∎

Jesus Is Hung on the Cross

²⁵It was about nine o'clock in the morning when the crucifixion took place.

²⁶A sign was put on the cross above his head. This sign told everyone what he had done wrong. It read, "The King of the Jews."

²⁷Two robbers were also crucified that morning. Their crosses were on either side of his. ²⁸And so the Scripture was fulfilled that said, "He was counted among evil men."

²⁹⁻³⁰The people laughed at him as they walked by. They shook their heads in mockery.

"Ha! Look at you now!" they yelled at him. "Sure, you can destroy the Temple and rebuild it in three days! If you're so wonderful, save yourself! Come down from the cross!"

³¹The chief priests and religious leaders were also joking about Jesus.

"He's quite clever at 'saving' others," they said. "But he can't save himself!"

³²"Hey there, Messiah!" they yelled at him. "You, 'King of Israel'! Come on down from the cross and we'll believe you!"

And even the two robbers dying with him cursed him.

Jesus Dies on the Cross

³³About noon, darkness fell across the land. It lasted until three o'clock that afternoon.

³⁴Then Jesus called out with a loud voice. He said, "My God, my God, why have you left me?"

³⁵There were many people standing there as he said this. Some thought he was calling for the prophet Elijah. ³⁶So one man ran and got a sponge. He filled

it with sour wine and held it up to him on a stick.

"Let's see if Elijah will come and take him down!" he said.

³⁷Then Jesus cried out in a loud voice and died.

³⁸And the curtain in the Temple was split apart from top to bottom.

³⁹The Roman officer standing beside his cross saw how Jesus had died. And he said, "Truly, this was the Son of God!"

⁴⁰Some women were there watching from a distance. Mary Magdalene and Salome were there. Mary, the mother of James the Younger and of Joses, was also there. ⁴¹They and many other Galilean women were his followers. They had served him while he was up in Galilee. Then they had come with him to Jerusalem.

The Burial of Jesus

⁴²⁻⁴³This all happened the day before the Sabbath. Late that afternoon Joseph from Arima-thea went to Pilate and asked for Jesus' body. Joseph was an honored member of the Jewish Supreme Court. He was eagerly looking for the coming of God's Kingdom.

⁴⁴Pilate couldn't believe that Jesus was already dead. So he called for the Roman officer in charge and asked him. ⁴⁵The officer told him that Jesus was dead. So Pilate told Joseph he could have the body.

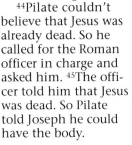

⁴⁶Joseph bought a long sheet of linen cloth. Then he took Jesus' body down from the cross. He wound it in the cloth and laid it in a tomb. And he rolled a stone in front of the door.

⁴⁷Mary Magdalene and Mary the mother of Joses watched as Jesus was buried.

Women Visit Jesus' Tomb

What would you think if an angel talked with you? What would you think if he said a dead person was alive? Would you be scared? These three women were. This is what happened.

16 The next evening, the Sabbath ended. And Mary Magdalene, Salome, and Mary the mother of James went out and bought spices. These were to be put on Jesus' body.

Early the following morning they carried them out to the tomb. It was just after sunrise. ³On the way they wondered how they would roll the huge stone from the door.

⁴But when they got there, they looked up and saw the stone. It was already moved away and the door was open! ⁵So they went into the tomb. And there on the right sat a young man clothed in white. The women were surprised. ⁶But the angel said, "Don't be so surprised. Aren't you looking for Jesus, the Nazarene who was crucified? He isn't here! He has come back to life! Look, that's where his body was lying. ⁷Now go and give this message to his disciples including Peter. Tell them, 'Jesus is going ahead of you to Galilee. You will see him there, just as he told you before he died!'"

⁸The women ran from the tomb. They were shaking and confused, and too afraid to talk.

- *Remember:* Which three women went to Jesus' tomb? (16:1) Who did they meet at the tomb? (16:5) What did the angel say to them? (16:6-7) What did the women think? What did they do? (16:8) What would you have done if you had been there?

- *Discover:* Jesus arose from the dead!

- *Apply:* Jesus is the only one who made dead people come back to life. He is the only one who came back to life himself. Jesus said we can live with him after we die. He showed us that he controls death. Believe him!

- *What's next?* Two men visit Jesus' tomb. But he is not there. Then they notice something in the tomb. What is it? Read John 20:1-10. ■

Mary Magdalene Talks with Jesus

⁹It was early on Sunday morning when Jesus came back to life. The first person to see him was Mary Magdalene. She was the woman from whom he had cast out seven demons. ¹⁰⁻¹¹After she saw Jesus, she went and found the disciples. They were very sad and were crying. She told them that she had seen Jesus! She told them that he was alive! But they didn't believe her.

Jesus Talks with Two Believers on the Road

¹²Later that day he showed himself to two of his followers. They were walking from Jerusalem into the country at the time. But they didn't recognize him at first. This was because he did not look the same as before. ¹³When they finally saw who he was, they rushed back to Jerusalem to tell the others. But no one believed them.

Jesus Appears to the Disciples

¹⁴Still later he showed himself to his 11 disciples. They were all eating together

at the time. He criticized them because they refused to believe he was alive. They would not believe the people who had seen him alive from the dead.

The Great Commission: A Job for Us All

15And then he told them, "You are to go into all the world. You are to preach the Good News to everyone, everywhere. 16Those who believe and are baptized will be saved. But those who refuse to believe will be judged.

17"And those who believe shall use my power to cast out demons. And they shall speak new languages. 18They will even be able to handle snakes with safety. And if they drink poison, it won't hurt them. They will be able to put their hands on the sick and heal them."

Jesus Is Taken Up into Heaven

19When Jesus had finished talking with them, he was taken up into Heaven. And there he sat down at God's right hand.

20Then the disciples went everywhere and preached the Good News. And the Lord was with them. They proved the truth of their words by the miracles they did.

LUKE

Would you like someone to write a book just for you? That's what Luke did. He wrote this book about Jesus for a friend. Sometimes this friend is called Theophilus. That means "friend of God." He was a friend who loved God. Luke wrote another book for this friend. It is called Acts. It tells what Christians did after Jesus went back to Heaven.

Luke was a doctor. He went to school to learn about medicine. Dr. Luke saw things others did not see. He takes us into adventures others would miss.

At Christmas, we read about Jesus' birth. Matthew tells us about the wise men. But Luke tells us how Jesus was born. He tells us about the angels and shepherds, too.

In Luke you'll meet one of the most important angels. You'll listen as he talks. You'll even hear a great angel choir. You'll go fishing with some men. You'll catch so many fish your boat almost sinks. You'll go to a funeral, but you'll watch the dead man get up and walk. You'll see the stable where Jesus was born. You'll see two men who died hundreds of years ago. You'll see Jesus rise up into Heaven. So join Dr. Luke for exciting adventure.

An Angel Visits Zacharias

What if you saw an angel in your house? Would you be afraid? Would you listen? This is a story about an angel. This angel told a man something special. Listen!

1 Dear friend who loves God:
¹⁻²Several accounts of Christ's life have already been written. They were records of the reports made by the early disciples and others who saw what happened. ³But I thought it would be good to check all these accounts. So I checked everything from first to last. And I decided to pass this summary on to you. ⁴This will reassure you that all you were taught is true.

⁵My story begins with a Jewish priest,

Zacharias. He lived when Herod was king of Judea. Zacharias was a member of the Abijah division of the Temple service corps. His wife was named Elizabeth. She was, like himself, a member of the priest tribe of the Jews. She was a descendant of Aaron. ⁶Zacharias and Elizabeth were godly people. They were careful to obey all of God's laws in spirit as well as in letter. ⁷But they had no children, for Elizabeth was barren. And now they were both very old.

⁸⁻⁹One day Zacharias was going about his work in the Temple. His division was on duty that week. And the honor fell to him by lot to enter the inner sanctuary. It

was his job to burn incense before the Lord. ¹⁰Meanwhile, a great crowd stood outside in the Temple court. They were praying as they always did while the incense was being burned.

¹¹⁻¹²Zacharias was doing his work in the sanctuary. Suddenly, an angel was there with him! The angel stood to the right of the altar of incense. Zacharias was surprised and very afraid.

¹³But the angel said, "Don't be afraid, Zacharias! For I have come to tell you that God has heard your prayer. Your wife, Elizabeth, will bear you a son! And you are to name him John. ¹⁴You will both have great joy and gladness at his birth. And many will rejoice with you. ¹⁵For he will be one of the Lord's great men. He must never touch wine or hard liquor. And he will be filled with the Holy Spirit, even from before his birth! ¹⁶He will bring many Jews back to the Lord his God. ¹⁷He will be a man of rugged spirit and power like Elijah, the prophet of old. And he will come before the Messiah. He will prepare the people for his coming. He will soften adult hearts to become like little children's. He will change disobedient minds to the wisdom of faith."

¹⁸Zacharias said to the angel, "But this is impossible! I'm an old man now. And my wife is also well along in years."

¹⁹Then the angel said, "I am Gabriel! I stand in the very presence of God. It was he who sent me to you with this good news! ²⁰And now, because you haven't believed me, you won't be able to talk until the child is born. For my words will surely come true at the proper time."

²¹Meanwhile the crowds outside were waiting for Zacharias to come out. They wondered why he was taking so long. ²²When he finally came out, he couldn't speak to them. But they saw from his motions that he must have seen a vision in the Temple. ²³He stayed on at the Temple until his term of duty was over. Then he went back home. ²⁴Soon after that Elizabeth his wife became pregnant. And she did not leave her house for five months.

²⁵"How kind the Lord is!" she exclaimed. "He has taken away my disgrace of having no children!"

- *Remember:* Who did the angel visit? (1:5) What kind of a person was Zacharias? (1:6) What did the angel say to Zacharias? (1:13) What was the angel's name? (1:19) What happened to Zacharias when he didn't believe the angel? (1:20) If you were Zacharias, would you believe the angel? Why?

- *Discover:* There really are angels! Most of us never see them. They are God's helpers (1:19).

- *Apply:* Think of some ways you can be God's helper. You can be like an angel!

- *What's next?* This same angel visits another person. Why does he do that? Read Luke 1:26-38. ∎

An Angel Visits Mary

Will you do anything God asks you to do? What if your friends and family will be angry? What if someone will hurt you when you do this? Will you still do what God wants? Mary did.

²⁶The following month God sent the angel Gabriel to Nazareth. This was a village in Galilee. ²⁷The angel went to a virgin named Mary. She was engaged to be married to a man named Joseph. Now Joseph was a descendant of King David.

²⁸Gabriel said to her, "Blessings on you, favored lady! The Lord is with you!"

²⁹Mary was very confused and troubled. She tried to think what the angel could mean.

³⁰"Don't be afraid, Mary," the angel

told her. "For God has decided to bless you in a special way! [31]Very soon now, you will become pregnant and have a baby boy. And you are to name him 'Jesus.' [32]He shall be very great and shall be called the Son of God. The Lord God shall give him the throne of his ancestor David. [33]And he shall reign over Israel forever. His Kingdom shall never end!"

[34]Mary asked the angel, "But how can I have a baby? I am a virgin."

[35]The angel replied, "The Holy Spirit shall come upon you. The power of God shall overshadow you. So the baby born to you will be holy, the Son of God. [36]Your cousin Elizabeth is going to have a baby in her old age. They once called her 'the barren one.' But now she is six months pregnant! [37]For every promise from God shall surely come true."

[38]Mary said, "I am the Lord's servant. I will do whatever he wants. May everything you said come true." And then the angel disappeared.

- *Remember:* Who did the angel Gabriel visit? (1:27) What were Mary and Joseph planning to do? (1:27) What special thing was going to happen to Mary? (1:30-31) What kind of person was Mary's baby to become? (1:32-33) Who was to be the baby's father? (1:35) Do you think Mary did what she should have done? Do you think she did what God wanted? Why?

- *Discover:* We should do what God wants.

- *Apply:* Why should we do what God wants? Which of these are true? (1) God knows more than we do. (2) God loves us. (3) God is wiser than we are. (4) God wants us to have what is best. Which of these should make us want to do things his way?

- *What's next?* "You are special," Mary's cousin told her. "God has given you something special. It is more special than any other gift." What was this gift? Read Luke 1:39-56. ■

Mary Visits Elizabeth

Elizabeth is Mary's cousin. She is quite old. Mary is quite young. But Elizabeth told Mary about Mary's special gift. No other woman had this special gift. What is it?

[39-40]A few days later Mary hurried to visit Elizabeth. She went to the highlands of Judea to the town where Zacharias lived.

[41]At the sound of Mary's greeting, Elizabeth's child jumped inside her. And she was filled with the Holy Spirit.

[42]She gave a happy cry. Then she said to Mary, "You are blessed by God above all other women. And your child will be blessed by God more than any other. [43]What an honor this is, that the mother of my Lord should visit me! [44]When you came in and greeted me, my baby moved in me for joy! [45]You believed that God would do what he said. That is why

he has given you this wonderful blessing."

[46]Mary responded, "Oh, how I praise the Lord! [47]How I rejoice in God my Savior! [48]For he took notice of his lowly servant girl. And now people will call me 'blessed of God' for all time. [49]For he, the mighty Holy One, has done great things to me. [50]His mercy goes on forever, to all who respect him.

[51]"How powerful is his mighty arm! How he scatters the proud ones! [52]He has torn princes from their thrones. And he has lifted up the lowly. [53]He has satisfied the hungry hearts. And he has sent the rich away with empty hands.

⁵⁴How he has helped his servant Israel! He has not forgotten his promise to be merciful. ⁵⁵For he made a promise to our fathers, Abraham and his children. He said he would be merciful to them forever."

⁵⁶Mary stayed with Elizabeth about three months. Then she went back to her own home.

- *Remember:* Who did Mary visit? (1:39-40) Elizabeth said Mary would be the mother of a special person. Who would that be? (1:43) How long did Mary stay with Elizabeth? (1:56) How do you think Mary felt about the things Elizabeth said?

- *Discover:* When God does something special for you, or gives you a great honor, what should you say? Find out what Mary said. (1:46-55)

- *Apply:* When you get to do something no one else can do, do you brag about it or thank God for that special honor? Have you told God how wonderful he is lately? When is the last time you said thank you to God? Has he done something special for you? Has he helped you do something? Has he given you a special gift? Remember to say "Praise God" or "Thank you, Lord."

- *What's next?* An angel tells a man to get married. Why would an angel do that? Read Matthew 1:18-25. ■

John the Baptist Is Born

⁵⁷By now Elizabeth's waiting was over. For the time had come for the baby to be born. And it was a boy! ⁵⁸The word spread quickly to her neighbors and relatives. They all heard about how kind the Lord had been to her. And everyone was full of joy.

⁵⁹On the eighth day, all the relatives and friends came over. And they all celebrated the boy's circumcision. They all thought the baby's name would be Zacharias, after his father.

⁶⁰But Elizabeth said, "No! He must be named John!"

⁶¹"What?" they said. "There is no one in all your family by that name." ⁶²So they asked the baby's father. They talked to him by making motions.

⁶³He motioned for a piece of paper. And he wrote, "His name is John!" This surprised everybody. ⁶⁴Right then Zacharias could speak again. And he began to praise God.

When something good happens to us, we should praise the Lord

Oh, how I praise the Lord!

Luke 1:46

---

⁶⁵Wonder fell upon the whole neighborhood. And the news of what had happened spread throughout the Judean hills. ⁶⁶Everyone who heard about it thought long and hard about it. They asked, "I wonder what this child will turn out to be? For the hand of the Lord is surely upon him in some special way."

⁶⁷Then his father, Zacharias, was filled with the Holy Spirit. And he gave this prophecy:

⁶⁸"Praise the Lord, the God of Israel! For he has come to visit his people and has redeemed them. ⁶⁹He is sending us a Mighty Savior from the royal line of his servant David. ⁷⁰It is just as he promised through his holy prophets long ago. ⁷¹Someone will come to save us from our enemies. He will deliver us from all who hate us.

⁷²⁻⁷³"The Lord has been merciful to our ancestors. Yes, he has been merciful to Abraham himself! For the Lord has remembered his holy promise to him. ⁷⁴He will free us from our enemies. We will be free to serve God without fear. ⁷⁵He will make us holy and acceptable. That way we will be ready to stand in his presence forever.

⁷⁶"And you, my little son, shall be called the prophet of the great God! For you will make the way ready for the Messiah. ⁷⁷You will tell people how to find salvation through forgiveness of their sins. ⁷⁸All this is because the mercy of our God is very tender. And Heaven's dawn is about to break upon us. ⁷⁹It will give light to those who sit in darkness and death's shadow. And it will guide us to the path of peace."

⁸⁰As the little boy grew up, he greatly loved God. He lived out in the desert until he began his public ministry to Israel.

Jesus Is Born

Millions of babies are born. Millions of stories are told. But the world remembers one baby and one story more than all others. Each Christmas your church talks about this baby. People sing about his birth. They act it out with plays. His birth was special. It still is. It always will be! Do you know why?

2 About this time Caesar Augustus was the emperor of Rome. He made a law that all the people should be counted throughout the empire. ²This took place when Quirinius was the governor of Syria.

³Everyone was told to go back to the home of his ancestors to be registered. ⁴Now Joseph was a member of the royal line. So he had to go to Bethlehem in Judea. This was King David's ancient home. He had to travel there from the Galilean village of Nazareth. ⁵He took with him Mary, his fiancée. She was very pregnant by this time.

⁶And while they were there, the time came for her baby to be born. ⁷So she gave birth to her first child, a son. She wrapped him in a blanket and laid him in a manger. This was because there was no room for them in the village inn.

- *Remember:* Where did Joseph and Mary live? (2:4) Where was Jesus born? (2:4) Why did Mary and Joseph go there? (2:1-5) Why did Mary put the baby Jesus in a manger? Who was Jesus? Why was his birth so important? If you had been there, what would you have said to Jesus? What would you have said to Mary and Joseph?

- *Discover:* Seven hundred years before Jesus came, God said that he would be born in Bethlehem. Read Micah 5:2. When God has special plans, they *will* happen!

- *Apply:* God may have special plans for you. He may want you to do something special for him.

- *What's next?* Would you be afraid to see one angel? How would you feel if you saw hundreds of them? What would you do if they began to sing? Read about some frightened shepherds in Luke 2:8-20. ■

Angels Appear to Shepherds

How many people are in your church choir? What would people say if 1,000 angels sang in your church choir? Here's a story about a choir like that.

⁸That night some shepherds were in the fields outside the village. They were guarding their flocks of sheep. ⁹Suddenly an angel was there with them! And the hills shone bright with the glory of the Lord. They were very afraid. ¹⁰But the angel comforted them.

"Don't be afraid!" he said. "I bring you the most joyful news ever told! And it's for everyone! ¹¹The Savior has been born tonight in Bethlehem! Yes, this is the Messiah, the Lord! ¹²How will you know him? You will find a baby wrapped in a blanket, lying in a manger!"

¹³Suddenly, the angel was joined by a great crowd of others. All the armies of Heaven were there! They were praising God.

¹⁴"Glory to God in the highest Heaven!" they sang. "May there be peace on earth for all those who please him."

¹⁵This great army of angels went back again to Heaven. So the shepherds said to each other, "Come on! Let's go to Bethlehem! Let's see this great thing that has happened, which the Lord has told us about."

¹⁶They ran to the village and found their way to Mary and Joseph. And there was the baby, lying in the manger. ¹⁷The shepherds told everyone what had happened. They told them what the angel had said to them about this child. ¹⁸All who heard the shepherds' story were amazed. ¹⁹But Mary quietly stored up these things in her heart. And she often thought about them.

²⁰Then the shepherds went back again to their fields and flocks. They praised God for the visit of the angels. And they praised him because they had seen the child. It had all happened just as the angel said it would.

● *Remember:* Where were the shepherds? (2:8) What did they see? Why were they afraid? (2:9) What news did the angel bring? (2:10-12) Who else did the shepherds see? (2:13) What did thes angels say or sing? (2:14) When the angel choir was gone, what did the shepherds do? (2:15-16) What do you think the shepherds told Mary and Joseph about the angels? When the shepherds left the manger, what did they do then? (2:17, 20)

● *Discover:* When we hear the Good News about Jesus, we must tell it to others.

- *Apply:* The shepherds wanted to tell others about Jesus. Why? You should tell your friends about Jesus, too, because it is the best news they will ever hear.

- *What's next?* Some important people went to see a baby. But they didn't know who the baby was. They didn't know where to find him. So why did they come so far? Read Matthew 2:1-12. ∎

Joseph and Mary Bring Jesus to the Temple

²¹Eight days later, the baby was circumcised. At that time, he was named Jesus. For this was the name given him by the angel before he was conceived.

²²The time came for Mary to give her offering at the Temple. This offering was to make her pure after she had her baby. The laws of Moses said she had to do this. At that time, his parents took Jesus along to Jerusalem. They wanted to present him to the Lord. ²³In the laws of Moses, God had said: "A woman's first child might be a boy. And if so, the child shall be dedicated to the Lord."

?????????????????????????????????
Who wanted to see the Messiah before he died?

(Read 2:25-26 for the answer.)
?????????????????????????????????

²⁴At that time Jesus' parents also gave a sacrifice so they would be made pure. They had to give either a pair of turtledoves or two young pigeons.

Simeon Holds Baby Jesus

²⁵That day a man named Simeon was in the Temple. He was a good man and very devout. He was filled with the Holy Spirit. And he was always looking for the Messiah to come soon. ²⁶For the Holy Spirit had shown him that he would not die until he had seen God's Messiah. ²⁷That very day, the Holy Spirit had told Simeon to go to the Temple. Now Mary and Joseph came to present the baby

Jesus to the Lord. They did this to obey the laws of Moses. ²⁸And Simeon was waiting there. He took the child in his arms, praising God.

²⁹⁻³¹"Lord," he said, "now I can die happy! For I have seen him as you promised I would. I have seen the Savior you have given to the world. ³²He is the Light that will shine upon the nations! And he will be the glory of your people Israel!"

Jesus' birth is good news for everyone

I bring you the most joyful news ever told! And it's for everyone! The Savior has been born tonight in Bethlehem!

Luke 2:10-11

---

³³Joseph and Mary just stood there. They were amazed at what was being said about Jesus.

³⁴⁻³⁵Simeon blessed them. But then he said to Mary, "A sword shall pierce your soul. For this child shall be rejected by many in Israel. And this will be their undoing. But he will be the greatest joy of many others. And the thoughts of many hearts shall be revealed."

Anna Tells Everyone about the Messiah

³⁶⁻³⁷Anna, a prophetess, was also there in the Temple that day. She was the daughter of Phanuel, of the Jewish tribe of Asher. She was very old, for she had been a widow for 84 years. And she had been married for seven years before her husband died. She never left the Temple but stayed there night and day. She worshiped God by praying and often fasting.

³⁸She came along just as Simeon was talking with Mary and Joseph. And she also began thanking God. She spoke to everyone in Jerusalem who had been waiting for the Savior. She told them that the Messiah had finally come.

The Boy Jesus at Nazareth

What kind of boy was Jesus? Would you like to play with him? What would your friends at school think of him? You'll learn something about him here.

³⁹Jesus' parents did all the things required by the Law of God. Then they went back home to Nazareth in Galilee. ⁴⁰There the child became a strong, robust lad. He was known for wisdom beyond his years. And God poured out his blessings on him.

- *Remember:* Where did Jesus grow up? (2:39) Did Jesus please God or was he always getting into trouble? (2:40) What was Jesus known for? (2:40) Why do you think this was?

- *Discover:* What kind of work did Jesus do when he was growing up? Read Mark 6:3 to find out.

- *Apply:* Jesus was a carpenter. He did not pretend he was a "big shot." He could have lived as a prince or a king. But he wanted to be one of us. That's what Jesus wants us to do, too. He doesn't want us to pretend that we're "big shots" either.

- *What's next?* Do any boys or girls teach at your school? Do any of them teach the teachers? You'll read about a boy who did. See Luke 2:41-52. ■

Jesus Teaches the Teachers

The teachers who taught at God's house were very smart people. Ordinary people would never try to teach them. They would never let a boy teach them. But one day they did! A boy taught the teachers. This is how it happened.

41-42When Jesus was 12 years old he went with his parents to Jerusalem. They traveled there for the yearly Passover Feast. They attended this feast each year. 43After the feast was over they started home to Nazareth. But Jesus stayed behind in Jerusalem. His parents didn't miss him the first day. 44They thought he was with friends among the other travelers. But then he didn't show up that evening. So they started to look for him among their relatives and friends. 45But they couldn't find him. So they went back to Jerusalem to look for him there.

???????????????????????????????????

Who was Jesus talking to at the Temple?

(Read 2:46-47 for the answer.)

???????????????????????????????????

46-47Three days later they finally found him. He was in the Temple, sitting among the teachers of the Law. He was talking about deep questions with them. And he amazed everyone with his answers.

48His parents didn't know what to think. "Son!" his mother said to him. "Why have you done this to us? Your father and I have been frantic! We have been looking for you everywhere!"

49"But why did you need to look?" he asked. "Didn't you know that I would be here at the Temple, in my Father's House?" 50But they didn't understand what he meant.

51Then he went back to Nazareth with them and obeyed them. And his mother stored away all these things in her heart.

Everyone loved Jesus

Jesus grew both tall and wise. And he was loved by both God and man.

Luke 2:52

52So Jesus grew both tall and wise. And he was loved by both God and man.

- *Remember:* How old was Jesus at this time? (2:41-42) Where did he go with his parents? How often did they go to this festival? (2:41-42) Why didn't Jesus' parents miss him on the way home? (2:44) What was Jesus doing at the Temple? (2:46-47) What did Jesus call the Temple? (2:49) How do you know that Jesus obeyed his parents? (2:51) If you could ask Jesus one question about Heaven, what would it be?

- *Discover:* Jesus knows more than anyone else about God and Heaven. That's because he is God's Son.

- *Apply:* Would you like to know what Jesus said about Heaven? Would you like to know what he said about God? Read Matthew, Mark, Luke, and John in your Bible. Jesus tells us many things about God and Heaven in those books.

- *What's next?* There was once a preacher who did not have a church. He preached near a river. Read about him in Luke 3:1-18. ■

John the Baptist Preaches

John the Baptist did not belong to a Baptist church. He didn't really belong to any church. That's because there were no churches then. So there were no Baptists, or Methodists, or Presbyterians. John preached near a river. Why did people come from everywhere to listen to him and ask him important questions? Read on to find out.

3 It was the 15th year of the reign of Emperor Tiberius Caesar. A message came from God to John, the son of Zacharias. At that time, John was living out in the deserts. Pilate was governor over Judea. Herod was ruling over Galilee. His brother Philip was ruling over Iturea and Trachonitis. Lysanias was ruling over Abilene. And Annas and Caiaphas were the High Priests. ³Now John went from place to place on both sides of the Jordan River. He preached that people should be baptized. This was to show that they had turned to God and away from their sins. They did this so they could be forgiven.

Share your gifts from God with those who need them

You might have extra food.
If so, give it away
to those who are hungry.

Luke 3:11

---

⁴Isaiah the prophet had written of this long before. He wrote, "There is a voice shouting in the wilderness. The voice says, 'Prepare a road for the Lord to travel on! Widen the pathway before him! ⁵Level the mountains! Fill up the valleys! Straighten the curves! Smooth out the ruts! ⁶And then all mankind shall see the Savior sent from God.'"

⁷Many people came to be baptized and to hear John preach. He said to them, "You snakes! You are trying to escape hell without truly turning to God! That is why you want to be baptized!

God loves his Son, Jesus

You are my much-loved Son.
Yes, you are my delight.

Luke 3:22

---

⁸First go and prove by the way you live that you really have repented. And don't think you are safe because you are descendants of Abraham. That isn't enough. God can produce children of Abraham from these desert stones! ⁹The axe of his judgment is lifted over you. It is ready to cut you down. Yes, every tree that does not produce good fruit will be chopped down. Then they will be thrown into the fire."

¹⁰The crowd replied, "What do you want us to do?"

¹¹"You might have two coats," he replied. "If so, give one to the poor. You might have extra food. If so, give it away to those who are hungry."

¹²Even tax collectors came to be baptized. They were well known for cheating people. They asked, "How shall we prove to you that we have stopped sinning?"

¹³"By your honesty," he replied. "Make sure you collect no more taxes than the Roman government tells you to."

¹⁴"And us," asked some soldiers, "what about us?"

John replied, "Don't take money by threats and violence. Don't accuse anyone of what you know he didn't do. And be content with your pay!"

¹⁵Everyone was expecting the Messiah to come soon. So they wanted to know if John was the Messiah. This topic was being talked about everywhere.

¹⁶John answered the question by saying, "I baptize only with water. But someone is coming soon who has far greater authority than I do. In fact, I am not even worthy of being his slave. He will baptize you with the Holy Spirit and fire. ¹⁷He will separate the chaff from the grain. He will burn up the chaff with eternal fire and store away the grain." ¹⁸He used many such warnings as he told the people the Good News of the Kingdom.

- *Remember:* Where did John live? (3:2) He preached near a river. Which river? (3:3) Why did John tell people to be baptized? (3:3) Why did John call some people snakes? What were they trying to do? (3:7) What should they do first? (3:8) Who was John talking about in verses 16 and 17? Why do you think people listened to John? Why didn't they stay away?

- *Discover:* Only God can forgive sins. That is why John told people to turn away from their sins and turn to God. Have you asked God to forgive you for your sins?

- *Apply:* Does your minister tell you about God? Listen! Does your Sunday school teacher tell you about God? Listen! Do your parents tell you about God? Listen! Do you have a friend who tells you about God? Listen! They can tell you how to live the right way and be forgiven for your sins. Then you can live with God forever in Heaven.

- *What's next?* Does your minister baptize people in your church? Long ago, Jesus asked a man to baptize him. Read Matthew 3:13-17. ■

Herod Arrests John the Baptist

¹⁹⁻²⁰At this time, Herod was the governor of Galilee. Now Herod had married Herodias, his brother's wife. He had also done many other bad things. So John spoke out against him in public. Because of this, Herod put John in prison. And so Herod added another sin to his many others.

Jesus Is Baptized

²¹Then one day, many people were being baptized. And Jesus himself came and was baptized. As he was praying, the heavens opened up. ²²The Holy Spirit settled upon him in the form of a dove. And a voice from Heaven said, "You are my much-loved Son. Yes, you are my delight."

Joseph's Family Tree

²³⁻³⁸Jesus was about 30 years old when he began his public ministry.

Jesus was known as the son of Joseph. Joseph's father was Heli. Heli's father was Matthat. Matthat's father was Levi. Levi's father was Melchi. Melchi's father was Jannai. Jannai's father was Joseph. Joseph's father was Mattathias. Mattathias's father was Amos. Amos's father was Nahum. Nahum's father was Esli. Esli's father was Naggai. Naggai's father was Maath. Maath's father was Mattathias. Mattathias's father was Semein. Semein's father was Josech. Josech's father was Joda. Joda's father was Joanan. Joanan's father was Rhesa. Rhesa's father was Zerubbabel. Zerubbabel's father was Shealtiel. Shealtiel's father was Neri.

Neri's father was Melchi. Melchi's father was Addi. Addi's father was Cosam. Cosam's father was Elmadam. Elmadam's father was Er. Er's father was Joshua. Joshua's father was Eliezer. Eliezer's father was Jorim. Jorim's father was Matthat. Matthat's father was Levi. Levi's father was Simeon. Simeon's father was Judah. Judah's father was Joseph. Joseph's father was Jonam. Jonam's father was Eliakim. Eliakim's father was Melea. Melea's father was Menna. Menna's father was Mattatha. Mattatha's father was Nathan. Nathan's father was David. David's father was Jesse. Jesse's father was Obed. Obed's father was Boaz. Boaz's father was Salmon. Salmon's father was Nahshon. Nahshon's father was Amminadab. Amminadab's father was Admin. Admin's father was Arni. Arni's father was Hezron. Hezron's father was Perez. Perez's father was Judah. Judah's father was Jacob. Jacob's father was Isaac. Isaac's father was Abraham. Abraham's father was Terah. Terah's father was Nahor. Nahor's father was Serug. Serug's father was Reu. Reu's father was Peleg. Peleg's father was Eber. Eber's father was Shelah. Shelah's father was Cainan.

Cainan's father was Arphaxad. Arphaxad's father was Shem. Shem's father was Noah. Noah's father was Lamech. Lamech's father was Methuselah. Methuselah's father was Enoch. Enoch's father was Jared. Jared's father was Mahalaleel. Mahalaleel's father was Cainan. Cainan's father was Enos. Enos's father was Seth. Seth's father was Adam. Adam's father was God.

Jesus Resists Temptation

4 Then Jesus, full of the Holy Spirit, left the Jordan River. He was sent by the Spirit out into the empty wastelands of Judea. And there, Satan tempted him for 40 days. He ate nothing all that time and was very hungry.

³Satan said, "If you are God's Son, tell this stone to become bread."

⁴But Jesus replied, "It is written in the Scriptures, 'Other things in life are much more important than bread!'"

⁵Then Satan showed him all the kingdoms of the world in a moment of time. ⁶⁻⁷The devil said to him, "I will give you all these kingdoms and their glory. For they are mine to give to anyone I wish. But you must get down on your knees and worship me."

⁸Jesus replied, "We must worship God, and him alone. So it is written in the Scriptures."

⁹⁻¹¹Then Satan took him to Jerusalem to a high roof of the Temple. He said, "If you are the Son of God, jump off! For the Scriptures say that God will send his angels to guard you. They will keep you from crashing to the ground below!"

¹²Jesus replied, "The Scriptures also say, 'Do not put the Lord your God to a foolish test.'"

¹³Now the devil had tempted Jesus in every way. So he left Jesus for a while and went away.

Jesus Preaches; People Are Amazed and Then Angry

¹⁴Then Jesus went back to Galilee, full of the Holy Spirit's power. Soon he became well known throughout all that region. ¹⁵He became famous for his sermons in the synagogues. Everyone praised him.

¹⁶Then he came to the village of Nazareth, his boyhood home. He went as usual to the synagogue on Saturday. And he stood up to read the Scriptures. ¹⁷The Book of Isaiah the prophet was handed to him. So he opened it to the place where it says:

¹⁸⁻¹⁹"The Spirit of the Lord is upon me. He has chosen me to preach Good News to the poor. He has sent me to heal those with broken hearts. He has sent me to tell the captives that they are free. The blind shall see. The abused shall be freed from those who treat them badly. And God is ready to give blessings to all who come to him."

²⁰He closed the book and handed it back to the attendant. Then he sat down, while everyone in the synagogue looked at him. ²¹Then he added, "These Scriptures came true today!"

²²All who were there spoke well of him. They were amazed by the beautiful words that fell from his lips. "How can this be?" they asked. "Isn't this Joseph's son?"

²³Then he said, "You will probably tell me that proverb, 'Doctor, heal yourself.' You want to ask, 'Why don't you do miracles here in your hometown? You have done many such things in Capernaum.' ²⁴But I tell you the truth! No prophet is accepted in his own hometown! ²⁵⁻²⁶Remember how Elijah the prophet used a miracle to help the widow of Zarephath? She was a foreigner from the land of Sidon. There were many Jewish widows needing help in those days of famine. There had been no rain for 3½ years, and hunger stalked the land. Yet Elijah was not sent to them. ²⁷Or think of the prophet Elisha. He healed Naaman, a Syrian. He did this even though many Jewish lepers needed help."

²⁸These remarks stung them to anger. ²⁹They jumped up and mobbed him. They took him to the edge of the hill on which the city was built. They wanted to push him over the cliff. ³⁰But he walked away through the crowd and left them.

An Evil Spirit Obeys Jesus

³¹Then he went back to Capernaum, a city in Galilee. He preached there in the synagogue every Saturday. ³²Here, too,

the people were amazed at the things he said. For he spoke as one who knew the truth. He didn't just quote the opinions of others as his authority.

33One day Jesus was teaching in the synagogue. And a man with a demon began shouting at him. 34"Go away!" the man said. "We want nothing to do with you, Jesus of Nazareth. You have come to destroy us. I know who you are! You are the Holy Son of God!"

35Jesus cut him short. "Be silent!" he told the demon. "Come out!" The demon threw the man to the floor as the crowd watched. But then the demon left the man without hurting him further.

36Amazed, the people asked, "What power does this man have? Even demons obey him!" 37The story of what he had done spread through the whole region.

Jesus Heals Simon's Mother-in-Law and Many Others

38After leaving the synagogue that day, he went to Simon's home. And there he found Simon's mother-in-law very sick with a high fever. "Please heal her," everyone begged.

39Standing at her bedside he commanded the fever to leave. Right away, the fever left her! So she got up and made a meal for them!

40As the sun went down, all the villagers brought their sick people to Jesus. The people had many different diseases. And the touch of his hands healed every one! 41Some of the people had demons. And the demons came out at his command. They shouted, "You are the Son of God!" But because they knew who he was, Jesus told them to be quiet.

42Early the next morning he went out into the desert. The crowds looked everywhere for him. They finally found him and begged him not to leave them. They asked him to stay at Capernaum. 43But he replied, "I must preach the Good News of the Kingdom of God in other places too. For that is why I was sent." 44So he traveled around, preaching in synagogues throughout Judea.

Catching Fish with Jesus

Have you ever gone fishing? Did you catch enough fish to fill two boats? That's a lot of fish. Here are some people who caught that many fish.

5 One day Jesus was preaching on the shore of the Sea of Galilee. And great crowds pressed in on him to listen to the Word of God. 2He saw two empty boats standing at the water's edge. The fishermen were on shore, washing their nets. 3Jesus stepped into one of the boats. And he asked Simon, its owner, to push out a little into the water. That way he could sit in the boat and speak to the crowds from there.

4When he had finished speaking, he turned to Simon. "Now go out where it is deeper," he said. "Let down your nets and you will catch a lot of fish!"

5"Sir," Simon replied, "we worked hard all last night. But we didn't catch a thing. But if you say so, we'll try again."

6And this time their nets were so full that they began to tear! 7A shout for help brought their partners in the other boat. And soon both boats were filled with fish. They were so full that they almost sank!

8When Simon Peter saw what had happened, he fell to his knees before Jesus. "Oh, sir, please leave us!" he cried. "I'm too much of a sinner for you to have around." 9Peter was amazed by the size of their catch. 10So were his partners, James and John, the sons of Zebedee. Jesus said to them, "Don't be afraid! From now on you'll be fishing for the souls of men!"

11And as soon as they landed, they left everything and went with him.

- *Remember:* Why did Jesus preach from a boat? (5:1-3). How many fish had Simon and his friends caught the night before? (5:5) How many fish did they catch when Jesus helped them? (5:6-7) Why did they catch more fish now? (5:4) How did Simon Peter feel about all these fish? (5:8-9) Jesus said they would fish for souls. What did he mean?

- *Discover:* Listen to Jesus. Do what his Word, the Bible, says. He will help you do more than you think you can.

- *Apply:* Do you ever say, "I can't"? If Jesus helps you, you can!

- *What's next?* "Give up all the things you have and follow me." How can anyone ask that? Jesus did. Read Mark 1:16-20. ■

Jesus Heals a Man with Leprosy

¹²One day Jesus was visiting in a certain village. And a man lived there who was very sick with leprosy. When he saw Jesus, he fell to the ground before him. He begged Jesus to heal him.

"Sir," he said, "please heal me! I know you can, if you want to."

¹³Jesus reached out and touched the man. "Of course I will," he said. "Be healed." And the leprosy left him right away! ¹⁴Then Jesus told him to go right away to see the Jewish priest. He also told the man not to tell anyone what had happened. "Give the sacrifice Moses' law requires for lepers who are healed," he said. "This will prove to everyone that you are well." ¹⁵Now the report of his power spread even faster. Great crowds came to hear him preach. They also came to be healed of their diseases. ¹⁶But Jesus often went into the wilderness to pray.

Jesus Heals and Forgives a Paralyzed Man

¹⁷One day Jesus was teaching the people. And the Lord was giving him the power to heal people. Some Jewish religious leaders and teachers of the Law were sitting nearby. It seemed that these men came from every village in all Galilee and Judea. They also came from Jerusalem.

¹⁸⁻¹⁹Then some men came carrying a paralyzed man on a sleeping mat. They tried to push through the crowd to Jesus. But they couldn't reach him. So they went up on the roof above him. They took off some tiles and lowered the sick man down into the crowd. The sick man was still on his sleeping mat. But his friends set him right in front of Jesus.

²⁰Jesus saw that they had great faith. So he said to the man, "My friend, your sins are forgiven!"

²¹The Pharisees and teachers of the Law heard this. "Who does this fellow think he is?" they asked. "This is blasphemy! Who but God can forgive sins?"

²²Jesus knew what they were thinking. So he said to them, "Why is it blasphemy? ²³⁻²⁴I, the Messiah, have the power on earth to forgive sins. But talk is cheap. Anybody could say that. So I'll prove it to you by healing this man." Then Jesus turned to the paralyzed man. He commanded, "Pick up your bed and go on home. For you are healed!"

²⁵And as everyone watched, the man jumped to his feet. He picked up his mat and went home praising God! ²⁶Everyone there was full of awe and fear, and they praised God. They said again and again, "We have seen strange things today."

Jesus Befriends a Tax Collector and His Friends

27Later when Jesus left the town he saw a tax collector. These men were known to be cheaters. This man was sitting at his tax collection booth. His name was Levi. Jesus said to him, "Come and be one of my disciples!" 28So Levi left everything, jumped up, and went with him.

29Soon Levi held a banquet in his home with Jesus as the guest of honor. Many of Levi's fellow tax collectors and other guests were there.

30But the Pharisees and teachers of the Law were angry about it. They complained to Jesus' disciples about his eating with such sinners.

31Jesus answered them, "It is the sick who need a doctor. Those in good health have no need for one. 32My purpose is to invite sinners to turn from their sins. I'm not here to spend my time with people who think they are good enough."

Why Don't You Do the Things We Do?

33They also complained that Jesus' disciples were feasting instead of fasting. "John the Baptist's disciples often pray and go without food," they said. "The disciples of the Pharisees do the same thing. Why are your disciples feasting and drinking?"

34Jesus asked, "Do happy men go without food? Do wedding guests go hungry while at a party for the groom? 35But the time will come when the bridegroom will be killed. Then they won't want to eat."

36Then Jesus told this story. "No one cuts a piece out of a new garment to make a patch for an old one," he said. "For then the new garment would be ruined! And the old garment would look worse with a new patch on it! 37And no one puts new wine into old wineskins. For the new wine bursts the old skins. This would ruin the skins and spill the wine! 38New wine must be put into new wineskins. 39But no one after drinking the old wine seems to want the fresh and the new. 'The old ways are best,' they say."

The Disciples Pick Wheat on the Sabbath

6One Sabbath Jesus and his disciples were walking through some fields. As they went, they broke off the heads of wheat. Then they rubbed off the husks in their hands and ate the grains.

2But some Pharisees said, "That's against the law! Your disciples are harvesting grain. And it's against the Jewish law to work on the Sabbath."

3Jesus replied, "Don't you read the Scriptures? Haven't you ever read what King David did when he and his men were hungry? 4He went into the Temple and took the special bread that was placed before the Lord. He ate it and shared it with others even though it was against the law." 5And Jesus added, "I am master even of the Sabbath."

Jesus Heals a Man's Hand on the Sabbath

6On another Sabbath he was in the synagogue teaching. A man was there whose right hand was crippled. 7The teachers of the Law and the Pharisees were watching Jesus closely. They wanted to see if he would heal the man that day, since it was the Sabbath. This was because they wanted to find some charge to bring against him.

8But Jesus knew what they were thinking. So he turned to the man with the crippled hand. He said, "Come and stand here where everyone can see." So he did.

9Then Jesus turned to the Pharisees and teachers of the Law. "I have a question for you," he said. "Is it right to do good on the Sabbath day, or to do harm? Is it right to save life, or to destroy it?"

10He looked around at them one by one. Then he said to the man, "Reach out your hand." And as he did, it became normal again. 11At this, the enemies of Jesus were very angry. And they began to plan his murder.

Jesus Picks the 12 Disciples

12One day soon after that he went out into the mountains to pray. He prayed there all night. 13At daybreak he called together his followers. He chose 12 of them to be the inner circle of his disciples. They were chosen as his "apostles," or "missionaries." 14-16Here are their names: There was Simon who was also called Peter. There was Andrew, Simon's brother. There were James, John, and Philip. There were Bartholomew, Matthew, and Thomas. There was James the son of Alphaeus. There was Simon who was a member of the Zealots, a rebellious political party. There was Judas, the son of James. And there was Judas Iscariot, who later betrayed him.

Jesus Preaches on the Mountainside

17-18Jesus and his disciples came down the slopes of the mountain. They stood with Jesus on a large, level area. And a crowd of his followers soon formed around him. Then another much greater crowd formed around them. For people from all over Judea had come to hear him or be healed. People came from Jerusalem. Some even came from as far north as the seacoasts of Tyre and Sidon. And Jesus cast out many demons. 19Everyone was trying to touch him. And when they did, they were healed. For healing power went out from him.

20Then he turned to his disciples. "Happy are those of you who are poor," he said. "For the Kingdom of God is yours! 21Happy are you who are now hungry. For you are going to be full! Happy are you who are crying. For the time will come when you shall laugh with joy! 22Happy are you when others hate you and exclude you because you know me! Happy are you when people insult you and smear your name because you are mine! 23Yes, when that happens, rejoice! Leap for joy! For you will have a great reward in Heaven. And you will be in good company. The ancient prophets were treated that way too!

24"But, oh, what sadness waits for the rich! For they have their only happiness down here. 25They are fat and wealthy now. But a time of awful hunger is before them. Their careless laughter now means sadness then. 26And what sadness is ahead for those praised by the crowds!

For *false* prophets have always been praised.

Jesus Teaches about Loving Your Enemies

27"Listen, all of you! Love your enemies. Do good to those who hate you. 28Pray for the happiness of those who curse you. Ask God to bless those who hurt you.

29"If someone slaps you on one cheek, let him slap the other too! If someone demands your coat, give him your shirt besides. 30Give what you have to anyone who asks you for it. And when things are taken away from you, don't worry about getting them back. 31Treat others as you want them to treat you.

32"Do you think you deserve praise for loving those who love you? Even the godless do that! 33And suppose you do good only to those who do you good. Is that so wonderful? Even sinners do that much! 34Suppose you lend money only to those who can pay you back. What good is that? Even the most wicked will lend to their own kind for full payment!

Others will treat you the way you treat them

Never criticize or condemn. If you do, it will all come back on you. Go easy on others. Then they will do the same for you.

Luke 6:37

35"Love your enemies! Do good to them! Lend to them! And don't worry about the fact that they won't pay you back. Then your reward from Heaven will be very great. And you will truly be acting like sons of God. For he is kind to the unthankful and those who are wicked.

36"Try to show as much mercy as your Father does.

Jesus Teaches about Criticizing Others

37"Never criticize or condemn. If you do, it will all come back on you. Go easy on others. Then they will do the same for you. ³⁸For if you give, you will get! Your gift will come back to you in full and overflowing measure. The measure you use to give will be used to measure what you get back."

³⁹Here are some of the stories Jesus used in his sermons. "What good is it for one blind man to lead another?" Jesus asked. "He will fall into a ditch and pull the other down with him. ⁴⁰How can a student know more than his teacher? But if he works hard, he may learn as much.

⁴¹"Don't worry about the speck in someone else's eye. Why worry about another person's little fault? You don't even see the board in your own eye! ⁴²How can you say to him, 'Brother, let me help you get rid of that speck in your eye'? You can't even see past the board in your own? Hypocrite! First get rid of the board. Then maybe you will see well enough to help him with his speck!

If You Are Good, You Will Do Good

⁴³"A tree from good stock doesn't produce bad fruit. And trees from poor stock don't produce good fruit. ⁴⁴A tree is known by the kind of fruit it produces. Figs never grow on thorns, and grapes never grow on bramble bushes. ⁴⁵A good man produces good deeds from a good heart. And an evil man produces evil deeds from his hidden wickedness. Whatever is in the heart overflows into speech.

A Foundation of Rock or Sand?

⁴⁶"So why do you call me 'Lord' when you won't obey me? ⁴⁷⁻⁴⁸People who listen to me and obey are like a man who builds a house on a rock. When the floodwaters rise and break against his house, it stands firm. For it stands on a strong foundation.

⁴⁹"But people who listen and don't obey are like a man who builds a house without a foundation. When the floods come against that house, it falls down. Soon it is just a heap of ruins."

A Man Is Healed Far Away

Do you believe in Jesus? Do you believe he can do anything? This is a story about a man who really believed Jesus could do anything.

7 Jesus finished his sermon and then went back to the city of Capernaum.

²At that time, a Roman army captain's slave was sick and near death. ³When the captain heard about Jesus, he sent some Jewish elders to speak to him. He told them to ask Jesus to come and heal his slave. ⁴So they begged Jesus to come with them and help the man. They told him what a good person the captain was.

"If anyone deserves your help, it is he," they said. ⁵"For he loves the Jews. He even built a synagogue for us!"

⁶⁻⁸Jesus went with them. But just before they got to the house, the captain sent some friends with a message. They said, "Sir, don't trouble yourself by coming to my home. For I am not worthy of any such honor. I am not even worthy to come and meet you. Just speak a word from where you are. If you do, I know that my servant boy will be healed! I know, because I am under the authority of my superior officers. And I have authority over my men. I only need to say, 'Go!' and they go. Or I might say, 'Come!' and they come. And to my slave, 'Do this or that,' and he does it. So just say, 'Be healed!' If you do, my servant will be well again!"

⁹When he heard this, Jesus was amazed. And he turned to the crowd

following him. "I have never met a man with faith like this," he said. "None of all the Jews in Israel have such faith!"

¹⁰Then the captain's friends went back to his house. And they found the slave completely healed.

- *Remember:* Who was sick? (7:2) Who asked Jesus to heal him? (7:3-4) How did he want Jesus to heal him? (7:6-8) What did Jesus think of this man? (7:9) Did Jesus heal the young man? (7:10) How do you know the Roman army officer had faith? How much faith did he

have? (7:9) What if the officer had not believed? Would Jesus still have healed the slave? Will Jesus do things for you if you don't believe?

- *Discover:* Do you want Jesus to help you? You must believe he can. You must believe he will.

- *Apply:* Did you pray last night? Did you ask Jesus to help you do something? Do you believe he can? Do you believe he will?

- *What's next?* Have you ever seen a dead person come back to life? You'll see this happen when you read Luke 7:11-17. ■

Jesus Helps a Boy Come Back to Life

Have you been at a funeral? Have you seen a dead person get up and walk? Jesus went to a funeral one day. He told the dead person to come back to life. Did it happen?

¹¹Not long after that Jesus went with his disciples to the village of Nain. He had the usual great crowd at his heels. ¹²A funeral procession was coming out as he came to the village gate. The boy who had died was the only son of his widowed mother. And many people from the village were with her.

¹³When the Lord saw her, he felt very sorry for her. "Don't cry!" he said. ¹⁴Then he walked over to the coffin and touched it. The men who were carrying it stopped. "Young man," he said, "come back to life again."

¹⁵Then the boy sat up and began to talk to those around him! And Jesus gave him back to his mother.

¹⁶Great fear and awe swept through the crowd. And they began to praise God. "A mighty prophet has risen among us," they said. "We have seen the hand of God at work today."

¹⁷The report of what he did that day raced from end to end of Judea. It even spread out across the borders.

- *Remember:* Where was the funeral? (7:11-12) Who had died? Why was this especially sad? (7:12) What did Jesus say to the boy who had died? (7:14) How did the

people there feel? What did they do? (7:16-17) How would you have felt if you had seen this? Would you have praised God, too?

- *Discover:* It is good to praise God when he does something special for us. Read Psalm 103:1-2.

- *Apply:* Think of something good God has done for you. Say thank you! You may also want to say "Praise God!"

- *What's next?* Has anyone ever kissed your feet while you ate lunch? Has anyone poured perfume on them? Has anyone wiped your feet with her hair? Someone did all of these things to Jesus. Read what Jesus did then in Luke 7:36-50. ■

Jesus Encourages John the Baptist

¹⁸The disciples of John the Baptist soon heard of all that Jesus was doing. When they told John about it, ¹⁹he sent two of his disciples to Jesus. He sent them to ask, "Are you really the Messiah? Or shall we keep on looking for him?"

²⁰⁻²²The two disciples went and found Jesus. At the time he was healing many sick people of their diseases. He was healing the lame and the blind. And he was casting out evil spirits. They asked him John's question. And Jesus said,

"Go back to John. Tell him all you have seen and heard here today. Tell him how those who were blind can now see. Tell him that the lame are walking without a limp. Tell him that the lepers are completely healed. Tell him that the deaf can hear again. Tell him that the dead come back to life. Tell him that the poor are hearing the Good News. 23And tell him, 'Blessed is the one who does not lose his faith in me.'"

24After they left, Jesus talked to the crowd about John. "Who is this man you went out into the Judean wilderness to see?" he asked. "Did you find him weak as grass, moved by every breath of wind? 25Did you find him dressed in fancy clothes? No! Men who live in luxury are found in palaces. They don't live out in the wilderness. 26But did you find a prophet? Yes! And he is more than a prophet. 27He is the one the Scriptures talked about: 'Look! I am sending my messenger ahead of you. He will make the way ready before you.' 28In all humanity there is no one greater than John. And yet the least important person of the Kingdom of God is greater than he."

29And all who heard Jesus' words agreed that God's way was right. Even the most wicked of them agreed. These people had already been baptized by John. 30Everyone agreed, that is, except the Pharisees and teachers of Moses' Law. They rejected God's plan for them and refused John's baptism.

31"What can I say about such men?" Jesus asked. "With what shall I compare them? 32They are like a group of children. They complain to their friends, 'You don't like it if we play "wedding." And you don't like it if we play "funeral."' 33For John the Baptist used to go without food. He never drank a drop of wine all his life. So you said, 'He must be crazy!' 34But I eat my food and drink my wine. So you say, 'What a glutton Jesus is! And he drinks! And he has the lowest sort of friends!' 35But wisdom is proved by the good things it does."

A Woman Kisses Jesus' Feet

Have you ever seen someone kiss your preacher's feet while he ate lunch? You probably won't. A woman did this one day. She poured perfume on Jesus' feet. She kissed them. She wiped his feet with her hair. Why do you think she did these things? Jesus tells us.

36One of the Pharisees asked Jesus to come to his home for lunch. And Jesus agreed to come. So they sat down to eat. 37But a prostitute heard Jesus was there. So she brought a flask filled with expensive perfume. 38Going in, she knelt behind him at his feet. She was crying and her tears fell down on his feet. She wiped them off with her hair and kissed them. Then she poured the perfume on them.

39Jesus' host, the Pharisee, saw what was happening. And he knew who the woman was. So he said to himself, "This proves that Jesus is no prophet. For if God had really sent him, he would know what kind of woman this one is!"

40Then Jesus spoke up and answered his thoughts. "Simon," he said to the Pharisee. "I have something to say to you."

"All right, Teacher," Simon replied. "Go ahead."

41Then Jesus told him this story. "A man loaned money to two people," Jesus began. "He loaned $5,000 to one and $500 to the other. 42But neither of them could pay him back. So he kindly forgave them both, letting them keep the money! Which do you suppose

loved him most after that?"

⁴³"I suppose the one who had owed him the most," Simon answered.

"Correct," Jesus agreed.

⁴⁴Then he turned to the woman and said to Simon, "Look! See this woman kneeling here! When I came to your home, you didn't offer me water to wash the dust from my feet. But she has washed them with her tears. And she wiped them off with her hair. ⁴⁵You did not give me the customary kiss of greeting. But she has kissed my feet from the time I first came in. ⁴⁶You did not give me the usual olive oil to anoint my head. But she has covered my feet with rare perfume. ⁴⁷Therefore, though her sins are many, she is forgiven. For she loved me much. But one who is forgiven little shows little love."

⁴⁸And he said to her, "Your sins are forgiven."

⁴⁹Then the men at the table spoke among themselves. "Who does this man think he is?" they muttered. "How can he go around forgiving sins?"

⁵⁰And Jesus said to the woman, "Your faith has saved you. Go in peace."

- *Remember:* What three things did the woman do to Jesus' feet? (7:38) Simon should have done three things when Jesus came to his house. What were they? (7:44-46) Who showed more love to Jesus, Simon or the woman? How? (7:47) How do you think Simon felt after Jesus told him these things? How would you have felt?

- *Discover:* When we love Jesus we do good things for him.

- *Apply:* Do you love Jesus? Don't just say you love him. Do things that show you love him. What could you do today to show Jesus that you love him?

- *What's next?* How important is dirt? You'll read what Jesus said in Matthew 13:1-23. ■

Women Go with Jesus

8 Not long after that Jesus began a tour of Galilee. He told the Good News about the Kingdom of God. And he took his 12 disciples with him. ²Some women went along, too. These woman had been healed of sicknesses or delivered from demons. Among them was Mary Magdalene. Jesus had cast out seven demons from her. ³There was also Joanna, Chuza's wife. Chuza was King Herod's business manager. He was in charge of Herod's palace and domestic affairs. There were also Susanna and many others. They all gave from their own money to support Jesus and his disciples.

A Story about Four Types of Soil

⁴One day Jesus told this story. He was speaking to a large crowd that was gathering to hear him. Other people were still on the way, coming from other towns.

⁵"A farmer went out to his field to plant grain. So he scattered the seed on the ground. Some of it fell on a footpath and was trampled on. And the birds came and ate it as it lay uncovered. ⁶Other seed fell on shallow soil with rock beneath. This seed began to grow quickly. But it soon withered and died because it didn't have enough water. ⁷Other seed landed in thistle patches. So the young grain stalks were soon choked out. ⁸Still other seed fell on good soil. This seed grew quickly. And it produced a crop 100 times as large as he had planted." Then he said, "If anyone has listening ears, use them now!"

Jesus Explains His Soil Story

⁹His apostles asked him what the story meant.

¹⁰He replied, "God wants you to know the meaning of these stories. For they tell a great deal about the Kingdom of God. But these crowds hear the words and do not understand. It is just as the ancient prophets said it would be.

¹¹"This is what it means. The seed is God's message to men. ¹²What does the hard path where some of the seed fell stand for? It stands for the hard hearts in some of those who hear the words of God. But then the devil comes and steals the words away. He does this before the people can believe and be saved. ¹³What does the stony ground stand for? It stands for those who enjoy listening to sermons. But somehow the message

never really takes root in their lives. They know the message is true. And they sort of believe for awhile. But when the hot winds of trouble blow, they lose interest. [14]What does the seed among the thorns stand for? It stands for those who listen and believe God's words. But later their faith is choked out by worry, riches, and the pleasures of life. And so they are never able to help anyone else to believe the Good News.

[15]"But the good soil stands for honest, good-hearted people. They listen to God's words and cling to them. And they steadily spread them to others who also soon believe.

A Story about a Lamp
[16]"People never light lamps and then cover them up to hide the light. Instead, lamps are set out in the open where they can be seen. [17]In the same way, someday everything shall be brought to light. The secrets of men's hearts will be made known to all. [18]So be careful how you listen. For whoever has, to him shall be given more. And whoever does not have, even what he thinks he has shall be taken away from him."

Those Who Hear and Obey Are Jesus' Family
[19]One day Jesus' mother and brothers came to see him. But they couldn't get into the house where he was teaching. This was because of the crowds. [20]Jesus was told they were standing outside and wanted to see him. [21]So he said, "My mother and brothers are those who hear God's message and obey it."

Even the Winds and Waves Obey Jesus!
[22]One day Jesus was with his disciples. He said to them, "Let's go across to the other side of the lake." So they got into a boat and set sail. [23]On the way across Jesus lay down for a nap. While he was sleeping the wind began to rise. A fierce storm came up on the lake. And the boat was in real danger of sinking.

[24]They rushed over and woke Jesus up. "Master, Master, we are sinking!" they screamed.

So he spoke to the storm. "Quiet down," he said. And the wind and waves stopped and all was calm! [25]Then he asked them, "Where is your faith?"

And they were filled with awe and fear of him. They said to one another, "Who is this man? Even the winds and waves obey him!"

Jesus Sends Demons Out of a Man and into Some Pigs
[26]So they came to the Gerasene country. This was across the lake from Galilee. [27]As Jesus climbed out of the boat, he was met by a man from the town. This man had been demon-possessed for a long time. He didn't live in a house and he didn't wear any clothes. He lived in a graveyard among the tombs. [28]As soon as he saw Jesus he screamed and fell to the ground before him. He cried, "What do you want with me, Jesus, Son of God Most High? Please, I beg you, don't torment me!"

[29]For Jesus was already commanding the demon to leave him. This demon often took control of the man. Even when he was bound with chains he just broke them. Then he would rush out into the desert. He did all this under the demon's power. [30]"What is your name?" Jesus asked the demon. "Legion," they replied. For the man was filled with thousands of them! [31]They kept begging Jesus not to order them into the Bottomless Pit.

[32]A herd of pigs was feeding on the mountain nearby. So the demons begged Jesus to let them enter into the pigs. And Jesus said they could. [33]So they left the man and went into the pigs. Then the whole herd rushed down the mountain. They fell over a cliff into the lake below, where they drowned. [34]The herdsmen rushed away to the nearby city. They spread the news as they ran.

[35]Soon a crowd came out to see for themselves what had happened. They saw the man who had been demon-possessed sitting quietly at Jesus' feet. He had clothes on and he wasn't crazy anymore! And the whole crowd was very afraid. [36]Some of them had seen it

happen. So they told the others how the man had been healed. ³⁷And everyone begged Jesus to go away and leave them alone. For a deep wave of fear had swept over them. So Jesus went back to the boat and left. He crossed back to the other side of the lake.

³⁸The man who had been demon-possessed begged to go too. But Jesus said no.

³⁹"Go back to your family," he told him. "Tell them what a great thing God has done for you."

So he went all through the city. And he told everyone about Jesus' miracle.

A Dead Girl Lives Again

Have you ever seen a dead person? People cry when someone dies. They know this person will never be with them here on earth again. They are gone. Jairus's daughter died. Everyone knew she was gone. Friends and family cried. Then Jesus came. How could he help a dead girl? Watch!

⁴⁰On the other side of the lake the crowds welcomed Jesus. They had been waiting for him to come back.

⁴¹Then a man named Jairus came and fell down at Jesus' feet. He was a leader of a Jewish synagogue. He begged Jesus to come home with him. ⁴²For his only child was dying, a little girl 12 years old. Jesus went with him, pushing through the crowds.

⁴³⁻⁴⁴As they went a woman came up behind Jesus and touched him. She had been slowly bleeding for 12 years and wanted to be healed. She could find no cure, though she had spent all she had on doctors. But when she touched the edge of Jesus' robe, the bleeding stopped.

⁴⁵"Who touched me?" Jesus asked.

All the people there denied it. And Peter said, "Master, so many are crowding against you. How could you ask such a question?"

⁴⁶But Jesus told him, "No, it was someone who touched me on purpose. For I felt healing power go out from me."

⁴⁷When the woman saw that Jesus knew, she began to shake. And she fell to her knees before him. Then she told him why she had touched him and that now she was well.

⁴⁸"Daughter," he said to her. "Your faith has healed you. Go in peace."

⁴⁹While he was still speaking to her, a messenger came from Jairus's home. He brought news that the little girl was dead. "She's gone," he told her father. "There's no use troubling the Teacher now."

⁵⁰Jesus heard what had happened. So he said to the father, "Don't be afraid! Just trust me, and she'll be all right."

⁵¹When they came to the house, Jesus went to the girl's room. He wouldn't let anyone come except Peter, James, John, and the girl's parents. ⁵²The home was filled with mourning people. But Jesus said, "Stop the crying! She isn't dead. She is only asleep!" ⁵³This brought scoffing and laughter. For they all knew she was dead.

⁵⁴Then he took her by the hand. And he said, "Get up, little girl!" ⁵⁵And at that moment her life came back. She jumped up! "Give her something to eat!" he said. ⁵⁶Her parents were overcome with joy. But Jesus told them not to tell anyone what had happened.

- *Remember:* What did Jairus ask Jesus to do? (8:41) When Jairus got bad news, what did Jesus tell him? (8:50) What was happening when Jesus got to Jairus's home? (8:52) What did Jesus do for the little girl then? (8:54-55) What would you have said to Jesus if you had been the girl's father?

- *Discover:* Can you bring a dead person back to life again? Do you know anyone who can? How could Jesus do this?

- *Apply:* Does this story help you trust Jesus more? Does it help you believe that Jesus is God's Son? The next time something bad happens, will you trust Jesus to help?

- *What's next?* Read about the strangest birthday party ever! Read Mark 6:14-29. ■

An Assignment for the Disciples

9 One day Jesus called together his 12 apostles. He gave them the power to cast out demons and heal diseases. ²Then he sent them away. They were to tell everyone about the coming of the Kingdom of God. And they were to heal the sick.

³"Don't even take along a walking stick," he told them. "Don't carry a beggar's bag, food, or money. Don't even bring an extra coat. ⁴Be a guest in only one home at each village.

⁵"The people of a town might not listen to you when you enter it. If so, turn around and leave. Show God's anger against it by shaking its dust from your feet as you go."

⁶So they began their tour of the villages. They preached the Good News and healed the sick.

Is John the Baptist Alive?

⁷Reports of Jesus' miracles soon reached Herod, the governor. He was worried and puzzled. For some were saying, "This is John the Baptist. He has come back to life again!" ⁸Others said, "It is Elijah or some other prophet risen from the dead." These rumors were spreading all over the land.

⁹"I beheaded John," Herod said. "So who is this man I am hearing so much about?" And he tried to see him.

Doctors
LUKE 8:43-44

When you get sick, your parents take you to a doctor. The doctor has gone to school many years. He has learned much about medicines and how to use them. Sometimes you must go to a hospital. You may even have surgery. Perhaps you have your appendix or tonsils taken out in an operation. Before long, you are well.

In Old Testament times there were doctors, but they didn't know very much about medicine and operations. People often thought diseases were caused by demons. So doctors often tried to drive out demons. Even in New Testament days there were only a few doctors. They knew very little compared to our doctors. They did not have most of our modern medicines. A Bible-time person with appendicitis had big trouble. There were no hospitals. So many people died when they got sick. Luke was a doctor. He heard about the wonderful ways Jesus healed people. He knew that only the Son of God could heal in such miraculous ways.

A Lunch of Five Loaves and Two Fish Fills 5,000 People

[10]Now the apostles went back to Jesus after their tour. And they reported what they had done. Then Jesus slipped quietly away with them toward the city of Bethsaida. [11]But the crowds found out where he was going and followed. And Jesus welcomed them. He taught them again about the Kingdom of God. And he healed those who were sick.

[12]Late in the afternoon all 12 of the disciples came to Jesus. They urged him to send the people away to the nearby villages and farms. There they could find food and places to stay for the night. "For there is nothing to eat here in this deserted spot," they said.

[13]But Jesus replied, "You feed them!"

"Why, we have only five loaves of bread and two fish!" they said. "Or do you want us to go and buy food for this crowd?" [14]For there were about 5,000 men there!

"Just tell them to sit down on the ground," Jesus said. "And tell them to divide into groups of about 50 each." [15]So they did what Jesus told them.

[16]Jesus took the five loaves and two fish. He looked up into the sky and gave thanks for the food. Then he broke off pieces for his disciples to give the crowd. [17]And everyone ate and ate. Still, 12 basketfuls of scraps were picked up after they were finished!

Peter Says Jesus Is the Messiah

[18]One day Jesus was alone, praying, and his disciples were with him. He asked them, "Who do the people say I am?"

[19]"John the Baptist," they told him. "Some also say you are Elijah. Others claim you are one of the other prophets risen from the dead."

[20]Then he asked them, "Who do you think I am?"

Peter replied, "You are the Messiah of God!"

Jesus Talks about His Death for the First Time

[21]He gave them strict orders not to speak of this to anyone. [22]"For I, the Messiah, must suffer much," he said. "I will be rejected by the Jewish leaders. The elders, chief priests, and teachers of the Law will not believe in me. And I will be killed. Then three days later I will come back to life again!"

[23]Then he said, "You might want to follow me. But if you do, you must put aside what you want. You must carry your cross with you every day. And you must keep close to me! [24]Whoever loses his life for my sake will save it. But whoever tries to keep his life will lose it. [25]What is the good of gaining the whole world when it means losing one's self?

[26]"I, the Messiah, will someday come in my glory. I will come in the glory of the Father and the holy angels. And I will be ashamed then of all who are ashamed of me now. [27]But this is the simple truth! Some of you will not die until you have seen the Kingdom of God."

Jesus Is Transfigured

Look! A person begins to shine like a bright light! His face shines. His clothes shine. What is happening?

[28]Eight days later Jesus went up into the hills to pray. He took Peter, James, and John with him. [29]And as he was praying, his face began to shine. His clothes became dazzling white and blazed with light. [30]Then two men appeared and be-gan talking with him. They were Moses and Elijah! [31]They appeared in heavenly glory. They were speaking of his death at Jerusalem. For this was part of God's plan.

[32]Peter and the others were drowsy

and had fallen asleep. Now they woke up and saw Jesus covered with brightness and glory. And they saw the two men standing with him. ³³Then Moses and Elijah began to leave. And Peter, all confused, spoke up. "Master, this is wonderful!" he blurted out. "We'll put up three shelters. One will be for you. One will be for Moses. And the other will be for Elijah!"

³⁴But even as he was saying this, a bright cloud formed above them. And they were filled with fear as it covered them. ³⁵And a voice from the cloud said, "This is my Son. He is my Chosen One. Listen to him."

³⁶Then, as the voice died away, Jesus was there alone with his disciples. They didn't tell anyone what they had seen until long afterwards.

- *Remember:* Who went with Jesus into the hills? (9:28) What happened to Jesus while he prayed? (9:29) Who came from Heaven to be with Jesus? (9:30) How did they look? What did they say? (9:31) How do you think they knew the way Jesus would die even though it had not happened yet? When God spoke from the cloud, who did he say was his Son? (9:35) What did God tell the disciples to do? (9:35) If God told you to do something, would you do it? Would you argue with him?

- *Discover:* We should do what God tells us.

- *Apply:* What do you think God wants you to do most today? Will you do it? Don't argue!

- *What's next?* Do you ever think you are better than someone else? Jesus wants to talk with you. Read Matthew 18:1-9. ■

Jesus Heals a Demon-Possessed Boy

³⁷The next day as they went down the hill, a huge crowd met them. ³⁸And a man in the crowd called out to Jesus. "Teacher," he said, "this boy here is my only son. ³⁹A demon keeps taking control of him, making him scream. And it makes him shake, roll around, and foam at the mouth. It is always hitting him and hardly ever leaves him alone. ⁴⁰I begged your disciples to cast the demon out. But they couldn't do it."

⁴¹"O you people of little faith," Jesus said to his disciples. "How long should I put up with you? Bring him here."

⁴²As the boy was coming, the demon knocked him to the ground. It caused him to shake violently. But Jesus ordered the demon to come out. He healed the boy and handed him over to his father.

⁴³Awe gripped the people as they saw this display of the power of God. The people were all amazed by the wonderful things Jesus was doing.

Jesus Predicts His Death a Second Time

Then Jesus said to his disciples, ⁴⁴"Listen to me. Remember what I say. I, the Messiah, am going to be betrayed." ⁴⁵But the disciples didn't know what he meant. For their minds had been sealed. And they were afraid to ask him what he meant.

The Disciples Argue about Who Will Be Greatest

⁴⁶Jesus' disciples began to argue about which of them was the greatest! ⁴⁷But Jesus knew their thoughts. So he stood a little child beside him. ⁴⁸And he said to them, "Take care of little children like this. For by caring for them you will be caring for me! And whoever cares for me is caring for God who sent me. Your care for others will prove how great you are."

The Disciples Forbid Someone Else from Using Jesus' Name

⁴⁹Now John said to Jesus, "Master, we saw someone using your name to cast out demons. And we told him not to. After all, he isn't in our group."

⁵⁰But Jesus said, "You shouldn't have done that! For anyone who is not against you is for you."

What Does It Cost to Follow Jesus?

⁵¹The time was coming near for Jesus to go back to Heaven. So he was determined to travel on toward Jerusalem.

⁵²One day as they traveled, Jesus sent messengers on ahead. They were to find a place for them to stay in a Samaritan village. ⁵³But they were turned away! The people of the village would have nothing to do with them. This was because they were going to Jerusalem.

⁵⁴Word soon came back of what had

happened. James and John were upset. They said to Jesus, "Master, shall we order fire down from Heaven to burn them up?" ⁵⁵But Jesus turned and scolded them. ⁵⁶And they went on to another village.

⁵⁷As they were walking along someone spoke to Jesus. He said, "I will always follow you no matter where you go."

⁵⁸But Jesus replied, "Remember, I don't even own a place to lay my head. Foxes have dens to live in. Birds have their nests. But I, the Messiah, have no earthly home at all."

⁵⁹Another time, Jesus asked a man to come with him to be his disciple. The man wanted to come. But he wanted to wait until his father's death.

⁶⁰Jesus replied, "Let those without eternal life worry about things like that. You have another job to do. You are to preach the coming of the Kingdom of God to all the world."

⁶¹Another said, "Yes, Lord, I will come. But first let me ask my family if I can come."

⁶²But Jesus told him, "Some start the work but then keep looking back. Such people are not fit for the Kingdom of God."

Jesus Sends Out 70 Messengers

10 The Lord now chose 70 other disciples. He sent them out in pairs to all the towns he planned to visit later.

²This is what he told them: "Ask the Lord of the harvest to send out more workers to help you. For the harvest is great, but the workers are so few. ³Go now, and remember that I am sending you out as lambs among wolves. ⁴Don't take any money with you. Don't take a beggar's bag or even an extra pair of shoes. And don't waste time along the way.

⁵"When you go into a home, give it your blessing. ⁶If it is worthy of the blessing, the blessing will stand. If not, the blessing will come back to you.

⁷"When you enter a village, don't move around from home to home. Stay in one place, eating and drinking whatever is set before you. And don't be afraid to take what they give you. For the workman is worthy of his wages!

⁸⁻⁹"If a town welcomes you, eat whatever is set before you. Heal the sick. And then say, 'The Kingdom of God is very near you now.'

¹⁰"But if a town refuses you, go out into its streets. Then say, ¹¹'We wipe the dust of your town from our feet. We do this to announce your doom. Never forget how close you were to the Kingdom of God!' ¹²Even wicked Sodom will be better off than such a city on the Judgment Day. ¹³What horrors wait for you, Chorazin and Bethsaida! For I did many miracles in you, but you still wouldn't believe. I might have done the same miracles in the cities of Tyre and Sidon. But if I had, their people would have turned from their sins long ago. They would have worn sackcloth to show they were sorry. They would have put ashes on their heads, too. ¹⁴Yes, Tyre and Sidon will be better off on the Judgment Day than you. ¹⁵And you people of Capernaum, what shall I say about you? Will you be brought up to Heaven? No, you shall be brought down to hell!"

¹⁶Then he said to the disciples, "Those who welcome you are welcoming me. And those who reject you are rejecting me. And those who reject me are rejecting God who sent me."

The 70 Messengers Return

¹⁷When the 70 disciples came back, they gave him a joyful report. They said, "Even the demons obey us when we use your name."

¹⁸"Yes," he told them. "I saw Satan falling from Heaven like a flash of light! ¹⁹I have given you the power to walk among snakes and scorpions. And I have given you authority over the power of the Enemy. Nothing shall hurt you! ²⁰But don't be full of joy because the demons obey you. Be full of joy because your names are written in Heaven."

²¹At that time, Jesus was filled with the joy of the Holy Spirit. He said, "I praise you, O Father, Lord of Heaven and earth! You have hidden these things from people who are smart and wise. But you have shown them to those who trust you like little children. Yes, thank you, Father! For that is the way

you wanted it. [22]The Father has put all things under my control. No one really knows the Son except the Father. And no one really knows the Father except the Son. The only people who know the Father are those the Son chooses to tell about him."

[23]Then Jesus turned to the 12 disciples. He said to them quietly, "You are blessed to see what you have seen. [24]Many prophets and kings of old have wished for these days. They also wanted to see and hear what you have now seen and heard!"

A Story about a Friend

Do you have some friends? Are they good friends? What is the difference between a friend and a good friend? Jesus tells us here.

[25]One day an expert in Jewish law came to test Jesus. He asked him, "Teacher, what does a man need to do to live forever in Heaven?"

[26]Jesus replied, "What does Moses' Law say about it?"

[27]He answered, "You must love the Lord your God with all your heart. You must love him with all your soul. You must love him with all your strength. You must love him with all your mind. And you must love your neighbor just as much as you love yourself."

[28]"Right!" Jesus told him. "Do this and you shall live!"

[29]The man wanted to justify his lack of love for some kinds of people. So he asked, "Who exactly is my neighbor?"

[30]Jesus answered him with a story. "A Jew went on a trip from Jerusalem to Jericho," Jesus began. "But on the way, he was attacked by robbers. They took away all of his clothes and money. Then they beat him up and left him lying half dead beside the road.

[31]"By chance a Jewish priest came along. He saw the man lying there. But he crossed to the other side of the road and passed him by. [32]Later, a Levite came along. His job was to serve in the Temple. He walked over and looked at the man lying there. But then he also just kept going. [33]"But then a hated Samaritan came along. When he saw the man, he felt deep pity. [34]So the Samaritan sat down beside him. He soothed his wounds with medicine and bandaged them. Then he put the man on his donkey and walked along beside him. They came to an inn, where the Samaritan nursed him through the night. [35]The next day he gave the innkeeper some money. And he told him to take care of the man. 'His bill might run higher than that,' the Samaritan said. 'But if it does, I'll pay the rest the next time I'm here.'

36"Now which of these three was a neighbor to the man who was beaten?"

37The man replied, "The one who showed him some pity."

Then Jesus said, "Yes, now go and do the same."

● *Remember:* What happened to the traveler? (10:30) Who came along the road first? What did he do for the man? (10:31) Who came along next? What did he do for the man? (10:32) Who was the third man to come along the road? What did the Samaritan do for the man? (10:33-35) You would expect a priest and a temple-worker to help, wouldn't you? But they didn't. They were not good friends. You would not expect a hated foreigner to help, would you? But he did. He was a good friend.

● *Discover:* Good friends do good things for their friends. They don't just talk about it.

● *Apply:* Are you a good friend? Do you really do good things for your friends? Or do you just say that you are a friend? Do your friends really do good things for you? Or do they just say they are friends?

● *What's next?* Would you rather feed a friend or listen to a friend? Read about two women who had to choose in Luke 10:38-42. ■

Jesus Visits Mary and Martha

Jesus came to see Mary and Martha. One talked with him. The other didn't have time to talk. Or at least she thought she didn't have time. Why was that?

38Now Jesus and the disciples continued on their way to Jerusalem. They came to a village where a woman named Martha asked them into her home. 39Her sister Mary sat on the floor. She listened to Jesus as he talked.

40But Martha was worried about the big dinner she was cooking. She came to Jesus and said, "Sir, my sister is just sitting here. I'm doing all the work. Doesn't that seem unfair to you? Tell her to come and help me!"

41But the Lord said to her, "Martha, dear friend, you are so upset over all these details! 42There is really only one thing worth worrying about. Mary has found it, and I won't take it away from her!"

● *Remember:* Which lady talked with Jesus? (10:39) Which got a big dinner for him? (10:40) Martha thought something was not fair. What? (10:40) Which lady did something more important than the other? (10:41-42) Why did Mary think it was more important to spend time with Jesus?

● *Discover:* Spending time with Jesus is more important than anything else we can do. Don't get so busy doing things that you stop spending time with Jesus.

● *Apply:* Do you spend time with Jesus each day? Do you talk with him? Or do other things take too much time? Are these other things really more important than Jesus?

● *What's next?* Who is the richest person in the world? Who is the poorest person in the world? Read Luke 12:13-34 for the answer. ■

Jesus Teaches about Prayer

11 One day Jesus was out praying in a certain place. One of his disciples came to him as he finished. He said, "Lord, teach us a prayer, just as John taught one to his disciples."

2And this is the prayer he taught them: "Father, may your name be honored for its holiness. Send your Kingdom soon. 3Give us our food day by day. 4And forgive our sins. For we have forgiven those who sinned against us. And don't allow us to be tempted."

5-6Then he told them this story to

teach them more about prayer. "Suppose you went to a friend's house at midnight," he began. "And suppose you wanted to borrow three loaves of bread. You would shout up to him, 'A friend of mine has just come for a visit. But I have nothing to give him to eat.' ⁷He would call down from his bedroom, 'Please don't ask me to get up. The door is locked for the night. We are all in bed. I just can't help you this time.'

You are either helping Jesus or hurting him

> *Anyone who is not for me is against me. If he isn't helping me, he is hurting me.*
>
> Luke 11:23

---

⁸"He might not get up and give you bread as a friend. But if you keep knocking, he will get up and give you what you want. ⁹And it's the same way with prayer. Keep on asking and you will keep on getting. Keep on looking and you will keep on finding. Knock and the door will be opened. ¹⁰Everyone who asks, receives. All who seek, find. And the door is opened to everyone who knocks.

¹¹"Now some of you men are fathers. If your boy asks for bread, do you give him a stone? If he asks for fish, do you give him a snake? ¹²If he asks for an egg, do you give him a scorpion? Of course not!

¹³"Even sinful persons like yourselves give children what they need. Don't you see that your heavenly Father will do at least as much as that for you? He will give the Holy Spirit to those who ask."

Jesus Answers Angry Words

¹⁴One day Jesus cast a demon from a man who couldn't speak. And the man's voice came back to him right away. The crowd was excited and amazed. ¹⁵But some said, "No wonder he can cast demons out. He gets his power from Satan, the king of demons!" ¹⁶Others asked Jesus to do some great miracle in the sky. They wanted him to prove he was the Messiah.

¹⁷He knew the thoughts of each of them. So he said, "Any kingdom filled with fighting is doomed. So is a home filled with argument and trouble. ¹⁸Now you say Satan gives me the power to cast out his demons. And by saying that, you claim he is fighting against himself. But if this is true, how can his kingdom survive? ¹⁹And suppose my power is from Satan. Then what about your own followers? For they cast out demons, too! Do you think this proves that their power is from Satan? Ask them if you are right! ²⁰But suppose I am casting out demons with power from God. If this is happening, it proves that the Kingdom of God has come.

²¹"For when Satan, strong and fully armed, guards his palace, it is safe. ²²But suppose someone stronger attacks his palace and defeats him. Then this stronger man will take away his weapons and all he owns.

²³"Anyone who is not for me is against me. If he isn't helping me, he is hurting me.

²⁴"When a demon is cast out of a man, it goes to the deserts. It looks there for a place to rest. But finding none, it goes back to the person it left. ²⁵It finds that its former home is all swept and clean. ²⁶Then it goes and gets seven other demons more evil than itself. And they all enter the man. So the poor fellow is seven times worse off than he was before."

²⁷As Jesus was speaking, a woman in the crowd called out. "God bless your mother," she said. "God bless the womb from which you came. God bless the breasts that gave you milk!"

²⁸"Yes," he replied. "But even more blessed are those who hear the Word of God and obey it."

Jesus Warns Those Who Don't Believe

²⁹⁻³⁰The crowd grew larger and pressed in upon him. Jesus said, "These are evil times, with evil people. They keep asking for some strange sign in the skies to prove I am the Messiah. But the only proof I will give them is a miracle like that of Jonah. What happened to Jonah proved to the people of Nineveh that

God had sent him. In the same way, what happens to me will prove that God has sent me.

[31]"At the Judgment Day the Queen of Sheba will stand up. She will point her finger at you people and judge you. For she went on a long, hard journey to listen to the wisdom of Solomon. But one far greater than Solomon is here and few listen to him.

[32]"The men of Nineveh, too, shall stand and judge this nation. For they turned from their sins when Jonah preached to them. And someone far greater than Jonah is here. But this nation won't listen.

Don't Hide Your Light!

[33]"No one lights a lamp and hides it! Instead, he puts it up on a lampstand. That way it will give light to all who enter the room. [34]Your eyes light up your inward being. A pure eye lets sunshine into your soul. A lustful eye shuts out the light and puts you into darkness. [35]So watch out that the sunshine isn't blotted out. [36]You should be filled with light within, with no dark corners. Then your face will shine, too. It will look as though a floodlight is shining on you."

Jesus Criticizes the Religious Leaders

[37-38]As he was speaking, one of the Pharisees asked him home for a meal. When Jesus got there, he sat down to eat. But he didn't wash first, as was demanded by Jewish custom. This greatly surprised his host.

[39]Then Jesus said to him, "You Pharisees wash the outside. But on the inside you are still dirty. You are full of greed and wickedness! [40]Fools! Didn't God make the inside as well as the outside? [41]Purity is best shown by being kind and generous.

[42]"How terrible it will be for you Pharisees! For you are careful to tithe even the smallest part of your money. But

Inns

LUKE 10:34

When was the last time you took a long trip in your car? Did you stay in a motel? Did it have a swimming pool? Did you eat in a restaurant? Travel in Bible times was much different from today. There were no cars, busses, planes, or trains. Travelers walked or rode a donkey. Only a few could afford to ride a camel. There were no restaurants or gas stations. There were no motels. There were only a few inns where travelers stayed. But an inn was much different from a motel. And there were only a few. These inns had no bathrooms, tubs, showers, or toilets. There was no running water. They had no beds or TVs. There were no pictures on the walls, no carpeting, no glass windows. There were no restaurants. It was merely a place to stay. Animals were kept in a big courtyard for the night. People slept inside. The next time you stay at a motel, remember Bible-time inns. You'll be thankful for what you have.

you completely forget about justice and the love of God. You should tithe, yes. But you should not leave these other things undone.

43"How terrible it will be for you Pharisees! For how you love the seats of honor in the synagogues! How you love the respect you get as you walk through the markets! 44Yes, great judgment is waiting for you. For you are like hidden graves in a field. Men go by you without knowing about the rot they are passing."

45An expert in religious law was standing there, too. "Sir," he said, "you have insulted me, too, in what you just said."

46"Yes," said Jesus, "the same terrors are waiting for you! For you crush men with impossible rules and laws. You tell others to do things that you yourselves would never try to do. 47How terrible it will be for you! For you are just like your ancestors who killed the prophets long ago. 48Murderers! You agree with your fathers that what they did was right. You would have done the same thing yourselves.

Do you want a good life?
You already have what you need!

Don't always be wishing for what you don't have. For real life and real living are not related to how rich we are.

Luke 12:15

49"This is what God says about you: 'I will send prophets and apostles to you. But you will kill some of them and chase away the others.'

50"You people will be guilty of the murder of God's servants from the beginning of the world. 51You will be guilty of the murder of Abel. You will be guilty of the murder of Zechariah, too. He died between the altar and the Temple. Yes, these murders will surely be charged against you.

52"How terrible it will be for you experts in religion! For you hide the truth from the people. You won't accept it for yourselves. And you keep others from having a chance to believe it."

53-54The Pharisees and legal experts were very angry. And from that time on they kept asking him questions. They were trying to trap him into saying something wrong. That way they could have him arrested.

Jesus Warns against Hypocrisy

12 Meanwhile the crowds grew until there were thousands of people. There were so many that they were crushing each other. Now Jesus turned to his disciples. "More than anything else, be careful of these Pharisees," he warned them. "They pretend to be good when they aren't. But such lies cannot be hidden forever. 2Everything that is hidden will become obvious. Everything that is done in secret will be made known. 3What you do in the dark shall be seen in the light. What you have whispered in the inner rooms shall be told for all to hear!

4"Dear friends, don't be afraid of these who want to murder you. They can only kill the body. They have no power over your souls. 5But I'll tell you whom to fear! Fear God who has the power to kill you and then put you into hell.

6"What is the price of five sparrows? A couple of pennies? Not much more than that. Yet God does not forget a single one of them. 7And he knows the number of hairs on your head! So don't be afraid. You are far more valuable to him than a whole flock of sparrows.

8"I tell you, if you stand before others here on earth and say you are my friend, I will honor you. I will say you belong to me in front of God's angels. 9But if you deny me among men, I will deny you before the angels. 10Those who speak against me may be forgiven. But those who speak against the Holy Spirit shall never be forgiven.

11"You will be brought to trial before these Jewish rulers in the synagogues. When this happens, don't worry about what to say in your defense. 12For the Holy Spirit will give you the right words to say."

A Story about Money

Who is the richest person in the world? Who is the poorest person in the world? You'll find the answer in this story.

¹³Then someone called from the crowd. "Sir," he said, "please tell my brother to divide my father's estate with me."

¹⁴But Jesus replied, "Man, who made me a judge over you? Who said I should divide property between you and your brother? ¹⁵Beware! Don't always be wishing for what you don't have. For real life and real living are not related to how rich we are."

¹⁶Then Jesus told a story. "A rich man had a fertile farm that produced fine crops," Jesus began. ¹⁷"In fact, his barns were full to overflowing. He couldn't get everything in them. He thought about this problem. ¹⁸And finally he said, 'I know! I'll tear down my barns and build bigger ones! Then I'll have enough room. ¹⁹Then I'll sit back and say to myself, "Friend, you have enough stored away for years to come. Now take it easy! Wine, women, and song for you!"'

²⁰"But God said to him, 'Fool! Tonight you die. Then who will get it all?'

²¹"Yes, every man is a fool who gets rich on earth but not in Heaven."

²²Then he turned to his disciples. "Don't worry about whether you have enough food to eat or clothes to wear," he said. ²³"For life is much more than food and clothes. ²⁴Look at the ravens. They don't plant or harvest. They don't have barns to store away their food. And yet they get along all right. For God feeds them. And you are far more important to him than any birds!

²⁵"And besides, what's the use of worrying? What good does it do? Will it add a single day to your life? Of course not! ²⁶And if worry can't even do little things, what's the use of worrying over bigger things?

²⁷"Look at the lilies! They don't sew and weave. And yet Solomon in all his glory was not dressed as well as they. ²⁸God provides clothing for the flowers that are here today and gone tomorrow. Don't you think that he will provide clothing for you? ²⁹And don't worry about food. Don't worry about what you eat and drink. Don't worry at all that God will provide it for you. ³⁰All mankind scratches for its daily bread. But your heavenly Father knows your needs. ³¹The thing you should worry about first is God's Kingdom. If you do this, God will always give you all you need.

³²"So don't be afraid, little flock. For it gives your Father great happiness to give you the Kingdom. ³³Sell what you have and give to those in need. This will bring you riches in Heaven! And the purses of Heaven have no rips or holes in them. Your treasures there will never disappear. No thief can steal them. No moth can destroy them. ³⁴Wherever your treasure is, there your heart and thoughts will be also.

- *Remember:* What kind of riches did the rich man have? (12:16-19) But what would happen to him that night? (12:20) What did Jesus say about riches on earth? (12:21) What did Jesus say about riches in Heaven? (12:33) Would you rather be rich on earth or rich in Heaven? Why?

- *Discover:* If you have riches on earth, but not in Heaven, you're really poor. There's nothing wrong with having riches on earth, but it is more important to store up riches in Heaven. Riches here don't last. Riches in Heaven last forever.

- *Apply:* How can you put riches in the Bank of Heaven? Here are some ways: (1) please Jesus, (2) help others come to know Jesus, (3) read your Bible so you can know God better, (4) pray often so you can know God better, (5) help others who need you. Can you think of other ways?

- *What's next?* A poor woman has been very sick for 18 years. Then Jesus heals her. So why should that make a man angry? Read Luke 13:10-17. ■

Prepare for Jesus' Return

³⁵"Be dressed and ready to serve. And keep your lamps burning. ³⁶Be ready for your Lord's return from the wedding feast. Then you will be able to let him in

the moment he knocks on the door. [37]There will be great joy for those who are ready for his coming. He himself will put on a waiter's uniform and serve them as they sit and eat! [38]He may come at nine o'clock at night, or even at midnight. But when he comes, there will be joy for his servants who are ready!

[39]"The house owner would be ready for a thief if he knew when the thief was coming. In the same way, everyone would be ready for me if they knew the exact hour of my return. [40]So be ready all the time. For I, the Messiah, will come when least expected."

[41]Peter asked, "Lord, are you talking just to us or to everyone?"

[42-44]And the Lord replied, "I'm talking to any man who is faithful. Now suppose the master of a house goes on a trip. And he chooses a faithful servant to feed his other servants. Then suppose his master comes back from his trip. If he finds that his servant has done a good job, there will be a reward. His master will put him in charge of all he owns.

[45]"But suppose the man begins to think, 'My Lord won't be back for a long time.' Suppose he begins to whip the men and women he is supposed to protect. And what if he spends his time getting drunk at parties? [46]Well, his master will come back without warning. And he will remove him from his position of trust. Then he will put him in the place of the unfaithful. [47]He will be punished. For he knew his duty, but he did not do it.

[48]"But some might not know they are doing wrong. If that is the case, they will only be punished lightly. Much is required from those to whom much is given.

Families Will Disagree about Jesus

[49]"I have come to bring fire to the earth. Oh, that my work was finished! [50]I must suffer a terrible baptism. And how I wish it had already happened!

[51]"Do you think I have come to give peace to the earth? No! Rather, I have come to bring trouble and division! [52]From now on families will be split apart. Three might be in favor of me, and two against. [53]A father will decide one way about me. His son will decide the other way. Mother and daughter will disagree. A daughter-in-law will laugh at the decision of her mother-in-law."

Learn to Interpret Signs from God

[54]Then he turned to the crowd. He said, "When you see clouds forming in the west, you say, 'Here comes a shower.' And you are right. [55]"When the south wind blows you say, 'Today it will be very hot.' And it is. [56]Hypocrites! You interpret the sky well enough when it comes to the weather. But you refuse to see the warnings all around you about the trouble ahead. [57]Why do you refuse to see for yourselves what is right?

[58]"Now suppose you meet your accuser on the way to court. If you do, try to settle the matter before it reaches the judge. Otherwise he might send you to jail. [59]If that happens, you won't be free until you pay the last penny you owe."

Jesus Tells the People to Repent

13 About this time some people brought Jesus some news. They told him that Pilate had killed some Jews from Galilee. The victims had been in Jerusalem, giving sacrifices at the Temple.

[2]"Do you think they were worse sinners than other men from Galilee?" Jesus asked. "Is that why they suffered? [3]Not at all! And unless you turn from your sins, you also will die!

[4]"And what about the 18 men who died when the Tower of Siloam fell on them? Were they the worst sinners in Jerusalem? [5]Not at all! And you, too, will die unless you turn from your sins."

[6]Then he taught them using this story. "A man planted a fig tree in his garden," Jesus began. "And he came again and again to see if he could find any fruit on it. But there was never any fruit. [7]Finally he told his gardener to cut it down. 'I've waited three years and there hasn't been a single fig!' he said. 'Why bother with it any longer? It's taking up space we can use for something else.'

[8]"'Give it one more chance,' the gardener said. 'Leave it another year. I'll dig around it and fertilize it. [9]If we get figs next year, fine. If not, I'll cut it down.'"

Jesus Heals on the Sabbath

Jesus healed a poor woman who was crippled. But a man was very angry about that. Why would anyone be angry that a poor woman had been healed?

¹⁰One Sabbath Jesus was teaching in a synagogue. ¹¹He saw a crippled woman there. She had been bent over for 18 years. And she was not able to straighten herself.

¹²Jesus called her over to him. He said, "Woman, you are healed of your sickness!" ¹³He touched her, and instantly she could stand straight. How she praised and thanked God!

¹⁴But the Jewish leader of the synagogue was very angry. This was because Jesus had healed her on the Sabbath day. "There are six days of the week to work," he shouted to the crowd. "Those are the days to come for healing. You should not come on the Sabbath!"

¹⁵But the Lord replied, "You hypocrite! You work on the Sabbath! Don't you untie your cattle from their stalls on the Sabbath? Don't you lead them out for water? ¹⁶This woman is a descendant of Abraham just like we are. But Satan has held her captive for 18 years. Surely it is not wrong for her to be set free on the Sabbath day!"

¹⁷This made his enemies ashamed. And all the people were full of joy because of the great things Jesus did.

- *Remember:* What day was it? (13:10) Where was Jesus teaching? (13:10) What was wrong with the sick woman? (13:11) What did Jesus do for her? (13:12-13) What did she do then? (13:13) Why was a man angry at Jesus? (13:14) What did Jesus say to him? (13:15-16) Do you think Jesus was right? Why?

- *Discover:* Don't criticize others for something you are doing. The man criticized Jesus for working on the Sabbath. But Jesus said that man also worked on the Sabbath!

- *Apply:* Have you criticized someone? You thought they were wrong. What were they doing? But are you also doing something like that?

- *What's next?* What must you do to become an important person? You might be surprised. Read Luke 13:22-30. ■

What Is the Kingdom of God Like?

¹⁸Now he began teaching them again about the Kingdom of God. "What is the Kingdom like?" he asked. "How can I tell you about it? ¹⁹It is like a tiny mustard seed planted in a garden. Soon it grows into a tall bush and the birds live among its branches.

²⁰⁻²¹"It is like yeast mixed into dough. It works unseen until it makes the dough rise high."

A Story about a Door

There is a door to Heaven. Some will go through it. Some will not. That's what Jesus said. Who will be able to go through? Who will be able to get into Heaven? How can you get into Heaven? Listen to Jesus!

²²He went from city to city and village to village. He taught people everywhere he went. But he was always pressing on toward Jerusalem.

²³Someone asked him, "Will only a few be saved?"

And he replied, ²⁴⁻²⁵"The door to Heaven is narrow. Work hard to get in! For the truth is that many will try to go in. But when the head of the house has locked the door, it will be too late. Then if you're still standing outside, he will say, 'I do not know you.' Then it won't help to beg, 'Lord, open the door for us.'

26"But we ate with you,' you will say. 'And you taught in our streets.'

27"And he will reply, 'I tell you, I don't know you. You can't come in here, guilty as you are. Go away.'

28"And there will be great crying and grinding of teeth as you stand outside. You will see Abraham, Isaac, Jacob, and all the prophets in the Kingdom of God. 29People will come from all over the world to take their places there. 30Some who are hated now will be greatly honored then. And some who are highly thought of now will be least important then."

- *Remember:* Is the door to Heaven wide? Will everyone go through it? (13:24-25) What happens when the door is locked? What about people who want to get in then? (13:24-28) Do you have to be important here on earth in order to enter Heaven? (13:30) What do you think you have to do to enter? It's a wonderful door to the most wonderful place! You want to go through it someday, don't you?

- *Discover:* Any person who accepts Jesus will go through the door into Heaven. It doesn't matter if you are rich or poor, pretty or not so pretty. It doesn't matter where you live or what friends you have. What matters is that you love Jesus. He must be your Savior.

- *Apply:* Do you want to go through the door to Heaven someday? Accept Jesus as your Savior now. Let him be your Savior.

- *What's next?* Is one bigger than 99? Sometimes it is. Jesus tells us when. Read Matthew 18:10-14. ■

O Jerusalem, Jerusalem!

31A few minutes later some Pharisees came to Jesus. They said to him, "Get out of here if you want to live! For King Herod is after you!"

32Jesus replied, "Bring a message to that fox, Herod. Tell him I will keep on casting out demons and healing people today and tomorrow. Then on the third day I will reach my goal. 33Yes, today, tomorrow, and the next day! Surely a

prophet of God shouldn't be killed anywhere except in Jerusalem!

34"O Jerusalem, Jerusalem! The city that murders the prophets. The city that stones those sent to help her. How often I have wanted to gather your children together. I have wanted to protect you as a hen protects her brood under her wings. But you wouldn't let me help you. 35And now your house will be left empty and destroyed. And you won't see me again until you say, 'Blessed is he who comes in the name of the Lord.'"

The Pharisees Criticize Jesus for Healing on the Sabbath

14 One Sabbath, Jesus went to eat at the home of an important Pharisee. The Pharisees were watching him very closely. There was a man present who was suffering from dropsy. They wanted to see if Jesus would heal him on the Sabbath.

3Jesus turned to the Pharisees and experts in the law who were there. He asked, "Is it all right to heal a man on the Sabbath day, or not?"

4They would not answer him. So Jesus took the sick man by the hand. Then he healed the man and sent him away.

5Then he turned to them. "Which of you doesn't work on the Sabbath?" he asked. "Suppose your cow falls into a pit. Don't you go right away to get it out?"

6Again they had no answer.

Jesus Teaches about Seeking Honor

7Jesus watched the people at the dinner. He saw how they were all trying to sit at the head of the table. So he gave them this advice: 8"Now suppose you are invited to a wedding feast. When dinnertime comes, don't always go for the best seat. For someone more respected than you might come. 9And the host will bring him over to where you are sitting. He will say, 'Let this man sit here instead.' Then you will be ashamed. And worse yet, you will have to take a seat at the foot of the table!

10"Do this instead. Sit down at the foot of the table. When your host sees you there he will come over. He will say, 'Friend, we have a better place than this for you!' Thus you will be honored in front of all the other guests. [11]For everyone who tries to honor himself will be humbled. And he who humbles himself will be honored." [12]Then he turned to his host. "When you put on a dinner," he said, "don't invite friends, brothers, relatives, and rich neighbors! For they will invite you to dinner in return. [13]Instead, invite the poor, the crippled, the lame, and the blind. [14]If you invite those who can't pay you back, you will be blessed. God will reward you at the resurrection of the godly."

A Story about a Great Feast

[15]A man sitting at the table heard what Jesus had said. He exclaimed, "What a privilege it would be to get into the Kingdom of God!"

[16]Jesus replied by telling them this story. "A man made a great feast and sent out many invitations," Jesus said. [17]"When all was ready, he sent out his servant to call his guests. [18]But they all began to make excuses. One said he had just bought a field. He asked to be excused because he wanted to look it over. [19]Another said he had just bought five pair of oxen. He wanted to go and try them out. [20]Another had just been married. And he wouldn't come for that reason.

[21]"The servant went home and told his master what they had said. His master was very angry. He told him to go quickly into the streets and alleys of the city. He was to invite the beggars, crippled, lame, and blind. [22]But even then, there was still room in the banquet hall.

[23]"'Well, then,' said his master, 'go out into the country lanes. Go out behind the hedges. Ask anyone you can find to come. That way the banquet hall will be full. [24]For none of those I invited first will be allowed to come. They won't get even the smallest taste of what I had made for them.'"

What It Means to Live for Jesus

[25]Great crowds were following Jesus, and he turned to them. [26]"Anyone who wants to be my follower must love me a great deal," he said. "In fact, he must love me far more than his own father, mother, wife, children, brothers, or sisters. Yes, he must love me more than his own life! If he doesn't, he cannot be my disciple. [27]And no one can be my disciple who does not carry his own cross and follow me.

[28]"But don't follow me until you have counted the cost. When a man builds a building, he first finds out how much it will cost. Then he checks to see if he has enough money to pay the bills. [29]Otherwise he might just finish the foundation and find he is out of money. And then everyone would laugh at him!

[30]"'See that fellow there?' they would say. 'He started that building. But he ran out of money before it was finished!'

Be humble, and God will honor you

Everyone who tries to honor himself will be humbled. And he who humbles himself will be honored.

Luke 14:11

---

[31]"When a king goes to war, he first sits down with his counselors. He talks with them about whether his army is strong enough to fight the enemy. He might have only 10,000 men, while the enemy has 20,000.

[32]"They might decide they are not strong enough to fight. If so, then he will send a team to make a peace treaty. And he will do this while the enemy is still far away. [33]So no one can become my disciple unless he first sits down and counts his blessings. Then he must give up all that he has for me.

[34]"What good is salt that has lost its saltiness? [35]Flavorless salt is fit for nothing. It isn't even good for fertilizing the ground. It is worthless and must be

thrown away. Listen well if you want to understand what I mean."

A Story about a Lost Sheep

15 Now tax collectors and other sinners often came to listen to Jesus' sermons. ²But the Pharisees and the experts on Jewish law complained about this. "This man spends time with sinners," they said. "He even eats with them!"

³-⁴So Jesus told a story. "Now suppose you had 100 sheep," Jesus began. "And suppose one of them ran away and was lost in the wilderness. If this happened, wouldn't you leave the 99 others? Wouldn't you go and look for the lost one until you found it? ⁵And then you would joyfully carry it home on your shoulders. ⁶When you got home you would call together your friends and neighbors. You would have a party because your lost sheep was found.

⁷"Well, the same thing happens in Heaven. There is great joy in Heaven over one lost sinner who comes back to God. In fact, there is more joy over that one than over the 99 others who haven't run away!

A Story about a Coin

A woman loses a coin. She wouldn't miss just one, would she? Why bother to find it? Let's see what this woman does.

8"Or suppose a woman has 10 silver coins and loses one. Won't she light a lamp and look in every corner of the house? Won't she sweep out every corner until she finds it? 9And then won't she call in her friends and neighbors to rejoice with her? 10In the same way there is joy among the angels of God when one sinner repents."

- *Remember:* How many coins did the woman have? How many did she lose? (15:8) Did she try to find her lost coin? (15:8) What did she do when she found it? (15:9) What does this have to do with angels? (15:10) Do you think the angels sing when you please God?

- *Discover:* When one person accepts Jesus, the angels are joyful. So is Jesus! Why is that?

- *Apply:* Would you like to bring great joy in Heaven? You can! Help a friend know about Jesus.

- *What's next?* A man has two sons. One runs away. What will happen when he decides to come back? Read Jesus' story about this in Luke 15:11-32. ■

A Story about Two Boys

Once upon a time there were two boys. One ran away. The other stayed home to help his father. Do you think the father hated the one who ran away and loved the one who stayed home? Let's see.

11Jesus continued, "There was a man who had two sons. 12The younger told his father, 'I want my share of your wealth now. I don't want to wait until you are dead!' So his father agreed to divide his wealth between his sons.

13"A few days later this younger son packed all his belongings. He took a trip to a faraway land. And there he wasted all his money on parties and prostitutes. 14Before long, all his money was gone. And about that time a great famine swept over the land. So he began to starve. 15He begged a local farmer to hire him to feed his pigs. 16And the boy was so hungry that even the pods he was feeding the pigs looked good. But no one gave him anything to eat.

17"Then he finally came to his senses. He said to himself, 'At home even the hired men have enough food. They even have more than they need! And here I am, dying of hunger! 18I will go home to my father. "Father," I will say. "I have sinned against both Heaven and you. 19I am no longer worthy of being called your son. Please take me on as a hired man."'

20"So he went back home to his father. And while he was still a long way off, his father saw him coming. His father was filled with loving pity. He ran out to meet his son. He hugged him and kissed him.

21"His son said to him, 'Father, I have sinned against Heaven and you. I am not worthy of being called your son.'

22"But his father said to the slaves, 'Quick! Bring the finest robe in the house. Put it on him. And bring a jeweled ring for his finger. Bring shoes, too! 23And kill the calf we have in the fattening pen. We must have a feast! 24For this son of mine was dead. But now he has come back to life. He was lost. But now he is found.' And so the party began.

25"Meanwhile, the older son was in the fields working. When he came back home, he heard dance music coming from the house. 26He asked one of the servants what was going on.

²⁷"'Your brother has come back,' he was told. 'And your father has killed the calf we were fattening. He has made a great feast to celebrate his coming home again unharmed.'

²⁸"The older brother was angry and wouldn't go in. His father came out and begged him to come in. ²⁹But the son replied, 'All these years I've worked hard for you. I have never once refused to do a single thing you told me to. And you never gave me even one young goat for a feast with my friends. ³⁰Yet this son of yours comes home. And he has spent much of your money on prostitutes. But you throw a great party! You kill the finest calf we have on the place!'

³¹"'Look, dear son,' his father said to him. 'You and I are very close. Everything I have is yours! ³²But it is right to have a party. For he is your brother. And he was dead and has come back to life! He was lost and is found!'"

- *Remember:* What did the younger son want from his father? Did the father do it? (15:11-12) What did this son do with the money? (15:13) Why did he go home? (15:14-20) How did his father receive him? (15:20-24) Why did the father celebrate? Why did he do something special for the runaway son? (15:32) What does this story tell you about how God forgives us?

- *Discover:* God is happy when a lost person comes back to him. He will receive that person with joy.

- *Apply:* There is a story in the newspaper. It is about a person who has done something terrible. If that person asks God to forgive him, will God do it? Will God accept him? Yes, he will.

- *What's next?* Can a person come back from Heaven to earth? Luke 16:19-31 tells us what Jesus said. ■

A Story about a Shrewd Accountant

16 Jesus now told this story to his disciples. "A rich man hired a manager to handle his affairs," Jesus began. "But soon a rumor went around that the manager was not honest.

²"So his employer called him in. 'What's this I hear about your stealing from me?' he asked. 'Get your report in order. For you are no longer my manager.'

³"The manager thought to himself, 'Now what? I can't work here anymore. I don't have the strength to go out and dig ditches. And I'm too proud to beg. ⁴I know just the thing! And then I'll have plenty of friends to take care of me when I leave!'

⁵⁻⁶"So he asked each one who owed money to his employer to come. He wanted to talk with them about the money they owed. He asked the first one, 'How much do you owe him?' 'My debt is 850 gallons of olive oil,' the man replied. 'Yes, here is the contract you signed,' the manager told him. 'Tear it up and write another one for half that much!'

⁷"'And how much do you owe him?' he asked the next man. 'A thousand bushels of wheat,' was the reply. 'Here,' the manager said. 'Take your note and replace it with one for only 800 bushels!'

⁸"The rich man had to admire the manager for being so smart. And it is true that the people of this world are more clever at cheating than the godly are. ⁹But shall I tell you to act that way? Shall I tell you to buy friendship through cheating? Will this make sure that you enter an everlasting home in Heaven? ¹⁰No! For unless you are honest in small matters, you won't be in large ones. If you cheat even a little, you won't be honest with greater things. ¹¹And if you can't be trusted with worldly riches, who will trust you with heavenly ones? ¹²And if you don't use other people's money wisely, why should you be trusted with money of your own?

You Cannot Love Both God and Money

¹³"For neither you nor anyone else can serve two masters. You will hate one and show loyalty to the other. You will love one and hate the other. You cannot serve both God and money."

¹⁴The Pharisees laughed at this teaching. For they dearly loved their money.

Do you want to learn to be honest? Start now with little things each day

Unless you are honest in small matters, you won't be in large ones.

Luke 16:10

---

¹⁵Then he said to them, "You act like you are pious in front of others. But God knows your evil hearts. Pretending you are holy brings you honor from the people. But God hates it when you just pretend to be holy. ¹⁶Before John the Baptist, the laws of Moses and the words of the prophets were your guides. But John told you the Good News that the Kingdom of God would come soon. And now many people are pressing to enter the Kingdom. ¹⁷But that doesn't mean that the Law has lost its force in even the smallest point. It is as strong and unshakable as heaven and earth.

¹⁸"So anyone who divorces his wife and marries someone else commits adultery. And anyone who marries a divorced woman commits adultery."

The Rich Man and Poor Lazarus

Can a person in Heaven come back to earth? Jesus tells us about some of these things.

¹⁹"There was a certain rich man," Jesus said. "He wore fancy clothes. And he lived each day in laughter and luxury. ²⁰One day Lazarus, a sick beggar, was laid at his door. ²¹He lay there wishing for scraps from the rich man's table. And

the dogs would come and lick his open sores. ²²Finally the beggar died. He was carried by the angels to be with Abraham. He was brought to the place of the righteous dead. The rich man also died and was buried. ²³But his soul went into hell. There, in torment, he saw Lazarus far away with Abraham.

²⁴"'Father Abraham!' the rich man shouted. 'Have some pity on me! Send Lazarus over here. Let him dip his finger in water to cool my tongue. For I am in great pain here in these flames.'

²⁵"But Abraham said to him, 'Son, remember how it was when you were living? You had everything you wanted, but Lazarus had nothing. So now he is here being comforted. But you are in great pain. ²⁶And besides, there is a great canyon that lies between us. Anyone wanting to come to you from here is stopped at its edge. And no one over there can cross to us.'

²⁷"Then the rich man said, 'O Father Abraham! Then please send him to my father's home. ²⁸For I have five brothers. Please warn them about this place of pain and suffering. That way they won't have to come here when they die.'

²⁹"But Abraham said, 'The Scriptures have warned them again and again. Your brothers can read them any time they want to.'

³⁰"The rich man replied, 'No, Father Abraham! They won't bother to read them. But if someone is sent from the dead, then they will turn from their sins.'

³¹"But Abraham said, 'They won't listen to Moses and the prophets. And they won't listen to someone who rises from the dead either.'"

- *Remember:* What did the rich man do with his money? Did he help others? (16:19-21) What happened to the beggar when he died? (16:22) Jesus was saying that the beggar went to Heaven. Where did the rich man go when he died? (16:23) What is between Heaven and hell? Can anyone in hell visit Heaven? Can anyone in Heaven visit hell? (16:26) The rich man begged for Lazarus to warn his brothers. Why didn't he? (16:27-31) What warns us about hell? What if a person came back from the dead? Would people listen to him more than the Bible? Jesus said they wouldn't.

- *Discover:* The Bible warns us about hell. It tells us how to get to Heaven. Read it! Listen to it!

- *Apply:* How often do you read your Bible? Do you try to learn what God says? Do you try to learn what he says to you?

- *What's next?* Must someone thank you for everything you do? Listen to what Jesus says in Luke 17:1-10. ■

A Story about a Servant

Do you expect to be thanked for each thing you do? Jesus talks here about times we shouldn't expect to be thanked.

17"There will always be things that tempt people to sin," Jesus said to his disciples. "But how terrible it will be for the man who does the tempting! ²⁻³For such a man will face a terrible punishment! It would be far better for him to be thrown into the sea with a rock tied to his neck. Yes, great trouble will be in store for those who harm these little children's souls. I am warning you!

"Rebuke your brother if he sins. But forgive him if he is sorry. ⁴He might even wrong you seven times a day. And each time he might turn again and ask you to forgive him. If this happens, then forgive him."

⁵One day the apostles said to the Lord, "We need more faith. Tell us how to get it."

⁶"Suppose your faith were only the size of a mustard seed," Jesus said. "If so, then it would be large enough to pull up

that mulberry tree over there. And it could send that tree flying into the sea! Your command would bring results right away! ⁷⁻⁹And suppose a servant comes in from plowing a field. Or perhaps he was taking care of the sheep. This servant doesn't just sit down and eat. But first, he cooks his master's meal and serves him his supper. Then he sits down to eat his own. And he is not even thanked for this. This is because he is just doing his duty. ¹⁰In the same way, if you obey me, you should not expect praise. For you have simply done your duty!"

● *Remember:* When the servant did the work he was supposed to do, was he thanked? (17:7-9) When we obey Jesus, as we are supposed to do, should we expect thanks? Why not? (17:10) Do you thank your parents every day for all the things they do? Do you expect them to thank you for everything you do?

● *Discover:* It's nice to say thanks. It's nice to be thanked. But don't expect to be thanked for doing what you should do.

● *Apply:* Make a list of things you should do each day. It would be nice if you were thanked for doing these things. But don't expect to be thanked for some of these things you do.

● *What's next?* A man has been dead several days. Suddenly he comes back to life again. How could that happen? Read John 11:1-53. ■

Jesus Heals Ten Lepers

Suppose you had a terrible disease. You had to stay away from your home. You could not be near your family. How would you feel? But suppose someone healed you? Shouldn't something so wonderful cause you to say thank you?

¹¹Jesus and his disciples continued their journey toward Jerusalem. They came to the border between Galilee and Samaria. ¹²And as they entered a village there, 10 lepers stood at a distance. ¹³They cried out, "Jesus, sir, have mercy on us!"

¹⁴He looked at them and said, "Go to the Jewish priest. Show him that you are healed!" And as they were going, their leprosy left them.

¹⁵One of them came back to Jesus. He shouted, "Glory to God, I'm healed!" ¹⁶He fell flat on the ground in front of Jesus. His face was down in the dust. He thanked Jesus for what he had done. This man was a hated Samaritan.

¹⁷Jesus asked, "Didn't I heal 10 men? Where are the other nine? ¹⁸Does only this Samaritan come to give glory to God?"

¹⁹And Jesus said to the man, "Stand up and go. Your faith has made you well."

● *Remember:* How many lepers asked Jesus to heal them? (17:12) Did Jesus touch them or speak to them? What did he say? (17:14) Were they healed? When? (17:14) How many thanked Jesus? How many did not thank him? (17:15-17) Why do you think the one man thanked Jesus? Why did the nine not thank him?

● *Discover:* We should thank God for special gifts. Why? Because it is a way to tell God how happy we are to receive his gifts.

● *Apply:* Make a list of special gifts God has given you. Did you remember sunshine, rain, clothing, food, your home, and your family? Now thank God for each one.

● *What's next?* Two men prayed in God's house. One did not say a good prayer. One did. What was the difference? Read Luke 18:9-14. ■

When Jesus Returns, What Will the World Be Like?

²⁰One day the Pharisees came to Jesus. They asked him, "When will the Kingdom of God begin?" Jesus replied, "The Kingdom of God can't be seen by looking for visible signs. ²¹You won't be able to say, 'The Kingdom has begun here in this place. Or it is there in that part of the country.' For the Kingdom of God is within you."

²²Later he talked again about this with his disciples. "The time is coming when you will long for me to be with you even for a single day," he said. "But I won't be here. ²³Reports will reach you that I have come back. People will say that I am in this place or that. But don't believe them or go out to look for me. ²⁴For when I come back, you will know it beyond all doubt. It will be as clear as lightning flashing across the sky. ²⁵But first I must suffer terribly. And I will be rejected by this whole nation.

²⁶"When I come back, the world will not be thinking about the things of God. They will be like the people were in Noah's day. ²⁷They ate and drank and married right up to the day when Noah went into the ark. Then the flood came and destroyed them all.

²⁸"And the world will be as it was in the days of Lot. People went about their daily business. They kept on eating and drinking, buying and selling, farming and building. ²⁹They did this right up until the morning Lot left Sodom. Then fire and brimstone rained down from Heaven and destroyed them all. ³⁰Yes, it will be 'business as usual' right up to the hour of my coming.

³¹"Those away from home that day must not go home to pack. Those in the fields must not go back to town. ³²Remember what happened to Lot's wife! ³³Whoever holds on to his life shall lose it. And whoever loses his life shall save it. ³⁴That night two men will be asleep in the same room. One will be taken away. The other will be left behind. ³⁵⁻³⁶Two women will be working together at household tasks. One will be taken. The other will be left behind. And so it will be with men working side by side in the fields."

³⁷"Lord, where will they be taken?" the disciples asked.

Jesus replied, "Where a dead body is, the vultures gather!"

A Story about a Persistent Widow

18 One day Jesus told his disciples a story. He did this to show them their need for constant prayer. He also wanted to show that they must keep praying until the answer comes.

²"There was a city judge," Jesus began. "He was a godless man who had great hate for everyone. ³A widow of that city came to him often. She always asked him for justice against a man who had harmed her. ⁴⁻⁵The judge did not listen to her for quite some time. But after awhile, she got on his nerves.

"'I don't fear God or man,' the judge said to himself. 'But this woman bothers me. I'm going to see that she gets justice. For she is wearing me out with her constant coming!'"

⁶Then the Lord said, "You see that even an evil judge can be worn down. ⁷So don't you think God will give justice to his people who beg with him? ⁸Yes! He will answer them quickly! But I wonder about this: I, the Messiah, will come back someday. But how many will I find who have faith and are still praying?"

When Two Men Prayed

One day two men went into God's house to pray. They said two different prayers. One was a good prayer. The other was not. Why was one not good?

⁹Then Jesus told a story to some people who bragged that they were godly. These people were proud and looked down on everyone else.

¹⁰"Two men went to the Temple to pray," Jesus said. "One was a proud, self-righteous Pharisee. The other was a cheating tax collector. ¹¹The proud Pharisee 'prayed' this prayer: 'Thank God, I am not a sinner like everyone else!

Thank God, I am not like that tax collector over there! For I never cheat. I don't commit adultery. [12]I go without food twice a week. And I give to God a tenth of all the money I earn.'

[13]"But the corrupt tax collector stood at a distance. He did not even dare to lift his eyes to Heaven as he prayed. But he beat his chest in sadness. And he said, 'God, be merciful to me, a sinner!' [14]I tell you, this sinner, not the Pharisee, went home forgiven! For the proud shall be humbled. But the humble shall be honored."

- *Remember:* What kind of person was the Pharisee? (18:10) What did he pray? (18:11-12) What kind of person was the tax collector? (18:10,13) What did he pray? (18:13) Which person was forgiven? Why? (18:14) What did you learn from these two prayers? What kind of prayer does God want to hear?

- *Discover:* We should not tell God how good we are. He knows better. We should beg him to forgive us for the bad things we do.

- *Apply:* Today when you pray, think about what you say to God. Are you bragging about how good you are? Are you complaining about how bad others are? Are you asking God to forgive you and to help you be the best person you can be for him?

- *What's next?* Some people try to chase children away from Jesus. Why? Read Mark 10:13-16. ■

Jesus Loves Children

[15]One day some mothers brought their babies to him to touch and bless. But the disciples told them to go away.

[16-17]Then Jesus called the children over to him. And he said to the disciples, "Let the little children come to me! Never send them away! For the Kingdom of God belongs to people who have hearts like these little children's. And those who don't have their kind of faith will never get into the Kingdom."

Jesus and the Rich Young Man

"What shall I do to get to Heaven?" a man asked. How would you answer? This is what Jesus said.

[18]Once a Jewish religious leader came to Jesus. He asked, "Good sir, what shall I do to get to Heaven?"

[19]"Do you know what you are saying when you call me 'good'?" Jesus asked him. "Only God is truly good, and no one else.

[20]"But as to your question, you know what the Ten Commandments say. Don't commit adultery. Don't murder. Don't steal. Don't lie. Honor your parents. And you know the other laws, too."
[21]The man replied, "I've obeyed every one of these laws since I was a small child."

[22]"There is still one thing you need to do," Jesus said. "Sell all you have and give the money to the poor. This will become treasure for you in Heaven. Then come and follow me."

[23]But when the man heard this he went sadly away. For he was very rich.

[24]Jesus watched the man go. Then he turned to his disciples. "How hard it is for the rich to enter the Kingdom of God!" he said. [25]"It is very hard for a camel to go through the eye of a needle. But it is even harder for a rich man to enter the Kingdom of God."

[26]Those who heard this asked, "If it is that hard, how can anyone be saved?"

[27]He replied, "God can do what men can't!"

[28]And Peter said, "We have left our homes and followed you."

[29-30]"Yes, you have," Jesus replied. "All who have done as you have will be paid back many times over. You will also receive eternal life in the world to come. For you have left home, wife, brothers, parents, and children. And you have done this for the sake of the Kingdom of God."

- *Remember:* Only one person is really good. Who is that? (18:19) How many of the Ten Commandments had this man obeyed? (18:21) What else did Jesus tell the man to do? (18:22) Did the man do what Jesus said? Why not? (18:23) What did Jesus say about this man? (18:24-25) Would you like to say something to this young man? What would you say?

- *Discover:* Don't let your things become more important to you than God.

- *Apply:* What is your favorite thing? If God asked you to give it up, could you? Would you? If something is more important to you than God, then you don't love God as much as you should. What can you do to show God you love him most?

- *What's next?* Is it fair to pay one person more than another for the same work? Read what Jesus said about this in Matthew 20:1-16. ◼

Jesus Predicts His Death for the Third Time

31Then Jesus called his 12 disciples together around him. He said to them, "As you know, we are going to Jerusalem. And when we get there, all the words of the prophets about me will come true. 32I will be handed over to the Gentiles to be laughed at. I will be treated badly and spat upon. 33I will be whipped and then killed. And on the third day I will rise again."

34But they didn't understand what he was saying. They thought he was just talking in riddles.

Jesus Heals a Blind Man

35As they came to Jericho, a blind man was sitting beside the road. He was begging from the travelers who went by. 36When he heard the noise of a crowd going past, he asked what was happening. 37He was told that Jesus from Nazareth was going by. 38So he began shouting, "Jesus, Son of David! Have mercy on me!"

39The crowds ahead of Jesus tried to quiet the man. But he only yelled the louder, "Son of David! Have mercy on me!"

40When Jesus got there, he stopped. "Bring the blind man over here," he said. 41Then Jesus asked the man, "What do you want?"

"Lord," he begged, "I want to see!"

42And Jesus said, "All right, begin seeing! Your faith has healed you."

43Right away the man could see, and he followed Jesus, praising God. And all the people who saw it happen praised God, too.

Jesus Gives Zacchaeus a New Life

Have you ever climbed up into a tree? Sometimes it's fun, isn't it? Here's a story about a man who climbed up into a tree. He didn't do it to have fun. Let's see why he did it.

19 Jesus went into Jericho and was passing through the town. A man named Zacchaeus lived there. He was a chief tax collector for the Romans and was very rich. 3He wanted to get a look at Jesus. But he was too short to see over the crowds. 4So he ran ahead and climbed into a sycamore tree beside the road. For he knew that Jesus would be passing that way.

5When Jesus came by, he looked up at Zacchaeus and called him by name! "Zacchaeus!" he said. "Quick! Come down! For I am going to be a guest in your home today!"

6Zacchaeus climbed down quickly! And he took Jesus to his house with great joy.

7But the crowds were angry. "He has gone to be the guest of a terrible sinner!" they said.

⁸Meanwhile, Zacchaeus stood before the Lord. He said, "Sir, from now on I will give half my wealth to the poor. Also, I might find I have charged someone too much for his taxes. If so, I will give him back four times as much as I took!"

⁹⁻¹⁰Jesus told him, "This shows that salvation has come to this home today. This man was one of the lost sons of Abraham. And I, the Messiah, have come to look for and to save such souls as his."

- *Remember:* What kind of work did Zacchaeus do? (19:1-2) Why couldn't Zacchaeus see Jesus? (19:3) Why did he climb a tree? (19:4) What did Jesus say to Zacchaeus? (19:5) Who was happy about this? Who wasn't happy? (19:6-7) How did Zacchaeus change? How did he show that he had changed? (19:8-10)

When Zacchaeus believed in Jesus, something happened! He changed the way he lived. Why do you think that was important?

- *Discover:* When we believe in Jesus, we should live differently. We should do things that are good and that please Jesus.

- *Apply:* Have you accepted Jesus as your Savior? Are you living the way Jesus wants? Are you doing some things Jesus does not like? What should you do about these things?

- *What's next?* A man becomes governor by using $2,000 the right way. Read Luke 19:11-27. ■

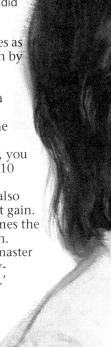

A Story about Investing

Suppose someone gave you the job of taking $2,000 and making more money from it. What would you do? This is a story about 10 men and what they did when they were given this job.

¹¹As they were listening Jesus told them a story. He told it because he was getting near to Jerusalem. And he wanted to make it clear that the Kingdom of God would not begin right away.

¹²"There once was a man of noble birth," Jesus said. "He was living in a certain province. But he was called away to the distant capital of the empire. While there, he was to be crowned king of his province. ¹³Before he left he called together 10 servants. He gave them each $2,000 to invest while he was gone. ¹⁴But some of his people hated him, so they sent him a message. They said they had turned against him and would not let him be their king. ¹⁵When he came back, he called in the men to whom he had given the money. He wanted to find out what they had done with it, and how much money they had made.

¹⁶"The first man had done very well.

He had made 10 times as much as he was given by the king!

¹⁷"'Fine!' the king exclaimed. 'You are a good man. You have been faithful with the little I gave to you. Now, as your reward, you shall be governor of 10 cities.'

¹⁸"The next man also reported an excellent gain. He had made five times the amount he was given.

¹⁹"'All right!' his master said. 'You can be governor over five cities.'

²⁰"But the third man brought back only the money he had started

with. 'I've kept it safe,' he said. ²¹'I did this because I was afraid you would demand my profits. For you are a hard man to deal with. You take what isn't yours and even take the crops that others plant.' ²²'You vile and wicked slave!' the king roared. 'Hard, am I? That's exactly how I'll be toward you! You say you know all about me. You say I am so hard. ²³If you thought this, then why didn't you put the money in the bank? That way I could at least get some interest on it!'

²⁴"Then turning to the others standing by he ordered, 'Take the money away from him. Give it to the man who earned the most.'

²⁵"'But, sir,' they said, 'he has enough already!'

²⁶"'Yes,' the king replied, 'but those who have will get more. And those who have little soon lose even that. ²⁷And now about these enemies of mine who broke from my rule. Bring them in and kill them in front of me.'"

- *Remember:* How much money did the nobleman give his assistants? (19:13) How many men received the money? What did he want the men to do with the money? (19:12-13) The man became king. He came back. He asked the 10 men to come to him. He asked what they did with the money. But how many men came? (19:16-20) Where were the other seven men? (19:14) What happened to the men who did what they should have with his money? (19:16-19) What happened to the man who did nothing? (19:20-24) What happened to the seven who kept the money? (19:27) This is a story about wise investing. It's a story about using wisely what God gives us.

- *Discover:* God gives us many special gifts. But he expects us to use them wisely for him. He expects us to share what he has given us with others, to help them or to bring them some happiness. This is how the things you have become more valuable.

- *Apply:* Make a list of God's good gifts to you. Beside each one write how you use it wisely for God. Then write how you should use it better for him.

- *What's next?* A man rides on a donkey. People throw their coats on the ground. They want him to ride over the coats. Why? Read Matthew 21:1-11. ∎

Jesus Rides into Jerusalem on a Donkey

²⁸After telling this story, Jesus went on toward Jerusalem. He walked along ahead of his disciples. ²⁹They came to the towns of Bethphage and Bethany, on the Mount of Olives. From there, Jesus sent two disciples on ahead. ³⁰He told them to go to the next village. And when they got there they were to look for a donkey tied beside the road. It would be a colt, not yet broken for riding.

"Untie him," Jesus said, "and bring him here. ³¹Someone might ask you what you are doing. If this happens, just say, 'The Lord needs him.'"

³²They found the colt just as Jesus said they would. ³³And as they were untying it, the owners stopped them.

"What are you doing?" they asked. "Why are you untying our colt?"

³⁴And the disciples simply replied, "The Lord needs him!" ³⁵So they brought the colt to Jesus. And they threw some of their clothing across its back for Jesus to sit on.

³⁶⁻³⁷Then the crowds spread out their robes along the road ahead of him. They came to the place where the road started down from the Mount of Olives. And there, the whole crowd began to shout and sing as they walked along. They praised God for all the great miracles Jesus had done.

³⁸"God has given us a King!" they shouted. "Long live the King! Let all Heaven rejoice! Glory to God in the highest Heavens!"

³⁹But there were some Pharisees in the crowd. They said to Jesus, "Sir, tell your followers to stop saying things like that!"

⁴⁰He replied, "I might tell them to keep quiet. But if I did, the stones along the road would burst into cheers!"

⁴¹Jesus and the crowd came closer and closer to Jerusalem. And when Jesus saw the city ahead, he began to cry. ⁴²"Eternal peace was within your reach," he cried. "But you turned it down and now it is too late. ⁴³Your enemies will pile up earth against your walls. They will surround you and close in on you. ⁴⁴They will crush you to the ground, and your

children within you. Your enemies will not leave one stone upon another. For you have rejected the chance God gave you."

Jesus Clears the Temple

⁴⁵Then he went into the Temple. And he began to drive out the merchants from their stalls. ⁴⁶He said to them, "The Scriptures say, 'My Temple is a place of prayer.' But you have turned it into a den of thieves!"

⁴⁷After that he taught in the Temple every day. The chief priests and other leaders were trying to find some way to get rid of him. ⁴⁸But they couldn't think of a way to stop him. This was because he was a hero to the people. The crowd listened to every word he said.

The Religious Leaders Challenge Jesus' Authority

20 One day Jesus was teaching and preaching the Good News in the Temple. And the chief priests and other religious leaders came to speak with him. ²They wanted to know how Jesus had the right to send the merchants from the Temple.

³"I'll ask you a question before I answer," he replied. ⁴"Was John sent by God, or was he just acting under his own authority?"

⁵They talked it over among themselves. "If we say John's message was from Heaven, then we are trapped. For he will ask, 'Then why didn't you believe him?' ⁶But if we say John was not sent from God, the people will mob us. For they are sure that he was a prophet." ⁷Finally they replied, "We don't know!"

⁸And Jesus said to them, "Then I won't answer your question either."

A Story about Wicked Farmers

⁹Now he turned to the people again and told them a story. "A man planted a vineyard and rented it out to some farmers," Jesus said. "Then he went away to a distant land to live for several years. ¹⁰When harvesttime came, he sent one of his men to the farm. He was to collect the owner's share of the crops. But the tenants beat him up and sent him back

empty-handed. ¹¹Then he sent another, but the same thing happened. He was beaten up and insulted and sent away with nothing. ¹²A third man was sent and the same thing happened. He, too, was wounded and chased away.

¹³"'What shall I do?' the owner asked himself. 'I know! I'll send my son. Surely they will show respect for him.'

¹⁴"But when the tenants saw his son, they said, 'This is our chance! This fellow will inherit all the land when his father dies. Come on! Let's kill him! Then it will be ours.' ¹⁵So they dragged him out of the vineyard and killed him.

"What do you think the owner will do? ¹⁶I'll tell you! He will come and kill them and rent the vineyard to others."

"But they would never do a thing like that," his listeners said.

¹⁷Then Jesus looked at them. He said, "Then what does the Scripture mean? For it says, 'The Stone rejected by the builders was made the cornerstone.'" ¹⁸And he added, "Whoever stumbles over that Stone shall be broken. And those on whom it falls will be crushed to dust."

¹⁹The chief priests and religious leaders heard about this story he had told. And they wanted to arrest him right away. For they knew that he was talking about them. They were the wicked tenants in his story. But they were afraid that if they arrested him, there would be a riot. So they tried to trick him into saying something that would get him in trouble. They hoped he would say something that would give the Roman governor a reason to arrest him.

The Religious Leaders Try to Trick Jesus

²⁰So they watched for their chance. And they sent secret agents pretending to be honest men. ²¹They said to Jesus, "Sir, we know what an honest teacher you are. You always tell the truth. You don't budge an inch in the face of what others think. You just teach the ways of God. ²²Now tell us this. Is it right to pay taxes to the Roman government or not?"

²³He saw that they were trying to trick him. So he said, ²⁴"Show me a coin.

Whose portrait is this on it? And whose name?"

They replied, "It is Caesar's portrait and name."

²⁵He said, "Then give Caesar all that is his. And give to God all that belongs to him!"

²⁶So this attempt at tricking him before the people failed. They were amazed at his answer, and were silent.

More Trick Questions for Jesus

²⁷⁻²⁸Then some Sadducees came to Jesus with another question. The Sadducees believed that there was no life after death. They didn't believe in the resurrection of the dead. They said to Jesus, "The laws of Moses include a law for a man who dies without children. This law says that the man's brother must marry the widow. Then their children will belong to the dead man and carry on his name. ²⁹We know of a family of seven brothers. The oldest married and then died without any children. ³⁰His brother married the widow. But then he, too, died. There were still no children. ³¹And so it went, one after the other. Each of the seven married her and died, leaving no children. ³²Finally the woman died also. ³³Now here is our question. Whose wife will she be in the resurrection? For all of them were married to her!"

³⁴⁻³⁵Jesus replied, "Marriage is for people here on earth. But when those who are raised from the dead get to Heaven, they will not marry. ³⁶And they will never die again. In these ways they are like angels and are sons of God. For they are raised up in new life from the dead.

³⁷⁻³⁸"But your real question is about the resurrection. You don't believe people will rise from the dead. Yet even the writings of Moses himself prove this! Haven't you read about the time when Moses saw the burning bush? There, Moses speaks of God as 'the God of Abraham, the God of Isaac, and the God of Jacob.' To say that the Lord is someone's God means that person is alive, not dead! So from God's point of view, all men are living."

³⁹"Well said, sir!" remarked some of the experts in the Jewish law. ⁴⁰And that ended all their questions. They didn't dare to ask him any more!

⁴¹Then he asked them a question. "Why is it," he asked, "that the Messiah is said to be a descendant of King David? ⁴²⁻⁴³For David himself wrote in the Book of Psalms: 'God said to my Lord, the Messiah, "Sit at my right hand. And I will put your enemies under your feet."' ⁴⁴How can the Messiah be both David's son and David's Lord at the same time?"

⁴⁵Then, with the crowds listening, he turned to his disciples. ⁴⁶"Beware of these experts in religion," he said. "For they love to walk around in fancy robes. They love it when the people bow to them as they walk along the street. And how they love the seats of honor in the synagogues and at feasts! ⁴⁷They pray long prayers with great outward piety. But at the same time, they make plans to cheat widows out of their property. So God's heaviest judgment will be given to these men."

The Widow's Small Coins

A widow gives two small copper coins to God. Some rich men gave lots of money. But Jesus said her coins were worth more. Why?

21 Now Jesus was standing in the Temple. He was watching the rich putting their gifts into the offering box. ²Then a poor widow came by. She dropped in two small copper coins.

³"I tell you the truth," he said. "This poor widow has given more than all the rest of them put together. ⁴For they have given a little of what they didn't need. But she, poor as she is, has given all she has."

- *Remember:* Where was Jesus? What was he watching there? (21:1) What did the poor widow give? (21:2) Why did she give more than the rich men? (21:4) What would you like to say to these rich men? What should they do?

- *Discover:* We give more to God when we give our best to God.

- *Apply:* Do you give your best to God? Or do you give your worst? Do you spend your best time with TV? Or do you spend it with God?

- *What's next?* Why would a lady pour perfume on Jesus' feet? Read John 12:1-11. ■

Jesus Describes the Future

5Some of his disciples began talking about the stonework of the Temple. They were taken with the beautiful decorations on the walls.

6But Jesus said, "Soon all these things will be knocked down. Not one stone will be left on top of another. All of it will become one great pile of rubble."

7"Master!" they exclaimed. "When? And will there be any warning ahead of time?"

8He replied, "Don't let anyone trick you. For many will come claiming they are the Messiah. They will say, 'The time has come.' But don't believe them! 9And when you hear of wars beginning, don't worry.

True, wars must come, but the end won't follow right away. 10For nation shall rise against nation and kingdom against kingdom. 11And there will be great earthquakes. There will be famines in many lands. There will be many plagues. And terrifying things will happen in the heavens.

12"But before this happens, there will be a time of great persecution. You will be dragged into synagogues and prisons. You will be taken before kings and governors for my name's sake. 13But as a result, the Messiah will be widely known and honored. 14So don't be worried about how to answer the charges against you. 15For I will give you the right words. None of your enemies will be able to reply! 16Even those closest to you will betray you. This might include your parents, brothers, relatives, and friends. They will have you arrested, and some of you will be killed. 17And everyone will hate you because you are mine and are called by my name. 18But not a hair of your head

will be destroyed! ¹⁹For if you stand firm, you will win your souls.

²⁰"But you will see Jerusalem surrounded by armies. And then you will know that the time of her destruction has come. ²¹Then let the people of Judea run to the hills. Let those in Jerusalem try to get away. And if you are outside the city, don't try to come back. ²²For those will be days of God's judgment. And the words written by the prophets will be fulfilled. ²³How terrible it will be for pregnant women in those days! How terrible it will be for those with tiny babies! For there will be great trouble upon this nation. And great anger will be directed at this people. ²⁴They will be brutally killed by enemy weapons. Or they will be sent away as exiles and captives. They will be taken to all the nations of the world. And Jerusalem shall be conquered and trampled down by the Gentiles. This shall continue until the period of Gentile triumph ends in God's good time.

²⁵"Then there will be strange events in the skies. There will be warnings and evil signs. There will be signs in the sun, moon, and stars. And down here on earth the nations will be in turmoil. They will be confused by the roaring seas and strange tides. ²⁶The courage of many people will break down. For they shall see the terrible fate coming upon the earth. The very heavens will be shaken up. ²⁷Then the peoples of the earth shall see me! I, the Messiah, shall come in a cloud with power and great glory. ²⁸So when all these things begin to happen, stand straight and look up! For your salvation is near."

²⁹Then he said, "Notice the fig tree, or any other tree. ³⁰When the leaves come out, you know without being told that summer is near. ³¹In the same way, you will see these things happening. And when you do, you will know the Kingdom of God is near.

³²"I tell you the truth. When these things happen, the end of this age has come. ³³All heaven and earth shall pass away. But my words remain forever true.

No One Knows When Jesus Will Return

³⁴⁻³⁵"Watch out! Don't let my sudden coming catch you when you aren't ready. Don't let me find you living in careless ease like all the rest of the world. Don't let me find you partying and drinking. Don't let me find you tied up with the problems of this life. ³⁶Keep on watching for me. And pray that you may come to my presence without having to suffer these things."

³⁷⁻³⁸Every day Jesus went to the Temple to teach. And the crowds began gathering early in the morning to hear him. Then each evening he went back to the Mount of Olives. It was there that he spent the night.

Religious Leaders Plan to Kill Jesus

22 And now the Passover Feast was drawing near. At this Jewish feast, only bread made without yeast was eaten. ²The chief priests and other religious leaders were actively planning Jesus' murder. They were trying to find a way to kill him without starting a riot. And they were very afraid this would happen if they tried to kill him.

Judas Agrees to Betray Jesus

Do you have a good friend? You wouldn't sell your friend, would you? Jesus had a friend. His name was Judas. Some men wanted to kill Jesus. They paid Judas to help them. This is what happened.

³Then Satan entered into Judas Iscariot. He was one of the 12 disciples. ⁴And Judas went over to the chief priests and captains of the Temple guards. He talked with them about the best way to betray Jesus to them. ⁵They were, of course,

happy to know that he was ready to help them. And they promised to give him a reward. 6So he began to look for a chance for them to arrest Jesus quietly. They would have to do it when the crowds weren't around.

- *Remember:* Who came into Judas? (22:3) Who did Judas visit? What did these people want to do to Jesus? (22:4-6) What do you think of Judas? What would you say if he wanted to be your friend?

- *Discover:* A friend who hurts you is not really a friend.

- *Apply:* Is there someone who tries to hurt you? Do you ever try to hurt someone else? That's not being a good friend. Good friends try to do good things for others. Do you?

- *What's next?* Jesus eats his last meal with his disciples. Read Mark 14:12-31. ■

The Disciples Prepare for the Passover

7Now the day of the Passover Feast came. This is when the Passover lamb was killed and eaten with the unleavened bread. 8Jesus sent Peter and John ahead to find a place to make their Passover meal.

9"Where do you want us to go?" they asked.

10And he replied, "Go into Jerusalem. You will see a man walking along carrying a pitcher of water. Follow this man into the house he enters. 11Then speak to the man who lives there. Say to him, 'Our Teacher says for you to show us your guest room. This is where he wants to eat the Passover meal with his disciples.' 12The man will take you upstairs to a large room. It will be all ready for us. That is the place. Then, go ahead and make the meal there."

13So they went off to the city. They found everything just as Jesus had said it would be. And they made the Passover supper there.

The Last Supper

14Then Jesus and the others came, too. And at the proper time, they all sat down together at the table. 15Jesus said, "I have looked forward to this hour with deep longing. I have wanted to eat this Passover meal with you before I suffer. 16For I won't eat it again until what it stands for has taken place in God's Kingdom."

17Then he took a cup of wine. He gave thanks for it. And he said, "Take this and share it among yourselves. 18For I will not drink wine again until the Kingdom of God has come."

19Then he took a loaf of bread. He had thanked God for it. And he broke it apart and gave it to them. He said, "This is my body, given for you. Eat it in remembrance of me."

20After supper he gave them another cup of wine. He said, "This wine is the token of God's new agreement to save you. It is an agreement sealed with the blood I shall pour out. And with it, I will buy back your souls. 21But here at this table is the man who will betray me. He is sitting among us as a friend. 22I must die. It is part of God's plan. But, oh, how terrible it will be for the man who betrays me!"

23Then the disciples whispered among themselves. They wondered which of them would ever do such a thing.

24And they began to argue among themselves about who was the greatest.

25Jesus told them, "In this world the kings and great men order their slaves around. And the slaves have no choice but to do what they are told! 26But among you, the one who serves you best will be your leader. 27Out in the world the master sits at the table and is served by his servants. But not here! For I am your servant. 28Yet you have stood by me in these terrible days. 29And my Father has given me a Kingdom to rule. So now I give you the right 30to eat and drink at my table in that Kingdom. And you will sit on thrones judging the 12 tribes of Israel.

Jesus Says Peter Will Deny Knowing Him

31"Simon, Satan has asked to have you. He wants to sift you like wheat. 32But I have begged in prayer for you. I have prayed that your faith will not completely fail. So when you have turned to me again, build up the faith of your brothers."

33Simon said, "Lord, I am ready to go to jail with you. I am even ready to die with you."

34But Jesus said, "Peter, let me tell you something. Before tomorrow morning when the rooster crows, you will deny me three times. You will claim that you don't even know me."

35Then Jesus said to them, "I once sent you out to preach the Good News. And you were without money, duffle bag, or extra clothing. During that time, how did you get along?"

"Fine," they replied.

36"But now," he said, "take a duffle bag if you have one. And take your money, too. If you don't have a sword, you had better sell your clothes and buy one! 37For the time has come for this prophecy about me to come true: 'He will be condemned as a criminal!' Yes, everything written about me by the prophets will come true."

38"Master," they replied, "we have two swords among us."

"That is enough," he said.

Jesus Prays

Are you ever tempted to do something wrong? Pray! But don't fall asleep when you should be praying. Even Jesus' friends had a problem. Here's what happened.

39Then, he left the upstairs room with his disciples. And they went as usual to the Mount of Olives. 40There he told them, "Pray to God that you will not give in to temptation."

41-42He walked away from them, perhaps a stone's throw. There he knelt down and prayed this prayer. "Father," he said. "If you are willing, please take away this cup of horror from me. But I want your will, not mine." 43Then an angel from Heaven came and gave him strength. 44Jesus was in such agony of spirit that he broke into a sweat of blood. Great drops fell to the ground as he prayed more and more earnestly. 45At last he stood up again and went back to the disciples. But he found them sound asleep. They were very tired from their sorrow.

46"Asleep!" he said. "Get up! Pray to God that you will not fall when you are tempted."

- *Remember:* What was the name of the mountain where Jesus and his disciples went? (22:39) Jesus asked his friends to pray for something. What? (22:39) What happened to Jesus' friends while he was praying? (22:45-46) Why did they fall

asleep? They were tempted to sleep. But they should have been praying. What should they have done?

- *Discover:* When you are tempted to do something wrong, pray!

- *Apply:* A friend asks you to look at some dirty magazines. Pray! A friend asks you to drink something wrong. Pray! A friend asks you to take some drugs. Pray! A friend asks you to do something bad. Pray!

- *What's next?* Why would anyone want to kill Jesus? Why would a friend of Jesus' want to help them? Read Matthew 26:47-56. ■

Jesus Is Betrayed and Arrested

47But even as he said this, a crowd came. It was led by Judas, one of Jesus' 12 disciples. Judas walked over to Jesus and kissed him on the cheek in friendly greeting.

48But Jesus said, "Judas, how can you do this? How can you betray the Messiah with a kiss?"

49The other disciples saw what was about to happen. So they said, "Master, shall we fight? We brought along the

swords!" ⁵⁰And one of them slashed at the High Priest's servant. He cut off his right ear.

⁵¹But Jesus said, "Don't fight any more." And he touched the man's ear and healed it. ⁵²Then Jesus spoke to the chief priests, the captains of the Temple guard, and the elders who led the crowd. "Am I a robber?" he asked. "Is that why you have come with swords and clubs to get me? ⁵³Why didn't you arrest me in the Temple? I was there every day. But this is your moment, when darkness reigns supreme."

Peter Denies Knowing Jesus

⁵⁴So they grabbed him and led him to the High Priest's house. Peter followed along at a distance. ⁵⁵The soldiers lit a fire in the courtyard and sat around it for warmth. And Peter joined them there.

⁵⁶A servant girl saw him in the firelight and began staring at him. Finally she said, "This man was with Jesus!"

⁵⁷Peter denied it. "Woman," he said, "I don't even know the man!"

⁵⁸After a while someone else looked at him. "You must be one of them!" he said.

"No sir, I am not!" Peter replied.

⁵⁹About an hour later someone else saw him. "I know this fellow is one of Jesus' disciples," he said. "For both of them are from Galilee."

⁶⁰But Peter said, "Man, I

don't know what you are talking about." And as he said the words, a rooster crowed.

⁶¹At that moment Jesus turned and looked at Peter. Then Peter remembered what he had said: "Before the rooster crows tomorrow morning, you will deny me three times." ⁶²And Peter walked out of the courtyard, crying bitterly.

⁶³⁻⁶⁴Now the guards in charge of Jesus began laughing at him. They covered his eyes and hit him with their fists. Then they asked, "Who hit you that time, prophet?" ⁶⁵And they threw all sorts of other insults at him.

Jesus Says He Is the Son of God; The Council Condemns Him

⁶⁶Early the next morning at daybreak the Jewish Supreme Court came. This included the chief priests and all the top religious leaders. Jesus was led before this Council. ⁶⁷⁻⁶⁸He was asked if he claimed to be the Messiah or not.

But he replied, "If I tell you, you won't believe me. You won't let me present my case. ⁶⁹But the time is soon coming when I, the Messiah, shall be seated beside Almighty God."

⁷⁰They all shouted, "Then you claim you are the Son of God?"

And he replied, "Yes, I am."

⁷¹"What need do we have for other witnesses?" they shouted. "For we ourselves have heard him say it."

Jesus Stands Before Pilate

23 Then the Council took Jesus over to Pilate, the governor. ²They began at once accusing him. They said, "This fellow has been leading our people astray. He tells them not to pay their taxes to the Roman government. And he claims he is our Messiah, a King."

³So Pilate asked him, "Are you their Messiah? Are you their King?"

"Yes," Jesus replied, "it is as you say."

⁴Then Pilate turned to the chief priests and the crowd. He said, "So? That isn't a crime!"

⁵Then they said, "But he is causing riots all over Judea! He started up in Galilee and has come all the way to Jerusalem."

Jesus Is Taken to Herod Antipas

King Herod was glad to meet Jesus. He thought Jesus would perform a miracle. Herod thought this would be a good show. Did Jesus do this for Herod?

⁶"Is he then a Galilean?" Pilate asked.

⁷When they told him yes, Pilate said to take him to King Herod. This was because Galilee was under Herod's rule. And Herod happened to be in Jerusalem at the time. ⁸Herod was happy for a chance to see Jesus, for he had heard a lot about him. He was hoping to see him do a miracle.

⁹He asked Jesus question after question. But he gave no answers. ¹⁰All the while, the chief priests and the other leaders accused him.

¹¹Now Herod and his soldiers began laughing at Jesus. They put a kingly robe on him. Then they sent him back to Pilate. ¹²That day Herod and Pilate became close friends. Before this time, they had been enemies.

- *Remember:* Where was Herod at this time? (23:7) Why did Herod want to meet Jesus? (23:8) How did Jesus answer Herod's questions? (23:9) How did Herod and his soldiers make fun of Jesus? (23:11) Why do you think this was wrong?

- *Discover:* We should never make fun of Jesus. He is God's Son.

- *Apply:* We make fun of Jesus when we make fun of people he loves. Do you ever do that?

• *What's next?* If a person doesn't want to do something, why do it? Ask Pilate. Read John 19:1-16. ■

Pilate Wants to Free Jesus but Listens to the Crowd

¹³Now Pilate called together the chief priests, the leaders, and the people. ¹⁴He gave them his decision.

"You brought this man to me," he said. "You accused him of leading a revolt against Rome. I have tested him on this point and find him innocent. ¹⁵Herod thought the same and sent him back to us. Nothing this man has done calls for the death penalty. ¹⁶So now I will have him punished and let him go."

¹⁷⁻¹⁸But a mighty roar rose from the crowd. They shouted with one voice, "Kill him! Give Barabbas to us!" ¹⁹Barabbas was in prison for starting a rebellion against the government. He was also there for murder. ²⁰Pilate argued with them, for he wanted to set Jesus free. ²¹But they shouted, "Crucify him! Crucify him!"

²²Once more, for the third time, he demanded, "Why? What crime has he done? I have found no reason to have him killed. I will therefore beat him and let him go." ²³But they shouted louder and louder for Jesus' death. And their voices won in the end.

²⁴So Pilate sentenced Jesus to die as they demanded. ²⁵And he set Barabbas free at their request. Barabbas was in prison for rebellion and murder. But he sent Jesus over to them to do with as they wanted.

Jesus Is Crucified

²⁶Then the crowd led Jesus away to his death. And Simon of Cyrene was forced to follow, carrying Jesus' cross. This man was just coming into Jerusalem from the country. ²⁷Great crowds followed along behind. Among them were women who cried and mourned for him.

²⁸But Jesus turned to them. "Daughters of Jerusalem, don't cry for me," he said. "Cry instead for yourselves and your children. ²⁹For soon women who have no children will thought to be lucky. ³⁰Mankind will beg the moun-

tains to fall on them and crush them. They will ask the hills to bury them. ³¹For they are doing terrible things when times are still good. How much worse do you think they will be when times are bad?"

³²⁻³³Two others, criminals, were led out to be killed with him. They were taken to a place called "The Skull." And there all three were crucified. Jesus was put on the center cross. The two criminals were hung on either side of him.

³⁴"Father, forgive these people," Jesus said. "For they don't know what they are doing."

And the soldiers gambled for his clothing, throwing dice for each piece. ³⁵The crowd watched. And the Jewish leaders laughed and made fun of him. "He was so good at helping others," they said. "Let's see him save himself. Let's see if he is really God's Chosen One, the Messiah."

³⁶The soldiers laughed at him, too. They offered him a drink of sour wine. ³⁷And they called to him, "If you are the King of the Jews, save yourself!"

³⁸A sign was nailed to the cross above him. It said, "This is the King of the Jews."

³⁹One of the criminals hanging beside him made fun of him. He said, "So you're the Messiah, are you? Prove it by saving yourself! And save us, too, while you're at it!"

⁴⁰⁻⁴¹But the other criminal stopped him. "Don't you even fear God when you are dying?" he said. "We deserve to die for what we did. But this man hasn't done one thing wrong." ⁴²Then he said, "Jesus, remember me when you come into your Kingdom."

⁴³And Jesus replied, "Today you will be with me in Paradise. This is a solemn promise."

Jesus Dies

⁴⁴By now it was noon and darkness fell across the whole land. The darkness lasted for three hours, until three o'clock. ⁴⁵The light from the sun was gone. And suddenly the thick veil hanging in the Temple split apart.

⁴⁶Then Jesus shouted, "Father, I

commit my spirit to you." And with those words he died.

⁴⁷The captain of the Roman unit in charge saw what had happened. And he praised God, saying, "Surely this was a good man."

⁴⁸And when the crowd saw that Jesus was dead they went home very sad. ⁴⁹Jesus' friends stood watching a little distance away. Among these were the women who had followed him down from Galilee.

Jesus Is Buried

The religious leaders hated Jesus. They were afraid that if people followed Jesus, the people would stop following them. They were jealous. So they had Jesus crucified. But one of these leaders did not hate Jesus. He even buried Jesus. Who was he?

⁵⁰⁻⁵²Then a man named Joseph went to Pilate and asked for Jesus' body. He was from the city of Arimathea in Judea. He was also a member of the Jewish Supreme Court. Now Joseph was a godly man. And he had been looking for the Messiah's coming. He had not agreed with the actions of the other Jewish leaders. ⁵³So he took down Jesus' body. He wrapped it in a long linen cloth. And he laid it in a new, unused tomb. It was cut into the rock at the side of a hill. ⁵⁴This was done late on Friday afternoon. This was the day used to get ready for the Sabbath.

⁵⁵As Jesus' body was taken away, the women from Galilee followed. And they saw him carried into the tomb. ⁵⁶Then they went home and bought spices for his burial. But by the time they were finished it was the Sabbath. So they rested all that day, as the Jewish law said they should.

- *Remember:* A religious leader buried Jesus. What was his name? Where was he from? (23:50) What did he do with Jesus' body? How did he bury it? (23:53) What day was this? (23:54) What did the women of Galilee do? Why did they wait? (23:55-56) Why do you think Joseph buried Jesus? Why did the women prepare the spices? Was it because they loved Jesus?

- *Discover:* When we love someone, we will do special things for him or her.

- *Apply:* Make a list of some people you love most. Who are they? Have you done something special for them today? Would you like to do that?

- *What's next?* An angel talks with some women. They are scared! Read Mark 16:1-8. ■

Jesus Is Alive!

24 But very early on Sunday morning they took the spices to the tomb. ²And they found that the huge stone covering the entrance had been rolled aside. ³So they went in, but the Lord Jesus' body was gone.

⁴They stood there confused. They tried to think of what could have happened to it. Suddenly two men appeared before them. They were dressed in shining robes that were so bright their eyes were dazzled. ⁵The women were terrified and bowed low before them.

Then the men asked, "Why are you looking in a tomb for someone who is alive? ⁶⁻⁷He isn't here! He has come back to life again! Don't you remember what he told you back in Galilee? He told you the Messiah would be betrayed into the power of evil men. He said he would be crucified. And he said he would rise again the third day."

⁸Then they remembered what Jesus had said. ⁹So they rushed back to Jerusalem to tell his 11 disciples what had happened. ¹⁰These women were Mary Magdalene, Joanna, Mary the mother of

James, and some others. [11]But their story sounded like a fairy tale to the men. They didn't believe it.

[12]However, Peter ran to the tomb to look. Stooping, he looked in and saw the empty linen cloth. Then he went back home again, wondering what had happened.

On the Road to Emmaus

A stranger joins two people. They walk together. They talk together. They don't know who he is. But he is actually their best friend. This is what happened.

[13]That same day two of Jesus' followers were going to the village of Emmaus. This was a town seven miles outside of Jerusalem. [14]As they walked along they were talking of Jesus' death. [15]Then suddenly Jesus himself came along and joined them. He began walking beside them. [16]But they didn't know who he was, for God kept them from it. [17]"You seem to be troubled about something," he said. "What are you so worried about?" They stopped short, sadness written across their faces. [18]One of them was named Cleopas. He said, "Some terrible things have happened in Jerusalem this last week. You must be the only person who hasn't heard about them."

[19]"What things?" Jesus asked.

"The things that happened to Jesus, the Man from Nazareth," they said. "He was a Prophet who did great miracles. He was a great Teacher, highly respected by both God and man. [20]But the chief priests and our religious leaders arrested him. They handed him over to the Romans to be condemned to death. And they killed him on a cross. [21]We had thought he was the Messiah. We were hoping he had come to save Israel.

"This all happened three days ago. [22-23]And now some women from our group have told us some amazing things. They were at his tomb early this morning. And they came back with an amazing report. They said his body was missing. And they claimed they had seen angels who told them Jesus is alive! ²⁴Some of our men ran out to see. And sure enough, Jesus' body was gone. It was just as the women had said."

²⁵Then Jesus said to them, "You are such foolish, foolish people! You find it so hard to believe all that the prophets wrote in the Scriptures! ²⁶They said the Messiah would suffer these things before entering his glory."

²⁷Then Jesus quoted the writings of the prophets. He began with the Book of Genesis and went right on through the Scriptures. He told them what the passages meant. And he told them what they said about himself.

²⁸By this time they were near Emmaus and the end of their journey. Jesus would have gone on. ²⁹But they begged him to stay the night with them. For by that time, it was getting late. So he went home with them. ³⁰As they sat down to eat, he asked God's blessing on the food. Then he took a small loaf of bread. He broke it and passed it over to them. ³¹Then suddenly their eyes were opened. They knew who he was! And at that moment he was gone!

³²They began telling each other how they had felt while walking with him. Their hearts had felt strangely warm. And they had been excited as he told them what the Scriptures meant. ³³⁻³⁴Within the hour they were on their way back to Jerusalem. The 11 disciples and the other followers of Jesus were there. They greeted them with these words, "The Lord has really risen! He appeared to Peter!"

³⁵Then the two from Emmaus told their story. They told of how Jesus had come to them as they were walking along the road. And they told how they knew who he was when he broke the bread.

- *Remember:* Where were the two people going? (24:13) Why didn't they know who Jesus was? (24:16) What did Jesus teach them? (24:25-27) What were they doing when they knew this was Jesus? (24:30-31) Where did they go then? (24:33-34) Why do you think they went back to Jerusalem? How would you feel if Jesus suddenly appeared to you in your back yard?

- *Discover:* The Old Testament teaches about Jesus, too. Many years before he came, it told what would happen.

- *Apply:* Would you like to read some Old Testament verses about Jesus? Look for these. Compare Isaiah 7:14 with Matthew 1:23. Compare Micah 5:2 with Matthew 2:6. Compare Zechariah 9:9 with Matthew 21:5. Compare Zechariah 11:12-13 with Matthew 27:9-10. There are many more.

- *What's next?* The doors are locked. But someone walks through the walls. Read John 20:19-31. ▪

Jesus Surprises the Disciples

³⁶And as they were telling about it, Jesus himself was suddenly there with them. And he greeted them. ³⁷But

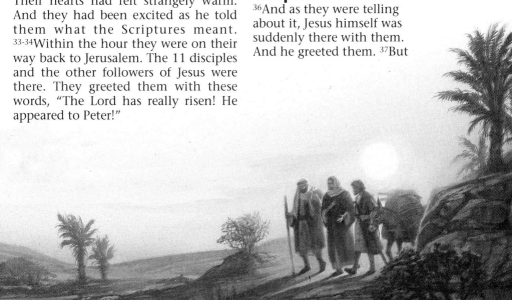

the whole group was very afraid. They thought they were seeing a ghost!

38"Why are you so afraid?" he asked. "Why do you doubt that it is really I? 39Look at my hands! Look at my feet! You can see that it is I, myself! Touch me and make sure that I am not a ghost! For ghosts don't have bodies, as you see that I do!" 40As he spoke, he held out his hands. They could see the marks of the nails. And he showed them the wounds in his feet.

41Still they stood there, unsure. They were filled with joy and doubt.

Then he asked them, "Do you have anything here to eat?"

42They gave him a piece of broiled fish. 43And he ate it as they watched!

44Then he said, "Remember when I was with you before? I told you that everything written about me must happen."

45Then Jesus opened their minds to understand at last these many Scriptures! 46And he said, "Yes, it was written long ago that the Messiah must suffer and die. It was also written that he must rise again from the dead on the third day. 47It said that this message of salvation should be taken from Jerusalem to all the nations. Yes, there is forgiveness of sins for all who turn to me! 48You have seen these prophecies come true.

49"And I am going to send the Holy Spirit upon you. It will happen just as my Father promised. Don't begin telling others yet. Stay here in the city until the Holy Spirit comes. He will fill you with power from Heaven."

Jesus Ascends into Heaven

Jesus is walking with his friends along the road. He stops. He begins rising into the sky. He goes all the way up into Heaven.

50Then Jesus led them out along the road to Bethany. He lifted up his hands toward Heaven and blessed them. 51Then he began rising into the sky, and went on to Heaven. 52And they worshiped him. Then they went back to Jerusalem filled with great joy. 53And they stayed continually in the Temple, praising God.

- *Remember:* Where were Jesus and his disciples? (24:50) What did he do to them? (24:50) Where did Jesus rise? How far did he go? (24:51) How did the disciples feel after this? Were they sad or happy? (24:53) Do you think you would have been excited to see Jesus rising into Heaven? Why?

- *Discover:* Walking with Jesus gives us much joy. Watching Jesus work makes us happy. Helping Jesus work also makes us happy.

- *Apply:* When you read your Bible, it will make you happy. When you share Jesus with others, it will make you happy. When you see the wonderful things Jesus can do, it will make you happy.

- *What's next?* A strong wind sweeps through the house. Little flames of fire appear on people's heads. What is happening? Read Acts 2:1-4.■

JOHN

If John lived on your street, you would want him as your friend. It's easy to love John. Jesus seemed to love John a little more than his other disciples. Perhaps John was a more loving person. Or perhaps John understood God's love more than others did.

John tells us much about love in this book. He tells us how much God loves us. He shows us what God did for us because he loves us so much. And he tells us how to love each other more.

John had been a fisherman until Jesus met him. Jesus asked John to become his disciple. John went wherever Jesus went. He heard Jesus teach. He watched Jesus do wonderful things. He learned that Jesus was God's Son. He learned how to get to Heaven. He tells us these things in his book.

John saw many exciting things. He wants to show them to us. Watch water turn into wine. Watch someone feed 5,000 people with only a little boy's lunch. Watch a blind man see. Watch a lame man walk. Look while a dead man comes to life. See a man sell his own friend for a few coins. Watch a man come into a room without opening the door. Read John's book and you'll see and learn wonderful things about God and his Son, Jesus.

God Becomes a Human

1 Before anything else existed, there was God's Son. He was the Word, and he was with God. He has always been alive and is himself God. ³He created everything there is. Nothing exists that he didn't make. ⁴Eternal life is in him. This life gives light to all mankind. ⁵His life is the light that shines through the darkness. And the darkness can never put it out.

⁶⁻⁷God sent John the Baptist as a

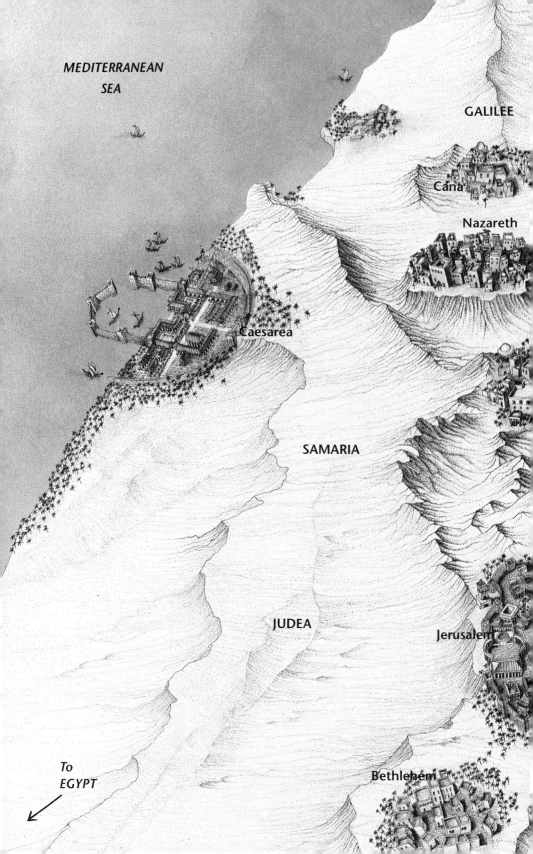

MEDITERRANEAN
SEA

GALILEE

Cana

Nazareth

Caesarea

SAMARIA

JUDEA

Jerusalem

To
EGYPT

Bethlehem

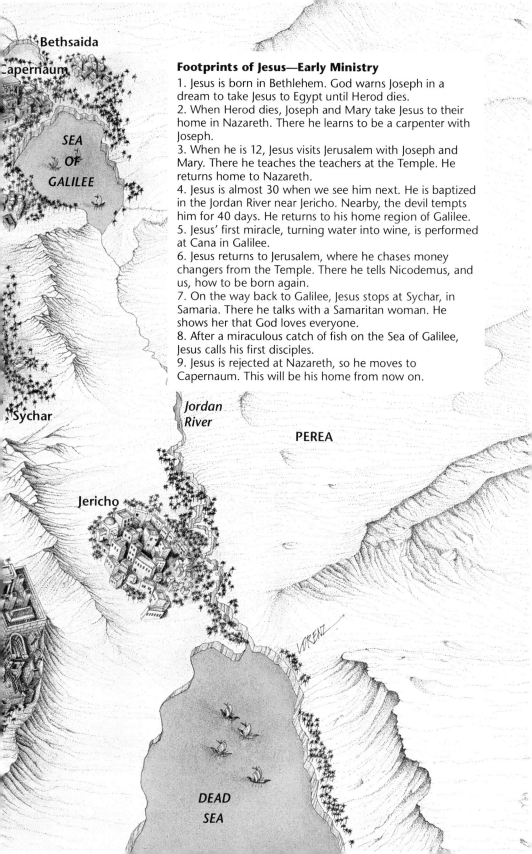

Bethsaida

Capernaum

SEA
OF
GALILEE

Footprints of Jesus—Early Ministry

1. Jesus is born in Bethlehem. God warns Joseph in a dream to take Jesus to Egypt until Herod dies.
2. When Herod dies, Joseph and Mary take Jesus to their home in Nazareth. There he learns to be a carpenter with Joseph.
3. When he is 12, Jesus visits Jerusalem with Joseph and Mary. There he teaches the teachers at the Temple. He returns home to Nazareth.
4. Jesus is almost 30 when we see him next. He is baptized in the Jordan River near Jericho. Nearby, the devil tempts him for 40 days. He returns to his home region of Galilee.
5. Jesus' first miracle, turning water into wine, is performed at Cana in Galilee.
6. Jesus returns to Jerusalem, where he chases money changers from the Temple. There he tells Nicodemus, and us, how to be born again.
7. On the way back to Galilee, Jesus stops at Sychar, in Samaria. There he talks with a Samaritan woman. He shows her that God loves everyone.
8. After a miraculous catch of fish on the Sea of Galilee, Jesus calls his first disciples.
9. Jesus is rejected at Nazareth, so he moves to Capernaum. This will be his home from now on.

Sychar

Jordan
River

PEREA

Jericho

LORENZ

DEAD
SEA

witness. He told people that Jesus Christ is the true Light. [8]John himself was not the Light. He was only a witness to tell others about it.

[9]Later on, the one who is the true Light came into the world. He came to shine on everyone.

[10]He was the one who made the world. But the world didn't know him when he came. [11-12]He was not accepted even in his own land and among his own people. Only a few would welcome and receive him. But to all who received him, he gave the right to become God's children. All they needed to do was to believe in him. [13]All those who believe this are reborn! This is not a physical rebirth. It doesn't result from human passion or plan. This birth comes from the will of God.

[14]And Christ became a human being and lived on earth among us. He was full of loving forgiveness and truth. And some of us have seen his glory. He has the glory of the only Son of the Father!

[15]John pointed him out to the people. He told the crowds, "This is the one I was talking about. He is the one of whom I said, 'Someone is coming who is greater than I am. For he existed long before I did!'" [16]We have all been blessed by what he brought to us. It has been given to us again and again! [17]For Moses gave us only the Law. But Jesus Christ brought us loving forgiveness. [18]No one has ever actually seen God. But his only Son is God and the Father's companion. And he has told us all about the Father.

John the Baptist Explains His Mission

[19]The Jewish leaders sent priests and Levites from Jerusalem to John. They asked John whether he claimed to be the Messiah.

[20]He said he wasn't. "I am not the Christ," he said.

[21]"Well then, who are you?" they asked. "Are you Elijah?"

"No," he replied.

"Are you the Prophet?"

"No."

[22]"Then who are you? Tell us, so we can give an answer to those who sent us. What do you have to say for yourself?"

[23]John replied with the words of the prophet Isaiah. He said, "I am a voice shouting from the barren desert. I say, 'Get ready for the coming of the Lord!'"

[24-25]Now some Pharisees were among this group. They said, "You say you aren't the Messiah or Elijah or the Prophet. Then what right do you have to baptize?"

Jesus created everything there is

*He created everything there is.
Nothing exists that
he didn't make.*

John 1:3

---

[26]John told them, "I merely baptize with water. But right here in the crowd is someone you do not know. [27]He will soon begin his work among you. And I am not even fit to be his slave."

[28]This event took place at Bethany. This is a village on the other side of the Jordan River where John was baptizing.

John the Baptist Proclaims Jesus as the Messiah

[29]The next day John saw Jesus coming toward him. He said, "Look! There is the Lamb of God who takes away the world's sin! [30]He is the one I was talking about earlier. Remember that I said, 'Soon a man greater than I am is coming. He existed long before me!' [31]I didn't know he was the one. But I am here baptizing with water. I do this to point him out to the nation of Israel."

[32]Then John told about the Holy Spirit coming upon Jesus. The Holy Spirit came down from Heaven in the form of a dove and rested upon Jesus.

[33]"I didn't know he was the one," John said again. "But God told me what to look for. He said, 'Look for the one you see the Holy Spirit resting upon. He is the one who baptizes with the Holy Spirit.' [34]I saw it happen to this man. So I tell you that he is the Son of God."

Jesus' First Followers

Do you know the names of Jesus' first followers? Why did they follow Jesus? This is the way it happened.

³⁵The following day John was standing with two of his disciples. ³⁶And Jesus walked by them. John looked at him and then said, "See! There is the Lamb of God!"

³⁷Then John's two disciples turned and followed Jesus.

³⁸Jesus looked around and saw them following. "What do you want?" he asked them.

"Sir," they replied, "where do you live?"

³⁹"Come and see," he said. So they went with him to the place where he was staying. They were with him from about four o'clock that afternoon until the evening. ⁴⁰One of these men was Andrew, Simon Peter's brother.

⁴¹Andrew then went to find his brother Peter. He told him, "We have found the Messiah!" ⁴²And he brought Peter to meet Jesus.

Jesus looked closely at Peter for a moment. Then he said, "You are Simon, John's son. But you will be called Peter, the rock!"

⁴³The next day Jesus decided to go to Galilee. He found Philip and told him, "Come with me." ⁴⁴Philip was from Bethsaida, Andrew and Peter's hometown.

⁴⁵Philip now went off to look for Nathanael. He told him, "We have found the Messiah! This is the one Moses and the prophets told about! His name is Jesus, the son of Joseph from Nazareth!"

⁴⁶"Nazareth!" exclaimed Nathanael. "Can anything good come from there?"

"Just come and see for yourself," Philip said.

⁴⁷As they drew near, Jesus said, "Here comes an honest man. He's a true son of Israel."

⁴⁸"How do you know what I am like?" Nathanael asked.

And Jesus replied, "I could see you under the fig tree. You were there before Philip found you."

⁴⁹Nathanael replied, "Sir, you are the Son of God! You are the King of Israel!"

⁵⁰Jesus asked him, "You believe me because I told you I saw you under the fig tree? But you will see much greater proofs than this! ⁵¹You will even see Heaven open. And you will see God's angels coming back and forth to me, the Messiah."

- *Remember:* What did John the Baptist call Jesus? (1:36) Who did Andrew bring to Jesus? (1:41-42) What was Peter's name at that time? (1:42) Who changed his name to Peter? (1:42) Who brought Nathanael to Jesus? (1:45-46) Jesus told Nathanael about a great miracle he would see. What was it? (1:51) What would you think if you saw angels coming out of Heaven? What would you say to a person who did not believe in Jesus?

- *Discover:* Did someone help you believe in Jesus? Who? Do you trust that person? Andrew brought his brother Peter to Jesus. Philip brought his friend Nathanael to Jesus. Do you have a friend who trusts you? They will listen as you tell them about Jesus. Then pray that they follow him.

- *Apply:* Would you like to tell a friend about Jesus? Try to do it this week! God will be with you when you try.

- *What's next?* Turn on the faucet. Water comes out. But what if it suddenly turned into a milkshake! What would you think? Read about something like this in John 2:1-12. ■

Jesus Turns Water into Wine

If you pour water into a glass, what do you have? You have water, don't you? It's always that way. But it's not always that way when Jesus is there. Jesus did things no one else could do. They were called miracles. Here is one you won't forget.

2Two days later Jesus' mother was a guest at a wedding. This wedding was in Cana of Galilee. 2And Jesus and his disciples were asked to come too. 3The wine supply ran out during the feast. And Jesus' mother came to him with the problem.

4"I can't help you now," he said. "It isn't yet my time for miracles."

5But his mother told the servants, "Do whatever he tells you."

6Six stone waterpots were standing there. They were used for the Jewish washing ceremony. They could hold 20 to 30 gallons each. 7-8Jesus told the servants to fill them to the brim with water. Then he said, "Take some of it to the master of the wedding."

9The master of the wedding tasted the water that had become wine. He wondered where it had come from. But of course, the servants knew. So he called the bridegroom over.

10"This is wonderful stuff!" he said. "You're different from most. Usually a host uses the best wine first. Then afterwards, when everyone is full, he gives the less expensive wine. But you have kept the best for the last!"

11This miracle at Cana in Galilee was the first one Jesus did. By doing it, he proved his glory. And his disciples believed in him.

12After the wedding he left for Capernaum for a few days. He went with his mother, brothers, and disciples.

- *Remember:* Why was Jesus in Cana? (2:1-2) Who asked Jesus to do a miracle there? (2:3) Did he? (2:7-9) How do you know this was his first miracle? (2:11) Can you turn water into wine? Why not?

- *Discover:* Jesus turned water into wine because he is God's Son. Only God and his Son Jesus can do miracles. Miracles show us that God is in charge of the whole world. He created it!

- *Apply:* Since Jesus is God's Son, listen to him! Listen to what he tells you! He knows everything! He can do anything! And he wants to show you how to truly enjoy life.

- *What's next?* Do you think Jesus would ever use a whip? He did. What would make him angry enough to use a whip? Read John 2:13-25. ■

Jesus Chases Bad Men from the Temple

How would you feel if some men tried to sell cows in your church? What if they set up stores in your church? What if they cheated people there? Would you get angry? Would you try to chase them out? The Temple was God's house. It was like your church. Do you see why Jesus did this?

¹³It was the time for the yearly Jewish Passover Feast. So Jesus went to Jerusalem.

¹⁴In the Temple area he saw merchants selling cattle, sheep, and doves for sacrifices. And he saw money changers behind their counters. ¹⁵Jesus made a whip from some ropes and chased them all out. He drove out the sheep and oxen. He scattered the money changers' coins over the floor. And he turned over their tables! ¹⁶Then he spoke to the men selling doves. He said, "Get these things out of here. Don't turn my Father's house into a market!"

¹⁷Then his disciples remembered this prophecy from the Scriptures. It said, "Concern for God's house will eat me up."

¹⁸"What right have you to order them out?" the Jewish leaders demanded. "If you have this authority from God, show us a miracle to prove it."

¹⁹Jesus replied, "This is the miracle I will do for you. Destroy this Temple and in three days I will build it up!"

²⁰"What!" they exclaimed. "It took 46 years to build this Temple! And you can do it in three days?" ²¹But by "this Temple" he meant his body. ²²After he came back to life again, the disciples remembered what he had said. Then they believed the words he had spoken.

²³Jesus did several miracles in Jerusalem at the Passover Feast. And as a result, many people believed he was the Messiah. ²⁴⁻²⁵But Jesus didn't trust them, for he knew what people were like. No one needed to tell him about human nature.

- *Remember:* What were the men selling in the Temple? (2:14) What did Jesus do about this? (2:15-16) Why did some people think he was the Messiah, God's Son? (2:23) What if you saw Jesus do something no one else could do? Would you think he is God's Son?

- *Discover:* Be sure you're angry at bad things, not good things.

- *Apply:* Are you angry at someone? Why? Is it because that person did not please God? Or is it because that person did not please you?

- *What's next?* When you came into the world, you were born. But you need to be born a second time. Read John 3:1-17. ■

Jesus Talks with Nicodemus

Would a Bible professor ask a carpenter to teach him about God? That's what Nicodemus did.

3 One night a Jewish religious leader named Nicodemus came to Jesus. Nicodemus was a member of the sect of the Pharisees. "Sir," he said, "we all know that God has sent you to teach us. Your miracles are proof enough of this."

³Jesus replied, "I tell you the truth. Unless you are born again, you can never see the Kingdom of God."

⁴"Born again!" exclaimed Nicodemus. "What do you mean? How can an old man go back to his mother's womb and be born again?"

⁵Jesus replied, "What I am telling you so earnestly is this. Unless one is born of water and the Spirit, he cannot enter the Kingdom of God. ⁶Men can only reproduce human life, but the Holy Spirit gives new spiritual life. ⁷So don't be surprised when I say you must be born again! ⁸You can hear the wind. But you can't tell where it comes from or where it will go next. So it is with those born of the Spirit."

⁹"What do you mean?" Nicodemus asked.

¹⁰⁻¹¹Jesus replied, "You are a respected Jewish teacher. And yet you don't understand these things? I am telling you what I know and have seen. And yet you all won't believe me. ¹²You don't even believe me when I tell you about such things on earth. How can you believe if I tell you what is going on in Heaven? ¹³For only I, the Messiah, have come to earth from Heaven. ¹⁴Moses in the wilderness lifted up the bronze image of a serpent on a pole. Even so I must be lifted up on a pole. ¹⁵I will do this so that anyone who believes in me will have eternal life. ¹⁶God loved the world so much that he gave his only Son. Anyone who believes in him will not die but have eternal life. ¹⁷God did not send his Son into the world to judge it. He sent his Son to save it.

● *Remember:* What kind of work did Nicodemus do? (3:1-2) What did Jesus tell Nicodemus he must do? (3:3) Did Jesus come from Heaven? Would he go back to Heaven? (3:13) Why did God send his Son into the world? (3:16-17) Do you wish you could have asked Jesus about Heaven? What would you have asked him?

● *Discover:* God wants you to live with him forever. That's because he loves you.

● *Apply:* Do you want to live with God in Heaven someday? You will if you ask Jesus to be your Savior.

● *What's next?* Jesus tells a woman some of her secrets. How does he know? Read John 4:1-42. ■

Those Who Trust in God Have Nothing to Fear

¹⁸"Eternal judgment does not wait for those who trust him to save them. But those who don't trust him have already been judged. But they do not believe in the only Son of God. ¹⁹The Light from Heaven came into the world. But they loved the darkness more than the Light. For their deeds were evil. ²⁰They hated the heavenly Light because they wanted to sin in the darkness. They stayed away from that Light. They feared their sins would be seen and they would be punished. ²¹But those doing right come to the Light. When they do so, they see they are doing what God wants."

John the Baptist Tells More about Jesus

²²Afterwards Jesus and his disciples left Jerusalem. They stayed for a while in Judea and baptized there.

²³⁻²⁴At this time John the Baptist was not yet in prison. He was baptizing at Aenon, near Salim. He baptized there

because there was plenty of water. [25]One day someone began an argument with John's disciples. He told them that Jesus' baptism was best. [26]So John's disciples went to speak with John. "Master, we want to talk to you," they said. "We need to know about the one you said was the Messiah. You told us about him when we were beyond the Jordan River. He is baptizing people too. Everyone is going over there instead of coming here to us."

God loves us and wants us to live with him forever

God loved the world so much that he gave his only Son. Anyone who believes in him will not die but have eternal life.

John 3:16

---

[27]John replied, "God in Heaven chooses each man's work. [28]My work is to prepare the way for that man. I do this so that everyone will go to him. You yourselves know how I told you that I am not the Messiah. I am here to make the way ready for him. [29]The crowds will naturally go to the main attraction. The bride will go where the bridegroom is! The bridegroom's friends are happy with him. And I am the Bridegroom's friend. I am filled with joy at his success. [30]He must become greater and greater. And I must become less and less.

[31]"He has come from Heaven and is greater than anyone else. I am of the earth. And my understanding is limited to the things of earth. [32]He tells what he has seen and heard. But how few believe what he tells them! [33-34]Those who believe him discover that God is a fountain of truth. For this one, sent by God, speaks God's words. For God's Spirit is upon him without measure or limit. [35]The Father loves this man because he is his Son. And God has given him everything there is. [36]And all who trust God's Son to save them have eternal life. Those who don't believe and obey him will never see life. But the anger of God will stay upon them."

Jesus Talks with a Woman at a Well

What if someone told you some of your secrets even though you hadn't told anyone? No one knew these things but you. What would you think about this person? Jesus told a woman some of her secrets one day. Do you think she was surprised? Here's what he told her.

4 The Pharisees heard that greater crowds were coming to Jesus than to John. Many were being baptized and becoming his disciples. Jesus himself didn't baptize them, but his disciples did. [3]Now Jesus knew that the Pharisees had noticed his growing popularity. So he left Judea and went back to Galilee.

[4]Now Jesus had to go through Samaria on the way. [5-6]And around noon he came to the village of Sychar. Jacob's Well was near this town. It was located on the plot of ground Jacob gave to his son Joseph. Jesus was tired from the long walk. So he sat beside the well to rest.

[7]Soon a Samaritan woman came to draw water. Jesus asked her for a drink. [8]He was alone because his disciples had gone into the village to buy some food. [9]The woman was surprised that a Jew would ask a Samaritan for anything. Usually they wouldn't even speak to them! And she remarked about this to Jesus.

[10]He replied, "You don't know who I am. And you don't know God's great gift for you. But if you knew these things, you would ask me for some living water!"

[11]"But you don't have a bucket," she said. "And this

is a very deep well! Where would you get this living water? [12]And besides, are you greater than our ancestor Jacob? How can you offer better water than that which he and his sons and cattle drank?"

[13]Jesus replied, "People who drink this water soon become thirsty again. [14]But those who drink the water I give them will never be thirsty. It becomes a spring of water inside them. And it waters them forever with eternal life."

[15]"Please, sir," the woman said, "give me some of that water! Then I'll never be thirsty again. And I won't have to make this long trip out here every day."

[16]"Go and get your husband," Jesus told her.

[17-18]"But I'm not married," the woman replied.

"All too true!" Jesus said. "For you have had five husbands. And you aren't even married to the man you're living with now."

[19]"Sir," the woman said, "you must be a prophet. [20]But tell me something. Why do you Jews say that Jerusalem is the only place of worship? We Samaritans claim it is here at Mount Gerizim. This was where our ancestors worshiped."

[21-24]Jesus replied, "Something new is coming. Then we will not worry about whether to worship here or in Jerusalem. For it's not where we worship that counts, but how we worship. We must worship in spirit and in truth. For God is Spirit, and we must worship him in truth. The Father wants this kind of worship from us. But you Samaritans know so little about him. We Jews know all about him. For salvation comes to the world through the Jews."

[25]The woman said, "Well, I know that the Messiah will come. They call him the Christ. And when he comes, he will explain everything to us."

[26]Then Jesus told her, "I am the Messiah!"

[27]Just then his disciples came up. They were surprised to find him talking to a woman. But none of them asked him why he was talking with her.

[28-29]Then the woman left her waterpot beside the well. She went back to the village and spoke to everyone. She said,

"Come and meet a man who told me everything I ever did! Can this be the Messiah?" [30]So the people came streaming from the village to see him.

[31]Meanwhile, the disciples were urging Jesus to eat. [32]"No," he said, "I have some food you don't know about."

[33]"Who brought it to him?" the disciples asked each other.

[34]Then Jesus explained. "My food comes from doing the will of God who sent me. It also comes from finishing his work. [35]Do you think the harvest will not begin until four months from now? Look around you! Great fields are ripening all around us. They are ready now for the harvest. [36]The harvesters will be paid good wages. They will be gathering souls into the granaries of eternal life! What joys await the planter and the harvester, both together! [37]For it is true that one plants and someone else harvests. [38]I sent you to harvest where you didn't plant. Others did the work, and you brought in the harvest."

[39]Many of the Samaritans believed he was the Messiah. This was because of the woman's report: "He told me everything I ever did!" [40-41]Then they came out to see him at the well. They begged him to stay at their village. And he did, for two days. During that time many of those who heard him believed in him. [42]Then they said to the woman, "Now we believe because we have heard him ourselves. We believe not just because of what you told us. He is indeed the Savior of the world."

- *Remember:* Where did Jesus meet this woman? (4:5-6) Jesus asked the woman for a drink of water. But what did he offer her? (4:10) Who did Jesus say he was? (4:26) Messiah means God's Son. Did any of the other Samaritans believe in Jesus? (4:42) Why do you think this woman believed in Jesus? What do you think she would tell you if she could talk with you today?

- *Discover:* We can worship God anywhere. That's what Jesus said. (4:21-24)

- *Apply:* Do you ever think about God when you are on a hike? Do you think about him at school? Do you think about him when you're riding in the car? Do you think about him on the playground? Where else do you think about him? You can think about him anywhere. Jesus said so.

• *What's next?* Jesus heals a child. But he is in one town and the child is in another town. How does Jesus do that? Read John 4:43-54. ■

Jesus Heals a Nobleman's Son

Only Jesus could touch people and heal them instantly. But could Jesus heal someone who was far away from him? Let's find out.

43-44At the end of the two days' stay he went on into Galilee. Jesus used to say, "A prophet is honored everywhere except in his own country!" 45But the Galileans welcomed him with open arms. For they had been in Jerusalem at the Passover Feast. And they had seen some of his miracles.

46-47As he traveled through Galilee, he came to the town of Cana. This was where he had turned the water into wine. While he was there, a government official came to him. His son, who was at home in Capernaum, was very sick. This official had heard that Jesus had come from Judea and was now in Galilee. So he went over to Cana to find Jesus. He begged him to come to Capernaum to heal his son. For he was right then at death's door.

48Jesus asked, "Won't any of you believe in me unless I do miracles?"

49The official begged, "Sir, please come now before my child dies."

50Then Jesus told him, "Go back home. Your son is healed!" And the man believed Jesus and started home. 51While he was on his way, some of his servants met him. They told him that all

was well. His son had gotten better. 52He asked them when the boy had begun to feel better. And they replied, "Yesterday afternoon! His fever left him at about one o'clock." 53The father saw it was the same time that Jesus had told him, "Your son is healed." And the officer and his whole family believed that Jesus was the Messiah.

54This was Jesus' second miracle in Galilee after coming from Judea.

• *Remember:* Where was Jesus? (4:46-47) Where was the boy he healed? (4:46-47) Did Jesus go to Capernaum to heal the boy? What did he do? (4:50) What did this man think about Jesus then? (4:53) How do you know this happened? If the Bible says it did, we know it did!

• *Discover:* No matter where we are, Jesus can help us.

• *Apply:* Are you ever lonely? Do you ever have to go someplace that might make you afraid? Remember to pray to Jesus. Why? Because he can help you, wherever you are.

• *What's next?* Some fishermen catch so many fish that their boat begins to sink. What will happen? Read Luke 5:1-11. ■

Jesus Heals a Sick Man

"I can't!" That's what a sick man said one day. He told Jesus, "I can't get well." The man had been sick for a long time. No one would help him. He really thought, "I can't." But Jesus did something special for him.

5 After this Jesus went back to Jerusalem for one of the Jewish holidays. ²Inside the city, near the Sheep Gate, was the Bethesda Pool. It had five covered platforms or porches around it. ³Crowds of sick folks lay on the platforms. There were lame, blind, and paralyzed people there. They were waiting for the water to move and bubble. ⁴An angel of the Lord came from time to time and stirred the water. And the first person to step down into it afterwards was healed.

⁵One of the men lying there had been sick for 38 years. ⁶Jesus saw him and knew how long he had been sick. He asked him, "Would you like to get well?"

⁷"I can't," the sick man said. "For I have no one to help me into the pool when the water moves. While I am trying to get there, someone else always gets in first."

⁸Jesus told him, "Stand up, roll up your sleeping mat, and go on home!"

⁹Right away, the man was healed! He rolled up his mat and began walking!

- *Remember:* How long had the man been sick? (5:5) Why did he tell Jesus, "I can't get well?" Why didn't he say, "I would love to get well?" (5:7) How did Jesus heal the man? What did he say to him? (5:8) How long did it take for the man to get well? (5:9) Do you think the man said, "I can't" anymore that day? Why not?

- *Discover:* Jesus wants to do many good things for us. Let's not say, "I can't do it." Let's say, "Thank you, Lord. I want to have your help."

- *Apply:* Make a list of all the good things Jesus wants to do for you. After each one write, "Thank you, Lord."

- *What's next?* Would you be happy to see a sick person healed? Most of us would. But some men hated Jesus because he healed a man. They wanted to kill Jesus. Why? Read Mark 3:1-6. ■

The Jewish Leaders Question the Healed Man

But it was on the Sabbath when this miracle was done. ¹⁰So the Jewish leaders objected. They said to the man who was healed, "You can't work on the Sabbath! You are not allowed to carry your sleeping mat today!"

¹¹"The man who healed me told me to," was his reply.

¹²"Who said such a thing as that?" they demanded.

¹³The man didn't know, and Jesus had gone into the crowd. ¹⁴But later Jesus found the man in the Temple. He said to him, "Now you are well. Don't sin as you did before. If you do, something even worse may happen to you."

¹⁵Then the man went to find the Jewish leaders. He told them it was Jesus who had healed him.

Jesus Claims to be the Son of God

¹⁶So they began bothering Jesus, saying that he broke the Sabbath.

¹⁷But Jesus replied, "My Father is always doing good. I'm following his example."

¹⁸Then the Jewish leaders were all the more eager to kill him. They were angry that he had disobeyed their Sabbath laws. And they were angry that he had spoken of God as his Father. In so doing, he made himself equal with God.

¹⁹Jesus replied, "The Son can do nothing by himself. He does only what he sees the Father doing. ²⁰For the Father loves the Son. He tells him everything he is doing. And the Son will do far more awesome miracles than this man's healing. ²¹He will even raise people from the dead, just as the Father does. ²²And the Father leaves all judgment of sin to his Son. ²³He did this so that everyone will honor the Son, just as they honor the Father. You might choose not to honor

God's Son, whom he sent. But if you do, then you are not honoring the Father.

²⁴"I have something serious to say. Anyone who listens to my message and believes in God who sent me has eternal life. Such a person will never be condemned. He has already passed out of death into life.

²⁵"And I tell you that a new time is coming soon. In fact, that time is already here. And during that time, the dead will hear the Son of God's voice. And those who listen will live. ²⁶The Father has life in himself. He has given his Son to have life in himself. ²⁷And he can judge the sins of all mankind because he is the Son of Man. ²⁸Don't be so surprised! Before long, all the dead in their graves will hear the voice of God's Son. ²⁹And they will rise again. Those who have done good will be given eternal life. And those who have walked in evil will be judged.

³⁰"But I pass no judgment without speaking with the Father. I judge as I am told. And my judgment is always fair and just. It is according to the will of God who sent me. It is not merely my own judgment.

Jesus' Miracles Prove That He Is God's Son

³¹"I make claims about myself. But those who hear them don't believe me. ³²⁻³³But someone else is making these claims for me, too. His name is John the Baptist. You have gone out to listen to his preaching. I can assure you that all he says about me is true! ³⁴But the truest witness I have is not from a man. I say this so that you will

believe in me and be saved. ³⁵John shone brightly for a while. And through him you were blessed and made glad. ³⁶But I have a greater witness than John. I am talking about the miracles I do. These have been given to me by the Father. And they are proof that the Father has sent me. ³⁷The Father himself has also testified about me. I don't mean he has come to you and spoken to you directly. ³⁸But you are not listening to him, for you refuse to believe me. And I am the one sent to you with God's message.

³⁹"You search the Scriptures, for you believe they give you eternal life. And the Scriptures point to me! ⁴⁰Yet you won't come to me so that I can give you life eternal!

⁴¹⁻⁴²"It is not important to me whether you praise me or not. But I know all about you. And I know that you don't have God's love within you. ⁴³I know this because I have come to you on my Father's behalf. And yet you refuse to welcome me. But you listen to those who aren't sent from him! ⁴⁴No wonder you can't believe! For you gladly honor each other. But you don't care about the honor that comes from the only God!

⁴⁵"Yet it is not I who will accuse you of this to the Father. Moses will! And Moses is the one you set your hopes on. ⁴⁶For you have refused to believe Moses. He wrote about me, but you refuse to believe him. So you refuse to believe in me. ⁴⁷You don't believe what he wrote. No wonder you don't believe in me!"

Jesus Feeds 5,000 People

There are 5,000 hungry people who need to be fed. But only one boy has a lunch. How can that feed 5,000 hungry people? What will Jesus do?

6 After this, Jesus crossed over the Sea of Galilee. This sea is also known as the Sea of Tiberias. ²⁻⁵And a huge crowd was following him wherever he went. Many of them were pilgrims on their way to Jerusalem for the Passover Feast. They watched him heal the sick. Then Jesus went up into the hills and sat down with his disciples. He soon saw a multitude of people climbing the hill, looking for him.

Jesus turned to Philip. "Philip," he said. "Where can we buy bread to feed all these people?" ⁶Now Jesus was testing Philip. For he already knew what he was going to do.

⁷Philip replied, "It would take a fortune to begin to do it!"

⁸⁻⁹Then Andrew, Simon Peter's brother, spoke up. "There's a youngster here with five barley loaves and two fishes! But what good is that with all this crowd?"

¹⁰"Tell everyone to sit down," Jesus ordered. And all of them sat down on the grassy slopes. There were about 5,000 men there all together. ¹¹Then Jesus took the loaves and gave thanks to God. And the bread was passed out to the people. After that he did the same with the fish. And everyone ate until full!

¹²"Now gather the scraps," Jesus told his disciples. "Nothing should be wasted." ¹³And 12 baskets were filled with the leftovers!

¹⁴The people saw that a great miracle had happened. They said, "Surely, he is the Prophet we have been looking for!"

¹⁵Jesus saw they wanted to take him by force and make him their king. So he went higher into the mountains alone.

● *Remember:* The lake where Jesus crossed had two names. What were they? (6:1) Why was there a big crowd there that day? (6:2-5) A boy had a lunch. What was in it? (6:8-9) How did Jesus feed the 5,000 with the boy's lunch? (6:10-12) What did the people think about this? (6:14) Could you feed 5,000 people with your lunch? Why not? What kind of person was Jesus?

- *Discover:* Jesus is God's Son. No one else can do what he can. Do you believe that? Why is it important to believe that?

- *Apply:* Do you want to know more about God? Read what Jesus, God's Son, said and did in the Bible.

- *What's next?* Can you walk across a lake? Matthew 14:22-33 tells about someone who did. ◼

Jesus Walks on the Water

[16]That evening his disciples went down to the shore to wait for him. [17]Darkness fell and Jesus still hadn't come back. So they got into the boat and headed out across the lake toward Capernaum. [18-19]But soon a storm swept down upon them as they rowed. The sea grew very rough. And they were in the middle of the lake. Suddenly they saw Jesus walking toward the boat! They were terrified. [20]So he called out to them and told them not to be afraid. [21]Then they were willing to let him come to them. And suddenly the boat was already at the place where they were going!

Jesus Is the Bread of Life from Heaven

[22-23]The next morning, back across the lake, crowds gathered on the shore. They were waiting to see Jesus. For they knew that Jesus and his disciples had come over in just one boat. And the disciples had taken that boat, leaving Jesus there. But Jesus was nowhere to be found. Several small boats from Tiberias were nearby. [24]So they took these boats to Capernaum to look for him.

[25]When they got there, they found him. "Sir, how did you get here?" they asked. [26]Jesus replied, "You want to be with me because I fed you. You haven't come because you saw the miracle. [27]But you shouldn't be so worried about things like food. They spoil and pass away very quickly. Spend your energy

looking for eternal life. Yes, I, the Messiah, can give it to you. For God the Father has sent me for this very reason."

[28]They replied, "What should we do to satisfy God?"

[29]Jesus told them, "God's will is that you believe in the one he has sent."

[30-31]They replied, "You must show us more miracles if you want us to believe. Give us free bread every day. Our ancestors had manna every day while they were in the wilderness! As the Scriptures say, 'Moses gave them bread from Heaven.'"

[32]Jesus said, "Moses didn't give it to them. My Father did. And now he offers you true Bread from Heaven. [33]The true Bread is a person, the one sent by God from Heaven. And he gives life to the world."

[34]"Sir," they said, "give us that bread every day of our lives!"

[35]Jesus replied, "I am the Bread of Life. No one coming to me will ever be hungry again. Those believing in me will never thirst. [36]But you haven't believed even though you have seen me. [37]But some will come to me. These are the ones the Father has given me. And I will never, never reject them. [38]For I have come here from Heaven to do the will of God who sent me. I am not doing things my own way. [39]It is God's will that I should not lose even one of all those he has given me. It is his will that I should raise them to eternal life at the Last Day. [40]For my Father wants everyone who sees his Son and believes in him to have eternal life. And I will raise up those who believe at the Last Day."

The Jews Disagree about What Jesus Is Saying

[41]Then the Jews began to murmur against him. For he had claimed to be the Bread from Heaven.

[42]"What?" they said. "Why, he is merely Jesus the son of Joseph. We know his father and mother. What is this he is saying, that he came down from Heaven?"

[43]But Jesus replied, "Don't murmur among yourselves about my saying that. [44]For no one can come to me unless the

Father who sent me draws him to me. And at the Last Day I will cause him to rise from the dead. ⁴⁵As it is written in the Scriptures, 'They will all be taught of God.' Those the Father speaks to will learn the truth from him. They will be drawn close to me. ⁴⁶Not that anyone actually sees the Father, for only I have seen him.

⁴⁷"How earnestly I tell you this. Anyone who believes in me already has eternal life! ⁴⁸⁻⁵¹Yes, I am the Bread of Life! Your fathers in the wilderness ate manna. But they all died. The Bread from Heaven gives eternal life to everyone who eats it. I am that Living Bread that came down out of Heaven. Anyone eating this Bread will live forever. This Bread is my flesh given for the sake of all people."

⁵²Then the Jews began arguing with each other about what he meant. "How can this man give us his flesh to eat?" they asked.

⁵³So Jesus said it again, "I tell you the truth. Unless you eat my flesh and drink my blood, you cannot have eternal life. ⁵⁴But anyone who does eat my flesh and drink my blood has eternal life. And I will raise him at the Last Day. ⁵⁵For my flesh is the true food, and my blood is the true drink. ⁵⁶Everyone who eats my flesh and drinks my blood is in me, and I in him. ⁵⁷I live by the power of the living Father who sent me. In the same way those who eat of me will live because of me! ⁵⁸I am the true Bread from Heaven. And anyone who eats this Bread will live forever. He will not die as your ancestors did." ⁵⁹He preached this message in the synagogue at Capernaum.

Many Followers Leave Jesus

⁶⁰Even his disciples said, "This is very hard to understand. Who can tell what he means?"

⁶¹Jesus knew within himself that his disciples were complaining. So he said to them, "Does this offend you? ⁶²Then what will you think if you see me, the Messiah, go back to Heaven? ⁶³Only the Spirit gives eternal life. The flesh is of no value. My message is spiritual and gives

life. ⁶⁴But some of you don't believe me." For Jesus knew from the beginning who didn't believe. And he knew the one who would betray him.

⁶⁵And Jesus said, "That is what I meant earlier. No one can come to me unless the Father draws him to me."

⁶⁶At this point many of his disciples turned away and left him.

⁶⁷Then Jesus asked the Twelve, "You aren't also leaving, are you?"

⁶⁸Simon Peter replied, "Master, to whom will we go? You alone have the words that give eternal life. ⁶⁹And we believe them and know you are God's Holy One."

⁷⁰Then Jesus said, "I chose the 12 of you. And one is a devil." ⁷¹He was speaking of Judas, son of Simon Iscariot. He was one of the 12 disciples. And he would be the one to betray Jesus.

Jesus' Brothers Make Fun of Him

7 After this, Jesus went to Galilee. He wanted to stay out of Judea where the Jewish leaders were planning his death. ²But soon it was time for the Feast of Tabernacles. This is one of the yearly Jewish holidays. ³And Jesus' brothers urged him to go to Judea for the feast.

"Go where more people can see your miracles!" they said. ⁴"You can't be famous when you hide like this! If you're so great, prove it to the world!" ⁵For even his brothers didn't believe in him.

⁶Jesus replied, "It is not the right time for me to go now. But you can go anytime. ⁷For the world doesn't hate you. But it does hate me, because I accuse it of sin and evil. ⁸You go on. I'll come later when it is the right time." ⁹So he stayed in Galilee.

Jesus Teaches at the Temple and Some Believe

¹⁰But after his brothers had left, then he went too. But he went secretly, staying out of the public eye. ¹¹The Jewish leaders tried to find him at the feast. They kept asking if anyone had seen him. ¹²There was a great deal of talk about him among the crowds. Some said, "He's a great man!" Others said, "No, he's fooling the people." ¹³But no one had the

courage to speak out for him. They were afraid of what the Jewish leaders might do to them.

¹⁴Then, halfway through the feast, Jesus went up to the Temple. And he spoke there openly. ¹⁵The Jewish leaders were surprised when they heard him. "How can he know so much when he's never been trained?" they asked.

¹⁶So Jesus told them, "I'm not teaching you my own thoughts. I speak the thoughts of God who sent me. ¹⁷Do any of you really want to do God's will? If so, then you will understand my teaching. You will know that is from God and not merely my own. ¹⁸Anyone who teaches his own ideas is looking for praise. But anyone seeking to honor the one who sent him is a true person. ¹⁹None of you obey the laws of Moses! So why accuse me of breaking them? Why do you try to kill me for this?"

²⁰The crowd replied, "You're out of your mind! Who's trying to kill you?"

²¹⁻²³Jesus replied, "I worked on the Sabbath by healing a man. And all of you were surprised. But you work on the Sabbath, too. Whenever you obey Moses' law to circumcise a child on the Sabbath you are working. (Actually, this law of circumcision is older than the laws of Moses.) Now suppose the right day for circumcising your child falls on the Sabbath. If this happens, you go right ahead and do it, as you should. So why should I be judged for healing a man on the Sabbath? ²⁴Think this through. You will see that I am right."

²⁵Some of the people who lived there in Jerusalem began asking questions. They asked, "Isn't this the man they are trying to kill? ²⁶But here he is preaching in public. And they say nothing to him. Can it be that our leaders think he really is the Messiah? ²⁷But how could he be? For we know where this man was born. When Christ comes, he will just appear. No one will know where he comes from."

²⁸So Jesus, still standing in the Temple, spoke to the crowd. "You should know about me and where I am from," he said. "I am not here on my own, but the one who sent me is true. ²⁹I know

him because I was with him. And he sent me to you."

³⁰Then the Jewish leaders looked for a way to arrest him. But no hand was laid on him, for God's time had not yet come.

³¹Many among the crowds at the Temple believed in him. They said, "What miracles would the Messiah do that this man hasn't done?"

The Jewish Leaders Try to Arrest Jesus

³²The Pharisees heard what the crowds were saying. So they and the chief priests sent officers to arrest Jesus. ³³But Jesus told them, "Not yet! I am supposed to be here a little longer. Then I will go back to the one who sent me. ³⁴You will look for me but not find me. And you won't be able to come where I am!"

³⁵The Jewish leaders were confused by this statement. "Where is he planning to go?" they asked. "Maybe he is thinking of leaving the country. Or perhaps he is going to the Jews in other lands. Or maybe he will go to the Gentiles! ³⁶What does he mean that we will not be able to find him? How can he say, 'You won't be able to come where I am'?"

³⁷On the last day of the feast, Jesus spoke loudly to the crowd. He said, "If anyone is thirsty, let him come to me and drink. ³⁸For the Scriptures spoke of this. They said that rivers of living water will flow from inside those who believe in me." ³⁹Now Jesus was speaking of the Spirit. The Spirit would be given to everyone who believed in him. But the Spirit had not yet been given because Jesus had not yet been glorified.

⁴⁰When they heard this, some said, "This man surely is the prophet." ⁴¹⁻⁴²Others said, "He is the Messiah." Still others, "But he can't be! Will the Messiah come from Galilee? For the Scriptures say the Messiah will be born in the line of David. They also say that he will be born in Bethlehem, David's town." ⁴³So the crowd was divided about him. ⁴⁴Some wanted to arrest him, but no one touched him.

The Pharisees Are Frustrated

45The Temple police had been sent to arrest Jesus. But they went back to the chief priests and Pharisees without him. "Why didn't you bring him in?" they demanded.

46"He says such great things!" they said. "We've never heard anything like it."

47"So you also have been led astray?" the Pharisees mocked. 48"Not one of us Jewish rulers or Pharisees has believed in him. 49These stupid crowds do. But what do they know about the Scriptures? They are cursed!"

50Then Nicodemus spoke up. He was the Jewish leader who came secretly to Jesus. 51"Is it legal to convict a man before he is even tried?" he asked.

52They replied, "Are you a Galilean too? Search the Scriptures and see for yourself. A prophet never comes out of Galilee!"

53Then everybody went home.

Jesus Forgives a Guilty Woman

8 Jesus went back to the Mount of Olives. 2But early the next morning he was back again at the Temple. A crowd soon gathered around him. Jesus sat down and talked to them. 3As he was speaking, the Jewish leaders and Pharisees came. They brought a woman caught in adultery. They placed her in front of the crowd.

4"Teacher," they said to Jesus, "this woman was caught in the act of adultery. 5Moses' law says to kill her. What do you say about it?"

6They were trying to trap him. They wanted him to say something they could use against him. But Jesus stooped down and wrote in the dust with his finger. 7They kept demanding an answer. So he stood up again and said, "All right. Throw the stones at her until she dies. But only he who never sinned may throw the first stone!"

8Then he stooped down again and wrote some more in the dust. 9And the Jewish leaders went away one by one, beginning with the eldest. Finally, only Jesus was left with the woman.

10Then Jesus said to her, "Where are the men who accused you? Didn't even one of them condemn you?"

11"No, sir," she said.

And Jesus said, "Neither do I. Go and sin no more."

Jesus Is the Light of the World

12Later, Jesus spoke to the people. He said, "I am the Light of the world. If you follow me, you won't stumble through the darkness. Living light will guide your path."

13The Pharisees replied, "You are bragging and lying!"

14Jesus told them, "What I say is true, even though I am talking about myself. For I know where I came from and where I am going. But you don't know this about me. 15You pass judgment on me without knowing the facts. I am not judging you now. 16But if I were, it would be completely fair and just. For I have with me the Father who sent me. 17Your laws say that the witness of two men is accepted as fact. 18Well, I am one witness. And my Father who sent me is the other."

19"Where is your father?" they asked.

Jesus answered, "You don't know who I am. So you don't know who my Father is. If you knew me, then you would know him too."

20Jesus said this while in the Treasury of the Temple. But he was not arrested, for his time had not yet run out.

The Jewish Leaders Do Not Understand

21Later he said to them again, "I am going away. You will look for me, but you will die in your sins. And you cannot come where I am going."

22The Jews asked, "Is he planning to kill himself? What does he mean, 'You cannot come where I am going'?"

23Then he said to them, "You are from below. I am from above. You are of this world. I am not. 24That is why I said that you will die in your sins. For unless you believe that I am the one, you will die in your sins."

25"Tell us who you are," they demanded.

He replied, "I am the one I have always claimed to be. 26I could condemn you for much, but I won't. For I say only what I am told to say by the one who sent me. And he is Truth." 27They still didn't understand that he was talking to them about God.

28So Jesus said, "You will kill the Messiah. And then you will know that I am he. And you will see that I have not been telling you my own ideas. I have spoken only what the Father taught me. 29And he who sent me is with me. He has not left me. For I always do the things that are pleasing to him."

Be a True Child of God

30-31Many of the Jews who heard him say these things believed in him.

Jesus said to them, "You are truly my disciples if you live as I tell you to. 32You will know the truth, and the truth will set you free."

33"But we are descendants of Abraham," they said. "We have never been slaves to anyone! What do you mean, 'set free'?"

34Jesus replied, "You are slaves of sin, every one of you. 35And slaves don't have rights. But a son has every right there is! 36So if the Son sets you free, you will indeed be free. 37Yes, I know you are descendants of Abraham! And yet some of you are trying to kill me. You want to do this because you do not accept my message. 38I am telling you what I saw when I was with my Father. But you are following the advice of your father."

39"Our father is Abraham," they declared.

"No!" Jesus replied, "for if he were, you would follow his example. 40But instead you are trying to kill me. And I told you the truth I heard from God! Abraham wouldn't do a thing like that! 41No, you are obeying your real father when you act that way."

They replied, "We were not born out of wedlock. Our true Father is God himself."

42Jesus told them, "If that were so, then you would love me. For I have come to you from God. I am not here on my own, but he sent me. 43Why can't you understand what I am saying? It is because you are prevented from doing

so! 44For you are the children of your father the devil. You love to do the evil things he does. He was a murderer from the beginning. There is no truth in him. When he lies, it is perfectly normal. For he is the father of lies. 45And so when I tell the truth, you just don't believe it!

46"Which of you can accuse me of one single sin? And since I am telling you the truth, why don't you believe me? 47Anyone whose Father is God listens gladly to the words of God. Since you don't, it proves you aren't his children."

Jesus Angers the Leaders by Claiming to Be God

48"You Samaritan!" the Jewish leaders said. "Didn't we say all along you had a demon?"

49"No," Jesus said, "I have no demon in me. For I honor my Father, and you dishonor me. 50I have no wish to make myself great. God wants this for me and judges those who reject me. 51I tell you the truth. No one who keeps my word will ever die!"

52The Jews said, "Now we know you have a demon in you! Even Abraham and the greatest prophets died. And yet you say that keeping your word will keep a man from dying! 53So you are greater than our father Abraham, who died? And greater than the prophets, who died? Who do you think you are?" 54Then Jesus said to them, "If I am merely bragging about myself, it doesn't count. But it is my Father who is saying these things about me. (And you claim that this Father is your God.) 55But you do not even know him. I do. If I said otherwise, I would be as great a liar as you! But it is true. I know him and fully obey him. 56Your father Abraham rejoiced to see my day. He knew I was coming and was glad."

57The Jews said, "You aren't even 50 years old! And you say you've seen Abraham?"

58Jesus said, "The truth is that I was in existence before Abraham was born!"

59At that point the Jewish leaders picked up stones to kill him. But Jesus was hidden from them, and he left the Temple.

Jesus Heals a Blind Man

How could a man get in trouble for healing a blind person? Jesus did! Then the man got in trouble, too. So did his parents! This is what happened.

9 As Jesus was walking along, he saw a man who had been blind from birth. 2"Master," his disciples asked him, "why was this man born blind? Was it because of his own sins or those of his parents?"

3"Neither," Jesus answered. "He was born blind to show the power of God. 4All of us must do the jobs given to us by the one who sent me. For there is little time left before the night falls and all work stops. 5But while I am still in the world, I give it my light."

6Then he spat on the ground and made mud from the spittle. He smoothed the mud over the blind man's eyes. 7And he told him, "Go and wash in the Pool of Siloam." The word *Siloam* means "Sent." So the man went where he was sent. He washed his eyes and came back seeing!

8His neighbors and others knew him as a blind beggar. When they saw him, they asked each other, "Is this the same man?"

9Some said yes, and some said no. "It can't be the same man," they thought. "But he surely looks like him!"

And the beggar said, "I am the same man!"

10Then they asked him what had happened.

11And he told them, "A man called Jesus made mud and smoothed it over my eyes. He told me to go to the Pool of Siloam and wash off the mud. I did, and now I can see!"

12"Where is he now?" they asked.

"I don't know," he replied.

13Then they took the man to the Pharisees. 14Now this all had happened on the Sabbath day. 15The Pharisees asked the man what had happened to him. So he told them how Jesus had smoothed the mud over his eyes. And he told them how he had washed the mud away, and then could see.

16Some of them said, "Then this Jesus is not from God. For he did this work on the Sabbath."

Others said, "But how could an ordinary sinner do such miracles?" So the people's opinions of Jesus were divided.

17Then the Pharisees turned on the man who had been blind. They said, "Who do you think this man is who opened your eyes?"

"I think he must be a prophet sent from God," the man replied.

18The Jews wouldn't believe he had been blind. So they called in his parents. 19They asked them, "Is this your son? Was he born blind? If so, how can he see?"

20His parents replied, "We know this is our son and that he was born blind. 21But we don't know what happened to make him see. And we don't know who did it. He is old enough to speak for himself. Ask him."

22-23They said this because they were afraid of the Jewish leaders. This was because the leaders had made an announcement. They had said that anyone saying Jesus was the Messiah would be expelled from the synagogue.

24So for the second time they called in the man who had been blind. They told him, "Give the glory to God. For we know Jesus is an evil person."

25"I don't know whether he is good or bad," the man replied. "But I know that I was blind and now I see!"

26"But what did he do?" they asked. "How did he heal you?"

27"Look!" the man exclaimed. "I told you once. Didn't you listen? Why do you want to hear it again? Do you want to become his disciples too?"

28Then they cursed him and said, "You are his disciple. We are disciples of Moses. 29We know God has spoken to Moses. But as for this man, we don't know anything about him."

30"Why, that's very strange!" the man replied. "He can heal blind men, and yet you don't know anything about him! 31Well, God doesn't listen to evil men. He listens to those who worship him and do his will. ³²Since the world began there has never been anyone who could open the eyes of someone born blind. ³³If this man were not from God, he couldn't do it."

³⁴"You were born in sin!" they shouted. "Are you trying to teach us?" And they threw him out.

³⁵When Jesus heard what had happened, he found the man. He said to him, "Do you believe in the Messiah?"

³⁶The man answered, "Who is he, sir? For I want to believe in him."

³⁷"You have seen him," Jesus said. "And he is speaking to you right now!"

³⁸"Yes, Lord!" the man said. "I believe!" And he worshiped Jesus.

³⁹Then Jesus told him, "I have come into the world to give sight to the blind. And I will show those who think they see that they are blind."

⁴⁰The Pharisees who were there asked, "Are you saying we are blind?"

⁴¹"If you were blind, you wouldn't be guilty," Jesus replied. "But your guilt remains because you claim to see."

- *Remember:* How long had this man been blind? (9:1) Why was he blind? (9:3) How did Jesus heal him? (9:6-7) Why were the Pharisees angry at Jesus? (9:14-16) Did the man who was blind think Jesus was from God? (9:17,32-33) Why did Jesus come into the world? (9:39) Jesus said he came to help spiritually blind people. Those are people who have not seen God's truth. They don't understand the Bible.

- *Discover:* Jesus wants us to understand what the Bible says. The Bible tells us God's truth.

- *Apply:* Do you read your Bible each day? Do you try to understand what God says? He wants you to.

- *What's next?* It's just one little coin that's lost. Why bother to look for it, right? Wrong! Read Luke 15:8-10. ■

Jesus: The Good Shepherd

10 "I tell you the truth. A man might refuse to walk through the gate into a sheepfold. Or he might sneak over the wall. But if he does this, he must surely be a thief! ²For the shepherd comes through the gate. ³The gatekeeper opens

the gate for him. The sheep hear his voice and come to him. And he calls his own sheep by name and leads them out. ⁴He walks ahead of them. And they follow him, for they know his voice. ⁵They won't follow a stranger but will run from him. For they don't know his voice."

Jesus died for us

I am the Good Shepherd. The Good Shepherd lays down his life for the sheep.

John 10:11

⁶Those who heard Jesus tell this story didn't know what he meant. ⁷So he explained it to them.

"I am the Gate for the sheep," he said. ⁸"All others who came before me were thieves and robbers. But the true sheep did not listen to them. ⁹Yes, I am the Gate. Those who come in by way of the Gate will be saved. They will go in and out and find green pastures. ¹⁰The thief's purpose is to steal, kill, and destroy. My purpose is to give life in all its fullness.

¹¹"I am the Good Shepherd. The Good Shepherd lays down his life for the sheep. ¹²A hired man will run when he sees a wolf coming. He will leave the sheep. For they aren't his and he isn't their shepherd. And so the wolf leaps on them and scatters the flock. ¹³The hired man runs because he has no real concern for the sheep.

¹⁴"I am the Good Shepherd and know my own sheep, and they know me. ¹⁵This is just as my Father knows me and I know the Father. And I lay down my life for the sheep. ¹⁶I have other sheep, too, that are not of this fold. I must bring them also, and they will listen to my voice. And there will be one flock with one Shepherd.

¹⁷"The Father loves me because I lay down my life. And in doing so, I will have it back again. ¹⁸No one can kill me without my consent. I lay down my life voluntarily. For I have the right and power to lay it down when I want to. And also I have the right and power to take it again. For the Father has given me this right."

[19]The Jews were again divided in their opinions about him. [20]Some of them said, "He has a demon, or else he is crazy. Why listen to a man like that?"

[21]Others said, "This doesn't sound to us like a man with a demon! Can a demon open the eyes of blind men?"

The Jewish Leaders Try to Stone Jesus Again

[22-23]It was winter. Jesus was in Jerusalem for the Feast of Dedication. He was at the Temple, walking through the section known as Solomon's Hall. [24]The Jewish leaders were all around him. They asked him, "How long are you going to keep us in suspense? If you are the Messiah, tell us plainly."

Jesus is God

I and the Father are one.

John 10:30

---

[25]"I have already told you, and you don't believe me," Jesus replied. "The proof is in the miracles I do in the name of my Father. [26]But you don't believe me because you are not in my flock. [27]My sheep know my voice. I know them, and they follow me. [28]I give them eternal life and they will never die. No one will take them away from me. [29]For my Father has given them to me. And he is more powerful than anyone else. So no one can kidnap them from me. [30]I and the Father are one."

[31]Then again the Jewish leaders picked up stones to kill him.

[32]Jesus said, "At God's direction I have done many miracles. For which one are you killing me?"

[33]They replied, "Not for any good work, but for blasphemy. You, a mere man, have said that you are God."

[34-36]"In your own Law it says that men are gods!" he replied. "The Scripture calls certain men gods. For God's message came to them. (And the Scripture is never untrue.) So do you call it blasphemy when the one sent into the world by the Father says, 'I am the Son of God'? [37]Don't believe me unless I do miracles of God. [38]But if I do, believe them even if you don't believe me. Then you will know that the Father is in me, and I in the Father."

[39]Once again they started to arrest him. But he walked away and left them. [40]He went beyond the Jordan River. He was near the place where John first baptized people. [41]And many followed him there.

"John didn't do miracles," they said to one another. "But all his predictions about this man have come true." [42]And many believed in him.

Jesus Raises Lazarus from the Dead

Lazarus was very sick. Then he died. He was buried in a cave. A few days later Jesus came to town. He went to the cave. He called to Lazarus to come back to life. Did he? Could he?

11 Now a man named Lazarus was sick. He lived in Bethany with his sisters Mary and Martha. (This was the Mary who put perfume on Jesus' feet. Then she wiped his feet with her hair.) [3]So the two sisters sent a message to Jesus. It said, "Sir, your good friend is very sick."

[4]But when Jesus heard about it he said, "This sickness will not result in death. It is for the glory

of God. I, the Son of God, will receive glory from this."

⁵Jesus was very fond of Martha, Mary, and Lazarus. ⁶But he stayed where he was for the next two days. ⁷Then he said to his disciples, "Let's go to Judea."

Anyone who believes in Jesus will live forever

I am the resurrection and the life. Anyone who believes in me, even though he dies, will live again.

John 11:25

---

⁸But his disciples objected. "Master," they said, "only a few days ago the Jewish leaders in Judea were trying to kill you. Are you going there again?"

⁹Jesus replied, "There are 12 hours of daylight each day. And during each hour of the day a man can walk safely and not stumble. ¹⁰Only at night is there danger of stumbling, because of the dark."

¹¹Then he said, "Our friend Lazarus has gone to sleep. But now I will go and waken him!"

¹²⁻¹³The disciples thought Jesus meant Lazarus was having a good rest. They said, "That means he is getting better!" But Jesus meant Lazarus had died.

¹⁴Then he told them plainly, "Lazarus is dead. ¹⁵And for your sake, I am glad I wasn't there. For this will give you another chance to believe in me. Come, let's go to him."

¹⁶Thomas was nicknamed "The Twin." He said to his fellow disciples, "Let's go too. Let us die with Jesus."

¹⁷They went to Bethany. And they were told that Lazarus had been in his tomb for four days. ¹⁸Bethany was only a few miles down the road from Jerusalem. ¹⁹And many of the Jews had come to comfort Martha and Mary. ²⁰Martha heard that Jesus was coming. So she went out to meet him. But Mary stayed at home.

²¹Martha said to Jesus, "Sir, you should have been here! Then my brother wouldn't have died. ²²And even now it's not too late. For I know that God will do whatever you ask him."

²³Jesus told her, "Your brother will come back to life again."

²⁴"Yes," Martha said, "he will rise in the resurrection at the last day."

²⁵Jesus told her, "I am the resurrection and the life. Anyone who believes in me, even though he dies, will live again. ²⁶He is given eternal life for believing in me and will never die. Do you believe this, Martha?"

²⁷"Yes, Master," she told him. "I believe you are the Messiah, the Son of God. You are the one we have waited for."

²⁸Then she left him and went back to Mary. Martha told her, "He is here and wants to see you." ²⁹So Mary went to him at once.

³⁰Now Jesus had stayed outside the village, at the place where Martha met him. ³¹The Jews who were at the house comforting Mary saw her leave. They thought she was going to Lazarus' tomb to cry. So they followed her.

³²When Mary went to where Jesus was, she fell down at his feet. She said, "Sir, if you had been here, my brother would not have died."

³³Jesus saw her crying and the Jews were crying with her. He was very moved and deeply troubled. ³⁴"Where is he buried?" he asked them.

They told him, "Come and see." ³⁵Tears came to Jesus' eyes.

³⁶"They were close friends," the Jewish leaders said. "See how much he loved him."

³⁷⁻³⁸But some said, "This man healed a blind man. Why couldn't he keep Lazarus from dying?"

And again Jesus was deeply moved. Then they came to the tomb. It was a cave with a stone rolled across its door. ³⁹"Roll the stone aside," Jesus told them.

But Martha, the dead man's sister, said, "By now the smell will be terrible. For he has been dead four days."

⁴⁰"But didn't I tell you that you will see God's glory?" Jesus asked her. "All you have to do is believe."

⁴¹So they rolled the stone aside. Then Jesus lifted up his eyes, "Father, thank you for hearing me. ⁴²(You always hear

me, of course. I said it because of all these people standing here. It will help them believe that you sent me.)" [43]Then he shouted, "Lazarus, come out!"

[44]And Lazarus came out! He was tied up in his graveclothes. His face was wrapped in a head covering. Jesus told them, "Unwrap him and let him go!"

[45]And many of the Jews who were with Mary saw this and believed in him. [46]But some went away to the Pharisees and told them about it.

[47]Then the chief priests and Pharisees called a meeting. They wanted to talk about what had happened.

"What are we going to do?" they asked each other. "For this man certainly does great miracles. [48]If we let him alone the whole nation will follow him. And then the Romans will come and take away our authority and Temple."

[49]One of them, Caiaphas, was High Priest that year. He said, "You don't know anything. [50]Let this one man die for the people. Why should the whole nation die?"

[51]This prophecy that Jesus should die for the whole nation came from Caiaphas. He was the High Priest at that time. He didn't think of it by himself, but was inspired to say it. [52]It was a prediction that Jesus' death would not be for Israel only. It would be for all the children of God scattered around the world. [53]From that time on the Jewish leaders began planning Jesus' death.

- *Remember:* Where did Lazarus live? (11:1-2) Who did he live with? (11:1-2)

Why did Lazarus get sick? (11:4) How long had Lazarus been dead when Jesus came to town? (11:17) What did Jesus say to Lazarus? (11:43) What did Lazarus do? (11:44) Can you make a dead person come back to life? Do you know anyone who can? How could Jesus do this? Who is he?

- *Discover:* Jesus is God's Son. He is the only one who can make dead people live again (see 11:25).

- *Apply:* Do you want to live in Heaven someday? Jesus is the one who can help you. Believe in him. Ask him to be your Savior.

- *What's next?* Jesus does something special for 10 people. Read Luke 17:11-19. ◼

Will Jesus Come to Passover?

[54]Jesus now stopped his public ministry and left Jerusalem. He went to the edge of the desert, to the village of Ephraim. He stayed there with his disciples.

[55]The Passover Feast, a Jewish holiday, was near. Many country people went to Jerusalem before the feast began. They did this to make themselves pure for the Passover Feast. [56]Now all these people wanted to see Jesus. They talked to one another in the Temple and asked each other, "What do you think? Will he come for the Passover?" [57]Meanwhile the chief priests and Pharisees had made an announcement. They said that anyone seeing Jesus must report him right away. That way they could arrest him.

Mary Anoints Jesus' Feet

Mary poured perfume on Jesus' feet. This perfume cost a lot of money. A man grumbled about this. He thought the woman should not have done this. But what did Jesus say?

12 Six days before the Passover Feast began, Jesus arrived in Bethany. Lazarus, the man Jesus had brought back to life, lived there. [2]A banquet was prepared in Jesus' honor. Martha served, and Lazarus sat at the table with him. [3]Then Mary took a jar of costly perfume made from nard. She poured it out on Jesus' feet. Then she wiped them off with her hair. And the house was filled with the sweet smell.

⁴But Judas Iscariot, one of his disciples, spoke up. This was the disciple who would soon betray Jesus. Judas said, ⁵"That perfume was worth a fortune! It should have been sold and the money given to the poor." ⁶Not that he cared for the poor. He was in charge of the disciples' funds. And he often dipped into them for his own use!

⁷Jesus replied, "Leave her alone. She did it to prepare me for my burial. ⁸You can always help the poor. But I won't be with you very long."

⁹The people of Jerusalem soon heard that Jesus was there. They flocked to see him and also to see Lazarus. Lazarus was the man who had come back to life again. ¹⁰Then the chief priests decided to kill Lazarus, too. ¹¹For many of the Jews now believed in Jesus. And it was because they had seen Lazarus raised from the dead.

- *Remember:* Where was Jesus? (12:1) How did Martha honor Jesus? (12:2) How did Mary honor Jesus? (12:3) Who grumbled about this? Why? (12:4-5) What did Judas often do that was wrong? (12:6) What did Jesus say about the perfume? (12:7) What would you say to Judas if you were there? Why?

- *Discover:* No gift is too good for Jesus.

- *Apply:* Do you ever think you are giving too much to Jesus? You can't!

- *What's next?* If someone gave you $5,000, what would you do with it? How would you use it? Read Matthew 25:14-30 to see what one man did when this happened to him. ∎

A Huge Crowd Salutes Jesus

¹²The next day, the crowd in Jerusalem heard that Jesus was coming. And a huge crowd of Passover visitors went out to meet him. ¹³They took palm branches and waved them. They shouted, "The Savior! God bless the King of Israel!"

¹⁴Jesus rode along on a young donkey. This fulfilled the prophecy that said, ¹⁵"Don't be afraid of your King, people of Israel. He will come to you meekly, sitting on a donkey's colt!"

¹⁶His disciples didn't know at the time that this fulfilled prophecy. But after Jesus rose from the dead, they saw that many prophecies had come true.

¹⁷There were people in the crowd who had seen Jesus call Lazarus back to life. And they were tell-

ing everyone all about it. [18]That was the main reason why so many went out to meet him. They had all heard about this great miracle.

[19]Then the Pharisees said to each other, "We've lost. Look! The whole world has gone after him!"

Jesus Explains Why He Must Die

[20]Some Greeks had come to Jerusalem to attend the Passover. [21]They came to Philip, who was from Bethsaida. They asked him, "Sir, we want to meet Jesus." [22]Philip told Andrew about it. And they went together to ask Jesus.

[23-24]Jesus told them that the time had come for him to be glorified. "I must fall and die," he said. "I will be like a kernel of wheat that falls into the earth. Unless I die I will be alone, a single seed. But my death will produce many new wheat kernels. It will result in a rich harvest of new lives. [25]If you love your life you will lose it. If you give up your life you will exchange it for eternal life.

[26]"If anyone wants to be my disciple, he must follow me. For my servants must be where I am. And if they follow me, the Father will honor them. [27]Now my soul is deeply troubled. Will I pray, 'Father, save me from what lies ahead'? But that is the very reason why I came! [28]Father, bring glory and honor to your name."

Then a voice spoke from Heaven saying, "I have already done this. And I will do it again." [29]When the crowd heard the voice, some of them thought it was thunder. Others declared an angel had spoken to him.

[30]Then Jesus told them, "The voice was to help you, not me. [31]The time of judgment for the world has come. The time has come when Satan, the prince of this world, will be cast out. [32]And when I am lifted up on the cross, I will draw everyone to me." [33]He said this to tell them how he was going to die.

[34]"Die?" asked the crowd. "We understood that the Messiah would live forever and never die. Why are you saying you will die? What Messiah are you talking about?"

[35]Jesus replied, "My light will shine out for you just a little while longer. Walk in it while you can before the darkness comes. For then it will be too late for you to find your way. [36]Make use of the Light while there is still time. Then you will become light bearers."

After saying these things, Jesus went away and was hidden from them.

Some Believe; Most Don't

[37]But despite all the miracles he had done, they would not believe in him. [38]This is exactly what Isaiah the prophet had said: "Lord, who will believe us? Who will accept God's mighty miracles as proof?" [39]But they couldn't believe. Isaiah also spoke about this. [40]He said, "God has blinded their eyes and hardened their hearts. They can neither see nor understand nor turn to me to heal them." [41]Isaiah was talking about Jesus when he said this. For he had seen a vision of the Messiah's glory.

[42]But even many of the Jewish leaders believed Jesus was the Messiah. However, they wouldn't admit it to anyone. They were afraid the Pharisees would expel them from the synagogue. [43]They loved the praise of men more than the praise of God.

God's Instructions Lead to Eternal Life

[44]Jesus shouted to the crowds, "If you trust me, you are really trusting God. [45]For when you see me, you are seeing the one who sent me. [46]I have come as a Light to shine in this dark world. All who put their trust in me will no longer wander in the darkness. [47]If anyone hears me and doesn't obey me, I am not his judge. For I have come to save the world and not to judge it. [48]But all who reject me and my message will be judged at the Day of Judgment. And they will be judged by the words I have spoken. [49]For these are not my own ideas. I have told you what the Father said to tell you. [50]And I know his instructions lead to eternal life. So whatever he tells me to say, I say!"

Jesus Washes His Disciples Feet

13 It was the evening of Passover Day. Jesus knew that it would be his last night on earth before going back to his Father. During supper the devil had already prompted Judas Iscariot to betray Jesus. (Judas was Simon's son.) Jesus knew that the Father had given him everything. And he knew that he had come from God and would go back to God. And how he loved his disciples! 4So he got up from the table and took off his robe. He wrapped a towel around him. 5Then he poured water into a basin and began to wash the disciples' feet. He wiped them with the towel he had around him.

6Then he came to Simon Peter. Peter said, "Master, you shouldn't be washing our feet!"

7Jesus replied, "You don't understand now why I am doing it. Someday you will."

8"No," Peter said, "you will never wash my feet!"

"But if I don't, you can't be my partner," Jesus replied.

9Simon Peter exclaimed, "Then wash my hands and head, not just my feet!"

Jesus wants us to love each other as much as he loves us

You must love one another just as much as I love you.

John 13:34

10Jesus replied, "If a person has bathed all over he is clean. He needs only to have his feet washed. Now you are clean. But that isn't true of everyone here." 11For Jesus knew who would betray him. That is what he meant when he said, "Not all of you are clean."

12After washing their feet he put on his robe again and sat down. Then he asked, "Do you understand what I was doing? 13You call me 'Master' and 'Lord.' And you do well to say it, for it is true. 14As I, the Lord and Teacher, have washed your feet, you ought to wash each other's feet. 15I have given you an example to follow. Do as I have done to you. 16A servant is not greater than his master. And the messenger is not more important than the one who sends him. 17You know these things. Now do them! That is the path of blessing.

18"I am not saying these things to all of you. I know each one of you so well! The Scripture says, 'One who eats supper with me will betray me.' And this will soon come true. 19I tell you this now so that when it happens, you will believe in me. 20"Truly, anyone who welcomes my messenger welcomes me. And to welcome me is to welcome the Father who sent me."

Jesus and the Disciples Eat Their Last Supper Together

21Now Jesus was very upset and in great pain of spirit. He said, "Yes, it is true! One of you will betray me." 22The disciples looked at each other. They wondered whom he could mean. 23The beloved disciple was sitting next to Jesus at the table. 24Simon Peter motioned to him to ask him who was the betrayer.

25The beloved disciple turned to Jesus. "Lord, who is it?" he asked.

26Jesus told him, "It is the one to whom I give the bread dipped in sauce."

And when he had dipped it, he gave it to Judas. Now Judas was the son of Simon Iscariot.

27As soon as Judas had eaten it, Satan entered into him. Then Jesus told him, "Hurry. Do it now."

28None of the others at the table knew what Jesus meant. 29Some thought that Jesus was telling him to buy food. Others thought Jesus told him to give some money to the poor. They thought these things because Judas was their treasurer. 30Judas left at once, going out into the night.

Jesus Predicts That Peter Will Deny Him

31As soon as Judas left the room, Jesus said, "My time has come. I will be glorified by God, and God will be glorified. 32And God will give me his own glory. And all this will happen very soon. 33Dear, dear children, how short are these moments before I go away! And then you will look for me. But you won't be able to come to me. This is also what I told the Jews.

³⁴"And so I am giving a new command to you now. You must love one another just as much as I love you. ³⁵Your love will prove to the world that you are my disciples."

³⁶Simon Peter said, "Master, where are you going?"

And Jesus replied, "You can't go with me now. But you will follow me later."

³⁷"But why can't I come now?" he asked. "I am ready to die for you."

³⁸Jesus answered, "Die for me? You will deny me three times. And you'll do it before the cock crows tomorrow morning."

Jesus Is the Way,
the Truth, and the Life

14 Jesus said, "Don't let your hearts be troubled. You trust in God, now trust in me. ²⁻³There are many homes in my Father's house. I am going to prepare a place for you. I will come again and take you to me. Then you will be with me where I am about to go. If this weren't so, I would tell you plainly. ⁴And you know the way to where I am going."

⁵"No, we don't," Thomas said. "We haven't any idea where you are going. So how can we know the way?"

⁶Jesus said, "I am the Way, the Truth, and the Life. No one can get to the Father except through me. ⁷If you really knew me, then you would know who my Father is. From now on you know him and have seen him!"

⁸Philip said, "Sir, show us the Father. Then we will be content."

⁹Jesus replied, "Don't you even yet know who I am, Philip? And I have been with you for all this time! Anyone who has seen me has seen the Father! So why are you asking to see him? ¹⁰Don't you believe that I am in the Father and the Father is in me? The words I say are not my own. They are from my Father who lives in me. And he does his work through me. ¹¹Just believe that I am in the Father and the Father is in me. Believe it because of the great miracles you have seen me do.

¹²⁻¹³"I tell you the truth. If you believe in me, you will do the same works I have done. You will do even greater ones, because I am going to the Father. You can ask him for anything, using my name. And I will do it! This will bring praise to the Father through his Son. ¹⁴Yes, ask anything, using my name! And I will do it!

Jesus Promises that
the Holy Spirit Will Come

¹⁵⁻¹⁶"If you love me, obey me. And I will ask the Father and he will give you another Comforter. He will never leave you. ¹⁷He is the Holy Spirit, the Spirit who leads into all truth. The world at large cannot receive him. The world isn't looking for him and doesn't know him. But you do, for he lives with you now and some day will be in you. ¹⁸No, I will not abandon you or leave you as orphans. I will come to you. ¹⁹In just a little while I will be gone from the world. But I will still be here with you. For I will live again, and you will too. ²⁰I will come back to life again. Then you will know that I am in my Father, and you in me, and I in you. ²¹The one who obeys me is the one who loves me. And because he loves me, my Father will love him. And I will, too. Furthermore, I will reveal myself to him."

Jesus is the only way to God

Jesus said, "I am the Way, the Truth, and the Life. No one can get to the Father except through me."

John 14:6

---

²²Judas had a question. This was not Judas Iscariot, but the other disciple with that name. He said, "Why are you going to reveal yourself only to us and not to the world?"

²³Jesus replied, "Because I will reveal myself only to those who love me and obey me. The Father will love them, too. And we will come to them and live with them. ²⁴Anyone who doesn't obey me doesn't love me. And remember, my words to you come from the Father who sent me.

25"I am telling you these things now while I am still with you. 26Then the Father will send the Comforter to you. The Comforter is the Holy Spirit. He will teach you much. And he will remind you of everything I myself have told you.

Jesus Leaves a Gift of Peace

27"I am leaving you my peace! And the peace I give isn't like the peace the world gives. So don't be troubled or afraid. 28Remember what I told you. I am going away, but I will come back to you again. If you really love me, you will be very happy for me. Now I can go to the Father, who is greater than I am. 29I have told you these things before they happen. I have done this so that when they do, you will believe.

30"I don't have much more time to talk to you. For the prince of this world is on his way. He has no power over me. 31But I will freely do what the Father asks of me. That way the world will know that I love the Father. Come, let's be going.

A Story about the Vine and the Branches

15 "I am the true Vine, and my Father is the Gardener. 2He cuts off all the branches that don't produce. He prunes those branches that bear fruit so that they will produce more. 3He has already pruned you back for greater fruitfulness. He did this by means of the commands I gave you. 4Take care to live in me. And let me live in you. For a branch can't produce fruit when it's cut from the vine. In the same way, you can't be fruitful apart from me.

5"Yes, I am the Vine. You are the branches. Whoever lives in me and I in him will produce much fruit. For apart from me you can't do anything. 6If anyone separates from me, he is thrown away like a useless branch. This branch withers and is gathered into a pile with others and burned. 7Stay in me and obey my commands. Then you may ask for anything you like, and it will be given to you! 8My true disciples produce rich harvests. This brings great glory to my Father.

9"I have loved you even as the Father has loved me. Live within my love. 10When you obey me you are living in my love. In the same way, I obey my Father and live in his love. 11I have told you this so that you will be filled with my joy. 12I demand that you love one another as much as I love you. 13And here is how to measure it. The greatest love is shown when a person lays down his life for his friends. 14And you are my friends if you obey me. 15I no longer call you slaves. For a master doesn't confide in his slaves. Now you are my friends. This is proved by the fact that I have told you all that the Father told me.

16"You didn't choose me! I chose you! I appointed you to go and produce fruit. Whatever you ask from the Father, using my name, he will give it to you.

Jesus Warns about the World's Hatred

17"I demand that you love one another. 18You will be hated by the world! But then, it hated me before it hated you. 19The world would love you if you belonged to it. But you don't, because I chose you to come out of the world. So it hates you. 20Do you remember what I told you? 'A slave isn't greater than his master!' Since they have treated me badly, they will do the same to you. And if they had listened to me, they would listen to you! 21The people of the world will persecute you because you belong to me. For they don't know God who sent me.

22"They would not be guilty if I had not come and spoken to them. But now they have no excuse for their sin. 23Anyone hating me is also hating my Father. 24If I hadn't done such miracles among them, they would not be guilty. But as it is, they saw these miracles but still they hated me and my Father. 25This has fulfilled the prophecy, 'They hated me without reason.'

26"But I will send you the Comforter, the Spirit of truth. He will come to you from the Father. He will tell you all about me. 27And you also must tell everyone about me. You will do this because you have been with me from the beginning.

16 "I have told you these things so you won't be confused by all that lies ahead. ²For you will be expelled from the synagogues. And the time is coming when those who kill you will think they are serving God. ³This is because they have never known the Father or me. ⁴Yes, I'm telling you these things now. When they happen you will remember I warned you. I didn't tell you earlier because I was with you.

Jesus Teaches about the Holy Spirit

⁵"But now I am going away to the one who sent me. And none of you ask where I am going. None of you wonder why. ⁶Instead you are only filled with sadness. ⁷But it is best for you that I go away. For if I don't, the Comforter won't come. If I do, he will. For I will send him to you.

⁸"And when he has come he will teach the world about sin, righteousness, and judgment. ⁹The world's sin is unbelief in me. ¹⁰There is righteousness because I go to the Father and you will see me no more. ¹¹There is deliverance from judgment because the prince of this world has been judged.

¹²"There is so much more I want to tell you. But you can't understand it now. ¹³When the Spirit of truth comes, he will guide you into all truth. He will not be giving you his own ideas. He will be passing on to you what he has heard. He will tell you about the future. ¹⁴He will praise me and bring me glory. ¹⁵All the Father's glory is mine. This is what I mean when I say that he will show you my glory.

¹⁶"In just a little while I will be gone. And you won't see me anymore. But just a little while after that, you will see me again!"

Jesus Teaches about Prayer and Encourages His Disciples

¹⁷⁻¹⁸"Whatever is he saying?" some of his disciples asked. "What is this 'little while' he is talking about? We don't know what he means."

¹⁹Jesus knew that they wanted to ask him. So he said, "Are you asking your-selves what I mean? ²⁰The world will greatly rejoice over what is going to happen to me. You will cry. But your crying will suddenly be turned to great joy. ²¹It will be like the joy of a woman when her child is finally born. Her pain gives place to joy. And soon the pain is forgotten. ²²You have sorrow now, but I will see you again. Then you will be full of joy. And no one will be able to rob you of that joy. ²³At that time you won't need to ask me for anything. You can go directly to the Father and ask him. And he will give you what you ask for because you use my name. ²⁴You haven't tried this before, but begin now. Ask, using my name, and you will receive and have great joy.

²⁵"I have spoken of these matters very cautiously. But the time will come when this will not be needed. And I will tell you clearly all about the Father. ²⁶Then you will ask for things in my name. And I won't need to ask the Father to give you these things. ²⁷The Father himself loves you dearly. For you love me and believe that I came from the Father. ²⁸Yes, I came from the Father into the world. And I will leave the world and go back to the Father."

²⁹"At last you are speaking clearly," his disciples said. "This is not a riddle. ³⁰Now we understand that you know everything. You don't need anyone to question you. From this we believe that you have come from God."

³¹"Do you finally believe this?" Jesus asked. ³²"But the time has now come when you will be scattered. Each one of you will go back to his own home. And you will leave me alone. Yet I will not be alone, for the Father is with me. ³³I have told you all this so that you will have peace. Here on earth you will have many trials and sorrows. But cheer up, for I have overcome the world!"

Jesus Prays for Himself

17 When Jesus had finished saying all these things he looked up to Heaven. Then he said, "Father, the time has come. Show the glory of your Son so that he can glorify you. ²For you have given him power over every person on earth. He gives eternal life to each one you have given him. ³And there is a way to have eternal life. It comes by knowing you, the only true God, and Jesus Christ, the one you sent to earth! ⁴I brought glory to you on earth by doing all that you wanted. ⁵And now, Father, glorify me with your presence. This is the glory we shared before the world began.

Jesus Prays for His Disciples

⁶"I have told these men all about you. They were in the world, but then you gave them to me. Actually, they were always yours, and you gave them to me. And they have obeyed you. ⁷Now they know that everything I have is a gift from you. ⁸For I have passed on to them the commands you gave me. They have accepted your commands. They know that I came down to earth from you. And they believe that you sent me.

⁹"My plea is not for the world. I ask for those you have given me because they belong to you. ¹⁰And all of them, since they are mine, belong to you. And you have given them back to me with everything else of yours. And so they are my glory! ¹¹Now I am leaving the world, and leaving them behind. And I am coming to you. Holy Father, keep them in your own care. Keep all those you have given me. May they be united just as we are. ¹²During my time here I guarded all of these you gave me. Not one died, except the son of destruction. And this happened as the Scriptures foretold.

¹³"And now I am coming to you. I have told them many things while I was with them. They should be filled with my joy. ¹⁴I have given them your commands. And the world hates them. This is because they don't belong in the world, just as I don't. ¹⁵I'm not asking you to take them out of the world. I am asking that you keep them from the evil one. ¹⁶They are not part of this world any more than I am. ¹⁷Make them pure and holy by teaching them your words of truth. ¹⁸As you sent me into the world, I am sending them into the world. ¹⁹And I give myself to meet their need for truth and holiness.

Jesus Prays for Future Christians

²⁰"I am not praying for these alone. I am praying also for those who will believe in me because of what these say. ²¹My prayer for all of them is that they will be one. May they be one, just as you and I are one. You are in me and I am in you. I pray that they also will be in us. And I pray that the world will believe you sent me.

²²"I have given them the glory you gave me. They have the glorious unity of being one, as we are. ²³With me in them and you in me, they will be made into one. Then the world will know you sent me. And the world will understand that you love them as much as you love me. ²⁴Father, I want these you've given me to be with me. I want them to see my glory. You gave me the glory because you loved me before the world began!

²⁵"O righteous Father, the world doesn't know you, but I do. And these disciples know you sent me. ²⁶And I have shown you to them and will keep on showing you. I pray that the love you have for me may be in them, and I in them."

The Soldiers and Police Arrest Jesus

18 After this prayer, Jesus and his disciples crossed the Kidron Valley. Then they went into a grove of olive trees. ²Judas, the betrayer, knew this place. For Jesus had gone there many times with his disciples.

³So Judas went to the grove, bringing some soldiers and police with him. The chief priests and Pharisees had sent these men along with Judas. With blazing torches, lanterns, and weapons they came to the olive grove.

⁴⁻⁵Jesus knew all

that was going to happen to him. So he stepped forward to meet them. "Whom are you looking for?" he asked.

"Jesus of Nazareth," they replied.

"I am he," Jesus said. 6And as he said it, they all fell backwards to the ground! 7Once more he asked them, "Whom are you looking for?"

And again they replied, "Jesus of Nazareth."

8"I told you I am he," Jesus said. "And since I am the one you are after, let these others go." 9He did this to carry out a prophecy. Jesus had said, "I have not lost a single one of those you gave me."

10Then Simon Peter drew a sword and cut off Malchus's right ear. Malchus was the High Priest's servant.

11But Jesus said to Peter, "Put your sword away. Will I not drink from the cup the Father has given me?"

Annas Questions Jesus

12So the Jewish police and the soldiers tied Jesus up. 13First they took him to Annas, the father-in-law of Caiaphas. Caiaphas was the High Priest that year. 14Caiaphas had told the other Jewish leaders, "Better that one should die for all."

Peter Denies Knowing Jesus

15Simon Peter followed along behind. So did another of the disciples who happened to know the High Priest. That other disciple was allowed into the courtyard along with Jesus. 16But Peter stood outside the gate. Then the other disciple spoke to the girl watching at the gate. And she let Peter in. 17The girl asked Peter, "Aren't you one of Jesus' disciples?"

"No," he said, "I am not!"

18It was a very cold night. So the police and the servants were standing around a fire. Peter stood there with them, warming himself.

19Inside, the High Priest began asking Jesus questions. He asked Jesus about his followers and his teachings.

20Jesus replied, "What I teach is widely known. I have preached regularly in the synagogues and Temple. I have been heard by all the Jewish leaders. I have taught nothing in private that I have not said in public. 21Why are you asking me this question? Ask those who heard me. You have some of them here. They know what I said."

22One of the soldiers standing there hit Jesus with his fist. "Is that the way to answer the High Priest?" he demanded.

23"If I lied, prove it," Jesus replied. "Should you hit a man for telling the truth?"

24Then Annas sent Jesus, bound, to Caiaphas the High Priest.

25Meanwhile, Simon Peter was still standing by the fire. He was asked again, "Aren't you one of his disciples?"

"Of course not," he replied.

26One of the slaves of the High Priest was standing there. He was a relative of the man whose ear Peter had cut off. He asked, "Didn't I see you out there in the olive grove with Jesus?"

27Again Peter denied it. And right then a rooster crowed.

Jesus Is Taken to Pilate

Pilate was a Roman governor. He did not want to kill Jesus. The priests were the religious leaders. They were Jesus' own people. They claimed to know God. They should not have wanted to kill Jesus. But they did.

28Jesus' trial before Caiaphas ended in the early hours of the morning. Next he was taken to the palace of the Roman governor. His accusers wouldn't go in themselves, for that would "defile" them. They said they wouldn't be allowed to eat the Passover lamb. 29So Pilate, the governor, went out to them.

He asked, "What is your charge against this man? What are you accusing him of doing?"

³⁰"We wouldn't have arrested him if he weren't a criminal!" they answered.

³¹"Then take him away and judge him yourselves by your own laws," Pilate said.

"But we want him killed on a cross," they said. "And you must agree to this first." ³²This fulfilled Jesus' prediction about how he would be killed.

³³Then Pilate went back into the palace. And he called for Jesus to be brought to him. "Are you the King of the Jews?" he asked him.

³⁴"'King' as you use the word or as the Jews use it?" Jesus asked.

³⁵"Am I a Jew?" Pilate answered. "Your own people and their chief priests brought you here. Why? What have you done?"

³⁶Then Jesus answered, "I am not an earthly king. If I were, my followers would have fought when I was arrested. My Kingdom is not of the world."

³⁷Pilate replied, "But you are a king then?"

"Yes," Jesus said. "I was born for that purpose. And I came to bring truth to the world. All who love the truth are my followers."

³⁸"What is truth?" Pilate exclaimed. Then he went out again to the people. He told them, "He is not guilty of any crime. ³⁹But you have a custom of asking me to set someone free from prison at Passover. So if you want me to, I'll release the 'King of the Jews.'"

⁴⁰But they screamed back. "No! Not this man, but Barabbas!" Now Barabbas was a rebel against the government.

- *Remember:* What did the people want Pilate to do with Jesus? (18:31) Jesus said he was a king. But what kind of king? (18:36) Pilate would release one man. Which man did the people choose? What kind of man was he? (18:40) Why would anyone choose a robber instead of Jesus?

- *Discover:* We should never choose anything bad instead of Jesus.

- *Apply:* It's time for Sunday school. Do you choose something else? It's time to read your Bible. Do you choose something else? It's time to pray. Do you choose something else? It's time to tell a friend about Jesus. Do you choose something else?

- *What's next?* Jesus was loving and kind. Who would dare make fun of Jesus? Read Luke 23:6-12. ∎

Pilate Judges Jesus

Pilate didn't want to crucify Jesus. So why did he order his soldiers to do it?

19 Then Pilate had Jesus beaten with a leaded whip. ²And the soldiers made a crown of thorns and put it on his head. They dressed him in a purple robe. ³"Hail, 'King of the Jews!'" they laughed. And they struck him with their fists.

⁴Pilate went outside again to speak to the Jews. He said, "I am going to bring him out to you now. But understand clearly that I do not find him guilty."

⁵Then Jesus came out wearing the crown of thorns and the purple robe. And Pilate said, "Behold the man!"

⁶At sight of him the chief priests and Jewish officials began yelling. They cried out, "Crucify him! Crucify him!"

"You crucify him," Pilate said. "I do not find him guilty."

⁷They replied, "By our laws he ought to die. For he claims he is the Son of God."

⁸When Pilate heard this, he was more afraid than ever. ⁹He took Jesus back into the palace again. He asked him, "Where are you from?" But Jesus gave no answer.

¹⁰"You won't talk to me?" Pilate demanded. "Don't you know that I have the power to set you free or have you killed?"

¹¹Then Jesus said, "You have no power at all unless it is given to you from above. So those who brought me to you have the greater sin."

¹²Then Pilate tried to set him free. But the Jewish leaders told him, "You might set this man free. But if you do, you're not Caesar's friend. Anyone who says he is a king is a rebel against Caesar."

¹³At these words Pilate brought Jesus out to them again. Then Pilate sat down at the judgment bench on a stone platform. ¹⁴It was now about noon of the day before Passover.

And Pilate said to the Jews, "Here is your king!"

¹⁵"Away with him," they yelled. "Away with him. Crucify him!"

"What? Crucify your king?" Pilate asked.

"We have no king but Caesar," the chief priests shouted back.

¹⁶Then Pilate gave Jesus to them to be crucified.

- *Remember:* What kind of crown and robe did Pilate make Jesus wear? (19:2) Who kept asking for Jesus to be crucified? (19:6,15) Do you think Pilate wanted to crucify Jesus? Pilate listened to the crowd, not to his own conscience.

- *Discover:* Be careful about listening to the crowd. It can lead you in the wrong way.

- *Apply:* If most of our friends are doing something, does that make it right?

Why not? How do you find out what is right? What do you think will happen if you know the right thing to do but don't do it?

- *What's next?* People spit on the most important person in the world. Why? Read Mark 15:16-24. ■

Jesus Is Nailed to the Cross

¹⁷He was taken out of the city. He carried his cross to the place known as "The Skull." In Hebrew it was called "Golgotha." ¹⁸There they crucified him and two others with him. One was on either side, with Jesus between them. ¹⁹And Pilate put a sign over him. It read, "Jesus of Nazareth, the King of the Jews." ²⁰The place where Jesus was crucified was near the city. And the signboard was written in Hebrew, Latin, and Greek.

²¹Then the chief priests came to Pilate. They said, "Change it from 'The King of the Jews' to 'He said, I am King of the Jews.'"

²²Pilate replied, "What I have written, I have written."

²³⁻²⁴So the soldiers crucified Jesus. Then they put his clothes into four piles. There was one piece of clothing for each of them. But they said, "Let's not tear up his robe," for it was seamless. "Let's throw dice to see who gets it." This fulfilled the Scriptures. It said, "They divided my clothes among them and cast lots for my robe." ²⁵So that is what they did.

Some women were standing near the cross. Jesus' mother, Mary, his aunt, the wife of Cleopas, and Mary Magdalene were among them. ²⁶Jesus saw his mother standing there beside his beloved disciple. He said to her, "He is your son."

²⁷And to the beloved disciple he said, "She is your mother!" And from then on the disciple took her into his home.

Jesus Dies and Is Buried

²⁸Jesus knew that everything was now finished. To fulfill the Scriptures he said, "I'm thirsty." ²⁹A jar of sour wine was sitting there. So a sponge was soaked in it. They put it on a hyssop branch and held it up to his lips.

³⁰When Jesus had tasted it, he said, "It is finished." Then he bowed his head and dismissed his spirit.

³¹The Jewish leaders didn't want the victims hanging there on the Sabbath.

GOLGOTHA

Herod's
Royal
Palace

Caiphas's
House?

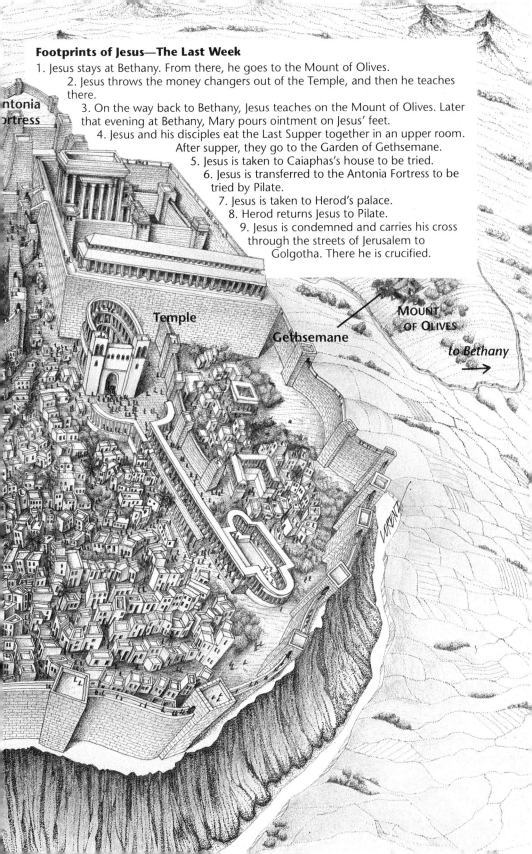

Footprints of Jesus—The Last Week

1. Jesus stays at Bethany. From there, he goes to the Mount of Olives.

2. Jesus throws the money changers out of the Temple, and then he teaches there.

3. On the way back to Bethany, Jesus teaches on the Mount of Olives. Later that evening at Bethany, Mary pours ointment on Jesus' feet.

4. Jesus and his disciples eat the Last Supper together in an upper room. After supper, they go to the Garden of Gethsemane.

5. Jesus is taken to Caiaphas's house to be tried.

6. Jesus is transferred to the Antonia Fortress to be tried by Pilate.

7. Jesus is taken to Herod's palace.

8. Herod returns Jesus to Pilate.

9. Jesus is condemned and carries his cross through the streets of Jerusalem to Golgotha. There he is crucified.

Antonia Fortress

Temple

Gethsemane

MOUNT OF OLIVES

to Bethany

That Sabbath was a special one, for it was during the Passover. So they asked Pilate to have the men's legs broken to quicken their deaths. Then their bodies could be taken down. ³²The soldiers broke the legs of the two men crucified with Jesus. ³³But when they came to him, they saw that he was dead already. So they didn't break his legs. ³⁴However, one of the soldiers pierced his side with a spear. As he did this, blood and water flowed out. ³⁵A witness saw all this and has given a true report. Therefore, you can believe it. ³⁶⁻³⁷The soldiers did this in fulfillment of the Scriptures. One said, "Not one of his bones will be broken." Another said, "They will look on him whom they pierced."

³⁸After that Joseph of Arimathea went boldly to Pilate. He asked if he could take Jesus' body down. Joseph had been a secret disciple of Jesus because he feared the Jewish leaders. Pilate told him to go and take the body. So he came and took it away. ³⁹Nicodemus, the man who had come to Jesus at night, came too. He brought 100 pounds of burial ointment made from myrrh and aloes. ⁴⁰Together they wrapped Jesus' body in a long linen cloth. The cloth was filled with the spices. This is the Jewish custom of burial. ⁴¹The place of crucifixion was near a grove of trees. There was a new tomb there, one never used before. ⁴²Because the tomb was near and the Sabbath was coming, they laid him there.

Peter and John Visit Jesus' Tomb

Jesus is not there! He arose from the dead. But look in the tomb. See the linen cloth. It is rolled neatly into a bundle. Jesus left it behind. He did not need it. It was for dead people only. Jesus is alive!

20 It was early Sunday morning, while it was still dark. At this time, Mary Magdalene went to the tomb. She found the stone rolled away from the door of the tomb.

²She ran and found Simon Peter and the beloved disciple. She said, "They have taken the Lord's body out of the tomb. I don't know where they have put him!"

³⁻⁴Peter and the beloved disciple ran to the tomb to see. The beloved disciple outran Peter and got there first. ⁵He stooped and looked in and saw the linen cloth lying there. But he didn't go in. ⁶Then Simon Peter came and went on inside. He also saw the cloth lying there. ⁷He saw the cloth that had covered Jesus' head. It was folded up and lying by itself. ⁸Then the beloved disciple went in too. He saw and believed that Jesus had risen.

⁹For then they still didn't know that the Scriptures said he would come to life again! ¹⁰They went on home.

- *Remember:* Which two men visited Jesus' tomb? (20:2-4) What did they find in the tomb? (20:5-7) What did they believe now for the first time? (20:8-9) Why is it important that Jesus is alive? What difference does it make?

- *Discover:* Jesus is a living Savior.

- *Apply:* A person says you will live with him forever. But he dies and does not come back to life. Would you trust him? A person says you will live with him forever. He comes back to life after he dies. Will you trust him?

- *What's next?* After Jesus arose, who was the first person to see him alive? Read John 20:11-18. ■

Mary Magdalene Sees Jesus

Jesus was alive! But no one had seen him yet. Mary Magdalene went to his tomb. A stranger spoke to her. Who was he? Did he know where Jesus was? Suddenly Mary was surprised. Something special happened.

[11]By that time Mary had gone back to the tomb. She was standing outside crying. And as she cried, she stooped and looked in. [12]She saw two white-robed angels. They were sitting at the head and foot of the place where Jesus' body had been.

[13]"Why are you crying?" the angels asked her.

"Because they have taken away my Lord," she replied. "And I don't know where they have put him."

[14]She glanced over her shoulder and saw someone standing behind her. It was Jesus, but she didn't recognize him!

[15]"Why are you crying?" he asked her. "Whom are you looking for?"

She thought he was the gardener. "Sir," she said, "Perhaps you have taken him away. If so, tell me where you have put him. And I will go and get him."

[16]"Mary!" Jesus said. Then she turned toward him.

"Master!" she exclaimed.

[17]"Don't touch me," he cautioned. "I haven't yet gone up to the Father. But go find my brothers. Tell them that I am going up to my Father and your Father, my God and your God." [18]Mary Magdalene found the disciples and told them, "I have seen the Lord!" Then she gave them his message.

- *Remember:* Whom did Mary see first at the tomb? (20:12) Who spoke to Mary outside the tomb? What did he ask? (20:14-15) When did she know he was Jesus? (20:16) Whom did Mary tell about this? (20:18) Why do you think she told the others? Why not keep it a secret?

- *Discover:* Good news is too good to keep. We must share it. We must tell others that Jesus is alive!

- *Apply:* At Easter we sing beautiful songs. They tell how Jesus came back to life. He arose from the dead. Why not sing one of these songs now? It will remind you that Jesus is alive. Perhaps your parents can help you.

- *What's next?* A friend walks along the road with two men. But they don't even know him. Read Luke 24:13-35. ■

Jesus Appears to His Disciples

The doors were locked. No one could get into the room. But suddenly Jesus stood there. How did he do that?

¹⁹That evening the disciples were meeting behind closed doors. They were still very afraid of the Jews. Suddenly Jesus was standing there among them! After greeting them, ²⁰he showed them his hands and side. How wonderful was their joy as they saw their Lord!

²¹He said, "As the Father has sent me, even so I am sending you." ²²Then he breathed on them and said, "Receive the Holy Spirit. ²³If you forgive anyone's sins, they are forgiven. If you refuse to forgive them, they are unforgiven."

²⁴One of the disciples, Thomas, was not there at that meeting. ²⁵They told him, "We have seen the Lord." He replied, "I won't believe it unless I see the nail wounds in his hands. And I must put my fingers into them and place my hand into his side."

²⁶Eight days later the disciples were together again. This time Thomas was with them. The doors were closed. Suddenly, Jesus was standing among them and greeting them.

²⁷Then he said to Thomas, "Put your finger into my hands. Put your hand into my side. Don't be faithless any longer. Believe!"

²⁸"My Lord and my God!" Thomas said to him.

²⁹Then Jesus told him, "You believe because you have seen me. But blessed are those who haven't seen me and believe anyway."

³⁰⁻³¹Jesus' disciples saw him do many other miracles besides the ones told about in this book. But these are recorded so that you will believe that Jesus is the Messiah, the Son of God. And when you believe this truth, you will have life.

- *Remember:* What did Jesus show to his disciples? (20:20) Why do you think he did this? Was it to show off? Or was it to show that it was really he who was crucified and who rose from the dead? How did they feel when they knew it was really Jesus? (20:20) Which disciple doubted? (20:24-25) How did Thomas come to believe? What did Jesus tell him to do? (20:26-28) Who are more blessed than Thomas? (20:29) How do we have life? (20:31) Do you sometimes doubt like Thomas? Why? What questions would you like to ask?

- *Discover:* When you doubt, don't stop there. Ask questions about Jesus until you have the answers. Then you will learn who Jesus really is and believe!

- *Apply:* Do you ever say that God doesn't love you? Do you ever say that your parents don't love you? Do you ever think that God should give more to you? Do you ever wonder if Jesus is who he says he is? These are some of the ways we doubt. Can you think of others? Ask your parents, your pastor, or a friend who believes in Jesus to help you answer these questions.

- *What's next?* Some men fish all night. But they catch nothing. Suddenly their nets are full. What happened? Read John 21. ■

Jesus Helps Catch Fish

Peter and his friends fished all night. They didn't catch one fish. Then a stranger said, "Throw your net on the other side of the boat." Suddenly their net was full of fish! How did he know? Who was he?

21 Jesus appeared again to the disciples beside the Lake of Galilee. This is how it happened.

2A group of disciples were together. Simon Peter and Thomas were there. Nathanael from Cana in Galilee was there. The sons of Zebedee, and two other disciples were there, too.

3Simon Peter said, "I'm going fishing."

"We'll come too," they all said. They did, but caught nothing all night. 4At dawn a man stood on the beach. But they couldn't see who he was.

5He called, "Any fish, boys?"

"No," they replied.

6Then he said, "Throw out your net on the right-hand side of the boat. Then you'll get plenty of them!" So they did. And they couldn't draw in the net because there were so many fish!

7Then the beloved disciple said to Peter, "It is the Lord!" At that, Simon Peter put on his tunic, for he was stripped to the waist. He jumped into the water and swam to the shore. 8The rest of the disciples stayed in the boat. They pulled the loaded net to the beach, about 300 feet away. 9When they got there, they saw a fire already burning. And fish were being cooked on it. There also was bread to eat.

10"Bring some of the fish you've just caught," Jesus said. 11So Simon Peter went out and pulled the net to shore. There were 153 large fish. And yet the net hadn't torn.

12"Now come and have some breakfast!" Jesus said. And none of them dared to ask him who he was. For they knew he was the Lord. 13Then Jesus gave them the bread and fish.

14This was the third time Jesus appeared to his disciples since his death.

15After breakfast Jesus spoke to Simon Peter. He said, "Simon, son of John, do you love me more than these others?"

"Yes," Peter replied, "you know I am your friend."

"Then feed my lambs," Jesus told him.

16Jesus repeated the question. "Simon, son of John, do you really love me?"

"Yes, Lord," Peter said, "you know I am your friend."

"Then take care of my sheep," Jesus said.

¹⁷Once more he asked him, "Simon, son of John, are you even my friend?"

Peter was upset at the way Jesus asked the question this third time. "Lord, you know everything," he said. "You know I am."

Jesus said, "Then feed my little sheep. ¹⁸When you were young, you were able to do as you liked. You could go wherever you wanted to. But when you are old, you will stretch out your hands. Others will take you where you don't want to go." ¹⁹Jesus said this to show Peter what kind of death he would suffer to bring glory to God. Then Jesus told him, "Follow me."

²⁰Peter turned around and saw the disciple Jesus loved following. This was the disciple who had asked Jesus during supper, "Master, who will betray you?" ²¹Peter asked Jesus, "What about him, Lord?"

²²Jesus replied, "If I want him to live until I return, what is that to you? You follow me."

²³So the rumor spread among the brothers that this disciple wouldn't die! But that isn't what Jesus said at all! He only said, "If I want him to live until I come, what is that to you?"

²⁴The writer of this account is that same disciple! He saw these events and has recorded them here. And we all know that his account of these things is true.

²⁵Jesus did many other things as well that aren't recorded here. And if all of them were written down, the whole world wouldn't hold all the books!

● *Remember:* Who went fishing? Where? (21:1-3) Who told them where to fish? Who was he? (21:4-7) What did Jesus ask Peter? How many times did he ask? (21:15-17) What did Jesus ask Peter to do? (21:15-17) Do you think Jesus wants you to feed his sheep too? What does that mean?

● *Discover:* Jesus wants us to help his friends. He wants us to help them grow.

● *Apply:* You can help others grow God's way. But first you must grow God's way. Read your Bible. Pray. Read good books about Jesus.

● *What's next?* A man is standing there. Suddenly he goes up into the sky. Where is he going? Luke 24:50-53. ▪

ACTS

*Pretend that you were there when Jesus was cruci-
fied. "What will happen now?" you wonder. Pretend
that you were there when Jesus rose from the dead.
"What will happen now?" you wonder. Pretend that
you saw Jesus going back to heaven. "What will
happen now?" you wonder. The Book of Acts answers your questions. After Jesus left, the Holy Spirit
came. This book tells us about his "acts" among the
first Christians. He does many wonderful things to
them and through them. This is how the church
started.*

*The Book of Acts is an exciting book. You'll see a
dead woman get up and greet her guests. You'll
watch a great sheet filled with animals come down
from the sky. You'll be there when a ship gets caught
in a storm. You'll watch the ship crash against an
island. You'll see an angel lead a man out of prison.
You'll see the prison doors open by themselves.
You'll watch a crowd of people burn their evil books.
Don't miss the exciting things to see and learn in
the Book of Acts!*

Jesus Goes Up to Heaven

1 Dear friend who loves God:
In my first letter I told you about
Jesus' life and teachings. I told you
about how Jesus went back to Heaven.
And I related how he gave his apostles
further teachings from the Holy Spirit.
³After Jesus died and rose again, he appeared to his apostles for a period of 40
days. He proved to them that he was
actually alive. He showed them in many
ways that he was really there with them.
During these times he talked to them
about the Kingdom of God.

⁴In one of these meetings he told
them not to leave Jerusalem. He told
them to wait there until the Holy Spirit
came upon them. This would fulfill the
Father's promise, a matter he had talked
about with them before.

⁵"John baptized you with water," he
reminded them. "But you shall be baptized with the Holy Spirit in just a few
days."

⁶Once, Jesus appeared to his apostles,
and they were talking together. They

asked him, "Lord, are you going to free Israel from Rome now? Are you planning to restore Israel as a free nation?"

⁷"The Father sets those dates," he replied. "Such things are not for you to know. ⁸But the Holy Spirit will come upon you. And you will receive power to speak about me with great effect. You will be my witnesses to the people in Jerusalem. You will also go throughout Judea, to Samaria, and to the ends of the earth. You will tell everyone that I died and then rose again from the dead."

Jesus will come back from Heaven someday

Jesus has gone to Heaven. And someday he will come back again, just as he went!

Acts 1:11

---

⁹Not long after this, Jesus rose into the sky. He went up into a cloud, leaving them staring after him. ¹⁰They were straining their eyes for another look at him. But suddenly two white-robed men were standing there with them. ¹¹They said, "Men of Galilee, why are you standing here staring at the sky? Jesus has gone to Heaven. And someday he will come back again, just as he went!"

¹²They were at the Mount of Olives when this happened. So they turned and walked the half mile back to Jerusalem. ¹³There they held a prayer meeting in an upstairs room of the house where they were staying.

¹⁴Here is the list of those who were at the meeting: Peter, John, James, Andrew, Philip, Thomas, Bartholomew, Matthew, James (son of Alphaeus), Simon (also called "The Zealot"), Judas (son of James), and the brothers of Jesus. Several women, including Jesus'

mother, were also there.

¹⁵This prayer meeting went on for several days. During this time, Peter stood up and spoke to them. On that day, there were about 120 people present.

¹⁶"Brothers," he began. "The Scriptures that spoke of Judas had to come true. He betrayed Jesus by guiding the crowd to him in the garden. This was predicted long ago by the Holy Spirit, speaking through King David. ¹⁷Judas was one of us. He was chosen to be an apostle just as we were. ¹⁸He bought a field with the money he was given for turning Jesus in. While he was there, he fell down and burst open, spilling out his bowels. ¹⁹The news of his death spread rapidly among all the people of Jerusalem. And they named the place 'The Field of Blood.' ²⁰King David spoke of this in the Book of Psalms. He said, 'Let his home become empty. Let no one live in it.' And again he said, 'Let his work be given to someone else to do.'

²¹⁻²²"So now we must choose someone else to take Judas's place. This person must join us as a witness of Jesus' resurrection. Let us choose someone who was with us when we first met the Lord. He must be a witness of Jesus' baptism by John. He must have seen everything until the day Jesus was taken into Heaven."

²³So the group there proposed two men. One was named Joseph Justus. He was also called Barsabbas. The other was named Matthias. ²⁴⁻²⁵Then they all prayed for the right man to be chosen. "O Lord," they said, "you know every heart. Show us which of these men you have chosen as an apostle. He will take the place of Judas the traitor, who has gone on to his proper place."

²⁶Then they drew straws. In this way Matthias was chosen. And he became an apostle with the other 11.

The Holy Spirit Comes

You hear a loud roar like rushing wind blowing through the house. Suddenly little flames of fire appear on people's heads! The people start talking all at once in different languages. What would you think? What would you do?

2 Seven weeks had gone by since Jesus' death and resurrection. And the Day of Pentecost had now arrived. The believers met together on that day. ²Suddenly there was a sound like the roaring of a mighty storm. The sound came from the skies above them. And it filled the house where they were meeting. ³Then, what looked like flames of fire settled on their heads. ⁴Everyone present was filled with the Holy Spirit. They began speaking in languages they didn't even know. For the Holy Spirit gave them the ability to do this.

⁵Many godly Jews were in Jerusalem that day for the religious feast. They had come there from many nations. ⁶The crowds heard the roaring in the sky above the house. So they came running to see what it was all about. And they were amazed to hear their own languages being spoken by the disciples.

⁷"How can this be?" they exclaimed. "For these men are all from Galilee. ⁸But we hear them speaking the languages of the lands where we were born! ⁹Some of us are Parthians, Medes, Elamites, and men from Mesopotamia. Some of us are from Judea, Cappadocia, Pontus, and Asia Minor. ¹⁰Others of us are from Phrygia, Pamphylia, Egypt, and the Cyrene language areas of Libya. Some of us even came from Rome, both Jews and Jewish converts. ¹¹Among us are also some Cretans and Arabians. We all hear these men speaking in our own languages! And they are telling about the mighty miracles of God!"

¹²They stood there amazed. "What can this mean?" they asked each other.

¹³But others in the crowd were laughing. "They're drunk, that's all!" they said.

¹⁴Then Peter stepped forward with the 11 apostles. He shouted to the crowd, "Listen, all of you! Listen, visitors and residents of Jerusalem alike! ¹⁵Some of you are saying these men are drunk! It isn't true! It's much too early for that! People don't get drunk by nine o'clock in the morning! ¹⁶No! What you see this morning was foretold by the prophet Joel many years ago. ¹⁷'This will happen in the last days,' God said. 'I will pour out my Holy Spirit upon all mankind. Your sons and daughters shall prophesy. Your young men shall see visions. And your old men shall dream dreams. ¹⁸Yes, the Holy Spirit shall come upon all my servants. He shall come upon men and women alike. And they shall prophesy. ¹⁹And I will cause strange things to happen in the heavens and on the earth. There will be blood and fire and clouds of smoke. ²⁰The sun shall turn black. The moon shall turn blood-red. Yes, this will happen before that awesome Day of the Lord gets here! ²¹But anyone who asks for mercy from the Lord shall have it and shall be saved.'

²²"O men of Israel, listen! Jesus of Nazareth was a very special man. God proved he was special by doing great miracles through him. You all know this. ²³Jesus was given to you. But you used the Romans to nail him to the cross and murder him. Yet God knew all this would happen. It all came about according to his plan. ²⁴Then God set him free from the horrors of death. He brought him back to life again. For death could not keep this man in the grave.

²⁵"King David quoted Jesus as saying:

'I know the Lord is always with me.
    He is helping me. God's mighty
    power supports me.
²⁶'No wonder my heart is filled with
    joy! No wonder my tongue
    shouts his praises! For I know all
    will be well with me in death.
²⁷'You will not leave my soul in
    hell. You will not let the body of
    your Holy Son decay.
²⁸'You will give me back my life.

You will give me great joy in your presence.'

29"Dear brothers, think! David wasn't talking about himself when he spoke these words. For David died and was buried. And his tomb is still here among us. 30But David was a prophet. He knew God's promise that one of his own descendants would be the Messiah. And God had promised that David's descendant would sit on David's throne. 31David was looking far into the future. He foresaw the Messiah's resurrection. He saw that the Messiah's soul would not be left in hell. He knew that the Messiah's body would not decay in the grave. 32He was speaking of Jesus. And we all are witnesses that Jesus rose from the dead.

33"And now he sits on the throne of highest honor in Heaven, next to God. And just as promised, the Father gave him authority to send the Holy Spirit. And today you are seeing and hearing the results of the Holy Spirit's coming.

34"No, David was not speaking about himself in the words I have quoted. For he never ascended into Heaven. But he said, 'God spoke to my Lord the Messiah. He said to him: Sit here in honor beside me. 35And I will put your enemies under your feet.'

36"So now let all the people in Israel listen to this! God has made this Jesus you crucified to be the Lord, the Messiah!"

37These words of Peter's moved them deeply. They said to him and to the other apostles, "Brothers, what should we do?"

38And Peter replied, "Each one of you must turn from sin and come back to God. Then you must be baptized in the name of Jesus Christ. For through him, you will find forgiveness for your sins. Then you also shall be given this gift, the Holy Spirit. 39For Christ promised him to each of you who has been called by the Lord our God. He has promised him to your children and

even to those in distant lands!"

40Then Peter preached a long sermon. He told the people all about Jesus. And he begged them, "Save yourselves from the evils of your nation." 41And all those who believed Peter were baptized. There were about 3,000 of them in all!

- *Remember:* How long had it been since Jesus was crucified? (2:1) What appeared on the disciples' heads? (2:3) Which new person came into the room? (2:4) Which apostle preached to the people? (2:14) How many people were baptized that day? (2:41) Peter was a fisherman, not a preacher. Why do you think people listened to him? Why do you think so many people became Christians?

- *Discover:* When God helps us talk, people listen!

- *Apply:* When you talk with others, do they listen? If not, ask God to help you talk.

- *What's next?* A man tells a crippled person to walk. Can he? Will he? Read Acts 3. ▓

The Believers Become the First Church

42These people joined with the other believers. They went to all the meetings where the apostles taught the people. They also shared in the Lord's Supper and went to prayer meetings.

43A deep sense of amazement was on them all. And the apostles did many miracles.

44All the believers met together constantly. And they shared everything they had with each other. 45They sold what they had and divided it among those in need. 46They worshiped together regularly at the Temple each day. They met in small groups in homes for the Lord's Supper. And they shared their meals with great joy and thankfulness, 47praising God. The whole city was favorable to them. And each day God added more to their number.

Peter and John Heal a Crippled Man

A crippled man can't walk. He has always been crippled. So he can't get a job and earn money. He must beg. Suddenly Peter tells him to get up and walk. How can a crippled man do that? Watch!

3 Peter and John went to the Temple one afternoon. They went there to take part in the three o'clock daily prayer meeting. ²As they came to the Temple, they saw a man who had been crippled from birth. He was being carried along the street to the Temple gate. This particular gate was called "Beautiful." This man was set there every day. And he begged from the people going to and from the Temple. ³As Peter and John were passing by, he asked them for some money.

⁴They stopped and looked at him intently. Then Peter said, "Look here!"

⁵The crippled man looked at them eagerly, expecting a gift.

⁶But Peter said, "We don't have any money for you! But I'll give you something else! I command you in the name of Jesus Christ of Nazareth, walk!"

⁷⁻⁸Then Peter took the crippled man by the hand. He pulled him to his feet. And as he did this, the man's feet and anklebones were healed! He came up with a jump! Then he stood there for a moment and began to walk! Then he ran after them into the Temple. He was walking and leaping and praising God!

⁹The people inside saw him walking. And they heard him praising God. ¹⁰They saw he was the beggar that had sat by the gate called "Beautiful." They were all very surprised and amazed! ¹¹They all rushed out to Solomon's Hall. And there he was, holding tightly to Peter and John! Everyone stood there amazed by the great thing that had happened.

¹²Peter saw his chance, so he spoke to the crowd. "Men of Israel!" he began. "What is so surprising about this? And why look at us as if we by our own power have made this man walk? ¹³For it is the God of Abraham, Isaac, and Jacob who has brought glory to his servant Jesus by doing this. I am talking about the Jesus whom you rejected before Pilate. And you did this even though Pilate begged you to set him free. ¹⁴He was the holy, righteous one. But you didn't want him set free. In his place, you asked Pilate to set a murderer free. ¹⁵And you killed the Author of Life. But God brought him back to life again. And John and I are witnesses of this fact. For after you killed him we saw him alive!

¹⁶"Jesus' name has healed this man. And you all know how crippled he was before. Faith in Jesus' name has caused this perfect healing. And this faith has been given to us from God.

¹⁷"Dear brothers, you did this to Jesus. But I know that you didn't understand what you were doing. And the same can be said of your leaders. ¹⁸But God let this happen to fulfill the prophecies of old. These prophecies said that the Messiah must suffer all these things. ¹⁹Now change your mind and attitude toward God. Turn to him so he can wash away your sins. And he will send you refreshment from the Lord's presence. ²⁰And he will send Jesus your Messiah back to you again. ²¹⁻²²For he must stay in Heaven until the time when God will restore all things. This has been foretold from ancient times by the holy prophets. Moses said long ago, 'The Lord God will raise up a prophet. This prophet will come from among your own people. And he will be like me! Listen carefully to all that he tells you. ²³Anyone who does not listen to him shall be destroyed.'

²⁴"Samuel spoke about the things that are going on today. So did every other prophet since his time! ²⁵You are the children of those prophets. And you are included in God's promise to your ancestors. God promised to bless the whole world through the Jewish race. Yes, that is the promise God gave to Abraham. ²⁶Now God brought his servant to life after he was killed. And he sent him first to you men of Israel. He wanted to bless you by turning you back from your sins."

- *Remember:* How long had the man been crippled? (3:2) What did the crippled man ask Peter and John to give him? (3:3) What better gift did Peter give? (3:6-8) How do you know that the man was healed? (3:7-8) Why do you think people were surprised? (3:9-11) Would you be surprised if a neighbor healed a cripple by speaking to him? Why? Would you be surprised if God did this? Why not?

- *Discover:* God works miracles. But people may sometimes help make a miracle happen. Peter helped God do a miracle. But God is the one who healed the cripple. We can't do God's work without God's help.

- *Apply:* God still works miracles today, but most are not this dramatic. That's how he wants it. Think about the birth of a child, or how a tree grows, or how sick people get well. People can help these things happen, but only God makes them happen. Do you need something special to happen? Can you do it all by yourself? Can God do it? If you can't and God can, pray! Ask him to help. But make sure you ask him to do something that helps others and not just yourself.

- *What's next?* You'll meet men who are not afraid of anyone. Read Acts 4:1-31. ■

Peter and John Are Brave for God

The Council was an important group of leaders. They were powerful men. They could make big trouble for someone. Who would dare stand against them? Peter and John did. They could not obey both the Council and God. Which would they obey?

4 Now Peter and John had been talking to the people for some time. And the chief priests, the captain of the Temple police, and some of the Sadducees came over to them. ²They were upset that Peter and John claimed that Jesus had risen from the dead. ³So they arrested them. And since it was already evening, they put them in jail overnight. ⁴But many of the people who heard their message believed it. As a result, the number of believers soon reached about 5,000 men!

Do you know wonderful things about Jesus? Tell someone!

We can't stop telling about the great things we saw Jesus do and heard him say.

Acts 4:20

⁵The next day, the Council of all the Jewish leaders met in Jerusalem. ⁶Annas the High Priest was there. So were Caiaphas, John, Alexander, and others of the High Priest's relatives. ⁷So the two disciples were brought in before them.

"By whose authority have you done this?" the Council demanded.

⁸Then Peter, filled with the Holy Spirit, spoke to them. "Honorable leaders and elders of our nation," he began. ⁹"You must be talking about the good deed done to the cripple. Yes, he has been healed! ¹⁰Let me state this clearly. And I say this to all the people of Israel. This miracle was done in the name and power of Jesus from Nazareth, the Messiah. He was the man you crucified. But God raised him back to life again. It is by his authority that this man stands here healed! ¹¹He is the one spoken of in the Scriptures: 'A stone is thrown away by the builders. But it will become the capstone of the arch.' ¹²There is salvation in no one else! Under all Heaven there is no other name for men

to call upon to save them."

¹³The Council saw how brave Peter and John were. And they could see that they had never been educated. So they were amazed by their wise words. They could see that Jesus had made a great change in them. ¹⁴The man that had been healed was standing right there beside them. So the Council couldn't pretend that Peter and John hadn't healed him. ¹⁵So next the Council sent them out of the room and spoke among themselves.

¹⁶"What shall we do with these men?" they asked each other. "We can't deny that they have done a great miracle. And everybody in Jerusalem knows about it. ¹⁷But we must stop their beliefs from spreading. Perhaps we can stop them from preaching their message. We will warn them not to speak in Jesus' name again." ¹⁸So they called Peter and John back into the room. And they told them never again to speak about Jesus.

¹⁹But Peter and John replied, "You decide for yourselves what we should do. Should we obey God? Or should we obey you? ²⁰We can't stop telling about the great things we saw Jesus do and heard him say."

²¹The Council then threatened them further. But finally they let Peter and John go. The Council didn't know how to punish them without starting a riot. For everyone was praising God for this great miracle. ²²A man who had been crippled for 40 years was now healed!

²³As soon as they were set free, Peter and John met with the other disciples. And they told them what the Council had said.

²⁴Then all the believers prayed. They said, "O Lord! You made the heavens and earth, the sea and everything in them. ²⁵⁻²⁶You spoke long ago by the Holy Spirit through our ancestor King David. He said, 'Why do the heathen rage against the Lord? Why do foolish

nations make their weak plans against Almighty God? The kings of the earth come together to fight against him. They unite to fight against the chosen Son of God!'

²⁷"That is what is happening here in this city today! For many have joined to fight against Jesus, your chosen Son and holy servant. Herod the king is fighting against him. And so is Pontius Pilate the governor, and all the Romans. Even the people of Israel are fighting against Jesus! ²⁸They won't stop at anything that you in your wise power will let them do. ²⁹And now, O Lord, hear their threats. Give to your servants great boldness in their preaching. ³⁰And send your healing power. May many miracles and wonders be done by the name of your holy servant Jesus!"

³¹After this prayer, the building where they were meeting shook. They were all filled with the Holy Spirit. And they boldly preached God's message.

- *Remember:* Why were Peter and John arrested? What did they say? (4:1-3) How many people believed in Jesus now? (4:4) Whose power healed the crippled man? (4:7-10) What had changed Peter and John? They were not educated. They were not trained. How could they preach so well? (4:8,13) The disciples asked someone for courage. Who? (4:29) How did God answer that prayer? (4:31) Would they have had courage without asking God for help? Why not?

- *Discover:* When you are afraid, ask God for courage. Only he can give you the kind of courage that can face anything.

- *Apply:* Think of something specific that you are afraid of. Ask God right now to give you courage. Do you believe he will give it to you? Should you believe?

- *What's next?* How would people treat each other if they really worked together? Read about it in Acts 4:32-37. ■

Christians Work Together

Do most families you know really work together? Do all the people in your church really work together? Does everyone at school really work together? Can people really work together? The disciples did! Here's what happened when they did.

³²All the believers were of one heart and mind. No one felt that what he owned was his own. Everyone shared everything he had. ³³And the apostles preached powerful sermons. They told everyone about the resurrection of the Lord Jesus. And there was warm fellowship among all the believers. ³⁴⁻³⁵No one was poor. For all who owned land or houses sold them. And they brought the money to the apostles to give to others in need.

³⁶For example, there was Joseph. The apostles called him "Barnabas, the encourager"! He was of the tribe of Levi, from the island of Cyprus. ³⁷He was one of those who sold a field he owned. He brought the money to the apostles to give to those in need.

● *Remember:* How do you know the disciples thought alike? (4:32) How do you know they felt the same? (4:32) What did they do because of this? (4:32-35) What did Joseph do? (4:36-37) How did loving each other change their giving to each other? Do you think they loved each other more because they thought and felt alike?

● *Discover:* Christians, and families, should work well together. They should love each other. Then they will share.

● *Apply:* Talk with your family. Do you share enough with each other? Are you united? Do you love each other? Then ask each other what you should do.

● *What's next?* Why are people punished when they give? You'll find out in Acts 5:1-11. ■

Ananias and Sapphira Lie to God

Ananias and Sapphira sold some property. They said they were going to give all of the money to the church. But instead they took some of it for themselves. Would they get away with it? Let's find out.

5 But there was also a man named Ananias. His wife was called Sapphira. They also sold some of their property. ²But they brought only part of the money, claiming it was the full price. His wife had agreed to lie about this.

³But Peter said, "Ananias, Satan has filled your heart. When you claimed this was the full price, you were lying to the Holy Spirit. ⁴The property was yours to sell or not, as you wished. And after selling it, it was yours to decide how much to give. How could you do a thing like this? You weren't lying to us, but to God."

⁵As soon as Ananias heard these words, he fell to the floor, dead! Everyone was terrified. ⁶The younger men covered him with a sheet. Then they took him out and buried him.

⁷About three hours later his wife came in. She did not know what had happened. ⁸Peter asked her, "Did you people sell your land for such and such a price?"

"Yes," she replied, "we did."

⁹And Peter said, "How could you and your husband even think of lying to us! Did you want to test God's power of knowing what is going on? Just outside that door are the young men who buried your husband. And they will carry you out, too."

¹⁰Right then she fell to the floor, dead. The young men came in and saw that she was dead. So they carried her out and buried her beside her husband. ¹¹Fear gripped the whole church and all others who heard what had happened.

Remember: Was Ananias the husband or the wife? (5:1) What did he give? (5:1-2) What did he do wrong? (5:1-3) How

should he have given his money? (5:4)
What happened to Ananias? (5:5-6)
What happened to Sapphira? (5:7-10)
Was it wrong for Ananias and Sapphira
to give? Was it wrong for them to lie
about what they gave? Were they lying
to Peter or to God? (5:4)

- *Discover:* Don't try to lie to God. He
knows everything you are thinking.

- *Apply:* Which of these is lying? (1) pre-

tending you did something you didn't
do, (2) pretending you didn't do something you did, (3) saying something that
isn't true, (4) thinking you are better
than you are. Can you think of other
ways people lie? What should we do
when we lie?

- *What's next?* Some preachers are beaten
by religious leaders. Why? Read Acts
5:12-42. ◼

Remarkable Miracles, Then Trouble

What would you think if someone beat your pastor with whips or
clubs? That is what happened to Peter and John.

12Meanwhile, the apostles were meeting regularly at the Temple. They had their meetings in the area known as Solomon's Hall. And they did many great miracles among the people. 13Most of the people were afraid to join them there. But all had the highest respect for them. 14More and more men and women believed in the Lord. And these joined the growing number of believers. 15Sick people were brought out into the streets on beds and mats. It was hoped that at least Peter's shadow would fall across some of them as he went by! 16And crowds came in from the Jerusalem suburbs. They brought their sick friends and those who had demons. And all of them were healed.

God comes first!

*We must obey God
rather than men.*

Acts 5:29

17Now the High Priest and his relatives soon became jealous of the apostles. And a group among the Sadducees also felt the same way. 18So they arrested the apostles and put them in the public jail.

19But an angel of the Lord came at night. He opened the gates of the jail and brought them out. Then he told them, 20"Go over to the Temple and preach about this new life!"

21So they went to the Temple about daybreak. And right away they began to preach! Later that morning the High Priest arrived at the Temple. He called the Jewish Council and the whole Senate to order. They sent for the apostles to be brought for trial. 22But when the police got to the jail, the men weren't there. So they went back to the Council with the report. 23They said, "The jail doors were locked and the guards were standing outside. But when we opened the gates, no one was there!"

24When the police captain and the chief priests heard this, they were very upset. They wondered what would happen next and where all this would end! 25Then someone came in with some news. He told them that the men they had jailed were out in the Temple! And they were preaching to the people!

26-27The police captain went with his officers and arrested them. They did this without violence. For they were afraid the people would kill them if they treated the apostles badly. Then they brought the apostles in before the Council.

28"Didn't we tell you never again to preach about this Jesus?" the High Priest demanded. "But instead you have filled all Jerusalem with your teaching. And you are bringing the blame for this man's death on us!"

29But Peter and the apostles replied, "We must obey God rather than men.

30Yes, you did kill him by hanging him on a cross. But the God of our ancestors brought Jesus back to life again. 31Then, with mighty power, God lifted him up to be a Prince and Savior. He did this so the people of Israel would have a chance to repent. He did this so all their sins could be forgiven. 32We are witnesses of all these things. And the Holy Spirit proves that all these things are true. The Holy Spirit is given by God to all who obey him."

33At this, the Council became very angry. And they decided to kill them. 34But then one of their members stood up. He was a Pharisee named Gamaliel. This Pharisee was an expert on religious law and very popular with the people. He asked that the apostles be sent outside the room while he talked.

35Then he spoke to the Council. "Men of Israel," he said. "Be careful about what you do to these men! 36Some time ago there was that fellow Theudas. He also pretended to be someone great. About 400 others joined him, but he was killed. Then his followers quickly scattered.

37"After him, at the time of the taxation, there was Judas of Galilee. He drew away some people as his disciples. But he also died, and his followers scattered.

38"And so my advice is, leave these men alone. Perhaps they teach and do things that are merely human. If this is the case, their cause will soon die out. 39But if it is of God, you will not be able to stop them. For you will find yourselves fighting against God."

40The Council accepted his advice. They called in the apostles and had them beaten. Then they told them never again to speak in the name of Jesus. And finally they let them go. 41The apostles left the Council chamber full of joy. They rejoiced that God had counted them worthy to suffer for his name. 42The apostles never stopped teaching and preaching about Jesus. Every day they taught people that Jesus was the Messiah. They held their meetings in the Temple and in homes.

- *Remember:* Why did the High Priest and his friends arrest the apostles and put them in jail? (5:17-18) Who let them out? Why? (5:19-20) Who wanted the apostles to stop preaching about Jesus? Why? (5:28) What did Peter tell the Council? How did the Council feel about this? (5:29-33) What was Gamaliel's advice? (5:34-39) Did the Council follow it? But what did they do that was wrong? (5:40) Why was it wrong to beat the apostles? What would you like to say to the Council? Why were the apostles happy that they were beaten?

- *Discover:* Be thankful you can please God, even if people hurt you for it. Why? Because pleasing God is more important than anything else you can do. It shows that you love him and want to do what is right and what helps others.

- *Apply:* Has someone made fun of you because you are a friend of Jesus? Be glad that you can please God, even if someone hurts you for it. One day the hurt will go away, but your friendship with Jesus will never end.

- *What's next?* Why were seven men chosen to feed people? Read Acts 6:1-7. ◾

Seven Men with Special Work

Christians in the early church gave food to people who needed it. But some people were unhappy about this. Why would anyone be unhappy about feeding needy people?

6 But as the church grew, new problems came up. Some of the believers were from a Greek background. Others were from a Jewish background. Those who were from a Greek background felt that their widows were not being treated fairly. They were not being given as much food as the widows from a Jewish

background. ²So the Twelve called a meeting of all the believers.

"We need to spend our time preaching," they said. "We don't have time to pass out the food. ³Now look around among yourselves, dear brothers. Choose seven men, wise and full of the Holy Spirit. They must be well respected by everyone. And we will put them in charge of this business. ⁴Then we can spend our time in prayer, preaching, and teaching."

⁵This sounded like a good idea to the whole church. So they chose seven men to do this work. They chose Stephen, who was full of faith and the Holy Spirit. They chose Philip, Prochorus, Nicanor, Timon, and Parmenas. And they also chose Nicolaus of Antioch. Nicolaus was a Gentile who had become a Christian. Before that, he had converted to the Jewish faith.

⁶These seven were brought to the apostles. And the apostles prayed for them and laid their hands on them in blessing.

⁷God's message was preached to more and more people. And in Jerusalem, the number of believers quickly grew. Many of the Jewish priests were converted too!

- *Remember:* People were being fed. But some were unhappy. Why? (6:1) What kind of work did the apostles do best? Why shouldn't they feed the needy people? (6:2) What were the seven new men supposed to do? (6:3) What could the apostles do then? (6:4) Who were the seven new helpers? (6:5) What happened to God's work then? (6:6) Do you think this was a good idea to find seven helpers? Why?

- *Discover:* God's helpers should do the kind of work they do best.

- *Apply:* Do you play an instrument well? Do you sing well? What do you do well? Do it to bring joy to others. Do it to help others. Then you will be doing it for God.

- *What's next?* Why would a man pray for people who are killing him? Read Acts 6:8–8:1. ■

Men Throw Stones at Stephen

God helped Stephen do great miracles. Stephen preached great sermons. He did great work for God. Some wicked people did not like that. So they killed Stephen. As he was dying, Stephen prayed for these people. Why would he do that?

⁸Now Stephen was a man full of faith and the Holy Spirit's power. And he did great miracles among the people.

⁹But one day some men came and started to argue with Stephen. These men were from the Jewish cult of "The Freedmen." They were Jews from Cyrene and Alexandria in Egypt. Some of them also came from the provinces of Cilicia and Asia Minor. ¹⁰But none of them was able to stand against Stephen's wisdom and spirit.

¹¹So they brought in some men to lie about him. They claimed they had heard Stephen curse Moses, and even God.

¹²These lies made the crowds very angry at Stephen. So the Jewish leaders arrested him and brought him before the Council. ¹³Then the liars again claimed that Stephen spoke against the Temple and the laws of Moses.

¹⁴They said, "We have heard him say that Jesus of Nazareth will destroy the Temple. And he claims that Moses' laws are no longer any good." ¹⁵At this point everyone looked over at Stephen. And his face had become as bright as an angel's!

7 Then the High Priest asked him, "Are these charges true?"

²This was Stephen's reply: "Brothers, listen to me! The glorious God spoke to our ancestor Abraham in Mesopotamia. This was before he moved to Haran. ³God told him to leave his native land

and to say good-bye to his relatives. He told him to start out for a country that God would show him. ⁴So he left the land of the Chaldeans and went to Haran, in Syria. He lived there until his father died. Then God brought him here to the land of Israel. ⁵But God gave him no land of his own.

"However, God promised that the whole land would be his. And he promised that it would belong to his descendants, too. But at that time, Abraham still had no children! ⁶But God also told him that these descendants of his would leave the land. He said they would live in a foreign land and become slaves for 400 years. ⁷'But I will punish the nation that enslaves them,' God told him. 'And then my people will go back to this land of Israel and worship me here.'

⁸"God also gave Abraham the ceremony of circumcision at that time. This showed that there was a covenant between God and Abraham's family. And so Isaac, Abraham's son, was circumcised when he was eight days old. Isaac became the father of Jacob. And Jacob was the father of the 12 patriarchs of Israel. ⁹These men were very jealous of their brother Joseph. So they sold him as a slave in Egypt. But God was with him. ¹⁰He brought Joseph out of all of his suffering. And he gave him favor before Pharaoh, king of Egypt. God also gave Joseph unusual wisdom. So Pharaoh chose him as the governor over all Egypt. He also put Joseph in charge of all the affairs of the palace.

¹¹"But a famine came to Egypt and Canaan. And there was great suffering for our ancestors. When their food was gone, ¹²Jacob heard that there was still grain in Egypt. So he sent his sons to buy some. ¹³The second time they went, Joseph told his brothers who he was. And they were introduced to Pharaoh. ¹⁴Then Joseph sent for his father Jacob to come to Egypt. He also sent for all his brothers' families. There were 75 persons in all. ¹⁵So Jacob came to Egypt, where he died. And all his sons died there, too. ¹⁶All of them were taken to Shechem. They were buried in the tomb Abraham bought from the sons of Hamor.

¹⁷⁻¹⁸"The time drew near when God would free Abraham's descendants from slavery. This would fulfill God's promise to Abraham. At this time, the Jewish people grew in number very quickly in Egypt. But then a king was crowned who had no respect for Joseph's memory. ¹⁹This king made plans against our race. He forced parents to leave their children in the fields.

²⁰"About that time Moses was born. He was a child with a special beauty. His parents hid him at home for three months. ²¹But at last they could no longer keep him hidden. So they had to get rid of him somehow. At that time, Pharaoh's daughter found him. And she adopted him as her own son. ²²Moses was taught all the wisdom of the Egyptians. And he became a mighty prince in Egypt.

²³"When Moses was 40 years old, he decided to visit the Israelites. ²⁴During this visit he saw an Egyptian treating a man of Israel badly. So Moses killed the Egyptian. ²⁵Moses thought his brothers would know that God had sent him to help them. But they didn't know this.

²⁶"The next day he visited them again. And he saw two men of Israel fighting. He tried to be a peacemaker. 'Gentlemen,' he said, 'you are brothers! You shouldn't be fighting like this! It is wrong!'

²⁷"But the man in the wrong told Moses to mind his own business. 'Who made you a ruler and judge over us?' he asked. ²⁸'Are you going to kill me as you killed that Egyptian yesterday?'

²⁹"At this, Moses left the country and lived in the land of Midian. And this was where his two sons were born.

³⁰"Forty years later he was still in the desert near Mount Sinai. And an Angel appeared to him in a burning bush. ³¹Moses saw it and wondered what it was. So he ran to see it up close. Then the voice of the Lord called out to him, ³²'I am the God of your ancestors! I am the God of Abraham, Isaac and Jacob.' Moses shook with terror and he didn't dare to look.

³³"And the Lord said to him, 'Take off your shoes. For you are standing on holy ground. ³⁴I have seen the suffering of my people in Egypt. I have heard their cries for help. So now I have come down to save them. Come, I will send you to

Egypt.' ³⁵And so God sent Moses back to Egypt to deliver the people of Israel. He did this even though his people had rejected Moses once before. They had asked, 'Who made you a ruler and judge over us?' So now Moses was sent to be their ruler and savior. ³⁶And by means of many great miracles he led them out of Egypt. He brought them through the Red Sea. And he led them in the wilderness for 40 years.

³⁷"Moses himself told the people of Israel, 'God will raise up a Prophet much like me from among your brothers.' ³⁸How true this proved to be! For in the wilderness, Moses stood between the Angel and the people of Israel. This Angel gave them the Law of God on Mount Sinai.

³⁹"But our fathers rejected Moses. They wanted to go back to Egypt. ⁴⁰They told Aaron, 'Make idols for us. Then we will have gods to lead us back. For we don't know what has become of this Moses, who brought us out of Egypt.' ⁴¹So they made an idol in the shape of a calf. Then they offered sacrifices to it. They were very happy with this thing they had made. ⁴²"Then God turned

away from them and gave them up. He did not stop them from worshiping the sun, moon, and stars! The Lord said in the book of Amos: 'Did you sacrifice to me during the 40 years in the desert, Israel? [43]No, your real interest was in your heathen gods. You worshiped Molech, and the star god Rephan. These were the images you made. So I will send you into captivity. I will send you far away beyond Babylon.'

[44]"Our ancestors carried the Tabernacle with them

through the wilderness. In it they kept the stone tablets with the Ten Commandments written on them. This building was made according to the plan shown to Moses by the Angel. [45]Years later Joshua led the battles against the Gentile nations. This same Tabernacle was taken with them into their new land. It was used until the time of King David.

[46]"God blessed David greatly. He asked if he could build a lasting Temple for the God of Jacob. [47]But it was Solomon who actually built it. [48-49]However, God doesn't live in temples made by human hands. 'The heavens are my throne,' says the Lord through his prophets. 'And the earth is my footstool. What kind of home could you build?' asks the Lord. 'Would I stay in it? [50]Didn't I make both the heavens and the earth?'

[51]"You stiff-necked people! Must you forever fight against the Holy Spirit? But your fathers did, and so do you! [52]Name one prophet your ancestors didn't persecute! They even killed the ones who foretold the coming of the Messiah. The Messiah finally came, but you betrayed and murdered him. [53]Yes, and you don't obey God's laws, even though they came from the hands of angels."

[54]The Jewish leaders became very angry at Stephen's words. They ground their teeth in rage. [55]But Stephen was filled with the Holy Spirit. He looked upward into Heaven and saw the glory of God. And he could see Jesus standing at God's right hand. [56]He said to them, "Look! I see the heavens opened. And I see Jesus the Messiah standing at the right hand of God!"

[57]The people in the crowd put their hands over their ears. And they drowned out his voice with their shouts. Then they went and mobbed him. [58]They dragged him out of the city and began to stone him. The people took off their coats. And they laid them at the feet of a young man named Saul.

[59]As the crowd threw stones at him, Stephen prayed, "Lord Jesus, receive my spirit." [60]Then he fell to his knees and cried out, "Lord, don't charge them with this sin!" And with those final words, he died.

8 Saul was there when they killed Stephen. And he agreed that killing him was a good thing.

- *Remember:* What kind of person was Stephen? (6:8,10) What kind of people lied about him? (6:9-14) Stephen preached a sermon. How did the Council leaders like it? (7:54-58) What did Stephen do as the people stoned him to death? (7:59-60) What kind of person would pray for people who were killing him? What did he ask God to do?

- *Discover:* Jesus prayed for the people who crucified him. He asked God to forgive them (see Luke 23:34). Stephen was like Jesus when he prayed for people who killed him. Instead of cursing our enemies, we should pray for them. Why? Because it shows we love them and want God to help them change. It shows we don't want them to be our enemies.

- *Apply:* Has someone tried to hurt you? Pray today for that person. Ask God to forgive that person. Ask God to help you feel love for that person.

- *What's next?* A religious leader tries to hurt all the Christians. Why? Read Acts 8:1-3. ■

Saul Tries to Hurt the Christians

Why would a religious leader try to hurt Christians? Why would he throw them into jail?

From that day, the Jews set out to hurt the church in Jerusalem. And all the believers except the apostles ran away into Judea and Samaria. ²But some godly Jews came, and with great sorrow they buried Stephen. ³Now Saul did everything he could to destroy the church. He went from house to house, dragging out men and women alike. Then he threw them in jail.

- *Remember:* What happened to the Christians as soon as Stephen died? (8:1) Where did the Christians go? (8:1) What did Saul do to the Christians? What kind of person was he? (8:3) Would you like Saul for a friend? Why not?

- *Discover:* Being a Christian doesn't keep you from getting hurt. You may even get hurt because you are a Christian. Many people who like to do bad don't like being around people who do good. The good they see shows them how bad they are.

- *Apply:* Has anyone ever made fun of you because you read your Bible or pray? Has anyone ever made fun of you because you go to church? Don't get angry. Pray for that person instead. Pray that he or she would see you doing good and would want to change. That's what Jesus would do. That's what Stephen would do.

- *What's next?* How can good news come from bad news? Read Acts 8:4-25. ■

Philip Preaches at Samaria

There was bad news. Christians had to run away from Jerusalem. Saul was hurting them. But there was good news. Everywhere they went they told others about Jesus. Sometimes good news can come from bad news!

⁴Many of the believers had left Jerusalem because of the trouble there. But they preached the Good News about Jesus wherever they went! ⁵Philip, for instance, went to the city of Samaria. He told the people there about Christ.

⁶Crowds listened to what he said because of the miracles he did. ⁷Many evil spirits were cast out, shrieking as they went. And many who were paralyzed or crippled were healed. ⁸As a result, there was much joy in that city!

⁹⁻¹¹There was a man in the city named Simon. He had been a sorcerer there for many years. He bragged that he was a great man. And he amazed the people with his magic. In fact, the Samaritan people often spoke of him as the "Great Power." ¹²But now they believed Philip's message that Jesus was the Messiah. They believed what he told them about the Kingdom of God. And many men and women were baptized. ¹³Then Simon himself believed and was baptized. And he began to follow Philip wherever he went. Simon was amazed by the miracles Philip did.

¹⁴The apostles in Jerusalem heard that Samaria had accepted God's message. So they sent Peter and John to visit them. ¹⁵When they got there, Peter and John began to pray for the new Christians. They prayed that they would receive the Holy Spirit. ¹⁶For as yet the Spirit had not come upon any of them. This was because they had only been baptized in the name of the Lord Jesus. ¹⁷Then Peter and John laid their hands upon these believers. And the Holy Spirit came upon them.

¹⁸Simon saw that the Holy Spirit was given when the apostles put their hands on people. So he offered them money to buy this power.

¹⁹"Let me have this power too!" he exclaimed. "I want to be able to give the Holy Spirit to people, too!"

²⁰But Peter replied, "You and your money should both be destroyed! For you have tried to buy God's gift with money! ²¹You can have no part in this. For your heart is not right before God. ²²Turn from this great wickedness and pray. Perhaps God will yet forgive your evil thoughts. ²³For I can see that there is jealousy and sin in your heart."

²⁴"Pray for me!" Simon exclaimed. "Pray that these bad things won't happen to me."

²⁵After preaching in Samaria, Peter and John went back to Jerusalem. Along the way, they stopped at several Samaritan villages. They preached the Good News to them, too.

- *Remember:* Why did Christians leave Jerusalem? Why did they go to other places to live? (8:3-4) What did they do in these places? (8:4-8) If Philip had stayed home in Jerusalem, would all this have happened in Samaria? Why not?

- *Discover:* We may want to stay where we are. But God may want us somewhere else. We can't go where God wants until we leave where we want to be.

- *Apply:* Are you moving to a new home? Would you rather stay where you are? God may want you to tell someone in your new school about Jesus. He may want you to tell a new neighbor about Jesus. Ask God to help you do what he wants in your new home.

- *What's next?* A preacher is preaching to hundreds. Why would God send him to a desert to preach to one person? Read Acts 8:26-40. ■

Philip Tells an Ethiopian about Jesus

Crowds came to hear Philip preach. Many accepted Christ. Demons were cast out. Lame people were healed. The whole city of Samaria was excited about Philip's ministry. Suddenly God sent him away. He sent him to the desert to meet one man. Why?

²⁶But an Angel of the Lord came and spoke to Philip. The Angel said, "Go over to the road that runs from Jerusalem through the Gaza Desert. Be there around noon." ²⁷So Philip did what the Angel told him to do. On the road, he

saw the Treasurer of Ethiopia, a eunuch. He had great authority under Candace the queen. He had gone to Jerusalem to worship. 28And now he was going home in his chariot. He was reading aloud from the book of the prophet Isaiah as he went.

Jesus is God's Son

I believe that Jesus Christ is the Son of God.

Acts 8:37

29The Holy Spirit said to Philip, "Go over and walk along beside the chariot."

30Philip ran over and heard what the Ethiopian was reading. "Do you understand it?" he asked.

31"Of course not!" the man replied. "How can I

when there is no one to teach me?" And he begged Philip to come up into the chariot and sit with him.

32The passage of Scripture he had been reading was this:

"He was led as a sheep about to be killed. He was like a lamb, silent before the shearers. He did not open his mouth to speak. 33He was shamed and was treated unfairly. And who can tell you how wicked the people of his generation are? For his life is taken from the earth."

34The eunuch asked Philip, "Was Isaiah talking about himself or someone else?"

35So Philip began with this same Scripture to tell him about Jesus. Then he used many others to tell him the Good News.

36As they rode along, they came to a small body of water. The eunuch said, "Look! Water! Why can't I be baptized?"

37"You can," Philip answered. "But you must

believe with all your heart."

And the eunuch replied, "I believe that Jesus Christ is the Son of God."

³⁸He stopped the chariot and went down into the water. And there Philip baptized him. ³⁹When they came up out of the water, the Spirit of the Lord took Philip away. The eunuch never saw him again. But he went on his way full of joy. ⁴⁰Meanwhile, Philip found himself at Azotus! He preached the Good News there. Then he traveled to Caesarea and preached in every city along the way.

- *Remember:* Where did God send Philip? (8:26) Whom did he meet there? (8:27) Where had this man been and where was he going? (8:27-28) What did the Holy Spirit send Philip to do? (8:29-35) What happened to the Ethiopian?

(8:36-38) Do you think the man told others in Ethiopia about Jesus? Do you think that's why the Lord wanted Philip there?

- *Discover:* Sharing Jesus with one person may really be sharing him with many. But be sure to share him with that one person.

- *Apply:* Is there someone you should tell about Jesus? Have you? What are you waiting for? That person may tell many others. They may tell many more. By sharing Jesus with one, you may be sharing him with a hundred.

- *What's next?* Think of the worst person in the world. Could he become a Christian? Could he help other people become Christians? It happened. Read Acts 9:1-9. ■

Saul Meets Jesus

Saul was one of the worst people in Jerusalem. He was a religious leader. But he wanted to destroy every Christian. How could a man like that ever become a Christian? It seemed even more impossible that he could become a preacher. Was it?

9 Now Saul was in Jerusalem, threatening to kill the believers there. But then he went to see the High Priest. ²He asked for a letter addressed to synagogues in Damascus. The letter told the Jews there to help Saul persecute the believers in their city. They were to arrest all the believers, both men and women. And then Saul would bring them in chains to Jerusalem.

³Saul was almost to Damascus to arrest the believers there. But suddenly a bright light from Heaven shone down on him! ⁴He fell to the ground. And he heard a voice saying to him, "Saul! Saul! Why are you trying to hurt me?"

⁵"Who is speaking, sir?" Saul asked.

And the voice replied, "I am Jesus, the one you are trying to hurt! ⁶Now get up and go into the city. Then wait there

for further orders from me."

⁷The men with Saul stood silent and amazed. For they heard the sound of someone's voice but saw no one! ⁸⁻⁹As Saul picked himself up off the ground, he found that he was blind. He had to be led into Damascus. He was there for three days, blind. And he went without food and water all that time.

- *Remember:* What kind of person was Saul? (9:1) What did he want to do to the Christians? (9:1-2) What happened on the road to Damascus? (9:3-9) Who talked to Saul there? (9:5) Who changed Saul? Do you think the greatest man in the world could have changed him? Only Jesus could do that.

- *Discover:* Jesus can make us new people. He is the only one who can. He can

change the worst person in the world. He can make that person a great Christian.

- *Apply:* Is there someone you want to tell about Jesus, but you don't know how Jesus could change that person? He can. Pray! Then share!

- *What's next?* Why would someone put an important man in a basket? Read Acts 9:10-31. ■

Saul Preaches in Damascus

Saul was a nasty man. He tried to put Christians in prison. He wanted to destroy them. He wanted to stop all preaching about Jesus. Then Saul met Jesus. Jesus changed him. He was filled with the Holy Spirit. Now look at the difference in Saul!

¹⁰Now there was in Damascus a believer named Ananias. The Lord spoke to him in a vision, calling, "Ananias!"

"Yes, Lord!" he replied.

¹¹And the Lord said, "Go over to Straight Street. Find the house of a man

named Judas. Ask there for a man named Saul of Tarsus. He is praying to me right now. ¹²For I have shown him a vision of a man named Ananias coming to him. This man laid his hands on him so that he could see again!"

¹³"But Lord!" exclaimed Ananias. "I have heard bad reports about this man. He has done terrible things to the believers in Jerusalem! ¹⁴And we hear that he has a letter with him from the chief priests. This letter gives him the power to arrest every believer here in Damascus!"

¹⁵But the Lord said, "Go and do what I say. For Saul is my chosen instrument. He will preach my message to the Gentiles and their kings. He also will preach to the people of Israel. ¹⁶And I will show him how much he must suffer for me."

¹⁷So Ananias went over and found Saul and laid his hands on him. "Brother Saul," he said, "the Lord Jesus

spoke to you on the road. And now he has sent me so that you may be filled with the Holy Spirit. I have also come to give you your sight back."

18Right away, something like scales fell from Saul's eyes. And he could see again! Saul was baptized without delay. 19Then he ate and was made strong.

He stayed with the believers in Damascus for a few days. 20Then he went at once to the synagogue to tell everyone there the Good News about Jesus. He told everyone that Jesus was indeed the Son of God!

21All who heard him were amazed. "Isn't this the same man who tried to hurt Jesus' followers in Jerusalem?" they asked. "And we understand that he came here to arrest them all. We were told he planned to take them in chains to the chief priests."

22Saul became more and more powerful in his preaching. And the Damascus Jews couldn't stand against his proofs that Jesus was the Messiah.

23After a while the Jewish leaders decided to kill him. 24But Saul was told about their plans to murder him. They were watching the city gates day and night in order to catch him. 25So during the night some of his converts put him in a large basket. Then they let him down through an opening in the city wall!

26When Saul got to Jerusalem he tried to meet with the believers. But they were all afraid of him. They thought he was trying to trick them! 27Then Barnabas brought him to the apostles. He told them how Saul had seen the Lord on the way to Damascus. He recounted what the Lord had said to him. And he told the believers all about Saul's powerful preaching in the name of Jesus. 28Then they accepted him. And after that he was always with the believers. 29He preached boldly in the name of the Lord. But then some Greek-speaking Jews with whom he had argued made plans to murder him. 30However, the other believers heard about his danger. So they took him to Caesarea and then sent him to his home in Tarsus.

31Meanwhile, the church had peace throughout Judea, Galilee, and Samaria. And it soon grew in strength and numbers. The believers learned how to walk in the fear of the Lord. And they lived with the comfort of the Holy Spirit.

- *Remember:* Whom did the Lord send to Saul? What did he want him to do? (9:10-12) Why didn't Ananias want to go? (9:13-14) How did Saul change when the Holy Spirit filled him? (9:15-22) Why did some people want to kill Saul? (9:21-23) Why did some people put Saul in a basket? (9:24-25) Which friends of Saul became enemies? Why?

- *Discover:* Jesus helps enemies become friends. The devil helps friends become enemies. Jesus helps you keep friends.

- *Apply:* Ask Jesus to help you change enemies and keep friends. He can do both.

- *What's next?* A dead woman gets up and greets her friends. How did this happen? Read Acts 9:32-43. ◼

Peter Brings Dorcas Back to Life

Everyone loved Dorcas. She was a kind helper. She did many kind things for others. She helped poor people. But Dorcas became sick. She died. Her friends cried. What could they do? Then Peter came. "Get up, Dorcas!" he said. Would she?

32Peter traveled from place to place to visit the believers. And in his travels, he came to the believers in the town of Lydda. 33There he met a man named Aeneas. He had been paralyzed and bound to his bed for eight years.

³⁴Peter said to him, "Aeneas! Jesus Christ has healed you! Get up and make your bed." And he was healed instantly. ³⁵Then all the people of Lydda and Sharon turned to the Lord. For they saw Aeneas walking around.

³⁶In the city of Joppa there was a woman named Dorcas. Her name means "Gazelle." She was a believer who always did kind things for others, especially the poor. ³⁷About this time she became sick and died. Her friends got her ready to be buried. And they laid her in an upstairs room. ³⁸But then they learned that Peter was nearby at Lydda. So they sent two men to beg him to come back with them to Joppa. ³⁹This he did. And when he got there, they took him upstairs where Dorcas lay. The room was filled with crying widows. They were showing each other the coats and other clothes Dorcas had made for them. ⁴⁰But Peter asked them all to leave the room. Then he knelt and prayed. Turning to the body he said, "Get up, Dorcas." And she opened her eyes! When she saw Peter, she sat up! ⁴¹He gave her his hand and helped her up. Then he called in the believers and widows, presenting her to them.

⁴²The news raced through the town. And many believed in the Lord. ⁴³After that Peter stayed a long time in Joppa. During this time, he lived with Simon, the tanner.

- *Remember:* What kind of person was Dorcas? (9:36) When Peter came, what did he do? (9:40) What happened to Dorcas? (9:40-41) When people heard about this, many believed in Jesus. Why do you think that happened? (9:42) Would you like to have known Dorcas? Why? Would you like to be a helper like Dorcas? Why?

- *Discover:* Helpers make many friends. If you want friends, be a helper.

- *Apply:* Do you want more friends? Ask how you can be a helper to someone today. But don't expect that person to be your friend because you help. Help

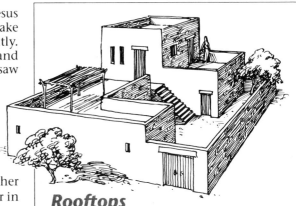

Rooftops and Courtyards
ACTS 10:9

Why did Peter go up to the rooftop to pray? Would you go up on the roof of your house to pray? Bible-time rooftops were not like yours. Your house probably has a roof covered with some kind of shingles. Does your roof rise at an angle? Bible-time houses had flat roofs. People often went up to the rooftop to sit. Sometimes they did chores up there. It was not fun to sit in the house. With few or no windows, houses got very hot by the end of the day. Remember, there was no air conditioning back then. The floors were dirt or stone. There was almost no furniture. It was dark inside. On a hot day, it was more pleasant sitting on the roof. It was also the best place to feel the cool evening breeze. There were steps to the roof. It was easy to get there.

Courtyards were also important. They were like yards, but people did not have grass lawns. A fence surrounded the courtyard. It had a gate. At night the gate was closed. That helped protect the people. If you lived in Bible times, you would like rooftops and courtyards. You could get out of the house. But you did not have to go out in the street. These were wonderful places to sit, work, or play.

because you want to help. Then you will have a friend.

● *What's next?* Starting a new church isn't easy. Here's how it should be done. Read Acts 11:19-30. ■

A Roman Captain Calls for Peter

10 In Caesarea there lived a Roman army officer named Cornelius. He was a captain in what was known as the Italian regiment. ²He was a godly man, very devout, as was his whole family. He gave generously to the poor and was a man of prayer. ³While wide awake one afternoon he had a vision. It came to him about three o'clock. And in this vision he saw an Angel of God coming toward him.

"Cornelius!" the Angel said.

⁴Cornelius stared at him in terror. "What do you want, sir?" he asked the angel.

And the Angel replied, "Your prayers and good deeds have been noticed by God! ⁵⁻⁶Now send some men to Joppa to find a man named Simon Peter. He is staying with Simon, the tanner, down by the shore. Ask him to come and visit you."

⁷As soon as the Angel was gone, Cornelius called two of his servants. He also called a godly soldier, one of his personal bodyguard. ⁸He told them what had happened and sent them off to Joppa.

Peter Goes to See Cornelius

⁹⁻¹⁰The next day about noon, they were getting close to the city. And Peter went up

on the flat roof of his house to pray. It was noon and he was hungry. But while lunch was being made, he fell into a trance. ¹¹He saw the sky open and a great canvas sheet settle to the ground. The sheet was held up by its four corners. ¹²In the sheet were all sorts of animals, snakes, and birds. Jews were not allowed to eat any of the things that were there.

¹³Then a voice said to him, "Go kill and eat any of them you wish."

¹⁴"Never, Lord," Peter declared. "I have never in all my life eaten such creatures. For they are forbidden by our Jewish laws."

¹⁵The voice spoke again, "Don't try to tell God what is pure or impure! If he says something is lawful to eat, then it is."

¹⁶Peter saw the same vision three times. Then the sheet was pulled up again to Heaven.

¹⁷Peter was very confused. What

could the vision mean? What was he supposed to do?

Just then the men sent by Cornelius had found the house. They were standing outside at the gate. [18]And they were asking if this was the place where Simon Peter lived!

[19]Meanwhile, Peter was thinking about the vision. Then the Holy Spirit said to him, "Three men have come to see you. [20]Go down and meet them and go with them. All is well, I have sent them."

[21]So Peter went down. "I'm the man you're looking for," he said. "Now what is it you want?"

[22]Then they told him about Cornelius, the Roman officer. They told him he was a good and godly man, well thought of by the Jews. And they told him how an angel had told him to send for Peter to come. The angel had said

that Peter would tell him what God wanted him to do.

23So Peter asked them in and they stayed overnight.

The next day Peter went with them. And several other believers from Joppa went along, too.

24They arrived in Caesarea the following day. And Cornelius was waiting for him. He had called together his relatives and close friends to meet Peter. 25As Peter entered his home, Cornelius fell to the floor before him.

?????????????????????????????????????

Who saw a big sheet full of animals, snakes, and birds?

Read 11:4-10

?????????????????????????????????????

26But Peter said, "Stand up! I'm not a god!"

27So he got up, and they talked together for a while. Then they went in to where the others were waiting.

28Peter told them, "You all know about the Jewish laws. They say it is wrong for me to come into a Gentile home like this. But God has shown me in a vision that I should never think of anyone as impure. 29So I came to you as soon as I was sent for. Now tell me what you want."

30Cornelius replied, "Four days ago I was praying as usual. It was at about this time of the afternoon. And suddenly a man was standing before me. He was dressed in a shining robe! 31He told me, 'Cornelius, God has heard your prayers. And your good deeds have been noticed by God! 32Now send some men to Joppa and call Simon Peter. He is staying in the home of Simon, a tanner, down by the shore.' 33So I sent for you at once. And you have done well to come so soon. Now here we are, waiting before the Lord. We want to hear what he has told you to tell us!"

Peter Preaches
in Cornelius's Home

34Then Peter replied, "I see that the Jews are not the only people God loves! 35In every nation he has those who worship him. They do good deeds and are accepted by him. 36-37I'm sure you have heard about the Good News for the people of Israel. It says that there is peace with God through Jesus, the Messiah. And yes, the Messiah is Lord of all creation! This message has spread all through Judea. It began with John the Baptist in Galilee. 38And you no doubt heard about Jesus of Nazareth. He was anointed by God with the Holy Spirit and with power. And he went around doing good deeds. He healed all who were controlled by demons, for God was with him.

39"And we apostles are witnesses of all he did in Israel and Jerusalem. We were there as he was murdered on a cross. 40-41But God brought him back to life again three days later. He came to certain people that God had chosen beforehand. He didn't appear to the general public. But he came to us and we ate and drank with him after he rose from the dead. 42And he sent us to preach the Good News everywhere. We are to tell everyone that Jesus is chosen by God to judge everyone, the living and the dead. 43And all the prophets have written about him. They say that all who believe in him will have their sins forgiven through his name."

44Even as Peter was saying these things, the Holy Spirit fell upon all those listening! 45The Jews who came with Peter were amazed. For the gift of the Holy Spirit was now given to the Gentiles, too! 46-47But there could be no doubt about it. For they heard them speaking in tongues and praising God.

Peter asked, "Can anyone object to my baptizing them? For they have received the Holy Spirit just as we did!" 48So he did, baptizing them in the name of Jesus, the Messiah. After that, Cornelius begged him to stay with them for several days.

Peter Tells Why
He Preaches to the Gentiles

11 Soon the news reached the apostles and other brothers in Judea. They all heard that Gentiles were also being converted! 2But when Peter got back to

Jerusalem, the Jewish believers argued with him.

³"You stayed with Gentiles and even ate with them!" they accused.

⁴Then Peter told them the whole story. ⁵"It all started one day in Joppa," he began. "While I was praying, I saw a vision. A huge sheet was let down from the sky by its four corners. ⁶Inside the sheet were all sorts of animals, reptiles, and birds. None of them were allowed by Jewish law as food. ⁷And I heard a voice say, 'Kill and eat whatever you wish.'

⁸"'Never, Lord,' I replied. 'For I have never yet eaten anything not allowed by our Jewish laws!'

⁹"But the voice came again, 'Don't say it isn't right when God says that it is!'

¹⁰"This happened three times before the sheet went back into Heaven. ¹¹Just then three men came to the house where I was staying! They had come to take me with them to Caesarea. ¹²The Holy Spirit told me to go with them! And he told me not to worry about their being Gentiles. These six brothers here went along with me. And we soon got to the home of the man who had sent the messengers. ¹³He told us how an angel had come to him. The angel had told him to send messengers to Joppa to find Simon Peter. ¹⁴'He will tell you how you and all your family can be saved!' the angel had said.

¹⁵"Well, I began telling them the Good News. I was just getting started with my sermon, and the Holy Spirit fell on them! The Spirit fell upon them just as he fell on us at the beginning! ¹⁶Then I thought of the Lord's words when he said, 'Yes, John baptized with water. But you shall be baptized with the Holy Spirit.' ¹⁷It was God who gave these Gentiles the gift of the Holy Spirit. It happened to them just as it did to us when we believed on the Lord Jesus Christ. So who was I to argue with God?"

¹⁸When the others heard this, all their arguments were answered. Then they began to praise God! "Yes," they said, "God has saved the Gentiles, too! He has given them the chance to come to him for eternal life!"

Christians Start a New Church

Do you know someone who is starting a new church where there are none? Do you know someone who is winning friends for Jesus? This is the way it's done.

¹⁹Now many believers had fled from Jerusalem soon after Stephen's death. And they had traveled as far as Phoenicia, Cyprus, and Antioch. They preached the Good News as they went, but only to the Jews. ²⁰However, there were some believers who went to Antioch from Cyprus and Cyrene. They also told the Good News about the Lord Jesus to some Greeks. ²¹The Lord blessed this effort to reach the Gentiles. And large numbers of them became believers.

²²The church at Jerusalem heard what had happened. So they sent Barnabas to Antioch to help the new converts. ²³When he got there, he saw the great things God was doing. And he was filled with excitement and joy. He encouraged the believers there to stay close to the Lord, whatever the cost. ²⁴Barnabas was a kindly person, full of the Holy Spirit and strong in faith. And because of his work, large numbers of people believed in the Lord.

²⁵Then Barnabas went on to Tarsus to hunt for Saul. ²⁶When he found him, he brought him back to Antioch. And both of them stayed there for a full year teaching the many new converts. It was there at Antioch that the believers were first called "Christians."

²⁷During this time some prophets came down from Jerusalem to Antioch. ²⁸One of them was named Agabus. He

stood up in
one of the meet-
ings to make a
prophecy by the
Spirit. He foretold
that a great famine
was coming upon
the land of Israel.
This was fulfilled
during the reign of
Claudius. ²⁹So the
believers decided to
send relief to the Christians in Judea.
Each gave as much as he could. ³⁰They
gave their gifts to Barnabas and Saul to
take to the church in Jerusalem.

- *Remember:* Where did the Christians go?
  (11:19) At first these Jewish Christians
  shared the Good News with their own
  people. Then they reached out to others.
  Who were these others? (11:20) What
  happened to the Greeks? (11:21) How
  did Barnabas help these new Christians?
  (11:22-23) How did this help the church?
  (11:24) What more did Barnabas do to
  help the church? (11:25-26) Would the

church have grown without helpers? Will
your church grow without helpers?

- *Discover:* We win friends for Jesus when
  we reach out for Jesus. Be a helper.

- *Apply:* This is the way to win friends for
  Jesus or build a church: (1) go to people
  who need Jesus, (2) tell them about
  Jesus, (3) show them that you are excited and happy about Jesus, (4) encourage them, (5) teach them. Can you think
  of other ways?

- *What's next?* An iron prison gate opens
  by itself. A prisoner walks free! How can
  this happen? Read Acts 12:1-19. ■

An Angel Lets Peter Out of Prison

Herod throws Peter into prison. He will kill him the next day. But an angel appears. Would you like to see how an angel takes someone from prison?

12 About that time King Herod moved against some of the believers. ²He killed the apostle James, John's brother. ³Now Herod saw how much this pleased the Jewish leaders. So he also arrested Peter during the Passover Feast. ⁴He put him in prison under the guard of 16 soldiers. Herod's plan was to give Peter to the Jews to be killed after the Passover. ⁵But while Peter was in prison, the church was praying to God for his safety.

⁶The night before he was to be killed, he was asleep. He was chained between two soldiers. And others were standing guard by the prison gate. ⁷But suddenly there was a light in the cell! And an Angel of the Lord stood beside Peter! The Angel slapped him on the side to wake him up. Then he said, "Quick! Get up!" And the chains fell off his wrists! ⁸Then the Angel told him, "Get dressed and put on your shoes." And he did. "Now put on your coat and follow me!" the Angel ordered.

⁹So Peter left the cell, following the Angel. But all the time he thought it was a dream or vision. He didn't believe it was really happening. ¹⁰They passed the first and second cell blocks. Then they came to the iron gate to the street. The gate swung open by itself! So they passed through and walked together for a little way. Then the Angel left him.

¹¹Peter finally saw what had happened! "It's really true!" he said to himself. "The Lord has sent his Angel. He has saved me from Herod! He has delivered me from what the Jews were hoping to do to me!"

¹²Then Peter went to the home of Mary, the mother of John Mark. Many were gathered there for a prayer meeting.

¹³He knocked at the door in the gate. And a girl named Rhoda came to open it. ¹⁴She heard Peter's voice and knew it was him. She was so happy that she ran back inside to tell everyone. And she left Peter standing outside in the street. ¹⁵They didn't believe her. "You're out of your mind," they said. When she insisted they decided, "It must be his angel. They must have killed him."

¹⁶Meanwhile Peter continued knocking. When they finally went out and opened the door, they were amazed. ¹⁷He motioned for them to quiet down and told them what had happened. He recounted how the Lord had brought him out of jail. "Tell James and the others what happened," he said. Then he left to find a safer place to stay.

¹⁸At dawn, the jail was in great confusion. What had happened to Peter? ¹⁹Herod had sent for Peter and found that he wasn't there. So he had the 16 guards arrested and sentenced to death.

After that, Herod went to live in Caesarea for a while.

● *Remember:* Why did Herod put Peter into prison? What did he plan to do with Peter? (12:4) What were the Christians doing about this? (12:5) What difference do you think this made? Who came to help Peter? (12:6-7) How did the angel take Peter from prison? (12:7-10) Friends were praying for Peter. Did they believe their prayers were answered? (12:12-16) What would you like to tell Peter's friends about answered prayer?

● *Discover:* When you pray, expect God to answer. Don't be surprised when he does.

● *Apply:* Are you praying for something? God will answer your prayer. Sometimes he sends what you ask. Sometimes he says no. Sometimes he tells you to wait. But he does answer.

● *What's next?* Maggots eat a king until he dies. Read Acts 12:20-23. ■

King Herod Dies

Herod was king. Some kings thought they were bigger and better than everyone else. Herod thought he was bigger than God. He was wrong. This is the way God showed he is bigger than any king.

²⁰While Herod was in Caesarea, a group from Tyre and Sidon came to see him. He was very upset with the people of those two cities. But this group had made friends with Blastus, the royal secretary. They had asked Herod for peace. This was because their cities needed to trade goods with Herod's country. ²¹A meeting with Herod was granted and the day soon arrived. Herod put on his royal robes, sat on his throne, and made a speech to them. ²²When he was finished, the people cheered loudly for him. They shouted, "It is the voice of a god and not of a man!"

²³Right then, an Angel of the Lord struck Herod with a sickness. Soon he was filled with maggots and died. This was because he let the people worship him instead of giving the glory to God.

● *Remember:* Why did the group of people come to see Herod? (12:20) How did Herod try to be a god? Why didn't he tell the people he wasn't a god? (12:21-22) Who caused Herod to be sick? What was the matter with him? (12:23) How do you know that God is bigger than King Herod?

● *Discover:* God is bigger and more powerful than we. We must never try to make ourselves look bigger than God.

● *Apply:* Have you ever thought you could do something better than God? Have you ever wanted to change the way God made things? Have you ever wanted to change the way God made you? Accept the way God does things. He knows best.

● *What's next?* How did the first foreign missionary trip begin? Read about it in Acts 12:24–13:5. ■

Saul's First Missionary Journey

Does your church support some missionaries? Are any of these working in foreign countries? This is the way the first foreign missionary journey began.

²⁴God's Good News was spreading quickly and there were many new believers.

²⁵Barnabas and Saul now visited Jerusalem. As soon as they had finished their business, they went back to Antioch. And they took John Mark with them.

13 In the church at Antioch, there were a number of prophets and teachers. Barnabus and Saul were among them. In addition, there was a man named Symeon, who was also known as "The Black Man." There was Lucius, who was from Cyrene. And there was Manaen, the foster-brother of King Herod. ²One day these men were worshiping and fasting together. And the Holy Spirit said to them, "Bless Barnabas and Saul for a special job I have for them." ³So these men fasted and prayed some more. Then they laid their hands on Barnabas and Saul and sent them on their way.

⁴Directed by the Holy Spirit, they went to Seleucia. And from there, they sailed for Cyprus. ⁵There, in the town of Salamis, they went to the Jewish synagogue and preached. John Mark went with them as their helper.

- *Remember:* Which prophets and teachers were in the church at Antioch? (13:1) Who told them to give Saul and Barnabas special work? (13:2) What did the men do first? (13:3) Who guided Saul and Barnabas on their journey? (13:4) Where did they go? How did these people plan this first journey?

- *Discover:* When we do God's work, we should do it God's way.

- *Apply:* Saul and Barnabas did God's work. They followed these steps. Before you work for God, follow these same steps: (1) Put God's work first. Don't let other things get in the way. (2) Pray. (3) Let the Holy Spirit lead you. (4) Go do it.

- *What's next?* A man tries to stop God's work. But he suddenly is struck blind. Read Acts 13:6-12. ■

Elymas Becomes Blind

A man named Elymas tries to stop God's work. Saul (whose name is now changed to Paul) is angry with him. Suddenly Elymas becomes blind. Now what will happen?

⁶⁻⁷After that they preached from town to town across the island. And they finally reached Paphos, where they met a Jewish sorcerer. He was a fake prophet named Bar-Jesus. (His name was Elymas in Greek.) This sorcerer had become friendly with the governor, Sergius Paulus. As it happened, the governor was a man of insight and knowledge. And he invited Barnabas and Saul to visit him. For he wanted to hear their message from God. ⁸But the sorcerer, Elymas, tried to stop him from meeting them. He told the governor not to listen to what Saul and Barnabas had to say. He was trying to keep the governor from trusting the Lord.

⁹But Saul was filled with the Holy Spirit. (Saul was also called Paul.) He glared angrily at the sorcerer. ¹⁰"You son of the devil!" Paul said. "You are full of all sorts of tricks and lies. You are an enemy of all that is good. Won't you ever stop fighting against the Lord? ¹¹And now God has laid his hand of judgment upon you. And you will be made blind for awhile."

Right then mist and darkness fell

upon him. And he began to wander around. He begged for someone to take his hand and lead him. [12]When the governor saw what happened, he believed. And he was amazed at the power of God's message.

- *Remember:* What kind of person was Elymas, or Bar-Jesus? (13:6-7) What kind of person was the governor? (13:6-7) What did Elymas try to stop? (13:8) What happened to him? (13:9-11) What did the governor do then? (13:12) Do you think Paul did what was right? Why?

- *Discover:* Sometimes God allows his enemies to win for a little while. At least it seems that way. But they are not really winning at all because in the end, God's side will win over all evil and sin.

- *Apply:* Do you know people who seem to fight God? Ask your parents if they know any. Sometimes these people seem to have more money. Or they seem to be more powerful. Or they may be more famous. Don't try to be like them. They may win for a little while. But if you really want to win, get on God's side. He will have the final victory.

- *What's next?* People think Paul and Barnabas are famous gods. Read Acts 14:1-20. ◼

Paul Preaches to the Jews in Antioch

[13]Now Paul and those with him left Paphos by ship for Asia Minor. They landed at the port town of Perga. There John Mark left them and went back to Jerusalem. [14]But Barnabas and Paul went on to Antioch. This was a city in the province of Pisidia.

On the Sabbath they went into the synagogue for the services. [15]They read the usual passages from the Books of Moses and from the Prophets. Then the men in charge of the service sent Paul and Barnabas a message. They said, "Brothers, do you have any special word of teaching for us? If you do, come and give it!"

[16]So Paul stood, waved a greeting to them, and began. "I greet you, men of Israel," he said. "I also greet any others here who respect God. Let me begin my remarks with a bit of history.

[17]"The God of this nation Israel chose our ancestors. Then he honored them in Egypt by leading them out of their slavery. [18]And he nursed them through 40 years of wandering in the wilderness. [19-20]Then he destroyed seven nations in Canaan. And he gave Israel their land as an inheritance. Judges ruled in Israel for about 450 years. And they were followed by Samuel the prophet.

[21]"Then the people begged for a king. And God gave them Saul, the son of Kish, as their king. He was a man of the tribe of Benjamin, and he reigned for 40 years. [22]But God removed him from the throne. And he made David the king in his place. God said, 'David, the son of Jesse, is a man after my own heart. For he will obey me.' [23]But now God has raised up one of King David's descendants. His name is Jesus. He is the One God promised would come to save Israel!

[24]"But before he came, John the Baptist preached to the people of Israel. He told them to turn from their sins and turn back to God. [25]As John was finishing his work he asked, 'Do you think I am the Messiah? No! But he is coming soon. And compared with him, I am nothing.'

[26]"Brothers, this salvation is for all of us! It is for you who are sons of Abraham. And it is also for you Gentiles here who respect God. [27]The Jews in Jerusalem killed Jesus on a cross. And by doing this, they did what the prophets of old foretold. For they didn't know who he was. They didn't realize that he was the one the prophets had written about. This happened even though they heard the prophets' words read every Sabbath! [28]They found no just cause to kill him. But they asked Pilate to have him killed anyway. [29]So they killed Jesus and did everything the prophets foretold about his death. Then he was taken from the cross and put in a tomb.

[30]"But God brought him back to life again! [31]And he was seen many times during the next few days. The men who had traveled with him to Jerusalem from Galilee spent time with him. And these

men have told people everywhere that Jesus is alive!

³²⁻³³"And now Barnabas and I are here to bring you this Good News. God's promise to our ancestors has come true in our own time! For God brought Jesus back to life again. The second Psalm talks about Jesus. It says, 'Today I have honored you as my Son.'

³⁴"God brought Jesus back to life again. And he will never again go back to the grave. This is written in the Scriptures. God said, 'I will do for you the great thing I promised David.' ³⁵In another Psalm he explained it more fully. He said, 'God will not let his Holy One decay.' ³⁶These words could not be talking about David. For David died and was buried, and his body decayed. ³⁷No, it was talking about someone else! It was someone that God brought back to life. It was someone whose body was not touched at all by death.

³⁸"Brothers! Listen! In this man Jesus there is forgiveness for your sins! ³⁹Everyone who trusts in him is freed from all guilt. He is declared to be righteous and holy. This is something the Jewish law could never do. ⁴⁰Oh, be careful! Don't let the prophets' words apply to you. For they said, ⁴¹'Look and die, you haters of the truth! For I am doing something in your day. It is something that you won't believe when you hear it announced.'"

⁴²As the people left the synagogue, they asked Paul to come back again. They wanted him to speak to them again the next week. ⁴³Many Jews and godly Gentiles who were at the synagogue followed Paul and Barnabas down the street. And the two men urged them to accept the mercies God was offering.

Now Paul Preaches to the Gentiles

⁴⁴The next week most of the city came to hear them preach the Word of God.

⁴⁵But when the Jewish leaders saw the crowds, they were jealous. So they cursed and argued against whatever Paul said.

⁴⁶Then Paul and Barnabas spoke out boldly. They said, "We must tell this Good News from God to you Jews first. But you have rejected it and shown yourselves unworthy of eternal life. So now, we will offer it to the Gentiles. ⁴⁷For this is just what the Lord commanded. He said, 'I have made you a light to the Gentiles. You will lead them from the farthest corners of the earth to my salvation.'"

⁴⁸When the Gentiles heard this, they were very glad. They rejoiced in the message that Paul preached. And all those who wanted eternal life, believed. ⁴⁹So God's message spread all through that region.

⁵⁰But the Jewish leaders stirred up the godly women and other city leaders. All of them turned against Paul and Barnabas, and ran them out of town. ⁵¹But they shook off the dust of their feet against the town. And they went on to the city of Iconium. ⁵²And the believers were filled with joy and with the Holy Spirit.

People Think Paul and Barnabas Are Gods

People thought Paul and Barnabas were famous gods. Paul and Barnabas could ask for anything! The people would give it to them. Will they?

14 At Iconium, Paul and Barnabas went together to the synagogue. They preached with such power that many Jews and Gentiles believed.

²But many of the Jews didn't believe God's message. And they caused the Gentiles to distrust Paul and Barnabas. They said all sorts of evil things about

them. ³But even so, they stayed there a long time, preaching boldly. And the Lord proved their message was true by helping them do great miracles. ⁴But the people of the city were divided. Some thought that the Jewish leaders were right. Others believed the apostles.

⁵⁻⁶Paul and Barnabas learned that some people wanted to kill them. The Jewish leaders with a crowd of Gentiles and Jews had a plan to stone them. So Paul and Barnabas ran for their lives. They went to the cities of Lycaonia, Lystra, Derbe, and the nearby areas. ⁷And they preached the Good News to the people there.

⁸While they were at Lystra, they came upon a man with crippled feet. He had been that way from birth. So all his life he had never walked. ⁹He was listening to Paul as he preached. Paul saw him and knew he had the faith to be healed. ¹⁰So Paul called to him, "Stand up!" And the man jumped to his feet and started walking!

¹¹The crowd there saw what Paul had done. So they shouted, "These men are gods in human bodies!" ¹²They decided that Barnabas was the Greek god Jupiter. And they thought Paul was Mercury. This was because Paul was the chief speaker. ¹³Now the temple of Jupiter was located at the edge of the city. And the priest from the temple brought them cartloads of flowers. He also prepared to sacrifice oxen to them at the city gates before the crowds.

¹⁴But Barnabas and Paul soon saw what was happening. They were very upset and ripped at their clothing. They ran out among the people, shouting, ¹⁵"Men! What are you doing? We are just human beings like yourselves! We have come to bring you Good News. We have come to invite you to turn from the worship of these foolish things. Come and pray instead to the living God. For he made the heavens and earth, and the sea and everything in them. ¹⁶In days past, God allowed the nations to follow their own ways. ¹⁷But he never left himself without a witness. He always reminded you that he was there. He sent you rain and good crops. He also gave you food and gladness."

¹⁸But even so, Paul and Barnabas could hardly stop the people from sacrificing to them!

¹⁹Yet only a few days later, some Jews came from Antioch and Iconium. They turned the crowds into an angry mob. And they stoned Paul and dragged him out of the city. They thought he was dead. ²⁰The believers went and stood around Paul. And he got up and went back into the city!

● *Remember:* Why did the people at Lystra think Paul and Barnabas were gods? What had Paul done? (14:8-10) What did the pagan priest there bring? (14:13) Did Paul and Barnabas claim to be gods? What did they say? Whom did they honor? (14:14-17) What did the same crowd do several days later? (14:19) Do you think Paul and Barnabas did what was right? Why?

● *Discover:* Don't let people praise you for what God does. Honor God. Tell them God did this.

● *Apply:* Your dog gets sick. You ask God to help him. Then you take care of him. People praise you for helping your dog get well. But God was the one who made your dog get well. Tell them you helped God.

● *What's next?* Paul and Barnabas were a great missionary team. But they stopped working together. Why? Read Acts 15:36-41. ∎

Paul and Barnabas Appoint Elders

The next day he left with Barnabas for Derbe. ²¹They preached the Good News there and made many disciples. Then they went back through Lystra, Iconium, and Antioch. ²²They helped the believers there to grow in love for God and each other. They encouraged the believers not to turn from their faith even though people treated them badly. And they reminded them that they must enter into the Kingdom of God through many troubles. ²³Paul and Barnabas also chose elders in every church. And they prayed for them with fasting. They turned them over to the care of the Lord, in whom they trusted.

24Then they traveled back through Pisidia to Pamphylia. 25They preached again in Perga, and went on to Attalia.

The First Journey Ends

26Finally they went by ship to Antioch, where their journey had begun. They had been devoted to God's work in the church there.

27When they got there, they called together the believers. They reported on the trip they had just completed. They told how God had opened the door of faith to the Gentiles. 28And they stayed there with the believers at Antioch for a long time.

A Church Conflict: Must Gentiles Follow the Jewish Law?

15 While Paul and Barnabas were at Antioch, some men came from Judea. They told the believers that they must obey the ancient Jewish customs. They told them that they had to be circumcised to be saved. 2Paul and Barnabas argued about this with them for a long time. But in the end, they decided to go to Jerusalem. And some local men went along, too. They wanted to discuss this question with the apostles and elders there. 3The whole church followed these men out of Antioch as they began their journey. After leaving the city, they went on to Jerusalem. They stopped along the way in the cities of Phoenicia and Samaria. They visited all the believers there. They told them that the Gentiles, too, were being converted. And everyone was full of joy.

A Church Council Meeting

4When they got to Jerusalem, they met with the church leaders. All the apostles and elders were there. And Paul and Barnabas reported on what God had been doing through their ministry. 5But some of the believers had been Pharisees before they became Christians. They stood up and they claimed that all Gentile believers must be circumcised. They wanted the Gentiles to follow all the Jewish customs and rules.

6So the apostles and church elders set a meeting to decide this question.

7At the meeting, there was a long debate on the question. And Peter stood and spoke to the people who were there. "Brothers," he said, "you all know what happened some years ago. God chose me from among you to preach to the Gentiles. For he wanted them to hear the Good News and believe. 8God knows men's hearts. And he proved that he accepts Gentiles by giving them the Holy Spirit. He gave them the Holy Spirit, just as he gave him to us. 9He showed that there is no difference between them and us. For he cleansed their lives through faith, just as he did ours. 10And now, are you going to correct God? Will you force the Gentiles to carry this heavy load? It is a load that neither we nor our fathers were able to carry! 11Don't you believe that all are saved the same way? Don't you believe we are saved by the free gift of the Lord Jesus?"

12There was no further debate. Everyone now listened as Barnabas and Paul told about their ministry. They told the council about the miracles God had done among the Gentiles.

James Says That Gentiles Don't Need to Obey Jewish Laws

13When they had finished, James took the floor. "Brothers," he said, "listen to me. 14Peter has told you about the time God first visited the Gentiles. God chose from among them people who now bring honor to his name. 15And the fact that Gentiles have become true believers was foretold by the prophets. Listen to this passage from the prophet Amos:

16"'Afterwards,' says the Lord, 'I will come back. I will renew the broken contract with David. 17And Gentiles, too, will find the Lord! Yes, the Lord will make it happen. 18That is what the Lord says. These things have been known for a long time.'

19"So I think we should not force the Gentiles who turn to God to obey our Jewish laws. 20Instead, we should write a letter to them. We should tell them not to eat meat sacrificed to idols. We should tell them not to eat meat that still has the blood in it. And we should tell them not to take part in any sexual sins. [21]These things have been preached against in Jewish synagogues for many years."

The Council Sends a Letter to the Gentile Believers

[22]Then the apostles and elders and all the people took a vote. They decided to send messengers to Antioch with Paul and Barnabas. They would report on this decision to the church there. The two church leaders chosen to go to Antioch were Judas, also called Barsabbas, and Silas.

[23]This is the letter they took along with them:

"*From:* The apostles, elders and brothers at Jerusalem.

"*To:* The Gentile brothers in Antioch, Syria, and Cilicia.

"Greetings!

[24]"We have heard that some believers from Jerusalem have upset you. They questioned whether you were saved or not. But they had no such orders from us. [25]We recently met to talk about this question and have made a decision. So it seemed wise to us to send to you two official messengers. They will come along with our beloved Barnabas and Paul. [26]These men, Judas and Silas, have risked their lives for the sake of our Lord Jesus Christ. And they will tell you what we decided in person.

[27-29]"For it seemed good to the Holy Spirit and to us not to burden you with all the Jewish laws. But we ask that you not eat food that has been offered to idols. We ask that you not eat unbled meat from strangled animals. And we ask that you not take part in any sexual sins. If you do these three things, it is enough. Farewell."

[30]The four messengers went at once to Antioch. And they called a general meeting of the Christians there. At this meeting, they gave them the letter from Jerusalem. [31]And there was great joy throughout the church that day as they read it.

[32]Now Judas and Silas were both gifted speakers. So they preached long sermons to the believers, building up their faith. [33]Judas and Silas stayed several days, and then went back to Jerusalem. They took greetings and thanks with them for the leaders in Jerusalem. [34-35]Paul and Barnabas stayed on at Antioch to help others who were preaching and teaching there.

Paul and Barnabas Separate

What would cause two great missionaries to stop working together? This did!

[36]Some time later Paul said to Barnabas, "We planted many churches in the cities of Asia Minor. Let's go back and visit each city where we preached before. Let's see how the new believers are getting along." [37]Barnabas agreed and wanted to take along John Mark. [38]But Paul didn't like that idea at all. This was because John Mark had left them in Pamphylia during their first trip. [39]They had a sharp disagreement over this and decided to separate. Barnabas took Mark with him and sailed for Cyprus. [40-41]But Paul chose Silas and left for Syria and Cilicia to encourage the churches there. They went out with the blessing of the believers in Antioch.

- *Remember:* Paul and Barnabas agreed to do something. What? (15:36-37) Why did they disagree? (15:37-39) What did Barnabas do? (15:39) What did Paul do? (15:40-41) Which man had the blessing of the believers? (15:40-41) Why do you think Paul had their blessing?

- *Discover:* Don't stop working because you can't do it your way. Don't stop playing because you can't play your way. Neither Paul nor Barnabas could have his own way. But they kept doing God's work anyway.

- *Apply:* Has a friend stopped playing because you didn't play her way? Has a friend gone home with his toys be-

cause you didn't play his way? Has a friend called you names because you didn't play his way? You may want to stop doing something good because you can't do it your way. Don't let that stop you.

- *What's next?* You would probably like to be like Timothy. Do you know why? Read Acts 16:1-5. ■

Timothy Is Paul's Helper

Who do you want to be like? Do you have a hero? Is she a movie star? Is he a professional athlete? Why do you want to be like this person? Timothy is a hero. He could be your hero. You might want to be like him. When you read this, you'll learn why.

16 Paul and Silas went first to Derbe. Then they went on to Lystra, where they met a believer named Timothy. Timothy's mother was a Christian Jewess, but his father was a Greek. ²Timothy was well thought of by the brothers in Lystra and Iconium. ³So Paul asked him to join them on their journey. And he circumcised Timothy before they left. Paul did this so he wouldn't offend any of the Jews of the area. For everyone knew that Timothy's father was Greek and hadn't allowed this before. ⁴Then they went from city to city. They told everyone about the decision concerning the Gentiles. They also related how the decision had been made by the apostles and elders in Jerusalem. ⁵So the church grew daily in faith and numbers.

- *Remember:* How do you know that Timothy was a Christian? (16:1) What did other Christians think of Timothy? (16:2) What did they do together? (16:4) What happened when Paul and Timothy worked together? (16:5) How do you think their work helped the church grow?

- *Discover:* A good helper is a real hero. Be a good helper. Good things will happen.

- *Apply:* When Mother asks you to help, do you grumble? Or do you help cheerfully? When Father asks you to help, do you do

your work well? Or do you do half of your job? When you help God do his work, do you remember that it's God's work?

- *What's next?* Why would people sing when they are thrown into prison? Read Acts 16:16-40. ■

God Speaks to Paul in a Vision

⁶Next they traveled through Phrygia and Galatia. The Holy Spirit had told them not to go into the province of Asia Minor at that time. ⁷Then they went along the borders of Mysia. And they headed north for the province of Bithynia. But again the Spirit of Jesus told them not to go there. ⁸So instead they went on through Mysia province to the city of Troas.

⁹That night Paul had a vision. In his dream he saw a man over in Macedonia, Greece. He was begging, "Come over here and help us." ¹⁰Well, that settled it! We would go on to Macedonia. For it seemed clear that God wanted us to preach the Good News there.

Lydia Becomes a Christian

¹¹We went aboard a boat at Troas and sailed straight across to Samothrace. On the next day we sailed to Neapolis. ¹²Then finally we reached Philippi. This is a Roman colony just inside the

Macedonian border. We stayed there for several days.

¹³On the Sabbath we went a little way outside the city to a riverbank. We had heard that some people met there for prayer. And we taught the Scriptures to some women who came. ¹⁴One of them was Lydia, a saleswoman from Thyatira. She was a merchant of purple cloth. She was already a wor- shiper of God.

And as she listened to us, the Lord opened her heart. She believed all that Paul was saying. ¹⁵She was baptized along with all her family. And she asked us to be her guests. "If you agree that I am faithful to the Lord," she said, "come and stay at my home." And she urged us until we did.

Paul and Silas Sing in Prison

Paul and Silas were beaten with wooden whips. They were thrown into prison. They were put in the dungeon. Then they were put in stocks so they couldn't move. What would you do if this happened to you? Would you complain? Would you be angry at God? Paul and Silas prayed and sang. Now look what happened.

¹⁶One day we went down to the place of prayer beside the river. On our way, we met a slave girl who was controlled by a demon. She was a fortune-teller and earned much money for her masters. ¹⁷She followed along behind us shouting, "These men are servants of God! They have come to tell you how to have your sins forgiven!"

¹⁸This went on day after day. This upset Paul, so he spoke to the demon within her. "I command you in the name of Jesus Christ to come out of her," he said. And right away the demon left her.

¹⁹Her masters' hopes of getting rich

by using this girl were now lost. So they grabbed Paul and Silas. And they took them before the judges at the marketplace.

You are saved by believing in Jesus

Believe on the Lord Jesus. Then you will be saved.

Acts 16:31

---

²⁰⁻²¹"These Jews are causing trouble in our city," they shouted. "They are teaching the people to do things that are against the Roman laws."

²²A crowd was quickly formed against Paul and Silas. So the judges ordered them stripped and beaten with wooden whips. ²³Again and again the rods slashed down across their bare backs. And after that they were thrown into prison. The jailer was told he would be killed if they got away. ²⁴So he took no chances, but put them into the inner dungeon. And there he clamped their feet into the stocks.

²⁵Around midnight, Paul and Silas were praying and singing hymns to the Lord. And all the other prisoners were listening to them. ²⁶But suddenly there was a great earthquake. The prison was shaken to its foundations. All the doors flew open. And the chains of every prisoner fell off! ²⁷The jailer woke up to see the prison doors wide open! He thought all the prisoners had gotten away! So he drew his sword to kill himself.

²⁸But Paul yelled to him, "Don't do it! We are all here!"

²⁹Shaking with fear, the jailer called for lights. Then he ran to the dungeon and fell down before Paul and Silas. ³⁰He brought them out and asked, "Sirs, what must I do to be saved?"

³¹They replied, "Believe on the Lord Jesus. Then you will be saved, and your whole family."

³²Then they told him and all his household the Good News from the Lord. ³³That same hour he washed their beaten backs. And he and all his family were baptized. ³⁴Then he brought them up into his house and set a meal before them. He and his family were full of joy because all of them believed! ³⁵The next morning the judges sent police officers over to the jailer. They said, "Let those men go!" ³⁶So the jailer told Paul they were free to leave.

³⁷But Paul replied, "Oh, no, they don't! They have publicly beaten us without trial and jailed us. And we are Roman citizens! So now they want us to leave secretly? Never! Let them come themselves and let us go!"

³⁸The police officers told this to the judges. They feared for their lives when they heard Paul and Silas were Roman citizens. ³⁹So they came to the jail and begged them to go. They brought them out and pled with them to leave the city.

⁴⁰Paul and Silas then went back to the home of Lydia. They met with the believers there. And they preached to them once more before leaving town.

● *Remember:* What kind of girl followed Paul and Silas each day? What did she say? (16:16-17) What did Paul do for this girl? (16:18) What happened in the prison at midnight? (16:25-26) How did the jailer become a Christian? (16:27-34) What if Paul and Silas had cursed God when they were put into prison? What if they had refused to pray? How do you think this story would end?

● *Discover:* When you're in trouble, pray and praise God. Don't turn against him. He is the one who can really help you.

● *Apply:* Next time you get into trouble, remember Paul and Silas. Turn to God, not away from him. Pray, don't grumble.

● *What's next?* Two towns hear the same story. But what a difference! Watch what these two towns do. Read Acts 17:1-15. ■

Paul Visits Two Towns

Two people hear about Jesus. One accepts him. The other rejects him. Two towns hear the same Gospel. One fights Paul. The other searches the Scriptures. Will it make a difference? Watch.

17 Now they traveled through the cities of Amphipolis and Apollonia. And then they came to Thessalonica, where there was a Jewish synagogue. ²As was Paul's custom, he went there to preach. And for three Sabbaths in a row he opened the Scriptures to the people. ³He explained the prophecies about the sufferings of the Messiah. He told them all about his coming back to life. In this way, he proved that Jesus was the Messiah. ⁴Some who listened believed and became Christians. Among them were a large number of godly Greek men. And many important women of the city also believed.

⁵But the Jewish leaders were jealous. So they asked some worthless fellows from the streets to start a riot. They attacked the home of Jason. For they planned to take Paul and Silas to the City Council for punishment.

⁶They didn't find them there. So they dragged out Jason and some of the other believers. They took them before the Council instead. "Paul and Silas have turned the rest of the world upside down. And now they are here disturbing our city," they shouted. ⁷"Jason has let them into his home. They are all guilty of treason. For they worship another king, Jesus, instead of Caesar."

⁸⁻⁹The people of the city, as well as the judges, were worried at these reports. And they let them go only after they had posted bail.

¹⁰That night the Christians hurried Paul and Silas to Beroea. And, as usual,

Study your Bible each day, and it will show you what is true

They read Scriptures day by day to check up on Paul and Silas. They wanted to make sure that what they said was true.

Acts 17:11

they went to the synagogue to preach. ¹¹But the people of Beroea were more open-minded than those in Thessalonica. They gladly listened to the message. They read Scriptures day by day to check up on Paul and Silas. They wanted to make sure that what they said was true. ¹²As a result, many of them believed. Among the believers were some important Greek women, and many men also.

¹³But the Jews in Thessalonica learned that Paul was preaching in Beroea. So they went over and stirred up trouble. ¹⁴The believers acted at once, sending Paul to the coast. Silas and Timothy stayed behind to continue the work. ¹⁵Those who were with Paul went on with him to Athens. Then Paul sent them back to Beroea with a message for Silas and Timothy. He wanted them to hurry and join him.

- *Remember:* When Paul shared the Gospel at Thessalonica, what happened? (17:2-9) When Paul shared the Gospel at Beroea, what happened? (17:10-12) There were some new believers in Thessalonica. But there were many in Beroea who believed in Jesus. Why was it different in Beroea? Does the way we listen matter?

- *Discover:* Listen to good Bible teaching. It will make a big difference in your life.

- *Apply:* How well do you listen in your Sunday school class? How well do you listen when the Bible is read? Next time, listen carefully! And read the Bible often! It will make a big difference in your life.

- *What's next?* The people at Athens did not believe in God. They believed in many gods. What would they do when Paul preached? Read Acts 17:16-34. ■

Paul Preaches on Mars Hill

Mars Hill was a different kind of place. Philosophers liked to go there. They talked about new ideas and new gods. Paul had not preached to Greek philosophers before. Did they listen to him?

¹⁶So Paul waited for them in Athens. While he was there, he was deeply troubled by all the idols he saw. They were everywhere throughout the city. ¹⁷He went to the synagogue to talk with the Jews and the godly Gentiles. And he spoke daily in the public square to all who were there.

¹⁸He also spoke with some of the Epicurean and Stoic philosophers. Paul told them about Jesus and his resurrection. Some of them said, "He's a dreamer." Others said, "He's pushing some foreign religion."

¹⁹But they invited him to the forum at Mars Hill. "Come and tell us more about this new religion," they said. ²⁰"For you are saying some rather amazing things. We want to hear more about this." ²¹All the people in Athens seemed to spend all their time talking about the latest new ideas. Even the visitors there joined in on the discussions.

²²So Paul stood before them at the Mars Hill forum. He spoke to them as follows:

"Men of Athens, I see that you are very religious. ²³For I was out walking and saw your many altars. One of them had this written on it: 'To the Unknown God.' You have been worshiping him without knowing who he is.

Now I wish to tell you about him!

24"He made the world and everything in it. And since he is Lord of the heavens and earth, he doesn't live in man-made temples. 25And human hands can't minister to his needs. This is because he has no needs! He himself gives life and breath to everything. He satisfies every need there is. 26He created all the people of the world from one man, Adam. And he scattered the nations across the face of the earth. He decided which nations should rise and fall, and when. He measured out and set all their borders.

27"God wanted them all to seek after him. He wanted them to feel their way toward him and find him. He is not far from any one of us. 28For in him we live and move and are! As one of your own poets says it, 'We are the sons of God.' 29If this is true, we shouldn't think of God as an idol. He is not made by men from gold or silver or chipped from stone. 30In years past, man did not know about God. But God put up with man's ignorance about these things. However, now he commands everyone to put away idols and worship only him. 31For he has set a day for justly judging the world. And God will do this through the man he has chosen. He has pointed this man out by bringing him back to life again."

32So Paul told them about the resurrection of Jesus from the dead. When they heard this, some of them laughed. But others said, "We want to hear more about this later." 33That ended Paul's discussion with them. 34But a few joined him and became believers. Among them was Dionysius, a member of the City Council. And there was a woman named Damaris, and others.

- *Remember:* What did Paul see in Athens that troubled him? Why? (17:16) Why did the philosophers invite Paul to Mars Hill? (17:18-21) When Paul preached, people did three different things. What were they? (17:32-34) Why do you think they did these three things?

- *Discover:* When you tell others about Jesus, some will accept him. Others will reject him. Some will say, "Some other time."

- *Apply:* Keep telling others about Jesus. But be ready to hear three kinds of answers.

- *What's next?* Why would a great preacher spend a lot of time sewing? Read Acts 18:1-11. ∎

Paul Works with Priscilla and Aquila

One of the greatest preachers in the world also sewed with needle and thread. Why did he do that?

18 Then Paul left Athens and went to Corinth. 2-3There he met a Jew named Aquila, born in Pontus. He had recently come from Italy with his wife, Priscilla. They had been expelled from Italy. This was because of Claudius Caesar's order to deport all Jews from Rome. Paul lived and worked with them. For they were tentmakers just as he was.

4Each Sabbath Paul went to the synagogue. He tried to convert the Jews and Greeks alike. 5Later, Silas and Timothy came back from Macedonia to join Paul. When they came, Paul spent his full time preaching to the Jews. He did all he could to convince them that Jesus was the Messiah. 6But the Jews wouldn't listen to him. And they threw insults at Jesus. So Paul shook the dust from his robe. "Your blood be upon your own heads!" he said. "I am innocent! From now on I will preach to the Gentiles."

7After that he stayed with Titus Justus. He was a Gentile who worshiped God and lived next door to the synagogue. 8Crispus was the leader of that synagogue. He and all his family believed in the Lord and were baptized.

And many others in Corinth believed, too.

⁹One night the Lord spoke to Paul in a vision. He told him, "Don't be afraid! Speak out! Don't quit! ¹⁰For I am with you and no one can hurt you. Many people here in this city belong to me." ¹¹So Paul stayed there the next year and a half. He spent most of his time teaching them the truths of God.

- *Remember:* What kind of work did Paul do? (18:3) Who were the other two tentmakers? (18:2-3) To whom did Paul preach first? (18:5-6) To whom did he preach when the Jews rejected Jesus? (18:6) Who was the Gentile believer? (18:7) Who was the Jewish believer? (18:8) What did the Lord tell Paul to do? How long did he preach at Corinth? (18:9-11) Do you think Paul was ever discouraged? Why do you think so? Do you think Paul stopped preaching when he was discouraged? Why not?

- *Discover:* Some people accept the Gospel. Some people reject it. But God wants us to keep sharing it.

- *Apply:* Have you told some friends about Jesus? Some listen. Some laugh. Don't give up. Don't let the ones who laugh discourage you.

- *What's next?* People build a big fire. They are burning expensive books. Why? Read Acts 19:13-20. ■

The Jews Take Paul to Court

¹²Gallio was made the governor of Achaia, in southern Greece. At that time, the Jews joined together against

Paul. And they brought him before the governor for judgment. ¹³They said, "Paul is telling people to worship God in ways that are against Roman law." ¹⁴Now Paul stood up to make his defense. But Gallio, the governor, turned to his accusers. "Listen, you Jews," he said. "If this was a criminal case, I would have to listen to you. ¹⁵But you are just arguing about words and names. You are just worried about your silly Jewish laws. So you take care of it! I don't want to have anything to do with it." ¹⁶And he sent them out of the courtroom.

¹⁷Then the crowd grabbed Sosthenes, the new leader of the synagogue. And they beat him outside the courtroom. But Gallio couldn't have cared less.

Paul Ends His Second Missionary Journey

¹⁸Paul stayed in the city several days after that. Then he said good-bye to the Christians and sailed for the coast of Syria. He took Priscilla and Aquila with him. At Cenchreae Paul had his head shaved according to Jewish custom. For he had made a special promise to God. ¹⁹When he got to the port of Ephesus, he left us aboard ship. Then he went over to the synagogue to talk with the Jews. ²⁰They asked him to stay for a few days. But he felt that he had no time to lose.

²¹"I must by all means be at Jerusalem for the holiday," he said. But he promised to come back to Ephesus later if God allowed it. And so he set sail again.

²²The next stop was at the port of Caesarea. And from there he visited the church at Jerusalem. After his visit, he sailed on to Antioch.

Paul Begins a Third Missionary Journey

²³He spent some time there, but then he went back to Asia Minor again. He went through Galatia and Phrygia visiting all the believers. He encouraged them and helped them grow in the Lord.

²⁴As it happened, a Jew named Apollos had just come to Ephesus. Apollos was a wonderful Bible teacher and preacher. He had come from Alexandria in Egypt. ²⁵⁻²⁶While he was in Egypt, someone had told him about John the Baptist. Apollos had heard about what John had said about Jesus. But that was all he knew. He had never heard the rest of the story! So he was preaching boldly in the synagogue, "The Messiah is coming! Get ready to receive him!" Priscilla and Aquila were there and heard him. And it was a powerful sermon. Afterwards they met with Apollos. They told him what had happened to Jesus since the time of John. And they explained what it all meant.

²⁷Apollos had been thinking about going to Greece.

And the believers encouraged him in this. They wrote to the believers there, telling them to welcome him. There in Greece, Apollos was greatly used by God to make the church stronger. ²⁸For he argued with strength and wisdom against the Jews in public debate. And he proved that the Jews were wrong. He used the Scriptures to prove that Jesus was indeed the Messiah.

Christians in Ephesus Receive the Holy Spirit

19 While Apollos was in Corinth, Paul traveled through Asia Minor. And Paul came to Ephesus, where he found several disciples. ²"Did you receive the Holy Spirit when you believed?" he asked them.

"No," they replied, "we don't know what you mean. What is the Holy Spirit?"

³"Then what beliefs did you acknowledge at your baptism?" he asked.

And they replied, "What John the Baptist taught."

⁴Then Paul explained to them about John's baptism. It was done to show a desire to repent from sin and turn to God. Paul showed them that those baptized by John also needed to believe in Jesus. For Jesus was the one John said would come later.

⁵When they heard this, they were baptized in the name of the Lord Jesus. ⁶Then Paul laid his hands upon their heads. And the Holy Spirit came upon them. They spoke in other languages and prophesied. ⁷There were about 12 men there in that group.

Paul Preaches Boldly and Does Unusual Miracles

⁸Then Paul went to the synagogue. He preached there boldly each Sabbath day for three months. He told them what he believed and why. And he caused many of the Jews to believe in Jesus. ⁹But some would not listen to his message. And they publicly spoke out against Christ. So Paul left, refusing to preach to them again. He pulled out all the believers. Then he began another meeting at the lecture hall of Tyrannus. And he preached there every day. ¹⁰This went on for the next two years. Paul preached to both Jews and Greeks. And everyone in the province of Asia Minor heard the Lord's message.

¹¹And God gave Paul the power to do great miracles. ¹²People took his handkerchiefs or parts of his clothing to sick people. And when they touched these things, they were healed. And the demons inside them came out.

Evil Books Are Burned

People burned a pile of books and charms. Why didn't they sell them instead? Why didn't they use the money for the Lord's work?

¹³Now there was a team of Jews who traveled from town to town. Their work was to cast out demons. So they tried to use the name of the Lord Jesus to do this. They decided they would say to the demons: "By the name of Jesus, whom Paul preaches, come out!" ¹⁴The seven sons of Sceva were doing this. (Sceva was a leading Jewish priest.) ¹⁵So they tried to say this to a man with a demon. And the demon said, "I know Jesus. And I know

Paul. But who are you?" ¹⁶And he jumped on two of them and beat them up. They ran out of his house with their clothes torn off. And they were badly hurt.

¹⁷The story of what happened spread quickly all through Ephesus. Jews and Greeks alike heard about it. And great fear came down on the city. After this, the name of the Lord Jesus was greatly honored. ¹⁸⁻¹⁹Many of the believers had

been doing black magic. They all confessed their deeds and brought their magic books and charms. They burned them in front of everyone at a great bonfire. Someone guessed that the books were worth at least $10,000. ²⁰This shows how deeply the whole area was stirred by God's message.

● *Remember:* Who tried to cast out a demon? How did they use Jesus' name? (19:13-15) What happened to these men? (19:15-16) What did this cause people to do with books of evil? (19:17-20) These Christians had been practicing black magic. Why was that wrong? Why can't we live for Jesus and the devil at the same time?

● *Discover:* Christians must get rid of things that might keep us from worshiping Jesus. Jesus and evil things can't live together in us.

● *Apply:* Have you accepted Jesus? Are you still keeping bad habits? Are you still saying dirty words? Are you still reading bad books or magazines? You can't have these and live for Jesus at the same time.

● *What's next?* A mob forms. People shout for two hours. But they don't know why they are shouting. Who can stop them? Read Acts 19:21-41. ■

The Silversmith Riot

Demetrius started the riot. He couldn't sell many silver statues anymore. His statues were idols. Paul said people shouldn't have idols. Demetrius didn't like that. So he got the other silversmiths mad, too. And they got other people mad. Before long there was a riot. Things got out of hand. Could anyone stop it?

²¹After that Paul decided to go back to Jerusalem. But he felt the Holy Spirit leading him to go to Greece before going there. "Then after Jerusalem," he said, "I must go on to Rome!" ²²He sent his two helpers, Timothy and Erastus, on ahead to Greece. And Paul stayed a little while longer in Asia Minor.

²³But at that time, trouble developed in Ephesus. And the trouble involved the Christians. ²⁴It all began with a man named Demetrius. He was a silversmith who employed many craftsmen. They made silver shrines of the Greek goddess Diana. ²⁵He called a meeting of his men, together with others in the same trade. He spoke to them like this:

"Gentlemen, we make our living by making idols. ²⁶But Paul has convinced many people that our idols aren't gods at all. You know this! You've all heard what he tells the people! As a result, our sales volume is going down! We can see this not only here in Ephesus, but throughout the province! ²⁷Of course,

I'm not just worried about our loss of business. I'm also worried that the temple of Diana will lose its influence. I'm afraid that the great goddess Diana will be forgotten! And she is not just worshiped here, but all around the world!"

²⁸At this the people became very angry. They began shouting, "Great is Diana of the Ephesians!"

²⁹A crowd began to gather, and soon the city was filled with confusion. Everyone went to the amphitheater. And they dragged along Gaius and Aristarchus to be tried. These two men were traveling with Paul. ³⁰Paul wanted to go in, but the believers wouldn't let him. ³¹Some of the Roman officers of the province were friends of Paul. They also sent a message to him, begging him not to risk his life by going there.

³²Inside the people were all shouting. Some were saying one thing and some another. Everything was in confusion. In fact, most of them didn't even know why they were there.

³³Alexander was spotted among the crowd by some of the Jews. And he was dragged forward. He motioned for silence and tried to speak. ³⁴But when the crowd saw that he was a Jew, they started shouting again. And they kept it up for two hours: "Great is Diana of the Ephesians! Great is Diana of the Ephesians!"

³⁵At last the mayor was able to quiet them down enough to speak. "Men of Ephesus!" he began. "Our city is the center of the religion of the great Diana. Long ago, her image fell down to us from Heaven. ³⁶Since we all know this, you shouldn't worry no matter what is said. You should do nothing violent or rash. ³⁷Yet you have brought these men here who have stolen nothing from her temple. These men have done nothing to hurt her. ³⁸Now Demetrius and the craftsmen might have a case against them. But if they do, the courts are now in session. And the judges can take the case at once. Let them go through legal channels. ³⁹And there might be some other complaints against them. But if so, they can be settled at the City Council meetings. ⁴⁰We are in danger of Rome's judgment for today's riot. For there is no real cause for it. And if Rome asks me to explain, I won't know what to say."

⁴¹Then he sent them away, and they all went home.

- *Remember:* What was Demetrius's business? (19:24) Why were he and his friends upset? (19:24-28) How did this start a riot? (19:28-34) Who calmed the crowd? How? (19:35-41) Which was a troublemaker, Demetrius or the mayor? Which was a peacemaker?

- *Discover:* It's much better to be a peacemaker than a troublemaker.

- *Apply:* Do you know a troublemaker at school? Do you know a peacemaker at school? Which would you rather have as a friend? Which would you rather be? Think of a way you can be a peacemaker today. What can you do?

- *What's next?* A young man is killed when he falls from an upstairs window. But Paul tells his family not to worry. Why would he say that? Read Acts 20:7-12. ■

On to Greece and Macedonia

20 When it was all over, Paul sent for the believers. He preached a farewell message to them. Then he said good-bye and left for Greece. ²He preached to the believers along the way in all the cities he passed through. ³He was in Greece for three months and was about to sail for Syria. At that time, he found out that the Jews were planning to kill him. So he decided to go north to Macedonia first.

⁴A number of men were traveling with Paul, going as far as Asia Minor. Among them was Sopater of Beroea, the son of Pyrrhus. Aristarchus and Secundus from Thessalonica were also with

How Do You Turn On the Lamp?
ACTS 20:8

Turn on the lamp! If you were in a Bible-time home, you could not turn it on. Bible-time homes had no electricity. The electric light bulb was not made yet. So how do you turn on the lamp? Bible-time lamps were made of clay. They looked like saucers with covers. There was a hole in the center of each cover. There was another hole at one end. People poured olive oil through the center hole. They put a wick in the other hole. The wick soaked up the oil. People lit the wick with some fire. There were no matches. They learned to make a fire without matches. The next time you turn on your light, think of Bible-time lamps. Are you glad for what you have?

him. Gaius from Derbe and Timothy went with him, too. And Tychicus and Trophimus went with him on the way to their homes in the provice of Asia. ⁵These men had gone on ahead and were waiting for us at Troas. ⁶We did not leave until the end of the Passover Feast. Then we boarded ship at Philippi in northern Greece. And five days later we arrived in Troas. We stayed there for a week.

Sleepy Eutychus Falls to His Death

Eutychus sat in an open window. The air was warm with flickering lamps. Paul preached on and on. Before long Eutychus fell asleep. Then he fell out of the window. He dropped three stories and died. But Paul told his friends not to worry. Why did he say that?

⁷On Sunday we gathered for a Communion service, with Paul preaching. And since he was leaving the next day, he talked until midnight! ⁸The upstairs room where we met was lighted with many lamps. ⁹Paul spoke on for a long time. And there was a young man named Eutychus sitting on the windowsill. He fell fast asleep and fell three stories to his death below. ¹⁰⁻¹²Paul went down and took him into his arms. "Don't worry," he said, "he's all right!" And he was! What a wave of awesome joy swept through the crowd! They all went back upstairs and ate the Lord's Supper together. Then Paul preached another long sermon. It was dawn when he finally left them!

- *Remember:* How long did Paul preach? (20:7) What made the room warmer? (20:8) What happened to Eutychus? (20:9) Was Paul right when he said not to worry? (20:10- 12) How much longer did the service last? (20:10-12) How do you know that God was with Paul? Can a man bring a dead person back to life without God's help?

- *Discover:* God shows he is with us by the things he does through us.

- *Apply:* Have you helped someone love God more? If you have, God helped you do it. Have you helped someone love the Bible more? If so, God helped you. What else has God helped you do?

- *What's next?* Hundreds of people want to kill a Christian preacher. Why? Read Acts 21:27–23:11. ∎

Paul Says Farewell to the Elders of Ephesus

¹³Paul was going by land to Assos. And we went on ahead by ship. ¹⁴He joined us there and we sailed together to Mitylene. ¹⁵The next day we passed Chios. The day after that, we touched at Samos. And a day later we arrived at Miletus.

¹⁶Paul had decided against stopping at Ephesus this time. For he was hurrying to get to Jerusalem. He wanted to get there for the Feast of Pentecost if possible.

¹⁷But when we landed at Miletus, he sent a message to the elders of the church at Ephesus. He asked them to come down to the boat to meet him.

¹⁸So the elders went down to see him. And he told them, "You men know how I lived while I was with you. ¹⁹I have done the Lord's work humbly. Yes, I have served him with tears. I have faced great danger from the plots of the Jews against my life. ²⁰Yet I never stopped telling you the truth, either publicly or in your homes. ²¹I have had one message for Jews and Gentiles alike. I have told you to turn from sin to God through faith in our Lord Jesus Christ.

²²"And now I am going to Jerusalem. I am being led there by the Holy Spirit. I don't know what is waiting for me there. ²³But I do know that jail and suffering lie ahead for me. I know this because the Holy Spirit has told me. ²⁴But life is worth nothing unless I use it for doing the work given me by the Lord Jesus. He has given me the work of tell-

ing others the Good News about God's kindness and love.

²⁵"While I was with you, I taught you about the Kingdom of God. But now I know that none of you will ever see me again. ²⁶Let me say plainly that I cannot be blamed for any man's unbelief. ²⁷For I didn't hold back from telling you God's message.

²⁸"And now be careful! Be sure that you feed and take care of God's flock. For they have been bought by his blood. And the Holy Spirit is holding you responsible as their leaders. ²⁹I know that after I leave you, false teachers will come. They will be like vicious wolves, not sparing the flock. ³⁰Some of you yourselves will twist the truth to get people to follow you. ³¹Watch out! Remember the three years I was with you. Don't forget how I watched over you night and day. Yes, and remember my many tears for you.

³²"And now I will trust God to take care of you. And I will trust his wonderful words to build your faith. They will give you all the blessings of those who are set apart for himself.

³³"I have never been hungry for money or fine clothing. ³⁴You know that these hands of mine worked to pay my own way. I even supplied the needs of those who were with me. ³⁵And I was a constant example to you in helping the poor. For I remembered the words of the Lord Jesus. He said, 'It is more blessed to give than to receive.'"

³⁶When he had finished speaking, he knelt and prayed with them. ³⁷They cried out loud as they hugged him in farewell. ³⁸They were very sad because he had said he would never see them again. Then they went with him down to the ship.

Paul Journeys to Jerusalem

21 After parting from the Ephesian elders, we sailed straight to Cos. The

next day we reached Rhodes and then went to Patara. ²There we boarded a ship sailing for the Syrian province of Phoenicia. ³We sighted the island of Cyprus and passed it on our left. And we landed at the harbor of Tyre, in Syria, where the ship was unloaded. ⁴We went ashore and found the local believers there. And we stayed with them for a week. These disciples warned Paul not to go on to Jerusalem. For they knew through the Holy Spirit that trouble awaited him there. ⁵At the end of the week we went back to the ship. All the believers including wives and children walked down to the beach with us. And there we prayed and said good-bye. ⁶Then we went aboard, and they went back home.

⁷The next stop after leaving Tyre was Ptolemais. We were greeted there by the believers but stayed only one day. ⁸Then we went on to Caesarea. While there, we stayed at the home of Philip the Evangelist. He was one of the first seven deacons. ⁹He had four unmarried daughters who had the gift of prophecy.

¹⁰During our stay of several days, a man named Agabus came from Judea. This man also had the gift of prophecy. ¹¹He took Paul's belt and tied up his own feet and hands with it. Then he said, "The Holy Spirit declares, 'This is how the Jews in Jerusalem will tie up the owner of this belt. Then they will turn him over to the Romans.'" ¹²Hearing this, all of us begged Paul not to go on to Jerusalem.

????????????????????????????????????
Which prophet tied his own hands and feet with a borrowed belt?

Read 21:10-11
????????????????????????????????????

¹³But he said, "Why all this crying? You are breaking my heart! For I am ready to be jailed at Jerusalem! What's more, I'm even ready to die for the sake of the Lord Jesus!" ¹⁴It soon became clear that Paul wouldn't change his mind. So we gave up and said, "May the Lord's will be done."

¹⁵So shortly after that we packed our things and left for Jerusalem. ¹⁶Some of the believers from Caesarea went with us. When we got there, we stayed at the home of Mnason. He was one of the early believers, and was originally from Cyprus. ¹⁷All the believers at Jerusalem welcomed us kindly.

Paul Shaves His Head

¹⁸The second day Paul took us to meet with James. All the other elders of the Jerusalem church were there, too. ¹⁹After greeting each other, Paul told them about his ministry. He recounted the many things God had done for the Gentiles through his work.

²⁰When they heard his report, they praised God. Then they said, "You know, dear brother, that many Jews have also believed. And they all think it is very important to obey the laws of Moses. ²¹Stories are going around among our Jewish Christians about your teachings. They have been told that you are against the laws of Moses and our Jewish customs. They have heard that you don't let Christians circumcise their children. ²²Now what can be done? For they will surely hear that you have come.

²³"We have a plan to help this situation. There are four men among us who are about to make special promises to God. They will soon shave their heads to show that they have made such promises. ²⁴Go with them to the Temple and have your head shaved, too. Also, pay the fee for their heads to be shaved.

"Then everyone will know that what they heard about you is not true. They will see that you yourself obey the laws of Moses.

²⁵"We don't ask the Gentile Christians to follow these Jewish customs. We wrote them a letter about this. It said, 'Do not eat food offered to idols. Do not eat unbled meat from strangled animals. And do not commit any sexual sins.'"

²⁶Paul agreed to do what they said. So the next day he went with the men for the ceremony. Then he went to the Temple to declare when the sacrifices would be made for the men. He declared that they would do this in seven days.

Paul Is Arrested

Paul was back from his third missionary journey. He went to the Temple to pray. But some men dragged Paul from the Temple. They beat him. They tried to kill him. The mob treated him violently. But Paul had not said a word. Why were so many people against him?

27The seven days were almost over. But some Jews from Asia Minor saw Paul in the Temple. They stirred up a crowd against him. They grabbed him, 28yelling, "Men of Israel! Help! Help! This is the man who preaches against our people. He tells everybody to disobey the Jewish laws. He even speaks out against the Temple. And he makes it impure by bringing Gentiles inside!" 29For they had seen him in the city with Trophimus earlier that day. Trophimus was a Gentile from Ephesus in Asia Minor. They thought that Paul had taken him into the Temple.

30All the people of the city became very upset. And a great riot followed. The people grabbed Paul and dragged him out of the Temple. And right away the gates were closed behind him. 31As they were about to kill him, word reached the commander of the Roman garrison. He was told that all Jerusalem was in an uproar. 32He quickly ordered out his soldiers and officers. And he ran down among the crowd. When the crowd saw the troops coming, they stopped beating Paul. 33The commander arrested him and ordered him tied up with double chains. Then he asked the crowd who he was and what he had done. 34Some shouted one thing and some another. He couldn't find out anything in all the uproar and confusion. So he ordered Paul to be taken to the armory. 35As they reached the stairs, the crowd grew very violent. The soldiers had to lift Paul to their shoulders to keep him safe. 36And the crowd shouted, "Away with him! Away with him!"

37-38As Paul was about to be taken inside, he turned to the commander. He asked, "May I have a word with you?"

"Do you speak Greek?" the commander asked. He was surprised at this. "I thought you were that Egyptian who led a rebellion a few years ago. He took 4,000 members of the Assassins with him into the desert."

39"No," Paul replied, "I am a Jew from Tarsus in Cilicia. And it is no small town. I wish you would let me talk to these people."

40The commander agreed, so Paul stood on the stairs. He motioned to the people to be quiet. Soon a deep silence spread across the crowd. Then Paul spoke to them in Hebrew as follows:

22 "Brothers and fathers, listen to me as I offer my defense." 2When they heard him speaking in Hebrew, they were even more quiet. 3"I am a Jew," he said. "I was born in Tarsus, a city in Cilicia. But I was educated here in Jerusalem under Gamaliel. I sat at his feet and learned to follow our Jewish laws very carefully. I wanted to honor God in everything I did. I did just as you have tried to do today. 4And I treated the Christians very badly, chasing them down. I caught them and threw them in prison. I did this to both men and women. 5The High Priest or members of the Council can tell you that this is true. For I asked them to write letters to the Jewish leaders in Damascus. They gave me orders to capture any Christians I found. And I was to bring them back to Jerusalem in chains to be punished.

6"Now I was on the road, getting close to Damascus. And suddenly about noon a very bright light from Heaven shone around me. 7I fell to the ground and heard a loud voice. It said, 'Saul, Saul, why are you trying to hurt me?'

8"'Who is it speaking to me, sir?' I asked. And he replied, 'I am Jesus of Nazareth, the one you are trying to hurt.' 9The men with me saw the light but didn't understand what was said.

10"And I said, 'What shall I do, Lord?'

"And the Lord told me, 'Get up and go into Damascus. There you will be told what awaits you in the years ahead.'

11"I was blinded by the intense light. And I had to be led into Damascus by my companions. ¹²There was a man there named Ananias. He was as godly a man as you could find for obeying the law. And he was well thought of by all the Jews of Damascus. ¹³He came to see me and stood beside me. Then he said, 'Brother Saul, receive your sight!' And that very hour I could see him!

Tell everyone you can about Jesus

You are to take his message everywhere.

Acts 22:15

---

¹⁴"Then he told me, 'The God of our fathers has chosen you to know his will. He wants you to see the Messiah and hear him speak. ¹⁵You are to take his message everywhere. You must tell everyone what you have seen and heard. ¹⁶And now, why wait? Go and be baptized and be cleansed from your sins. Yes, call on the name of the Lord!'

¹⁷⁻¹⁸"Well, I came back to Jerusalem and went to pray in the Temple. Suddenly, I fell into a trance. And I saw a vision of God. He said to me, 'Hurry! Leave Jerusalem. For the people here won't listen to the truth about me.'

¹⁹"'But Lord,' I argued, 'they know that I once caught and beat Christians from every synagogue. ²⁰And when your witness Stephen was killed, I was standing there. I watched the coats they laid aside as they stoned him.'

²¹"But God said to me, 'Leave Jerusalem. For I will send you far away to the Gentiles!'"

²²The crowd listened until Paul told them this. Then with one voice they shouted, "Away with such a fellow! Kill him! He isn't fit to live!" ²³They yelled and threw their coats in the air. And they tossed up handfuls of dust.

²⁴So the commander brought him inside. He ordered him to be lashed with whips to make him confess his crime. He wanted to find out why the crowd had become so angry!

²⁵They were tying Paul down to whip him. But Paul spoke to an officer standing there. "Is it legal to whip a Roman citizen without a trial?" he asked.

²⁶The officer went to the commander. "What are you doing?" he asked. "This man is a Roman citizen!"

²⁷So the commander went over to Paul. He asked him, "Tell me, are you a Roman citizen?"

"Yes, I certainly am."

²⁸"I am too," the commander muttered. "And it cost me plenty!"

"But I am a citizen by birth!"

²⁹The soldiers were about to whip Paul. But when they heard he was a Roman citizen, they quickly backed away. The commander was afraid because he had ordered him bound and whipped.

³⁰The next day the commander freed Paul from his chains. And he ordered the chief priests into session with the Jewish Council. He brought Paul in to speak before them. He wanted to find out what the trouble was all about.

23 Paul looked straight at the Council and began:

"Brothers, I have always lived a clean life before God! I have never had a dirty conscience."

²Then Ananias the High Priest told those near Paul to slap him on the mouth.

³Paul said to him, "God shall slap you, you whitewashed pigpen! What kind of judge are you? You break the law yourself by ordering me struck like that!"

⁴Those standing near Paul asked him, "Is that the way to talk to God's High Priest?"

⁵"I didn't know he was the High Priest, brothers," Paul replied. "For the Scriptures say, 'Never speak evil of any of your rulers.'"

⁶Then Paul thought of something! Part of the Council were Sadducees, and part were Pharisees! So he shouted, "Brothers, I am a Pharisee, as were all my ancestors! And I am being tried here today because I believe in the resurrection of the dead!"

⁷This divided the Council right down the middle. The Pharisees were set up against the Sadducees. ⁸For the Sadducees don't believe in the resurrection. They don't believe in angels either. And they don't believe people have an

eternal spirit. But the Pharisees believe in all of these things.

⁹So a great argument arose. Some of the Jewish leaders jumped up to argue that Paul was all right. "We see nothing wrong with him," they shouted. "Perhaps a spirit or angel did speak to him there on the Damascus road."

¹⁰The shouting grew louder and louder. The men were tugging at Paul from both sides, pulling him this way and that. The commander was afraid they would tear him apart. So he ordered his soldiers to take him away from them by force. Then they brought him back to the armory.

¹¹That night the Lord stood beside Paul. "Don't worry, Paul," he said. "You have told the people about me here in Jerusalem. In the same way, you must also be my witness in Rome."

● *Remember:* Did Paul do something wrong? Or did people only accuse him

of doing wrong? (21:27-29) Did these people give him a fair trial? Or did they just try to kill him? (21:30-31) Who tried to beat Paul with whips? (22:24) Who wanted Paul slapped? (23:2) Which people tugged at Paul from both sides, almost tearing him apart? (23:10) Who comforted Paul? Who told Paul not to worry? (23:11) Paul must have thought the whole world was against him. Think how much God's comfort meant to him.

● *Discover:* Sometimes it seems that everyone is against us. But God is still for us!

● *Apply:* When is the last time you were discouraged? When did you think everyone was against you? Did you remember that God is for you? Next time you feel that way, stop! Remember that God will comfort you.

● *What's next?* Some men vow that they will not eat until they kill a man. Why? Read Acts 23:12-35. ■

Paul's Nephew Warns Him

A boy hears a plot. He must tell the Roman army commander. Will a boy be taken to the commander? Will the commander listen?

¹²⁻¹³The next morning some 40 or more of the Jews got together. They promised that they wouldn't eat or drink until they had killed Paul! ¹⁴Then they went to the chief priests and elders. They told them about the promise they had made. ¹⁵"Ask the commander to bring Paul back to the Council again," they told them. "Pretend you want to ask a few more questions. We will kill him on the way."

¹⁶But Paul's nephew heard about their plan. So he came to the armory and told Paul.

¹⁷Paul called one of the officers. "Take this boy to the commander," Paul said. "He has something important to tell him."

¹⁸So the officer did this. "Paul, the prisoner, called me over," the officer explained to the commander. "He asked

me to bring this young man to you to tell you something."

¹⁹The commander took the boy by the hand. He led him aside and asked, "What is it you want to tell me?"

²⁰"Tomorrow," he told him, "the Jews will ask you to bring Paul to the Council again. They will pretend they want to hear more of what he has to say. ²¹But don't do it! There will be more than 40 men hiding along the road. They will be ready to jump him and kill him. They have promised not to eat or drink till he is dead. They are out there now, hoping you will agree to what they ask."

²²"Don't tell anyone you told me this," the commander warned the boy as he left. ²³⁻²⁴Then the commander called two of his officers. "Get 200 soldiers ready to leave for Caesarea at nine o'clock tonight!" he ordered. "Take 200

spearmen and 70 mounted cavalry. Give Paul a horse to ride and get him safely to Governor Felix."

²⁵Then he wrote this letter to the governor:

²⁶"*From:* Claudius Lysias.

"*To:* His Excellency, Governor Felix.

"Greetings!

²⁷"This man was seized by the Jews. They were about to kill him when I sent the soldiers to rescue him. For I learned that he was a Roman citizen. ²⁸Then I took him to their Council to try to find out what he had done. ²⁹I soon found out it had something to do with their Jewish beliefs. He has done nothing that deserves prison or death. ³⁰But then I was told about a secret plan to kill him. So I decided to send him on to you. I will tell the Jews to bring their charges before you."

³¹So that night, as ordered, the soldiers took Paul to Antipatris. ³²They came back to the armory the next morning. They left the cavalry with him to take him on to Caesarea.

³³When they came to Caesarea, they gave Paul into the governor's charge. They also gave him the letter. ³⁴He read it and then asked Paul where he was from.

"Cilicia," Paul answered.

³⁵"I will hear your case fully when your accusers come," the governor told him. Then he ordered him kept in the prison at King Herod's palace.

- *Remember:* What vow did the men make? (23:12) Who was part of the plot to kill Paul? (23:14-15) What do you think of this? Which boy heard about the plot? (23:16) Whom did he tell? (23:16) What did the commander do about this? (23:17-35) Do you think Paul's nephew did what was right? Do you think he was brave?

- *Discover:* We should be brave when we have important work to do. We should pray for courage.

- *Apply:* Do you have something important to do? What is it? Should you tell someone about Jesus? Should you say no to something friends want you to do? Pray for courage. Be brave. God will help you.

- *What's next?* Read about a strange trial in Acts 24. A religious leader tries to get a preacher killed. A Roman governor protects the preacher. Why? ■

Paul Before Felix

Paul was accused of crimes. What were they? (1) Starting riots, (2) getting people to rebel against the Roman government, and (3) defiling the Temple. Not one of these was true. Did Felix, the Roman governor, listen to these charges? Or did he believe Paul?

24 Five days later Ananias the High Priest came. He brought some of the Jewish leaders and the lawyer Tertullus with him. They wanted to make their charges against Paul. ²Tertullus was called forward by the governor. So he gave this speech to accuse Paul:

"Governor Felix! You have brought a great peace to our land. And you have treated the Jews fairly during your time of rule. ³And for this we are very, very thankful to you. ⁴But I don't want to bore you. Please be kind and listen as I bring our charges against this man. ⁵For we have found him to be a trouble-maker. He has caused riots among the Jews throughout the Roman world. And he encourages them to rebel against the Roman government. He is a ringleader of the sect known as the Nazarenes. ⁶Moreover, he was trying to make our Temple impure when we arrested him.

"We would have given him what he justly deserved. ⁷But Lysias, the commander of the garrison, came and took him away from us. ⁸He demanded that he be tried by Roman law. You can find out the truth of what we say by asking him yourself."

⁹Then all the other Jews spoke up. They agreed that everything Tertullus said was true.

¹⁰Now it was Paul's turn to speak. So the governor motioned for him to rise.

Paul began, "I know, sir, that you have judged Jewish cases for many years. For this reason, I am happy to make my defense before you. ¹¹It was no more than 12 days ago that I went to Jerusalem. I wanted to worship at the Temple there. ¹²You will find that I never caused a riot in any synagogue. I have never caused trouble on the streets of any city. ¹³And these men cannot prove the things they charge me of doing.

¹⁴"But one thing I do admit! I believe in the way of salvation, which they refer to as a sect. I follow that system of serving the God of our ancestors. I firmly believe in the Jewish law. And I believe everything written in the books of prophecy. ¹⁵I believe, just as these men do! I believe that both the righteous and the ungodly will rise from the dead. ¹⁶Because of this, I try to keep my conscience clean before God and man.

¹⁷"After several years away, I came back to Jerusalem. I brought money with me to help the Jews there. And I wanted to offer a sacrifice to God. ¹⁸My accusers saw me in the Temple as I was giving my thank offering. I had shaved my head as their laws said I should. There was no crowd around me, and no rioting! But some Jews from Asia Minor were there. ¹⁹And they should be here if they have anything against me! ²⁰But look! Ask these men right here what the Council found I had done. ²¹I did say one thing I shouldn't have. For I said, 'I stand before the Council because I believe that the dead will rise again!'"

²²Now Felix knew Christians didn't go around starting riots. So he told the Jews to wait for Lysias, the garrison commander, to come. Then he would decide the case. ²³He ordered Paul to prison but told the guards to treat him well. He told them to allow his friends to visit him and bring him gifts. That way his stay in prison would be more comfortable.

²⁴A few days later Felix came with Drusilla. She was his legal wife, and a Jewess. Sending for Paul, they listened as he told them about faith in Christ Jesus. ²⁵He talked to them about being righteous and self-controlled. And he told them about the judgment to come. When Felix heard these things, he was very afraid.

"Go away for now," he replied. "When I have more time, I'll call for you again."

²⁶He also hoped that Paul would bribe him. So he sent for him from time to time and talked with him. ²⁷Two years

went by in this way. Then Felix was replaced by Porcius Festus. And because Felix wanted to gain favor with the Jews, he left Paul in prison.

- *Remember:* Who accused Paul of crimes? (24:1-8) What were the crimes? Did Paul really do any of these? (24:5-6) Did Felix listen to Paul talk about Jesus? (24:24-25) How did he respond? (24:25-26) Why didn't Felix set Paul free? How long did he leave Paul in prison? (24:27) What do you think of Felix? Whom did he try to

please more, God or others? Do you think God was pleased with what he did? Why not?

- *Discover:* We should please God more than others.

- *Apply:* A friend asks you to do something you know is wrong. Will you please your friend or God?

- *What's next?* A new governor judges Paul. Will he do what he knows is right? Or will he try to please people instead? Read Acts 25:1-12. ■

Paul Before Festus

Judges should do what is fair. Festus became Paul's judge. Was he fair?

25 Festus arrived in Caesarea to become the new governor. And just three days later, he left for Jerusalem. ²There the chief priests and other Jewish leaders spoke to him. They gave him their story about Paul. ³They begged him to bring Paul to Jerusalem at once. Their plan was to capture him and kill him. ⁴But Paul was at Caesarea and Festus was going back there soon. ⁵So he told the Jews who knew about the case to come back with him for the trial.

⁶Eight or ten days later he went back to Caesarea. And on the next day, he opened Paul's trial.

⁷When Paul got to the court the Jews from Jerusalem gathered around. They said Paul had done many wrong things. But they couldn't prove any of them. ⁸Paul denied that he had done these things. "I am not guilty," he said. "I have not gone against the Jewish laws. I have not made the Temple unclean. And I have not rebelled against the Roman government."

⁹Now Festus wanted to please the Jewish leaders. So he asked Paul, "Will you go to Jerusalem and stand trial before me?"

¹⁰⁻¹¹But Paul replied, "No! I want my

privilege of being judged by Caesar himself. You know very well I am not guilty. If I have done something worthy of death, I don't refuse to die! But if I am innocent, no one has the right to turn me over to these men to kill me. I appeal to Caesar!"

¹²Festus talked with his advisors. Then he said, "Very well! You have asked to be judged by Caesar. So I will send you to Caesar!"

- *Remember:* What did the religious leaders want Festus to do? Why? (25:1-3) What did Festus do instead? (25:4-6) Whom did Festus try to please more, God or Paul's accusers? (25:9) Do you think this was wrong? Why?

- *Discover:* Pleasing others more than God is wrong. It makes them seem more important than God.

- *Apply:* God wants you to read your Bible and pray. A friend makes fun of you for doing this. Whom will you please? Will you let the friend talk you out of what is right? Is this person really a friend?

- *What's next?* Paul goes on trial before a king. What will happen to him now? Read Acts 25:13–26:32. ■

King Agrippa Wants to Hear Paul

What would you say to a king? Would you have the courage to tell him about Jesus? Did Paul?

¹³A few days later King Agrippa came with Bernice to visit Festus. ¹⁴During their stay Festus talked about Paul's case with the king. "There is a prisoner here," he told him. "His case was left for me by Felix. ¹⁵When I was in Jerusalem, the chief priests and other Jewish leaders spoke to me. They gave me their side of the story. And they asked me to have him killed. ¹⁶Of course I quickly told them about Roman law. It does not allow a man to be convicted before he is tried. So I gave him a chance to defend himself face to face with his accusers.

¹⁷"The Jewish leaders came here for the trial. So I called the case the very next day. And I ordered Paul to be brought in. ¹⁸But the charges they made against him weren't at all what I thought they would be. ¹⁹It was something about their religion. It was about someone called Jesus whom the Jews say is dead. But Paul claims this man is alive! ²⁰I was confused as to how to decide a case of this kind. I asked Paul if he would stand trial on these charges in Jerusalem. ²¹But Paul appealed to Caesar! So I ordered him back to jail. And now I must arrange to get him to the emperor."

²²"I'd like to hear the man myself," Agrippa said.

And Festus replied, "You shall! We'll call him tomorrow!"

²³So the next day the king and Bernice went to the courtroom with great pomp. Many military officers and important men of the city went with them. Then Festus ordered Paul to be brought in.

²⁴Then Festus spoke to the audience. "King Agrippa and all who are here today, you see this man before you," he began. "This man's death is demanded both by the local Jews and by those in Jerusalem! ²⁵But in my opinion he has done nothing worthy of death. However, he asked for Caesar to be his judge. And I have no choice but to send him to Caesar. ²⁶But what shall I write the emperor? For there is no real charge against him! So I have brought him before you

all. I bring this case especially to you, King Agrippa. I want you to listen to him and then tell me what to write. ²⁷For how can I send a prisoner to Caesar without any charges against him?"

26 Then Agrippa said to Paul, "Go ahead. Tell us your story."

So Paul, with many gestures, presented his case.

²"I am fortunate, King Agrippa," he began. "For I have a chance to present my answer before you. ³I know you are an expert on Jewish laws and customs. Now please listen patiently!

⁴"The Jews know all about my background. I was given good Jewish training from my earliest childhood in Tarsus. Then later I was trained in Jerusalem. And I have always lived by the Jewish law. ⁵The Jews have known me for a long time. They know that I have always been a strict Pharisee. And I have obeyed all the Jewish laws and customs. ⁶But the real reason behind their charges is something else. It is because I look forward to the fulfillment of God's promise made to our ancestors. ⁷The 12 tribes of Israel work night and day to get this same hope I have! Yet, O King, for me it is a crime, they say! ⁸But is it a crime to believe that the dead will rise again? Does it seem impossible to you that God can bring men back to life again?

⁹"I used to believe that I should punish the followers of Jesus of Nazareth. ¹⁰I put many of the saints in Jerusalem into prison. The High Priests gave me the authority to do this. And when they were condemned to death, I cast my vote against them. ¹¹I used torture to try to make Christians curse Christ. I even chased them to distant cities in foreign lands.

¹²"I was on such a mission to Damascus. I was armed with the authority and commission of the chief priests. ¹³But one day about noon, sir, a light from Heaven shone down on me and my men. The light was brighter than the sun! ¹⁴We all fell down. And I heard a

voice speaking to me in Hebrew. The voice said, 'Saul, Saul, why are you trying to hurt me? You are only hurting yourself.'

¹⁵"'Who are you, sir?' I asked.

"And the Lord replied, 'I am Jesus, the one you are trying to hurt. ¹⁶Now stand up! For I have chosen you as my servant and my witness. You are to tell the world about this experience. And you will tell them about the many other times I will appear to you. ¹⁷I will keep you safe from both your own people and the Gentiles. Yes, I am going to send you to the Gentiles. ¹⁸Through you, I will open their eyes to their sins. That way they will be given the chance to repent. They will have a chance to live in the light of God instead of in Satan's darkness. They will have a chance to be forgiven of their sins. They will be able to receive God's blessings along with all the people whose sins are washed away. And they will have a chance to be blessed like all those who have faith in me.'

¹⁹"And so, O King Agrippa, I did not disobey that vision from Heaven! ²⁰I preached first to those in Damascus. Then I went to Jerusalem and through Judea. And I went to the Gentiles, too. I told them to leave their sins and turn to God. I told them to prove they had repented by doing good deeds. ²¹The Jews arrested me in the Temple for preaching this. And they tried to kill me. ²²But God kept me safe. And I am alive today to tell these facts to everyone, both great and small. I teach nothing except what the Prophets and Moses said. ²³They said that the Messiah would suffer. And they said he would be the first to rise from the dead. They said he would bring light to Jews and Gentiles alike."

²⁴Suddenly Festus shouted, "Paul, you are insane! Your long studying has broken your mind!"

²⁵But Paul replied, "I am not insane, Most Excellent Festus. I speak words of sober truth. ²⁶And King Agrippa knows about these things. I speak frankly for I am sure these events are all familiar to him. For they were not done in a corner! ²⁷King Agrippa, do you believe the Prophets? But I know you do!"

²⁸Agrippa said to him. "Do you expect me to become a Christian? You haven't given nearly enough proof for me to believe!"

²⁹And Paul replied, "It doesn't matter if my proofs are weak or strong. But I wish that you and everyone here might become the same as I am. Yes, I wish you would be like me—except for these chains!"

³⁰Then the king, the governor, Bernice, and all the others stood and left. ³¹They talked it all over afterwards. "This man hasn't done anything worthy of death or prison," they agreed.

³²And Agrippa said to Festus, "We could have set him free! But he asked to be judged by Caesar."

- *Remember:* Who was judging Paul now? (25:24) Did King Agrippa want to hear Paul's story? (26:1) What did Paul say to him? Did he tell him what he believed about Jesus? Or did he say what he thought the king wanted? (26:2-27) Do you think Paul was brave? Why?

- *Discover:* We should say bravely what we believe about Jesus. We should do this even to important people.

- *Apply:* Do you believe in Jesus? Do you love him? Do you read your Bible and pray? Do you go to church? Would you be afraid to tell anyone these things?

- *What's next?* A great storm rages across the ocean. A ship is caught in the storm. It is wrecked on an island. Read about this in Acts 27. ■

Paul's Ship Is Wrecked

Everything is going wrong. Paul is a prisoner. He is on a ship to Rome. He will be tried there. He could be executed. A storm rages across the ocean. The ship is caught in the storm. Sailors are throwing the cargo overboard. People can't eat. It looks hopeless. But God tells Paul that no one will die. Will people believe God? What will happen now?

27 Plans were finally made to start us on our way to Rome by ship. So Paul and several other prisoners were put under the guard of an officer named Julius. He was a member of the imperial guard. ²We left on a boat that was scheduled to make several stops along the coast of Asia Minor. I should add that Aristarchus, a Greek from Thessalonica, was with us.

³The next day we docked at Sidon. Julius was very kind to Paul. He let him go ashore to visit with friends. ⁴Setting sail from there, we met headwinds that made it hard to keep the ship on course. So we sailed north of Cyprus between the island and the mainland. ⁵We passed along the coast of the provinces of Cilicia and Pamphylia. And we landed at Myra, in the province of Lycia. ⁶There our officer found an Egyptian ship from Alexandria. It was sailing for Italy, so he put us on board.

⁷⁻⁸We had several days of rough sailing, and finally neared Cnidus. But the winds had become too strong. So we sailed across to Crete, passing the port of Salome. From there we sailed into the wind and it was very slow going. We went slowly along the southern coast and finally came to Fair Havens. This port town is near the city of Lasea. ⁹There we stayed for several days. The weather was becoming dangerous for long voyages by then. It was late in the year, and most ships didn't sail at that time. Paul spoke to the ship's officers about this.

¹⁰"Sirs," he said, "I believe there is trouble ahead if we go on. We will probably suffer shipwreck, loss of cargo, injuries, or even death." ¹¹But the officers guarding the prisoners listened to the ship's captain. They didn't listen to what Paul had to say. ¹²Fair Havens had an open harbor and was a poor place to spend the winter. Most of the crew wanted to go up the coast to Phoenix. It was a better harbor to spend the winter. Phoenix had a good harbor which was open to the northwest and southwest.

¹³Just then a light wind began blowing from the south. And it looked like a perfect day for the trip. So they pulled up anchor and sailed along close to shore.

¹⁴⁻¹⁵But shortly after that the weather changed. A heavy wind of typhoon strength caught the ship. They called it a "northeaster." It blew our ship out to sea. They tried at first to face back to shore, but they couldn't. So they gave up and let the ship run before the gale.

¹⁶We finally sailed behind a small island named Clauda. And there we managed to pull the lifeboat on board. We had been towing it along behind us. ¹⁷And then we banded the ship with ropes to keep it from falling apart. The sailors were afraid of being driven across to the quicksands of the African coast. So they lowered the topsails and were thus driven before the wind.

¹⁸The next day the seas grew higher. So the crew began throwing the cargo overboard. ¹⁹The following day they

threw out the tackle and anything else they could find. ²⁰The terrible storm blew for many days without stopping. And in the end, all hope was gone.

²¹No one had eaten for a long time. But finally Paul called the crew together. "Men, you should have listened to me in the first place," he said. "You should not have left Fair Havens. If you had listened, you would not have suffered all this loss! ²²But cheer up! Not one of us will lose our lives. However, the ship will go down.

²³"For last night an angel stood beside me. This angel was from the God whom I serve. ²⁴He said, 'Don't be afraid, Paul. For you will surely stand trial before Caesar! What's more, God will do what you have asked. He will save the lives of all those sailing with you.' ²⁵So take courage! For I believe God! It will be just as he said! ²⁶But we will be shipwrecked on an island."

²⁷Now it was about midnight on the 14th night of the storm. We were being driven to and fro on the Adriatic Sea. And the sailors thought that land must be near. ²⁸They threw a rope into the water with a weight on it. And they found 120 feet of water below them. A little later they threw the rope in again. And they found only 90 feet of water. ²⁹At that rate they knew they would soon be driven ashore. They were afraid of rocks along the coast. So they threw out four anchors from the stern and prayed for daylight.

³⁰Some of the sailors planned to leave the ship. So they lowered the lifeboat. They pretended that they were going to put out anchors from the prow. ³¹But Paul spoke to the soldiers and commanding officer. He said, "You will all die unless everyone stays on the ship." ³²So the soldiers cut the ropes and let the boat fall off.

³³Soon the darkness gave way to the early morning light. And Paul begged everyone to eat. "You haven't touched food for two weeks," he said. ³⁴"Please eat something now for your own good! For not a hair of your heads shall be destroyed!"

³⁵Then he took some hardtack and gave thanks to God before them all. He broke off a piece and ate it. ³⁶Suddenly everyone felt better and began eating. ³⁷There were 276 of us in all. ³⁸After eating, the crew made the ship lighter. They did this by throwing all the wheat overboard.

³⁹When it was day, they didn't know where they were. But they saw a bay with a beach. They wondered if they could get between the rocks and be washed onto the beach. ⁴⁰They finally decided to try. So they cut off the anchors and left them in the sea. They lowered the rudders. Then they raised the foresail and headed for the shore. ⁴¹But the ship hit a sandbar and ran aground. The front of the ship stuck fast in the sand. And the back of the ship was caught in the waves and began to break apart.

⁴²The soldiers told their commander to let them kill the prisoners. This was because they didn't want any of them to swim ashore and get away. ⁴³But Julius wanted to save Paul, so he told them no. Then he ordered all who could swim to jump overboard and make for land. ⁴⁴He told the rest to try for it on planks and boards from the broken ship. So everyone made it to the shore safely!

- *Remember:* Who was Paul's guard? What was he like? (27:1-3) Paul warned about future danger. What did he say? Did the officers listen? (27:10-11) How bad was the storm? (27:14-20) How did Paul encourage the crew? (27:21-26) How was the ship wrecked? (27:27-41) Is it hard to be brave in danger? God asked the people to do this.

- *Discover:* We can be brave in danger if God is with us. He knows what will happen. He can change what will happen.

- *Apply:* Have you ever been afraid of something? What was it? Was it a storm? God is in charge of weather. Were you afraid of the dark? God makes darkness and light. Were you afraid of a dog? God can protect you. Ask God to be with you. He will.

- *What's next?* A poisonous snake bites Paul. How can he live? Read Acts 28:1-10. ◼

Paul Is Shipwrecked on Malta

Paul was shipwrecked on Malta. At first, the people thought he was a criminal. Later they showered him with gifts. Why the difference? What happened?

28 We soon learned that we were on the island of Malta. The people of the island were very kind to us. They made a bonfire on the beach to welcome and warm us in the rain and cold.

³Paul was gathering an armful of sticks to lay on the fire. And a deadly snake bit his hand and hung there! The snake had been driven out by the heat. ⁴The people of the island saw it hanging there. They said to each other, "A murderer, no doubt! He got away from the sea. But justice will not allow him to live!"

⁵But Paul shook off the snake into the fire and was unhurt. ⁶The people waited for him to begin swelling or to suddenly fall dead. But they waited a long time and no harm came to him. So they changed their minds and decided he was a god.

⁷Near the shore where we landed was some land belonging to Publius. He was the governor of the island. He welcomed us kindly and fed us for three days. ⁸Now Publius's father was sick with fever and dysentery. So Paul went in and prayed for him. He laid his hands on him and healed him! ⁹Then all the other sick people in the island came and were healed. ¹⁰As a result the people gave us many gifts. And when it was time to sail, the people gave us all we needed for the trip.

- *Remember:* Why did the people think Paul was a murderer? (28:3-4) What changed their minds? (28:5-9) How did the people show their love to Paul? (28:10) What if Paul had not helped the people? What would they have thought of him then?

- *Discover:* People will love us more when we help them more.

- *Apply:* Do you want someone to like you better? Be a helper.

What's next? What was it like to be a prisoner at Rome? Acts 28:11-31 will tell you. ■

Paul Is a Prisoner at Rome

How would you feel if you were a prisoner? What if you were a prisoner because you believe in Jesus? Would you turn against Jesus? Would you stop telling others about Jesus? What would you do? This is what Paul did.

¹¹It was three months after the shipwreck before we set sail again. This time we rode in *The Twin Brothers* of Alexandria. It was a ship that had spent the winter on the island. ¹²Our first stop was Syracuse, where we stayed three days. ¹³From there we circled around to Rhegium. A day later a south wind began blowing. So the next day we came to Puteoli. ¹⁴And there we found some believers! They begged us to stay with them seven days. Then we went on to Rome.

¹⁵The brothers in Rome had heard we were coming. So they came to meet us at the Forum on the Appian Way. Others joined us at The Three Taverns. When Paul saw them, he thanked God and took courage.

Paul Under House Arrest in Rome

¹⁶When we got to Rome, Paul was allowed to live wherever he wanted to. However, he was guarded by a soldier at all times.

¹⁷Three days after he got there, he called together the local Jewish leaders. He said to them, "Brothers, I was arrested by the Jews in Jerusalem. They handed me over to the Roman government to be punished. They did this even though I hadn't hurt anyone. And I never showed disrespect for the customs of our ancestors. ¹⁸The Romans gave me a trial and wanted to set me free. They couldn't see why the Jewish leaders wanted to kill me. ¹⁹The Jews were upset that the Romans didn't find me guilty. So I decided, with no hate against them, to appeal to Caesar. ²⁰I asked you to come here today so we could meet each other. And I wanted to tell you why I am a prisoner. It is because I believe the Messiah has already come!"

²¹They replied, "We have heard nothing against you! We have had no letters from Judea. No reports about you have come from our brothers in Jerusalem. ²²But we want to hear what you believe. We know that people everywhere are speaking against these Christians!"

²³So a time was set, and on that day many people came to his house. He told them about the Kingdom of God. And he taught them about Jesus from the five books of Moses and the books of prophecy. He began teaching in the morning and went on into the evening!

²⁴Some believed and some didn't. ²⁵They argued back and forth among themselves for some time. Then they left with a final word from Paul ringing in their ears. Paul said, "The Holy Spirit was right when he spoke through Isaiah the prophet. The Holy Spirit said, ²⁶'Say to the Jews, "You will hear and see but not understand. ²⁷For your hearts are too fat and your ears don't listen! You have closed your eyes against understanding. For you don't want to see and hear. You don't want to understand either. You refuse to turn to me so I can heal you."'

²⁸⁻²⁹"I want you to know that this salvation from God is for the Gentiles too. Yes, and they will accept it!"

³⁰Paul lived for the next two years in his rented house. He welcomed all who came to visit him. ³¹He told them boldly about God's Kingdom and the Lord Jesus Christ. And no one tried to stop him.

- *Remember:* How did Christians greet Paul? Do you think they loved him? Why? (28:13-15) What did Paul tell the local Jewish leaders? (28:17-20) Did they listen to him? (28:21-23) Did some believe in Jesus? Did some reject Jesus? (28:24)

- *Discover:* When the Gospel is given, some will accept Jesus. Some will reject Jesus.

- *Apply:* Are you afraid to tell others about Jesus? Are you afraid no one will accept him? Some will accept Jesus. Some will reject him. Don't let those who reject him stop you. Keep telling others about Jesus.

- *What's next?* A runaway slave could be punished. But this runaway is different. Read the Book of Philemon. ∎

ROMANS

Paul was a special Bible-time missionary. He traveled to many different cities telling people about Jesus, God's Son. Paul also wrote letters to many people and churches. In these letters he explained things that Christians should know. Many of these letters are part of the New Testament. The Book of Romans is a letter Paul wrote to the church at Rome. Rome was the capital of the Roman Empire. This Empire controlled almost all of the Bible-time world. The church at Rome was a group of Christians. Some were Jews. Others were Gentiles. Paul's letter helped Roman Christians know what to believe. It helps us know what to believe, too. There are no adventure stories in the Book of Romans. But it is an important book. There are some important verses in this book. Can you find some of them?

Paul Writes a Letter with Good News

1 Dear friends in Rome: ¹This letter is from Paul, Jesus Christ's slave. I was chosen to be a missionary. And I was sent out to preach God's Good News. ²This Good News was promised long ago by God's prophets in the Old Testament. ³It is the Good News about God's Son, Jesus Christ our Lord. He came as a human baby, born into King David's royal family line. ⁴By rising from the dead, Jesus proved he was God's Son. He showed that he was God.

⁵Because of Christ, all of God's kindness has been poured out upon us sinners. Now he is sending us out around the world. We are telling all people about the great things God has done for them. Then they, too, will believe and obey him.

⁶⁻⁷And you, dear friends in Rome, are among those he dearly loves. You, too, are invited by Jesus Christ to be God's very own holy people. May all God's mercies and peace be yours from God our Father and from Jesus Christ our Lord.

God's Good News Is Powerful

⁸Wherever I go you are being talked about! For your faith in God is becoming known around the world. I thank God through Jesus Christ for this good report. I thank him for each one of you. ⁹God knows how often I pray for you. Day and night I bring you and your needs in prayer to him. I serve him with

all my might. I tell others the Good News about his Son.

¹⁰I pray for a chance, God willing, to come to see you. And I pray that I will have a safe trip. ¹¹⁻¹²I want to visit you so that I can give you faith. This will help your church grow strong in the Lord. I want to share my faith with you. But I want to be encouraged by your faith, too. Each of us will be a blessing to the other.

We know that Jesus is God's Son because he rose from the dead

By rising from the dead, Jesus proved he was God's Son. He showed that he was God.

Romans 1:4

---

¹³I want you to know, dear brothers, that I planned to come many times before. But I couldn't. I wanted to work among you and see good results. I have seen great blessings among the other Gentile churches. ¹⁴I owe a great debt to you all. I owe this debt to polite people and people who are not polite. I owe it to people who have gone to school. I owe it to people who have not gone to school. ¹⁵So I am ready to come to you in Rome to preach God's Good News.

¹⁶I am not ashamed about Christ's Good News. It is God's powerful way to bring all who believe it to Heaven. This message was first preached only to the Jews. But now everyone is asked to come to God in the same way. ¹⁷This Good News tells us that God makes us ready for Heaven. He makes us right in God's sight. This happens when we put our faith and trust in Christ to save us. This happens from start to finish by faith. As the Bible says, "The man who finds life will find it by trusting God."

God's Anger with Sinful People Is Powerful

¹⁸But God shows his anger from Heaven. It is against all sinful, evil men who push away the truth. ¹⁹These men know the truth about God. God has taught them in their hearts. ²⁰Since earliest times men have seen the earth and sky and all God made. That is how they know about God and his great eternal power. So they will have no excuse when they stand before God at Judgment Day.

²¹Yes, they knew about him. But they wouldn't admit it or worship him. They wouldn't even thank him for all his care for them. They thought up silly ideas about what God was like and what he wanted them to do. So their foolish minds became dark and confused. ²²They thought they were wise without God. So they became fools instead. ²³They didn't worship the great, ever-living God. Instead, they took wood and stone and made idols for themselves. They carved them to look like birds and animals and snakes and men.

²⁴So God let them go ahead into every sort of sex sin. He let them do whatever they wanted. They did vile and sinful things with each other's bodies. ²⁵They didn't believe in the truth they knew was from God. Instead they chose to believe lies. So they prayed to the things God made. But they wouldn't obey the blessed God who made these things.

I will not be ashamed to tell people about Jesus

I am not ashamed about Christ's Good News. It is God's powerful way to bring all who believe it to Heaven. This message was first preached only to the Jews. But now everyone is asked to come to God in the same way.

Romans 1:16

---

²⁶That is why God let go of them. He let them go and do these evil things. Even their women turned against God's natural plan for them. They had sex sin with each other. ²⁷And the men didn't have normal sex with women. Instead they burned with lust for each other. They did shameful things with other men. As a result, their own souls paid the penalty they so richly deserved.

²⁸They gave God up and would not say they knew him. So God gave them

up to do everything their evil minds could think of. [29]Their lives became full of every kind of wickedness and sin. They were full of greed and hate, envy, murder, fighting, lying, bitterness, and gossip.

[30]They were backbiters, haters of God, insolent, proud, and braggarts. They could always think of new ways of sinning. They never obeyed their parents. [31]They didn't want to understand. They broke their promises, and were heartless and without pity. [32]They knew about God's death penalty for these crimes. But they went ahead and did them anyway. They helped other people to do them, too.

God Will Judge Us All

2 You may say, "What terrible people you have been talking about!" But wait a minute! You are just as bad. You say they are wicked and should be punished. But you do these very same things. [2]We know that God will punish anyone who does things like these. [3]God will judge and condemn others for doing these things. Do you think he will overlook you when you do them, too? [4]Don't you know how patient he is being with you? Or don't you care? Can't you see that he has been waiting all this time without punishing you? He is giving you time to turn from your sin. His kindness is meant to lead you to change. [5]But you won't listen. You are stubborn. You refuse to turn from your sin. So you are saving up terrible punishment for yourselves. There is going to come a day of anger. That is when God will be the Judge of all the world. [6]He will give each one whatever his deeds deserve. [7]He will give eternal life to those who patiently do the will of God. They seek for the unseen glory and honor and eternal life that he offers. [8]But he will terribly punish those who fight against the truth of God. God's anger will be poured out on people who walk in evil ways. [9]There will be sorrow and suffering for Jews and Gentiles who keep on sinning. [10]There will be glory and honor and peace from God for all who obey him. He will give this to the Jews and the Gentiles. [11]God

treats everyone the same.

[12-15]He will punish sin wherever it is found. The heathen never had God's written laws. But he will punish them when they sin. Down in their hearts they know right from wrong. God's laws are written within them. Their own heart accuses them, or sometimes excuses them. God will punish the Jews for sinning because they have his laws but don't obey them. They know what is right but don't do it. Salvation isn't given to those who know what to do, unless they do it. [16]The day will come when God will command Jesus Christ to judge everyone's secret life. He will judge their inmost thoughts and motives. This is all part of God's great plan, which I am telling you about.

Knowing God's Law Isn't Enough

[17]You Jews have God's law. You brag that you are his special friends. [18]Yes, you know what he wants. You know right from wrong. You have been taught his laws since you were young. So you want to do what is right. [19]You are so sure of the way to God. You think you can point it out to a blind man. You think you are lights that bring men out of darkness to God. [20]You think that you can guide the simple. You think you can even teach children about God. You really know his laws. They are full of all knowledge and truth.

[21]You teach others, then why don't you teach yourselves? You tell others not to steal. Do you steal? [22]You say it is wrong to commit adultery. Do you do it? You say, "Don't pray to idols." But then you make money your god, and worship it instead.

[23]You are so proud of knowing God's laws. But you shame him by breaking them. [24]No wonder the Bible says that the world speaks evil of God because of you.

[25]Being a Jew is worth something if you obey God's laws. But if you don't, then you are no better off than the heathen. [26]God planned to give the Jews his rights and honors. If the heathen obey God's laws, won't he give them these things instead? [27]Those heathen will be

much better off than you Jews. You know so much about God. You have his promises but you don't obey his laws.

²⁸For you were born of Jewish parents. You have gone through the Jewish ceremony of circumcision. But that doesn't make you a real Jew. ²⁹No, a real Jew is anyone whose heart is right with God. For God is not looking for those who cut their bodies in circumcision. He is looking for people with changed hearts and minds. Whoever has that kind of change will be praised not by you but by God.

God Remains Faithful

3 Then what's the use of being a Jew? Are they special to God? Is Jewish circumcision worth anything? ²Yes, being a Jew is good. First of all, God trusted them with his laws. That way they could know and do his will. ³True, some of them were not faithful. They broke their promises to God. But does that mean God will break his promises? ⁴Of course not! Even if everyone else in the world is a liar, God is not. Do you remember what the Book of Psalms says about this? God's words will always be true and right, no matter who asks questions about them.

Everyone has sinned

No one is good without God. Every person in the world has sinned.

Romans 3:10

---

⁵Some people say, "It is good that we broke our promises to God. Our sins serve a good purpose. People will notice how good God is when they see how bad we are. Is it fair for him to punish us when our sins are helping him?" This is the way some people talk. ⁶God forbid! Then what kind of God would he be, to overlook sin? How could he ever judge anyone? ⁷What if my lies brought God glory by showing how honest he is? Then he could not judge and condemn me as a sinner. ⁸But you are really saying, "The worse we are, the better God likes it!" Some people say that this is what I preach! It is right that they be judged!

All People Are Sinners and Deserve Punishment

⁹Well then, are we Jews better than others? No, not at all! We have already shown that all people are sinners. It doesn't matter if they are Jews or Gentiles. ¹⁰The Bible says, "No one is good without God. Every person in the world has sinned."

¹¹No one has ever really followed God's paths or even truly wanted to.

¹²Everyone has turned away from God. All have gone wrong. No one anywhere has kept on doing what is right.

¹³Their talk is foul and dirty like the smell from an open grave. Their tongues are loaded with lies. Everything they say is like the sting and poison of deadly snakes.

¹⁴Their mouths are full of cursing and bitterness.

¹⁵They are quick to kill. They hate anyone who does not agree with them.

¹⁶Wherever they go they leave sadness and trouble behind them. ¹⁷They have never known what it is to feel secure. They don't know what it means to enjoy God's blessing.

¹⁸They don't care about God or what he thinks of them.

¹⁹The Jews have to keep God's laws instead of doing all these evil things. Not one of them has any excuse for not keeping the law. In fact, all the world stands hushed and guilty before Almighty God.

²⁰Now do you see it? No one can be right in God's sight by doing what the law commands. The more we know God's laws, the more we see that we aren't obeying them. His laws only show us that we are sinners.

Christ Took Our Punishment for Us

²¹⁻²²But now God has shown us another way to Heaven. It is not by "being good enough" and trying to keep his laws. It is by a new way. It is not really new. Because the Scriptures told about it long ago. Now God says he will accept us and declare us "not guilty." He will do this if we trust Jesus Christ to take away our sins. We all can be saved by

coming to Christ. It doesn't matter who we are or what we have been like. ²³Yes, all have sinned. All fall short of God's perfect glory. ²⁴But if we trust in Jesus Christ, God says we are "not guilty." In his kindness he freely takes away our sins.

²⁵God sent Christ Jesus to take the punishment for our sins. He ended all God's anger against us. Christ's blood and our faith saves us from God's anger. This is the way he could be fair to everybody. He did not punish the people who sinned before Christ came. He was looking forward to the time when Christ would come and take away those sins. ²⁶And now in these days he can welcome sinners in this same way. Because Jesus took away their sins.

But isn't this unfair for God to say criminals are not guilty of sin? No, he does it because they trust in Jesus who took away their sins.

²⁷Then what can we brag about doing to earn our salvation? Nothing at all! Why? Because we were not forgiven because of our good deeds. Instead, we were forgiven because of what Christ has done and our faith in him. ²⁸So we are saved by faith in Christ, not by the good things we do.

²⁹And does God save only the Jews in this way? No, the Gentiles, too, may come to him in this same way. ³⁰God treats us all the same. Jews and Gentiles are forgiven if they have faith. ³¹We are saved by faith. Does this mean that we no longer need to obey God's laws? Just the opposite! In fact, only when we trust Jesus can we really obey him.

Abraham Believed God

4 Abraham was the father of the Jewish nation. What did he learn about being saved by faith? Was it because of his good deeds that God welcomed him? If so, then he would have something to brag about. But from God's point of view Abraham had no basis at all for pride. ³The Bible tells us Abraham *believed God.* That is why God canceled his sins and declared him "not guilty."

⁴⁻⁵Didn't he earn his right to Heaven by all the good things he did? No, be-

cause being saved is a gift. If a person could earn it by being good, then it wouldn't be free! It is given to those who do not work for it. For God says sinners are good in his sight if they have faith in Christ to save them from God's anger.

⁶King David spoke about this. He showed the happiness of a sinner whom God says is "not guilty." ⁷He said, "Blessed are those whose sins are forgiven and put out of sight. ⁸There is joy for anyone whose sins aren't counted against him by the Lord."

⁹Is this blessing given only to those who keep the Jewish laws? Or is the blessing also given to those who only trust in Christ? Well, what about Abraham? We say that he was given these blessings because of his faith. Was it by faith alone, or because he also kept the Jewish rules?

¹⁰When did God give this blessing to Abraham? It was before he became a Jew. It was before he was circumcised.

¹¹After God had promised to bless him because of his faith, he was circumcised. Circumcision was a sign that Abraham already had faith. It showed that God had already accepted him. God said he was just and good in his sight before he was circumcised. So Abraham is the spiritual father of people who believe. They are saved without obeying Jewish laws. People who do not keep these rules are justified by God because of faith. ¹²Abraham is also the father of those Jews who have been circumcised. They can see from his example that circumcision does not save them. Because Abraham found favor with God by faith alone before he was circumcised.

¹³God promised to give the whole earth to Abraham and his children. God's promise was not because Abraham obeyed God's laws. It was because Abraham trusted God to keep his promise. ¹⁴If God's blessings go to those who are "good enough," then faith is foolish. ¹⁵When we try to gain God's blessing by keeping his laws we make him angry. We always fail to keep the laws. The way to keep from breaking laws is not to have any to break!

¹⁶So God's blessings are a free gift. They are given to us by faith. We will get them if we follow Jewish customs. And we will get them if we have faith like Abraham's. Because Abraham is the father of all of us who have faith. ¹⁷That's why the Bible says that God made Abraham the father of many nations. God makes the dead live again and creates things out of nothing. So he will welcome all people in every nation who trust God as Abraham did.

¹⁸God told Abraham that he would give him a son. That son would have many children and become a great nation. Abraham believed God even though such a promise just couldn't happen! ¹⁹His faith was strong. He didn't worry that he was 100 years old and couldn't be a father. He didn't care that Sarah his wife could not have a baby.

²⁰But Abraham never doubted. His faith and trust always grew stronger. So he praised God for this blessing even before it happened. ²¹He was sure that God was able to do anything he promised. ²²And because of Abraham's faith God forgave his sins and declared him "not guilty."

²³All this wasn't just for Abraham's benefit. ²⁴It was for us too. We believe in God who brought back Jesus our Lord from the dead. So God will accept us the same way he accepted Abraham. ²⁵He died for our sins and rose again to make us right with God.

Believing God
Can Make You Joyful

5 We have been made right in God's sight by faith in his promises. So we can have real peace with him. Why? Because of what Jesus Christ our Lord has done for us. ²Our faith has brought us into this wonderful place where we now stand. Here we joyfully look forward to becoming all that God wants us to be.

³Here we can rejoice when we run into problems and trials. We know that they are good for us. They help us learn to be patient. ⁴And patience helps us become better people. This helps us trust God. Finally our hope and faith are strong and steady. ⁵Then we are able to hold our heads high and know that all is well. Why? Because we know how dearly God loves us. He has given us the Holy Spirit to fill our hearts with his love.

⁶We were helpless sinners who had no use for God. Then Christ came at just the right time and died for us. ⁷Even if we were good, we really wouldn't expect anyone to die for us. That would be barely possible. ⁸But God showed his great love for us. He sent Christ to die for us while we were still sinners. ⁹He died a bloody death and made us right with God. Now he will do much more for us. He will save us from God's anger which is coming. ¹⁰When we were God's enemies we were brought back by the death of his Son. We are now his friends, so God can do much more for us. He can rescue us because his eternal life is in us!

¹¹Now we rejoice in our wonderful new relationship with God. It is all because of what our Lord Jesus Christ has done by dying for our sins. He made us friends with God.

Adam Brought Sin;
Christ Brought Forgiveness

¹²When Adam sinned, sin entered the whole human race. His sin spread death through all the world. Everything began to grow old and die because all sinned. ¹³We know that it was Adam's sin that made this happen. Of course, people were sinning from the time of Adam until Moses. But God did not judge them guilty of death for breaking his laws. He had not yet given his laws to them. ¹⁴So when their bodies died it was not for their own sins. They had never sinned the same way Adam had sinned.

What a contrast between Adam and Christ who was yet to come! ¹⁵And what a difference between man's sin and God's forgiveness!

For this one man, Adam, brought death to many through his sin. But this one man, Jesus Christ, brought forgiveness to many through God's mercy. ¹⁶Adam's one sin brought the penalty of death to many. But Christ freely takes away many sins and gives new life in-

stead. [17]The sin of this one man, Adam, caused death to be king over all. But all who will take God's gift of forgiveness are kings of life. Why? Because of this one man, Jesus Christ. [18]Yes, Adam's sin brought punishment to all. But what Christ did was right and good. This makes men right with God, so that they can live. [19]Adam caused many to be sinners because he disobeyed God. Christ caused many to be welcome to God because he obeyed.

[20]God's laws were given so that everybody could know how much they had failed. But the more we see our sin, the more we see God's grace forgiving us. [21]Before, sin ruled over all men and brought them to death. But now God's kindness rules instead. This gives us a right standing with God. This results in eternal life through Jesus Christ our Lord.

Christ Broke Sin's Power Over You

6 Should we keep on sinning? Will this make God give us more and more kindness and forgiveness?

[2-3]Of course not! Should we keep on sinning when we don't have to? Sin's power over us was broken. This happened when we were baptized to become a part of Jesus Christ. Through his death the power of your sinful nature was broken. [4]Your old sin-loving nature was buried with him by baptism when he died. God the Father, with great power, brought him back to life again. That was when you were given his wonderful new life to enjoy.

[5]You have become a part of him. So you died with him, so to speak, when he died. Now you share his new life and will rise as he did. [6]Your old evil desires were nailed to the cross with him. The part of you that loves to sin was crushed. Now your sin-loving body is no longer under sin's control. It no longer needs to be a slave to sin. [7]When you are dead to sin you are free from its power over you. [8]Your old sin-loving nature "died" with Christ. So we know that you will share his new life. [9]Christ rose from the dead and will never die again. Death no longer has any power over him. [10]He died once for all to end sin's power. But now he lives forever in fellowship with God. [11]So look upon your old sin nature as dead to sin. Instead be alive to God through Jesus Christ our Lord.

Sin makes us die, but Christ helps us have life forever

Sin makes us die. Through Christ, God gives us life that never ends.

Romans 6:23

---

[12]Do not let sin control your body anymore. Do not give in to its sinful desires. [13]Do not let any part of your bodies become tools of wickedness. Do not let them be used for sinning. Give every part of yourself to God. You are back from death. Give yourself to be a tool in the hands of God. Let him use you for his good purposes. [14]Sin doesn't ever have to be your master. You are not tied to the law where sin makes you its slave. You are free under God's favor and mercy.

You Are Free to Obey

[15]Our salvation does not depend on keeping the law. Instead, it depends on receiving God's grace. Does this mean that now we can go ahead and sin? Of course not!

[16]Don't you know that you can choose your own master? You can choose sin which ends in death. Or you can choose to obey. This will make you right and good. The one you choose will take you and be your master. You will be his slave. [17]Once you chose to be slaves of sin. But, thank God, now you have obeyed! You have obeyed with all your heart the teaching God has given you. [18]And now you are free from your old master, sin. You have become slaves to what is right and good.

[19]I use the example of slaves and masters because it is easy to understand. You used to be slaves to all kinds of sin. Now you must let yourselves be slaves to all that is right and holy.

[20]In the days when you were slaves to sin you didn't bother with goodness.

21What was the result? It must not have been good. Why? Because you are now ashamed even to think about those things you used to do. All of them end in eternal doom. 22But now you are free from the power of sin. You are slaves of God. So you will have holiness and everlasting life. 23Sin makes us die. Through Christ, God gives us life that never ends.

You Can Serve God

7Don't you understand, brothers? When a person dies the law no longer holds him in its power.

2It is like when a woman marries a man. The law says he is her husband as long as he is alive. But if he dies, she is not his wife anymore. She doesn't have to keep the laws of marriage anymore. 3She can marry someone else if she wants to. That would be wrong while her husband was alive. But it is all right after he dies.

If we're God's children, his Spirit will lead us

Everybody who is led by God's Spirit is a son of God.

Romans 8:14

4Your "husband" used to be the Jewish law. But you "died" with Christ on the cross. Since you are "dead," you are no longer "married to the law." It has no more control over you. You came back to life again when Christ came back to life. You are a new person. Now you are "married" to the one who rose from the dead. You can grow good fruit in your life. That means you do good deeds for God. 5When your old nature was still active, sinful desires were at work in you. They made you want to do whatever God said not to do. They produced sinful things. Those things are the rotting fruit of death. 6But now you don't need to worry about the Jewish laws. You "died" while you were captured by them. Now you can really serve God. Not in the old way by obeying a set of rules. But in the new way, with all of your hearts and minds.

God's Law Shows Us Our Sin

7Am I saying that these laws of God are evil? Of course not! No, the law is not sinful. But it was the law that showed me my sin. I wouldn't have known the sin in my heart. The law told me about it. It said, "You must not have evil desires in your heart." 8Sin used this law against evil desires. It reminded me that those desires are wrong. This made me desire all kinds of forbidden things! Only if there were no laws to break would there be no sinning.

9I felt fine so long as I didn't understand what the law really demanded. But then I learned the truth. I found out that I had broken the law. I was a sinner, doomed to die. 10So, the good law was supposed to show me the way of life. But instead it gave me the death penalty. 11Sin fooled me. It took God's good laws and used them to make me guilty of death. 12But the law is still right and good.

13But how can that be? Didn't the law cause my doom? How can it be good? It was sin that used what was good to bring about my doom. So you can see how tricky and deadly sin is. It uses God's good laws for its own evil purposes.

Why Can't I Do What Is Right?

14The law is good. The trouble is not the Law. The trouble is with me! I am sold into slavery and sin is my owner.

15I don't understand myself at all. I really want to do what is right, but I can't. Instead I do what I don't want to do. I do the things I hate. 16I know what I am doing is wrong. I know that these laws I am breaking are right and good. 17But I can't help myself because I'm no longer doing it. Sin inside me is stronger than I am. It makes me do these evil things.

18I know that my old sinful nature is rotten. No matter which way I turn I can't make myself do right. I want to but I can't. 19When I want to do good, I don't. When I try not to do wrong, I do it anyway. 20I am doing what I don't want to do. So it is easy to see where the trouble is. Sin still has me in its evil grip. 21When I want to do what is right, I

stead. [17]The sin of this one man, Adam, caused death to be king over all. But all who will take God's gift of forgiveness are kings of life. Why? Because of this one man, Jesus Christ. [18]Yes, Adam's sin brought punishment to all. But what Christ did was right and good. This makes men right with God, so that they can live. [19]Adam caused many to be sinners because he disobeyed God. Christ caused many to be welcome to God because he obeyed.

[20]God's laws were given so that everybody could know how much they had failed. But the more we see our sin, the more we see God's grace forgiving us. [21]Before, sin ruled over all men and brought them to death. But now God's kindness rules instead. This gives us a right standing with God. This results in eternal life through Jesus Christ our Lord.

Christ Broke Sin's Power Over You

6 Should we keep on sinning? Will this make God give us more and more kindness and forgiveness?

[2-3]Of course not! Should we keep on sinning when we don't have to? Sin's power over us was broken. This happened when we were baptized to become a part of Jesus Christ. Through his death the power of your sinful nature was broken. [4]Your old sin-loving nature was buried with him by baptism when he died. God the Father, with great power, brought him back to life again. That was when you were given his wonderful new life to enjoy.

[5]You have become a part of him. So you died with him, so to speak, when he died. Now you share his new life and will rise as he did. [6]Your old evil desires were nailed to the cross with him. The part of you that loves to sin was crushed. Now your sin-loving body is no longer under sin's control. It no longer needs to be a slave to sin. [7]When you are dead to sin you are free from its power over you. [8]Your old sin-loving nature "died" with Christ. So we know that you will share his new life. [9]Christ rose from the dead and will never die again. Death no longer has any power over him. [10]He died once for all to end sin's power. But now he lives forever in fellowship with God. [11]So look upon your old sin nature as dead to sin. Instead be alive to God through Jesus Christ our Lord.

Sin makes us die, but Christ helps us have life forever

Sin makes us die. Through Christ, God gives us life that never ends.

Romans 6:23

[12]Do not let sin control your body anymore. Do not give in to its sinful desires. [13]Do not let any part of your bodies become tools of wickedness. Do not let them be used for sinning. Give every part of yourself to God. You are back from death. Give yourself to be a tool in the hands of God. Let him use you for his good purposes. [14]Sin doesn't ever have to be your master. You are not tied to the law where sin makes you its slave. You are free under God's favor and mercy.

You Are Free to Obey

[15]Our salvation does not depend on keeping the law. Instead, it depends on receiving God's grace. Does this mean that now we can go ahead and sin? Of course not!

[16]Don't you know that you can choose your own master? You can choose sin which ends in death. Or you can choose to obey. This will make you right and good. The one you choose will take you and be your master. You will be his slave. [17]Once you chose to be slaves of sin. But, thank God, now you have obeyed! You have obeyed with all your heart the teaching God has given you. [18]And now you are free from your old master, sin. You have become slaves to what is right and good.

[19]I use the example of slaves and masters because it is easy to understand. You used to be slaves to all kinds of sin. Now you must let yourselves be slaves to all that is right and holy.

[20]In the days when you were slaves to sin you didn't bother with goodness.

21What was the result? It must not have been good. Why? Because you are now ashamed even to think about those things you used to do. All of them end in eternal doom. 22But now you are free from the power of sin. You are slaves of God. So you will have holiness and everlasting life. 23Sin makes us die. Through Christ, God gives us life that never ends.

You Can Serve God

7 Don't you understand, brothers? When a person dies the law no longer holds him in its power.

2It is like when a woman marries a man. The law says he is her husband as long as he is alive. But if he dies, she is not his wife anymore. She doesn't have to keep the laws of marriage anymore. 3She can marry someone else if she wants to. That would be wrong while her husband was alive. But it is all right after he dies.

If we're God's children, his Spirit will lead us

Everybody who is led by God's Spirit is a son of God.

Romans 8:14

4Your "husband" used to be the Jewish law. But you "died" with Christ on the cross. Since you are "dead," you are no longer "married to the law." It has no more control over you. You came back to life again when Christ came back to life. You are a new person. Now you are "married" to the one who rose from the dead. You can grow good fruit in your life. That means you do good deeds for God. 5When your old nature was still active, sinful desires were at work in you. They made you want to do whatever God said not to do. They produced sinful things. Those things are the rotting fruit of death. 6But now you don't need to worry about the Jewish laws. You "died" while you were captured by them. Now you can really serve God. Not in the old way by obeying a set of rules. But in the new way, with all of your hearts and minds.

God's Law Shows Us Our Sin

7Am I saying that these laws of God are evil? Of course not! No, the law is not sinful. But it was the law that showed me my sin. I wouldn't have known the sin in my heart. The law told me about it. It said, "You must not have evil desires in your heart." 8Sin used this law against evil desires. It reminded me that those desires are wrong. This made me desire all kinds of forbidden things! Only if there were no laws to break would there be no sinning.

9I felt fine so long as I didn't understand what the law really demanded. But then I learned the truth. I found out that I had broken the law. I was a sinner, doomed to die. 10So, the good law was supposed to show me the way of life. But instead it gave me the death penalty. 11Sin fooled me. It took God's good laws and used them to make me guilty of death. 12But the law is still right and good.

13But how can that be? Didn't the law cause my doom? How can it be good? It was sin that used what was good to bring about my doom. So you can see how tricky and deadly sin is. It uses God's good laws for its own evil purposes.

Why Can't I Do What Is Right?

14The law is good. The trouble is not the Law. The trouble is with me! I am sold into slavery and sin is my owner.

15I don't understand myself at all. I really want to do what is right, but I can't. Instead I do what I don't want to do. I do the things I hate. 16I know what I am doing is wrong. I know that these laws I am breaking are right and good. 17But I can't help myself because I'm no longer doing it. Sin inside me is stronger than I am. It makes me do these evil things.

18I know that my old sinful nature is rotten. No matter which way I turn I can't make myself do right. I want to but I can't. 19When I want to do good, I don't. When I try not to do wrong, I do it anyway. 20I am doing what I don't want to do. So it is easy to see where the trouble is. Sin still has me in its evil grip.

21When I want to do what is right, I

stead. [17]The sin of this one man, Adam, caused death to be king over all. But all who will take God's gift of forgiveness are kings of life. Why? Because of this one man, Jesus Christ. [18]Yes, Adam's sin brought punishment to all. But what Christ did was right and good. This makes men right with God, so that they can live. [19]Adam caused many to be sinners because he disobeyed God. Christ caused many to be welcome to God because he obeyed.

[20]God's laws were given so that everybody could know how much they had failed. But the more we see our sin, the more we see God's grace forgiving us. [21]Before, sin ruled over all men and brought them to death. But now God's kindness rules instead. This gives us a right standing with God. This results in eternal life through Jesus Christ our Lord.

Christ Broke Sin's Power Over You

6 Should we keep on sinning? Will this make God give us more and more kindness and forgiveness?

[2-3]Of course not! Should we keep on sinning when we don't have to? Sin's power over us was broken. This happened when we were baptized to become a part of Jesus Christ. Through his death the power of your sinful nature was broken. [4]Your old sin-loving nature was buried with him by baptism when he died. God the Father, with great power, brought him back to life again. That was when you were given his wonderful new life to enjoy.

[5]You have become a part of him. So you died with him, so to speak, when he died. Now you share his new life and will rise as he did. [6]Your old evil desires were nailed to the cross with him. The part of you that loves to sin was crushed. Now your sin-loving body is no longer under sin's control. It no longer needs to be a slave to sin. [7]When you are dead to sin you are free from its power over you. [8]Your old sin-loving nature "died" with Christ. So we know that you will share his new life. [9]Christ rose from the dead and will never die again. Death no longer has any power over him. [10]He

died once for all to end sin's power. But now he lives forever in fellowship with God. [11]So look upon your old sin nature as dead to sin. Instead be alive to God through Jesus Christ our Lord.

Sin makes us die, but Christ helps us have life forever

Sin makes us die. Through Christ, God gives us life that never ends.

Romans 6:23

[12]Do not let sin control your body anymore. Do not give in to its sinful desires. [13]Do not let any part of your bodies become tools of wickedness. Do not let them be used for sinning. Give every part of yourself to God. You are back from death. Give yourself to be a tool in the hands of God. Let him use you for his good purposes. [14]Sin doesn't ever have to be your master. You are not tied to the law where sin makes you its slave. You are free under God's favor and mercy.

You Are Free to Obey

[15]Our salvation does not depend on keeping the law. Instead, it depends on receiving God's grace. Does this mean that now we can go ahead and sin? Of course not!

[16]Don't you know that you can choose your own master? You can choose sin which ends in death. Or you can choose to obey. This will make you right and good. The one you choose will take you and be your master. You will be his slave. [17]Once you chose to be slaves of sin. But, thank God, now you have obeyed! You have obeyed with all your heart the teaching God has given you. [18]And now you are free from your old master, sin. You have become slaves to what is right and good.

[19]I use the example of slaves and masters because it is easy to understand. You used to be slaves to all kinds of sin. Now you must let yourselves be slaves to all that is right and holy.

[20]In the days when you were slaves to sin you didn't bother with goodness.

²¹What was the result? It must not have been good. Why? Because you are now ashamed even to think about those things you used to do. All of them end in eternal doom. ²²But now you are free from the power of sin. You are slaves of God. So you will have holiness and everlasting life. ²³Sin makes us die. Through Christ, God gives us life that never ends.

You Can Serve God

7Don't you understand, brothers? When a person dies the law no longer holds him in its power.

²It is like when a woman marries a man. The law says he is her husband as long as he is alive. But if he dies, she is not his wife anymore. She doesn't have to keep the laws of marriage anymore. ³She can marry someone else if she wants to. That would be wrong while her husband was alive. But it is all right after he dies.

If we're God's children, his Spirit will lead us

Everybody who is led by God's Spirit is a son of God.

Romans 8:14

---

⁴Your "husband" used to be the Jewish law. But you "died" with Christ on the cross. Since you are "dead," you are no longer "married to the law." It has no more control over you. You came back to life again when Christ came back to life. You are a new person. Now you are "married" to the one who rose from the dead. You can grow good fruit in your life. That means you do good deeds for God. ⁵When your old nature was still active, sinful desires were at work in you. They made you want to do whatever God said not to do. They produced sinful things. Those things are the rotting fruit of death. ⁶But now you don't need to worry about the Jewish laws. You "died" while you were captured by them. Now you can really serve God. Not in the old way by obeying a set of rules. But in the new way, with all of your hearts and minds.

God's Law Shows Us Our Sin

⁷Am I saying that these laws of God are evil? Of course not! No, the law is not sinful. But it was the law that showed me my sin. I wouldn't have known the sin in my heart. The law told me about it. It said, "You must not have evil desires in your heart." ⁸Sin used this law against evil desires. It reminded me that those desires are wrong. This made me desire all kinds of forbidden things! Only if there were no laws to break would there be no sinning.

⁹I felt fine so long as I didn't understand what the law really demanded. But then I learned the truth. I found out that I had broken the law. I was a sinner, doomed to die. ¹⁰So, the good law was supposed to show me the way of life. But instead it gave me the death penalty. ¹¹Sin fooled me. It took God's good laws and used them to make me guilty of death. ¹²But the law is still right and good.

¹³But how can that be? Didn't the law cause my doom? How can it be good? It was sin that used what was good to bring about my doom. So you can see how tricky and deadly sin is. It uses God's good laws for its own evil purposes.

Why Can't I Do What Is Right?

¹⁴The law is good. The trouble is not the Law. The trouble is with me! I am sold into slavery and sin is my owner.

¹⁵I don't understand myself at all. I really want to do what is right, but I can't. Instead I do what I don't want to do. I do the things I hate. ¹⁶I know what I am doing is wrong. I know that these laws I am breaking are right and good. ¹⁷But I can't help myself because I'm no longer doing it. Sin inside me is stronger than I am. It makes me do these evil things.

¹⁸I know that my old sinful nature is rotten. No matter which way I turn I can't make myself do right. I want to but I can't. ¹⁹When I want to do good, I don't. When I try not to do wrong, I do it anyway. ²⁰I am doing what I don't want to do. So it is easy to see where the trouble is. Sin still has me in its evil grip.

²¹When I want to do what is right, I

always do what is wrong. This seems to be a fact of life. 22My new nature loves to do God's will. 23-25But my lower nature is at war with my mind. It always wins the fight. It makes me a slave to the sin that is still within me. In my mind I want to be God's servant. But instead I am sin's slave.

So my new life tells me to do right. But the old nature that is still inside me loves to sin. Oh, this is terrible! Who will free me from being a slave to this deadly lower nature? Thank God! It has been done by Jesus Christ our Lord. He has set me free!

The Holy Spirit Frees Us from Sin

8 God won't judge people who belong to Christ Jesus. 2Because the life-giving Spirit has set me free from sin and death. 3We aren't saved from sin because we know God's laws. We can't keep them. But God had a different plan to save us. He sent his own Son. Jesus Christ had a body like ours, except he didn't use his for sin. Instead he destroyed sin by dying on the cross for our sins. 4So now we can obey God's laws. How? By following the Holy Spirit and not obeying the old evil nature within us.

5Some people are controlled by their lower natures. They live only to make themselves happy. But the people who follow the Holy Spirit do the things that please God. 6Following the Holy Spirit leads to life and peace. But following the old nature leads to death. 7For the old sinful nature in us is against God. It never did obey God's laws and it never will. 8So people who are under the control of their sinful selves can't please God.

9But you are not like that. Your new nature controls you. Why? Because you have the Spirit of God living in you. Anybody who doesn't have the Spirit of Christ living in him is not a Christian. 10Even though Christ lives within you, your body will die because of sin. But your spirit will live because Christ made you right with God. 11The Spirit of God raised up Jesus from the dead. This Spirit lives in you. He will make your bodies live again after you die. How? Because this same Holy Spirit lives in you.

We Are God's Children

12So, dear brothers, you don't have to do what your sinful nature begs you to do. 13If you keep on following your sinful nature, you are lost. But if you follow the Holy Spirit, you will live. 14Because everybody who is led by God's Spirit is a son of God.

15So we are not fearful slaves, but we are God's very own children. We have been adopted into his family. So when we call out to him we can say "Father, Father." 16His Spirit speaks to us in our hearts and says we are God's children. 17Since we are his children, we will share his treasures. All God gives to his Son Jesus is ours too. But if we share his glory, we have to share his suffering, too.

Our Future Reward

18Our suffering now is nothing compared to the glory he will give us later. 19All creation is waiting patiently for the day when God will resurrect his children. 20-21On that day the things that overcame the world will disappear. The world will share in the glorious freedom from sin which God's children enjoy.

22We know that the animals and plants suffer as they wait for this great event. 23We have the Holy Spirit within us as a taste of future glory. But we also groan to be set free from pain and suffering. We are waiting for the day when God will make us his sons. He will give us new bodies. They are bodies that will never be sick again and will never die.

Learning to Trust God

24We are saved by trusting. And trusting means looking forward to getting something we don't have yet. A man who already has something doesn't need to hope to get it later. 25But we must keep trusting God for something that hasn't happened yet. This teaches us to wait patiently and with confidence.

Letting the Holy Spirit Help Us

26And in the same way the Holy Spirit helps us with our prayers. We don't know what we should pray. So the Holy Spirit prays for us. He has feelings that can't be spoken with words. 27God knows all our hearts. He also knows what the Spirit is praying. Because the Spirit prays the way God wants. [28]Everything that happens to us is working for our good. We know this is true if we love God and fit into his plans.

Nothing Can Separate Us from God's Love

[29]From the very beginning God knew who would come to him. He decided that they would become like his Son. That way his Son would be the First, with many brothers. [30]After he chose us, he called us to come to him. When we came, he declared us "not guilty." He filled us with Christ's goodness. He gave us right standing and promised us his glory.

??????????????????????????????????

Which of these can separate us from Christ's love—death, life, angels, powers of hell, fears, worries?

(Read 8:38 for the answer.)

??????????????????????????????????

[31]What can we ever say to such wonderful things as these? If God is on our side, who can ever be against us? [32]God did not hold back even his own Son from us. He gave him up for us all. Won't he also surely give us everything else?

[33]Who dares accuse us whom God has chosen for his own? Will God? No! He is the one who has forgiven us. He has given us right standing with himself.

[34]Who then will condemn us? Will Christ? No! For he is the one who died for us. He came back to life again for us. He is sitting at the place of highest honor next to God. And he is praying for us there.

[35]Who then can ever keep Christ's love from us? Sometimes we have troubles or disasters. Sometimes we are hunted down or destroyed. Is this because he doesn't love us anymore? Sometimes we are hungry and poor. Sometimes we are in danger or close to death. Does this mean that God has left us?

[36]No! The Bible tells us that we face death every day for him. We are like sheep waiting to die. [37]But despite all this, victory is ours through Christ. He loved us enough to die for us. [38]I am sure that nothing can ever separate us from his love. Death can't, and life can't. The angels won't. All the powers of hell can't keep God's love away. Our fears for today, and our worries about tomorrow can't either. [39]It doesn't matter if we are high above the sky, or deep in the ocean. Nothing can carry us away from God's love that is in our Lord Jesus Christ.

God Is Sovereign; He Has the Right to Do What He Wants

9 O Israel, my people! O my Jewish brothers! How I wish you would come to Christ! My heart is heavy and I cry day and night because of you. I have prayed to be forever damned if that would save you. [4]God has given you so much, but still you won't listen to him. He took you as his own special people. He led you with a bright cloud of glory. He told you how very much he wanted to bless you. He gave you his laws. He let you worship him and gave you mighty promises. [5]Great men of God were your fathers. Christ himself was one of you. He was a Jew in his human nature. He now rules over all things. Praise God forever!

[6]Well then, has God failed to fulfill his promises to the Jews? No! For these promises are only to people who are truly Jews. And not everyone born into a Jewish family is truly a Jew! [7]Just because they come from Abraham doesn't make them truly Abraham's children. Abraham had many children. But the Bible says the promises are only to Abraham's son Isaac and Isaac's children. [8]This means that not all of Abraham's children are children of God. Only those who believe the promise God made to Abraham are God's children.

[9]God promised, "Next year I will give you and Sarah a son." [10-13]And years later Isaac was grown up and married Rebecca. His wife was about to bear him twin children. God told her that the child born first would serve his twin brother. The Bible says, "I chose to bless Jacob but not Esau." And God said this

world will share when the Jews come to Christ.

¹³As you know, God has chosen me as a special messenger to you Gentiles. I remind the Jews about this as often as I can. ¹⁴I want to make them want what you Gentiles have. In that way God can save some of them. ¹⁵How wonderful it will be when they become Christians! God turned away from them. This means he turned to the rest of the world to offer his salvation. Now it is even more wonderful when the Jews come to Christ. It will be like dead people coming back to life. ¹⁶And since Abraham and the prophets are God's people, their children will belong to God too. Because if the roots of the tree are holy, the branches will be too.

¹⁷But some of the branches from Abraham's tree, the Jews, have been broken off. You Gentiles who were branches from a wild olive tree were grafted in. So now you, too, receive the blessing God has promised Abraham and his children. You share in God's rich nourishment of his own special olive tree.

¹⁸But be careful. Don't brag about being put in to replace the branches that were broken off. Remember, you are important only because you are now a part of God's tree. You are just a branch, not a root.

¹⁹You may be saying, "Those branches were broken off to make room for me. I must be pretty good."

²⁰Watch out! Remember that those branches, the Jews, were broken off because they didn't believe God. You are there only because you believe. Do not be proud. Be humble, grateful, and careful. ²¹God did not spare the branches he put there in the first place. So he won't spare you either.

²²Notice how God is both kind and severe. He is very hard on those who disobey. But he is very good to you if you continue to love and trust him. If you don't, you will be cut off too. ²³If the Jews come back to God, God will graft them back into the tree again. He has the power to do it.

²⁴You were part of a wild olive tree. You were far away from God. God grafted you into his own good tree. This is a very unusual thing to do. The Jews were there in the first place. So God will be more ready to put the Jews back than to keep you there.

God's Kindness and Forgiveness for Everyone

²⁵I want you to know about this truth from God, dear brothers. I don't want you to feel proud and start bragging. Yes, it is true. Some of the Jews are against the Good News now. But this will last only until all of you Gentiles have come to Christ. ²⁶And then all Israel will be saved.

Do you remember what the prophets said about this? "There shall come out of Zion a Deliverer. He shall turn the Jews from all ungodliness. ²⁷At that time I will take away their sins, just as I promised."

²⁸Now many of the Jews are enemies of the Good News. They hate it! But this has been good for you. God has given his gifts to you Gentiles. Yet the Jews are still loved by God. Why? Because he gave his promises to Abraham, Isaac, and Jacob. ²⁹God's gifts and his call can never be taken away. He will never go back on his promises. ³⁰Once you were rebels against God. But when the Jews refused his gifts, God was merciful to you instead. ³¹And now the Jews are the rebels. But someday they, too, will share in God's mercy. ³²God gave them all up to sin so he could have mercy on everybody.

³³Oh, what a wonderful God we have! How great are his wisdom and knowledge and riches! We can't know his decisions and his methods! ³⁴For who among us can know the mind of the Lord? Who knows enough to be his guide? ³⁵And who could ever offer to the Lord enough to cause him to act? ³⁶For everything comes from God alone. Everything lives by his power. Everything is for his glory. To him be glory evermore!

Give Your Life to God

12 And so, dear brothers, I beg with you to give your bodies to God. Let them be a holy, living sacrifice, the kind he can accept. When you think of what he has done for you, is this too much to ask? [2]Don't copy the world. Be a different person with a fresh newness in all you do and think. Then you will learn how his ways will really satisfy you.

Get excited when you work for God

Never be lazy in your work. You should get excited when you serve God.

Romans 12:11

---

[3]I am God's messenger. So I want to give each of you God's warning. Be honest when you think about yourself. Measure your value by how much faith God has given you. [4-5]There are many parts to our bodies. It is the same with Christ's body. We are all parts of his body. It takes every one of us to make it complete. We each have different work to do. We belong to each other, and each needs all the others.

[6]God has given each of us the ability to do certain things well. God may have given you the ability to prophesy. If so, you should prophesy as often as your faith is strong enough to do it. [7]If your gift is that of serving others, serve them well. If you are a teacher, do a good job of teaching. [8]If you are a preacher, your sermons should be strong and helpful. If God has given you money, be generous in helping others with it. If God has put you in charge of the work of others, do this job well. Those who comfort people who are sad should do it with cheer.

[9]Don't just pretend that you love others, really love them! Hate what is wrong. Stand on the side of the good. [10]Love each other like brothers. Enjoy giving each other honor. [11]Never be lazy in your work. You should get excited when you serve God. [12]Be glad for all God is planning for you. Be patient in trouble, and always pray. [13]When God's children are in need, you be the one to help them out. And get into the habit of inviting guests to your home for dinner.

[14]If someone hurts you because you are a Christian, don't curse him. Pray that God will bless him. [15]When others are happy, be happy with them. If they are sad, share their sadness. [16]Work happily together. Don't try to act big. Don't try to be important. Enjoy the company of plain folks. And don't think you know it all!

[17]Never pay back evil for evil. Do things in a way that everyone can see you are honest. [18]Don't argue with anyone. Be at peace with everyone as much as you can.

[19]Dear friends, if people are mean to you, don't try to get even. Leave that to God. He has said that he will pay them back. [20]Instead, feed your enemy if he is hungry. If he is thirsty give him something to drink. If you do this you will be "heaping coals of fire on his head." That means he will feel bad about what he has done to you. [21]Don't let evil be the winner. Crush evil by doing good.

Obey the Government

13 Obey the rulers because God is the one who has put them there. There are no rulers anywhere that God has not put in power. [2]So those who refuse to obey the laws of the land are refusing to obey God. They will be punished. [3]For the policeman does not scare people who are doing right. But people who do evil will always fear him. So if you don't want to be afraid, keep the laws. [4]The policeman is sent by God to help you. But if you are doing something wrong, you should be afraid. He will have you punished. He is sent by God to do that. [5]Obey the laws to keep from being punished. Also, obey because you know you should.

Let good win in your life

Don't let evil be the winner. Crush evil by doing good.

Romans 12:21

---

[6]This is why you should pay your taxes, too. Rulers need to be paid so that they can keep on serving you. [7]Pay everyone whatever he should have. Pay what you owe and be happy about it. Obey the people you should obey. Give honor and respect to everybody who should have it.

Loving Others Fulfills God's Requirements

8Pay all your debts except the debt of love for others. You should never finish paying that! If you love them, you will obey all of God's laws. 9You should love your neighbor as much as you love yourself. Then you will not want to harm or cheat him. You will not want to kill him or steal from him. And you won't sin with his wife or want what is his. You won't do anything else the Ten Commandments say is wrong. All ten are part of this one, love your neighbor as you love yourself. 10Love does no wrong to anyone. That's why it keeps all of God's laws. It is the only law you need.

11Also, you know how late it is. Time is running out. Wake up! The coming of the Lord is nearer now than when we first believed. 12-13The night is far gone. The day of his return will soon be here. So quit the evil deeds of darkness. Put on the armor of right living. We who live in the daylight should do this! Be decent and true in everything you do. That way, everybody can agree with your way of life. Don't spend your time in wild parties and getting drunk. Don't live in adultery and lust or fighting or jealousy. 14Ask the Lord Jesus Christ to help you live as you should. Don't make plans to enjoy evil.

Don't Criticize Other Christians

14 Give a warm welcome to any brother who wants to join you. Do this even though his faith is weak. Don't worry if his ideas are different from yours. 2For example, some eat meat that has been offered to idols. Don't argue about this. You may believe there is no harm in it. But other people's faith is weaker. They might think it is wrong. Perhaps they have chosen to eat only vegetables. 3People who eat this kind of meat shouldn't look down on people who don't. If you don't eat meat, don't find fault with those who do. Because God has accepted them to be his children. 4They are God's servants, not yours. Let him tell them whether they are right or wrong. And God is able to make them do as they should.

How Do You Treat Guests?
ROMANS 12:13

Suppose a stranger knocks on your door today. The stranger asks to stay at your house. He won't pay you. He asks you to feed him for a few days. But you can't charge him. What would you do? You'd probably tell him to find a motel and restaurant. In Bible times there were no motels or restaurants. On caravan routes there were only a few inns. But inns had no restaurants. They had no beds. They had no bathrooms. So travelers depended on strangers to take care of them in their own homes. Hosts were not to charge travelers. Guests were very important people in a Bible-time home. The host gave the guest water to wash his feet. Sometimes he even washed the guest's feet. He fed the guest and let him sleep in his home. He protected the guest while he was in the home. He took care of the guest and served him. The guest could have almost anything he wanted. Why did people do all these things? That was the way people did it at that time. Everyone was expected to be a good host. Each host knew that someday he might be the guest. He expected to be treated well, too.

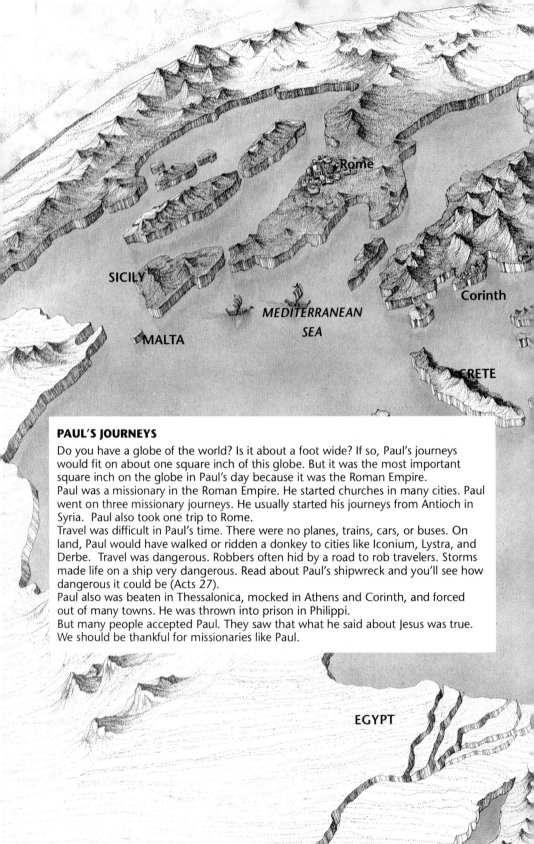

SICILY

MALTA

MEDITERRANEAN SEA

Rome

Corinth

CRETE

EGYPT

PAUL'S JOURNEYS

Do you have a globe of the world? Is it about a foot wide? If so, Paul's journeys would fit on about one square inch of this globe. But it was the most important square inch on the globe in Paul's day because it was the Roman Empire.

Paul was a missionary in the Roman Empire. He started churches in many cities. Paul went on three missionary journeys. He usually started his journeys from Antioch in Syria. Paul also took one trip to Rome.

Travel was difficult in Paul's time. There were no planes, trains, cars, or buses. On land, Paul would have walked or ridden a donkey to cities like Iconium, Lystra, and Derbe. Travel was dangerous. Robbers often hid by a road to rob travelers. Storms made life on a ship very dangerous. Read about Paul's shipwreck and you'll see how dangerous it could be (Acts 27).

Paul also was beaten in Thessalonica, mocked in Athens and Corinth, and forced out of many towns. He was thrown into prison in Philippi.

But many people accepted Paul. They saw that what he said about Jesus was true. We should be thankful for missionaries like Paul.

before the children were even born. He said it before they had done anything either good or bad. This proves that God was doing what he had decided from the beginning. It was not because of what the children did. It was because of what God wanted and chose.

¹⁴Was God being unfair? Of course not! ¹⁵For God had said to Moses, "If I want to be kind to someone, I will. And I will take pity on anyone I want to." ¹⁶God's blessings are not given because someone wants them or works hard to get them. They are given because God takes pity on those he wants to.

¹⁷Pharaoh, king of Egypt, was an example of this fact. God told him he had given him the kingdom of Egypt for a purpose. God wanted to show his awesome power against Pharaoh. That way all the world would hear about God's name. ¹⁸So God is kind to some people because he wants to be. He makes some people refuse to listen.

¹⁹Well then, why does God blame them for not listening? Haven't they done what he made them do?

²⁰No, don't say that. Who are you to question God? Should the thing that is made question the one who made it? Should it say, "Why have you made me like this?" ²¹A man can use some clay to make a beautiful jar for flowers. He can use the same clay and make a jar for garbage. ²²God has been patient with some people for a long time. Those people are only good to be thrown away. Doesn't God have a right to show his anger against those people? ²³⁻²⁴And he can be kind to us so that everyone can see how very great his glory is. This is why he made us. It doesn't matter if we are Jews or Gentiles.

²⁵Remember what the prophet Hosea says? "God will find other children for himself who are not from his Jewish family. He will love them even though no one had ever loved them before. ²⁶Once he said, "You are not my people." But now they are called "sons of the Living God."

²⁷Isaiah the prophet cried out about the Jews. He told them that out of millions of Jews only a few would be saved.

²⁸"For the Lord will do what he said he would do to the earth," he said. "He will finish it and cut it short."

²⁹And Isaiah also said, "If God did not have mercy all the Jews would be destroyed. It will be just like the cities of Sodom and Gomorrah were destroyed.

Some People Don't Understand the Good News

³⁰Well then, what shall we say about these things? Just this, that God has given the Gentiles a chance. They can be saved by faith, even though they had not been seeking God. ³¹But the Jews tried so hard to get right with God by keeping his laws. But they never succeeded. ³²Why not? Because they wanted to be saved by keeping the law instead of by faith. They have tripped over the great stumbling stone. ³³God warned them about this in the Bible. He said, "I have put a Rock in the path of the Jews. Many will stumble over Jesus. People who believe in him will never be disappointed."

10 Dear brothers, I hope and pray that the Jewish people will be saved. ²I know how excited they are about the honor of God. But they don't know what they are doing. ³They don't understand that Christ has died to make them right with God. Instead they try to gain God's favor by keeping the Jewish laws and customs. But that is not God's way of salvation. ⁴They don't understand that Christ is the end of all that. People who believe in him are right with God.

⁵Moses wrote that if a person could be perfectly good and never sin, he could be forgiven and saved. ⁶But what does the salvation that comes through faith say? It says, "You don't need to bring Christ down from Heaven to help you." It also says, ⁷"You don't need to go to the grave to bring Christ back to life."

⁸We preach about the salvation that comes from trusting Christ. It is already within easy reach of each of us. In fact, it is as near as our own hearts and mouths. ⁹This is how you will be saved. Tell others with your own mouth that Jesus Christ is your Lord. Also, believe in your own heart that God has raised him

from the dead. [10]Because it is by believing in his heart that a man becomes right with God. With his mouth he tells others about his faith and is saved.

[11]The Bible says that God won't fail anyone who believes in Christ. [12]Jew and Gentile are the same. They have the same Lord. He gives his riches to anybody who asks him for them. [13]Anybody who calls upon the name of the Lord will be saved.

[14]But how shall they ask him to save them unless they believe in him? And how can they believe in him if they have never heard about him? And how can they hear about him unless someone tells them? [15]And how will anyone go and tell them unless someone sends him? That is why the Bible says, "People who preach the Good News of peace have beautiful feet. They bring glad tidings of good things." In other words, how welcome are those who come preaching God's Good News!

[16]But not everyone who hears the Good News has welcomed it. Isaiah the prophet said, "Lord, who has believed me when I told them?" [17]Yet faith comes from listening to the Good News about Christ.

[18]But what about the Jews? Have they heard God's Word? Yes, for it has gone wherever they are. The Good News has been told to the ends of the earth. [19]And did they understand? Did they know that God would give his salvation to others if they refused to take it? Yes, they knew! Even in the time of Moses God said he would make his people jealous. He said that he would do this by giving his salvation to the heathen. [20]Later, Isaiah was very brave. He said that God would be found by people who weren't looking for him. [21]Now, he keeps on reaching out his hands to the Jews. But they keep arguing and refusing to come to him.

God's Kindness and Forgiveness for Israel

11 I ask then, has God rejected and left his people the Jews? Oh no, not at all! Remember that I myself am a Jew. I am a child of Abraham and a member of Benjamin's family.

[2-3]God has not thrown away his own people whom he chose from the beginning. Do you remember what the Bible says about this? Elijah the prophet was complaining to God about the Jews. He told God how they had killed the prophets and torn down God's altars. Elijah said he was the only one left in Israel who still loved God. They were trying to kill him, too.

[4]Do you remember how God replied? God said, "No, you are not the only one left. I have 7,000 others who love me and haven't bowed to idols!"

[5]It is the same today. Not all the Jews have turned away from God. There are a few being saved because of God's kindness in choosing them. [6]If it's by God's kindness, then it's not because they are good enough. Then the free gift wouldn't be free. It isn't free when it is earned.

[7]Most of the Jews have not found the favor of God they are looking for. A few have. They are the ones God has picked out. But the eyes of the others have been blinded. [8]This is why the Bible says that God has put them to sleep. He has shut their eyes and ears. Now they don't understand what we are talking about when we tell them about Christ. And so it is to this very day.

[9]King David spoke of this same thing. He said, "Let their good food and other blessings trap them. Then they will think that all is well between themselves and God. Let these good things come back against them. Let them fall back on their heads to crush them. [10]Let their eyes be dim," he said. "Then they cannot see. Let them walk bent-backed forever with a heavy load."

[11]Does this mean that God has rejected his Jewish people forever? Of course not! His purpose was to bring his salvation to the Gentiles. Then the Jews would be jealous and begin to want God's salvation for themselves. [12]The whole world became rich as a result of God's offer of salvation. The Jews stumbled over God's salvation and turned it down. Think how great a blessing the

Thessalonica

Philippi

Athens

Troas

Iconium

Ephesus

Lystra

Antioch
in PISIDIA

Derbe

Perga

CYPRUS

Salamis

Antioch

Paphos

Ptolemais

Caesarea

ISRAEL

⁵Some think that Christians should observe the Jewish holidays. Others say it is wrong and foolish to go to all that trouble. They say that every day alike belongs to God. On questions of this kind everyone must decide for himself. ⁶If you have special days for worshiping the Lord, you honor him. This is a good thing. The person who eats meat offered to idols is thankful to the Lord. He is doing right. The person who won't touch such meat wants to please the Lord. ⁷We are not our own bosses to live or die as we choose. ⁸Living or dying we follow the Lord. Either way we are his. ⁹Christ died and rose again for this purpose: So he can be our Lord both while we live and when we die.

¹⁰You have no right to hate your brother or look down on him. Remember, each of us will stand in front of God's Judgment Seat. ¹¹The Bible says, "Every knee shall bow to me and every tongue confess to God." ¹²Yes, each of us will tell everything about himself to God.

Try to please others

Let's try to please other people, not ourselves.

Romans 15:2

¹³So don't judge each other anymore. Instead, live so that you will never make your brother stumble. Don't do the things your brother thinks are wrong. ¹⁴I know there is nothing wrong with eating meat offered to idols. I know this because I believe in Jesus Christ. But if someone believes it is wrong, then he shouldn't do it. ¹⁵If your brother is bothered by what you eat, don't eat it. If you do, you are not showing love to your brother. Christ died for him. So don't let your eating ruin him. ¹⁶Don't do anything that will make people hate you. ¹⁷The important thing is not what we eat or drink. It is goodness and peace and joy from the Holy Spirit. ¹⁸If you let Christ be Lord in these things, God will be glad, and so will others. ¹⁹This is the way to have peace in the church. So try to build each other up.

²⁰Don't undo the work of God for a chunk of meat. Remember, there is nothing wrong with the meat. It is wrong to eat it if it makes somebody stumble. ²¹What is the right thing to do? Quit eating meat or drinking wine or doing anything that makes your brother sin. ²²You may know that there is nothing wrong with what you do. But keep it to yourself. Don't show off your faith in front of people who might be hurt by it. Happy is the man who doesn't sin by doing what he knows is right. ²³Anyone who believes that something he wants to do is wrong shouldn't do it. He sins if he does. He thinks it is wrong, and so for him it is wrong. Anything that is done apart from what he feels is right is sin.

Think of Others First

15We cannot just go ahead and do these things to please ourselves. We must care for the people who feel these things are wrong. ²Let's try to please other people, not ourselves. Do what is good for them. Build them up in the Lord. ³Christ didn't please himself. The Bible says, "He came to suffer the insults of people who were against God." ⁴These things were written in the Bible long ago. They are there to teach us patience and to make us strong. Then we will look forward to the time when God will conquer sin and death.

⁵May God who gives patience and comfort help you live in peace with each other. May you each live like Christ toward each other. ⁶Then all of us can praise the Lord with one voice. We can give glory to God, the Father of our Lord Jesus Christ.

⁷So warmly welcome each other into the church. For Christ has warmly welcomed you. Then God will be glorified. ⁸Jesus Christ came because God is true to his promises to help the Jews. ⁹Remember that he came also that the Gentiles might be saved. Then they can give glory to God for his mercies to them. That is why the psalmist wrote: "I will praise you among the Gentiles. I will sing to your name."

¹⁰In another place he said, "You Gentiles be glad with his people the Jews."

¹¹And yet again, "Praise the Lord, O you Gentiles! Let everyone praise him."

¹²The prophet Isaiah said, "There shall be an Heir in the house of Jesse. He will be King over the Gentiles. They will pin their hopes on him alone."

¹³So I pray for you Gentiles. I pray to the God who gives hope. I pray he will give you joy and peace because you believe. I pray you will overflow with hope through the Holy Spirit's power in you.

Paul Explains Why He Writes and Preaches

¹⁴I know that you are wise and good, my brothers. You know these things so well that you can teach them to others. ¹⁵⁻¹⁶But I have been bold to write you some of these points. I know that all you need is this reminder from me. Because I am, by God's grace, a messenger from Jesus Christ to you Gentiles, I bring you the Good News. I offer you up as a sweet-smelling sacrifice to God. You have been made pure and pleasing to him by the Holy Spirit. ¹⁷I am proud of what Christ Jesus has done through me. ¹⁸I dare not judge how he has used others. But I know that he has used me to win the Gentiles to God. ¹⁹I have won them by my words and by the way I have lived. I have also won them by the miracles I have done as signs from God. All this is by the Holy Spirit's power. In this way I have preached the full Good News of Christ. I have preached all the way from Jerusalem clear over into Illyricum.

²⁰But my ambition has been to go still farther. I want to preach where the name of Christ has never been heard. I don't want to preach where a church has been started by someone else. ²¹I have been following the plan spoken of in the Bible. Isaiah says, "People who have never heard about him will see and understand." ²²That is why I have been so long in coming to visit you.

Paul Explains His Travel Plans

²³But now at last I have finished my work here. I am ready to come after all these long years of waiting. ²⁴I am planning to take a trip to Spain. When I do, I will stop off there in Rome. After we have

Reading and Writing
ROMANS 16:22

Can you read? Can you write? Today, most people learn to read and write at school. They learn when they are very young. In Bible times, few people knew how to read and write. There were not many schools. And not many people went to school. Only a few could learn things like reading and writing. What if a person wanted to write a letter? He had to hire a scribe. Scribes were trained to write. They were educated about other things, too. Sometimes they knew law. Or they knew something special about government. A scribe helped Paul write some of his letters. Paul was an educated man. He knew how to write. But the scribe may have helped Paul as a favor. You probably could not read any Bible-time writing. Hebrews and Greeks had languages very different from ours.

been together for a while, you can send me on my way.

²⁵But before I come, I must go up to Jerusalem. I have to take a gift to the Jewish Christians there. ²⁶The Christians in Macedonia and Achaia have taken an offering for the poor in Jerusalem. ²⁷They were very glad to do this. They

feel they owe a real debt to the Jerusalem Christians. Why? Because the news about Christ came to these Gentiles from the church in Jerusalem. They received this gift of the Good News from there. So they feel that the least they can do is give them some money. 28I will deliver this money and complete this good deed of theirs. Then I will come to see you on my way to Spain. 29I am sure when I come I will bring a great blessing for you.

???????????????????????????????????
Who was the very first person in Asia to become a Christian?
(Read 16:5 for the answer.)
???????????????????????????????????

30Will you be my prayer partners? Pray much with me for my work. Do this for the Lord Jesus Christ's sake. Do it because of your love for me. This love was given to you by the Holy Spirit. 31Pray that I will be safe in Jerusalem from those who are not Christians. Pray also that the Christians there will accept the money I am bringing. 32Then I will be able to come with joy and in God's will. Then we can refresh each other.

33And now may our God, who gives peace, be with you all. Amen.

Paul Greets His Friends

16 Phoebe, a woman from the town of Cenchreae, will be coming to see you. She has worked hard in the church there. Receive her as your sister in the Lord. Give her a warm Christian welcome. Help her in every way you can. She has helped many people, including me. 3Tell Priscilla and Aquila hello. They have been my fellow workers in the work of Christ Jesus. 4In fact, they risked their lives for me. I am not the only one who is thankful to them. All the Gentile churches are thankful, too.

5Please greet all those who meet to worship in Priscilla and Aquila's home. Greet my good friend Epaenetus. He was the very first person to become a Christian in Asia. 6Remember me to Mary. She has worked so hard to help us. 7Then there are Andronicus and Junias. They are my relatives who were in prison with

me. They are known by the apostles and became Christians before I did. Please give them my greetings. 8Say hello to Ampliatus, whom I love as one of God's own children. 9Say hello to Urbanus, our fellow worker, and Stachys whom I love.

10Then there is Apelles, a good man whom the Lord knows. Greet him for me. And give my best regards to those working at the house of Aristobulus. 11Remember me to Herodion my relative. Remember me to the Christian slaves over at Narcissus House. 12Say hello to Tryphaena and Tryphosa, the Lord's workers. Say hello to dear Persis, who has worked so hard for the Lord. 13Greet Rufus for me, whom the Lord picked out to be his very own. Also greet his dear mother who has been such a mother to me. 14Give my greetings to Asyncritus, Phlegon, Hermes, Patrobas, Hermas, and the brothers with them. 15Give my love to Philologus, Julia, Nereus, and his sister. Give my love to Olympas, and all the Christians who are with him. 16Shake hands warmly with each other. All the churches here send you their greetings.

One Last Instruction

17And now there is one more thing to say before I end this letter. Stay away from those who cause divisions and are upsetting people's faith. They teach things that are not the same as what you have been taught. 18Such teachers are not working for our Lord Jesus. They only want gain for themselves. They are good speakers, and simple people are fooled by them. 19But everyone knows that you stand loyal and true. This makes me very happy. I want you to keep in mind what is right. I want you to stay innocent of any wrong. 20The God of peace will soon crush Satan under your feet. Blessings from our Lord Jesus Christ be upon you.

Paul Says Good-bye

21Timothy my fellow worker, and Lucius and Jason and Sosipater, my relatives, greet you. 22Tertius is the one who is writing this letter for Paul. He sends his greetings too, as a Christian brother. 23Gaius says to say hello to you for him.

I am his guest, and the church meets here in his home. Erastus, the city treasurer, sends you his greetings. So does Quartus, a Christian brother. [24]Goodbye. May the grace of our Lord Jesus Christ be with you all.

[25-27]I commit you to God. He is able to make you strong and steady in the Lord. This is part of the Good News, just as I have told you. This is God's plan of salvation for you Gentiles. It has been kept secret from the beginning of time. The prophets foretold it. And God commanded that this message be preached everywhere. That way people around the world will have faith in Christ and obey him. To God who alone is wise be the glory forever through Jesus Christ our Lord. Amen.

Sincerely, Paul

FIRST CORINTHIANS

Corinth was a beautiful city. Travelers and merchants came from many places. They bought and sold. People made lots of money. They had money to buy many things. But they spent too much money and time on their things. Having fun and owning things became too important to them. Even the Christians lived like their pagan neighbors. Some of them even thought it was exciting to find sinful ways to have fun. People had trouble with their marriages and home lives. People looked for the wrong leaders to lead them. Does this sound like what also happens today? Paul wrote this letter to the Christians at Corinth. Living like their pagan neighbors was tearing the church apart. He urged them to live as Christians should.

Paul: Chosen to Be a Missionary

1 *From:* Paul, chosen by God to be Jesus Christ's missionary, and from brother Sosthenes.

²*To:* The Christians in Corinth. You have been invited by God to be his people. He welcomes you because of Christ Jesus. *And to:* All Christians everywhere. To anybody who calls upon the name of Jesus Christ, our Lord and theirs.

³May God our Father and the Lord Jesus Christ give you his blessings. May he give you great peace of heart and mind.

Paul Thanks God for Keeping His Word

⁴I can never stop thanking God for all the gifts he has given you. They are yours now that you are Christ's. ⁵He has made your whole life rich. He has helped you speak out for him. He has given you a full understanding of the truth. ⁶The things I told you Christ could do for you have happened! ⁷Now you have every grace and blessing. You have every spiritual gift and power for doing his will. These things are yours while you wait for our Lord Jesus Christ to return. ⁸He will help you grow right up to the end. That way you will be free from sin and guilt when he returns. ⁹God will surely do this for you. He always does just what he says. For he invited you into this wonderful friendship with his Son Jesus Christ our Lord.

Stop Arguing with One Another

¹⁰I beg you, brothers, in the name of the Lord Jesus Christ, stop arguing with each other. Let there be real peace among you. Then there won't be splits in the church.

I beg with you to be of one mind, united in thought and purpose. [11]Dear brothers, those who live at Chloe's house have told me about your arguments. [12]Some of you are saying, "I am a follower of Paul." Others say that they are for Apollos or for Peter. Some say that they alone are the true followers of Christ. [13]And so you have broken Christ into many pieces.

But did I, Paul, die for your sins? Were any of you baptized in my name? [14]I am glad that I didn't baptize any of you except Crispus and Gaius. [15]Now no one can think I have been trying to start "The Church of Paul." [16]Oh, yes, and I baptized the family of Stephanas. I don't remember ever baptizing anyone else. [17]For Christ didn't send me to baptize, but to preach the Good News. Even my preaching sounds poor. I don't fill my sermons with profound words and high sounding ideas. I don't want to water down the message of the cross of Christ.

Christ Brings Us Life from God

[18]When those who are lost hear that Jesus died to save them, it sounds foolish. But we who are saved know this message is the very power of God. [19]God says, "I will destroy all human plans of salvation. It doesn't matter how wise they seem to be. I ignore the best ideas of men, even the smartest of them."

[20]So what about these wise men? What about these scholars? What about these men who argue about this world's great affairs? God has made them all look foolish. He has shown their wisdom to be useless nonsense. [21]God is wise. He decided that the world would never find God through human wisdom. Then he stepped in and saved everybody who believed his message. The world calls his message foolish and silly. [22]It seems foolish to the Jews because they want a sign from Heaven. This would be proof that what is preached is true. It is foolish to the Gentiles, too. They only agree with what seems wise to them. [23]So we preach about Christ dying to save all people. But the Jews are offended and

the Gentiles say it's all nonsense. [24]However, God has opened the eyes of those called to salvation. He has opened the eyes of both Jews and Gentiles. They can see that Christ is the mighty power of God to save them. Christ himself is the center of God's wise plan for their salvation. [25]This so-called "foolish" plan of God is wiser than the plan of the wisest man. God in his weakness is far stronger than any man.

God lives in you

You are God's house.
The Spirit of God lives among
you in his house.

1 Corinthians 3:16

---

[26]Look at yourselves, dear brothers. Few of you who follow Christ have big names or power or wealth. [27]Instead, God has chosen people the world considers foolish. He uses them to shame the people who are wise and great. [28]He has chosen a plan the world hates. He used it to bring down to nothing those the world considers great. [29]That way no one anywhere can ever brag in front of God.

[30]For it is from God alone that you have your life through Christ Jesus. He showed us God's plan of salvation. He was the one who made us welcome to God. He made us pure and holy and gave himself to buy our salvation. [31]The Bible says, "If anyone is proud, let him be proud of what the Lord has done."

The Holy Spirit Gives Us Wisdom

2 Brothers, remember when I first came to you? I didn't use big words and great ideas to tell you God's message. [2]I decided to only speak of Jesus Christ and his death on the cross. [3]I came to you in weakness. I was timid and shaking. [4]My preaching was very plain. I didn't use a lot of big words and human wisdom. The Holy Spirit's power was in my words. This proved to those who heard them that the message was from God. [5]I wanted your faith to stand firmly upon God, not on man's great ideas.

⁶When I am among mature Christians I do speak with words of great wisdom. But they are not the kind of words that come from here on earth. They are not the kind that appeal to the great men of this world. These men are doomed to fall. ⁷Our words are wise because they are from God. They tell of God's wise plan to bring us into the glories of Heaven. This plan was hidden in former times. It was made for our benefit before the world began. ⁸But the great men of the world have not understood it. If they had, they wouldn't have killed the Lord of Glory on the cross.

⁹The Bible says nobody has seen, heard, or known what God has ready for those who love him. ¹⁰But we know about these things. God has sent his Spirit to tell us. His Spirit searches out and shows us all of God's deepest secrets. ¹¹No one can really know what anyone else is thinking. Nobody knows what he is really like except that person himself. And no one can know God's thoughts except God's own Spirit. ¹²And God has actually given us his Spirit. We don't have the world's spirit. God's Spirit tells us about the free gifts of grace and blessing God has given us. ¹³We are telling you about these gifts. We have used the very words given to us by the Holy Spirit. We do not use the words that we as men might choose. So we use the Holy Spirit's words to explain the Holy Spirit's facts. ¹⁴But the man who isn't a Christian can't accept these thoughts from God. The things of the Spirit sound foolish to him. Only those who have the Holy Spirit can understand what the Holy Spirit means. Others just can't take it in. ¹⁵But the man with the Spirit knows about all things. The man of the world can't understand him at all. ¹⁶How could he? He has never been one to know the Lord's thoughts. He has never discussed them with him. He doesn't move the hands of God by prayer. But we Christians have in us the thoughts and mind of Christ.

3 Brothers, I've been talking to you like you are babies in the Christian life. You are not following the Lord. You are doing what you want to do. I can't talk to you like you are filled with the Spirit.

²I have had to feed you with milk and not with solid food. You can't eat stronger food. You still have to be fed on milk. ³You are still only baby Christians. You do what you want to do. You don't do what God wants. You are jealous of one another and divide up into groups and argue. That proves you are still babies, wanting your own way. In fact, you are acting like people who don't belong to the Lord at all. ⁴You are quarreling about whether I am greater than Apollos. You are breaking up the church. Doesn't this show how little you have grown in the Lord?

⁵Who am I? And who is Apollos? Should we be the cause of a fight? We're just God's servants. Each of us can do different things. With our help you believed. ⁶My work was to plant the seed in your hearts. Apollos' work was to water it. But it was God who made the garden grow in your hearts. ⁷The person who does the planting or watering isn't very important. God is important because he is the one who makes things grow. ⁸Apollos and I are working as a team with the same aim. Each of us will be rewarded for his own hard work. ⁹We only work together with God. You are God's garden, not ours. You are God's building, not ours.

¹⁰God, in his kindness, has taught me how to be an expert builder. I have started the building and Apollos has built on it. But he who builds must be very careful. ¹¹No one can start a building other than the one we already have. That is Jesus Christ. ¹²But there are different things that can be used to build with. Some use gold and silver and jewels. Some build with sticks and hay or even straw! ¹³There is going to come a time of testing at Christ's Judgment Day. This test will show what kind of material each builder has used. Everyone's work will be put through the fire. Then all can see whether or not it keeps its value. ¹⁴Then every workman whose work still stands will get his pay. ¹⁵But if the house he has built burns up, he will have a great loss. He himself will be saved. But it will be like a man escaping through a wall of flames.

16You are God's house. The Spirit of God lives among you in his house. 17If someone spoils God's home, God will destroy him. For God's home is holy and clean, and you are that home.

18Stop fooling yourselves. If you are smart, you should be a fool. Then you can have the true wisdom from above. 19The wisdom of this world is foolishness to God. The Book of Job says that God uses man's own brilliance to trap him. He stumbles over his own "wisdom" and falls. 20The Book of Psalms says that the Lord knows how the human mind thinks. He knows how foolish and futile it is.

21Don't be proud of following the wise men of this world. God has already given you everything you need. 22He has given you Paul and Apollos and Peter as your helpers. He has given you the whole world to use. Life and even death are your servants. He has given you all of the present and all of the future. All are yours, 23and you belong to Christ, and Christ is God's.

The Church Shouldn't Be a Bunch of Bickering Groups

4 So Apollos and I should be looked upon in this way. We are Christ's servants who give God's blessings by explaining God's secrets. 2A servant should do just what his master tells him to. 3What about me? Have I been a good servant? I don't worry about what you think about this or what anyone else thinks. I don't even trust what I think about this. 4My conscience is clear, but even that isn't final proof. It is the Lord who must decide.

5Be careful not to jump to conclusions before the Lord returns. You should not decide if someone is a good servant or not. When the Lord comes he will turn on the lights. Everyone will see what each one of us is like deep in our hearts. And everyone will know why we have been doing the Lord's work. Then God will give to each one whatever praise is coming to him.

6I have used Apollos and myself as examples to show what I have been saying. You must not have favorites. You must not be proud of one of God's teachers more than another. 7What are you so puffed up about? What do you have that God hasn't given you? If all you have is from God, why act like you are so great? Why act like you have done something on your own?

???????????????????????????????????
Paul never had children. But he called one young man a beloved and trusted child in the Lord. Who was this young man?
(Read 4:17 for the answer.)
???????????????????????????????????

8You seem to think you already have all the spiritual food you need. You are full, rich kings on your thrones, leaving us far behind! I wish you really were already on your thrones. When that time comes we will be there, too, reigning with you. 9Sometimes I think God has put us apostles at the end of the line. We are like prisoners soon to be killed. We are put on display at the end of a victor's parade. We are stared at by men and angels alike.

10Religion has made us foolish, you say. But of course you are all such wise and sensible Christians! We are weak, but not you! You are well thought of, while we are laughed at. 11To this very hour we have gone hungry and thirsty. We don't have enough clothes to keep us warm. We have been kicked around without homes of our own. 12We have worked with our hands to earn our living. We have blessed those who cursed us. We have been patient with those who hurt us. 13We have answered quietly when evil things have been said about us. Yet right up to now we are like dirt under people's feet, like garbage.

14I am not writing about these things to make you ashamed. I want to warn you like the children that I love. 15You may have 10,000 others to teach you about Christ. But remember that you have only me as your father. I was the one who brought you to Christ when I preached the Good News. 16So I beg you to follow my example and do as I do.

[17]I am sending Timothy to help you do this. He is one of those I won to Christ. He is a beloved and trusted child in the Lord. He will remind you of what I teach in all the churches everywhere.

[18]I know that some of you will have become proud. You think that I am afraid to come to deal with you. [19]But I will come, and soon, if the Lord will let me. Then I'll learn if these proud men are talkers or if they have God's power. [20]The Kingdom of God is not just talking. It is living by God's power. [21]Which do you choose? Shall I come to punish and scold you? Or shall I come gently with quiet love?

Paul Speaks against Sin in the Church

5 Everyone is talking about the awful thing that has happened there among you. It is something so evil even the heathen don't do it. You have a man there who is living in sin with his father's wife. [2]And are you still so proud, so blind? Why aren't you crying in sorrow and shame? Why don't you see to it that this man is removed from the church?

[3-4]I am not there with you but I have been thinking about this. In the name of the Lord Jesus Christ I have decided what to do. It is just as though I were there. You are to call a meeting of the church. The power of the Lord Jesus will be with you as you meet. I will be there in spirit. [5]Throw out this man from the church and into Satan's hands, to punish him. Then his soul will be saved when our Lord Jesus Christ returns.

[6]It is terrible that you are proud of yourselves and yet you let this go on. Don't you know that if one person goes on sinning, all will be hurt? [7]Take away this wicked person from among you. Then you can stay pure. Christ, God's Lamb, has been killed for us. [8]So let us feast upon him and grow strong in the Christian life. Leave behind the old life with its wicked hatred. Let us feast instead upon the pure bread of honor and purity and truth.

[9]When I wrote to you before I said not to mix with evil people. [10]When I said

that, I wasn't talking about unbelievers. I didn't mean people who live in sexual sin or are greedy cheats. I wasn't talking about thieves and idol worshipers. You can't live in this world without being with people like that. [11]I meant that you aren't to be with a Christian who is in sexual sins. Don't be with a Christian who is greedy, or is a cheat. Stay away from Christians who worship idols, are drunkards, or nasty. Don't even eat lunch with such people.

[12]It isn't our job to judge people who are outside the church. It is our job to judge those who are members of the church. We judge them if they are sinning in these ways. [13]God alone is the Judge of those on the outside. But you must deal with this man and put him out of your church.

Christians Should Not Take Each Other to Court

6 Do any of you have a problem with another Christian? Do you "go to law" and ask a heathen court to decide the matter? Why don't you take it to other Christians to decide which of you is right? [2]Don't you know that someday we Christians are going to judge the world? So why can't you decide even these little things together? [3]Don't you know that we will judge the angels in Heaven? You should be able to decide your problems here on earth easily enough. [4]Why then go to outside judges who are not even Christians? [5]I am trying to make you ashamed. Isn't there anyone in the church who is wise enough to decide these arguments? [6]Instead, one Christian sues another Christian brother in front of people who don't believe.

[7]To do this is a defeat for you as Christians. Why not just accept the wrong and leave it at that? It would bring more honor to the Lord to let yourselves be cheated. [8]Instead, you yourselves are the ones who do wrong. You cheat others, even your own brothers.

[9-10]Don't you know that those doing such things can't share in God's Kingdom? Don't fool yourselves. If you live in sin, worship idols, are an adulterer or

homosexual you can't share his Kingdom. Neither can thieves or greedy people, drunkards, slanderers, or robbers. [11]There was a time when some of you were like this. But now your sins are washed away. You are set apart for God. He has accepted you. Why? Because of what the Lord Jesus Christ and the Spirit of God have done.

[12]I can do anything I want to if Christ has not said no. But some of these things aren't good for me. I may be allowed to do them. But I'll refuse to if I think that I can't stop when I want to. [13]For example, God has given us food and stomachs to digest it. But that doesn't mean we should eat more than we need. Don't think of eating as important. Someday God will do away with both stomachs and food.

But sexual sin is never right. Our bodies were not made for that, but for the Lord. The Lord wants to fill our bodies with himself. [14]God is going to raise our bodies from the dead by his power. He will do this just as he raised up the Lord Jesus Christ. [15]Don't you know that your bodies are actually parts and members of Christ? So should I take a part of Christ and join him to a prostitute? Never! [16]What happens if a man joins himself to a prostitute? She becomes a part of him and he becomes a part of her. God tells us in the Bible that the two become one person. [17]If you give yourself to the Lord, you join him as one person.

[18]That is why I tell you to run from sex sin. No other sin hurts the body as this one does. When you sin this sin it is against your own body. [19]Don't you know that your body is the home of the Holy Spirit? The Holy Spirit lives within you! Your own body does not belong to you. [20]God has bought you with a great price. So use your body to give glory back to God because he owns it.

Questions about Marriage

[7]Now about those questions you asked in your last letter. My answer is that if you do not marry, it is good. [2]But usually it is best to be married. Each man should have his own wife. Each woman should have her own husband. If you don't marry you might fall back into sin.

[3]The man should give his wife everything she should have. The wife should do the same for her husband. [4]A girl who marries no longer has full right to her own body. Her husband then has his rights to it, too. In the same way the husband doesn't have full right to his body either. It belongs also to his wife. [5]So do not refuse these rights to each other. The husband and wife could agree to give up these rights for a short time. Then they can give themselves more to prayer. After this, they should come together again. That way Satan won't be able to tempt them because they can't control themselves.

[6]I'm not saying you must marry. But you certainly may if you wish. [7]I wish everyone could get along without marrying, just as I do. But we are not all the same. God gives some the gift of a husband or wife. To others he gives the gift of being able to stay happily unmarried. [8]If you aren't married or are widowed, it's better to stay unmarried like me. [9]But if you can't control yourselves, go ahead and marry. It is better to marry than to burn with lust.

[10]Now, for those who are married I have a command. And it is not a command from me, it is from the Lord. A wife must not leave her husband. [11]If she has already left him, let her stay single or go back to him. And the husband must not leave his wife.

[12]Here I want to say some things. These are not commands from the Lord, but they seem right to me. A Christian might have a wife who is not a Christian. If she wants to stay with him he must not leave her. [13]A Christian woman may have a husband who isn't a Christian. If he wants her to stay with him, she must not leave him. [14]The husband who isn't a Christian may become a Christian because of his wife. And the wife who isn't a Christian may become a Christian because of her husband. If the family splits up, the children might never know the Lord. A family that stays together in God's plan will result in the children's salvation.

¹⁵If the husband or wife who isn't a Christian wants to leave, they should leave. The Christian husband or wife should not insist that the other stay. God wants his children to live in peace. ¹⁶Because how can a wife know if her husband will believe? How can a husband know if his wife will be saved?

Be Content Where God Has Placed You

¹⁷But be sure that you are living the way God wants. Accept the life God has put you into. This is my rule for all the churches.

¹⁸A man might have been circumcised before he became a Christian. If so, he shouldn't worry about it. And if he hasn't been circumcised, he shouldn't do it now. ¹⁹It doesn't matter if a Christian has done this or not. But it does matter if he is keeping God's commands. That is the important thing.

²⁰A person should do the work he was doing when God called him. ²¹Are you a slave? Don't let that worry you. If you get a chance to be free, take it. ²²If the Lord calls you as a slave, to Christ you are free. If he has called you as a free man, you are now Christ's slave. ²³You have been bought and paid for by Christ. You belong to him. Be free now from all the pride and fears found on earth. ²⁴Brothers, whatever life a person had when called, let him stay there. Now the Lord is there to help him.

Questions about Being Single

²⁵Now I will try to answer your other question. What about girls who are not yet married? I have no special command from the Lord about them. But the Lord in his kindness has given me wisdom that can be trusted. So I will be glad to tell you what I think.

²⁶We Christians are facing great dangers to our lives right now. So I think it is best for a person not to be married. ²⁷Of course, if you are married now, don't split up because of this. But if you aren't, don't rush into it at this time. ²⁸If you men decide to get married now, it is all right. If a girl gets married in times like these, it is no sin. Marriage will bring extra problems that I don't want you to face right now.

²⁹Time is very short. So those who have wives should stay free for the Lord. ³⁰Happiness or sadness or wealth should not keep anyone from doing God's work. ³¹Those who use the things the world offers should use them without enjoying them. Why? Because the world as it is now will soon be gone.

³²In all you do, I want you to be free from worry. A man who is not married can do the Lord's work and please him. ³³But a married man can't do that as well. He has to think about the things of the world. He has to please his wife. ³⁴His interests are divided. It is the same with a girl who marries. She faces the same problem. A girl who is not married wants to please the Lord. She wants him to be happy in all she is and does. But a married woman must think of the things of the world. She must please her husband.

³⁵I am saying this to help you. I am not trying to keep you from marrying. I want to help you serve the Lord best. I want to help you keep your eyes on him.

³⁶But if anyone wants to marry and control his lust, it is all right. It is not a sin for him to marry. ³⁷A man may have the power not to marry. He may decide that he doesn't need to and won't. He has made a wise decision. ³⁸The person who marries does well. The person who doesn't marry does even better.

³⁹The wife is part of her husband as long as he lives. If her husband dies, she may marry again, if she marries a Christian. ⁴⁰I think she will be happier if she doesn't marry again. I think it is from God's Spirit when I say this.

Food Offered to Idols

8Next is your question about eating food that has been offered to idols. Everyone thinks that only he has the right answer to this question! Being a "know-it-all" makes us feel important. But what is really needed to build the church is love. ²If anyone thinks he knows all the answers, he is being stupid. ³The person who loves God is the one who is open to God's knowledge.

4So now, what about it? Should we eat meat that has been offered to idols? Well, we all know that an idol is not really a god. There is only one God, and no other. 5Some people think there are many gods, both in Heaven and on earth. 6But we know that there is only one God, the Father. He created all things and made us to be his own. And there is one Lord Jesus Christ. He made everything and gives us life.

7Some Christians don't know this. All their lives they have been thinking that idols are alive. They have believed that food offered to the idols is offered to gods. When they eat such food it bothers them and hurts their tender consciences. 8Remember that God doesn't care if we eat it or not. We are no worse off if we don't eat it. We are no better off if we do. 9But be careful not to use your freedom to eat it. You might cause some Christian brother to sin whose conscience is weaker than yours.

10He may see you eating at an idol's temple. For you know there is no harm in this. Then he will become bold and eat there too. He will do this even though he still feels it is wrong. 11You know it is all right to do it. But you will hurt the brother with a tender conscience for whom Christ died. 12You will sin against your brother because he will do something he thinks is wrong. 13I don't want to make my brother sin. So I won't eat meat offered to idols as long as I live.

The Rights of an Apostle

9 I am an apostle, God's messenger. I am a free man. I have seen Jesus our Lord with my own eyes. And your changed lives are because of my hard work for him. 2If others think that I am not an apostle, I know I am to you. You have been won to Christ through me. 3This is my answer to those who question my rights.

4Or don't I have any rights at all? Can't I be like the other apostles and be a guest in your homes? 5If I had a wife couldn't I bring her with me like the other disciples do? The Lord's brothers do this and so does Peter. 6Must Barna-

bas and I work for our living while you supply these others? 7What soldier in the army has to pay his own way? What farmer harvests his crop and doesn't eat some of it? What shepherd isn't allowed to drink some of the milk of the flock? 8This is not only what men think is right. I'm telling you what God's law says. 9It says don't muzzle an ox while it is working in the wheat. Why? So it can eat some of the wheat. Do you think God only cared about oxen when he said this? 10Wasn't he also thinking about us? Of course he was! He said this to show that Christian workers should be paid by those they help. Those who plow and harvest should have a share of the crop.

11We have planted good seed in your souls. Is it too much to ask for food and clothing in return? 12You give them to others who preach to you, and you should. But shouldn't we have an even greater right to them? Yet we have never used this right. We meet our own needs without your help. We have never asked for pay of any kind. We are afraid you won't welcome our message to you from Christ.

13Don't you know about the people working in God's temple? They take some of the foods that are gifts to God. What about those who work at the altar of God? They get some of the food brought by those offering it to the Lord. 14It is the same for those who preach the Good News. The Lord has ordered that the people who believe the Good News support their leaders.

15Yet I have never asked you for one penny. I am not writing this to hint that I would like to start now. I would rather die than have someone say this is true. 16Preaching the Good News isn't any special credit to me. I couldn't keep from preaching it if I wanted to. I would be very unhappy. How terrible it would be for me if I stopped!

17I am not preaching the Good News because I want to do it. If I were, the Lord would give me a special reward. But that is not the way it is. God has picked me out and given me this holy trust. I have no choice. 18So what am I being paid? My pay is the special joy I get from preaching the Good News for free. I don't ask for what is mine.

¹⁹So I don't have to obey anyone because he pays me. Yet I've become a servant of all so I can win them to Christ. ²⁰When I'm with the Jews I'm like them so I can win them to Christ. When I'm with people who follow Jewish laws I don't agree but I don't argue. I am like them because I want to help them. ²¹When with the heathen I agree with them as much as I can. I always do what is right as a Christian. But by agreeing I can win them and help them too.

²²Sometimes I am with people whose consciences bother them easily. I don't act like I know it all. I don't say they are foolish. And because of this, they are willing to let me help them. Whatever a person is like, I try to be like him. Then he will let me tell him about Christ and let Christ save him. ²³I do this to get the Good News to them. I also have a blessing when I see them come to Christ.

²⁴In a race everyone runs, but only one person gets first prize. So run your race to win. ²⁵To win you must deny many things that keep you from doing your best. An athlete goes to all this trouble just to win a blue ribbon. But we do it for a heavenly reward that never disappears. ²⁶So I run for the goal with a plan for every step. I fight to win. I'm not just shadow-boxing or playing around. ²⁷Like an athlete, I make my body work hard. I treat it roughly. I train it to do what it should. I don't want to fail when I ask others to work hard for Jesus.

Lessons about Idol Worship

10 Brothers, remember what happened to our people in the wilderness long ago. God led them by sending a cloud that moved along ahead of them. He brought them all safely through the waters of the Red Sea. ²This might be called their "baptism." They were baptized both in sea and cloud! This showed their commitment to Moses as their leader. ³⁻⁴By a miracle God sent them food to eat and water to drink

Plowing
1 CORINTHIANS 9:10

Have you watched a farmer plow his field? How did he do it? Did he use a tractor? Or was the plow pulled by oxen? A farmer plows his fields so that seeds can be planted in the soil. A farmer today has a big tractor. The tractor has an engine. It may pull a dozen plow blades behind it. These blades are made of steel. But plowing was different in Bible times. A farmer made his own plow. Or he hired a carpenter to make one. His plow was made out of a sharp piece of wood. It was pulled by donkeys or oxen. The farmer walked behind the plow. He guided the plow as he held the handles. Would you like to plow this way? A Bible-time farmer would have been amazed to see a modern tractor and plow. But he could not have used it. There wasn't any gasoline or diesel fuel in Bible times. Plows were as important then as they are now. The hard soil had to be broken up so that seeds would grow. Crops grew from seeds. And bread was made from crops. People ate bread because farmers plowed. You eat bread because farmers plow. Let's be thankful that farmers plow their fields.

in the desert. They drank the water that Christ gave them. He was there with them as a Rock that followed them. ⁵Yet after all this most of them did not obey God. So they died in the desert.

⁶This is a warning that we must not desire evil things as they did. ⁷We shouldn't worship idols as they did. The Bible says, "The people sat down to eat and drink and then got up to dance." This happened when they worshiped the golden calf.

⁸Remember what happened when some of them sinned with other men's wives. In just one day, 23,000 fell dead! ⁹And don't tempt the Lord. They did and died from snake bites. ¹⁰Don't murmur against God as some of them did. That is why God sent his Angel to destroy them.

¹¹All these things happened to them as examples to us. They warn us not to do the same things. They were written so we could learn from them as the world nears its end.

¹²So be careful. You may be thinking, "Oh, I would never behave like that." But let this be a warning to you. You, too, may fall into sin. ¹³Remember, the wrong desires in your life aren't anything new. Many others have faced the same problems before you. You can trust God. He won't let you be carried away by sin. He will show you how to escape. You will survive the test.

Don't do anything that might make someone else sin

Don't cause anyone else to sin.
1 Corinthians 10:32

---

¹⁴So, dear friends, stay away from idol worship of every kind.

¹⁵You are smart people. Look now and see if what I am about to say is true. ¹⁶We ask the Lord's blessing on the cup of wine at the Lord's Table. This means that all who drink it are sharing the blessing of Christ's blood. And when we eat the bread it shows that we are sharing his body. ¹⁷It doesn't matter how many of us there are. We all eat from the same loaf of bread. This shows that we are all parts of the one body of Christ. ¹⁸All the

Jewish people eat the offerings. They are united by that act.

¹⁹What am I trying to say? Are the idols real gods? Are their offerings of some value? No, not at all! ²⁰But those who offer to these idols are united in offering to demons. I don't want you to be partners with demons by eating their food. ²¹You cannot drink the cup at the Lord's Table and at Satan's table, too. You can't eat bread both at the Lord's Table and at Satan's table.

²²What? Are you tempting the Lord to be angry with you? Are you stronger than he is?

When Deciding What Is Best, Think of Others

²³You are free to eat food offered to idols if you want to. It's not against God's laws to eat such meat. But that doesn't mean that you should go ahead and do it. It may be legal, but it may not be best and helpful. ²⁴Don't think only of yourself. Try to do what is best for others.

²⁵Take any meat you want that is sold at the market. Don't ask if it was offered to idols. The answer might hurt your conscience. ²⁶The earth and everything in it belongs to the Lord. They are yours to enjoy.

²⁷If someone who isn't a Christian asks you out to dinner, go ahead. Eat what is on the table and don't ask any questions about it. Then you won't know if it has been used as an offering to idols. That way you won't risk having a bad conscience over eating it. ²⁸Someone may warn you that this meat has been offered to idols. If so, don't eat it for the sake of the man who told you. You should take care of his conscience. ²⁹His feeling about it is the important thing, not yours.

You may ask, why should I be limited by what someone else thinks? ³⁰I can thank God for the food and enjoy it. Why should I let someone spoil everything because he thinks I am wrong? ³¹Well, I'll tell you why. Because you must do everything for God's glory, even your eating and drinking. ³²So don't cause anyone else to sin. It doesn't matter if they are Jews or Gentiles or Christians. [33]That is the plan I follow, too. I try to please everyone in everything I do. I don't do what I like or what is best for me. I do what is best for them, so that they may be saved.

11 You should follow my example, just as I follow Christ's.

Worship God with Honor and Respect

[2] I am glad, brothers, that you remember and do everything I taught you. [3]But I want to remind you that a wife follows her husband. Her husband follows Christ, and Christ follows God. [4]So, if a man won't remove his hat while praying, he doesn't honor Christ. [5]And if a woman prays without covering her head, she doesn't honor her husband. Her covering is a sign that she follows him. [6]If she won't wear a head covering she should cut off all her hair. You may think it's a shame for a woman to have her head shaved. If you think this, then she should wear a covering. [7]But a man should not wear anything on his head. His hat is a sign he follows men.

God's glory is man made in his image. A man's glory is the woman. [8]The first man didn't come from woman, but the first woman came out of man. [9]Adam, the first man, was not made for Eve. She was made for Adam. [10]So a woman should wear a covering on her head. It is a sign that she follows a man's leading. This is a fact for all the angels to see and rejoice in.

[11]But remember that in God's plan men and women need each other. [12]The first woman came out of man. All men have been born from women ever since. Both men and women came from God their Creator.

[13]What do you really think about this? Is it right for a woman to pray in public without covering her head? [14-15]Doesn't nature teach us that women's heads should be covered? Women are proud of their long hair. A man with long hair tends to be ashamed. [16]Someone may want to argue about this. Tell him that we never teach anything but this. All the churches feel the same way about it.

The Right Way to Have Communion

[17]There is something else I cannot agree with. More harm than good is done when you meet together for your communion services. [18]I have heard about the arguing that goes on in these meetings. I know there are splits among you. I believe these reports to a certain extent. [19]There should be some differences so that the people who are right will be known.

[20]When you come together to eat, it isn't the Lord's Supper you are eating. [21]You are eating your own supper. For I am told that each one gobbles all the food he can. You don't wait to share with the others. So one doesn't get enough while another has too much and gets drunk. [22]What? Is this really true? Can't you do your eating and drinking at home? Do you hate God's church and the poor who have no food? What am I supposed to say about these things? Do you want me to praise you? Well, I do not!

[23]I have told you what the Lord told me about his Table. It was on the night when Judas betrayed him. The Lord Jesus took bread. [24]When he had given thanks, he broke it and gave it to his disciples. He said, "Take this and eat it. This is my body, which is given for you. Do this to remember me." [25]In the same way, he took the cup of wine after supper. He said, "This cup is the new promise God has given you. He will keep his promise because I shed my blood. Do this to remember me when you drink it." [26]Every time you eat this bread and drink this cup you show the Lord's death. Do this until he comes again.

[27]Some of you may eat this bread and drink from this cup in the wrong way. But such people are sinning against the body and blood of the Lord. [28]So a man should think carefully before eating the bread and drinking from the cup. [29]If he doesn't, he is eating and drinking God's judgment upon himself. Why? He doesn't think about the body of Christ and what it means. [30]That is why many of you are weak and sick. Some of you have even died.

³¹If you are careful before eating you will not be judged and punished. ³²Why are we judged and punished by the Lord? It is so that we will not be punished with the rest of the world. ³³So brothers, when you gather for the Lord's Supper, wait for each other. ³⁴If anyone is really hungry he should eat at home. That way he won't be punished when you meet together.

I'll talk to you about the other matters after I come to you.

Everyone Has Special Abilities

12 Now, brothers, about the special gifts the Holy Spirit gives you. I want you to understand them. ²Remember before you became Christians? You went around from one idol to another. Not one of them could speak a single word. ³Now you are meeting people who claim to speak from God's Spirit. How can you know they are from God or if they are fakes? No one speaking in God's Spirit can curse Jesus. No one can say "Jesus is Lord" unless the Holy Spirit is helping him.

⁴God gives us many kinds of special gifts. It is the same Holy Spirit who is the source of them all. ⁵There are different kinds of service to God. But it is the same Lord we are serving. ⁶There are many ways in which God works in our lives. But it is the same God who works in all of us. ⁷The Holy Spirit shows God's power through each of us. It is a way of helping the whole church.

⁸To one person the Spirit gives the ability to give wise advice. Someone else may be good at studying and teaching. This is his gift from the same Spirit. ⁹He gives special faith to another. To someone else he gives the power to heal the sick. ¹⁰He gives power for doing miracles to some. To others he gives power to prophesy and preach. Another knows if a spirit is of God or not. Another person is able to speak in languages he never learned. Others are given power to understand what he is saying. ¹¹It is the same Spirit who gives all these gifts and powers. The Spirit decides which each one of us should have.

Many Parts But One Body

¹²Our bodies have many parts. Those many parts make up only one body when they are all put together. It is the same with the "body" of Christ. ¹³Each of us is a part of the one body of Christ. Some of us are Jews, some are Gentiles. Some are slaves, and some are free. But the Holy Spirit has fitted us all together into one body. We have been baptized into Christ's body by the one Spirit. We have all been given that same Holy Spirit.

¹⁴Yes, the body has many parts, not just one part. ¹⁵The foot may say, "I am not part of the body. I am not a hand." That does not make it any less a part of the body. ¹⁶An ear might say, "I am not part of the body. I am only an ear and not an eye." Would that make it any less a part of the body? ¹⁷Suppose the whole body were an eye? How would you hear? Or if your whole body were one big ear, how could you smell?

¹⁸But that isn't the way God has made us. He has made many parts for our bodies. He has put each part just where he wants it. ¹⁹What a strange thing a body would be if it had only one part! ²⁰So he has made many parts, but still there is only one body.

²¹The eye can never say to the hand, "I don't need you." The head can't say to the feet, "I don't need you."

²²The parts that seem weakest and least important are needed the most. ²³Yes, we are glad to have some parts that seem odd! We cover those parts that should not be seen. ²⁴Of course, the parts that may be seen do not need this special care. God has put the body together. He has given honor and care to those parts that might seem less needed. ²⁵This makes for happiness among the parts. All the parts have the same care for each other that they do for themselves. ²⁶If one part suffers, all parts suffer with it. If one part is honored, all the parts are glad.

²⁷All of you together are the one body of Christ. Each one of you is a separate and needed part of it. ²⁸He has placed some of these parts in his Church:

Apostles,
Prophets—those who preach God's
　　Word,
Teachers,
Those who do miracles,
Those who have the gift of healing,
Those who can help others,
Those who can get others to work
　　together,
Those who speak in languages they
　　have never learned.

²⁹Is everyone an apostle? Of course not! Is everyone a preacher? No! Are all teachers? Does everyone have the power to do miracles? ³⁰Can everyone heal the sick? Of course not! Are all of us able to speak in languages we've never learned? Can anyone know what those are saying who have that gift of foreign speech? ³¹No, but try your best to have the more important of these gifts.

Now, let me tell you about something that is better than any of them!

What Is Love?

13I may be able to speak in every language in Heaven and earth. But if I didn't love others, I would only be making noise. ²I may have prophecy. I may know everything about *everything*. But if I didn't love others, what good would it do? I may have so much faith I could move mountains. I would still be worth nothing at all without love. ³I could give everything I have to poor people. I could be burned alive for preaching the Good News. But if I didn't love others, it would be of no value.

⁴Love is very patient and kind. It is never jealous or envious. It never boasts or is proud. ⁵It is never haughty or selfish or rude. Love does not demand its own way. It is not angry. It does not hold grudges. It will hardly notice when others do it wrong. ⁶It is never glad about things that are wrong. It is happy when truth wins out. ⁷If you love someone, you will be loyal to him no matter what the cost. You will always believe in him. You will always expect the best of him. You will always stand your ground and defend him.

⁸All the gifts and powers from God will someday come to an end. But love

goes on forever. Someday prophecy, speaking in different languages, and special knowledge will end. ⁹Now we know so little, even with our special gifts. The preaching of those most gifted is still so poor. ¹⁰But when we have been made perfect, these gifts will disappear.

Be loyal to the people you love

*If you love someone,
you will be loyal to him
no matter what the cost.*

1 Corinthians 13:7

---

¹¹When I was a child I thought like a child does. When I became a man I put away the childish things. ¹²We can see and understand only a little about God now. It is like we were looking at his reflection in a poor mirror. Someday we are going to see him face to face. Now all that I know is hazy and blurred. But then I will see everything clearly. I will see as clearly as God sees into my heart right now.

¹³Three things remain: faith, hope, and love. The greatest of these is love.

The Gifts of Prophecy and Speaking in Tongues

14Let love be your goal. Ask also for the gifts the Holy Spirit gives. Ask especially for the gift of prophecy.

²Is your gift to speak in different languages? If so, you will be talking to God, not to others. They won't be able to understand you. You will be speaking by the Spirit's power. It will all be a secret. ³But one who preaches the messages of God is helping others grow in the Lord. ⁴So a person "speaking in tongues" helps himself grow. But one who preaches messages from God helps all the church grow.

⁵I wish you all had the gift of "speaking in tongues." Even more I wish you were all able to prophesy, preaching God's messages. That is greater than speaking in different languages. You should be able to tell everyone what you were saying. Then they can get some good out of it, too.

⁶Dear friends, what if I came to you

talking in some language you don't understand. How would that help you? I should speak what God has shown me. I should tell you the things I know and what is going to happen. I should teach the great truths of God's Word. That is what you need. That is what will help you. 7The flute or the harp are good examples. They show the need for speaking in plain, simple language. No one will know the tune unless each note is sounded clearly. 8What if the army bugler doesn't play the right notes? How will the soldiers know they are being called to battle? 9What if you talk to someone in some language he doesn't understand? How will he know what you mean? You might as well be talking to an empty room.

10I suppose that there are hundreds of different languages in the world. All of them are good for those who understand them. 11But to me they mean nothing. A person talking in one of these languages will be a stranger to me. I will be a stranger to him, too. 12You want so badly to have special gifts from the Holy Spirit. Ask him for the very best. Ask for those that will be of real help to the whole church.

13Someone may have the gift of speaking in unknown tongues. He should pray also for the gift of knowing what he has said. Then he can tell people afterwards plainly. 14If I pray in a language I don't understand, my spirit is praying. But I don't know what I am saying.

15Well, then, what shall I do? I will do both. I will pray with my spirit and my mind at the same time. I will sing with my spirit and with my mind, too. Then everyone will be able to understand me. 16What if you praise and thank God with the spirit alone, using another language? How can those who don't understand you praise God with you? How can they join you when they don't know what you are saying? 17You will be giving thanks very nicely, no doubt. But the other people present won't be helped.

18I thank God that I "speak in tongues" privately more than any of you. 19But in public worship I would much rather speak five words with my mind. That way people will be able to understand and be helped. This is better than 10,000 words in a different language.

20Brothers, don't be childish when you understand these things. Be innocent babies when it comes to planning evil. But be men to understand these things. 21The Bible says that God would send men to speak in different languages. But even then his people wouldn't listen. 22So "speaking in tongues" is not a sign to God's children. It is a sign to the people who are not saved. But prophecy is what the Christians need. People who don't believe aren't yet ready for it. 23However, what if an unsaved person comes to church and hears you talking in other languages? He will think you are crazy. 24But what will happen if you prophesy instead? If an unsaved person comes in he will know he is a sinner. His conscience will be pricked by all he hears. 25As he listens, his secret thoughts will be laid bare. He will fall down on his knees and worship God. He will say that God is really there among you.

Worship in an Orderly Way

26 Well, my brothers, let's add up what I am saying. When you meet together some will sing. Another will teach, or tell you something about God. Someone may speak in a different language. Someone else will explain that language. Everything that is done must be useful to all. It should build them up in the Lord. 27No more than two or three should speak in a different language. They must speak one at a time. Someone must be ready to explain what they are saying. 28But if no one can explain, they must not speak out loud. They must talk silently to themselves and to God in the different language.

29-30Two or three may prophesy, one at a time, while all the others listen. Someone listening may be given a message or idea from the Lord. Then the one who is speaking should stop. 31This way all who have the gift of prophecy can speak, one after the other. Everyone will learn and be encouraged and helped. ³²Remember, a person who has a message from God has the power to stop himself. He can wait his turn. ³³God doesn't like things to be mixed-up. He likes harmony, and he finds it in all the other churches.

³⁴Women should be silent during the church meetings. They are not to speak. They should follow the men like the Bible says. ³⁵If they have any questions they should ask their husbands at home. It is not right for women to speak in church meetings.

³⁶You disagree? Do you think that the knowledge of God begins and ends with you? Well, you are wrong! ³⁷You claim to have the gift of prophecy and can follow God's Spirit. You should know that what I am saying is from the Lord. ³⁸If anyone still disagrees, then you should ignore him.

³⁹So, brothers, wish to be prophets. Then you can preach God's message plainly. Never say it is wrong to "speak in tongues." ⁴⁰But be sure that everything is done in a good and orderly way.

Christ Rose from the Dead

15 Let me remind you, brothers, about what the Good News really is. It has not changed. It is the same Good News I preached to you before. You welcomed it then and still do now. Your faith is built upon this message. ²It is this Good News that saves you if you still firmly believe it. But it won't save you if you never believed it in the first place.

³I passed on to you from the first what had been told to me. Christ died for our sins just as the Bible said he would. ⁴He was buried, and three days later he rose from the grave. This happened just as the prophets said it would. ⁵He was seen by Peter. Later he was seen by the rest of the Twelve. ⁶After that, more than 500 Christian brothers saw him at one time. Most of them are still alive, though some have died by now. ⁷Then James saw him, and later all the apostles. ⁸Last of all I saw him too, long after the others. It was as though I had been born almost too late for this. ⁹For I am the least worthy of all

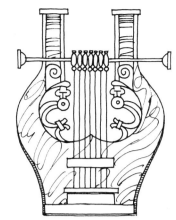

Musical Instruments

1 CORINTHIANS 14:7

Do you play a musical instrument? Which one? Do you take lessons? Perhaps you play in the school orchestra or band. Do you play your instrument at church? There were many musical instruments in Bible times. How many of them do you know? Have you seen a sackbut, a psaltery, or a timbrel? What about a dulcimer or a taboret? You would recognize a harp or a flute. A lyre was a type of harp. You would also know a trumpet or drums. Musical instruments were wind, string, or percussion instruments just like they are today. People blew on them, plucked their strings, or beat on them. In 1 Corinthians 14:7, Paul compares music to saying things clearly. Unless notes are played well, we don't hear the right music. Unless we speak the Gospel clearly, people can't hear what we are saying. When we tell others about Jesus, let's make sure they clearly understand what we are saying.

the apostles. I shouldn't be called an apostle after the way I treated the church of God.

¹⁰But what I am is all because of God's kindness and grace upon me. This was not for nothing. I have worked harder than all the other apostles. Yet I wasn't

doing it. It was God working in me to bless me. [11]It doesn't matter who worked the hardest. It is most important that we preached the Good News to you and you believed.

We Will Come Alive Again

[12] But tell me this! We preach that *Christ* rose from the dead. So why are some of you saying that dead people never come back to life? [13]If there is no resurrection of the dead, then Christ must still be dead. [14]If he is still dead, then all our preaching is useless. Your trust in God is empty, worthless, and hopeless. [15]This means that we apostles are all liars. Why? Because we have said that God raised Christ from the grave. Of course that isn't true if the dead don't come back to life again. [16]If they don't, then Christ is still dead. [17]If they don't, you are foolish to trust God to save you. It means your sins are not forgiven. [18]So all Christians who have died are lost! [19]We should hope for more from Christ than just things in this life. If we don't, we are sad and poor. The rest of the world should pity us.

Jesus will give us new bodies someday

The bodies we have on earth will die and become dust. When Jesus gives us new life, our bodies will be different. They will never die.

1 Corinthians 15:42

---

[20]The fact is that Christ did rise from the dead. He has become the first of millions who will come back to life.

[21]Death came into the world because of what Adam did. It is because of what Christ has done that there is the resurrection from the dead. [22]Everyone dies because all of us are related to Adam. But all who are related to Christ will rise again. [23]Each takes his own turn. Christ rose first. And when Christ comes back, all his people will live again.

[24]After that the end will come. He will turn the Kingdom over to God the Father. This will happen after he has put down all enemies of every kind. [25]Christ will be King until he has defeated all his enemies. [26]The last enemy is death. This, too, must be defeated and ended. [27]For the rule over all things has been given to Christ by his Father. Of course, Christ does not rule over the Father himself. The Father gave him this power to rule. [28]God put everything under Christ. And when everything is under Christ then Christ himself will be under God. This will happen so that God will be everything to everybody.

[29]What is the point of people being baptized for those who are dead? Why do it unless you believe that the dead will someday rise again?

[30]Why do we face death hour by hour? [31]It is a fact that I face death everyday. This is as true as my pride in your growth in the Lord. [32]What value was there in fighting wild beasts—those men of Ephesus? Was it only for what I gain in this life down here? Some of you say we will never live again after we die. If this is true, then we might as well go and have a good time. Let's eat, drink, and be merry. What's the difference? For tomorrow we die, and that ends it all!

[33]Don't be fooled by those who say such things. If you listen to them you will start acting like them. [34]Get some sense and quit your sinning. To your shame I say that some of you are not Christians at all. You have never really known God.

What Will We Look Like after the Resurrection?

[35]Someone may ask, "How will the dead be brought back to life again? What kind of bodies will they have?" [36]What a silly question! You will find the answer in your own garden! When you plant a seed it doesn't grow unless it "dies" first. [37]The plant that grows is very different from the seed you first planted. You put a dry little seed into the ground. [38]When it grows, God gives it a beautiful new body. A different kind of plant grows from each kind of seed. [39]There are different kinds of seeds and plants. So there are different kinds of flesh, too. Hu-

mans, animals, fish, and birds are all different.

⁴⁰The angels in Heaven have bodies far different from ours. The glory of their bodies is different from the glory of ours. ⁴¹The sun has one kind of glory, the moon and stars have another kind. And the stars differ from each other in their beauty.

Give God part of what you earn each week

On the Lord's Day each week, give part of what you have earned to the Lord.

1 Corinthians 16:2

---

⁴²The bodies we have on earth will die and become dust. When Jesus gives us new life, our bodies will be different. They will never die. ⁴³The bodies we have now shame us. They become sick and die. But they will be full of glory when we come back to life again. Yes, they are weak, dying bodies now. But when we live again they will be strong. ⁴⁴They are just human bodies at death. But when they come back to life they will be superhuman bodies. There are natural, human bodies. There are also spiritual bodies.

⁴⁵That is why the Bible says, "The first man was named Adam. He was made a living person." So the last Adam, Christ, became a Spirit who gives us eternal life.

⁴⁶First, we have these human bodies. Later on, God gives us spiritual bodies. ⁴⁷Adam was made from the dust of the earth, but Christ came from Heaven. ⁴⁸Every human being has a body just like Adam's, made of dust. But all who become Christ's will have the same kind of body as his. It is a body from Heaven. ⁴⁹Each of us now has a body like Adam's. In the same way, each shall some day have a body like Christ's.

⁵⁰Brothers, an earthly body made of flesh and blood cannot get into God's Kingdom. These bodies of ours will rot. They are not the right kind to live forever.

⁵¹But I am telling you a secret. We will not all die, but we shall all be given new bodies! ⁵²It will all happen in a moment, in the twinkling of an eye. It will happen when the last trumpet is blown. There will be a trumpet blast. Then all the Christians who have died will suddenly become alive. We will have new bodies that will never, never die. Then we who are still alive shall have new bodies, too. ⁵³For our bodies that can die must be changed. They will become heavenly bodies that cannot die but will live forever.

⁵⁴When this happens, the words of the Bible will come true. They say, "Death is swallowed up in victory." ⁵⁵⁻⁵⁶O death, where then your victory? Where then is your sting? For sin is the sting that causes death. The law shows us our sin. ⁵⁷How we thank God for all of this! He makes us the winners because of Jesus Christ our Lord!

⁵⁸So brothers, future victory is sure! Be strong and steady. Overflow with the Lord's work. You know that nothing you do for the Lord is ever wasted.

Directions for Giving an Offering

16 I have told the churches in Galatia about collecting money for the brothers and sisters. Now I will tell you the same thing. ²On the Lord's Day each week, give part of what you have earned to the Lord. The amount depends on how much the Lord has helped you earn. Don't wait until I get there to collect it all at once. ³When I come I will send your loving gift with a letter to Jerusalem. It should be taken there by messengers you will choose. ⁴If it seems wise for me to go along, then we can travel together.

Paul's Travel Plans

⁵I am coming to visit you after I have been to Macedonia first. But I will be staying there only for a little while. ⁶It could be that I will stay longer with you, perhaps all winter. Then you can send me on to where I plan to go. ⁷I don't want to make just a passing visit and then go right on. I want to come and stay awhile, if the Lord will let me. ⁸I will be staying here at Ephesus until the holiday of Pentecost. ⁹There is a wide open

door for me to preach and teach here. But there are many enemies, too.

[10]If Timothy comes, make him feel at home. He is doing the Lord's work just as I am. [11]Don't let anyone hate or ignore him because he is young. Send him back to me happy with his time among you. I am waiting to see him and the other brothers.

[12]I begged Apollos to visit you along with the others. He thought that it was not God's will for him to go now. He will be seeing you later on when he has a chance.

Paul's Final Instructions

[13]Be careful. Stand true to the Lord. Act like men. Be strong. [14]Do everything with kindness and love.

[15]Do you remember Stephanas and his family? They were the first to become Christians in Greece. They are spending their lives helping and serving Christians everywhere. [16]Please do what they ask. Do everything you can to help them. Help others like them who work hard at your side. [17]I am glad that Stephanas, Fortunatus, and Achaicus have come here. They have been making up for the help you aren't here to give me. [18]They have cheered me greatly. I am sure they were helpful to you, too. I hope you know how special they are.

[19]The churches here in Asia greet you. Aquila and Priscilla send you their love. The others who meet in their home greet you, too. [20]All the friends here asked me to say hello to you for them. Give each other a loving handshake when you meet.

[21]I will write these final words of this letter with my own hand. [22]If anyone does not love the Lord, that person is cursed. Lord Jesus, come! [23]May the love and favor of the Lord Jesus Christ rest upon you. [24]I give my love to all of you. For we all belong to Christ Jesus.

Sincerely, Paul

SECOND CORINTHIANS

This is the second letter Paul wrote to the church at Corinth. He probably wrote it the same year as his first letter. The church was having some problems. They were living like their non-Christian neighbors. Living this way was tearing the church apart. Paul wrote about the way Christians should live. He said that they should be honest about their problems. They should share what they have with others. They should stay away from false teachers. They should serve others. And he said that they should be more like Christ. This is good advice for us today, isn't it?

Paul: A Messenger of God

1 Dear friends: This letter is from Paul. I was chosen by God to be Jesus Christ's messenger. It is from our dear brother Timothy, too. We are writing to you Christians in Corinth and all around Greece. ²May God our Father and the Lord Jesus Christ bless you and give you peace.

God Comforts Us All

³⁻⁴What a wonderful God we have! He is the Father of our Lord Jesus Christ, the source of every mercy. He comforts us in our troubles. Why does he do this? So when others are troubled we can give them the comfort God has given us. ⁵The more we suffer for Christ, the more he will comfort us. ⁶⁻⁷We are in deep trouble for bringing you God's comfort and salvation. But in our trouble God has showered us with comfort. He does this so we can help you. We can show you how God will comfort you when you suffer. He will give you the power to stick with it.

⁸I want you to know, brothers, about the hard time we had in Asia. We were really crushed and beaten. We feared we would never live through it. ⁹We felt we were doomed to die. We saw that we didn't have the power to help ourselves. But that was good. For then we put it all into the hands of God. Only he could save us. He can even raise the dead. ¹⁰And he did help us and save us from a terrible death. We expect him to do it again and again. ¹¹But you must help us too by praying for us. Thanks and praise will go to God from you. Why? Because you see his wonderful answers to your prayers for our safety!

Paul Changes His Plans

¹²We are so glad that we can say that we have been pure and sincere. We depend on the Lord for his help and not on our own skills. This is even more true about the way we have acted toward you. ¹³⁻¹⁴My letters have been honest. Nothing is written between the lines! Even though you don't know me very well I hope someday you will. I want you to be proud of me. You already are to some

extent. And I will be proud of you on the day when our Lord Jesus comes back. [15-16]I was so sure of this that I planned to visit you twice. First, I planned to stop on the way to Macedonia. And second, I planned to see you again when I came back through. That way I could be a double blessing to you. Then you could send me on my way to Judea.

[17]Then why, you may be asking, did I change my plan? Hadn't I made up my mind yet? Or am I like a man of the world? Do I say yes when I really mean no? [18]Never! As sure as God is true, I am not that sort of person. My yes means yes.

[19]Timothy and Silvanus and I have told you about Jesus Christ the Son of God. He isn't one to say yes when he means no. He always does exactly what he says. [20]He carries out all of God's promises. It doesn't matter how many of them there are. So we say "Amen" to God, giving glory to his name. [21]God has anchored both you and us in Christ. He has poured the Holy Spirit on us like oil. He called us apostles to preach the Good News. [22]He has put his brand upon us. It is a mark that shows he owns us. He has given us his Holy Spirit in our hearts. This proves that we belong to him. It is the first taste of all that he is going to give us.

To be more like God, we should let God work in us more

We reflect the wonderful things of the Lord. As God works in us, we become more like him.

2 Corinthians 3:18

---

[23]God will speak against me if I am not telling the truth. Why haven't I come to visit you yet? Because I don't want to sadden you with a rebuke. [24]I can't do much to help your faith. It is strong already. I want to be able to do something about your joy. I want to make you happy, not sad.

2 "No," I said to myself, "I won't do it. I'll not make them sad during my next visit." [2]For if I make you sad, who is going to make me happy? You are the ones to do it. How can you if I cause you pain? [3]That is why I wrote my last letter to you. I want you to get things right before I come. When I do come, the people who should give me joy won't make me sad. I am sure that your joy is the same as mine.

[4]Oh, how I hated to write that strong letter! It almost broke my heart. I tell you honestly that I cried over it. I didn't want to hurt you. I had to show you how very much I love you.

Forgive and Accept the Sorry Sinner

[5-6]Remember the man I wrote about who caused all the trouble? He has not made me as sad as he has made you. I have my share of sadness, though. I don't want to be harder on him than I should. He has been punished by you all. That is enough. [7]Now it is time to forgive him and comfort him. Otherwise he may become so bitter that his heart won't heal. [8]Please show him now that you still do love him very much.

[9]I wrote you as I did to find out if you would obey me. [10]When you forgive anyone, I do too. When I forgive, if I forgive anything, it is because Christ has forgiven. I do it for your good. [11]Another reason to forgive is to keep from being tricked by Satan. We know what he is trying to do.

[12]I traveled as far as the city of Troas. It was like the Lord opened the door for me to preach the Good News there. [13]But Titus, my brother, wasn't there to meet me. So I couldn't rest. I wondered where he was and what had happened to him. So I said good-bye and went to Macedonia to try to find him.

Be Like a Sweet Perfume

[14]But thanks be to God because of what Christ has done! He is the winner over us. Now, wherever we go he uses us to tell others about the Lord. We spread the Good News like a sweet perfume. [15]God is a sweet smell in our lives. It is the scent of Christ within us. It is an aroma to both the saved and the unsaved all around us. [16]Those who are not being saved smell death and doom. But to those who know Christ we are a life-giving perfume. But who can do such a

task as this? [17]Only those who, like ourselves, are honest men, sent by God. We are speaking with Christ's power, with God's eye upon us. We are not like those men. Their idea in spreading the Good News is to get rich from it.

Our Success Comes from God

3 Are we starting to be like those false teachers of yours? They must tell you all about themselves. They bring long letters to introduce themselves. I don't think you need a letter to tell you about us, do you? And we don't need a letter from you, either! [2]The only letter I need is you yourselves! Look at the good change in your hearts. Everyone can see that we have done a good work among you. [3]They can see that you are a letter from Christ, written by us. It is not a letter written with pen and ink. It was written by the Spirit of the living God. It was not carved on stone, but in human hearts.

[4]Why do we dare to say these good things about ourselves? Only because of our great trust in God through Christ. He will help us be true to what we say. [5]This is not because we think we can do anything by ourselves. Our only power and success comes from God. [6]He has helped us tell others about his new agreement to save them. We don't tell them to obey every law of God or die. We tell them there is life for them from the Holy Spirit. The old way is trying to be saved by keeping the Ten Commandments. But this way ends in death. In the new way, the Holy Spirit gives them life.

A New Plan for Our Salvation

[7] Yet that old way of law that led to death began with such glory. People could not bear to look at Moses' face. He gave them God's law to obey. When he did this his face shone out with the very glory of God. The glory was already fading away. [8]Shall we not expect greater glory when the Holy Spirit is giving life? [9]The plan that leads to doom was glorious. The plan that makes men right with God is much greater. [10]The glory that shone from Moses' face is worth nothing at all. It can't compare with the overflowing

glory of the new agreement. [11]The old way that faded into nothing was full of the glory of Heaven. But the glory of God's new plan is far greater. It is eternal.

[12]We know that this new glory will never fade away. So we can preach with great boldness. [13]We don't preach like Moses did. He put a veil over his face. That way Israel could not see the glory fade away.

[14]So Moses' face was veiled. But his people's minds were veiled and blinded, too. Now, when the Bible is read the Jewish hearts are covered by a veil. They can't see and understand the real meaning of the Bible. This veil can be taken away only by believing in Christ. [15]Today, when they read Moses' writings, their hearts are blind. They think that obeying the Ten Commandments is the way to be saved.

Tell people the truth about Jesus

We do not try to trick people into believing in Jesus. We do not teach what the Bible doesn't teach. We tell the truth.

2 Corinthians 4:2

[16]But when anyone turns to the Lord from sins, the veil is taken away. [17]The Lord is the Spirit who gives them life. Where the Spirit is there is freedom from keeping the Jewish laws. [18]We Christians have no veil over our faces. We reflect the wonderful things of the Lord. As God works in us, we become more like him.

Satan Blinds, but God Gives Light

4 God, in his mercy, has given us this work of telling his Good News. So we never give up. [2]We do not try to trick people into believing in Jesus. We are not interested in fooling anyone. We do not teach what the Bible doesn't teach. We have given up the hidden things of shame. We stand in front of God as we speak, so we tell the truth. Everybody who knows us will agree that this is true.

[3]The Good News we preach may be hidden to some people. They are the ones who are on the road to eternal

death. ⁴Satan is the god of this evil world. He has made them blind. So they can't see the light of the Good News that is shining upon them. They can't know the message we preach about the glory of Christ, who is God. ⁵We don't preach about ourselves but about Christ Jesus as Lord. We say that we are your slaves because of what Jesus has done. ⁶God said, "Let there be light in the darkness." He has made us know what that light is. It is the glory that is seen in the face of Jesus Christ.

⁷This is a rich treasure. But it is held in jars that can break, our weak bodies. Everyone can see that this power in us is from God. It is not our own.

⁸We are pressed on every side by troubles, but not crushed and broken. We don't know why things happen as they do. But we don't give up and quit. ⁹We are hunted down, but God never leaves us. We get knocked down, but we get up again and keep going. ¹⁰These bodies of ours are always facing death just as Jesus did. So all can see that it is the living Christ within who keeps us safe.

We become new people when we accept Jesus as our Savior

When someone becomes a Christian, he becomes a brand new person inside. He is not the same anymore. A new life has begun!

2 Corinthians 5:17

---

¹¹Yes, we are always in danger because we serve the Lord. But this always shows the power of Jesus Christ in our dying bodies. ¹²Because of our preaching we face death. But this brings eternal life to you. ¹³We say what we believe because we trust. Like the Psalm writer said, "I believe, so I speak." ¹⁴God brought the Lord Jesus back from death. We know that he will also bring us back to life again with Jesus. He will present us to him along with you. ¹⁵These sufferings of ours are for you. When more are won to Christ, then more can thank him for his kindness. And then, the Lord is given even more glory.

¹⁶That is why we never give up. Our bodies are dying, but we are growing strong in the Lord every day. ¹⁷These troubles are quite small and won't last very long. This short time of trouble will bring God's richest blessing upon us forever! ¹⁸So we don't look at the troubles we can see right now. We look forward to the joys in Heaven which we have not yet seen. The troubles will soon be over, but the joys to come will last forever.

We Will Have New Bodies in Heaven

5 When we die and leave these bodies, this tent we live in now is taken down. Then we will have wonderful new bodies in Heaven. They are homes that will be ours forever. They are made for us by God himself and not by human hands. ²How tired we grow of our present bodies. That is why we look forward to the day when we will have bodies from Heaven. We will put them on like new clothes. ³For we shall not be spirits without bodies. ⁴These earthly bodies make us groan and sigh. But we wouldn't like to die and have no bodies at all. We want to slip into our new bodies. Then these dying bodies will be swallowed up by eternal life. ⁵This is what God has prepared for us. To prove it, he has given us his Holy Spirit.

⁶Now we bravely look forward to our heavenly bodies. We know that when we are in our bodies we are away from the Lord. ⁷We know this is true because we believe. It doesn't matter what we see around us. ⁸We are not afraid. We are willing to die. And then we will be at home with the Lord. ⁹So we want to always make him happy. It doesn't matter if we are in this body or with him in Heaven. ¹⁰For we must all stand before Christ to be judged. We will have our lives laid bare before him. Each of us will be paid for what he has done in his body. They may be good things or they may be bad.

We Are God's Ambassadors

¹¹We fear the Lord. So we work hard to win others. God knows that our hearts

are pure in this matter. I hope that, deep within, you really know it too.

¹²Are we trying to pat ourselves on the back again? No! Those preachers of yours brag about how they look but don't have honest hearts. You can tell them that we, at least, are honest.

¹³⁻¹⁴Are we crazy to say such things about ourselves? If so, it is to bring glory to God. And if we are in our right minds, it is for you. The things we do are not for ourselves. Christ's love controls us now. We believe that Christ died for all of us. We should also believe we have died to the life we used to live. ¹⁵He died for all so that all who live should not live for themselves. They should spend their lives pleasing Christ who died and rose again for them. ¹⁶So don't think of Christians the way the world thinks about them. Don't look at what they seem to be like on the outside. Once I thought of Christ that way. I thought he was a human being like myself. But I feel different now! ¹⁷When someone becomes a Christian, he becomes a brand new person inside. He is not the same anymore. A new life has begun!

¹⁸All these new things are from God. He brought us back to himself because of what Christ Jesus did. And God has given us the work of making everyone his friend. ¹⁹God was in Christ, bringing the world back to himself. He didn't count men's sins against them anymore. Instead, he washed away all their sins. This is the message he has given us to tell others. ²⁰We are Christ's agents. God is using us to speak to you. We beg you as if Christ himself were here begging you. Take the love he offers you and be friends with God. ²¹For God took the sinless Christ and poured into him our sins. Then, he poured God's goodness into us!

6 We are God's partners. We beg you not to throw away this message of God's great kindness. ²For God says, "Your cry came to me at a good time. The doors of welcome were wide open. I helped you on a day when salvation was being offered." Right now God is ready to welcome you. Today he is ready to save you.

³We don't want to do anything that will keep people from finding the Lord. No one can find fault with us and blame it on the Lord. ⁴In fact, everything we do is to show we are true servants of God.

When Life is Hard, Lean on God

We are patient and suffer trouble of every kind. ⁵We have been beaten and put in jail. We have faced angry crowds. We have worked very hard. We stayed awake through sleepless nights of prayer. And we have gone without food. ⁶We have proved to be what we claim to be. How? We have lived pure lives. We have a strong knowledge of the Good News. And we have patience. We have been kind and truly loving and filled with the Holy Spirit. ⁷We have been honest, with God's power helping us in all we do. All of God's weapons of defense have been ours. So have all his weapons of attack.

⁸We stand true to the Lord, whether others honor us or hate us. We don't give up, whether they blame us or praise us. And we are honest, but they call us liars.

⁹The world ignores us, but we are known to God. We live close to death, but here we are. We are still very much alive! We have been hurt but kept from death. ¹⁰Our hearts ache, but at the same time we have the joy of the Lord. We are poor, but we have the riches of the Spirit to give. We own nothing, and yet we enjoy everything.

¹¹Oh, my dear Corinthian friends! I have told you all my feelings. I love you with all my heart. ¹²Any coldness still between us is not because of any lack of love on my part. It is because your love is too small. It does not reach out to me and draw me in. ¹³I am talking to you now as if you were my very own children. Open your hearts to us! Return our love!

Don't Hang Around with the Wrong People

¹⁴Don't be teamed up with those who do not love the Lord. What do the people of God have in common with the people of sin? How can light live with darkness? ¹⁵How can Christ and the devils sing the

same song? How can a Christian be a partner with one who doesn't believe? [16]And what union can there be between God's temple and idols? For you are God's temple, the home of the living God. God has said, "I will live in them and walk among them. I will be their God and they shall be my people." [17]That is why the Lord has said, "Leave them, cut yourselves off from them. Don't touch their dirty things. I will welcome you [18]and be a Father to you. You will be my sons and daughters."

[7]Dear friends, we have these great promises. Let's turn away from all things wrong of body or spirit. Let's make ourselves pure. Live in the fear of God. Give yourselves to him alone.

Paul Is Proud of the Christians

[2]Please open your hearts to us again. Not one of you has suffered wrong from us. Not one of you was led astray. We have cheated no one. [3]I'm not saying this to scold or blame you. As I said before, you are in my heart forever. I live and die with you. [4]I have the highest hope in you. My pride in you is great. You have encouraged me. You have made me happy in spite of all my suffering.

[5]When we arrived in Macedonia there was no rest for us. Outside, trouble was on every hand and all around us. Within us, our hearts were full of dread and fear. [6]But God cheers those who are beaten. He cheered us when Titus came. [7]His coming was a joy. So was the news he brought of the time he had with you. He told me how much you were looking forward to my visit. He said you were sorry about what had happened. I learned about your warm love for me. This made me overflow with joy!

[8]I am no longer sorry that I sent that letter to you. I was very sorry for a time. I knew how much it would hurt you. But it hurt you only for a little while. [9]Now I am glad I sent it. Not because it hurt you but because the pain turned you to God. It was a good kind of sadness you felt. It was the kind of sadness God wants his people to have. So I don't need to come to you and be rough. [10]God sometimes uses sadness to help us turn away

from sin and seek eternal life. We should never be angry that he has sent it. But the sadness of the man who is not a Christian doesn't change him. It brings him more death.

[11]See how much good this grief from the Lord did for you! You became honest and real. You want to get rid of the sin that I wrote you about. You were afraid about what had happened and longed for me to come help. You went to work on the problem and cleared it up. You punished the man who sinned. You have done all you could to make it right.

[12]I wrote as I did so the Lord could show how much you care for us. It wasn't to help the man who sinned or the man sinned against.

[13]Your love cheered us up. But we were made happier by Titus's joy. You gave him such a fine welcome and set his mind at ease. [14]I told him how it would be there with you. I told him before he left me of my pride in you. You didn't let me down. I have always told you the truth. Now my boast to Titus has also proved true! [15]He loves you more than ever. He remembers the way you listened to him. He remembers how you welcomed him with such fear and care. [16]How happy this makes me! Now I am sure all is well between us again. Once again I can trust you.

Generous Giving Pleases God

[8]I want to tell you what God's grace has done for the churches in Macedonia.

[2]They have been going through much trouble and hard times. They have mixed their wonderful joy with their deep poverty. The result has been an overflow of giving to others. [3]They gave not only what they could afford but far more. I tell you that they did it because they wanted to. They didn't do it because of nagging on my part. [4]They begged us to let them share their gift with the Christians in Jerusalem. [5]But they went beyond our highest hopes. Their first action was to give themselves to the Lord and to us. They did this because God wanted them to do it. [6]Titus urged your giving in the first

place. So I asked him to visit you. I wanted him to urge you to finish your share in this ministry of giving. [7]You people there are leaders in so many ways. You have so much faith, so many good preachers, and so much learning. You are so excited and show so much love for us. Now I want you to be leaders also in the spirit of cheerful giving.

[8]I am not giving you an order. I am not saying you must do it. But others are eager for it. This is one way to prove that your love is real.

[9]You know how full of love and kindness our Lord Jesus was. He was so very rich yet to help you he became so very poor. When he became poor he made you rich.

[10]I would like you to finish what you started to do a year ago. You were the first to think of this. You were also the first to begin doing something about it. [11]You started the ball rolling. So you should finish this project. Give what you can out of what you have. Let your idea at the start be equal to your action now. [12]If you are eager to give, it isn't important how much you give. God wants you to give what you have, not what you haven't got.

[13]I don't think others should have an easy time of it at your expense. [14]You should divide with them. Right now you have plenty and can help them. At some other time they can share with you when you need it. In this way, each will have as much as he needs. [15]That is why the Bible says, "He that gathered much had nothing left over. He that gathered little had enough." So you also should share with those in need.

[16]I am thankful to God. He has given Titus the same real care for you that I have. [17]He is glad to do what I say and visit you again. But I think he would have come anyway, for he is very eager to see you! [18]I am sending another well-known brother with him. This brother is praised as a preacher of the Good News in all the churches. [19]He was elected by the churches to travel with us. We together will take their gift to Jerusalem. This will glorify the Lord and show we are eager to help each other. [20]By travel-

ing together we will guard against any doubts. We don't want anyone to blame us for the way we handle their gift. [21]God knows we are honest, but I want everyone else to know it, too. That is why we have made this plan.

God wants us to give cheerfully

If you give little, you will get little. Each person should decide how much he should give. No one should force him to give. God loves cheerful givers.

2 Corinthians 9:6-7

---

[22]I am sending you still another brother. We know he is a hardworking Christian. He looks forward to this trip because I have told him that you want to help.

[23]If anyone asks who Titus is, say that he is my partner and helper. You can also say that the other two brothers are sent by the churches. They are an honor to the Lord.

[24]Please show your love for me to these men. Do for them all that I have boasted you would.

God Likes People Who Give Happily

9 I know I don't need to tell you to help God's people. [2]I know you want to do it. I have boasted to our friends in Macedonia about this. I said that you were ready to send a gift a year ago. It was your zeal that stirred them up to begin helping. [3]But I am sending these men to be sure that you really are ready. I told them you would have your money all collected. I don't want to be wrong in my boasting about you. [4]What if some Macedonians come with me and find you aren't ready? I would be ashamed, and so would you. Especially after all I have told them!

[5]So I have asked these other brothers to go ahead of me. They can see to it that the gift you promised is ready. I want it to be a real gift. It should not be given under pressure.

[6]But remember, if you give little, you

will get little. A farmer who plants just a few seeds will get a small crop. But if he plants much, he will harvest much.

⁷Each person should decide how much he should give. No one should force him to give. God loves cheerful givers. ⁸God is able to make it up to you. He can give you all you need and more. Then there will be enough for your needs. There will be plenty left over to give joyfully to others, too. ⁹As the Bible says: "The godly man gives to the poor. His good deeds will be an honor to him forever."

¹⁰God gives seed to the farmer to plant. Later he gives good crops to harvest and eat. So he will give you more and more seed to plant. He will make it grow. Then you can give away more and more fruit from your harvest.

¹¹Yes, God will give you much so that you can give away much. When we take your gifts to the needy they will give thanks to God. ¹²So two good things happen as a result of your gifts. Those in need are helped, and they overflow with thanks to God. ¹³Those you help will be glad because of your gifts to them and to others. They will praise God that your deeds are as good as your doctrine. ¹⁴And they will pray for you with deep feeling. Why? Because of the grace God has shown through you.

¹⁵Thank God for his Son—his Gift too wonderful for words.

Where Does Paul Get His Authority?

10 I, Paul, beg with you gently, as Christ himself would do. Yet some of you say, "Paul's letters are bold when he is far away. But when he gets here he will be afraid to raise his voice!"

²I hope I won't need to show you how rough I can be. Some of you think my deeds and words are like those of any man. I don't want to carry out my present plans against them. ³It is true that I am like any man. But I don't use human plans and methods to win my battles. ⁴I use God's mighty weapons, not those made by men. I use them to knock down the devil's forts. ⁵These weapons can break down every proud argument

against God. They can bring down every wall built to keep men from finding him. With these weapons I can capture rebels. I can bring them back to God. I can change them into men whose hearts obey Christ. ⁶I will use these weapons against every rebel. But first I will use them on you until you obey Christ.

⁷When you look at me I seem weak and powerless. But you don't look under the surface. Yet if anyone can claim the power of Christ, I can too. ⁸I may seem to be bragging more than I should about my power. It is power to help you, not to hurt you. But I shall make good every claim. ⁹Why do I say this? So you won't think I only scold you in my letters.

¹⁰"Don't bother about his letters," some say. "He sounds big, but it's all noise. When he gets here you will see that there is nothing great about him. And you have never heard a worse preacher!" ¹¹When I'm with you this time I will be as rough as my letters!

¹²I wouldn't say I am like these men who tell you how good they are! Their trouble is they compare themselves with each other. They measure themselves against their own little ideas. How stupid!

¹³But we will not brag of power we do not have. Our goal is to measure up to God's plan for us. This plan includes our working there with you. ¹⁴We are not going too far when we reach out to you. We were the first to come to you with the Good News concerning Christ. ¹⁵We are not claiming credit for work someone else has done among you. Instead, we hope that your faith will grow. We hope that our work among you will become bigger.

¹⁶Then we hope to preach the Good News to cities that are beyond you. These are places where no one else is working. Then there will be no question about being in someone else's field. ¹⁷The Bible says, "If anyone is going to boast, let him boast about the Lord." ¹⁸When someone boasts about himself it doesn't count for much. But when the Lord praises him, that's different!

Watch Out for Smooth Talkers and Phony Teachers

11 I hope you will be patient with me as I talk like a fool. Do bear with me and let me say what is on my heart. ²I am worried about you. I have the care of God himself. I am worried that your love be for Christ alone. You should love him like a pure maiden loves only one man. He is the one who will be her husband. ³Eve was fooled by Satan in the Garden of Eden. I am afraid that you will be fooled, too. I am afraid you will be led away from your love for our Lord. ⁴You believe whatever anyone tells you. You believe even if he is preaching another Jesus than the one we preach. You welcome a different spirit than the Holy Spirit you received. If he shows you a different way to be saved, you swallow it all.

⁵I don't feel that these "messengers from God" are better than I am. ⁶If I am a poor speaker, at least I know what I'm talking about. I think you know this, because we have proved it again and again.

⁷Did I do wrong? Did I make you look down on me? Did this happen because I preached God's Good News to you without charge? ⁸⁻⁹Instead I "robbed" other churches. I took what they sent me and used it while I was with you. That way I could serve you without cost. When that money was gone and I was hungry, I didn't ask you for anything. The Christians from Macedonia brought me another gift. I have never asked you for one cent, and I never will. ¹⁰I promise this with every ounce of truth I possess. I will tell everyone in Greece about it! ¹¹Why? Because I don't love you? God knows I do. ¹²But I will do it so "God's messengers" can't boast. They say that they work for God the same way we do.

¹³God never sent those men at all. They are "phonies" who have fooled you into thinking they are Christ's apostles. ¹⁴Yet I am not surprised! Satan can change himself into an angel of light. ¹⁵So it is no wonder his servants can seem like godly ministers. In the end they will be punished for their wicked deeds.

The Devil and His Helpers
2 CORINTHIANS 11:12-15

The devil is also called Satan. He is very wicked. Everything bad comes from Satan. Everything good comes from God. The devil was once an angel. But he turned against God. He wanted to rule everything. He wanted to be God. He still does. Satan has much power. He has the power to tempt each of us. He tries to make us do bad things. But he tries to make these bad things look good. He wants to turn you away from God. He wants you to think other things are more important than God. Satan always lies. He might say that God doesn't love you. Don't listen to him! Satan has many helpers. Demons help him. People who do bad things help the devil. You can see these people. You can't see the devil and his other helpers. But they are here! Does the devil have a red suit, horns, and a pitchfork? The Bible doesn't say that he has those things. When you are tempted to do something bad, stop! Don't do it. That will not please God. How can you say no to the devil? Read your Bible. Pray. Let God help you. He will.

16I beg you, don't think I have lost my wits to talk like this. If you do, listen to me anyway. I want to boast a little like they do. 17Such bragging isn't what the Lord told me to do. I am just acting like a fool. 18Those other men keep telling you how wonderful they are, so I will too. 19-20You think you are wise, but you listen to those fools. You don't mind when they make you their slaves. You are patient when they take all that you have. They trick you, put on airs, and slap you in the face. But you are patient. 21I'm ashamed to say that I'm not strong and daring like that!

Whatever they can boast about I can boast about, too. Remember, I am talking like a fool.

22They brag that they are Hebrews, do they? Well, so am I. And they say that they are Israelites, God's chosen people? So am I. They say they are in Abraham's family? Well, I am too.

Paul Faces All Kinds of Problems

23They say they serve Christ? But I have served him far more! Do you think I have gone mad to boast like this? I have worked harder. I have been put in jail more often. I have been whipped times without number. I have faced death again and again and again. 24Five different times the Jews gave me their terrible 39 lashes. 25Three times I was beaten with rods. Once I was stoned.

???????????????????????????????????
Which famous man was ship-wrecked three times?

(Read 11:25 for the answer.)

???????????????????????????????????

Three times my ship was wrecked. Once I was in the open sea all night and the whole next day. 26I have traveled many weary miles. I am often in danger from flooded rivers, from robbers, and from the Jews. I am in danger from the hands of people who are not Jews, too. I have faced danger in the cities, in the deserts, and in the seas. I have been in danger from men who pretend to believe in Christ. 27I have lived with weariness and pain and sleepless nights. I have been

hungry and thirsty and have gone without food. Often I have shivered with cold because I had no clothes to keep me warm.

28Besides all this, I have the constant worry about all the churches. 29Who makes a mistake and I do not feel his sadness? Who falls without my longing to help him? Who is hurt in his spirit and I don't burn with anger?

30These are the things I brag about. I brag about the things that show how weak I am. 31God, the Father of our Lord Jesus Christ, is to be praised forever. He knows I tell the truth. 32In Damascus the governor under King Aretas kept guards in the city to catch me. 33But I was let down in a basket from a hole in the city wall. So I got away!

Paul Has Some Physical Problems

12 To boast is so foolish, but let me go on. Let me tell about the visions I've had. Let me tell you what I have found out about the Lord.

2-3Fourteen years ago I was taken up to Heaven for a visit. I don't know if my body was there or just my spirit. Only God can answer that. But I was in paradise! 4And I heard things that are beyond a man's power to put in words. I am not allowed to tell them to others. 5This is worth bragging about, but I am not going to do it. I am going to boast only about how weak I am. 6I have plenty to boast about. I would not be a fool to do it. But I don't want people to think more highly of me than they should. They should know me only from my life and my words.

7I shouldn't be puffed up by these things. So God gave me pain in my body like a thorn in my flesh. It is a messenger from Satan to bother me and prick my pride. 8I begged God three times to make me well again.

9Each time he said, "No. But I am with you. That is all you need. My power shows up best in weak people." Now I am glad to brag about how weak I am. I am glad to show off Christ's power instead of my own. 10Now I know it is all for Christ's good. So I am happy about insults and hard times. I am happy when people treat me badly. Why? Because when I am weak, then I am strong. The less I have, the more I depend on God.

Paul Is Concerned for the Corinthians

[11]You have made me act like a fool. You people should be writing about me. I shouldn't have to write about myself. There isn't anything these other fellows have that I don't have, too. I am really worth nothing at all but I am still better than them. [12]When I was there I proved I was an apostle, sent by God. I did many wonders and signs and mighty works with patience. [13]But there is one thing I didn't do for you. I didn't ask you to give me food to eat and a place to stay. I do this in the other churches. Please forgive me for this wrong!

[14]Now I am coming to you again, the third time. It is still not going to cost you anything. I don't want your money. I want you! And anyway, you are my children. Little children don't pay for their father's and mother's food. It's the other way around. Parents supply food for their children. [15]I am glad to give you myself. I give all I have for your souls. It doesn't matter that the more I love you, the less you love me.

[16]Some of you say, "His visits didn't seem to cost us anything. He is a sneaky fellow, that Paul, and he fooled us. As sure as anything he must have made money from us some way."

[17]But how? Did any of the men I sent to you cheat you? [18]I urged Titus to visit you and sent our other brother with him. Did they make any profit? No, of course not! We have the same Holy Spirit and walk in each other's steps. We do things the same way.

[19]Do you think I am saying this to get back into your good graces? That isn't it at all. God is listening as I say that I have said this to help you, dear friends. I have said it to build you up and not to help myself. [20]I'm afraid when I come to visit you I won't like what I find. And then you won't like the way I will have to act. I'm afraid I will find you arguing and envying each other. You might be angry

with each other and acting big. You might be saying wicked things about each other, whispering behind each other's backs. I am afraid I will find you filled with pride and disunity. [21]Yes, I am afraid that when I come God will humble me before you. I will be sad and mourn. Why? Because many of you have sinned. You don't care about the wicked things you have done. You won't turn away from lust, immorality, and the taking of other men's wives.

Check Up on Yourselves

13 This is the third time I am coming to visit you. The Bible says if two or three have seen a wrong, it must be punished. This is my third warning as I come now for this visit. [2]I have already warned those who had been sinning when I was there last. Now I warn them again and all others, just as I did then. This time I come ready to punish harshly and I will not spare them.

[3]I will give you all the proof you want that Christ speaks through me. Christ is not weak in his dealings with you. He is a mighty power within you. [4]His weak, human body died on the cross. But now he lives by the mighty power of God. We, too, are weak in our bodies, as he was. But now we live and are strong, as he is. We have all of God's power to use in dealing with you.

[5]Check up on yourselves. Are you really Christians? Do you pass the test? Do you feel Christ more and more within you? Or are you pretending to be Christians when actually you aren't at all? [6]I hope you can agree I have passed that test and belong to the Lord.

[7]I pray you will live good lives. I don't pray this to get a feather in our caps. I am not trying to prove that what we teach is right. No! We want you to do right even if we are hated. [8]We work for the truth at all times. We don't work against the truth. [9]We are glad to be weak and hated if you are really strong. Our prayer is that you will become mature Christians.

[10]I am writing this while I am away from you. I hope that I won't need to scold and punish you when I come. The

Lord gave me power. I don't want to use it to punish you. I want to use it to make you strong.

[11]Now brothers, be happy. Grow in Christ. Listen to what I have said. Live in harmony and peace. And may the God of love and peace be with you.

[12]Greet each other warmly in the Lord. [13]All the Christians here send you their best regards. [14]May the grace of our Lord Jesus Christ be with you all. May God's love and the Holy Spirit's friendship be yours.

Sincerely, Paul

GALATIANS

Galatia was a large region, not a city. Today this is part of the country of Turkey. In Paul's time it included several cities. Iconium, Lystra, Derbe, and Antioch in Pisidia were in Galatia. Paul visited these places on his first and second missionary journeys. He started churches in Galatia. He wrote this letter to them. People were starting trouble in the church. They were teaching that Gentiles must first become Jews to become Christians. They taught that all Christians must follow the Jewish law and Jewish customs. Paul wrote to tell them the truth. He told them that people don't become Christians by obeying laws. People become Christians through faith in Jesus Christ. Then the Holy Spirit lives in them. He keeps them from sinning. Christians should also help each other please God.

Paul: A Missionary of Jesus Christ

1 *From:* Paul the missionary and all the other Christians here.

To: The churches of Galatia.

I was not called to be a missionary by any group or agency. My call is from Jesus Christ. It is also from God the Father who raised him from the dead. ³May peace and blessing be yours. This comes from God the Father and from the Lord Jesus Christ. ⁴Jesus died for our sins. God planned for him to do this. He rescued us from our wicked world. ⁵All glory to God forever! Amen.

There Is Only One Gospel

⁶I am amazed that you are turning away so soon from God. He invited you to share the eternal life he gives through Christ. But you have decided to follow a different path to be saved. And that way won't save you! ⁷For there is no other way than the one we showed you. You are being fooled by those who twist and change the truth about Christ.

God planned for Jesus to die for us

*Jesus died for our sins.
God planned for him to do this.
He rescued us from our
wicked world.*

Galatians 1:4

---

⁸We told you the way to be saved. Let God curse anyone, even myself, who preaches another way to be saved. Even if an angel from Heaven preaches any other message, let him be cursed. ⁹Again, if anyone preaches another message than the one you welcomed, let God curse him.

¹⁰Am I trying to please you by sweet

talk and flattery? No! I am trying to please God. If I were still trying to please men I could not be Christ's servant.

Paul's Message Comes from God

¹¹Friends, I told you that the Good News I preach is not a human message. ¹²My message comes from Jesus Christ himself. He was the one who told me what to say. No one else has taught me.

¹³You know what I was like when I followed the Jewish religion. I went after the Christians with no mercy. I hunted them down and did my best to get rid of them all. ¹⁴I was one of the most religious Jews of my age in the whole country. I tried hard to follow all the old traditions of my religion.

¹⁵But then something happened! Even before I was born, God called me to be his. That was his kindness and grace. ¹⁶He revealed his Son within me so I could preach the Good News to the Gentiles.

When this happened to me I didn't talk it over with anyone for a while. ¹⁷I didn't go to Jerusalem to talk with those who were apostles before me. No, I went away into the deserts of Arabia. Then I came back to the city of Damascus. ¹⁸It was not until three years later that I finally went to Jerusalem. I visited with Peter and stayed there with him for 15 days. ¹⁹The only other apostle I met at that time was James, our Lord's brother. ²⁰I am telling you this in the very presence of God. This is exactly what happened. I am not lying to you. ²¹Then after this visit I went to Syria and Cilicia. ²²And still the Christians in Judea didn't even know what I looked like. ²³But they knew that their former enemy was preaching the faith he had tried to wreck. ²⁴And they gave glory to God because of me.

The Church Leaders Accepted Paul

2 Then 14 years later I went back to Jerusalem again. This time I went with Barnabas and Titus. ²I went there with orders from God. I talked with the brothers there about the message I was preaching to the Gentiles. I talked to the leaders of the church alone. I wanted them to understand what I had been teaching. I hoped they would agree that it was right. ³And they did agree. They didn't even force Titus to be circumcised, even though he was a Gentile.

⁴That question wouldn't have come up except for some false "Christians" there. They came to spy on us. They wanted to see the freedom we enjoyed in Christ Jesus. They wanted to know if we obeyed the Jewish laws or not. They tried to tie us up in their rules, like slaves in chains. ⁵But we did not listen to them for a single moment. We didn't want to confuse you about the truth of the Good News.

⁶The leaders of the church had nothing to add to what I was preaching. If they were great leaders it made no difference to me. All people are the same to God. ⁷⁻⁹Peter, James, and John were known as the pillars of the church. They saw how God had used me in winning the Gentiles. In the same way, Peter had been blessed in his preaching to the Jews. The same God gave us each our special gifts. So they shook hands with Barnabas and me. They were happy that we would preach to the Gentiles. They would keep on working with the Jews. ¹⁰They did suggest that we always remember to help the poor. I, too, was eager for that.

Peter and Paul Disagree

¹¹But when Peter came to Antioch I had to argue with him in public. I spoke strongly against what he was doing. It was very wrong. ¹²When he first came, he ate with the Gentile Christians. These people don't bother with circumcision and the many other Jewish laws. Later on, some Jewish Christians came to visit. These men were friends of James. After they came, Peter wouldn't eat with the Gentiles anymore. He was afraid of what these Jewish lawkeepers would say. ¹³Then all the other Jewish Christians followed Peter. Even Barnabas became dishonest about the truth. ¹⁴I saw that they weren't being honest about the truth of the Good News. So I said to Peter in front of all the others, "You are a Jew by birth. But you have thrown away the

Jewish laws. So why are you trying to make these Gentiles obey them? [15]You and I are Jews by birth, not Gentile sinners. [16]Yet we know that we can't become right with God by obeying our Jewish laws. We know that our sins are forgiven only by faith in Jesus Christ. So we have trusted Jesus Christ, too. Now we are welcomed by God because of faith. He doesn't welcome us because we obey the Jewish laws. For no one will ever be saved by obeying them."

[17]But what if we trust Christ to save us and then find that we are wrong? What if we can't be saved without obeying all the Jewish laws? Wouldn't we need to say that faith in Christ had ruined us? God forbid that anyone should dare to think such things about our Lord. [18]If I rebuild the Jewish laws I have destroyed, I am a real sinner. [19]I read the Bible. That's how I found out I couldn't find God's favor by obeying the laws. I learned that God welcomes me because I believe in Christ.

[20]I have been crucified with Christ. I myself no longer live, but Christ lives in me. I now have life in this body. But it is because I trust in the Son of God. He loved me and gave himself for me. [21]I am not one of those who throws away Christ's death. We can't be saved by keeping Jewish laws. If we could, then there would have been no need for Christ to die.

The Jewish Law and Faith in Christ

3 Oh, foolish Galatians! What magician has cast an evil spell over you? For you used to see the meaning of Jesus Christ's death. It was clear to you. It was like I had shown you a picture of Christ dying on the cross. [2]I have one question to ask you. Did you receive the Holy Spirit by trying to keep the Jewish laws? Of course not! The Holy Spirit came upon you after you heard about Christ and trusted him. [3]Then have you gone completely crazy? Obeying the Jewish laws never gave you spiritual life in the first place. So why do you think that obeying them now will make you stronger Christians? [4]You have suffered

so much for the Good News. Now are you going to just throw it all away? I can hardly believe it!

[5]Why does God give you the Holy Spirit and work miracles among you? Is it because you try to obey the Jewish laws? No, of course not! These things come when you believe in Christ and fully trust him.

[6]Abraham had the same experience. God said he was fit for Heaven because he believed God's promises. [7]You can see from this who are the real children of Abraham. They are the people who truly trust in God.

[8-9]The Bible knew that God would save the Gentiles by their faith. God told Abraham about this long ago. He said, "I will bless those in every nation who trust in me as you do." And so all who trust in Christ share the same blessing Abraham was given.

[10]Those who depend on the Jewish laws to save them are under God's curse. The Bible says, "Cursed is everyone who breaks one of God's laws." [11]It is clear that no one can win God's favor by keeping the Jewish laws. God has said that the only way we can be right in his sight is by faith. The prophet Habakkuk says, "The man who finds life will find it by trusting God." [12]How different is the way of law from this way of faith! It says that a man is saved by obeying every law of God. [13]But Christ has bought us out from under the doom of the law. He took the curse for our sins upon himself. The Bible says, "Anyone who is hanged on a tree is cursed."

[14]Now God can bless the Gentiles with this same blessing he promised to Abraham. All of us as Christians can have the promised Holy Spirit through this faith.

The Jewish Law and God's Promises

[15]Brothers, in everyday life, a promise that is written down and signed can't be changed. No one can decide afterward to do something else instead.

[16]Now, God gave some promises to Abraham and his Child. It doesn't say the promises were to his children. It

would say this if all his sons were being spoken about. But it says, "his Child." That, of course, means Christ. [17]I am saying that the promise God wrote down could not be changed. It was not even changed 430 years later when God gave the law. [18]What if obeying those laws could save us? Then this would be a different way of pleasing God than Abraham's way. All Abraham did was believe God's promise.

The Holy Spirit grows good fruit in us

With the Holy Spirit in our lives there will be different kinds of fruit. They are love, joy, peace, patience, kindness, goodness, and faith. People with the Spirit are gentle and have self-control.

Galatians 5:22-23

---

[19]Well then, why were the laws given? They were added after the promise was given. They showed men that they are sinners when they break God's laws. But the law was to last only until the coming of Christ. He was the Child to whom God's promise was made. God gave his laws to angels to give to Moses. Moses then gave them to the people. [20]But when God gave his promise to Abraham, he did it by himself alone. He did not use angels or Moses as go-betweens.

[21-22]Well then, are God's laws and God's promises against each other? Of course not! What if we could be saved by his laws? Then God wouldn't have given us a different way to get out of sin. The Bible says that we are all prisoners of sin. The only way out is through faith in Jesus Christ. This way of escape is open to all who believe him.

[23]Until Christ came we were guarded by the law. We were kept by the law until we could believe in the coming Savior.

[24]Let me put it another way. The Jewish laws were our teacher and guide until Christ came. He gave us right standing with God through our faith. [25]Now that Christ has come we don't need those laws to guard us.

We Are God's Children

[26]Now we are all children of God through faith in Jesus Christ. [27]We have been baptized into union with Christ. We are covered by him. [28]We are no longer Jews or Gentiles. We are no longer slaves or free men. We are not even men or women. We are all the same, we are Christians. We are one in Christ Jesus. [29]Now that we are Christ's we are the true children of Abraham. All of God's promises to him belong to us.

4 Remember, when a father dies he leaves his wealth for his little son. But that child is not better off than a slave until he grows up. It doesn't matter that he owns everything his father had. [2]He has to do what his guardians tell him. He has to wait until he reaches the age his father set.

[3]And that is the way it was with us before Christ came. We were slaves to Jewish laws and rituals. We thought they could save us. [4]But when the right time came, God sent his Son. He was born of a woman and as a Jew. [5]God sent him to buy freedom for us who were slaves to the law. God did this so that he could adopt us as his very own sons. [6]We are God's sons. So God has sent the Spirit of his Son into our hearts. Now we can say that God is our dear Father. [7]Now we are no longer slaves but God's own sons. Since we are his sons, everything he has belongs to us. This is the way God planned it to be.

Paul Is Concerned for the Galatians

[8]Before you Gentiles knew God you were slaves to gods that didn't exist. [9]Now you have found God, and God has found you. So how can you go back and become slaves to a useless religion? [10]You are trying to please God by keeping days or months or seasons or years. [11]I fear for you. I am afraid that all my hard work for you was worth nothing.

[12]Dear brothers, please feel as I do about these things. I am as free from these chains as you used to be. You did not hate me when I first preached to you. [13]I was sick when I first brought you the Good News of Christ. [14]My sickness

was horrid to you. But you didn't reject me and turn me away. No, you took me in and cared for me. It was like I was an angel from God or even Jesus Christ himself.

15Where is that happy spirit that we felt together then? I know you would have taken out your own eyes and given them to me.

16And now have I become your enemy because I tell you the truth?

????????????????????????????????
How many kinds of fruit does the Holy Spirit produce in us?
(Read 5:22-23 for the answer.)
????????????????????????????????

17Those false teachers want to win your favor. But they are not doing it for your good. They are just trying to shut you off from me. That way you will pay more attention to them. 18It is a fine thing when people are nice to you with pure hearts. But they shouldn't do it just when I am with you! 19Oh, my children, how you are hurting me! I am once again suffering for you. It is like the pains of a mother waiting for her child to be born. I am longing for the time when you will finally be filled with Christ. 20How I wish I could be there with you right now. I wish I didn't have to reason with you like this. But I am far away and I frankly don't know what to do.

A Lesson about the Law from Sarah and Hagar
21Listen to me! Some of you think you have to obey the Jewish laws to be saved. Why don't you find out what those laws really mean? 22For it is written that Abraham had two sons. One was from his slave-wife and one was from his freeborn wife. 23The slave-wife's baby was born like every other baby. But the baby of the freeborn wife was born because God had promised he would come.

24-25Now this true story shows God's two ways of helping people. One way was by giving them his laws to obey. He did this on Mount Sinai, when he gave the Ten Commandments to Moses.

Mount Sinai, by the way, is called Mount Hagar by the Arabs. Abraham's slave-wife Hagar stands for Jerusalem, the city of the Jews. The Jews are her slave children. 26But our city is the heavenly Jerusalem. It is not a slave to Jewish laws.

27That is why Isaiah said, "Now you can rejoice, O childless woman. You can shout with joy though you never before had a child. I am going to give you more children than the slave-wife has."

28You and I, brothers, are the children that God promised, just as Isaac was. 29We are born of the Holy Spirit. So we are treated badly by those who want us to keep the Jewish laws. This is just like Isaac. He was the child of promise. So he was treated badly by Ishmael, the slave-wife's son.

The Lord wants us to help each other

Share each other's troubles and problems. That's what our Lord commands.

Galatians 6:2

30But what does the Bible say? God told Abraham to send away the slave-wife and her son. Why? Because the slave-wife's son could not be given Abraham's home and lands. They would be given to the free woman's son. 31Dear brothers, we are not slave children. We don't have to keep the Jewish laws. We are children of the free woman. God welcomes us because of our faith.

Freedom:
A Special Gift from Christ
5 So Christ has made us free. Now make sure that you stay free. Don't get tied up again in the chains of slavery to Jewish laws. 2Listen to me, this is serious. If you try to keep Jewish laws, then Christ cannot save you. 3I'll say it again. Anyone trying to please God by being circumcised must obey every other Jewish law. 4Are you counting on clearing your debt to God by keeping those laws? Then Christ is useless to you and you are lost from God's grace.

5We have the help of the Holy Spirit. So we believe that Christ's death will make us right with God. ⁶Christ has given us eternal life. So we don't need to worry if we keep the law or not. All we need is faith working through love.

Do your best and you will be glad

Let everyone be sure that he is doing his very best. Then he can be proud of himself for work well done. He won't need to compare himself with someone else.

Galatians 6:4

---

⁷You were getting along so well. Who has kept you from following the truth? ⁸It certainly isn't God who has done it. He is the one who has called you to freedom in Christ. ⁹But it takes only one wrong person among you to infect all the others.

¹⁰I'm trusting the Lord that you still believe as I do about these things. God will deal with whoever has been troubling and confusing you.

¹¹Some people even say that I am preaching Jewish laws. Well, if I preached that, I wouldn't be treated badly anymore. That message doesn't offend anyone. But I am still being treated badly for what I preach. This proves I am still preaching salvation through faith in the cross of Christ.

No one is perfect

Each of us has faults and problems. Not one of us is perfect.

Galatians 6:5

---

¹²These teachers want you to cut yourselves by being circumcised. I wish they would cut themselves off from you and leave you alone!

¹³For, dear brothers, you have been given freedom. It is not freedom to do wrong. It is freedom to love and serve each other. ¹⁴For the whole Law can be summed up in one command. It is, "Love others as you love yourself." ¹⁵But watch out! Don't always argue and fight with each other. If you do you will ruin each other.

Letting the Holy Spirit Guide You Will Produce Good Fruit

¹⁶I advise you to obey only the Holy Spirit's teachings. He will tell you where to go and what to do. Then you won't be doing the wrong things your evil nature wants you to. ¹⁷For we love to do evil things. And these things are against the things the Holy Spirit tells us to do. But we do good things when the Spirit has his way with us. They are against our natural desires. These two forces in us are always fighting to win control over us. Our wishes are never free from their demands. ¹⁸When you're guided by the Holy Spirit, you don't need to obey Jewish laws.

We will be rewarded or punished by what we do

Don't fool yourself! Remember, you can't ignore God and get away with it. A man will always harvest the kind of crop he plants!

Galatians 6:7

---

¹⁹But when you follow your own natural desires there will be evil results. There are impure thoughts, lustful pleasures, ²⁰idolatry, spiritism, hatred, and fighting. There are jealousy and anger, arguments and criticism. People feel that everyone else is wrong except those in their own little group. There will be wrong doctrine, ²¹envy, and murder. People will be drunk at wild parties and do all these sorts of things. Let me tell you again what I have told you before. Anyone living that sort of life will not enter the Kingdom of God.

²²But with the Holy Spirit in our lives there will be different kinds of fruit. They are love, joy, peace, patience, kindness, goodness, and faith. ²³People with the Spirit are gentle and have self-control. None of these things are against the Jewish laws.

²⁴Those who belong to Christ have killed their natural evil desires on the cross.

²⁵We are living now by the Holy

Spirit's power. So let's follow the Holy Spirit's leading in every part of our lives. [26]Let's not look for honors or try to be popular. These things make people jealous and cause hard feelings.

We Reap What We Sow

6 Brothers, do you know what to do if a Christian is overcome by sin? You who are godly should humbly help him back onto the right path. Remember that next time it might be one of you who sins. [2]Share each other's troubles and problems. That's what our Lord commands. [3]If anyone thinks he is too great to do this, he is fooling himself. He is really a nobody.

[4]Let everyone be sure that he is doing his very best. Then he can be proud of himself for work well done. He won't need to compare himself with someone else. [5]Each of us has faults and problems. Not one of us is perfect.

[6]Those who are taught the Word of God should pay their teachers.

Keep doing what you should

Let's not get tired of doing what is right. After a while we will harvest a rich crop of blessing. So don't give up.

Galatians 6:9

---

[7]Don't fool yourself! Remember, you can't ignore God and get away with it. A man will always harvest the kind of crop he plants! [8]If he plants to please his own desires, he is planting seeds of evil. He will surely harvest a crop of spiritual decay and death. But if he plants the things of the Spirit, he will harvest eternal life. [9]Let's not get tired of doing what is right. After a while we will harvest a rich crop of blessing. So don't give up. [10]Always try to be kind to others. Especially be kind to other Christians.

Paul Gives More Advice

[11]I will write these closing words in my own handwriting. See how large I have to make the letters! [12]Why do your teachers want you to be circumcised?

Planting Grain
GALATIANS 6:7

If you plant wheat seeds, will carrots come up? If you plant radish seeds, will corn come up? Wheat grows from wheat seeds. Radishes grow from radish seeds. If you plant three grains of wheat, will you have a large field of plants? The Bible says you will grow and harvest only what you plant. Bible-time farmers planted seeds by hand. They hung a bag of seeds on their shoulder. As they walked, they reached into the bag for seeds. They scattered the seeds on the ground. This was called sowing. Farmers threw the seeds so that they would fall evenly on the ground. Farmers sowed mostly wheat and barley. Bread was made from these two grains. If a farmer wanted bread, he had to plant wheat or barley. Do you want a good life? Do things that bring a good life. That's like planting the right seeds.

They want to be popular. They don't want to be treated badly because they believe the cross of Christ. [13]Those teachers who submit to circumcision don't try to keep the other Jewish laws.

They want you to be circumcised so they can boast that you are their disciples.

Be kind to others

Always try to be kind to others. Especially be kind to other Christians.

Galatians 6:10

¹⁴God forbid that I should boast about anything except the cross of our Lord Jesus Christ. The cross stopped me from wanting the nice things of the world. The world's interest in me was also killed on the cross. ¹⁵It doesn't matter if we have been circumcised or not. What counts is if we really have been changed into new and different people.

¹⁶May God's mercy and peace be upon all of you who live by this rule. May they be upon everybody who is really God's own.

¹⁷From now on please don't argue with me about these things. I carry on my body the scars of the wounds from Jesus' enemies. These scars mark me as Jesus Christ's slave.

¹⁸Dear brothers, may the grace of our Lord Jesus Christ be with you all.

Sincerely, Paul

EPHESIANS

Ephesus was an important city. It was a seaport. Ships came from many places. Two great roads went through Ephesus. Many merchants and travelers went there. Ephesus had a big, beautiful temple. It was one of the largest buildings in the world. People worshiped the goddess Diana there. They also bought little silver idols from this temple. Making and selling these idols was big business in Ephesus. The story of the silversmith riot in Acts 19 will tell you more about this business. Paul preached in Ephesus for three years. The last time he saw the Christians of Ephesus they had a sad good-bye. You can read about it in Acts 20:17-38. Paul wrote this letter to them from prison in Rome. Paul told them that the Christian life is different. Beautiful buildings are not important. Riches are not important. Friendship with God is important. The church is made up of people. A strong church is made up of strong families and godly people. Strong churches today are made of these same things, aren't they?

Paul: A Loyal Follower of Christ

1 This is Paul writing to the Christians at Ephesus who are loyal to the Lord. I have been chosen by God to be Jesus Christ's messenger. ²May his blessings and peace be yours. These are sent to you from God our Father and Jesus Christ our Lord.

God Showers His Kindness on All of Us

³How we praise God, the Father of our Lord Jesus Christ! He has blessed us with every blessing in Heaven because we belong to Christ.

⁴Long ago, before he made the world, God chose us to be his very own. He did this because of what Christ would do for us. He decided then to make us holy in his eyes, without a single fault. We stand before him covered with his love. ⁵His plan has always been to adopt us into his own family. He would do this by sending Jesus Christ to die for us. And he did this because he wanted to!

⁶Now all praise to God for his wonderful kindness to us! He poured his favor upon us because we belong to his dearly loved Son. ⁷He has so much kindness! He took away all our sins through

the blood of his Son. This saved us. [8]He has showered upon us the richness of his grace. He understands us and knows what is best for us at all times.

[9]God has told us his secret reason for sending Christ. He has a plan he decided on in mercy long ago. [10]He plans to gather us all together when the time is ripe. He will gather his people in Heaven and on earth. They will be with him in Christ forever. [11]Also, we have become gifts to God that he delights in. As part of God's plan we were chosen from the beginning to be his. All things happen just as he decided long ago. [12]We were the first to trust in Christ. God wants us to praise and give glory to him for doing these things.

[13]You also heard the Good News about how to be saved. You trusted Christ. Then you were marked as belonging to Christ by the Holy Spirit. Long ago the Spirit had been promised to all of us Christians. [14]The Spirit is God's pledge that he will give us all that he promised. The Spirit's seal upon us means that we belong to God. It is his pledge to bring us to himself. This is just one more reason for us to praise our great God.

Paul Prays for the Ephesian Believers

[15]I heard of your strong faith in the Lord Jesus. I know you love Christians everywhere. [16-17]So I have never stopped thanking God for you. I pray for you all the time. I ask God, the Father of our Lord Jesus Christ, to give you wisdom. Then you will see and understand who Christ is and what he has done. [18]I pray that your hearts will be flooded with light. Then you can see something of the future he has called you to share. You can see that God is rich because we have been given to him! [19]I pray you will know how great his power is for those who believe him. It is that same mighty power [20]that raised Christ from the dead. It seated him in the place of honor at God's right hand in Heaven. [21]He is far above any other king or ruler or dictator or leader. His name is above anyone else's in this world or in the world to come. [22]And God has put all things un-

der his feet. He made Christ the Head of the Church. [23]The Church is his body. It is filled with himself. He is the Author and Giver of everything everywhere.

Our Lives Before and After Christ

2 Once you were under God's curse, doomed forever for your sins. [2]You went along with the crowd and were just like all the others. You were full of sin, obeying Satan, the prince of the power of the air. He is at work right now in those who are against the Lord. [3]All of us used to be just as they are. Our lives expressed the evil within us. We did every wicked thing that our passions and thoughts might lead us into. We started out bad by being born with evil natures. We were under God's anger just like everyone else.

[4]But God is so rich in mercy. He loved us so much. [5]We were dead in our spirit and doomed by our sins. But he gave us back our lives again when he raised Christ from the dead. Only by his favor and grace have we ever been saved. [6]He lifted us up from the grave into glory along with Christ. Now we sit with him in the heavenly realms. This is all because of what Christ Jesus did. [7]Now God can point to us to show how rich his kindness is. It is shown in all he has done for us through Jesus Christ.

[8]Because of his kindness, you have been saved through trusting Christ. And even that trust is not your own. It, too, is a gift from God. [9]Salvation is not a reward for the good we have done. So none of us can take any credit for it. [10]It is God himself who has made us what we are. He has given us new lives from Christ Jesus. Long ago he planned that we should spend our lives in helping others.

[11]Never forget that once you were heathen. You were called godless and "unclean" by the Jews. Their hearts, too, were still unclean. They circumcised themselves as a sign of godliness. But it didn't matter that they were going through the rituals of the godly. [12]Remember, in those days you were living apart from Christ. You were enemies of God's children. He had promised you no

help. You were lost, without God, without hope.

¹³But now you belong to Christ Jesus. You once were far away from God. But now you have been brought near to him. This happened because of what Jesus Christ has done for you with his blood.

Christ: The Way to Peace

¹⁴For Christ himself is our way of peace. He has made peace between us Jews and you Gentiles. He made us all one family. He broke down the wall of hate that used to separate us. ¹⁵By his death he ended the anger between us. This anger was caused by the Jews' laws that shut out the Gentiles. He died to end that whole system of Jewish laws. Then he took the two arguing groups and made them parts of himself. That is how he put us together to become one new person. So at last there was peace. ¹⁶As parts of the same body, our anger against each other is gone. Both of us have become friends with God again. So the fighting ended at last at the cross. ¹⁷You Gentiles were very far away from him. But he has brought this Good News of peace to you. And, he brought it to us Jews who were near him. ¹⁸Now, both Jews and Gentiles may come to God the Father. We do this with the Holy Spirit's help because of what Christ has done.

¹⁹Now you are no longer strangers to God and foreigners in Heaven. You are members of God's very own family. You are citizens of God's country. You belong in God's household with every other Christian.

²⁰Your faith is built on the apostles and the prophets. The strongest stone of the building is Jesus Christ himself! ²¹We who believe are carefully joined together with Christ. We are parts of a beautiful, growing temple for God. ²²And you also are joined with him and with each other by the Spirit. You are part of this dwelling place of God.

God's Gift of Salvation Is for Everyone

3 I, Paul, the servant of Christ, am here in jail because of you. I am here for preaching that you Gentiles are a part of God's house. ²⁻³You know that God gave me this work of showing his favor to you Gentiles. I briefly mentioned this before in one of my letters. God showed me this secret plan of his. He showed me that the Gentiles are included in his kindness, too. ⁴I say this to explain how I know about these things. ⁵In olden times God did not share this plan with his people. But now he has shown it to his apostles and prophets by the Spirit.

⁶The secret is that the Gentiles will share with the Jews in all God's riches. They are invited to belong to his Church. All of God's promises through Christ are theirs too. This happens when they accept the Good News about Christ. ⁷God has made me the person to tell everyone about his plan. He has given me his power and special ability to do it well.

?????????????????????????????????
Who was thrown into jail for preaching that Gentiles are part of God's house?

(Read 3:1 for the answer.)
?????????????????????????????????

⁸Just think! I did nothing to deserve it. I am the most useless Christian there is! Yet I was the one chosen for this joy. I tell the Gentiles the Glad News. It is full of endless treasures which are theirs in Christ. ⁹I explain to everyone that God is the Savior of the Gentiles too. He secretly planned this in the beginning when he made all things.

¹⁰And why did he do this? He wanted to show all the rulers in Heaven how perfectly wise he is. They will see the Jews and Gentiles joined together in his Church. ¹¹This is the way he had always planned it through Jesus Christ our Lord.

¹²Now we can come fearlessly right into God's presence. Why? Because we are sure to be welcomed because we believe in Christ.

¹³So please don't lose heart at what they are doing to me here. It is for you I am suffering. You should feel honored and happy.

God's Love Has No End

14-15Sometimes I think of the wisdom and scope of his plan. Then I fall down on my knees and pray to God. He is the Father of every family in Heaven and on earth. 16I pray that his glorious riches will strengthen you inwardly. He will do this through his Holy Spirit. 17I pray that Christ will be more and more at home in your hearts. He will live within you as you trust in him. May your roots go down deep into the soil of God's love. 18-19May you be able to know, with all God's children, God's love. May you know how long, how wide, how deep, and how high his love is. May you taste this love for yourselves. It is so great you will never see the end of it. You won't fully know or understand it. But at last you will be filled up with God himself.

God's power in us helps us do more than we thought we could

Praise God! When his power works in us we do much more than we prayed that we would. We do more than we hoped that we would.

Ephesians 3:20

20Praise God! When his power works in us we do much more than we prayed that we would. We do more than we hoped that we would. 21May he be given glory in the Church and in Jesus Christ forever.

Why So Many Different People with Different Abilities?

4 I am a prisoner here in jail for serving the Lord. I beg you to live in a proper way. Live like those who have been chosen for these blessings. 2Be humble and gentle. Be patient with each other. Allow for each other's faults because of your love. 3Try always to be led together by the Holy Spirit. Then you can be at peace with one another.

4We are all parts of one body. We have the same Spirit. And we've all been called to the same future. 5For us there is only one Lord, one faith, and one baptism. 6We all have the same God and Father. He is over us all, in us all, and living through us all. 7However, Christ has given each of us special abilities. They are whatever he wants us to have in his rich storehouse of gifts.

We hurt each other when we lie

Stop lying to each other. Tell the truth. We are part of each other. So when we lie to each other we are hurting ourselves.

Ephesians 4:25

8The Psalmist tells about this. He says that Christ went back to Heaven after his resurrection and victory over Satan. Then he gave generous gifts to men. 9Notice that it says he went back to Heaven. This means that he had first come down from Heaven. He went far down to the lowest parts of the earth. 10The same one who came down is the one who went back up. He did that so he might fill all things with himself.

11Some of us have been given special ability as apostles. To others he has given the gift of being able to preach well. Some have special ability in winning people to Christ. They help people to trust him as their Savior. Others have a gift for caring for God's people like a shepherd does sheep. He leads them and teaches them in the ways of God.

12Why does he make us able to do certain things best? It is so that God's people will be ready to do better work for him. They will build up the Church, the body of Christ. It will be strong and grown up. 13Finally we all will have the same beliefs. We will all become full-grown in the Lord. We will come to the point of being filled full with Christ.

14Then we will no longer be like children. We won't always change our minds about what we believe. Some do this because someone has told them a new doctrine. Sometimes someone lies and makes the lie sound like the truth. 15-16Instead, we will lovingly follow the truth at all times. We will speak truly, deal truly, and live truly. So we will become more in every way like Christ. He is the Head of his body, the Church. Under his direction, the whole body is put together perfectly. Each part helps the other parts in its own special way. Then the whole body is healthy and growing and full of love.

Living Like a New Person

17-18I am speaking for the Lord. Don't live like the unsaved do anymore. They are blinded and confused. Their closed hearts are full of darkness. They are far away from the life of God. Why? Because they have shut their minds against him. They can't understand his ways. 19They don't care anymore about right and wrong. They have given themselves over to doing wrong things. They stop at nothing. They are driven by their evil minds and reckless lusts.

20But that isn't the way Christ taught you! 21Have you really heard his voice and learned the truth from him? 22Then throw off your old evil nature. It is the old you that was a partner in your evil ways. It is rotten through and through, full of lust and lies.

23Now your attitudes and thoughts are all changing for the better. 24Yes, you must be new and different people, holy and good. Dress yourself with this new nature.

Don't steal

If anyone is stealing he must stop it. Let him begin by using his hands for honest work. Then he can give to others in need.

Ephesians 4:28

25Stop lying to each other. Tell the truth. We are part of each other. So when we lie to each other we are hurting ourselves. 26If you are angry, don't sin by staying angry. Don't let the sun go down with you still angry. Get over it quickly. 27When you are angry, you give a mighty foothold to the devil.

28If anyone is stealing he must stop it.

Let him begin by using his hands for honest work. Then he can give to others in need. 29Don't use bad language. Say only what is good and helpful to those you are talking to. That will give them a blessing.

Don't be mean or argue

Stop being mean, bad-tempered, and angry. Fighting, harsh words, and dislike of others should have no place in your lives.

Ephesians 4:31

30Don't cause the Holy Spirit sorrow by the way you live. Remember, he has marked you until the day when salvation will be complete.

31Stop being mean, bad-tempered, and angry. Fighting, harsh words, and dislike of others should have no place in your lives. 32Instead, be kind to each other and tenderhearted. Forgive one another just as God has forgiven you because you belong to Christ.

Learn What Pleases God

5 Follow God's example in everything you do. Be like a much loved child who follows his father. 2Be full of love for others. Follow the example of Christ. He loved you and gave himself to God as a sacrifice for your sins. And God was pleased about this. Christ's love for you was like sweet perfume to him.

3Let there be no sex sin, impurity, or greed among you. Let no one be able to accuse you of any such things. 4Dirty stories, foul talk, and coarse jokes are not for you. Instead, remind each other of God's goodness and be thankful.

5There is one thing you can be sure of. The Kingdom of Christ and of God can't belong to an impure or greedy man. A greedy person is really an idol worshiper. He loves and worships the good things of this life more than God. 6Don't be fooled by those who try to excuse these sins. The terrible anger of God is upon all those who do them. 7Don't even spend time with such people. ⁸Once your heart was full of darkness. Now it is full of light from the Lord. Your life should show it! ⁹You have this light within you. So you should do only what is good and right and true.

Live like God's child

*Follow God's example
in everything you do.
Be like a much loved child
who follows his father.*

Ephesians 5:1

¹⁰Learn as you go along what pleases the Lord. ¹¹Take no part in the worthless pleasures of evil and darkness. Instead, rebuke them and bring them out into the light. ¹²It would be shameful even to mention here those pleasures of darkness. ¹³But when you expose them, the light shines in upon their sin. When they see how wrong they are, some of them may become children of light! ¹⁴That is why God says, "Awake, O sleeper! Rise up from the dead. Christ shall give you light."

¹⁵⁻¹⁶So be careful how you act. These are difficult days. Don't be fools, but instead be wise. Make the most of every chance you have for doing good. ¹⁷Don't act foolishly. Try to find out and do whatever the Lord wants you to. ¹⁸Don't drink too much wine. Many evils lie along that path. Be filled instead with the Holy Spirit and be controlled by him.

¹⁹Talk with each other about the Lord. Quote psalms and hymns and sing sacred songs. Make music in your hearts to the Lord. ²⁰Thank God for everything. Thank him in Jesus' name.

Advice for Husbands and Wives

²¹Honor Christ by submitting to each other. ²²Wives, submit to your husbands' leadership the way you submit to the Lord. ²³A husband is in charge of his wife. And in the same way, Christ is in charge of the Church. He gave his very life to take care of it and be its Savior! ²⁴So you wives must obey your husbands

in everything, like the Church obeys Christ.

²⁵Husbands, love your wives like Christ loved the Church when he died for her. ²⁶He did that to make her holy and clean, washed by the water in God's Word. ²⁷That way he could give her to himself as a glorious Church. She would be without a spot or wrinkle or any other blemish. She would be holy and without a single fault. ²⁸That is how husbands should treat their wives, loving them as parts of themselves. A man and his wife are now one. So a man is doing himself a favor when he loves his wife! ²⁹⁻³⁰No one hates his own body but lovingly cares for it. It is just as Christ cares for the Church, of which we are parts.

³¹The husband and wife are one body. This is proved by the Bible. It says, "A man must leave his father and mother when he marries. Then he can be joined to his wife, and the two shall be one." ³²I know this is hard to understand. It shows us the way we are parts of the body of Christ.

Thank God for all he has done for you

*Thank God for everything.
Thank him in Jesus' name.*

Ephesians 5:20

³³So again I say, a man must love his wife as a part of himself. The wife must deeply respect her husband by obeying, praising, and honoring him.

Advice for Children and Parents

6 Children, obey your parents. This is the right thing to do. ²Honor your father and mother. This is the first of God's Ten Commandments that ends with a promise. ³The promise is that you will have a long life, full of blessing.

⁴And now a word to you parents. Don't keep on scolding and nagging your children. This makes them angry and bitter. Rather, bring them up with the Lord's loving discipline and godly advice.

Be Responsible Workers and Fair Bosses

⁵Slaves, obey your masters. Be eager to give them your very best. Serve them as you would Christ. ⁶⁻⁷Don't work only when your master is watching. For then you will be lazy when he isn't looking. Work hard and with gladness all the time. Do everything as if you are working for Christ. Do the will of God with all your hearts. ⁸Remember, the Lord will pay you for each good thing you do. It doesn't matter if you are slave or free.

⁹And you slave owners must treat your slaves right. Do just as I have told them to treat you. Don't keep threatening them. Remember, you are slaves to Christ. You have the same Master they do, and he has no favorites.

Wear God's Armor

¹⁰Last of all, let your strength come from the Lord's power within you. ¹¹Put on all of God's armor. Then you will be safe from Satan's attacks. ¹²We are not fighting against people made of flesh and blood. We are fighting against persons without bodies. They are the evil rulers of the unseen world. They are the satanic beings and evil princes of darkness who rule this world. They are the huge numbers of wicked spirits in the spirit world.

¹³So use every piece of God's armor to fight the enemy whenever he attacks. Then when it is all over, you will still be standing up.

God wants you to obey your parents

Children, obey your parents.
This is the right thing to do.

Ephesians 6:1

---

¹⁴You will need to wear the strong belt of truth. And put on the breastplate of righteousness, too. ¹⁵Wear shoes that are the Good News of peace with God. ¹⁶In every battle you will need faith as your shield. It will stop the fiery arrows aimed at you by Satan. ¹⁷And you will need the helmet of salvation and the sword of the Spirit. The Spirit is the Word of God. ¹⁸Pray all the time. Ask God for

Bible-time Families
EPHESIANS 5:21–6:4

A Bible-time family usually had a mother, a father, and children just like we do today. Parents expected children to honor and obey them. Most women took care of the home and children. They did not go out to work. Very few children went to school. So mothers taught girls household chores. Girls also helped take care of younger children. Boys learned their father's trade. Men were farmers, shepherds, carpenters, masons, shopkeepers, or silversmiths. Families ate all meals together. They did not have Little League, school plays, music lessons, or things like that. Sometimes children married as young as age 13. Often they would live next door to their parents or in the same village. Clans were groups of relatives that kept strong family ties. They all lived close to each other. Tribes were made up of many clans that were all related. Travel was hard. So families did not take trips for fun as you do. Most of life was hard work. Feasts and weddings were times for fun. Bible-time families spent lots of time together.

anything in line with the Holy Spirit's wishes. Beg with him, reminding him of your needs. Pray for all Christians everywhere. [19]Pray for me, too. Ask God to give me the right words. That way I can boldly speak about the Lord and his salvation for the Gentiles. [20]I am in chains now for preaching this message from God. But pray that I will speak boldly for him in prison, as I should.

Paul Signs Off with a Blessing
[21]Tychicus is a much-loved brother and faithful helper in the Lord's work. He

---

Show respect to your parents

Honor your father and mother.

Ephesians 6:2

---

will tell you all about how I am getting along. [22]I am sending him to you for this reason. He will let you know how we are. Be encouraged by his report.

Ask God to help you fight Satan

Put on all of God's armor. Then you will be safe from Satan's attacks.

Ephesians 6:11

---

[23]May God give peace to you, my Christian brothers. I send you my love, with faith from God the Father and the Lord Jesus Christ. [24]May God's grace be upon all who purely love our Lord Jesus Christ.

Sincerely, Paul

PHILIPPIANS

Pretend that you are a prisoner. You can't go where you want. Someone guards you at all times. You have to wear chains on your wrists and ankles. Now pretend that you are writing a letter to a friend. What would you say? Would you complain about the chains and the guard?

Paul was a prisoner in Rome. He wrote this letter to the church at Philippi. His letter is filled with joy. Why? How can he be so joyful when he is a prisoner? He is joyful because he is a Christian. Even though he is a prisoner, Jesus Christ fills him with joy. Paul wants others to have that same joy. The next time you start to complain, remember Paul's letter to the Philippians.

Paul started the church at Philippi. He was on his second missionary journey. One night he had a vision. In the vision a man asked him to come to Europe. He asked Paul for help. Paul did go to Europe. The first stop was Philippi. He led Lydia, a seller of purple cloth, to Christ. He commanded a demon to come out of a little girl. For that, he was thrown into prison. There he and Silas sang and prayed. He led the jailer and his family to Christ. These people became part of the Philippian church. Paul was writing to them. You'll want to read Acts 16:9-40 again. You'll want to remember to be joyful.

Paul: A Slave of Jesus Christ

1 *From:* Paul and Timothy, slaves of Jesus Christ.

To: The pastors and deacons and all the Christians in the city of Philippi.

²May God bless you all. I pray that God our Father and the Lord Jesus Christ will give you peace.

Paul's Prayer: Keep Growing in Spiritual Things

³All my prayers for you are full of praise to God! ⁴When I pray for you, my heart is full of joy. ⁵Why? Because of all your wonderful help in making known the Good News about Christ! You have done this from the time you first heard the

Good News until now. 6God began the good work within you. I am sure he will finish it until Jesus Christ comes back.

Put others first

Don't be selfish. Don't live to impress others. Be humble. Think of others as better than yourself.

Philippians 2:3

7How natural it is that I should feel as I do about you. You have a very special place in my heart. We have shared together the blessings of God. You shared with me when I was in prison. And when I was out we defended the truth together. 8Only God knows how I long for you with the tenderness of Jesus Christ. 9My prayer for you is that you will overflow more and more with love for others. I pray that you grow in spiritual knowledge and insight. 10I want you to see the difference between right and wrong. And I pray that you will be inwardly clean. No one should be able to blame you from now until our Lord comes back. 11May you always do those good, kind things that show you are a child of God. This will bring much praise and glory to the Lord.

The Good News Is Being Preached

12And I want you to know something, brothers. Everything that has happened to me here has helped the Good News concerning Christ. 13Everyone here knows that I am in chains because I am a Christian. This includes all the soldiers at the barracks. 14Because I am in prison, many here seem to have lost their fear of chains! Somehow my patience has cheered them up. They have become more and more bold in telling others about Christ.

15Some, of course, are preaching the Good News because they are jealous of me. They want to be known as fearless preachers! But others are more pure. 16-17They preach because they love me. They know the Lord has brought me here to defend the Truth. Some preach to make me jealous. They think that their success will add to my sadness here

in jail! 18I don't care why they do it. The fact is, the Good News about Christ is being preached, and I am glad.

19I am going to keep on being glad. I know that you pray for me and the Spirit helps me. So this is all going to turn out for my good. 20I eagerly expect and hope that I will never be ashamed of what I do. I expect that I will always be ready to speak boldly for Christ. Even now, just as in the past, I hope that I will be an honor to Christ. This is true whether I live or die. 21For to me, living is Christ, and dying—well, that's better yet! 22But if I live I can win people to Christ. So I don't know which is better. Should I live or die? 23Sometimes I want to live, and at other times I don't. For I long to go and be with Christ. How much happier for *me* than being here! 24But I can be of more help to *you* by staying!

Try to think the way Jesus does

Your attitude should be the kind that was shown us by Jesus Christ.

Philippians 2:5

25Yes, I am still needed here. So I feel certain I will be staying on earth a little longer. That way I can help you grow and become happy in your faith. 26My staying will make you glad. It will give you reason to glorify Christ when I come back to visit you.

27But whatever happens to me, remember always to live as Christians should. That way, even if I never see you again, I will hear good reports about you. I will be told that you are standing side by side. I will hear that you share the one strong purpose of telling the Good News. 28Do it without fear, no matter what your enemies may do. They will see this as a sign of their downfall. But for you it is a sign from God that he is with you. It means that he has given you eternal life with him. 29For you have been given not only trust in him but also suffering for him. 30We are in this fight together. You have seen me suffer for him in the past. I am still in the midst of a great and terrible struggle now, as you know so well.

Have an Attitude Like Christ's

2 Is there any such thing as Christians cheering each other up? Do you love me enough to want to help me? Are we brothers in the Lord, sharing the same Spirit? Are your hearts tender and kind at all? [2]Then make me truly happy by loving each other. Agree with each other. Work together with one heart and mind and purpose.

[3]Don't be selfish. Don't live to impress others. Be humble. Think of others as better than yourself. [4]Don't just think about your own affairs. Be interested in others and in what they are doing.

[5]Your attitude should be the kind that was shown us by Jesus Christ. [6]He was God, but he did not demand and hold on to his rights as God. [7]He put aside his power and glory. He put on the costume of a slave and became like men. [8]He humbled himself even more. He went so far as to die a criminal's death on a cross.

[9]Yet it was because of this that God raised him up to Heaven. God gave him a name which is above every other name. [10]At the name of Jesus every knee shall bow in Heaven and on earth and under the earth. [11]Every tongue shall confess that Jesus Christ is Lord. This is to the glory of God the Father.

God Is There to Help You

[12]Dearest friends, when I was with you, you were careful to do what I said. Now I am far away from you. So even more you must do the things that come from being saved. Obey God with honor. Shrink back from all that might not please him. [13]For God is at work within you. He helps you want to obey him. And he helps you do what he wants.

Each of us should worship Jesus

At the name of Jesus every knee shall bow in Heaven and on earth and under the earth.

Philippians 2:10

---

[14]Don't complain or argue in anything you do. [15]Then no one will be able to speak a word of blame against you. You are to live pure lives as children of God around tough and crooked people. Shine out among them like beacon lights. [16]Hold out to them the Word of Life.

Stop arguing and complaining

Don't complain or argue in anything you do.

Philippians 2:14

When Christ comes back, I will be glad that my work among you was worthwhile. [17]My lifeblood may be poured out over your faith as an offering to God. Even then I will be glad and will share my joy with each of you. [18]You should be happy about this. Rejoice with me for having this privilege of dying for you.

Timothy and Epaphroditus Are Coming Soon

[19]If the Lord is willing, I will send Timothy to see you soon. Then when he comes back, he can cheer me up. He can tell me all about you and how you are getting along. [20]There is no one like Timothy for really caring about you. [21]Everyone else worries about his own plans and not those of Jesus Christ. [22]But you know Timothy. He has been just like a son to me, helping me to preach the Good News. [23]I hope to send him to you. I will do this when I find out what will happen to me here. [24]And I am trusting the Lord that soon I may come to see you.

[25]Meanwhile, I thought I ought to send Epaphroditus back to you. You sent him to help me in my need. He and I have been real brothers, working and battling side by side. [26]Now I am sending him home again. He has been homesick for all of you. He is upset because you heard that he was ill. [27]He was so sick that he almost died. But God had mercy on him and on me too. He didn't allow me to have this sorrow with so much other sadness.

[28]So, all the more, I want to get him back to you again. I know how thankful you will be to see him. That will make me happy and lighten all my cares. [29]Welcome him in the Lord with great joy, and show your thanks. [30]He risked

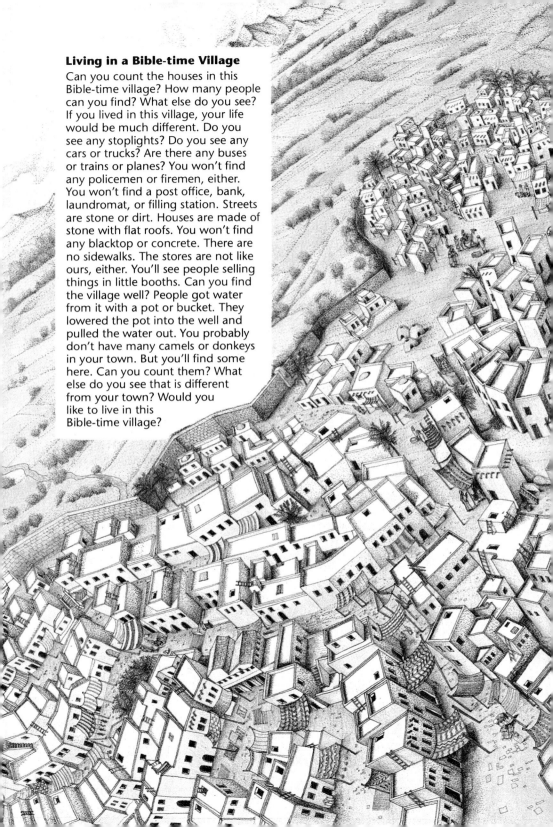

Living in a Bible-time Village

Can you count the houses in this Bible-time village? How many people can you find? What else do you see? If you lived in this village, your life would be much different. Do you see any stoplights? Do you see any cars or trucks? Are there any buses or trains or planes? You won't find any policemen or firemen, either. You won't find a post office, bank, laundromat, or filling station. Streets are stone or dirt. Houses are made of stone with flat roofs. You won't find any blacktop or concrete. There are no sidewalks. The stores are not like ours, either. You'll see people selling things in little booths. Can you find the village well? People got water from it with a pot or bucket. They lowered the pot into the well and pulled the water out. You probably don't have many camels or donkeys in your town. But you'll find some here. Can you count them? What else do you see that is different from your town? Would you like to live in this Bible-time village?

his life for the work of Christ. He was near death while doing things for me that you couldn't do.

Knowing Jesus Is Worth Everything

3 Whatever happens, dear friends, be glad in the Lord. I never get tired of telling you this. It is good for you to hear it again and again.

²Watch out for those wicked men. I call them "dangerous dogs." They say you must be circumcised to be saved. ³It isn't the *cutting of our bodies* that makes us children of God. We are made his children by *worshiping him with our spirits*. That is the only true "circumcision." We Christians glory in what Christ Jesus has done for us. We know that we are helpless to save ourselves.

????????????????????????????????

Which two women did Paul beg to stop quarreling?

(Read 4:2 for the answer.)

????????????????????????????????

⁴If anyone has reason to hope he could save himself, it would be I. If others could be saved by what they are, I could too! ⁵I was circumcised when I was eight days old. I was born into a pure Jewish home. It was a branch of the old original Benjamin family. So I was a real Jew if there ever was one! I was a member of the Pharisees. They demand strict obedience to every Jewish law and custom. ⁶And honest? Yes, so much so that I tried to destroy the Church. I tried to obey every Jewish law down to the very last point.

⁷I once thought all these things were important. But now I've thrown them all away. Now I can put my trust and hope in Christ alone. ⁸Everything else is worthless. It can't be compared with the priceless gain of knowing Christ Jesus my Lord. I have put aside all else. I count it worth less than nothing, in order that I can have Christ. ⁹Then I can become one with him. I no longer count on being saved by obeying God's laws. I am trusting Christ to save me. God's way of making us right with himself depends

on faith in Christ. ¹⁰I have given up everything else. I have found it to be the only way to really know Christ. It is the way to experience the power that brought him back to life. It is the way to find out what it means to suffer with him. ¹¹It doesn't matter to me what it takes. I will live in the new life of those who are alive from the dead.

Forget the Past and Reach for the Future

¹²I don't mean to say I am perfect. I haven't learned all I should yet. But I keep running the race. At the end I will finally be all that Christ saved me to be.

¹³No, dear brothers, I am still not all I should be. But I am bringing all my energies to bear on one thing. I am forgetting the past and looking forward to what lies ahead. ¹⁴I am running to reach the end of the race. Then I will receive the prize for which God has called us in Christ.

¹⁵I hope all of you who are grown Christians will agree with me. If you disagree on some point, God will make it plain to you. ¹⁶For now, obey the truth you have.

¹⁷Dear brothers, pattern your lives after mine. Pay attention to those who live up to my example. ¹⁸I have told you before, now I say it again with tears in my eyes. There are many who live like they are enemies of the cross of Christ.

Pray instead of worrying

Don't worry about anything. Instead, pray about everything.

Philippians 4:6

---

¹⁹Their future is eternal loss, for their god is their enjoyment. They are proud of what they should be ashamed of. All they think about is this life here on earth. ²⁰But our homeland is in Heaven, where our Savior, the Lord Jesus Christ, is. We are looking forward to his return from there. ²¹When he comes back, he will change these dying bodies of ours. He will make them into glorious bodies like his own. He will use the same mighty power that he uses to rule all things.

Think about What Is True, Good, and Right

4 Dear brothers, I love you and long to see you. You are my joy and the reward for my work. My beloved friends, stay true to the Lord.

²And now I want to beg with those two dear women, Euodias and Syntyche. Please, with the Lord's help, stop arguing. Be friends again. ³And I ask you, my true friend, to help these women. They worked side by side with me in telling the Good News to others. They worked with Clement and the rest of my fellow workers. Their names are written in the Book of Life.

⁴Always be full of joy in the Lord. I'll say it again—rejoice! ⁵Let everyone see that you have mercy in all you do. Remember that the Lord is coming soon. ⁶Don't worry about anything. Instead, pray about everything. Tell God your needs, and don't forget to thank him for his answers. ⁷If you do this, you will find God's peace. It is far more wonderful than the human mind can understand. God's peace will keep your thoughts and your hearts as you trust in Christ Jesus.

God will help you obey him

I can do everything God asks me to with the help of Christ. He gives me strength and power.

Philippians 4:13

---

⁸And now, brothers, as I close this letter, let me say one more thing. Fix your thoughts on what is true and good and right. Think about things that are pure and lovely. Dwell on the fine, good things in others. Think about all you can praise God for and be glad about. ⁹Put into practice all you learned from me and saw me doing. Then the God of peace will be with you.

God Gives Us What We Need to Serve Him

¹⁰I praise the Lord that you are helping me again. I know you have always been anxious to send what you could. But for a while you didn't have the chance.

¹¹Not that I was ever in need. I have learned how to get along happily if I have much or little. ¹²I know how to live on almost nothing or with everything. I have learned a secret. I can be content and happy in every situation. It doesn't matter if I have a full stomach or am hungry. I am content if I have plenty or am in need. ¹³I can do everything God asks me to with the help of Christ. He gives me strength and power. ¹⁴But even so, you have done right in helping me in my present time of trouble.

God will take care of all your needs

And it is he who will supply all your needs from his riches in glory. He does this because of what Christ Jesus has done for us.

Philippians 4:19

---

¹⁵You know that I brought the Good News to you. Then I went on my way, leaving Macedonia. Only you Philippians became my partners in giving and receiving. No other church did this. ¹⁶Even when I was over in Thessalonica you sent help twice. ¹⁷I am thankful for your gifts. But what makes me happiest is the reward you will have because of your kindness.

¹⁸At the moment I have all I need. I have more than I need! I am supplied with the gifts you sent me when Epaphroditus came. They are a sweet-smelling sacrifice that pleases God well. ¹⁹And it is he who will supply all your needs from his riches in glory. He does this because of what Christ Jesus has done for us. ²⁰Now unto God our Father be glory forever and ever. Amen.

Sincerely, Paul

A P.S. from Paul

P.S. ²¹Say hello for me to all the Christians there. The brothers with me send their greetings, too. ²²All the other Christians here want to greet you. Those who work in Caesar's palace especially say "hello." ²³The blessings of our Lord Jesus Christ be upon your spirits.

COLOSSIANS

Why is it important to read your Bible? The Bible is God's book. It tells us what God says. Do you want to know the truth about God? He tells you in the Bible. The Bible tells us what Christians should believe.

But some Christians forget this. They listen to other teachings. They add these strange teachings to Bible teachings. They still call themselves Christians. But they believe many things Christians should not believe! This was the problem with the Colossians. They were mixing other teachings with God's teachings. So Paul wrote this letter to help them. This is what Paul said they should do: First, believe in Jesus. Believe that he died for us. Believe that he rose from the dead. That is the foundation for all we believe. Second, know your Bible. Know what God says. Let his teaching guide your life each day. Third, live the way God wants. Help others live the way he wants. Stay away from false teachings.

Paul wrote to the church at Colosse while he was a prisoner at Rome. He had not been at Colosse on his missionary journeys. But Paul knew how to help these people. He helped them know what they should believe. He helps us know what we should believe, too.

Paul: Chosen by God

1 *From:* Paul, chosen by God to be Jesus Christ's messenger, and from Brother Timothy.

²*To:* The faithful Christian brothers and sisters in the city of Colosse.

May God our Father shower you with blessings and fill you with his peace.

Paul's Prayer for the Colossians

³When we pray for you, we give thanks to God. He is the Father of our Lord Jesus Christ. ⁴We have heard how you trust the Lord and how you love his people. ⁵We know you are looking forward to the joys of Heaven. You have looked forward to it ever since the Good News

first was preached to you. ⁶The same Good News that came to you is going out all over the world. It is changing lives everywhere. It changed yours since the day you heard about God's great kindness to sinners.

⁷Epaphras, our much-loved fellow worker, was the one who brought you this Good News. He is Jesus Christ's faithful slave, here to help us in your place. ⁸He told us about the love that the Holy Spirit has given you.

Jesus made everything there is

Christ is the exact copy of the unseen God. He lived before God made anything at all. Christ created everything in Heaven and earth. He was before all else began. His power holds everything together.

Colossians 1:15-17

---

⁹Ever since we heard about you we have been praying. We ask God to help you understand what he wants you to do. We ask him to make you wise about spiritual things. ¹⁰We ask that the way you live will please the Lord and honor him. That way you will always be doing kind things for others. At the same time you are learning to know God better and better.

¹¹We are praying, too, that you will be filled with his mighty, glorious strength. That way you can keep going no matter what happens. You will always be full of the joy of the Lord. ¹²We pray that you will be thankful to the Father. He has made us fit to share the things given to those who live in God's light. ¹³For he has rescued us out of Satan's kingdom. He has brought us into the Kingdom of his dear Son. ¹⁴His Son bought our freedom with his blood and forgave us all our sins.

Who Is Jesus Christ?

¹⁵Christ is the exact copy of the unseen God. He lived before God made any-thing at all. ¹⁶Christ created everything

in Heaven and earth. He created the things we can see and the things we can't see. All kings and kingdoms, rulers and powers were made by Christ. He made them for his own use and glory. ¹⁷He was before all else began. His power holds everything together. ¹⁸He is the Head of the body which is his Church. He is the beginning. He is the Leader of all those who rise from the dead. So he is first in everything. ¹⁹Why? Because God wanted all of himself to be in his Son.

²⁰Because of what his Son did, God cleared a path for everything to come to him. Everything means all things in Heaven and on earth. Christ's death on the cross has made peace with God for all by his blood. ²¹This includes you who were once so far away from God. You were his enemies and hated him. You were separated from him by your evil thoughts and actions. Yet now he has brought you back as his friends. ²²He has done this through the death on the cross of his own human body. As a result, Christ has brought you into the very presence of God. You are standing before him holy, with nothing left against you. ²³The only condition is that you fully believe the Truth. Stand in it steadfast and firm. Be strong in the Lord. Be sure of the Good News that Jesus died for you. Never shift from trusting him to save you. This is the wonderful news that came to each of you. It is now spreading all over the world. And I, Paul, have the joy of telling it to others.

Paul's Job

²⁴But part of my work is to suffer for you. I am glad to do it. I am helping to finish up Christ's sufferings for his body, the Church.

²⁵God has sent me to help his Church and to tell his secret plan. ²⁶⁻²⁷He has kept this secret for centuries and gener-ations past. But now he is pleased to tell it to the brothers and sisters. The riches and glory of his plan are for you Gen-tiles, too. This is the secret: *Christ in your hearts is your only hope of glory.*

²⁸So everywhere we go we talk about Christ to all who will listen. We warn them and teach them as well as we know

how. We want to present each one to God. We want them to be perfect because of what Christ has done for each of them. ²⁹This is my work. I can do it only because Christ's mighty power is at work within me.

2 I wish you could know how much I have struggled for you. I've struggled for the church at Laodicea and for many others who don't know me. ²I have prayed that you will be encouraged and knit together in love. I have prayed that you will have the rich experience of knowing Christ. I want you to know him with clear understanding. For God's secret plan, now at last made known, is Christ himself. ³In him lie hidden all the treasures of wisdom and knowledge.

⁴I am saying this so no one can fool you with smooth talk. ⁵For though I am far away from you my heart is with you. I am happy because you are getting along so well. I am happy because of your strong faith in Christ.

A New Life in Christ

⁶You trusted Christ to save you. So now trust him, too, for each day's problems. Live in close union with him. ⁷Let your roots grow down into him and draw up strength from him. See that you go on growing in the Lord. Become strong and vigorous in the truth you were taught. Let your lives overflow with joy and thanksgiving for all he has done.

⁸Don't let others spoil your faith and joy with their philosophies. They give wrong and shallow answers built on men's thoughts and ideas. The things they teach are not built on what Christ has said. ⁹For in Christ there is all of God in a human body. ¹⁰So you have everything when you have Christ! Then you are filled with God through your union with Christ. He is the highest Ruler. And he is over every other power.

¹¹When you came to Christ, he set you free from your evil desires. He didn't do this by the work of circumcision. He used the baptism of your souls. ¹²In baptism your old, evil nature died and was buried with him. Then you came up out of death with him into a new life. Why? Because you trusted the Word of the mighty God who raised Christ from the dead.

¹³You were dead in sins, and your sinful desires were not yet cut away. Then he gave you a share in the life of Christ when he forgave all your sins. ¹⁴He erased the charges against you. Those charges are the commands which you did not obey. He took this list of sins and destroyed it by nailing it to Christ's cross. ¹⁵In this way God took away Satan's power to say you sinned. God showed the world Christ's victory at the cross where he took your sins away.

These Rules Were Made to Be Broken

¹⁶So don't let anyone blame you for what you eat or drink. It doesn't matter if you celebrate holidays and feasts or new moons or Sabbaths. ¹⁷These rules ended when Christ came. They were only shadows of the real thing which is Christ himself. ¹⁸Don't let anyone blame you when you refuse to worship angels. They say they have seen a vision. They think you should, too. These proud men are blinded by their own ideas. ¹⁹But they are not connected to Christ. He is the Head to which all of us who are his body are joined. We are joined together by his strong cords. We grow only as we get our food and strength from God.

????????????????????????????????????
Which Christian doctor was Paul's friend?

(Read 4:14 for the answer.)

????????????????????????????????????

²⁰You died with Christ. This has set you free from following the world's ideas of how to be saved. So why do you keep on following them anyway? Why are you still bound by rules like ²¹not holding, tasting, or touching certain foods? ²²These rules are human teachings. Food was made to be eaten and used up. ²³These rules may seem good. People need to be loyal and humble to keep these rules. They are hard on the body. But they can't conquer a person's evil thoughts and desires. They only make him proud.

Some Rules to Obey

3 You became alive again when Christ rose from the dead. So now set your sights on the rich treasures and joys of Heaven. He sits there beside God in the place of honor and power. ²Let Heaven fill your thoughts. Don't spend your time worrying about things down here. ³You should have as little desire for this world as a dead person does. Your real life is in Heaven with Christ and God. ⁴Christ is our real life. When he comes back, you will shine with him in all his glory.

Heavenly things are more important than earthly things

Let Heaven fill your thoughts. Don't spend your time worrying about things down here.

Colossians 3:2

---

⁵Put away sinful, earthly things. Deaden the evil desires in you. Have nothing to do with sexual sin, impurity, lust, and shameful desires. Don't worship the good things of life, for that is idolatry. ⁶God's terrible anger is upon those who do such things. ⁷You used to do them when your life was still part of this world. ⁸But now is the time to throw away anger, hatred, cursing, and dirty language.

Remember what Jesus has taught and share it with others

Remember what Christ taught. Let his words enrich your lives and make you wise. Teach each other. Sing psalms and hymns and spiritual songs. Sing to the Lord with thankful hearts.

Colossians 3:16

---

⁹Don't tell lies to each other. It was your old life with all its evil that did that sort of thing. Now it is dead and gone. ¹⁰You are living a brand new kind of life. You are always learning more and more of what is right. This life is always trying to be more like Christ who created it. ¹¹In this new life your nation or race or education or social group means nothing. Christ is what matters, and he has been given to all.

¹²God has chosen you and given you this new kind of life. He has deep love and concern for you. So you should have a heart full of mercy and kindness to others. Be humble and ready to suffer quietly and patiently. ¹³Be gentle and ready to forgive. Never hold grudges. Remember, the Lord forgave you, so you must forgive others.

¹⁴Most of all, let love guide your life. Then the whole church will stay together in perfect harmony. ¹⁵Let the peace that comes from Christ be always present in your hearts and lives. Because, as members of his body, you should have peace with each other. And always be thankful.

¹⁶Remember what Christ taught. Let his words enrich your lives and make you wise. Teach each other. Sing psalms and hymns and spiritual songs. Sing to the Lord with thankful hearts. ¹⁷And whatever you do or say, be a model of the Lord Jesus. Come with him to God the Father to give him your thanks.

Some Rules for Families and Friends

¹⁸You wives, submit yourselves to your husbands. That is what the Lord has planned for you. ¹⁹You husbands must love your wives. Do not be bitter against them or harsh.

²⁰You children must always obey your fathers and mothers. For this pleases the Lord. ²¹Fathers, don't scold your children so much that they quit trying.

²²You slaves must always obey your earthly masters. Don't only try to please them when they are watching you. Obey them because of your love for the Lord and because you want to please him. ²³Work hard and with good cheer at all you do. Do everything like you were working for the Lord and not only for your masters. ²⁴Remember, it is the Lord Christ who is going to pay you. He will give you your full portion of all he owns.

He is the one you are really working for. ²⁵If you don't do your best for him, he will pay you in a way that you won't like. He has no favorite people who can be lazy.

4 You slave owners must be just and fair to all your slaves. Always remember that you have a Master in Heaven who is closely watching you.

²Don't be weary in prayer. Keep at it! Watch for God's answers, and remember to be thankful when they come. ³Don't forget to pray for us, too. Pray that God will give us a chance to preach the Good News of Christ. That is why I am here in jail. ⁴Pray that I will be bold enough to make it plain, as I should.

⁵Make the most of your chances to tell others the Good News. Be wise in all your contacts with them. ⁶Let your words be kind as well as real. Then you will have the right answer for everyone.

Paul Says Good-bye

⁷Tychicus, our much-loved brother, will tell you how I am getting along. He is a hard worker and serves the Lord with me. ⁸I have sent him on this special trip. He has come to see how you are and to comfort and cheer you. ⁹I am also sending Onesimus, a faithful and much-loved brother. He is one of your own people. He and Tychicus will give you all the latest news.

**When you do any work,
do it for the Lord**

Work hard and with good cheer at all you do. Do everything like you were working for the Lord.

Colossians 3:23

---

¹⁰Aristarchus, who is with me here as a prisoner, sends you his love. So does Mark, a relative of Barnabas. And as I said before, welcome Mark if he comes your way. ¹¹Jesus Justus also sends his love. These are the only Jewish Christians working with me here. What a comfort they have been!

¹²Epaphras, from your city, a servant of Christ Jesus, sends you his love. He is

Prisons

COLOSSIANS 4:10

In Bible times, prisons were much worse than they are today. Chains were often fastened to a prisoner's hands, feet, or neck. Some chains were very short. This kept the prisoner from moving. Prisoners sometimes were put in wooden stocks. A prisoner in stocks could not move. Prisons were dark, often without windows. So the air was stuffy. There were no toilets like ours and no running water. So prisons smelled. Rats were common. The small amount of food was bad. Guards sometimes forced families of prisoners to pay money. If they didn't, the prisoner was tortured. People were put into prison for crimes. But they also went to prison if they owed money and could not pay it back. Many went to prison for no good reason. They were blamed for crimes they did not commit. Christians were sometimes sent to prison just because they told others about Jesus. How would you feel if you got sent to prison for telling people about Jesus?

always praying for you. He asks God to make you strong and perfect. He asks God to help you know his will in everything you do. [13]I can tell you that he has worked hard for you with his prayers. He also prays for the Christians in Laodicea and Hierapolis.

[14]Our dear doctor Luke sends his love, and so does Demas.

[15]Please give my greeting to the Christian friends at Laodicea. Greet Nymphas and those who meet in his home. [16]After you have read this letter, pass it on to the church at Laodicea. And read the letter I wrote to them. [17]Tell Archippus, "Be sure that you do all the Lord has told you to."

[18]Here is my own greeting in my own handwriting. Remember me here in jail. May God's blessings surround you.

Sincerely, Paul

FIRST THESSALONIANS

Thessalonica was a big city. It had about 200,000 people. Thessalonica also had a good seaport. Merchants came in ships to buy and sell in the city. Merchants also traveled the main road, buying and selling. After Paul and Silas were beaten and thrown into prison at Philippi, they went to Thessalonica. As he usually did, Paul preached first at the synagogue. Some Jewish people believed. Many Greeks and women believed. These people, and others, became the church that Paul wrote this letter to. Some people did not like Paul's preaching about Jesus. They stirred up others and started a riot. Paul had to leave the city. These people kept attacking the Christians who stayed. Paul was concerned. So he sent Timothy back to see how things were going. Timothy returned to Paul with good news. Paul wrote this letter to the Thessalonian Christians. He was thankful for Timothy's good news. But he was concerned about the lies people were telling about Paul and his missionary friends. He tried to answer each one. Paul urges the people there to love each other. They should live so they will please God.

1 *From:* Paul, Silas, and Timothy.
To: The church at Thessalonica. You belong to God the Father and the Lord Jesus Christ. May blessings and peace of heart be your rich gifts. They are from God our Father and from Jesus Christ our Lord.

God Has Chosen You; Be an Example to Others

²We thank God for you and pray for you always. ³We never forget your loving deeds as we pray to our God and Father. We remember your strong faith and patient hope in our Lord Jesus Christ.

⁴We know that God has chosen you, dear brothers, much beloved of God. ⁵When we brought you the Good News, it was not just words to you. No, you listened and wanted to understand. What we told you produced a powerful effect upon you. The Holy Spirit made you sure that what we said was true. Our lives were more proof to you of the truth of our message. ⁶So you became followers of us and of the Lord. You welcomed our message with joy from the Holy Spirit. It didn't matter what trials and sorrows it brought you.

[7]Then you became an example to all the other Christians in Greece. [8]Now the Word of the Lord has spread out from you to others everywhere. It has gone far beyond your city. Wherever we go we find people telling us about your faith in God. We don't need to tell *them* about it. [9]*They* keep telling *us* about the wonderful welcome you gave us. They tell us how you turned away from your idols to God. Now the living and true God is your only Master. [10]They speak of how you are waiting for the return of God's Son from Heaven. He is Jesus, whom God brought back to life. He is our only Savior from God's terrible anger against sin.

Paul Remembers His Friends

2 You know, dear brothers, how helpful that visit was. [2]You know how badly we were treated at Philippi just before we came. You know how much we suffered there. Yet God gave us the courage to boldly repeat the same message to you. We did this even though we were surrounded by enemies. [3]We were not preaching to trick you, or with evil reasons in mind.

The Lord helps our love grow so that it spills over to other people

May the Lord make your love grow and overflow to each other. And may you love everyone else, just as we love you.

1 Thessalonians 3:12

---

[4]For we speak as messengers from God, trusted by him to tell the truth. We don't change his message so that those who hear will like it. We serve God alone. He knows our hearts' deepest thoughts. [5]Never once did we try to win you with flattery. You know we weren't pretending to be your friends so you would give us money! God knows this is true. [6]As for praise, we have never asked for it from you or anyone else. As apostles of Christ we did have a right to some honor from you. [7]But we were as gentle among you as a mother caring for her children. [8]We loved you dearly. And we gave you not only God's message, but our own lives too.

[9]Don't you remember, dear brothers, how hard we worked among you? Night and day we toiled and sweated to earn enough to live on. That way we would not be a burden to anyone there. That is how we preached God's Good News among you. [10]You and God are our witnesses. We have been pure and honest toward every one of you. [11]We talked to you as a father to his own children. We begged of you, encouraged you, and even demanded of you. [12]We didn't want your daily lives to make God ashamed. We wanted you to bring joy to him. Why? Because he invited you into his Kingdom to share his glory.

[13]We will never stop thanking God. For when we preached, you didn't think the words we spoke were our own. You accepted what we said as the very Word of God. It was God's Word. And it changed your lives when you believed it.

[14]Then, dear brothers, you suffered like the churches in Judea. You were hurt by your own people. The same thing happened to them. They suffered from their own people, the Jews. [15]The Jews killed their own prophets. They even killed the Lord Jesus! Now they have hurt us and driven us out. They are against both God and man. [16]They try to keep us from preaching to the Gentiles. They are afraid some might be saved. So their sins continue to grow. But God's anger has caught up with them at last.

[17]Brothers, we were away from you for a little while but our hearts never left you. We tried hard to come back to see you once more. [18]We wanted very much to come. I, Paul, tried again and again, but Satan stopped us. [19]What do we live for? What gives us hope and joy? What is our proud reward and crown? It is you when we stand together before our Lord Jesus Christ. [20]For you are our trophy and joy.

A Job Well Done

3 When I could stand it no longer, I decided to stay alone in Athens. [2-3]I sent Timothy, our brother and fellow worker, God's minister, to visit you. I

sent him to strengthen your faith and encourage you. He was to keep you from becoming weak in the troubles you were going through. You know that such troubles are a part of God's plan for us Christians. 4Even while we were still with you we warned you. We told you ahead of time that suffering would soon come. And it did come!

5I couldn't wait any more. That is why I sent Timothy to find out if your faith was still strong. I was afraid that Satan had gotten the best of you. I was afraid that all our work had been useless. 6Now Timothy has just come back. He brings the welcome news that your faith and love are as strong as ever. He says you remember us with joy and want to see us. We want to see you too. 7So we are greatly comforted, dear brothers. Our own troubles and suffering here crush us. But now we know you are standing true to the Lord. 8So we can bear anything as long as we know that you remain strong in him.

9How can we thank God enough? You have given us joy and delight in our prayers for you. 10Night and day we pray on and on for you. We ask God to let us see you again. We want to fill up any cracks there may yet be in your faith.

11May God our Father and our Lord Jesus send us back to you again. 12May the Lord make your love grow and overflow to each other. And may you love everyone else, just as we love you. 13May God make your hearts strong, sinless, and holy. Then you will stand before him with no guilt. You will do this on the day when our Lord Jesus comes back with his holy ones.

How Can I Please God?

4 Dear brothers, I would like to tell you more. You already know how to please God in your daily living. You know the commands we gave you from the Lord Jesus himself. Now we beg you in the name of the Lord Jesus. You must live more and more closely to that ideal. 3-4God wants you to be holy and pure and to keep clear of all sexual sin. Then each of you will marry in holiness and honor. 5Your marriage won't be in lustful passion like the heathen's. They don't know God and his ways.

6God's will is that you never cheat in this matter by taking another man's wife. The Lord will punish you terribly for this. We have seriously told you about this before. 7God has not called us to be dirty-minded and full of lust. He wants us to be holy and clean. 8Does anyone refuse to live by these rules? Then he is not disobeying the rules of men but of God. He gives his *Holy* Spirit to you.

??????????????????????????????????
When Christ returns, whose voice will be heard?

(Read 4:16 for the answer.)
??????????????????????????????????

9I don't need to say very much to you about loving the brothers. God himself is teaching you to love one another. 10You love all the Christian brothers throughout your whole nation. Even so, dear friends, we beg you to love them more and more. 11Your ambition should be to live a quiet life. Mind your own business and do your own work, as we told you before. 12Then people who aren't Christians will trust and respect you. You won't need to depend on others for the money to pay your bills.

What Will Happen When Christ Returns?

13Brothers, I want you to know what happens when a Christian dies. Then, when it happens, you will not be full of sorrow. For that is what happens to those who have no hope. 14We believe that Jesus died and then came back to life again. So, when Jesus comes back, God will bring back with him all the dead Christians.

15The Lord has told us to tell you about this. Some of us will be living when the Lord comes back. But we won't rise to meet him before those who are in their graves. 16The Lord himself will come down from Heaven. This will happen with a mighty shout. There will be the voice of the archangel and a trumpet of God. The believers who are dead will be the first to rise to meet the Lord. [17]Then we who are alive and remain on the earth will be caught up with them. We will go to the clouds to meet the Lord in the air. We will stay with him forever. [18]So comfort and cheer each other with this news.

Are You Ready for Christ's Return?

5 When is all this going to happen? I really don't need to say anything about that, brothers. [2]You know perfectly well that no one knows. That day of the Lord will come when you don't expect it. It will come like a thief in the night. [3]When people say, "Everything is quiet and peaceful," then disaster will fall on them. It will happen as suddenly as a woman's birth pains begin when her child is born. There will be no place to hide.

Don't try to get even; instead, do something good

See that no one pays back evil for evil. Always try to do good to each other and to everyone else.

1 Thessalonians 5:15

---

[4]But, dear brothers, you are not in the dark about these things. You won't be surprised as by a thief when that day of the Lord comes. [5]You are all children of the light and of the day. You do not belong to darkness and night. [6]So be on your guard, not asleep like the others. Watch for his coming, and stay sober. [7]Night is the time for sleep and the time when people get drunk. [8]But let us who live in the light keep sober. Let us be protected by the armor of faith and love. Let us wear as our helmet the happy hope of salvation.

Keep praying

Always keep on praying.

1 Thessalonians 5:17

---

[9]God has not chosen to pour out his anger upon us. He wants to save us through our Lord Jesus Christ. [10]Christ died for us so that we can live with him forever. It won't matter if we are dead or alive at the time of his return. [11]So support each other and build each other up, just as you are already doing.

More Words of Wisdom

[12]Brothers, honor those who work hard among you. They lead you and warn you against all that is wrong. [13]Think highly of them and give them your honest love. They are working to help you. And remember, no arguing among yourselves.

Stay away from bad things

Keep away from every kind of evil.

1 Thessalonians 5:22

---

[14]Dear brothers, warn those who are lazy. Comfort those who are afraid. Take tender care of those who are weak. And be patient with everyone. [15]See that no one pays back evil for evil. Always try to do good to each other and to everyone else. [16]Always be joyful. [17]Always keep on praying. [18]No matter what happens, always be thankful. This is God's will for you who belong to Christ Jesus.

[19]Do not smother the Holy Spirit. [20]Do not tease those who prophesy. [21]But do test everything they say to be sure it is true. If it is, then accept it. [22]Keep away from every kind of evil. [23]May the God of peace himself make you entirely pure and devoted to God. May your spirit and soul and body be kept blameless. May they be blameless until that day when our Lord Jesus Christ comes back. [24]God called you to become his child. He will do all this for you, just as he promised. [25]Dear brothers, pray for us. [26]Shake hands for me with all the brothers there. [27]I command you in the Lord to read this letter to all the Christians. [28]And may rich blessings from our Lord Jesus Christ be with you, every one.

Sincerely, Paul

SECOND THESSALONIANS

Paul was on his second missionary journey when he visited Thessalonica. But his preaching about Jesus angered some Jews. They stirred up a riot and drove him out of town. From there he went to Beroea, then Athens, and then Corinth. He preached in Corinth for 18 months. While there, he wrote the two letters to the Thessalonian church. This letter was written only two or three months after his first letter.

In his first letter, Paul said that Jesus would come back soon. So some of the Christians quit working. "Why work," they asked, "if Jesus is coming back soon?" This kind of attitude caused problems among the people.

Also, evil people were still hurting the Christians. Some said this also showed that Jesus would come soon. Paul corrected these mistakes. He said Jesus would not come back before other things happened. While they wait, Christians should live in a way that will please Jesus when he does return. They should tell others about Jesus. They should stay true to Jesus, no matter how much others hurt them. Jesus will come back someday. But while we are waiting, let's do our best work for him. Being ready for Jesus means obeying him.

Another Letter for the Thessalonians

1 *From:* Paul, Silas, and Timothy.
To: The church of Thessalonica. You are in God our Father and in the Lord Jesus Christ.

²May God the Father and the Lord Jesus Christ give you blessings and peace.

God Is There When the Going Gets Tough

³Dear brothers, giving thanks to God for you is the right thing to do. But it is also our duty to God. Why? Because your faith has grown so much! Also because your love for each other is growing. ⁴We are happy to tell other churches about your patience and faith in God. This is

yours in spite of all the crushing troubles you have.

⁵This shows how fair and just God is. He is using your sufferings to make you ready for his Kingdom. ⁶It is right for him to pay back those who are hurting you with punishment.

The Lord protects us from Satan

But the Lord is faithful.
He will make you strong and
guard you from Satan's
attacks of every kind.

2 Thessalonians 3:3

---

⁷You are suffering. But God will give you rest along with us. This will happen when the Lord Jesus appears suddenly from Heaven. He will come in flaming fire with his mighty angels. ⁸He will bring judgment on those who do not wish to know God. He will judge those who refuse the Good News of our Lord Jesus Christ. ⁹They will be punished in everlasting hell. They will be forever separated from the Lord. They will never see the glory of his power. ¹⁰This will happen when he comes back. Then he will receive praise because of all he has done for his people. And you will be among those praising him. Why? Because you have believed what we told you about him.

¹¹So we keep on praying for you. We pray that our God will make you the kind of children he wants to have. We ask him to make you as good as you wish you could be! He will reward your faith with his power. ¹²Then everyone will be praising the name of the Lord Jesus Christ. Why? Because of the results they see in you. Your greatest glory will be that you belong to him. The mercy of God and of the Lord Jesus Christ has made this possible.

Paul Talks about the Antichrist

2 Now, we have something to say about the coming of our Lord Jesus Christ. Don't be upset, brothers, if you hear that this day of the Lord has already begun. You may hear of people having

visions and special messages from God about this. They may say they have letters that are supposed to have come from me. If this happens, don't believe them. ³Don't be carried away and tricked no matter what they say.

For that day will not come until two things happen. First, there will be a time when many people leave God. Then the lawless man will come. He is the son of hell. ⁴He will be against every god there is. He will tear down everything people worship. He will go in and sit as God in the temple of God. He will do this claiming that he is God. ⁵Don't you remember that I told you this when I was with you? ⁶And you know what is keeping him from being here already. He can come only when his time is ready.

???????????????????????????????
What does Paul put at the end of each letter?

(Read 3:17 for the answer.)
???????????????????????????????

⁷His work is already going on. He won't come until the one holding him back steps out of the way. ⁸Then this wicked one will appear. The Lord Jesus will burn him up with the breath of his mouth. He will destroy him by his presence when he returns. ⁹This man of sin will come as Satan's tool, full of satanic power. He will trick everyone with strange magical shows and miracles. ¹⁰He will fool those who are lost from God. For they have not believed the Truth. They won't believe it and love it and let it save them. ¹¹So God will allow them to believe lies with all their hearts. ¹²They all will be judged for believing lies, refusing the Truth, and enjoying their sins.

Stand Firm and
Keep a Grip on the Truth

¹³But we must forever give thanks to God for you. You are our brothers, loved by the Lord. God chose you from the very first to give you salvation. He cleansed you by the Holy Spirit and by your trusting in the Truth. ¹⁴Through us he told

you the Good News. Through us he called you to share in the glory of our Lord Jesus Christ.

¹⁵So, brothers, stand firm and hold on to the truth. It is the truth we taught you with our letters and our words.

¹⁶I pray to our Lord Jesus Christ. And I pray to God our Father. He has loved us and given us eternal comfort and hope and grace. ¹⁷I ask them to comfort your hearts with all comfort. I pray that they help you in every good thing you say and do.

God Makes Us Strong and Protects Us from Satan

3 Dear brothers, I come to the end of this letter. I ask you to pray for us. Pray that the Lord's message will spread and triumph wherever it goes. Pray that it will win converts everywhere as it did when it came to you. ²Pray, too, that we will be saved out of the hands of evil men. Not everyone loves the Lord. ³But the Lord is faithful. He will make you strong and guard you from Satan's attacks of every kind. ⁴We trust the Lord that you are practicing the things we taught you. We trust that you always will. ⁵May the Lord bring your hearts into a deeper understanding of the love of God and Christ's patience.

No Laziness or Gossiping Allowed

⁶This command, brothers, is given in the name of our Lord Jesus Christ. Stay away from any lazy Christian who doesn't follow the ideal we gave you. ⁷You know that you ought to follow our example. You never saw us loafing. ⁸We never accepted food from anyone without buying it. We worked hard day and night for the money we needed to live

on. We don't want to be a burden to any of you. ⁹We had the right to ask you to feed us. But we wanted to show you firsthand how you should work for your living. ¹⁰While we were with you, we gave you the rule, "He who doesn't work won't eat."

Don't be lazy

While we were with you, we gave you the rule, "He who doesn't work won't eat."

2 Thessalonians 3:10

---

¹¹Yet we hear that some of you are living in laziness. You refuse to work and waste your time in gossip. ¹²We have a command for you in the name of the Lord Jesus Christ. Quiet down, get to work, and earn your own living. ¹³To the rest of you I say, brothers, never be tired of doing right.

¹⁴Watch if anyone refuses to obey what we say in this letter. Notice who he is and stay away from him. That way he may be ashamed of himself. ¹⁵Don't think of him as an enemy. Speak to him as you would to a brother who needs to be warned.

Paul Signs Off with a Blessing

¹⁶May the Lord of peace himself give you his peace no matter what happens. The Lord be with you all.

¹⁷I am writing my greeting with my own hand. I do this at the end of all my letters. It is my proof that the letter is really from me. This is in my own handwriting. ¹⁸May the blessing of our Lord Jesus Christ be upon you all.

Sincerely, Paul

FIRST TIMOTHY

Timothy was a young man who followed God. He had good training. His mother, Eunice, taught him about God. So did his grandmother, Lois. When Timothy became a Christian, he became Paul's helper. He went to many faraway places with Paul. He helped Paul tell others about Jesus. As he helped, Paul taught him.

But Timothy had his share of trouble. It was not easy to be a Christian at that time. Paul wrote this letter to encourage Timothy. He wrote to give him good advice. Paul says to follow leaders who follow God. Watch out for leaders who tell you to do things the Bible says are wrong. Keep your faith in Jesus strong. Keep praying. Live so you will please Jesus.

A Letter to Paul's Son in the Lord

1 *From:* Paul, a missionary of Jesus Christ. I've been sent by the command of God our Savior and by Jesus Christ our hope.

²*To:* Timothy.

Timothy, you are like a son to me in the things of the Lord. Kindness, mercy, and peace to you from God the Father and Jesus Christ our Lord.

Watch Out for False Teachers!

3-4When I left for Macedonia, I asked you to stay there in Ephesus. I want you to stop the men who are teaching wrong doctrine. Put an end to their myths and fables. Stop their talk of endless chains of angels leading up to God. These wild ideas stir up questions and arguments. They don't help people accept God's plan of faith. ⁵I am eager that all the Christians there be filled with love from pure hearts. I want their minds to be clean and their faith to be strong.

⁶But these teachers have missed this whole idea. They spend their time arguing and talking foolishness. ⁷They want to become famous as teachers of the laws of Moses. But they haven't any idea what those laws really show us. ⁸Those laws are good when used as God wanted. ⁹But they were not made for us, whom God has saved. They are for sinners who hate God. These people aren't holy. They curse and swear, attack their fathers and mothers, and murder. 10-11Yes, these laws are made for immoral and impure sinners. They are for homosexuals, kidnappers, and liars. They are against the Good News of our blessed God, whose messenger I am.

Kings

1 TIMOTHY 2:2

The Bible tells us about many kings. Some ruled over big empires like the Roman Empire. They were very powerful men. They controlled many thousands of lives. Others ruled over cities and the surrounding land. They were also powerful. But they did not rule over as many people. They were more like what mayors are today. Kings could do what they wanted. Usually no one told a king what to do. Prophets like Samuel told Israelite kings what God said. But kings did not always listen. Samuel appointed Saul and David as kings. He anointed them with perfumed olive oil. That showed that God had chosen them. David was one of the best warrior kings. Solomon was one of the richest kings of all. He had vast amounts of gold and silver. Egyptian rulers called themselves Pharaoh. Roman rulers called themselves Emperor. They thought they were gods. In most lands, the oldest prince became king when his father died. People did not elect kings. They just obeyed them.

God's Kindness and Mercy for All

¹²I am thankful to Christ Jesus our Lord. He chose me as one of his messengers. He also gave me the strength to be faithful to him. ¹³I used to scoff at the name of Christ. I hunted down his people. I hurt them in every way I could. But God had mercy on me because I didn't know what I was doing. I didn't know Christ at that time. ¹⁴Oh, how kind our Lord was! He gave me so much faith and love in Christ Jesus.

¹⁵There is a true saying. I long that everyone would know it. Christ Jesus came into the world to save sinners. I was the greatest of them all. ¹⁶But God had mercy on me. That way Christ Jesus could use me as an example. He could show everyone how patient he is with even the worst sinners. Then others will know that they, too, can have eternal life. ¹⁷Glory and honor to God forever and ever. He is the King of the ages, the unseen one who never dies. He alone is God, and full of wisdom. Amen.

Hold On to Your Faith

¹⁸Now, Timothy, my son, I have a command for you. Fight well in the Lord's battles. The Lord told us through his prophets that you would. ¹⁹Cling tightly to your faith in Christ. Always keep your conscience clear, doing what you know is right. Some people have not obeyed their consciences. They know they have done what was wrong. So they lost their faith in Christ. ²⁰Hymenaeus and Alexander are two men like this. I had to give them over to Satan to punish them. I did this so they could learn not to bring shame to the name of Christ.

Some Guidelines for Worship

2 ¹I direct you to pray much for others. Beg for God's mercy on them. Give thanks for all he is going to do for them.

²Pray for kings and all who have power over us. Then we can live in peace and quietness. We can spend our time in godly living and thinking much about the Lord. ³This is good and pleases God our Savior. ⁴He longs for all to be saved and to understand the truth. ⁵God is on one side and all the people are on the

other side. The man Christ Jesus is between them to bring them together. ⁶He did this by giving his life for all mankind.

This is the message that God gave to the world. And he gave this message at just the right time. ⁷And I have been chosen as God's minister and missionary. I am to teach the Gentiles about faith and truth.

⁸So I want men everywhere to pray with holy hands lifted up to God. Let them pray free from sin and anger and bad feelings. ⁹⁻¹⁰The women should be the same way. They should be quiet and wear simple clothing. Christian women should be noticed for being kind and good. They should not be seen for their hair or their jewels or fancy clothes. ¹¹Women should listen and learn quietly and meekly.

¹²I never let women teach men or lord it over them. Let them be silent in your church meetings. ¹³Why? Because God made Adam first. And after that he made Eve. ¹⁴And it was not Adam who was fooled by Satan, but Eve. Sin was the result. ¹⁵So God sent pain and suffering to women when their children are born. But he will save their souls if they are faithful, quiet, good, and loving.

Guidelines for Church Leaders

3 If a man wants to be a pastor he has a good ambition. This is a true saying. ²A pastor must be a good man whose life cannot be spoken against. He must have only one wife. He must be hardworking and unselfish. He must be orderly and do many good deeds. He must enjoy having guests in his home. And he must be a good Bible teacher. ³He must not be a drinker or a man who quarrels a lot. But he must be gentle and kind. And he must not be one who loves money. ⁴He must have a well-behaved family, with children who obey quickly and quietly. ⁵If a man can't make his own family behave, how can he help the church?

⁶The pastor must not be a new Christian. For if he is, he might become proud of being chosen so soon. This may cause him to fall like Satan. ⁷Also, he must be well spoken of by people who aren't

Christians. Then Satan can't trap him because of people's complaints.

⁸The deacons must be the same sort of good, steady men as the pastors. They must not be heavy drinkers. And they must not be greedy for money. ⁹They must follow Christ with all their hearts. He is the hidden Source of their faith. ¹⁰Before they are deacons, they should be given other jobs in the church. This will test their character and ability. If they do well, then they may be chosen as deacons.

??????????????????????????????????
Which two men did Paul give to Satan to punish?
(Read 1:20 for the answer.)
??????????????????????????????????

¹¹Their wives must be serious, not heavy drinkers, and not gossipers. But they must be faithful in everything. ¹²Deacons should have only one wife. They should have happy, obedient families. ¹³Those who do well as deacons will be well rewarded by respect from others. They will also develop their own confidence and bold trust in the Lord.

¹⁴I am writing these things to you now, though I hope to be there soon. ¹⁵But I may not come for awhile. And I wanted you to know how one should live in the church of the living God. For his church contains and holds high the truth of God.

¹⁶It is true that living a godly life is not an easy matter. But the answer lies in Christ. He came to earth as a man and was proved pure in his Spirit. He was served by angels and was preached among the nations. The world believed in him, and he was received up to his glory in Heaven.

Ignore False Teachers: They Lie

4 The Holy Spirit tells us clearly about the last times. Some in the church will turn away from Christ. They will become followers of teachers with devilish ideas. ²These teachers will tell lies with straight faces. They will do it so often that their consciences won't bother them.

³They will say it is wrong to be married and wrong to eat meat. But God gave these things to us. They should be taken with thanks by Christians who know the truth. ⁴Everything God made is good. We may eat it gladly if we are thankful for it. ⁵It is made good by the Word of God and prayer.

⁶Explain this to the others. Then you will be doing your duty as a worthy pastor. It shows you are fed by faith and by the teaching you have followed.

⁷Don't waste time arguing over foolish ideas and silly myths and legends. Spend your time and energy in the exercise of keeping spiritually fit. ⁸Bodily exercise is all right. But spiritual exercise is much more important. It helps you in everything you do. So exercise your spirit. Practice being a better Christian. This will help you now in this life and in the next life, too. ⁹⁻¹⁰This is the truth and everyone should accept it. We work hard and suffer much in order that people will believe it. Our hope is in the living God who died for all. He especially died for those who have accepted his salvation.

God can use you even if you're young

Don't let anyone think little of you because you are young.
Be their example.
Let them follow the way you teach and live.

1 Timothy 4:12

---

¹¹Teach these things and make sure everyone learns them well. ¹²Don't let anyone think little of you because you are young. Be their example. Let them follow the way you teach and live. Be a pattern for them in your love, your faith, and your clean thoughts. ¹³Until I get there, read and explain the Bible to the church. Preach God's Word.

¹⁴Be sure to use the abilities God has given you through his prophets. He gave them to you when the church elders laid their hands upon your head. ¹⁵Put these abilities to work. Work hard at what you do so everyone will notice your growth. ¹⁶Keep a close watch on all you do and think. Stay true to what is right. Then God will bless you and use you to help others.

Do Your Part to Help God's Family

5 Never speak sharply to an older man. Plead with him with respect just as if he were your own father. Talk to the younger men as you would to much-loved brothers. ²Treat the older women as mothers. Treat the girls as your sisters. Think only pure thoughts about them.

³The church should take care of widows if they have no one to help them. ⁴But if they have children or grandchildren they should help the church. Kindness should begin at home, caring for needy parents. This is something that pleases God very much.

⁵The church should care for widows who are poor and alone in the world. But the widows should be hoping in God and spending much time in prayer. ⁶Don't help them if they are gossiping and seeking only pleasure. This will ruin their souls. ⁷This should be your church rule. That way the Christians will know and do what is right.

⁸Some won't even care for their own relatives. They won't even take care of those living in their own family. But they have no right to say they are Christians. Such people are worse than the heathen.

⁹Now a widow might want to become one of the special church workers. If so, she should be at least 60 years old and have been married only once. ¹⁰She must be well thought of by everyone because of the good she has done. Has she brought up her children well? Has she been kind to strangers as well as to other Christians? Has she helped those who are sick and hurt? Is she always ready to show kindness?

¹¹The younger widows should not become members of this special group. After awhile they are likely to forget their promise to Christ and marry again. ¹²Then they will stand condemned be-

cause they broke their first promise. [13]Besides, they are likely to be lazy. They may spend their time gossiping around from house to house. They get into other people's business. [14]So I think it is better for these younger widows to marry again. They should have children and take care of their own homes. Then no one will be able to say anything against them. [15]I am afraid that some of them have already turned away from the church. They have been led astray by Satan.

[16]Let me remind you again that a widow's relatives must take care of her. They should not leave this to the church. Then the church can spend its money for the care of women who are really widows.

[17]Pastors who do their work well should be paid well and highly honored. This is especially true of those who work hard at both preaching and teaching. [18]The Bible says, "Never tie up the mouth of an ox that is treading out the grain. Let him eat as he goes along!" And in another place it says, "Those who work deserve their pay!"

[19]Don't listen to complaints against the pastor. Only listen if there are two or three witnesses to accuse him. [20]If he has sinned, then he should be rebuked in front of the whole church. That will keep others from following his example.

[21]I solemnly command you before God and Jesus Christ and the holy angels. Do this whether the pastor is a special friend of yours or not. All must be treated just the same. [22]Never be in a hurry about choosing a pastor. You may overlook his sins. And it will look as if you approve of them. Be sure that you yourself stay away from all sin. [23]This doesn't mean you should completely give up drinking wine. You ought to take a little as medicine for your stomach and your other weaknesses.

[24]Remember that some men lead sinful lives, and everyone knows it. In such situations you can do something about it. But in other cases only the Judgment Day will reveal the terrible truth. [25]In the same way, everyone knows how much good some pastors do. But sometimes

their good deeds aren't known until long afterward.

Money Isn't Everything

6 Christian slaves should work hard for their owners and respect them. Never let it be said that Christ's people are poor workers. Don't let the name of God or his teaching be laughed at because of this.

[2]If their owner is a Christian, that is no excuse for slowing down. Rather they should work all the harder. Why? A brother in the faith is being helped by their efforts.

Teach these truths, Timothy, and encourage all to obey them.

[3]Some may deny these things. But they are the sound, wholesome teachings of the Lord Jesus Christ. They are the foundation for a godly life. [4]Anyone who says anything different is both proud and stupid. He is arguing over the meaning of Christ's words. He is stirring up arguments that end in jealousy and anger. They only lead to name-calling, accusations, and evil suspicions. [5]These people's minds are warped by sin. They don't know how to tell the truth.

Always think and do what is right

Keep a close watch on all you do and think. Stay true to what is right. Then God will bless you and use you to help others.

1 Timothy 4:16

To them the Good News is just a means of making money. Keep away from them.

[6]Do you want to be truly rich? You already are if you are happy and good. [7]After all, we didn't bring any money with us when we came into the world. We can't carry away a single penny when we die. [8]So we should be satisfied without money if we have enough food and clothing. [9]But people who long to be rich do all kinds of wrong things for money. They do things that hurt them and make them evil-minded. Finally these things send them to hell itself.

¹⁰The love of money is the first step toward all kinds of sin. Some people have even turned away from God because of their love for it. As a result they have pierced themselves with many sorrows.

Keep Up the Good Fight!

¹¹O Timothy, you are God's man. Run from evil things. Work instead at doing what is right and good. Learn to trust him and love others and to be patient and gentle. ¹²Fight on for God. Hold tightly to the eternal life that God has given you. Hold on to the good confession you have spoken before many people.

Do good and stay away from evil

Run from evil things. Work instead at doing what is right and good. Learn to trust him and love others and to be patient and gentle.

1 Timothy 6:11

---

¹³I command you before God, who gives life to all. I command you before Christ Jesus, who gave a fearless testimony before Pontius Pilate. ¹⁴I command that you do all he has told you to do. Do this from now until our Lord Jesus Christ comes back. ¹⁵For in his own time Christ will be revealed from Heaven. The blessed and only Almighty God will do this. He is the King of kings and Lord of lords. ¹⁶He alone can never die. He lives in light so terrible that no human being can come near him. No man has ever seen him or ever will. Unto him be honor and everlasting power and dominion forever and ever! Amen.

¹⁷Tell those who are rich not to be proud. Tell them not to trust in their money. It will soon be gone. Their pride and trust should be in the living God. He richly gives us all we need for our enjoyment. ¹⁸Tell them to use their money to do good. They should be rich in good works and give happily to those in need. They should always be ready to share with others whatever God has given them. ¹⁹By doing this they will be storing up real treasure for themselves in Heaven. This is the only safe way to save for the future! And then they will be living a truly fruitful Christian life.

²⁰Oh, Timothy, don't fail to do these things that God entrusted to you. Keep out of foolish arguments with those who brag about what they know. This proves their lack of knowledge. ²¹Some of these people have missed the most important thing in life. They don't know God. May God's mercy be upon you.

Sincerely, Paul

SECOND
TIMOTHY

Timothy was a young man. Some people thought he was too young to do important work. They looked down on him. But Paul didn't. He gave Timothy many important jobs. He gave Timothy some of his own work. Timothy became one of Paul's closest friends. He became one of his most important helpers. In this letter, Paul urges Timothy to be faithful to God, to tell others the Good News about Jesus, to live like a Christian, and to be strong like a good soldier. This is one of Paul's last letters. Within a year, Paul would die. He seemed to know this. He had fought well. He was near the end. But he knew there would be a crown waiting for him in Heaven.

A Letter to Encourage Timothy

1 *From:* Paul, Jesus Christ's missionary. I have been sent by God to tell men and women everywhere about eternal life. He has promised it to them through faith in Jesus Christ.

²*To:* Timothy, my dear son. May God the Father and Christ Jesus our Lord give you kindness, mercy, and peace.

Keep Up the Good Work!

³How I thank God for you, Timothy. I pray for you every day. Many times during the long nights I beg my God to bless you richly. He is the God my ancestors served, and mine as well. My only purpose in life is to please him.

⁴How I long to see you again! How happy I would be! I remember your tears as we left each other.

⁵I know how much you trust the Lord. You trust him just as your mother, Eunice, and your grandmother, Lois, do.

I feel sure you are still trusting him as much as ever.

⁶So, I want to remind you to stir into flame the strength and boldness that is in you. It entered into you when I laid my hands upon you and blessed you. ⁷The Holy Spirit doesn't want you to be afraid of people. He wants you to be wise and strong, and to love them.

⁸Stir up this inner power. Then you will never be afraid to tell others about our Lord. You won't be afraid to tell them I'm your friend even though I am in jail. You will be ready to suffer with me for the Lord. He will give you strength in suffering.

⁹He saved us and chose us for his holy work. He didn't do this because we deserved it. It was because that was his plan long before the world began. His plan was to show his love and kindness to us through Christ. ¹⁰Now he has shown this to us by the coming of our Savior

Jesus Christ. He broke the power of death. He showed us the way of everlasting life through trusting him. ¹¹And God has chosen me to be his missionary. I am to preach to the Gentiles and teach them.

We should teach God's truth to others

Teach others those things you and many others have heard me speak about. Teach these great truths to trustworthy men who will pass them on to others.

2 Timothy 2:2

---

¹²That is why I am suffering here in jail. I am not ashamed of it, for I know the one in whom I trust. I am sure that he is able to guard all I have given him. He will do this until the day of his return. ¹³Hold tightly to the pattern of truth I taught you. Hold on to the faith and love Christ Jesus offers you. ¹⁴Guard the ability you were given by the Holy Spirit who lives within you.

Work hard for God

Work hard so God can say to you, "Well done." Be a good workman. Then you won't be ashamed when God examines your work.

2 Timothy 2:15

---

¹⁵As you know, all the Christians who came here from Asia have left me. Even Phygellus and Hermogenes are gone. ¹⁶May the Lord bless Onesiphorus and all his family. He visited me and encouraged me often. His visits revived me like a breath of fresh air. He was never ashamed of my being in jail. ¹⁷When he came to Rome he looked everywhere trying to find me. He finally did. ¹⁸May the Lord give him a special blessing at the day of Christ's return. You know very well how much he helped me at Ephesus.

Be a Good Soldier

2 O Timothy, my son, be strong with the strength Christ Jesus gives you. ²Teach others those things you and many others have heard me speak about. Teach these great truths to trustworthy men who will pass them on to others.

³Take your share of suffering as a good soldier of Jesus Christ. ⁴As Christ's soldier, do not let yourself become tied up in worldly affairs. Then you cannot satisfy the one who has enlisted you in his army. ⁵Follow the Lord's rules for doing his work. An athlete either follows the rules or is thrown out of the game. ⁶Work hard like a farmer who gets paid if he raises a large crop. ⁷Think over these three examples. May the Lord help you to understand how they apply to you.

⁸Don't ever forget the wonderful fact that Jesus Christ was a man. He was born into King David's family. And remember that he was God. This was shown by the fact that he rose again from the dead. ⁹I have preached these truths. So I am in trouble and have been put in jail like a criminal. But the Word of God is not chained, even though I am. ¹⁰I am willing to suffer. I do this so salvation and eternal glory in Christ Jesus will come to God's chosen.

¹¹I am comforted by this truth. When we suffer for Christ it means that we will begin living with him. ¹²We may think that our present service for him is hard. But remember that we are going to rule with him. But if we give up and turn against Christ, then he must turn against us. ¹³When we are weak in faith, he is faithful to us. He cannot disown us if we are a part of himself. He will always carry out his promises to us.

Be a Good Worker

¹⁴Remind your people of these great facts. Command them in the name of the Lord not to argue over unimportant things. Such arguments are confusing and useless and even harmful. ¹⁵Work hard so God can say to you, "Well done." Be a good workman. Then you won't be ashamed when God examines your

work. Know what his Word says and means. [16]Stay away from discussions that lead people into the sin of anger with each other. [17]Things will be said that will burn and hurt for a long time to come. Hymenaeus and Philetus love to argue. They are men like that. [18]They have left the path of truth. They preach the lie that the resurrection of the dead has already happened. They have weakened the faith of some who believe them.

[19]But God's truth stands firm like a great rock. Nothing can shake it! It is a foundation stone. On it is written, "The Lord knows those who are really his." It also says, "A person who calls himself a Christian should stay away from wrong."

[20]In a wealthy home there are dishes made of gold and silver. There are also some made from wood and clay. The expensive dishes are used for guests. The cheap ones are used in the kitchen or to put garbage in. [21]If you stay away from sin you will be a dish made of gold. Then Christ can use you for his highest purposes.

[22]Run from anything that gives you the evil thoughts that young men often have. Stay close to anything that makes you want to do right. Have faith and love with those who love the Lord and have pure hearts.

[23]Again I say, don't get involved in foolish arguments. They only upset people and make them angry. [24]God's people must not argue. They must be gentle, patient teachers of those who are wrong. [25]Be humble when you teach those who are against the truth. If you are humble, God may turn them back to what is true. [26]Then they will come to their senses and escape from Satan's trap. He uses it to catch them whenever he likes. Then they can begin doing the will of God.

Being a Christian Can Be Tough

3 Please understand that the last days will be very hard times for Christians. [2]People will love only themselves and their money. They will be proud and boastful, laughing at God. They will not obey their parents. They will be ungrateful, and bad through and through. [3]They will be hardheaded and never give in to others. They will be liars and troublemakers. They will think nothing of being immoral. They will be rough and cruel. They will sneer at those who try to be good. [4]They will betray their friends. They will be hotheaded, puffed up with pride. They will want to have a good time rather than worship God. [5]They will go to church, but they won't believe anything they hear. Don't be taken in by people like that.

[6]They sneak into homes and make friends with silly, sin-burdened women. They teach them their new doctrines. [7]Women of that kind are forever following new teachers. They never understand the truth. [8]These teachers fight truth just as Jannes and Jambres fought against Moses. They have dirty, twisted minds. They have turned against the Christian faith.

[9]But they won't get away with all this forever. Someday their ways will be well known to everyone, just like Jannes and Jambres.

[10]But you know from watching me

Christians should not argue

God's people must not argue. They must be gentle, patient teachers of those who are wrong.

2 Timothy 2:24

---

that I am not that kind of person. You know what I believe and the way I live and what I want. You know my faith in Christ and how I have suffered. You know my love for you, and my patience. [11]You know how many troubles I have had because of preaching the Good News. You know what was done to me in Antioch, Iconium, and Lystra. But the Lord has delivered me. [12]Those who live godly lives for Christ will be hurt by those who hate him. [13]In fact, evil men and false teachers will become worse and worse. They will trick many because they have been tricked by Satan.

Crowns

2 TIMOTHY 4:8

Do you ever wear a crown on your head? In Bible times, an athlete who won a race or game was sometimes given a crown. It was like winning a trophy today. Sometimes a warrior was given a crown. It was like being given a medal today. These crowns showed that someone had done something special. Roman soldiers put a crown of thorns on Jesus. They were making fun of Jesus being "King of the Jews." A crown was put on the head of a person when he became king. This was called coronation. People still do this in certain countries today. Kings' crowns were often made of gold and jewels. A king couldn't have an ordinary crown. Israel's High Priest wore a cap or turban, something like a crown. It was white with a gold band. On the gold band were the words, "Holiness to the Lord." This showed that the priest was to do only God's work. Some Israelite kings also had the same words on their crowns. This showed that they would serve the Lord. They were appointed by him. You may never wear a king's crown. But the Bible says you can wear special crowns in Heaven (2 Tim. 4:8; 1 Pet. 5:4; James 1:12; Rev. 2:10). You can't see these crowns now. But they are trophies for living the way God wants. God will crown you with them if you please him.

Keep Believing
What You Have Been Taught

[14]But you must keep on believing the things you have been taught. You know they are true. You know that you can trust those of us who have taught you. [15]When you were a small child, you were taught the holy Bible. It makes you wise to accept God's salvation by trusting in Christ Jesus. [16]The whole Bible was given to us by inspiration from God. It is useful to teach us what is true. It helps us to know what is wrong in our lives. It straightens us out and helps us do what is right. [17]It makes us well prepared and fully equipped to do good to everyone.

Share Your Faith

4 Before God and before Christ Jesus I give you a command. Christ Jesus is the one who will judge the living and the dead when he comes in his Kingdom. [2]Preach the Word of God at all times. Do it whenever you get the chance. Do it in season and out. Do it when it is convenient and when it is not. Correct and rebuke people when they need it. Encourage them to do right. All the time feed them patiently with God's Word.

[3]There is going to come a time when people won't listen to the truth. They will look for teachers to tell them just what they want to hear. [4]They won't listen to the Bible. They will happily follow their own ideas.

[5]Stand steady, and don't be afraid of suffering for the Lord. Bring others to Christ. Leave nothing undone that you ought to do.

The Lord will reward his faithful workers

In Heaven a crown is waiting for me. The Lord, the righteous Judge, will give it to me on the day he comes back.

2 Timothy 4:8

---

[6]I say this because I won't be around to help you very much longer. My time has almost run out. Very soon now I will

be on my way to Heaven. [7]I have fought long and hard for my Lord. Through it all I have kept true to him. Now the time has come for me to stop fighting and rest. [8]In Heaven a crown is waiting for me. The Lord, the righteous Judge, will give it to me on the day he comes back. He won't only give it to me. He will give it to all those who are happy he is coming back.

Some Final Words for Timothy

[9]Please come as soon as you can. [10]Demas has left me. He loved the good things of this life and went to Thessalonica. Crescens has gone to Galatia. Titus has gone to Dalmatia. [11]Only Luke is with me. Bring Mark with you when you come, for I need him. [12]Tychicus is gone too. I sent him to Ephesus. [13]When you come, bring the coat I left at Troas with Carpus. Also bring the books, but especially bring the parchments.

[14]Alexander the coppersmith has done me much harm. The Lord will punish him. [15]But be careful of him, for he fought against everything we said.

[16]The first time I was brought before the judge, no one here helped me. Everyone had run away. I hope that they will not be blamed for it. [17]But the Lord stood with me and gave me power. He gave me the chance to boldly preach for all the world to hear. And he saved me from being thrown to the lions. [18]Yes, and the Lord will always deliver me from all evil. He will bring me into his heavenly Kingdom. To God be the glory forever and ever. Amen.

[19]Please say hello for me to Priscilla and Aquila. Greet those living at the home of Onesiphorus. [20]Erastus stayed at Corinth, and I left Trophimus sick at Miletus.

???????????????????????????????
What did Paul want Timothy to bring to him in prison?
(Read 4:13 for the answer.)
???????????????????????????????

[21]Try to be here before winter. Eubulus sends you greetings. So do Pudens, Linus, Claudia, and all the others. [22]May the Lord Jesus Christ be with your spirit.

Farewell, Paul

TITUS

Does your church have a pastor? Someone trained him to be a pastor. Perhaps he went to a Bible school or seminary. In Paul's time there were few Bible schools. Usually older men like Paul trained younger men. Two of the young men Paul trained were Timothy and Titus. Paul wanted them to be leaders. Titus was Greek. Paul had probably helped him to know Jesus. Titus traveled with Paul. He learned much from him. Titus was the one who delivered Paul's first letter to the Corinthians. A few years before he died, Paul went to the island of Crete with Titus. A church was already there. Someone else had started it. Paul helped organize this church. But he had to leave. He could not finish the job. When Paul left, Titus stayed. He became the leader of this church. Later, Paul sent this letter to Titus. The letter teaches Titus how to lead the church.

Paul: A Messenger Sent to Bring Faith

1 *From:* Paul, the slave of God and the messenger of Jesus Christ.

I have been sent to bring faith to those God has chosen. I am to teach them to know God's truth. For it is the truth that changes lives. And by that truth they can have eternal life. God promised eternal life to them before the world began, and he cannot lie. ³Now, in his own time he has revealed this Good News. He also allows me to tell it to everyone. By the command of God our Savior, I have been trusted to do this work.

⁴*To:* Titus, who is truly my son in the work of the Lord.

May God the Father and Christ Jesus our Savior give you blessings and peace.

Guidelines for Church Leaders

⁵I left you on the island of Crete. I asked you to stay there to strengthen the churches. And you were to choose pastors in every city. ⁶The men you appoint must be well thought of for their good lives. They must have only one wife. Their children must love the Lord and not be wild or disobedient.

⁷These pastors must be men of blameless lives. For they are to be God's ministers. They must not be proud or impatient. They must not be drunkards or fighters or greedy for money. ⁸They must enjoy

having guests in their homes and must love all that is good. They must be sensible men, and fair. They must be clean-minded and levelheaded. [9]Their belief in the truth that they have been taught must be strong. That way they will be able to teach it to others. They will be able to show those who disagree with them where they are wrong.

Watch Out for False Teachers

[10]For there are many who refuse to obey. This is especially true among those who say that Christians must obey the Jewish laws. But this is foolish talk. It blinds people to the truth. [11]It must be stopped. Already whole families have been turned away from the grace of God. Such teachers are only after your money. [12]One of their own men, a prophet from Crete, has spoken about them. He said, "These men of Crete are all liars. They are like lazy animals. They live only to satisfy their stomachs." [13]And this is true. So speak to the Christians there to make them strong in the faith. [14]Stop them from listening to Jewish folk tales. Don't let them follow the commands of men who turn their backs on the truth.

If your heart is clean, you will see the good in everything

A person who is pure of heart sees goodness and purity in everything. But a person whose own heart is evil and untrusting finds evil in everything.

Titus 1:15

---

[15]A person who is pure of heart sees goodness and purity in everything. But a person whose own heart is evil and untrusting finds evil in everything. His dirty mind and rebellious heart color all he sees and hears. [16]Such persons claim they know God. But from seeing the way they act, it is clear that they don't. They are rotten and disobedient. They are worthless so far as doing anything good is concerned.

Guidelines for People of Every Age

2 As for you, speak about the right living that goes along with true Christianity. [2]Teach the older men to be serious and unruffled. They must be sensible, knowing and believing the truth. They must do everything with love and patience.

[3]Teach the older women to be quiet and respectful in all they do. They must not speak evil of others and must not be heavy drinkers. They should be teachers of goodness. [4]These older women must train the younger women to live quietly. They should train them to love their husbands and their children. [5]The young women should be sensible and clean-minded. They should spend their time in their own homes. They should be kind and obedient to their husbands. That way people who know them won't speak against the Christian faith.

[6]In the same way, urge the young men to behave carefully. Tell them to take life seriously. [7]You must be an example of good deeds of every kind. Let all you do reflect your love of the truth. Show that you are serious about it. [8]Your talk should be so sensible that anyone who wants to argue will be ashamed. Why? There won't be anything to criticize in anything you say!

[9]Tell slaves to obey their masters. Tell them to do their best to make them happy. They must not talk back. [10]And they must not steal. They must show themselves to be worthy of trust. That way they will make people want to believe in our Savior and God.

[11]For the free gift of eternal salvation is now being offered to everyone. [12]It teaches us that God wants us to turn from godless living. He wants us to leave behind sinful pleasures. He wants us to live good, God-fearing lives day after day. [13]We should be looking forward to that wonderful time we've been expecting. It is the time when his glory shall be seen. It is the glory of our great God and Savior Jesus Christ. [14]He died under God's judgment against our sins. That way he could save us from falling into sin. He could make us his very own people. Now we can have clean hearts.

We can have real joy as we do kind things for others. 15You must teach your people these things. Encourage them to do right. Correct them when they need it as one who has every right to do so. Don't let anyone think that what you say is not important.

Obey the Government

3 Remind your people to obey the government and its officers. Tell them to always be obedient and ready for any honest work. 2They must not speak evil of anyone. They must not quarrel and argue. They should be gentle and truly kind to all.

3Once we, too, were foolish and disobedient. We were led astray by others. And we became slaves to many evil pleasures and wicked desires. Our lives were full of ill will and envy. We hated others, and they hated us.

4Then the time came for the kindness and love of God our Savior to appear. 5He saved us. He didn't save us because we were good enough to be saved. He saved us because of his kindness and pity. He washed away our sins and gave us the joy of the Holy Spirit inside us. 6He poured the Spirit out upon us with wonderful fullness. This is all because of what Jesus Christ our Savior did. 7Then he could declare us good in God's eyes. And he did this all because of his great kindness. Now we can share in the riches of the eternal life he gives us. We are eagerly looking forward to receiving it. 8These things I have told you are all true. Insist on them so that Christians will do good deeds all the time. This is not only right, but it brings results.

Avoid Useless Arguments

9Don't argue about foolish questions and ideas. And don't argue and quarrel about obeying the Jewish laws. This kind of thing isn't worthwhile. It only does harm. 10If anyone is causing divisions, he should be given a first and second warning. After that have nothing more to do with him. 11Such a person has a wrong sense of values. He is sinning and he knows it.

Paul's Final Instructions

12I am planning to send either Artemas or Tychicus to you. When one of them comes, please meet me at Nicopolis as quickly as you can. I have decided to stay there for the winter. 13Do everything you can to help Zenas the lawyer and Apollos with their trip. See that they are given everything they need. 14Our people must learn to help all who need their help. Then their lives will be fruitful.

Be a good example, and love the truth

You must be an example of good deeds of every kind. Let all you do reflect your love of the truth. Show that you are serious about it.

Titus 2:7

15Everybody here sends greetings. Please say hello to all of the Christian friends there. May God's blessings be with you all.

Sincerely, Paul

PHILEMON

In Bible times it was common for a man to own slaves. This man was called a master. If a slave disobeyed his master, the master could punish him any way he wanted. If a slave ran away, the master might even kill him. Onesimus was a slave who ran away. Then he met Paul. He became a Christian. His master was also a Christian. Paul had helped both men know Jesus. Now what was Onesimus to do? What was Philemon to do? Paul wrote this letter to Philemon. He sent it back with Onesimus. What do you think Paul said?

Onesimus Comes Home

Think how surprised Philemon was when his runaway slave Onesimus came home. Think how surprised he was that Onesimus had a letter from his friend Paul. Where had he met Paul? How had Onesimus become a Christian? What had Paul written in the letter? Philemon must have had a dozen questions. Paul's letter answered each one. You'll find the answers, too, as you read.

1 *From:* Paul. I am in jail for preaching the Good News about Jesus Christ. This letter is also from Brother Timothy.

To: Philemon, our much-loved fellow worker. This letter is also for the church that meets in your home. It is for Apphia, our sister. And it is for Archippus who, like myself, is the Lord's soldier.

³May God our Father and the Lord Jesus Christ give you blessings and peace.

⁴I always thank God when I pray for you, dear Philemon. ⁵I hear of your love and trust in the Lord Jesus and in his people. ⁶I pray that as you share your faith with others, faith will grip their lives too. I pray that they will see the good things in you that come from Christ Jesus. ⁷I have gained much joy and comfort from your love, my brother. Your kindness has so often refreshed the hearts of God's people.

⁸⁻⁹Now I want to ask a favor of you. I could demand it of you in the name of Christ. Why could I demand it? Because it is the right thing for you to do! But I love you and prefer just to ask you. I am Paul, an old man in jail for the sake of Jesus Christ. ¹⁰My plea is that you show kindness to my child Onesimus. I won

Slaves

PHILEMON 1:15-16

Onesimus was a slave. Philemon owned him.

Some people became slaves when they were captured in battle. These slaves worked hard building things. They did the hard, dirty work for their new king. The Hebrew slaves in Egypt built cities for Pharaoh.

Rich people sometimes bought slaves. Onesimus was a household slave. Joseph was a household slave in Egypt. These slaves were treated better than people captured in war. But slaves were still slaves. They had to obey their masters. Their masters owned them. In most countries masters could do anything they wanted to a slave. If a person owed money, but could not pay it, he might become a slave.

The Israelites had laws about slaves. Israelite slave owners had to treat their slaves well. Israelite slaves were not to work on the Sabbath. That was one of the Ten Commandments (Exod. 20:10). Israelite slaves could go free in six years (Exod. 21:2). They also could go free in the Year of Jubilee (a special year every 50th year). It was no fun to be a slave. Be thankful you live today!

him to the Lord while here in my chains. [11]Onesimus's name means "Useful." But he hasn't been of much use to you in the past. Now, however, he is going to be of real use to both of us. [12]I am sending him back to you, and with him comes my own heart.

[13]I am here in chains for preaching the Good News. And I wanted to keep him here with me. That way you would have been helping me through him. [14]But I didn't want to do it without your permission. I didn't want you to be kind because you had to. You should be kind because you want to. [15]He ran away from you for a little while. But now he can be yours forever. [16]He will no longer be only a slave. He will be something much better—a beloved brother! He is already such a brother to me. Now he will mean much more to you, too. He is not only a servant. Now he is also your brother in Christ.

You should want to be kind

You should be kind because
you want to.

Philemon 1:14

---

[17]If I am really your friend, give him the same welcome you would give to me. [18]If he has harmed you or stolen anything, charge me for it. [19]I will pay it back. I, Paul, personally guarantee this by writing it here with my own hand. I won't mention how much you owe me! The fact is, you even owe me your very soul! [20]Yes, dear brother, give me joy by doing this loving act. If you do, my weary heart will praise the Lord.

[21]I've written you this letter because I am sure you will do what I ask. In fact I know you will do even more!

[22]Please keep a guest room ready for me. I am hoping God will answer your prayers and let me come to you soon.

[23]Epaphras my fellow prisoner is also here for preaching Christ Jesus. He sends you his greetings. [24]So do Mark, Aristarchus, Demas, and Luke, my fellow workers.

[25]The blessings of our Lord Jesus Christ be upon your spirit.

Paul

- *Remember:* Who was the slave, Philemon or Onesimus? (1:11) How do you know Philemon was a Christian? (1:4-7) Who won Philemon to Christ? (1:19) Who won Onesimus to Christ? (1:10) What did Paul want Philemon to do? (1:8-12,17) Why should Philemon be kind to Onesimus? Should he do it because he has to? Or should he do it because he wants to? (1:14) Why should we be kind to others?

- *Discover:* We should be kind because we want to, not because we have to.

- *Apply:* Have you been unkind to your brother or sister? You should be kind. But you should be kind because you want to.

- *What's next?* An old man sits on a lonely island. He writes to seven churches. He has an important message for each of them. You can read these messages in Revelation 1:4–3:22. ■

HEBREWS

Your friend becomes a Christian. He is excited. This is wonderful! But then other friends tease him. They want him to do bad things that look like fun. But he knows Christians shouldn't do them. No one else in his family is a Christian. Family members don't understand. One day your friend has doubts. He wonders if the old way is better.

This is what the Book of Hebrews is about. Jewish people had become Christians. They were excited. They thought Christ would come back soon. Other people made fun of them. Other people even hurt them just because they believed in Jesus. These new Christians had family members who didn't believe in Jesus. These Jewish Christians began to have doubts. Should they go back to their old religion? Should they give up Christianity?

The author of Hebrews tries to help these new Christians. He tells them to make a complete break with Temple worship and sacrifices. Jesus Christ is a greater High Priest than the one at the Temple. His sacrifice on the cross is much better than Temple sacrifices. Living for Jesus is better than following religious laws. Do you ever doubt? Remember the Book of Hebrews! Living with Jesus is the only way to really live!

Jesus Christ Is God's Son

1 Long ago God spoke in many different ways to our fathers. He spoke through the prophets in visions, dreams, and even face to face. Little by little he told them about his plans.

²But now in these days he has spoken to us through his Son. He has given his Son everything. Through his Son he made the world and everything there is.

³God's Son shines out with God's glory. All that God's Son is and does marks him as God. He controls the universe by the power of his command. He is the one who died to cleanse us of all sin. Then he sat down in highest honor beside the great God of Heaven.

Jesus Christ Is Greater than the Angels

4Thus he became far greater than the angels. This is proved because his name is "Son of God." This name was passed on to him from his Father. It is far greater than the names and titles of the angels. 5-6God never said to any angel, "You are my Son." He didn't tell them, "Today I have given you the honor of that name." But God did say this about Jesus. Another time he said, "I am his Father and he is my Son." And when his firstborn Son came to earth what did God say? He said, "Let all the angels of God worship him."

7God speaks of his angels as messengers. They are as fast as the wind. They are servants made of flaming fire. 8But of his Son he says, "Your Kingdom, O God, will last forever and ever. Its commands are always just and right. 9You love right and hate wrong. So God, your God, has poured out more gladness on you than on anyone else."

10God also called him "Lord." He said, "Lord, in the beginning you made the earth. The heavens are the work of your hands. 11They will disappear into nothingness. But you will remain forever. They will become worn-out like old clothes. 12Someday you will fold them up and replace them. But you will never change, and your years will never end."

13Did God say to an angel, "Sit beside me until I crush your enemies under your feet"? No! But he said that to his Son.

14The angels are spirits who serve God. They are messengers sent to care for those who will receive his salvation.

Listen Carefully and Obey God

2 So we must listen very carefully to the truths we have heard. If we don't, we may drift away from them. 2The messages from angels have always proved true. People have always been punished for disobeying them. 3So how can we escape if we are careless about this great salvation? It was announced by the Lord Jesus himself. It was passed on to us by those who heard him speak.

4God always has shown us that these messages are true. He does this by signs and wonders and miracles. He gives special abilities from the Holy Spirit to those who believe. God has given such gifts to each of us.

Christ Became a Human Being

5The future world we are talking about will not be controlled by angels. 6Remember what David says to God in the Book of Psalms. "What is man that you care about him?" he said. "And who is this Son of Man you honor so highly? 7You made him lower than the angels for a little while. Now you have crowned him with glory and honor. 8And you have put him in complete charge of everything there is. Nothing is left out."

We have not yet seen all of this take place. 9But we see Jesus. For awhile he was a little lower than the angels. But now he is crowned by God with glory and honor. Why? Because he suffered death for us. This was because of God's great kindness. Jesus tasted death for everyone in all the world.

10God made everything for his own glory. So it was right that God should allow Jesus to suffer. In doing this he was bringing many of God's people to Heaven. His suffering made Jesus a perfect Leader. He was fit to bring them into their salvation.

11We have been made holy by Jesus. Now we have the same Father he has. That is why Jesus is not ashamed to call us his brothers. 12He says in the Psalms, "I will talk to my brothers about God my Father. Together we will sing his praises." 13Another time he said, "I will trust in God along with my brothers." And at another time he said, "See, here am I and the children God gave me."

14God's children are human beings, made of flesh and blood. He became flesh and blood too by being born in human form. Only as a human being could he die. And in dying he broke the power of the devil, who held the power of death. 15Only in that way could he deliver those who were living in fear of death.

16We all know he did not come as an angel but as a Jew. 17And it was necessary for Jesus to be like us, his brothers. That way he could be our merciful and faithful High Priest before God. He was a Priest who would be both merciful to us and faithful to God. He did this while dealing with the sins of the people. ¹⁸For Jesus has been through suffering and temptation. He knows what it is like when we suffer and are tempted. So now he is wonderfully able to help us.

Jesus Christ Is Greater than Moses

3 Dear brothers, God has set you apart for himself. You are chosen for Heaven. So think about Jesus, God's Messenger and the High Priest of our faith.

²For Jesus was faithful to God who chose him as High Priest. He was faithful just as Moses was when he served in God's house. ³But Jesus has far more honor than Moses! Jesus has more honor than Moses, just as a builder gets more honor than the house he builds. ⁴And many people can build houses, but only God made everything.

⁵Moses did a fine job working in God's house. But he was only a servant. His work was meant to show us those things that would happen later on. ⁶But Christ is God's faithful Son. He is in complete charge of God's house. And we are God's house, if we hold our courage and hope firm to the end.

Listen to God

⁷⁻⁸Christ is much better than Moses! So the Holy Spirit warns us to listen to him. Be careful to hear his voice today. Don't let your hearts become set against him, as the people of Israel did. Their hearts were hard. They complained against him in the desert while he was testing them. ⁹God was patient with them for 40 years, though they tested his patience sorely. He kept right on doing his mighty miracles for them to see. ¹⁰"But," God says, "I was very angry with them. Their hearts were always looking somewhere else instead of up to me. So they never found the paths I wanted them to follow."

¹¹God was full of this anger against them. So he made a promise that they would never come to his place of rest.

¹²So, dear brothers, be careful of your own hearts. They might be evil and unbelieving too. They might lead you away from the living God. ¹³Speak to each other about these things every day while there is still time. That way none of you will become hardened against God and blinded by sin. ¹⁴Hold the faith you had in the beginning all the way to the end. Then we will share in all that belongs to Christ.

¹⁵It is said, "*Today* if you hear God's voice, don't harden your hearts. The people of Israel did this when they rebelled against him in the desert."

**Jesus knows how we feel
when we hurt**

*For Jesus has been through
suffering and temptation.
He knows what it is like when
we suffer and are tempted.
So now he is wonderfully able
to help us.*

Hebrews 2:18

---

¹⁶Who were those who heard God's voice and then rebelled against him? They were the ones who came out of Egypt with Moses, their leader. ¹⁷And who was it who made God angry for all those 40 years? These were the same people who sinned and as a result died in the wilderness. ¹⁸And to whom did God swear that they could never go into the Promised Land? He was speaking to all those who disobeyed him. ¹⁹And why couldn't they go in? Because they didn't trust him.

God Promises Rest for Everyone Who Needs It

4 Now God still promises that all may enter his place of rest. But you need to be very careful. Why? Because some of you may fail to get there after all. ²The Good News has been given to us. It was also given to those who lived in the time of Moses. But it didn't do them any good because they didn't believe it. They did

not accept it with faith. ³Only we who believe God can enter into his place of rest. He has said, "I have promised that those without faith will never get in." This is true even though he has been ready for them since the world began.

⁴We know he is ready and waiting. How? Because it is written that God rested on the seventh day of creation. He had finished all that he had planned to make.

⁵Even so, they didn't get in. God finally said, "They shall never enter my rest." ⁶Yet the promise remains and some get in. But those who had the first chance did not. They disobeyed God and failed to enter.

????????????????????????????????????

Who is the great High Priest who has gone to Heaven to help us?

(Read 4:14 for the answer.)

????????????????????????????????????

⁷But he has set another time for coming in. And that time is now! He announced this through King David years after man's first failure to enter. He said, "Today you will hear him calling. And when you do, don't harden your hearts against him."

⁸He is talking about a new place of rest. He doesn't mean the land of Israel that Joshua led them into. That is not what God meant. If it was he wouldn't have said later that "today" is the time to get in. ⁹So there is a full complete rest still waiting for the people of God. ¹⁰Christ has already entered there. He is resting from his work, just as God did after the creation. ¹¹Let us do our best to go into that place of rest. Let's be careful not to disobey God as the children of Israel did. For then we would fail to get in.

¹²For whatever God says to us is full of living power. It is sharper than the sharpest sword. It cuts swift and deep into our innermost thoughts and desires. It shows us for what we really are. ¹³God knows about everyone everywhere. Everything about us is wide open to the eyes of our living God. Nothing is hidden from him to whom we must explain all we have done.

Jesus Christ Is Our High Priest

¹⁴But Jesus the Son of God is our great High Priest. He has gone to Heaven itself to help us. Therefore let us never stop trusting him. ¹⁵This High Priest of ours understands how weak we are. He had the same temptations we do. But he never once gave way to them and sinned. ¹⁶So let us come boldly to the throne of God. There he will give us his mercy. And there we will find grace to help in times of need.

5 The Jewish High Priest is a man like anyone else. But he is chosen to speak for all other men in their dealings with God. He presents their gifts to God. He offers to him the blood of animals that are sacrificed. This blood is for the sins of the people and his own sins too. And because he is a man, he can deal gently with other men. It doesn't matter that they are foolish and ignorant. He, too, has the same temptations. So he understands their problems very well.

⁴No one can be a High Priest just because he wants to be. He must be called by God in the same way God chose Aaron.

⁵That is why Christ didn't choose himself to be the High Priest. No, he was chosen by God. God said to him, "My Son, today I have honored you." ⁶Another time God said to him, "You have been chosen to be a priest forever. You have the same rank as Melchizedek."

⁷Yet while Christ was here on earth he begged with God. He prayed, crying with tears, to the only one who could save him from death. And God heard his prayers because of his strong desire to obey.

⁸Jesus was God's Son. But he still had to learn what it was like to obey. He learned to obey even when obeying meant suffering. ⁹Jesus proved himself perfect through suffering. Then he became the Giver of eternal salvation to all those who obey him. ¹⁰Remember, God chose him to be High Priest just like Melchizedek.

Listen and Learn So
You Can Understand

[11]There is much more I would like to say along these lines. But you don't seem to listen. So it's hard to make you understand.

[12-13]You have been Christians a long time now. You ought to be teaching others. Instead you have dropped back to the place where you need someone to teach you. You need to be taught all over again the basics of God's Word. You are like babies who can drink only milk. You are not old enough for solid food. When a person is living on milk it shows he's not grown as a Christian. It shows he doesn't know the difference between right and wrong. He is still a baby Christian! [14]When will you be able to eat solid spiritual food? When will you understand the deeper things of God's Word? This will happen when you learn right from wrong by doing right.

6 Let us stop going over the same old ground again and again. We are always teaching those first lessons about Christ. Let us go on to other things. Let us become mature in our understanding, as strong Christians ought to be. Surely we don't need to speak further about being saved by being good. We don't have to mention the need for faith in God. [2]You already learned about baptism and spiritual gifts. You know about the resurrection of the dead and eternal judgment.

[3]The Lord willing, we will go on now to other things.

[4]There is no use trying to bring some people back to the Lord again. They have once understood the Good News. They have tasted for themselves the good things of Heaven. They have shared in the Holy Spirit. [5]They know how good the Word of God is. They have felt the mighty powers of the world to come. [6]But then they have turned against God. They cannot repent again. They have nailed the Son of God to the cross again by rejecting him. They hold him up to laughter and public shame.

[7]When a farmer's land has had many showers upon it, good crops come up. That land has been given God's blessing.

[8]But what if it keeps on having crops of thistles and thorns? If this happens, the land is thought to be no good. It is thought to be ready for condemnation and burning.

[9]Dear friends, I really don't think that what I am saying applies to you. I'm sure you have the fruit that comes with your salvation. [10]God is not unfair. How can he forget your hard work for him? Can he forget the way you have shown your love for him? No! You have been helping his children and you still are. [11]And we want you to keep on loving others to the end. That way you will get your full reward.

[12]Then you won't become bored with being a Christian. You won't become spiritually dull and indifferent. But you will follow those who receive all that God has promised them. Why? Because of their strong faith and patience.

You Can Count on God's Promises

[13]For instance, there was God's promise to Abraham. God made a promise in his own name. And there is no one greater to make a promise by. [14]He promised that he would bless Abraham again and again. He would give him a son and make him the father of a great nation. [15]Then Abraham waited patiently. Finally God gave him a son, Isaac, just as he had promised.

Do not be afraid to come to God when you need help

So let us come boldly to the throne of God. There he will give us his mercy. And there we will find grace to help in times of need.

Hebrews 4:16

---

[16]When a man makes a promise, he is calling upon someone greater than himself. This forces him to do what he has promised. He will be punished if he doesn't do it. The promise ends all argument about it. [17]God also bound himself with a promise. That way those he promised to help would be confident. They

would never need to wonder whether he might change his plans.

¹⁸Now God has given us his promise. This is something we can count on! For it is impossible for God to tell a lie. Now all those who go to him to be saved can take new courage. They can hear about the promises from God. And they can know for sure that he will save them as he promised.

¹⁹This hope of being saved is a strong anchor for our souls. It connects us with God himself behind the holy curtains of Heaven. ²⁰Christ has gone ahead of us there. He pleads for us from his position as our High Priest. He has the same honor and rank as Melchizedek.

Melchizedek:
King of Justice and Peace

7 This Melchizedek was king of the city of Salem. He was also a priest of the Most High God. Once, Abraham was going home after winning a great battle against many kings. Melchizedek met him and blessed him. ²Abraham took a tenth of all he won in battle and gave it to Melchizedek.

Melchizedek's name means "Justice." So he is the King of Justice. He is also the King of Peace. Why? Because the name of his city is Salem, which means "Peace." ³Melchizedek had no father or mother. There is no record of any of his ancestors. He was never born and he never died. His life is like that of the Son of God. He is a priest forever.

⁴Melchizedek was a great man. Abraham was the first of God's chosen people. Even he gave Melchizedek a tenth of what he took from the kings he fought. ⁵Abraham should have done this only if Melchizedek was a priest of God. Later on the law told God's people to give gifts to their priests. But the priests were part of their own family. ⁶Melchizedek was not a part of the family. But still Abraham paid him.

Then Melchizedek placed a blessing upon mighty Abraham. ⁷Everyone knows the person who blesses is greater than the person who is blessed.

⁸The Jewish priests were men who would someday die. Even so, they were given a tenth of all the people had. But we are told that Melchizedek lives on.

⁹Levi was the first of all Jewish priests. One might even say that Levi himself paid tithes to Melchizedek through Abraham. ¹⁰Levi wasn't born when this happened. But the seed from which he came was in Abraham. It was in him when Abraham paid Melchizedek.

¹¹What if the Jewish priests and laws could save us? Why would God send Christ as a priest like Melchizedek? He could have sent a priest who was the same as Aaron. That was what all the other priests were.

¹²⁻¹⁴When God sends a new kind of priest, his law must change to allow it. We all know that Christ didn't belong to the tribe of Levi. He came from the tribe of Judah. That tribe had not been chosen for priesthood. Moses had never given them that work.

Christ Is Like Melchizedek

¹⁵So we can plainly see that God's method changed. Christ, the new High Priest, came with the rank of Melchizedek. ¹⁶Did he become a priest by belonging to the tribe of Levi? No! Christ was a priest because of the power flowing from a life that cannot end. ¹⁷As the Psalmist says of Christ, "You are a priest forever like Melchizedek."

¹⁸Yes, the priesthood based on family lines has ended because it didn't work. It was weak and useless for saving people. ¹⁹It never made anyone really right with God. But now we have a far better hope. Christ makes it so God welcomes us. Now we can come close to God.

²⁰God promised that Christ would always be a Priest. ²¹He never said that of other priests. To Christ he said, "The Lord has made a promise. He will never change his mind. You are a Priest forever like Melchizedek." ²²That is why Christ can guarantee forever this new and better plan.

²³Under the old plan there had to be many priests. Then, when the older ones died, the system could still carry on with others.

²⁴But Jesus lives forever. He continues to be a Priest so that no one else is

needed. ²⁵He is able to totally save all who come to God through him. He will live forever. So he will always be there to pray to God for us.

²⁶So he is exactly the kind of High Priest we need. He is holy and can't be blamed. He is unstained by sin, not ruined by sinners. To him has been given the place of honor in Heaven. ²⁷He never needs the daily blood of animal offerings as other priests did. They had to cover their own sins and then the sins of the people. But Christ finished all sacrifices, once and for all. This happened when he sacrificed himself on the cross. ²⁸In the old way, even the High Priests were weak and sinful men. They could not keep from doing wrong. But the word of God's promise came later than the law. It made God's Son our High Priest. And that Son is perfect forever.

A New High Priest for a New Covenant

8 This is what we are saying. Christ is our High Priest. He is in Heaven at the place of greatest honor next to God himself. ²He serves in the Temple in Heaven. It is the true Temple, built by the Lord and not by human hands.

³Every High Priest is appointed to offer gifts and sacrifices. So Christ must make an offering too. ⁴The sacrifice he offers is far better than those offered by the earthly priests. If he were here on earth he wouldn't be allowed to be a priest. Why? Because down here the priests still follow the old Jewish way of offerings. ⁵Their work is part of an earthly model of the real Temple in Heaven. Moses was getting ready to build the house of God. Then God warned him to follow the plans shown to him on Mount Sinai. ⁶But Christ is a minister in Heaven. He has been rewarded with a far more important work. The new agreement that he gives to us from God contains far better promises.

⁷The old agreement didn't even work. If it had, there would have been no need for another to take its place. ⁸But God found fault with the old one. He said, "The day will soon come. I will make a new agreement with the people of Israel and Judah. ⁹It will not be like the old one I gave to their fathers. That was the day I took them by the hand to lead them out of Egypt. They did not keep their part in that agreement. So I had to cancel it. ¹⁰This is the new agreement I will make with Israel, says the Lord. I will write my laws in their minds and in their hearts. I will be their God and they shall be my people. ¹¹No one will need to tell his neighbor or brother, 'You should know the Lord.' Everyone, great and small, will know me already. ¹²And I will be merciful to them in the wrong things they do. I will remember their sins no more."

¹³God says the new promises of this new agreement take the place of the old. The old one is out of date now and has been put aside forever.

Old Rules about Worship

9 In the first agreement between God and his people there were rules for worship. There was a holy tent down here on earth. Inside this tent there were two rooms. The first one contained the golden candlestick. It had a table with special loaves of holy bread upon it. This part was called the Holy Place. ³Then there was a curtain. Behind the curtain was a room called the Holy of Holies. ⁴In that room there were a golden altar for incense and the golden chest. That chest was called the Ark of the Covenant. It was covered on all sides with pure gold. Inside the Ark were the tablets of stone with the Ten Commandments written on them. There was a golden jar with manna in it. Aaron's rod that budded was also there. ⁵Above the golden chest were statues of angels called the cherubim. They are the guardians of God's glory. They had their wings stretched out over the Ark's golden cover. The cover of the Ark was called· the mercy seat. But enough of such details.

⁶When all was ready, the priests went into the first room whenever they wanted to. That is where they did their work. ⁷But only the High Priest went into the inner room. He only went in once a year, all alone. He took blood to

sprinkle on the mercy seat as an offering to God. This was to cover his own mistakes and the mistakes of all the people.

⁸The Holy Spirit uses all this to show us something. Under the old way the people could not go into the Holy of Holies. They stayed out as long as the outer room was still in use.

⁹This has an important lesson for us today. Under the old way, gifts and sacrifices were offered. But these failed to cleanse the hearts of the people who brought them. ¹⁰The old system dealt only with special things. It dealt with eating and drinking, washing, and rules about this and that. The people had to keep these rules until Christ came with God's better way.

Christ Is the Perfect Sacrifice

¹¹He came as High Priest of this better way we now have. He went into that greater, perfect holy tent in Heaven. It was not made by men. It was not even a part of this world. ¹²Once for all he took blood into the Holy of Holies. He sprinkled it on the mercy seat. But it was not the blood of goats and calves. No, he took his own blood. With it he made sure of our eternal salvation.

¹³The old way used the blood of bulls and goats and ashes of young cows. These things could cleanse men's bodies from sin. ¹⁴So how much more will the blood of Christ cleanse our lives and hearts. His sacrifice frees us from the old rules so we can serve the living God. Christ was perfect, without a single sin or fault. By the eternal Spirit, he gave himself to God to die for our sins. ¹⁵Christ came with this new agreement. Now all who are invited may have all of what God promised them forever. Christ died to save them from their sins under that old way.

¹⁶When someone dies he leaves a list of things to be given away. This is called a will. But no one gets anything until the person who wrote the will is dead. ¹⁷The will goes into effect after the death of the person who wrote it. While he is alive no one can get the things he has promised them.

¹⁸That is why blood was sprinkled before the first agreement could begin. ¹⁹First Moses gave the people all of God's laws. Then he took blood of calves and goats, along with water. He sprinkled the blood over the book of God's laws and over all the people. He used branches of hyssop bushes and scarlet wool to sprinkle with. ²⁰Then he said, "This is the blood that marks the beginning of the agreement between you and God. It is the agreement God commanded me to make with you." ²¹In the same way he sprinkled the holy tent and the things used for worship. ²²In the old agreement almost everything was cleansed by sprinkling it with blood. Unless blood is shed there is no forgiveness of sins.

²³The holy tent and everything in it were all copied from things in Heaven. They all had to be made pure by being sprinkled with the blood of animals. The real things in Heaven were made pure with better offerings.

²⁴Christ has gone into Heaven itself. He stands now before God as our Friend. It was not in the earthly place of worship that he did this. That was only a copy of the real Temple in Heaven. ²⁵And he has not offered himself again and again. The High Priest on earth offers animal blood in the Holy of Holies each year. ²⁶If that was needed, Christ would have died again and again since the world began. But no! He came once for all, at the end of the age. He put away the power of sin forever by dying for us.

²⁷It is planned that men die only once. And after that comes judgment. ²⁸So Christ died only once as an offering for the sins of many people. He will come again, but not to deal again with our sins.

This time he will come to rescue all who are waiting for him.

Christ's One Offering Brings Forgiveness for All

10 The Jewish laws were a shadow of the good things Christ would do for us. The Jewish offerings were repeated again and again, year after year. But they could never save those who lived under their rules. ²If they could have, one offering would have been enough. The offerers would have been made clean once for all. Their feeling of guilt would have been gone.

³But just the opposite happened. Those offerings reminded them of their sins instead of easing their minds. ⁴It is not possible for the blood of bulls and goats to take away sins.

⁵So Christ came into the world. That's when he said, "O God, the blood of bulls and goats cannot satisfy you. So you made this body for me to offer on your altar. ⁶You weren't happy with animals, killed and burnt as offerings for sin. ⁷Then I said, 'See, I have come to do your will. Like the Bible said, I have come to lay down my life.'"

⁸First Christ said that God was not happy with the offerings and sacrifices. They were needed in the Jewish laws. ⁹Then he said, "Here I am. I have come to give my life."

He ended the first way in favor of a far better one. ¹⁰Under this new plan we have been forgiven. We were made clean by Christ's dying for us once for all.

¹¹Under the old plan the priests stood before the altar day after day. They offered sacrifices that could never take away our sins. ¹²But Christ gave himself for our sins as one offering for all time. Then he sat down in the place of highest honor by God's right hand. ¹³Now he is waiting for his enemies to be put under his feet. ¹⁴By that one offering he made all those who are holy to be perfect forever.

¹⁵The Holy Spirit promises that this is true. He has said, ¹⁶"The people of Israel broke their first contract with me. But this is the understanding I will have with them now. I will write my laws into their minds and put them in their hearts." ¹⁷Then he added, "I will never again remember their sins and lawless deeds."

¹⁸When sins have been forgiven, there is no need for more offerings for sin.

Keep Trusting God

¹⁹So brothers, now we may walk right into the Holy of Holies! Why? Because of the blood of Jesus. ²⁰This is a fresh,

The Ark of the Covenant

HEBREWS 9:1-5

There has never been another box like the Ark of the Covenant. It was about four feet long, two feet wide, and two feet high. It was covered inside and outside with pure gold. It had golden rings at each corner. Golden poles slipped through these rings. People held these poles to carry the Ark. The lid was made of pure gold. Two angel-like figures stood on top. They were called cherubim. The Lord was there between the cherubim in some special way. There were three items in the Ark. The stones with the Ten Commandments were in it. A little pot of manna and Aaron's rod were in it. The Israelites carried the Ark through the wilderness to the Promised Land. Then the Israelites came into the Promised Land. They put the Ark in the Tabernacle at Shiloh. One time the Philistines captured the Ark. But they had so much trouble because of it that they sent it home. Nobody knows what happened to the Ark. The Babylonians may have captured it. Or it may still be hidden somewhere. Don't you wish you could see the Ark of the Covenant?

new, life-giving way. Christ opened it by tearing the curtain into the Holy of Holies. That curtain is his body.

²¹This great High Priest of ours rules over God's household. ²²So let's go in, to God himself, with true hearts fully trusting him. He will welcome us. We have been sprinkled with Christ's blood. So now our bodies have been washed with pure water.

Work hard to love each other and do good

Let us outdo each other in loving each other and doing good.

Hebrews 10:24

---

²³Now we can look forward to the salvation God has promised us. There is no longer any room for doubt. We can tell others that salvation is ours. There is no question that God will do what he says.

²⁴So let us outdo each other in loving each other and doing good.

²⁵Let us not neglect our church meetings, as some people do. Encourage and warn each other. Do this especially now that his day of coming is near.

²⁶Some people may sin on purpose after knowing the truth of forgiveness. This sin is not covered by Christ's death. There is no way to get rid of it. ²⁷There will be nothing to look forward to. There will only be the terrible punishment of God's anger. It will burn up all his enemies. ²⁸A man who refused to obey the laws given by Moses was killed without mercy. But there had to be two or three witnesses to his sin. ²⁹But what if people trample underfoot the Son of God? What if they treat his blood as though it were common? What if they insult the Holy Spirit, who brings God's mercy? Think how much more terrible the punishment will be for them.

³⁰For we know him who said, "Justice belongs to me. I will repay them!" He also said, "The Lord himself will handle these cases." ³¹It is a fearful thing to fall into the hands of the living God.

³²Don't ever forget those great days when you first learned about Christ. Remember, you kept right on with the Lord. And you did it even though it meant terrible suffering. ³³Sometimes you were laughed at and beaten. Sometimes you were made sad as you saw others suffering the same things. ³⁴You suffered with those thrown into jail. You were joyful when all you owned was taken from you. You knew that better things were waiting for you in Heaven. They are things that would be yours forever.

³⁵Don't let this happy trust in the Lord die away, no matter what happens. Remember your reward! ³⁶You need to keep on patiently doing God's will. Do this if you want him to do all he has promised. ³⁷His coming will not be delayed much longer. ³⁸And those whose faith has made them good in God's sight must live by faith. They trust him in everything. But if they turn back, God will have no joy in them.

³⁹But we have never turned our backs on God and sealed our fate. No! Our faith in him makes the salvation of our souls sure.

Great Heroes of the Faith

11 What is faith? It is the confident knowlege that something we want is going to happen. It is the confidence that what we hope for is waiting for us. We know it is there even though we cannot see it up ahead. ²Men of God in days of old were famous for their faith.

Faith is believing God when you can't see what he is doing

What is faith?
It is the confidence that what we hope for is waiting for us. We know it is there even though we cannot see it up ahead.

Hebrews 11:1

---

³By faith we know that all things were made at God's command. It shows us that they were all made from things that can't be seen.

⁴It was by faith that Abel obeyed God.

He brought an offering that pleased God more than Cain's offering did. God accepted Abel and proved it by accepting his gift. Abel died a long time ago. But we can still learn lessons from him about trusting God.

⁵Enoch trusted God too. That is why God took him away to Heaven without dying. Suddenly he was gone because God took him. Before this happened God had said how pleased he was with Enoch. ⁶You can never please God without faith. You cannot please him without depending on him. Anyone who wants to come to God must believe that there is a God. They also must believe that he rewards those who truly look for him.

⁷Noah was another who trusted God. He heard God's warning about the future. Noah believed him even though there was then no sign of a flood. Noah wasted no time. He built the ark and saved his family. Noah's belief in God was different from the disbelief of the world. Because of his faith he became one of those whom God has welcomed.

⁸Abraham trusted in God. God told him to leave home. He told Abraham to go far away to another land. He promised to give that land to Abraham. So Abraham obeyed. Away he went, not even knowing where he was going. ⁹When he reached God's promised land, he lived in tents like a visitor. Isaac and Jacob lived in tents too. God gave them the same promise. ¹⁰Abraham was waiting for the city whose designer and builder is God.

¹¹Sarah, too, had faith. Because of this she was able to become a mother in her old age. She knew that God, who promised, would certainly do what he said. ¹²And so a whole nation came from Abraham. He was too old to have even one child. Yet he began a nation with millions of people. They are like the stars of the sky! They are like the sand on the ocean shores! There is no way to count them all.

¹³These men of faith died without ever seeing all that God had promised them. But they saw it all waiting for them and were glad. They agreed that this earth was not their real home. They knew that they were just strangers here. ¹⁴People who say such things show they are seeking a place of their own.

¹⁵If they had wanted to, they could have gone back to the world. ¹⁶But they didn't want to. They were living for Heaven. And now God is not ashamed to be called their God. He has made a heavenly city for them.

¹⁷While God was testing him, Abraham still trusted in God and his promises. So he offered his son Isaac. He was ready to kill him on the altar of sacrifice. ¹⁸God had promised to give Abraham a big family. And he had promised to do this through his son, Isaac. Yet, by faith, Abraham would even kill Isaac!

???????????????????????????????
Who chose to suffer instead of being treated as the grandson of a king?
(Read 11:24-25 for the answer.)
???????????????????????????????

¹⁹He believed that if Isaac died God would bring him back to life. That is just about what happened. As far as Abraham knew, Isaac was doomed to death. But he came back again, alive! ²⁰By faith, Isaac knew God would bless his two sons, Jacob and Esau.

²¹By faith Jacob blessed Joseph's sons. He did this when he was old and dying. And he worshiped, leaning on the top of his cane.

²²By faith, Joseph spoke of God bringing the people of Israel out of Egypt. He did this as he neared the end of his life. By faith he told them to take his bones with them when they left!

²³Moses' parents had faith too. They saw that God had given them an unusual child. They trusted that God would save him from the death the king commanded. So they hid him for three months and were not afraid.

²⁴⁻²⁵Now Moses grew up. And by faith, he refused to be treated as the king's grandson. He chose to suffer with God's people instead of enjoying the pleasures of sin. ²⁶He would rather suffer for Christ than own the treasures of Egypt. He was looking forward to the great reward that

God would give him. ²⁷He trusted God. So he left the land of Egypt and wasn't afraid of the king's anger. Moses kept right on going. It seemed like he could see God right there with him. ²⁸He believed God would save his people. So he commanded them to kill a lamb as God had told them. He told them to sprinkle the blood on the doorposts of their homes. That way the Angel of Death could not touch the oldest child in those homes.

**Work hard at what
God has given you to do**

*Let us run with patience the race
that God has set before us.*

Hebrews 12:1

---

²⁹The people of Israel trusted God. So they went through the Red Sea as though they were on dry ground. But when the Egyptians chasing them tried it, they all were drowned.

³⁰It was faith that brought the walls of Jericho tumbling down. God had commanded Israel to walk around the walls for seven days. And when they did, the walls fell down. ³¹By faith, Rahab the prostitute did not die with all the others in her city. They refused to obey God. But she gave a friendly welcome to the spies.

³²Well, how much more do I need to say? It would take too long to tell the stories of Gideon and Barak. I have no time to tell of Samson, Jephthah, David, Samuel, and other prophets. ³³These people all trusted God. As a result they won battles and overthrew kingdoms. They ruled their people well. And they were given what God had promised them. They were kept from harm in a den of lions. ³⁴They were kept safe in a fiery furnace. Some, through their faith, escaped death by the sword. Some were made strong again after they had been weak or sick. Others were given great power in battle. They made whole armies turn and run away. ³⁵Some women, through faith, received their loved ones back again from death. But others trusted God and were beaten to death. They would rather die than turn from

God and be free. They trusted that they would rise from death to a better life.

³⁶Some were laughed at and their backs cut open with whips. Others were chained in prisons. ³⁷⁻³⁸Some died by stoning. Others were killed by being sawed in two. Still others were promised freedom if they would give up their faith. Then they were killed with the sword. Some walked around in skins of sheep and goats. They wandered over deserts and mountains. They hid in dens and caves. They were hungry and sick and badly treated. They were too good for this world. ³⁹These men of faith trusted God and won his approval. But none of them received all that God had promised them. ⁴⁰God wanted them to wait and share the better rewards that were prepared for us.

Let God Train You

12 There is a huge crowd of men of faith watching us from the grandstands. So let us strip off anything that slows us down or holds us back. Let us drop those sins that wrap around our feet and trip us up. Let us run with patience the race that God has set before us.

²Keep your eyes on Jesus, our Leader and Instructor. He was willing to die a shameful death on the cross. Why? Because of the joy he knew would be his afterwards. Now he sits in the place of honor by the throne of God.

³Think about his patience when sinful men did such terrible things to him. That way you can keep from becoming fainthearted and weary. ⁴After all, you have never yet struggled against sin until you shed your blood.

Love others like they are your family

*Keep loving each other like
brothers.*

Hebrews 13:1

---

⁵Have you forgotten the encouraging words God spoke to you? He said, "My son, don't be angry when the Lord punishes you. Don't be defeated when he has to show you where you are wrong. ⁶For when he punishes you, it proves

that he loves you. When he whips you, it proves you are really his child."

⁷Let God train you. He is doing what any loving father does for his children. Whoever heard of a son who was never corrected? ⁸Other fathers punish their sons. If God doesn't punish you, it means you aren't really in his family. ⁹We respect our fathers here on earth, and they punish us. Shouldn't we cheerfully submit to God's training so that we can really live?

¹⁰Our earthly fathers trained us for a few brief years. They did the best for us that they knew how. But God's training is always for our good. He does it so that we may share his holiness. ¹¹We don't like being punished while it is happening. But afterwards we can see the result, a quiet growth in grace and character.

¹²So take a new grip with your tired hands. Stand firm on your shaky legs. ¹³Mark out a straight, smooth path for your feet. Then the weak and lame will not fall and hurt themselves, but will become strong.

Listen to God and Obey

¹⁴Stay out of arguments, and seek to live a clean and holy life. One who is not holy will not see the Lord. ¹⁵Look after each other. That way not one of you will fail to find God's best blessings. Watch out that no bitterness takes root among you. When it springs up it causes deep trouble, hurting many in their spiritual lives. ¹⁶Watch out that no one becomes involved in sexual sin. They should not become careless about God as Esau did. He traded his rights as the oldest son for a single meal. ¹⁷Afterwards, when he wanted those rights back again, it was

too late. It didn't matter that he wept bitter tears of repentance. So remember, and be careful.

¹⁸You haven't come to the mountain where the Israelites stood face to face with terror. At Mount Sinai, they saw flaming fire, gloom, darkness, and a terrible storm. This happened when God gave them his laws. ¹⁹There was an awesome trumpet blast and a voice. It spoke a message so terrible that the people

Sheep and Shepherds
HEBREWS 13:20-21

Bible-time shepherds took care of sheep. That was their job. They fed them. They found water for them. They protected them from wild animals. If a sheep got lost, the shepherd looked for it. Each morning a shepherd took his sheep to pasture. He went before them. He called them by name. He did not walk behind them and make them move. He led them. Jesus is called the Great Shepherd, or Good Shepherd. He takes care of us. He feeds us. He protects us. He leads us. He knows our names. When we are lost, he looks for us. Would you like to thank him for doing all these things?

begged God to stop speaking. ²⁰They staggered back under God's command. He said that if even an animal touched the mountain it must die. ²¹Moses himself was so frightened at the sight that he shook with terrible fear.

²²But you have come to Mount Zion. It is the city of the living God, the heavenly Jerusalem. You have come to the gathering of countless angels. ²³And you have come to the church. It is composed of all those registered in Heaven. You have come to God, the Judge of all. You have come to the spirits of men who are not guilty of sin. They are men who have been made perfect. ²⁴And you have come to Jesus himself. He has brought us his wonderful new agreement. You have come to the sprinkled blood. It graciously forgives instead of crying out for vengeance like the blood of Abel.

²⁵So see to it that you obey him who is speaking to you. The people of Israel did not escape when they refused to listen to Moses. He was the earthly messenger. We are in terrible danger if we refuse to listen to God. And he speaks to us from Heaven! ²⁶When he spoke from Mount Sinai his voice shook the earth. But, "Next time," he says, "I will shake the earth and the heavens too." ²⁷This means that he will sift out everything without a solid base. That means that only unshakable things will be left.

Be happy with what you have

Don't love money. Be happy with what you have.

Hebrews 13:5

---

²⁸We have a Kingdom nothing can destroy. So let's serve God with thankful hearts and with holy fear and awe. ²⁹For our God is a consuming fire.

Live Good and Obedient Lives

13 Keep loving each other like brothers. ²Don't forget to be kind to strangers. Some who have done this have served angels without knowing it! ³Don't forget about those in jail. Suffer with them as though you were there

yourself. Share the sorrow of those being treated wrongly. You know what they are going through.

⁴Honor your marriage and its vows, and be pure. God will punish all those who are immoral or commit adultery.

⁵Don't love money. Be happy with what you have. For God has said, "I will never fail you nor forsake you." ⁶That is why we can say without any doubt or fear, "The Lord is my Helper. I am not afraid of anything that man can do to me."

Jesus is always the same

Jesus Christ is the same yesterday, today, and forever.

Hebrews 13:8

---

⁷Remember your leaders who have taught you the Word of God. Think of all the good that has come from their lives. Try to trust the Lord as they do.

⁸Jesus Christ is the same yesterday, today, and forever. ⁹So do not be attracted by strange new ideas. Your strength is a gift from God, not from rules about eating certain foods. This hasn't helped those who have tried it!

¹⁰We have an altar. It is the cross where Christ was sacrificed. Those who seek salvation by obeying Jewish laws can never be helped by the cross. ¹¹The Jewish High Priest brought the blood of animals into the Holy of Holies. It was a sacrifice for sin. Then the bodies of the animals were burned outside the city. ¹²That is why Jesus suffered outside the city, where his blood washed our sins away.

¹³So let us go out to him beyond the city walls. Let's suffer with him there, bearing his shame. ¹⁴This world is not our home. We are looking forward to our everlasting home in Heaven.

¹⁵With Jesus' help we will always offer our sacrifice of praise to God. We will do this by telling others of the glory of his name. ¹⁶Don't forget to do good. Share what you have with those in need. Such sacrifices are very pleasing to God. ¹⁷Obey your leaders and be willing to do what they say. For their

work is to watch over your souls. God will judge them on how well they do this. Give them reason to report joyfully to the Lord and not with sorrow. For if you don't do this, then you will suffer for it.

Final Words

[18]Pray for us. Our conscience is clear and we want to keep it that way. [19]I especially need your prayers so that I can come back to you sooner.

[20-21]The God of peace brought again from the dead our Lord Jesus. May he equip you with all you need for doing his will. Jesus Christ became the great Shepherd of the sheep. This happened by an everlasting agreement sealed with his blood. May God produce in you through Christ all that is pleasing to him. To him be glory forever and ever. Amen.

[22]Brethren, please listen patiently to what I have said in this short letter. [23]I want you to know that Brother Timothy is now out of jail. If he comes here soon, I will come with him to see you. [24-25]Give my greetings to all your leaders and to the other believers there. The Christians from Italy who are here with me send you their love. God's grace be with you all. Good-bye.

God is pleased when we share with those in need

Share what you have with those in need. Such sacrifices are very pleasing to God.

Hebrews 13:16

JAMES

Do you tell people you like to pray? That's great. But how much do you pray? Do you tell people you like to read your Bible? Great! But how much do you read your Bible? Do you tell people you love Jesus? Wonderful! But do you live the way Jesus wants you to live? James is a book about living God's way. If you say you're a Christian, live as a Christian should. Talk like a Christian should. Treat others the way a Christian should. Think as a Christian should. You may be a Christian. But your neighbors need to see how a Christian lives. That's what this book is about.

James: A Servant of God

1 *From:* James, a servant of God and of the Lord Jesus Christ.

To: Jewish Christians scattered everywhere. Greetings!

Have Patience When Life Gets Tough

²Dear brothers, is your life full of trouble and trials? Then be happy. ³When the way is rough, your patience has a chance to grow. ⁴So let it grow! And don't try to get out of your problems. One day, your patience will finally be in full bloom. Then you will be ready for anything. You will be strong in character, full, and perfect.

Ask God for Wisdom; He'll Give It to You

⁵If you want to know what God wants you to do, ask him. He will gladly tell you. He is ready to give wisdom to all who ask him. He will not scold you.

⁶When you ask him, be sure that you really expect him to answer you. A doubtful mind is like a wave of the sea. It is driven and tossed by the wind. ⁷⁻⁸Your thoughts will be unsure. You will turn first this way and then that. If you don't ask with faith, don't expect the Lord to give you an answer.

????????????????????????????????????
Does God ever tempt us?
(Read 1:13 for the answer.)
????????????????????????????????????

⁹A Christian who doesn't amount to much in this world should be glad. He is great in the Lord's sight. ¹⁰⁻¹¹But a rich man should be glad that his riches mean nothing to the Lord. That man will soon be gone. He is like a flower that has lost its beauty and fades away. It is dried out and killed by the hot summer sun. So it is with rich men. They will soon die and leave behind all their busy work.

God Gives Good and Perfect Gifts, Not Temptation

12A man is happy if he doesn't give in when he is tempted. Then later he will get his reward. He will get the crown of life God has promised those who love him. 13Remember this! When someone wants to do wrong, God is not tempting him. God never wants to do wrong. And he never tempts anyone else to do it. 14Temptation is the pull of man's own evil thoughts and wishes. 15Evil thoughts lead to evil deeds. Then evil deeds lead to the death penalty from God. 16So don't let yourselves be tricked, dear brothers.

Listen more than you talk

*It is best to listen much,
speak little,
and not become angry.*

James 1:19

17Whatever is good and perfect comes to us from God. He is the Creator of all light. He shines forever without change or shadow. 18He decided to give us our new lives through the truth of his Word. We became the first children in his new family.

Listen and Obey

19Dear brothers, remember this! It is best to listen much, speak little, and not become angry. 20Anger doesn't make us good. And God demands that we be good.

Any sin makes you a sinner

*What if someone keeps every
law but makes one little slip?
He is just as guilty as the person
who has broken every law.*

James 2:10

21So get rid of all that is wrong in your life, both inside and outside. Humbly be glad for the message we have been given. It is able to save our souls as it takes hold of our hearts.

22And remember, it is a message to obey. It is not just something to listen to. So don't fool yourselves. 23What kind of person just listens and doesn't obey? He is like a man looking at his face in a mirror. 24When he walks away, he quickly forgets what he looks like! 25But some people keep looking into God's law that sets people free. They don't walk away and forget about it. Such people will not just remember it. They will also do what it says. Then God will greatly bless them in all they do.

26Anyone who says he's a Christian but doesn't control his tongue is fooling himself. His religion isn't worth much. 27What kind of Christian is pure and without fault? God the Father sees that he takes care of orphans and widows. He remains true to the Lord. Such a person isn't made dirty by his contacts with the world.

Don't Give the Rich Man Special Treatment

2 Brothers, do you say you belong to the Lord Jesus Christ, the Lord of glory? You shouldn't if you love rich people and look down on poor people.

2Now suppose a man comes dressed in fine clothes and gold rings. At the same time another man comes in who is poor and dressed in rags. 3Then you fuss over the rich man. You give him the best seat in the house. But you say to the poor man, "Stand over there." Or you say, "Sit on the floor." 4You judge those men by their wealth. This shows that you judge for evil reasons.

5Listen to me, dear brothers! God has chosen poor people to be rich in faith. The Kingdom of Heaven is theirs. That is the gift God has promised to all those who love him. 6And yet, of the two strangers, you have hated the poor man. Don't the rich men pick on you? Don't they drag you into court? 7And they laugh at Jesus Christ, whose name you hold.

8It is good when you obey our Lord's command. He said, "You must love your neighbors as much as you love yourself." 9You break this law when you love the rich. It is a great sin.

¹⁰What if someone keeps every law but makes one little slip? He is just as guilty as the person who has broken every law. ¹¹God said you must not marry a woman who already has a husband. He also said you must not murder. You may not have broken the marriage laws. But if you have murdered someone, you have broken God's laws. So you stand guilty before him.

¹²You will be judged by whether you do what Christ wants you to or not. So watch what you do and what you think. ¹³There will be no mercy to those who have shown no mercy. But if you have been merciful, then God's mercy will win over his judgment.

Faith and Good Works Go Together

¹⁴Brothers, why pretend you have faith if you aren't proving it by helping others? Will *that* kind of faith save anyone? ¹⁵You may have a friend who is in need of food and clothing. ¹⁶What if you say to him, "Good-bye and God bless you. Stay warm and eat well"? If you don't give him clothes or food, what good does that do?

¹⁷So you see, it isn't enough just to have faith. You must also do good to prove that you have it. Faith that doesn't show itself by good works is dead and useless.

¹⁸But someone may argue, "You say the way to God is by faith alone. Well, I say that good works are important too. Without good works you can't prove whether you have faith or not. But anyone can see that I have faith by the way I act."

¹⁹Are there still some among you who hold that "only believing" is enough? Is believing in one God enough? Well, remember that the demons believe this. And they shake with fear! ²⁰Fool! Don't you know that "believing" is useless unless you *do* what God wants? Faith that does not result in good deeds is not real faith.

²¹Remember, our father Abraham was declared good because of what he *did*. He was willing to obey God. He even went as far as giving his son Isaac to die on the

Clothing
JAMES 2:1-4

Almost everything you and your family wear is different from Bible-time clothing. There were no blue jeans then. Women did not go to the store to buy clothing. They made it. They even made the threads to weave into cloth. Threads were woven on a loom to make cloth. Different colors were woven together to make designs. To get colors, people had to use special dyes from plants or rocks. Men and boys wore tunics. A tunic was like a long T-shirt, reaching below the knees. A wide band of cloth was wrapped around the waist. A man wore a cloak over all this. A woman wore about the same thing as a man but in much brighter colors. She also wore a scarf. Sometimes it covered her face. She could also wrap the scarf on top of her head. Clothing was hard to make, so people did not have much clothing. Would you like to wear Bible-time clothing to school? Be glad for the clothing you have and how easy it is to get it.

altar. ²²He had enough faith to do whatever God told him. His faith was made complete by what he did. ²³So it happened just as the Bible says. Abraham trusted God, and the Lord declared him good. He was even called "the friend of God." ²⁴So, a man is saved by what he does. He is not just saved by what he believes.

Be careful what you say

The tongue is a small thing.
But what huge damage it can do.

James 3:5

---

²⁵Rahab, the prostitute, is another example of this. She was saved because of what she did. She hid the messengers and sent them safely away by a different way. ²⁶Our body is dead when there is no spirit in it. So faith is dead if it is not the kind that results in good deeds.

Control What You Say

3 Brothers, don't be too eager to tell others their faults. We all make many mistakes. When teachers do wrong, their punishment will be greater than it would be for others.

If anyone can control his tongue, it proves he has control over himself. ³We use a small bit to make a large horse go where we want. ⁴And a tiny rudder makes a huge ship turn where the pilot wants. It doesn't matter that the winds are strong.

Do not give in to Satan

Resist the devil and
he will run from you.

James 4:7

---

⁵So also the tongue is a small thing. But what huge damage it can do. A great forest can be set on fire by one tiny spark. ⁶And the tongue is a flame of fire. It is full of evil. It poisons every part of the body. The tongue is set on fire by hell itself. It can turn our whole lives into a blazing flame of doom and ruin.

⁷Men can train every kind of animal, bird, reptile, and fish. ⁸But no human being can tame the tongue. It is always ready to pour out its deadly poison. ⁹Sometimes it praises our heavenly Father. Sometimes it breaks out into curses against men who are made like God. ¹⁰And so blessing and cursing come pouring out of the same mouth. Dear brothers, surely this is not right! ¹¹Does a spring of water bubble with fresh water and then with bitter water? ¹²Can you pick olives from a fig tree, or figs from a grape vine? No! And you can't draw fresh water from a salty pool.

Real Wisdom Comes from Heaven

¹³If you are wise, live a life of steady goodness. Then only good deeds will pour forth. And if you don't brag about them, then you will be truly wise! ¹⁴Don't brag about being wise if you are bitter and jealous and selfish. That is the worst sort of lie. ¹⁵Jealousy and selfishness are not God's kind of wisdom. Such things are earthly, unspiritual, and inspired by the devil. ¹⁶Wherever there is jealousy or ambition, there will be disorder and every kind of evil.

¹⁷But the wisdom that comes from Heaven is pure. It is full of quiet gentleness. And so it is peace-loving and polite. It allows debate and is willing to give in to others. It is full of mercy and good deeds. It is real and direct and heartfelt. ¹⁸Those who are peacemakers will plant seeds of peace and harvest a crop of goodness.

How Can You Get Close to God?

4 What is causing the fights among you? Isn't it because there is a whole army of evil desires within you? ²You want what you don't have. So you kill to get it! You long for what others have. So you start a fight to take it away! Why don't you have what you want? Because you don't ask God for it. ³When you do ask you don't get it because your whole aim is wrong. You want only what will make *you* happy.

⁴You are like an unfaithful wife who loves her husband's enemies. Don't you know that making friends with this world makes you an enemy of God? If you enjoy the pleasure of the world, you

cannot be a friend of God. ⁵The Bible says that the Holy Spirit within us watches over us with jealousy. ⁶He gives us strength to stand against evil wishes. The Bible says God gives strength to the humble. But he sets himself against the proud.

?????????????????????????????????

How is the length of our lives like morning fog?

(Read 4:14 for the answer.)

?????????????????????????????????

⁷So give yourselves humbly to God. Resist the devil and he will run from you. ⁸And when you draw close to God, God will draw close to you. Wash your hands, sinners! Let your hearts be filled with God. He will make them pure and true to him. ⁹Let there be tears for the wrong things you have done. Let there be sorrow and real grief. Let there be sadness instead of laughter. Let there be gloom instead of joy. ¹⁰When you understand you are useless before the Lord, he will lift you up. He will encourage and help you.

¹¹Don't speak against each other, dear brothers. If you do, you are fighting against God's law. In fact, you are saying it is wrong. Your job is not to decide whether this law is right or wrong. You are to obey it. ¹²Only he who made the law can rightly judge among us. He alone decides to save or destroy us. So what right do you have to judge or scold others?

God Has a Plan for You

¹³Some of you say, "Today or tomorrow we are going to this town. We will stay there a year, and make a profit." Listen! ¹⁴How do you know what is going to happen tomorrow? For the length of your lives is like the morning fog. Now you see it. But soon it is gone. ¹⁵You should say, "If the Lord lets us, we shall live. We will do this or that." ¹⁶Otherwise you will be bragging about your own plans. Such pride never pleases God.

¹⁷And remember this! Do you do what you know is right? If you don't, you are sinning.

A Warning to the Rich

5 Look here, you rich men! Now is the time to cry and groan with grief. You have terrible troubles ahead of you. ²Your wealth is even now rotting away. Your fine clothes are becoming moth-eaten rags. ³The value of your gold and silver is dropping fast. It will stand as proof against you. It will eat your flesh like a fire. That is what you have stored up for the Day of Judgment. ⁴For listen! Hear the cries of the field workers you have cheated of their pay. Their cries have reached the ears of the Lord of Heaven's armies.

Do what you know is right

Do you do what you know is right? If you don't, you are sinning.

James 4:17

---

⁵You have spent your years here on earth having fun. You have satisfied your every desire. Now your fat hearts are ready to be killed. ⁶You have condemned and killed good men. They had no power to defend themselves against you.

Be Patient and Take Courage

⁷You, dear brothers, are waiting for the Lord's return. Be patient, like a farmer waits until autumn for his harvest to ripen. ⁸Yes, be patient. Take courage, for the coming of the Lord is near.

⁹Don't grumble about each other, brothers. Are you yourselves above scolding? For look! The great Judge is coming. He is almost here. Let him do whatever scolding must be done.

¹⁰For examples of patience in suffering, look at the Lord's prophets. ¹¹We know how happy they are because they stayed true to him. They suffered greatly for it. Job is an example of a man who continued to trust the Lord in sorrow. From his life we can see how the Lord's

plan finally ended in good. God is full of tenderness and mercy.

Pray for each other when you sin

Tell each other when you do wrong. Pray for each other. Then you will be healed.

James 5:16

---

¹²Most of all, brothers, don't swear by Heaven or earth or anything else. Just say a simple yes or no. That way you won't sin and be guilty for it.

The Right Kind of Prayer Has Power and Brings Results

¹³Is anyone among you suffering? If so, he should pray about it. And those who are thankful should sing praises to the Lord.

¹⁴Is anyone sick? He should call for the elders of the church. They should pray over him and pour a little oil upon him. They should call on the Lord to heal him. ¹⁵If their prayer is offered in faith, it will heal him. The Lord will make him well. If his sickness was caused by some sin, the Lord will forgive him.

¹⁶Tell each other when you do wrong. Pray for each other. Then you will be healed. The earnest prayer of a righteous man has great power and wonderful results. ¹⁷Elijah was as human as we are. He prayed that no rain would fall. None fell for the next three and a half years! ¹⁸Then he prayed again, this time that it *would* rain. Down the rain poured! The grass turned green and the gardens began to grow again.

Helping Those Who Wander Away from God

¹⁹Now suppose, brothers, someone slips away from God. Such a person no longer trusts in the Lord. But then someone helps him understand the Truth again. ²⁰The person who brings him back to God will have saved a soul from death. He will bring about the forgiveness of his many sins.

Sincerely, James

FIRST PETER

A friend of yours accepts Jesus. His other friends laugh at him. Bigger boys take him behind your school and beat him up. A policeman sees this. He laughs. He also beats your friend with his club and throws him in jail. Your friend is tortured there. He may even be killed. Why? Because he accepted Jesus.

This won't happen to you or your friends, of course. Be glad you live in a free country! But it did happen to Christians in Peter's time. Nero, the Roman emperor, hated Christians. He threw them in jail. He tortured them. He killed them. Many religious leaders also hated them. They did all they could to hurt the Christians.

Peter wrote a letter to the Christians. He told them to keep on believing in Jesus. Christians should live like Jesus. Jesus suffered much for them. They may have to suffer some for him. Before long Peter would suffer and be killed. Why? Because he believed in Jesus. You don't suffer that much for Jesus, do you? But what if friends make fun of you because you're a Christian? Would you pretend that you don't know him? What would you do?

A Letter from Peter, God's Missionary

1 *From:* Peter, Jesus Christ's missionary. *To:* The Jewish Christians driven out of Jerusalem. You are scattered throughout Pontus, Galatia, Cappadocia, Asia Minor, and Bithynia.

²Dear friends, God the Father chose you long ago. He knew you would become his children. The Holy Spirit has been at work in your hearts. He is cleansing you with the blood of Jesus Christ. This makes you pleasing to him. May God bless you richly. May he grant you more and more freedom from anxiety and fear.

The Priceless Gift of Eternal Life

³All honor to God, the God and Father of our Lord Jesus Christ. It is his great mercy that has given us the privilege of being born again. Now we are members of God's own family. Now we live in the hope of eternal life. Why? Because Christ rose again from the dead. ⁴God has reserved for his children the priceless gift of eternal life. It is kept in Heaven for you. It is pure and spotless.

It is beyond the reach of change and decay. [5]God's power will guard it because you are trusting him. It will be yours in the last day for all to see. [6]So be truly glad! There is wonderful joy ahead! This is true, even though the going is rough for a while.

[7]These trials test your faith. They will prove whether it is strong and pure. It is being tested as fire tests gold and purifies it. Your faith is far more precious to God than gold. Your strong faith will bring you praise and glory and honor when he returns.

[8]You love him even though you have never seen him. You haven't seen him, but you trust him. So you are happy with joy that can't be explained. This joy comes from Heaven itself. [9]The end of it all will be the salvation of your souls.

[10]This salvation was something the prophets did not understand. They wrote about it, but they wondered what it all could mean. [11]They wondered what the Spirit of Christ was talking about. He told them to write about what would happen to Christ. They wrote about his suffering and his great glory afterwards. And they wondered when and to whom all this would happen.

[12]They were told that these things would not happen during their lifetime. But it happened a long time later, during yours. Now this Good News has been announced to all of us. It was preached by the Holy Spirit from Heaven. Even the angels in Heaven would want to know more about it.

[13]So be sober and be smart. Look forward to more of God's kindness when Jesus Christ returns.

Live a Holy Life

[14]Obey God because you are his children. Don't slip back into your old ways. For then you did evil because you didn't know better. [15]But be holy now in everything you do. The Lord is holy, who invited you to be his child. [16]He himself has said, "You must be holy, for I am holy."

[17]Your heavenly Father to whom you pray has no favorites when he judges. He will judge you with perfect justice for all you do. So act with respect for him from now on until you get to Heaven. [18]God paid a ransom to save you from the impossible way your fathers tried to take. The ransom he paid wasn't gold or silver as you very well know. [19]But he paid for you with the precious blood of

---

God's Word lasts forever

But the Word of the Lord will last forever. And his message is the Good News that was preached to you.

1 Peter 1:25

Christ. He was the sinless, spotless Lamb of God. [20]God chose him for this purpose long before the world began. Only recently was he brought into public view as a blessing to you.

[21]Because of this, your trust can be in God. He raised Christ from the dead and gave him great glory. Now your faith and hope can rest in him alone. [22]Now you can have real love for everyone. Your souls were cleansed from hatred when you trusted Christ to save you. So be sure that you love each other warmly, with all your hearts.

[23]For you have a new life. It was not passed on to you from your parents. The life they gave you will fade away. This new one will last forever. It comes from Christ, God's living Message to men. [24]Our lives will fade like dried grass. All our greatness is like a flower that droops and falls. [25]But the Word of the Lord will last forever. And his message is the Good News that was preached to you.

2 So get rid of your feelings of hatred. Don't just pretend to be good! Be done with dishonesty and jealousy. Stop talking about others behind their backs. [2-3]You know how kind the Lord has been to you. So put away all evil, lying, envy, and fraud. Long to grow up into the fullness of your salvation. Cry for this as a baby cries for his milk.

Be a Living Stone for God's House

[4]Come to Christ. He is the living Foundation Rock upon which God builds.

Men have thrown him out. But he is very precious to God who has chosen him above all others.

⁵You have become living stones for God's use in building his house. What's more, you are his holy priests. So come to him. You are acceptable to him because of Jesus Christ. Offer to God those things that please him. ⁶The Bible says, "I am sending Christ to be the chosen and honored Cornerstone of my church. I will never fail those who trust in him."

⁷Yes, he is very precious to you who believe. To the builders who reject him the same Stone has become the Cornerstone. It is the most honored and important part of the building. ⁸The Bible also says, "He is the Stone that some will stumble over. He is the Rock that will make them fall." They will stumble because they will not listen to God's Word or obey it. Their punishment is that they will fall.

Heaven is our real home

Your real home is in Heaven. So I beg you to keep away from the evil pleasures of this world.

1 Peter 2:11

---

⁹But you are not like that. You have been chosen by God himself. You are priests of the King. You are holy and pure. You are God's very own. Now you can tell how God called you out of darkness into his wonderful light. ¹⁰Once you were less than nothing. Now you are God's own. Once you knew very little of God's kindness. Now your lives have been changed by it.

Obey Those in Authority and Follow Christ's Example

¹¹Dear brothers, you are only visitors here. Your real home is in Heaven. So I beg you to keep away from the evil pleasures of this world. They are not for you. For they fight against your very souls.

¹²Your unsaved neighbors may talk against you. They may say you are evil. So be careful how you behave among them. They will end up praising God

Prophets
1 PETER 1:10-12

A prophet told people what God said. God helped the prophet know what he should say. Then he helped the prophet know how to say it. Sixteen Bible books were written by prophets. Isaiah, Jeremiah, Daniel, Ezekiel, Jonah, Joel, and Amos are a few of them. All are in the Old Testament. Sometimes God showed a prophet what would happen many years later. Isaiah wrote about Jesus. But Isaiah lived about 700 years before Jesus. How did he know what Jesus would do? God told him. Some prophets worked miracles. They did things that no one else could do because God worked through them. God called people to be prophets. They did not just decide to do this work. Being a prophet meant that you had to speak up for God in front of others. You had to stand up for what was good and right, even if people made fun of you. Would you have been that brave? Would you have made a good prophet?

for your good works when Christ returns.

¹³For the Lord's sake, obey every law of your government. Obey the laws of the king as head of the state. ¹⁴Also obey the king's officers. They have been sent by the king to punish all who do wrong. They also honor those who do right.

?????????????????????????????????

What makes a woman more beautiful than jewelry, lovely clothes, and a perm?

(Read 3:3-5 for the answer.)

?????????????????????????????????

¹⁵God wants your good lives to silence foolish men. ¹⁶You are free from the law. But that doesn't mean you are free to do wrong. Live as those who are free to do only God's will at all times. ¹⁷Show respect for everyone. Love Christians everywhere. Fear God and honor the government.

Christians should love one another like family

You should be like one big family. You should be full of kindness toward each other. Love one another with tender hearts and humble minds.

1 Peter 3:8

---

¹⁸Servants, you must respect your masters. Do whatever they tell you. Don't do it only if they are kind and pleasant. But do it even if they are tough and cruel. ¹⁹Praise the Lord if you are punished for doing right! ²⁰You get no credit for being patient if you are beaten for doing wrong. But if you do right and suffer, and are patient, God is well pleased.

²¹This suffering is all part of the work God has given you. Christ, who suffered for you, is your example. Follow in his steps. ²²He never sinned. He never told a lie. ²³He never answered back when insulted. When he suffered he did not

threaten to get even. He left his case in the hands of God who always judges fairly. ²⁴He carried our sins in his own body when he died on the cross. That way we can be finished with sin and live a good life. For his wounds have healed ours! ²⁵Like sheep you wandered away from God. But now you have come back to your Shepherd. He guards your souls and keeps you safe from all attacks.

Good Advice for Husbands and Wives

3 Wives, fit in with your husbands' plans. They might refuse to listen when you talk to them about the Lord. But they will be won by your respectful, pure behavior. Your godly lives will speak to them better than any words.

³Don't worry about the beauty that depends on jewelry, or clothes, or fancy hair. ⁴Be beautiful inside, in your hearts. Have the lasting charm of a gentle and quiet spirit that is so precious to God. ⁵That kind of deep beauty was seen in the saintly women of old. They trusted God and fitted in with their husbands' plans.

⁶Sarah obeyed her husband Abraham. She honored him as head of the house. You have become her children in doing what is right. You don't need to fear offending your husbands.

⁷You husbands must be careful of your wives. Be thoughtful of their needs. Honor them as the weaker sex. Remember that you and your wife are partners in receiving God's blessings. If you don't treat her as you should, your prayers will not be answered.

Do What Is Right, No Matter What Others Say and Do

⁸Also, you should be like one big family. You should be full of kindness toward each other. Love one another with tender hearts and humble minds. ⁹Don't repay evil for evil. Don't snap back at those who say unkind things about you. Instead, pray for God's help for them. We are to be kind to others. And if we are, God will bless us for it.

¹⁰If you want a happy, good life, keep control of your tongue. Guard your lips

from telling lies. ¹¹Turn away from evil and do good. Try to live in peace. Run after it to catch and hold it! ¹²For the Lord is watching his children and listening to their prayers. But the Lord's face is hard against those who do evil.

¹³Usually no one will hurt you for wanting to do good. ¹⁴But even if they should, you are to be envied. God will reward you for it. ¹⁵Quietly trust yourself to Christ your Lord. If anybody asks why you believe as you do, be ready to tell him. Do it in a gentle and respectful way.

¹⁶Do what is right. If you do, men still might speak against you. They still might call you evil names. But they will be ashamed of themselves. ¹⁷If God gives you suffering, it is better to suffer for good than for evil!

Christ Is Our Partner Even When We Suffer

¹⁸Christ also suffered. He died once for the sins of all. He was innocent of any sin at any time. He wanted to bring us safely home to God. But though his body died, his spirit lived on. ¹⁹In the spirit he visited the spirits in prison and preached to them. ²⁰They were those who, in the days of Noah, refused to listen to God. He waited patiently for them while Noah was building the ark. Yet only eight persons were saved from drowning in that terrible flood. ²¹That is what baptism pictures for us. Baptism shows that we have been saved by the resurrection of Christ. It is not because our bodies are washed clean by the water. It is because we are turning to God and asking him to cleanse our hearts. ²²Now Christ is in Heaven. He is sitting in the place of honor next to God the Father. All the angels and powers of Heaven are bowing before him and obeying him.

4 Christ suffered great pain. So you must have the same attitude he did. You must be ready to suffer, too. For remember, when your body suffers, sin loses its power. ²You won't be spending the rest of your life chasing after evil desires. Instead you will be anxious to do the will of God. ³You have had enough in the past of the evil things the godless enjoy. You have enjoyed sex sins, lust, drunkenness, wild parties, drinking bouts, and idol worship.

⁴Your friends will be surprised when you don't join them in their wickedness. They will laugh at you in contempt and scorn. ⁵But remember, they must face the Judge of the living and the dead. They will be punished for the way they have lived. ⁶That is why the Good News was preached even to those who were killed by the flood. Their bodies were punished with death. But they could still live in their spirits as God lives.

Continue to Love One Another

⁷The end of the world is coming soon. Therefore be earnest, thoughtful men of prayer. ⁸Most important of all, continue to show deep love for each other. Love makes up for many of your faults. ⁹Cheerfully share your homes and your food with those who have need.

Help others with the talents God has given you

God has given each of you special abilities. Be sure to use them to help each other. Pass on to others God's many kinds of blessings.

1 Peter 4:10

---

¹⁰God has given each of you special abilities. Be sure to use them to help each other. Pass on to others God's many kinds of blessings. ¹¹Are you called to preach? Then preach as though God himself were speaking through you. Are you called to help others? Do it with all the strength and energy that God supplies. Then God will be glorified through Jesus Christ. To him belongs glory and power forever and ever. Amen.

Hard Times Bring Reward

¹²Dear friends, don't be surprised when you go through the fiery trials ahead. This is no strange, unusual thing that is going to happen to you. ¹³Instead, be really glad. These trials will make you partners with Christ in his suffering.

Afterwards you will joyfully share his glory in the day when it is displayed.

¹⁴Be happy if you are cursed and insulted for being a Christian. When that happens the Spirit of God will come upon you with great glory. ¹⁵Don't any of you suffer for murdering or stealing or making trouble. May none of you be a busybody, prying into other people's affairs. ¹⁶But it is no shame to suffer for being a Christian. Praise God for the privilege of being in Christ's family. You are called by his wonderful name! ¹⁷For the time has come for judgment. It must begin first among God's own children. We who are Christians must be judged. So what terrible fate awaits those who have never believed in the Lord. ¹⁸If the righteous are barely saved, what chance will the godless have?

¹⁹If you are suffering according to God's will, keep on doing what is right. Trust yourself to the God who made you. For he will never fail you.

Some Advice for Teachers and Students

5 And now, a word to you elders of the church. I, too, am an elder. With my own eyes I saw Christ dying on the cross. I, too, will share his glory and his honor when he returns. Fellow elders, I have a plea for you. ²Feed the flock of God. Care for it willingly, not because you have to. Don't do it for what you will get out of it. Do it because you are eager to serve the Lord. ³Don't be dictators. But lead them by your good example. ⁴For soon the Head Shepherd will come. And then your reward will be a never-ending share in his glory and honor.

????????????????????????????????????

Who is called the Head Shepherd?

(Read 5:1-4 for the answer.)

????????????????????????????????????

⁵You younger men, follow the leadership of those who are older. And all of you serve each other with humble spirits. God gives special blessings to those who are humble. But he sets himself against those who are proud. ⁶Humble yourselves under the mighty hand of God. In his good time he will lift you up.

⁷Let God have all your worries and cares. He is always thinking about you and watching everything that concerns you.

Watch Out for Your Great Enemy

⁸Watch out for attacks from Satan, your great enemy. He prowls around like a hungry, roaring lion. He is always looking for someone to tear apart. ⁹Stand firm when he attacks. Trust the Lord. Remember that other Christians all around the world are going through these sufferings too.

Give God all your worries

Let God have all your worries and cares. He is always thinking about you and watching everything that concerns you.

1 Peter 5:7

---

¹⁰You will have to suffer a little while. But our God is full of kindness through Christ. He will give you eternal glory. He will come and pick you up. He will set you firmly in place. You will be stronger than ever. ¹¹To him be all power over all things, forever and ever. Amen.

Peace to All of You

¹²I am sending this note to you through the courtesy of Silvanus. He is, in my opinion, a very faithful brother. I hope I have encouraged you by this letter. I have given you a true statement of the way God blesses. What I have told you here should help you stand firmly in his love.

¹³The church here in Rome is your sister in the Lord. She sends you her greetings. So does my son Mark. ¹⁴Give each other the handshake of Christian love. Peace be to all of you who are in Christ.

SECOND PETER

The Book of 2 Peter is about false teachers. A false teacher is someone who tries to tell you it's okay to do something wrong. False teachers teach things that aren't true. They teach things that will hurt you. They try to make bad things look good. Sometimes they even pretend their words are God's words! They teach things that will not please God.

Peter wrote this book about false teachers. There were many of them in Bible times. There are many today. False teachers don't care if they hurt you. They care more about money than about you. Some even make fun of God. They think they are bigger than God. But God will punish them. Listen to God. Don't listen to them. That's what Peter says in this book.

A Letter for All of You

1 *From:* Simon Peter, a servant and missionary of Jesus Christ.

To: All of you who have our kind of faith. That faith is the kind that Jesus Christ our God and Savior gives to us. How precious it is. How just and good he is to give this faith to us.

Steps to Spiritual Growth

²Do you want more and more of God's kindness and peace? Then learn to know God better and better. ³Then his great power will give you all you need for living a good life. He even shares his own glory and his own goodness with us! ⁴He uses that power to give you all the rich blessings he promised. And you can be rescued from the rottenness around us. Then he will give you his own character.

⁵But to obtain these gifts, you need more than faith. You must also work hard to be good, and even that is not enough. You must know God better and find out what he wants you to do. ⁶Next, learn to put aside your own desires. That

---

God gives his friends everything they need

Learn to know God better and better. Then his great power will give you all you need for living a good life.

2 Peter 1:2-3

---

way you will become patient and godly. You will gladly let God have his way with you. ⁷This will make possible the next step. This step is for you to enjoy other people and to like them. Finally you will grow to love them deeply. ⁸When you go on in this way, you will grow strong spiritually. You will become fruitful and useful to our Lord Jesus Christ. ⁹But anyone who fails to go after these additions to faith is blind. He is unwise and has forgotten that God saved him from his sins. He did this so he could live a strong, good life for the Lord.

¹⁰So, brothers, work to prove you really are those God has called and chosen. Then you will never stumble or fall away. ¹¹You will enter into the eternal Kingdom of our Lord and Savior Jesus Christ.

Pay Attention to God's Word

¹²You already know these things and are really getting along quite well! But I plan to keep on reminding you of them. ¹³⁻¹⁴The Lord Jesus Christ has showed me that my days on earth are numbered. I am soon to die. As long as I am still here I will keep on reminding you. ¹⁵I hope to impress these things upon you. Then you will remember them long after I have gone.

¹⁶We explained to you the power of our Lord Jesus Christ. And we told you about his return. We have not been telling you fairy tales. My own eyes have seen his glory. ¹⁷⁻¹⁸I was on the holy mountain when he shone out with honor. It was given him by God his Father. I heard that great, majestic voice calling down from Heaven. It said, "This is my much-loved Son. I am well pleased with him."

¹⁹So we have seen and proved that what the prophets said came true. You will be wise to listen to all they have written. Their words are like lights shining into dark corners. They help us to understand many things. Consider the truth of the prophets' words. Then the light will dawn and Christ the Morning Star will shine in your hearts. ²⁰⁻²¹No prophecy in the Bible was thought up by the prophet himself. The Holy Spirit within these godly men gave them true messages from God.

Beware of False Teachers

2 But there were false prophets in those days. And there will be false teachers among you, too. They will cleverly tell their lies about God. They will even turn against their Master who bought them. But theirs will be a swift and terrible end. ²Many will follow them in sexual sin. And because of them Christ and his truth will be laughed at.

³These greedy teachers will tell you anything to get your money. But God condemned them long ago. Their destruction is on the way. ⁴For God did not spare even the angels who sinned. He threw them into hell. They are chained in gloomy caves and darkness until the Judgment Day. ⁵He did not spare any of the people who lived in ancient times. But he guarded Noah and his family of seven. He was the one man who spoke up for God. At that time God destroyed the ungodly world with the flood. ⁶Later, he turned the cities of Sodom and Gomorrah into heaps of ashes. He erased them off the face of the earth. They were an example for people who want to live ungodly lives.

⁷⁻⁸At the same time the Lord saved Lot out of Sodom because he was a good man. He was sick of the wickedness he saw around him every day. ⁹So the Lord can rescue us from the temptations that are around us. He can punish the ungodly until the day of final judgment comes. ¹⁰He will especially punish those who follow their own evil, lustful thoughts. He will punish those who are proud and willful. They even dare to laugh at the angels in Heaven without fear. ¹¹The angels in Heaven stand in the very presence of the Lord. They are far greater in power and strength than these false teachers. But the angels never speak out against the false teachers before the Lord.

¹²But false teachers are fools. They are no better than animals. They do whatever they feel like. They are born only to be caught and killed. They laugh at the powers of the underworld which they know so little about. They will be destroyed along with all the demons and powers of hell.

¹³That is the pay these teachers will have for their sin. They live in evil pleasures day after day. They are a disgrace and a stain among you. They trick you

by living in sin. And they join your feasts as if they are honest men. ¹⁴No woman can escape their sinful stare. They never have enough of adultery. They make a game of tempting unstable women. They train themselves to be greedy and are doomed and cursed. ¹⁵They've gone off the road and become lost like Balaam, the son of Beor. He fell in love with the money he could make by doing wrong. ¹⁶Balaam was stopped from his sin when his donkey spoke with a human voice. The donkey scolded and rebuked him.

¹⁷These men are as useless as dried-up springs of water. They promise much and deliver nothing. They are as unstable as clouds driven by the storm winds. They are doomed to the eternal pits of darkness. ¹⁸They proudly brag about their sins and conquests. Using lust, they lure those who have escaped from wicked living back into sin.

¹⁹These teachers who offer "freedom" from law are slaves to sin. For a man is a slave to whatever controls him. ²⁰A person can escape from the wicked ways of the world. This happens by learning about our Lord and Savior Jesus Christ. But what if he gets tangled up with sin and becomes its slave again? He is worse off than he was before! ²¹He should have never known God's way. For that would be better than knowing it, and then turning from God's holy commands. ²²There is an old saying, "A dog comes back to what he has vomited. A pig is washed only to come back and roll in the mud again." That is the way it is with those who turn again to their sin.

Hope for Growing Christians

3 This is my second letter to you, dear brothers. In both of them I have reminded you about facts you already know. These are facts you learned from the holy prophets. You also learned them from us apostles. We brought you the words of our Lord and Savior.

³First, in the last days there will come scoffers. They will do every wrong they can think of. And they will laugh at the truth. ⁴They will say, "So Jesus promised to come back, did he? Then where is he?

He'll never come! Everything has stayed just as it was since the first day of creation."

⁵⁻⁶They forget that God destroyed the world with a mighty flood. This happened long after God made the heavens by the word of his command. That was when he used the waters to form the earth and surround it. ⁷God commanded that the earth and heavens be stored away for a great fire. This will happen at the Judgment Day, when all ungodly men will die.

??????????????????????????????????

How will Jesus return to earth like a thief?

(Read 3:10 for the answer.)

??????????????????????????????????

⁸But don't forget this, dear friends! A day is like 1,000 years to the Lord. ⁹It may seem like he is slow in coming back as he promised. But he isn't. He is waiting because he does not want anyone to die. He is giving more time for sinners to repent. ¹⁰The day of the Lord is surely coming. It will come as suddenly as a thief in the night. Then the heavens will pass away with a terrible noise. The heavenly bodies will disappear in fire. The earth and everything on it will be burned up.

¹¹Yes, everything is going to melt! So now, what holy lives we should be living! ¹²You should look forward to that day and hurry it along. It is the day when God will set the heavens on fire. Then the heavenly bodies will melt and disappear in flames. ¹³But we are looking forward to God's promise of new heavens and a new earth. Only goodness will be there.

¹⁴Dear friends, you are waiting for these things to happen. You are waiting for him to come back. So try to live without sinning. Be at peace with everyone. Then he will be pleased with you when he returns.

¹⁵⁻¹⁶And remember why he is waiting. He is giving us time to get his message of salvation out to others. Our wise and beloved brother Paul has talked about

these things in his letters. Some of them are not easy to understand.

There are unlearned people who have twisted his letters around. They want them to mean something different from what he wanted. They do this to the rest of the Bible, too. The result is disaster for them.

[17]I am warning you ahead of time, dear brothers. I want you to be careful. Don't be carried away by the mistakes of these wicked men. If you do, you will become mixed up too. [18]But grow in spiritual strength. And learn more about our Lord and Savior Jesus Christ. To him be all glory and honor, both now and forever. Good-bye.

Peter

FIRST JOHN

An old man sits down to write a letter. He wants to tell his young friends about Jesus. These young Christians were not even born when Jesus died on the cross. They had only heard about him from people like John. False teachers tried to tell them strange things about Jesus. But John said, "Listen to me. I saw Jesus. I touched him. I listened to him." John was one of Jesus' disciples. He was there when Jesus taught. He was there when Jesus healed sick people. He was there when Jesus brought people back from the dead. He was there when Jesus was crucified. He was there when the disciples found the tomb empty. Who would you want to teach you, someone who was there or someone who just wanted to argue? Let's listen to John. He has some important things to tell us about Jesus.

Jesus Christ Is Eternal Life

1 Christ was alive when the world began. I have seen him with my own eyes and listened to him speak. I have touched him with my own hands. He is God's message of life. ²This one who is life from God has been shown to us. We have seen him. I am speaking of Christ, who is eternal Life. He was with the Father and then was shown to us. ³We are telling you about what we ourselves have seen and heard. That way you may share our fellowship. Our fellowship is with the Father and with Jesus Christ his Son. ⁴We are writing this letter so we all will be full of joy.

The Light of God Wipes Out Darkness

⁵God has given us a message to pass on to you. It is that God is Light and in him is no darkness at all. ⁶If we say we are God's friends but live in darkness, we are lying. ⁷We should live in the light, as Christ does. Then we will have fellowship with each other. Also, the blood of Jesus his Son cleanses us from every sin.

⁸If we say that we have no sin, we are fooling ourselves. We are refusing to accept the truth. ⁹If we confess our sins, he can be depended on to forgive us. He will cleanse us from every wrong. It is proper for God to do this because Christ died for our sins. ¹⁰If we say we haven't sinned, we make God a liar. For he says we have sinned.

2 My little children, I'm telling you this so you will stay away from sin. But if you sin, there is someone to beg for you before the Father. His name is Jesus Christ. He is all that is good, and he pleases God completely. ²He took

God's anger against our sins upon himself. He brought us into fellowship with God. He is the forgiveness for our sins. And he brings forgiveness to all the sins of the world.

³How can we be sure that we belong to him? By looking within ourselves. Are we really trying to do what he wants us to?

⁴Someone may say, "I am a Christian. I am on my way to Heaven. I belong to Christ." But if he doesn't do what Christ tells him, he's a liar. ⁵But those who do what Christ tells them will love God more and more. That is the way to know whether or not you are a Christian. ⁶Anyone who says he is a Christian should live as Christ did.

⁷Dear brothers, I am not writing out a new rule for you to obey. This rule is an old one you have had from the start. You have heard it all before. ⁸Yet it is always new. It works for you just as it did for Christ. Why? Because the darkness is going away. The true light is already shining.

God's friends live like Christ

If we say we are God's friends but live in darkness, we are lying. We should live in the light, as Christ does.

1 John 1:6-7

---

⁹What if someone says he is in the light but dislikes his fellow man? He is still in darkness. ¹⁰But whoever loves his fellow man is "walking in the light." He can see his way without stumbling around in darkness and sin. ¹¹For he who dislikes his brother is wandering in spiritual darkness. He doesn't know where he is going. The darkness has made him blind so that he cannot see the way.

Know and Love God, Not This Evil World

¹²I am writing these things to you, my little children. Why? Because your sins have been forgiven in the name of Jesus our Savior. ¹³I am saying these things to

you older men, too. Why? Because you know Christ, the one who has been alive from the beginning. Young men, I'm talking to you because you've won your battle with Satan. And I am writing to you younger boys and girls, too. Why? Because you have learned to know God our Father.

Loving bad things keeps us from loving God

Stop loving this evil world and all it offers you. When you love these things you show you don't really love God.

1 John 2:15

---

¹⁴I have written to you fathers because you know the eternal God. I have written to you young men because you are strong. You have kept God's Word in your hearts. You have won your struggle against Satan. ¹⁵Stop loving this evil world and all it offers you. When you love these things you show you don't really love God. ¹⁶What are these worldly things? One is the lust for sex. Another is the desire to buy everything that charms you. The third is the pride that comes from riches and power. None of these are from God. They are from this evil world. ¹⁷This world is fading away. These evil, forbidden things will go with it. But whoever keeps doing the will of God will live forever.

Beware of False Teachers Who Are against God

¹⁸Dear children, this world's last hour has come. You have heard about the Antichrist who is coming. He is the one who is against Christ. Already many such persons have appeared. This is why we are certain that the end of the world is near. ¹⁹These people used to be members of our churches. But they never belonged with us or else they would have stayed. When they left us it proved that they were not of us.

²⁰But you are not like that. The Holy Spirit has come upon you, and you know the truth. ²¹I am not writing to you

because you need to know the truth. But I warn you because you know the difference between true and false.

²²And who is the greatest liar? The one who says that Jesus is not the Christ. Such a person is antichrist. He does not believe in God the Father and in his Son. ²³A person who doesn't believe in God's Son doesn't have the Father. But he who believes in God's Son has God the Father also.

²⁴So keep believing what you have been taught from the beginning. Then you will be in fellowship with both God the Father and his Son. ²⁵And he has promised us eternal life.

²⁶I am writing about those who want to blindfold you and lead you astray. ²⁷But you have received the Holy Spirit. He lives within you. So you don't need anyone to teach you what is right. He teaches you all things. He is the Truth, and no liar. So, as he said, you must live in Christ and never leave him.

²⁸Now, little children, stay in fellowship with the Lord. Then when he comes you will know all is well. You will not be ashamed and shrink back from meeting him. ²⁹We know that God is always good and does only right. So all those who do right are his children.

We Are God's Children

3 See how very much our heavenly Father loves us. He allows us to be called his children, and we really are! Most people don't know God. So they don't understand that we are his children. ²Yes, dear friends, we are already God's children. We can't imagine what it is going to be like later on. But we do know that when he comes we will be like him. We shall see him as he really is. ³Everyone who believes this will stay pure because Christ is pure.

⁴But those who keep on sinning are against God. Every sin is done against the will of God. ⁵You know he became a man so that he could take away our sins. There is no sin in him. He never missed God's will at any time. ⁶So if we stay close to him, we won't sin either. Everyone who sins has never known him.

⁷Dear children, don't let anyone trick

Poor People
1 JOHN 3:16-17

Do you know anyone who is poor? How poor is that person? Does he have enough to eat? Does she have enough to pay rent? There are many poor people today. There were many poor people in Bible times. The government did not give a blind person money for food and clothing. So a blind person had to beg. People who were sick or lame could not get good jobs. There were not even enough good jobs for strong, healthy people. Sick or lame people often became beggars. Most farms were very small. People barely had enough to eat from their farms. Old people had no Social Security or retirement programs like we do today. Younger people often supported them. People were paid very little for their work then. It was easy to be poor in Bible times. It was hard to get enough money for everyday needs. The Bible says Christians must help poor people. If we don't, we are not showing God's love. Would we want help if we were poor? We should help others in the same way we would want others to help us. That's the Golden Rule.

you. If you do what's good, it's because you are good, even as he is. [8]But if you keep on sinning, it shows you belong to Satan. He has been sinning from the beginning. But the Son of God came to destroy the works of the devil. [9]Anyone born into God's family doesn't practice sin. God's life is in him, so he can't keep on sinning. This new life has been born into him and controls him. He has been *born again.*

Love One Another

[10]Now we can tell who is a child of God and who belongs to Satan. Whoever lives a life of sin and doesn't love his brother is not of God. [11]The message to us from the beginning is that we should love one another.

[12]We are not to be like Cain. He belonged to Satan and killed his brother. Why did he kill him? Because Cain had been doing wrong. He knew very well that his brother's life was better than his. [13]So don't be surprised, dear friends, if the world hates you.

Your actions should show that you love others

Let us stop just saying we love people. Let us really love them and prove it by our actions.

1 John 3:18

---

[14]Loving Christians proves we have come out of death and into eternal life. But a person who doesn't have love for others is headed for eternal death. [15]Anyone who hates his Christian brother is really a murderer at heart. You know that no murderer has eternal life. [16]We know what real love is from Christ's example in dying for us. So we also ought to lay down our lives for our Christian brothers. [17]Now suppose a Christian has plenty of money. And suppose he sees a needy brother but won't help him. If this happens, how can God's love be within him? [18]Little children, let us stop just saying we love people. Let us really love them and prove it by our actions. [19]Then we will know, by our actions, that we are

on God's side. Our consciences will be clear, even when we stand before the Lord. [20]If we feel we've done wrong, the Lord will feel it even more. He knows everything we do.

[21]Dearly loved friends, listen to me. If our consciences are clear, we can come to the Lord with perfect safety. [22]He will give us whatever we ask for. Why? Because we are obeying him and doing the things that please him. [23]God has a command for us. He tells us to believe on the name of his Son Jesus Christ. And he tells us to love one another. [24]Those who do what God says are living with God, and he with them. We know this is true because the Spirit he gave us tells us so.

Can You Tell What's True and What's Not?

4 Dearly loved friends, don't believe everything you hear. Be careful even if someone says it is a message from God. Test it first to see if it really is. For there are many false teachers around. [2]There is a way to find out if their message is from the Holy Spirit. Ask if they agree that Jesus Christ came to earth. Ask if they believe he was a man with a human body. If they believe this, then their message is from God. [3]But if not, their message is not from God. It is from one who is against Christ. This is the "Antichrist" you have heard is going to come. His hate against Christ is already abroad in the world.

[4]Dear young friends, you belong to God. You have already won your fight with those who are against Christ. There is someone in you who is stronger than any evil teacher in this world. [5]These men belong to this world. So they are concerned about worldly things, and the world listens to them. [6]But we are children of God. That is why only those who know God will listen to us. Others won't. That is another way to know whether a message is from God. If it is, the world won't listen to it.

[7]Dear friends, let us practice loving each other. Love comes from God. Everyone who loves is a child of God and knows God. [8]But a person who doesn't

love doesn't know God, because God is love.

⁹God has shown us how much he loved us. He sent his only Son into the world to bring us eternal life. ¹⁰In this act we see what real love is. It is not that we love God but that he loved us. He sent his Son to satisfy God's anger against our sins.

Love Comes from God

¹¹Dear friends, God loved us as much as that. We surely ought to love each other too. ¹²We have never seen God. When we love each other God lives in us and his love in us grows. ¹³He has put his own Holy Spirit into our hearts. This proves that we are living with him and he with us. ¹⁴We have seen and now tell that God sent his Son to save the world. ¹⁵Anyone who says Jesus is the Son of God has God living in him. He is also living with God.

¹⁶We know how much God loves us. We believe him when he tells us that he loves us dearly. God is love. Anyone who lives in love lives with God and God lives in him. ¹⁷And our love grows more perfect and complete. So we will not be ashamed at the Day of Judgment. We will face him with joy because he loves us and we love him.

You can't love God and hate others

If someone says, "I love God,"
but hates his brother, he is a liar.

1 John 4:20

---

¹⁸We need have no fear of someone who loves us perfectly. His perfect love for us ends all dread of what he might do to us. If we are afraid, it is fear of what he might do to us. This shows that we are not sure that he loves us. ¹⁹So, our love for him comes because he loved us first.

²⁰If someone says, "I love God," but hates his brother, he is a liar. He doesn't love his brother who is right there in front of him. So how can he love God whom he has never seen? ²¹And God said that one must love not only God but his brother too.

If You Love God, You Can Obey Him

5 If you believe Jesus is the Christ then you are a child of God. And all who love the Father love his children too. ²You can know you love God's children by how much you love and obey God. ³If you love God, do what he says. That isn't hard at all. ⁴Every child of God can obey him. They can defeat sin and evil pleasure by trusting Christ.

⁵Who could fight and win this battle? It is only done by believing that Jesus is truly the Son of God. ⁶⁻⁸And we know he is. God said so with a voice from Heaven when Jesus was baptized. He said it again as Jesus was facing death. He said it not only at his baptism but also at his death.

Obey God if you love him

If you love God, do what he says.

1 John 5:3

And the Holy Spirit, forever truthful, says it too. So we have these three witnesses. One is the voice of the Holy Spirit in our hearts. The second is the voice from Heaven at Christ's baptism. The third is the voice before he died. And they all say that Jesus Christ is the Son of God. ⁹We believe men who witness in our courts. So surely we can believe whatever God declares. And God declares that Jesus is his Son. ¹⁰All who believe this know in their hearts that it is true. Anyone who doesn't believe this is calling God a liar. Why? Because he doesn't believe what God has said about his Son.

¹¹And what is it that God has said? He said he has given us eternal life, and this life is in his Son. ¹²So whoever has God's Son has life. Whoever does not have his Son does not have life.

God Is Life

¹³I have written this to you who believe in the Son of God. That way you may know you have eternal life. ¹⁴We are sure he will hear us when we ask in line with his will. ¹⁵We know he is listening when we talk to him and make our requests. So we can be sure that he will answer us.

¹⁶What if you see a Christian in a sin that doesn't end in death? You should ask God to forgive him. Then God will give him life unless he has sinned that one fatal sin. But there is one sin which ends in death. If he has done that, there is no use praying for him. ¹⁷Every wrong is a sin, of course. I'm not talking about these ordinary sins. I am speaking of that one that ends in death.

¹⁸No one who has become part of God's family makes a practice of sinning. Christ, God's Son, holds him tight. So the devil cannot get his hands on him. ¹⁹We know that we are children of God. We also know that the rest of the world is under Satan's power and control. ²⁰And we know that Christ, God's Son, has come. He helps us understand and find the true God. Now we are in God because we are in Jesus Christ his Son. He is the only true God and eternal Life.

²¹Dear children, keep away from anything that might take God's place in your hearts. Amen.

Sincerely, John

SECOND JOHN

Your mother looks at you and says, "Tell the truth." What does she want? Don't lie. Don't pretend. Don't add to the story. Don't tell her what sounds good. Tell her what really happened. Tell her what you really think. Tell her what you really said. Tell her what you really did.

John writes about the truth in this book. What is the truth? It's what God really is. It's what God really thinks. It's what God really says. It's what God really does. It's all in the Bible. That's his book of truth. False teachers add to it. They get us off track. They say what sounds good but really isn't good. John tells us not to listen to them. Do you want to tell the truth? That's good. Do you want to live the truth? That's even better. Christians should try to do this. When they do, they live the way the Bible says. That pleases Jesus.

A Short Letter from John

1 *From:* John, the old Elder of the church. *To:* That dear woman Cyria, one of God's very own. Also to her children, whom I love so much. Everyone else in the church loves them too. ²The Truth is in our hearts forever. ³So God the Father and Jesus Christ his Son will bless us. They will give us mercy, peace, truth, and love.

God wants us to love each other

If we love God, we will obey him. And he has told us to love each other.

2 John 1:6

Beware of False Teachers

⁴How happy I am to find some of your children here following the Truth.

⁵I remind you, friends, of the old rule God gave us from the beginning. That rule is that Christians should love one another. ⁶If we love God, we will obey him. And he has told us to love each other.

⁷There are many false teachers around. They don't believe Jesus Christ came with a real body. Such people are against the truth and against Christ. ⁸Be careful not to act like them. For if you do, you might lose the prize that we have been working to get. See to it that you win your full reward from the Lord. ⁹If you wander beyond the teaching of Christ, you will leave God behind. But if

you are loyal to Christ's teachings, you will have God too. Then you will have both the Father and the Son.

[10]Someone may come to teach you yet not believe what Christ taught. Don't even invite him into your home. Don't encourage him in any way. [11]If you do, you will be a partner with him in his wickedness.

A Final Word from John

[12]I have much more to say, but I don't want to write it to you. I hope to come to see you soon. Then we can talk over these things together and have a joyous time.

[13]Greetings from the children of your sister, who is chosen by God.

Sincerely, John

THIRD JOHN

You'll meet three men in this book. Demetrius was a faithful Christian. He did God's work. He may have been a traveling evangelist or missionary. People said many good things about him. Traveling missionaries usually had to give up their jobs so they could tell others about Jesus. They spent their time serving God. They had no money. So when they traveled, they needed help from other Christians. There were no motels or restaurants, so they needed places to stay and food to eat. They needed Christian friends.

Gaius was just such a helper. When missionaries came to town, they stayed at his house. He gave them rooms to sleep in. He fed them. He was their friend. He even gave them gifts when they left. But Diotrephes was nasty. He tried to control others. He would not share his house and food with these missionaries. He was angry at people who shared with them. He even tried to drive them out of the church.

Which person would you like as a friend? Which would you like in your church?

Another Letter from John

1 *From:* John, the Elder.
To: Dear Gaius, whom I truly love.

Hospitality Pleases God

[2]Dear friend, I am praying all is well with you. I pray that your body is as healthy as I know your soul is. [3]Some of the brothers traveling by have made me very happy. They told me that your life stays clean and true. They say that you are living by the standards of the Good News. [4]I could have no greater joy than to hear such things about my children.

[5]Dear friend, you are doing a good work. You are being faithful to take care of the traveling teachers and missionaries. [6]They have told the church here of your friendship and your loving deeds. I am glad when you send them on their way with a generous gift. [7]They are traveling for the Lord. So they take nothing from those who are not Christians. [8]So we should take care of them. That way

we become partners with them in the Lord's work.

⁹I sent a brief letter to the church about this. But Diotrephes loves to push himself forward as the leader there. So

---

Helping missionaries is good

You are doing a good work.
You are being faithful
to take care of
the traveling teachers
and missionaries.

3 John 1:5

Letters

3 JOHN 1:9

Did you write a letter this week? Did you buy colorful stationery at a store? Did you write with a ballpoint pen? You probably put a stamp on the envelope and put it in a mailbox. Your letter can go anywhere in the world. That's because there are post offices in almost every town and city. There is a mailbox at almost every house. But in Bible times there were no post offices. There were no postmen. No one had a mailbox. A letter could be sent with a friend. But only if that friend was going to a certain place. Kings and rich people sent messengers. Paul wrote letters to churches he had visited. He sent his letters with friends. John wrote this letter to a man named Gaius. Demetrius probably carried it to Gaius. John did not have colorful stationery. He did not even have paper like ours. So he probably wrote on animal skins. He rolled these into scrolls. Sometimes people wrote on broken pieces of pottery. Or they made papyrus by pressing stalks from the papyrus plant together. Their ink was often made of soot from a fire mixed with olive oil. Next time you send a letter, remember Bible-time people. They would have been glad for what you have.

he doesn't listen to me. ¹⁰When I come I will tell you some of the things he is doing. You will learn what wicked things he is saying. He refuses to welcome the missionary travelers. He also tells others not to. When they do he tries to put them out of the church.

Follow the example of good people

Follow only what is good.
Those who do what is right
prove they are God's children.

3 John 1:11

---

¹¹Dear friend, don't let his bad example control you. Follow only what is good. Those who do what is right prove they are God's children. Those who continue in evil prove that they are far from God. ¹²But everyone, including Truth itself, speaks highly of Demetrius. I can say the same for him, and you know I speak the truth.

John Says Good-Bye

¹³I have much to say, but I don't want to write it. ¹⁴I hope to see you soon. Then we will have much to talk about together. ¹⁵So good-bye for now. Friends here send their love. Please give each of the people there a special greeting from me.

Sincerely, John

JUDE

Jude was Jesus' half brother. At first, Jude didn't believe that Jesus was God's Son. But then he began to see the truth. He became a strong Christian leader. Jude wrote this letter to all Christians. Why? Jude was concerned about false teachers. These people were not teaching Bible truth. They were pretending that their teachings were more important than what the Bible teaches. Jude warns believers to stand against these false teachers. Don't listen to them. Don't follow them. There are many false teachers today, too. They don't teach what the Bible says. We must not listen to them! That's what Jude wants to tell us.

A Letter to Christians Everywhere

1 *From:* Jude, a servant of Jesus Christ and a brother of James.

To: Christians everywhere who are beloved of God and chosen by him. ²May you be given more and more of God's kindness, peace, and love.

Watch Out for False Teachers

³Friends, I had been planning to write you about the salvation we share. But now I must write of something else instead. I urge you to defend the truth that God gave to his people. He gave it once for all for us to keep without change. ⁴Some godless teachers have wormed their way in among you. They say that after we become Christians we can do what we like. They say we don't have to fear God's punishment. The fate of such people was written long ago. They have turned against our only Master and Lord, Jesus Christ.

⁵Remember what you know already. The Lord saved a whole nation of people out of the land of Egypt. Then he killed every one of them who didn't trust and obey him. ⁶I remind you of the angels who were pure and holy. But they turned to a life of sin. Now God has them chained up in prisons of darkness. They are waiting for the Judgment Day. ⁷And don't forget the cities of Sodom and Gomorrah and their neighboring towns. They were full of lust of every kind, including lust of men for other men. Those cities were destroyed by fire. They continue to warn us that there is a hell in which sinners are punished.

⁸Yet these false teachers go on living their evil, immoral lives. They degrade their bodies and laugh at those in authority over them. They even laugh at the Glorious Ones. ⁹Michael is one of the mightiest of the angels. Once he was arguing with Satan about Moses' body.

But he didn't dare to accuse Satan or laugh at him. He simply said, "The Lord rebuke you." [10]But these men laugh and curse at anything they don't understand. They are like animals. They do whatever they feel like and ruin their own souls.

?????????????????????????????????
Who argued with Satan about Moses' body?
(Read 1:9 for the answer.)
?????????????????????????????????

[11]How terrible it will be for them! They follow the example of Cain, who killed his brother. Like Balaam, they will do anything for money. Like Korah, they have disobeyed God and will die under his curse.

[12]These men are hidden smears in your love feasts. They stuff themselves without a thought for others. They are like clouds blowing over dry land without giving rain. They promise much but produce nothing. They are like fruit trees without any fruit at picking time. They are not only dead, but doubly dead. Why? Because they have been pulled out, roots and all. They are about to be burned.

[13]All they leave behind them is shame and disgrace. It is like the dirty foam left along the beach by the wild waves. They wander around looking as bright as stars. But ahead of them is eternal gloom and darkness. God has prepared this for them.

[14]Enoch lived seven generations after Adam. He knew about these men. He said, "See, the Lord is coming with millions of his holy ones. [15]He will bring the people of the world before him in judgment. They will be given fair punishment. This will prove the terrible things they have done against God. It will reveal all they have said against him." [16]These men complain all the time. They are never content and satisfied. They do whatever evil they feel like. They are loudmouthed "show-offs." When they show respect for others, it is only to get something from them.

Fight for God's Truth
[17]Dear friends, remember what the apostles of our Lord Jesus Christ told you. [18]They said in the last times these scoffers would come. Their whole purpose in life is to enjoy their ungodly pleasures. [19]They stir up arguments. They love the evil things of the world. They do not have the Holy Spirit living in them.

[20]But you, dear friends, build up your lives in your holy faith. Learn to pray in the power and strength of the Holy Spirit.

Don't run from God's love

Stay in God's love. Wait for the mercy of our Lord Jesus Christ and the eternal life he is going to give to you.

Jude 1:21

---

[21]Stay in God's love. Wait for the mercy of our Lord Jesus Christ and the eternal life he is going to give to you. [22]Try to help those who argue against you. Be merciful to those who doubt. [23]Save some by snatching them as from the very flames of hell itself. And as for others, help them find the Lord by being kind to them. But be careful that you aren't pulled along into their sins. Hate every trace of their sin while being merciful to them as sinners.

A Doxology
[24-25]All glory to him who alone is God. He saves us through Jesus Christ our Lord. Yes, splendor, majesty, and power are his from the beginning. They are his, and they will be forever. He is able to keep you from slipping and falling away. He will bring you, perfect, into his presence with mighty shouts of joy. Amen.

Sincerely, Jude

REVELATION

One day you turn on your TV. You start to watch your favorite program. Suddenly you see the future of the world on your TV. You even watch the end of the world. What would you think? How would you feel? John must have felt that way when he had a vision from God. In that vision God showed him the future. God showed him what will happen someday.

When John was a young man, he was a fisherman. Then he quit his job and followed Jesus. He was one of Jesus' twelve disciples. When Jesus went back to Heaven, John became a leader in the early church. The Romans did not like John telling others about Jesus. They sent him to the island of Patmos as a prisoner. But there God showed him something no other person has ever seen. God told John to write down everything he saw.

This book tells us about many of the things God showed John when he was an old man. He showed John what will happen when the world ends. He also showed him what Heaven will be like. Imagine yourself sitting next to John as you read this incredible book.

A Revelation about the Future and the Present

1 This book uncovers some of the future events in the life of Jesus Christ. God gave this information to Jesus. That way he could show his people the things that will soon happen. So Jesus sent his angel from Heaven to explain the vision's meaning to his servant John. ²In this book John tells about everything he saw. This is his report about what Jesus Christ told him. It is a message from God.

³Read this prophecy aloud to the church. Then you will receive a special blessing from the Lord. Those who listen to it and do what it says will also be blessed. For the time is near when these things will all come true.

John Writes to Seven Churches

John writes a letter to seven churches. But it is really Jesus' letter. He shows John what to write. The letter is also written for us. It tells us many wonderful things. If Jesus wrote you a personal letter, would you read it? This is his letter to you. Be sure to read it!

⁴*From:* John

To: The seven churches in the Roman province of Asia.

Dear Friends:

May grace and peace be given to you. This is from God who is, and was, and is to come. It is also from the seven Spirits before his throne. ⁵And it is from Jesus Christ, who faithfully shows all truth to us. He was the first to rise from death to die no more. He is far greater than any king in all the earth. Praise to him who loves us and set us free from our sins. He did this by pouring out his blood for us. ⁶He brought us into his Kingdom. He made us priests of God his Father. Give to him everlasting glory! He rules forever! Amen!

⁷See! He is coming, surrounded by clouds. Every eye shall see him, and also those who pierced him. The nations will cry in sorrow and terror when he comes. Yes! Amen! Let it be so!

⁸The Lord God says, "I am the A and the Z. I am the Beginning and the Ending of all things. I am the Lord, the All Powerful One. I am the one who is, and was, and is coming again!"

⁹I am your brother John, a fellow sufferer for the Lord's sake. I have shared the patience Jesus gives. And now we shall share his Kingdom!

I was on the island of Patmos. I was sent there for preaching the Word of God and telling about Jesus Christ. ¹⁰I was worshiping on the Lord's Day. And suddenly, I heard a loud voice behind me. The voice sounded like a trumpet blast. ¹¹It said, "I am A and Z, the First and Last!" And then I heard him say, "Write down everything you see. Send your letter to the seven churches in Asia. Send it to Ephesus, Smyrna, Pergamos, Thyatira, Sardis, Philadelphia, and Laodicea."

¹²I turned to see who was speaking. And I saw seven candlesticks of gold.

¹³Standing among them was one who looked like Jesus. He called himself the Son of Man. He was wearing a long robe circled with a golden band across his chest. ¹⁴His hair was white as wool or snow. His eyes penetrated like flames of fire. ¹⁵His feet gleamed like burnished bronze. His voice thundered like waves against the shore. ¹⁶He held seven stars in his right hand. A sharp, double-edged sword was in his mouth. His face shone like the power of the sun.

¹⁷⁻¹⁸When I saw him, I fell at his feet as dead. But he laid his right hand on me. Then he said, "Don't be afraid! I am the First and Last. I am the Living One who died and is now alive forever. I have the keys of hell and death. So don't be afraid! ¹⁹Write down what you have seen and what will soon be shown to you. ²⁰There is a meaning to the seven stars you saw in my right hand. And there is a meaning to the seven golden candlesticks. The seven stars are the leaders of the seven churches. The seven candlesticks are the churches themselves.

2 "Write a letter to the leader of the church at Ephesus. Tell him this is a message from him who walks among the churches. He holds their leaders in his right hand.

²"I know how many good things you are doing. I have watched your hard work and your patience. I know you don't tolerate sin among your members. You have tested those who say they are apostles but aren't. You have found out how they lie. ³You have patiently suffered for me without quitting.

⁴"Yet there is one thing wrong. You don't love me like you did at first! ⁵Think about those times of your first love. Turn back to me again and work as you did before. If you don't, I will come and remove your candlestick from its place.

⁶"But there is something about you

that is good. You hate the deeds of the Nicolaitans, just as I do.

7"May all who can hear listen to what the Spirit says to the churches. To the victors I will give fruit from the Tree of Life. This tree is in the Paradise of God.

8"Write to the leader of the church in Smyrna.

"This message is from him who is the First and Last. He is the one who was dead and then came back to life.

9"I know how much you suffer for the Lord. I know all about your poverty. But you have heavenly riches! I know the slander of those who are against you. They say that they are Jews, but they aren't. They really support the cause of Satan. 10Stop being afraid of what you are about to suffer. The devil will soon throw some of you into prison to test you. You will be persecuted for 'ten days.' Remain faithful even when facing death. Then I will give you the crown of life. 11Let everyone who can hear listen to what the Spirit says to the churches. He who is victorious shall not be hurt by the Second Death.

12"Write this letter to the leader of the church in Pergamos.

"This message is from him who has the sharp and double-bladed sword. 13I know you live in the city where Satan's throne is. It is the center of satanic worship. Yet you have stayed loyal to me. You didn't deny me even when Antipas, my faithful witness, was martyred.

14"Yet I have a few things against you. You tolerate some who do as Balaam did. He taught Balak how to ruin the people of Israel. He involved them in sexual sin. And he encouraged them to go to idol feasts. 15Yes, you have some of these very same followers of Balaam among you!

16"Change your mind and attitude. If not, I will come to you suddenly. I will fight against them with the sword of my mouth.

17"Let everyone who can hear listen to what the Spirit says to the churches! Everyone who is victorious shall eat of the hidden manna. It is the secret food from Heaven. I will give to each of them a white stone. And on each stone will be written a new name. No one else will know that name except the one receiving it.

18"Write this letter to the leader of the church in Thyatira.

"This is a message from the Son of God. His eyes are like flames of fire. His feet are like glowing brass.

19"I am aware of all your good deeds. You are kind to the poor and serve them. Also I know your love and faith and patience. I can see you have improved in all these things.

20"Yet I have something against you. You put up with the woman Jezebel. She calls herself a prophetess. She teaches my servants that sex sin is not serious. She urges them to eat meat that has been offered to idols. 21I gave her time to change her mind and attitude, but she refused. 22Listen to what I am saying. I will lay her upon a sickbed of great suffering. Her immoral followers will be with her. This will happen unless they turn to me, repenting of their sin with her. 23I will strike her children dead. And all the churches shall know that I am he who searches men's hearts. I will give to each of you whatever you deserve.

24-25"Some of you in Thyatira have not followed this false teaching. They call the false teachings 'deeper truths.' But they are really from the depths of Satan. I will ask nothing further of you. Hold tightly to what you have until I come.

26"To everyone who overcomes I will give power over the nations. 27You will rule them with a rod of iron. This authority was given to me by my Father. These nations will be shattered like a pot of clay, broken into tiny pieces. 28And I will give you the Morning Star!

29"Let all who can hear listen to what the Spirit says to the churches.

3 "Write this letter to the leader of the church in Sardis.

"This is from him who has the seven Spirits of God and the seven stars.

"I have heard you are a live and active church, but you are dead. 2Now wake up! Strengthen the little that is left, for even that is near death. Your deeds are far from right in the sight of God. 3Go back to what you heard and believed at first. Hold on to it firmly and turn to me again. Unless you do, I will come suddenly upon you. I will be unexpected like a thief. Then I will punish you.

⁴"There are some in Sardis who haven't become dirty with the world's filth. They shall walk with me in white,

---

Jesus waits for us to hear his voice

I have been standing at the door. And I am always knocking. If anyone hears my voice and opens the door, I will come in. I will fellowship with him and he with me.

Revelation 3:20

---

for they are worthy. ⁵All who conquer will be dressed in white. I will not erase their names from the Book of Life. I will announce before my Father and his angels that they are mine.

⁶"Let all who can hear listen to what the Spirit is saying to the churches.

⁷*"Write this letter to the leader of the church in Philadelphia.*

"This message is sent to you by the one who is holy and true. He holds the key of David. He can open what no one can shut. And he can shut what no one can open.

⁸"I know you well. You aren't strong, but you have obeyed. And you have not denied my Name. Therefore I have opened a door to you that no one can shut.

⁹"Watch out! Some support the causes of Satan while claiming to be mine. But they aren't mine. They are lying! I will force them to fall at your feet. They will know that you are the ones I love.

¹⁰"You have patiently obeyed me despite the persecution. So I will protect you from the time of Great Tribulation and temptation. It will come upon the world to test everyone alive. ¹¹Look, I am coming soon! Hold tightly to the little strength you have. Then no one will take away your crown.

¹²"I will make the one who conquers a pillar in the Temple of my God. He will be secure and never again leave it. He will be a citizen in the city of my God.

That city is the New Jerusalem. It will come down from Heaven from my God. And he will have my new name written on him.

¹³"Let all who can hear listen to what the Spirit says to the churches.

¹⁴*"Write this letter to the leader of the church in Laodicea.*

"This message is from the one who stands firm. He is the faithful and true Witness. And he is the source of God's creation.

¹⁵"I know you well. You are neither hot nor cold. I wish you were one or the other! ¹⁶But you are merely lukewarm. So I will spit you out of my mouth!

¹⁷"You say, 'I am rich. I have everything I want. I don't need a thing!' You don't know that you are wretched and miserable. You don't realize that you are poor, blind, and naked.

¹⁸"My advice is to buy pure gold from me, gold purified by fire. Only then will you truly be rich. Buy from me white garments, clean and pure. Then you won't be naked and ashamed. Get medicine from me to heal your eyes and give you back your sight. ¹⁹I discipline and punish everyone I love. So turn from your dullness and become excited about the things of God.

²⁰"Look! I have been standing at the door. And I am always knocking. If anyone hears my voice and opens the door, I will come in. I will fellowship with him and he with me. ²¹Everyone who conquers will sit beside me on my throne. I also took my place with my Father on his throne when I conquered. ²²Let those who can hear listen to what the Spirit says to the churches."

- *Remember:* Who is this letter from? (1:13,19) Who wrote it for Jesus? (1:4) Which seven churches is it for? (1:11) Who stands at the door of our lives and knocks? What does he want us to do? (3:20-21) Who should listen to what Jesus says to the seven churches? (3:22)

- *Discover:* When we listen to Jesus teach others we can learn what he wants to teach us.

- *Apply:* Can you find three things Jesus wanted the churches to do? Which of these are things he wants us to do? ■

The Glorious Throne

4 Then I looked and saw a door standing open in Heaven. I heard the same voice I had heard before. It was the one that sounded like a mighty trumpet blast. It said, "Come up! I will show you what must happen in the future!"

²And instantly I was in the spirit. And I saw a throne and someone sitting on it! ³Great bursts of light flashed forth from him. It was like light from a glittering diamond or from a shining ruby. There was a rainbow glowing like an emerald around his throne. ⁴Twenty-four smaller thrones surrounded his throne. There were 24 Elders sitting on them. All of them were clothed in white. They had golden crowns upon their heads. ⁵Lightning and thunder came from the throne. And there were voices in the thunder. Directly in front of his throne were seven lighted lamps. They are the sevenfold Spirit of God. ⁶Spread out before it was a shining crystal sea. Four Living Beings, dotted front and back with eyes, stood at the throne's four sides. ⁷The first of these Living Beings was in the form of a lion. The second one looked like an ox. The third had the face of a man. And the fourth had the form of a flying eagle. ⁸Each of these Living Beings had six wings. The central sections of their wings were covered with eyes. They didn't rest day or night. They said, "Holy, holy, holy, Lord God Almighty! He was, and is, and is coming."

⁹The Living Beings gave honor and thanks to the one sitting on the throne. He is the one who lives forever and ever. ¹⁰Then the 24 Elders fell down before him. They all worshiped the Eternal Living One. They threw down their crowns before the throne. Then they sang, ¹¹"O Lord, you are worthy. You should receive the glory and the honor and the power. You have created all things. They were created and called into being by your act of will."

Scrolls
REVELATION 5:1-9

Suppose someone had never seen a book before. How would you describe it to that person? Bible-time people did not have books like ours. In Abraham's time books were smooth hunks of clay. They were called clay tablets. People pressed wedge-shaped letters in the clay when it was soft. The clay hardened. People could still read these books hundreds of years later. Clay tablets were short books. But some libraries had hundreds of them. Later, people wrote books on scrolls. These were made of long strips of animal skin or papyrus. Papyrus was made by pressing flat the stems of the papyrus plant. There was no paper like ours. People then did not have ink like ours, either. There was no printing then, so books had to be written by hand. Each end of a scroll was rolled onto a stick. Readers rolled the scroll from one end to the other as they read. A scroll might be 35 feet long. If your whole Bible was written by hand on a scroll, it would be hundreds of feet long. How would you like to carry a scroll that big to church each week?

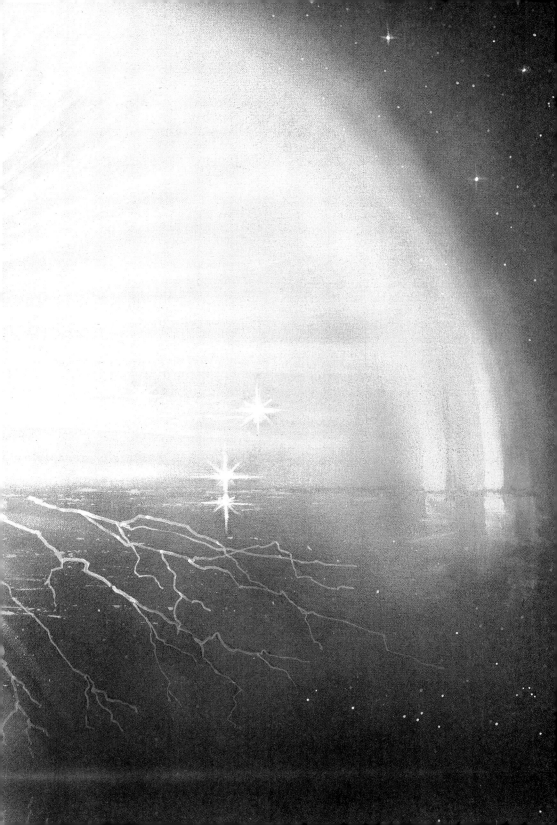

The Sealed Scroll and the Lamb

5 And I saw a scroll in the right hand of the one who was sitting on the throne. It had writing on the inside and on the back. It was sealed with seven seals. ²A mighty angel with a loud voice was shouting. It asked, "Who is worthy to break the seals? Who is worthy to open the scroll?" ³But no one in Heaven, on earth, or under the earth could open and read it.

⁴Then I cried because no one was worthy. No one could tell us what it said.

⁵But one of the 24 Elders said to me, "Stop crying. Look! The Lion of the tribe of Judah, the Root of David, has conquered. He is worthy to open the scroll! He is worthy to break its seven seals!"

⁶I looked and saw a Lamb standing before the 24 Elders. He was in front of the throne and the Living Beings. On the Lamb were wounds that once had caused his death. He had seven horns and seven eyes, which are the sevenfold Spirit of God. This spirit has been sent out into every part of the world. ⁷He took the scroll from the right hand of the one sitting upon the throne. ⁸As he took the scroll, the 24 Elders fell down before the Lamb. Each one had a harp and golden vials filled with incense. The incense is the prayers of God's people.

⁹They were singing him a new song. They sang, "You are worthy to take the scroll and open its seals. You were slain. Your blood has bought people from every nation as gifts for God. ¹⁰And you have gathered them into a kingdom. You made them priests of our God. And they shall reign upon the earth."

¹¹Then I heard the singing of many angels. They were surrounding the throne and the Living Beings and the Elders. ¹²They sang with a loud voice, "The Lamb is worthy. He has been slain. He is worthy to receive the power, the riches, the wisdom, and the strength. He is worthy to receive the honor, the glory, and the blessing."

¹³Then I heard everyone in Heaven, on earth, under the earth, and in the sea. They were saying, "Blessing, honor, glory, and power belong to the one on the throne. And they belong to the Lamb forever and ever." ¹⁴And the four Living Beings kept saying, "Amen!" And the 24 Elders fell down and worshiped him.

Breaking the Seals One by One

6 As I watched, the Lamb broke the first seal on the scroll. Then one of the four Living Beings spoke with a voice like thunder. He said, "Come!"

²I looked, and there in front of me was a white horse. Its rider carried a bow. And a crown was placed upon his head. He rode out to conquer in many battles and win the war.

³Then he opened the second seal. And I heard the second Living Being say, "Come!"

⁴This time a red horse rode out. Its rider was given a long sword. He had the power to take peace away from the earth. War and killing broke out everywhere.

⁵Then he opened the third seal. I heard the third Living Being say, "Come!" And I saw a black horse. Its rider was holding a pair of balances in his hand. ⁶And a voice came from among the four Living Beings. It said, "A loaf of bread for $20, or three pounds of barley flour. But there is no olive oil or wine."

⁷Then the fourth seal was opened. And I heard the fourth Living Being say, "Come!" ⁸Now I saw a pale horse. And its rider's name was Death. And after him followed Hell. They were given control of one-fourth of the earth. They could kill with war and famine and disease and wild animals.

⁹And when he broke open the fifth seal, I saw an altar. Underneath it were the souls of those who were killed for the Word of God. They were also killed for their witness. ¹⁰They called loudly to the Lord. They said, "O Sovereign Lord, you are holy and true. How long until you judge people on earth for what they've done to us? When will you avenge our blood against those living on the earth?" ¹¹White robes were given to each of them. They were told to rest a little longer. They were to wait until their brothers, fellow servants, had been martyred like them. Then their number would be complete.

¹²I watched as he broke the sixth seal. Then there was a vast earthquake. The

sun became dark like black cloth, and the moon was blood-red. ¹³The stars of the heavens appeared to be falling to earth. They fell like green fruit falls from fig trees shaken by strong winds. ¹⁴The heavens disappeared as if they were rolled up like a scroll. Every mountain and island shook and shifted. ¹⁵I saw the kings of the earth, world leaders, rich and strong men. I saw all men great and small, slaves and free. They all hid themselves in the caves and rocks of the mountains. ¹⁶They cried to the mountains to crush them. "Fall on us," they begged. "Hide us from the face of the One sitting on the throne. Hide us from the anger of the Lamb. ¹⁷Because the great day of their anger has come. And who can survive it?"

The 144,000 Chosen by God

7 Then I saw four angels standing at the four corners of the earth. They were holding back the four winds from blowing. Not a leaf rustled in the trees. And the ocean became as smooth as glass. ²I saw another angel coming from the east. He was carrying the seal of the Living God. He shouted to those four angels who had power to injure earth and sea. ³"Wait!" He shouted, "Don't do anything yet. Don't hurt the earth or the sea or the trees. Wait until we have put the Seal of God on the foreheads of his servants."

⁴⁻⁸How many were given this mark? I heard the number. It was 144,000. They were from the 12 tribes of Israel:

12,000 from the tribe of Judah
12,000 from the tribe of Naphtali
12,000 from the tribe of Issachar
12,000 from the tribe of Reuben
12,000 from the tribe of Manasseh
12,000 from the tribe of Zebulun
12,000 from the tribe of Gad
12,000 from the tribe of Simeon
12,000 from the tribe of Joseph
12,000 from the tribe of Asher
12,000 from the tribe of Levi
12,000 from the tribe of Benjamin

A Great Crowd

⁹After this I saw a great crowd, too big to count. They were from all nations and lands and languages. I saw them stand-ing in front of the throne and before the Lamb. They were dressed in white. And they had palm branches in their hands. ¹⁰They were shouting with a mighty shout. They said, "Salvation comes from our God upon the throne, and from the Lamb."

¹¹The angels crowded around the throne. They were around the Elders and the four Living Beings. They fell face-down before the throne and worshiped God. ¹²"Amen!" they said. "Blessing, glory, wisdom, thanksgiving, honor, power, and might! These all belong to our God forever and forever. Amen!"

¹³Then one of the 24 Elders spoke. He asked me, "Do you know who these are, who are dressed in white? Do you know where they come from?"

¹⁴"No, sir," I replied. "Please tell me."

"These are the ones coming out of the Great Tribulation," he said. "They washed their robes and whitened them by the blood of the Lamb. ¹⁵That is why they are here before the throne of God. They serve him day and night in his Temple. The one sitting on the throne will shelter them. ¹⁶They will never be hungry again, or thirsty. And they will be fully protected from the scorching noontime heat. ¹⁷For the Lamb standing in front of the throne will feed them. He will be their Shepherd and lead them to the springs of Water of Life. And God will wipe their tears away."

The Seventh Seal Is Broken

8 Then the Lamb opened the seventh seal. After that, there was silence in Heaven for about half an hour. ²I saw the seven angels that stand before God. They were given seven trumpets.

³Then another angel with a golden censer came. He stood at the altar. Incense was given to him to mix with the prayers of God's people. He offered it upon the golden altar before the throne. ⁴And the smoke of the incense went up to God from the hand of the angel.

⁵Then the angel filled the censer with fire from the altar. He threw it down upon the earth. Thunder crashed and rumbled! Lightning flashed! And there was a terrible earthquake.

Seven Mighty Trumpets

⁶Then the seven angels with the seven trumpets got ready to blow their mighty blasts.

⁷The first angel blew his trumpet. Hail and fire mixed with blood were thrown down upon the earth. One-third of the earth was set on fire. One-third of the trees were burned, and all the green grass.

⁸⁻⁹Then the second angel blew his trumpet. What looked like a huge burning mountain was thrown into the sea. It destroyed a third of all the ships. A third of the sea turned red as blood. A third of the fish were killed.

¹⁰The third angel blew. A great flaming star fell from Heaven upon a third of the rivers and springs. ¹¹The star was called "Bitterness." It poisoned a third of the water on the earth, and many people died.

¹²The fourth angel blew his trumpet. Right away, a third of the sun was darkened. A third of the moon and the stars were darkened. So the daylight was dimmed by a third. And the nighttime darkness deepened. ¹³I saw a single eagle flying through the heavens crying loudly. He said, "How terrible it will be for the people of the earth! Terrible things will soon happen when the last three angels blow their trumpets."

9 Then the fifth angel blew his trumpet. And I saw one who fell to earth from Heaven. To him was given the key to the bottomless pit. ²When he opened it, smoke poured out like from a huge furnace. The sun and air were darkened by the smoke.

³Then locusts came from the smoke. They descended onto the earth and were given power to sting like scorpions. ⁴They were told not to hurt the grass or plants or trees. They were to attack people who didn't have the mark of God on their foreheads. ⁵They were not to kill them, but to torture them for five months. They suffered with agony like the pain of scorpion stings. ⁶In those days men will try to kill themselves but won't be able to. They will long to die, but death will flee away!

⁷The locusts looked like horses armored for battle. They had what looked like golden crowns on their heads. Their faces looked like men's. ⁸Their hair was long like women's. Their teeth were those of lions. ⁹They wore breastplates that seemed to be made of iron. Their wings roared like an army of chariots rushing into battle. ¹⁰They had stinging tails like scorpions. Their power to hurt was in their tails. This power was given to them for five months. ¹¹Their king is the Prince of the bottomless pit. His name in Hebrew is *Abaddon*. In Greek it is *Apollyon*. In English that means the *Destroyer*.

¹²One terror now ends, but there are two more coming!

¹³The sixth angel blew his trumpet. I heard a voice from the four horns of the golden altar. This altar stands before the throne of God. ¹⁴The voice spoke to the sixth angel. It said, "Release the four mighty demons held bound at the great River Euphrates." ¹⁵They had been made ready for that year and month and day and hour. Now they were turned loose to kill a third of all mankind. ¹⁶They led an army of 200,000,000 warriors. I heard an announcement of how many there were.

¹⁷⁻¹⁸I saw their horses spread out before me in my vision. Their riders wore fiery breastplates. Some were blue and others were yellow. The horses' heads looked much like the heads of lions. Smoke and fire and flaming sulfur billowed from their mouths. They killed one-third of all mankind. ¹⁹Their power of death was not only in their mouths. It was also in their tails. Their tails were like serpents' heads. They struck and bit with deadly wounds.

²⁰The men left alive after these plagues *still would not worship God!* They would not leave their demon-worship. They wouldn't turn from their idols of gold, silver, brass, stone, and wood. And these things neither see nor hear nor walk! ²¹They wouldn't change their mind about their murders, witchcraft, immorality, and theft.

A Tall Angel with a Scroll to Eat

10 Then I saw another mighty angel coming down from Heaven. He

was surrounded by a cloud, with a rainbow over his head. His face shone like the sun and his feet flashed with fire. ²He held in his hand a small scroll that was open. He set his right foot on the sea and his left foot on the earth. ³Then he gave a great shout like the roar of a lion. The seven thunders crashed their reply.

⁴I was about to write what the thunders said. But a voice from Heaven called to me, "Don't do it. Their words are not to be revealed."

⁵Then the angel standing on the sea and land lifted his right hand to Heaven. ⁶He swore by him who lives forever. Yes, he swore by the one who created the heavens and everything in them. He is the one who created the earth and all that it contains. He is the one who made the sea and its dwellers. The angel swore that there should be no more delay. ⁷He said that the seventh angel would blow his trumpet. Then God's mystery would be finished. This is just as it had been told by his servants the prophets.

⁸Then the voice from Heaven spoke to me again. It said, "Go get the unrolled scroll from the angel standing on the sea and land."

⁹So I went to him and asked him to give me the scroll. "Yes, take it and eat it," he said. "At first it will taste like honey. But when you swallow it, it will make your stomach sour!" ¹⁰So I took it from his hand and ate it! It was just as he had said. The scroll was sweet in my mouth, but it gave me a stomachache.

¹¹Then he told me, "You must prophesy more. You will tell about many peoples, nations, tribes, and kings."

Two Prophets

11 Now I was given a measuring stick. I was and told to go and measure the Temple of God. This included the inner court where the altar stands. And I was to count the number of worshipers. ²"But do not measure the outer court," I was told. "It has been turned over to the nations. They will trample the Holy City for 42 months. ³And I will give power to my two witnesses. That way they can prophesy 1,260 days clothed in sackcloth."

Trumpets
REVELATION 8:6

Do you have a friend who plays a trumpet? Perhaps you play one. Today some people play trumpets in orchestras and bands. Trumpets are made of metal. Players change notes by pressing valves. Some Bible-time trumpets were made of metal, too. But they did not have valves to change notes. Other Bible-time trumpets were made of animal horns. Some were made of large seashells. Trumpets were used mostly to send signals. There was a signal to break camp (Num. 10:2). Another signal called people to battle (Judges 3:27). Watchmen blew trumpets when a city was in danger (Neh. 4:18). Priests blew trumpets as part of worship (1 Chron. 16:6). Trumpets were blown at the coronations of kings (2 Sam. 15:10). In Revelation we see seven angels blowing seven trumpets. These angels blow their trumpets to signal seven terrible punishments.

⁴These two prophets are the two olive trees. They are also the two candlesticks standing before the God of all the earth. ⁵Anyone trying to harm them will be killed by fire from their mouths. ⁶They have power to shut the skies. That way no rain will fall during the 3½ years they prophesy. They will turn rivers and oceans to blood. They can send plagues on the earth as often as they wish.

7They will complete the 3½ years of their testimony. Then the tyrant who comes from the bottomless pit will declare war against them. He will conquer and kill them. 8-9For 3½ days their bodies will lie in the streets of Jerusalem. It is the city called "Sodom" or "Egypt." It is the place where their Lord was crucified. No one will be allowed to bury them. People from many nations will crowd around to look at them. 10And there will be a worldwide holiday. People everywhere will rejoice and give presents to each other. They will throw parties to celebrate the death of the two prophets. The two prophets had tormented them so much!

11But after 3½ days the parties will end. The spirit of life from God will enter the two prophets. They will stand up! And great fear will fall on everyone. 12Then a loud voice will shout from Heaven. It will say, "Come up!" And they will rise to Heaven in a cloud as their enemies watch.

13The same hour there will be a terrible earthquake. It will level a tenth of the city, leaving 7,000 dead. Then everyone left will, in their terror, give glory to the God of Heaven.

14The second terror is past, but the third quickly follows.

The Seventh Trumpet Blast

15For just then the seventh angel blew his trumpet. Loud voices shouted down from Heaven. They said "The Kingdom of this world belongs to our Lord, and his Christ. He shall reign forever and ever."

16And the 24 Elders sitting on their thrones before God fell down in worship. They said, 17"We give thanks to you, Lord God Almighty who is and was. Now you have taken your great power and have begun to reign. 18The nations were angry with you. But now it is your turn to be angry with them. It is time to judge the dead and reward your servants. You will reward both the prophets and the people. You will reward all who fear your Name, both great and small. Now you will destroy those who have caused destruction upon the earth."

19Then, in Heaven, the Temple of God was opened. The Ark of his covenant could be seen inside. Lightning flashed and thunder crashed and roared. There was a great hailstorm. And the world was shaken by a mighty earthquake.

The Woman and the Dragon

12 Then a great symbol appeared in the heavens. I saw a woman clothed with the sun. And the moon was beneath her feet. A crown of 12 stars was on her head. 2She was pregnant and screamed in the pain of her labor. She was waiting for her baby to be born.

3Suddenly a red Dragon appeared. He had seven heads and ten horns. And seven crowns were on his heads. 4His tail pulled behind him a third of the stars. And he plunged the stars to the earth. He stood before the woman as she was about to give birth. He was ready to eat the baby as soon as it was born.

5She gave birth to a boy. He was to shepherd all nations with an iron rod. He was caught up to God and to his throne. 6The woman fled into the wilderness, where God had made a place for her. She would be taken care of there for 1,260 days.

7Then there was war in Heaven. Michael and his angels fought the Dragon and his army of fallen angels. 8And the Dragon lost the battle and was forced from Heaven. 9This great Dragon is the ancient serpent called the devil, or Satan. He is the one deceiving the whole world. He was thrown down onto the earth with all his angels.

10Then I heard a loud voice in Heaven saying, "It has happened at last! God's salvation and power have won! The Kingdom and authority of Christ have come! Our brothers' Accuser has been thrown down from Heaven to the earth. He accused them day and night before our God. 11They defeated him by the blood of the Lamb and by their testimony. They did not love their lives but laid them down for him. 12Rejoice, O heavens! You citizens of Heaven, rejoice! Be glad! But how terrible it will be for you people of the world. The devil has come down to you in great anger. He knows that he has little time left."

¹³When the Dragon was thrown down to earth, he persecuted the woman. She is the one who had given birth to the child. ¹⁴But she was given two wings like those of a great eagle. She was to fly into the wilderness to the place prepared for her. There she was fed and protected from the Dragon for 3½ years.

¹⁵A great flood of water gushed out from the Serpent's mouth. The flood swept toward the woman in an effort to get rid of her. ¹⁶But the earth helped her by opening its mouth and swallowing the flood! ¹⁷Then the furious Dragon set out to attack the rest of her children. They are the ones who keep God's commands and confess they belong to Jesus. He stood waiting on an ocean beach.

The Two Strange Creatures

13 In my vision, I saw a strange Creature rising up out of the sea. It had seven heads, and ten horns. It had ten crowns upon its horns. Written on each head were ungodly names. Each name defied and insulted God. ²This Creature looked like a leopard but had bear's feet and a lion's mouth! And the Dragon gave him his own power and throne and great authority.

³I saw that one of his heads seemed wounded beyond recovery. But the fatal wound was healed! All the world marveled at this miracle. So they followed the Creature in awe. ⁴They worshiped the Dragon for giving him such power. They also worshiped the strange Creature. "Where is there anyone as great as he?" they exclaimed. "Who is able to fight against him?"

⁵The Dragon helped the Creature to speak great curses against the Lord. He gave the Creature authority to control the earth for 42 months. ⁶The Creature cursed God's Name and his Temple and all those living in Heaven. ⁷The Dragon gave him power to fight against God's people and to overcome them. The Creature had power to rule over all nations and languages in the world. ⁸And all mankind worshiped the evil Creature. They are those whose names were not written in the Lamb's Book of Life. The Lamb was killed before the founding of the world.

⁹Anyone who can hear, listen carefully. ¹⁰The people of God who are destined for prison will go to prison. Those destined for death will be killed. This is their time for endurance and confidence.

¹¹Then I saw another strange animal. This one was coming up out of the earth. He had two horns like a lamb but a voice like a dragon. ¹²He used the power of the Creature whose death-wound had been healed. He required all the world to worship the Creature. ¹³He did unbelievable miracles. He made fire flame down to earth from the skies while everyone was watching. ¹⁴By doing these miracles, he tricked people everywhere. He could do these fantastic things whenever the first Creature was there watching. He ordered the people of the world to make a statue of the first Creature. He was the one who was fatally wounded and then came back to life. ¹⁵He was allowed to give breath to this statue and even make it speak! Then the statue ordered that anyone refusing to worship it must die!

?????????????????????????????????
The Bible talks about a great Dragon. Who is he?

(Read 12:9 for the answer.)

?????????????????????????????????

¹⁶He gave a command to everyone, great and small, rich and poor, slave and free. They had to put a certain mark on their right hand or on their forehead. ¹⁷No one could buy or sell without that mark. It was either the name of the Creature or the number of his name. ¹⁸Here is a puzzle that calls for careful thought to solve. Let those who are able figure out the number of the Creature. For it is the number of a man. The number of his name is 666!

The Lamb and a Tremendous Choir

14 Then I saw a Lamb standing on Mount Zion in Jerusalem. With him were 144,000 people. They had his Name and his Father's Name written on their foreheads. ²And I heard a sound from Heaven. It was like the roaring of a great waterfall or the rolling of mighty thunder. It was the singing of a choir accompanied by harps.

³They sang a new song. They sang in front of the throne, the four Living Beings and the 24 Elders. No one else could sing this song. Only the 144,000 who had been redeemed from the earth could sing it. ⁴For they are spiritually undefiled, pure as virgins. They follow the Lamb wherever he goes. They have been bought from among men. They are the first offering to God and the Lamb. ⁵No falsehood can be charged against them. They are blameless.

Three Angels and a Call from God

⁶And I saw another angel flying through the heavens. He was carrying the everlasting Good News to preach to those on earth. It was for every nation, tribe, language, and people.

⁷"Fear God," he shouted, "and celebrate his greatness. For the time has come when he will sit as Judge. Worship him who made the heavens and earth, the sea and all its sources."

⁸Then another angel followed him through the skies. He was saying, "The great Babylon is fallen, is fallen. She trapped and ruined the nations of the world. She made them share the wine of her sexual sin."

⁹Then a third angel followed them. He was shouting, "Don't worship the Creature from the sea and his statue. Don't accept his mark on the forehead or the hand. ¹⁰Anyone who does must drink the wine of God's anger. It is poured out straight into God's cup of wrath. And they will be tortured with fire and burning sulfur. This will happen in the presence of the holy angels and the Lamb. ¹¹The smoke of their torture rises forever and ever. They will have no relief day or night. They have worshiped the Creature and his statue. They have taken the mark of his name. ¹²Let this help God's people endure patiently every trial and torture. They are his saints, staying to the end. They obey his commands and trust in Jesus."

The Judgment Time

¹³And I heard a voice in the heavens above me. It said, "Write that the time has come for his martyrs to get their reward. Yes, says the Spirit, they are blessed indeed. Now they shall rest from all their toils and trials. Their good deeds follow them to Heaven!" ¹⁴Then the scene changed. I saw a white cloud. Someone was sitting on it, and he looked like Jesus. He was called "The Son of Man." He had a crown of gold on his head and a sickle in his hand.

¹⁵Then an angel came from the Temple and called out to him. He said, "Begin to use the sickle. The time has come for you to harvest. The harvest is ripe on the earth." ¹⁶So the one sitting on the cloud swung his sickle over the earth. The harvest was gathered in. ¹⁷After that another angel came from the Temple in Heaven. He also had a sharp sickle.

¹⁸Then the angel with power to destroy the world with fire shouted. He said to the angel with the sickle, "Use your sickle now. Cut off the clusters of grapes from the vines of the earth. They are fully ripe for judgment." ¹⁹So the angel swung his sickle on the earth. Then he loaded the grapes into the great winepress of God's anger. ²⁰And the grapes were crushed in the winepress outside the city. Blood flowed out in a stream 200 miles long. It was as deep as a horse's bridle.

15 And I saw another symbol in Heaven. It was great and wonderful. Seven angels had brought the seven last plagues. Then at last God's anger was finished.

²Spread out before me was what seemed to be an ocean of fire and glass. I saw the victors over the Evil Creature, his statue, his mark, and number. They were standing on the sea of glass and fire holding harps of God. ³⁻⁴They were singing. They sang the song of Moses, the servant of God. And they sang the song of the Lamb.

"Great and marvelous
Are your doings,
Lord God Almighty.
Just and true
Are your ways,

O King of Ages.
Who will not fear, O Lord?
And who will not glorify your
    Name?
For you alone are holy.
All nations will come
And worship before you.
For your righteous deeds
Have been disclosed."

⁵Then I saw that the Holy of Holies in the Temple in Heaven was open! ⁶The seven angels with the seven plagues then came from the Temple. They were dressed in spotless white linen. They had golden belts across their chests. ⁷One of the four Living Beings handed each of them a golden jar. Each jar was filled with the wrath of God, who lives forever and forever. ⁸The Temple was filled with smoke from his glory and power. No one could enter until the seven angels finished pouring out the seven plagues.

Seven Flasks of Wrath

16 And I heard a mighty voice shouting from the Temple to the seven angels. It said, "Go your ways. Empty out the seven flasks of God's wrath upon the earth."

²So the first angel went out and poured out his jar over the earth. Horrible, hurtful sores came from it. These sores hurt everyone with the Creature's mark and who worshiped his statue.

³The second angel poured out his jar upon the oceans. They became like the watery blood of a dead man. Everything in all the oceans died.

⁴The third angel poured out his jar upon the rivers and springs. They became blood. ⁵And I heard this angel of the waters. He said, "You are fair in sending this judgment, O Holy One who is and was. ⁶Your saints and prophets have been martyred. Their blood has been poured out upon the earth. Now you have poured out the blood of those who murdered them. This is the right reward for them."

⁷I heard the angel of the altar. He said, "Yes, Lord God Almighty, your punishments are just and true."

⁸Then the fourth angel poured out his jar upon the sun. This caused it to scorch all men with its fire. ⁹Everyone was burned by this blast of heat. So they cursed the name of God who sent the plagues. But they didn't change their mind and give him glory.

¹⁰The fifth angel poured out his jar upon the throne of the Creature from the sea. The Creature's kingdom was darkened. And his subjects gnawed their tongues in pain. ¹¹They cursed the God of Heaven for their pains and sores. But they refused to repent of all their evil deeds.

¹²The sixth angel poured out his flask upon the great River Euphrates. It dried up. That made it easy for the kings from the east to march their armies west. ¹³I saw three evil spirits that looked like frogs. They jumped from the mouths of the Dragon, the Creature, and his False Prophet. ¹⁴These are demons who can do miracles. They went out to the rulers of the world. They gathered them for battle on that great Day of God Almighty.

¹⁵"Remember, I will come like a thief in the night. You don't know when I will come. Blessed are all who are waiting for me. They keep their robes clean and will not walk naked and ashamed."

¹⁶They gathered the armies of the world to a place called Armageddon.

¹⁷Then the seventh angel poured out his jar into the air. A mighty shout came from the throne of the Temple in Heaven. It said, "It is finished!" ¹⁸Then the thunder crashed and rolled. The lightning flashed. There was a great earthquake bigger than any ever seen before. ¹⁹The great city of "Babylon" split into three sections. Cities around the world fell in heaps of rubble. So all of "Babylon's" sins were remembered in God's thoughts. He punished her with the cup of the wine of his fierce anger. ²⁰Islands vanished, and mountains flattened out. ²¹There was an incredible hailstorm from Heaven. Hailstones weighing 100 pounds fell from the sky onto the people. And they cursed God because of the terrible hail.

A Drunken Woman
and a Strange Animal

17 One of the seven angels who poured out the plagues talked with me. "Come with me," he said. "I will show you the punishment of the great Prostitute. She sits on many waters of the world. ²The kings of the world have had immoral relations with her. The people of the earth have been made drunk by the wine of her sin."

³So the angel took me in spirit into the wilderness. There I saw a woman sitting on a red animal. It had seven heads and ten horns. Written all over it were curses against God. ⁴The woman wore purple and red clothing. She had beautiful jewelry made of gold and precious gems and pearls. She held in her hand a golden goblet full of obscene things.

⁵A name was written on her forehead. It was "Babylon the Great, Mother of Prostitutes and Idol Worship of the World."

⁶I could see that she was drunk. She was drunk with the blood of the martyrs of Jesus she had killed. I stared at her in horror.

⁷"Why are you so surprised?" the angel asked. "I'll tell you who she is. And I'll tell you what the animal stands for that she is riding. ⁸He was once alive, but isn't now. Soon he will come up out of the bottomless pit and go to destruction. The people of earth will be amazed at his return from death. The names of these people haven't been written in the Book of Life.

⁹"And now think hard. His seven heads stand for a city on seven hills where this woman lives. ¹⁰They also stand for seven kings. Five have already fallen. The sixth now reigns, and the seventh is yet to come. But his reign will be short. ¹¹The red animal that died is the eighth king. He reigned before as one of the seven. After his second reign, he too, will go to his doom. ¹²His ten horns are ten kings who have not yet risen to power. They will be given kingdoms for one hour, to reign with him. ¹³They will all sign a treaty giving their power and strength to him. ¹⁴Together they will fight against the Lamb. The Lamb will conquer them because he is Lord of lords, and King of kings. His people are the called and chosen and faithful ones.

¹⁵"The waters the woman is sitting on are people of every race and nation. ¹⁶"The red animal and his ten horns all hate the woman. The ten horns stand for ten kings who will reign with him. They will attack her and leave her naked and ravaged by fire. ¹⁷God will put a plan into their minds. It is a plan that will carry out his purposes. They all will agree to give their power to the red animal. That way the words of God will be fulfilled. ¹⁸This woman you saw is the great city that rules the kings of the earth."

The Fall of Babylon

18 After all this I saw another angel come down from Heaven with great power. The earth grew bright with his shining glory.

²He gave a mighty shout, "Babylon the Great is fallen, is fallen. She has become a den of demons. She is a den of devils and every kind of evil spirit. ³All the nations have drunk the wine of her sin. The rulers of earth have enjoyed themselves with her. Businessmen of the world have grown rich from all her lush living."

⁴Then I heard another voice calling from Heaven. It said, "Come away from her, my people. Do not take part in her sins, or you will be punished with her. ⁵For her sins are piled as high as Heaven. God is ready to judge her for her crimes. ⁶Do to her as she has done to you, and more. Give double penalty for all her evil deeds. She brewed many a cup of terror for others. Give twice as much to her. ⁷She has lived in luxury and pleasure. Match it now with torments and with sorrows. She brags, 'I am queen upon my throne. I am no helpless widow. I will not experience sorrow.' ⁸So the sorrows of death, mourning and famine shall overtake her in one day. She will be burned by fire because the Lord who judges her is mighty."

⁹The world leaders took part in her immoral acts and enjoyed her favors.

They will mourn for her as they see the smoke rising from her burning. ¹⁰They will stand far off and shake with fear. They will cry out, "Alas, Babylon, that mighty city! In one moment her judgment came."

¹¹The merchants of the earth will cry and mourn for her. There is no one left to buy their goods. ¹²She bought gold, silver, precious stones, pearls, fine linen, purple, and red. They sold her perfumed wood, ivory, wooden carvings, brass, iron, and marble. ¹³She bought spices, perfumes, incense, ointment, frankincense, wine, olive oil, fine flour, and wheat. Their goods were cattle, sheep, horses, chariots, slaves, and even the souls of men.

¹⁴"All the fancy things you loved so much are gone," they cry. "The choice treats that you loved so much will never be yours again. They are gone forever."

¹⁵These merchants who have become rich from her shall stand at a distance. They will fear danger to themselves. They will weep and cry. ¹⁶They will say, "Alas, that great city was so beautiful. She was like a woman clothed in finest purple and red linens. She wore gold and precious stones and pearls! ¹⁷In one moment, all the wealth of the city is gone!"

All the shipowners and captains and crews will stand a long way off. ¹⁸They will cry as they watch the smoke go up. They will say, "Where in the world is another city such as this?" ¹⁹They will throw dust on their heads in sorrow. They will say, "Alas, alas, for that great city! She made us all rich from her great wealth. And now in a single hour all is gone!"

²⁰But you, O Heaven, children of God, prophets, and apostles, rejoice over her. For at last God has given judgment against her for you.

²¹Then a mighty angel picked up a boulder shaped like a millstone. He threw it into the ocean and shouted. He said, "Babylon, that great city, shall be thrown away like this stone. She shall disappear forever. ²²Never again will the sound of music be in her. There will be no more pianos, saxophones, and trumpets. No industry of any kind will ever

again exist there. There will be no more milling of the grain. ²³Her nights will be very dark. Not even a lamp in a window will ever be seen again. No more will joyous wedding bells ring. And no more will the happy voices of bridegrooms and brides be heard. Her businessmen were known around the world. She tricked all nations with her sorceries. ²⁴She was guilty for the blood of all the martyred prophets and the saints."

A Hallelujah Chorus

19 After this I heard the shouting of a great crowd in Heaven. "Hallelujah!" they said. "Praise the Lord! Salvation is from our God. Honor and power belong to him alone. ²His judgments are just and true. He has punished the Great Prostitute who has corrupted the earth with her sin. He has repaid the murder of his servants."

³Again and again their voices rang, "Praise the Lord! The smoke from her burning ascends forever and forever!"

⁴Then the 24 Elders and four Living Beings fell down and worshiped God. He was sitting upon the throne. They said, "Amen! Hallelujah! Praise the Lord!"

⁵Out of the throne came a voice. It said, "Praise our God, all his servants! Praise him, small and great, who fear him!"

The Wedding Banquet of the Lamb

⁶Then I heard again what sounded like the voice of a huge crowd. It was like the waves of 100 oceans crashing on the shore. It was like the mighty rolling of great thunder. They said, "Praise the Lord! For the Lord our God, the Almighty, reigns. ⁷Let us be glad and rejoice and honor him. The time has come for the wedding banquet of the Lamb. His bride has prepared herself. ⁸She is to wear the cleanest and whitest and finest of linens." Fine linen stands for the good deeds done by the people of God.

⁹And the angel spoke to me. He said, "Blessed are those who are invited to the wedding feast of the Lamb." And he added, "God himself has said this."

¹⁰Then I fell down at his feet to

worship him. But he said, "No! Don't! I am a servant of God like you, and your brothers. You all testify your faith in Jesus. Worship God. The purpose of this prophecy is to tell others about Jesus."

The Rider of the White Horse

11Then I saw Heaven opened and a white horse standing there. The one sitting on the horse was named Faithful and True. He is the one who justly punishes and makes war. 12His eyes were like flames, and on his head were many crowns. A name was written on his forehead, and only he knew its meaning. 13He was clothed with garments dipped in blood. His title was "The Word of God." 14The armies of Heaven followed him on white horses. They were dressed in finest linen, white and clean.

?????????????????????????????????

Someday Heaven will open. A rider will come out on a white horse. What is the name of the rider?

(Read 19:11 for the answer.)

?????????????????????????????????

15In his mouth he held a sharp sword to strike down the nations. He ruled them with an iron grip. He trod the winepress of the wrath of Almighty God. 16On his robe and thigh was written, "King of kings and Lord of lords."

17Then I saw an angel standing in the sunshine, shouting loudly to the birds. "Come!" he said. "Gather together for the supper of the Great God! 18Come and eat the flesh of kings, and captains, and great generals. Eat horses and riders and all humanity, great and small, slave and free."

19Then I saw the Evil Creature, the kings of the earth, and their armies coming. They were meeting to fight against the one sitting on the horse and his army. 20And the Evil Creature was captured, and with him the False Prophet. He could do mighty miracles when the Evil Creature was present. His miracles tricked people with the Evil Creature's mark who worshiped his statue. The Evil Creature and his False Prophet were thrown alive into the Lake of Fire. It burns with sulfur. 21Their whole army was killed. They died by the sword in the mouth of the one riding the white horse. All the birds of the heavens were filled with their flesh.

20 Then I saw an angel come down from Heaven. He had the key to the bottomless pit and a heavy chain in his hand. 2He seized the Dragon, that old Serpent, the devil, Satan. He bound him in chains for 1,000 years. 3The angel threw him into the bottomless pit. Then he shut and locked it. That way he couldn't fool the nations until the 1,000 years were finished. Afterwards he would be set free again for a little while.

4Then I saw thrones. Sitting on them were those who had been given the right to judge. I saw the souls of those who had been beheaded. Their heads were cut off for their testimony about Jesus and the Word of God. They had not worshiped the Creature or his statue. They didn't have his mark on their foreheads or their hands. They had come to life again. Now they ruled with Christ for 1,000 years.

5This is the First Resurrection. The rest of the dead didn't live until the 1,000 years had ended. 6Blessed and holy are those who share in the First Resurrection. For them the Second Death holds no terrors. They will be priests of God and of Christ. They shall rule with him 1,000 years.

The 1,000 Years

7When the 1,000 years end, Satan will be let out of his prison. 8He will trick the nations of the world and gather them together. They will join Gog and Magog for battle. They will be a mighty army, numberless as sand along the shore. 9They will go up across the broad plain of the earth. They will surround God's people and the beloved city of Jerusalem. But fire from Heaven will flash down and destroy them.

10Then the devil who tricked them will be thrown into the Lake of Fire. It is burning with sulfur where the Creature

and False Prophet are. They will be tormented day and night forever and ever.

The Final Judgment

¹¹I saw a great white throne and the one who sat upon it. The earth and sky fled away from his face. But they found no place to hide. ¹²I saw the dead, great and small, standing before God. And the books were opened, including the Book

---

There won't be pain, crying, sadness, or death in Heaven

He will wipe away all tears from their eyes. There shall be no more death, sorrow, crying, or pain. All of that has gone forever.

Revelation 21:4

---

of Life. And the dead were judged according to the things written in the books. Each one was judged according to the deeds he had done. ¹³The oceans surrendered the bodies buried in them. The earth and the underworld gave up the dead in them. Each was judged according to his deeds. ¹⁴And Death and Hell were thrown into the Lake of Fire. This is the Second Death. ¹⁵Anyone whose name wasn't in the Book of Life was thrown into the Lake of Fire.

A New Heaven and New Earth

21 Then I saw a new earth and a new Heaven. The first earth and Heaven had disappeared. And there was no more sea. ²And I, John, saw the Holy City, the new Jerusalem. It was coming down from God out of Heaven. It was like a bride ready for her husband.

³I heard a loud shout from the throne. It was saying, "Look, the home of God is now among men. He will live with them and they will be his people. Yes, God himself will be among them. ⁴He will wipe away all tears from their eyes. There shall be no more death, sorrow, crying, or pain. All of that has gone forever."

⁵And the one sitting on the throne said, "See, I am making all things new!"

And then he said to me, "Write all this down. What I tell you is faithful and true. ⁶It is finished! I am the A and the Z, the Beginning and the End. I will freely give to the thirsty the spring of the Water of Life. ⁷Everyone who conquers will inherit all these blessings. I will be his God and he will be my son. ⁸But there are cowards who turn back from following me. There are those who are unfaithful to me. There are corrupt men, murderers, immoral men, those who speak with demons, idol worshipers and liars. Their doom is in the Lake that burns with fire and sulfur. This is the Second Death."

The New Jerusalem

⁹Then one of the seven angels who had the jars of the seven last plagues came. He said to me, "Come with me. I will show you the bride, the Lamb's wife."

¹⁰In a vision he took me to a towering mountain peak. There I watched the holy city, Jerusalem, descending out of Heaven from God. ¹¹It was filled with the glory of God. Her light was like a precious gem, crystal clear like jasper. ¹²Its walls were wide and high, with 12 gates guarded by 12 angels. And the names of the 12 tribes of Israel were written on the gates. ¹³There were three gates on each side—north, south, east, and west. ¹⁴The walls had 12 foundation stones. On them were written the names of the 12 apostles of the Lamb.

¹⁵The angel held in his hand a golden measuring stick. He was about to measure the city and its gates and walls. ¹⁶The city was a square as wide as it was long. In fact it was in the form of a cube. Its height was exactly the same as its length and width. It was 1,500 miles each way. ¹⁷Then he measured the thickness of the walls. They were 216 feet across. The angel called out these measurements to me, using standard units.

¹⁸⁻²⁰The city itself was pure, clear gold like glass! The wall was made of jasper. It was built on 12 layers of foundation stones inlaid with gems. The first layer was jasper. The second was sapphire. The third was chalcedony. The fourth was emerald. The fifth was sardonyx. The

sixth layer was sardus. The seventh was chrysolite. The eighth was beryl. The ninth was topaz. The tenth was chrysoprase. The eleventh layer was jacinth. The twelfth was amethyst.

²¹The 12 gates were made of pearls. Each gate was made from a single pearl! And the main street was pure, clear gold, like glass.

²²No temple could be seen in the city. Why? Because the Lord God Almighty and the Lamb are worshiped in it everywhere. ²³And the city has no need of sun or moon to light it. The glory of God and of the Lamb give it light. ²⁴Its light will light the nations of the earth. The rulers of the world will come and bring their glory to it. ²⁵Its gates will never close. They will stay open all day long because there is no night! ²⁶The glory and honor of all the nations shall be brought into it. ²⁷Nothing evil will be allowed into it. No one immoral or dishonest can be there. Only those who are written in the Lamb's Book of Life can enter the city.

The River of Life

22 And he showed me a river of pure Water of Life, clear as crystal. It was flowing from the throne of God and the Lamb. ²The river ran down the center of the main street. On each side of the river grew the Tree of Life. It had 12 crops of fruit, a fresh crop each month. The leaves of the tree were used for medicine to heal the nations.

³There shall be nothing in the city that is evil. The throne of God and of the Lamb will be there. His servants will worship him. ⁴They shall see his face. And his name shall be written on their foreheads. ⁵And there will be no night there. So there will be no need for lamps or sun. The Lord God will be their light, and they shall reign forever and ever.

The Promise of Jesus' Return

⁶⁻⁷Then the angel said to me, "These words are trustworthy and true. 'I am coming soon!' God tells his prophets what the future holds. He has sent his angel to tell you this will happen soon. Blessed are those who believe it and all else written in the scroll."

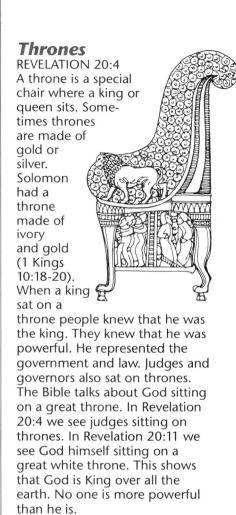

Thrones

REVELATION 20:4
A throne is a special chair where a king or queen sits. Sometimes thrones are made of gold or silver. Solomon had a throne made of ivory and gold (1 Kings 10:18-20). When a king sat on a throne people knew that he was the king. They knew that he was powerful. He represented the government and law. Judges and governors also sat on thrones. The Bible talks about God sitting on a great throne. In Revelation 20:4 we see judges sitting on thrones. In Revelation 20:11 we see God himself sitting on a great white throne. This shows that God is King over all the earth. No one is more powerful than he is.

⁸I, John, saw and heard all these things. I fell down to worship the angel who showed them to me. ⁹But he said, "No, don't do anything like that. I am a servant of Jesus like you, and like your brothers the prophets. I am like all those who hear and act on the truth stated in this book. Only worship God."

¹⁰Then he instructed me, "Do not seal up what you have written. The time of their fulfillment is near. ¹¹When that time comes, people who do wrong will do it more and more. The wicked will become more wicked. Good men will be

better. Those who are holy will continue on in greater holiness."

¹²"See, I am coming soon, and my reward is with me. I will repay everyone according to the deeds he has done. ¹³I am the A and the Z. I am the Beginning and the End. I am the First and Last. ¹⁴Blessed are all who are washing their robes. They have the right to enter in through the gates of the city. They can eat the fruit from the Tree of Life.

¹⁵"Outside the city are those who have strayed away from God. Outside are sorcerers and immoral people. And there are murderers, idolaters, and all who tell lies.

¹⁶"I, Jesus, have sent my angel to you to tell the churches these things. I am both David's Root and his Offspring. I am the bright Morning Star. ¹⁷The Spirit and the bride say, 'Come.' Let each one who hears them say the same, 'Come.' Let the thirsty one come. Anyone who wants to, let him come and drink the Water of Life for free. ¹⁸I have serious words for everyone who reads this book. Don't add anything to what is written here. If you do, God will give you the plagues described in this book. ¹⁹Don't take away any part of these prophecies. If you do God will take away your share in the Tree of Life. He will also take away your part in the Holy City. These things are explained in this book.

²⁰"He who has said all these things declares, 'Yes, I am coming soon!'"

Amen! Come, Lord Jesus!

²¹The grace of our Lord Jesus Christ be with you all. Amen!

100 Interesting, Exciting Bible Look-ups
Who, What, Where, When Were These?

1. Taking a walk in a hot furnace—*Daniel 3:25*
2. Lonely prayer meeting inside a fish—*Jonah 2:1*
3. Dining with the pigs—*Luke 15:16*
4. A salty woman—*Genesis 19:26*
5. Green jeans—*Genesis 3:7*
6. Making a calf from golden earrings—*Exodus 32:2-4*
7. Spies on the roof—*Joshua 2:1-6*
8. Baby basket boat—*Exodus 2:1-6*
9. Blind sorcerer—*Acts 13:6-12*
10. Making a washbasin with mirrors—*Exodus 38:8*
11. Taking a nap in the land of Nod—*Genesis 4:16*
12. A lake of fire—*Revelation 20:15*
13. Angel argument with the devil—*Jude 1:9*
14. Dining with the birds—*1 Kings 17:1-6*
15. Saving a family with a scarlet rope—*Joshua 2:1,18*
16. His fat swallowed a dagger—*Judges 3:15-25*
17. Killing 600 Philistines with an ox goad—*Judges 3:31*
18. Teasing a bald man—*2 Kings 2:22-24*
19. Little king—*2 Kings 22:1*
20. A queen's blood sprinkled on horses—*2 Kings 9:30-33*
21. A talking donkey—*Numbers 22:28-30*
22. Seven baths to get well—*2 Kings 5:14*
23. Moses' nurse—*Exodus 2:7-10*
24. Fire on my lips—*Isaiah 6:6-7*
25. Five husbands—*John 4:7, 17-18*
26. Hanging by my hair—*2 Samuel 18:9*
27. Throwing money away—*Matthew 27:5*
28. Twelve barrels of water to help start a fire—*1 Kings 18:33,38*
29. Blasting walls down with a trumpet—*Joshua 6:15,20*
30. Dreaming about a king's grape juice—*Genesis 40:1-13*
31. Dreaming about a basket of baked goods—*Genesis 40:16-19*
32. Dreaming about fourteen cows—*Genesis 41:1-4*
33. The sun, moon, and stars bow down—*Genesis 37:5,9*
34. People like a half-baked cake—*Hosea 7:8*
35. Throwing a man's head over a wall—*2 Samuel 20:21-22*
36. Boils from head to foot—*Job 2:7*
37. 700 left-handed sharpshooters who never missed—*Judges 20:16*
38. Sleeping in a bed 13 feet long—*Deuteronomy 3:11*
39. Hiding a prince in a storeroom for 6 years—*2 Kings 11:1-3*
40. A king eats grass—*Daniel 4:33*
41. This lady drove a tent-peg through a man's head—*Judges 4:21*
42. A donkey's head and dove's manure for dinner—*2 Kings 6:25*
43. Five golden rats—*1 Samuel 6:1-5*
44. A giant with 12 fingers and 12 toes—*2 Samuel 21:20-21*
45. 300 fiery fox tails—*Judges 15:3-5*
46. A haircut took away his strength—*Judges 16:16-20*
47. Three pounds of hair on his head—*2 Samuel 14:25-26*
48. The oldest old man ever—*Genesis 5:25-27*
49. Falling asleep, falling down dead—*Acts 20:7-12*
50. Dreaming about a stairway to Heaven—*Genesis 28:10-12*

51. River of blood—*Exodus 7:20*
52. Burning books of black magic—*Acts 19:17-20*
53. They died because they lied—*Acts 5:1-11*
54. Ear off, ear on—*Luke 22:49-51*
55. An angel choir with good news—*Luke 2:8-14*
56. Eat rocks!—*Matthew 4:1-4*
57. Stop storm!—*Mark 4:35-41*
58. Sleeping with hungry lions—*Daniel 6*
59. Stand still, sun and moon!—*Joshua 10:12-13*
60. Escape in a basket—*Acts 9:23-25*
61. Water becomes wine—*John 2:1-11*
62. 5,000 for lunch—*Matthew 14:15-21*
63. Fantastic fishing fun—*Luke 5:1-11*
64. A house on a rock—*Matthew 7:24-27*
65. A big party for a runaway—*Luke 15:11-32*
66. Baker on a stake at a birthday party—*Genesis 40:20-22*
67. Preacher's head on a tray at a birthday party—*Mark 6:21-29*
68. An angel goes up to Heaven in a fire—*Judges 13:19-20*
69. A prophet goes to Heaven in a whirlwind—*2 Kings 2:11*
70. Walking through the sea—*Exodus 14:21-22*
71. The sun's shadow moves backward—*Isaiah 38:1-8*
72. Rain for 40 days and nights—*Genesis 7:5-12*
73. Murdered by his brother—*Genesis 4:2-8*
74. Burned himself to death—*1 Kings 16:18*
75. Died when he touched a golden box—*2 Samuel 6:6-7*
76. Dying with royal worms—*Acts 12:21-23*
77. A tree sweetens bitter water—*Exodus 15:22-25*
78. A sheet full of animals—*Acts 11:4-10*
79. The first child born on earth—*Genesis 4:1*
80. The longest name in the Bible—*Isaiah 8:1*
81. The first rainbow—*Genesis 9:8-17*
82. A bush that would not stop burning—*Exodus 3:2*
83. Stole $1000 from his mother—*Judges 17:2*
84. The first cattleman—*Genesis 4:20*
85. The first musician—*Genesis 4:21*
86. Throwing dice for a seamless robe—*John 19:23-24*
87. Two men who wrapped Jesus' body—*John 19:38-40*
88. Wrestling with God all night—*Genesis 32:21-31*
89. The Bronze Snake Clinic—*Numbers 21:4-9*
90. Killing a lion with bare hands—*Judges 14:5-6*
91. Thief freed instead of Jesus—*Matthew 27:15-22*
92. A "good Samaritan"—*Luke 10:25-37*
93. Purple cloth for sale!—*Acts 16:14*
94. Writing on a wall—*Daniel 5:1-5*
95. Dining on locusts and wild honey—*Matthew 3:1-4*
96. Gold, frankincense, and what?—*Matthew 2:1,11*
97. A giant killer—*1 Samuel 17*
98. Hundred-pound hailstones—*Revelation 16:21*
99. Reaching for the skies with a tower—*Genesis 11:1-9*
100. A silver cup in a sack of grain—*Genesis 44:1-2*

HOW TO BECOME A CHRISTIAN

Many Bible-time people became Christians. Paul was a very famous Christian. At first, he hated Jesus and hurt Christians. But Jesus spoke from Heaven to Paul on the Damascus Road. He told Paul to stop fighting him. Paul became a Christian. He was sorry for the terrible things he had done. From that day on he worked for Jesus. He became a great missionary.

The jailer at Philippi asked Paul, "What must I do to be saved?" Paul told him, "Believe on the Lord Jesus and you will be saved." The jailer believed. He was saved. He became a Christian.

One day Jesus saw Simon Peter and his brother Andrew. They were fishermen. "Come, follow me! And I will make you fishermen for the souls of men," Jesus told them. They followed Jesus. They became great Christian leaders. They helped other people follow Jesus. That was much better than catching fish!

When Jesus met Levi the tax collector he said, "Come with me. Come be my disciple." He did. Levi gave up his job. He gave up lots of money. Levi's name was changed to Matthew. He became Jesus' disciple. He wrote the Book of Matthew in our Bible. He had something worth much more than money and a big job.

There were many more who became Christians. When Peter preached on the day of Pentecost, 3,000 people became Christians. Christians were called "believers" at that time. The word "Christian" was not used until later.

In the Bible, people who accepted Jesus as Savior were called Christians, believers, followers of Jesus, or disciples. The names may be different, but they all mean the same thing. A Christian believed that Jesus was God's Son, the Messiah, the Savior. They asked him to be their Savior, to forgive their sins, to give them a new life. They became his helpers, followed him, and served him. They tried to win others to accept him, too.

So why should you want to be a Christian?

1. Jesus forgives your sins. Have you done things you wish you had not done? If you ask him, Jesus forgives you. He will not hold them against you. If you've hurt someone, you have hurt Jesus and that person. Jesus will forgive you for hurting him.

2. Jesus helps you live the way you should. He knows what is best for you. Each day he goes with you. He becomes your best friend. He helps you stay away from things you shouldn't do. He helps you have the courage to say "I'm sorry" to the person you hurt. He helps you have the courage to say, "Please forgive me." He helps you have the courage to say, "I'm a Christian." He helps you to please him.

3. Jesus helps you win others to him. That's very special. You want your best friend, Jesus, and your other friends to know each other, don't you? You want everyone to know Jesus, even people you have never met.

4. You will be happier. Christians who please Jesus stay away from bad things. They do good things. Doing good things makes people happy. Doing bad things makes people sad. Christians who please Jesus will be happy people.

5. You will know that you will be in Heaven after you die. All the Christians who ever lived will be with God and his Son, Jesus, forever in his home. Heaven is a special home.

This is how you can become a Christian:

1. Decide to turn from all the bad things you have done. Decide that you want to stop sinning.

2. Ask Jesus to forgive your sins and become your Savior. He will. You will be a new Christian. He will also help you want to live for him.When you become a Christian, follow Jesus, live for him, do what he wants, please him, serve him.

Becoming a Christian is wonderful. Would you like to become a Christian? If you would, pray this prayer: "Jesus, please forgive my sins and be my Savior. Help me love you, please you, and follow you each day. Amen."

When you become a Christian, you may want to record your decision on the page provided in this section.

How should a Christian live?

How should a Christian live? What does Jesus expect you to do?

When you accept Jesus as Savior you are different. Jesus forgives your sins. You know you will live with him forever in Heaven. He helps you do good things, not bad things. Doing good things is good for you. This helps you be a better you. You want to be his helper. You don't want to hurt him. You don't want to help the devil or his people. You want to please Jesus.

Jesus helps Christians get ready to live in Heaven. That's where Christians will live for millions and millions of years. Accepting Jesus is the way to get to Heaven. But living for Jesus here on earth preares you to live in Heaven. How? By living for Jesus, you get to know him better each day.

The most important reason to live in Heaven is to live with God and his Son Jesus. Wonderful things are there. Heaven is a special place, much better than earth. These things are all right, but you really want to live there to be with the Lord. So you want to get to know him while you are here on earth. When you get to Heaven, he will already be your friend.

Here are some ways to get to know him better now:

1. *Read your Bible.* God wrote the Bible for you. It's his love letter to you. He tells you about Heaven. He tells you how to get there. He tells you how to be a Christian. He tells you how to live here on earth. He tells you many other things, too.

But the most important thing that God tells you is about himself. He helps you get to know him better. A Christian should read the Bible each day. That's one important way you will know God better. It's even more important than eating and sleeping each day.

2. *Pray.* Some people think you should pray to get things. There are times when you will ask God to help you get something. But there is a much more important reason to pray. Praying is talking with God. You get to know him when you talk with him each day. It's just as important as breathing.

Sometimes you will want to thank God when you pray. You like to thank people you love, don't you? You like to thank them for special things. Be sure to thank God for food, clothing, a home, a car, and other things he gives you.

Sometimes you will want to praise God when you pray. That's telling God how special he is. When you love someone, you like to tell that person how special he or she is. Do you ever tell Mom how special she is to you? Do you ever tell Dad how special he is to you? Tell God each day how special he is to you. Praise him! The more you talk with friends, the better you know them. The more you talk with God, the better you know him. When you get to Heaven, you will meet him as a good friend.

3. *Please Jesus.* The Bible tells you how you can do that. You like to please your parents, don't you? You do if you love them. You also want to please Jesus if you love him. Jesus is pleased when you do good things instead of bad things. He is pleased when you do what he says. He knows what is best for you. What he says is best for you. Pleasing Jesus is helping yourself.

4. *Follow Jesus.* People who follow Jesus are sometimes called disciples. Learning to follow Jesus is called discipleship. Following Jesus is walking where he would go. It's following in his steps. It's doing what he would do. Following Jesus is trying to be like Jesus. It's walking where you should go.

He wants you to do what he knows is best for you. Following Jesus pleases him, but it's also best for you. It's not easy to follow Jesus. But the Bible shows you how to do it.

5. *Tell others about Jesus.* Help others accept Jesus. Help them love him as you do. Tell them how he will be their Savior. When you have something wonderful, you want to share it with others. Are you glad that you will live in Heaven with Jesus? You will want to share Heaven with others. You will want others to know joy in being Jesus' friend.

6. *Help Jesus do his work.* Jesus wants you to be his helper. He lets you share his work here on earth. Jesus shares his work with special people. When you share his work, you are a special person.

There are many things you can do to be his helper. Do you help keep your Sunday school room neat and clean? If you do, you are Jesus' helper. Do you ever sing at church or play your instrument? Do you ever take part in a church program? Do you ever read the Bible to others in Sunday school class? You're being Jesus' helper. Do you help your parents at home? That pleases Jesus and helps him do his work, too. Can you think of other ways?

7. *Help Jesus' friends grow the way he wants.* It's important to help a friend accept Jesus. It's also important to help that friend grow as a Christian. Have you learned something special about praying? Share it with another Christian.

Have you learned something special from the Bible? Share it with another Christian.

Have you learned something special about living for Jesus? Share it with another Christian.

As you help others grow, you will also grow.

Living the way a Christian should will make you happy. It will please Jesus. It will win friends for Jesus and help them grow. And it will get you ready to live with Jesus forever.

MY DECISION

My name

_____

Date

_____

Why I want to follow Jesus

_____

_____

_____

_____

_____

Each Bible story highlighted in this Bible has an important Bible truth that can be applied to daily living. Truth applied is a teaching/learning value. All important teaching/learning values are listed below topically. If you are reading this Bible yourself, you will want to use this section to help you apply the Bible to daily living. If you are a parent or teacher, you will want to use this section as a topical resource guide for Bible learning and Bible teaching. Story titles and page numbers are given so you can quickly find the Bible story where each teaching/learning value is found.

Accepting

How can God help us if we don't let him? God wanted to help Lot's family. But most of them wouldn't let him. Let him help you! *God Destroys Sodom, page 29*

God has a good reason for doing what he does. Accept God's ways. Don't tell God to change. God did what was best for the Hebrews and he does what is best for you. *The Longest Night, page 102*

God has many good gifts for us. We must be willing to accept them. We must also be willing to earn some of them. The Israelites wanted the Promised Land. But they didn't trust God to help them fight for it. *The Twelve Spies, page 196*

Advice

When you're in trouble, whose advice do you want? You will show what kind of person you are by the advice you seek. Saul showed his poor character by asking a witch to guide him. *Saul Visits a Witch, page 392*

When Saul needed advice he asked a witch. When David needed advice he asked the Lord. Saul lost. David won. The Lord has the best answer. Follow him. *David Leaves the Philistines, page 394*

Don't listen to your best friend if he is wrong. Don't do something wrong just because a friend says to do it. Saul's armor bearer refused to kill his king, even though his king told him to. *Saul Dies in Battle, page 396*

Listen to good advice. It will keep you from trouble. Good advice always tries to help people. Bad advice tries to hurt them. Rehoboam listened to bad advice. His kingdom split in two. *The Kingdom Splits in Two, page 454*

Listen to God's advice. He knows exactly what you should do. You'll find his good advice in the Bible. Read it each day. King Ahab died in battle because he did not listen to God's good advice. *Ahab Dies in Battle, page 471*

Anger

Don't get angry at every bad thing that happens. Ask God to bring good from it. *Joseph Tells the Meaning of Two Dreams, page 66*

Be sure you're angry at bad things, not good things. Jesus was angry at the bad things merchants did at the Temple. *Jesus Chases Bad Men from the Temple, page 1230*

Appearance

Do you ever wish you were more handsome or more beautiful? Handsome people sin or do good things. Beautiful people sin or do good things. Hand-

some Absalom did many terrible things. You can do wonderful things for God no matter how you look. *Absalom Rebels, page 417*

Bad words

Be careful not to say bad things. Your words may come back to punish you. Judah once said, "Let's sell Joseph." Now he begs Joseph for his life. *Joseph Tests His Brothers, page 73*

Cheerfulness

Accept a new leader cheerfully. Lead cheerfully. Joshua did. *Joshua Becomes Israel's New Leader, page 222*

Choosing

Good choices bring good things. Bad choices bring bad things. Samson made too many bad choices. *Samson's Foolish Choices, page 327*

We should never choose anything bad instead of Jesus. Some people chose to free the criminal Barabbas instead of Jesus. *Jesus Is Taken to Pilate, page 1262*

Commitment

Sometimes God has a special job for you to do. Will you do it? Are you ready? God gave Saul a special job as king. *Saul Becomes King, page 357*

When God gives you a job, he will also give you the power to do it. So do it! God gave young David the power to be king. *Samuel Anoints David, page 368*

Complaining

When you think something is bad, stop grumbling. Be thankful it isn't worse. You could be a Hebrew slave in Egypt. *The Hebrews Become Slaves, page 85*

The Israelites complained about water, but they should have prayed about it. God helps us more when we pray than when we complain. *Bitter Water at Marah, page 117*

Do you need help? Don't grumble and complain. Pray! The Israelites grumbled. Moses prayed. God listened to Moses. *Someone to Help Moses, page 193*

Courage

Are you ever afraid? You are braver when you know that God is with you. Jonathan was! *Jonathan's Brave Fight, page 363*

When you are afraid, ask God for courage. Only he can give the kind of courage you need. Peter and John were brave because God was with them. *Peter and John Are Brave for God, page 1284*

We should be brave when we have important work to do. Paul's nephew was. If we lack courage, we should pray for it. *Paul's Nephew Warns Him, page 1331*

We should say bravely what we believe about Jesus. We should be brave for Jesus even before important people. Paul told King Agrippa what he believed about Jesus. Would you tell a king or president these things? *King Agrippa Wants to Hear Paul, page 1335*

We can be brave in danger if we know that God is with us. He knows what will happen. He will change what will happen. Paul knew that God was with him. This helped him be brave during the shipwreck. *Paul's Ship Is Wrecked, page 1337*

Criticism

Don't criticize others for something you are doing. Jesus healed a woman. But

a leader criticized him for doing this on the Sabbath. Jesus said the man worked on the Sabbath, too. He did much less important things. *Jesus Heals on the Sabbath, page 1191*

Deceiving

Trying to deceive family members will tear your family apart. Jacob deceived Isaac. He got the birthright. But he lost the right to use it. *Jacob Deceives Isaac, page 44*

When we deceive others, others may deceive us. Jacob deceived his father. Now his uncle deceives him. *Jacob Marries Rachel, page 50*

Demons

Demons are afraid of Jesus. When he spoke, they ran away. If you are ever scared, thinking about Satan or demons, pray to Jesus. *Jesus Heals a Man with Demons, page 1115*

Doubt

If you ever have doubts about Jesus, ask questions about Jesus until you have the answers. Then you will learn who Jesus really is. Thomas doubted. But he touched Jesus and talked with him. His doubts disappeared. *Jesus Appears to His Disciples, page 1273*

Fairness

We must always do as much as we promise. That's fair. But it's also fair to give some people more than others. The vineyard owner was fair when he paid some workers more than they deserved. God also gives us more than we deserve when we accept him. *A Story about a Vineyard, page 1081*

Faith

Jesus has special power. He can do many things that we can't do. He will do these special things. But we must

believe. The woman who touched Jesus' clothes believed that he would heal her. He did. *A Woman Touches Jesus' Clothes, page 1116*

The Roman army captain believed that Jesus would heal his slave. His slave was healed. Believe Jesus. Things will happen. *A Man Is Healed Far Away, page 1172*

Faithfulness

Always take the right side, even if you could get hurt. Jeremiah took God's side and he was hurt for it. But God took care of him. *Ebed-Melech Rescues Jeremiah, page 882*

Worship God and don't think about your reward. Think about pleasing him. Please him even if you get hurt. Shadrach, Meshach, and Abednego pleased God even though they would be burned in a fiery furnace. *The Fiery Furnace, page 961*

Will you do what God wants? Will you do it even if people make fun of you? Joseph did. *An Angel Visits Joseph, page 1046*

Would you like to hear God say that you please him? Start by pleasing him, as Jesus did. *John Baptizes Jesus, page 1052*

Is Jesus worth more than TV? Is he worth more than toys? He is worth more than anything in the world. If so we should be willing to give up anything for him. The pearl merchant was willing to give everything for the one great pearl. *A Story about a Pearl, page 1070*

Following

A great leader, like Moses, must first be a great follower. Learn to follow God. *The Exodus, page 108*

Someday David would be king instead of Saul. Now he was content to serve Saul as king. Before we can be a leader we must learn to follow and serve. *David Plays Music for Saul, page 369*

Who are your heroes? What kind of people are they? Be like godly people. Don't be like ungodly people. Be like Daniel who was always faithful to God. *Strange Writing on the Wall, page 965*

Following Jesus is more important than anything else we do. The four disciples left everything they were doing to follow him. *Jesus Calls Four Followers, page 1105*

Forgiveness

When someone hurts us, we can get even or forgive. God wants us to forgive, just as Esau forgave Jacob. *Jacob Meets Esau, page 55*

Joseph's brothers felt guilty for selling Joseph. Doing wrong makes us feel guilty. Ask God and others to forgive. *Joseph's Brothers Buy Grain, page 70*

Are you holding a grudge against someone? Joseph could have held a grudge against his brothers for selling him. But he didn't. He forgave them. Forgive, as you want God to forgive you. *Joseph Forgives His Brothers, page 75*

Joseph forgave his brothers for selling him as a slave. When someone is sorry and asks for your forgiveness, do what God would do and forgive. *Joseph Forgives His Brothers, page 83*

Would you like to do something special for God? First God wants to forgive you and make you clean. Then you can work for him. Isaiah was called to serve God. But first he was forgiven and cleansed. *God Calls Isaiah, page 790*

We must forgive others when they ask for forgive-

ness. Jesus said we must forgive many times. *A Story about Forgiving, page 1079*

Only God can forgive sins. He wants to. Will you let him? That's what John preached. *John the Baptist Preaches, page 1163*

Pray for those who try to hurt you. Ask God to forgive them. Ask God to help you love them. Stephen prayed for those who stoned him. *Men Throw Stones at Stephen, page 1290*

Friendship

Jonathan showed he was a best friend by giving his best gifts to David. Best friends do nice things for each other. *David and Jonathan Become Friends, page 374*

Jonathan helped his best friend, even when it could hurt him. A good friend is always a good friend, even when it hurts him. *Jonathan Warns David, page 379*

Good friends do good things. They don't just talk about it. The Good Samaritan did good things for a stranger. So he was a good friend, even though he was a stranger. *A Story about a Friend, page 1183*

Jesus helps enemies become friends. The devil helps friends become enemies. Jesus helps you keep friends. Ask Jesus to help you change enemies and keep friends. Saul's friends became his enemies. His enemies became his new friends. *Saul Preaches in Damascus, page 1298*

Generosity

Ruth and Boaz were very unselfish people. Be generous, even though you may not want to. God will do good things for you. *Ruth Marries Boaz, page 341*

Giving

It's better to be a giver than a taker. It's better to be

like Abram than Lot. God loves a giver. God is a giver! *Lot Leaves Abram, page 22*

God loves a cheerful giver. Those who gave to the Tabernacle did it cheerfully. Give to God with a smile. *Gifts for the Tabernacle, page 144*

When God gives us his best, why shouldn't we give God our best? God gave Samuel to Hannah, so Hannah gave Samuel to God. *Samuel Is Born, page 345*

Do you have a special talent? Is it a gift from God? Use it for God. Honor him with it. David honored God with the Bethlehem water his men gave him. *David's Men Bring Water from Bethlehem, page 429*

Do you love to give to God? You should! God loves to give to you. God gave much to the couple at Shunem. They gave to Elisha, God's prophet. *A Room for Elisha, page 480*

Do you give Jesus your best gifts? The wise men did. *Wise Men Visit Baby Jesus, page 1048*

We give more to God when we give our best to God. The widow gave her best. Even though it seemed less, it was really more. *The Widow's Small Coins, page 1208*

Do you ever think you are giving too much to Jesus? You can't. You will never give him more than he gave you. Mary gave Jesus very expensive perfume. *Mary Anoints Jesus' Feet, page 1253*

God the Creator

God made our wonderful world. He is the only one who can make something from nothing. We can't. *God Makes Everything, page 1*

God was creative to make so many kinds of birds and animals. He also made each of us to be different. God made Adam and Eve different from each other. *God*

Makes Adam and Eve, page 4
There are some things that only God could make. Thank him for each one. Even though the Egyptians' magicians said that God sent the plagues, Pharaoh would not believe it. *Pharaoh Learns about God's Power, page 100*

God's Care
When you do God's work, he will take care of you. God called Jeremiah to work for him. Then he took care of Jeremiah. Don't be afraid. Trust God. *God Calls Jeremiah, page 841*

God's House
The Tabernacle was God's special tent for worship. Your church is God's house. God wants us to make special places where we can worship him. *The Tabernacle Is Built, page 150*
You can help make God's house a special place. Solomon did. *Solomon Builds the Temple, page 441*

God's Plans
God had special plans to send his Son. He told about this hundreds of years before Jesus came. God's special plans will always happen. Would you like to help him? *Jesus Is Born, page 1156*

God's Son
Jesus' miracles show that he is God's Son. The disciples knew that. God's Son knows about God better than anyone. We should listen to him. *Jesus Walks on Water, page 1071*
Jesus is King over all kings. He rules over everything. We should praise him as the people did at the Triumphal Entry. *Jesus Rides into Jerusalem, page 1083*
The winds and seas obey Jesus. All nature obeys him. He is God's Son. *Jesus Stops a Storm, page 1114*

Jesus is God's Son. Only God's Son could do the miracles he did. When Jesus said he was God's Son, some men thought he made fun of God. Believe him! He is! *Jesus Is Taken before the Rulers, page 1144*
Only God's Son could come from Heaven to earth. Jesus could tell people about Heaven because he had been there. Listen to him! The rulers and soldiers didn't. They beat him and had him killed. *Roman Soldiers Beat Jesus, page 1145*
Only God's Son could feed 5,000 with a boy's lunch. If you want to know more about God, listen to God's Son. He tells you much about God in God's Word. *Jesus Feeds 5,000, page 1240*
Jesus is the only one who can bring a dead person back to life. He raised Lazarus from the dead. *Jesus Raises Lazarus from the Dead, page 1250*

God's Way
Do God's work God's way. Doing it your way will get you into trouble. David got into trouble when he tried to carry the Ark his way. He got out of trouble when he did it God's way. *David Brings the Ark to Jerusalem, page 405*

God's Word
God doesn't talk to us from burning bushes, as he did to Moses. But he does talk to us through his Word, the Bible. *The Burning Bush, page 90*
Bible-time people, like Manoah, needed a special visit from God to know what he wanted. We can read our Bible. *Samson Is Born, page 323*
God spoke to Samuel with his voice. God speaks to us through the Bible, his Word.

God Speaks to Samuel, page 348
We please God when we obey his Word. We will be punished when we disobey his Word. Josiah wanted to please God by obeying his Word. *The Book of the Law Is Found, page 583*
No one can destroy God's Word. Someone can burn a Bible, but they can't burn every Bible. King Jehoiakim foolishly thought he could destroy God's Word by burning Jeremiah's scroll. But we have the Book of Jeremiah today. *The King Burns Jeremiah's Scroll, page 880*
God's Word grows in our hearts when we accept it. It is like seed in good soil. Ask God to show you something special when you read his Word. *A Story about a Farmer, page 1068*
God's Word is like the lamp which was lit. It gave out light. We are not to hide the light of God's Word. Reading your Bible each day is a good start. *A Story about a Lamp, page 1113*
Jesus said he came to help spiritually blind people see just as he helped a blind man see. God's Word helps us see spiritually. Do you read it each day? *Jesus Heals a Blind Man, page 1248*
The people of Beroea listened to good Bible teaching. They studied God's Word to see what he said. This will make a big difference in your life. *Paul Visits Two Towns, page 1318*

Godliness
Spending time with God makes us more like him. When Moses talked with God, his face began to shine. *Moses Talks with God, page 142*
When God is with you, you will be different from other people. But you will be

different in good ways. Be different God's way as Moses was. *Moses Dies, page 269*

Good News

Some news is too good to keep, especially news about Jesus. We must share it with others. The man who was healed had to share the good news. *Jesus Helps a Man Hear, page 1123*

The shepherds heard the good news about Jesus from an angel choir. Then they saw Jesus. The news was too good to keep. It's too good for us to keep, too. We must tell others. *Angels Appear to Shepherds, page 1159*

If good news is really good, it is too good to keep. We must share it. We must tell others the good news that Jesus is alive. Mary Magdalene ran to tell the disciples that she had seen Jesus alive. She couldn't keep that news to herself. *Mary Magdalene Sees Jesus, page 1271*

Greatness

The greatest people in the world are those who please Jesus. *Who Is the Greatest?, page 1078*

Healing

Who really heals us when we are sick? Doctors and others help. But God heals. Jesus healed many sick people. Next time you're sick, ask God to help. *Jesus Heals Many Sick People, page 1122*

Heaven

Jesus knows more about Heaven than anyone else. That's because Heaven is his home. Important teachers listened to him. So should we. *Jesus Teaches the Teachers, page 1162*

The Bible warns us about hell. It tells us how to get to Heaven. Read it! Listen to it! The rich man learned too late about Heaven and hell.

The Rich Man and Poor Lazarus, page 1197

Helping

We should help those who need us. We should help them even if they are not our friends. Abram rescued Lot after Lot turned against him. God rescues us even when we have sinned. *Abram Rescues Lot, page 24*

Help God do his work even if someone yells at you. Moses and Aaron did what God wanted but the Hebrews and Egyptians yelled at them. *Making Bricks without Straw, page 94*

Are you trying to do something alone? Moses could not hold up his hands without help. So Aaron and Hur helped him. There are some things we can't do alone. Ask God or others to help you. *Aaron and Hur Help Moses, page 121*

God wants to help us. But we must do what he says. God gave Moses laws to help him and his people know what to do. *God Talks to Moses on a Mountain, page 123*

God gave us his commandments to help us, not hurt us. Why? Because he loves us. The Ten Commandments tell us how to keep from getting hurt. They also tell us how to please God. *The Ten Commandments, page 125*

We can help each other, even though we aren't even friends. Rahab helped the enemy spies. She and her family would later be safe because she did. *Spies Visit Jericho, page 272*

The Lord helps us do things we could never do by ourselves. Ask him. God helped Gideon win an impossible battle. *God Calls Gideon to Lead Israel, page 310*

Do you need help? Ask

God! He is more powerful than armies. The Philistines learned that. *God Sends Thunder, page 355*

You can do God's work better if you let others help you. Elisha let Elijah help him. He became even greater than Elijah. *Elijah Gives His Coat to Elisha, page 467*

When you pray for God to do something, be willing to help him do it. Get ready to help God when you pray. Nehemiah prayed. Then he helped God answer his prayer. *Nehemiah Begs to Go Home, page 603*

Is there something you want to do for God? If you think God really wants you to do it, get going! Nehemiah prepared to build walls after God gave him the desire to do it. *A Night Visit at the Walls, page 605*

When you help someone in need, you are like the four who brought their friend to Jesus. You may even bring this person to Jesus, too. *A Hole in the Roof, page 1107*

Any time is the right time to help someone. Jesus healed a man on the Sabbath. Some people didn't like that. But Jesus said the Sabbath was a good day to help a person in need. *Jesus Heals a Crippled Hand, page 1109*

The angel Gabriel brought good news from God. He was God's helper. You can be like an angel by being a good helper. *An Angel Visits Zacharias, page 1151*

Jesus wants to help you do many good things. Say, "thank you, Lord." He helped a sick man. He will help you. *Jesus Heals a Sick Man, page 1238*

Dorcas had many friends. That's because she was a helper. Helpers make many friends. If you want friends, be a helper. *Peter Brings Dorcas Back to Life, page 1300*

Timothy was Paul's special helper. A good helper is a real hero. Be a hero. Be a good helper like Timothy. *Timothy Is Paul's Helper, page 1315*

The people on Malta loved Paul when he helped them. Do you want someone to like you better? Be a helper. People will love us more when we help them more. *Paul Is Shipwrecked on Malta, page 1340*

Honoring God

When God does something good for you, don't brag that you did it. Joseph told what Pharaoh's dreams meant. But he said God actually did it. *Joseph Becomes Ruler of Egypt, page 67*

The Philistines thought they defeated God by capturing his Ark. But they learned later that God would defeat them. No one can defeat God. *Philistines Are Punished, page 352*

Do you love anything more than God? Do you love TV or other things more? If so, those things are idols. They have taken God's place. God helped Elijah defeat the prophets of Baal, an idol. Let God, not idols, have first place in your life. *Elijah Defeats the Prophets of Baal, page 463*

Have you or your family lost something? Don't get angry at God. He is the one who gave it to you. He can help you the most. Job honored God when he had much. He honored God when he lost everything. *Job Loses Everything, page 635*

God rewards and honors those who honor him. God will honor you if you please him and honor him. Daniel honored God by refusing the king's food and wine.

Daniel Refuses to Eat the King's Food, page 957

Has God done something special for you? Did you take the credit? Don't! Honor God by saying he did it. Daniel honored God. He told the king that God helped him know his dream. *Daniel Tells the King What He Dreamed, page 959*

When God did something special for Mary and Elizabeth, they honored him. They praised him. Has God done something special for you? Honor him. Praise him. *Mary Visits Elizabeth, page 1154*

Don't let people praise you for what God does. Honor God. Tell them God did this. Paul and Barnabas could have taken the honor for healing the man with crippled feet. But they honored God. *People Think Paul and Barnabas Are Gods, page 1311*

Honoring Jesus

We must never make fun of Jesus. He is God's Son. We must never make fun of people he loves. Herod made fun of Jesus. *Jesus Is Taken to Herod Antipas, page 1214*

When we love someone, we will do special things for him or her. Joseph loved Jesus. He wanted to do one last act of kindness and wrap his body. *Jesus Is Buried, page 1217*

Honoring Special Days

God set the Passover aside as a special day for the Hebrews to honor. He wants us to honor special days, too. *The First Passover, page 106*

Humility

When God gives you an important job to do, don't think he is making you important. He wants you to be helpful to others. God blessed David for Israel's sake, not David's. *David Becomes King of All Israel, page 403*

God uses ordinary people for extraordinary tasks. He may give you a job too big for yourself. Accept it. Do it. Thank him. Esther was a Jewish orphan in a strange land. But God made her become a powerful queen. *Esther Becomes Queen, page 625*

Jesus worked as a carpenter. He did not pretend to be a "big shot" in his work. We shouldn't either. *The Boy Jesus at Nazareth, page 1161*

Herod tried to look bigger than God. He died a terrible death. Don't try to look bigger than God. He is much bigger and more powerful than we. *King Herod Dies, page 1308*

Jealousy

Jealousy and refusing to share build ugly feelings. That's what tore Abraham's family apart. *Isaac Is Born, page 33*

Saul's jealousy of David made him less like a king. Jealousy always hurts you more than the other person. *Saul Becomes Jealous of David, page 375*

Saul's jealousy became so bad that he tried to kill David. Jealousy eats away at us until we do foolish and terrible things. *Saul Tries to Kill David, page 377*

Saul did not kill because of his jealousy, but he allowed people to be murdered. That's just as bad as doing it himself. Are you jealous of someone? It's just as bad to want that person hurt as to hurt that person. *The Murder of the Priests, page 381*

Joyfulness

Would you like to bring great joy in Heaven? You can. Help a friend know about Jesus. That's like the joy of finding a lost coin. *A Story about a Coin, page 1195*

God is happy when a lost

person comes back to him. He will receive that person with joy. It is like the joy the father felt when his prodigal son came home. *A Story about Two Boys, page 1195*

Walking with Jesus gives us much joy. Watching Jesus work makes us happy. Helping Jesus work also makes us happy. Reading your Bible will make you happy. Jesus' wonderful works will make you happy. We should try to be happy, shouldn't we? After the ascension, the disciples were filled with great joy. They had walked with Jesus. *Jesus Ascends into Heaven, page 1220*

Kindness

Would you like to be called kind, serving and helping? Be like Rebekah! *Isaac Gets Married, page 37*

Kind people are often rewarded with kindness. If you want others to be kind to you, be kind to others first. Boaz showed kindness to kind Ruth. *Ruth Gleans in the Fields, page 339*

Mephibosheth was King Saul's grandson. He could start trouble for David. But David was kind to him anyway. We should be kind to others, even our enemies. *David Is Kind to Mephibosheth, page 409*

Sometimes you win by being kind instead of fighting. Elisha defeated an army with kindness. *The Blind Army, page 488*

We should be kind because we want to, not because we have to. Paul asked Philemon to be kind to Onesimus, but hoped he would want to do it. *Onesimus Comes Home, page 1449*

Leading

When God wants us to meet someone, he helps us do it. He helped Jacob meet Rachel. He will help you

meet new friends and helpers. Jacob Meets Rachel, page 48

God led Moses and his people with a pillar of cloud and fire. God guides us each day. Wherever you go, God has already been there, so he knows which way is best. *A Pillar of Cloud and Fire, page 111*

When you're in trouble, ask God for the way out. If he can take the people of Israel through the sea, he can lead you, too. *Crossing the Red Sea, page 112*

We should support our government leaders. We should support God's work. Both are important. That's what Jesus taught. *Jesus Talks about Caesar and God, page 1137*

Listening

Listen to God's special messengers. Joshua listened to the commander-in-chief of God's army. *Commander-in-Chief of God's Army, page 278*

Listen to Jesus. He is God's Son. He did many miracles. He even turned water into wine. *Jesus Turns Water into Wine, page 1228*

Be careful. Don't listen to the crowd. It can lead you the wrong way. Pilate listened to the crowd and sent Jesus to the cross. *Pilate Judges Jesus, page 1263*

Loneliness

Are you ever lonely? Jesus is there with you. He can help you anywhere. He even helped a nobleman's son far away. *Jesus Heals a Nobleman's Son, page 1237*

Love

Do you hate someone? Does Jesus love that person? You should love that person too! Some people hated Matthew. But Jesus loved him. He even called Matthew to be his disciple. *Jesus Asks*

Matthew to Follow Him, page 1061

When you love someone, don't hurt that person. Judas hurt Jesus by betraying him. *Judas Betrays Jesus, page 1095*

Jesus loves children. Some children learned that one day when they came to him. *Jesus and the Children, page 1131*

Loyalty

Don't turn against God when he helps you get something special. The Israelites turned against God when he offered them the Promised Land. *Forty Years in the Wilderness, page 198*

When we rebel against God and his leaders, we can get into bad trouble. Korah and his friends did! *Korah Rebels, page 203*

A true friend is a loyal friend. A true family member is a loyal family member. Ruth was loyal to Naomi. She was a true friend and a true family member. *Ruth Goes Home with Naomi, page 337*

A traitor pretends to be a friend but will hurt you to help himself. Traitors turned against David, even after he helped them. *Traitors Turn against David, page 383*

On the night of the Last Supper, some of Jesus' friends would pretend they did not know him. Judas had already betrayed him. Peter would deny him. Others would run away. That night they forgot to be true friends. True friends are true friends always. *The Last Supper, page 1140*

Judas betrayed Jesus. He sold his friend for a few coins. A friend who hurts you is not a true friend. Be sure you never hurt a friend. *Judas Agrees to Betray Jesus, page 1210*

Lying

You can't get by with a little lie any more than a big

lie. Abram didn't! *Abram and Sarai Visit Egypt, page 21*

You may need a second sin to cover the first, and another to cover the second. Stop before you start the first sin! Joseph's brothers had to lie to cover up their sin of selling Joseph. *Joseph's Brothers Sell Him, page 61*

When you lie, you may need a bigger lie to cover up the first one. Elisha's servant lied a second time to cover his first lie. Don't lie the first time, then you won't need to lie the second time. *Elisha's Greedy Servant, page 484*

Don't try to lie to God. He knows everything you are thinking. Ananias and Sapphira died because they lied. *Ananias and Sapphira Lie to God, page 1287*

Meanness

When Miriam said mean things about Moses, she got leprosy. We probably won't get leprosy. But saying mean things will hurt the other person, God, and us. *Miriam Gets Leprosy, page 195*

Miracles

Miracles are special. Only God can work a miracle. That's because he is God. He held back the Jordan River. No other person could do that. *Crossing the Jordan River, page 275*

God shows us miracles each day in his creation. Honor him for his miracles as Elisha and the prophets did. *A Whirlwind Takes Elijah Away, page 476*

God works miracles. But we may help him do it. Peter helped God heal a crippled man. But God did the healing. *Peter and John Heal a Crippled Man, page 1283*

Obeying

God would give Canaan to Abram only if Abram obeyed him and went to Canaan. God knows what is best for you. But he can't give you his best unless you obey. *Abram Moves to New Lands, page 21*

Would you do ANYTHING for God? Why not start with the most simple things right now? Abraham showed God he would do anything for him. *Abraham Offers Isaac, page 35*

Disobedience brings punishment. It hurts you, your parents, and God. Disobeying isn't worth it, is it? Moses learned this when he disobeyed God. He got the honor for getting water. But he lost the greater honor of going into the Promised Land. *Moses Disobeys God, page 209*

It is better to obey God than to obey a king. That's because God is more important than a king. Balaam learned that God was more important than King Balak. *Who Will Balaam Obey?, page 216*

Saul made a foolish mistake. He did not obey God when things got tough. Obey God at all times, especially when things get tough. Disobeying God only makes things worse. *Saul's Foolish Mistake, page 361*

God can do wonderful things for us if we obey his commands. The young widow saved her sons from slavery by obeying. *Elisha Helps a Poor Widow, page 480*

Do you want God to help you? Do what he says. Sometimes you may think what he wants is foolish. Naaman thought bathing in the Jordan River was a foolish way to be healed. But when he obeyed, he was healed. *Naaman Is Healed, page 483*

Obeying God brings happiness. Disobeying him brings punishment and sadness. Jerusalem was destroyed because its people disobeyed God. *Jerusalem Is Destroyed, page 587*

We should do what God wants. Mary did. *An Angel Visits Mary, page 1153*

God said that Jesus was his Son. He said we should listen to him. Do you? Do you obey him? *Jesus Is Transfigured, page 1180*

We should please God more than others. That's what Paul did. He may have been released from prison if he had pleased others. But he didn't. *Paul Before Felix, page 1333*

Pleasing others more than God makes them seem more important than God. Paul believed God was more important than Festus. So he pleased God more than Festus. *Paul Before Festus, page 1334*

Patience

Learn to wait for good gifts. God knows the best timing. It was hard for Abraham and Sarah to wait many years for a promised son. *Angels Visit Abraham, page 28*

Adonijah was David's oldest son. He could have become king after David. But he couldn't wait! He tried to become king while David was alive. So David made Solomon king instead. Be patient! Wait! *Solomon Becomes King, page 433*

Did you pray for something yesterday? Do you think you should have it today? Be patient. Wait for God. The Israelites waited many years for God to send them home from captivity. *The Israelites Return Home, page 591*

Peacemaking

Sometimes it's better to give up something than get something. Sometimes it's better to be quiet than win an argument. Isaac refused to fight to keep his wells. He lost some wells. But he won a peaceful homeland. *Isaac Gives Up His Wells, page 43*

A wise person knows when to fight for something. A wise person knows when to walk away without fighting. Moses was wise not to fight Edom. *Edom Says No, page 210*

Be a peacemaker, not a troublemaker. Peacemaking brings happiness. Troublemaking brings sadness. Abigail was a peacemaker. *Abigail Stops a Fight, page 386*

Don't stop working or playing because you can't have your way. Paul and Barnabas each wanted to work his own way. They couldn't. So they each worked God's way. But they worked apart. *Paul and Barnabas Separate, page 1314*

It's much better to be a peacemaker than a troublemaker. Which would you rather be? The silversmith and his friends were troublemakers. The mayor was a peacemaker. *The Silversmith Riot, page 1324*

Persecution

Be thankful you can please God, even if people hurt you for it. Friendship with others is short. Friendship with God is forever. *Remarkable Miracles, Then Trouble, page 1288*

Being a Christian does not keep you from getting hurt. You may even get hurt because you are a Christian. Saul persecuted the Christians because they followed Jesus. *Saul Tries to Hurt the Christians, page 1294*

Sometimes it seems that everyone is against us. When Paul was arrested, he could have thought that. But he knew that God was still for him. We should remember that, too. *Paul Is Arrested, page 1329*

Perseverance

Has anyone made fun of you for being a Christian? Never stop helping God because someone makes fun of you or tries to hurt you. Nehemiah didn't. He kept on building the walls. *Nehemiah Builds the Walls, page 607*

Bad people will do bad things to stop God's work. Don't listen to them. Nehemiah listened to God. But he didn't listen to the neighbors. *Nehemiah Finishes the Walls, page 610*

Pleasing God

When you pray, ask God to give you what will please him most. He may give you more, but don't expect it. Solomon prayed for wisdom. God gave him more. *Solomon Asks for Wisdom, page 437*

Prayer

When you pray, don't expect God to answer your way. Expect him to surprise you his way. Moses' mother could never expect Moses to be rescued by the princess who would hire her as Moses' nurse. *Moses Is Born, page 88*

God hears and answers our prayers. But he answers the way he knows is best. Accept his answer. Thank him for it. God answered Hezekiah's prayer, but he answered his way. *Hezekiah Gets Sick, page 508*

Are you ever too tired to pray? Are you ever too busy to pray? Are you too interested in TV to pray? Remember Daniel. He prayed, even when he knew he could be killed for it. *Daniel in the Lions' Den, page 968*

Is something bothering you? Is something wrong? Ask Jesus to help you. One minute makes a big difference when Jesus is with you. The blind man learned that! *Jesus Heals a Blind Man, page 1127*

Jesus can do special things. Before you ask, be sure God would want this. Then believe! Blind Bartimaeus believed, then asked. He saw. *Jesus Heals Blind Bartimaeus, page 1133*

When we pray we should not try to tell God how good we are, as the Pharisee did. We should confess how bad we are and how much we need him, as the tax collector did. *When Two Men Prayed, page 1201*

When you pray, expect God to answer. Don't be surprised when he does. Peter's friends were surprised when their prayers for Peter's release were answered. *An Angel Lets Peter Out of Prison, page 1307*

Presence

God is with us everywhere. When we do right, he is there to help us. When we do wrong, he is there to watch over us. *Jacob's Ladder, page 47*

Wherever we go, God is already there. The Israelites learned this as they moved the Tabernacle, God's house. *Moving Day for God's House, page 192*

God is not with us when we refuse to invite him. The Israelites brought the Ark into battle, but forgot to ask God to come, too. *The Ark Is Stolen, page 350*

Don't try to run away from God. You can't. He is everywhere. He sees all things. Jonah tried to run away from God. But he couldn't. *A Big Fish Swallows Jonah, page 1003*

Spending time with Jesus is more important than anything else we can do. Mary wanted to spend time with Jesus. Martha let dinner become more important. *Jesus Visits Mary and Martha, page 1185*

Pride

The builders at the Tower of Babel were proud. God doesn't like pride. When we think we're big, we think others are small. We may even think God is small. *Building a Tower to Touch the Sky, page 17*

Be careful when you are proud. God may put you down. Joseph's proud brothers bowed before him. When they sold him, they never thought they would do this. *Joseph's Brothers Return to Egypt, page 72*

Pharaoh saw God's miracles, but didn't think God was doing them. We are proud and stubborn when we see the things God makes but don't think they are special. *The River That Turned to Blood, page 97*

David was proud of his army. He depended on his army for strength. This time he forgot to depend on God. So he was punished. The next time you are tempted to be proud, stop. Give honor to God. *David Buys a Threshing Floor, page 430*

Promises

God keeps his promises. He kept his promises to Noah. The rainbow reminds us of that. We should keep our promises, too. *God Sends a Great Flood, page 14*

God always keeps his promises. He kept his promises to Abram. So should you! *God Makes a Promise to Abram, page 25*

Keep your promises, even if the person you promised isn't around. Joseph kept his promise to his father, even after his father died. *Jacob Dies and Is Buried, page 82*

Keeping promises is important to us, others, and God. God did exactly what he promised the Israelites. *The Battle for Jericho, page 278*

Joshua promised the Gibeonites protection. He kept his promise, even though they did not deserve it. Keep your promises, even when you don't want to. *Gibeonites Trick Joshua, page 284*

Don't make foolish promises, as Jephthah did. You will need to keep them and that may hurt you. *Jephthah's Foolish Vow, page 319*

Promises should not be broken, so be careful what vows or promises you make. Saul made a foolish vow. He had to break it or kill his son. *Saul's Foolish Promise, page 365*

King Herod made a foolish promise. He didn't want to keep it. But he had to! Don't make foolish promises. You will be sorry when you have to keep them. *Herod Kills John the Baptist, page 1119*

Prophecy

The Old Testament teaches about Jesus. Many years before he came, it told what would happen. The people on the road to Emmaus heard Jesus teach these things. *On the Road to Emmaus, page 1218*

Provision

God gave the Israelites manna and quail in the wilderness. He causes all food to grow and gives us what we need. Remember to thank him. *God Sends Manna and Quail, page 117*

God gave the Israelites water from a rock. He gives us good gifts, even when we don't deserve them. Thank him. *Water from a Rock, page 120*

Punishment

The "fun" of sin is never worth the punishment for it. Eating the fruit was not worth losing the garden. *Adam and Eve Are Tempted, page 5*

God punishes people when they do wrong. He punished the Philistines for capturing his Ark and made them send it back. *The Ark Comes Back, page 353*

Are you about to do something wrong? Think first about the possible punishment. Then you won't do it. The Ammonites and Syrians lost 40,000 horsemen and 700 chariot drivers. They should have thought of that before they picked a fight with David. *A King Makes Fun of David's Men, page 410*

Sin brings punishment. Even the great King David was punished for his sin. If you don't want to be punished, don't sin. *Nathan Scolds David, page 413*

People will be punished for bad things they do. Athaliah was punished for all the wicked things she did as queen. *Joash Becomes King, page 496*

The bad things we plan for others may come back to hurt us. Haman was hanged on his own gallows. *Queen Esther Defeats Haman, page 628*

Rebellion

The next time you feel rebellious, remember Absalom. He rebelled against his father. That hurt him, his father, the army, the nation, and God. Absalom also died because of it. *Absalom Is Defeated, page 421*

Repentance

When we have done something wrong, we should be sorry. Even Judas was sorry that he had betrayed Jesus. *Judas Hangs Himself, page 1098*

Responsibility

Esther learned that she was queen for a good reason, God's reason. God may give you an important job for an important reason. Do what he wants. *Haman Tricks the King, page 626*

Resurrection

Jesus is the only one who can make dead people live again. Why? He is God's Son. He arose from the dead. An angel at Jesus' empty tomb told this good news to the women who came there. *Women Visit Jesus' Tomb, page 1148*

Revenge

Getting even, or revenge, can hurt us as much as the other person. Don't do it! Forgive. Samson killed himself with the Philistines. *Samson Pulls Down a Temple, page 329*

Anyone can get even. Only a special person will refuse to get even. David refused to get even when Saul tried to kill him. *David Refuses to Get Even, page 384*

Has someone hurt you or made fun of you? Do you want to hurt that person or make fun of him? Don't. Shimei insulted David. He said terrible things to David. But David would not get even. *Shimei Insults David, page 419*

Would you really like for God to hurt someone who has hurt you? Pray for that person instead. Jonah foolishly wanted God to destroy Nineveh. But God told him why he was wrong. *Jonah Preaches at Nineveh, page 1005*

Salvation

Some fish are not accepted by fishermen. Wicked people will not live with God in Heaven. People who accept Jesus as Savior live with him. Jesus takes their sins away. He gives them a new life. *A Story about Some Fish, page 1070*

Jesus does not want one person lost. He is like the shepherd who looked for the lost lamb. *A Story about a Lamb, page 1078*

We must go to Heaven God's way, as the guests had to come to the wedding the king's way. We cannot get there our own way. *A Story about a Wedding, page 1087*

Jesus died on the cross because he loves us and wants to be our Savior. We should accept him as our Savior. He will give us a new life. He will help us live in Heaven. *Jesus Is Crucified, page 1099*

Do you want to go to Heaven some day? Accept Jesus as your Savior now. Jesus said he is the door to Heaven. He is the only way to get in. *A Story about a Door, page 1191*

When we accept Jesus we have a new life. We live differently than before. That's what happened to Zacchaeus. *Jesus Gives Zacchaeus a New Life, page 1203*

Nicodemus wanted to know more about Heaven. So Jesus told him how to get there. Jesus can help you get to Heaven, too. Accept him as your Savior. *Jesus Talks with Nicodemus, page 1232*

Jesus can change the worst person in the world. He can make that person a great Christian. Look at Saul! *Saul Meets Jesus, page 1297*

Satisfaction

Are you satisfied with what God has given you? Or do you always want more? Solomon sinned. God gave him great riches. But he turned from God because he wanted more. *Solomon Turns from God, page 452*

Be satisfied with what God has given you. If you want more, be sure it's something God wants you to have. King Uzziah had everything a king could want. But he wanted to do a priest's work,

too. God was not pleased. Look what happened. *A King Turns into a Leper, page 574*

Do you have less than some friends have? Thank God for what you have. Don't cry for what you don't have. The Israelites cried for the Temple they once had. But their new Temple was still God's house. *The New Temple, page 594*

Be grateful for what you have. Job praised God when he was rich. He praised God when he lost everything. Job was grateful no matter what he had. *God Gives Job Good Gifts, page 659*

Self-Control

Cain killed Abel because he didn't control his anger. Control your anger. Stay out of trouble. *Cain Kills Abel, page 6*

Self-Pity

Do you ever feel sorry for yourself? Elijah did. But God showed Elijah that he was still with him. The next time you feel sorry for yourself, stop. Praise God and ask for his help. *God Whispers to Elijah, page 466*

Shame

Are you ever ashamed of Jesus? Peter was the morning Jesus was arrested. Peter cried when he realized what he had done. You'll be sad too if you are ever ashamed of him. If you are, someday he will be ashamed of you. *Peter Denies that He Knows Jesus, page 1097*

Stealing

When we want something too much, we may try to steal it. We may lie and cheat too! Ahab wanted Naboth's vineyard. He was happy to see Naboth murdered to get that vineyard. *Ahab Steals Naboth's Vineyard, page 470*

Stewardship

When God gives you good gifts, use them wisely. God gave Samson great strength and he used it foolishly. *Samson Gets Married, page 324*

Never try to hurt God, especially with a wonderful gift he has given you. God made Jeroboam king. But Jeroboam used his kingship to hurt God. *Jeroboam Makes Two Golden Calves, page 455*

God gives each person special talents. Use them well or you will lose them. *A Story about Talents, page 092*

God can make big things come from tiny things. Your smallest prayer, your smallest work, like the tiny mustard seed, can do big things. *A Story about a Tiny Seed, page 1113*

God gave us a wonderful world. We should use it wisely. God gave us his Word. We should share it. God gave us his Son. We should follow him. The tenants in the story were poor stewards. They did not honor the owner. We must honor the owner of our world, the Lord himself. *A Story about a Farm, page 1136*

Would you rather be rich on earth or in Heaven? The rich fool couldn't take his money with him when he died. Neither can we. But we can send riches ahead by serving God. *A Story about Money, page 1189*

Don't let your things become more important to you than God. That's what happened to the rich young man. *Jesus and the Rich Young Man, page 1102*

God gives us many good gifts. We must use them wisely. Good stewards of God's gifts use them wisely. *A Story about Investing, page 1204*

Temptation

Don't let people tempt you to do something God says is wrong. If you sin, blame yourself, not them. It was you who decided to sin, just as the Israelites decided to worship the Golden Calf. *The Golden Calf, page 138*

Say no to temptation and obey God, no matter what the reward. God told Balaam to obey him, no matter what. *King Balak Offers Balaam Money, page 214*

A second sin is often needed to cover the first. When you are tempted, don't sin the first time. Then you won't need to sin the second time. David had to murder Uriah to cover his sin with Uriah's wife. *David and Bathsheba, page 411*

Jesus showed us how to resist temptation. Let God's Word help you. *Jesus Is Tempted 1052*

When you are tempted to do something wrong, pray! That's what Jesus did. *Jesus Prays, page 1212*

Thankfulness

Say "thank you" when someone does special things for you. The woman who was healed said "thank you" to Jesus by getting dinner for him. *Jesus Heals a Sick Woman, page 1060*

When Jesus does something special, we should thank him. Has Jesus forgiven your sins? Be sure to thank him. The leper Jesus healed was so thankful that he told everyone the good news. *Jesus Heals a Leper, page 1106*

Thank God and praise him when he does something special for you. The people praised God when the boy was brought back to life. *Jesus Helps a Boy Come Back to Life, page 1173*

Do you love Jesus? Do things that show that you love him. The woman did something special for Jesus. We should too. *A Woman Kisses Jesus' Feet, page 1174*

It's nice to say thanks. It's nice to be thanked. But don't expect to be thanked for doing certain things. We are expected to do some things, such as brushing our teeth. That's what Jesus said. *A Story about a Servant, page 1198*

Jesus healed ten lepers. One said thanks. The others didn't. We need to be thankful, don't we? *Jesus Heals Ten Lepers, page 1200*

Trouble

When you're in trouble, don't turn against God. He can help you. Like Paul and Silas, pray, don't grumble. *Paul and Silas Sing In Prison, page 1317*

Trust

Listen to God more than your friends. Trust him more than them. Noah did what God said because he believed what God would do. *Noah Builds the Ark, page 10*

When we trust God to help us, let's trust him to do it his way. Abram and Sarai forgot to do this. They got into a lot of trouble. *Sarai Becomes Jealous, page 26*

God can do anything. When we pray, we must trust him to do anything. That doesn't mean he WILL do anything. He will do what is best. When Aaron's rod budded, the Israelites saw that God could do impossible things. *A Rod Like a Fruit Tree, page 206*

We should listen to God, even when his advice seems strange. It must have seemed strange to cure snakebite by looking at a snake. But it was God's way for the Israelites to show they trusted him. Those who did it were healed. Those who didn't died. *The Bronze Snake, page 211*

God can use small things like Jael's tent pegs to win big victories. God can use our pennies, nickels, dimes, and quarters to do his work. But we must trust him to do it. *Deborah and Barak, page 308*

It is better to have less with God than more without God. David was stronger with a little sling and God's help than Goliath was with great weapons alone. *David Fights Goliath, page 370*

We trust people who show they can be trusted. David showed he could be trusted. *David Sneaks into Saul's Camp at Night, page 389*

Trust God to give you what you need, not what you want. The widow's food was simple, but she always had enough. *Elijah Helps a Poor Widow, page 462*

God knew about Jesus' trip to Egypt 600 years before it happened. Actually he knew it long before that. You can trust a God who knows that much, can't you? *Escape to Egypt, page 1051*

Jesus brought Jairus's daughter back from the dead. Can you trust him to help you? You can! *A Dead Girl Lives Again, page 1178*

Andrew brought his brother Peter to Jesus. You can help a friend know Jesus too. A friend who trusts you may learn to trust Jesus, too. *Jesus' First Followers, page 1227*

Jesus is a living Savior. He is not dead. He is not in a tomb. He is alive in Heaven. In most religions people worship an idol or a dead god.

We worship a living God. We can trust him. Will you? *Peter and John Visit Jesus' Tomb, page 1269*

Unity

Christians, and families, work best when they are united and work together. Ask each other how you can be more united. The early Christians worked well because they worked together. *Christians Work Together, page 1286*

Wisdom

Being smart doesn't make you wise. You show that you are wise when you make the right choices. Choose what will please God most. Solomon showed he was wise when he made the right choices. *Solomon Shows How Wise He Is, page 438*

People like to be with a truly wise person. You can be wise if you know what God says and what he wants. That's why Solomon was wise. *The Queen of Sheba Visits Solomon, page 450*

Witnessing

When the Holy Spirit is in us, we have something to say. We also have the power to say it. The disciples became strong witnesses when they were filled with the Holy Spirit. *The Holy Spirit Comes, page 1279*

Sharing Jesus with one person may actually be sharing him with many. The Ethiopian could go home to tell many there about Jesus. *Philip Tells an Ethiopian about Jesus, page 1295*

We win friends for Jesus when we reach out for Jesus. Be a helper. The early Christians won friends for Jesus by being helpers. *Christians Start a New Church, page 1305*

When you tell others about Jesus, some will accept him. Some will reject him. Some will put it off. But keep telling them about Jesus. Let him do his own work in their hearts. *Paul Preaches on Mars Hill, page 1319*

Some people who hear the Gospel laugh at it. Don't let that discourage you. Keep telling. *Paul Works with Priscilla and Aquila, page 1320*

When you tell others about Jesus, some will accept him and some will reject him. Keep telling others about him. That's what Paul did at Rome. *Paul Is a Prisoner at Rome, page 1341*

Worry

In new places, you may find a new friend of God to help you. Ask God to help you find that person. Moses found Jethro and his family in a faraway land. *Moses Runs Away, page 90*

God fed Elijah, even during a famine. Do you ever worry about food or clothes or something else? God will take care of you. He may not do it your way. But he will take care of you. He will do it his way, which is the best way. *Ravens Feed Elijah, page 460*

Do you ever worry? Do you wonder how God could help you? He will. But he may help in unusual ways. Look how God provided food in a great famine. *Four Lepers Visit an Enemy Camp, page 489*

Worship

We can worship God anywhere. That's what Jesus told the woman at the well. *Jesus Talks with a Woman at a Well, page 234*